Scholarships
2014

RELATED TITLES FOR COLLEGE-BOUND STUDENTS

College Admissions and Financial Aid

Your College Admissions Game Plan

You're Accepted: A Stress-Free and Proven Approach to Getting Into College

Test Preparation

ACT Premier with CD-ROM

ACT: Strategies, Practice, and Review

SAT Premier with CD-ROM

SAT: Strategies, Practice, and Review

12 Practice Tests for the SAT

Essay Writing for High School Students

Scholarships

2014

by Gail Schlachter, R. David Weber, and the Staff of Reference Service Press

Introduction by Douglas Bucher

New York

This publication is designed to provide accurate and authoritative information in regard to the subject matter covered. It is sold with the understanding that the publisher is not engaged in rendering legal, accounting, or other professional service. If legal advice or other expert assistance is required, the services of a competent professional should be sought.

Published by Kaplan Publishing, a division of Kaplan, Inc.
395 Hudson Street
New York, NY 10014

Printed in the United States of America

10 9 8 7 6 5 4 3 2 1

ISBN 13: 978-1-61865-061-0

Kaplan Publishing books are available at special quantity discounts to use for sales promotions, employee premiums, or educational purposes. For more information or to purchase books, please call the Simon & Schuster special sales department at 866-506-1949.

CONTENTS

Lots of books list scholarships. What makes this book different?

1. The funding opportunities described here can be used at any number of schools.
Look through other scholarship books, and you'll see that most of them contain large numbers of scholarships that can be used only at a particular college or university. So even if you're lucky, only a handful of these school-specific scholarships will be for the schools you're considering. And even this handful of scholarship listings is of little value because the schools you apply to (or are considering applying to) will gladly send you information about all their scholarship programs free of charge.

But, not one of the scholarships listed in this book is limited to only one particular school. The result: more listings in this book have the potential to be of use to you.

2. Only the biggest and the best funding programs are covered in this book.
Most of the other scholarship books are bulked up with awards that may be worth only a few hundred dollars. While any free money you can get your hands on for college is good, you will have to be careful that you don't waste your time and money chasing scholarships that will hardly put a dent in your overall college cost burden. And, to make your search even easier, we've specially marked the scholarships that offer the most money.

The scholarships in this book all offer students the chance to receive at least $1,000 per year. So more of the scholarships in this book will really be worth the investment of your time.

3. Not one dollar of the programs listed in this book needs to be repaid.
Most scholarship books list awards that are really loans. We're not against loans, especially college loans with reduced interest rates or delayed repayment. *But of the funding opportunities covered in this book, not one dollar has to be repaid, provided stated requirements are met.* Accepting one of these scholarships need not add to the debt burden you'll face when you finish school.

In fact, we're so convinced this book contains the most helpful and most accurate scholarship information on the market that we offer satisfaction guaranteed or your money back (details on the inside front cover).

About the Authors

PART ONE

Douglas Bucher

Douglas Bucher is the Vice President of Enrollment Services and Planning at New York University (NYU), the largest private university in the United States. He also formerly served as president of the Eastern Association of Student Financial Aid Administrators and is a member of the New York Association of Student Financial Aid Administrators. He teaches seminars for the U.S. Department of Education and has conducted a variety of sessions on financial aid at many professional conferences. He also teaches a graduate seminar course in NYU's School of Education and acts as a consultant for public, private, and proprietary two- and four-year schools.

PART TWO

Gail Schlachter

Dr. Gail Schlachter is president of Reference Service Press, a publishing company specializing in the development of electronic and print directories of financial aid. Dr. Schlachter has taught library-related courses on the graduate-school level and has presented dozens of workshops and lectures in the field. Dr. Schlachter has served on the councils of the American Library Association (ALA) and the California Library Association, is a past president of the ALA's Reference and User Services Association, and has served as editor-in-chief of *Reference and User Services Quarterly*, the official journal of ALA's Reference and User Services Association. In recognition of her outstanding contributions to the field of reference librarianship, Dr. Schlachter has been a recipient of both the Isadore Gilbert Mudge Award and the Louis Shores–Oryx Press Award and was named the "Outstanding Alumna" by the University of Wisconsin's School of Library and Information Studies. In addition, her financial aid print resources have won numerous awards, including the *Choice*'s "Outstanding Reference Book" award, *Library Journal*'s "Best Reference Book of the Year" award, the National Education and Information Center Advisory Committee's "Best of the Best" award, and the Knowledge Industry Publications "Award for Library Literature."

R. David Weber

Dr. R. David Weber has served as Reference Service Press's (RSP's) chief editor since 1988. In that capacity, he has been involved in building, refining, and maintaining RSP's award-winning financial aid database. In addition, Dr. Weber has taught at East Los Angeles College, where he was named "Teacher of the Year" on several occasions, and Harbor College. Besides his work in the area of financial aid, Dr. Weber has written a number of critically acclaimed reference books, including *Dissertations in Urban History* and the three-volume *Energy Information Guide.*

Reference Service Press

Reference Service Press (RSP) began in 1977 with a single financial aid publication, *Directory of Financial Aids for Women,* and now specializes in the development of financial aid resources in multiple formats, including books, large-print books, ebooks, print-on-demand reports, electronic databases, and online sources. RSP is committed to collecting, organizing, and disseminating—in both print and electronic format—the most current and accurate information available on scholarships, fellowships, loans, grants, awards, internships, and other types of funding opportunities. The company has compiled one of the largest financial aid databases currently available—with up-to-date information on more than 45,000 portable programs (not restricted to any one school) that are open to high school students, high school graduates, undergraduates, graduate students, professionals, and postdoctorates. The database identifies billions of dollars in funding opportunities that will be awarded to millions of recipients each year. Using that information, RSP publishes a number of award-winning financial aid directories aimed at specific groups.

After you've mined the resources described in this book, you might be interested in continuing your funding search by looking through other RSP books. You may be able to find these titles in your local public or academic library. Or, contact RSP to order your own copy:

Reference Service Press
5000 Windplay Drive, Suite 4
El Dorado Hills, CA 95762-9319
Phone: (916) 939-9620; Fax: (916) 939-9626
Email: info@rspfunding.com
Website: www.rspfunding.com

Specialized Financial Aid Directories from Reference Service Press

College Student's Guide to Merit and Other No-Need Funding
Named "best of the best" by *Choice.* The focus here is on 1,300 merit scholarships and other no-need funding programs open specifically to students currently in or returning to college. 490 pages. ISBN 1-58841-212-1. $32.50, plus $7 shipping.

Directory of Financial Aids for Women
Published since 1977, this is the only comprehensive and current source of information on 1,400 scholarships, fellowships, grants, and other awards designed primarily or exclusively for women. *Guide to Reference* calls this "the best available reference source." 552 pages. ISBN 1-58841-216-4. $45, plus $7 shipping.

Financial Aid for African Americans
Selected as the "Editor's Choice" by *Reference Books Bulletin,* this unique directory describes 1,300 scholarships, fellowships, grants, and awards for African Americans. 490 pages. ISBN 1-58841-242-3. $42.50, plus $7 shipping.

Financial Aid for Asian Americans
Use this award-winning source to find funding for Americans of Chinese, Japanese, Korean, Vietnamese, Filipino, or other Asian origin. Nearly 1,000 opportunities are described here. 350 pages. ISBN 1-58841-243-1. $40, plus $7 shipping.

Financial Aid for Hispanic Americans
Called a "landmark resource" by *Reference Books Bulletin*, this directory describes nearly the 1,100 biggest and best funding programs open to Americans of Mexican, Puerto Rican, Central American, or other Latin American heritage. 446 pages. ISBN 1-58841-244-X. $42.50, plus $7 shipping.

Financial Aid for Native Americans
Detailed information is provided in this award-winning directory on more than 1,300 funding opportunities open to American Indians, Native Alaskans, and Native Hawaiians. 506 pages. ISBN 1-58841-245-8. $45, plus $7 shipping.

Financial Aid for Research and Creative Activities Abroad
Nearly 1,100 funding programs (scholarships, fellowships, grants, etc.) available to support research, professional, or creative activities abroad are described here. 422 pages. ISBN 1-58841-206-7. $45, plus $7 shipping.

Financial Aid for Study and Training Abroad
Called "the best available reference source" by *Guide to Reference*, this directory covers more than 1,000 financial aid opportunities available to support structured or independent study abroad. 362 pages. ISBN 1-58841-205-9. $40, plus $7 shipping.

Financial Aid for the Disabled and Their Families
Chosen one of the "Best Reference Books of the Year" by *Library Journal*, this directory describes in detail more than 1,200 funding opportunities for these groups. 530 pages. ISBN 1-58841-247-4. $40, plus $7 shipping.

Financial Aid for Veterans, Military Personnel, and Their Dependents
According to *Reference Book Review*, this directory, with its 1,400 entries, is "the most comprehensive guide available on the subject." 488 pages. ISBN 1-58841-248-2. $40, plus $7 shipping.

High School Senior's Guide to Merit and Other No-Need Funding
Here's your guide to 1,100 merit awards and other no-need funding programs that never look at income when awarding money to high school seniors for college. 424 pages. ISBN 1-58841-210-5. $29.95, plus $7 shipping.

How to Pay for Your Degree in Business & Related Fields
Described here are more than 800 scholarships, fellowships, grants, and awards available to support undergraduate and graduate students working on a degree in business or a related field. 302 pages. ISBN 1-58841-237-7. $30, plus $7 shipping.

How to Pay for Your Degree in Education & Related Fields
Use this directory to identify 1,000 funding opportunities available to support undergraduate and graduate students preparing for a career in teaching, guidance, etc. 298 pages. ISBN 1-58841-240-7. $30, plus $7 shipping.

How to Pay for Your Degree in Engineering
Check here for the 900+ biggest and best scholarships, fellowships, awards, grants, and other funding opportunities available to support undergraduate or graduate studies in all types of engineering. 324 pages. ISBN 1-58841-249-0. $30, plus $7 shipping.

How to Pay for Your Degree in Nursing
More than 800 scholarships, fellowships, and other funding programs that support study or research for nursing students (both undergraduate and graduate) are described—more than twice the number of programs listed in any other directory. 250 pages. ISBN 1-58841-239-3. $30, plus $7 shipping.

How to Pay for Your Law Degree
Here's information on more than 625 fellowships, loans, grants, awards, internships, and bar exam stipends available to law students working on a J.D., LL.M., or other law-related degree. There's no other guide like this one. 262 pages. ISBN 1-58841-241-5. $30, plus $7 shipping.

Money for Christian College Students
This is the only directory to describe more than 800 funding opportunities available to support Christian students working on an undergraduate or graduate degree (secular or religious). 264 pages. ISBN 1-58841-225-3. $30, plus $7 shipping.

Money for Graduate Students in the Arts & Humanities
This directory identifies nearly 1,100 funding opportunities available to support graduate study, training, research, and creative activities in the arts and humanities. "Highly recommended" by *Choice.* 292 pages. ISBN 1-58841-229-6. $42.50, plus $7 shipping.

Money for Graduate Students in the Biological Sciences
This unique directory focuses specifically on funding for graduate study and research in the biological sciences. More than 800 funding opportunities are described. 248 pages. ISBN 1-58841-230-X. $37.50, plus $7 shipping.

Money for Graduate Students in the Health Sciences
Described here are the 1,000 fellowships, grants, awards, and traineeships set aside just for students interested in working on a graduate degree in dentistry, genetics, medicine, nutrition, pharmacology, etc. 304 pages. ISBN 1-58841-231-8. $42.50, plus $7 shipping.

Money for Graduate Students in the Physical & Earth Sciences
Nearly 900 funding opportunities for graduate study or research in the physical or earth sciences are described in detail and accessed through five indexes. 276 pages. ISBN 1-58841-232-6. $40, plus $7 shipping.

Money for Graduate Students in the Social & Behavioral Sciences
This directory covers 1,100 funding opportunities for graduate study and research in the social and behavioral sciences that are indexed by title, sponsor, subject, geographic coverage, and deadline. 316 pages. ISBN 1-58841-233-4. $42.50, plus $7 shipping.

Preface

While getting a college degree may be the best investment you will ever make, paying for it is another matter. Going to college is expensive. It can cost $100,000 or more just to complete a bachelor's degree. That's more than most students can afford to pay on their own, especially in these tough economic times. So what can you do?

Fortunately, money is available. According to the College Board, there is more than $185 billion in financial aid available to undergraduates each year. Of this, at least $119 billion comes from federal loans and grants, $32 billion from the colleges, $16 billion from education tax credits, $10 billion from the states, and $6 billion from employer grants and private scholarships.

How can you find out about financial aid that might be available to you? For some sources of funding, it's not difficult at all. To learn about federal resources, call 800-4-FEDAID or visit the U.S. Department of Education's website at studentaid.ed.gov. To find out what your state is offering, go to www.rspfunding.com/finaidinfo_stateaid.html to link to your state higher education agency. Similarly, you can write to the colleges of your choice or check with your employer to learn about funding from those sources.

Information on private sources of funding is much more elusive. That's where this book can help. Here, in one place, you'll find detailed information on more than 3,000 of the biggest and best scholarships available to fund education after high school. These programs are open to high school seniors, high school graduates, currently enrolled college students, and those returning to college after a break. They can be used to support study in any area, in junior and community colleges, vocational and technical institutes, four-year colleges, and universities. No other source can match the scope, currency, and detail provided in this book. That's why we have a satisfaction guaranteed or your money back offer (see details on the inside front cover).

What's Unique about This Book?

All scholarship directories identify funding opportunities. But this directory is unique in several ways:

- **This directory covers only programs open to support college studies.** Most other directories mix together programs for a number of groups—high school students, college students, and even graduate students or post doctorates. Here, you won't spend your time sifting through programs that aren't aimed at you.

- **Only free money is identified.** If a program requires repayment or charges interest, it's not listed. Here's your chance to find out about billions of dollars in aid, knowing that not one dollar will ever need to be repaid, provided stated requirements are met.

- **Not every funding opportunity is based on need or on academics.** Many sources award money based on career plans, writing ability, research skills, religious or ethnic background, military or organizational activities, athletic success, personal characteristics, and even pure luck in random drawings.

- **The money awarded by these scholarships can be taken to any number of schools.** Unlike other financial aid directories that often list large numbers of scholarships available only to students enrolled at one specific school, all of the entries in this book are "portable."

- **Only the biggest and best funding programs are covered.** To be listed here, a program has to offer at least $1,000 per year. Many go way beyond that, paying $20,000 or more each year, or covering the full cost of college attendance. (Look for the $ or $$ after the entry numbers to identify these higher paying programs.) Other scholarship books are often bulked up with awards that may be worth only a few hundred dollars. While any free money you can get your hands on for college is good, you will have to be careful that you don't waste your time and energy chasing scholarships that will hardly put a dent in your overall college cost burden.

- **Searching for scholarships couldn't be easier.** You can identify funding programs by discipline, specific subject, sponsoring organization, most money awarded (look for the $ or $$ after the program entry number), where you live, where you want to go to school, and when you want to apply. Plus, you'll find all the information you need to decide if a program is right for you: eligibility requirements, financial data, duration, number awarded, and application date. You even get fax numbers, toll-free numbers, email addresses, and website locations (when available), along with complete contact information.

What's Not Covered?

While this book is intended to be the most current and comprehensive source of free money available to college students in the United States, there are some things we have specifically excluded:

- **Funding not aimed at incoming, currently enrolled, or returning college students.** If a program is open only to graduate school students, for instance, or to adults of any age interested in photography, it is not covered. If a scholarship is not specifically for college students, it has not been included.

- **Individual school-based programs.** Financial aid given by individual schools solely for the benefit of their own students is not covered. Instead, the directory identifies "portable" programs—ones that can be used at any number of schools.

- **Money for study outside the United States.** Only funding that supports study in the United States is covered. For information on sources of funding to go abroad, see the titles listed in the Reference Service Press section in this directory.

- **Very restrictive programs.** In general, programs are excluded if they are open only to a limited geographic area (students in specific cities or counties), are available only to members of a union, social organization, or professional association, or offer only limited financial support (less than $1,000 per year).

- **Programs that did not respond to our research inquiries.** Despite our best efforts—up to four letters and three follow-up phone calls—some organizations did not supply information. Consequently, their programs have not been included.

How to Use This Book

We've divided this book into three sections: introductory materials; a detailed list of free money available for college, organized by discipline; and a set of indexes to help you pinpoint appropriate funding programs.

Getting Started

The first section of the directory, written by Douglas Bucher, Vice President of Enrollment Services and Planning at New York University, offers tips on searching for scholarships, applying for aid, and avoiding scholarship search scams.

Scholarship Listings

The main section (part two) of the directory, prepared by Gail Schlachter, R. David Weber, and the staff of Reference Service Press, describes more than 3,000 scholarships, competitions, and awards that provide free money for college. The programs listed are sponsored by federal and state government agencies, professional organizations, foundations, educational associations, and military/veterans organizations. All areas of the sciences, social sciences, and humanities are covered.

To help you tailor your search, the entries in this section are grouped into four main categories:

1. **Unrestricted by Subject Area.** Described here are funding opportunities that can be used to support study in any subject area (though the programs may be restricted in other ways).

2. **Humanities.** Described here are programs that 1) reward outstanding artistic and creative work by students or 2) support college studies in the humanities, including architecture, art, creative writing, design, history, journalism, languages, literature, music, and religion.

3. **Sciences.** Described here are sources of free money that 1) reward student speeches, essays, inventions, organizational involvement, and other activities in the sciences or 2) support college studies in a number of scientific fields, including agricultural sciences, chemistry, computer science, engineering, environmental sciences, food science, horticulture, mathematics, marine sciences, nursing, nutrition, pharmacology, and technology.

4. **Social Sciences.** Described here are programs that 1) reward outstanding speeches, essays, organizational involvement, and other activities in the social sciences or 2) support college studies in various social science fields, including accounting, business administration, criminology, economics, education, geography, home economics, international relations, labor relations, political science, sales and marketing, sociology, social services, sports and recreation, and tourism.

Each program entry in part two has been prepared to give you a concise but clear picture of the available funding. Information, as available, is provided on organizational points of contact, program title, eligibility, money awarded, duration, number of awards, and application deadline.

Indexes

To help you find the aid you need, we have included five indexes; these will let you access the listings by specific subject, residency, tenability (where you want to study), sponsoring organization, and deadline date. These indexes use a word-by-word alphabetical arrangement. Note: Numbers in the index refer to *entry* numbers, not to page numbers.

1. **Subject Index.** Use this index when you want to identify funding programs by specific subject.

2. **Residency Index.** Some programs listed in this book are restricted to residents of a particular state, region, or other geographic location. Others are open to students wherever they live. This index helps you identify programs available only to residents in your area, as well as programs that have no residency restrictions.

3. **Tenability Index.** Some programs described in this book are restricted to persons attending schools in specific cities, counties, states, or regions. This index will help you locate funding specifically for the geographic area where you attend or plan to attend school.

4. **Sponsoring Organization Index.** This index makes it easy to identify agencies that offer free money for college. Sponsoring organizations are listed alphabetically, word by word. In addition, we've used a code to help you identify which programs sponsored by these organizations fall within your general area of interest (Unrestricted by Subject Area, Humanities, Sciences, or Social Sciences).

5. **Calendar Index.** Because most financial aid programs have specific deadline dates, some may have already closed by the time you begin to look for funding. You can use the Calendar Index to identify which programs are still open.

How to Get the Most Out of This Book

To Locate Financial Aid by Discipline. If you want to get an overall picture of the funding available for any area of college study, turn to the first category, Unrestricted by Subject Area. You'll find nearly 1,100 general programs that support study in any area (though they may be restricted in other ways). If you've decided on your area of specialization, turn next to the appropriate chapter (Humanities, Sciences, or Social Sciences) and browse through the listings there.

To Find Information on a Particular Financial Aid Program. If you know the name and disciplinary focus of a particular financial aid program, you can go directly to the appropriate category in part two, where you'll find program profiles grouped by discipline and arranged alphabetically by title.

To Find Programs with the Largest Awards. Want to target the programs that offer you the most money? Look for the dollar signs after the program entry number: $ means the scholarship is between $2,000 and $4,999; $$ means the scholarship pays at least $5,000 or covers part or all of your tuition costs; no dollar sign means the scholarship is worth from $1,000 to $1,999 (our minimum to be included in this book).

To Browse Quickly Through the Listings. Turn to the section in part two that interests you (Unrestricted by Subject Area, Humanities, Sciences, Social Sciences) and read the Summary field in each entry. In seconds, you'll know if this is an opportunity that might apply to you. If it is, be sure to read the entire entry to make sure you meet all of the requirements. Don't apply if you don't qualify!

To Locate Financial Aid for Studies in a Particular Subject Area. Turn to the subject index first if you are interested in identifying funding by specific subject area. Be sure also to check the listings under the "General Programs" heading; these programs support studies in any area (though they may be restricted in other ways).

To Locate Financial Aid Based on Where You Live. Use the Residency Index to identify funding that supports applicants in your area. The index is subdivided by broad subject area. When using this index, be sure also to check the listings under the term "United States," because the programs indexed there have no geographic restrictions and can be used in any area.

To Locate Financial Aid Based on Where You Want to Study. Use the Tenability Index to identify funding that supports study in a particular geographic location. The index is subdivided by broad subject area. When using this index, be sure also to check the listings under the term "United States," because the programs indexed there have no geographic restrictions and can be used in any area in the country.

To Locate Financial Aid Programs Sponsored by a Particular Organization. The Sponsoring Organization Index makes it easy to determine which groups are providing free money for college and to identify specific financial aid programs offered by a particular sponsor. Each entry number in the index is coded to indicate broad subject coverage, to help you target appropriate entries.

Let Us Hear from You

We'd like to hear from you. Send your comments, suggestions, questions, problems, or success stories to: Gail Schlachter, Kaplan Scholarships Editor, 5000 Windplay Drive, Suite 4, El Dorado Hills, CA 95762, or email her at GailSchlachter@rspfunding.com.

SAMPLE ENTRY

① ② ③ **71 $$ AXA ACHIEVEMENT SCHOLARSHIPS**

④ Scholarship America
Attn: Scholarship Management Services
One Scholarship Way
P.O. Box 297
St. Peter, MN 56082
Phone: (507) 931-1682; (800) 537-4180; Fax: (507) 931-9168;
Email: axaachievement@scholarshipamerica.org
Web: www.axa-equitable.com

⑤ **Summary:** To provide financial assistance for college to high school seniors who demonstrate outstanding achievement.

⑥ **Eligibility:** Open to graduating high school seniors who plan to enroll full time in an accredited 2- or 4-year college or university in the United States. Applicants must demonstrate ambition and self-drive as demonstrated by outstanding achievement in school, community, or work-related activities. In selecting finalists, primary consideration is given to the applicant's non-academic outstanding achievement as described in the online application essays. The achievement may be a long-term accomplishment or an activity or project that occurred in their school, community, or workplace. Other factors considered in include extracurricular activities in school and community, work experience, and academic record. Finalists are then invited to submit transcripts and an appraisal from an unrelated adult who can confirm the achievement. Selection of recipients is based on demonstrated achievement. From among the recipients, students whose achievements are especially noteworthy are designated as national AXA Achievers.

⑦ **Financial data:** The stipend is $10,000. Funds may be used only for undergraduate educational expenses. Students selected as national AXA Achievers receive an additional stipend of $15,000 and the offer of an internship.

⑧ **Duration:** 1 year. Awards are not renewable, but recipients may arrange to receive payment in installments over multiple years as long as they continue to meet eligibility requirements.

⑨ **Number awarded:** 52 each year: 1 from each state, the District of Columbia, and Puerto Rico. Of those 52, 10 are designated as national AXA Achievers.

⑩ **Deadline:** November of each year.

Definitions

① **Entry number:** Consecutive number assigned to the references and used to index the entry.

② **Award category:** $ means the award is between $2,000 and $4,999; $$ means it is at least $5,000 or pays part or all of your tuition; if there is no dollar sign there, the amount awarded is between $1,000 and $1,999.

③ **Program title:** Title of scholarship, competition, or award.

④ **Sponsoring organization:** Name, address, telephone number, toll-free number, fax number, email address, and website location (when information was supplied) for the organization sponsoring the program.

⑤ **Summary:** Identifies the major program requirements; read the rest of the entry for additional detail.

⑥ **Eligibility:** Qualifications required of applicants and factors considered in the selection process.

⑦ **Financial data:** Financial details of the program, including fixed sum, average amount, or range of funds offered, expenses for which funds may and may not be applied, and cash-related benefits supplied (e.g., room and board).

⑧ **Duration:** Time period for which support is provided; renewal prospects.

⑨ **Number awarded:** Total number of recipients each year or other specified period.

⑩ **Deadline:** The month by which applications must be submitted. When the sponsor has not specified a deadline date for a program, this field is not included in our entry description.

Note: The information provided for the funding opportunities covered in this book was verified when the entries were prepared. Since then, it is possible that some changes may have occurred (for example, in the address or website URL). If you have any questions about the information provided in a specific entry, send an email to GailSchlachter@rspfunding.com. Be sure to include the name of the program and its entry number as part of your query.

PART ONE

GETTING STARTED

by Douglas Bucher

Searching for Scholarships

If you are reading this book, it's a good bet that you're looking for money to help you achieve your higher-education goals. As you will see, the key to success in this area is motivated, energetic research—a process that you have already started by reading these very words. There are numerous sources of aid available; many of these are listed in this volume. In addition, this book includes other strategies for finding resources, locally and globally, using both technology, such as computers and the Internet, and old-fashioned methods, such as talking to people who may be able to help.

All of the information we will discuss is available to you in books or other easily obtainable sources that will cost you little or nothing to use. Any company that says you have to pay them to research the same data you could research on your own is not worthy of your dollars. Ignore all of the promises. In most cases, the companies will provide no more information than you could have gleaned yourself.

Scholarship Scams

For years, in fact, students' desire to finance their educations has been fodder for those who would take advantage of people with trusting natures. Financial aid personnel at colleges and universities have been aware of such unethical approaches for some time now, and recently the Federal Trade Commission (FTC) issued a warning about these "scholarship scams." Among the telltale signs you should look for—and then stay far away from—are the following:

"We guarantee you'll get a scholarship or your money back." In reality, almost every financial aid applicant is eligible for something. A guarantee like this is, therefore, worth nothing.

"You can't get this information anywhere else." Nonsense. We live in an information-rich society. Any legitimate source of financial aid will make information widely available through a number of means and media. Don't pay a premium for what is free or readily available in an inexpensive format—like this book!

"Credit card or bank account number required to hold scholarship." Don't even think about it. Legitimate scholarship providers do not require this information as a condition for you to receive funds.

"We'll do all the work." Okay, this one is tempting. We are all very busy people with a million things to do who feel that we can't possibly find the time to do this kind of research. But there is only one person who is going to benefit from the kind of work that this entails, and that is you. A pitch like this appeals to the lazy instincts in all of us, but there is no one you can expect to be more motivated to do the research than yourself.

"The scholarship will cost you some money." This one hardly deserves comment. There is a strong preconception in this country that, as a general rule, you need to spend money to make money. While this may be true on Wall Street, it doesn't apply here. The investment you are making is in your education, and the best resource you can invest is your time.

"You are a finalist" or *"You have been selected"* in a contest you never entered. The absurdity of this is clear once you think about it for a moment. It is very flattering to think that some organization pored through the records of every person in the country to find that you are the most qualified to receive its generous award—and you didn't even apply! Remember, if it seems too good to be true, it is.

In other words, *caveat emptor!*

Setting a Timetable for Your Search

If there is one piece of advice that can be a key to a successful search for scholarship funding, it is to start early. In fact, keep in mind that each step described in this book requires a good deal of time. Furthermore, many small sources of funding have deadlines some 9 to 12 months before the beginning of the term for which you will be applying.

When should you start? The answer depends on your personal pace. If you have the time and energy to research a subject extensively for a short period of time, you could start some 14 months before the beginning of school. If, on the other hand, you wish to make this a more leisurely process, give yourself a good 18 months. In any case, the bottom line is that you can never begin too early. When you are done reading this, sit down with a calendar and make a plan. When can you start? How much time can you devote each week?

Here is a summary timetable to help you plan:

- *24–18 months before money is needed:* Perform the extensive searches discussed in this chapter.
- *18–12 months before money is needed:* Write for applications; follow up if necessary.
- *12–9 months before money is needed:* Mail all applications with required documentation.
- *9–6 months before money is needed:* Follow up with any organization from which you have not heard a decision (if deadline has passed).
- *Summer before school:* Notify the financial aid office of any scholarships you have been awarded. Be sure to ask what effect this will have on earlier awards and your options.
- *Late summer right before school:* Write thank-you notes to organizations.
- *Fall:* Begin the process again for renewing scholarships and finding new sources of aid.

Types of Scholarships

The types of scholarships you may receive for your education can be broken down into three general categories: individual scholarships, state scholarships, and loans.

Individual Scholarships

While going through your college search, be sure to ask admissions officers about scholarships. Each school has different rules for scholarship consideration. Be sure to find out about all scholarships available, what must be done to be considered, and—very important—the deadline by which to apply. More and more schools are offering scholarships for reasons other than athletic or academic achievement. Some scholarships are reserved for very specific types of students. See if any of these exist at the colleges to which you are applying. Much of this information might be on their home page, so you can research on your own.

Become familiar with your college's financial aid office, which might be able to provide additional information on scholarship sources. At some schools, the financial aid officers are more familiar with scholarship sources than the admissions officers.

Another great source of scholarship information might be the academic departments with which you are affiliated. Many of the faculty members know about scholarships specifically for your major. Some departments have their own scholarships that other offices on campus might not even know about. Professors also have many contacts outside of the college that might be sources of scholarship information.

State Scholarships

Some state education authorities and other state agencies offer assistance above and beyond the usual tuition-assistance programs. Some states offer aid for particular fields of study to residents of the state who remain in-state to complete their studies. You should contact your state's higher-education agency to investigate opportunities.

Loans and Forgivable Loans

There is another form of aid that predominates in certain fields, particularly those with a shortage of qualified professionals. Often called *forgivable loans,* these arrangements provide funding for school and a guaranteed job after graduation.

Sometimes offered by private employers, sometimes by government agencies, forgivable loans work in the following way: An organization provides funding for a student's academic expenses in the form of a loan. In return, the student agrees to work for the organization (under terms usually outlined in a contract) for a given period of time. If the student keeps up his or her part of the bargain, the loan will be forgiven or reduced. If the student chooses not to work for the organization, he or she is given a repayment schedule and must pay back the entire balance with interest. Depending on the field, the jobs provided are usually competitively paid, though more often than not, they are located in areas that are underserved or understaffed.

Some organizations offer regular loans as well as scholarships. Some philanthropic agencies even offer interest-free loans to students. These can be very good opportunities to save money on interest you would otherwise pay on federal or private loans. Again, consider carefully the terms of any loan agreement you sign.

Getting On with the Search

There are a number of sources of aid to consider and several strategies for finding them. Some sources may be obscure, while others may be quite obvious to you. Who might have money to give? Unions, professional organizations, high schools, clubs, lodges, foundations, and local and state governments might have resources to share with you. At the very least, they are worth exploring.

A parent can easily check with his or her union or professional organization regarding available opportunities. A teacher, guidance counselor, or professor might know of opportunities with a variety of organizations.

Many high school guidance offices have a list of scholarships that have been secured by former students. These scholarships often are provided by local agencies that lack the resources to publicize them in other ways. Contacting guidance offices at local high schools is an effective way to canvass the entire community. While the local scholarships might be small, they can add up to larger sums of money.

You might even consider contacting civic, fraternal, religious, and business organizations in your community. Many of them have scholarships that are not well publicized. These awards are also usually small, but they add up quickly. These organizations enjoy supporting the future of their communities through education and make themselves visible in the yellow pages or on lists at local chambers of commerce. Even if you don't know anyone at a given organization, you should still contact it about the possibility of a scholarship.

I have met students in my career who actually talked some of these organizations into creating scholarships. A few hundred dollars may not be much to an organization, but it can really help an individual recipient. Soliciting these organizations might make you that lucky recipient. They might like your tenacity and award you a scholarship for this. Don't be pushy, but do be aggressive.

Employers represent another major local source of scholarships. You might be working part-time or full-time for a company that offers scholarships to its employees. If it is a national chain, your boss might not even know if a scholarship exists. Ask your boss to check with the central office. If you are planning to attend school locally and keep your job, you might want to check out tuition remission scholarships from your employer.

Many parents or relatives have employers that offer scholarships to dependents. Have your parents check with their benefits/personnel office to see if any programs exist. Don't assume you have to be a high school student or live at home to qualify; you'll find out if such restrictions exist when you ask. Many of these scholarships can be awarded to dependents other than just sons or daughters. Ask all your family members to check out the possibilities.

Graduate Funding

A graduate student is one who is pursuing an advanced degree beyond the bachelor's. When an individual has not yet received a bachelor's degree, he or she is referred to as an undergraduate student. While some aid resources are specifically geared toward undergraduate students, others are earmarked solely for graduate students involved in advanced study of a given field. Knowing this will help you avoid wasting your time on resources for which you are not eligible. Concentrate only on scholarships available to you.

Books

There are many places to search for scholarships. This book contains extensive lists of scholarships, but no book can be totally inclusive. Therefore, as with any research project, you should not depend on only one source. Multiple sources will yield the most extensive data and thus the most scholarship dollars.

There is usually a scholarship section in the reference room of any public library. Many of these books focus exclusively on particular types of scholarships for majors, grade levels, and so on, saving you time you would otherwise spend reading fruitlessly. Of course, there is always the chance that human error may enter into the picture, and you may overlook a valuable source. Having family members look through the same books you're reading will allow you to compare lists and eliminate duplicates. Many people also do group searches with friends. The possibility of your friends applying for the same scholarships should not deter you, because most scholarships offer more than one award, and having more eyes search the same books will reduce the chance of overlooking resources.

Online Resources

Students are increasingly turning to the Internet for scholarship searches, many of which allow you to access data free of charge. The great advantage of using the Internet is that it is less labor-intensive than using books; the computer can match details about yourself with criteria in the database faster than you can, saving valuable time. Another advantage is that most of these sites are up-to-date and have the most current information. Criteria for scholarships change, and using the Internet will allow you to search for the most current criteria. In addition, many schools list their own scholarships with these services, so you may discover special scholarships at schools you might attend. In some cases, you can apply online for scholarships.

There's a good deal of overlap among these databases, but you'll find exclusive listings in each one. Try, then, to search a number of databases; eliminate duplicates by checking the application information on the listings. If you get duplicates, use the application information from the most recently updated scholarship listing.

It's important to have a good basic knowledge about financial aid before searching for scholarships. The Kaplan website at www.kaptest.com is a good place to begin.

Another excellent reference is the "Parents and Students" page on the National Association of Student Financial Aid Administrators (NASFAA) website at www.nasfaa.org. This organization is the professional association for financial aid administrators, and it has links to extensive resources for financial aid.

Many colleges now have websites that contain important information about aid. You may be able to get information about scholarships offered through the college and how to apply. Many of these sites also have links to other financial aid information or scholarship search databases. Check the sites of all colleges you are considering.

Some other sites that might be helpful in your research include the following:

- U.S. Department of Education; www.ed.gov/students
- U.S. Department of Education: Federal Student Aid; www.studentaid.ed.gov
- FastWeb—Scholarship Search; www.fastweb.com
- Scholarship Resource Network Express; www.srnexpress.com
- Scholarships.com; www.scholarships.com
- Reference Service Press Funding; www.rspfunding.com
- Sallie Mae College Answer: www.collegeanswer.com

Many high schools, colleges, and libraries have purchased scholarship databases that you can use to broaden your search. They may not be as up-to-date as the Internet sources, but they should not be overlooked.

How to Apply

As previously mentioned, early planning is important to a successful scholarship search. Once you have your list of addresses of possible donors, you must contact them. Be sure to check the application deadlines for the scholarships you have discovered. Eliminate any for which the deadline has passed or will soon pass (usually within six to eight weeks). This way, you will not waste the donor's or your time. Scholarships that you eliminate now could be resources for following years. Remember, the college experience lasts more than one year; your scholarship research should extend for the number of years you need to complete your degree.

Writing the First Letter

Your first letter to a scholarship provider should be a very simple letter of introduction. Some providers require the initial processing to be done online through a scholarship database. If you must write a letter, it probably will not be read by the actual committee that will choose the scholarship recipient, so there is no need to go into great detail about yourself or why you are applying. Keep it simple so the request moves quickly. Use a regular business letter format, similar to the sample letter below.

Sample Letter of Introduction

Today's Date

AAA Foundation
999 7th Avenue
New York, NY 10000

Attn: Talent Scholarship Office

Dear AAA Foundation,

I am a high school student at ABC High School and am applying to attend XYZ College for fall 2014.

I would like to receive application forms for the Talent Scholarship that I read about in Kaplan's *Scholarships 2014*.

Also, I would like to receive any other scholarship or fellowship program information that is available through your organization. Enclosed is a self-addressed, stamped envelope for your convenience. I have also provided a phone number and email address if you would like to contact me.

Thank you in advance for your assistance and information.

Sincerely,

Suzy Student
123 High Street
Philadelphia, PA 19100
(555) 444-4444
suzys@xxx.com

Try to address the letter to a specific individual. If you have a phone number, call to make sure the letter is going directly to the right office. If there is no phone number or specific office, send your letter to the attention of the scholarship's name. Someone in the organization will know which office should receive your request.

Be sure to date your letter so you remember when it was sent. Include your return address so that the organization can easily send you the application. Keep your letter brief; its purpose is simply to request an application. It will not be used to make any recipient decisions; that is the purpose of the application.

The text should mention the specific scholarships for which you are applying. Some agencies administer more than one scholarship, so this will help ensure that they send you the correct application. If an organization administers more than one scholarship, and you are applying for more than one of them, you should use a separate letter for each scholarship. Mail these letters in separate envelopes.

The letter should briefly describe how you will use the scholarship money (e.g., to attend a certain college, to conduct research, etc.) and it should also mention how you found out about the scholarship. Many agencies like to know how their information is disseminated. They want to make sure it is going to the correct "market" and to a diverse population. They will appreciate this data as they plan future cycles. You should also tell them when you intend to use the money so that they send you information for the right year and ask them to send any other scholarship applications that they administer that might be appropriate for you. Include a phone number and/or an email address in case the organization wants to contact you.

There is no need to send the letter by certified mail, but be sure to include a self-addressed, stamped envelope with the letter. Many of these organizations are nonprofit and will appreciate the help to reduce postage costs. A self-addressed envelope will also get you an earlier response, because the organization won't have to type an envelope. Remember, time is critical!

The Follow-up Letter

Once the initial letters have been mailed, carefully keep track of responses. Be sure to note the application deadline (if known) of each scholarship for your records. Obviously, those due the soonest should be watched very carefully.

If you still have not received anything after six to eight weeks, it is appropriate to send a second letter. You should send your original letter (with a new date) again as if it had never been sent to the organization. It is not wise to send a different letter that says something about the organization not getting or not answering your first request. That could be perceived as being too pushy. You don't want to turn off any possible donors.

If you send a second letter and still receive no response, you might not want to send another letter. Even if the organization's listing contains the most up-to-date information, there's a chance the organization is no longer offering scholarships. You might want to call to ask if the organization has your application and will mail it soon, or if the organization is no longer offering the scholarship. If you don't have a contact number, use directory assistance.

When you call, remember to be polite. You might want to begin your conversation by asking general questions about the scholarship. This way, you can discreetly find out if it is still being offered. If it isn't being offered, ask if the organization has any new scholarship programs for which you qualify. If so, have them send you an application. If the scholarship is still being offered, tell them you have sent a request and want to make sure that they have received it (remember, don't be too aggressive). You might find that it is not easy to confirm that they have the request. If this is the case, ask if you can fax a copy of the letter. Some agencies will be able to tell you if they have the letter, in which case you should ask when you can expect to receive the application. Be sure to confirm the deadline for submission.

Be sure to keep good records on the progress of each individual search. Record notes and conversations on the file copy of the letter so you can easily check the status of the search. Organizations that drop out along the way should be considered when you begin your search again the following year.

The Application

Once you have secured the applications, it's time to begin the process of completing them. You should approach this step as if you are applying for a job. Initial impressions on paper are very important, so you want your application to stand out from all the others. Neatness is very important. You should type your application but first make several photocopies so you can go through some drafts before the final edition. Use all personal resources to review your various drafts. The application should be your own, but seeking input from others can improve it.

Be sure to read the entire application and any accompanying instructions before completing it, because failing to answer as instructed might eliminate you from consideration. For most scholarships, there are many more applicants than recipients. It is easy to eliminate the applicants who did not provide all requested information. Don't lose out because of a mistake that could have been avoided with proper planning.

Many applications require supplemental information from other sources. If such information is needed, be sure to plan your time to secure what is requested. Some items, such as academic transcripts and letters of reference, might take some time to obtain. Don't wait until the last minute; it might be too late to send in a complete application. The importance of planning cannot be overemphasized.

If letters of recommendation are needed, seek people who will provide the most positive influence on your application. You might need recommendations for many of the applications. If this is the case, it is best to have these recommendations tailored to the specific application, because general recommendations do not make as much of an impact. Find out if the recommendations are to be sealed and included with the application or if they are to be sent in separately by the recommendation writers. If the recommendations must be separate, tell the writers not to send them until the day you expect your application to reach the organization, because it is easier for the scholarship provider to match up documents if the application arrives first. If any of the documents are misplaced, you could be eliminated from consideration.

If the instructions say nothing about enclosing other documents, consider including a cover letter with your application. This letter should be short and precise, highlighting the reasons why you would make an excellent recipient of the scholarship. A letter with bullet points often is most effective. You might also want to include a statement of your academic and career objectives and how the donor's scholarship would influence these. A cover letter might help differentiate your application from the others, but don't overdo it. A quick summary is all that is needed.

In mailing your application, there are different techniques that can be used to ensure that it is received. A simple approach is to send the application via certified mail so that you can be sure the envelope gets to the organization. Another approach is to send a response form for the organization with a self-addressed, stamped envelope. This could be a check-off letter to acknowledge that all necessary documents have been received. This approach is particularly helpful if documents are being sent under separate cover. If you send the application via first-class mail, you might want to call the scholarship office (if you have the phone number) a few weeks later to make sure it was received.

When You Get Your Scholarship(s)

Congratulations! You've done the hard work and are now receiving aid from one or a number of organizations. What should you do next?

Thank-You Letters

If you are awarded a scholarship by an organization, foundation, or individual, an important final step is the thank-you letter. After all, many of these organizations award scholarships for purely philanthropic reasons, and the only immediate reward they can expect is sincere thanks. Thank-you letters are an effective method to communicate gratitude, lay groundwork for future renewal, and encourage the continuation of these programs for future recipients.

The letter itself need not be a terribly complicated affair. Short, simple, sincere, and to the point will do just fine (see the sample letter below). You do not need to, nor should you, copy this version verbatim. Your thank-you letter should, like your initial letters and application, let your own personality shine through. If you have nice penmanship, a handwritten version may help achieve the desired personal effect. Remember, you are receiving an award because you deserve it and because someone is willing to grant it. Don't be afraid to let your happiness show!

Sample Thank-You Letter

Today's Date

AAA Foundation
999 7th Avenue
New York, NY 10000

To Whom It May Concern (or, if you have a contact name, by all means use it!),

I am taking this occasion to express my deep appreciation for the opportunity that your generous (grant, loan, etc.) has given me. I know that it will allow me to achieve my goals, and I hope that the results will justify your faith in me.

Thank you for your time and attention.

Sincerely,

Your name

Notifying the School

You must tell your school about any outside scholarships you receive. Most financial aid packages need to be adjusted in order to "make room" for outside sources of aid. This is because most packages contain federal aid and therefore have to follow federal guidelines as to how much aid a student who receives other forms of aid can receive. The internal policies of various schools might also require changes to your package. Most financial aid offices will reduce the least desirable forms of aid first (e.g., loans with higher interest rates, work-study).

If your school guarantees its own scholarship over your academic period and the outside award does not, or it is explicitly one-time-only, it may make more financial sense to turn down the outside offer in order to keep the money your school is offering.

Depending on the kind of outside aid you are receiving, you might also have to make arrangements with the business or bursar's office of your college. Depending on the documentation you have, your school might extend credit to you based upon a certain expectation of funds.

Finally, remember that the aid you are receiving may be contingent on certain aspects of your enrollment; you may have to register for a certain number of credits or a certain major, for example. Keep any requirements for the award in mind as you enroll in school.

Renewing Scholarships for Subsequent Years

Renewal procedures vary depending on the kind of award you receive. Some groups offer one-time-only forms of aid, while others automatically renew previous recipients as long as they are enrolled in an eligible program. More commonly, scholarship programs require new applications each year from all interested parties. Remember that you've done it before; use your knowledge of the process to your advantage. Start early in gathering applications, recommendations, and other supporting materials to reapply for your hard-won award. At this time, you should also consider using the research you have already done to reapply for aid for which you may not have been eligible the previous year. There is no reason to limit your options and waste your hard work from the year before.

Once you are in school, there are usually many announcements of large-scale scholarship competitions. Most schools have specific offices that coordinate these prestigious awards. Sometimes this coordination is done at the financial aid office, but not always. Begin at the aid office; if they don't coordinate or know about these awards, check with the academic dean. Academic deans administer applications for the many awards that are associated with strong academic performance.

Summary

If you remember nothing else from this chapter, be sure to recall the following key points:

Start Early

Give yourself plenty of time to find what you are looking for and apply for it. Missed deadlines are nobody's fault but your own, and even the most benevolent organization will usually not make exceptions to its deadline rules.

Use All Resources and Strategies Available to You

Don't hobble your search by ignoring possibilities you don't know much about. Investigate everything, because you never know when an unlikely source of funding may decide to grant you a scholarship. Look everywhere you can, using every tool available to you. Be sure to use the power of the Internet. Anything else would be cheating yourself.

Know What You Are Looking For

On the other hand, when it becomes clear that a particular source is not appropriate for you, move on. If you are going to be an undergraduate student and you find a listing for graduate aid, it is probably pointless to follow that path any farther.

Follow All Steps and Instructions

You would be surprised at how many people ignore this simple advice. Remember, you are asking for assistance with your education. The least you can do is precisely follow the instructions given to you. One of the qualities these organizations might be looking for is an ability to read and understand instructions and deadlines.

Be Confident and Self-Assured but Polite and Respectful

You need to have a good self-image, a high level of confidence in your abilities, and pride in your past achievements. But remember, nobody owes you anything, and if you treat people with anything less than polite respect, you are almost automatically proving yourself to be unworthy of their assistance. Just show folks the same respect and courtesy that you expect to be shown yourself.

Remember to Thank Those Who Have Helped

Remember, the most that many of these organizations and individuals receive in return for their generosity is the occasional thank you (and maybe a tax deduction!). An expression of gratitude will confirm that they have made the right choice, and it will lay the groundwork for possible renewals.

Don't Pay Anyone to Do This Work for You

No need to dwell on this any further. You have been warned, but if you want to learn more about this subject, the FTC in 1996 inaugurated "Project $cholar$cam," an educational campaign to alert students and parents about fraudulent scholarship companies. These warnings can be found on its website at www.ftc.gov/bcp/conline/edcams/scholarship.

With that, good luck in your search for financial aid and, more importantly, best wishes in all of your academic endeavors.

A Special Note for International Students

In our quickly shrinking world, cross-border education has become an ever more important feature of American colleges. Large and small schools alike are sending students abroad in increasing numbers and have opened at least part of their U.S. enrollment to students from around the world.

If you are a non-U.S. student who is considering coming here to study, you probably already know that while American colleges and universities are highly regarded around the world, the American custom of actually paying for an education is truly a foreign notion. Many countries provide free or heavily subsidized higher education for their citizens. Study in the United States, in contrast, requires careful financial planning—especially for international students, who are cut off from most need-based U.S. government aid programs.

While some students who come here receive funding from their college or university—or from the U.S. government—and others are supported by their home government, the vast majority are here without support other than their savings and family back home. The rules governing those residing in the United States on a student visa largely prohibit or limit the ability to work. The result is that for all but the wealthiest families, study in the United States requires a great deal of sacrifice, and for many it is not even in the realm of possibility.

Fortunately, many of the resources discussed in this book are not necessarily limited to U.S. students. Most of the advice within these pages applies to the international student just as much as to the domestic student. In fact, the one piece of advice that this book hopes to drive home more than any other—start early!—applies to international students even more. Despite the Internet revolution (a technology that you should certainly take advantage of), much business continues to be transacted through the mail. As you may know, international post brings a whole new meaning to the term *snail mail.*

Of course, a key part of your research should be to look for financial assistance at the school you plan to attend. The admissions and financial aid offices may have information on both institutional and external sources of assistance. Many schools also have offices that specialize in assisting international students in all facets of the enrollment process, including finding or facilitating sources of funding. Check your college's website for a guide to services it offers.

There are other sources of information particularly designed for international students, as well:

In addition to administering the Fulbright program, the Institute of International Education (IIE) is a particularly rich source of information on all aspects of international education in the United States:

Institute of International Education
809 United Nations Plaza
New York, NY 10017-3580 USA
Phone: (212) 984-5400
Fax: (212) 984-5452
Website: www.iie.org

Another source of information for international students is NAFSA: Association of International Educators. This is the professional association of those who administer the college international student offices mentioned above.

NAFSA: Association of International Educators
1307 New York Avenue, N.W., 8th Floor
Washington, DC 20005-4701 USA
Phone: (202) 737-3699
Fax: (202) 737-3657
Website: www.nafsa.org

You may also visit the Financial Aid Information Page (FinAid) at www.edupass.org for more general information about financing a U.S. education.

While financial resources for international students are by no means plentiful, opportunities do exist. As international education becomes an ever more important feature of American higher education, you can be sure that more sources of funding will become available. Some schools have begun to work with banks to develop financing tools for this key population. More developments are sure to follow.

Unrestricted

1 $ ACCESS MISSOURI FINANCIAL ASSISTANCE PROGRAM

Missouri Department of Higher Education
Attn: Student Financial Assistance
205 Jefferson Street
P.O. Box 1469
Jefferson City, MO 65102–1469
Phone: (573) 526–7958; (800) 473–6757; Fax: (573) 751–6635;
Email: info@dhe.mo.gov
Web: www.dhe.mo.gov/ppc/grants/accessmo.php

Summary: To provide financial assistance to college students in Missouri who demonstrate financial need.

Eligibility: Open to residents of Missouri who are full–time students working on their first baccalaureate degree at a participating postsecondary school in the state. Applicants must have an expected family contribution (EFC) of $12,000 or less. Students working on a degree or certificate in theology or divinity are not eligible. U.S. citizenship or permanent resident status is required.

Financial data: At public 2–year colleges, stipends range from $300 to $1,000; at public 4–year colleges and universities, stipends range from $1,000 to $2,150; at private institutions, stipends range from $2,000 to $4,600.

Duration: 1 year; may be renewed, provided the recipient maintains a GPA of 2.5 or higher and meets the financial need limitation.

Number awarded: Varies each year; recently, 38,958 of these scholarships, worth more than $72 million, were awarded.

Deadline: March of each year.

2 $ A.D. OSHERMAN SCHOLARSHIP FUND

Greater Houston Community Foundation
Attn: Scholarship Coordinator
5120 Woodway Drive, Suite 6000
Houston, TX 77056
Phone: (713) 333–2205; Fax: (713) 333–2220;
Email: lgardner@ghcf.org
Web: www.ghcf.org/Receive/Scholarships/AD–Osherman–Scholarship–Fund

Summary: To provide financial assistance to residents of Texas who are members of designated groups and are interested in attending college in any state.

Eligibility: Open to Texas residents who are graduating high school seniors or full–time freshmen, sophomores, or juniors at an accredited public 2– or 4–year college or university in any state. Applicants must qualify as a member of a recognized minority group, the first in their family to attend college, or a veteran with active service, particularly service in Iraq or Afghanistan. They must have a GPA of 2.75 or higher and a history of community service. Financial need is considered in the selection process.

Financial data: The stipend is $2,500 per year for students at 4–year universities or $1,500 per year for students at 2–year colleges.

Duration: 1 year; recipients may reapply.

Number awarded: 2 each year.

Deadline: March of each year.

3 ADO MEMORIAL SCHOLARSHIPS

American Darts Organization
230 North Crescent Way, Suite K
Anaheim, CA 92801–6707
Phone: (714) 254–0212; Fax: (714) 254–0214;
Email: office@adodarts.com
Web: www.adodarts.com/?s=scholarship

Summary: To provide financial aid for college to players in the American Darts Organization (ADO) Youth Playoff Program.

Eligibility: Open to ADO members who are area or national winners in the Youth Playoff Program and under 21 years of age. Applicants must be enrolled or accepted at an accredited U.S. college as a full–time student with a GPA of 2.0 or higher. They must be U.S. citizens or have lived in the United States for at least 2 years.

Financial data: Stipends are: $500 for quarter finalists in the National Championship; $750 for each semifinalist; $1,000 for each runner–up; and $1,500 for each National Champion. Any participant/winner who is eligible to compete in more than 1 area/national championship may repeat as a scholarship winner, up to $8,000 in prizes. Funds may be used for any legitimate college expense, including fees for parking stickers, library fees, student union fees, tuition, and books.

Duration: The funds are awarded annually.

Number awarded: 8 each year: 4 quarter finalists, 2 semifinalists, 1 runner–up, and 1 National Champion.

Deadline: Deadline not specified.

4 $ "ADVICE TO YOUR HIGH SCHOOL SELF" SCHOLARSHIP

CampusDiscovery.com
c/o WiseChoiceBrands, LLC
3020 Hartley Road, Suite 220
Jacksonville, FL 32257
Email: info@campusdiscovery.com
Web: www.campusdiscovery.com/college–scholarships

Summary: To recognize and reward college students and recent graduates who complete an online essay on college.

Eligibility: Open to students currently enrolled at an accredited 2– or 4–year college or university and to recent graduates of those institutions. Applicants must complete an online survey about their college and also submit a 200–word essay on advice about college they would give themselves if they were still in high school. Selection is based on writing ability (25%), wisdom (25%), originality (25%), and overall excellence (25%). U.S. citizenship or permanent resident status is required.

Financial data: The award is $2,500. If the recipient is still attending college, funds are disbursed directly to the institution. If the recipient has already graduated, funds are paid directly to the individual.

Duration: The award is presented annually.

Number awarded: 1 each year.

Deadline: January of each year.

5 $ AFA AIR FORCE SPOUSE SCHOLARSHIPS

Air Force Association
Attn: Manager, National Aerospace Awards
1501 Lee Highway
Arlington, VA 22209–1198
Phone: (703) 247–5800, ext. 4807; (800) 727–3337, ext. 4807; Fax: (703) 247–5853;
Email: lcross@afa.org
Web: www.afa.org/aef/aid/spouse.asp

Summary: To provide financial assistance for undergraduate or graduate study to spouses of Air Force members.

Eligibility: Open to spouses of active–duty Air Force, Air National Guard, or Air Force Reserve members. Spouses who are themselves military members or in ROTC are not eligible. Applicants must have a GPA of 3.5 or higher in college (or high school if entering college for the first time) and be able to provide proof of acceptance into an accredited undergraduate or graduate degree program. They must submit a 2–page essay on their academic and career goals, the motivation that led them to that decision, and how Air Force and other local community activities in which they are involved will enhance their goals. Selection is based on the essay and 2 letters of recommendation.

Financial data: The stipend is $2,500; funds are sent to the recipients' schools to be used for any reasonable cost related to working on a degree.

Duration: 1 year; nonrenewable.

Number awarded: Varies each year; recently, 3 of these scholarships were awarded.

Deadline: April of each year.

6 AFRICAN AMERICAN FUTURE ACHIEVERS SCHOLARSHIP PROGRAM

Ronald McDonald House Charities
Attn: U.S. Scholarship Program
One Kroc Drive
Oak Brook, IL 60523
Phone: (630) 623–7048; Fax: (630) 623–7488;
Email: info@rmhc.org
Web: rmhc.org/what–we–do/rmhc–u–s–scholarships

Summary: To provide financial assistance for college to African American high school seniors in specified geographic areas.

Eligibility: Open to high school seniors in designated McDonald's market areas who are legal residents of the United States and have at least 1 parent of African American or Black Caribbean heritage. Applicants must be planning to enroll full time at an accredited 2– or 4–year college, university, or vocational/technical school. They must have a GPA of 2.7 or higher. Along with their application, they must submit a personal statement, up to 2 pages in length, on their African American or Black Caribbean background, career goals, and desire to contribute to their community; information about unique, personal, or financial circumstances may be added. Selection is based on that statement, high school transcripts, a letter of recommendation, and financial need.

Financial data: Most awards are $1,000 per year. Funds are paid directly to the recipient's school.

Duration: 1 year; nonrenewable.

Number awarded: Varies each year; since RMHC began this program, it has awarded more than $44 million in scholarships.

Deadline: January of each year.

7 $ AIEF SCHOLARSHIP PROGRAM

American Indian Education Foundation
2401 Eglin Street
Rapid City, SD 57703
Phone: (866) 866–8642;
Email: mlee@nrc1.org
Web: www.nrcprograms.org

Summary: To provide financial assistance for college to American Indian and Alaskan Native students.

Eligibility: Open to full–time students of Native American or Alaskan Native descent who are currently attending or planning to attend a 2–year college, a 4–year college or university, or a vocational/technical school. Applicants may be either graduating high school seniors or undergraduates who are entering, continuing, or returning to school. Along with their application, they must submit a 4–page essay in which they describe themselves as a student, their ultimate career goals, their plans for working in or with the Indian community, and their participation in leadership and/or community service activities. A GPA between 2.0 to 3.4 is desirable, but all current or future undergraduate students are encouraged to apply. An ACT score of 14 or higher is desirable. Financial need is considered in the selection process.

Financial data: The stipend is $2,000 per year. Funds are paid directly to the recipient's college or university.

Duration: 1 year; may be renewed, provided the recipient maintains a GPA of 2.0 or higher.

Number awarded: More than 225 each year.

Deadline: April of each year.

8 $ AIRMEN MEMORIAL FOUNDATION SCHOLARSHIP PROGRAM

Air Force Sergeants Association
Attn: Scholastic Coordinator
5211 Auth Road
Suitland, MD 20746
Phone: (301) 899–3500; (800) 638–0594; Fax: (301) 899–8136;
Email: balsobrooks@hqafsa.org
Web: www.hqafsa.org

Summary: To provide financial assistance for college to the dependent children of enlisted Air Force personnel.

Eligibility: Open to the unmarried children (including stepchildren and legally adopted children) of active–duty, retired, or veteran members of the U.S. Air Force, Air National Guard, or Air Force Reserves. Applicants must be attending or planning to attend an accredited academic institution. They must have an unweighted GPA of 3.5 or higher. Along with their application, they must submit 1) a paragraph on their life objectives and what they plan to do with the education they receive; and 2) an essay on the most urgent problem facing society today. High school seniors must also submit a transcript of all high school grades and a record of their SAT or ACT scores. Selection is based on academic record, character, leadership skills, writing ability, versatility, and potential for success. Financial need is not a consideration.

Financial data: Stipends are $2,000, $1,500, or $1,000; funds may be used for tuition, room and board, fees, books, supplies, and transportation.

Duration: 1 year; may be renewed if the recipient maintains full–time enrollment.

Number awarded: Varies each year; recently, 30 of these scholarships were awarded: 18 at $2,000, 4 at $1,500, and 8 at $1,000, including 3 sponsored by the United Services Automobile Association (USAA) Insurance Corporation. Since this program began, it has awarded more than $421,000 in financial aid.

Deadline: March of each year.

9 $$ ALABAMA FIRST IN FAMILY SCHOLARSHIPS

J. Craig and Page T. Smith Scholarship Foundation
Attn: Foundation Administrator
400 Caldwell Trace Park
Indian Springs, AL 35242
Phone: (205) 202–4076;
Email: ahrian@smithscholarships.com
Web: smithscholarships.com

Summary: To provide financial assistance to high school seniors in Alabama planning to attend college in the state, especially those who are the first in their family to attend college.

Eligibility: Open to seniors graduating from high schools in Alabama who have a grade average of "C+" or higher. Applicants must be planning to enroll full time at a 4–year college or university in the state. They must submit an essay on their future plans or goals of accomplishment for themselves, an essay documenting community and civic–oriented activities or assistance to family members, an official transcript, ACT or SAT scores (no minimum is required), and documentation of financial need. Special consideration is given to applicants who will be the first in either their mother's or father's (or both parents') families to attend college.

Financial data: Funding covers full payment of tuition, campus room, board, and books.

Duration: 4 years, provided the recipient remains enrolled full time, makes significant progress toward completion of an undergraduate degree, verifies community service during the school year, and maintains a GPA of at least "C+."

Number awarded: Approximately 10 each year.

Deadline: January of each year.

10 $$ ALABAMA G.I. DEPENDENTS' SCHOLARSHIP PROGRAM

Alabama Department of Veterans Affairs
770 Washington Avenue, Suite 470
Montgomery, AL 36102–1509
Phone: (334) 242–5077; Fax: (334) 242–5102;
Email: willie.moore@va.state.al.us
Web: www.va.state.al.us/scholarship.htm

Summary: To provide educational benefits to the dependents of disabled, deceased, and other Alabama veterans.

Eligibility: Open to children, spouses, and unremarried widow(er)s of veterans who are currently rated as 20% or more service–connected disabled or were so rated at time of death, were a former prisoner of war, have been declared missing in action, died as the result of a service–connected disability, or died while on active military duty in the line of duty. The veteran must have been a permanent civilian resident of Alabama for at least 1 year prior to entering active military service and served honorably for at least 90 days during war time (or less, in case of death or service–connected disability). Veterans who were not Alabama residents at the time of entering active military service may also qualify if they have a 100% disability and were permanent residents of Alabama for at least 5 years prior to filing the application for this program or prior to death, if deceased. Children and stepchildren must be under the age of 26, but spouses and widow(er)s may be of any age. Spouses cease to be eligible if they become divorced from the qualifying veteran. Widow(er)s cease to be eligible if they remarry.

Financial data: Eligible dependents may attend any state–supported Alabama institution of higher learning or enroll in a prescribed course of study at any Alabama state–supported trade school without payment of any tuition, book fees, or laboratory charges.

Duration: This is an entitlement program for 5 years of full–time undergraduate or graduate study or part–time equivalent for all qualifying children and for spouses and unremarried widow(er)s who veteran spouse is or was rated 100% disabled or meets other qualifying requirements. Spouses and unremarried widow(er)s whose veteran spouse is or was rated between 20% and 90% disabled may attend only 3 standard academic years.

Number awarded: Varies each year.

Deadline: Applications may be submitted at any time.

11 $$ ALABAMA JUNIOR AND COMMUNITY COLLEGE ATHLETIC SCHOLARSHIPS

Alabama Commission on Higher Education
Attn: Grants Coordinator
100 North Union Street
P.O. Box 302000
Montgomery, AL 36130–2000
Phone: (334) 242–2273; Fax: (334) 242–0268;
Email: cheryl.newton@ache.alabama.gov
Web: www.ache.alabama.gov/StudentAsst/Programs.htm

Summary: To provide financial assistance to athletes in Alabama interested in attending a junior or community college in the state.

Eligibility: Open to full–time students enrolled in public junior and community colleges in Alabama. Selection is based on athletic ability as determined through try–outs.

Financial data: Awards cover the cost of tuition and books.

Duration: Scholarships are available as long as the recipient continues to participate in the designated sport or activity.
Number awarded: Varies each year.
Deadline: Deadline not specified.

12 $$ ALABAMA POLICE OFFICER'S AND FIREFIGHTER'S SURVIVOR'S EDUCATIONAL ASSISTANCE PROGRAM

Alabama Commission on Higher Education
Attn: Grants Coordinator
100 North Union Street
P.O. Box 302000
Montgomery, AL 36130–2000
Phone: (334) 242–2273; Fax: (334) 242–0268;
Email: cheryl.newton@ache.alabama.gov
Web: www.ache.alabama.gov/StudentAsst/Programs.htm

Summary: To provide financial assistance to the spouses and dependents of deceased police officers and firefighters in Alabama interested in attending college in the state.
Eligibility: Open to the unremarried spouses and children of police officers and firefighters killed in the line of duty in Alabama. Applicants may be high school seniors or currently–enrolled undergraduates in Alabama.
Financial data: Grants are offered to cover tuition, fees, books, and supplies. There is no limit on the amount awarded to recipients.
Duration: 1 year; may be renewed.
Number awarded: Varies each year.
Deadline: Deadline not specified.

13 $ ALABAMA STUDENT ASSISTANCE PROGRAM

Alabama Commission on Higher Education
Attn: Grants Coordinator
100 North Union Street
P.O. Box 302000
Montgomery, AL 36130–2000
Phone: (334) 242–2273; Fax: (334) 242–0268;
Email: cheryl.newton@ache.alabama.gov
Web: www.ache.alabama.gov/StudentAsst/Programs.htm

Summary: To provide financial assistance to undergraduate students who are residents of Alabama and interested in attending college in the state.
Eligibility: Open to residents of Alabama who are attending or planning to attend eligible Alabama institutions (nearly 80 schools participate in this program). Applicants must be able to demonstrate financial need. Eligible students are required to submit the Free Application for Federal Student Aid (FAFSA).
Financial data: Stipends range from $300 to $2,500 per academic year.
Duration: 1 year; may be renewed.
Deadline: Deadline not specified.

14 ALABAMA STUDENT GRANT PROGRAM

Alabama Commission on Higher Education
Attn: Grants Coordinator
100 North Union Street
P.O. Box 302000
Montgomery, AL 36130–2000
Phone: (334) 242–2273; Fax: (334) 242–0268;
Email: cheryl.newton@ache.alabama.gov
Web: www.ache.alabama.gov/StudentAsst/Programs.htm

Summary: To provide financial assistance to undergraduates at designated private colleges or universities in Alabama.
Eligibility: Open to undergraduate students who are attending 1 of 14 designated private colleges or universities in Alabama on at least a half–time basis. Alabama residency is required, but financial need is not considered.
Financial data: Stipends up to $1,200 per year are available.
Number awarded: Varies each year.
Deadline: Each participating institution sets its own deadline date.

15 $$ ALABAMA TWO–YEAR COLLEGE ACADEMIC SCHOLARSHIP PROGRAM

Alabama Commission on Higher Education
Attn: Grants Coordinator
100 North Union Street
P.O. Box 302000
Montgomery, AL 36130–2000
Phone: (334) 242–2273; Fax: (334) 242–0268;
Email: cheryl.newton@ache.alabama.gov
Web: www.ache.alabama.gov/StudentAsst/Programs.htm

Summary: To provide financial assistance to entering junior college students in Alabama.
Eligibility: Open to students who have been accepted for enrollment at any Alabama public 2–year postsecondary educational institution. Selection is based on academic merit. Preference is given to Alabama residents.
Financial data: Scholarships are available to cover the cost of in–state tuition and books.
Duration: 1 year; may be renewed if the recipient maintains a high level of academic achievement.
Number awarded: Varies each year.
Deadline: Deadline not specified.

16 $$ ALASKA FREE TUITION FOR SPOUSE OR DEPENDENT OF ARMED SERVICES MEMBER

Department of Military and Veterans Affairs
Attn: Office of Veterans Affairs
P.O. Box 5800
Fort Richardson, AK 99505–5800
Phone: (907) 428–6016; Fax: (907) 428–6019;
Email: jerry_beale@ak–prepared.com
Web: veterans.alaska.gov/state_benefits.htm

Summary: To provide financial assistance for college to dependents and spouses in Alaska of servicemembers who died or were declared prisoners of war or missing in action.
Eligibility: Open to the spouses and dependent children of Alaska residents who died in the line of duty, died of injuries sustained in the line of duty, or were listed by the Department of Defense as a prisoner of war or missing in action. Applicants must be in good standing at a state–supported educational institution in Alaska.
Financial data: Those eligible may attend any state–supported educational institution in Alaska without payment of tuition or fees.
Duration: 1 year; may be renewed.
Number awarded: Varies each year.
Deadline: Deadline not specified.

17 ALASKA LEGION AUXILIARY SCHOLARSHIP

American Legion Auxiliary
Department of Alaska
Attn: Secretary/Treasurer
P.O. Box 670750
Chugiak, AK 99567
Phone: (907) 688–0241; Fax: (907) 688–0241;
Email: aladepak@qci.net
Web: alaskalegionauxiliary.org/Scholarship.htm

Summary: To provide financial assistance to veterans' children in Alaska who plan to attend college in any state.
Eligibility: Open to the children of veterans who served during eligibility dates for membership in the American Legion. Applicants must be between 17 and 24 years of age, high school seniors or graduates who have not yet attended an institution of higher learning, and residents of Alaska. They must be planning to attend a college or university in any state.
Financial data: The stipend is $1,500, half of which is payable each semester toward tuition, matriculation, laboratory, or similar fees.
Duration: 1 year.
Number awarded: 1 each year.Thurgood Marshall College Fund.
Deadline: March of each year.

18 $ ALASKA PERFORMANCE SCHOLARSHIPS

Alaska Commission on Postsecondary Education
Attn: AlaskAdvantage Programs
3030 Vintage Boulevard
P.O. Box 110505
Juneau, AK 99811–0505
Phone: (907) 465–6779; (866) 427–5683; Fax: (907) 465–5316; TDD: (907) 465–3143;
Email: customer_service@alaska.gov
Web: acpe.alaska.gov/STUDENT–PARENT/Grants_Scholarships.aspx

Summary: To provide financial assistance to high school seniors in Alaska residents who complete a rigorous curriculum in high school and plan to attend college in the state.

Eligibility: Open to seniors graduating from high schools in Alaska who have completed a defined academic curriculum. Applicants must be planning to attend a college or university in the state and be able to demonstrate unmet costs of attendance at the school where they plan to enroll. To receive the highest level of support, they must have a GPA of 3.5 or higher and a score of at least 25 on the ACT or 1680 on the SAT; for the second–highest level, they must have a GPA of 3.0 and a score of at least 23 on the ACT or 1560 on the SAT; for the third–highest level, they must have a GPA of 2.5 or higher and a score of at least 21 on the ACT or 1450 on the SAT. Students planning to enroll in a career and technical education certificate program may substitute equivalent WorkKeys scores for ACT or SAT scores.

Financial data: Stipends may not exceed the students' unmet cost of attendance, ranging up to $4,755 per year for the highest level of support, $3,566 per year for the second–highest level of support, or $2,378 for the third–highest level of support. Stipends are prorated for students enrolled less than full time. Funds are disbursed directly to the postsecondary institution.

Duration: 1 year; may be renewed up to 3 additional years, provided the recipient remains enrolled at least half time, makes satisfactory academic progress, and continues to meet residency and financial need requirements.

Number awarded: Varies each year; recently, the program awarded more than $3 million in assistance to more than 900 high school seniors.

Deadline: Deadline not specified.

19 ALASKA SEA SERVICES SCHOLARSHIPS

Navy League of the United States
Attn: Scholarships
2300 Wilson Boulevard, Suite 200
Arlington, VA 22201–5424
Phone: (703) 528–1775; (800) 356–5760; Fax: (703) 528–2333;
Email: scholarships@navyleague.org
Web: www.navyleague.org/corporate/donate/scholarship.html

Summary: To provide financial assistance to spouses and dependent children of naval personnel in Alaska who are interested in attending college in any state.

Eligibility: Open to the spouses and dependent children of personnel serving in the Navy, Marine Corps, or Coast Guard (active duty or Reserve), retired from those services, or were serving at the time of death or missing in action status. Applicants must be residents of Alaska enrolled or planning to enroll full time at an accredited 4–year college or university in any state to work on an undergraduate degree. Selection is based on academic proficiency, character, leadership ability, community involvement, and financial need.

Financial data: The stipend is $1,000 per year; funds are paid directly to the academic institution for tuition, books, and fees.

Duration: 1 year; may be renewed 1 additional year.

Number awarded: Up to 4 each year.

Deadline: February of each year.

20 ALBERT BAKER FUND STUDENT FINANCIAL AID

Albert Baker Fund
777 Campus Commons Road, Suite 165
Sacramento, CA 95825–8309
Phone: (916) 643–9999; (800) 269–0388; Fax: (916) 568–1372;
Email: admin@albertbakerfund.org
Web: www.albertbakerfund.org

Summary: To provide financial aid (in the form of grants and loans) to undergraduate, graduate, and vocational students in the United States and Canada who are Christian Scientists.

Eligibility: Open to students who are Christian Scientists and members of The Mother Church (the First Church of Christ, Scientist in Boston, Massachusetts) or a branch church. Applicants must be enrolled or planning to enroll at least half time as an undergraduate or graduate student at an accredited college, university, or accredited vocational school in the United States or Canada. They must have a GPA of 2.5 or higher and be able to demonstrate financial need. U.S. or Canadian citizenship is required.

Financial data: Financial aid is provided in the form of grants and loans (amount not specified). For loans, interest rates are fixed at 3%; they must be repaid within 10 years.

Duration: 1 year; may be renewed.

Number awarded: Varies each year; recently, the program awarded $370,000 in grants and $515,000 in loans to 557 North American students (including 407 undergraduates, 71 graduate students, and 79 vocational students).

Deadline: February, May, September, or November of each year.

21 $ ALBERT YANNI SCHOLARSHIP PROGRAM

West Virginia Department of Education
Attn: Office of Career and Technical Innovation
1900 Kanawha Boulevard, East
Building 6, Room 221
Charleston, WV 25305
Phone: (304) 558–2389; Fax: (304) 558–0048;
Email: gcoulson@access.k12.wv.us
Web: careertech.k12.wv.us

Summary: To provide financial assistance to high school seniors in West Virginia who plan to enroll in a postsecondary technical program in any state.

Eligibility: Open to seniors graduating from public high schools in West Virginia who have completed at least 4 units in a single technical concentration. Applicants must be planning to attend an accredited postsecondary institution or technical center in any state to work on a certificate or degree in a career field related to their high school technical concentration. They must rank in the top 25% of their class and have a GPA of 3.0 or higher with no grades below a "C." Along with their application, they must submit a 500–word essay on how their participation in high school career and technical education relates to the course of study they will be pursuing in postsecondary school, their career goal, their plan for achieving their career goal, and any paid or unpaid work experience they have and how those experiences have influenced their career plans. Selection is based on the essay (50 points for content and 50 points for form); recommendations from an academic teacher (25 points), a technical teacher (25 points), and a peer (10 points); and awards, honors, and school and community involvement (40 points).

Financial data: The stipend is $2,000.

Duration: 1 year.

Number awarded: 20 each year.

Deadline: March of each year.

22 $$ ALEXANDER GRAHAM BELL COLLEGE SCHOLARSHIP AWARDS PROGRAM

Alexander Graham Bell Association for the Deaf and Hard of Hearing
Attn: College Scholarship Program
3417 Volta Place, N.W.
Washington, DC 20007–2778
Phone: (202) 337–5220; Fax: (202) 337–8314; TDD: (202) 337–5221;
Email: financialaid@agbell.org
Web: nc.agbell.org/page.aspx?pid=493

Summary: To provide financial assistance to undergraduate students with moderate to profound hearing loss.

Eligibility: Open to full–time undergraduate students who have been diagnosed with a moderate to profound bilateral hearing loss prior to their fourth birthday (hearing loss averages 60dB or greater in the better ear in the speech frequencies of 500, 1000, and 2000 Hz). Applicants must be committed to using spoken language as their primary mode of communication. They must be accepted or enrolled at a mainstream college or university and have a GPA of 3.25 or higher. Along with their application, they must submit a 1–page essay on 1 of the following topics: 1) if they could invent or improve upon a product, what it would be and why; 2) if they could change 1 thing to improve society on a local or global level, what it would be and why; or 3) their goals, how or why they became their goals, and the impact they hope to have over the course of their life. Financial need is not considered in the selection process.

Financial data: Stipends range from $1,000 to $10,000 per year.

Duration: 1 year; may be renewed 1 additional year.

Number awarded: Varies each year; recently, 18 of these scholarships were awarded.

Deadline: February of each year.

23 ALICE DODD MEMORIAL SCHOLARSHIP FOR OUTSTANDING COMMUNITY SERVICE

Georgia District Civitan Foundation, Inc.
c/o Kenny Martin, Scholarship Chair
2063 Julianne Road
Rentz, GA 31075–3354
Phone: (478) 275–0506;
Email: kmartin@nlamerica.com
Web: www.georgiacivitan.org

Summary: To provide financial assistance to high school seniors in Georgia who have an outstanding record of community service and plan to attend college in any state.

Eligibility: Open to seniors graduating from high schools in Georgia and planning to attend an accredited college or university in any state. Membership in

Civitan International is not required, but Junior Civitan Club members are encouraged to apply. Interested students must submit a 500–word essay on their community activities and how those experiences have prepared them for life. In the selection process, academic achievement and financial need are considered, but the overwhelming factor is community service involvement.
Financial data: The winner receives $1,200 and the runner–up receives $800. Funds are paid directly to the student.
Duration: 1 year.
Number awarded: 2 each year.
Deadline: January of each year.

24 $$ ALL IOWA OPPORTUNITY SCHOLARSHIPS

Iowa College Student Aid Commission
603 East 12th Street, Fifth Floor
Des Moines, IA 50319
Phone: (515) 725–3400; (877) 272–4456; Fax: (515) 725–3401;
Email: info@iowacollegeaid.gov
Web: www.iowacollegeaid.gov/ScholarshipsGrants/scholarshipsgrants.html
Summary: To provide financial assistance to high school seniors and graduates in Iowa who demonstrate financial need and plan to attend college in the state.
Eligibility: Open to 1) seniors graduating from high schools in Iowa who have a GPA of 2.5 or higher and plan to attend an eligible Iowa college or university; and 2) Iowa residents who are entering an eligible Iowa college or university within 2 years of graduating from high school. Applicants must complete the Free Application for Federal Student Aid (FAFSA). Priority is given to students who participated in the federal TRIO programs and to applicants who graduated from alternative high schools or alternative high school programs.
Financial data: Stipends range up to the average tuition and fee rate at Iowa Regent Universities; recently, that was $7,806 per year.
Duration: 1 year; may be renewed.
Number awarded: Varies each year.
Deadline: Priority is given to students who apply before the end of February of each year. Applications received after that date are considered only if funds remain available.

25 ALL–INK COLLEGE SCHOLARSHIPS

All–Ink.com
1460 North Main Street, Suite 2
Spanish Fork, UT 84660
Phone: (801) 794–0123; (888) 567–6511; Fax: (801) 794–0124;
Email: CSP@all–ink.com
Web: www.all–ink.com/scholarship.aspx
Summary: To provide financial assistance for college or graduate school to students who submit a scholarship application online.
Eligibility: Open to U.S. citizens and permanent residents who are enrolled or planning to enroll at an accredited college or university at any academic level from freshman through graduate student. Applicants must have a GPA of 2.5 or higher. They must submit, through an online process, an essay of 50 to 200 words on a person who has had the greatest impact on their life and another essay of the same length on what they hope to achieve in their personal and professional life after graduation. Applications are not accepted through the mail.
Financial data: The stipend is $1,000.
Duration: 1 year.
Number awarded: Varies each year; recently 5 of these scholarships were awarded.
Deadline: December of each year.

26 $ ALL–USA COLLEGE ACADEMIC TEAM

USA Today
Attn: Communications Director
7950 Jones Branch Drive
McLean, VA 22108–9995
Phone: (703) 854–5304;
Email: hzimmerman@usatoday.com
Web: www.usatoday.com/marketing/academic_teams/index.html
Summary: To recognize and reward outstanding college students in the United States.
Eligibility: Open to full–time college or university students of at least junior standing at accredited 4–year institutions in the United States. Candidates must be nominated by college presidents or faculty members. U.S. citizenship is not required. Nominees submit a 500–word essay describing their most outstanding original academic or intellectual product. Selection is based primarily on the students' ability to describe their endeavor in their own words.
Financial data: Winners receive $2,500 in cash prizes and are guests of *USA Today* at a special awards luncheon.
Duration: This competition is held annually.
Number awarded: 20 students receive recognition in *USA Today;* and receive cash prizes.
Deadline: May of each year.

27 $ ALL–USA COMMUNITY COLLEGE ACADEMIC TEAM

Phi Theta Kappa
Attn: Scholarship Programs Department
1625 Eastover Drive
Jackson, MS 39211
Phone: (601) 987–5741; (800) 946–9995; Fax: (601) 984–3550;
Email: scholarship.programs@ptk.org
Web: www.ptkfoundation.org/become–a–member/scholarships/academic–teams
Summary: To recognize and reward the outstanding achievements of community college students.
Eligibility: Open to students who have completed at least 36 hours at a community college in the United States (including 30 hours completed within the past 5 years) and are on track to earn an associate or bachelor's degree. Candidates must be nominated by a designated official at their college. Nominees must have a cumulative GPA of at least 3.5 for all college course work completed in the last 5 years, regardless of institution attended. They must submit a 2–page essay describing their most significant endeavor since attending community college in which they applied their academic or intellectual skills from their community college education to benefit their school, community, or society. Selection is based on information in the essay; awards, honors, and recognition for academic achievement; academic rigor and GPA; participation in honors programs; and service to the college and the community.
Financial data: The award is $2,500.
Duration: The competition is held annually.
Number awarded: 20 each year.
Deadline: November of each year.

28 ALPHA GAMMA DELTA ETA ALUMNAE SCHOLARSHIP

Putnam County Community Foundation
Attn: Scholarship Manager
2 South Jackson Street
P.O. Box 514
Greencastle, IN 46135
Phone: (765) 653–4978; Fax: (765) 653–6385;
Email: mwhited@pcfoundation.org
Web: www.pcfoundation.org/scholar_listings_home.html
Summary: To provide financial assistance to upper–division students from any state enrolled at colleges in Indiana.
Eligibility: Open to residents of any state entering their junior or senior year at an accredited college or university in Indiana. Applicants must have a GPA of 3.0 or higher. Along with their application, they must submit an essay on their plans for the future, who or what influenced those plans, and the reason they seek this scholarship. Selection is based on academic ability, intellectual and social commitment, extracurricular achievements, and ability to articulate a career plan that shows motivation, initiative, and commitment.
Financial data: A stipend is awarded (amount not specified).
Duration: 1 year; recipients may reapply.
Number awarded: 1 or more each year.
Deadline: March of each year.

29 $ ALPHA KAPPA ALPHA UNDERGRADUATE SCHOLARSHIPS

Alpha Kappa Alpha Sorority, Inc.
Attn: Educational Advancement Foundation
5656 South Stony Island Avenue
Chicago, IL 60637
Phone: (773) 947–0026; (800) 653–6528; Fax: (773) 947–0277;
Email: akaeaf@akaeaf.net
Web: www.akaeaf.org/undergraduate_scholarships.htm
Summary: To provide financial assistance to students (especially African American women) who are working on an undergraduate degree in any field.
Eligibility: Open to undergraduate students who are enrolled full time as sophomores or higher in an accredited degree–granting institution and are

planning to continue their program of education. Applicants may apply either for a scholarship based on merit (requires a GPA of 3.0 or higher) or on financial need (requires a GPA of 2.5 or higher). Along with their application, they must submit 1) a list of honors, awards, and scholarships received; 2) a list of organizations in which they have memberships, especially minority organizations; and 3) a statement of their personal and career goals, including how this scholarship will enhance their ability to attain those goals. The sponsor is a traditionally African American women's sorority.
Financial data: Stipends range from $750 to $2,500.
Duration: 1 year; nonrenewable.
Number awarded: Varies each year; recently, 69 of these scholarships, with a total value of $74,700 were awarded.
Deadline: April of each year.

30 ALPHONSE A. MIELE SCHOLARSHIP

UNICO National
Attn: UNICO Foundation, Inc.
271 U.S. Highway 46 West, Suite A–108
Fairfield, NJ 07004
Phone: (973) 808–0035; (800) 877–1492; Fax: (973) 808–0043;
Email: uniconational@unico.org
Web: www.unico.org/scholarships.asp
Summary: To provide financial assistance for college to Italian American high school seniors.
Eligibility: Open to high school seniors of Italian origin (i.e., at least 1 parent or grandparent of Italian origin) who are planning to attend an accredited college or university. Applicants must have a GPA of 3.0 or higher and be U.S. citizens. Along with their application, they must submit SAT or ACT test scores and a letter of recommendation from a UNICO chapter in the city or town where they live. Selection is based on citizenship, leadership, character, personality, community service, and financial need.
Financial data: The stipend is $1,500 per year.
Duration: 4 years.
Number awarded: 1 each year.
Deadline: April of each year.

31 $ AMANDA "BABE" SLATTERY SCHOLARSHIPS

Western Athletic Scholarship Association
Attn: Scholarship Coordinator
13730 Loumont Street
Whittier, CA 90601
Summary: To provide financial assistance for college to outstanding softball players.
Eligibility: Open to graduating high school seniors who have played an active role in amateur softball. Applicants must be planning to attend an accredited 2– or 4–year college or university. They need not have played on a high school team and are not required to play softball in college. Along with their application, they must submit an essay describing the role softball has played in their life, why they think they should receive this scholarship, and where they learned about it. Selection is based on academic achievement, community service, participation in softball, and financial need.
Financial data: The stipend is $2,000 per year.
Duration: 1 year; may be renewed.
Number awarded: Up to 10 each year.
Deadline: February of each year.

32 $ AMERICAN ATHEISTS SCHOLARSHIPS

American Atheists
Attn: Youth and Family Director
P.O. Box 204
Boise, ID 83701–0204
Phone: (208) 860–7738;
Email: yfdirector@atheists.org
Web: www.atheists.org/youth_&_family/scholarship
Summary: To provide financial assistance for college to students who identify themselves as atheists.
Eligibility: Open to college–bound high school seniors and current college students. Applicants must be atheists and have a cumulative GPA of 2.5 or higher. Along with their application, they must submit an essay of 500 to 1,000 words describing their record of activism. Selection is based on activism, with special attention given to students who show activism in their schools (e.g., starting atheist/freethinker groups, fighting against violations of the separation of church and state in the school).
Financial data: Stipends are $2,000 or $1,000.
Duration: 1 year.
Number awarded: 3 each year: 1 at $2,000 and 2 at $1,000.
Deadline: January of each year.

33 AMERICAN BAPTIST UNDERGRADUATE SCHOLARSHIPS

American Baptist Churches USA
National Ministries
Attn: Office of Financial Aid for Studies
P.O. Box 851
Valley Forge, PA 19482–0851
Phone: (610) 768–2067; (800) ABC–3USA, ext. 2067; Fax: (610) 768–2453;
Email: Financialaid.Web@abc-usa.org
Web: www.nationalministries.org
Summary: To provide financial assistance to undergraduate students who are members of American Baptist–related churches.
Eligibility: Open to students planning to enroll as a full–time freshman at a college or university in the United States or Puerto Rico. Applicants must be U.S. citizens who have been a member of a church affiliated with American Baptist Churches USA for at least 1 year. Along with their application, they must submit a 500–word essay on the gifts they believe God has given them. Preference is given to students attending a college or university affiliated with American Baptist Churches USA and to dependents of American Baptist pastors. Students receiving assistance from other American Baptist scholarship programs are not eligible.
Financial data: Stipends range from $500 to $1,000 per year. Funds are paid directly to the recipient's school and credited towards tuition.
Duration: 1 year; may be renewed if the recipient maintains a GPA of 2.75 or higher.
Number awarded: Varies each year.
Deadline: May of each year.

34 $$ AMERICAN COLLEGE FOUNDATION VISIONARY SCHOLARSHIPS

American College Foundation
955 Massachusetts Avenue, Suite 525
Cambridge, MA 02139–3233
Phone: (617) 395–6757; Fax: (617) 395–6743;
Email: Admin@AmericanCollegeFoundation.org
Web: americancollegefoundation.org
Summary: To provide financial assistance to high school students who are interested in studying any field at a college in any state.
Eligibility: Open to high school freshmen, sophomores, juniors, and seniors from all income levels. Applicants must be planning to enroll at a college or university in the United States and major in the field of their choice. They must be U.S. citizens or eligible noncitizens. Along with their application, they must submit a 500–word essay on why college is important to them. Selection is based on ability to follow guidelines (25%), grammar and punctuation (25%), and merit of the essay (50%).
Financial data: Stipends are $5,000 or $1,000. Funds must be used for the first year of college.
Duration: 1 year; nonrenewable.
Number awarded: Varies each year; recently, 7 of these scholarships were awarded: 1 at $5,000 and 6 at $1,000.
Deadline: March of each year.

35 $ AMERICAN LEGION JUNIOR AIR RIFLE NATIONAL CHAMPIONSHIP SCHOLARSHIPS

American Legion
Attn: Americanism and Children & Youth Division
700 North Pennsylvania Street
P.O. Box 1055
Indianapolis, IN 46206–1055
Phone: (317) 630–1249; Fax: (317) 630–1223;
Email: acy@legion.org
Web: legion.org/shooting/championship
Summary: To provide college scholarships to the top competitors in the American Legion Junior Position Air Rifle Tournament.
Eligibility: Open to students between the ages of 14 and 20 who compete in air rifle tournaments sponsored by local posts of the American Legion. Based on posted scores in the precision and sporter categories, the top 30 competitors and state and regional champions compete in a qualification round and a postal

tournament. The top 15 shooters then participate in a shoulder–to–shoulder match in August at the Olympic Training Center, Colorado Springs, Colorado.
Financial data: The awards are $2,500 college scholarships.
Duration: The awards are presented annually.
Number awarded: 2 each year: 1 in the precision category and 1 in the sporter category.
Deadline: Deadline not specified.

36 AMERICAN LEGION LEGACY SCHOLARSHIPS

American Legion
Attn: Americanism and Children & Youth Division
700 North Pennsylvania Street
P.O. Box 1055
Indianapolis, IN 46206–1055
Phone: (317) 630–1212; Fax: (317) 630–1223;
Email: acy@legion.org
Web: legion.org/scholarships/legacy

Summary: To provide financial assistance for college to children of U.S. military personnel killed on active duty on or after September 11, 2001.
Eligibility: Open to the children (including adopted children and stepchildren) of active–duty U.S. military personnel (including federalized National Guard and Reserve members) who died on active duty on or after September 11, 2001. Applicants must be high school seniors or graduates planning to enroll full time at an accredited institution of higher education in the United States. Selection is based on academic achievement, school and community activities, leadership skills, and financial need.
Financial data: The stipend depends on the availability of funds.
Duration: 1 year; may be renewed.
Number awarded: Varies each year.
Deadline: April of each year.

37 AMERICAN PATRIOT FREEDOM SCHOLARSHIP AWARD

Homefront America
27375 Paseo La Serna
San Juan Capistrano, CA 92675
Phone: (949) 248–9468;
Email: info@homefrontamerica.org
Web: www.homefrontamerica.org

Summary: To provide financial assistance to children of active, Reserve, disabled, deceased, or retired military personnel.
Eligibility: Open to students between 18 and 21 years of age who are children of 1) full–time active duty or Reserve servicemembers; 2) servicemembers disabled as a direct result of injuries sustained during a military operation; 3) deceased servicemembers killed in action during a military operation; or 4) servicemembers who are retired with an honorable discharge. Applicants must be enrolled or planning to enroll at an accredited college, university, or vocational/technical institute to work on an undergraduate degree. Selection is based primarily on a 500–word essay on significant contributions of America's greatest generation to our country.
Financial data: The stipend is $1,000.
Duration: 1 year.
Number awarded: 5 each year.
Deadline: Applications may be submitted at any time, but they must be received in time for the announcement of recipients at the end of May of each year.

38 $ AMERICAN RADIO RELAY LEAGUE GENERAL FUND SCHOLARSHIPS

American Radio Relay League
Attn: ARRL Foundation
225 Main Street
Newington, CT 06111–1494
Phone: (860) 594–0397; Fax: (860) 594–0259;
Email: foundation@arrl.org
Web: www.arrl.org/scholarship–descriptions

Summary: To provide financial assistance to licensed radio amateurs who are interested in working on an undergraduate or graduate degree in any field.
Eligibility: Open to undergraduate or graduate students at accredited institutions in any subject area who are licensed radio amateurs (any class). Applicants must submit an essay on the role amateur radio has played in their lives and provide documentation of financial need.
Financial data: The stipend is $2,000.
Duration: 1 year.
Number awarded: Varies each year; recently, 2 of these scholarships were awarded. In addition, the sponsor also awards several named scholarships.
Deadline: January of each year.

39 AMERICAS CHILDRENS EDUCATION FOUNDATION SCHOLARSHIPS

Americas Childrens Education Foundation
119 West Sixth Street, Suite 203
Pueblo, CO 81003
Phone: (719) 583–7860;
Email: info@acefoundation.net
Web: www.acefoundation.net/scholarship_programs.html

Summary: To provide financial assistance to high school seniors and graduates who are interested in working on a college degree in any field.
Eligibility: Open to citizens of the United States or its territories who are high school graduates (or equivalents) or who will graduate during the current year. Applicants must be attending or planning to attend an accredited postsecondary institution of higher learning. Along with their application, they must submit a 1–page narrative that details their future goals and objectives. Selection is based on that narrative (15%), academic ability (30%), financial need (30%), volunteer and community service (15%), special achievements and academic honors (5%), and extracurricular activities (5%).
Financial data: A stipend is awarded (amount not specified).
Duration: 1 year.
Number awarded: Varies each year; recently, 4 of these scholarships were awarded.
Deadline: April of each year.

40 $$ AMERICA'S NATIONAL TEENAGER SCHOLARSHIP PROGRAM

America's National Teenager Scholarship Organization
1132 Frenchtown Lane
Franklin, TN 37067
Phone: (615) 771–7478; (866) NAT–TEEN; Fax: (888) 370–2075;
Email: jennytelwar@mac.com
Web: www.nationalteen.com/pageants.php

Summary: To recognize (locally and nationally) the scholastic and leadership achievements of America's teenage girls and to provide cash, tuition scholarships, and awards to the participants.
Eligibility: Open to girls who are 13 to 15 years of age. They are eligible to enter the Miss Junior National Teenager competition. Girls who are 16 to 18 may enter the Miss National Teenager competition. Entrants must have no children and never have been married. Selection is based on academic excellence (15%), school and community involvement (15%), social and conversational skills in an interview (30%), poise and personality in an evening gown (15%), personal expression (15%), and response to an on–stage question (10%). There is no swimsuit competition.
Financial data: This program awards approximately $100,000 in scholarships at state and national levels each year.
Duration: The contest is held annually.
Deadline: Deadline dates vary. Check with the sponsors of your local and state pageant.

41 $$ AMERICORPS NATIONAL CIVILIAN COMMUNITY CORPS

Corporation for National and Community Service
1201 New York Avenue, N.W.
Washington, DC 20525
Phone: (202) 606–5000, ext. 144; (800) 942–2677; Fax: (202) 565–2791; TDD: (800) 833–3722;
Email: info@cns.gov
Web: www.americorps.gov/about/programs/nccc.asp

Summary: To enable young Americans to earn funds for higher education while gaining experience and training by participating in a residential national service program.
Eligibility: Open to U.S. citizens, nationals, or permanent residents between the ages of 18 and 24. Members work in teams of 8 to 12 people on a variety of projects in 6 different areas: environment, education, public safety, unmet needs, homeland security, and disaster relief. Selection is based on an application, personal references, and a telephone interview.
Financial data: Corps members receive a living allowance of approximately $4,000, housing, meals, limited medical insurance, up to $400 per month for

child care (if necessary), member uniforms, and an education award of $5,550 for future education costs or repayment of student loans.

Duration: To complete a term, participants must serve 10 months and complete 1,700 hours of community service, including 80 hours of independent service. They may serve a total of 2 terms and receive 2 education awards.

Number awarded: Varies each year.

Deadline: March of each year for the fall cycle; July of each year for the winter cycle.

42 $$ AMERICORPS STATE AND NATIONAL PROGRAM

Corporation for National and Community Service
1201 New York Avenue, N.W.
Washington, DC 20525
Phone: (202) 606–5000; (800) 942–2677; Fax: (202) 565–2784; TDD: (800) 833–3722;
Email: info@cns.gov
Web: www.americorps.gov/about/programs/state_national.asp

Summary: To enable Americans to earn money for college or graduate school while serving as volunteers for public or nonprofit organizations that work to meet the nation's education, public safety, human, or environmental needs.

Eligibility: Open to applicants who are at least 17 years old; be U.S. citizens, nationals, or permanent residents, and have completed at least their high school diploma or agree to obtain the diploma before using the education award. They must be interested in working on community projects in 1 of 4 areas: education, public safety, health, and the environment. Additional qualifications are set by participating agencies.

Financial data: Full–time participants (at least 1,700 service hours) receive a modest living allowance of approximately $9,300, limited health care, and a post–service education award of $5,550 to pay for college, graduate school, or repayment of student loans. Part–time participants receive pro–rated amounts.

Duration: The length of the term is established by each participating agency but ranges from 9 to 12 months. Participants may serve up to 4 terms, but they may receive education awards for only 2 terms.

Number awarded: Varies each year; recently, approximately 44,000 members served in this program.

Deadline: Each participating organization sets its own deadline.

43 $$ AMERICORPS VISTA

Corporation for National and Community Service
1201 New York Avenue, N.W.
Washington, DC 20525
Phone: (202) 606–5000; (800) 942–2677; Fax: (202) 565–2784; TDD: (800) 833–3722;
Email: info@cns.gov
Web: www.americorps.gov/about/programs/vista.asp

Summary: To enable Americans to earn money for higher education or other purposes while working as volunteers for public or nonprofit organizations that serve low–income communities.

Eligibility: Open to U.S. citizens, nationals, or permanent residents 18 years of age or older who either have a baccalaureate degree or at least 3 years of related volunteer/job experience and skills. Participants serve at approved public or nonprofit sponsoring organizations in low–income communities located in the United States, Virgin Islands, or Puerto Rico. Assignments may include working to fight illiteracy, improve health services, create businesses, increase housing opportunities, or bridge the digital divide. Sponsors may also establish particular skill, education, or experience requirements; Spanish language skills are desirable for some assignments.

Financial data: Participants receive a monthly living allowance for housing, food, and incidentals; the allowance does not affect Social Security, veterans', or public assistance benefits but is subject to taxation. Health insurance is also provided for participants, but not for family members. Upon completion of service, participants also receive an educational award of $5,550 per year of service that may be used to pay for educational expenses, repay student loans, or pay the expenses of participating in a school–to–work program. In lieu of the educational award, participants may elect to receive an end–of–service stipend of $1,500.

Duration: Full–time service of at least 1 year is required to earn educational benefits. Participants may serve up to 3 terms, but they may receive education awards for only 2 terms.

Number awarded: Varies each year; recently, approximately 6,000 volunteers served in this program.

Deadline: March of each year for first consideration; October of each year for fall replacements.

44 $ ANCHOR SCHOLARSHIP FOUNDATION AWARD

Anchor Scholarship Foundation
4966 Euclid Road, Suite 109
Virginia Beach, VA 23462
Phone: (757) 671–3200, ext. 116; Fax: (757) 671–3300;
Email: admin@anchorscholarship.com
Web: anchorscholarship.com

Summary: To provide financial assistance for college to dependents of active–duty or retired personnel serving in the Naval Surface Forces.

Eligibility: Open to dependents of active–duty or retired personnel who have served at least 6 years (need not be consecutive) in a unit under the administrative control of Commanders, Naval Surface Forces, U.S. Atlantic Fleet or U.S. Pacific Fleet. Applicants must be high school seniors or students already attending an accredited 4–year college or university and working on a bachelor's degree as a full–time student. Spouses are eligible if they are working full time on a first bachelor's degree. Selection is based on academic proficiency, extracurricular activities, character, all–around ability, and financial need.

Financial data: Stipends range up to $2,000.

Duration: 1 year; may be renewed.

Number awarded: Varies each year; recently, 34 students received new or renewal scholarships.

Deadline: February of each year.

45 $$ ANDRE SOBEL AWARD

Andre Sobel River of Life Foundation
Attn: Awards
8581 Santa Monica Boulevard, Suite 80
P.O. Box 361640
Los Angeles, CA 90036
Phone: (310) 276–7111; Fax: (310) 276–0244;
Email: info@andreriveroflife.org
Web: andreriveroflife.org/participate/award

Summary: To recognize and reward young survivors of life–threatening illnesses who submit outstanding essays on their illness.

Eligibility: Open to survivors of life–threatening illnesses between 12 and 21 years of age. Applicants are allowed to define themselves as a survivor; no medical definition or certain amount of time is required. They must submit an essay, up to 1,500 words in length, on a topic that changes annually but relates to their illness.

Financial data: First prize is $5,000. Other cash prizes are awarded to second– and third–place winners.

Duration: The competition is held annually.

Number awarded: 3 cash prizes are awarded each year.

Deadline: March of each year.

46 $$ ANNE FRANK OUTSTANDING SCHOLARSHIP AWARD

The Anne Frank Center USA
Attn: Spirit of Anne Frank Awards
44 Park Place
New York, NY 10007
Phone: (212) 431–7993, ext. 302; Fax: (212) 431–8375
Web: www.annefrank.com/fileadmin/safa/categories.html

Summary: To provide financial assistance for college to high school seniors who demonstrate the commitment, ideals, and courage of Anne Frank.

Eligibility: Open to graduating high school seniors who have been accepted at a 4–year college or university. Applicants must be able to demonstrate the qualities of Anne Frank by 1) acting as spokespersons for tolerance; 2) having the courage, on a daily basis, to be bridge builders and peacemakers; 3) creating programs that address intolerance, violence prevention, and conflict resolution; and 4) standing up against intolerance by leading or participating in community–based organizations. Along with their application, they must submit a 1,000–word essay describing contributions they have made to their community and how their goals are inspired by Anne Frank.

Financial data: The stipend is $10,000.

Duration: 1 year.

Number awarded: 1 or more each year.

Deadline: February of each year.

47 APARTMENT INVESTMENT AND MANAGEMENT COMPANY (AIMCO) CARES OPPORTUNITY SCHOLARSHIPS

National Leased Housing Association
Attn: NLHA Education Fund
1900 L Street, N.W., Suite 300

Washington, DC 20036
Phone: (202) 785–8888; Fax: (202) 785–2008;
Email: info@hudnlha.com
Web: www.hudnlha.com/education_fund/index.asp
Summary: To provide financial assistance for college to residents of federally–assisted rental housing properties and members of families receiving rental subsidy through federal housing programs.
Eligibility: Open to U.S. citizens and permanent residents who reside in a federally–assisted rental housing property or whose families receive rental subsidy through a recognized federal housing program (e.g., Section 8, Rent Supplement, Rental Assistance Payments, Low Income Housing Tax Credit). Applicants must be graduating high school seniors, current undergraduates, or GED recipients entering an accredited undergraduate program. They must have a GPA of 2.5 or higher and be able to demonstrate financial need and community leadership through volunteer work at school or in the community. Along with their application, they must submit a 1–page essay on what education means to their future.
Financial data: A stipend is awarded (amount not specified). Funds are disbursed directly to the recipient's institution of higher learning for partial payment of tuition, books, room and board, or other activities directly related to the student's education.
Duration: 1 year.
Number awarded: Varies each year; recently, 37 of these scholarships were awarded.
Deadline: February of each year.

48 APHF SCHOLARSHIPS

American Police Hall of Fame and Museum
Attn: American Federation of Police & Concerned Citizens
6350 Horizon Drive
Titusville, FL 32780
Phone: (321) 264–0911; Fax: (321) 264–0033;
Email: policeinfo@aphf.org
Web: www.aphf.org/scholarships.html
Summary: To provide financial assistance for college to children of deceased law enforcement officers.
Eligibility: Open to the sons and daughters of law enforcement officers killed in the line of duty. They must be attending or planning to attend a private or public college or a vocational program. Along with their application, they must submit a high school transcript, ACT/SAT scores, and a copy of the acceptance letter from the institution they plan to attend. Financial need is not considered in the selection process.
Financial data: The stipend is $1,000 per year.
Duration: 1 year; may be renewed up to 3 additional years, provided the recipient remains enrolled in at least 6 credit hours per semester and maintains a GPA of 2.0 or higher.
Number awarded: Varies each year, depending on the availability of funds.
Deadline: Deadline not specified.

49 $ APIASF/SARA LEE FOUNDATION SCHOLARSHIP

Asian & Pacific Islander American Scholarship Fund
1900 L Street, N.W., Suite 210
Washington, DC 20036–5002
Phone: (202) 986–6892; (877) 808–7032; Fax: (202) 530–0643;
Email: info@apiasf.org
Web: www.apiasf.org/scholarship_apiasf_saralee.html
Summary: To provide financial assistance to female Asian and Pacific Islander Americans who are entering college for the first time.
Eligibility: Open to women who are U.S. citizens, nationals, permanent residents, or citizens of the Freely Associated States and of Asian or Pacific Islander heritage. Applicants must be enrolling full time at an accredited 2– or 4–year college or university in the United States as a first–year student. They must have a GPA of 2.7 or higher or the GED equivalent. In addition, they must complete the FAFSA and apply for federal financial aid.
Financial data: The stipend is $2,500.
Duration: 1 year; nonrenewable.
Number awarded: 1 each year.
Deadline: January of each year.

50 $$ APIASF SCHOLARSHIPS

Asian & Pacific Islander American Scholarship Fund
1900 L Street, N.W., Suite 210
Washington, DC 20036–5002
Phone: (202) 986–6892; (877) 808–7032; Fax: (202) 530–0643;
Email: info@apiasf.org
Web: www.apiasf.org/scholarship_apiasf_list.html
Summary: To provide financial assistance to Asian and Pacific Islander Americans who are entering college for the first time.
Eligibility: Open to U.S. citizens, nationals, permanent residents, and citizens of the Freely Associated States who are first–time incoming college students and of Asian or Pacific Islander heritage. Applicants must be enrolling full time at an accredited 2– or 4–year college or university in the United States. They must have a GPA of 2.7 or higher or the GED equivalent. In addition, they must complete the FAFSA and apply for federal financial aid.
Financial data: The stipends range from $2,500 to $5,000.
Duration: 1 year.
Number awarded: Varies each year; recently, 256 of these scholarships were awarded.
Deadline: January of each year.

51 ARAB AMERICAN INSTITUTE FOUNDATION/HELEN ABBOTT COMMUNITY SERVICE AWARDS

Arab American Institute Foundation
Attn: Executive Director
1600 K Street, N.W., Suite 601
Washington, DC 20006
Phone: (202) 429–9210; Fax: (202) 429–9214;
Email: aaif@aaiusa.org
Web: www.aaiusa.org/pages/student–resource–center
Summary: To recognize and reward Arab American college and high school students who can demonstrate a strong record of community service.
Eligibility: Open to U.S. citizens and permanent residents of Arab descent who are currently enrolled as either high school students or college/university students. Applicants must have a GPA of 3.0 or higher. Along with their application, they must submit 1) a resume that indicates a strong interest and commitment to community service; and 2) a 500–word essay on how their field of study is a springboard for a life of community service.
Financial data: Awards are $1,000 for college/university students or $500 for high school students.
Duration: The awards are granted annually.
Number awarded: 3 each year: 2 to college/university students and 1 to a high school student.
Deadline: March of each year.

52 $ ARIZONA LEVERAGING EDUCATIONAL ASSISTANCE PARTNERSHIP GRANTS

Arizona Commission for Postsecondary Education
2020 North Central Avenue, Suite 650
Phoenix, AZ 85004–4503
Phone: (602) 258–2435; Fax: (602) 258–2483;
Email: help@azhighered.gov
Web: www.azhighered.gov/LEAP_Grant.html
Summary: To provide financial assistance to undergraduate students in Arizona who can demonstrate financial need.
Eligibility: Open to Arizona residents who are attending or planning to attend a participating Arizona postsecondary educational institution on at least a half–time basis. Applicants must be U.S. citizens or eligible noncitizens and able to demonstrate substantial financial need.
Financial data: Awards range from $100 to $2,500 per year and average $1,000 per year.
Duration: 1 year; may be renewed, provided the recipient maintains satisfactory academic progress.
Number awarded: Varies each year; recently, approximately $3.4 million in these grants was awarded.
Deadline: Each participating institution in Arizona sets its own deadline.

53 $ ARKANSAS ACADEMIC CHALLENGE SCHOLARSHIP

Arkansas Department of Higher Education
Attn: Financial Aid Division
114 East Capitol Avenue
Little Rock, AR 72201–3818
Phone: (501) 371–2050; (800) 54–STUDY; Fax: (501) 371–2001;
Email: finaid@adhe.edu
Web: www.adhe.edu/divisions/financialaid/Pages/fa_programs.aspx

Summary: To provide financial assistance to residents of Arkansas who are traditional, current, or nontraditional students and interested in attending college in the state.
Eligibility: Open to Arkansas residents who are either traditional or nontraditional students. Traditional students must be graduating high school seniors, have completed the Smart Core curriculum requirements, have a GPA of 2.5 or higher, have an ACT score of at least 19 or an equivalent SAT score, and be planning to enroll full time in an associate or baccalaureate degree program at an approved institution in the state. Current students must have begun post-secondary education as a full–time first–time freshman within 12 months after graduating from high school, have been continuously enrolled since then, and have maintained a college GPA of 2.5 or higher. Nontraditional students must 1) have graduated from an Arkansas high school with a GPA of 2.5 or higher and an ACT score of at least 19 or an equivalent SAT score; 2) have completed at least 12 semester hours of credit at an approved institution of higher education with a postsecondary GPA of 2.5 or higher; or 3) have graduated from a home school or a private or out–of–state high school and have an ACT score of at least 19 or an equivalent SAT score. They must be enrolled or planning to enroll full or part time in an associate or baccalaureate degree program at an approved institution in the state. U.S. citizenship or permanent resident status is required.
Financial data: The maximum stipend is $4,500 per year for students at 4–year colleges and universities or $2,250 per year for students at 2–year institutions.
Duration: 1 year; may be renewed until the recipient earns a baccalaureate degree or attempts a total of 130 semester hours in 8 semesters (or 16 semesters for part–time nontraditional students). Renewal requires that the recipient maintain full–time enrollment (or part–time if a nontraditional student) and a GPA of 2.5 or higher.
Number awarded: Approximately 28,000 each year.
Deadline: May of each year.

54 ARKANSAS AMERICAN LEGION AUXILIARY ACADEMIC SCHOLARSHIP

American Legion Auxiliary
Department of Arkansas
Attn: Department Secretary
1415 West Seventh Street
Little Rock, AR 72201–2903
Phone: (501) 374–5836; Fax: (501) 372–0855;
Email: arkaux@att.net
Web: auxiliary.arlegion.org/scholarships.html
Summary: To provide financial assistance to descendants of veterans who are high school seniors in Arkansas and planning to attend college in any state.
Eligibility: Open to the descendants of veterans in Arkansas who served during eligibility dates for membership in the American Legion. Both the student and the parent must be residents of Arkansas. Their total family income must be less than $55,000. The student must be a high school senior planning to attend college in any state. Along with their application, they must submit an essay of 800 to 1,000 words on what their country's flag means to them. Selection is based on character (15%), Americanism (15%), leadership (15%), financial need (15%), and scholarship (40%).
Financial data: The stipend is $1,000; funds are paid in 2 equal installments.
Duration: 1 year.
Number awarded: 1 each year.
Deadline: February of each year.

55 ARKANSAS GOVERNOR'S COMMISSION ON PEOPLE WITH DISABILITIES SCHOLARSHIPS

Arkansas Governor's Commission on People with Disabilities
Attn: Scholarship Committee
26 Corporate Hill Drive
Little Rock, AR 72205
Phone: (501) 296–1637; Fax: (501) 296–1883; TDD: (501) 296–1637
Web: ace.arkansas.gov
Summary: To provide financial assistance to Arkansas students with disabilities who are interested in attending college or graduate school in any state.
Eligibility: Open to high school seniors, high school graduates, undergraduates, and graduate students who have a disability and are residents of Arkansas. Applicants must be attending or planning to attend a college or university in any state. Selection is based on a description of their disability (20 points), present and past school involvement (10 points), a brief statement on their career goals (15 points), community and volunteer activities (10 points), a brief essay on the positive or negative effects their disability has had on their life thus far (20 points), 3 letters of recommendation (10 points), and financial need (10 points).
Financial data: The stipend varies, up to $1,000 per year.
Duration: 1 year; recipients may reapply.
Number awarded: Several each year.
Deadline: February of each year.

56 $$ ARKANSAS GOVERNOR'S DISTINGUISHED SCHOLARS PROGRAM

Arkansas Department of Higher Education
Attn: Financial Aid Division
114 East Capitol Avenue
Little Rock, AR 72201–3818
Phone: (501) 371–2050; (800) 54–STUDY; Fax: (501) 371–2001;
Email: finaid@adhe.edu
Web: www.adhe.edu/divisions/financialaid/Pages/fa_govscholars.aspx
Summary: To provide financial assistance to exceptional high school seniors in Arkansas.
Eligibility: Open to high school seniors who are U.S. citizens or permanent residents, are residents of Arkansas, can demonstrate leadership, and are planning to enroll in a college or university in Arkansas. Applicants must have an SAT combined critical reading and mathematics score of 1410 or higher, have an ACT score of 32 or higher, be a National Merit Finalist or a National Achievement Scholar, or have a GPA of 3.5 or higher in academic classes. Selection is based on high school GPA (35%), class rank (10%), ACT or SAT score (45%), and school and community leadership (10%).
Financial data: Stipends up to $10,000 per year are provided.
Duration: 1 year; may be renewed for up to 3 additional years, provided the recipient maintains a cumulative GPA of 3.25 or higher and completes at least 30 semester hours each year.
Number awarded: Up to 300 each year.
Deadline: January of each year.

57 $ ARKANSAS GOVERNOR'S SCHOLARS PROGRAM

Arkansas Department of Higher Education
Attn: Financial Aid Division
114 East Capitol Avenue
Little Rock, AR 72201–3818
Phone: (501) 371–2050; (800) 54–STUDY; Fax: (501) 371–2001;
Email: finaid@adhe.edu
Web: www.adhe.edu/divisions/financialaid/Pages/fa_govscholars.aspx
Summary: To provide financial assistance to outstanding high school seniors in Arkansas.
Eligibility: Open to high school seniors who are U.S. citizens or permanent residents, are residents of Arkansas, can demonstrate leadership, and are planning to enroll in a college or university in the state. Applicants must have an SAT combined critical reading and mathematics score of 1220 or higher, an ACT score of 27 or higher, or a GPA of 3.5 or higher in academic classes. Selection is based on high school GPA (35%), class rank (10%), ACT or SAT score (45%), and school and community leadership (10%).
Financial data: The stipend is $4,000 per year.
Duration: 1 year; may be renewed for up to 3 additional years, provided the recipient maintains a 3.0 cumulative GPA and completes at least 30 semester hours each year.
Number awarded: Up to 75 each year (1 in each Arkansas county).
Deadline: January of each year.

58 ARKANSAS HIGHER EDUCATION OPPORTUNITIES GRANT

Arkansas Department of Higher Education
Attn: Financial Aid Division
114 East Capitol Avenue
Little Rock, AR 72201–3818
Phone: (501) 371–2050; (800) 54–STUDY; Fax: (501) 371–2001;
Email: finaid@adhe.edu
Web: www.adhe.edu/divisions/financialaid/Pages/fa_gogrant.aspx
Summary: To provide financial assistance to high school seniors in Arkansas who come from a low–income family and plan to attend college in the state.
Eligibility: Open to high school seniors in Arkansas who have been residents of the state for at least 1 year and plan to attend an eligible Arkansas institution. Applicants must come from a family with an annual income of less than $25,000 per year for a 1–member family, rising by $5,000 for each additional family member to a maximum of $75,000. They must be U.S. citizens or permanent residents.
Financial data: The stipend is $1,000 per year for full–time students or $500 per year for part–time students.

Duration: 1 year; may be renewed up to 3 additional years, provided the recipient maintains a GPA of 2.0 or higher and continues to demonstrate financial need.
Number awarded: 10 each year.
Deadline: August of each year.

59 $$ ARKANSAS LAW ENFORCEMENT OFFICERS' DEPENDENTS' SCHOLARSHIPS

Arkansas Department of Higher Education
Attn: Financial Aid Division
114 East Capitol Avenue
Little Rock, AR 72201–3818
Phone: (501) 371–2050; (800) 54–STUDY; Fax: (501) 371–2001;
Email: finaid@adhe.edu
Web: www.adhe.edu/divisions/financialaid/Pages/fa_leod.aspx
Summary: To provide financial assistance for undergraduate education to the dependents of deceased or disabled Arkansas law enforcement officers, firefighters, or other designated public employees.
Eligibility: Open to the spouses and/or children (natural, adopted, or step) of Arkansas residents who were killed or permanently disabled in the line of duty as law enforcement officers, municipal and/or college or university police officers, sheriffs and deputy sheriffs, constables, state correction employees, game wardens, state park employees who are commissioned law enforcement officers or emergency response employees, full–time or volunteer firefighters, state forestry employees engaged in fighting forest fires, certain Arkansas Highway and Transportation Department employees, emergency medical technicians, or Department of Community Punishment employees. Children must be less than 23 years of age. Spouses may not have remarried. All applicants must have been Arkansas residents for at least 6 months.
Financial data: The scholarship covers tuition, on–campus room charges, and fees (but not books, school supplies, food, materials, or dues for extracurricular activities) at any state–supported college or university in Arkansas.
Duration: Up to 8 semesters, as long as the student is working on a baccalaureate or associate degree and maintains a GPA of 2.0 or higher.
Number awarded: Varies each year.
Deadline: May of each year for late summer and fall terms; October of each year for spring and early summer terms.

60 $$ ARKANSAS MILITARY DEPENDENTS' SCHOLARSHIP PROGRAM

Arkansas Department of Higher Education
Attn: Financial Aid Division
114 East Capitol Avenue
Little Rock, AR 72201–3818
Phone: (501) 371–2050; (800) 54–STUDY; Fax: (501) 371–2001;
Email: finaid@adhe.edu
Web: www.adhe.edu/divisions/financialaid/Pages/fa_mds.aspx
Summary: To provide financial assistance for educational purposes to dependents of certain categories of Arkansas veterans.
Eligibility: Open to the natural children, adopted children, stepchildren, and spouses of Arkansas residents who have been declared to be a prisoner of war, killed in action, missing in action, killed on ordnance delivery, or 100% totally and permanently disabled during, or as a result of, active military service. Applicants and their parent or spouse must be residents of Arkansas. They must be working on, or planning to work on, a bachelor's degree or certificate of completion at a public college, university, or technical school in Arkansas.
Financial data: The program pays for tuition, general registration fees, special course fees, activity fees, room and board (if provided in campus facilities), and other charges associated with earning a degree or certificate.
Duration: 1 year; undergraduates may obtain renewal as long as they make satisfactory progress toward a baccalaureate degree; graduate students may obtain renewal as long as they maintain a minimum GPA of 2.0 and make satisfactory progress toward a degree.
Number awarded: Varies each year; recently, 4 of these scholarships were awarded.
Deadline: May of each year for late summer and fall terms; October of each year for spring and early summer terms.

61 ARKANSAS SECOND EFFORT SCHOLARSHIP

Arkansas Department of Higher Education
Attn: Financial Aid Division
114 East Capitol Avenue
Little Rock, AR 72201–3818
Phone: (501) 371–2050; (800) 54–STUDY; Fax: (501) 371–2001;
Email: finaid@adhe.edu
Web: www.adhe.edu/divisions/financialaid/Pages/fa_ses.aspx
Summary: To provide financial assistance for undergraduate study to students in Arkansas who have earned a General Educational Development (GED) certificate.
Eligibility: Open to Arkansas residents who did not graduate from high school but completed their GED certificate in the previous year. Applicants must be attending or planning to attend an approved Arkansas 2– or 4–year public or private postsecondary institution. They must be at least 18 years of age or a former member of a high school class that has graduated. The students who received the highest GED scores are awarded this scholarship. Financial need is not considered. Students do not apply for this award; eligible candidates are contacted directly by the Arkansas Department of Higher Education if they achieve the highest scores.
Financial data: The stipend is $1,000 per year or the cost of tuition, whichever is less.
Duration: 1 year; may be renewed for an additional 3 years (or equivalent for part–time students) or until completion of a baccalaureate degree, provided the recipient maintains a GPA of 2.5 or higher.
Number awarded: 10 each year.
Deadline: Deadline not specified.

62 ARLINE ANDREWS LOVEJOY SCHOLARSHIP

Maine Federation of Business and Professional Women's Clubs
Attn: BPW/Maine Futurama Foundation
c/o Susan Tardie, Co–President
25 Hall Street
Fort Kent, ME 04743
Email: susan.tardie@maine.edu
Web: www.bpwmefoundation.org/files/index.php?id=10
Summary: To provide financial assistance to female high school seniors and recent graduates in Maine who plan to attend college in any state.
Eligibility: Open to women who are seniors graduating from high schools in Maine or recent graduates of those schools. Applicants must be planning to attend an accredited college or university in any state. They must have a realistic goal for the educational plans. Along with their application, they must submit a statement describing their educational and personal goals, including their financial need.
Financial data: The stipend is $1,200. Funds are paid directly to the recipient's school.
Duration: 1 year.
Number awarded: 1 or more each year.
Deadline: April of each year.

63 ARMED SERVICES YMCA ANNUAL ESSAY CONTEST

Armed Services YMCA
Attn: Essay Contest
6359 Walker Lane, Suite 200
Alexandria, VA 22310
Phone: (703) 313–9600, ext. 106; (800) 597–1260; Fax: (703) 313–9668;
Email: tharper@asymca.org
Web: www.asymca.org
Summary: To recognize and reward outstanding essays by children of armed service personnel.
Eligibility: Open to children of active–duty and retired military personnel in the Army, Navy, Marines, Air Force, Coast Guard, and National Guard/Reserve. Applicants must submit an essay on a topic that changes annually; recently, students were asked to write on "My Military Hero." Essays by students in grades 1–8 must be from 100 to 300 words and essays by students in grades 9–12 must be from 300 to 500 words.
Financial data: For grades 1–8, first prize is a $500 savings bond and second prize is a $100 savings bond. For grades 9–12, first prize is a $1,000 savings bond and second prize is a $200 savings bond.
Duration: The contest is held annually.
Number awarded: A total of 12 prizes are awarded each year. A first prize and a second prize are awarded for 6 categories: first and second grade, third and fourth grade, fifth and sixth grade, seventh and eighth grade, ninth and tenth grade, and eleventh and twelfth grade.
Deadline: March of each year.

64 $ ARMENIAN MISSIONARY ASSOCIATION SCHOLARSHIP PROGRAM

Armenian Missionary Association of America, Inc.
Attn: Scholarship Committee
31 West Century Road

Paramus, NJ 07652
Phone: (201) 265–2607; Fax: (201) 265–6015;
Email: amaa@amaa.org
Web: www.amaa.org/education.htm

Summary: To provide financial assistance to undergraduate and graduate students of Armenian descent.

Eligibility: Open to full–time undergraduate and graduate students of Armenian descent. Proof of enrollment must be provided. Selection is based on financial need, academic accomplishments, leadership potential, and character references.

Financial data: The stipend is $2,000 per year. Funds are paid directly to the recipient's institution and may be used for tuition only.

Duration: 1 year; recipients may reapply.

Number awarded: Varies; approximately 130 students are supported each year.

Deadline: May of each year.

65 $ ARMY SCHOLARSHIP FOUNDATION SCHOLARSHIPS

Army Scholarship Foundation
11700 Preston Road, Suite 660–301
Dallas, TX 75230
Email: ContactUs@armyscholarshipfoundation.org
Web: www.armyscholarshipfoundation.org/scholarships.html

Summary: To provide financial assistance for undergraduate study to the children and spouses of Army personnel.

Eligibility: Open to 1) children of regular active–duty, active–duty Reserve, and active–duty Army National Guard members in good standing; 2) spouses of serving enlisted regular active–duty, active–duty Reserve, and active–duty Army National Guard members in good standing; and 3) children of former U.S. Army members who received an honorable or medical discharge or were killed while serving in the U.S. Army. Applicants must be high school seniors, high school graduates, or undergraduates enrolled at an accredited college, university, or vocational/technical institute. They must be U.S. citizens and have a GPA of 2.0 or higher; children must be younger than 24 years of age. Financial need is considered in the selection process.

Financial data: Stipends range from $500 to $2,000 per year.

Duration: 1 year; recipients may reapply.

Number awarded: 1 or more each year. The sponsor also offers 1 or more Sponsored Scholarships, which are funded by a number of companies (including Hamilton Sundstrand, KBR, and BAE Systems).

Deadline: April of each year.

66 $$ ARNOLD SOBEL SCHOLARSHIPS

U.S. Coast Guard
Attn: Office of Work–Life (CG–111)
2100 Second Street, S.W., Stop 7902
Washington, DC 20593–7902
Phone: (202) 475–5140; (800) 872–4957; Fax: (202) 475–5907;
Email: HQS.SMB.FamilySupportServices@uscg.mil
Web: www.uscg.mil/worklife/scholarship.asp

Summary: To provide financial assistance for college to the dependent children of Coast Guard enlisted personnel.

Eligibility: Open to the dependent children of enlisted members of the U.S. Coast Guard on active duty, retired, or deceased, and of enlisted personnel in the Coast Guard Reserve currently on extended active duty 180 days or more. Applicants must be high school seniors or current undergraduates enrolled or planning to enroll full–time at a 4–year college, university, or vocational school. They must be under 24 years of age and registered in the Defense Enrollment Eligibility Reporting System (DEERS) system. Along with their application, they must submit their SAT or ACT scores, a letter of recommendation, transcripts, a financial information statement, and a 500–word essay on their personal and academic achievements, extracurricular activities, contributions to the community, and academic plans and career goals.

Financial data: The stipend is $5,000 per year.

Duration: 1 year; may be renewed up to 3 additional years.

Number awarded: 4 each year.

Deadline: March of each year.

67 ASIA SCHOLARSHIP PROGRAM

Ronald McDonald House Charities
Attn: U.S. Scholarship Program
One Kroc Drive
Oak Brook, IL 60523
Phone: (630) 623–7048; Fax: (630) 623–7488;
Email: info@rmhc.org
Web: rmhc.org/what–we–do/rmhc–u–s–scholarships

Summary: To provide financial assistance for college to Asian Pacific high school seniors in specified geographic areas.

Eligibility: Open to high school seniors in designated McDonald's market areas who are legal residents of the United States and have at least 1 parent of Asian Pacific heritage. Applicants must be planning to enroll full time at an accredited 2– or 4–year college, university, or vocational/technical school. They must have a GPA of 2.7 or higher. Along with their application, they must submit a personal statement, up to 2 pages in length, on their Asian Pacific background, career goals, and desire to contribute to their community; information about unique, personal, or financial circumstances may be added. Selection is based on that statement, high school transcripts, a letter of recommendation, and financial need.

Financial data: Most awards are $1,000 per year. Funds are paid directly to the recipient's school.

Duration: 1 year; nonrenewable.

Number awarded: Varies each year; since RMHC began this program, it has awarded more than $44 million in scholarships.

Deadline: January of each year.

68 ASSOCIATED COLLEGES OF ILLINOIS/ED HORNER SCHOLARSHIP

Associated Colleges of Illinois
Attn: Director, Scholarship Program
70 East Lake Street, Suite 1418
Chicago, IL 60601
Phone: (312) 263–2391; Fax: (312) 263–3424;
Email: aci@acifund.org
Web: acigrantsadministration.org/Scholarships

Summary: To provide financial assistance to students from any state who are enrolled at institutions affiliated with the Associated Colleges of Illinois (ACI) and can demonstrate financial need.

Eligibility: Open to students from any state enrolled full time at the 22 private colleges and universities that are members of ACI. Applicants must have unmet financial need.

Financial data: The stipend is $1,000.

Duration: 1 year.

Number awarded: 1 each year.

Deadline: Deadline not specified.

69 $ ATLANTA BRAVES HIGH SCHOOL SCHOLARSHIP PROGRAM

Atlanta Braves
Attn: Scholarship Program
755 Hank Aaron Drive
P.O. Box 4064
Atlanta, GA 30302–4064
Phone: (404) 522–7630
Web: atlanta.braves.mlb.com/atl/community/scholarship.jsp

Summary: To provide financial assistance to high school seniors in Georgia who have a strong record of community service and plan to attend college in any state.

Eligibility: Open to seniors graduating from high schools in Georgia and planning to enroll at an accredited college or university in any state. Applicants must have a GPA of 3.2 or higher and a record of strong community service during their high school years. Along with their application, they must submit a 500–word essay on how they have made a positive impact in their community. Financial need is not considered in the selection process.

Financial data: The stipend is $2,000.

Duration: 1 year.

Number awarded: 6 each year.

Deadline: April of each year.

70 $ AURA NEELY–GARY MEMORIAL SCHOLARSHIP

Community Foundation of Greater Jackson
525 East Capitol Street, Suite 5B
Jackson, MS 39201
Phone: (601) 974–6044; Fax: (601) 974–6045;
Email: info@cfgj.org
Web: www.cfgreaterjackson.org/scholarships.html

Summary: To provide financial assistance to students at colleges and universities in Mississippi who have resumed their studies after an absence.
Eligibility: Open to residents of any state who are enrolled or planning to enroll at a college or university in Mississippi. Preference is given to students who desire to resume their education following a period of personal difficulties. Special consideration is given to young women who had previously dropped out of school and are now enrolled at a postsecondary institution. Applicants must be able to demonstrate financial need and potential contribution to society.
Financial data: The stipend is $2,000.
Duration: 1 year.
Number awarded: 1 each year.
Deadline: June of each year.

71 $$ AXA ACHIEVEMENT SCHOLARSHIPS

Scholarship America
Attn: Scholarship Management Services
One Scholarship Way
P.O. Box 297
St. Peter, MN 56082
Phone: (507) 931–1682; (800) 537–4180; Fax: (507) 931–9168;
Email: axaachievement@scholarshipamerica.org
Web: www.axa–equitable.com/axa–foundation/about.html

Summary: To provide financial assistance for college to high school seniors who demonstrate outstanding achievement.
Eligibility: Open to graduating high school seniors who plan to enroll full time in an accredited 2– or 4–year college or university in the United States. Applicants must demonstrate ambition and self–drive as demonstrated by outstanding achievement in school, community, or work–related activities. In selecting finalists, primary consideration is given to the applicant's non–academic outstanding achievement as described in the online application essays. The achievement may be a long–term accomplishment or an activity or project that occurred in their school, community, or workplace. Other factors considered in include extracurricular activities in school and community, work experience, and academic record. Finalists are then invited to submit transcripts and an appraisal from an unrelated adult who can confirm the achievement. Selection of recipients is based on demonstrated achievement. From among the recipients, students whose achievements are especially noteworthy are designated as national AXA Achievers.
Financial data: The stipend is $10,000. Funds may be used only for undergraduate educational expenses. Students selected as national AXA Achievers receive an additional stipend of $15,000 and the offer of an internship.
Duration: 1 year. Awards are not renewable, but recipients may arrange to receive payment in installments over multiple years as long as they continue to meet eligibility requirements.
Number awarded: 52 each year: 1 from each state, the District of Columbia, and Puerto Rico. Of those 52, 10 are designated as national AXA Achievers.
Deadline: November of each year.

72 $ AXA COMMUNITY SCHOLARSHIP PROGRAM

Scholarship America
Attn: Scholarship Management Services
One Scholarship Way
P.O. Box 297
St. Peter, MN 56082
Phone: (507) 931–1682; (800) 537–4180; Fax: (507) 931–9168;
Email: axacommunity@scholarshipamerica.org
Web: www.axa–equitable.com/axa–foundation/about.html

Summary: To provide financial assistance for college to high school seniors who demonstrate outstanding achievement in their local community.
Eligibility: Open to seniors graduating from high schools in the United States and Puerto Rico and planning to enroll full time at an accredited 2– or 4–year college or university. Applicants must demonstrate ambition and motivation, as evidenced by outstanding achievement in school, community, or work activities. In selecting finalists, primary consideration is given to the applicant's non–academic achievement as described in the online application essays. The achievement may be a long–term accomplishment or an activity or project that occurred in their school, community, or workplace. Other factors considered include extracurricular activities in school and community, work experience, and academic record. Finalists are then invited to submit transcripts and an appraisal from an unrelated adult who can confirm the achievement. Selection of recipients is based on demonstrated achievement.
Financial data: The stipend is $2,000. Funds may be used only for undergraduate educational expenses.
Duration: 1 year; nonrenewable.
Number awarded: Varies each year; each branch office of the sponsoring organization selects up to 12 recipients in their area. Recently, a total of 288 of these scholarships were awarded.
Deadline: January of each year.

73 BABE RUTH LEAGUE SCHOLARSHIPS

Babe Ruth League, Inc.
1770 Brunswick Pike
P.O. Box 5000
Trenton, NJ 08638
Phone: (609) 695–1434; Fax: (609) 695–2505;
Email: scholarships@baberuthleague.org
Web: www.baberuthleague.org/side–indexes/scholarships.html

Summary: To provide financial assistance for college to high school seniors who played Babe Ruth League baseball or softball.
Eligibility: Open to graduating high school seniors who played Babe Ruth League baseball or softball previously. Applicants must be planning to attend college. Along with their application, they must submit a 100–word essay on how playing Babe Ruth League baseball or softball has affected their life. Financial need is not considered in the selection process.
Financial data: The stipend is $1,000.
Duration: 1 year.
Number awarded: Varies each year; recently, 12 of these scholarships were awarded.
Deadline: June of each year.

74 BASEBALL SCHOLARSHIPS

American Legion Baseball
700 North Pennsylvania Street
Indianapolis, IN 46204
Phone: (317) 630–1249; Fax: (317) 630–1369;
Email: acy@legion.org
Web: baseball.legion.org/scholarships

Summary: To provide financial assistance to participants in the American Legion baseball program who plan to attend college.
Eligibility: Open to participants in the American Legion baseball program who are high school graduates or college freshmen; students still in high school are not eligible. In each American Legion department, candidates may be nominated by a team manager or head coach. The department baseball committee selects a player who demonstrates outstanding leadership, citizenship, character, scholarship, and financial need.
Financial data: The stipend ranges from $600 to $5,000.
Duration: Students have 8 years to utilize the scholarship funds from the date of the award, excluding any time spent on active military duty.
Number awarded: Up to 51 each year: 1 in each state and Puerto Rico. Recently, $22,000 in scholarships was awarded by this program.
Deadline: July of each year.

75 $ BEGO FUND SCHOLARSHIPS

Community Foundation of New Jersey
Attn: Donor Services
35 Knox Hill Road
P.O. Box 338
Morristown, NJ 07963–0338
Phone: (973) 267–5533, ext. 221; (800) 659–5533; Fax: (973) 267–2903;
Email: mrivera@cfnj.org
Web: www.cfnj.org/funds/scholarship/index.php

Summary: To provide financial assistance for college to residents of New Jersey, New York, and Pennsylvania, especially those from immigrant families.
Eligibility: Open to residents of New Jersey, New York, and Pennsylvania who are either graduating high school seniors or current college students. Preference is given to students who are from immigrant families and are either U.S. residents, naturalized citizens, or first–generation U.S. citizens. Applicants must submit a copy of official school transcripts; a resume outlining work experience, activities, and achievements; a 1–page statement of career goals and the reasons for those goals; and 1 character reference.
Financial data: The stipend is $1,000 per year for high school seniors or $4,000 per year for college students.
Duration: 1 year; recipients may reapply if they maintain a GPA of at least 3.0.
Number awarded: 1 each year: 1 high school senior and 1 college student.
Deadline: May of each year.

76 $ BEN SELLING SCHOLARSHIP

Oregon Student Access Commission
Attn: Grants and Scholarships Division
1500 Valley River Drive, Suite 100
Eugene, OR 97401–2146
Phone: (541) 687–7395; (800) 452–8807, ext. 7395; Fax: (541) 687–7414; TDD: (800) 735–2900;
Email: awardinfo@osac.state.or.us
Web: www.oregonstudentaid.gov/scholarships.aspx

Summary: To provide financial assistance to residents of Oregon who are attending college in any state.

Eligibility: Open to residents of Oregon who are entering their sophomore or higher years at a college or university in any state. Applicants must have a cumulative GPA of 3.5 or higher and be able to demonstrate financial need.

Financial data: Stipends for scholarships offered by the Oregon Student Access Commission (OSAC) range from $200 to $10,000 but recently averaged $2,300.

Duration: 1 year.

Number awarded: Varies each year.

Deadline: February of each year.

77 $ BENJAMIN FRANKLIN/EDITH GREEN SCHOLARSHIP

Oregon Student Access Commission
Attn: Grants and Scholarships Division
1500 Valley River Drive, Suite 100
Eugene, OR 97401–2146
Phone: (541) 687–7395; (800) 452–8807, ext. 7395; Fax: (541) 687–7414; TDD: (800) 735–2900;
Email: awardinfo@osac.state.or.us
Web: www.oregonstudentaid.gov/scholarships.aspx

Summary: To provide financial assistance to graduating high school seniors in Oregon who plan to attend college in the state.

Eligibility: Open to seniors graduating from high schools in Oregon. Applicants must be planning to attend a 4–year public college or university in the state. They must have a GPA between 3.45 and 3.55 and be able to demonstrate financial need.

Financial data: Stipends for scholarships offered by the Oregon Student Access Commission (OSAC) range from $200 to $10,000 but recently averaged $2,300.

Duration: 1 year; nonrenewable.

Number awarded: Varies each year; recently, 14 of these scholarships were awarded.

Deadline: February of each year.

78 BEST BUY SCHOLARSHIP PROGRAM

Scholarship America
Attn: Scholarship Management Services
One Scholarship Way
P.O. Box 297
St. Peter, MN 56082
Phone: (507) 931–1682; (800) 537–4180; Fax: (507) 931–9168;
Email: bestbuy@scholarshipamerica.org
Web: bestbuy.scholarshipamerica.org

Summary: To provide financial assistance for college to high school students who demonstrate outstanding volunteer community service.

Eligibility: Open to high school students in grades 9–12 at public, private, alternative, or home schools in the United States or Puerto who have a GPA of 2.5 or higher. Applicants must be planning to enroll full time at an accredited 2– or 4–year college, university, vocational/technical school, or online school/ program in the United States or Puerto Rico after graduation. They must be able to demonstrate "solid academic performance and exemplary community volunteer service or work experience." Consideration may also be given to participation and leadership in school activities, but financial need is not considered. Applications are only available at Best Buy stores throughout the country.

Financial data: The stipend is $1,000.

Duration: 1 year; nonrenewable.

Number awarded: 1,200 each year.

Deadline: February of each year.

79 BETTY MULLINS JONES SCHOLARSHIP

National Panhellenic Conference
Attn: NPC Foundation
3901 West 86th Street, Suite 398
Indianapolis, IN 46268
Phone: (317) 876–7802; Fax: (317) 876–7904;
Email: npcfoundation@npcwomen.org
Web: www.npcwomen.org/foundation/scholarships.aspx

Summary: To provide financial assistance to undergraduate women who are members of Greek–letter societies.

Eligibility: Open to Greek–affiliated women at colleges and universities in the United States. Applicants must be able to demonstrate that they have worked to further their Greek community's reputation on their campus. In the selection process, emphasis is placed on financial need and participation in university, Panhellenic, chapter, and other activities.

Financial data: The stipend is $1,000.

Duration: 1 year.

Number awarded: 1 each year.

Deadline: January of each year.

80 $$ BIA HIGHER EDUCATION GRANT PROGRAM

Bureau of Indian Affairs
Attn: Bureau of Indian Education
1849 C Street, N.W.
Mail Stop 3609 MIB
Washington, DC 20240
Phone: (202) 208–6123; Fax: (202) 208–3312
Web: www.bie.edu/ParentsStudents/Grants/index.htm

Summary: To provide financial assistance to undergraduate students who belong to or are affiliated with federally–recognized Indian tribes.

Eligibility: Open to 1) members of American Indian tribes who are eligible for the special programs and services provided through the Bureau of Indian Affairs (BIA) because of their status as Indians; and 2) individuals who are at least one–quarter degree Indian blood descendants of those members. Applicants must be 1) enrolled or planning to enroll at an accredited college or university in a course of study leading to an associate of arts or bachelor's degree; and 2) able to demonstrate financial need. Most tribes administer the grant program directly for their members, but other tribal members may contact the BIA Bureau of Indian Education to learn the name and address of the nearest Education Line Officer who can provide an application and assistance in completing it.

Financial data: Individual awards depend on the financial need of the recipient; they range from $300 to $5,000 and average $2,800 per year. Recently, a total of $20,290,000 was available for this program.

Duration: 1 year; may be renewed for up to 4 additional years.

Number awarded: Approximately 9,500 students receive assistance through this program annually.

Deadline: June of each year for fall term; October of each year for spring term; April of each year for summer school.

81 BIACS SCHOLARSHIPS

Bluegrass Indo–American Civic Society
Attn: Chair, Scholarship Endowment Fund
P.O. Box 910666
Lexington, KY 40591–0666
Email: scholarship@biacs.org
Web: biacs.org/11746.html

Summary: To provide financial assistance to high school seniors in Kentucky who plan to attend college in any state.

Eligibility: Open to seniors graduating from high schools in Kentucky and planning to enroll full time at a recognized educational institution in any state. Students of all races and national origins are eligible. Along with their application, they must submit 1–page essays on 1) their civic, volunteer, athletic, academic, and other activities and accomplishments; and 2) their educational goals, plans to accomplish those goals, and their future career ambitions. Selection is based on academic excellence, extracurricular activities, demonstrated potential for successful completion of higher education, and financial need.

Financial data: The stipend is $1,000.

Duration: 1 year.

Number awarded: Varies each year; recently, 12 of these scholarships were awarded.

Deadline: April of each year.

82 $ BIG 33 ACADEMIC SCHOLARSHIPS

Big 33 Scholarship Foundation
Attn: Scholarship Coordinator
4750 Lindle Road

Harrisburg, PA 17111
Phone: (717) 774–3303; (877) PABIG–33; Fax: (717) 774–1749;
Email: leckenrode@big33.org
Web: www.big33.org

Summary: To provide financial assistance to graduating high school seniors in Pennsylvania who plan to attend college in any state.

Eligibility: Open to seniors graduating from public and accredited private high schools in Pennsylvania. Applicants must be planning to attend a college or university in any state. Selection is based on special talents, leadership, obstacles overcome, academic achievement (at least a 2.0 GPA), community service, unique endeavors, financial need, and a 1–page essay on why the applicant deserves the scholarship.

Financial data: Stipends range up to $4,000, but most are $1,000.

Duration: 1 year; nonrenewable.

Number awarded: Varies each year; recently, a total of 79 of these scholarships was awarded.

Deadline: February of each year.

83 BIG Y 50TH ANNIVERSARY EMPLOYEE COMMEMORATIVE SCHOLARSHIPS

Big Y Foods, Inc.
Attn: Scholarship Committee
2145 Roosevelt Avenue
P.O. Box 7840
Springfield, MA 01102–7840
Phone: (413) 504–4080
Web: www.bigy.com/education/y_scholarships.php

Summary: To provide financial assistance to outstanding undergraduate and graduate students in the Big Y Foods market area in Massachusetts and Connecticut.

Eligibility: Open to high school seniors, undergraduates, graduate students, and nontraditional students of any age who reside within western or central Massachusetts, Norfolk County in Massachusetts, or the state of Connecticut. Big Y employees and their dependents are also eligible. Applicants must submit a transcript, standardized test scores (SAT, ACT, GRE, GMAT, or LSAT), 2 letters of recommendation, and a resume. Selection is based on academic merit and achievement.

Financial data: The stipend is $1,000.

Duration: 1 year; nonrenewable.

Number awarded: 6 each year.

Deadline: January of each year.

84 $ BILL MCADAM SCHOLARSHIP FUND

Hemophilia Foundation of Michigan
c/o Cathy McAdam
22226 Doxtator
Dearborn, MI 48128
Phone: (313) 563–1412;
Email: mcmcadam@comcast.net

Summary: To provide financial assistance for college to students with a bleeding disorder or members of their families.

Eligibility: Open to 1) students with a hereditary bleeding disorder (hemophilia, von Willebrand, etc.) or 2) members of their families (spouse, partner, child, sibling). Applicants must be U.S. citizens and enrolled or planning to enroll at an accredited 2– or 4–year college, trade or technical school, or other certification program. Along with their application, they must submit 2 letters of recommendation and 3 essays: 1) what they would like the scholarship committee to know about their dream career and the passion that moves them toward furthering their education; 2) how they would describe a favorite painting or photograph to someone who is blind; and 3) how they will make a difference in the fight against stigma, fear, and discrimination for people facing chronic illness or disability. Financial need is not considered in the selection process.

Financial data: The stipend is $2,000. Funds are paid directly to the recipient's institution.

Duration: 1 year; nonrenewable.

Number awarded: 1 each year.

Deadline: May of each year.

85 $ BIORX/HEMOPHILIA OF NORTH CAROLINA EDUCATIONAL SCHOLARSHIPS

Hemophilia of North Carolina
Attn: Scholarship Committee
260 Town Hall Drive, Suite A
Morrisville, NC 27560–5544
Phone: (919) 319–0014; (800) 990–5557; Fax: (919) 319–0016;
Email: info@hemophilia–nc.org
Web: www. hemophilia–nc.org/scholarships.html

Summary: To provide financial assistance for college to people with hemophilia, their caregivers, and their families.

Eligibility: Open to caregivers of children affected with bleeding disorders, people who have been diagnosed with hemophilia, and siblings and parents of people diagnosed with hemophilia. Residents of all states are eligible. Applicants must be enrolled or planning to enroll at an accredited college, university, or certified training program. Along with their application, they must submit an essay of 1 to 2 pages describing their occupational goals and objectives in life and how their or their family's experiences with bleeding disorders have affected their choices. Preference is given to applicants who are studying or planning to study a health care–related field. Selection is primarily based on merit, although financial need may be considered as well.

Financial data: The stipend is $2,000.

Duration: 1 year.

Number awarded: 4 each year, of which at least 1 of which is reserved for an applicant studying in a health–related field.

Deadline: April of each year.

86 BLANCH ABELS BURRELL SCHOLARSHIP

United Daughters of the Confederacy–Mississippi Division
c/o Sallie L. Roberts, Second Vice President
40 West Julius Carter Road
Woodville, MS 39669–4232
Web: mississippiudc.homestead.com/Scholarships.html

Summary: To provide financial assistance for college to Confederate descendants from Mississippi.

Eligibility: Open to residents of Mississippi who are 1) lineal descendants of Confederates; or 2) collateral descendants and also members of the Children of the Confederacy or the United Daughters of the Confederacy (UDC). Applicants must submit proof of the Confederate military record of at least 1 ancestor, with the company and regiment in which he served.

Financial data: A stipend is awarded (amount not specified).

Duration: 1 year.

Number awarded: 1 each year.

Deadline: February of each year.

87 $$ BLOGGING SCHOLARSHIP

College Scholarships Foundation
5506 Red Robin Road
Raleigh, NC 27613
Phone: (919) 630–4895; (888) 501–9050;
Email: info@collegescholarships.org
Web: www.collegescholarships.org/our–scholarships/blogging.htm

Summary: To recognize and reward, with college scholarships, students who maintain a weblog.

Eligibility: Open to U.S. citizens and permanent residents currently enrolled full time at a postsecondary institution in the United States. Applicants must be maintaining a weblog while they are in school. Selection is based on a 1,000–word essay they submit online. The essay should cover such questions as the most interesting or inspiring blog post they have ever read, why they found it inspiring, how they have used blogging to help themselves or others, the most powerful social change they have seen come out of blogging, why they started blogging, what blogging means to them, and why blogging is important to them.

Financial data: The prize is a $10,000 scholarship.

Duration: The prize is awarded annually.

Number awarded: 1 each year.

Deadline: November of each year.

88 $ BLOSSOM KALAMA EVANS MEMORIAL SCHOLARSHIPS

Hawai'i Community Foundation
Attn: Scholarship Department
827 Fort Street Mall
Honolulu, HI 96813
Phone: (808) 537–6333; (888) 731–3863; Fax: (808) 521–6286;
Email: scholarships@hcf–hawaii.org
Web: www.hawaiicommunityfoundation.org/scholarships

Summary: To provide financial assistance to residents of Hawaii of native ancestry who are interested in working on an undergraduate or graduate degree at a school in any state.

Eligibility: Open to residents of Hawaii who are of Native Hawaiian ancestry and enrolled as full–time juniors, seniors, or graduate students at a college or university in any state. Applicants must be able to demonstrate academic achievement (GPA of 2.7 or higher), good moral character, and financial need. Along with their application, they must submit a short statement indicating their reasons for attending college, their planned course of study, their career goals, what community service means to them, and how they plan to use their knowledge to serve the needs of the Native Hawaiian community.

Financial data: The amounts of the awards depend on the availability of funds and the need of the recipient. Recently, the average value of each of the scholarships awarded by the foundation was more than $2,000.

Duration: 1 year.

Number awarded: Varies each year; recently, 9 of these scholarships were awarded.

Deadline: February of each year.

89 BOBBY DODD MEMORIAL SCHOLARSHIP FOR OUTSTANDING COMMUNITY SERVICE

Georgia District Civitan Foundation, Inc.
c/o Kenny Martin, Scholarship Chair
2063 Julianne Road
Rentz, GA 31075–3354
Phone: (478) 275–0506;
Email: kmartin@nlamerica.com
Web: www.georgiacivitan.org

Summary: To provide financial assistance to high school seniors in Georgia who are physically challenged, have an outstanding record of community service, and plan to attend college in any state.

Eligibility: Open to physically–challenged seniors graduating from high schools in Georgia and planning to attend an accredited college or university in any state. Membership in Civitan International is not required, but Junior Civitan Club members are encouraged to apply. Interested students must submit a 500–word essay on their community activities and how those experiences have prepared them for life. In the selection process, academic achievement and financial need are considered, but the overwhelming factor is community service involvement.

Financial data: The winner receives $1,200 and the runner–up receives $800. Funds are paid directly to the student.

Duration: 1 year.

Number awarded: 2 each year.

Deadline: January of each year.

90 $ BOBBY SOX HIGH SCHOOL SENIOR SCHOLARSHIP PROGRAM

Bobby Sox Softball
Attn: Scholarship
P.O. Box 5880
Buena Park, CA 90622–5880
Phone: (714) 522–1234; Fax: (714) 522–6548
Web: www.bobbysoxsoftball.org/scholar.html

Summary: To provide financial assistance for college to high school seniors who have participated in Bobby Sox Softball.

Eligibility: Open to girls graduating from high school with a GPA of 2.0 or higher. Applicants must have participated in Bobby Sox Softball for at least 5 seasons. They must submit an essay on "The Value of Participation in Bobby Sox Softball." Selection is based on the essay (60 points), academic excellence (20 points), and letters of recommendation from Bobby Sox officials, community leaders, and school representatives (20 points).

Financial data: Stipends range from $100 to $2,500.

Duration: 1 year.

Number awarded: Approximately 45 each year.

Deadline: April of each year.

91 $$ BONNER SCHOLARS PROGRAM

Corella and Bertram F. Bonner Foundation
10 Mercer Street
Princeton, NJ 08540
Phone: (609) 924–6663; Fax: (609) 683–4626;
Email: info@bonner.org
Web: bonnernetwork.pbworks.com/w/page/13112067/Bonner–Program

Summary: To provide scholarships to high school seniors who need help paying for college and who have a commitment to strengthening their communities through service.

Eligibility: Open to graduating high school seniors planning to attend a participating college throughout the southeastern and midwestern United States (check with the sponsor for the latest list). Applicants must have significant financial need, a solid academic performance in high school (graduating in the top 40% of their class), acceptance at a participating college, and demonstrated responsibility and good citizenship at home, school, church/synagogue, or in the community. A goal of the program is to increase the racial or ethnic diversity of the incoming class, so that the Bonner Scholars will have at least double the number of students of color as the college as a whole. Interested students must contact the admissions office at the participating Bonner college they wish to attend.

Financial data: Scholars receive a grant of $2,500 during the school year in recognition of their service during that time and another grant of $5,000 to support 2 full–time summer service internships. Scholars who successfully complete the program and graduate from college receive $2,000 to reduce their student loans or to pay for future educational opportunities. The program also provides additional funds to support service trips and enrichment activities for scholars.

Duration: 1 year; may be renewed up to 3 additional years.

Number awarded: Approximately 1,500 each year.

Deadline: Deadline not specified.

92 $ BOOMER ESIASON FOUNDATION GENERAL ACADEMIC SCHOLARSHIPS

Boomer Esiason Foundation
c/o Jerry Cahill
483 Tenth Avenue, Suite 300
New York, NY 10018
Phone: (646) 292–7930; Fax: (646) 292–7945;
Email: jcahill@esiason.org
Web: esiason.org/thriving–with–cf/scholarships.php

Summary: To provide financial assistance to undergraduate and graduate students who have cystic fibrosis (CF).

Eligibility: Open to CF patients who are working on an undergraduate or graduate degree. Applicants must submit a letter from their doctor confirming the diagnosis of CF and a list of daily medications, information on financial need, a detailed breakdown of tuition costs from their academic institution, transcripts, and a 2–page essay on 1) their postgraduation goals; and 2) the importance of compliance with CF therapies and what they practice on a daily basis to stay healthy. Selection is based on academic ability, character, leadership potential, service to the community, and financial need. Finalists are interviewed by telephone.

Financial data: Stipends range from $500 to $2,500. Funds are paid directly to the academic institution to assist in covering the cost of tuition and fees.

Duration: 1 year; nonrenewable.

Number awarded: 10 to 15 each year.

Deadline: March, June, September, or December of each year.

93 $$ BP PRINCIPAL AND COMMISSIONER SCHOLARSHIPS

Alaska Association of Secondary School Principals
Attn: Executive Director, Alaska Principal Foundation
P.O. Box 83530
Fairbanks, AK 99708
Phone: (907) 458–8880; Fax: (907) 458–8889;
Email: scholarships@alaskaprincipal.org
Web: www.alaskaprincipal.org/domain/29

Summary: To provide financial assistance to high school seniors in Alaska who plan to attend college in any state.

Eligibility: Open to seniors graduating from high schools in Alaska who are nominated by their principal and who plan to enroll full–time at a 4–year college or university in any state. Letters of nomination must describe the student's academic achievement, community and school involvement, leadership potential, financial need, and strengths compared to other students eligible for nomination, as well as describing how the scholarship will assist the student in meeting personal goals and aspirations. In addition to the letter of nomination, the application packet must include a 1–page letter from the student explaining why he or she is seeking this scholarship, SAT and/or ACT scores, and transcripts.

Financial data: Stipends are $5,000 or $1,000 per year.

Duration: 1 year; may be renewed up to 3 additional years, provided the recipient remains enrolled full time at a 4–year college or university with a GPA of 2.0 or higher.
Number awarded: 25 each year (including 10 from large schools and 25 from small schools), of whom 24 receive $1,000 per year and 1 (the most outstanding applicant) receives an additional $4,000 per year.
Deadline: February of each year.

94 BRIGADIER GENERAL ROSCOE C. CARTWRIGHT AWARDS

The ROCKS, Inc.
c/o WSC Associates, LLP
7700 Old Branch Avenue, Suite A202
Clinton, MD 20735
Phone: (301) 856–9319; (877) 762–5732; Fax: (301) 856–5220;
Email: therocks@aol.com
Web: www.rocksinc.org
Summary: To provide financial assistance to students enrolled in ROTC programs at Historically Black Colleges and Universities (HBCUs).
Eligibility: Open to Army and Air Force Cadets and Navy Midshipmen at HBCUs. Applicants must be planning to enter military service as officers following graduation from college. They must submit a letter of recommendation from their professor of military science evaluating their appearance, attitude, character, dedication, initiative, integrity, judgment, leadership potential, and written and oral communication ability. Financial need is not considered in the selection process.
Financial data: The stipend is $1,200.
Duration: 1 year.
Number awarded: Varies each year.
Deadline: February of each year.

95 $$ BRUCE LEE SCHOLARSHIP

US Pan Asian American Chamber of Commerce
Attn: Scholarship Coordinator
1329 18th Street, N.W.
Washington, DC 20036
Phone: (202) 296–5221; (800) 696–7818; Fax: (202) 296–5225;
Email: info@uspaacc.com
Web: celebrasianconference.com/about–celebrasian/scholarships/overview
Summary: To provide financial assistance for college to high school seniors who have persevered over adversity.
Eligibility: Open to high school seniors of any ethnicity who are U.S. citizens or permanent residents. Applicants must be planning to enroll full time at an accredited postsecondary educational institution in the United States. Along with their application, they must submit a 500–word essay on the adversities they have overcome. Selection is based on academic excellence (GPA of 3.3 or higher), character, ability to persevere and prevail over adversity, community service involvement, and financial need.
Financial data: The maximum stipend is $5,000. Funds are paid directly to the recipient's college or university.
Duration: 1 year.
Number awarded: 1 each year.
Deadline: March of each year.

96 $$ BRYANT–JORDAN FOUNDATION OUTSTANDING SCHOLAR–ATHLETE AWARDS

Alabama High School Athletic Association
Attn: Bryant–Jordan Foundation
7325 Halcyon Summit Drive
P.O. Box 242367
Montgomery, AL 36124–2367
Phone: (334) 263–6994; Fax: (334) 387–0075;
Email: staff@ahsaa.com
Web: www.ahsaa.com
Summary: To recognize and reward, with scholarships for college in any state, high school seniors in Alabama who have demonstrated excellence in academics and athletics.
Eligibility: Open to seniors graduating from high schools in Alabama who have been involved in the interscholastic athletic program of the school and have also demonstrated academic excellence. Students must be nominated by their school. They first compete within the state's 6 athletic classes (based on enrollment) and the 8 regions into which each class is divided. Selection is based on academic standing, athletic honors, student leadership, and civic and church leadership. Regional winners are selected by school administrators in each region; a state committee then selects winners in each of the athletic classes from among the regional winners for that class; the state committee then selects the overall state winner from among the class winners.
Financial data: The award is a $2,500 college scholarship for each of the regional winners. Each class winner receives an additional $3,000 college scholarship. The overall state winner receives an additional $3,000 college scholarship. The school of each class winner receives $2,000 and the school of the overall state winner receives an additional $1,000.
Duration: The awards are presented annually.
Number awarded: 48 regional winners are selected each year. Of those, 6 are chosen as class winners and 1 of those class winners is selected as the overall state winner.
Deadline: January of each year.

97 $ BRYON RIESCH SCHOLARSHIPS

Bryon Riesch Paralysis Foundation
P.O. Box 1388
Waukesha, WI 53187–1388
Phone: (262) 547–2083;
Email: briesch@brpf.org
Web: www.brpf.org/Grants/ApplicationScholarships.html
Summary: To provide financial assistance to undergraduate and graduate students who have a neurological disability or the children of people with such a disability.
Eligibility: Open to students entering or enrolled at a 2– or 4–year college or university as an undergraduate or graduate student. Applicants must have a neurological disability or be the child of a person with such a disability. They must have a GPA of 2.5 or higher in high school or college. Along with their application, they must submit a 200–word essay on why they deserve the scholarship, a statement of their 5– and 10–year goals, and a list of work experience. Financial need is not considered in the selection process.
Financial data: Stipends range from $1,000 to $2,000.
Duration: 1 year; may be renewed.
Number awarded: Varies each semester; recently, 5 scholarships (all at $1,000) were awarded for the fall semester and 3 (including 1 at $2,000 and 2 at $1,000) were awarded for the spring semester.
Deadline: May of each year for fall semester; December of each year for spring semester.

98 $$ BURGER KING SCHOLARS PROGRAM

Burger King Corporation
Attn: Have It Your Way Foundation
5505 Blue Lagoon Drive
Miami, FL 33126
Phone: (303) 378–3186; Fax: (303) 378–7017;
Email: BK–HIYWFoundation@whopper.com
Web: www.haveityourwayfoundation.org/burger_king_scholars_program.html
Summary: To provide financial assistance for college to high school seniors in the United States, Canada, and Puerto Rico.
Eligibility: Open to seniors graduating from high schools or home schools in the United States, Canada, and Puerto Rico who are planning to enroll full time at an accredited 2– or 4–year college, university, or vocational/technical school. Applicants must have a cumulative GPA of 2.5 or higher. Selection is based on academic achievements and records (50%) and participation in school and community activities (50%).
Financial data: The stipend is $25,000 for the King Award, $5,000 for regional awards, and $1,000 for all other scholarships.
Duration: 1 year; nonrenewable.
Number awarded: Varies each year; recently, 1,255 of these scholarships were awarded, including 1 King Award, 5 regional awards, and 1,249 other scholarships.
Deadline: January of each year.

99 $ BUTLER–WELLS SCHOLARSHIP

Muskingum County Community Foundation
Attn: Scholarship Central
534 Putnam Avenue
Zanesville, OH 43701–4933
Phone: (740) 453–5192; Fax: (740) 453–5734;
Email: scholarshipcentral@mccf.org
Web: www.mccf.org

Summary: To provide financial assistance to residents of Illinois, Indiana, Ohio, and Pennsylvania who are attending college in those states.
Eligibility: Open to residents of Illinois, Indiana, Ohio, and Pennsylvania who are currently attending an accredited college, university, community college, vocational/technical school, or trade school in those states; preference is given to residents of Piqua, Ohio, Cincinnati, Ohio, or Miami County, Ohio. Applicants must have a GPA of 2.0 or higher. They may be majoring in any field, but their course of study must relate to specific career objectives, a terminal degree, or eventual job certification. Selection is based on financial need, commitment to pursuing and completing their course of study, and commitment to "giving back to the community" through volunteerism, community service, or religious activity.
Financial data: Stipends range from $250 to $2,500.
Duration: 1 year; recipients may reapply.
Number awarded: 1 or more each year.
Deadline: March of each year.

100 $ C. EUGENE CATO MEMORIAL SCHOLARSHIP

Indiana High School Athletic Association, Inc.
9150 Meridian Street
P.O. Box 40650
Indianapolis, IN 46240
Phone: (317) 846–6601; Fax: (317) 575–4244
Web: www.ihsaa.org
Summary: To provide financial assistance to high school seniors in Indiana who have participated in athletics and plan to attend college in any state.
Eligibility: Open to seniors graduating from high schools in Indiana that are members of the Indiana High School Athletic Association (IHSAA) and planning to attend a college or university in any state. Applicants must have won a varsity letter in at least 1 of the 20 IHSAA sanctioned athletic programs. They must have no violations of their school's athletic code of conduct and may not have been ejected from an IHSAA contest due to unsportsmanlike behavior. Selection is based on academic achievement (GPA of 3.0 or higher) and participation in athletics.
Financial data: The stipend is $2,500. Funds are paid directly to the student.
Duration: 1 year.
Number awarded: 12 each year.
Deadline: January of each year.

101 C. RAYMOND AND DELSIA R. COLLINS FUND SCHOLARSHIP

Greater Kanawha Valley Foundation
Attn: Scholarship Program Officer
1600 Huntington Square
900 Lee Street East, 16th Floor
Charleston, WV 25301
Phone: (304) 346–3620; (800) 467–5909; Fax: (304) 346–3640;
Email: shoover@tgkvf.org
Web: www.tgkvf.org/page.aspx?pid=409
Summary: To provide financial assistance for college to residents of West Virginia.
Eligibility: Open to residents of West Virginia who are attending or planning to attend a college or university in any state. Applicants must have an ACT score of 20 or higher; be able to demonstrate good moral character, academic excellence, and financial need; and have a GPA of 2.5 or higher.
Financial data: The stipend is $1,000 per year.
Duration: 1 year; may be renewed.
Number awarded: Varies each year; recently, 10 of these scholarships were awarded.
Deadline: January of each year.

102 $$ CAL GRANT A

California Student Aid Commission
Attn: Student Support Services Branch
10811 International Drive, Suite 100
P.O. Box 419027
Rancho Cordova, CA 95741–9027
Phone: (888) CA–GRANT; Fax: (916) 446–8002;
Email: studentsupport@csac.ca.gov
Web: www.csac.ca.gov/doc.asp?id=105
Summary: To provide financial assistance to low– and middle–income students in California who need help to pay tuition/fee costs.
Eligibility: Open to California residents who are U.S. citizens or eligible noncitizens, have financial need, are attending a qualifying college in California at least half time, are in a program of study leading directly to an undergraduate degree or certificate, do not possess a bachelor's degree prior to receiving a Cal Grant award, and do not owe a refund on any state or federal educational grant or have not defaulted on a student loan. They must complete and file both the Free Application for Federal Student Aid and GPA verification forms. Selection is based on financial need and GPA. The income ceiling for dependent students and independent students with dependents other than a spouse is $92,600 with 6 or more family members, $85,900 with 5 family members, $80,100 with 4 family members, $73,700 with 3 family members, or $72,000 with 2 family members. For independent students, the income ceiling is $33,600 for married students with no dependents other than a spouse or $29,400 for single students. The asset ceiling is $62,000 for dependent students or $29,500 for independent students. All graduating high school seniors in California who have a GPA of 3.0 or higher, meet the Cal Grant financial and academic requirements, and apply on time receive a Cal Grant A Entitlement Award. Other eligible students who have a GPA of 3.0 or higher may apply for a Cal Grant A Competitive Award; selection of those is based on family income, parents' educational level, GPA, time out of high school, and whether or not the applicant comes from a single–parent household. The performance standards and resources available to the applicant's high school may also be taken into account.
Financial data: Stipends cover the full payment of tuition and fees at public 4–year universities in California (currently, $12,192 at campuses of the University of California or $5,472 at components of the California State University system). For students at independent colleges and universities in California, the maximum stipend is $9,708. Students who qualify for a Cal Grant A and want to attend a California community college may reserve a tuition/fee award for up to 3 years, until they transfer to a tuition/fee charging college.
Duration: 1 year; may be renewed up to 3 additional years. Students in a teaching credential or mandatory 5–year program may apply for a fifth year of support.
Number awarded: Varies each year; recently, more than 112,000 Cal Grant A and B entitlement awards were provided and 11,500 Cal Grant A and B competitive awards (up to half reserved for students transferring from community colleges) were provided.
Deadline: High school seniors must apply for an entitlement grant by February of each year. Students entering a community college and applying for a competitive grant must do so by the end of August of each year.

103 $$ CAL GRANT B

California Student Aid Commission
Attn: Student Support Services
10811 International Drive
P.O. Box 419027
Rancho Cordova, CA 95741–9027
Phone: (916) 526–7590; (888) CA–GRANT; Fax: (916) 526–8002;
Email: studentsupport@csac.ca.gov
Web: www.csac.ca.gov/doc.asp?id=106
Summary: To provide financial assistance to disadvantaged and low–income students in California who need help to pay tuition/fee costs.
Eligibility: Open to California residents who are U.S. citizens or eligible noncitizens, have financial need, are attending a qualifying college in California at least half time, are in a program of study leading directly to an undergraduate degree or certificate, do not possess a bachelor's degree prior to receiving a Cal Grant award, and do not owe a refund on any state or federal educational grant or have not defaulted on a student loan. They must complete and file both the Free Application for Federal Student Aid and GPA verification forms. Selection is based on financial need and GPA. The income ceiling for dependent students and independent students with dependents other than a spouse is $50,900 with 6 or more family members, $47,100 with 5 family members, $42,100 with 4 family members, $37,900 with 3 family members, or $33,600 with 2 family members. For independent students, the income ceiling is $33,600 for married students with no dependents other than a spouse or $29,400 for single students. The asset ceiling is $62,000 for dependent students or $29,500 for independent students. All graduating high school seniors in California who have a GPA of 2.0 or higher, meet the Cal Grant financial and academic requirements, and apply on time receive a Cal Grant B Entitlement Award. Other eligible students who have a GPA of 2.0 or higher may apply for a Cal Grant B Competitive Award; selection of those is based on family income, parents' educational level, GPA, time out of high school, whether or not the applicant comes from a single–parent household, and the performance standards and resources available to the applicant's high school.
Financial data: In the first year of college, these grants provide only an allowance of $1,551 for books and living expenses. When renewed or applied for after the freshman year, grants provide that living allowance plus full payment of tuition and fees at University of California campuses (currently $12,192 per year) or components of the California State University system (currently $5,472

per year) or up to $9,708 for students at independent colleges and universities in California.

Duration: 1 year; may be renewed up to 3 additional years. Students in a teaching credential or mandatory 5–year program may apply for a fifth year of support.

Number awarded: Varies each year; recently, more than 112,000 Cal Grant A and B entitlement awards were provided and 11,500 Cal Grant A and B competitive awards (up to half reserved for students transferring from community colleges) were provided.

Deadline: High school seniors must apply for an entitlement grant by February of each year. Students entering a community college and applying for a competitive grant must do so by the end of August of each year.

104 $ CAL GRANT C

California Student Aid Commission
Attn: Student Support Services
10811 International Drive
P.O. Box 419027
Rancho Cordova, CA 95741–9027
Phone: (916) 526–7590; (888) CA–GRANT; Fax: (916) 526–8002;
Email: studentsupport@csac.ca.gov
Web: www.csac.ca.gov/doc.asp?id=107

Summary: To provide financial assistance to vocational school students in California who need help with tuition and training costs.

Eligibility: Open to California residents who are U.S. citizens or eligible noncitizens, have financial need, have a high school GPA of 2.0 or higher, are attending a qualifying occupational or vocational training program in California at least half time, are in a program of study that is at least 4 months in length, do not possess a bachelor's degree prior to receiving a Cal Grant award, and do not owe a refund on any state or federal educational grant or have not defaulted on a student loan. They must complete and file both the Free Application for Federal Student Aid and GPA verification forms. The income ceiling for dependent students and independent students with dependents other than a spouse is $92,600 with 6 or more family members, $85,900 with 5 family members, $80,100 with 4 family members, $73,700 with 3 family members, or $72,000 with 2 family members. For independent students, the income ceiling is $33,600 for married students with no dependents other than a spouse or $29,400 for single students. The asset ceiling is $62,000 for dependent students or $29,500 for independent students.

Financial data: Grants provide $576 for books, tools, and equipment. Students who attend a school other than a California community college may also receive up to $2,592 in assistance.

Duration: 1 year; may be renewed.

Number awarded: Varies each year; recently, 7,761 new grants were awarded.

Deadline: February of each year.

105 $$ CALIFORNIA CHAFEE GRANT PROGRAM

California Student Aid Commission
Attn: Specialized Programs Operations Branch
10811 International Drive, Suite 100
P.O. Box 419029
Rancho Cordova, CA 95741–9029
Phone: (916) 526–8276; (888) CA–GRANT; Fax: (916) 464–7977;
Email: specialized@csac.ca.gov
Web: www.chafee.csac.ca.gov

Summary: To provide financial assistance for college to residents of California who have been in foster care.

Eligibility: Open to residents of California who have been in foster care between their 16th and 18th birthday and are currently younger than 22 years of age. Applicants must be enrolled at least half time in a college or vocational school in any state. They must be able to demonstrate financial need.

Financial data: The stipend depends on the need of the recipient, to a maximum of $5,000 per year.

Duration: 1 year; may be renewed if the recipient maintains at least half time enrollment and satisfactory academic progress.

Number awarded: Varies each year; recently, a total of $14.5 million was paid to 2,897 recipients.

Deadline: Deadline not specified.

106 $$ CALIFORNIA FEE WAIVER PROGRAM FOR CHILDREN OF VETERANS

California Department of Veterans Affairs
Attn: Division of Veterans Services
1227 O Street, Room 105
P.O. Box 942895
Sacramento, CA 94295
Phone: (916) 653–2573; (877) 741–8532; Fax: (916) 653–2563; TDD: (800) 324–5966
Web: www.cdva.ca.gov/VetServices/Education.aspx

Summary: To provide financial assistance for college to the children of disabled or deceased veterans in California.

Eligibility: Open to the children of veterans who 1) died of a service–connected disability; 2) had a service–connected disability at the time of death; or 3) currently have a service–connected disability of any level of severity. Applicants must plan to attend a community college in California, branch of the California State University system, or campus of the University of California. Their income, including the value of support received from parents, cannot exceed $11,369. The veteran is not required to have a connection to California for this program. Dependents in college who are eligible to receive federal education benefits from the U.S. Department of Veterans Affairs are not eligible for these fee waivers.

Financial data: This program provides for waiver of registration fees to students attending any publicly–supported community or state college or university in California.

Duration: 1 year; may be renewed.

Number awarded: Varies each year.

Deadline: Deadline not specified.

107 $$ CALIFORNIA FEE WAIVER PROGRAM FOR DEPENDENTS OF TOTALLY DISABLED VETERANS

California Department of Veterans Affairs
Attn: Division of Veterans Services
1227 O Street, Room 105
P.O. Box 942895
Sacramento, CA 94295
Phone: (916) 653–2573; (877) 741–8532; Fax: (916) 653–2563; TDD: (800) 324–5966
Web: www.cdva.ca.gov/VetServices/Education.aspx

Summary: To provide financial assistance for college to dependents of disabled and other California veterans.

Eligibility: Open to the spouses, children, and unremarried spouses or registered domestic partners (RDPs) of veterans who are currently totally service–connected disabled (or are being compensated for a service–connected disability at a rate of 100%) or who died of a service–connected cause or disability. The veteran parent must have served during a qualifying war period and must have been discharged or released from military service under honorable conditions. Children must be younger than 27 years of age (extended to 30 if the child is a veteran); there are no age restrictions for spouses, surviving spouses, or RDPs. This program does not have an income limit. Dependents in college are not eligible if they are qualified to receive educational benefits from the U.S. Department of Veterans Affairs. Applicants must be attending or planning to attend a community college, branch of the California State University system, or campus of the University of California.

Financial data: Full–time college students receive a waiver of tuition and registration fees at any publicly–supported community or state college or university in California.

Duration: Children of eligible veterans may receive postsecondary benefits until the needed training is completed or until the dependent reaches 27 years of age (extended to 30 if the dependent serves in the armed forces). Spouses and surviving spouses are limited to a maximum of 48 months' full–time training or the equivalent in part–time training.

Number awarded: Varies each year.

Deadline: Deadline not specified.

108 $$ CALIFORNIA FEE WAIVER PROGRAM FOR RECIPIENTS OF THE MEDAL OF HONOR AND THEIR CHILDREN

California Department of Veterans Affairs
Attn: Division of Veterans Services
1227 O Street, Room 101
P.O. Box 942895
Sacramento, CA 94295
Phone: (916) 653–2573; (877) 741–8532; Fax: (916) 653–2563; TDD: (800) 324–5966
Web: www.cdva.ca.gov/VetServices/Education.aspx

Summary: To provide financial assistance for college to veterans in California who received the Medal of Honor and their children.

Eligibility: Open to recipients of the Medal of Honor and their children younger than 27 years of age who are residents of California. Applicants must be

attending or planning to attend a community college, branch of the California State University system, or campus of the University of California.
Financial data: Full–time college students receive a waiver of tuition and registration fees at any publicly–supported community or state college or university in California.
Duration: 1 year; may be renewed.
Number awarded: Varies each year.
Deadline: Deadline not specified.

109 CALIFORNIA LEGION AUXILIARY EDUCATIONAL ASSISTANCE

American Legion Auxiliary
Department of California
Veterans War Memorial Building
401 Van Ness Avenue, Room 113
San Francisco, CA 94102–4586
Phone: (415) 861–5092; Fax: (415) 861–8365;
Email: calegionaux@calegionaux.org
Web: www.calegionaux.org/scholarships.htm
Summary: To provide financial assistance to high school seniors in California who are the children of veterans or military personnel and require assistance to continue their education.
Eligibility: Open to seniors graduating from high schools in California who are the children of active–duty military personnel or veterans who served during war time. Applicants must be planning to continue their education at a college, university, or business/trade school in California. Each high school in California may nominate only 1 student for these scholarships; the faculty selects the nominee if more than 1 student wishes to apply. Selection is based on the application (25%), scholarship (25%), character and leadership (25%), and financial need (25%).
Financial data: Stipends are $1,000 or $500 per year.
Duration: 1 year; 1 of the scholarships may be renewed 1 additional year.
Number awarded: 8 each year: 1 at $1,000 that may be renewed 1 additional year, 4 at $1,000 that are nonrenewable, and 3 at $500 that are nonrenewable.
Deadline: March of each year.

110 CALIFORNIA LEGION AUXILIARY SCHOLARSHIPS FOR CONTINUING AND/OR REENTRY STUDENTS

American Legion Auxiliary
Department of California
Veterans War Memorial Building
401 Van Ness Avenue, Room 113
San Francisco, CA 94102–4586
Phone: (415) 861–5092; Fax: (415) 861–8365;
Email: calegionaux@calegionaux.org
Web: www.calegionaux.org/scholarships.htm
Summary: To provide financial assistance to California residents who are active–duty military personnel, veterans, or children of veterans and require assistance to continue their education.
Eligibility: Open to California residents who are 1) active–duty military personnel; 2) veterans of World War I, World War II, Korea, Vietnam, Grenada/Lebanon, Panama, or Desert Shield/Desert Storm; and 3) children of veterans who served during those periods of war. Applicants must be continuing or reentry students at a college, university, or business/trade school in California. Selection is based on the application (25%), scholarship (25%), character and leadership (25%), and financial need (25%).
Financial data: The stipend is $1,000 or $500.
Duration: 1 year.
Number awarded: 5 each year: 3 at $1,000 and 2 at $500.
Deadline: March of each year.

111 $ CALIFORNIA SCOTTISH RITE FOUNDATION SPECIAL SCHOLARSHIPS

California Scottish Rite Foundation
Attn: Secretary
855 Elm Avenue
Long Beach, CA 90813–4414
Phone: (562) 435–6061; Fax: (562) 435–3302;
Email: secy.csrf@verizon.net
Web: www.casr–foundation.org/scholarships/special–scholarship
Summary: To provide financial assistance to California residents interested in attending college in any state to major in any field.
Eligibility: Open to California residents between 17 and 25 years of age who are attending or planning to attend an accredited college or university in any state as a full–time student and major in any field. Applicants must be able to demonstrate high ideals and ability, strong grades in school (GPA of 3.0 or higher), financial need, and part–time employment. No affiliation with a Masonic–related organization is required. Along with their application, they must submit brief statements on their 1) belief in a Supreme Being; 2) ideas about separation of church and state; and 3) career goals.
Financial data: The stipend is $2,000 per year.
Duration: 1 year; may be renewed up to 3 additional years.
Number awarded: Varies each year.
Deadline: February of each year.

112 CALIFORNIA YOUTH LEADERSHIP SCHOLARSHIP PROGRAM

California Narcotic Officer's Association
28245 Avenue Crocker, Suite 230
Santa Clarita, CA 91355–1201
Phone: (661) 775–6960; (877) 775–NARC; Fax: (661) 775–1648;
Email: info@cnoa.org
Web: www.ncoa.org/awards/overview
Summary: To provide financial assistance to high school seniors who are the children of California peace officers and interested in studying any field at a college in the state.
Eligibility: Open to seniors graduating from high schools in California who are the children or wards of active or retired peace officers, as defined under California Penal Code Section 830. Applicants must be planning to enroll full time at a recognized postsecondary educational institution in the state. They must have volunteered for at least 16 hours of verified community service and submit an essay of 500 to 600 words on the importance of community service. Selection is based on that essay, citizenship, and leadership.
Financial data: The stipend is $1,000.
Duration: 1 year.
Number awarded: 5 each year.
Deadline: June of each year.

113 CALIFORNIA–HAWAII ELKS ASSOCIATION VOCATIONAL GRANTS

California–Hawaii Elks Association
Attn: Scholarship Committee
5450 East Lamona Avenue
Fresno, CA 93727–2224
Phone: (559) 255–4531; Fax: (559) 456–2659
Web: www.chea–elks.org/vocationalgrant.html
Summary: To provide financial assistance for vocational school to residents of California and Hawaii.
Eligibility: Open to residents of California or Hawaii who are high school seniors or older. Applicants must be enrolled or planning to enroll in a vocational/technical program of 2 years or less that leads to a terminal associate degree, diploma, or certificate, but less than a bachelor's degree. Students planning to transfer to a 4–year school to work on a bachelor's degree are not eligible. Selection is based on motivation, financial need, aptitude toward chosen vocation, grades, and completeness and neatness of the application brochure. Applications are available from an Elks Lodge in California or Hawaii; they must be endorsed by the lodge. U.S. citizenship is required.
Financial data: The stipend is $1,000 per year. Funds may be used for tuition and fees, room and board (if living on campus), and books and supplies. They may not be used for general living expenses or child care costs.
Duration: 1 year; may be renewed for 1 additional year.
Number awarded: 58 each year: 55 to residents of California and 3 to residents of Hawaii.
Deadline: Applications may be submitted at any time.

114 $ CALIFORNIA–HAWAII ELKS UNDERGRADUATE SCHOLARSHIP PROGRAM FOR STUDENTS WITH DISABILITIES

California–Hawaii Elks Association
Attn: Scholarship Committee
5450 East Lamona Avenue
Fresno, CA 93727–2224
Phone: (559) 255–4531; Fax: (559) 456–2659
Web: www.chea–elks.org/uspsd.html

Summary: To provide financial assistance to residents of California and Hawaii who have a disability and are interested in attending college in any state.
Eligibility: Open to residents of California or Hawaii who have a physical impairment, neurological impairment, visual impairment, hearing impairment, and/or speech/language disorder. Applicants must be a senior in high school, be a high school graduate, or have passed the GED test. They must be planning to attend a college, university, community college, or vocational school in any state. U.S. citizenship is required. Selection is based on financial need, GPA, severity of disability, seriousness of purpose, and depth of character. Applications are available from an Elks Lodge in California or Hawaii; students must first request an interview with the lodge's scholarship chairman, secretary, or Exalted Ruler.
Financial data: The stipend is $2,000 per year for 4–year colleges or universities or $1,000 for community colleges and vocational schools.
Duration: 1 year; may be renewed for up to 3 additional years or until completion of an undergraduate degree, whichever occurs first.
Number awarded: 20 to 30 each year.
Deadline: March of each year.

115 CAPED GENERAL EXCELLENCE SCHOLARSHIP

California Association for Postsecondary Education and Disability
Attn: Executive Assistant
71423 Biskra Road
Rancho Mirage, CA 92270
Phone: (760) 346–8206; Fax: (760) 340–5275; TDD: (760) 341–4084;
Email: caped2000@aol.com
Web: www.caped.net/scholarships.html
Summary: To provide financial assistance to undergraduate and graduate students in California who have a disability and can demonstrate academic achievement and involvement in community and campus activities.
Eligibility: Open to students at public and private colleges and universities in California who have a disability. Undergraduates must have completed at least 6 semester credits and have a GPA of 2.5 or higher. Graduate students must have completed at least 3 semester units and have a GPA of 3.0 or higher. Applicants must submit a 1–page personal letter that demonstrates their writing skills, progress towards meeting their educational and vocational goals, management of their disability, and involvement in community activities. They must also submit a letter of recommendation from a faculty member, verification of disability, official transcripts, proof of current enrollment, and documentation of financial need. This award is presented to the applicant who demonstrates the highest level of academic achievement and involvement in community and campus life.
Financial data: The stipend is $1,500.
Duration: 1 year.
Number awarded: 1 each year. The sponsor also offers a number of named scholarships, including the Betty Bacon Memorial Scholarship, the Cindy Kolb Memorial Scholarship, the Lynn M. Smith Memorial Scholarship, the Steve Fasteau Past President's Scholarship, and the William May Memorial Scholarship.
Deadline: September of each year.

116 CAPPEX "A GPA ISN'T EVERYTHING" SCHOLARSHIP

Cappex.com, LLC
2008 St. Johns Avenue
Highland Park, IL 60035
Web: www.cappex.com/scholarships
Summary: To provide financial assistance for college to high school seniors who complete a profile for Cappex.com but whose GPA is not outstanding.
Eligibility: Open to applicants who must first complete an online profile for Cappex.com that will enable colleges and universities to contact them for recruiting purposes. They must be U.S. citizens or permanent residents planning to attend an accredited college or university in the United States. In completing their profile, they must describe their extracurricular, leadership, and volunteer activities. This scholarship is reserved for high school seniors who want to "get some cash for getting an A in street smarts."
Financial data: The stipend is $1,000.
Duration: 1 year.
Number awarded: 5 or 6 each year.
Deadline: Deadline dates are set periodically.

117 CAPTURE THE DREAM SINGLE PARENT SCHOLARSHIP

Capture the Dream, Inc.
Attn: Scholarship Program
484 Lake Park Avenue, Suite 15
Oakland, CA 94610
Phone: (510) 343–3635;
Email: info@capturethedream.org
Web: www.capturethedream.org/programs/scholarship.php
Summary: To provide financial assistance to residents of California who are single parents and planning to attend college in any state.
Eligibility: Open to California residents who are graduating high school seniors or current full–time undergraduates at 2– or 4–year colleges and universities in any state. Applicants must be U.S. citizens or permanent residents and have at least 1 birth child in their custody. Along with their application, they must submit a 1,000–word essay on why they should be selected to receive this scholarship, using their experiences within school, work, and home to display the challenges they have faced as a single parent and how they overcame adversity to exemplify a leader. They should also explain how their career goals and future aspirations will build them as a future community leader. Selection is based on academic performance, community service, leadership history, professional recommendations, and financial need.
Financial data: The stipend is $1,000.
Duration: 1 year.
Number awarded: 1 or more each year.
Deadline: July of each year.

118 $ CAREER AID FOR TECHNICAL STUDENTS PROGRAM

New Hampshire Charitable Foundation
37 Pleasant Street
Concord, NH 03301–4005
Phone: (603) 225–6641; (800) 464–6641; Fax: (603) 225–1700;
Email: info@nhcf.org
Web: www.nhcf.org/page.aspx?pid=475
Summary: To provide financial assistance to New Hampshire residents preparing for a vocational or technical career.
Eligibility: Open to residents of New Hampshire entering a 2– or 3–year degree program or a shorter–term technical degree training program that leads to an associate degree, a trade license, or certification. Applicants must be dependent students younger than 24 years of age and planning to enroll at least half time at a community college, vocational school, trade school, or other short–term training program. They must be able to demonstrate financial need. Although academic excellence is not considered in the selection process, applicants should be able to document reasonable achievement and a commitment to their chosen field of study.
Financial data: Stipends range from $100 to $3,500, depending on the needs of the recipient.
Duration: 1 year.
Number awarded: Varies each year. A total of $250,000 is distributed annually.
Deadline: May of each year.

119 CAREER COLLEGE ASSOCIATION ADULT SKILLS EDUCATION PROGRAM

Career College Association
Attn: Imagine America Foundation
1101 Connecticut Avenue, N.W., Suite 901
Washington, DC 20036
Phone: (202) 336–6719; Fax: (202) 408–8102;
Email: scholarships@imagine–america.org
Web: www.imagine–america.org/scholarshipsforadults
Summary: To provide financial assistance to adults interested in attending a career college.
Eligibility: Open to adults over 19 years of age who have a high school diploma, have a GED, or can pass an Ability to Benefit test. Applicants must be interested in attending 1 of the more than 500 career colleges that participate in the program. They must complete a student assessment provided by the National Center for Competency Testing (NCCT). All applications are submitted to the college that the student wishes to attend. Selection is based on the results of the NCCT assessment. U.S. citizenship or permanent resident status is required.
Financial data: The stipend is $1,000. Funds must be used for payment of tuition at a participating career college.
Duration: 1 year; nonrenewable.
Number awarded: Varies each year; each participating career college determines how many scholarships it wishes to award.
Deadline: June of each year.

120 $ CARNEGIE HERO AWARD

Carnegie Hero Fund Commission
436 Seventh Avenue, Suite 1101
Pittsburgh, PA 15219–1841
Phone: (412) 281–1302; (800) 447–8900; Fax: (412) 281–5751;
Email: carnegiehero@carnegiehero.org
Web: www.carnegiehero.org

Summary: To recognize and reward outstanding acts of selfless heroism performed in the United States or Canada.

Eligibility: Open to persons who risk their lives to an extraordinary degree while saving or attempting to save the lives of others. There must be no measure of responsibility between the rescuer and rescued. The heroic act must have been performed in the United States or Canada and must be brought to the attention of the commission within 2 years of the date of the act. Persons not eligible for these awards are: those whose duties in following their regular vocations require them to perform such acts, unless the rescues are clearly beyond the line of duty; members of the armed services; children considered by the commission to be too young to comprehend the risks involved; and members of the same family, except in cases of outstanding heroism where the rescuer loses his or her life or is severely injured.

Financial data: Amounts of the cash awards vary. Funds may be used as a 1–time grant, scholarship aid for college or university education, death benefits, or continuing assistance.

Duration: The award is presented annually.

Number awarded: Varies each year; recently, 83 were awarded. To date, nearly 9,500 awards have been presented, totaling more than $33 million.

Deadline: Nominations may be submitted at any time.

121 CAROL NIGUS LEADERSHIP SCHOLARSHIP

Kansas Federation of Business & Professional Women's Clubs, Inc.
Attn: Kansas BPW Educational Foundation, Inc.
c/o Kathy Niehoff, Executive Secretary
605 East 15th
Ottawa, KS 66067
Phone: (785) 242–9319; Fax: (785) 242–1047;
Email: kathyniehoff@sbcglobal.net
Web: kansasbpw.memberlodge.org/Default.aspx?pageId=450103

Summary: To provide financial assistance for college to residents of Kansas who can demonstrate a record of public and community service.

Eligibility: Open to Kansas residents (men and women) who are enrolled in a school of higher education in the state and have demonstrated an extensive record of public service and outstanding leadership potential. Applicants must submit 1) a written summary of their involvement in community affairs; and 2) a 3–page personal biography in which they express their career goals, the direction they want to take in the future, their proposed field of study, their reason for selecting that field, the institutions they plan to attend and why, their circumstances for reentering school (if a factor), and what makes them uniquely qualified for this scholarship. They must also be able to document financial need. Applications must be submitted through a local organization of the sponsor.

Financial data: A stipend is awarded (amount not specified).

Duration: 1 year.

Number awarded: 1 or more each year.

Deadline: December of each year.

122 $ CAROLINE H. NEWHOUSE SCHOLARSHIP FUND

Career Transition for Dancers
Attn: Grants Administrator
165 West 46th Street, Suite 701
New York, NY 10036–2501
Phone: (212) 764–0172, ext. 224; Fax: (212) 764–0343;
Email: info@careertransition.org
Web: www.careertransition.org/Programs/ScholarshipsAndGrants

Summary: To provide financial assistance to current and former professional dancers interested in acquiring an academic degree or a new skill in any field.

Eligibility: Open to current and former professional dancers who can demonstrate paid employment as a dancer under union jurisdiction for at least 100 weeks over a period of 7 years or more and earnings of at least $56,000 from dance employment in the 7 best years of their performing career; the performing years need not be consecutive or current. They must be interested in obtaining funding for 1) tuition for an academic degree; 2) retraining for the acquisition of a new skill; or 3) seed money to begin a business enterprise.

Financial data: Recipients are entitled to grants totaling $2,000 over their lifetime. Funds may be used for tuition, fees, books, and materials at schools, institutes, and specialized certificate programs.

Duration: Funding may extend over a period of years, as long as the total awarded does not exceed $2,000.

Number awarded: Varies each year; recently, a total of $300,000 was available for this program.

Deadline: January, March, April, July, August, or October of each year.

123 $$ CARVER SCHOLARS PROGRAM

Roy J. Carver Charitable Trust
202 Iowa Avenue
Muscatine, IA 52761–3733
Phone: (563) 263–4010; Fax: (563) 263–1547;
Email: info@carvertrust.org
Web: www.carvertrust.org

Summary: To provide financial assistance for college to students in Iowa who have overcome significant obstacles to attend college.

Eligibility: Open to students attending the 3 public universities in Iowa, the 18 participating private 4–year colleges and universities in the state, or a community college in Iowa and planning to transfer to 1 of those 4–year institutions. Applicants must be sophomores seeking support for their junior year. They must present evidence of unusual social and/or other barriers to attending college full time; examples include, but are not limited to, students who 1) are from 1–parent families; 2) are attending college while working full time; 3) have social, mental, or physical disabilities; or 4) have families to support. They must have graduated from a high school in Iowa or have been residents of the state for at least 5 consecutive years immediately prior to applying, be full–time students, have at least a 2.8 GPA, be U.S. citizens, and submit a financial profile indicating insufficient personal, family, and institutional resources to pay full–time college tuition. A particular goal of the program is to assist students "who fall between the cracks of other financial aid programs." Applications must be submitted to the financial aid office at the Iowa college or university the applicant attends.

Financial data: Stipends generally average $5,200 at public universities or $7,600 at private colleges in Iowa.

Duration: 1 year; may be renewed 1 additional year.

Number awarded: Varies each year; since the program's establishment, it has awarded more than 2,240 scholarships worth more than $16.8 million.

Deadline: March of each year.

124 CATHERINE T. MURRAY MEMORIAL SCHOLARSHIP

Ocean State Center for Independent Living
Attn: Office Manager
1944 Warwick Avenue
Warwick, RI 02889
Phone: (401) 738–1013, ext. 10; (866) 857–1161; Fax: (401) 738–1083; TDD: (401) 738–1015;
Email: cmckenna@oscil.org
Web: www.oscil.org/murray_scholarship.htm

Summary: To provide financial assistance to residents of Rhode Island who have a disability and are interested in attending college in any state.

Eligibility: Open to residents of Rhode Island who have a significant disability. Applicants must be enrolled or planning to enroll in an academic, trade, or vocational educational program in any state and/or to acquire assistive or adaptive equipment or devices to access such an educational opportunity. Along with their application, they must submit a 1–page essay describing their career goals and plans. Selection is based on that essay (15 points), activities (5 points), accurate completion of the application (5 points), and financial need (5 points).

Financial data: The stipend is $1,000.

Duration: 1 year.

Number awarded: 1 each year.

Deadline: March of each year.

125 $$ CFCAREFORWARD SCHOLARSHIPS

Abbott Laboratories
c/o Ruder Finn
Attn: CFCareForward Scholarship Program
301 East 57th Street
New York, NY 10022
Web: www.cfcareforwardscholarship.com

Summary: To provide financial assistance for college or graduate school to students with cystic fibrosis (CF).

Eligibility: Open to high school seniors, vocational school students, college students, and graduate students with CF. U.S. citizenship is required. Applicants must submit 1) a creative presentation (e.g., a written work, piece of art, craft, collage, photograph) on what sets them apart from their peers, what inspires them to live life to the fullest, or anything else that they think makes them unique; 2) a photograph; and 3) a 250–word essay on the topic, "My dream for the future is..." Selection is based on academic excellence, creativity, community involvement, and ability to serve as a role model to others with CF. Information on all winners is posted on the sponsor's web site to allow the public to select a Thriving Undergraduate Student and a Thriving Graduate Student.

Financial data: The stipend is $2,500. The Thriving Students receive an additional award (recently, $16,500 for a total award of $19,000 to honor the program's 19th year).

Duration: 1 year.

Number awarded: 40 each year, of whom 1 is designated the Thriving Undergraduate Student and 1 the Thriving Graduate Student.

Deadline: May of each year.

126 $$ CFSRF COLLEGE GRANTS

Children of Fallen Soldiers Relief Fund
P.O. Box 3968
Gaithersburg, MD 20885–3968
Phone: (301) 685–3421; (866) 96–CFSRF; Fax: (301) 630–0592;
Email: grants@cfsrf.org
Web: www.cfsrf.org

Summary: To provide financial assistance for college to children and spouses of military personnel killed or severely disabled during service in Iraq or Afghanistan.

Eligibility: Open to spouses and children of military personnel killed or severely disabled as a result of service in Operation Iraqi Freedom or Operation Enduring Freedom. Applicants must be enrolled or planning to enroll at a college or university. They must have a GPA of 2.75 or higher and be able to demonstrate financial need.

Financial data: Grants have ranged from $1,000 to $28,000, depending on the need of the recipient.

Duration: These are 1–time grants.

Number awarded: Varies each year; since the organization was founded, it has awarded 14 of these college grants.

Deadline: Applications may be submitted at any time.

127 $$ CHAIRSCHOLARS FOUNDATION NATIONAL SCHOLARSHIPS

ChairScholars Foundation, Inc.
16101 Carencia Lane
Odessa, FL 33556–3278
Phone: (813) 926–0544; (888) 926–0544; Fax: (813) 920–7661;
Email: chairscholars@tampabay.rr.com
Web: www.chairscholars.org/national.html

Summary: To provide financial assistance for college to physically challenged students.

Eligibility: Open to high school seniors and college freshmen who have a significant physical challenge, although they are not required to be in a wheelchair. Applicants should be able to demonstrate financial need, have a GPA of 3.0 or higher, and show some form of community service or social contribution in the past. Along with their application, they must submit an essay of 300 to 500 words on how they became physically challenged, how their situation has affected them and their family, and their goals and aspirations for the future. Graduate students and all students over 21 years of age are not eligible.

Financial data: Stipends range from $1,000 to $5,000 per year. Funds are to be used for tuition and school expenses.

Duration: Up to 4 years for high school seniors; up to 3 years for college freshmen. The maximum total award is $20,000.

Number awarded: 15 to 20 each year.

Deadline: February of each year.

128 $$ CHARLES AND MELVA T. OWEN MEMORIAL SCHOLARSHIPS

National Federation of the Blind
Attn: Scholarship Committee
200 East Wells Street
Baltimore, MD 21230
Phone: (410) 659–9314, ext. 2415; Fax: (410) 685–5653;
Email: scholarships@nfb.org
Web: www.nfb.org/nfb/scholarship_program.asp

Summary: To provide financial assistance to entering or continuing undergraduate or graduate students who are blind.

Eligibility: Open to legally blind students who are working on or planning to work full time on an undergraduate or graduate degree. Scholarships, however, are not awarded for the study of religion or solely to further general or cultural education; the academic program should be directed towards attaining financial independence. Along with their application, they must submit transcripts, standardized test scores, proof of legal blindness, 2 letters of recommendation, and a letter of endorsement from their National Federation of the Blind state president or designee. Selection is based on academic excellence, service to the community, and financial need.

Financial data: Stipends are $10,000 or $3,000.

Duration: 1 year; recipients may resubmit applications up to 2 additional years.

Number awarded: 2 each year: 1 at $10,000 and 1 at $3,000.

Deadline: March of each year.

129 $$ CHEVY SCHOLAR PROGRAM SCHOLARSHIPS

Chevy Scholar Program
c/o Odney Advertising Agency
7 Third Street S.E., Suite 101
Minot, ND 58701
Phone: (701) 857–7205
Web: www.chevyscholar.com

Summary: To recognize and reward, with funding for college or other purposes, high school juniors and seniors in North Dakota and Minnesota who are selected in an online voting competition.

Eligibility: Open to juniors and seniors at high schools in North Dakota and Minnesota and home–schooled students at the equivalent grade level. Students must be nominated by a relative, teacher, friend, or anyone else, including themselves. Nominations must be submitted to participating Chevrolet dealers in the area. Finalists are selected on the basis of academic achievement, community involvement, and extracurricular activities. Information on the finalists is posted on the sponsor's website; winners are selected by public voting.

Financial data: Prizes are $5,000. A goal of the program is to enable winners to continue their education, but they are free to spend the money in any way they wish.

Duration: The competition is held annually.

Number awarded: 10 finalists are chosen each year and each receives a $500 prize; 4 winners are chosen from among those finalists and each receives a $5,000 prize; 1 nominator is selected at random and receives a $500 prize.

Deadline: February of each year.

130 $ CHICK AND SOPHIE MAJOR MEMORIAL DUCK CALLING CONTEST

Stuttgart Chamber of Commerce
507 South Main Street
P.O. Box 1500
Stuttgart, AR 72160
Phone: (870) 673–1602; Fax: (870) 673–1604;
Email: stuttgartchamber@centurytel.net
Web: stuttgartarkansas.org/index.php?fuseaction=p0004.&mod=45

Summary: To recognize and reward, with college scholarships, high school seniors who are outstanding duck callers.

Eligibility: Open to high school seniors interested in entering a duck calling contest. Contestants are allowed 90 seconds in which to present 1) hail or long distance call; 2) mating or lonesome duck call; 3) feed or clatter call; and 4) comeback call.

Financial data: The prizes are a $2,000 scholarship for the winner, a $1,000 scholarship for second place, a $750 scholarship for third place, and a $500 scholarship for fourth place. Funds must be applied toward higher education.

Duration: The competition is held annually.

Number awarded: 4 prizes are presented each year.

Deadline: The competition is held annually on the Friday and Saturday following Thanksgiving.

131 $ CHIEF MASTER SERGEANTS OF THE AIR FORCE SCHOLARSHIPS

Air Force Sergeants Association
Attn: Scholarship Coordinator
5211 Auth Road
Suitland, MD 20746
Phone: (301) 899–3500; (800) 638–0594; Fax: (301) 899–8136;
Email: balsobrooks@hqafsa.org
Web: www.hqafsa.org

Summary: To provide financial assistance for college to the dependent children of enlisted Air Force personnel.

Eligibility: Open to the unmarried children (including stepchildren and legally adopted children) of enlisted active–duty, retired, or veteran members of the U.S. Air Force, Air National Guard, or Air Force Reserves. Applicants must be attending or planning to attend an accredited academic institution. They must have an unweighted GPA of 3.5 or higher. Along with their application, they must submit 1) a paragraph on their life objectives and what they plan to do with the education they receive; and 2) an essay on the most urgent problem facing society today. High school seniors must also submit a transcript of all high school grades and a record of their SAT or ACT scores. Selection is based on academic record, character, leadership skills, writing ability, versatility, and potential for success. Financial need is not a consideration. A unique aspect of these scholarships is that applicants may supply additional information regarding circumstances that entitle them to special consideration; examples of such circumstances include student disabilities, financial hardships, parent disabled and unable to work, parent missing in action/killed in action/prisoner of war, or other unusual extenuating circumstances.

Financial data: Stipends range from $1,000 to $3,000; funds may be used for tuition, room and board, fees, books, supplies, and transportation.

Duration: 1 year; may be renewed if the recipient maintains full–time enrollment.

Number awarded: Varies each year; recently, 11 of these scholarships were awarded: 1 at $3,000, 1 at $2,500, 1 at $2,000, 1 at $1,500 and 7 at $1,000. Since this program began, it has awarded more than $250,000 in scholarships.

Deadline: March of each year.

132 CHILDREN OF FALLEN PATRIOTS FOUNDATION ASSISTANCE

Children of Fallen Patriots Foundation
P.O. Box 181
Old Greenwich, CT 06870
Phone: (866) 917–CFPF; Fax: (203) 547–6243;
Email: contact@fallenpatriots.org
Web: fallenpatriots.org/for–families/faqs

Summary: To provide financial assistance to the children of military personnel killed in combat or training.

Eligibility: Open to the children (natural, by marriage, or adopted) of military personnel who died in the line of duty. Applicants must be enrolled or planning to enroll at a college, university, community college, or vocational school. Applicants must submit documentation of their relationship to the deceased military member, bills or receipts for all covered expenses, transcripts that include GPA, and information on their U.S. Department of Veterans Affairs benefits.

Financial data: The foundation attempts to pay for all costs of higher education not covered by other grants or scholarships.

Duration: Until completion of a college degree or certificate.

Number awarded: Varies each year.

Deadline: Applications may be submitted at any time.

133 $ CHILDREN OF WARRIORS NATIONAL PRESIDENTS' SCHOLARSHIP

American Legion Auxiliary
8945 North Meridian Street
Indianapolis, IN 46260
Phone: (317) 569–4500; Fax: (317) 569–4502;
Email: alahq@alaforveterans.org
Web: www.alaforveterans.org/what_we_do/scholarships/Pages/default.aspx

Summary: To provide financial assistance for college to the descendants of war veterans.

Eligibility: Open to children, stepchildren, grandchildren, and great–grandchildren of veterans who served during war time. Applicants must be high school seniors who have completed at least 50 hours of volunteer service within their community and plan to attend an accredited 4–year college or university. Each Department (state) organization of the American Legion Auxiliary nominates 1 candidate for this scholarship annually. Nominees must submit a 1,000–word essay on a topic that changes annually; recently, students were asked to write on "The Importance of Helping Military Families in Your Community." Selection is based on the essay (25%), character and leadership (25%), scholarship, (25%), and financial need (25%).

Financial data: Stipends are $2,500, $2,000, or $1,500. Funds are paid directly to the recipient's school.

Duration: 1 year; recipients may not reapply.

Number awarded: 15 each year: in each of the 5 divisions of the Auxiliary, 1 scholarship at $2,500, 1 at $2,000, and 1 at $1,500 are awarded.

Deadline: February of each year.

134 CHINESE AMERICAN CITIZENS ALLIANCE FOUNDATION ESSAY CONTEST

Chinese American Citizens Alliance
1044 Stockton Street
San Francisco, CA 94108
Phone: (415) 434–2222;
Email: info@cacanational.org
Web: www.cacanational.org/Essay–Contest

Summary: To recognize and reward high school students of Chinese descent who write outstanding essays on a topic related to Asian Americans.

Eligibility: Open to high school students of Chinese descent. Candidates apply through their local lodge of the Chinese American Citizens Alliance and meet at a site arranged by that lodge, usually on the first Saturday in March. They are given a topic and devote the next 2 hours to writing a 500–word essay, in English, on that topic. The topic is assigned at the time of the competition (always relates to the Chinese and Asian American communities). Selection is based on originality, clarity of thought, and expression.

Financial data: Prizes are $1,000 for first place, $700 for second place, $500 for third place, and $100 for merit awards.

Duration: The competition is held annually.

Number awarded: Varies each year; recently, prizes included 1 first place, 1 second place, 1 third place, and 10 merit awards.

Deadline: February of each year.

135 CHRISTIAN RECORD SERVICES SCHOLARSHIPS

Christian Record Services
4444 South 52nd Street
P.O. Box 6097
Lincoln, NE 68506–0097
Phone: (402) 488–0981; Fax: (402) 488–7582;
Email: info@christianrecord.org
Web: services.christianrecord.org/scholarships/index.php

Summary: To provide financial assistance for college to blind students.

Eligibility: Open to students who are legally blind and attending or planning to attend college full time on the undergraduate level to secure training that will result in independence and self–support. Financial need is considered in the selection process. U.S. citizenship is required.

Financial data: A stipend is awarded (amount not specified).

Duration: 1 year; may be renewed.

Number awarded: Varies each year; recently, 10 of these scholarships were awarded.

Deadline: March of each year.

136 $ CHRISTIAN REFORMED CHURCH RACE RELATIONS SCHOLARSHIP

Christian Reformed Church
Attn: Office of Race Relations
2850 Kalamazoo Avenue, S.E.
Grand Rapids, MI 49560–0200
Phone: (616) 241–1691; (877) 279–9994; Fax: (616) 224–0803;
Email: crcna@crcna.org
Web: www.crcna.org/pages/racerelations_scholar.cfm

Summary: To provide financial assistance to undergraduate and graduate minority students interested in attending colleges related to the Christian Reformed Church in North America (CRCNA).

Eligibility: Open to students of color in the United States and Canada. Normally, applicants are expected to be members of CRCNA congregations who plan to pursue their educational goals at Calvin Theological Seminary or any of the colleges affiliated with the CRCNA. Students who have no prior history with the CRCNA must attend a CRCNA–related college or seminary for a full academic year before they are eligible to apply for this program. Students entering their sophomore year must have earned a GPA of 2.0 or higher as freshmen; students entering their junior year must have earned a GPA of 2.3 or higher as sophomores; students entering their senior year must have earned a GPA of 2.6 or higher as juniors.

Financial data: First–year students receive $500 per semester. Other levels of students may receive up to $2,000 per academic year.

Duration: 1 year.
Number awarded: Varies each year; recently, 31 students received a total of $21,000 in support.
Deadline: March of each year.

137 $$ CIA UNDERGRADUATE SCHOLARSHIP PROGRAM

Central Intelligence Agency
Attn: Human Resource Management
Recruitment and Retention Center, 4B14–034 DD1
Washington, DC 20505
Phone: (703) 371–2107
Web: https://www.cia.gov/careers/student–opportunities/index.html

Summary: To provide funding and work experience to high school seniors and college sophomores, especially minorities and people with disabilities, who would be interested in working for the Central Intelligence Agency (CIA) after graduation from college.
Eligibility: Open to U.S. citizens who are either high school seniors or college freshmen or sophomores. Seniors must be at least 18 years of age by April of the year they apply and have minimum scores of 1500 on the SAT (1000 on critical reading and mathematics and 500 on writing) or 21 on the ACT. College students must have a GPA of 3.0 or higher. All applicants must be able to demonstrate financial need (household income of $70,000 or less for a family of 4 or $80,000 or less for a family of 5 or more) and be able to meet the same employment standards as permanent employees of the CIA. This program was developed, in part, to assist minority and disabled students, but it is open to all students who meet the requirements.
Financial data: Scholars are provided a salary, an optional benefits package (health, dental, and vision insurance, life insurance, and retirement), and up to $18,000 per year for tuition, fees, books, and supplies. They must agree to continue employment with the CIA after college graduation for a period 1.5 times the length of their college support.
Duration: 1 year; may be renewed if the student maintains a GPA of 3.0 or higher and full–time enrollment in a 4– or 5–year college program.
Number awarded: Varies each year.
Deadline: October of each year.

138 CIVILIAN MARKSMANSHIP PROGRAM SCHOLARSHIPS

Corporation for the Promotion of Rifle Practice and Firearms Safety, Inc.
Attn: Civilian Marksmanship Program
Camp Perry Training Site, Building 3
P.O. Box 576
Port Clinton, OH 43452
Phone: (419) 635–2141, ext. 1101; Fax: (419) 635–2573;
Email: competitions@odcmp.com
Web: www.odcmp.com/Competitions/Scholarships.htm

Summary: To provide financial assistance to high school seniors who have participated in a team or club rifle or pistol marksmanship competition and plan to attend college.
Eligibility: Open to high school seniors who are currently enrolled in a team or club that is participating in rifle or pistol marksmanship competitions. Examples include the JROTC Service Championships, high school teams or clubs, or programs sponsored by 4–H, Boy Scouts, or the American Legion. Applicants must be able to document acceptance at a college, university, or trade school; good moral character; academic achievement (GPA of 2.5 or higher); and U.S. citizenship. They must be nominated by a coach, instructor, or adult leader.
Financial data: The stipend is $1,000.
Duration: 1 year; nonrenewable.
Number awarded: Approximately 100 each year.
Deadline: March of each year.

139 CLAIRE OLIPHANT MEMORIAL SCHOLARSHIP

American Legion Auxiliary
Department of New Jersey
c/o Lucille M. Miller, Secretary/Treasurer
1540 Kuser Road, Suite A–8
Hamilton, NJ 08619
Phone: (609) 581–9580; Fax: (609) 581–8429

Summary: To provide financial assistance to New Jersey residents who are the descendants of veterans and planning to attend college in any state.
Eligibility: Open to the children, grandchildren, and great–grandchildren of veterans who served in the U.S. armed forces during specified periods of war time. Applicants must be graduating high school seniors who have been residents of New Jersey for at least 2 years. They must be planning to attend a college or university in any state. Along with their application, they must submit a 1,000–word essay on a topic that changes annually; recently, students were asked to write on the topic, "The Importance of Helping Military Families in Your Community " Selection is based on academic achievement (40%), character (15%), leadership (15%), Americanism (15%), and financial need (15%).
Financial data: The stipend is $1,800.
Duration: 1 year.
Number awarded: 1 each year.
Deadline: April each year.

140 CLARKE SINCLAIR MEMORIAL ARCHERY COLLEGE SCHOLARSHIPS

Clarke Sinclair Memorial Archery Scholarship Corporation
c/o Dakota Sinclair
P.O. Box 1827
Ridgecrest, CA 93555
Phone: (760) 384–8886;
Email: barbazu2003@yahoo.com
Web: www.clarkesinclair.org

Summary: To provide financial assistance to undergraduate students who have participated in archery–related activities.
Eligibility: Open to students currently enrolled in college who have at least 1 year remaining until graduation. Applicants must have a record of participation in archery–related activities and be a member of an archery team. They must have a GPA of 3.0 or higher. Along with their application, they must submit a short essay on 1) growing a college club and their participation; 2) things archery has taught them; or 3) the most important thing about a competition. Financial need is not considered in the selection process.
Financial data: Stipends are $1,000 or $500.
Duration: 1 year.
Number awarded: Varies each year; recently, 3 of these scholarships were awarded: 1 at $1,000 and 2 at $500.
Deadline: March of each year.

141 $$ CLEAP: COLORADO LEVERAGING EDUCATIONAL ASSISTANCE PARTNERSHIP

Colorado Commission on Higher Education
1560 Broadway, Suite 1600
Denver, CO 80202
Phone: (303) 866–2723; Fax: (303) 866–4266;
Email: cche@state.co.us
Web: highered.colorado.gov

Summary: To provide financial assistance for college to residents of Colorado who can demonstrate financial need.
Eligibility: Open to residents of Colorado who are enrolled or accepted for enrollment in eligible postsecondary institutions in Colorado. Applicants must be able to demonstrate substantial financial need.
Financial data: The amount of assistance varies, to a maximum of $5,000 per year.
Duration: 1 year; renewable.
Number awarded: Varies each year.
Deadline: Each participating institution sets its own deadlines.

142 $ CMOH SCHOLARSHIPS

Congressional Medal of Honor Society
40 Patriots Point Road
Mt. Pleasant, SC 29464
Phone: (843) 884–8862; Fax: (843) 884–1471;
Email: medalhq@earthlink.net
Web: www.cmohfoundation.org/educational–outreach/scholarship–program

Summary: To provide financial assistance to dependents of Congressional Medal of Honor winners who are interested in pursuing postsecondary education.
Eligibility: Open to sons and daughters of Congressional Medal of Honor recipients. They must be high school seniors or graduates and have been accepted by an accredited college or university.
Financial data: The stipend is $2,000 per year.
Duration: 1 year; may be renewed for up to 3 additional years.
Number awarded: Varies; approximately 15 each year.
Deadline: August or December of each year.

143 $$ COCA–COLA FIRST GENERATION SCHOLARSHIP

American Indian College Fund
Attn: Scholarship Department
8333 Greenwood Boulevard
Denver, CO 80221
Phone: (303) 426–8900; (800) 776–FUND; Fax: (303) 426–1200;
Email: scholarships@collegefund.org
Web: www.collegefund.org/content/full_circle_scholarships_listings

Summary: To provide financial assistance to Native Americans who are attending a Tribal College or University (TCU) and are the first in their famiiy to attend college.

Eligibility: Open to American Indians or Alaska Natives who are enrolled full time in their freshman year at an eligible TCU. Applicants must have a GPA of 3.0 or higher and be able to demonstrate exceptional academic achievement or financial need. They must be the first in their immediate family to attend college. Applications are available only online and include required essays on specified topics. U.S. citizenship is required.

Financial data: The stipend is $5,000 per year.

Duration: 1 year; may be renewed, provided the recipient maintains a GPA of 3.0 or higher and participates actively in campus and community life.

Number awarded: 1 or more each year.

Deadline: May of each year.

144 $$ COCA–COLA SCHOLARSHIPS

Coca–Cola Scholars Foundation, Inc.
P.O. Box 442
Atlanta, GA 30301–0442
Phone: (800) 306–COKE; Fax: (404) 733–5439;
Email: scholars@na.ko.com
Web: www.coca–colascholars.org/page.aspx?pid=388

Summary: To provide financial assistance for college to meritorious students.

Eligibility: Open to high school and home–school seniors who are planning to attend an accredited U.S. college or university. Applicants must have a GPA of 3.0 or higher at the end of their junior year in high school. They must be a U.S. citizen, national, permanent resident, temporary resident in a legalization program, refugee, asylee, Cuban–Haitian entrant, or humanitarian parolee. Selection is based on demonstrated leadership in academics, school, community, and civic activities, as well as personal character and the motivation to serve and succeed.

Financial data: The stipend is $5,000 per year (for National Scholars) or $2,500 per year (for Regional Scholars).

Duration: All scholarships are for 4 years.

Number awarded: 250 each year: 50 National Scholars and 200 Regional Scholars.

Deadline: October of each year; approximately 2,200 semifinalists are chosen and they submit an additional application, including detailed biographical data, an essay, secondary school report, and recommendations, by the end of January.

145 $ COLBURN–KEENANFOUNDATION/BETH CAREW MEMORIAL SCHOLARSHIPS

Colburn–Keenan Foundation, Inc.
31 Moody Road
P.O. Box 811
Enfield, CT 06083–0811
Phone: (800) 966–2431; Fax: (888) 345–0259;
Email: admin@colkeen.org
Web: www.colkeen.org/?page_id=123

Summary: To provide financial assistance for college to students who have a bleeding disorder.

Eligibility: Open to high school seniors and college freshmen, sophomores, and juniors who have hemophilia, von Willebrand Disease, or another related inherited bleeding disorder. Applicants must be attending or planning to attend an accredited 2– or 4–year college or university in the United States as a full–time student. Along with their application, they must submit essays on their academic goals, what they would like to be able to do after they receive their undergraduate degree, why they would be a good choice for this scholarship, their participation in volunteer activities in the bleeding disorder community, their greatest challenge as a person living with a bleeding disorder, and examples of choices they have made that demonstrate good and poor judgment on their part.

Financial data: The stipend is $4,000 per year.

Duration: 1 year; recipients may reapply.

Number awarded: 10 each year.

Deadline: April of each year.

146 $ COLLEGE ASSISTANCE MIGRANT PROGRAM (CAMP) SCHOLARSHIPS

Migrant Students Foundation
305 Prospect Avenue, Suite 4
Lewiston, ID 83501
Phone: (509) 368–7132;
Email: support@migrantstudents.org
Web: www.migrantstudents.org/scholarships/campscholarship.html

Summary: To provide financial assistance for college to high school seniors from migrant or seasonal farmworker families.

Eligibility: Open to migrant and seasonal farmworkers and their families working in agricultural activities directly related to the production of crops, dairy products, poultry, or livestock; the cultivation or harvesting of trees; or fish farms. Applicants may verify eligibility in 1 of 3 ways: 1) participation during high school or eligibility to participate in a Title 1 Migrant Education Program; 2) participation or eligibility to participate in the Workforce Investment Act (WIA); or 3) verification that they or their parents have spent at least 75 days during the past 24 months as a migrant and/or seasonal (not year–round) farmworker as their primary employment. They must also plan to enroll as a freshman at a 4–year college or university that participates in the College Assistance Migrant Program (CAMP) of the U.S. Department of Education to complete a bachelor's degree, be a U.S. citizen or permanent resident, and be able to document financial need.

Financial data: The stipends range from $750 to $4,000, depending on the need of the recipients and the school they attend.

Duration: 1 year.

Number awarded: Approximately 2,000 each year.

Deadline: February of each year.

147 $$ COLLEGE–BOUND AWARD OF LIGHTHOUSE INTERNATIONAL

Lighthouse International
Attn: Scholarship and Career Awards
111 East 59th Street
New York, NY 10022–1202
Phone: (212) 821–9428; (800) 829–0500; Fax: (212) 821–9703; TDD: (212) 821–9713;
Email: sca@lighthouse.org
Web: www.lighthouse.org/services–and–assistance

Summary: To provide financial assistance to legally blind high school seniors who plan to attend college.

Eligibility: Open to high school seniors or recent high school graduates now planning to begin college who are legally blind and U.S. citizens. Applicants must be planning to attend an accredited college or university in 1 of the 50 states, the District of Columbia, or a U.S. territory. Along with their application, they must submit essays of 400 to 600 words on 1) their academic focus and extracurricular activities and what inspires their interest in each area; 2) their passion and how they express that passion; 3) key academic and personal accomplishments and the challenges they overcome to be successful; and 4) how this scholarship will support their academic and/or career development. Selection is based on academic and personal achievements; financial need is not considered.

Financial data: The stipend is $10,000.

Duration: 1 year.

Number awarded: 2 each year.

Deadline: January of each year.

148 $ COLLEGEBOUNDFUND ACADEMIC PROMISE SCHOLARSHIP

Rhode Island Higher Education Assistance Authority
Attn: Scholarship and Grant Division
560 Jefferson Boulevard, Suite 100
Warwick, RI 02886–1304
Phone: (401) 736–1170; (800) 922–9855; Fax: (401) 732–3541; TDD: (401) 734–9481;
Email: scholarships@riheaa.org
Web: www.riheaa.org/sng/ap_prog_detail.php

Summary: To provide financial assistance to high school seniors in Rhode Island who can demonstrate academic promise and plan to attend college in any state.

Eligibility: Open to U.S. citizens and permanent residents who have been residents of Rhode Island since the beginning of the year prior to the academic year in which they enroll in college. Applicants must be high school seniors accepted

for full–time enrollment in a program that leads to a certificate or degree, have a federal estimated family contribution (EFC) of $5,550 or lower, and not already possess a bachelor's degree. They must file a Free Application for Federal Student Aid (FAFSA) and take the SAT or ACT test. Selection is based on a formula that utilizes EFC and SAT or ACT scores.
Financial data: The stipend is $2,500 per year.
Duration: 1 year; may be renewed for up to 3 additional years, provided the recipient maintains a cumulative GPA of 2.50 or higher for the first year, 2.62 or higher for the second year, and 2.75 or higher for the third year.
Number awarded: 100 each year.
Deadline: February of each year.

149 COLONA SCHOLARSHIP GRANT

Chief Warrant and Warrant Officers Association
Attn: Executive Director
200 V Street, S.W.
Washington, DC 20024
Phone: (202) 554–7753; (800) 792–8447; Fax: (202) 484–0641;
Email: cwoauscg@verizon.net
Web: www.cwoauscg.org/scholarship.htm
Summary: To provide financial assistance for college to children of active or retired enlisted personnel of the U.S. Coast Guard.
Eligibility: Open to the dependent sons and daughters of members of the U.S. Coast Guard (active duty or retired) or the Coast Guard Reserve serving on active duty. Applicants must be high school seniors or currently–enrolled full–time college students and have at least a 2.0 GPA. Along with their application, they must submit transcripts, a letter of acceptance, an essay on their reasons for attending or desiring to attend an accredited institution of higher learning, support documentation if applicable, and a photograph (optional). Their parents' financial status is not considered in the selection process.
Financial data: The stipend is $1,000 per year.
Duration: 1 year; may be renewed up to 3 additional years.
Number awarded: 1 or more each year.
Deadline: May of each year.

150 $$ COLORADO DEPENDENTS TUITION ASSISTANCE PROGRAM

Colorado Commission on Higher Education
1560 Broadway, Suite 1600
Denver, CO 80202
Phone: (303) 866–2723; Fax: (303) 866–4266;
Email: cche@state.co.us
Web: highered.colorado.gov
Summary: To provide financial assistance for college to the dependents of disabled or deceased Colorado National Guardsmen, law enforcement officers, and firefighters.
Eligibility: Open to dependents of Colorado law enforcement officers, firefighters, and National Guardsmen disabled or killed in the line of duty, as well as dependents of prisoners of war or service personnel listed as missing in action. Students must be Colorado residents under 22 years of age enrolled at 1) a state–supported 2– or 4–year Colorado college or university; 2) a private college, university, or vocational school in Colorado approved by the commission; or 3) an out–of–state 4–year college. Financial need is considered in the selection process.
Financial data: Eligible students receive free tuition at Colorado public institutions of higher education. If the recipient wishes to attend a private college, university, or proprietary school, the award is limited to the amount of tuition at a comparable state–supported institution. Students who have applied to live in a dormitory, but have not been accepted because there is not enough space, may be provided supplemental assistance. Students who choose to live off–campus are not eligible for room reimbursement or a meal plan. Students who attend a non–residential Colorado institution and do not live at home are eligible for a grant of $1,000 per semester to assist with living expenses. Students who attend an out–of–state institution are eligible for the amount of tuition equivalent to that at a comparable Colorado public institution, but they are not eligible for room and board.
Duration: Up to 6 years or until completion of a bachelor's degree, provided the recipient maintains a GPA of 2.5 or higher.
Number awarded: Varies each year; recently, nearly $365,000 was allocated to this program.
Deadline: Deadline not specified.

151 COLORADO LEGION AUXILIARY DEPARTMENT PRESIDENT'S SCHOLARSHIPS

American Legion Auxiliary
Department of Colorado
7465 East First Avenue, Suite D
Denver, CO 80230
Phone: (303) 367–5388; Fax: (303) 367–5388;
Email: dept–sec@alacolorado.com
Web: www.alacolorado.com/index_files/Forms.htm
Summary: To provide financial assistance to children and grandchildren of veterans in Colorado who plan to attend college in the state.
Eligibility: Open to children and grandchildren of veterans who served in the armed forces during wartime eligibility dates for membership in the American Legion. Applicants must be residents of Colorado who are high school seniors planning to attend a college in the state. Along with their application, they must submit a 1,000–word essay on the topic, "My Obligations as an American." Selection is based on character (15%), Americanism (15%), leadership (15%), scholarship (15%), and financial need (40%).
Financial data: Stipends are $1,000 or $500.
Duration: 1 year.
Number awarded: 4 each year: 2 at 1,000 and 2 at $500.
Deadline: March of each year.

152 $$ COLORADO STUDENT GRANTS

Colorado Commission on Higher Education
1560 Broadway, Suite 1600
Denver, CO 80202
Phone: (303) 866–2723; Fax: (303) 866–4266;
Email: cche@state.co.us
Web: highered.colorado.gov
Summary: To provide financial assistance for college to residents of Colorado who can demonstrate financial need.
Eligibility: Open to residents of Colorado who are enrolled or accepted for enrollment in participating postsecondary institutions in Colorado. Selection is based on financial need, as indicated by the student's Expected Family Contribution (EFC) from their Free Application for Federal Student Aid (FAFSA). Students whose EFC is between zero and $6,926 are in level 1, students whose EFC is between $6,926 and 200% of that required for the minimum Pell Grant (or $9,234) are in level 2, and all other students who demonstrate financial need are in level 3.
Financial data: The amount of assistance varies. Students in level 1 receive from $850 to the maximum amount of unmet need, up to $5,000; students in level 2 receive from $600 to $2,500 or the maximum amount of unmet need, whichever is less; students in level 3 receive from $300 to $500.
Duration: 1 year; renewable.
Number awarded: Varies each year.
Deadline: Each participating institution sets its own deadlines.

153 COLUMBIAN CLUB SCHOLARSHIPS

Columbian Club Charitable Foundation
c/o Dr. Frank Trocchio
7310 West North Avenue, Suite 3A
Elmwood Park, IL 60707
Phone: (708) 456–2800
Web: www.columbianclub.org/scholarship.htm
Summary: To provide financial assistance to Illinois residents of Italian descent who are attending or planning to attend college in any state.
Eligibility: Open to Illinois residents who are entering their first, second, third, or fourth year of college. Applicants must be at least 25% of Italian lineage. Along with their application, they must submit a personal information summary that includes a biographical sketch of their Italian ancestry, schools attended and years graduated, school now attending, GPA or class rank, 2 most recent awards or honors received, and summary of their personal and professional goals. They must also submit a sample of their writing skill with an original narrative about an Italian or Italian–American public figure of historic prominence. U.S. citizenship is required.
Financial data: The stipend is $1,000.
Duration: 1 year.
Number awarded: Varies each year; recently, 15 of these scholarships were awarded.
Deadline: October of each year.

154 $ COMMANDER RONALD J. CANTIN SCHOLARSHIP

U.S. Coast Guard
Attn: Office of Work–Life (CG–111)
2100 Second Street, S.W., Stop 7902
Washington, DC 20593–7902
Phone: (202) 475–5140; (800) 872–4957; Fax: (202) 475–5907;
Email: HQS.SMB.FamilySupportServices@uscg.mil
Web: www.uscg.mil/worklife/scholarship.asp

Summary: To provide financial assistance for college to the dependent children of Coast Guard enlisted personnel.

Eligibility: Open to the dependent children of enlisted members of the U.S. Coast Guard on active duty, retired, or deceased and of enlisted personnel in the Coast Guard Reserve currently on extended active duty 180 days or more. Applicants must be high school seniors or current undergraduates enrolled or planning to enroll full–time at a 4–year college, university, or vocational school. They must be under 24 years of age and registered in the Defense Enrollment Eligibility Reporting System (DEERS) system. Along with their application, they must submit their SAT or ACT scores, a letter of recommendation, transcripts, a financial information statement, and a 500–word essay on their personal and academic achievements, extracurricular activities, contributions to the community, and academic plans and career goals.

Financial data: The stipend is $2,500.

Duration: 1 year; nonrenewable.

Number awarded: 1 each year.

Deadline: March of each year.

155 COMMANDER WILLIAM S. STUHR SCHOLARSHIPS

Commander William S. Stuhr Scholarship Fund
Attn: Executive Director
P.O. Box 1138
Kitty Hawk, NC 27949–1138
Phone: (252) 255–3013; Fax: (252) 255–3014;
Email: stuhrstudents@earthlink.net

Summary: To provide financial assistance for college to the dependent children of retired or active–duty military personnel.

Eligibility: Open to the dependent children of military personnel who are serving on active duty or retired with pay after 20 years' service (not merely separated from service). Applicants must be high school seniors who rank in the top 10% of their class and have an SAT score of at least 1250 or an ACT score of at least 27. They must plan to attend a 4–year accredited college. Selection is based on academic performance, extracurricular activities, demonstrated leadership potential, and financial need.

Financial data: The stipend is $1,200 per year.

Duration: 4 years, provided the recipient makes the dean's list at their college at least once during their first 2 years.

Number awarded: 6 each year: 1 for a child of a military servicemember from each of the 6 branches (Air Force, Army, Coast Guard, Marine Corps, Navy, and Reserves/National Guard).

Deadline: January of each year.

156 $ COMMON KNOWLEDGE SCHOLARSHIPS

Common Knowledge Scholarship Foundation
P.O. Box 290361
Davie, FL 33329–0361
Phone: (954) 262–8395;
Email: info@cksf.org
Web: www.cksf.org/index.cfm?Page=Scholarships

Summary: To recognize and reward, with college scholarships, students who achieve the highest scores on online quizzes on a range of subjects.

Eligibility: Open to high school students in grades 9–12 and college students from freshmen through seniors. Contestants must register with the Common Knowledge Scholarship Foundation and take online quizzes on topics that change periodically. Topics range from general knowledge to specific subjects selected by participating sponsors. For each question students answer correctly, they receive 500 points, minus 1 point for each second they require to answer the question. The students with the highest scores win the scholarships. No questions about financial need or GPA are included. Winners are selected solely on the basis of the quiz scores.

Financial data: Prizes range from $250 to $2,500. Funds are paid directly to the winners' postsecondary schools.

Duration: Contest are held on an ongoing basis.

Number awarded: Varies each year. Since the program began, it has awarded more than $300,000 to more than 700 students.

Deadline: The quiz questions are available online at all times.

157 $$ COMMONWEALTH SCHOLARSHIPS

Kentucky Community and Technical College System
Attn: Financial Aid
300 North Main Street
Versailles, KY 40383
Phone: (859) 256–3100; (877) 528–2748 (within KY)
Web: www.kctcs.edu

Summary: To provide financial assistance to outstanding students at participating institutions within the Kentucky Community and Technical College System (KCTCS).

Eligibility: Open to Kentucky residents who are 1) current–year valedictorians in their high school class; 2) valedictorians who graduated from high school during the previous academic year; and 3) salutatorians or the top 10% of the current high school graduating class. Applicants must be attending or planning to attend a participating KCTCS institution. They must be able to demonstrate unmet financial need. Most colleges require full–time enrollment.

Financial data: Stipends vary at each participating college, but are intended to provide full payment of tuition and required fees.

Duration: 1 year; may be renewed 1 additional year.

Number awarded: Varies each year.

Deadline: Each college sets its own deadline.

158 COMMUNITY COLLEGE TRANSFER SCHOLARS FUND

Independent College Fund of Maryland
Attn: Director of Programs and Scholarships
3225 Ellerslie Avenue, Suite C–160
Baltimore, MD 21218–3519
Phone: (443) 997–5700; Fax: (443) 997–2740;
Email: Ifund@jhu.edu
Web: i–fundinfo.org

Summary: To provide financial assistance to students graduating from community colleges in Maryland and planning to transfer to member institutions of the Independent College Fund of Maryland.

Eligibility: Open to students who have an associate degree from an accredited Maryland community college. Applicants must have been admitted as a full time student at a member institution. They must have a GPA of 3.0 or higher and be able to demonstrate financial need. U.S. citizenship is required.

Financial data: A stipend is awarded (amount not specified).

Duration: 1 year.

Number awarded: 1 or more each year.

Deadline: Deadline not specified.

159 COMMUNITY CONTRIBUTION SCHOLARSHIP

Educational Research Center of America, Inc.
Attn: Scholarship Committee
777 Sunrise Highway
P.O. Box 9012
Lynbrook, NY 11563
Phone: (561) 882–9800;
Email: info@studentresearch.org
Web: www.studentresearch.org/application

Summary: To provide financial assistance for college to high school seniors who have provided outstanding service to their community.

Eligibility: Open to college–bound high school seniors. Applicants must have recognized a need or problem in their community, have determined a way to address that need or solve that problem, have developed an action plan, and have worked to put the plan in place so as to address the need or solve the problem. Selection is based on that description, honors or awards received, GPA, and a letter of reference.

Financial data: The stipend is $1,000.

Duration: 1 year.

Number awarded: 25 each year.

Deadline: July of each year.

160 CONGRESSIONAL BLACK CAUCUS SPOUSES EDUCATION SCHOLARSHIP

Congressional Black Caucus Foundation, Inc.
Attn: Director, Educational Programs
1720 Massachusetts Avenue, N.W.
Washington, DC 20036

Phone: (202) 263–2800; (800) 784–2577; Fax: (202) 775–0773;
Email: info@cbcfinc.org

Summary: To provide financial assistance to minority and other undergraduate and graduate students who reside in a Congressional district represented by an African American.

Eligibility: Open to 1) minority and other graduating high school seniors planning to attend an accredited institution of higher education; and 2) currently–enrolled full–time undergraduate, graduate, and doctoral students in good academic standing with a GPA of 2.5 or higher. Applicants must reside or attend school in a Congressional district represented by a member of the Congressional Black Caucus. Along with their application, they must a personal statement of 500 to 1,000 words on 1) their future goals, major field of study, and how that field of study will help them to achieve their future career goals; 2) involvement in school activities, community and public service, hobbies, and sports; 3) how receiving this award will affect their current and future plans; and 4) other experiences, skills, or qualifications. They must also be able to demonstrate financial need, leadership ability, and participation in community service activities.

Financial data: A stipend is awarded (amount not specified).

Duration: 1 year.

Number awarded: Varies each year.

Deadline: June of each year.

161 $$ CONGRESSIONAL HISPANIC CAUCUS INSTITUTE SCHOLARSHIP AWARDS

Congressional Hispanic Caucus Institute, Inc.
911 Second Street, N.E.
Washington, DC 20002
Phone: (202) 543–1771; (800) EXCEL–DC; Fax: (202) 546–2143;
Email: chci@chci.org
Web: www.chci.org/scholarships

Summary: To provide financial assistance for college or graduate school to students of Hispanic descent.

Eligibility: Open to U.S. citizens and permanent residents who are Hispanic as defined by the U.S. Census Bureau (individuals of Mexican, Puerto Rican, Cuban, Central and South American, and other Spanish and Latin American descent). Applicants must be attending or planning to attend an accredited community college, 4–year university, or professional or graduate program as a full–time student. Along with their application, they must submit a 1–page essay on the field of study they plan to pursue and how the Latino community will benefit. Selection is based on demonstrated financial need, consistent active participation in public and/or community service activities, and good writing skills.

Financial data: The stipend is $5,000 for graduate students, $2,500 for students at 4–year institutions, or $1,000 for students at 2–year community colleges. Funds are intended to cover tuition, room and board, textbooks, and other educational expenses associated with college enrollment. Undergraduate students also receive a DELL Notebook Computer and Microsoft Package.

Duration: 1 year.

Number awarded: Varies each year; recently, 136 of these scholarships were awarded: 17 to community college students, 99 to undergraduates, and 20 to graduate students.

Deadline: April of each year.

162 $$ CONNECTICUT AID FOR PUBLIC COLLEGE STUDENTS

Connecticut Office of Financial and Academic Affairs for Higher Education
Attn: Student Financial Aid
61 Woodland Street
Hartford, CT 06105–2326
Phone: (860) 947–1855; (800) 842–0229 (within CT); Fax: (860) 947–1311;
Email: sfa@ctdhe.org
Web: www.ctohe.org/SFA/default.htm

Summary: To provide financial assistance to Connecticut residents attending public colleges in the state.

Eligibility: Open to residents of Connecticut who are attending a public college in the state. Selection is based on financial need.

Financial data: Awards up to the amount of unmet financial need are provided.

Duration: 1 year.

Number awarded: Varies each year.

Deadline: Deadline not specified.

163 $$ CONNECTICUT INDEPENDENT COLLEGE STUDENT GRANTS

Connecticut Office of Financial and Academic Affairs for Higher Education
Attn: Student Financial Aid
61 Woodland Street
Hartford, CT 06105–2326
Phone: (860) 947–1855; (800) 842–0229 (within CT); Fax: (860) 947–1311;
Email: sfa@ctdhe.org
Web: www.ctohe.org/SFA/default.htm

Summary: To provide financial assistance for undergraduate education to students attending independent colleges in Connecticut.

Eligibility: Open to residents of Connecticut who are attending an independent college in the state. Selection is based on financial need.

Financial data: Grants up to $8,166 per year are provided.

Duration: 1 year.

Number awarded: Varies each year.

Deadline: Deadline not specified.

164 $ CONNECTICUT NATIONAL GUARD FOUNDATION SCHOLARSHIPS

Connecticut National Guard Foundation, Inc.
Attn: Scholarship Committee
360 Broad Street
Hartford, CT 06105–3795
Phone: (860) 241–1550; Fax: (860) 293–2929;
Email: scholarship.committee@ctngfoundation.org
Web: www.ctngfoundation.org/Scholarship.asp

Summary: To provide financial assistance for college to members of the Connecticut National Guard and their families.

Eligibility: Open to members of the Connecticut Army National Guard and Organized Militia, their children, and their spouses. Applicants must be enrolled or planning to enroll in an accredited college or technical program. Along with their application, they must submit a letter of recommendation, a list of extracurricular activities, high school or college transcripts, and a 200–word statement on their educational and future goals. Selection is based on achievement and citizenship.

Financial data: Stipends are $2,000 or $1,000.

Duration: 1 year.

Number awarded: 10 each year: 5 at $2,000 and 5 at $1,000.

Deadline: March of each year.

165 CONNECTICUT TEACHERS OF ENGLISH TO SPEAKERS OF OTHER LANGUAGES SCHOLARSHIPS

Connecticut Teachers of English to Speakers of Other Languages
P.O. Box 304
Norwich, CT 06360–0304
Email: ConnTESOL@gmail.com
Web: www.conntesol.net

Summary: To provide financial assistance to Connecticut residents whose native language is not English and who are attending or planning to attend college in any state.

Eligibility: Open to residents of Connecticut whose first language is not English. Awards are presented in 4 categories: 1) high school seniors entering a 2–year college; 2) high school seniors entering a 4–year college or university; 3) community college students transferring to a 4–year college or university; and 4) adult education students entering a college or university. Applicants must submit an essay of 250 to 500 words on how the education they are receiving in the United States is influencing their life.

Financial data: The stipend is $1,000.

Duration: 1 year.

Number awarded: At least 4 each year (1 in each category).

Deadline: April of each year.

166 $$ CONNECTICUT TUITION WAIVER FOR VETERANS

Connecticut Office of Financial and Academic Affairs for Higher Education
Attn: Student Financial Aid
61 Woodland Street
Hartford, CT 06105–2326
Phone: (860) 947–1855; (800) 842–0229 (within CT); Fax: (860) 947–1311;
Email: sfa@ctdhe.org

Web: www.ctohe.org/SFA/default.htm

Summary: To provide financial assistance for college to certain Connecticut veterans and military personnel and their dependents.

Eligibility: Open to 1) honorably–discharged Connecticut veterans who served at least 90 days during specified periods of war time; 2) active members of the Connecticut Army and Air National Guard; 3) Connecticut residents who are a dependent child or surviving spouse of a member of the armed forces killed in action on or after September 11, 2001 who was also a Connecticut resident; and 4) Connecticut residents who are dependent children of a person officially declared missing in action or a prisoner of war while serving in the armed forces after January 1, 1960. Applicants must be attending or planning to attend a public college or university in the state.

Financial data: The program provides a waiver of 100% of tuition for students working on an undergraduate or graduate degree at the University of Connecticut, 100% of tuition for general fund courses at campuses of Connecticut State University, 50% of tuition for extension and summer courses at campuses of Connecticut State University, 100% of tuition at all Connecticut community colleges, and 50% or fees at Charter Oak State College.

Duration: Up to 4 years.

Number awarded: Varies each year.

Deadline: Deadline not specified.

167 COURAGE CENTER SCHOLARSHIP FOR PEOPLE WITH DISABILITIES

Courage Center
Attn: Vocational Services Department
3915 Golden Valley Road
Minneapolis, MN 55422
Phone: (763) 520–0553; (888) 8–INTAKE; Fax: (763) 520–0392; TDD: (763) 520–0245;
Email: vocationalservices@couragecenter.org
Web: www.couragecenter.org/PreviewPages/disabilities_scholarship.aspx

Summary: To provide financial assistance to Minnesota residents who have a disability and are interested in attending college in any state.

Eligibility: Open to U.S. citizens who are residents of Minnesota or have received Courage Center services. Applicants must have a sensory impairment or physical disability and a desire to gain technical expertise beyond high school. They must be attending or planning to attend a college or technical school in any state. Along with their application, they must submit a concise essay that reflects their educational aspirations, career goals, and how a scholarship will help meet their needs. Selection is based on that essay, employment history, honors and awards, leadership experience, and financial need. Graduation ranking is not considered.

Financial data: The stipend is $1,000.

Duration: 1 year.

Number awarded: 1 or more each year.

Deadline: May of each year.

168 $$ CRISTIN ANN BAMBINO MEMORIAL SCHOLARSHIP

New York Schools Insurance Reciprocal
Attn: Executive Director
333 Earle Ovington Boulevard, Suite 1030
Uniondale, NY 11553–3624
Phone: (516) 393–2329; (800) 476–9747;
Email: jgoncalves@nysir.org
Web: nysir.org/nysir–student–asbo–scholarships

Summary: To provide financial assistance to special education seniors graduating from high schools that subscribe to the New York Schools Insurance Reciprocal (NYSIR) who plan to attend college in any state.

Eligibility: Open to seniors graduating from NYSIR–subscriber high schools who have been enrolled in special education and have worked through special challenges to complete high school. Applicants must be planning to attend a college or university in any state. Along with their application, they must submit a 650–word essay on their accomplishments, how they overcame their challenges, how they can serve as a role model for other young people with special challenges, and what they plan to study in college. Financial need is not considered in the selection process.

Financial data: The grand award winner receives $5,000. Regional winners receive $4,000 or $3,000.

Duration: 1 year.

Number awarded: 9 each year: the grand award winner and 8 regional winners, of whom 1 receives $4,000 and 7 receive $3,000.

Deadline: March of each year.

169 $$ CROHN'S SCHOLARSHIP PROGRAM

UCB, Inc.
c/o Summit Medical Communications
1421 East Broad Street, Suite 340
Fuquay–Varina, NC 27526
Phone: (866) 757–4440;
Email: ucbcrohnsscholarship@summitmedcomm.com
Web: www.crohnsandme.com/crohns–scholarship

Summary: To provide financial assistance to undergraduate and graduate students who have Crohn's disease.

Eligibility: Open to students who are working on or planning to work on an associate, undergraduate, or graduate degree or are enrolled in a trade school educational program. Applicants must have been diagnosed with Crohn's disease by a physician. They may be of any age. Along with their application, they must submit an essay of 1 to 2 pages describing how they are living beyond the boundaries of Crohn's disease (to demonstrate academic ambition and personal achievement) and how the scholarship would impact their life.

Financial data: Stipends range up to $5,000.

Duration: 1 year; nonrenewable.

Number awarded: 30 each year.

Deadline: February of each year.

170 CRUMLEY ROBERTS CHAIRMAN'S SCHOLARSHIPS

Crumley Roberts Attorneys at Law
Attn: Director of Community Relations
2400 Freeman Mill Road, Suite 200
Greensboro, NC 27406
Phone: (336) 333–0044; (866) 336–4547; Fax: (336) 333–9894
Web: www.crumleyroberts.com

Summary: To provide financial assistance to high school seniors in North Carolina who plan to attend college in any state.

Eligibility: Open to seniors graduating from high schools in North Carolina and planning to attend an accredited 4–year college or university in any state. Applicants must have a GPA of 2.8 or higher and a record of aptitude and passion for service to their local or global communities. Along with their application, they must submit an essay on a topic of current concern that changes annually; recently, students were asked to write on reducing distracted driving. Financial need is not considered in the selection process.

Financial data: Awards include a $1,000 scholarship and an iPad.

Duration: 1 year; nonrenewable.

Number awarded: 5 each year.

Deadline: February of each year.

171 CRUMLEY ROBERTS NEXT–STEP SCHOLARSHIPS

Crumley Roberts Attorneys at Law
Attn: Director of Community Relations
2400 Freeman Mill Road, Suite 200
Greensboro, NC 27406
Phone: (336) 333–0044; (866) 336–4547; Fax: (336) 333–9894
Web: www.crumleyroberts.com

Summary: To provide financial assistance to community college students in North Carolina who are planning to transfer to a 4–year university in the state.

Eligibility: Open to students at community colleges in North Carolina who are planning to transfer to a 4–year university in the state. Selection is based on community service and an essay on their educational and career goals.

Financial data: Awards include a $1,000 scholarship and an iPad.

Duration: 1 year; nonrenewable.

Number awarded: 5 each year.

Deadline: February of each year.

172 $ CVS CAREMARK/ERIC DELSON MEMORIAL SCHOLARSHIP

CVS Caremark
c/o Scholarship America
Scholarship Management Services
One Scholarship Way
P.O. Box 297
St. Peter, MN 56082
Phone: (507) 931–1682
Web: cvscaremarkspecialtyrx.com

Summary: To provide financial assistance for high school, college, or graduate school to students with a bleeding disorder.
Eligibility: Open to students diagnosed with a bleeding disorder who are 1) high school seniors, high school graduates or equivalent (GED), college students, or graduate students currently enrolled or planning to enroll full time at an accredited 2– or 4–year college, university, or vocational/technical school; or 2) students entering grades 7–12 at a private secondary school in the United States. Selection is based on academic record, demonstrated leadership and participation in school and community activities, work experience, a statement of educational and career goals, unusual personal or family circumstances, and an outside appraisal.
Financial data: The stipend is $2,500 for college students or $1,500 for high school students. Funds are paid in 2 equal installments directly to the recipient.
Duration: 1 year; may be renewed for up to 3 additional years, provided the recipient maintains a GPA of 2.5 or higher for the freshman year and 3.0 or higher for subsequent years.
Number awarded: 4 each year: 3 for college students and 1 for a high school student.
Deadline: June of each year.

173 CYNTHIA RUTH RUSSELL MEMORIAL GRANTS

Kansas Masonic Foundation, Inc.
2909 S.W. Maupin Lane
Topeka, KS 66614–5335
Phone: (785) 357–7646; Fax: (785) 357–7406;
Email: kmf@kmfonline.org
Web: www.kmfonline.org/content/view/15/36
Summary: To provide financial assistance to physically challenged Kansas residents attending a college or university in the state.
Eligibility: Open to residents of Kansas who are physically challenged. Applicants must be attending or planning to attend an institution of higher education in the state as a full–time undergraduate or graduate student. Along with their application, they must submit a 300–word statement of their educational goals, a short autobiography that includes a discussion of their physical challenge, a list of extracurricular activities, their latest grade transcript, letters of reference, ACT and/or SAT scores, and documentation of financial need.
Financial data: A stipend is awarded (amount not specified).
Duration: 1 year; may be renewed, provided the recipient remains enrolled full time and maintains a GPA of 2.5 or higher.
Number awarded: 1 or more each year.
Deadline: March of each year.

174 CYSTIC FIBROSIS SCHOLARSHIPS

Cystic Fibrosis Scholarship Foundation
1555 Sherman Avenue, Suite 116
Evanston, IL 60201
Phone: (847) 328–0127; Fax: (847) 328–0127;
Email: mkbcfsf@aol.com
Web: www.cfscholarship.org
Summary: To provide financial assistance to undergraduate students who have cystic fibrosis (CF).
Eligibility: Open to students enrolled or planning to enroll in college (either a 2– or 4–year program) or vocational school. Applicants must have CF. Along with their application, they must submit an essay on a topic that changes annually; recently, students were asked to select a personal or historical situation they would like to observe as a "fly on the wall," what they would hope to learn, and how it would benefit them. Selection is based on academic achievement, leadership, and financial need.
Financial data: Most stipends are $1,000 per year, although some designated awards (funded by single–year donations) may range up to $2,500. Funds are sent directly to the student's institution to be used for tuition, books, room, and board.
Duration: 1 year; some awards may be renewed up to 3 additional years.
Number awarded: Varies each year; recently, 45 of these scholarships were awarded.
Deadline: March of each year.

175 DAN AND LUCILLE WOOD ATHLETIC SCHOLARSHIPS

New Mexico Activities Association
Attn: Administrative Assistant
6600 Palomas Avenue, N.E.
Albuquerque, NM 87109
Phone: (505) 923–2380; (888) 820–NMAA; Fax: (505) 923–3114;
Email: mindy@nmact.org
Web: www.nmact.org/scholarship_information_forms
Summary: To provide financial assistance to high school seniors in New Mexico who have participated in sports and plan to attend college in any state.
Eligibility: Open to seniors graduating from high schools in New Mexico with a GPA of 3.0 or higher. Applicants must have participated in at least 1 sport sanctioned by the New Mexico Activities Association (NMAA) during their sophomore and junior year and at least 2 sports during their senior year. They must be planning to attend a college or university in any state. Along with their application, they must submit transcripts, ACT and/or SAT scores, 3 letters of recommendation, and a personal statement on how involvement in athletics impacted their high school career. Applicants may request that financial need be considered in the selection process.
Financial data: The stipend is $1,000.
Duration: 1 year.
Number awarded: 2 each year.
Deadline: February of each year.

176 $$ DANA CHRISTMAS SCHOLARSHIP FOR HEROISM

New Jersey Higher Education Student Assistance Authority
Attn: Grants and Scholarships
4 Quakerbridge Plaza
P.O. Box 540
Trenton, NJ 08625–0540
Phone: (609) 588–2349; (800) 792–8670; Fax: (609) 588–3450;
Email: ClientServices@hesaa.org
Web: www.hesaa.org/Pages/GrantsandScholarshipsDetails.aspx
Summary: To provide financial assistance for college or graduate school to residents of New Jersey who have performed an act of heroism.
Eligibility: Open to U.S. citizens and eligible noncitizens who are New Jersey residents and have performed an act of heroism when they were 21 years of age or younger. Both applications and nominations from others are required. Letters of nomination must be accompanied by a description of the act of heroism, including such additional documentation as newspaper articles. Nominees must be enrolled or planning to enroll as an undergraduate or graduate student at an institution eligible to participate in the federal Title IV student aid programs.
Financial data: The stipend is $10,000.
Duration: 1 year; nonrenewable.
Number awarded: Up to 5 each year.
Deadline: October of each year.

177 DANIEL E. LAMBERT MEMORIAL SCHOLARSHIP

American Legion
Department of Maine
P.O. Box 900
Waterville, ME 04903–0900
Phone: (207) 873–3229; Fax: (207) 872–0501;
Email: legionme@mainelegion.org
Web: www.mainelegion.org/pages/programs/scholarships.php
Summary: To provide financial assistance to the children of veterans in Maine who plan to attend college in any state.
Eligibility: Open to residents of Maine who are the child or grandchild of a veteran. Applicants must be attending or planning to attend an accredited college or vocational/technical school in any state. They must have demonstrated, by their past behavior, that they believe in the American way of life. U.S. citizenship is required. Financial need is considered in the selection process.
Financial data: The stipend is $1,000.
Duration: 1 year.
Number awarded: 1 or 2 each year.
Deadline: April of each year.

178 DANIELS SCHOLARSHIP PROGRAM

Daniels Fund
Attn: Scholarship Program
101 Monroe Street
Denver, CO 80206
Phone: (303) 941–4453; (877) 791–4726; Fax: (720) 941–4208;
Email: scholars@danielsfund.org
Web: www.danielsfund.org/Scholarships/Index.asp

Summary: To provide financial assistance to high school students in Colorado, Utah, Wyoming, and New Mexico who can demonstrate financial need and plan to attend college in any state.
Eligibility: Open to seniors graduating from high schools in Colorado, Utah, Wyoming, and New Mexico. Applicants must be planning to attend an accredited 2– or 4–year college or university in any state, but they must intend to complete a bachelor's degree. They must have a composite ACT score of 17 or higher or a combined critical reading and mathematics SAT score of 830 or higher. Selection is based primarily on financial need, although strength of character, academic performance and promise, leadership potential, emotional maturity, potential to contribute to the community, and a well–rounded personality are also considered. Students may not apply directly for these scholarships; they must be nominated by a designated referral agency, which may be a youth service agency in their home community or their high school. They must have U.S. citizenship or status as a permanent resident, refugee, or asylum–holder. Semifinalists are interviewed.
Financial data: Stipends cover the recipient's unmet financial need, and pay for tuition and fees, room and board, books and supplies, and miscellaneous educational expenses.
Duration: 1 year; may be renewed up to 3 additional years, provided the recipient makes satisfactory academic progress and holds a job that entails at least 125 hours per academic year for the first year and 250 hours per academic year for the remaining 3 years.
Number awarded: Approximately 250 each year.
Deadline: December of each year.

179 $ DARLENE HOOLEY SCHOLARSHIP FOR OREGON VETERANS

Oregon Student Access Commission
Attn: Grants and Scholarships Division
1500 Valley River Drive, Suite 100
Eugene, OR 97401–2146
Phone: (541) 687–7395; (800) 452–8807, ext. 7395; Fax: (541) 687–7414; TDD: (800) 735–2900;
Email: awardinfo@osac.state.or.us
Web: www.oregonstudentaid.gov/scholarships.aspx
Summary: To provide financial assistance to veterans in Oregon who served during the Global War on Terror and are interested in working on an undergraduate or graduate degree at a college in the state.
Eligibility: Open to Oregon veterans who served during the Global War on Terror; there is no minimum length of service requirement. Preference is given to members of active–duty Reserves and the National Guard who were deployed to an overseas conflict. Applicants must be enrolled or planning to enroll at least half time as an undergraduate or graduate student at a college or university in Oregon. Financial need is considered in the selection process.
Financial data: Stipends for scholarships offered by the Oregon Student Access Commission (OSAC) range from $200 to $10,000 but recently averaged $2,300.
Duration: 1 year; recipients may reapply.
Number awarded: Varies each year.
Deadline: February of each year.

180 $ DAUGHTERS OF THE CINCINNATI SCHOLARSHIP PROGRAM

Daughters of the Cincinnati
Attn: Scholarship Administrator
20 West 44th Street, Suite 508
New York, NY 10036
Phone: (212) 991–9945;
Email: scholarships@daughters1894.org
Web: www.daughters1894.org
Summary: To provide financial assistance for college to high school seniors who are the daughters of active–duty, deceased, or retired military officers.
Eligibility: Open to high school seniors who are the daughters of career commissioned officers of the regular Army, Navy, Air Force, Coast Guard, or Marine Corps on active duty, deceased, or retired. Applicants must be planning to enroll at a college or university in any state. Along with their application, they must submit an official school transcript, SAT or ACT scores, a letter of recommendation, and documentation of financial need.
Financial data: Scholarship amounts have recently averaged $4,000 per year. Funds are paid directly to the college of the student's choice.
Duration: 1 year; may be renewed up to 3 additional years, provided the recipient remains in good academic standing.
Number awarded: Approximately 12 each year.
Deadline: March of each year.

181 $ DAVE MADEIROS CONTINUED EDUCATION SCHOLARSHIPS

Factor Foundation of America
Attn: Scholarship Committee
P.O. Box 812542
Boca Raton, FL 33481–2542
Phone: (561) 504–6531;
Email: kmadeiros@factorfoundation.org
Web: www.factorfoundation.org/programs.htm
Summary: To provide financial assistance for college to people with a bleeding disorder and their families.
Eligibility: Open to people with a bleeding disorder and their siblings, parents, and children. Applicants must be attending or planning to attend an accredited 2– or 4–year college or university or technical school. They must be recommended by a local hemophilia chapter, physician, and/or hemophilia treatment center. Along with their application, they must submit a 500–word letter describing their goals and aspirations and how the bleeding disorders community has played a part in their life. Financial need is also considered in the selection process.
Financial data: The stipend is $2,000 per year.
Duration: 1 year; may be renewed if the recipient remains in good academic standing.
Number awarded: Varies each year; recently, 12 of these scholarships were awarded.
Deadline: June of each year.

182 DAVE WARD MEMORIAL SCHOLARSHIP

Monumental Rifle and Pistol Club, Inc.
c/o Bryant Cramer, Scholarship Committee Chair
10990 Frederick Road
Ellicott City, MD 21042
Phone: (410) 465–6906;
Email: dbcramer@comcast.net
Web: www.monumental.org
Summary: To provide financial assistance to high school juniors and seniors in Maryland who submit an outstanding essay on citizenship and plan to attend college in any state.
Eligibility: Open to juniors and seniors at high schools in Maryland who plan to continue on to college in any state. Applicants must submit an essay, 3 to 5 pages in length, on "What Citizenship Means to Me." Selection is based primarily on the essay, although consideration is also given to academic achievement, participation in activities related to the shooting sports, and participation in activities related to the study and support of citizenship and the second amendment.
Financial data: The stipend is $1,000.
Duration: 1 year.
Number awarded: 1 each year.
Deadline: July of each year.

183 DAVID GALL MEMORIAL SCHOLARSHIP

Ohio Transfer Council
c/o Celestine Goodloe
Xavier University
3800 Victory Parkway
Cincinnati, OH 45207–5131
Phone: (513) 745–3163;
Email: goodloe@xavier.edu
Web: www.ohiotransfer.org
Summary: To provide financial assistance to residents of any state transferring from a college or university that belongs to the Ohio Transfer Council to another.
Eligibility: Open to students enrolled at a 4–year college or university, 2–year community college, or vocational/technical institute that belongs to the Ohio Transfer Council. Applicants must have completed at least 24 semester credit hours or 36 quarter hours with a GPA of 3.0 or higher. They must be planning to transfer to another member institution. Along with their application, they must submit a 300–word essay on their short– and long–term educational goals, what led them to transfer schools, any special circumstances that led to that decision, and what motivates them to continue with their education. Selection is based on academic performance, written communication skills, academic and career goals, initiative and responsibility, and persistence toward completing a degree program. Ohio residency is not required.
Financial data: The stipend is $1,000.

Duration: 1 year; nonrenewable.
Number awarded: 3 each year.
Deadline: June of each year.

184 DAVID KNAUS MEMORIAL SCHOLARSHIP

American Radio Relay League
Attn: ARRL Foundation
225 Main Street
Newington, CT 06111–1494
Phone: (860) 594–0397; Fax: (860) 594–0259;
Email: foundation@arrl.org
Web: www.arrl.org/scholarship–descriptions

Summary: To provide financial assistance to licensed radio amateurs in Illinois who are interested in working on an undergraduate degree in any area.
Eligibility: Open to licensed radio amateurs of any class who are residents of Wisconsin and who are working on or planning to work on a bachelor's or associate degree in any field at an educational institution in any state. If no qualified resident of Wisconsin applies, residents of Indiana or Illinois may also be considered. Applicants must submit an essay on the role amateur radio has played in their lives and provide documentation of financial need.
Financial data: The stipend is $1,500.
Duration: 1 year.
Number awarded: 1 each year.
Deadline: January of each year.

185 $$ DAVIDSON FELLOWS AWARDS

Davidson Institute for Talent Development
Attn: Davidson Fellows Program
9665 Gateway Drive, Suite B
Reno, NV 89521
Phone: (775) 852–3483, ext. 435; Fax: (775) 852–2184;
Email: DavidsonFellows@davidsongifted.org
Web: www.davidsongifted.org/fellows

Summary: To recognize and reward, with college scholarships, young people who complete significant pieces of work in designated areas.
Eligibility: Open to U.S. citizens, permanent residents, and students stationed overseas because of active–duty military service who are under 18 years of age. Applicants must have completed a "significant piece of work" in 1 of the following submission categories: 1) philosophy: a portfolio presenting analyses of fundamental assumptions or beliefs relating to human thought or culture; 2) music: a portfolio demonstrating the applicant's talent as a composer, vocalist, classical instrumentalist, or other instrumentalist; 3) literature: a portfolio displaying a number of literary styles and genres; 4) science: a project in a specific area or science, such as biology, chemistry, earth science, engineering, environmental science, medicine, physics, or space science; 5) mathematics: a project in a specific area of mathematics, such as calculus, fractals, or number theory; 6) technology: a project in a specific area of technology, such as computer programming or artificial intelligence; or 7) "outside the box:" university graduate level or comparable work completed with the supervision of an expert or experts. Selection is based on the quality and scope of the entry (50 points), the level of significance of the work (30 points), and the applicant's depth of knowledge and understanding of the work and the related domain area (20 points).
Financial data: Awards are $50,000, $25,000, or $10,000. Funds must be used for tuition and related expenses at an accredited college or university. Scholarship money is available for 10 years after the date of the award.
Duration: The awards are presented annually.
Number awarded: Varies each year; recently, 18 of these awards were presented: 1 at $50,000, 9 at $25,000, and 8 at $10,000.
Deadline: A screening form for the "outside the box" category is due in late January. Preliminary submissions for all other categories are due in mid–February. Completed applications for all categories are due in early March of each year.

186 $$ DAVIS–PUTTER SCHOLARSHIPS

Davis–Putter Scholarship Fund
P.O. Box 7307
New York, NY 10116–7307
Email: administrator@davisputter.org
Web: dpsf.davisputter.org

Summary: To provide financial assistance to undergraduate and graduate student activists.
Eligibility: Open to undergraduate and graduate students who are involved in "struggles for civil rights, economic justice, international solidarity or other progressive issues." While U.S. citizenship is not required, applicants must be living in the United States and planning to enroll in school here. They must submit a completed application, a personal statement that describes their activism and their perspective on social change, financial need reports, recommendation letters, transcripts, and a photograph.
Financial data: Grants range up to $10,000 per year, depending upon need.
Duration: 1 year; recipients may reapply.
Number awarded: Varies each year; recently, 22 of these scholarships were awarded.
Deadline: March of each year.

187 DELAWARE DEPARTMENT OF EDUCATION DIAMOND STATE SCHOLARSHIPS

Delaware Department of Education
Attn: Higher Education Office
401 Federal Street
Dover, DE 19901–3639
Phone: (302) 735–4120; (800) 292–7935; Fax: (302) 739–4654;
Email: dheo@doe.k12.de.us
Web: www.doe.k12.de.us/infosuites/students_family/dheo/default.shtml

Summary: To provide financial assistance to Delaware high school seniors who have outstanding academic records and plan to attend college in any state.
Eligibility: Open to seniors graduating from high schools in Delaware residents who have a combined score of 1800 on the SAT and a rank in the upper quarter of their class. Applicants must be planning to enroll full time at an accredited college or university in any state. U.S. citizenship or permanent resident status is required.
Financial data: The stipend is $1,250 per year.
Duration: 1 year; may be renewed up to 3 additional years, provided the recipient maintains a GPA of 3.0 or higher.
Number awarded: Approximately 50 each year.
Deadline: March of each year.

188 $$ DELAWARE EDUCATIONAL BENEFITS FOR CHILDREN OF DECEASED VETERANS AND OTHERS

Delaware Department of Education
Attn: Higher Education Office
401 Federal Street
Dover, DE 19901–3639
Phone: (302) 735–4120; (800) 292–7935; Fax: (302) 739–4654;
Email: dheo@doe.k12.de.us
Web: www.doe.k12.de.us/infosuites/students_family/dheo/default.shtml

Summary: To provide financial assistance for undergraduate education to dependents of deceased Delaware veterans, state police officers, and Department of Transportation employees and members of the armed forces declared prisoners of war or missing in action.
Eligibility: Open to applicants who have been Delaware residents for at least 3 consecutive years and are the children, between 16 and 24 years of age, of members of the armed forces 1) whose cause of death was service–related; 2) who are being held or were held as a prisoner of war; or 3) who are officially declared missing in action. The parent must have been a resident of Delaware at the time of death or declaration of missing in action or prisoner of war status. Also eligible are children of Delaware state police officers whose cause of death was service–related and employees of the state Department of Transportation routinely employed in job–related activities upon the state highway system whose cause of death was job related. U.S. citizenship or eligible noncitizen status is required.
Financial data: Eligible students receive full tuition at any state–supported institution in Delaware or, if the desired educational program is not available at a state–supported school, at any private institution in Delaware. If the desired educational program is not offered at either a public or private institution in Delaware, this program pays the full cost of tuition at the out–of–state school the recipient attends. Students who wish to attend a private or out–of–state school even though their program is offered at a Delaware public institution receive the equivalent of the average tuition and fees at the state school.
Duration: 1 year; may be renewed for 3 additional years.
Number awarded: Varies each year.
Deadline: Applications may be submitted at any time, but they must be received at least 4 weeks before the beginning of classes.

189 $ DELAWARE GOVERNOR'S EDUCATION GRANTS FOR UNEMPLOYED WORKERS

Delaware Department of Education
Attn: Higher Education Office
401 Federal Street

Dover, DE 19901–3639
Phone: (302) 735–4120; (800) 292–7935; Fax: (302) 739–4654;
Email: dheo@doe.k12.de.us
Web: www.doe.k12.de.us/infosuites/students_family/dheo/default.shtml

Summary: To provide financial assistance to Delaware residents who are unemployed and wish to receive additional training.

Eligibility: Open to residents of Delaware who are 18 years of age or older and high school graduates or GED recipients. Applicants must have lost their jobs due to the current economic climate, have been unsuccessful in obtaining employment within their current career field, have been actively seeking employment for at least 90 days, be registered with the Department of Labor's Division of Employment and Training (DET), be recommended by a DET career counselor, and be ineligible for the Department of Labor's Dislocated Worker Training Program. They must be enrolled as a part–time undergraduate at a participating Delaware college or adult education center. U.S. citizenship or eligible noncitizen status is required.

Financial data: Grants cover 80% of tuition and fees, to a maximum of $2,000 per year. The participating institution agrees to provide 10% of tuition and fees and the student is expected to pay the remaining 10%.

Duration: 1 year; renewable.

Number awarded: Varies each year.

Deadline: Applications may be submitted at any time, but they must be received by the end of the drop/add date at the participating college.

190 $ DELAWARE GOVERNOR'S EDUCATION GRANTS FOR WORKING ADULTS

Delaware Department of Education
Attn: Higher Education Office
401 Federal Street
Dover, DE 19901–3639
Phone: (302) 735–4120; (800) 292–7935; Fax: (302) 739–4654;
Email: dheo@doe.k12.de.us
Web: www.doe.k12.de.us/infosuites/students_family/dheo/default.shtml

Summary: To provide financial assistance for part–time education to Delaware working adults with financial need.

Eligibility: Open to residents of Delaware who are at least 18 years of age and high school graduates or GED recipients. Applicants must be employed by a company in Delaware; if employed full time, they must work for an eligible small business with 100 or fewer employees. They must be enrolled as a part–time undergraduate at a participating Delaware college or adult education center. Their income may not exceed $32,670 for a single individual or $44,130 for a family of 2, rising to $124,350 for a family of 9. U.S. citizenship or eligible noncitizen status is required.

Financial data: Grants cover 65% of tuition and fees, to a maximum of $2,000 per year. The participating institution agrees to provide 10% of tuition and fees and the student or employer is expected to pay the remaining 25%.

Duration: 1 year; renewable.

Number awarded: Varies each year.

Deadline: Applications may be submitted at any time, but they must be received by the end of the drop/add date at the participating college.

191 $ DELAWARE SCHOLARSHIP INCENTIVE PROGRAM

Delaware Department of Education
Attn: Higher Education Office
401 Federal Street
Dover, DE 19901–3639
Phone: (302) 735–4120; (800) 292–7935; Fax: (302) 739–4654;
Email: dheo@doe.k12.de.us
Web: www.doe.k12.de.us/infosuites/students_family/dheo/default.shtml

Summary: To provide financial assistance for undergraduate or graduate study to Delaware residents with financial need.

Eligibility: Open to Delaware residents who are 1) enrolled full time in an undergraduate degree program at a Delaware or Pennsylvania college or university; or 2) enrolled full time in an undergraduate or graduate degree program at an accredited out–of–state institution or at a private institution in Delaware if their major is not offered at the University of Delaware, Delaware State University, or Delaware Technical and Community College. Applicants must be able to demonstrate financial need and have a GPA of 2.5 or higher. U.S. citizenship or eligible noncitizen status is required.

Financial data: The amount awarded depends on the need of the recipient but does not exceed the cost of tuition, fees, and books. Currently, the maximum for undergraduates ranges from $700 to $2,200 per year, depending on GPA; that includes a need–based award of $700 and a merit supplement up to $1,500; the maximum for graduate students is $1,000 per year.

Duration: 1 year; nonrenewable.

Number awarded: Approximately 1,500 each year.

Deadline: April of each year.

192 $$ DELL SCHOLARS PROGRAM

Michael & Susan Dell Foundation
Attn: Scholarships
P.O. Box 163867
Austin, TX 78716
Phone: (512) 347–1744; (800) 294–2039; Fax: (512) 600–5501;
Email: apply@dellscholars.org
Web: www.dellscholars.org

Summary: To provide financial assistance for college to high school seniors who have participated in a college readiness program sponsored by the Michael & Susan Dell Foundation (MSDF).

Eligibility: Open to graduating high school seniors who have participated in an MSDF approved college readiness program for at least 2 years. Applicants must have a GPA of 2.4 or higher and be able to demonstrate financial need. They must be planning to enroll at an accredited college or university in the following fall to work on a bachelor's degree. Selection is based on individual determination to succeed, future goals and plans to achieve them, ability to communicate the hardships they have overcome or currently face, self–motivation in completing challenging course work, and financial need. U.S. citizenship or permanent resident status is required.

Financial data: The stipend is $5,000 per year. Funds may be used for tuition, fees, books, and on–campus room and board. With approval of the sponsor, they may also be used for approved internships and study abroad programs.

Duration: 4 years.

Number awarded: 300 each year.

Deadline: January of each year.

193 DEPARTMENT OF ILLINOIS AMVETS SERVICE FOUNDATION SCHOLARSHIPS

AMVETS–Department of Illinois
2200 South Sixth Street
Springfield, IL 62703
Phone: (217) 528–4713; (800) 638–VETS (within IL); Fax: (217) 528–9896
Web: www.ilamvets.org/prog_scholarships.cfm

Summary: To provide financial assistance for college to high school seniors in Illinois, especially children and grandchildren of veterans.

Eligibility: Open to seniors graduating from high schools in Illinois who have taken the ACT or SAT. Financial need is considered in the selection process. Priority is given to children and grandchildren of veterans.

Financial data: The stipend is $1,000.

Duration: 1 year; nonrenewable.

Number awarded: Up to 30 each year: 6 in each of the sponsor's 5 divisions.

Deadline: February of each year.

194 DEPARTMENT OF ILLINOIS AMVETS TRADE SCHOOL SCHOLARSHIPS

AMVETS–Department of Illinois
2200 South Sixth Street
Springfield, IL 62703
Phone: (217) 528–4713; (800) 638–VETS (within IL); Fax: (217) 528–9896
Web: www.ilamvets.org/prog_scholarships.cfm

Summary: To provide financial assistance to high school seniors in Illinois, especially children and grandchildren of veterans, who are interested in attending trade school.

Eligibility: Open to seniors graduating from high schools in Illinois who have been accepted at an approved trade school. Financial need is considered in the selection process. Priority is given to children and grandchildren of veterans.

Financial data: The stipend is $5,000.

Duration: 1 year; nonrenewable.

Number awarded: 5 each year: 1 in each of the sponsor's divisions.

Deadline: February of each year.

195 $$ DIABETES SCHOLARS FOUNDATION SCHOLARSHIPS

Diabetes Scholars Foundation
2118 Plum Grove Road, Suite 356
Rolling Meadows, IL 60008

Phone: (312) 215–9861; Fax: (847) 991–8739;
Email: collegescholarships@diabetesscholars.org
Web: www.diabetesscholars.org/college.html
Summary: To provide financial assistance for college to high school seniors who have diabetes.
Eligibility: Open to graduating high school seniors who have Type 1 diabetes and plan to attend an accredited 4–year university, college, or technical/trade school in any state. Applicants must be able to demonstrate active involvement in the diabetes community, academic performance, participation in community and/or extracurricular activities, and successful management of the challenges of living with diabetes. Financial need is not considered in the selection process. U.S. citizenship or permanent resident status is required.
Financial data: Stipends are $5,000.
Duration: 1 year.
Number awarded: At least 5 each year.
Deadline: May of each year.

196 DIAMONDS IN THE ROUGH MINISTRY SCHOLARSHIP

Diamonds in the Rough Ministry International
Attn: Scholarship Fund
2414 East Highway 80, Suite 302
Mesquite, TX 75150
Phone: (972) 288–0112;
Email: aparker@diamondsntherough.org
Web: diamondsntherough.org/scholarship.html
Summary: To provide financial assistance to female high school seniors from Texas who are "allowing God to develop them into precious diamonds" by attending college in any state.
Eligibility: Open to women who are graduating from high schools in Texas and planning to attend college in any state. Applicants must be able to demonstrate that they understand the goal of the sponsoring organization to "empower women down the road of self–discovery and self–worth in Jesus Christ." They must have a GPA of 2.5 or higher. Along with their application, they must submit a 500–word essay on how they see God using a challenging situation or circumstance to polish them into a precious diamond.
Financial data: A stipend is awarded (amount not specified).
Duration: 1 year.
Number awarded: 1 or 2 each year.
Deadline: April of each year.

197 $$ DINAH SHORE SCHOLARSHIP

Ladies Professional Golf Association
Attn: LPGA Foundation
100 International Golf Drive
Daytona Beach, FL 32124–1082
Phone: (386) 274–6200; Fax: (386) 274–1099;
Email: foundation.scholarships@lpga.com
Web: www.lpgafoundation.org/Scholarships/scholarshipgeneral.aspx
Summary: To provide financial assistance for college to female graduating high school seniors who played golf in high school.
Eligibility: Open to female high school seniors who have a GPA of 3.2 or higher. Applicants must have played in at least 50% of their high school golf team's scheduled events or have played golf "regularly" for the past 2 years. They must be planning to enroll full time at a college or university in the United States, but they must not be planning to play collegiate golf. Along with their application, they must submit a letter that describes how golf has been an integral part of their lives and includes their personal, academic, and professional goals; chosen discipline of study; and how this scholarship will be of assistance. Financial need is not considered in the selection process.
Financial data: The stipend is $5,000.
Duration: 1 year.
Number awarded: 1 each year.
Deadline: May of each year.

198 $$ DISABLED WORKERS COMMITTEE SCHOLARSHIP

Disabled Workers Committee
Attn: Joanna Y. Lazarus, Scholarship Committee Chair
Suisman Shapiro Attorneys At Law
2 Union Plaza, Suite 200
P.O. Box 1591
New London, CT 06320
Phone: (860) 442–4416; Fax: (860) 442–0495
Summary: To provide financial assistance to children of people with disabilities in Connecticut who are interested in attending college in any state.
Eligibility: Open to seniors graduating from high schools in Connecticut whose parent is totally and permanently disabled as the result of an injury. The injury must arise out of the workplace. Applicants must be interested in attending a college or university in any state. Selection is based on academic achievement and financial need.
Financial data: The stipend is $5,000.
Duration: 1 year.
Number awarded: 2 each year.
Deadline: April of each year.

199 $$ DISCOVER CARD TRIBUTE AWARDS

Discover Financial Services
c/o International Scholarship and Tuition Services, Inc.
200 Crutchfield Avenue
Nashville, TN 37210
Phone: (615) 320–3149; (866) 756–7932; Fax: (615) 320–3151;
Email: info@applyists.com
Web: www.discoverfinancial.com/community/scholarship.shtml
Summary: To provide financial assistance for college to high school juniors who have demonstrated excellence in many areas of their lives, in addition to academics.
Eligibility: Open to high school juniors who are enrolled in public or accredited private schools in the 50 United States and the District of Columbia. Both U.S. citizens and noncitizens are eligible if they plan to graduate from their U.S. high school and continue their education or training at a U.S. postsecondary institution (including certification or license, trade or technical school, 2– or 4–year college, or university). Applicants must have a cumulative GPA of 2.75 or higher. Along with their application, they must submit statements on their leadership, obstacles they have overcome, and community service. Awards are presented to applicants who 1) have diverse and outstanding accomplishments; 2) have faced a significant obstacle or challenge; and 3) display initiative, creativity, determination, and personal results.
Financial data: State scholarships are $2,500 each. National scholarships are $25,000 each.
Duration: 1 year.
Number awarded: Up to 300 state scholarships are awarded each year; 10 of those winners are selected to receive national scholarships.
Deadline: January of each year.

200 $ DISCUS AWARDS SCHOLARSHIPS

Discus Awards
7101 Wisconsin Avenue, Suite 750
Bethesda, MD 20814
Phone: (301) 907–2390, ext. 19;
Email: info@discusawards.com
Web: www.discusawards.com
Summary: To recognize and reward, with college scholarships, high school students who demonstrate outstanding achievement in diverse areas of activity.
Eligibility: Open to graduating high school seniors who plan to attend college and are nominated by themselves or by another individual. Nominees must identify 3 areas from a list of 10 attributes that they believe they possess: 1) academics, for grades, honors, and competitions; 2) arts, for drama, writing, music, film, photography, or other artistic endeavors; 3) athletics, for sports, training, coaching, cheerleading, or other athletic accomplishment; 4) community service, for volunteering, tutoring, mentoring, or other ways in which they make an impact; 5) faith, for youth groups, mission, retreat, or other leadership activities in church, synagogue, or other house of worship; 6) for student government, politics, campaigning, or other involvement with the way the world is governed; 7) green, for clean–ups, recycling, building awareness, or other environmental activism; 8) technology, for web, programming, science, blogging, or Internet innovation; 9) work, for part–time jobs, involvement in a family business, or entrepreneurship; or 10) other, for clubs, student activities, overcoming obstacles, or other personal achievements. For each of the 3 areas they select, students must write 750 characters or less describing their activities; they may also include images and videos. Students whose entries are judged outstanding are recognized with Discus Awards. Each month, the award winner considered most excellent receives a scholarship.
Financial data: Scholarship stipends are $2,000.
Duration: The scholarship is for 1 year.
Number awarded: 10 each year: 1 each month from September through June.
Deadline: Applications may be submitted at any time during the school year.

201 DISTANCE LEARNING SCHOLARSHIP

Christian Connector, Inc.
627 24 1/2 Road, Suite D
Grand Junction, CO 81501
Phone: (970) 256–1610; (800) 667–0600
Web: www.christianconnector.com

Summary: To provide financial assistance to students interested in working on an undergraduate or graduate degree from a Christ–centered distance learning program.

Eligibility: Open to students planning to enroll through a distance learning program at a Christ–centered Christian college, Bible college, seminary, or Christian graduate school. Schools that are members of the CCCU, NACCAP, or AABC automatically qualify. Applicants enter the competition by registering online with the sponsoring organization, providing personal information and indicating the distance learning program they are considering. The recipient of the scholarship is selected in a random drawing.

Financial data: The award is $1,000. Funds are sent directly to the winner's school.

Duration: The award is presented annually.

Number awarded: 1 each year. The sponsor also awards scholarships for students to attend Christian colleges and seminaries.

Deadline: May of each year.

202 $$ DISTINGUISHED YOUNG WOMEN SCHOLARSHIPS

Distinguished Young Women
Attn: Foundation Administrator
751 Government Street
Mobile, AL 36602
Phone: (251) 438–3621; Fax: (251) 431–0063;
Email: foundation@distinguishedyw.org
Web: www.distinguishedyw.org/about/scholarships

Summary: To recognize and reward, with college scholarships, female high school seniors who participate in the Distinguished Young Women competition.

Eligibility: Open to girls who are seniors in high school, are U.S. citizens, have never been married, and have never been pregnant. Contestants first enter local competitions, from which winners advance to the state level. The winner in each state is invited to the national competition, held in Mobile, Alabama in June of each year. Prior to the contestants' arrival for the national competition, the judges evaluate their high school academic records and test scores for the scholastics score (20% of the overall score). At the competition, girls are given scores on the basis of their personality, ability to relate to others, maturity, and ability to express themselves in an interview (25% of overall score); their performing arts talent presented during a 90–second audition on stage in front of an audience (25% of overall score); their fitness as demonstrated during a choreographed group aerobic routine (15% of overall score); and their self–expression, grace, poise, demeanor, carriage, posture, and speaking ability (15% of overall score). The girls with the highest scores in each of the 5 categories receive awards. Overall scores are used for selection of 10 finalists, from whom the "Distinguished Young Woman of America" and 2 runners–up are selected. In addition, "satellite awards" are presented to girls who excel in special activities.

Financial data: The "Distinguished Young Woman of America" receives a $40,000 scholarship; other scholarships are $25,000 for the first runner–up, $15,000 for the second runner–up, $3,000 for each of the 7 other finalists, $1,000 for each of the category winners, and "satellite awards" ranging from $500 to $1,500 for other activities.

Duration: The competition is held annually.

Number awarded: More than $140,000 in scholarships is awarded at the national finals each year.

Deadline: Each local competition sets its own deadline.

203 $$ DISTRICT OF COLUMBIA TUITION ASSISTANCE GRANT PROGRAM (DC TAG)

Office of the State Superintendent of Education
Attn: Higher Education Financial Services
810 First Street, N.E., Ninth Floor
Washington, DC 20002
Phone: (202) 727–2824; (877) 485–6751;
Email: osse@dc.gov
Web: osse.dc.gov/service/dctag–get–funding–college

Summary: To provide financial assistance to residents of the District of Columbia who are interested in attending a public college or university anywhere in the United States, a private institution in the Washington metropolitan area, or a study abroad program.

Eligibility: Open to all residents of the District of Columbia who are high school seniors or recent graduates (under 24 years of age), regardless of where they attended high school. Applicants must be interested in attending 1) a public 4–year college or university anywhere in the United States (except in the District of Columbia), Puerto Rico, or Guam; 2) a private nonprofit college or university in the Washington metropolitan area (defined as the District of Columbia, the cities of Alexandria, Falls Church, and Fairfax, and the counties of Arlington, Fairfax, Montgomery, and Prince George's); 3) a private Historically Black College or University (HBCU) in any state; or 4) a 2–year community college in any state. Students attending proprietary institutions are not eligible. Study abroad programs do qualify if they are approved for credit by the institution attended. Financial need is not required. U.S. citizenship or eligible noncitizen status is required.

Financial data: Awards at 4–year public institutions are equal to the difference between the in–state and out–of–state tuition, to an annual maximum of $10,000 or a lifetime maximum of $50,000. At private institutions in the Washington Metropolitan area and at HBCUs in any state, the maximum award is $2,500 per year or $12,500 over a lifetime. At 2–year community colleges, the maximum award is the difference between in–state or out–of–state tuition, or $2,500 per year, to a lifetime maximum of $10,000. All those amounts are for full–time enrollment; awards for part–time enrollment are reduced proportionally, with no support for less than half–time enrollment. Funds are sent directly to the eligible school and may be used for tuition and fees only.

Duration: 1 year. Awards are limited to a maximum of 6 years at public colleges and universities in the United States, Puerto Rico, and Guam, at private institutions in the Washington Metropolitan area, and at HBCUs. The maximum time at a 2–year community college is 4 years.

Number awarded: Varies each year; recently, approximately 4,700 of these grants were awarded.

Deadline: June of each year.

204 DIXIE SOFTBALL SCHOLARSHIPS

Dixie Softball, Inc.
Attn: President
1101 Skelton Drive
Birmingham, AL 35224
Phone: (205) 785–2255; Fax: (205) 785–2258;
Email: OBIEDSI@aol.com
Web: softball.dixie.org/scholarships9876.htm

Summary: To provide financial assistance for college to high school senior women who have participated in the Dixie Softball program.

Eligibility: Open to high school senior women who played in the Dixie Softball program for at least 2 seasons. Applicants must submit academic data (GPA, SAT/ACT scores, class rank), a letter explaining why they are seeking this assistance, verification from a Dixie Softball local official of the number of years the applicant participated in the program, and documentation of financial need. Ability as an athlete is not considered in the selection process.

Financial data: The stipend is $1,500.

Duration: 1 year.

Number awarded: 6 each year.

Deadline: February of each year.

205 $ DIXIE YOUTH BASEBALL SCHOLARSHIPS

Dixie Youth Baseball, Inc.
Attn: Scholarship Committee
P.O. Box 877
Marshall, TX 75671–0877
Phone: (903) 927–2255; Fax: (903) 927–1846;
Email: dyb@dixie.org
Web: youth.dixie.org/Main_Navigation/Scholarships/scholarshipslc78.htm

Summary: To provide financial assistance for college to high school seniors who have participated in a Dixie Youth Baseball franchised league.

Eligibility: Open to high school seniors (males and females) who played in a Dixie Youth Baseball franchised league when they were 12 years of age or younger. Applicants must submit academic information (GPA, ACT/SAT scores, class rank), a letter explaining why they are seeking this assistance, verification from a Dixie Youth local official of participation in a franchised league, and documentation of financial need. Ability as an athlete is not considered in the selection process.

Financial data: The stipend is $2,000.

Duration: 1 year.

Number awarded: Varies each year; recently, 70 of these scholarships were awarded.

Deadline: February of each year.

206 $$ DKF VETERANS ASSISTANCE FOUNDATION SCHOLARSHIPS

DKF Veterans Assistance Foundation
P.O. Box 7166
San Carlos, CA 94070
Phone: (650) 595–3896;
Email: admin@dkfveterans.com
Web: www.dkfveterans.com

Summary: To provide financial assistance for college in any state to California residents who are veterans of Operation Enduring Freedom (OEF) in Afghanistan or Operation Iraqi Freedom (OIF) or the dependents of deceased or disabled veterans of those actions.

Eligibility: Open to 1) veterans of the U.S. armed forces (including the Coast Guard) who served in support of OEF or OIF within the central command area of responsibility; and 2) dependents of those veterans who were killed in action or incurred disabilities rated as 75% or more. Applicants must be residents of California enrolled or planning to enroll full time at a college, university, community college, or trade institution in any state. Along with their application, they must submit a cover letter introducing themselves and their educational goals.

Financial data: The stipend is $5,000 per year for students at universities and state colleges or $1,500 per year for students at community colleges and trade institutions.

Duration: 1 year; may be renewed up to 3 additional years, provided the recipient maintains a GPA of 3.0 or higher.

Number awarded: A limited number of these scholarships are awarded each year.

Deadline: Deadline not specified.

207 DO SOMETHING SCHOLARSHIPS

Do Something, Inc.
24–32 Union Square East, Fourth Floor
New York, NY 10003
Phone: (212) 254–2390
Web: www.dosomething.org/scholarships/campaignfaq

Summary: To recognize and reward, with college scholarships, high school, college, and graduate students who participate in Do Something campaigns to improve their community.

Eligibility: Open to U.S. and Canadian citizens under 25 years of age who participate in 1 of Do Something's monthly campaigns. Applicants must be enrolled or planning to enroll at an accredited 2– or 4–year institution of higher education to work on an undergraduate or graduate degree. There is no application form; each campaign has specific rules for participation and students follow those rules to submit reports on their involvement. In general, awards are presented for projects that 1) are creative and demonstrate a commitment to social change; 2) focus on improving community problems by engaging and involving the community in the project; and 3) address a problem within the participant's community and has a measurable impact.

Financial data: Awards range from $500 to $1,000, depending on the campaign. Funds must be used prior to the recipient's 26th birthday.

Duration: Awards are presented annually.

Number awarded: Varies each year. Each campaign's rules define the number of awards available through it.

Deadline: Each campaign sets its own deadline.

208 $ DOLPHIN SCHOLARSHIPS

Dolphin Scholarship Foundation
Attn: Scholarship Administrator
4966 Euclid Road, Suite 109
Virginia Beach, VA 23462
Phone: (757) 671–3200, ext. 111; Fax: (757) 671–3330;
Email: scholars@dolphinscholarship.org
Web: www.dolphinscholarship.org

Summary: To provide financial assistance for college to the children of members or former members of the Submarine Force.

Eligibility: Open to the unmarried children and stepchildren under 24 years of age of 1) members or former members of the Submarine Force who qualified in submarines and served in the submarine force for at least 8 years; 2) Navy members who served in submarine support activities for at least 10 years; and 3) Submarine Force members who died on active duty. Applicants must be working or intending to work toward a bachelor's degree at an accredited 4–year college or university. Selection is based on academic proficiency, commitment and excellence in school and community activities, and financial need.

Financial data: The stipend is $3,400 per year.

Duration: 1 year; may be renewed for 3 additional years.

Number awarded: Varies each year; recently, 27 new and 100 renewal scholarships were awarded.

Deadline: March of each year.

209 DONALD AND ITASKER THORNTON MEMORIAL SCHOLARSHIP

Thornton Sisters Foundation
P.O. Box 21
Atlantic Highlands, NJ 07716–0021
Phone: (732) 872–1353;
Email: tsfoundation2001@yahoo.com
Web: www.thornton–sisters.com/ttsf.htm

Summary: To provide financial assistance for college to women of color in New Jersey.

Eligibility: Open to women of color (defined as African Americans, Latino Americans, Caribbean Americans, and Native Americans) who are graduating from high schools in New Jersey. Applicants must have a grade average of "C+" or higher and be able to document financial need. They must be planning to attend an accredited 4–year college or university. Along with their application, they must submit a 500–word essay describing their family background, personal and financial hardships, honors or academic distinctions, and community involvement and activities.

Financial data: A stipend is awarded (amount not specified). Funds are to be used for tuition and/or books.

Duration: 1 year; nonrenewable.

Number awarded: 1 or more each year.

Deadline: May of each year.

210 $ DOROTHY AND ROBERT DEBOLT SCHOLARSHIP

Adopt A Special Kid
Attn: Scholarship Committee
8201 Edgewater Drive, Suite 103
Oakland, CA 94621–3020
Phone: (510) 553–1748; (888) 680–7349; Fax: (510) 553–1747;
Email: info@aask.org
Web: www.aask.org

Summary: To provide financial assistance to residents of California who have been in foster care and are interested in attending college in any state.

Eligibility: Open to residents of California who are younger than 25 years of age and have been adopted after having been in foster care as a dependent of the juvenile court. Applicants must have been accepted or be enrolled at an accredited 2– or 4–year college, university, or trade/vocational school in any state. Along with their application, they must submit a 2–page essay that includes their background, how they came to be in the foster care system, how they became a part of their adoptive family, how those experiences have led them to where they are now in life, their extracurricular and volunteer community activities, how this scholarship will be beneficial to them, and their short– and long–term goals. Selection is based on academic achievement, promise of success in the institution they have selected, community service, extracurricular activities, and financial need.

Financial data: Stipends range up to $3,000.

Duration: 1 year.

Number awarded: 1 or more each year.

Deadline: June of each year.

211 $ DOROTHY KELLERMAN SCHOLARSHIP

American Legion Auxiliary
Department of New Jersey
c/o Lucille M. Miller, Secretary/Treasurer
1540 Kuser Road, Suite A–8
Hamilton, NJ 08619
Phone: (609) 581–9580; Fax: (609) 581–8429

Summary: To provide financial assistance to New Jersey residents who are the descendants of veterans and planning to attend college in any state.

Eligibility: Open to the children, grandchildren, and great–grandchildren of veterans who served in the U.S. armed forces during specified periods of war time. Applicants must be graduating high school seniors who have been residents of New Jersey for at least 2 years. They must be planning to attend a college or university in any state. Along with their application, they must submit a 1,000–word essay on a topic that changes annually; recently, students were asked to write on the topic, "The Importance of Helping Military Families in

Your Community " Selection is based on academic achievement (40%), character (15%), leadership (15%), Americanism (15%), and financial need (15%).
Financial data: Stipends range from $1,000 to $2,500.
Duration: 1 year; nonrenewable.
Number awarded: 1 each year.
Deadline: April of each year.

212 DPSTF SCHOLARSHIP PROGRAM

Texas Department of Public Safety Officers' Association
Attn: Texas DPS Troopers Foundation
5821 Airport Boulevard
Austin, TX 78752
Phone: (512) 451–0582; (800) 933–7762; Fax: (512) 451–0709;
Email: info@dpstf.org
Web: www.dpstf.org/programs–2/scholarship–grants
Summary: To provide financial assistance to high school seniors and graduates in Texas who plan to attend college in any state.
Eligibility: Open to seniors graduating from high schools in Texas and to residents of the state who graduated from high school within the past 4 years. Applicants must be planning to enter a college or university in any state as a full–time student. They must have a high school GPA of 2.0 or higher. Along with their application, they must submit a narrative description of their achievements, leadership skills, extracurricular activities, career goals, and need for financial assistance.
Financial data: Stipends generally range up to $1,000.
Duration: 1 year; may be renewed, provided the recipient maintains a GPA of 2.75 or higher.
Number awarded: Varies each year; recently, 123 new and renewal scholarships were awarded.
Deadline: June of each year.

213 DR. ARNITA YOUNG BOSWELL SCHOLARSHIP

National Hook–Up of Black Women, Inc.
Attn: Scholarship Committee
1809 East 71st Street, Suite 205
Chicago, IL 60649–2000
Phone: (773) 667–7061; Fax: (773) 667–7064;
Email: info@nhbwinc.com
Web: nhbwinc.com/scholarships.html
Summary: To provide financial assistance to African American high school and college students who are interested in earning an undergraduate degree.
Eligibility: Open to African American high school seniors or currently–enrolled college students. They must be attending or preparing to attend an accredited school and have a GPA of 2.75 or higher. They must demonstrate written communication skills by preparing an essay of 300 to 500 words on a topic that changes annually but relates to current events of national interest. Selection is based on academic record, financial need, community service, concern for the African American family, and a desire to complete a college degree.
Financial data: The stipend is $1,000. Funds are paid directly to the college or university of the recipient's choice.
Duration: 1 year.
Number awarded: 5 each year.
Deadline: February of each year.

214 $$ DRS GUARDIAN SCHOLARSHIP FUND

National Guard Educational Foundation
Attn: Scholarship Fund
One Massachusetts Avenue, N.W.
Washington, DC 20001
Phone: (202) 789–0031; Fax: (202) 682–9358;
Email: ngef@ngaus.org
Web: www.drsfoundation.net/guard
Summary: To provide financial assistance for college to children of members of the National Guard who died in service.
Eligibility: Open to 1) high school juniors and seniors who have been accepted to an accredited community college, technical school, or 4–year college or university and have a GPA of 3.0 or higher; and 2) students who are currently enrolled full time at an accredited community college, technical school, or 4–year college or university and have a GPA of 2.5 or higher. Applicants must be the dependent child of a National Guard member who died in an operational or training mission in support of Operation Enduring Freedom, Operation Iraqi Freedom, or Operation New Dawn. The educational institution they are attending or planning to attend must be located in the 50 states, the District of Columbia, Puerto Rico, the U.S. Virgin Islands, or Guam. Along with their application, they must submit a 1–page essay on their deceased parent, transcripts, and documentation of financial need.
Financial data: The stipend is $6,250 per year.
Duration: 1 year; may be renewed 1 additional year by students at community colleges and technical schools and up to 3 additional years by students at 4–year colleges and universities.
Number awarded: Varies each year.
Deadline: June of each year.

215 DUANE BUCKLEY MEMORIAL SCHOLARSHIP

American Council of the Blind
Attn: Coordinator, Scholarship Program
2200 Wilson Boulevard, Suite 650
Arlington, VA 22201
Phone: (202) 467–5081; (800) 424–8666; Fax: (703) 465–5085;
Email: info@acb.org
Web: www.acb.org/scholarship
Summary: To provide financial assistance for college to blind high school seniors.
Eligibility: Open to graduating high school seniors who are legally blind in both eyes. Applicants must submit verification of legal blindness in both eyes; SAT or ACT scores; information on extracurricular activities (including involvement in the American Council of the Blind); employment record; and a 500–word autobiographical sketch that includes their personal goals, strengths, weaknesses, hobbies, honors, achievements, and reasons for choice of field or courses of study. A cumulative GPA of 3.3 or higher is generally required. Financial need is not considered in the selection process.
Financial data: The stipend is $1,000.
Duration: 1 year.
Number awarded: 1 each year.
Deadline: February of each year.

216 DUNKIN' DONUTS SCHOLARSHIPS

Scholarship America
Attn: Scholarship Management Services
One Scholarship Way
P.O. Box 297
St. Peter, MN 56082
Phone: (507) 931–1682; (800) 537–4180; Fax: (507) 931–9168
Web: www.dunkindonuts.com/content/dunkindonuts/en/scholarship.html
Summary: To provide financial assistance to residents of selected areas in eastern states who are attending or planning to attend college in any state.
Eligibility: Open to seniors graduating from high schools in Connecticut; the Delaware counties of Kent and New Castle; the Massachusetts counties of Bristol, Franklin, Hamden, and Hampshire; the New Jersey counties of Atlantic, Burlington, Camden, Cape May, Cumberland, Gloucester, Mercer, and Salem; the Pennsylvania counties of Berks, Bucks, Chester, Delaware, Lehigh, Montgomery, Northampton, and Philadelphia; and Rhode Island. Applicants must be able to demonstrate academic excellence, leadership, involvement in school and community activities, experience in a work environment, and other features of a "well–rounded" character. Financial need is not considered in the selection process.
Financial data: The stipend is $1,000.
Duration: 1 year.
Number awarded: 75 each year. Since the program was established, it has awarded more than $2 million in scholarships.
Deadline: March of each year for applications from Connecticut, Massachusetts, and Rhode Island; April of each year for applications from Delaware, New Jersey, and Pennsylvania.

217 $ E. WAYNE COOLEY SCHOLARSHIP AWARD

Iowa Girls High School Athletic Union
Attn: Scholarships
5000 Westown Parkway
West Des Moines, IA 50266
Phone: (515) 288–9741; Fax: (515) 284–1969;
Email: jasoneslinger@ighsau.org
Web: www.ighsau.org/aspx/cooley_award.aspx
Summary: To provide financial assistance to female high school seniors in Iowa who have participated in athletics and plan to attend college in the state.

Eligibility: Open to women graduating from high schools in Iowa who have a GPA of 3.75 or higher and an ACT score of 23 or higher. Applicants must have earned a varsity letter in at least 2 different sports and have participated in at least 2 sports each year of high school. They must be planning to attend a college or university in Iowa. Each high school in the state may nominate 1 student. Selection is based on academic achievements, athletic accomplishments, non–sports extracurricular activities, and community involvement.
Financial data: The winner's stipend is $3,750 per year. Finalists receive a $1,000 scholarship.
Duration: 4 years for the winner, provided she maintains at least a 2.5 GPA while enrolled in college. The scholarships for finalists are for 1 year.
Number awarded: 6 each year: 1 winner and 5 finalists.
Deadline: December of each year.

218 $$ EDUCATION ADVANTAGE UNIVERSITY SCHOLARSHIP

Baxter Healthcare Corporation
c/o Scholarship America
Scholarship Management Services
One Scholarship Way
P.O. Box 297
St. Peter, MN 56082
Phone: (877) 544–3018;
Email: baxter@scholarshipamerica.org
Web: www.myeducationadvantage.com/education/scholarship
Summary: To provide financial assistance to people who have hemophilia A and are interested in working on a bachelor's degree.
Eligibility: Open to people who have hemophilia A or hemophilia with inhibitors and are enrolled or planning to enroll full time at a 4–year college or university. Applicants must submit a personal statement that focuses on their unique experiences that make them stand out from other students (e.g., their experiences of living with hemophilia, how it impacts their education or career goals, noteworthy volunteer activities within the hemophilia community). They must have a GPA of 2.0 or higher. Both merit–based and need–based scholarships are available. U.S. citizenship or permanent resident status is required.
Financial data: The stipend ranges up to $15,000 per year for need–based scholarships or $1,000 per year for merit–based scholarships.
Duration: 1 year; may be renewed up to 3 additional years, provided the recipient remains enrolled full time, maintains a GPA of 2.0 or higher, provides evidence of participation in annual comprehensive clinic and routine dental care, performs 20 hours of community service, and submits a 250–word essay on their academic progress, their career goals and developments, and the value of funding assistance.
Number awarded: Varies each year; recently, 30 of these scholarships were awarded. A similar program, Education Advantage Community College or Technical Scholarship, also awards another 10 scholarships to students who have hemophilia A and are interested in working on a community college or technical degree.
Deadline: April of each year.

219 EDUCATION FOUNDATION FOR THE COLORADO NATIONAL GUARD GRANTS

National Guard Association of Colorado
Attn: Education Foundation, Inc.
P.O. Box 440889
Aurora, CO 80044–0889
Phone: (303) 909–6369; Fax: (720) 535–5925;
Email: BernieRogoff@comcast.net
Web: efcong.org/Grants
Summary: To provide financial assistance to members of the Colorado National Guard and their families who are interested in attending college or graduate school in any state.
Eligibility: Open to current and retired members of the Colorado National Guard and their dependent unmarried children and spouses. Applicants must be enrolled or planning to enroll full or part time at a college, university, trade school, business school, or graduate school in any state. Along with their application, they must submit an essay, up to 2 pages in length, on their desire to continue their education, what motivates them, their financial need, their commitment to academic excellence, and their current situation. Selection is based on academic achievement, community involvement, and financial need.
Financial data: Stipends are generally at least $1,000 per year.
Duration: 1 year; may be renewed.
Number awarded: Varies each year; recently, 38 of these grants, with a total value of $50,000, were awarded.
Deadline: July of each year for fall semester; January of each year for spring semester.

220 EDWARD J. BLOUSTEIN DISTINGUISHED SCHOLARS PROGRAM

New Jersey Higher Education Student Assistance Authority
Attn: Grants and Scholarships
4 Quakerbridge Plaza
P.O. Box 540
Trenton, NJ 08625–0540
Phone: (609) 588–2349; (800) 792–8670; Fax: (609) 588–3450;
Email: ClientServices@hesaa.org
Web: www.hesaa.org/Pages/GrantsandScholarshipsDetails.aspx
Summary: To provide financial assistance to outstanding high school seniors in New Jersey who are interested in attending college.
Eligibility: Open to high school students in New Jersey. High school staff in New Jersey are invited to nominate candidates for this award. Nominees must be seniors at New Jersey high schools who rank in the top 10% of their class and have combined critical reading and mathematics SAT scores of 1260 or higher. They must be planning to attend a college or university in New Jersey as a full–time undergraduate. Students may not apply directly for this program; they must be nominated by their high school. U.S. citizenship or eligible noncitizen status is required.
Financial data: Scholars receive $1,000 per year, regardless of financial need.
Duration: Up to 5 semesters at a 2–year institution; up to 8 semesters at a 4–year institution; up to 10 semesters if enrolled in a bona fide 5–year program.
Number awarded: Varies each year.
Deadline: Participating secondary schools must submit nominations by the end of September of each year.

221 $$ EDWARD T. CONROY MEMORIAL SCHOLARSHIP PROGRAM

Maryland Higher Education Commission
Attn: Office of Student Financial Assistance
6 North Liberty Street, Ground Suite
Baltimore, MD 21201
Phone: (410) 767–3300; (800) 974–0203; Fax: (410) 332–0250; TDD: (800) 735–2258;
Email: osfamail@mhec.state.md.us
Web: www.mhec.state.md.us/financialAid/descriptions.asp
Summary: To provide financial assistance for college or graduate school in Maryland to children and spouses of victims of the September 11, 2001 terrorist attacks and specified categories of veterans, public safety employees, and their children or spouses.
Eligibility: Open to entering and continuing undergraduate and graduate students in the following categories: 1) children and surviving spouses of victims of the September 11, 2001 terrorist attacks who died in the World Trade Center in New York City, in the Pentagon in Virginia, or on United Airlines Flight 93 in Pennsylvania; 2) veterans who have, as a direct result of military service, a disability of 25% or greater and have exhausted or are no longer eligible for federal veterans' educational benefits; 3) children of armed forces members whose death or 100% disability was directly caused by military service; 4) POW/MIA veterans of the Vietnam Conflict and their children; 5) state or local public safety officers or volunteers who became 100% disabled in the line of duty; and 6) children and unremarried surviving spouses of state or local public safety employees or volunteers who died or became 100% disabled in the line of duty. The parent, spouse, veteran, POW, or public safety officer or volunteer must have been a resident of Maryland at the time of death or when declared disabled. Financial need is not considered.
Financial data: The amount of the award is equal to tuition and fees at a Maryland postsecondary institution, to a maximum of $19,000 for children and spouses of the September 11 terrorist attacks or $9,000 for all other recipients.
Duration: Up to 5 years of full–time study or 8 years of part–time study.
Number awarded: Varies each year.
Deadline: July of each year.

222 ELAINE CHAPIN FUND SCHOLARSHIPS

Elaine Chapin Fund
4367 Humber Circle
St. Louis, MO 63129
Email: ElaineMemorial@sbcglobal.net
Web: www.elainememorial.com
Summary: To provide financial assistance for college to people who have multiple sclerosis (MS) and their families.
Eligibility: Open to people whose lives have been affected by MS, either directly or as a family member. Applicants must be enrolled or planning to enroll as full–time undergraduates at an accredited 2– or 4–year college, university, or

vocational/technical school in the United States. They must be U.S. citizens. Along with their application, they must submit a 500–word essay on the impact of MS on their life. Selection is based on that essay, academic standing, and financial need.

Financial data: The stipend is $1,000.

Duration: 1 year.

Number awarded: At least 8 each year.

Deadline: April of each year.

223 $$ ELECTRONIC SECURITY ASSOCIATION YOUTH SCHOLARSHIP PROGRAM

Electronic Security Association
Attn: Youth Scholarship Program
6333 North State Highway 161, Suite 350
Irving, TX 75038
Phone: (972) 807–6800; (888) 447–1689, ext. 209; Fax: (972) 807–6883;
Email: Lauri.Knox@esaweb.org
Web: www.esaweb.org/?page=youthscholarship

Summary: To provide financial assistance for college to high school seniors whose parents are active–duty law enforcement or fire service personnel.

Eligibility: Open to seniors graduating from high school who are the children of full–time active–duty (not on disability) law enforcement and fire service personnel. Applicants must submit an essay of 500 to 1,000 words on what it means to them to have their parent or guardian involved in securing our community. Selection is based on that essay (25 points), grade average (25 points), SAT or ACT scores (30 points), and extracurricular participation (20 points). State chapters of the sponsor in 16 states hold their own competitions; each awards its own prizes, but each state winner is automatically nominated for this program. Students in other states may apply directly to the national organization; those applications will be judged, and 1 of those will be entered with the 14 state winners to compete for the national awards.

Financial data: Stipends are $7,500 or $2,500. The student residing in a state without a chapter or in a non–participating state who is selected to compete with the 16 state winners receives an award of $1,000.

Duration: 1 year.

Number awarded: 2 each year: 1 at $7,500 and 1 at $2,500.

Deadline: March of each year.

224 $ ELIZABETH AHLEMEYER QUICK/GAMMA PHI BETA SCHOLARSHIP

National Panhellenic Conference
Attn: NPC Foundation
3901 West 86th Street, Suite 398
Indianapolis, IN 46268
Phone: (317) 876–7802; Fax: (317) 876–7904;
Email: npcfoundation@npcwomen.org
Web: www.npcwomen.org/foundation/scholarships.aspx

Summary: To provide financial assistance to undergraduate women who are members of Greek–letter societies.

Eligibility: Open to women enrolled full time as juniors or seniors at colleges and universities in the United States. Applicants must have a GPA of 3.0 or higher and be able to demonstrate financial need. They must be nominated by their college Panhellenic and have demonstrated outstanding service to that organization. Selection is based on campus, chapter, and community service; financial need; academic standing; and nomination by the applicant's college Panhellenic.

Financial data: The stipend is $2,000.

Duration: 1 year.

Number awarded: 1 each year.

Deadline: January of each year.

225 $ ELIZABETH NASH FOUNDATION SCHOLARSHIP PROGRAM

Elizabeth Nash Foundation
P.O. Box 1260
Los Gatos, CA 95031–1260
Email: scholarships@elizabethnashfoundation.org
Web: www.elizabethnashfoundation.org/scholarshipprogram.html

Summary: To provide financial assistance for college or graduate school to individuals with cystic fibrosis (CF).

Eligibility: Open to undergraduate and graduate students who have CF. Applicants must be able to demonstrate clear academic goals and a commitment to participate in activities outside the classroom. U.S. citizenship is required. Selection is based on academic record, character, demonstrated leadership, service to CF–related causes and the broader community, and financial need.

Financial data: Stipends range from $1,000 to $2,500. Funds are paid directly to the academic institution to be applied to tuition and fees.

Duration: 1 year; recipients may reapply.

Number awarded: Varies each year; recently, 17 of these scholarships were awarded. Since the program was established, it has awarded 78 scholarships.

Deadline: April of each year.

226 $$ ELKS "MOST VALUABLE STUDENT" SCHOLARSHIP AWARD

Elks National Foundation
Attn: Scholarship Department
2750 North Lakeview Avenue
Chicago, IL 60614–2256
Phone: (773) 755–4732; Fax: (773) 755–4729;
Email: scholarship@elks.org
Web: www.elks.org/enf/scholars/mvs.cfm

Summary: To provide financial assistance to outstanding high school seniors who can demonstrate financial need and are interested in attending college.

Eligibility: Open to graduating high school students (or the equivalent) who are U.S. citizens residing within the jurisdiction of the B.P.O. Elks of the U.S.A. Applicants must be planning to work on a 4–year degree on a full–time basis at a college or university within the United States. Along with their application, they must submit 1) a 500–word essay on their choice of 3 assigned topics; and 2) exhibits, up to 20 pages, on their achievements in scholarship, leadership, athletics, performing arts, community service, or other activities. Selection is based on that essay and exhibits, transcripts, SAT and/or ACT scores, a report from their school counselor, letters of recommendation, and financial need. Male and female students compete separately.

Financial data: First place is $15,000 per year; second place is $10,000 per year; third place is $5,000 per year; fourth place is $4,000 per year; fifth place is $3,000 per year, sixth place is $2,500 per year, seventh place is $2,000 per year, and runners–up receive $1,000 per year. Nearly $2.3 million is distributed through this program each year.

Duration: 4 years.

Number awarded: 500 each year: 2 first awards (1 male and 1 female), 2 second awards (1 male and 1 female), 2 third awards (1 male and 1 female), 2 fourth awards (1 male and 1 female), 2 fifth awards (1 male and 1 female), 4 sixth awards (2 males and 2 females), 4 seventh awards (2 males and 2 females), and 482 runners–up (241 males and 241 females).

Deadline: January of each year.

227 ELSIE G. RIDDICK SCHOLARSHIP

North Carolina Federation of Business and Professional Women's Club, Inc.
Attn: BPW/NC Foundation
P.O. Box 276
Carrboro, NC 27510
Web: www.bpw–nc.org/Default.aspx?pageId=837230

Summary: To provide financial assistance to women attending North Carolina colleges, community colleges, or graduate schools.

Eligibility: Open to women who are currently enrolled in a community college, 4–year college, or graduate school in North Carolina. Applicants must be endorsed by a local BPW unit. Along with their application, they must submit a 1–page statement that summarizes their career goals, previous honors, or community activities and justifies their need for this scholarship. U.S. citizenship is required.

Financial data: The stipend is $1,000. Funds are paid directly to the recipient's school.

Duration: 1 year; recipients may reapply.

Number awarded: 1 each year.

Deadline: April of each year.

228 ELSIE MAE WHITE MEMORIAL SCHOLARSHIP FUND

Columbus Foundation
Attn: Scholarship Manager
1234 East Broad Street
Columbus, OH 43205–1453
Phone: (614) 251–4000; Fax: (614) 251–4009;
Email: dhigginb@columbusfoundation.org

Web: columbusfoundation.org/grants/columbus–foundation
Summary: To provide financial assistance for college or graduate school to African American high school seniors and college students from any state.
Eligibility: Open to African American high school seniors and college students. High school seniors must rank in the top third of their class; college students must have a GPA of 2.8 or higher. Applicants must be attending or planning to attend an accredited college or university in the United States as a full– or part–time undergraduate or graduate student. Preference is given to students at land grant colleges and universities. Along with their application, they must submit 300–word essays on 1) their educational and career plans and goals, why they have chosen their particular field, and why they think they will be a success; 2) why they feel they need this scholarship, especially as related to financial need; and 3) any other information that will assist the selection committee in making its decision.
Financial data: The stipend is $1,000.
Duration: 1 year.
Number awarded: Varies each year.
Deadline: May of each year.

229 $$ EMERGE SCHOLARSHIPS

Emerge Scholarships, Inc.
3535 Peachtree Road, Suite 520–121
Atlanta, GA 30326
Phone: (770) 905–5175;
Email: info@emergescholarships.org
Web: www.emergescholarships.org
Summary: To provide financial assistance to women interested in returning to college or graduate school after a delay or interruption.
Eligibility: Open to women who are at least 25 years of age and who have interrupted or delayed their education because they are changing careers, seeking advancement in their career or work life, looking for personal growth, or returning to school after caring for children. Applicants must have been accepted as an undergraduate or graduate student at an educational institution. They must be current residents of the United States or Puerto Rico (including foreign nationals who plan to study in the United States) or U.S. citizens living abroad applying to study in the United States. Along with their application, they must submit a 2–page essay on how beginning or continuing their education will positively impact their life. Selection is based on that essay, leadership and participation in community activities, honors and awards received, career and life goals, financial need, and other funding received. Preference is given to women from Georgia.
Financial data: Stipends range from $2,000 to $5,000.
Duration: 1 year.
Number awarded: Varies each year; recently, 10 of these scholarships were awarded.
Deadline: January of each year.

230 $ EMPIRE STATE DIVERSITY HONORS SCHOLARSHIP PROGRAM

State University of New York
Attn: Office of Diversity, Equity and Inclusion
State University Plaza
353 Broadway
Albany, NY 12246
Phone: (518) 320–1189
Web: www.suny.edu/provost/odee/programs.cfm
Summary: To provide financial assistance to residents of New York who are attending campuses of the State University of New York (SUNY) and contribute to the diversity of the student body.
Eligibility: Open to U.S. citizens and permanent residents who are New York residents and enrolled as undergraduate students at any of the participating SUNY colleges. Applicants must be able to demonstrate 1) how they will contribute to the diversity of the student body, primarily by having overcome a disadvantage or other impediment to success in higher education; and 2) high academic achievement. Economic disadvantage, although not a requirement, may be the basis for eligibility. Membership in a racial or ethnic group that is underrepresented at the applicant's school or program may serve as a plus factor in making awards, but may not form the sole basis of selection.
Financial data: The maximum stipend provided by the SUNY system is half the student's cost of attendance or $3,000, whichever is less. The individual campus must match the SUNY award in an equal amount.
Duration: 1 year; renewable.
Number awarded: Varies each year; recently, nearly 1,000 students at 46 SUNY institutions received support from this program.
Deadline: Deadline not specified.

231 EPSILON SIGMA ALPHA (ESA) FOUNDATION GENERAL SCHOLARSHIPS

Epsilon Sigma Alpha International
Attn: ESA Foundation
363 West Drake Road
Fort Collins, CO 80526
Phone: (970) 223–2824; Fax: (970) 223–4456;
Email: esainfo@epsilonsigmaalpha.org
Web: www.epsilonsigmaalpha.org/scholarships–and–grants
Summary: To provide financial assistance to students from any state interested in majoring in any field in college.
Eligibility: Open to students who are 1) graduating high school seniors who have minimum scores of 22 on the ACT or 1030 on the combined critical reading and mathematics SAT; 2) enrolled in college with a GPA of 2.0 or higher; 3) enrolled at a technical school or returning to school after an absence for retraining of job skills or obtaining a degree; or 4) engaged in online study through an accredited college, university, or vocational school. Applicants may be attending or planning to attend an accredited school anywhere in the United States and major in any field. Awards are presented to students with a GPA of 2.0 to 2.49, of 2.5 to 2.99, of 3.0 to 3.49, and of 3.5 or higher Selection is based on character (20%), leadership (20%), service (20%), financial need (20%), and scholastic ability (20%).
Financial data: The stipend is $1,000.
Duration: 1 year; may be renewed.
Number awarded: Varies each year, depending on the availability of funds. Recently, 20 of these scholarships were awarded: 1 to a student with a GPA of 2.0 to 2.49, 1 to a student with a GPA of 2.5 to 2.99, 10 to students with GPAs of 3.0 to 3.49, and 8 to students with GPAs of 3.5 or higher.
Deadline: January of each year.

232 $ ERIC C. MARDER SCHOLARSHIP PROGRAM

Immune Deficiency Foundation
Attn: Scholarship Programs
40 West Chesapeake Avenue, Suite 308
Towson, MD 21204–4803
Phone: (410) 321–6647; (800) 296–4433; Fax: (410) 321–9165;
Email: idf@primaryimmune.org
Web: primaryimmune.org/patients_and_families/idf–scholarship–programs
Summary: To provide financial assistance to undergraduates with a primary immune deficiency disease.
Eligibility: Open to undergraduates entering or attending college or technical training school who have a primary immune deficiency disease. Applicants must submit an autobiographical essay, 2 letters of recommendation, a family financial statement, and a letter of verification from their immunologist. Financial need is the main factor considered in selecting the recipients and the size of the award.
Financial data: Stipends range from $750 to $2,000, depending on the recipient's financial need.
Duration: 1 year; may be renewed.
Number awarded: Varies each year.
Deadline: March of each year.

233 ERIC DOSTIE MEMORIAL COLLEGE SCHOLARSHIP

NuFACTOR Specialty Pharmacy
Attn: Scholarship Administrator
41093 Country Center Drive, Suite B
Temecula, CA 92591
Phone: (951) 296–2516; (800) 323–6832, ext. 1300; Fax: (877) 432–6258;
Email: info@kelleycom.com
Web: www.nufactor.com/EricDostieMemorial.aspx?Section=Patients
Summary: To provide financial assistance for college to students with hemophilia or members of their families.
Eligibility: Open to 1) students with hemophilia or a related bleeding disorder; or 2) members of their families. Applicants must be U.S. citizens and enrolled or planning to enroll full time at an accredited 2– or 4–year college or university. They must have a GPA of 2.5 or higher. Along with their application, they must submit an essay on how their education will be used to serve humankind and to encourage self–improvement and enrichment. Selection is based on academic achievement, community service, and financial need.
Financial data: The stipend is $1,000.
Duration: 1 year.
Number awarded: 10 each year.
Deadline: February of each year.

234 ESSAY COMPETITION FOR CHILDREN OF PUBLIC EMPLOYEES

Civil Service Employees Insurance Group
Attn: Scholarship Contest
2121 North California Boulevard, Suite 555
Walnut Creek, CA 94596–3501
Phone: (925) 817–6394; (800) 282–6848;
Email: SFerrucci@cseinsurance.com
Web: www.cse–insurance.com/scholarship.htm

Summary: To recognize and reward, with college scholarships, the best essays written on teenage automobile safety by the children of full–time public employees (including military personnel) in selected states.

Eligibility: Open to high school seniors in 3 geographic regions: southern California, northern California, and Arizona/Nevada/Utah. Applicants must have been accepted as a full–time student at an accredited 4–year college, university, or trade school in the United States. They must have a cumulative GPA of 3.0 or higher. Their parent or legal guardian must be currently employed full time (or if retired or deceased, must have been employed full time) by a government entity, including, but not limited to, peace officers, firefighters, educators, postal employees, military personnel, or federal, state, and local government workers. Qualified students are invited to write an essay (up to 500 words) that discusses the ways the teenage automobile accident rate can be reduced. Essays are evaluated on the basis of practicality, creativity, and written skill. Also required in the application process are an official transcript and letters of recommendation.

Financial data: Prizes in each region are $1,500 scholarships for first place, $1,000 scholarships for second place, and $500 scholarships for third place, and $250 scholarships for fourth place.

Duration: The prizes are awarded annually.

Number awarded: 12 each year: 4 in each region.

Deadline: April of each year.

235 ETHEL AND EMERY FAST SCHOLARSHIP

Ethel and Emery Fast Scholarship Foundation, Inc.
12620 Rolling Road
Potomac, MD 20854
Phone: (301) 762–1102; Fax: (301) 279–0201;
Email: qccarol@erols.com

Summary: To provide financial assistance to qualified Native Americans enrolled as undergraduates or graduate students.

Eligibility: Open to applicants who 1) are Native Americans enrolled in a federally–recognized tribe; 2) have successfully completed 1 year of their undergraduate or graduate school program; 3) are enrolled in school full time; and 4) are able to demonstrate financial need. Along with their application, they must submit documentation of Native American eligibility, an original transcript, a letter confirming enrollment, a federal income tax return, a statement of financial need, and a personal statement (up to 2 pages) describing their current situation, their future aspirations in terms of their academic pursuits, and how this scholarship will assist them in attaining their goals.

Financial data: A stipend is awarded (amount not specified). Funds are paid directly to the recipient's college or university and can only be used to pay for tuition, room, board, and fees.

Duration: 1 year.

Number awarded: Varies each year.

Deadline: August of each year for the fall semester; December of each year for the spring semester.

236 EVANS MEMORIAL FUND SCHOLARSHIPS

Greater Kanawha Valley Foundation
Attn: Scholarship Program Officer
1600 Huntington Square
900 Lee Street East, 16th Floor
Charleston, WV 25301
Phone: (304) 346–3620; (800) 467–5909; Fax: (304) 346–3640;
Email: shoover@tgkvf.org
Web: www.tgkvf.org/page.aspx?pid=409

Summary: To provide financial assistance to residents of West Virginia who are interested in attending college in the state.

Eligibility: Open to residents of West Virginia who are attending or planning to attend a college or university in the state. Applicants must have an ACT score of 20 or higher; be able to demonstrate good moral character, academic excellence, and financial need; and have a GPA of 2.5 or higher.

Financial data: Stipends average $1,000 per year.

Duration: 1 year; may be renewed.

Number awarded: Varies each year; recently, 24 of these scholarships were awarded.

Deadline: January of each year.

237 $ EVE KRAFT EDUCATION AND COLLEGE SCHOLARSHIPS

United States Tennis Association
Attn: USTA Serves
70 West Red Oak Lane
White Plains, NY 10604
Phone: (914) 696–7223;
Email: foundation@usta.com
Web: www.usta.com/About–USTA/USTA–Serves

Summary: To provide financial assistance for college to high school seniors who have participated in an organized community tennis program.

Eligibility: Open to high school seniors who have excelled academically, demonstrated achievements in leadership, and participated extensively in an organized community tennis program. Applicants must be planning to enroll as a full–time undergraduate student at a 4–year college or university. They must be able to demonstrate financial need. Along with their application, they must submit an essay of 1 to 2 pages about how their participation in a tennis and education program has influenced their life, including examples of special mentors, volunteer service, and future goals. Males and females are considered separately.

Financial data: The stipend is $2,500. Funds are paid directly to the recipient's college or university.

Duration: 1 year; nonrenewable.

Number awarded: 2 each year: 1 male and 1 female.

Deadline: February of each year.

238 $$ EWI SCHOLARSHIP PROGRAM

Executive Women International
Attn: Scholarship Coordinator
7414 South State Street
Midvale, UT 84047
Phone: (801) 355–2800; (877) 4EWI–NOW; Fax: (801) 355–2852;
Email: ewi@ewiconnect.com
Web: ewiconnect.com

Summary: To provide financial assistance for college to high school juniors with outstanding business and general leadership potential.

Eligibility: Open to high school juniors attending public, private, and parochial schools located in Executive Women International (EWI) chapter cities. Applicants must be planning to attend college in the United States or Canada to prepare for a career in a business or professional field of study. They must have a GPA of 3.0 or higher and be able to demonstrate financial need. Along with their application, they must submit a 750–word essay on how their course of study will contribute to their future career plans and why they have chosen this path, a time they failed and what they learned from the experience, and the person who has impacted their life the most and how it has changed them. Selection is based on academic performance and financial need.

Financial data: Stipends are $5,000 for the first–place winner, $3,000 for the second–place winner, $2,000 for the third–place winner, and $1,000 for finalists. These funds are paid to the winners' colleges. Individual chapters also award scholarships. A total of $200,000 is distributed through this program each year.

Duration: The scholarship funds are disbursed over a period of no more than 5 years.

Number awarded: 8 national winners are selected each year: 1 first place, 1 second place, 1 third place, and 5 other finalists.

Deadline: Applications must be received by local chapters by the end of March so they can select their winners by mid–April.

239 $$ EXEMPTION FOR DEPENDENTS OF TEXAS VETERANS

Texas Higher Education Coordinating Board
Attn: Grants and Special Programs
1200 East Anderson Lane
P.O. Box 12788
Austin, TX 78711–2788
Phone: (512) 427–6340; (800) 242–3062; Fax: (512) 427–6420;
Email: grantinfo@thecb.state.tx.us
Web: www.collegeforalltexans.com/apps/financialaid/tofa2.cfm?ID=579

Summary: To exempt children and spouses of disabled or deceased U.S. veterans from payment of tuition at public universities in Texas.

Eligibility: Open to residents of Texas whose parent or spouse was a resident of the state at the time of entry into the U.S. armed forces, the Texas National Guard, or the Texas Air National Guard. The veteran parent or spouse must have died as a result of service–related injuries or illness, be missing in action, or have become totally disabled as a result of service–related injury or illness. Applicants must have no remaining federal education benefits. They must be attending or planning to attend a public college or university in the state. Children of veterans must be 25 years of age or younger.
Financial data: Eligible students are exempt from payment of tuition, dues, fees, and charges at state–supported colleges and universities in Texas.
Duration: 1 year; may be renewed.
Number awarded: Varies each year; recently, 9 of these awards were granted.
Deadline: Deadline not specified.

240 $$ EXEMPTION FOR ORPHANS OF TEXAS MEMBERS OF THE U.S. ARMED FORCES OR NATIONAL GUARD

Texas Higher Education Coordinating Board
Attn: Grants and Special Programs
1200 East Anderson Lane
P.O. Box 12788
Austin, TX 78711–2788
Phone: (512) 427–6340; (800) 242–3062; Fax: (512) 427–6420;
Email: grantinfo@thecb.state.tx.us
Web: www.collegeforalltexans.com/apps/financialaid/tofa2.cfm?ID=507
Summary: To exempt residents of Texas whose parent died in service to the U.S. military or National Guard from payment of tuition at public universities in the state.
Eligibility: Open to residents of Texas who are the dependent children of a parent who died as a result of injury or illness directly related to service in the U.S. military or the National Guard. Applicants must have used up all federal education benefits for which they are eligible. They must be attending or planning to attend a public college or university in the state.
Financial data: Eligible students are exempt from payment of tuition, dues, fees, and charges at state–supported colleges and universities in Texas.
Duration: 1 year; may be renewed.
Number awarded: Varies each year.
Deadline: Deadline not specified.

241 $$ EXEMPTION FROM TUITION FEES FOR DEPENDENTS OF KENTUCKY VETERANS

Kentucky Department of Veterans Affairs
Attn: Field Operations Branch
321 West Main Street, Suite 390
Louisville, KY 40202
Phone: (502) 595–4447; (800) 928–4012 (within KY); Fax: (502) 595–4448;
Email: Pamela.Cypert@ky.gov
Web: www.veterans.ky.gov/benefits/tuitionwaiver.htm
Summary: To provide financial assistance for undergraduate or graduate studies to the children or unremarried widow(er)s of deceased Kentucky veterans.
Eligibility: Open to the children, stepchildren, adopted children, and unremarried widow(er)s of veterans who were residents of Kentucky when they entered military service or joined the Kentucky National Guard. The qualifying veteran must have been killed in action during a wartime period or died as a result of a service–connected disability incurred during a wartime period. Applicants must be attending or planning to attend a state–supported college or university in Kentucky to work on an undergraduate or graduate degree.
Financial data: Eligible dependents and survivors are exempt from tuition and matriculation fees at any state–supported institution of higher education in Kentucky.
Duration: There are no age or time limits on the waiver.
Number awarded: Varies each year.
Deadline: Deadline not specified.

242 $$ EXERCISE FOR LIFE ATHLETIC SCHOLARSHIPS

Boomer Esiason Foundation
c/o Jerry Cahill
483 Tenth Avenue, Suite 300
New York, NY 10018
Phone: (646) 292–7930; Fax: (646) 292–7945;
Email: jcahill@esiason.org
Web: esiason.org/thriving–with–cf/scholarships.php
Summary: To provide financial assistance for college to high school seniors who have been involved in athletics and who have cystic fibrosis (CF).
Eligibility: Open to CF patients who are college–bound high school seniors. Applicants must have been involved in athletics. They should be jogging on a regular basis and training for a 1.5 mile run. Along with their application, they must submit a letter from their doctor confirming the diagnosis of CF and a list of daily medications, information on financial need, a detailed breakdown of tuition costs from their academic institution, a completed running log, transcripts, and a 2–page essay on 1) their postgraduation goals; and 2) the importance of compliance with CF therapies and what they practice on a daily basis to stay healthy. Selection is based on academic ability, athletic ability, character, leadership potential, service to the community, financial need, and daily compliance to CF therapy. Male and female students compete separately.
Financial data: The stipend is $10,000. Funds are paid directly to the academic institution to assist in covering the cost of tuition and fees.
Duration: 1 year; nonrenewable.
Number awarded: 2 each year: 1 to a male and 1 to a female.
Deadline: June of each year.

243 $$ FAMILIES OF FREEDOM SCHOLARSHIP FUND

Scholarship America
Attn: Scholarship Management Services
One Scholarship Way
P.O. Box 297
St. Peter, MN 56082
Phone: (507) 931–1682; (877) 862–0136; Fax: (507) 931–9168;
Email: info@familiesoffreedom.org
Web: www.familiesoffreedom.org
Summary: To provide college scholarships to financially–needy individuals and the families of individuals who were victims of the terrorist attacks on September 11, 2001.
Eligibility: Open to the individuals who were disabled as a result of the terrorist attacks on September 11, 2001 and to the relatives of those individuals who were killed or permanently disabled during the attacks. Primarily, the fund will benefit dependents (including spouses and children) of the following groups: airplane crew and passengers; World Trade Center workers and visitors; Pentagon workers and visitors; and rescue workers, including firefighters, emergency medical personnel, and law enforcement personnel. Applicants must be enrolled or planning to enroll in an accredited 2– or 4–year college, university, or vocational/technical school in the United States. They must be able to demonstrate financial need.
Financial data: Stipends range from $1,000 to $28,000 per year, depending upon the need of the recipient. Recently, awards averaged $17,100 per academic year. Funds are distributed annually, in 2 equal installments. Checks are made payable jointly to the student and the student's school.
Duration: 1 year; may be renewed.
Number awarded: This is an entitlement program; all eligible students will receive funding. Recently 1,876 students had received more than $74 million in scholarship funds, including 641 students who received more than $11 million in the most recent single year.
Deadline: Applications may be submitted at any time.

244 $$ FAMILY EPILEPSY SCHOLARSHIP PROGRAM

UCB, Inc.
Family Scholarship Program
c/o Hudson Medical Communications
200 White Plains Road, Second Floor
Tarrytown, NY 10591
Phone: (866) 825–1920;
Email: UCBScholarship@hudsongloballlc.com
Web: www.ucbepilepsyscholarship.com/ProgramInformation.aspx
Summary: To provide financial assistance for college or graduate school to epilepsy patients and their family members and caregivers.
Eligibility: Open to epilepsy patients and their family members and caregivers. Applicants must be working on or planning to work on an undergraduate or graduate degree at an institution of higher education in the United States. They must be able to demonstrate academic achievement, a record of participation in activities outside of school, and service as a role model. Along with their application, they must submit a 1–page essay explaining why they should be selected for the scholarship, how epilepsy has impacted their life either as a patient or as a family member or caregiver, and how they will benefit from the scholarship. U.S. citizenship or permanent resident status is required.
Financial data: The stipend is $5,000.

Duration: 1 year; nonrenewable.
Number awarded: 30 each year.
Deadline: April of each year.

245 $$ FAPSC SCHOLARSHIP PROGRAM

Florida Association of Postsecondary Schools and Colleges
150 South Monroe Street, Suite 303
Tallahassee, FL 32301
Phone: (850) 577–3139; Fax: (850) 577–3133;
Email: scholarship@fapsc.org
Web: flcareers.org/scholarship.php

Summary: To provide financial assistance to Florida residents interested in attending a career or vocational school in the state.
Eligibility: Open to seniors graduating from high schools in Florida and recipients of a GED credential during the current year. Applicants must be interested in attending a participating Florida career or vocational school. They must have a GPA of 2.0 or higher. Along with their application, they must submit a 300–word essay that explains why they have chosen this particular career, how this program of study will help them obtain that career, and why they want to attend this particular institution.
Financial data: Scholarships provide either 1) full payment of tuition or 2) stipends of $5,000 or $1,000 as partial payment of tuition.
Duration: 1 academic term.
Number awarded: More than 600 each year.
Deadline: April of each year.

246 $$ FEDERAL PELL GRANTS

Department of Education
Attn: Federal Student Aid Information Center
P.O. Box 84
Washington, DC 20044–0084
Phone: (319) 337–5665; (800) 4–FED–AID; TDD: (800) 730–8913
Web: studentaid.ed.gov/types/grants–scholarships

Summary: To provide financial assistance for undergraduate education to students with financial need.
Eligibility: Open to students who have not yet earned a bachelor's or professional degree. They must meet specified financial need qualifications and be U.S. citizens or eligible noncitizens working toward a degree in an eligible program. In addition, they must have a valid Social Security number and have completed registration with the Selective Service if required.
Financial data: The amount of the grant is based on the cost of attendance at the recipient's college or university, minus the Expected Family Contribution (EFC), up to a specified maximum, currently set at $4,995. Recently, grants ranged from $575 to $5,550 per year.
Duration: Up to 5 years of undergraduate study.
Number awarded: Varies each year; under this program, the federal government guarantees that each participating school will receive enough money to pay the Pell grants of its eligible students. Recently, 9.1 million grants, worth more than $34.7 billion, were awarded.
Deadline: Students may submit applications between January of the current year through June of the following year.

247 $ FEDERAL SUPPLEMENTAL EDUCATIONAL OPPORTUNITY GRANTS

Department of Education
Attn: Federal Student Aid Information Center
P.O. Box 84
Washington, DC 20044–0084
Phone: (319) 337–5665; (800) 4–FED–AID; TDD: (800) 730–8913
Web: studentaid.ed.gov/types/grants–scholarships

Summary: To provide financial assistance for undergraduate education to students with exceptional financial need.
Eligibility: Open to students who have not earned a bachelor's or professional degree. They must meet specified financial need qualifications and be U.S. citizens or eligible noncitizens working toward a degree in an eligible program. In addition, they must have a valid Social Security number and have completed registration with the Selective Service if required. Applicants for federal Pell Grants who demonstrate the greatest financial need qualify for these grants.
Financial data: The amount of the award is based on the cost of attendance at the recipient's college or university, minus the Expected Family Contribution (EFC). Grants range between $100 and $4,000 per year and recently averaged $736.
Duration: Up to 5 years of undergraduate study.
Number awarded: Varies each year, depending on the availability of funds; under this program, the federal government does not guarantee that each participating school will receive enough money to pay the FSEOG grants of all of its eligible students. Recently, more than 1,300,000 grants, worth nearly $1 billion, were awarded by this program.
Deadline: Each participating school sets its own deadline.

248 FIRST MARINE DIVISION ASSOCIATION SCHOLARSHIPS

First Marine Division Association
403 North Freeman Street
Oceanside, CA 92054
Phone: (760) 967–8561; (877) 967–8561; Fax: (760) 967–8567;
Email: oldbreed@sbcglobal.net
Web: www.1stmarinedivisionassociation.org/scholarships.php

Summary: To provide financial assistance for college to dependents of deceased or disabled veterans of the First Marine Division.
Eligibility: Open to dependents of veterans who served in the First Marine Division or in a unit attached to that Division, are honorably discharged, and now are either totally and permanently disabled or deceased from any cause. Applicants must be attending or planning to attend an accredited college, university, or trade school as a full–time undergraduate student. Graduate students and students still in high school or prep school are not eligible.
Financial data: The stipend is $1,750 per year.
Duration: 1 year; may be renewed up to 3 additional years.
Number awarded: Varies each year; recently, 28 of these scholarships were awarded.
Deadline: Deadline not specified.

249 FIRST SERGEANT DOUGLAS AND CHARLOTTE DEHORSE SCHOLARSHIP

Catching the Dream
8200 Mountain Road, N.E., Suite 203
Albuquerque, NM 87110–7835
Phone: (505) 262–2351; Fax: (505) 262–0534;
Email: NScholarsh@aol.com
Web: www.catchingthedream.org/First_Sergeant_Douglas_Scholarship.htm

Summary: To provide financial assistance to American Indians who have ties to the military and are working on an undergraduate or graduate degree.
Eligibility: Open to American Indians who 1) have completed 1 year of an Army, Navy, or Air Force Junior Reserve Officer Training (JROTC) program; 2) are enrolled in an Army, Navy, or Air Force Reserve Officer Training (ROTC) program; or 3) are a veteran of the U.S. Army, Navy, Air Force, Marines, Merchant Marine, or Coast Guard. Applicants must be enrolled in an undergraduate or graduate program of study. Along with their application, they must submit a personal essay, high school transcripts, and letters of recommendation.
Financial data: A stipend is awarded (amount not specified).
Duration: 1 year.
Number awarded: 1 or more each year.
Deadline: April of each year for fall semester or quarter; September of each year for spring semester or winter quarter.

250 $ FIRST STATE MANUFACTURED HOUSING ASSOCIATION SCHOLARSHIP

Delaware Department of Education
Attn: Higher Education Office
401 Federal Street
Dover, DE 19901–3639
Phone: (302) 735–4120; (800) 292–7935; Fax: (302) 739–4654;
Email: dheo@doe.k12.de.us
Web: www.doe.k12.de.us/infosuites/students_family/dheo/default.shtml

Summary: To provide financial assistance to Delaware residents who have lived in a manufactured home and plan to attend college in any state.
Eligibility: Open to Delaware residents who have lived in a manufactured home for at least 1 year. Applicants may be planning to enroll full or part time in an accredited degree, training, licensing, or certification program at a school in any state. Selection is based on academic record, an essay, recommendations, and financial need.
Financial data: The maximum stipend is $2,000 per year.
Duration: 1 year; recipients may reapply.

Number awarded: 2 each year (usually 1 for a traditional student and 1 for a nontraditional student).
Deadline: April of each year.

251 $ FISHER CATS FOUNDATION SCHOLAR–ATHLETE SCHOLARSHIPS

New Hampshire Charitable Foundation
37 Pleasant Street
Concord, NH 03301–4005
Phone: (603) 225–6641; (800) 464–6641; Fax: (603) 225–1700;
Email: info@nhcf.org
Web: www.nhcf.org/page.aspx?pid=958
Summary: To provide financial assistance to high school seniors in New Hampshire and Massachusetts who have participated in athletics and plan to attend college in any state.
Eligibility: Open to seniors graduating from high schools in New Hampshire and Massachusetts and planning to enroll at a 4–year college or university in any state or a local community college or technical school. Applicants must have participated in athletics while in high school. Selection is based on academic performance, athletic achievement, and citizenship.
Financial data: The stipend is $2,500.
Duration: 1 year.
Number awarded: 12 each year: 10 to students from New Hampshire and 2 to students from Massachusetts.
Deadline: April of each year.

252 FLEETWOOD MEMORIAL FOUNDATION GRANTS

Fleetwood Memorial Foundation
501 South Fielder Road
Arlington, TX 76013
Phone: (817) 825–6699; Fax: (817) 542–0839;
Email: fleetwood@fleetwoodmemorial.org
Web: www.fleetwoodmemorial.org/form.php
Summary: To provide no–strings–attached grants to injured law enforcement or fire protection personnel in Texas or to the families of deceased or disabled personnel.
Eligibility: Open to certified Texas law enforcement or fire protection personnel who have been injured in the performance of their duties or to the families of personnel who were killed or permanently disabled in the performance of their duties. For the purposes of this program, "line of duty" does not automatically mean "on duty;" for example, no injuries considered Section V or strains during normal exercise, automobile accidents while going to lunch, etc. are viewed as "line of duty" by this program.
Financial data: These grants, of varying amounts, are designed to provide immediate financial relief to meet unexpected expenses until insurance or more permanent sources of funds can be arranged. Grants may be used to re-educate qualified personnel if they are unable to return to their normal duties after an accident. Educational funds are also available to the dependent children of deceased or disabled peace and fire personnel as long as they attend a public junior or senior college in Texas. Those funds are intended to provide support for housing and other needs not covered by funding from the Texas Higher Education Coordinating Board.
Duration: These are 1–time grants.
Number awarded: Since its inception in 1974, the foundation has provided more than 500 grants to qualified recipients, totaling nearly $2.0 million.
Deadline: Applications may be submitted at any time.

253 FLICKER OF HOPE SCHOLARSHIPS

Flicker of Hope Foundation
Attn: Scholarship Committee
8624 Janet Lane
Vienna, VA 22180
Phone: (703) 698–1626; Fax: (703) 698–6225;
Email: info@flickerofhope.org
Web: www.flickerofhope.org/whatwedo.htm
Summary: To provide financial assistance for college to burn survivors.
Eligibility: Open to high school seniors and graduates who are burn survivors and enrolled or planning to enroll in college. Applicants must submit a 500–word essay describing the circumstances of how they were burned, how that injury has affected their life, and the benefits to be derived from their planned course of study. Selection is based on severity of burn injury, academic performance, community service, and financial need.
Financial data: A stipend is awarded (amount not specified). Funds are paid directly to the postsecondary institution.
Duration: 1 year.
Number awarded: Varies each year; recently, 14 of these scholarships were awarded.
Deadline: May of each year.

254 FLORENCE ALLEN SCHOLARSHIPS

The Allen Endowment
c/o Holly S. Goodyear
3500 Granger Road
Medina, OH 44256–8602
Phone: (330) 725–3333;
Email: allenendowmen@gmail.com
Summary: To provide financial assistance to women from Ohio who are interested in attending college in any state.
Eligibility: Open to women from Ohio who are either traditional students (graduating high school seniors or recent GED recipients) or nontraditional students (at least 30 years of age). Traditional students must be enrolled or planning to enroll full time at a 4–year college or university in Ohio; nontraditional students must also attend a 4–year college or university in Ohio, but they are not required to enroll full time. All applicants must submit a 500–word essay describing their short–term goals and how the proposed training will help them to accomplish those goals and make a difference in their professional career. Selection is based on that essay; academic, employment, and/or volunteer record; and financial need. Special consideration is given to members of the Ohio Federation of Business and Professional Women (BPW/Ohio) and/or applicants endorsed by a BPW/Ohio local organization. U.S. citizenship is required.
Financial data: A stipend is awarded (amount not specified).
Duration: 1 year.
Number awarded: 1 or more each year.
Deadline: February of each year.

255 FLORIDA ACADEMIC SCHOLARS AWARD PROGRAM

Florida Department of Education
Attn: Office of Student Financial Assistance
325 West Gaines Street
Tallahassee, FL 32399–0400
Phone: (850) 410–5160; (888) 827–2004; Fax: (850) 487–1809;
Email: osfa@fldoe.org
Web: www.floridastudentfinancialaid.org/SSFAD/factsheets/BF.htm
Summary: To provide financial assistance for college to outstanding high school seniors in Florida.
Eligibility: Open to seniors in Florida public and private high schools who have been Florida residents for at least 1 year and will attend eligible Florida institutions of higher education. Applicants must have 1) earned a GPA of 3.5 or higher in a specified high school academic curriculum; 2) achieved scores of at least 1270 combined mathematics and critical reading on the SAT or 28 on the ACT; and 3) completed at least 100 hours of community service. Also eligible are National Merit and Achievement scholars and finalists, National Hispanic Scholars, IB Diploma recipients, and home–schooled students and GED recipients who achieve the same minimum SAT or ACT scores. U.S. citizenship or eligible noncitizen status is required.
Financial data: Stipends are $101 per semester hour for students at 4–year institutions, $62 per semester hour for students at 2–year institutions, $70 per semester hour for students enrolled in community college baccalaureate programs, or $51 per semester hour for students at career and technical centers.
Duration: Recipients may use this award 1) for up to 132 credit hours required to complete a standard undergraduate degree at their institution; 2) for up to 7 years from high school graduation (if initially funded within 3 years after high school graduation); or 3) until completion of their first baccalaureate degree program, whichever comes first. Renewal requires a GPA of 3.0 or higher.
Number awarded: Varies each year; recently, this program awarded 11,501 new and 27,668 renewal awards.
Deadline: March of each year.

256 FLORIDA ACADEMIC TOP SCHOLARS AWARD PROGRAM

Florida Department of Education
Attn: Office of Student Financial Assistance
325 West Gaines Street
Tallahassee, FL 32399–0400

Phone: (850) 410–5160; (888) 827–2004; Fax: (850) 487–1809;
Email: osfa@fldoe.org
Web: www.floridastudentfinancialaid.org/SSFAD/factsheets/BF.htm

Summary: To provide financial assistance for college to the top high school seniors in Florida.

Eligibility: Open to seniors in Florida public and private high schools who have been Florida residents for at least 1 year and will attend eligible Florida institutions of higher education. They must have completed a specified curriculum while in high school. U.S. citizenship or eligible noncitizen status is required. The Academic Top Scholars Award is presented to the student with the highest academic ranking in each county, based on GPA and SAT/ACT test scores.

Financial data: The Academic Top Scholars awardees receive an annual stipend of $43 per semester hour in addition to their Academic Scholars Award.

Duration: Recipients may use this award 1) for up to 132 credit hours required to complete a standard undergraduate degree at their institution; 2) for up to 7 years from high school graduation (if initially funded within 3 years after high school graduation); or 3) until completion of their first baccalaureate degree program, whichever comes first. Renewal requires a GPA of 3.0 or higher.

Number awarded: Varies each year; recently, this program awarded 65 new and 187 renewal scholarships.

Deadline: March of each year.

257 $$ FLORIDA CHAIRSCHOLARS PROGRAM

ChairScholars Foundation, Inc.
16101 Carencia Lane
Odessa, FL 33556–3278
Phone: (813) 926–0544; (888) 926–0544; Fax: (813) 920–7661;
Email: chairscholars@tampabay.rr.com
Web: www.chairscholars.org/florida.html

Summary: To provide financial assistance to physically challenged students in Florida who plan to attend college in the state.

Eligibility: Open to residents of Florida who are enrolled in grades 7–11 at a public school and have a serious physical disability. Qualifying disabilities include cerebral palsy, muscular dystrophy, spinal muscular atrophy, amputations, congenital missing or shortened limbs, multiple sclerosis, profound deafness, hearing impairments requiring FM modulator, blindness, various forms of cancer, any condition that permanently places the student in a wheelchair, or other illnesses, diseases, or conditions that severely impair mobility or motor skills. Applicants must have at least a "B" average and be able to demonstrate significant financial need (annual income less than $20,137 for a family of 1, rising to $69,616 for a family of 8). They must be planning to attend a college, university, community college, or vocational school in the state. Along with their application, they must submit a 1–page essay outlining how they became physically challenged, how their situation has affected them or their family, their family situation, things they like to do, why they need this scholarship, and their goals and dreams for the future.

Financial data: The awards provide full payment of tuition at any public college, university, or community college in Florida, or support for vocational training at a school in the state.

Duration: Up to 4 years.

Number awarded: Varies each year; recently, 24 of these scholarships were awarded. Since the program was established, it has awarded 502 scholarships.

Deadline: January of each year.

258 FLORIDA FIRST GENERATION MATCHING GRANT PROGRAM

Florida Department of Education
Attn: Office of Student Financial Assistance
325 West Gaines Street
Tallahassee, FL 32399–0400
Phone: (850) 410–5160; (888) 827–2004; Fax: (850) 487–1809;
Email: osfa@fldoe.org
Web: www.floridastudentfinancialaid.org/SSFAD/factsheets/FGMG.htm

Summary: To provide financial assistance to residents of Florida who are first–generation students at colleges in the state.

Eligibility: Open to residents of Florida who are enrolled or planning to enroll for at least 6 credit hours at a public university or community college in the state. The parents of applicants may not have earned a baccalaureate or higher degree. Financial need is considered in the selection process. U.S. citizenship or eligible noncitizen status is required.

Financial data: The amount of the grant depends on the need of the recipient and the availability of funds. Recently, grants averaged $1,768 at state universities and $716 at community colleges.

Duration: 1 year; may be renewed.

Number awarded: Varies each year; recently, this program awarded 6,090 new and 4,084 renewal grants.

Deadline: Each institution sets its own deadline.

259 $$ FLORIDA GOLD SEAL VOCATIONAL SCHOLARS AWARDS

Florida Department of Education
Attn: Office of Student Financial Assistance
325 West Gaines Street
Tallahassee, FL 32399–0400
Phone: (850) 410–5160; (888) 827–2004; Fax: (850) 487–1809;
Email: osfa@fldoe.org
Web: www.floridastudentfinancialaid.org/SSFAD/factsheets/BF.htm

Summary: To provide financial assistance for vocational education to outstanding high school seniors in Florida.

Eligibility: Open to graduating high school seniors in Florida who plan to attend a vocational, technical, trade, or business school in the state. Applicants must have earned a GPA of 3.0 or higher in their required academic program and 3.5 or higher in their vocational classes in high school. They must also have achieved the following minimum scores: 1) on the CPT, 83 in reading, 83 in sentence skills, and 72 in algebra; 2) on the SAT, 440 in critical reading and 440 in mathematics; or 3) on the ACT, 17 in English, 18 in reading, and 19 in mathematics. U.S. citizenship or eligible noncitizen status is required.

Financial data: Stipends are $76 per semester hour for students at 4–year institutions, $47 per semester hour for students at 2–year institutions, $52 per semester hour for students enrolled in community college baccalaureate programs, or $38 per semester hour for students at career and technical centers.

Duration: Recipients may use this award 1) for up to 90 semester hours; 2) for up to 7 years from high school graduation (if initially funded within 3 years after high school graduation); or 3) until completion of their first baccalaureate degree program, whichever comes first. Renewal requires a GPA of 2.75 or higher.

Number awarded: Varies each year; recently, this program awarded 1,342 new and 1,595 renewal scholarships.

Deadline: March of each year.

260 FLORIDA JCI SENATE FOUNDATION SCHOLARSHIPS

Florida JCI Senate Foundation
c/o Paul Chesler, Scholarship Chair
11125 Park Boulevard, Suite 104–169
P.O. Box 1242
Pinellas Park, FL 33780–1242
Email: info@fljcifoundation.org
Web: fljcifoundation.org

Summary: To provide financial assistance to high school seniors in Florida who plan to attend college in any state.

Eligibility: Open to seniors graduating from high schools in Florida and planning to enroll full time at an accredited college, university, or vocational school in any state. Applicants must be able to demonstrate financial need. Along with their application, they must submit an essay of 100 to 300 words on their chosen field of college study, their reasons for that choice, and any experiences, activities, or accomplishments that may have influenced their choice.

Financial data: The stipend is $1,000.

Duration: 1 year.

Number awarded: Varies each year.

Deadline: January or May of each year.

261 $ FLORIDA LEGION AUXILIARY DEPARTMENT SCHOLARSHIP

American Legion Auxiliary
Department of Florida
1912A Lee Road
P.O. Box 547917
Orlando, FL 32854–7917
Phone: (407) 293–7411; Fax: (407) 299–6522;
Email: contact@alafl.org
Web: alafl.org/index.php?department–scholarship

Summary: To provide financial assistance to the children of Florida veterans who are interested in attending college in the state.

Eligibility: Open to children and stepchildren of honorably–discharged veterans who are Florida residents. Applicants must be enrolled or planning to enroll full time at a postsecondary school in the state. Financial need is considered in the selection process.

Financial data: The stipends are up to $2,000 for a 4–year university or up to $1,000 for a community college or vocational/technical school. All funds are paid directly to the institution.
Duration: 1 year; may be renewed if the recipient needs further financial assistance and has maintained a GPA of 2.5 or higher.
Number awarded: Varies each year, depending on the availability of funds.
Deadline: January of each year.

262 FLORIDA MEDALLION SCHOLARS AWARDS

Florida Department of Education
Attn: Office of Student Financial Assistance
325 West Gaines Street
Tallahassee, FL 32399–0400
Phone: (850) 410–5160; (888) 827–2004; Fax: (850) 487–1809;
Email: osfa@fldoe.org
Web: www.floridastudentfinancialaid.org/SSFAD/factsheets/BF.htm
Summary: To provide financial assistance for college to outstanding high school seniors in Florida.
Eligibility: Open to seniors in Florida public and private high schools who have been Florida residents for at least 1 year and who plan to attend eligible Florida institutions of higher education. Applicants must have 1) earned a GPA of 3.0 or higher in a specified high school academic curriculum; and 2) achieved combined mathematics and critical reading scores of at least 980 on the SAT or 21 on the ACT. Also eligible are National Medallion and Achievement scholars and finalists who complete 75 hours of community service, National Hispanic Scholars who complete 75 hours of community service, home–schooled students who achieve scores of at least 1070 combined mathematics and critical reading on the SAT or 23 on the ACT, and GED recipients who achieve test scores of at least 980 combined mathematics and critical reading on the SAT or 21 on the ACT and a GPA of 3.0 or higher.
Financial data: Stipends are $76 per semester hour for students at 4–year institutions, $47 per semester hour for students at 2–year institutions, $52 per semester hour for students enrolled in community college baccalaureate degree programs, $62 per semester hour for students enrolled in community college associate degree programs, or $38 per semester hour for students at career and technical centers.
Duration: Recipients may use this award 1) for up to 132 semester hours; 2) for up to 7 years from high school graduation (if initially funded within 3 years after high school graduation); or 3) until completion of their first baccalaureate degree program, whichever comes first. Renewal requires a GPA of 2.75 or higher.
Number awarded: Varies each year; recently, this program awarded 40,957 new and 96,013 renewal scholarships.
Deadline: March of each year.

263 $ FLORIDA PUBLIC POSTSECONDARY CAREER EDUCATION STUDENT ASSISTANCE GRANTS

Florida Department of Education
Attn: Office of Student Financial Assistance
325 West Gaines Street
Tallahassee, FL 32399–0400
Phone: (850) 410–5160; (888) 827–2004; Fax: (850) 487–1809;
Email: osfa@fldoe.org
Web: www.floridastudentfinancialaid.org/SSFAD/factsheets/FSAG–CE.htm
Summary: To provide financial assistance to Florida residents enrolled at a community college or career center in the state.
Eligibility: Open to Florida residents enrolled in certificate programs of at least 450 clock hours at community colleges and career centers operated by district school boards. Applicants must be U.S. citizens or eligible noncitizens. A minimum of 1 year of Florida residency is required. Financial need must be documented; applicants must submit the Free Application for Federal Student Aid (FAFSA) and demonstrate substantial financial need. Priority is given to students who rank in the top 20% of their high school class and plan to attend 1 of the 11 state universities.
Financial data: Stipends range from $200 to a maximum that varies each year but recently was $2,413 per year.
Duration: Grants may be received until completion of 110% of the number of clock hours required to complete a program.
Number awarded: Varies each year; recently, this program awarded 3,431 new and 481 renewal scholarships.
Deadline: Each participating institution sets its own deadline.

264 $$ FLORIDA ROAD–TO–INDEPENDENCE PROGRAM

Florida Department of Children and Families
Attn: Office of Family Safety
1317 Winewood Boulevard, Building 1, Room 202
Tallahassee, FL 32399–0700
Phone: (850) 487–1111; Fax: (850) 922–2993;
Email: osfa@fldoe.org
Web: www.dcf.state.fl.us/programs/fostercare
Summary: To provide financial assistance for college or vocational training to Florida residents who have been in foster care.
Eligibility: Open to Florida residents between 18 and 23 years of age who have spent at least 6 months living in foster care prior to their 18th birthday. Applicants must be enrolled full time at a Florida public state university, public community college or career center, or eligible Florida private college, university, technical school, high school, or GED program.
Financial data: The amount of the award is based on the living and educational needs of the recipients and may be up to the amount they should have earned if they had worked 40 hours per week at a federal minimum wage job. Recently, the maximum grant was $892 per month ($10,704 per year).
Duration: 1 year; may be renewed until the recipient reaches 23 years of age.
Number awarded: Varies each year.
Deadline: Deadline not specified.

265 $$ FLORIDA SCHOLARSHIPS FOR CHILDREN AND SPOUSES OF DECEASED OR DISABLED VETERANS

Florida Department of Education
Attn: Office of Student Financial Assistance
325 West Gaines Street
Tallahassee, FL 32399–0400
Phone: (850) 410–5160; (888) 827–2004; Fax: (850) 487–1809;
Email: osfa@fldoe.org
Web: www.floridastudentfinancialaid.org/SSFAD/factsheets/CDDV.htm
Summary: To provide financial assistance for college to the children and spouses of Florida veterans who are disabled, deceased, or officially classified as prisoners of war (POW) or missing in action (MIA).
Eligibility: Open to residents of Florida who are U.S. citizens or eligible noncitizens and the dependent children or spouses of veterans or servicemembers who 1) died as a result of service–connected injuries, diseases, or disabilities sustained while on active duty during a period of war; 2) have a service–connected 100% total and permanent disability; or 3) were classified as POW or MIA by the U.S. armed forces or as civilian personnel captured while serving with the consent or authorization of the U.S. government during wartime service. The veteran or servicemember must have been a U.S. citizen or eligible noncitizens and a resident of Florida for at least 1 year before death, disability, or POW/MIA status. Children must be between 16 and 22 years of age. Spouses of deceased veterans or servicemembers must be unremarried and must apply within 5 years of their spouse's death. Spouses of disabled veterans must have been married for at least 1 year.
Financial data: Awards provide payment of tuition and registration fees at public institutions in Florida or an equivalent sum at private institutions.
Duration: 1 quarter or semester; may be renewed for up to 110% of the required credit hours of an initial associate, baccalaureate, diploma, or certificate program, provided the student maintains a GPA of 2.0 or higher.
Number awarded: Varies each year; recently, 233 new and 553 renewal scholarships were awarded.
Deadline: March of each year.

266 $$ FLORIDA STATE ELKS ASSOCIATION HOPE SCHOLARSHIP PROGRAM

Florida State Elks Association
Attn: Administrator
P.O. Box 49
Umatilla, FL 32784–0049
Phone: (352) 669–2241; Fax: (352) 669–1236;
Email: fsea@mpinet.net
Web: www.floridaelks.org/HOPE/index.html
Summary: To provide financial assistance to high school seniors in Florida who plan to attend college in any state.
Eligibility: Open to seniors graduating from high schools in Florida and planning to attend a college or university in any state. Applicants must submit an essay of 250 to 300 words on the area of study where the scholarship would be applied, why they selected that area, and how their education will benefit

society. Selection is based on that essay, academic achievement, work experience, leadership and extracurricular activities, community service, honors and awards, and financial need. U.S. citizenship is required.

Financial data: Stipends range from $1,000 to $6,000.

Duration: 1 year.

Number awarded: Varies each year; recently, 20 of these scholarships were awarded: 2 at $6,000, 4 at $3,000, 6 at $1,500, and 8 at $1,000.

Deadline: November of each year.

267 $ FLORIDA STUDENT ASSISTANCE GRANTS

Florida Department of Education
Attn: Office of Student Financial Assistance
325 West Gaines Street
Tallahassee, FL 32399–0400
Phone: (850) 410–5160; (888) 827–2004; Fax: (850) 487–1809;
Email: osfa@fldoe.org
Web: www.floridastudentfinancialaid.org/SSFAD/factsheets/FSAG.htm

Summary: To provide financial assistance for undergraduate studies to needy Florida residents.

Eligibility: Open to 1) undergraduate students who are enrolled full or part time at public Florida universities and community colleges; 2) full time students at eligible private, nonprofit 4–year colleges and universities; and 3) full–time students at other postsecondary degree–granting private colleges and universities not eligible under the private institution program. Applicants must be U.S. citizens or eligible noncitizens who have at least 1 year of Florida residency. They must submit the Free Application for Federal Student Aid (FAFSA) and demonstrate substantial financial need. Priority is given to students who rank in the top 20% of their high school class and plan to attend 1 of the 11 state universities.

Financial data: Stipends range from $200 to a maximum that varies each year but recently was $2,413 per year.

Duration: Grants may be received for up to 9 semesters or 14 quarters or until receipt of a bachelor's degree, whichever comes first. Renewal requires that the student earn a GPA of 2.0 or higher each semester.

Number awarded: Varies each year; recently, this program supported 89,063 students at public institutions (44,579 new and 44,484 renewal), 13,517 students at private institutions (5,776 new and 7,741 renewal), and 14,320 students at other postsecondary institutions (8,822 new and 5,498 renewal).

Deadline: Each participating institution sets its own deadline.

268 $ FLOYD QUALLS MEMORIAL SCHOLARSHIPS

American Council of the Blind
Attn: Coordinator, Scholarship Program
2200 Wilson Boulevard, Suite 650
Arlington, VA 22201
Phone: (202) 467–5081; (800) 424–8666; Fax: (703) 465–5085;
Email: info@acb.org
Web: www.acb.org/scholarship

Summary: To provide financial assistance to entering and continuing undergraduate and graduate students who are blind.

Eligibility: Open to legally blind students in 4 categories: entering freshmen in academic programs, undergraduates (sophomores, juniors, and seniors) in academic programs, graduate students in academic programs, and vocational school students or students working on an associate's degree from a community college. Applicants must submit verification of legal blindness in both eyes; SAT, ACT, GRE, or similar scores; information on extracurricular activities (including involvement in the American Council of the Blind); employment record; and a 500–word autobiographical sketch that includes their personal goals, strengths, weaknesses, hobbies, honors, achievements, and reasons for choice of field or courses of study. A cumulative GPA of 3.3 or higher is generally required. Financial need is not considered in the selection process.

Financial data: The stipend is $2,500.

Duration: 1 year.

Number awarded: At least 4 each year: 1 in each of the 4 categories.

Deadline: February of each year.

269 $$ FOOT LOCKER SCHOLAR ATHLETE PROGRAM

Do Something, Inc.
24–32 Union Square East, Fourth Floor
New York, NY 10003
Phone: (212) 254–2390;
Email: footlocker@dosomething.org
Web: www.dosomething.org/footlocker/about

Summary: To provide financial assistance to high school seniors who have been involved in sports and plan to attend college.

Eligibility: Open to graduating high school seniors who are currently involved in sports at the high school, intramural, or community level. Applicants must be planning to attend an accredited 4–year college or university. They must have a GPA of 3.0 or higher. Along with their application, they must submit essays of 200 to 350 words each on 1) how they exemplify sportsmanship on and off the field; 2) how sports have help them to grow into a strong leader; and 3) how a college degree will help them grow both professionally and personally. In the selection process, judges consider if applicants are good Foot Locker Scholar Athlete material (proactive and highly motivated, inspiring and charismatic, honest and trustworthy, genuine), if they embody good sportsmanship and strong moral character, and if they are passionate and enthusiastic about being a leader. A goal of the program is to select scholar athletes who come from diverse backgrounds, are from different places, have varied academic ambitions, and play different sports. U.S. citizenship or permanent resident status is required. Financial need is not considered. Semifinalists are interviewed via Skype.

Financial data: The stipend is $5,000 per year.

Duration: 4 years.

Number awarded: 20 each year.

Deadline: January of each year.

270 FRA NON–MEMBER SCHOLARSHIPS

Fleet Reserve Association
Attn: FRA Education Foundation
125 North West Street
Alexandria, VA 22314–2754
Phone: (703) 683–1400; (800) FRA–1924; Fax: (703) 549–6610;
Email: scholars@fra.org
Web: www.fra.org/Content/AM/Template.cfm?Section=About_FRA

Summary: To provide financial assistance for college or graduate school to sea service personnel and their families.

Eligibility: Open to 1) active–duty, Reserve, honorably–discharged veterans, and retired members of the U.S. Navy, Marine Corps, and Coast Guard; and 2) their spouses, children, and grandchildren. Applicants must be enrolled as full–time undergraduate or graduate students, but they are not required to be members of the sponsoring organization. Along with their application, they must submit an essay on why they want to go to college and what they intend to accomplish with their degree. Selection is based on academic record, financial need, extracurricular activities, leadership skills, and participation in community activities. U.S. citizenship is required.

Financial data: A stipend is awarded (amount not specified).

Duration: 1 year; may be renewed.

Number awarded: 1 or more each year.

Deadline: April of each year.

271 FRANCES SHUGART ENDOWMENT SCHOLARSHIP

Epsilon Sigma Alpha International
Attn: ESA Foundation
363 West Drake Road
Fort Collins, CO 80526
Phone: (970) 223–2824; Fax: (970) 223–4456;
Email: esainfo@epsilonsigmaalpha.org
Web: www.epsilonsigmaalpha.org/esa–foundation/scholarships

Summary: To provide financial assistance to residents of Florida planning to attend college in any state.

Eligibility: Open to residents of Florida who are 1) graduating high school seniors with a GPA of 3.0 or higher or with minimum scores of 22 on the ACT or 1030 on the combined critical reading and mathematics SAT; 2) enrolled in college with a GPA of 3.0 or higher; 3) enrolled at a technical school or returning to school after an absence for retraining of job skills or obtaining a degree; or 4) engaged in online study through an accredited college, university, or vocational school. Applicants may be attending or planning to attend an accredited school anywhere in the United States and major in any field. Selection is based on character (10%), leadership (20%), service (10%), financial need (30%), and scholastic ability (30%).

Financial data: The stipend is $1,500.

Duration: 1 year; may be renewed.

Number awarded: 2 each year.

Deadline: January of each year.

272 $ FRANK O'BANNON GRANT PROGRAM

State Student Assistance Commission of Indiana
Attn: Grants and Scholarships
W462 Indiana Government Center South
402 West Washington Street
Indianapolis, IN 46204
Phone: (317) 232–2355; (888) 528–4719 (within IN); Fax: (317) 232–3260;
Email: grants@ssaci.in.gov
Web: www.in.gov/ssaci/2346.htm

Summary: To provide financial assistance to Indiana residents who are working full time on an undergraduate degree.

Eligibility: Open to Indiana residents who are high school seniors, high school graduates, or GED certificate recipients. Applicants must be attending or planning to attend an eligible Indiana postsecondary institution as a full–time undergraduate student working on an associate or first bachelor's degree. They must be able to demonstrate financial need for tuition assistance. U.S. citizenship or eligible noncitizen status is required.

Financial data: This program offers tuition assistance from $200 to several thousand dollars per year, depending on the level of appropriations, the number of eligible students making application, the calculation of student's financial need, and the cost of tuition and fees at the schools of choice.

Duration: 1 year.

Number awarded: Varies each year.

Deadline: March of each year.

273 $ FRED AND MARIE CHRISTOPHERSON SCHOLARSHIP

Sioux Falls Area Community Foundation
Attn: Scholarship Coordinator
300 North Phillips Avenue, Suite 102
Sioux Falls, SD 57104–6035
Phone: (605) 336–7055, ext. 20; Fax: (605) 336–0038;
Email: pgale@sfacf.org
Web: www.sfacf.org/ScholarshipDetails.aspx?CategoryID=1

Summary: To provide financial assistance to high school seniors in South Dakota who plan to attend college in the state.

Eligibility: Open to seniors graduating from high schools in South Dakota. Applicants must be interested in attending a 4–year college or university in the state. They must have a GPA of 3.9 or higher and an ACT score of at least 28. Along with their application, they must submit a 500–word essay on their educational and career goals. Financial need is considered in the selection process.

Financial data: The stipend is $2,500 the first year and $1,000 in subsequent years. Funds are paid annually in 2 equal installments and are to be used for tuition, fees, and/or books.

Duration: 1 year; may be renewed for 3 additional years, provided the recipient maintains a GPA of 3.0 or higher and full–time enrollment.

Number awarded: Varies each year; recently, 3 of these scholarships were awarded.

Deadline: March of each year.

274 $ FRED SCHEIGERT SCHOLARSHIPS

Council of Citizens with Low Vision International
c/o American Council of the Blind
2200 Wilson Boulevard, Suite 650
Arlington, VA 22201
Phone: (202) 467–5081; (800) 733–2258; Fax: (703) 465–5085;
Email: scholarship@cclvi.org
Web: www.cclvi.org/schguide.htm

Summary: To provide financial assistance to entering and continuing undergraduate and graduate students with low vision.

Eligibility: Open to full–time undergraduate and graduate students who have been certified by an ophthalmologist as having low vision (acuity of 20/70 or worse in the better seeing eye with best correction or side vision with a maximum diameter of no greater than 30 degrees). Applicants may be entering freshmen, undergraduates, or graduate students. They must have a GPA of 3.2 or higher and a record of involvement in their school and/or local community.

Financial data: The stipend is $3,000.

Duration: 1 year.

Number awarded: 3 each year: 1 each to an entering freshman, undergraduate, and graduate student.

Deadline: February of each year.

275 $$ FREDERICK C. BRANCH MARINE CORPS LEADERSHIP SCHOLARSHIPS

U.S. Navy
Attn: Naval Education and Training Command
NSTC OD2
250 Dallas Street, Suite A
Pensacola, FL 32508–5268
Phone: (850) 452–4941, ext. 29395; (800) NAV–ROTC, ext. 29395; Fax: (850) 452–2486;
Email: pnsc_nrotc.scholarship@navy.mil
Web: www.nrotc.navy.mil/hist_black.aspx

Summary: To provide financial assistance to students who are entering or enrolled at specified Historically Black Colleges or Universities (HBCUs) and interested in joining Navy ROTC to prepare for service as an officer in the U.S. Marine Corps.

Eligibility: Open to students attending or planning to attend 1 of 17 specified HBCUs with a Navy ROTC unit on campus. Applicants may either apply through their local Marine recruiter for a 4–year scholarship or be nominated by the professor of naval science at their institution and meet academic requirements set by each school for 2– or 3–year scholarships. They must be U.S. citizens between 17 and 23 years of age who are willing to serve for 4 years as active–duty Marine Corps officers following graduation from college. They must not have reached their 27th birthday by the time of college graduation and commissioning; applicants who have prior active–duty military service may be eligible for age adjustments for the amount of time equal to their prior service, up to a maximum of 36 months. The qualifying scores are 1000 composite on the SAT or 22 composite on the ACT. Current enlisted and former military personnel are also eligible if they will complete the program by the age of 30.

Financial data: These scholarships provide payment of full tuition and required educational fees, as well as a specified amount for textbooks, supplies, and equipment. The program also provides a stipend for 10 months of the year that is $250 per month as a freshman, $300 per month as a sophomore, $350 per month as a junior, and $400 per month as a senior.

Duration: Scholarships are available for 2–, 3–, or 4–year terms.

Number awarded: Varies each year.

Deadline: January of each year for students applying for a 4–year scholarship through their local Marine recruiter; July of each year if applying for a 2– or 3–year scholarship through the Navy ROTC unit at their institution.

276 $$ FREEDOM ALLIANCE SCHOLARSHIPS

Freedom Alliance
Attn: Scholarship Fund
22570 Markey Court, Suite 240
Dulles, VA 20166–6915
Phone: (703) 444–7940; (800) 475–6620; Fax: (703) 444–9893
Web: freedomalliance.org/programs/scholarship–fund

Summary: To provide financial assistance for college to the children of deceased and disabled military personnel.

Eligibility: Open to high school seniors, high school graduates, and undergraduate students under 26 years of age who are dependent children of military personnel (soldier, sailor, airman, Marine, or Guardsman). The military parent must 1) have been killed or permanently disabled as a result of an operational mission or training accident; or 2) be currently classified as a POW or MIA. For disabled parents, the disability must be permanent, service–connected, and rated at 100% by the U.S. Department of Veterans Affairs. Applicants must submit a 500–word essay on what their parent's service means to them.

Financial data: Stipends range up to $6,000 per year.

Duration: 1 year; may be renewed up to 3 additional years, provided the recipient remains enrolled full time with a GPA of 2.0 or higher.

Number awarded: Varies each year; recently, 240 of these scholarships were awarded.

Deadline: July of each year.

277 FRESH START SCHOLARSHIP

Wilmington Women in Business
Attn: Fresh Start Scholarship Foundation, Inc.
P.O. Box 7784
Wilmington, DE 19803
Phone: (302) 656–4411;
Email: fsscholar@comcast.net
Web: www.wwb.org?page_id=11

Summary: To provide financial assistance to women from any state who have experienced an interruption in their education and are interested in attending college in Delaware.

Eligibility: Open to women from any state who are at least 20 years of age, have a high school diploma or GED, and have been admitted to an accredited Delaware college in a 2– or 4–year undergraduate degree program. Applicants must have had at least a 2–year break in education either after completing high school or during college studies. They must have at least a "C" average if currently enrolled in college and be recommended by a social service agency (or a college representative if a social service agency is not available). U.S. citizenship or permanent resident status is required. Financial need is considered in the selection process.

Financial data: The stipend varies annually, depending on the availability of funds. Awards are paid to the college at the beginning of each semester.

Duration: 1 year.

Number awarded: Varies each year. Since the program was established, it has awarded more than $425,000 to 120 women.

Deadline: May of each year.

278 $ FRS COLLEGE SCHOLARSHIP PROGRAM

Foundation for Rural Service
Attn: Selection Committee
4121 Wilson Boulevard, Tenth Floor
Arlington, VA 22203
Phone: (703) 351–2026; Fax: (703) 351–2027;
Email: foundation@frs.org
Web: www.frs.org/youth–programs/college–scholarship–program

Summary: To provide financial assistance for college to high school seniors who live in rural areas of the United States.

Eligibility: Open to graduating high school seniors who receive local telecommunications service from a current member of the National Telecommunications Cooperative Association (NTCA) that serves as a sponsor; associate NTCA members (businesses that provide goods and services to the telecommunications industry) may also sponsor a student. Applicants must live in a rural area and be interested in returning to rural America following graduation. They must have a GPA of 2.0 or higher and have been accepted by an accredited 2– or 4–year college, university, or vocational/technical school. Along with their application, they must submit transcripts, letters of recommendation, an endorsement by their sponsor, and a 300–word essay on an assigned topic. Financial need is not considered in the selection process. U.S. citizenship is required.

Financial data: The stipend is $2,500 (of which $500 is provided by the sponsoring NTCA member cooperative).

Duration: 1 year; nonrenewable.

Number awarded: 30 each year.

Deadline: February of each year.

279 $$ FULL CIRCLE SCHOLARSHIPS

American Indian College Fund
Attn: Scholarship Department
8333 Greenwood Boulevard
Denver, CO 80221
Phone: (303) 426–8900; (800) 776–FUND; Fax: (303) 426–1200;
Email: scholarships@collegefund.org
Web: www.collegefund.org/content/full_circle_scholarships_listings

Summary: To provide financial assistance to American Indian college students from any state who are enrolled at non–tribal colleges and universities.

Eligibility: Open to American Indians registered as a member of a tribe or a descendant of at least 1 grandparent or parent who is an enrolled tribal member. Applicants must be enrolled at a non–tribal college or university in any state. They must have a GPA of 2.0 or higher and be able to demonstrate exceptional academic achievement or financial need. This program includes many scholarships offered by corporate and other donors, many of whom impose additional requirements. U.S. citizenship is required.

Financial data: Stipends range up to $10,000.

Duration: 1 year.

Number awarded: Varies each year.

Deadline: May of each year.

280 $ G. JASON AND MARCIA VANCE CONWAY MEMORIAL SCHOLARSHIP

Vermont Student Assistance Corporation
Attn: Scholarship Programs
10 East Allen Street
P.O. Box 2000
Winooski, VT 05404–2601
Phone: (802) 654–3798; (888) 253–4819; Fax: (802) 654–3765; TDD: (800) 281–3341 (within VT);
Email: info@vsac.org
Web: services.vsac.org

Summary: To provide financial assistance to residents of Vermont who are interested in attending college in any state and face significant obstacles that limit their access to higher education.

Eligibility: Open to residents of Vermont who are high school seniors, high school graduates, or students currently enrolled at a college or university in any state. Applicants must face significant barriers or obstacles that limit their access to higher education. Along with their application, they must submit 1) a 250 word–essay on their short– and long–term academic, educational, career, vocational, and/or employment goals; and 2) a 100–word essay on the barriers that limit their access to education. Selection is based on those essays, letters of recommendation, and financial need (estimated family contribution less than $23,360).

Financial data: The stipend is $2,000.

Duration: 1 year.

Number awarded: 1 or more each year.

Deadline: March of each year.

281 GEN AND KELLY TANABE SCHOLARSHIP

Gen and Kelly Tanabe
3286 Oak Court
Belmont, CA 94002
Phone: (650) 618–2221;
Email: tanabe@gmail.com
Web: www.gkscholarship.com

Summary: To provide financial assistance for undergraduate or graduate study to U.S. citizens and permanent residents.

Eligibility: Open to U.S. citizens and permanent residents who are high school students (grades 9–12), college undergraduates, or graduate students. Applicants must submit an essay, up to 250 words, on 1) why they deserve to win this scholarship; 2) their academic or career goals; or 3) a topic of their choice. Selection is based primarily on that essay.

Financial data: The stipend is $1,000.

Duration: 1 year.

Number awarded: 2 or more each year.

Deadline: July of each year for the spring competition; December of each year for the fall competition.

282 GENERAL FEDERATION OF WOMEN'S CLUBS OF WEST VIRGINIA SCHOLARSHIPS

General Federation of Women's Clubs of West Virginia
Attn: Scholarship Fund Board
P.O. Box 75
Bethany, WV 26032–0075
Email: information@gfwcwestvirginia.org
Web: gfwcwestvirginia.org

Summary: To provide financial assistance to residents of West Virginia who are interested in attending college in any state.

Eligibility: Open to U.S. citizens who have been residents of West Virginia for at least 3 years. Applicants must be enrolled or planning to enroll full time at an accredited college or professional, vocational, or technical program offered by an institution in the state; enrollment at an institution outside West Virginia is allowed only if the desired course is not offered within the state. Both men and women are eligible. Selection is based on work experience (volunteer or paid) within the past year, extracurricular activities within the past year, and financial need.

Financial data: Stipends range up to $1,000 per year.

Duration: 1 year; recipients may reapply, but priority is given to first–time applicants.

Number awarded: 1 or more each year.

Deadline: March of each year.

283 $ GENERAL HENRY H. ARNOLD EDUCATION GRANT PROGRAM

Air Force Aid Society
Attn: Education Assistance Department
241 18th Street South, Suite 202

Arlington, VA 22202–3409
Phone: (703) 607–3072, ext. 51; (800) 769–8951; Fax: (703) 607–3022
Web: www.afas.org/Education/ArnoldEdGrant.cfm
Summary: To provide financial assistance for college to dependents of active–duty, retired, disabled, or deceased Air Force personnel.
Eligibility: Open to 1) dependent children of Air Force personnel who are active duty, Reservists on extended active duty, retired due to length of active–duty service or disability, or deceased while on active duty or in retired status; 2) spouses of active–duty Air Force members and Reservists on extended active duty; and 3) surviving spouses of Air Force members who died while on active duty or in retired status. Applicants must be enrolled or planning to enroll as full–time undergraduate students at an accredited college, university, or vocational/trade school. Spouses must be attending school within the 48 contiguous states. Selection is based on family income and education costs.
Financial data: The stipend is $2,000.
Duration: 1 year; may be renewed if the recipient maintains a GPA of 2.0 or higher.
Number awarded: Varies each year.
Deadline: March of each year.

284 GEOFFREY FOUNDATION SCHOLARSHIPS

Geoffrey Foundation
Ocean Avenue
P.O. Box 1112
Kennebunkport, ME 04046
Phone: (207) 967–5798
Summary: To provide financial assistance to deaf students who attend school with hearing students and communicate using spoken language.
Eligibility: Open to U.S. citizens who are hearing impaired (severe to profound hearing loss greater than 80 dB) and are utilizing an auditory–verbal approach to communication. Applicants must be currently enrolled or planning to attend a preschool, elementary school, junior high or high school, or college for hearing students on a full–time basis in the forthcoming year. They must submit a current audiogram plus 3 letters of recommendation.
Financial data: The amount awarded varies, depending upon the needs of the recipient.
Duration: 1 year or longer.
Number awarded: Varies each year. The foundation awards grants in excess of $30,000 each year to children and college students.
Deadline: March of each year.

285 $ GEORGE BARTOL MEMORIAL SCHOLARSHIPS

George Bartol Memorial Scholarship Fund
c/o Kari Bartol Romano
4616 Edgewater Drive
Orlando, FL 32804
Phone: (407) 718–7601;
Email: livebait3@gmail.com
Web: www.mindsmatterusa.org/Scholarship.html
Summary: To provide financial assistance for college to children of brain tumor patients.
Eligibility: Open to students who are enrolled full time at an accredited 2– or 4–year college or university and have a GPA of 2.5 or higher. Applicants must have a parent battling a primary brain tumor or a parent who has passed away as a result of a primary brain tumor. They must be between 18 and 23 years of age. Along with their application, they must submit 5 essays on the following topics: 1) their parent who has lost their battle to a primary brain tumor or who is currently battling a primary brain tumor; 2) their academic and professional goals; 3) the person who has motivated and inspired them the most in their life; 4) their current financial status and how their parent's medical condition has increased their financial need for this scholarship; and 5) how their parent's medical condition has changed their outlook on life. Selection is based on the essays, grades, letters of recommendation, and financial need. Children of Vietnam veterans who have not been awarded VA Chapter 35 benefits are strongly encouraged to apply.
Financial data: The stipend is $1,000 per semester ($3,000 per year, including summer semester). Students at schools on the quarter system may receive $750 per quarter ($3,000 per year, including summer quarter). Funds are paid directly to the financial aid office at the school the recipient is attending.
Duration: 1 semester or quarter; may be renewed if the recipient maintains a GPA of 2.5 or higher.
Number awarded: Varies each year; recently, 3 of these scholarships were awarded.
Deadline: September of each year.

286 $ GEORGE COLEMAN SCHOLARSHIP

New England Association of Collegiate Registrars and Admissions Officers
c/o Kathy A. Posey, Scholarship Committee
Mount Ida College
Office of the Registrar
777 Dedham Street
Newton, MA 02459
Phone: (617) 928–4503; Fax: (617) 928–4728;
Email: pastpresident@neacrao.org
Web: www.neacrao.org/scholarship_info.html
Summary: To provide financial assistance to high school seniors in New England who plan to attend a college or university that is a member of the New England Association of Collegiate Registrars and Admissions Officers (NEACRAO).
Eligibility: Open to seniors graduating from high schools in New England who are recommended by their guidance counselor. Applicants must be planning to attend a NEACRAO member institution. They must have a GPA of 3.0 or higher. Along with their application, they must submit a 250–word essay on their career goals. Selection is based on academic record and potential of the applicant to succeed in a postsecondary academic environment.
Financial data: The stipend is $2,000.
Duration: 1 year.
Number awarded: 3 each year.
Deadline: April of each year.

287 GEORGE GENG ON LEE MINORITIES IN LEADERSHIP SCHOLARSHIP

Capture the Dream, Inc.
Attn: Scholarship Program
484 Lake Park Avenue, Suite 15
Oakland, CA 94610
Phone: (510) 343–3635;
Email: info@capturethedream.org
Web: www.capturethedream.org/programs/scholarship.php
Summary: To provide financial assistance to minorities in California who can demonstrate leadership and are interested in attending college in any state.
Eligibility: Open to residents of California who are members of minority groups and either graduating high school seniors or current full–time undergraduates at 4–year colleges and universities in any state. Applicants must submit a 1,000–word essay on why they should be selected to receive this scholarship, using their experiences within school, work, and home to display the challenges they have faced as a minority and how they overcame adversity to assume a leadership role. They should also explain how their career goals and future aspirations will build them as a future minority leader. Selection is based on academic performance, community service, leadership history, professional recommendations, and financial need. U.S. citizenship or permanent resident status is required.
Financial data: The stipend is $1,000.
Duration: 1 year.
Number awarded: 1 or more each year.
Deadline: July of each year.

288 $ GEORGE "SLATS" O'BRIEN SCHOLARSHIPS

Western Athletic Scholarship Association
Attn: Scholarship Coordinator
13730 Loumont Street
Whittier, CA 90601
Summary: To provide financial assistance for college to outstanding volleyball players.
Eligibility: Open to graduating high school seniors who have played an active role in amateur volleyball. Applicants must be planning to attend an accredited 2– or 4–year college or university. They need not have played on a high school team and are not required to play volleyball in college. Along with their application, they must submit an essay describing the role volleyball has played in their life, why they think they should receive this scholarship, and where they learned about it. Selection is based on academic achievement, community service, participation in volleyball, and financial need.
Financial data: The stipend is $2,000 per year.
Duration: 1 year; may be renewed.
Number awarded: Up to 10 each year.
Deadline: February of each year.

289 $$ GEORGIA STUDENT FINANCE COMMISSION ACCEL PROGRAM

Georgia Student Finance Commission
Attn: Scholarships and Grants Division
2082 East Exchange Place, Suite 200
Tucker, GA 30084–5305
Phone: (770) 724–9000; (800) 505–GSFC; Fax: (770) 724–9089;
Email: gacollege411@gsfc.org
Web: www.gacollege411.org

Summary: To provide financial assistance to high school students in Georgia who are enrolled concurrently in college–level courses.

Eligibility: Open to Georgia residents who are enrolled simultaneously as a junior or senior at an eligible public or private high school in the state and at an eligible Georgia public or private postsecondary institution. Applicants must be taking college degree–level courses in English language arts, mathematics, social studies, science, or foreign language. U.S. citizenship or permanent resident status is required.

Financial data: Accel Scholars who attend public colleges or universities receive full tuition and payment of mandatory fees plus a book allowance of $300 per academic year. The stipend for Accel Scholarships at private colleges and universities is $4,000 per year; funds may be used only for tuition and mandatory fees.

Duration: 1 year; may be renewed for 1 additional year.

Number awarded: Varies each year.

Deadline: Applications must be submitted on or before the last day of the academic term.

290 GEORGIA TUITION EQUALIZATION GRANTS

Georgia Student Finance Commission
Attn: Scholarships and Grants Division
2082 East Exchange Place, Suite 200
Tucker, GA 30084–5305
Phone: (770) 724–9000; (800) 505–GSFC; Fax: (770) 724–9089;
Email: gacollege411@gsfc.org
Web: www.gacollege411.org

Summary: To provide financial assistance to students who wish to attend a private college or university in Georgia or an adjoining state.

Eligibility: Open to Georgia residents who are attending 1 of 38 accredited private colleges or universities in Georgia. Applicants must be U.S. citizens, nationals, or permanent residents and in compliance with the Georgia Drug–Free Postsecondary Education Act. Financial need is not considered in the selection process.

Financial data: The stipend is currently $350 per semester, or up to $1,050 per year.

Duration: 1 year; may be renewed.

Number awarded: Varies each year; recently, 32,457 of these grants were awarded.

Deadline: Applications must be submitted on or before the last day of the academic term.

291 $ GEORGIA'S HERO SCHOLARSHIP PROGRAM

Georgia Student Finance Commission
Attn: Scholarships and Grants Division
2082 East Exchange Place, Suite 200
Tucker, GA 30084–5305
Phone: (770) 724–9000; (800) 505–GSFC; Fax: (770) 724–9089;
Email: gacollege411@gsfc.org
Web: www.gacollege411.org

Summary: To provide financial assistance for college to members of the National Guard or Reserves in Georgia and their children and spouses.

Eligibility: Open to Georgia residents who are active members of the Georgia National Guard or U.S. Military Reserves, were deployed outside the United States for active–duty service on or after February 1, 2003 to a location designated as a combat zone, and served in that combat zone for at least 181 consecutive days. Also eligible are 1) the children, younger than 25 years of age, of Guard and Reserve members who completed at least 1 term of service (of 181 days each) overseas on or after February 1, 2003; 2) the children, younger than 25 years of age, of Guard and Reserve members who were killed or totally disabled during service overseas on or after February 1, 2003, regardless of their length of service; and 3) the spouses of Guard and Reserve members who were killed in a combat zone, died as a result of injuries, or became 100% disabled as a result of injuries received in a combat zone during service overseas on or after February 1, 2003, regardless of their length of service. Applicants must be interested in attending a unit of the University System of Georgia, a unit of the Georgia Department of Technical and Adult Education, or an eligible private college or university in Georgia.

Financial data: The stipend for full–time study is $2,000 per academic year, not to exceed $8,000 during an entire program of study. The stipend for part–time study is prorated appropriately.

Duration: 1 year; may be renewed (if satisfactory progress is maintained) for up to 3 additional years.

Number awarded: Varies each year.

Deadline: June of each year.

292 GERALD AND PAUL D'AMOUR FOUNDERS' FELLOWSHIPS FOR ACADEMIC EXCELLENCE

Big Y Foods, Inc.
Attn: Scholarship Committee
2145 Roosevelt Avenue
P.O. Box 7840
Springfield, MA 01102–7840
Phone: (413) 504–4080
Web: www.bigy.com/education/y_scholarships.php

Summary: To provide financial assistance to outstanding undergraduate and graduate students in the Big Y Foods market area in Massachusetts and Connecticut.

Eligibility: Open to high school seniors, undergraduates, graduate students, and nontraditional students of any age who reside within western or central Massachusetts, Norfolk County in Massachusetts, or the state of Connecticut. Big Y employees and their dependents are also eligible. Applicants must submit a transcript, standardized test scores(SAT, ACT, GRE, GMAT, or LSAT), 2 letters of recommendation, and a resume. Selection is based on academic merit and achievement.

Financial data: The stipend is $1,000.

Duration: 1 year; nonrenewable.

Number awarded: Varies each year; recently, 128 of these scholarships were awarded.

Deadline: January of each year.

293 $$ GE–REAGAN FOUNDATION SCHOLARSHIP

Reagan Presidential Foundation
40 Presidential Drive
Simi Valley, CA 93065
Phone: (805) 522–2977; Fax: (805) 520–970;
Email: info@reaganfoundation.org
Web: www.reaganlibrary.com/GE–RFScholarships.aspx

Summary: To provide financial assistance for college to high school seniors who demonstrate outstanding leadership and integrity.

Eligibility: Open to seniors graduating from high schools in the United States who have a GPA of 3.0 or higher and plan to work on a bachelor's degree at a college or university. Applicants must demonstrate such characteristics as leadership, integrity, drive, and citizenship. They must be nominated by a community leader, such as a high school principal, elected official, or nonprofit executive. Along with their application, they must submit an essay of 500 to 750 words describing how their leadership and service have made a positive difference in their school, community, family, and/or job, and how they will continue to make a difference in college and beyond. U.S. citizenship is required. Financial need is also considered in the selection process.

Financial data: The stipend is $10,000 per year.

Duration: 4 years.

Number awarded: Up to 20 each year.

Deadline: February of each year.

294 $ GILBERT MATCHING STUDENT GRANT PROGRAM

Massachusetts Office of Student Financial Assistance
454 Broadway, Suite 200
Revere, MA 02151
Phone: (617) 391–6070; Fax: (617) 727–0667;
Email: osfa@osfa.mass.edu
Web: www.osfa.mass.edu/default.asp?page=gilbert

Summary: To provide financial assistance for college to Massachusetts residents who are attending accredited independent institutions.

Eligibility: Open to applicants who have been permanent legal residents of Massachusetts for at least 1 year and are working full time on an associate or bachelor's degree at an independent, regionally–accredited college or university in Massachusetts. U.S. citizenship or permanent resident status is required. Selection is based on financial need.

Financial data: Awards range from $200 to $2,500 per year, depending on the need of the recipient.

Duration: 1 year; may be renewed.
Number awarded: Varies each year.
Deadline: Deadlines are established by the school the student attends.

295 GIVE KIDS A CHANCE SCHOLARSHIPS

Give Kids A Chance
c/o Brian J. McDonough
150 West Flagler Street, Suite 2200
Miami, FL 33130
Phone: (305) 789–3350;
Email: bmcdonough@stearnsweaver.com
Web: www.gkac@scholarshipapplication.html
Summary: To provide financial assistance to high school seniors in Florida who can demonstrate significant financial need and plan to attend college in any state.
Eligibility: Open to seniors graduating from public high schools in Florida and planning to enroll at a college or university in any state. Applicants must have a GPA of 2.5 or higher and a family income less than 60% of the median income in the area where they reside. Along with their application, they must submit a 150–word essay about themselves, their educational and career goals, how this award can help them to achieve those goals, and why they should receive this award.
Financial data: The stipend is $1,000 per year.
Duration: 1 year; may be renewed up to 3 additional years, provided the recipient maintains a GPA of 2.5 or higher.
Number awarded: Approximately 25 each year; since the program was established, it has provided support to 188 students.
Deadline: April of each year.

296 $ GLADYS MCPARTLAND SCHOLARSHIPS

United States Marine Corps Combat Correspondents Association
Attn: Executive Director
110 Fox Court
Wildwood, FL 34785
Phone: (352) 748–4698;
Email: usmccca@cfl.rr.com
Web: www.usmccca.org/archives/4941
Summary: To provide financial assistance to members of the U.S. Marine Corps Combat Correspondents Association (USMCCCA) or their dependents and Marines in designated occupational fields who are interested in studying any field in college.
Eligibility: Open to 1) members of USMCCCA, their dependents, and their spouses; and 2) active–duty Marines in Occupational Fields 4300 and 4600 and their dependents who are USMCCCA members or will agree to become members if awarded a scholarship. Applicants must be enrolled or planning to enroll in an undergraduate program in any field. Along with their application, they must submit 500–word essays on 1) their noteworthy achievements and long–range goals; and 2) the United States I want to see in 15 years and my role in the transformation. Financial need is not considered in the selection process.
Financial data: Stipends range up to $3,000; funds are disbursed directly to the recipient's institution to be used exclusively for tuition, books, and/or fees.
Duration: 1 year.
Number awarded: 1 or more each year.
Deadline: May of each year.

297 $$ GLAMOUR'S TOP TEN COLLEGE WOMEN COMPETITION

Glamour Magazine
4 Times Square, 16th Floor
New York, NY 10036–6593
Phone: (800) 244–GLAM; Fax: (212) 286–6922;
Email: TTCW@glamour.com
Web: www.glamour.com/about/top–10–college–women
Summary: To recognize and reward outstanding college women.
Eligibility: Open to women enrolled full time in their junior year at accredited colleges and universities in the United States and Canada. Applications must be approved and signed by the appropriate members of the school's faculty and administration (i.e., faculty adviser, the director of public relations, the director of student activities, or the dean of students). There is no limit on the number of applicants from any 1 school. Applicants must submit an essay (up to 500 words) describing their most meaningful achievements and how those relate to their field of study and future goals. Selection is based on leadership experience (34%), personal involvement in campus and community affairs (33%), and academic excellence (33%).
Financial data: The grand prize is $20,000 and other prizes are $3,000. Each winner also receives a trip to New York City and recognition in the October issue of *Glamour* magazine.
Duration: The competition is held annually.
Number awarded: 10 each year: 1 grand prize and 9 other prizes.
Deadline: July of each year for the early deadline; September of each year for the late deadline.

298 $ GLORIA BARRON PRIZE FOR YOUNG HEROES

The Barron Prize
545 Pearl Street
Boulder, CO 80302
Email: ba_richman@barronprize.org
Web: www.barronprize.org
Summary: To recognize and reward young people from diverse backgrounds who have "shown extraordinary leadership in making our world better."
Eligibility: Open to students between the ages of 8 and 18 who have shown leadership in making the world a better place: by helping people, protecting the environment, halting violence, or leading other important service work. They must be residents of the United States or Canada. They must be nominated by an adult who is familiar with their service activity. In all cases, nominees must have been the prime mover of the service activity; the service activity cannot have been done solely to complete an assignment for school or work. Selection is based on the nominees' positive spirit, courage, intelligence, generosity, and high moral purpose.
Financial data: Winners receive $2,500. Funds may be used for higher education or completion of the service project.
Duration: The competition is held annually.
Number awarded: 25 each year: half have focused on helping their communities and fellow beings and half have focused on protecting the health and sustainability of the environment.
Deadline: Nominations must be submitted by the end of April of each year.

299 $ GOLD STAR SCHOLARSHIP PROGRAMS

Navy–Marine Corps Relief Society
Attn: Education Division
875 North Randolph Street, Suite 225
Arlington, VA 22203–1757
Phone: (703) 696–4960; Fax: (703) 696–0144;
Email: education@nmcrs.org
Web: www.nmcrs.org/education.html
Summary: To provide financial assistance for college to the children and spouses of Navy or Marine Corps personnel who died while serving on active duty or after retirement.
Eligibility: Open to children under 23 years of age and unremarried spouses of members of the Navy or Marine Corps who died while serving on active duty or after retirement. Applicants must be enrolled or planning to enroll full time at a college, university, or vocational/technical school. They must have a GPA of 2.0 or higher and be able to demonstrate financial need.
Financial data: Stipends range from $500 to $2,500 per year. Funds are disbursed directly to the financial institution.
Duration: 1 year; recipients may reapply.
Number awarded: Varies each year.
Deadline: March of each year.

300 $$ GOVERNOR'S COALITION FOR YOUTH WITH DISABILITIES SCHOLARSHIPS

Governor's Coalition for Youth with Disabilities
P.O. Box 2485
Hartford, CT 06146–2485
Phone: (860) 263–6018;
Email: gcydinfo@gmail.com
Web: www.gcyd.org/scholarship.html
Summary: To provide financial assistance for college to Connecticut residents who have a disability.
Eligibility: Open to seniors graduating from high schools in Connecticut who have a disability. Applicants must be planning to attend 1) a college or university in Connecticut or any other state; 2) any of the 4 campuses of the Connecticut State University System; or 3) any of the 12 Connecticut community colleges. Along with their application, they must submit an essay of 500 to 600 words

describing the nature of their disability, how it has impacted their life experiences, how they will use what they have learned from those experiences, and the intended major or specific occupational skill they wish to pursue in college. Selection is based on 1) the manner in which applicants have overcome the obstacles created by their disability; 2) the degree to which they have contributed to their school and community through service, leadership, and being a positive role model; and 3) their desire for a successful career.

Financial data: For students at colleges and universities nationwide, the stipend ranges from $500 to $5,000. For students at Connecticut State Universities, the stipend is $500 per semester. For students at Connecticut community colleges, the award provides full payment of tuition and fees.

Duration: 1 year. National scholarships are nonrenewable, Connecticut State University scholarships may be renewed for a total of 8 semesters, and Connecticut community college scholarships may be renewed for a total of 3 years.

Number awarded: Varies each year; recently, 18 of these scholarships, with a value of $30,950, were awarded.

Deadline: February of each year.

301 $ GRAEME CLARK SCHOLARSHIPS

Cochlear Americas
Attn: Scholarships
13059 East Peakview Avenue
Centennial, CO 80111
Phone: (303) 790–9010; (800) 523–5798; Fax: (303) 790–1157;
Email: Recipients@Cochlear.com
Web: www.cochlearamericas.com/support/168.asp

Summary: To provide financial assistance for college to students who have received a cochlear nucleus implant.

Eligibility: Open to graduating high school seniors, current university students, and older students who have been accepted into a university course. Applicants must have received a cochlear nucleus implant. They must have a GPA of 2.5 or higher. Along with their application, they must submit a 1,000–word personal statement on their academic aspirations and other interests, including why they chose their proposed area of study, their postgraduate aspirations, their definition of success, and why they wish to receive this scholarship. Selection is based on academic achievement and demonstrated commitment to the ideals of leadership and humanity.

Financial data: The stipend is $2,000 per year.

Duration: 1 year; may be renewed up to 3 additional years, provided the recipient maintains a GPA of 2.5 or higher.

Number awarded: Varies each year; recently, 5 of these scholarships were awarded.

Deadline: October of each year.

302 $ GRANVILLE P. MEADE SCHOLARSHIPS

Virginia Department of Education
Attn: CTE Resource Center
2002 Bremo Road, Lower Level
Richmond, VA 23226
Phone: (804) 225–3370;
Email: Joseph.Whartt@doe.virginia.gov
Web: www.doe.virginia.gov

Summary: To provide financial assistance to needy high school seniors in Virginia who are interested in attending college in the state.

Eligibility: Open to Virginia high school seniors who have achieved academically but who are financially unable to attend college without assistance. Applicants must be interested in attending a public or private college or university in the state. They must submit their application for this scholarship to their high school principal. The principals forward the applications to their division superintendent. Each division superintendent selects the 5 most qualified applicants and submits those applications to the regional chairs, who then submit their 5 best applications to the Virginia Department of Education. Home–schooled and private school students are also eligible to compete; they should submit their applications to the department directly. Selection is based on financial need and academic record.

Financial data: The stipend is $2,000 per year.

Duration: 4 years, provided the recipient maintains at least a 2.5 GPA and attends school full time.

Number awarded: 1 or more each year.

Deadline: February of each year.

303 $$ GUARDIAN SCHOLARSHIPS

Workforce Safety & Insurance
1600 East Century Avenue, Suite 1
P.O. Box 5585
Bismarck, ND 58506–5585
Phone: (701) 328–5936; (800) 440–3796; Fax: (701) 328–3820; TDD: (800) 366–6888;
Email: ndwsi@nd.gov
Web: www.workforcesafety.com/workers/typesofbenefits.asp

Summary: To provide financial assistance for college to children and spouses of workers who died in work–related accidents in North Dakota.

Eligibility: Open to spouses and dependent children of workers who lost their lives in work–related accidents in North Dakota. Applicants must be attending or planning to attend an accredited college, university, or technical school.

Financial data: The maximum stipend is $10,000 per year.

Duration: 1 year; may be renewed up to 4 additional years.

Number awarded: Varies each year; recently, 32 of these scholarships were awarded.

Deadline: Deadline not specified.

304 $$ GUILDSCHOLAR PROGRAM

Jewish Guild for the Blind
Attn: GuildScholar Program
15 West 65th Street
New York, NY 10023
Phone: (212) 769–7801; (800) 284–4422; Fax: (212) 769–6266;
Email: guildscholar@jgb.org
Web: www.jgb.org/guildscholar.asp?GS=TRue

Summary: To provide financial assistance for college to blind high school seniors.

Eligibility: Open to college–bound high school seniors who can document legal blindness. Applicants must submit copies of school transcripts and SAT or ACT scores, proof of U.S. citizenship, 3 letters of recommendation, proof of legal blindness, a 500–word personal statement describing their educational and personal goals, a 500–word essay describing the influence of an outstanding teacher on their education, and documentation of financial need (if they wish that to be considered in the selection process).

Financial data: The stipend ranges up to $15,000.

Duration: 1 year.

Number awarded: 12 to 16 each year.

Deadline: June of each year (the end of the junior year of high school).

305 $ GUTHRIE–KOCH PKU SCHOLARSHIP

National PKU News
6869 Woodlawn Avenue, N.E., Suite 116
Seattle, WA 98115–5469
Phone: (206) 525–8140; Fax: (206) 525–5023;
Email: schuett@pkunews.org
Web: www.pkunews.org/guthrie/guthrie.htm

Summary: To provide financial assistance for college to students with phenylketonuria (PKU).

Eligibility: Open to college–age people from any country who have PKU and are on the required diet. Applicants must be accepted as an undergraduate at an accredited college or technical school before the scholarship is awarded, but they may apply before acceptance is confirmed. Along with their application, they must submit a statement that includes why they are applying for the scholarship, educational objectives and career plans, school and community activities, honors and awards, work history, current diet and how they cope with it on a daily basis, overall experience with PKU, attitudes toward the PKU diet now and in the past, and the influence PKU has had on their life. Selection is based on that statement, academic record, educational and career goals, extracurricular activities, volunteer work, and letters of recommendation. Financial need is considered but is not required; students can be awarded a scholarship without having significant financial need.

Financial data: Stipends vary but recently have been $2,000.

Duration: 1 year.

Number awarded: Varies each year; recently, 6 of these scholarships were awarded.

Deadline: October of each year.

306 HACER SCHOLARSHIP PROGRAM

Ronald McDonald House Charities
Attn: U.S. Scholarship Program
One Kroc Drive
Oak Brook, IL 60523

Phone: (630) 623–7048; Fax: (630) 623–7488;
Email: info@rmhc.org
Web: rmhc.org/what–we–do/rmhc–u–s–scholarships

Summary: To provide financial assistance for college to Hispanic high school seniors in specified geographic areas.

Eligibility: Open to high school seniors in designated McDonald's market areas who are legal residents of the United States and have at least 1 parent of Hispanic heritage. Applicants must be planning to enroll full time at an accredited 2– or 4–year college, university, or vocational/technical school. They must have a GPA of 2.7 or higher. Along with their application, they must submit a personal statement, up to 2 pages in length, on their Hispanic background, career goals, and desire to contribute to their community; information about unique, personal, or financial circumstances may be added. Selection is based on that statement, high school transcripts, a letter of recommendation, and financial need.

Financial data: Most awards are $1,000 per year. Funds are paid directly to the recipient's school.

Duration: 1 year; nonrenewable.

Number awarded: Varies each year; since RMHC began this program, it has awarded more than $44 million in scholarships.

Deadline: January of each year.

307 HALL/MCELWAIN MERIT SCHOLARSHIPS

Boy Scouts of America
Attn: National Eagle Scout Association, S322
1325 West Walnut Hill Lane
P.O. Box 152079
Irving, TX 75015–2079
Phone: (972) 580–2431
Web: nesa.org/scholarships.html

Summary: To provide financial assistance for college to Eagle Scouts.

Eligibility: Open to Eagle Scouts who are graduating high school seniors or currently–enrolled college freshmen, sophomores, or juniors. Applicants must be able to demonstrate leadership ability in Scouting and a strong record of participation in activities outside of Scouting. Financial need is not considered.

Financial data: The stipend is $1,000. Awards may be used only for tuition, room, board, and books.

Duration: 1 year; nonrenewable.

Number awarded: Varies each year; recently, 84 of these scholarships (21 in each region) were awarded.

Deadline: January of each year.

308 $$ HANA SCHOLARSHIPS

United Methodist Church
Attn: General Board of Higher Education and Ministry
Office of Loans and Scholarships
1001 19th Avenue South
P.O. Box 340007
Nashville, TN 37203–0007
Phone: (615) 340–7344; Fax: (615) 340–7367;
Email: umscholar@gbhem.org
Web: www.gbhem.org

Summary: To provide financial assistance to upper–division and graduate Methodist students who are of Hispanic, Asian, Native American, or Pacific Islander ancestry.

Eligibility: Open to full–time juniors, seniors, and graduate students at accredited colleges and universities in the United States who have been active, full members of a United Methodist Church (UMC) for at least 1 year prior to applying. Applicants must have at least 1 parent who is Hispanic, Asian, Native American, or Pacific Islander. They must be able to demonstrate involvement in their Hispanic, Asian, or Native American (HANA) community in the UMC. Selection is based on that involvement, academic ability (GPA of at least 2.85), and financial need. U.S. citizenship or permanent resident status is required.

Financial data: The maximum stipend is $3,000 for undergraduates or $5,000 for graduate students.

Duration: 1 year; recipients may reapply.

Number awarded: 50 each year.

Deadline: February of each year.

309 HAPA COLLEGIATE SCHOLARSHIPS

Honolulu Alumnae Panhellenic Association
Attn: Vice President Scholarship
94–253 Hokulewa Loop
Mililani, HI 96789
Email: hapascholarship@earthlink.net
Web: www.greekhawaii.com/HAPA/hawaiiaphscholarships.htm

Summary: To provide financial assistance to female college student from Hawaii who are members of a National Panhellenic Conference (NPC) sorority.

Eligibility: Open to women who are initiated and active members of an NPC–affiliated sorority at a college or university where they are working on an undergraduate degree. Their permanent home address or college address must be in Hawaii. Along with their application, they must submit 1) a brief essay on the part sorority membership has played in their life and why they feel this scholarship will benefit their future goals; 2) a list of all school, sorority, and community activities and offices; and 3) letters of recommendation from a professor, sorority officer, and another person in the community. Financial need is not considered in the selection process.

Financial data: A stipend is awarded (amount not specified).

Duration: 1 year.

Number awarded: 1 or more each year.

Deadline: March of each year.

310 HAPA HIGH SCHOOL SCHOLARSHIPS

Honolulu Alumnae Panhellenic Association
Attn: Vice President Scholarship
94–253 Hokulewa Loop
Mililani, HI 96789
Email: hapascholarship@earthlink.net
Web: www.greekhawaii.com/HAPA/hawaiiaphscholarships.htm

Summary: To provide financial assistance to female high school seniors in Hawaii who are interested in going to a college with National Panhellenic Conference (NPC) sororities on campus.

Eligibility: Open to females graduating from high schools in Hawaii. Applicants must be interested in attending 1 of the more than 500 colleges and universities with NPC sororities. Along with their application, they must submit 1) a brief essay on the expectations they have of becoming part of a sorority and the qualities they can bring to the sisterhood; 2) SAT and/or ACT scores; 3) a list of all class and school offices, other offices and responsibilities, school and athletic activities, extracurricular and community activities, honors, and awards; and 4) letters of recommendation from their high school senior counselor and another person in the community. Financial need is also considered in the selection process, but the program gives priority to well–rounded students who have balanced scholastics with school and/or community activities. Interviews are included.

Financial data: A stipend is awarded (amount not specified).

Duration: 1 year.

Number awarded: 1 or more each year.

Deadline: February of each year.

311 $ HAPPY CHANDLER FOUNDATION SCHOLARSHIPS

Happy Chandler Scholarship Foundation
Attn: Executive Director
1718 Alexandria Drive, Suite 203
P.O. Box 8393
Lexington, KY 40533–8393
Phone: (859) 278–5550; Fax: (859) 276–2090;
Email: Info@KyFutureLeaders.org
Web: www.kyfutureleaders.org/scholarships.php

Summary: To provide financial assistance to Kentucky high school seniors who are interested in attending college in the state.

Eligibility: Open to seniors graduating from high schools in Kentucky who have a GPA of 3.0 or higher or an ACT score of 25 or higher. Applicants must be planning to enroll full time at a college or university in Kentucky. Along with their application, they must submit a 500–word essay on their professional plans after college. Financial need is not considered in the selection process. U.S. citizenship is required.

Financial data: The stipend is $4,000 per year. Funds are paid directly to the recipient's college or university.

Duration: 1 year; may be renewed up to 3 additional years.

Number awarded: 3 each year.

Deadline: February of each year.

312 HARD OF HEARING OR DEAF STUDENTS SCHOLARSHIPS

Sertoma International
Attn: Director of Finance and Administration
1912 East Meyer Boulevard

Kansas City, MO 64132–1174
Phone: (816) 333–8300, ext. 214; Fax: (816) 333–4320; TDD: (816) 333–8300;
Email: infosertoma@sertomahq.org
Web: www.sertoma.org/Scholarships

Summary: To provide financial assistance for college to hearing impaired students.

Eligibility: Open to students who have a minimum 40dB bilateral hearing loss and are interested in working full time on a bachelor's degree at a 4–year college or university in the United States. Students working on a graduate degree, community college degree, associate degree, or vocational program degree are ineligible. Applicants must have a GPA of 3.2 or higher. Along with their application, they must submit a statement of purpose on how this scholarship will help them achieve their goals. U.S. citizenship is required. Selection is based on academic achievement, honors and awards received, community volunteer activities, interscholastic activities, extracurricular activities, and 2 letters of recommendation.

Financial data: The stipend is $1,000 per year.

Duration: 1 year; may be renewed up to 4 times.

Number awarded: 20 each year.

Deadline: April of each year.

313 HARVEY SIMON MEMORIAL SCHOLARSHIP

The Simon Cancer Foundation
P.O. Box 25093
Tamarac, FL 33320
Phone: (954) 288–8455;
Email: thescf@gmail.com
Web: www.thescf.org/Scholarships.html

Summary: To provide financial assistance to cancer patients and survivors who are currently attending college.

Eligibility: Open to cancer patients and survivors who are currently enrolled at a 4–year college or university. Applicants must have a GPA of 3.0 or higher and a record of strong leadership and community service.

Financial data: The stipend is $1,000.

Duration: 1 year; nonrenewable.

Number awarded: Varies each year; recently, 5 of these scholarships were awarded.

Deadline: January of each year.

314 $ HATHAWAY SCHOLARSHIPS

Wyoming Department of Education
Attn: School Improvement Unit
2020 Grand Avenue, Suite 500
Laramie, WY 82070
Phone: (307) 721–1905; Fax: (307) 777–6719;
Email: smoore@educ.state.wy.us
Web: www.hathawayscholarships.com

Summary: To provide financial assistance to high school seniors in Wyoming who plan to attend a public college or university in the state.

Eligibility: Open to graduating seniors and recent graduates of high schools in Wyoming who plan to attend the University of Wyoming or a community college in the state. U.S. citizenship is required. Applicants may qualify for 4 levels of support: 1) honors, for students with a GPA of 3.5 or higher and a minimum ACT score of 25 (or GED of 575); 2) performance, for students with a GPA of 3.0 or higher and a minimum ACT score of 21 (or GED of 540); 3) opportunity, for students with a GPA of 2.5 or higher and a minimum ACT score of 19 (or GED of 500); or 4) provisional opportunity, for students entering community colleges with a GPA of 2.5 or higher and a minimum ACT of 17, GED of 500, or WorkKeys of 12. Honors and performance scholarships also require that students have completed prescribed advanced courses in science, mathematics, social studies, and foreign languages. Applicants who can demonstrate financial need receive additional assistance.

Financial data: Honors students receive $1,600 per semester or, if they demonstrate financial need, 100% of annual unmet need plus $100 per semester. Performance students receive $1,200 per semester plus, if they demonstrate financial need, 25% of annual unmet need (to a maximum of an additional $750 per semester) plus $100 per semester. Opportunity and provisional opportunity students receive $800 per semester plus, if they demonstrate financial need, 25% of annual unmet need (to a maximum of an additional $750 per semester) plus $100 per semester. Part–time students receive proportional awards.

Duration: Up to 8 full–time semesters or part–time equivalent. Honors and performance recipients must maintain a GPA of 2.5 or higher. Opportunity and provisional opportunity recipients must maintain a GPA of 2.25 or higher.

Number awarded: Varies each year; recently, a total of 2,519 of these scholarships were awarded, including 548 at the honors level, 919 at the performance level, 683 at the opportunity level, and 369 at the provisional opportunity level.

Deadline: Deadline not specified.

315 $ HATTIE TEDROW MEMORIAL FUND SCHOLARSHIP

American Legion
Department of North Dakota
405 West Main Street, Suite 4A
P.O. Box 5057
West Fargo, ND 58078
Phone: (701) 293–3120; Fax: (701) 293–9951;
Email: Programs@ndlegion.org
Web: www.ndlegion.org/children_youth.html

Summary: To provide financial assistance to high school seniors in North Dakota who are direct descendants of veterans and interested in attending college in any state.

Eligibility: Open to seniors graduating from high schools in North Dakota and planning to attend a college, university, trade school, or technical school in any state. Applicants must be the children, grandchildren, or great–grandchildren of veterans who served honorably in the U.S. armed forces. Along with their application, they must submit a 500–word essay on why they should receive this scholarship. Selection is based on the essay and academic performance; financial need is not considered.

Financial data: The stipend is $2,000.

Duration: 1 year; nonrenewable.

Number awarded: 1 each year.

Deadline: April of each year.

316 $ HAWAII HIGH SCHOOL HALL OF HONOR SCHOLARSHIPS

Hawaii High School Athletic Association
P.O. Box 62029
Honolulu, Hawaii 96839
Phone: (808) 587–4495
Web: www.sportshigh.com/resources/scholarship/hall_of_honor

Summary: To provide financial assistance to high school seniors in Hawaii who have participated in athletics and plan to attend college in any state.

Eligibility: Open to seniors graduating from high schools in Hawaii who have participated in a sport approved by the Hawaii High School Athletic Association. Coaches, athletic directors, other school personnel, or anyone else in a position to recognize outstanding high school athletes may submit the names of selection committee members for consideration; those committee members may then nominate students for these scholarships. Nominees must be planning to attend a college or university in any state. Selection is based primarily on athletic achievement; other factors considered include contributions to the team, versatility in sports, character and behavior on and off the playing field, sportsmanship and dedication, character and behavior on and off the playing field or court, academic achievement, role in school activities outside sports, and involvement in the community.

Financial data: The stipend is $2,000.

Duration: 1 year.

Number awarded: 12 each year.

Deadline: April of each year.

317 HAZEL KNAPP ENDOWMENT SCHOLARSHIP

Epsilon Sigma Alpha International
Attn: ESA Foundation
363 West Drake Road
Fort Collins, CO 80526
Phone: (970) 223–2824; Fax: (970) 223–4456;
Email: esainfo@epsilonsigmaalpha.org
Web: www.epsilonsigmaalpha.org/esa–foundation/scholarships

Summary: To provide financial assistance to residents of Oregon planning to attend college in any state.

Eligibility: Open to residents of Oregon who are 1) graduating high school seniors with a GPA of 3.0 or higher or with minimum scores of 22 on the ACT or 1030 on the combined critical reading and mathematics SAT; 2) enrolled in college with a GPA of 3.0 or higher; 3) enrolled at a technical school or returning to school after an absence for retraining of job skills or obtaining a degree; or 4) engaged in online study through an accredited college, university, or vocational school. Applicants may be attending or planning to attend a school in any state

and major in any field. Selection is based on character (10%), leadership (20%), service (10%), financial need (30%), and scholastic ability (30%).
Financial data: The stipend is $1,000.
Duration: 1 year; may be renewed.
Number awarded: 1 each year.
Deadline: January of each year.

318 HBCUCONNECT MEMBER SCHOLARSHIPS

HBCUConnect.com, LLC.
Attn: Scholarship Administrator
750 Cross Pointe Road, Suite Q
Columbus, OH 43230
Phone: (877) 864–4446;
Email: culpepper@hbcuconnect.com
Web: hbcuconnect.com/scholarships/1998/hbcu–connect–member–scholarship
Summary: To provide financial assistance to underrepresented minority students attending or planning to attend an Historically Black College or University (HBCU).
Eligibility: Open to high school seniors and current full–time college students who are members of an underrepresented minority group (African American, Hispanic American, Native American). Applicants must be attending or interested in attending an HBCU to work on a 4–year degree. Along with their application, they must submit a 350–word essay on why they chose to attend an HBCU. Selection is based on quality of content in their online registration with HBCUConnect and financial need.
Financial data: The stipend is $1,000.
Duration: 1 year.
Number awarded: Up to 4 each year.
Deadline: May of each year.

319 HEATHER JOY MEMORIAL SCHOLARSHIP

The Resource Center
16362 Wilson Boulevard
Masaryktown, FL 34604–7335
Phone: (352) 799–1381;
Email: dblaha@innet.com
Summary: To provide financial assistance for college to students, regardless of their GPA or financial need.
Eligibility: Open to students currently enrolled or planning to enroll in college. Along with their application, they must submit a 250–word essay on why they should be selected. GPA and financial need are not considered in the selection process.
Financial data: The stipend is $1,000.
Duration: 1 year.
Number awarded: 2 each year: 1 in spring and 1 in fall.
Deadline: April of each year for fall; October of each year for spring.

320 $ HEBREW IMMIGRANT AID SOCIETY SCHOLARSHIPS

Hebrew Immigrant Aid Society
Attn: Scholarship Department
333 Seventh Avenue, 16th Floor
New York, NY 10001–5004
Phone: (212) 613–1358; Fax: (212) 967–4483;
Email: scholarship@hias.org
Web: us.hias.org/en/pages/scholarships
Summary: To provide financial assistance for educational purposes to Jewish refugees and asylees.
Eligibility: Open to Jewish refugees and asylees who arrived in the United States after January 1, 1992 and who have attended high school, college, or graduate school in the United States for at least 1 year. Applicants must have been assisted by the Hebrew Immigrant Aid Society (HIAS). They may be either high school seniors planning to pursue postsecondary education or students already enrolled in college or graduate school. Previous recipients are not eligible to apply. Selection is based on academic excellence, financial need, and Jewish community service.
Financial data: The stipend is $4,000.
Duration: 1 year; nonrenewable.
Number awarded: Varies each year; recently, 60 of these scholarships were awarded.
Deadline: March of each year.

321 HELEN KLIMEK STUDENT SCHOLARSHIP

American Legion Auxiliary
Department of New York
112 State Street, Suite 1310
Albany, NY 12207
Phone: (518) 463–1162; (800) 421–6348; Fax: (518) 449–5406;
Email: alanyterry@nycap.rr.com
Web: www.deptny.org/Scholarships.htm
Summary: To provide financial assistance to New York residents who are the descendants of veterans and interested in attending college in any state.
Eligibility: Open to residents of New York who are high school seniors or graduates and attending or planning to attend an accredited college or university in any state. Applicants must be the children, grandchildren, or great–grandchildren of veterans who served during specified periods of wartime. Along with their application they must submit a 700–word statement on the significance or value of volunteerism as a resource towards the positive development of their personal and professional future. Selection is based on character (20%), Americanism (15%), volunteer involvement (20%), leadership (15%), scholarship (15%), and financial need (15%). U.S. citizenship is required.
Financial data: The stipend is $1,000. Funds are paid directly to the recipient's school.
Duration: 1 year.
Number awarded: 1 each year.
Deadline: February of each year.

322 HELLENIC TIMES SCHOLARSHIPS

Hellenic Times Scholarship Fund
Attn: Nick Katsoris
823 11th Avenue, Fifth Floor
New York, NY 10019–3535
Phone: (212) 986–6881; Fax: (212) 977–3662;
Email: HTSFund@aol.com
Web: www.htsfund.org/guidelines.html
Summary: To provide financial assistance to undergraduate or graduate students of Greek descent.
Eligibility: Open to undergraduate and graduate students of Greek descent who are between 17 and 25 years of age and enrolled at an accredited college or university. Students who are receiving other financial aid that exceeds 50% of their annual tuition are ineligible. Selection is based on need and merit.
Financial data: A stipend is awarded (amount not specified).
Number awarded: Varies; approximately $100,000 is available for this program each year.
Deadline: February of each year.

323 HELPING HANDS BOOK SCHOLARSHIP PROGRAM

Helping Hands Foundation
Attn: Scholarship Director
4480–H South Cobb Drive
PMB 435
Smyrna, GA 30080
Summary: To provide high school seniors, undergraduates, and graduate students with funds to purchase textbooks and other study materials.
Eligibility: Open to students who are 16 years of age or older and who are planning to attend or are currently attending a 2– or 4–year college, university, or vocational/technical institute. Applicants must be enrolled as a high school, college, or graduate student in the United States, Canada, or Mexico. Along with their application, they must submit a 500–word essay describing their educational plans as they relate to their career objectives and why they feel this scholarship will help them achieve those goals. Selection is based on academic record and career potential.
Financial data: Stipends range from $100 to $1,000 per semester. Funds are intended to be used to purchase textbooks and study materials. Checks are sent directly to the recipient.
Duration: These are 1–time nonrenewable awards.
Number awarded: Up to 50 each year.
Deadline: July of each year for fall semester; December of each year for spring semester.

324 HEMOPHILIA FEDERATION OF AMERICA EDUCATIONAL SCHOLARSHIPS

Hemophilia Federation of America
Attn: Scholarship Committee
210 Seventh Street, S.E., Suite 200B
Washington, DC 20003
Phone: (202) 675–6984; (800) 230–9797; Fax: (202) 675–6983;
Email: info@hemophiliafed.org
Web: hemophiliafed.org

Summary: To provide financial assistance for college to students who have a blood clotting disorder.

Eligibility: Open to high school seniors and current college students who have a blood clotting disorder. Applicants must be attending or planning to attend an accredited 2– or 4–year college, university, or trade school in the United States. Along with their application, they must submit a 1–page essay on their goals and aspirations and how the blood clotting community has played a part in their lives. Financial need is also considered in the selection process.

Financial data: The stipend is $1,500 per year.

Duration: 1 year; may be renewed.

Number awarded: 6 each year.

Deadline: April of each year.

325 $ HEMOPHILIA FOUNDATION OF MINNESOTA/DAKOTAS SCHOLARSHIPS

Hemophilia Foundation of Minnesota/Dakotas
Attn: Scholarship Program
750 South Plaza Drive, Suite 207
Mendota Heights, MN 55120
Phone: (651) 406–8655; (800) 994–HFMD; Fax: (651) 406–8656;
Email: hemophiliafound@visi.com
Web: www.hfmd.org/Scholarships/Scholarships.html

Summary: To provide financial assistance to residents of Minnesota, North Dakota, and South Dakota who have a bleeding disorder and are interested in attending college in any state.

Eligibility: Open to residents of Minnesota, North Dakota, and South Dakota who have an inherited bleeding disorder and/or are patients at a hemophilia treatment center in those states. Applicants must be participating in programs and services of the Hemophilia Foundation of Minnesota/Dakotas. They must be attending or planning to attend a college or university in any state. Financial need is considered in the selection process.

Financial data: The stipend is $1,000. Funds are paid to the academic institution.

Duration: 1 year.

Number awarded: 10 each year.

Deadline: May of each year.

326 HEMOPHILIA HEALTH SERVICES MEMORIAL SCHOLARSHIPS

Accredo's Hemophilia Health Services
Attn: Scholarship Committee
201 Great Circle Road
Nashville, TN 37228
Phone: (615) 850–5210; (800) 800–6606; Fax: (615) 261–6730;
Email: lisa.dabrowiak@accredo.com
Web: www.hemophiliahealth.com/Scholarships.html

Summary: To provide financial assistance for college or graduate school to people who have hemophilia or other bleeding disorders.

Eligibility: Open to individuals with hemophilia (factor VIII or IX), von Willebrand Disease (type 1, 2, 2A, 2B, 2M, 2N, or 3), factor I (fibrinogen), factor II (prothrombin), factor V (proaccelerin), factor VII (proconvertin), factor X, factor XI, factor XIII, or Glanzmann's thrombasthenia. Applicants must be 1) high school seniors; 2) college freshmen, sophomores, or juniors; or 3) college seniors planning to attend graduate school or students already enrolled in graduate school. Applicants must be enrolled or planning to enroll full time at an accredited nonprofit college, university, or vocational/technical school in the United States or Puerto Rico. Along with their application, they must submit an essay, up to 250 words, on the following topic: "What has been your own personal challenge in living with a bleeding disorder?" U.S. citizenship is required. Selection is based on the essay, academic achievements and records, community involvement, and financial need.

Financial data: The stipend is at least $1,500. Funds are issued payable to the recipient's school.

Duration: 1 year; recipients may reapply.

Number awarded: Several each year.

Deadline: April of each year.

327 HERB KOHL EDUCATIONAL FOUNDATION INITIATIVE SCHOLARSHIPS

Herb Kohl Educational Foundation, Inc.
Attn: Kim Marggraf
P.O. Box 877
Sheboygan, WI 53082–0877
Phone: (920) 457–1727;
Email: marggraf@excel.net
Web: www.kohleducation.org/aboutus

Summary: To provide financial assistance to Wisconsin high school seniors who are unlikely to be eligible for other academic–based scholarships and plan to attend college in any state.

Eligibility: Open to seniors graduating from designated high schools in Wisconsin and planning to attend college in any state. Students should 1) be unlikely to be eligible for other academic–based scholarships; 2) have achieved an academic record that represents their maximum effort; 3) have shown strong promise of succeeding in college and beyond; 4) have demonstrated a high level of motivation to achieve; and 5) may have overcome significant personal obstacles or adversity. Recipients are selected by their teachers and school administrators.

Financial data: The stipend is $1,000. Funds may be used to pay for tuition and fees during the first year of college only and are paid directly to the recipient's postsecondary institution.

Duration: 1 year (the first year of college); nonrenewable.

Number awarded: Each year, the foundation designates approximately 85 high schools throughout Wisconsin to select a recipient. Since the program was established, it has awarded nearly 1,200 scholarships.

Deadline: January of each year.

328 $ HERBERT LEHMAN EDUCATION FUND

NAACP Legal Defense and Educational Fund
Attn: Director of Scholarship Programs
99 Hudson Street, Suite 1600
New York, NY 10013–2897
Phone: (212) 965–2265; Fax: (212) 219–1595;
Email: scholarships@naacpldf.org
Web: www.naacpldf.org/scholarships

Summary: To provide financial assistance for college to high school seniors and recent graduates who are committed to civil rights.

Eligibility: Open to high school seniors, high school graduates, and college freshmen attending or planning to attend 4–year colleges and universities. Applicants must be dedicated to advancing the cause of civil rights, excel academically, show exceptional leadership potential, and have made an impact on their communities through service to others. They must also be able to demonstrate financial need.

Financial data: The stipend is $2,000 per year.

Duration: 1 year; may be renewed for up to 3 additional years if the student remains enrolled full time, maintains good academic standing, and fulfills all program requirements.

Number awarded: Varies each year; recently, a total of 79 new and renewal scholarships were awarded.

Deadline: March of each year.

329 $$ HERFF JONES PRINCIPAL'S LEADERSHIP AWARDS

National Association of Secondary School Principals
Attn: Department of Student Programs
1904 Association Drive
Reston, VA 20191–1537
Phone: (703) 860–7242; (800) 253–7746, ext. 242; Fax: (703) 476–5432;
Email: carrollw@principals.org
Web: www.principals.org/Awards–and–Recognition/Student–Awards

Summary: To recognize and reward, with college scholarships, high school seniors who demonstrate outstanding leadership.

Eligibility: Open to high school seniors. Each principal of a public, private, or parochial high school in all 50 states, the District of Columbia, the U.S. Virgin Islands, or Puerto Rico may nominate 1 student leader from the top 20% of the senior class. Nominees must submit an original essay. Selection is based primarily on leadership qualities, as judged by participation in service organizations and clubs, achievements in the arts and sciences, employment experience, and academic record. U.S. citizenship is not required.

Financial data: Stipends range from $1,000 to $12,000.

Duration: The awards are presented annually.

Number awarded: 100 each year: the national winner at $12,000, the national finalist at $8,500, the national semifinalist at $5,000, 5 regional winners at $1,500 each, and 92 other winners at $1,000 each.
Deadline: Principals must submit their nomination by December of each year.

330 $ HERITAGE SCHOLARSHIP AWARDS

Grand Lodge of Minnesota, A.F. & A.M.
Attn: Minnesota Masonic Charities
11501 Masonic Home Drive
Bloomington, MN 55437–3699
Phone: (952) 948–6004; (800) 245–6050 (within MN); Fax: (952) 948–6710;
Email: grandlodge@qwest.net
Web: www.mn–masons.org/masonic–programs/scholarships
Summary: To provide financial assistance to high school seniors in Minnesota who plan to attend college in any state.
Eligibility: Open to seniors graduating from high schools in Minnesota and planning to attend college in any state. Applicants must have a GPA between 3.0 and 3.79. Selection is based on academic and personal achievement, community participation or service, and overall excellence. No consideration is given to age, gender, religion, national origin, or Masonic affiliation.
Financial data: The stipend is $2,500 per year.
Duration: 1 year; may be renewed up to 3 additional years.
Number awarded: 10 each year.
Deadline: February of each year.

331 HEROES LEGACY SCHOLARSHIPS

Fisher House Foundation
111 Rockville Pike, Suite 420
Rockville, MD 20850
Phone: (888) 294–8560;
Email: bgawne@fisherhouse.org
Web: www.militaryscholar.org/legacy/index.html
Summary: To provide financial assistance for college to the children of deceased and disabled veterans and military personnel.
Eligibility: Open to the unmarried sons and daughters of U.S. military servicemembers (including active duty, retirees, Guard/Reserves, and survivors) who are high school seniors or full–time freshmen at an accredited college, university, or community college and younger than 23 years of age. Applicants must have at least 1 parent who, while serving on active duty after September 11, 2001, either died or became disabled, defined as qualified for receipt of Traumatic Servicemembers Group Life Insurance (TSGLI) or rated as 100% permanently and totally disabled by the U.S. Department of Veterans Affairs. They must have a GPA of 2.5 or higher. Along with their application, they must submit a 500–word essay on a topic that changes annually; recently, students were asked to identify the 4 persons whose faces they would place on a 21st century Mount Rushmore type of monument and why. Selection is based on merit.
Financial data: A stipend is awarded (amount not specified).
Duration: 1 year.
Number awarded: Varies each year, depending on the availability of funds.
Deadline: March of each year.

332 $$ HEROES TRIBUTE SCHOLARSHIPS

Marine Corps Scholarship Foundation, Inc.
Attn: Scholarship Office
909 North Washington Street, Suite 400
Alexandria, VA 22314
Phone: (703) 549–0060; (866) 496–5462; Fax: (703) 549–9474;
Email: students@mcsf.org
Web: www.mcsf.org
Summary: To provide financial assistance for college to the children of Marines and Navy Corpsmen serving with the Marines who were killed on September 11, 2001 or in combat since that date.
Eligibility: Open to the children of 1) Marines and former Marines killed in the terrorist attacks on September 11, 2001; and 2) Marines and U.S. Navy Corpsmen serving with the Marines who were killed in combat since September 11, 2001. Applicants must be high school seniors, high school graduates, or current undergraduates in an accredited college, university, or post-secondary vocational/technical school. They must submit academic transcripts (GPA of 2.0 or higher), documentation of their parent's service, and a 500–word essay on a topic that changes periodically. Only undergraduate study is supported. There is no maximum family income limitation. All qualified applicants receive scholarships.
Financial data: The stipend is $7,500 per year.
Duration: 4 years.
Number awarded: Varies each year; recently, 4 of these scholarships were awarded.
Deadline: February of each year.

333 HICKAM OFFICERS' SPOUSES' CLUB SCHOLARSHIPS

Hickam Officers' Spouses' Club
Attn: Scholarship Chair
PMB 168
P.O. Box 30800
Honolulu, HI 96820–0800
Email: scholarships@hickamosc.com
Web: www.hickamosc.com
Summary: To provide financial assistance to dependents of current and former military personnel in Hawaii who are interested in attending college or graduate school in any state.
Eligibility: Open to dependents of 1 of the following: 1) active–duty military members permanently stationed in Hawaii; 2) active–duty military members on a remote assignment from Hawaii; 3) retired military members resident in Hawaii; 4) full–time Hawaii National Guard and U.S. military Reserve members residing in Hawaii; and 5) survivors of deceased military members residing in Hawaii. Applicants must be seniors graduating from a Hawaii high school or accredited home school program based in Hawaii and planning to enroll at an accredited 2– or 4–year college, university, or vocational/technical school in any state; dependent children currently working on an undergraduate or graduate degree at a college or university in any state; or spouses currently working on an undergraduate or graduate degree at a college or university in any state. High school seniors must submit a 1–page essay on their greatest challenge, how they overcame it, and what lessons they learned. Spouses and other continuing students must submit a 1–page essay on what it means to live passionately and how they demonstrate it in their daily life. Selection is based on the essay, academic ability, extracurricular activities and work experience, service activities and citizenship, and a letter of recommendation.
Financial data: A stipend is awarded (amount not specified).
Duration: 1 year.
Number awarded: 1 or more each year.
Deadline: March of each year.

334 $$ HISPANIC COLLEGE FUND/DARDEN FOUNDATION SCHOLARSHIP PROGRAM

Hispanic College Fund
Attn: Scholarship Processing
1300 L Street, N.W., Suite 975
Washington, DC 20005
Phone: (202) 296–5400; (800) 644–4223; Fax: (202) 296–3774;
Email: hcf–info@hispanicfund.org
Web: scholarships.hispanicfund.org/applications
Summary: To provide financial assistance to Hispanic American undergraduate and graduate students working on a degree in any field.
Eligibility: Open to U.S. citizens and permanent residents of Hispanic background (at least 1 grandparent must be 100% Hispanic) who are enrolled or planning to enroll full time at an accredited college or university in the 50 states or Puerto Rico. Applicants must have a GPA of 3.0 or higher and be able to demonstrate financial need. They may be interested in working on an undergraduate or graduate degree in any academic discipline. Preference is given to alumni and resident advisers of the Hispanic Youth Institute.
Financial data: Stipends range from $500 to $5,000, depending on need and academic achievement. Funds are paid directly to the recipient's college or university to help cover tuition and fees.
Duration: 1 year; recipients may reapply.
Number awarded: Varies each year.
Deadline: February of each year.

335 $$ HISPANIC SCHOLARSHIP FUND GENERAL COLLEGE SCHOLARSHIPS

Hispanic Scholarship Fund
Attn: Selection Committee
55 Second Street, Suite 1500
San Francisco, CA 94105
Phone: (415) 808–2300; (877) HSF–INFO; Fax: (415) 808–2301;
Email: scholar1@hsf.net
Web: www.hsf.net/innercontent.aspx?id=460

Summary: To provide financial assistance for college or graduate school to Hispanic American students.

Eligibility: Open to U.S. citizens and permanent residents (must have a permanent resident card or a passport stamped I–551). Applicants must be of Hispanic heritage and enrolled or planning to enroll full time in a degree program at an accredited community college, 4–year university, or graduate school in the United States, Puerto Rico, Guam, or the U.S. Virgin Islands. They must have a GPA of 3.0 or higher and have applied for federal financial aid. Selection is based on academic achievement, personal strengths, leadership, and financial need.

Financial data: Stipends normally range from $1,000 to $5,000 per year.

Duration: 1 year; recipients may reapply.

Number awarded: Varies each year; recently, this program awarded more than $28 million in scholarships to more than 4,400 students.

Deadline: December of each year.

336 $$ HMSA KAIMANA SCHOLARSHIPS

Hawaii High School Athletic Association
P.O. Box 62029
Honolulu, Hawaii 96839
Phone: (808) 587–4495
Web: www.sportshigh.com/resources/scholarship/kaimana_awards

Summary: To provide financial assistance to high school seniors in Hawaii who have participated in athletics and plan to attend college in any state.

Eligibility: Open to seniors graduating from high schools in Hawaii who have a GPA of 2.75 or higher. Applicants must have played on at least 1 school athletic team in a sport sanctioned by the Hawaii High School Athletic Association. They must be planning to attend a college or university in any state. Special consideration is given to student athletes in lower–profile sports. Selection is based on athletic and academic achievement, community involvement, sportsmanship, and letters of recommendation.

Financial data: The stipend is $3,000; recipients of distinguished scholarships receive an additional $2,000.

Duration: 1 year.

Number awarded: Varies each year; recently, 22 students received these scholarships, including 5 who received distinguished scholarships.

Deadline: February of each year.

337 $$ HOPE GRANTS FOR CERTIFICATE AND DIPLOMA PROGRAMS

Georgia Student Finance Commission
Attn: Scholarships and Grants Division
2082 East Exchange Place, Suite 200
Tucker, GA 30084–5305
Phone: (770) 724–9000; (800) 505–GSFC; Fax: (770) 724–9089;
Email: gacollege411@gsfc.org
Web: www.gacollege411.org

Summary: To provide financial assistance to residents of Georgia who are interested in earning a certificate or diploma at a public technical institute in the state.

Eligibility: Open to Georgia residents who are working on a certificate or diploma in a non–degree program of study at a public institution in the state. The certificate or degree program must be approved by the Technical College System of Georgia or be a comparable program approved by the Board of Regents of the University System of Georgia. Continuing education programs are not eligible. U.S. citizenship or eligible noncitizen status is required.

Financial data: These grants pay tuition and mandatory fees at public technical institutes in Georgia, along with a book allowance of up to $300 per year.

Duration: This assistance may be used for a total of 63 semester hours of study.

Number awarded: Varies each year; recently, 108,387 of these grants were awarded.

Deadline: Applications must be submitted on or before the last day of the academic term.

338 $ HOPE SCHOLARSHIPS FOR DEGREE–SEEKING STUDENTS

Georgia Student Finance Commission
Attn: Scholarships and Grants Division
2082 East Exchange Place, Suite 200
Tucker, GA 30084–5305
Phone: (770) 724–9000; (800) 505–GSFC; Fax: (770) 724–9089;
Email: gacollege411@gsfc.org
Web: www.gacollege411.org

Summary: To provide financial assistance to outstanding students who are attending or planning to attend a college or university in Georgia.

Eligibility: Open to residents of Georgia who are enrolled or planning to enroll at a college or university within the state. Students who are applying as seniors at eligible high schools or home schools must have at least a 3.0 cumulative GPA. Students who graduate from an ineligible high school or home study program may also be eligible if they 1) score in the national composite 85th percentile or higher on the SAT or ACT tests; and then 2) complete the first year of college with a GPA of 3.0 or higher. Students who are applying for the first time as college students must have earned a GPA of 3.0 or higher in college regardless of their high school GPA. U.S. citizenship or eligible noncitizen status is required.

Financial data: HOPE Scholars who attend University System of Georgia institutions receive stipends that vary by institution and number of units completed, to a maximum of $3,181 for full–time enrollment at designated universities. At institutions in the Technical College System of Georgia, the stipend is $911 per year. The stipend for HOPE Scholarships at private colleges and universities is $3,600 per year for full–time study or $1,800 per year for half–time study. Funds may be used only for tuition and mandatory fees.

Duration: 1 year; may be renewed for up to 3 additional years if the recipient maintains a cumulative GPA of 3.0 or higher in college.

Number awarded: Varies each year.

Deadline: Applications must be submitted on or before the last day of the academic term.

339 $$ HORATIO ALGER NATIONAL SCHOLARSHIP PROGRAM

Horatio Alger Association of Distinguished Americans, Inc.
99 Canal Center Plaza, Suite 320
Alexandria, VA 22314
Phone: (703) 684–9444; (866) 763–9228; Fax: (703) 548–3822
Web: www.horatioalger.org/scholarships/sp.cfm

Summary: To provide financial assistance for college to high school seniors who can demonstrate integrity and perseverance in overcoming adversity.

Eligibility: Open to seniors at high schools in all 50 states, the District of Columbia, and Puerto Rico. Applicants must be planning to enroll at a college in any state to work on a bachelor's degree (they may begin at a 2–year college and then transfer to a 4–year institution). They must be U.S. citizens, be able to demonstrate critical financial need ($50,000 or less adjusted gross income per family), have a GPA of 2.0 or higher, and have a record of involvement in co–curricular and community activities. Along with their application, they must submit information on the adversities they have encountered. Examples of adversity include having been in foster care or a ward of the state; having been homeless; experiencing the death, incarceration, or abandonment of a parent or guardian; living in a household where alcohol or drugs are or were abused; having a physical or mental disability or serious illness; or suffering from physical or mental abuse.

Financial data: The stipend is $5,000 per year.

Duration: 4 years.

Number awarded: 104 each year: 2 in each state, the District of Columbia, and Puerto Rico.

Deadline: October of each year.

340 $$ HORNSTEIN SCHOLARSHIP FUND

Central Scholarship Bureau
1700 Reisterstown Road, Suite 220
P.O. Box 37064
Baltimore, MD 21297–3064
Phone: (410) 415–5558; Fax: (410) 415–5501;
Email: contact@centralsb.org
Web: www.central–scholarship.org/scholarships

Summary: To provide financial assistance to residents of Maryland interested in working on an undergraduate or graduate degree at a college in any state.

Eligibility: Open to residents of Maryland who are enrolled or planning to enroll full time at a college, university, or vocational school in any state. Undergraduates and graduate students must have a cumulative GPA of 3.0 or higher; vocational students must have a cumulative GPA of 2.0 or higher. All applicants must have a family income less than $90,000 per year. Financial need is considered in the selection process. U.S. citizenship or permanent resident status is required.

Financial data: The stipend is $5,000.

Duration: 1 year.

Number awarded: 1 or more each year.

Deadline: May of each year.

341 HOVLAND SCHOLARSHIP

Sioux Falls Area Community Foundation
Attn: Scholarship Coordinator
300 North Phillips Avenue, Suite 102
Sioux Falls, SD 57104–6035
Phone: (605) 336–7055, ext. 20; Fax: (605) 336–0038;
Email: pgale@sfacf.org
Web: www.sfacf.org/ScholarshipDetails.aspx?CategoryID=6

Summary: To provide financial assistance to undergraduate students of Norwegian descent.

Eligibility: Open to students of Norwegian descent who are entering their junior year at an accredited college or university in any state. Applicants must have a cumulative GPA of 2.0 or higher and be able to demonstrate financial need. Along with their application, they must submit 500–word essays on 1) their educational and career goals; and 2) how Norwegian ancestry has enriched their life and how they intend to pass on their heritage.

Financial data: The stipend is $1,000. Funds are to be used for tuition, fees, and/or books.

Duration: 1 year; may be renewed by sophomores if they maintain a GPA of 2.5 or higher in their major and 2.0 or higher overall.

Number awarded: Varies each year.

Deadline: July of each year.

342 $ HOWARD P. RAWLINGS EDUCATIONAL ASSISTANCE GRANTS

Maryland Higher Education Commission
Attn: Office of Student Financial Assistance
6 North Liberty Street, Ground Suite
Baltimore, MD 21201
Phone: (410) 767–3300; (800) 974–0203; Fax: (410) 332–0250; TDD: (800) 735–2258;
Email: osfamail@mhec.state.md.us
Web: www.mhec.state.md.us/financialAid/descriptions.asp

Summary: To provide financial assistance to undergraduate students in Maryland.

Eligibility: Open to Maryland residents who are high school seniors or full–time undergraduates at Maryland 2– or 4–year colleges or universities. Applicants must be able to document financial need.

Financial data: At 4–year institutions, the amount of the grant equals 40% of the financial need as calculated by the Office of Students Financial Assistance (OSFA); at community colleges, the amount of the grant equals 60% of the financial need. Awards are limited to a minimum of $400 and a maximum of $3,000 per year. The total amount of all state awards may not exceed the cost of attendance as determined by the school's financial aid office or $19,000, whichever is less.

Duration: 1 year; recipients may reapply for up to 3 additional years if they maintain satisfactory academic progress and continue to demonstrate financial need.

Number awarded: Varies each year.

Deadline: February of each year.

343 $$ HOWARD P. RAWLINGS GUARANTEED ACCESS GRANTS

Maryland Higher Education Commission
Attn: Office of Student Financial Assistance
6 North Liberty Street, Ground Suite
Baltimore, MD 21201
Phone: (410) 767–3300; (800) 974–0203; Fax: (410) 332–0250; TDD: (800) 735–2258;
Email: osfamail@mhec.state.md.us
Web: www.mhec.state.md.us/financialAid/descriptions.asp

Summary: To provide financial assistance to needy undergraduate students in Maryland.

Eligibility: Open to seniors graduating from high schools in Maryland and planning to enroll as full–time undergraduate students in a program leading to a degree, diploma, or certificate at a 2– or 4–year college or university in the state. Applicants must have a high school GPA of 2.5 or higher and be able to demonstrate financial need. Currently, the maximum allowable total income is $14,157 for a family of 1, rising to $48,919 for a family of 8 plus $4,966 for each additional family member.

Financial data: Awards equal 100% of financial need, ranging from $400 to $15,500 per year. The total amount of all state awards may not exceed the cost of attendance as determined by the school's financial aid office or $19,000, whichever is less.

Duration: 1 year; recipients may reapply for up to 3 additional years if they maintain satisfactory academic progress and continue to demonstrate financial need.

Number awarded: Varies each year.

Deadline: February of each year.

344 HOWARD STILES NUCHOLS SCHOLARSHIP

United Daughters of the Confederacy–Virginia Division
c/o Barbara Joyner, Second Vice President
8219 Seaview Drive
Chesterfield, VA 23838–5163
Email: bobbielou–udc@comcast.net
Web: vaudc.org/gift.html

Summary: To provide financial assistance to Confederate descendants from Virginia who are interested in attending college in the state.

Eligibility: Open to residents of Virginia who are 1) lineal descendants of Confederates; or 2) collateral descendants and also members of the Children of the Confederacy or the United Daughters of the Confederacy (UDC). Applicants must submit proof of the Confederate military record of at least 1 ancestor, with the company and regiment in which he served. They must also submit a personal letter pledging to make the best possible use of the scholarship; describing their health, social, family, religious, and fraternal connections within the community; and reflecting on what a Southern heritage means to them (using the term "War Between the States" in lieu of "Civil War"). They must have a GPA of 3.0 or higher and be able to demonstrate financial need. Preference is given to applicants who are current or former members of the Virginia division of the Children of the Confederacy.

Financial data: The amount of the stipend depends on the availability of funds. Payment is made directly to the college or university the recipient attends.

Duration: 1 year; may be renewed up to 3 additional years if the recipient maintains a GPA of 3.0 or higher.

Number awarded: This scholarship is offered whenever a prior recipient graduates or is no longer eligible.

Deadline: April of the years in which the scholarship is available.

345 H.S. AND ANGELINE LEWIS SCHOLARSHIPS

American Legion Auxiliary
Department of Wisconsin
Attn: Education Chair
2930 American Legion Drive
P.O. Box 140
Portage, WI 53901–0140
Phone: (608) 745–0124; (866) 664–3863; Fax: (608) 745–1947;
Email: alawi@amlegionauxwi.org
Web: www.amlegionauxwi.org/Scholarships.htm

Summary: To provide financial assistance to Wisconsin residents who are related to veterans or members of the American Legion Auxiliary and interested in working on an undergraduate or graduate degree at a school in any state.

Eligibility: Open to the children, wives, and widows of veterans who are high school seniors or graduates and have a GPA of 3.5 or higher. Grandchildren and great–grandchildren of members of the American Legion Auxiliary are also eligible. Applicants must be residents of Wisconsin and interested in working on an undergraduate or graduate degree at a school in any state. Along with their application, they must submit a 300–word essay on "Education—An Investment in the Future." Financial need is considered in the selection process.

Financial data: The stipend is $1,000.

Duration: 1 year; nonrenewable.

Number awarded: 6 each year: 1 to a graduate student and 5 to undergraduates.

Deadline: March of each year.

346 HUMAN CAPITAL SCHOLARSHIPS

Asian Pacific Fund
Attn: Scholarship Coordinator
225 Bush Street, Suite 590
San Francisco, CA 94104

Phone: (415) 433–6859; (800) 286–1688; Fax: (415) 433–2425;
Email: scholarship@asianpacificfund.org
Web: www.asianpacificfund.org/information–for–student–applicants

Summary: To provide financial assistance to minority students enrolling at any campus of the University of California who are the first member of their family to attend college.

Eligibility: Open to members of minority groups (African American, Asian American, Latino American, or other underrepresented heritage) who are full–time incoming freshmen at a campus of the University of California. Applicants must be first–generation college students. They must have a GPA of 2.7 or higher and be able to demonstrate financial need. Preference is given to students planning to major in the liberal arts. Along with their application, they must submit essays of 250 to 500 words each on 1) their family background and the experiences or values that have led to their plans to become a college graduate; 2) a project, experience, or person related to their academic and career goals that inspired them; and 3) any unusual family or personal circumstances that have affected their achievement in school, work, or extracurricular activities.

Financial data: The stipend is $1,500.

Duration: 1 year; nonrenewable.

Number awarded: 2 each year.

Deadline: March of each year.

347 $ HUMBLE ARTESIAN CHAPTER ABWA SCHOLARSHIP GRANTS

American Business Women's Association–Humble Artesian Chapter
c/o Caroline Smith, Education Committee
1702 Baldsprings Trail
Kingwood, TX 77345–1997
Phone: (281) 360–6226;
Email: californiasmith@earthlink.net
Web: www.abwahumble.org/scholarships

Summary: To provide financial assistance to women from any state who have completed at least the sophomore year of college.

Eligibility: Open to all women who are U.S. citizens. Applicants must be enrolled as juniors, seniors, or graduate students at a college or university in any state and have a GPA of 2.5 or higher.

Financial data: The stipend is $2,000.

Duration: 1 year.

Number awarded: 1 each year.

Deadline: January of each year.

348 $ IDA M. CRAWFORD SCHOLARSHIP

Oregon Student Access Commission
Attn: Grants and Scholarships Division
1500 Valley River Drive, Suite 100
Eugene, OR 97401–2146
Phone: (541) 687–7395; (800) 452–8807, ext. 7395; Fax: (541) 687–7414; TDD: (800) 735–2900;
Email: awardinfo@osac.state.or.us
Web: www.oregonstudentaid.gov/scholarships.aspx

Summary: To provide financial assistance to graduates of Oregon high schools who plan to attend college in any state.

Eligibility: Open to graduates of accredited high schools in Oregon who are attending or planning to attend college in any state. Applicants must have a cumulative GPA of 3.5 or higher and be able to demonstrate financial need. They must submit documentation of birth within the continental United States. Students planning to study law, medicine, music, theology, or teaching are not eligible.

Financial data: Stipends for scholarships offered by the Oregon Student Access Commission (OSAC) range from $200 to $10,000 but recently averaged $2,300.

Duration: 1 year.

Number awarded: Varies each year; recently, 63 of these scholarships were awarded.

Deadline: February of each year.

349 $$ IDAHO FREEDOM SCHOLARSHIPS

Idaho State Board of Education
Len B. Jordan Office Building
650 West State Street, Room 307
P.O. Box 83720
Boise, ID 83720–0037
Phone: (208) 332–1574; Fax: (208) 334–2632;
Email: scholarshiphelp@osbe.idaho.gov
Web: www.boardofed.idaho.gov/scholarship/freedom.asp

Summary: To provide financial assistance for college to dependent children of Idaho veterans who are deceased or listed as prisoners of war or missing in action.

Eligibility: Open to dependent children of Idaho veterans who have been determined by the federal government to have been 1) killed in action or died of injuries or wounds sustained in action; 2) prisoners of war (POW); or 3) missing in action (MIA) in southeast Asia (including Korea) or any area of armed conflict in which the United States is a party.

Financial data: Each scholarship provides a full waiver of tuition and fees at public institutions of higher education or public vocational schools within Idaho, an allowance of $500 per semester for books, and on–campus housing and subsistence.

Duration: Benefits are available for a maximum of 36 months.

Number awarded: Varies each year.

Deadline: Deadline not specified.

350 $ IDAHO GOVERNOR'S CUP SCHOLARSHIP

Idaho State Board of Education
Len B. Jordan Office Building
650 West State Street, Room 307
P.O. Box 83720
Boise, ID 83720–0037
Phone: (208) 332–1574; Fax: (208) 334–2632;
Email: scholarshiphelp@osbe.idaho.gov
Web: www.boardofed.idaho.gov/scholarship/gov_cup.asp

Summary: To provide financial assistance to outstanding high school seniors in Idaho who wish to attend a postsecondary institution in the state.

Eligibility: Open to graduating high school seniors who are U.S. citizens, Idaho residents, and planning to enroll full time at an eligible postsecondary educational institution in the state. Applicants must have maintained a GPA of 2.8 or better, must take the ACT or SAT examinations if entering an academic program, and should have demonstrated a commitment to public service.

Financial data: The stipend is $3,000 per year.

Duration: 1 year; may be renewed for up to 3 additional years for academic programs or up to 2 years for professional and technical programs.

Number awarded: Varies each year; recently, 19 of these scholarships were awarded.

Deadline: January of each year.

351 $ IDAHO MINORITY AND "AT RISK" STUDENT SCHOLARSHIP

Idaho State Board of Education
Len B. Jordan Office Building
650 West State Street, Room 307
P.O. Box 83720
Boise, ID 83720–0037
Phone: (208) 332–1574; Fax: (208) 334–2632;
Email: scholarshiphelp@osbe.idaho.gov
Web: www.boardofed.idaho.gov/scholarship/minority.asp

Summary: To provide financial assistance to "at risk" high school seniors in Idaho who plan to attend college in the state.

Eligibility: Open to residents of Idaho who are graduates of high schools in the state. Applicants must meet at least 3 of the following 5 requirements: 1) have a disability; 2) be a member of an ethnic minority group historically underrepresented in higher education in Idaho (Native Americans, African Americans, Hispanic Americans); 3) have substantial financial need; 4) be a first–generation college student; 5) be a migrant farm worker or a dependent of a farm worker. U.S. citizenship is required.

Financial data: The maximum stipend is $3,000 per year.

Duration: 1 year; may be renewed for up to 3 additional years.

Number awarded: Approximately 40 each year.

Deadline: Deadline not specified.

352 IDAHO OPPORTUNITY SCHOLARSHIP

Idaho State Board of Education
Len B. Jordan Office Building
650 West State Street, Room 307
P.O. Box 83720
Boise, ID 83720–0037

Phone: (208) 332–1574; Fax: (208) 334–2632;
Email: scholarshiphelp@osbe.idaho.gov
Web: www.boardofed.idaho.gov/scholarship/opportunity.asp

Summary: To provide financial assistance to high school seniors in Idaho who have significant financial need and wish to attend a postsecondary institution in the state.

Eligibility: Open to seniors graduating from high schools in Idaho and recipients of GED certification in the state. Applicants must be planning to enroll full time at an eligible postsecondary educational institution in Idaho. They must have applied for federal financial aid but still demonstrate need for further assistance.

Financial data: A stipend is awarded (amount not specified). This program is designed to be a "last dollar" mechanism, so it provides support only after students have been awarded federal financial aid and have contributed their own or their families' funding.

Duration: 1 year; may be renewed, provided the recipient maintains satisfactory academic progress.

Number awarded: Varies each year.

Deadline: February of each year.

353 IDAHO STATE ELKS ASSOCIATION STUDENT OF THE YEAR SCHOLARSHIP

Idaho State Elks Association
c/o Darrel Green, State Scholarship Chair
2318 East 3600 South
Gooding, ID 83338
Email: darrel_jen@filertel.com
Web: idahoelks.org/welcome–idaho–state–elks–association?page=1

Summary: To provide financial assistance to high school seniors in Idaho who plan to attend college in any state.

Eligibility: Open to seniors graduating from high schools in Idaho and planning to enroll at a 4–year college or university in any state. Applicants must submit an essay of 1 to 3 pages on what volunteering has meant to them and how they feel their participation has made a difference in their community. Selection is based on that essay, a list of their volunteer work in their community, information on their high school extracurricular activities, transcripts, and 3 letters of recommendation. Men and women are judged separately.

Financial data: The stipend is $1,250. Funds are sent directly to the recipient's college or university.

Duration: 1 year.

Number awarded: 2 each year: 1 man and 1 woman.

Deadline: Applications must be submitted to the local lodge by March of each year.

354 ILLINOIS AMVETS JUNIOR ROTC SCHOLARSHIPS

AMVETS–Department of Illinois
2200 South Sixth Street
Springfield, IL 62703
Phone: (217) 528–4713; (800) 638–VETS (within IL); Fax: (217) 528–9896
Web: www.ilamvets.org/prog_scholarships.cfm

Summary: To provide financial assistance for college to high school seniors in Illinois who have participated in Junior ROTC (JROTC), especially children and grandchildren of veterans.

Eligibility: Open to seniors graduating from high schools in Illinois who have taken the ACT or SAT and have participated in the JROTC program. Financial need is considered in the selection process. Priority is given to children and grandchildren of veterans.

Financial data: The stipend is $1,000.

Duration: 1 year; nonrenewable.

Number awarded: 5 each year: 1 in each of the sponsor's divisions.

Deadline: February of each year.

355 $$ ILLINOIS GRANT PROGRAM FOR DEPENDENTS OF CORRECTIONAL OFFICERS

Illinois Student Assistance Commission
Attn: Scholarship and Grant Services
1755 Lake Cook Road
Deerfield, IL 60015–5209
Phone: (847) 948–8550; (800) 899–ISAC; Fax: (847) 831–8549; TDD: (800) 526–0844;
Email: isac.studentservices@isac.illinois.gov
Web: www.collegeillinois.org

Summary: To provide financial assistance to the children or spouses of disabled or deceased Illinois correctional workers who plan to attend college in the state.

Eligibility: Open to the spouses and children of Illinois correctional officers who were at least 90% disabled or killed in the line of duty. Applicants must be enrolled on at least a half–time basis as an undergraduate at an approved Illinois public or private 2– or 4–year college or university. They need not be Illinois residents at the time of application. U.S. citizenship or eligible noncitizen status is required.

Financial data: The grants provide full payment of tuition and mandatory fees at approved public colleges in Illinois or an equivalent amount at private colleges.

Duration: Up to 8 academic semesters or 12 academic quarters of study.

Number awarded: Varies each year.

Deadline: September of each year for the academic year; February of each year for spring semester or winter or spring quarter; June of each year for summer term.

356 $$ ILLINOIS GRANT PROGRAM FOR DEPENDENTS OF POLICE OR FIRE OFFICERS

Illinois Student Assistance Commission
Attn: Scholarship and Grant Services
1755 Lake Cook Road
Deerfield, IL 60015–5209
Phone: (847) 948–8550; (800) 899–ISAC; Fax: (847) 831–8549; TDD: (800) 526–0844;
Email: isac.studentservices@isac.illinois.gov
Web: www.collegeillinois.org

Summary: To provide financial assistance to the children or spouses of disabled or deceased Illinois police or fire officers who plan to attend college or graduate school in the state.

Eligibility: Open to the spouses and children of Illinois police and fire officers who were at least 90% disabled or killed in the line of duty. Applicants must be enrolled on at least a half–time basis in either undergraduate or graduate study at an approved Illinois public or private 2– or 4–year college, university, or hospital school. They need not be Illinois residents at the time of application. U.S. citizenship or eligible noncitizen status is required.

Financial data: The grants provide full payment of tuition and mandatory fees at approved public colleges in Illinois or an equivalent amount at private colleges.

Duration: Up to 8 academic semesters or 12 academic quarters of study.

Number awarded: Varies each year.

Deadline: September of each year for the academic year; February of each year for spring semester or winter or spring quarter; June of each year for summer term.

357 $$ ILLINOIS MIA/POW SCHOLARSHIP

Illinois Department of Veterans' Affairs
833 South Spring Street
P.O. Box 19432
Springfield, IL 62794–9432
Phone: (217) 782–6641; (800) 437–9824 (within IL); Fax: (217) 524–0344; TDD: (217) 524–4645;
Email: webmail@dva.state.il.us
Web: www2.illinois.gov/veterans/benefits/Pages/education.aspx

Summary: To provide financial assistance for 1) the undergraduate education of Illinois dependents of disabled or deceased veterans or those listed as prisoners of war or missing in action; and 2) the rehabilitation or education of disabled dependents of those veterans.

Eligibility: Open to the spouses, natural children, legally adopted children, or stepchildren of a veteran or servicemember who 1) has been declared by the U.S. Department of Defense or the U.S. Department of Veterans Affairs to be permanently disabled from service–connected causes with 100% disability, deceased as the result of a service–connected disability, a prisoner of war, or missing in action; and 2) at the time of entering service was an Illinois resident or was an Illinois resident within 6 months of entering such service. Special support is available for dependents who are disabled.

Financial data: An eligible dependent is entitled to full payment of tuition and certain fees at any Illinois state–supported college, university, or community college. In lieu of that benefit, an eligible dependent who has a physical, mental, or developmental disability is entitled to receive a grant to be used to cover the cost of treating the disability at 1 or more appropriate therapeutic, rehabilitative, or educational facilities. For all recipients, the total benefit cannot exceed the cost equivalent of 4 calendar years of full–time enrollment, including summer terms, at the University of Illinois.

Duration: This scholarship may be used for a period equivalent to 4 calendar years, including summer terms. Dependents have 12 years from the initial term of study to complete the equivalent of 4 calendar years. Disabled dependents who elect to use the grant for rehabilitative purposes may do so as long as the total benefit does not exceed the cost equivalent of 4 calendar years of full–time enrollment at the University of Illinois.
Number awarded: Varies each year.
Deadline: Deadline not specified.

358 $ ILLINOIS MONETARY AWARD PROGRAM

Illinois Student Assistance Commission
Attn: Scholarship and Grant Services
1755 Lake Cook Road
Deerfield, IL 60015–5209
Phone: (847) 948–8550; (800) 899–ISAC; Fax: (847) 831–8549; TDD: (800) 526–0844;
Email: isac.studentservices@isac.illinois.gov
Web: www.collegeillinois.org
Summary: To provide financial assistance to undergraduate students in Illinois.
Eligibility: Open to Illinois residents who are enrolled for at least 3 credit hours per term as an undergraduate student at an approved institution of higher education in the state. Applicants must be able to demonstrate financial need. High school grades and test scores are not considered in the selection process. U.S. citizenship or eligible noncitizenship status is required.
Financial data: The actual dollar amount of the award depends on financial need and the cost of the recipient's schooling; in no case does the award exceed the actual cost of tuition and fees or $4,720 per year, whichever is less. The funds may be used only for tuition and mandatory fees; funds cannot be spent on books, travel, or housing. All awards are paid directly to the recipient's school.
Duration: 1 year; may be renewed until completion of 135 credit hours.
Number awarded: Varies each year.
Deadline: Funding for this program is limited. To increase your chances of receiving funding, apply as soon after the beginning of January as possible.

359 ILLINOIS PATRIOT EDUCATION FUND

Student Veterans of America
P.O. Box 77673
Washington, DC 20013
Email: SVA@studentveterans.org
Web: www.studentveterans.org/?page=Programs
Summary: To provide financial assistance to veterans from Illinois who are working on a bachelor's or graduate degree at a college or university in the state.
Eligibility: Open to veterans who are working on an undergraduate or graduate degree at a college or university in Illinois. Applicants must have a strong Illinois connection (e.g., lived in the state prior to service). Selection is based on academic achievement, participation in Student Veterans of America (SVA), community involvement, and a personal essay.
Financial data: The stipend is $1,000.
Duration: 1 year.
Number awarded: Varies each year; recently 7 of these scholarships were awarded.
Deadline: January of each year.

360 ILLINOIS SONS OF CONFEDERATE VETERANS/MILITARY ORDER OF THE STARS AND BARS

Illinois SCV/MOS&B Scholarship
c/o James F. Barr, Scholarship Chair
3162 North Broadway, Suite 200
Chicago, IL 60657
Phone: (773) 755–2748;
Email: jim@tax–acct.net
Summary: To provide financial assistance to high school seniors in Illinois who are descendants of Confederate veterans and plan to attend college in any state.
Eligibility: Open to seniors (male or female) graduating from high schools in Illinois and planning to attend a college, university, or community college in any state. Applicants must be a descendant of a male who served honorably in the army, navy, judicial, executive, or civil service of the Confederate States of America. Along with their application, they must submit 1) a transcript of grades; 2) an autobiography that includes a genealogical chart showing lineal or collateral family lines to a Confederate ancestor; and 3) a 500–word essay on an event, person, philosophy, or ideal associated with the Confederate Cause during the War Between the States. Financial need is not considered in the selection process.
Financial data: The stipend is $1,000.
Duration: 1 year.
Number awarded: 1 each year.
Deadline: March of each year.

361 $$ ILLINOIS VETERAN GRANT PROGRAM

Illinois Student Assistance Commission
Attn: Scholarship and Grant Services
1755 Lake Cook Road
Deerfield, IL 60015–5209
Phone: (847) 948–8550; (800) 899–ISAC; Fax: (847) 831–8549; TDD: (800) 526–0844;
Email: isac.studentservices@isac.illinois.gov
Web: www.collegeillinois.org
Summary: To provide financial assistance to Illinois veterans Guard who are interested in attending college or graduate school in the state.
Eligibility: Open to Illinois residents who served in the U.S. armed forces (including members of the Reserves and the Illinois National Guard) for at least 1 year on active duty and have been honorably discharged. The 1–year service requirement does not apply to veterans who 1) served in a foreign country in a time of hostilities in that country; 2) were medically discharged for service–related reasons; or 3) were discharged prior to August 11, 1967. Applicants must have been Illinois residents for at least 6 months before entering service and they must have returned to Illinois within 6 months after separation from service. Current members of the Reserve Officer Training Corps are not eligible.
Financial data: This program pays all tuition and certain fees at all Illinois public colleges, universities, and community colleges.
Duration: This scholarship may be used for the equivalent of up to 4 years of full–time enrollment, provided the recipient maintains the minimum GPA required by their college or university.
Number awarded: Varies each year.
Deadline: Applications may be submitted at any time.

362 IMAGINE AMERICA SCHOLARSHIPS

Career College Association
Attn: Imagine America Foundation
1101 Connecticut Avenue, N.W., Suite 901
Washington, DC 20036
Phone: (202) 336–6719; Fax: (202) 408–8102;
Email: scholarships@imagine–america.org
Web: www.imagine–america.org/highschoolscholarships
Summary: To provide financial assistance to high school seniors interested in attending a career college.
Eligibility: Open to seniors graduating from high schools that are enrolled in the Imagine America program. Applicants must be interested in attending 1 of the more than 500 career colleges that participate in the program. They must have a GPA of 2.5 or higher. All applications are submitted online to the college that the student wishes to attend. Selection is based on likelihood of successful completion of postsecondary education, demonstrated voluntary community service during senior year of high school, and financial need.
Financial data: The stipend is $1,000. Funds must be used for payment of tuition at a participating career college.
Duration: 1 year.
Number awarded: Varies each year; up to 3 students at each enrolled high school may receive a scholarship.
Deadline: December of each year.

363 $ INCIGHT SCHOLARSHIPS

Incight Education
Attn: Scholarship Coordinator
310 S.W. Fourth Avenue, Suite 630
Portland, OR 97204
Phone: (971) 244–0305; Fax: (971) 244–0304;
Email: lauren@incight.org
Web: www.incighteducation.org/new–scholarship–application

Summary: To provide financial assistance for college to students who have a physical disability or impairment.
Eligibility: Open to students who have a documented disability or impairment, including a physical, cognitive, or learning disability. Applicants must have a GPA of 2.5 or higher and be entering or attending college as a full–time student. Along with their application, they must submit a 250–word essay on the word "handicrap," a term that the sponsoring organization feels is prevalent in the disabled and non–disabled communities and what they have done to conquer it. They must also submit 2 other 250–word essays on 1) their involvement in their community in the past and what they will continue to do in the future; and 2) other information about themselves.
Financial data: Stipends range from $500 to $2,500.
Duration: 1 year; may be renewed up to 3 additional years.
Number awarded: Up to 100 each year.
Deadline: March of each year.

364 $$ INDEPENDENT COLLEGE FUND OF MARYLAND LEADERSHIP SCHOLARSHIPS

Independent College Fund of Maryland
Attn: Director of Programs and Scholarships
3225 Ellerslie Avenue, Suite C–160
Baltimore, MD 21218–3519
Phone: (443) 997–5700; Fax: (443) 997–2740;
Email: Ifund@jhu.edu
Web: i–fundinfo.org/scholarships/business–scholarships.html
Summary: To provide financial assistance to students from any state at member institutions of the Independent College Fund of Maryland who have demonstrated outstanding leadership on campus or in the community.
Eligibility: Open to students from any state currently enrolled at member institutions. Applicants must have demonstrated outstanding leadership qualities on campus and/or in the community. They must have a GPA of 3.2 or higher and be able to demonstrate financial need.
Financial data: The stipend is $5,000.
Duration: 1 year.
Number awarded: 10 each year: 1 at each member institution.
Deadline: Deadline not specified.

365 $$ INDIANA CHILD OF VETERAN AND PUBLIC SAFETY OFFICER SUPPLEMENTAL GRANT PROGRAM

State Student Assistance Commission of Indiana
Attn: Grants and Scholarships
W462 Indiana Government Center South
402 West Washington Street
Indianapolis, IN 46204
Phone: (317) 232–2355; (888) 528–4719 (within IN); Fax: (317) 232–3260;
Email: grants@ssaci.in.gov
Web: www.in.gov/ssaci/2338.htm
Summary: To provide financial assistance to residents of Indiana who are the children or spouses of specified categories of deceased or disabled veterans or public safety officers and interested in attending college or graduate school in the state.
Eligibility: Open to 1) children of deceased or disabled Indiana veterans, children of Purple Heart recipients, and children of Vietnam War veterans who were listed as POW or MIA; 2) children and spouses of members of the Indiana National Guard who suffered a service–connected death while serving on state active duty; 3) Indiana veterans who received a Purple Heart; 4) current and former students at the Indiana Soldiers' and Sailors' Children's Home (Morton Memorial High School); and 5) children and spouses of Indiana police officers, firefighters, or emergency medical technicians killed in the line of duty or Indiana state police troopers permanently and totally disabled in the line of duty. The veterans and National Guard portions of this program are open to Indiana residents who are the natural or adopted children or spouses of veterans who served in the active–duty U.S. armed forces during a period of war time.
Financial data: Qualified applicants receive a 100% remission of tuition and all mandatory fees for undergraduate or graduate work at state–supported postsecondary schools and universities in Indiana. Support is not provided for such fees as room and board.
Duration: Up to 124 semester hours of study.
Number awarded: Varies each year.
Deadline: Applications must be submitted at least 30 days before the start of the college term.

366 INDIANA PART–TIME GRANT PROGRAM

State Student Assistance Commission of Indiana
Attn: Grants and Scholarships
W462 Indiana Government Center South
402 West Washington Street
Indianapolis, IN 46204
Phone: (317) 232–2355; (888) 528–4719 (within IN); Fax: (317) 232–3260;
Email: grants@ssaci.in.gov
Web: www.in.gov/ssaci/2362.htm
Summary: To provide financial assistance to Indiana residents who are working part time on an undergraduate degree at a school in the state.
Eligibility: Open to Indiana residents who are high school seniors, high school graduates, or GED certificate recipients. Applicants must be attending or planning to attend an eligible Indiana postsecondary institution as a part–time undergraduate student working on an associate or first bachelor's degree. They must be able to demonstrate financial need for tuition assistance.
Financial data: The amount of the award depends on the availability of funds and the number of credit hours taken.
Duration: 1 term (quarter or semester); may be renewed.
Number awarded: Varies each year.
Deadline: Most schools require applications to be submitted no later than 30 days prior to the end of the applicable academic term.

367 IOWA BETTER BUSINESS BUREAU STUDENT OF INTEGRITY SCHOLARSHIP

Better Business Bureau of Des Moines
Attn: Education Foundation
505 Fifth Avenue, Suite 950
Des Moines, IA 50309
Phone: (515) 243–8137, ext. 305; (800) 222–1600; Fax: (515) 243–2227;
Email: info@iowa.bbb.org
Web: www.iowa.bbb.org
Summary: To provide financial assistance to high school seniors in Iowa who submit an essay on ethics and plan to attend college in any state.
Eligibility: Open to seniors graduating from high schools in Iowa and planning to attend a college or university in any state. Applicants must submit a 1,000–word essay describing a life lesson they have learned from an ethical situation they have faced. Selection is based on that essay (30%), leadership (25%), community service (25%), academic achievement (15%), and letters of recommendation (5%).
Financial data: The stipend is $1,000.
Duration: 1 year.
Number awarded: 5 each year.
Deadline: December of each year.

368 $$ IOWA EDUCATION AND TRAINING VOUCHER GRANTS

Iowa College Student Aid Commission
603 East 12th Street, Fifth Floor
Des Moines, IA 50319
Phone: (515) 725–3400; (877) 272–4456; Fax: (515) 725–3401;
Email: info@iowacollegeaid.gov
Web: www.iowacollegeaid.gov/ScholarshipsGrants/scholarshipsgrants.html
Summary: To provide financial assistance to residents of Iowa who have been involved in foster care and plan to attend college in any state.
Eligibility: Open to residents of Iowa who 1) are under 18 years of age and currently in licensed foster care under the care and custody of the Iowa Department of Human Services or Iowa Juvenile Court Services and will remain in placement to within 30 days of their 18th birthday; 2) are under 18 years of age and currently under Juvenile Court order to live with a relative or suitable person and will remain in placement to within 30 days of their 18th birthday; 3) are currently between 18 and 21 years of age and were in a living situation described in the previous categories until the age of 18; or 4) were previously in Iowa foster care and were legally adopted after 16 years of age. Applicants must be planning to enroll at a college, university, or vocational school in any state and enter before they reach 21 years of age.
Financial data: Grants range up to $5,000. Funds are sent directly to the recipient's college or university to be used to pay for tuition, fees, room, board, books, supplies, and personal living expenses.
Duration: 1 year; may be renewed.
Number awarded: Varies each year.
Deadline: Priority is given to students who apply before the end of February of each year.

369 IOWA GRANTS

Iowa College Student Aid Commission
603 East 12th Street, Fifth Floor
Des Moines, IA 50319
Phone: (515) 725–3400; (877) 272–4456; Fax: (515) 725–3401;
Email: info@iowacollegeaid.gov
Web: www.iowacollegeaid.gov/ScholarshipsGrants/scholarshipsgrants.html

Summary: To provide financial assistance for undergraduate study to needy Iowa residents.

Eligibility: Open to residents of Iowa who are enrolled or planning to enroll at least part time in an undergraduate degree program at an eligible state university, independent college or university, or area community college in the state. Selection is based on financial need, with priority given to the neediest applicants. U.S. citizenship or permanent resident status is required.

Financial data: The maximum grant is $1,000 per year (may be adjusted for less than full–time study).

Duration: Up to 4 years of undergraduate study.

Number awarded: More than 1,600 each year.

Deadline: Applicants must submit a FAFSA form as early as possible after January 1.

370 $ IOWA TUITION GRANTS

Iowa College Student Aid Commission
603 East 12th Street, Fifth Floor
Des Moines, IA 50319
Phone: (515) 725–3400; (877) 272–4456; Fax: (515) 725–3401;
Email: info@iowacollegeaid.gov
Web: www.iowacollegeaid.gov/ScholarshipsGrants/scholarshipsgrants.html

Summary: To provide financial assistance to Iowa residents who are interested in attending a private college or university in the state.

Eligibility: Open to residents of Iowa who are enrolled or planning to enroll at least part time in an undergraduate degree program at an eligible independent college or university in the state. Selection is based on financial need, with priority given to the neediest applicants. U.S. citizenship or permanent resident status is required.

Financial data: The maximum grant is $4,000 per year (may be adjusted for less than full–time study).

Duration: Up to 4 years of full–time undergraduate study.

Number awarded: More than 14,000 each year.

Deadline: Applicants must submit a FAFSA form as early as possible after January 1. For priority consideration, the form must be completed and mailed in time to reach the processing center by the end of June.

371 IOWA VOCATIONAL/TECHNICAL TUITION GRANTS

Iowa College Student Aid Commission
603 East 12th Street, Fifth Floor
Des Moines, IA 50319
Phone: (515) 725–3400; (877) 272–4456; Fax: (515) 725–3401;
Email: info@iowacollegeaid.gov
Web: www.iowacollegeaid.gov/ScholarshipsGrants/scholarshipsgrants.html

Summary: To provide financial assistance for study in vocational/technical programs at community colleges to needy Iowa residents.

Eligibility: Open to residents of Iowa who are enrolled or planning to enroll for at least 3 credit hours in vocational/technical or career option programs at community colleges in the state. The program must last at least 12 weeks. Applicants must be able to demonstrate financial need. U.S. citizenship or permanent resident status is required.

Financial data: The maximum grant is $1,200 per year (may be adjusted for less than full–time study.

Duration: Up to 2 years of full–time vocational study.

Number awarded: Varies each year.

Deadline: Applicants must submit a FAFSA form as early as possible after January 1. For priority consideration, the form must be completed and mailed in time to reach the processing center by the end of June.

372 $$ IRAQ AND AFGHANISTAN SERVICE GRANTS

Department of Education
Attn: Federal Student Aid Information Center
P.O. Box 84
Washington, DC 20044–0084
Phone: (319) 337–5665; (800) 4–FED–AID; TDD: (800) 730–8913
Web: studentaid.ed.gov/types/grants–scholarships

Summary: To provide financial assistance for undergraduate education to students whose parent was killed as a result of service in Iraq or Afghanistan.

Eligibility: Open to students younger than 24 years of age whose parent or guardian was a member of the U.S. armed forces and died as a result of service performed in Iraq or Afghanistan after September 11, 2001. Applicants must be enrolled at least part time. The program is designed for students who do not qualify for Federal Pell Grants because of their family's financial situation.

Financial data: The amount of the grant ranges up to that of a Federal Pell Grant, currently $5,550 per year.

Duration: Up to 5 years of undergraduate study.

Number awarded: Varies each year; recently, approximately 1,000 students qualified for this program.

Deadline: Students may submit applications between January of the current year through June of the following year.

373 ISABELLE CHRISTENSON MEMORIAL SCHOLARSHIP

Izzie's Gifts of Hope Foundation
c/o C.O.R.E.
204 Sigma Drive
RIDC Park
Pittsburgh, PA 15238
Email: izziesgifts@gmail.com
Web: www.izziesgifts.org/scholarships.php

Summary: To provide financial assistance for college to organ transplant candidates, donors, recipients, and their families.

Eligibility: Open to organ transplant candidates, recipients, donor family members, and immediate family members of a transplant candidate or recipient. Applicants must be attending or planning to attend a college, university, or trade/technical school. Along with their application, they must submit 1) a statement of 250 to 500 words on their educational goals; and 2) a 500–word statement of how donation/transplantation has influenced their life.

Financial data: A stipend is awarded (amount not specified).

Duration: 1 year; nonrenewable.

Number awarded: 1 or 2 each year.

Deadline: March of each year.

374 ISABELLE M. HICKMAN COLLEGE SCHOLARSHIP

New Jersey Retirees' Education Association
Attn: Scholarship Committee
P.O. Box 1211
Trenton, NJ 08607–1211

Summary: To provide financial assistance to high school seniors in New Jersey who rank in the top 10% of their class and plan to attend college in any state.

Eligibility: Open to seniors graduating from public high schools in New Jersey and planning to enroll at a 4–year college or university in any state. Applicants must rank in the top 10% of their class. Along with their application, they must submit 1) a brief statement of their goals, hobbies, and interests; 2) a high school transcript with SAT scores, GPA, and class rank; 3) a list of extracurricular activities, athletics, community services, honors, and employment; and 4) 2 letters of recommendation.

Financial data: The stipend is $1,000 per year.

Duration: 1 year; recipients may reapply for up to 3 additional years, provided they maintain a college GPA of 3.0 or higher.

Number awarded: 1 or more each year.

Deadline: March of each year.

375 ITALIAN AMERICAN EXECUTIVES OF TRANSPORTATION SCHOLARSHIPS

Italian American Executives of Transportation Club
c/o Charlotte Sorci
306 South Salem Drive
Schaumburg, IL 60193
Phone: (630) 272–3947;
Email: scholarship@iaet–chicago.org
Web: www.iaet–chicago.org/id11.html

Summary: To provide financial assistance to high school seniors in Illinois who are of Italian ancestry and interested in attending college in any state.

Eligibility: Open to seniors graduating from high schools in Illinois and planning to attend a college or university in any state. Applicants must be of Italian American heritage, in whole or in part. Along with their application, they must submit a 1–page essay on their educational goals and what their Italian heritage

has meant to them. Selection is based on academic achievement and financial need.
Financial data: A stipend is awarded (amount not specified).
Duration: 1 year.
Number awarded: Varies each year; recently, 19 of these scholarships were awarded.
Deadline: September of each year.

376 $ JACK AND JILL SCHOLARSHIPS

Jack and Jill Foundation of America
1930 17th Street, N.W.
Washington, DC 20009
Phone: (202) 232–5290; Fax: (202) 232–1747
Web: www.jackandjillfoundation.org/scholarships
Summary: To provide financial assistance to African American high school seniors who plan to attend college in any state.
Eligibility: Open to African American seniors graduating from high schools in any state with a GPA of 3.0 or higher. Applicants must be planning to enroll full time at an accredited 4–year college or university. Dependents of members of Jack and Jill of America are not eligible.
Financial data: Stipends range from $1,500 to $2,500. Funds may be used for tuition or room and board.
Duration: 1 year.
Number awarded: Varies each year.
Deadline: March of each year.

377 $$ JACK KENT COOKE UNDERGRADUATE TRANSFER SCHOLARSHIPS

Jack Kent Cooke Foundation
44325 Woodridge Parkway
Lansdowne, VA 20176–5199
Phone: (703) 723–8000; (800) 310–4053; Fax: (703) 723–8030
Web: www.jkcf.org/scholarships/undergraduate–transfer–scholarships
Summary: To provide financial assistance to students at 2–year colleges planning to transfer to a 4–year college or university.
Eligibility: Open to students who are currently enrolled as sophomores at accredited U.S. community or 2–year colleges (or who graduated from such a college within the past 5 years). Candidates must be interested in transferring to a full–time baccalaureate program at an accredited college or university in the United States. They must be nominated by their college and have a GPA of 3.5 or higher. Selection is based on academic achievement, critical thinking ability, financial need, will to succeed, and breadth of interest and activities.
Financial data: Stipends up to $30,000 per year are provided. Funds are paid directly to the institution.
Duration: 1 year; may be renewed until completion of an undergraduate degree, as long as the fellow continues to meet the eligibility requirements.
Number awarded: Approximately 60 each year.
Deadline: Campus faculty representatives must submit applications by December of each year.

378 $$ JACKIE ROBINSON FOUNDATION SCHOLARSHIPS

Jackie Robinson Foundation
Attn: Education and Leadership Development Program
75 Varick Street, Second Floor
New York, NY 10013–1917
Phone: (212) 290–8600; Fax: (212) 290–8081;
Email: general@jackierobinson.org
Web: www.jackierobinson.org
Summary: To provide financial assistance for college to minority high school seniors.
Eligibility: Open to members of an ethnic minority group who are high school seniors accepted at a 4–year college or university. Applicants must have a mathematics and critical reading SAT score of 1000 or higher or ACT score of 21 or higher. Selection is based on academic achievement, financial need, dedication towards community service, and leadership potential. U.S. citizenship is required.
Financial data: The maximum stipend is $7,500 per year.
Duration: 4 years.
Number awarded: 100 or more each year.
Deadline: March of each year.

379 $$ JACOBSEN FUND SCHOLARSHIPS

Jacobsen Scholarship Fund
1400 Foothill Drive, Suite 25
Salt Lake City, UT 84108
Phone: (801) 592–7314
Web: www.jacobsenscholarshipfund.com
Summary: To provide financial assistance for college to members of the Church of Jesus Christ of Latter–day Saints (LDS).
Eligibility: Open to worthy and active members of the LDS who are enrolled or planning to enroll full time at an accredited postsecondary institution in any state. Applicants must have a GPA of 2.75 or higher and be able to demonstrate financial need. U.S. citizenship is required.
Financial data: Awards are equal to the full–time undergraduate resident tuition, plus a standardized amount for books, supplies, and fees. All funds are paid directly to the student's institution.
Duration: 1 semester; may be renewed up to 7 additional semesters, provided the recipient continues to demonstrate financial need and activity in the LDS church.
Number awarded: Varies each year.
Deadline: May of each year for fall semester; October of each year for winter semester.

380 JAMES R. OLSEN MEMORIAL SCHOLARSHIP

American Council of the Blind
Attn: Coordinator, Scholarship Program
2200 Wilson Boulevard, Suite 650
Arlington, VA 22201
Phone: (202) 467–5081; (800) 424–8666; Fax: (703) 465–5085;
Email: info@acb.org
Web: www.acb.org/scholarship
Summary: To provide financial assistance to outstanding blind college students.
Eligibility: Open to legally blind students enrolling or continuing in an undergraduate program. Applicants must submit verification of legal blindness in both eyes; SAT or ACT scores; information on extracurricular activities (including involvement in the American Council of the Blind); employment record; and a 500–word autobiographical sketch that includes their personal goals, strengths, weaknesses, hobbies, honors, achievements, and reasons for choice of field or courses of study. A cumulative GPA of 3.3 or higher is generally required. Financial need is not considered in the selection process.
Financial data: The stipend is at least $1,000.
Duration: 1 year.
Number awarded: 1 each year.
Deadline: February of each year.

381 $$ JAMES W. MCLAMORE WHOPPER SCHOLARSHIPS

Burger King Corporation
Attn: Have It Your Way Foundation
5505 Blue Lagoon Drive
Miami, FL 33126
Phone: (303) 378–3186; Fax: (303) 378–7017;
Email: BK–HIYWFoundation@whopper.com
Web: www.haveityourwayfoundation.org/burger_king_scholars_program.html
Summary: To provide financial assistance for college to high school seniors in the United States, Canada, and Puerto Rico.
Eligibility: Open to U.S. and Canadian citizens who are seniors graduating from public, private, parochial, or alternative high schools or home schools in the United States, Canada, and Puerto Rico or who graduated from such a school within the last 3 years. Applicants must be planning to enroll as a full–time freshman at an accredited 4–year college or university in the United States. They must have a cumulative unweighted GPA of 3.3 or higher; scores of at least 25 on the ACT or 1700 on the SAT; a record of active leadership in community service, athletics, and/or similar co–curricular activities; and substantial work experience. Selection is based on academic achievements and records (50%) and participation in school and community activities and work experience (50%); financial need is also considered.
Financial data: The stipend is $50,000.
Duration: 1 year; nonrenewable.
Number awarded: 3 each year.
Deadline: January of each year.

382 $ JANET LOGAN DAILY SCHOLARSHIP

Janet Logan Daily Foundation
c/o Founders Education, LLC
1105 Taylorsville Road, Suite 1
Washington Crossing, PA 18977
Phone: (215) 305–8794; Fax: (888) 391–9949;
Email: application@janetlogandailyfoundation.org
Web: www.janetlogandailyfoundation.org

Summary: To provide financial assistance to high school seniors in New Jersey who are not in the top of their class but who have demonstrated responsibility, motivation, and character and plan to attend college in any state.

Eligibility: Open to seniors graduating from high schools in New Jersey and planning to enroll full time at an accredited college or university in any state. Applicants are not required to be at the top of their class, but they must have a GPA of 2.5 or higher, participation in at least 1 extracurricular activity, an employment record of an average of 30 hours per week during the summer since they became 16 years of age, and demonstrated financial need. Along with their application, they must submit an essay of 250 to 500 words in which they describe an instance or instances in which they have done something positive for another person without expecting to receive anything in return.

Financial data: The stipend is $2,500 per year.

Duration: 4 years, provided the recipient maintains a GPA of 2.5 or higher.

Number awarded: 1 each year.

Deadline: May of each year.

383 JEANNE L. HAMMOND MEMORIAL SCHOLARSHIP

Maine Federation of Business and Professional Women's Clubs
Attn: BPW/Maine Futurama Foundation
c/o Susan Tardie, Co–President
25 Hall Street
Fort Kent, ME 04743
Email: susan.tardie@maine.edu
Web: www.bpwmefoundation.org/files/index.php?id=10

Summary: To provide financial assistance to female high school seniors and recent graduates in Maine who plan to attend college in any state.

Eligibility: Open to women who are seniors graduating from high schools in Maine or recent graduates of those schools. Applicants must be planning to enroll at least half time for their first year of postsecondary study at an accredited college or university in any state. They must have a realistic goal for the educational plans. Along with their application, they must submit a statement describing their educational and personal goals, including their financial need. First priority is given to women who can demonstrate a record of school and/or community involvement. Second priority is given to applicants who are interested in working on a journalism degree, members of the Maine Federation of Business and Professional Women's Clubs (BPW/Maine) and their dependents, and members of the American Association of University Women (AAUW) and their dependents.

Financial data: The stipend is $1,200. Funds are paid directly to the recipient's school.

Duration: 1 year.

Number awarded: 1 or more each year.

Deadline: April of each year.

384 $ JEANNETTE RANKIN AWARD

Jeannette Rankin Foundation, Inc.
1 Huntington Road, Suite 701
Athens, GA 30606
Phone: (706) 208–1211; Fax: (706) 548–0202;
Email: info@rankinfoundation.org
Web: www.rankinfoundation.org

Summary: To provide financial assistance for college to women who are 35 years of age or older.

Eligibility: Open to women who are 35 years of age or older and working on a technical or vocational certificate, associate degree, or first bachelor's degree. Applicants must meet standards of a low–income household, currently defined as net income less than $13,958 for a family of 1, rising to $53,491 for a family of 6. Along with their application, they must submit a 2–page essay that includes a description of their academic and career goals, what they have done of which they are the most proud, and how their education will benefit themselves, their family, and their community. Selection is based on the applicants' goals, plan for reaching those goals, challenges they have faced, and their financial situation. U.S. citizenship is required.

Financial data: The stipend is $2,000.

Duration: 1 year; nonrenewable.

Number awarded: Varies each year; recently, 80 of these scholarships were awarded.

Deadline: February of each year.

385 $$ JEFF KROSNOFF SCHOLARSHIP

Jeff Krosnoff Scholarship Fund
P.O. Box 8585
La Crescenta, CA 91224–0585
Email: jeffrey5788@gmail.com
Web: www.krosnoffscholarship.com/Scholarship.htm

Summary: To provide financial assistance to high school seniors in California who submit outstanding essays and plan to attend college in any state.

Eligibility: Open to seniors graduating from high schools in California who plan to attend a 4–year college or university in any state. Applicants must be able to demonstrate excellent academic credentials, a breadth of interests, a driving desire to succeed in their chosen endeavors, outstanding community citizenship, and the ability to share their experiences through the written word. They must have a GPA of 3.0 or higher. Selection is based on an essay on a topic that changes annually; recently, applicants were asked to select something that inspires them and to explain why. Financial need is not considered.

Financial data: The stipend is $10,000.

Duration: 1 year.

Number awarded: 1 each year.

Deadline: January of each year.

386 $ JEROME B. STEINBACH SCHOLARSHIP

Oregon Student Access Commission
Attn: Grants and Scholarships Division
1500 Valley River Drive, Suite 100
Eugene, OR 97401–2146
Phone: (541) 687–7395; (800) 452–8807, ext. 7395; Fax: (541) 687–7414; TDD: (800) 735–2900;
Email: awardinfo@osac.state.or.us
Web: www.oregonstudentaid.gov/scholarships.aspx

Summary: To provide financial assistance to residents of Oregon who are attending college in any state.

Eligibility: Open to residents of Oregon who are entering their sophomore or higher year at a college or university in any state. Applicants must have a cumulative GPA of 3.5 or higher. They must submit proof of birth within the United States. Financial need is considered in the selection process.

Financial data: Stipends for scholarships offered by the Oregon Student Access Commission (OSAC) range from $200 to $10,000 but recently averaged $2,300.

Duration: 1 year.

Number awarded: Varies each year.

Deadline: February of each year.

387 $ JERRY HARVEY ENDOWMENT SCHOLARSHIP

Epsilon Sigma Alpha International
Attn: ESA Foundation
363 West Drake Road
Fort Collins, CO 80526
Phone: (970) 223–2824; Fax: (970) 223–4456;
Email: esainfo@epsilonsigmaalpha.org
Web: www.epsilonsigmaalpha.org/esa–foundation/scholarships

Summary: To provide financial assistance to residents of Texas who plan to attend college in any state.

Eligibility: Open to residents of Texas who are 1) graduating high school seniors with a GPA of 3.0 or higher or with minimum scores of 22 on the ACT or 1030 on the combined critical reading and mathematics SAT; 2) enrolled in college with a GPA of 3.0 or higher; 3) enrolled at a technical school or returning to school after an absence for retraining of job skills or obtaining a degree; or 4) engaged in online study through an accredited college, university, or vocational school. Applicants may be attending or planning to attend a school in any state and major in any field. Selection is based on character (10%), leadership (20%), service (10%), financial need (30%), and scholastic ability (30%).

Financial data: The stipend is $2,000.

Duration: 1 year; may be renewed.

Number awarded: 1 each year.

Deadline: January of each year.

388 $$ JESSE BROWN MEMORIAL YOUTH SCHOLARSHIP PROGRAM

Disabled American Veterans
Attn: Voluntary Service Department
P.O. Box 14301
Cincinnati, OH 45250–0301
Phone: (859) 441–7300; (877) 426–2838; Fax: (859) 441–1416
Web: www.dav.org/volunteers/Scholarship.aspx

Summary: To provide financial assistance to college students who demonstrate outstanding volunteer service to hospitalized disabled veterans.

Eligibility: Open to students who are 21 years of age or younger and have volunteered at least 100 hours for the Department of Veterans Affairs Voluntary Service (VAVS) programs to assist disabled veterans. They may be attending an accredited college, university, community college, or vocational school. Nominations must be submitted by Chiefs of Voluntary Services at VA medical centers. Self–nominations are also accepted if the student includes a 750–word essay on what volunteering has meant to them.

Financial data: Stipends range up to $20,000.

Duration: Funds must be used before the recipient's 25th birthday.

Number awarded: Varies each year; recently, 8 of these scholarships were awarded: 1 at $20,000, 1 at $15,000, 1 at $10,000, 2 at $7,500, and 3 at $5,000.

Deadline: February of each year.

389 $$ JESSE L. JACKSON SR. FELLOWS SCHOLARSHIP AWARD

PUSH Excel
Attn: General Offices
930 East 50th Street
Chicago, IL 60615
Phone: (773) 373–3366;
Email: pushexcel@rainbowpush.org
Web: www.pushexcel.org/?page_id=61

Summary: To provide financial assistance to high school seniors who plan to attend college and are willing to help promote the scholarship program of PUSH–Excel.

Eligibility: Open to seniors graduating from high school and planning to enroll at an accredited 4–year college or university. Applicants must be U.S. citizens and have a GPA of 3.0 or higher. Along with their application, they must submit a 500–word essay that identifies 5 prerequisites for success, explains their personal philosophy for the pursuit of excellence, and explains how they will use their college education to achieve this pursuit of excellence. They must also agree to cooperate with the scholarship committee of PUSH–Excel by promoting its program, participating in its public relations activities, and attending its Annual National Conference luncheon and Education Leadership Conference. Selection is based on the essay, academic preparation to attend college and succeed, and ability to overcome obstacles to achieve academic and personal goals.

Financial data: The stipend is $5,000 per year.

Duration: 1 year; nonrenewable.

Number awarded: 1 or more each year.

Deadline: June of each year.

390 $ JEWELL HILTON BONNER SCHOLARSHIP

Navy League of the United States
Attn: Scholarships
2300 Wilson Boulevard, Suite 200
Arlington, VA 22201–5424
Phone: (703) 528–1775; (800) 356–5760; Fax: (703) 528–2333;
Email: scholarships@navyleague.org
Web: www.navyleague.org/corporate/donate/scholarship.html

Summary: To provide financial assistance for college to dependent children of sea service personnel, especially Native Americans.

Eligibility: Open to U.S. citizens who are 1) dependents or direct descendants of an active, Reserve, retired, or honorably discharged member of the U.S. sea service (including the Navy, Marine Corps, Coast Guard, or Merchant Marines); or 2) current active members of the Naval Sea Cadet Corps. Applicants must be entering their freshman year at an accredited college or university. They must have a GPA of 3.0 or higher. Along with their application, they must submit transcripts, 2 letters of recommendation, SAT/ACT scores, documentation of financial need, proof of qualifying sea service duty, and a 1–page personal statement on why they should be considered for this scholarship. Preference is given to applicants of Native American heritage.

Financial data: The stipend is $2,500 per year.

Duration: 4 years, provided the recipient maintains a GPA of 3.0 or higher.

Number awarded: 1 each year.

Deadline: March of each year.

391 J.F. SCHIRMER SCHOLARSHIP

American Mensa Education and Research Foundation
1229 Corporate Drive West
Arlington, TX 76006–6103
Phone: (817) 607–5577; (800) 66–MENSA; Fax: (817) 649–5232;
Email: info@mensafoundation.org
Web: www.mensafoundation.org/what–we–do/scholarships

Summary: To provide financial assistance for undergraduate or graduate study in any field to qualified students.

Eligibility: Open to students who are enrolled or will enroll in a degree program in any field at an accredited American institution of postsecondary education. Membership in Mensa is not required, but applicants must be U.S. citizens or permanent residents. There are no restrictions as to age, race, gender, level of postsecondary education, GPA, or financial need. Selection is based on a 550–word essay that describes the applicant's career, vocational, or academic goals. These awards are reserved for the applicants who rank highest among applicants for national Mensa scholarships.

Financial data: The stipend is $1,000.

Duration: 1 year; may be renewed for up to 3 additional years if the recipient remains in school and achieves satisfactory grades.

Number awarded: 4 each year.

Deadline: January of each year.

392 JIMMY RANE FOUNDATION SCHOLARSHIPS

Jimmy Rane Foundation
1100 Highway 431 North
P.O. Box 40
Abbeville, AL 36310
Phone: (334) 585–9505; (866) 606–2470;
Email: info@jimmyranefoundation.org
Web: www.jimmyranefoundation.org

Summary: To provide financial assistance to residents of designated states who are interested in attending college in any state.

Eligibility: Open to residents of Alabama, Arkansas, Florida, Georgia, Iowa, Kansas, Kentucky, Louisiana, Mississippi, Missouri, Nebraska, North Carolina, Oklahoma, South Carolina, Tennessee, and Texas. Applicants must be younger than 20 years of age and high school seniors, college freshmen or sophomores, or GED recipients. They must be enrolled or planning to enroll at a college or university in any state. High school seniors must have a GPA of 3.0 or higher; college students must have a GPA of 2.75 or higher. Along with their application, they must submit a biography that includes school and unpaid community activities, special awards, honors, and offices held; an essay on why they feel they should be awarded this scholarship, including their plans as they relate to their education, career, and long–term goals; 3 letters of recommendation; and documentation of financial need.

Financial data: The stipend depends on the need of the recipient.

Duration: 1 year; may be renewed up to 3 additional years.

Number awarded: Varies each year; recently, 21 of these scholarships were awarded.

Deadline: February of each year.

393 JOAN BUCKLEY SCHOLARSHIP

Alabama Association of Federal Program Administrators
c/o Karen Calvert
Blount County Board of Education
204 Second Avenue East
P.O. Box 578
Oneonta, AL 35121
Phone: (205) 625–4102;
Email: kcalvert@blountboe.net
Web: www.aafepa.org

Summary: To provide financial assistance to high school seniors and college freshmen from Alabama interested in working on a college degree in any field.

Eligibility: Open to students currently enrolled as seniors at high schools in Alabama or freshmen at accredited colleges or universities in the state. Applicants may be interested in working on a degree in any field. They must be able to demonstrate 1) a GPA of 3.0 or higher; 2) a commitment to learning; and 3) a successful experience working with children or young people. Financial need is considered in the selection process.

Financial data: The stipend is $1,500.
Duration: 1 year.
Number awarded: 1 each year.
Deadline: October of each year.

394 JOANNE HOLBROOK PATTON MILITARY SPOUSE SCHOLARSHIP PROGRAM

National Military Family Association, Inc.
Attn: Spouse Scholarship Program
2500 North Van Dorn Street, Suite 102
Alexandria, VA 22302–1601
Phone: (703) 931–NMFA; (800) 260–0218; Fax: (703) 931–4600;
Email: scholarships@militaryfamily.org
Web: www.militaryfamily.org/our–programs/military–spouse–scholarships
Summary: To provide financial assistance for postsecondary study to spouses of active and retired military personnel.
Eligibility: Open to the spouses of military personnel (active, retired, Reserve, Guard, or survivor). Applicants must be attending or planning to attend an accredited postsecondary institution to work on an undergraduate or graduate degree, professional certification, vocational training, GED or ESL, or other postsecondary training. They may enroll part or full time and on–campus or online. Along with their application, they must submit an essay on a question that changes annually; recently, applicants were asked to write about what they like most about the health care they are receiving as a military family member, what they like the least, and what they would recommend to change it. Selection is based on that essay, community involvement, and academic achievement.
Financial data: The stipend is $1,000. Funds are paid directly to the educational institution to be used for tuition, fees, and school room and board. Support is not provided for books, rent, or previous education loans.
Duration: 1 year; recipients may reapply.
Number awarded: Varies each year; recently, 484 of these scholarships were awarded.
Deadline: January of each year.

395 JOE FOSS, AN AMERICAN HERO SCHOLARSHIP

Sioux Falls Area Community Foundation
Attn: Scholarship Coordinator
300 North Phillips Avenue, Suite 102
Sioux Falls, SD 57104–6035
Phone: (605) 336–7055, ext. 20; Fax: (605) 336–0038;
Email: pgale@sfacf.org
Web: www.sfacf.org/ScholarshipDetails.aspx?CategoryID=1
Summary: To provide financial assistance to high school seniors in South Dakota who plan to attend college in any state.
Eligibility: Open to seniors graduating from high schools in South Dakota and planning to attend an accredited college, university, or vocational/technical school in any state. Applicants must have a GPA of 3.5 or higher and an ACT score of at least 21. They must be able to demonstrate the characteristics of an American patriot. Along with their application, they must submit a 500–word essay either on their definition of an American patriot or an event or individual that was helpful to them in forming their value system. Financial need is considered in the selection process.
Financial data: The stipend is $1,000. Funds are paid in 2 equal installments and are to be used for tuition, fees, and/or books.
Duration: 1 year.
Number awarded: Varies each year; recently, 6 of these scholarships were awarded.
Deadline: March of each year.

396 $ JOHN A. PFAFF SCHOLARSHIP

National Association of Federal Education Program Administrators
c/o Rick Carder, President
125 David Drive
Sutter Creek, CA 95685
Phone: (916) 669–5102; Fax: (888) 487–6441;
Email: rickc@sia–us.com
Web: www.nafepa.org
Summary: To provide financial assistance to high school seniors and college freshmen who are interested in working on a degree in any field other than education.
Eligibility: Open to graduating high school seniors and graduates already enrolled in the first year of college. Applicants must be working on or planning to work on a degree in any field other than education. They must be nominated by their state affiliate of the sponsoring organization. Along with their application, they must submit a 300–word personal narrative explaining why they are applying for this scholarship, including their awards, interests, leadership activities within the community, and future goals. Selection is based on that essay (20 points), a high school or college transcript from the current semester (20 points), extracurricular and leadership activities within the community or church (20 points), 3 letters of recommendation (20 points), and financial need (20 points).
Financial data: The stipend is $2,500.
Duration: 1 year.
Number awarded: 1 each year.
Deadline: Each state affiliate sets its own deadline; for a list of those, contact the sponsor.

397 $$ JOHN AND ABIGAIL ADAMS SCHOLARSHIP PROGRAM

Massachusetts Office of Student Financial Assistance
454 Broadway, Suite 200
Revere, MA 02151
Phone: (617) 391–6070; Fax: (617) 727–0667;
Email: osfa@osfa.mass.edu
Web: www.osfa.mass.edu/default.asp?page=adamsScholarship
Summary: To provide financial assistance for college to Massachusetts residents who earn high scores on the MCAS tests.
Eligibility: Open to permanent Massachusetts residents who are U.S. citizens or permanent residents. Applicants must score "Advanced" in either the mathematics or the English language section of the grade 10 MCAS and score either "Advanced" or "Proficient" in the other of those 2 sections. They must also have a combined MCAS score on those assessments that ranks in the top 25% in their school district and be planning to enroll full time at a Massachusetts public college or university. Financial need is not considered.
Financial data: Recipients of these scholarships are eligible for an award of a non–need–based tuition waiver for state–supported undergraduate courses in Massachusetts.
Duration: Up to 4 academic years, provided the student maintains a college GPA of 3.0 or higher.
Number awarded: Varies each year.
Deadline: April of each year.

398 $ JOHN B. LYNCH SCHOLARSHIP

John B. Lynch Scholarship Foundation
P.O. Box 4248
Wilmington, DE 19807–0248
Phone: (302) 654–3444;
Email: info@johnblynchfoundation.com
Web: www.johnblynchfoundation.com
Summary: To provide financial assistance for college to students who reside or attend school in Delaware or nearby areas.
Eligibility: Open to 1) seniors graduating from high schools in Delaware and planning to attend college in any state; 2) students currently attending college in Delaware (regardless of place of permanent residence); and 3) students who live in an adjoining state (Pennsylvania, New Jersey, or Maryland) within 20 miles of Delaware and attending college in any state. Graduating high school seniors must have a GPA of 3.0 or higher and a recent SAT score of at least 1650. Current undergraduate students must have a GPA of 2.75 or higher. Priority is given to students already enrolled in college. Students working on a second bachelor's degree are eligible if they received no support from this foundation for their first undergraduate degree. Applicants must be younger than 30 years of age and attending or planning to attend college on a full–time basis. Selection is based on academic achievement and financial need.
Financial data: The stipend is normally $2,500 per year.
Duration: Up to 4 years.
Number awarded: Varies each year.
Deadline: March of each year.

399 JOHN B. MCLENDON SCHOLARSHIP FUND

North Carolina State Education Assistance Authority
Attn: Grants, Training, and Outreach Department
P.O. Box 13663
Research Triangle Park, NC 27709–3663
Phone: (919) 549–8614; (800) 700–1775; Fax: (919) 248–4687;
Email: information@ncseaa.edu
Web: www.ncseaa.edu/McLendon.htm

Summary: To provide financial assistance to residents of North Carolina who are varsity athletes enrolled at designated Historically Black Colleges and Universities (HBCUs) in the state.
Eligibility: Open to residents of North Carolina who have been enrolled for at least 2 semesters at Bennett College for Women, Elizabeth City State University, Fayetteville State University, Johnson C. Smith University, Livingstone College, North Carolina A&T State University, North Carolina Central University, Shaw University, St. Augustine's College, or Winston–Salem State University. Applicants must be varsity athletes at their campus. Selection is made by the institution and based on leadership qualities, academics, and involvement in the institution's community. Men and women are considered separately.
Financial data: The stipend is $1,250.
Duration: 1 year; nonrenewable.
Number awarded: 20 each year: 2 (1 man and 1 woman) at each participating institution (except Bennett College for Women, which selects 2 women).
Deadline: Each institution sets its own deadline.

400 JOHN C. YOUNGBLOOD SCHOLARSHIPS

Virginia Interscholastic Athletic Administrators Association
c/o Steve Heon, Scholarship Chair
Western Albemarle High School
5941 Rockfish Gap Turnpike
Crozet, VA 22932
Phone: (434) 823–8705;
Email: sheon@k12albemarle.org
Web: www.viaaa.org/ssp/scholarship_information
Summary: To provide financial assistance to high school seniors in Virginia who have been involved in athletics and plan to attend college in any state.
Eligibility: Open to seniors graduating from high schools in Virginia where the athletic director is a member of the Virginia Interscholastic Athletic Administrators Association. Students must be nominated by their athletic director. Nominees must have made a significant contribution to athletics (have received at least 1 varsity monogram during their high school career and have participated in a varsity athletic program for at least 2 years), be planning to continue on to higher education at a school in any state, and be able to demonstrate financial need. They must submit a 100–word essay on how the award would be of special assistance to them and a 200–word essay on how their participation in high school athletics positively impacted their school and community.
Financial data: The stipend is $1,500.
Duration: 1 year.
Number awarded: 4 each year.
Deadline: January of each year.

401 $ JOHN D. GRAHAM SCHOLARSHIP

Public Relations Student Society of America
Attn: Vice President of Member Services
33 Maiden Lane, 11th Floor
New York, NY 10038–5150
Phone: (212) 460–1474; Fax: (212) 995–0757;
Email: prssa@prsa.org
Web: www.prssa.org/scholarships_competitions/individual
Summary: To provide financial assistance to upper–division students preparing for a career in public relations.
Eligibility: Open to students entering their senior year who are enrolled in a program of journalism, public relations, or other field that will prepare them for a career in public relations. Applicants must submit a 1–page resume, letters of recommendation from faculty members, and a statement on their views of the public relations profession and their public relations career goals. Selection is based on writing skills as demonstrated by the statement; commitment to public relations, particularly as expressed in the statement; practical experience (e.g., internships, other work or service); demonstrated leadership; letters of recommendation; and academic achievement in public relations and overall studies.
Financial data: Stipends are $3,000 or $1,000.
Duration: 1 year.
Number awarded: 3 each year: 1 at $3,000 and 2 at $1,000.
Deadline: June of each year.

402 $$ JOHN LEPPING MEMORIAL SCHOLARSHIP

Lep Foundation for Youth Education
Attn: Scholarship Selection Committee
9 Whispering Spring Drive
Millstone Township, NJ 08510
Email: lepfoundation@aol.com
Web: www.lepfoundation.org/application.htm
Summary: To provide financial assistance to high school seniors in New Jersey, New York, or Pennsylvania who have a physical disability or psychological handicap and plan to attend college in any state.
Eligibility: Open to seniors graduating from high schools in New Jersey, New York, or Pennsylvania and planning to enroll at a college, university, community college, or vocational school in any state. Applicants must have a disability, including (but not limited to) physical disabilities (e.g., spinal cord injury, loss of limb, birth defects, Lyme disease) or psychological handicaps (e.g., autism, cerebral palsy, post–traumatic stress). Along with their application, they must submit a brief statement of their career goals and ambitions for the future and a 500–word essay on why they feel they are the best candidate for this award. Financial need is considered in the selection process.
Financial data: The stipend is $5,000. Funds are paid directly to the recipient's school.
Duration: 1 year.
Number awarded: At least 4 each year.
Deadline: April of each year.

403 $ JOHN W. PERRY FUND

Coalition for HEA Reform
Attn: DRCNet Foundation
1623 Connecticut Avenue, N.W., Third Floor
Washington, DC 20009
Phone: (202) 362–0030; Fax: (202) 293–8344;
Email: perryfund@raiseyourvoice.com
Web: www.raiseyourvoice.com/Perry–index.html
Summary: To provide financial assistance for college or graduate school to students who are otherwise ineligible for aid because of a drug conviction.
Eligibility: Open to students who are ineligible for financial aid under the terms of the 1998 Higher Education Act that denies loans and grants to people who have drug convictions. Applicants must be entering or enrolled in college or graduate school. Along with their application, they must submit 1) a 1–page statement describing their drug conviction history, including the date of the offense, conviction date, conviction type, the amounts and type of drugs involved, and their role in the offense; and 2) an essay describing any special circumstances that increase their dependence on financial aid and/or obstacles to education they face or have faced. Financial need is considered in the selection process.
Financial data: Stipends range up to $2,000.
Duration: 1 year.
Number awarded: 1 or more each year.
Deadline: Deadline not specified.

404 $ JON M. PRITSCH MEMORIAL FUND GOLF SCHOLARSHIPS

Jon M. Pritsch Memorial Fund
8111 Carnoustie Place
Port St. Lucie, FL 34986
Summary: To provide financial assistance to high school seniors who have played on their golf team and plan to attend college in any state to prepare for a career as a professional golfer.
Eligibility: Open to seniors graduating from high schools in any state who have played golf as a member of their high school team. Applicants must be planning to enroll at a college or university and prepare for a career as a professional golfer. Along with their application, they must submit 1) an endorsement and letter of recommendation from their high school golf coach; 2) a letter of recommendation from the golf pro at the course where they play most of their golf; and 3) a 1–page essay on how they plan to prepare for a career as a professional golfer. Financial need is not considered in the selection process.
Financial data: Stipends range from $500 to $2,000.
Duration: 1 year.
Number awarded: 1 or more each year.
Deadline: May of each year.

405 $$ JOSEPHINE DE KARMAN FELLOWSHIPS

Josephine de Karman Fellowship Trust
Attn: Judy McClain, Secretary
P.O. Box 3389
San Dimas, CA 91773

Phone: (909) 592–0607;
Email: info@dekarman.org
Web: www.dekarman.org

Summary: To provide financial assistance to outstanding college seniors or students in their last year of a Ph.D. program.

Eligibility: Open to students in any discipline who will be entering their senior undergraduate year or their terminal year of a Ph.D. program in the fall of the next academic year. Postdoctoral students are not eligible. Foreign students may apply if they are already enrolled in a university in the United States. Applicants must be able to demonstrate exceptional ability and seriousness of purpose. Along with their application, they must submit a statement of 250 to 300 words on their intellectual interest in which undergraduates emphasize their long–term objectives and graduate students emphasize their current and proposed research.

Financial data: The stipend is $22,000 per year for graduate students or $14,000 per year for undergraduates. Funds are paid in 2 installments to the recipient's school. No funds may be used for travel.

Duration: 1 year; may not be renewed or postponed.

Number awarded: At least 10 each year.

Deadline: January of each year.

406 $ JOSHUA DAVID GARDNER MEMORIAL SCHOLARSHIP

Joshua David Gardner Memorial Scholarship Endowment, Inc.
4196 Merchant Plaza, Suite 816
Lake Ridge, VA 22192–5085
Phone: (719) 433–8101;
Email: gardner@joshgardnerendowment.org
Web: www.joshgardnerendowment.org

Summary: To provide financial assistance to undergraduates enrolled or planning to enroll at an Historically Black College or University (HBCU).

Eligibility: Open to U.S. citizens between 17 and 25 years of age who are enrolled or planning to enroll at an accredited 4–year HBCU. Applicants must have a GPA of 3.0 or higher and scores of at least 1000 on the critical reading and mathematics SAT or 19 on the ACT. Along with their application, they must submit a 500–word essay on the importance of personal integrity for leaders. Financial need is considered in the selection process.

Financial data: The stipend is $2,000.

Duration: 1 year; nonrenewable.

Number awarded: At least 1 each year.

Deadline: April of each year.

407 K. LEROY IRVIS UNDERGRADUATE SCHOLARSHIPS

Pennsylvania Black Conference on Higher Education
c/o Judith A.W. Thomas, Scholarship Committee Chair
Lincoln University, School of Social Sciences and Behavioral Studies
1570 Old Baltimore Pike
P.O. Box 179
Lincoln University, PA 19352
Phone: (484) 365–8159;
Email: scholarships@pbcohe.org
Web: www.phcohe.org

Summary: To provide financial assistance to African American residents of any state who are enrolled as undergraduates at colleges in Pennsylvania.

Eligibility: Open to African Americans from any state who have completed at least the first semester as an undergraduate at a college or university in Pennsylvania. Applicants must have a GPA of 3.0 or higher. Along with their application, they must submit an essay, up to 5 pages in length, on why they should receive this scholarship. Selection is based on that essay, academics, extracurricular activity participation, leadership qualities, and interpersonal qualities.

Financial data: The stipend is $1,000.

Duration: 1 year.

Number awarded: 6 each year: 2 in each of 3 regions (eastern, central, and western) in Pennsylvania.

Deadline: January of each year.

408 KANSAS BPW EDUCATIONAL FOUNDATION UNDERGRADUATE SCHOLARSHIP

Kansas Federation of Business & Professional Women's Clubs, Inc.
Attn: Kansas BPW Educational Foundation, Inc.
c/o Kathy Niehoff, Executive Secretary
605 East 15th
Ottawa, KS 66067
Phone: (785) 242–9319; Fax: (785) 242–1047;
Email: kathyniehoff@sbcglobal.net
Web: kansasbpw.memberlodge.org/Default.aspx?pageId=450103

Summary: To provide financial assistance to residents of Kansas who are attending a college in any state.

Eligibility: Open to Kansas residents (men and women) who are college sophomores, juniors, or seniors enrolled in a 4–year academic program at an accredited college or university in any state. Applicants must submit a 3–page personal biography in which they express their career goals, the direction they want to take in the future, their proposed field of study, their reason for selecting that field, the institutions they plan to attend and why, their circumstances for reentering school (if a factor), and what makes them uniquely qualified for this scholarship. They must also be able to document financial need. Applications must be submitted through a local unit of the sponsor.

Financial data: A stipend is awarded (amount not specified).

Duration: 1 year.

Number awarded: 1 or more each year.

Deadline: December of each year.

409 $ KANSAS COMPREHENSIVE GRANTS

Kansas Board of Regents
Attn: Student Financial Assistance
1000 S.W. Jackson Street, Suite 520
Topeka, KS 66612–1368
Phone: (785) 296–3518; Fax: (785) 296–0983;
Email: dlindeman@ksbor.org
Web: www.kansasregents.org/scholarships_and_grants

Summary: To provide need–based grants to Kansas residents who are attending college in the state.

Eligibility: Open to residents of Kansas who are enrolled full time at 1) the 18 private colleges and universities located in the state; 2) the 6 public universities; or 3) Washburn University. Financial need must be demonstrated.

Financial data: Stipends range from $200 to $3,500 per year at the private institutions and from $100 to $1,500 at the public institutions.

Duration: 1 year; may be renewed as long as the recipient remains in academic "good standing" and is able to demonstrate financial need.

Number awarded: Varies; generally, 7,000 or more each year. The funding level allows about 1 in 3 eligible students to be assisted.

Deadline: March of each year.

410 KANSAS ETHNIC MINORITY SCHOLARSHIP PROGRAM

Kansas Board of Regents
Attn: Student Financial Assistance
1000 S.W. Jackson Street, Suite 520
Topeka, KS 66612–1368
Phone: (785) 296–3518; Fax: (785) 296–0983;
Email: dlindeman@ksbor.org
Web: www.kansasregents.org/scholarships_and_grants

Summary: To provide financial assistance to minority students in Kansas who are interested in attending college in the state.

Eligibility: Open to Kansas residents who fall into 1 of these minority groups: American Indian, Alaskan Native, African American, Asian, Pacific Islander, or Hispanic. Applicants may be current college students (enrolled in community colleges, colleges, or universities in Kansas), but high school seniors graduating in the current year receive priority consideration. Minimum academic requirements include 1 of the following: 1) ACT score of 21 or higher or combined mathematics and critical reading SAT score of 990 or higher; 2) cumulative GPA of 3.0 or higher; 3) high school rank in upper 33%; 4) completion of the Kansas Scholars Curriculum (4 years of English, 3 years of mathematics, 3 years of science, 3 years of social studies, and 2 years of foreign language); 5) selection by the National Merit Corporation in any category; or 6) selection by the College Board as a Hispanic Scholar. Selection is based primarily on financial need.

Financial data: A stipend of up to $1,850 is provided, depending on financial need and availability of state funds.

Duration: 1 year; may be renewed for up to 3 additional years (4 additional years for designated 5–year programs), provided the recipient maintains a 2.0 cumulative GPA and has financial need.

Number awarded: Approximately 200 each year.

Deadline: April of each year.

411 KANSAS FOSTER AND ADOPTIVE CHILDREN SCHOLARSHIP FUND

Greater Kansas City Community Foundation
Attn: Scholarship Coordinator
1055 Broadway, Suite 130
Kansas City, MO 64105–1595
Phone: (816) 842–0944; Fax: (816) 842–8079;
Email: scholarships@gkccf.org
Web: www.gkccf.org/scholarships

Summary: To provide financial assistance to residents of Kansas who are current or former foster children and planning to attend college in any state.

Eligibility: Open to residents of Kansas who are or have been foster children, including those who have been adopted. Applicants must be attending or planning to attend a college, university, junior college, vocational/technical school, or other trade school in any state. Along with their application, they must submit brief statements on their intended field of study, what they hope to do with their education, the school and community organizations with which they have been involved, and which of those has been most important to them.

Financial data: A stipend is awarded (amount not specified).

Duration: 1 year.

Number awarded: 1 or more each year.

Deadline: Applications may be submitted at any time, but awards are made in June and November of each year.

412 $$ KANSAS FOSTER CHILD EDUCATION ASSISTANCE PROGRAM

Kansas Board of Regents
Attn: Student Financial Assistance
1000 S.W. Jackson Street, Suite 520
Topeka, KS 66612–1368
Phone: (785) 296–3518; Fax: (785) 296–0983;
Email: dlindeman@ksbor.org
Web: www.kansasregents.org/scholarships_and_grants

Summary: To provide financial assistance for college to residents of Kansas who have been in foster care.

Eligibility: Open to residents of Kansas who were 1) foster care children in the custody of the Department of Social and Rehabilitation Services at age 18; 2) in foster care placement while graduating from high school or completing their GED requirements prior to their 18th birthday; 3) adopted from foster care after 16 years of age; or 4) left a foster care placement subject to a guardianship after 16 years of age. Applicants must be enrolled or planning to enroll full time at educational institutions in Kansas, including area vocational/technical schools, community colleges, the municipal university, or state educational institutions or technical colleges. Enrollment must begin within 2 years following graduation from high school or completion of GED requirements.

Financial data: Qualifying students are permitted to enroll at an approved Kansas institution without payment of tuition or fees. They are responsible for other costs, such as books, room, and board.

Duration: 1 year; may be renewed as long as the recipient remains enrolled as a full–time undergraduate and employed an average of at least 10 hours per week.

Number awarded: Varies each year; no institution is required to honor more than 5 waivers in any academic year.

Deadline: Deadline not specified.

413 $$ KANSAS MILITARY SERVICE SCHOLARSHIPS

Kansas Board of Regents
Attn: Student Financial Assistance
1000 S.W. Jackson Street, Suite 520
Topeka, KS 66612–1368
Phone: (785) 296–3518; Fax: (785) 296–0983;
Email: dlindeman@ksbor.org
Web: www.kansasregents.org/scholarships_and_grants

Summary: To provide financial assistance for college to residents of Kansas who have served or are still serving in the military.

Eligibility: Open to students who graduated from high school in Kansas or received a GED credential and have been a resident of the state for at least 2 years. Applicants must have served in the U.S. armed forces in Iraq or Afghanistan, or in international waters or on foreign soil in support of military operations in Iraq or Afghanistan, for at least 90 days after September 11, 2001 or for less than 90 days because of injuries received during such service. They must still be in military service or have received an honorable discharge with orders that indicate they served after September 11, 2001 in Operations Enduring Freedom, Nobel Eagle, and/or Iraqi Freedom. Qualified veterans and military personnel may enroll at a public postsecondary institution in Kansas, including area vocational schools, area vocational/technical schools, community colleges, the municipal university, state educational institutions, or technical colleges. In the selection process, priority is given to applicants who can demonstrate financial need.

Financial data: Qualifying students are permitted to enroll at an approved Kansas institution without payment of tuition or fees. If they receive any federal military tuition assistance, that money must be applied to their tuition and fees and they are eligible only for the remaining balance in scholarship assistance.

Duration: 1 year; may be renewed for a total of 10 semesters as long as the recipient remains in good academic standing.

Number awarded: Varies each year.

Deadline: April of each year.

414 KANSAS STATE SCHOLARSHIPS

Kansas Board of Regents
Attn: Student Financial Assistance
1000 S.W. Jackson Street, Suite 520
Topeka, KS 66612–1368
Phone: (785) 296–3518; Fax: (785) 296–0983;
Email: dlindeman@ksbor.org
Web: www.kansasregents.org/scholarships_and_grants

Summary: To provide need–based assistance to students who are in the top of their high school class in Kansas and planning to attend college.

Eligibility: Open to high school seniors in Kansas who are designated as State Scholars. Applicants must be planning to enroll full time at a college or university in the state. Selection for this program is based on ACT Assessment scores (recently, the average score of designees was 29), completion of the Kansas Scholars Curriculum (4 years of English, 4 years of mathematics, 3 years of science, 3 years of social studies, 2 years of foreign language, and 1 year of computer technology), and academic record (recently, the average GPA of designees was 3.89). State Scholars who demonstrate financial need are eligible for these scholarships.

Financial data: The stipend ranges up to $1,000 per year, depending upon the recipient's financial need.

Duration: Up to 4 academic years (unless enrolled in a designated 5–year program), provided the recipient maintains a 3.0 GPA and financial need.

Number awarded: Varies; generally, at least 1,200 each year. Generally, between 20 and 40% of high school seniors who complete the Kansas Scholars Curriculum are designated as Kansas State Scholars.

Deadline: April of each year.

415 $$ KANSAS TUITION WAIVER FOR DEPENDENTS AND SPOUSES OF DECEASED MILITARY PERSONNEL

Kansas Board of Regents
Attn: Student Financial Assistance
1000 S.W. Jackson Street, Suite 520
Topeka, KS 66612–1368
Phone: (785) 296–3518; Fax: (785) 296–0983;
Email: dlindeman@ksbor.org
Web: www.kansasregents.org/scholarships_and_grants

Summary: To provide financial assistance for college to residents of Kansas whose parent or spouse died on active military service after September 11, 2001.

Eligibility: Open to residents of Kansas who are the dependent children or spouses of members of the U.S. armed forces who died on or after September 11, 2001 while, and as a result of, serving on active military duty. The deceased military member must have been a resident of Kansas at the time of death. Applicants must be enrolled or planning to enroll at a public educational institution in Kansas, including area vocational/technical schools and colleges, community colleges, the state universities, and Washburn University.

Financial data: Qualifying students are permitted to enroll at an approved Kansas institution without payment of tuition or fees. They are responsible for other costs, such as books, room, and board.

Duration: 1 year; may be renewed for a total of 10 semesters of undergraduate study.

Number awarded: Varies each year.

Deadline: Deadline not specified.

416 $$ KANSAS TUITION WAIVER FOR DEPENDENTS AND SPOUSES OF DECEASED PUBLIC SAFETY OFFICERS

Kansas Board of Regents
Attn: Student Financial Assistance
1000 S.W. Jackson Street, Suite 520

Topeka, KS 66612–1368
Phone: (785) 296–3518; Fax: (785) 296–0983;
Email: dlindeman@ksbor.org
Web: www.kansasregents.org/scholarships_and_grants

Summary: To provide financial assistance for college to residents of Kansas whose parent or spouse died in the line of duty as a public safety officer.

Eligibility: Open to residents of Kansas who are the dependent children or spouses of public safety officers (law enforcement officers, firefighters, and emergency medical services attendants) who died as the result of injuries sustained in the line of duty. Applicants must be enrolled or planning to enroll at a public educational institution in Kansas, including area vocational/technical schools and colleges, community colleges, the state universities, and Washburn University.

Financial data: Qualifying students are permitted to enroll at an approved Kansas institution without payment of tuition or fees. They are responsible for other costs, such as books, room, and board.

Duration: 1 year; may be renewed for a total of 10 semesters of undergraduate study.

Number awarded: Varies each year.

Deadline: Deadline not specified.

417 $$ KANSAS TUITION WAIVER FOR PRISONERS OF WAR

Kansas Board of Regents
Attn: Student Financial Assistance
1000 S.W. Jackson Street, Suite 520
Topeka, KS 66612–1368
Phone: (785) 296–3518; Fax: (785) 296–0983;
Email: dlindeman@ksbor.org
Web: www.kansasregents.org/scholarships_and_grants

Summary: To provide financial assistance for college to residents of Kansas who have been a prisoner of war.

Eligibility: Open to current residents of Kansas who entered active service in the U.S. armed forces as a resident of the state. Applicants must have been declared a prisoner of war after January 1, 1960 while serving in the armed forces. They must be enrolled or planning to enroll at a public educational institution in Kansas, including area vocational/technical schools and colleges, community colleges, the state universities, and Washburn University.

Financial data: Qualifying students are permitted to enroll at an approved Kansas institution without payment of tuition or fees. They are responsible for other costs, such as books, room, and board.

Duration: 1 year; may be renewed for a total of 10 semesters of undergraduate study.

Number awarded: Varies each year.

Deadline: Deadline not specified.

418 $ KATHERN F. GRUBER SCHOLARSHIPS

Blinded Veterans Association
477 H Street, N.W.
Washington, DC 20001–2694
Phone: (202) 371–8880; (800) 669–7079; Fax: (202) 371–8258;
Email: bva@bva.org
Web: www.bva.org/services.html

Summary: To provide financial assistance for undergraduate or graduate study to spouses and children of blinded veterans.

Eligibility: Open to dependent children and spouses of blinded veterans of the U.S. armed forces. The veteran must be legally blind; the blindness may be either service–connected or nonservice–connected. Applicants must have been accepted or be currently enrolled as a full–time student in an undergraduate or graduate program at an accredited institution of higher learning. Along with their application, they must submit a 300–word essay on their career goals and aspirations. Financial need is not considered in the selection process.

Financial data: The stipend is $2,000; funds are intended to be used to cover the student's expenses, including tuition, other academic fees, books, dormitory fees, and cafeteria fees. Funds are paid directly to the recipient's school.

Duration: 1 year; recipients may reapply for up to 3 additional years.

Number awarded: 6 each year.

Deadline: April of each year.

419 $$ KENNETH JERNIGAN SCHOLARSHIP

National Federation of the Blind
Attn: Scholarship Committee
200 East Wells Street
Baltimore, MD 21230
Phone: (410) 659–9314, ext. 2415; Fax: (410) 685–5653;
Email: scholarships@nfb.org
Web: www.nfb.org/nfb/scholarship_program.asp

Summary: To provide financial assistance to entering or continuing undergraduate and graduate blind students.

Eligibility: Open to legally blind students who are working on or planning to work full time on an undergraduate or graduate degree. Along with their application, they must submit transcripts, standardized test scores, proof of legal blindness, 2 letters of recommendation, and a letter of endorsement from their National Federation of the Blind state president or designee. Selection is based on academic excellence, service to the community, and financial need.

Financial data: The stipend is $12,000.

Duration: 1 year; recipients may resubmit applications up to 2 additional years.

Number awarded: 1 each year.

Deadline: March of each year.

420 KENNY C. GUINN MEMORIAL MILLENNIUM SCHOLARSHIP

Nevada State Treasurer
Attn: Governor Guinn Millennium Scholarship
101 North Carson Street, Suite 4
Carson City, NV 89701
Phone: (702) 486–3383; (888) 477–2667; Fax: (702) 486–3246
Web: www.nevadatreasurer.gov

Summary: To provide financial assistance to high school seniors in Nevada who complete a required core curriculum and plan to attend college in the state.

Eligibility: Open to seniors graduating from public or private high schools in Nevada who complete a required core curriculum with a GPA of 3.25 or higher. Applicants must be planning to enroll at an approved institution of higher education in the state in a program that leads to a recognized associate degree, baccalaureate degree, or pre–baccalaureate certificate. Along with their application, they must submit a resume that includes their school and community involvement, awards, and achievements; a 500–word essay describing what this scholarship means to them and how they will use their degree to benefit the citizens of Nevada; a statement of community service; and letters of recommendation. Financial need is not considered in the selection process.

Financial data: Students at community colleges receive $40 per semester for each lower–division hour or $60 per semester for each upper–division hour; students at state colleges receive $60 per semester credit hour; students at other universities in the state receive $80 per semester credit. Support is provided up to 12 hours per semester. The lifetime maximum for each student is $10,000.

Duration: Support is available for a maximum of 6 years following graduation from high school. Continuation of support requires the student to enroll in at least 12 units per semester in a degree program at a university or state college or 6 units per semester in a degree program at a community college and maintain a GPA of 2.6 or higher for up to 30 units or 2.75 or higher for 30 units or more.

Number awarded: Varies each year; recently, more than 9,200 students qualified for these scholarships and more than 4,700 utilized them.

Deadline: March of each year.

421 KENTUCKY COLLEGE ACCESS PROGRAM GRANTS

Kentucky Higher Education Assistance Authority
Attn: Student Aid Branch
100 Airport Road
P.O. Box 798
Frankfort, KY 40602–0798
Phone: (502) 696–7397; (800) 928–8926, ext. 7397; Fax: (502) 696–7373;
TDD: (800) 855–2880;
Email: studentaid@kheaa.com
Web: www.kheaa.com/website/kheaa/cap?main=1

Summary: To provide financial assistance to college students in Kentucky who have financial need.

Eligibility: Open to Kentucky residents enrolled in 2– or 4–year public or private nonprofit colleges, proprietary schools, or vocational/technical schools for a minimum of 6 semester hours in an academic program that takes at least 2 years to complete. Applicants must be able to demonstrate financial need (the total Expected Family Contribution toward educational expenses cannot exceed $5,273). Students majoring in divinity, theology, or religious education are not eligible.

Financial data: The maximum stipend is $1,900 per year. Eligible part–time college students receive an award calculated at the rate of $79 per credit hour.

Duration: Students at 2–year schools may receive the equivalent of 5 semesters of grants; students at 4–year schools may receive the equivalent of 9 semesters of grants.

Number awarded: Varies each year; awards are made to eligible students until funds are depleted. Recently, approximately 43,650 students received these grants.
Deadline: Applications may be submitted at any time, but students who file by March of each year have the best chance of receiving funds.

422 $ KENTUCKY COLONELS BETTER LIFE SCHOLARSHIPS

Kentucky Community and Technical College System
Attn: Financial Aid
300 North Main Street
Versailles, KY 40383
Phone: (859) 256–3100; (877) 528–2748 (within KY)
Web: www.kctcs.edu
Summary: To provide financial assistance to single parents attending or planning to attend 1 of the schools within the Kentucky Community and Technical College System (KCTCS).
Eligibility: Open to Kentucky residents who are single working parents with at least 1 child under 12 years of age. Applicants must be attending or planning to attend a KCTCS institution and able to demonstrate unmet financial need. Selection is based on demonstrated enthusiasm for learning and potential for academic success.
Financial data: The stipend is $2,500 per year.
Duration: 1 year; may be renewed 1 additional year if the recipient maintains full–time enrollment and satisfactory academic progress.
Number awarded: 16 each year: 1 in each of the KCTCS districts.
Deadline: Deadline not specified.

423 $$ KENTUCKY COMMUNITY AND TECHNICAL COLLEGE SYSTEM PRESIDENT'S SCHOLARSHIPS

Kentucky Community and Technical College System
Attn: Financial Aid
300 North Main Street
Versailles, KY 40383
Phone: (859) 256–3100; (877) 528–2748 (within KY)
Web: www.kctcs.edu
Summary: To provide financial assistance to students at participating institutions within the Kentucky Community and Technical College System (KCTCS).
Eligibility: Open to students entering or attending participating KCTCS institutions. Each college establishes its own selection criteria, but most are based on academic excellence and financial need.
Financial data: Stipends vary at each participating college, but are intended to provide full payment of tuition and required fees.
Duration: 1 year; may be renewed 1 additional year.
Number awarded: Varies each year.
Deadline: Each college sets its own deadline.

424 $$ KENTUCKY DECEASED OR DISABLED LAW ENFORCEMENT OFFICER AND FIRE FIGHTER DEPENDENT TUITION WAIVER

Kentucky Fire Commission
Attn: Executive Director
300 North Main Street
Versailles, KY 40383
Phone: (859) 256–3478; (800) 782–6823; Fax: (859) 256–3125;
Email: ronnie.day@kctcs.net
Web: kyfirecommission.kcts.edu
Summary: To provide financial assistance for college to the children and spouses of Kentucky police officers or firefighters deceased or disabled in the line of duty.
Eligibility: Open to spouses, widow(er)s, and children of Kentucky residents who became a law enforcement officer, firefighter, or volunteer firefighter and who 1) were killed while in active service or training for active service; 2) died as a result of a service–connected disability; or 3) became permanently and totally disabled as a result of active service or training for active service. Children must be between 17and 23 years of age; spouses and widow(er)s may be of any age.
Financial data: Recipients are entitled to a waiver of tuition at state–supported universities, community colleges, and technical training institutions in Kentucky.
Duration: 1 year; may be renewed up to a maximum total of 36 months.
Number awarded: Varies each year; all qualified applicants are entitled to this aid.
Deadline: Deadline not specified.

425 $ KENTUCKY EDUCATIONAL EXCELLENCE SCHOLARSHIPS

Kentucky Higher Education Assistance Authority
Attn: Student Aid Branch
100 Airport Road
P.O. Box 798
Frankfort, KY 40602–0798
Phone: (502) 696–7397; (800) 928–8926, ext. 7397; Fax: (502) 696–7373;
TDD: (800) 855–2880;
Email: kees@kheaa.com
Web: www.kheaa.com/website/kheaa/kees?main=1
Summary: To provide financial assistance to Kentucky residents who achieve high GPAs and ACT scores in high school and plan to attend college in the state.
Eligibility: Open to Kentucky high school students who achieve at least a 2.5 GPA each year in high school and a score of at least 15 on the ACT or 710 on the critical reading and mathematics SAT. Students must graduate from a high school in Kentucky and fulfill the state's core curriculum requirements. They must attend an accredited public or private institution in Kentucky, including community and technical colleges, or a school in another state that participates in the Academic Common Market. Other requirements apply to students who have a GED, are home schooled, or graduated from high school previously. U.S. citizenship or status as a permanent resident or national is required.
Financial data: For each year in high school that students achieve at least a 2.5 GPA, they receive at least $125 per year for college. Higher GPAs mean larger scholarships, rising to $500 per year for a 4.0 GPA. In addition, students receive a bonus award based on their best ACT score, starting at $36 for 15 and rising to $500 for a score of 28 or higher. The maximum potential award is $2,500 per year of college for a student who achieves a 4.0 GPA for each of 4 years of high school (thus earning an annual college scholarship of $2,000—$500 for each of the years with a 4.0 GPA) plus a bonus of $500 for an ACT score of 28 or higher. Recently, awards averaged approximately $1,520 per year.
Duration: Up to 4 years, provided the recipient earns a GPA of 2.5 or higher during the first year of college and 3.0 or higher during each succeeding year. Students in designated programs that require 5 years for a bachelor's degree (architecture, landscape architecture, and engineering) are entitled to 5 years of support from this program.
Number awarded: Varies each year; recently, more than 47,000 students received more than $72 million in these awards.
Deadline: Deadline not specified.

426 KENTUCKY GO HIGHER GRANT PROGRAM

Kentucky Higher Education Assistance Authority
Attn: Go Higher Grant Coordinator
100 Airport Road
P.O. Box 798
Frankfort, KY 40602–0798
Phone: (502) 696–7397; (800) 928–8926, ext. 7397; Fax: (502) 696–7373;
TDD: (800) 855–2880;
Email: grants@kheaa.com
Web: www.kheaa.com/website/kheaa/gohighergrant?main=1
Summary: To provide financial assistance to adult Kentucky residents who are interested in attending college in the state on less than a half–time basis.
Eligibility: Open to Kentucky residents who are 24 years of age or older and do not currently have a bachelor's degree. Applicants must be interested in enrolling at a college or university in the state for fewer than 6 credit hours. They must be able to demonstrate financial need. U.S. citizenship or status as a permanent resident or national is required.
Financial data: The program provides a stipend of $1,000 per year to be applied to tuition and a book allowance of $50 per credit hour.
Duration: 1 year.
Number awarded: Varies each year.
Deadline: Deadline not specified.

427 $ KENTUCKY TUITION GRANTS

Kentucky Higher Education Assistance Authority
Attn: Student Aid Branch
100 Airport Road
P.O. Box 798
Frankfort, KY 40602–0798
Phone: (502) 696–7397; (800) 928–8926, ext. 7397; Fax: (502) 696–7373;
TDD: (800) 855–2880;
Email: studentaid@kheaa.com
Web: www.kheaa.com/website/kheaa/ktg?main=1

Summary: To provide financial assistance to Kentucky residents who are attending independent colleges in the state.
Eligibility: Open to Kentucky residents enrolled in eligible Kentucky independent nonprofit institutions as full–time undergraduate students in eligible courses of study. They must be able to demonstrate financial need. Programs in divinity, theology, or religious education are not eligible.
Financial data: Grants range from $200 to $2,964 per academic year.
Duration: Students at 2–year schools may receive the equivalent of 5 semesters of grants; students at 4–year schools may receive the equivalent of 9 semesters of grants.
Number awarded: Varies each year; awards are made to eligible students until funds are depleted. Recently, approximately 11,270 students received these grants.
Deadline: Applications may be submitted at any time, but students who file by March of each year have the best chance of receiving funds.

428 $$ KENTUCKY VETERANS TUITION WAIVER PROGRAM

Kentucky Department of Veterans Affairs
Attn: Field Operations Branch
321 West Main Street, Suite 390
Louisville, KY 40202
Phone: (502) 595–4447; (800) 928–4012 (within KY); Fax: (502) 595–4448;
Email: Pamela.Cypert@ky.gov
Web: www.veterans.ky.gov/benefits/tuitionwaiver.htm
Summary: To provide financial assistance for college to the children, spouses, or unremarried widow(er)s of disabled or deceased Kentucky veterans.
Eligibility: Open to the children, stepchildren, spouses, and unremarried widow(er)s of veterans who are residents of Kentucky (or were residents at the time of their death). The qualifying veteran must meet 1 of the following conditions: 1) died on active duty (regardless of wartime service); 2) died as a result of a service–connected disability (regardless of wartime service); 3) has a 100% service–connected disability; 4) is totally disabled (nonservice–connected) with wartime service; or 5) is deceased and served during war time. The military service may have been as a member of the U.S. armed forces, the Kentucky National Guard, or a Reserve component; service in the Guard or Reserves must have been on state active duty, active duty for training, inactive duty training, or active duty with the U.S. armed forces. Children of veterans must be under 26 years of age; no age limit applies to spouses or unremarried widow(er)s. All applicants must be attending or planning to attend a 2–year, 4–year, or vocational technical school operated and funded by the Kentucky Department of Education.
Financial data: Eligible dependents and survivors are exempt from tuition and matriculation fees at any state–supported institution of higher education in Kentucky.
Duration: Tuition is waived until the recipient completes 45 months of training, receives a college degree, or (in the case of children of veterans) reaches 26 years of age, whichever comes first. Spouses and unremarried widow(er)s are not subject to the age limitation.
Number awarded: Varies each year.
Deadline: Deadline not specified.

429 KEVIN CHILD SCHOLARSHIP

National Hemophilia Foundation
Attn: Information Resource Center
116 West 32nd Street, 11th Floor
New York, NY 10001–3212
Phone: (212) 328–3700; (800) 42–HANDI, ext. 2; Fax: (212) 328–3777;
Email: handi@hemophilia.org
Web: hemophilia.org
Summary: To provide financial assistance for college to students with hemophilia.
Eligibility: Open to high school seniors entering their first year of undergraduate study as well as those currently enrolled in college. Applicants must have hemophilia A or B. Along with their application, they must submit a 1–page essay on their occupational objectives and goals in life and how the educational program they have planned will meet those objectives. Selection is based on that essay, academic performance, and participation in school and community activities.
Financial data: The stipend is $1,000.
Duration: 1 year.
Number awarded: 1 each year.
Deadline: May of each year.

430 $$ KFC COLONEL'S SCHOLARS

KFC Corporation
Attn: Kentucky Fried Chicken Foundation
P.O. Box 725489
Atlanta, GA 31139
Phone: (866) KFC–7240;
Email: scholars@kfc.com
Web: www.kfcscholars.org/scholarships
Summary: To provide financial assistance to high school seniors who plan to attend a college or university in their state.
Eligibility: Open to graduating high school seniors planning to attend a 2– or 4–year public college or university in their home state with plans to complete a bachelor's degree. They must have a GPA of 2.75 or higher and be able to demonstrate financial need. U.S. citizenship or permanent resident status is required.
Financial data: The stipend is $5,000 per year.
Duration: 1 year; may be renewed up to 3 additional years, provided the recipients remain enrolled full time with a GPA of 2.75 or higher.
Number awarded: Approximately 75 each year.
Deadline: February of each year.

431 $ KIM AND HAROLD LOUIE FAMILY FOUNDATION SCHOLARSHIPS

Kim and Harold Louie Family Foundation
102 Fey Drive
Burlingame, CA 94010
Phone: (650) 491–3434; Fax: (650) 490–3153;
Email: louiefoundation@gmail.com
Web: www.louiefamilyfoundation.org
Summary: To provide financial assistance for college to high school seniors who have faced special challenges in completing their education.
Eligibility: Open to graduating high school seniors who plan to enroll either full time or at least substantial part time at an accredited college, university, or vocational program in any state. Applicants must be able to demonstrate outstanding personal achievements, academic merit, leadership qualities, and/or community service. They must have a GPA of 3.0 or higher and an SAT score of at least 1700 or an ACT score of at least 24. Special consideration is given to students who have a demonstrated financial need, whose parents who did not attend college, who have a documented disability, who have overcome significant adversity, or who have parents that are U.S. veterans or are currently in the U.S. military. U.S. citizenship or legal resident status is required.
Financial data: Stipends vary each year; recently, they averaged $4,000.
Duration: 1 year.
Number awarded: Varies each year; recently, 25 of these scholarships were awarded. The foundation expects to award $100,000 in scholarships each year.
Deadline: March of each year.

432 KOHL EXCELLENCE SCHOLARSHIPS

Herb Kohl Educational Foundation, Inc.
Attn: Kim Marggraf
P.O. Box 877
Sheboygan, WI 53082–0877
Phone: (920) 457–1727;
Email: marggraf@excel.net
Web: www.kohleducation.org/students
Summary: To provide financial assistance to Wisconsin high school seniors who plan to attend college in any state.
Eligibility: Open to seniors graduating from high schools in Wisconsin and planning to attend college in any state. Applications are available from the Wisconsin Department of Public Instruction (DPI) for public school students, the Wisconsin Council of Religious and Independent Schools (WCRIS) for religious and independent school students, or from the Wisconsin Parents Association (WPA) for home–schooled students. Along with their application, they must submit an essay of 300 to 500 words describing their goals in future education, personal life, community and society service, and career. Selection is based on the essay (35 points); 3 letters of recommendation (15 points); leadership and participation in music and speech activities (10 points); leadership and participation in athletic activities (10 points); leadership and participation in other school and community activities (10 points); work experience, hobbies, outside interests, and special talents (10 points); and overall quality of application (8 points).
Financial data: The stipend is $1,000. Funds may be used to pay for tuition and fees during the first year of college only and are paid directly to the recipient's postsecondary institution.

Duration: 1 year (the first year of college); nonrenewable.
Number awarded: 100 each year; awards are distributed proportionally to students in public schools, religious and independent schools, and home schools. Since the program was established, it has awarded 2,200 scholarships.
Deadline: November of each year.

433 $$ KOHL'S CARES SCHOLARSHIP PROGRAM

Kohl's Department Stores, Inc.
Attn: Community Relations Department
N56 W17000 Ridgewood Drive
Menomonee Falls, WI 53051
Phone: (262) 703–7000; Fax: (262) 703–6305;
Email: community.relations@kohls.com
Web: www.kohlscorporation.com/CommunityRelations/scholarship/index.asp

Summary: To recognize and reward kids who volunteer in their communities.
Eligibility: Open to kids who volunteer and have made a difference in their communities within the past 12 months. They must be between 6 and 18 years of age and have not yet graduated from high school. They must have conducted a community service project within the past 12 months that resulted in a positive community outcome. Students must be nominated. Awards are presented on the individual store level, on the regional level, and on the national level. Selection is based on the project, benefits, and outcome; financial need and academic performance are not considered.
Financial data: Awards are presented in all age groups. Store–level winners receive a $50 Kohl's gift card and a certificate. Regional winners receive a $1,000 college scholarship, a certificate, and appearance on an in–store poster. National winners receive a $10,000 college scholarship, a plaque, national recognition on an in–store poster, and a $1,000 grant to the charity of their choice.
Duration: The competition is held annually.
Number awarded: Each year, more than 2,100 awards are presented on the store level, more than 200 on the regional level, and 10 on the national level.
Deadline: March of each year.

434 $$ KOREAN ANCESTRY GRANTS

William Orr Dingwall Foundation
2201 N Street, N.W., Suite 117
Washington, DC 20037
Email: apply@dingwallfoundation.org
Web: www.dingwallfoundation.org/

Summary: To provide financial assistance to undergraduates of Asian (preferably Korean) ancestry.
Eligibility: Open to graduating high school seniors and undergraduates currently enrolled at a college or university in the United States. Applicants should be of Korean ancestry, although exceptional students of other Asian ancestry may also be considered. They must have a GPA of 3.5 or higher but may be majoring in any field. Selection is based on academic record, written statements, and letters of recommendation.
Financial data: The stipend is $20,000 per year.
Duration: 1 year; may be renewed up to 3 additional years, provided the recipient maintains a GPA of 3.5 or higher.
Number awarded: Varies each year; recently, 26 of these grants were awarded.
Deadline: January of each year.

435 KYLE LEE FOUNDATION SCHOLARSHIP

Kyle Lee Foundation, Inc.
3843 South Bristol Street, Number 293
Santa Ana, CA 92704
Phone: (714) 433–3204;
Email: foundation@kylelee28.com
Web: www.kylelee28.com

Summary: To provide financial assistance for college to cancer survivors.
Eligibility: Open to high school seniors and current college students who have had cancer, especially Ewing's sarcoma. Applicants must submit a letter from their doctor confirming their cancer diagnosis, copies of academic transcripts, 2 letters of recommendation, and a 700–word essay outlining their goals in college and how their fight with cancer has affected their life and goals.
Financial data: Stipends are $1,000 or $500.
Duration: 1 year.
Number awarded: Varies each year; recently, 5 of these scholarships were awarded.
Deadline: May of each year.

436 $$ KYLE PATRICK WANKMILLER SCHOLARSHIP FUND

Central Scholarship Bureau
1700 Reisterstown Road, Suite 220
P.O. Box 37064
Baltimore, MD 21297–3064
Phone: (410) 415–5558; Fax: (410) 415–5501;
Email: contact@centralsb.org
Web: www.centralsb.org/html/KylePatrickWankmillerScholarshipFund.htm

Summary: To provide financial assistance to residents of Maryland interested in working on an undergraduate or graduate degree at a college in any state.
Eligibility: Open to residents of Maryland who are enrolled or planning to enroll full time at a college, university, or vocational school in any state. Undergraduates and graduate students must have a cumulative GPA of 3.0 or higher; vocational students must have a cumulative GPA of 2.0 or higher. All applicants must have a family income less than $90,000 per year. Financial need is considered in the selection process. U.S. citizenship or permanent resident status is required.
Financial data: The stipend is $5,000 per year.
Duration: 1 year; recipients may reapply.
Number awarded: 1 or more each year.
Deadline: May of each year.

437 $ LA FRA NATIONAL PRESIDENT'S SCHOLARSHIP

Ladies Auxiliary of the Fleet Reserve Association
Attn: Membership Service Administrator
P.O. Box 2086
Shingle Springs, CA 95682–2086
Phone: (530) 677–3925;
Email: laframsa@att.net
Web: www.la–fra.org/scholarship.html

Summary: To provide financial assistance for college to the children and grandchildren of naval personnel.
Eligibility: Open to the children and grandchildren of Navy, Marine, Coast Guard, active Fleet Reserve, Fleet Marine Corps Reserve, and Coast Guard Reserve personnel on active duty, retired with pay, or deceased while on active duty or retired with pay. Applicants must submit an essay on their life experiences, career objectives, and what motivated them to select those objectives. Selection is based on academic record, financial need, extracurricular activities, leadership skills, and participation in community activities. U.S. citizenship is required.
Financial data: The stipend is $2,500.
Duration: 1 year; may be renewed.
Number awarded: 1 each year.
Deadline: April of each year.

438 LA UNIDAD LATINA SCHOLARSHIPS

La Unidad Latina Foundation, Inc.
132 East 43rd Street, Suite 358
New York, NY 10017
Email: info@lulfoundation.org
Web: www.lulfoundation.org

Summary: To provide financial assistance to Hispanic students who are working on a bachelor's or master's degree in any field.
Eligibility: Open to students of Hispanic background who have completed at least 1 year of full–time undergraduate study or 1 semester of full–time graduate school. Undergraduates must have a GPA between 2.8 and 3.6 (college students with a GPA higher than 3.6 are not eligible). Applicants must be enrolled at an accredited 4–year college or university in the United States and working on a bachelor's or master's degree. Along with their application, they must submit brief essays on their financial need, their academic plans and career goals, an instance in which they have demonstrated exceptional leadership during their college or graduate experience, the impact they have had or plan to have on improving or supporting their Latino/Hispanic community, their extracurricular activities, any honors or awards they have received, and their special interests or hobbies.
Financial data: Stipends range from $250 to $1,000.
Duration: 1 year.
Number awarded: Varies each year.
Deadline: March of each year for spring semester; October of each year for fall semester.

439 $ LARRY STREETER MEMORIAL SCHOLARSHIP

National Federation of the Blind
Attn: Scholarship Committee
200 East Wells Street
Baltimore, MD 21230
Phone: (410) 659–9314, ext. 2415; Fax: (410) 685–5653;
Email: scholarships@nfb.org
Web: www.nfb.org/nfb/scholarship_program.asp

Summary: To provide financial assistance to blind students working on an undergraduate or graduate degree in any field.

Eligibility: Open to legally blind students who are working on or planning to work full time on an undergraduate or graduate degree in any field. Applicants must be attempting to "elevate their quality of life, equipping them to be active, productive participants in their family, community, and the workplace." Along with their application, they must submit transcripts, standardized test scores, proof of legal blindness, 2 letters of recommendation, and a letter of endorsement from their National Federation of the Blind state president or designee. Selection is based on academic excellence, service to the community, and financial need.

Financial data: The stipend is $3,000.

Duration: 1 year; recipients may resubmit applications up to 2 additional years.

Number awarded: 1 each year.

Deadline: March of each year.

440 LAURA BLACKBURN MEMORIAL SCHOLARSHIP

American Legion Auxiliary
Department of Kentucky
P.O. Box 5435
Frankfort, KY 40602–5435
Phone: (502) 352–2380; Fax: (502) 352–2381
Web: www.kyamlegionaux.org

Summary: To provide financial assistance to descendants of veterans in Kentucky who plan to attend college in any state.

Eligibility: Open to the children, grandchildren, and great–grandchildren of veterans who served in the armed forces during eligibility dates for membership in the American Legion. Applicants must be Kentucky residents enrolled in their senior year at an accredited high school. They must be planning to attend a college or university in any state. Selection is based on academic achievement (40%), character (20%), leadership (20%), and Americanism (20%).

Financial data: The stipend is $1,000.

Duration: 1 year.

Number awarded: 1 each year.

Deadline: March of each year.

441 LAWRENCE C. YEARDLEY FUND SCHOLARSHIP

Greater Kanawha Valley Foundation
Attn: Scholarship Program Officer
1600 Huntington Square
900 Lee Street East, 16th Floor
Charleston, WV 25301
Phone: (304) 346–3620; (800) 467–5909; Fax: (304) 346–3640;
Email: shoover@tgkvf.org
Web: www.tgkvf.org/page.aspx?pid=409

Summary: To provide financial assistance to residents of West Virginia who are interested in attending college in any state.

Eligibility: Open to residents of West Virginia who are attending or planning to attend a college or university anywhere in the country. Applicants must have an ACT score of 20 or higher; be able to demonstrate good moral character, academic excellence, and extreme financial need; and have a GPA of 2.5 or higher.

Financial data: The stipend is $1,500 per year.

Duration: 1 year; may be renewed.

Number awarded: 1 or 2 each year.

Deadline: January of each year.

442 LAWRENCE MADEIROS SCHOLARSHIP

Lawrence Madeiros Scholarship Program
Attn: Scholarship Panel
P.O. Box 11
Mayfield, NY 12117
Phone: (518) 863–8998
Web: www.adirondackspintacular.com

Summary: To provide financial assistance for college to high school seniors who have a bleeding or other chronic disorder.

Eligibility: Open to seniors graduating from high school who have been accepted at an accredited college or university. Applicants must be diagnosed with a bleeding or other chronic disorder. Along with their application, they must submit brief essays on 1) how living with or around a chronic disorder has impacted their life; 2) their goals and aspirations in life; and 3) their passion. Financial need may also be considered.

Financial data: The stipend is $1,000.

Duration: 1 year.

Number awarded: Varies each year.

Deadline: April of each year.

443 $ LEAD WITH YOUR HEART SCHOLARSHIP

Cappex.com, LLC
2008 St. Johns Avenue
Highland Park, IL 60035
Web: www.cappex.com/scholarships

Summary: To provide financial assistance for college to high school seniors who complete a profile for Cappex.com and who have contributed selfless service to others.

Eligibility: Open to students who complete an online profile for Cappex.com that will enable colleges and universities to contact them for recruiting purposes. They must be U.S. citizens or permanent residents planning to attend an accredited college or university in the United States. In completing their profile, they must describe their extracurricular, leadership, and volunteer activities. This scholarship is reserved for high school seniors who have contributed selfless service that has made a big impact on their school, town, or beyond.

Financial data: The stipend is $2,500.

Duration: 1 year.

Number awarded: 1 each year.

Deadline: December of each year.

444 LEADERS AND ACHIEVERS SCHOLARSHIP PROGRAM

Comcast Foundation
One Comcast Center
1500 Market Street
Philadelphia, PA 19102–2148
Phone: (215) 665–1700; (800) COMCAST;
Email: comcast@applyists.com
Web: corporate.comcast.com

Summary: To provide financial assistance for college to high school seniors in communities served by Comcast Digital Cable.

Eligibility: Open to seniors graduating from high schools in communities served by Comcast Digital Cable (although they are not required to subscribe to that service). Students must be nominated by their principals. They must have a GPA of 2.8 or higher and a record of community service and leadership abilities in school activities or through work experience. Each school can nominate only 1 student. Financial need is not considered in the selection process.

Financial data: The stipend is $1,000.

Duration: 1 year; nonrenewable.

Number awarded: Approximately 1,700 each year.

Deadline: January of each year.

445 LEGACY OF LEARNING SCHOLARSHIPS

Workers Compensation Fund
100 West Towne Ridge Parkway
Sandy, UT 84070
Phone: (385) 351–8051; (800) 446–2667; Fax: (385) 351–8372
Web: www.wcfgroup.com/legacy–learning

Summary: To provide financial assistance to children and spouses of workers who died in work–related accidents in Utah and are interested in attending college or graduate school in any state.

Eligibility: Open to Utah residents who are the children and spouses of workers who died in accidents that occurred on job sites covered by the sponsoring company. Applicants must be attending or planning to attend an accredited college or university in any state to work on an undergraduate or graduate degree. Selection is based on GPA, SAT/ACT scores, general character, community involvement, and financial need.

Financial data: The stipend is $1,500 per year.

Duration: 1 year; may be renewed as long as the recipient remains in college.

Number awarded: Varies each year; since this program was established, it has awarded more than 1,000 scholarships valued in excess of $1.3 million.
Deadline: Deadline not specified.

446 $ LEGACY SCHOLARSHIPS

U.S. Army Women's Foundation
Attn: Scholarship Committee
P.O. Box 5030
Fort Lee, VA 23801–0030
Phone: (804) 734–3078;
Email: info@awfdn.org
Web: www.awfdn.org/programs/legacyscholarships.shtml
Summary: To provide financial assistance for college to women who are serving or have served in the Army and their children.
Eligibility: Open to 1) women who have served or are serving honorably in the U.S. Army, U.S. Army Reserve, or Army National Guard; and 2) children of women who served honorably in the U.S. Army, U.S. Army Reserve, or Army National Guard. Applicants must be 1) upper–division students at an accredited college or university and have a GPA of 3.0 or higher; or 2) high school graduates or GED recipients enrolled at a community college and have a GPA of 2.5 or higher. Along with their application, they must submit a 2–page essay on why they should be considered for this scholarship, their future plans as related to their program of study, and information about their community service, activities, and work experience. Selection is based on merit, academic potential, community service, and financial need.
Financial data: The stipend is $2,500 for college and university students or $1,000 for community college students.
Duration: 1 year.
Number awarded: 5 to 10 each year.
Deadline: January of each year.

447 $$ LEGISLATIVE INCENTIVE FOR FUTURE EXCELLENCE (LIFE) SCHOLARSHIP PROGRAM

South Carolina Commission on Higher Education
Attn: LIFE Scholarship Program Manager
1122 Lady Street, Suite 300
Columbia, SC 29201
Phone: (803) 737–4397; (877) 349–7183; Fax: (803) 737–2297;
Email: ghampton@che.sc.gov
Web: www.che.sc.gov/New_Web/GoingToCollege/LIFE_Hm.htm
Summary: To provide financial assistance for college to residents of South Carolina.
Eligibility: Open to residents of South Carolina who graduate from high school or complete a home school program and attend an eligible South Carolina public or private college or university. As an entering freshman at a 4–year college or university, they must meet any 2 of the following requirements: 1) have earned a GPA of 3.0 or higher in high school; 2) score at least 1100 on the mathematics and critical reading sections of the SAT or 24 on the ACT; and/or 3) graduate in the top 30% of their high school class. Students entering a 2–year or technical institution must have a high school GPA of 3.0 or higher. Continuing college students must have completed an average of 30 credit hours for each academic year and maintained a GPA of 3.0 or higher. Students transferring must have completed 30 credit hours for a second–year transfer, 60 for a third–year transfer, or 90 for a fourth–year transfer; their cumulative GPA must be 3.0 or higher. U.S. citizenship or permanent resident status is required. Applicants may not have been convicted of any felonies or alcohol– or drug–related charges. Students at 4–year institutions who complete at least 14 credit hours of mathematics and physical sciences qualify for an enhanced mathematics and sciences award.
Financial data: The stipend is $4,700 per year, plus a $300 book allowance, at 4–year colleges or universities. Students at public and private 2–year colleges receive a stipend of the cost of tuition at a regional campus of the University of South Carolina plus a $300 book allowance. Technical school students receive the cost of tuition plus a $300 book allowance. Students at 4–year institutions who qualify for the enhanced mathematics and sciences award receive an additional stipend of $2,500 per year beginning with their sophomore year.
Duration: 1 year; may be renewed up to a total of 10 semesters for a 5–year program, 8 semesters for a 4–year program, 4 semesters for a 2–year program, or 2 semesters for a 1–year certificate or diploma program.
Number awarded: Varies each year; recently, 29,182 of these scholarships, worth nearly $75.3 million, were awarded.
Deadline: Deadline not specified.

448 $$ LEOPOLD SCHEPP FOUNDATION SCHOLARSHIPS

Leopold Schepp Foundation
551 Fifth Avenue, Suite 3000
New York, NY 10176–2597
Phone: (212) 692–0191
Web: www.scheppfoundation.org
Summary: To provide financial assistance to undergraduate and graduate students.
Eligibility: Open to undergraduates under 30 years of age and graduate students under 40 years of age. Applicants must either be currently enrolled full time or be high school seniors applying for their first year in college. They must have a GPA of 3.2 or higher. Graduate students completing a dissertation but not enrolled in class and students working on a second degree at the same level are not eligible. U.S. citizenship or permanent resident status is required. Selection is based on character, ability, and financial need.
Financial data: The maximum stipend is $8,500 per year.
Duration: 1 year; may be renewed.
Number awarded: Approximately 200 each year.
Deadline: The foundation stops accepting applications when a sufficient number has been received, usually in January.

449 $ LESBIAN, BISEXUAL, GAY AND TRANSGENDER UNITED EMPLOYEES (LEAGUE) FOUNDATION ACADEMIC SCHOLARSHIPS

Lesbian, Bisexual, Gay and Transgender United Employees (LEAGUE) at AT&T Foundation
Attn: LEAGUE Foundation
c/o Charles Eader, Executive Director
One AT&T Way, Room 4B214J
Bedminster, NJ 07921–2694
Phone: (571) 354–4525; TDD: (800) 855–2880;
Email: info@leaguefoundation.org
Web: www.leaguefoundation.org/scholarships/apply.cfm
Summary: To provide financial assistance for college to high school seniors who identify with the gay, lesbian, bisexual, or transgender (GLBT) communities.
Eligibility: Open to high school seniors who have been accepted for full–time study at an accredited 2– or 4–year college or university. Applicants must identify as a gay, lesbian, bisexual, or transgender person. They must have at least a 3.0 GPA and a record of active involvement in community service. Along with their application, they must submit 250–word essays on 1) their academic, career, and personal goals and plans for service to the community, especially on how they plan to increase respect for the individual and aid inclusion of human differences; and 2) their choice of another assigned topic related to the GLBT community. Selection is based on academic record, personal plans, community service, leadership, and concern for others.
Financial data: Stipends are $2,500 (for the Matthew Shepard Memorial Scholarship and the Laurel Hester Memorial Scholarship) or $1,500.
Duration: 1 year.
Number awarded: Varies each year; recently, 7 of these scholarships were awarded: 1 Matthew Shepard Memorial Scholarship, 1 Laurel Hester Memorial Scholarship, and 5 others.
Deadline: April of each year.

450 LESLIE DELK, SR. ACADEMIC SCHOLARSHIP

Taylor Delk Sickle Cell Foundation
418 Chapel Cove
Brownsville, TN 38012
Phone: (731) 694–8727;
Email: tiffanydelk@tdscf.org
Web: tdscf.org/program.html
Summary: To provide financial assistance for college to high school seniors who have sickle cell disease.
Eligibility: Open to seniors graduating from high school in any state and planning to enroll at a 4–year college or university. Applicants must be U.S. citizens or permanent residents who have sickle cell disease. Finalists are interviewed by telephone. Selection is based primarily on academic achievement.
Financial data: The stipend is $1,000.
Duration: 1 year.
Number awarded: 1 each year.
Deadline: Deadline not specified.

451 LESSANS FAMILY SCHOLARSHIP

Central Scholarship Bureau
1700 Reisterstown Road, Suite 220
P.O. Box 37064
Baltimore, MD 21297–3064
Phone: (410) 415–5558; Fax: (410) 415–5501;
Email: contact@centralsb.org
Web: www.centralsb.org/html/lessans.htm

Summary: To provide financial assistance to Jewish students of Maryland who are attending college in any state.

Eligibility: Open to Jewish residents of Maryland who have already applied for an interest–free loan from the sponsoring organization. Applicants must have a GPA of 3.0 or higher and be currently enrolled as an undergraduate student at an accredited college, university, or vocational school in any state. They are eligible if they have not received or been notified of their loan. Their family may have an income up to $90,000 per year. Along with their application, they must submit a 500–word essay describing their achievements, career and educational goals, and personal or family circumstances demonstrating exceptional need or merit. U.S. citizenship or permanent resident status is required.

Financial data: A stipend is awarded (amount not specified). Funds are paid directly to the school.

Duration: 1 year. May be renewed if the recipient remains in school and meets eligibility criteria.

Number awarded: Varies each year.

Deadline: May of each year.

452 $$ LIFE LESSONS SCHOLARSHIP PROGRAM

Life and Health Insurance Foundation for Education
1655 North Fort Myer Drive, Suite 610
Arlington, VA 22209
Phone: (202) 464–5000, ext. 4446; (888) LIFE–777; Fax: (202) 464–5011;
Email: scholarship@lifehappens.org
Web: lifehappens.org/life–lessons/scholarship–program–rules

Summary: To recognize and reward (with college scholarships) students whose parent has died and who submit outstanding essays or videos about the experience.

Eligibility: Open to college–bound high school seniors and current college students between 17 and 24 years of age. Applicants must submit 1) an essay, up to 500 words in length; or 2) a video, up to 3 minutes in length. The entry must describe how the death of a parent or legal guardian affected their life financially and emotionally, especially how that death impacted their college plans and how the lack of adequate life insurance coverage affected their family's financial situation. Selection is based on 1) the compelling nature of the story; 2) the instructiveness of the story with regards to the need for proper insurance planning; and 3) the determination of the student not to allow their loss from preventing them from realizing the goal of obtaining a college education. The grand prize is awarded to the creator of the outstanding essay or video; runners–up are selected for outstanding essays and videos.

Financial data: The grand prize is a $10,000 scholarship. In both the essay and the video competition, first runners–up prizes are $5,000, second $2,500, and third $1,000. Funds are paid directly to the winners' college, university, or trade school.

Duration: The competition is held annually.

Number awarded: 1 grand prize is awarded each year. For the essay competition, 49 runner–up prizes are awarded each year: 5 for first, 4 for second, and 40 for third. For the video competition, 9 runner–up prizes are awarded each year, 2 for first, 2 for second, and 5 for third.

Deadline: March of each year.

453 $$ LILLY ENDOWMENT COMMUNITY SCHOLARSHIP PROGRAM

Independent Colleges of Indiana
3135 North Meridian Street
Indianapolis, IN 46208
Phone: (317) 236–6090; Fax: (317) 236–6086;
Email: info@icindiana.org
Web: www.icindiana.org/lecsp/lilly.asp

Summary: To provide financial assistance to residents of Indiana entering a 4–year college in the state.

Eligibility: Open to seniors graduating from high schools in Indiana and planning to attend a 4–year college or university in the state. Community foundations in each county administer the program locally and determine additional eligibility requirements for that county. Independent Colleges of Indiana (ICI) oversees statewide administration of the program. For the name and address of the community foundation in each county, contact ICI.

Financial data: Awards provide full payment of tuition plus required fees and an annual book stipend of $800.

Duration: 1 year; may be renewed up to 3 additional years.

Number awarded: Approximately 92 each year: 1 from each county in Indiana.

Deadline: Each county community foundation sets its own deadline.

454 LILLY REINTEGRATION SCHOLARSHIPS

The Center for Reintegration, Inc.
Attn: Lilly Secretariat
310 Busse Highway
PMB 327
Park Ridge, IL 60068–3251
Phone: (800) 809–8202;
Email: lillyscholarships@reintegration.com
Web: www.reintegration.com/resources/scholarships/apply.asp

Summary: To provide financial assistance to undergraduate and graduate students diagnosed with schizophrenia.

Eligibility: Open to U.S. citizens diagnosed with bipolar disorder, schizophrenia, schizophreniform disorder, or schizoaffective disorder. Applicants must be receiving medical treatment for the disease and be actively involved in rehabilitative or reintegrative efforts. They must be interested in pursuing postsecondary education, including trade or vocational school programs, high school equivalency programs, associate degrees, bachelor's degrees, and graduate programs. Along with their application, they must submit an essay on their career goal and their rationale for choosing that goal, how this course of study will help them achieve their career goal, obstacles they have faced in life and how they have overcome them, steps they have taken to prepare for pursuit of this education, rationale for the specific school chosen, and their plans to continue treatment while pursuing an education. Selection is based on the quality of the essay, academic success, 3 references, thoughtfulness and appropriateness of academic and vocational/career goals, rehabilitation involvement, success in dealing with the disease, recent volunteer and/or vocational experience, and completion of application requirements.

Financial data: The amount awarded varies, depending upon the specific needs of the recipient. Funds may be used to pay for tuition and related expenses, such as textbooks and laboratory fees.

Duration: 1 year; may be renewed.

Number awarded: Varies each year; generally, 70 to 120 of these scholarships (including renewals) are awarded annually.

Deadline: January of each year.

455 LINDY CALLAHAN SCHOLAR ATHLETE

Mississippi High School Activities Association
1201 Clinton/Raymond Road
P.O. Box 127
Clinton, MS 39060
Phone: (601) 924–6400; Fax: (601) 924–1725;
Email: mhsaa@netdoor.com
Web: www.misshsaa.com

Summary: To provide financial assistance to graduating high school scholar–athletes in Mississippi who plan to attend college in any state.

Eligibility: Open to seniors graduating from high schools that belong to the Mississippi High School Activities Association. Applicants must have won at least 1 varsity letter prior to their senior year and have a GPA of 3.3 or higher. They must be planning to attend a college or university in any state. Along with their application, they must submit a 500–word essay on how athletics and other extracurricular activities have influenced their life. Selection is based on academic achievement, involvement in sports, leadership in school and community, and volunteerism. Males and females compete separately.

Financial data: The stipend is $1,500.

Duration: 1 year.

Number awarded: 16 each year: 1 female and 1 male graduating high school senior in each of the association's 8 districts.

Deadline: February of each year.

456 $ LISA SECHRIST MEMORIAL FOUNDATION SCHOLARSHIP

Lisa Sechrist Memorial Foundation
Attn: Kim Mackmin, Scholarship Selection Committee
Brookfield Homes

8500 Executive Park Avenue, Suite 300
Fairfax, VA 22031–2225
Phone: (703) 270–1400
Web: lisasechrist.com/scholarship.html

Summary: To provide financial assistance to female high school seniors from Virginia who come from disadvantaged backgrounds and plan to attend college in any state.

Eligibility: Open to women graduating from high schools in Virginia who come from a disadvantaged background. Applicants must be planning to attend an accredited college, university, community college, or technical school in any state. Preference is given to applicants who are members of honor societies, participate in sports or other extracurricular activities, demonstrate citizenship and service within the community, and/or exhibit leadership skills within the school or community. Selection is based on merit, integrity, academic potential, and financial need.

Financial data: The stipend is $2,500 per year.

Duration: 4 years, provided the recipient maintains a GPA of 2.5 or higher.

Number awarded: 1 each year.

Deadline: March of each year.

457 $ LIVING BREATH FOUNDATION SCHOLARSHIPS

Living Breath Foundation
2031 Marsala Circle
Monterey, CA 93940
Phone: (831) 392–5285;
Email: LivingBreathFoundation@gmail.com
Web: thelivingbreathfoundation.com/aid.html

Summary: To provide financial assistance to individuals who have cystic fibrosis and are interested in attending college or graduate school.

Eligibility: Open to U.S. citizens who have cystic fibrosis and are graduating high school seniors or undergraduate or graduate students continuing their education at a 2– or 4–year college, university, or trade school in any state. Applicants must submit an essay on how continuing their education will benefit their future. Selection is based on academic record, leadership, community service, and financial need.

Financial data: The stipend ranges from $500 to $2,000. Funds are disbursed directly to the student to assist in payment of tuition, books, or the expenses of going to school while having cystic fibrosis (e.g., private rooms, food, rooms with running water, bathrooms, parking).

Duration: 1 year.

Number awarded: 1 or more each year.

Deadline: February of each year.

458 LOUIS B. RUSSELL, JR. MEMORIAL SCHOLARSHIP

Indiana State Teachers Association
Attn: Scholarships
150 West Market Street, Suite 900
Indianapolis, IN 46204–2875
Phone: (317) 263–3369; (800) 382–4037; Fax: (800) 777–6128;
Email: mshoup@ista–in.org
Web: www.ista–in.org/dynamic.aspx?id=1038

Summary: To provide financial assistance to ethnic minority high school seniors in Indiana who are interested in attending vocational school in any state.

Eligibility: Open to ethnic minority high school seniors in Indiana who are interested in continuing their education in the area of industrial arts, vocational education, or technical preparation at an accredited postsecondary institution in any state. Selection is based on academic achievement, leadership ability as expressed through co–curricular activities and community involvement, recommendations, and a 300–word essay on their educational goals and how they plan to use this scholarship.

Financial data: The stipend is $1,000.

Duration: 1 year; may be renewed for 1 additional year, provided the recipient maintains a GPA of "C+" or higher.

Number awarded: 1 each year.

Deadline: February of each year.

459 LOUISE TUMARKIN ZAZOVE SCHOLARSHIPS

Louise Tumarkin Zazove Foundation
c/o Phillip Zazove
2903 Craig Road
Ann Arbor, MI 48103
Email: phillip@ltzfoundation.org
Web: www.ltzfoundation.org/scholarships.php

Summary: To provide financial assistance for college (and possibly for high school or graduate school) to people with hearing loss.

Eligibility: Open to U.S. citizens and permanent residents who have a significant bilateral hearing loss. Strong preference is given to undergraduate students, but support may be provided for graduate school or high school tuition in certain situations. Applicants must submit a transcript of high school and/or college grades, 3 letters of recommendation, documentation of the severity of the hearing loss, information on any special circumstances by or about the family, and documentation of financial need.

Financial data: A stipend is awarded (amount not specified). Funds are paid directly to schools.

Duration: 1 year; may be renewed up to 3 additional years, provided the recipient continues to do well in school and demonstrate financial need.

Number awarded: Varies each year; since the program was established, it has awarded 19 scholarships.

Deadline: May of each year.

460 $$ LOUISIANA EDUCATIONAL BENEFITS FOR CHILDREN, SPOUSES, AND SURVIVING SPOUSES OF VETERANS

Louisiana Department of Veterans Affairs
Attn: Education Program
1885 Wooddale Boulevard, Room 1013
P.O. Box 94095, Capitol Station
Baton Rouge, LA 70804–9095
Phone: (225) 219–5000; (877) GEAUXVA; Fax: (225) 219–5590;
Email: veteran@la.gov
Web: vetaffairs.la.gov/education

Summary: To provide financial assistance to children, spouses, and surviving spouses of certain disabled or deceased Louisiana veterans who plan to attend college in the state.

Eligibility: Open to children (between 16 and 25 years of age), spouses, or surviving spouses of veterans who served during specified periods of war time and 1) were killed in action or died in active service; 2) died of a service–connected disability; 3) are missing in action (MIA) or a prisoner of war (POW); 4) sustained a disability rated as 90% or more by the U.S. Department of Veterans Affairs; or 5) have been determined to be unemployable as a result of a service–connected disability. Deceased, MIA, and POW veterans must have resided in Louisiana for at least 12 months prior to entry into service. Living disabled veterans must have resided in Louisiana for at least 24 months prior to the child's or spouse's admission into the program.

Financial data: Eligible persons accepted as full–time students at Louisiana state–supported colleges, universities, trade schools, or vocational/technical schools are admitted free and are exempt from payment of tuition, laboratory, athletic, medical, and other special fees. Free registration does not cover books, supplies, room and board, or fees assessed by the student body on themselves (such as yearbooks and weekly papers).

Duration: Support is provided for a maximum of 4 school years, to be completed in not more than 5 years from date of original entry.

Number awarded: Varies each year.

Deadline: Applications must be received no later than 3 months prior to the beginning of a semester.

461 LOUISIANA GO GRANT PROGRAM

Louisiana Office of Student Financial Assistance
602 North Fifth Street
P.O. Box 91202
Baton Rouge, LA 70821–9202
Phone: (225) 219–1012; (800) 259–LOAN, ext. 1012; Fax: (225) 208–1496;
Email: custserv@osfa.state.la.us
Web: www.osfa.state.la.us

Summary: To provide financial assistance to residents of Louisiana who are enrolled or planning to enroll at a college in the state and can demonstrate financial need.

Eligibility: Open to residents of Louisiana who are entering or attending a public or private college or university in the state. Applicants must be eligible for a federal Pell grant or other need–based assistance when they enter college or become eligible after they have already enrolled. Students over 25 years of age are also eligible for this program if they entered college more than 5 years previously and qualify for a Pell grant.

Financial data: The stipend is $1,000 per year for full–time students, $500 per year for half–time students, or $250 per year for students enrolled less than half time.

Duration: 1 year; may be renewed for up to 4 additional years or a maximum of $10,000 in funds from this program; provided the recipient remains eligible for a Pell grant.

Number awarded: Varies each year.

Deadline: Deadline not specified.

462 $ LOUISIANA STATE MATCHING FUND GRANTS

Louisiana Office of Student Financial Assistance
602 North Fifth Street
P.O. Box 91202
Baton Rouge, LA 70821–9202
Phone: (225) 219–1012; (800) 259–LOAN, ext. 1012; Fax: (225) 208–1496;
Email: custserv@osfa.state.la.us
Web: www.osfa.state.la.us

Summary: To provide need–based funds to academically qualified high school seniors and graduates in Louisiana who are planning to attend college.

Eligibility: Open to applicants who have been Louisiana residents for at least 1 year; have substantial financial need (at least $199); are enrolled as a full–time undergraduate student; are a U.S. citizen or eligible noncitizen; have earned at least a 2.0 GPA in high school, a minimum average score of 450 on the GED, or a composite score of at least 20 on the ACT; have applied for federal aid; do not owe a refund on federal aid; and are not in default on federal aid. The Louisiana Office of Student Financial Assistance allocates award funds to Louisiana post-secondary schools based on prior fall enrollment. Students are selected for the award by the financial aid officers at their participating schools.

Financial data: Individual grants range up to $2,000 per year. Funds may be used for educational expenses, including tuition, fees, supplies, and living expenses (e.g., room and board, transportation).

Duration: 1 year; may be renewed if the recipient continues to meet all eligibility requirements and maintains a GPA of 2.0 or higher.

Number awarded: Approximately 4,000 each year.

Deadline: Deadline not specified.

463 $$ LOUISIANA TOPS TECH AWARD

Louisiana Office of Student Financial Assistance
602 North Fifth Street
P.O. Box 91202
Baton Rouge, LA 70821–9202
Phone: (225) 219–1012; (800) 259–LOAN, ext. 1012; Fax: (225) 208–1496;
Email: custserv@osfa.state.la.us
Web: www.osfa.state.la.us

Summary: To provide financial assistance to graduating high school seniors in Louisiana who are interested in pursuing a technical or vocational education in the state.

Eligibility: Open to seniors graduating from high schools in Louisiana who have completed a core curriculum of 13 units plus either 1) an option of 4 additional units in fine arts, foreign language, or computer education; or 2) an option of 6 additional units in career education, technical courses, and base computer courses. Applicants must have a GPA of 2.5 or higher and an ACT score of at least 17 (or an ACT score of 19 or higher for home–schooled students). They must be registered with Selective Service (if required), have no criminal convictions, be a U.S. citizen or permanent resident, and enter an eligible postsecondary institution as a first–time freshman by the first semester following the first anniversary of their high school graduation (unless entering into military service). Independent students or at least 1 parent or legal guardian of dependent students must have been a Louisiana resident for at least 24 months prior to the date of high school graduation. Applicants must plan to attend a school within the Louisiana Community and Technical College System, an approved proprietary or cosmetology school, or a component of the Louisiana Public Colleges and Universities that does not offer a baccalaureate degree. They may also attend a component of the Louisiana Public Colleges and Universities that does offer a baccalaureate degree or a private college or university that is a member of the Louisiana Association of Independent Colleges and Universities (LAICA), but only to take skills or occupational training; students who plan to pursue an academic program or degree are not eligible.

Financial data: At community and technical colleges, proprietary and cosmetology schools, and public colleges and universities that do not offer baccalaureate degrees, this program provides full payment of tuition for skills or occupational training. At public colleges and universities that do offer baccalaureate degrees and at private institutions, the program provides payment of the average of awards paid to students at public schools that do not offer baccalaureate degrees.

Duration: 1 year; may be renewed for 1 additional year if the recipient earns at least 24 credits per academic year and maintains a GPA of 2.5 or higher at the end of each spring semester or 2.0 or higher at the end of all other semesters.

Number awarded: Varies each year.

Deadline: June of each year.

464 $$ LOWE'S SCHOLARSHIPS

Lowe's Companies, Inc.
Attn: Scholarship Program
P.O. Box 1111
North Wilkesboro, NC 28656
Phone: (336) 658–4104; (800) 44–LOWES
Web: careers.lowes.com/college_recruiting_scholarship.aspx

Summary: To provide financial assistance for college to high school seniors in communities where Lowe's stores are located.

Eligibility: Open to seniors graduating from high schools in communities where Lowe's does business. Applicants must be planning to attend an accredited 2– or 4–year college or university in any state. They must have a GPA of 3.25 or higher. Selection is based on academic performance, leadership, community involvement, and/or work experience.

Financial data: The stipend is $2,500.

Duration: 1 year.

Number awarded: 140 each year.

Deadline: February of each year.

465 LULAC GENERAL AWARDS

League of United Latin American Citizens
Attn: LULAC National Education Service Centers
1133 19th Street, N.W., Suite 1000
Washington, DC 20036
Phone: (202) 835–9646; Fax: (202) 835–9685;
Email: scholarships@lnesc.org
Web: www.lnesc.org/site/296/Scholarships

Summary: To provide financial assistance to Hispanic American undergraduate and graduate students.

Eligibility: Open to Hispanic Americans who are U.S. citizens or permanent residents currently enrolled or planning to enroll at an accredited college or university as a graduate or undergraduate student. Although grades are considered in the selection process, emphasis is placed on the applicant's motivation, sincerity, and community involvement, as revealed through a personal interview and in an essay on their personal and career goals. Need, community involvement, and leadership activities are also considered. Candidates must live near a participating local council of the League of United Latin American Citizens (LULAC) and must apply directly to that council.

Financial data: The stipend ranges from $250 to $1,000 per year, depending on the need of the recipient.

Duration: 1 year.

Number awarded: Varies; approximately 500 each year.

Deadline: March of each year.

466 LUSO–AMERICAN EDUCATION FOUNDATION GENERAL SCHOLARSHIPS

Luso–American Education Foundation
Attn: Administrative Director
7080 Donlon Way, Suite 202
P.O. Box 2967
Dublin, CA 94568
Phone: (925) 828–3883; Fax: (925) 828–3883;
Email: education@luso–american.org
Web: www.luso–american.org/laef

Summary: To provide financial assistance to high school seniors in designated states who are of Portuguese descent or taking classes in Portuguese in high school and planning to attend college in any state.

Eligibility: Open to seniors graduating from high schools in the states in which the Luso–American Life Insurance Society (LALIS) is licensed to operate. Applicants must be planning to attend a trade school, business school, junior college, or 4–year college or university in any state. They must 1) be of Portuguese descent and have a GPA of 3.5 or higher; or 2) be taking Portuguese language classes in high school and have a GPA of 3.0 or higher. Along with their application, they must submit transcripts, SAT or ACT scores, and 2 letters of recommendation. Selection is based on promise of success in college, financial need, leadership, vocational promise, and sincerity of purpose.

Financial data: The stipend is $1,500, $750, or $500.

Duration: 1 year; nonrenewable.

Number awarded: 13 to 17 each year: 1 at $1,500, 6 to 8 at $750, and 6 to 8 at $500.
Deadline: February of each year.

467 $$ LUTHERAN COMMUNITY FOUNDATION SCHOLARSHIP

Lutheran Community Foundation
Attn: Senior Associated, Donor Services
625 Fourth Avenue South, Suite 1500
Minneapolis, MN 55415
Phone: (612) 844–4110; (800) 365–4172; Fax: (800) 844–4109;
Email: rebecca.westermeyer@thelcf.org
Web: www.thelcf.org/grants/grants_services/scholarship_applications

Summary: To provide financial assistance to high school seniors who belong to a congregation that has an active Lutheran Community Foundation (LCF) Organizational Fund and who plan to attend a Lutheran college.
Eligibility: Open to graduating high school seniors who are members of a congregation that has an active LCF Organizational Fund. Applicants must be planning to enroll full time at an accredited Lutheran–affiliated college or university. They must have a GPA of 3.5 or higher and be able to demonstrate financial need. Along with their application, they must submit a 200–word essay on why they are uniquely qualified for this award and a 500–word essay related to the mission of the LCF.
Financial data: The stipend is $5,000. Funds must be used for tuition, room and board, books, laboratory expenses, and/or other educational expenditures.
Duration: 1 year.
Number awarded: 1 each year.
Deadline: May of each year.

468 $ MAASFEP GENERAL SCHOLARSHIPS

Minnesota Association of Administrators of State and Federal Education Programs
c/o Matthew Mohs, Treasurer
2140 Timmy Street
St. Paul, MN 55120
Phone: (651) 632–3787;
Email: matthew.mohs@spps.org
Web: www.maasfep.org/scholarships.shtml

Summary: To provide financial assistance to high school seniors in Minnesota who have participated in a Title I program and plan to attend college in any state.
Eligibility: Open to seniors graduating from high schools in Minnesota who have participated in a Title I program while in high school. Applicants must be planning to attend a 2– or 4–year college, university, or vocational/technical school in any state. They must have a GPA of 2.5 or higher. Along with their application, they must submit 1) a 100–word essay on how the Title I program helped them with their education; 2) a 100–word essay on their plans for the future; and 3) a 250–word essay on a challenging experience they have had in their life and how they overcame it. Selection is based on those essays, desire for education beyond high school, study habits, positive attitude, and interest in school, community, and/or work–related activities.
Financial data: The stipend is $2,000.
Duration: 1 year.
Number awarded: 2 each year: 1 to a student attending a 4–year college or university and 1 to a student attending a 2–year college or vocational/technical school.
Deadline: January of each year.

469 $$ MAINE FOSTER CARE TUITION WAIVER PROGRAM

Finance Authority of Maine
Attn: Education Finance Programs
5 Community Drive
P.O. Box 949
Augusta, ME 04332–0949
Phone: (207) 623–3263; (800) 228–3734; Fax: (207) 623–0095; TDD: (207) 626–2717;
Email: education@famemaine.com
Web: www.famemaine.com/Education_Home.aspx

Summary: To provide financial assistance to foster and adopted children in Maine who are interested in attending college in the state.
Eligibility: Open to residents of Maine who have graduated from an approved secondary school or successfully completed a GED examination. Applicants must 1) have been a foster child under the custody of the Maine Department of Health and Human Services when they graduated from high school; or 2) be an adopted person or minor ward of a permanency guardian whose adoptive parent or guardian receives a subsidy from the Maine Department of Health and Human Services. They must be enrolled in or accepted for enrollment in a branch of the University of Maine system, the Maine Community College System, or the Maine Maritime Academy. Awards are granted on a first–come, first–served basis.
Financial data: Eligible students receive waivers of tuition and fees.
Duration: 1 year; may be renewed up to 3 additional years.
Number awarded: A total of 30 slots are available for this program.
Deadline: Applications may be submitted at any time.

470 MAINE LEGISLATIVE MEMORIAL SCHOLARSHIP FUND

Maine Education Services
Attn: MES Foundation
131 Presumpscot Street
Portland, ME 04103
Phone: (207) 791–3600; (800) 922–6352; Fax: (207) 791–3616;
Email: info@mesfoundation.com
Web: www.mesfoundation.com

Summary: To provide financial assistance to residents of Maine planning to attend or currently attending a college or university in the state.
Eligibility: Open to residents of Maine who are either seniors graduating from high schools in the state or already in college. Applicants must be planning to enroll or be currently enrolled in an accredited 2– or 4–year degree–granting Maine college, university, or technical school as an undergraduate or graduate student. Selection is based on academic excellence as demonstrated by transcripts and GPA, contributions to community and employment, letters of recommendation, a 300–word essay on educational goals and intentions, and financial need.
Financial data: The stipend is $1,000.
Duration: 1 year.
Number awarded: 16 each year: 1 from each county in Maine.
Deadline: April of each year.

471 $$ MAINE PUBLIC SERVICE TUITION WAIVER PROGRAM

Finance Authority of Maine
Attn: Education Finance Programs
5 Community Drive
P.O. Box 949
Augusta, ME 04332–0949
Phone: (207) 623–3263; (800) 228–3734; Fax: (207) 623–0095; TDD: (207) 626–2717;
Email: education@famemaine.com
Web: www.famemaine.com/Education_Home.aspx

Summary: To provide financial assistance to children and spouses of deceased law enforcement officers, firefighters, and emergency medical services personnel in Maine who are interested in attending college in the state.
Eligibility: Open to children and spouses of firefighters, law enforcement officers, and emergency medical services personnel who have been killed in the line of duty or died as a result of injuries received during the performance of their duties. Applicants must be enrolled in or accepted for enrollment in a branch of the University of Maine system, the Maine Community College System, or the Maine Maritime Academy. Awards are granted on a first–come, first–served basis.
Financial data: Eligible students receive waivers of tuition and fees.
Duration: 1 year; may be renewed up to 3 additional years.
Number awarded: Varies each year.
Deadline: Applications may be submitted at any time.

472 MAINE STATE CHAMBER OF COMMERCE SCHOLARSHIPS

Maine Education Services
Attn: MES Foundation
One City Center, 11th Floor
Portland, ME 04101
Phone: (207) 791–3600; (800) 922–6352; Fax: (207) 791–3616;
Email: info@mesfoundation.com
Web: www.mesfoundation.com/scholarships/scholarships_mes_chamber.asp

Summary: To provide financial assistance for a college–level technical, education, or business program to residents of Maine.

Eligibility: Open to residents of Maine who are 1) high school seniors planning to work on a technical associate degree at a 2–year college; 2) high school seniors planning to work on a business–related bachelor's degree at a 4–year college or university; and 3) adult learners planning to attend a 2–year college to work on a degree in a business– or education–related field (those applicants must meet federal financial aid criteria for independent student status, i.e., be 24 years of age or older, or be married, or have legal dependents other than a spouse, or be an orphan or ward of the court, or be a veteran of the U.S. armed forces). Preference is given to applicants planning to attend college in Maine. Selection is based on academic achievement, employment and community activities, a letter of recommendation from a high school or community official, an essay describing challenges that businesses face in Maine, and financial need.

Financial data: The stipend is $1,500.

Duration: 1 year.

Number awarded: 3 each year: 1 to a high school senior pursuing a technical degree at a 2–year college, 1 to a high school senior pursuing a business degree at a 4–year institution, and 1 to an adult learner working on a 2–year degree in business or education.

Deadline: April of each year.

473 MAINE STATE SOCIETY OF WASHINGTON, D.C. FOUNDATION SCHOLARSHIP PROGRAM

Maine State Society of Washington, D.C.
c/o Joan M. Beach, Vice President
4718 Columbia Road
Annandale, VA 22003–6110
Phone: (703) 256–4524;
Email: JoanMBeach@aol.com
Web: www.mainestatesociety.org/MSSFoundation.htm

Summary: To provide financial assistance to students who are currently enrolled full time at a university or 4–year degree–granting, nonprofit institution of higher learning within Maine.

Eligibility: Open to full–time students enrolled at a 4–year degree–granting, nonprofit institution of higher learning in Maine. High school seniors are not eligible to apply. Applicants must have been legal residents of Maine for at least 4 years (or have at least 1 parent who has been a resident of Maine for at least 4 years). They must be under 25 years of age, be enrolled in at least 12 semester hours or the equivalent, have at least a 3.0 GPA, be working on a baccalaureate degree, and submit an essay (up to 500 words) with background information on their qualifications for this scholarship, including academic credentials, outside interests, and community service. Financial need is not considered in the selection process.

Financial data: The stipend is at least $1,000.

Duration: 1 year; nonrenewable.

Number awarded: Varies each year; recently, 10 of these scholarships were awarded.

Deadline: March of each year.

474 $$ MAINE VETERANS DEPENDENTS EDUCATIONAL BENEFITS

Bureau of Veterans' Services
117 State House Station
Augusta, ME 04333–0117
Phone: (207) 430–6035; (800) 345–0116 (within ME); Fax: (207) 626–4471;
Email: mainebvs@maine.gov
Web: www.maine.gov/dvem/bvs/educational_benefits.htm

Summary: To provide financial assistance for undergraduate or graduate education to dependents of disabled and other Maine veterans.

Eligibility: Open to children (high school seniors or graduates under 22 years of age), non–divorced spouses, or unremarried widow(er)s of veterans who meet 1 or more of the following requirements: 1) living and determined to have a total permanent disability resulting from a service–connected cause; 2) killed in action; 3) died from a service–connected disability; 4) died while totally and permanently disabled due to a service–connected disability but whose death was not related to the service–connected disability; or 5) a member of the armed forces on active duty who has been listed for more than 90 days as missing in action, captured, forcibly detained, or interned in the line of duty by a foreign government or power. The veteran parent must have been a resident of Maine at the time of entry into service or a resident of Maine for 5 years preceding application for these benefits. Children may be working on an associate or bachelor's degree. Spouses, widows, and widowers may work on an associate, bachelor's, or master's degree.

Financial data: Recipients are entitled to free tuition at institutions of higher education supported by the state of Maine.

Duration: Children may receive up to 8 semesters of support; they have 6 years from the date of first entrance to complete those 8 semesters. Continuation in the program is based on their earning a GPA of 2.0 or higher each semester. Spouses are entitled to receive up to 120 credit hours of educational benefits and have 10 years from the date of first entrance to complete their program.

Number awarded: Varies each year.

Deadline: Deadline not specified.

475 $$ MAINELY CHARACTER SCHOLARSHIP

Mainely Character
P.O. Box 11131
Portland, ME 04103
Email: info@mainelycharacter.org
Web: www.mainelycharacter.org

Summary: To provide financial assistance to Maine residents who demonstrate principles of character and plan to attend college in any state.

Eligibility: Open to residents of Maine who are high school seniors or have received a high school diploma and are entering the first year of postsecondary education at a school in any state. Selection is based on character, determined by an assessment process that includes a written essay describing how the applicants have demonstrated the principles of courage, integrity, responsibility, and concern for others. A personal interview is also required.

Financial data: The stipend is $5,000 or $2,500.

Duration: 1 year; nonrenewable.

Number awarded: 3 each year: 2 at $5,000 and 1 at $2,500.

Deadline: March of each year.

476 MAJOR DON S. GENTILE SCHOLARSHIP

UNICO National
Attn: UNICO Foundation, Inc.
271 U.S. Highway 46 West, Suite A–108
Fairfield, NJ 07004
Phone: (973) 808–0035; (800) 877–1492; Fax: (973) 808–0043;
Email: uniconational@unico.org
Web: www.unico.org/scholarships.asp

Summary: To provide financial assistance for college to Italian American high school seniors.

Eligibility: Open to high school seniors of Italian origin (i.e., at least 1 parent or grandparent of Italian origin) who are planning to attend an accredited college or university. Applicants must have a GPA of 3.0 or higher and be U.S. citizens. Along with their application, they must submit SAT or ACT test scores and a letter of recommendation from a UNICO chapter in the city or town where they live. Selection is based on citizenship, leadership, character, personality, community service, and financial need.

Financial data: The stipend is $1,500 per year.

Duration: 4 years.

Number awarded: 1 each year.

Deadline: April of each year.

477 $ MAJOR JAMES W. LOVELL SCHOLARSHIP

100th Infantry Battalion Legacy Organization
Attn: Scholarship Committee
520 Kamoku Street
Honolulu, HI 96826–5120
Phone: (808) 637–5324;
Email: hondan001@hawaii.rr.com
Web: www.100thlegacy.org

Summary: To provide financial assistance to high school seniors in Hawaii who plan to attend college in any state.

Eligibility: Open to seniors graduating from high schools in Hawaii and planning to attend an institution of higher education in any state. Applicants must submit an essay about James W. Lovell, how he gained such high esteem from veterans who served in the 100th Infantry Battalion (which was comprised mainly of Japanese Americans), his service to Hawaii, and his service to the 100th Infantry Battalion Legacy Organization. Selection is based on that essay (50%), academics (20%), community service (15%), and leadership (15%).

Financial data: The stipend is $3,000.

Duration: 1 year; nonrenewable.

Number awarded: 1 each year.

Deadline: March of each year.

478 MAJOR SAMUEL WOODFILL CHAPTER AUSA SCHOLARSHIP PROGRAM

Association of the United States Army–Major Samuel Woodfill Chapter
c/o LTC Robert F. Sprague, Retired
1326 Cayton Road
Florence, KY 41042–9335
Phone: (859) 525–1082;
Email: spraguer@fuse.net
Web: www3.ausa.org/chapweb/wcc/index.html

Summary: To provide financial assistance to Army personnel and their families, especially those from Indiana, Kentucky, and Ohio, who have served in the Global War on Terror and are interested in attending college in any state.

Eligibility: Open to 1) children of U.S. Army soldiers (active–duty, Reserve, or National Guard) who have fallen, been wounded, are currently serving, or have served in the Global War on Terrorism; 2) medically or honorably discharged Army veterans of Operation Enduring Freedom or Operation Iraqi Freedom; 3) spouses of fallen soldiers in the Global War on Terrorism; and 4) Army soldiers who are currently serving or have served in the Global War on Terrorism. Priority is given to residents of Indiana, Kentucky, and Ohio. Applicants may be attending or accepted at an accredited college or university in any state. Along with their application, they must submit a 500–word essay on the greatest challenge they have faced and how it has impacted them. High school seniors must also submit information on their GPA, extracurricular activities, honors and/or awards, and SAT/ACT scores. Financial need is not considered in the selection process.

Financial data: The stipend is $1,000. Funds are disbursed directly to the recipient's college or university.

Duration: 1 year.

Number awarded: 1 or more each year.

Deadline: March of each year.

479 $$ MAMORU AND AIKO TAKITANI FOUNDATION SCHOLARSHIPS

Mamoru and Aiko Takitani Foundation
P.O. Box 10687
Honolulu, HI 96816–0687
Phone: (808) 228–0209;
Email: info@takitani.org
Web: www.takitani.org

Summary: To provide financial assistance to needy high school seniors in Hawaii who plan to attend college in any state.

Eligibility: Open to seniors graduating from high schools in Hawaii and planning to attend a college, university, community college, or trade school in any state. Applicants must prepare a 500–word essay describing their personal goals and how this scholarship would help them attain those, how their plans will benefit Hawaii and its community after graduation, and any financial or related circumstances that the sponsor should consider. They must submit that essay and other application materials to the college counselor or senior adviser at their high school. Selection is based on academic achievement, the qualities of hard work, commitment to excellence, proven dedication to the community, and financial need. Each school selects its winner. From among those, 10 finalists are selected (1 from each of the 7 school districts, 1 from the Hawaii Catholic Schools, and 2 from the Hawaii Association of Independent Schools). From among those finalists, the sponsor's board of directors selects the top scholarship awardees.

Financial data: The stipend for each high school winner is $1,000. Finalists receive an additional $2,000 scholarship. The top scholarship awards are $10,000 or $5,000.

Duration: 1 year.

Number awarded: Each qualifying high school in the state (approximately 60) awards 1 of these scholarships. Finalist awards are presented to 10 students, of whom 3 receive the top scholarship awards.

Deadline: February of each year.

480 MARA CRAWFORD PERSONAL DEVELOPMENT SCHOLARSHIP

Kansas Federation of Business & Professional Women's Clubs, Inc.
Attn: Kansas BPW Educational Foundation, Inc.
c/o Kathy Niehoff, Executive Secretary
605 East 15th
Ottawa, KS 66067
Phone: (785) 242–9319; Fax: (785) 242–1047;
Email: kathyniehoff@sbcglobal.net
Web: kansasbpw.memberlodge.org/Default.aspx?pageId=450103

Summary: To provide financial assistance to women in Kansas who are already in the workforce but are interested in pursuing additional education.

Eligibility: Open to women residents of Kansas who graduated from high school more than 5 years previously and are already in the workforce. Applicants may be seeking a degree in any field of study and may be attending a 2–year, 4–year, vocational, or technological program. They must submit a 3–page personal biography in which they express their career goals, the direction they want to take in the future, their proposed field of study, their reason for selecting that field, the institutions they plan to attend and why, their circumstances for reentering school (if a factor), and what makes them uniquely qualified for this scholarship. Preference is given to applicants who demonstrate they have serious family responsibilities and obligations. Applications must be submitted through a local unit of the sponsor.

Financial data: A stipend is awarded (amount not specified).

Duration: 1 year.

Number awarded: 1 or more each year.

Deadline: December of each year.

481 MARGARET COSFIELD COLLEGE GRANTS

California Association for the Gifted
Attn: California Foundation for Gifted Education
9278 Madison Avenue
Orangevale, CA 95662
Phone: (916) 988–3999; Fax: (916) 988–5999;
Email: judithr11@aol.com
Web: www.cfge.org/grants_student.php

Summary: To provide financial assistance to high school students in California who have participated in gifted and talented programs and plan to attend college in any state.

Eligibility: Open to seniors graduating from high schools in California and juniors at those schools who expect to participate in an early entrance program at a participating college or university. Applicants must be planning to enter a recognized institution of higher education in any state. They must be able to demonstrate outstanding achievement in a chosen area of talent or giftedness and be nominated by a teacher, mentor, or member of a gifted association. Letters of nomination must include 1) an essay of 1 to 3 pages on the student's intellectual or artistic passion; 2) a sample of demonstrated excellence in the gifted or talented area (e.g., portfolio, school or sample projects, honors awarded); 3) 2 letters of reference; and 4) a transcript. Financial need is not considered in the selection process.

Financial data: The stipend is $1,000.

Duration: 1 year.

Number awarded: Varies each year.

Deadline: February of each year.

482 $$ MARGUERITE ROSS BARNETT MEMORIAL SCHOLARSHIP

Missouri Department of Higher Education
Attn: Student Financial Assistance
205 Jefferson Street
P.O. Box 1469
Jefferson City, MO 65102–1469
Phone: (573) 526–7958; (800) 473–6757; Fax: (573) 751–6635;
Email: info@dhe.mo.gov
Web: www.dhe.mo.gov/ppc/grants/rossbarnett.php

Summary: To provide financial assistance for college to students in Missouri who are employed while attending school part time.

Eligibility: Open to residents of Missouri who are enrolled at least half time but less than full time at participating Missouri postsecondary institutions. Applicants must be able to demonstrate financial need and must be employed at least 20 hours per week. Students working on a degree or certificate in theology or divinity are not eligible. U.S. citizenship or permanent resident status is required.

Financial data: The maximum annual award is the lesser of the actual tuition charged at the school the recipient is attending part time or the amount of tuition charged to a Missouri undergraduate resident enrolled part time in the same class level at the University of Missouri at Columbia.

Duration: 1 semester; may be renewed, provided the recipient maintains a GPA of 2.5 or higher.

Number awarded: Varies each year; recently, 184 of these scholarships, worth $420,580, were awarded.

Deadline: July of each year.

483 $ MARIA C. JACKSON/GENERAL GEORGE A. WHITE SCHOLARSHIP

Oregon Student Access Commission
Attn: Grants and Scholarships Division
1500 Valley River Drive, Suite 100
Eugene, OR 97401–2146
Phone: (541) 687–7395; (800) 452–8807, ext. 7395; Fax: (541) 687–7414; TDD: (800) 735–2900;
Email: awardinfo@osac.state.or.us
Web: www.oregonstudentaid.gov/scholarships.aspx

Summary: To provide financial assistance to veterans and children of veterans and military personnel in Oregon who are interested in attending college or graduate school in the state.
Eligibility: Open to residents of Oregon who served, or whose parents are serving or have served, in the U.S. armed forces. Applicants or their parents must have resided in Oregon at the time of enlistment. They must be enrolled or planning to enroll at a college or graduate school in the state. College and university undergraduates must have a GPA of 3.75 or higher, but there is no minimum GPA requirement for graduate students or those attending a technical school. Selection is based on scholastic ability and financial need.
Financial data: Stipends for scholarships offered by the Oregon Student Access Commission (OSAC) range from $200 to $10,000 but recently averaged $2,300.
Number awarded: Varies each year.
Deadline: February of each year.

484 $ MARIAN WOOD BAIRD SCHOLARSHIP

United States Tennis Association
Attn: USTA Serves
70 West Red Oak Lane
White Plains, NY 10604
Phone: (914) 696–7223;
Email: foundation@usta.com
Web: www.usta.com/About–USTA/USTA–Serves/baird_scholarship

Summary: To provide financial assistance for college to high school seniors who have participated in an organized community tennis program.
Eligibility: Open to high school seniors who have excelled academically, demonstrated achievements in leadership, and participated extensively in an organized community tennis program. Applicants must be planning to enroll as a full–time undergraduate student at a 4–year college or university. They must have a GPA of 3.0 or higher and be able to demonstrate financial need and sportsmanship. Along with their application, they must submit an essay of 1 to 2 pages about how their participation in a tennis and education program has influenced their life, including examples of special mentors, volunteer service, and future goals.
Financial data: The stipend is $3,750 per year. Funds are paid directly to the recipient's college or university.
Duration: 4 years.
Number awarded: 1 each year.
Deadline: February of each year.

485 $ MARIE L. ROSE HUGUENOT SCHOLARSHIPS

Huguenot Society of America
Attn: Office of the Scholarship Committee
20 West 44th Street, Suite 510
New York, NY 10036
Phone: (212) 755–0592; Fax: (212) 317–0676;
Email: hugsoc@verizon.net
Web: huguenotsocietyofamerica.org/?page=Scholarships

Summary: To provide financial assistance for undergraduate education to the descendants of Huguenots.
Eligibility: Open to applicants able to submit proof of descent from a Huguenot who emigrated from France and either settled in what is now the United States or left France for other countries before 1787. The scholarships are available to students at 1 of 50 participating universities; for a list, contact the Huguenot Society.
Financial data: The award is $3,000 per year.
Duration: 1 year.
Number awarded: Varies each year.
Deadline: Deadline not specified.

486 $ MARILYN YETSO MEMORIAL SCHOLARSHIP

Ulman Cancer Fund for Young Adults
Attn: Scholarship Committee
10440 Little Patuxent Parkway, Suite G1
Columbia, MD 21044
Phone: (410) 964–0202; (888) 393–FUND; Fax: (410) 964–0402;
Email: scholarship@ulmanfund.org
Web: www.ulmanfund.org/scholarship.aspx

Summary: To provide financial assistance for college or graduate school to students who have or have lost a parent to cancer.
Eligibility: Open to students who have or have lost a parent or guardian to cancer. Applicants must be 35 years of age or younger and attending, or planning to attend, a 2– or 4–year college, university, or vocational program to work on an undergraduate or graduate degree. The parent or guardian must have been first diagnosed with cancer after the applicant was 15 years of age. Along with their application, they must submit an essay of at least 1,000 words on how their parent's cancer experience has impacted their outlook on life and the legacy that they desire to leave behind. Selection is based on demonstrated dedication to community service, commitment to educational and professional goals, use of their cancer experience to impact the lives of other young adults affected by cancer, medical hardship, and financial need.
Financial data: The stipend is $2,500. Funds are paid directly to the educational institution.
Duration: 1 year.
Number awarded: 1 each year.
Deadline: March of each year.

487 $$ MARILYNN SMITH SCHOLARSHIP

Ladies Professional Golf Association
Attn: LPGA Foundation
100 International Golf Drive
Daytona Beach, FL 32124–1082
Phone: (386) 274–6200; Fax: (386) 274–1099;
Email: foundation.scholarships@lpga.com
Web: www.lpgafoundation.org/Scholarships/scholarshipgeneral.aspx

Summary: To provide financial assistance to female graduating high school seniors who played golf in high school and plan to continue playing in college.
Eligibility: Open to female high school seniors who have a GPA of 3.2 or higher. Applicants must have played in at least 50% of their high school golf team's scheduled events or have played golf "regularly" for the past 2 years. They must be planning to enroll full time at a college or university in the United States and play competitive golf. Along with their application, they must submit a letter that describes how golf has been an integral part of their lives and includes their personal, academic, and professional goals; their chosen discipline of study; and how this scholarship will be of assistance. Financial need is not considered in the selection process.
Financial data: The stipend is $10,000.
Duration: 1 year.
Number awarded: 10 each year.
Deadline: May of each year.

488 MARINE CORPS LEAGUE SCHOLARSHIPS

Marine Corps League
Attn: National Executive Director
P.O. Box 3070
Merrifield, VA 22116–3070
Phone: (703) 207–9588; (800) MCL–1775; Fax: (703) 207–0047;
Email: mcl@mcleague.org
Web: www.mcleague.org

Summary: To provide college aid to students whose parents served in the Marines and to members of the Marine Corps League or Marine Corps League Auxiliary.
Eligibility: Open to 1) children of Marines who lost their lives in the line of duty; 2) spouses, children, grandchildren, great–grandchildren, and stepchildren of active Marine Corps League and/or Auxiliary members; and 3) members of the Marine Corps League and/or Marine Corps League Auxiliary who are honorably discharged and in need of rehabilitation training not provided by government programs. Applicants must be seeking further education and training as a full–time student and be recommended by the commandant of an active chartered detachment of the Marine Corps League or the president of an active chartered unit of the Auxiliary. Financial need is not considered in the selection process.
Financial data: A stipend is awarded (amount not specified). Funds are paid directly to the recipient.
Duration: 1 year; may be renewed up to 3 additional years (all renewals must complete an application and attach a transcript from the college or university).
Number awarded: Varies, depending upon the amount of funds available each year.
Deadline: June of each year.

489 $$ MARINE CORPS SCHOLARSHIPS

Marine Corps Scholarship Foundation, Inc.
Attn: Scholarship Office
909 North Washington Street, Suite 400
Alexandria, VA 22314
Phone: (703) 549–0060; (866) 496–5462; Fax: (703) 549–9474;
Email: students@mcsf.org
Web: www.mcsf.org

Summary: To provide financial assistance for college to the children of present or former members of the U.S. Marine Corps.

Eligibility: Open to the children of 1) Marines on active duty or in the Reserves who have served at least 90 days; 2) veteran Marines who have received an honorable discharge, received a medical discharge, were wounded, or were killed while serving in the U.S. Marines; 3) active–duty or Reserve U.S. Navy Corpsmen who are serving or have served with a U.S. Marine unit; and 4) U.S. Navy Corpsmen who have served with a U.S. Marine unit, have received an honorable discharge or medical discharge, were wounded, or were killed while serving in the U.S. Navy. Applicants must be high school seniors, high school graduates, or current undergraduates in an accredited college, university, or postsecondary vocational/technical school. They must submit academic transcripts (GPA of 2.0 or higher); a written statement of service from their parent's commanding officer or a copy of their parent's honorable discharge; and a 500–word essay on a topic that changes periodically. Only undergraduate study is supported. The family income of applicants must be less than $90,000 per year.

Financial data: Stipends range from $1,500 to $10,000 per year.

Duration: 1 year; may be renewed upon reapplication.

Number awarded: Varies each year; recently, 1,636 of these scholarships were awarded.

Deadline: February of each year.

490 $$ MARINE GUNNERY SERGEANT JOHN DAVID FRY SCHOLARSHIP

Department of Veterans Affairs
Attn: Veterans Benefits Administration
810 Vermont Avenue, N.W.
Washington, DC 20420
Phone: (202) 418–4343; (888) GI–BILL1
Web: www.gibill.va.gov

Summary: To provide financial assistance to children of military personnel who died in the line of duty on or after September 11, 2001.

Eligibility: Open to the children of active–duty members of the Armed Forces who have died in the line of duty on or after September 11, 2001. Applicants must be planning to enroll as undergraduates at a college or university. They must be at least 18 years of age, even if they have completed high school.

Financial data: Eligible students receive full payment of tuition and fees at public schools in their state of residence. For students attending a private or foreign university, the maximum payment for tuition and fees in most states is $17,500; students at private institutions in Arizona, Michigan, New Hampshire, New York, Pennsylvania, South Carolina, and Texas may be eligible for a higher tuition reimbursement rate. A monthly living stipend based on the military housing allowance for the zip code where the school is located and an annual book and supplies allowance of $1,000 are also provided.

Duration: Participants receive up to 36 months of entitlement. They have 15 years in which to utilize the benefit.

Number awarded: Varies each year.

Deadline: Deadline not specified.

491 $$ MARION HUBER LEARNING THROUGH LISTENING AWARDS

Learning Ally
Attn: Training and Support Center
20 Roszel Road
Princeton, NJ 08540
Phone: (609) 243–7087; (800) 221–4792; Fax: (609) 987–8116;
Email: mGreenwald@LearningAlly.org
Web: www.learningally.org/awards

Summary: To provide financial assistance to outstanding high school students with learning disabilities who plan to continue their education.

Eligibility: Open to seniors graduating from public or private high schools in the United States or its territories who have a specific learning disability (visual impairment or physical disability alone does not satisfy this requirement). Applicants must be planning to continue their education at a 2– or 4–year college or vocational school. They must have been registered members of Learning Ally for at least 1 year and have earned a GPA of 3.0 or higher in grades 9–12. Selection is based on academic excellence, leadership, and service to others.

Financial data: Stipends are $6,000 or $2,000.

Duration: 1 year.

Number awarded: 6 each year: 3 at $6,000 and 3 at $2,000.

Deadline: March of each year.

492 MARION J. BAGLEY SCHOLARSHIP

American Legion Auxiliary
Department of New Hampshire
State House Annex
25 Capitol Street, Room 432
Concord, NH 03301–6312
Phone: (603) 271–2212; (800) 778–3816; Fax: (603) 271–5352;
Email: nhalasec@amlegion.state.nh.us
Web: www.nhlegion.org/Legion%20Scholarships/Index%20PAGE.htm

Summary: To provide financial assistance to New Hampshire residents who plan to attend college in any state.

Eligibility: Open to New Hampshire residents and to members of a unit of the American Legion Auxiliary, Department of New Hampshire, who have been members for at least 3 consecutive years. Applicants must be graduating high school seniors, graduates of a high school or equivalent, or students currently attending an institution of higher learning in any state. Along with their application, they must submit 3 letters of recommendation; a list of school, church, and community activities or organizations in which they have participated; transcripts; and a 1,000–word essay on "My Obligations as an American." Financial need is considered in the selection process.

Financial data: The stipend is $1,000.

Duration: 1 year.

Number awarded: 1 each year.

Deadline: April of each year.

493 MARJORIE RUSHFORD ENDOWMENT SCHOLARSHIPS

Epsilon Sigma Alpha International
Attn: ESA Foundation
363 West Drake Road
Fort Collins, CO 80526
Phone: (970) 223–2824; Fax: (970) 223–4456;
Email: esainfo@epsilonsigmaalpha.org
Web: www.epsilonsigmaalpha.org/esa–foundation/scholarships

Summary: To provide financial assistance to residents of South Carolina and Virginia who plan to attend college in any state.

Eligibility: Open to residents of South Carolina and Virginia who are enrolled at a college or university in any state and have a GPA of 3.0 or higher. Applicants may be majoring in any field. Selection is based on character (10%), leadership (10%), service (5%), financial need (50%), and scholastic ability (25%).

Financial data: The stipend is $1,000.

Duration: 1 year; may be renewed.

Number awarded: 2 each year: 1 to a student who graduated from high school in South Carolina and 1 who graduated from high school in Virginia.

Deadline: January of each year.

494 $$ MARTHA C. JOHNSON TUITION SCHOLARSHIPS

Kentucky Community and Technical College System
Attn: Financial Aid
300 North Main Street
Versailles, KY 40383
Phone: (859) 256–3100; (877) 528–2748 (within KY)
Web: www.kctcs.edu

Summary: To provide financial assistance to sophomores attending a school within the Kentucky Community and Technical College System (KCTCS).

Eligibility: Open to KCTCS students entering their sophomore year with a GPA of 3.0 or higher. Applicants must have completed at least 30 hours of a pre–baccalaureate program for transfer to a 4–year college or university. They must be able to demonstrate financial need and outside community service and involvement. Along with their application, they must submit a 1–page essay on their career choice, personal values, and community service. Preference is given to women.

Financial data: Stipends vary at each participating college but are intended to provide full payment of tuition and required fees.

Duration: 1 year.

Number awarded: Varies each year.

Deadline: Deadline not specified.

495 MARTHA MAXWELL DEVELOPMENTAL EDUCATION STUDENT SCHOLARSHIP

National Association for Developmental Education
500 North Estrella Parkway, Suite B2
PMB 412
Goodyear, AZ 85338
Phone: (877) 233–9455; Fax: (623) 792–5747;
Email: office@nade.net
Web: www.nade.net/awards.html

Summary: To provide financial assistance to college students who have participated in a developmental education program.

Eligibility: Open to students who have completed at least 2 developmental courses in college or participated in at least 2 of the following developmental program activities: TRIO Upward Bound, TRIO Student Support Services, high school–to–college bridge program, special admissions program, or enrollment in developmental classes (e.g., mathematics, writing, study skills, reading). Applicants must have a cumulative GPA of 3.0 or higher and plans to enroll in or continue enrollment in a postsecondary educational institution during the next academic year. They must submit a 500–word autobiographical essay on the topic, "How my involvement in developmental education has helped me prepare for regular college courses." Other information that may be submitted along with the essay include educational background, goals and aspirations, creative abilities, leadership skills, and any other facts that the applicant wishes to present. interested in pursuing such professional development activities as instructional design; research or evaluation; or individual, departmental, or institutional growth. Applicants must have been members of the association for 1 or more years, have served 1 or more years as an educator or administrator in a developmental education program, and be currently employed as an educator or administrator in such a program. They must submit a description of a proposed professional development project with an explanation of how it will contribute to professional development for the applicant, the applicant's department, the applicant's institution, or the professional of developmental education.

Financial data: The stipend is $1,000.

Duration: 1 year; nonrenewable.

Number awarded: 1 or more each year.

Deadline: November of each year.

496 MARTIN BARNES SCHOLARSHIPS

Martin Barnes Scholarship Fund
P.O. Box 448
Oxon Hill, MD 20750

Summary: To provide financial assistance for college to high school seniors and current undergraduates.

Eligibility: Open to high school seniors or currently–enrolled full–time undergraduate students. They must be U.S. citizens, have at least a 2.5 GPA, and have performed at least 100 hours of community service within the current academic year in the field of human outreach. Along with their application, they must submit a 250–word essay on an assigned topic related to their religious beliefs and moral judgments. Selection is based on leadership in school, civic, and other extracurricular activities; academic achievement; motivation to serve and succeed; and individual character.

Financial data: The stipend is $1,500.

Duration: 1 year.

Number awarded: 2 each year.

Deadline: June of each year.

497 MARY BARRETT MARSHALL SCHOLARSHIP

American Legion Auxiliary
Department of Kentucky
P.O. Box 5435
Frankfort, KY 40602–5435
Phone: (502) 352–2380; Fax: (502) 352–2381
Web: www.kyamlegionaux.org

Summary: To provide financial assistance to female dependents of veterans in Kentucky who plan to attend college in the state.

Eligibility: Open to the daughters, wives, sisters, widows, granddaughters, or great–granddaughters of veterans eligible for membership in the American Legion who are high school seniors or graduates and 5–year residents of Kentucky. Applicants must be planning to attend a college or university in Kentucky.

Financial data: The stipend is $1,000. The funds may be used for tuition, registration fees, laboratory fees, and books, but not for room and board.

Duration: 1 year.

Number awarded: 1 each year.

Deadline: March of each year.

498 MARY KARELE MILLIGAN SCHOLARSHIP

Czech Center Museum Houston
Attn: Scholarship Coordinator
4920 San Jacinto Street
Houston, TX 77004
Phone: (713) 528–2060; Fax: (713) 528–2017;
Email: czech@czechcenter.org
Web: www.czechcenter.org/scholarships/scholarships.asp

Summary: To provide financial assistance for college to students of Czech descent.

Eligibility: Open to full–time undergraduate students currently enrolled at a 4–year college or university. Applicants must be born of Czech parentage (at least 1 parent), be able to identify and communicate with the Czech community, be U.S. citizens, and be able to demonstrate financial need. Preference is given to residents of Texas, but applications are accepted from residents of other states who are children of members of the Czech Center Museum Houston.

Financial data: The stipend is $1,000 per year.

Duration: 1 year; may be renewed up to 3 additional years.

Number awarded: 3 each year.

Deadline: February of each year.

499 $ MARY M. GOOLEY HEMOPHILIA SCHOLARSHIP

Mary M. Gooley Hemophilia Center
Attn: Scholarship Selection Committee
1415 Portland Avenue, Suite 500
Rochester, NY 14621
Phone: (585) 922–5700; Fax: (585) 922–5775;
Email: Kristina.Ritchie@rochestergeneral.org
Web: www.hemocenter.org/site/PageServer?pagename=programs_scholarships

Summary: To provide financial assistance to people with a bleeding disorder and their families who plan to attend college.

Eligibility: Open to people who are affected directly or indirectly by hemophilia, von Willebrand Disease, hereditary bleeding disorder, or hemochromatosis. Applicants must be enrolled or planning to enroll at an accredited 2– or 4–year college or university, vocational/technical school, or certified training program. Along with their application, they must submit 1) a 1,000–word essay on their goals and aspirations, their biggest challenge and how they met it, and anything else they want the selection committee to know about them; and 2) a 250–word essay on any unusual family or personal circumstances have affected their achievement in school, work, or participation in school and community activities, including how the bleeding disorder has affected their life. Selection is based on the essays, academic performance, participation in school and community activities, work or volunteer experience, personal or family circumstances, recommendations, and financial need.

Financial data: The maximum stipend is $2,000.

Duration: 1 year.

Number awarded: 1 or 2 each year.

Deadline: March of each year.

500 $$ MARY P. OENSLAGER SCHOLASTIC ACHIEVEMENT AWARDS

Learning Ally
Attn: Training and Support Center
20 Roszel Road
Princeton, NJ 08540
Phone: (609) 243–7087; (800) 221–4792; Fax: (609) 987–8116;
Email: mGreenwald@LearningAlly.org
Web: www.learningally.org/awards

Summary: To recognize and reward the outstanding academic achievements of blind college seniors and graduate students.

Eligibility: Open to candidates who 1) are legally blind; 2) have received, or will receive, a bachelor's, master's, or doctoral degree from a 4–year accredited college or university in the United States or its territories during the year the award is given; 3) have an overall academic average of 3.0 or higher; and 4) have been registered members of Learning Ally for at least 1 year. Selection is based on academic excellence, leadership, and service to others.

Financial data: Top winners receive $6,000 each, special honors winners $3,000 each, and honors winners $1,000 each.

Duration: The awards are presented annually.

Number awarded: 9 each year: 3 top winners, 3 special honors winners, and 3 honors winners.

Deadline: March of each year.

501 MARYANN K. MURTHA MEMORIAL SCHOLARSHIP

American Legion Auxiliary
Department of New York
112 State Street, Suite 1310
Albany, NY 12207
Phone: (518) 463–1162; (800) 421–6348; Fax: (518) 449–5406;
Email: alanyterry@nycap.rr.com
Web: www.deptny.org/Scholarships.htm

Summary: To provide financial assistance to New York residents who are the descendants of veterans and interested in attending college in any state.

Eligibility: Open to residents of New York who are high school seniors or graduates and attending or planning to attend an accredited college or university in any state. Applicants must be the children, grandchildren, or great–grandchildren of veterans who served during specified periods of war time. Along with their application, they must submit a 700–word article describing their plans and goals for the future and how they hope to use their talent and education to help others. Selection is based on character (20%), Americanism (15%), community involvement (15%), leadership (15%), scholarship (20%), and financial need (15%). U.S. citizenship is required.

Financial data: The stipend is $1,000. Funds are paid directly to the recipient's school.

Duration: 1 year.

Number awarded: 1 each year.

Deadline: February of each year.

502 $ MARYELLEN LOCHER FOUNDATION SCHOLARSHIP

MaryEllen Locher Foundation
Attn: Cindy Pare
P.O. Box 4032
Chattanooga, TN 37405
Phone: (423) 490–4555;
Email: cindy@melfoundation.org
Web: www.melfoundation.org/scholarships.html

Summary: To provide financial assistance for college to students who have a parent who died from or survived breast cancer.

Eligibility: Open to students who have been accepted as a full–time enrollee at an accredited 2– or 4–year college or university. Applicants must have lost a parent to breast cancer or complication resulting from breast cancer, or have a parent who has survived breast cancer. They must have a GPA of 2.0 or higher and be a legal resident of the United States. Along with their application, they must submit 2 essays on assigned topics related to the impact of breast cancer on their family. Selection is based on those essays, grades, and financial need.

Financial data: Stipends are $3,000 or $1,500.

Duration: 1 year; may be renewed up to 3 additional years.

Number awarded: Varies each year; recently, 30 of these scholarships were awarded.

Deadline: January of each year.

503 $$ MARYLAND COMMUNITY COLLEGE TUITION WAIVER FOR STUDENTS WITH DISABILITIES

Maryland Higher Education Commission
Attn: Office of Student Financial Assistance
6 North Liberty Street, Ground Suite
Baltimore, MD 21201
Phone: (410) 767–3300; (800) 974–0203; Fax: (410) 332–0250; TDD: (800) 735–2258;
Email: osfamail@mhec.state.md.us
Web: www.mhec.state.md.us/financialAid/descriptions.asp

Summary: To provide financial assistance to residents of Maryland who have a disability and plan to attend a community college in the state.

Eligibility: Open to Maryland residents who have a disability and are receiving Supplemental Security Income (SSI) or Social Security Disability Insurance (SSDI) benefits. Applicants must be taking or planning to take credit classes at a community college in the state; non–credit courses do not qualify. They must complete and submit a FAFSA.

Financial data: Recipients are exempt from paying tuition and mandatory fees at community colleges in Maryland for up to 12 credits per semester if they are taking classes as part of a degree or certificate program designed to lead to employment or for up to 6 credits if they are enrolled in a community college for any other reason.

Duration: 1 semester; may be renewed.

Number awarded: Varies each year.

Deadline: February of each year.

504 $$ MARYLAND DELEGATE SCHOLARSHIP PROGRAM

Maryland Higher Education Commission
Attn: Office of Student Financial Assistance
6 North Liberty Street, Ground Suite
Baltimore, MD 21201
Phone: (410) 767–3300; (800) 974–0203; Fax: (410) 332–0250; TDD: (800) 735–2258;
Email: osfamail@mhec.state.md.us
Web: www.mhec.state.md.us/financialAid/descriptions.asp

Summary: To provide financial assistance to vocational, undergraduate, and graduate students in Maryland.

Eligibility: Open to students enrolled or planning to enroll either part time or full time in a vocational, undergraduate, or graduate program in Maryland. Applicants and their parents must be Maryland residents. Awards are made by state delegates to students in their district. Financial need must be demonstrated if the Office of Student Financial Assistance makes the award for the delegate.

Financial data: The minimum annual award is $200. The total amount of all state awards may not exceed the cost of attendance as determined by the school's financial aid office or $19,000, whichever is less.

Duration: 1 year; may be renewed for up to 3 additional years if the recipient maintains satisfactory academic progress.

Number awarded: Varies each year.

Deadline: February of each year.

505 $ MARYLAND PART–TIME GRANTS

Maryland Higher Education Commission
Attn: Office of Student Financial Assistance
6 North Liberty Street, Ground Suite
Baltimore, MD 21201
Phone: (410) 767–3300; (800) 974–0203; Fax: (410) 332–0250; TDD: (800) 735–2258;
Email: osfamail@mhec.state.md.us
Web: www.mhec.state.md.us/financialAid/descriptions.asp

Summary: To provide financial assistance to students in Maryland who are attending college on a part–time basis.

Eligibility: Open to students at Maryland colleges who are enrolled for at least 6 but no more than 11 credits each semester. Applicants must be able to demonstrate financial need. Both they and their parents must be Maryland residents.

Financial data: Grants range from $200 to $2,000 per year.

Duration: 1 year; may be renewed for up to 7 additional years.

Number awarded: Varies each year.

Deadline: February of each year.

506 $$ MARYLAND SCHOLARSHIPS FOR VETERANS OF THE AFGHANISTAN AND IRAQ CONFLICTS

Maryland Higher Education Commission
Attn: Office of Student Financial Assistance
6 North Liberty Street, Ground Suite
Baltimore, MD 21201
Phone: (410) 767–3300; (800) 974–0203; Fax: (410) 332–0250; TDD: (800) 735–2258;
Email: osfamail@mhec.state.md.us
Web: www.mhec.state.md.us/financialAid/descriptions.asp

Summary: To provide financial assistance for college to residents of Maryland who served in the armed forces in Afghanistan or Iraq and their children and spouses.

Eligibility: Open to Maryland residents who are 1) a veteran who served at least 60 days in Afghanistan on or after October 24, 2001 or in Iraq on or after March 19, 2003; 2) an active–duty member of the armed forces who served at least 60 days in Afghanistan or Iraq on or after those dates; 3) a member of a Reserve component of the armed forces or the Maryland National Guard who was activated as a result of the Afghanistan or Iraq conflicts and served at least 60 days; and 4) the children and spouses of such veterans, active–duty armed forces personnel, or members of Reserve forces or Maryland National Guard. Applicants must be enrolled or accepted for enrollment in a regular undergraduate program at an eligible Maryland institution. In the selection process, veterans are given priority over dependent children and spouses.

Financial data: The stipend is equal to 50% of the annual tuition, mandatory fees, and room and board of a resident undergraduate at a 4–year public institution within the University System of Maryland, currently capped at $9,430 per year. The total amount of all state awards may not exceed the cost of attendance as determined by the school's financial aid office or $19,000, whichever is less.

Duration: 1 year; may be renewed for an additional 4 years of full–time study or 7 years of part–time study, provided the recipient remains enrolled in an eligible program with a GPA of 2.5 or higher.
Number awarded: Varies each year.
Deadline: February of each year.

507 $$ MARYLAND SENATORIAL SCHOLARSHIPS

Maryland Higher Education Commission
Attn: Office of Student Financial Assistance
6 North Liberty Street, Ground Suite
Baltimore, MD 21201
Phone: (410) 767–3300; (800) 974–0203; Fax: (410) 332–0250; TDD: (800) 735–2258;
Email: osfamail@mhec.state.md.us
Web: www.mhec.state.md.us/financialAid/descriptions.asp
Summary: To provide financial assistance to vocational, undergraduate, and graduate students in Maryland.
Eligibility: Open to students enrolled either part time or full time in a vocational, undergraduate, or graduate program in Maryland. Applicants and their parents must be Maryland residents and able to demonstrate financial need. Awards are made by state senators to students in their districts. Some senators ask the Office of Student Financial Assistance to make awards for them; those awards are made on the basis of financial need.
Financial data: Stipends range from $400 to $9,450 per year, depending on the need of the recipient. The total amount of all state awards may not exceed the cost of attendance as determined by the school's financial aid office or $19,000, whichever is less.
Duration: 1 year; may be renewed for up to 3 additional years of full–time study or 7 additional years of part–time study, provided the recipient maintains satisfactory academic progress.
Number awarded: Varies each year.
Deadline: February of each year.

508 $$ MARYLAND TUITION WAIVER FOR FOSTER CARE RECIPIENTS

Maryland Higher Education Commission
Attn: Office of Student Financial Assistance
6 North Liberty Street, Ground Suite
Baltimore, MD 21201
Phone: (410) 767–3300; (800) 974–0203; Fax: (410) 332–0250; TDD: (800) 735–2258;
Email: osfamail@mhec.state.md.us
Web: www.mhec.state.md.us/financialAid/descriptions.asp
Summary: To provide financial assistance to residents of Maryland who have lived in foster care and plan to attend college in the state.
Eligibility: Open to Maryland residents under 21 years of age who either 1) resided in a foster care home in the state at the time they graduated from high school or completed a GED examination; or 2) resided in a foster care home in the state on their 13th birthday and were then adopted. Applicants must be planning to enroll as a degree candidate at a public 2– or 4–year higher educational institution in Maryland.
Financial data: Recipients are exempt from paying tuition and mandatory fees at public colleges and universities in Maryland.
Duration: 1 year; may be renewed for an additional 4 years or until completion of a bachelor's degree, whichever comes first, provided the recipient maintains satisfactory academic progress.
Number awarded: Varies each year.
Deadline: February of each year.

509 $$ MASSACHUSETTS CASH GRANT PROGRAM

Massachusetts Office of Student Financial Assistance
454 Broadway, Suite 200
Revere, MA 02151
Phone: (617) 391–6070; Fax: (617) 727–0667;
Email: osfa@osfa.mass.edu
Web: www.osfa.mass.edu/default.asp?page=cashGrant
Summary: To provide financial assistance to Massachusetts residents who are attending state–supported colleges and universities.
Eligibility: Open to applicants who have been permanent legal residents of Massachusetts for at least 1 year and are an undergraduate at a state–supported college or university. They must be enrolled in at least 3 credits per semester. U.S. citizenship or permanent resident status is required. Financial need must be demonstrated.
Financial data: These awards provide assistance in meeting institutionally–held charges, such as mandatory fees and non–state–supported tuition. The amount of the award depends on the need of the recipient.
Duration: 1 year; may be renewed.
Number awarded: Varies each year.
Deadline: Deadlines are established by the financial aid office of each participating Massachusetts institution.

510 $$ MASSACHUSETTS DSS ADOPTED CHILDREN TUITION WAIVER

Massachusetts Office of Student Financial Assistance
454 Broadway, Suite 200
Revere, MA 02151
Phone: (617) 391–6070; Fax: (617) 727–0667;
Email: osfa@osfa.mass.edu
Web: www.osfa.mass.edu/default.asp?page=adoptedChildWaiver
Summary: To provide financial assistance for college to students adopted through the Massachusetts Department of Social Services (DSS).
Eligibility: Open to students 24 years of age or younger who were adopted through DSS by state employees or eligible Massachusetts residents, regardless of the date of adoption. Applicants must be U.S. citizens or permanent residents attending or planning to attend a Massachusetts public institution of higher education as an undergraduate student.
Financial data: All tuition for state–supported courses is waived.
Duration: Up to 4 academic years.
Number awarded: Varies each year.
Deadline: April of each year.

511 $$ MASSACHUSETTS DSS TUITION WAIVER FOR FOSTER CARE CHILDREN

Massachusetts Office of Student Financial Assistance
454 Broadway, Suite 200
Revere, MA 02151
Phone: (617) 391–6070; Fax: (617) 727–0667;
Email: osfa@osfa.mass.edu
Web: www.osfa.mass.edu/default.asp?page=fosterChildWaiver
Summary: To provide financial assistance for college to foster children in the custody of the Massachusetts Department of Social Services (DSS).
Eligibility: Open to students 24 years of age or younger who have been in the custody of the DSS for at least 12 consecutive months. Applicants may not have been adopted or returned home. They must be U.S. citizens or permanent residents attending or planning to attend a college or university in Massachusetts as a full–time undergraduate student.
Financial data: All tuition for state–supported courses is waived.
Duration: Up to 4 academic years.
Number awarded: Varies each year.
Deadline: April of each year.

512 MASSACHUSETTS FEDERATION OF POLISH WOMEN'S CLUBS SCHOLARSHIPS

Kosciuszko Foundation
Attn: Grants Department
15 East 65th Street
New York, NY 10021–6595
Phone: (212) 734–2130, ext. 210; Fax: (212) 628–4552;
Email: addy@thekf.org
Web: www.thekf.org/scholarships/about
Summary: To provide financial assistance to undergraduate students of Polish ancestry from Massachusetts who are attending college in any state.
Eligibility: Open to residents of Massachusetts who are U.S. citizens of Polish ancestry or Polish citizens with permanent resident status in the United States. Applicants must be enrolled in the second, third, or fourth year of undergraduate study at an accredited college or university in the United States and have a GPA of 3.0 or higher. If no residents of Massachusetts apply, qualified residents of New England may be considered. Selection is based on academic excellence; the applicant's academic achievements, interests, and motivation; the applicant's interest in Polish subjects or involvement in the Polish American community; and financial need.
Financial data: The stipend is $1,000.

Duration: 1 year; nonrenewable.
Number awarded: 1 or more each year.
Deadline: January of each year.

513 $$ MASSACHUSETTS FOSTER CHILD GRANT PROGRAM

Massachusetts Office of Student Financial Assistance
454 Broadway, Suite 200
Revere, MA 02151
Phone: (617) 391–6070; Fax: (617) 727–0667;
Email: osfa@osfa.mass.edu
Web: www.osfa.mass.edu/default.asp?page=fosterChild
Summary: To provide financial assistance for college to foster children in the custody of the Massachusetts Department of Social Services (DSS).
Eligibility: Open to students 24 years of age or younger who are current or former foster children placed in the custody of the DSS through a care and protection petition. Applicants must have signed a voluntary agreement with DSS establishing terms and conditions for receiving this aid. They must be U.S. citizens or permanent residents attending or planning to attend a college or university in the continental United States as a full–time undergraduate student.
Financial data: The stipend is $6,000 per year.
Duration: Up to 5 academic years.
Number awarded: Varies each year.
Deadline: April of each year.

514 $$ MASSACHUSETTS JOINT ADMISSIONS TUITION ADVANTAGE WAIVER PROGRAM

Massachusetts Office of Student Financial Assistance
454 Broadway, Suite 200
Revere, MA 02151
Phone: (617) 391–6070; Fax: (617) 727–0667;
Email: osfa@osfa.mass.edu
Web: www.osfa.mass.edu/default.asp?page=jointAdmissionsWaiver
Summary: To provide financial assistance to Massachusetts students who transfer from a community college to a public 4–year institution in the state.
Eligibility: Open to students who completed an associate degree at a public community college in Massachusetts within the prior calendar year as a participant in a Joint Admissions Program. Applicants must have earned a GPA of 3.0 or higher and be transferring to a state college or participating university.
Financial data: Eligible students receive a waiver of tuition equal to 33% of the resident tuition rate at the college or university they attend.
Duration: Up to 2 academic years, provided the recipient maintains a cumulative GPA of 3.0 or higher.
Number awarded: Varies each year.
Deadline: April of each year.

515 $$ MASSACHUSETTS NEED BASED TUITION WAIVER PROGRAM

Massachusetts Office of Student Financial Assistance
454 Broadway, Suite 200
Revere, MA 02151
Phone: (617) 391–6070; Fax: (617) 727–0667;
Email: osfa@osfa.mass.edu
Web: www.osfa.mass.edu/default.asp?page=needBasedWaiver
Summary: To provide financial assistance for college to Massachusetts residents who demonstrate financial need.
Eligibility: Open to applicants who have been permanent legal residents of Massachusetts for at least 1 year, are U.S. citizens or permanent residents, are in compliance with Selective Service registration, are not in default on any federal student loan, are enrolled for at least 3 undergraduate units in an eligible program at a Massachusetts institution of higher learning, and are able to document financial need.
Financial data: Eligible students are exempt from any tuition payments for an undergraduate degree or certificate program at public colleges or universities in Massachusetts. These awards, in combination with other resources in the student's financial aid package, may not exceed the student's demonstrated financial need.
Duration: Up to 4 academic years, for a total of 130 semester hours.
Number awarded: Varies each year.
Deadline: April of each year.

516 $$ MASSACHUSETTS PART–TIME GRANT PROGRAM

Massachusetts Office of Student Financial Assistance
454 Broadway, Suite 200
Revere, MA 02151
Phone: (617) 391–6070; Fax: (617) 727–0667;
Email: osfa@osfa.mass.edu
Web: www.osfa.mass.edu/default.asp?page=partTimeGrant
Summary: To provide financial assistance to Massachusetts residents who are attending colleges and universities on a part–time basis.
Eligibility: Open to applicants who have been permanent legal residents of Massachusetts for at least 1 year and are a part–time undergraduate at a public, private, independent, for profit, or nonprofit institution in Massachusetts. U.S. citizenship or permanent resident status is required. Financial need must be demonstrated.
Financial data: Awards range from $200 to a maximum that depends on the type of institution the student attends.
Duration: 1 year; may be renewed.
Number awarded: Varies each year.
Deadline: Deadlines are established by the financial aid office of each participating Massachusetts institution.

517 $ MASSACHUSETTS PUBLIC SERVICE GRANT PROGRAM

Massachusetts Office of Student Financial Assistance
454 Broadway, Suite 200
Revere, MA 02151
Phone: (617) 391–6070; Fax: (617) 727–0667;
Email: osfa@osfa.mass.edu
Web: www.osfa.mass.edu/default.asp?page=publicServiceGrant
Summary: To provide financial assistance for college to children or widow(er)s of deceased public service officers and others in Massachusetts.
Eligibility: Open to Massachusetts residents who are enrolled or planning to enroll full time at a college or university in the state. Applicants must be 1) the children or spouses of firefighters, police officers, or corrections officers who were killed or died from injuries incurred in the line of duty; 2) children of prisoners of war or military service personnel missing in action in southeast Asia whose wartime service was credited to Massachusetts and whose service was between February 1, 1955 and the termination of the Vietnam campaign; or 3) children of veterans whose service was credited to Massachusetts and who were killed in action or died as a result of their service. U.S. citizenship or permanent resident status is required. This is an entitlement program; support is provided to all qualifying students, regardless of their academic achievement or financial need.
Financial data: Scholarships provide up to the cost of tuition at a state–supported college or university in Massachusetts; if the recipient attends a private Massachusetts college or university, the scholarship is equivalent to tuition at a public institution, up to $2,500.
Duration: 1 year; renewable.
Number awarded: Varies each year.
Deadline: April of each year.

518 $$ MASSACHUSETTS SOLDIERS LEGACY FUND SCHOLARSHIPS

Massachusetts Soldiers Legacy Fund
P.O. Box 962061
Milk Street Post Office
Boston, MA 02196
Phone: (866) 856–5533;
Email: info@mslfund.org
Web: www.mslfund.org
Summary: To provide financial assistance for college or professional school to the children of servicemembers from Massachusetts who were killed in Afghanistan or Iraq.
Eligibility: Open to children of members of the U.S. armed forces who died while deployed on operations Enduring Freedom or Iraqi Freedom. The parent's home of record must have been Massachusetts. Applicants must be enrolled or planning to enroll at a 2– or 4–year college or university, professional school, or trade school in any state. All qualified children receive this assistance; there is no selection process.
Financial data: The stipend is $10,000 per year.
Duration: 1 year; may be renewed up to 3 additional years.
Number awarded: Varies each year.
Deadline: Deadline not specified.

519 MASSACHUSETTS SONS OF ITALY SCHOLARSHIPS

Order Sons of Italy in America–Grand Lodge of Massachusetts
Attn: Charitable and Education Trust
93 Concord Avenue
Belmont, MA 02478–4061
Phone: (617) 489–5234; Fax: (617) 489–5371
Web: osiama.org/charitable.html

Summary: To provide financial assistance to high school seniors in designated New England states who are interested in attending college in any state.

Eligibility: Open to seniors graduating from high schools in Maine, Massachusetts, New Hampshire, and Vermont who plan to attend an accredited 4–year college or university in any state. Applicants are not required to be of Italian heritage or members of the Order Sons of Italy. Selection is based on academic ability, character, and activities.

Financial data: The stipend is $1,000.

Duration: 1 year.

Number awarded: At least 40 each year.

Deadline: March of each year.

520 $$ MASSACHUSETTS VALEDICTORIAN TUITION WAIVER PROGRAM

Massachusetts Office of Student Financial Assistance
454 Broadway, Suite 200
Revere, MA 02151
Phone: (617) 391–6070; Fax: (617) 727–0667;
Email: osfa@osfa.mass.edu
Web: www.osfa.mass.edu/default.asp?page=valedictorianWaiver

Summary: To provide financial assistance for college to Massachusetts residents who have been designated as valedictorians at their high school.

Eligibility: Open to seniors designated by a public or private high school in Massachusetts as a valedictorian. Applicants must have been permanent legal residents of Massachusetts for at least 1 year and be planning to enroll at a public higher education institution in the state. They must be in compliance with Selective Service registration and may not be in default on any federal student loan.

Financial data: Eligible students are exempt from any tuition payments for an undergraduate degree or certificate program at public colleges or universities in Massachusetts.

Duration: Up to 4 academic years, for a total of 130 semester hours.

Number awarded: Varies each year.

Deadline: Deadline not specified.

521 $$ MASSACHUSETTS VETERANS TUITION WAIVER PROGRAM

Massachusetts Office of Student Financial Assistance
454 Broadway, Suite 200
Revere, MA 02151
Phone: (617) 391–6070; Fax: (617) 727–0667;
Email: osfa@osfa.mass.edu
Web: www.osfa.mass.edu/default.asp?page=categoricalwaiver

Summary: To provide financial assistance for college to Massachusetts residents who are veterans.

Eligibility: Open to applicants who are permanent legal residents of Massachusetts for at least 1 year and veterans who served actively during the Spanish–American War, World War I, World War II, Korea, Vietnam, the Lebanese peace keeping force, the Grenada rescue mission, the Panamanian intervention force, the Persian Gulf, or Operation Restore Hope in Somalia. They may not be in default on any federal student loan.

Financial data: Eligible veterans are exempt from any tuition payments for an undergraduate degree or certificate program at public colleges or universities in Massachusetts.

Duration: Up to 4 academic years, for a total of 130 semester hours.

Number awarded: Varies each year.

Deadline: Deadline not specified.

522 MASSGRANT PROGRAM

Massachusetts Office of Student Financial Assistance
454 Broadway, Suite 200
Revere, MA 02151
Phone: (617) 391–6070; Fax: (617) 727–0667;
Email: osfa@osfa.mass.edu
Web: www.osfa.mass.edu/default.asp?page=massGrant

Summary: To provide financial assistance to Massachusetts residents who are attending college in designated states.

Eligibility: Open to students enrolled in a certificate, associate, or bachelor's degree program. Applicants must have been permanent legal residents of Massachusetts for at least 1 year and attending state–approved postsecondary schools (public, private, independent, for profit, or nonprofit) as full–time undergraduate students in Connecticut, Maine, Massachusetts, New Hampshire, Pennsylvania, Rhode Island, Vermont, or Washington, D.C. U.S. citizenship or permanent resident status is required. Selection is based on financial need, with an expected family contribution between zero and $5,273.

Financial data: Award amounts vary, depending on the type of institution.

Duration: 1 year; may be renewed for up to 4 additional years.

Number awarded: Varies each year.

Deadline: April of each year.

523 $ MAXPREPS CITIZEN ATHLETE AWARD CONTEST

MaxPreps, Inc.
4080 Plaza Goldorado Circle, Suite A
Cameron Park, CA 95682
Phone: (800) 329–7324; Fax: (530) 672–8559
Web: www.maxpreps.com/events/citizenathlete/default.aspx

Summary: To recognize and reward high school students who participate in athletics and are registered users of the MaxPreps Service.

Eligibility: Open to high school students over 13 years of age who are registered users of the MaxPreps Service. Contestants must prepare a 3–minute video or photographs of themselves displaying their athletic abilities and submit that as an entry. Based on those videos, judges select 1 male and 1 female athlete from each of 5 regions (northwest, southwest, Midwest, northeast, and southeast). The videos of the 10 regional winners are then displayed online, and viewers are invited to vote to select the national winners.

Financial data: Each regional winner selected by the judges receives a prize of $2,500. The national winners receive an additional $500 to be awarded to their high school athletic department.

Duration: The contest is held annually.

Number awarded: Each year, 10 regional winners (1 male and 1 female in each region) are selected. Of those, 2 are voted as national winners.

Deadline: Entries must be submitted by March of each year.

524 MAY T. HENRY SCHOLARSHIP

May T. Henry Scholarship Fund
c/o Central National Bank and Trust Company
Attn: Trust Department
P.O. Box 3448
Enid, OK 73702–3448
Phone: (580) 233–3535

Summary: To provide financial assistance to high school seniors who are interested in attending a state–supported college, university, or technical school in Oklahoma.

Eligibility: Open to student entering any field of study, if the following requirements are met: the student must plan to attend a college, university, or technical school supported by the state of Oklahoma; the student has graduated or will be graduating from an accredited high school or equivalent institution. Both financial need and scholastic performance are considered in the selection process.

Financial data: The stipend is $1,000 per year. Funds are paid directly to the recipient.

Duration: 1 year; may be renewed for up to 3 additional years.

Deadline: March of each year.

525 ME ENCANTA SCHOLARSHIP PROGRAM

Hispanic College Fund
Attn: Scholarship Processing
1300 L Street, N.W., Suite 975
Washington, DC 20005
Phone: (202) 296–5400; (800) 644–4223; Fax: (202) 296–3774;
Email: hcf–info@hispanicfund.org
Web: scholarships.hispanicfund.org/applications

Summary: To provide financial assistance to Hispanic American high school seniors from designated states who plan to attend college in the United States or Puerto Rico.

Eligibility: Open to U.S. citizens and permanent residents of Hispanic background (at least 1 grandparent must be 100% Hispanic) who are seniors graduating from high schools in the District of Columbia, Maryland, Virginia, or West Virginia. Applicants must be planning to enroll full time at a college or university in the United States or Puerto Rico and major in any field. They must have a GPA of 3.0 or higher and be able to demonstrate financial need.
Financial data: This stipend is $1,500. Funds are paid directly to the recipient's college or university to help cover tuition and fees.
Duration: 1 year.
Number awarded: 1 or more each year.
Deadline: February of each year.

526 MEDALLION FUND

New Hampshire Charitable Foundation
37 Pleasant Street
Concord, NH 03301–4005
Phone: (603) 225–6641; (800) 464–6641; Fax: (603) 225–1700;
Email: info@nhcf.org
Web: www.nhcf.org/page.aspx?pid=484
Summary: To provide financial assistance to New Hampshire residents preparing for a vocational or technical career.
Eligibility: Open to residents of New Hampshire of any age who are enrolling in an accredited vocational or technical program that does not lead to a 4–year baccalaureate degree. Applicants must be planning to attend a community college, vocational school, trade school, apprenticeship, or other short–term training program. They must be able to demonstrate financial need as well as competence and a commitment to their chosen field of study. Preference is given to applicants 1) whose fields are in the traditional manufacturing trade sector (e.g., plumbing, electrical, constructing, machining); 2) who have a clear vision for how their education will help them achieve or improve their employment goals; 3) who have had little or no other educational or training opportunities; and 4) who have made a commitment to their educational program both financially and otherwise.
Financial data: Stipends are provided (amount not specified).
Duration: 1 year.
Number awarded: Varies each year.
Deadline: Applications may be submitted at any time.

527 MEDIACOM COMMUNICATIONS WORLD CLASS SCHOLARSHIPS

Mediacom Communications Corporation
Attn: Scholarship Program
3737 Westown Parkway, Suite A
West Des Moines, IA 50266
Phone: (866) 755–2225;
Email: scholarship@mediacomcc.com
Web: www.mediacomworldclass.com
Summary: To provide financial assistance for college to high school seniors in areas serviced by Mediacom.
Eligibility: Open to seniors graduating from high schools in areas of Arizona, California, Illinois, Indiana, Iowa, Kansas, Kentucky, Michigan, Minnesota, Missouri, Ohio, Oklahoma, South Dakota, Tennessee, and Wisconsin that are serviced by Mediacom. Applicants must be planning to attend an accredited 2– or 4–year college, university, technical, or vocational school in the United States. Along with their application, they must submit an essay of 400 to 500 words on how they exhibit leadership in their school and community. Selection is based on academic achievement, leadership, participation in school activities, honors received, participation in community activities, and references from 2 educators at their school; financial need is not considered.
Financial data: The stipend is $1,000.
Duration: 1 year; nonrenewable.
Number awarded: Varies each year; recently, 50 of these scholarships were awarded.
Deadline: February of each year.

528 $ MEDPRORX EDUCATION IS POWER SCHOLARSHIPS

MedProRx, Inc.
Attn: Scholarship Coordinator
140 Northway Court
Raleigh, NC 27615–4916
Phone: (866) KATHY–MD;
Email: educationispower@medprorx.com
Web: www.medprorx.com/scholarship.html
Summary: To provide financial assistance for college to people with a bleeding disorder.
Eligibility: Open to residents of the United States who are living with hemophilia or von Willebrand Disease. Applicants must be entering or attending a community college, junior college, 4–year college, university, or vocational school. They must be able to demonstrate a record of community involvement and/or volunteer work. Along with their application, they must submit a 250–word essay on their dreams and aspirations, what they are most passionate about, how living with a bleeding disorder has affected their life, and what they would change if they had the power to change something in the world.
Financial data: Stipends range from $500 to $2,500.
Duration: 1 year.
Number awarded: At least 20 each year.
Deadline: April of each year.

529 MEN'S SCHOLARSHIP PROGRAM

USA Gymnastics
Attn: Men's Scholarship Program
132 East Washington Street, Suite 700
Indianapolis, IN 46204
Phone: (317) 237–5050; (800) 345–4719; Fax: (317) 237–5069;
Email: dmcin@usa–gymnastics.org
Web: www.usa–gymnastics.org/pages/men/pages/scholarship_program.html
Summary: To provide financial assistance for college to male elite–level gymnasts.
Eligibility: Open to high school seniors and currently–enrolled college students who are gymnasts working on a college or postsecondary degree. Applicants must be training at the elite level, with an emphasis on international competition, and enrolled or planning to enroll in an undergraduate educational program with a GPA of 2.0 or higher. Along with their application, they must submit information on their gymnastics accomplishments, athletic goals for the current and next 5 years, academic goals, probable career goals, how a scholarship would contribute to their goals, honors and activities, and financial need. U.S. citizenship is required.
Financial data: The size of the scholarship varies, depending upon the funds raised throughout the year in support of the program. Funds must be used for college or postsecondary educational expenses.
Duration: 1 year; may be renewed if the recipient maintains a GPA of 2.0 or higher.
Number awarded: Varies each year.
Deadline: April or October of each year.

530 $ MERFELD FAMILY FOUNDATION SCHOLARSHIPS

Ventura County Community Foundation
Attn: Scholarships
1317 Del Norte Road, Suite 150
Camarillo, CA 93010–8364
Phone: (805) 988–0196, ext. 119; Fax: (805) 988–3379;
Email: vweber@vccf.org
Web: www.vccf.org/funds/scholarship_fund/list.shtml
Summary: To provide financial assistance to college students who parents have been diagnosed with amyotrophic lateral sclerosis (ALS).
Eligibility: Open to students currently enrolled in college who have a parent diagnosed with ALS. Applicants may be residents of any state, but preference is given to those from Iowa and southern California.
Financial data: The stipend is $2,500.
Duration: 1 year.
Number awarded: 4 to 6 each year.
Deadline: January of each year.

531 $$ MG JAMES URSANO SCHOLARSHIP FUND

Army Emergency Relief
200 Stovall Street
Alexandria, VA 22332–0600
Phone: (703) 428–0000; (866) 878–6378; Fax: (703) 325–7183;
Email: ursano@aerhq.org
Web: www.aerhq.org/dnn563/EducationalAssistance/DependentChildren.aspx
Summary: To provide financial assistance for college to the dependent children of Army personnel.
Eligibility: Open to dependent unmarried children under 23 years of age (including stepchildren and legally adopted children) of soldiers on active duty,

retired, or deceased while on active duty or after retirement. Applicants must be working or planning to work full time on a 4–year degree at an accredited college or university. They must have a GPA of 2.0 or higher. Selection is based primarily on financial need, but academic achievements and individual accomplishments are also considered.

Financial data: The amount varies, depending on the needs of the recipient, but ranges from $1,000 to $5,200 per academic year. Recently, awards averaged more than $3,000.

Duration: 1 year; may be renewed for up to 3 additional years, provided the recipient maintains a GPA of 2.0 or higher.

Number awarded: Varies each year; recently, 3,310 of these scholarships, with a value of $9,961,826, were awarded.

Deadline: March of each year.

532 MGA PROFECT 21 MISSOURI SCHOLARSHIP PROGRAM

Missouri Gaming Association
Attn: Executive Director
109A East High Street
P.O. Box 305
Jefferson City, MO 65102
Phone: (573) 634–4001; Fax: (573) 634–7117;
Email: info@missouricasinos.org
Web: www.missouricasinos.org

Summary: To recognize and reward, with scholarships for college in any state, high school seniors in Missouri who submit outstanding articles, posters, or videos on the topic of underage gambling.

Eligibility: Open to seniors at high schools in Missouri who plan to attend a college, university, or vocational/technical school in the United States. Applicants must submit 1) an article published in the newspaper, magazine, or other publication of their school; 2) a poster displayed in a public area of their school; or 3) a video of 5 minutes or less in length that has been viewed in a school forum or meeting. Entries must have been published or displayed during January or February of the year. They must attempt to inform the general public that the legal age for casino gaming in Missouri is 21, and to deter underage gambling. Winners are selected on the basis of originality, content, style, and educational value.

Financial data: Prizes are $1,500 and $1,000 college scholarships. Funds are issued jointly to the winning authors and the institutions they attend.

Duration: The competition is held annually.

Number awarded: 6 each year: 2 at $1,500 and 4 at $1,000.

Deadline: March of each year.

533 MHSAA SCHOLAR–ATHLETE AWARDS

Michigan High School Athletic Association
1661 Ramblewood Drive
East Lansing, MI 48823–7392
Phone: (517) 332–5046; Fax: (517) 332–4071;
Email: afrushour@mhsaa.com
Web: www.mhsaa.com/Schools/Students/ScholarAthleteAward.aspx

Summary: To provide financial assistance for college to seniors who have participated in athletics at high schools that are members of the Michigan High School Athletic Association (MHSAA).

Eligibility: Open to seniors graduating from high schools that are members of the MHSAA. Applicants must be planning to attend an accredited college, university, or trade school and have a GPA of 3.5 or higher. They must have won a varsity letter in 1 of the sports in which post–season tournaments are sponsored by MHSAA: baseball, boys' and girls' basketball, boys' and girls' bowling, girls' competitive cheer, boys' and girls' cross country, football, boys' and girls' golf, girls' gymnastics, ice hockey, boys' and girls' lacrosse, boys' and girls' soccer, softball, boys' and girls' skiing, boys' and girls' swimming and diving, boys' and girls' tennis, boys' and girls' track and field, girls' volleyball, and wrestling. Along with their application, they must submit a long essay on the importance of sportsmanship in educational athletics and short essays on how they have benefited by activity in school sports and outside school activities. Selection is based on the long essay (40%), involvement in extracurricular activities (30%), the short essays (20%), and 2 letters of recommendation (10%).

Financial data: The stipend is $1,000.

Duration: 1 year; nonrenewable.

Number awarded: 32 each year: 12 from Class A schools (6 boys and 6 girls), 8 from Class B schools (4 boys and 4 girls), 6 from Class C schools (3 boys and 3 girls), 4 from Class D schools (2 boys and 2 girls), and 2 selected at large to minority students.

Deadline: Students must submit applications to their school by November of each year. The number of nominations each school may submit depends on the size of the school; Class A schools may nominate 6 boys and 6 girls, Class B schools may nominate 4 boys and 4 girls, Class C schools may nominate 3 boys and 3 girls, and Class D schools may nominate 2 boys and 2 girls.

534 $ MICHAEL A. HUNTER MEMORIAL SCHOLARSHIP

Orange County Community Foundation
Attn: Scholarship Associate
4041 MacArthur Boulevard, Suite 510
Newport Beach, CA 92660
Phone: (949) 553–4202, ext. 46; Fax: (949) 553–4211;
Email: alee@oc–cf.org
Web: www.oc–cf.org/Page.aspx?pid=869

Summary: To provide financial assistance for college to leukemia and lymphoma patients and the children of non–surviving leukemia and lymphoma patients.

Eligibility: Open to graduating high school seniors, community college students, and 4–year university students nationwide. Applicants must be leukemia or lymphoma patients and/or the children of non–surviving leukemia or lymphoma patients who are enrolled or planning to enroll full time. They must have a GPA of 3.0 or higher and be able to document financial need.

Financial data: Stipends range from $1,000 to $2,500.

Duration: 1 year.

Number awarded: 2 each year.

Deadline: March of each year.

535 MICHAEL BAKER CORPORATION IRAQ SURVIVORS SCHOLARSHIP FUND

Pittsburgh Foundation
Attn: Scholarship Coordinator
Five PPG Place, Suite 250
Pittsburgh, PA 15222–5414
Phone: (412) 394–2649; Fax: (412) 391–7259;
Email: turnerd@pghfdn.org
Web: www.pittsburghfoundation.org/node/1669

Summary: To provide financial assistance for college in any state to children and spouses of military servicemembers killed in the war in Iraq.

Eligibility: Open to children and surviving spouses of servicemembers who died during active military service in, or as the direct result of service in, the war in Iraq. Applicants must be enrolled or planning to enroll at a 2– or 4–year college, university, or technical school in any state. They must have a GPA of 2.8 or higher. Along with their application, they must submit a 1–page essay on how this scholarship would help them achieve their long–term career goals.

Financial data: A stipend is awarded (amount not specified).

Duration: 1 year.

Number awarded: 1 or more each year.

Deadline: April of each year.

536 $ MICHAEL "PUGSTER" SILOVICH SCHOLARSHIPS

Western Athletic Scholarship Association
Attn: Scholarship Coordinator
13730 Loumont Street
Whittier, CA 90601

Summary: To provide financial assistance for college to outstanding baseball players.

Eligibility: Open to graduating high school seniors who have played an active role in amateur baseball. Applicants must be planning to attend an accredited 2– or 4–year college or university. They need not have played on a high school team and are not required to play baseball in college. Along with their application, they must submit an essay describing the role baseball has played in their life, why they think they should receive this scholarship, and where they learned about it. Selection is based on academic achievement, community service, participation in baseball, and financial need.

Financial data: The stipend is $2,000 per year.

Duration: 1 year; may be renewed.

Number awarded: Up to 10 each year.

Deadline: February of each year.

537 $$ MICHAEL WILSON SCHOLARSHIPS

Air Force Association
Attn: Scholarship Manager
1501 Lee Highway

Arlington, VA 22209–1198
Phone: (703) 247–5800, ext. 4807; (800) 727–3337, ext. 4807; Fax: (703) 247–5853;
Email: lcross@afa.org
Web: www.afa.org/MichaelWilson
Summary: To provide financial assistance to Air Force ROTC cadets who are entering their junior or senior year of college.
Eligibility: Open to Air Force ROTC cadets entering their junior or senior year as full–time students with a GPA of 2.8 or higher. Applicants must be enrolled in the Professional Air Force ROTC Officer Course program and attending both the Aerospace Studies class and the Leadership Laboratory each semester. Along with their application, they must submit essays of 500 words each on the following topics: 1) how their choice of a major or career will support the mission of the Air Force; 2) what single issue affecting the military would they bring to the attention of the President if they had the opportunity to speak with him; and 3) who or what inspired them to make the choice to become a leader in the Air Force and why.
Financial data: The stipend is $15,000.
Duration: 1 year.
Number awarded: 2 each year.
Deadline: Deadline not specified.

538 MICHELLE AND PETER WILLMOTT FUND FOR MINORITY LEADERSHIP

Associated Colleges of Illinois
Attn: Director, Scholarship Program
70 East Lake Street, Suite 1418
Chicago, IL 60601
Phone: (312) 263–2391; Fax: (312) 263–3424;
Email: aci@acifund.org
Web: acigrantsadministration.org/Scholarships
Summary: To provide financial assistance to minority students from any state who are enrolled at institutions affiliated with the Associated Colleges of Illinois (ACI).
Eligibility: Open to minority students from any state enrolled as freshmen or sophomores at the 22 private colleges and universities that are members of ACI. Applicants must be outstanding volunteers and leaders who have unmet financial need.
Financial data: The stipend is $1,000.
Duration: 1 year.
Number awarded: 2 each year.
Deadline: Deadline not specified.

539 $ MICHIGAN CHILDREN OF VETERANS TUITION GRANTS

Michigan Department of Treasury
Michigan Higher Education Assistance Authority
Attn: Office of Scholarships and Grants
P.O. Box 30462
Lansing, MI 48909–7962
Phone: (517) 373–0457; (888) 4–GRANTS; Fax: (517) 241–5835;
Email: osg@michigan.gov
Web: www.michigan.gov/mistudentaid
Summary: To provide financial assistance for college to the children of Michigan veterans who are totally disabled or deceased as a result of service–connected causes.
Eligibility: Open to natural and adopted children of veterans who have been totally and permanently disabled as a result of a service–connected illness or injury prior to death and have now died, have died or become totally and permanently disabled as a result of a service–connected illness or injury, have been killed in action or died from another cause while serving in a war or war condition, or are listed as missing in action in a foreign country. The veteran must have been a legal resident of Michigan immediately before entering military service and did not reside outside of Michigan for more than 2 years, or must have established legal residency in Michigan after entering military service. Applicants must be between 16 and 26 years of age and must have lived in Michigan at least 12 months prior to the date of application. They must be enrolled or planning to enroll at least half time at a community college, public university, or independent degree–granting college or university in Michigan. U.S. citizenship or permanent resident status is required.
Financial data: Recipients are exempt from payment of the first $2,800 per year of tuition or any other fee that takes the place of tuition.
Duration: 1 year; may be renewed for up to 3 additional years if the recipient maintains full–time enrollment and a GPA of 2.25 or higher.
Number awarded: Varies each year; recently, 400 of these grants were awarded.
Deadline: Deadline not specified.

540 MICHIGAN COMPETITIVE SCHOLARSHIP PROGRAM

Michigan Department of Treasury
Michigan Higher Education Assistance Authority
Attn: Office of Scholarships and Grants
P.O. Box 30462
Lansing, MI 48909–7962
Phone: (517) 373–3394; (888) 4–GRANTS; Fax: (517) 241–5835;
Email: osg@michigan.gov
Web: www.michigan.gov/mistudentaid
Summary: To provide financial assistance for college to residents of Michigan.
Eligibility: Open to Michigan residents who are attending or planning to attend an eligible Michigan college at least half time. Applicants must demonstrate financial need, achieve a qualifying score on the ACT test (recently, the qualifying score was 23 or higher), and be a U.S. citizen, permanent resident, or approved refugee. Students working on a degree in theology, divinity, or religious education are ineligible.
Financial data: Awards are restricted to tuition and fees, recently to a maximum of $575 per academic year at public universities or $1,512 at independent colleges and universities.
Duration: 1 year; the award may be renewed until 1 of the following circumstances is reached: 1) 10 years following high school graduation; 2) completion of an undergraduate degree; or 3) receipt of 10 semesters or 15 quarters of undergraduate aid. Renewals are granted only if the student maintains a GPA of 2.0 or higher and meets the institution's satisfactory academic progress policy.
Number awarded: Varies each year; recently, 27,885 students received these scholarships.
Deadline: Priority is given to students who apply by February of each year.

541 $ MICHIGAN LEGION AUXILIARY NATIONAL PRESIDENT'S SCHOLARSHIP

American Legion Auxiliary
Department of Michigan
212 North Verlinden Avenue, Suite B
Lansing, MI 48915
Phone: (517) 267–8809; Fax: (517) 371–3698;
Email: info@michalaux.org
Web: www.michalaux.org
Summary: To provide financial assistance to children of veterans in Michigan who plan to attend college in any state.
Eligibility: Open to Michigan residents who are the children of veterans who served during designated periods of war time. Applicants must be in their senior year or graduates of an accredited high school and may not yet have attended an institution of higher learning. They must have completed 50 hours of community service during their high school years. Selection is based on scholarship, character, leadership, Americanism, and financial need. The winner competes for the American Legion National President's Scholarship. If the Michigan winners are not awarded the national scholarship, then they receive this departmental scholarship.
Financial data: The stipend ranges from $1,000 to $2,500.
Duration: 1 year.
Number awarded: 1 each year.
Deadline: February of each year.

542 $$ MICHIGAN POLICE OFFICER'S AND FIRE FIGHTER'S SURVIVOR TUITION GRANT

Michigan Department of Treasury
Michigan Higher Education Assistance Authority
Attn: Office of Scholarships and Grants
P.O. Box 30462
Lansing, MI 48909–7962
Phone: (517) 373–0457; (888) 4–GRANTS; Fax: (517) 241–5835;
Email: osg@michigan.gov
Web: www.michigan.gov/mistudentaid
Summary: To provide financial assistance to children and spouses of deceased Michigan police officers and firefighters who plan to attend college in the state.
Eligibility: Open to children and spouses of Michigan police officers (including sheriffs, deputy sheriffs, village or township marshals, police officers of any city or other local jurisdiction, or officer of the state police) or firefighter

(including a member, volunteer or paid, of a fire department or other organization who was directly involved in fire suppression) killed in the line of duty. Children must have been younger than 21 at the time of death of the police officer or firefighter and must apply for this assistance before the age of 21. Applicants must have been residents of Michigan for 12 consecutive months prior to applying. Their family income must be less than 400% of the federal poverty level.

Financial data: This program provides waiver of tuition at Michigan public colleges, universities, and community colleges.

Duration: Until completion of 124 credit hours or 9 semesters of study.

Number awarded: Varies each year.

Deadline: April of each year.

543 MICHIGAN TUITION GRANT PROGRAM

Michigan Department of Treasury
Michigan Higher Education Assistance Authority
Attn: Office of Scholarships and Grants
P.O. Box 30462
Lansing, MI 48909–7962
Phone: (517) 373–3394; (888) 4–GRANTS; Fax: (517) 241–5835;
Email: osg@michigan.gov
Web: www.michigan.gov/mistudentaid

Summary: To provide financial assistance to residents of Michigan who plan to work on an undergraduate or graduate degree at a private college in the state.

Eligibility: Open to Michigan residents who are attending or planning to attend an independent, private, nonprofit degree–granting Michigan college or university at least half time as an undergraduate or graduate student. Applicants must demonstrate financial need and be a U.S. citizen, permanent resident, or approved refugee. Students working on a degree in theology, divinity, or religious education are ineligible.

Financial data: Awards are limited to tuition and fees, to a maximum of $1,512 per academic year.

Duration: 1 year; the award may be renewed for a total of 10 semesters or 15 quarters of undergraduate aid or 6 semesters or 9 quarters of graduate aid.

Number awarded: Varies each year; recently, 35,518 of these grants were awarded.

Deadline: Priority is given to students who apply by February of each year.

544 $$ MICHIGAN TUITION INCENTIVE PROGRAM

Michigan Department of Treasury
Michigan Higher Education Assistance Authority
Attn: Office of Scholarships and Grants
P.O. Box 30462
Lansing, MI 48909–7962
Phone: (517) 373–0457; (888) 4–GRANTS; Fax: (517) 241–5835;
Email: osg@michigan.gov
Web: www.michigan.gov/mistudentaid

Summary: To provide financial assistance to high school seniors in Michigan.

Eligibility: Open to Michigan residents who have (or have had) Medicaid coverage for 24 months within a 36 consecutive month period as identified by the Michigan Department of Human Services (DHS), formerly the Family Independence Agency (FIA). That financial eligibility can be established as early as sixth grade. Students who meet the financial eligibility guidelines are then eligible for this assistance if they graduate from high school or complete a GED prior to becoming 20 years of age. All applicants must be U.S. citizens or permanent residents. Phase I is for students who enroll in a program leading to an associate degree or certificate. Phase II is for students who enroll at least half time at a Michigan degree–granting college or university in a 4–year program other than theology or divinity. Participants must have earned at least 56 transferable semester credits or an associate degree or certificate in Phase I before admission to Phase II.

Financial data: Phase I provides payment of tuition and mandatory fees. Phase II pays tuition and mandatory fees up to $500 per semester to a lifetime maximum of $2,000.

Duration: Students may participate in Phase I for up to 80 semester credits. Course work for Phase II must be completed within 30 months of completion of Phase I requirements.

Number awarded: Varies each year; recently, 11,710 of these awards were granted.

Deadline: Deadline not specified.

545 MIDWEST AREA REGIONAL COUNCIL (MARC) ENDOWMENT SCHOLARSHIP

Epsilon Sigma Alpha International
Attn: ESA Foundation
363 West Drake Road
Fort Collins, CO 80526
Phone: (970) 223–2824; Fax: (970) 223–4456;
Email: esainfo@epsilonsigmaalpha.org
Web: www.epsilonsigmaalpha.org/esa–foundation/scholarships

Summary: To provide financial assistance to residents of designated midwestern states who plan to attend college in any state.

Eligibility: Open to residents of Illinois, Indiana, Iowa, Michigan, Minnesota, Missouri, Nebraska, Ohio, South Dakota, or Wisconsin who are 1) graduating high school seniors with a GPA of 3.0 or higher or with minimum scores of 22 on the ACT or 1030 on the combined critical reading and mathematics SAT; 2) enrolled in college with a GPA of 3.0 or higher; 3) enrolled at a technical school or returning to school after an absence for retraining of job skills or obtaining a degree; or 4) engaged in online study through an accredited college, university, or vocational school. Applicants may be attending or planning to attend a school in any state and major in any field. Selection is based on character (10%), leadership (20%), service (10%), financial need (30%), and scholastic ability (30%).

Financial data: The stipend is $1,000.

Duration: 1 year; may be renewed.

Number awarded: 1 each year.

Deadline: January of each year.

546 $$ MIDWEST STUDENT EXCHANGE PROGRAM

Midwestern Higher Education Commission
Attn: Midwest Student Exchange Program
1300 South Second Street, Suite 130
Minneapolis, MN 55454–1079
Phone: (612) 625–4368; Fax: (612) 626–8290;
Email: msep@mhec.org
Web: www.mhec.org/MidwestStudentExchangeProgram

Summary: To provide a tuition discount to undergraduate and graduate students from selected midwestern states who are attending schools affiliated with the Midwest Student Exchange Program.

Eligibility: Open to students who are attending schools affiliated with the Midwest Student Exchange Program, an interstate initiative established to increase interstate educational opportunities for students in the member states. The Tuition Discount Program includes the 9 participating states of Illinois, Indiana, Kansas, Michigan, Minnesota, Missouri, Nebraska, North Dakota, and Wisconsin. Residents of these states may enroll in programs in the other participating states, but only at the level at which their home state admits students. All of the enrollment and eligibility decisions for the program are made by the institution.

Financial data: Participants in this program pay no more than 150% of the regular resident tuition, plus any required fees, at public colleges and universities in the state where they are enrolled. Students attending designated independent colleges and universities participating in the program receive at least a 10% reduction in their tuition. Recently, the average savings per student was $5,457.

Duration: Students receive these benefits as long as they are enrolled in the program to which they were originally admitted and are making satisfactory progress towards a degree.

Number awarded: Varies each year; recently, 3,276 students were participating in this program.

Deadline: Deadline not specified.

547 MIKE HYLTON AND RON NIEDERMAN SCHOLARSHIPS

Factor Support Network Pharmacy
Attn: Scholarship Committee
900 Avenida Acaso, Suite A
Camarillo, CA 93012–8749
Phone: (805) 388–9336; (877) 376–4968; Fax: (805) 482–6324;
Email: Scholarships@FactorSupport.com
Web: www.factorsupport.com/scholarships.htm

Summary: To provide financial assistance for college to men with hemophilia and their immediate families.

Eligibility: Open to men with bleeding disorders and their immediate family members. Applicants must be entering or attending a college, university, juniors college, or vocational school. They must submit 3 short essays: 1) their

career goals; 2) how hemophilia or von Willebrand Disease has affected their life; and 3) their efforts to be involved in the bleeding disorder community and what they can do to education their peers and others outside their family about bleeding disorders. Selection is based on academic goals, volunteer work, school activities, other pertinent experience and achievements, and financial need.
Financial data: The stipend is $1,000. Funds are paid directly to the recipient.
Duration: 1 year.
Number awarded: 10 each year.
Deadline: April of each year.

548 $$ MILITARY CHILD OF THE YEAR AWARDS

Operation Homefront
8930 Fourwinds Drive, Suite 340
San Antonio, TX 78239
Phone: (210) 659–7756; (800) 722–6098; Fax: (210) 566–7544
Web: www.operationhomefront.net
Summary: To recognize and reward outstanding military children.
Eligibility: Open to children of military personnel in each branch of the armed forces (Air Force, Army, Coast Guard, Marine Corps, Navy). Nominees must have demonstrated resilience, strength of character, leadership within their families and communities, and ability to thrive in the face of the challenges of military life. They must be between 8 and 18 years of age and enrolled in the Defense Enrollment Eligibility Reporting System (DEERS).
Financial data: The award is $5,000.
Duration: The awards are presented annually.
Number awarded: 5 each year: 1 from each branch.
Deadline: Nominations must be submitted by January of each year.

549 $$ MILITARY COMMANDERS' SCHOLARSHIP FUND

Scholarship America
Attn: Scholarship Management Services
One Scholarship Way
P.O. Box 297
St. Peter, MN 56082
Phone: (507) 931–1682; (800) 537–4180; Fax: (507) 931–9168;
Email: militarycommanders@scholarshipamerica.org
Web: sms.scholarshipamerica.org/militarycommanders
Summary: To provide financial assistance for college to children of active and retired military personnel.
Eligibility: Open to children of active–duty, Reserve, National Guard, and retired members of the U.S. military. Applicants must be high school seniors or graduates who plan to enroll full time as entering freshmen at an accredited 2– or 4–year college or university. They must have a cumulative GPA of 3.5 or higher. Selection is based on academic record, demonstrated leadership and participation in school and community activities, honors, work experience, a statement of goals and aspirations, unusual personal or family circumstances, an outside appraisal, and financial need.
Financial data: The stipend is $5,000.
Duration: 1 year; nonrenewable.
Number awarded: Up to 15 each year: 3 from each branch of the armed forces (Air Force, Army, Coast Guard, Marines, Navy).
Deadline: February of each year.

550 $ MILITARY FAMILY SUPPORT TRUST SCHOLARSHIPS

Military Family Support Trust
1010 American Eagle Boulevard
P.O. Box 301
Sun City Center, FL 33573
Phone: (813) 634–4675; Fax: (813) 633–2412;
Email: president@mobc–online.org
Web: www.mobc–online.org/scholarships.html
Summary: To provide financial assistance for college to children and grandchildren of retired and deceased officers who served in the military or designated public service agencies.
Eligibility: Open to graduating high school seniors who have a GPA of 3.0 and a minimum score of 21 on the ACT or 1500 on the 3–part SAT. Applicants must have a parent, guardian, or grandparent who is 1) a retired active–duty, National Guard, or Reserve officer or former officer of the U.S. Army, Navy, Marine Corps, Air Force, Coast Guard, Public Health Service, or National Oceanic and Atmospheric Administration, at the rank of O–1 through O–10, WO–1 through WO–5, or E–5 through E–9; 2) an officer who died while on active duty in service to the country; 3) a recipient of the Purple Heart, regardless of pay grade or length of service; 4) a World War II combat veteran of the Merchant Marine; 5) a federal employee at the grade of GS–7 or higher; 6) a Foreign Service Officer at the grade of FSO–8 or lower; or 7) an honorably discharged or retired foreign military officer of friendly nations meeting the service and disability retirement criteria of the respective country and living in the United States. Applicants must have been accepted to an accredited program at a college or university. Selection is based on leadership (40%), scholarship (30%), and financial need (30%).
Financial data: Stipends range from $500 to $3,000 per year.
Duration: 4 years, provided the recipient maintains a GPA of 3.0 or higher.
Number awarded: 16 each year: 4 at $3,000 per year, 1 at $2,500 per year, 1 at $2,000 per year, 2 at $1,500 per year, 1 at $1,000 per year, and 7 at $500 per year.
Deadline: February of each year.

551 $$ MILITARY NON–RESIDENT TUITION WAIVER AFTER ASSIGNMENT IN TEXAS

Texas Higher Education Coordinating Board
Attn: Grants and Special Programs
1200 East Anderson Lane
P.O. Box 12788
Austin, TX 78711–2788
Phone: (512) 427–6340; (800) 242–3062; Fax: (512) 427–6420;
Email: grantinfo@thecb.state.tx.us
Web: www.collegeforalltexans.com/apps/financialaid/tofa2.cfm?ID=463
Summary: To provide educational assistance to the spouses and children of Texas military personnel assigned elsewhere.
Eligibility: Open to the spouses and dependent children of members of the U.S. armed forces or commissioned officers of the Public Health Service who remain in Texas when the member is reassigned to duty outside of the state. The spouse or dependent child must reside continuously in Texas. Applicants must be attending or planning to attend a Texas public college or university.
Financial data: Eligible students are entitled to pay tuition and fees at the resident rate at publicly–supported colleges and universities in Texas.
Duration: The waiver remains in effect for the duration of the member's first assignment outside of Texas.
Number awarded: Varies each year.
Deadline: Deadline not specified.

552 $$ MILITARY NON–RESIDENT TUITION WAIVER FOR MEMBERS, SPOUSES OR CHILDREN ASSIGNED TO DUTY IN TEXAS

Texas Higher Education Coordinating Board
Attn: Grants and Special Programs
1200 East Anderson Lane
P.O. Box 12788
Austin, TX 78711–2788
Phone: (512) 427–6340; (800) 242–3062; Fax: (512) 427–6420;
Email: grantinfo@thecb.state.tx.us
Web: www.collegeforalltexans.com/apps/financialaid/tofa2.cfm?ID=452
Summary: To exempt military personnel stationed in Texas and their dependents from the payment of non–resident tuition at public institutions of higher education in the state.
Eligibility: Open to members of the U.S. armed forces and commissioned officers of the Public Health Service from states other than Texas, their spouses, and dependent children. Applicants must be assigned to Texas and attending or planning to attend a public college or university in the state.
Financial data: Although persons eligible under this program are classified as non–residents, they are entitled to pay the resident tuition at Texas institutions of higher education, regardless of their length of residence in Texas.
Duration: 1 year; may be renewed.
Number awarded: Varies each year.
Deadline: Deadline not specified.

553 $$ MILITARY NON–RESIDENT TUITION WAIVER FOR MEMBERS, SPOUSES OR CHILDREN WHO REMAIN CONTINUOUSLY ENROLLED IN HIGHER EDUCATION IN TEXAS

Texas Higher Education Coordinating Board
Attn: Grants and Special Programs
1200 East Anderson Lane
P.O. Box 12788
Austin, TX 78711–2788

Phone: (512) 427–6340; (800) 242–3062; Fax: (512) 427–6420;
Email: grantinfo@thecb.state.tx.us
Web: www.collegeforalltexans.com/apps/financialaid/tofa2.cfm?ID=436

Summary: To waive non–resident tuition at Texas public colleges and universities for members of the armed forces and their families who are no longer in the military.

Eligibility: Open to members of the U.S. armed forces, commissioned officers of the Public Health Service (PHS), their spouses, and their children. Applicants must have previously been eligible to pay tuition at the resident rate while enrolled in a degree or certificate program at a Texas public college or university because they were a member, spouse, or child of a member of the armed forces or PHS. This waiver is available after the servicemember, spouse, or parent is no longer a member of the armed forces or a commissioned officer of the PHS. The student must remain continuously enrolled in the same degree or certificate program in subsequent terms or semesters.

Financial data: The student's eligibility to pay tuition and fees at the rate provided for Texas students does not terminate because the member, spouse, or parent is no longer in the service.

Duration: 1 year.

Number awarded: Varies each year.

Deadline: Deadline not specified.

554 MILITARY ORDER OF THE STARS AND BARS SCHOLARSHIPS

Military Order of the Stars and Bars
P.O. Box 1700
White House, TN 37188–1700
Web: www.militaryorderofthestarsandbars.org/programs–services

Summary: To provide financial assistance to high school seniors and currently–enrolled college and graduate students who are the descendants of Confederate officers or public servants.

Eligibility: Open to graduating high school seniors and currently–enrolled undergraduate and graduate students who are the genealogically proven descendants of 1) a Confederate officer; 2) a member of the Confederate executive or legislative branches of government; or 3) a member of the Confederate legislative, judiciary, or executive branches of state government. Applicants must submit a personal letter of application (describing academic and career aspirations), genealogical proof of Confederate ancestor, a completed and signed application form, and 3 letters of recommendation. Selection is based on academic performance (70%), extracurricular activities (10%), the personal statement (10%), and letters of recommendation (10%).

Financial data: The stipend is $1,000.

Duration: 1 year; nonrenewable.

Number awarded: Varies each year, but at least 1 in each of the 3 Confederate Army departments.

Deadline: February of each year.

555 MILITARYVALOAN.COM DISABILITY SCHOLARSHIPS

United States Military V.A. Loan
200 112th Avenue N.E., Suite 204
Bellevue, WA 98004
Phone: (888) 516–9990; Fax: (425) 454–7547;
Email: scholarship@MilitaryVALoan.com
Web: www.militaryvaloan.com/disability–scholarships.html

Summary: To recognize and reward, with college scholarships, high school seniors (disabled or not) who submit outstanding essays about overcoming disability.

Eligibility: Open to students completing study in a public high school, private high school, or home school and planning to enroll at a college or other institution of higher education. Applicants must submit an essay of 500 to 1,000 words on how they or someone they know overcame disability to do something great. They must be at least 17 years of age and have a GPA of 3.0 or higher.

Financial data: The stipend is $1,000.

Duration: 1 year.

Number awarded: 2 each year: 1 for spring and 1 for fall.

Deadline: January of each year for spring applicants; July of each year for fall applicants.

556 $ MILLIE BROTHER SCHOLARSHIPS

Children of Deaf Adults Inc.
c/o Jennie E. Pyers, Scholarship Committee
Wellesley College
106 Central Street, SCI480
Wellesley, MA 02842
Phone: (781) 283–3736; Fax: (781) 283–3730;
Email: coda.scholarship@gmail.com
Web: coda–international.org/blog/scholarship

Summary: To provide financial assistance for college to the children of deaf parents.

Eligibility: Open to the hearing children of deaf parents who are high school seniors or graduates attending or planning to attend college. Applicants must submit a 2–page essay on 1) how their experience as the child of deaf parents has shaped their life and goals; and 2) their future career aspirations. Essays are judged on organization, content, and creativity. In addition to the essay, selection is based on a high school and/or college transcript and 2 letters of recommendation.

Financial data: The stipend is $3,000.

Duration: 1 year; recipients may reapply.

Number awarded: 2 each year.

Deadline: March of each year.

557 MILLIE GONZALEZ MEMORIAL SCHOLARSHIPS

Factor Support Network Pharmacy
Attn: Scholarship Committee
900 Avenida Acaso, Suite A
Camarillo, CA 93012–8749
Phone: (805) 388–9336; (877) 376–4968; Fax: (805) 482–6324;
Email: Scholarships@FactorSupport.com
Web: www.factorsupport.com/scholarships.htm

Summary: To provide financial assistance to women with a bleeding disorder.

Eligibility: Open to women with hemophilia or von Willebrand Disease who are entering or attending a college, university, juniors college, or vocational school. Applicants must submit 3 short essays: 1) their career goals; 2) how hemophilia or von Willebrand Disease has affected their life; and 3) their efforts to be involved in the bleeding disorder community and what they can do to education their peers and others outside their family about bleeding disorders. Selection is based on academic goals, volunteer work, school activities, other pertinent experience and achievements, and financial need.

Financial data: The stipend is $1,000. Funds are paid directly to the recipient.

Duration: 1 year.

Number awarded: 5 each year.

Deadline: April of each year.

558 $$ MILTON FISHER SCHOLARSHIP FOR INNOVATION AND CREATIVITY

Community Foundation for Greater New Haven
Attn: Administrative Assistant
70 Audubon Street
New Haven, CT 06510–9755
Phone: (203) 777–7079; Fax: (203) 777–6584;
Email: gackeifi@cfgnh.org
Web: www.cfgnh.org/Grantmaking/Scholarships/tabid/200/Default.aspx

Summary: To provide financial assistance to residents of Connecticut and New York City who demonstrate outstanding innovation and creativity and plan to attend college in any state.

Eligibility: Open to residents of Connecticut and New York City who are high school juniors or seniors, recent high school graduates entering college in any state for the first time, or first–year students at colleges in any state. Students from other states attending or planning to attend a college, university, vocational school, or technical school in Connecticut or New York City are also eligible. Applicants must have demonstrated innovation and creativity, as in 1) solving artistic, scientific, or technical problems in new or unusual ways; 2) coming up with a distinctive solution to problems faced by their school, community, or family; or 3) creating a new group, organization, or institution that serves an important need. Along with their application, they must submit 1) a 400–word essay on their college plans and long–term goals, including what they hope to accomplish, how their goals build on what they have already accomplished, and special circumstances or obstacles in their lives; and 2) an 800–word essay on their innovative and creative activities. Selection is based primarily on those activities. Financial need is not considered, but it is used to determine the amount of the stipend.

Financial data: Stipends range up to $5,000 per year, depending on the need of the recipient.

Duration: 4 years.

Number awarded: 3 to 5 each year.

Deadline: April of each year.

559 $ MINNESOTA CHILD CARE GRANT PROGRAM

Minnesota Office of Higher Education
Attn: Manager of State Financial Aid Programs
1450 Energy Park Drive, Suite 350
St. Paul, MN 55108–5227
Phone: (651) 642–0567; (800) 657–3866; Fax: (651) 642–0675; TDD: (800) 627–3529;
Email: info@ohe.state.mn.us
Web: www.ohe.state.mn.us/mPg.cfm?pageID=891

Summary: To provide financial assistance for child care to students in Minnesota who are not receiving Minnesota Family Investment Program (MFIP) benefits.

Eligibility: Open to Minnesota residents who are working on an undergraduate degree or vocational certificate in the state and have children age 12 and under (14 and under if disabled). They may apply to receive money for child care expenses. Recipients must demonstrate financial need, but they must not be receiving MFIP benefits. U.S. citizenship or eligible noncitizen status is required.

Financial data: The amount of the assistance depends on the income of applicant and spouse, number of day care hours necessary to cover education and work obligations, student's enrollment status, and number of eligible children in applicant's family. The maximum available is $2,600 per eligible child per academic year.

Duration: 1 year; may be renewed as long as the recipient remains enrolled on at least a half–time basis in an undergraduate program.

Number awarded: Varies each year; recently, a total of $1.1 million was provided for this program.

Deadline: Deadline not specified.

560 $ MINNESOTA G.I. BILL PROGRAM

Minnesota Office of Higher Education
Attn: Manager of State Financial Aid Programs
1450 Energy Park Drive, Suite 350
St. Paul, MN 55108–5227
Phone: (651) 642–0567; (800) 657–3866; Fax: (651) 642–0675; TDD: (800) 627–3529;
Email: info@ohe.state.mn.us
Web: www.ohe.state.mn.us/mPg.cfm?pageID=891

Summary: To provide financial assistance for college or graduate school in the state to residents of Minnesota who served in the military after September 11, 2001 and the families of deceased or disabled military personnel.

Eligibility: Open to residents of Minnesota enrolled at colleges and universities in the state as undergraduate or graduate students. Applicants must be 1) a veteran who is serving or has served honorably in a branch of the U.S. armed forces at any time on or after September 11, 2001; 2) a non–veteran who has served honorably for a total of 5 years or more cumulatively as a member of the Minnesota National Guard or other active or Reserve component of the U.S. armed forces, and any part of that service occurred on or after September 11, 2001; or 3) a surviving child or spouse of a person who has served in the military at any time on or after September 11, 2001 and who has died or has a total and permanent disability as a result of that military service. Financial need is also considered in the selection process.

Financial data: The stipend is $1,000 per semester for full–time study or $500 per semester for part–time study. The maximum award is $3,000 per fiscal year or $10,000 per lifetime.

Duration: 1 year; may be renewed, provided the recipient continues to make satisfactory academic progress.

Number awarded: Varies each year.

Deadline: Deadline not specified.

561 MINNESOTA LEGION AUXILIARY DEPARTMENT SCHOLARSHIPS

American Legion Auxiliary
Department of Minnesota
State Veterans Service Building
20 West 12th Street, Room 314
St. Paul, MN 55155–2069
Phone: (651) 224–7634; (888) 217–9598; Fax: (651) 224–5243;
Email: deptoffice@mnala.org
Web: www.mnala.org/ala/scholarship.asp

Summary: To provide financial assistance to the children and grandchildren of Minnesota veterans who are interested in attending college in the state.

Eligibility: Open to the children and grandchildren of veterans who served during designated periods of war time. Applicants must be a resident of Minnesota or a member of an American Legion post, American Legion Auxiliary unit, or Sons of the American Legion detachment in the Department of Minnesota. They must be high school seniors or graduates, have a GPA of 2.0 or higher, be able to demonstrate financial need, and be planning to attend a vocational or business school, college, or university in Minnesota. Along with their application, they must submit a brief essay, telling of their plans for college, career goals, and extracurricular and community activities.

Financial data: The stipend is $1,000. Funds are to be used to pay for tuition or books and are sent directly to the recipient's school.

Duration: 1 year.

Number awarded: 7 each year.

Deadline: March of each year.

562 $ MINNESOTA MASONIC CHARITIES LEGACY SCHOLARSHIPS

Grand Lodge of Minnesota, A.F. & A.M.
Attn: Minnesota Masonic Charities
11501 Masonic Home Drive
Bloomington, MN 55437–3699
Phone: (952) 948–6004; (800) 245–6050 (within MN); Fax: (952) 948–6710;
Email: grandlodge@qwest.net
Web: www.mn–masons.org/masonic–programs/scholarships

Summary: To provide financial assistance to high school seniors in Minnesota who demonstrate academic excellence and plan to attend college in any state.

Eligibility: Open to seniors graduating from high schools in Minnesota and planning to attend college in any state. Applicants must have a GPA of 3.8 or higher. Selection is based on academic and personal achievement, community participation or service, and overall excellence. No consideration is given to age, gender, religion, national origin, or Masonic affiliation.

Financial data: The stipend is $4,000 per year.

Duration: 1 year; may be renewed up to 3 additional years.

Number awarded: 3 each year.

Deadline: February of each year.

563 $$ MINNESOTA PUBLIC SAFETY OFFICERS' SURVIVOR GRANT

Minnesota Office of Higher Education
Attn: Manager of State Financial Aid Programs
1450 Energy Park Drive, Suite 350
St. Paul, MN 55108–5227
Phone: (651) 642–0567; (800) 657–3866; Fax: (651) 642–0675; TDD: (800) 627–3529;
Email: info@ohe.state.mn.us
Web: www.ohe.state.mn.us/mPg.cfm?pageID=891

Summary: To provide financial assistance for college to survivors of deceased Minnesota public safety officers.

Eligibility: Open to dependent children (under 23 years of age) and surviving spouses of public safety officers killed in the line of duty on or after January 1, 1973. Applicants must be Minnesota residents who are enrolled at least half time in an undergraduate degree or certificate program at a Minnesota public postsecondary institution or at a private, residential, 2– or 4–year, liberal arts, degree–granting college or university in Minnesota.

Financial data: Scholarships cover tuition and fees at state–supported institutions or provide an equivalent amount at private colleges and universities. Recently, the maximum grant was $10,488 at 4–year colleges or universities or $5,808 at 2–year colleges.

Duration: 1 year; may be renewed for a maximum of 8 semesters or 12 quarters.

Number awarded: Varies each year; recently, a total of $100,000 was available for this program.

Deadline: Deadline not specified.

564 $$ MINNESOTA STATE GRANT PROGRAM

Minnesota Office of Higher Education
Attn: Manager of State Financial Aid Programs
1450 Energy Park Drive, Suite 350
St. Paul, MN 55108–5227
Phone: (651) 642–0567; (800) 657–3866; Fax: (651) 642–0675; TDD: (800) 627–3529;
Email: info@ohe.state.mn.us
Web: www.ohe.state.mn.us/mPg.cfm?pageID=891

Summary: To provide financial assistance to undergraduate students in Minnesota who demonstrate financial need.

Eligibility: Open to Minnesota residents who are enrolled for at least 3 credits as undergraduate students at 1 of more than 130 eligible schools in Minnesota. They must be 1) an independent student who has resided in Minnesota for purposes other than postsecondary education for at least 12 months; 2) a dependent student whose parent or legal guardian resides in Minnesota; 3) a student who graduated from a Minnesota high school, if the student was a resident of the state during high school; or 4) a student who, after residing in Minnesota for a minimum of 1 year, earned a high school equivalency certificate in Minnesota. Students in default on a student loan or more than 30 days behind for child support owed to a public agency are not eligible.
Financial data: Applicants are required to contribute at least 46.3% of their cost of attendance (tuition and fees plus allowances for room and board, books and supplies, and miscellaneous expenses) from savings, earnings, loans, or other assistance from school or private sources. The other 53.7% is to be contributed by parents (for dependent students) or by independent students, along with a federal Pell Grant and these State Grants. Recently, maximum grants ranged from $6,537 at public 2–year colleges to $9,391 at private 4–year colleges; the average was approximately $1,350.
Duration: Assistance continues until the student has completed a baccalaureate degree or full–time enrollment of 8 semesters or 12 quarters, whichever comes first.
Number awarded: Varies each year; recently, nearly 89,000 undergraduate students received $120 million in support through this program.
Deadline: June of each year.

565 MINNESOTA STATE HIGH SCHOOL COACHES ASSOCIATION SCHOLARSHIPS

Minnesota State High School Coaches Association
c/o Gregg Martig, Scholarship Committee Co–Chair
3118 Partridge Court
St. Cloud, MN 56301
Phone: (320) 252–8770; Fax: (320) 252–8483;
Email: Gregg.Martig@isd742.org
Web: www.mshsca.org/scholarship_information.htm
Summary: To provide financial assistance to high school seniors in Minnesota who have participated in athletics and plan to attend college in any state.
Eligibility: Open to seniors graduating from high schools in Minnesota who have participated in athletics through their final year of school. Applicants must be planning to enroll at a college or university in any state. They must have a GPA that is equivalent to the standard of an honor student. Along with their application, they must submit an official high school transcript that includes ACT and/or SAT scores, a letter of recognition from 1 of their coaches, and a 1–page letter outlining the role athletics has played in their life.
Financial data: The stipend is $1,000.
Duration: 1 year.
Number awarded: Approximately 6 each year.
Deadline: March.

566 $ MINNESOTA STATE MEMORIAL ENDOWMENT SCHOLARSHIP

Epsilon Sigma Alpha International
Attn: ESA Foundation
363 West Drake Road
Fort Collins, CO 80526
Phone: (970) 223–2824; Fax: (970) 223–4456;
Email: esainfo@epsilonsigmaalpha.org
Web: www.epsilonsigmaalpha.org/esa–foundation/scholarships
Summary: To provide financial assistance to residents of Minnesota who plan to attend college in any state.
Eligibility: Open to residents of Minnesota who are 1) graduating high school seniors with a GPA of 3.0 or higher or with minimum scores of 22 on the ACT or 1030 on the combined critical reading and mathematics SAT; 2) enrolled in college with a GPA of 3.0 or higher; 3) enrolled at a technical school or returning to school after an absence for retraining of job skills or obtaining a degree; or 4) engaged in online study through an accredited college, university, or vocational school. Applicants may be attending or planning to attend a school in any state and major in any field. Selection is based on character (10%), leadership (20%), service (10%), financial need (30%), and scholastic ability (30%).
Financial data: The stipend is $2,500.
Duration: 1 year; may be renewed.
Number awarded: 4 each year.
Deadline: January of each year.

567 MINNESOTAJOBS.COM SCHOLARSHIP

MinnesotaJobs.com
c/o Trumor Inc.
21435 Johnson Street N.E., Suite 200
East Bethel, MN 55011–5028
Phone: (763) 784–9393; (800) 632–1576; Fax: (763) 784–1090
Web: www.minnesotajobs.com/scholarships/index.php?js_zone=true
Summary: To provide financial assistance to students at colleges and universities in Minnesota who are preparing for a career in the state.
Eligibility: Open to students enrolled or planning to enroll at a 2– or 4–year college or university in Minnesota. Applicants must be planning a program of study that will enable them to provide future Minnesota employers with necessary skills. They must be at least 18 years of age. At least 75% of their proposed credits must be earned through classroom training. Selection is based on a random drawing from among all qualified applicants.
Financial data: The stipend is $1,000. Funds are disbursed directly to the recipient's school and applied to tuition.
Duration: 1 year; nonrenewable.
Number awarded: 4 each year.
Deadline: March, June, September, or December.

568 MINNIE PEARL SCHOLARSHIP PROGRAM

Hearing Bridges
Attn: Scholarship Program
415 Fourth Avenue South, Suite A
Nashville, TN 37201
Phone: (615) 248–8828; (866) 385–6524; Fax: (615) 248–4797; TDD: (615) 248–8828;
Email: ap@hearingbridges.org
Web: hearingbridges.org/scholarships
Summary: To provide financial assistance to hearing impaired high school seniors who want to attend college.
Eligibility: Open to high school seniors who have severe to profound bilateral hearing loss and a GPA of 3.0 or higher. Applicants must be planning to enroll full time at a college, university, junior college, or technical school. Along with their application, they must submit brief essays on what a college education means to them, their goals after graduating from college, why they are a good candidate for this scholarship, and a difficult situation in their life and how they handled it. Selection is based on those essays, academic performance, extracurricular activities, an audiology report, and letters of recommendation. U.S. citizenship is required.
Financial data: The stipend is $1,000 per year. Payment is made directly to the recipient's college, university, or school.
Duration: 1 year; may be renewed up to 3 additional years, provided the recipient maintains a GPA of 3.0 or higher.
Number awarded: 1 each year.
Deadline: March of each year.

569 $$ MISS AMERICA COMPETITION AWARDS

Miss America Pageant
Attn: Scholarship Department
222 New Road, Suite 700
Linwood, NJ 08221
Phone: (609) 653–8700, ext. 127; Fax: (609) 653–8740;
Email: info@missamerica.org
Web: www.missamerica.org/scholarships
Summary: To provide educational scholarships to participants in the Miss America Pageant on local, state, and national levels.
Eligibility: Open to women who participated in the Miss America Pageant on the local, state, and national levels. Among the qualifications required to participate are that the applicant must be female, between the ages of 17 and 24, a resident of the town or state in which they first compete, in good health, of good moral character, and a citizen of the United States. A complete list of all eligibility requirements is available from each local and state pageant. Separate scholarships are awarded to the winners of the talent competition and the lifestyle and fitness in swimsuit competition. Other special awards may be presented on a 1–time basis.
Financial data: More than $45 million in cash and tuition assistance is awarded annually at the local, state, and national Miss America Pageants. At the national level, nearly $500,000 is awarded: Miss America receives $50,000 in scholarship money, the first runner–up $25,000, second runner–up $20,000, third runner–up $15,000, fourth runner–up $10,000, 5 other top 10 finalists $7,000 each, 2 other top 12 semifinalists $5,000 each, 3 other top 15 semifinalists $4,000 each, and other national contestants $3,000 each. Other awards

include those for the 3 preliminary talent winners at $2,000 each, the 3 preliminary lifestyle and fitness in swimsuit winners at $1,000 each, and the 5 non–finalist talent winners at $1,000 each. Recent special awards included the Miracle Maker Award of $5,000, the Fourpoints Award of $2,000, the Miss Congeniality Award of $2,000, the Ric Ferentz Non–Finalist Interview Award of $2,000, the Louanne Gamba Instrumental Award of $1,000, and the Marion A. Crooker Award of $1,000.
Duration: The pageants are held every year.
Number awarded: At the national level, 52 contestants (1 from each state, the District of Columbia, and the Virgin Islands) share the awards.
Deadline: Varies, depending upon the date of local pageants leading to the state and national finals.

570 MISS AMERICA SCHOLAR AWARDS

Miss America Pageant
Attn: Scholarship Department
222 New Road, Suite 700
Linwood, NJ 08221
Phone: (609) 653–8700, ext. 127; Fax: (609) 653–8740;
Email: info@missamerica.org
Web: www.missamerica.org/scholarships/missstate.aspx
Summary: To recognize and reward, with college scholarships, women who participate in the Miss America Pageant at the state level and demonstrate academic excellence.
Eligibility: Open to women who compete at the state level of the Miss America Pageant. Selection is based on academic excellence (grades, course content, and academic standing of the institution).
Financial data: The stipend is $1,000.
Duration: 1 year.
Number awarded: Up to 52 each year: 1 for each of the states, the District of Columbia, and the Virgin Islands.
Deadline: Varies, depending upon the date of local pageants leading to the state finals.

571 $$ MISS TEEN USA

Miss Universe Organization
1370 Avenue of the Americas, 16th Floor
New York, NY 10019
Phone: (212) 373–4999; Fax: (212) 315–5378;
Email: pr@missuniverse.com
Web: www.missuniverse.com/missteenusa
Summary: To recognize and reward beautiful and talented women between 14 and 19 years of age in the United States.
Eligibility: Open to women between 14 and 19 years of age who reside in the United States. Some cities and all states have preliminary pageants. The winner of the city pageant goes on to compete in the state pageant for her home city. A delegate may also enter a state pageant without having won a city title. One delegate from each of the 50 states and the District of Columbia is selected to compete in the pageant. Participants must be between 14 and 19 years of age. They must never have been married or pregnant. Selection is based on beauty, intelligence, and ability to handle an interview.
Financial data: Miss Teen USA receives cash and prizes whose value varies each year.
Duration: The national pageant is held annually, usually at the end of the summer.
Number awarded: 1 national winner each year.
Deadline: June of each year.

572 $$ MISS USA

Miss Universe Organization
1370 Avenue of the Americas, 16th Floor
New York, NY 10019
Phone: (212) 373–4999; Fax: (212) 315–5378;
Email: pr@missuniverse.com
Web: www.missuniverse.com/missusa
Summary: To identify and reward the most beautiful women selected in a competition among women from each state.
Eligibility: Open to women between 18 and 27 years of age who have never been married or pregnant. Entrants are first selected in state competitions, and then 51 women (1 from each state and the District of Columbia) compete in the Miss USA Pageant. Selection of the winner is based on interviews by pageant judges (on successes, talents, goals, and ambitions), a swimsuit competition (with swimsuit styles provided by the pageant), and an evening gown competition (with gowns chosen by the competitors). The Photogenic Award is presented to the delegate voted on and selected by the television audience, and the Congeniality Award is presented to the delegate selected by her sister delegates as the most charismatic and inspirational.
Financial data: Miss USA receives cash and prizes whose value varies each year.
Duration: The national pageant is held annually, in February or March.
Number awarded: 1 each year.
Deadline: January of each year.

573 $$ MISSISSIPPI EDUCATIONAL ASSISTANCE FOR MIA/POW DEPENDENTS

Mississippi State Veterans Affairs Board
3466 Highway 80
P.O. Box 5947
Pearl, MS 39288–5947
Phone: (601) 576–4850; (877) 203–5632; Fax: (601) 576–4868
Web: www.vab.ms.gov
Summary: To provide financial assistance for college to the children of Mississippi residents who are POWs or MIAs.
Eligibility: Open to the children of members of the armed services whose official home of record and residence is in Mississippi and who are officially reported as being either a prisoner of a foreign government or missing in action. Applicants must be attending or planning to attend a state–supported college or university in Mississippi.
Financial data: This assistance covers all costs of college attendance.
Duration: Up to 8 semesters.
Number awarded: Varies each year.
Deadline: Deadline not specified.

574 $ MISSISSIPPI EMINENT SCHOLARS GRANTS

Mississippi Office of Student Financial Aid
3825 Ridgewood Road
Jackson, MS 39211–6453
Phone: (601) 432–6997; (800) 327–2980 (within MS); Fax: (601) 432–6527;
Email: sfa@mississippi.edu
Web: www.mississippi.edu/riseupms/financialaid–state.php
Summary: To provide financial assistance to residents of Mississippi who have exceptional academic records and plan to attend college in the state.
Eligibility: Open to seniors graduating from high schools in Mississippi, home–schooled students in the state with less than 12 college hours, and college students who graduated from high school or completed a home school program within the past 3 years and have completed 12 or more college hours. Applicants must have been residents of Mississippi for at least 1 year prior to enrolling in college and have a high school or college GPA of 3.5 or higher and a score of 29 or higher on the ACT, 1290 or higher on the SAT I, or 1940 or higher on the new SAT; if they qualified as a semifinalist or finalist in the National Merit Scholarship Competition or the National Achievement Scholarship Competition, they are not required to have the minimum ACT score. They must be enrolled or planning to enroll as a full–time student at an approved college or university in the state.
Financial data: The stipend is $2,500 per year, not to exceed tuition and required fees.
Duration: 1 year; may be renewed for up to 4 additional years or completion of an undergraduate degree, as long as the recipient maintains continuous full–time enrollment and a cumulative GPA of 3.5 or higher.
Number awarded: Varies each year; recently, more than 2,000 of these grants were awarded.
Deadline: September of each year.

575 $$ MISSISSIPPI HIGHER EDUCATION LEGISLATIVE PLAN FOR NEEDY STUDENTS

Mississippi Office of Student Financial Aid
3825 Ridgewood Road
Jackson, MS 39211–6453
Phone: (601) 432–6997; (800) 327–2980 (within MS); Fax: (601) 432–6527;
Email: sfa@mississippi.edu
Web: www.mississippi.edu/riseupms/financialaid–state.php
Summary: To provide financial assistance for college to residents of Mississippi who demonstrate financial need.
Eligibility: Open to applicants who have been residents of Mississippi for at least 2 years and have graduated from high school within the immediate past 2 years. They must be enrolled or planning to enroll full time at a college or

university in the state. High school seniors entering their freshman year in college must have a cumulative high school GPA of 2.5 or higher and have completed specific high school core curriculum requirements. College freshmen entering their sophomore year must have achieved a cumulative GPA of 2.5 or higher on all college course work previously completed. All applicants must have scored 20 or higher on the ACT and be able to demonstrate financial need with an average family adjusted gross income of $36,500 or less over the prior 2 years for a family with no dependent members under 21 years of age other than the student, and rising by $5,000 for each sibling in the family under 21 years of age.

Financial data: Students in this program receive a full waiver of tuition at eligible Mississippi public institutions of higher learning or eligible Mississippi public community/junior colleges. Students attending private institutions receive an award amount equal to the award of a student attending the nearest comparable public institution.

Duration: 1 year; may be renewed up to 4 additional years, provided the recipient continues to meet all program requirement and maintains a GPA of 2.5 or higher.

Number awarded: Varies each year; recently, 316 of these awards, worth more than $1.5 million, were granted.

Deadline: March of each year.

576 $$ MISSISSIPPI LAW ENFORCEMENT OFFICERS AND FIREMEN SCHOLARSHIP PROGRAM

Mississippi Office of Student Financial Aid
3825 Ridgewood Road
Jackson, MS 39211–6453
Phone: (601) 432–6997; (800) 327–2980 (within MS); Fax: (601) 432–6527;
Email: sfa@mississippi.edu
Web: www.mississippi.edu/riseupms/financialaid–state.php

Summary: To provide financial assistance to the spouses and children of disabled or deceased Mississippi law enforcement officers and firefighters who are interested in attending college in the state.

Eligibility: Open to children and spouses of law enforcement officers, full–time firefighters, and volunteer firefighters who became permanently and totally disabled or who died in the line of duty and were Mississippi residents at the time of death or injury. Applicants must be high school seniors or graduates interested in attending a state–supported postsecondary institution in Mississippi on a full–time basis. Children may be natural, adopted, or stepchildren up to 23 years of age; spouses may be of any age.

Financial data: Students in this program receive full payment of tuition fees, the average cost of campus housing, required fees, and applicable course fees at state–supported colleges and universities in Mississippi. Funds may not be used to pay for books, food, school supplies, materials, dues, or fees for extracurricular activities.

Duration: Up to 8 semesters.

Number awarded: Varies each year; recently, 21 of these awards, worth more than $178,000, were granted.

Deadline: September of each year.

577 MISSISSIPPI TUITION ASSISTANCE GRANTS

Mississippi Office of Student Financial Aid
3825 Ridgewood Road
Jackson, MS 39211–6453
Phone: (601) 432–6997; (800) 327–2980 (within MS); Fax: (601) 432–6527;
Email: sfa@mississippi.edu
Web: www.mississippi.edu/riseupms/financialaid–state.php

Summary: To provide financial assistance to Mississippi residents who demonstrate significant financial need and are interested in attending college in the state.

Eligibility: Open to students entering their freshman, sophomore, junior, or senior year as a full–time student at an eligible Mississippi college or university. Applicants must have been Mississippi residents for at least 1 year and be receiving less than the full federal Pell Grant for college. High school seniors must have a GPA of 2.5 or higher and an ACT score of 15 or higher. Home–schooled students must submit a transcript showing the course work corresponding to that of a high school graduate for grades 9–12 and an ACT score of 15 or higher. Students already enrolled in college must have a cumulative GPA of 2.5 or higher. All applicants must be attending or planning to attend a 2– or 4–year public or private accredited college or university in Mississippi.

Financial data: Awards depend on the availability of funds and the need of the recipient; the maximum award for a freshman or sophomore is $500 per year; the maximum award for a junior or senior is $1,000 per year.

Duration: 1 year; may be renewed for up to 4 additional years or completion of an undergraduate degree, as long as the recipient maintains continuous full–time enrollment and a GPA of 2.5 or higher.

Number awarded: Varies each year; recently, more than 23,000 Mississippi residents received nearly $14 million in support from this program.

Deadline: September of each year.

578 $ MISSOURI A+ SCHOLARSHIP PROGRAM

Missouri Department of Higher Education
Attn: Student Financial Assistance
205 Jefferson Street
P.O. Box 1469
Jefferson City, MO 65102–1469
Phone: (573) 526–7958; (800) 473–6757; Fax: (573) 751–6635;
Email: info@dhe.mo.gov
Web: www.dhe.mo.gov/ppc/grants/aplusscholarship.php

Summary: To provide financial assistance to high school seniors who graduate from a designated "A+ School" in Missouri and are interested in attending a community college or vocational institute in the state.

Eligibility: Open to students who graduate from a designated "A+ School" in Missouri. Applicants must meet the following requirements: have attended a designated A+ School for 3 consecutive years prior to graduation, have a GPA of at least 2.5, have at least a 95% attendance record, perform at least 50 hours of unpaid tutoring or mentoring, maintain a record of good citizenship and avoid the unlawful use of drugs or alcohol, have a score of proficient or advanced on the algebra I end–of–course examination, and be planning to enroll full time at a community college or postsecondary vocational/technical school in Missouri.

Financial data: Scholarships provide reimbursement of the unpaid balance of tuition and general fees after all available, non–loan federal assistance has been applied to the account; the amount eligible for reimbursement is capped at $149 per credit hour or $4 per clock hour.

Duration: 1 year; may be renewed if the recipient maintains a GPA of 2.5 or higher.

Number awarded: Varies each year.

Deadline: Deadline not specified.

579 MISSOURI AMERICAN LEGION COMMANDER'S SCHOLARSHIPS

American Legion
Department of Missouri
3341 American Avenue
P.O. Box 179
Jefferson City, MO 65102–0179
Phone: (573) 893–2353; (800) 846–9023; Fax: (573) 893–2980;
Email: info@missourilegion.org
Web: www.missourilegion.org/default_016.htm

Summary: To provide financial assistance to veterans in Missouri who are interested in attending college in the state.

Eligibility: Open to residents of Missouri who served at least 90 days in the U.S. armed forces and received an honorable discharge. Applicants must be enrolled or planning to enroll full time at an accredited vocational/technical school, college, or university in Missouri.

Financial data: The stipend is $1,000.

Duration: 1 year.

Number awarded: 2 each year.

Deadline: April of each year.

580 MISSOURI GICC ENDOWMENT SCHOLARSHIP

Epsilon Sigma Alpha International
Attn: ESA Foundation
363 West Drake Road
Fort Collins, CO 80526
Phone: (970) 223–2824; Fax: (970) 223–4456;
Email: esainfo@epsilonsigmaalpha.org
Web: www.epsilonsigmaalpha.org/esa–foundation/scholarships

Summary: To provide financial assistance to residents of Missouri who plan to attend college in any state.

Eligibility: Open to residents of Missouri who are 1) graduating high school seniors with a GPA of 3.0 or higher or with minimum scores of 22 on the ACT or 1030 on the combined critical reading and mathematics SAT; 2) enrolled in college with a GPA of 3.0 or higher; 3) enrolled at a technical school or returning to school after an absence for retraining of job skills or obtaining a degree;

or 4) engaged in online study through an accredited college, university, or vocational school. Applicants may be attending or planning to attend an accredited school anywhere in the United States and major in any field. Selection is based on character (20%), leadership (20%), service (20%), financial need (20%), and scholastic ability (20%).
Financial data: The stipend is $1,000.
Duration: 1 year; may be renewed.
Number awarded: 1 each year.
Deadline: January of each year.

581 MISSOURI HIGHER EDUCATION ACADEMIC "BRIGHT FLIGHT" SCHOLARSHIP PROGRAM

Missouri Department of Higher Education
Attn: Student Financial Assistance
205 Jefferson Street
P.O. Box 1469
Jefferson City, MO 65102–1469
Phone: (573) 526–7958; (800) 473–6757; Fax: (573) 751–6635;
Email: info@dhe.mo.gov
Web: www.dhe.mo.gov/ppc/grants/brightflight.php
Summary: To provide financial assistance to high school seniors in Missouri who achieve high scores on standardized tests and plan to attend college in the state.
Eligibility: Open to seniors graduating from high schools in Missouri who plan to enroll full time at a participating college or university in the state. Applicants with SAT scores of 800 or higher in critical reading and 790 or higher in mathematics or composite ACT scores of 31 or higher qualify for the highest level of awards. Applicants with SAT scores of 770 to 799 in critical reading and 780 to 789 in mathematics or composite ACT scores of 30 qualify for the second level of awards. Students working on a degree or certificate in theology or divinity are not eligible. U.S. citizenship or permanent resident status is required.
Financial data: The statutory maximum for students in the highest level of SAT or ACT scores is $3,000 per year and for students in the second level of SAT or ACT scores $1,000 per year. Because of financial limitations on the program, recent awards were $1,750 per year for students in the highest level; no funding was available for students in the second level.
Duration: 1 year; may be renewed for up to 4 additional years or until completion of a baccalaureate degree, provided the recipient maintains full–time status and satisfactory academic progress.
Number awarded: Varies each year; recently, 8,823 of these scholarships, worth more than $16 million, were awarded.
Deadline: July of each year.

582 $$ MISSOURI PUBLIC SERVICE OFFICER OR EMPLOYEE'S CHILD SURVIVOR GRANT PROGRAM

Missouri Department of Higher Education
Attn: Student Financial Assistance
205 Jefferson Street
P.O. Box 1469
Jefferson City, MO 65102–1469
Phone: (573) 526–7958; (800) 473–6757; Fax: (573) 751–6635;
Email: info@dhe.mo.gov
Web: www.dhe.mo.gov/ppc/grants/publicserviceofficer.php
Summary: To provide financial assistance to disabled public safety officers in Missouri and the spouses and children of disabled or deceased officers who are interested in attending college in the state.
Eligibility: Open to residents of Missouri who are 1) public safety officers who were permanently and totally disabled in the line of duty; 2) spouses of public safety officers who were killed or permanently and totally disabled in the line of duty; or 3) children of Missouri public safety officers or Department of Transportation employees who were killed or permanently and totally disabled while engaged in the construction or maintenance of highways, roads, and bridges. Applicants must be Missouri residents enrolled or accepted for enrollment as a full–time undergraduate student at a participating Missouri college or university; children must be younger than 24 years of age. Students working on a degree or certificate in theology or divinity are not eligible. U.S. citizenship or permanent resident status is required.
Financial data: The maximum annual grant is the lesser of 1) the actual tuition charged at the school where the recipient is enrolled; or 2) the amount of tuition charged to a Missouri undergraduate resident enrolled full time in the same class level and in the same academic major as an applicant at the University of Missouri at Columbia.
Duration: 1 year; may be renewed.
Number awarded: Varies each year; recently, 11 students received $47,045 in support from this program.
Deadline: There is no application deadline, but early submission of the completed application is encouraged.

583 MISSOURI TORCHBEARERS ENDOWMENT SCHOLARSHIP

Epsilon Sigma Alpha International
Attn: ESA Foundation
363 West Drake Road
Fort Collins, CO 80526
Phone: (970) 223–2824; Fax: (970) 223–4456;
Email: esainfo@epsilonsigmaalpha.org
Web: www.epsilonsigmaalpha.org/esa–foundation/scholarships
Summary: To provide financial assistance to residents of Missouri who plan to attend college in any state.
Eligibility: Open to residents of Missouri who are 1) graduating high school seniors with a GPA of 3.0 or higher or with minimum scores of 22 on the ACT or 1030 on the combined critical reading and mathematics SAT; 2) enrolled in college with a GPA of 3.0 or higher; 3) enrolled at a technical school or returning to school after an absence for retraining of job skills or obtaining a degree; or 4) engaged in online study through an accredited college, university, or vocational school. Applicants may be attending or planning to attend a school in any state and major in any field. Selection is based on character (25%), leadership (25%), service (20%), financial need (15%), and scholastic ability (15%).
Financial data: The stipend is $1,000.
Duration: 1 year; may be renewed.
Number awarded: 3 each year.
Deadline: January of each year.

584 $$ MISSOURI VIETNAM VETERAN SURVIVOR GRANT PROGRAM

Missouri Department of Higher Education
Attn: Student Financial Assistance
205 Jefferson Street
P.O. Box 1469
Jefferson City, MO 65102–1469
Phone: (573) 526–7958; (800) 473–6757; Fax: (573) 751–6635;
Email: info@dhe.mo.gov
Web: www.dhe.mo.gov/ppc/grants/vietnamveterans.php
Summary: To provide financial assistance to survivors of certain deceased Missouri Vietnam veterans who plan to attend college in the state.
Eligibility: Open to surviving spouses and children of veterans who served in the military in Vietnam or the war zone in southeast Asia, who were residents of Missouri when first entering military service and at the time of death, whose death was attributed to or caused by exposure to toxic chemicals during the Vietnam conflict, and who served in the Vietnam Theater between 1961 and 1972. Applicants must be Missouri residents enrolled in a program leading to a certificate, associate degree, or baccalaureate degree at an approved postsecondary institution in the state. Students working on a degree or certificate in theology or divinity are not eligible. U.S. citizenship or permanent resident status is required.
Financial data: The maximum annual grant is the lesser of 1) the actual tuition charged at the school where the recipient is enrolled; or 2) the amount of tuition charged to a Missouri undergraduate resident enrolled full time in the same class level and in the same academic major as an applicant at the Missouri public 4–year regional institutions.
Duration: 1 semester; may be renewed until the recipient has obtained a baccalaureate degree, has received the award for 10 semesters, or has completed 150 semester credit hours, whichever comes first. Dependent children remain eligible until they reach 25 years of age. Spouses remain eligible until the fifth anniversary of the veteran's death.
Number awarded: Up to 12 each year.
Deadline: There is no application deadline, but early submission of the completed application is encouraged.

585 $$ MISSOURI WARTIME VETERAN'S SURVIVOR GRANT PROGRAM

Missouri Department of Higher Education
Attn: Student Financial Assistance
205 Jefferson Street
P.O. Box 1469
Jefferson City, MO 65102–1469

Phone: (573) 526–7958; (800) 473–6757; Fax: (573) 751–6635;
Email: info@dhe.mo.gov
Web: www.dhe.mo.gov/ppc/grants/wartimevetsurvivor.php

Summary: To provide financial assistance to survivors of deceased or disabled Missouri post–September 11, 2001 veterans who plan to attend college in the state.

Eligibility: Open to spouses and children of veterans whose deaths or injuries were a result of combat action or were attributed to an illness that was contracted while serving in combat action, or who became 80% disabled as a result of injuries or accidents sustained in combat action since September 11, 2001. The veteran must have been a Missouri resident when first entering military service or at the time of death or injury. The spouse or child must be a U.S. citizen or permanent resident or otherwise lawfully present in the United States; children of veterans must be younger than 25 years of age. All applicants must be enrolled or accepted for enrollment at least half time at participating public college or university in Missouri.

Financial data: The maximum annual grant is the lesser of 1) the actual tuition charged at the school where the recipient is enrolled; or 2) the amount of tuition charged to a Missouri resident enrolled in the same number of hours at the University of Missouri at Columbia. Additional allowances provide up to $2,000 per semester for room and board and the lesser of the actual cost for books or $500.

Duration: 1 year. May be renewed, provided the recipient maintains a GPA of 2.5 or higher and makes satisfactory academic progress; children of veterans are eligible until they turn 25 years of age or receive their first bachelor's degree, whichever occurs first.

Number awarded: Up to 25 each year.

Deadline: There is no application deadline, but early submission of the completed application is encouraged.

586 $ MITCH DANIELS EARLY GRADUATION SCHOLARSHIP

State Student Assistance Commission of Indiana
Attn: Grants and Scholarships
W462 Indiana Government Center South
402 West Washington Street
Indianapolis, IN 46204
Phone: (317) 232–2355; (888) 528–4719 (within IN); Fax: (317) 232–3260;
Email: grants@ssaci.in.gov
Web: www.in.gov/ssaci/2504.htm

Summary: To provide financial assistance to high school seniors in Indiana who graduate early and plan to attend college in the state.

Eligibility: Open to seniors who graduate from a publicly–supported high school in Indiana at least 1 year early. Applicants must be planning to attend an approved public or private college or university in the state in a program that will lead to an approved postsecondary degree or credential.

Financial data: The stipend is $4,000. Funds may be used only for tuition and regularly assessed fees. If any scholarship balance exists, it must be remitted to the student.

Duration: 1 year; nonrenewable.

Number awarded: Varies each year.

Deadline: September of each year.

587 $ MOAA AMERICAN PATRIOT SCHOLARSHIPS

Military Officers Association of America
Attn: Educational Assistance Program
201 North Washington Street
Alexandria, VA 22314–2539
Phone: (703) 549–2311; (800) 234–MOAA; Fax: (703) 838–5819;
Email: edassist@moaa.org
Web: www.moaa.org/loans

Summary: To provide financial assistance for undergraduate education to children of members of the uniformed services who have died.

Eligibility: Open to children under 24 years of age of active, Reserve, and National Guard uniformed service personnel (Army, Navy, Air Force, Marines, Coast Guard, Public Health Service, or National Oceanographic and Atmospheric Administration) whose parent has died on active service. Applicants must be working on an undergraduate degree. They must have a GPA of 3.0 or higher. Selection is based on academic ability, activities, and financial need.

Financial data: The stipend is currently $2,500 per year.

Duration: 1 year; may be renewed up to 4 additional years.

Number awarded: Varies each year; recently, 57 of these scholarships were awarded. Since the program was established, it has awarded $1,770,000 to 225 children of deceased military personnel.

Deadline: February of each year.

588 $$ MONTANA 2 PLUS 2 HONOR SCHOLARSHIPS

Office of the Commissioner of Higher Education
Attn: Montana University System
State Scholarship Coordinator
2500 Broadway
P.O. Box 203201
Helena, MT 59620–3201
Phone: (406) 444–0638; (800) 537–7508; Fax: (406) 444–1469;
Email: mtscholarships@montana.edu
Web: www.mus.edu

Summary: To provide financial assistance to students graduating from 2–year institutions in Montana and planning to transfer to a 4–year university in the state.

Eligibility: Open to residents of Montana who are graduating from a community college or 2–year branch of the Montana University System and planning to transfer to a 4–year branch of the System as a full–time student. Applicants must have earned an associate degree with a GPA of 3.4 or higher. Along with their application, they must submit a 250–word essay on how receiving this scholarship would help them obtain their short–term (next 2 years) and long–term (next 10 years) goals. Selection is based on GPA; if 2 or more students at the same 2–year college are tied, the tie is broken on the basis of financial need. If a tie still exists, it is broken by an evaluation of the essay. U.S. citizenship is required.

Financial data: Students selected to receive this benefit are entitled to attend 4–year branches of the Montana University System without payment of undergraduate tuition.

Duration: 1 year; may be renewed 1 additional year, provided the recipient remains enrolled full time and maintains a GPA of 3.4 or higher.

Number awarded: The number of scholarships awarded at each 2–year college is based on the size of the graduating class, up to 5 from each college.

Deadline: June of each year.

589 $$ MONTANA COMMUNITY COLLEGE HONOR SCHOLARSHIPS

Office of the Commissioner of Higher Education
Attn: Montana University System
State Scholarship Coordinator
2500 Broadway
P.O. Box 203201
Helena, MT 59620–3201
Phone: (406) 444–0638; (800) 537–7508; Fax: (406) 444–1469;
Email: snewlun@montana.edu
Web: www.mus.edu/Prepare/Pay/Tuition_and_Fee_Waivers.asp

Summary: To provide financial assistance to outstanding community college students in Montana planning to transfer to a university in the state.

Eligibility: Open to residents of Montana who are graduating from a community college in the state and planning to transfer to a branch of the Montana University System. Their college must verify that they are 1 of the highest ranking members of their class desiring to attend a Montana University System unit.

Financial data: Students eligible for this benefit are entitled to attend any unit of the Montana University System without payment of undergraduate registration or incidental fees.

Duration: 1 year; nonrenewable.

Number awarded: The number of scholarships awarded at each community college is based on the size of the graduating class.

Deadline: Deadline not specified.

590 $ MONTANA GOVERNOR'S "BEST AND BRIGHTEST" HIGH SCHOOL MERIT SCHOLARSHIPS

Office of the Commissioner of Higher Education
Attn: Montana University System
State Scholarship Coordinator
2500 Broadway
P.O. Box 203201
Helena, MT 59620–3201
Phone: (406) 444–0638; (800) 537–7508; Fax: (406) 444–1469;
Email: mtscholarships@montana.edu
Web: www.mus.edu

Summary: To provide financial assistance to high school seniors in Montana who are planning to attend designated institutions in the state and can demonstrate academic merit.

Eligibility: Open to graduating high school seniors in Montana who have been accepted as a full–time student at components of the Montana University

System, community colleges, or Indian colleges in the state. Applicants must have a GPA of 3.0 or higher and a score of at least 20 on the ACT or 1440 on the SAT. They must be nominated by officials at their high school.

Financial data: The stipend is $2,000 per year.

Duration: 1 year; may be renewed 1 additional year for students at community colleges or 3 additional years for students at 4–year campuses. Renewal requires satisfactory academic progress and full–time enrollment.

Number awarded: Each high school in Montana may award 1 of these scholarships.

Deadline: March of each year.

591 $ MONTANA GOVERNOR'S "BEST AND BRIGHTEST" MERIT AT–LARGE SCHOLARSHIPS

Office of the Commissioner of Higher Education
Attn: Montana University System
State Scholarship Coordinator
2500 Broadway
P.O. Box 203201
Helena, MT 59620–3201
Phone: (406) 444–0638; (800) 537–7508; Fax: (406) 444–1469;
Email: mtscholarships@montana.edu
Web: www.mus.edu

Summary: To provide financial assistance to Montana residents who are attending or planning to attend designated institutions in the state and can demonstrate academic merit.

Eligibility: Open to residents of Montana who have been accepted or are enrolled as a full–time student at components of the Montana University System, community colleges, or Indian colleges in the state. Applicants must have a GPA of 3.0 or higher and a score of at least 20 on the ACT or 1440 on the SAT. Nontraditional and home–schooled students are encouraged to apply.

Financial data: The stipend is $2,000 per year.

Duration: 1 year; may be renewed 1 additional year for students at community colleges or 3 additional years for students at 4–year campuses. Renewal requires satisfactory academic progress and full–time enrollment.

Number awarded: Varies each year; recently, this program awarded 121 new and 119 renewal scholarships.

Deadline: March of each year.

592 MONTANA GOVERNOR'S "BEST AND BRIGHTEST" NEED–BASED SCHOLARSHIPS

Office of the Commissioner of Higher Education
Attn: Montana University System
State Scholarship Coordinator
2500 Broadway
P.O. Box 203201
Helena, MT 59620–3201
Phone: (406) 444–0638; (800) 537–7508; Fax: (406) 444–1469;
Email: mtscholarships@montana.edu
Web: www.mus.edu

Summary: To provide financial assistance to Montana residents who are attending or planning to attend designated institutions in the state and can demonstrate financial need.

Eligibility: Open to residents of Montana who have been accepted or are enrolled as a full–time student at the 12 components of the Montana University System, the 3 community colleges, or the 7 Indian colleges in the state. Each institution is allocated a specific number of general, health science, technology, or trade/green scholarships. Selection is based only on financial need.

Financial data: The stipend is $1,000 per year.

Duration: 1 year; may be renewed 1 additional year provided the recipient maintains satisfactory academic progress and continues to demonstrate financial need.

Number awarded: Each participating institution may award up to 5 of these scholarships.

Deadline: March of each year.

593 $$ MONTANA HONOR SCHOLARSHIPS FOR NATIONAL MERIT SCHOLARSHIP SEMIFINALISTS

Office of the Commissioner of Higher Education
Attn: Montana University System
State Scholarship Coordinator
2500 Broadway
P.O. Box 203201
Helena, MT 59620–3201
Phone: (406) 444–0638; (800) 537–7508; Fax: (406) 444–1469;
Email: mtscholarships@montana.edu
Web: www.mus.edu

Summary: To provide financial assistance for undergraduate education to National Merit Scholarship semifinalists in Montana.

Eligibility: Open to residents of Montana who are National Merit Scholarship semifinalists. Students must enroll at a campus of the Montana University System or community college in the state within 9 months of high school graduation.

Financial data: Students eligible for this benefit are entitled to attend any unit of the Montana University System without payment of undergraduate registration or incidental fees.

Duration: The waiver is valid through the completion of the first academic year of enrollment.

Number awarded: Varies each year.

Deadline: Deadline not specified.

594 $$ MONTANA HONORABLY DISCHARGED VETERAN WAIVER

Office of the Commissioner of Higher Education
Attn: Montana University System
State Scholarship Coordinator
2500 Broadway
P.O. Box 203201
Helena, MT 59620–3201
Phone: (406) 444–0638; (800) 537–7508; Fax: (406) 444–1469;
Email: snewlun@montana.edu
Web: www.mus.edu/Prepare/Pay/Tuition_and_Fee_Waivers.asp

Summary: To provide financial assistance for undergraduate or graduate studies to selected Montana veterans.

Eligibility: Open to honorably–discharged veterans who served with the U.S. armed forces and who are residents of Montana. Only veterans who at some time qualified for U.S. Department of Veterans Affairs (VA) educational benefits, but who are no longer eligible or have exhausted their benefits, are entitled to this waiver. Veterans who served any time prior to May 8, 1975 are eligible to work on undergraduate or graduate degrees. Veterans whose service began after May 7, 1975 are eligible only to work on their first undergraduate degree. They must have received an Armed Forces Expeditionary Medal for service in Lebanon, Grenada, or Panama; served in a combat theater in the Persian Gulf between August 2, 1990 and April 11, 1991 and received the Southwest Asia Service Medal; were awarded the Kosovo Campaign Medal; or served in a combat theater in Afghanistan or Iraq after September 11, 2001 and received the Global War on Terrorism Expeditionary Medal, the Afghanistan Campaign Medal, or the Iraq Campaign Medal. Financial need must be demonstrated.

Financial data: Veterans eligible for this benefit are entitled to attend any unit of the Montana University System without payment of registration or incidental fees.

Duration: Students are eligible for continued fee waiver as long as they make reasonable academic progress as full–time students.

Number awarded: Varies each year.

Deadline: Deadline not specified.

595 $ MONTANA NATIONAL GUARD SCHOLARSHIPS

Montana National Guard
Attn: Education Service Officer
P.O. Box 4789
Fort Harrison, MT 59636–4789
Phone: (406) 324–3237;
Email: Julie.benson1@us.army.mil
Web: www.montanaguard.com/hro/html/educationpg2.cfm

Summary: To provide financial assistance for college to members of the Montana National Guard.

Eligibility: Open to members of the Montana National Guard who are enrolled or accepted for enrollment at a college, university, vocational/technical college, or other VA–approved training program in the state. Applicants must be in pay grades E–1 through E–7, W–1 through W–3, or O–1 through O–2; have completed Initial Active Duty for Training; have a high school diploma or GED; be eligible for Montgomery GI Bill Selected Reserve Benefits or be under a 6–year obligation to the Montana National Guard; and not have completed more than 16 years of military service. Funds are awarded on a first–come, first–served basis until exhausted.

Financial data: Stipends are $1,500 per semester for study at a college or university or $400 per semester at a community college.

Duration: 1 year; may be renewed.
Number awarded: Varies each year.
Deadline: Deadline not specified.

596 MONTANA STATE ESA COUNCIL ENDOWMENT SCHOLARSHIP

Epsilon Sigma Alpha International
Attn: ESA Foundation
363 West Drake Road
Fort Collins, CO 80526
Phone: (970) 223–2824; Fax: (970) 223–4456;
Email: esainfo@epsilonsigmaalpha.org
Web: www.epsilonsigmaalpha.org/esa–foundation/scholarships

Summary: To provide financial assistance to residents of Montana interested in attending college in the state.

Eligibility: Open to residents of Montana who are 1) graduating high school seniors with a GPA of 3.0 or higher or with minimum scores of 22 on the ACT or 1030 on the combined critical reading and mathematics SAT; 2) enrolled in college with a GPA of 3.0 or higher; 3) enrolled at a technical school or returning to school after an absence for retraining of job skills or obtaining a degree; or 4) engaged in online study through an accredited college, university, or vocational school. Applicants must be attending or planning to attend a school in Montana and major in any field. Selection is based on character (10%), leadership (10%), service (5%), financial need (50%), and scholastic ability (25%).

Financial data: The stipend is $1,500.
Duration: 1 year; may be renewed.
Number awarded: 1 each year.
Deadline: January of each year.

597 MONTANA TUITION ASSISTANCE PROGRAM BAKER GRANTS

Office of the Commissioner of Higher Education
Attn: Montana University System
State Scholarship Coordinator
2500 Broadway
P.O. Box 203201
Helena, MT 59620–3201
Phone: (406) 444–0638; (800) 537–7508; Fax: (406) 444–1469;
Email: mtscholarships@montana.edu
Web: www.mus.edu/Prepare/Pay/Scholarships/Montana_State_Grants.asp

Summary: To provide financial assistance to Montana residents who are attending college in the state and working to support themselves.

Eligibility: Open to residents of Montana who are attending units of the Montana University System, community colleges, Indian colleges, or designated private institutions in the state full time. Applicants must be working and have at least $3,275 in earned income during the prior calendar year. (That amount is based on the minimum wage multiplied by 500 hours; if the minimum wage is increased, the amount a student must earn is increased accordingly.) They must be making satisfactory academic progress toward their first undergraduate degree and have an expected family contribution from the results of their Free Application for Federal Student Aid (FAFSA) of $8,050 or less.

Financial data: The grant is intended to offset any federal Pell Grant dollars the student may have lost due to earned wages. Recently, grants ranged from $100 to $1,000.
Duration: 1 year.
Number awarded: Varies each year; recently, 2,400 students received more than $2.0 million in grants through this program.
Deadline: Deadline not specified.

598 $$ MONTANA UNIVERSITY SYSTEM HONOR SCHOLARSHIPS

Office of the Commissioner of Higher Education
Attn: Montana University System
State Scholarship Coordinator
2500 Broadway
P.O. Box 203201
Helena, MT 59620–3201
Phone: (406) 444–0638; (800) 537–7508; Fax: (406) 444–1469;
Email: mtscholarships@montana.edu
Web: www.mus.edu/Prepare/Pay/Scholarships/MUS_Honor_Scholarship.asp

Summary: To provide financial assistance to high school students in Montana who have outstanding academic records and plan to attend a public college in the state.

Eligibility: Open to residents of Montana who are graduating from high school and planning to attend a branch of the Montana University System or a community college in the state. Applicants must have been enrolled at an accredited high school for at least 3 years prior to graduation, meet the college preparatory requirements, submit ACT or SAT scores to their high school, and have a GPA of 3.4 or higher. They must be nominated by their high school. Selection is based on class rank and ACT or SAT score. U.S. citizenship is required.

Financial data: Students eligible for this benefit are entitled to attend any unit of the Montana University System or any community college in the state without payment of tuition or registration fees.
Duration: 1 year; may be renewed for up to 3 additional years if the recipient maintains full–time enrollment and a GPA of 3.4 or higher.
Number awarded: Up to 200 each year.
Deadline: March of each year.

599 $$ MONTANA WAR ORPHANS WAIVER

Office of the Commissioner of Higher Education
Attn: Montana University System
State Scholarship Coordinator
2500 Broadway
P.O. Box 203201
Helena, MT 59620–3201
Phone: (406) 444–0638; (800) 537–7508; Fax: (406) 444–1469;
Email: snewlun@montana.edu
Web: www.mus.edu/Prepare/Pay/Tuition_and_Fee_Waivers.asp

Summary: To provide financial assistance for undergraduate education to the children of Montana veterans who died in the line of duty or as a result of service–connected disabilities.

Eligibility: Open to children of members of the U.S. armed forces who served on active duty during World War II, the Korean Conflict, the Vietnam Conflict, the Afghanistan Conflict, or the Iraq Conflict; were legal residents of Montana at the time of entry into service; and were killed in action or died as a result of injury, disease, or other disability while in the service. Applicants must be no older than 25 years of age. Financial need is considered in the selection process.

Financial data: Students eligible for this benefit are entitled to attend any unit of the Montana University System without payment of undergraduate registration or incidental fees.
Duration: Undergraduate students are eligible for continued fee waiver as long as they maintain reasonable academic progress as full–time students.
Number awarded: Varies each year.
Deadline: Deadline not specified.

600 $$ MONTGOMERY GI BILL (ACTIVE DUTY)

Department of Veterans Affairs
Attn: Veterans Benefits Administration
810 Vermont Avenue, N.W.
Washington, DC 20420
Phone: (202) 418–4343; (888) GI–BILL1
Web: www.gibill.va.gov/benefits/montgomery_gibill/active_duty.html

Summary: To provide financial assistance for college, graduate school, and other types of postsecondary schools to new enlistees in any of the armed forces after they have completed their service obligation.

Eligibility: Open to veterans who received an honorable discharge and have a high school diploma, a GED, or, in some cases, up to 12 hours of college credit; veterans who already have a bachelor's degree are eligible to work on a master's degree or higher. Applicants must also meet the requirements of 1 of the following categories: 1) entered active duty for the first time after June 30, 1985, had military pay reduced by $100 per month for the first 12 months, and continuously served for 3 years, or 2 years if that was their original enlistment, or 2 years if they entered Selected Reserve within a year of leaving active duty and served 4 years (the 2 by 4 program); 2) entered active duty before January 1, 1977, had remaining entitlement under the Vietnam Era GI Bill on December 31, 1989, served at least 1 day between October 19, 1984 and June 30, 1985, and stayed on active duty through June 30, 1988 (or June 30, 1987 if they entered Selected Reserve within 1 year of leaving active duty and served 4 years); 3) on active duty on September 30, 1990 and separated involuntarily after February 2, 1991, involuntarily separated on or after November 30, 1993, or voluntarily separated under either the Voluntary Separation Incentive (VSI) or Special Separation Benefit (SSB) program, and before separation had military pay reduced by $1,200; or 4) on active duty on October 9, 1996, had money remaining in an account from the Veterans Educational Assistance Program (VEAP), elected Montgomery GI Bill (MGIB) by October 9, 1997, and paid $1,200. Certain

National Guard members may also qualify under category 4 if they served on full–time active duty between July 1, 1985 and November 28, 1989, elected MGIB between October 9, 1996 and July 8, 1997, and paid $1,200. Following completion of their service obligation, participants may enroll in colleges or universities for associate, bachelor, or graduate degrees; in courses leading to a certificate or diploma from business, technical, or vocational schools; for apprenticeships or on–the–job training programs; in correspondence courses; in flight training; for preparatory courses necessary for admission to a college or graduate school; for licensing and certification tests approved for veterans; or in state–approved teacher certification programs. Veterans who wish to enroll in certain high–cost technology programs (life science, physical science, engineering, mathematics, engineering and science technology, computer specialties, and engineering, science, and computer management) may be eligible for an accelerated payment.

Financial data: For veterans in categories 1, 3, and 4 who served on active duty for 3 years or more, the current monthly stipend for college or university work is $1,473 for full–time study. For enlistees whose initial active–duty obligation was less than 3 years, the current monthly stipend for college or university work is $1,196. For veterans in category 2 with remaining eligibility, the current monthly stipend for institutional study full time is $1,661 for no dependents, $1,697 with 1 dependent, $1,728 with 2 dependents, and $16 for each additional dependent. Lower rates apply for less than full–time study, apprenticeships and on–the–job training, cooperative education, correspondence courses, and flight training.

Duration: 36 months; active–duty servicemembers must utilize the funds within 10 years of leaving the armed services; Reservists may draw on their funds while still serving.

Number awarded: Varies each year.

Deadline: Deadline not specified.

601 $ MONTGOMERY GI BILL (SELECTED RESERVE)

Department of Veterans Affairs
Attn: Veterans Benefits Administration
810 Vermont Avenue, N.W.
Washington, DC 20420
Phone: (202) 418–4343; (888) GI–BILL1
Web: www.gibill.va.gov

Summary: To provide financial assistance for college or graduate school to members of the Reserves or National Guard.

Eligibility: Open to members of the Reserve elements of the Army, Navy, Air Force, Marine Corps, and Coast Guard, as well as the Army National Guard and the Air National Guard. To be eligible, a Reservist must 1) have a 6–year obligation to serve in the Selected Reserves signed after June 30, 1985 (or, if an officer, to agree to serve 6 years in addition to the original obligation); 2) complete Initial Active Duty for Training (IADT); 3) meet the requirements for a high school diploma or equivalent certificate before completing IADT; and 4) remain in good standing in a drilling Selected Reserve unit. Reservists who enlisted after June 30, 1985 can receive benefits for undergraduate degrees, graduate training, or technical courses leading to certificates at colleges and universities. Reservists whose 6–year commitment began after September 30, 1990 may also use these benefits for a certificate or diploma from business, technical, or vocational schools; cooperative training; apprenticeship or on–the–job training; correspondence courses; independent study programs; tutorial assistance; remedial, deficiency, or refresher training; flight training; or state–approved alternative teacher certification programs.

Financial data: The current monthly rate is $345 for full–time study, $258 for three–quarter time study, $171 for half–time study, or $86.25 for less than half–time study. For apprenticeship and on–the–job training, the monthly stipend is $258.75 for the first 6 months, $189.75 for the second 6 months, and $120.75 for the remainder of the program. Other rates apply for cooperative education, correspondence courses, and flight training.

Duration: Up to 36 months for full–time study, 48 months for three–quarter study, 72 months for half–time study, or 144 months for less than half–time study. Benefits end 10 years from the date the Reservist became eligible for the program.

Number awarded: Varies each year.

Deadline: Applications may be submitted at any time.

602 $$ MOOSE YOUTH AWARENESS PROGRAM

Moose International, Inc.
Attn: Department of Fraternal Programs
155 South International Drive
Mooseheart, IL 60539–1183
Phone: (630) 966–2224; Fax: (630) 966–2225
Web: www.mooseintl.org/Public/Area/YouthAware.asp

Summary: To recognize and reward, with college scholarships, high school students who deliver talks to children about current issues.

Eligibility: Open to U.S. and Canadian high school students who develop brief talks to deliver to groups of children 4 to 9 years of age whom they identify in their community. The talks must deal with such current issues as drug and alcohol abuse, child abuse, "stranger danger," bullying and peer pressure, and healthy habits and nutrition. Students must make at least 3 talks in their community and submit written reports on their presentations. School officials select 2 participating students to attend a local student congress; selection is based on academic ability and leadership qualities. At those congresses, participants present their talks to fellow students, and 60 of them are selected by their peers to attend the International Student Congress. At that Congress, participating students vote to select the winners of the scholarships.

Financial data: First prize is a $12,000 scholarship, second an $8,000 scholarship, third a $5,000 scholarship, fourth a $3,000 scholarship, and fifth a $2,000 scholarship. All expenses to attend the International Student Congress are paid by local Moose Lodges.

Duration: The competition is held annually.

Number awarded: 5 each year.

Deadline: Local student congresses are held in October and November of each year.

603 MOTHER ELNORA JOHNSON VISIONARY AWARD

David and Dovetta Wilson Scholarship Fund, Inc.
115–67 237th Street
Elmont, NY 11003–3926
Phone: (516) 285–4573;
Email: DDWSF4@aol.com
Web: www.wilsonfund.org/Elnora_Johnson.html

Summary: To provide financial assistance to high school seniors who are interested in going to college and demonstrate a commitment to the values of its namesake.

Eligibility: Open to graduating high school seniors who have actively participated in community and religious projects and can demonstrate financial need. Applicants must be U.S. citizens or permanent residents and have a GPA of 3.0 or higher. Along with their application, they must submit 3 letters of recommendation, high school transcripts, and an essay (up to 250 words) on "How My College Education Will Help Me Make a Positive Impact on My Community." This award is presented to applicants who demonstrate that the values of Mother Elnora Johnson, a "love of God, hard work, and education," are the means to a successful life.

Financial data: The stipend is $1,000.

Duration: 1 year; nonrenewable.

Number awarded: 1 or more each year.

Deadline: March of each year.

604 MOULTON–FARNSWORTH SCHOLARSHIPS

American Deficit Disorder Association
P.O. Box 7557
Wilmington, DE 19803–9997
Phone: (800) 939–1019; Fax: (800) 939–1019;
Email: info@add.org
Web: www.add.org/?page=MoultonFarnsworth

Summary: To provide financial assistance for college to students who have attention deficit/hyperactivity disorder (ADHD).

Eligibility: Open to students who have been diagnosed with ADHD by a licensed physician or mental health professional. Applicants must be enrolled or planning to enroll at an approved college or university as an undergraduate student. Along with their application, they must submit a 500–word essay on why they would like to be considered for this scholarship, the ways in which ADHD has been a challenge for them in the educational setting, and the strategies they have used to meet the challenge.

Financial data: The stipend is $1,000 per year. Funds are paid directly to the recipient's college.

Duration: 1 year; recipients may reapply.

Number awarded: 2 each year.

Deadline: March of each year.

605 $ MOUSE HOLE SCHOLARSHIPS

Blind Mice, Inc.
16810 Pinemoor Way
Houston, TX 77058

Phone: (713) 893–7277;
Email: blindmicemart@att.net
Web: www.blindmicemegamall.com/bmm/Mouse_Hole_Scholarships

Summary: To provide financial assistance for college to blind students and the children of blind parents.

Eligibility: Open to visually impaired students and to sighted students who have visually impaired parents. Applicants must be high school seniors or graduates who have never been enrolled in college. Along with their application, they must submit an essay, between 4 and 15 pages in length, on a topic that changes annually; recently, students were asked to speculate on what their life will be like in 10 years. Essays are judged on originality, creativity, grammar, spelling, and the judge's overall impression of the applicant.

Financial data: Stipends are $2,000 for the winner and $1,000 for the first runner–up.

Duration: 1 year.

Number awarded: 2 each year.

Deadline: May of each year.

606 MYBOOKBUYER.COM TEXTBOOKS FOR A YEAR SCHOLARSHIP

MyBookBuyer.com
1451 Doolittle Drive
San Leandro, CA 94577
Phone: (408) 890–5155; (800) 345–4350; Fax: (408) 942–2828
Web: www.mybookbuyer.com/textbooks–for–a–year–scholarship.htm

Summary: To recognize and reward college students who submit outstanding essays to the MyBookBuyer.com web site.

Eligibility: Open to legal residents of the United States who are 18 years of age and older and currently attending a college or university in any state. Applicants must submit an essay, of 500 to 1,000 words, through the sponsor's web site. The topic varies each semester; recently, students were asked to identify 1 person who has had a significant and positive impact on their life and explain how some of those influences have changed their life. Those essays are judged on the basis of writing ability, creativity, originality, and overall excellence and 10 finalists are selected. The finalists must then submit supporting documents (an affidavit of eligibility, publicity/liability release, copyright assignment, IRS W–9 form, copy of driver's license, and a photograph) and a grand prize winner and runner–up are named.

Financial data: Awards are $1,250 as the grand prize and $250 for the runner–up. The grand prize is intended to cover the cost of college textbooks for 1 year.

Duration: The competition is held each semester.

Number awarded: 1 grand prize and 1 runner–up prize are awarded each semester.

Deadline: April of each year for spring; October of each year for fall.

607 NANOR KRIKORIAN HIGH SCHOOL STUDENT SCHOLARSHIPS

Armenian Youth Federation
104 North Belmont Street, Suite 313
Glendale, CA 91206
Phone: (818) 507–1933; Fax: (818) 240–3442;
Email: ayf@ayfwest.org
Web: www.ayfwest.org/programs/scholarship

Summary: To provide financial assistance for college to high school seniors of Armenian descent.

Eligibility: Open to college–bound high school seniors of Armenian descent. Applicants must be able to demonstrate involvement in community service activities, clubs and organizations on campus, and athletics. Along with their application, they must submit a 1,000–word essay on how their major and/or future plans will benefit the Armenian community. Financial need is not considered in the selection process.

Financial data: Stipends are $1,000, $500, or $250.

Duration: 1 year.

Number awarded: 4 each year: 1 at $1,000, 1 at $500, and 2 at $250.

Deadline: April of each year.

608 $ NATIONAL ACHIEVEMENT SCHOLARSHIP PROGRAM

National Merit Scholarship Corporation
Attn: National Achievement Scholarship Program
1560 Sherman Avenue, Suite 200
Evanston, IL 60201–4897
Phone: (847) 866–5100; Fax: (847) 866–5113
Web: www.nationalmerit.org/nasp.php

Summary: To provide financial assistance for college to Black American high school seniors with exceptional scores on the SAT and/or PSAT/NMSQT.

Eligibility: Open to Black American seniors who are enrolled full time in a secondary school and progressing normally toward graduation or completion of high school requirements. Applicants must be U.S. citizens (or intend to become a citizen as soon as qualified) and be planning to attend an accredited college or university in the United States. They must take the PSAT/NMSQT at the proper time in high school (no later than the 11th grade) and mark section 14 on the PSAT/NMSQT answer sheet, which identifies them as a Black American who is requesting consideration in the Achievement Program. Final selection is based on the student's academic record, a self–description, PSAT/NMSQT and SAT scores, and a recommendation written by the principal or another official. Financial information is not considered, nor are college choice, course of study, or career plans.

Financial data: The stipend is $2,500.

Duration: 1 year.

Number awarded: Approximately 700 each year.

Deadline: Applicants must take the PSAT/NMSQT no later than October of their junior year.

609 NATIONAL ASSOCIATION OF NEGRO BUSINESS AND PROFESSIONAL WOMEN'S CLUBS NATIONAL SCHOLARSHIPS

National Association of Negro Business and Professional Women's Clubs
Attn: Scholarship Committee
1806 New Hampshire Avenue, N.W.
Washington, DC 20009–3206
Phone: (202) 483–4206; Fax: (202) 462–7253;
Email: education@nanbpwc.org
Web: www.nanbpwc.org/scholarship_applications0.aspx

Summary: To provide financial assistance for college to African American high school seniors.

Eligibility: Open to African American high school seniors planning to enroll in an accredited college or university. Applicants must have a GPA of 3.0 or higher. Along with their application, they must submit an essay (at least 300 words) on "Why Education is Important to Me." Financial need is not considered in the selection process. U.S. citizenship is required.

Financial data: The stipend is $1,000.

Duration: 1 year.

Number awarded: 10 each year.

Deadline: February of each year.

610 $ NATIONAL CENTER FOR LEARNING DISABILITIES ALLEGRA FORD SCHOLARSHIP

National Center for Learning Disabilities
Attn: Scholarship
381 Park Avenue South, Suite 1401
New York, NY 10016–8806
Phone: (212) 545–7510; (888) 575–7373; Fax: (212) 545–9665;
Email: afscholarship@ncld.org
Web: www.ncld.org

Summary: To provide financial assistance to high school seniors who have a learning disability and plan to attend a community college or vocational training program.

Eligibility: Open to high school seniors who have a documented learning disability and plan to attend a 2–year community college, vocational/technical training program, or specialized program for students with learning disabilities. Applicants must be able to demonstrate financial need. They must 1) articulate their learning disability and recognize the need for self–advocacy; 2) be committed to postsecondary academic study or career training and have begun to set realistic career goals; 3) participate in school and community activities; and 4) have demonstrated perseverance and commitment to achieving personal goals despite the challenges of learning disabilities. U.S. citizenship is required.

Financial data: The stipend is $2,500.

Duration: 1 year; nonrenewable.

Number awarded: 1 each year.

Deadline: December of each year.

611 NATIONAL COLLEGIATE CANCER FOUNDATION SCHOLARSHIP

National Collegiate Cancer Foundation
Attn: Scholarship Committee
4858 Battery Lane, Suite 216
Bethesda, MD 20814

Phone: (240) 515–6262;
Email: info@collegiatecancer.org
Web: www.collegiatecancer.org/scholarships.html

Summary: To provide financial assistance for college or graduate school to cancer survivors.

Eligibility: Open to students between 18 and 35 years of age who are cancer survivors or currently undergoing treatment for cancer. Applicants must be enrolled or planning to enroll at a college or university to work on a certificate or an associate, bachelor's, master's, or doctoral degree. Along with their application, they must submit a 1,000–word essay on 1 of 4 assigned topics related to their experiences with cancer and college. Selection is based on the essay, letters of recommendation, displaying a "Will Win" attitude, overall story of cancer survivorship, commitment to education, and financial need.

Financial data: The stipend is $1,000.

Duration: 1 year.

Number awarded: 1 or more each year.

Deadline: May of each year.

612 $$ NATIONAL COMMISSION FOR COOPERATIVE EDUCATION SCHOLARSHIPS

National Commission for Cooperative Education
360 Huntington Avenue, 384 CP
Boston, MA 02115–5096
Phone: (617) 373–3770; Fax: (617) 373–3463;
Email: ncce@co–op.edu
Web: www.co–op.edu/scholarships.htm

Summary: To provide financial assistance to students participating or planning to participate in cooperative education projects at designated colleges and universities.

Eligibility: Open to high school seniors and community college transfer students entering 1 of the 7 partner colleges and universities. Applicants must be planning to participate in college cooperative education. They must have a GPA of 3.5 or higher. Along with their application, they must submit a 1–page essay describing why they have chosen to enter a college cooperative education program. Applications are especially encouraged from minorities, women, and students interested in science, mathematics, engineering, and technology. Selection is based on merit; financial need is not considered.

Financial data: The stipend is $6,000 per year.

Duration: 1 year; may be renewed up to 3 additional years or (for some programs) up to 4 additional years.

Number awarded: Varies each year; recently, 155 of these scholarships were awarded: 30 at Drexel, 30 at Johnson & Wales, 20 at Kettering, 15 at Rochester Tech, 15 at Cincinnati, 15 at Toledo, and 30 at Wentworth Tech.

Deadline: February of each year.

613 NATIONAL CORNERSTONE HEALTHCARE SERVICES SCHOLARSHIPS

National Cornerstone Healthcare Services Inc.
24747 Redlands Boulevard, Suite B
Loma Linda, CA 92354
Phone: (877) 616–6247; Fax: (877) 777–5717;
Email: inquiry@nc–hs.com
Web: www.nc–hs.com

Summary: To provide financial assistance for college to people who have a bleeding disorder and members of their family.

Eligibility: Open to graduating high school seniors who are planning to attend an accredited technical school, college, or university. Applicants must have been diagnosed with a bleeding disorder or be the parent, spouse, partner, child, or sibling of a person with such a disorder. They must have a GPA of 2.5 or higher during their entire senior year of high school. Along with their application, they must submit a brief essay on their dreams, goals, and objectives for attending postsecondary education. Selection is based on that statement, academic merit, employment status, reference letters, impact of the bleeding disorders community, and financial need.

Financial data: Stipends range from $500 to $1,000.

Duration: 1 year.

Number awarded: 1 or more each year.

Deadline: March of each year.

614 $ NATIONAL EAGLE SCOUT ASSOCIATION SCHOLARSHIPS

Boy Scouts of America
Attn: National Eagle Scout Association, S322
1325 West Walnut Hill Lane
P.O. Box 152079
Irving, TX 75015–2079
Phone: (972) 580–2431
Web: nesa.org/scholarships.html

Summary: To provide financial assistance for college to Eagle Scouts who demonstrate financial need and academic excellence.

Eligibility: Open to Eagle Scouts who are graduating high school seniors planning to enroll as a full–time student at an accredited 4–year college or university. They must have an SAT score of at least 1200 and/or an ACT score of 28. Selection is based on academic achievement, demonstrated leadership ability in Scouting, participation in activities outside of Scouting, and financial need.

Financial data: The stipend is $3,000. Funds are paid directly to the recipients' universities.

Duration: 1 year; nonrenewable.

Number awarded: 28 each year: 7 in each region.

Deadline: January of each year.

615 $$ NATIONAL EXCHANGE CLUB ACCEPTING THE CHALLENGE OF EXCELLENCE AWARD

National Exchange Club
Attn: Foundation
3050 Central Avenue
Toledo, OH 43606–1700
Phone: (419) 535–3232; (800) XCHANGE; Fax: (419) 535–1989
Web: www.exchangeclubfoundation.org/scholarship.htm

Summary: To recognize and reward, with college scholarships, outstanding high school seniors who have overcome obstacles.

Eligibility: Open to high school students who have made a dramatic change in their attitude and performance sometime during their high school years and are now eligible for high school graduation. Candidates should have overcome great physical, emotional, or social obstacles, including physical difficulties, language difficulties, child abuse, delinquency, or substance abuse. They must first be selected by their local Exchange Club, and the club's award chair must submit a 500–word description of the candidate's problem and how it was overcome. The students must also submit 2 essays of 250 words each: 1) the event or events in their life that they are most proud of; and 2) their plans for the future to make their community and world a better place to live. Other selection criteria include community service activities and volunteer service hours. District winners are selected from among the local club nominees, and the national winner is chosen from among the district winners.

Financial data: The winner receives a $10,000 scholarship.

Duration: The award is presented annually.

Number awarded: 1 each year.

Deadline: Districts must submit their candidates by May of each year.

616 $ NATIONAL FEDERATION OF REPUBLICAN WOMEN'S NATIONAL PATHFINDER SCHOLARSHIPS

National Federation of Republican Women
Attn: Scholarships and Internships
124 North Alfred Street
Alexandria, VA 22314–3011
Phone: (703) 548–9688; Fax: (703) 548–9836;
Email: mail@nfrw.org
Web: www.nfrw.org/programs/scholarships.htm

Summary: To provide financial assistance for college or graduate school to Republican women.

Eligibility: Open to women currently enrolled as college sophomores, juniors, seniors, or master's degree students. Recent high school graduates and first–year college women are not eligible. Applicants must submit 3 letters of recommendation, an official transcript, a 1–page essay on why they should be considered for the scholarship, and a 1–page essay on career goals. Applications must be submitted to the Republican federation president in the applicant's state. Each president chooses 1 application from her state to submit for scholarship consideration. Financial need is not a factor in the selection process. U.S. citizenship is required.

Financial data: The stipend is $2,500.

Duration: 1 year; nonrenewable.

Number awarded: 3 each year.

Deadline: Applications must be submitted to the state federation president by May of each year.

617 $$ NATIONAL ITALIAN AMERICAN FOUNDATION GENERAL CATEGORY I SCHOLARSHIPS

National Italian American Foundation
Attn: Education Director
1860 19th Street, N.W.
Washington, DC 20009
Phone: (202) 387–0600; Fax: (202) 387–0800;
Email: scholarships@niaf.org
Web: www.niaf.org/scholarships

Summary: To provide financial assistance to Italian American college and graduate students.

Eligibility: Open to Italian Americans (defined as having at least 1 ancestor who has immigrated from Italy) who are U.S. citizens or permanent residents. Applicants must be currently enrolled at or entering an accredited college or university in the United States and have a GPA of 3.5 or higher. They may be high school seniors, undergraduates, graduate students, or doctoral candidates. Selection is based on academic performance, field of study, career objectives, and the potential, commitment, and abilities applicants have demonstrated that would enable them to make significant contributions to their chosen field of study. Some scholarships also require financial need, but most do not.

Financial data: Stipends range from $2,000 to $12,000.

Duration: 1 year. Recipients are encouraged to reapply.

Number awarded: Varies each year.

Deadline: February of each year.

618 $ NATIONAL MERIT SCHOLARSHIP CORPORATION COLLEGE–SPONSORED MERIT SCHOLARSHIP AWARDS

National Merit Scholarship Corporation
Attn: Department of Educational Services and Selection
1560 Sherman Avenue, Suite 200
Evanston, IL 60201–4897
Phone: (847) 866–5100; Fax: (847) 866–5113
Web: www.nationalmerit.org/nmsp.php

Summary: To provide financial assistance from participating colleges to finalists for the National Merit Scholarship Program but who are not awarded Merit Scholarships.

Eligibility: Open to high school seniors who are high scorers in the National Merit Scholarship Program but are not awarded scholarships. After recipients of National Merit Scholarships and Corporate–Sponsored Merit Scholarships have been chosen, the remaining National Merit finalists are contacted and asked to report their current college choice. Those who reply that a sponsor college or university is their first choice are referred to officials of that institution as candidates for the College–Sponsored Merit Scholarship Program. College officials select the award winners.

Financial data: College officials determine each winner's stipend within a range of $500 to $2,000 per year. The college may meet part of a winner's financial need with loans, employment, and grants; however, unless the student's total need (as calculated by the college) is met with gift aid, the Merit Scholarship must represent at least half the winner's need, up to an annual maximum stipend of $2,000.

Duration: 1 year; renewable for up to 3 additional years.

Number awarded: Approximately 4,800 each year.

Deadline: To qualify for the National Merit Scholarship Program, applicants must take the PSAT/NMSQT no later than October of their junior year.

619 $$ NATIONAL MERIT SCHOLARSHIP CORPORATION CORPORATE–SPONSORED ACHIEVEMENT SCHOLARSHIPS

National Merit Scholarship Corporation
Attn: National Achievement Scholarship Program
1560 Sherman Avenue, Suite 200
Evanston, IL 60201–4897
Phone: (847) 866–5100; Fax: (847) 866–5113
Web: www.nationalmerit.org/nasp.php

Summary: To provide financial assistance from corporate sponsors to African American finalists for the National Achievement Scholarship Program who are not awarded Achievement Scholarships.

Eligibility: Open to African American high school seniors who are high scorers in the National Achievement Scholarship Program but who not awarded scholarships. Because winners of these scholarships must meet preferential criteria specified by sponsors, not all finalists for the National Achievement Scholarship Program are considered for this award, and the awards are not subject to regional allocation. Further, corporate sponsors frequently offer their awards to finalists who are children of their employees or residents of an area where a plant or office is located. Some companies offer scholarships to students who plan to pursue particular college majors or careers. Finalists who have qualifications that especially interest a sponsor are identified and winners are selected from among eligible candidates. Financial need is considered for some of the awards.

Financial data: Most of these scholarships provide stipends that are individually determined, taking into account college costs and family financial circumstances. Variable stipend awards of this type range from at least $500 to $2,000 per year, although some have a higher annual minimum and a few range as high as $10,000 per year. Some renewable awards provide a fixed annual stipend (between $1,000 and $5,000) that is the same for every recipient of the sponsor's awards. Other corporate–sponsored scholarships are nonrenewable and provide a single payment (from $2,500 to $5,000) for the recipient's first year of college study.

Duration: 1 year; most awards are renewable up to 3 additional years.

Number awarded: Approximately 100 each year.

Deadline: Applicants must take the PSAT/NMSQT no later than October of their junior year.

620 $$ NATIONAL MERIT SCHOLARSHIP CORPORATION CORPORATE–SPONSORED MERIT AND SPECIAL SCHOLARSHIPS

National Merit Scholarship Corporation
Attn: Department of Educational Services and Selection
1560 Sherman Avenue, Suite 200
Evanston, IL 60201–4897
Phone: (847) 866–5100; Fax: (847) 866–5113
Web: www.nationalmerit.org/nmsp.php

Summary: To provide financial assistance from corporate sponsors to finalists for the National Merit Scholarship Program but who are not awarded Merit Scholarships.

Eligibility: Open to high school seniors who are high scorers in the National Merit Scholarship Program but are not awarded scholarships are considered for this program. Those who are named as finalists receive these Merit Scholarships, awarded by corporate sponsors to students who fulfill preferential criteria specified by the award sponsor; usually, the criteria require that the recipient be the child of an employee of the sponsoring corporation, although some are offered to residents of a service area or community where a business has plants or offices or to students with career plans the sponsor wishes to encourage. Some corporate sponsors also offer Special Scholarships; those are offered to students who did not qualify as finalists in the National Merit Scholarship Program but may receive these awards because the corporate sponsor wishes to award scholarships to the specified groups, even though not all have achieved status as Merit Scholars. Some of the Corporate and Special Scholarships are merit–based; others consider financial need.

Financial data: Most of these scholarships provide stipends that are individually determined, taking into account college costs and family financial circumstances. Variable stipend awards of this type range from at least $500 to $2,000 per year, although some have a higher annual minimum and a few range as high as $10,000 per year. Some renewable awards provide a fixed annual stipend (between $1,000 and $5,000) that is the same for every recipient of the sponsor's awards. Other corporate–sponsored scholarships are nonrenewable and provide a single payment (from $2,500 to $5,000) for the recipient's first year of college study.

Duration: 1 year; many may be renewed up to 3 additional years.

Number awarded: Approximately 1,000 Corporate–Sponsored Merit Scholarships and 1,300 Corporate–Sponsored Special Scholarships are awarded each year.

Deadline: To qualify for the National Merit Scholarship Program, applicants must take the PSAT/NMSQT no later than October of their junior year.

621 $ NATIONAL MERIT SCHOLARSHIP PROGRAM

National Merit Scholarship Corporation
Attn: Department of Educational Services and Selection
1560 Sherman Avenue, Suite 200
Evanston, IL 60201–4897
Phone: (847) 866–5100; Fax: (847) 866–5113
Web: www.nationalmerit.org/nmsp.php

Summary: To provide financial assistance for college to high school seniors who achieve outstanding scores on standardized tests.

Eligibility: Open to students who are enrolled full time in a secondary school, progressing normally toward graduation or completion of high school, and planning to enter college in the fall following high school graduation. Applicants must be a U.S. citizen or a permanent resident in the process of becoming a U.S. citizen and be taking the PSAT/NMSQT at the proper time in the high school program and no later than the third year in grades 9 through 12, regardless of grade classification or educational pattern. On the basis of the PSAT/NMSQT results, approximately 16,000 of the highest scorers are designated as semifinalists; they are apportioned among states based on the number of graduating seniors in each state, to ensure equitable geographical representation. Finalists for National Merit Scholarships must be graduating seniors who are selected from among the semifinalists on the basis of SAT scores, academic performance in all of grades 9–12, and recommendations by high school principals.

Financial data: The award is $2,500.

Duration: 1 year.

Number awarded: Up to 2,500 each year.

Deadline: Applicants must take the PSAT/NMSQT no later than October of their junior year.

622 $ NATIONAL MS SOCIETY SCHOLARSHIP PROGRAM

National Multiple Sclerosis Society
Attn: Scholarship Fund
900 South Broadway, Suite 200
Denver, CO 80209
Phone: (303) 698–6100, ext. 15259;
Email: nmss@act.org
Web: www.nationalmssociety.org

Summary: To provide financial assistance for college to students who have Multiple Sclerosis (MS) or are the children of people with MS.

Eligibility: Open to 1) high school seniors who have MS and will be attending an accredited postsecondary school for the first time; 2) high school seniors who are the children of parents with MS and will be attending an accredited postsecondary school for the first time; 3) high school (or GED) graduates of any age who have MS and will be attending an accredited postsecondary school for the first time; and 4) high school (or GED) graduates of any age who have a parent with MS and will be attending an accredited postgraduate school for the first time. Applicants must be U.S. citizens or permanent residents who plan to enroll for at least 6 credit hours per semester in an undergraduate course of study at an accredited 2– or 4–year college, university, or vocational/technical school in the United States or its territories to work on a degree, license, or certificate. Along with their application, they must submit a 1–page personal statement on the impact MS has had on their life. Selection is based on that statement, academic record, leadership and participation in school or community activities, work experience, goals and aspirations, an outside appraisal, special circumstances, and financial need.

Financial data: Stipends range from $1,000 to $3,000 per year.

Duration: 1 year; may be renewed.

Number awarded: Varies each year; recently, 639 of these scholarships (439 new awards and 200 renewals), with a total value of $1,166,350, were awarded.

Deadline: January of each year.

623 NATIONAL PRESBYTERIAN COLLEGE SCHOLARSHIP

Presbyterian Church (USA)
Attn: Office of Financial Aid for Studies
100 Witherspoon Street, Room M–052
Louisville, KY 40202–1396
Phone: (502) 569–5224; (888) 728–7228, ext. 5224; Fax: (502) 569–8766;
TDD: (800) 833–5955;
Email: finaid@pcusa.org
Web: gamc.pcusa.org

Summary: To provide financial assistance to high school seniors planning to attend a Presbyterian college.

Eligibility: Open to high school seniors preparing to enroll as full–time incoming freshmen at a participating college related to the Presbyterian Church (USA). Applicants must be members of the PCUSA, have a GPA of 3.0 or higher, be U.S. citizens or permanent residents, and be able to demonstrate financial need. Along with their application, they must submit a 500–word essay on what they plan to study and their plans for their education or career after college. Selection is based on that essay; personal qualities of character and leadership as reflected in contributions to church, school, and community; academic achievements; and recommendations from school and church officials.

Financial data: Stipends range up to $1,500 per year, depending upon the financial need of the recipient.

Duration: 1 year; may be renewed up to 3 additional years, provided the recipient maintains of GPA of 2.5 or higher, regularly participates in campus ministry or attends church, and participates in discernment of vocation through a series of essay questions that ask them to consider who God is calling them to be.

Number awarded: 25 to 30 each year.

Deadline: January of each year.

624 NATIVE AMERICAN EDUCATION GRANTS

Presbyterian Church (USA)
Attn: Office of Financial Aid for Studies
100 Witherspoon Street, Room M–052
Louisville, KY 40202–1396
Phone: (502) 569–5224; (800) 728–7228, ext. 5224; Fax: (502) 569–8766;
TDD: (800) 833–5955;
Email: finaid@pcusa.org
Web: gamc.pcusa.org

Summary: To provide financial assistance to Native American students interested in continuing their college education.

Eligibility: Open to Alaska Native and Native American students who are enrolled or planning to enroll full time at an accredited institution in the United States. Applicants must be able to provide documentation of membership in a Native American or Alaska Native tribe. They must have a GPA of 2.5 or higher and be able to demonstrate financial need. Along with their application, they must submit a 500–word essay on what they plan to study and their plans for their education or career after college. Students from all faith traditions are encouraged to apply, but preference is given to members of the PCUSA.

Financial data: Stipends range up to $1,500 per year, depending upon the recipient's financial need.

Duration: 1 year; may be renewed up to 3 additional years.

Number awarded: Up to 30 each year.

Deadline: April of each year.

625 NAVIANCE MSCA HIGH SCHOOL SCHOLARSHIP PROGRAM

Minnesota School Counselors Association
c/o Dawn Brown, President
Sartell High School
213 Third Avenue North
Sartell, MN 56377
Phone: (320) 656–3701, ext. 3409;
Email: brown@sartell.k12.mn.us
Web: www.mnschoolcouneslors.org

Summary: To provide financial assistance to high school seniors in Minnesota who plan to attend college in any state.

Eligibility: Open to seniors who are graduating from public and private high schools in Minnesota and planning to attend a college, university, technical college, or trade school in any state. Applicants must submit a 500–word essay describing how a licensed school counselor at any level has supported them in 1 or more of the following areas: career development, education planning, and/or dealing with a social or emotional challenge. The counselor must endorse the application and must be a member of the Minnesota School Counselors Association (MSCA). Selection is based primarily on the essay; financial need is not considered.

Financial data: The stipend is $1,000.

Duration: 1 year.

Number awarded: 11 each year: 1 in each MSCA division.

Deadline: February of each year.

626 $ NAVY LEAGUE FOUNDATION SCHOLARSHIPS

Navy League of the United States
Attn: Scholarships
2300 Wilson Boulevard, Suite 200
Arlington, VA 22201–5424
Phone: (703) 528–1775; (800) 356–5760; Fax: (703) 528–2333;
Email: scholarships@navyleague.org
Web: www.navyleague.org/corporate/donate/scholarship.html

Summary: To provide financial assistance for college to dependent children of sea service personnel.

Eligibility: Open to U.S. citizens who are 1) dependents or direct descendants of an active, Reserve, retired, or honorably discharged member of the U.S. sea service (including the Navy, Marine Corps, Coast Guard, or Merchant Marine); or 2) currently an active member of the Naval Sea Cadet Corps. Applicants must be entering their freshman year at an accredited college or university. They must have a GPA of 3.0 or higher. Along with their application, they must submit transcripts, 2 letters of recommendation, SAT/ACT scores, documentation of financial need, proof of qualifying sea service duty, and a 1–page personal statement on why they should be considered for this scholarship.

Financial data: The stipend is $2,500 per year.

Duration: 4 years, provided the recipient maintains a GPA of 3.0 or higher.

Number awarded: Approximately 25 each year.

Deadline: March of each year.

627 NAVY/MARINE CORPS/COAST GUARD ENLISTED DEPENDENT SPOUSE SCHOLARSHIP

Navy Wives Clubs of America
c/o NSA Mid–South
P.O. Box 54022
Millington, TN 38054–0022
Phone: (866) 511–NWCA;
Email: nwca@navywivesclubsofamerica.org
Web: www.navywivesclubsofamerica.org/scholarships

Summary: To provide financial assistance for undergraduate or graduate study to spouses of naval personnel.

Eligibility: Open to the spouses of active–duty Navy, Marine Corps, or Coast Guard members who can demonstrate financial need. Applicants must be 1) a high school graduate or senior planning to attend college full time next year; 2) currently enrolled in an undergraduate program and planning to continue as a full–time undergraduate; 3) a college graduate or senior planning to be a full–time graduate student next year; or 4) a high school graduate or GED recipient planning to attend vocational or business school next year. Along with their application, they must submit a brief statement on why they feel they should be awarded this scholarship and any special circumstances (financial or other) they wish to have considered. Financial need is also considered in the selection process.

Financial data: The stipends range from $500 to $1,000 each year (depending upon the donations from chapters of the Navy Wives Clubs of America).

Duration: 1 year.

Number awarded: 1 or more each year.

Deadline: May of each year.

628 NAVY WIVES CLUBS OF AMERICA NATIONAL SCHOLARSHIPS

Navy Wives Clubs of America
c/o NSA Mid–South
P.O. Box 54022
Millington, TN 38054–0022
Phone: (866) 511–NWCA;
Email: nwca@navywivesclubsofamerica.org
Web: www.navywivesclubsofamerica.org/scholarships

Summary: To provide financial assistance for college or graduate school to the children of naval personnel.

Eligibility: Open to the children (natural born, legally adopted, or stepchildren) of enlisted members of the Navy, Marine Corps, or Coast Guard on active duty, retired with pay, or deceased. Applicants must be attending or planning to attend an accredited college or university as a full–time undergraduate or graduate student. They must have a GPA of 2.5 or higher. Along with their application, they must submit an essay on their career objectives and the reasons they chose those objectives. Selection is based on academic standing, moral character, and financial need. Some scholarships are reserved for students majoring in special education, medical students, and children of members of Navy Wives Clubs of America (NWCA).

Financial data: The stipend is $1,500.

Duration: 1 year; may be renewed up to 3 additional years.

Number awarded: 30 each year, including at least 4 to freshmen, 4 to current undergraduates applying for the first time, 2 to medical students, 1 to a student majoring in special education, and 4 to children of NWCA members.

Deadline: May of each year.

629 $$ NAVY–MARINE CORPS ROTC 2–YEAR SCHOLARSHIPS

U.S. Navy
Attn: Naval Education and Training Command
NSTC OD2
250 Dallas Street, Suite A
Pensacola, FL 32508–5268
Phone: (850) 452–4941, ext. 29395; (800) NAV–ROTC, ext. 29395; Fax: (850) 452–2486;
Email: pnsc_nrotc.scholarship@navy.mil
Web: www.nrotc.navy.mil/scholarships.aspx

Summary: To provide financial assistance to upper–division students who are interested in joining Navy ROTC in college.

Eligibility: Open to students who have completed at least 2 years of college (or 3 years if enrolled in a 5–year program) with a GPA of 2.5 or higher overall and 2.0 or higher in calculus and physics. Preference is given to students at colleges with a Navy ROTC unit on campus or at colleges with a cross–enrollment agreement with a college with an NROTC unit. Applicants must be U.S. citizens between the ages of 17 and 21 who plan to pursue an approved course of study in college and complete their degree before they reach the age of 27. Former and current enlisted military personnel are also eligible if they will complete the program by the age of 30.

Financial data: These scholarships provide payment of full tuition and required educational fees, as well as a specified amount for textbooks, supplies, and equipment. The program also provides a stipend for 10 months of the year that is $350 per month as a junior and $400 per month as a senior.

Duration: 2 years, until the recipient completes the bachelor's degree.

Number awarded: Approximately 800 each year.

Deadline: March of each year.

630 $$ NAVY–MARINE CORPS ROTC 4–YEAR SCHOLARSHIPS

U.S. Navy
Attn: Naval Education and Training Command
NSTC OD2
250 Dallas Street, Suite A
Pensacola, FL 32508–5268
Phone: (850) 452–4941, ext. 29395; (800) NAV–ROTC, ext. 29395; Fax: (850) 452–2486;
Email: pnsc_nrotc.scholarship@navy.mil
Web: www.nrotc.navy.mil/scholarships.aspx

Summary: To provide financial assistance to graduating high school seniors who are interested in joining Navy ROTC in college.

Eligibility: Open to graduating high school seniors who have been accepted at a college with a Navy ROTC unit on campus or a college with a cross–enrollment agreement with such a college. Applicants must be U.S. citizens between 17 and 23 years of age who are willing to serve for 4 years as active–duty Navy officers following graduation from college. They must not have reached their 27th birthday by the time of college graduation and commissioning; applicants who have prior active–duty military service may be eligible for age adjustments for the amount of time equal to their prior service, up to a maximum of 36 months. The qualifying scores for the Navy option are 530 critical reading and 520 mathematics on the SAT or 22 on English and 21 on mathematics on the ACT; for the Marine Corps option they are 1000 composite on the SAT or 22 composite on the ACT. Eligible academic majors are classified as Tier 1 for engineering programs of Navy interest (aerospace, aeronautical, astronautical, chemical, electrical, mechanical, naval, nuclear, ocean, and systems); Tier 2 for other engineering, mathematics, and science programs (e.g., general engineering and other engineering specialties; biochemistry and other specialties within biology; chemistry; mathematics; oceanography; pharmacology and toxicology; physics; quantitative economics; physics); or Tier 3 for selected regional and cultural area studies, designated foreign languages, or other academic majors.

Financial data: These scholarships provide payment of full tuition and required educational fees, as well as a specified amount for textbooks, supplies, and equipment. The program also provides a stipend for 10 months of the year that is $250 per month as a freshman, $300 per month as a sophomore, $350 per month as a junior, and $400 per month as a senior.

Duration: 4 years.

Number awarded: Approximately 2,200 each year; approximately 85% of the scholarships are awarded to students with Tier 1 or 2 majors.

Deadline: January of each year.

631 $ NAVY–MARINE CORPS ROTC COLLEGE PROGRAM

U.S. Navy
Attn: Naval Education and Training Command
NSTC OD2
250 Dallas Street, Suite A
Pensacola, FL 32508–5268
Phone: (850) 452–4941, ext. 29395; (800) NAV–ROTC, ext. 29395; Fax: (850) 452–2486;
Email: PNSC_NROTC.scholarship@navy.mil
Web: www.nrotc.navy.mil/scholarships.aspx

Summary: To provide financial assistance to lower–division students who are interested in joining Navy ROTC in college.

Eligibility: Open to U.S. citizens between the ages of 17 and 21 who are already enrolled as non–scholarship students in naval science courses at a college or university with a Navy ROTC program on campus. They must apply before the spring of their sophomore year. All applications must be submitted through the professors of naval science at the college or university attended.

Financial data: Participants in this program receive free naval science textbooks, all required uniforms, and a stipend for 10 months of the year that is $350 per month as a junior and $400 per month as a senior.

Duration: 2 or 4 years.

Deadline: March of each year.

632 $$ NCAA DIVISION II DEGREE–COMPLETION AWARD PROGRAM

National Collegiate Athletic Association
Attn: Leadership Advisory Board
1802 Alonzo Watford Sr. Drive
P.O. Box 6222
Indianapolis, IN 46206–6222
Phone: (317) 917–6222; Fax: (317) 917–6364;
Email: esummers@ncaa.org
Web: www.ncaa.org

Summary: To provide financial assistance to student–athletes at Division II colleges and universities who have exhausted their eligibility for aid from the institutions they attend.

Eligibility: Open to student–athletes who have exhausted their eligibility for institutional aid at a Division II member institution of the National Collegiate Athletic Association (NCAA). Applicants must be within their first 10 semesters or 15 quarters of full–time college attendance. They must have a GPA of 2.5 or higher and be within 32 semester hours of their first undergraduate degree. Selection is based on financial circumstances, athletic achievement, and involvement in campus and community activities.

Financial data: The award is the lesser of 1) the recipient's athletics aid for the final year of eligibility; 2) tuition for the remaining credits toward completing an undergraduate degree; or 3) $6,000.

Duration: Until completion of an undergraduate degree.

Number awarded: Varies each year; recently, 72 of these awards were granted. Since the program was established, it has awarded more than $3 million to 830 student–athletes.

Deadline: April of each year.

633 $$ NCCA DIVISION I DEGREE–COMPLETION AWARD PROGRAM

National Collegiate Athletic Association
Attn: Leadership Advisory Board
1802 Alonzo Watford Sr. Drive
P.O. Box 6222
Indianapolis, IN 46206–6222
Phone: (317) 917–6307; Fax: (317) 917–6364;
Email: esummers@ncaa.org
Web: www.ncaa.org

Summary: To provide financial assistance to student–athletes at Division I colleges and universities who have exhausted their eligibility for aid from the institutions they attend.

Eligibility: Open to student–athletes who have exhausted their 5 years of eligibility for institutional aid at a Division I member institution of the National Collegiate Athletic Association (NCAA). Applicants must be entering at least their sixth year of college and be within 30 semester hours of their degree requirements. They must submit documentation of financial need.

Financial data: Awards provide payment of the actual cost of tuition and fees plus a book allowance ($400 per semester for full–time students or an equivalent amount for part–time students).

Duration: 1 academic term; may be renewed if the recipient earns a GPA of 2.0 or higher.

Number awarded: Varies each year.

Deadline: April of each year for fall; September of each year for winter, spring, or summer.

634 NCFOP FOUNDATION SCHOLARSHIPS

North Carolina Fraternal Order of Police
Attn: NCFOB Foundation, Inc.
1500 Walnut Street
Cary, NC 27511–5927
Phone: (919) 461–4939; (877) 628–8063;
Email: ncfop@nc.rr.com
Web: www.ncfop.com/ht/d/sp/i/204/pid/204

Summary: To provide financial assistance for college to families of disabled or deceased law enforcement officers in North Carolina.

Eligibility: Open to North Carolina residents who are enrolled in an appropriate postsecondary institution, including colleges and vocational schools. Applicants must be the child or spouse of a North Carolina law enforcement officer killed or disabled in the line of duty.

Financial data: A stipend is awarded (amount not specified).

Duration: 1 year.

Number awarded: Varies each year; recently, 3 of these scholarships were awarded.

Deadline: Deadline not specified.

635 $ NCLD ANNE FORD SCHOLARSHIP

National Center for Learning Disabilities
Attn: Scholarship
381 Park Avenue South, Suite 1401
New York, NY 10016–8806
Phone: (212) 545–7510; (888) 575–7373; Fax: (212) 545–9665;
Email: afscholarship@ncld.org
Web: www.ncld.org

Summary: To provide financial assistance to high school seniors who have a learning disability and plan to attend a 4–year college or university.

Eligibility: Open to high school seniors who have a documented learning disability and plan to work full time on a bachelor's degree at a 4–year college or university. Applicants must have a GPA of 3.0 or higher and be able to demonstrate financial need. They must 1) articulate their learning disability and recognize the importance of self–advocacy; 2) be committed to completing a 4–year college degree and have begun to set realistic career goals; 3) participate in school and community activities; 4) have demonstrated academic achievements consistent with college and career goals; 5) plan to contribute to society in ways that increase opportunities for other individuals with learning disabilities; and 6) excel as a role model and spokesperson for others who struggle with learning disabilities. U.S. citizenship is required.

Financial data: The stipend is $2,500 per year.

Duration: 4 years.

Number awarded: 1 each year.

Deadline: December of each year.

636 NEBRASKA DIVISION SCHOLARSHIPS

Midwest Dairy Association–Nebraska Division
Attn: Industry Relations Manager
6409 Tanglewood Lane
Lincoln, NE 68516
Phone: (402) 853–2028; (800) 642–3895;
Email: rjohnson@midwestdairy.com
Web: www.midwestdairy.com

Summary: To provide financial assistance to family members of dairy farmers in Nebraska who are interested in attending college in any state.

Eligibility: Open to producers who fund Midwest Dairy Association, their spouses, their children, and their grandchildren. The producer must have an active dairy operation and must reside in Nebraska. Applicants must be enrolled or planning to enroll full time at an accredited college or university in any state; students planning to major in the dairy field and students working on a degree in any field are considered separately. Along with their application, they must submit essays on 1) their career aspirations and what stimulates their interest in that career; 2) their involvement in the dairy industry and/or participation in their family farm; and 3) their work experience or involvement in special dairy projects. Financial need is not considered in the selection process.

Financial data: Stipends are $1,500, $1,000, or $500 per year.

Duration: 1 year; recipients may reapply.

Number awarded: 7 each year: 2 for students majoring in the dairy field (1 at $1,500 and 1 at $1,000) and 5 at $500 for students majoring in any field.

Deadline: May of each year.

637 $ NEBRASKA OPPORTUNITY GRANT PROGRAM

Coordinating Commission for Postsecondary Education
Attn: Financial Aid Coordinator
140 North Eighth Street, Suite 300
P.O. Box 95005
Lincoln, NE 68509–5005
Phone: (402) 471–0032; Fax: (402) 471–2886;
Email: Ritchie.Morrow@nebraska.gov
Web: www.ccpe.state.ne.us/PublicDoc/Ccpe/financialaid.asp

Summary: To provide financial assistance to residents of Nebraska who demonstrate financial need and are interested in attending college in the state.

Eligibility: Open to residents of Nebraska who demonstrate financial need. Applicants must be attending or planning to attend a public or private institution of higher education in the state.

Financial data: The amount of the grant is determined by each participating institution; recently, grants ranged up to $3,400 and averaged $961.

Duration: 1 year.

Number awarded: Varies each year; recently, more than 15,000 students received nearly $15 million in these grants.

Deadline: Each participating institution establishes its own deadline.

638 $$ NEBRASKA WAIVER OF TUITION FOR VETERANS' DEPENDENTS

Department of Veterans' Affairs
State Office Building
301 Centennial Mall South, Sixth Floor
P.O. Box 95083
Lincoln, NE 68509–5083
Phone: (402) 471–2458; Fax: (402) 471–2491;
Email: john.hilgert@nebraska.gov
Web: www.vets.state.ne.us/benefits.html

Summary: To provide financial assistance for college to dependents of deceased and disabled veterans and military personnel in Nebraska.

Eligibility: Open to spouses, widow(er)s, and children who are residents of Nebraska and whose parent, stepparent, or spouse was a member of the U.S. armed forces and 1) died of a service–connected disability; 2) died subsequent to discharge as a result of injury or illness sustained while in service; 3) is permanently and totally disabled as a result of military service; or 4) is classified as missing in action or as a prisoner of war during armed hostilities. Applicants must be attending or planning to attend a branch of the University of Nebraska, a state college, or a community college in Nebraska.

Financial data: Tuition is waived at public institutions in Nebraska.

Duration: The waiver is valid for 1 degree, diploma, or certificate from a community college and 1 baccalaureate degree.

Number awarded: Varies each year; recently, 311 of these grants were awarded.

Deadline: Deadline not specified.

639 $$ NED MCWHERTER SCHOLARS PROGRAM

Tennessee Student Assistance Corporation
Parkway Towers
404 James Robertson Parkway, Suite 1510
Nashville, TN 37243–0820
Phone: (615) 741–1346; (800) 342–1663; Fax: (615) 741–6101;
Email: TSAC.Aidinfo@tn.gov
Web: www.tn.gov/collegepays/mon_college/ned_mc_shcolar.htm

Summary: To provide financial assistance to outstanding Tennessee high school seniors who plan to attend college in the state.

Eligibility: Open to seniors graduating from high schools in Tennessee who have scores of at least 29 on the ACT or 1280 on the mathematics and critical reading SAT and a GPA of 3.5 or higher. Applicants must be planning to enroll full time at an eligible college or university in Tennessee. The selection process includes consideration of difficulty of courses and leadership positions held while in high school, but financial need is not considered. U.S. citizenship or permanent resident status is required.

Financial data: Stipends up to $6,000 per year are provided.

Duration: 1 year; may be renewed for up to 3 additional years if the recipient remains a full–time student and maintains a minimum GPA of 3.2.

Number awarded: Approximately 50 each year.

Deadline: February of each year.

640 $ NEW CENTURY SCHOLARS PROGRAM

Phi Theta Kappa
Attn: Scholarship Programs Department
1625 Eastover Drive
Jackson, MS 39211
Phone: (601) 987–5741; (800) 946–9995; Fax: (601) 984–3550;
Email: scholarship.programs@ptk.org
Web: www.ptkfoundation.org/become–a–member/scholarships/academic–teams

Summary: To recognize and reward the outstanding achievements of community college students.

Eligibility: Open to students who have completed at least 36 hours at a community college in the United States, Alberta (Canada), or the 5 nations where Phi Theta Kappa has a chapter. Candidates must be nominated by a designated official at their college. Students at colleges in the United States are not required to be members of Phi Theta Kappa, but membership is required for students at colleges outside the country. Nominees must have a cumulative GPA of at least 3.5 for all college course work completed in the last 5 years, regardless of institution attended, and be on track to earn an associate or bachelor's degree. They must submit a 2–page essay describing their most significant endeavor since attending community college in which they applied their academic or intellectual skills from their community college education to benefit their school, community, or society. Selection is based on information in the essay; awards, honors, and recognition for academic achievement; academic rigor and GPA; participation in honors programs; and service to the college and the community.

Financial data: The award is $2,000.

Duration: The competition is held annually.

Number awarded: 52 each year: 1 from each state, 1 from Alberta, Canada, and 1 from outside Canada and the United States.

Deadline: November of each year.

641 NEW ENGLAND FEMARA SCHOLARSHIPS

American Radio Relay League
Attn: ARRL Foundation
225 Main Street
Newington, CT 06111–1494
Phone: (860) 594–0397; Fax: (860) 594–0259;
Email: foundation@arrl.org
Web: www.arrl.org/scholarship–descriptions

Summary: To provide financial assistance to licensed radio amateurs, especially those from the New England states, who are interested in working on an undergraduate or graduate degree in any field.

Eligibility: Open to undergraduate or graduate students in any subject area who are enrolled at accredited institutions in any state and are licensed radio amateurs of technician class or higher. Applicants must submit an essay on the role amateur radio has played in their lives and provide documentation of financial need. Preference is given to residents of the New England states.

Financial data: The stipend is $1,000.

Duration: 1 year.

Number awarded: Varies, depending upon the availability of funds; recently, 3 of these scholarships were awarded.

Deadline: January of each year.

642 $$ NEW ENGLAND REGIONAL STUDENT PROGRAM

New England Board of Higher Education
45 Temple Place
Boston, MA 02111
Phone: (617) 357–9620; Fax: (617) 338–1577;
Email: tuitionbreak@nebhe.org
Web: www.nebhe.org

Summary: To enable students in New England to attend a college or graduate school within the region at reduced tuition when their area of study is not offered at their own state's public institutions.

Eligibility: Open to residents of the 6 New England states: Connecticut, Maine, Massachusetts, New Hampshire, Rhode Island, and Vermont. Students may apply for this support when their chosen field of study is not offered at any of the public institutions within their own state. Contact the New England Board of Higher Education for a catalog of degree programs and states that qualify for this program. Undergraduate program eligibility is based on entire degree programs only, not on concentrations or options within degree programs. Some highly specialized graduate programs might be available even if they are not listed in the catalog. Eligibility is not based on financial need.

Financial data: With this program, students accepted at a public college or university in New England (but outside their own state) generally pay 150% of the in–state tuition for residents of the state. The average tuition savings is approximately $7,000.

Duration: Up to 4 years.

Number awarded: Varies each year; recently, more than 9,000 New England students took advantage of this program.

Deadline: Deadline not specified.

643 NEW HAMPSHIRE CHARITABLE FOUNDATION ADULT STUDENT AID PROGRAM

New Hampshire Charitable Foundation
37 Pleasant Street
Concord, NH 03301–4005
Phone: (603) 225–6641; (800) 464–6641; Fax: (603) 225–1700;
Email: info@nhcf.org
Web: www.nhcf.org/page.aspx?pid=473

Summary: To provide funding for undergraduate study to adults in New Hampshire who are returning to school in the state.

Eligibility: Open to New Hampshire residents who are 24 years of age or older, have served in the military, are a ward of the court, have not been claimed by their parents for 2 consecutive years and have earned at least $4,000 in each of those 2 years, or are married or have dependent children. Applicants should 1) have had little or no education beyond high school; and 2) be now returning to school to upgrade skills for employment or career advancement, to qualify

for a degree program, or to make a career change. They must demonstrate that they have secured all available financial aid and still have a remaining unmet need. Preference for funding is given in the following order: 1) students who have previously received funding through this program and have successfully completed prior work; 2) students with the least amount of higher education or training; and 3) single parents. Only undergraduate students are eligible.
Financial data: The maximum award is $500 per term, or a total of $1,500 per recipient. Most awards are in the form of grants, although interest–free loans may also be provided.
Duration: 1 academic term; may be renewed up to 2 additional terms.
Number awarded: Varies each year.
Deadline: May, August, or December of each year.

644 NEW HAMPSHIRE HOUSING AUTHORITIES CORPORATION SCHOLARSHIPS

New Hampshire Housing Authorities Corporation
c/o Vernon Sherman, Scholarship Committee
Exeter Housing Authority
277 Water Street
Exeter, NH 03833
Phone: (603) 778–8110, ext. 10
Web: www.nhhac.org/scholarship_program.php
Summary: To provide financial assistance to high school seniors and adults who have been subsidized by a New Hampshire housing authority and plan to attend college in any state.
Eligibility: Open to residents of New Hampshire who are graduating high school seniors or adults returning to education. Applicants must be interested in attending a college or university in any state. They must have been residents of an assisted housing program in New Hampshire for at least 12 months prior to applying. Along with their application, they must submit an essay of 250 to 500 words on how living in subsidized housing has impacted their life.
Financial data: Stipends range from $500 to $1,500. Funds are paid directly to the recipient's school to assist in payment of tuition, room, board, books, and laboratory or approved activity fees.
Duration: 1 year; may be renewed.
Number awarded: 1 or more each year.
Deadline: May of each year.

645 $ NEW HAMPSHIRE LEGION DEPARTMENT SCHOLARSHIP

American Legion
Department of New Hampshire
State House Annex
25 Capitol Street, Room 431
Concord, NH 03301–6312
Phone: (603) 271–2211; (800) 778–3816; Fax: (603) 271–5352;
Email: adjutantnh@amlegion.state.nh.us
Web: www.nhlegion.org/Legion%20Scholarships/Index%20Page.htm
Summary: To provide financial assistance to residents of New Hampshire entering a college or university in any state.
Eligibility: Open to seniors graduating from high schools in New Hampshire who have been residents of the state for at least 3 years. Applicants must be entering their first year of a bachelor's degree program at a 4–year college or university in any state. They must have a GPA of 3.0 or higher for their junior and senior years of high school. Along with their application, they must submit a brief narrative of the vocation they intend to pursue. Financial need is considered in the selection process.
Financial data: The stipend is $2,000.
Duration: 1 year.
Number awarded: 2 each year.
Deadline: April of each year.

646 $ NEW HAMPSHIRE LEGION DEPARTMENT VOCATIONAL EDUCATION SCHOLARSHIP

American Legion
Department of New Hampshire
State House Annex
25 Capitol Street, Room 431
Concord, NH 03301–6312
Phone: (603) 271–2211; (800) 778–3816; Fax: (603) 271–5352;
Email: adjutantnh@amlegion.state.nh.us
Web: www.nhlegion.org/Legion%20Scholarships/Index%20Page.htm
Summary: To provide financial assistance to residents of New Hampshire entering a vocational training program at a school in any state.
Eligibility: Open to seniors graduating from high schools in New Hampshire who have been residents of the state for at least 3 years. Applicants must be entering their first year of vocational training at a school in any state to work on an associate degree. They must have a GPA of 3.0 or higher for their junior and senior years of high school. Along with their application, they must submit a brief narrative of the vocation they intend to pursue. Financial need is considered in the selection process.
Financial data: The stipend is $2,000.
Duration: 1 year.
Number awarded: 1 each year.
Deadline: April of each year.

647 $ NEW HAMPSHIRE SCHOLARSHIPS FOR ORPHANS OF VETERANS

New Hampshire Department of Education
Attn: Higher Education Commission
Walker Building, Suite 20
21 Fruit Street
Concord, NH 03301–2450
Phone: (603) 271–2695; (888) 747–2382, ext. 119; Fax: (603) 271–1953;
Email: Amy.Slattery@doe.nh.gov
Web: www.education.nh.gov/highered/finanical/index.htm
Summary: To provide financial assistance for college in the state to the children of New Hampshire veterans who died of service–connected causes.
Eligibility: Open to New Hampshire residents between 16 and 25 years of age whose parent(s) died while on active duty or as a result of a service–related disability incurred during World War II, the Korean Conflict, the southeast Asian Conflict (Vietnam), or the Gulf Wars. Parents must have been residents of New Hampshire at the time of death. Applicants must be enrolled at least half time as undergraduate students at a public college or university in New Hampshire. Financial need is not considered in the selection process.
Financial data: The stipend is $2,500 per year, to be used for the payment of room, board, books, and supplies. Recipients are also eligible to receive a tuition waiver from the institution.
Duration: 1 year; may be renewed for up to 3 additional years.
Number awarded: Varies each year; recently, 2 of these scholarships were awarded.
Deadline: Deadline not specified.

648 NEW JERSEY BANKERS EDUCATION FOUNDATION SCHOLARSHIPS

New Jersey Bankers Association
Attn: New Jersey Bankers Education Foundation, Inc.
411 North Avenue East
Cranford, NJ 07016–2436
Phone: (908) 272–8500, ext. 614; Fax: (908) 272–6626;
Email: j.meredith@njbankers.com
Web: www.njbankers.com
Summary: To provide financial assistance to dependents of deceased and disabled military personnel who have a connection to New Jersey and are interested in attending college in any state.
Eligibility: Open to the spouses, children, stepchildren, and grandchildren of members of the armed services who died or became disabled while on active duty; it is not required that the military person died in combat. Applicants must have a high school or equivalency diploma and be attending college in any state. Adult dependents who wish to obtain a high school equivalency diploma are also eligible. Either the dependent or the servicemember must have a connection to New Jersey; the applicant's permanent address must be in New Jersey or the servicemember's last permanent address or military base must have been in the state. Financial need is considered in the selection process.
Financial data: A stipend is awarded (amount not specified).
Duration: 1 year; may be renewed if the recipient maintains a "C" average.
Number awarded: 1 or more each year.
Deadline: June of each year.

649 $ NEW JERSEY EDUCATIONAL OPPORTUNITY FUND GRANTS

New Jersey Commission on Higher Education
Attn: Educational Opportunity Fund
20 West State Street, Fourth Floor

P.O. Box 542
Trenton, NJ 08625–0542
Phone: (609) 984–2709; Fax: (609) 292–7225;
Email: audrey.bennerson@njhe.state.nj.us
Web: www.state.nj.us/highereducation/EOF/index.html

Summary: To provide financial assistance for undergraduate or graduate study in New Jersey to students from disadvantaged backgrounds.

Eligibility: Open to students from economically and educationally disadvantaged backgrounds who have been legal residents of New Jersey for at least 12 consecutive months. Applicants must be from families with annual incomes below specified limits, ranging from $21,780 for a household size of 1 to $75,260 for a household size of 8. They must be attending or accepted for attendance as full–time undergraduate or graduate students at institutions of higher education in New Jersey. Along with their application, they must submit the Free Application for Federal Student Aid. Some colleges may also require students to complete the College Scholarship Service's (CSS) Financial Aid Form to apply for institutional aid.

Financial data: Undergraduate grants range from $200 to $2,500 and graduate grants from $200 to $4,350, depending on college costs and financial need.

Duration: 1 year; renewable annually (based on satisfactory academic progress and continued eligibility).

Deadline: September of each year.

650 NEW JERSEY PART–TIME TUITION AID GRANTS FOR COUNTY COLLEGE STUDENTS

New Jersey Higher Education Student Assistance Authority
Attn: Grants and Scholarships
4 Quakerbridge Plaza
P.O. Box 540
Trenton, NJ 08625–0540
Phone: (609) 588–2349; (800) 792–8670; Fax: (609) 588–3450;
Email: ClientServices@hesaa.org
Web: www.hesaa.org/Pages/GrantsandScholarshipsDetails.aspx

Summary: To provide financial assistance to residents of New Jersey enrolled as part–time students at county colleges in the state.

Eligibility: Open to U.S. citizens and eligible noncitizens who have been residents of New Jersey for at least 12 consecutive months before receiving the grant. Applicants must be, or planning to be, enrolled in 6 to 11 credits per term at New Jersey county colleges. They must be able to demonstrate financial need.

Financial data: The stipend is $419 per term ($828 per year) for students enrolled half time (6 to 8 credits) or $628 per term ($1,256 per year) for students enrolled three–quarter time (9 to 11 credits).

Duration: 1 academic term; may be renewed if the recipient maintains satisfactory academic progress and continued eligibility.

Number awarded: Varies each year.

Deadline: May of each year for students who received a Tuition Aid Grant in the preceding year; September of each year for new applicants for fall term; February of each year for new applicants for spring term only.

651 $$ NEW JERSEY POW/MIA TUITION BENEFIT PROGRAM

New Jersey Department of Military and Veterans Affairs
Attn: Division of Veterans Programs
101 Eggert Crossing Road
P.O. Box 340
Trenton, NJ 08625–0340
Phone: (609) 530–7045; (800) 624–0508 (within NJ); Fax: (609) 530–7075
Web: www.state.nj.us/military/veterans/programs.html

Summary: To provide financial assistance for college to the children of New Jersey military personnel reported as missing in action or prisoners of war during the southeast Asian conflict.

Eligibility: Open to New Jersey residents attending or accepted at a New Jersey public or independent postsecondary institution whose parents were military service personnel officially declared prisoners of war or missing in action after January 1, 1960.

Financial data: This program entitles recipients to full undergraduate tuition at any public or independent postsecondary educational institution in New Jersey.

Duration: Assistance continues until completion of a bachelor's degree.

Number awarded: Varies each year.

Deadline: February of each year for the spring term and September for the fall and spring terms.

652 $ NEW JERSEY PRINCIPALS AND SUPERVISORS ASSOCIATION STUDENT LEADERSHIP SCHOLARSHIPS

New Jersey Principals and Supervisors Association
Attn: Student Activities Committee
12 Centre Drive
Monroe Township, NJ 08831–1564
Phone: (609) 860–1200; Fax: (609) 860–2999;
Email: NJPSA@aol.com
Web: www.njpsa.org/membership/student–awards.aspx

Summary: To provide financial assistance to high school seniors in New Jersey who have participated in non–athletic extracurricular activities and plan to attend college in any state.

Eligibility: Open to seniors graduating from high schools in New Jersey and planning to attend college in any state. Applicants must have demonstrated leadership through participation in co–curricular activities other than athletics. Along with their application, they must submit a 1–page essay on the importance of student involvement in school activities. Financial need is not considered in the selection process.

Financial data: The stipend is $2,000.

Duration: 1 year.

Number awarded: 25 each year.

Deadline: April of each year.

653 NEW JERSEY SCHOOL COUNSELOR ASSOCIATION SCHOLARSHIPS

New Jersey School Counselor Association, Inc.
c/o Sheila Brewer, Scholarship Chair
Towns Pemberton
125 Trenton Road
Browns Mills, NJ 08015–3249
Phone: (609) 893–8141, ext. 2047;
Email: sbrewer@pemb.org
Web: njsca.org/content.php?sid=26&mID=5

Summary: To provide financial assistance to high school seniors in New Jersey who submit outstanding essays on their school counselor and plan to attend college in any state.

Eligibility: Open to seniors graduating from high schools in New Jersey who plan to attend college in any state. Applicants must submit an essay of 300 to 500 words on how a school counselor has influenced their life in a positive way. The counselor must be a member of the New Jersey School Counselor Association. Along with the essay and the application, students must submit, through their counselor, copies of their high school transcript, high school profile, and letter of acceptance to a postsecondary institution. Financial need is not considered in the selection process.

Financial data: The stipend is $1,000.

Duration: 1 year.

Number awarded: 3 each year.

Deadline: March of each year.

654 NEW JERSEY STATE LATINO PEACE OFFICERS ASSOCIATION ACADEMIC SCHOLARSHIPS

Latino Peace Officers Association–New Jersey State Chapter
7 Glenwood Avenue, Suite 203
East Orange, NJ 07017
Phone: (877) 4–LPOANJ
Web: www.lpoanj.org/programs/scholarships

Summary: To provide financial assistance to residents of New Jersey who are interested in working on an undergraduate degree in any field.

Eligibility: Open to residents of New Jersey who are graduating high school seniors or students currently enrolled at a college or university in any state. Applicants must be planning to work on a degree in any academic field. They must have a GPA of 2.5 or higher. Along with their application, they must submit a 250–word essay on their achievements, career goals, community work, leadership skills, financial need, and any special circumstances that warrant consideration.

Financial data: The stipend is $1,000.

Duration: 1 year.

Number awarded: Varies each year.

Deadline: June of each year.

655 $$ NEW JERSEY STUDENT TUITION ASSISTANCE REWARD SCHOLARSHIPS II (NJSTARS II)

New Jersey Higher Education Student Assistance Authority
Attn: Grants and Scholarships
4 Quakerbridge Plaza
P.O. Box 540
Trenton, NJ 08625–0540
Phone: (609) 588–2349; (800) 792–8670; Fax: (609) 588–3450;
Email: ClientServices@hesaa.org
Web: www.njstars.net

Summary: To provide financial assistance to residents of New Jersey who are graduating from a county college in the state and planning to transfer to a New Jersey 4–year institution.

Eligibility: Open to U.S. citizens and eligible noncitizens who have been attending a New Jersey county college with support from a New Jersey Student Tuition Assistance Reward Scholarship (NJSTARS). Applicants must have a GPA of 3.25 or higher for their county college courses. They must be planning to transfer to a 4–year college or university in the state and enroll full time. Students whose family income is greater than $250,000 per year are not eligible.

Financial data: The stipend is $6,000 per year for students who earn an associate degree with a GPA of 3.25 to 3.49 or $7,000 per year for students who earn an associate degree with a GPA of 3.5 or higher.

Duration: 1 year; may be renewed for 1 additional year, provided the recipient maintains a GPA of 3.25 or higher.

Number awarded: Varies each year.

Deadline: May of each year for students who received a Tuition Aid Grant in the preceding year; September of each year for new applicants for the academic year; February of each year for new applicants for spring term only.

656 $$ NEW JERSEY STUDENT TUITION ASSISTANCE REWARD SCHOLARSHIPS (NJSTARS)

New Jersey Higher Education Student Assistance Authority
Attn: Grants and Scholarships
4 Quakerbridge Plaza
P.O. Box 540
Trenton, NJ 08625–0540
Phone: (609) 588–2349; (800) 792–8670; Fax: (609) 588–3450;
Email: ClientServices@hesaa.org
Web: www.njstars.net

Summary: To provide financial assistance to high school seniors in New Jersey who have an outstanding academic record and plan to attend a county college in the state.

Eligibility: Open to U.S. citizens and eligible noncitizens who have been residents of New Jersey for at least 12 consecutive months and are graduating from a high school in the state. Applicants must rank in the top 15% of their class, must have completed a prescribed program of high school classes, and must achieve a passing score on a college placement test administered by the New Jersey Council of County Colleges. They must be planning to enroll full time at 1 of the 19 New Jersey county colleges.

Financial data: The program provides full payment of tuition.

Duration: 1 year; may be renewed for a total of 5 semesters, provided the recipient maintains a GPA of 3.0 or higher.

Number awarded: Varies each year.

Deadline: May of each year for students who received a Tuition Aid Grant in the preceding year; September of each year for new applicants for the academic year; February of each year for new applicants for spring term only.

657 $$ NEW JERSEY SURVIVOR TUITION BENEFITS PROGRAM

New Jersey Higher Education Student Assistance Authority
Attn: Grants and Scholarships
4 Quakerbridge Plaza
P.O. Box 540
Trenton, NJ 08625–0540
Phone: (609) 588–2349; (800) 792–8670; Fax: (609) 588–3450;
Email: ClientServices@hesaa.org
Web: www.hesaa.org/Pages/GrantsandScholarshipsDetails.aspx

Summary: To provide financial assistance to the spouses and children of New Jersey emergency service personnel, firefighters, or law enforcement officers killed in the performance of their duties.

Eligibility: Open to surviving spouses, daughters, and sons of law enforcement officials, firefighters, and emergency service personnel killed in the line of duty. Applicants must be residents of New Jersey enrolled or planning to enroll at least half time at a private or public undergraduate institution in the state. Surviving spouses must apply within 8 years of the date of death; children must apply within 8 years following high school graduation. U.S. citizenship or eligible noncitizen status is required.

Financial data: Grants pay the actual cost of tuition up to the highest tuition charged at a New Jersey public institution of higher education.

Duration: 1 year; may be renewed for up to 7 additional years as long as the recipient attends a New Jersey institution of higher education as an undergraduate student on at least a half–time basis.

Number awarded: Varies each year.

Deadline: September of each year for fall and spring term; February of each year for spring term only.

658 $$ NEW JERSEY TUITION AID GRANTS

New Jersey Higher Education Student Assistance Authority
Attn: Grants and Scholarships
4 Quakerbridge Plaza
P.O. Box 540
Trenton, NJ 08625–0540
Phone: (609) 588–2349; (800) 792–8670; Fax: (609) 588–3450;
Email: ClientServices@hesaa.org
Web: www.hesaa.org/Pages/GrantsandScholarshipsDetails.aspx

Summary: To provide financial assistance for college to students in New Jersey.

Eligibility: Open to U.S. citizens and eligible noncitizens who have been residents of New Jersey for at least 12 consecutive months before receiving the grant. Applicants must be, or planning to be, full–time undergraduates at approved New Jersey colleges, universities, and degree–granting proprietary schools. They must be able to demonstrate financial need.

Financial data: Stipends depend on the financial need of the recipient, to a maximum of $2,458 at county colleges, $6,512 at state colleges and universities, $10,980 at independent colleges and universities, $10,980 at proprietary degree–granting institutions, $8,812 at Rutgers/University of Medicine and Dentistry of New Jersey, or $9,984 at New Jersey Institute of Technology.

Duration: 1 year; may be renewed if the recipient maintains satisfactory academic progress and continued eligibility.

Number awarded: Varies each year.

Deadline: May of each year for students who received a grant in the preceding year; September of each year for new applicants for fall term; February of each year for new applicants for spring term only.

659 NEW JERSEY URBAN SCHOLARS PROGRAM

New Jersey Higher Education Student Assistance Authority
Attn: Grants and Scholarships
4 Quakerbridge Plaza
P.O. Box 540
Trenton, NJ 08625–0540
Phone: (609) 588–2349; (800) 792–8670; Fax: (609) 588–3450;
Email: ClientServices@hesaa.org
Web: www.hesaa.org/Pages/GrantsandScholarshipsDetails.aspx

Summary: To provide financial assistance to outstanding high school seniors from urban areas in New Jersey who are interested in attending college.

Eligibility: Open to high school seniors at New Jersey high schools in urban and economically distressed areas (Type A and B school districts as defined by the New Jersey Department of Education) who are U.S. citizens or eligible noncitizens and have been residents of New Jersey for at least 12 months. They must be planning to attend a college or university in New Jersey as a full–time undergraduate. Students may not apply directly for this program; they must be nominated by their high school.

Financial data: Scholars receive $1,000 per year, regardless of financial need.

Duration: Up to 5 semesters at a 2–year institution; up to 8 semesters at a 4–year institution; up to 10 semesters if enrolled in an official 5–year program.

Number awarded: Varies each year.

Deadline: Participating secondary schools must submit nominations by the end of September of each year.

660 NEW JERSEY UTILITIES ASSOCIATION EXCELLENCE IN DIVERSITY SCHOLARSHIPS

New Jersey Utilities Association
50 West State Street, Suite 1117
Trenton, NJ 08608
Phone: (609) 392–1000; Fax: (609) 396–4231;
Email: info@njua.com
Web: www.njua.com/html/njua_eeo_scholarship.cfm

Summary: To provide financial assistance to minority, female, and disabled high school seniors in New Jersey interested in attending college in any state.
Eligibility: Open to seniors graduating from high schools in New Jersey who are women, minorities (Black or African American, Hispanic or Latino, American Indian or Alaska Native, Asian, Native Hawaiian or Pacific Islander, or 2 or more races), and persons with disabilities. Applicants must be planning to work on a bachelor's degree at a college or university in any state. Along with their application, they must submit a 500–word essay explaining their career ambition and why they have chosen that career. Children of employees of any New Jersey Utilities Association–member company are ineligible. Selection is based on overall academic excellence and demonstrated financial need. U.S. citizenship or permanent resident status is required.
Financial data: The stipend is $1,500 per year. Funds are paid to the recipient's college or university.
Duration: 4 years.
Number awarded: 2 each year.
Deadline: March of each year.

661 $$ NEW JERSEY WORLD TRADE CENTER SCHOLARSHIP

New Jersey Higher Education Student Assistance Authority
Attn: Grants and Scholarships
4 Quakerbridge Plaza
P.O. Box 540
Trenton, NJ 08625–0540
Phone: (609) 588–2349; (800) 792–8670; Fax: (609) 588–3450;
Email: ClientServices@hesaa.org
Web: www.hesaa.org/Pages/GrantsandScholarshipsDetails.aspx
Summary: To provide financial assistance to residents of New Jersey whose parent or spouse was killed in the terrorist attacks of September 11, 2001 and are interested in attending college in any state.
Eligibility: Open to the dependent children and surviving spouses of New Jersey residents who were killed in the terrorist attacks against the United States on September 11, 2001, or who died as the result of injuries received in the attacks, or who are missing and officially presumed dead as a direct result of the attacks. Applicants must be attending or planning to attend a college or university (may be in any state) as a full–time undergraduate. The sponsor assumes that all applicants have financial need. Surviving spouses must apply within 8 years of the date of death; children must apply within 8 years following high school graduation. U.S. citizenship or eligible noncitizen status is required.
Financial data: The maximum stipend is $6,500 per year. Funds must be used for tuition, fees, room, and board.
Duration: 1 year; may be renewed.
Number awarded: Varies each year.
Deadline: September of each year for fall and spring term; February of each year for spring term only.

662 NEW MEXICO ACTIVITIES ASSOCIATION ACTIVITIES SCHOLARSHIPS

New Mexico Activities Association
Attn: Administrative Assistant
6600 Palomas Avenue, N.E.
Albuquerque, NM 87109
Phone: (505) 923–2380; (888) 820–NMAA; Fax: (505) 923–3114;
Email: mindy@nmact.org
Web: www.nmact.org/scholarship_information_forms
Summary: To provide financial assistance to high school seniors in New Mexico who have participated in sanctioned extracurricular activities and plan to attend college in any state.
Eligibility: Open to seniors graduating from high schools in New Mexico with a GPA of 3.0 or higher. Applicants must have participated in at least 1 extracurricular activity sanctioned by the New Mexico Activities Association (NMAA) during their sophomore and junior years and at least 2 activities during their senior year. They must be planning to attend a college or university in any state. Along with their application, they must submit transcripts, ACT and/or SAT scores, 3 letters of recommendation, and a personal statement on how involvement in extracurricular activities impacted their high school career. Applicants may request that financial need be considered in the selection process.
Financial data: The stipend is $1,000.
Duration: 1 year.
Number awarded: 2 each year.
Deadline: February of each year.

663 $ NEW MEXICO ACTIVITIES ASSOCIATION EXTRAORDINARY PARTICIPATION SCHOLARSHIPS

New Mexico Activities Association
Attn: Administrative Assistant
6600 Palomas Avenue, N.E.
Albuquerque, NM 87109
Phone: (505) 923–2380; (888) 820–NMAA; Fax: (505) 923–3114;
Email: mindy@nmact.org
Web: www.nmact.org/scholarship_information_forms
Summary: To provide financial assistance to high school seniors in New Mexico who have participated in sanctioned sports and extracurricular activities and plan to attend college in any state.
Eligibility: Open to seniors graduating from high schools in New Mexico with a GPA of 3.0 or higher. Applicants must have participated in at least 1 sport and at least 1 extracurricular activity sanctioned by the New Mexico Activities Association (NMAA) throughout their high school career. They must be planning to attend a college or university in any state. Along with their application, they must submit transcripts, ACT and/or SAT scores, 3 letters of recommendation, and a personal statement on how involvement in athletics and extracurricular activities impacted their high school career. Financial need is not considered in the selection process.
Financial data: The stipend is $2,500.
Duration: 1 year.
Number awarded: 2 each year.
Deadline: February of each year.

664 $$ NEW MEXICO CHILDREN OF DECEASED MILITARY AND STATE POLICE PERSONNEL SCHOLARSHIPS

New Mexico Department of Veterans' Services
Attn: Benefits Division
407 Galisteo Street, Room 142
P.O. Box 2324
Santa Fe, NM 87504–2324
Phone: (505) 827–6374; (866) 433–VETS; Fax: (505) 827–6372;
Email: alan.martinez@state.nm.us
Web: www.dvs.state.nm.us/benefits.html
Summary: To provide financial assistance for college or graduate school to the children of deceased military and state police personnel in New Mexico.
Eligibility: Open to the children of 1) military personnel killed in action or as a result of such action during a period of armed conflict; 2) members of the New Mexico National Guard killed while on active duty; and 3) New Mexico State Police killed on active duty. Applicants must be between the ages of 16 and 26 and enrolled in a state–supported school in New Mexico. Children of deceased veterans must be nominated by the New Mexico Veterans' Service Commission; children of National Guard members must be nominated by the adjutant general of the state; children of state police must be nominated by the New Mexico State Police Board. Selection is based on merit and financial need.
Financial data: The scholarships provide full waiver of tuition at state–funded postsecondary schools in New Mexico. A stipend of $150 per semester ($300 per year) provides assistance with books and fees.
Duration: 1 year; may be renewed.
Deadline: Deadline not specified.

665 $$ NEW MEXICO COMPETITIVE SCHOLARSHIPS

New Mexico Higher Education Department
Attn: Financial Aid Division
2048 Galisteo Street
Santa Fe, NM 87505–2100
Phone: (505) 476–8411; (800) 279–9777; Fax: (505) 476–8454;
Email: karen.kennedy@state.nm.us
Web: hed.state.nm.us/Comp.aspx
Summary: To provide financial assistance to residents of other states who wish to attend a college or university in New Mexico.
Eligibility: Open to students who are not residents of New Mexico but who wish to enroll full time at public 4–year institutions of higher education in the state. They are not required to be U.S. citizens or residents. Applicants to the University of New Mexico and New Mexico State University must have either 1) a high school GPA of 3.5 or higher and an ACT score of 23 or higher; or 2) a high school GPA of 3.0 or higher and an ACT score of 26 or higher. Applicants to other public 4–year institutions in the state must have either 1) a high school GPA of 3.5 or higher and an ACT score of 20 or higher; or 2) a high school GPA of 3.0 or higher and an ACT score of 23 or higher. Equivalent SAT scores may be used in lieu of ACT scores.

Financial data: For recipients, the out–of–state portion of tuition is waived and a stipend of at least $100 is paid.
Duration: 1 year; may be renewed up to 3 additional years.
Number awarded: Varies each year, depending on the availability of funds.
Deadline: Deadlines are established by the participating institutions.

666 $ NEW MEXICO LEGISLATIVE ENDOWMENT SCHOLARSHIPS

New Mexico Higher Education Department
Attn: Financial Aid Division
2048 Galisteo Street
Santa Fe, NM 87505–2100
Phone: (505) 476–8411; (800) 279–9777; Fax: (505) 476–8454;
Email: karen.kennedy@state.nm.us
Web: hed.state.nm.us/LegisEndo.aspx
Summary: To provide financial assistance to needy residents of New Mexico who plan to attend a public college or university in the state.
Eligibility: Open to residents of New Mexico enrolled or planning to enroll at least half time at a public institution of higher education in the state. Applicants must be able to demonstrate substantial financial need. Preference is given to 1) at all institutions, renewing students who have met the continuing eligibility requirements; 2) at 4–year institutions, returning students and students transferring from New Mexico 2–year public postsecondary institutions; and 3) at 2–year institutions, returning students. U.S. citizenship or permanent resident status is required.
Financial data: Full–time students receive up to $2,500 per year at 4–year institutions or up to $1,000 per year at 2–year institutions. Part–time students are eligible for prorated awards.
Duration: 1 year; may be renewed.
Number awarded: Varies each year.
Deadline: Deadlines are established by the participating institutions.

667 $$ NEW MEXICO LEGISLATIVE LOTTERY SCHOLARSHIPS

New Mexico Higher Education Department
Attn: Financial Aid Division
2048 Galisteo Street
Santa Fe, NM 87505–2100
Phone: (505) 476–8411; (800) 279–9777; Fax: (505) 476–8454;
Email: karen.kennedy@state.nm.us
Web: hed.state.nm.us/Lottery.aspx
Summary: To provide financial assistance to residents of New Mexico who plan to attend a public college or university in the state.
Eligibility: Open to full–time students at New Mexico public colleges and universities who graduated from a public or private high school in New Mexico or obtained a New Mexico GED. Home–schooled students are eligible if they pass the New Mexico GED. Applicants who earn at least a 2.5 GPA during their first college semester are eligible to begin receiving the award for their second semester of full–time enrollment.
Financial data: Scholarships are equal to 100% of tuition at the New Mexico public postsecondary institution where the student is enrolled.
Duration: Up to 8 consecutive semesters.
Number awarded: Varies each year, depending on the availability of funds.
Deadline: Deadlines are established by the participating institutions.

668 NEW MEXICO MANUFACTURED HOUSING SCHOLARSHIP FUND

Albuquerque Community Foundation
Attn: Scholarship Program
624 Tijeras Avenue, N.W.
P.O. Box 25266
Albuquerque, NM 87125–5266
Phone: (505) 883–6240; Fax: (505) 883–3629;
Email: foundation@albuquerquefoundation.org
Web: www.albuquerquefoundation.org/student_aid
Summary: To provide financial assistance to residents of New Mexico who live in mobile homes and plan to attend college in the state.
Eligibility: Open to graduating seniors who reside in mobile/manufactured housing in New Mexico. Applicants must be planning to enroll full time at a 2– or 4–year college, university, or vocational institution in New Mexico. They must be able to demonstrate financial need and have a high school GPA of 3.0 or higher. Along with their application, they must submit a personal statement describing why they are going to college, what they plan to study, their career goals, and any unusual challenges they face in continuing their education.
Financial data: The stipend is $1,000.
Duration: 1 year.
Number awarded: 1 or 2 each year.
Deadline: March of each year.

669 $$ NEW MEXICO SCHOLARS PROGRAM

New Mexico Higher Education Department
Attn: Financial Aid Division
2048 Galisteo Street
Santa Fe, NM 87505–2100
Phone: (505) 476–8411; (800) 279–9777; Fax: (505) 476–8454;
Email: karen.kennedy@state.nm.us
Web: hed.state.nm.us
Summary: To provide financial assistance to graduating high school seniors in New Mexico who plan to attend a public college or university or designated private college in the state.
Eligibility: Open to graduating high school seniors in New Mexico who plan to enroll full time at a public institution of higher education or selected private college in the state. Applicants must be in the top 5% of their high school graduating class or have an ACT score of at least 25. The family income may be no greater than $30,000 a year.
Financial data: This program provides recipients with tuition, fees, and books at a participating college or university in New Mexico. Awards at private colleges do not exceed an amount equal to the resident tuition rate charged by a public institution.
Duration: 1 year; may be renewed.
Number awarded: Varies each year, depending on the availability of funds.
Deadline: Deadlines are established by the participating institutions.

670 NEW MEXICO STATE COUNCIL ROADRUNNER ENDOWMENT SCHOLARSHIP

Epsilon Sigma Alpha International
Attn: ESA Foundation
363 West Drake Road
Fort Collins, CO 80526
Phone: (970) 223–2824; Fax: (970) 223–4456;
Email: esainfo@epsilonsigmaalpha.org
Web: www.epsilonsigmaalpha.org/esa–foundation/scholarships
Summary: To provide financial assistance to residents of New Mexico or neighboring cities who plan to attend college in any state.
Eligibility: Open to residents of New Mexico who are 1) graduating high school seniors with a GPA of 3.0 or higher or with minimum scores of 22 on the ACT or 1030 on the combined critical reading and mathematics SAT; 2) enrolled in college with a GPA of 3.0 or higher; 3) enrolled at a technical school or returning to school after an absence for retraining of job skills or obtaining a degree; or 4) engaged in online study through an accredited college, university, or vocational school. Applicants may be attending or planning to attend a school in any state and major in any field. Residents of El Paso and Farwell, Texas are also eligible. Selection is based on character (10%), leadership (10%), service (35%), financial need (35%), and scholastic ability (10%).
Financial data: The stipend is $1,500.
Duration: 1 year; may be renewed.
Number awarded: 1 each year.
Deadline: January of each year.

671 $ NEW MEXICO STUDENT INCENTIVE GRANTS

New Mexico Higher Education Department
Attn: Financial Aid Division
2048 Galisteo Street
Santa Fe, NM 87505–2100
Phone: (505) 476–8411; (800) 279–9777; Fax: (505) 476–8454;
Email: karen.kennedy@state.nm.us
Web: hed.state.nm.us/Grants
Summary: To provide financial assistance to needy residents of New Mexico attending public or private nonprofit colleges in the state.
Eligibility: Open to full–time and half–time undergraduate students at public or designated private colleges and universities in New Mexico who can demonstrate substantial financial need. Applicants must be U.S. citizens and New Mexico residents.

Financial data: The amount of the award is set by the participating college or university; generally, the awards range from $200 to $2,500 per year.
Duration: 1 year; may be renewed.
Number awarded: Varies each year, depending on the availability of funds.
Deadline: Deadlines are established by the participating institutions.

672 $$ NEW MEXICO VIETNAM VETERAN SCHOLARSHIPS

New Mexico Department of Veterans' Services
Attn: Benefits Division
407 Galisteo Street, Room 142
P.O. Box 2324
Santa Fe, NM 87504–2324
Phone: (505) 827–6374; (866) 433–VETS; Fax: (505) 827–6372;
Email: alan.martinez@state.nm.us
Web: www.dvs.state.nm.us/benefits.html
Summary: To provide financial assistance to Vietnam veterans in New Mexico who are interested in working on an undergraduate or master's degree at a public college in the state.
Eligibility: Open to Vietnam veterans who have been residents of New Mexico for at least 10 years. Applicants must have been honorably discharged and have been awarded the Vietnam Service Medal or the Vietnam Campaign Medal. They must be planning to attend a state–supported college, university, or community college in New Mexico to work on an undergraduate or master's degree. Awards are granted on a first–come, first–served basis.
Financial data: The scholarships provide full payment of tuition and purchase of required books at any state–funded postsecondary institution in New Mexico.
Duration: 1 year.
Deadline: Deadline not specified.

673 NEW YORK LEGION AUXILIARY DEPARTMENT SCHOLARSHIP

American Legion Auxiliary
Department of New York
112 State Street, Suite 1310
Albany, NY 12207
Phone: (518) 463–1162; (800) 421–6348; Fax: (518) 449–5406;
Email: alanyterry@nycap.rr.com
Web: www.deptny.org/Scholarships.htm
Summary: To provide financial assistance to New York residents who are the descendants of veterans and interested in attending college in any state.
Eligibility: Open to residents of New York who are high school seniors or graduates and attending or planning to attend an accredited college or university in any state. Applicants must be the children, grandchildren, or great–grandchildren of veterans who served during specified periods of war time. Along with their application, they must submit a 500–word essay on a subject of their choice. Selection is based on character (20%), Americanism (20%), leadership (20%), scholarship (15%), and financial need (25%). U.S. citizenship is required.
Financial data: The stipend is $1,000. Funds are paid directly to the recipient's school.
Duration: 1 year.
Number awarded: 1 each year.
Deadline: February of each year.

674 NEW YORK LEGION AUXILIARY DISTRICT SCHOLARSHIPS

American Legion Auxiliary
Department of New York
112 State Street, Suite 1310
Albany, NY 12207
Phone: (518) 463–1162; (800) 421–6348; Fax: (518) 449–5406;
Email: alanyterry@nycap.rr.com
Web: www.deptny.org/Scholarships.htm
Summary: To provide financial assistance to descendants of veterans in New York who are interested in attending college in any state.
Eligibility: Open to residents of New York who are high school seniors or graduates and attending or planning to attend an accredited college or university in any state. Applicants must be the children, grandchildren, or great–grandchildren of veterans who served during specified periods of war time. Along with their application, they must submit a 500–word essay on why they chose to further their education. Selection is based on character (30%), Americanism (20%), leadership (10%), scholarship (30%), and financial need (20%). U.S. citizenship is required.
Financial data: The stipend is $1,000. Funds are paid directly to the recipient's school.
Duration: 1 year.
Number awarded: 10 each year: 1 in each of the 10 judicial districts in New York.
Deadline: February of each year.

675 $$ NEW YORK MEMORIAL SCHOLARSHIPS

New York State Higher Education Services Corporation
Attn: Student Information
99 Washington Avenue
Albany, NY 12255
Phone: (518) 473–1574; (888) NYS–HESC; Fax: (518) 473–3749; TDD: (800) 445–5234;
Email: webmail@hesc.com
Web: www.hesc.com/content.nsf/SFC/Grants_Scholarships_and_Awards
Summary: To provide financial aid for college in the state to the children or spouses of public service officers in New York who died as the result of injuries sustained in the line of duty.
Eligibility: Open to New York residents whose parent or spouse was a police officer, peace officer (including corrections officer), firefighter, volunteer firefighter, or emergency medical service worker in New York and died as the result of injuries sustained in the line of duty. Applicants must be accepted or enrolled as a full–time undergraduate at a public college or university or private institution in New York.
Financial data: At public colleges and universities, this program provides payment of actual tuition and mandatory educational fees; actual room and board charged to students living on campus or an allowance for room and board for commuter students; and allowances for books, supplies, and transportation. At private institutions, the award is equal to the amount charged at the State University of New York (SUNY) for 4–year tuition and average mandatory fees (or the student's actual tuition and fees, whichever is less) plus allowances for room, board, books, supplies, and transportation.
Duration: This program is available for 4 years of full–time undergraduate study (or 5 years in an approved 5–year bachelor's degree program).
Number awarded: Varies each year; recently, more than 60 students received $558,000 in assistance through this program.
Deadline: April of each year.

676 $ NEW YORK PART–TIME TAP PROGRAM

New York State Higher Education Services Corporation
Attn: Student Information
99 Washington Avenue
Albany, NY 12255
Phone: (518) 473–1574; (888) NYS–HESC; Fax: (518) 473–3749; TDD: (800) 445–5234;
Email: webmail@hesc.com
Web: www.hesc.com/content.nsf/SFC/Grants_Scholarships_and_Awards
Summary: To provide financial assistance to residents of New York who are enrolled part time at a college in the state.
Eligibility: Open to residents of New York who are enrolled part time (at least 6 but less than 12 hours per semester) in an undergraduate degree program in the state. Applicants must be charged at least $200 in tuition per year. They must meet the net taxable income limits established for the New York Tuition Assistance Program (TAP); currently, those are $80,000 per year for dependent students or those who are married or have tax dependents, or $10,000 per year for single independent students with no dependents. U.S. citizenship or eligible noncitizenship status is required.
Financial data: The stipend depends on the number of units the recipient is taking, ranging from 50% of full TAP awards for those taking 6 semester hours to 91.67% of full TAP awards for those taking 11 semester hours. For dependent students or those who are married or have tax dependents, full TAP awards range from $500 to $5,000. For single independent students with no dependents and for married independent students with no other dependents, full TAP awards range from $500 to $3,025.
Duration: 1 year; recipients may reapply for up to 8 years of part–time study if they maintain a GPA of at least 2.0.
Number awarded: Varies each year.
Deadline: Deadline not specified.

677 $ NEW YORK STATE AID FOR PART–TIME STUDY (APTS) PROGRAM

New York State Higher Education Services Corporation
Attn: Student Information
99 Washington Avenue
Albany, NY 12255
Phone: (518) 473–1574; (888) NYS–HESC; Fax: (518) 473–3749; TDD: (800) 445–5234;
Email: webmail@hesc.com
Web: www.hesc.com/content.nsf/SFC/Grants_Scholarships_and_Awards

Summary: To provide financial assistance to students who are attending college on a part–time basis in New York.

Eligibility: Open to students who are enrolled part time (at least 3 but less than 12 hours per semester) in an undergraduate degree program in New York; meet the income limits established for this program (students whose parents could not claim them as dependents may earn no more than $34,250 per year; the total family income if parents do claim the student as a dependent may not exceed $50,550 per year); be a New York resident and a U.S. citizen or eligible noncitizen; have a tuition bill of at least $100 per year; not have used up their Tuition Assistance Program (TAP) eligibility; and not be in default on a student loan.

Financial data: Stipends range up to $2,000 per year; awards may not exceed actual tuition charges.

Duration: 1 year; recipients may reapply for up to 8 years of part–time study if they maintain a GPA of at least 2.0.

Number awarded: Varies each year; recently, more than 20,000 students received more than $12 million in assistance through this program.

Deadline: Deadline not specified.

678 $$ NEW YORK STATE MILITARY SERVICE RECOGNITION SCHOLARSHIPS

New York State Higher Education Services Corporation
Attn: Student Information
99 Washington Avenue
Albany, NY 12255
Phone: (518) 473–1574; (888) NYS–HESC; Fax: (518) 473–3749; TDD: (800) 445–5234;
Email: webmail@hesc.com
Web: www.hesc.com/content.nsf/SFC/Grants_Scholarships_and_Awards

Summary: To provide financial assistance to disabled veterans and the family members of deceased or disabled veterans who are residents of New York and interested in attending college in the state.

Eligibility: Open to New York residents who served in the armed forces of the United States or state organized militia at any time on or after August 2, 1990 and became severely and permanently disabled as a result of injury or illness suffered or incurred in a combat theater or combat zone or during military training operations in preparation for duty in a combat theater or combat zone of operations. Also eligible are the children, spouses, or financial dependents of members of the armed forces of the United States or state organized militia who at any time after August 2, 1990 1) died, became severely and permanently disabled as a result of injury or illness suffered or incurred, or are classified as missing in action in a combat theater or combat zone of operations; 2) died as a result of injuries incurred in those designated areas; or 3) died or became severely and permanently disabled as a result of injury or illness suffered or incurred during military training operations in preparation for duty in a combat theater or combat zone of operations. Applicants must be attending or accepted at an approved program of study as full–time undergraduates at a public college or university or private institution in New York.

Financial data: At public colleges and universities, this program provides payment of actual tuition and mandatory educational fees; actual room and board charged to students living on campus or an allowance for room and board for commuter students; and allowances for books, supplies, and transportation. At private institutions, the award is equal to the amount charged at the State University of New York (SUNY) for 4–year tuition and average mandatory fees (or the student's actual tuition and fees, whichever is less) plus allowances for room, board, books, supplies, and transportation.

Duration: This program is available for 4 years of full–time undergraduate study (or 5 years in an approved 5–year bachelor's degree program).

Number awarded: Varies each year.

Deadline: April of each year.

679 NEW YORK STATE SCHOLARSHIPS FOR ACADEMIC EXCELLENCE

New York State Higher Education Services Corporation
Attn: Student Information
99 Washington Avenue
Albany, NY 12255
Phone: (518) 473–1574; (888) NYS–HESC; Fax: (518) 473–3749; TDD: (800) 445–5234;
Email: webmail@hesc.com
Web: www.hesc.com/content.nsf/SFC/Grants_Scholarships_and_Awards

Summary: To provide financial assistance to high school seniors in New York who have a record of academic excellence and plan to attend a college or university in the state.

Eligibility: Open to seniors graduating from high schools in New York who plan to enroll full time in an approved undergraduate program in the state. U.S. citizenship or qualifying noncitizenship status is required. Selection is based on student grades in certain Regents examinations. The top graduating scholar at each registered high school in New York receives 1 of these awards, and the others are distributed to other outstanding high school graduates in the same ratio of total students graduating from each high school in the state as compared to the total number of students who graduated during the prior school year.

Financial data: Stipends are $1,500 or $500. Recipients can accept other non–loan student aid, but the total of that assistance and this scholarship cannot exceed the cost of attendance.

Duration: This program is available for 4 years of full–time undergraduate study (or 5 years in an approved 5–year bachelor's degree program).

Number awarded: 8,000 each year: 2,000 at $1,500 and 6,000 at $500.

Deadline: April of each year.

680 $$ NEW YORK STATE WORLD TRADE CENTER MEMORIAL SCHOLARSHIPS

New York State Higher Education Services Corporation
Attn: Student Information
99 Washington Avenue
Albany, NY 12255
Phone: (518) 473–1574; (888) NYS–HESC; Fax: (518) 473–3749; TDD: (800) 445–5234;
Email: webmail@hesc.com
Web: www.hesc.com/content.nsf/SFC/Grants_Scholarships_and_Awards

Summary: To provide financial assistance to undergraduates in New York who are survivors or victims of the terrorist attacks on September 11, 2001 or their relatives.

Eligibility: Open to 1) the children, spouses, and financial dependents of deceased or severely and permanently disabled victims of the September 11, 2001 terrorist attacks or the subsequent rescue and recovery operations; and 2) survivors of the terrorist attacks who are severely and permanently disabled as a result of injuries sustained in the attacks or the subsequent rescue and recovery operations. Applicants must be attending or accepted at an approved program of study as full–time undergraduates at a public college or university or private institution in New York.

Financial data: At public colleges and universities, this program provides payment of actual tuition and mandatory educational fees; actual room and board charged to students living on campus or an allowance for room and board for commuter students; and allowances for books, supplies, and transportation. At private institutions, the award is equal to the amount charged at the State University of New York (SUNY) for 4–year tuition and average mandatory fees (or the student's actual tuition and fees, whichever is less) plus allowances for room, board, books, supplies, and transportation.

Duration: This program is available for 4 years of full–time undergraduate study (or 5 years in an approved 5–year bachelor's degree program).

Number awarded: Varies each year.

Deadline: April of each year.

681 $$ NEW YORK TUITION ASSISTANCE PROGRAM (TAP)

New York State Higher Education Services Corporation
Attn: Student Information
99 Washington Avenue
Albany, NY 12255
Phone: (518) 473–1574; (888) NYS–HESC; Fax: (518) 473–3749; TDD: (800) 445–5234;
Email: webmail@hesc.com
Web: www.hesc.com/content.nsf/SFC/Grants_Scholarships_and_Awards

Summary: To provide financial assistance to New York residents enrolled as undergraduate students at postsecondary institutions in the state.

Eligibility: Open to residents of New York who are U.S. citizens or eligible noncitizens. Applicants' income may not exceed the limitations for this program: for dependent students and independent students (married or unmarried) who have tax dependents, the limit is $80,000 net taxable family income; for independent students who are married but have no other tax dependents, the limit is $40,000 net taxable family income; for single independent students with no dependents, the limit is $10,000 net taxable income. Applicants must be enrolled in school full time in New York (at least 12 credits per semester); have tuition charges of at least $200 per year; and not be in default on a federal or state loan.

Financial data: TAP awards are based on net taxable income, tuition charges, and type of institution attended. At public and nonprofit private institutions, the award range is $500 to $5,000 for dependent students and independent students (married or unmarried) who have tax dependents; for independent students who are married and have no other tax dependents and for single independent students, the award range is $500 to $3,025. For students at proprietary registered non–degree private business schools, the award range is $100 to $800 for dependent students or independent students who are married or have tax dependents, or $100 to $640 for independent students who are single with no dependents.

Duration: Up to 4 years for undergraduate students (or 5 years in approved 5–year baccalaureate programs); up to 4 years for graduate or professional students. The combined undergraduate–graduate total cannot exceed 8 years.

Number awarded: Varies each year; recently, nearly 342,000 students received approximately $636 million in assistance through this program.

Deadline: April of each year.

682 $$ NEW YORK VETERANS TUITION AWARDS

New York State Higher Education Services Corporation
Attn: Student Information
99 Washington Avenue
Albany, NY 12255
Phone: (518) 473–1574; (888) NYS–HESC; Fax: (518) 473–3749; TDD: (800) 445–5234;
Email: webmail@hesc.com
Web: www.hesc.com/content.nsf/SFC/Grants_Scholarships_and_Awards

Summary: To provide tuition assistance to eligible veterans enrolled in an undergraduate or graduate program in New York.

Eligibility: Open to veterans who served in the U.S. armed forces in 1) Indochina between February 28, 1961 and May 7, 1975; 2) hostilities that occurred after February 28, 1961 as evidenced by receipt of an Armed Forces Expeditionary Medal, Navy Expeditionary Medal, or Marine Corps Expeditionary Medal; 3) the Persian Gulf on or after August 2, 1990; or 4) Afghanistan on or after September 11, 2001. Applicants must have been discharged from the service under honorable conditions, must be a New York resident, must be a U.S. citizen or eligible noncitizen, must be enrolled full or part time at an undergraduate or graduate degree–granting institution in New York or in an approved vocational training program in the state, must be charged at least $200 tuition per year, and must apply for a New York Tuition Assistance Program (TAP) award.

Financial data: For full–time study, the maximum stipend is tuition or $5,295, whichever is less. For part–time study, the stipend is based on the number of credits certified and the student's actual part–time tuition.

Duration: For undergraduate study, up to 8 semesters, or up to 10 semesters for a program requiring 5 years for completion; for graduate study, up to 6 semesters; for vocational programs, up to 4 semesters. Award limits are based on full–time study or equivalent part–time study.

Number awarded: Varies each year.

Deadline: April of each year.

683 $$ NFB SCHOLARSHIPS

National Federation of the Blind
Attn: Scholarship Committee
200 East Wells Street
Baltimore, MD 21230
Phone: (410) 659–9314, ext. 2415; Fax: (410) 685–5653;
Email: scholarships@nfb.org
Web: www.nfb.org/nfb/scholarship_program.asp

Summary: To provide financial assistance for college or graduate school to blind students.

Eligibility: Open to legally blind students who are working on or planning to work on an undergraduate or graduate degree. In general, full–time enrollment is required, although 1 scholarship may be awarded to a part–time student who is working full time. Along with their application, they must submit transcripts, standardized test scores, proof of legal blindness, 2 letters of recommendation, and a letter of endorsement from their National Federation of the Blind state president or designee. Selection is based on academic excellence, service to the community, and financial need.

Financial data: Stipends are $7,000, $5,000, or $3,000.

Duration: 1 year; recipients may resubmit applications up to 2 additional years.

Number awarded: 26 each year: 2 at $7,000, 4 at $5,000, and 20 at $3,000.

Deadline: March of each year.

684 $$ NINA BELLE REDDITT MEMORIAL SCHOLARSHIP

American Business Women's Association–Pirate Charter Chapter
Attn: Nicole Betschman, Secretary
P.O. Box 20498
Greenville, NC 27858
Email: secretary@pirateabwa.org
Web: pirateabwa.org/scholarship.html

Summary: To provide financial assistance to female residents of North Carolina working on an undergraduate or graduate degree at a school in the state.

Eligibility: Open to women who are residents of North Carolina and U.S. citizens. Applicants must be juniors, seniors, or graduate students at an accredited college or university in North Carolina and have a GPA of 2.5 or higher. Along with their application, they must submit a 2–page biographical sketch that includes information about their background, school activities, outside interests, honors and awards, work experience, community service, and long–term goals. Financial need is not considered in the selection process.

Financial data: The stipend is $5,000.

Duration: 1 year.

Number awarded: 2 or 3 each year.

Deadline: May of each year.

685 $$ NISSAN MISSISSIPPI SCHOLARSHIPS

Mississippi Office of Student Financial Aid
3825 Ridgewood Road
Jackson, MS 39211–6453
Phone: (601) 432–6997; (800) 327–2980 (within MS); Fax: (601) 432–6527;
Email: sfa@mississippi.edu
Web: www.mississippi.edu/riseupms/financialaid–state.php

Summary: To provide financial assistance for college to high school seniors in Mississippi who plan to attend a public college in the state.

Eligibility: Open to residents of Mississippi who are graduating seniors at high schools in the state. Applicants must have been accepted for enrollment at a public 2– or 4–year college or university in the state. They must have a GPA of 2.5 or higher after 7 semesters of high school and minimum scores of 20 on the ACT or 940 on the combined critical reading and mathematics SAT. Along with their application, they must submit a 200–word essay on the topic, "How do my plans for the future and my college major support the automotive industry in Mississippi?" Selection is based on the essay (15%); academic achievement (50%); extracurricular activities, work, leadership, and community involvement (15%); and demonstrated financial need (20%).

Financial data: Students in this program receive full payment of tuition and required fees plus an allowance for books.

Duration: 1 year; may be renewed 1 additional year for students at 2–year public colleges (followed by up to 3 years of support if the recipient transfers to a 4–year college or university) or up to 4 additional years for students at 4–year public colleges and universities. Renewal requires that the recipient reapplies each year; maintains a GPA of 2.5 or higher; displays leadership skills through participation in community service, extracurricular, or other activities; demonstrates full–time enrollment and satisfactory academic progress toward completion of a degree; maintains Mississippi residency; and maintains good standing at the college or university.

Number awarded: Varies each year; recently, 3 of these scholarships were awarded.

Deadline: February of each year.

686 $ NOIAW SCHOLARSHIPS

National Organization of Italian American Women
25 West 43rd Street, Suite 1005
New York, NY 10036
Phone: (212) 642–2003; Fax: (212) 642–2006;
Email: noiaw@noiaw.org
Web: www.noiaw.org/ct/html/ta/me/scholarships/ti/scholarships

Summary: To provide financial assistance for college or graduate school to women of Italian descent.

Eligibility: Open to women who have at least 1 parent of Italian American descent and are working on an associate, bachelor's, or master's degree. Applicants must be enrolled full time and have a GPA of 3.5 or higher. Along with their application, they must submit a 2–page essay on how being an Italian

American has impacted them personally and professionally. Financial need is considered in the selection process.

Financial data: The stipend is $2,000.

Duration: 1 year; nonrenewable.

Number awarded: 4 each year, including 1 reserved for an undergraduate or graduate student at the City University of New York system.

Deadline: April of each year.

687 $$ NON–RESIDENT TUITION WAIVERS FOR VETERANS AND THEIR DEPENDENTS WHO MOVE TO TEXAS

Texas Higher Education Coordinating Board
Attn: Grants and Special Programs
1200 East Anderson Lane
P.O. Box 12788
Austin, TX 78711–2788
Phone: (512) 427–6340; (800) 242–3062; Fax: (512) 427–6420;
Email: grantinfo@thecb.state.tx.us
Web: www.collegeforalltexans.com/apps/financialaid/tofa2.cfm?ID=502

Summary: To exempt veterans who move to Texas and their dependents from the payment of non–resident tuition at public institutions of higher education in the state.

Eligibility: Open to former members of the U.S. armed forces and commissioned officers of the Public Health Service who are retired or have been honorably discharged, their spouses, and dependent children. Applicants must have moved to Texas upon separation from the service and be attending or planning to attend a public college or university in the state. They must have indicated their intent to become a Texas resident by registering to vote and doing 1 of the following: owning real property in Texas, registering an automobile in Texas, or executing a will indicating that they are a resident of the state.

Financial data: Although persons eligible under this program are still classified as non–residents, they are entitled to pay the resident tuition at Texas institutions of higher education on an immediate basis.

Duration: 1 year.

Number awarded: Varies each year.

Deadline: Deadline not specified.

688 NORMAN WILENSKY SCHOLARSHIP

USA Racquetball
Attn: Scholarship Program
1685 West Uintah, Suite 103
Colorado Springs, CO 80904–2906
Phone: (719) 635–5396, ext. 123; Fax: (719) 635–0685
Web: www.usra.org/Programs/Scholarships.aspx

Summary: To provide financial assistance to students who compete in intercollegiate racquetball.

Eligibility: Open to students who compete in intercollegiate racquetball and participate in the current year's Intercollegiate National Racquetball Championships. Applicants must submit college transcripts, a biography of their racquetball accomplishments, an essay describing the reason they should be selected for this scholarship, and 2 letters of recommendation. Selection is based on academic achievement; racquetball accomplishments; team spirit, dedication, and loyalty; conduct and values on and off the racquetball court; and focus towards the needs of others.

Financial data: A stipend is awarded (amount not specified). Funds are paid directly to the recipient's college or university.

Duration: 1 year.

Number awarded: 1 each year.

Deadline: January of each year.

689 NORTH CAROLINA ASSOCIATION OF EDUCATIONAL OFFICE PROFESSIONALS STUDENT SCHOLARSHIPS

North Carolina Association of Educational Office Professionals, Inc.
c/o Kathy Newman, Scholarship Chair
S.W. Snowden Elementary School
693 North Seventh Avenue
Aurora, NC 27806
Phone: (252) 322–5351; Fax: (252) 322–4372;
Email: knewman@beaufort.k12.nc.us
Web: www.ncaeop.org/scholarships.html

Summary: To provide financial assistance to residents of North Carolina who are high school seniors or college freshmen and attending or planning to attend college in any state.

Eligibility: Open to residents of North Carolina who are either 1) graduating high school seniors planning to enroll full time at a college or university in any state; or 2) freshmen already enrolled. Applicants may be planning to major in any field. Along with their application, they must submit a 1–page biographical sketch on why they are choosing to further their education (including a statement of financial need); an official high school transcript; and verification of acceptance or enrollment from their college. U.S. citizenship is required. Selection is based on academic achievement (35 points); character, extracurricular activities, and employment (35 points); and financial need (30 points).

Financial data: Stipends range from $200 to $1,200.

Duration: 1 year.

Number awarded: 14 each year: 1 at $1,200, 1 at $1,000, 2 at $800, 1 at $600, 1 at $500, 1 at $400, and 7 at $200.

Deadline: Districts must submit applications to the state chair by November of each year.

690 $ NORTH CAROLINA BAR ASSOCIATION SCHOLARSHIPS

North Carolina Bar Association
Attn: Young Lawyers Division Scholarship Committee
8000 Weston Parkway
P.O. Box 3688
Cary, NC 27519–3688
Phone: (919) 677–0561; (800) 662–7407; Fax: (919) 677–0761;
Email: jterrell@ncbar.org
Web: younglawyers.ncbar.org

Summary: To provide financial assistance for college or graduate school to the children of disabled or deceased law enforcement officers in North Carolina.

Eligibility: Open to the natural or adopted children of North Carolina law enforcement officers who were permanently disabled or killed in the line of duty. Applicants must be younger than 27 years of age and enrolled or planning to enroll full time at an accredited institution of higher learning (including community colleges, trade schools, colleges, universities, and graduate programs) in North Carolina. Selection is based on academic performance and financial need.

Financial data: The stipend is $2,000 per academic year.

Duration: Up to 4 years.

Number awarded: Varies each year; recently, 17 of these scholarships were awarded.

Deadline: March of each year.

691 NORTH CAROLINA BUSINESS AND PROFESSIONAL WOMEN'S FOUNDATION SCHOLARSHIPS

North Carolina Federation of Business and Professional Women's Club, Inc.
Attn: BPW/NC Foundation
P.O. Box 276
Carrboro, NC 27510
Web: www.bpw–nc.org/Default.aspx?pageId=837230

Summary: To provide financial assistance to women attending North Carolina colleges, community colleges, or graduate schools.

Eligibility: Open to women who are currently enrolled in a community college, 4–year college, or graduate school in North Carolina. Applicants must be endorsed by a local BPW unit. Along with their application, they must submit a 1–page statement that summarizes their career goals, previous honors, or community activities and justifies their need for this scholarship. U.S. citizenship is required.

Financial data: The stipend is $1,000. Funds are paid directly to the recipient's school.

Duration: 1 year; recipients may reapply.

Number awarded: 2 each year.

Deadline: April of each year.

692 $ NORTH CAROLINA EDUCATION LOTTERY SCHOLARSHIP

College Foundation of North Carolina
Attn: College Foundation, Inc.
2917 Highwoods Boulevard
P.O. Box 41966
Raleigh, NC 27629–1966
Phone: (888) 234–6400; Fax: (919) 821–3139
Web: www.cfnc.org/paying/schol/info_schol.jsp

Summary: To provide financial assistance to residents of North Carolina who can demonstrate financial need and are interested in attending college in the state.
Eligibility: Open to North Carolina residents who are enrolled or planning to enroll in at least 6 credit hours per semester at a community college, campus of the University of North Carolina system, or eligible private college or university in the state. Applicants must be able to demonstrate financial need using the same criteria as for federal Pell Grants (with the exception that students ineligible for a Pell Grant with an estimated family contribution of $5,000 or less are eligible for this program).
Financial data: Stipends depend on the need of the recipient, ranging from $100 to $3,400 per year.
Duration: 1 year; may be renewed as long as the recipient continues to make satisfactory academic progress.
Number awarded: Varies each year; recently, a total of 31,768 students were receiving $32,852,215 through this program.
Deadline: Deadline not specified.

693 NORTH CAROLINA LEGISLATIVE TUITION GRANTS

North Carolina State Education Assistance Authority
Attn: Grants, Training, and Outreach Department
10 T.W. Alexander Drive
P.O. Box 13663
Research Triangle Park, NC 27709–3663
Phone: (919) 549–8614; (800) 700–1775; Fax: (919) 248–4687;
Email: information@ncseaa.edu
Web: www.ncseaa.edu/NCLTG.htm
Summary: To provide financial assistance to students enrolled in private colleges in North Carolina.
Eligibility: Open to North Carolina residents attending a legislatively–designated private college in the state on a full–time basis. Financial need is not considered in the selection process. Students of theology, divinity, religious education, or any other course of study designed primarily for career preparation in a religious vocation are not eligible.
Financial data: The maximum stipend is $1,850 per year. Funds are paid to the institution on behalf of the recipient.
Duration: 1 year; may be renewed.
Number awarded: Varies each year; recently, a total of 36,091 students were receiving $57,757,183 through this program.
Deadline: Deadline not specified.

694 $ NORTH CAROLINA SCHOLARSHIPS FOR CHILDREN OF WAR VETERANS

Division of Veterans Affairs
Albemarle Building
325 North Salisbury Street, Suite 1065
1315 Mail Service Center
Raleigh, NC 27699–1315
Phone: (919) 733–3851; Fax: (919) 733–2834;
Email: ncdva.aso@ncmail.net
Web: www.ncveterans.com/benefitlist.aspx
Summary: To provide financial assistance to the children of disabled and other classes of North Carolina veterans who plan to attend college in the state.
Eligibility: Open to applicants in these 5 categories: Class I–A: the veteran parent died in wartime service or as a result of a service–connected condition incurred in wartime service; Class I–B: the veteran parent is rated by the U.S. Department of Veterans Affairs (VA) as 100% disabled as a result of wartime service and currently or at the time of death was drawing compensation for such disability; Class II: the veteran parent is rated by the VA as much as 20% but less than 100% disabled due to wartime service, or was awarded a Purple Heart medal for wounds received, and currently or at the time of death drawing compensation for such disability; Class III: the veteran parent is currently or was at the time of death receiving a VA pension for total and permanent disability, or the veteran parent is deceased but does not qualify under any other provisions, or the veteran parent served in a combat zone or waters adjacent to a combat zone and received a campaign badge or medal but does not qualify under any other provisions; Class IV: the veteran parent was a prisoner of war or missing in action. For all classes, applicants must 1) be under 25 years of age and have a veteran parent who was a resident of North Carolina at the time of entrance into the armed forces; or 2) be the natural child, or adopted child prior to age 15, who was born in North Carolina, has been a resident of the state continuously since birth, and is the child of a veteran whose disabilities occurred during a period of war.
Financial data: Students in Classes I–A, II, III, and IV receive $4,500 per academic year if they attend a private college or junior college; if attending a public postsecondary institution, they receive free tuition, a room allowance, a board allowance, and exemption from certain mandatory fees. Students in Class I–B receive $1,500 per academic year if they attend a private college or junior college; if attending a public postsecondary institution, they receive free tuition and exemption from certain mandatory fees.
Duration: 4 academic years.
Number awarded: An unlimited number of awards are made under Classes I–A, I–B, and IV. Classes II and III are limited to 100 awards each year in each class.
Deadline: Applications for Classes I–A, I–B, and IV may be submitted at any time; applications for Classes II and III must be submitted by February of each year.

695 $ NORTH CAROLINA STATE CONTRACTUAL SCHOLARSHIP FUND PROGRAM

North Carolina State Education Assistance Authority
Attn: Grants, Training, and Outreach Department
10 T.W. Alexander Drive
P.O. Box 13663
Research Triangle Park, NC 27709–3663
Phone: (919) 549–8614; (800) 700–1775; Fax: (919) 248–4687;
Email: information@ncseaa.edu
Web: www.ncseaa.edu/SCSF.htm
Summary: To provide financial assistance to residents of North Carolina enrolled at private colleges and universities in the state.
Eligibility: Open to North Carolina residents who are enrolled full or part time at approved North Carolina private colleges and universities. Applicants must normally be undergraduates, although they may have a bachelor's degree if they are enrolled in a licensure program for teachers or nurses. Students enrolled in a program of study in theology, divinity, religious education, or any other program of study designed primarily for career preparation in a religious vocation are not eligible. Financial need is considered in the selection process.
Financial data: Stipends depend on the need of the recipient and the availability of funds. Recently, they averaged more than $2,600 per year.
Duration: 1 year.
Number awarded: Varies each year; recently, a total of 18,349 students received $46,397,693 through this program.
Deadline: Deadline not specified.

696 NORTH DAKOTA ACADEMIC SCHOLARSHIP

North Dakota Department of Public Instruction
600 East Boulevard Avenue, Department 201
Bismarck, ND 58505–0440
Phone: (701) 328–2755; Fax: (701) 328–0201;
Email: comittleider@nd.gov
Web: www.dpi.state.nd.us/resource/act/act.shtm
Summary: To provide financial assistance to high school seniors in North Dakota who complete a prescribed curriculum and plan to attend college in the state.
Eligibility: Open to seniors graduating from high schools in North Dakota who complete a prescribed graduation curriculum. Applicants must have a cumulative GPA of 3.0 or higher with no grade lower than a "C" in any unit, a score of 24 or higher on the ACT, and a completed AP course. Applicants must have a cumulative GPA of 3.0 or higher with no grade lower than a "C" in any unit, a score of 24 or higher on the ACT, and a completed AP course. They must be planning to attend a public or private college or university in North Dakota. Financial need is not considered in the selection process.
Financial data: The stipend is $1,500 per year.
Duration: 1 year; may be renewed up to 3 additional years, provided the recipient maintains a GPA of 2.75 or higher.
Number awarded: Varies each year.
Deadline: June of each year.

697 NORTH DAKOTA CAREER AND TECHNICAL EDUCATION SCHOLARSHIP

North Dakota Department of Public Instruction
600 East Boulevard Avenue, Department 201
Bismarck, ND 58505–0440
Phone: (701) 328–2755; Fax: (701) 328–0201;
Email: comittleider@nd.gov
Web: www.dpi.state.nd.us/resource/act/act.shtm

Summary: To provide financial assistance to high school seniors in North Dakota who complete a prescribed curriculum and plan to attend vocational school in the state.
Eligibility: Open to seniors graduating from high schools in North Dakota who complete a prescribed graduation curriculum. Applicants must have a cumulative GPA of 3.0 or higher with no grade lower than a "C" in any unit and a score of 24 or higher on the ACT or 3 scores of 5 on the WorkKeys tests. They must be planning to attend a vocational or technical school in North Dakota. Financial need is not considered in the selection process.
Financial data: The stipend is $1,500 per year.
Duration: 1 year; may be renewed up to 3 additional years, provided the recipient maintains a GPA of 2.75 or higher.
Number awarded: Varies each year.
Deadline: June of each year.

698 $$ NORTH DAKOTA EDUCATIONAL ASSISTANCE FOR DEPENDENTS OF VETERANS

Department of Veterans Affairs
4201 38th Street S.W., Suite 104
P.O. Box 9003
Fargo, ND 58106–9003
Phone: (701) 239–7165; (866) 634–8387; Fax: (701) 239–7166
Web: www.nd.gov/veterans/benefits/waiver.html
Summary: To provide financial assistance for college to the spouses, widow(er) s, and children of disabled and other North Dakota veterans and military personnel.
Eligibility: Open to the spouses, widow(er)s, and dependent children of veterans who were killed in action, died from wounds or other service–connected causes, were totally disabled as a result of service–connected causes, died from service–connected disabilities, were a prisoners of war, or were declared missing in action. Veteran parents must have been born in and lived in North Dakota until entrance into the armed forces (or must have resided in the state for at least 6 months prior to entrance into military service) and must have served during war time.
Financial data: Eligible dependents receive free tuition and are exempt from fees at any state–supported institution of higher education, technical school, or vocational school in North Dakota.
Duration: Up to 45 months or 10 academic semesters.
Number awarded: Varies each year.
Deadline: Deadline not specified.

699 $$ NORTH DAKOTA FEE WAIVER FOR SURVIVORS OF DECEASED PUBLIC SERVICE OFFICIALS

North Dakota University System
Attn: Director of Financial Aid
State Capitol, Tenth Floor
600 East Boulevard Avenue, Department 215
Bismarck, ND 58505–0230
Phone: (701) 328–4114; Fax: (701) 328–2961;
Email: nathan.stratton@ndus.edu
Web: www.ndus.nodak.edu
Summary: To waive tuition and fees for survivors of deceased firefighters, emergency medical services personnel, and peace officers at public institutions in North Dakota.
Eligibility: Open to residents of North Dakota who are the survivors of firefighters, emergency medical services personnel, and peace officers who died as a direct result of injuries received in the performance of official duties. Applicants must be attending or planning to attend a public college or university in North Dakota.
Financial data: Qualified students are entitled to a waiver of all tuition and fees (except fees charged to retire outstanding bonds).
Duration: 1 academic year; renewable.
Number awarded: Varies each year.
Deadline: Deadline not specified.

700 $$ NORTH DAKOTA SCHOLARS PROGRAM

North Dakota University System
Attn: Director of Financial Aid
State Capitol, Tenth Floor
600 East Boulevard Avenue, Department 215
Bismarck, ND 58505–0230
Phone: (701) 328–4114; Fax: (701) 328–2961;
Email: nathan.stratton@ndus.edu
Web: www.ndus.nodak.edu
Summary: To provide financial assistance to outstanding high school seniors in North Dakota who are interested in attending college in the state.
Eligibility: Open to seniors at high schools in North Dakota who took the ACT test in their junior year and scored in the upper fifth percentile of all North Dakota ACT test takers. Applicants must be interested in attending a college or university in North Dakota.
Financial data: Students who attend a public or tribal college receive full payment of tuition. Students who attend a private institution in North Dakota receive a stipend equivalent to tuition at North Dakota State University or the University of North Dakota.
Duration: 1 academic year; renewable up to 3 additional years, provided the recipient maintains a cumulative GPA of 3.5 or higher.
Number awarded: 45 to 50 each year.
Deadline: Deadline not specified.

701 NORTH DAKOTA STATE STUDENT INCENTIVE GRANT PROGRAM

North Dakota University System
Attn: Director of Financial Aid
State Capitol, Tenth Floor
600 East Boulevard Avenue, Department 215
Bismarck, ND 58505–0230
Phone: (701) 328–4114; Fax: (701) 328–2961;
Email: nathan.stratton@ndus.edu
Web: www.ndus.nodak.edu
Summary: To provide financial assistance to residents of North Dakota who need additional funding to attend a college or university in the state.
Eligibility: Open to residents of North Dakota who are high school graduates (or have a GED) and are eligible for admission as a full–time student at a public, private, or tribal college in the state. Applicants must be U.S. citizens or permanent residents and able to demonstrate financial need.
Financial data: Stipends range from $800 to $1,500 per year.
Duration: 1 academic year; renewable.
Number awarded: From 7,900 to 8,500 each year.
Deadline: March of each year.

702 $$ NORTH DAKOTA VETERANS DEPENDENTS FEE WAIVER

North Dakota University System
Attn: Director of Financial Aid
State Capitol, Tenth Floor
600 East Boulevard Avenue, Department 215
Bismarck, ND 58505–0230
Phone: (701) 328–4114; Fax: (701) 328–2961;
Email: nathan.stratton@ndus.edu
Web: www.ndus.edu/students/military–veterans–families
Summary: To waive tuition and fees for dependents of deceased or other veterans at public institutions in North Dakota.
Eligibility: Open to the dependents of veterans who were North Dakota residents when they entered the armed forces and died of service–related causes, were killed in action, were prisoners of war, or were declared missing in action. Applicants must be attending or planning to attend a public college or university in North Dakota.
Financial data: Qualified students are entitled to a waiver of all tuition and fees (except fees charged to retire outstanding bonds) at public institutions in North Dakota.
Duration: 1 academic year; renewable.
Number awarded: Varies each year.
Deadline: Deadline not specified.

703 NORTH DAKOTA WOMEN'S OPPORTUNITY SCHOLARSHIP FUND

North Dakota Council on Abused Women's Services
Attn: Scholarship Review Committee
525 North Fourth Street
Bismarck, ND 58501
Phone: (701) 255–6240; (888) 255–6240; Fax: (701) 255–1904
Web: www.ndcaws.org/what_we_do/scholarships

Summary: To provide financial assistance to women in North Dakota who are interested in attending a college or university in the state.
Eligibility: Open to female residents of North Dakota who plan to enroll full time at a college, university, or certification program in the state. Applicants must be able to demonstrate income lower than established financial guidelines (currently less than $13,612 for a single person, rising to $47,035 for a family of 8). Along with their application, they must submit an essay of 500 to 1,000 words on their motivation for attending college and their plans for the future. Priority is given to 1) first–time students and current students in special circumstances that may prevent them from completing a pending degree or program; and 2) students who may not be eligible for sources of funding normally available to low–income applicants.
Financial data: A stipend is awarded (amount not specified).
Duration: 1 year; may be renewed.
Number awarded: Varies each year.
Deadline: June of each year.

704 $$ NORWEGIAN COMMERCIAL CLUB SCHOLARSHIPS

Norwegian Commercial Club
2245 N.W. 57th Street
Seattle, WA 98107
Phone: (206) 783–1274
Web: www.norwegiancommercialclub.com
Summary: To provide financial assistance for study in the Pacific Northwest or in Scandinavia.
Eligibility: Open to college students in the Pacific Northwest who "have a background in American–Norwegian ideals." Applicants must be requesting funds to study in the area or to travel to study in Scandinavia. Along with their application, they must submit a 300–word essay on their plans for furthering their education or vocation and why they think they qualify for this scholarship. Selection is based on financial need, academic capability, and activities of the applicant.
Financial data: The stipend is approximately $5,000. Funds are paid directly to the recipient's school. For students who wish to travel to Scandinavia to study, a round–trip airline ticket to Oslo, Norway is also provided.
Duration: Up to 1 year.
Number awarded: 2 each year: 1 cash only award and 1 award of cash plus an airline ticket to Oslo.
Deadline: March of each year.

705 $$ NOVO NORDISK DONNELLY AWARDS

World Team Tennis, Inc.
Attn: Billie Jean King WTT Charities
1776 Broadway, Suite 600
New York, NY 10019
Phone: (212) 586–3444, ext. 20; Fax: (212) 586–6277;
Email: dstone@wtt.com
Web: www.wtt.com/page.aspx?article_id=1429
Summary: To recognize and reward young tennis players who have diabetes.
Eligibility: Open to scholar/athletes between 12 and 21 years of age who play tennis competitively either on a school team or as a ranked tournament player and have type I diabetes. Applicants must submit a 500–word essay on the significance of diabetes in their lives. Selection is based on values, commitment, sportsmanship, community involvement, and financial need.
Financial data: Awards are $5,000 for winners or $2,500 for regional finalists; funds may be used for education, tennis development, and/or medical care.
Duration: The nonrenewable awards are presented annually.
Number awarded: 8 each year: 2 winners and 6 regional finalists.
Deadline: April of each year.

706 $$ NOVOTNI COLLEGE SCHOLARSHIP FUND

American Deficit Disorder Association
P.O. Box 7557
Wilmington, DE 19803–9997
Phone: (800) 939–1019; Fax: (800) 939–1019;
Email: info@add.org
Web: www.add.org/?page=NovotniScholarship
Summary: To provide financial assistance for college to students who have attention deficit/hyperactivity disorder (ADHD).
Eligibility: Open to students who have been diagnosed with ADHD by a licensed physician or mental health professional. Applicants must be enrolled or planning to enroll at an approved college or university as an undergraduate student. Along with their application, they must submit a 500–word essay on why they would like to be considered for this scholarship, the ways in which ADHD has been a challenge for them in the educational setting, and the strategies they have used to meet the challenge.
Financial data: Stipends are $5,000, $3,000, or $1,000 per year. Funds are paid directly to the recipient's college.
Duration: 1 year; recipients may reapply.
Number awarded: 1 or more each year.
Deadline: March of each year.

707 O'HAIR FUND SCHOLARSHIP

Greater Kanawha Valley Foundation
Attn: Scholarship Program Officer
1600 Huntington Square
900 Lee Street East, 16th Floor
Charleston, WV 25301
Phone: (304) 346–3620; (800) 467–5909; Fax: (304) 346–3640;
Email: shoover@tgkvf.org
Web: www.tgkvf.org/page.aspx?pid=409
Summary: To provide financial assistance to residents of West Virginia who are interested in attending college in any state.
Eligibility: Open to residents of West Virginia who are attending or planning to attend a college or university anywhere in the country. Applicants must have an ACT score of 20 or higher; be able to demonstrate good moral character, academic excellence, and financial need; and have a GPA of 2.5 or higher.
Financial data: Recently, the stipend was $1,500 per year.
Duration: 1 year; may be renewed.
Number awarded: Varies each year; recently, 1 of these scholarships was awarded.
Deadline: January of each year.

708 OHIO COLLEGE OPPORTUNITY GRANT PROGRAM

Ohio Board of Regents
Attn: State Grants and Scholarships
30 East Broad Street, 36th Floor
Columbus, OH 43215–3414
Phone: (614) 466–6000; (888) 833–1133; Fax: (614) 466–5866;
Email: hotline@regents.state.oh.us
Web: ohiohighered.org/ocog
Summary: To provide financial assistance for college to students in Ohio who demonstrate financial need.
Eligibility: Open to Ohio residents who are attending or planning to attend public and private colleges and universities in the state. Applicants must be able to demonstrate financial need, with an expected family contribution up to $2,190 and a family income of $75,000 or less.
Financial data: Maximum stipends for full–time enrollment are $856 per year for students at public institutions or $2,280 for students at private institutions. Part–time stipends are prorated appropriately.
Duration: 1 year; may be renewed up to 4 additional years or until degree completion, whichever comes first.
Number awarded: Varies each year.
Deadline: September of each year.

709 OHIO HIGH SCHOOL ATHLETIC ASSOCIATION MINORITY SCHOLAR ATHLETE SCHOLARSHIPS

Ohio High School Athletic Association
Attn: Foundation
4080 Roselea Place
Columbus, OH 43214
Phone: (614) 267–2502; Fax: (614) 267–1677
Web: www.ohsaa.org/members/scholar/application.htm
Summary: To provide financial assistance to minority high school seniors in Ohio who have participated in athletics and plan to attend college in any state.
Eligibility: Open to minority seniors graduating from high schools in Ohio that are members of the Ohio High School Athletic Association (OHSAA). Applicants must have received at least 3 varsity letters in 1 sport or 4 letters in 2 sports and have a GPA of 3.25 or higher. They must be planning to attend a college or university in any state. Along with their application, they must submit a 1–page essay on the role that interscholastic athletics has played in their life and how such participation will benefit them in the future. Selection is based on that essay, GPA, ACT and SAT scores, varsity letters earned, and athletic honors.
Financial data: The stipend is $1,000.

Duration: 1 year.
Number awarded: 6 each year: 1 in each OHSSA District.
Deadline: April of each year.

710 $ OHIO HIGH SCHOOL ATHLETIC ASSOCIATION SCHOLAR ATHLETE SCHOLARSHIPS

Ohio High School Athletic Association
Attn: Foundation
4080 Roselea Place
Columbus, OH 43214
Phone: (614) 267–2502; Fax: (614) 267–1677
Web: www.ohsaa.org/members/scholar/application.htm

Summary: To provide financial assistance to high school seniors in Ohio who have participated in athletics and plan to attend college in any state.
Eligibility: Open to seniors graduating from high schools in Ohio that are members of the Ohio High School Athletic Association (OHSAA). Applicants must have received at least 3 varsity letters in 1 sport or 4 letters in 2 sports and have a GPA of 3.25 or higher. They must be planning to attend a college or university in any state. Along with their application, they must submit a 1–page essay on the role that interscholastic athletics has played in their life and how such participation will benefit them in the future. Selection is based on that essay, GPA, ACT and SAT scores, varsity letters earned, and athletic honors.
Financial data: Stipends are $2,000 or $1,000.
Duration: 1 year.
Number awarded: 48 each year: 12 at $2,000 (2 in each OHSSA District) and 36 at $1,000 (6 in each OHSAA District).
Deadline: April of each year.

711 OHIO LEGION AUXILIARY DEPARTMENT PRESIDENT'S SCHOLARSHIP

American Legion Auxiliary
Department of Ohio
1100 Brandywine Boulevard, Suite D
P.O. Box 2760
Zanesville, OH 43702–2760
Phone: (740) 452–8245; Fax: (740) 452–2620;
Email: ala_katie@rrohio.com
Web: www.alaohio.org/Scholarships

Summary: To provide financial assistance to veterans and their descendants in Ohio who are interested in attending college in any state.
Eligibility: Open to honorably–discharged veterans and the children, grandchildren, and great–grandchildren of living, deceased, or disabled honorably–discharged veterans who served during designated periods of war time. Applicants must be residents of Ohio, seniors at an accredited high school, planning to enter a college in any state, and sponsored by an American Legion Auxiliary Unit. Along with their application, they must submit an original article (up to 500 words) written by the applicant on a topic that changes annually. Recently, students were asked to write on "Education and the American Dream." Selection is based on character, Americanism, leadership, scholarship, and financial need.
Financial data: Stipends are $1,500 or $1,000. Funds are paid to the recipient's school.
Duration: 1 year.
Number awarded: 2 each year: 1 at $1,500 and 1 at $1,000.
Deadline: February of each year.

712 $ OHIO LEGION SCHOLARSHIPS

American Legion
Department of Ohio
60 Big Run Road
P.O. Box 8007
Delaware, OH 43015
Phone: (740) 362–7478; Fax: (740) 362–1429;
Email: legion@ohiolegion.com
Web: www.ohiolegion.com/scholarships/info.htm

Summary: To provide financial assistance to residents of Ohio who are members of the American Legion, their families, or dependents of deceased military personnel and interested in attending college in any state.
Eligibility: Open to residents of Ohio who are Legionnaires, direct descendants of living or deceased Legionnaires, or surviving spouses or children of deceased U.S. military personnel who died on active duty or of injuries received on active duty. Applicants must be attending or planning to attend colleges, universities, or other approved postsecondary schools in any state with a vocational objective. Selection is based on academic achievement as measured by course grades, scholastic test scores, difficulty of curriculum, participation in outside activities, and the judging committee's general impression.
Financial data: Stipends are $2,500 or $1,500.
Duration: 1 year.
Number awarded: Varies each year; recently, 9 of these scholarships were awarded: 1 at $2,500 and 8 at $1,500.
Deadline: April of each year.

713 $$ OHIO SAFETY OFFICERS COLLEGE MEMORIAL FUND

Ohio Board of Regents
Attn: State Grants and Scholarships
30 East Broad Street, 36th Floor
Columbus, OH 43215–3414
Phone: (614) 466–6000; (888) 833–1133; Fax: (614) 466–5866;
Email: hotline@regents.state.oh.us
Web: ohiohighered.org/safety–officers–college–fund

Summary: To provide financial assistance to Ohio residents who are interested in attending college in the state and whose parent or spouse was killed in the line of duty as a safety officer or member of the armed forces.
Eligibility: Open to Ohio residents whose parent or spouse was 1) a peace officer, firefighter, or other safety officer killed in the line of duty anywhere in the United States; or 2) a member of the U.S. armed forces killed in the line of duty during Operation Enduring Freedom, Operation Iraqi Freedom, or other designated combat zone. Applicants must be interested in attending a participating Ohio college or university. Children and spouses of military personnel are eligible for this program only if they do not qualify for the Ohio War Orphans Scholarship.
Financial data: At Ohio public colleges and universities, the program provides full payment of tuition. At Ohio private colleges and universities, the stipend is equivalent to the average amounts paid to students attending public institutions, currently $3,990 per year.
Duration: 1 year; may be renewed up to 3 additional years.
Number awarded: Varies each year; recently, 54 students received benefits from this program.
Deadline: Application deadlines are established by each participating college and university.

714 $ OHIO WAR ORPHANS SCHOLARSHIP

Ohio Board of Regents
Attn: State Grants and Scholarships
30 East Broad Street, 36th Floor
Columbus, OH 43215–3414
Phone: (614) 752–9528; (888) 833–1133; Fax: (614) 466–5866;
Email: jabdullah–simmons@regents.state.oh.us
Web: ohiohighered.org/ohio–war–orphans

Summary: To provide financial assistance to the children of deceased or disabled Ohio veterans who plan to attend college in the state.
Eligibility: Open to residents of Ohio who are under 25 years of age and interested in enrolling full time at an eligible college or university in the state. Applicants must be the child of a veteran who 1) was a member of the U.S. armed forces, including the organized Reserves and Ohio National Guard, for a period of 90 days or more (or discharged because of a disability incurred after less than 90 days of service); 2) served during specified periods of war time; 3) entered service as a resident of Ohio; and 4) as a result of that service, either was killed or became at least 60% service–connected disabled. Also eligible are children of veterans who have a permanent and total nonservice–connected disability and are receiving disability benefits from the U.S. Department of Veterans Affairs. If the veteran parent served only in the organized Reserves or Ohio National Guard, the parent must have been killed or became permanently and totally disabled while at a scheduled training assembly, field training period (of any duration or length), or active duty for training, pursuant to bona fide orders issued by a competent authority. Financial need is considered in the selection process.
Financial data: At Ohio public colleges and universities, the program provides payment of 80% of tuition and fees. At Ohio private colleges and universities, the stipend is $4,797 per year (or 80% of the average amount paid to students attending public institutions).
Duration: 1 year; may be renewed up to 4 additional years, provided the recipient maintains a GPA of 2.0 or higher.
Number awarded: Varies, depending upon the funds available. If sufficient funds are available, all eligible applicants are given a scholarship. Recently, 861 students received benefits from this program.
Deadline: June of each year.

715 OKLAHOMA BW FOUNDATION SCHOLARSHIPS

Oklahoma Federation of Business Women, Inc.
Attn: Oklahoma Business Women's Foundation
P.O. Box 160
Maud, OK 74854–0160
Phone: (405) 374–2866; Fax: (405) 374–2316;
Email: askkathy@oklahomabusinesswomen.org
Web: www.oklahomabusinesswomen/obw_foundation.htm

Summary: To provide financial assistance to women from any state who are working on an undergraduate or graduate degree in any field at a school in Oklahoma.

Eligibility: Open to women from any state who are working on an undergraduate or graduate degree at a college, university, or technical school in Oklahoma. Applicants must submit a 500–word essay on their career goals and how receiving this scholarship will help them to accomplish those goals and make a difference in their professional career. Selection is based on that essay, academic record, employment and volunteer record, and financial need.

Financial data: Stipends are $1,000, $750, or $500.

Duration: 1 year.

Number awarded: Varies each year; recently, 9 of these scholarships were awarded.

Deadline: February of each year.

716 OKLAHOMA DAR SCHOLARSHIPS

Daughters of the American Revolution–Oklahoma Society
c/o Jean VanDelinder, Scholarship Chair
Oklahoma State University–Graduate College
202 Whitehurst
Stillwater, OK 74078–1019
Phone: (405) 744–6368; Fax: (405) 744–0355;
Email: jean.van_delinder@okstate.edu
Web: www.oklahomadar.org

Summary: To provide financial assistance to students attending or planning to attend Oklahoma colleges and universities.

Eligibility: Open to high school seniors and students currently enrolled at an Oklahoma college or university with plans to continue at an Oklahoma institution in the following year. Scholarships are awarded without regard to race, religion, sex, or national origin.

Financial data: The stipend is $1,000.

Duration: 1 year.

Number awarded: 5 each year.

Deadline: January of each year.

717 OKLAHOMA FOUNDATION FOR EXCELLENCE ACADEMIC ALL–STATE SCHOLARSHIPS

Oklahoma Foundation for Excellence
120 North Robinson, Suite 1420–W
Oklahoma City, OK 73102–7400
Phone: (405) 236–0006; Fax: (405) 236–8590;
Email: info@ofe.org
Web: www.ofe.org/awards/index.htm

Summary: To provide financial assistance for college to seniors at public high schools in Oklahoma who demonstrate academic excellence.

Eligibility: Open to seniors at public high schools in Oklahoma who are nominated by their principal or superintendent. Nominees must meet at least 1 of the following criteria: ACT score of 30 or higher, combined critical reading and mathematics SAT score of 1340 or higher, National Merit Scholarship Program semifinalist, National Achievement Scholarship Program semifinalist, or National Hispanic Scholar Awards Program semifinalist. In addition to those minimum criteria, selection is based on academic achievement, extracurricular activities, community involvement, and an essay.

Financial data: The stipend is $1,000.

Duration: 1 year.

Number awarded: 100 each year.

Deadline: November of each year.

718 OKLAHOMA HALL OF FAME SCHOLARSHIP

Oklahoma Heritage Association
Attn: Scholarship Committee
1400 Classen Drive
Oklahoma City, OK 73106
Phone: (405) 523–3202; (888) 501–2059; Fax: (405) 235–2714;
Email: gmc@oklahomaheritage.com
Web: oklahomaheritage.com

Summary: To provide financial assistance to high school seniors in Oklahoma who have a record of outstanding community involvement and plan to attend college in the state.

Eligibility: Open to seniors graduating from high schools in Oklahoma who plan to attend a college or university in the state. Students may be nominated by a teacher, administrator, or other responsible adult who is not a relative. Nominees must submit brief essays on 1) why they are proud to be from Oklahoma, why it is important to them to receive their education from an Oklahoma institution of higher education, and what they hope to contribute to the state in their lifetime; 2) their demonstrated characteristics of leadership positions, leadership potential, and corresponding leadership roles; 3) their demonstrated characteristics of good citizenship, service in student or community clubs, and other acts of volunteerism; and 4) their overall academic achievement. Selection is based on information in those essays.

Financial data: The stipend is $1,250 per year.

Duration: 4 years, provided the recipient remains enrolled full time and maintains a GPA of 3.5 or higher.

Number awarded: 1 each year.

Deadline: September of each year.

719 $$ OKLAHOMA HIGHER LEARNING ACCESS PROGRAM

Oklahoma State Regents for Higher Education
Attn: Director of Scholarship and Grant Programs
655 Research Parkway, Suite 200
P.O. Box 108850
Oklahoma City, OK 73101–8850
Phone: (405) 225–9152; (800) 858–1840; Fax: (405) 225–9230;
Email: okpromise@osrhe.edu
Web: www.okhighered.org/okpromise

Summary: To provide financial assistance to Oklahoma residents who complete a specified high school curriculum.

Eligibility: Open to students who sign up during grades 8–10 at Oklahoma high schools or ages 13–15 if homeschooled. If they complete a specified college preparatory curriculum and demonstrate a commitment to academic success, they receive assistance when they attend college. Applicants must 1) demonstrate financial need (currently defined as a family income less than $50,000 at the time of application and less than $100,000 at the time of entering college); 2) achieve a GPA of 2.5 or higher both cumulatively and in the required curriculum; 3) fulfill an agreement to attend school, do homework regularly, refrain from substance abuse and criminal or delinquent acts, and have school work and records reviewed by school officials; and 4) be admitted as a regular entering freshman at an Oklahoma college, university, or area vocational technical school. U.S. citizenship or permanent resident status is required.

Financial data: Students enrolled at an institution in the Oklahoma State System of Higher Education receive resident tuition, paid to the institution on their behalf. Students enrolled at an accredited private institution have tuition paid at an amount equivalent to the resident tuition at a comparable institution of the state system. Students enrolled in eligible vocational/technical programs have their tuition paid. No provision is made for other educational expenses, such as books, supplies, room, board, or other special fees.

Duration: Up to 5 years or until completion of a bachelor's degree, whichever occurs first. The award must be taken up within 3 years of high school graduation. Renewal requires that the student achieves a GPA of 2.0 or higher during the sophomore year of college and 2.5 or higher during the junior and senior years.

Number awarded: Varies each year; recently, approximately 19,000 students received $54 million in support from this program.

Deadline: Applications must be submitted by June following completion of the student's grade 8–10 year.

720 $$ OKLAHOMA INDEPENDENT LIVING ACT TUITION WAIVERS

Oklahoma State Regents for Higher Education
Attn: Director of Scholarship and Grant Programs
655 Research Parkway, Suite 200
P.O. Box 108850
Oklahoma City, OK 73101–8850
Phone: (405) 225–9239; (800) 858–1840; Fax: (405) 225–9230;
Email: studentinfo@osrhe.edu
Web: www.okcollegestart.org

Summary: To provide financial assistance to residents in Oklahoma who have been in a foster care program of the Department of Human Services (DHS) and are interested in attending college in the state.

Eligibility: Open to residents of Oklahoma who graduated within the previous 3 years from an accredited high school in the state or from a high school bordering Oklahoma as approved by the State Board of Education, or who have completed the GED requirements. Applicants must be younger than 21 years of age and have been in DHS custody for at least 9 months between 16 and 18 years of age. They must currently be enrolled at an Oklahoma public college or university or in certain programs at technology centers.

Financial data: Under this program, all resident tuition fees are waived.

Duration: 1 year; may be renewed until the student reaches 26 years of age or completes a baccalaureate degree or program certificate, whichever comes first.

Number awarded: Varies each year.

Deadline: Deadline not specified.

721 OKLAHOMA KNIGHTS TEMPLAR SCHOLARSHIPS

Knights Templar of Oklahoma
Attn: District of Oklahoma Educational Foundation
620 West Cherry Street
P.O. Box 1223
Drumright, OK 74030–1223
Phone: (918) 352–2382;
Email: grandsecrec@sbcglobal.net
Web: www.okyorkrite.org/charities.htm

Summary: To provide financial assistance to residents of Oklahoma interested in attending college or graduate school in any state.

Eligibility: Open to residents of Oklahoma who are graduating high school seniors or students currently enrolled at an accredited 2– or 4–year college or university, vocational school, or graduate school in any state. Applicants must be U.S. citizens and have a GPA of 2.5 or higher. They must provide information on their financial situation, but the scholarship is available to all students regardless of their financial circumstances. In the selection process, no consideration is given to age, race, religion, national origin, gender, or Masonic ties or affiliation.

Financial data: A stipend is awarded (amount not specified); funds are deposited with the recipient's school of choice.

Duration: 1 year.

Number awarded: 4 each year.

Deadline: January of each year.

722 $$ OKLAHOMA STATE REGENTS ACADEMIC SCHOLARS PROGRAM

Oklahoma State Regents for Higher Education
Attn: Director of Scholarship and Grant Programs
655 Research Parkway, Suite 200
P.O. Box 108850
Oklahoma City, OK 73101–8850
Phone: (405) 225–9239; (800) 858–1840; Fax: (405) 225–9230;
Email: cwadsworth@osrhe.edu
Web: www.okcollegestart.org

Summary: To provide financial assistance to outstanding high school seniors and graduates who wish to attend a college or university in Oklahoma.

Eligibility: Open to high school seniors who plan to attend a college or university in Oklahoma and students already enrolled at such a school. Residents of Oklahoma automatically qualify by 1) being designated a National Merit Scholar, a National Merit Finalist, or a United States Presidential Scholar; or 2) achieving an ACT or SAT score that is at least at the 99.5 percentile level (currently, at least 134 in all ACT skill areas or 1560 on the mathematics and critical reading SAT). Out–of–state students are considered if they are designated as a National Merit Scholar, a National Merit Finalist, or a United States Presidential Scholar. In addition, public colleges and universities may nominate students attending their institution if they meet criteria established by the institution.

Financial data: The program provides funding for tuition, fees, room and board, and textbooks. The exact amount of funding awarded varies each year; for "automatic qualifiers" from Oklahoma, it is currently $5,500 per year for students at the 3 comprehensive universities, $4,000 per year for students at other 4–year public or private colleges or universities in Oklahoma, or $3,500 per year for students at Oklahoma 2–year colleges. For institutional nominees, the current rate is $2,800 per year at the 3 comprehensive universities, $2,000 per year at other 4–year institutions, or $1,800 at 2–year colleges. Students who enroll at public universities and colleges are also eligible for a tuition waiver.

Duration: Up to 4 years of undergraduate study, as long as the recipient remains a full–time student with a GPA of 3.25 or higher.

Number awarded: Varies each year; recently, 667 entering freshmen received this support (including 427 "automatic qualifiers" and 240 institutional nominees). A total of 2,213 students were enrolled in the program.

Deadline: Deadline not specified.

723 OKLAHOMA TUITION AID GRANT PROGRAM

Oklahoma State Regents for Higher Education
Attn: Director of Scholarship and Grant Programs
655 Research Parkway, Suite 200
P.O. Box 108850
Oklahoma City, OK 73101–8850
Phone: (405) 225–9456; (800) 858–1840; Fax: (405) 225–9476;
Email: studentinfo@osrhe.edu
Web: www.okcollegestart.org

Summary: To provide financial assistance to Oklahoma residents who demonstrate financial need and plan to attend college in the state.

Eligibility: Open to residents of Oklahoma who are attending or planning to attend public or private institutions in Oklahoma. Applicants must complete the Free Application for Federal Student Aid (FAFSA) and demonstrate financial need with an expected family contribution that varies each year. Undocumented immigrants are eligible if they 1) have graduated from a public or private high school in Oklahoma or have successfully completed the GED in Oklahoma; and 2) will have resided in Oklahoma with a parent or guardian for at least 2 years prior to graduation from high school or successful completion of the GED in Oklahoma.

Financial data: At public colleges, universities, and technology centers, the annual stipend is $1,000 or 75% of enrollment costs, whichever is less. At private colleges and universities, the annual stipend is $1,300 or 75% of enrollment costs, whichever is less.

Duration: 1 year; renewable.

Number awarded: Varies each year.

Deadline: For best consideration, applications should be submitted by February of each year.

724 $ OKLAHOMA TUITION EQUALIZATION GRANT PROGRAM

Oklahoma State Regents for Higher Education
Attn: Director of Scholarship and Grant Programs
655 Research Parkway, Suite 200
P.O. Box 108850
Oklahoma City, OK 73101–8850
Phone: (405) 225–9456; (877) 662–6231; Fax: (405) 225–9230;
Email: studentinfo@osrhe.edu
Web: www.okcollegestart.org

Summary: To provide financial assistance to Oklahoma residents who meet financial need requirements and are entering a private college in the state as first–time freshmen.

Eligibility: Open to residents of Oklahoma entering a nonprofit private or independent institution of higher education in the state as a full–time undergraduate for the first time. Applicants must have a family income of $50,000 or less.

Financial data: The stipend is $2,000 per year.

Duration: 1 year; may be renewed up to 4 additional years.

Number awarded: Varies each year.

Deadline: Deadline not specified.

725 $$ OKLAHOMA TUITION WAIVER FOR DEPENDENTS OF PEACE OFFICERS AND FIRE FIGHTERS

Oklahoma State Regents for Higher Education
Attn: Director of Scholarship and Grant Programs
655 Research Parkway, Suite 200
P.O. Box 108850
Oklahoma City, OK 73101–8850
Phone: (405) 225–9239; (800) 858–1840; Fax: (405) 225–9230;
Email: studentinfo@osrhe.edu
Web: www.okcollegestart.org

Summary: To provide financial assistance for college to the children of deceased Oklahoma peace officers and firefighters.

Eligibility: Open to the children of Oklahoma peace officers or firefighters who lost their lives in the line of duty. Selection is based on financial need, academic aptitude and achievement, student activity participation, academic level, and academic discipline or field of study.

Financial data: Eligible applicants are entitled to receive free tuition at any Oklahoma state–supported postsecondary educational, technical, or vocational school.
Duration: Assistance continues for 5 years or until receipt of a bachelor's degree, whichever occurs first.
Number awarded: Varies each year.
Deadline: Deadline not specified.

726 $$ OKLAHOMA TUITION WAIVER FOR PRISONERS OF WAR, PERSONS MISSING IN ACTION, AND DEPENDENTS

Oklahoma State Regents for Higher Education
Attn: Director of Scholarship and Grant Programs
655 Research Parkway, Suite 200
P.O. Box 108850
Oklahoma City, OK 73101–8850
Phone: (405) 225–9239; (800) 858–1840; Fax: (405) 225–9230;
Email: studentinfo@osrhe.edu
Web: www.okcollegestart.org
Summary: To provide financial assistance for college to Oklahoma residents (or their dependents) who were declared prisoners of war or missing in action.
Eligibility: Open to veterans who were declared prisoners of war or missing in action after January 1, 1960 and were residents of Oklahoma at the time of entrance into the armed forces or when declared POW/MIA. Dependent children of those veterans are also eligible as long as they are under 24 years of age. Selection is based on financial need, academic aptitude and achievement, student activity participation, academic level, and academic discipline or field of study.
Financial data: Eligible applicants are entitled to receive free tuition at any Oklahoma state–supported postsecondary educational, technical, or vocational school.
Duration: Assistance continues for 5 years or until receipt of a bachelor's degree, whichever occurs first.
Number awarded: Varies each year.
Deadline: Deadline not specified.

727 OMAHA VOLUNTEERS FOR HANDICAPPED CHILDREN SCHOLARSHIPS

Omaha Volunteers for Handicapped Children
c/o Lois Carlson
2010 Country Club Avenue
Omaha, NE 68104
Phone: (402) 553–0378
Summary: To provide financial assistance to Nebraska residents who have a physical disability or are preparing for a career related to people with orthopedic impairments or physical disabilities and are interested in attending college in any state.
Eligibility: Open to residents of Nebraska who are U.S. citizens. First priority applicants must have an orthopedic impairment or physical disability and be 1) high school seniors with a GPA of 2.25 or higher and accepted into the school of their choice or 2) college students making satisfactory progress toward graduation. Second priority applicants must be enrolled in the college of their choice and preparing for a teaching or health–related career of service to people with orthopedic impairments or physical disabilities. All applicants must submit a 250–word essay on their future goals in relation to the orthopedically impaired and/or physically disabled and their need for the scholarship.
Financial data: The stipend is $1,000 per year.
Duration: 1 year; may be renewed.
Number awarded: 5 to 10 each year.
Deadline: July of each year.

728 ONE FAMILY SCHOLARS PROGRAM

One Family, Inc.
Attn: Director, One Family Scholars Program
186 South Street, Fourth Floor
Boston, MA 02111
Phone: (617) 423–0504; Fax: (617) 588–0441;
Email: scholars@onefamilyinc.org
Web: www.onefamilyinc.org/scholar–application
Summary: To provide financial assistance to residents of Massachusetts who are single heads of households and interested in attending college in the state.
Eligibility: Open to residents of Massachusetts who are single heads of household with dependent children younger than 18 years of age. Applicants must be attempting to enter or reenter college in Massachusetts to work on an associate or bachelor's degree. They must apply through a participating social service organization at sites in Massachusetts. Along with their application, they must submit a personal essay and 3 letters of reference. They must also apply for financial aid and participate in an interview. U.S. citizenship or permanent resident status is required. Selection is based on financial need (family earnings below 200% of the federal poverty level), clear and realistic academic and career goals, potential for success in chosen academic program, and desire to participate actively in all aspects of the program.
Financial data: A stipend is awarded (amount not specified).
Duration: 1 year; may be renewed until completion of a degree, provided the scholar successfully completes 6 to 9 credits per semester; participates in mandatory leadership development retreats, seminars, and activities; maintains a GPA of 3.0 or higher; remains a Massachusetts resident; and maintains contact with site coordinators.
Number awarded: Varies each year; recently, 23 scholars received support from this program.
Deadline: July of each year for fall; November of each year for spring; April of each year for summer.

729 $ ONE SCHOLARSHIP COMPETITION

Higher One
115 Munson Street
New Haven, CT 06511
Phone: (866) 444–4379
Web: www.higherone.com
Summary: To provide financial assistance to students entering or enrolled at colleges and universities that utilize services of Higher One.
Eligibility: Open to 1) full– and part–time undergraduate and graduate students enrolled at 2– and 4–year colleges and universities that partner with Higher One for specialized financial services; and 2) high school seniors accepted at such an institution. Applicants must prepare and submit a 2–minute video in which they discuss the philosophy of Higher One, how they have overcome obstacles in the past, and their future goals. They must have a GPA of 3.0 or higher. Selection is based primarily on their video.
Financial data: The stipend is $2,500.
Duration: 1 year.
Number awarded: 20 each year.
Deadline: April of each year.

730 ONIPA'A CHAPTER ABWA SCHOLARSHIPS

American Business Women's Association–Onipa'a Chapter
c/o Julie Dugan, Education Committee Chair
P.O. Box 43
Waimanalo, HI 96795
Web: www.onipaa.hawaiiabwa.org/Scholarship.htm
Summary: To provide financial assistance to female residents of Hawaii who are working on an undergraduate degree at a college or university in the state.
Eligibility: Open to residents of Hawaii who have completed at least 2 semesters as a full–time undergraduate student at an accredited university, community college, or business school in the state. Applicants must have a GPA of 3.0 or higher. Along with their application, they must submit a 1–page biographical summary that includes educational background and career objective. Financial need is also considered in the selection process. U.S. citizenship is required.
Financial data: The stipend is $1,000.
Duration: 1 year.
Number awarded: 2 each year.
Deadline: April of each year.

731 $ OPTIMIST INTERNATIONAL COMMUNICATION CONTEST FOR THE DEAF AND HARD OF HEARING

Optimist International
Attn: Programs Department
4494 Lindell Boulevard
St. Louis, MO 63108
Phone: (314) 371–6000; (800) 500–8130, ext. 235; Fax: (314) 371–6006;
Email: programs@optimist.org
Web: optimist.org/e/member/scholarships2.cfm
Summary: To recognize and reward, with college scholarships, outstanding presentations made by hearing impaired high school students.
Eligibility: Open to young people up to and including grade 12 in the United States and Canada, to CEGEP in Quebec, and to grade 13 in the Caribbean.

Applicants must be identified by a qualified audiologist as deaf or hard of hearing with a hearing loss of 40 decibels or more. They are invited to make a presentation (using oral communication, sign language, or a combination of both) from 4 to 5 minutes on a topic that changes annually; a recent topic was "How my Optimism Helps me Overcome Obstacles." Competition is first conducted at the level of individual clubs, with winners advancing to zone and then district competitions. Selection is based on material organization (40 points), delivery and presentation (30 points), and overall effectiveness (30 points).
Financial data: Each district winner receives a $2,500 college scholarship, payable to an educational institution of the recipient's choice, subject to the approval of Optimist International.
Duration: The competition is held annually.
Number awarded: Nearly 300 Optimist International clubs participate in this program each year. Each participating district offers 1 scholarship; some districts may offer a second award with separate competitions for signing and oral competitors, or for male and female entrants.
Deadline: Each club sets its own deadline. Districts must submit materials to the national office by June of each year.

732 $ OPTIMIST INTERNATIONAL ESSAY CONTEST

Optimist International
Attn: Programs Department
4494 Lindell Boulevard
St. Louis, MO 63108
Phone: (314) 371–6000; (800) 500–8130, ext. 235; Fax: (314) 371–6009;
Email: programs@optimist.org
Web: optimist.org/e/member/scholarships3.cfm
Summary: To recognize and reward, with college scholarships, outstanding essays by high school students on a topic that changes annually.
Eligibility: Open to high school students in the United States, the Caribbean, or Canada who are younger than 18 years of age. Applicants are invited to write an essay of 700 to 800 words on a topic that changes each year; a recent topic was "How my Positive Outlook Benefits my Community." They first compete on the local club level; club winners advance to district competitions. Essays may be written in the official language of the area where the club is located (English, Spanish, or French). Selection is based on material organization (40 points); vocabulary and style (30 points); grammar, punctuation, and spelling (20 points); neatness (5 points); and adherence to contest rules (5 points).
Financial data: District winners are awarded $2,500 college scholarships.
Duration: The competition is held annually.
Number awarded: More than 1,200 Optimist International local clubs participate in the program each year.
Deadline: Clubs must submit their winning essay to the district chair by the end of February of each year. Districts must submit their winner's information to the national office in April.

733 $ OPTIMIST INTERNATIONAL ORATORICAL CONTEST

Optimist International
Attn: Programs Department
4494 Lindell Boulevard
St. Louis, MO 63108
Phone: (314) 371–6000; (800) 500–8130, ext. 235; Fax: (314) 371–6009;
Email: programs@optimist.org
Web: optimist.org/e/member/scholarships4.cfm
Summary: To recognize and reward, with college scholarships, outstanding orators at the high school or younger level.
Eligibility: Open to all students in public, private, or parochial elementary, junior high, and senior high schools in the United States, Canada, or the Caribbean who are under 18 years of age. All contestants must prepare their own orations of 4 to 5 minutes, but they may receive advice and make minor changes or improvements in the oration at any time. Each year a different subject is selected for the orations; a recent topic was "How my Optimism Helps me Overcome Obstacles." The orations may be delivered in a language other than English if that language is an official language of the country in which the sponsoring club is located. Selection is based on poise (20 points), content of speech (35 points), delivery and presentation (35 points), and overall effectiveness (10 points). Competition is first conducted at the level of individual clubs, with winners advancing to zone and then district competitions. At the discretion of the district, boys may compete against boys and girls against girls in separate contests.
Financial data: Each district awards either 2 scholarships of $2,500 (1 for a boy and 1 for a girl) or (if the district chooses to have a combined gender contest) a first–place scholarship of $2,500, a second–place scholarship of $1,500, and a third–place scholarship of $1,000.
Duration: The competition is held annually.
Number awarded: Each year, more than $150,000 is awarded in scholarships.
Deadline: Each local club sets its own deadline. The district deadline is the end of June.

734 ORA LEE SANDERS SCHOLARSHIP

PUSH Excel
Attn: General Offices
930 East 50th Street
Chicago, IL 60615
Phone: (773) 373–3366;
Email: pushexcel@rainbowpush.org
Web: www.pushexcel.org/?page_id=64
Summary: To provide financial assistance to high school seniors who plan to attend college and are willing to help promote the scholarship program of PUSH–Excel.
Eligibility: Open to seniors graduating from high school and planning to enroll at an accredited 4–year college or university. Applicants must be U.S. citizens and have a GPA of 2.5 or higher. Along with their application, they must submit a 500–word essay that identifies 5 prerequisites for success, explains their personal philosophy for the pursuit of excellence, and explains how they will use their college education to achieve this pursuit of excellence. They must also agree to cooperate with the scholarship committee of PUSH–Excel by promoting its program, participating in its public relations activities, and attending its Annual National Conference luncheon and Education Leadership Conference. Selection is based on the essay, academic preparation to attend college and succeed, ability to overcome obstacles to achieve academic and personal goals, and financial need.
Financial data: The stipend is $1,000 per year.
Duration: 1 year; may be renewed up to 3 additional years if the recipient maintains a GPA of 2.5 or higher and fulfills the obligations to PUSH–Excel.
Number awarded: Varies each year; recently, 50 of these scholarships were awarded.
Deadline: June of each year.

735 $ OREGON CHAFEE EDUCATION AND TRAINING GRANTS

Oregon Student Access Commission
Attn: Public Programs
1500 Valley River Drive, Suite 100
Eugene, OR 97401–2148
Phone: (541) 687–7443; (800) 452–8807, ext. 7443; Fax: (541) 687–7414; TDD: (800) 735–2900;
Email: peggy.d.cooksey@osac.state.or.us
Web: www.oregonstudentaid.gov/chafeetv.html
Summary: To provide financial assistance for college to Oregon residents who are or have been in foster care.
Eligibility: Open to residents of Oregon who 1) currently are in a foster care placement with Oregon's Department of Human Services (DHS) or 1 of the 9 federally–recognized tribes in the state; or 2) have been in foster care for at least 180 days after their 14th birthday and exited substitute care at 16 years of age or older. Applicants must be younger than 21 years of age. Along with their application, they must submit essays of 250 to 350 words on 1) their most significant challenge or accomplishment and its value to their life; and 2) their long–range goals and what they need to achieve them.
Financial data: The stipend is $3,000 for a full academic year (3 or 4 terms), $2,000 for 2 terms, or $1,000 for 1 term.
Duration: 1 year; may be renewed until recipient reaches 23 years of age.
Number awarded: 1 or more each year.
Deadline: July of each year for fall term; October of each year for winter term; January of each year for spring term; April of each year for summer term.

736 $$ OREGON DECEASED OR DISABLED PUBLIC SAFETY OFFICER GRANT PROGRAM

Oregon Student Access Commission
Attn: Public Programs
1500 Valley River Drive, Suite 100
Eugene, OR 97401–2130
Phone: (541) 687–7443; (800) 452–8807, ext. 7443; Fax: (541) 687–7414; TDD: (800) 735–2900;
Email: awardinfo@osac.state.or.us
Web: www.oregonstudentaid.gov/ddpso–grant.aspx
Summary: To provide financial assistance for college or graduate school in the state to the children of disabled or deceased Oregon public safety officers.

Eligibility: Open to the natural, adopted, or stepchildren of Oregon public safety officers (firefighters, state fire marshals, chief deputy fire marshals, deputy state fire marshals, police chiefs, police officers, sheriffs, deputy sheriffs, county adult parole and probation officers, correction officers, and investigators of the Criminal Justice Division of the Department of Justice) who, in the line of duty, were killed or disabled. Applicants must be enrolled or planning to enroll as a full–time undergraduate student at a public or private college or university in Oregon. Children of deceased officers are also eligible for graduate study. Financial need must be demonstrated.
Financial data: At a public 2– or 4–year college or university, the amount of the award is equal to the cost of tuition and fees. At an eligible private college, the award amount is equal to the cost of tuition and fees at the University of Oregon.
Duration: 1 year; may be renewed for up to 3 additional years of undergraduate study, if the student maintains satisfactory academic progress and demonstrates continued financial need. Children of deceased public safety officers may receive support for 12 quarters of graduate study.
Number awarded: Varies each year.
Deadline: Deadline not specified.

737 OREGON EDUCATIONAL AID FOR VETERANS

Oregon Department of Veterans' Affairs
Attn: Educational Aid Program
700 Summer Street N.E., Suite 150
Salem, OR 97301–1285
Phone: (503) 373–2085; (800) 828–8801 (within OR); Fax: (503) 373–2362; TDD: (503) 373–2217;
Email: orvetsbenefits@odva.state.or.us
Web: www.oregon.gov/ODVA/BENEFITS/OregonEducationBenefit.shtml
Summary: To provide financial assistance for college to certain Oregon veterans.
Eligibility: Open to veterans who served on active duty in the U.S. armed forces for not less than 90 days during the Korean War or subsequent to June 30, 1958. Applicants must be residents of Oregon released from military service under honorable conditions. They must be enrolled or planning to enroll in classroom instruction, home study courses, or vocational training from an accredited educational institution. U.S. citizenship is required.
Financial data: Full–time students are entitled to receive up to $150 per month and part–time students up to $100 per month.
Duration: Benefits are paid for as many months as the veteran spent in active service, up to a maximum of 36 months. One month of entitlement will be charged for each month paid, regardless of the amount paid.
Number awarded: Varies each year.
Deadline: Applications must be submitted at the time of enrollment.

738 OREGON LEGION AUXILIARY DEPARTMENT SCHOLARSHIPS

American Legion Auxiliary
Department of Oregon
30450 S.W. Parkway Avenue
P.O. Box 1730
Wilsonville, OR 97070–1730
Phone: (503) 682–3162; Fax: (503) 685–5008;
Email: contact@alaoregon.org
Web: www.alaoregon.org
Summary: To provide financial assistance to the dependents of Oregon veterans who are interested in attending college in any state.
Eligibility: Open to Oregon residents who are children or wives of disabled veterans or widows of veterans. Applicants must be interested in obtaining education beyond the high school level at a college, university, business school, vocational school, or any other accredited postsecondary school in the state of Oregon. Selection is based on ability, aptitude, character, seriousness of purpose, and financial need.
Financial data: The stipend is $1,000.
Duration: 1 year; nonrenewable.
Number awarded: 3 each year; 1 of these is to be used for vocational or business school.
Deadline: March of each year.

739 OREGON OCCUPATIONAL SAFETY AND HEALTH DIVISION WORKERS MEMORIAL SCHOLARSHIPS

Oregon Student Access Commission
Attn: Grants and Scholarships Division
1500 Valley River Drive, Suite 100
Eugene, OR 97401–2146
Phone: (541) 687–7395; (800) 452–8807, ext. 7395; Fax: (541) 687–7414; TDD: (800) 735–2900;
Email: awardinfo@osac.state.or.us
Web: www.oregonstudentaid.gov/scholarships.aspx
Summary: To provide financial assistance to the children and spouses of disabled or deceased workers in Oregon who are interested in attending college or graduate school in any state.
Eligibility: Open to residents of Oregon who are U.S. citizens or permanent residents. Applicants must be high school seniors or graduates who 1) are dependents or spouses of an Oregon worker who has suffered permanent total disability on the job; or 2) are receiving, or have received, fatality benefits as dependents or spouses of a worker fatally injured in Oregon. They may be attending a college or graduate school in any state. Along with their application, they must submit an essay of up to 500 words on how the injury or death of their parent or spouse has affected or influenced their decision to further their education. Financial need is not required, but it is considered in the selection process.
Financial data: Stipends range up to $1,000.
Duration: 1 year.
Number awarded: Varies each year; recently, 7 of these scholarships were awarded.
Deadline: February of each year.

740 OREGON OPPORTUNITY GRANTS

Oregon Student Access Commission
1500 Valley River Drive, Suite 100
Eugene, OR 97401–2130
Phone: (541) 687–7400; (800) 452–8807; Fax: (541) 687–7414; TDD: (800) 735–2900;
Email: awardinfo@osac.state.or.us
Web: www.oregonstudentaid.gov/oregon–opportunity–grant.aspx
Summary: To provide financial assistance to residents of Oregon who have financial need and are interested in attending college in the state.
Eligibility: Open to residents of Oregon who are enrolled or planning to enroll at a nonprofit college or university in the state on at least a half–time basis. Applicants must have an annual family income below specified levels with an unmet need of at least $1,950. They must be U.S. citizens or eligible noncitizens and not in default on any federal student loan. Grants are awarded on a first–come, first–served basis until funds are exhausted.
Financial data: Currently, the maximum award is $1,950, regardless of the type of institution the student attends.
Duration: 1 year; may be renewed for up to 3 additional years, if the student maintains satisfactory academic progress and demonstrates continued financial need.
Number awarded: Varies each year; recently, more than 13,000 of these grants, with a value of nearly $19 million, were awarded.
Deadline: January of each year.

741 $ OREGON SPORTS HALL OF FAME SCHOLARSHIPS

Oregon Sports Hall of Fame and Museum
Attn: Scholarship Chair
8500 S.E. McLoughlin Boulevard, Suite 101
Portland, OR 97222
Phone: (503) 227–7466; Fax: (503) 227–6925;
Email: info@oregonsportshall.org
Web: www.oregonsportshall.org/programs.htm
Summary: To provide financial assistance for college to high school seniors in Oregon who have been involved in sports.
Eligibility: Open to seniors graduating from high schools in Oregon who are planning to attend an institution of higher education in the state. Applicants must have participated in sports. They must have a GPA of 3.3 or higher, an ACT score of at least 21, and an SAT score of 1350 or higher. Selection is based on academic achievement, community involvement, athletic accomplishment, and financial need.
Financial data: The stipend is $3,000.
Duration: 1 year.
Number awarded: Up to 6 each year.
Deadline: April of each year.

742 $ ORION FUND GRANTS

The Orion Fund
P.O. Box 11518
Piedmont, CA 94611

Phone: (510) 482–2226;
Email: theorionfund@gmail.com
Web: theorionfund.org/OrionGrants.htm

Summary: To provide financial assistance to California college and graduate students who have a serious illness or injury.

Eligibility: Open to undergraduate and graduate students at colleges and universities in California who are younger than 30 years of age and have a serious medical condition that affects their ability to stay in school. Applicants must submit a personal statement describing the purpose of the grant and providing justification for the request, a letter of support from a campus administrator or a medical provider, unofficial transcripts, and information on financial resources.

Financial data: Stipends range from $300 to $3,000. Funds may be used for unpaid medical bills, medical technology, and educational and living expenses.

Duration: 1 year.

Number awarded: 1 or more each year.

Deadline: Applications normally must be submitted by April of each year. In special circumstances, they may be accepted at any time.

743 OUTSTANDING JROTC CADET AWARD

National Society Sons of the American Revolution
1000 South Fourth Street
Louisville, KY 40203–3208
Phone: (502) 589–1776; Fax: (502) 589–1671
Web: www.sar.org/node/260

Summary: To recognize and reward outstanding high school students who are participating in the Junior Reserve Officers' Training Corps (JROTC) program.

Eligibility: Open to JROTC cadets in their next to last year (a third–year cadet in a 4–year program or a second–year cadet in a 2–year program), normally in grade 11. Each chapter of the National Society of the Sons of the American Revolution (SAR) selects an outstanding cadet and nominates him or her for their state society program. For the state competition, each cadet must submit an essay on how JROTC has prepared them to be a better citizen of the United States. Each state winner is entered into the national competition, where the essay is also considered. Selection is based on patriotism, leadership, military bearing, scholarship, and general excellence.

Financial data: The Outstanding Cadet in the nation receives a prize of $1,000 and up to $1,000 to attend the national SAR convention where the prize is presented. The award is presented annually.

Number awarded: 1 each year.

Deadline: Each chapter and state sets the date for its competition. The nominations of each state organization must be submitted to national by the end of April of each year.

744 P. BUCKLEY MOSS SOCIETY/ANNE AND MATT HARBISON SCHOLARSHIP

P. Buckley Moss Society
74 Poplar Grove Lane
Mathews, VA 23109
Phone: (540) 932–1728; (800) 430–1320;
Email: society@mosssociety.org
Web: www.mosssociety.org/page.php?id=30

Summary: To provide financial assistance for college to high school seniors with language–related learning disabilities.

Eligibility: Open to high school seniors with language–related learning disabilities. They must be nominated by a member of the P. Buckley Moss Society. The nomination packet must include verification of a language–related learning disability from a counselor or case manager, a high school transcript, 2 letters of recommendation, and 4 essays by the nominees (on themselves; their learning disability and its effect on their lives; their extracurricular, community, work, and church accomplishments; and their plans for next year).

Financial data: The stipend is $1,500. Funds are paid to the recipient's college or university.

Duration: 1 year; may be renewed for up to 3 additional years.

Number awarded: 1 each year.

Deadline: March of each year.

745 PALCUS SCHOLARSHIP PROGRAM

Portuguese American Leadership Council of the United States, Inc.
Attn: Administrative Assistant
9255 Center Street, Suite 404
Manassas, VA 20110
Phone: (202) 466–4664; Fax: (202) 466–4661;
Email: palcus@palcus.org
Web: www.palcus.org/programs/education/scholarships

Summary: To provide financial assistance to undergraduate and graduate students of Portuguese ancestry.

Eligibility: Open to students accepted or enrolled in a baccalaureate or graduate degree program who are of at least 25% Portuguese ancestry. Applicants must have a GPA of 3.0 or higher. Along with their application, they must submit a 1–page essay on the impact of their Portuguese ancestry on their personal development, the role they anticipate that their Portuguese ancestry will play in their future, and their career goals and community involvement. Selection is based on that essay, academic record, extracurricular activities, and community service.

Financial data: The stipend is $1,000.

Duration: 1 year; recipients may reapply.

Number awarded: September or more each year.

Deadline: April of each year.

746 $$ PALMER B. CARSON MEMORIAL SCHOLARSHIP

Parents, Families and Friends of Lesbians and Gays
Attn: Safe Schools and Diversity Outreach Coordinator
1828 L Street, N.W., Suite 660
Washington, DC 20036
Phone: (202) 467–8180, ext. 212; Fax: (202) 349–0788;
Email: mlucas@pflag.org
Web: community.pflag.org/page.aspx?pid=370

Summary: To provide financial assistance for college to high school seniors and recent graduates who have a connection to Parents, Families and Friends of Lesbians and Gays (PFLAG).

Eligibility: Open to high school seniors and prior–year graduates who have not attended college. Applicants must have applied to an accredited higher education institution to work on 1) an associate degree leading to transfer to complete a bachelor's degree; or 2) a bachelor's degree at a 4–year college or university. They must self–identify either as a gay, lesbian, bisexual, or transgender (GLBT) person or as a supporter of GLBT people. Along with their application, they must submit a high school transcript showing a GPA of 3.0 or higher, 2 letters of recommendation, and a 2–page essay discussing either their life as an GLBT student or how they have been involved with and supported the GLBT community. Financial need is also considered in the selection process.

Financial data: The stipend is $5,000.

Duration: 1 year; nonrenewable.

Number awarded: 1 each year.

Deadline: March of each year.

747 $$ PALMETTO FELLOWS SCHOLARSHIPS

South Carolina Commission on Higher Education
Attn: Student Services
1122 Lady Street, Suite 300
Columbia, SC 29201
Phone: (803) 737–2262; (877) 349–7183; Fax: (803) 737–2297;
Email: ecaulder@che.sc.gov
Web: www.che.sc.gov/New_Web/GoingToCollege/FinAst.htm

Summary: To provide financial assistance for college to high school seniors in South Carolina who have achieved a high score on a college entrance examination.

Eligibility: Open to residents of South Carolina who are enrolled in a public or private high school or an approved home school program. Applicants must be planning to attend a 4–year public or private college or university in South Carolina during the fall immediately following graduation. They must either 1) score at least 1200 on the mathematics and critical reading sections of the SAT or 27 on the ACT, have a GPA of 3.5 or higher, and rank in the top 6% of their class; or 2) score at least 1400 on the mathematics and critical reading sections of the SAT or 32 on the ACT and have a GPA of 4.0. Early awards are based on test scores, GPA, and class rank at the end of the junior year; final awards are based on test scores, GPA, and class rank at the end of the senior year. U.S. citizenship or permanent resident status is required. Students who complete at least 14 credit hours of mathematics and life and physical sciences qualify for an enhanced mathematics and sciences award. Financial need is not considered in the selection process.

Financial data: The stipend is $6,700 for the freshman year and $7,500 per year for sophomore and later years. Students who qualify for the enhanced mathematics and sciences award receive an additional $2,500 per year beginning with their sophomore year.

Duration: 1 year; may be renewed for 3 additional years, provided the recipient maintains full–time enrollment and a GPA of 3.0 or higher.

Number awarded: Varies each year; recently, 5,506 of these scholarships, worth more than $22 million, were awarded.
Deadline: December of each year for early awards; June of each year for final awards.

748 PAR OR BETTER SCHOLARSHIP

Par or Better Golf Club
c/o Craig V. Smith, President
145 Lee Haven Drive
St. Charles, MO 63303
Web: parorbetter.org/par–or–better–scholarship
Summary: To provide financial assistance to high school seniors planning to attend college in any state.
Eligibility: Open to seniors graduating from high school and planning to enroll at a 2– or 4–year institution of higher education in any state. Applicants must have a GPA of 2.0 or higher. Along with their application, they must submit an essay of 200 to 400 words on the importance of receiving this scholarship for their anticipated major. Financial need is not considered in the selection process.
Financial data: The stipend is $1,000. Funds are disbursed to the recipient's college or university.
Duration: 1 year.
Number awarded: 1 each year.
Deadline: July of each year.

749 PARENTS, FAMILIES AND FRIENDS OF LESBIANS AND GAYS (PFLAG) NATIONAL SCHOLARSHIPS

Parents, Families and Friends of Lesbians and Gays
Attn: Safe Schools and Diversity Outreach Coordinator
1828 L Street, N.W., Suite 660
Washington, DC 20036
Phone: (202) 467–8180, ext. 212; Fax: (202) 349–0788;
Email: mlucas@pflag.org
Web: community.pflag.org/page.aspx?pid=370
Summary: To provide financial assistance for college to high school seniors and recent graduates who have a connection to Parents, Families and Friends of Lesbians and Gays (PFLAG).
Eligibility: Open to high school seniors and prior–year graduates who have not attended college. Applicants must have applied to an accredited higher education institution to work on 1) an associate degree leading to transfer to complete a bachelor's degree; or 2) a bachelor's degree at a 4–year college or university. They must self–identify either as a gay, lesbian, bisexual, or transgender (GLBT) person or as a supporter of GLBT people. Along with their application, they must submit a high school transcript showing a GPA of 3.0 or higher, 2 letters of recommendation, and a 2–page essay discussing either their life as an GLBT student or how they have been involved with and supported the GLBT community. Financial need is also considered in the selection process.
Financial data: The stipend is $1,000.
Duration: 1 year; nonrenewable.
Number awarded: Varies each year; recently, 11 of these scholarships were awarded.
Deadline: March of each year.

750 $ PARR FAMILY MEMORIAL ENDOWMENT SCHOLARSHIP

Epsilon Sigma Alpha International
Attn: ESA Foundation
363 West Drake Road
Fort Collins, CO 80526
Phone: (970) 223–2824; Fax: (970) 223–4456;
Email: esainfo@epsilonsigmaalpha.org
Web: www.epsilonsigmaalpha.org/esa–foundation/scholarships
Summary: To provide financial assistance for college to students from designated states whose grades are in the "C" range.
Eligibility: Open to residents of Illinois, Indiana, Iowa, Michigan, Minnesota, Missouri, Nebraska, Ohio, South Dakota, or Wisconsin. Applicants may be 1) graduating high school seniors with a GPA of 2.5 to 3.0; 2) enrolled in college with a GPA of 2.5 to 3.0; 3) enrolled at a technical school or returning to school after an absence for retraining of job skills or obtaining a degree; or 4) engaged in online study through an accredited college, university, or vocational school. They may be attending or planning to attend a school in any state and major in any field. Selection is based on character (10%), leadership (10%), service (35%), financial need (35%), and scholastic ability (10%).
Financial data: The stipend is $2,000.
Duration: 1 year; may be renewed.
Number awarded: 2 each year.
Deadline: January of each year.

751 $$ PATRICK KERR SKATEBOARDING SCHOLARSHIP

Patrick Kerr Skateboarding Scholarship Fund
P.O. Box 2054
Jenkintown, PA 19046
Phone: (215) 663–9329; Fax: (215) 663–5897;
Email: info@skateboardscholarship.org
Web: skateboard.about.com/od/money/a/PatKerScholarsh.htm
Summary: To provide financial assistance for college to high school seniors who are skateboarders.
Eligibility: Open to graduating high school seniors who are skateboarders planning to enroll full time at an accredited 2–year or 4–year college or university. Applicants must have a GPA of 2.5 or higher and be able to demonstrate financial need. Along with their application, they must submit a 300–word essay on how skateboarding has been a positive influence in their life. Special consideration is given to applicants who have been actively promoting skateboarding in their community, but skateboarding skill is not considered in the selection process. U.S. citizenship is required.
Financial data: Stipends are $5,000 or $1,000.
Duration: 1 year.
Number awarded: 4 each year: 1 at $5,000 and 3 at $1,000.
Deadline: April of each year.

752 $ PATSY TAKEMOTO MINK EDUCATION FOUNDATION EDUCATION SUPPORT AWARD

Patsy Takemoto Mink Education Foundation for Low–Income Women and Children
P.O. Box 479
Honolulu, HI 96809
Email: admin@ptmfoundation.net
Web: www.patsyminkfoundation.org/edsupport.html
Summary: To provide financial assistance for college or graduate school to low–income mothers.
Eligibility: Open to women who are at least 17 years of age and are from a low–income family (less than $17,500 annually for a family of 2, $22,000 for a family of 3, or $26,500 for a family of 4). Applicants must be mothers with minor children. They must be 1) enrolled in a skills training, ESL, or GED program; or 2) working on an associate, bachelor's, master's, professional, or doctoral degree. Along with their application, they must submit brief essays on what this award will help them accomplish, the program in which they are or will be enrolled, how they decided on that educational pursuit, their educational goals, their educational experience, and their personal and educational history.
Financial data: The stipend is $2,000.
Duration: 1 year.
Number awarded: 5 each year.
Deadline: July of each year.

753 PATTY AND MELVIN ALPERIN FIRST GENERATION SCHOLARSHIP

Rhode Island Foundation
Attn: Funds Administrator
One Union Station
Providence, RI 02903
Phone: (401) 427–4017; Fax: (401) 331–8085;
Email: lmonahan@rifoundation.org
Web: www.rifoundation.org
Summary: To provide financial assistance to high school seniors in Rhode Island whose parents did not attend college and who plan to attend college in any state.
Eligibility: Open to seniors graduating from high schools in Rhode Island whose parents did not have the benefit of attending college. Applicants must be planning to enroll at an accredited 2– or 4–year college or university in any state. Along with their application, they must submit an essay (up to 300 words) on what it means to them to be of the first generation in their family to work on a college degree. Selection is based on academic excellence, character, and financial need.
Financial data: The stipend ranges up to $1,000.

Duration: 1 year; may be renewed for up to 3 additional years if the recipient maintains good academic standing.
Number awarded: Varies each year.
Deadline: April of each year.

754 $$ PAUL F. RONCI MEMORIAL SCHOLARSHIPS

Paul F. Ronci Memorial Trust
c/o Mary Lou Fonseca
P.O. Box 515
Harmony, RI 02829–0515
Phone: (401) 349–4400
Web: www.paulfroncischolarship.org
Summary: To provide financial assistance to undergraduate and graduate students from Rhode Island.
Eligibility: Open to full–time undergraduate and graduate students who have been residents of Rhode Island for at least 10 of the last 12 years. Applicants must rank in the top 10% of their class. Along with their application, they must submit documentation of financial need and an essay on their goals, ambitions, and desires, with specific reference to what they intend to accomplish for the good of humanity.
Financial data: Stipends range from $500 up to full payment of tuition.
Duration: 1 year; recipients may reapply.
Number awarded: 1 each year.
Deadline: March of each year.

755 $ PAUL H. D'AMOUR FOUNDER'S FELLOWSHIPS

Big Y Foods, Inc.
Attn: Scholarship Committee
2145 Roosevelt Avenue
P.O. Box 7840
Springfield, MA 01102–7840
Phone: (413) 504–4080
Web: www.bigy.com/education/y_scholarships.php
Summary: To provide financial assistance to outstanding undergraduate and graduate students in the Big Y Foods market area in Massachusetts and Connecticut.
Eligibility: Open to high school seniors, undergraduates, graduate students, and nontraditional students of any age who reside within western or central Massachusetts, Norfolk County in Massachusetts, or the state of Connecticut. Big Y employees and their dependents are also eligible. Applicants must submit a transcript, standardized test scores (SAT, ACT, GRE, GMAT, or LSAT), 2 letters of recommendation, and a resume. Selection is based on academic merit and achievement.
Financial data: The stipend is $2,000.
Duration: 1 year; nonrenewable.
Number awarded: 7 each year.
Deadline: January of each year.

756 $$ PAUL TSONGAS SCHOLARSHIP PROGRAM

Massachusetts Office of Student Financial Assistance
454 Broadway, Suite 200
Revere, MA 02151
Phone: (617) 391–6070; Fax: (617) 727–0667;
Email: osfa@osfa.mass.edu
Web: www.osfa.mass.edu/default.asp?page=tsongasScholarship
Summary: To provide financial assistance to Massachusetts students who attend 1 of the state colleges in Massachusetts.
Eligibility: Open to residents of Massachusetts who have graduated from high school within 5 years and are attending or planning to attend a state college in Massachusetts. Applicants must be U.S. citizens or permanent residents and have a GPA of 3.75 or higher and a highly competitive SAT or ACT score.
Financial data: Eligible students receive a waiver of tuition and mandatory fees.
Duration: Up to 4 academic years, if the recipient maintains a GPA of 3.3 or higher in college.
Number awarded: 45 each year: 5 at each state college in Massachusetts.
Deadline: April of each year.

757 $$ PEARSON PRIZE FOR HIGHER EDUCATION

Pearson Foundation
1330 Avenue of the Americas, Ninth Floor
New York, NY 10019
Phone: (800) 745–8489;
Email: info@pearsonfoundation.org
Web: www.pearsonfoundation.org/pearsonprize
Summary: To provide merit–based scholarships to students who have completed their first year of college.
Eligibility: Open to full–time students who have completed at least 1 year at an accredited 2– or 4–year college, university, or career school. Applicants must be U.S. citizens or permanent residents and have a GPA of 2.5 or higher. They must submit online essays regarding their community and volunteer service while in college; finalists submit video essays. Financial need is not considered in the selection process.
Financial data: Stipends are $5,000 or $500 per year.
Duration: 1 or 2 years.
Number awarded: 70 each year: 20 at $5,000 per year for 2 years and 50 at $500 per year for 1 year.
Deadline: March of each year.

758 $ PELLEGRINI SCHOLARSHIP FUND

Swiss Benevolent Society of New York
Attn: Scholarship Committee
500 Fifth Avenue, Room 1800
New York, NY 10110
Phone: (212) 246–0655; Fax: (212) 246–1366;
Email: scholarships@sbsny.org
Web: www.sbsny.org/sbs_scholarships.html
Summary: To provide financial assistance to undergraduate and graduate students of Swiss descent in the Northeast.
Eligibility: Open to undergraduate and graduate students who are residents of Connecticut, New Jersey, Pennsylvania, Delaware, or New York. Applicants must demonstrate a strong academic record (GPA of 3.0 or higher), aptitude in their chosen field of study, and financial need. Either the applicant or at least 1 parent must be a Swiss national.
Financial data: The stipend ranges from $500 to $4,000 per year. Funds are paid directly to the recipient's school in 2 installments (beginning of fall semester and beginning of spring semester).
Duration: 1 year; recipients may reapply.
Number awarded: Approximately 55 each year.
Deadline: March of each year.

759 PENNSYLVANIA ASSOCIATION OF MEDICAL SUPPLIERS SCHOLARSHIP

Pennsylvania Association of Medical Suppliers
777 East Park Drive, Suite 300
Harrisburg, PA 17111
Phone: (717) 909–1958; Fax: (717) 236–8767
Web: www.pamsonline.org
Summary: To provide financial assistance to high school seniors in Pennsylvania and Delaware who use home medical equipment and services to overcome a physical challenge and are interested in attending college in any state.
Eligibility: Open to seniors graduating from high school in Pennsylvania and Delaware who are planning to enroll in a postsecondary educational program in any state. Applicants must have been successful in their educational pursuits while overcoming physical challenges with the help of home medical equipment and services (e.g., wheelchairs, respiratory devices). Along with their application, they must submit a short essay that describes their experiences with home medical equipment and how it will help them work on a college degree.
Financial data: The stipend is $1,000.
Duration: 1 year.
Number awarded: 1 each year.
Deadline: March of each year.

760 $ PENNSYLVANIA BPW FOUNDATION SCHOLARSHIPS

Business and Professional Women of Pennsylvania
Attn: Pennsylvania BPW Foundation
c/o Teresa A. Miller, Vice Chair
8 West Front Street
Media, PA 19063
Phone: (610) 566–5035; Fax: (610) 566–2954;
Email: tmiller@frontrowlaw.com
Web: www.bpwpa.org
Summary: To provide financial assistance to women from Pennsylvania who are interested in attending college in any state.

Eligibility: Open to female residents of Pennsylvania who are attending or planning to attend a college or university in any state. Applicants must submit an essay that 1) discusses their specific short–term career goals and how the proposed training will help them accomplish those goals; 2) explains how those short–term goals apply to their long–range career goals; and 3) includes a summary of issues that are important to working women in today's world. In the selection process, strong emphasis is placed on financial need.
Financial data: The stipend is $2,500.
Duration: 1 year.
Number awarded: 6 each year: 3 in the fall semester and 3 in the spring semester.
Deadline: April of each year for fall semester; September of each year for spring semester.

761 $ PENNSYLVANIA CHAFEE EDUCATION AND TRAINING GRANT PROGRAM

Pennsylvania Higher Education Assistance Agency
Attn: Special Programs
1200 North Seventh Street
P.O. Box 8157
Harrisburg, PA 17105–8157
Phone: (717) 720–2800; (800) 692–7392; Fax: (717) 720–5786; TDD: (800) 654–5988;
Email: paetg@pheaa.org
Web: www.pheaa.org
Summary: To provide financial assistance to residents of Pennsylvania who have been in foster care and plan to attend college in the state.
Eligibility: Open to residents of Pennsylvania who are eligible for services under the Pennsylvania John H. Chafee Foster Care Independence Program, were adopted from foster care after their 16th birthday, or were participating in this program on their 21st birthday (until they turn 23 years of age). Applicants must be enrolled or planning to enroll in an approved college or career school in Pennsylvania on at least a half time basis.
Financial data: The maximum stipend is $2,500 per year. Awards may not exceed the actual cost of attendance, minus other financial aid the student receives.
Duration: 1 year; may be renewed if the recipient remains enrolled at least half time and makes satisfactory academic progress.
Number awarded: Varies each year.
Deadline: April of each year.

762 PENNSYLVANIA EDUCATIONAL GRATUITY FOR VETERANS' DEPENDENTS

Office of the Deputy Adjutant General for Veterans Affairs
Building S–0–47, FTIG
Annville, PA 17003–5002
Phone: (717) 865–8910; (800) 54 PA VET (within PA); Fax: (717) 861–8589;
Email: RA–VA–Info@pa.gov
Web: www.dmva.state.pa.us
Summary: To provide financial assistance for college to the children of disabled or deceased Pennsylvania veterans.
Eligibility: Open to children (between 16 and 23 years of age) of honorably–discharged veterans who are rated totally and permanently disabled as a result of wartime service or who have died of such a disability. Applicants must have lived in Pennsylvania for at least 5 years immediately preceding the date of application, be able to demonstrate financial need, and have been accepted or be currently enrolled in a Pennsylvania state or state–aided secondary or post-secondary educational institution.
Financial data: The stipend is $500 per semester ($1,000 per year). The money is paid directly to the recipient's school and is to be applied to the costs of tuition, board, room, books, supplies, and/or matriculation fees.
Duration: The allowance is paid for up to 4 academic years or for the duration of the course of study, whichever is less.
Number awarded: Varies each year.
Deadline: Deadline not specified.

763 PENNSYLVANIA GRANTS FOR CHILDREN OF SOLDIERS DECLARED POW/MIA

Pennsylvania Higher Education Assistance Agency
Attn: Special Programs
1200 North Seventh Street
P.O. Box 8157
Harrisburg, PA 17105–8157
Phone: (717) 720–2800; (800) 692–7392; Fax: (717) 720–5786; TDD: (800) 654–5988
Web: www.pheaa.org
Summary: To provide financial assistance for college to the children of POWs/MIAs from Pennsylvania.
Eligibility: Open to dependent children of members or former members of the U.S. armed services who served on active duty after January 31, 1955, who are or have been prisoners of war or are or have been listed as missing in action, and who were residents of Pennsylvania for at least 12 months preceding service on active duty. Eligible children must be enrolled in a program of at least 1 year in duration on at least a half–time basis at an approved school. Financial need is not considered in the selection process.
Financial data: The maximum grant is $1,200.
Duration: 1 year; may be renewed for 3 additional years.
Number awarded: Varies each year.
Deadline: April of each year for students at colleges, universities, and transferable programs at community colleges; July of each year for students at business schools, trade/technical schools, hospital schools of nursing, and non–transferable programs at community colleges.

764 $$ PENNSYLVANIA HOUSE OF REPRESENTATIVES SCHOLARSHIP

The Foundation for Enhancing Communities
Attn: Program Officer
200 North Third Street
P.O. Box 678
Harrisburg, PA 17108–0678
Phone: (717) 236–5040; Fax: (717) 231–4463;
Email: allison@tfec.org
Web: www.tfec.org/index.cfm?act=funds_scholarship
Summary: To provide financial assistance to high school seniors in Pennsylvania who plan to attend a college or university in the state.
Eligibility: Open to seniors graduating from high schools in Pennsylvania with a GPA of 3.0 or higher. Applicants must be planning to enroll full time at a college, university, or career school in Pennsylvania. Selection is based on academic achievement, commitment to community, demonstrated leadership qualities, extracurricular activities, a 500–word personal essay, and financial need.
Financial data: The program provides full payment of tuition at member institutions of the State System of Higher Education. Students who attend other Pennsylvania colleges and universities receive an equivalent amount (approximately $2,500 per year) paid jointly to them and their institution.
Duration: 4 years, provided the recipient maintains a GPA of 2.5 in the first year of college and 3.0 or higher in each subsequent year.
Number awarded: 2 each year.
Deadline: February of each year.

765 $$ PENNSYLVANIA POSTSECONDARY EDUCATIONAL GRATUITY PROGRAM

Pennsylvania Higher Education Assistance Agency
Attn: Special Programs
1200 North Seventh Street
P.O. Box 8157
Harrisburg, PA 17105–8157
Phone: (717) 720–2800; (800) 692–7392; Fax: (717) 720–5786; TDD: (800) 654–5988;
Email: pegp@pheaa.org
Web: www.pheaa.org
Summary: To provide financial assistance for college to the children of Pennsylvania public service personnel who died in the line of service.
Eligibility: Open to residents of Pennsylvania who are the children of 1) Pennsylvania police officers, firefighters, rescue and ambulance squad members, corrections facility employees, or National Guard members who died in the line of duty after January 1, 1976; or 2) Pennsylvania sheriffs, deputy sheriffs, National Guard members, and certain other individuals on federal or state active military duty who died after September 11, 2001 as a direct result of performing their official duties. Applicants must be 25 years of age or younger and enrolled or accepted at a Pennsylvania community college, state–owned institution, or state–related institution as a full–time student working on an associate or baccalaureate degree. They must have already applied for other scholarships, including state and federal grants and financial aid from the post-secondary institution to which they are applying.
Financial data: Grants cover tuition, fees, room, and board charged by the institution, less awarded scholarships and federal and state grants.

Duration: Up to 5 years.
Number awarded: Varies each year.
Deadline: March of each year.

766 $ PENNSYLVANIA STATE GRANTS

Pennsylvania Higher Education Assistance Agency
Attn: State Grants
1200 North Seventh Street
P.O. Box 8157
Harrisburg, PA 17105–8157
Phone: (717) 720–2800; (800) 692–7392; Fax: (717) 720–5786; TDD: (800) 654–5988;
Email: info@pheaa.org
Web: www.pheaa.org

Summary: To provide financial assistance to high school seniors in Pennsylvania who have financial need and are interested in attending college in Pennsylvania or most other states.

Eligibility: Open to seniors graduating from high schools in Pennsylvania who plan to attend a postsecondary school in Pennsylvania on at least a half–time basis. Applicants may also attend accredited colleges in other states, except those states that border Pennsylvania and do not allow their grant recipients to attend Pennsylvania schools (i.e., Maryland, New Jersey, and New York). They must be able to demonstrate financial need.

Financial data: Grants depend on financial need and the type of school attended. Recently, annual grants at Pennsylvania institutions ranged from $1,400 to $4,348 at 4–year private schools, from $1,100 to $3,700 at state system schools, from $1,600 to $3,950 at state–related schools, from $1,000 to $3,978 at junior colleges, from $450 to $1,400 at community colleges, from $1,200 to $3,700 at nursing schools, and from $950 to $3,800 at business, trade, and technical schools. For students at out–of–state institutions, the maximum grant was $400, or $600 if enrolled in a state that permits their students to carry their state grants to Pennsylvania, or $800 for veterans.

Duration: 1 year; may be renewed for 3 additional years.

Number awarded: Varies each year.

Deadline: April of each year for renewal applicants, new applicants who plan to enroll in a baccalaureate degree program, and students in college transfer programs at 2–year public or junior colleges; July of each year for first–time applicants for business, trade, or technical schools, hospital schools of nursing, or 2–year terminal programs at community, junior, or 4–year colleges.

767 $ P.E.O. PROGRAM FOR CONTINUING EDUCATION

P.E.O. Sisterhood
Attn: Executive Office
3700 Grand Avenue
Des Moines, IA 50312–2899
Phone: (515) 255–3153; Fax: (515) 255–3820
Web: www.peointernational.org/peo–projectsphilanthropies

Summary: To provide financial assistance to women interested in resuming or continuing their academic or technical education.

Eligibility: Open to mature women who are citizens of the United States or Canada and have experienced an interruption in their education that has lasted at least 24 consecutive months during their adult life. Applicants are frequently single parents who must acquire marketable skills to support their families. They must be within 2 years of completing an academic or technical course of study. Applicants must be sponsored by a local P.E.O. chapter. Students enrolled in a doctoral degree program are not eligible.

Financial data: The maximum stipend is $3,000.

Duration: 1 year; nonrenewable.

Number awarded: Varies each year; for a recent biennium, 3,242 of these awards, with a total value of nearly $4.3 million, were granted.

Deadline: Applications may be submitted at any time.

768 $ P.E.O. STAR SCHOLARSHIPS

P.E.O. Sisterhood
Attn: Scholar Awards Office
3700 Grand Avenue
Des Moines, IA 50312–2899
Phone: (515) 255–3153; Fax: (515) 255–3820;
Email: psa@peodsm.org
Web: www.peointernational.org/peo–projectsphilanthropies

Summary: To provide financial assistance for college to female high school seniors in the United States or Canada.

Eligibility: Open to women who are graduating from high schools in the United States or Canada and planning to enroll full or part time at an accredited postsecondary educational institution. Applicants must have an unweighted GPA of 3.0 or higher. They must be sponsored by a local P.E.O. chapter. Selection is based on leadership, extracurricular activities, community service, and potential for success; financial need is not considered. U.S. or Canadian citizenship or permanent resident status is required.

Financial data: The stipend is $2,500.

Duration: 1 year; nonrenewable.

Number awarded: Varies each year.

Deadline: November of each year.

769 $ PEOPLE'S UNITED BANK SCHOLARSHIP

Vermont Student Assistance Corporation
Attn: Scholarship Programs
10 East Allen Street
P.O. Box 2000
Winooski, VT 05404–2601
Phone: (802) 654–3798; (888) 253–4819; Fax: (802) 654–3765; TDD: (800) 281–3341 (within VT);
Email: info@vsac.org
Web: services.vsac.org/wps/wcm/connect/VSAC/vsac/pay+for+college

Summary: To provide financial assistance to high school seniors in Vermont who plan to attend college in the state.

Eligibility: Open to seniors graduating from high schools in Vermont who are planning to attend an accredited 2– or 4–year college or university in the state. Applicants must have a GPA of 3.5 or higher and a record of school and community involvement. Along with their application, they must submit 1) a 100–word essay on the school, church, and community activities in which they have participated; 2) a 250–word essay on their short– and long–term academic, educational, career, vocational, and/or employment goals; and 3) a 250–word essay on what they believe distinguishes their application from others that may be submitted. Selection is based on those essays, academic achievement, letters of recommendation, and financial need.

Financial data: The stipend is $2,500 per year.

Duration: 1 year; may be renewed up to 3 additional years.

Number awarded: 2 each year.

Deadline: March of each year.

770 $ PETER CONNACHER MEMORIAL SCHOLARSHIPS

Oregon Student Access Commission
Attn: Grants and Scholarships Division
1500 Valley River Drive, Suite 100
Eugene, OR 97401–2146
Phone: (541) 687–7395; (800) 452–8807, ext. 7395; Fax: (541) 687–7414; TDD: (800) 735–2900;
Email: awardinfo@osac.state.or.us
Web: www.oregonstudentaid.gov/scholarships.aspx

Summary: To provide financial assistance for college or graduate school to ex–prisoners of war and their descendants.

Eligibility: Open to U.S. citizens who 1) were military or civilian prisoners of war; or 2) are the descendants of ex–prisoners of war. They must be full–time undergraduate or graduate students. A copy of the ex–prisoner of war's discharge papers from the U.S. armed forces must accompany the application. In addition, written proof of POW status must be submitted, along with a statement of the relationship between the applicant and the ex–prisoner of war (father, grandfather, etc.). Selection is based on academic record and financial need. Preference is given to Oregon residents or their dependents.

Financial data: Stipends for scholarships offered by the Oregon Student Access Commission (OSAC) range from $200 to $10,000 but recently averaged $2,300.

Duration: 1 year; may be renewed for up to 3 additional years for undergraduate students or 2 additional years for graduate students. Renewal is dependent on evidence of continued financial need and satisfactory academic progress.

Number awarded: Varies each year; recently, 4 of these scholarships were awarded.

Deadline: February of each year.

771 $ PETER CROSSLEY MEMORIAL SCHOLARSHIP

Oregon Student Access Commission
Attn: Grants and Scholarships Division
1500 Valley River Drive, Suite 100
Eugene, OR 97401–2146

Phone: (541) 687–7395; (800) 452–8807, ext. 7395; Fax: (541) 687–7414; TDD: (800) 735–2900;
Email: awardinfo@osac.state.or.us
Web: www.oregonstudentaid.gov/scholarships.aspx
Summary: To provide financial assistance to seniors graduating from public alternative high schools in Oregon and planning to attend college in any state.
Eligibility: Open to seniors graduating from public alternative high schools in Oregon. Applicants must be planning to enroll at least half time at a college or university in any state. They must be able to demonstrate financial need. Along with their application, they must submit an essay on why they chose an alternative school and what that experience has done for them.
Financial data: Stipends for scholarships offered by the Oregon Student Access Commission (OSAC) range from $200 to $10,000 but recently averaged $2,300.
Duration: 1 year; may be renewed if the recipient makes normal progress.
Number awarded: 1 or more each year.
Deadline: February of each year.

772 $ PGE FOUNDATION SCHOLARSHIP AWARD FOR INDEPENDENT COLLEGES

Oregon Independent College Foundation
c/o Marylhurst University
17600 Pacific Highway
Davignon Hall
P.O. Box 23
Marylhurst, OR 97036–0023
Phone: (503) 496–3422; Fax: (503) 496–0292;
Email: oicf@oicf.org
Web: www.oicf.org
Summary: To provide financial assistance to high school seniors planning to study at an independent college in Oregon.
Eligibility: Open to Oregon high school seniors who plan to enroll full time as first–year students at a college or university that is a member of the Oregon Independent College Foundation (OICF). Selection is based on academic record in high school, achievements in school or community activities, and a written statement, up to 500 words, on the meaning of good citizenship and how the fulfillment of their personal goals will help applicants live up to that definition.
Financial data: The stipend is $2,500 per year.
Duration: 4 years for entering freshmen.
Number awarded: 20 each year: 2 at each of the participating institutions.
Deadline: March of each year.

773 PHI THETA KAPPA/COCA–COLA COMMUNITY COLLEGE ACADEMIC TEAM

Phi Theta Kappa
Attn: Scholarship Programs Department
1625 Eastover Drive
Jackson, MS 39211
Phone: (601) 987–5741; (800) 946–9995; Fax: (601) 984–3550;
Email: scholarship.programs@ptk.org
Web: www.ptkfoundation.org/become–a–member/scholarships/academic–teams
Summary: To recognize and reward the outstanding achievements of community college students.
Eligibility: Open to students who have completed at least 36 hours at a community college in the United States (including 30 hours completed within the past 5 years) and are on track to earn an associate or bachelor's degree. Candidates must be nominated by a designated official at their college. Nominees must have a cumulative GPA of at least 3.5 for all college course work completed in the last 5 years, regardless of institution attended. They must submit a 2–page essay describing their most significant endeavor since attending community college in which they applied their academic or intellectual skills from their community college education to benefit their school, community, or society. Selection is based on information in the essay; awards, honors, and recognition for academic achievement; academic rigor and GPA; participation in honors programs; and service to the college and the community.
Financial data: Gold Awards are $1,500, Silver Awards are $1,250, and Bronze Awards are $1,000.
Duration: The competition is held annually.
Number awarded: 150 each year: 50 Gold Awards (1 from each state), 50 Silver Awards (1 from each state), and 50 Bronze Awards (1 from each state).
Deadline: November of each year.

774 PHILIP HROBAK SCHOLARSHIP

First Catholic Slovak Union of the United States and Canada
Jednota Benevolent Foundation, Inc.
Attn: Scholarship Program
6611 Rockside Road, Suite 300
Independence, OH 44131
Phone: (216) 642–9406; (800) JEDNOTA; Fax: (216) 642–4310;
Email: FCSU@aol.com
Web: www.fcsu.com/scholarships
Summary: To provide financial assistance for college to male high school seniors who are of Slovak descent and the Catholic faith.
Eligibility: Open to men graduating from high schools in the United States and Canada and planning to attend an approved institution of higher education. Applicants must be of Slovak descent and the Catholic faith. They must have had at least $5,000 of reserve insurance with the sponsoring organization for at least 4 years. Along with their application, they must submit 1) a transcript of grades that includes ACT or SAT scores; 2) a list of volunteer community activities in which they have participated; 3) a list of awards received for academic excellence and leadership ability; 4) a description of their career objectives; 5) an essay on why they think they should receive this scholarship; and 6) information on their financial need.
Financial data: The stipend is $1,000. The winner also receives a $3,000 single premium life insurance policy upon proof of graduation from college.
Duration: 1 year; nonrenewable.
Number awarded: 1 each year.
Deadline: March of each year.

775 PHYLLIS G. MEEKINS SCHOLARSHIP

Ladies Professional Golf Association
Attn: LPGA Foundation
100 International Golf Drive
Daytona Beach, FL 32124–1082
Phone: (386) 274–6200; Fax: (386) 274–1099;
Email: foundation.scholarships@lpga.com
Web: www.lpgafoundation.org/Scholarships/scholarshipgeneral.aspx
Summary: To provide financial assistance to minority female graduating high school seniors who played golf in high school and plan to continue to play in college.
Eligibility: Open to female high school seniors who are members of a recognized minority group. Applicants must have a GPA of 3.0 or higher and a background in golf. They must be planning to enroll full time at a college or university in the United States and play competitive golf. Along with their application, they must submit a letter that describes how golf has been an integral part of their lives and includes their personal, academic, and professional goals; their chosen discipline of study; and how this scholarship will be of assistance. Financial need is considered in the selection process. U.S. citizenship or legal resident status is required.
Financial data: The stipend is $1,250.
Duration: 1 year.
Number awarded: 1 each year.
Deadline: May of each year.

776 PINKROSE BREAST CANCER SCHOLARSHIP

PinkRose Foundation, Inc.
P.O. Box 4025
Dedham, MA 02027
Email: info@pinkrose.org
Web: www.pinkrose.org/scholarship.htm
Summary: To provide financial assistance for college to high school graduates who have lost a parent to breast cancer.
Eligibility: Open to legal residents of the United States who are younger than 25 years of age and have lost a parent or legal guardian to breast cancer. Applicants must have a high school diploma or equivalent and be planning to enroll in a postsecondary education or certificate training program. Along with their application, they must submit a 2–page statement that includes 1) autobiographical information describing the significant impact of breast cancer on their life and how it altered their academic motivation and interests, professional and volunteer experience, and career objectives; and 2) their interest in this scholarship, especially how obtaining a postsecondary degree or certificate will benefit their future by helping to fulfill their goals and dreams. Financial need is not considered in the selection process.
Financial data: The stipend is $1,000.

Duration: 1 year.
Number awarded: Varies each year.
Deadline: August of each year.

777 $ PIRATE CHARTER CHAPTER ABWA OUTRIGHT GRANT

American Business Women's Association–Pirate Charter Chapter
Attn: Nicole Betschman, Secretary
P.O. Box 20498
Greenville, NC 27858
Email: secretary@pirateabwa.org
Web: pirateabwa.org/scholarship.html

Summary: To provide financial assistance to female residents of North Carolina working on an undergraduate or graduate degree at a school in any state.
Eligibility: Open to women who are residents of North Carolina and U.S. citizens. Applicants must be graduating high school seniors, undergraduates, or graduate students at an accredited college, university, community college, or licensed technical or vocational school in any state. They must have a GPA of 2.5 or higher. Along with their application, they must submit a 2–page biographical sketch that includes information about their background, school activities, outside interests, honors and awards, work experience, community service, and long–term goals. Financial need is not considered in the selection process.
Financial data: The stipend is $2,000.
Duration: 1 year.
Number awarded: 1 each year.
Deadline: October of each year.

778 PNC/KHSAA SWEET 16 SCHOLARSHIPS

Kentucky High School Athletic Association
Attn: Assistant Commissioner
2280 Executive Drive
Lexington, KY 40505
Phone: (859) 299–5472; Fax: (859) 293–5999;
Email: bcope@khsaa.org
Web: www.khsaa.org

Summary: To provide financial assistance to student–athletes in Kentucky high schools who plan to attend college in the state.
Eligibility: Open to high school seniors in Kentucky who have participated in athletics or cheerleading and plan to attend college in the state. The awards are presented in conjunction with the state basketball tournament, but all student–athletes, not just basketball players, are eligible. Students must be nominated by a school representative. Letters of nomination must explain why the student is an exemplary leader and should receive the scholarship. Selection is based on academic achievement, leadership at school, and community service. Men and women are judged separately.
Financial data: The stipend is $1,000.
Duration: 1 year; nonrenewable.
Number awarded: 32 each year: 1 female and 1 male in each of 16 regions in Kentucky.
Deadline: February of each year.

779 $$ POINT FOUNDATION SCHOLARSHIPS

Point Foundation
5757 Wilshire Boulevard, Suite 370
Los Angeles, CA 90036
Phone: (323) 933–1234; (866) 33–POINT; Fax: (866) 39–POINT;
Email: info@pointfoundation.org
Web: www.thepointfoundation.org/scholarships.html

Summary: To provide financial assistance for college or graduate school to students who have been marginalized because of their sexual orientation.
Eligibility: Open to citizens of any country who are attending or planning to attend a college or university in the United States to work on an undergraduate or graduate degree. Applicants must be able to demonstrate that they have been marginalized because of their sexual orientation, gender expression, or gender identity. Along with their application, they must submit 250–word essays on 1) either what they are most looking forward to gaining from their college experience or why they chose their intended graduate course of study and how they hope to make a difference in their field; 2) specific instances in which they were successful in bringing about positive change and what they learned from those experiences; 3) their experience with marginalization; and 4) any additional information. Selection is based on academic achievement, personal merit, leadership, involvement in the LGBTQ community, professional experiences, personal and future goals, and financial need.
Financial data: Stipends recently averaged $22,360.
Duration: 1 year; may be renewed if the recipient maintains a GPA of 3.3 or higher.
Number awarded: Varies each year; recently, 25 of these named and corporate scholarships were awarded.
Deadline: February of each year.

780 POLANKI COLLEGE ACHIEVEMENT AWARDS

Polanki, The Polish Women's Cultural Club of Milwaukee
Attn: College Achievement Awards
P.O. Box 341458
Milwaukee, WI 53234
Phone: (414) 858–9357;
Email: polanki@polanki.org
Web: www.polanki.org/scholar–main.html

Summary: To recognize and reward upper–division and graduate students in Wisconsin who have a Polish connection and demonstrate academic excellence.
Eligibility: Open to college juniors, seniors, and graduate students who are Wisconsin residents or attending college in the state. Applicants must be 1) of Polish heritage; 2) non–Polish students of Polish language, history, society, or culture; or 3) significantly engaged with Polish culture. They must have a GPA of 3.0 or higher. Along with their application, they must submit 1) an essay of 500 to 600 words on a topic that changes annually but relates to Poland; and 2) a paragraph of 100 to 150 words on their personal, academic, and professional plans for the future. U.S. citizenship or permanent residence is required.
Financial data: Awards range from $750 to $1,500.
Duration: The awards are presented annually.
Number awarded: Varies each year; recently, 11 of these awards were presented. Additionally, an award was presented jointly with Marquette University and 3 with the University of Wisconsin at Milwaukee.
Deadline: January of each year.

781 POLISH HERITAGE ASSOCIATION OF MARYLAND SCHOLARSHIP GRANTS

Polish Heritage Association of Maryland, Inc.
c/o Victoria T. Leshinskie
1101 St. Paul Street, Apartment 1202
Baltimore, MD 21202
Phone: (410) 962–8611;
Email: vleshinskie@anes.umm.edu
Web: www.pha–md.org/main.php?page=scholarships

Summary: To provide financial assistance to residents of Maryland who are of Polish descent and interested in attending college in any state.
Eligibility: Open to residents of Maryland who are of Polish descent (i.e., have at least 2 Polish ancestors). Applicants must be graduating high school seniors or students currently enrolled full time at a college or university in any state. Selection is based primarily on financial need; other factors considered are academic standing, leadership potential, and the students' pride in their Polish heritage.
Financial data: The stipend is $1,500.
Duration: 1 year.
Number awarded: 10 each year.
Deadline: March of each year.

782 POLISH ROMAN CATHOLIC UNION OF AMERICA EDUCATION FUND SCHOLARSHIPS

Polish Roman Catholic Union of America
Attn: Education Fund Scholarship Program
984 North Milwaukee Avenue
Chicago, IL 60622–4101
Phone: (773) 782–2600; (800) 772–8632; Fax: (773) 278–4595;
Email: info@prcua.org
Web: www.prcua.org/benefits/educationfundscholarship.htm

Summary: To provide financial assistance to undergraduate and graduate students of Polish heritage.
Eligibility: Open to students enrolled full time as sophomores, juniors, and seniors in an undergraduate program or full or part time as a graduate or professional school students. Along with their application, they must submit brief statements on 1) the Polonian organization(s) that benefited from their membership and how; 2) the organized volunteer community or other group(s) that benefited from their membership or service and how; and 3) their career goals.

Selection is based on academic achievement, Polonia involvement, and community service.
Financial data: A stipend is awarded (amount not specified). Funds are paid directly to the institution.
Duration: 1 year.
Number awarded: 1 or more each year.
Deadline: June of each year.

783 PONY BASEBALL AND SOFTBALL ALUMNI SCHOLARSHIPS

PONY Baseball and Softball
Attn: Scholarship Committee
1951 Pony Place
P.O. Box 225
Washington, PA 15301
Phone: (724) 225–1060; Fax: (724) 225–9852;
Email: info@pony.org
Web: www.pony.org
Summary: To provide financial assistance for college to high school seniors who have played PONY League baseball or softball.
Eligibility: Open to high school seniors who have played on a PONY affiliated Pony, Colt, or Palomino team for at least 2 years. Applicants must be planning to attend a college or university. Along with their application, they must submit a 100–word essay on the value that PONY, an acronym for Protect Our Nation's Youth, has had on their personal growth and development. Selection is based on that essay, a transcript, and participation in school, community, and PONY activities.
Financial data: The stipend is $1,500.
Duration: 1 year.
Number awarded: 8 each year: 4 in each of the 4 U.S. PONY zones plus 1 each in the Asia Pacific Zone, the Caribbean Zone, Canada, and Mexico.
Deadline: April of each year.

784 PORTUGUESE AMERICAN CITIZENS COMMITTEE OF RHODE ISLAND SCHOLARSHIPS

Portuguese American Citizens Committee of Rhode Island
Attn: Scholarship Co–Chair
P.O. Box 9175
Pawtucket, RI 02862
Phone: (401) 309–9816
Web: www.paccri.com/about.htm
Summary: To provide financial assistance to high school seniors in Rhode Island who are of Portuguese descent and interested in attending college in any state to major in any field.
Eligibility: Open to seniors graduating from high schools in Rhode Island who have at least 1 parent of 100% Portuguese ethnicity. Applicants must be planning to enroll at a college or university in any state. Along with their application, they must submit transcripts that include SAT scores, documentation of financial need, a letter describing how their Portuguese heritage has influenced them and how they plan to use their higher education to better the Portuguese community, a statement of their reasons for applying for this scholarship and furthering their education, and information on their extracurricular activities and work experience.
Financial data: The stipend is $1,000.
Duration: 1 year; nonrenewable.
Number awarded: Several each year.
Deadline: March of each year.

785 PORTUGUESE FOUNDATION SCHOLARSHIPS

Portuguese Foundation of Connecticut
690 Flatbush Avenue
P.O. Box 331441
West Hartford, CT 06133–1441
Phone: (860) 236–9350;
Email: info@pfict.org
Web: www.pfict.org/scholarship–program.html
Summary: To provide financial assistance to students of Portuguese ancestry in Connecticut who are interested in attending college or graduate school in any state.
Eligibility: Open to residents of Connecticut who are U.S. citizens or permanent residents of Portuguese ancestry. Applicants must be attending, or planning to attend, a 4–year college or university in any state as a full–time undergraduate or full– or part–time graduate student. Along with their application, they must submit an essay describing financial need; an essay detailing proof of Portuguese ancestry, interest in the Portuguese language and culture, and plans for contributing to the Portuguese–American community after completion of their studies; 2 letters of recommendation; their high school or college transcripts; a copy of the FAFSA form or their most recent federal income tax return; and their SAT report. Selection is based on financial need and academic record.
Financial data: Stipends are at least $1,250 per year.
Duration: 1 year; may be renewed up to 3 additional years.
Number awarded: 4 each year.
Deadline: March of each year.

786 $$ PORTUGUESE–AMERICAN SCHOLARSHIP FOUNDATION OF NEW JERSEY SCHOLARSHIPS

Portuguese–American Scholarship Foundation of New Jersey
Attn: Scholarship Review Board
P.O. Box 3848
Union, NJ 07083
Email: pasf@vivaportugal.com
Web: www.vivaportugal.com
Summary: To provide financial assistance for college to New Jersey residents of Portuguese ancestry.
Eligibility: Open to New Jersey high school seniors who are Portuguese born or whose parent or grandparent was Portuguese born (proof may be required). Applicants must be U.S. citizens or permanent residents (Alien Registration Card may be required) and have been continuous residents of New Jersey for the 12–month period immediately preceding receipt of the award. They must have at least a 3.0 GPA and be applying for admission to a 4–year college or university in any state. Financial need must be demonstrated.
Financial data: The stipend is $8,000.
Duration: 1 year; may be renewed for up to 3 additional years.
Number awarded: 8 each year.
Deadline: February of each year.

787 $$ POST–9/11 GI BILL

Department of Veterans Affairs
Attn: Veterans Benefits Administration
810 Vermont Avenue, N.W.
Washington, DC 20420
Phone: (202) 418–4343; (888) GI–BILL1
Web: www.gibill.va.gov/benefits/post_911_gibill/index.html
Summary: To provide financial assistance to veterans or military personnel who entered service on or after September 11, 2001.
Eligibility: Open to current and former military personnel who 1) served on active duty for at least 90 aggregate days after September 11, 2001; or 2) were discharged with a service–connected disability after 30 days. Applicants must be planning to enroll in an educational program, including work on an undergraduate or graduate degree, vocational/technical training, on–the–job training, flight training, correspondence training, licensing and national testing programs, entrepreneurship training, and tutorial assistance.
Financial data: Participants working on an undergraduate or graduate degree at public institutions in their state receive full payment of tuition and fees. For participants who attend private institutions in most states, tuition and fee reimbursement is capped at $17,500 per academic year; the reimbursement rate is higher at private schools in Arizona, Michigan, New Hampshire, New York, Pennsylvania, South Carolina, and Texas. Benefits for other types of training programs depend on the amount for which the veteran qualified under prior educational programs. Veterans also receive a monthly housing allowance based on the national average Basic Allowance for Housing (BAH) for an E–5 with dependents (currently $673.50) or $1,347 per month at schools in foreign countries); an annual book allowance of $1,000; and (for participants who live in a rural county remote from an educational institution) a rural benefit payment of $500 per year.
Duration: Most participants receive up to 36 months of entitlement under this program. Benefits are payable for up to 15 years following release from active duty.
Number awarded: Varies each year; since the program began, it has awarded nearly $4 billion in benefits to more than 295,000 veterans.
Deadline: Deadline not specified.

788 PRESIDENTIAL CHOICE SCHOLARSHIP AWARD

PUSH Excel
Attn: General Offices
930 East 50th Street

Chicago, IL 60615
Phone: (773) 373–3366;
Email: pushexcel@rainbowpush.org
Web: www.pushexcel.org/?page_id=540
Summary: To provide financial assistance for college to high school seniors who have demonstrated a commitment to social justice and are willing to help promote the scholarship program of PUSH–Excel.
Eligibility: Open to seniors graduating from high school and planning to enroll at an accredited 4–year college or university. Applicants must be U.S. citizens and have a GPA of 3.0 or higher. They must have demonstrated 1) a commitment to addressing and advocating for social justice issues; and 2) an understanding and practice of the gift of service. Along with their application, they must submit a 500–word essay that identifies 5 prerequisites for success, explains their personal philosophy for the pursuit of excellence, and explains how they will use their college education to achieve this pursuit of excellence. They must also agree to cooperate with the scholarship committee of PUSH–Excel by promoting its program, participating in its public relations activities, and attending its Annual National Conference luncheon and Education Leadership Conference. Selection is based on the essay, academic preparation to attend college and succeed, ability to overcome obstacles to achieve academic and personal goals, character, persistence and dedication to service, and financial need.
Financial data: The stipend is $1,000 per year.
Duration: 1 year; may be renewed up to 3 additional years if the recipient maintains a GPA of 3.0 or higher and fulfills the obligations to PUSH–Excel.
Number awarded: Varies each year.
Deadline: June of each year.

789 PRISCILLA R. MORTON SCHOLARSHIPS

United Methodist Higher Education Foundation
Attn: Scholarships Administrator
60 Music Square East, Suite 350
P.O. Box 340005
Nashville, TN 37203–0005
Phone: (615) 649–3990; (800) 811–8110; Fax: (615) 649–3980;
Email: umhefscholarships@umhef.org
Web: www.umhef.org/scholarship–info
Summary: To provide financial assistance to members of the United Methodist Church who are interested in working on an undergraduate, graduate, or professional degree.
Eligibility: Open to undergraduate, graduate, and professional students who have been active, full members of a United Methodist Church for at least 1 year prior to applying. Applicants must have a GPA of 3.5 or higher and be able to demonstrate financial need. Along with their application, they must submit a 200–word essay on their involvement and/or leadership responsibilities in their church, school, and community within the last 3 years. U.S. citizenship or permanent resident status is required. Preference is given to students enrolled or planning to enroll full time at a United Methodist–related college, university, seminary, or theological school.
Financial data: The stipend is at least $1,000 per year.
Duration: 1 year; recipients may reapply.
Number awarded: Varies each year; recently, 14 of these scholarships were awarded.
Deadline: February of each year.

790 PROFESSOR CHEN WEN–CHEN SCHOLARSHIPS

Professor Chen Wen–Chen Memorial Foundation
Attn: Scholarship Committee
P.O. Box 136
Kingston, NJ 08528
Phone: (609) 936–1352;
Email: cwcmfusa@gmail.com
Web: cwcmf.net
Summary: To provide financial assistance to students at North American colleges and universities who have been involved in the Taiwanese community.
Eligibility: Open to students who have participated in Taiwanese social–political movements or have made significant contributions to the Taiwanese community in North America. Applicants must be currently enrolled at a college or university in North America. Selection is based on character, academic ability, financial need, and participation in Taiwanese American community affairs.
Financial data: The stipend ranges from $1,000 to $1,500.
Duration: 1 year.
Number awarded: 4 to 6 each year.
Deadline: July of each year.

791 $$ PROFESSOR ULLA HEDNER SCHOLARSHIPS

Novo Nordisk Inc.
Attn: Customer Care
100 College Road West
Princeton, NJ 08540
Phone: (609) 987–5800; (877) NOVO–777; Fax: (800) 826–6993
Web: www.changingpossibilities–us.com/SupportPrograms/Education.aspx
Summary: To provide financial assistance to high school seniors and current college students who have a bleeding disorder.
Eligibility: Open to high school seniors and students under 23 years of age currently enrolled in college or vocational school. Applicants must have hemophilia with an inhibitor or factor VII deficiency. Along with their application, they must submit a 500–word essay on how changes in the health care landscape will affect their life with a bleeding disorder.
Financial data: Stipends range from $2,000 to $7,000 per year.
Duration: 1 year; recipients may reapply.
Number awarded: Varies each year.
Deadline: May of each year.

792 $$ PRUDENTIAL SPIRIT OF COMMUNITY AWARDS

National Association of Secondary School Principals
Attn: Department of Student Programs
1904 Association Drive
Reston, VA 20191–1537
Phone: (703) 860–7242; (877) 525–8491; Fax: (703) 476–5432;
Email: spirit@principals.org
Web: www.principals.org/Awards–and–Recognition/Student–Awards
Summary: To recognize and reward middle level and high school students who demonstrate exemplary community service.
Eligibility: Open to students in grades 5–12 at public and private schools in the United States. Students must submit 500–word essays on 1) what motivated them to do their volunteer work; 2) the effort required to do their volunteer work; 3) what their volunteer activity accomplished; and 4) what they got out of their volunteer work. Each school may select 1 honoree for every 1,000 students. At the local level, honorees are chosen on the basis of their individual community service activity or significant leadership in a group activity that has taken place during the previous year. Local honorees are then certified by their school principal, Girl Scout council executive director, county 4–H agent, American Red Cross chapter official, YMCA representative, or HandsOn Network of the Points of Light Institute to compete at the state level. As a result of that judging, 1 high school and 1 middle level student in each state and the District of Columbia are named state honorees. The state honorees then compete for national awards.
Financial data: Each state honoree receives $1,000, a silver medallion, and an all–expense paid trip to Washington, D.C. to compete at the national level. National honorees receive an additional $5,000, a gold medallion, a crystal trophy for their school or organization, and a $5,000 grant for the nonprofit, charitable organization of their choice.
Duration: The competition is held annually.
Number awarded: 102 state honorees are chosen each year: 1 middle level student and 1 high school student from each state and the District of Columbia; 10 of those (5 middle level students and 5 high school students) are named national honorees.
Deadline: Students must submit applications to their principal, Girl Scout council, county 4–H agent, American Red Cross chapter, YMCA, or HandsOn Network by October of each year.

793 PURSUING VICTORY WITH HONOR SCHOLARSHIPS

New Mexico Activities Association
Attn: Administrative Assistant
6600 Palomas Avenue, N.E.
Albuquerque, NM 87109
Phone: (505) 923–2380; (888) 820–NMAA; Fax: (505) 923–3114;
Email: mindy@nmact.org
Web: www.nmact.org/scholarship_information_forms
Summary: To provide financial assistance to high school seniors in New Mexico who have demonstrated outstanding sportsmanship through participation in interscholastic activities and plan to attend college in any state.
Eligibility: Open to seniors graduating from high schools in New Mexico who have participated in interscholastic activities throughout their high school career. They must be planning to attend a college or university in any state. Along with their application, they must submit a 1–page personal statement on the importance of sportsmanship and its relevance in interscholastic activities

and life. Awards are presented to students who have exhibited true sportsmanship by pursuing victory with honor. Financial need is not considered.
Financial data: Stipends are $2,500 or $1,000.
Duration: 1 year.
Number awarded: 8 each year: 2 at $2,500 and 6 at $1,000.
Deadline: February of each year.

794 $$ QUALITY OF LIFE AWARDS

Miss America Pageant
Attn: Scholarship Department
222 New Road, Suite 700
Linwood, NJ 08221
Phone: (609) 653–8700, ext. 127; Fax: (609) 653–8740;
Email: info@missamerica.org
Web: www.missamerica.org/scholarships/quality.aspx
Summary: To recognize and reward, with college scholarships, women who participate in the Miss America Pageant at the national level and demonstrate outstanding community service.
Eligibility: Open to women who compete at the national level of the Miss America Pageant and demonstrate a commitment to enhancing the quality of life for others through volunteerism and community service. Applicants must demonstrate that they have fulfilled a legitimate need in their community through the creation, development, and/or participation in a community service project. Selection is based on the depth of service, creativity of the project, and effects on the lives of others.
Financial data: The awards are college scholarships of $6,000 for the winner, $4,000 for the first runner–up, and $2,000 for the second runner–up.
Duration: The awards are presented annually.
Number awarded: 3 each year.
Deadline: Deadline not specified.

795 RACHEL E. LEMIEUX YOUTH SCHOLARSHIP

Maine Federation of Business and Professional Women's Clubs
Attn: BPW/Maine Futurama Foundation
c/o Susan Tardie, Co–President
25 Hall Street
Fort Kent, ME 04743
Email: susan.tardie@maine.edu
Web: www.bpwmefoundation.org/files/index.php?id=10
Summary: To provide financial assistance to female high school seniors and recent graduates in Maine who plan to attend college in any state.
Eligibility: Open to women who are seniors graduating from high schools in Maine or recent graduates of those schools. Applicants must be planning to attend an accredited college or university in any state. They must have a realistic goal for the educational plans. Along with their application, they must submit a statement describing their educational and personal goals, including their financial need.
Financial data: The stipend is $1,200. Funds are paid directly to the recipient's school.
Duration: 1 year.
Number awarded: 1 or more each year.
Deadline: April of each year.

796 $ RARE "EVERYDAY HERO" WRITING SCHOLARSHIPS

Winning Futures
Attn: RARE Everyday Hero Scholarship
27500 Cosgrove
Warren, MI 48092
Phone: (586) 698–4387; Fax: (586) 698–4532;
Email: info@winningfutures.org
Web: www.winningfutures.org/RARE_Scholarship.html
Summary: To recognize and reward, with scholarships to attend college in the state, high school seniors in Michigan who submit outstanding essays on "everyday heroes."
Eligibility: Open to seniors graduating from high schools in Michigan who plan to attend a college, university, or other postsecondary school in the state. Applicants must submit a 1–page essay on the topic, "An Everyday Hero in Our Community—A True Difference Maker." Special consideration is given to students who focus on individuals in their communities who do more than what is required of them and go above and beyond in making a difference in the world around them. Selection is based on quality of the everyday hero (how they have excelled at work and/or in the community), quality of the essay, specific examples supporting why the person is an everyday hero, and creativity of the essay.
Financial data: The award is a $2,500 scholarship, paid directly to the Michigan institution where the winner enrolls.
Duration: The competition is held annually.
Number awarded: Varies each year; recently, 8 of these scholarships were awarded.
Deadline: November of each year.

797 RAYMOND T. WELLINGTON, JR. MEMORIAL SCHOLARSHIP

American Legion Auxiliary
Department of New York
112 State Street, Suite 1310
Albany, NY 12207
Phone: (518) 463–1162; (800) 421–6348; Fax: (518) 449–5406;
Email: alanyterry@nycap.rr.com
Web: www.deptny.org/Scholarships.htm
Summary: To provide financial assistance to New York residents who are the descendants of veterans and interested in attending college in any state.
Eligibility: Open to residents of New York who are high school seniors or graduates and attending or planning to attend an accredited college or university in any state. Applicants must be the children, grandchildren, or great–grandchildren of veterans who served during specified periods of war time. Along with their application, they must submit a 700–word autobiography that includes their interests, experiences, long–range plans, and goals. Selection is based on character (15%), Americanism (15%), community involvement (15%), leadership (15%), scholarship (20%), and financial need (20%). U.S. citizenship is required.
Financial data: The stipend is $1,000. Funds are paid directly to the recipient's school.
Duration: 1 year.
Number awarded: 1 each year.
Deadline: February of each year.

798 REGIONAL COUNCIL STUDENT LEADER SCHOLARSHIPS

National Association for Campus Activities
Attn: NACA Foundation
13 Harbison Way
Columbia, SC 29212–3401
Phone: (803) 732–6222; Fax: (803) 749–1047;
Email: scholarships@naca.org
Web: www.naca.org/Scholarships/Pages/ScholarshipListings.aspx
Summary: To provide financial assistance to outstanding college student leaders.
Eligibility: Open to full–time undergraduate students who have made significant contributions to their campus communities, have played leadership roles in campus activities, and have demonstrated leadership skills and abilities. Financial need is not considered in the selection process. U.S. citizenship is required.
Financial data: The amounts of the awards vary each year; scholarships are to be used for educational expenses, including tuition, books, fees, or other related expenses.
Number awarded: 7 each year: 1 in each of the association's regions.
Deadline: April of each year.

799 $$ REGIONAL UNIVERSITY BACCALAUREATE SCHOLARSHIP PROGRAM

Oklahoma State Regents for Higher Education
Attn: Director of Scholarship and Grant Programs
655 Research Parkway, Suite 200
P.O. Box 108850
Oklahoma City, OK 73101–8850
Phone: (405) 225–9239; (800) 858–1840; Fax: (405) 225–9230;
Email: studentinfo@osrhe.edu
Web: www.okcollegestart.org
Summary: To provide financial assistance to Oklahoma residents who are attending designated publicly–supported regional universities in the state.
Eligibility: Open to residents of Oklahoma who are attending 1 of 11 designated regional public institutions in the state and working on an undergraduate degree. Applicants must 1) be designated a National Merit Semifinalist or Commended Student; or 2) have an ACT score of at least 30 and have an

exceptional GPA and class ranking as determined by the collegiate institution. Selection is based on academic promise.
Financial data: The stipend is $3,000 per year. Awardees also receive a resident tuition waiver from the institution.
Duration: Up to 4 years if the recipient maintains a cumulative GPA of 3.25 or higher and full–time enrollment.
Number awarded: Up to 165 each year: 15 at each of the 11 participating regional universities.
Deadline: Deadline not specified.

800 REHABGYM SCHOLARSHIP

Vermont Student Assistance Corporation
Attn: Scholarship Programs
10 East Allen Street
P.O. Box 2000
Winooski, VT 05404–2601
Phone: (802) 654–3798; (888) 253–4819; Fax: (802) 654–3765; TDD: (800) 281–3341 (within VT);
Email: info@vsac.org
Web: services.vsac.org/wps/wcm/connect/VSAC/vsac/pay+for+college
Summary: To provide financial assistance to residents of Vermont who have undergone a significant physical challenge and plan to attend college in any state.
Eligibility: Open to residents of Vermont who are attending or planning to attend a college or university in any state. Applicants must be able to demonstrate that they have undergone a significant physical challenge or illness and have met the challenge with courage and perseverance. Along with their application, they must submit 1) a 100–word essay on any significant barriers that limit their access to education; and 2) a 250–word essay on what they believe distinguishes their application from others that may be submitted. Selection is based on those essays and financial need.
Financial data: The stipend is $1,000.
Duration: 1 year.
Number awarded: 1 each year.
Deadline: March of each year.

801 $ RENEE FELDMAN SCHOLARSHIPS

Blinded Veterans Association Auxiliary
c/o Hazel C. Compton, Scholarship Chair
P.O. Box 267
Richlands, VA 24641
Phone: (276) 963–3745
Web: www.bvaaux.org
Summary: To provide financial assistance for college to spouses and children of blinded veterans.
Eligibility: Open to children and spouses of blinded veterans who are enrolled or planning to enroll full time at a college, university, community college, or vocational school. The veteran is not required to be a member of the Blinded Veterans Association. Applicants must submit a 300–word essay on their career goals and aspirations. Selection is based on that essay, academic achievement, and letters of reference.
Financial data: Stipends are $2,000 or $1,000 per year. Funds are paid directly to the recipient's school to be applied to tuition, books, and general fees.
Duration: 1 year; may be renewed up to 3 additional years.
Number awarded: 3 each year: 2 at $2,000 and 1 at $1,000.
Deadline: April of each year.

802 $ RESERVE EDUCATIONAL ASSISTANCE PROGRAM

Department of Veterans Affairs
Attn: Veterans Benefits Administration
810 Vermont Avenue, N.W.
Washington, DC 20420
Phone: (202) 418–4343; (888) GI–BILL1
Web: www.gibill.va.gov/benefits/other_programs/reap.html
Summary: To provide financial assistance for college or graduate school to members of the Reserves or National Guard who are called to active duty during a period of national emergency.
Eligibility: Open to members of the Selected Reserve and Individual Ready Reserve (including Reserve elements of the Army, Navy, Air Force, Marine Corps, and Coast Guard, as well as the Army National Guard and the Air National Guard) who have served on active duty on or after September 11, 2001 for at least 90 consecutive days. Applicants must be interested in working on an undergraduate or graduate degree, vocational or technical training, on–the–job or apprenticeship training, correspondence training, or flight training.
Financial data: For full–time study at a college or university, the current monthly rate is $589.20 for personnel with consecutive service of 90 days but less than 1 year, $883.80 for personnel with consecutive service of more than 1 year but less than 2 years, or $1,178.40 for those with consecutive service of 2 years or more. Reduced rates apply for part–time college or university study, apprenticeship and on–the–job training, licensing and certification training, cooperative education, correspondence courses, and flight training.
Duration: Up to 36 months for full–time study. There is no fixed time for persons eligible for this program to utilize its benefits (except in the case of a member separated from the Ready Reserve for a disability, who are entitled to benefits for 10 years after the date of eligibility).
Number awarded: Varies each year.
Deadline: Applications may be submitted at any time.

803 REV. DR. KAREN LAYMAN GIFT OF HOPE: 21ST CENTURY SCHOLARS PROGRAM

United Methodist Church
Attn: General Board of Higher Education and Ministry
Office of Loans and Scholarships
1001 19th Avenue South
P.O. Box 340007
Nashville, TN 37203–0007
Phone: (615) 340–7344; Fax: (615) 340–7367;
Email: umscholar@gbhem.org
Web: www.gbhem.org
Summary: To provide financial assistance to undergraduate Methodist students who can demonstrate leadership in the church.
Eligibility: Open to full–time undergraduate students at United Methodist institutions who have been active, full members of a United Methodist Church for at least 3 years prior to applying. Applicants must have a GPA of 3.0 or higher and be able to show evidence of leadership and participation in religious activities during college either through their campus ministry or through local United Methodist Churches in the city where their college is located. They must also show how their education will provide leadership for the church and society and improve the quality of life for others. U.S. citizenship, permanent resident status, or membership in the Central Conferences of the United Methodist Church is required. Financial need is considered in the selection process.
Financial data: The stipend is $1,000.
Duration: 1 year; recipients may reapply.
Number awarded: Varies each year.
Deadline: February of each year.

804 RHODE ISLAND ASSOCIATION OF FORMER LEGISLATORS SCHOLARSHIP

Rhode Island Foundation
Attn: Funds Administrator
One Union Station
Providence, RI 02903
Phone: (401) 427–4017; Fax: (401) 331–8085;
Email: lmonahan@rifoundation.org
Web: www.rifoundation.org
Summary: To provide financial assistance to graduating high school seniors in Rhode Island who have been involved in public service activities and plan to attend college in any state.
Eligibility: Open to seniors graduating from high schools in Rhode Island who plan to attend a college or university in any state. Applicants must have distinguished themselves by their outstanding involvement in community service and be able to demonstrate financial need. Along with their application, they must submit an essay (up to 300 words), explaining the nature of their community service participation, the work's influence on them, and how they plan to continue their public service work into the future.
Financial data: The stipend is $1,500.
Duration: 1 year; nonrenewable.
Number awarded: 5 each year.
Deadline: April of each year.

805 $$ RHODE ISLAND EDUCATIONAL BENEFITS FOR DISABLED AMERICAN VETERANS

Division of Veterans Affairs
480 Metacom Avenue
Bristol, RI 02809–0689

Phone: (401) 254–8350; Fax: (401) 254–2320; TDD: (401) 254–1345;
Email: devangelista@dhs.ri.gov
Web: www.dhs.ri.gov/VeteransServices/tabid/307/Default.aspx
Summary: To provide assistance to disabled veterans in Rhode Island who wish to pursue higher education at a public institution in the state.
Eligibility: Open to permanent residents of Rhode Island who have been verified by the Department of Veterans Affairs (DVA) as having a disability of at least 10% resulting from military service.
Financial data: Eligible veterans are entitled to take courses at any public institution of higher education in Rhode Island without the payment of tuition, exclusive of other fees and charges.
Number awarded: Varies each year.
Deadline: Deadline not specified.

806 $$ RICHARD AND ELIZABETH DEAN SCHOLARSHIP

Daughters of the American Revolution–National Society
Attn: Committee Services Office, Scholarships
1776 D Street, N.W.
Washington, DC 20006–5303
Phone: (202) 628–1776
Web: www.dar.org/natsociety/edout_scholar.cfm
Summary: To provide financial assistance to high school seniors who have exceptional GPAs and plan to attend college in any state.
Eligibility: Open to high school seniors who plan to attend a college or university in any state. Applicants must have a GPA of 3.75 or higher. Selection is based on academic achievement and financial need.
Financial data: The stipend is $5,000 per year.
Duration: 1 year; may be renewed up to 3 additional years; provided the recipient maintains a GPA of 3.25 or higher.
Number awarded: 1 or more each year.
Deadline: February of each year.

807 RICHARD D. JORDAN MEMORIAL SCHOLARSHIP

American Legion
Department of Alaska
1550 Charter Circle
Anchorage, AK 99508
Phone: (907) 278–8598; Fax: (907) 278–0041;
Email: legion@anch.net
Web: www.alaskalegion.org
Summary: To provide financial assistance to high school seniors in Alaska who plan to attend college in any state.
Eligibility: Open to seniors graduating from high schools in Alaska who plan to attend college in any state. Applicants should 1) have at least average grades (2.0 to 3.0 GPA); 2) have been improving academically but they do not need to be at the top; and 3) not be eligible for an academic or athletic scholarship. Along with their application, they must submit a 500–word essay on their involvement in school, church, and community activities and why patriotic organizations (such as the American Legion) are important to the world today. Selection is based on that essay, clearly defined goals for the future, community or American Legion Post involvement, and financial need.
Financial data: The stipend is $1,000, payable directly to the school.
Duration: 1 year.
Number awarded: 1 each year.
Deadline: February of each year.

808 $ RICHARD H. PIERCE MEMORIAL SCHOLARSHIPS

Maine Education Services
Attn: MES Foundation
131 Presumpscot Street
Portland, ME 04103
Phone: (207) 791–3600; (800) 922–6352; Fax: (207) 791–3616;
Email: info@mesfoundation.com
Web: www.mesfoundation.com
Summary: To provide financial assistance to residents of Maine who are attending college in any state.
Eligibility: Open to residents of Maine who are enrolled at a college or university in any state and have completed at least 1 year of a 2–year program or 2 years of a 4– or 5–year program. Applicants must submit a 300–word essay on a time or event when they faced a personal challenge, how they persevered for something in which they believed, and how the experience influenced them. Selection is based on that essay, academic excellence, contributions to community and employment, letters of recommendation, and financial need.
Financial data: The stipend is $2,500.
Duration: 1 year.
Number awarded: 2 each year.
Deadline: April of each year.

809 $ RICHARD R. TUFENKIAN MEMORIAL SCHOLARSHIP

Armenian Educational Foundation, Inc.
Attn: Scholarship Committee
600 West Broadway, Suite 130
Glendale, CA 91204
Phone: (818) 242–4154; Fax: (818) 242–4154;
Email: Hermine@aefweb.org
Web: www.aefweb.org/aefscholarships.php
Summary: To provide financial assistance to undergraduate students of Armenian descent.
Eligibility: Open to students of Armenian descent who are enrolled or planning to enroll full time at an accredited college or university in the United States. Applicants must have a GPA of 3.0 or higher. Along with their application, they must submit a 1–page essay on 1) why they believe they are deserving of this scholarship and how they will utilize their college education to benefit the community; and 2) their need for financial assistance. Selection is based on honors and awards, extracurricular activities, financial need, and Armenian community service and volunteer work.
Financial data: The stipend is $2,000; fund are sent to the recipient upon presenting proof of registration for the upcoming fall semester/quarter.
Duration: 1 year.
Number awarded: 5 each year.
Deadline: July of each year.

810 RISE SCHOLARSHIPS

Rise Scholarship Foundation, Inc.
Attn: Awards Selection Committee
P.O. Box 422417
Atlanta, GA 30342
Web: www.risescholarshipfoundation.org/rise–award
Summary: To provide financial assistance for college to high school seniors who have a learning disability.
Eligibility: Open to graduating high school seniors who have a documented learning disability (a diagnosis of ADHD or ADD alone does not qualify). Applicants must be planning to enroll in at least 2 or more core classes each semester at an accredited college or university. They must have a GPA of 2.5 or higher. Along with their application, they must submit a high school transcript, documentation of a learning disability (e.g., an I.E.P. and/or 504 plan), letters of recommendation, and an essay on the advice they would give a child newly diagnosed as a student with a learning difference. Financial need is not considered in the selection process. U.S. citizenship is required.
Financial data: A stipend is awarded (amount not specified).
Duration: 1 year.
Number awarded: Varies each year; recently, 3 of these scholarships were awarded.
Deadline: February of each year.

811 RISING STAR SCHOLARSHIP OF THE JUVENILE DIABETES RESEARCH FOUNDATION

Diabetes Scholars Foundation
2118 Plum Grove Road, Suite 356
Rolling Meadows, IL 60008
Phone: (312) 215–9861; Fax: (847) 991–8739;
Email: collegescholarships@diabetesscholars.org
Web: www.diabetesscholars.org/college.html
Summary: To provide financial assistance for college to high school seniors who have diabetes.
Eligibility: Open to graduating high school seniors who have Type 1 diabetes and plan to attend an accredited 4–year university, college, or technical/trade school in any state. Applicants must be able to demonstrate active involvement in the diabetes community, academic performance, participation in community and/or extracurricular activities, and successful management of the challenges of living with diabetes. Financial need is not considered in the selection process. U.S. citizenship or permanent resident status is required.
Financial data: The stipend is $1,000.

Duration: 1 year.
Number awarded: 1 each year.
Deadline: May of each year.

812 $ ROADWAY WORKER MEMORIAL SCHOLARSHIPS

American Traffic Safety Services Foundation
Attn: Foundation Director
15 Riverside Parkway, Suite 100
Fredericksburg, VA 22406–1022
Phone: (540) 368–1701; (800) 272–8772; Fax: (540) 368–1717;
Email: foundation@atssa.com
Web: www.atssa.com

Summary: To provide financial assistance for college to children of roadway workers killed or permanently disabled in work zones.

Eligibility: Open to students enrolled or planning to enroll at a 4–year college or university, 2–year accredited college, or vocational/technical school or training institution. Applicants must be children of roadway workers killed or permanently disabled in work zones, including mobile operations and the installation of roadway safety features. They must submit a statement, up to 200 words, explaining their reasons for wanting to continue their education and listing any volunteer activities or accomplishments. Selection is based on that statement, academic performance, 2 letters of recommendation, and financial need.

Financial data: The stipend is $2,000. The Chuck Bailey Scholarship provides an additional $1,000 to recipients who demonstrate a strong commitment to volunteerism.

Duration: 1 year.
Number awarded: Varies each year; recently, 5 of these scholarships were awarded.
Deadline: February of each year.

813 ROBERT D. BLUE SCHOLARSHIP

Treasurer of State
State Capitol Building
Des Moines, IA 50319–0005
Phone: (515) 242–5270; Fax: (515) 281–6962;
Email: rdbluescholarship@iow.gov
Web: www.rdblue.org

Summary: To provide financial assistance to Iowa residents who are currently attending or planning to attend a college or university in the state.

Eligibility: Open to graduating high school seniors and students currently attending a college or university as an undergraduate student. Applicants must have spent the majority of their lives in Iowa and be attending or planning to attend a college or university in the state. They must "demonstrate literary and scholastic ability, exhibit qualities of truth, courage, and fellowship, and display moral force of character." Along with their application they must submit an official transcript, 3 letters of recommendation, a statement of expenses and awards from their college financial aid office, and a 500–word essay on an individual from their community who has demonstrated the responsibilities of being a citizen in that community. Selection is based on that essay (25%), financial need (45%), academic performance (20%), and recommendations (10%).

Financial data: Stipends range from $500 to $1,000.

Duration: 1 year.
Number awarded: Varies each year; recently, 7 of these scholarships (all at $1,000) were awarded.
Deadline: May of each year.

814 ROBERT D. LYNCH LEADERSHIP SCHOLARSHIP

Pennsylvania Black Conference on Higher Education
c/o Judith A.W. Thomas, Scholarship Committee Chair
Lincoln University, School of Social Sciences and Behavioral Studies
1570 Old Baltimore Pike
P.O. Box 179
Lincoln University, PA 19352
Phone: (484) 365–8159;
Email: scholarships@pbcohe.org
Web: www.phcohe.org

Summary: To provide financial assistance to African American residents of any state who are enrolled as undergraduates at colleges in Pennsylvania and have demonstrated outstanding leadership skills.

Eligibility: Open to African Americans from any state who have completed at least the first semester as an undergraduate at a college or university in Pennsylvania. Applicants must have a GPA of 3.0 or higher. Along with their application, they must submit an essay, up to 5 pages in length, on why they should receive this scholarship. Selection is based on leadership skills and academic record.

Financial data: The stipend is $1,000.

Duration: 1 year.
Number awarded: 1 each year.
Deadline: January of each year.

815 ROBERT E. (BOBBY) THOMAS MEMORIAL SCHOLARSHIP

Kentucky Sheriffs Association
c/o Charlie Williams, Hardin County Sheriff
100 Public Square
Elizabethtown, KY 42701
Phone: (270) 765–5133; Fax: (270) 737–4574
Web: kentuckysheriffs.ky.gov/Conference+and+Scholarship+Information

Summary: To provide financial assistance to residents of Kentucky who are interested in attending college in any state.

Eligibility: Open to residents of Kentucky who are graduating high school seniors or students currently enrolled at an accredited institution of higher education in any state. Applicants must submit an essay of 200 to 300 words on their career goals and why they feel they are deserving of this scholarship. Financial need is considered in the selection process.

Financial data: The stipend is $1,000.

Duration: 1 year.
Number awarded: Up to 5 each year.
Deadline: July of each year.

816 ROBERT GLENN RAPP FOUNDATION ENDOWMENT SCHOLARSHIP

Epsilon Sigma Alpha International
Attn: ESA Foundation
363 West Drake Road
Fort Collins, CO 80526
Phone: (970) 223–2824; Fax: (970) 223–4456;
Email: esainfo@epsilonsigmaalpha.org
Web: www.epsilonsigmaalpha.org/scholarships–and–grants

Summary: To provide financial assistance to residents of Oklahoma who plan to attend college in the state.

Eligibility: Open to residents of Oklahoma who are 1) graduating high school seniors with a GPA of 3.0 or higher or with minimum scores of 22 on the ACT or 1030 on the combined critical reading and mathematics SAT; 2) enrolled in college with a GPA of 3.0 or higher; 3) enrolled at a technical school or returning to school after an absence for retraining of job skills or obtaining a degree; or 4) engaged in online study through an accredited college, university, or vocational school. Applicants must be attending or planning to attend school in Oklahoma. They may major in any field. Selection is based on character (10%), leadership (10%), service (5%), financial need (50%), and scholastic ability (25%).

Financial data: The stipend is $1,000.

Duration: 1 year; may be renewed.
Number awarded: 4 each year.
Deadline: January of each year.

817 $ ROBERT R. LEE PROMISE CATEGORY A SCHOLARSHIP

Idaho State Board of Education
Len B. Jordan Office Building
650 West State Street, Room 307
P.O. Box 83720
Boise, ID 83720–0037
Phone: (208) 332–1574; Fax: (208) 334–2632;
Email: scholarshiphelp@osbe.idaho.gov
Web: www.boardofed.idaho.gov/scholarship/promise_a.asp

Summary: To provide financial assistance for college or professional/technical school to outstanding high school seniors in Idaho.

Eligibility: Open to graduating high school seniors who are Idaho residents planning to enroll full time in academic or professional/technical programs in public or private institutions in the state. Academic applicants must have a cumulative GPA of 3.5 or higher and an ACT score of 28 or higher. Professional/technical applicants must have a cumulative GPA of 2.8 or higher and must take the COMPASS test (reading, writing, and algebra scores are required). U.S. citizenship is also required.

Financial data: The stipend is $3,000 per year.

Duration: 1 year. Academic scholarships may be renewed for up to 3 additional years and professional/technical scholarships may be renewed for up to 2 additional years; renewal is granted only if the recipient remains enrolled full time with a rank in the top 50% of the students in the class and a GPA of 3.0 or higher.
Number awarded: Approximately 25 each year; academic students receive 75% of the awards and professional/technical students receive 25%.
Deadline: January of each year.

818 ROBERT SMILEY SCHOLARSHIP

Iowa Girls High School Athletic Union
Attn: Scholarships
5000 Westown Parkway
West Des Moines, IA 50266
Phone: (515) 288–9741; Fax: (515) 284–1969;
Email: jasoneslinger@ighsau.org
Web: www.ighsau.org

Summary: To provide financial assistance to female high school seniors in Iowa who have participated in athletics and plan to attend college in the state.
Eligibility: Open to women graduating from high schools in Iowa who have lettered in 1 varsity sport sponsored by the Iowa Girls High School Athletic Union (IGHSAU) each year of high school and have a GPA of 2.5 or higher. Applicants must be planning to attend a college or university in Iowa. Each high school in the state may nominate 1 student. Selection is based on academic achievements, athletic accomplishments, non–sports extracurricular activities, and community involvement.
Financial data: The stipend is $1,000.
Duration: 1 year.
Number awarded: 1 each year.
Deadline: March of each year.

819 $ ROCK CATS SCHOLAR–ATHLETE AWARDS

New Britain Rock Cats Baseball Club
Attn: Rock Cats Foundation
230 John Karbonic Way
P.O. Box 1718
New Britain, CT 06050
Phone: (860) 224–8383, ext. 23; Fax: (860) 225–6267;
Email: ahelbling@rockcats.com
Web: www.rockcats.com

Summary: To provide financial assistance to high school seniors in Connecticut who have participated in sports and plan to attend college in any state.
Eligibility: Open to seniors graduating from high schools in Connecticut and planning to attend a college or university in any state. Applicants must be a member of at least 1 sports team at their high school and participate in extracurricular activities. They must have a GPA of 3.0 or higher and minimum scores of 1300 on the 2400–scale SAT, 850 on the 1600–scale SAT, or 19 on the ACT. Along with their application, they must submit a 500–word essay that describes who they are, how they view themselves, and any other information they wish to have considered. Males and females are judged separately. Financial need is not considered in the selection process.
Financial data: The stipend is $2,500.
Duration: 1 year.
Number awarded: 2 each year: 1 for a female and 1 for a male.
Deadline: May of each year.

820 $$ RON BROWN SCHOLAR PROGRAM

CAP Charitable Foundation
Attn: Ron Brown Scholar Program
1160 Pepsi Place, Suite 206
Charlottesville, VA 22901
Phone: (434) 964–1588; Fax: (434) 964–1589;
Email: info@ronbrown.org
Web: www.ronbrown.org

Summary: To provide financial assistance for college to African American high school seniors.
Eligibility: Open to academically–talented African American high school seniors who have demonstrated social commitment and leadership potential. They must be interested in attending a 4–year college or university as a full–time student. U.S. citizenship or permanent resident status is required. Finalists are invited to participate in a weekend selection program in Washington, D.C.; their expenses are reimbursed. Final selection is based on academic excellence, leadership, skills, school and community involvement, and financial need.
Financial data: The stipend is $10,000 per year. Funds may be used to cover tuition, fees, books, room, board, and other college–related expenses. Payment is made directly to the recipient's school.
Duration: 4 years.
Number awarded: 10 to 20 each year.
Deadline: January of each year.

821 RONALD MCDONALD HOUSE CHARITIES SCHOLARS PROGRAM

Ronald McDonald House Charities
Attn: U.S. Scholarship Program
One Kroc Drive
Oak Brook, IL 60523
Phone: (630) 623–7048; Fax: (630) 623–7488;
Email: info@rmhc.org
Web: rmhc.org/what–we–do/rmhc–u–s–scholarships

Summary: To provide financial assistance for college to high school seniors in specified geographic areas.
Eligibility: Open to high school seniors in designated McDonald's market areas who are legal residents of the United States. Applicants must be planning to enroll full time at an accredited 2– or 4–year college, university, or vocational/technical school. They must have a GPA of 2.7 or higher. Along with their application, they must submit a personal statement, up to 2 pages in length, on their career goals and desire to contribute to their community; information about unique, personal, or financial circumstances may be added. Selection is based on that statement, high school transcripts, a letter of recommendation, and financial need.
Financial data: Most awards are $1,000 per year. Funds are paid directly to the recipient's school.
Duration: 1 year; nonrenewable.
Number awarded: Varies each year; since RMHC began this program, it has awarded more than $44 million in scholarships.
Deadline: January of each year.

822 $ RONALD N. DAVIS ACADEMIC ALL–STATE TEAM

Florida High School Athletic Association
Attn: Director of Special Programs
1801 N.W. 80th Boulevard
Gainesville, FL 32606
Phone: (352) 372–9551, ext. 170; (800) 461–7895; Fax: (352) 373–1528;
Email: lring@fhsaa.org
Web: www.fhsaa.org

Summary: To provide financial assistance to student–athletes in Florida who have excelled in academics and athletics and plan to attend college in any state.
Eligibility: Open to seniors graduating from high schools in Florida and planning to attend college in any state. Each high school in the state may nominate 1 boy and 1 girl. Nominees must have a cumulative unweighted GPA of 3.5 or higher and have earned a varsity letter in at least 2 different sports during each of their junior and senior years. Boys and girls are judged separately.
Financial data: Each honoree receives a $1,000 award. From among those honorees, the Scholar–Athletes of the Year receive an additional $3,000 scholarship.
Duration: The awards are presented annually.
Number awarded: 24 honorees (12 boys and 12 girls) are selected each year. From among those, 2 Scholar–Athletes of the Year (1 boy and 1 girl) are selected annually.
Deadline: Schools must submit nominations by February of each year.

823 $$ RONALD REAGAN COLLEGE LEADERS SCHOLARSHIP PROGRAM

Phillips Foundation
1 Massachusetts Avenue, N.W., Suite 620
Washington, DC 20001
Phone: (202) 250–3887, ext. 628;
Email: jhollingsworth@thephillipsfoundation.org
Web: www.thephillipsfoundation.org/#ronald_reagan_scholarships.cfm

Summary: To provide financial assistance to college students who "demonstrate leadership on behalf of the cause of freedom, American values, and constitutional principles."
Eligibility: Open to U.S. citizens enrolled as full–time students at accredited 4–year degree–granting institutions in the United States or its possessions who are applying during their sophomore or junior year. Applicants must submit an essay of 500 to 750 words describing their personal background, career objectives, and scope of participation in activities that promote the cause of freedom,

American values, and constitutional principles. Selection is based on merit, although financial need may be taken into consideration.
Financial data: Stipends currently are $7,500, $5,000, $2,500, or $1,000 per year.
Duration: 1 year. Recipients who apply as sophomores use the scholarship during their junior year and may apply for renewal for their senior year. Recipients who apply as juniors use the scholarship during their senior year.
Number awarded: Varies each year; recently, 46 of these scholarships, with a total value of $163,500, were awarded.
Deadline: January of each year.

824 $ ROOTHBERT FUND SCHOLARSHIPS AND GRANTS

Roothbert Fund, Inc.
475 Riverside Drive, Room 1830
New York, NY 10115
Phone: (212) 870–3116;
Email: mail@roothbertfund.org
Web: www.roothbertfund.org/scholarships.php
Summary: To provide financial assistance for college or graduate school to residents of designated eastern states who are primarily motivated by spiritual values.
Eligibility: Open to undergraduate and graduate students who are current residents of or planning to move to the following states: Connecticut, Delaware, District of Columbia, Maine, Maryland, Massachusetts, New Hampshire, New Jersey, New York, North Carolina, Ohio, Pennsylvania, Rhode Island, Vermont, Virginia, or West Virginia. Applicants are not required to be adherents of any particular form of religious practice or worship, but they must be motivated by spiritual values. They may be studying any field at a college or university in the United States. Preference is given to applicants with outstanding academic records who are considering teaching as a vocation. Finalists are invited to New York, New Haven, Philadelphia, or Washington, D.C. for an interview; applicants must affirm their willingness to attend the interview if invited. The fund does not pay transportation expenses for those asked to interview. Being invited for an interview does not guarantee a scholarship, but no grants are awarded without an interview.
Financial data: Grants range from $2,000 to $3,000 per year.
Duration: 1 year; may be renewed.
Number awarded: Approximately 20 each year.
Deadline: January of each year.

825 ROSAMOND P. HAEBERLE MEMORIAL SCHOLARSHIP

Daughters of the American Revolution–Michigan State Society
c/o Toni Barger, Memorial Scholarship Committee
130 Lake Region Circle
Winter Haven, FL 33881–9535
Phone: (863) 326–1687;
Email: tonibarger@aol.com
Web: www.michigandar.org/scholarships.htm
Summary: To provide financial assistance to Michigan veterans and military personnel interested in attending college in the state.
Eligibility: Open to residents of Michigan who have served on active duty in the U.S. armed forces (including Reserves and National Guard) for at least 6 continuous months and are either currently serving in the armed forces or have received a separation from active duty under honorable conditions. Applicants must be currently accepted to and/or enrolled at a 2– or 4–year accredited college, university, or technical/trade school in Michigan. They must be enrolled at least half time and have a cumulative high school or undergraduate GPA of 2.5 or higher. Along with their application, they must submit a 1–page essay on what serving their country has meant to them and how it has influenced their future goals and priorities. Selection is based on academic performance, extracurricular activities, community service, potential to succeed in an academic environment, financial need, and military service record.
Financial data: The stipend is $1,500.
Duration: 1 year.
Number awarded: 1 each year.
Deadline: March of each year.

826 ROY WEBSTER MEMORIAL SCHOLARSHIP

The Fruit Company
2900 Van Horn Drive
Hood River, OR 97031
Phone: (541) 387–3100; (800) 387–3100; Fax: (541) 387–3104;
Email: scholarship@thefruitcompany.com
Web: www.thefruitcompany.com/page/scholarship
Summary: To provide financial assistance to residents of Oregon and Washington who are attending college in any state.
Eligibility: Open to graduates of Oregon and Washington high schools who are currently enrolled at a college or university in any state. Applicants must submit a 500–word statement of career objectives and a 1,000–word essay on how the urbanization of rural farming communities in the Northwest has changed the political and socioeconomic landscape and what they would change to support both the sustainability of agricultural areas and the growing high–tech industrial population. Financial need is not considered in the selection process.
Financial data: The stipend is $1,000. Funds are paid directly to the recipient's college or university.
Duration: 1 year.
Number awarded: 1 each year.
Deadline: April of each year.

827 RUTH ANN JOHNSON FUND SCHOLARSHIPS

Greater Kanawha Valley Foundation
Attn: Scholarship Program Officer
1600 Huntington Square
900 Lee Street East, 16th Floor
Charleston, WV 25301
Phone: (304) 346–3620; (800) 467–5909; Fax: (304) 346–3640;
Email: shoover@tgkvf.org
Web: www.tgkvf.org/page.aspx?pid=409
Summary: To provide financial assistance to residents of West Virginia who are interested in attending college in any state.
Eligibility: Open to residents of West Virginia who are attending or planning to attend a college or university anywhere in the country. Applicants must have an ACT score of 20 or higher; be able to demonstrate good moral character, academic excellence, and extreme financial need; and have a GPA of 2.5 or higher.
Financial data: The stipend is $1,000 per year.
Duration: 1 year; may be renewed.
Number awarded: Varies each year; recently, 44 of these scholarships were awarded.
Deadline: January of each year.

828 RYAN MULLALY SECOND CHANCE SCHOLARSHIPS

Ryan Mullaly Second Chance Fund
26 Meadow Lane
Pennington, NJ 08534
Phone: (609) 737–1800;
Email: The2dChanceFund@aol.com
Web: www.ryans2dchancefund.org
Summary: To provide financial assistance for college to high school seniors who are fighting lymphoma.
Eligibility: Open to U.S. citizens and permanent residents who were diagnosed with lymphoma or a recurrence of lymphoma between age 13 and graduation from high school. Applicants must have a treatment history that includes chemotherapy and/or radiation and must be able to demonstrate that their high school years were substantially impacted by treatment and/or side effects of treatment. They must be high school seniors planning to 1) work on an associate or bachelor's degree at an accredited 2– or 4–year college or university; or 2) enroll in an accredited postsecondary vocational or trade program that will culminate in certification. Priority is given to students still undergoing treatment and those with permanent effects from treatment.
Financial data: The stipend is $1,000.
Duration: 1 year; nonrenewable.
Number awarded: Up to 15 each year.
Deadline: July of each year.

829 SAKAE TAKAHASHI SCHOLARSHIP

100th Infantry Battalion Legacy Organization
Attn: Scholarship Committee
520 Kamoku Street
Honolulu, HI 96826–5120
Phone: (808) 637–5324;
Email: hondan001@hawaii.rr.com
Web: www.100thlegacy.org
Summary: To provide financial assistance to high school seniors in Hawaii who plan to attend college in any state.

Eligibility: Open to seniors graduating from high schools in Hawaii and planning to attend an institution of higher in any state. Applicants must submit an essay about the challenges faced by veterans of the 100th Infantry Battalion after World War II, how they were influenced by the cultural values they learned from their Issei parents, and the 4 most significant Issei values that contributed to the accomplishments of Sakae Takahashi. Selection is based on that essay (50%), academics (20%), community service (15%), and leadership (15%).
Financial data: The stipend is $3,000.
Duration: 1 year; nonrenewable.
Number awarded: 1 each year.
Deadline: March of each year.

830 $ SALVATORE E. QUINCI SCHOLARSHIPS

Salvatore E. Quinci Foundation
178 Florence Street
Melrose, MA 02176–3710
Phone: (781) 760–7138
Web: www.seqfoundation.org

Summary: To provide financial assistance for college to people who have a bleeding disorder.
Eligibility: Open to people who have been diagnosed with hemophilia or another bleeding disorder. Applicants must be attending or accepted at an accredited college, university, or vocational/technical school. Along with their application, they must submit a 1–page statement that discusses their future educational and career goals and how they plan to use the scholarship money. Selection is based on that statement, the quality of the application, high school and/or college grades, and financial need.
Financial data: The stipend is $2,000. Funds must be used for tuition, fees, books, or other education–related expenses.
Duration: 1 year.
Number awarded: 2 each year.
Deadline: April of each year.

831 $$ SAMMY AWARDS

Milk Processor Education Program
Attn: Scholar Athlete Milk Mustache of the Year (SAMMY)
1250 H Street, N.W., Suite 950
Washington, DC 20005
Phone: (202) 737–0153; (800) WHY–MILK; Fax: (202) 737–0156
Web: www.sammyapplication.com

Summary: To provide financial assistance for college to outstanding high school scholar–athletes.
Eligibility: Open to residents of the 48 contiguous United States and the District of Columbia who are currently high school seniors and who participate in a high school or club sport. Applicants must have a GPA of 3.2 or higher. They must submit a 250–word essay on how they refuel with milk while excelling in academics, athletics, community service, and leadership. The country is divided into 25 geographic regions, and 3 finalists are selected from each region. From those, 1 winner from each region is chosen. Selection is based on academic achievement (35%), athletic excellence (35%), leadership (15%), community service (10%), and a 75–word essay on how drinking milk is part of their life and training regimen (5%).
Financial data: College scholarships of $7,500 each are awarded. In addition, each winner plus 2 guests are invited to attend the winners' ceremony at Disney World in Orlando, Florida.
Duration: The awards are presented annually.
Number awarded: 25 each year (1 from each of 25 geographic districts).
Deadline: March of each year.

832 $$ SAMSUNG AMERICAN LEGION SCHOLARSHIPS

American Legion
Attn: Americanism and Children & Youth Division
700 North Pennsylvania Street
P.O. Box 1055
Indianapolis, IN 46206–1055
Phone: (317) 630–1202; Fax: (317) 630–1223;
Email: acy@legion.org
Web: legion.org/scholarships/samsung

Summary: To provide financial assistance for college to descendants of veterans who participate in Girls State or Boys State.
Eligibility: Open to students entering their senior year of high school who are selected to participate in Girls State or Boys State, sponsored by the American Legion Auxiliary or American Legion in their state. Applicants must be the child, grandchild, or great–grandchild of a veteran who saw active–duty service during specified periods of war time. Finalists are chosen at each participating Girls and Boys State, and they are then nominated for the national awards. Selection is based on academic record, community service, involvement in school and community activities, and financial need. Special consideration is given to descendants of U.S. veterans of the Korean War.
Financial data: Stipends are $20,000 or $1,100.
Duration: 4 years.
Number awarded: Varies each year; recently, 9 scholarships at $20,000 and 89 at $1,100 were awarded.
Deadline: Deadline not specified.

833 $ SARBANES SCHOLARSHIP PROGRAM

National Fallen Firefighters Foundation
Attn: Scholarship Committee
P.O. Drawer 498
Emmitsburg, MD 21727
Phone: (301) 447–1365; Fax: (301) 447–1645
Web: firehero.org/resources/families/scholarships/sarbanes.html

Summary: To provide financial assistance for college or graduate school to the spouses and children of deceased firefighters.
Eligibility: Open to the spouses, life partners, children, and stepchildren of fallen firefighters honored at the National Fallen Firefighters Memorial in Emmitsburg, Maryland. Children must currently be under 30 years of age and have been under 22 years of age at the time of their firefighter's death; there is no age cutoff for spouses or partners. Applicants must have a high school diploma or the equivalent; be pursuing or planning to pursue undergraduate, graduate, or job skills training at an accredited university, college, community college, or technical school; and be able to demonstrate academic and personal potential. Along with their application, they must submit a personal statement, up to 400 words, explaining why they want the scholarship; their personal, educational, and career goals; their extracurricular, community, and/or volunteer activities; any special circumstances (such as financial hardship or family responsibilities); and any other information they want the scholarship committee to know about them. Selection is based on academic standing (GPA of 2.0 or higher); involvement in extracurricular activities, including community and volunteer activities; the personal statement; and 2 letters of recommendation, at least 1 of which should be from a member of the fire service.
Financial data: Stipends average more than $2,600.
Duration: 1 year; may be renewed.
Number awarded: Varies each year; recently, 78 of these scholarships (38 new and 40 renewal) worth more than $205,000 were awarded. Since the program was established, it has awarded 648 scholarships worth more than $1,500,000.
Deadline: March of each year.

834 $$ SARLO EMIGRE YOUTH FUND SCHOLARSHIPS

Jewish Community Federation of San Francisco, the Peninsula, Marin and Sonoma Counties
Attn: Scholarship Program Manager
121 Steuart Street
San Francisco, CA 94105
Phone: (415) 777–0411; Fax: (415) 495–6635;
Email: MeganK@sfjcf.org
Web: jewishfed.org/see–how–we–help/college–scholarships

Summary: To provide financial assistance for college or graduate school to Jewish residents of any state who are emigres or families of immigrants.
Eligibility: Open to foreign–born or first– or second–generation immigrant Jewish residents of any state. Applicants must be working full time on an undergraduate or (on occasion) graduate degree at an accredited institution of higher learning and/or the arts and have a GPA of 3.0 or higher. They must be the first member of their family to attend college. Along with their application, they must submit a 1,000–word essay on what drives them to achieve in academics, community or Jewish service, and career goals. Selection is based on academic and/or artistic excellence and achievements and financial need.
Financial data: Stipends range from $1,000 to $10,000.
Duration: 1 year.
Number awarded: 6 or more each year.
Deadline: April of each year.

835 $$ SCHOLARSHIP TO HONOR BARRY GOLDWATER, K7UGA

American Radio Relay League
Attn: ARRL Foundation
225 Main Street

Newington, CT 06111–1494
Phone: (860) 594–0397; Fax: (860) 594–0259;
Email: foundation@arrl.org
Web: www.arrl.org/scholarship–descriptions
Summary: To provide financial assistance to licensed radio amateurs who are interested in working on an undergraduate or graduate degree in any field.
Eligibility: Open to undergraduate or graduate students at accredited institutions who are licensed radio amateurs at the novice class or higher. Applicants may be working on a degree in any academic discipline. Along with their application, they must submit an essay on the role amateur radio has played in their lives and provide documentation of financial need.
Financial data: The stipend is $5,000.
Duration: 1 year.
Number awarded: 1 each year.
Deadline: January of each year.

836 SCHOLARSHIPS FOR MILITARY CHILDREN

Fisher House Foundation
111 Rockville Pike, Suite 420
Rockville, MD 20850
Phone: (888) 294–8560;
Email: JWeiskopf@fisherhouse.org
Web: www.militaryscholar.org/sfmc/index.html
Summary: To provide financial assistance for college to the children of veterans and military personnel.
Eligibility: Open to sons and daughters of U.S. military servicemembers (including active duty, retirees, Guard/Reserves, and survivors of deceased members) who are enrolled or accepted for enrollment as a full–time undergraduate at a college or university. Applicants must be younger than 23 years of age and enrolled in the Defense Enrollment Eligibility Reporting System (DEERS). They must have a GPA of 3.0 or higher. Along with their application, they must submit a 500–word essay on a topic that changes annually; recently, students were asked to identify the 4 persons whose faces they would place on a 21st century Mount Rushmore type of monument and why. Selection is based on merit.
Financial data: The stipend is $1,500.
Duration: 1 year; recipients may reapply.
Number awarded: At least 1 scholarship is allocated for each of the commissaries worldwide operated by the Defense Commissary Agency (DeCA); more than 1 scholarship per commissary may be available, depending on donations from suppliers and manufacturers whose products are sold at commissaries. Recently, the program awarded more than $1 million to 670 students.
Deadline: February of each year.

837 SCHOLARSHIPS FOR STUDENT LEADERS

National Association for Campus Activities
Attn: NACA Foundation
13 Harbison Way
Columbia, SC 29212–3401
Phone: (803) 732–6222; Fax: (803) 749–1047;
Email: scholarships@naca.org
Web: www.naca.org/Scholarships/Pages/ScholarshipListings.aspx
Summary: To provide financial assistance to outstanding college student leaders.
Eligibility: Open to full–time undergraduate students who have made significant contributions to their campus communities, have played leadership roles in campus activities, and have demonstrated leadership skills and abilities. Financial need is not considered in the selection process. U.S. citizenship is required.
Financial data: A stipend is awarded (amount not specified).
Duration: 1 year.
Number awarded: 7 each year, of which 6 are designated.
Deadline: October of each year.

838 SCHOLARSHIPS FOR USPHS COMMISSIONED CORPS DEPENDENTS

Commissioned Officers Association of the USPHS Inc.
Attn: PHS Commissioned Officers Foundation for the Advancement of Public Health
8201 Corporate Drive, Suite 200
Landover, MD 20785
Phone: (301) 731–9080; Fax: (301) 731–9084;
Email: info@phscof.org
Web: www.phscof.org/education.html
Summary: To provide financial assistance for college or graduate school to dependents of officers of the United States Public Health Service (USPHS) Commissioned Corps.
Eligibility: Open to dependent children and dependent spouses of active–duty, retired, or deceased officers of the USPHS Commissioned Corps. Applicants must be entering or continuing full–time students at a college or graduate school. They must be U.S. citizens and have a GPA of 3.0 or higher. Along with their application, they must submit an essay on why they want to go to college and what they intend to accomplish with their degree. Financial need is not considered in the selection process.
Financial data: Stipends range up to $1,000.
Duration: 1 year.
Number awarded: Varies each year; recently, 12 of these scholarships were awarded.
Deadline: May of each year.

839 SCHOOL PRIDE SCHOLARSHIP

CenturyLinkQuote
5202 West Douglas Corrigan Way, Suite 300
Salt Lake City, UT 84116
Phone: (888) 561–9173
Web: www.centurylinkquote.com/scholarship
Summary: To recognize and reward, with college scholarships, students who submit outstanding essays on how their college has or will contribute to the career path.
Eligibility: Open to seniors who will graduate in the current year from high school or home school, students who will earn a GED in the current year, and full–time college freshmen, sophomores, juniors, and seniors. Applicants must have a GPA of 2.5 or higher; high school seniors must have taken the ACT or SAT. All applicants must be U.S. citizens or permanent residents enrolled or planning to enroll at a 2– or 4–year college or university. They must write an essay of 350 to 500 words on how their college has or will specifically contribute to their career path and post that essay on their blog or web site; any blogging platform qualifies, but Facebook and other social mediums are not acceptable. Selection is based on creativity, thoughtfulness, and insight, as well as how well they promoted their post.
Financial data: The award is a $1,000 scholarship paid directly to the winner's institution.
Duration: The competition is held annually.
Number awarded: 1 each year.
Deadline: May of each year.

840 $ SCHWALLIE FAMILY SCHOLARSHIPS

Organization for Autism Research
Attn: Scholarship
2000 North 14th Street, Suite 710
Arlington, VA 22201
Phone: (703) 243–9710
Web: www.researchautism.org/news/otherevents/scholarship.asp
Summary: To provide financial assistance for college to individuals with autism or Asperger's Syndrome.
Eligibility: Open to individuals with an established autism or Asperger's Syndrome diagnosis who are attending or planning to attend an accredited 2– or 4–year college, university, or vocational/technical institute. Applicants must be enrolled at least part time and be working toward certification or accreditation in a particular field. Along with their application, they must submit a 1,000–word autobiographical essay that includes their reasons for applying for this scholarship. Selection is based on originality of content, previous challenges overcome, future aspirations, and financial need.
Financial data: The stipend is $3,000.
Duration: 1 year; nonrenewable.
Number awarded: Varies each year; recently, 22 of these scholarships were awarded. Since the program was established, it has awarded $178,500 in scholarships to 55 students.
Deadline: April of each year.

841 SCOTT DELGADILLO SCHOLARSHIP

Friends of Scott Foundation
Attn: Scholarship Fund
6977 Navajo Road, Number 168

San Diego, CA 92119
Phone: (619) 223–7268; Fax: (619) 223–7002;
Email: aztec.graphics@yahoo.com
Web: www.friendsofscott.org/scholarship.aspx
Summary: To provide financial assistance for college or graduate school to childhood cancer survivors.
Eligibility: Open to survivors of childhood cancer and to patients currently receiving treatment. Applicants must be attending or planning to attend a technical school, vocational school, junior college, or 4–year college or university as an undergraduate or graduate student. Along with their application, they must submit a 500–word essay on how their experience with cancer has impacted their life. Selection is based on financial need and personal hardship.
Financial data: The stipend is $1,000.
Duration: 1 year.
Number awarded: Varies each year; recently, 4 of these scholarships were awarded.
Deadline: April of each year.

842 SDATAT SCHOLARSHIP

South Dakota Association of Towns and Townships
Attn: Scholarship Program
351 Wisconsin, S.W., Suite 101
P.O. Box 903
Huron, SD 57350–0903
Phone: (605) 353–1439; Fax: (605) 352–5322;
Email: sdtstaff@sdtownships.com
Web: sdtownships.com/7.html
Summary: To provide financial assistance to high school seniors in South Dakota who plan to attend college in the state.
Eligibility: Open to seniors graduating from high schools in South Dakota or who are home schooled. Applicants must be planning to attend a university, college, or vocational school in South Dakota. Along with their application, they must submit a 500–word essay on a topic that changes annually but relates to government; recently, students were asked to discuss the "Alive at 25" program sponsored by the South Dakota Department of Public Safety and the South Dakota Safety Council. The application may be accompanied by up to 2 letters of support; financial need is not considered in the selection process.
Financial data: The stipend is $1,000.
Duration: 1 year.
Number awarded: 1 each year.
Deadline: March of each year.

843 SEABEE MEMORIAL SCHOLARSHIP ASSOCIATION PROGRAM

Seabee Memorial Scholarship Association
P.O. Box 6574
Silver Spring, MD 20916
Phone: (301) 570–2850; Fax: (301) 570–2873;
Email: smsa@erols.com
Web: www.seabee.org/scholarships.shtml
Summary: To provide financial assistance for college to the children or grandchildren of active or deceased members of the Naval Construction Battalion (Seabees) or Navy Civil Engineering Corps.
Eligibility: Open to the children, stepchildren, and grandchildren of regular, Reserve, retired, or deceased officers and enlisted members who are now serving in or have been honorably discharged from the Naval Construction Force (Seabees) or Navy Civil Engineering Corps. Applicants may be high school seniors, high school graduates, or students currently enrolled full–time at a 4–year college or university. Selection is based on financial need, citizenship, leadership, and scholastic record.
Financial data: The stipend is $1,900 per year.
Duration: 1 year; may be renewed for 3 additional years.
Number awarded: Varies each year; recently, 20 new scholarships were awarded through this program.
Deadline: April of each year.

844 $ SEAN SILVER MEMORIAL SCHOLARSHIP

Ulman Cancer Fund for Young Adults
Attn: Scholarship Committee
10440 Little Patuxent Parkway, Suite G1
Columbia, MD 21044
Phone: (410) 964–0202; (888) 393–FUND; Fax: (410) 964–0402;
Email: scholarship@ulmanfund.org
Web: www.ulmanfund.org/scholarship.aspx
Summary: To provide financial assistance for college or graduate school to young adults who have cancer.
Eligibility: Open to students who are younger than 30 years of age and currently undergoing active treatment for cancer. Applicants must be attending or planning to attend a 4–year college or university to work on an undergraduate or graduate degree. They must be U.S. citizens or permanent residents. Along with their application, they must submit an essay of at least 1,000 words on what they have discovered about themselves while attending school as a young adult receiving treatment for or living with cancer. Selection is based on demonstrated dedication to community service, commitment to educational and professional goals, use of their cancer experience to impact the lives of other young adults affected by cancer, medical hardship, and financial need.
Financial data: The stipend is $2,500. Funds are paid directly to the educational institution.
Duration: 1 year.
Number awarded: 1 each year.
Deadline: March of each year.

845 SENATOR ROBERT J. DOLE PUBLIC SERVICE SCHOLARSHIP

University of Kansas
Attn: Robert J. Dole Institute of Politics
2350 Petefish Drive
Lawrence, KS 66045
Phone: (785) 864–4900; Fax: (785) 864–1414;
Email: doleinstitute@ku.edu
Web: www.sms.scholarshipamerica.org/senatordolepublicservice
Summary: To provide financial assistance to high school seniors in Kansas who have demonstrated involvement in volunteer community and public service and plan to attend college in the state.
Eligibility: Open to seniors graduating from public and private high schools in Kansas with a GPA of 3.0 or higher. Applicants must be able to demonstrate significant involvement in volunteer community service projects or public service activities. They must be planning to attend the University of Kansas, Kansas State University, Pittsburg State University, Fort Hays State University, Wichita State University, Emporia State University, or Washburn University. Selection is based on demonstrated leadership and participation in school and community activities, involvement in volunteer community service, work experience, a statement of career and educational aspirations and goals, unusual personal or family circumstances, and an outside appraisal. Special consideration is given to volunteerism, community, and public service, paid or otherwise. Financial need is not considered.
Financial data: The stipend is $1,000 per year.
Duration: 1 year; nonrenewable.
Number awarded: Up to 60 each year.
Deadline: March of each year.

846 $ SERGEANT ANDREW EDMUND TOPHAM MEMORIAL SCHOLARSHIP

Army Scholarship Foundation
11700 Preston Road, Suite 660–301
Dallas, TX 75230
Email: ContactUs@armyscholarshipfoundation.org
Web: www.armyscholarshipfoundation.org/scholarships.html
Summary: To provide financial assistance for undergraduate study to the children and spouses of Army personnel, especially those who served in the Global War on Terrorism.
Eligibility: Open to 1) children of regular active–duty, active–duty Reserve, and active–duty Army National Guard members in good standing; 2) spouses of serving enlisted regular active–duty, active–duty Reserve, and active–duty Army National Guard members in good standing; and 3) children of former U.S. Army members who received an honorable or medical discharge or were killed while serving in the U.S. Army. Preference is given to students who are family members of soldiers who served in either Afghanistan or Iraq as part of the Global War on Terrorism. Applicants must be high school seniors, high school graduates, or undergraduates enrolled at an accredited college, university, or vocational/technical institute. They must be U.S. citizens and have a GPA of 2.0 or higher; children must be younger than 24 years of age. Financial need is considered in the selection process.
Financial data: The stipend ranges from $500 to $2,000 per year.
Duration: 1 year; recipients may reapply.
Number awarded: 1 each year.
Deadline: April of each year.

847 $ SERGEANT FELIX M. DELGRECO, JR. SCHOLARSHIP FUND

Connecticut Community Foundation
43 Field Street
Waterbury, CT 06702–1906
Phone: (203) 753–1315; Fax: (203) 756–3054;
Email: grants@conncf.org
Web: www.conncf.org/scholarships

Summary: To provide financial assistance to high school seniors and current college students whose parents are members of the Connecticut Army National Guard.

Eligibility: Open to the children of members of the Connecticut Army National Guard who are attending or planning to attend college in any state. Applicants must have a grade average of "B–" or higher. Selection is based on academic motivation, extracurricular activities, work experience, a letter of recommendation, financial need, and an essay. U.S. citizenship is required.

Financial data: The stipend is $4,000 per year. Funds are paid directly to the recipient's school.

Duration: 1 year; recipients may reapply up to the minimum number of years required to complete an undergraduate degree in their course of study, provided they maintain a grade average of "C+" or higher.

Number awarded: Varies each year.

Deadline: March of each year.

848 $$ S.E.T. EDUCATIONAL FUND SCHOLARSHIPS

S.E.T. Educational Fund
P.O. Box 36656
Grosse Pointe Farms, MI 48236
Email: contact@setfund.org
Web: www.setfund.org

Summary: To provide financial assistance to underprivileged residents of Michigan attending or planning to attend a public college or university in the state.

Eligibility: Open to Michigan residents who can demonstrate financial need. Applicants must submit 1) proof of Michigan residence; 2) letter of acceptance or current transcript from a Michigan public university; 3) their parents' latest tax return; 4) a letter from a non–family member describing their community service; and 5) a 200–word statement on why they are going to college to obtain their chosen degree.

Financial data: The stipend varies, but recently was $6,500.

Duration: 1 year.

Number awarded: Varies each year; recently, 2 of these scholarships were awarded.

Deadline: May of each year.

849 $ SEVENSECURE ADULT EDUCATION GRANTS

Novo Nordisk Inc.
Attn: Customer Care
100 College Road West
Princeton, NJ 08540
Phone: (609) 987–5800; (877) NOVO–777; Fax: (800) 826–6993
Web: www.changingpossibilities–us.com/SupportPrograms/Education.aspx

Summary: To provide financial assistance for college to adults who have a bleeding disorder.

Eligibility: Open to adults over 23 years of age currently enrolled in college or vocational school. Applicants must have hemophilia with an inhibitor or factor VII deficiency. They must be working on a certificate or associate or bachelor's degree to get more training to help improve their career or transition to a new field.

Financial data: Stipends range up to $2,500 per year. Funds are paid directly to the university or institution.

Duration: 1 year.

Number awarded: Varies each year.

Deadline: Applications may be submitted at any time.

850 $$ SFM FOUNDATION SCHOLARSHIP

SFM Foundation
P.O. Box 582992
Minneapolis, MN 55458–2992
Phone: (952) 838–4323; Fax: (952) 838–2055;
Email: info@sfm–foundation.org
Web: www.sfmic.com/foundation/application_information.cfm

Summary: To provide financial assistance to residents of Minnesota and Wisconsin whose parent was injured or killed in a work–related accident and who are interested in attending college, preferably in those state.

Eligibility: Open to residents of Minnesota and Wisconsin between 16 and 25 years of age who are high school students, GED recipients, or high school graduates. Applicants must be the natural, adopted, or stepchild of a worker injured or killed in a work–related accident during the course and scope of employment with a Minnesota– or Wisconsin–based employer and entitled to receive benefits under the Minnesota Workers' Compensation Act or Worker's Compensation Act of Wisconsin. They must be planning to work on an associate or bachelor's degree or a certificate or license from any accredited school; preference is given to students attending institutions within the Minnesota State Colleges and Universities system or the University of Wisconsin system. Financial need is considered in the selection process.

Financial data: Stipends range from $1,000 to $5,000 per year. Funds are paid directly to the educational institution.

Duration: 1 year; may be renewed, provided the recipient maintains a GPA of 2.0 or higher.

Number awarded: Varies each year.

Deadline: March of each year.

851 SHEPHERD SCHOLARSHIP

Ancient and Accepted Scottish Rite of Freemasonry–Southern Jurisdiction
Supreme Council, 33
Attn: Office of the Grand Executive Director
1733 16th Street, N.W.
Washington, DC 20009–3103
Phone: (202) 232–3579; Fax: (202) 464–0487;
Email: council@scottishrite.org
Web: scottishrite.org/about/philanthropy–scholarships/scholarships

Summary: To provide financial assistance to undergraduate and graduate students who are working on degrees in areas associated with public service.

Eligibility: Open to undergraduate and graduate students who have taken part in social, civic, religious, or fraternal activities in their communities. Applicants must be working on a baccalaureate or graduate degree in a field "associated with service to country and generally perceived as benefiting the human race." U.S. citizenship is required. Selection is based on dedication, ambition, academic record, financial need, and promise of outstanding performance at the advanced level. No Masonic affiliation is required.

Financial data: The stipend is $1,500 per year.

Duration: 4 years.

Number awarded: 1 or more each year.

Deadline: March of each year.

852 SHERMAN AND NANCY REESE SCHOLARSHIPS

Epsilon Sigma Alpha International
Attn: ESA Foundation
363 West Drake Road
Fort Collins, CO 80526
Phone: (970) 223–2824; Fax: (970) 223–4456;
Email: esainfo@epsilonsigmaalpha.org
Web: www.epsilonsigmaalpha.org/esa–foundation/scholarships

Summary: To provide financial assistance to residents of South Carolina and Virginia who plan to attend college in any state.

Eligibility: Open to residents of South Carolina and Virginia who are enrolled at a college or university in any state and have a GPA of 3.0 or higher. Applicants may be majoring in any field. Selection is based on character (10%), leadership (10%), service (5%), financial need (50%), and scholastic ability (25%).

Financial data: The stipend is $1,000.

Duration: 1 year; may be renewed.

Number awarded: 2 each year: 1 to a student who graduated from high school in South Carolina and 1 who graduated from high school in Virginia.

Deadline: January of each year.

853 $ SHIRE ADHD SCHOLARSHIP PROGRAM

Shire US Inc.
Attn: ADHD Scholarship Program
860 High Street
P.O. Box 562
Chestertown, MD 21620
Phone: (484) 595–8248; (855) 474–4732;
Email: mcabrey@shire.com

Web: www.shireadhdscholarship.com

Summary: To provide financial assistance for college to students who have attention deficit/hyperactivity disorder (ADHD).

Eligibility: Open to legal residents of the United States who have been diagnosed with ADHD and are enrolled or accepted in an undergraduate program at an accredited 2– or 4–year college, university, or trade/technical/vocational school. Applicants must be under the care of a licensed health professional, although they are not required to be taking medication or to have a specific future or ongoing plan of management for treatment of their ADHD. Along with their application, they must submit a 500–word essay on how ADHD has impacted their life, the challenges they have faced, and how they managed them or what you are doing to manage them. Selection is based on that essay (50%), letters of recommendation (20%), a 100–word statement on how having an ADHD coach will help them transition to higher education (15%), and a list of community, volunteer, and extracurricular activities (15%).

Financial data: The stipend is $2,000. Funds are paid directly to the recipient's institution.

Duration: 1 year; nonrenewable.

Number awarded: 50 each year.

Deadline: March of each year.

854 SHIRLEY A. DREYER MEMORIAL ENDOWMENT SCHOLARSHIP

Epsilon Sigma Alpha International
Attn: ESA Foundation
363 West Drake Road
Fort Collins, CO 80526
Phone: (970) 223–2824; Fax: (970) 223–4456;
Email: esainfo@epsilonsigmaalpha.org
Web: www.epsilonsigmaalpha.org/esa–foundation/scholarships

Summary: To provide financial assistance to residents of North Carolina who plan to attend college in any state.

Eligibility: Open to residents of North Carolina who are 1) graduating high school seniors with a GPA of 3.0 or higher or with minimum scores of 22 on the ACT or 1030 on the combined critical reading and mathematics SAT; 2) enrolled in college with a GPA of 3.0 or higher; 3) enrolled at a technical school or returning to school after an absence for retraining of job skills or obtaining a degree; or 4) engaged in online study through an accredited college, university, or vocational school. Applicants may be attending or planning to attend an accredited school in any state and major in any field. Selection is based on character (10%), leadership (20%), service (10%), financial need (30%), and scholastic ability (30%).

Financial data: The stipend is $1,000.

Duration: 1 year; may be renewed.

Number awarded: 2 each year.

Deadline: January of each year.

855 SHOE CITY–WB54/WB50 SCHOLARSHIPS

Central Scholarship Bureau
1700 Reisterstown Road, Suite 220
P.O. Box 37064
Baltimore, MD 21297–3064
Phone: (410) 415–5558; Fax: (410) 415–5501;
Email: contact@centralsb.org
Web: www.centralsb.org/html/wb54.htm

Summary: To provide financial assistance to high school seniors in Maryland and Washington, D.C. who plan to attend college in any state.

Eligibility: Open to residents of Maryland and Washington, D.C. who are high school seniors planning to attend an accredited college in any state full time in the following fall. Preference is given to residents of Baltimore City and Washington, D.C. Applicants must submit their high school transcript, a letter of recommendation, a copy of their SAR or FAFSA, and a 500–word essay on their achievements, career and educational goals, and personal or family circumstances demonstrating exceptional merit or need. U.S. citizenship or permanent resident status is required.

Financial data: The stipend is $1,500.

Duration: 1 year; nonrenewable.

Number awarded: 4 each year.

Deadline: May of each year.

856 SICKLE CELL THALASSEMIA PATIENTS NETWORK UNDERGRADUATE SCHOLARSHIPS

Sickle Cell Thalassemia Patients Network
Attn: Scholarships
1139 St. Johns Place
Brooklyn, NY 11213
Phone: (347) 533–8485; Fax: (718) 789–5767;
Email: scholarships@sctpn.org
Web: sctpn.net/scholarship.php

Summary: To provide financial assistance to high school seniors and current college students who are living with an inherited blood disorder and are interested in attending college in any state.

Eligibility: Open to high school seniors and current college students who have been diagnosed with sickle cell disease or thalassemia (Cooley's anemia). Applicants must be attending or planning to attend an accredited 2– or 4–year college or university in any state. Along with their application, they must submit statements on their extracurricular activities, their future educational and career goals, and how they plan to use this scholarship.

Financial data: A stipend is awarded (amount not specified).

Duration: 1 year; recipients may reapply.

Number awarded: 1 or more each year.

Deadline: May of each year.

857 SIGMA GAMMA RHO SCHOLARSHIPS/FELLOWSHIPS

Sigma Gamma Rho Sorority, Inc.
Attn: National Education Fund
1000 Southhill Drive, Suite 200
Cary, NC 27513
Phone: (919) 678–9720; (888) SGR–1922; Fax: (919) 678–9721;
Email: info@sgrho1922.org
Web: www.sgrho1922.org/nef

Summary: To provide financial assistance for undergraduate or graduate study to applicants who can demonstrate financial need.

Eligibility: Open to high school seniors, undergraduates, and graduate students who can demonstrate financial need. The sponsor is a traditionally African American sorority, but support is available to males and females of all races. Applicants must have a GPA of "C" or higher.

Financial data: A stipend is awarded (amount not specified).

Duration: 1 year.

Number awarded: Varies each year.

Deadline: April of each year.

858 $$ SIGNATURE SCHOLARSHIP AWARDS

Grand Lodge of Minnesota, A.F. & A.M.
Attn: Minnesota Masonic Charities
11501 Masonic Home Drive
Bloomington, MN 55437–3699
Phone: (952) 948–6004; (800) 245–6050 (within MN); Fax: (952) 948–6710;
Email: grandlodge@qwest.net
Web: www.mn–masons.org/masonic–programs/scholarships

Summary: To provide financial assistance to high school seniors in Minnesota who demonstrate academic excellence and plan to attend college in any state.

Eligibility: Open to seniors graduating from high schools in Minnesota and planning to attend college in any state. Applicants must have a GPA of 3.8 or higher. Selection is based on academic and personal achievement, community participation or service, and overall excellence. No consideration is given to age, gender, religion, national origin, or Masonic affiliation.

Financial data: The stipend is $5,000 per year.

Duration: 1 year; may be renewed up to 3 additional years.

Number awarded: 5 each year.

Deadline: February of each year.

859 $$ SILENT KEY MEMORIAL SCHOLARSHIPS

Foundation for Amateur Radio, Inc.
Attn: Scholarship Committee
P.O. Box 911
Columbia, MD 21044–0911
Phone: (410) 552–2652; Fax: (410) 981–5146;
Email: dave.prestel@gmail.com
Web: www.farweb.org/scholarships

Summary: To provide funding to licensed radio amateurs who are interested in attending college.

Eligibility: Open to residents of the United States who have an amateur radio license. Applicants must be interested in working full time on a bachelor's degree in any field at a college or university in any state. Financial need is considered in the selection process.

Financial data: The stipend is $5,000.
Duration: 1 year.
Number awarded: 2 each year.
Deadline: April each year.

860 SMART PROGRAM SCHOLARSHIPS

United States Bowling Congress
Attn: SMART Program
621 Six Flags Drive
Arlington, TX 76011
Phone: (800) 514–BOWL, ext. 3168;
Email: smart@bowl.com
Web: www.bowl.com/smart/index.aspx

Summary: To recognize and reward, with scholarships for college and other educational activities, young bowlers who compete in state and local tournaments or leagues.

Eligibility: Open to bowlers who compete at state and local levels throughout the United States and Canada. Some scholarships are presented to winners of bowling tournaments, but others require written applications. Some require demonstrations of financial need, but others are based on bowling and/or academic accomplishments. Some are limited to students, but others are open to bowlers at other levels. All scholarships must conform to the standards of the Scholarship Management and Accounting Reports for Tenpins (SMART) program of the United States Bowling Congress (USBC).

Financial data: The stipends vary. Funds may be used for tuition, fees, textbooks, meal plans, housing plans, or required class supplies and equipment necessary for the successful completion of a course or program at a university, college, business school, technical school, trade school, vocational school, or continuing education course. Support is not available for transportation expenses, clothing expenses, sport camp or lessons, sports equipment or supplies, private tutor fees, or elementary or high school tuition or fees.

Duration: Funds must be used within 6 years from high school graduation or, if the recipient has already graduated from high school, from the date they won the scholarship.

Number awarded: Varies each year; recently, more than 35,000 bowlers received more than $2.7 million in scholarships. For a complete list of all these scholarship opportunities, contact the sponsor.

Deadline: Deadline not specified.

861 SOCIETY OF DAUGHTERS OF THE UNITED STATES ARMY SCHOLARSHIPS

Society of Daughters of the United States Army
c/o Janet B. Otto, Scholarship Chair
7717 Rockledge Court
Springfield, VA 21152

Summary: To provide financial assistance for college to daughters and granddaughters of active, retired, or deceased career Army warrant and commissioned officers.

Eligibility: Open to the daughters, adopted daughters, stepdaughters, or granddaughters of career commissioned officers or warrant officers of the U.S. Army (active, regular, or Reserve) who 1) are currently on active duty; 2) retired after 20 years of active duty or were medically retired; or 3) died while on active duty or after retiring from active duty with 20 or more years of service. Applicants must have at least a 3.0 GPA and be studying or planning to study at the undergraduate level. Selection is based on depth of character, leadership, seriousness of purpose, academic achievement, and financial need.

Financial data: Scholarships, to a maximum of $1,000, are paid directly to the college or school for tuition, laboratory fees, books, or other expenses.

Duration: 1 year; may be renewed up to 4 additional years if the recipient maintains at least a 3.0 GPA.

Number awarded: Varies each year.

Deadline: February of each year.

862 $$ SONIA STREULI MAGUIRE OUTSTANDING SCHOLASTIC ACHIEVEMENT AWARD

Swiss Benevolent Society of New York
Attn: Scholarship Committee
500 Fifth Avenue, Room 1800
New York, NY 10110
Phone: (212) 246–0655; Fax: (212) 246–1366;
Email: scholarships@sbsny.org
Web: www.sbsny.org/sbs_scholarships.html

Summary: To provide financial assistance to college seniors and graduate students of Swiss descent in the Northeast.

Eligibility: Open to college seniors and graduate students who are residents of Connecticut, New Jersey, Pennsylvania, Delaware, or New York. Applicants must be able to demonstrate sustained academic excellence (at least a 3.8 GPA) in a demanding course of study. Either the applicant or at least 1 parent must be a Swiss national. Financial need is not considered in the selection process.

Financial data: The stipend ranges from $4,000 to $6,000 per year. Funds are paid directly to the recipient's school in 2 installments (beginning of fall semester and beginning of spring semester).

Duration: 1 year; nonrenewable.

Number awarded: 1 or 2 each year.

Deadline: March of each year.

863 $$ SONLIGHT SCHOLARSHIPS

Sonlight Curriculum, Ltd.
Attn: Scholarship Committee
8042 South Grant Way
Littleton, CO 80122–2705
Phone: (303) 730–6292; Fax: (303) 730–6509;
Email: scholarship@sonlight.com
Web: www.sonlight.com/scholarships.html

Summary: To provide financial assistance for college to home–schooled students who have utilized Sonlight Core programs.

Eligibility: Open to high school seniors and current college students who have been home schooled and used at least 5 Sonlight Core programs for at least 3 years. Applicants must submit 1) measures of academic performance, such as ACT or SAT scores; 2) a list of extracurricular activities; 3) a 2–page personal essay on how their future plans and aspirations fit in with the purposes of God (including references to seeking God's Kingdom, asserting the crown rights of King Jesus, and how their future plans or purposes will help extend His Kingdom); 4) a 3–page project (e.g., review, digest, portfolio) on a mathematics, science, performing arts, or visual arts discipline of interest or concern to them; and 5) a 3–page argumentative essay on a topic of their choice. For some of the awards (which the sponsor designates as the "Green Criteria"), selection is based on these factors in the following order: creativity, mission–mindedness, or acts of kindness; spiritual–mindedness; leadership; academic performance; heart for learning; and activities and interests. For other awards (which the sponsor designates as the "Blue Criteria"), selection is based on the same criteria but in the following order: academic performance; spiritual–mindedness; leadership; creativity, mission–mindedness, or acts of kindness; heart for learning; and activities and interests. Students indicate on their applications the criteria by which they wish to be judged.

Financial data: Stipends are $20,000 ($5,000 per year), $10,000 ($2,500 per year), or $4,000 ($1,000 per year).

Duration: 4 years, provided the recipients maintain a GPA of 3.5 or higher and provide the sponsor with a copy of their college transcript.

Number awarded: 13 each year: 1 at $5,000 per year, 4 at $2,500 per year, and 8 at $1,000 per year, awarded in this way: 2 at $2,500 per year and 2 at $1,000 per year selected according to the "Green Criteria" and 1 at $5,000 per year, 2 at $2,500 per year, and 6 at $1,000 per year selected according to the "Blue Criteria."

Deadline: December of each year.

864 $$ SONS OF ITALY NATIONAL LEADERSHIP GRANTS

Order Sons of Italy in America
Attn: Sons of Italy Foundation
219 E Street, N.E.
Washington, DC 20002
Phone: (202) 547–2900; (800) 552–OSIA; Fax: (202) 546–8168;
Email: scholarships@osia.org
Web: www.osia.org/students/scholarships.php

Summary: To provide financial assistance to undergraduate and graduate students of Italian descent.

Eligibility: Open to U.S. citizens of Italian descent who are enrolled as full–time students in an undergraduate or graduate program at an accredited 4–year college or university. Both high school seniors and students already enrolled in college are eligible for the undergraduate awards. Applications must be accompanied by essays, from 500 to 750 words in length, on a personal experience that demonstrated or generated pride in their Italian heritage. These merit–based awards are presented to students who have demonstrated exceptional leadership qualities and distinguished scholastic abilities.

Financial data: Stipends range from $5,000 to $25,000.

Duration: 1 year; nonrenewable.

Number awarded: 10 to 12 each year.

Deadline: February of each year.

865 $ SOOZIE COURTER SHARING A BRIGHTER TOMORROW HEMOPHILIA SCHOLARSHIP

Pfizer Inc.
Attn: Hemophilia Scholarship Program (QD Healthcare Group)
One Dock Street, Suite 520
Stamford, CT 06902
Phone: (888) 999–2349
Web: www.hemophiliavillage.com

Summary: To provide financial assistance for college or graduate school in any field to persons with hemophilia.

Eligibility: Open to persons with hemophilia (A or B) who are high school seniors, have a GED, or are currently attending an accredited college, university, junior college, vocational school, or graduate school. Along with their application, they must submit a 2–page essay on 1 of the following topics: 1) how hemophilia has affected their school life and how they have overcome those challenges; 2) the advice they would give to a child with hemophilia who is beginning school; or 3) the time in history they would travel back to if they could and why. Financial need is not considered in the selection process.

Financial data: The stipends are $2,500 for undergraduate students or $4,000 for graduate students.

Duration: 1 year.

Number awarded: 17 each year: 12 to undergraduates and 5 to graduate students.

Deadline: July of each year.

866 SOPHIA L. GOKEY SCHOLARSHIP AWARD

Sophia's Heart
Attn: Scholarships
544 East Ogden Avenue, Suite 700–262
Milwaukee, WI 53202
Email: info@sophiasheart.org
Web: www.sophiasheart.org/SophiaLGokeyScholarshipAward.php

Summary: To provide financial assistance for college to high school seniors who have been challenged with a roadblock or set back (including a disability) to completing their education.

Eligibility: Open to graduating high school seniors who plan to enroll at a college or university. Applicants must have been challenged with a significant roadblock or setback, such as a disability, that could stifle their desire to pursue their dream of a higher education. They must have a GPA of 2.75 or higher. Along with their application, they must submit a 500–word essay describing the dream they are pursuing and the significant roadblock, setback, or challenge they have faced along the way. Selection is based on that essay, GPA, accomplishments in community service, and participation in extracurricular activities.

Financial data: The stipend is $1,000.

Duration: 1 year.

Number awarded: 1 or more each year.

Deadline: December of each year.

867 SOUTH CAROLINA CAREER AND TECHNOLOGY EDUCATION ADMINISTRATION ASSOCIATION SCHOLARSHIP

South Carolina Career and Technology Education Administration Association
c/o Chet Horton, Scholarship Committee
874 Vocational Lane
Camden, SC 29020

Summary: To provide financial assistance to high school seniors in South Carolina who are completing a career and technology program and planning to attend college in any state.

Eligibility: Open to seniors graduating from high schools in South Carolina who are classified as a career and technology education completer by having earned 4 or more CATE Carnegie units of site–based credit. Applicants must be planning to enroll at a college or technical school in any state. Along with their application, they must submit an essay on why they need financial assistance to complete their educational and career goals. Selection is based on financial need (30%), career plans and goals (20%), course work related to career goals (20%), awards and activities (10%), work experience (10%), and completeness of application (10%).

Financial data: The stipend is $1,500.

Duration: 1 year; nonrenewable.

Number awarded: 1 or more each year.

Deadline: March of each year.

868 $ SOUTH CAROLINA HOPE SCHOLARSHIPS

South Carolina Commission on Higher Education
Attn: Student Services
1122 Lady Street, Suite 300
Columbia, SC 29201
Phone: (803) 737–4397; (877) 349–7183; Fax: (803) 737–2297;
Email: ghampton@che.sc.gov
Web: www.che.sc.gov/New_Web/GoingToCollege/HOPE_Hm.htm

Summary: To provide financial assistance to high school seniors in South Carolina who plan to attend a 4–year institution in the state.

Eligibility: Open to seniors graduating from high schools or completing a home school program in South Carolina who are planning to enroll full time at a 4–year public or private college or university in the state, Applicants must have a GPA of 3.0 or higher. They cannot have been convicted of any felony or drug– or alcohol–related misdemeanor during the past academic year and cannot be eligible for the Palmetto Fellows or LIFE Scholarship Programs. U.S. citizenship or permanent resident status is required. Selection is based on merit.

Financial data: The maximum stipend is $2,800, including a $300 book allowance.

Duration: 1 year; nonrenewable.

Number awarded: Varies each year; recently, 2,556 students received support from this program.

Deadline: Deadline not specified.

869 SOUTH CAROLINA LOTTERY TUITION ASSISTANCE PROGRAM

South Carolina Commission on Higher Education
Attn: Lottery Tuition Assistance Program
1122 Lady Street, Suite 300
Columbia, SC 29201
Phone: (803) 737–2262; (877) 349–7183; Fax: (803) 737–2297;
Email: ecaulder@che.sc.gov
Web: www.che.sc.gov/New_Web/GoingToCollege/LTA_Hm.htm

Summary: To provide financial assistance to needy students at 2–year colleges in South Carolina.

Eligibility: Open to students at 2–year public and private colleges and technical schools in South Carolina who meet the qualifications of financial need as established by the financial aid office at the institution they are attending. Applicants must be U.S. citizens or permanent residents and residents of South Carolina. They may not be receiving other scholarship assistance from the South Carolina Commission on Higher Education.

Financial data: The amount of the assistance varies each year; recently, full–time students were eligible for up to $936 per semester and part–time students were eligible for up to $78 per credit hour.

Duration: 1 semester; may be renewed.

Number awarded: Varies each year; recently, 28,269 students received support from this program.

Deadline: Deadline not specified.

870 $$ SOUTH CAROLINA NATIONAL GUARD COLLEGE ASSISTANCE PROGRAM

South Carolina Commission on Higher Education
Attn: Student Services
1122 Lady Street, Suite 300
Columbia, SC 29201
Phone: (803) 737–2144; (877) 349–7183; Fax: (803) 737–2297;
Email: mbrown@che.sc.gov
Web: www.che.sc.gov/New_Web/GoingToCollege/FinAsst.htm

Summary: To provide financial assistance to members of the South Carolina National Guard who are interested in attending college in the state.

Eligibility: Open to members of the South Carolina National Guard who are in good standing and have not already received a bachelor's or graduate degree. Applicants must be admitted, enrolled, and classified as a degree–seeking full– or part–time student at an eligible institution in South Carolina. They may not be taking continuing education or graduate course work. U.S. citizenship or permanent resident status is required.

Financial data: This program provides full payment of the cost of attendance, including tuition, fees, and textbooks, to a maximum of $9,000 per year for members of the Air National Guard or $4,500 for members of the Army National Guard. The cumulative total of all benefits received from this program may not exceed $18,000.

Duration: Support is provided for up to 130 semester hours of study, provided the Guard member maintains satisfactory academic progress as defined by the institution.
Number awarded: Varies each year.
Deadline: Deadline not specified.

871 $ SOUTH CAROLINA NEED–BASED GRANTS PROGRAM

South Carolina Commission on Higher Education
Attn: Need–Based Grant Coordinator
1122 Lady Street, Suite 300
Columbia, SC 29201
Phone: (803) 737–2262; (877) 349–7183; Fax: (803) 737–2297;
Email: ecaulder@che.sc.gov
Web: www.che.sc.gov/New_Web/GoingToCollege/NBG_Hm.htm
Summary: To provide financial assistance to South Carolina residents who have financial need and plan to attend college in the state.
Eligibility: Open to residents of South Carolina who meet the qualifications of financial need as established by the financial aid office at the college or university in South Carolina that they are attending or planning to attend. Assistance is provided at participating South Carolina public or private 2– or 4–year colleges and universities. Applicants must be enrolled for their first 1–year program, first associate degree, first 2–year program leading to a bachelor's degree, first bachelor's degree, or first professional degree. U.S. citizenship or legal resident status is required.
Financial data: Grants up to $2,500 per academic year are available to full–time students and up to $1,250 per academic year to part–time students.
Duration: 1 year; may be renewed for up to 8 full–time equivalent terms.
Number awarded: Varies each year; recently, 25,175 students received support from this program.
Deadline: Deadline not specified.

872 $ SOUTH CAROLINA TUITION GRANTS PROGRAM

South Carolina Higher Education Tuition Grants Commission
Attn: Executive Director
800 Dutch Square Boulevard, Suite 260A
Columbia, SC 29210–7317
Phone: (803) 896–1120; Fax: (803) 896–1126;
Email: info@sctuitiongrants.org
Web: www.sctuitiongrants.com
Summary: To provide financial assistance to students at independent colleges and universities in South Carolina.
Eligibility: Open to residents of South Carolina who are attending or accepted for enrollment as full–time students at eligible private institutions in the state. Applicants must 1) graduate in the upper 75% of their high school class; 2) score 900 or above on the mathematics and critical reading SAT or 19 or above on the ACT; or 3) graduate with a high school GPA of 2.0 or higher. Selection is based on financial need.
Financial data: The amounts of the awards depend on the need of the recipient and the tuition and fees at the institution to be attended. Recently, the maximum grant was $2,600 and the average grant was approximately $2,350. Funds may not be used for part–time enrollment, room and board charges, summer school enrollment, or graduate school enrollment.
Duration: 1 year; may be renewed.
Number awarded: Varies each year; recently, approximately 14,200 students were receiving in excess of $33 million in support from this program.
Deadline: June of each year.

873 $$ SOUTH CAROLINA TUITION PROGRAM FOR CHILDREN OF CERTAIN WAR VETERANS

South Carolina Office of Veterans Affairs
c/o VA Regional Office Building
6437 Garners Ferry Road, Suite 1126
Columbia, SC 29209
Phone: (803) 647–2434; Fax: (803) 647–2312;
Email: va@oepp.sc.gov
Web: www.govoepp.state.sc.us/va/benefits.html
Summary: To provide free college tuition to the children of disabled and other South Carolina veterans.
Eligibility: Open to the children of war time veterans who were legal residents of South Carolina both at the time of entry into military or naval service and during service, or who have been residents of South Carolina for at least 1 year. Veteran parents must 1) be permanently and totally disabled as determined by the U.S. Department of Veterans Affairs; 2) have been a prisoner of war; 3) have been killed in action; 4) have died from other causes while in service; 5) have died of a disease or disability resulting from service; 6) be currently missing in action; 7) have received the Congressional Medal of Honor; 8) have received the Purple Heart Medal from wounds received in combat; or 9) now be deceased but qualified under categories 1 or 2 above. The veteran's child must be 26 years of age or younger and working on an undergraduate degree.
Financial data: Children who qualify are eligible for free tuition at any South Carolina state–supported college, university, or postsecondary technical education institution. The waiver applies to tuition only. The costs of room and board, certain fees, and books are not covered.
Duration: Students are eligible to receive this support as long as they are younger than 26 years of age and working on an undergraduate degree.
Number awarded: Varies each year.
Deadline: Deadline not specified.

874 SOUTH DAKOTA JUMP START SCHOLARSHIPS

South Dakota Board of Regents
Attn: Scholarship Committee
306 East Capitol Avenue, Suite 200
Pierre, SD 57501–3159
Phone: (605) 773–3455; Fax: (605) 773–5320;
Email: info@sdbor.edu
Web: www.sdbor.edu/students/JumpStart.htm
Summary: To provide financial assistance to high school students in South Dakota who graduate early and attend college in the state.
Eligibility: Open to public high school students in South Dakota who completed all graduation graduates before the start of their fourth year. Applicants must plan to enroll full time at an accredited 2– or 4–year public or private college or university in the state.
Financial data: The stipend is $1,812.
Duration: 1 year; nonrenewable.
Number awarded: Varies each year.
Deadline: Deadline not specified.

875 $ SOUTH DAKOTA OPPORTUNITY SCHOLARSHIP

South Dakota Board of Regents
Attn: Vice President for Research and Economic Development
306 East Capitol Avenue, Suite 200
Pierre, SD 57501–2545
Phone: (605) 773–3455; Fax: (605) 773–2422;
Email: pault@sdbor.edu
Web: sdos.sdbor.edu
Summary: To provide financial assistance to South Dakota high school seniors who plan to attend college in the state.
Eligibility: Open to seniors who are graduating from high schools in South Dakota and have completed specified curriculum requirements. Applicants must be interested in attending designated public and private institutions of higher education in the state. They may have received no grade below a "C" and must have a cumulative high school GPA of 3.0 or higher as well as a score of at least 24 on the ACT or 1090 on the critical reading and mathematics portions of the SAT.
Financial data: The stipend is $1,000 per year for the first 3 years and $2,000 for the fourth year.
Duration: 4 years, provided recipients maintain a GPA of 3.0 or higher and full–time enrollment.
Number awarded: Varies each year; recently, 1,229 students received initial awards from this program.
Deadline: August of each year for fall term; January of each year for spring term.

876 $$ SOUTH DAKOTA REDUCED TUITION FOR CHILDREN OF DECEASED FIREFIGHTERS, POLICE OFFICERS OR EMTS

South Dakota Board of Regents
Attn: Scholarship Committee
306 East Capitol Avenue, Suite 200
Pierre, SD 57501–2545
Phone: (605) 773–3455; Fax: (605) 773–2422;
Email: info@sdbor.edu
Web: www.sdbor.edu/students/redtuit_childsurvivor.htm

Summary: To provide free tuition at South Dakota public colleges and universities to children of deceased firefighters, law enforcement officers, and emergency medical technicians (EMTs).

Eligibility: Open to residents of South Dakota who are the survivor of a firefighter, certified law enforcement officer, or EMT who died as a direct result of injuries received in performance of official duties. Applicants must have been accepted for enrollment at a state–supported institution of higher education or technical or vocational school. The death of the parent must have occurred before the child reached 21 years of age.

Financial data: Eligible students receive a 100% tuition waiver. The waiver applies only to tuition, not fees.

Duration: Until completion of a bachelor's or vocational degree; the degree must be earned within 36 months or 8 semesters.

Number awarded: Varies each year.

Deadline: Deadline not specified.

877 $$ SOUTH DAKOTA REDUCED TUITION FOR CHILDREN OF DECEASED SERVICEMEN/WOMEN

South Dakota Board of Regents
Attn: Scholarship Committee
306 East Capitol Avenue, Suite 200
Pierre, SD 57501–2545
Phone: (605) 773–3455; Fax: (605) 773–2422;
Email: info@sdbor.edu
Web: www.sdbor.edu/students/redtuit_childservice.htm

Summary: To provide free tuition at South Dakota public colleges and universities to children of military personnel who died while in service.

Eligibility: Open to residents of South Dakota younger than 25 years of age. The applicant's parent must have been killed in action or died of other causes while on active duty and must have been a resident of South Dakota for at least 6 months immediately preceding entry into active service.

Financial data: Qualifying applicants are granted a 100% tuition waiver at state–supported postsecondary institutions in South Dakota. The waiver applies only to tuition, not fees.

Duration: 8 semesters or 12 quarters of either full– or part–time study.

Number awarded: Varies each year.

Deadline: Deadline not specified.

878 $$ SOUTH DAKOTA REDUCED TUITION FOR DEPENDENTS OF PRISONERS OF WAR OR MISSING IN ACTION

South Dakota Board of Regents
Attn: Scholarship Committee
306 East Capitol Avenue, Suite 200
Pierre, SD 57501–2545
Phone: (605) 773–3455; Fax: (605) 773–2422;
Email: info@sdbor.edu
Web: www.sdbor.edu/students/redtuit_deppowmia.htm

Summary: To provide free tuition at South Dakota public colleges and universities to dependents of prisoners of war (POWs) and persons missing in action (MIAs).

Eligibility: Open to residents of South Dakota who are the dependents of POWs or of MIAs who are officially listed as residents of the state. Dependents include 1) children born before or during the period of time when the parent was declared MIA or POW; 2) children legally adopted or in legal custody of the parent during the period of time when the parent was declared MIA or POW; and 3) the spouse (if not legally separated) of the individual who is MIA or POW. Applicants must be attending or planning to attend a state–supported school in South Dakota.

Financial data: For those who qualify, tuition and mandatory fees are waived.

Duration: 8 semesters or 12 quarters of either full– or part–time study.

Number awarded: Varies each year.

Deadline: Deadline not specified.

879 $$ SOUTH DAKOTA REDUCED TUITION FOR VETERANS

South Dakota Board of Regents
Attn: Scholarship Committee
306 East Capitol Avenue, Suite 200
Pierre, SD 57501–2545
Phone: (605) 773–3455; Fax: (605) 773–2422;
Email: info@sdbor.edu
Web: www.sdbor.edu/students/redtuit_Veterans.htm

Summary: To provide free tuition at South Dakota public colleges and universities to certain veterans.

Eligibility: Open to current residents of South Dakota who have been discharged from the military forces of the United States under honorable conditions. Applicants must meet 1 of the following criteria: 1) served on active duty at any time between August 2, 1990 and March 3, 1991; 2) received an Armed Forces Expeditionary Medal, Southwest Asia Service Medal, or other U.S. campaign or service medal for participation in combat operations against hostile forces outside the boundaries of the United States: or 3) have a service–connected disability rating of at least 10%. They may not be eligible for any other educational assistance from the U.S. government. Qualifying veterans must apply for this benefit within 20 years after the date proclaimed for the cessation of hostilities or within 6 years from and after the date of their discharge from military service, whichever is later. They must be attending or planning to attend a South Dakota state–supported institution of higher education or state–supported technical or vocational school.

Financial data: Eligible veterans receive a waiver of tuition. The waiver applies only to tuition, not fees.

Duration: Eligible veterans are entitled to receive 1 month of tuition waiver for each month of qualifying service, from a minimum of 1 year to a maximum of 4 years.

Number awarded: Varies each year.

Deadline: Deadline not specified.

880 SOVEREIGN GRAND COMMANDER'S SCHOLARSHIP PROGRAM

Ancient and Accepted Scottish Rite of Freemasonry–Southern Jurisdiction
Supreme Council, 33
Attn: Director of Education
1733 16th Street, N.W.
Washington, DC 20009–3103
Phone: (202) 232–3579; Fax: (202) 464–0487;
Email: council@scottishrite.org
Web: scottishrite.org/about/philanthropy–scholarships/scholarships

Summary: To provide financial assistance to high school seniors who plan to attend college in the United States.

Eligibility: Open to graduating high school seniors who plan to attend an accredited university, college, or vocational school in the United States. Applicants must be able to demonstrate volunteer experience; participation in social, civic, religious, and fraternal activities of the community; or other demonstrated leadership ability. They must have a GPA of 2.8 or higher, but GPA is not of the greatest importance in the selection process. No Masonic affiliation is required. Emphasis is placed on financial need, volunteer experience, leadership qualities, special circumstances, ambition, dedication, and academic preparation. U.S. citizenship is required.

Financial data: The amount of the stipend varies each year.

Duration: 4 years, or until completion of a bachelor's degree or vocational license or certification, whichever comes first. Renewal depends on the recipient's maintaining a GPA of 3.0 or higher.

Number awarded: 1 or more each year.

Deadline: March of each year.

881 $ SOVEREIGN NATIONS SCHOLARSHIP FUND FOR MAINSTREAM UNIVERSITIES

American Indian College Fund
Attn: Scholarship Department
8333 Greenwood Boulevard
Denver, CO 80221
Phone: (303) 426–8900; (800) 776–FUND; Fax: (303) 426–1200;
Email: scholarships@collegefund.org
Web: www.collegefund.org/content/full_circle_scholarships_listings

Summary: To provide financial assistance to Native American students who are interested in attending a mainstream university.

Eligibility: Open to American Indians and Alaska Natives who can document proof of enrollment or descendancy. Applicants must be enrolled or planning to enroll full time in a bachelor's degree program at a mainstream institution. They must have a GPA of 2.0 or higher and be able to demonstrate exceptional academic achievement. Applications are available only online and include required essays on specified topics. U.S. citizenship is required.

Financial data: The stipend is $2,000 per year.

Duration: 1 year; may be renewed.

Number awarded: Varies each year.

Deadline: May of each year.

882 $ SOVEREIGN NATIONS SCHOLARSHIP FUND FOR TRIBAL COLLEGES

American Indian College Fund
Attn: Scholarship Department
8333 Greenwood Boulevard
Denver, CO 80221
Phone: (303) 426–8900; (800) 776–FUND; Fax: (303) 426–1200;
Email: scholarships@collegefund.org
Web: www.collegefund.org/content/full_circle_scholarships_listings

Summary: To provide financial assistance for college to Native American students who are interested in attending a Tribal College or University (TCU) and working for a tribe or Indian organization after graduation.

Eligibility: Open to American Indians and Alaska Natives who can document proof of enrollment or descendancy. Applicants must be planning to 1) enroll full time at a TCU; and 2) work for their tribe or an Indian organization after graduation. They must have a GPA of 3.0 or higher and be able to demonstrate exceptional academic achievement. Applications are available only online and include required essays on specified topics. U.S. citizenship is required.

Financial data: The stipend is $2,000 per year.

Duration: 1 year; may be renewed.

Number awarded: Varies each year.

Deadline: May of each year.

883 $$ SPARE FUNDS SCHOLARSHIP

SpareFoot, Inc.
720 Brazos Street, Suite 300
Austin, TX 78701
Phone: (512) 705–6208;
Email: matt@sparefoot.com
Web: www.sparefoot.com/scholarship.html

Summary: To provide financial assistance to undergraduates who use the online service of SpareFoot to locate a self–storage unit.

Eligibility: Open to full–time undergraduate students who locate and use a temporary self–storage unit through the online service of SpareFoot. Applicants must submit 100–word statements about 1) themselves, their passions, and their future plans; 2) why they needed storage and how their experience went; and 3) what they thought of SpareFoot and how the service could be improved. Selection is based on those statements, academic performance, and extracurricular involvement.

Financial data: The winner receives a stipend of $5,000 and reimbursement of rent paid for the self–storage unit.

Duration: 1 year.

Number awarded: 1 each year.

Deadline: May of each year.

884 $ SPORTSMANSHIP RECOGNITION PROGRAM SCHOLARSHIP

Kentucky High School Athletic Association
Attn: Assistant Commissioner
2280 Executive Drive
Lexington, KY 40505
Phone: (859) 299–5472; Fax: (859) 293–5999;
Email: bcope@khsaa.org
Web: www.khsaa.org/sportsmanship

Summary: To recognize and reward, with college scholarships, outstanding student–athletes (including cheerleaders) in Kentucky high schools.

Eligibility: Open to high school seniors in Kentucky who have participated in athletics or cheerleading. Applicants must have at least a 2.5 GPA, 3 letters of recommendation from coaches and administrators illustrating the student's traits of good sportsmanship, demonstrated leadership within the school and the community, and a 2–page essay on a topic that changes annually (recently, students were asked to discuss why they play sports, how their participation prepares them for their future, and the impact of sports participation on themselves, their school, and their community). They must be planning to attend a college or university in Kentucky. A male and a female are recognized from each school in the state. They are chosen on the basis of these traits: playing the game by the rules; treating game officials, coaches, and competitors with due respect; shaking hands with opponents at the end of each contest; taking victory and defeat without undue emotionalism; controlling their tempers; being positive with officials, coaches, and competitors who criticize them; cooperating with officials, coaches, and fellow players in trying to promote good sportsmanship; being positive with opponents; letting student and adult audiences know that inappropriate behavior reflects poorly on the team; and serving as a role model for future student–athletes. These students are awarded a certificate and are entered into a regional competition. Males and females continue to compete separately. The regional winners are given a plaque and are considered for the Sportsmanship Recognition Program Scholarship. Selection is based on GPA, recommendations, leadership roles and honors, and the case study essay.

Financial data: The stipend is $3,000.

Duration: 1 year.

Number awarded: 2 each year: 1 for a female and 1 for a male.

Deadline: Applications must be submitted to the school's athletic director in March.

885 $$ SPORTSMANSHIP SCHOLARSHIP

HP Hood LLC
Attn: Sportsmanship Scholarship
Six Kimball Lane
Lynnfield, MA 01940
Phone: (800) 662–4468
Web: www.hood.com

Summary: To provide financial assistance to high school seniors in New England who have participated in a varsity sport and plan to attend college in any state.

Eligibility: Open to seniors graduating from high schools in the New England states who have participated in at least 1 varsity sport. Applicants must be planning to attend an accredited 2– or 4–year college or university in any state. They must have a GPA of 3.0 or higher and a record of volunteer work in their community. Along with their application, they must submit a 250–word essay on why they are a "good sport" on and off the field. Entries are posted online and the public votes for the outstanding students. The 10 students in each state who receive the most votes are then interviewed to select the winners. Financial need is not considered.

Financial data: The stipend is $5,000.

Duration: 1 year.

Number awarded: 18 each year: 3 in each of the New England states.

Deadline: February of each year.

886 $$ SPOUSE/CAREGIVER SCHOLARSHIPS

Hope for the Warriors
Attn: Spouse/Caregiver Scholarships Director
1011 South MacDill Avenue, Suite 812
Tampa, FL 33629
Phone: (877) 246–7349;
Email: scholarship@hopeforthewarriors.org
Web: www.hopeforthewarriors.org/spouse.html

Summary: To provide financial assistance for college to the spouses and caregivers of wounded or deceased military personnel or veterans.

Eligibility: Open to spouses and caregivers of current and former servicemembers who were wounded or killed in the line of duty since September 11, 2001. Applicants must be enrolled or planning to enroll full or part time at an accredited college, university, or trade school to work on a bachelor's degree, master's degree, or vocational certification. They must have a high school GPA of 2.6 or higher or a GED score of 650 or higher. Along with their application, they must submit a 500–word essay on how their life has been impacted by the Global War on Terror and how that impact played a role in their pursuit of higher education. Selection is based on that essay, academic achievement, personal goals, and letters of recommendation.

Financial data: The stipend is $5,000 or $1,250 per year.

Duration: 1 year; may be renewed up to 3 additional years.

Number awarded: 5 each year: 4 at $5,000 and 1 at $1,250.

Deadline: March of each year.

887 $ SPOUSE EDUCATION ASSISTANCE PROGRAM

Army Emergency Relief
200 Stovall Street
Alexandria, VA 22332–0600
Phone: (703) 428–0000; (866) 878–6378; Fax: (703) 325–7183;
Email: Spouse@aerhq.org
Web: www.aerhq.org/dnn563/EducationalAssistance/Spouses.aspx

Summary: To provide financial assistance for college to the dependent spouses of Army personnel.

Eligibility: Open to spouses of Army soldiers on active duty, widow(er)s of soldiers who died while on active duty, spouses of retired soldiers, and widow(er)s of soldiers who died while in a retired status. Applicants may be residing in the United States or overseas. They must be working full or part time on a 4–year college degree and have a GPA of 2.0 or higher. Study for a second undergraduate or graduate degree is not supported. Selection is based primarily on financial need.

Financial data: The maximum stipend is $2,800 per academic year.

Duration: 1 year; may be renewed up to 3 additional years of full–time study or up to 7 additional years of part–time study.

Number awarded: Varies each year; recently, approximately 2,000 spouses received support annually.

Deadline: March of each year.

888 $$ SREB ACADEMIC COMMON MARKET

Southern Regional Education Board
592 Tenth Street N.W.
Atlanta, GA 30318–5776
Phone: (404) 875–9211; Fax: (404) 872–1477;
Email: acm–rcp@sreb.org
Web: www.sreb.org/page/1304/academic_common_market.html

Summary: To enable undergraduate and graduate students from southern states to attend a public college or university in another southern state at reduced tuition.

Eligibility: Open to residents of the following southern states: Alabama, Arkansas, Delaware, Georgia, Kentucky, Louisiana, Maryland, Mississippi, Oklahoma, South Carolina, Tennessee, Virginia, and West Virginia; Florida and Texas also participate but only at the graduate level. Applicants must be interested in studying in a program not available at any public institution of higher education in their home state. If their state has made arrangements to send students to another state, they may participate in this program.

Financial data: Participants pay only the in–state tuition at the institution outside their home state while they are studying in a program not available in their home state.

Duration: 1 year; may be renewed.

Number awarded: Varies each year; recently, more than 2,200 students participated in this program.

Deadline: Deadline not specified.

889 $ ST. ANDREW'S SOCIETY OF WASHINGTON SCHOLARSHIPS

St. Andrew's Society of Washington, D.C.
Attn: Washington Scots Charity and Education Fund
c/o T.J. Holland, Scholarships Committee Chair
1443 Laurel Hill Road
Vienna, VA 22182–1711
Email: tjholland@wmalumni.com
Web: www.saintandrewsociety.org/scholarships.htm

Summary: To provide financial assistance for college or graduate school to students in Scotland and to U.S. students of Scottish descent who live in the mid–Atlantic states.

Eligibility: Open to 1) U.S. citizens who reside in the mid–Atlantic region (defined as the District of Columbia and the states of Delaware, Maryland, New Jersey, North Carolina, Pennsylvania, Virginia, and West Virginia); and 2) British subjects who were born in Scotland. Applicants must be enrolled full time as a junior, senior, or graduate student at a college or university in the United States or Scotland. They may be attending school in their own country or in the other country. The proposed course of study must contribute to their intellectual development and economic independence. Special attention is given to applicants whose study relates to Scottish history or culture. Along with their application, they must submit genealogical data to establish their Scottish descent, 2 letters of recommendation, a statement of their goals and plans, and documentation of financial need.

Financial data: Stipends are $2,500 or $2,000.

Duration: 1 year.

Number awarded: Varies each year; recently, 6 of these scholarships were awarded: 1 at $2,500 and 5 at $2,000.

Deadline: April of each year.

890 $$ STANLEY L. AND DOROTHY LOBE CAHN GRANT FUND

Central Scholarship Bureau
1700 Reisterstown Road, Suite 220
P.O. Box 37064
Baltimore, MD 21297–3064
Phone: (410) 415–5558; Fax: (410) 415–5501;
Email: contact@centralsb.org
Web: www.centralsb.org/html/CahnGrantFund.htm

Summary: To provide financial assistance to residents of Maryland who are attending or planning to attend college in any state.

Eligibility: Open to residents of Maryland who are attending or planning to attend an accredited U.S. college or university as a full–time student. They must have a family income less than $90,000 per year. Along with their application, they must submit a 500–word essay on their achievements, career and educational goals, and personal or family circumstances demonstrating exceptional merit or need. U.S. citizenship or permanent resident status is required.

Financial data: The stipend is $10,000.

Duration: 1 year; nonrenewable.

Number awarded: 1 each year.

Deadline: May of each year.

891 $$ STANLEY Z. KOPLIK CERTIFICATE OF MASTERY TUITION WAIVER PROGRAM

Massachusetts Office of Student Financial Assistance
454 Broadway, Suite 200
Revere, MA 02151
Phone: (617) 391–6070; Fax: (617) 727–0667;
Email: osfa@osfa.mass.edu
Web: www.osfa.mass.edu/default.asp?page=koplikWaiver

Summary: To provide financial assistance for college to Massachusetts residents who earn a Stanley Z. Koplik Certificate of Mastery while in high school.

Eligibility: Open to permanent Massachusetts residents who are U.S. citizens or permanent residents. In order to become a candidate for the Stanley Z. Koplik Certificate of Mastery, students must score "Advanced" on at least 1 grade 10 MCAS test subject and score "Proficient" on the remaining sections of the grade 10 MCAS. Once they become candidates, they must then fulfill additional requirements through 1 of the following combinations covering both arts/humanities and mathematics/science: 2 AP exams; 2 SAT II exams; 1 SAT II exam and 1 AP exam; 1 SAT II exam and 1 other achievement; or 1 AP exam and 1 other achievement. They must score at least 3 on any AP exam; if there are SAT II and AP exams in the same subject area, they must receive a score on the SAT II exam determined by the Department of Education to be comparable to a score of 3 on the AP exam. In subject areas where there are no corresponding AP exams, a student must achieve an SAT II score designated by the Department of Education.

Financial data: Recipients of Koplik Certificates are eligible for an award of a non–need–based tuition waiver for state–supported undergraduate courses in Massachusetts.

Duration: Up to 4 academic years, provided the student maintains a college GPA of 3.3 or higher.

Number awarded: Varies each year.

Deadline: April of each year.

892 $ STATE EMPLOYEES' CREDIT UNION FOUNDATION HIGH SCHOOL SCHOLARSHIP PROGRAM

State Employees' Credit Union
Attn: SECU Foundation
P.O. Box 25966
Raleigh, NC 27611–5966
Phone: (919) 839–5180; (800) 634–8017;
Email: SECUFoundation@ncsecu.org
Web: https://www.scsecufoundation.org/Scholarships.html

Summary: To provide financial assistance to high school seniors in North Carolina who plan to attend a campus of the University of North Carolina system.

Eligibility: Open to seniors graduating from traditional public high schools in North Carolina who plan to enroll full time at 1 of the 16 campuses of the University of North Carolina system. Applicants must have a GPA of 2.5 or higher and be deserving of financial aid. They must be able to demonstrate leadership, excellence of character, integrity, and community involvement. There is no formal application process; all graduating seniors who meet the eligibility criteria are considered by their high schools. Preference is given to students who parents or guardians and family members are public sector employees living and working in the state. U.S. citizenship is required.

Financial data: The stipend is $2,500 per year.

Duration: 4 years at the same university.

Number awarded: 1 to a student at every traditional public high school in North Carolina.

Deadline: Each high school selects its recipient and submits that name to the sponsor by May of each year.

893 STATE OF MAINE GRANT PROGRAM

Finance Authority of Maine
Attn: Education Finance Programs
5 Community Drive
P.O. Box 949
Augusta, ME 04332–0949
Phone: (207) 623–3263; (800) 228–3734; Fax: (207) 623–0095; TDD: (207) 626–2717;
Email: education@famemaine.com
Web: www.famemaine.com/Education_Home.aspx

Summary: To provide financial assistance to Maine residents interested in working on a college degree.

Eligibility: Open to residents of Maine who have lived in the state for at least 1 year, have graduated from an approved secondary school, have an Estimated Family Contribution from their FAFSA of less than $5,000, and are enrolled at least half time at an approved institution for their first undergraduate degree. Approved schools include all accredited 2– and 4–year colleges and universities in Connecticut, Maine, Massachusetts, Pennsylvania, Rhode Island, Vermont, and Washington, D.C.

Financial data: The maximum annual full–time stipend is $1,250 at private schools in Maine, $1,000 at public schools in Maine, $1,000 at private schools outside of Maine, or $500 at public schools outside of Maine.

Duration: 1 year; may be renewed up to 4 additional years if the recipient remains a Maine resident and maintains satisfactory academic progress.

Number awarded: Scholarships are presented to students who demonstrate the greatest financial need. The award process continues until all available funds have been exhausted.

Deadline: April of each year.

894 $ STATE VOCATIONAL REHABILITATION SERVICES PROGRAM

Department of Education
Office of Special Education and Rehabilitative Services
Attn: Rehabilitation Services Administration
500 12th Street, S.W., Room 5032
Washington, DC 20202–2800
Phone: (202) 245–7313; Fax: (202) 245–7590;
Email: Steven.Zwillinger@ed.gov
Web: www.ed.gov/programs/rsabvrs/index.html

Summary: To provide financial assistance to individuals with disabilities for undergraduate or graduate study pursued as part of their program of vocational rehabilitation.

Eligibility: Open to individuals who 1) have a physical or mental impairment that is a substantial impediment to employment; 2) will be able to benefit in terms of employment from vocational rehabilitation services; and 3) require vocational rehabilitation services to prepare for, enter, engage in, or retain gainful employment. Priority is given to applicants with the most significant disabilities. Persons accepted for vocational rehabilitation develop an Individualized Written Rehabilitation Program (IWRP) in consultation with a counselor for the vocational rehabilitation agency in the state in which they live. The IWRP may include a program of postsecondary education, if the disabled person and counselor agree that such a program will fulfill the goals of vocational rehabilitation. In most cases, the IWRP will provide for postsecondary education only to a level at which the disabled person will become employable, but that may include graduate education if the approved occupation requires an advanced degree as a minimum condition of entry. Students accepted to a program of postsecondary education as part of their IWRP must apply for all available federal, state, and private financial aid.

Financial data: Funding for this program is provided by the federal government through grants to state vocational rehabilitation agencies. Grants under the basic support program currently total more than $3 billion per year. States must supplement federal funding with matching funds of 21.3%. Persons who are accepted for vocational rehabilitation by the appropriate state agency receive financial assistance based on the cost of their education and other funds available to them, including their own or family contribution and other sources of financial aid. Allowable costs in most states include tuition, fees, books, supplies, room, board, transportation, personal expenses, child care, and expenses related to disability (special equipment, readers, attendants, interpreters, or notetakers).

Duration: Assistance is provided until the disabled person achieves an educational level necessary for employment as provided in the IWRP.

Number awarded: Varies each year; recently, more than 1.2 million people (of whom more than 80% have significant disabilities) were participating in this program.

Deadline: Deadline not specified.

895 $ STATEWIDE STUDENT AID PROGRAM

New Hampshire Charitable Foundation
37 Pleasant Street
Concord, NH 03301–4005
Phone: (603) 225–6641; (800) 464–6641; Fax: (603) 225–1700;
Email: info@nhcf.org
Web: www.nhcf.org/page.aspx?pid=487

Summary: To provide financial assistance to residents of New Hampshire who are attending or planning to attend college or graduate school in any state.

Eligibility: Open to residents of New Hampshire who are either between 17 and 23 years of age or attending graduate school. Applicants must be enrolled or planning to enroll full or part time in a 4–year baccalaureate degree program or a graduate program at a school in any state. Selection is based on financial need, academic merit, and other non–academic factors, such as community service, school activities, and work experience; priority is given to students with the fewest financial resources.

Financial data: Stipends range from $500 to $3,500 and average $1,800.

Duration: 1 year.

Number awarded: Varies each year; approximately $1 million is awarded through this program annually.

Deadline: April of each year.

896 $$ STAY FIT'S HEALTHY LIFESTYLES SCHOLARSHIP

Stay Fit
6393 Penn Avenue
Pittsburgh, PA 15206
Phone: (412) 943–7113;
Email: stayfit@fitnessexercises.tv
Web: www.fitnessexercises.tv/scholarships.php

Summary: To recognize and reward, with college scholarships, high school seniors and college freshmen interested in majoring in any subject who submit outstanding essays on a healthy lifestyle.

Eligibility: Open to high school seniors and first–year college students who are residents of the United States or Canada. Applicants must be younger than 25 years of age. They must submit 1) a 1,000–word essay on why a healthy lifestyle is important in school; and 2) a 500–word description of their career plans, goals, and personal ambitions. Selection is based entirely on those essays.

Financial data: The prize is a $5,000 scholarship.

Duration: The scholarship is presented annually.

Number awarded: 1 each year.

Deadline: December of each year.

897 STEPHANIE HUSEK SCHOLARSHIP

First Catholic Slovak Union of the United States and Canada
Jednota Benevolent Foundation, Inc.
Attn: Scholarship Program
6611 Rockside Road, Suite 300
Independence, OH 44131
Phone: (216) 642–9406; (800) JEDNOTA; Fax: (216) 642–4310;
Email: FCSU@aol.com
Web: www.fcsu.com/scholarships

Summary: To provide financial assistance for college to female high school seniors who are of Slovak descent and the Catholic faith.

Eligibility: Open to women graduating from high schools in the United States and Canada and planning to attend an approved institution of higher education. Applicants must be of Slovak descent and the Catholic faith. They must have had at least $5,000 of reserve insurance with the sponsoring organization for at least 4 years. Along with their application, they must submit 1) a transcript of grades that includes ACT or SAT scores; 2) a list of volunteer community activities in which they have participated; 3) a list of awards received for academic excellence and leadership ability; 4) a description of their career objectives; 5) an essay on why they think they should receive this scholarship; and 6) information on their financial need.

Financial data: The stipend is $1,000. The winner also receives a $3,000 single premium life insurance policy upon proof of graduation from college.

Duration: 1 year; nonrenewable.

Number awarded: 1 each year.

Deadline: March of each year.

898 STEPHEN BUFTON MEMORIAL EDUCATION FUND OUTRIGHT GRANTS PROGRAM

American Business Women's Association
Attn: Stephen Bufton Memorial Educational Fund

11050 Roe Avenue, Suite 200
Overland Park, KS 66211
Phone: (800) 228–0007
Web: www.sbmef.org/Opportunities.cfm

Summary: To provide financial assistance to women undergraduate and graduate students in any field who are sponsored by a chapter of the American Business Women's Association (ABWA).

Eligibility: Open to women who are at least juniors at an accredited college or university. Applicants must be working on an undergraduate or graduate degree and have a GPA of 2.5 or higher. They are not required to be ABWA members, but they must be sponsored by an ABWA chapter that has contributed to the fund in the previous chapter year. U.S. citizenship is required.

Financial data: The maximum grant is $1,500. Funds are paid directly to the recipient's institution to be used only for tuition, books, and fees.

Duration: 1 year. Grants are not automatically renewed, but recipients may reapply.

Number awarded: Varies each year; since the inception of this program, it has awarded more than $14 million to more than 14,000 students.

Deadline: May of each year.

899 $$ STEPHEN J. BRADY STOP HUNGER SCHOLARSHIPS

Sodexo Foundation
9801 Washingtonian Boulevard
Gaithersburg, MD 20878
Phone: (800) 763–3946;
Email: STOPHunger@sodexofoundation.org
Web: sodexofoundation.org/hunger_us/scholarships/scholarships.asp

Summary: To provide financial assistance for college or graduate school to students at all academic levels who provide outstanding community service to organizations that are involved in the fight against hunger.

Eligibility: Open to U.S. citizens and permanent residents who are enrolled at all academic levels from kindergarten through graduate school. Applicants must have performed unpaid volunteer services impacting hunger within the past 12 months to an organization in their community. They must submit a letter of recommendation from a representative of the organization. Selection is based on that letter and the volunteer services performed by the student. Special consideration is given to students working to fight childhood hunger.

Financial data: Regional winners receive a grant of $1,000 to be donated to the hunger–related charity of their choice in their local community. National winners receive a $5,000 scholarship for college or graduate school and a $5,000 grant to be donated to the hunger–related charity of their choice in their local community. If winners are not yet enrolled in college, the $5,000 scholarship is contributed to a 529 Plan established by their family for their benefit when they reach college age. National winners are also recognized at a Sodexo Foundation Dinner in Washington in June; all expenses for the winner and 2 family members are paid.

Duration: College scholarships are for 1 year.

Number awarded: Up to 20 regional winners and up to 5 national winners are selected each year.

Deadline: December of each year.

900 $ STERLING SCHOLAR AWARDS OF UTAH

Deseret News
Attn: Marketing/Promotions/Special Events Department
5 North 300 West
Salt Lake City, UT 84101
Phone: (801) 237–2900
Web: deseretnews.com/scholars

Summary: To provide financial assistance for college to outstanding high school seniors in Utah.

Eligibility: Open to graduating seniors at high schools in Utah. Candidates must be nominated by their principals in 1 of the following categories: English, mathematics, social science, science, foreign language, computer technology, trade and technical education, family and consumer sciences, business and marketing, speech and drama, visual arts, music, and dance. Each school may nominate only 1 student per category. Nominees submit portfolios demonstrating their work; the contents of the portfolio depend on the category for which they have been nominated. Selection is based on overall scholarship (25 points), scholarship within the category (25 points), leadership (25 points), and community service and citizenship (25 points). The program is conducted in 5 regions throughout Utah: Wasatch Front (Box Elder, Cache, Weber, Davis, Salt Lake, Tooele, and Utah counties), Northeast (Rich, Morgan, Summit, Wasatch, Duchesne, Dagget, and Uintah counties), Central (Juab, Sanpete, Millard, Sevier, Piute, and Wayne counties), Southwest (Beaver, Iron, Garfield, Washington, and Kane counties), and Southeast (Carbon, Emery, Grand, and San Juan counties).

Financial data: In the Wasatch Front region, a total of $21,000 is awarded, including a general scholarship award of $1,500 and category awards of $1,000 for first place and $250 for each runner–up. In the Northeast region, each category winner receives $500 plus a scholarship to a Utah college and each category runner–up receives $300 plus a scholarship to a Utah college. For information on the awards in the other regions, contact your high school principal or counselor. Many Utah colleges and universities also designate special awards exclusively for Sterling Scholars.

Duration: 1 year.

Number awarded: Varies by region. For example, in the Wasatch Front region, 39 awards are presented (a winner and 2 runners–up in each category); 1 of those recipients is selected to receive the additional general scholarship award, 1 to receive the Douglas Bates Community Service Award, and 1 to receive the Philo T. Farnsworth Excellence in Education Award.

Deadline: In the Wasatch Front region, schools must submit nominations by January of each year and nominees must complete their portfolios by February.

901 STEVEN M. PEREZ FOUNDATION SCHOLARSHIPS

Steven M. Perez Foundation
P.O. Box 955
Melville, NY 11747
Phone: (631) 367–9016; Fax: (631) 367–3848;
Email: info@smpfoundation.org
Web: www.smpfoundation.org

Summary: To provide financial assistance for college to high school seniors who have survived leukemia or lost a family member to cancer or a related disease.

Eligibility: Open to graduating high school seniors who have survived leukemia or who have lost a parent or sibling to cancer or a related disease. Applicants must be planning to attend a college or university in any state. Along with their application, they must submit medical certification, a recommendation from a counselor, and an essay that describes their connection to leukemia.

Financial data: Stipend amounts vary; recently, they averaged approximately $1,450.

Duration: 1 year.

Number awarded: Varies each year; recently, 17 of these scholarships were awarded.

Deadline: April of each year.

902 $$ STRAUS SCHOLARS GRANTS

Central Scholarship Bureau
1700 Reisterstown Road, Suite 220
P.O. Box 37064
Baltimore, MD 21297–3064
Phone: (410) 415–5558; Fax: (410) 415–5501;
Email: contact@centralsb.org
Web: www.centralsb.org/html/StrausScholarsGrantProgram.htm

Summary: To provide financial assistance to residents of Maryland who are attending college in any state.

Eligibility: Open to residents of Maryland who are entering their sophomore, junior, or senior year at an accredited U.S. college or university as a full–time student. They must have a GPA of 3.0 or higher and a family income less than $90,000 per year. Along with their application, they must submit a 500–word essay on their achievements, career and educational goals, and personal or family circumstances demonstrating exceptional merit or need. Preference is given to residents of Baltimore city who attend public colleges in Maryland, but all Maryland residents are encouraged to apply. U.S. citizenship or permanent resident status is required.

Financial data: The stipend is $5,000 per year.

Duration: 1 year; may be renewed up to 3 additional years. Students who graduate within 4 years with a cumulative GPA of 3.0 or higher receive an additional $5,000 grant to help repay any student loans.

Number awarded: 1 or more each year.

Deadline: May of each year.

903 $$ STUCK AT PROM SCHOLARSHIP CONTEST

ShurTech Brands, LLC
32150 Just Imagine Drive
Avon, OH 44011–1355
Phone: (800) 321–1733
Web: www.duckbrand.com/Promotions/stuck–at–prom.aspx

Summary: To recognize and reward (with college scholarships) high school students who wear duct tape to their spring prom.
Eligibility: Open to residents of the United States and Canada who are 14 years of age or older. Applicants must enter as a couple who attend a high school (or home school association) spring prom wearing complete attire or accessories made from duct tape. They must submit a color photograph (professional or amateur) of themselves together in their prom attire. Judges select 10 finalists on the basis of workmanship (30%), originality (25%), use of color (25%), accessories (10%), and quantity of duct tape used (10%). Photographs are then posted on the sponsor's web site. Online votes determine the winners.
Financial data: Each member of the first–place couple receives a $5,000 cash scholarship, each member of the second–place couple receives a $3,000 cash scholarship, each member of the third–place couple receives a $2,000 cash scholarship, and each member of the runner–up couples receives a cash prize of $500. The schools that host the prize winners receive cash prizes of $5,000, $3,000, $2,000, and $500 respectively.
Duration: The competition is held annually.
Number awarded: 20 students receive cash scholarships each year: 1 first place, 1 second place, 1 third place, and 7 runners–up; 10 schools receive cash prizes.
Deadline: June of each year.

904 $$ STUDENT AID FUND FOR NON–REGISTRANTS

Mennonite Church USA
Executive Board
Attn: Student Aid Fund for Non–registrants
P.O. Box 1245
Elkhart, IN 46515–1245
Phone: (574) 523–3041;
Email: KathrynR@MennoniteUSA.org
Web: peace.mennolink.org/safnr.html
Summary: To provide financial assistance for college or graduate school to men who are ineligible to receive government grants and loans because they have declined to register with the U.S. Selective Service System for reasons of Christian conscience.
Eligibility: Open to students who have declined to register with the U.S. Selective Service because of their Christian conscience. They must be either 1) attending a Mennonite Church USA college or seminary; or 2) attending a congregation of Mennonite Church USA and enrolled in undergraduate or graduate studies in other–than–Mennonite institutions.
Financial data: Aid is available in the form of both grants and loans. The amount of assistance is based on formulas that would have been used if the student were eligible for government aid. For loans, no interest is charged until 6 months following completion of undergraduate study; at that time (even if the recipient continues on to graduate school), the loan must be repaid with a fixed interest rate based upon the long–term 120% AFR monthly rate, set 90 days after the student graduates or discontinues school; the minimum payment is $50 per month and the total repayment period cannot exceed 10 years.
Number awarded: Varies each year.
Deadline: August of each year.

905 STUDENT ATHLETE OF THE YEAR SCHOLARSHIP

Cappex.com, LLC
2008 St. Johns Avenue
Highland Park, IL 60035
Web: www.cappex.com/scholarships
Summary: To provide financial assistance for college to high school seniors who complete a profile for Cappex.com and have participated in athletics.
Eligibility: Open to applicants who first complete an online profile for Cappex.com that will enable colleges and universities to contact them for recruiting purposes. They must be U.S. citizens or permanent residents planning to attend an accredited college or university in the United States. In completing their profile, they must describe their athletic, leadership, and volunteer activities. This scholarship is reserved for high school seniors who have demonstrated outstanding athletic accomplishments.
Financial data: The stipend is $1,000.
Duration: 1 year.
Number awarded: 1 each year.
Deadline: December of each year.

906 $$ STUDENT OF INTEGRITY SCHOLARSHIPS

Better Business Bureau of Minnesota and North Dakota
Attn: Student of Integrity Program
2706 Gannon Road
St. Paul, MN 55116
Phone: (651) 695–2482; (888) 646–6222, ext. 2482;
Email: mkelley@thefirstbbb.org
Web: Minnesota.bbb.org/scholarship
Summary: To provide financial assistance to high school seniors in Minnesota and North Dakota who plan to attend college in any state and submit essays on integrity.
Eligibility: Open to seniors graduating from high schools in Minnesota and North Dakota and planning to attend a college or university in any state. Applicants must submit essays, up to 1,000 words in length, that give a specific, personal example of how they were challenged through a difficult situation and how they overcame the situation by the application of high character and personal ethics. They must also submit a letter of recommendation, a list of their high school extracurricular activities, a copy of their high school transcript, and a short paragraph describing their postsecondary plans and goals. Selection is based primarily on the essay, but information in the other application information may also be considered.
Financial data: Stipends are $5,000 or $2,500. Funds are paid directly to the recipient's institution.
Duration: 1 year; nonrenewable.
Number awarded: 2 each year: 1 at $5,000 and 1 at $2,500.
Deadline: September of each year.

907 $ STUDENT OPPORTUNITY SCHOLARSHIPS OF THE PRESBYTERIAN CHURCH (USA)

Presbyterian Church (USA)
Attn: Office of Financial Aid for Studies
100 Witherspoon Street, Room M–052
Louisville, KY 40202–1396
Phone: (502) 569–5224; (800) 728–7228, ext. 5224; Fax: (502) 569–8766; TDD: (800) 833–5955;
Email: finaid@pcusa.org
Web: gamc.pcusa.org
Summary: To provide financial assistance to Presbyterian college students, especially those of racial/ethnic minority heritage.
Eligibility: Open to active members of the Presbyterian Church (USA) who are entering their sophomore, junior, or senior year of college as full–time students. Preference is given to applicants who are members of racial/ethnic minority groups (Asian American, African American, Hispanic American, Native American, Alaska Native). Applicants must have a GPA of 2.5 or higher and be able to demonstrate financial need.
Financial data: Stipends range up to $2,000 per year, depending upon the financial need of the recipient.
Duration: 1 year; may be renewed for up to 3 additional years if the recipient continues to need financial assistance and demonstrates satisfactory academic progress.
Number awarded: Varies each year.
Deadline: May of each year.

908 STUDENTS WITH DISABILITIES ENDOWED SCHOLARSHIPS HONORING ELIZABETH DALEY JEFFORDS

Vermont Student Assistance Corporation
Attn: Scholarship Programs
10 East Allen Street
P.O. Box 2000
Winooski, VT 05404–2601
Phone: (802) 654–3798; (888) 253–4819; Fax: (802) 654–3765; TDD: (800) 281–3341 (within VT);
Email: info@vsac.org
Web: services.vsac.org/wps/wcm/connect/VSAC/vsac/pay+for+college
Summary: To provide financial assistance to high school seniors with disabilities in Vermont who are interested in enrolling at a college in any state.
Eligibility: Open to graduating high school seniors in Vermont who have a documented disability. Applicants must be planning to attend a college or university in any state. Along with their application, they must submit documentation of their disability (school 504 or IEP plan) and a 250–word essay on what they believe distinguishes their application from others that may be submitted. Selection is based on the essay, a letter of recommendation, a personal interview, and financial need.
Financial data: The stipend is $1,500.
Duration: 1 year; nonrenewable.
Number awarded: 1 or more each year.
Deadline: March of each year.

909 STUDENTS WITHOUT MOTHERS SCHOLARSHIPS

Students Without Mothers
4500 Hugh Howell Road, Suite 790
Tucker, GA 30084
Phone: (770) 724–0648; Fax: (770) 234–6811;
Email: support@studentswithoutmothers.org
Web: www.studentswithoutmothers.org/scholarshipProgram.htm

Summary: To provide financial assistance for college studies in any state to high school seniors from Georgia whose mother is no longer living or available.

Eligibility: Open to seniors graduating from high schools in Georgia whose mother is not at home, either because of death or other unfortunate circumstances. Priority is given to residents of the metropolitan Atlanta area. Applicants must be planning to enroll at a 2– or 4–year institution of higher learning in any state. Along with their application, they must submit a 250–word essay on their hobbies and interests, hardships, future plans, and why they should be awarded a scholarship. Priority is given to applicants whose guardian earns less than $50,000 per year.

Financial data: The stipend is $1,000 per year.

Duration: 4 years.

Number awarded: Varies each year.

Deadline: December of each year.

910 $$ SUBSIDIZED STAFFORD LOANS

Department of Education
Attn: Federal Student Aid Information Center
P.O. Box 84
Washington, DC 20044–0084
Phone: (319) 337–5665; (800) 4–FED–AID; TDD: (800) 730–8913
Web: studentaid.ed.gov/types/loans

Summary: To provide loans, some of which may be forgiven, to college students in the United States who demonstrate financial need.

Eligibility: Open to U.S. citizens or eligible noncitizens who have or will have at least a high school diploma or GED certificate, are registered with the Selective Service if required, are enrolled as regular students working toward a degree or certificate in an eligible program, and have a valid Social Security number. This program is available to both dependent and independent students. Independent students are those who meet at least 1 of the following requirements: 1) are 22 years of age or older; 2) are married; 3) are enrolled in a master's or doctoral program; 4) have children for whom they provide more than half the support; 5) have dependents (other than their children or spouses) who live with them and for whom they provide more than half the support; 6) are orphans or wards of a court; or 7) are veterans of the U.S. armed forces. Students who meet none of those requirements are considered dependents. Financial need is required for this program.

Financial data: All loans are issued directly by the federal government. Undergraduate students, both dependent and independent, may borrow subsidized loans up to $3,500 for the first full year of study, up to $4,500 for the second year, and up to $5,500 per year for the third and subsequent years. Graduate students may borrow up to $8,500 per academic year in subsidized loans. The total subsidized debt that may be incurred under this program is $23,000 for undergraduates or $65,500 for graduate students. A loan origination fee of 1.0% is deducted from each disbursement of the loan. The interest rate is fixed, currently at 3.4% for undergraduates or 6.8% for graduate students. For these loans, the federal government pays the interest while the student is enrolled in school at least half time, during a grace period, or during authorized periods of deferment.

Duration: Plans for repayment over 10 to 25 years are available.

Number awarded: Varies each year; in recent years, approximately 7 million new loans, worth more than $36 billion, have been issued annually.

Deadline: June of each year.

911 SUPERSIBS! SCHOLARSHIPS

SuperSibs!
Attn: Scholarship Committee
660 North First Bank Drive
Palatine, IL 60067
Phone: (847) 462–4SIB; (888) 417–4704; Fax: (847) 984–9292;
Email: info@supersibs.org
Web: supersibs.org/programs–and–services/scholarship–program–main.html

Summary: To provide financial assistance for college to siblings of children with cancer.

Eligibility: Open to seniors who are graduating from high schools in the United States, Puerto Rico, or the Virgin Islands and have a GPA of 2.0 or higher. Applicants must be the siblings of children who have or have had cancer. They must be planning to enroll full time at an accredited college, university, or vocational institution in the following fall. Half–siblings and stepsiblings who reside in the same home as the cancer patient are also eligible. Along with their application, they must submit an essay, up to 1,000 words, on 1 of the following: 1) what they learned from their personal "sibling journey;" 2) how the experience as the sibling of a brother or sister with cancer may impact their future; or 3) the advice they can share with other siblings living this journey and those who support them. Financial need is not considered in the selection process.

Financial data: The stipend is $1,000.

Duration: 1 year.

Number awarded: Varies each year; recently, 10 of these scholarships were awarded.

Deadline: January of each year.

912 $$ SURVIVING DEPENDENTS OF MONTANA FIRE FIGHTERS/PEACE OFFICERS WAIVER

Office of the Commissioner of Higher Education
Attn: Montana University System
State Scholarship Coordinator
2500 Broadway
P.O. Box 203201
Helena, MT 59620–3201
Phone: (406) 444–0638; (800) 537–7508; Fax: (406) 444–1469;
Email: snewlun@montana.edu
Web: www.mus.edu/Prepare/Pay/Tuition_and_Fee_Waivers.asp

Summary: To provide financial assistance for college to dependents of deceased firefighters or peace officers in Montana.

Eligibility: Open to residents of Montana who are surviving spouses or children of Montana firefighters or peace officers killed in the course and scope of employment. Financial need is considered.

Financial data: Students eligible for this benefit are entitled to attend any unit of the Montana University System without payment of undergraduate registration or incidental fees.

Duration: Undergraduate students are eligible for continued fee waiver as long as they maintain reasonable academic progress as full–time students.

Number awarded: Varies each year.

Deadline: Deadline not specified.

913 $$ SURVIVING DEPENDENTS OF MONTANA NATIONAL GUARD MEMBER WAIVER

Office of the Commissioner of Higher Education
Attn: Montana University System
State Scholarship Coordinator
2500 Broadway
P.O. Box 203201
Helena, MT 59620–3201
Phone: (406) 444–0638; (800) 537–7508; Fax: (406) 444–1469;
Email: snewlun@montana.edu
Web: www.mus.edu/Prepare/Pay/Tuition_and_Fee_Waivers.asp

Summary: To provide financial assistance for undergraduate study to dependents of deceased National Guard members in Montana.

Eligibility: Open to residents of Montana who are surviving spouses or children of Montana National Guard members killed as a result of injury, disease, or other disability incurred in the line of duty while serving on state active duty. Financial need is considered.

Financial data: Students eligible for this benefit are entitled to attend any unit of the Montana University System without payment of undergraduate registration or incidental fees.

Duration: Undergraduate students are eligible for continued fee waiver as long as they maintain reasonable academic progress as full–time students.

Number awarded: Varies each year.

Deadline: Deadline not specified.

914 $$ SURVIVORS' AND DEPENDENTS' EDUCATIONAL ASSISTANCE PROGRAM

Department of Veterans Affairs
Attn: Veterans Benefits Administration
810 Vermont Avenue, N.W.
Washington, DC 20420
Phone: (202) 418–4343; (888) GI–BILL1
Web: www.gibill.va.gov/benefits/other_programs/dea.html

Summary: To provide financial assistance for undergraduate or graduate study to children and spouses of deceased and disabled veterans, MIAs, and POWs.
Eligibility: Open to spouses and children of 1) veterans who died or are permanently and totally disabled as the result of active service in the armed forces; 2) veterans who died from any cause while rated permanently and totally disabled from a service–connected disability; 3) servicemembers listed as missing in action or captured in the line of duty by a hostile force; 4) servicemembers listed as forcibly detained or interned by a foreign government or power; and 5) servicemembers who are hospitalized or receiving outpatient treatment for a service–connected permanent and total disability and are likely to be discharged for that disability. Children must be between 18 and 26 years of age, although extensions may be granted. Spouses and children over 14 years of age with physical or mental disabilities are also eligible.
Financial data: Monthly stipends for study at an academic institution are $957 for full time, $718 for three–quarter time, or $476 for half–time. Other rates apply for apprenticeship and on–the–job training, farm cooperative training, and special restorative training.
Duration: Up to 45 months (or the equivalent in part–time training). Spouses must complete their training within 10 years of the date they are first found eligible. For spouses of servicemembers who died on active duty, benefits end 20 years from the date of death.
Number awarded: Varies each year.
Deadline: Applications may be submitted at any time.

915 $$ SUSAN G. KOMEN BREAST CANCER FOUNDATION COLLEGE SCHOLARSHIP AWARDS

Susan G. Komen Breast Cancer Foundation
Attn: Scholarship Program Office
5005 LBJ Freeway, Suite 250
Dallas, TX 75244
Phone: (972) 855–1616; (877) GO–KOMEN; Fax: (972) 855–1605;
Email: collegescholarships@komen.org
Web: ww5.komen.org/ResearchGrants/AwardsampScholarships.html

Summary: To provide financial assistance for college to high school seniors and college students who lost a parent to breast cancer or are breast cancer survivors.
Eligibility: Open to high school seniors and college freshmen, sophomores, and juniors who have lost a parent to breast cancer or are a breast cancer survivor diagnosed at 25 years of age or younger. Applicants must be under 25 years of age, be U.S. citizens or permanent residents, have a high school and/or college GPA of 2.8 or higher, and be enrolled or planning to enroll full time at a state–supported college or university in the state where they permanently reside. Along with their application, they must submit 2 essays of 500 words each on 1) how breast cancer has changed them; and 2) how their education will help them achieve their career objectives and personal goals. Selection is based on the essay, academic achievements or records, community involvement, letters of reference, and financial need.
Financial data: Stipends up to $10,000 per year are available. Funds may be used for tuition, books, fees, and on–campus room and board.
Duration: 4 years, provided the recipient remains enrolled full time and makes reasonable progress toward completion of a baccalaureate degree.
Number awarded: 5 each year.
Deadline: January of each year.

916 $ SUSSMAN–MILLER EDUCATIONAL ASSISTANCE FUND

Albuquerque Community Foundation
Attn: Scholarship Program
624 Tijeras Avenue, N.W.
P.O. Box 25266
Albuquerque, NM 87125–5266
Phone: (505) 883–6240; Fax: (505) 883–3629;
Email: foundation@albuquerquefoundation.org
Web: www.albuquerquefoundation.org/student_aid

Summary: To provide financial assistance to undergraduate students from New Mexico.
Eligibility: Open to students who have been residents of New Mexico for at least 1 year and are able to demonstrate financial need. They may be either graduating high school seniors (who apply during the spring semester of their senior year) or current full–time college students (who apply after completing 1 semester of undergraduate study). U.S. citizenship or permanent resident status is required. High school applicants must have a GPA of 3.0 or higher in academic subjects; current college students must have a GPA of 2.5 or higher. Selection is based primarily on financial need.
Financial data: The minimum stipend is $500 per year. The maximum stipend is 20% of the student's total budget or $2,000, whichever is less.
Duration: 1 year; may be renewed up to 3 additional years.
Number awarded: Varies each year; recently, 9 of these scholarships were awarded.
Deadline: April of each year for high school seniors planning to attend college outside New Mexico or in–state private schools; June of each year for current undergraduate students and high school seniors planning to attend public schools in New Mexico.

917 SWIM WITH MIKE

University of Southern California
Athletic Department
Heritage Hall
MC 0602
Los Angeles, CA 90089–0602
Phone: (213) 740–4155; Fax: (213) 740–1306;
Email: swimwithmike@gmail.com
Web: swimwithmike.org

Summary: To provide financial assistance for college or graduate school to physically challenged athletes.
Eligibility: Open to athletes who participated in organized competitive youth, high school, or collegiate athletics and subsequently have sustained a life–changing accident or illness (e.g., paralysis, blindness, cancer, amputation, head injuries). Applicants must meet the admission standards of a 4–year or graduate–level institution of higher learning. Along with their application, they must submit a personal statement with an emphasis on their athletic history and experience and their educational goals, 3 letters of recommendation, verification of disability, and documentation of financial need.
Financial data: Stipends depend on the need of the recipient.
Duration: 1 year; may be renewed, provided the recipient.
Number awarded: Varies each year; recently, 50 athletes received $796,000 in scholarships.
Deadline: April of each year.

918 SWISS BENEVOLENT SOCIETY OF CHICAGO SCHOLARSHIPS

Swiss Benevolent Society of Chicago
Attn: Education Committee
P.O. Box 2137
Chicago, IL 60690–2137
Email: education@sbschicago.org
Web: sbschicago.org/scholarship–announcement.html

Summary: To provide financial aid for college to Swiss students in Illinois or southern Wisconsin.
Eligibility: Open to 1) Swiss nationals with permanent U.S. residency status; and 2) people of documented Swiss descent; Swiss students studying in the United States on a student or visitor's visa are not eligible. Applicants must reside in Illinois or southern Wisconsin (Dane, Grant, Green, Iowa, Jefferson, Kenosha, Lafayette, Milwaukee, Ozaukee, Racine, Rock, Walworth, Washington, and Waukesha counties) and intend to attend college on a full–time basis during the following school year. High school seniors must have test scores of at least 26 on the ACT or equivalent on the SAT; college freshmen must have the same minimum test scores and at least a 3.3 GPA in college work completed through the current semester; current college sophomores and juniors must have a minimum cumulative GPA of 3.3 in all college work completed through the current semester. Selection is based on academic merit only; financial need is not considered.
Financial data: Stipends are $1,000 or $500.
Duration: 1 year; may be renewed for up to 3 additional years of full–time undergraduate study.
Number awarded: Varies each year. Recently, scholarships were awarded to 7 high school seniors (1 at $1,000 and 6 at $500); 4 college freshmen (1 at $1,000 and 3 at $500); and 7 college sophomores or juniors (1 at $1,000 and 6 at $500).
Deadline: April of each year.

919 $ T. ROWE PRICE FOUNDATION SCHOLARSHIPS

Independent College Fund of Maryland
Attn: Director of Programs and Scholarships
3225 Ellerslie Avenue, Suite C–160
Baltimore, MD 21218–3519
Phone: (443) 997–5700; Fax: (443) 997–2740;
Email: Ifund@jhu.edu
Web: i–fundinfo.org/scholarships/business–scholarships.html

Summary: To provide financial assistance to students from Maryland at member institutions of the Independent College Fund of Maryland who have demonstrated outstanding leadership on campus or in the community.
Eligibility: Open to students from Maryland currently enrolled at member institutions. Applicants must have demonstrated outstanding leadership qualities on campus and/or in the community. They must have a GPA of 3.0 or higher and be able to demonstrate financial need.
Financial data: The stipend is $3,500.
Duration: 1 year.
Number awarded: 1 or more each year.
Deadline: Deadline not specified.

920 $$ TAILHOOK EDUCATIONAL FOUNDATION SCHOLARSHIPS

Tailhook Educational Foundation
9696 Businesspark Avenue
P.O. Box 26626
San Diego, CA 92196–0626
Phone: (858) 689–9223; (800) 322–4665;
Email: tag@tailhook.net
Web: www.tailhook.org/Foundation.html
Summary: To provide financial assistance for college to personnel associated with naval aviation and their children.
Eligibility: Open to 1) the children (natural, step, and adopted) of current or former U.S. Navy or Marine Corps personnel who served as an aviator, flight officer, or air crewman; or 2) personnel and children of personnel who are serving or have served on board a U.S. Navy aircraft carrier as a member of the ship's company or air wing. Applicants must be enrolled or accepted for enrollment at an accredited college or university. Selection is based on educational and extracurricular achievements, merit, and citizenship.
Financial data: The stipend ranges from $1,500 to $15,000.
Duration: 1 to 2 years.
Number awarded: Varies each year; recently, 71 of these scholarships were awarded.
Deadline: March of each year.

921 $$ TALBOTS WOMEN'S SCHOLARSHIP FUND

Talbots Charitable Foundation
c/o Scholarship America
Scholarship Management Services
One Scholarship Way
P.O. Box 297
St. Peter, MN 56082
Phone: (507) 931–1682; (800) 537–4180; Fax: (507) 931–9168;
Email: talbotswomen@scholarshipamerica.org
Web: www1.talbots.com
Summary: To provide financial assistance to women returning to college after an absence of at least 10 years.
Eligibility: Open to women who earned their high school diploma or GED at least 10 years ago and are now enrolled or planning to enroll full or part time at an accredited 2– or 4–year college, university, or vocational/technical school. Applicants must have at least 2 full–time semesters remaining to complete their undergraduate degree. They must be currently residing in the United States or Canada. Along with their application, they must submit an essay on their plans as they relate to their educational and career objectives and long–term goals. Selection is based on the essay, academic record, leadership and participation in community activities, honors, work experience, an outside appraisal, and financial need.
Financial data: Stipends are either $30,000 or $15,000. Checks are mailed to the recipient's home address and are made payable jointly to the student and the school.
Duration: 1 year; nonrenewable.
Number awarded: 11 each year: 1 at $30,000 (named the Nancy Talbot Scholarship Award in honor of the firm's founder) and 10 at $15,000.
Deadline: December of each year.

922 TALL CLUBS INTERNATIONAL STUDENT SCHOLARSHIPS

Tall Clubs International
8466 North Lockwood Ridge Road 188
Sarasota, FL 34243
Phone: (888) I–M–TALL–2
Web: www.tall.org/scholarships.cfm?CFID=220367&CFTOKEN=27879259
Summary: To provide financial assistance for college to students entering their first year of college who meet the minimum height requirements of the Tall Clubs International (TCI).
Eligibility: Open to students who are younger than 21 years of age and planning to enter their first year of college. Applicants must live within a geographic area served by a participating TCI and must meet the minimum TCI height requirements: 5'10" for females or 6'2" for males. Applications must be submitted to the local TCI club, which nominates the most outstanding applicant for the national competition. Selection is based on academic record and achievements, involvement in school clubs and activities, personal achievements, involvement in clubs and activities outside the school community, and an essay on "What being tall means to me."
Financial data: The stipend is $1,000.
Duration: 1 year.
Number awarded: 2 or 3 each year.
Deadline: Local clubs must submit their nominations by May of each year.

923 TAYLOR J. ERTEL SCHOLARSHIPS

First Community Foundation Partnership of Pennsylvania
Attn: Program Officer
330 Pine Street, Suite 400
Williamsport, PA 17701
Phone: (570) 321–1500; (888) 901–2372; Fax: (570) 321–6434;
Email: bettyg@fcfpartnership.org
Web: www.fcfpa.org/content/award–opportunities
Summary: To provide financial assistance to residents of Pennsylvania who have been in foster care and are interested in attending college or graduate school in any state.
Eligibility: Open to Pennsylvania residents who have been placed in foster care by a child welfare agency. Applicants must be enrolled or planning to enroll in a program of study, ranging from short vocational courses through college or graduate degrees, in any state. They must be able to demonstrate financial need. Along with their application, they must submit an essay on their reason for choosing their desired career.
Financial data: The stipend is $1,000 per year.
Duration: 1 year; recipients may reapply.
Number awarded: Varies each year.
Deadline: Applications may be submitted at any time; scholarships are awarded on a first–come, first–served basis until all available funds for the current year are committed.

924 $$ TENNESSEE ASPIRE AWARDS

Tennessee Student Assistance Corporation
Parkway Towers
404 James Robertson Parkway, Suite 1510
Nashville, TN 37243–0820
Phone: (615) 741–1346; (800) 342–1663; Fax: (615) 741–6101;
Email: TSAC.Aidinfo@tn.gov
Web: www.tn.gov/collegepays/mon_college/need_based_award.htm
Summary: To provide supplemental financial assistance to high school seniors in Tennessee who qualify for the Tennessee HOPE Scholarships and also demonstrate financial need.
Eligibility: Open to seniors graduating from public and private high schools in Tennessee and other residents of the state who qualify for a Tennessee HOPE Scholarship. Applicants must have an annual family income of $36,000 or less. They must be planning to attend an accredited public or private college or university in Tennessee.
Financial data: The stipend is an additional $2,500, so the total award is $8,500 per year for students at 4–year colleges and universities or $5,500 per year for students at 2–year schools.
Duration: 1 year; students may receive this supplemental funding only once.
Number awarded: Varies each year; recently, 18,601 students received nearly $88 million in scholarships from this program.
Deadline: August of each year for fall semester; January of each year for spring and summer semesters.

925 $$ TENNESSEE DEPENDENT CHILDREN SCHOLARSHIP

Tennessee Student Assistance Corporation
Parkway Towers
404 James Robertson Parkway, Suite 1510
Nashville, TN 37243–0820

Phone: (615) 741–1346; (800) 342–1663; Fax: (615) 741–6101;
Email: TSAC.Aidinfo@tn.gov
Web: www.tn.gov/collegepays/mon_college/depend_child_scholar.htm

Summary: To provide financial assistance to the dependent children of disabled or deceased Tennessee law enforcement officers, firefighters, or emergency medical service technicians who plan to attend college in the state.

Eligibility: Open to Tennessee residents who are the dependent children of a Tennessee law enforcement officer, firefighter, or emergency medical service technician who was killed or totally and permanently disabled in the line of duty. Applicants must be enrolled or accepted for enrollment as a full–time undergraduate student at a college or university in Tennessee.

Financial data: The award covers tuition and fees, books, supplies, and room and board, minus any other financial aid for which the student is eligible.

Duration: 1 year; may be renewed for up to 3 additional years or until completion of a program of study.

Number awarded: Varies each year; recently, 19 students received $77,786 in support from this program.

Deadline: July of each year.

926 TENNESSEE DUAL ENROLLMENT GRANTS

Tennessee Student Assistance Corporation
Parkway Towers
404 James Robertson Parkway, Suite 1510
Nashville, TN 37243–0820
Phone: (615) 741–1346; (800) 342–1663; Fax: (615) 741–6101;
Email: TSAC.Aidinfo@tn.gov
Web: www.tn.gov

Summary: To provide financial assistance to high school students in Tennessee who have a dual enrollment at a college or university in the state.

Eligibility: Open to juniors and seniors at high schools in Tennessee and home–schooled students in the state at an equivalent level. Applicants must also be enrolled in college courses at eligible postsecondary institutions for which they will receive college credit. All college enrollments qualify, regardless of course delivery location or method.

Financial data: The maximum award is $300 per semester for 1 course or $600 per semester ($1,200 per year) for an additional course.

Duration: Until completion of a high school diploma.

Number awarded: Varies each year; recently, 16,404 of these grants, worth nearly $7.2 million, were awarded.

Deadline: At colleges and universities, deadlines are August of each year for fall enrollment, January of each year for spring, or April of each year for summer. At Tennessee Technology Centers, deadlines are October of each year for fall enrollment, February of each year for spring, or April of each year for summer.

927 $$ TENNESSEE GENERAL ASSEMBLY MERIT SCHOLARSHIPS

Tennessee Student Assistance Corporation
Parkway Towers
404 James Robertson Parkway, Suite 1510
Nashville, TN 37243–0820
Phone: (615) 741–1346; (800) 342–1663; Fax: (615) 741–6101;
Email: TSAC.Aidinfo@tn.gov
Web: www.tn.gov/collegepays/mon_college/gams.htm

Summary: To provide supplemental financial assistance to high school seniors in Tennessee who meet academic requirements in excess of those for the Tennessee HOPE Scholarships and plan to attend college in the state.

Eligibility: Open to seniors graduating from public and private high schools in Tennessee and other residents of the state who qualify for a Tennessee HOPE Scholarship. Applicants for this supplemental funding must have higher levels of academic achievement: ACT scores of at least 29 (instead of 21), SAT scores of at least 1280 (instead of 980), and GPA of 3.75 or higher (instead of 3.0). The GPA may be weighted to include extra credit for AP or other advanced courses. They must be planning to attend an accredited public or private college or university in Tennessee.

Financial data: The stipend is an additional $1,500, so the total award is $7,500 per year for students at 4–year colleges and universities or $4,500 per year for students at 2–year schools.

Duration: 1 year; students may receive this supplemental funding only once.

Number awarded: Varies each year; recently, 5,810 students received more than $23 million in scholarships from this program.

Deadline: August of each year for fall semester; January of each year for spring and summer semesters.

928 $ TENNESSEE HELPING HEROES GRANTS

Tennessee Student Assistance Corporation
Parkway Towers
404 James Robertson Parkway, Suite 1510
Nashville, TN 37243–0820
Phone: (615) 741–1346; (800) 342–1663; Fax: (615) 741–6101;
Email: TSAC.Aidinfo@tn.gov
Web: www.tn.gov/collegepays/mon_college/hh_grant.htm

Summary: To provide financial assistance to veterans and current Reservists or National Guard members who are residents of Tennessee and enrolled at a college or university in the state.

Eligibility: Open to residents of Tennessee who are veterans honorably discharged from the U.S. armed forces and former or current members of a Reserve or Tennessee National Guard unit who were called into active military service. Applicants must have been awarded, on or after September 11, 2001, the Iraq Campaign Medal, the Afghanistan Campaign Medal, or the Global War on Terrorism Expeditionary Medal. They must be enrolled at least half time at an eligible college or university in Tennessee and receive no final failing grade in any course. No academic standard or financial need requirements apply.

Financial data: Grants are $1,000 per semester for full–time study or $500 per semester for part–time study. Funds are awarded after completion of each semester of work.

Duration: Grants are awarded until completion of the equivalent of 8 full semesters of work, completion of a baccalaureate degree, or the eighth anniversary of honorable discharge from military service, whichever comes first.

Number awarded: Varies each year; recently, 503 students received $680,000 in scholarships through this program.

Deadline: August of each year for fall enrollment, January of each year for spring, or April of each year for summer.

929 $ TENNESSEE HOPE ACCESS GRANTS

Tennessee Student Assistance Corporation
Parkway Towers
404 James Robertson Parkway, Suite 1510
Nashville, TN 37243–0820
Phone: (615) 741–1346; (800) 342–1663; Fax: (615) 741–6101;
Email: TSAC.Aidinfo@tn.gov
Web: www.tn.gov/collegepays/mon_college/hope_grant.htm

Summary: To provide financial assistance to high school seniors in Tennessee who do not qualify for the Tennessee HOPE Scholarships but meet other academic and income requirements and plan to attend college in the state.

Eligibility: Open to seniors graduating from public and private high schools in Tennessee who have a weighted GPA of 2.75 or more and an ACT score from 18 to 20 or an SAT score from 860 to 970. Applicants must have an annual family income of $36,000 or less. They must be planning to attend an accredited public or private college or university in Tennessee.

Financial data: The stipend is $2,750 per year for students at 4–year colleges and universities or $1,375 per year for students at 2–year schools. Awards to part–time students are prorated.

Duration: 1 year; this grant is nonrenewable but recipients may apply for a Tennessee HOPE Scholarship after 1 year of college if they have a cumulative GPA of 2.75 or higher.

Number awarded: Varies each year; recently, more than 400 of these grants, worth nearly $870,000, were awarded.

Deadline: August of each year for fall semester; January of each year for spring and summer semesters.

930 $$ TENNESSEE HOPE FOSTER CHILD TUITION GRANT

Tennessee Student Assistance Corporation
Parkway Towers
404 James Robertson Parkway, Suite 1510
Nashville, TN 37243–0820
Phone: (615) 741–1346; (800) 342–1663; Fax: (615) 741–6101;
Email: TSAC.Aidinfo@tn.gov
Web: www.tn.gov/collegepays/mon_college/hope_foster_grant.html

Summary: To provide financial assistance to high school seniors in Tennessee who have been in foster care and are interested in attending college in the state.

Eligibility: Open to seniors graduating from public and private high schools in Tennessee who have been in the custody of the Tennessee Department of Children's Services 1) for at least 1 year after reaching 14 years of age; 2) for at least 1 year after reaching 14 years of age, were placed for adoption by the department or an adoption contract agency, and the adoption was finalized; or 3) for at least 1 year and were placed in permanent guardianship by the department after reaching 14 years of age. Applicants must qualify for either a Tennessee HOPE

Scholarship (which requires a weighted GPA of 3.0 or higher and either an ACT score of at least 21 or an SAT score of at least 980) or a Tennessee HOPE Access Grant (which requires a weighted GPA of 2.75 or higher, an ACT score from 18 to 20 or an SAT score from 860 to 970, and an annual family income of $36,000 or less). They must be planning to attend an accredited public or private college or university in Tennessee.

Financial data: For students at public postsecondary institutions, awards cover all costs of tuition and associated fees remaining after applying all other student assistance from all sources towards the student's cost of attendance. For students at independent 2– and 4–year institutions, awards provide the average of full tuition and associated fees charged at 2– or 4–year public postsecondary institutions.

Duration: 1 year; may be renewed up to 3 additional years (or 5 additional years, provided the student maintains satisfactory academic progress as defined by their institution).

Number awarded: Varies each year; recently, 51 of these grants, worth more than $250,000, were awarded.

Deadline: August of each year for fall semester; January of each year for spring and summer semesters.

931 $$ TENNESSEE HOPE SCHOLARSHIPS

Tennessee Student Assistance Corporation
Parkway Towers
404 James Robertson Parkway, Suite 1510
Nashville, TN 37243–0820
Phone: (615) 741–1346; (800) 342–1663; Fax: (615) 741–6101;
Email: TSAC.Aidinfo@tn.gov
Web: www.tn.gov/collegepays/mon_college/hope_scholar.htm

Summary: To provide financial assistance to high school seniors in Tennessee who plan to attend college in the state.

Eligibility: Open to seniors graduating from public and private high schools in Tennessee, students in Tennessee who have completed a home school program, and residents of Tennessee who have attained a GED. High school seniors must have an ACT score of at least 21 (or SAT score of at least 980) or a weighted GPA of 3.0 or higher; home school students must have an ACT score of at least 21 (or SAT score of at least 980); and GED recipients must have a GED score of at least 525 and an ACT score of at least 21 (or SAT score of at least 980). Applicants must be planning to attend an accredited public or private college or university in Tennessee.

Financial data: The stipend is $6,000 per year for students at 4–year colleges and universities or $3,000 per year for students at 2–year schools.

Duration: 1 year; may be renewed up to 4 additional years if the recipient maintains a cumulative GPA of 2.75 or higher after 24 and 48 attempted semester hours and 3.0 or higher after 72 attempted semester hours and beyond.

Number awarded: Varies each year; recently, 43,282 students received more than $148.4 million in scholarships from this program.

Deadline: August of each year for fall semester; January of each year for spring and summer semesters.

932 $$ TENNESSEE STUDENT ASSISTANCE AWARDS

Tennessee Student Assistance Corporation
Parkway Towers
404 James Robertson Parkway, Suite 1510
Nashville, TN 37243–0820
Phone: (615) 741–1346; (800) 342–1663; Fax: (615) 741–6101;
Email: TSAC.Aidinfo@tn.gov
Web: www.tn.gov/collegepays/mon_college/tsa_award.htm

Summary: To provide funding to students in Tennessee who have financial need.

Eligibility: Open to residents of Tennessee who are enrolled at least half time at a public or eligible private college or university in the state and can demonstrate financial need (expected family contribution of $2,100 or less). Awards are presented on a first–come, first–served basis; priority is given to U.S. citizens.

Financial data: Recently, the maximum annual award for full–time study was $4,000 at eligible Tennessee 2– and 4–year private institutions, $2,000 at public 4–year institutions, $1,300 at public 2–year institutions, $2,000 at career schools, or $1,000 at technology centers.

Duration: 1 year; nonrenewable.

Number awarded: Varies each year; recently, $3.2 million was available for this program.

Deadline: February of each year.

933 $$ TEXAS ARMED SERVICES SCHOLARSHIP PROGRAM

Texas Higher Education Coordinating Board
Attn: Grants and Special Programs
1200 East Anderson Lane
P.O. Box 12788
Austin, TX 78711–2788
Phone: (512) 427–6340; (800) 242–3062; Fax: (512) 427–6420;
Email: grantinfo@thecb.state.tx.us
Web: www.collegeforalltexans.com/apps/financialaid/tofa2.cfm?ID=581

Summary: To provide funding to high school seniors in Texas who plan to participate in an ROTC program at a college in the state and then serve in the U.S. armed forces, the Texas National Guard, or the Texas Air National Guard.

Eligibility: Open to seniors graduating from high schools in Texas who can meet any 2 of the following requirements: 1) are on track to graduate with the Distinguished Achievement Program (DAP) or International Baccalaureate (IB) Program; 2) have a high school GPA of 3.0 or higher; 3) have an SAT score of 1590 or higher or an ACT score of 23 or higher; or 4) rank in the top third of their class. Applicants must plan to attend a public or private college or university in Texas and enter into a written agreement to complete 4 years of ROTC training, graduate within 5 years, and serve 4 years as a member of the Texas Army or Air Force National Guard or as a commissioned officer in the U.S. armed services. They must apply through their state senator or representative.

Financial data: The current stipend is $10,000 per year. If recipients fail to fulfill their service agreement, they must repay all funds received.

Duration: 1 year; may be renewed up to 3 additional years.

Number awarded: Up to 185 each year.

Deadline: Legislators must submit nominations by August of each year.

934 $$ TEXAS CHILDREN OF DISABLED OR DECEASED FIREMEN, PEACE OFFICERS, GAME WARDENS, AND EMPLOYEES OF CORRECTIONAL INSTITUTIONS EXEMPTION PROGRAM

Texas Higher Education Coordinating Board
Attn: Grants and Special Programs
1200 East Anderson Lane
P.O. Box 12788
Austin, TX 78711–2788
Phone: (512) 427–6340; (800) 242–3062; Fax: (512) 427–6420;
Email: grantinfo@thecb.state.tx.us
Web: www.collegeforalltexans.com/apps/financialaid/tofa2.cfm?ID=548

Summary: To provide educational assistance to the children of disabled or deceased Texas firefighters, peace officers, game wardens, and employees of correctional institutions.

Eligibility: Open to children of Texas paid or volunteer firefighters; paid municipal, county, or state peace officers; custodial employees of the Department of Corrections; or game wardens. The parent must have suffered an injury in the line of duty, resulting in disability or death. Applicants must be under 21 years of age.

Financial data: Eligible students are exempted from the payment of all dues, fees, and tuition charges at publicly–supported colleges and universities in Texas.

Duration: Support is provided for up to 120 semester credit hours of undergraduate study or until the recipient reaches 26 years of age, whichever comes first.

Number awarded: Varies each year; recently, 140 students received support through this program.

Deadline: Deadline not specified.

935 $$ TEXAS CHILDREN OF U.S. MILITARY WHO ARE MISSING IN ACTION OR PRISONERS OF WAR EXEMPTION PROGRAM

Texas Higher Education Coordinating Board
Attn: Grants and Special Programs
1200 East Anderson Lane
P.O. Box 12788
Austin, TX 78711–2788
Phone: (512) 427–6340; (800) 242–3062; Fax: (512) 427–6420;
Email: grantinfo@thecb.state.tx.us
Web: www.collegeforalltexans.com/apps/financialaid/tofa2.cfm?ID=421

Summary: To provide educational assistance to the children of Texas military personnel declared prisoners of war or missing in action.

Eligibility: Open to dependent children of Texas residents who are either prisoners of war or missing in action. Applicants must be under 21 years of age, or under 25 if they receive the majority of support from their parent(s).
Financial data: Eligible students are exempted from the payment of all dues, fees, and tuition charges at publicly–supported colleges and universities in Texas.
Duration: Up to 8 semesters.
Number awarded: Varies each year; recently, 4 of these exemptions were granted.
Deadline: Deadline not specified.

936 $$ TEXAS COMPETITIVE SCHOLARSHIP WAIVERS

Texas Higher Education Coordinating Board
Attn: Grants and Special Programs
1200 East Anderson Lane
P.O. Box 12788
Austin, TX 78711–2788
Phone: (512) 427–6323; (800) 242–3062, ext. 6323; Fax: (512) 427–6420;
Email: grantinfo@thecb.state.tx.us
Web: www.collegeforalltexans.com/apps/financialaid/tofa2.cfm?ID=435
Summary: To provide waivers of non–resident tuition at Texas public institutions to students from outside the state who receive other competitive scholarships.
Eligibility: Open to non–resident and foreign students who receive a competitive scholarship of at least $1,000 to attend a public institution in Texas. Applicants must have competed with other students, including Texas residents, for the award.
Financial data: Eligible students are able to attend Texas public institutions and pay the resident tuition rate.
Duration: 1 year; may be renewed.
Number awarded: Varies each year; recently, 13,417 of these waivers were awarded.
Deadline: Deadline not specified.

937 $$ TEXAS ECONOMIC DEVELOPMENT AND DIVERSIFICATION WAIVERS

Texas Higher Education Coordinating Board
Attn: Grants and Special Programs
1200 East Anderson Lane
P.O. Box 12788
Austin, TX 78711–2788
Phone: (512) 427–6323; (800) 242–3062, ext. 6323; Fax: (512) 427–6420;
Email: grantinfo@thecb.state.tx.us
Web: www.collegeforalltexans.com/apps/financialaid/tofa2.cfm?ID=567
Summary: To provide waivers of non–resident tuition at Texas public institutions to students from outside the state whose families come to the state as part of Texas' promotional activities.
Eligibility: Open to students from outside the state whose families come to the state as part of the promotional activities of the Economic Development and Tourism division of the Office of the Governor. They are entitled to attend public colleges and universities in the state as state residents even before they have established residency. Applicants must be non–residents of Texas but U.S. citizens, permanent residents, or eligible non–immigrants.
Financial data: Eligible students are able to attend Texas public institutions and pay the resident tuition rate.
Duration: 1 year; if the family is still residing in Texas, students may request a change in classification in order to pay resident tuition.
Number awarded: Varies each year; recently, 236 of these waivers were awarded.
Deadline: Deadline not specified.

938 $$ TEXAS EDUCATION AND TRAINING VOUCHERS FOR YOUTHS AGING OUT OF FOSTER CARE

Texas Higher Education Coordinating Board
Attn: Grants and Special Programs
1200 East Anderson Lane
P.O. Box 12788
Austin, TX 78711–2788
Phone: (512) 427–6340; (800) 242–3062; Fax: (512) 427–6420;
Email: grantinfo@thecb.state.tx.us
Web: www.collegeforalltexans.com/apps/financialaid/tofa2.cfm?ID=480
Summary: To provide financial assistance for college to students in Texas who have been in foster care.
Eligibility: Open to residents of Texas who 1) are between 16 and 21 years of age, have a high school diploma or equivalent, and are attending a Texas public or private college that provides a bachelor's degree or not less than a 2–year program that provides credit toward an associate degree or certificate; 2) are beyond the age of compulsory school attendance (age 18) and are attending an accredited or preaccredited program that provides not less than 1 year of training toward gainful employment; 3) are in foster care of the Texas Department of Family and Protective Services (TDFPS), are at least 16 years of age, and are likely to remain in foster care until turning 18; 4) have aged out of TDFPS foster care but have not yet turned 21; or 5) are adopted from TDFPS foster care after turning 16 years of age but are not yet 21. Applicants must be attending or planning to attend a Texas public or private educational institution that is accredited or granted preaccredited status.
Financial data: Vouchers can be used to cover the cost of attendance (tuition and fees, books and supplies, room and board, transportation, child care, and some personal expenses) or $5,000 per year, whichever amount is less.
Duration: 1 year. Participants in the program remain eligible until age 23 as long as they are enrolled and making satisfactory progress toward completing their postsecondary education or training program.
Number awarded: Varies each year.
Deadline: Deadline not specified.

939 $$ TEXAS EDUCATIONAL OPPORTUNITY GRANT PROGRAM

Texas Higher Education Coordinating Board
Attn: Grants and Special Programs
1200 East Anderson Lane
P.O. Box 12788
Austin, TX 78711–2788
Phone: (512) 427–6340; (800) 242–3062; Fax: (512) 427–6420;
Email: grantinfo@thecb.state.tx.us
Web: www.collegeforalltexans.com/apps/financialaid/tofa2.cfm?ID=529
Summary: To provide financial assistance to students entering a public 2–year college in Texas.
Eligibility: Open to residents of Texas enrolled at least half time in the first 30 credit hours at a public community college, public technical college, or public state college in the state. Applicants must have an Expected Family Contribution (EFC) of no more than $2,000.
Financial data: Full–time stipends are approximately $3,390 per semester for public state college students, $890 per semester for community college students, or $1,575 per semester for technical college students.
Duration: 1 year. Students can receive awards for up to 75 semester credit hours, for 4 years, or until they receive an associate degree, whichever occurs first. Renewal requires completion of at least 75% of the hours taken in the prior year plus a cumulative college GPA of 2.5 or higher.
Number awarded: Varies each year; recently, 3,906 of these grants were awarded.
Deadline: Deadline not specified.

940 $$ TEXAS EXEMPTION FOR HIGHEST RANKING HIGH SCHOOL GRADUATE PROGRAM

Texas Higher Education Coordinating Board
Attn: Grants and Special Programs
1200 East Anderson Lane
P.O. Box 12788
Austin, TX 78711–2788
Phone: (512) 427–6340; (800) 242–3062; Fax: (512) 427–6420;
Email: grantinfo@thecb.state.tx.us
Web: www.collegeforalltexans.com/apps/financialaid/tofa2.cfm?ID=431
Summary: To recognize and reward the top students in Texas high schools.
Eligibility: Open to the highest ranking graduate (i.e., valedictorians) of accredited high schools in Texas. Applicants may be Texas residents, non–residents, or foreign students.
Financial data: Tuition is waived for award winners at any public college or university in Texas.
Duration: 1 year; nonrenewable.
Number awarded: Varies each year; recently, 1,014 of these exemptions were granted.
Deadline: Deadline not specified.

941 $$ TEXAS EXEMPTION FOR PEACE OFFICERS DISABLED IN THE LINE OF DUTY

Texas Higher Education Coordinating Board
Attn: Grants and Special Programs
1200 East Anderson Lane
P.O. Box 12788
Austin, TX 78711–2788
Phone: (512) 427–6340; (800) 242–3062; Fax: (512) 427–6420;
Email: grantinfo@thecb.state.tx.us
Web: www.collegeforalltexans.com/apps/financialaid/tofa2.cfm?ID=508

Summary: To provide educational assistance to disabled Texas peace officers.

Eligibility: Open to Texas residents who are permanently disabled as a result of an injury suffered as a peace officer and are unable to continue employment as a peace officer because of the disability. Applicants must be planning to attend a publicly–supported college or university in Texas as an undergraduate student.

Financial data: Eligible students are exempted from the payment of all dues, fees, and tuition charges at publicly–supported colleges and universities in Texas.

Duration: Up to 12 semesters.

Number awarded: Varies each year; recently, 31 of these exemptions were awarded.

Deadline: Deadline not specified.

942 $$ TEXAS EXEMPTION FOR STUDENTS UNDER CONSERVATORSHIP OF THE DEPARTMENT OF FAMILY AND PROTECTIVE SERVICES

Texas Higher Education Coordinating Board
Attn: Grants and Special Programs
1200 East Anderson Lane
P.O. Box 12788
Austin, TX 78711–2788
Phone: (512) 427–6340; (800) 242–3062; Fax: (512) 427–6420;
Email: grantinfo@thecb.state.tx.us
Web: www.collegeforalltexans.com/apps/financialaid/tofa2.cfm?ID=429

Summary: To exempt students in Texas who have been in foster care under specified conditions from payment of tuition at public colleges and universities in the state.

Eligibility: Open to students who have been in the care or conservatorship of the Texas Department of Family and Protective Services 1) on the day before their 18th birthday; 2) on the day they graduated from high school or received the equivalent of a high school diploma; 3) on the day after their 14th birthday, if they were also eligible for adoption on or after that day; 4) on the day preceding the date they are adopted or the date permanent managing conservatorship of the student is awarded to a person other than their parent; or 5) during an academic term in which the student was enrolled in a dual credit course or other course for which they may earn joint high school and college credit. Applicants must enroll as an undergraduate at a public college or university in Texas.

Financial data: Eligible students are exempted from the payment of all dues, fees, and tuition charges at publicly–supported colleges and universities in Texas.

Duration: 1 year.

Number awarded: Varies each year.

Deadline: Deadline not specified.

943 $$ TEXAS EXEMPTION FOR SURVIVING SPOUSES AND DEPENDENT CHILDREN OF CERTAIN DECEASED PUBLIC SERVANTS

Texas Higher Education Coordinating Board
Attn: Grants and Special Programs
1200 East Anderson Lane
P.O. Box 12788
Austin, TX 78711–2788
Phone: (512) 427–6340; (800) 242–3062; Fax: (512) 427–6420;
Email: grantinfo@thecb.state.tx.us
Web: www.collegeforalltexans.com/apps/financialaid/tofa2.cfm?ID=476

Summary: To provide educational assistance to the children and spouses of certain deceased Texas public employees.

Eligibility: Open to residents of Texas whose parent or spouse was killed in the line of duty in certain public service positions after September 1, 2000. Eligible public service positions include peace officers, probation officers, parole officers, jailers, members of organized police reserve and auxiliary units, juvenile correctional employees, paid and volunteer firefighters, and emergency medical service volunteers and paid personnel. Applicants must be enrolled or planning to enroll full time at a Texas public college or university.

Financial data: Eligible students are exempted from the payment of all dues, fees, and tuition charges at publicly–supported colleges and universities in Texas. In addition, the institution provides them with an allowance for textbooks. If the student qualifies to live in the institution's housing, the institution must provide either free room and board or an equivalent room and board stipend.

Duration: 1 year; may be renewed.

Number awarded: Varies each year; recently, 167 students received support through this program.

Deadline: Deadline not specified.

944 $$ TEXAS EXEMPTION PROGRAM FOR ADOPTED STUDENTS FORMERLY IN FOSTER OR OTHER RESIDENTIAL CARE

Texas Higher Education Coordinating Board
Attn: Grants and Special Programs
1200 East Anderson Lane
P.O. Box 12788
Austin, TX 78711–2788
Phone: (512) 427–6340; (800) 242–3062; Fax: (512) 427–6420;
Email: grantinfo@thecb.state.tx.us
Web: www.collegeforalltexans.com/apps/financialaid/tofa2.cfm?ID=551

Summary: To provide educational assistance to students in Texas who once were in foster or other residential care and have been adopted.

Eligibility: Open to students who have been in foster care or other residential care under the conservatorship of the Texas Department of Family and Protective Services and have been adopted. Applicants must be attending or planning to attend a public college or university in Texas.

Financial data: Eligible students are exempted from the payment of all dues, fees, and tuition charges at publicly–supported colleges and universities in Texas.

Duration: 1 year; may be renewed.

Number awarded: Varies each year; recently, 52 students received support through this program.

Deadline: Deadline not specified.

945 $$ TEXAS EXEMPTION PROGRAM FOR CHILDREN OF PROFESSIONAL NURSING PROGRAM FACULTY AND STAFF

Texas Higher Education Coordinating Board
Attn: Grants and Special Programs
1200 East Anderson Lane
P.O. Box 12788
Austin, TX 78711–2788
Phone: (512) 427–6340; (800) 242–3062; Fax: (512) 427–6420;
Email: grantinfo@thecb.state.tx.us
Web: www.collegeforalltexans.com/apps/financialaid/tofa2.cfm?ID=390

Summary: To exempt from tuition the children of nursing faculty and staff at public colleges and universities in Texas.

Eligibility: Open to residents of Texas whose parents are employed as a full–time faculty or staff members in an undergraduate or graduate professional nursing program at a public college or university in Texas. Eligibility includes children of contract employees in nursing programs and of full–time teaching assistants. Applicants must be working on or planning to work on an undergraduate degree in any field at the same Texas institution where their parent is currently employed or with which the parent has contracted as a professional nursing faculty, staff member, or teaching assistant.

Financial data: Eligible students are exempted from the payment of tuition charges (but not fees).

Number awarded: Varies each year.

Deadline: Deadline not specified.

946 TEXAS EXEMPTION PROGRAM FOR CLINICAL PRECEPTORS AND THEIR CHILDREN

Texas Higher Education Coordinating Board
Attn: Grants and Special Programs
1200 East Anderson Lane
P.O. Box 12788
Austin, TX 78711–2788
Phone: (512) 427–6340; (800) 242–3062; Fax: (512) 427–6420;
Email: grantinfo@thecb.state.tx.us

Web: www.collegeforalltexans.com/apps/financialaid/tofa2.cfm?ID=546

Summary: To provide financial assistance for additional study at institutions in Texas to residents of the state who are working as clinical preceptors in nursing programs in the state and to their children.

Eligibility: Open to residents of Texas who are either 1) registered nurses serving at least 1 day per week as a clinical preceptor for students enrolled in an undergraduate professional nursing program in the state; or 2) the children of such clinical preceptors. Applicants must be attending or planning to attend a Texas public college or university. Clinical preceptors must be taking classes related to their work. Their children may be majoring in any subject field.

Financial data: The stipend is $500 per semester or actual tuition, whichever is less.

Duration: Clinical preceptors may take classes as long as they meet program requirements. Children of clinical preceptors may enroll for up to 10 semester or until they receive their bachelor's degree.

Number awarded: Varies each year.

Deadline: Deadline not specified.

947 $$ TEXAS GRANT

Texas Higher Education Coordinating Board
Attn: Grants and Special Programs
1200 East Anderson Lane
P.O. Box 12788
Austin, TX 78711–2788
Phone: (512) 427–6340; (800) 242–3062; Fax: (512) 427–6420;
Email: grantinfo@thecb.state.tx.us
Web: www.collegeforalltexans.com/apps/financialaid/tofa.cfm?Kind=GS

Summary: To provide financial assistance to undergraduate students entering college in Texas from high school or a community college.

Eligibility: Open to Texas residents who 1) graduated from a high school in the state no earlier than the 1998–99 school year, completed the recommended or distinguished achievement high school curriculum or its equivalent, enrolled at a public Texas college or university within 16 months of high school graduation, and have accumulated no more than 30 semester credit hours; or 2) earned an associate degree from a public technical, state, or community college in Texas and enrolled at a public university in Texas no more than 12 months after receiving their associate degree. Applicants must be able to demonstrate financial need and have an Expected Family Contribution (EFC) of $4,000 or less.

Financial data: Full–time stipends are approximately $6,780 per year for public university and state college students, $1,780 per year for community college students, or $3,150 per year for technical college students.

Duration: 1 year. Students who qualify on the basis of their high school curriculum can receive awards for up to 150 semester credit hours, for 6 years, or until their receive their bachelor's degree, whichever occurs first. Students who qualify on the basis of an associate degree can receive awards for up to 90 semester credit hours, for 4 years, or until they complete a baccalaureate degree, whichever occurs first. Renewal requires completion of at least 75% of the hours taken in the prior year plus a cumulative college GPA of 2.5 or higher.

Number awarded: Varies each year; recently, 61,086 of these grants were awarded.

Deadline: Deadline not specified.

948 $$ TEXAS NATIONAL GUARD TUITION ASSISTANCE PROGRAM

Texas Higher Education Coordinating Board
Attn: Grants and Special Programs
1200 East Anderson Lane
P.O. Box 12788
Austin, TX 78711–2788
Phone: (512) 427–6340; (800) 242–3062; Fax: (512) 427–6420;
Email: grantinfo@thecb.state.tx.us
Web: www.collegeforalltexans.com/apps/financialaid/tofa2.cfm?ID=430

Summary: To provide financial assistance for college or graduate school to members of the Texas National Guard.

Eligibility: Open to Texas residents who are active, drilling members of the Texas National Guard, the Texas Air Guard, or the State Guard. Applicants may be undergraduate or graduate students attending or planning to attend a public or private college or university in Texas; attendance at career colleges or universities is not supported.

Financial data: Eligible Guard members receive exemption from tuition at Texas public colleges and universities. For students who attend a private, nonprofit institution, the award is based on public university tuition charges for 12 semester credit hours at the resident rate.

Duration: Tuition assistance is available for up to 12 semester credit hours per semester for up to 10 semesters or 5 academic years, whichever occurs first.

Number awarded: Varies each year; recently, 864 Guard members participated in this program.

Deadline: June of each year for the fall semester; November of each year for the spring semester.

949 TEXAS PUBLIC EDUCATIONAL GRANT PROGRAM

Texas Higher Education Coordinating Board
Attn: Grants and Special Programs
1200 East Anderson Lane
P.O. Box 12788
Austin, TX 78711–2788
Phone: (512) 427–6340; (800) 242–3062; Fax: (512) 427–6420;
Email: grantinfo@thecb.state.tx.us
Web: www.collegeforalltexans.com/apps/financialaid/tofa2.cfm?ID=406

Summary: To provide financial assistance to undergraduate and graduate students in Texas.

Eligibility: Open to residents of Texas, non–residents, and foreign students. Applicants may be undergraduate or graduate students. They must be attending a public college or university in Texas. Financial need is considered as part of the selection process.

Financial data: The amount awarded varies, depending upon the financial need of the recipient. No award may exceed the student's unmet financial need. Each institution sets its own maximum award amounts.

Duration: 1 year; may be renewed.

Number awarded: Varies each year.

Deadline: Deadline not specified.

950 $$ TEXAS TANF EXEMPTION PROGRAM

Texas Higher Education Coordinating Board
Attn: Grants and Special Programs
1200 East Anderson Lane
P.O. Box 12788
Austin, TX 78711–2788
Phone: (512) 427–6340; (800) 242–3062; Fax: (512) 427–6420;
Email: grantinfo@thecb.state.tx.us
Web: www.collegeforalltexans.com/apps/financialaid/tofa2.cfm?ID=559

Summary: To provide educational assistance to students in Texas whose families are receiving Temporary Assistance to Needy Families (TANF).

Eligibility: Open to students who graduated from a public high school in Texas and are dependent children whose parents received, during the year of their high school graduation, TANF for at least 6 months. Applicants must be younger than 22 years of age at the time of enrollment in college and must enroll in college within 24 months of high school graduation.

Financial data: Eligible students are exempt from the payment of all fees (other than building use fees) and tuition charges at publicly–supported colleges and universities in Texas.

Duration: 1 year; nonrenewable.

Number awarded: Varies each year; recently, 128 students received this assistance.

Deadline: Deadline not specified.

951 $ TEXAS TOP 10% SCHOLARSHIP PROGRAM

Texas Higher Education Coordinating Board
Attn: Grants and Special Programs
1200 East Anderson Lane
P.O. Box 12788
Austin, TX 78711–2788
Phone: (512) 427–6340; (800) 242–3062; Fax: (512) 427–6420;
Email: grantinfo@thecb.state.tx.us
Web: www.collegeforalltexans.com/apps/financialaid/tofa2.cfm?ID=385

Summary: To provide financial assistance to residents of Texas who graduate in the top 10% of their high school class and plan to attend a public university in the state.

Eligibility: Open to seniors graduating from high schools in Texas who are ranked in the top 10% of their class and have completed the recommended or distinguished achievement high school curriculum. Applicants must be planning to enroll full time at a public 2– or 4–year college or university in Texas. They must be able to demonstrate financial need. Additional support is available to students who major in a critical workforce shortage field (teaching, nursing, allied health, science, technology, engineering, and mathematics).

Financial data: The stipend is $2,000 per year or $4,000 per year for students majoring in a critical workforce shortage field.
Duration: 1 year; may be renewed, provided the recipient completes at least 75% of the semester credit hours attempted, remains enrolled full time, and maintains a cumulative GPA of 3.25 or higher.
Number awarded: Varies each year.
Deadline: Deadline not specified.

952 $$ TEXAS TUITION EQUALIZATION GRANT PROGRAM

Texas Higher Education Coordinating Board
Attn: Grants and Special Programs
1200 East Anderson Lane
P.O. Box 12788
Austin, TX 78711–2788
Phone: (512) 427–6340; (800) 242–3062; Fax: (512) 427–6420;
Email: grantinfo@thecb.state.tx.us
Web: www.collegeforalltexans.com/apps/financialaid/tofa2.cfm?ID=534
Summary: To provide financial assistance to undergraduate and graduate students attending private postsecondary schools in Texas.
Eligibility: Open to 1) residents of Texas; and 2) residents of other states who are National Merit Scholarship finalists. Applicants must be enrolled full time as an undergraduate or graduate student at an eligible nonprofit independent college in the state. They may not be receiving an athletic scholarship. Financial need is considered in the selection process.
Financial data: The maximum awarded (currently $3,518 per academic year) may not exceed the student's financial need or the amount of tuition the student is paying in excess of what he or she would pay at a public institution. Students with exceptional financial need (those with an Expected Family Contribution of less than or equal to $1,000) may receive awards up to $5,277 per academic year.
Duration: 1 year; may be renewed, provided the recipient remains enrolled full time and maintains a GPA of 2.5 or higher.
Number awarded: Varies each year.
Deadline: Deadline not specified.

953 $$ TEXAS WAIVERS OF NON–RESIDENT TUITION FOR MILITARY SURVIVORS

Texas Higher Education Coordinating Board
Attn: Grants and Special Programs
1200 East Anderson Lane
P.O. Box 12788
Austin, TX 78711–2788
Phone: (512) 427–6340; (800) 242–3062; Fax: (512) 427–6420;
Email: grantinfo@thecb.state.tx.us
Web: www.collegeforalltexans.com/apps/financialaid/tofa2.cfm?ID=501
Summary: To provide a partial tuition exemption to the surviving spouses and dependent children of deceased military personnel who move to Texas following the servicemember's death.
Eligibility: Open to the surviving spouses and dependent children of members of the U.S. armed forces and commissioned officers of the Public Health Service who died while in service. Applicants must move to Texas within 60 days of the date of the death of the servicemember. They must be attending or planning to attend a public college or university in the state. Children are eligible even if the surviving parent does not accompany them to Texas.
Financial data: Although persons eligible under this program are still classified as non–residents, they are entitled to pay the resident tuition at Texas institutions of higher education on an immediate basis.
Duration: 1 year.
Number awarded: Varies each year.
Deadline: Deadline not specified.

954 $ THANKSUSA SCHOLARSHIPS

ThanksUSA
1390 Chain Bridge Road, Suite 260
McLean, VA 22101
Phone: (877) THX–USAS
Web: www.thanksusa.org/main/scholarships.html
Summary: To provide financial assistance for college to children and spouses of military personnel who served after September 11, 2001.
Eligibility: Open to dependent children 24 years of age or younger and spouses of active–duty military personnel. The parent or spouse must 1) have served on active duty for at least 180 days since September 11, 2001; 2) have been killed or wounded in action since that date; 3) be a member of the military Reserves activated to full–time duty; or 4) be a member of the National Guard who have been federalized. Applicants must be entering or attending an accredited 2– or 4–year college, university, vocational school, or technical school as a full–time student. They must have a GPA of 2.0 or higher. Selection is based on financial need, academic record, and demonstrated leadership and participation in school and community activities.
Financial data: The stipend is $3,000.
Duration: 1 year.
Number awarded: Varies each year; recently, more than 250 of these scholarship were awarded. Since the program was established, it has awarded 2,200 scholarships with a value of nearly $6.5 million.
Deadline: May of each year.

955 $ THE BIG DIG SCHOLARSHIP

Antique Trader TV
4216 Pacific Coast Highway, Suite 302
Torrance, CA 90505
Phone: (310) 294–9981;
Email: contact@antiquetrader.tv
Web: www.antiquetrader.tv/studentscholarship.php
Summary: To recognize and reward, with college scholarships, high school seniors and current college undergraduates who submit outstanding essays on an assigned topic related to burying artifacts from today for discovery in the future.
Eligibility: Open to high school seniors and students enrolled in their first or second year of college. Applicants must submit an essay of 500 to 1,000 words for which they are asked to assume that they will bury an object in their back yard and that it will be discovered by a relative 200 years from now. The object must be currently sold in a store today and cost less than $500. In their essay, they must explain why they chose that item and why they believe the object will have immense value in 200 years. Selection is based on originality (35%); depth of content (50%); and grammar, punctuation, and spelling (15%).
Financial data: The award is a $3,000 scholarship.
Duration: 1 year.
Number awarded: 1 each year.
Deadline: December of each year.

956 $$ THE FOUNTAINHEAD ESSAY CONTEST

Ayn Rand Institute
Attn: Essay Contests
2121 Alton Parkway, Suite 250
P.O. Box 57044
Irvine, CA 92619–7044
Phone: (949) 222–6550, ext. 247; Fax: (949) 222–6558;
Email: essays@aynrand.org
Web: essaycontest.aynrandnovels.com/TheFountainhead.aspx?theme=blue
Summary: To recognize and reward outstanding essays written by high school students on Ayn Rand's novel, *The Fountainhead.*
Eligibility: Open to juniors or seniors in high school. Applicants must submit an essay on questions selected each year from Ayn Rand's novel, *The Fountainhead.* The essay must be between 800 and 1,600 words. Selection is based on style and content. Judges look for writing that is clear, articulate, and logically organized. To win, an essay must demonstrate an outstanding grasp of the philosophical meaning of the novel.
Financial data: First prize is $10,000; second prizes are $2,000; third prizes are $1,000; finalist prizes are $100; and semifinalist prizes are $50.
Duration: The competition is held annually.
Number awarded: 236 each year: 1 first prize, 5 second prizes, 10 third prizes, 45 finalist prizes, and 175 semifinalist prizes.
Deadline: April of each year.

957 THEODORE MAZZA SCHOLARSHIP

UNICO National
Attn: UNICO Foundation, Inc.
271 U.S. Highway 46 West, Suite A–108
Fairfield, NJ 07004
Phone: (973) 808–0035; (800) 877–1492; Fax: (973) 808–0043;
Email: uniconational@unico.org
Web: www.unico.org/scholarships.asp
Summary: To provide financial assistance for college to Italian American high school seniors.

Eligibility: Open to high school seniors of Italian origin (i.e., at least 1 parent or grandparent of Italian origin) who are planning to attend an accredited college or university. Applicants must have a GPA of 3.0 or higher and be U.S. citizens. Along with their application, they must submit SAT or ACT test scores and a letter of recommendation from a UNICO chapter in the city or town where they live. Selection is based on citizenship, leadership, character, personality, community service, and financial need.
Financial data: The stipend is $1,500 per year.
Duration: 4 years.
Number awarded: 1 each year.
Deadline: April of each year.

958 THOMAS A. BRADY, MD COMEBACK AWARDS

Methodist Sports Medicine/The Orthopedic Specialists
Attn: Research and Education Foundation
201 Pennsylvania Parkway, Suite 100
Indianapolis, IN 46280
Phone: (317) 817–1258; Fax: (317) 817–1220;
Email: dthornton@methodistsports.com
Web: www.methodistsports.com/researchfoundation/comebackawards.html
Summary: To recognize and reward, with scholarships, high school and college athletes in Indiana who have overcome adversity or injury and returned to excel in competition in their respective sport.
Eligibility: Open to student athletes who are nominated by a high school, college, or university in Indiana. Each school may nominate 1 male and 1 female athlete. Nominees must have distinguished themselves by overcoming adversity or injury and returned and excelled beyond expectations in their respective sport. They must have demonstrated good sportsmanship and ethical behavior on and off the playing field.
Financial data: The award is a $1,000 college scholarship.
Duration: The awards are presented annually.
Number awarded: 4 each year: 2 high school athletes (1 male and 1 female) and 2 college athletes (1 male and 1 female).
Deadline: February of each year.

959 $ THOMAS "SARGE" JOHNSON SCHOLARSHIPS

USA Boxing, Inc.
Attn: Foundation
One Olympic Plaza
Colorado Springs, CO 80909
Phone: (719) 866–2315; Fax: (719) 866–2310;
Email: cthompson@usaboxing.org
Web: usaboxing.org/programs/scholarship–program
Summary: To provide financial assistance for college to athlete members of USA Boxing.
Eligibility: Open to students currently enrolled and making satisfactory academic progress at 2– and 4–year colleges and universities or at technical or vocational schools. Applicants must have been registered USA Boxing athletes for at least 3 consecutive years with at least 2 bouts at sanctioned events each year. They must be recommended by the chair of the Local Boxing Committee (LBC). Selection is based on information in the application (including financial need), not on boxing achievement.
Financial data: The stipend is $1,000 for first–year recipients, $1,000 for continuing recipients enrolled in 6 to 8 units with a GPA of 2.0 or higher, $2,000 for continuing recipients enrolled in 9 or more units with a GPA of 2.0 or higher, and $3,000 for continuing recipients enrolled in 12 or more units with a GPA of 3.0 or higher.
Duration: 1 year; may be renewed.
Number awarded: Varies each year; recently, 12 new and 11 renewal scholarships, with a total value of $33,000, were awarded.
Deadline: July of each year.

960 THOMAS W. PORTER, W8KYZ, SCHOLARSHIP

American Radio Relay League
Attn: ARRL Foundation
225 Main Street
Newington, CT 06111–1494
Phone: (860) 594–0397; Fax: (860) 594–0259;
Email: foundation@arrl.org
Web: www.arrl.org/scholarship–descriptions
Summary: To provide financial assistance to licensed radio amateurs, particularly from Ohio and West Virginia, who are interested in working on an undergraduate degree in any field.
Eligibility: Open to licensed radio amateurs of technician class or higher. Preference is given to residents of Ohio or West Virginia who are attending an accredited 2– or 4–year college, university, or technical school in any state. Applicants may be majoring in any field. Along with their application, they must submit an essay on the role amateur radio has played in their lives and provide documentation of financial need.
Financial data: The stipend is $1,000.
Duration: 1 year.
Number awarded: 1 each year.
Deadline: January of each year.

961 THROUGH THE LOOKING GLASS SCHOLARSHIPS

Through the Looking Glass
3075 Adeline Street, Suite 120
Berkeley, CA 94703
Phone: (510) 848–1112; (800) 644–2666; Fax: (510) 848–4445; TDD: (510) 848–1005;
Email: scholarships@lookingglass.org
Web: lookingglass.org/announcements/scholarships
Summary: To provide financial assistance for college to high school seniors who have a parent with a disability.
Eligibility: Open to graduating high school seniors and full–time college students who are 21 years of age or younger. Applicants must have at least 1 parent who has a physical, sensory, intellectual, medical, or mental health disability. Along with their application, they must submit a 3–page essay describing the experience of growing up with a parent with a disability. Selection is based on that essay, academic performance, community service, and letters of recommendation; financial need is considered for some of the scholarships.
Financial data: The stipend is $1,000.
Duration: 1 year.
Number awarded: 15 each year, of which 5 are awarded to students who can demonstrate extreme financial need.
Deadline: March of each year.

962 $ THURGOOD MARSHALL SCHOLARSHIPS

Thurgood Marshall College Fund
Attn: Campus Relations Associate
901 F Street, N.W., Suite 300
Washington, DC 20004
Phone: (202) 747–7183; Fax: (202) 652–2934;
Email: janay.hawkins@tmcfund.org
Web: www.thurgoodmarshallfund.net
Summary: To provide financial assistance to high school seniors or graduates who are interested in working on a degree at a college or university that is a member of the Thurgood Marshall College Fund (TMCF).
Eligibility: Open to full–time students enrolled or accepted at 1 of 47 designated TMCF institutions, most of which are public Historically Black Colleges and Universities (HBCUs) or other schools with large African American enrollments. Applicants must be U.S. citizens or permanent residents with a valid permanent resident card or passport stamped I–551. They must have a current GPA of 3.0 or higher and be able to demonstrate financial need. Along with their application, they must submit 1) a resume that includes community service, leadership activities, and employment/internship experience; 2) their Student Aid report from their FAFSA; 3) their most recent transcript; 4) a recommendation from a current school faculty member; and 5) a 500–word essay on their choice of 3 assigned topics.
Financial data: Stipends average $2,200 per semester ($4,400 per year), depending on the need of the recipient. Funds are awarded through the institution to be used for tuition, room, board, books, and fees.
Duration: 1 year; may be renewed for up to 3 additional years if the recipient maintains a GPA of 3.0 or higher in college.
Number awarded: Varies each year; recently, nearly 1,000 students were receiving support from this program.
Deadline: April of each year.

963 TILLMAN MILITARY SCHOLARS PROGRAM

Pat Tillman Foundation
2121 South Mill Avenue, Suite 214
Tempe, AZ 85282

Phone: (480) 621–4074; Fax: (480) 621–4075;
Email: scholarships@pattillmanfoundation.org
Web: www.pattillmanfoundation.org/tillman–military–scholars

Summary: To provide financial assistance to veterans, active servicemembers, and their spouses who are interested in working on an undergraduate or graduate degree.

Eligibility: Open to veterans and active servicemembers of all branches of the armed forces from both the pre– and post–September 11 era and their spouses; children are not eligible. Applicants must be enrolled or planning to enroll full time at a 4–year public or private college or university to work on an undergraduate, graduate, or postgraduate degree. Current and former servicemembers must submit 400–word essays on 1) their motivation and decision to serve in the U.S. military and how that decision and experience has changed their life and ambitions; and 2) their educational and career goals, how they will incorporate their military service experience into those goals, and how they intend to continue their service to others and the community. Spouses must submit 400–word essays on 1) their previous service to others and the community; and 2) their educational and career goals, how they will incorporate their service experiences and the impact of their spouse's military service into those goals, and how they intend to continue their service to others and the community. Selection is based on those essays, educational and career ambitions, record of military service, record of personal achievement, demonstration of service to others in the community, desire to continue such service, and leadership potential.

Financial data: The stipend depends on the need of the recipient and the availability of funds.

Duration: 1 year; may be renewed, provided the recipient maintains a GPA of 3.0 or higher, remains enrolled full time, and documents participation in civic action or community service.

Number awarded: Varies each year; recently, 60 students received a total of $916,000 through this program.

Deadline: March of each year.

964 TOBY WRIGHT SCHOLARSHIP FUND

Workers' Compensation Association of New Mexico
Attn: Brock Carter
3207 Matthew Avenue, N.E., Suite A
Albuquerque, NM 87107
Phone: (505) 881–1112; (800) 640–0724;
Email: brock@safetycounseling.com
Web: www.wcaofnm.com/i6/Toby_Wright_Scholarship/information.html

Summary: To provide financial assistance for college to residents of New Mexico whose parent was permanently disabled or killed in an employment–related accident.

Eligibility: Open to residents of New Mexico between 16 and 25 years of age who are attending or planning to attend a college, university, or trade school in the state. Applicants must have a parent who was permanently or catastrophically injured or killed in an employment–related accident that resulted in a New Mexico workers' compensation claim. The parent's death or injury must have resulted in a substantial decline in the family income.

Financial data: A stipend is awarded (amount not specified). Funds may be used for tuition, books, housing, meals, and course fees.

Duration: 1 semester or quarter; may be renewed if the recipient maintains a GPA of 2.5 or higher and full–time enrollment.

Number awarded: Varies each year; recently, 8 of these scholarships were awarded.

Deadline: Deadline not specified.

965 $ TONI K. ALLEN SCHOLARSHIP

Association of Legal Administrators–Capital Chapter
1250 Connecticut Avenue, N.W., Suite 700
Washington, DC 20036
Phone: (202) 419–1539;
Email: info@alacapchap.org
Web: www.alacapchap.org/community/scholarship.cfm

Summary: To provide financial assistance to high school seniors in Washington, D.C. area who plan to attend college in any state.

Eligibility: Open to seniors graduating from high schools in Washington, D.C. who plan to attend a college or university in any state. Applicants must submit an essay on their personal and career goals. Selection is based on that essay, academic achievement, extracurricular activities, community involvement as a volunteer, and an interview.

Financial data: The stipend is $15,000. Funds are disbursed over the college career of the recipient.

Duration: 4 years.

Number awarded: 1 each year.

Deadline: April of each year.

966 $$ TRAMPOLINE AND TUMBLING SCHOLARSHIP PROGRAM

USA Gymnastics
Attn: Trampoline and Tumbling Program
132 East Washington Street, Suite 700
Indianapolis, IN 46204
Phone: (317) 237–5050; (800) 345–4719; Fax: (317) 237–5069;
Email: mobaka@usagym.org
Web: www.usa–gymnastics.org/pages/tt/pages/scholarship_program.html

Summary: To provide financial assistance for college to gymnasts who participate in trampoline and tumbling activities.

Eligibility: Open to high school seniors and currently–enrolled college students who are registered athletes training and competing with USA Gymnastics trampoline and tumbling. Applicants must be enrolled or planning to enroll full or part time at an accredited college or university. They must have a GPA of 2.5 or higher. Along with their application, they must submit information on their athletic accomplishments, athletic goals for the current and next 5 years, academic goals, probable career goals, how a scholarship would contribute to their goals, honors and activities, and financial need.

Financial data: Stipends range from $1,500 to $5,000. Funds must be used for college or postsecondary educational expenses.

Duration: 1 year.

Number awarded: Varies each year; recently, 11 of these scholarships were awarded: 3 at $5,000, 5 at $2,500, and 3 at $1,500.

Deadline: May of each year.

967 $$ TRANSFER OF POST–9/11 GI–BILL BENEFITS TO DEPENDENTS

Department of Veterans Affairs
Attn: Veterans Benefits Administration
810 Vermont Avenue, N.W.
Washington, DC 20420
Phone: (202) 418–4343; (888) GI–BILL1
Web: www.gibill.va.gov

Summary: To provide financial assistance to dependents of military personnel who qualify for Post–9/11 GI Bill benefits and agree to transfer unused benefits to their spouse or child.

Eligibility: Open to dependents of current military personnel whose parent or spouse 1) has at least 6 years of service in the armed forces (active duty and/or Selected Reserve) and agrees to serve 4 additional years; 2) has at least 10 years of service, is precluded by either standard policy or statute from committing to 4 additional years, but agrees to serve for the maximum amount of time allowed by such policy or statute; or 3) is or becomes retirement eligible during the period following August 1, 2009 and agrees to serve for an additional period up to 3 years, depending on the date of retirement eligibility. The military parent or spouse must agree to transfer unused months of educational benefits to a dependent while still serving on active duty. Dependents must be enrolled or planning to enroll in an educational program, including work on an undergraduate or graduate degree, vocational/technical training, on–the–job training, flight training, correspondence training, licensing and national testing programs, entrepreneurship training, and tutorial assistance.

Financial data: Dependents working on an undergraduate or graduate degree at public institutions in their state receive full payment of tuition and fees. For dependents who attend private institutions in most states, tuition and fee reimbursement is capped at $17,500 per academic year; the reimbursement rate is higher at private schools in Arizona, Michigan, New Hampshire, New York, Pennsylvania, South Carolina, and Texas. Benefits for other types of training programs depend on the amount for which the spouse or parent qualified under prior educational programs. Dependents also receive a monthly housing allowance based on the national average Basic Allowance for Housing (BAH) for an E–5 with dependents (currently $673.50) or $1,347 per month at schools in foreign countries); an annual book allowance of $1,000; and (for participants who live in a rural county remote from an educational institution) a rural benefit payment of $500 per year.

Duration: Military members may transfer all or a portion of their 36 months of entitlement to a dependent. Spouses may start to use the benefit immediately, may use the benefit while the member remains in the armed forces or after separation from active duty, are not eligible for the housing or book allowances while the member is still serving on active duty, and can use the benefit for up to 15 years after the servicemember's last separation from active duty. Children may

use the benefit only after they have completed high school (or equivalency certificate) or reached 18 years of age, may use the benefit only after the parent has completed 10 years of service, may use the benefit while the member remains in the armed forces or after separation from active duty, are entitled to the housing and book allowances even while the parent is on active duty, and are not subject to the 15–year limit but may not use the benefit after reaching 26 years of age.
Number awarded: Varies each year.
Deadline: Deadline not specified.

968 $$ TRANSPLANT SCHOLARS AWARDS

Astellas Pharma US, Inc.
Attn: Transplant Scholars Award
Three Parkway North
Deerfield, IL 60015–2548
Phone: (800) 888–7704
Web: astellastransplant.com/events_scholar.php

Summary: To recognize and reward, with scholarships for college or graduate school, transplant recipients and donors who submit outstanding essays on their transplant experience.
Eligibility: Open to liver, kidney, or heart transplant recipients who are taking Prograf and to organ donors who have donated a portion of their liver or a kidney. Applicants must be beginning higher education, returning to school after their surgery, or working on an advanced degree. They must submit a 500–word essay that describes their transplant or donation experience, how the experience has changed their life, and how they would use the scholarship award to further their education and give back to the transplant community. Selection is based on the compelling nature of the story, the educational goals of the applicant and how those were affected by transplantation, and the applicant's intention to impact the transplant community positively.
Financial data: The award is a $5,000 scholarship to be used for educational expenses.
Duration: The awards are presented annually.
Number awarded: Varies each year; recently, 12 of these scholarships were awarded.
Deadline: June of each year.

969 $ TRAUB–DICKER RAINBOW SCHOLARSHIPS

Stonewall Community Foundation
Attn: Bee's Fund
446 West 33rd Street, Sixth Floor
New York, NY 10001
Phone: (212) 367–1155; Fax: (212) 367–1157;
Email: stonewall@stonewallfoundation.org
Web: stonewallfoundation.org

Summary: To provide financial assistance to undergraduate and graduate students who identify as lesbians.
Eligibility: Open to lesbian–identified students who are 1) graduating high school seniors planning to attend a recognized college or university; 2) currently–enrolled undergraduates; and 3) graduate students. Applicants must submit 400–word essays on 1) their personal history, including a significant challenge or achievement in terms of community service, academic excellence, or dynamic leadership; 2) a particularly important experience they have had as a lesbian and how it has affected them; and 3) their plans or goals to give back to or focus on the lesbian, gay, bisexual, and transgender (LGBT) community while in school or after graduating. Selection is based on academic excellence, community service, and commitment to impacting LGBT issues. Financial need is not considered.
Financial data: The stipend is $3,000. Funds are paid directly to the recipient's school to help pay for tuition, books, or room and board.
Duration: 1 year.
Number awarded: 3 each year.
Deadline: April of each year.

970 $$ TRIBAL COLLEGE UNDERGRADUATE SCHOLARSHIPS

American Indian College Fund
Attn: Scholarship Department
8333 Greenwood Boulevard
Denver, CO 80221
Phone: (303) 426–8900; (800) 776–FUND; Fax: (303) 426–1200;
Email: scholarships@collegefund.org
Web: www.collegefund.org/content/full_circle_scholarships_listings

Summary: To provide financial assistance to American Indian college students from any state who are enrolled at tribal colleges and universities.
Eligibility: Open to American Indians registered as a member of a tribe or a descendant of at least 1 grandparent or parent who is an enrolled tribal member. Applicants must be enrolled at a tribal college or university in any state. They must have a GPA of 2.0 or higher and be able to demonstrate exceptional academic achievement or financial need. This program includes many scholarships offered by corporate and other donors, many of whom impose additional requirements. U.S. citizenship is required.
Financial data: Stipends range up to $8,000.
Duration: 1 year.
Number awarded: Varies each year.
Deadline: Each tribal college sets its own deadline.

971 TRIPLE "A" AWARDS

Minnesota State High School League
2100 Freeway Boulevard
Brooklyn Center, MN 55430–1735
Phone: (763) 560–2262; Fax: (763) 569–0499
Web: www.mshsl.org/mshsl/recognition.asp?program=5

Summary: To provide financial assistance to high school seniors in Minnesota who excel in the Triple "A" activities of academics, arts, and athletics and plan to attend college in any state.
Eligibility: Open to seniors graduating from high schools in Minnesota and planning to attend college in any state. Each school may nominate 2 students, a female and a male. Selection of state winners is based on academic performance; involvement in athletic programs sponsored by the Minnesota State High School League (badminton, baseball, basketball, cross country running, competitive dance, football, golf, gymnastics, hockey, lacrosse, skiing, soccer, softball, swimming and diving, synchronized swimming, tennis, track, volleyball, wrestling, and adapted soccer, bowling, floor hockey, and softball); involvement in League–sponsored fine arts activities (state, section, sub–section, school, or community–sponsored activities in instrumental or vocal music, drama, debate, speech, or visual arts); and involvement in other school and community activities. Nominees must have a GPA of 3.0 or higher and be in compliance with the League's Student Code of Conduct. They must submit 3 100–word essays on how their participation in each of the components of the program (academics, arts, and athletics) has influenced them and others and how they benefited from the experience. Students from Class A and Class AA schools are judged separately, as are females and males.
Financial data: The stipend is $1,000 per year.
Duration: 4 years.
Number awarded: 4 each year: a female and a male from each of the 2 classes of schools.
Deadline: January of each year.

972 $$ TRUFIT GOOD CITIZEN SCHOLARSHIPS

Citizens Financial Group
One Citizens Plaza
Providence, RI 02903
Phone: (401) 456–7000; Fax: (401) 456–7819
Web: www.citizensbank.com/scholarship

Summary: To recognize and reward, with scholarships for additional study, high school seniors, undergraduates, and graduate students who submit outstanding essays or videos on community service.
Eligibility: Open to graduating high school seniors, undergraduates currently enrolled at 4–year colleges and universities, and graduate students. Applicants must submit either a 250–word essay (and may include an optional photograph) or a 1–minute video on how they demonstrate good citizenship through community volunteerism and leadership; entries should include demonstrated leadership in their community, the number of hours per week/month/year that they are involved, and how they will continue to stay involved in the community as they continue their education. The sponsor selects 3,000 entries in a random drawing and then judges those on the basis of depiction of leadership and initiative (33%); relevance to theme, including type of service and amount of time spent doing service (33%); and compelling quality of essay or video (34%).
Financial data: Grand prize is $5,000, first prizes are $2,500, and second prizes are $1,000. Funds are awarded in the form of checks, co–payable to the students and their colleges.
Duration: The competition is held annually.
Number awarded: 40 each year: 1 grand prize, 4 first prizes, and 35 second prizes.
Deadline: April of each year.

973 $$ TUITION WAIVER FOR DISABLED CHILDREN OF KENTUCKY VETERANS

Kentucky Department of Veterans Affairs
Attn: Field Operations Branch
321 West Main Street, Suite 390
Louisville, KY 40202
Phone: (502) 595–4447; (800) 928–4012 (within KY); Fax: (502) 595–4448;
Email: Pamela.Cypert@ky.gov
Web: www.veterans.ky.gov/benefits/tuitionwaiver.htm

Summary: To provide financial assistance for college to the children of Kentucky veterans who have a disability related to their parent's military service.

Eligibility: Open to the children of veterans who have acquired a disability as a direct result of their parent's military service. The disability must have been designated by the U.S. Department of Veterans Affairs as compensable (currently defined as spina bifida). The veteran parent must 1) have served on active duty with the U.S. armed forces or in the National Guard or Reserve component on state active duty, active duty for training, or inactive duty training; and 2) be (or if deceased have been) a resident of Kentucky. Applicants must have been admitted to a state–supported university, college, or vocational training institute in Kentucky.

Financial data: Eligible children are exempt from payment of tuition at state–supported institutions of higher education in Kentucky.

Duration: There are no age or time limits on the waiver.

Number awarded: Varies each year.

Deadline: Deadline not specified.

974 $ UMHEF DOLLARS FOR SCHOLARS PROGRAM

United Methodist Higher Education Foundation
Attn: Scholarships Administrator
60 Music Square East, Suite 350
P.O. Box 340005
Nashville, TN 37203–0005
Phone: (615) 649–3990; (800) 811–8110; Fax: (615) 649–3980;
Email: umhefscholarships@umhef.org
Web: www.umhef.org/UMDFSapp.php

Summary: To provide financial assistance to students at Methodist colleges, universities, and seminaries whose home churches agree to contribute to their support.

Eligibility: Open to students attending or planning to attend a United Methodist–related college, university, or seminary as a full–time student. Applicants must have been an active, full member of a United Methodist Church for at least 1 year prior to applying. Their home church must nominate them and agree to contribute to their support. Many of the United Methodist colleges and universities have also agreed to contribute matching funds for a Triple Your Dollars for Scholars Program, and a few United Methodist conference foundations have agreed to contribute additional matching funds for a Quadruple Your Dollars for Scholars Program. Awards are granted on a first–come, first–served basis. Some of the awards are designated for Hispanic, Asian, and Native American (HANA) students funded by the General Board of Higher Education and Ministry.

Financial data: The sponsoring church contributes $1,000 and the United Methodist Higher Education Foundation (UMHEF) contributes a matching $1,000. Students who attend a participating United Methodist college or university receive an additional $1,000 for the Triple Your Dollars for Scholars Program, and those from a participating conference receive a fourth $1,000 increment for the Quadruple Your Dollars for Scholars Program.

Duration: 1 year; may be renewed as long as the recipients maintain satisfactory academic progress as defined by their institution.

Number awarded: 350 each year, including 25 designated for HANA students.

Deadline: Local churches must submit applications in February of each year for senior colleges, universities, and seminaries or May of each year for 2–year colleges.

975 $$ UNDERGRADUATE AWARD OF LIGHTHOUSE INTERNATIONAL

Lighthouse International
Attn: Scholarship and Career Awards
111 East 59th Street
New York, NY 10022–1202
Phone: (212) 821–9428; (800) 829–0500; Fax: (212) 821–9703; TDD: (212) 821–9713;
Email: sca@lighthouse.org
Web: www.lighthouse.org

Summary: To provide financial assistance to legally blind students working on an undergraduate degree.

Eligibility: Open to undergraduate students who are legally blind and U.S. citizens. Applicants must be attending an accredited college or university in 1 of the 50 states, the District of Columbia, or a U.S. territory. Along with their application, they must submit essays of 400 to 600 words on 1) their academic focus and extracurricular activities and what inspires their interest in each area; 2) their passion and how they express that passion; 3) key academic and personal accomplishments and the challenges they overcome to be successful; and 4) how this scholarship will support their academic and/or career development. Selection is based on academic and personal achievements; financial need is not considered.

Financial data: The stipend is $10,000.

Duration: 1 year.

Number awarded: 1 each year.

Deadline: January of each year.

976 UNITED METHODIST ETHNIC MINORITY SCHOLARSHIPS

United Methodist Church
Attn: General Board of Higher Education and Ministry
Office of Loans and Scholarships
1001 19th Avenue South
P.O. Box 340007
Nashville, TN 37203–0007
Phone: (615) 340–7344; Fax: (615) 340–7367;
Email: umscholar@gbhem.org
Web: www.gbhem.org

Summary: To provide financial assistance to undergraduate Methodist students who are of ethnic minority ancestry.

Eligibility: Open to full–time undergraduate students at accredited colleges and universities in the United States who have been active, full members of a United Methodist Church for at least 1 year prior to applying. Applicants must have at least 1 parent who is African American, Hispanic, Asian, Native American, or Pacific Islander. They must have a GPA of 2.5 or higher and be able to demonstrate financial need. U.S. citizenship, permanent resident status, or membership in a central conference of the United Methodist Church is required. Selection is based on church membership, involvement in church and community activities, GPA, and financial need.

Financial data: Stipends range from $500 to $1,000.

Duration: 1 year; recipients may reapply.

Number awarded: Varies each year.

Deadline: February of each year.

977 UNITED METHODIST FOUNDATION COLLEGE AND UNIVERSITY MERIT SCHOLARS PROGRAM

United Methodist Higher Education Foundation
Attn: Scholarships Administrator
60 Music Square East, Suite 350
P.O. Box 340005
Nashville, TN 37203–0005
Phone: (615) 649–3990; (800) 811–8110; Fax: (615) 649–3980;
Email: umhefscholarships@umhef.org
Web: www.umhef.org/scholarship–info/foundation–merit–scholars–program

Summary: To provide financial assistance to undergraduate students attending colleges and universities affiliated with the United Methodist Church.

Eligibility: Open to freshmen, sophomores, juniors, and seniors at United Methodist–related 4–year colleges and universities and to freshmen and sophomores at 2–year colleges. Nominees must have been active members of the United Methodist Church for at least 1 year prior to application. They must be planning to enroll full time and have a GPA of 3.0 or higher. Financial need is considered in the selection process. U.S. citizenship or permanent resident status is required.

Financial data: The stipend is $1,000.

Duration: 1 year; nonrenewable.

Number awarded: 420 each year: 1 to a member of each class at each school.

Deadline: Nominations from schools must be received by August of each year.

978 $ UNITED METHODIST GENERAL SCHOLARSHIP PROGRAM

United Methodist Church
Attn: General Board of Higher Education and Ministry
Office of Loans and Scholarships

1001 19th Avenue South
P.O. Box 340007
Nashville, TN 37203–0007
Phone: (615) 340–7344; Fax: (615) 340–7367;
Email: umscholar@gbhem.org
Web: www.gbhem.org

Summary: To provide financial assistance to undergraduate and graduate students who are members of United Methodist Church congregations.

Eligibility: Open to undergraduate and graduate Methodist students who have these characteristics: 1) U.S. citizenship or permanent resident status; 2) active, full membership in a United Methodist Church for at least 1 year prior to applying; 3) GPA of 2.5 or higher; 4) demonstrated financial need; and 5) full–time enrollment in an undergraduate or graduate degree program at an accredited educational institution in the United States. Students from the Central Conferences must be enrolled at a United Methodist–related institution. Most graduate scholarships are designated for persons working on a degree in theological studies (M.Div., D.Min., Ph.D.) or higher education administration.

Financial data: Undergraduate stipends range from $500 to $1,000; graduate stipends range from $1,000 to $2,000.

Duration: 1 year; renewal policies are set by participating universities.

Number awarded: Varies each year.

Deadline: February of each year.

979 $$ UNITED STATES SENATE YOUTH PROGRAM SCHOLARSHIPS

William Randolph Hearst Foundation
90 New Montgomery Street, Suite 1212
San Francisco, CA 94105–4504
Phone: (415) 908–4540; (800) 841–7048, ext. 4540; Fax: (415) 243–0760;
Email: ussyp@hearstfdn.org
Web: www.ussenateyouth.org

Summary: To recognize and reward, with a trip to Washington, D.C. and college scholarships, outstanding high school student leaders.

Eligibility: Open to high school juniors and seniors who are currently serving in 1 of the following student government offices: student body president, vice president, secretary, or treasurer; class president, vice president, secretary, or treasurer; student council representative; or student representative to a district, regional, or state–level civic or educational organization. Applications are available only through high school principals and state education administrators. Selection is based on ability and demonstrated leadership. Recipients must, within 2 years after high school graduation, enroll at an accredited U.S. college or university, pledging to include courses in government or related subjects in their undergraduate program.

Financial data: Winners receive an all–expense paid trip to Washington, D.C. for 1 week (to be introduced to the operation of the federal government and Congress) and are presented with a $5,000 college scholarship.

Duration: The awards are presented annually.

Number awarded: 104 each year: 2 from each state, Washington, D.C., and the Department of Defense Education Activity.

Deadline: September of each year.

980 $ UNITED STATES SKI AND SNOWBOARD ASSOCIATION TUITION ASSISTANCE

United States Ski and Snowboard Association
Attn: Director of Athletic Career and Education
1 Victory Lane
P.O. Box 100
Park City, UT 84060–0100
Phone: (435) 647–2085; Fax: (435) 940–2825;
Email: llobert@ussa.org
Web: ussa.org/global/ussa–tuition–assistance–program

Summary: To provide financial assistance for college to skiing and snowboarding athletes.

Eligibility: Open to members of the U.S. Ski Team, U.S. Snowboarding Team, and U.S. Freeskiing Team. Alumni are eligible for 2 years after retirement. Applicants must be in good standing with the United States Ski and Snowboard Association (USSA) and earn less than $50,000 per year. They must be working on a bachelor's degree at a 4–year college or university and have a GPA of 2.0 or higher. Athletes must first apply for assistance from the USOC Special Assistance/Tuition Program. All qualified applicants receive assistance.

Financial data: Stipends up to $2,500 are available. Funds may be used for tuition only and are awarded as reimbursement for completed terms.

Duration: 1 year.

Number awarded: Varies each year.

Deadline: July of each year.

981 UNITED STATES TENNIS ASSOCIATION SERVES COLLEGE EDUCATION SCHOLARSHIPS

United States Tennis Association
Attn: USTA Serves
70 West Red Oak Lane
White Plains, NY 10604
Phone: (914) 696–7223;
Email: foundation@usta.com
Web: www.usta.com

Summary: To provide financial assistance for college to high school seniors who have participated in an organized community tennis program.

Eligibility: Open to high school seniors who have excelled academically, demonstrated achievements in leadership, and participated extensively in an organized community tennis program. Applicants must be planning to enroll as a full–time undergraduate student at a 2– or 4–year college or university. They must have a GPA of 3.0 or higher and be able to demonstrate financial need. Along with their application, they must submit an essay of 1 to 2 pages about how their participation in a tennis and education program has influenced their life, including examples of special mentors, volunteer service, and future goals.

Financial data: The stipend is $1,500 per year. Funds are paid directly to the recipient's college or university.

Duration: 2 years for students at community colleges; 4 years for students at 4–year colleges and universities.

Number awarded: Varies each year; recently, 55 of these scholarships were awarded.

Deadline: February of each year.

982 UNITED STATES TENNIS ASSOCIATION SERVES COLLEGE TEXTBOOK SCHOLARSHIPS

United States Tennis Association
Attn: USTA Serves
70 West Red Oak Lane
White Plains, NY 10604
Phone: (914) 696–7223;
Email: foundation@usta.com
Web: www.usta.com/About–USTA/USTA–Serves/college_textbook_scholarship

Summary: To provide financial assistance for the purchase of college textbooks and supplies to high school seniors who have participated in an organized community tennis program.

Eligibility: Open to high school seniors who have excelled academically, demonstrated achievements in leadership, and participated extensively in an organized community tennis program. Applicants must be planning to enroll as a full–time undergraduate student at a 2– or 4–year college or university. Along with their application, they must submit an essay of 1 to 2 pages about how their participation in a tennis and education program has influenced their life, including examples of special mentors, volunteer service, and future goals.

Financial data: The stipend is $1,000. Funds are paid directly to the recipient's college or university bookstore to assist students in purchasing textbooks or supplies.

Duration: 1 year; nonrenewable.

Number awarded: 10 each year.

Deadline: February of each year.

983 $$ UNSUBSIDIZED STAFFORD LOANS

Department of Education
Attn: Federal Student Aid Information Center
P.O. Box 84
Washington, DC 20044–0084
Phone: (319) 337–5665; (800) 4–FED–AID; TDD: (800) 730–8913
Web: studentaid.ed.gov/types/loans

Summary: To provide loans, some of which may be forgiven, to college students in the United States who demonstrate financial need.

Eligibility: Open to U.S. citizens or eligible noncitizens who have or will have at least a high school diploma or GED certificate, are registered with the Selective Service if required, are enrolled as regular students working toward a degree or certificate in an eligible program, and have a valid Social Security number. This program is available to both dependent and independent students. Independent students are those who meet at least 1 of the following requirements: 1) are 22 years of age or older; 2) are married; 3) are enrolled in a master's or doctoral program; 4) have children for whom they provide more than half the support; 5) have dependents (other than their children or spouses) who live with them and for whom they provide more than half the support; 6) are orphans or wards of a court; or 7) are veterans of the U.S. armed forces. Students who meet none of those requirements are considered dependents. This program is available to students who cannot demonstrate financial need.

Financial data: All loans are issued directly by the federal government. Dependent undergraduate students may borrow up to $2,000 per year in unsubsidized loans, in addition to the subsidized loans for which they may be eligible (up to $3,500 for the first full year of study, up to $4,500 for the second year, and up to $5,500 per year for the third and subsequent years). Independent undergraduate students and those whose parents are unable to obtain a loan through the Federal PLUS Program may borrow unsubsidized loans up to $6,000 per year for the first and second full years of study and $7,000 per year for the third and subsequent years. Those amounts are in addition to the subsidized loans of $3,500 for the first year, $4,500 for the second year, and $5,500 per year for the third and subsequent years. Graduate students may borrow up to $12,000 per academic year in unsubsidized loans, in addition to the $8,500 in subsidized loans they may borrow. The total unsubsidized debt that may be incurred under this program is $8,000 for dependent undergraduate students (along with $23,000 in subsidized loans), $34,500 for independent undergraduate students (along with $23,000 in subsidized loans), or $73,000 for graduate or professional students (along with $65,500 in subsidized loans). A loan fee of 1.0% is deducted from each disbursement of the loan. The interest rate recently was 6.8%. Interest is charged from the day the loan is disbursed, including in-school, grace, and deferment periods.

Duration: Plans for repayment over 10 to 25 years are available.

Number awarded: Varies each year; in recent years, nearly 7 million new loans, worth more than $42 billion, have been issued annually.

Deadline: June of each year.

984 $$ U.S. AIR FORCE ROTC HIGH SCHOOL SCHOLARSHIPS

U.S. Air Force
Attn: Headquarters AFROTC/RRUC
551 East Maxwell Boulevard
Maxwell AFB, AL 36112–6106
Phone: (334) 953–2091; (866) 4–AFROTC; Fax: (334) 953–6167;
Email: afrotc1@maxwell.af.mil
Web: afrotc.com/scholarships/high–school

Summary: To provide financial assistance to high school seniors or graduates who are interested in joining Air Force ROTC in college and are willing to serve as Air Force officers following completion of their bachelor's degree.

Eligibility: Open to high school seniors who are U.S. citizens at least 17 years of age and have been accepted at a college or university with an Air Force ROTC unit on campus or a college with a cross–enrollment agreement with such a college. Applicants must have a cumulative GPA of 3.0 or higher and an ACT composite score of 24 or higher or an SAT score of 1100 or higher (mathematics and critical reading portion only). They must agree to serve for at least 4 years as active–duty Air Force officers following graduation from college. Recently, scholarships were offered to students planning to major (in order or priority) in 1) the science and technical fields of architecture, chemistry, computer science, engineering (aeronautical, aerospace, astronautical, architectural, civil, computer, electrical, environmental, or mechanical), mathematics, meteorology and atmospheric sciences, nuclear physics, operations research, or physics; 2) foreign languages (Chinese, Dutch, French, German, Japanese, Italian, Korean, Spanish American, Polish, Persian–Farsi, Brazilian, Spanish–Castilian, Russian, Tagalog, Turkish, Vietnamese, southeast Asian languages, or Slavic languages); 3) all other fields.

Financial data: Type 1 scholarships provide payment of full tuition and most laboratory fees, as well as $900 per year for books. Type 2 scholarships pay the same benefits except tuition is capped at $18,000 per year; students who attend an institution where tuition exceeds $18,000 must pay the difference. Type 7 scholarships pay full tuition and most laboratory fees, but students must attend a public college or university where they qualify for the in–state tuition rate or a college or university where the tuition is less than the in–state rate; they may not attend an institution with higher tuition and pay the difference. Approximately 5% of scholarship offers are for Type 1, approximately 20% are for Type 2, and approximately 75% are for Type 7. All recipients are also awarded a tax–free subsistence allowance for 10 months of each year that is $300 per month as a freshman, $350 per month as a sophomore, $450 per month as a junior, and $500 per month as a senior.

Duration: 4 years.

Number awarded: Approximately 2,000 each year.

Deadline: November of each year.

985 $$ U.S. ARMY ROTC COLLEGE SCHOLARSHIP PROGRAM

U.S. Army
ROTC Cadet Command
Attn: Scholarship Branch
204 1st Cavalry Regiment Road, Building 1002
Fort Knox, KY 40121
Phone: (502) 624–7371; (888) 550–ARMY; Fax: (502) 624–6937;
Email: train2lead@usacc.army.mil
Web: www.rotc.usaac.army.mil/scholarships.aspx

Summary: To provide financial assistance to students who are or will be enrolled in Army ROTC.

Eligibility: Open to U.S. citizens between 17 and 26 years of age who have already completed 1 or 2 years in a college or university with an Army ROTC unit on campus or in a college with a cross–enrollment agreement with a college with an Army ROTC unit on campus. Applicants must have 2 or 3 years remaining for their bachelor's degree (or 4 years of a 5–year bachelor's program) and must be able to complete that degree before their 31st birthday. They must have a high school GPA of 2.5 or higher and scores of at least 920 on the combined mathematics and critical reading SAT or 19 on the ACT.

Financial data: These scholarships provide financial assistance for college tuition and educational fees, up to an annual amount of $20,000. In addition, a flat rate of $1,200 is provided for the purchase of textbooks, classroom supplies, and equipment. Recipients are also awarded a stipend for up to 10 months of each year that is $350 per month during their sophomore year, $450 per month during their junior year, and $500 per month during their senior year.

Duration: 2 or 3 years, until the recipient completes the bachelor's degree.

Number awarded: Varies each year; a recent allocation provided for 700 4–year scholarships, 1,800 3–year scholarships, and 2,800 2–year scholarships.

Deadline: December of each year.

986 $$ U.S. COAST GUARD FOUNDATION SCHOLARSHIPS

U.S. Coast Guard
Attn: Office of Work–Life (CG–111)
2100 Second Street, S.W., Stop 7902
Washington, DC 20593–7902
Phone: (202) 475–5140; (800) 872–4957; Fax: (202) 475–5907;
Email: HQS.SMB.FamilySupportServices@uscg.mil
Web: www.uscg.mil/worklife/scholarship.asp

Summary: To provide financial assistance for college to the dependent children of Coast Guard enlisted personnel.

Eligibility: Open to the dependent children of enlisted members of the U.S. Coast Guard on active duty, retired, or deceased, and of enlisted personnel in the Coast Guard Reserve currently on extended active duty 180 days or more. Applicants must be high school seniors or current undergraduates enrolled or planning to enroll full–time at a 4–year college, university, or vocational school. They must be under 24 years of age and registered in the Defense Enrollment Eligibility Reporting System (DEERS) system. Along with their application, they must submit their SAT or ACT scores, a letter of recommendation, transcripts, a financial information statement, and a 500–word essay on their personal and academic achievements, extracurricular activities, contributions to the community, and academic plans and career goals.

Financial data: Stipends range from $2,500 to $5,000 per year.

Duration: 1 year; may be renewed up to 3 additional years.

Number awarded: Varies each year; recently, 14 of these scholarships were awarded.

Deadline: March of each year.

987 $$ US PAN ASIAN AMERICAN CHAMBER OF COMMERCE SCHOLARSHIP PROGRAM

US Pan Asian American Chamber of Commerce
Attn: Scholarship Coordinator
1329 18th Street, N.W.
Washington, DC 20036
Phone: (202) 296–5221; (800) 696–7818; Fax: (202) 296–5225;
Email: info@uspaacc.com
Web: celebrasianconference.com/about–celebrasian/scholarships/overview

Summary: To provide financial assistance for college to Asian Pacific American high school seniors who demonstrate financial need.

Eligibility: Open to high school seniors of Asian or Pacific Islander heritage who are U.S. citizens or permanent residents. Applicants must be planning to enroll full time at an accredited postsecondary educational institution in the United States. Along with their application, they must submit a 500–word essay on their background, achievements, and personal goals. Selection is based on

academic excellence (GPA of 3.3 or higher), leadership in extracurricular activities, community service involvement, and financial need.
Financial data: The maximum stipend is $5,000. Funds are paid directly to the recipient's college or university.
Duration: 1 year.
Number awarded: Several named scholarships are awarded each year, including the Paul Shearman Allen & Associates Hallmark Scholarship, the Coca–Cola Company Hallmark Scholarship, Denny's Hallmark Scholarship, Enterprise Holdings Hallmark Scholarship, Exxon Mobil Corporation Hallmark Scholarship, PepsiCo Hallmark Scholarships, and UPS Hallmark Scholarships.
Deadline: March of each year.

988 USTA SERVES/DWIGHT F. DAVIS MEMORIAL SCHOLARSHIPS

United States Tennis Association
Attn: USTA Serves
70 West Red Oak Lane
White Plains, NY 10604
Phone: (914) 696–7223;
Email: foundation@usta.com
Web: www.usta.com/About–USTA/USTA–Serves/davis_memorial_scholarship
Summary: To provide financial assistance for college to high school seniors who have participated in an organized community tennis program.
Eligibility: Open to high school seniors who have excelled academically, demonstrated achievements in leadership, and participated extensively in an organized community tennis program. Applicants must be planning to enroll as a full–time undergraduate student at a 4–year college or university. They must have a GPA of 3.0 or higher and be able to demonstrate financial need. Along with their application, they must submit an essay of 1 to 2 pages about how their participation in a tennis and education program has influenced their life, including examples of special mentors, volunteer service, and future goals. Women and men are judged separately in the selection process.
Financial data: The stipend is $1,875 per year. Funds are paid directly to the recipient's college or university.
Duration: 4 years.
Number awarded: 2 each year: 1 to a woman and 1 to a man.
Deadline: February of each year.

989 $ UTAH ELKS ASSOCIATION SCHOLARSHIP PROGRAM

Utah Elks Association
c/o Linda Gaines, Scholarship Chair
Provo Lodge 849
1000 South University Avenue
Provo, UT 84601
Phone: (801) 796–6069
Web: www.elksinutah.org
Summary: To provide financial assistance for college to high school seniors in Utah.
Eligibility: Open to seniors graduating from high schools in Utah. Applicants must submit a 500–word essay on their career and life goals and their plan to achieve those. Selection is based on that essay, academic achievement, community service, honors and awards, leadership, and financial need. U.S. citizenship is required. Females and males compete separately.
Financial data: Stipends are $4,000, $800, or $700.
Duration: 1 year.
Number awarded: Varies each year; recently, the program awarded 4 scholarships (2 to males and 2 to females) at $4,000, 16 (8 to males and 8 to females) at $800, and 16 (8 to males and 8 to females) at $700.
Deadline: January of each year.

990 UTAH ELKS ASSOCIATION SPECIAL NEEDS STUDENT SCHOLARSHIP AWARD

Utah Elks Association
c/o Linda Gaines, Scholarship Chair
Provo Lodge 849
1000 South University Avenue
Provo, UT 84601
Phone: (801) 796–6069
Web: www.elksinutah.org
Summary: To provide financial assistance for college to high school seniors in Utah who have a disability or other special need.
Eligibility: Open to seniors graduating from high schools in Utah who have a special need, such as a disability. Applicants must submit 1) a supporting letter from a doctor or professional person stating the nature of the special need; and 2) a 500–word essay on their career and life goals and their plan to achieve those. Selection is based on that essay, academic achievement, community service, honors and awards, leadership, and financial need. U.S. citizenship is required.
Financial data: A stipend is awarded (amount not specified).
Duration: 1 year.
Number awarded: Varies each year, depending upon the funds available.
Deadline: January of each year.

991 UTAH ELKS ASSOCIATION VOCATIONAL GRANT PROGRAM

Utah Elks Association
c/o Linda Gaines, Scholarship Chair
Provo Lodge 849
1000 South University Avenue
Provo, UT 84601
Phone: (801) 796–6069
Web: www.elksinutah.org
Summary: To provide financial assistance to high school seniors in Utah who plan to attend a technical/vocational school.
Eligibility: Open to seniors graduating from high schools in Utah who plan to attend a 2–year or less vocational or technical program that leads to an associate degree, diploma, or certificate and will enable them to become gainfully employed in their chosen vocational career. Applicants must be planning to enroll full time. Students enrolled in an associate degree program that is a stepping stone to a bachelor's degree, a part–time program, or night school are not eligible. Along with their application, they must submit a 500–word essay on their career and life goals and their plan to achieve those. Selection is based on that essay, academic achievement, community service, honors and awards, leadership, and financial need. U.S. citizenship is required.
Financial data: The stipend is $1,000.
Duration: 2 years; nonrenewable.
Number awarded: Varies each year, depending upon the funds available.
Deadline: January of each year.

992 $ UTAH LEGION AUXILIARY NATIONAL PRESIDENT'S SCHOLARSHIP

American Legion Auxiliary
Department of Utah
350 North State Street, Suite 80
P.O. Box 148000
Salt Lake City, UT 84114–8000
Phone: (801) 539–1015; (877) 345–6780; Fax: (801) 521–9191;
Email: alaut@yahoo.com
Web: www.utlegion.org/Auxiliary/aux1.htm
Summary: To provide financial assistance to children of veterans in Utah who plan to attend college in any state.
Eligibility: Open to Utah residents who are the children of veterans who served during specified periods of war time. They must be high school seniors or graduates who have not yet attended an institution of higher learning. Selection is based on character, Americanism, leadership, scholarship, and financial need. The winners then compete for the American Legion Auxiliary National President's Scholarship. If the Utah winners are not awarded a national scholarship, then they receive this departmental scholarship.
Financial data: The stipend is $1,500.
Duration: 1 year.
Number awarded: 1 each year.
Deadline: February of each year.

993 $ UTAH NEW CENTURY SCHOLARSHIP PROGRAM

Utah System of Higher Education
State Board of Regents
Attn: New Century Scholarship Program
P.O. Box 145116
Salt Lake City, UT 84114–5116
Phone: (801) 321–7221; (800) 418–8757, ext. 7221; Fax: (801) 321–7168;
Email: newcentury@utahsbr.edu
Web: www.higheredutah.org/scholarship_info

Summary: To provide financial assistance to Utah residents who complete an associate degree while still enrolled in high school and plan to work on a bachelor's degree at a college or university in the state.

Eligibility: Open to high school students in Utah who take classes at a local community college and complete an associate degree by September of the year their class graduates from high school. Applicants must complete specified college courses while earning their associate degree and have a cumulative high school GPA of 3.5 or higher and a GPA for their associate degree work of 3.0 or higher. They must be planning to enroll full time at an accredited 4–year college or university in the state to work on a bachelor's degree. Home–schooled students are eligible if they take the ACT test and score 26 or higher. Financial need is not considered in the selection process.

Financial data: The stipend is $1,250 per semester ($2,500 per year).

Duration: 1 semester; may be renewed up to 3 additional semesters, provided the student maintains at least a 3.0 GPA.

Number awarded: Varies each year.

Deadline: January of each year.

994 UTAH REGENTS' SCHOLARSHIP PROGRAM

Utah System of Higher Education
State Board of Regents
Attn: Regents' Scholarship Program
P.O. Box 145114
Salt Lake City, UT 84114–5114
Phone: (801) 321–7159; (877) 336–7378; Fax: (801) 321–7168;
Email: regentsscholarship@utahsbr.edu
Web: www.higheredutah.org/scholarship_info

Summary: To provide financial assistance to Utah residents who complete a core course of study in high school and plan to attend college in the state.

Eligibility: Open to seniors graduating from high schools in Utah who have completed the curriculum of the Utah Scholars Core Course of Study. Applicants must be planning to enroll full time at an accredited 2– or 4–year college or university in the state. Students who have a cumulative weighted GPA of 3.0 or higher and no individual grade lower than a "C" in required core courses qualify for the Base Award. Students who have a weighted cumulative GPA of 3.5 or higher, an ACT score of 26 or higher, and no individual grade lower than a "B" in required core courses qualify for the Exemplary Academic Achievement Award. Financial need is not considered in the selection process. U.S. citizenship or eligible noncitizen status is required.

Financial data: The Base Award is $1,000. The Exemplary Academic Achievement Award is $900 per semester.

Duration: The Base Award is a nonrenewable 1–time grant. The Exemplary Academic Achievement Award may be renewed for a total of 4 semesters, provided the recipient verifies full–time enrollment and a GPA of 3.0 or higher each semester.

Number awarded: Varies each year.

Deadline: The priority deadline is December of each year; the final deadline is January of each year.

995 $$ VEGETARIAN RESOURCE GROUP COLLEGE SCHOLARSHIPS

Vegetarian Resource Group
P.O. Box 1463
Baltimore, MD 21203
Phone: (410) 366–8343;
Email: vrg@vrg.org
Web: www.vrg.org/student/scholar.htm

Summary: To provide financial assistance for college to high school students who have promoted vegetarianism.

Eligibility: Open to high school seniors who have promoted vegetarianism in their schools and/or communities. Applicants must submit an essay that covers 16 assigned topics, including how they expect to promote vegetarianism in college and beyond, their future goals, why they should receive this scholarship, how they became vegetarian and why they are vegetarian, how they define vegetarianism, and why vegetarianism is important to them. The award is presented to applicants who have "shown compassion, courage, and a strong commitment to promoting a peaceful world through a vegetarian diet/lifestyle." Financial need is not considered in the selection process.

Financial data: The stipend is $5,000. Funds are paid directly to the recipient's college.

Duration: 1 year.

Number awarded: 2 each year.

Deadline: February of each year.

996 $ VERA TRAN MEMORIAL SCHOLARSHIP

Vietnamese American Scholarship Foundation
P.O. Box 429
Stafford, TX 77497
Email: scholarships@vietscholarships.org
Web: www.vietscholarships.org/scholarships.html

Summary: To provide financial assistance to high school seniors of Vietnamese descent who plan to attend college in any state.

Eligibility: Open to seniors graduating from high schools in any state who are of Vietnamese descent. Applicants must be planning to enroll at an accredited 4–year college or university in any state. Along with their application, they must submit a 2,000–word essay on the most valuable lesson they have learned about the world or about themselves through community service. Selection is based on dedication to academic excellence, commitment to community service, passion for learning, and compassion and desire to help others.

Financial data: The stipend is $2,000.

Duration: 1 year; nonrenewable.

Number awarded: 1 each year.

Deadline: April of each year.

997 $$ VERMONT INCENTIVE GRANTS

Vermont Student Assistance Corporation
Attn: Scholarship Programs
10 East Allen Street
P.O. Box 2000
Winooski, VT 05404–2601
Phone: (802) 654–3798; (888) 253–4819; Fax: (802) 654–3765; TDD: (800) 281–3341 (within VT);
Email: info@vsac.org
Web: services.vsac.org

Summary: To provide financial assistance for college to needy residents of Vermont.

Eligibility: Open to residents of Vermont who wish to enroll as a full–time undergraduate student in a degree or certificate program in any state. U.S. citizenship or permanent resident status is required. Selection is based on financial need.

Financial data: Stipends depend on the need of the student and the cost of attendance at the school; recently, they ranged from $700 to $11,200 per year.

Duration: 1 year; may be renewed.

Number awarded: Varies each year.

Deadline: Applications are accepted on a first–come, first–served basis as long as funding is available.

998 VERMONT NONDEGREE GRANTS

Vermont Student Assistance Corporation
Attn: Scholarship Programs
10 East Allen Street
P.O. Box 2000
Winooski, VT 05404–2601
Phone: (802) 654–3798; (888) 253–4819; Fax: (802) 654–3765; TDD: (800) 281–3341 (within VT);
Email: info@vsac.org
Web: services.vsac.org

Summary: To provide financial assistance to needy residents of Vermont who are enrolled in an educational program but not seeking a degree.

Eligibility: Open to residents of Vermont who are enrolled in a non–degree course that will improve employability or encourage further study. Applicants must be interested in taking classes in Vermont or any other state at a college, an educational institution such as a high school or technical center that offers a continuing education program, or a private organization that offers training courses. Financial need must be demonstrated.

Financial data: The amount of the grant depends on the need of the recipient and the cost of the course, to a maximum that varies each year; recently, the maximum grant was $885 per term.

Duration: 1 academic term; may be renewed.

Number awarded: Varies each year.

Deadline: Deadline not specified.

999 $$ VERMONT PART–TIME GRANTS

Vermont Student Assistance Corporation
Attn: Scholarship Programs
10 East Allen Street

P.O. Box 2000
Winooski, VT 05404–2601
Phone: (802) 654–3798; (888) 253–4819; Fax: (802) 654–3765; TDD: (800) 281–3341 (within VT);
Email: info@vsac.org
Web: services.vsac.org

Summary: To provide financial assistance to needy residents of Vermont who wish to attend college in any state on a part–time basis.

Eligibility: Open to residents of Vermont who are enrolled or accepted for enrollment in an undergraduate degree, diploma, or certificate program at a postsecondary institution in any state. Applicants must be taking fewer than 12 credits per semester and not have already received a baccalaureate degree. Financial need is considered in the selection process.

Financial data: The amounts of the awards depend on the number of credit hours and the need of the recipient; recently, they ranged from $350 to $8,400 per year.

Duration: 1 year; may be renewed.

Number awarded: Varies each year.

Deadline: Applications are accepted on a first–come, first–served basis as long as funding is available.

1000 VETERANS EDUCATIONAL ASSISTANCE PROGRAM (VEAP)

Department of Veterans Affairs
Attn: Veterans Benefits Administration
810 Vermont Avenue, N.W.
Washington, DC 20420
Phone: (202) 418–4343; (888) GI–BILL1
Web: www.gibill.va.gov/benefits/other_programs/veap.html

Summary: To provide financial assistance for college to veterans who first entered active duty between January 1, 1977 and June 30, 1985.

Eligibility: Open to Veterans who served and military servicemembers currently serving, if they 1) entered active duty between January 1, 1977 and June 30, 1985; 2) were released under conditions other than dishonorable or continue on active duty; 3) served for a continuous period of 181 days or more (or were discharged earlier for a service–connected disability); and 4) have satisfactorily contributed to the program. No individuals on active duty could enroll in this program after March 31, 1987. Veterans who enlisted for the first time after September 7, 1980 or entered active duty as an officer or enlistee after October 16, 1981 must have completed 24 continuous months of active duty. Benefits are available for the pursuit of an associate, bachelor, or graduate degree at a college or university; a certificate or diploma from a business, technical, or vocational school; apprenticeship or on–the–job training programs; cooperative courses; correspondence school courses; tutorial assistance; remedial, refresher, and deficiency training; flight training; study abroad programs leading to a college degree; nontraditional training away from school; and work–study for students enrolled at least three–quarter time.

Financial data: Participants contribute to the program, through monthly deductions from their military pay, from $25 to $100 monthly, up to a maximum of $2,700. They may also, while on active duty, make a lump sum contribution to the training fund. At the time the eligible participant elects to use the benefits to pursue an approved course of education or training, the Department of Veterans Affairs (VA) will match the contribution at the rate of $2 for every $1 made by the participant.

Duration: Participants receive monthly payments for the number of months they contributed or for 36 months, whichever is less. The amount of the payments is determined by dividing the number of months benefits will be paid into the participant's training fund total. Participants have 10 years from the date of last discharge or release from active duty within which to use these benefits.

Number awarded: Varies each year.

Deadline: Applications may be submitted at any time.

1001 $ VETERANS UNITED FOUNDATION SCHOLARSHIPS

VA Mortgage Center.com
2101 Chapel Plaza Court, Suite 107
Columbia, MO 65203
Phone: (573) 876–2729; (800) 405–6682;
Email: jbuerck@vamc.com
Web: www.vamortgagecenter.com/scholarships.html

Summary: To provide financial assistance for college to students who have a tie to the military.

Eligibility: Open to 1) active–duty military personnel with plans to attend college; 2) honorably–discharged veterans of the U.S. military; 3) spouses of military members or veterans; 4) surviving spouses of fallen soldiers; and 5) children of veterans or active–duty military. Applicants must be attending or planning to attend college as a full–time student. They must have a GPA of 2.5 or higher. Selection is based primarily on an essay.

Financial data: The stipend is $2,000.

Duration: 1 year.

Number awarded: 10 each year: 5 each term.

Deadline: April or October of each year.

1002 VIAAA/CLAUDIA DODSON AWARD

Virginia Interscholastic Athletic Administrators Association
c/o Steve Heon, Scholarship Chair
Western Albemarle High School
5941 Rockfish Gap Turnpike
Crozet, VA 22932
Phone: (434) 823–8705;
Email: sheon@k12albemarle.org
Web: www.viaaa.org/ssp/scholarship_information

Summary: To provide financial assistance to high school seniors in Virginia who have been involved in athletics and plan to attend college in any state.

Eligibility: Open to seniors graduating from high schools in Virginia where the athletic director is a member of the Virginia Interscholastic Athletic Administrators Association. Applicants must have earned at least 4 varsity athletic letters, be planning to attend an institution of higher learning in any state, have a GPA of 3.0 or higher, have achieved a leadership position in school and community activities, have extensive service to school and community, have received no full athletic scholarship, and be able to demonstrate financial need. Along with their application, they must submit a 100–word essay on how the award would be of special assistance to them and a 200–word essay on how their participation in high school athletics has impacted their life.

Financial data: The stipend is $1,500.

Duration: 1 year.

Number awarded: 1 each year.

Deadline: January of each year.

1003 $ VICTORY FOR WOMEN ACADEMIC SCHOLARSHIP FOR WOMEN WITH BLEEDING DISORDERS

National Hemophilia Foundation
Attn: Manager of Education
P.O. Box 971483
Ypsilanti, MI 48197
Phone: (734) 890–2504;
Email: pflax@hemophilia.org
Web: www.hemophilia.org

Summary: To provide financial assistance for college or graduate school to women who have a bleeding disorder.

Eligibility: Open to women who are entering or already enrolled in an undergraduate or graduate program at a university, college, or accredited vocational school. Applicants must have von Willebrand Disease, hemophilia or other clotting factor deficiency, or carrier status. Along with their application, they must submit a 250–word essay that describes how their education and future career plans will benefit others in the bleeding disorders community. Selection is based on that essay, achievements, and community service to the bleeding disorders community.

Financial data: The stipend is $2,500.

Duration: 1 year.

Number awarded: 2 each year.

Deadline: May of each year.

1004 VINCENT J. DOOLEY AWARDS

Athletes for a Better World
Attn: Program Director
1401 Peachtree Street N.E., Suite 500
Atlanta, GA 30309
Phone: (404) 892–2328;
Email: sajigirvan@abw.org
Web: www.abw.org/awards

Summary: To recognize and reward, with scholarships for college study in any field, high school senior athletes in Georgia who demonstrate outstanding sportsmanship.

Eligibility: Open to all high schools students in Georgia who are nominated on the basis of character, teamwork, and citizenship. Each school may nominate up to 2 students (1 girl and 1 boy). A selection committee then chooses 10 males and 10 females as finalists and invites them to a banquet at Turner Field in Atlanta, where they are interviewed and winners are selected.

Financial data: The award is a scholarship of $1,000 per year.

Duration: 4 years.

Number awarded: 2 each year: 1 male and 1 female.

Deadline: Schools must submit their nominations by March of each year.

1005 $ VINCENT STEFANO SCHOLARSHIP AWARD

Kidney & Urology Foundation of America
Attn: Program Director
2 West 47th Street, Suite 401
New York, NY 10036
Phone: (212) 629–9770; (800) 633–6628; Fax: (212) 629–5652;
Email: info@kidneyurology.org
Web: www.kidneyurology.org/Patient_Resources/scholarships.php

Summary: To provide financial assistance for college to patients who have been diagnosed with kidney disease.

Eligibility: Open to young adults between 17 and 25 years of age who are attending or planning to attend college. Applicants must have been diagnosed with kidney disease. Along with their application, they must submit an essay of 1 to 2 pages on how kidney disease has impacted their life; their educational background, extracurricular activities, hobbies, and personal interests; their educational goals and how this scholarship will help them to achieve those goals; their contributions to the renal or transplant community; any extenuating circumstances involving them or their family; and why they should be selected to receive this scholarship. Selection is based on achievements, commitment to working on a college degree, and financial need. Priority is given to applicants from the sponsoring organization's participating partner centers.

Financial data: The stipend is $2,000 per year. Funds are paid directly to the recipient's institution.

Duration: 1 year; may be renewed up to 3 additional years.

Number awarded: 1 or more each year.

Deadline: May of each year.

1006 $$ VIRGINIA COLLEGE SCHOLARSHIP ASSISTANCE PROGRAM

State Council of Higher Education for Virginia
Attn: Financial Aid Office
James Monroe Building
101 North 14th Street, Tenth Floor
Richmond, VA 23219–3659
Phone: (804) 225–2600; (877) 515–0138; Fax: (804) 225–2604; TDD: (804) 371–8017;
Email: communications@schev.edu
Web: www.schev.edu/students/undergradFinancialaidPrograms.asp

Summary: To provide financial assistance to residents of Virginia who demonstrate extreme financial need and plan to attend college in the state.

Eligibility: Open to residents of Virginia who have been admitted into a Virginia public 2– or 4–year college or university or a participating Virginia private nonprofit 4–year college or university. Applicants must be enrolled or planning to enroll at least half time, be a U.S. citizen or eligible noncitizen, and have a computed expected family contribution that is less than half the total cost of attendance.

Financial data: The amount awarded ranges from $400 to $5,000 per year, depending on the need of the recipient.

Duration: 1 year; may be renewed for up to 3 additional years if the recipient maintains at least half–time status and satisfactory academic progress.

Number awarded: Varies each year.

Deadline: Deadline not specified.

1007 VIRGINIA DIVISION GIFT SCHOLARSHIPS

United Daughters of the Confederacy–Virginia Division
c/o Barbara Joyner, Second Vice President
8219 Seaview Drive
Chesterfield, VA 23838–5163
Email: bobbielou–udc@comcast.net
Web: vaudc.org/gift.html

Summary: To provide financial assistance to Confederate descendants from Virginia who are interested in attending college in the state.

Eligibility: Open to residents of Virginia who are 1) lineal descendants of Confederates; or 2) collateral descendants and also members of the Children of the Confederacy or the United Daughters of the Confederacy. Applicants must submit proof of the Confederate military record of at least 1 ancestor, with the company and regiment in which he served. They must also submit a personal letter pledging to make the best possible use of the scholarship; describing their health, social, family, religious, and fraternal connections within the community; and reflecting on what a Southern heritage means to them (using the term "War Between the States" in lieu of "Civil War"). They must have a GPA of 3.0 or higher and be able to demonstrate financial need.

Financial data: The amount of the stipend depends on the availability of funds. Payment is made directly to the college or university the recipient attends.

Duration: 1 year; may be renewed up to 3 additional years if the recipient maintains a GPA of 3.0 or higher.

Number awarded: These scholarships are offered whenever a prior recipient graduates or is no longer eligible.

Deadline: April of years in which any of the scholarships are available.

1008 $ VIRGINIA M. WAGNER EDUCATIONAL GRANT

Soroptimist International of the Americas–Midwestern Region
c/o Alexandra Nicholis
2117 Quayle Drive
Akron, OH 44312–2332
Phone: (330) 524–7113;
Email: soroptimist@simwr.org
Web: simwr.org/id61.html

Summary: To provide financial assistance to women working on an undergraduate or graduate degree at a college or university in midwestern states.

Eligibility: Open to women who reside in Illinois, Indiana, Kentucky, Michigan, Ohio, or Wisconsin and are attending college or graduate school in any state. Applicants must be working on a bachelor's, master's, or doctoral degree in the field of their choice. Awards are first presented at the club level, then in districts, and finally for the entire region. Selection is based on the effort toward education by the applicant and her family, cumulative GPA, extracurricular activities, general impression, and financial need.

Financial data: Club level awards vary at the discretion of the club. District finalists receive a $500 award and are then judged at the regional level. The regional winner receives a $3,000 award.

Duration: 1 year.

Number awarded: 4 district winners are selected each year; 1 of those receives the regional award.

Deadline: January of each year.

1009 $$ VIRGINIA MILITARY SURVIVORS AND DEPENDENTS EDUCATION PROGRAM

Virginia Department of Veterans Services
270 Franklin Road, Room 810
Roanoke, VA 24011–2215
Phone: (540) 597–1730; Fax: (540) 857–7573
Web: www.dvs.virginia.gov/veterans–benefits.shtml

Summary: To provide educational assistance to the children and spouses of disabled and other Virginia veterans or service personnel.

Eligibility: Open to residents of Virginia whose parent or spouse served in the U.S. armed forces (including the Reserves, the Virginia National Guard, or the Virginia National Guard Reserves) during any armed conflict subsequent to December 6, 1941, as a result of a terrorist act, during military operations against terrorism, or on a peacekeeping mission. The veterans must have been killed, missing in action, taken prisoner of war, or become at least 90% disabled as a result of such service. Applicants must have been accepted at a public college or university in Virginia as an undergraduate or graduate student. Children must be between 16 and 29 years of age; there are no age restrictions for spouses. The veteran must have been a resident of Virginia at the time of entry into active military service or for at least 5 consecutive years immediately prior to the date of application or death. Surviving spouses must have been residents of Virginia for at least 5 years prior to marrying the veteran or for at least 5 years immediately prior to the date on which the application was submitted.

Financial data: The program provides 1) waiver of tuition and all required fees at public institutions of higher education in Virginia; and 2) a stipend up to $1,500 per year to offset the costs of room, board, books, and supplies at those institutions. If more students qualify, the stipend is reduced; recently, it was $675 per semester ($1,350 per year) for full–time enrollment, $450 per semester for enrollment less than full–time but at least half–time, or $225 per semester for enrollment less than half–time.

Duration: Entitlement extends to a maximum of 36 months (4 years).

Number awarded: Varies each year; recently, funding allowed for a total of 667 stipends at $1,500, but 740 students actually qualified and received a reduced stipend.

Deadline: Applications may be submitted at any time, but they must be received at least 30 days prior to the start of the term.

1010 $ VIRGINIA PUBLIC SAFETY FOUNDATION SCHOLARSHIPS

Virginia Public Safety Foundation
2201 West Main Street
Richmond, VA 23220
Phone: (804) 648–6299, ext. 1004; Fax: (804) 359–9680;
Email: vpsf@alliancegroupltd.com
Web: vpsf.org/About.html

Summary: To provide financial assistance to the children and surviving spouses of deceased Virginia public safety officers who are interested in attending college in any state.

Eligibility: Open to the children and surviving spouses and life partners of all active–duty Virginia public safety officers killed in the line of duty. "Public safety" officers are defined as state and local police, sheriffs, their deputies, corrections and jail officers, firefighters, agents of the Alcoholic Beverage Control Department, and volunteer members of a fire company or rescue squad. Applicants may be high school seniors or currently enrolled at a college or university in any state. Along with their application, they must submit a 1–page statement that includes their personal or career goals, what being a "survivor" means to them, and other relevant information about their parent or spouse. Children must be under 25 years of age; spouses and partners must apply within 5 years of the death of the officer. Financial need is not considered in the selection process.

Financial data: Stipends range up to $2,000 per year.

Duration: 1 year; nonrenewable.

Number awarded: Varies each year.

Deadline: Deadline not specified.

1011 VIRGINIA STATE COUNCIL ENDOWMENT SCHOLARSHIP

Epsilon Sigma Alpha International
Attn: ESA Foundation
363 West Drake Road
Fort Collins, CO 80526
Phone: (970) 223–2824; Fax: (970) 223–4456;
Email: esainfo@epsilonsigmaalpha.org
Web: www.epsilonsigmaalpha.org/esa–foundation/scholarships

Summary: To provide financial assistance to students of Virginia studying any field at a college in any state.

Eligibility: Open to residents of Virginia who are 1) graduating high school seniors with a GPA of 3.0 or higher or with minimum scores of 22 on the ACT or 1030 on the combined critical reading and mathematics SAT; 2) enrolled in college with a GPA of 3.0 or higher; 3) enrolled at a technical school or returning to school after an absence for retraining of job skills or obtaining a degree; or 4) engaged in online study through an accredited college, university, or vocational school. Applicants may be majoring in any field at a school in any state. Selection is based on character (10%), leadership (10%), service (5%), financial need (50%), and scholastic ability (25%).

Financial data: The stipend is $1,000.

Duration: 1 year; may be renewed.

Number awarded: 1 each year.

Deadline: January of each year.

1012 $ VIRGINIA TUITION ASSISTANCE GRANT PROGRAM

State Council of Higher Education for Virginia
Attn: Financial Aid Office
James Monroe Building
101 North 14th Street, Tenth Floor
Richmond, VA 23219–3659
Phone: (804) 225–2600; (877) 515–0138; Fax: (804) 225–2604; TDD: (804) 371–8017;
Email: communications@schev.edu
Web: www.schev.edu/students/undergradFinancialaidPrograms.asp

Summary: To provide financial assistance to undergraduate and graduate students attending private colleges or universities in Virginia.

Eligibility: Open to residents of Virginia enrolled full time at a private college or university in the state. Undergraduates may be majoring in any field except religious training or theological education. Graduate students must be working on a degree in a health–related profession. Financial need is not considered in the selection process. Students pursuing are not eligible.

Financial data: The amount awarded varies, depending on annual appropriations and number of applicants; recently, the maximum award was $2,800 for undergraduates or $1,300 for graduate students.

Duration: 1 year; may be renewed for 1 additional year for associate programs, 3 additional years for undergraduate study, 3 additional years for graduate study of medicine or pharmacy, or 2 additional years for all other graduate study.

Number awarded: Varies each year.

Deadline: July of each year.

1013 VIRGINIA'S FUTURE LEADERS SCHOLARSHIP

Virginia Cable Telecommunications Association
Attn: Director of Office Operations
1001 East Broad Street, Suite 210
Richmond, VA 23219
Phone: (804) 780–1776; (877) 861–5464; Fax: (804) 225–8036;
Email: kvoxland@vcta.com
Web: www.vcta.com

Summary: To provide financial assistance to residents of Virginia interested in working on an undergraduate degree in any field at a college in the state.

Eligibility: Open to Virginia residents who are attending or planning to attend a 2– or 4–year college or university in Virginia. Applicants must submit a 500–word essay on either 1) a recent leadership experience they have had in an area of their life, their role in the situation, how they were effective, and what they learned; or 2) a situation in which they exhibited the ability to make a difference under difficult circumstances. Selection is based on the essay, academic transcripts, and extracurricular activities; financial need is not considered. U.S. citizenship is required.

Financial data: A stipend is awarded (amount not specified).

Duration: 1 year; nonrenewable.

Number awarded: Varies each year; recently, 72 students received approximately $100,000 in scholarships from this program.

Deadline: April of each year.

1014 $$ VISINE STUDENTS WITH VISION SCHOLARSHIPS

Johnson & Johnson Healthcare Products
Attn: Information Center
199 Grandview Road
Skillman, NJ 08558–9418
Phone: (888) 734–7648; TDD: (880) 722–1322
Web: www.visine.com/scholarship

Summary: To provide financial assistance for college to high school seniors and current undergraduates who can demonstrate a clear vision or goal for their future.

Eligibility: Open to graduating high school seniors and college freshmen, sophomores, and juniors who "demonstrate a clear and unique vision, strong ambition and determination to bring their dream to life." Applicants must have a GPA of 2.8 or higher. Along with their application, they must submit a 300–word essay or 2–minute video describing their vision or goal. Selection is based on their demonstrated vision or goal, academic achievement, school and community involvement, and financial need.

Financial data: The stipend is $5,000.

Duration: 1 year.

Number awarded: 10 each year.

Deadline: April of each year.

1015 VIVIAN SCOTT SCHOLARSHIPS

Florida Association of State and Federal Educational Program Administrators
c/o Celia Elrod, Scholarship Committee
Fulton–Holland Educational Services Center, Suite C 206
3300 Forest Hill Boulevard
West Palm Beach, FL 33406
Phone: (561) 434–8446;
Email: celia.elrod@palmbeachschools.org
Web: www.fasfepa.org/membership_scholarship

Summary: To provide financial assistance to high school seniors in Florida who plan to study any field at a college in any state.

Eligibility: Open to seniors graduating from high schools in Florida and planning to enroll full time at a college or university in any state. Applicants may be planning to major in any field of the arts and sciences. They must have a GPA of 3.0 or higher. Along with their application, they must submit a 200–word essay on how this scholarship would enhance their ability to continue their education. Selection is based on academic achievement, contribution to society, and financial need.

Financial data: The stipend is $1,000.

Duration: 1 year.

Number awarded: 15 each year: 3 in each district of Florida.

Deadline: February of each year.

1016 $$ VOCATIONAL REHABILITATION AND EMPLOYMENT VETSUCCESS PROGRAM

Department of Veterans Affairs
Attn: Veterans Benefits Administration
Vocational Rehabilitation and Employment Service
810 Vermont Avenue, N.W.
Washington, DC 20420
Phone: (202) 418–4343; (800) 827–1000
Web: www.vba.va.gov/bin/vre/index.htm

Summary: To provide funding to veterans with service–connected disabilities who need assistance to find employment or, if seriously disabled, to live independently.

Eligibility: Open to veterans who have a service–connected disability of at least 10% or a memorandum rating of 20% or more from the Department of Veterans Affairs (VA). They must qualify for services provided by the VA VetSuccess that include assistance finding and keeping a job, including the use of special employer incentives and job accommodations; on–the–job training, apprenticeships, and unpaid work experiences; postsecondary training at a college, vocational, technical, or business school; supportive rehabilitation services such as case management, counseling, and medical referrals; independent living services for veterans unable to work due to the severity of their disabilities.

Financial data: While in training and for 2 months after, eligible disabled veterans may receive subsistence allowances in addition to their disability compensation or retirement pay. For most training programs, the current full–time monthly rate is $566.97 with no dependents, $703.28 with 1 dependent, $828.76 with 2 dependents, and $60.41 for each additional dependent; proportional rates apply for less than full–time training.

Duration: Veterans remain eligible for these services up to 12 years from either the date of separation from active military service or the date the veteran was first notified by VA of a service–connected disability rating (whichever came later).

Number awarded: Varies each year.

Deadline: Applications are accepted at any time.

1017 VOLUNTEERISM/COMMUNITY SERVICE SCHOLARSHIPS

Colorado Council on High School and College Relations
Attn: Scholarship Committee
P.O. Box 3383
Pagosa Springs, CO 81147
Phone: (970) 264–2231, ext. 226;
Email: mthompson@pagosa.k12.co.us
Web: www.coloradocouncil.org/resources/scholarship.php

Summary: To provide financial assistance for college to high school seniors in Colorado who have been involved in community service activities.

Eligibility: Open to high school seniors who have been Colorado residents for at least their final 2 years of high school. Applicants must have a GPA of 2.5 or higher and acceptance at a college or university that is a member of the Colorado Council on High School and College Relations as a full–time student. They must submit a 2–page essay on a significant experience or achievement that has special meaning to them in their past volunteer work. Selection is based on volunteerism and community service, extracurricular activities, and dedication to serving others. U.S. citizenship or permanent resident status is required.

Financial data: The stipend is $1,500.

Duration: 1 year; nonrenewable.

Number awarded: 14 each year.

Deadline: January of each year.

1018 $$ WAIVER FOR NON–RESIDENTS ENROLLED IN TEXAS PUBLIC UNIVERSITIES LOCATED WITHIN 100 MILES OF THE TEXAS BORDER

Texas Higher Education Coordinating Board
Attn: Grants and Special Programs
1200 East Anderson Lane
P.O. Box 12788
Austin, TX 78711–2788
Phone: (512) 427–6340; (800) 242–3062; Fax: (512) 427–6420;
Email: grantinfo@thecb.state.tx.us
Web: www.collegeforalltexans.com/apps/financialaid/tofa2.cfm?ID=451

Summary: To enable residents of adjoining states to attend designated Texas public institutions at reduced rates.

Eligibility: Open to residents of Arkansas, Louisiana, New Mexico, and Oklahoma who are attending designated public institutions in Texas. The institution must be within 100 miles of the Texas border.

Financial data: Eligible students are able to attend Texas public institutions and pay a reduced tuition rate.

Duration: 1 year; may be renewed.

Number awarded: Varies each year; recently, 770 of these waivers were awarded.

Deadline: Deadline not specified.

1019 $$ WAIVERS OF NON–RESIDENT TUITION FOR DEPENDENTS OF MILITARY PERSONNEL MOVING TO TEXAS

Texas Higher Education Coordinating Board
Attn: Grants and Special Programs
1200 East Anderson Lane
P.O. Box 12788
Austin, TX 78711–2788
Phone: (512) 427–6340; (800) 242–3062; Fax: (512) 427–6420;
Email: grantinfo@thecb.state.tx.us
Web: www.collegeforalltexans.com/apps/financialaid/tofa2.cfm?ID=405

Summary: To exempt dependents of military personnel who move to Texas from the payment of non–resident tuition at public institutions of higher education in the state.

Eligibility: Open to the spouses and dependent children of members of the U.S. armed forces and commissioned officers of the Public Health Service who move to Texas while the servicemember remains assigned to another state. Applicants must be attending or planning to attend a public college or university in the state. They must indicate their intent to become a Texas resident. For dependent children to qualify, the spouse must also move to Texas.

Financial data: Although persons eligible under this program are still classified as non–residents, they are entitled to pay the resident tuition at Texas institutions of higher education on an immediate basis.

Duration: 1 year.

Number awarded: Varies each year.

Deadline: Deadline not specified.

1020 $$ WAIVERS OF NON–RESIDENT TUITION FOR DEPENDENTS OF MILITARY PERSONNEL WHO PREVIOUSLY LIVED IN TEXAS

Texas Higher Education Coordinating Board
Attn: Grants and Special Programs
1200 East Anderson Lane
P.O. Box 12788
Austin, TX 78711–2788
Phone: (512) 427–6340; (800) 242–3062; Fax: (512) 427–6420;
Email: grantinfo@thecb.state.tx.us
Web: www.collegeforalltexans.com/apps/financialaid/tofa2.cfm?ID=536

Summary: To provide a partial tuition exemption to the spouses and dependent children of military personnel who are Texas residents but are not assigned to duty in the state.

Eligibility: Open to the spouses and dependent children of members of the U.S. armed forces who are not assigned to duty in Texas but have previously resided in the state for at least 6 months. Servicemembers must verify that they remain Texas residents by designating Texas as their place of legal residence for income tax purposes, registering to vote in the state, and doing 1 of the following: owning real property in Texas, registering an automobile in Texas, or executing a will indicating that they are a resident of the state. The spouse or dependent child must be attending or planning to attend a Texas public college or university.

Financial data: Although persons eligible under this program are classified as non–residents, they are entitled to pay the resident tuition at Texas institutions of higher education, regardless of their length of residence in Texas.

Duration: 1 year.

Number awarded: Varies each year.

Deadline: Deadline not specified.

1021 $$ WALMART SCHOLARSHIPS OF THE THURGOOD MARSHALL COLLEGE FUND

Thurgood Marshall College Fund
Attn: Campus Relations Associate
901 F Street, N.W., Suite 300
Washington, DC 20004
Phone: (202) 747–7183; Fax: (202) 652–2934;
Email: janay.hawkins@tmcfund.org
Web: www.thurgoodmarshallfund.net/current–scholarships

Summary: To provide financial assistance to African American students enrolled at any of the public Historically Black Colleges and Universities (HBCUs) that are members of the Thurgood Marshall College Fund (TMCF).

Eligibility: Open to African American students currently enrolled full time at 1 of the 47 colleges and universities that are TMCF members. Applicants must be the first member of their family to attend college. They must have a GPA of 2.5 or higher and be able to demonstrate financial need. Along with their application, they must submit a 500–word essay on 1 of the following topics: 1) a significant setback, challenge, or opportunity in their life and the impact it has had on them; 2) what inspired them to pursue a degree in their current field of study and the impact it will have on our society; or 3) what it means to be the first person in their family to receive a college degree. U.S. citizenship or permanent resident status is required.

Financial data: The stipend is $3,100 per semester ($6,200 per year).

Duration: 1 year.

Number awarded: Approximately 100 each year.

Deadline: April of each year.

1022 $ WALTER U. LUM UNDERGRADUATE SCHOLARSHIP

Chinese American Citizens Alliance
1044 Stockton Street
San Francisco, CA 94108
Phone: (415) 434–2222;
Email: info@cacanational.org
Web: www.cacanational.org/purpose

Summary: To provide financial assistance to Chinese American undergraduate students.

Eligibility: Open to students of Chinese descent who have completed the sophomore year of college. Preference is given to U.S. citizens. Applicants must submit a copy of their college transcripts; copies of their and their parents' latest income tax returns; copies of successful applications for financial aid; an essay (up to 500 words) that describes their community activities, career goals, and personal outlook; and 2 reference letters. Selection is based on academic achievement, campus and community extracurricular activities, career goals and personal outlook, quality of the essay, and financial need.

Financial data: The stipend is $2,000.

Duration: 1 year; nonrenewable.

Number awarded: 2 each odd–numbered year.

Deadline: April of each odd–numbered year.

1023 $$ WASHINGTON REALIZE THE DREAM SCHOLARSHIPS

College Success Foundation
1605 N.W. Sammamish Road, Suite 200
Issaquah, WA 98027–5388
Phone: (425) 416–2000; (877) 655–4097; Fax: (425) 416–2001;
Email: info@collegesuccessfoundation.org
Web: www.collegesuccessfoundation.org/Page.aspx?pid=377

Summary: To provide financial assistance to high school seniors in Washington who are undocumented residents and planning to attend college in the state.

Eligibility: Open to seniors graduating from high schools in Washington who are undocumented residents of the United States and have lived in Washington for at least 3 years. Applicants must be planning to enroll full time at a 2– or 4–year college or university in the state. They must have a GPA of 2.0 or higher and be able to demonstrate financial need (family income of $39,000 or less for a family of 1, rising to $94,000 or less for a family of 7). Along with their application, they must submit an affidavit verifying their status and pledging to seek permanent resident status when legally permitted to do so.

Financial data: The stipend is $5,000 per year.

Duration: 1 year; may be renewed up to 3 additional years.

Number awarded: Varies each year.

Deadline: June of each year.

1024 $ WASHINGTON STATE ASSOCIATION FOR JUSTICE PRESIDENTS' SCHOLARSHIP

Washington State Association for Justice
1809 Seventh Avenue, Suite 1500
Seattle, WA 98101–1328
Phone: (206) 464–1011; Fax: (206) 464–0703;
Email: wsja@washingtonjustice.org
Web: www.washingtonjustice.org

Summary: To provide financial assistance to Washington high school seniors who have a disability or have been a victim of injury and plan to attend college in any state.

Eligibility: Open to seniors at high schools in Washington who are planning to work on a bachelor's degree at an institution of higher education in any state. Applicants must be able to demonstrate 1) financial need; 2) a history of achievement despite having been a victim of injury or overcoming a disability, handicap, or similar challenge; 3) a record of serving others; and 4) a commitment to apply their education toward helping others.

Financial data: Stipends average $2,000. Funds are paid directly to the recipient's chosen institution of higher learning to be used for tuition, room, board, and fees.

Duration: 1 year.

Number awarded: 1 or more each year.

Deadline: March of each year.

1025 WASHINGTON STATE BUSINESS AND PROFESSIONAL WOMEN'S FOUNDATION MATURE WOMAN EDUCATIONAL SCHOLARSHIP

Washington State Business and Professional Women's Foundation
Attn: Virginia Murphy, Scholarship Committee Chair
P.O. Box 631
Chelan, WA 98816–0631
Phone: (509) 682–4747;
Email: vamurf@nwi.net
Web: www.bpwwa.org/scholarships.htm

Summary: To provide financial assistance to mature women from Washington interested in attending postsecondary school in the state for retraining or continuing education.

Eligibility: Open to women over 35 years of age who have been residents of Washington for at least 2 years. Applicants must be planning to enroll at a college or university in the state for a program of retraining or continuing education. Along with their application, they must submit a 500–word essay on their specific short–term goals and how the proposed training will help them accomplish those goals and make a difference in their professional career. Financial need is considered in the selection process. U.S. citizenship is required.

Financial data: The stipend is $1,000.

Duration: 1 year.

Number awarded: 1 or more each year.

Deadline: March of each year.

1026 WASHINGTON STATE BUSINESS AND PROFESSIONAL WOMEN'S FOUNDATION SINGLE PARENT SCHOLARSHIP

Washington State Business and Professional Women's Foundation
Attn: Virginia Murphy, Scholarship Committee Chair
P.O. Box 631
Chelan, WA 98816–0631
Phone: (509) 682–4747;
Email: vamurf@nwi.net
Web: www.bpwwa.org/scholarships.htm

Summary: To provide financial assistance to women from Washington who are single parents interested in returning to college to continue their education.

Eligibility: Open to women of any age who have been residents of Washington for at least 2 years. Applicants must have at least 1 dependent child, under 18 years of age, living at home. They must be interested in returning to school in the state to continue their education beyond the high school level. Along with their application, they must submit a 500–word essay on their specific short–term goals and how the proposed training will help them accomplish those goals and make a difference in their professional career. Financial need is considered in the selection process. U.S. citizenship is required.

Financial data: The stipend is $1,000.

Duration: 1 year.

Number awarded: 1 or more each year.

Deadline: March of each year.

1027 $$ WASHINGTON STATE NEED GRANT

Washington Student Achievement Council
917 Lakeridge Way
P.O. Box 43430
Olympia, WA 98504–3430
Phone: (360) 753–7850; (888) 535–0747; Fax: (360) 753–7808; TDD: (360) 753–7809;
Email: finaid@wsac.wa.gov
Web: www.wsac.wa.gov/PayingForCollege/FinancialAidPrograms

Summary: To provide financial assistance to Washington residents who come from a low–income or disadvantaged family and plan to attend college in the state.

Eligibility: Open to applicants enrolled or planning to enroll at least half time in an eligible certificate, first bachelor's degree, or first associate degree program at an academic institution in the state. They may not be working on a degree in theology. This program provides 1) maximum grants to residents of Washington whose family income is equal to or less than 50% of the state median (currently defined as $21,500 for a family of 1 ranging to $56,500 for a family of 8); or 2) smaller grants for students from families with higher incomes. Consideration is automatic with the institution's receipt of the student's completed financial aid application.

Financial data: The maximum grant depends on the type of institution the recipient attends. Recently, it was $10,868 per year at public research universities, from $7,196 to $7,882 per year at public comprehensive universities, $3,696 per year at public community and technical colleges, $8,517 at private 4–year colleges and universities, $4,259 per year at 4–year proprietary colleges, or from $1,412 to $2,823 at 2–year propriety colleges. Students whose family income falls between 51% and 55% of the state median are eligible for 70% of those maximums, family income between 56% and 60% for 65% of those maximums, family income between 61% and 65% for 60% of those maximums, or family income between 66% and 70% for 50% of those maximums.

Duration: 1 academic year; may be renewed up to 4 additional years or up to 125% of program length.

Number awarded: Varies each year; recently, more than 65,000 students received about $155 million in benefits from this program.

Deadline: Varies according to the participating institution; generally in October of each year.

1028 $ W.C. AND PEARL CAMPBELL SCHOLARSHIP

Oregon Student Access Commission
Attn: Grants and Scholarships Division
1500 Valley River Drive, Suite 100
Eugene, OR 97401–2146
Phone: (541) 687–7395; (800) 452–8807, ext. 7395; Fax: (541) 687–7414; TDD: (800) 735–2900;
Email: awardinfo@osac.state.or.us
Web: www.oregonstudentaid.gov/scholarships.aspx

Summary: To provide financial assistance to high school seniors in Oregon who have outstanding academic records and plan to attend college in the state.

Eligibility: Open to seniors graduating from high schools in Oregon who have a GPA of 3.85 or higher and test scores of at least 1220 on the combined mathematics and critical reading SAT or 27 on the ACT. Applicants must be planning to attend a college or university in the state. They must be able to demonstrate financial need.

Financial data: Stipends for scholarships offered by the Oregon Student Access Commission (OSAC) range from $200 to $10,000 but recently averaged $2,300.

Duration: 1 year; nonrenewable.

Number awarded: Varies each year.

Deadline: February of each year.

1029 $ WE THE LIVING ESSAY CONTEST

Ayn Rand Institute
Attn: Essay Contests
2121 Alton Parkway, Suite 250
P.O. Box 57044
Irvine, CA 92619–7044
Phone: (949) 222–6550, ext. 247; Fax: (949) 222–6558;
Email: essays@aynrand.org
Web: essaycontest.aynrandnovels.com/WeTheLiving.aspx?theme=blue

Summary: To recognize and reward outstanding essays written by high school students on Ayn Rand's novel, *We the Living.*

Eligibility: Open to sophomores, juniors, or seniors in high school. Applicants must submit an essay on questions selected each year from Ayn Rand's novel, *We the Living.* The essay must be between 700 and 1,500 words. Selection is based on style and content. Judges look for writing that is clear, articulate, and logically organized. To win, an essay must demonstrate an outstanding grasp of the philosophical meaning of the novel.

Financial data: First prize is $3,000; second prizes are $1,000; third prizes are $300; finalist prizes are $50; and semifinalist prizes are $25.

Duration: The competition is held annually.

Number awarded: 116 each year: 1 first prize, 5 second prizes, 5 third prizes, 25 finalist prizes, and 80 semifinalist prizes.

Deadline: May of each year.

1030 WEST VIRGINIA ENDOWMENT SCHOLARSHIP

Epsilon Sigma Alpha International
Attn: ESA Foundation
363 West Drake Road
Fort Collins, CO 80526
Phone: (970) 223–2824; Fax: (970) 223–4456;
Email: esainfo@epsilonsigmaalpha.org
Web: www.epsilonsigmaalpha.org/esa–foundation/scholarships

Summary: To provide financial assistance to residents of West Virginia who plan to attend college in any state.

Eligibility: Open to residents of West Virginia who are 1) graduating high school seniors with a GPA of 3.0 or higher or with minimum scores of 22 on the ACT or 1030 on the combined critical reading and mathematics SAT; 2) enrolled in college with a GPA of 3.0 or higher; 3) enrolled at a technical school or returning to school after an absence for retraining of job skills or obtaining a degree; or 4) engaged in online study through an accredited college, university, or vocational school. Applicants may be attending or planning to attend an accredited school in any state and major in any field. Selection is based on character (20%), leadership (20%), service (20%), financial need (20%), and scholastic ability (20%).

Financial data: The stipend is $1,000.

Duration: 1 year; may be renewed.

Number awarded: 1 each year.

Deadline: January of each year.

1031 $ WEST VIRGINIA HIGHER EDUCATION GRANT PROGRAM

West Virginia Higher Education Policy Commission
Attn: College Foundation of West Virginia
Financial Aid Program Staff
1018 Kanawha Boulevard, East, Suite 700
Charleston, WV 25301–2827
Phone: (304) 558–4618; (877) 987–7664; Fax: (304) 558–4622
Web: https://secure.cfwv.com/Financial_Aid_Planning/_default.aspx

Summary: To provide financial assistance to West Virginia residents who wish to attend an approved institution of higher education in West Virginia or Pennsylvania.

Eligibility: Open to U.S. citizens who have been residents of West Virginia for at least 1 year prior to applying. Applicants must plan to enroll as full–time undergraduate students at an approved college or university in West Virginia or Pennsylvania. Selection is based on financial need and academic performance.

Financial data: Awards are limited to payment of tuition and fees. Recently, grants ranged up to $2,400 per year. Funds are sent directly to the institution.

Duration: 1 year; may be renewed for up to 3 additional years.

Number awarded: Varies each year; recently, approximately 13,000 students received assistance worth $34.6 million.

Deadline: April of each year.

1032 $$ WEST VIRGINIA PROMISE SCHOLARSHIPS

West Virginia Higher Education Policy Commission
Attn: PROMISE Scholarship Program
1018 Kanawha Boulevard, East, Suite 700
Charleston, WV 25301–2827
Phone: (304) 558–4618; (877) 987–7664; Fax: (304) 558–4622;
Email: promise@hepc.wvnet.edu
Web: www.wvhepc.org/DataExchange/Applications/Promise

Summary: To provide financial assistance to high school seniors in West Virginia who have complied with core academic requirements and plan to attend college in the state.

Eligibility: Open to high school seniors in West Virginia who have earned a GPA of 3.0 or higher in core courses (4 credits of English/language arts, 4 credits of mathematics, 4 credits of social sciences, and 3 credits of natural sciences) and overall. Applicants must attain a composite score of 22 or higher on the ACT (including 20 or higher on each of the 4 subject areas of English, mathematics, science, and reading) or a combined score of 1020 or higher on the SAT (including at least 490 in critical reading and at least 480 in mathematics). Home–schooled students who can document completion of grades 11 and 12 in West Virginia and GED recipients who completed high school no more than 2 years previously are also eligible; members of both groups must earn a score of 2500 or higher on the GED examination. All applicants must have lived in West Virginia for at least 12 months immediately preceding application for this program. Half of the credits required for high school graduation must have been completed in a public or private high school in West Virginia. Selection is based on merit; financial need is not considered.

Financial data: Students who attend a West Virginia state college or university receive a full tuition scholarship. Students who attend a West Virginia private college receive an equivalent dollar scholarship, recently for $4,750.

Duration: 1 year; may be renewed for 1 additional year in an associate degree program or for 3 additional years in a baccalaureate degree program. Recipients must earn at least 30 college credits each year and maintain a GPA of 2.75 or higher during the first year of college and at least 3.0 cumulatively in successive years.

Number awarded: Varies each year; recently, the program received $10.9 million in general revenue funding and $27 million from the state video lottery. A total of approximately 9,300 students were receiving support from the program, including 3,300 incoming freshmen.

Deadline: February of each year.

1033 $$ WEST VIRGINIA STATE WAR ORPHANS EDUCATIONAL PROGRAM

West Virginia Department of Veteran's Assistance
Attn: Executive Secretary
1321 Plaza East, Suite 109
Charleston, WV 25301–1400
Phone: (304) 558–3661; (866) WV4–VETS (within WV); Fax: (304) 558–3662;
Email: Angela.S.Meadows@wv.gov
Web: www.veterans.wv.gov

Summary: To provide financial assistance for college to the children and spouses of deceased West Virginia veterans.

Eligibility: Open to residents of West Virginia who are children between 16 and 25 years of age or spouses of deceased veterans. The veteran must have entered service as a resident of West Virginia; served during specified periods of war time; and died during that wartime period or, if subsequent to discharge, as a result of disability incurred in that wartime service. Applicants must be attending or planning to attend a college or university in West Virginia.

Financial data: The state appropriates $5,000 per year for the educational expenses of each qualifying child or spouse. That includes a waiver of tuition and fees at state–supported colleges and universities.

Duration: 1 year; may be renewed upon reapplication if the student maintains a cumulative GPA of at least 2.0.

Number awarded: Varies each year.

Deadline: July of each year for the fall semester; November of each year for the spring semester.

1034 WEST VIRGINIA VETERAN'S RE–EDUCATION SCHOLARSHIP PROGRAM

West Virginia Department of Veteran's Assistance
Attn: Scholarship Program
1321 Plaza East, Suite 109
Charleston, WV 25301–1400
Phone: (304) 558–3661; (866) WV4–VETS (within WV); Fax: (304) 558–3662;
Email: Angela.S.Meadows@wv.gov
Web: www.veterans.wv.gov/Pages/Veteran'sRe–Education.aspx

Summary: To provide financial assistance to veterans in West Virginia who wish to return to college after completing their military service.

Eligibility: Open to residents of West Virginia who have been honorably discharged after at least 181 consecutive days of military service; Reservists with active duty for training only are not eligible. Applicants must be eligible for federal Pell grants or be unemployed and have exhausted all federal educational benefits from the Department of Veterans Affairs (VA). They must be attending or planning to attend a college or university in West Virginia and apply through their institution.

Financial data: The stipend is $500 per term for full–time students or $250 per term for part–time students. The maximum award per calendar year is $1,500.

Duration: 1 year; may be renewed upon reapplication if the student maintains a cumulative GPA of at least 2.0.

Number awarded: Varies each year.

Deadline: July of each year for the fall semester; November of each year for the spring semester.

1035 $ WESTBROOK SCHOLARSHIP FUND

U.S. Coast Guard
Attn: Office of Work–Life (CG–111)
2100 Second Street, S.W., Stop 7902
Washington, DC 20593–7902
Phone: (202) 475–5140; (800) 872–4957; Fax: (202) 475–5907;
Email: HQS.SMB.FamilySupportServices@uscg.mil
Web: www.uscg.mil/worklife/scholarship.asp

Summary: To provide financial assistance for college to the dependent children of Coast Guard enlisted personnel.

Eligibility: Open to the dependent children of enlisted members of the U.S. Coast Guard on active duty, retired, or deceased and of enlisted personnel in the Coast Guard Reserve currently on extended active duty 180 days or more. Applicants must be high school seniors or current undergraduates enrolled or planning to enroll full–time at a 4–year college, university, or vocational school. They must be under 24 years of age and registered in the Defense Enrollment Eligibility Reporting System (DEERS) system. Along with their application, they must submit their SAT or ACT scores, a letter of recommendation, transcripts, a financial information statement, and a 500–word essay on their personal and academic achievements, extracurricular activities, contributions to the community, and academic plans and career goals.

Financial data: The stipend is $2,500.

Duration: 1 year; nonrenewable.

Number awarded: 1 each year.

Deadline: March of each year.

1036 $$ WESTERN UNDERGRADUATE EXCHANGE

Western Interstate Commission for Higher Education
Attn: Student Exchange Programs
3035 Center Green Drive, Suite 200
Boulder, CO 80301–2204
Phone: (303) 541–0270; Fax: (303) 541–0291;
Email: info–sep@wiche.edu
Web: www.wiche.edu/wue

Summary: To underwrite some of the cost of out–of–state undergraduate schooling for students in selected western states.

Eligibility: Open to residents of states that participate in the Western Undergraduate Exchange (WUE): Alaska, Arizona, California, Colorado, Hawaii, Idaho, Montana, Nevada, New Mexico, North Dakota, Oregon, South Dakota, Utah, Washington, and Wyoming. To be eligible, students should be residents of 1 of those states for at least 1 year before applying and be interested in enrolling in a participating 2– or 4–year college or university in 1 of the other states. The financial status of the applicants is not considered. Interested students apply for admission and for WUE assistance directly from the institution of their choice.

Financial data: Participants in this program attend out–of–state institutions but pay only 150% of resident tuition instead of the regular full non–refundable resident tuition.

Duration: 1 year; may be renewed.

Number awarded: Varies each year; recently, more than 29,000 students (approximately 4,700 at 2–year colleges and 24,300 at 4–year universities) were enrolled at 148 campuses in the 15 states.

Deadline: Deadline dates vary; check with the institution you wish to attend.

1037 $$ WESTERN UNION FOUNDATION FAMILY SCHOLARSHIP PROGRAM

Western Union Foundation
c/o Institute of International Education
1400 K Street, N.W., Suite 700
Washington, DC 20005
Phone: (202) 326–7861; Fax: (202) 326–7696;
Email: wufoundaton@iie.org
Web: foundation.westernunion.com/education_programs.html

Summary: To provide financial assistance to pairs of students from the same family of immigrants in designated cities, both of whom wish to attend college in any state.

Eligibility: Open to pairs of students from the same family of immigrants. Applications must be submitted jointly by the 2 students (parent and child, siblings). Both applicants must be 18 years of age or older, have been born outside of the United States, have been in this country for 7 years or less, and be planning to attend an accredited institution of higher education or nonprofit training institute in any state. They must be residents of Chicago, Denver, Los Angeles, Miami, New York, San Francisco, or Washington, D.C. Funding is available for college or university tuition, language acquisition classes, technical or skill training, and/or financial literacy; graduate study is not supported.
Financial data: Stipends range from $1,000 to $5,000 per family. Funds are paid directly to the educational institution.
Duration: 1 year.
Number awarded: Varies each year.
Deadline: October of each year.

1038 $ WILDER–NAIFEH TECHNICAL SKILLS GRANTS

Tennessee Student Assistance Corporation
Parkway Towers
404 James Robertson Parkway, Suite 1510
Nashville, TN 37243–0820
Phone: (615) 741–1346; (800) 342–1663; Fax: (615) 741–6101;
Email: TSAC.Aidinfo@tn.gov
Web: www.tn.gov/collegepays/mon_college/wilder_naifeh.htm
Summary: To provide financial assistance to students enrolled at Tennessee Technology Centers.
Eligibility: Open to students working on a certificate or diploma at a Tennessee Technology Center. Applicants must be enrolled full time, but they are not required to meet any GPA or ACT minimum scores. They may not have previously received a Tennessee HOPE Scholarship.
Financial data: The stipend is $2,000 per year.
Duration: 1 year.
Number awarded: Varies each year; recently, nearly 13,000 of these grants were awarded.
Deadline: August of each year for fall semester; January of each year for spring and summer semesters.

1039 WILLIAM C. DAVINI SCHOLARSHIP

UNICO National
Attn: UNICO Foundation, Inc.
271 U.S. Highway 46 West, Suite A–108
Fairfield, NJ 07004
Phone: (973) 808–0035; (800) 877–1492; Fax: (973) 808–0043;
Email: uniconational@unico.org
Web: www.unico.org/scholarships.asp
Summary: To provide financial assistance for college to Italian American high school seniors.
Eligibility: Open to high school seniors of Italian origin (i.e., at least 1 parent or grandparent of Italian origin) who are planning to attend an accredited college or university. Applicants must have a GPA of 3.0 or higher and be U.S. citizens. Along with their application, they must submit SAT or ACT test scores and a letter of recommendation from a UNICO chapter in the city or town where they live. Selection is based on citizenship, leadership, character, personality, community service, and financial need.
Financial data: The stipend is $1,500 per year.
Duration: 4 years.
Number awarded: 1 each year.
Deadline: April of each year.

1040 $ WILLIAM D. SQUIRES SCHOLARSHIPS

William D. Squires Educational Foundation, Inc.
P.O. Box 2940
Jupiter, FL 33468–2940
Phone: (561) 741–7751;
Email: info@wmdsquiresfoundation.org
Web: www.wmdsquiresfoundation.org
Summary: To provide financial assistance to high school seniors in Ohio who plan to attend college in any state.
Eligibility: Open to seniors graduating from high schools in Ohio and planning to enroll full time at a 4–year college or university in any state. Applicants must have a GPA of 3.2 or higher and a clear idea of their career goal. They must be able to demonstrate financial need with an Expected Family Contribution of less than $8,000. Along with their application, they must submit a 1–page essay about their career choice. Selection is based primarily on financial need.
Financial data: The stipend is $3,000 per year.
Duration: 1 year; may be renewed up to 3 additional years; provided that the recipient maintains a GPA of 2.5 or higher.
Number awarded: 15 each year.
Deadline: April of each year.

1041 WILLIAM F. GANDERT MEMORIAL SCHOLARSHIPS

National Leased Housing Association
Attn: NLHA Education Fund
1900 L Street, N.W., Suite 300
Washington, DC 20036
Phone: (202) 785–8888; Fax: (202) 785–2008;
Email: info@hudnlha.com
Web: www.hudnlha.com/education_fund/index.asp
Summary: To provide financial assistance for trade school to residents of federally–assisted rental housing properties and members of families receiving rental subsidy through federal housing programs.
Eligibility: Open to U.S. citizens and permanent residents who reside in a federally–assisted rental housing property or whose families receive rental subsidy through a recognized federal housing program (e.g., Section 8, Rent Supplement, Rental Assistance Payments, Low Income Housing Tax Credit). Applicants must be graduating high school seniors, students currently enrolled full time in a certified training program for a specific trade, or GED recipients entering such a program. They must be able to demonstrate financial need and community leadership through volunteer work at school or in the community. Along with their application, they must submit a 1–page essay on their goals with respect to their education they are seeking.
Financial data: A stipend is awarded (amount not specified). Funds are disbursed directly to an accredited trade school to be used for partial payment of tuition, books, equipment and tools, or other expenses directly related to the student's education.
Duration: 1 year.
Number awarded: Varies each year; recently, 2 of these scholarships were awarded.
Deadline: February of each year.

1042 $ WILLIAM L. BOYD, IV, FLORIDA RESIDENT ACCESS GRANTS

Florida Department of Education
Attn: Office of Student Financial Assistance
325 West Gaines Street
Tallahassee, FL 32399–0400
Phone: (850) 410–5160; (888) 827–2004; Fax: (850) 487–1809;
Email: osfa@fldoe.org
Web: www.floridastudentfinancialaid.org/SSFAD/factsheets/FRAG.htm
Summary: To provide financial assistance to students at private colleges and universities in Florida.
Eligibility: Open to full–time undergraduate students who are attending any of 31 eligible private nonprofit colleges or universities in Florida and who have been Florida residents for at least 1 year. Applicants must be U.S. citizens or eligible noncitizens. Financial need is not considered in the selection process.
Financial data: The amount of the award is specified by the state legislature annually; recently, the stipend was $2,149.
Duration: Up to 9 semesters or 14 quarters, provided the student maintains full–time enrollment and a GPA of 2.0 or higher.
Number awarded: Varies each year; recently, 16,405 new and 23,022 renewal grants were awarded.
Deadline: Deadline not specified.

1043 $ WILLIAM M. EVANS SCHOLARSHIP

Bose McKinney & Evans LLP
Attn: Scholarship Award Committee
111 Monument Circle, Suite 2700
Indianapolis, IN 46204
Phone: (317) 684–5000; Fax: (317) 684–5173
Web: www.boselaw.com
Summary: To provide financial assistance to high school seniors in Indiana who are classified as special education students and who plan to attend college in any state.

Eligibility: Open to seniors graduating from high schools in Indiana who have been classified as special education students. Applicants must be planning to attend a university, college, junior college, or vocational training program in any state. Selection is based on personal achievement, future goals, and financial need.
Financial data: The stipend is $2,000.
Duration: 1 year.
Number awarded: 1 each year.
Deadline: March of each year.

1044 WINGS OVER AMERICA SCHOLARSHIPS

Wings Over America Scholarship Foundation
Attn: Scholarship Administrator
4966 Euclid Road, Suite 109
Virginia Beach, VA 23462
Phone: (757) 671–3200, ext. 118;
Email: scholarship@wingsoveramerica.us
Web: www.wingsoveramerica.us
Summary: To provide financial assistance for college to dependents of naval aviators.
Eligibility: Open to 1) children of a military sponsor who are graduating high school seniors planning to enroll in college full time to work on a bachelor's degree or who are already enrolled in such a program; and 2) spouses of a military sponsor currently enrolled full or part time and working on an associate or bachelor's degree at an accredited college or university. Children must be unmarried and younger than 23 years of age. The military sponsor must have completed at least 8 years of active–duty service in a Naval air forces or subordinate command and be currently on active duty, retired, or deceased. Also eligible are children of members of the U.S. Navy who died while on active duty serving with a Naval air force unit, regardless of the length of service of the deceased parent. Selection is based on academic proficiency, extracurricular activities, community contributions, and life experience and character of the applicant. The highest ranked applicant receives the CAPT Neil Kinnear Scholarship.
Financial data: The CAPT Neil Kinnear Scholarship is $3,000 per year. Other stipend amounts depend on the availability of funds.
Duration: 1 year; may be renewed.
Number awarded: Varies each year; recently, 43 of these scholarships were awarded: 20 high school seniors, 16 college students, and 7 spouses. Since the program was established, it has awarded more than $440,000 in scholarships.
Deadline: March of each year.

1045 $ WISCONSIN ACADEMIC EXCELLENCE SCHOLARSHIP PROGRAM

Wisconsin Higher Educational Aids Board
131 West Wilson Street, Suite 902
P.O. Box 7885
Madison, WI 53707–7885
Phone: (608) 267–2213; Fax: (608) 267–2808;
Email: nancy.wilkison@wisconsin.gov
Web: heab.state.wi.us/programs.html
Summary: To provide financial assistance to Wisconsin high school seniors who have the highest GPAs in their schools and plan to attend college in the state.
Eligibility: Open to seniors at each public and private high school throughout Wisconsin who have the highest GPAs. Applicants must plan to attend a branch of the University of Wisconsin, a Wisconsin technical college, or an independent institution in the state as a full–time student in the following fall.
Financial data: The awards provide full tuition, up to $2,250 per year, during the first 3 years of undergraduate study; for subsequent years, the maximum award is equal to full tuition and fees at a campus of the University of Wisconsin.
Duration: Up to 10 semesters.
Number awarded: The number of scholarships allotted to each high school is based on total student enrollment, ranging from 1 scholarship for schools with enrollment of 80 to 499 up to 6 scholarships for schools with enrollment greater than 2,500. Students at schools with enrollment of less than 80 compete statewide for an additional 10 scholarships.
Deadline: High schools must nominate their top–ranked student by February of each year.

1046 $$ WISCONSIN G.I. BILL TUITION REMISSION PROGRAM

Wisconsin Department of Veterans Affairs
201 West Washington Avenue
P.O. Box 7843
Madison, WI 53707–7843
Phone: (608) 266–1311; (800) WIS–VETS; Fax: (608) 267–0403;
Email: WDVAInfo@dva.state.wi.us
Web: www.dva.state.wi.us/Ben_education.asp
Summary: To provide financial assistance for college or graduate school to Wisconsin veterans and their dependents.
Eligibility: Open to current residents of Wisconsin who 1) were residents of the state when they entered or reentered active duty in the U.S. armed forces; or 2) have moved to the state and have been residents for any consecutive 12–month period after entry or reentry into service. Applicants must have served on active duty for at least 2 continuous years or for at least 90 days during specified wartime periods. Also eligible are 1) qualifying children and unremarried surviving spouses of Wisconsin veterans who died in the line of duty or as the direct result of a service–connected disability; and 2) children and spouses of Wisconsin veterans who have a service–connected disability rated by the U.S. Department of Veterans Affairs as 30% or greater. Children must be between 17 and 25 years of age (regardless of the date of the veteran's death or initial disability rating) and be a Wisconsin resident for tuition purposes. Spouses remain eligible for 10 years following the date of the veteran's death or initial disability rating; they must be Wisconsin residents for tuition purposes but they may enroll full or part time. Students may attend any institution, center, or school within the University of Wisconsin (UW) System or the Wisconsin Technical College System (WCTS). There are no income limits, delimiting periods following military service during which the benefit must be used, or limits on the level of study (e.g., vocational, undergraduate, professional, or graduate).
Financial data: Veterans who qualify as a Wisconsin resident for tuition purposes are eligible for a remission of 100% of standard academic fees and segregated fees at a UW campus or 100% of program and material fees at a WCTS institution. Veterans who qualify as a Wisconsin veteran for purposes of this program but for other reasons fail to meet the definition of a Wisconsin resident for tuition purposes at the UW system are eligible for a remission of 100% of non–resident fees. Spouses and children of deceased or disabled veterans are entitled to a remission of 100% of tuition and fees at a UW or WCTS institution.
Duration: Up to 8 semesters or 128 credits, whichever is greater.
Number awarded: Varies each year.
Deadline: Applications must be submitted within 14 days from the office start of the academic term: in October for fall, March for spring, or June for summer.

1047 $ WISCONSIN HIGHER EDUCATION GRANT

Wisconsin Higher Educational Aids Board
131 West Wilson Street, Suite 902
P.O. Box 7885
Madison, WI 53707–7885
Phone: (608) 266–0888; Fax: (608) 267–2808;
Email: cindy.cooley@wisconsin.gov
Web: heab.state.wi.us/programs.html
Summary: To provide financial assistance to financially needy undergraduate students attending public institutions of higher education in Wisconsin.
Eligibility: Open to Wisconsin residents enrolled at least half time at any branch of the University of Wisconsin, at any Wisconsin technical college, or at any Tribal College or University (TCU) in the state. Selection is based on financial need.
Financial data: The stipend ranges from $250 to $3,000 per year.
Duration: Up to 10 semesters.
Number awarded: Varies each year.
Deadline: Deadline not specified.

1048 $ WISCONSIN JOB RETRAINING GRANTS

Wisconsin Department of Veterans Affairs
201 West Washington Avenue
P.O. Box 7843
Madison, WI 53707–7843
Phone: (608) 266–1311; (800) WIS–VETS; Fax: (608) 267–0403;
Email: WDVAInfo@dva.state.wi.us
Web: www.dva.state.wi.us/Ben_retraininggrants.asp

Summary: To provide funds to recently unemployed Wisconsin veterans or their families who need financial assistance while being retrained for employment.

Eligibility: Open to current residents of Wisconsin who 1) were residents of the state when they entered or reentered active duty in the U.S. armed forces; or 2) have moved to the state and have been residents for any consecutive 12–month period after entry or reentry into service. Applicants must have served on active duty for at least 2 continuous years or for at least 90 days during specified wartime periods. Unremarried spouses and minor or dependent children of deceased veterans who would have been eligible for the grant if they were living today may also be eligible. The applicant must, within the year prior to the date of application, have become unemployed (involuntarily laid off or discharged, not due to willful misconduct) or underemployed (experienced an involuntary reduction of income). Underemployed applicants must have current annual income from employment that does not exceed federal poverty guidelines (currently $14,521 for a family of 1, rising to $50,557 for a family of 8). All applicants must be retraining at accredited schools in Wisconsin or in a structured on–the–job program. Course work toward a college degree does not qualify. Training does not have to be full time, but the program must be completed within 2 years and must reasonably be expected to lead to employment.

Financial data: The maximum grant is $3,000 per year; the actual amount varies, depending upon the amount of the applicant's unmet need. In addition to books, fees, and tuition, the funds may be used for living expenses.

Duration: 1 year; may be renewed 1 additional year.

Number awarded: Varies each year.

Deadline: Applications may be submitted at any time.

1049 WISCONSIN LEGION AUXILIARY MERIT AND MEMORIAL SCHOLARSHIPS

American Legion Auxiliary
Department of Wisconsin
Attn: Education Chair
2930 American Legion Drive
P.O. Box 140
Portage, WI 53901–0140
Phone: (608) 745–0124; (866) 664–3863; Fax: (608) 745–1947;
Email: alawi@amlegionauxwi.org
Web: www.amlegionauxwi.org/Scholarships.htm

Summary: To provide financial assistance to Wisconsin residents who are related to veterans or members of the American Legion Auxiliary and interested in working on an undergraduate degree at a school in any state.

Eligibility: Open to the children, wives, and widows of veterans who are high school seniors or graduates and have a GPA of 3.5 or higher. Grandchildren and great–grandchildren of members of the American Legion Auxiliary are also eligible. Applicants must be residents of Wisconsin and interested in working on an undergraduate degree at a school in any state. Along with their application, they must submit a 300–word essay on "Education—An Investment in the Future." Financial need is considered in the selection process.

Financial data: The stipend is $1,000.

Duration: 1 year; nonrenewable.

Number awarded: 7 each year.

Deadline: March of each year.

1050 $ WISCONSIN MINORITY UNDERGRADUATE RETENTION GRANTS

Wisconsin Higher Educational Aids Board
131 West Wilson Street, Suite 902
P.O. Box 7885
Madison, WI 53707–7885
Phone: (608) 267–2212; Fax: (608) 267–2808;
Email: deanna.schulz@wisconsin.gov
Web: heab.state.wi.us/programs.html

Summary: To provide financial assistance to minorities in Wisconsin who are currently enrolled at a college in the state.

Eligibility: Open to residents of Wisconsin who are African Americans, Hispanic Americans, American Indians, or southeast Asians (students who were admitted to the United States after December 31, 1975 and who are a former citizen of Laos, Vietnam, or Cambodia or whose ancestor was a citizen of 1 of those countries). Applicants must be enrolled at least half time as sophomores, juniors, seniors, or fifth–year undergraduates at a Wisconsin technical college, tribal college, or independent college or university in the state. They must be nominated by their institution and be able to demonstrate financial need.

Financial data: Stipends range from $250 to $2,500 per year, depending on the need of the recipient.

Duration: Up to 4 years.

Number awarded: Varies each year.

Deadline: Deadline dates vary by institution; check with your school's financial aid office.

1051 $ WISCONSIN STUDENT OF INTEGRITY INDUSTRY AND TRADES SCHOLARSHIP

Better Business Bureau of Wisconsin Foundation, Inc.
Attn: Scholarship Committee
10101 West Greenfield Avenue, Suite 125
Milwaukee, WI 53214
Phone: (414) 847–6016; (800) 273–1002;
Email: scholarship@wisconsin.bbb.org
Web: Wisconsin.bbb.org/scholarship

Summary: To provide financial assistance to high school seniors in Wisconsin who have demonstrated integrity and plan to attend vocational school in any state.

Eligibility: Open to seniors graduating from high schools in Wisconsin who plan to attend an accredited industrial or trade institution of higher education or training program in any state. Applicants must have demonstrated character, leadership, and ethical values. They must have a GPA of 2.5 or higher. Along with their application, they must submit a 500–word essay on 1) how they will promote and demonstrate ethics and integrity in their chosen field; and 2) an example of when they have been presented with an ethical dilemma and how they responded. U.S. citizenship is required.

Financial data: The stipend is $2,500.

Duration: 1 year.

Number awarded: 1 each year.

Deadline: March of each year.

1052 WISCONSIN TALENT INCENTIVE PROGRAM (TIP) GRANTS

Wisconsin Higher Educational Aids Board
131 West Wilson Street, Suite 902
P.O. Box 7885
Madison, WI 53707–7885
Phone: (608) 266–1665; Fax: (608) 267–2808;
Email: colettem1.brown@wi.gov
Web: heab.state.wi.us/programs.html

Summary: To provide financial assistance for college to needy and educationally disadvantaged students in Wisconsin.

Eligibility: Open to residents of Wisconsin entering a college or university in the state who meet the requirements of both financial need and educational disadvantage. Financial need qualifications include 1) family contribution (a dependent student whose expected parent contribution is $200 or less or an independent student whose maximum academic year contribution is $200 or less); 2) Temporary Assistance to Needy Families (TANF) or Wisconsin Works (W2) benefits (a dependent student whose family is receiving TANF or W2 benefits or an independent student who is receiving TANF or W2 benefits); or 3) unemployment (a dependent student whose parents are ineligible for unemployment compensation and have no current income from employment, or an independent student and spouse, if married, who are ineligible for unemployment compensation and have no current income from employment). Educational disadvantage qualifications include students who are 1) minorities (African American, Native American, Hispanic, or southeast Asian); 2) enrolled in a special academic support program due to insufficient academic preparation; 3) a first–generation college student (neither parent graduated from a 4–year college or university); 4) disabled according to the Department of Workforce Development, the Division of Vocational Rehabilitation, or a Wisconsin college or university that uses the Americans with Disabilities Act definition; 5) currently or formerly incarcerated in a correctional institution; or 6) from an environmental and academic background that deters the pursuit of educational plans. Students already in college are not eligible.

Financial data: Stipends range up to $1,800 per year.

Duration: 1 year; may be renewed up to 4 additional years, provided the recipient continues to be a Wisconsin resident enrolled at least half time in a degree or certificate program, makes satisfactory academic progress, demonstrates financial need, and remains enrolled continuously from semester to semester and from year to year. If recipients withdraw from school or cease to attend classes for any reason (other than medical necessity), they may not reapply.

Number awarded: Varies each year.

Deadline: Deadline not specified.

1053 $ WISCONSIN TUITION GRANT

Wisconsin Higher Educational Aids Board
131 West Wilson Street, Suite 902
P.O. Box 7885
Madison, WI 53707–7885
Phone: (608) 267–2212; Fax: (608) 267–2808;
Email: Deanne.schulz@wisconsin.gov
Web: heab.state.wi.us/programs.html

Summary: To provide assistance to financially needy undergraduate students attending private institutions of higher education in Wisconsin or abroad.

Eligibility: Open to Wisconsin residents enrolled in independent nonprofit colleges and universities in the state. Students may study abroad if the tuition cost of the program is paid directly to the Wisconsin institution and the credits earned are acceptable by the institution as credit for the degree on which the student is working. Selection is based on financial need.

Financial data: Awards are based on financial need, but may not exceed tuition charged at the University of Wisconsin at Madison.

Duration: Up to 10 semesters.

Number awarded: Varies each year.

Deadline: Deadline not specified.

1054 $$ WISCONSIN VETERANS EDUCATION (VETED) REIMBURSEMENT GRANTS

Wisconsin Department of Veterans Affairs
201 West Washington Avenue
P.O. Box 7843
Madison, WI 53707–7843
Phone: (608) 266–1311; (800) WIS–VETS; Fax: (608) 267–0403;
Email: WDVAInfo@dva.state.wi.us
Web: www.dva.state.wi.us/Ben_VetEd.asp

Summary: To provide financial assistance for undergraduate education to Wisconsin veterans.

Eligibility: Open to current residents of Wisconsin who 1) were residents of the state when they entered or reentered active duty in the U.S. armed forces; or 2) have moved to the state and have been residents for any consecutive 12–month period after entry or reentry into service. Applicants must have served on active duty for at least 2 continuous years or for at least 90 days during specified wartime periods. They must be working full or part time on a degree, certificate of graduation, or course completion at an eligible campus of the University of Wisconsin, technical college, or approved private institution of higher education in Wisconsin or Minnesota. Their household income must be below $50,000 plus $1,000 for each dependent in excess of 2 dependents. Veterans seeking reimbursement through this program must first apply for Wisconsin G.I. Bill benefits. To qualify for reimbursement, they must achieve at least a 2.0 GPA or an average grade of "C" in the semester for which reimbursement is requested. Veterans may use this program up to 10 years after leaving active duty. Once a veteran reaches the 10–year delimiting date, he or she may "bank" up to 60 unused credits for part–time study.

Financial data: Eligible veterans are entitled to reimbursement of 100% of the costs of tuition and fees not covered by other grants, scholarships, or remissions, to a maximum of the UW–Madison rate for the same number of credits.

Duration: The amount of reimbursement depends on the time the veteran served on active duty: 30 credits or 2 semesters for 90 to 180 days of active service, 60 credits or 4 semesters for 181 to 730 days of active service, or 120 credits or 8 semesters for 731 days or more of active service.

Number awarded: Varies each year.

Deadline: Applications must be received within 60 days of the start of the course, semester, or term.

1055 WISCONSIN WOMEN'S ALLIANCE FOUNDATION SCHOLARSHIP

Community Foundation for the Fox Valley Region, Inc.
Attn: Scholarships
4455 West Lawrence Street
P.O. Box 563
Appleton, WI 54912–0563
Phone: (920) 830–1290; Fax: (920) 830–1293;
Email: scholarships@cffoxvalley.org
Web: www.cffoxvalley.org/page.aspx?pid=246

Summary: To provide financial assistance to mature women in Wisconsin who are working on an undergraduate or graduate degree at a school in any state.

Eligibility: Open to Wisconsin women who are 25 years of age or older. Applicants must be attending an accredited 2– or 4–year college, university, or technical college to work on an undergraduate or graduate degree. They must submit a personal statement of their reasons for working on a degree in their chosen field, including their special professional interests, goals, and purposes within that field. Selection is based on that statement, employment history, volunteer activities, professional and community activities, and financial need.

Financial data: The stipend ranges up to $1,000.

Duration: 1 year.

Number awarded: Normally, 3 each year.

Deadline: February of each year.

1056 $$ WOKSAPE OYATE: "WISDOM OF THE PEOPLE" DISTINGUISHED SCHOLAR AWARD

American Indian College Fund
Attn: Scholarship Department
8333 Greenwood Boulevard
Denver, CO 80221
Phone: (303) 426–8900; (800) 776–FUND; Fax: (303) 426–1200;
Email: scholarships@collegefund.org
Web: www.collegefund.org/content/full_circle_scholarships_listings

Summary: To provide financial assistance to Native American high school seniors who are the valedictorian or salutatorian of their class and planning to attend a Tribal College or University (TCU).

Eligibility: Open to American Indians or Alaska Natives who are graduating from high school as the valedictorian or salutatorian of their class. Applicants must be planning to enroll full time at an eligible TCU. Applications are available only online and include required essays on specified topics. Selection is based on exceptional academic achievement. U.S. citizenship is required.

Financial data: The stipend is $8,000. Funding is available only if the recipient maintains a GPA of 3.5 or higher.

Duration: 1 year.

Number awarded: 1 each year.

Deadline: May of each year.

1057 $$ WOKSAPE OYATE: "WISDOM OF THE PEOPLE" KEEPERS OF THE NEXT GENERATION AWARD

American Indian College Fund
Attn: Scholarship Department
8333 Greenwood Boulevard
Denver, CO 80221
Phone: (303) 426–8900; (800) 776–FUND; Fax: (303) 426–1200;
Email: scholarships@collegefund.org
Web: www.collegefund.org/content/full_circle_scholarships_listings

Summary: To provide financial assistance to Native Americans who are single parents and attending or planning to attend a Tribal College or University (TCU).

Eligibility: Open to American Indians or Alaska Natives who are single parents and enrolled or planning to enroll full time at an eligible TCU. Applicants must have a GPA of 2.0 or higher. Applications are available only online and include required essays on specified topics. Selection is based on exceptional academic achievement. U.S. citizenship is required.

Financial data: The stipend is $8,000.

Duration: 1 year.

Number awarded: 1 each year.

Deadline: May of each year.

1058 WOMEN MARINES ASSOCIATION SCHOLARSHIP PROGRAM

Women Marines Association
P.O. Box 377
Oaks, PA 19456–0377
Phone: (888) 525–1943;
Email: scholarship@womenmarines.org
Web: www.womenmarines.org/scholarships.aspx

Summary: To provide financial assistance for college or graduate school to students sponsored by members of the Women Marines Association (WMA).

Eligibility: Open to students who are sponsored by a WMA member and fall into 1 of the following categories: 1) have served or are serving in the U.S. Marine Corps, regular or Reserve; 2) are a direct descendant by blood or legal adoption or a stepchild of a Marine on active duty or who has served honorably in the U.S. Marine Corps, regular or Reserve; 3) are a sibling or a descendant of a sibling by blood or legal adoption or a stepchild of a Marine on active duty or who has served honorably in the U.S. Marine Corps, regular or Reserve; or 4) have completed 2 years in a Marine Corps JROTC program. WMA members

may sponsor an unlimited number of applicants per year. High school seniors must submit transcripts (GPA of 3.0 or higher) and SAT or ACT scores. Undergraduate and graduate students must have a GPA of 3.0 or higher.
Financial data: The stipend is $1,500 per year.
Duration: 1 year; may be renewed 1 additional year.
Number awarded: Varies each year.
Deadline: January of each year.

1059 WOMEN WHO MADE A DIFFERENCE SCHOLARSHIPS

Arizona Business and Professional Women's Foundation
Attn: Administrator
P.O. Box 32596
Phoenix, AZ 85064
Web: www.arizonabpwfoundation.com/scholarships.html
Summary: To provide financial assistance to women in Arizona who are attending or interested in attending a community college or university in the state.
Eligibility: Open to women, at least 25 years of age, who are attending a community college or university in Arizona. Applicants must fall into 1 of the following categories: women who have been out of the workforce and wish to upgrade their skills; women with no previous experience in the workforce who are seeking a marketable skill, and women who are currently employed who are interested in career advancement or change. Along with their application, they must submit 2 letters of recommendation, a statement of financial need (latest income tax return must be provided), a career goal statement, and their most recent transcript (when available). Preference is given to women who have been members of Arizona Business and Professional Women for 2 or more years.
Financial data: The stipend is $1,000.
Duration: 1 year.
Number awarded: 1 or more each year.
Deadline: February of each year.

1060 WOMEN'S ARMY CORPS VETERANS' ASSOCIATION SCHOLARSHIP

Women's Army Corps Veterans' Association
P.O. Box 5577
Fort McClellan, AL 36205–5577
Phone: (256) 820–6824;
Email: info@armywomen.org
Web: www.armywomen.org
Summary: To provide financial assistance for college to the relatives of Army military women.
Eligibility: Open to high school seniors who are the children, grandchildren, nieces, or nephews of Army service women. Applicants must have a cumulative GPA of 3.5 or higher and be planning to enroll full time at an accredited college or university in the United States. They must submit a 500–word biographical sketch that includes their future goals and how the scholarship would be used. Selection is based on academic achievement, leadership ability as expressed through co–curricular activities and community involvement, the biographical sketch, and recommendations. Financial need is not considered. U.S. citizenship is required.
Financial data: The stipend is $1,500.
Duration: 1 year.
Number awarded: 1 or more each year.
Deadline: April of each year.

1061 $ WOMEN'S INDEPENDENCE SCHOLARSHIP PROGRAM

Women's Independence Scholarship Program, Inc.
Attn: WISP Program
4900 Randall Parkway, Suite H
Wilmington, NC 28403
Phone: (910) 397–7742; (866) 255–7742; Fax: (910) 397–0023;
Email: nancy@wispinc.org
Web: www.wispinc.org/Programs/WISP/tabid/62/Default.aspx
Summary: To provide financial assistance for college or graduate school to women who are victims of partner abuse.
Eligibility: Open to women who are victims of partner abuse and have worked for at least 6 months with a nonprofit domestic violence victim services provider that is willing to sponsor them. Applicants must be interested in attending a vocational school, community college, 4–year college or university, or (in exceptional circumstances) graduate school as a full– or part–time student. They should have left an abusive partner at least 1 year previously; women who have been parted from their batterer for more than 5 years are also eligible, but funding for such applicants may be limited. Preference is given to single mothers with young children. Special consideration is given to applicants who plan to use their education to further the rights of, and options for, women and girls. Selection is based primarily on financial need. U.S. citizenship or permanent resident status is required.
Financial data: Stipends depend on the need of the recipient, but they are at least $250 and average $2,000 per academic term. First priority is given to funding for direct educational expenses (tuition, books, and fees), which is paid directly to the educational institution. Second priority is for assistance in reducing indirect financial barriers to education (e.g., child care, transportation), which is paid directly to the sponsoring agency.
Duration: 1 year; may be renewed if the recipient maintains a GPA of 2.75 or higher.
Number awarded: Varies each year.
Deadline: Applications may be submitted at any time, but they must be received at least 2 months before the start of the intended program.

1062 $$ WOMEN'S OPPORTUNITY AWARDS PROGRAM

Soroptimist International of the Americas
Attn: Program Department
1709 Spruce Street
Philadelphia, PA 19103–6103
Phone: (215) 893–9000; Fax: (215) 893–5200;
Email: siahq@soroptimist.org
Web: www.soroptimist.org/awards/awards.html
Summary: To provide financial assistance to women reentering the job market to upgrade their employment status through education.
Eligibility: Open to women who provide the primary financial support for their family. Applicants must have been accepted to a vocational/skills training program or an undergraduate degree program. They must reside in 1 of the 20 countries or territories (divided into 28 regions) that are part of Soroptimist International of the Americas. Along with their application, they must submit 1) a 300–word description of their career goals and how their education and/or skills training support those goals; 2) a 750–word essay on the economic and personal hardships they have faced and their plans to gain additional skills, training, and education; and 3) documentation of financial need.
Financial data: The award is $10,000.
Duration: The awards are issued each year and are nonrenewable.
Number awarded: In each of the 28 regions, the winner receives an award of $5,000; most regions grant additional $3,000 awards. From among the regional winners, 3 receive an additional award of $10,000 from Soroptimist International of the Americas. Since the program was established, it has awarded approximately $20 million in scholarships to more than 25,000 women.
Deadline: Applications must be submitted to regional contacts by November of each year.

1063 WOSL SCHOLARSHIPS FOR WOMEN

Women's Overseas Service League
Attn: Scholarship Committee
P.O. Box 124
Cedar Knolls, NJ 07927–0124
Email: kelsey@openix.com
Web: www.wosl.org/scholarships.htm
Summary: To provide financial assistance for college to women who are committed to a military or other public service career.
Eligibility: Open to women who are committed to a military or other public service career. Applicants must have completed at least 12 semester or 18 quarter hours of postsecondary study with a GPA of 2.5 or higher. They must be working on an academic degree (the program may be professional or technical in nature) and must agree to enroll for at least 6 semester or 9 quarter hours of study each academic period. Along with their application, they must submit a 250–word essay on their career goals. Financial need is considered in the selection process.
Financial data: Stipends range from $500 to $1,000 per year.
Duration: 1 year; may be renewed 1 additional year.
Deadline: February of each year.

1064 W.P. BLACK FUND SCHOLARSHIPS

Greater Kanawha Valley Foundation
Attn: Scholarship Program Officer
1600 Huntington Square

900 Lee Street East, 16th Floor
Charleston, WV 25301
Phone: (304) 346–3620; (800) 467–5909; Fax: (304) 346–3640;
Email: shoover@tgkvf.org
Web: www.tgkvf.org/page.aspx?pid=409

Summary: To provide financial assistance to residents of West Virginia who are interested in attending college in any state.

Eligibility: Open to residents of West Virginia who are attending or planning to attend a college or university anywhere in the country. Applicants must have an ACT score of 20 or higher, be able to demonstrate good moral character and extreme financial need, and have a GPA of 2.5 or higher.

Financial data: The stipend is $1,000 per year.

Duration: 1 year; may be renewed.

Number awarded: Varies each year; recently, 96 of these scholarships were awarded.

Deadline: January of each year.

1065 WSCA/CAREER CRUISING HIGH SCHOOL SCHOLARSHIPS

Wisconsin School Counselor Association
2830 Agriculture Drive
Madison, WI 53718
Phone: (608) 204–9825;
Email: admin@wscaweb.org
Web: www.wscaweb.org/site/scholarshipsandawards.asp

Summary: To provide financial assistance to high school seniors in Wisconsin who plan to attend college in any state.

Eligibility: Open to graduating seniors at public and private high schools in Wisconsin. Applicants must be planning to attend a 2– or 4–year college or university in any state. Along with their application, they must submit a 1–page essay describing how a school counselor or school counseling program has helped them plan, decide, resolve, or grow in some area of their life. Financial need is not considered in the selection process.

Financial data: The stipend is $1,000.

Duration: 1 year.

Number awarded: 4 each year.

Deadline: November of each year.

1066 $$ WYOMING COMBAT VETERAN SURVIVING ORPHAN TUITION BENEFIT

Wyoming Veterans Commission
Attn: Executive Director
5410 Bishop Boulevard
Cheyenne, WY 82009
Phone: (307) 777–8151; (800) 833–5987; Fax: (307) 777–8150;
Email: larry.barttelbort@wyo.gov
Web: sites.google.com

Summary: To provide financial assistance to children of deceased, POW, or MIA Wyoming veterans who are interested in attending college in the state.

Eligibility: Open to children of veterans whose parent had been a resident of Wyoming for at least 1 year at the time of entering service and received the armed forces expeditionary medal or a campaign medal for service in an armed conflict in a foreign country. The veteran parent must 1) have died during active service during armed conflict in a foreign country; 2) be listed officially as being a POW or MIA as a result of active service with the military forces of the United States; or 3) have been honorably discharged from the military and subsequently died of an injury or disease incurred while in service and was a Wyoming resident at the time of death. Applicants must have been younger than 21 years of age when the veteran died or was listed as POW or MIA and younger than 22 years of age when they enter college. They must be attending or planning to attend the University of Wyoming or a community college in the state.

Financial data: Qualifying veterans' children are eligible for free resident tuition at the University of Wyoming or at any of the state's community colleges.

Duration: Up to 10 semesters.

Number awarded: Varies each year.

Deadline: Applications may be submitted at any time, but they should be received 2 or 3 weeks before the beginning of the semester.

1067 $$ WYOMING COMBAT VETERAN SURVIVING SPOUSE TUITION BENEFIT

Wyoming Veterans Commission
Attn: Executive Director
5410 Bishop Boulevard
Cheyenne, WY 82009
Phone: (307) 777–8151; (800) 833–5987; Fax: (307) 777–8150;
Email: larry.barttelbort@wyo.gov
Web: sites.google.com

Summary: To provide financial assistance to surviving spouses of deceased, POW, or MIA Wyoming veterans who are interested in attending college in the state.

Eligibility: Open to spouses of veterans whose spouse had been a resident of Wyoming for at least 1 year at the time of entering service and received the armed forces expeditionary medal or a campaign medal for service in an armed conflict in a foreign country. The veteran spouse must 1) have died during active service during armed conflict in a foreign country; 2) be listed officially as being a POW or MIA as a result of active service with the military forces of the United States; or 3) have been honorably discharged from the military and subsequently died of an injury or disease incurred while in service and was a Wyoming resident at the time of death. Applicants must enroll at the University of Wyoming or a community college in the state within 10 years following the death of the combat veteran.

Financial data: Qualifying veterans' spouses are eligible for free resident tuition at the University of Wyoming or at any of the state's community colleges.

Duration: Up to 10 semesters.

Number awarded: Varies each year.

Deadline: Applications may be submitted at any time, but they should be received 2 or 3 weeks before the beginning of the semester.

1068 $$ WYOMING OVERSEAS COMBAT VETERAN TUITION BENEFIT

Wyoming Veterans Commission
Attn: Executive Director
5410 Bishop Boulevard
Cheyenne, WY 82009
Phone: (307) 777–8151; (800) 833–5987; Fax: (307) 777–8150;
Email: larry.barttelbort@wyo.gov
Web: sites.google.com

Summary: To provide financial assistance to Wyoming veterans who served in overseas combat anytime except during the Vietnam era and are interested in attending college in the state.

Eligibility: Open to Wyoming veterans who served anytime except during the Vietnam era and were residents of Wyoming for at least 1 year before entering military service. Applicants must have received an honorable discharge and have been awarded the armed forces expeditionary medal or other authorized service or campaign medal indicating service to the United States in an armed conflict in a foreign country. They must enroll at the University of Wyoming or a community college in the state within 10 years following completion of military service.

Financial data: Qualifying veterans are eligible for free resident tuition at the University of Wyoming or at any of the state's community colleges.

Duration: Up to 10 semesters.

Number awarded: Varies each year.

Deadline: Applications may be submitted at any time, but they should be received 2 or 3 weeks before the beginning of the semester.

1069 $$ WYOMING VIETNAM VETERAN SURVIVING CHILD TUITION BENEFIT

Wyoming Veterans Commission
Attn: Executive Director
5410 Bishop Boulevard
Cheyenne, WY 82009
Phone: (307) 777–8151; (800) 833–5987; Fax: (307) 777–8150;
Email: larry.barttelbort@wyo.gov
Web: sites.google.com

Summary: To provide financial assistance to children of deceased, POW, or MIA Wyoming veterans of the Vietnam era who are interested in attending college in the state.

Eligibility: Open to children of veterans whose parent had been a resident of Wyoming for at least 1 year at the time of entering service, served between August 5, 1964 and May 7, 1975, and received the Vietnam service medal. The veteran parent must 1) have died as a result of service–connected causes; 2) be listed officially as being a POW or MIA as a result of active service with the military forces of the United States; or 3) have been honorably discharged from the military and subsequently died of an injury or disease incurred while in service and was a Wyoming resident at the time of death. Applicants must be attending or planning to attend the University of Wyoming or a community college in the state.

Financial data: Qualifying veterans' children are eligible for free resident tuition at the University of Wyoming or at any of the state's community colleges.
Duration: Up to 10 semesters.
Number awarded: Varies each year.
Deadline: Applications may be submitted at any time, but they should be received 2 or 3 weeks before the beginning of the semester.

1070 $$ WYOMING VIETNAM VETERAN SURVIVING SPOUSE TUITION BENEFIT

Wyoming Veterans Commission
Attn: Executive Director
5410 Bishop Boulevard
Cheyenne, WY 82009
Phone: (307) 777–8151; (800) 833–5987; Fax: (307) 777–8150;
Email: larry.barttelbort@wyo.gov
Web: sites.google.com

Summary: To provide financial assistance to surviving spouses of deceased, POW, or MIA Wyoming veterans of the Vietnam era who are interested in attending college in the state.
Eligibility: Open to spouses of veterans whose spouse had been a resident of Wyoming for at least 1 year at the time of entering service, served between August 5, 1964 and May 7, 1975, and received the Vietnam service medal. The veteran spouse must 1) have died as a result of service–connected causes; 2) be listed officially as being a POW or MIA as a result of active service with the military forces of the United States; or 3) have been honorably discharged from the military and subsequently died of an injury or disease incurred while in service and was a Wyoming resident at the time of death. Applicants must be attending or planning to attend the University of Wyoming or a community college in the state.
Financial data: Qualifying veterans' surviving spouses are eligible for free resident tuition at the University of Wyoming or at any of the state's community colleges.
Duration: Up to 10 semesters.
Number awarded: Varies each year.
Deadline: Applications may be submitted at any time, but they should be received 2 or 3 weeks before the beginning of the semester.

1071 $$ WYOMING VIETNAM VETERAN TUITION BENEFIT

Wyoming Veterans Commission
Attn: Executive Director
5410 Bishop Boulevard
Cheyenne, WY 82009
Phone: (307) 777–8151; (800) 833–5987; Fax: (307) 777–8150;
Email: larry.barttelbort@wyo.gov
Web: sites.google.com

Summary: To provide financial assistance to Wyoming veterans who served during the Vietnam era and are interested in attending college in the state.
Eligibility: Open to Wyoming veterans who 1) served on active duty with the U.S. armed forces between August 5, 1964 and May 7, 1975; 2) received a Vietnam service medal between those dates; 3) received an honorable discharge; 4) have lived in Wyoming for at least 1 year; and 5) have exhausted their veterans' benefits entitlement or for some other reason are no longer eligible for U.S. Department of Veterans Affairs benefits. Applicants must be attending or planning to attend the University of Wyoming or a community college in the state.
Financial data: Qualifying veterans are eligible for free resident tuition at the University of Wyoming or at any of the state's community colleges.
Duration: Up to 10 semesters.
Number awarded: Varies each year.
Deadline: Applications may be submitted at any time, but they should be received 2 or 3 weeks before the beginning of the semester.

1072 $$ YELLOW RIBBON PROGRAM OF THE POST–9/11 GI BILL

Department of Veterans Affairs
Attn: Veterans Benefits Administration
810 Vermont Avenue, N.W.
Washington, DC 20420
Phone: (202) 418–4343; (888) GI–BILL1
Web: www.gibill.va.gov

Summary: To provide financial assistance to veterans and their dependents who qualify for the Post–9/11 GI Bill and wish to attend a high cost private or out–of–state public institution.
Eligibility: Open to veterans who 1) served on active duty for at least 36 aggregate months after September 11, 2001; or 2) were honorably discharged for a service–connected disability and served at least 30 continuous days after September 11, 2001. Military personnel currently on active duty and their spouses may qualify for Post–9/11 GI Bill benefits but are not eligible for the Yellow Ribbon Program. This program is available to veterans who qualify for those benefits at the 100% rate, the children of those veterans to whom they wish to transfer their benefits, and the children and spouses of active–duty personnel who qualify for benefits at the 100% rate to whom they wish to transfer those benefits. Applicants must be working on or planning to work on an undergraduate or graduate degree at a private or out–of–state public institution that charges tuition in excess of the $17,500 cap imposed by the Post–9/11 GI Bill and that has agreed with the Department of Veterans Affairs (VA) to participate in this program.
Financial data: Colleges and universities that charge more than $17,500 per academic year in tuition and fees (or a higher amount at schools in Arizona, Michigan, New Hampshire, New York, Pennsylvania, South Carolina, and Texas) agree to waive tuition (up to 50%) for qualifying veterans and dependents. The amount that the college or university waives is matched by VA.
Duration: Most participants receive up to 36 months of entitlement under this program. Benefits are payable for up to 15 years following release from active duty.
Number awarded: Varies each year.
Deadline: Deadline not specified.

1073 YOUNG HEROES SCHOLARSHIPS

Wipe Out Kids' Cancer
Attn: Young Heroes Scholarships
1349 Empire Central, Suite 240
Dallas, TX 75247
Phone: (214) 987–4662; Fax: (214) 987–4668;
Email: ecostolo@wokc.org
Web: www.wokc.org/YoungHeroesScholarships_16.aspx

Summary: To provide financial assistance for college to pediatric cancer survivors.
Eligibility: Open to pediatric cancer survivors who are enrolled or planning to enroll at a college or university. Applicants must submit a 500–word essay on how their personal journey with cancer has prepared them for college. Selection is based on the content, originality, and overall impression of the essay (80%), and school and community recommendations (20%).
Financial data: The stipend is $1,000. Winners also receive a laptop and printer.
Duration: 1 year.
Number awarded: 10 each year.
Deadline: February of each year.

1074 $$ YOUNG HUMANITARIAN AWARD

YouthLINC
1140 East Brickyard Road, Suite 76
Salt Lake City, UT 84106
Phone: (801) 467–4417; Fax: (801) 467–1982;
Email: youthlink@xmission.com
Web: www.youthlinc.org/yha/index.html

Summary: To provide financial assistance to high school and undergraduate students in Utah who demonstrate outstanding community service.
Eligibility: Open to students enrolled at high schools, colleges, and universities in Utah. Candidates must have excelled in their efforts to provide humanitarian service to their communities. Their activities must have been coordinated through the Utah nonprofit organization YouthLINC (Youth serving the Local and International Needs Community).
Financial data: The winner receives a $5,000 scholarship to be used for tuition at an undergraduate or graduate college or university. Runners–up receive $1,000 scholarships for the same purpose.
Duration: The awards are presented annually.
Number awarded: 1 winner and 3 runners–up are selected each year.
Deadline: October of each year.

1075 YOUNG LADIES' RADIO LEAGUE SCHOLARSHIPS

Foundation for Amateur Radio, Inc.
Attn: Scholarship Committee
P.O. Box 911
Columbia, MD 21044–0911
Phone: (410) 552–2652; Fax: (410) 981–5146;
Email: dave.prestel@gmail.com
Web: www.farweb.org/scholarships

Summary: To provide funding to female licensed radio amateurs who are interested in earning a bachelor's or graduate degree in the United States.
Eligibility: Open to female radio amateurs who have at least an FCC Technician Class license or equivalent foreign authorization. Applicants must intend to work full time on a bachelor's or graduate degree at a college or university in the United States. There are no restrictions on the course of study or residency location. Non–U.S. amateurs are eligible. Preference is given to students working on a degree in communications, electronics, or related arts and sciences. Financial need is considered in the selection process.
Financial data: The stipend is $1,500.
Duration: 1 year.
Number awarded: 2 each year.
Deadline: April of each year.

1076 YOURLOCALSECURITY.COM BLOGGING SCHOLARSHIP

Clear Link Technologies, LLC
Attn: YourLocalSecurity.com
5202 West Douglas Corrigan Way, Suite 300
Salt Lake City, UT 84116
Phone: (866) 238–9934
Web: yourlocalsecurity.com/scholarship
Summary: To recognize and reward, with scholarships, high school seniors and college students who submit outstanding blogs on topics of current interest.
Eligibility: Open to graduating high school seniors and full–time students at 2– or 4–year colleges and universities who are U.S. citizens or permanent residents. Applicants must have a GPA of 2.5 or higher; high school seniors must also submit SAT and/or ACT scores. They must post on their blog platform an essay of 300 words or more on a topic that changes each semester; recently, students were asked to pick their favorite presidential candidate and explain why that candidate has their vote. Judges select the winner on the basis of creativity, thoughtfulness, and insight.
Financial data: The award is a $1,000 scholarship.
Duration: The competition is held each semester (fall and spring).
Number awarded: 2 each year (1 each semester).
Deadline: June of each year for fall semester; December of each year for spring semester.

1077 $$ YOUTH COURAGE AWARDS

Colin Higgins Foundation
Attn: Youth Courage Awards
c/o Tides Foundation New York Office
55 Exchange Place, Suite 402
New York, NY 10005
Phone: (212) 509–4975; Fax: (212) 509–1059;
Email: garyschwartz@colinhiggins.org
Web: www.colinhiggins.org/courageawards/index.cfm
Summary: To recognize and reward young people who have shown courage in the face of adversity related to discrimination against members of the lesbian, gay, bisexual, transgender, and questioning (LGBTQ) communities.
Eligibility: Open to young people under 24 years of age who are 1) LGBTQ youth who have "bravely stood up to hostility and intolerance based on their sexual orientation and triumphed over bigotry;" or 2) allies who are working to end homophobia and discrimination against LGBTQ communities. They must be nominated; letters of nomination must include 350–word essays describing why the nominee represents the ideals of this award. Self–nominations are not accepted.
Financial data: The award is a $10,000 grant.
Duration: The awards are presented annually.
Number awarded: 2 or 3 each year.
Deadline: February of each year.

1078 $$ YOUTH OF THE YEAR AWARD

National Exchange Club
Attn: Foundation
3050 Central Avenue
Toledo, OH 43606–1700
Phone: (419) 535–3232; (800) XCHANGE; Fax: (419) 535–1989
Web: www.exchangeclubfoundation.org/scholarship.htm
Summary: To recognize and reward, with college scholarships outstanding high school seniors.
Eligibility: Open to outstanding high school seniors. This competition starts at the local level, where Exchange Clubs select their own Youth of the Month and (from them) Youth of the Year winners. Then, clubs nominate their Youth of the Year winners for a district competition. The district winners then compete on the national level. National candidates must be high school seniors who are qualified for graduation from public, parochial, or private schools and who have been selected Youth of the Year winners on both the club and district levels. Along with their application, they must submit an essay (from 800 to 1,200 words) on a topic that changes annually. Selection is based on school participation , including student government, newspaper or annual, athletic teams, musical activities, debate activities, stage productions (160 points), community service activities (40 points), grades (200 points), personal achievements and awards (160 points), and the essay (300 points).
Financial data: The winner receives $10,000, to be used for educational purposes. Half the award is paid at the sponsor's national convention in the year of the competition and the second installment when the winner registers for his or her second year of college.
Duration: The award is presented annually.
Number awarded: 1 each year.
Deadline: May of each year.

1079 $ ZELL MILLER SCHOLARSHIPS

Georgia Student Finance Commission
Attn: Scholarships and Grants Division
2082 East Exchange Place, Suite 200
Tucker, GA 30084–5305
Phone: (770) 724–9000; (800) 505–GSFC; Fax: (770) 724–9089;
Email: gacollege411@gsfc.org
Web: www.gacollege411.org
Summary: To provide financial assistance to exceptionally outstanding students who are attending or planning to attend a college or university in Georgia.
Eligibility: Open to residents of Georgia who are enrolled or planning to enroll at a college or university within the state. Students who are applying as seniors at eligible high schools or home schools must have at least a 3.7 cumulative GPA and minimum scores of 1200 on the mathematics and critical reading portions of the SAT or 26 on the ACT. Students who graduate from an ineligible high school or home study program may also be eligible if they 1) score at least 1200 on the mathematics and critical reading SAT or 26 on the ACT; and then 2) complete the first year of college with a GPA of 3.3 or higher. Students who are applying for the first time as college students must have earned a GPA of 3.3 or higher in college regardless of their high school GPA. U.S. citizenship or eligible noncitizen status is required.
Financial data: HOPE Scholars who attend University System of Georgia institutions receive stipends that vary by institution and number of units completed, to a maximum of $3,641 for full–time enrollment at designated universities. At institutions in the Technical College System of Georgia, the stipend is $1,125 per year. The stipend for HOPE Scholarships at private colleges and universities is $4,000 per year for full–time study or $2,000 per year for half–time study. Funds may be used only for tuition and mandatory fees.
Duration: 1 year; may be renewed for up to 3 additional years if the recipient maintains a cumulative GPA of 3.3 or higher in college.
Number awarded: Varies each year.
Deadline: Applications must be submitted on or before the last day of the academic term.

1080 ZONTA CLUB OF BANGOR SCHOLARSHIPS

Zonta Club of Bangor
c/o Barbara A. Cardone
P.O. Box 1904
Bangor, ME 04402–1904
Web: www.zontaclubofbangor.org/?area=scholarship
Summary: To provide financial assistance to women attending or planning to attend college in Maine and major in any field.
Eligibility: Open to women who are attending or planning to attend an accredited 2– or 4–year college in Maine. Applicants may major in any field. Along with their application, they must submit brief essays on 1) their goals in seeking higher education and their plans for the future; and 2) any school and community activities that have been of particular importance to them and why they found them worthwhile. Financial need may be considered in the selection process.
Financial data: The stipend is $1,000.
Duration: 1 year.
Number awarded: 2 each year.
Deadline: March of each year.

1081 $ AAF MINORITY/DISADVANTAGED SCHOLARSHIP PROGRAM

American Institute of Architects
Attn: American Architectural Foundation
1799 New York Avenue, N.W.
Washington, DC 20006–5292
Phone: (202) 626–7511; Fax: (202) 626–7420;
Email: scholarships@aia.org
Web: www.archfoundation.org

Summary: To provide financial assistance to high school and college students from minority and/or disadvantaged backgrounds who are interested in studying architecture in college.

Eligibility: Open to students from minority and/or disadvantaged backgrounds who are high school seniors, students in a community college or technical school transferring to an accredited architectural program, or college freshmen entering a professional degree program at an accredited program of architecture. Students who have completed 1 or more years of a 4–year college curriculum are not eligible. Initially, candidates must be nominated by 1 of the following organizations or persons: an individual architect or firm, a chapter of the American Institute of Architects (AIA), a community design center, a guidance counselor or teacher, the dean or professor at an accredited school of architecture, or the director of a community or civic organization. Nominees are reviewed and eligible candidates are invited to complete an application form in which they write an essay describing the reasons they are interested in becoming an architect and provide documentation of academic excellence and financial need. Selection is based primarily on financial need.

Financial data: Stipends range from $3,000 to $4,000 per year, depending upon individual need. Students must apply for supplementary funds from other sources.

Duration: 9 months; may be renewed for up to 2 additional years.

Number awarded: Up to 5 each year.

Deadline: April of each year.

1082 $$ ABE VORON SCHOLARSHIP

Broadcast Education Association
Attn: Scholarships
1771 N Street, N.W.
Washington, DC 20036–2891
Phone: (202) 429–3935; (888) 380–7222; Fax: (202) 775–2981;
Email: BEAMemberServices@nab.org
Web: www.beaweb.org/scholarships.htm

Summary: To provide financial assistance to upper–division and graduate students who are interested in preparing for a career in radio broadcasting.

Eligibility: Open to juniors, seniors, and graduate students enrolled full time at a college or university where at least 1 department is an institutional member of the Broadcast Education Association. Applicants must be studying for a career in radio. Selection is based on evidence that the applicant possesses integrity, superior academic ability, potential to be an outstanding electronic media professional, and a sense of personal and professional responsibility.

Financial data: The stipend is $5,000.

Duration: 1 year; nonrenewable.

Number awarded: 2 each year.

Deadline: October of each year.

1083 ACADEMY OF SPECIAL DREAMS FOUNDATION COLLEGE SCHOLARSHIP FUND

Academy of Special Dreams Foundation
115 West California Boulevard, Suite 326
Pasadena, CA 91105
Email: specialacademy@gmail.com
Web: www.specialacademy.org/scholarships

Summary: To provide financial assistance to college students who have a disability and are majoring in a field of art.

Eligibility: Open to students who have a disability and are enrolled or planning to enroll full or part time at a college, university, trade school, art school, or other art degree program. Applicants must be majoring or planning to major in any field of art (e.g., design, painting, drawing, photography, sculpture, video, animation). They must be lawful residents of the United States. Along with their application, they must submit 1) a statement from their physician or other medical provider describing their disability; 2) a portfolio of at least 5 unique works of art; 3) a personal statement describing their commitment to art.

Financial data: Stipends are $1,000, $500, or $250.

Duration: 1 year.

Number awarded: Varies each year.

Deadline: Applications may be submitted at any time.

1084 $ ACADEMY OF TELEVISION ARTS & SCIENCES COLLEGE TELEVISION AWARDS

Academy of Television Arts & Sciences Foundation
Attn: Education Department
5220 Lankershim Boulevard
North Hollywood, CA 91601–3109
Phone: (818) 754–2820; Fax: (818) 761–ATAS;
Email: ctasupport@emmys.org
Web: www.emmysfoundation.org/college–television–awards

Summary: To recognize and reward outstanding college student videos.

Eligibility: Open to undergraduate and graduate students currently enrolled at a college, university, or community college. U.S. citizenship is not required, but all applicants must be enrolled at schools in the United States. All entries must have been produced for school–related classes, groups, or projects. Competitions are held in the following categories: 1) alternative; 2) animation (all forms); 3) children's; 4) comedy; 5) commercial; 6) documentary; 7) drama; 8) magazine; 9) music (best composition); 10) music (best use of music); 11) narrative series (comedy or drama); and 12) newscast. Entries in the comedy, documentary, drama, and narrative series category may not exceed 1 hour. Entries in the animation, music, children's, newscast, and magazine categories may not exceed 30 minutes. Commercial entries may not exceed 1 minute and must advertise a product or service. For the narrative series category, at least 6 episodes must have been produced and 2 episodes must be submitted. The alternative category is open to various programming genres such as nonfiction, reality, dating/relationship, game shows, talk shows, hidden camera, or variety; at least 6 episodes must have been produced during the eligibility period and the running time may not exceed 1 hour. The children's category must be targeted for preschool through 11 years of age.

Financial data: In each category, first place is $2,000, second $1,000, and third $500. The Directing Award is $1,000 and the Seymour Bricker Family Humanitarian Award of $4,000 is presented to the first–place winner from any category whose work best represents a humanitarian concern.

Duration: The competition is held annually.

Number awarded: Up to 38 each year: 1 first–place winner, 1 second–place winner, and 1 third–place winner in each category plus the 2 special awards.

Deadline: January of each year.

1085 ACP REPORTER OF THE YEAR AWARDS

Associated Collegiate Press
Attn: ACP Contest
2221 University Avenue S.E., Suite 121
Minneapolis, MN 55414
Phone: (612) 625–8335; Fax: (612) 626–0720;
Email: info@studentpress.org
Web: www.studentpress.org/acp/contests.html

Summary: To recognize and reward outstanding reporting by journalism students at college newspapers that are members of the Associated Collegiate Press (ACP).

Eligibility: Open to reporters enrolled as full–time students and working on the staff of an ACP member publication. Applicants must submit copies of their 3 best single news or feature stories published during the preceding academic year. Stories must be the work of 1 reporter, although 1 of the 3 may have been published under a shared byline. The stories may be of any length. Only 1 student from each newspaper may enter the contest. Reporters compete in separate categories for 2–year colleges and 4–year colleges and universities. Selection is based on significance and news worthiness of the stories, quality and depth of reporting, quality of quotes, quality of writing, quality of editing, and AP style usage.

Financial data: For each category, first prize is $1,000, second $500, and third $250.

Duration: The competition is held annually.

Number awarded: 6 each year: 3 in each category.

Deadline: June of each year.

1086 $$ ACT POSTER CONTEST

American College Testing
Attn: Student Services
2727 Scott Boulevard
P.O. Box 414

Iowa City, IA 52243–0414
Phone: (319) 337–1270
Web: www.actstudent.org/postercontest
Summary: To recognize and reward, with college scholarships, high school students who submit outstanding posters on taking the ACT examination.
Eligibility: Open to juniors and seniors at high schools in the United States who plan to attend a 2– or 4–year college or university in the next 2 years. Applicants must submit a poster that features the ACT logo and promotes the theme of attending college and taking the ACT examination as their college entrance test. Selection is based on creativity (25%), visual appeal (25%), and overall content (50%).
Financial data: Awards are $5,000 for first, $2,500 for second, and $1,000 for third. Funds may be used as scholarships for books and tuition only.
Duration: Awards are presented annually.
Number awarded: 3 each year.
Deadline: January of each year.

1087 $ AD CLUB SCHOLARSHIP
Community Foundation for the Greater Capital Region
Attn: Scholarship Coordinator
Six Tower Place
Albany, NY 12203
Phone: (518) 446–9638; Fax: (518) 446–9708;
Email: info@cfgcr.org
Web: www.cfgcr.org/scholarships.php
Summary: To provide financial assistance to high school seniors and current undergraduate students from any state who are attending or planning to attend colleges in the capital region of New York and major in fields related to communications.
Eligibility: Open to 1) high school seniors who plan to enroll as a full–time student at an accredited 4–year college in the capital region; and 2) full–time undergraduate and graduate students currently enrolled at an accredited college in the region. Applicants must be studying or planning to study in a communications–related field of study, such as advertising, electronic media, marketing, graphic arts, public relations, or journalism. Along with their application, they must submit 3 project samples, a letter on their personal goals and how those related to the communications field, 2 letters of recommendation, transcripts, and financial date. Selection is based on creativity as demonstrated in work samples (30%), the applicant's letter (20%) GPA (10%), financial need (20%), and letters of recommendation (20%).
Financial data: The stipend is $3,000. Funds are paid directly to the recipient's school.
Duration: 1 year.
Number awarded: 1 or 2 each year.
Deadline: March of each year.

1088 ADVERTISING EDUCATION FOUNDATION OF HOUSTON SCHOLARSHIPS
American Advertising Federation–Houston
Attn: Advertising Education Foundation of Houston
P.O. Box 27592
Houston, TX 77227
Phone: (713) ADS–9999; Fax: (713) 522–8327;
Email: adclub@aaf–houston.org
Web: www.houstonadscholarships.com
Summary: To provide financial assistance to undergraduate and graduate students at colleges and universities in designated states who are preparing for a career in a field related to advertising.
Eligibility: Open to students working on an undergraduate or graduate degree in advertising, commercial art, communications, interactive marketing, journalism, public relations, radio/TV, or a related field. Applicants must be attending a college or university in Arkansas, Louisiana, Oklahoma, or Texas. They must have a GPA of 3.0 or higher in their major and 2.75 or higher overall and a demonstrated record of commitment to the communications industry with internship and work experience, industry activities, and participation in communications–focused professional or campus organizations. Along with their application, they must submit a brief essay that describes their career goals, where they see themselves 5 years after graduation, and how this scholarship will help them achieve their goals. Selection is based primarily on the essay and GPA; secondary consideration is given to the steps taken to prepare for participation in the industry, financial need, community and collegiate activities, relevant organizations joined, and internships or work experience.
Financial data: The stipend is $1,500.
Duration: 1 year.
Number awarded: 11 each year.
Deadline: February of each year.

1089 AFFMA GRANTS
Arpa Foundation for Film, Music and Art
2919 Maxwell Street
Los Angeles, CA 90027
Phone: (323) 663–1882; Fax: (323) 663–1882
Web: affma.org/film–festival/winners
Summary: To provide funding to student and professional filmmakers, writers, musicians, photographers, and artists of Armenian descent.
Eligibility: Open to students and professionals of Armenian descent. Applicants must be preparing for a career as a filmmaker, writer, artist, photographer, or musician.
Financial data: Grants are typically $1,000.
Duration: 1 year; nonrenewable.
Number awarded: Varies each year; recently, 4 of these grants were awarded.
Deadline: March of each year.

1090 AFRO–ACADEMIC, CULTURAL, TECHNOLOGICAL AND SCIENTIFIC OLYMPICS (ACT–SO)
National Association for the Advancement of Colored People
Attn: ACT–SO Director
4805 Mt. Hope Drive
Baltimore, MD 21215
Phone: (410) 580–5650; (877) NAACP–98;
Email: ACTSO@naacpnet.org
Web: www.naacp.org/programs/entry/act–so
Summary: To recognize and reward (with college scholarships) outstanding African American high school students who distinguish themselves in the Afro–Academic, Cultural, Technological and Scientific Olympics (ACT–SO) program.
Eligibility: Open to high school students (grades 9–12) of African descent who are U.S. citizens and amateurs in the category in which they wish to participate. Competitions are held in 26 categories in 5 general areas: humanities (music composition, original essay, playwriting, and poetry), sciences (biology and microbiology, chemistry and biochemistry, computer science, earth and space science, engineering, mathematics, medicine and health, and physics), performing arts (dance, dramatics, music instrumental/classical, music instrumental/contemporary, music vocal/classical, music vocal/contemporary, and oratory), visual arts (architecture, drawing, filmmaking, painting, photography, and sculpture), and business (entrepreneurship). Competition is first conducted by local chapters of the NAACP; winners in each event at the local level then compete at the national level.
Financial data: In each category, the first–prize winner receives a gold medal and a $1,000 scholarship, the second–prize winner receives a silver medal and a $750 scholarship, and the third–prize winner receives a bronze medal and a $500 scholarship.
Duration: The competition is held annually.
Number awarded: 78 each year: 3 in each of 26 categories.
Deadline: Local competitions usually take place between February and April. The national finals are held each year in July.

1091 AGO/QUIMBY REGIONAL COMPETITIONS FOR YOUNG ORGANISTS
American Guild of Organists
475 Riverside Drive, Suite 1260
New York, NY 10115
Phone: (212) 870–2310; Fax: (212) 870–2163;
Email: info@agohq.org
Web: www.agohq.org/competitions/index.html
Summary: To recognize and reward outstanding student organists.
Eligibility: Open to student organists 23 years of age or younger. Competitions are held in each of the 9 regions of the American Guild of Organists (AGO); contestants may enter the region either where they reside or where they attend school. Applicants must play an assigned repertoire with a total performance time up to 40 minutes. Students first compete in their local chapter; winners advance to the regional competitions.
Financial data: Each region awards a cash prize of $1,000 to the first–place winner and $500 to the second–place winner.
Duration: The competition is held biennially, in odd–numbered years.
Number awarded: 18 each year: a first and second prize in each AGO region.

Deadline: Competitors must register with their chapter by mid–January of each odd–numbered year.

1092 AINA SWAN CUTLER NEW ENGLAND MUSIC SCHOLARSHIP

Finlandia Foundation–Boston Chapter
c/o Edith Eash
80 Potter Road
Lexington, MA 02421
Phone: (781) 652–0154;
Email: syrjalaeash@rcn.net
Web: sites.google.com/site/finlandiafoundationboston/scholarships

Summary: To provide financial assistance to residents of New England who are of Finnish heritage and studying music.

Eligibility: Open to students from the New England states who have a Finnish–American heritage. Applicants must be studying music, either classical or jazz. Hard rock and electronic music without a melody are not eligible. Along with their application, they must submit information on their college experience, background and performances, extracurricular and work activities (especially those related to their musical talents), language proficiency, and Finnish ancestry.

Financial data: The stipend is $1,500.

Duration: 1 year.

Number awarded: 1 each year.

Deadline: May of each year.

1093 $ AIR FORCE BAND OF LIBERTY MUSICAL EXCELLENCE SCHOLARSHIP

Hanscom Spouses' Club
Attn: Scholarship Committee Chair
P.O. Box 557
Bedford, MA 01730
Phone: (781) 429–2977;
Email: scholarship@hanscomsc.org
Web: www.hanscomsc.org/HSC/HSC_Scholarship.html

Summary: To provide financial assistance to high school seniors who are children of military personnel or veterans in New England, have demonstrated proficiency in music, and plan to attend college in any state.

Eligibility: Open to dependents of active–duty, retired, and deceased members of any branch of the armed forces, including Reservists and National Guard members who were activated during the school year. Applicants must be graduating high school seniors who 1) have a valid military identification card and reside in New England or 2) are a dependent whose military sponsor is stationed at Hanscom Air Force Base. They must be planning to attend a 2– or 4–year college or university in any state; they are not required to major in music, but they must be able to demonstrate accomplishment in at least 1 of the following categories: brass, classical guitar, jazz, mallet percussion, piano, strings, woodwinds, or voice. Along with their application, they must submit 1) a 2–page essay on their educational goals, how their educational experience will help prepare them to pursue future goals, and how they intend to apply their education to better their community; 2) a 2–page essay specifically addressing their music background, experience, and goals; and 3) a solo recording of their playing or singing in digital format (CD, DVD, flash drive) with or without accompaniment. Selection is based on merit.

Financial data: Recently, stipends of all scholarships offered by this sponsor averaged more than $2,000.

Duration: 1 year; nonrenewable.

Number awarded: Varies each year; recently, the sponsor awarded a total of 16 high school senior scholarships.

Deadline: March of each year.

1094 AL NEUHARTH FREE SPIRIT SCHOLARSHIP AND CONFERENCE PROGRAM

Freedom Forum
Attn: Manager, Free Spirit Program
555 Pennsylvania Avenue, N.W.
Washington, DC 20001
Phone: (202) 292–6271; Fax: (202) 292–6265;
Email: freespirit@freedomforum.org
Web: www.freespirit.org

Summary: To provide financial assistance for college to high school journalists who demonstrate a "free spirit."

Eligibility: Open to high school juniors who are active in high school journalism. Applicants must be planning to attend college to prepare for a career in journalism. They must demonstrate qualities of a "free spirit" in their academic or personal life. A "free spirit" is defined as "a risk–taker, a visionary, an innovative leader, an entrepreneur, or a courageous achiever who accomplishes great things beyond his or her normal circumstances." Along with their application, they must submit 2 essays of 500 words each: 1) explaining why they want to prepare for a career in journalism; and 2) describing their specific qualities as a free spirit and their experiences and/or challenges that make them a free spirit. U.S. citizenship or permanent resident status is required. Financial need is not considered in the selection process.

Financial data: The stipend is $1,000.

Duration: 1 year.

Number awarded: 51 each year: 1 from each state and the District of Columbia.

Deadline: February of each year.

1095 $ AL SPRAGUE MEMORIAL SCHOLARSHIP OF MASSACHUSETTS

Massachusetts Broadcasters Association
43 Riverside Avenue
PMB 401
Medford, MA 02155
Phone: (800) 471–1875; Fax: (800) 471–1876;
Email: info@massbroadcasters.org
Web: www.massbroadcasters.org/students/index.cfm

Summary: To provide financial assistance to Massachusetts residents interested in attending college in any state to prepare for a career in broadcasting.

Eligibility: Open to residents of Massachusetts who are in the process of enrolling or are currently enrolled full time at an accredited institution of higher learning in any state. Applicants must be preparing for a career in broadcasting. Along with their application, they must submit 150–word essays on 1) why they have chosen to prepare for a career in a broadcast–related field; and 2) why they believe they are a good candidate for this scholarship. The award is presented to the applicant who shows the most promise in industry advocacy, leadership, and entrepreneurship. Financial need is also considered.

Financial data: The stipend is $3,000. Checks are made payable to the recipient and the recipient's school.

Duration: 1 year.

Number awarded: 1 each year.

Deadline: March of each year.

1096 $$ AL SPRAGUE MEMORIAL SCHOLARSHIP OF NEW HAMPSHIRE

New Hampshire Association of Broadcasters
707 Chestnut Street
Manchester, NH 03104
Phone: (603) 627–9600; Fax: (603) 627–9603;
Email: info@nhab.org
Web: www.nhab.org/students/index.cfm

Summary: To provide financial assistance to New Hampshire residents interested in attending college in any state to prepare for a career in broadcasting.

Eligibility: Open to residents of New Hampshire who are in the process of enrolling or are currently enrolled full time at an accredited institution of higher learning in any state. Applicants must be preparing for a career in broadcasting. Along with their application, they must submit 150–word essays on 1) why they have chosen to prepare for a career in a broadcast–related field; and 2) why they believe they are a good candidate for this scholarship. The award is presented to the applicant who shows the most promise in industry advocacy, leadership, and entrepreneurship. Financial need is also considered in the selection process.

Financial data: The stipend is $5,000. Checks are made payable to the recipient and the recipient's school.

Duration: 1 year.

Number awarded: 1 each year.

Deadline: March of each year.

1097 $$ ALABAMA CONCRETE INDUSTRIES ASSOCIATION SCHOLARSHIPS

Alabama Concrete Industries Association
Attn: President
1745 Platt Place
Montgomery, AL 36117

Phone: (334) 265–0501; (800) 732–9118; Fax: (334) 265–2250;
Email: jsorrell@alconcrete.org
Web: www.alconcrete.org/scholarships.aspx
Summary: To provide financial assistance to students from any state majoring in architecture, building sciences, or engineering in Alabama.
Eligibility: Open to students from any state entering their senior year at colleges and universities in Alabama. Applicants must be enrolled in an accredited program in architecture, engineering, or building sciences. Selection is based on academic and extracurricular activity record.
Financial data: The stipend is $8,000.
Duration: 1 year.
Number awarded: 2 each year.
Deadline: November of each year.

1098 $$ ALABAMA JUNIOR AND COMMUNITY COLLEGE PERFORMING ARTS SCHOLARSHIPS

Alabama Commission on Higher Education
Attn: Grants Coordinator
100 North Union Street
P.O. Box 302000
Montgomery, AL 36130–2000
Phone: (334) 242–2273;
Email: cheryl.newton@ache.alabama.gov
Web: www.ache.alabama.gov/StudentAsst/Programs.htm
Summary: To provide financial assistance to performing artists in Alabama interested in attending a junior or community college in the state.
Eligibility: Open to full–time students enrolled in public junior and community colleges in Alabama. Selection is based on artistic talent as determined through competitive auditions.
Financial data: Awards cover up to the cost of in–state tuition.
Number awarded: Varies each year.
Deadline: Deadline not specified.

1099 ALASKA PROFESSIONAL COMMUNICATORS MEMORIAL SCHOLARSHIP

Alaska Professional Communicators
c/o Connie Huff, Scholarship Manager
P.O. Box 100441
Anchorage, AK 99510–0441
Phone: (907) 550–8464;
Email: chuff@alaskapublic.org
Web: www.akpresswomen.com/scholarships.php
Summary: To provide financial assistance to residents of Alaska enrolled as undergraduate students at a school in any state and majoring in journalism or public communications fields.
Eligibility: Open to residents of Alaska enrolled at 4–year colleges and universities in any state as undergraduates. Applicants must be majoring in a phase of public communications, including advertising, public relations, print, radio–television, or video. Students with other majors may be eligible if they have a definite commitment to enter the media profession. Along with their application, they must submit a resume, a transcript covering all college work in Alaska or elsewhere, a statement of their career goals and why they desire the scholarship, at least 3 letters of recommendation, and up to 3 samples of their work. Selection is based on promise in the journalism or public communications fields and the likelihood that the applicant will enter those fields, financial need, and academic progress.
Financial data: The stipend is $1,000.
Duration: 1 year.
Number awarded: 2 each year.
Deadline: March of each year.

1100 $ ALBERT K. MURRAY FINE ARTS EDUCATIONAL FUND SCHOLARSHIP

Albert K. Murray Fine Arts Educational Fund
Attn: Chair, Scholarship Committee
9665 Young America Road
P.O. Box 367
Adamsville, OH 43802–0367
Phone: (740) 796–4797; Fax: (740) 796–4799
Summary: To provide financial aid to students enrolled or entering an art program in college or graduate school.
Eligibility: Open to full–time students working on a bachelor's, master's, or doctoral degree in fine arts at accredited colleges and universities in the United States. Applicants must have a GPA of 2.5 or higher and be able to demonstrate financial need. Along with their application, they must submit a portfolio of their work; a brief essay on the reasons for selecting the college or university and the art program into which they have been accepted, their specific field of study, and the degree they will receive; and a statement of their personal background, reasons for working on a degree in art, intended career goals, and why they think they should be awarded this scholarship. Selection is based on academic merit, the quality of the portfolio, and financial need. U.S. citizenship is required.
Financial data: Recently, stipends ranged from $450 to $4,100. Funds must be used for tuition and related educational expenses (fees, books, supplies), not for room or board. Funds are paid directly to the recipient's school.
Duration: 1 quarter; recipients may reapply.
Number awarded: Varies each year; recently, 36 of these scholarships, with a total value of $64,805, were awarded.
Deadline: July of each year for September grants; October of each year for December grants; January of each year for March grants; or April of each year for June grants.

1101 $$ ALEXANDER M. TANGER SCHOLARSHIP

Broadcast Education Association
Attn: Scholarships
1771 N Street, N.W.
Washington, DC 20036–2891
Phone: (202) 429–3935; (888) 380–7222; Fax: (202) 775–2981;
Email: BEAMemberServices@nab.org
Web: www.beaweb.org/scholarships.htm
Summary: To provide financial assistance to upper–division and graduate students who are interested in preparing for a career in broadcasting.
Eligibility: Open to juniors, seniors, and graduate students enrolled full time at a college or university where at least 1 department is an institutional member of the Broadcast Education Association. Applicants may be studying any area of broadcasting. Selection is based on evidence that the applicant possesses high integrity, superior academic ability, potential to be an outstanding electronic media professional, and a sense of personal and professional responsibility.
Financial data: The stipend is $5,000.
Duration: 1 year; nonrenewable.
Number awarded: 1 each year.
Deadline: October of each year.

1102 $ ALFRED G. AND ELMA M. MILOTTE SCHOLARSHIP

Alfred G. and Elma M. Milotte Scholarship Fund
c/o Bank of America Trust Services
1201 Main Street, Eighth Floor
Dallas, TX 75202
Phone: (866) 461–7282;
Email: info@milotte.org
Web: www.milotte.org
Summary: To provide financial assistance to high school seniors or graduates from Washington who wish to attend college or graduate school in any state to work on a degree in a field related to the artistic portrayal of wilderness areas.
Eligibility: Open to high school seniors, high school graduates, or students who hold a GED certificate and have been residents of Washington for at least 5 years. Applicants must have been accepted at a trade school, art school, 2–year college, or 4–year college or university in any state for either undergraduate or graduate study. They must submit 1) samples of work they have done expressing their observations of the natural world around them (the work may be either written or visual and be communicated in images, word, song, or by use of contemporary technology); 2) high school or college transcripts (cumulative GPA of 3.0 or higher); and 3) 2 letters of reference. Successful candidates are those who are "profoundly fascinated by nature, have been a careful observer of it and have successfully expressed [their] observations in an artistic way that engages the everyday person."
Financial data: Grants up to $4,000 are available.
Duration: 1 year.
Deadline: March of each year.

1103 $$ ALFRED T. GRANGER STUDENT ART FUND

Vermont Student Assistance Corporation
Attn: Scholarship Programs
10 East Allen Street

P.O. Box 2000
Winooski, VT 05404–2601
Phone: (802) 654–3798; (888) 253–4819; Fax: (802) 654–3765; TDD: (800) 281–3341 (within VT);
Email: info@vsac.org
Web: services.vsac.org

Summary: To provide financial assistance to residents of Vermont who are interested in working on an undergraduate or graduate degree in a field related to design at a school in any state.

Eligibility: Open to residents of Vermont who are graduating high school seniors, high school graduates, GED recipients, or current undergraduate or graduate students. Applicants must be interested in attending an accredited postsecondary institution in any state to work on a degree in architecture, interior design, studio art, architectural engineering, mechanical drawing, or lighting design. Along with their application, they must submit a 100–word essay on their interest in and commitment to pursuing their chosen degree or vocation. Selection is based on academic achievement (GPA of 3.1 or higher), a portfolio, letters of recommendation, and financial need (expected family contribution of $23,360 or less).

Financial data: The stipend is $5,000 per year for graduate students or $2,500 per year for undergraduates.

Duration: 1 year; recipients may reapply.

Number awarded: 2 graduate scholarships and 4 undergraduate scholarships are awarded each year.

Deadline: March of each year.

1104 $ ALLIANCE FOR WOMEN IN MEDIA–DALLAS/FORT WORTH CHAPTER SCHOLARSHIP

Alliance for Women in Media–Dallas/Fort Worth Chapter
c/o Carrie Rudnicki, Past President
KTVT–TV
10111 North Central Expressway
Dallas, TX 75231
Phone: (214) 245–5542; Fax: (214) 743–2150;
Email: carrier@KTXA.TV
Web: www.allwomeninmedia_dfw.org/content/awm_scholarships

Summary: To provide financial assistance to undergraduate and graduate students from any state who are enrolled at universities in Texas that offer degrees in broadcasting, broadcast journalism, or advertising.

Eligibility: Open to full–time juniors, seniors, and graduate students who have completed at least 75 hours of course work at a public or private university in Texas. Applicants must have a GPA of 3.25 or higher and a declared major in radio, television, film, public relations, advertising, communications, or broadcasting. Selection is based on educational and career goals, activities and honors, service to community, and references.

Financial data: The stipend is $2,500. Funds are paid directly to the university's financial aid office to be used for tuition only.

Duration: 1 year.

Number awarded: 1 each year.

Deadline: March of each year.

1105 ALOIS AND MARIE GOLDMANN SCHOLARSHIPS

Idaho Community Foundation
Attn: Scholarship Coordinator
210 West State Street
Boise, ID 83702
Phone: (208) 342–3535; (800) 657–5357; Fax: (208) 342–3577;
Email: edavis@idcomfdn.org
Web: www.idcomfdn.org/pages/scho_general.htm

Summary: To provide financial assistance to high school seniors in Idaho who submit outstanding essays on the Holocaust and plan to attend college in the state.

Eligibility: Open to seniors graduating from high schools or home schools in Idaho who are planning to attend an accredited institution of higher learning in the state. Applicants must have a grade average of "C" or higher. Along with their application, they must submit an original essay of 2 to 6 pages in length on a specific aspect of the Holocaust. Selection is based primarily on that essay; academic achievement, financial need, and extracurricular or community activities are not considered.

Financial data: The stipend is approximately $1,000.

Duration: 1 year.

Number awarded: 1 or more each year.

Deadline: March of each year.

1106 ALYCE SHEETZ OREGON HIGH SCHOOL JOURNALIST OF THE YEAR SCHOLARSHIP

Oregon Journalism Education Association
c/o Lisa Lacy, President
Tualatin High School
22300 Southwest Boones Ferry Road
Tualatin, OR 97062
Phone: (503) 431–5751;
Email: llacy@ttsd.k12.or.us
Web: www.oregonjea.org/awards

Summary: To recognize and reward, with college scholarships, outstanding high school journalists in Oregon.

Eligibility: Open to seniors graduating from high schools in Oregon who have been involved in journalism for at least 2 years. Applicants must be planning to study journalism and/or mass communications at a college or university in any state and prepare for a career in that field. Along with their application, they must submit examples of their work that show the following 4 characteristics: 1) skilled and creative use of media content; 2) inquiring mind and investigative persistence resulting in an in–depth study of issues important to the local high school audience, high school students in general, or society; 3) courageous and responsible handling of controversial issues despite threat or imposition of censorship; and 4) variety of journalistic experiences, each handled in a quality manner, on a newspaper, yearbook, broadcast, or other medium.

Financial data: The winner receives a $1,000 scholarship and the runner–up receives a $500 scholarships.

Duration: The competition is held annually.

Number awarded: 1 winner and 1 runner–up is selected each year.

Deadline: February of each year.

1107 AMERICAN ACADEMY OF CHEFS COLLEGE SCHOLARSHIPS

American Culinary Federation, Inc.
Attn: American Academy of Chefs
180 Center Place Way
St. Augustine, FL 32095
Phone: (904) 824–4468; (800) 624–9458, ext. 102; Fax: (904) 825–4758;
Email: academy@acfchefs.net
Web: www.acfchefs.org/AM/Template.cfm?Section=Education4

Summary: To provide financial assistance to students enrolled in a culinary program.

Eligibility: Open to students who are currently enrolled at an accredited college with a major in culinary or pastry arts. Applicants must have completed at least 1 grading or marking period. They must have a GPA of 2.5 or higher and be able to demonstrate financial need. Along with their application, they must submit 5 brief essays on: 1) their leadership ability and team building skills; 2) an example of when they have utilized their leadership skills in a culinary work environment; 3) what they hope to contribute to the culinary industry; 4) the importance and benefits of becoming a member of a professional organization; and 5) how important community service is to them. Selection is based on the essays (25 points), academic GPA (30 points), participation in culinary competitions (20 points), volunteer for school and industry activities (10 points), American Culinary Foundation involvement (10 points), and 2 letters of recommendation (5 points).

Financial data: The stipend is $1,000.

Duration: 1 year.

Number awarded: Varies each year; recently, 16 of these scholarships were awarded.

Deadline: April or August of each year.

1108 AMERICAN ACADEMY OF CHEFS HIGH SCHOOL STUDENT SCHOLARSHIPS

American Culinary Federation, Inc.
Attn: American Academy of Chefs
180 Center Place Way
St. Augustine, FL 32095
Phone: (904) 824–4468; (800) 624–9458, ext. 102; Fax: (904) 825–4758;
Email: academy@acfchefs.net
Web: www.acfchefs.org/AM/Template.cfm?Section=Education4

Summary: To provide financial assistance to high school seniors planning to attend college to prepare for a career as a chef or pastry chef.

Eligibility: Open to graduating high school seniors who plan to attend an accredited college and major in culinary or pastry arts. Applicants must have a GPA of 2.5 or higher and be able to demonstrate financial need. Along with their application, they must submit 5 brief essays on: 1) their leadership ability and teamwork building skills; 2) an example of when they have utilized their leadership skills in a culinary work environment; 3) what they hope to contribute to the culinary industry; 4) the importance and benefits of becoming a member of a professional organization; and 5) how important community service is to them. Selection is based on the essays (25 points), academic GPA (30 points), participation in culinary competitions (20 points), volunteer for school and industry activities (10 points), American Culinary Foundation involvement (10 points), and 2 letters of recommendation (5 points).

Financial data: A stipend is awarded (amount not specified).

Duration: 1 year.

Number awarded: Varies each year; recently, 6 of these scholarships were awarded.

Deadline: March of each year.

1109 AMERICAN ADVERTISING FEDERATION FOURTH DISTRICT CLUB PRESIDENT'S SCHOLARSHIP

American Advertising Federation–District 4
c/o Maria Lucas, Governor
Farah & Farah
10 West Adams Street
Jacksonville, FL 32202
Phone: (904) 807–3113; (800) 533–5555; Fax: (904) 355–5599;
Email: mlucas@farahandfarah.com
Web: 4aaf.com/education/scholarships

Summary: To provide financial assistance to undergraduate and graduate students at colleges and universities in Florida who are residents of any state, interested in entering the field of advertising, and able to demonstrate outstanding service to the community.

Eligibility: Open to undergraduate and graduate students from any state currently enrolled at accredited colleges and universities in Florida. Applicants must be working on a bachelor's or master's degree in advertising, marketing, communications, public relations, art, graphic arts, or a related field. They must have a GPA of 3.0 or higher overall and 3.5 or higher in their major field. Along with their application, they must submit a 250–word essay on 1 of the following topics: 1) is advertising a profession, and why or why not; 2) if everyone should lead, then why learn to follow; or 3) if you were asked to serve your community, what single thing would you do. Selection is based on academic excellence, leadership, and service to the community.

Financial data: The stipend is $1,000.

Duration: 1 year.

Number awarded: 1 each year.

Deadline: February of each year.

1110 AMERICAN ADVERTISING FEDERATION FOURTH DISTRICT GOVERNOR'S SCHOLARSHIP

American Advertising Federation–District 4
c/o Maria Lucas, Governor
Farah & Farah
10 West Adams Street
Jacksonville, FL 32202
Phone: (904) 807–3113; (800) 533–5555; Fax: (904) 355–5599;
Email: mlucas@farahandfarah.com
Web: 4aaf.com/education/scholarships

Summary: To provide financial assistance to undergraduate and graduate students at colleges and universities in Florida who are residents of any state, interested in entering the field of advertising, and able to demonstrate outstanding service to the profession.

Eligibility: Open to undergraduate and graduate students from any state currently enrolled at accredited colleges and universities in Florida. Applicants must be working on a bachelor's or master's degree in advertising, marketing, communications, public relations, art, graphic arts, or a related field. They must have a GPA of 3.0 or higher overall and 3.5 or higher in their major field. Along with their application, they must submit a 250–word essay on 1 of the following topics: 1) what single community problem do you feel most strongly about correcting and why; 2) if everyone should lead, then why learn to follow; or 3) if you were asked to serve your profession, what single thing would you do. Selection is based on academic excellence, service to the community, and service to the profession.

Financial data: The stipend is $1,000.

Duration: 1 year.

Number awarded: 1 each year.

Deadline: February of each year.

1111 AMERICAN ADVERTISING FEDERATION FOURTH DISTRICT MOSAIC SCHOLARSHIP

American Advertising Federation–District 4
c/o Maria Lucas, Governor
Farah & Farah
10 West Adams Street
Jacksonville, FL 32202
Phone: (904) 807–3113; (800) 533–5555; Fax: (904) 355–5599;
Email: mlucas@farahandfarah.com
Web: 4aaf.com/education/scholarships

Summary: To provide financial assistance to minority undergraduate and graduate students from any state who are enrolled at colleges and universities in Florida and interested in entering the field of advertising.

Eligibility: Open to undergraduate and graduate students from any state enrolled at accredited colleges and universities in Florida who are U.S. citizens or permanent residents of African, African American, Hispanic, Hispanic American, Indian, Native American, Asian, Asian American, or Pacific Islander descent. Applicants must be working on a bachelor's or master's degree in advertising, marketing, communications, public relations, art, graphic arts, or a related field. They must have an overall GPA of 3.0 or higher. Along with their application, they must submit a 250–word essay on why multiculturalism, diversity, and inclusion are important in the advertising, marketing, and communications industry today. Preference is given to members of the American Advertising Federation.

Financial data: The stipend is $1,000.

Duration: 1 year.

Number awarded: 1 or more each year.

Deadline: February of each year.

1112 $ AMERICAN EDUCATIONAL LEADERS INVESTIGATIVE JOURNALISM CONTEST

American Educational Leaders
P.O. Box 1287
Monrovia, CA 91017
Phone: (626) 357–7733;
Email: aelmain@americanism.org
Web: www.americanism.org/investigative–journalism.htm

Summary: To recognize and reward journalism students who submit samples of their investigative work.

Eligibility: Open to full– and part–time undergraduate students currently enrolled at colleges and universities in the United States and majoring in journalism, mass media, or electronic communication. Applicants must submit samples of their work published or broadcast prior to the application deadline. Radio and television taped submissions must be shorter than 15 minutes. All entries must be of general interest; subject may include (but are not limited to) politics, government, economics, education, social issues, community activism, or health care. Entries should involve documentary research, the use of public and private records, interviewing, and other journalistic skills with a focus on the accountability of individuals and institutions wielding power.

Financial data: Prizes are $2,000 for first, $1,000 for second, and $500 for third.

Duration: The competition is held annually.

Number awarded: 3 each year.

Deadline: March of each year.

1113 $ AMERICAN INDIAN ARTS COUNCIL SCHOLARSHIP PROGRAM

American Indian Arts Council, Inc.
Attn: Scholarship Committee
725 Preston Forest Shopping Center, Suite B
Dallas, TX 75230
Phone: (214) 265–0071; Fax: (214) 265–0071;
Email: aiac@flash.net
Web: www.americanindianartscouncil.org/scholarship.html

Summary: To provide financial assistance to American Indian undergraduate or graduate students planning a career in the arts or arts administration.

Eligibility: Open to American Indian undergraduate and graduate students who are preparing for a career in fine arts, visual and performing arts, communication arts, creative writing, or arts administration or management. Applicants must be currently enrolled in and attending a fully–accredited college or university. They must provide official tribal documentation verifying American Indian heritage and have a GPA of 2.5 or higher. Students majoring

in the visual or performing arts (including writing) must submit slides, photographs, videotapes, audio tapes, or other examples of their work. All applicants must submit letters of recommendation and brief essays on their long–term goals, their opinion on the role of arts relative to American Indians, and why they would appreciate receiving this scholarship. Awards are based on either merit or merit and financial need. If the applicants wish to be considered for a need–based award, a letter from their financial aid office is required to verify financial need.
Financial data: Stipends range from $250 to $1,000 per semester.
Duration: 1 semester; may be renewed if the recipient maintains a GPA of 2.5 or higher.
Number awarded: Varies each year.
Deadline: September of each year for the fall semester; March of each year for the spring semester.

1114 $ AMERICAN INSTITUTE OF ARCHITECTS CORPORATE ARCHITECTS AND FACILITY MANAGEMENT SCHOLARSHIP

American Institute of Architects
Attn: Corporate Architects and Facility Management Scholarship Advisory Group
1735 New York Avenue, N.W.
Washington, DC 20006–5292
Phone: (202) 626–7366; (800) AIA–3837; Fax: (202) 626–7547;
Email: cafm@aia.org
Web: www.aia.org/practicing/groups/kc/AIAB080402
Summary: To provide financial assistance to upper–division and graduate students in architecture interested in studying corporate architecture and facility management.
Eligibility: Open to students at accredited schools of architecture in the United States and Canada who are 1) in the third or fourth year of a 5–year program that results in a B.Arch. degree; 2) in the fourth or fifth year of a 6–year program (4+2 or other combination) that results in an M.Arch. degree; or 3) in the second or third year of a 3– to 4–year program that results in an M.Arch. degree and with an undergraduate degree in a discipline other than architecture. Applicants must be interested in specializing in corporate architecture and facility management. Along with their application, they must submit a 500–word essay on how their education has prepared them to design projects for and with corporate clients. Selection is based on that essay, a letter of recommendation, and academic performance.
Financial data: The stipend is $2,000.
Duration: 1 year.
Number awarded: 2 each year.
Deadline: March of each year.

1115 $$ AMERICANS FOR THE ARTS POSTER DESIGN COMPETITION

The Art Institutes International, Inc.
Free Markets Center
210 Sixth Avenue, 33rd Floor
Pittsburgh, PA 15222–2603
Phone: (412) 995–7685; (888) 624–0300; Fax: (412) 918–2598
Web: www.artinstitutes.edu/competition/graphic–design–posters.aspx
Summary: To recognize and reward (with scholarships to participating Art Institutes) high school seniors and graduates who participate in a poster design competition.
Eligibility: Open to high school seniors and graduates (over 16 years of age) in the United States, Puerto Rico, and Canada who are planning to attend a participating Art Institute to study graphic design or other field. Applicants must have a GPA of 2.0 or higher. Along with their application, they must submit 1) an original poster that illustrates the concepts of a specified theme (recently, the theme was "You Can Create Tomorrow"); 2) a current transcript (for high school seniors) or proof of high school graduation; and 3) a written statement of 300 to 500 words describing their design concept and why they want to enter a design field. Entries are first submitted to the Art Institute the applicant wishes to attend. Each institute then forwards its winning design to the national competition. Selection is based on originality of concept (25%), visual impact of poster (25%), basic design skills (25%), and conformity with specified theme (25%).
Financial data: In the high school senior category, local prizes are $3,000 scholarships for first place and $1,000 scholarships for second; national prizes are a full tuition scholarship at the Art Institute through which the winner applied as the grand prize, a half tuition scholarship as a first prize, and a quarter tuition scholarship as a second prize. In the high school graduate/adult category, local finalist prizes are $1,000 and the national grand prize is a $10,000 tuition scholarship to attend the Art Institute through which the winner applied.
Duration: The competition is held annually.
Number awarded: In the high school senior category, 50 local first prizes (1 for each participating Art Institute), 50 local second prizes, and 3 national prizes are awarded. In the high school graduate/adult category, 50 local finalist prizes (1 for each participating Art Institute) and 1 national grand prize are awarded.
Deadline: Entries must be submitted for local competitions by February of each year.

1116 $$ ANNE SOWLES CALHOUN MEMORIAL SCHOLARSHIP

Print and Graphics Scholarship Foundation
Attn: Scholarship Competition
200 Deer Run Road
Sewickley, PA 15143–2600
Phone: (412) 259–1740; (800) 910–GATF; Fax: (412) 741–2311;
Email: pgsf@printing.org
Web: www.printing.org/pgsf
Summary: To provide financial assistance for college to women who want to prepare for a career in the printing or publishing industry.
Eligibility: Open to women who are high school seniors or full–time college students. Applicants must be interested in preparing for a career in graphic communications or printing. This is a merit–based program; financial need is not considered.
Financial data: The stipend ranges from $1,000 to $5,000, depending upon the funds available each year.
Duration: 1 year; may be renewed for up to 3 additional years, provided the recipient maintains a GPA of 3.0 or higher.
Number awarded: 1 or more each year.
Deadline: February of each year for high school seniors; March of each year for students already in college.

1117 $$ AP–GOOGLE JOURNALISM AND TECHNOLOGY SCHOLARSHIP PROGRAM

Online News Association
Attn: Scholarship Manager
P.O. Box 65741
Washington, DC 20035
Phone: (646) 290–7900;
Email: irving@journalists.org
Web: journalists.org/next–gen/ap–google–scholarship
Summary: To recognize and reward undergraduate and graduate students, especially those from diverse backgrounds, who propose outstanding projects "at the intersection of journalism and technology."
Eligibility: Open to full–time undergraduates (at least sophomores) and graduate students at U.S. institutions who have at least 1 year of study remaining and a GPA of 3.0 or higher. Students from diverse backgrounds (defined as ethnic and racial minorities, members of the lesbian, gay, bisexual, and transgender (LGBT) community, and students with disabilities) and those attending rural area institutions are strongly encouraged to apply. Some scholarships are reserved for students who can demonstrate financial need. Applicants must develop original journalistic content with computer science elements; they should explain how their strategy moves digital journalism forward or provides valuable lessons or outcomes. Examples include data visualization, data mining, mobile devices and applications, 3–D storytelling, digital ethics, or microcomputers. In the selection process, emphasis is placed on innovation and creativity. U.S. citizenship is required.
Financial data: The award is a $20,000 scholarship, of which half is paid to the winner's institution at the beginning of the first semester and half at the beginning of the second semester, provided the recipient earns a GPA of 3.0 or higher for the first semester.
Duration: The competition is held annually.
Number awarded: 6 each year.
Deadline: February of each year.

1118 APTRA MEMORIAL JOURNALISM SCHOLARSHIP AWARD

Associated Press Television and Radio Association
c/o Chris Havlik
AP West Broadcast Editor
1850 North Central Avenue, Suite 640
Phoenix, AZ 85004

Phone: (602) 354–7690;
Email: chavlik@ap.org
Web: www.aptra.com/scholar_about.htm
Summary: To provide financial assistance to students from any state who are enrolled at colleges and universities in designated western states and are interested in broadcast journalism careers.
Eligibility: Open to residents of any state currently enrolled at colleges and universities in Alaska, Arizona, California, Colorado, Hawaii, Idaho, Montana, Nevada, New Mexico, Oregon, Utah, Washington, and Wyoming. Applicants must have a broadcast journalism career objective. Selection is based on a 500–word essay on why the students wish to pursue broadcast journalism; another 500–word essay on their honors, awards, and broadcast experience; 3 letters of recommendation; and a statement of how they are financing their education.
Financial data: The stipend is $1,500.
Duration: 1 year.
Number awarded: 1 each year.
Deadline: February of each year.

1119 $ ARCHIBALD RUTLEDGE SCHOLARSHIP PROGRAM

South Carolina State Department of Education
Attn: Office of Teacher Effectiveness
1429 Senate Street, Suite 607–B
Columbia, SC 29201
Phone: (803) 734–0323; Fax: (803) 734–5953;
Email: shockman@ed.sc.gov
Web: ed.sc.gov
Summary: To recognize and reward, with scholarships for college in the state, high school seniors in South Carolina who participate in a competition in art, creative writing, dance, drama, or music.
Eligibility: Open to U.S. citizens who have attended South Carolina public high schools for at least 2 years, are currently seniors, and are planning to attend a South Carolina college or university. Applicants compete by submitting samples of their work in 1 of 5 areas: 1) visual arts, limited to 2–dimensional work such as drawing, painting, mixed media, printmaking, and collage; no 3–dimensional works, photographs, or computer–generated images are accepted; 2) creative writing, a sonnet, lyric, or narrative poem, up to 1 page; 3) theater, a 1–act play with a performing time of 10 to 15 minutes; 4) dance, an original short dance composition of 3 to 10 minutes composed for solo or ensemble dancers in any appropriate movement style; or 5) music, a composition of 3 to 10 minutes for solo or small ensemble, vocal or instrumental, in any appropriate style. In addition to the work, they must submit a process folio that contains documentation of the planning and development of the project and a 1–page reflection statement addressing the intent of the work and comparing the final product with the original concept. A panel of professionals in the field selects up to 10 finalists, based on originality, creativity, and the correlation and implications of the process folio for the final composition. Finalists must attend the scholarship competition, where they present a portfolio of a number of selected works as specified by the judges.
Financial data: The award consists of a $2,000 scholarship, paid directly to the South Carolina institution to be used for tuition, room, board, and instructional resource expenses.
Duration: 1 year.
Number awarded: 5 each year: 1 in each of the 5 categories.
Deadline: February of each year.

1120 $ ARKANSAS POST SAME SCHOLARSHIPS

Society of American Military Engineers–Arkansas Post
Attn: Scholarship and Camp Committee Chair
P.O. Box 867
Little Rock, AR 72203–0867
Web: posts.same.org/Arkansas/scholarship
Summary: To provide financial assistance to Arkansas high school seniors interested in studying architecture or engineering at a college in any state.
Eligibility: Open to seniors graduating from high schools in Arkansas and planning to attend a college or university in any state. Applicants must be interested in studying architecture or a field of engineering related to construction (e.g., civil, electrical, environmental, geotechnical, mechanical, structural). Along with their application, they must submit a 200–word essay explaining why they want to study architecture or construction–related engineering and why receiving this scholarship is critical to achieving their continuing educational goals. Financial need is not considered in the selection process. U.S. citizenship or permanent resident status is required.
Financial data: The stipend is $2,000.
Duration: 1 year.
Number awarded: 2 each year.
Deadline: March of each year.

1121 $$ ARMENIAN GENERAL BENEVOLENT UNION PERFORMING ARTS FELLOWSHIPS

Armenian General Benevolent Union
Attn: Scholarship Program
55 East 59th Street, Seventh Floor
New York, NY 10022–1112
Phone: (212) 319–6383; Fax: (212) 319–6507;
Email: scholarship@agbu.org
Web: www.agbu–scholarship.org/opportunities
Summary: To provide financial assistance to undergraduate and graduate students of Armenian heritage worldwide working on a degree in performing arts at universities in any country.
Eligibility: Open to full–time undergraduate and graduate students of Armenian heritage from any country (except Armenians studying in Armenia). Applicants must be working on a degree in performing arts at a university in any country. They must have a GPA of 3.5 or higher, as measured by the U.S. grading system. Selection is based on academic excellence, public and community service (especially involvement in the Armenian community), and financial need.
Financial data: Stipends range from $2,500 to $7,500 per year.
Duration: Up to 5 years.
Number awarded: 1 or more each year.
Deadline: May of each year.

1122 $$ ARTHUR N. TUTTLE, JR. GRADUATE FELLOWSHIP IN HEALTH FACILITY PLANNING AND DESIGN

American Institute of Architects
Attn: Academy of Architecture for Health
1735 New York Avenue, N.W.
Washington, DC 20006–5292
Phone: (202) 626–7366; (800) AIA–3837; Fax: (202) 626–7547;
Email: aah@aia.org
Web: www.aia.org/practicing/groups/kc/AIAS074546
Summary: To provide financial assistance to upper–division and graduate students in architecture interested in studying health facility planning and design.
Eligibility: Open to 1) undergraduates entering the fifth year of a 5–year program leading to a professional degree in architecture with a program that focuses on health care design; 2) graduate students at an accredited school of architecture that has a program of health care architecture or a school of health care–focused design, planning, or management; or 3) doctoral candidates in the health facilities field or conducting an independent study that is near completion with the intent to present the results and publish in the *Academy Journal.* Undergraduates and graduate students must submit a plan listing course that will permit them to concentrate on the planning and design of health care facilities. Doctoral candidates must be prepared and in a position to devote adequate time to complete the proposed research during the allotted period. All applicants must be enrolled at an accredited school of architecture in the United States, Mexico, or Canada. They must have a command of the English language and a record of past academic performance that strongly indicates an ability to complete the fellowship successfully. Selection is based on significance of the proposed research, qualifications of the applicant, content of the letters of recommendation, completeness and clarity of the application, and potential of the applicant to make significant future professional contributions.
Financial data: Stipends for undergraduate or graduate study range from $4,500 to $10,000. Grants for doctoral level graduate research range from $3,000 to $5,000.
Duration: 1 year.
Number awarded: Normally, 2 each year.
Deadline: May of each year.

1123 ARTS AND SCIENCES AWARDS

Alexander Graham Bell Association for the Deaf and Hard of Hearing
Attn: Financial Aid Coordinator
3417 Volta Place, N.W.
Washington, DC 20007–2778
Phone: (202) 337–5220; Fax: (202) 337–8314; TDD: (202) 337–5221;
Email: financialaid@agbell.org

Web: nc.agbell.org/page.aspx?pid=496
Summary: To provide financial aid to hearing impaired students who are participating in extracurricular activities in arts and sciences.
Eligibility: Open to residents of the United States or Canada who have been diagnosed prior to their fourth birthday as having a moderate to profound bilateral hearing loss and who use spoken language as their primary form of communication. They must be between 6 and 19 years of age and enrolled in an art or science program as an extracurricular activity during after–school time, summer, or weekends. Programs can be offered through museums, nature centers, art or music centers, zoological parks, space and science camps, dance and theater studios, martial arts studios, or any other program with a focus on the arts or sciences. Recreational summer camps, sports camps or sports, and travel and study abroad programs that do not have an explicit arts or science focus are not eligible. Membership in the Alexander Graham Bell Association is not required, but preference is given to members.
Financial data: The amount of the award varies, depending upon the cost of the program in which the recipient is enrolled.
Duration: 1 year; may be renewed upon reapplication.
Number awarded: Varies each year.
Deadline: April of each year.

1124 $ ASCAP/LOTTE LEHMANN FOUNDATION SONG CYCLE COMPETITION

Lotte Lehmann Foundation
545 Eighth Avenue, Suite 401
New York, NY 10018
Phone: (347) 684–1640;
Email: daron@daronhagen.com
Web: www.lottelehmann.org/llf/programs
Summary: To recognize and reward, with commissions for further work, outstanding student and other composers of art songs.
Eligibility: Open to composers under 30 years of age who are U.S. citizens, permanent residents of the United States, or enrolled students with student visas. Applicants must submit an original art song with English text. Arrangements of pre–existing music are ineligible. They must submit a printed copy of the English text, a 200–word biography, and a CD or cassette recording of a live performance of the work.
Financial data: First prize is $3,500 and a commission to compose a song cycle for voice and piano, to be published by E.C. Schirmer and performed in 3 major American cities. Second prize is $1,000 and a commission to compose an art song for voice and piano. Third prize is $500 and a commission to compose an art song for voice and piano. Fourth prize is $500 and a commission to compose an art song for voice and piano on poetry by Andre Brunin and premiered at the Albert Roussel International Festival in France.
Duration: The competition is held biennially, in odd–numbered years.
Number awarded: 4 every other year.
Deadline: September of odd–numbered years.

1125 $ ASID FOUNDATION LEGACY SCHOLARSHIP FOR UNDERGRADUATES

American Society of Interior Designers
Attn: ASID Foundation
608 Massachusetts Avenue, N.E.
Washington, DC 20002–6006
Phone: (202) 546–3480; Fax: (202) 546–3240;
Email: education@asid.org
Web: www.asidfoundation.org
Summary: To provide financial assistance to upper–division students working on an undergraduate degree in interior design.
Eligibility: Open to juniors and seniors enrolled in at least a 3–year program in interior design. Applicants must submit a portfolio of 8 to 12 components; each component may be a lighting plan, furniture or cabinetry detail, lifecycle cost analysis presentation, furniture layout, or perspective rendering. Selection is based on academic accomplishments, presentation skills, design and planning competency, and conceptual creativity.
Financial data: The stipend is $4,000.
Duration: 1 year.
Number awarded: 1 each year.
Deadline: March of each year.

1126 $ ASLA COUNCIL OF FELLOWS SCHOLARSHIPS

Landscape Architecture Foundation
Attn: Leadership in Landscape Scholarship Program
818 18th Street, N.W., Suite 810
Washington, DC 20006–3520
Phone: (202) 331–7070; Fax: (202) 331–7079;
Email: scholarships@lafoundation.org
Web: www.lafoundation.org
Summary: To provide financial assistance to upper–division students, especially those from disadvantaged and underrepresented groups, working on a degree in landscape architecture.
Eligibility: Open to landscape architecture students in the third, fourth, or fifth year of undergraduate work. Preference is given to, and 1 scholarship is reserved for, members of underrepresented ethnic or cultural groups. Applicants must submit a 500–word essay on how they envision themselves contributing to the profession of landscape architecture, 2 letters of recommendation, documentation of financial need, and (for students applying for the scholarship reserved for underrepresented groups) a statement identifying their association with a specific ethnic or cultural group. U.S. citizenship or permanent resident status is required.
Financial data: The stipend is $4,000. Students also receive a 1–year membership in the American Society of Landscape Architecture (ASLA), general registration fees for the ASLA annual meeting, and a travel stipend to attend the meeting.
Duration: 1 year.
Number awarded: 2 each year, of which 1 is reserved for a member of an underrepresented group.
Deadline: February of each year.

1127 ASPIRING MUSIC TEACHER SCHOLARSHIP

Vermont Student Assistance Corporation
Attn: Scholarship Programs
10 East Allen Street
P.O. Box 2000
Winooski, VT 05404–2601
Phone: (802) 654–3798; (888) 253–4819; Fax: (802) 654–3765; TDD: (800) 281–3341 (within VT);
Email: info@vsac.org
Web: services.vsac.org
Summary: To provide financial assistance to residents of Vermont who are interested in attending college in any state to study music education or piano pedagogy.
Eligibility: Open to residents of Vermont who are graduating high school seniors, high school graduates, or current college students. Applicants must be attending or planning to attend an accredited postsecondary institution in any state to study music education or piano pedagogy. Along with their application, they must submit 1) a 100–word essay on the school, church, and community activities in which they have participated; and 2) a 100–word essay on their interest in and commitment to pursuing their chosen career or vocation. Selection is based on those essays, a letter of recommendation, and academic achievement (GPA of 3.1 or higher).
Financial data: The stipend ranges from $1,000 to $1,500.
Duration: 1 year.
Number awarded: 1 each year.
Deadline: March of each year.

1128 $ ASSOCIATED CHINESE UNIVERSITY WOMEN SCHOLARSHIPS

Associated Chinese University Women, Inc.
Attn: Dorothy Mau, Scholarship Committee Chair
P.O. Box 62264
Honolulu, HI 96822
Web: www.acuwhawaii.org/scholarship
Summary: To provide financial assistance to residents of Hawaii who are of Chinese ancestry and interested in majoring in education or Chinese studies at a college in any state.
Eligibility: Open to residents of Hawaii who are of Chinese ancestry or interested in Chinese culture. Applicants must be attending or planning to attend an accredited 4–year U.S. college or university as a full–time student with the objective of earning a baccalaureate degree. They must have a GPA of 3.8 or higher and be planning to major in education or Chinese studies (e.g., history, language, music, art, dance, and/or theater). Along with their application, they must submit a personal statement on why they should be awarded this scholarship, including their plans for serving their community after graduation. Selection is based on academic achievement (including GPA and SAT score), character, extracurricular activities, school and/or community service, and financial need. U.S. citizenship or permanent resident status is required.

Financial data: The stipend is $2,000 for regular scholarships or $1,000 for special scholarships.
Duration: 1 year.
Number awarded: Varies each year; recently, 6 were awarded.
Deadline: March of each year.

1129 ASSOCIATED MALE CHORUSES OF AMERICA SCHOLARSHIPS

Associated Male Choruses of America
c/o Weldon Wilson, Scholarship Chair
5143 South 40th Street
St. Cloud, MN 56301
Phone: (320) 251–1317;
Email: scholarships@amcofa–sing.org
Web: amcofa–sing.org/scholarships.html

Summary: To provide financial assistance for undergraduate education to music majors who are sponsored by a chorus that is a member of the Associated Male Choruses of America (AMCA).
Eligibility: Open to undergraduates enrolled full time in music programs at colleges and universities in the United States and Canada. Preference is given to students specializing in vocal music studies, although students of instrumental music are also eligible. Applicants must be sponsored by an AMCA member. Along with their application, they must submit a detailed letter of support from their sponsoring chorus; an audition CD for voice and performance evaluation; a personal letter describing their musical background, goals, and career objectives; 3 letters of recommendation; and their most recent transcript. Selection is based on academic record, musical skills, and involvement in the community.
Financial data: Stipends range from $1,000 to $1,200 per year; funds are paid to the recipient's college for tuition, books, music texts, or private lessons.
Duration: 1 year; recipients may reapply.
Number awarded: Varies each year; recently, 4 of these scholarships were awarded.
Deadline: February of each year.

1130 ASSOCIATION FOR WOMEN IN ARCHITECTURE SCHOLARSHIPS

Association for Women in Architecture
Attn: Scholarship Chair
22815 Frampton Avenue
Torrance, CA 90501–5034
Phone: (310) 534–8466; Fax: (310) 257–6885;
Email: scholarship@awa–la.org
Web: www.awa–la.org/scholarships.php

Summary: To provide financial assistance to women undergraduates in California who are interested in preparing for a career in architecture.
Eligibility: Open to women who have completed at least 18 college units of study in any of the following fields: architecture; civil, structural, mechanical, or electrical engineering as related to architecture; landscape architecture; urban and land planning; interior design; architectural rendering and illustration; or environmental design. Applicants must be residents of California or attending school in the state. Students in their final year of study are also eligible and may use the funds for special projects (such as a trip abroad). Selection is based on grades, a personal statement, recommendations, and the quality and organization of materials submitted; financial need is not considered.
Financial data: The stipend is $1,000.
Duration: 1 year.
Number awarded: 5 each year.
Deadline: April of each year.

1131 $ ASSOCIATION FOR WOMEN IN SPORTS MEDIA SCHOLARSHIP/INTERNSHIP PROGRAM

Association for Women in Sports Media
Attn: Scholarship and Internship Coordinator
161 West Sylvania Avenue
Neptune City, NJ 07753
Email: lindsay.jones@awsmonline.org
Web: awsmonline.org/internship–scholarship

Summary: To provide financial assistance and work experience to women undergraduate and graduate students who are interested in preparing for a career in sports writing.
Eligibility: Open to women who are enrolled in college or graduate school full time and preparing for a career in sports writing, sports copy editing, sports broadcasting, or sports public relations. Applicants must submit a 750–word essay describing their most memorable experience in sports or sports media, a 1–page resume highlighting their journalism experience, a letter of recommendation, up to 5 samples of their work, and a $20 application fee. They must apply for and accept an internship with a sports media organization.
Financial data: Winners receive a stipend up to $1,000 and placement in a paid internship.
Duration: 1 year; nonrenewable.
Number awarded: Varies each year; recently, 6 students received support from this program.
Deadline: October of each year.

1132 $$ ASTA NATIONAL SOLO COMPETITION–SENIOR DIVISION

American String Teachers Association
Attn: Competitions
4153 Chain Bridge Road
Fairfax, VA 22030
Phone: (703) 279–2113; Fax: (703) 279–2114;
Email: asta@astaweb.com
Web: www.astaweb.com

Summary: To recognize and reward outstanding performers on stringed instruments.
Eligibility: Open to students between 19 and 25 years of age who have graduated from high school. Competitions are held for violin, viola, cello, double bass, classical guitar, and harp. Candidates must be members of the American String Teachers Association (ASTA) or current students of ASTA members. They first enter their state competitions; they may enter either in their state of residency or the state in which they are studying. The state chairs then submit CDs of the winners in their state to the national chair. Musicians who live in states that do not have a state competition may submit CDs directly to the national chair. The repertoire must consist of a required work and a work of the competitor's choice; CDs of performances should run from 17 to 20 minutes. Based on those CDs, finalists are invited to the national competition, where the winners are selected. First–place prizes are awarded to the winner for each instrument; the grand prize is awarded to the first–place winner selected as most outstanding.
Financial data: Prizes vary; in the past, the grand prize has been as high as $7,000.
Duration: The competition is held biennially, in odd–numbered years.
Number awarded: 6 first–place winners are selected each odd–numbered year; of those, 1 is selected as the grand prize winner.
Deadline: Each state sets the date of its competition, but all state competitions must be completed by October of even–numbered years so the winning tapes or CDs reach the national chair by the middle of November. The national competition is in March.

1133 AUDREY TANZER SCHOLARSHIP

Alliance for Women in Media–New York City Chapter
c/o Kathleen M. Brommer
75 Broad Street, 15th Floor
New York, NY 10004
Phone: (646) 839–5119; Fax: (646) 839–5178;
Email: kbrommer@newsbroadcastnetwork.com
Web: www.awrtnyc.org/tanzer.php

Summary: To provide financial assistance to students from any state majoring in broadcast communications at colleges and universities in the New York tri–state area.
Eligibility: Open to students from any state majoring in broadcast communications at colleges and universities in New York City, New Jersey, and Connecticut. Applicants must have a GPA of 3.0 or higher. Along with their application, they must submit a 300–word essay on their career goals. Financial need is not considered in the selection process.
Financial data: The stipend is $1,000.
Duration: 1 year.
Number awarded: 1 or more each year.
Deadline: May of each year.

1134 AWEBER EMAIL MARKETING SCHOLARSHIP

AWeber Communications, Inc.
3103 Philmont Avenue, Suite 200
Huntingdon Valley, PA 19006
Phone: (877) 293–2371;
Email: scholarship@aweber.com
Web: www.aweber.com/email–marketing–scholarship.htm

Summary: To recognize and reward, with scholarships for further study, students who submit outstanding essays on modern communication tools.

Eligibility: Open to graduating high school seniors and full–time college freshmen, sophomores, and juniors. Applicants must 1) take a 5–question online survey on how they use different communication technologies; and 2) submit a 500–word essay on the modern communication tools they use, which of those they use the most and why, how their communication habits would change if that tool went away forever, how they would cope with the loss of that tool, and whether they would still do the things that they did with that tool.

Financial data: The stipend is $1,000.

Duration: The competition is held annually.

Number awarded: 1 each year.

Deadline: February of each year.

1135 B. PHINIZY SPALDING SCHOLARSHIP

Georgia Trust
Attn: Scholarship Committee
1516 Peachtree Street, N.W.
Atlanta, GA 30309
Phone: (404) 881–9980; Fax: (404) 875–2205;
Email: kryan@georgiatrust.org
Web: www.georgiatrust.org/preservation/opportunities.php

Summary: To provide financial assistance to Georgia residents majoring in a field related to historical preservation at a college or university in the state.

Eligibility: Open to Georgia residents who are enrolled full time in their first year of undergraduate study at a college or university in the state. Applicants must be working on a degree in historic preservation or a related field (e.g., archaeology, architecture, history, planning). U.S. citizenship is required. Selection is based on academic achievement and past and planned involvement within preservation–related fields.

Financial data: The stipend is $1,000.

Duration: 1 year.

Number awarded: 1 each year.

Deadline: February of each year.

1136 $ BARBARA L. FRYE SCHOLARSHIP

Capital Press Club of Florida
336 East College Avenue, Suite 303
Tallahassee, FL 32301
Phone: (850) 224–7263;
Email: barbarafryescholarship@gmail.com
Web: barbarafryescholarship.wordpress.com

Summary: To provide financial assistance to high school seniors and college students in Florida who are planning to prepare for a career in journalism.

Eligibility: Open to applicants who are 1) attending or expecting to attend a Florida college or university; or 2) graduates or prospective graduates of a Florida high school attending or expecting to attend a college in any state. College seniors are not eligible to apply. Along with their application, they must submit an essay (of 300 to 500 words) describing their reason for choosing a career in journalism, their experience in the field, and other factors that should be considered in the selection process; samples of their work (either clips, CDs, or links); and at least 1 letter of recommendation from a teacher, professor, or professional journalist. Selection is based on merit, dedication to journalism, and demonstrated aptitude for print or broadcast journalism. An applicant's racial minority status or financial need may be considered by the selection committee, but those are not required for eligibility.

Financial data: The stipend is $2,000.

Duration: 1 year; recipients may reapply.

Number awarded: 10 to 12 each year.

Deadline: June of each year.

1137 $ BARNUM FESTIVAL FOUNDATION/JENNY LIND COMPETITION FOR SOPRANOS

Barnum Festival Foundation
Attn: Director
1070 Main Street
Bridgeport, CT 06604
Phone: (203) 367–8495; (866) 867–8495; Fax: (203) 367–0212;
Email: barnumfestival@aol.com
Web: www.barnumfestival.com

Summary: To recognize and reward (with scholarships and a concert trip to Sweden) outstanding young female singers who have not yet reached professional status.

Eligibility: Open to sopranos between 20 and 30 years of age who have not yet attained professional status. They must be U.S. citizens. Past finalists may reapply, but former first–place winners and mezzo–sopranos are not eligible. Applicants must submit a CD or audio cassette tape with 2 contrasting arias and 1 art song. Based on the CD or tape, 12 semifinalists are selected for an audition at the Barnum Festival in Bridgeport, Connecticut every April. From that audition, 6 finalists are chosen. Selection of the winner is based on technique, musicianship, diction, interpretation, and stage presence.

Financial data: The winner of the competition is presented with a $2,000 scholarship award to further her musical education at a recognized voice training school, academy, or college or with a recognized voice teacher or coach. She is featured in a concert in June with the Swedish Jenny Lind at a locale in Connecticut and is sent to Sweden with her Swedish counterpart to perform in concerts for 2 weeks in July and August. The runner–up receives a $500 scholarship.

Duration: The competition is held annually.

Number awarded: 2 each year: 1 winner and 1 runner–up.

Deadline: March of each year.

1138 BEA TWO–YEAR/COMMUNITY COLLEGE AWARD

Broadcast Education Association
Attn: Scholarships
1771 N Street, N.W.
Washington, DC 20036–2891
Phone: (202) 429–3935; (888) 380–7222; Fax: (202) 775–2981;
Email: BEAMemberServices@nab.org
Web: www.beaweb.org/scholarships.htm

Summary: To provide financial assistance to current or former community college students who are interested in preparing for a career in broadcasting.

Eligibility: Open to students who are either 1) enrolled full time at a community college; or 2) graduates of a community college enrolled full time at a 4–year college or university. Their current or former community college must be an institutional member of the Broadcast Education Association. Applicants must be studying for a career in broadcasting. Selection is based on evidence that the applicant possesses high integrity, superior academic ability, potential to be an outstanding electronic media professional, and a sense of personal and professional responsibility.

Financial data: The stipend is $1,500.

Duration: 1 year; nonrenewable.

Number awarded: 2 each year.

Deadline: October of each year.

1139 $$ BEATRICE S. DEMERS FOREIGN LANGUAGE FELLOWS PROGRAM

Rhode Island Foundation
Attn: Funds Administrator
One Union Station
Providence, RI 02903
Phone: (401) 427–4017; Fax: (401) 331–8085;
Email: lmonahan@rifoundation.org
Web: www.rifoundation.org

Summary: To provide financial assistance to residents of Rhode Island (regardless of age or educational level) and students at colleges in the state who are interested in a program of study in a foreign language.

Eligibility: Open to 1) residents of Rhode Island who are undergraduates, graduate students, professors, educators, or other persons of any age; and 2) residents of other states enrolled as students at Rhode Island colleges and universities. Applicants must be interested in studying a foreign language at a school in the state; preference is given to applicants proposing to study at the University of Rhode Island. Selection is based on the applicant's dedication to foreign language learning; the likelihood that the proposed program of study will promote a high level of foreign language fluency; and the extent to which the award will promote a diversity of languages studied, program types, and individuals receiving fellowships.

Financial data: Stipends range from $1,000 to $25,000; funds, paid directly to the fellow, are to support the costs of tuition, fee, travel, housing, etc.

Duration: 1 year.
Number awarded: Varies each year.
Deadline: January of each year.

1140 $ BENNY BOOTLE SCHOLARSHIP

American Society of Heating, Refrigerating and Air–Conditioning Engineers
Attn: Scholarship Administrator
1791 Tullie Circle, N.E.
Atlanta, GA 30329–2305
Phone: (404) 539–1120; Fax: (404) 539–2120;
Email: lbenedict@ashrae.org
Web: www.ashrae.org/students/page/1271

Summary: To provide financial assistance to undergraduate architecture and engineering students at schools in selected states who are interested in heating, ventilating, air conditioning, and refrigeration (HVAC&R).

Eligibility: Open to undergraduate architecture and engineering students working on a bachelor's degree in an NAAB– or ABET–accredited program in Georgia, North Carolina, or South Carolina. Applicants must be enrolled full time in a course of study that has traditionally been preparatory for the profession of HVAC&R. They must have a GPA of 3.0 or higher and a standing in the top 30% of their class. Selection is based on potential service to the HVAC&R profession, financial need, leadership ability, recommendations from instructors, and work ethics.

Financial data: The stipend is $3,000.
Duration: 1 year.
Number awarded: 1 each year.
Deadline: November of each year.

1141 $ BENNY GOODMAN FOUNDATION SCHOLARSHIP

Sacramento Region Community Foundation
740 University Avenue, Suite 110
Sacramento, CA 95825
Phone: (916) 921–7723; Fax: (916) 921–7725;
Email: scholarships@sacregcf.org
Web: sacregcf.org/index.cfm/receive/scholarships

Summary: To provide financial assistance to residents of any state who are enrolled at a campus of the University of California and working on a degree in music with an emphasis on jazz or classical.

Eligibility: Open to residents of any state who are currently enrolled at a campus of the University of California. Applicants must be majoring in music with an emphasis on jazz or classical; preference is given to clarinet musicians. They must have a GPA of 3.0 or higher. Along with their application, they must submit a 1–page essay on how music has played a role in their life and their future goals in music. Selection is based on that essay (25%), past music performance (25%), career and musical objectives (25%), and letters of reference (25%).

Financial data: The stipend ranges from $1,000 to $3,500 per year.
Duration: 1 year; may be renewed up to 3 additional years.
Number awarded: 1 or more each year.
Deadline: April of each year.

1142 $ BERKELEY PRIZE ARCHITECTURAL DESIGN FELLOWSHIP

University of California at Berkeley
Department of Architecture
Attn: Raymond Lifchez
474 Wurster Hall
Berkeley, CA 94720
Phone: (510) 642–7585; Fax: (510) 643–5607;
Email: info@berkeleyprize.org
Web: www.berkeleyprize.org/fellowship

Summary: To recognize and reward undergraduate students from any country who submit outstanding essays describing an architectural design competition to be conducted at their own school.

Eligibility: Open to undergraduates currently enrolled at accredited schools of architecture worldwide. Applicants must submit a 1,250–word proposal for an architectural competition to be conducted at their school. The competition should relate to a theme selected annually; recently, the theme was housing for homeless in your community. In their proposal, students should provide a complete description and rules of the competition, including its title, format (e.g., essay, sketch, design problem), time competitors have to complete it, publicity, members of the jury, criteria for evaluating the entries, schedule, and prizes. The competition must be endorsed by the applicant's academic institution; its winning design should be potentially built, assembled, and/or actually used by the public.

Financial data: The student who submits the most outstanding competition proposal receives a prize of $2,500. An additional $2,500 is awarded for use as prizes for the students who actually enter the competition at the winner's institution, to be distributed according to the rules described in the proposal.

Duration: The prize for the best proposal is awarded annually. The architectural competition described in the winning proposal must be organized and completed within the calendar year of the award.
Number awarded: 1 each year.
Deadline: March of each year.

1143 $ BERKELEY PRIZE ESSAY COMPETITION

University of California at Berkeley
Department of Architecture
Attn: Raymond Lifchez
474 Wurster Hall
Berkeley, CA 94720
Phone: (510) 642–7585; Fax: (510) 643–5607;
Email: info@berkeleyprize.org
Web: www.berkeleyprize.org/essay

Summary: To recognize and reward undergraduate students from any country who submit outstanding essays on architecture as a social art.

Eligibility: Open to undergraduates currently enrolled at accredited schools of architecture worldwide. An architecture student may team up with another undergraduate in architecture, urban studies, or the social sciences. Applicants must submit a 500–word proposal for an essay on a question that changes annually but relates to architecture as a social art; recently, students were invited to write on what is being done in their city to make it accessible to people who have physical disabilities and what they, as an architect, believe can be done additionally. On the basis of those proposals, semifinalists are invited to submit 2,500–word essays.

Financial data: A total of $12,500 is available for prizes each year; recently, the jury awarded $4,000 as first prize, $3,500 as second prize, and $2,500 as third prizes to 2 entries judged to be tied. For essays submitted by teams, the prize money is divided equally among the members.

Duration: The competition is held annually.
Number awarded: Varies each year; recently, 4 prizes were awarded.
Deadline: Initial proposals must be submitted by October of each year.

1144 $ BEST TEEN CHEF CULINARY SCHOLARSHIP COMPETITION

The Art Institutes International, Inc.
Free Markets Center
210 Sixth Avenue, 33rd Floor
Pittsburgh, PA 15222–2603
Phone: (412) 995–7685; (888) 624–0300; Fax: (412) 918–2598
Web: www.artinstitutes.edu

Summary: To recognize and reward (with scholarships to participating Art Institutes) high school seniors who are winners in a culinary competition.

Eligibility: Open to seniors graduating from high schools in the United States, Puerto Rico, and Canada who have a GPA of 2.0 or higher and are interested in attending an Art Institute that offers a culinary arts program. Applicants must submit 1) their favorite recipe in standardized format; 2) a 250–word essay on why they would like to study the culinary arts at their participating Art Institute; and 3) a current high school transcript. Those entries are judged on the basis of presentation, creative use of ingredients, ease of preparation, quality of the essay in conveying the applicant's desire to study the culinary arts, and academic performance. Semifinalists are selected at each Art Institute to compete in local cook–offs. In the cook–offs, winners are selected on the basis of technical skills (such as knife skills), safety and sanitation, mise en place, cooking techniques, and clean–up (45%); and judges' scores in taste and flavor, texture and doneness, portion size, temperature, and presentation (55%).

Financial data: The first–prize winner at each participating Arts Institutes International culinary school receives a $4,000 tuition scholarship to that school. The second–prize winner receives a $1,000 tuition scholarship.

Duration: The competition is held annually.
Number awarded: Recently, 38 Art Institutes (37 in the United States and 1 in Canada) participated in this program and each awarded 2 scholarships.
Deadline: February of each year.

1145 $$ BLOUNT–SLAWSON YOUNG ARTISTS COMPETITION

Montgomery Symphony Orchestra
Attn: Young Artists Competition Committee

301 North Hull Street
P.O. Box 1864
Montgomery, AL 36102
Phone: (334) 240–4004;
Email: montgomerysymphony@gmail.com
Web: www.montgomerysymphony.org/comp_Blount.htm

Summary: To recognize and reward talented young musicians who perform at a competition in Montgomery, Alabama.

Eligibility: Open to musicians in grades 7–12 who reside in and attend school in the United States. Students of strings, winds, brass, percussion, and piano are eligible to enter. Acceptable music for the competition includes 1 movement from any work in the standard concerto repertoire. Memorization is preferred but not required.

Financial data: First prize is $2,500 in cash, a $7,500 scholarship (to pay for music education at any institution of higher learning, summer music festival, seminar, etc.), and the opportunity to perform with the Montgomery Symphony Orchestra. Second prize is $4,000, third $1,000, fourth $500, and merit prizes are $250. The second– through fourth–place winners perform at the Young Artists recital.

Duration: The competition is held annually.

Number awarded: 9 cash prizes (including 5 merit prizes) and 1 scholarship are awarded each year.

Deadline: December of each year.

1146 $$ BLUE AWARD

Vienna University of Technology
Attn: Faculty for Architecture and Planning
Attn: Department of Spatial and Sustainable Design
Karlsplatz 13/253–3
A–1040 Vienna
Austria
Phone: 43 1 58801 253301; Fax: 43 1 58801 253399;
Email: office@blueaward.at
Web: www.blueaward.at/about/information.html

Summary: To recognize and reward architectural students from any country who submit outstanding designs relating to sustainable architecture.

Eligibility: Open to students of architecture, regional planning, and urbanism at universities in any country. Applicants must submit a project that addresses the topic of sustainability, particularly in hot and dry climates. Awards are presented in 3 categories: 1) urban development and transformation, landscape development; 2) ecological building; and 3) building in existing structures. Projects located in crisis areas and in areas environmentally threatened are given special consideration.

Financial data: A total of 20,000 Euros is awarded in prizes each year; awards are distributed to the winners of the 3 categories at the discretion of the jury.

Duration: The competition is held biennially, in even–numbered years.

Number awarded: 3 each year: 1 in each category.

Deadline: January of each even–numbered year.

1147 $ BOB BAXTER SCHOLARSHIP

National Press Photographers Foundation
3200 Croasdaile Drive, Suite 306
Durham, NC 27705–2586
Phone: (919) 383–7246; (800) 289–6772; Fax: (919) 383–7261;
Email: info@nppa.org
Web: nppf.org

Summary: To provide financial assistance to undergraduate and graduate students who are interested in preparing for a career in photojournalism.

Eligibility: Open to undergraduate and graduate students enrolled full time at an accredited 4–year college or university in the United States or Canada. Applicants must be preparing for a career in photojournalism. Along with their application, they must submit a portfolio of their work with 6 to 12 entries (single photographs, multiple picture stories, or multimedia stories). Selection is based on aptitude for photojournalism, academic ability, and financial need.

Financial data: The stipend is $2,000.

Duration: 1 year; nonrenewable.

Number awarded: 1 each year.

Deadline: February of each year.

1148 $ BOB EAST SCHOLARSHIP

National Press Photographers Foundation
3200 Croasdaile Drive, Suite 306
Durham, NC 27705–2586
Phone: (919) 383–7246; (800) 289–6772; Fax: (919) 383–7261;
Email: info@nppa.org
Web: nppf.org

Summary: To provide financial assistance to college photojournalists who are interested in continuing college or going to graduate school.

Eligibility: Open to full–time undergraduate and graduate students at 4–year colleges and universities in the United States and Canada. Applicants must be preparing for a career in photojournalism. Along with their application, they must submit a portfolio of their work with 6 to 12 entries (single photographs, multiple picture stories, or multimedia stories). Selection is based on aptitude for photojournalism, academic ability, and financial need.

Financial data: The stipend is $2,000.

Duration: 1 year.

Number awarded: 1 each year.

Deadline: February of each year.

1149 $$ BODIE MCDOWELL SCHOLARSHIPS

Outdoor Writers Association of America
615 Oak Street, Suite 201
Missoula, MT 59801
Phone: (406) 728–7434; (800) 692–2477; Fax: (406) 728–7445;
Email: owaa@montana.com
Web: owaa.org

Summary: To provide financial assistance for college or graduate school to students interested in a career in outdoor writing.

Eligibility: Open to undergraduates entering their junior or senior year of study and graduate students. Applicants must be majoring in a field related to outdoor communications, including print, photography, film, art, or broadcasting. Selection is based on 1) career goals in outdoor communications; 2) examples of work; and 3) letters of recommendation; academic achievement is also considered but is not among the top 3 selection criteria.

Financial data: Stipends range from $1,000 to $5,000 per year.

Number awarded: Varies each year; recently, 6 of these scholarships were awarded: 3 to undergraduates (1 each at $4,500, $3,500, and $3,000) and 3 to graduate students (1 each at $4,500, $3,500, and $3,000).

Deadline: February of each year.

1150 BOHDAN "BO" KOLINSKY MEMORIAL SCHOLARSHIP

Connecticut Sports Writers Alliance
Attn: Scholarship Chair
P.O. Box 70
Unionville, CT 06085
Phone: (860) 677–0087;
Email: RbrtBarton@aol.com
Web: www.ctsportswriters.org

Summary: To provide financial assistance to high school seniors in Connecticut who are interested in attending college in any state to prepare for a career as a sports journalist.

Eligibility: Open to seniors graduating from high schools in Connecticut who are interested in attending a 4–year college or university in any state to study sports journalism. Applicants must submit a resume showing good academic standing, involvement in journalism, extracurricular involvement, and awards; a 1–page essay on why they wish to prepare for a career in print journalism; a letter of recommendation; and 3 samples of their writing published in a daily or weekly newspaper, an online site, a magazine, or a school publication. Selection is based on promise as a journalist and ability to complete college–level academic work.

Financial data: The stipend is $1,000 for the first year; the amount increases annually so the total award is $6,500.

Duration: 1 year; may be renewed up to 3 additional years.

Number awarded: 1 each year.

Deadline: February of each year.

1151 BOSTON AIWF CULINARY SCHOLARSHIP PROGRAM

American Institute of Wine & Food–Boston Chapter
c/o Patricia Metcalf, Scholarship Co–Chair
321 Beach Avenue
Hull, MA 02045
Email: pmbythesea@comcast.net
Web: www.aiwf.org/boston/scholarships.html

Summary: To provide financial assistance to seniors at vocational high schools in Massachusetts who are interested in studying culinary arts at a school in any state.

Eligibility: Open to seniors graduating from the 10 vocational high school programs in Massachusetts. Applicants must be planning to enroll at a postsecondary institution in any state to prepare for a career in the culinary field. Along with their application, they must submit a 250–word essay explaining why they should be chosen as a recipient of this scholarship, why they are preparing for a career in the culinary field, how they would personally apply their knowledge and skills, and how the sponsor could benefit from their selection. Financial need is not considered in the selection process.
Financial data: The stipend is $1,000.
Duration: 1 year.
Number awarded: 2 each year.
Deadline: March of each year.

1152 $$ BOSTON SWEA SCHOLARSHIP

Swedish Women's Educational Association International–Boston Chapter
Scholarship Committee
c/o Gittan Lehman, Secretary
128 Old Lancaster road
Sudbury, MA 01776
Email: GittanL@aol.com
Web: www.sweaboston.org/scholarship
Summary: To provide financial assistance to women who are working on an undergraduate or graduate degree in Swedish studies at a university in New England and interested in visiting Sweden for a study, work/study, or research program.
Eligibility: Open to women currently enrolled as undergraduate or graduate students at a university in New England. Applicants must be interested in participating in a study, work/study, or research program in Sweden. Their project must relate to Swedish culture and society. Along with their application, they must submit 1) a curriculum vitae; 2) a 500–word project proposal describing their interests and goals for their studies in Sweden; 3) letters of recommendation from college instructors who can comment on their planned activities in Sweden and their ability to achieve their goals; and 4) college transcript.
Financial data: A total of $7,000 is available for this program each year.
Duration: At least 1 semester.
Number awarded: 1 or 2 each year.
Deadline: March of each year.

1153 BRASLER PRIZE

National Scholastic Press Association
2221 University Avenue, S.E., Suite 121
Minneapolis, MN 55414
Phone: (612) 625–8335; Fax: (612) 626–0720;
Email: contests@studentpress.org
Web: www.studentpress.org/nspa/contests.html
Summary: To recognize and reward outstanding high school journalists.
Eligibility: Open to high school journalists who submit samples of stories that they have written in 5 categories: news, diversity, feature, sports, and editorial/commentary. In each category, 1 student is selected as the author of the Story of the Year. Selection of those stories is based on quality of writing, sensitivity, and fairness. The first–place winners in each category then compete for this prize.
Financial data: The prize is $1,000.
Duration: The competition is held annually.
Number awarded: 1 each year.
Deadline: June of each year.

1154 $ BRIAN BOLTON GRADUATE/MATURE STUDENT ESSAY CONTEST

Freedom from Religion Foundation
P.O. Box 750
Madison, WI 53701
Phone: (608) 256–8900; Fax: (608) 204–0422;
Email: gradessay@ffrf.org
Web: www.ffrf.org/outreach/student–essay–contests
Summary: To recognize and reward essays on the separation of church and state submitted by graduate or mature undergraduate students.
Eligibility: Open to graduate students of any age and undergraduate students over 25 years of age currently enrolled at colleges and universities in North America. Applicants write an essay on topics that change annually but involve rejecting religion; recent topics were "Why God and Government are a Dangerous Mix—Especially in an Election Year." They may include current examples of religious pandering, church politicking, or political litmus tests. Essays should be from 850 to 1,000 words, accompanied by a paragraph biography identifying the student's college or university, year in school, previous degrees earned, major, and interests.
Financial data: First prize is $3,000, second $2,000, third $1,000, fourth $500, fifth $300, and honorable mentions $200.
Duration: The competition is held annually.
Number awarded: 5 prizes and a varying number of honorable mentions are awarded each year.
Deadline: July of each year.

1155 BRIAN MORDEN MEMORIAL SCHOLARSHIP

Brian Morden Foundation
2809 Columbia Drive
Altoona, PA 16602
Email: fdj@brianmordenfoundation.org
Web: www.brianmordenfoundation.org/scholarship.htm
Summary: To provide financial assistance to students, including cancer survivors, who are interested in studying computer science, medicine, or music in college.
Eligibility: Open to U.S. citizens who, by summer of the year they apply, will have graduated from high school. Applicants must be majoring or planning to major in computer–related fields, medicine, or music. They are not required to be cancer survivors, but cancer survivors are asked to share information on their treatment and to explain how their cancer experience has affected their life. All applicants are asked to submit 5 other brief statements on assigned topics. Selection is based on those statements, GPA, extracurricular activities, awards and honors, and their plan of study.
Financial data: The stipend is $1,000.
Duration: 1 year.
Number awarded: 1 or more each year.
Deadline: March of each year.

1156 BROOME AND ALLEN SCHOLARSHIP FUND

American Sephardi Federation
Attn: Scholarship Committee
15 West 16th Street
New York, NY 10011
Phone: (212) 294–8350; Fax: (212) 294–8348;
Email: info@americansephardifederation.org
Web: www.americansephardifederation.org/scholarship.html
Summary: To provide financial assistance to Sephardic Jews for undergraduate or graduate study in America.
Eligibility: Open to undergraduate and graduate students who are either Sephardic Jews or working on a degree in Sephardic studies. Applicants may be engaged in a program of study or research. They may be citizens or residents of any country, but they must be studying or conducting research in the United States. Selection is based on academic achievement, extracurricular activities, school commendations, and financial need.
Financial data: A stipend is awarded (amount not specified).
Duration: 1 year; recipients may reapply.
Number awarded: Varies each year.
Deadline: May of each year.

1157 $$ BUICK ACHIEVERS SCHOLARSHIP PROGRAM

Scholarship America
Attn: Scholarship Management Services
One Scholarship Way
P.O. Box 297
St. Peter, MN 56082
Phone: (507) 931–1682; (866) 243–4644; Fax: (507) 931–9168;
Email: buickachievers@scholarshipamerica.org
Web: www.buickachievers.com
Summary: To provide financial assistance to students entering college for the first time and planning to major in specified fields related to design, engineering, or business.
Eligibility: Open to high school seniors and graduates who are planning to enroll full time at an accredited 4–year college or university as first–time freshmen. Applicants must be planning to major in fields of engineering (chemical, computer, controls, electrical, energy, environmental, industrial, manufacturing, materials, mechanical, plastic/polymers, or software); technology (automotive technology, computer science, engineering technology, information technology); design (graphic, industrial, product, transportation); or business (accounting, business administration, ergonomics, finance, industrial hygiene, international business, labor and industrial relations, management information

systems, marketing, mathematics, occupational health and safety, production management, statistics, or supply chain/logistics). U.S. citizenship or permanent resident status is required. Selection is based on academic achievement, financial need, participation and leadership in community and school activities, work experience, educational and career goals, and other unusual circumstances. Special consideration is given to first–generation college students, women, minorities, military veterans, and dependents of military personnel.

Financial data: Stipends are $25,000 or $2,000 per year.

Duration: 1 year. The $25,000 awards may be renewed up to 3 additional years (or 4 years for students entering a 5–year engineering program), provided the recipient remains enrolled full time, continues to major in an eligible field, and maintains a GPA of 3.0 or higher. The $2,000 awards are nonrenewable.

Number awarded: 1,100 each year: 100 at $25,000 and 1,000 at $2,000.

Deadline: February of each year.

1158 $ BUILD A FUTURE SCHOLARSHIP

Construction Writers Association
Attn: Executive Director
P.O. Box 14784
Chicago, IL 60614
Phone: (773) 687–8726;
Email: info@constructionwriters.org
Web: www.constructionwriters.org/awards/scholarship

Summary: To provide financial assistance to undergraduates studying journalism, public relations, or communications as applied to fields related to construction.

Eligibility: Open to students currently enrolled as sophomores, juniors, or seniors at an accredited college or university in the United States or Canada. Applicants must be majoring or minoring in journalism, public relations, or communications as applied to architecture, engineering, construction, or construction management. They must have a GPA of 2.5 or higher. Along with their application, they must submit a 1,000–word essay on how this scholarship would benefit them and why they are applying for it; the essay should include a statement of why they would be the best candidate for this scholarship, what it would allow them to accomplish that they would have been unable to do without it, and any financial aspects to their situation that should be considered.

Financial data: The stipend is $2,000. Winners also receive free registration to the sponsor's annual conference and a travel stipend up to $500.

Duration: 1 year.

Number awarded: 1 or more each year.

Deadline: April of each year.

1159 CESAR E. CHAVEZ MEMORIAL EDUCATION AWARD

California Teachers Association
Attn: CTA Foundation for Teaching and Learning
1705 Murchison Drive
P.O. Box 921
Burlingame, CA 94011–0921
Phone: (650) 697–1400;
Email: scholarships@cta.org
Web: www.cta.org/About–CTA/CTA–Foundation/Scholarships.aspx

Summary: To recognize and reward students in California who submit outstanding artwork or essays on themes related to the legacy of Cesar Chavez.

Eligibility: Open to California students in grades preK through college sophomores. Applicants must submit 1) visual arts projects (paintings, drawings, collages, posters, original technologically generated art); or 2) written essays (no biographies). Essays must be of any age–appropriate length for grades preK–2, 200 to 300 words for grades 3–4, 400 to 600 words for grades 5–8, 800 to 1,100 words for grades 9–12, or 1,000 to 1,500 for college freshmen and sophomores. If written in a language other than English, an English translation is required. The theme of the artwork or essay must relate to a principle of Cesar Chavez's legacy: principles of non–violence; self–determination through unionization; social justice for farm workers; safe food, health, environmental issues; human and civil rights issues; teamwork, cooperation, collaboration, and service to others; empowerment of the disenfranchised; or innovation and education. A teacher or professor at the school or college who is a member of the California Teachers Association (CTA) must sponsor the work; each member may sponsor up to 5 entries.

Financial data: Awards are $1,000.

Duration: This competition is held annually.

Number awarded: Varies each year; recently, 47 of these awards were presented: 34 for visual arts and 13 for written essays.

Deadline: January of each year.

1160 $ CALIFORNIA RESTAURANT ASSOCIATION EDUCATIONAL FOUNDATION SCHOLARSHIPS

California Restaurant Association
Attn: CRAEF Scholarship Program
621 Capitol Mall, Suite 2000
Sacramento, CA 95814
Phone: (916) 447–5793; (800) 765–4842; Fax: (916) 447–6182;
Email: craefinfo@calrest.org
Web: www.calrest.org/foundation/our–programs/scholarships

Summary: To provide financial assistance to California residents enrolled or planning to enroll in a postsecondary culinary program at a school in any state.

Eligibility: Open to residents of California who are high school seniors or undergraduates currently enrolled full time in a college or university (may be in any state) in a culinary program. Applicants must have completed at least 1 academic term and have a GPA of 2.75 or higher. They must have work experience in a hospitality–related field of at least 250 hours as a high school senior, 400 hours as a freshman entering the sophomore year, or 550 hours field as a student beyond the freshman year. Along with their application, they must an essay of 500 to 750 words on their motivation for preparing for a career in the restaurant and hospitality industry. Selection is based on the essay, presentation of the application, industry–related work experience, and a personal interview. U.S. citizenship or permanent resident status is required.

Financial data: The stipend is $2,000 per year.

Duration: 1 year; recipients may reapply.

Number awarded: Varies each year.

Deadline: May of each year.

1161 $$ CARLOZZI FAMILY SCHOLARSHIP

New York Women in Communications, Inc.
Attn: NYWICI Foundation
355 Lexington Avenue, 15th Floor
New York, NY 10017–6603
Phone: (212) 297–2133; Fax: (212) 370–9047;
Email: nywicipr@nywici.org
Web: www.nywici.org/foundation/scholarships

Summary: To provide financial assistance to female residents of designated eastern states who are working on an undergraduate degree in communications at a college in any state.

Eligibility: Open to women who are residents of New York, New Jersey, Connecticut, or Pennsylvania and currently enrolled as undergraduates at a college or university in any state. Also eligible are women who reside outside the 4 states but are currently enrolled at a college or university within 1 of the 5 boroughs of New York City. All applicants must be working on a degree in a communications–related field (e.g., advertising, broadcasting, communications, English, film, journalism, marketing, new media, public relations) and be an accomplished writer. They must have a GPA of 3.2 or higher. Along with their application, they must submit a 2–page resume that includes school and extracurricular activities, significant achievements, academic honors and awards, and community service work; a personal essay of 300 to 500 words on their choice of an assigned topic that changes annually; 2 letters of recommendation; and an official transcript. Selection is based on academic record, need, demonstrated leadership, participation in school and community activities, honors, work experience, goals and aspirations, and unusual personal and/or family circumstances. U.S. citizenship is required.

Financial data: The stipend ranges up to $10,000.

Duration: 1 year.

Number awarded: 1 each year.

Deadline: January of each year.

1162 $ CAROLE SIMPSON RTDNF SCHOLARSHIP

Radio Television Digital News Foundation
Attn: Programs, Awards, and Membership Manager
529 14th Street, N.W., Suite 425
Washington, DC 20045
Phone: (202) 725–8318; Fax: (202) 223–4007;
Email: katies@rtdna.org
Web: www.rtdna.org/pages/education/scholarship–info.php

Summary: To provide financial assistance to minority undergraduate students who are interested in preparing for a career in electronic journalism.

Eligibility: Open to sophomore or more advanced minority undergraduate students enrolled in an electronic journalism sequence at an accredited or nationally–recognized college or university. Applicants must submit 1 to 3 examples of their journalistic skills on audio CD or DVD (no more than 15 minutes total, accompanied by scripts); a description of their role on each story

and a list of who worked on each story and what they did; a 1–page statement explaining why they are preparing for a career in electronic journalism with reference to their specific career preference (radio, television, online, reporting, producing, or newsroom management); a resume; and a letter of reference from their dean or faculty sponsor explaining why they are a good candidate for the award and certifying that they have at least 1 year of school remaining.
Financial data: The stipend is $2,000, paid in semiannual installments of $1,000 each.
Duration: 1 year.
Number awarded: 1 each year.
Deadline: May of each year.

1163 CARVILLE M. AKEHURST MEMORIAL SCHOLARSHIP

American Nursery and Landscape Association
Attn: Horticultural Research Institute
1200 G Street, N.W., Suite 800
Washington, DC 20005
Phone: (202) 695–2474; Fax: (888) 761–7883;
Email: scholarships@hriresearch.org
Web: www.hriresearch.org/index.cfm?page=Content&categoryID=167
Summary: To provide financial assistance to residents of Maryland, Virginia, and West Virginia working on an undergraduate or graduate degree in landscape architecture or horticulture at a school in any state.
Eligibility: Open to students enrolled full time in a landscape or horticulture undergraduate or graduate program at an accredited 2– or 4–year college or university. Applicants must be residents of Maryland, Virginia, or West Virginia, although they are not required to attend an institution within those states. Undergraduates must be enrolled as a junior in a 4–year program or a sophomore in a 2–year program and have a minimum GPA of 2.7 overall and 3.0 in their major. Preference is given to applicants who plan to work within the nursery industry, including nursery operations; landscape architecture, design, construction, or maintenance; interiorscape; horticultural distribution; or retail garden center.
Financial data: The stipend is $1,000 per year.
Duration: 1 year; may be renewed.
Number awarded: 2 each year.
Deadline: May of each year.

1164 $ CBC SCHOLARSHIPS

Connecticut Building Congress
Attn: Scholarship Fund
P.O. Box 107
Rocky Hill, CT 06067–0107
Phone: (860) 228–0163;
Email: cbc@cbc–ct.org
Web: www.cbc–ct.org/pages/CBC_Scholarship
Summary: To provide financial assistance to high school seniors in Connecticut who are interested in studying a field related to the construction industry at a college in any state.
Eligibility: Open to seniors graduating from high schools in Connecticut. Applicants must be interested in enrolling at a 2– or 4–year college or university in any state with the goal of completing an associate, bachelor's, or master's degree in a field related to construction (e.g., architecture, construction–related engineering, construction management, surveying, planning, drafting). They must submit an essay (up to 500 words) that explains how their planned studies will relate to a career in the construction industry. Selection is based on academic merit, extracurricular activities, potential, and financial need.
Financial data: Stipends range from $500 to $2,000 per year.
Duration: Up to 4 years.
Number awarded: Varies each year.
Deadline: March of each year.

1165 $ CBC SPOUSES HEINEKEN USA PERFORMING ARTS SCHOLARSHIP

Congressional Black Caucus Foundation, Inc.
Attn: Director, Educational Programs
1720 Massachusetts Avenue, N.W.
Washington, DC 20036
Phone: (202) 263–2800; (800) 784–2577; Fax: (202) 775–0773;
Email: scholarships@cbcfinc.org
Web: www.cbcfinc.org/scholarships.html
Summary: To provide financial assistance to undergraduate students who are interested in studying the performing arts.
Eligibility: Open to graduating high school seniors and current undergraduates enrolled or planning to enroll full time at an accredited college or university. Applicants must be interested in preparing for a career in the performing arts, including theater, motion pictures, drama, comedy, music, dance, opera, marching bands, and other musical ensembles. They must have a GPA of 2.5 or higher. Along with their application, they must submit a 2–minute recorded sample of their performance; a 1–page resume listing their extracurricular activities, honors, employment, community service, and special skills; and a personal statement of 500 to 1,000 words on themselves and their interests. They must also be able to demonstrate financial need, leadership ability, and participation in community service activities.
Financial data: The stipend is $3,000.
Duration: 1 year.
Number awarded: Up to 10 each year.
Deadline: April of each year.

1166 $ CBC SPOUSES VISUAL ARTS SCHOLARSHIP

Congressional Black Caucus Foundation, Inc.
Attn: Director, Educational Programs
1720 Massachusetts Avenue, N.W.
Washington, DC 20036
Phone: (202) 263–2800; (800) 784–2577; Fax: (202) 775–0773;
Email: scholarships@cbcfinc.org
Web: www.cbcfinc.org/scholarships.html
Summary: To provide financial assistance to undergraduate students who are interested in studying the visual arts.
Eligibility: Open to graduating high school seniors and current undergraduates enrolled or planning to enroll full time at an accredited college or university. Applicants must be interested in preparing for a career in the visual arts, including architecture, ceramics, drawing, fashion, graphic design, illustration, interior design, painting, photography, sketching, video production, or other decorative arts. They must have a GPA of 2.5 or higher. Along with their application, they must submit 5 samples of their work in the art genre for which they are applying; a 1–page resume listing their extracurricular activities, honors, employment, community service, and special skills; and a personal statement of 500 to 1,000 words on themselves and their interests. They must also be able to demonstrate financial need, leadership ability, and participation in community service activities.
Financial data: The stipend is $3,000.
Duration: 1 year.
Number awarded: Up to 10 each year.
Deadline: April of each year.

1167 $ CHARLES AND LUCILLE KING FAMILY FOUNDATION UNDERGRADUATE SCHOLARSHIPS

Charles and Lucille King Family Foundation, Inc.
c/o Charles Brucia & Co.
1212 Avenue of the Americas, Seventh Floor
New York, NY 10036
Phone: (212) 682–2913;
Email: KingScholarships@aol.com
Web: www.kingfoundation.org
Summary: To provide financial assistance to undergraduate students who are majoring in television or film.
Eligibility: Open to full–time students who are entering their junior or senior year at a 4–year U.S. college or university and majoring in television or film. U.S. citizenship is not required. Applicants must submit a 2–page personal statement that describes their goals and why they feel that furthering their education will help them accomplish those goals. Selection is based on academic excellence, professional potential, and financial need.
Financial data: Stipends range up to $3,500 per year.
Duration: 1 year; students who receive an award as a junior may renew the award in their senior year if they earn at least a 3.0 GPA.
Number awarded: Varies each year; recently, 13 of these scholarships were awarded.
Deadline: March of each year.

1168 $ CHARLES E. PETERSON PRIZE

National Park Service
Attn: Historic American Buildings Survey
1201 Eye Street, N.W. (2270)

Washington, DC 20005
Phone: (202) 354–2166; Fax: (202) 371–6473
Web: www.cr.nps.gov/hdp/competitions/peterson.htm

Summary: To recognize and reward sets of measured drawings prepared by students or teams of students that meet standards of the Historic American Buildings Survey (HABS) of the National Park Service.

Eligibility: Open to students or teams of students in architecture, architectural history, interior design, and American studies who have faculty sponsorship. Participants are required to produce a set of measured drawings made to HABS standards. The drawings must be of a building that has not yet been recorded by HABS through measured drawings, or it must be an addendum to existing HABS drawings that makes a substantial contribution to the understanding of significant features of the building. Applicants should contact the HABS office to determine if a structure has already been recorded. Selection is based on a short–form historical report (5 points), significance of building being documented (5 points), field records (25 points), appropriate level of documentation (30 points), and presentation (35 points).

Financial data: First prize is $3,000, second $2,500, and third $2,000.

Duration: The competition is held annually.

Number awarded: 3 prizes are awarded each year.

Deadline: Entry forms must be submitted by May of each year. Completed entries are due in June.

1169 CHOPIN FOUNDATION OF THE UNITED STATES SCHOLARSHIP PROGRAM FOR YOUNG PIANISTS

Chopin Foundation of the United States, Inc.
Attn: Scholarship Committee
1440 79th Street Causeway, Suite 117
Miami, FL 33141
Phone: (305) 868–0624; Fax: (305) 865–5150;
Email: info@chopin.org
Web: www.chopin.org

Summary: To recognize and reward (with scholarships) outstanding young American pianists who demonstrate "a special affinity for the interpretation of Chopin's music."

Eligibility: Open to any qualified American pianist (citizen or legal resident) between the ages of 14 and 17 whose field of study is music and whose major is piano. Enrollment at the secondary or undergraduate school level as a full–time student is required. Applicants must submit a formal application, along with a statement of career goals, a minimum of 2 references from piano teachers or performers, and a performance DVD of 20 to 30 minutes of Chopin's works. Each piece must be an unedited performance.

Financial data: The award is $1,000.

Duration: 1 year; renewable for up to 4 years, as long as the recipient continues to study piano, maintains satisfactory academic progress, and submits an annual audiocassette of unedited performances of designated works by Chopin for evaluation.

Number awarded: Up to 10 each year.

Deadline: April of each year.

1170 $ CHRISTIAN REFORMED CHURCH RACE RELATIONS SCHOLARSHIP

Summary: To provide financial assistance to undergraduate and graduate minority students interested in attending colleges related to the Christian Reformed Church in North America (CRCNA).

See Listing #136.

1171 CHRISTOPHER COLUMBUS ESSAY CONTEST

Daughters of the American Revolution–National Society
Attn: American History Committee
1776 D Street, N.W.
Washington, DC 20006–5303
Phone: (202) 628–1776;
Email: historian@dar.org
Web: www.dar.org/natsociety/essays.cfm

Summary: To recognize and reward high school students who submit essays on a topic related to Christopher Columbus.

Eligibility: Open to students in grades 9–12. Applicants must submit an essay, from 800 to 1,200 words, on a topic that changes annually but relates to Christopher Columbus. Recently, the topic was "How did the faith and courage of Christopher Columbus give to mankind a new world?" Selection is based on historical accuracy, adherence to topic, organization of material, interest, originality, spelling, grammar, punctuation, and neatness. Competitions are held at the chapter, state, division, and then national level.

Financial data: The national winner receives an award of $1,200 and paid lodging and transportation for the winner and a parent to visit Washington, D.C. for the award ceremony. The national second–place winner receives $500 and the third–place winner receives $300.

Duration: The competition is held annually.

Number awarded: 3 national winners are selected each year.

Deadline: Each local chapter sets its own deadline; some are as early as November.

1172 CHRISTOPHER J. GEORGES AWARD

Nieman Foundation
Walter Lippmann House
One Francis Avenue
Cambridge, MA 02138–2098
Phone: (617) 495–2237; Fax: (617) 495–8976;
Email: nieman@harvard.edu
Web: www.nieman.harvard.edu

Summary: To recognize and reward college journalists who submit outstanding stories as part of the Georges Collegiate Weekend at the Nieman Foundation of Harvard University.

Eligibility: Open to student journalists at campus newspapers that are accepted for participation in the Georges Collegiate Weekend. Each school may submit 1 entry, which may be either a single story or a multipart series. Entries must have been written and published in the student newspaper during the preceding calendar year. The work should reflect the values of the journalist for whom the award is named, to "represent in–depth reporting on a policy issue of importance affecting the campus, community, or beyond."

Financial data: The award is $1,000 for the principal reporter and an additional $500 for the principal editor of the winning piece. If a team of 2 reporters co–authored the winning piece, each receives $1,000. If the winning entry is co–authored by more than 2 reporters, the total award remains capped at $2,500, to be shared equally among the winning reporters.

Duration: The award is presented annually.

Number awarded: 1 reporter or team of co–reporters and 1 editor receive awards each year.

Deadline: March of each year.

1173 CHRISTOPHERS POSTER CONTEST

The Christophers
Attn: Youth Department Coordinator
5 Hanover Square, 11th Floor
New York, NY 10004
Phone: (212) 759–4050; (888) 298–4050; Fax: (212) 838–5073;
Email: youth@christophers.org
Web: www.christophers.org/Page.aspx?pid=274

Summary: To recognize and reward posters drawn by high school students that best illustrate the motto of The Christophers: "It's better to light one candle than to curse the darkness."

Eligibility: Open to all students in grades 9–12 who prepare posters on the theme: "You Can Make a Difference." The posters must be 15" × 20" and the original work of 1 student. Selection is based on overall impact, effectiveness in conveying the theme, originality, and artistic merit.

Financial data: First prize is $1,000, second $500, third $250, and honorable mentions $100.

Duration: The competition is held annually.

Number awarded: 8 each year: 1 each for first, second, and third place plus 5 honorable mentions.

Deadline: January of each year.

1174 CIVIL WAR HIGH SCHOOL ESSAY CONTEST

Gilder Lehrman Institute of American History
Attn: Civil War Essay Contest
19 West 44th Street, Suite 500
New York, NY 10036
Phone: (646) 366–9666; Fax: (646) 366–9669;
Email: affiliates@gilderlehrman.org
Web: www.gilderlehrman.org/affiliate/civil_war.php

Summary: To recognize and reward students at selected high schools who write outstanding essays on topics related to the Civil War.

Eligibility: Open to students at high schools that participate in the Gilder Lehrman Institute (GLI) Network. Candidates must submit essays at least 1,500 words in length on Civil War topics.
Financial data: First prize is $1,000, second $750, third $500, and honorable mentions $100. The school of the first–prize winner also receives a $500 honorarium.
Duration: The competition is held annually.
Number awarded: Up to 10 prizes are awarded each year: 3 main prizes and up to 7 honorable mentions.
Deadline: February of each year.

1175 $ CLAMPITT PAPER SCHOLARSHIP

Electronic Document Systems Foundation
Attn: EDSF Scholarship Awards
1845 Precinct Line Road, Suite 212
Hurst, TX 76054
Phone: (817) 849–1145; Fax: (817) 849–1185;
Email: info@edsf.org
Web: www.edsf.org/what_we_do/scholarships/index.html
Summary: To provide financial assistance to undergraduate and graduate students at schools in designated states, especially those who are working on a degree in the field of document management and graphic communications.
Eligibility: Open to full–time undergraduate and graduate students at colleges and universities in Arkansas, New Mexico, Oklahoma, and Texas. Special consideration is given to student who demonstrate a strong interest in preparing for a career in the document management and graphic communications industry, including computer science and engineering (e.g., web design, webmaster, software development, materials engineer, applications specialist, information technology designer, systems analyst); graphic and media communications (e.g., graphic designer, illustrator, color scientist, print production, prepress imaging specialist, workflow specialist, document preparation, production and/or document distribution, content management, e–commerce, imaging science, printing, web authoring, electronic publishing, archiving, security); or business (e.g., sales, marketing, trade shows, customer service, project or product development, management). Preference is given to graduate students and upper–division undergraduates, but freshmen and sophomores who can show interest, experience, and/or commitment to the document management and graphic communication industry are encouraged to apply. Applicants must have a GPA of 3.0 or higher. Along with their application, they must submit 2 essays on assigned topics that change annually but relate to the document management and graphic communication industries. Selection is based on the essays, academic excellence, participation in school activities, community service, honors and organizational affiliations, education goals, and recommendations; financial need is not considered.
Financial data: The stipend is $2,500.
Duration: 1 year.
Number awarded: 1 each year.
Deadline: April of each year.

1176 $$ CLAN MACBEAN FOUNDATION GRANTS

Clan MacBean Foundation
Attn: Director
7475 West Fifth Avenue, Suite 201Z
Lakewood, CO 80226
Phone: (303) 233–6002;
Email: macbean@ecentral.com
Web: www.clanmacbean.net/scholarships.html
Summary: To provide financial assistance to college students interested in studying subjects or conducting research relating to 1) Scottish culture; or 2) the liberal arts and sciences as related to the "Human Family."
Eligibility: Open to students who have completed at least 2 years of college. Applicants may be either working on a degree or conducting a specific project. If they are working on a degree, their course of study must relate directly to Scottish culture or be in a field of the liberal arts and sciences that leads directly to the improvement and benefit of the "Human Family." If they are conducting a specific project, it must reflect direct involvement in the preservation or enhancement of Scottish culture or contribute directly to the improvement and benefit of the "Human Family." Financial need is not considered in the selection process.
Financial data: Grants up to $5,000 are available. Funds may be used for tuition, fees, books, room and board, printing and publishing costs, historical research fees, and/or initial costs in establishing a project.
Duration: 1 year.
Number awarded: 1 or more each year.
Deadline: April of each year.

1177 $ COLBURN–PLEDGE MUSIC SCHOLARSHIP

Colburn–Pledge Music Scholarship Foundation
Attn: Secretary
6322 Cornplanter
San Antonio, TX 78238–1514
Email: cleoviolin@satx.rr.com
Summary: To provide financial assistance to Texas residents who are interested in studying classical music at a school in any state.
Eligibility: Open to residents of Texas at the pre–high school, high school, or college level. Applicants must be interested in studying a string instrument (violin, viola, cello, bass) in classical music with the intention of becoming a professional musician. They must be attending or planning to attend a college, music school, or music camp in any state. Financial need must be demonstrated, but selection is based primarily on musical talent.
Financial data: Stipends range up to $4,000.
Duration: 1 year.
Deadline: April of each year.

1178 COLLEGE PHOTOGRAPHER OF THE YEAR

National Press Photographers Foundation
c/o University of Missouri at Columbia
Attn: CPOY Director
101B Lee Hills Hall
Columbia, MO 65211
Phone: (573) 884–2118; Fax: (573) 884–4999;
Email: info@cpoy.org
Web: www.cpoy.org
Summary: To recognize and reward the outstanding photojournalism work of undergraduate and graduate students.
Eligibility: Open to students currently working on an undergraduate or graduate degree. Applicants may submit work completed during the previous academic year in up to 16 different categories. Single picture categories are: 1) spot news; 2) general news; 3) feature; 4) sports action; 5) sports feature; 6) portrait; 7) interpretive eye; and 8) illustration. Multiple picture categories are: 9) interpretive project; 10) domestic picture story; 11) international picture story; and 12) documentary. Portfolio categories are 13 sports portfolio; and 14) portfolio. Multimedia categories are 15) large group multimedia project; 16) individual multimedia story or essay; 17) multimedia project; and 18) solo journalist multimedia story or essay. Professional photographers, videographers, or web producers who have worked 2 years or more are not eligible.
Financial data: In the portfolio competition, the first–place winner receives a 14–week internship at *National Geographic Magazine* and the Colonel William J. Lookadoo Award of $1,000. The second–place winner receives the Milton Freier Award of $500. Winners in other categories receive equipment and additional educational opportunities.
Duration: The competition is held annually, in the fall.
Deadline: October of each year.

1179 $ COLORADO FEDERATION OF GARDEN CLUBS SCHOLARSHIPS

Colorado Federation of Garden Clubs
c/o Jessie Boyer, Scholarship Chair
5596 South Lewiston Street
Centennial, CO 80015–4068
Phone: (303) 693–1168;
Email: boyerjessie@hotmail.com
Web: www.coloradogardenclubs.org/education/scholarships.html
Summary: To provide financial assistance to upper–division and graduate students in horticulture, landscape design, and related disciplines.
Eligibility: Open to residents of Colorado currently enrolled as full–time juniors, seniors, and graduate students (master's only) at a college or university in any state. Applicants must be working on a degree in agricultural education, agronomy, botany, biology, city (rural and urban) planning, environmental concerns, environmental conservation (including environmental engineering and environmental law), floriculture, forestry, habitat or forest systems ecology, horticulture, land management, landscape design, plant pathology, wildlife science, or allied subjects. They must have at least a 3.25 GPA and be able to demonstrate financial need. Along with their application, they must submit a personal letter discussing their background, future goals, financial need, and commitment to their chosen career. Selection is based on academic record (40%), applicant's letter (30%), listing of honors, extracurricular activities, and work experience (10%), financial need (15%), and recommendations (5%). U.S. citizenship or permanent resident status is required; international and foreign exchange students are not eligible.

Financial data: The stipend is $2,000.
Duration: 1 year.
Number awarded: 1 each year.
Deadline: February of each year.

1180 COLORADO STATE THESPIAN SCHOLARSHIPS

Colorado State Thespians
Attn: Brittany Wallis, Audition Coordinator
2001 Lincoln Street, Suite 1611
Denver, CO 80202
Phone: (720) 972–4501;
Email: info@cothespians.com
Web: www.cothespians.com/scholarships.htm
Summary: To provide financial assistance to high school seniors in Colorado, New Mexico, and Wyoming who have been active in theater and plan to attend college in any state.
Eligibility: Open to seniors graduating from high schools in Colorado, New Mexico, or Wyoming who have a GPA of 2.75 or higher. Applicants must be active members of their thespian troupe and registered for the Colorado State Thespian Conference. At the conference, they must present 1) a 2–minute audition in acting, musical theater, or dance; or 2) a portfolio with designs, renderings, plots, pictures, or other materials that illustrate their expertise in technical theater. Selection is based on the audition or portfolio.
Financial data: The stipend is $1,000. Funds are sent directly to the recipient's college or university.
Duration: 1 year.
Number awarded: 3 each year.
Deadline: Students must register for the conference by November of each year.

1181 $$ COLVIN SCHOLARSHIP PROGRAM

Certified Angus Beef LLC
Attn: Trudi Hoyle
206 Riffel Road
Wooster, OH 44691–8588
Phone: (330) 345–2333; (800) 225–2333, ext. 211; Fax: (330) 345–0808;
Email: thoyle@certifiedangusbeef.com
Web: www.certifiedangusbeef.com/press/colvin/index.php
Summary: To provide financial assistance to upper–division students working on a degree related to the beef industry.
Eligibility: Open to students entering their junior or senior year of college. Applicants must have demonstrated a commitment to the beef industry through work on a degree in meat science, food science, animal science, marketing, business, communications, journalism, or other field related to the industry. Along with their application, they must submit a 1,000–word essay on a topic that changes annually but relates to the beef industry. Selection is based on, in this order of importance, activities and scholastic achievement, communication skills (both essay and verbal), and reference letters.
Financial data: Stipends range from $1,000 to $5,000. Funds are paid directly to the recipient for tuition, fees, books, room and board, or other direct college expenses.
Duration: 1 year.
Number awarded: 5 each year: 1 each at $5,000, $4,000, $3,000, $2,000, and $1,000.
Deadline: November of each year.

1182 CONNECTICUT HOSPITALITY EDUCATIONAL FOUNDATION SCHOLARSHIPS

Connecticut Restaurant Association
Attn: Connecticut Hospitality Educational Foundation
40 Hungerford Street
Hartford, CT 06106
Phone: (860) 278–8008, ext. 108; Fax: (860) 278–8006;
Email: conkling@ctrestaurant.org
Web: www.cthef.org
Summary: To provide financial assistance to Connecticut high school seniors interested in preparing for a career in the food service industry at a school in any state.
Eligibility: Open to seniors graduating from high schools in Connecticut who have participated in the ProStart Program and are entering an accredited college, university, or culinary school in any state. Applicants must be preparing for a career in culinary arts or culinary management. They must have a GPA of 2.65 or higher. Along with their application, they must submit a 300–word essay explain why they are the best candidate for this scholarship, including their experience or desire for a career in the culinary arts and their financial need. Selection is based on academic achievement, participation in extracurricular activities, employment while attending school, and financial need.
Financial data: The stipend is $1,000.
Duration: 1 year.
Number awarded: Varies each year.
Deadline: June of each year.

1183 $ COPY EDITING SCHOLARSHIPS

American Copy Editors Society
Attn: Education Fund Vice President
7 Avenida Vista Grande, Suite B7 467
Santa Fe, MN 87508
Email: alex@execpc.com
Web: www.copydesk.org/edfund/apply
Summary: To provide financial assistance to undergraduate and graduate students interested in becoming copy editors.
Eligibility: Open to college juniors, seniors, and graduate students who are interested in a career as a copy editor. Graduating students who will take full–time jobs or internships as copy editors are also eligible. Applicants must submit 1) a resume that includes significant activities and honors related to editing; 2) an essay, up to 500 words, on the aspects of copy editing that are and will be the most important in a multimedia world; 3) 3 letters of recommendation; and 4) as many as 6 headlines they have written. Selection is based on commitment to copy editing as a career, work experience in copy editing, academic achievement, and recommendations. Financial need is not considered. The highest ranked applicant receives the Merv Aubespin Scholarship.
Financial data: Stipends are $2,500 (for the Merv Aubespin Scholarship) or $1,000.
Duration: 1 year.
Number awarded: 5 each year: 1 at $2,500 and 4 at $1,000.
Deadline: November of each year.

1184 CORINNE JEANNINE SCHILLINGS FOUNDATION ACADEMIC SCHOLARSHIPS

Corinne Jeannine Schillings Foundation
10645 Nebraska Street
Frankfort, IL 60423–2223
Phone: (815) 534–5598;
Email: dschillings1@comcast.net
Web: www.cjsfoundation.org/html/academic_study.html
Summary: To provide financial assistance to Girl Scouts who plan to study a foreign language in college.
Eligibility: Open to members of the Girl Scouts who have earned the Silver or Gold Award. Applicants must be enrolled or planning to enroll full time at a 4–year college or university and major or minor in a foreign language. They must have a GPA of 3.0 or higher. Along with their application, they must submit a 5–page essay about themselves, including the impact of Girl Scouting on their life, why they have chosen to major or minor in a foreign language, how they plan to utilize their language skills, and why they feel they should receive this scholarship. Financial need is not considered in the selection process.
Financial data: The stipend is $1,500 per year.
Duration: 1 year; may be renewed up to 3 additional years, provided the recipient maintains a GPA of 3.0 or higher, both overall and in foreign language classes.
Number awarded: Varies each year; recently, this program awarded 13 new and renewal scholarships.
Deadline: May of each year.

1185 $$ COURTLAND PAUL SCHOLARSHIP

Landscape Architecture Foundation
Attn: Leadership in Landscape Scholarship Program
818 18th Street, N.W., Suite 810
Washington, DC 20006–3520
Phone: (202) 331–7070; Fax: (202) 331–7079;
Email: scholarships@lafoundation.org
Web: www.lafoundation.org
Summary: To provide financial assistance to upper–division students working on a degree in landscape architecture.
Eligibility: Open to landscape architecture students in the final 2 years of undergraduate study. Applicants must be able to demonstrate financial need

and a GPA of 2.0 or higher. Along with their application, they must submit a 500–word essay describing their aspirations, ability to surmount obstacles, high level of drive, and need for financial assistance. U.S. citizenship is required.
Financial data: The stipend is $5,000. Funds may be used only for tuition and books.
Duration: 1 year.
Number awarded: 1 each year.
Deadline: February of each year.

1186 $$ CREATE–A–GREETING–CARD SCHOLARSHIP CONTEST

Prudent Publishing Company, Inc.
The Gallery Collection
Attn: Scholarship Administrator
65 Challenger Road
P.O. Box 150
Ridgefield Park, NJ 07660
Phone: (800) 950–7064;
Email: scholarshipadmin@gallerycollection.com
Web: www.gallerycollection.com/greetingcardscontests.htm
Summary: To recognize and reward (with college scholarships) students and military personnel who submit artwork for use on a greeting card.
Eligibility: Open to legal residents (including international students who have a valid visa) of the United States and its territories. Applicants must be 1) high school, home school, college, or university students who are at least 14 years of age; or 2) military personnel who are younger than 35 years of age. They must submit an original photograph, artwork, or computer graphics appropriate for the front of a greeting card. Both digital and paper submissions are accepted. Selection is based on overall aesthetic appeal, quality of execution, creativity and originality, incorporation of design elements, appropriateness for use as a greeting card, attractiveness to the sponsor's corporate and consumer customers, and suitability as a design in the sponsor's greeting card line.
Financial data: The award is $10,000. For students currently enrolled at a college or university, funds are sent directly to the institution as payment toward tuition, fees, books, and supplies. For students who are still minors, funds are paid to the winner's parent or guardian as custodian. The winner's school receives a grant of $1,000.
Duration: The competition is held annually.
Number awarded: 1 each year.
Deadline: January of each year.

1187 $ CTBA SCHOLARSHIPS

Connecticut Broadcasters Association
Attn: Scholarships
90 South Park Street
Willimantic, CT 06226
Phone: (860) 633–5031; Fax: (860) 456–5688;
Email: mcrice@prodigy.net
Web: www.ctba.org/page.cfm?page=17
Summary: To provide financial assistance to Connecticut residents who are interested in attending college in any state to prepare for a career in broadcasting.
Eligibility: Open to Connecticut residents who are entering their first, second, third, or fourth year at a 2– or 4–year college, university or technical school in any state. Applicants must be majoring in broadcasting, communications, marketing, or a related field. Selection is based on academic achievement, community service, goals in the chosen field, and financial need.
Financial data: The stipend is $2,500.
Duration: 1 year.
Number awarded: Varies each year.
Deadline: March of each year.

1188 $$ CULINARY EDUCATION SCHOLARSHIPS

The Culinary Trust
Attn: Scholarship Program
P.O. Box 5485
Portland, OR 97208
Phone: (347) 284–6415;
Email: scholarships@theculinarytrust.com
Web: www.theculinarytrust.org/scholarships–and–grants
Summary: To provide financial assistance to students interested in pursuing training in the United States or abroad in the culinary arts.
Eligibility: Open to residents of any country who are at least 18 years of age and have at least a high school diploma or equivalent. There is no maximum age limit. Applicants must be enrolled or planning to enroll in specified culinary arts educational programs. They must be able to meet the admission requirements of the school they plan to attend, including language proficiency. If they have been students in the last 5 years, they must have a GPA of 3.0 or higher or international equivalent. Along with their application, they must submit a 2–page essay on their educational and career goals. Selection is based on that essay, awards and honors, volunteer activities and community service, 2 letters of recommendation, and financial need.
Financial data: Stipends range from $1,500 to $5,000 or equivalent amounts in foreign currencies.
Duration: 1 year.
Number awarded: Varies each year.
Deadline: February of each year.

1189 $ CYNTHIA AND ALAN BARAN FINE ARTS AND MUSIC SCHOLARSHIP

Community Foundation of Middle Tennessee
Attn: Scholarship Committee
3833 Cleghorn Avenue, Suite 400
Nashville, TN 37215–2519
Phone: (615) 321–4939; (888) 540–5200; Fax: (615) 327–2746;
Email: grants@cfmt.org
Web: www.cfmt.org/request/scholarships/allscholarships
Summary: To provide financial assistance to residents of Tennessee who are working on an undergraduate or graduate degree in fine arts or music at a school in any state.
Eligibility: Open to residents of Tennessee who are full– or part–time rising sophomores, juniors, seniors, or graduate students at an accredited college, university, or institute in any state. Applicants must be working on 1) a B.F.A. (bachelor of fine arts), B.A. in studio art (defined to include painting, drawing, sculpture, ceramics, photography, or printmaking), or M.F.A. (master of fine arts); or 2) a bachelor's or master's degree in music, with preference to those studying acoustic mandolin or acoustic guitar. They must have a GPA of 3.0 or higher. Along with their application, they must submit an essay describing their educational plans and how those plans will help them reach their career goals. Financial need is considered in the selection process.
Financial data: Stipends range from $500 to $2,500 per year. Funds are paid to the recipient's school and must be used for tuition, fees, books, supplies, room, board, or miscellaneous expenses.
Duration: 1 year.
Number awarded: 2 each year: 1 for fine arts and 1 for music.
Deadline: March of each year.

1190 $$ DANIEL LADNER SCHOLARSHIPS

New York Women in Communications, Inc.
Attn: NYWICI Foundation
355 Lexington Avenue, 15th Floor
New York, NY 10017–6603
Phone: (212) 297–2133; Fax: (212) 370–9047;
Email: nywicipr@nywici.org
Web: www.nywici.org/foundation/scholarships
Summary: To provide financial assistance to female upper–division and graduate students who reside in designated eastern states and are interested in preparing for a career in financial or political communications at a college or graduate school in any state.
Eligibility: Open to female residents of New York, New Jersey, Connecticut, or Pennsylvania who are attending a college or university in any state. Also eligible are women who reside outside the 4 states but are currently enrolled at a college or university within 1 of the 5 boroughs of New York City. Applicants must be college juniors, seniors, or graduate students who are preparing for a career in either 1) financial communications (e.g., marketing, advertising, investor relations, public relations, corporate communications, media/journalism); or 2) political communications (e.g., political journalism; advertising; analysis; consulting; public, government, or international affairs; diplomacy; speechwriting; advocacy). They must have a GPA of 3.2 or higher. Graduate students must be members of New York Women in Communications, Inc. (NYWICI). Along with their application, they must submit a 2–page resume that includes school and extracurricular activities, significant achievements, academic honors and awards, and community service work; a personal essay of 300 to 500 words on their choice of an assigned topic that changes annually; 2 letters of recommendation; and an official transcript. Selection is based on academic record, need, demonstrated leadership, participation in school and community activities,

honors, work experience, goals and aspirations, and unusual personal and/or family circumstances. U.S. citizenship is required.
Financial data: The stipend ranges up to $10,000.
Duration: 1 year.
Number awarded: 2 each year.
Deadline: January of each year.

1191 $$ DAVID BARRETT MEMORIAL SCHOLARSHIP

American Society of Interior Designers
Attn: ASID Foundation
608 Massachusetts Avenue, N.E.
Washington, DC 20002–6006
Phone: (202) 546–3480; Fax: (202) 546–3240;
Email: education@asid.org
Web: www.asidfoundation.org
Summary: To provide financial assistance to undergraduate and graduate students working on a degree in interior design with an emphasis on classical designs and traditional materials.
Eligibility: Open to undergraduate and graduate students enrolled in an interior design program at a degree–granting institution. Applicants must be able to demonstrate a continuing interest and ability in utilizing classical designs and traditional materials, inclusive of furniture and fabrics. Along with their application, they must submit 1) a design portfolio of 8 to 12 components with a written description detailing how classical designs and traditional materials are used in each design component; 2) a personal statement; and 3) a letter of recommendation.
Financial data: The stipend is $12,000.
Duration: 1 year.
Number awarded: 1 each even–numbered year.
Deadline: November of each odd–numbered year.

1192 DAVID HONEYCUTT MEMORIAL SCHOLARSHIP

Prime Contractors, Inc.
525 North Belt, Suite 172
Houston, TX 77060
Phone: (281) 999–0875; Fax: (281) 999–0885
Web: www.primecontractorsinc.com/Careers.html
Summary: To provide financial assistance to students preparing for a career in a field related to construction.
Eligibility: Open to students who are enrolled or planning to enroll at a college or university in any state. Applicants must be preparing for a career in construction management, architecture, or civil engineering. They must have a GPA of 3.0 or higher. Along with their application, they must submit an essay of 3 to 5 pages describing why they want to be awarded this scholarship, what value it would have for them, and why they have chosen a career in a construction–related field. Financial need is not considered in the selection process.
Financial data: The stipend is $1,000.
Duration: 1 year.
Number awarded: 5 each year.
Deadline: April of each year.

1193 $ DAVID HOODS MEMORIAL SCHOLARSHIP

Electronic Document Systems Foundation
Attn: EDSF Scholarship Awards
1845 Precinct Line Road, Suite 212
Hurst, TX 76054
Phone: (817) 849–1145; Fax: (817) 849–1185;
Email: info@edsf.org
Web: www.edsf.org/what_we_do/scholarships/index.html
Summary: To provide financial assistance to undergraduate and graduate students from any country interested in preparing for a career in document management and graphic communications, especially those interested in marketing and public relations.
Eligibility: Open to full–time undergraduate and graduate students from any country who demonstrate a strong interest in preparing for a career in the document management and graphic communications industry, including computer science and engineering (e.g., web design, webmaster, software development, materials engineer, applications specialist, information technology designer, systems analyst); graphic and media communications (e.g., graphic designer, illustrator, color scientist, print production, prepress imaging specialist, workflow specialist, document preparation, production and/or document distribution, content management, e–commerce, imaging science, printing, web authoring, electronic publishing, archiving, security); or business (e.g., sales, marketing, trade shows, customer service, project or product development, management). Preference is given to graduate students and upper–division undergraduates, but freshmen and sophomores who can show interest, experience, and/or commitment to the document management and graphic communication industry are encouraged to apply. Special consideration is given to students interested in marketing and public relations. Applicants must have a GPA of 3.0 or higher. Along with their application, they must submit 2 essays on assigned topics that change annually but relate to the document management and graphic communication industries. Selection is based on the essays, academic excellence, participation in school activities, community service, honors and organizational affiliations, education goals, and recommendations; financial need is not considered.
Financial data: The stipend is $2,000.
Duration: 1 year.
Number awarded: 1 each year.
Deadline: April of each year.

1194 DAVID L. WOLPER STUDENT DOCUMENTARY ACHIEVEMENT AWARD

International Documentary Association
1201 West Fifth Street, Suite M270
Los Angeles, CA 90017–2029
Phone: (213) 534–3600; Fax: (213) 534–3610;
Email: programming@documentary.org
Web: www.documentary.org
Summary: To recognize and reward outstanding documentaries produced by college students.
Eligibility: Open to full–time college students. Applicants must submit (on 5 DVDs) a nonfiction film or video. Selection is based on overall creative excellence.
Financial data: The prize is a $1,000 honorarium and a $1,000 certificate toward the purchase of motion picture film (courtesy of the Eastman Kodak Company).
Duration: The competition is held annually, in the fall.
Deadline: The early and regular deadlines are in June of each year. The late deadline is in July.

1195 DAVID S. BARR AWARDS

Newspaper Guild–Communications Workers of America
501 Third Street, N.W., Sixth Floor
Washington, DC 20001–2797
Phone: (202) 434–7177; Fax: (202) 434–1472;
Email: guild@cwa–union.org
Web: www.newsguild.org/time–start–preparing–broun–barr–entries
Summary: To recognize and reward student journalists whose work has helped to promote social justice.
Eligibility: Open to high school students (including those enrolled in vocational, technical, or special education programs) and part– and full–time college students (including those in community colleges and in graduate programs). Applicants must submit work published or broadcast during the preceding calendar year; entries should help to right a wrong, correct an injustice, or promote justice and fairness.
Financial data: The award is $1,500 for college students or $500 for high school students.
Duration: The awards are presented annually.
Number awarded: 2 each year.
Deadline: January of each year.

1196 $ DAVID W. MILLER AWARD FOR STUDENT JOURNALISTS

Chronicle of Higher Education
Attn: Deputy Managing Editor
1255 23rd Street, N.W.
Washington, DC 20037
Phone: (202) 466–1000; Fax: (202) 452–1033;
Email: milleraward@chronicle.com
Web: chronicle.com
Summary: To recognize and reward college journalists who submit outstanding samples of their published work.
Eligibility: Open to undergraduate students in any country. Applicants are invited to submit up to 3 samples of their published work (in English),

accompanied by a 1–page letter describing the articles and why they were chosen for submission. Entries must have appeared in a campus publication during the previous academic year. Each piece should be journalistic, using expository, explanatory, narrative, or other techniques to report evenhandedly on a topic of intellectual interest. Opinion essays, personal columns, scholarly or research papers, and articles that present the author's own research findings are ineligible.
Financial data: The award is $3,000.
Duration: The award is presented annually.
Number awarded: 1 each year.
Deadline: June of each year.

1197 DEEN TERRY MEMORIAL SCHOLARSHIP

American Institute of Wine & Food–Atlanta Chapter
c/o Karen Losin
2827 Overlook Trace
Atlanta, GA 30324
Phone: (404) 846–5940;
Email: aiwfatlanta@gmail.com
Web: www.aiwf.org/atlanta/scholarships.html
Summary: To provide financial assistance to residents of Georgia interested in studying culinary arts or hospitality at a school in any state.
Eligibility: Open to residents of Georgia who are enrolled in or accepted to an accredited culinary arts or hospitality program in any state as a full–time student. Applicants must have either at least 1 year of experience in the hospitality field or 2 years of college. Students already enrolled in college must have a GPA of 3.0 or higher. Along with their application, they must submit a 750–word essay on why they are a good candidate for this scholarship, including a summary of their short– and long–term hospitality/culinary career goals. Financial need is also considered in the selection process.
Financial data: The stipend is $1,000.
Duration: 1 year.
Number awarded: 1 or more each year.
Deadline: May of each year.

1198 DELTA OMICRON TRIENNIAL COMPOSITION COMPETITION

Delta Omicron International Music Fraternity
Attn: Debbie Beckner, Executive Secretary
910 Church Street
P.O. Box 752
Jefferson City, TN 37760
Phone: (865) 471–6155; Fax: (865) 475–9716;
Email: DOExecSec@att.net
Web: www.delta–omicron.org/?q=node/131
Summary: To recognize and reward composers of college age and older who enter a competition sponsored by Delta Omicron (the international music fraternity).
Eligibility: Open to composers from any country who are of college age or older. Applicants are not required to have any music fraternity affiliation. They must submit a composition, from 7 to 15 minutes in length, for solo piano.
Financial data: The award is $1,000.
Duration: The competition is held triennially (2015, 2018, etc.).
Number awarded: 1 every 3 years.
Deadline: March of the year prior to the competition.

1199 DENDEL SCHOLARSHIPS

Handweavers Guild of America, Inc.
Attn: Scholarship Committee
1255 Buford Highway, Suite 211
Suwanee, GA 30024
Phone: (678) 730–0010; Fax: (678) 730–0836;
Email: hga@weavespindye.org
Web: www.weavespindye.org
Summary: To provide financial assistance to undergraduate and graduate students working on a degree in the field of fiber arts.
Eligibility: Open to undergraduate and graduate students enrolled in accredited colleges and universities in the United States, its possessions, and Canada. Applicants must be working on a degree in the field of fiber arts, including training for research, textile history, and conservation. Along with their application, they must submit 1) a brief essay on their study goals and how those fit into their future plans; and 2) 5 to 16 digital images of their work. Selection is based on artistic and technical merit; financial need is not considered.
Financial data: The stipend ranges up to $1,000. Recipients may use the funds for tuition, materials (e.g., film for photographs), or travel.
Duration: Funds must be spent within 1 year.
Number awarded: 1 each year.
Deadline: March of each year.

1200 DIVISION OF ENGINEERING SERVICES ENGINEERING/ARCHITECTURAL SCHOLARSHIP

California Department of Transportation
Attn: Division of Engineering Services
MS 9 5/2J
P.O. Box 168041
Sacramento, CA 95816–8041
Phone: (916) 227–9525; Fax: (916) 227–8041;
Email: Kathy_S_Stewart@dot.ca.gov
Web: www.dot.ca.gov/hq/esc/scholarships
Summary: To provide financial assistance to high school seniors in California who plan to study engineering or architecture at a college or university in the state.
Eligibility: Open to seniors graduating from high schools in California and planning to enroll in an engineering or architectural program at a community college, state college, or university in the state. Applicants must submit 1) a 100–word personal statement on their college and career plans and how they believe they can make a contribution to Caltrans; 2) a 500–word essay on how they would improve California's current transportation system; 3) a list of community and school activities; 4) information on work and/or volunteer experience; and 5) letters of recommendation.
Financial data: The stipend is $1,000.
Duration: 1 year.
Number awarded: At least 1 each year.
Deadline: March of each year.

1201 DOROTHY DYER VANEK ENDOWMENT SCHOLARSHIP

Epsilon Sigma Alpha International
Attn: ESA Foundation
363 West Drake Road
Fort Collins, CO 80526
Phone: (970) 223–2824; Fax: (970) 223–4456;
Email: esainfo@epsilonsigmaalpha.org
Web: www.epsilonsigmaalpha.org/scholarships–and–grants
Summary: To provide financial assistance to students from any state interested in majoring in architecture or interior design in college.
Eligibility: Open to students who are 1) graduating high school seniors with a GPA of 3.0 to 3.5 or with minimum scores of 22 on the ACT or 1030 on the combined critical reading and mathematics SAT; 2) enrolled in college with a GPA of 3.0 to 3.5; 3) enrolled at a technical school or returning to school after an absence for retraining of job skills or obtaining a degree; or 4) engaged in online study through an accredited college, university, or vocational school. Applicants may be attending or planning to attend an accredited school in any state and major in architecture or interior design. Selection is based on character (20%), leadership (20%), service (20%), financial need (20%), and scholastic ability (20%).
Financial data: The stipend is $1,000.
Duration: 1 year; may be renewed.
Number awarded: 3 each year.
Deadline: January of each year.

1202 $ DOUG INGALLS ACTING SCHOLARSHIPS

Massachusetts Educational Theater Guild
P.O. Box 93
Chelmsford, MA 01824
Phone: (978) 456–3454;
Email: metg@metg.org
Web: metg.org/contests/scholarship–auditions
Summary: To recognize and reward high school seniors in Massachusetts who demonstrate outstanding talent in an acting audition and plan to major in any field at a college or university in any state.
Eligibility: Open to seniors at high schools that are members of the Massachusetts Educational Theater Guild. Applicants must register to perform in an acting audition held in conjunction with the annual guild festival.

They must perform 2 contrasting pieces with a total performance time that may not exceed 4 minutes. Selection is based on presentation and performance; financial need is not considered.

Financial data: Stipends range from $200 to $2,000.

Duration: Auditions are held annually.

Number awarded: Varies each year; since this program was established, it has awarded $70,600 to 120 students.

Deadline: October of each year.

1203 $$ DR. ALMA S. ADAMS SCHOLARSHIP

American Legacy Foundation
1724 Massachusetts Avenue, N.W.
Washington, DC 20036
Phone: (202) 454–5555;
Email: adamsscholarship@legacyforhealth.org
Web: www.legacyforhealth.org/adams–scholarship.aspx

Summary: To provide financial assistance to undergraduate or graduate students in selected fields who have engaged in community service or visual arts activities to reduce smoking in communities designated as especially vulnerable to the tobacco industry.

Eligibility: Open to students entering or enrolled in college or graduate school and working on a degree in public health, education, social work, communications, or other field related to reducing tobacco use. Applicants must be able to demonstrate experience working in an underserved community (American Indian, Native Hawaiian, Alaska Native, Hispanic/Latino, African American, Asian, Pacific Islander, lesbian/gay/bisexual, and other populations that have significantly higher than average smoking prevalence rates) that the sponsor has identified as disproportionately targeted by the tobacco industry or lacking the tools and resources to combat smoking in their communities. They must have a GPA of 3.0 or higher. Along with their application, they must submit 1) a 500–word essay on their career aspirations, interest in tobacco control, and/or experience and record of community service in an underserved community setting; 2) a sample of their originally–developed health communication material aimed at conveying a health message or raising community awareness of the harmful effects of tobacco or other drugs (e.g., poetry, essays, lyrics, scripts, sketches for murals or paintings, recordings for musical scores or dance performances); 3) copies of all college transcripts (or high school transcripts for high school seniors); 4) 2 letters of recommendation; and 5) information on financial need.

Financial data: The stipend is $5,000.

Duration: 1 year.

Number awarded: 2 each year.

Deadline: April of each year.

1204 $ DR. AURA–LEE A. AND JAMES HOBBS PITTENGER AMERICAN HISTORY SCHOLARSHIP

Daughters of the American Revolution–National Society
Attn: Committee Services Office, Scholarships
1776 D Street, N.W.
Washington, DC 20006–5303
Phone: (202) 628–1776
Web: www.dar.org/natsociety/edout_scholar.cfm

Summary: To provide financial assistance to high school seniors planning to major in American history or government in college.

Eligibility: Open to graduating high school seniors who plan to major in American history or government. Applicants must be sponsored by a local chapter of the Daughters of the American Revolution (DAR). Judging first takes place at the state level; 2 state winners then enter the national competition. Selection is based on academic excellence, commitment to field of study, and financial need. U.S. citizenship is required.

Financial data: The stipend is $2,000 per year.

Duration: 4 years, provided the recipient maintains a GPA of 3.25 or higher.

Number awarded: 1 each year.

Deadline: February of each year.

1205 DR. CHESTER A. MCPHEETERS SCHOLARSHIP

United Methodist Higher Education Foundation
Attn: Scholarships Administrator
60 Music Square East, Suite 350
P.O. Box 340005
Nashville, TN 37203–0005
Phone: (615) 649–3990; (800) 811–8110; Fax: (615) 649–3980;
Email: umhefscholarships@umhef.org
Web: www.umhef.org/scholarship–info

Summary: To provide financial assistance to undergraduate and graduate Methodist students who are preparing for ministry.

Eligibility: Open to full–time undergraduate and graduate students who are preparing for a career as a minister in the United Methodist Church. Applicants must have been active, full members of a United Methodist Church for at least 1 year prior to applying and be attending or planning to attend a seminary or theological school affiliated with that denomination. They must have a GPA of 3.0 or higher and be able to demonstrate financial need. U.S. citizenship or permanent resident status is required.

Financial data: The stipend is at least $1,000 per year.

Duration: 1 year; recipients may reapply.

Number awarded: Varies each year; recently, 3 of these scholarships were awarded.

Deadline: February of each year.

1206 DR. JULIANNE MALVEAUX SCHOLARSHIP

National Association of Negro Business and Professional Women's Clubs
Attn: Scholarship Committee
1806 New Hampshire Avenue, N.W.
Washington, DC 20009–3206
Phone: (202) 483–4206; Fax: (202) 462–7253;
Email: education@nanbpwc.org
Web: www.nanbpwc.org/scholarship_applications0.aspx

Summary: To provide financial assistance to African American women studying journalism, economics, or a related field in college.

Eligibility: Open to African American women enrolled at an accredited college or university as a sophomore or junior. Applicants must have a GPA of 3.0 or higher and be majoring in journalism, economics, or a related field. Along with their application, they must submit an essay, up to 1,000 words in length, on their career plans and their relevance to the theme of the program: "Black Women's Hands Can Rock the World." U.S. citizenship is required.

Financial data: The stipend is $1,000.

Duration: 1 year.

Number awarded: 1 or more each year.

Deadline: February of each year.

1207 $$ DWIGHT DAVID EISENHOWER HISTORICALLY BLACK COLLEGES AND UNIVERSITIES TRANSPORTATION FELLOWSHIP PROGRAM

Department of Transportation
Federal Highway Administration
Attn: Office of PCD, HPC–32
4600 North Fairfax Drive, Suite 800
Arlington, VA 22203–1553
Phone: (703) 235–0538; (877) 558–6873; Fax: (703) 235–0593;
Email: transportationedu@dot.gov
Web: www.fhwa.dot.gov/ugp/index.htm

Summary: To provide financial assistance to undergraduate and graduate students working on a degree in a transportation–related field at an Historically Black College or University (HBCU).

Eligibility: Open to students working on a bachelor's, master's, or doctoral degree at a federally–designated 4–year HBCU. Applicants must be working on a degree in a transportation–related field (i.e., engineering, accounting, business, architecture, environmental sciences). They must be U.S. citizens or have an I–20 (foreign student) or I–551 (permanent resident) identification card. Undergraduates must be entering at least their junior year and have a GPA of 3.0 or higher. Graduate students must have a GPA of at least 3.25. Selection is based on their proposed plan of study, academic achievement (based on class standing, GPA, and transcripts), transportation work experience, and letters of recommendation.

Financial data: Fellows receive payment of full tuition and fees (to a maximum of $10,000) and a monthly stipend of $1,450 for undergraduates, $1,700 for master's students, or $2,000 for doctoral students. They are also provided with a 1–time allowance of up to $1,500 to attend the annual Transportation Research Board (TRB) meeting.

Duration: 1 year.

Number awarded: Varies each year. The sponsor also offers similar scholarships for Hispanic American, Native American, and disabled students, but only at a small number (less than 10) schools.

Deadline: January of each year.

1208 E. LUCILLE MILLER MEMORIAL SCHOLARSHIP

General Federation of Women's Clubs of Iowa
Attn: Scholarship Chair
3839 Merle Hay Road, Suite 201
Des Moines, IA 50310–1321
Phone: (515) 276–0510;
Email: gfwciowa@qwestoffice.net
Web: www.gfwciowa.org/id21.html

Summary: To provide financial assistance to high school seniors in Iowa who plan to study music at a college in the state.
Eligibility: Open to seniors graduating from high schools in Iowa and planning to enroll at a college or university in the state. Applicants must be planning to work on a degree in music. Along with their application, they must submit a personal letter about themselves and their family, reasons for applying, goals, and accomplishments; transcripts; letter of sponsorship from a local club member of the General Federation of Women's Clubs of Iowa; ACT or SAT scores; and information on their financial situation.
Financial data: The stipend is $1,000.
Duration: 1 year.
Number awarded: 1 each year.
Deadline: February of each year.

1209 $$ ED BRADLEY SCHOLARSHIP

Radio Television Digital News Foundation
Attn: Programs, Awards, and Membership Manager
529 14th Street, N.W., Suite 425
Washington, DC 20045
Phone: (202) 725–8318; Fax: (202) 223–4007;
Email: katies@rtdna.org
Web: www.rtdna.org/pages/education/scholarship–info.php

Summary: To provide financial assistance to minority undergraduate students who are preparing for a career in electronic journalism.
Eligibility: Open to sophomore or more advanced minority undergraduate students enrolled in an electronic journalism sequence at an accredited or nationally–recognized college or university. Applicants must submit 1 to 3 examples of their journalistic skills on audio CD or DVD (no more than 15 minutes total, accompanied by scripts); a description of their role on each story and a list of who worked on each story and what they did; a 1–page statement explaining why they are preparing for a career in electronic journalism with reference to their specific career preference (radio, television, online, reporting, producing, or newsroom management); a resume; and a letter of reference from their dean or faculty sponsor explaining why they are a good candidate for the award and certifying that they have at least 1 year of school remaining.
Financial data: The stipend is $10,000, paid in semiannual installments of $5,000 each.
Duration: 1 year.
Number awarded: 1 each year.
Deadline: May of each year.

1210 $$ EDSA MINORITY SCHOLARSHIP

Landscape Architecture Foundation
Attn: Leadership in Landscape Scholarship Program
818 18th Street, N.W., Suite 810
Washington, DC 20006–3520
Phone: (202) 331–7070; Fax: (202) 331–7079;
Email: scholarships@lafoundation.org
Web: www.lafoundation.org

Summary: To provide financial assistance to minority college students who are interested in studying landscape architecture.
Eligibility: Open to African American, Hispanic, Native American, and minority college students of other cultural and ethnic backgrounds. Applicants must be entering their final 2 years of undergraduate study in landscape architecture. Along with their application, they must submit a 500–word essay on a design or research effort they plan to pursue (explaining how it will contribute to the advancement of the profession and to their ethnic heritage), 3 work samples, and 2 letters of recommendation. Selection is based on professional experience, community involvement, extracurricular activities, and financial need.
Financial data: The stipend is $5,000.
Number awarded: 1 each year.
Deadline: February of each year.

1211 EDUCATION FOR ALL PHOTOGRAPHY CONTEST

Fagen Friedman & Fulfrost LLP
Attn: F3 Education Awards Foundation
6300 Wilshire Boulevard, Suite 1700
Los Angeles, CA 90048
Phone: (323) 330–6300; Fax: (323) 330–6311;
Email: nmchugh@fagenfriedman.com
Web: www.fagenfriedman.com/page.php?id=85

Summary: To recognize and reward high school juniors and seniors in California who submit outstanding photographs on specified themes.
Eligibility: Open to juniors and seniors at high schools in California. Applicants must submit photographs, up to 10 MB in size, that are solely their original work. They must also submit a 200–word statement explaining how their photograph speaks to the themes of the contest: diversity, collaboration, and/or achievement. Each student may submit only 1 photograph. Selection is based on originality, technical excellence, composition, overall impact, and artistic merit.
Financial data: Prizes are $1,000. Funds must be used for educational purposes.
Duration: The contest is held annually.
Number awarded: 3 each year.
Deadline: December of each year.

1212 EDWARD J. NELL MEMORIAL SCHOLARSHIPS

Quill and Scroll
c/o University of Iowa
School of Journalism and Mass Communications
100 Adler Journalism Building, Room E346
Iowa City, IA 52242–2004
Phone: (319) 335–3457; Fax: (319) 335–3989;
Email: quill–scroll@uiowa.edu
Web: quillandscroll.org/scholarships

Summary: To provide financial assistance for college to high school journalists who are national winners of contests sponsored by Quill and Scroll (the international honor society for high school journalists).
Eligibility: Open to high school seniors who are winners in either of 2 contests conducted by Quill and Scroll for high school journalists: 1) the International Writing/Photography Contest, open to all high school students, with competitions in editorial, editorial cartoon, general columns, review columns, in-depth reporting (individual and team), news story, feature story, sports story, advertisement, and photography (news feature and sports); or 2) the Yearbook Excellence Contest, open to all Quill and Scroll charter high schools. In addition to being a winner of 1 of the contests, candidates for the scholarships must be planning to major in journalism or mass communications at a college or university in any state. Along with their application, they must submit 2 letters of recommendation, 3 examples of their journalistic work, and a 500–word personal statement on their journalistic experience, future plans, activities, honors, volunteer service, and how they plan to finance their college education.
Financial data: Stipends range up to $1,500.
Duration: 1 year; nonrenewable.
Number awarded: Varies each year; recently, 4 of these scholarships were awarded.
Deadline: Entries in the International Writing/Photo Contest are due in February; entries in the Yearbook Excellence Contest must be submitted by the end of October. Scholarship applications must be submitted in May.

1213 $ ELECTRONIC DOCUMENT SYSTEMS FOUNDATION BOARD OF DIRECTORS SCHOLARSHIPS

Electronic Document Systems Foundation
Attn: EDSF Scholarship Awards
1845 Precinct Line Road, Suite 212
Hurst, TX 76054
Phone: (817) 849–1145; Fax: (817) 849–1185;
Email: info@edsf.org
Web: www.edsf.org/what_we_do/scholarships/index.html

Summary: To provide financial assistance to undergraduate and graduate students from any country interested in preparing for a career in document management and graphic communications.
Eligibility: Open to full–time undergraduate and graduate students from any country who demonstrate a strong interest in preparing for a career in the document management and graphic communications industry, including computer science and engineering (e.g., web design, webmaster, software development, materials engineer, applications specialist, information technology designer, systems analyst); graphic and media communications (e.g., graphic designer, illustrator, color scientist, print production, prepress imaging

specialist, workflow specialist, document preparation, production and/or document distribution, content management, e–commerce, imaging science, printing, web authoring, electronic publishing, archiving, security); or business (e.g., sales, marketing, trade shows, customer service, project or product development, management). Preference is given to graduate students and upper–division undergraduates, but freshmen and sophomores who can show interest, experience, and/or commitment to the document management and graphic communication industry are encouraged to apply. Applicants must have a GPA of 3.0 or higher. Along with their application, they must submit 2 essays on assigned topics that change annually but relate to the document management and graphic communication industries. Selection is based on the essays, academic excellence, participation in school activities, community service, honors and organizational affiliations, education goals, and recommendations; financial need is not considered.

Financial data: The stipend ranges from $500 to $3,000.

Duration: 1 year.

Number awarded: Varies each year; recently, 39 of these scholarships were awarded: 2 at $3,000, 7 at $2,500, 8 at $2,000, 2 at $1,500, 19 at $1,000, and 1 at $500.

Deadline: April of each year.

1214 $$ ELIE WIESEL PRIZE IN ETHICS

Elie Wiesel Foundation for Humanity
Attn: Prize in Ethics
555 Madison Avenue, 20th Floor
New York, NY 10022
Phone: (212) 490–7788; Fax: (212) 490–6006;
Email: info@eliewieselfoundation.org
Web: www.eliewieselfoundation.org/prizeinethics.aspx

Summary: To recognize and reward upper–division students who submit outstanding essays on a topic related to ethics.

Eligibility: Open to full–time juniors and seniors at accredited colleges and universities in the United States. Students are invited to submit an essay, between 3,000 and 4,000 words in length, on the recommended topic: "Articulate with clarity an ethical issue that you have encountered and analyze what it has taught you about ethics and yourself." That topic is only a recommendation; students may write on any topic of their choice, provided it explores the theme of ethics. They must have a faculty sponsor review their essay and sign their entry form. Readers look for adherence to guidelines, carefully proofread essays, observance of rules for standard English usage, thoroughly thought–out essays that remain tightly focused, clear articulation and genuine grappling with an ethical dilemma, originality and imagination, eloquence of writing style, and intensity and unity in the essay.

Financial data: First prize is $5,000, second $2,500, third $1,500, and each honorable mention $500.

Duration: The competition is held annually.

Number awarded: 5 prizes each year: a first, second, and third prize as well as 2 honorable mentions.

Deadline: November of each year.

1215 ELIZABETH BARICEVIC/JOSEFINA BOTTA MEMORIAL SCHOLARSHIPS

Confederation in Oregon for Language Teaching
P.O. Box 1044
Salem, OR 97308–1044
Phone: (503) 375–5447; Fax: (503) 375–5448;
Email: coflt@chemeketa.edu
Web: cofltoregon.ning.com/page/scholarships–1

Summary: To provide financial assistance to high school and college students in Oregon taking second–language classes.

Eligibility: Open to high school and college students in Oregon. High school students must be currently enrolled in the third–year or higher level of second–language study, must rank in the upper third of their senior class, and must have earned a GPA of 3.5 or higher in their second–language classes. College or university students must be currently enrolled in at least the second year of the language. Applicants must submit a 300–word personal statement on why the study of second languages is important to them, the ways in which they use their second language outside of the classroom setting, their goals and plans for the use of their second language in the future, and their interests outside of the classroom that are not language related. Selection is based on that statement (50 points); second language grade point average (5 points); letters of recommendation (10 points); personal interests and qualities, motivation, dedication to language study (20 points); and language–related activities and future language–related goals (20 points).

Financial data: The stipend is $1,000.

Duration: 1 year.

Number awarded: 4 each year: 1 to a student at a high school with 500 students or less; 2 for students at high schools of any size; and 1 for a student at the college/university level.

Deadline: February of each year.

1216 ENID HALL GRISWOLD MEMORIAL SCHOLARSHIP

Daughters of the American Revolution–National Society
Attn: Committee Services Office, Scholarships
1776 D Street, N.W.
Washington, DC 20006–5303
Phone: (202) 628–1776
Web: www.dar.org/natsociety/edout_scholar.cfm

Summary: To provide financial assistance to upper–division college students majoring in selected social science fields.

Eligibility: Open to undergraduate students entering their junior or senior year with a major in political science, history, government, or economics. Applicants must be sponsored by a local chapter of the Daughters of the American Revolution (DAR). Selection is based on academic excellence, commitment to the field of study, and financial need. U.S. citizenship is required.

Financial data: The stipend is $1,000.

Duration: 1 year; nonrenewable.

Number awarded: Varies each year.

Deadline: February of each year.

1217 ERNEST I. AND EURICE MILLER BASS SCHOLARSHIP

United Methodist Higher Education Foundation
Attn: Scholarships Administrator
60 Music Square East, Suite 350
P.O. Box 340005
Nashville, TN 37203–0005
Phone: (615) 649–3990; (800) 811–8110; Fax: (615) 649–3980;
Email: umhefscholarships@umhef.org
Web: www.umhef.org/scholarship–info

Summary: To provide financial assistance to undergraduate Methodist students, especially those who are preparing for a career in ministry or other religious vocation.

Eligibility: Open to undergraduate students who are enrolled or planning to enroll full time in a degree program at an accredited institution. Applicants must have been active, full members of a United Methodist Church for at least 1 year prior to applying. They must have a GPA of 2.5 or higher and be able to demonstrate financial need. Preference is given to 1) students preparing for ministry or other religious vocations; and 2) students enrolled or planning to enroll at a United Methodist–related college or university. U.S. citizenship or permanent resident status is required.

Financial data: The stipend is at least $1,000 per year.

Duration: 1 year; recipients may reapply.

Number awarded: Varies each year; recently, 24 of these scholarships were awarded.

Deadline: February of each year.

1218 $$ ESPERANZA SCHOLARSHIP

New York Women in Communications, Inc.
Attn: NYWICI Foundation
355 Lexington Avenue, 15th Floor
New York, NY 10017–6603
Phone: (212) 297–2133; Fax: (212) 370–9047;
Email: nywicipr@nywici.org
Web: www.nywici.org/foundation/scholarships

Summary: To provide financial assistance to Hispanic women who are residents of designated eastern states and interested in preparing for a career in communications at a college or graduate school in any state.

Eligibility: Open to Hispanic women who are seniors graduating from high schools in New York, New Jersey, Connecticut, or Pennsylvania or undergraduate or graduate students who are permanent residents of those states; they must be attending or planning to attend a college or university in any state. Graduate students must be members of New York Women in Communications, Inc. (NYWICI). Also eligible are Hispanic women who reside outside the 4 states but are currently enrolled at a college or university within 1 of the 5 boroughs of New York City. All applicants must be working on a degree in a communications–related field (e.g., advertising, broadcasting, communications, English, film, journalism, marketing, new media, public relations) and have a GPA of 3.2

or higher. Along with their application, they must submit a 2–page resume that includes school and extracurricular activities, significant achievements, academic honors and awards, and community service work; a personal essay of 300 to 500 words on their choice of an assigned topic that changes annually; 2 letters of recommendation; and an official transcript. Selection is based on academic record, need, demonstrated leadership, participation in school and community activities, honors, work experience, goals and aspirations, and unusual personal and/or family circumstances. U.S. citizenship is required.
Financial data: The stipend ranges up to $10,000.
Duration: 1 year.
Number awarded: 1 each year.
Deadline: January of each year.

1219 $$ EVELYN KEEDY MEMORIAL SCHOLARSHIP

The Art Institutes International, Inc.
Free Markets Center
210 Sixth Avenue, 33rd Floor
Pittsburgh, PA 15222–2603
Phone: (412) 995–7685; (888) 624–0300; Fax: (412) 918–2598
Web: www.artinstitutes.edu/financialaid_scholarships.aspx
Summary: To provide financial assistance to high school seniors who are planning to enroll in a participating Art Institute.
Eligibility: Open to high school seniors planning to attend a participating Art Institute. Applicants must demonstrate "dedication to their education and a desire for a creative career." Along with their application, they must submit an official high school transcript; letters of recommendation; a resume including their educational background, extracurricular activities, hobbies, work experience, community involvement, and awards; and a 200–word essay about their career choice. Financial need is not considered in the selection process.
Financial data: The stipend is $30,000. The recipient may use the funds for tuition at the Art Institute of his or her choice.
Duration: 1 year.
Number awarded: 1 each year.
Deadline: May of each year.

1220 EVERT CLARK/SETH PAYNE AWARD FOR YOUNG SCIENCE WRITERS

National Press Foundation
1211 Connecticut Avenue, N.W., Suite 310
Washington, DC 20036
Phone: (202) 663–7280; Fax: (202) 530–2855;
Email: npf@nationalpress.org
Web: nationalpress.org/awards
Summary: To recognize and reward young science writers and reporters.
Eligibility: Open to young writers of non–technical print and online articles. Items published in newspapers (including college newspapers), magazines, web sites, and newsletters are eligible. Both freelancers and staff writers may enter. Books, as well as articles in technical journals and trade association publications, are not considered. Since the prize is managed by *Businessweek* staffers, stories in that magazine will not be accepted. Science writing is broadly defined. It includes, but is not limited to, writing in the biological, physical, environmental, computer, and space sciences, along with technology, mathematics, health, and science policy. Entries are judged on the basis of accuracy, clarity, insightfulness, fairness, resourcefulness, and timeliness. Applicants must be 30 years of age or younger. They may submit a single article or series, up to 4 individual pieces. Applications may be submitted by the author or on the author's behalf.
Financial data: The winner receives $1,000 and expenses to attend the annual meeting of the National Association of Science Writers and the New Horizons briefing of the Council for the Advancement of Science Writing.
Duration: The award is presented annually.
Number awarded: 1 each year.
Deadline: June of each year.

1221 $ FARMER, LUMPE AND MCCLELLAND EXCELLENCE IN COMMUNICATIONS SCHOLARSHIP

Ohio Soybean Council
Attn: Foundation
918 Proprietors Road, Suite A
Worthington, OH 43085
Phone: (614) 476–3100; (888) SOY–OHIO; Fax: (614) 476–9576;
Email: tfontana@soyohio.org
Web: associationdatabase.com/aws/OHSOY/pt/sp/osc_foundation_programs
Summary: To provide financial assistance to residents of Ohio enrolled at a college in the state and majoring in a field related to communications.
Eligibility: Open to residents of Ohio enrolled full time at colleges and universities in the state as sophomores or higher. Applicants must be majoring in agricultural or business communications. They must have a GPA of 3.0 or higher. Selection is based on merit.
Financial data: The stipend is $3,000. Funds are paid directly to the recipient's institution.
Duration: 1 year; recipients may reapply.
Number awarded: 1 each year.
Deadline: January of each year.

1222 $$ FEDERAL JUNIOR DUCK STAMP PROGRAM AND SCHOLARSHIP COMPETITION

Fish and Wildlife Service
Attn: Federal Duck Stamp Office
4401 North Fairfax Drive
MB–4070
Arlington, VA 22203–1622
Phone: (703) 358–2073; Fax: (703) 358–2009;
Email: duckstamps@fws.gov
Web: www.fws.gov/juniorduck/junior.htm
Summary: To recognize and reward student artwork submitted to the Junior Duck Stamp Program.
Eligibility: Open to students in public or private kindergartens through high schools in the United States; home–schooled students are also eligible. U.S. citizenship, nationality, or permanent resident status is required. Applicants must submit paintings of ducks as part of the federal government's Junior Duck Stamp program, which supports awards and scholarships for conservation education. Students are also encouraged to include a short conservation message that expresses the spirit of what they have learned through classroom discussions, research, and planning for their entries. They must submit their applications to a designated receiving site in their home state. Each state selects 12 first–place winners (3 in each of 4 grade level groups: K–3, 4–6, 7–9, and 10–12), and then designates 1 of those 12 as best of show to compete in the national competition. Artwork is judged on the basis of design, anatomical accuracy, artistic composition, and suitability for reproduction. The conservation messages are also judged for quality.
Financial data: First prize for artwork at the national level is $5,000. The winner also receives a free trip to Washington, D.C. in the fall to attend the (adult) Federal Duck Stamp Contest, along with an art teacher, a parent, and a state coordinator. Second prize is $3,000 and third prize is $2,000. The conservation message first prize is $500.
Duration: The competition is held annually.
Number awarded: 6 national prizes are awarded each year: 3 for artwork and 3 for conservation message.
Deadline: Applications must be submitted to the respective state receiving site by March of each year (or January for South Carolina, February for Arizona and Ohio).

1223 FERNANDO MADEIRA MEMORIAL SCHOLARSHIP

Portuguese Foundation of Connecticut
690 Flatbush Avenue
P.O. Box 331441
West Hartford, CT 06133–1441
Phone: (860) 236–9350;
Email: info@pfict.org
Web: www.pfict.org/scholarship–program.html
Summary: To provide financial assistance to students of Portuguese ancestry in Connecticut who are studying music at a school in any state.
Eligibility: Open to residents of Connecticut who are U.S. citizens or permanent residents of Portuguese ancestry. Applicants must be enrolled as a full–time student in a music conservatory or a junior or senior in the music department of an accredited college or university in any state. Along with their application, they must submit an essay describing financial need; an essay detailing proof of Portuguese ancestry, interest in the Portuguese language and culture, and plans for contributing to the Portuguese–American community with their music degree after completion of their studies; 2 letters of recommendation; their high school or college transcripts; a copy of the FAFSA form or their most recent federal income tax return; and their SAT report. Selection is based on financial need and academic record.
Financial data: The stipend is at least $1,250 per year.
Duration: 1 year; may be renewed up to 3 additional years.
Number awarded: 1 each year.
Deadline: March of each year.

1224 $ FFTA SCHOLARSHIP COMPETITION

Flexographic Technical Association
Attn: Educational Program Coordinator
3920 Veterans Memorial Highway
Bohemia, NY 11716
Phone: (631) 737–6020, ext. 36; Fax: (631) 737–6813;
Email: srubin@flexography.org
Web: www.flexography.org/04Education/scholar_fta.html

Summary: To provide financial assistance for college to students interested in a career in flexography.

Eligibility: Open to 1) high school seniors enrolled in a Flexo in Education program and planning to attend a postsecondary school; and 2) students currently enrolled at a college offering a course of study in flexography. Applicants must demonstrate interest in a career in flexography, exhibit exemplary performance in their studies (particularly in the area of graphic communications), and have an overall GPA of 3.0 or higher. Along with their application, they must submit an essay of 200 to 250 words providing personal information about themselves (including special circumstances, interests, and activities); career and/or educational goals and how those relate to the flexo industry; employment and internship experience; and reasons why they feel they should be selected for this scholarship. Financial need is not considered.

Financial data: Stipends are $3,000 per year.

Duration: 1 year; may be renewed.

Number awarded: Varies each year; recently, 14 of these scholarships were awarded.

Deadline: February of each year.

1225 $$ FIERI POPE ITALIAN LANGUAGE SCHOLARSHIP

FIERI–Bronx/Westchester Chapter
c/o Dr. Donna M. Alfieri
4226 Bruner Avenue
Bronx, NY 10466
Phone: (718) 325–6487
Web: wiccny.org/about–us/fieri–young–professionals–group

Summary: To provide financial assistance to Italian American undergraduate students who are working on a degree in Italian language.

Eligibility: Open to undergraduate students of Italian American origin who are majoring in Italian language. High school seniors are not eligible, but part–time and evening students are encouraged to apply. Students who believe they face unusual financial hardships may describe those and include copies of relevant income tax forms. All applicants must submit a 2–page essay on what led them to the study of Italian and how they plan to utilize their Italian language skills in the future. Selection is based on academic achievement and merit; involvement in community, professional, academic, and/or social activities; recommendations; and the essay.

Financial data: The stipend is $5,000.

Duration: 1 year.

Number awarded: 1 each year.

Deadline: April of each year.

1226 $ FINALE NATIONAL COMPOSITION CONTEST

American Composers Forum
Attn: Vice President of Programs
332 Minnesota Street, Suite E–145
St. Paul, MN 55101–1300
Phone: (651) 251–2833; Fax: (651) 291–7978;
Email: ccarnahan@composersforum.org
Web: www.composersforum.org

Summary: To recognize and reward undergraduate and graduate students who submit outstanding compositions for string quartet.

Eligibility: Open to undergraduate and graduate students who may be of any age and nationality as long as they are enrolled at an institution in the United States and are currently living in the country. Applicants are not required to be formal students of composition or music, but they must submit a piece of chamber music they have written within the past 3 years that represents their best work. On the basis of those submissions, 3 finalists are announced in January and required to compose a string quartet, from 8 to 10 minutes in length, that utilizes the full ensemble and is acoustic only (i.e., no duos or trios and no additional instruments). Those finalists travel to New York City in early September, where their works are workshopped and performed by the JACK Quartet. A winner is selected to receive an additional prize.

Financial data: Each finalist receives an award of $1,000 plus $750 to help defray expenses associated with attending the studio performance in New York. The composer of the winning piece receives an additional $2,000; JACK Quartet will give the piece additional performances.

Duration: This competition is held annually.

Number awarded: 3 finalists are selected each year; 1 of those is selected as the winner.

Deadline: Original entries must be submitted by November of each year. The compositions of the 3 finalists must be submitted by May of the following year.

1227 $ FINLANDIA FOUNDATION TRUST SCHOLARSHIPS

Finlandia Foundation National
P.O. Box 92298
Pasadena, CA 91109–2298
Phone: (626) 795–2081; Fax: (626) 795–6533;
Email: office@finlandiafoundation.org
Web: www.finlandiafoundation.org/Scholarships

Summary: To provide financial assistance to undergraduate and graduate students in the United States and Finland, especially those studying Finnish studies.

Eligibility: Open to citizens of the United States and Finland who have been accepted to an accredited institution of higher learning. Applicants may be full–time undergraduate (sophomore or higher) or graduate students. They must have a GPA of 3.0 or higher. Students can work on a degree in any subject area, but those studying subjects related to Finnish culture receive special consideration. Selection is based on financial need, course of study, and citizenship.

Financial data: Stipends range from $500 to $3,000.

Duration: 1 year; nonrenewable.

Number awarded: Varies each year; recently 20 of these scholarships were awarded.

Deadline: January of each year.

1228 FIRST FREEDOM STUDENT COMPETITION

First Freedom Center
Attn: Student Competition Coordinator
1321 East Main Street
Richmond, VA 23219–3629
Phone: (804) 643–1786; Fax: (804) 644–5024;
Email: competition@firstfreedom.org
Web: firstfreedom.org/education/students.html

Summary: To recognize and reward high school students who submit outstanding essays or videos on religious freedom.

Eligibility: Open to students in grades 9–12 in public, private, parochial, and home schools in the United States and U.S. territories, along with U.S. students attending high schools overseas, students attending American high schools overseas, foreign exchange students in the United States, and legal aliens and visitors studying in the United States. GED students under 20 years of age are also eligible. Applicants must be interested in submitting an essay (from 750 to 1,450 words) or a video (from 5 to 7 minutes in play length) on a topic that changes annually but relates to freedom of religion. Selection of the winning essay is based on knowledge of subject matter and historical accuracy (20 points), analysis and interpretation of the topic (15 points), use of supporting evidence (15 points), grammatical conventions (20 points), organization and clarity (15 points), and originality and creativity (15 points). Selection of the winning essay is based on knowledge of subject matter and historical accuracy (20 points), analysis and interpretation of the topic (15 points), use of supporting evidence (15 points), organization and clarity (15 points), originality and creativity (15 points), video quality (15 points), and video script (5 points).

Financial data: The prizes are $2,500.

Duration: The competition is held annually.

Number awarded: 2 each year: 1 for an essay and 1 for a video.

Deadline: November of each year.

1229 $ FIRST LIEUTENANT SCOTT MCCLEAN LOVE MEMORIAL SCHOLARSHIP

Army Scholarship Foundation
11700 Preston Road, Suite 660–301
Dallas, TX 75230
Email: ContactUs@armyscholarshipfoundation.org
Web: www.armyscholarshipfoundation.org/scholarships.html

Summary: To provide financial assistance for undergraduate study to the children and spouses of Army personnel, especially those who major in the fine arts.

Eligibility: Open to 1) children of regular active–duty, active–duty Reserve, and active–duty Army National Guard members in good standing; 2) spouses of serving enlisted regular active–duty, active–duty Reserve, and active–duty Army National Guard members in good standing; and 3) children of former

U.S. Army members who received an honorable or medical discharge or were killed while serving in the U.S. Army. Preference is given to students who are majoring or planning to major in the fine arts. Applicants must be high school seniors, high school graduates, or undergraduates enrolled at an accredited college, university, or vocational/technical institute. They must be U.S. citizens and have a GPA of 2.0 or higher; children must be younger than 24 years of age. Financial need is considered in the selection process.
Financial data: The stipend ranges from $500 to $2,000 per year.
Duration: 1 year; recipients may reapply.
Number awarded: 1 each year.
Deadline: April of each year.

1230 FLORIDA OUTDOOR WRITERS ASSOCIATION SCHOLARSHIP FOR OUTDOOR COMMUNICATORS

Florida Outdoor Writers Association
c/o Dorothy Zimmerman, Scholarship Committee Chair
P.O. Box 110409
Gainesville, FL 32611–0409
Phone: (352) 392–2801;
Email: dozimmer@ufl.edu
Web: www.fowa.org
Summary: To provide financial assistance to students at colleges in Florida who are preparing for a career in outdoor communication.
Eligibility: Open to students currently enrolled at colleges and universities in Florida or whose application is endorsed by a member of the Florida Outdoor Writers Association (FOWA). Applicants must have a career goal of communicating to the public a love and appreciation for hunting, fishing, and other outdoor activities. Preference is given to journalism and communication majors. Along with their application, they must submit an essay of 500 to 1,000 words that expresses their appreciation for the outdoor experience. Selection is based on that essay, academic merit, extracurricular activities, and an endorsement by an FOWA member or the applicant's faculty adviser.
Financial data: Stipends range from $500 to $1,000.
Duration: 1 year.
Number awarded: 1 or more each year.
Deadline: May of each year.

1231 $$ FOCUS ON DIVERSITY AND GENDER EQUALITY IN CHILDREN'S MEDIA SCHOLARSHIP

Academy of Television Arts & Sciences Foundation
Attn: Education Department
5220 Lankershim Boulevard
North Hollywood, CA 91601–3109
Phone: (818) 754–2820; Fax: (818) 761–ATAS;
Email: ctasupport@emmys.org
Web: www.emmysfoundation.org/college–television–awards
Summary: To recognize and reward outstanding college student videos for children that have a focus on gender equality.
Eligibility: Open to undergraduate and graduate students currently enrolled at a college, university, or community college. U.S. citizenship is not required, but all applicants must be enrolled at schools in the United States. All entries must have been produced for school–related classes, groups, or projects. This award is presented to an entry targeted for children from preschool through 11 years of age. Live action, comedy, drama, animation, educational, and musical entries are eligible provided they 1) challenge popular culture for how females and males are portrayed; 2) show diversity and dispel stereotypes for how male and female characters are portrayed; and 3) show a balance in quantity between male and female roles. Running time may not exceed 30 minutes.
Financial data: The award is a $5,000 scholarship.
Duration: The award is presented annually.
Number awarded: 1 each year.
Deadline: January of each year.

1232 $$ FOOTWEAR DESIGN SCHOLARSHIPS

Two Ten Footwear Foundation
Attn: Scholarship Director
1466 Main Street
Waltham, MA 02451
Phone: (781) 736–1512; (800) FIND–210, ext. 1512; Fax: (781) 736–1555;
Email: scholarship@twoten.org
Web: www.twoten.org/What–We–Do/Scholarships.aspx
Summary: To provide financial assistance to undergraduate students working on a degree in a field related to footwear design.
Eligibility: Open to students attending or planning to attend an accredited college, university, or vocational/technical school. Applicants must be able to demonstrate an interest and commitment to footwear design. Along with their application, they must submit a motivational statement, footwear design portfolio, transcripts, a letter of recommendation, and documentation of financial need. They must be U.S. citizens or eligible noncitizens. Selection is based on design potential and financial need.
Financial data: Stipends range from $1,000 to $3,000 per year, depending on the need of the recipient. Funds are sent directly to the recipient's school.
Duration: 1 year; may be renewed up to 3 additional years.
Number awarded: 1 or more each year.
Deadline: January of each year.

1233 FORREST BASSFORD STUDENT AWARD

Livestock Publications Council
910 Currie Street
Fort Worth, TX 76107
Phone: (817) 336–1130; Fax: (817) 232–4820;
Email: dianej@flash.net
Web: www.livestockpublications.com/awards_forrestbassford.php
Summary: To provide financial assistance to students majoring in agricultural communications or related fields.
Eligibility: Open to college juniors and seniors majoring in agricultural journalism, agricultural communications, or agricultural public relations. Applicants must have at least 1 semester of school remaining at the time they receive the award. Along with their application, they must submit a 200–word essay on the future of agricultural communications and how they fit in that career. Selection is based on that essay, a transcript of college work completed and a list of courses in progress, scholarships and awards received, employment record, and a 1–page press release announcing that they have won this award.
Financial data: The winner receives a $1,500 scholarship, plus a $500 travel scholarship (to attend the council's annual meeting). The runners–up receive $750 travel scholarships to attend the meeting.
Duration: 1 year.
Number awarded: 1 winner and up to 3 runners–up are selected each year.
Deadline: February of each year.

1234 FORT DETRICK POST SAME SCHOLARSHIPS

Society of American Military Engineers–Fort Detrick Post
c/o Jonathan Kruft, Scholarship Committee
Analytical Services, Inc.
8600 Snowden River Parkway, Suite 300
Columbia, MD 21045
Phone: (410) 312–3535
Web: www.samefortdetrick.org
Summary: To provide financial assistance to students working on a bachelor's degree in specified fields related to architecture or engineering, especially at colleges and universities in the service area of the Fort Detrick Post of the American Society of Military Engineers (SAME).
Eligibility: Open to full–time undergraduate students at accredited colleges and universities, preferably in the Fort Detrick SAME area of Frederick, Baltimore, and Washington, D.C. Applicants must be working on a bachelor's degree in engineering, architecture, or a related science, planning, or construction field. Along with their application, they must submit a 600–word narrative that covers their academic and professional goals, extracurricular activities, previous military service (if any), and other comments to assist the selection process. Financial need is not considered. U.S. citizenship is required.
Financial data: The stipend is $1,000.
Duration: 1 year.
Number awarded: 1 or more each year.
Deadline: April of each year.

1235 FORT WORTH POST SAME SCHOLARSHIP

Society of American Military Engineers–Fort Worth Post
P.O. Box 17300
Fort Worth, TX 76102–0300
Phone: (817) 886–1653
Web: www.same–fortworth.org/scholarships.htm

Summary: To provide financial assistance to engineering, architecture, and science college and graduate students, especially those at colleges and universities in Texas.

Eligibility: Open to U.S. citizens who are college–bound high school seniors or students currently in college or graduate school; preference is given to students at colleges and universities in Texas. Applicants must be working on or planning to work full time on a degree in an engineering, architecture, or science–related field. They must have a GPA of 3.0 or higher. Along with their application, they must submit a 500–word essay that covers why they are preparing for a career in engineering, architecture, or a related science, their understanding of the Society of American Military Engineers (SAME) and how involvement with the organization will help them to achieve their academic and professional aspirations and objectives, and what distinguishes them from other candidates. Selection is based on academic achievement, character, personal merit, and commitment to the field of engineering.

Financial data: A stipend is awarded (amount not specified).

Duration: 1 year.

Number awarded: Varies each year.

Deadline: Deadline not specified.

1236 $$ FREDERICK FENNELL PRIZE

American Society of Composers, Authors and Publishers
Attn: ASCAP Foundation
ASCAP Building
One Lincoln Plaza
New York, NY 10023–7142
Phone: (212) 621–6219; Fax: (212) 621–6236;
Email: ascapfoundation@ascap.com
Web: www.ascapfoundation.org/awards.html

Summary: To recognize and reward outstanding young composers of music for bands.

Eligibility: Open to U.S. citizens and permanent residents who are between 18 and 30 years of age. Enrolled students with visas are also eligible. Applicants may be undergraduates, graduate students, or doctorates with a D.M.A. degree. They must submit completely original compositions for concert band that have not previously earned awards or prizes in major national competitions. Arrangements are not eligible. Entries must include a completed application form; the notated score of 1 composition; a cassette or CD of the composition; and biographical information that includes prior music studies, background and experience, and a list of compositions to date.

Financial data: The prize is $5,000.

Duration: The prize is presented biennially, in even–numbered years.

Number awarded: 1 each even–numbered year.

Deadline: October of each even–numbered year.

1237 $ FREEDOM OF SPEECH PSA CONTEST

National Association of Broadcasters
Attn: Education Foundation
1771 N Street, N.W.
Washington, DC 20036–2891
Phone: (202) 429–5424; Fax: (202) 429–4199
Web: www.freedomofspeechpsa.org

Summary: To recognize and reward, with scholarships for additional study, undergraduate and graduate communications students who create outstanding public service announcements (PSAs) for radio, television, or interactive media on the importance of free speech.

Eligibility: Open to full–time and part–time undergraduate and graduate students enrolled at colleges, universities, and community/technical colleges who have a major or minor in a field related to communications. Applicants must create a 1) a 30–second PSA for radio on why freedom of speech matters to them; 2) a 30–second PSA for television on the same subject; or 3) an interactive media piece that includes a combination of some or all of the following: text, audio, animation, video, and interactivity content, all on the same subject. They must have maintained significant control over the content and aesthetics of the PSA or interactive media piece (e.g., producing, directing, writing, editing). Winners in the 2 PSA categories are chosen by judges; the winner in the interactive media category are selected by student voting.

Financial data: Winners in all 3 categories receive $3,000 scholarships, payable directly to their college or university. In each of the 2 PSA categories, second prizes of $2,000 scholarships and third prizes of $1,000 scholarships are also awarded.

Duration: The competition is held annually.

Number awarded: 7 winners are selected each year (3 each for the radio and television categories) plus 1 for the interactive media category.

Deadline: April of each year.

1238 FREEDOM OF THE PRESS HIGH SCHOOL ESSAY CONTEST

Society of Professional Journalists
Attn: High School Essay Contest
3909 North Meridian Street
Indianapolis, IN 46208
Phone: (317) 927–8000; Fax: (317) 920–4789;
Email: awards@spj.org
Web: www.spj.org/a–hs.asp

Summary: To recognize and reward, with college scholarships, high school students who write outstanding essays on the importance of a free press.

Eligibility: Open to students in grades 9–12 in the United States. Applicants must submit an essay (300 to 500 words) on "Why is it important that we have news media that are independent of the government" to their local chapter of the Society of Professional Journalists. Selection is based on material organization (40 points); vocabulary and style (30 points); grammar, punctuation, and spelling (20 points); neatness (5 points); and adherence to contest rules (5 points).

Financial data: Winners receive scholarships of $1,000 for first place, $500 for second place, and $300 for third place.

Duration: The competition is held annually.

Number awarded: 3 each year.

Deadline: March of each year.

1239 $ GAERF STUDENT DESIGN COMPETITION

Graphic Arts Education and Research Foundation
1899 Preston White Drive
Reston, VA 20191
Phone: (703) 264–7200; (866) 381–9839; Fax: (703) 620–3165;
Email: gaerf@npes.org
Web: www.graphiccommcentral.org/sdc/student–design–competition.html

Summary: To recognize and reward high school and college students who submit outstanding graphic designs of marketing materials.

Eligibility: Open to students in 2 categories: secondary and postsecondary. Applicants submit marketing pieces for a subject or firm that changes annually; recently, students were asked to promote themselves, explaining why they are the ideal candidate for the career of their choice in the graphic communications industry. They must download templates for a web site banner, postcard, or display ad and complete designs for their choice of those formats.

Financial data: Winners receive $2,000, plus a 2–day all–expense paid trip for the student and an instructor to attend GRAPHEXPO. Second prize is $1,500 and third prize is $1,000.

Duration: The competition is held annually.

Number awarded: 6 each year: 3 in each category.

Deadline: June of each year.

1240 GARDEN CLUB COUNCIL OF WINSTON–SALEM AND FORSYTH COUNTY SCHOLARSHIP

Winston–Salem Foundation
Attn: Student Aid Department
860 West Fifth Street
Winston–Salem, NC 27101–2506
Phone: (336) 714–3445; (866) 227–1209; Fax: (336) 727–0581;
Email: StudentAid@wsfoundation.org
Web: www.wsfoundation.org/netcommunity/page.aspx?pid=854

Summary: To provide financial assistance to residents of North Carolina who are interested in working on an undergraduate degree in horticulture or landscape architecture at a school in the state.

Eligibility: Open to residents of North Carolina who are attending or planning to attend an accredited 2– or 4–year college or university in the state. Applicants must be planning to work full time on an associate or bachelor's degree in horticulture technology or landscape architecture. They may be of traditional or nontraditional student age. Selection is based on academic potential and financial need. U.S. citizenship is required.

Financial data: The stipend is $1,500 per year.

Duration: 1 year; may be renewed 1 additional year if the recipient remains enrolled full time with a GPA of 2.0 or higher.

Number awarded: 1 or more each year.

Deadline: August of each year.

1241 $ GARDEN WRITERS ASSOCIATION FOUNDATION GENERAL SCHOLARSHIPS

Garden Writers Association
Attn: Foundation

7809 North FM 179
Shallowater, TX 79363
Phone: (806) 832–1870; Fax: (806) 832–5244;
Email: info@gardenwriters.org
Web: www.gardenwriters.org

Summary: To provide financial assistance to upper–division students working on a degree in horticulture, plant science, or journalism.

Eligibility: Open to juniors and seniors enrolled full time at a 4–year college or university. Applicants must be majoring in horticulture, plant science, or journalism, with an interest in garden communications (including garden photography). They must have a GPA of 3.0 or higher. Along with their application, they must submit 2 written compositions or photographs. Selection is based on academic record and writing or photographic skills.

Financial data: The stipend ranges from $250 to $2,000, depending on the availability of funds. Funds are paid directly to the recipient's institution.

Duration: 1 year.

Number awarded: 2 to 6 each year.

Deadline: November of each year.

1242 GEORGE AND OPHELIA GALLUP SCHOLARSHIPS

Quill and Scroll
c/o University of Iowa
School of Journalism and Mass Communications
100 Adler Journalism Building, Room E346
Iowa City, IA 52242–2004
Phone: (319) 335–3457; Fax: (319) 335–3989;
Email: quill–scroll@uiowa.edu
Web: quillandscroll.org/scholarships

Summary: To provide financial assistance for college to high school journalists who are national winners of contests sponsored by Quill and Scroll (the international honor society for high school journalists).

Eligibility: Open to high school seniors who are winners in either of 2 contests conducted by Quill and Scroll for high school journalists: 1) the International Writing/Photography Contest, open to all high school students, with competitions in editorial, editorial cartoon, general columns, review columns, in-depth reporting (individual and team), news story, feature story, sports story, advertisement, and photography (news feature and sports); or 2) the Yearbook Excellence Contest, open to all Quill and Scroll charter high schools. In addition to being a winner of 1 of the contests, candidates for the scholarships must be planning to major in journalism or mass communications at a college or university in any state. Along with their application, they must submit 2 letters of recommendation, 3 examples of their journalistic work, and a 500–word personal statement on their journalistic experience, future plans, activities, honors, volunteer service, and how they plan to finance their college education.

Financial data: The stipend is $1,500.

Duration: 1 year; nonrenewable.

Number awarded: 2 each year.

Deadline: Entries in the International Writing/Photo Contest are due in February; entries in the Yearbook Excellence Contest must be submitted by the end of October. Scholarship applications must be submitted in May.

1243 $ GEORGE S. AND STELLA M. KNIGHT ESSAY CONTEST

National Society Sons of the American Revolution
Attn: Education Director
1000 South Fourth Street
Louisville, KY 40203–3208
Phone: (502) 589–1776, ext. 30; Fax: (502) 589–1671;
Email: cwilson@sar.org
Web: www.sar.org/Youth/Knight_Essay

Summary: To recognize and reward outstanding high school essays on the American Revolution.

Eligibility: Open to juniors and seniors in all public, parochial, and private high schools in the United States who are U.S. citizens or legal residents. Applicants must write an essay of 800 to 1,200 words on an event, person, philosophy, or idea associated with the American Revolution, the Declaration of Independence, or the framing of the U.S. constitution. Selection is based on historical accuracy, clarity of thought, organization, grammar and spelling, and documentation. Winners at state and district levels advance to the national contest.

Financial data: At the national level, first prize is $2,000, a plaque, and airfare and hotel for 1 night to attend the sponsor's annual congress; second prize is $1,000; third prize is $500.

Duration: The competition is held annually.

Number awarded: 3 national scholarships are awarded each year.

Deadline: December of each year.

1244 GLADYS C. ANDERSON MEMORIAL SCHOLARSHIP

American Foundation for the Blind
Attn: Scholarship Committee
2 Penn Plaza, Suite 1102
New York, NY 10121
Phone: (212) 502–7661; (800) AFB–LINE; Fax: (888) 545–8331;
Email: afbinfo@afb.net
Web: www.afb.org/Section.asp?Documentid=2962

Summary: To provide financial assistance to legally blind women who are studying classical or religious music on the undergraduate or graduate school level.

Eligibility: Open to women who are legally blind, U.S. citizens, and enrolled in an undergraduate or graduate degree program in classical or religious music. Along with their application, they must submit 200–word essays on 1) their past and recent achievements and accomplishments; 2) their intended field of study and why they have chosen it; and 3) the role their visual impairment has played in shaping their life. They must also submit a sample performance tape or CD of up to 30 minutes. Financial need is considered in the selection process.

Financial data: The stipend is $1,000.

Duration: 1 academic year.

Number awarded: 1 each year.

Deadline: April of each year.

1245 $ GLENN MILLER SCHOLARSHIP COMPETITION

Glenn Miller Birthplace Society
Attn: Scholarship Program
122 West Clark Street
P.O. Box 61
Clarinda, IA 51632
Phone: (712) 542–2461; Fax: (712) 542–2868;
Email: gmbs@glennmiller.org
Web: www.glennmiller.org/scholarships.html

Summary: To recognize and reward, with college scholarships, present and prospective college music majors.

Eligibility: Open to 1) graduating high school seniors planning to major in music in college; and 2) freshmen music majors at an accredited college, university, or school of music. Both instrumentalists and vocalists may compete. Those who entered as high school seniors and did not win first place are eligible to enter again as college freshmen. Each entrant must submit an audition tape or CD, from which 10 instrumentalist finalists and 10 vocalist finalists are selected. Finalists audition in person. They must perform a composition of concert quality, up to 5 minutes in length, sight read selections chosen by the judges, and perform technical exercises. They must also submit a statement that they intend to make music performance or teaching a central part of their future life. Selection is based on talent in any field of applied music; the competition is not intended to select Glenn Miller look–alikes or sound–alikes.

Financial data: Awards are $4,000 for first place, $2,000 for second, or $1,000 for third. The funds are to be used for any school–related expense.

Duration: The competition is held annually, in June.

Number awarded: 6 each year: 3 for instrumentalists and 3 for vocalists.

Deadline: February of each year.

1246 $ GORDON STAFFORD SCHOLARSHIP IN ARCHITECTURE

Gordon Stafford Scholarship
Attn: Scholarship Selection Committee
622 20th Street
Sacramento, CA 95814
Phone: (916) 930–5900; Fax: (916) 930–5800;
Email: scholarship@gsscholarship.com
Web: www.gsscholarship.com

Summary: To provide financial assistance to members of minority groups from California interested in studying architecture at a college in any state.

Eligibility: Open to California residents accepted by an accredited school of architecture in any state as first–year or transfer students. Applicants must be U.S. citizens or permanent residents who are persons of color (defined as Black, Hispanic, Native American, Pacific–Asian, or Asian–Indian). They must submit a 500–word statement expressing their desire to study architecture. Finalists are interviewed and must travel to Sacramento, California at their own expense for the interview.

Financial data: The stipend is $2,000 per year. That includes $1,000 deposited in the recipient's school account and $1,000 paid to the recipient directly.

Duration: 1 year; may be renewed up to 4 additional years.

Number awarded: Up to 5 of these scholarships may be active at a time.

Deadline: June of each year.

1247 $ GRADY–RAYAM PRIZE IN SACRED MUSIC

"Negro Spiritual" Scholarship Foundation
P.O. Box 547728
Orlando, FL 32854–7728
Phone: (407) 841–NSSF
Web: www.negrospiritual.org/competition

Summary: To recognize and reward, with college scholarships, African American high school students in selected eastern states who excel at singing "Negro spirituals."

Eligibility: Open to high school juniors and seniors of Afro–ethnic heritage in 6 districts: 1) Florida; 2) Southeast (Georgia, North Carolina, and South Carolina); 3) Mid–south (Alabama, Arkansas, Louisiana, Mississippi, and Tennessee); 4) Northeast (New Jersey, New York, and Pennsylvania; 5) New England (Connecticut, Maine, Massachusetts, New Hampshire, Rhode Island, and Vermont); and 6) Capital (Delaware, Maryland, Virginia, Washington, D.C., and West Virginia). Participants must perform 2 "Negro spiritual" songs, 1 assigned and 1 selected. Selection is based on technique (tone quality, intonation, and vocal production), musicianship and artistry (inflection, diction, authenticity, rhythmic energy, and memorization), and stage presence (demeanor, posture, and sincerity of delivery). U.S. citizenship or permanent resident status is required.

Financial data: Winners earn tuition assistance grants for college of $3,000 and cash prizes of $300. Other finalists receive cash prizes of $100.

Duration: The competition is held annually at a site in each of the 5 regions.

Number awarded: 12 tuition assistance grants and cash prizes (1 to a male and 1 to a female in each of the 6 districts). The number of other cash prizes awarded to finalists varies each year.

Deadline: December of each year.

1248 $ GRANDMA MOSES SCHOLARSHIP

Western Art Association
Attn: Foundation
13730 Loumont Street
Whittier, CA 90601

Summary: To provide financial assistance for art school to female high school seniors whose art demonstrates a "congruence with the art of Grandma Moses."

Eligibility: Open to female graduating high school seniors. Applicants must be planning to study art in a college, university, or specialized school of art. Preference is given to applicants from the western United States. Candidates must submit samples of their artwork; selection is based on the extent to which their work "manifests a congruence with the work of the famed folk artist, Grandma Moses." Financial need is not considered.

Financial data: The stipend is $3,000 per year.

Duration: 1 year; may be renewed up to 3 additional years.

Number awarded: 1 each year.

Deadline: March of each year.

1249 $ GREAT FALLS ADVERTISING FEDERATION COLLEGIATE SCHOLARSHIP

Great Falls Advertising Federation
Attn: Advertising Scholarship Committee
609 Tenth Avenue South, Suite B
P.O. Box 634
Great Falls, MT 59403
Phone: (406) 761–6453; (800) 803–3351; Fax: (406) 453–1128;
Email: gfaf@gfaf.com
Web: www.gfaf.com/Scholarships.html

Summary: To provide financial assistance to residents of Montana majoring in fields related to advertising at colleges and universities in the state.

Eligibility: Open to residents of Montana who 1) have completed a 2–year college program and have been admitted to a 4–year college or university in the state; and 2) are currently enrolled at least as a junior at a 4–year college or university in the state. Applicants must be majoring in advertising, communications, fine arts, marketing, or another field related to advertising. They must have a cumulative GPA of 3.0 or higher. Along with their application, they must submit a personal statement that covers such topics as why they chose their field of study, obstacles overcome, short– and long–term goals, recent honors and awards, and financial need.

Financial data: The stipend is $2,000.

Duration: 1 year.

Number awarded: 1 or more each year.

Deadline: March of each year.

1250 $ GREAT FALLS ADVERTISING FEDERATION HIGH SCHOOL ART SCHOLARSHIP

Great Falls Advertising Federation
Attn: Advertising Scholarship Committee
609 Tenth Avenue South, Suite B
P.O. Box 634
Great Falls, MT 59403
Phone: (406) 761–6453; (800) 803–3351; Fax: (406) 453–1128;
Email: gfaf@gfaf.com
Web: www.gfaf.com/Scholarships.html

Summary: To provide financial assistance to high school seniors in Montana planning to attend college in any state to prepare for a career in art.

Eligibility: Open to seniors graduating from high schools in Montana who plan to enroll at a postsecondary educational or training program in any state. Applicants must intend to pursue a program of study that will prepare them for a career in art or a related field. Along with their application, they must submit 1) a resume that includes work experience, volunteer experience, extracurricular activities, and honors and awards; 2) letters of recommendation; and 3) a portfolio of 10 color photographs or printed outputs of their work. Financial need is not considered in the selection process.

Financial data: The stipend is $2,000.

Duration: 1 year.

Number awarded: 1 each year.

Deadline: February of each year.

1251 GREEN/SUSTAINABLE DESIGN SCHOLARSHIP

International Furnishings and Design Association
Attn: IFDA Educational Foundation
2700 East Grace Street
Richmond, VA 23223
Phone: (804) 644–3946; Fax: (804) 644–3834;
Email: colleaguesinc@earthlink.net
Web: www.ifdaef.org/scholarships.php

Summary: To provide financial assistance to undergraduate students who are working on a degree in interior design with an emphasis on green or sustainable design.

Eligibility: Open to students enrolled at an accredited school, college, or university who have completed 4 design courses and are majoring in interior design or a related field. Applicants must be focusing on green or sustainable design, defined as the development of innovative ways to create living spaces that are energy efficient and feature green or sustainable materials, fabrications, and products. They must be able to demonstrate creative use of green products and eco–friendly furnishings in class projects, familiarity with current information with the green/sustainable field, the application of this knowledge in class work, and a goal of seeking a Leadership in Energy and Environmental Design (LEED) accreditation. Along with their application, they must submit an essay of 200 to 400 words on their long– and short–term goals, special interests, volunteer and community service, and what inspired them to a career in green or sustainable design; samples of their work featuring 1 or more aspects of green or sustainable design with detailed explanations; a transcript; and a letter of recommendation from a professor or instructor. Financial need is not considered.

Financial data: The stipend is $1,500.

Duration: 1 year.

Number awarded: At least 1 each year.

Deadline: March of each year.

1252 $ HAROLD AND MIMI STEINBERG NATIONAL STUDENT PLAYWRITING AWARD

John F. Kennedy Center for the Performing Arts
Education Department
Attn: Kennedy Center American College Theater Festival
2700 F Street, N.W.
Washington, DC 20566
Phone: (202) 416–8857; Fax: (202) 416–8860;
Email: KCACTF@kennedy–center.org
Web: www.kcactf.org/KCACTF.ORG_NATIONAL/Kanin_Playwriting.html

Summary: To recognize and reward outstanding undergraduate and graduate student playwrights.

Eligibility: Open to students at any accredited junior or senior college in the United States, provided their college agrees to participate in the Kennedy Center American College Theater Festival (KCACTF). Undergraduate students must be carrying at least 6 semester hours, graduate students must be enrolled in at least 3 semester hours, and continuing part–time students must be enrolled in a regular degree or certificate program. For the Michael Kanin

Playwriting Awards Program, students must submit either 1 major work or 2 or more shorter works based on a single theme or encompassed within a unifying framework; all entries must provide a full evening of theater. The work must be written while the student was enrolled, and the production must be presented during that period or within 2 years after enrollment ends. The play selected as the best by the judges is presented at the national festival and its playwright receives this award.

Financial data: The winning playwright receives 1) production of the play as part of the KCACFT national festival with all expenses paid for the playwright; 2) a cash prize of $2,500; 3) the Dramatists Guild Award of active membership in the Guild; 4) the Samuel French Award of a contract for publication of the play by Samuel French, Inc., which will send the playwright royalties received for production of the play worldwide; and 5) an all–expense paid professional development opportunity.

Duration: The competition is held annually.

Number awarded: 1 each year.

Deadline: November of each year.

1253 HARRIET IRSAY SCHOLARSHIP GRANT

American Institute of Polish Culture, Inc.
Attn: Scholarship Committee
1440 79th Street Causeway, Suite 117
Miami, FL 33141–3555
Phone: (305) 864–2349; Fax: (305) 865–5150;
Email: info@ampolinstitute.org
Web: www.ampolinstitute.org/index2.html

Summary: To provide financial assistance to Polish American and other students interested in working on an undergraduate or graduate degree in selected fields.

Eligibility: Open to students working full time on an undergraduate or graduate degree in the following fields: communications, education, film, history, international relations, journalism, liberal arts, Polish studies, or public relations. Also eligible are graduate students in business programs whose thesis is directly related to Poland and to graduate students in all majors whose thesis is on a Polish subject. U.S. citizenship or permanent resident status is required. Preference is given to applicants of Polish heritage. Along with their application, they must submit an essay of 200 to 400 words on why they should receive the scholarship, an article (up to 700 words) on any subject about Poland, transcripts, a detailed resume, and 3 letters of recommendation. Selection is based on merit.

Financial data: The stipend is $1,000.

Duration: 1 year.

Number awarded: Varies each year; recently, 7 of these scholarships were awarded.

Deadline: June of each year.

1254 $ HARRY BARFIELD SCHOLARSHIPS

Kentucky Broadcasters Association
101 Enterprise Drive
Frankfort, KY 40601
Phone: (502) 848–0426; (888) THE–KBA1; Fax: (502) 848–5710;
Email: kba@kba.org
Web: www.kba.org

Summary: To provide financial assistance to residents of Kentucky who are majoring in broadcasting at a school in the state.

Eligibility: Open to Kentucky residents who are currently enrolled at a college or university in the state and majoring in broadcasting or telecommunications. Applicants must be preparing for a career in broadcasting. They must submit a college transcript (GPA of 3.0 or higher), a list of extracurricular activities, and a faculty recommendation. Financial need is not considered in the selection process. Preference is given to rising juniors.

Financial data: The stipend is $2,500 per year.

Duration: 1 year; may be renewed for 1 additional year if the recipient maintains a GPA of 3.0 or higher.

Number awarded: Up to 4 each year.

Deadline: April of each year.

1255 $ HAWAII CHAPTER/DAVID T. WOOLSEY SCHOLARSHIP

Landscape Architecture Foundation
Attn: Leadership in Landscape Scholarship Program
818 18th Street, N.W., Suite 810
Washington, DC 20006–3520
Phone: (202) 331–7070; Fax: (202) 331–7079;
Email: scholarships@lafoundation.org
Web: www.lafoundation.org

Summary: To provide financial assistance to residents of Hawaii who are working on an undergraduate or graduate degree in landscape architecture at a school in any state.

Eligibility: Open to third–, fourth–, or fifth–year undergraduate students and graduate students in landscape architecture who are residents of Hawaii enrolled at a college or university in any state. Applicants are required to submit 2 letters of recommendation (1 from a design instructor), a 500–word autobiographical essay that addresses personal and professional goals, and 3 samples of design work. Selection is based on professional experience, community involvement, extracurricular activities, and financial need.

Financial data: The stipend is $2,000.

Number awarded: 1 each year.

Deadline: February of each year.

1256 $ HB DESIGN SCHOLARSHIP

Oregon Student Access Commission
Attn: Grants and Scholarships Division
1500 Valley River Drive, Suite 100
Eugene, OR 97401–2146
Phone: (541) 687–7395; (800) 452–8807, ext. 7395; Fax: (541) 687–7414; TDD: (800) 735–2900;
Email: awardinfo@osac.state.or.us
Web: www.oregonstudentaid.gov/scholarships.aspx

Summary: To provide financial assistance to residents of Oregon who are interested in working on an undergraduate or graduate degree related to graphic or web design at a school in any state.

Eligibility: Open to residents of Oregon who are enrolled as juniors, seniors, or graduate students at a college or university in any state. Applicants must be working on a degree in graphic design or interactive/web design. They must have a GPA of 3.0 or higher. Semifinalists are required to e–mail a design sample along with a 200–word description that includes the communication objective, intended audience, and the central idea behind the concept.

Financial data: Stipends for scholarships offered by the Oregon Student Access Commission (OSAC) range from $200 to $10,000 but recently averaged $2,300.

Duration: 1 year; recipients may reapply.

Number awarded: Varies each year.

Deadline: February of each year.

1257 $$ HEARST JOURNALISM AWARDS PROGRAM BROADCAST NEWS COMPETITIONS

William Randolph Hearst Foundation
90 New Montgomery Street, Suite 1212
San Francisco, CA 94105–4504
Phone: (415) 908–4560; (800) 841–7048, ext. 4560;
Email: journalism@hearstfdn.org
Web: www.hearstfdn.org/hearst_journalism/about.php

Summary: To recognize and reward, with scholarships for additional study, outstanding college student broadcast news journalists.

Eligibility: Open to full–time undergraduate students majoring in journalism at accredited colleges and universities that are members of the Association of Schools of Journalism and Mass Communication (ASJMC). For each of the 2 semifinal competitions, each student submits an online entry of 2 distinct reports, totaling no more than 5 minutes, originating with and produced by the undergraduate student with primary responsibility for the entry. Entries must have been "aired" in the sense of having been made available to an anonymous audience of substantial size. The first competition of each year, for both radio and television, is for "features;" entries must be soft news: non–deadline reporting of personalities, events, or issues. They may be based on, but not limited to, public affairs, business, investigations, science, sports, or weather. The second competition of each year, for television only, is for "news;" entries must be based on coverage of breaking or developing news stories related to campus, community, national, or international issues, sports, business, investigative, science, weather, or other current newsworthy matter. Reports must have a hard news focus. All entries must have been aired since September of the previous year. Broadcast entries are judged on the basis of writing, understandability, clarity, depth, focus, editing, knowledge of subject, broadcast skills, originality, visual storytelling, graphics, human interest, and reporting. Radio and television entries are judged separately. The top 5 winners in each of the 2 television competitions are then entered into the television semifinals, from which 5 finalists are selected. The 5 television finalists, along with the top 5 radio entries, are flown to San Francisco for the finals of on–the–spot assignments.

Financial data: The 5 television finalists and the 5 radio winners receive awards of $2,600 for first, $2,000 for second, $1,500 for third, and $1,000 for fourth and fifth. Their schools are awarded matching grants. For the finals competitions for both radio and television, additional scholarships are awarded of $5,000 for first place, $4,000 for second, $3,000 for third, and $1,500 for each of the other 2 finalists; in addition, the students who make the best use of radio for news coverage and the best use of television for news coverage each receive another scholarship of $1,000. Scholarship funds are paid to the college or university and credited to the recipients' educational costs (tuition, matriculation and other fees, and room and board provided by or approved by the college or university). The total amount awarded in scholarships and grants in this and the other competitions is nearly $500,000 per year.

Duration: The competition is held annually.

Number awarded: For the radio competition, there are no semifinal competitions; 5 finalists are selected. For the television competitions, 5 semifinalists are selected from each of the 2 competitions; from those 10 semifinalists, 5 finalists are selected. In addition, 1 scholarship is awarded each year for best use of radio and 1 for best use of television.

Deadline: The deadline for the first competition is in November of each year and for the second competition in January of each year. Additional entries by finalists must be submitted by February of each year for the first competition or April of each year for the second competition. The competition among the top 10 finalists takes place in San Francisco in June.

1258 $$ HEARST JOURNALISM AWARDS PROGRAM MULTIMEDIA COMPETITIONS

William Randolph Hearst Foundation
90 New Montgomery Street, Suite 1212
San Francisco, CA 94105–4504
Phone: (415) 908–4560; (800) 841–7048, ext. 4560;
Email: journalism@hearstfdn.org
Web: www.hearstfdn.org/hearst_journalism/about.php

Summary: To recognize and reward, with scholarships for additional study, outstanding college student journalists who submit multimedia entries.

Eligibility: Open to full–time undergraduate students majoring in journalism at accredited colleges or universities that are members of the Association of Schools of Journalism and Mass Communication (ASJMC). Each entry consists of a project produced and posted on the Internet sometime after September of the year the competition begins. Entrants must have completed at least 3 of the following components: writing, photographs, audio slideshows, interactivity, Flash, video, animation, graphics, or other visual tool; they could also have used social media, including blogging. For the preliminaries, 4 separate competitions are held; 1) narrative multimedia storytelling—a feature story for an online audience using linear multimedia techniques, with an emphasis on storytelling; 2) the human condition—a multimedia piece for an online audience using visual storytelling techniques, with an emphasis on human interest or human condition projects; 3) news—an emphasis on data and information storytelling, including hard or breaking news events; entries can be based on but are not limited to public affairs, business, science, or sports news; feature stories are not accepted; and 4) team multimedia storytelling—for teams of up to 15 undergraduates, producing news that can be based on but is not limited to public affairs, business, science, or sports news; team entries do not compete for awards. The first–place winners from the first 3 competitions and the 2 highest–scoring finalists in those preliminary competitions qualify for the national championship held in San Francisco in June. Multimedia entries are judged on the basis of visual storytelling, writing, reporting, photography, audio and video, graphics, versatility, human interest, news value, originality, editing, navigation and structure, and design.

Financial data: In each of the first 3 preliminary competitions, winners receive awards of $2,600 for first, $2,000 for second, $1,500 for third, and $1,000 for fourth and fifth. Their schools are awarded matching grants. For the finalists whose articles are judged best in the national multimedia championship, additional scholarships of $5,000 are awarded for first place, $4,000 for second, $3,000 for third, and $1,500 for each of the other finalists. Scholarship awards are paid to the college or university and credited to the recipients' educational costs (tuition, matriculation and other fees, and room and board provided by or approved by the college or university). The total amount awarded in scholarships and grants in this and the other competitions is nearly $500,000 per year.

Duration: The competition is held annually.

Number awarded: Each year, 15 scholarships are awarded to the preliminary winners, and an additional 5 are presented to the national finalists.

Deadline: Multimedia entries for the preliminary competitions must be submitted by December of each year for narrative multimedia storytelling, January of each year for the human condition, February of each year for news, and April of each year for team multimedia storytelling. The championship is held in June of each year.

1259 $$ HEARST JOURNALISM AWARDS PROGRAM PHOTOJOURNALISM COMPETITIONS

William Randolph Hearst Foundation
90 New Montgomery Street, Suite 1212
San Francisco, CA 94105–4504
Phone: (415) 908–4560; (800) 841–7048, ext. 4560;
Email: photos@hearstfdn.org
Web: www.hearstfdn.org/hearst_journalism/about.php

Summary: To recognize and reward, with scholarships for additional study, outstanding college student photojournalists.

Eligibility: Open to full–time undergraduate students enrolled at accredited colleges and universities that are members of the Association of Schools of Journalism and Mass Communication (ASJMC); they are not required to be majoring in journalism. For each of the 2 semifinal competitions, each student submits photographs from newspapers, magazines, online media, or web sites. For the first competition of each year, the categories are news and features; entries consist of at least 2 images for the news category and 2 in the features category, or a maximum of 8 images. News includes breaking news, general news, or news photos relating to sporting events. Features includes portraits, sports, or documentary photography. For the second competition of each year, the categories are picture stories and series; each entry must include 1 picture story/series, with up to 15 images on any subject. All photographs must have been taken since September of the previous year and disseminated in print or online. Photography is judged on the basis of quality, visual storytelling, versatility, consistency, human interest, news value, originality, editing, writing, and reporting. The judges select the top 5 entrants in each of the 2 competitions plus 2 entrants with the highest scores. Those 12 finalists must submit a portfolio consisting of additional entries. Based on those portfolios, judges select the top 5 finalists to go to San Francisco for on–the–spot assignments to rank the winners.

Financial data: In each of the 2 semifinal competitions, winners receive awards of $2,600 for first, $2,000 for second, $1,500 for third, and $1,000 for fourth and fifth. Their schools are awarded matching grants. For the finals competition, additional scholarships are awarded of $5,000 for first place, $4,000 for second, $3,000 for third, $1,500 for each of the other finalists, and $1,000 for each of the other semifinalists. In addition, the photographers who submit the best single photo and the best portfolio each receive another scholarship of $1,000. Scholarship funds are paid to the college or university and credited to the recipients' educational costs (tuition, matriculation and other fees, and room and board provided by or approved by the college or university). The total amount awarded in scholarships and grants in this and the other competitions is nearly $500,000 per year.

Duration: The competition is held annually.

Number awarded: 12 semifinal and 5 final winners are chosen each year; 2 additional scholarships are awarded each year for the best single photo and best picture story.

Deadline: The deadline for the first competition is in November of each year and for the second competition in February of each year. Additional entries by finalists must be submitted by April of each year. The competition among the top 5 finalists takes place in San Francisco in June.

1260 $$ HEARST JOURNALISM AWARDS PROGRAM WRITING COMPETITIONS

William Randolph Hearst Foundation
90 New Montgomery Street, Suite 1212
San Francisco, CA 94105–4504
Phone: (415) 908–4560; (800) 841–7048, ext. 4560;
Email: journalism@hearstfdn.org
Web: www.hearstfdn.org/hearst_journalism/about.php

Summary: To recognize and reward, with scholarships for additional study, outstanding college student journalists.

Eligibility: Open to full–time undergraduate students majoring in journalism at accredited colleges or universities that are members of the Association of Schools of Journalism and Mass Communication (ASJMC). Each entry consists of a single article written by the student with primary responsibility for the work and published in a campus or professional publication. For the preliminaries, 5 separate competitions are held; 1) feature writing—a color or mood article covering news, business, feature, or entertainment, as opposed to a conventional news story or personality profile; 2) enterprise reporting—original reporting, including explanatory and investigative journalism across any topic; 3) sports writing—a news, feature, or commentary in sports, relevant to an event or issue, not to a sports personality; 4) personality profile—a personality sketch of someone on or off campus; and 5) breaking news writing—major coverage of the event, not a sidebar or analysis. The 5 first–place winners and the 3 highest–scoring finalists in the preliminary competitions qualify for the national writing championship held in San Francisco in June; at that time, competition assignments consist of an on–the–spot assignment and a news story and personality

profile from a press interview of a prominent individual in the San Francisco area. Writing is judged on the basis of knowledge of subject, understandability, clarity, color, reporting in depth, and construction. Additional awards are presented for article of the year and best reporting technique.
Financial data: In each of the 5 semifinal competitions, winners receive awards of $2,600 for first, $2,000 for second, $1,500 for third, and $1,000 for fourth and fifth. Their schools are awarded matching grants. For the finalists whose articles are judged best in the national writing championship, additional scholarships of $5,000 are awarded for first place, $4,000 for second, $3,000 for third, and $1,500 for each of the other finalists. The additional awards for article of the year and best reporting technique are each $1,000. Scholarship awards are paid to the college or university and credited to the recipients' educational costs (tuition, matriculation and other fees, and room and board provided by or approved by the college or university). The total amount awarded in scholarships and grants in this and the other competitions is nearly $500,000 per year.
Duration: The competition is held annually.
Number awarded: Each year, 25 scholarships are awarded to the preliminary winners, and an additional 8 are presented to the national finalists.
Deadline: Articles for the preliminary competitions must be submitted by October of each year for feature writing, January of each year for enterprise reporting, February of each year for sports writing, early March of each year for personality profile, and late March of each year for breaking news writing. The championship is held in June of each year.

1261 $ HEIDELBERG USA SCHOLARSHIP

Electronic Document Systems Foundation
Attn: EDSF Scholarship Awards
1845 Precinct Line Road, Suite 212
Hurst, TX 76054
Phone: (817) 849–1145; Fax: (817) 849–1185;
Email: info@edsf.org
Web: www.edsf.org/what_we_do/scholarships/index.html
Summary: To provide financial assistance to undergraduate and graduate students from any country interested in preparing for a career in document management and graphic communications, especially those who have experience with printing equipment.
Eligibility: Open to full–time undergraduate and graduate students from any country who demonstrate a strong interest in preparing for a career in the document management and graphic communications industry, including computer science and engineering (e.g., web design, webmaster, software development, materials engineer, applications specialist, information technology designer, systems analyst); graphic and media communications (e.g., graphic designer, illustrator, color scientist, print production, prepress imaging specialist, workflow specialist, document preparation, production and/or document distribution, content management, e–commerce, imaging science, printing, web authoring, electronic publishing, archiving, security); or business (e.g., sales, marketing, trade shows, customer service, project or product development, management). Preference is given to graduate students and upper–division undergraduates, but freshmen and sophomores who can show interest, experience, and/or commitment to the document management and graphic communication industry are encouraged to apply. Special consideration is given to students who have experience with printing equipment. Applicants must have a GPA of 3.0 or higher. Along with their application, they must submit 2 essays on assigned topics that change annually but relate to the document management and graphic communication industries. Selection is based on the essays, academic excellence, participation in school activities, community service, honors and organizational affiliations, education goals, and recommendations; financial need is not considered.
Financial data: The stipend is $2,000.
Duration: 1 year.
Number awarded: 1 each year.
Deadline: April of each year.

1262 HERB ALPERT YOUNG JAZZ COMPOSER AWARDS

American Society of Composers, Authors and Publishers
Attn: ASCAP Foundation
ASCAP Building
One Lincoln Plaza
New York, NY 10023–7142
Phone: (212) 621–6219; Fax: (212) 621–6236;
Email: ascapfoundation@ascap.com
Web: www.ascapfoundation.org/awards.html
Summary: To recognize and reward outstanding original compositions by college students, graduate students, and other young jazz composers.
Eligibility: Open to U.S. citizens and permanent residents who are younger than 30 years of age. Enrolled students with visas are also eligible. Applicants may be students in grades K–12, college undergraduates, graduate students, or recipients of a D.M.A. or Ph.D. degree. They must submit completely original jazz compositions that have not previously earned awards or prizes in major national competitions. Arrangements are not eligible. Entries must include a completed application form; the notated score of 1 composition; a cassette or CD of the composition; and biographical information that includes prior music studies, background, and experience.
Financial data: Winners share $30,000 in prizes.
Duration: The prizes are presented annually.
Number awarded: Varies each year; recently, 22 composers shared these awards.
Deadline: December of each year.

1263 $ HERBERT BUSHONG ANNUAL ESSAY CONTEST

Freedom from Religion Foundation
P.O. Box 750
Madison, WI 53701
Phone: (608) 256–8900; Fax: (608) 204–0422;
Email: highschoolessay@ffrf.org
Web: www.ffrf.org/outreach/student–essay–contests
Summary: To recognize and reward outstanding essays written by high school students on freethought or state/church separation themes.
Eligibility: Open to college–bound seniors at high schools in North America. They are invited to write an essay on a topic that changes annually but relates to freethinking and separation of church and state; recently, the topic was "Describe a Moment When You Stood Up for Freethought and/or That Made You Proud to Be a Freethinker." Essays should be from 500 to 700 words in length and deal with the role of freethinking in their life. Students should include a paragraph biography that includes their hometown, the college or university they will be attending, their intended major, and their interests or high school achievements.
Financial data: First prize is $3,000, second $2,000, third $1,000, fourth $500, fifth $300, and honorable mentions $200.
Duration: The competition is held annually.
Number awarded: 5 prizes and a varying number of honorable mentions are awarded each year.
Deadline: May of each year.

1264 HERBERT FERNANDES SCHOLARSHIP

Luso–American Education Foundation
Attn: Administrative Director
7080 Donlon Way, Suite 202
P.O. Box 2967
Dublin, CA 94568
Phone: (925) 828–3883; Fax: (925) 828–3883;
Email: education@luso–american.org
Web: www.luso–american.org/laef
Summary: To provide financial assistance for undergraduate study in Portuguese language to students in California.
Eligibility: Open to students of Portuguese descent who are sophomores, juniors, or seniors at 4–year colleges or universities with a GPA of 3.0 or higher. Applicants must be California residents who are actively involved in the Luso–American community and have taken or will enroll in Portuguese language classes. Selection is based on promise of success in college, financial need, leadership, vocational promise, and sincerity of purpose.
Financial data: The stipend is $1,000.
Duration: 1 year; nonrenewable.
Number awarded: 1 each year.
Deadline: February of each year.

1265 HGA SCHOLARSHIPS

Handweavers Guild of America, Inc.
Attn: Scholarship Committee
1255 Buford Highway, Suite 211
Suwanee, GA 30024
Phone: (678) 730–0010; Fax: (678) 730–0836;
Email: hga@weavespindye.org
Web: www.weavespindye.org
Summary: To provide financial assistance to undergraduate and graduate students working on a degree in the field of fiber arts.

Eligibility: Open to undergraduate and graduate students enrolled in accredited colleges and universities in the United States, its possessions, and Canada. Applicants must be working on a degree in the field of fiber arts, including training for research, textile history, and conservation. Along with their application, they must submit 1) a brief essay on their study goals and how those fit into their future plans; and 2) 5 to 16 digital images of their work. Selection is based on artistic and technical merit; financial need is not considered.
Financial data: The stipend ranges up to $1,000. Use of funds is restricted to tuition.
Duration: Funds must be spent within 1 year.
Number awarded: 1 each year.
Deadline: March of each year.

1266 HISTORY AND PHILOSOPHY OF GEOLOGY STUDENT AWARD

Geological Society of America–History and Philosophy of Geology Division
c/o Jane P. Davidson, Secretary
University of Nevada at Reno
Art Department 224
Reno, NV 89557
Phone: (775) 784–6561; Fax: (775) 784–6655;
Email: jdhexen@unr.edu
Web: gsahist.org/HoGaward/awards.htm
Summary: To recognize and reward undergraduate and graduate students who submit outstanding papers on the history of geology.
Eligibility: Open to undergraduate and graduate students working on a degree in a field related to the history of geology. Applicants must submit a proposal for an oral or poster presentation at the History of Geology division session at the annual meeting of the Geological Society of America; oral presentations are preferred. Entries may be 1) a paper in the history of geology; 2) a literature review of ideas for a technical work or thesis/dissertation; or 3) another paper on an imaginative aspect of the history of geology. Students must be able to present their paper at the meeting.
Financial data: The award includes an honorarium of $1,000 plus $500 to be applied to the student's expenses to attend the annual GSA meeting.
Duration: The award is presented annually.
Number awarded: 1 each year.
Deadline: April of each year.

1267 $$ HOLOCAUST REMEMBRANCE PROJECT

Holland & Knight Charitable Foundation, Inc.
201 North Franklin Street, 11th Floor
P.O. Box 2877
Tampa, FL 33601–2877
Phone: (813) 227–8500; (866) HK–CARES;
Email: holocaust@hklaw.com
Web: holocaust.hklaw.com
Summary: To recognize and reward, with college scholarships in any subject area, high school students who submit outstanding essays on a topic related to the Holocaust.
Eligibility: Open to high school students in grades 9–12 (including graduating seniors), home–school students, and students under 19 years of age enrolled in a high school equivalency program. Applicants must be residents of the United States, the Virgin Islands, or Guam or be U.S. citizens living abroad. They are expected to study the Holocaust and then, in a 1,200–word essay, analyze why it is vital to remember and pass to a new generation the history and lessons of the Holocaust, and suggest what they, as students, can do to combat and prevent prejudice, discrimination, and violence in our world today. In preparation for writing, students are encouraged to research their essay using a variety of sources, including historical and reference material, interviews, eyewitness accounts, oral testimonies, official documents and other primary sources, readings from diaries, letters, autobiographies, works of poetry, video or audio tapes, films, art, CD–ROMs, and Internet sources. Selection is based on 1) evidence of relevant reading and thoughtful use of resource materials; 2) treatment of the assigned theme; 3) clear and effective language, mechanics, and grammar; 4) a coherent plan of organization; and 5) creative use of literary devices.
Financial data: First–place winners receive scholarships that range from $2,500 to $5,000; funds are paid to the recipients' institutions after high school graduation and documentation of enrollment at a college or university. They also receive a 1–week, all–expense paid trip to Boston that includes a visit to the New England Holocaust Memorial. Second–place winners receive $500 grants and third–place winners receive $250 grants.
Duration: The competition is held annually. Former first–place winners are not eligible to enter in subsequent years.
Number awarded: 30 each year: 10 first–place winners, 10 second–place winners, and 10 third–place winners.
Deadline: April of each year.

1268 $ HONORABLE ERNESTINE WASHINGTON LIBRARY SCIENCE/ENGLISH LANGUAGE ARTS SCHOLARSHIP

African–American/Caribbean Education Association, Inc.
P.O. Box 1224
Valley Stream, NY 11582–1224
Phone: (718) 949–6733;
Email: aaceainc@yahoo.com
Web: www.aaceainc.com/Scholarships.html
Summary: To provide financial assistance to high school seniors of African American or Caribbean heritage who plan to study a field related to library science or English language arts in college.
Eligibility: Open to graduating high school seniors who are U.S. citizens of African American or Caribbean heritage. Applicants must be planning to attend a college or university and major in a field related to library science or English language arts. They must have completed 4 years of specified college preparatory courses with a grade of 90 or higher and have an SAT score of at least 1790. They must also have completed at least 200 hours of community service during their 4 years of high school, preferably in the field that they plan to study in college. Financial need is not considered in the selection process. New York residency is not required, but applicants must be available for an interviews in the Queens, New York area.
Financial data: The stipend ranges from $1,000 to $2,500. Funds are paid directly to the recipient.
Duration: 1 year.
Number awarded: 1 each year.
Deadline: April of each year.

1269 HOUSTON SUN SCHOLARSHIP

National Association of Negro Business and Professional Women's Clubs
Attn: Scholarship Committee
1806 New Hampshire Avenue, N.W.
Washington, DC 20009–3206
Phone: (202) 483–4206; Fax: (202) 462–7253;
Email: education@nanbpwc.org
Web: www.nanbpwc.org/scholarship_applications0.aspx
Summary: To provide financial assistance to African Americans from designated states studying journalism at a college in any state.
Eligibility: Open to African Americans (men or women) who are residents of Arkansas, Kansas, Louisiana, Missouri, New Mexico, Oklahoma, or Texas. Applicants must be enrolled at an accredited college or university in any state as a sophomore or junior. They must have a GPA of 3.0 or higher and be majoring in journalism. Along with their application, they must submit an essay, up to 750 words in length, on the topic, "Credo of the Black Press." U.S. citizenship is required.
Financial data: The stipend is $1,000.
Duration: 1 year.
Number awarded: 1 or more each year.
Deadline: February of each year.

1270 HUBERT B. OWENS SCHOLARSHIP

Georgia Trust
Attn: Scholarship Committee
1516 Peachtree Street, N.W.
Atlanta, GA 30309
Phone: (404) 881–9980; Fax: (404) 875–2205;
Email: kryan@georgiatrust.org
Web: www.georgiatrust.org/preservation/opportunities.php
Summary: To provide financial assistance to Georgia residents majoring in a field related to historical preservation at a college or university in the state.
Eligibility: Open to Georgia residents who are enrolled full time in their first year of undergraduate study at a college or university in the state. Applicants must be working on a degree in historic preservation or a related field (e.g., archaeology, architecture, history, planning). U.S. citizenship is required. Selection is based on academic achievement and past and planned involvement within preservation–related fields.
Financial data: The stipend is $1,000.
Duration: 1 year.

Number awarded: 1 each year.
Deadline: February of each year.

1271 $ HUFFSTUTTER FAMILY STYLIST SCHOLARSHIP

Oregon Student Access Commission
Attn: Grants and Scholarships Division
1500 Valley River Drive, Suite 100
P.O. Box 40370
Eugene, OR 97404
Phone: (541) 687–7395; (800) 452–8807, ext. 7395; Fax: (541) 687–7414; TDD: (800) 735–2900;
Email: awardinfo@osac.state.or.us
Web: www.oregonstudentaid.gov/scholarships.aspx
Summary: To provide financial assistance to Oregon and Washington residents who wish to prepare for a career as a barber or hairdresser.
Eligibility: Open to residents of Oregon and Washington who are attending or planning to attend a school in Oregon that offers a degree or certificate in cosmetology or hair design. Applicants must be preparing for a career as a cosmetologist, beautician, barber, or hairdresser. They must be able to demonstrate financial need.
Financial data: Stipends for these scholarships range from $200 to $10,000 but recently averaged $2,300.
Duration: 1 year.
Number awarded: Varies each year.
Deadline: February of each year.

1272 $$ HUMANE STUDIES FELLOWSHIPS

Institute for Humane Studies at George Mason University
3301 North Fairfax Drive, Suite 440
Arlington, VA 22201–4432
Phone: (703) 993–4880; (800) 697–8799; Fax: (703) 993–4890;
Email: ihs@gmu.edu
Web: www.theihs.org/humane–studies–fellowships
Summary: To provide financial assistance to undergraduate and graduate students in the United States or abroad who intend to prepare for scholarly careers and have demonstrated an interest in classical liberal principles.
Eligibility: Open to students who will be full–time graduate students (including law students) or undergraduate juniors and seniors. Applicants must be able to demonstrate a "research interest in the intellectual and institutional foundations of a free society." Relevant fields of study include economics, history, law, philosophy, political science, and sociology. Along with their application, they must submit 1) essays of 750 to 1,000 words on their personal intellectual history, the nature of their academic discipline, and their current research interests; 2) a 30–page writing sample; and 3) transcripts. Applications from students outside the United States or studying abroad receive equal consideration. Selection is based on academic or professional performance, relevance of work to the advancement of a free society, and potential for success.
Financial data: Stipends range from $2,000 to $15,000.
Duration: 1 year; may be renewed upon reapplication.
Number awarded: Recently, the program has been awarding between 110 and 195 of these fellowships each year.
Deadline: January of each year.

1273 $$ IALD EDUCATION TRUST SCHOLARSHIPS

International Association of Lighting Designers
Attn: Education Trust Fund
440 North Wells Street, Suite 210
Chicago, IL 60654
Phone: (312) 527–3677; Fax: (312) 527–3680;
Email: iald@iald.org
Web: www.iald.org/trust/programs.asp?altlink=152
Summary: To provide financial assistance to students in any country pursuing a program in architectural lighting design.
Eligibility: Open to students who are pursuing architectural lighting design as a course of study at a college or university in any country. Applicants must submit 1) a 2–page resume; 2) an official transcript; 3) 2 letters of reference; 4) up to 10 images of their artwork that show their design ability; and 5) a personal statement, up to 2 pages, on their experience with lighting, why they want to study lighting, or why they should receive this scholarship. Selection is based on those submissions; financial need is not considered.
Financial data: Stipends range from $500 to $5,000.
Duration: 1 year.
Number awarded: Varies each year; recently, 9 students received a total of $28,000 in these scholarships.
Deadline: March of each year.

1274 IFDA LEADERS COMMEMORATIVE SCHOLARSHIP

International Furnishings and Design Association
Attn: IFDA Educational Foundation
2700 East Grace Street
Richmond, VA 23223
Phone: (804) 644–3946; Fax: (804) 644–3834;
Email: colleaguesinc@earthlink.net
Web: www.ifdaef.org/scholarships.php
Summary: To provide financial assistance to undergraduate students who are working on a degree in interior design and have been involved in volunteer or community service.
Eligibility: Open to full–time undergraduates who have completed at least 4 courses in interior design or a related field. Applicants must have a record of involvement in volunteer or community service and have held leadership positions during the past 5 years. Along with their application, they must submit an essay of 300 to 400 words on their long– and short–term goals, special interests, volunteer and community service, and what inspired them to prepare for a career in this field; samples of their design work; a transcript; and a letter of recommendation from a professor or instructor. Financial need is not considered.
Financial data: The stipend is $1,500.
Duration: 1 year.
Number awarded: At least 1 each year.
Deadline: March of each year.

1275 IFDA PART TIME STUDENT SCHOLARSHIP

International Furnishings and Design Association
Attn: IFDA Educational Foundation
2700 East Grace Street
Richmond, VA 23223
Phone: (804) 644–3946; Fax: (804) 644–3834;
Email: colleaguesinc@earthlink.net
Web: www.ifdaef.org/scholarships.php
Summary: To provide financial assistance to undergraduate students working part time on a degree in interior design.
Eligibility: Open to part–time undergraduates currently enrolled in at least 2 courses. Applicants must have completed at least 4 courses in interior design or a related field. Along with their application, they must submit an essay of 200 to 400 words on their long– and short–term goals, special interests, volunteer and community service, and what inspired them to prepare for a career in this field; samples of their design work; a transcript; and a letter of recommendation from a professor or instructor. Financial need is not considered.
Financial data: The stipend is $1,500.
Duration: 1 year.
Number awarded: At least 1 each year.
Deadline: March of each year.

1276 $ IFEC SCHOLARSHIPS

International Foodservice Editorial Council
7 Point Place
P.O. Box 491
Hyde Park, NY 12538
Phone: (845) 229–6973; Fax: (845) 229–6973;
Email: ifec@ifenonline.com
Web: www.ifeconline.com/scholarship_info.cfm
Summary: To provide financial assistance to undergraduate or graduate students who are interested in preparing for a career in communications in the food service industry.
Eligibility: Open to currently–enrolled college students who are working on an associate, bachelor's, or master's degree. Applicants should be preparing for a career as a writer, editor, public relations and marketing communication practitioner, or closely–related area in the food service industry. They must be enrolled full time with a combination of studies (and/or work experience) in both the food service and communication arts. Appropriate food service majors include culinary arts; hospitality management; hotel, restaurant, and institutional management; dietetics; food science and technology; and nutrition. Applicable communications areas include journalism, English, mass communications, public relations, marketing, broadcast journalism, graphic arts, and photography. Selection is based on academic record, character references, and demonstrated financial need.

Financial data: Stipends range from $500 to $4,000.
Duration: 1 year.
Number awarded: 4 to 8 each year.
Deadline: March of each year.

1277 $$ IFMA FOUNDATION SCHOLARSHIPS

International Facility Management Association
Attn: IFMA Foundation
1 East Greenway Plaza, Suite 1100
Houston, TX 77046–0104
Phone: (281) 974–5601; Fax: (479) 696–9494;
Email: foundation@ifmafoundation.org
Web: www.ifmafoundation.org/grants–scholarships
Summary: To provide financial assistance to undergraduate and graduate students working on a degree in facility management or a related field.
Eligibility: Open to students enrolled full time at an accredited 4–year college or university in an undergraduate or graduate program in facility management or a related field (e.g., architecture, business operations, construction, engineering, environmental design, interior design). Undergraduates must have completed at least 2 years of study for a bachelor's degree or 1 year of study for an associate degree and have a GPA of 3.2 or higher. Graduate students must have a GPA of 3.5 or higher. Applicants may not be currently employed full time in facility management. Selection is based on 1) a 250– to 500–word letter of professional intent describing their short– and long–term goals in facility management; 2) resume; 3) academic achievement; 4) a description in their own words of facility management and how they see it being used in the normal flow of business; 5) involvement in facility management related activities; 6) leadership qualities; and 7) letters of recommendation.
Financial data: Stipends range from $1,500 to $5,000.
Duration: 1 year.
Number awarded: Varies each year; recently, 36 of these scholarships were awarded: 8 at $5,000, 4 at $4,000, 4 at $2,500, 8 at $2,000, and 12 at $1,500.
Deadline: May of each year.

1278 $ IHA STUDENT DESIGN COMPETITION

International Housewares Association
Attn: Design Programs Coordinator
6400 Shafer Court, Suite 650
Rosemont, IL 60018
Phone: (847) 292–4200; Fax: (847) 292–4211;
Email: vmatranga@nhma.com
Web: www.housewares.org/show/info/sdc
Summary: To recognize and reward outstanding young designers of housewares products.
Eligibility: Open to sophomores, juniors, seniors, or graduate students at a college or university in any country. They are invited to design a housewares product in any of the following categories: household small electric appliances; personal care and home health care products; tableware, serving products, and accessories; cook and bakeware; kitchenware; outdoor products and home maintenance; organization and storage; cleaning products; furniture; decorative accessories; juvenile and pet products; and electronic products that enhance home activities. Students may submit more than 1 entry, but they may not be awarded more than 1 prize. Selection is based on design research, design, and technical skills and presentation organization.
Financial data: First place is $2,500, second place is $1,800, and third place is $1,300. Winners also receive transportation and lodging for the International Housewares Show.
Duration: The competition is held annually.
Number awarded: Each year, 2 first places, 2 second places, and 2 third places are awarded.
Deadline: December of each year.

1279 ILBA STUDENT SCHOLARSHIPS

Illinois Broadcasters Association
Attn: Foundation
200 Missouri Avenue
Carterville, IL 62918
Phone: (618) 985–5555; Fax: (618) 985–6070;
Email: iba@ilba.org
Web: ilba.org/about–us/ibfoundation
Summary: To provide funding to high school seniors in Illinois who are planning to major in a field related to broadcasting at a college in the state.
Eligibility: Open to seniors graduating from high schools in the state and planning to enroll at a college or university in the state that offers a major in telecommunications or broadcast journalism or that has a radio or television facility on campus. Applicants must be interested in majoring in broadcast–related field (e.g., journalism, broadcast engineering, programming, on–air). They must have a GPA of 3.0 or higher. Along with their application, they must submit information on how they are financing their college education, their employment experience, any special recognitions they have received, and their extracurricular activities.
Financial data: Each participating Illinois broadcast station determines the amount of its awards. The Illinois Broadcasters Foundation matches whatever the station awards, to a maximum of $500 per grant. All funds are paid directly to the recipient's school.
Duration: 1 year.
Number awarded: Varies each year; the Foundation has $100,000 available for this program each year.
Deadline: March of each year.

1280 $ INDIANA BROADCASTERS ASSOCIATION COLLEGE SCHOLARSHIPS

Indiana Broadcasters Association
Attn: Scholarship Administrator
3003 East 98th Street, Suite 161
Indianapolis, IN 46280
Phone: (317) 573–0119; (800) 342–6276 (within IN); Fax: (317) 573–0895;
Email: iba@indianabroadcasters.org
Web: www.indianabroadcasters.org/scholarship
Summary: To provide financial assistance to college students in Indiana who are interested in preparing for a career in a field related to broadcasting.
Eligibility: Open to residents of Indiana who are attending a college or university in the state that is a member of the Indiana Broadcasters Association (IBA) or that has a radio/TV facility on campus. Applicants must be majoring in telecommunications or broadcast journalism and have a GPA of 3.0 or higher. They must be actively participating on a college broadcast facility or working for a commercial broadcast facility while attending college. Along with their application, they must submit an essay on their interest in continuing their education in telecommunications or broadcast journalism. Financial need is not considered in the selection process.
Financial data: The stipend is $2,700.
Duration: 1 year.
Number awarded: Varies each year: recently, 10 of these scholarships were awarded.
Deadline: February of each year.

1281 $$ INDIANAPOLIS PRESS CLUB FOUNDATION SCHOLARSHIPS

Indianapolis Press Club Foundation Inc.
Attn: Executive Director
P.O. Box 40923
Indianapolis, IN 46240–0923
Phone: (317) 701–1130; Fax: (317) 844–5805;
Email: jlabalme.indypress@att.net
Web: indypressfoundation.typepad.com/blog/scholarships.html
Summary: To provide financial assistance to college students in Indiana who are interested in preparing for a career in journalism.
Eligibility: Open to students who are enrolled in an Indiana college or university and interested in a career in the news business. Preference is given to students who are majoring in journalism or broadcast journalism. Along with their application, students must submit a 1–page essay in which they describe their career goals, how they plan to achieve those goals, why they are important to them, and how the scholarship will assist them in reaching their goal of a career in journalism. Financial need is considered, but career interest, writing ability, ethics, news judgment, and potential for success are the chief concerns in the selection process.
Financial data: Recently, the stipend was $5,000.
Duration: 1 year.
Number awarded: Varies each year; recently, 2 of these scholarships were awarded.
Deadline: April of each year.

1282 $$ INTELLIGENCE AND CYBER SECURITY SCHOLARSHIPS

Armed Forces Communications and Electronics Association
Attn: AFCEA Educational Foundation

4400 Fair Lakes Court
Fairfax, VA 22033–3899
Phone: (703) 631–6138; (800) 336–4583, ext. 6138; Fax: (703) 631–4693;
Email: scholarshipsinfo@afcea.org
Web: www.afcea.org

Summary: To provide financial assistance to undergraduate and graduate students working on a degree in a field related to intelligence.

Eligibility: Open to full–time undergraduate or graduate students at 2– and 4–year colleges and universities. Applicants must be working on a degree in a field directly related to the support of U.S. intelligence or homeland security enterprises, such as cyber security, cyber attack, computer science, information technology, digital forensics, electronic engineering, and/or foreign languages. They must have a GPA of 3.0 or higher. Selection is based primarily on demonstrated academic excellence, leadership, and financial need. U.S. citizenship is required.

Financial data: The stipend is $2,250 for undergraduates or $5,000 for graduate students.

Duration: 1 year.

Number awarded: Varies each year; recently, 5 of these scholarships were awarded: 2 to undergraduate and 3 to graduate students.

Deadline: October of each year.

1283 $$ INTERMARKETS–LUCIDO JOURNALISM SCHOLARSHIPS

Community Foundation for Northern Virginia
Attn: Director of Grants
8283 Greensboro Drive
McLean, VA 22102
Phone: (703) 902–3158; Fax: (703) 902–3564;
Email: MacDonald_Lesley@ne.bah.com
Web: www.novacf.org/page10003427.cfm

Summary: To provide financial assistance to high school seniors in Virginia who plan to attend college in any state to major in journalism.

Eligibility: Open to seniors graduating from public or private high schools in Virginia who plan to enroll at an accredited 4–year college or university in any state. Applicants must be planning to major in journalism. Along with their application, they must submit 1) a 200–word essay on 3 character traits that a journalist should have and why; 2) 2 published articles or graded essays that reflect their writing style; and 3) a 500–word essay that takes a current article from a major U.S. newspaper that the candidate views as biased, explains why it is biased, and describes how it should be changed. Selection is based on those submissions, extracurricular activities, and academic excellence. U.S. citizenship is required.

Financial data: The stipend is $5,000.

Duration: 1 year.

Number awarded: 3 each year.

Deadline: April of each year.

1284 INTERNATIONAL SCHOLARSHIP PROGRAM FOR COMMUNITY SERVICE

Memorial Foundation for Jewish Culture
50 Broadway, 34th Floor
New York, NY 10004
Phone: (212) 425–6606; Fax: (212) 425–6602;
Email: office@mfjc.org
Web: www.mfjc.org/support/howto.html

Summary: To assist well–qualified individuals to train for careers in a field related to Jewish community service.

Eligibility: Open to any individual, regardless of country of origin, who is presently receiving or plans to undertake training in his/her chosen field at a recognized yeshiva, teacher training seminary, school of social work, university, or other educational institution. Applicants must be interested in pursuing professional training for careers in Jewish education, Jewish social service, the Rabbinate, or as religious functionaries (e.g., shohatim, mohalim) in Diaspora Jewish communities in need of such personnel. Students planning to serve in the United States, Canada, or Israel are not eligible.

Financial data: The amount of the grant varies, depending on the country in which the student will be trained and other considerations.

Duration: 1 year; may be renewed.

Deadline: November of each year.

1285 $$ INTERNATIONAL SOLO COMPETITION

Walter W. Naumburg Foundation, Inc.
120 Claremont Avenue
New York, NY 10027–4698
Phone: (212) 362–9877
Web: www.naumburg.org

Summary: To recognize and reward outstanding student and other young singers and instrumentalists of all nationalities.

Eligibility: Open to musicians who are at least 20 but not more than 35 years of age. Applicants must submit a tape recording of no less than 30 minutes of satisfactory listenable quality. Based on those tapes, judges select contestants for live preliminary auditions, followed by semifinals and finals. Musicians may be of any nationality.

Financial data: Prizes vary; recently, they were $15,000 for first, $10,000 for second, and $5,000 for third.

Duration: The competition is held approximately annually.

Number awarded: Varies each year; recently, 3 prizes were awarded.

Deadline: February of each year.

1286 $$ INTERPUBLIC GROUP SCHOLARSHIP AND INTERNSHIP

New York Women in Communications, Inc.
Attn: NYWICI Foundation
355 Lexington Avenue, 15th Floor
New York, NY 10017–6603
Phone: (212) 297–2133; Fax: (212) 370–9047;
Email: nywicipr@nywici.org
Web: www.nywici.org/foundation/scholarships

Summary: To provide financial assistance and work experience to women from ethnically diverse groups who are residents of designated eastern states and enrolled as juniors at a college in any state to prepare for a career in advertising or public relations.

Eligibility: Open to female residents of New York, New Jersey, Connecticut, or Pennsylvania who are from ethnically diverse groups and currently enrolled as juniors at a college or university in any state. Also eligible are women who reside outside the 4 states but are currently enrolled at a college or university within 1 of the 5 boroughs of New York City. Applicants must be preparing for a career in advertising or public relations and have a GPA of 3.2 or higher. They must be available for a summer internship with Interpublic Group (IPG) in New York City. Along with their application, they must submit a 2–page resume that includes school and extracurricular activities, significant achievements, academic honors and awards, and community service work; a personal essay of 300 to 500 words on their choice of an assigned topic that changes annually; 2 letters of recommendation; and an official transcript. Selection is based on academic record, need, demonstrated leadership, participation in school and community activities, honors, work experience, goals and aspirations, and unusual personal and/or family circumstances. U.S. citizenship is required.

Financial data: The scholarship stipend ranges up to $10,000; the internship is salaried (amount not specified).

Duration: 1 year.

Number awarded: 1 each year.

Deadline: January of each year.

1287 IOWA BARBER AND COSMETOLOGY ARTS AND SCIENCES TUITION GRANTS

Iowa College Student Aid Commission
603 East 12th Street, Fifth Floor
Des Moines, IA 50319
Phone: (515) 725–3400; (877) 272–4456; Fax: (515) 725–3401;
Email: info@iowacollegeaid.gov
Web: www.iowacollegeaid.gov/ScholarshipsGrants/scholarshipsgrants.html

Summary: To provide financial assistance to Iowa residents interested in studying at a barber and cosmetology college in the state.

Eligibility: Open to residents of Iowa who are enrolled or planning to enroll at a participating barber and cosmetology college in the state. Priority is given to applicants with the greatest financial need. U.S. citizenship or permanent resident status is required.

Financial data: The maximum grant is $1,200 per year (may be adjusted for less than full–time study.

Duration: 1 year.

Number awarded: Varies each year.

Deadline: Applicants must submit a FAFSA form as early as possible after January 1, but no later than the end of June.

1288 IOWA SCHOLARSHIPS FOR THE ARTS

Iowa Arts Council
Attn: Iowa Scholarships for the Arts
600 East Locust
Des Moines, IA 50319–0290
Phone: (515) 281–3293; Fax: (515) 242–6498; TDD: (800) 735–2942;
Email: Veronica.OHern@iowa.gov
Web: www.iowaartscouncil.org

Summary: To provide financial assistance to Iowa high school seniors who plan to study the arts at a college or university in the state.
Eligibility: Open to graduating seniors at high schools in Iowa who have been accepted as full–time undergraduate students at an accredited college or university in the state. Applicants must be planning to major in music, dance, visual arts, folk or traditional arts, theater, or literature. Along with their application, they must submit samples of their work and a 2–page essay on the themes or concepts that inspire their work, why their art form is significant, what they value about being an artist, and what they hope to gain from an education in their particular field. Selection is based on 1) artistic abilities; 2) clear vision for their art work; and 3) future goals and objectives relating to the intended field of study.
Financial data: The stipend is $1,500.
Duration: 1 year.
Number awarded: Varies each year; recently, 3 of these scholarships were awarded.
Deadline: January of each year.

1289 $ IRENE RYAN ACTING SCHOLARSHIPS

John F. Kennedy Center for the Performing Arts
Education Department
Attn: Kennedy Center American College Theater Festival
2700 F Street, N.W.
Washington, DC 20566
Phone: (202) 416–8857; Fax: (202) 416–8860;
Email: KCACTF@kennedy–center.org
Web: www.kcactf.org/KCACTF.ORG_NATIONAL/Irene_Ryans.html

Summary: To recognize and reward outstanding college actors.
Eligibility: Open to students enrolled at an accredited junior or senior college in the United States. Participants must appear as actors in plays produced by their college and entered in 1 of the 8 regional festivals of the Kennedy Center American College Theater Festival (KCACTF). Undergraduate students must be carrying at least 6 semester hours, graduate students must be enrolled in at least 3 semester hours, and continuing part–time students must be enrolled in a regular degree or certificate program. From each of the regional festivals, 2 winners and their acting partners are invited to the national festival at the John F. Kennedy Center for the Performing Arts in Washington, D.C. to participate in an "Evening of Scenes." Scholarships are awarded to outstanding student performers at each regional festival and from the "Evening of Scenes."
Financial data: Regional winners receive $500 scholarships and payment of expenses (transportation, lodging, and per diem) to attend the national festival. National winners receive $3,000 scholarships; the best partner receives the Kingsley Colton Award of $500. All scholarship funds are paid directly to the institutions designated by the recipients and may be used for any field of study.
Duration: The competition is held annually.
Number awarded: 16 regional winners receive awards each year; at the national festival "Evening of Scenes," 2 performers receive scholarships. Several other awards are also presented.
Deadline: The regional festivals are held in January and February of each year; the national festival is held in April of each year. Application deadlines are set within each region.

1290 $ JACKSON FOUNDATION JOURNALISM SCHOLARSHIP

Oregon Student Access Commission
Attn: Grants and Scholarships Division
1500 Valley River Drive, Suite 100
Eugene, OR 97401–2146
Phone: (541) 687–7395; (800) 452–8807, ext. 7395; Fax: (541) 687–7414; TDD: (800) 735–2900;
Email: awardinfo@osac.state.or.us
Web: www.oregonstudentaid.gov/scholarships.aspx

Summary: To provide financial assistance to students in Oregon interested in majoring in journalism at a college in the state.
Eligibility: Open to graduates of Oregon high schools who are studying or planning to study journalism at a college or university in the state. Preference is given to students who have taken the SAT examination and have good scores on the writing section. Financial need is considered in the selection process.
Financial data: Stipends for scholarships offered by the Oregon Student Access Commission (OSAC) range from $200 to $10,000 but recently averaged $2,300.
Duration: 1 year; may be renewed.
Number awarded: Varies each year.
Deadline: February of each year.

1291 $ JAMES ALAN COX FOUNDATION SCHOLARSHIPS

James Alan Cox Foundation for Student Photographers
P.O. Box 9158
Austin, TX 78766
Phone: (512) 459–8515
Web: www.jamesalancoxfoundation.org/application.php

Summary: To provide financial assistance to college students interested in photography or photojournalism.
Eligibility: Open to students who have completed at least 1 year at a recognized college, university, or professional school and have taken courses in photography or photojournalism. Applicants must have at least 1 semester of school remaining. They must submit either 5 images as digital still photography entries or 2 videos up to 3 minutes in length. Financial need is considered in the selection process. U.S. citizenship is required.
Financial data: The stipend is $2,500.
Duration: 1 year.
Number awarded: 5 each year: 4 for video work and 1 for still photography.
Deadline: November of each year.

1292 JAMES J. WYCHOR SCHOLARSHIPS

Minnesota Broadcasters Association
Attn: Scholarship Program
3033 Excelsior Boulevard, Suite 440
Minneapolis, MN 55416
Phone: (612) 926–8123; (800) 245–5838; Fax: (612) 926–9761;
Email: llasere@minnesotabroadcasters.com
Web: www.minnesotabroadcasters.com/membership

Summary: To provide financial assistance to Minnesota residents interested in studying broadcasting at a college in any state.
Eligibility: Open to residents of Minnesota who are accepted or enrolled at an accredited postsecondary institution in any state offering a broadcast–related curriculum. Applicants must have a high school or college GPA of 3.0 or higher and must submit a 500–word essay on why they wish to prepare for a career in broadcasting or electronic media. Employment in the broadcasting industry is not required, but students who are employed must include a letter from their general manager describing the duties they have performed as a radio or television station employee and evaluating their potential for success in the industry. Financial need is not considered in the selection process. Some of the scholarships are awarded only to minority or women candidates.
Financial data: The stipend is $1,500.
Duration: 1 year; recipients who are college seniors may reapply for an additional 1–year renewal as a graduate student.
Number awarded: 10 each year, distributed as follows: 3 within the 7–county metro area, 5 allocated geographically throughout the state (northeast, northwest, central, southeast, southwest), and 2 reserved specifically for women and minority applicants.
Deadline: June of each year.

1293 JAMES L. GOLDEN OUTSTANDING STUDENT ESSAY IN RHETORIC AWARD

National Communication Association
Attn: Executive Assistant
1765 N Street, N.W.
Washington, DC 20036–2802
Phone: (202) 464–4622; Fax: (202) 464–4600;
Email: hfranklin@natcom.org
Web: www.natcom.org/awards

Summary: To recognize and reward undergraduate and graduate students who submit outstanding essays on the history, theory, or criticism of rhetoric.

Eligibility: Open to 1) undergraduates; and 2) graduate students who have not yet completed a master's degree. Applicants must submit an essay, up to 20 pages in length, on the history, theory, or criticism of rhetoric. Selection is based on contribution to the understanding of rhetorical process and outcomes, excellence of conception and grounding, weight of argument, strength of evidence, and eloquence of expression.
Financial data: The winner receives a cash prize of $1,000, an award certificate, and travel support to present the essay at the annual convention of the National Communication Association.
Duration: The award is granted annually.
Number awarded: 1 each year.
Deadline: March of each year.

1294 $ JAMES M. AND VIRGINIA M. SMYTH SCHOLARSHIP FUND

Community Foundation for Greater Atlanta, Inc.
50 Hurt Plaza, Suite 449
Atlanta, GA 30303
Phone: (404) 688–5525; Fax: (404) 688–3060;
Email: scholarships@cfgreateratlanta.org
Web: www.cfgreateratlanta.org/Grants–Support/Scholarships.aspx
Summary: To provide financial assistance to high school seniors, especially those from designated states, who are interested in majoring in selected fields at colleges in any state.
Eligibility: Open to graduating high school seniors, with special consideration given to residents of Georgia, Illinois, Mississippi, Missouri, Oklahoma, Tennessee, and Texas. Applicants must have a GPA of 3.0 or higher and be interested in attending a college, university, or community college in any state to work on a degree in the arts and sciences, human services, music, or ministry. They must be able to demonstrate financial need and a commitment to community service through school, community, or religious organizations. Adults returning to school to increase employability are also eligible.
Financial data: The stipend is $2,000 per year.
Duration: 1 year; may be renewed up to 3 additional years.
Number awarded: 12 to 15 each year.
Deadline: February of each year.

1295 JAMES O. THOMASON SCHOLARSHIP

Harry Hampton Memorial Wildlife Fund, Inc.
P.O. Box 2641
Columbia, SC 29202
Phone: (803) 600–1570;
Email: jim.goller@hamptonwildlifefund.org
Web: www.hamptonwildlifefund.org/scholarship.html
Summary: To provide financial assistance to high school seniors in South Carolina who plan to major in a field related to journalism or communications at a college or university in the state.
Eligibility: Open to seniors graduating from high schools in South Carolina who plan to attend an institution of higher learning in the state. Applicants must be planning to major in electronic, print, or photo journalism; advertising; public relations; or mass communications. Along with their application, they must submit 1) a 1,200–word essay on a topic that changes annually; recently, students were asked to write on the advantages and disadvantages of developing wind energy along the coast of South Carolina; and 2) a brief autobiography that includes a description of their career ambitions in the natural resources field; why they desire a college education; their interest in wildlife resources, the environment, coastal resources, or related topics; and why they will be a good investment if they are awarded this scholarship. Financial need is also considered in the selection process.
Financial data: The stipend is $1,000 per year.
Duration: 1 year; may be renewed up to 3 additional years, provided the recipient maintains a GPA of 2.5 or higher.
Number awarded: 1 each year.
Deadline: January of each year.

1296 JANET DZIADULEWICZ BRANDEN MEMORIAL AWARD

Polanki, The Polish Women's Cultural Club of Milwaukee
Attn: College Achievement Awards
P.O. Box 341458
Milwaukee, WI 53234
Phone: (414) 858–9357;
Email: polanki@polanki.org
Web: www.polanki.org/scholar–main.html
Summary: To recognize and reward upper–division and graduate students in Wisconsin who have a Polish connection and demonstrate academic excellence in Polish studies.
Eligibility: Open to college juniors, seniors, and graduate students who are Wisconsin residents or attending college in the state. Applicants must be 1) of Polish heritage; 2) non–Polish students of Polish language, history, society, or culture; or 3) significantly engaged with Polish culture. They must have a GPA of 3.0 or higher. Along with their application, they must submit 1) an essay of 500 to 600 words on a topic that changes annually but relates to Poland; and 2) a paragraph of 100 to 150 words on their personal, academic, and professional plans for the future. This award is reserved for a student of Polish studies. U.S. citizenship or permanent residence is required.
Financial data: Awards range from $750 to $1,500.
Duration: The awards are presented annually.
Number awarded: 1 each year.
Deadline: January of each year.

1297 $$ JAPANESE AMERICAN ASSOCIATION OF NEW YORK MUSIC SCHOLARSHIP AWARDS

Japanese American Association of New York, Inc.
Attn: Scholarship Committee
15 West 44th Street, 11th Floor
New York, NY 10036
Phone: (212) 840–6942; Fax: (212) 840–0616;
Email: info@jaany.org
Web: www.jaany.org/music_scholarship.html
Summary: To recognize and reward Japanese and Japanese American students who participate in a music competition.
Eligibility: Open to students who are Japanese or Americans of Japanese descent. Recently, the competition was limited to ensembles from trio to quintet; applicants performed 1 piece from the Classical era and another from the Romantic era or the 20th century at the recital in New York.
Financial data: Awards range from $2,000 to $5,000.
Duration: The competition is held annually.
Number awarded: 2 each year.
Deadline: September of each year.

1298 $$ JAY FRANKE SCHOLARSHIPS

Diabetes Scholars Foundation
2118 Plum Grove Road, Suite 356
Rolling Meadows, IL 60008
Phone: (312) 215–9861; Fax: (847) 991–8739;
Email: collegescholarships@diabetesscholars.org
Web: www.diabetesscholars.org/college.html
Summary: To provide financial assistance to high school seniors who have diabetes and plan to major in the arts in college.
Eligibility: Open to graduating high school seniors who have Type 1 diabetes and plan to attend an accredited 4–year university, college, or technical/trade school in any state. Applicants must be planning to major in the arts (e.g., music, theater, dance). They must be able to demonstrate active involvement in the diabetes community, academic performance, participation in community and/or extracurricular activities, and successful management of the challenges of living with diabetes. Financial need is not considered in the selection process. U.S. citizenship or permanent resident status is required.
Financial data: Stipends are $5,000 or $3,500.
Duration: 1 year.
Number awarded: 2 each year: 1 at $5,000 and 1 at $3,500.
Deadline: May of each year.

1299 $$ JAY KENNEDY MEMORIAL SCHOLARSHIP

National Cartoonists Society
Attn: Foundation
341 North Maitland Avenue, Suite 130
Maitland, FL 32751
Phone: (407) 647–8839; Fax: (407) 629–2502
Web: www.cartoonistfoundation.org/jay–kennedy–scholarship.html
Summary: To provide financial assistance to upper–division students who are interested in cartooning.
Eligibility: Open to juniors and seniors at 4–year colleges and universities in the United States, Canada, or Mexico. Applicants must be interested in cartooning, although they are not required to be art majors. Along with their application, they must submit 1) a brief statement on what they have done with car-

tooning so far; 2) a brief statement on their future plans for cartooning; and 3) 8 samples of their work. Financial need is not considered in the selection process.
Financial data: The stipend is $5,000.
Duration: 1 year.
Number awarded: 1 each year.
Deadline: December of each year.

1300 $ J.B. STEVENSON SCHOLARSHIP

Alabama Scholastic Press Association
c/o University of Alabama
490 Reese Phifer
P.O. Box 870172
Tuscaloosa, AL 35487–0172
Phone: (205) 348–ASPA; Fax: (205) 348–2780;
Email: aspa@ua.edu
Web: aspa1.ua.edu/contests–and–critiques
Summary: To provide financial assistance to high school seniors in Alabama who are interested in studying journalism at a college in any state.
Eligibility: Open to seniors graduating from high schools in Alabama who have been involved in journalism for at least 2 years. Applicants must be interested in attending college in any state to prepare for a career in journalism or mass communications. They must have a GPA of 3.0 or higher. Along with their application, they must submit an official transcript, a self–analytical evaluation of their "journalistic life," letters of recommendation, a portfolio showing examples of their best published work, and an issue of their newspaper or magazine or photocopies of relevant yearbook spreads. Items to be covered in their self–analytical evaluation include how they feel about journalism, how they got started in the field, what they have had to go through to achieve, what they have contributed to journalism, and their journalism plans for the future. Based on those submissions, winners are selected for 3 awards: Journalist of the Year, Rick Bragg Award for Feature Writing, and Bailey Thompson Award for Editorial Writing. The winners of those awards are then considered for this scholarship.
Financial data: Each of the awards is $500. The stipend of the scholarship is an additional $2,500.
Duration: 1 year.
Number awarded: 3 awards and 1 scholarship are awarded each year.
Deadline: January of each year.

1301 JEAN KENNEDY SMITH PLAYWRITING AWARD

John F. Kennedy Center for the Performing Arts
Education Department
Attn: Kennedy Center American College Theater Festival
2700 F Street, N.W.
Washington, DC 20566
Phone: (202) 416–8857; Fax: (202) 416–8860;
Email: KCACTF@kennedy–center.org
Web: www.kcactf.org/KCACTF.ORG_NATIONAL/Kanin_Playwriting.html
Summary: To recognize and reward the student authors of plays on the theme of disability.
Eligibility: Open to students at any accredited junior or senior college in the United States, provided their college agrees to participate in the Kennedy Center American College Theater Festival (KCACTF). Undergraduate students must be carrying at least 6 semester hours, graduate students must be enrolled in at least 3 semester hours, and continuing part–time students must be enrolled in a regular degree or certificate program. This award is presented to the best student–written script that explores the human experience of living with a disability.
Financial data: The winning playwright receives a cash award of $1,000, active membership in the Dramatists Guild, Inc., and a fellowship providing transportation, housing, and per diem to attend a prestigious playwriting program.
Duration: The award is presented annually.
Number awarded: 1 each year.
Deadline: November of each year.

1302 JEAN LEE/JEFF MARVIN COLLEGIATE SCHOLARSHIPS

Indiana Association for Health, Physical Education, Recreation, and Dance
c/o Karen Hatch, Executive Director
2007 Wilno Drive
Marion, IN 46952
Phone: (765) 664–8319;
Email: hatch@comteck.com
Web: www.inahperd.org/grants–scholarships
Summary: To provide financial assistance to upper–division students in Indiana who are majoring in health education, physical education, recreation, or dance.
Eligibility: Open to juniors and seniors at colleges and universities in Indiana who are majoring in health education, physical education, recreation, dance education, or related areas (including sports administration). Applicants must submit a statement in which they describe their plans for after graduation, why they need this scholarship, their extracurricular activities, and their personal philosophy relating to their future profession. Selection is based on participation in collegiate activities, professional competencies, GPA, potential as a professional, financial need, and recommendations.
Financial data: The stipend is $1,000.
Duration: 1 year.
Number awarded: 4 each year.
Deadline: November of each year.

1303 JEANNE L. HAMMOND MEMORIAL SCHOLARSHIP

Summary: To provide financial assistance to female high school seniors and recent graduates in Maine who plan to attend college in any state.
See Listing #383.

1304 JEANNE MOWLDS DISTINGUISHED LIFETIME SERVICE AWARD

Electronic Document Systems Foundation
Attn: EDSF Scholarship Awards
1845 Precinct Line Road, Suite 212
Hurst, TX 76054
Phone: (817) 849–1145; Fax: (817) 849–1185;
Email: info@edsf.org
Web: www.edsf.org/what_we_do/scholarships/index.html
Summary: To provide financial assistance to undergraduate and graduate students from any country interested in preparing for a career in document management and graphic communications.
Eligibility: Open to full–time undergraduate and graduate students from any country who demonstrate a strong interest in preparing for a career in the document management and graphic communications industry, including computer science and engineering (e.g., web design, webmaster, software development, materials engineer, applications specialist, information technology designer, systems analyst); graphic and media communications (e.g., graphic designer, illustrator, color scientist, print production, prepress imaging specialist, workflow specialist, document preparation, production and/or document distribution, content management, e–commerce, imaging science, printing, web authoring, electronic publishing, archiving, security); or business (e.g., sales, marketing, trade shows, customer service, project or product development, management). Preference is given to graduate students and upper–division undergraduates, but freshmen and sophomores who can show interest, experience, and/or commitment to the document management and graphic communication industry are encouraged to apply. Applicants must have a GPA of 3.0 or higher. Along with their application, they must submit 2 essays on assigned topics that change annually but relate to the document management and graphic communication industries. Selection is based on the essays, academic excellence, participation in school activities, community service, honors and organizational affiliations, education goals, and recommendations; financial need is not considered.
Financial data: The stipend is $1,000.
Duration: 1 year.
Number awarded: 1 each year.
Deadline: April of each year.

1305 JEFF HENDERSON SCHOLARSHIP FOR JOURNALISM EXCELLENCE

Texas Intercollegiate Press Association
c/o Texas A&M University at Commerce
2600 South Neal
Box 4104
Commerce, TX 75429
Phone: (903) 886–5231; Fax: (903) 468–3128
Web: www.texasipa.org/default.asp?pageName=scholarships
Summary: To provide financial assistance to journalism students at colleges and universities in Texas.
Eligibility: Open to students majoring in journalism at 2– and 4–year colleges and universities in Texas. Applicants must have a GPA of 3.0 or higher. Each school may nominate 1 student.

Financial data: The stipend is $1,000.
Duration: 1 year.
Number awarded: 1 each year.
Deadline: February of each year.

1306 JEFF ZASLOW COLLEGE COLUMNIST AWARD

National Society of Newspaper Columnists
Attn: Education Foundation
P.O. Box 411532
San Francisco, CA 94141–1532
Phone: (415) 488–NSNC; Fax: (484) 297–0336
Web: www.columnists.com

Summary: To recognize and reward, with college scholarships, undergraduate journalism students who write outstanding columns.
Eligibility: Open to undergraduates who write bylined general interest, editorial page, or Op–Ed page columns for their college newspapers. It is not open to columnists writing on sports, arts, health, or other specialized topics. Candidates must submit 3 columns published during the 12–month period prior to the deadline. Columns published online are eligible if they also appeared in print editions.
Financial data: First prize is a $1,000 scholarship; second prize is a $500 scholarship; and third prize is a $250 scholarship.
Duration: The prizes are presented annually.
Number awarded: 3 each year.
Deadline: February of each year.

1307 $ JENA AND STEPHEN B. HALL SCHOLARSHIPS

WithIt, Inc.
Attn: Scholarship Foundation
2125 Eastchester Drive, Suite 103
P.O. Box 16264
High Point, NC 27261
Phone: (336) 882–9373;
Email: director@withit.org
Web: www.withit.org/scholarship.asp

Summary: To provide financial assistance to upper–division students interested in preparing for a career in the home furnishings industry.
Eligibility: Open to full–time students currently enrolled as sophomores or juniors at accredited institutions of higher learning. Applicants must be preparing for a career in the home furnishings industry; relevant majors include accessory design, architectural design, forestry, furniture design, textile design, graphic design, interior architecture, sustainable design, or other fields related to home and furnishing industries. Along with their application, they must submit a 300–word essay on why they are a candidate for a career in home furnishings. Selection is based primarily on academic performance, as reflected by GPA, SAT and/or ACT scores, the essay, and letters of recommendation. Special emphasis is placed on involvement in extracurricular activities and the community. Financial need may be considered.
Financial data: The stipend is $2,500. Funds are paid directly to the recipient's institution.
Duration: 1 year.
Number awarded: 1 or more each year.
Deadline: March of each year.

1308 JIM AND CAROLYN FERN MUSIC EDUCATION SCHOLARSHIP

Kentucky Music Educators Association
2106 Lexington Road, Harper Square, Suite F
P.O. Box 1058
Richmond, KY 40476–1058
Phone: (859) 626–5635; Fax: (859) 626–1115
Web: www.kmea.org/FernScholarship/default.htm

Summary: To provide financial assistance to residents of any state who are working on a degree in music education at a college in Kentucky.
Eligibility: Open to U.S. citizens from any state who are currently enrolled at a college or university in Kentucky. Applicants must be at least of junior standing and have been admitted to the teacher education program at their school with a declared major in music education. Their GPA must be sufficient to qualify for scholarship consideration at their institution. Financial need is not considered in the selection process.
Financial data: The stipend is $1,000 per year.
Duration: 1 year; recipients may reapply.
Number awarded: 1 each year.
Deadline: May of each year.

1309 $ JIMI LOTT SCHOLARSHIP

National Press Photographers Foundation
3200 Croasdaile Drive, Suite 306
Durham, NC 27705–2586
Phone: (919) 383–7246; (800) 289–6772; Fax: (919) 383–7261;
Email: info@nppa.org
Web: nppf.org

Summary: To provide financial assistance to undergraduate students who are interested in preparing for a career in photojournalism.
Eligibility: Open to full–time undergraduates at 4–year colleges and universities in the United States or Canada. Applicants must be preparing for a career in photojournalism. Along with their application, they must submit a portfolio of their work with 6 to 12 entries (single photographs, multiple picture stories, or multimedia stories). Selection is based on aptitude for photojournalism, academic ability, and financial need.
Financial data: The stipend is $2,000.
Duration: 1 year; nonrenewable.
Number awarded: 1 each year.
Deadline: February of each year.

1310 JOE FRANCIS HAIRCARE SCHOLARSHIPS

Joe Francis Haircare Scholarship Foundation
P.O. Box 50625
Minneapolis, MN 55405
Phone: (651) 769–1757; Fax: (651) 459–8371;
Email: kimlarsonmn@gmail.com
Web: www.joefrancis.com

Summary: To provide financial assistance to students interested in a career in cosmetology.
Eligibility: Open to students enrolled in, or planning to enroll in, a cosmetology school. Applicants must submit an essay of 1 to 2 pages that includes their ambitions and interests, a brief family history, why they want to be a cosmetologist, and their financial need.
Financial data: The stipend is $1,000.
Duration: 1 year.
Number awarded: Varies each year; recently, 26 of these scholarships were awarded.
Deadline: May of each year.

1311 JOEL CARTUN SCHOLARSHIP

Electronic Document Systems Foundation
Attn: EDSF Scholarship Awards
1845 Precinct Line Road, Suite 212
Hurst, TX 76054
Phone: (817) 849–1145; Fax: (817) 849–1185;
Email: info@edsf.org
Web: www.edsf.org/what_we_do/scholarships/index.html

Summary: To provide financial assistance to undergraduate and graduate students from any country interested in preparing for a career in document management and graphic communications.
Eligibility: Open to full–time undergraduate and graduate students from any country who demonstrate a strong interest in preparing for a career in the document management and graphic communications industry, including computer science and engineering (e.g., web design, webmaster, software development, materials engineer, applications specialist, information technology designer, systems analyst); graphic and media communications (e.g., graphic designer, illustrator, color scientist, print production, prepress imaging specialist, workflow specialist, document preparation, production and/or document distribution, content management, e–commerce, imaging science, printing, web authoring, electronic publishing, archiving, security); or business (e.g., sales, marketing, trade shows, customer service, project or product development, management). Preference is given to graduate students and upper–division undergraduates, but freshmen and sophomores who can show interest, experience, and/or commitment to the document management and graphic communication industry are encouraged to apply. Applicants must have a GPA of 3.0 or higher. Along with their application, they must submit 2 essays on assigned topics that change annually but relate to the document management and graphic communication industries. Selection is based on the essays, academic excellence, participation in school activities, community service, honors

and organizational affiliations, education goals, and recommendations; financial need is not considered.
Financial data: The stipend is $1,000.
Duration: 1 year.
Number awarded: 1 each year.
Deadline: April of each year.

1312 $$ JOHANSEN INTERNATIONAL COMPETITION FOR YOUNG STRING PLAYERS

Friday Morning Music Club, Inc.
Attn: FMMC Foundation
801 K Street, N.W.
Washington, DC 20001
Phone: (202) 333–2075;
Email: JohansenComp@fmmc.org
Web: www.fmmc.org
Summary: To recognize and reward outstanding young string players from any state.
Eligibility: Open to young string players (13 through 17 years of age) from any state. Applicants must submit an audiocassette or CD with 1) 5 minutes or less of an unaccompanied sonata, partita, or suite of J.S. Bach; 2) 12 minutes or less of a sonata with piano from the classical, romantic, impressionist, or contemporary period; 3) 13 minutes or less of a concerto or major work for soloist or orchestra by a composer other than Bach; 4) a short work or a movement from a longer work that shows virtuosity; and 5) a new work commissioned for this competition. Based on those recordings, semifinalists are invited to compete in Washington, D.C. They must be prepared to play any selection from their preliminary repertoire as well as a new work commissioned for this competition and sent to them prior to the semifinals. Finalists are selected from those auditions and compete the following day. All repertoire must be performed from memory. Separate awards are presented for violin, viola, and cello.
Financial data: In each category, first prize is $10,000, second $7,000, and third $5,000. The prize for the best performance on the commissioned piece is $500.
Duration: The competition is held triennially (2015, 2018, etc.).
Number awarded: 3 first prizes (1 each for violin, viola, and cello) are awarded in each competition.
Deadline: November of the year prior to the competition.

1313 $$ JOHN BAYLISS BROADCAST FOUNDATION SCHOLARSHIPS

John Bayliss Broadcast Foundation
Attn: Scholarship Chair
c/o Broadcast Education Association
1771 N Street, N.W.
Washington, DC 20036
Phone: (202) 429–5355; Fax: (202) 775–2981
Web: www.beaweb.org/bayliss/radio.html
Summary: To provide financial assistance to upper–division students who are preparing for a career in the radio industry.
Eligibility: Open to juniors and seniors who are preparing for a career in the radio industry, preferably commercial radio. Applicants must have a GPA of 3.0 or higher and a record of participation in radio–related activities. Along with their application, they must submit transcripts, 3 letters of recommendation, and a 2–page essay describing their broadcasting goals as they relate to radio and the ways in which they hope to achieve those goals. Although financial need is a consideration, students of merit with an extensive history of radio–related activities are given preference.
Financial data: The stipend is $5,000.
Duration: 1 year.
Number awarded: Up to 15 each year. Since this program was established, it has awarded more than 345 scholarships.
Deadline: April of each year.

1314 JOHN BAYLISS SCHOLARSHIP AWARD

Broadcast Education Association
Attn: Scholarships
1771 N Street, N.W.
Washington, DC 20036–2891
Phone: (202) 429–3935; (888) 380–7222; Fax: (202) 775–2981;
Email: BEAMemberServices@nab.org
Web: www.beaweb.org/scholarships.htm
Summary: To provide financial assistance to upper–division and graduate students who are interested in preparing for a career in radio.
Eligibility: Open to juniors, seniors, and graduate students enrolled full time at a college or university where at least 1 department is an institutional member of the Broadcast Education Association (BEA). Applicants must be studying for a career in radio. Selection is based on evidence that the applicant possesses high integrity, superior academic ability, potential to be an outstanding electronic media professional, and a sense of personal and professional responsibility.
Financial data: The stipend is $1,500.
Duration: 1 year; nonrenewable.
Number awarded: 1 each year.
Deadline: October of each year.

1315 $$ JOHN F. AND ANNA LEE STACEY SCHOLARSHIP FOR ART EDUCATION

National Cowboy and Western Heritage Museum
Attn: Art Director
1700 N.E. 63rd Street
Oklahoma City, OK 73111
Phone: (405) 478–2250; Fax: (405) 478–4714;
Email: info@nationalcowboymuseum.org
Web: www.nationalcowboymuseum.org/education/staceyfund/default.aspx
Summary: To provide financial assistance to students of conservative or classical art interested in further education.
Eligibility: Open to U.S. citizens between 18 and 35 years of age. Applicants must be artists whose works (paintings and drawings) have their roots in the classical tradition of western culture and favor realism or naturalism. Artists working in related fields (e.g., sculpture, collage, fashion design, decoration) are ineligible. Applicants must submit 4 to 6 digital images of their best work in any of the following categories: painting from life, drawing from the figure (nude), composition, or landscape. Financial need is not considered in the selection process.
Financial data: Scholarships are $5,000; funds must be used to pursue art education along "conservative" lines.
Duration: 1 year.
Number awarded: 1 or more each year.
Deadline: January of each year.

1316 $$ JOHN LENNON SCHOLARSHIPS

Broadcast Music Inc.
Attn: BMI Foundation, Inc.
7 World Trade Center
250 Greenwich Street
New York, NY 10007–0030
Phone: (212) 220–3000;
Email: JohnLennon@bmifoundation.org
Web: www.bmifoundation.org/program/john_lennon_scholarships
Summary: To recognize and reward outstanding student composers attending designated institutions.
Eligibility: Open to musicians between 17 and 24 years of age who are current students or graduates of colleges, universities, or schools of music. Applicants may not have had any musical work commercially recorded or distributed or have been a prior winner in this competition. They must submit (on CD or MP3 with a typed copy of the lyrics) an original song with lyrics and accompanied by any instrumentation. Both lyrics and music must be original and not based on any prior work.
Financial data: Prizes range up to $10,000.
Duration: The competition is held annually.
Number awarded: A total of $20,000 is available for this program each year. Recently, that was awarded in 4 prizes: 1 at $10,000, 1 at $5,000, and 2 at $2,500.
Deadline: April of each year.

1317 $ JOHN SWAIN MEMORIAL SCHOLARSHIP

Direct Marketing Association of Washington
Attn: Educational Foundation
c/o Karen Depew
4414 Walsh Street
Chevy Chase, MD 20815
Phone: (301) 652–7074;
Email: karen@northwoodconsulting.com
Web: www.dmawef.org/Awards/John_Swain/John_Swain_Award.html

Summary: To provide financial assistance to residents of any state who are enrolled as upper–division students at colleges and universities in the mid–Atlantic region and have an interest in direct marketing.
Eligibility: Open to juniors and seniors from any state enrolled at a college or university in Delaware, Maryland, Virginia, Washington, D.C., or Wet Virginia. Applicants must have a GPA of 3.0 or higher and a desire to preparing for a career in the field of direct and interactive marketing, including Web design, online, search engine marketing, creative, telemarketing, database, direct mail, and direct response. Along with their application, they must submit a statement on their interest in the field of direct or interactive marketing, how this scholarship would benefit them, and the geographic area in which they would like to work after graduation. Selection is based on that statement, academics, extracurricular activities, and work experience.
Financial data: The stipend is $2,000.
Duration: 1 year.
Number awarded: 1 each year.
Deadline: November of each year.

1318 $ JOHN W. AND MARY D. NICHOLS SCHOLARSHIP

Oklahoma Heritage Association
Attn: Scholarship Committee
1400 Classen Drive
Oklahoma City, OK 73106
Phone: (405) 523–3202; (888) 501–2059; Fax: (405) 235–2714;
Email: gmc@oklahomaheritage.com
Web: oklahomaheritage.com
Summary: To provide financial assistance to high school seniors in Oklahoma who demonstrate knowledge and appreciation of the state's history and geography and plan to attend college in the state.
Eligibility: Open to seniors graduating from high schools in Oklahoma who plan to attend a college or university in the state. Students may be nominated by a teacher, administrator, or other responsible adult who is not a relative. Nominators should list all relevant activities and achievements relating to Oklahoma history and geography from the time the student began school until the date of application. Selection is based primarily on those activities; other factors considered include overall academic achievement, citizenship, and leadership.
Financial data: The stipend is $2,500 per year.
Duration: 4 years, provided the recipient remains on the Oklahoma college or university Dean's Honor Roll or receives equivalent recognition.
Number awarded: 1 each year.
Deadline: February of each year.

1319 $ JOSEPH AND MARION GREENBAUM JUDAIC STUDIES SCHOLARSHIP

Jewish Federation of Delaware
Attn: Jewish Fund for the Future
101 Garden of Eden Road
Wilmington, DE 19803
Phone: (302) 427–2100, ext. 20; Fax: (302) 427–2438;
Email: Gina.Kozicki@ShalomDel.org
Web: www.shalomdelaware.org/page.aspx?id=159112
Summary: To provide financial assistance to 1) Jewish residents of Delaware and adjacent communities interested in taking courses in Jewish studies at a college in any state and 2) Jewish residents of other states interested in studying in Delaware.
Eligibility: Open to 1) Jewish residents of Delaware who wish to study at a college or university in any state; 2) Jewish residents of adjacent communities (including, but not limited to, Elkton, Maryland or the Pennsylvania towns of Avondale, Chadds Ford, Kennett Square, Landenberg, Lincoln University, or Westchester) who wish to study at a college or university in any state; and 3) Jewish residents of other states interested in studying at a college or university in Delaware. Applicants must be interested in taking courses in Judaic studies, preferably as part of a major or minor in the field. Along with their application, they must submit a brief essay on what they have learned or hope to learn during the proposed course of study and what they hope to be able to carry with them throughout their lifetime as a result of the courses they plan to take. Selection is based on the essay, GPA, references, volunteer and community activities, and information about the courses the applicant plans to take. Financial need is considered only if there are more applicants than available funds or if the applicant is seeking funds beyond the amount of the current guideline award; lack of financial need does not disqualify any applicant.
Financial data: The stipend is $83 per credit, based on the rate of $2,500 per year.
Duration: Funding is provided on a per credit basis for each course in Judaic studies the student completes as part of an undergraduate degree.
Number awarded: Varies each year.
Deadline: March of each year.

1320 $ JOSEPH S. RUMBAUGH HISTORICAL ORATION CONTEST

National Society Sons of the American Revolution
Attn: Education Director
1000 South Fourth Street
Louisville, KY 40203–3208
Phone: (502) 589–1776, ext. 30; Fax: (502) 589–1671;
Email: cwilson@sar.org
Web: www.sar.org/Youth/Oration_Contest
Summary: To recognize and reward outstanding high school oratory on the American Revolution.
Eligibility: Open to freshmen, sophomore, junior, or senior class students in all public, parochial, private, and home high schools in the United States. Applicants must compose and present an original oration of 5 to 6 minutes on an event, a document, or a personality within the context of the Revolutionary War, showing the relationship it bears to America today. Winners are selected on the basis of composition, delivery, logic, significance, and history. Winners at state and district levels advance to the national contest.
Financial data: At the national level, first prize is a $3,000 scholarship, second prize is a $2,000 scholarship, and third prize is a $1,000 scholarship. All other finalists receive $300 and all other national contestants receive $200.
Duration: The competition is held annually.
Number awarded: 3 national scholarships are awarded each year.
Deadline: All local contests must be completed by June of each year to qualify winners for the national competition.

1321 $$ JOSEPHINE DE KARMAN FELLOWSHIPS

Summary: To provide financial assistance to outstanding college seniors or students in their last year of a Ph.D. program.
See Listing #405.

1322 $ JOSH TURNER SCHOLARSHIP FUND

Community Foundation of Middle Tennessee
Attn: Scholarship Committee
3833 Cleghorn Avenue, Suite 400
Nashville, TN 37215–2519
Phone: (615) 321–4939; (888) 540–5200; Fax: (615) 327–2746;
Email: grants@cfmt.org
Web: www.cfmt.org/request/scholarships/allscholarships
Summary: To provide financial assistance to high school seniors in rural areas of South Carolina who are interested in attending college in any state to prepare for a career in the music business or the arts.
Eligibility: Open to seniors graduating from high schools in rural areas of South Carolina. Applicants must be preparing for a career that will introduce them to various opportunities in the music business or a discipline of the arts. Along with their application, they must submit an essay describing their educational plans and how those plans will help them reach their career goals. Financial need is considered in the selection process.
Financial data: Stipends range from $500 to $2,500. Funds are paid to the recipient's school and must be used for tuition, fees, books, supplies, room, board, or miscellaneous expenses.
Duration: 1 year.
Number awarded: 1 or more each year.
Deadline: March of each year.

1323 JOURNALISM EDUCATION ASSOCIATION FUTURE TEACHER SCHOLARSHIP

Journalism Education Association
c/o Kansas State University
103 Kedzie Hall
Manhattan, KS 66506–1505
Phone: (785) 532–5532; (866) JEA–5JEA; Fax: (785) 532–5563;
Email: jea@spub.ksu.edu
Web: jea.org/category/awards

Summary: To provide financial assistance to upper–division and master's degree students working on a degree in education who intend to teach journalism.

Eligibility: Open to upper–division undergraduates and master's degree students in a college program designed to prepare them for teaching journalism at the secondary school level. Current secondary school journalism teachers who are in a degree program to improve their journalism teaching skills are also eligible. Applicants must submit a 250–word essay explaining their desire to teach high school journalism, 2 letters of recommendation, and college transcripts. They must also provide information on the journalism courses they have completed and their grade in each, their high school journalism experience, and their experiences working with high school journalists since they graduated from high school.

Financial data: The stipend is $1,000.

Duration: 1 year.

Number awarded: Up to 3 each year.

Deadline: February of each year.

1324 $ JTG SCHOLARSHIP IN SCIENTIFIC AND TECHNICAL TRANSLATION OR INTERPRETATION

American Foundation for Translation and Interpretation
c/o ATA Headquarters
225 Reinekers Lane, Suite 590
Alexandria, VA 22314
Phone: (703) 683–6100, ext. 3006; Fax: (703) 683–6122;
Email: walter@atanet.org
Web: www.afti.org/award_jtg.php

Summary: To provide financial assistance to undergraduate and graduate students in translator or interpreter education programs.

Eligibility: Open to students enrolled in graduate or undergraduate programs in scientific and technical translation on in interpretation at accredited U.S. colleges and universities. Applicants must be full–time students who have completed at least 1 year of postsecondary education and have at least 1 year of academic work remaining to complete their program of study. They must have a GPA of 3.0 or higher overall and 3.5 or higher in translation and interpretation related courses. U.S. citizenship is required. Along with their application, they must submit an essay of 300 to 500 words on their interests and goals as they relate to the field of translation or interpretation. Selection is based on the essay, demonstrated achievement in translation and interpretation, academic record, and 3 letters of recommendation.

Financial data: The stipend is $2,500.

Duration: 1 year; nonrenewable.

Number awarded: 1 each year.

Deadline: June of each year.

1325 $$ JUDY CORMAN MEMORIAL SCHOLARSHIP AND INTERNSHIP

New York Women in Communications, Inc.
Attn: NYWICI Foundation
355 Lexington Avenue, 15th Floor
New York, NY 10017–6603
Phone: (212) 297–2133; Fax: (212) 370–9047;
Email: nywicipr@nywici.org
Web: www.nywici.org/foundation/scholarships

Summary: To provide financial assistance and work experience to female residents of designated eastern states who are interested in preparing for a career in public relations at a college or graduate school in any state.

Eligibility: Open to women who are seniors graduating from high schools in New York, New Jersey, Connecticut, or Pennsylvania or undergraduate or graduate students who are permanent residents of those states; they must be attending or planning to attend a college or university in any state. Graduate students must be members of New York Women in Communications, Inc. (NYWICI). Also eligible are women who reside outside the 4 states but are currently enrolled at a college or university within 1 of the 5 boroughs of New York City. Applicants must be preparing for a career in public relations and be interested in a summer internship with Scholastic. They must have a GPA of 3.2 or higher. Along with their application, they must submit a 2–page resume that includes school and extracurricular activities, significant achievements, academic honors and awards, and community service work; a personal essay of 300 to 500 words on their choice of an assigned topic that changes annually; 2 letters of recommendation; and an official transcript. Selection is based on academic record, need, demonstrated leadership, participation in school and community activities, honors, work experience, goals and aspirations, and unusual personal and/or family circumstances. U.S. citizenship is required.

Financial data: The scholarship stipend ranges up to $10,000; the internship is salaried (amount not specified).

Duration: 1 year.

Number awarded: 1 each year.

Deadline: January of each year.

1326 $$ JUDY VAN NOSTRAND ARTS AWARD

Lighthouse International
Attn: Scholarship and Career Awards
111 East 59th Street
New York, NY 10022–1202
Phone: (212) 821–9428; (800) 829–0500; Fax: (212) 821–9703; TDD: (212) 821–9713;
Email: sca@lighthouse.org
Web: www.lighthouse.org

Summary: To provide financial assistance to legally blind high school seniors, recent graduates, undergraduates, or graduate students who are interested in working on a degree in the arts.

Eligibility: Open to legally blind U.S. citizens who are graduating high school seniors, recent graduates, current undergraduates, or current graduate students. Applicants must be attending or planning to attend an accredited college or university in 1 of the 50 states, the District of Columbia, or a U.S. territory. They must be working on or planning to work on a degree in the arts (including graphic arts, music, visual arts, and writing). Along with their application, they must submit essays of 400 to 600 words on 1) their academic focus and extracurricular activities and what inspires their interest in each area; 2) their passion and how they express that passion; 3) key academic and personal accomplishments and the challenges they overcome to be successful; and 4) how this scholarship will support their academic and/or career development. Selection is based on academic and personal achievements; financial need is not considered.

Financial data: The stipend is $10,000.

Duration: 1 year.

Number awarded: 1 each year.

Deadline: January of each year.

1327 JULIA SEGALL–DERFLER SCHOLARSHIP IN ARABIC OR HEBREW TRANSLATION AND INTERPRETING

American Foundation for Translation and Interpretation
c/o ATA Headquarters
225 Reinekers Lane, Suite 590
Alexandria, VA 22314
Phone: (703) 683–6100, ext. 3006; Fax: (703) 683–6122;
Email: walter@atanet.org
Web: www.afti.org/award_julia.php

Summary: To provide financial assistance to undergraduate and graduate students working on a degree in Arabic or Hebrew with a focus on translation and/or interpreting.

Eligibility: Open to students enrolled in graduate or undergraduate programs in Arabic or Hebrew with a focus on translation and/or interpreting at accredited U.S. colleges and universities. Applicants must be full–time students who have completed at least 1 year of postsecondary education and have at least 1 year of academic work remaining to complete their program of study. They must have a GPA of 3.0 or higher overall and 3.5 or higher in translation and interpretation related courses. U.S. citizenship is required. Along with their application, they must submit an essay of 300 to 500 words on their interests and goals as they relate to the field of translation or interpretation. Selection is based on the essay, demonstrated achievement in translation and interpretation, academic record, and 3 letters of recommendation.

Financial data: The stipend is $1,000.

Duration: 1 year; nonrenewable.

Number awarded: 1 each year.

Deadline: September of each year.

1328 KAB BROADCAST SCHOLARSHIP PROGRAM

Kansas Association of Broadcasters
Attn: Scholarship Committee
214 S.W. 16th Street, Suite 300
Topeka, KS 66603
Phone: (785) 235–1307; Fax: (785) 233–3052;
Email: kent@kab.net
Web: www.kab.net/Programs/StudentServices/default.aspx

Summary: To provide financial assistance to residents of Kansas who are interested in attending college in the state to prepare for a career in broadcasting.
Eligibility: Open to residents of Kansas who are entering their junior year or above at a 4–year college or university in the state or their sophomore year at a 2–year college or vocational/technical trade school in the state. Applicants must be enrolled in a broadcast or related program as a full–time student. They must have a GPA of 2.5 or higher. Along with their application, they must submit a 3–page essay explaining why they selected broadcasting as a career, the specific area of broadcasting that most interests them and why, their eventual career goal, what they have learned during school that reinforced their decision to prepare for a career in broadcasting, their feeling about broadcast advertising and its importance to a station, whether the FCC's role in broadcasting has helped or hurt, how they think broadcasting could better serve society, the radio or television station they most admire, and their most rewarding broadcast–related experience. Selection is based on the depth of thought, clarity of expression, and commitment to broadcasting as revealed in the essay; extracurricular activities; community involvement; and financial need.
Financial data: The stipend is awarded (amount not specified).
Duration: 1 year; may be renewed.
Number awarded: Varies each year; recently, a total of $16,000 was available for this program.
Deadline: April of each year.

1329 KANSAS AMERICAN LEGION MUSIC COMMITTEE SCHOLARSHIP

American Legion
Department of Kansas
1314 S.W. Topeka Boulevard
Topeka, KS 66612–1886
Phone: (785) 232–9315; Fax: (785) 232–1399
Web: www.ksamlegion.org/programs.htm
Summary: To provide financial assistance to students of music at institutions in Kansas.
Eligibility: Open to residents of Kansas who are high school seniors or college freshmen or sophomores. Applicants must be studying or planning to major or minor in music at an approved college, university, or community college in Kansas. They must have an average or better academic record. Financial need is considered in the selection process.
Financial data: The stipend is $1,000.
Duration: 1 year; nonrenewable.
Number awarded: 1 each year.
Deadline: February of each year.

1330 $$ KANSAS CITY IFMA SCHOLARSHIP

International Facility Management Association–Kansas City Chapter
Attn: Scholarship Chair
P.O. Box 412591
Kansas City, MO 64141
Phone: (816) 822–4260;
Email: kcifmascholarship@gmail.com
Web: www.kcifma.com/scholarship.cfm
Summary: To provide financial assistance to students from any state who are working on an undergraduate or graduate degree in a field related to facility management at a school in Kansas or Missouri.
Eligibility: Open to residents of any state who are enrolled full time at a college or university in Kansas or Missouri. Applicants must be working on an undergraduate or graduate degree in a field related to facility management, including (but not limited to) architecture, business operations, construction science, engineering, environmental design, or interior design. Along with their application, they must submit a letter of professional intent that describes their short– and long–term career goals and explains how their understanding of facility management relates to their career goals. Selection is based on that letter, academic excellence, other accomplishments, appraisals and recommendations, and a personal interview.
Financial data: Stipends range from $500 to $5,000.
Duration: 1 year.
Number awarded: Varies each year; recently, 3 of these scholarships were awarded.
Deadline: April of each year.

1331 KANSAS HIGH SCHOOL JOURNALIST OF THE YEAR SCHOLARSHIPS

Kansas Scholastic Press Association
Attn: Executive Director
University of Kansas
William Allen White School of Journalism and Mass Communications
317 Stauffer–Flint Hall
1435 Jayhawk Boulevard
Lawrence, KS 66045–7515
Phone: (785) 864–7625; Fax: (785) 864–5945;
Email: jeffbrowne@ku.edu
Web: www.kspaonline.org/awards/hs–journalist–of–the–year
Summary: To recognize and reward, with college scholarships, high school seniors in Kansas who demonstrate excellence as a journalist.
Eligibility: Open to seniors graduating from high schools in Kansas who have been involved in journalism for at least 2 years with an adviser who is a member of the Journalism Education Association (JEA). Applicants must be planning to study journalism and/or mass communications in college and to prepare for a career in those fields. They must have a GPA of 3.0 or higher. Along with their application, they must submit a self–analytical essay 40–page portfolio of their work on the newspaper, yearbook, or broadcast. Winners are selected in 3 categories, for schools in divisions 1A/2A, 3A/4A, and 5A/6A. An overall winner is selected from among those.
Financial data: The winner in each category receives a $750 scholarship and the overall winner receives an additional $500.
Duration: 1 year.
Number awarded: 3 category winners are selected each year, of whom 1 is selected as the overall winner.
Deadline: February of each year.

1332 $ KAREN ANN SHOPIS–FOX MEMORIAL SCHOLARSHIP

American Society of Landscape Architects–Connecticut Chapter
Attn: Scholarship Committee
370 James Street, Fourth Floor
New Haven, CT 06513
Phone: (800) 878–1474;
Email: executivedirector@ctasla.org
Web: www.ctasla.org/scholarships.htm
Summary: To provide financial assistance to residents of Connecticut interested in working on an undergraduate or graduate degree in landscape architecture at a college or university in any state.
Eligibility: Open to Connecticut residents entering or enrolled in an accredited undergraduate or graduate landscape architecture of environmental education program at a college or university in any state. Applicants must submit a brief statement explaining why they desire this financial aid and why they have chosen landscape architecture as their field of study.
Financial data: The stipend ranges from $1,500 to $2,500.
Duration: 1 year.
Number awarded: 1 or 2 each year.
Deadline: March of each year.

1333 KEN LUDWIG PLAYWRITING SCHOLARSHIP

John F. Kennedy Center for the Performing Arts
Education Department
Attn: Kennedy Center American College Theater Festival
2700 F Street, N.W.
Washington, DC 20566
Phone: (202) 416–8857; Fax: (202) 416–8860;
Email: KCACTF@kennedy–center.org
Web: www.kcactf.org/KCACTF.ORG_NATIONAL/Kanin_Playwriting.html
Summary: To provide financial assistance to undergraduate and graduate students preparing for a career as a playwright.
Eligibility: Open to students enrolled as continuing undergraduates or entering or continuing graduate students at a college or university that has an associate or participating entry for the Kennedy Center American College Theater Festival. Applicants must be working on a degree in a field related to playwriting. Along with their application, they must submit a resume of their writing and the scripts of 3 plays, at least 1 of which must be at least 60 minutes in length. Selection is based on their body of work.
Financial data: A stipend is awarded (amount not specified).
Duration: 1 year.
Number awarded: 1 each year.
Deadline: January of each year.

1334 KENNEDY CENTER AMERICAN COLLEGE THEATER FESTIVAL LATINO PLAYWRITING AWARD

John F. Kennedy Center for the Performing Arts
Education Department

Attn: Kennedy Center American College Theater Festival
2700 F Street, N.W.
Washington, DC 20566
Phone: (202) 416–8857; Fax: (202) 416–8860;
Email: KCACTF@kennedy–center.org
Web: www.kennedy–center.org/education/actf/actfsitv.html
Summary: To recognize and reward outstanding plays by Latino student playwrights.
Eligibility: Open to Latino students at any accredited junior or senior college in the United States, provided their college agrees to participate in the Kennedy Center American College Theater Festival (KCACTF). Undergraduate students must be carrying at least 6 semester hours, graduate students must be enrolled in at least 3 semester hours, and continuing part–time students must be enrolled in a regular degree or certificate program. This award is presented to the best student–written play by a Latino.
Financial data: The prizes are $1,000 for first place and $500 for second place.
Duration: The award is presented annually.
Number awarded: 2 each year.
Deadline: November of each year.

1335 $$ KENNETH E. BEHRING NATIONAL HISTORY DAY CONTEST

National History Day
Attn: Director
University of Maryland
4511 Knox Road, Suite 102
College Park, MD 20742
Phone: (301) 314–9739; Fax: (301) 314–9767;
Email: info@nhd.org
Web: www.nationalhistoryday.org/KennethBehring.htm
Summary: To recognize and reward outstanding history papers, exhibits, performances, and media presentations prepared by middle and high school students around the country.
Eligibility: Open to middle and high school students in the United States. Each year, the competition revolves around a theme that changes annually; recently, students were invited to select a topic related to "Turning Points in History: People, Ideas, Events." Contests are held in 2 divisions (junior, for grades 6–8, and senior, for grades 9–12) and, within each division, in 9 categories: paper, individual exhibit, group exhibit, individual performance, group performance, individual documentary, group documentary, individual web site, and group web site. Following local school and district contests, winners compete in state contests, where 2 entries in each category are selected to compete at the national level. Selection is based on historical quality (60%), relation to theme (20%), and clarity of presentation (20%). Special awards are presented to the best entries on designated topics. History Channel awards are presented to high school seniors who submit the best entries in the individual documentary and group documentary categories.
Financial data: At the national level, winners in each category of the 2 divisions receive prizes of $1,000 for first place, $500 for second place, and $250 for third place. The amounts of the special awards vary. The History Channel awards are $5,000.
Duration: The competition is held annually.
Number awarded: At the local level, more than 500,000 students and 50,000 teachers participate in the competition. Nearly 2,000 students each year advance to the national competition where 3 prizes are presented in each of the 2 divisions and 9 categories. The number of special awards varies. There are 2 History Channel awards.
Deadline: Each local contest sets its own deadline.

1336 $ KEVIN AND KELLY PERDUE MEMORIAL SCHOLARSHIP

Foundation for Amateur Radio, Inc.
Attn: Scholarship Committee
P.O. Box 911
Columbia, MD 21044–0911
Phone: (410) 552–2652; Fax: (410) 981–5146;
Email: dave.prestel@gmail.com
Web: www.farweb.org/scholarships
Summary: To provide funding to licensed radio amateurs who are interested in studying humanities or the social sciences in college.
Eligibility: Open to licensed radio amateurs who are interested in working full time on a bachelor's degree in the liberal arts, humanities, or social sciences. Financial need is considered in the selection process.
Financial data: The stipend is $2,000.
Duration: 1 year.
Number awarded: 1 each year.
Deadline: April of each year.

1337 $ KIMBALL OFFICE SCHOLARSHIP

International Interior Design Association
Attn: IIDA Foundation
222 Merchandise Mart, Suite 567
Chicago, IL 60654
Phone: (312) 467–1950; (888) 799–4432; Fax: (312) 467–0779;
Email: iidahq@iida.org
Web: www.iida.org/content.cfm/kimball–office–scholarship–fund
Summary: To provide financial assistance to minority students enrolled in the senior year of an interior design program.
Eligibility: Open to college seniors of African, Asian, Latino, or Native American heritage. Applicants must be working on a degree in interior design. Selection is based on excellence in academics and promising design talent.
Financial data: The stipend is $4,000.
Duration: 1 year.
Number awarded: 1 each year.
Deadline: Deadline not specified.

1338 $ KIRCHHOFF FAMILY FINE ARTS SCHOLARSHIP

Oregon Student Access Commission
Attn: Grants and Scholarships Division
1500 Valley River Drive, Suite 100
Eugene, OR 97401–2146
Phone: (541) 687–7395; (800) 452–8807, ext. 7395; Fax: (541) 687–7414; TDD: (800) 735–2900;
Email: awardinfo@osac.state.or.us
Web: www.oregonstudentaid.gov/scholarships.aspx
Summary: To provide financial assistance to residents of Oregon who are enrolled as undergraduate or graduate students at a school in the state and working on a degree in fine arts or graphic arts.
Eligibility: Open to residents of Oregon who are enrolled at a 4–year college or university in the state. Applicants must be working on a degree in fine arts or graphic arts. First preference is given to upper–division students, then to candidates for an M.F.A. degree. Semifinalists may be asked to submit non–returnable slides or photographs of their art samples. Financial need is not required, but it is considered in the selection process.
Financial data: Stipends for scholarships offered by the Oregon Student Access Commission (OSAC) range from $200 to $10,000 but recently averaged $2,300.
Duration: 1 year; recipients may reapply.
Number awarded: Varies each year.
Deadline: February of each year.

1339 KITSAP QUILTERS' SCHOLARSHIP

Kitsap Quilters' Quilt Guild
c/o Eileen Veals
20343 N.W. Cedar Lane
Poulsbo, WA 98370
Email: toquilt@embarqmail.com
Web: www.kitsapquilters.com/scholarship.html
Summary: To provide financial assistance to residents of Washington working on an undergraduate degree in a field related to fiber art at a college in the state.
Eligibility: Open to residents of Washington who graduated from a high school in the state at least 4 years previously. Applicants must be enrolled at an accredited college, university, or technical institution in the state and have completed course work above the 100 level with a GPA of 2.0 or higher. They must be majoring in a field related to fiber arts, including (but not limited to) sewing, weaving, clothing design, quilting, dyeing, basketry, curatorship and preservation, or history and technical production of textiles; art courses that include design, composition, surface design, and art history are also considered. Financial need is not considered in the selection process.
Financial data: The stipend is $1,000.
Duration: 1 year.
Number awarded: 1 each year.
Deadline: May of each year.

1340 $ KODAK STUDENT CINEMATOGRAPHY SCHOLARSHIP AWARD

University Film and Video Foundation
c/o Michele DeLano
343 State Street
Rochester, NY 14650–0315
Phone: (585) 724–6751;
Email: michele.delano@kodak.com
Web: www.ufva.org/grants/kodak

Summary: To recognize and reward, with funding for payment of educational expenses and other products, undergraduate and graduate cinematography students.

Eligibility: Open to students working on a bachelor's or master's degree in cinematography. Candidates must be enrolled full time at a college or university in the United States, Canada, or a participating foreign country. Each school may nominate 1 candidate. Nominees must submit samples of their work that communicate a story or theme in some fashion; clips or short vignettes are not acceptable. Selection is based solely on quality of cinematography skills.

Financial data: First place is a $3,000 scholarship and $5,000 in Kodak motion picture product; honorably mention is a $1,500 scholarship and $3,000 in Kodak motion picture product. Scholarships are paid directly to the recipient's institution.

Duration: The competition is held annually.

Number awarded: 2 each year: 1 first place and 1 honorable mention.

Deadline: Nominations must be submitted by June of each year.

1341 $ KODAK STUDENT SCHOLARSHIP AWARD

University Film and Video Foundation
c/o Michele DeLano
343 State Street
Rochester, NY 14650–0315
Phone: (585) 724–6751;
Email: michele.delano@kodak.com
Web: www.ufva.org/grants/kodak

Summary: To recognize and reward, with funding for payment of educational expenses and other products, undergraduate and graduate film students who submit outstanding samples of their work.

Eligibility: Open to students working on a bachelor's or master's degree in film or film production. Candidates must be enrolled full time at a college or university in the United States, Canada, or a participating foreign country. Each school may nominate up to 2 candidates. Nominees must submit samples of their work that communicate a story or theme in some fashion; clips or short vignettes are not acceptable. Selection is based on academic achievement, creative and technical ability, communications ability, and range of filmmaking experience.

Financial data: The Gold Prize is a $4,000 scholarship and $5,000 in Kodak motion picture product; the Silver Prize is a $3,000 scholarship (paid directly to the institution) and $4,000 in Kodak motion picture product; the Bronze Prize is a $2,000 scholarship and $3,000 in Kodak motion picture product. Scholarships are paid directly to the recipient's institution.

Duration: The competition is held annually.

Number awarded: 3 each year: 1 Gold Prize, 1 Silver Prize, and 1 Bronze Prize.

Deadline: Nominations must be submitted by June of each year.

1342 $$ KOSCIUSZKO FOUNDATION CHOPIN PIANO COMPETITION

Kosciuszko Foundation
Attn: Director of Cultural Affairs
15 East 65th Street
New York, NY 10021–6595
Phone: (212) 734–2130, ext. 214; (800) 287–9956; Fax: (212) 628–4552;
Email: culture@thekf.org
Web: www.thekf.org/programs/competitions/chopin

Summary: To recognize and reward outstanding pianists.

Eligibility: Open to U.S. citizens, permanent residents of the United States, and international full–time students with valid student visas; all entrants must be between 16 and 22 years of age. Contestants prepare a program of 60 to 75 minutes encompassing a selection of works by Chopin, a mazurka by Szymanowski, a major work by J.S. Bach, a complete classical (Beethoven, Haydn, Mozart, or Schubert) sonata, a major 19th–century work by a composer other than Chopin, and a substantial work by an American, Polish, or Polish American composer written after 1950; jurors choose works from the program for the auditions. Preliminary competitions take place in Chicago and New York; winners advance to the national competitions in New York.

Financial data: The preliminary competitions provide small cash prizes and round–trip airfare to the national finals. In the national competitions, first place is $5,000, second place $2,500, and third place $1,500.

Duration: The competition is held annually; the preliminaries are held in March and the national finals in April.

Number awarded: 3 national prizes are awarded each year.

Deadline: September of each year.

1343 $$ KOSCIUSZKO FOUNDATION WIENIAWSKI VIOLIN COMPETITION

Kosciuszko Foundation
Attn: Director of Cultural Affairs
15 East 65th Street
New York, NY 10021–6595
Phone: (212) 734–2130, ext. 214; (800) 287–9956; Fax: (212) 628–4552;
Email: culture@thekf.org
Web: www.thekf.org/programs/competitions/violen

Summary: To recognize and reward outstanding young violinists.

Eligibility: Open to U.S. citizens, permanent residents of the United States, and international full–time students with valid student visas; all entrants must be between 16 and 22 years of age. Contestants prepare a program of 60 to 75 minutes encompassing a concerto by Wieniawski or Szymanowski, the first 2 movements of a Bach sonata, a sonata by Beethoven or Mozart, a virtuosic 19th–century work, a Paganini caprice, and a substantial work by an American, Polish, or Polish American composer written after 1950. They must submit an audition CD of approximately 15 minutes with selections from their program. Based on those CDs, finalists are invited to the competition in New York.

Financial data: First place is $5,000, second $2,500, and third $1,500.

Duration: The competition is held biennially, in April.

Number awarded: 3 national prizes are awarded each odd–numbered year.

Deadline: March of each odd–numbered year.

1344 $ LANDSCAPE EDUCATIONAL ADVANCEMENT FOUNDATION SCHOLARSHIPS

California Landscape Contractors Association
Attn: Landscape Educational Advancement Foundation
1491 River Park Drive, Suite 100
Sacramento, CA 95815
Phone: (916) 830–2780; Fax: (916) 830–2788;
Email: leaf@clca.org
Web: www.clca.org/clca/about/wapply.php

Summary: To provide financial assistance to students in California who are majoring in ornamental horticulture.

Eligibility: Open to undergraduate students enrolled in at least 6 credits at an accredited California community college or state university and majoring in ornamental horticulture. Applications must submit brief essays on their educational objectives, occupational goals as they relate to the landscape industry, reasons for choosing that field, and reasons for requesting financial assistance. Selection is based on those essays, GPA in their major, career goals, outside activities, work experience, letters of recommendation, and financial need.

Financial data: Stipend amounts vary, but recently averaged nearly $2,000.

Duration: 1 year.

Number awarded: Varies each year; recently, 17 of these scholarships, with a total value of $32,800, were awarded.

Deadline: April of each year.

1345 $ LANDSCAPE FORMS DESIGN FOR PEOPLE SCHOLARSHIP

Landscape Architecture Foundation
Attn: Leadership in Landscape Scholarship Program
818 18th Street, N.W., Suite 810
Washington, DC 20006–3520
Phone: (202) 331–7070; Fax: (202) 331–7079;
Email: scholarships@lafoundation.org
Web: www.lafoundation.org

Summary: To provide financial assistance to undergraduate landscape architecture students who demonstrate interest in design of public spaces.

Eligibility: Open to landscape architecture students entering the final year of full–time undergraduate study. Applicants must be able to demonstrate a proven contribution to the design of public spaces that integrates landscape design and the use of amenities to promote social interaction. Along with their application, they must submit 2 letters of recommendation, 3 academic or internship work samples, and a 300–word essay on the qualities essential to the creation of great and successful public spaces. Selection is based on financial need, creative ability, and academic accomplishment.

Financial data: The stipend is $3,000.

Duration: 1 year.

Number awarded: 1 each year.

Deadline: February of each year.

1346 $ LARRY FULLERTON PHOTOJOURNALISM SCHOLARSHIP

The Dayton Foundation
Attn: Scholarship Program Officer
500 Kettering Tower
Dayton, OH 45423
Phone: (937) 225–9955; (877) 222–0410; Fax: (937) 222–0636;
Email: ehorner@daytonfoundation.org
Web: www.daytonfoundation.org/sresults2.php

Summary: To provide financial assistance to residents of Ohio working on an undergraduate degree in photojournalism at a college in the state.

Eligibility: Open to Ohio residents who are currently enrolled as full–time undergraduates at a college, university, junior college, or other school offering a structured 2–year curriculum in the state. Applicants must be majoring in photojournalism and have a GPA of 2.5 or higher. Along with their application, they must submit 10 to 15 images of their work that demonstrate creativity, technical excellence, versatility, and the ability to communicate visually. They must also include a statement discussing their philosophy of photojournalism, current career goals, work experience, and financial need.

Financial data: Stipends are $3,000 or $1,500.

Duration: 1 year.

Number awarded: 2 each year: 1 at $3,000 and 1 at $1,500.

Deadline: February of each year.

1347 LAWRENCE ALAN SPIEGEL REMEMBRANCE SCHOLARSHIP

Holocaust and Human Rights Center of Maine
c/o University of Maine at Augusta
Michael Klahr Center
46 University Drive
Augusta, ME 04330
Phone: (207) 621–3530;
Email: infohhrc@maine.edu
Web: www.hhrc.org/awards–scholarships

Summary: To recognize and reward, with college scholarships, high school seniors in Maine who write outstanding essays about the Holocaust.

Eligibility: Open to high school seniors and home–schooled students who are Maine residents and who have been accepted at an accredited college, university, or technical school in any state. Applicants must write an essay, up to 4 pages in length, on "Why is it important that the remembrance, history and lessons of the Holocaust be passed to a new generation?"

Financial data: The award is a $1,000 scholarship.

Duration: The competition is held annually.

Number awarded: 1 each year.

Deadline: April of each year.

1348 $ LEADING EDGE STUDENT DESIGN COMPETITION

New Buildings Institute
Attn: Program Manager
142 East Jewett Boulevard
P.O. Box 2349
White Salmon, WA 98672
Phone: (509) 493–4468, ext. 12; Fax: (509) 493–4078;
Email: pat@newbuildings.org
Web: www.leadingedgecompetition.org

Summary: To recognize and reward undergraduate and graduate students who submit outstanding zero–net energy entries in a design competition.

Eligibility: Open to undergraduate and graduate students enrolled in architecture, engineering, drafting, or environmental design programs at 2–year colleges, 4– or 5–year colleges or programs, graduate programs, and technical schools. The first category is for students in their third, fourth, or fifth year of undergraduate study and all graduate and post–baccalaureate students; the second category is for students in the first or second year of their undergraduate design education. Entries may be submitted by individuals or teams. Participants are invited to submit designs for a problem at an actual site. Complete information is provided on site history, demographics, climate, utilities, site description, and special requirements. Each design must be accompanied by a 750–word narrative that describes the overall energy efficiency and environmental sustainability aspects of the design.

Financial data: In each category, first prize is $3,000 and second prize is $2,000. If winning entries are submitted by teams of students, the prizes must be divided equally among them. The schools of the winning teams receive $1,500 for first prize and $1,000 for second prize.

Duration: The competition is held annually.

Number awarded: 4 cash prizes are awarded each year: 2 in each category.

Deadline: Registration must be completed by April of each year. Completed entries are due in June.

1349 LEE A. LYMAN MEMORIAL MUSIC SCHOLARSHIP

Vermont Student Assistance Corporation
Attn: Scholarship Programs
10 East Allen Street
P.O. Box 2000
Winooski, VT 05404–2601
Phone: (802) 654–3798; (888) 253–4819; Fax: (802) 654–3765; TDD: (800) 281–3341 (within VT);
Email: info@vsac.org
Web: services.vsac.org

Summary: To provide financial assistance to residents of Vermont who are interested in working on a degree in music at a college in any state.

Eligibility: Open to the residents of Vermont who are seniors in high school, high school graduates, or currently enrolled in college. Applicants must be enrolled or planning to enroll at a college or university in any state and work on a degree in music, including (but not limited to) musical performing arts, musical recording arts, instrumentation, sound engineering, studio recording, or music history. Along with their application, they must submit 100–word essays on 1) the school, church, and community activities in which they have participated; 2) their interest in and commitment to pursuing their chosen career or vocation; and 3) any significant barriers that limit their access to education. Selection is based on those essays; participation in music–related activities, performances, and/or groups; academic achievement (GPA of 3.1 or higher); letters of recommendation; and financial need (expected family contribution of $23,360 or less).

Financial data: The stipend is $1,000.

Duration: 1 year; recipients may reapply.

Number awarded: 4 each year.

Deadline: March of each year.

1350 LEE PATTERSON SCHOLARSHIP FOR CLASSICAL VOICE TRAINING

Maine Community Foundation
Attn: Program Director
245 Main Street
Ellsworth, ME 04605
Phone: (207) 667–9735; (877) 700–6800; Fax: (207) 667–0447
Email: info@mainecf.org
Web: www.mainecf.org/HancockScholars.aspx

Summary: To provide financial assistance to Maine residents interested in pursuing classical voice training.

Eligibility: Open to residents of Maine who are at least 14 years of age. Applicants must be interested in pursuing classical voice training (opera, operettas, and art song literature composed between 1600 and 1920) with a certified voice teacher or at a school in the state. Financial need is considered in the selection process.

Financial data: A stipend is awarded (amount not specified).

Duration: 1 year.

Number awarded: Varies each year.

Deadline: March of each year.

1351 $$ LEE–JACKSON FOUNDATION SCHOLARSHIP

Lee–Jackson Foundation
P.O. Box 8121
Charlottesville, VA 22906

Phone: (434) 977–1861; Fax: (434) 977–6083;
Email: leejacksonfoundation@yahoo.com
Web: www.lee–jackson.org

Summary: To recognize and reward high school students in Virginia who enter an historical essay contest and plan to attend a college or university in the United States.

Eligibility: Open to juniors and seniors at Virginia secondary schools who plan to enroll full time at a 4–year college or university in any state. Applicants must write an essay that demonstrates an appreciation of the character and virtues of Generals Robert E. Lee and Thomas J. "Stonewall" Jackson. The length of the papers is not specified, but most are between 7 and 10 pages. Selection is based on historical accuracy, quality of research, and clarity of written expression. Students first compete in the 8 high school regions in the state or as private high school or home–schooled students. Within each region plus the private/home–schooled category, first– and second–place winners are selected. A grand prize is awarded to the author of the essay judged best of all the essays submitted.

Financial data: Within each of the 8 public high school regions in the state plus the private/home–schooled category, first prize is $2,000 and second is $1,000. The grand prize winner receives an additional $8,000. A $1,000 award is given to schools or home school regions that encourage the most participation. Funds are mailed to the financial aid director of the college the winner attends; they may be used only for payment of tuition and required fees.

Duration: The competition is held annually.

Number awarded: 18 each year: 2 winners in each of the 8 public high school regions of the state plus 2 to private and home school students. The grand prize is awarded to 1 of those students whose essay is judged to be the best in the state. In addition, 9 schools (1 in each public school region plus 1 in the private/home–school category) receive the awards for encouraging the most participation.

Deadline: February of each year.

1352 LEMUEL C. SUMMERS SCHOLARSHIP

United Methodist Higher Education Foundation
Attn: Scholarships Administrator
60 Music Square East, Suite 350
P.O. Box 340005
Nashville, TN 37203–0005
Phone: (615) 649–3990; (800) 811–8110; Fax: (615) 649–3980;
Email: umhefscholarships@umhef.org
Web: www.umhef.org/scholarship–info

Summary: To provide financial assistance to undergraduate and graduate Methodist students who are preparing for ministry.

Eligibility: Open to full–time undergraduate, graduate, and professional students at United Methodist–related colleges, universities, seminaries, and theological schools. Applicants must have been active, full members of a United Methodist Church for at least 1 year prior to applying and be preparing for Christian ministry. They must have a GPA of 3.0 or higher and be able to demonstrate financial need. U.S. citizenship or permanent resident status is required.

Financial data: The stipend is at least $1,000 per year.

Duration: 1 year; recipients may reapply.

Number awarded: Varies each year; recently, 3 of these scholarships were awarded.

Deadline: February of each year.

1353 LILLIAN GORELL SCHOLARSHIP FUND

Pittsburgh Foundation
Attn: Scholarship Coordinator
Five PPG Place, Suite 250
Pittsburgh, PA 15222–5414
Phone: (412) 394–2649; Fax: (412) 391–7259;
Email: turnerd@pghfdn.org
Web: www.pittsburghfoundation.org/node/1655

Summary: To provide financial assistance to entering or continuing undergraduate and graduate students, especially those who are blind or studying the arts.

Eligibility: Open to all applicants, but preference is given to blind students and to those working on a degree in the arts. Applicants must be enrolled or planning to enroll at a college or university in any state. Along with their application, they must submit 1) a brief essay explaining their educational goals; 2) official transcripts; and 3) a statement of the amount they need and the purpose for which the award will be used.

Financial data: A stipend is awarded (amount not specified). Funds are intended to be used for maintenance, supplies, instructions, tuition, room, board, and any other expenses related to attending an educational institution.

Duration: 1 year; recipients may reapply until completion of their educational program.

Number awarded: 1 or more each year.

Deadline: April of each year.

1354 $$ LIN MEDIA MINORITY SCHOLARSHIP AND TRAINING PROGRAM

LIN Television Corporation
Attn: Vice President, Human Resources
One West Exchange Street, Suite 5A
Providence, RI 02903–1064
Phone: (401) 454–2880; Fax: (401) 454–6990
Web: www.linmedia.com/contact–us/minority–scholarship–program

Summary: To provide scholarship/loans to minority undergraduates interested in earning a degree in a field related to broadcast journalism and working at a station owned by LIN Television Corporation.

Eligibility: Open to U.S. citizens and permanent residents of non–white origin who are enrolled as a sophomore or higher at a college or university. Applicants must have a declared major in broadcast journalism, digital multimedia, mass/speech/digital communication, television production, or marketing and a GPA of 3.0 or higher. Along with their application, they must submit a list of organizations and activities in which they have held leadership positions, 3 references, a 50–word description of their career goals, a list of personal achievements and honors, and a 500–word essay about themselves. Financial need is not considered in the selection process.

Financial data: The program pays for tuition and fees, books, and room and board, to a maximum of $10,000 per year. Recipients must sign an employment agreement that guarantees them part–time employment as an intern during school and a 2–year regular position at a television station owned by LIN Television Corporation following graduation. If they fail to honor the employment agreement, they must repay all scholarship funds received.

Duration: 2 years.

Number awarded: 2 each year: 1 for a student in broadcast television and 1 for a student in digital media.

Deadline: March of each year.

1355 $$ LINCOLN–JUAREZ LITERARY ESSAY CONTEXT

Military Order of the Loyal Legion of the United States
c/o Eric Rojo, Chancellor–in–Chief
4430 Tindall Street, N.W.
Washington, DC 20016–2718
Email: eric@er–x.com
Web: suvcw.org/mollus/mollus.htm

Summary: To recognize and reward college students who submit outstanding essays on the Battle of Puebla during the French intervention in Mexico and its effect on the U.S. Civil War.

Eligibility: Open to students who are currently enrolled full time at a college or university anywhere in the United States, regardless of citizenship or place of study. Applicants must submit an essay, from 1,250 to 1,500 words in length, on the Battle of Puebla on May 5, 1862, its effect on the U.S. Civil War, and the relationship between Presidents Benito Juarez and Abraham Lincoln. Selection is based on originality, historical accuracy, and detail of the analysis.

Financial data: Prizes are $5,000 for first, $3,000 for second, and $1,000 for third.

Duration: The competition is held annually.

Number awarded: 3 each year.

Deadline: February of each year.

1356 $$ LLEWELLYN L. CAYVAN STRING INSTRUMENT SCHOLARSHIP

Grand Rapids Community Foundation
Attn: Education Program Officer
185 Oakes Street S.W.
Grand Rapids, MI 49503–4008
Phone: (616) 454–1751, ext. 103; Fax: (616) 454–6455;
Email: rbishop@grfoundation.org
Web: www.grfoundation.org/scholarshipslist

Summary: To provide financial assistance to undergraduate and graduate students working on a degree in string instruments at a college in any state.
Eligibility: Open to undergraduate and graduate students at a college or university in any state. Applicants must be working on a degree in violin, viola, violoncello, or bass viol. They must be U.S. citizens or permanent residents, but there are no residency or financial need requirements.
Financial data: The stipend depends on the need of the recipient and the availability of funds, but ranges from $500 to $5,000 and averages $1,000. Funds are paid directly to the recipient's institution.
Duration: 1 year.
Number awarded: 1 each year.
Deadline: March of each year.

1357 $$ LOREEN ARBUS FOCUS ON DISABILITY SCHOLARSHIP

Academy of Television Arts & Sciences Foundation
Attn: Education Department
5220 Lankershim Boulevard
North Hollywood, CA 91601–3109
Phone: (818) 754–2820; Fax: (818) 761–ATAS;
Email: ctasupport@emmys.org
Web: www.emmysfoundation.org/college–television–awards
Summary: To recognize and reward outstanding college student videos that have a focus on disability.
Eligibility: Open to undergraduate and graduate students currently enrolled at a college, university, or community college. U.S. citizenship is not required, but all applicants must be enrolled at schools in the United States. All entries must have been produced for school–related classes, groups, or projects. This award is presented to the entry that best 1) sheds light on people with disabilities by having a main character with a disability; 2) helps emerging artists within this community gain recognition; or 3) increases visibility for artists with disabilities.
Financial data: The award is a $10,000 scholarship.
Duration: The award is presented annually.
Number awarded: 1 each year.
Deadline: January of each year.

1358 LORRAINE HANSBERRY PLAYWRITING AWARD

John F. Kennedy Center for the Performing Arts
Education Department
Attn: Kennedy Center American College Theater Festival
2700 F Street, N.W.
Washington, DC 20566
Phone: (202) 416–8857; Fax: (202) 416–8860;
Email: KCACTF@kennedy–center.org
Web: www.kcactf.org/KCACTF.ORG_NATIONAL/Kanin_Playwriting.html
Summary: To recognize and reward student authors of plays on the African American experience in America.
Eligibility: Open to students at any accredited junior or senior college in the United States, provided their college agrees to participate in the Kennedy Center American College Theater Festival (KCACTF). Undergraduate students must be carrying at least 6 semester hours, graduate students must be enrolled in at least 3 semester hours, and continuing part–time students must be enrolled in a regular degree or certificate program. These awards are presented to the best plays written by students of African or Diasporan descent on the subject of the African American experience.
Financial data: The first–place award is $1,000 and the second–place award is $500. In addition, grants of $750 and $500 are made to the theater departments of the colleges or universities producing the first– and second–place plays. The winning playwright also receives an all–expense paid professional development opportunity.
Duration: The awards are presented annually.
Number awarded: 2 students and 2 sponsoring institutions receive awards each year.
Deadline: November of each year.

1359 $$ LOTTE LENYA COMPETITION FOR SINGERS

Kurt Weill Foundation for Music, Inc.
7 East 20th Street, Third Floor
New York, NY 10003–1106
Phone: (212) 505–5240; Fax: (212) 353–9663;
Email: kwfinfo@kwf.org
Web: www.kwf.org/grants–a–prizes
Summary: To recognize and reward outstanding singers who reside in the United States or Canada.
Eligibility: Open to singers, including students, between 19 and 32 years of age who reside in the United States or Canada. Contestants must prepare 4 selections: 1 theatrical selection (any genre) by Kurt Weill; 1 selection from the operatic or operetta repertoire (not by Kurt Weill); 1 song from the "Golden Age" (pre–1968) of the American musical theater repertoire (may include another work by Kurt Weill); and 1 song from the American musical theater repertoire from 1968 or later. They must perform the selections from memory and in their original language (although English versions of selected works by Weill are allowed). The competition begins when singers submit video DVDs of a complete performance of all works from all 4 categories. Based on those recordings, semi–finalists are invited to New York City for auditions at which finalists are selected. Those finalists then participate in the national finals at Rochester, New York, where winners are selected.
Financial data: Finalists receive an award of $1,000 plus a stipend to help pay travel costs to compete in the national finals. In the national competition, first prize is $15,000, second $10,000, and third $7,500.
Duration: This competition is held annually.
Number awarded: 3 national winners are selected each year.
Deadline: January of each year.

1360 LOU AND CAROLE PRATO SPORTS REPORTING SCHOLARSHIP

Radio Television Digital News Foundation
Attn: Programs, Awards, and Membership Manager
529 14th Street, N.W., Suite 425
Washington, DC 20045
Phone: (202) 725–8318; Fax: (202) 223–4007;
Email: katies@rtdna.org
Web: www.rtdna.org/pages/education/scholarship–info.php
Summary: To provide financial assistance for undergraduate education to students whose career objective is radio or television sports reporting.
Eligibility: Open to sophomores, juniors, and seniors who are enrolled full time in electronic journalism at a college or university where such a major is offered. Applicants must submit 1 to 3 examples of their journalistic skills on audio CD or DVD (no more than 15 minutes total, accompanied by scripts); a description of their role on each story and a list of who worked on each story and what they did; a 1–page statement explaining why they are preparing for a career as a sports reporter in television or radio; a resume; and a letter of reference from their dean or faculty sponsor explaining why they are a good candidate for the award and certifying that they have at least 1 year of school remaining.
Financial data: The stipend is $1,000.
Duration: 1 year.
Number awarded: 1 each year.
Deadline: May of each year.

1361 LOVETTE HOOD JR. SCHOLARSHIP

Sigma Gamma Rho Sorority, Inc.
Attn: National Education Fund
1000 Southhill Drive, Suite 200
Cary, NC 27513
Phone: (919) 678–9720; (888) SGR–1922; Fax: (919) 678–9721;
Email: info@sgrho1922.org
Web: www.sgrho1922.org/nef
Summary: To provide financial assistance to undergraduate students working on a degree in theology.
Eligibility: Open to undergraduates working on a degree in theology. The sponsor is a traditionally African American sorority, but support is available to males and females of all races. Applicants must have a GPA of "C" or higher and be able to demonstrate financial need.
Financial data: A stipend is awarded (amount not specified).
Duration: 1 year.
Number awarded: 1 each year.
Deadline: April of each year.

1362 $ LUCINDA BENEVENTI FINDLEY HISTORY SCHOLARSHIP

Daughters of the American Revolution–National Society
Attn: Committee Services Office, Scholarships
1776 D Street, N.W.
Washington, DC 20006–5303

Phone: (202) 628–1776
Web: www.dar.org/natsociety/edout_scholar.cfm
Summary: To provide financial assistance to high school seniors who plan to major in history in college.
Eligibility: Open to graduating high school seniors who plan to enroll full time at an accredited college or university in the United States and major in history. Applicants must be sponsored by a local chapter of the Daughters of the American Revolution (DAR). They must have a GPA of 3.25 or higher. Selection is based on academic excellence, commitment to the field of study, and financial need. U.S. citizenship is required.
Financial data: The stipend is $2,000.
Duration: 1 year; nonrenewable.
Number awarded: Varies each year.
Deadline: February of each year.

1363 $ M. LOUISE MILLER SCHOLARSHIP

American Guild of Organists–Greater Bridgeport Chapter
c/o Jeffrey Wood, Scholarship Coordinator
Saint Mary Church
70 Gulf Street
Milford, CT 06516
Phone: (978) 407–9074;
Email: musicdirector@saintmarychurchmilford.org
Web: www.agohq.org/chapter/?handle=greaterbridgeport
Summary: To provide financial assistance to undergraduate students interested in preparing for a career in organ performance and church music.
Eligibility: Open to undergraduates enrolled or planning to enroll at a college, university, or conservatory in the United States. Applicants must be preparing for a career in organ performance or church music. They must submit a recording of 2 standard organ pieces and an essay of 100 to 300 words about their life, musical philosophy, goals for life as an organist and musician in the concert field or in religious venues, and musical activities. Selection is based on skills as an organist and musician, musical sensitivity, playing style, appropriate registration for each piece, potential for future growth and development, and financial need.
Financial data: The stipend is $2,000.
Duration: 1 year.
Number awarded: 1 each year.
Deadline: June of each year.

1364 MAKE ART SAVE ART AWARD

Do Something, Inc.
24–32 Union Square East, Fourth Floor
New York, NY 10003
Phone: (212) 254–2390;
Email: photos@dosomething.org
Web: www.dosomething.org/make–art–save–art
Summary: To recognize and reward, with college scholarships, school and college students who submit outstanding artwork via online social networks.
Eligibility: Open to U.S. citizens and permanent residents between 13 and 25 years of age who submit visual art, including drawing, painting, printmaking, photography, and graphic design; strong preference is given to digital artwork in formats .jpg, .png, or .gif. Applicants submit their entries online (e.g., Facebook, Twitter) and encourage family, friends, and social networks to share it. The 10 most shared works are designated finalists and judges select the most outstanding art as the winner of this award.
Financial data: The winner receives a $1,000 college scholarship and a personal laptop computer. The winner's school receives a $5,000 grant for its art program.
Duration: The award is presented annually.
Number awarded: 1 each year.
Deadline: November of each year.

1365 MALCOLM HAYES AWARD FOR ARTISTS

David and Dovetta Wilson Scholarship Fund, Inc.
115–67 237th Street
Elmont, NY 11003–3926
Phone: (516) 285–4573;
Email: DDWSF4@aol.com
Web: www.wilsonfund.org/Malcolm_Hayes.html
Summary: To provide financial assistance to high school seniors who are interested in going to college and studying a field of the arts.
Eligibility: Open to graduating high school seniors who plan to attend an accredited college or university and study the arts. Applicants must be U.S. citizens or permanent residents and have a GPA of 3.0 or higher. Along with their application, they must submit 3 letters of recommendation, high school transcripts, and an essay (up to 250 words) on "How My College Education Will Help Me Make a Positive Impact on My Community." Selection is based on community involvement, desire to prepare for a career in the arts, and financial need.
Financial data: The stipend is $1,000.
Duration: 1 year; nonrenewable.
Number awarded: 1 each year.
Deadline: March of each year.

1366 MANSON A. STEWART SCHOLARSHIPS

Classical Association of the Middle West and South
c/o Monmouth College
Department of Classics
700 East Broadway
Monmouth, IL 61462
Phone: (309) 457–2284; Fax: (815) 346–2565;
Email: camws@camws.org
Web: www.camws.org/awards/index.php
Summary: To provide financial assistance to undergraduate students majoring in classics at a college or university in the area of the Classical Association of the Middle West and South (CAMWS).
Eligibility: Open to undergraduate students who are majoring in classics at the sophomore or junior level at a college or university in the geographic area served by the association. Candidates must be nominated by the chair of their department or program; students then fill out an application and send it along with transcripts and letters of recommendation from 2 members of the association. Nominees are expected to take at least 2 courses in Latin or Greek during the junior or senior year in which the scholarship is held.
Financial data: The award is $1,000.
Duration: 1 year.
Number awarded: 6 each year.
Deadline: January of each year.

1367 $ MARCELLA SEMBRICH MEMORIAL VOICE SCHOLARSHIP COMPETITION

Kosciuszko Foundation
Attn: Director of Cultural Affairs
15 East 65th Street
New York, NY 10021–6595
Phone: (212) 734–2130, ext. 214; (800) 287–9956; Fax: (212) 628–4552;
Email: culture@thekf.org
Web: www.thekf.org/programs/competitions/voice
Summary: To recognize and reward, with college scholarships, outstanding singers.
Eligibility: Open to U.S. citizens, permanent residents of the United States, and international full–time students with valid student visas; all entrants must be between 18 and 35 years of age and preparing for professional singing careers. They must submit a CD of a proposed program if they are selected for the competition; the program must include an 18th century aria (Bach to Mozart), a 19th or 20th century opera area, a song by Stanislaw Moniuszko, a contemporary American aria or song, a 19th century lied, a contemporary Polish song, and 2 additional 20th century songs.
Financial data: The first–prize winner receives a $3,000 cash scholarship; round–trip airfare from New York City to Warsaw, accommodations, and meals in Poland to perform in the International Moniuszko Competition; a recital at the Moniuszko Festival in Poland; and an invitation to perform at the Sembrich Memorial Association in Lake George, New York. Second and third prizes are $1,500 and $1,000 scholarships, respectively.
Duration: The competition is held biennially, in March.
Number awarded: 3 prizes are awarded each year of the competition.
Deadline: February of each even–numbered year.

1368 MARCIA S. HARRIS LEGACY FUND SCHOLARSHIP

Restaurant Association of Maryland Education Foundation
Attn: Senior Director of Development and ProStart
6301 Hillside Court
Columbia, MD 21046

Phone: (410) 290–6800, ext. 1015; Fax: (410) 290–6882;
Email: LaDeana@ramef.org

Summary: To provide financial assistance to Maryland residents who are students or teachers of culinary arts or hospitality management and interested in attending a college or university in any state.

Eligibility: Open to residents of Maryland who are 1) high school seniors; 2) college students; or 3) high school or postsecondary instructors who teach culinary arts or hospitality management. Applicants must be interested in attending a college or university in any state to study culinary arts or hospitality management. Along with their application, they must submit essays on 1) why they have chosen to study for a career in the food service and/or hospitality industries and what they hope to accomplish in their chose career; 2) an especially memorable culinary experience; and 3) their thoughts on a quotation from the scholarship's namesake. Selection of student finalists is based on the essays (25%), grades in food service course work (25%), food service work experience and/or extracurricular activities (25%), and financial need (25%). Finalists are invited to an interview, and scholarship recipients are selected on the basis of the essays (25%), food service work experience and/or extracurricular activities (25%), and the interview (50%). Selection of teachers is judged separately on the basis of the essays (50%), financial need (25%), and recommendations (25%).

Financial data: A stipend is awarded (amount not specified).

Duration: 1 year.

Number awarded: 1 or more each year.

Deadline: April of each year.

1369 $$ MARCIA SILVERMAN MINORITY STUDENT AWARD

Public Relations Student Society of America
Attn: Vice President of Member Services
33 Maiden Lane, 11th Floor
New York, NY 10038–5150
Phone: (212) 460–1474; Fax: (212) 995–0757;
Email: prssa@prsa.org
Web: www.prssa.org/scholarships_competitions/individual

Summary: To provide financial assistance to minority college seniors who are interested in preparing for a career in public relations.

Eligibility: Open to minority (African American/Black, Hispanic/Latino, Asian, Native American, Alaskan Native, or Pacific Islander) students who are entering their senior year at an accredited 4–year college or university. Applicants must have a GPA of 3.0 or higher and be working on a degree in public relations, journalism, or other field to prepare for a career in public relations. Along with their application, they must submit an essay on their view of the public relations profession and their public relations career goals. Selection is based on academic achievement, demonstrated leadership, practical experience, commitment to public relations, writing skills, and letters of recommendation.

Financial data: The stipend is $5,000.

Duration: 1 year.

Number awarded: 1 each year.

Deadline: June of each year.

1370 $ MARK TWAIN PRIZE FOR COMIC PLAYWRITING

John F. Kennedy Center for the Performing Arts
Education Department
Attn: Kennedy Center American College Theater Festival
2700 F Street, N.W.
Washington, DC 20566
Phone: (202) 416–8857; Fax: (202) 416–8860;
Email: KCACTF@kennedy–center.org
Web: www.kcactf.org/KCACTF.ORG_NATIONAL/Kanin_Playwriting.html

Summary: To recognize and reward the student authors of comedy plays.

Eligibility: Open to students at any accredited junior or senior college in the United States, provided their college agrees to participate in the Kennedy Center American College Theater Festival (KCACTF). Undergraduate students must be carrying at least 6 semester hours, graduate students must be enrolled in at least 3 semester hours, and continuing part–time students must be enrolled in a regular degree or certificate program. This award is presented to the best student–written full–length comedy play.

Financial data: Awards are $1,000 for first place and $500 for second place. The first–place winner also receives an all–expense paid professional development opportunity.

Duration: The award is presented annually.

Number awarded: 2 each year.

Deadline: November of each year.

1371 $$ MARRIOTT SCHOLARS PROGRAM

Hispanic College Fund
Attn: Scholarship Processing
1300 L Street, N.W., Suite 975
Washington, DC 20005
Phone: (202) 296–5400; (800) 644–4223; Fax: (202) 296–3774;
Email: hcf–info@hispanicfund.org
Web: scholarships.hispanicfund.org/applications

Summary: To provide financial assistance to Hispanic American undergraduate students who are interested in preparing for a career in the hospitality industry.

Eligibility: Open to U.S. citizens and permanent residents of Hispanic background (at least 1 grandparent must be 100% Hispanic) who are enrolled full time at an accredited 4–year college or university in the 50 states or Puerto Rico or planning to transfer from a community college to a 4–year school. Applicants must be entering their freshman or sophomore year and working on or planning to work on a degree within the hospitality management, hotel management, culinary, or food and beverage field. They must have a GPA of 3.0 or higher and be able to demonstrate financial need.

Financial data: Stipends provide for full payment of tuition, to a maximum of $9,000 per year.

Duration: 4 years.

Number awarded: Varies each year.

Deadline: February of each year.

1372 $ MARSHALL E. MCCULLOUGH SCHOLARSHIPS

National Dairy Shrine
Attn: Executive Director
P.O. Box 725
Denmark, WI 54208
Phone: (920) 863–6333; Fax: (920) 863–6333;
Email: info@dairyshrine.org
Web: www.dairyshrine.org/scholarships.php

Summary: To provide financial assistance to graduating high school students interested in a career in dairy journalism.

Eligibility: Open to high school seniors planning to enter a 4–year college or university and major in 1) dairy/animal science with a communications emphasis; or 2) agricultural journalism with a dairy/animal science emphasis. U.S. citizenship is required. Applicants must submit 1) essays of 100 to 200 words on their farm experiences, dairy–related participation, and communications–related experiences; 2) a 250–word essay on how they would assure a concerned consumer that a carton of milk is safe to drink; and 3) a 1,000–word essay on what they see as the future of the U.S. dairy industry and their role in it. Based on those written applications, 3 or 4 finalists are selected; they must submit a video on which they respond to specific questions about the dairy industry. Winners are selected from this group.

Financial data: Scholarships are $2,500 or $1,000.

Duration: 1 year.

Number awarded: 2 each year: 1 at $2,500 and 1 at $1,000.

Deadline: April of each year.

1373 $$ MARYLAND ASSOCIATION OF PRIVATE COLLEGES AND CAREER SCHOOLS SCHOLARSHIPS

Maryland Association of Private Colleges and Career Schools
Attn: Scholarship Committee
6470 Freetown Road, Suite 200–62
Columbia, MD 21044
Phone: (410) 282–4012;
Email: info@mapccs.org
Web: www.mapccs.org/scholarships.html

Summary: To provide financial assistance to students interested in attending selected private career schools in Maryland.

Eligibility: Open to high school seniors and graduates who are interested in attending a participating private career school in Maryland. Applicants should be interested in working on a degree in such business or technical areas as cosmetology, barbering, diesel mechanics, automotive technology, massage therapy, allied health, secretarial sciences, or drafting. The H.R. Leslie Scholarship is open to any student who applies to a member school. Selection is based on GPA, involvement in school and community activities, recommendations from school officials, desire, and potential to succeed in their career field. Financial need is not considered in the selection process.

Financial data: Individual awards range from $1,000 to $17,700. Funds must be applied for full or partial payment of tuition.

Duration: 1 year.

Number awarded: Varies each year; since the program was established in 1983, more than $2,650,000 in scholarships has been awarded.
Deadline: March of each year.

1374 MAS FAMILY SCHOLARSHIP PROGRAM

Jorge Mas Canosa Freedom Foundation
P.O. Box 14–1898
Miami, FL 33144
Phone: (305) 529–0075, ext. 135;
Email: dlafuente@canf.org
Web: www.jorgemascanosa.org/pages/MFS–Overview_&_Objectives.htm

Summary: To provide financial assistance to students of Cuban descent who are working on an undergraduate or graduate degree in selected subject areas.
Eligibility: Open to students who are direct descendants of those who left Cuba or were born in Cuba themselves. Applicants must have a GPA of 3.5 or higher and an SAT test score (mathematics and critical reading) of at least 1000. They must be able to meet federal standards of financial need. At least 1 parent or 2 grandparents must have been born in Cuba. Both undergraduate and graduate students may apply, provided they are working on a degree in 1 of the following subjects: engineering, business, international relations, economics, communications, or journalism. Selection is based on academic performance, leadership qualities, financial need, potential to contribute to the advancement of a free society, and likelihood of succeeding in their chosen field. Finalists may be interviewed.
Financial data: The amount of the award depends on the cost of tuition at the recipient's selected institution, on the family's situation, and on the amount of funds received from other sources. Full scholarships are not awarded to students who will be receiving full tuition scholarships and/or stipendiary support from other sources.
Duration: 1 year; may be renewed up to 3 additional years.
Deadline: April of each year.

1375 $ MASSACHUSETTS STUDENT BROADCASTER SCHOLARSHIPS

Massachusetts Broadcasters Association
43 Riverside Avenue
PMB 401
Medford, MA 02155
Phone: (800) 471–1875; Fax: (800) 471–1876;
Email: info@massbroadcasters.org
Web: www.massbroadcasters.org/students/index.cfm

Summary: To provide financial assistance to Massachusetts residents interested in attending college in any state to prepare for a career in broadcasting.
Eligibility: Open to residents of Massachusetts who are in the process of enrolling or are currently enrolled full time at an accredited institution of higher learning in any state. Applicants must be preparing for a career in broadcasting. Along with their application, they must submit a 150–word essay on why they have chosen to prepare for a career in a broadcast–related field. Selection is based on financial need, academic merit, community service, extracurricular activities, and work experience. Highest priority is given to students with the most limited financial resources.
Financial data: The stipend is $2,000. Checks are made payable to the recipient and the recipient's school.
Duration: 1 year.
Number awarded: 1 or more each year.
Deadline: March of each year.

1376 MEDIA FELLOWS PROGRAM

Washington Media Scholars Foundation
815 Slaters Lane, Suite 201
Alexandria, VA 22314
Phone: (703) 299–4399;
Email: Kara.Watt@mediascholars.org
Web: mediascholars.org/media–fellows–program–requirements

Summary: To provide financial assistance to upper–division students who are preparing for a career in a media–related field.
Eligibility: Open to full–time juniors and seniors whose major or minor will prepare them for a career in strategic public policy advertising research, management, planning, and buying. Eligible fields include (but are not limited to) mass communications, journalism, marketing, and political science. Applicants must have a GPA of 3.0 or higher and be able to demonstrate financial need. Along with their application, they must submit a statement of career goals, what most appeals to them about the strategic media advertising field, and how their academic plan boosts their ability to achieve their goals. In the selection process, special consideration is given to students who 1) have completed or are engaged in an internship in advertising research, sales, or strategic planning in the public policy or corporate industry areas; 2) have experience in other facets of the cable or broadcast television, radio, print, or online media industries; or 3) can demonstrate an extraordinary achievement in the field, such as an award–winning advertising or public relations club project.
Financial data: The stipend recently averaged $1,500.
Duration: 1 year.
Number awarded: Varies each year; recently, 20 of these scholarships were awarded.
Deadline: July of each year.

1377 $ MEDIA PLAN CASE COMPETITION

Washington Media Scholars Foundation
815 Slaters Lane, Suite 201
Alexandria, VA 22314
Phone: (703) 299–4399;
Email: Kara.Watt@mediascholars.org
Web: mediascholars.org/case–competition

Summary: To recognize and reward, with scholarships for continuing study, undergraduate students who develop outstanding strategic media plans in a case competition.
Eligibility: Open to undergraduate students working on a degree related to strategic media planning. Eligible majors include (but are not limited to) mass communications, journalism, marketing, and political science. Applicants first enter a qualifying round in which they demonstrate their knowledge of the basics of media planning; they may work individually or as a team of 2. Based on the results of that round, 30 teams of 2 students each are invited to participate in the media plan case competition. They are required to complete a media plan for a hypothetical special election referendum issue with real–world data from leading national research and ratings firms and a budget of $2.5 million. Based on those plans, 6 teams are invited to Washington D.C. for Media Scholars Week in early June. Winners are selected through events during that week.
Financial data: Awards are $3,000 scholarships for each member of the winning team and $2,000 scholarships for each member of the first runner–up team.
Duration: The competition is held annually; qualifying teams have 4 weeks to prepare their media plan.
Number awarded: 2 teams of 2 students each win scholarships each year.
Deadline: Applications for the qualifying round must be submitted by November of each year. The 30 qualifying teams are notified in mid–February and have until mid–March to complete their plans.

1378 MERLE J. ISAAC SENIOR COMPOSITION CONTEST

American String Teachers Association
Attn: Competitions
4153 Chain Bridge Road
Fairfax, VA 22030
Phone: (703) 279–2113; Fax: (703) 279–2114;
Email: asta@astaweb.com
Web: www.astaweb.com

Summary: To recognize and reward composers of outstanding works for school orchestra programs.
Eligibility: Open to composers of original unpublished works suitable for elementary, middle/junior high school, and high school orchestras who are 19 years of age and older. Works may be intended for string or full orchestras. Compositions written for commission or that have been submitted for publication are not eligible. The length of the composition should be appropriate to the age level. The manuscript must be clear and legible and include the title and rehearsal numbers or letters. The string parts should be thoroughly edited with bowings and fingerings appropriate to the age level. Manuscripts are evaluated by score analysis and a live performance.
Financial data: The prize is $1,500.
Duration: The competition is held annually.
Number awarded: 1 each year.
Deadline: January of each year.

1379 METG COSTUME DESIGN CONTEST

Massachusetts Educational Theater Guild
P.O. Box 93
Chelmsford, MA 01824
Phone: (978) 456–3454;
Email: metg@metg.org

Web: metg.org/contests/costume–design
Summary: To recognize and reward high school students in Massachusetts who submit outstanding costume designs for a play.
Eligibility: Open to students in grades 7–12 at middle and high schools in Massachusetts. Applicants must prepare a costume design for each of 4 separate characters who appear in a play of their choice. Designs may have a clear overlay to show a coat or outerwear and should have actual swatches of fabric to be used in making the costume. Selection is based on the quality of the design's concept and execution, its originality, and it appropriateness to the selected play.
Financial data: Cash prizes are awarded (amount not specified).
Duration: The contest is held annually.
Number awarded: Varies each year; recently, 2 of these awards were presented.
Deadline: October of each year.

1380 METG SET DESIGN CONTEST

Massachusetts Educational Theater Guild
P.O. Box 93
Chelmsford, MA 01824
Phone: (978) 456–3454;
Email: metg@metg.org
Web: metg.org/contests/set–design–contest
Summary: To recognize and reward high school seniors in Massachusetts who design outstanding theatrical sets and plan to major in any field at a college or university in any state.
Eligibility: Open to seniors at high schools that are members of the Massachusetts Educational Theater Guild (METG). Applicants must register to present a set design in conjunction with the annual guild festival. They must select a scene from a published play and design a set for that choice. Selection is based on the quality of the design's concept and execution and its appropriateness to the selected play; financial need is not considered.
Financial data: A scholarship stipend is awarded (amount not specified).
Duration: The contest is held annually.
Number awarded: Varies each year; recently, 2 of these scholarships were awarded.
Deadline: October of each year.

1381 $$ METROPOLITAN OPERA NATIONAL COUNCIL AUDITIONS

Metropolitan Opera
Attn: National Council Auditions
Lincoln Center
New York, NY 10023
Phone: (212) 870–4515; Fax: (212) 870–7648;
Email: ncouncil@metopera.org
Web: www.metoperafamily.org/metopera/auditions/national–council.aspx
Summary: To recognize and reward singers who have the potential to appear in the Metropolitan Opera.
Eligibility: Open to singers between 20 and 30 years of age who have a voice with operatic potential (exceptional quality, range, projection, charisma, communication, and natural beauty) as well as musical training and background. They must be able to sing correctly in more than 1 language and show artistic aptitude. Applicants should be citizens of the United States or Canada; foreign applicants must show proof of a 1–year residency or full–time enrollment at a university or conservatory in the United States or Canada. Singers must present 5 arias of their choice and of no more than 8 minutes' duration, in contrasting languages and styles. The competition begins at the district level, with winners advancing to regional auditions. The winners from each of the 15 regions represent their region at the national semifinals in New York and then 10 of those singers are selected as national finalists. At the National Grand Finals concert, which is held exactly 1 week later, the 10 National Grand Finalists perform 2 arias each on the stage of the Metropolitan Opera accompanied by the MET Orchestra in a nationally–broadcast concert. The national winners are selected at that concert.
Financial data: At the regional level, each first–place winner receives the $800 Mrs. Edgar Tobin Award; some regions award additional prizes or encouragement awards. At the national level, each winner receives $15,000, each finalist receives $5,000, and each semifinalist receives $1,500. All national winners, finalists, and semifinalists are eligible to apply for grants of $5,000 to be disbursed over 3 years for additional musical training.
Duration: The competition is held annually.
Number awarded: The United States and Canada are divided into 13 regions, which in turn are divided into 40 districts. Singers first compete at the district level, from which winners advance to regional competitions. The 13 regional winners are national semifinalists, from whom 10 national finalists are selected. From those finalists, up to 5 national winners are chosen.
Deadline: Deadlines are chosen by local districts and regions; most of them are in the fall of each year. District auditions usually occur in October or November, with the winners advancing to the regional auditions, usually in December or January. The national competition in New York usually takes place in late February.

1382 $ MICHAEL HAKEEM MEMORIAL COLLEGE ESSAY CONTEST

Freedom from Religion Foundation
P.O. Box 750
Madison, WI 53701
Phone: (608) 256–8900; Fax: (608) 204–0422;
Email: collegeessay@ffrf.org
Web: www.ffrf.org/outreach/student–essay–contests
Summary: To recognize and reward outstanding college student essays on the separation of church and state.
Eligibility: Open to undergraduate students under 25 years of age currently enrolled at colleges and universities in North America. Applicants write an essay on topics that change annually but involve rejecting religion; recently, the topic was "Why I Am an Out of the Closet Atheist." They may write about their own experiences as a non–believer, why they encourage others to come "out of the closet," and their best arguments for rejecting religious belief. Essays should be from 750 to 900 words, accompanied by a paragraph biography identifying the student's college or university, year in school, major, and interests.
Financial data: First prize is $3,000, second $2,000, third $1,000, fourth $500, fifth $300, and honorable mentions $200.
Duration: The competition is held annually.
Number awarded: 5 prizes and a varying number of honorable mentions are awarded each year.
Deadline: June of each year.

1383 MICHAEL S. POWELL HIGH SCHOOL JOURNALIST OF THE YEAR AWARD

Maryland–Delaware–DC Press Association
Attn: MDDC Press Foundation
2000 Capital Drive
Annapolis, MD 21401–3151
Phone: (410) 295–1581; (855) 721–NDDC; Fax: (855) 721–NDDC;
Email: service@mddcpress.com
Web: www.mddcpress.com/index.php?option=com_contact&view=article&id=70
Summary: To recognize and reward, with a scholarship for study at a college in any state, outstanding high school senior journalists in Maryland, Delaware, or the District of Columbia.
Eligibility: Open to high school seniors working on a Maryland, Delaware, or District of Columbia high school newspaper. Applicants must submit 5 samples of their work, a letter of recommendation from their adviser, and an autobiographical statement. They must be interested in majoring in journalism at a college in any state.
Financial data: The award is a $1,500 scholarship.
Duration: The award is presented annually.
Number awarded: 1 each year.
Deadline: January of each year.

1384 MIKE REYNOLDS JOURNALISM SCHOLARSHIP

Radio Television Digital News Foundation
Attn: Programs, Awards, and Membership Manager
529 14th Street, N.W., Suite 425
Washington, DC 20045
Phone: (202) 725–8318; Fax: (202) 223–4007;
Email: katies@rtdna.org
Web: www.rtdna.org/pages/education/scholarship–info.php
Summary: To provide financial assistance for undergraduate education to students whose career objective is radio or television news.
Eligibility: Open to sophomores, juniors, and seniors who are enrolled full time in electronic journalism at a college or university where such a major is offered. Applicants must submit 1 to 3 examples of their journalistic skills on audio CD or DVD (no more than 15 minutes total, accompanied by scripts); a description of their role on each story and a list of who worked on each story and what they did; a 1–page statement explaining why they are preparing for a career in electronic journalism with reference to their specific career preference (radio, television, online, reporting, producing, or newsroom management); a resume; and a letter of reference from their dean or faculty sponsor explaining why they

are a good candidate for the award and certifying that they have at least 1 year of school remaining. They must also document financial need and list media-related jobs held and contributions made to funding their own education.
Financial data: The stipend is $1,000.
Duration: 1 year.
Number awarded: 1 each year.
Deadline: May of each year.

1385 MIRIAM HOFFMAN SCHOLARSHIPS

United Methodist Church
Attn: General Board of Higher Education and Ministry
Office of Loans and Scholarships
1001 19th Avenue South
P.O. Box 340007
Nashville, TN 37203-0007
Phone: (615) 340-7344; Fax: (615) 340-7367;
Email: umscholar@gbhem.org
Web: www.gbhem.org
Summary: To provide financial assistance to undergraduate and graduate Methodist students who are preparing for a music-related career.
Eligibility: Open to undergraduate and graduate students who are enrolled full time and preparing for a career in music. Applicants must have been active, full members of a United Methodist Church for at least 1 year prior to applying and have a GPA of 2.5 or higher. Preference is given to students interested in music education or music ministry. U.S. citizenship or permanent resident status is required.
Financial data: The stipend is $1,000.
Duration: 1 year; recipients may reapply.
Number awarded: Varies each year; recently, 12 of these scholarships were awarded.
Deadline: February of each year.

1386 $ MISSISSIPPI ASSOCIATION OF BROADCASTERS SCHOLARSHIP PROGRAM

Mississippi Association of Broadcasters
Attn: Scholarship Committee
855 South Pear Orchard Road, Suite 403
Ridgeland, MS 39157
Phone: (601) 957-9121; Fax: (601) 957-9175;
Email: email@msbroadcasters.org
Web: www.msbroadcasters.org/index.php/resources/scholarships
Summary: To provide financial assistance to residents of Mississippi enrolled in broadcast programs at colleges and universities in the state.
Eligibility: Open to residents of Mississippi enrolled in accredited broadcast programs at 2- and 4-year colleges and universities in the state. Applicants must submit a 3-page statement that covers why they selected broadcasting as their career choice, the specific area of broadcasting that most interests them and why, their first job preference after college, their career goal 10 years after graduation, their eventual career goal, the broadcast activities in which they have participated, how they feel about broadcast advertising and its importance to a station, how they feel about broadcast advertising and its obligation to consumers, how they think broadcasting could better serve society, the radio or television station they respect most, how their college career could improve their value as a broadcaster, and their most rewarding broadcast-related experience. Selection is based on the essay, extracurricular activities, community involvement, commitment to broadcasting, 3 letters of recommendation, and financial need.
Financial data: Up to $4,000 is available for this program each year.
Duration: 1 year.
Number awarded: 1 or more each year.
Deadline: April of each year.

1387 $ MISSOURI BROADCASTERS ASSOCIATION SCHOLARSHIPS

Missouri Broadcasters Association
Attn: Scholarship Committee
1025 Northeast Drive
P.O. Box 104445
Jefferson City, MO 65110-4445
Phone: (573) 636-6692; Fax: (573) 634-8258;
Email: mba@mbaweb.org
Web: www.mbaweb.org/scholarship-program
Summary: To provide financial assistance to Missouri residents interested in studying broadcasting at a college in the state.
Eligibility: Open to Missouri residents who are currently attending a college, university, or accredited technical/trade school in the state or graduating high school seniors who have been admitted to a Missouri institution of higher education. Applicants must be enrolled or planning to enroll as a full-time student in a broadcast or related program that provides training and expertise applicable to broadcast operation. They must have a GPA of 3.0 or higher and submit their application to a radio or television station that is a member of the Missouri Broadcasters Association. Each station selects its top candidate to forward to the association for statewide consideration. Selection is based on curriculum and career goals, clarity of thought and expression, letters of recommendation, community involvement, extracurricular activities, and financial need. Finalists are invited for personal interviews.
Financial data: A stipend is awarded (amount not specified).
Duration: 1 year; may be renewed if the recipient continues to meet eligibility requirements.
Number awarded: Varies each year.
Deadline: March of each year.

1388 $ MJSA EDUCATION FOUNDATION JEWELRY SCHOLARSHIP

Rhode Island Foundation
Attn: Funds Administrator
One Union Station
Providence, RI 02903
Phone: (401) 427-4017; Fax: (401) 331-8085;
Email: lmonahan@rifoundation.org
Web: www.rifoundation.org
Summary: To provide financial assistance to undergraduate and graduate students working on a degree in a field related to jewelry.
Eligibility: Open to undergraduate and students at colleges, universities, and postsecondary nonprofit technical schools in the United States. Applicants must be studying tool making, design, metals fabrication, or other field related to jewelry. Along with their application, they must submit an essay (up to 300 words), in which they describe their program of study, how far along they are towards completion, their reason for choosing the program, and their professional goal. Selection is based on course of study, career objectives, samples of work (if appropriate), jewelry industry experience, academic achievement, recommendations, and financial need.
Financial data: Stipends range from $500 to $2,000 per year.
Duration: 1 year; may be renewed for up to 3 additional years if the recipient maintains good academic standing.
Number awarded: Varies each year; recently, 5 of these scholarships were awarded.
Deadline: June of each year.

1389 MONTANA ASSOCIATION OF SYMPHONY ORCHESTRAS YOUNG ARTIST COMPETITION

Montana Association of Symphony Orchestras
P.O. Box 1872
Bozeman, MT 59715-1872
Phone: (406) 585-9551;
Email: info@montanasymphonies.org
Web: www.montanasymphonies.org/competition.htm
Summary: To recognize and reward outstanding young musicians in Montana.
Eligibility: Open to residents of Montana between the ages of 13 and 22 who play any of the standard orchestral instruments. Competitions are held in a junior division (ages 13 through 15), a senior division (age 16 through high school graduate), and a college division (post-high school through age 22). Students who are attending college out of Montana are eligible if they have retained their Montana resident status. Past winners are ineligible to compete in the same division in future competitions. Applicants must submit a CD (up to 15 minutes in length)of a concerto or work for solo instrument and orchestra. Pianists should perform without accompaniment; other instrumentalists should have a piano or orchestra accompaniment. On the basis of the CDs, finalists are invited to auditions on the campus of Montana State University in Bozeman where they perform from memory the same work as on the CD.
Financial data: Prizes are $1,000 for the college division, $650 for the senior division, and $450 for the junior division.
Duration: The competition is held biennially, in odd-numbered years.
Number awarded: 3 every other year: 1 in each of the divisions.
Deadline: October of even-numbered years.

1390 MONTANA BROADCASTERS ASSOCIATION SCHOLARSHIPS PROGRAM

Montana Broadcasters Association
3914 Rainbow Bend Drive
Bonner, MT 59823
Phone: (406) 244–4622; Fax: (406) 244–5518;
Email: mba@mtbroadcasters.org
Web: www.mtbroadcasters.org/scholarships

Summary: To provide financial assistance to college students in Montana who are preparing for a career in the broadcast industry.

Eligibility: Open to residents of any state enrolled at a college or university in Montana. Applicants must be majoring in broadcasting, media, advertising, engineering, broadcast journalism, or a related field. Along with their application, they must submit a 1–page statement summarizing their professional abilities, career goals, and extracurricular activities; 2 letters of recommendation; and their most recent transcript.

Financial data: A stipend is awarded (amount not specified).

Duration: 1 year.

Number awarded: Varies each year.

Deadline: January of each year.

1391 MORRIS J. AND BETTY KAPLUN FOUNDATION ESSAY CONTEST

Morris J. and Betty Kaplun Foundation
Attn: Essay Contest Committee
P.O. Box 234428
Great Neck, NY 11023
Email: essays@kaplunfoundation.org
Web: www.kaplunfoundation.org

Summary: To recognize and reward outstanding essays on topics related to being Jewish.

Eligibility: Open to students in grades 10–12 who write an essay of 250 to 1,500 words on a topic that changes annually but is related to being Jewish. A recent topic was "Remembering the Holocaust: What can you do so that we Never Forget?" For students in junior high school (grades 7–9), the essay must be 250 to 1,000 words; a recent topic was "Honoring Thy Father and Mother: How and why, from your own perspective."

Financial data: Prizes are $1,800 or $750.

Duration: The competition is held annually.

Number awarded: Each year, 1 prize of $1,800 and 5 prizes of $750 are awarded at both the high school and junior high levels.

Deadline: March of each year.

1392 MORTON GOULD YOUNG COMPOSER AWARDS

American Society of Composers, Authors and Publishers
Attn: ASCAP Foundation
ASCAP Building
One Lincoln Plaza
New York, NY 10023–7142
Phone: (212) 621–6320; Fax: (212) 621–6236;
Email: concertmusic@ascap.com
Web: www.ascapfoundation.org/programs/awards.aspx

Summary: To recognize and reward outstanding young American composers.

Eligibility: Open to U.S. citizens, permanent residents, or enrolled students with proper visas who are younger than 30 years of age, including students in grades K–12, undergraduates, graduate students, and recipients of a D.M.A. or Ph.D. degree. Original music of any style is considered. However, works that have earned awards or prizes in other national competitions are ineligible, as are arrangements. To compete, each applicant must submit a completed application form, 1 reproduction of a manuscript or score, biographical information, a list of compositions to date, and 2 professional recommendations. Only 1 composition per composer may be submitted. A cassette tape or CD of the composition may be included. So that music materials may be returned, each entry must be accompanied by a self–addressed envelope with sufficient postage.

Financial data: The winners share cash awards of more than $40,000.

Duration: The award is presented annually.

Number awarded: Varies each year; recently, 37 students received these awards.

Deadline: January of each year.

1393 $ MTNA SENIOR PERFORMANCE COMPETITIONS

Music Teachers National Association
Attn: MTNA Foundation
441 Vine Street, Suite 3100
Cincinnati, OH 45202–3004
Phone: (513) 421–1420; (888) 512–5278; Fax: (513) 421–2503;
Email: mtnanet@mtna.org
Web: www.mtna.org

Summary: To recognize and reward outstanding performances by high school musicians.

Eligibility: Open to musicians between 15 and 18 years of age who participate in a performance competition. Prizes are awarded in 4 categories: 1) brass, strings, and woodwinds; 2) voice; 3) piano; and 4) piano duet. Participants first compete in state and division levels and then in the national finals. The required repertoire includes works of different styles and periods. The entrants must be students of members of the Music Teachers National Association (MTNA).

Financial data: The national winners each receive a cash prize of $2,000 and the second–place winners each receive a cash prize of $1,000. The teachers of the national winners each receive $200. All national finalists receive a $100 merit award.

Duration: The competition is held annually.

Number awarded: 6 first prizes (1 in each category) and 6 second prizes (1 in each category) are awarded each year. The number of merit awards varies.

Deadline: September of each year.

1394 MTNA STUDENT COMPOSITION COMPETITIONS

Music Teachers National Association
Attn: MTNA Foundation
441 Vine Street, Suite 3100
Cincinnati, OH 45202–3004
Phone: (513) 421–1420; (888) 512–5278; Fax: (513) 421–2503;
Email: mtnanet@mtna.org
Web: www.mtna.org/programs/competitions/composition–guidelines

Summary: To recognize and reward outstanding musical compositions by students.

Eligibility: Open to students from elementary school through college level whose teachers are members of the Music Teachers National Association (MTNA). Applicants must submit original musical compositions in state competitions; winners advance to the national level. Performance times may not exceed 10 minutes. Compositions may be in any style for any medium. Competitions are held in 4 age–level divisions: elementary for 5 to 10 years of age, junior for 11 to 14 years of age, senior for 15 to 18 years of age, and young artist for 19 to 26 years of age.

Financial data: The national winners receive a certificate, plaque, and the following cash prizes: $500 for the elementary division, $1,000 for the junior division, $2,000 for the senior division, and $3,000 for the young artist division. Second–place winners receive $250 in the elementary division, $500 in the junior division, $1,000 in the senior division, and $1,500 in the young adult division. The teachers of all national winners receive $200.

Duration: The competition is held annually.

Number awarded: 4 first prizes (1 in each division) and 4 second prizes (1 in each division) are awarded each year.

Deadline: September of each year.

1395 $ MTNA YOUNG ARTIST PERFORMANCE COMPETITION

Music Teachers National Association
Attn: MTNA Foundation
441 Vine Street, Suite 3100
Cincinnati, OH 45202–3004
Phone: (513) 421–1420; (888) 512–5278; Fax: (513) 421–2503;
Email: mtnanet@mtna.org
Web: www.mtna.org

Summary: To recognize and reward outstanding performances by college musicians.

Eligibility: Open to musicians between 19 and 26 years of age who participate in a performance competition. Prizes are awarded in 3 categories: 1) brass, strings, and woodwinds; 2) voice; and 3) piano. Participants first compete in state and division levels and then in the national finals. The required repertoire includes works of different styles and periods. The entrants must be students of members of the Music Teachers National Association (MTNA).

Financial data: The national winners (except piano) each receive a cash prize of $3,000 and the second–place winners each receive a cash prize of $1,500. The national winner in the piano category receives a Steinway grand piano with a retail value of more than $49,000. The teachers of the national winners each receive $200. All national finalists receive a $100 merit award.

Duration: The competition is held annually.

Number awarded: 3 first prizes (1 in each category) and 3 second prizes (1 in each category) are awarded each year. The number of merit awards varies.
Deadline: September of each year.

1396 MUGGETS SCHOLARSHIP

American Nursery and Landscape Association
Attn: Horticultural Research Institute
1200 G Street, N.W., Suite 800
Washington, DC 20005
Phone: (202) 695–2474; Fax: (888) 761–7883;
Email: scholarships@hriresearch.org
Web: www.hriresearch.org/index.cfm?page=Content&categoryID=167

Summary: To provide financial assistance to students working on an undergraduate or graduate degree in landscape architecture or horticulture.
Eligibility: Open to students enrolled full time in a landscape or horticulture undergraduate or graduate program at an accredited 2– or 4–year college or university. Students enrolled in a vocational agriculture program are also eligible. Applicants must be at least in their sophomore year of undergraduate study or any year of graduate study and have a minimum GPA of 2.25 overall and 2.7 in their major. Preference is given to applicants who plan to work within the nursery industry, including nursery operations; landscape architecture, design, construction, or maintenance; interiorscape; horticultural distribution; or retail garden center.
Financial data: The stipend is $1,000.
Duration: 1 year; may be renewed.
Number awarded: 1 each year.
Deadline: May of each year.

1397 $$ MUSICAL MERIT FOUNDATION OF GREATER SAN DIEGO SCHOLARSHIP AWARDS

Musical Merit Foundation of Greater San Diego
c/o Connie Almond, Auditions Chair
8331 Mono Lake Drive
San Diego, CA 92119
Web: www.musicalmerit.org

Summary: To recognize and reward, with college scholarships, outstanding musicians from the San Diego (California) area.
Eligibility: Open to 1) residents of San Diego County, Imperial County, or the Mexican state of Baja California del Norte; and 2) residents of any state enrolled full time at a college or university in that area. Applicants must be interested in participating in a competition in voice, keyboard, strings, winds, brass, or percussion. Instrumentalists must have reached 16 years or age or be a graduating high school senior, and not have reached 24 years of age. Vocalists must have reached 18 years of age or be a graduating high school senior, and not have reached 32 years of age. All applicants must submit 1) a letter of recommendation from their private music teacher; 2) a short statement of their musical goals; and 3) a transcript of credit from the school they last attended. They must provide a repertoire sheet listing the precise title of all works to be performed at the preliminary auditions. Those works must meet prescribed requirements for each category of performer. Based on the preliminary auditions, finalists are selected to compete for the scholarship prizes.
Financial data: Awards are presented in the form of scholarships to the college or university of the recipient's choice. They range from $3,000 to $12,000.
Duration: The competition is held annually.
Number awarded: Varies each year. Recently, 15 of these awards were presented: 1 at $12,000, 3 at $8,000, 3 at $5,000, 7 at $4,000, and 1 at $3,000.
Deadline: Applications for the preliminary auditions must be submitted by April of each year.

1398 NAAFA FASHION DESIGN SCHOLARSHIP

National Association to Advance Fat Acceptance
P.O. Box 4662
Foster City, CA 94404–0662
Phone: (916) 558–6880
Web: www.naafaonline.com/dev2/community/scholarship.html

Summary: To provide financial assistance to fashion design students who are interested in specializing in work for the plus–size body.
Eligibility: Open to students currently enrolled at an accredited fashion design school. Applicants must be interested in specializing in the design of fashions for the plus–size body (women's sizes 16 to 32). Along with their application, they must submit 3 drawings of plus–size designs and a 750–word essay on why their fashion entries are unique or innovative and their interest and motivation for a career in the plus–size fashion industry.
Financial data: The stipend is $1,000.
Duration: 1 year.
Number awarded: 1 each year.
Deadline: June of each year.

1399 NAMTA FOUNDATION VISUAL ART MAJOR SCHOLARSHIPS

International Art Materials Trade Association
Attn: NAMTA Foundation
20200 Zion Avenue
Cornelius, NC 28031
Phone: (704) 892–6244; (800) 746–2682; Fax: (704) 892–6247;
Email: scholarship@namta.org
Web: www.namta.org/i4a/pages/index.cfm?pageid=3450

Summary: To provide financial assistance to college students working on a degree in the studio arts.
Eligibility: Open to students currently enrolled as freshmen, sophomores, or juniors at a college, university, or technical institute. Applicants must be majoring or planning to major in the studio arts (including art, ceramics, drawing, fine arts, graphic design, illustration, painting, printmaking, and sculpture) or art education in college. They must have a GPA of 3.0 or higher. Along with their application, they must submit 1) a 1–page statement on why they are seeking this scholarship and what it will do for their education; and 2) a CD with 2 or 3 samples of their work. Both domestic and international students are eligible. Selection is based primarily on artistic talent and/or potential and degree of interest and enthusiasm for the fine arts; some consideration is given to extracurricular activities, GPA, and financial need.
Financial data: A stipend is awarded (amount not specified).
Duration: 1 year; nonrenewable.
Number awarded: Varies each year; recently, 4 of these scholarships were awarded.
Deadline: March of each year.

1400 $$ NAOMI BERBER MEMORIAL SCHOLARSHIP

Print and Graphics Scholarship Foundation
Attn: Scholarship Competition
200 Deer Run Road
Sewickley, PA 15143–2600
Phone: (412) 259–1740; (800) 910–GATF; Fax: (412) 741–2311;
Email: pgsf@printing.org
Web: www.printing.org/pgsf

Summary: To provide financial assistance for college to women who want to prepare for a career in the printing or publishing industry.
Eligibility: Open to women who are high school seniors or full–time college students. Applicants must be interested in preparing for a career in graphic communications or printing. This is a merit–based program; financial need is not considered.
Financial data: The stipend ranges from $1,000 to $5,000, depending upon the funds available each year.
Duration: 1 year; may be renewed for up to 3 additional years, provided the recipient maintains a GPA of 3.0 or higher.
Number awarded: 1 or more each year.
Deadline: February of each year for high school seniors; March of each year for students already in college.

1401 NARRAGANSETT BAY POST SAME SCHOLARSHIP

Society of American Military Engineers–Narragansett Bay Post
Attn: Scholarship Committee
15 Mohegan Avenue
New London, CT 06320
Phone: (860) 444–8312; Fax: (860) 444–8219;
Email: Gregory.j.carabine@uscg.mil
Web: posts.same.org/Narragansett/scholarship.htm

Summary: To provide financial assistance to residents of New England interested in working on a bachelor's degree in construction–related fields at colleges in any state.
Eligibility: Open to residents of New England (preferably Connecticut, Massachusetts, and Rhode Island) who are graduating high school seniors or students currently enrolled at a college or university in any state. Applicants must be interested in working on a bachelor's degree in an accredited engineering or architectural program, preferably in civil engineering, environmental engineering, architecture, or other construction–related program. Preference

is given to students who 1) are dependents of or sponsored by a member of the Narragansett Bay Post of the Society of American Military Engineers (SAME); 2) are enrolled in ROTC (preferably not a recipient of an ROTC scholarship); or 3) have prior U.S. military service and/or public service. Along with their application, they must submit a 500–word essay about themselves, their achievements, or their situation. Selection is based on that essay, grades and class rank, school or community honors, extracurricular activities, leadership, volunteer activities, and completeness and quality of the application. U.S. citizenship is required.
Financial data: The stipend is $1,000.
Duration: 1 year.
Number awarded: 1 each year.
Deadline: May of each year.

1402 NATIONAL ART SCHOLARSHIP CONTEST

Chapel of Four Chaplains
The Navy Yard, Building 649
1201 Constitution Avenue
Philadelphia, PA 19112–1307
Phone: (215) 218–1943; (866) 400–0975; Fax: (215) 218–1949;
Email: chapel@fourchaplains.org
Web: www.fourchaplains.org/programs.html
Summary: To recognize and reward, with college scholarships, high school seniors who submit outstanding works of art on a topic related to public service.
Eligibility: Open to seniors at public and private high schools. Students are invited to submit any form of flat art (except photography) on a theme that changes periodically; recently, students were invited to depict a compelling problem, need, or unresolved conflict (e.g., racial discrimination, religious intolerance, community injustice, public indifference, civic discord, societal ignorance) that, through caring intervention, demonstrates the high ideals of unity without uniformity. They are encouraged to capture the spirit of the theme in whatever manner they wish, through representational, stylized, or abstract means of expression. The medium may be watercolor, crayon, tempera, collage, pen and ink, or computer art. The maximum size is 24" × 30". The artwork should not contain any wording, including slogans, descriptions, narrative, or dialogue balloons. Selection is based on originality, meaning, and imaginative creativity.
Financial data: First prize is a $1,000 scholarship, second a $750 scholarship, and third a $500 scholarship.
Duration: The competition is held annually.
Number awarded: 3 each year.
Deadline: December of each year.

1403 $$ NATIONAL ASSOCIATION OF FARM BROADCASTING SCHOLARSHIPS

National Association of Farm Broadcasting
Attn: NAFB Foundation
1100 Platte Falls Road
P.O. Box 500
Platte City, MO 64079
Phone: (816) 431–4032; Fax: (816) 431–4087;
Email: info@nafb.com
Web: www.nafb.com/index.aspx?mid=9376
Summary: To provide financial assistance to upper–division and graduate students working on a degree in agricultural communications.
Eligibility: Open to college juniors, seniors, and graduate students who are enrolled in or transferring to an agricultural communications program with concentration and/or application in broadcast media (which may include Internet/online media distribution). Applicants must submit a 2–minute personal statement on audio CD that includes a description of their communications experience, reasons for choosing a career in agricultural communications, long–term career goals, and how they anticipate using electronic communications skills. Selection is based on agricultural communications aptitude and leadership achievements, academic record, and career plans.
Financial data: Stipends are $5,000 or $4,000. Expense–paid trips to the annual convention of the National Association of Farm Broadcasting are also provided.
Duration: 1 year.
Number awarded: 3 each year: 1 at $5,000 (the Glenn Kummerow Memorial Scholarship) and 2 at $4,000.
Deadline: June of each year.

1404 $ NATIONAL ASSOCIATION OF NEGRO MUSICIANS SCHOLARSHIP CONTEST

National Association of Negro Musicians, Inc.
Attn: National Scholarship Chair
11551 South Laflin Street
P.O. Box 43053
Chicago, IL 60643
Phone: (773) 568–3818; Fax: (773) 785–5388;
Email: nanm@nanm.org
Web: www.nanm.org/Scholarship_competition.htm
Summary: To recognize and reward (with scholarships for additional study) young musicians who are sponsored by a branch of the National Association of Negro Musicians.
Eligibility: Open to musicians between 18 and 30 years of age. Contestants must be sponsored by a branch in good standing, although they do not need to be a member of a local branch or the national organization. For each category of the competition, they must select 2 compositions from assigned lists to perform, of which 1 list consists of works by African American composers. People ineligible to compete include former first–place winners of this competition; full–time public school teachers and college faculty (although graduate students holding teaching assistantships are still eligible if they receive less than 50% of their employment from that appointment); vocalists who have contracts as full–time solo performers in operatic, oratorio, or other types of professional singing organizations; instrumentalists with contractual full–time orchestral or ensemble jobs; and professional performers under management. Local branches nominate competitors for regional competitions. Regional winners advance to the national competition. Selection is based on musical accuracy (20 points), intonation (20 points), interpretation (20 points), tone quality (20 points), technical proficiency (10 points), and memorization (10 points). The category of the competition rotates on a 5–year schedule as follows: 2013: organ; 2014: winds and percussion; 2015: piano; 2016: voice; 2017: strings.
Financial data: In the national competition, awards are at least $2,000 for first place, $1,500 for second, $1,000 for third, $750 for fourth, and $500 for fifth. All funds are paid directly to the winner's teacher/coach or institution.
Duration: The competition is held annually.
Number awarded: 5 each year.
Deadline: Deadline not specified.

1405 NATIONAL FFA SCHOLARSHIPS FOR UNDERGRADUATES IN THE HUMANITIES

National FFA Organization
Attn: Scholarship Office
6060 FFA Drive
P.O. Box 68960
Indianapolis, IN 46268–0960
Phone: (317) 802–4419; Fax: (317) 802–5419;
Email: scholarships@ffa.org
Web: www.ffa.org
Summary: To provide financial assistance to FFA members who wish to study agricultural journalism and related fields in college.
Eligibility: Open to current and former members of the organization who are working or planning to work full time on a degree in fields related to agricultural journalism and communications, floriculture, and landscape design. For most of the scholarships, applicants must be high school seniors; others are open to students currently enrolled in college. The program includes a large number of designated scholarships that specify the locations where the members must live, the schools they must attend, the fields of study they must pursue, or other requirements. Some consider family income in the selection process, but most do not. Selection is based on academic achievement (10 points for GPA, 10 points for SAT or ACT score, 10 points for class rank), leadership in FFA activities (30 points), leadership in community activities (10 points), and participation in the Supervised Agricultural Experience (SAE) program (30 points). U.S. citizenship is required.
Financial data: Stipends vary, but most are at least $1,000.
Duration: 1 year or more.
Number awarded: Varies; generally, a total of approximately 1,000 scholarships are awarded annually by the association.
Deadline: February of each year.

1406 $ NATIONAL GARDEN CLUBS SCHOLARSHIPS

National Garden Clubs, Inc.
4401 Magnolia Avenue
St. Louis, MO 63110–3492

Phone: (314) 776–7574; Fax: (314) 776–5108;
Email: headquarters@gardenclub.org
Web: www.gardenclub.org/Youth/Scholarships.aspx

Summary: To provide financial assistance to upper–division and graduate students in horticulture, landscape design, and related disciplines.

Eligibility: Open to full–time juniors, seniors, and graduate students (master's only) who are working on a degree in agricultural education, agronomy, botany, biology, city (rural and urban) planning, environmental concerns, environmental conservation (including environmental engineering and environmental law), floriculture, forestry, habitat or forest systems ecology, horticulture, land management, landscape design, plant pathology, wildlife science, or allied subjects. Applicants must have at least a 3.25 GPA and be able to demonstrate financial need. Along with their application, they must submit a personal letter discussing their background, future goals, financial need, and commitment to their chosen career. All applications must be submitted to the state garden club affiliate and are judged there first; then 1 from each state is submitted to the national competition. Selection is based on academic record (40%), applicant's letter (30%), listing of honors, extracurricular activities, and work experience (10%), financial need (15%), and recommendations (5%). U.S. citizenship or permanent resident status is required; international and foreign exchange students are not eligible.

Financial data: The stipend is $3,500.

Duration: 1 year.

Number awarded: 35 each year.

Deadline: Applications must be submitted to the appropriate state organization by February of each year.

1407 $$ NATIONAL ITALIAN AMERICAN FOUNDATION GENERAL CATEGORY II SCHOLARSHIPS

National Italian American Foundation
Attn: Education Director
1860 19th Street, N.W.
Washington, DC 20009
Phone: (202) 387–0600; Fax: (202) 387–0800;
Email: scholarships@niaf.org
Web: www.niaf.org/scholarships

Summary: To provide financial assistance for college or graduate school to students interested in majoring in Italian language, Italian studies, or Italian American studies.

Eligibility: Open to students of any nationality who are currently enrolled at or entering an accredited college or university in the United States with a GPA of 3.5 or higher. Applicants must be majoring or planning to major in Italian language, Italian studies, Italian American studies, or a related field. They may be high school seniors, undergraduates, graduate students, or doctoral candidates. Selection is based on academic performance, field of study, career objectives, and the potential, commitment, and abilities applicants have demonstrated that would enable them to make significant contributions to their chosen field of study. Some scholarships also require financial need, but most do not. U.S. citizenship or permanent resident status is required.

Financial data: Stipends range from $2,000 to $12,000.

Duration: 1 year. Recipients are encouraged to reapply.

Number awarded: Varies each year.

Deadline: February of each year.

1408 NATIONAL LATIN EXAMINATION SCHOLARSHIPS

National Latin Examination
c/o University of Mary Washington
1301 College Avenue
Fredericksburg, VA 22401
Phone: (888) 378–7721; Fax: (540) 654–1567;
Email: nle@umw.edu
Web: www.nle.org/awards.html

Summary: To recognize and reward, with college scholarships, high school seniors who achieve high scores on the National Latin Examination.

Eligibility: Open to high school students who are enrolled or have completed a Latin course during the current academic year. They are invited to take the National Latin Examination. The examinations consist of 40 multiple choice questions on comprehension, grammar, historical background, classical literature, and literary devices. Different examinations are given for Introduction to Latin, Latin I, Latin II, Latin III, Latin III–IV Prose, Latin III–IV Poetry, and Latin V–VI. The top scorers in each category receive gold medals; gold medal winners in Latin III, Latin III–IV Prose, Latin III–IV Poetry, and Latin V–VI who are high school seniors are invited to apply for these scholarships.

Financial data: The award is a $1,000 scholarship.

Duration: 1 year; may be renewed if the recipient continues to study classical Greek or Latin in college.

Number awarded: 21 each year.

Deadline: The examinations must be ordered by January of each year.

1409 NATIONAL MAKE IT WITH WOOL FASHION/APPAREL DESIGN COMPETITION

American Sheep Industry Women
c/o Marie Lehfeldt
P.O. Box 175
Lavina, MT 59046
Phone: (406) 636–2036; Fax: (406) 636–2731;
Email: levi@midrivers.com
Web: www.makeitwithwool.com/fashiondesigncontest.html

Summary: To recognize and reward, with college scholarships, students who submit outstanding designs for wool garments.

Eligibility: Open to students who are currently enrolled in a college–level fashion or apparel design program. Applicants must create an original design for a garment and then construct it for themselves or another; all garments must be made from loomed, knitted, or felted fabric or yarn with a minimum of 60% wool and no more than 40% synthetic fiber. Selection is based on creativity; effectiveness of design, including beautiful use of wool, appropriate presentation of wool product, and workmanship; fit; and marketability.

Financial data: The award is a $1,000 college scholarship.

Duration: The competition is held annually.

Number awarded: 1 each year.

Deadline: October of each year.

1410 $ NATIONAL MAKE IT YOURSELF WITH WOOL CONTEST

American Sheep Industry Women
c/o Marie Lehfeldt
P.O. Box 175
Lavina, MT 59046
Phone: (406) 636–2036; Fax: (406) 636–2731;
Email: levi@midrivers.com
Web: www.makeitwithwool.com/home.html

Summary: To recognize and reward, with college scholarships, students who sew, knit, or crochet fashionable wool garments.

Eligibility: Open to all persons between 13 and 16 years of age for the junior division and 17 through 24 years of age for the senior division. In addition, many states also have a pre–teen division for competitors 12 years of age and younger and an adult division for persons over 24 years of age. Competitors enter machine or hand–knitted, woven, or crocheted garments, or garments containing any part that has been knitted or crocheted; all entries must be made from loomed, knitted, or felted fabric or yarn with a minimum of 60% wool and no more than 40% synthetic fiber. All entrants must select, construct, and model the garment themselves. Selection is based on appropriateness of the garment to the contestant's lifestyle, coordination of fabric/yarn with garment style and design, contestant's presentation, creativity, and construction quality. Contestants must participate in the state where they live or attend school. State winners in the junior and senior divisions advance to the national competition. Scholarships are awarded to national junior and senior division winners.

Financial data: Scholarships awarded at the national level are $2,000 or $1,000, to be used for tuition, books, and fees; funds are paid directly to registrars of approved accredited colleges.

Duration: The competition is held annually.

Number awarded: 6 national scholarships are awarded each year: 2 at $2,000 (1 for the junior winner and 1 for the senior winner) and 4 at $1,000 (2 from the Mohair Council of America for the junior and senior winners of complete garments made of mohair, the Pendleton Woolen Mills award for the junior winner, and the American Wool Council Fashion/Apparel Design Award).

Deadline: November of each year.

1411 $ NATIONAL OPERA ASSOCIATION SCHOLARSHIP DIVISION AWARDS

National Opera Association
Attn: Executive Director
2305 Russell Long Boulevard
P.O. Box 60869
Canyon, TX 79016–0869
Phone: (806) 651–2857; Fax: (806) 651–2958;
Email: rhansen@noa.org

Web: www.noa.org/competitions.html

Summary: To recognize and reward outstanding undergraduate and graduate opera students.

Eligibility: Open to opera students between 18 and 24 years of age who are currently enrolled in an undergraduate or graduate program or equivalent. Their teacher or coach must be a member of the National Opera Association. Applicants must submit a CD with 2 arias and judges select the finalists on the basis of those recordings. Finalists are then invited to auditions where they present 4 arias in contrasting styles and periods, in 3 languages (including 1 originally in English). The singer chooses the first selection, after which the judges request 1 or more selections.

Financial data: The first–place award is $2,000; second– and third–place awards range from $500 to $1,250. In addition, the first–place winner receives a scholarship for summer study at the American Institute of Musical Studies (AIMS) Graz Experience in Austria.

Duration: The competition is held annually.

Number awarded: 3 each year.

Deadline: October of each year.

1412 $$ NATIONAL SCULPTURE COMPETITION PRIZES

National Sculpture Society
Attn: National Sculpture Competition
75 Varick Street, Floor 11
New York, NY 10013
Phone: (212) 764–5645, ext. 10; Fax: (212) 764–5651;
Email: nss1893@aol.com
Web: www.sculpturecompetition.info

Summary: To recognize and reward outstanding creative work by students and other young sculptors.

Eligibility: Open to sculptors who are between 18 and 39 years of age and citizens or residents of the United States. Artists who wish to be considered only for the Dexter Jones Award must submit images of up to 3 bas–reliefs (2 views of each bas–relief); the award is presented for the best work of sculpture in bas–relief. Artists who wish to enter the figure modeling contest must submit images of 2 separate views of up to 10 works of sculpture. On the basis of those images, the jury invites up to 15 entrants to travel to the site of the contest where they work for 28 hours over 5 days to create a sculpture of a full–figure model from life. Selection of winners is based on the following criteria: mastery of the figure in sculptural form; comprehension of the action, unity, and rhythm of the pose; and how well the artist gives evidence of understanding proportion, stance, solidity, and continuity of line. The Charlotte Gefken Prize is awarded to the most outstanding competitor, the Roger T. Williams Prize is awarded to the sculptor "who reaches for excellence in representational sculpture," the Walter and Michael Lantz Prize is presented to another outstanding competitor, and the Edward Fenno Hoffman Prize is awarded to the sculptor "who strives to uplift the human spirit through the medium of his/her art."

Financial data: The Dexter Jones Award is $5,000, the Charlotte Gefken Prize is $5,000, the Roger T. Williams Prize is $1,500, the Walter and Michael Lantz Prize is $750, and the Edward Fenno Hoffman Prize is $350.

Duration: The competition is held annually.

Number awarded: Each year, 1 prize is awarded on the basis of images of bas–reliefs and 4 prizes are awarded to winners of the figure modeling contest.

Deadline: March of each year.

1413 $ NATIONAL SCULPTURE SOCIETY SCHOLARSHIPS

National Sculpture Society
Attn: Education Committee
75 Varick Street, Floor 11
New York, NY 10013
Phone: (212) 764–5645; Fax: (212) 764–5651;
Email: nss1893@aol.com
Web: www.nationalsculpture.org/nssN/index.cfm/fa/cProg.scholarships

Summary: To provide financial assistance for college to student sculpturers.

Eligibility: Open to students entering or enrolled in a college or master's degree program in figurative or representational sculpture. They must submit a letter of application that includes a brief biography and an explanation of their background in sculpture, 2 letters of recommendation, 6 to 15 images of at least 5 of their works (figurative, realist, or representational sculpture is preferred), and proof of financial need.

Financial data: The stipend is $2,000. Funds are paid directly to the academic institution through which the student applies, to be credited towards tuition.

Duration: 1 year.

Number awarded: 4 each year.

Deadline: May of each year.

1414 $$ NATIONAL SECURITY SCHOLARSHIPS OF THE INDEPENDENT COLLEGE FUND OF MARYLAND

Independent College Fund of Maryland
Attn: Director of Programs and Scholarships
3225 Ellerslie Avenue, Suite C–160
Baltimore, MD 21218–3519
Phone: (443) 997–5700; Fax: (443) 997–2740;
Email: Ifund@jhu.edu
Web: i–fundinfo.org/scholarships/national–security–scholarships.html

Summary: To provide financial assistance to students from any state enrolled at member institutions of the Independent College Fund of Maryland and majoring in a field related to national security.

Eligibility: Open to students from any state who are enrolled as sophomores or juniors at member institutions and have a GPA of 3.0 or higher. Applicants must be preparing for a career in the national security field. Preferred majors are computer science, engineering (software, computer, systems), information assurance, information systems, information technology, mathematics, and physics; consideration is also given to students majoring in accounting, economics, finance, languages, liberal arts, and political science. U.S. citizenship is required.

Financial data: The stipend is $15,000.

Duration: 1 year.

Number awarded: 1 or more each year.

Deadline: September of each year.

1415 NATIONAL SOCIETY OF THE COLONIAL DAMES OF AMERICA IN THE STATE OF GEORGIA SCHOLARSHIPS

Georgia Trust
Attn: Scholarship Committee
1516 Peachtree Street, N.W.
Atlanta, GA 30309
Phone: (404) 881–9980; Fax: (404) 875–2205;
Email: kryan@georgiatrust.org
Web: www.georgiatrust.org/preservation/opportunities.php

Summary: To provide financial assistance to Georgia residents majoring in a field related to historical preservation at a college or university in the state.

Eligibility: Open to Georgia residents who are enrolled full time in their first year of undergraduate study at a college or university in the state. Applicants must be working on a degree in historic preservation or a related field (e.g., archaeology, architecture, history, planning). They may not have a family affiliation to the National Society of the Colonial Dames of America. U.S. citizenship is required. Selection is based on academic achievement and past and planned involvement within preservation–related fields.

Financial data: The stipend is $1,500.

Duration: 1 year.

Number awarded: 2 each year.

Deadline: February of each year.

1416 $$ NATIONAL SPEAKERS ASSOCIATION SCHOLARSHIPS

National Speakers Association
Attn: NSA Foundation
1500 South Priest Drive
Tempe, AZ 85281
Phone: (480) 968–2552; Fax: (480) 968–0911;
Email: Mandy@nsaspeaker.org
Web: www.nsafoundation.org/Scholarships.aspx

Summary: To provide financial assistance to students interested in focusing on speech communication in college.

Eligibility: Open to full–time college juniors, seniors, and graduate students majoring or minoring in speech communications. Students majoring in speech pathology, television, radio, mass media, public relations, law, or human resources are not eligible. Applicants must intend to 1) become professional speakers, trainers, or speech educators; or 2) use their speaking talents for improving the lives of others. Along with their application, they must submit a 500–word essay on their career objective, their desire to be a professional speaker, and how they will use their skills in oral communications. Selection is based on that essay; a letter of recommendation from a speech teacher or the speech department head or dean; a list of awards, honors, extracurricular activities, and outside work interests; and an official transcript. Hardship and financial need may be considered, although the final decision is not based solely on financial need.

Financial data: The stipend is $5,000.

Duration: 1 year.

Number awarded: 4 each year.
Deadline: May of each year.

1417 $$ NATIONAL STUDENT JOURNALIST OF THE YEAR SCHOLARSHIPS

Journalism Education Association
c/o Kansas State University
103 Kedzie Hall
Manhattan, KS 66506–1505
Phone: (785) 532–5532; (866) JEA–5JEA; Fax: (785) 532–5563;
Email: jea@spub.ksu.edu
Web: jea.org/category/awards

Summary: To recognize and reward, with college scholarships, outstanding high school journalists.
Eligibility: Open to graduating high school seniors who are planning to study journalism and/or mass communications in college and prepare for a career in that field, have a GPA of 3.0 or higher, and have participated in high school journalism for at least 2 years. Applicants must submit examples of their work that show the following 4 characteristics: 1) skilled and creative use of media content; 2) inquiring mind and investigative persistence resulting in an in–depth study of issues important to the local high school audience, high school students in general, or society; 3) courageous and responsible handling of controversial issues despite threat or imposition of censorship; and 4) variety of journalistic experiences, each handled in a quality manner, on a newspaper, yearbook, broadcast, or other medium. Applications are to be sent to the applicant's state contest coordinator; winners from the state Journalist of the Year competitions are sent to the national level for judging.
Financial data: The award is $5,000 for the top winner and $2,000 for each runner–up. Funds are released when the recipient enrolls in a college journalism program.
Duration: The competition is held annually.
Number awarded: Approximately 7 each year: 1 top winner and approximately 6 runners–up.
Deadline: Applications must be submitted to state coordinators in February of each year.

1418 NATIONAL UNDERGRADUATE PLAYWRITING AWARD

John F. Kennedy Center for the Performing Arts
Education Department
Attn: Kennedy Center American College Theater Festival
2700 F Street, N.W.
Washington, DC 20566
Phone: (202) 416–8857; Fax: (202) 416–8860;
Email: KCACTF@kennedy–center.org
Web: www.kcactf.org/KCACTF.ORG_NATIONAL/Kanin_Playwriting.html

Summary: To recognize and reward outstanding undergraduate playwrights.
Eligibility: Open to students at any accredited junior or senior college in the United States, provided their college agrees to participate in the Kennedy Center American College Theater Festival (KCACTF). Applicants must be carrying at least 6 semester hours. For the Michael Kanin Playwriting Awards Program, students must submit either 1 major work or 2 or more shorter works based on a single theme or encompassed within a unifying framework; all entries must provide a full evening of theater. This award is presented to the author of best play written by an undergraduate.
Financial data: The winning playwright receives 1) a cash prize of $1,000; 2) the Dramatists Guild Award of active membership in the Guild; and 3) a 2–week all–expense paid professional development opportunity at the Eugene O'Neill Theater Center in Waterford, Connecticut. Second prize is $500.
Duration: The competition is held annually.
Number awarded: 1 each year.
Deadline: November of each year.

1419 $ NEDMA FOUNDATION DIRECT MARKETING SCHOLARSHIP

New England Direct Marketing Association
Attn: NEDMA Foundation, Inc.
193 Haverhill Street
North Reading, MA 01864
Phone: (978) 664–3877; Fax: (978) 664–2835;
Email: nedmafdn@comcast.net
Web: www.nedma.com/resources/foundation–scholarships.asp

Summary: To provide financial assistance and work experience to upper–division students in New England who are preparing for a career in direct marketing.
Eligibility: Open to students who have completed their sophomore or junior year at a college or university in New England. Applicants must be majoring in marketing, advertising, communications, or other field designed to prepare them for a career in direct marketing. Along with their application, they must submit essays covering why they are applying for this scholarship, what courses in their major have interested them the most and why, the extracurricular activities in which they have participated, their employment or internship experiences (especially those related to marketing, advertising, or journalism), their special interest in the field, how they believe this scholarship will affect their short– and long–term goals, and what direct marketing means to them. Financial need is not considered in the selection process.
Financial data: The award includes a stipend of $3,000 to be applied to college tuition, attendance at a nationally sponsored seminar on the basics of direct marketing, a paid summer internship at a New England firm that represents a segment of the direct marketing industry, and attendance at the annual conference of the New England Direct Marketing Association (NEDMA).
Duration: 1 year.
Number awarded: 1 each year.
Deadline: January of each year.

1420 $$ NELLIE LOVE BUTCHER MUSIC SCHOLARSHIP

Daughters of the American Revolution–National Society
Attn: Committee Services Office, Scholarships
1776 D Street, N.W.
Washington, DC 20006–5303
Phone: (202) 628–1776
Web: www.dar.org/natsociety/edout_scholar.cfm

Summary: To provide financial assistance to students working on an undergraduate degree in music.
Eligibility: Open to students who are working on or planning to work on a degree in piano or voice. Applicants must be sponsored by a local chapter of the Daughters of the American Revolution (DAR). Special consideration is given to students currently attending the Duke Ellington School of the Performing Arts in Washington, D.C. Selection is based on academic excellence, commitment to the field of study, and financial need. U.S. citizenship is required.
Financial data: The stipend is $5,000 per year.
Duration: 1 year; may be renewed up to 3 additional years, provided the recipient maintains a GPA of 3.0 or higher.
Number awarded: 1 each year.
Deadline: February of each year.

1421 $$ NELSON BROWN AWARD

Connecticut Broadcasters Association
Attn: Scholarships
90 South Park Street
Willimantic, CT 06226
Phone: (860) 633–5031; Fax: (860) 456–5688;
Email: mcrice@prodigy.net
Web: www.ctba.org/page.cfm?page=17

Summary: To provide financial assistance to Connecticut residents who are interested in attending college in any state to prepare for a career in broadcasting.
Eligibility: Open to Connecticut residents who are entering their first, second, third, or fourth year at a 2– or 4–year college, university or technical school in any state. Applicants must be majoring in broadcasting, communications, marketing, or a related field. Selection is based on academic achievement, community service, goals in the chosen field, and financial need.
Financial data: The stipend is $5,000.
Duration: 1 year.
Number awarded: 1 each year.
Deadline: March of each year.

1422 $ NEW ENGLAND COX COMMUNICATIONS SCHOLARSHIPS

Cox Communications–New England
Attn: Community Relations Coordinator
9 JP Murphy Highway
West Warwick, RI 02893

Phone: (401) 383–2000;
Email: rosie.fernandez@cox.com
Web: ww2.cox.com/myconnection/rhodeisland/community/editorial2.cox

Summary: To provide financial assistance to high school seniors in Connecticut and Rhode Island who plan to major in communications in college.

Eligibility: Open to seniors graduating from high schools in Rhode Island or in selected towns in Connecticut. Applicants must be planning to attend a college or university to major in communications or a communications–related field (e.g., telecommunications, technology, engineering). Along with their application, they must submit an essay describing the greatest impact they have made on their community through a community service project. Selection is based on academic achievement, community involvement, and desire to prepare for a career in communications, telecommunications, engineering, or technology; financial need is not considered.

Financial data: The stipend is $2,000.

Duration: 1 year.

Number awarded: 16 each year: 8 for students from Rhode Island and 8 for students from Connecticut.

Deadline: February of each year.

1423 $ NEW ENGLAND GRAPHIC ARTS SCHOLARSHIP

Printing and Publishing Council of New England
c/o Jay Smith, Scholarship Chair
166 New Boston Street
Woburn, MA 01801
Email: jay@mhcp.com
Web: www.ppcne.org/scholarships.html

Summary: To provide financial assistance to high school seniors, graduates, and currently–enrolled college students from New England who are preparing for a career in printing or the graphic arts.

Eligibility: Open to residents of New England who are high school seniors or recent graduates. Applicants must be attending or planning to attend a 2– or 4–year college or university in any state that offers a certificate or degree related to printing or the graphic arts. Selection is based on academic achievement, extracurricular activities, personal qualifications, and financial need.

Financial data: The maximum stipend is $2,500 per year. Funds are paid directly to the recipient's college or university.

Duration: Up to 4 years, provided the recipient maintains a GPA of 2.5 or higher.

Number awarded: 1 or more each year; nearly $100,000 in scholarships is awarded annually.

Deadline: May of each year.

1424 $ NEW HAMPSHIRE ASSOCIATION OF BROADCASTERS STUDENT BROADCASTER SCHOLARSHIP PROGRAM

New Hampshire Association of Broadcasters
707 Chestnut Street
Manchester, NH 03104
Phone: (603) 627–9600; Fax: (603) 627–9603;
Email: info@nhab.org
Web: www.nhab.org/students/index.cfm

Summary: To provide financial assistance to New Hampshire residents interested in attending college in any state to prepare for a career in broadcasting or communications.

Eligibility: Open to residents of New Hampshire who are enrolled or planning to enroll full time in a broadcast program at a 2– or 4–year college or university in any state. Applicants must submit a 150–word statement on why they have chosen to prepare for a career in a broadcast–related field. Selection is based on financial need, academic merit, community service, extracurricular activities, and work experience. Highest priority is given to students with the most limited financial resources.

Financial data: The stipend is $2,500.

Duration: 1 year.

Number awarded: At least 6 each year.

Deadline: March of each year.

1425 NEW JERSEY POST SAME SCHOLARSHIP

Society of American Military Engineers–New Jersey Post
c/o John Booth
CTSC
P.O. Box 60
Fort Monmouth, NJ 07703
Phone: (732) 544–0995, ext. 102;
Email: boothjl@aol.com
Web: posts.same.org/newjersey/scholarships.html

Summary: To provide financial assistance to students in New Jersey working on an undergraduate degree in architecture, engineering, or a related field.

Eligibility: Open to undergraduate students working on a degree in architecture, engineering, or a related field. Candidates must be nominated by a member of the New Jersey Post of the Society of American Military Engineers (SAME). Selection is based on school and community activities, educational goals, academics, recommendations, and employment experience.

Financial data: The stipend is $1,000.

Duration: 1 year; nonrenewable.

Number awarded: Varies each year; recently, 5 of these scholarships were awarded.

Deadline: March of each year.

1426 $ NEW JERSEY VIETNAM VETERANS' MEMORIAL SCHOLARSHIPS

New Jersey Vietnam Veterans' Memorial
Attn: Scholarship Committee
1 Memorial Lane
P.O. Box 648
Holmdel, NJ 07733
Phone: (732) 335–0033; (800) 648–8387; Fax: (732) 335–1107
Web: www.njvvmf.org/Scholarship

Summary: To recognize and reward, with scholarships for college in any state, New Jersey high school seniors who have visited the New Jersey Vietnam Veterans' Memorial and written an essay about the experience.

Eligibility: Open to seniors graduating from high schools in New Jersey who have visited the New Jersey Vietnam Veterans' Memorial. Applicants must submit an essay in which they reflect upon their visit. They must submit proof of acceptance to a college or trade school in any state, but letters of recommendation and transcripts are not required.

Financial data: The award is a $2,500 scholarship.

Duration: The awards are granted annually.

Number awarded: 2 each year.

Deadline: April of each year.

1427 NICK ADAMS SHORT STORY COMPETITION

Associated Colleges of the Midwest
Attn: Coordinator of Projects & Administration
205 West Wacker Drive, Suite 1300
Chicago, IL 60606
Phone: (312) 263–5000; Fax: (312) 263–5879;
Email: acm@acm.edu
Web: www.acm.edu

Summary: To recognize and reward outstanding short stories written by college students at schools belonging to the Associated Colleges of the Midwest (ACM).

Eligibility: Open to students at colleges that belong to ACM. They may submit up to 2 stories to their campus's English department. The story need not have been written especially for the competition, but it cannot have been previously published off–campus. Each department selects the 4 best stories submitted and sends them to ACM's national office. The finalist is selected from that group.

Financial data: The prize is $1,000.

Duration: The prize is awarded annually.

Number awarded: 1 each year.

Deadline: March of each year.

1428 NORTH AMERICAN SURVEYING HISTORY SCHOLARSHIP

Museum of Surveying
220 South Museum Drive
Lansing, MI 48933
Phone: (517) 484–6605;
Email: museumofsurvey@acd.net
Web: www.surveyhistory.org

Summary: To provide financial assistance to upper–division surveying students in North America who have demonstrated an interest in history.

Eligibility: Open to juniors and seniors at accredited colleges and universities in North America who are majoring in surveying, geomatics, or a similar field. Applicants must have a GPA of 3.0 or higher. They must have demonstrated an

interest in surveying history in ways that include, but are not limited to, the following: participating in a re–enactment group on a regular basis; participating in a significant historical survey retracement; preparing a paper (preferably published) about an historical surveying event, person, or technological development in equipment; or performing a service project related to surveying history for a museum.
Financial data: The stipend is $1,000.
Duration: 1 year.
Number awarded: 1 each year.
Deadline: October of each year.

1429 $ NPPF STILL AND MULTIMEDIA PHOTOGRAPHER SCHOLARSHIP

National Press Photographers Foundation
3200 Croasdaile Drive, Suite 306
Durham, NC 27705–2586
Phone: (919) 383–7246; (800) 289–6772; Fax: (919) 383–7261;
Email: info@nppa.org
Web: nppf.org
Summary: To provide financial assistance to undergraduate photojournalism students who are concentrating on still and multimedia work.
Eligibility: Open to full–time undergraduate students at 4–year colleges and universities in Canada and the United States. Applicants must be preparing for a career in photojournalism with an emphasis on still and multimedia. Along with their application, they must submit a portfolio of their work with 6 to 12 entries (single photographs, multiple picture stories, or multimedia stories). Selection is based on aptitude for photojournalism, academic ability, and financial need.
Financial data: The stipend is $2,000.
Duration: 1 year.
Number awarded: 1 each year.
Deadline: February of each year.

1430 $ NPPF TELEVISION NEWS SCHOLARSHIP

National Press Photographers Foundation
3200 Croasdaile Drive, Suite 306
Durham, NC 27705–2586
Phone: (919) 383–7246; (800) 289–6772; Fax: (919) 383–7261;
Email: info@nppa.org
Web: nppf.org
Summary: To provide financial assistance to undergraduate students interested in a career in television photojournalism.
Eligibility: Open to full–time undergraduates at 4–year colleges and universities in the United States or Canada. Applicants must be preparing for a career in television photojournalism. Along with their application, they must submit a portfolio of their work with 6 to 12 entries (single photographs, multiple picture stories, or multimedia stories). Selection is based on aptitude for photojournalism, academic ability, and financial need.
Financial data: The stipend is $2,000.
Duration: 1 year.
Number awarded: 1 each year.
Deadline: February of each year.

1431 $$ NPPF–NPPA CAREER EXPANSION SCHOLARSHIPS

National Press Photographers Foundation
3200 Croasdaile Drive, Suite 306
Durham, NC 27705–2586
Phone: (919) 383–7246; (800) 289–6772; Fax: (919) 383–7261;
Email: info@nppa.org
Web: nppf.org
Summary: To provide financial assistance to professional still photojournalists who have returned to college to obtain new skills.
Eligibility: Open to professional still photographers who have at least 3 years of experience and whose work has been published in a newspaper, book, or magazine. Applicants must be enrolled full time at a college or university to expand their skills in order to change their career path. Along with their application, they must submit brief statements on their reasons for returning to school and their financial need.
Financial data: The stipend is $5,000.
Duration: 1 year.
Number awarded: 5 each year.
Deadline: November of each year.

1432 $ NRAEF ACADEMIC SCHOLARSHIPS FOR FIRST–TIME FRESHMEN, GED GRADUATES AND PROSTART STUDENTS

National Restaurant Association Educational Foundation
Attn: Scholarships Program
175 West Jackson Boulevard, Suite 1500
Chicago, IL 60604–2814
Phone: (312) 715–1010, ext. 738; (800) 765–2122, ext. 6738; Fax: (312) 566–9733;
Email: scholars@nraef.org
Web: www.nraef.org/scholarships
Summary: To provide financial assistance to high school seniors, GED graduates, ProStart students, and first–time freshmen entering college to prepare for a career in the hospitality industry.
Eligibility: Open to graduating high school seniors, GED graduates enrolling in college for the first time, students who have participated in the ProStart program of the National Restaurant Association, and high school graduates enrolling in college for the first time. Applicants must be planning to enroll either full time or substantial part time at an accredited culinary school, college, or university to major in culinary, restaurant management, or other food service–related field of study. They must be U.S. citizens or permanent residents. Along with their application, they must submit an essay of 350 to 1,000 words on their career goals in the restaurant/food service industry, their background and educational and work experience, how their background and experience will help them to achieve their career goals, what they need to do to reach their career goals, and the person or experience that most influenced them in selecting restaurant and food service as a career. Selection is based on the essays, presentation of the application, industry–related work experience, letters of recommendation, and food service certificates (such as the ProStart National Certificate of Achievement).
Financial data: The stipend is $2,500.
Duration: 1 year.
Number awarded: Varies each year.
Deadline: August of each year.

1433 NSPA JOURNALISM HONOR ROLL AWARD

National Scholastic Press Association
2221 University Avenue, S.E., Suite 121
Minneapolis, MN 55414
Phone: (612) 625–8335; Fax: (612) 626–0720;
Email: contests@studentpress.org
Web: www.studentpress.org/nspa/contests.html
Summary: To recognize and reward outstanding high school journalists.
Eligibility: Open to high school seniors who have earned a GPA of 3.75 or higher and have worked in student media for 1 or more years. The publication on which the student works must have a current membership in the National Scholastic Press Association (NSPA). Candidates must be nominated by their teacher. The nominee judged most outstanding receives this award. Selection is based on cumulative GPA, publication experience (including years on staff, positions held, and workshops/conventions attended), college plans, and an essay of 500 words or less that explains "Why I'm choosing a career in journalism."
Financial data: The award is a $1,000 scholarship.
Duration: The competition is held annually.
Number awarded: 1 each year.
Deadline: February of each year.

1434 NVTA SCHOLARSHIP PROGRAM

NVTA
c/o Zina Bleck
McLean Community Players
P.O. Box 160
McLean, VA 22101
Phone: (703) 615–6626;
Email: zbleck@aol.com
Web: www.nvtaweb.org/scholarship
Summary: To provide financial assistance to high school seniors in the Washington, D.C. metropolitan area who are interested in studying theater in college.
Eligibility: Open to seniors graduating from high schools in Washington D.C. or the metropolitan areas of northern Virginia and suburban Maryland. Applicants must plan to enroll as a student in a dramatic/musical theater performance or technical theater program. They must have a GPA of 2.5 or higher. Along with their application, they must submit a resume that describes their performance or technical training and experience, a high school transcript,

and a 200–word personal statement relating to their career objectives. For the performance scholarship, they must also present a 5–minute audition. For the technical scholarship, they must also submit a 3–dimensional presentation of a set design or a 2–dimensional presentation of lighting design, costume design, makeup, or hair design. They must be sponsored by an NVTA member theater. Financial need is not considered in the selection process.

Financial data: The stipend is $1,000. Funds are sent directly to the recipient's college or drama school.

Duration: 1 year.

Number awarded: Varies each year; recently, 3 of these scholarships were awarded.

Deadline: April of each year.

1435 $$ NYWICI FOUNDATION SCHOLARSHIPS

New York Women in Communications, Inc.
Attn: NYWICI Foundation
355 Lexington Avenue, 15th Floor
New York, NY 10017–6603
Phone: (212) 297–2133; Fax: (212) 370–9047;
Email: nywicipr@nywici.org
Web: www.nywici.org/foundation/scholarships

Summary: To provide financial assistance to female residents of designated eastern states who are interested in preparing for a career in communications at a college or graduate school in any state.

Eligibility: Open to women who are seniors graduating from high schools in New York, New Jersey, Connecticut, or Pennsylvania or undergraduate or graduate students who are permanent residents of those states; they must be attending or planning to attend a college or university in any state. Graduate students must be members of New York Women in Communications, Inc. (NYWICI). Also eligible are women who reside outside the 4 states but are currently enrolled at a college or university within 1 of the 5 boroughs of New York City. All applicants must be working on a degree in a communications–related field (e.g., advertising, broadcasting, communications, English, film, journalism, marketing, new media, public relations) and have a GPA of 3.2 or higher. Along with their application, they must submit a 2–page resume that includes school and extracurricular activities, significant achievements, academic honors and awards, and community service work; a personal essay of 300 to 500 words on their choice of an assigned topic that changes annually; 2 letters of recommendation; and an official transcript. Selection is based on academic record, need, demonstrated leadership, participation in school and community activities, honors, work experience, goals and aspirations, and unusual personal and/or family circumstances. U.S. citizenship is required.

Financial data: The maximum stipend is $10,000.

Duration: 1 year; recipients may reapply.

Number awarded: Varies each year; recently, 19 of these scholarships, with a total value of $103,000, were awarded.

Deadline: January of each year.

1436 OCCUPATIONAL/PHYSICAL THERAPY SCHOLARSHIP

Daughters of the American Revolution–National Society
Attn: Committee Services Office, Scholarships
1776 D Street, N.W.
Washington, DC 20006–5303
Phone: (202) 628–1776
Web: www.dar.org/natsociety/edout_scholar.cfm

Summary: To provide financial assistance to students working on an undergraduate degree in occupational, physical, art, or music therapy.

Eligibility: Open to students who are enrolled in an accredited program of occupational or physical therapy. Programs in art and music therapy also qualify. Applicants must be sponsored by a local chapter of the Daughters of the American Revolution (DAR). Selection is based on academic excellence, commitment to field of study, and financial need. U.S. citizenship is required.

Financial data: The stipend is $1,000 per year.

Duration: 1 year; may be renewed.

Number awarded: Varies each year.

Deadline: February of each year.

1437 OHIO CLASSICAL CONFERENCE SCHOLARSHIP FOR PROSPECTIVE LATIN TEACHERS

Ohio Classical Conference
c/o Kelly Kusch, Scholarship Committee
Covington Latin School
21 East 11th Street
Covington, KY 41011
Phone: (513) 227–6847;
Email: Kelly.kusch@covingtonlatin.org
Web: www.xavier.edu/occ/occ–scholarships.cfm

Summary: To provide financial assistance to Ohio residents preparing for a career as a Latin teacher.

Eligibility: Open to college students at least at the sophomore level who are either residents of Ohio enrolled at a college or university in any state or residents of other states enrolled at a college or university in Ohio. Applicants must be taking courses leading to a career in the teaching of Latin at the K–12 level in a public, private, or parochial school. They must submit college transcripts, 2 letters of recommendation (including 1 from a member of their classics department), a prospectus of courses completed and to be taken as part of the program, and a 1–page statement of their academic goals and reasons for applying for the scholarship.

Financial data: The stipend is $1,500.

Duration: 1 year; nonrenewable.

Number awarded: 1 each year.

Deadline: March of each year.

1438 OHIO CLASSICAL CONFERENCE SCHOLARSHIP FOR THE STUDY OF LATIN OR GREEK

Ohio Classical Conference
c/o Kelly Kusch, Scholarship Committee
Covington Latin School
21 East 11th Street
Covington, KY 41011
Phone: (513) 227–6847;
Email: Kelly.kusch@covingtonlatin.org
Web: www.xavier.edu/occ/occ–scholarships.cfm

Summary: To provide financial assistance to Ohio high school seniors planning to study Latin or Greek at a college in any state.

Eligibility: Open to seniors graduating from high schools in Ohio and entering a college or university in any state. Applicants must be planning to study Latin or Greek. Their high school teacher must be a member of the Ohio Classical Conference. Along with their application, they must submit an official high school transcript, 2 letters of recommendation (including 1 from their high school Latin teacher), and a 1–page statement on their reasons for studying Latin or the classics.

Financial data: The stipend is $1,500 for the first year, $1,000 for the second year, and $500 for the third year.

Duration: Up to 3 years, provided the recipient maintains a GPA of 3.0 or higher.

Number awarded: 1 each year.

Deadline: March of each year.

1439 OKLAHOMA CITY CHAPTER SCHOLARSHIPS

Association for Women in Communications–Oklahoma City Chapter
c/o Mandi Briggs, Byliner Committee Co–Chair
Heritage Trust
2802 West Country Club Drive
P.O. Box 21708
Oklahoma City, OK 73156
Phone: (405) 848–8899; (877) 887–8899; Fax: (405) 848–8805;
Email: mandi@heritagetrust.com
Web: www.okcawc.org/p/2399/Default.aspx

Summary: To provide financial assistance to women from any state studying journalism or a related field at a school in Oklahoma.

Eligibility: Open to women who are residents of any state working on a degree in a communications–related field (e.g., public relations, journalism, advertising, photography) at a 2– or 4–year college or university in Oklahoma. Applicants must submit a 250–word statement explaining why they are applying for the scholarship, why they chose to study communications, their goals after graduation, and related topics. Selection is based on aptitude, interest in preparing for a career in journalism or communications, academic achievement, community service, extracurricular activities, and financial need. Preference is given to student or professional members of the Association of Women in Communications.

Financial data: Stipends range from $1,000 to $1,500.

Duration: 1 year.

Number awarded: Varies each year; recently, 5 of these scholarships were awarded: 1 at $1,500, 2 at $1,250, and 2 at $1,000.

Deadline: April of each year.

1440 OKLAHOMA HERITAGE COUNTY SCHOLARSHIPS

Oklahoma Heritage Association
Attn: Scholarship Committee
1400 Classen Drive
Oklahoma City, OK 73106
Phone: (405) 523–3202; (888) 501–2059; Fax: (405) 235–2714;
Email: gmc@oklahomaheritage.com
Web: oklahomaheritage.com

Summary: To recognize and reward, with college scholarships, high school students in Oklahoma who achieve high scores on a test about the state's history and geography.

Eligibility: Open to students in grades 9–12 at high schools in Oklahoma. Applicants take a 2–hour test on the state's history and geography at their choice of 12 sites around the state. Students in each county who achieve high scores on the test are awarded these scholarships for use at a college, university, community college, or vocational/technical school. Some scholarships may be used only at designated postsecondary institutions in Oklahoma; others may be used at any college or university in the country.

Financial data: Most awards are $1,000; a few are smaller. Funds are held in trust until the winner graduates from high school and enrolls at a postsecondary institution, when they are disbursed directly to that school.

Duration: The competition is held annually.

Number awarded: Varies each year; more than $400,000 in scholarships is awarded each year.

Deadline: March of each year.

1441 $$ OLMSTED SCHOLARS PROGRAM

Landscape Architecture Foundation
Attn: Olmsted Scholarship Program
818 18th Street, N.W., Suite 810
Washington, DC 20006–3520
Phone: (202) 331–7070; Fax: (202) 331–7079;
Email: scholarships@lafoundation.org
Web: www.lafoundation.org/scholarship/olmsted–scholars

Summary: To provide financial assistance to upper–division and graduate students in landscape architecture who demonstrate outstanding potential for leadership.

Eligibility: Open to landscape architecture students in the United States and Canada in the final 2 years of undergraduate study or in graduate school in an LAAB–accredited program. Each institution may nominate 1 student. Nominees must submit a 2–page essay describing their personal development and how it has influenced their direction and vision for the future, how they see their role in advancing sustainable planning and design and fostering human and societal health and well–being, how they would use the funds to advance their leadership in their areas of interest, and how their work could further the mission of the sponsor. Selection is based on the nominee's leadership potential in 1) the advancement of sustainable planning and design; and 2) fostering human and societal benefits, as assessed through a demonstration of leadership and vision, engagement with current issues, critical thinking, communication skill, and personal characteristics and values.

Financial data: The National Olmsted Scholar receives a stipend is $25,000. Finalists receive $1,000.

Duration: 1 year.

Number awarded: 1 National Olmsted Scholar and 4 finalists are selected each year.

Deadline: Nominations must be submitted by February of each year.

1442 OREGON BARBER AND HAIRDRESSER GRANT PROGRAM

Oregon Student Access Commission
Attn: Grants and Scholarships Division
1500 Valley River Drive, Suite 100
P.O. Box 40370
Eugene, OR 97404
Phone: (541) 687–7395; (800) 452–8807, ext. 7395; Fax: (541) 687–7414; TDD: (800) 735–2900;
Email: awardinfo@osac.state.or.us
Web: www.oregonstudentaid.gov/barbers–grant.aspx

Summary: To provide financial assistance to Oregon residents who wish to prepare for a career as a barber or hairdresser.

Eligibility: Open to residents of Oregon who are attending or planning to attend a licensed school of barbering, hair design, cosmetology, or manicure in the state. Applicants must enroll full time in a program that is at least 9 months long or 900 clock hours and must be able to demonstrate significant financial need. Students are not eligible if they are currently in prison, are concurrently enrolled in high school and a beauty or barbering program, or are in default on any prior educational loan.

Financial data: The stipend is $1,000.

Duration: This is a 1–time award.

Number awarded: Approximately 30 to 40 each year.

Deadline: January of each year.

1443 OUTPUTLINKS GRAPHIC ARTS EDUCATORS SCHOLARSHIP

Electronic Document Systems Foundation
Attn: EDSF Scholarship Awards
1845 Precinct Line Road, Suite 212
Hurst, TX 76054
Phone: (817) 849–1145; Fax: (817) 849–1185;
Email: info@edsf.org
Web: www.edsf.org/what_we_do/scholarships/index.html

Summary: To provide financial assistance to undergraduate students at schools in any country who are nominated by a graphic arts educator for studies related to the graphic arts and communications industries.

Eligibility: Open to full–time undergraduate students at 2– and 4–year colleges and universities in any country. Applicants must be interested in preparing for a career in the graphic arts and communications industry, including graphic designer, illustrator, color scientist, print production, prepress imaging specialist, workflow specialist, document preparation, production and/or document distribution, content management, e–commerce, imaging science, printing, web authoring, electronic publishing, archiving, or security. They must be nominated by a graphic arts educator and have a GPA of 3.0 or higher. Along with their application, they must submit 2 essays on assigned topics that change annually but relate to the graphic arts and communication industries. Selection is based on the essays, academic excellence, participation in school activities, community service, honors and organizational affiliations, education goals, and recommendations; financial need is not considered.

Financial data: The stipend is $1,000.

Duration: 1 year.

Number awarded: 1 each year.

Deadline: April of each year.

1444 OUTPUTLINKS INDUSTRY ANALYSTS SCHOLARSHIPS HONORING STEVE REYNOLDS

Electronic Document Systems Foundation
Attn: EDSF Scholarship Awards
1845 Precinct Line Road, Suite 212
Hurst, TX 76054
Phone: (817) 849–1145; Fax: (817) 849–1185;
Email: info@edsf.org
Web: www.edsf.org/what_we_do/scholarships/index.html

Summary: To provide financial assistance to undergraduate students at schools in any country who are nominated by analysts or media representatives for studies related to the graphic arts and corporate communications industries.

Eligibility: Open to full–time undergraduate students at 2– and 4–year colleges and universities in any country. Applicants must be interested in preparing for a career in the graphic arts and corporate communications industry, including graphic designer, illustrator, color scientist, print production, prepress imaging specialist, workflow specialist, document preparation, production and/or document distribution, content management, e–commerce, imaging science, printing, web authoring, electronic publishing, archiving, or security. They must be nominated by corporate analysts or media representatives and have a GPA of 3.0 or higher. Along with their application, they must submit 2 essays on assigned topics that change annually but relate to the graphic arts and communication industries. Selection is based on the essays, academic excellence, participation in school activities, community service, honors and organizational affiliations, education goals, and recommendations; financial need is not considered.

Financial data: The stipend is $1,000.

Duration: 1 year.

Number awarded: 2 each year.

Deadline: April of each year.

1445 OUTPUTLINKS SUSTAINABILITY/STEWARDSHIP AWARD

Electronic Document Systems Foundation
Attn: EDSF Scholarship Awards
1845 Precinct Line Road, Suite 212

Hurst, TX 76054
Phone: (817) 849–1145; Fax: (817) 849–1185;
Email: info@edsf.org
Web: www.edsf.org/what_we_do/scholarships/index.html

Summary: To provide financial assistance to undergraduate and graduate students from any country who are working on a degree in the field of document management and graphic communications, especially those who are involved in environmental sustainability project or who have a record of leadership and community involvement.

Eligibility: Open to full–time undergraduate and graduate students from any country who demonstrate a strong interest in preparing for a career in the document management and graphic communications industry, including computer science and engineering (e.g., web design, webmaster, software development, materials engineer, applications specialist, information technology designer, systems analyst); graphic and media communications (e.g., graphic designer, illustrator, color scientist, print production, prepress imaging specialist, workflow specialist, document preparation, production and/or document distribution, content management, e–commerce, imaging science, printing, web authoring, electronic publishing, archiving, security); or business (e.g., sales, marketing, trade shows, customer service, project or product development, management). Preference is given to graduate students and upper–division undergraduates, but freshmen and sophomores who can show interest, experience, and/or commitment to the document management and graphic communication industry are encouraged to apply. Special consideration is given to students who 1) are involved in environmental sustainability projects; or 2) can demonstrate leadership and community involvement through school, volunteer, and community activities. Applicants must have a GPA of 3.0 or higher. Along with their application, they must submit 2 essays on assigned topics that change annually but relate to the document management and graphic communication industries. Selection is based on the essays, academic excellence, participation in school activities, community service, honors and organizational affiliations, education goals, and recommendations; financial need is not considered.

Financial data: The stipend is $1,000.

Duration: 1 year.

Number awarded: 1 each year.

Deadline: April of each year.

1446 $$ OUTPUTLINKS WOMAN OF DISTINCTION AWARD

Electronic Document Systems Foundation
Attn: EDSF Scholarship Awards
1845 Precinct Line Road, Suite 212
Hurst, TX 76054
Phone: (817) 849–1145; Fax: (817) 849–1185;
Email: info@edsf.org
Web: www.edsf.org/what_we_do/scholarships/index.html

Summary: To provide financial assistance to female undergraduate and graduate students from any country interested in preparing for a career in document management and graphic communications.

Eligibility: Open to full–time female undergraduate and graduate students from any country who demonstrate a strong interest in preparing for a career in the document management and graphic communications industry, including computer science and engineering (e.g., web design, webmaster, software development, materials engineer, applications specialist, information technology designer, systems analyst); graphic and media communications (e.g., graphic designer, illustrator, color scientist, print production, prepress imaging specialist, workflow specialist, document preparation, production and/or document distribution, content management, e–commerce, imaging science, printing, web authoring, electronic publishing, archiving, security); or business (e.g., sales, marketing, trade shows, customer service, project or product development, management). Preference is given to graduate students and upper–division undergraduates, but freshmen and sophomores who can show interest, experience, and/or commitment to the document management and graphic communication industry are encouraged to apply. Applicants must have a GPA of 3.0 or higher. Along with their application, they must submit 2 essays on assigned topics that change annually but relate to the document management and graphic communication industries. Selection is based on the essays, academic excellence, participation in school activities, community service, honors and organizational affiliations, education goals, and recommendations; financial need is not considered.

Financial data: The stipend is $5,000.

Duration: 1 year.

Number awarded: 1 each year.

Deadline: April of each year.

1447 $ OVERSEAS PRESS CLUB FOUNDATION SCHOLARSHIPS

Overseas Press Club
Attn: Director, Overseas Press Club Foundation
40 West 45th Street
New York, NY 10036
Phone: (212) 626–9220; Fax: (212) 626–9210;
Email: foundation@opcofamerica.org
Web: opcofamerica.org/overseas–press–club–foundation

Summary: To provide financial assistance to undergraduate and graduate students who are preparing for a career as a foreign correspondent.

Eligibility: Open to undergraduate and graduate students who are studying in the United States and are interested in working as a foreign correspondent after graduation. Applicants are invited to submit an essay (up to 500 words) on an area of the world or an international topic that is in keeping with their interest. Also, they should attach a 1–page autobiographical letter that addresses such questions as how they developed their interest in that particular part of the world or issue and how they would use a scholarship to further their journalistic ambitions. U.S. citizenship is not required.

Financial data: The stipend is $2,000.

Duration: 1 year.

Number awarded: 12 each year.

Deadline: November of each year.

1448 P. BUCKLEY MOSS ENDOWED SCHOLARSHIP

P. Buckley Moss Society
74 Poplar Grove Lane
Mathews, VA 23109
Phone: (540) 932–1728; (800) 430–1320;
Email: society@mosssociety.org
Web: www.mosssociety.org/page.php?id=69

Summary: To provide financial assistance to high school seniors with language–related learning disabilities who plan to study visual arts in college.

Eligibility: Open to high school seniors with language–related learning disabilities and visual arts talent. They must be nominated by a member of the P. Buckley Moss Society. Nominees must be planning to attend a 4–year college or university or a 2–year community college and prepare for a career in a visual art field. The nomination packets must include evidence of financial need, verification of a language–related learning disability from a counselor or case manager, a high school transcript, 2 letters of recommendation, and 3 essays by the nominees: 1) themselves; 2) their learning disability, how it has challenged them, specific strategies they have used to cope, and its effect on their lives; and 3) where they intend to go to school and why, how they plan to use their artistic talent, and what they see themselves doing with their art in 10 years.

Financial data: The stipend is $1,500. Funds are paid to the recipient's college or university.

Duration: 1 year; may be renewed for up to 3 additional years.

Number awarded: 1 each year.

Deadline: March of each year.

1449 PACIFIC NORTHWEST CHAPTER AIWF SCHOLARSHIP

American Institute of Wine & Food–Pacific Northwest Chapter
c/o Brian Steinmetz, Chapter Chair
2104 N.W. Boulder Way Drive
Issaquah, WA 98027–5643
Phone: (425) 427–8608;
Email: bsteinmetz100@hotmail.com
Web: www.aiwf.org/pnw/scholarships.html

Summary: To provide financial assistance to students in Washington working on a degree in the culinary arts.

Eligibility: Open to students enrolled in a Washington accredited culinary or winemaking arts program who have been residents of the state for at least 2 years. Applicants must have a GPA of at least 3.0. Selection is based on merit, as measured by a resume, references, and GPA.

Financial data: The stipend is $1,500.

Duration: 1 year.

Number awarded: 4 each year.

Deadline: Deadline not specified.

1450 $$ PALADIN BUILDING SCIENCES SCHOLARSHIP

Kentucky Community and Technical College System
Attn: Financial Aid
300 North Main Street
Versailles, KY 40383
Phone: (859) 256–3100; (877) 528–2748 (within KY)
Web: www.kctcs.edu

Summary: To provide financial assistance to students transferring from an institution within the Kentucky Community and Technical College System (KCTCS) to a 4–year university in Kentucky and majoring in the building sciences.

Eligibility: Open to Kentucky residents who are transferring from a KCTCS institution to a 4–year college or university in Kentucky. Applicants must be majoring in architecture or engineering (civil, electrical, mechanical, or structural). They must have a GPA of 3.0 or higher. Applications must be submitted through the financial aid office at their local community college.

Financial data: The stipend is $5,000 per year.

Duration: 1 year.

Number awarded: 1 or more each year.

Deadline: Each college sets its own deadline.

1451 $$ PASSION FOR FASHION COMPETITION

The Art Institutes International, Inc.
Free Markets Center
210 Sixth Avenue, 33rd Floor
Pittsburgh, PA 15222–2603
Phone: (412) 995–7685; (888) 624–0300; Fax: (412) 918–2598
Web: www.artinstitutes.edu

Summary: To recognize and reward (with scholarships to participating Art Institutes) high school seniors who participate in competitions in fashion design and in fashion marketing and merchandising.

Eligibility: Open to high school seniors who are planning to attend a participating Art Institute to study either fashion design or fashion marketing and merchandising and retail management. Applicants in the fashion design category must submit 1) a finished, originally designed evening wear garment product; 2) a description of their design process summary, from original idea to finished product; and 3) an 600–word essay outlining why their fashion entry is unique and innovative and explaining their interest and motivation for a career in fashion. Applicants in the fashion marketing and merchandising and retail management category must submit 1) a finished and original fashion marketing, fashion merchandising, or retail management product or plan in categories of merchandising of a fashion product line or brand, marketing of a fashion product line or brand, or a store concept; and 2) a 600–word description of their product or plan that includes a mission statement, a description of how they aspire to contribute to the fashion industry, a review of influences on their entry, evidence of marketing research, and a statement of how the plan or concept would be executed. All applicants must have a GPA of 2.0 or higher. They first enter local competitions, from which winners advance to the national finals.

Financial data: Each local winner receives a $3,000 scholarship to be applied to tuition at the Art Institute of their choice. The national winners in each category receive a half–tuition scholarship at the Art Institute of their choice as a grand prize, a $5,000 tuition scholarship as a second prize, and a $4,000 tuition scholarship as a third prize. The grand prize winners in each category also earn a trip to New York that includes lunch and a $500 shopping spree at DKNY with a *Seventeen* style professional and a $500 gift care to shop anywhere in the city.

Duration: The competitions are held annually.

Number awarded: 22 Art Institutes accept entries for the fashion design category and 49 for the fashion marketing and merchandising and retail management category. From among those local winners, 6 national winners (3 in each category) are selected.

Deadline: January of each year.

1452 PAUL AND HELEN L. GRAUER SCHOLARSHIP

American Radio Relay League
Attn: ARRL Foundation
225 Main Street
Newington, CT 06111–1494
Phone: (860) 594–0397; Fax: (860) 594–0259;
Email: foundation@arrl.org
Web: www.arrl.org/scholarship–descriptions

Summary: To provide financial assistance to licensed radio amateurs, especially those from designated midwestern states, who are interested in working on an undergraduate or graduate degree, preferably in electronics or communications.

Eligibility: Open to undergraduate or graduate students at accredited institutions who are licensed radio amateurs of the novice class or higher. Preference is given to students who are 1) residents of Iowa, Kansas, Missouri, or Nebraska and attending schools in those states; and 2) working on a degree in electronics, communications, or related fields. Applicants must submit an essay on the role amateur radio has played in their lives and provide documentation of financial need.

Financial data: The stipend is $1,000.

Duration: 1 year.

Number awarded: 1 each year.

Deadline: January of each year.

1453 $$ PAUL JENSEN MEMORIAL SCHOLARSHIP

New York Schools Insurance Reciprocal
Attn: Executive Director
333 Earle Ovington Boulevard, Suite 1030
Uniondale, NY 11553–3624
Phone: (516) 393–2329; (800) 476–9747;
Email: jgoncalves@nysir.org
Web: nysir.org/nysir–student–asbo–scholarships

Summary: To provide financial assistance to seniors graduating from high schools that subscribe to the New York Schools Insurance Reciprocal (NYSIR) who plan to attend college in any state and study design.

Eligibility: Open to seniors graduating from NYSIR–subscriber high schools who have excelled in design. Applicants must be planning to attend a college or university in any state and continue their study of design. Along with their application, they must submit a 650–word essay on a way they would design, or adapt an existing design, for a specific purpose; how this design or adaptation would be accomplished; and why this design or adaptation would be useful. Financial need is not considered in the selection process.

Financial data: Stipends are $5,000 or $3,000.

Duration: 1 year.

Number awarded: 2 each year: 1 at $5,000 and 1 at $3,000.

Deadline: March of each year.

1454 $ PAUL K. TAFF SCHOLARSHIP AWARD

Connecticut Broadcasters Association
Attn: Scholarships
90 South Park Street
Willimantic, CT 06226
Phone: (860) 633–5031; Fax: (860) 456–5688;
Email: mcrice@prodigy.net
Web: www.ctba.org/page.cfm?page=17

Summary: To provide financial assistance to Connecticut residents who are interested in attending college in any state to prepare for a career in broadcasting.

Eligibility: Open to Connecticut residents who are entering their first, second, third, or fourth year at a 2– or 4–year college, university, or technical school in any state. Applicants must be majoring in broadcasting, communications, marketing, or a related field. Selection is based on academic achievement, community service, goals in the chosen field, and financial need.

Financial data: The stipend is $2,500 per year.

Duration: 4 years.

Number awarded: 1 each year.

Deadline: March of each year.

1455 PAUL STEPHEN LIM ASIAN–AMERICAN PLAYWRITING AWARD

John F. Kennedy Center for the Performing Arts
Education Department
Attn: Kennedy Center American College Theater Festival
2700 F Street, N.W.
Washington, DC 20566
Phone: (202) 416–8857; Fax: (202) 416–8860;
Email: KCACTF@kennedy–center.org
Web: www.kcactf.org/KCACTF.ORG_NATIONAL/Kanin_Playwriting.html

Summary: To recognize and reward outstanding Asian America student playwrights.

Eligibility: Open to students at any accredited junior or senior college in the United States, provided their college agrees to participate in the Kennedy Center American College Theater Festival (KCACTF). Undergraduate students must be carrying at least 6 semester hours, graduate students must be enrolled in at least 3 semester hours, and continuing part–time students must be enrolled in a regular degree or certificate program. This award is presented to the author of the best play on any subject who is of Asian heritage.

Financial data: The winning playwright receives a cash award of $1,000 for a full–length play or $500 for a 1–act play. The award includes an all–expense paid professional development opportunity.

Duration: The award is presented annually.

Number awarded: 2 students and 2 sponsoring institutions receive awards each year.

Deadline: November of each year.

1456 PAULA VOGEL AWARD IN PLAYWRITING

John F. Kennedy Center for the Performing Arts
Education Department
Attn: Kennedy Center American College Theater Festival
2700 F Street, N.W.
Washington, DC 20566
Phone: (202) 416–8857; Fax: (202) 416–8860;
Email: KCACTF@kennedy–center.org
Web: www.kcactf.org/KCACTF.ORG_NATIONAL/Kanin_Playwriting.html

Summary: To recognize and reward the student authors of plays that relate to gender, diversity, and sexual orientation.

Eligibility: Open to students at any accredited junior or senior college in the United States, provided their college agrees to participate in the Kennedy Center American College Theater Festival (KCACTF). Undergraduate students must be carrying at least 6 semester hours, graduate students must be enrolled in at least 3 semester hours, and continuing part–time students must be enrolled in a regular degree or certificate program. This award is presented to the best student–written script that explores issues of gender, diversity, and sexual orientation.

Financial data: Awards are $1,000 for first place and $500 for second place. The first–place winner also receives an all–expense paid professional development opportunity.

Duration: The award is presented annually.

Number awarded: 2 each year.

Deadline: November of each year.

1457 $ PCI STUDENT ARCHITECTURAL DESIGN COMPETITION

Precast/Prestressed Concrete Institute
Attn: Director of Research and Development
200 West Adams Street, Suite 2100
Chicago, IL 60606
Phone: (312) 360–3213; Fax: (312) 621–1114;
Email: rbecker@pci.org
Web: www.pci.org/cms/index.cfm/education/arch_design

Summary: To recognize and reward architecture students who submit outstanding entries in a design competition utilizing precast and prestressed concrete.

Eligibility: Open to students currently enrolled in an architecture–related program, including landscape architecture, construction management, interior design, or other program with an emphasis on the build environment. Applicants submit drawings of projects (either site–specific or non–site–specific) that make 100% utilization of precast and prestressed concrete. Selection is based on such design criteria as ability to design creatively and integrate technically architectural and structural total precast concrete systems; utilization of the many forms of precast concrete in building design and site development; elegant and expressive use of precast concrete as a material; response to specific architectural concepts of the program; integration of landscape features, site lighting, vehicular storage, waste management, pedestrian access, and other exterior features; level of attention paid to preserving and enhancing the surrounding environment; effectiveness of the solution in meeting the stated goals of the program; and ability to integrate functional aspects of the challenge in an appropriate manner.

Financial data: Prizes are $2,500 for the first–place team, $1,500 for second–place, and $750 for third–place. The adviser of the first–place team receives $750, of the second–place team $500, and of the third–place team $250.

Duration: The competition is held annually.

Number awarded: 3 student prizes and 3 adviser prizes are awarded each year.

Deadline: May of each year.

1458 $$ PEERMUSIC LATIN SCHOLARSHIP

Broadcast Music Inc.
Attn: BMI Foundation, Inc.
7 World Trade Center
250 Greenwich Street
New York, NY 10007–0030
Phone: (212) 220–3000;
Email: latinscholarship@bmifoundation.org
Web: www.bmifoundation.org/program/peermusic_latin_scholarship

Summary: To recognize and reward students at colleges and universities who submit outstanding songs or instrumental works in a Latin genre.

Eligibility: Open to students between 16 and 24 years of age enrolled at colleges and universities in the United States and Puerto Rico. Applicants may not have had any musical work commercially recorded or distributed. They must submit an original song or instrumental work in a Latin genre. The entry must be submitted on CD or MP3, accompanied by 3 typed copies of the lyric.

Financial data: The award is $5,000.

Duration: The award is presented annually.

Number awarded: 1 each year.

Deadline: February of each year.

1459 $$ PHOENIX POST SAME SCHOLARSHIPS

Society of American Military Engineers–Phoenix Post
c/o Michelle Obregon
The Durrant Group
410 North 44th Street, Suite 800
Phoenix, AZ 85008
Phone: (602) 275–6830; Fax: (602) 275–4331;
Email: mobregon@durrant.com
Web: www.samephxaz.org/about–same/education–and–mentoring

Summary: To provide financial assistance to residents of Arizona who are interested in working on an undergraduate degree in a field related to the built environment at a college in the state.

Eligibility: Open to residents of Arizona who are either graduating high school seniors or college freshmen or sophomores enrolled or planning to enroll at an institution of higher learning in the state. Applicants must be working on or planning to work on a degree in engineering or a similar field related to the built environment (e.g., construction, architecture, civil engineering, electrical/mechanical/structural engineering for facilities). They must have a GPA of 3.0 or higher. Along with their application, they must submit brief essays on what distinguishes them from other candidates and why they are preparing for a career in engineering, architecture, or related sciences. Selection is based on those essays, academic achievement, leadership ability, and community service. U.S. citizenship is required.

Financial data: Stipends range from $1,500 to $5,000.

Duration: 1 year.

Number awarded: Varies each year; recently, 4 of these scholarships were awarded: 1 at $5,000, 1 at $3,000, and 2 at $1,500.

Deadline: April of each year.

1460 $$ PIANOARTS NORTH AMERICAN BIENNIAL COMPETITION

PianoArts
Attn: Sue Medford
2642 North Summit Avenue
Milwaukee, WI 53211–3849
Phone: (414) 962–3055; Fax: (414) 962–3211;
Email: info@pianoarts.org
Web: www.pianoarts.org/competition.html

Summary: To recognize and reward outstanding pianists between 15 and 20 years of age.

Eligibility: Open to pianists between the age of 15 and 20. In the preliminary round, contestants perform on DVD a solo of their choice and the first movement of a selected concerto. The 12 semifinalists are asked to come to Milwaukee where they perform solo recitals. Based on those recitals, 3 finalists are chosen to perform in the prize round. Those finalists perform concertos by Beethoven, Mendelssohn, Schumann, Chopin, or Mozart with the Milwaukee Chamber Orchestra to compete for prizes. Separate competitions for duos of piano and violin and for piano and cello are also conducted.

Financial data: Awards are $10,000 for first, $6,000 for second, and $4,000 for third. Winners have an opportunity to win a scholarship to attend the International Keyboard Institute and Festival. Other awards include $1,000 for the best performance of a prelude and fugue by Johann Sebastian Bach, $750 for the best contestant from Wisconsin, $500 for the best performance of a duo, $500 for the audience communication prize, and $300 for the junior jury prize.

Duration: The competition is held biennially, in even–numbered years.

Number awarded: 3 major prizes and at least 5 smaller prizes are awarded each year.

Deadline: Initial applications must be submitted by January of even–numbered years. Preliminary DVDs are due the following February. The semifinal round and finals take place in June.

1461 PICA/TREADAWAY SCHOLARSHIP

Printing Industry of the Carolinas Foundation, Inc.
Attn: Vice President, Education and Member Services
3601 Rose Lake Drive
P.O. Box 19488
Charlotte, NC 28219–9488
Phone: (704) 357–1150; (800) 849–7422; Fax: (704) 357–1154;
Email: cjepps@picanet.org
Web: www.picanet.org/about/foundation.asp

Summary: To provide financial assistance to community college students who are working on a graphic communications degree in North Carolina or South Carolina.
Eligibility: Open to students working on a graphic communications degree at designated community colleges in North or South Carolina. Candidates must be nominated by their school.
Financial data: The stipend is $500 for the first year and $1,000 for the second year.
Duration: 1 year; may be renewed for 1 additional year, provided the recipients improve their overall and major GPA.
Number awarded: 1 each year.
Deadline: Deadline not specified.

1462 PIEF GENERAL SCHOLARSHIPS

Printing Industries of Ohio and Northern Kentucky
Attn: Printing Industries Education Funds, Inc.
88 Dorcester Square
P.O. Box 819
Westerville, OH 43086–0819
Phone: (614) 794–2300; (888) 576–1971; Fax: (614) 794–2049;
Email: info@pianko.org
Web: www.pianko.org/aws/PIAKO/pt/sp/scholarships

Summary: To provide financial assistance to residents of Kentucky and Ohio who are interested in preparing for a career in the graphic communications industry.
Eligibility: Open to residents of Kentucky and Ohio who are high school seniors, high school graduates, or college freshmen, sophomores, or juniors and have a GPA of 2.5 or higher. Applicants must 1) be enrolled at a 2– or 4–year college in northern Kentucky or Ohio with an accredited graphic communications program, or 2) be a professional working in an Ohio or northern Kentucky graphic communications company seeking to increase their industry knowledge. They must be preparing for a career in the graphic communications industry, preferably in Ohio or northern Kentucky. Financial need is not considered in the selection process.
Financial data: The stipend is generally $1,000.
Duration: 1 year; may be renewed provided the recipient maintains a GPA of 3.0 or higher.
Number awarded: Varies each year; recently 22 of these scholarships were awarded.
Deadline: February of each year.

1463 PISCATAQUA POST SAME SCHOLARSHIPS

Society of American Military Engineers–Piscataqua Post
c/o Noah Elwood, Post Secretary
Public Works Officer
Code 910, Building 59
Portsmouth Naval Shipyard
Portsmouth, NH 03804–5000
Phone: (207) 438–1000;
Email: nelwood@appledoremarine.com
Web: posts.same.org/piscataqua

Summary: To provide financial assistance to residents of Maine, New Hampshire, and Vermont, especially those with ties to the military, who are majoring in designated fields at their state universities.
Eligibility: Open to residents of Maine, New Hampshire, and Vermont who are sophomores or juniors at any campus of the University of Maine, the University of New Hampshire, or the University of Vermont. Applicants must be majoring in architecture, engineering, environmental sciences or a related field and have a GPA of 2.75 or higher. They must apply through their university. Preference is given to students who are enrolled in ROTC, have prior U.S. military service and/or public service, or have an immediate family member currently serving in the armed forces. Along with their application, they must submit a 1–page essay on why they deserve this scholarship. Selection is based on that essay; academic achievement; extracurricular, volunteer, community, and public service; and financial need. U.S. citizenship is required.
Financial data: The stipend is $1,500.
Duration: 1 year.
Number awarded: Up to 2 each year.
Deadline: Each university sets its own deadline, but they must forward the applications to the sponsor by April of each year.

1464 $ PLANET AEF SCHOLARSHIPS

Professional Landcare Network
Attn: PLANET Academic Excellence Foundation
950 Herndon Parkway, Suite 450
Herndon, VA 20170
Phone: (703) 736–9666; (800) 395–ALCA; Fax: (703) 736–9668;
Email: scholarship@landcarenetwork.org
Web: www.landcarenetwork.org/foundation/scholarships/about.cfm

Summary: To provide financial assistance to students at colleges and universities that have a connection to the Professional Landcare Network (PLANET).
Eligibility: Open to students at colleges and universities that 1) have an accredited PLANET landscape contracting curriculum; 2) have a PLANET student chapter; and/or 3) participate in PLANET student career days activities. Applicants must provide information on awards, honors, and scholarships received in high school or college; high school, college, and community activities related to horticulture; PLANET events attended; work experience; and brief essays on what they have learned about financial management as part of their education that will help them in their career, how their landscape industry–related curriculum has helped them in achieving their career goals, the kind of training and work experience they will need to attain their goals, their plan to attain more leadership and human relations skills, their reasons for desiring the scholarship, their career objectives as they relate to the field of landscape contracting and horticulture, and where they see their career 5 years after graduation.
Financial data: Stipends range from $500 to $2,500.
Duration: 1 year.
Number awarded: Varies each year; recently, 62 of these scholarships were awarded: 4 at $2,500, 1 at $2,000, 1 at $1,500, 2 at $1,200, 53 at $1,000, and 1 at $500.
Deadline: November of each year.

1465 $ PLAYBOY COLLEGE FICTION CONTEST

Playboy Magazine
Attn: Fiction Contest
9346 Civic Center Drive
Beverly Hills, CA 90210
Email: support@submittable.com
Web: playboymagazine.submittable.com/

Summary: To recognize and reward outstanding fiction written by undergraduate or graduate students.
Eligibility: Open to undergraduate and graduate students of any age. They are invited to enter this contest. Applicants must submit a work of fiction no more than 25 pages in length.
Financial data: First prize is $3,000 and publication in *Playboy* magazine; second prize is $500 and a 1–year subscription to *Playboy;* third prize is $250 and a 1–year subscription to *Playboy.*
Duration: The competition is held annually.
Number awarded: 3 prizes are awarded each year.
Deadline: February of each year.

1466 POLANKI COLLEGE ACHIEVEMENT AWARDS

Summary: To recognize and reward upper–division and graduate students in Wisconsin who have a Polish connection and demonstrate academic excellence.
See Listing #780.

1467 $$ PRINT AND GRAPHICS SCHOLARSHIP FOUNDATION SCHOLARSHIPS

Print and Graphics Scholarship Foundation
Attn: Scholarship Competition

200 Deer Run Road
Sewickley, PA 15143–2600
Phone: (412) 259–1740; (800) 910–GATF; Fax: (412) 741–2311;
Email: pgsf@gatf.org
Web: www.gain.net

Summary: To provide financial assistance to college students interested in preparing for a career in the graphic communications industries.

Eligibility: Open to high school seniors, high school graduates who have not yet started college, and currently–enrolled college students. Applicants must be interested in a career in the graphic communications industry and be willing to attend school on a full–time basis (scholarships are not awarded for part–time study). High school students must take the SAT or ACT and arrange for their test scores to be sent to the Graphic Arts Technical Foundation. Current college students are requested to submit transcripts and a letter of recommendation from their major area adviser. College freshmen also need to submit a high school transcript. Semifinalists are interviewed. Selection is based on academic records and honors, extracurricular activities, and letters of recommendation.

Financial data: Stipends range from $1,000 to $5,000 per year. Funds are paid directly to the college selected by the award winner; the college will be authorized to draw upon the award to pay for tuition and other fees.

Duration: 1 year; may be renewed for up to 3 additional years if the recipient maintains a GPA of 3.0 or higher and full–time enrollment.

Number awarded: Approximately 200 per year.

Deadline: February of each year for high school seniors; March of each year for students already in college.

1468 $$ PROFILE IN COURAGE ESSAY CONTEST

John F. Kennedy Library Foundation
Attn: Profile in Courage Essay Contest
Columbia Point
Boston, MA 02125–3313
Phone: (617) 514–1550; Fax: (617) 436–3395;
Email: profiles@nara.gov
Web: www.jfklibrary.org

Summary: To recognize and reward high school authors of essays on public officials who have demonstrated political courage.

Eligibility: Open to 1) U.S. students in grades 9–12 attending public, private, parochial, or home schools; 2) U.S. students under 20 years of age enrolled in a high school correspondence course or GED program in any of the 50 states, the District of Columbia, or the U.S. territories; and 3) U.S. citizens attending schools overseas. Applicants must submit an essay, up to 1,000 words, that identifies an elected public official in the United States, either serving currently or since 1956, who is acting or has acted courageously to address a political issue at the local, state, national, or international level. Selection is based on content of the essay (55%) and presentation (45%).

Financial data: The first–place winner receives $10,000 ($5,000 in cash and $5,000 in a John Hancock Freedom 529 College Savings Plan), the second–place winner receives $1,000, and the other finalists receive $500. The nominating teacher of the first–place winner receives $500 for school projects encouraging student leadership and civic engagement.

Duration: The awards are presented annually.

Number awarded: 7 each year: 1 first place, 1 second place, and 5 other finalists.

Deadline: January of each year.

1469 "PROJECT LIFESAVER" SCHOLARSHIP CONTEST

Chapel of Four Chaplains
The Navy Yard, Building 649
1201 Constitution Avenue
Philadelphia, PA 19112–1307
Phone: (215) 218–1943; (866) 400–0975; Fax: (215) 218–1949;
Email: chapel@fourchaplains.org
Web: www.fourchaplains.org/programs.html

Summary: To recognize and reward, with college scholarships outstanding high school senior teams that develop projects related to the work of the sponsoring organization.

Eligibility: Open to seniors in public and private high schools. They are invited to form teams to participate in this program. A team consists of a team leader, 5 team members, and a faculty adviser. The team develops a project on a theme that changes periodically; recently, students were invited to identify a compelling problem, need, or unresolved conflict (e.g., racial discrimination, religious intolerance, community injustice, public indifference, civic discord, societal ignorance) that, through caring intervention, can be transformed and corrected. Selection is based on originality and creativity of the project, community impact and involvement, organizational skills, and correct grammar and spelling in the project paper.

Financial data: The prizes for the winning project include a $1,000 scholarship to the student leader, $750 scholarships to each of the 5 team members, and $1,000 to the faculty adviser.

Duration: The competition is held annually.

Number awarded: 1 project receives an award each year.

Deadline: December of each year.

1470 PUBLIC RELATIONS SOCIETY OF AMERICA DIVERSITY MULTICULTURAL SCHOLARSHIPS

Public Relations Student Society of America
Attn: Vice President of Member Services
33 Maiden Lane, 11th Floor
New York, NY 10038–5150
Phone: (212) 460–1474; Fax: (212) 995–0757;
Email: prssa@prsa.org
Web: www.prssa.org/scholarships_competitions/individual

Summary: To provide financial assistance to minority college students who are interested in preparing for a career in public relations.

Eligibility: Open to minority (African American/Black, Hispanic/Latino, Asian, Native American, Alaskan Native, or Pacific Islander) students who are at least juniors at an accredited 4–year college or university. Applicants must be enrolled full time, be able to demonstrate financial need, and have a GPA of 3.0 or higher. Membership in the Public Relations Student Society of America is preferred but not required. A major or minor in public relations is preferred; students who attend a school that does not offer a public relations degree or program must be enrolled in a communications degree program (e.g., journalism, mass communications).

Financial data: The stipend is $1,500.

Duration: 1 year.

Number awarded: 2 each year.

Deadline: May of each year.

1471 $ QUESTEX MEDIA GROUP SCHOLARSHIP

Electronic Document Systems Foundation
Attn: EDSF Scholarship Awards
1845 Precinct Line Road, Suite 212
Hurst, TX 76054
Phone: (817) 849–1145; Fax: (817) 849–1185;
Email: info@edsf.org
Web: www.edsf.org/what_we_do/scholarships/index.html

Summary: To provide financial assistance to undergraduate and graduate students from any country who are working on a degree in the field of document management and graphic communications, especially those who are interested in journalism, trade show management, or marketing communications.

Eligibility: Open to full–time undergraduate and graduate students from any country who demonstrate a strong interest in preparing for a career in the document management and graphic communications industry, including computer science and engineering (e.g., web design, webmaster, software development, materials engineer, applications specialist, information technology designer, systems analyst); graphic and media communications (e.g., graphic designer, illustrator, color scientist, print production, prepress imaging specialist, workflow specialist, document preparation, production and/or document distribution, content management, e–commerce, imaging science, printing, web authoring, electronic publishing, archiving, security); or business (e.g., sales, marketing, trade shows, customer service, project or product development, management). Preference is given to graduate students and upper–division undergraduates, but freshmen and sophomores who can show interest, experience, and/or commitment to the document management and graphic communication industry are encouraged to apply. Special consideration is given to students who are preparing for a career in journalism, trade show management, or marketing communications. Applicants must have a GPA of 3.0 or higher. Along with their application, they must submit 2 essays on assigned topics that change annually but relate to the document management and graphic communication industries. Selection is based on the essays, academic excellence, participation in school activities, community service, honors and organizational affiliations, education goals, and recommendations; financial need is not considered.

Financial data: The stipend is $2,000.

Duration: 1 year.

Number awarded: 1 each year.

Deadline: April of each year.

1472 $$ R. REID VANCE SCHOLARSHIP

Printing Industries of Ohio and Northern Kentucky
Attn: Printing Industries Education Funds, Inc.
88 Dorcester Square
P.O. Box 819
Westerville, OH 43086–0819
Phone: (614) 794–2300; (888) 576–1971; Fax: (614) 794–2049;
Email: info@pianko.org
Web: www.pianko.org/aws/PIAKO/pt/sp/scholarships

Summary: To provide financial assistance to high school seniors in Kentucky and Ohio who are interested in preparing for a career in the graphic communications industry.

Eligibility: Open to seniors graduating from high schools in Kentucky and Ohio with a GPA of 2.5 or higher. Applicants must be planning to attend a college or university with a graphic communications program approved by the Printing Industries Education Funds (PIEF). They must be preparing for a career in the graphic communications industry, preferably in Ohio or northern Kentucky. Financial need is not considered in the selection process.

Financial data: The stipend is $5,000.

Duration: 1 year.

Number awarded: 1 or 2 each year.

Deadline: February of each year.

1473 $ RADIO TELEVISION DIGITAL NEWS FOUNDATION PRESIDENTS' SCHOLARSHIPS

Radio Television Digital News Foundation
Attn: Programs, Awards, and Membership Manager
529 14th Street, N.W., Suite 425
Washington, DC 20045
Phone: (202) 725–8318; Fax: (202) 223–4007;
Email: katies@rtdna.org
Web: www.rtdna.org/pages/education/scholarship–info.php

Summary: To provide financial assistance to undergraduate students who are preparing for a career in electronic journalism.

Eligibility: Open to sophomores, juniors, and seniors who are enrolled full time in electronic journalism at a college or university where such a major is offered. Applicants must submit 1 to 3 examples of their journalistic skills on audio CD or DVD (no more than 15 minutes total, accompanied by scripts); a description of their role on each story and a list of who worked on each story and what they did; a 1–page statement explaining why they are preparing for a career in electronic journalism with reference to their specific career preference (radio, television, online, reporting, producing, or newsroom management); a resume; and a letter of reference from their dean or faculty sponsor explaining why they are a good candidate for the award and certifying that they have at least 1 year of school remaining.

Financial data: The stipend is $2,500.

Duration: 1 year.

Number awarded: 2 each year.

Deadline: May of each year.

1474 $ RAIN BIRD INTELLIGENT USE OF WATER SCHOLARSHIP

Landscape Architecture Foundation
Attn: Leadership in Landscape Scholarship Program
818 18th Street, N.W., Suite 810
Washington, DC 20006–3520
Phone: (202) 331–7070; Fax: (202) 331–7079;
Email: scholarships@lafoundation.org
Web: www.lafoundation.org

Summary: To provide financial assistance to landscape architecture, horticulture, and irrigation science students who demonstrate commitment to those professions.

Eligibility: Open to landscape architecture, horticulture, and irrigation science students in the final 2 years of undergraduate study and in need of financial assistance. Applicants must submit a 300–word essay describing their career goals and explaining how they will contribute to the advancement of the profession of landscape architecture, horticulture, or irrigation science. Selection is based on demonstrated commitment to the profession, extracurricular activities, and scholastic record.

Financial data: The stipend is $2,500.

Number awarded: 1 each year.

Deadline: February of each year.

1475 RALPH V. "ANDY" ANDERSON–K0NL SCHOLARSHIP

Foundation for Amateur Radio, Inc.
Attn: Scholarship Committee
P.O. Box 911
Columbia, MD 21044–0911
Phone: (410) 552–2652; Fax: (410) 981–5146;
Email: dave.prestel@gmail.com
Web: www.farweb.org/scholarships

Summary: To provide funding to licensed radio amateurs who are interested in earning a bachelor's degree, particularly in the field of journalism.

Eligibility: Open to residents of the United States and its territories who have an amateur radio license of at least general class. Applicants must be working full time on a bachelor's degree. There is no restriction on the course of study, but preference is given to students majoring in journalism. Financial need is considered in the selection process.

Financial data: The stipend is $1,000.

Duration: 1 year.

Number awarded: 1 each year.

Deadline: April of each year.

1476 $ RALPH WALDO EMERSON PRIZES

Concord Review
Attn: TCR Submissions
730 Boston Post Road, Suite 24
Sudbury, MA 01776
Phone: (978) 443–0022; (800) 331–5007;
Email: fitzhugh@tcr.org
Web: www.tcr.org/tcr/emerson.htm

Summary: To recognize and reward outstanding historical essays written by high school seniors in any country.

Eligibility: Open to high school students from any country. They are invited to submit historical essays to the *Concord Review,* the first and only quarterly journal in the world that publishes essays written by high school students from any country. Essays should be from 4,000 to 6,000 words, on any historical topic.

Financial data: The prize is $3,000.

Duration: The prizes are awarded annually.

Number awarded: 6 each year.

Deadline: Deadline not specified.

1477 $ RDW GROUP, INC. MINORITY SCHOLARSHIP FOR COMMUNICATIONS

Rhode Island Foundation
Attn: Funds Administrator
One Union Station
Providence, RI 02903
Phone: (401) 427–4017; Fax: (401) 331–8085;
Email: lmonahan@rifoundation.org
Web: www.rifoundation.org

Summary: To provide financial assistance to Rhode Island undergraduate and graduate students of color interested in preparing for a career in communications at a school in any state.

Eligibility: Open to undergraduate and graduate students at colleges and universities in any state who are Rhode Island residents of color. Applicants must intend to work on a degree in communications (including computer graphics, art, cinematography, or other fields that would prepare them for a career in advertising). They must be able to demonstrate financial need and a commitment to a career in communications. Along with their application, they must submit an essay (up to 300 words) on the impact they would like to have on the communications field.

Financial data: The stipend is approximately $2,000 per year.

Duration: 1 year; recipients may reapply.

Number awarded: 1 each year.

Deadline: April of each year.

1478 $ REID BLACKBURN SCHOLARSHIP

National Press Photographers Foundation
3200 Croasdaile Drive, Suite 306
Durham, NC 27705–2586
Phone: (919) 383–7246; (800) 289–6772; Fax: (919) 383–7261;
Email: info@nppa.org
Web: nppf.org

Summary: To provide financial assistance to undergraduate students who are interested in preparing for a career in photojournalism.
Eligibility: Open to full–time undergraduates at 4–year colleges and universities in the United States or Canada. Applicants must be preparing for a career in photojournalism. Along with their application, they must submit a portfolio of their work with 6 to 12 entries (single photographs, multiple picture stories, or multimedia stories). Selection is based on aptitude for photojournalism, academic ability, and financial need.
Financial data: The stipend is $2,000.
Duration: 1 year; nonrenewable.
Number awarded: 1 each year.
Deadline: February of each year.

1479 REID SOUND SCHOLARSHIP

Reid Sound
92 North Main Street, Building 16
P.O. Box 54
Windsor, NJ 08561
Phone: (609) 259–9495; Fax: (609) 858–7434;
Email: info@reidsound.com
Web: www.reidsound.com
Summary: To provide financial assistance to high school seniors in New Jersey who plan to major in technical theater at a college in any state.
Eligibility: Open to seniors graduating from high schools in New Jersey who have been active participants in technical theater activities, either at their high school or through outside groups. Qualifying activities include participation with sound, lighting, costume or set design, stage management, or running crew. Applicants must be planning to enroll full time at a 2– or 4–year college or university in any state and major in technical theater. Along with their application, they must submit a resume of their technical theater activities, a transcript, and 2 letters of recommendation. Selection is based on skill and dedication to the art of technical theater.
Financial data: The stipend is $1,500.
Duration: 1 year.
Number awarded: 1 or more each year.
Deadline: April of each year.

1480 RICHARD EATON FOUNDATION AWARD

Broadcast Education Association
Attn: Scholarships
1771 N Street, N.W.
Washington, DC 20036–2891
Phone: (202) 429–3935; (888) 380–7222; Fax: (202) 775–2981;
Email: BEAMemberServices@nab.org
Web: www.beaweb.org/scholarships.htm
Summary: To provide financial assistance to upper–division and graduate students who are interested in preparing for a career in broadcasting.
Eligibility: Open to juniors, seniors, and graduate students enrolled full time at a college or university where at least 1 department is an institutional member of the Broadcast Education Association (BEA). Applicants may be studying in any area of broadcasting. Selection is based on evidence that the applicant possesses high integrity, superior academic ability, potential to be an outstanding electronic media professional, and a sense of personal and professional responsibility.
Financial data: The stipend is $1,500.
Duration: 1 year; nonrenewable.
Number awarded: 2 each year.
Deadline: October of each year.

1481 RICK PANKOW FOUNDATION SCHOLARSHIP

Rick Pankow Foundation
Attn: Scholarship Program
18654 N.W. Bernina Court
Issaquah, WA 98027
Phone: (425) 392–6164;
Email: chuck@pacificplants.com
Web: www.rickpankowfoundation.org
Summary: To provide financial assistance to high school seniors in Washington who are interested in majoring in horticulture or landscape architecture at a college in any state.
Eligibility: Open to seniors graduating from high schools in Washington who are planning to enter a 2– or 4–year program in horticulture or landscape architecture at a college in any state. Selection is based on academic achievement, community and school involvement, leadership, recommendations, and financial need.
Financial data: The stipend is $1,000.
Duration: 1 year.
Number awarded: 1 or 2 each year.
Deadline: March of each year.

1482 R.L. GILLETTE SCHOLARSHIPS

American Foundation for the Blind
Attn: Scholarship Committee
2 Penn Plaza, Suite 1102
New York, NY 10121
Phone: (212) 502–7661; (800) AFB–LINE; Fax: (888) 545–8331;
Email: afbinfo@afb.net
Web: www.afb.org/Section.asp?Documentid=2962
Summary: To provide financial assistance to legally blind undergraduate women who are studying literature or music.
Eligibility: Open to women who are legally blind, U.S. citizens, and enrolled full time in a 4–year baccalaureate degree program in literature or music. Along with their application, they must submit 200–word essays on 1) their past and recent achievements and accomplishments; 2) their intended field of study and why they have chosen it; and 3) the role their visual impairment has played in shaping their life. They must also submit a sample performance tape or CD (not to exceed 30 minutes) or a creative writing sample. Financial need is considered in the selection process.
Financial data: The stipend is $1,000.
Duration: 1 academic year.
Number awarded: 2 each year.
Deadline: April of each year.

1483 ROB BRANHAM SCHOLARSHIP

Advertising Club of Connecticut
Attn: Sandra Brangiero, Executive Director
P.O. Box 298
Marlborough, CT 06447
Phone: (860) 295–8929;
Email: admin@adclubct.org
Web: www.adclubct.org/scholarship
Summary: To provide financial assistance to residents of Connecticut interested in attending college in any state to study fields related to advertising.
Eligibility: Open to Connecticut residents entering or attending an accredited university or technical/trade school in any state. Applicants must be interested in studying advertising, marketing, broadcast media, web design, graphic design, communications, or print production. They must have a GPA of 3.0 or higher. Along with their application, they must submit a 500–word essay on their interest in advertising, marketing, and/or print production; the occupation they propose to pursue after graduating; their long–term goals; and how they plan to achieve those. They must be sponsored by a member of the Advertising Club of Connecticut. Selection is based on the essay (30 points), activities and work experience (30 points), GPA (20 points), and SAT/ACT scores (20 points).
Financial data: The stipend is $1,000.
Duration: 1 year.
Number awarded: Varies each year; recently, 2 of these scholarships were awarded.
Deadline: April of each year.

1484 $$ ROBERT C. BYRD MEMORIAL SCHOLARSHIPS

Turkish Coalition of America
1510 H Street, N.W., Suite 900
Washington, DC 20005
Phone: (202) 370–1399; Fax: (202) 370–1398;
Email: info@tc–america.org
Web: www.turkishcoalition.org/scholarships
Summary: To provide financial assistance to Turkish–Americans from Appalachian area states who are entering or continuing an undergraduate or graduate program in fields related to public affairs.
Eligibility: Open to Turkish Americans who are graduating high school seniors, current undergraduates, or entering or continuing graduate students and residents of Alabama, Georgia, Kentucky, Maryland, Mississippi, New York, North Carolina, Ohio, Pennsylvania, South Carolina, Tennessee, Virginia, or West

Virginia. Applicants must be enrolled or planning to enroll full time to work on a degree in law, public policy, public affairs, political science, international relations, communications, journalism, or public relations. They must have a GPA of 3.3 or higher. Along with their application, they must submit an essay of 500 words or less on how they have been able to achieve success both academically and socially, the major obstacles they have faced, how they have been able to overcome those obstacles, and how they plan to contribute to the Turkish American community, to U.S.–Turkey relations, and to Turkey. Selection is based on academic achievement, interest in Turkish American issues as demonstrated by involvement in Turkish American community affairs, and individual leadership qualities conducive to preparing for a career in public affairs, media, or public relations. Financial need is not required, but special consideration is given to applicants who provide information about and prove financial need. Preference is given to students who are admitted to top national universities or liberal arts colleges. U.S. citizenship or permanent resident status is required.

Financial data: The stipend is $5,000 per year.

Duration: 1 year; may be renewed as long as the recipient maintains a GPA of 3.3 or higher.

Number awarded: Up to 15 each year.

Deadline: June of each year.

1485 ROBERT J. LEONARD MEMORIAL AWARD

Polanki, The Polish Women's Cultural Club of Milwaukee
Attn: College Achievement Awards
P.O. Box 341458
Milwaukee, WI 53234
Phone: (414) 858–9357;
Email: polanki@polanki.org
Web: www.polanki.org/scholar–main.html

Summary: To recognize and reward upper–division and graduate students in Wisconsin who have a Polish connection and demonstrate academic excellence in dance or theater.

Eligibility: Open to college juniors, seniors, and graduate students who are Wisconsin residents or attending college in the state. Applicants must be 1) of Polish heritage; 2) non–Polish students of Polish language, history, society, or culture; or 3) significantly engaged with Polish culture. They must have a GPA of 3.0 or higher. Along with their application, they must submit 1) an essay of 500 to 600 words on a topic that changes annually but relates to Poland; and 2) a paragraph of 100 to 150 words on their personal, academic, and professional plans for the future. This award is reserved for a student in dance or theater. U.S. citizenship or permanent residence is required.

Financial data: Awards range from $750 to $1,500.

Duration: The awards are presented annually.

Number awarded: 1 each year.

Deadline: January of each year.

1486 $$ ROBERT LEWIS BAKER SCHOLARSHIP

Federated Garden Clubs of Maryland, Inc.
Attn: Scholarship Chair
4915 Greenspring Avenue
Baltimore, MD 21209–4542
Phone: (410) 396–4842;
Email: office@fgcofmd.org
Web: www.fgcofmd.org/SCHOLARSHIP_PROGRAMS.html

Summary: To provide financial assistance to Maryland residents who are interested in working on an undergraduate or graduate degree in ornamental horticulture or landscape design at a school in any state.

Eligibility: Open to high school seniors, currently–enrolled college students, and graduate students who are Maryland residents. Applicants must be interested in working on a degree in ornamental horticulture, landscape design, or an allied subject at a college or university in any state. Along with their application, they must submit a 2–page personal letter discussing their background, career goals, commitment to the chosen field of study, and financial need.

Financial data: Stipends range up to $5,000.

Duration: 1 year.

Number awarded: 1 or more each year.

Deadline: June of each year.

1487 $ ROSA PARKS PLAYWRITING AWARD

John F. Kennedy Center for the Performing Arts
Education Department
Attn: Kennedy Center American College Theater Festival
2700 F Street, N.W.
Washington, DC 20566
Phone: (202) 416–8857; Fax: (202) 416–8860;
Email: KCACTF@kennedy–center.org
Web: www.kcactf.org/KCACTF.ORG_NATIONAL/Kanin_Playwriting.html

Summary: To recognize and reward the student and faculty authors of plays that relate to civil rights and/or social justice.

Eligibility: Open to students and faculty at any accredited junior or senior college in the United States. They are eligible to compete, provided their college agrees to participate in the Kennedy Center American College Theater Festival (KCACTF). Undergraduate students must be carrying at least 6 semester hours, graduate students must be enrolled in at least 3 semester hours, and continuing part–time students must be enrolled in a regular degree or certificate program. This award is presented to the best faculty– or student–written script on the subject of social justice and/or civil rights.

Financial data: The winning playwright receives a cash award of $1,000 for a full–length play or $500 for a 1–act play. The award includes an all–expense paid professional development opportunity.

Duration: The award is presented annually.

Number awarded: 1 each year.

Deadline: November of each year.

1488 $$ ROSSINI FLEXOGRAPHIC SCHOLARSHIP COMPETITION

Flexographic Technical Association
Attn: Educational Program Coordinator
3920 Veterans Memorial Highway
Bohemia, NY 11716
Phone: (631) 737–6020, ext. 36; Fax: (631) 737–6813;
Email: srubin@flexography.org
Web: www.flexography.org/04Education/scholar_rossini.html

Summary: To recognize and reward, with funding for research, undergraduate students who propose an outstanding project related to flexography.

Eligibility: Open to 1) full–time sophomores and juniors at 4–year colleges and universities; and 2) full–time second–year students at technical and 2–year colleges transferring to a 4–year college or university. Applicants must be majoring in graphic communications with a focus on flexography and have a GPA of 3.0 or higher. They must submit a proposal for a research project in the field of flexography. The project must address an issue, topic, or problem facing the flexographic industry; the focus of the project must be directed at finding results that will benefit the flexographic industry; and the research must be conducted by an individual student. In addition to their research proposal, students must submit transcripts, a statement of educational and personal goals, and 3 letters of recommendation.

Financial data: Awards for students are $7,500 for first place, $4,500 for second, and $3,000 for third. The institutions of winners receive grants of $2,500 for the first–place winner, $1,500 for second, and $1,000 for third. Funds are to be used to conduct the proposed research project. Winners also receive an all–expense paid trip to the Foundation of Flexographic Technical Association (FFTA) annual forum where they will outline their projects.

Duration: The competition is held annually.

Number awarded: 3 each year.

Deadline: Applications must be submitted by February of each year.

1489 $ RUTH CLARK FURNITURE DESIGN SCHOLARSHIP

International Furnishings and Design Association
Attn: IFDA Educational Foundation
2700 East Grace Street
Richmond, VA 23223
Phone: (804) 644–3946; Fax: (804) 644–3834;
Email: colleaguesinc@earthlink.net
Web: www.ifdaef.org/scholarships.php

Summary: To provide financial assistance to undergraduate and graduate students working on a degree in residential furniture design.

Eligibility: Open to full–time undergraduate and graduate students enrolled in a design program at an accredited college or design school with a focus on residential upholstered and/or wood furniture design. Applicants must have completed at least 4 design courses. Along with their application, they must submit an essay of 200 to 400 words on their long– and short–term goals, special interests, volunteer and community service, and what inspired them to prepare for a career in this field; 5 examples of their original residential furniture designs; a transcript; and a letter of recommendation from a professor or instructor. Financial need is not considered.

Financial data: The stipend is $3,000.

Duration: 1 year.

Number awarded: 1 each year.
Deadline: March of each year.

1490 RUTH I. CLEVELAND SCHOLARSHIP

Garden Club Federation of Massachusetts, Inc.
Attn: Scholarship Secretary
219 Washington Street
Wellesley Hills, MA 02481
Phone: (781) 237–0336; Fax: (781) 237–0336;
Email: gcfmscholarship@aol.com
Web: www.gcfm.org/Education/Scholarships/GCFMScholarships.aspx

Summary: To provide financial assistance to residents of Massachusetts interested in working on an undergraduate or graduate degree in the arts and/or sciences.

Eligibility: Open to high school seniors, undergraduates, and graduate students who have been residents of Massachusetts for at least 1 year. Applicants must be working on or planning to work on a degree in any field of the arts and/or sciences. They must have a GPA of 3.0 or higher. Along with their application, they must submit official transcripts; a brief essay about their goals, aspirations, and career plans; a list of their activities, including special honors and/or leadership positions; 3 letters of recommendation; and documentation of financial need.

Financial data: The stipend is $1,000.
Duration: 1 year.
Number awarded: Varies each year.
Deadline: February of each year.

1491 RUTH JACOBS MEMORIAL SCHOLARSHIP

Choristers Guild
Attn: Memorial Scholarship Committee
12404 Park Central Drive, Suite 100
Dallas, TX 75251–1803
Phone: (469) 398–3606; (800) CHORISTER; Fax: (469) 398–3611;
Email: Scholarships@mailcg.org
Web: www.choristersguild.org/scholarships.html

Summary: To provide financial assistance to upper–division and graduate students majoring in church music.

Eligibility: Open to juniors, seniors, and graduate students working full time on a degree in church music. Applicants must submit a 2–page essay explaining why they have chosen to prepare for a career in choral church music, how children and youth choirs will be a part of their career, their choral experience as a singer and as a conductor, and their music background, both formal and informal. Selection is based on academic merit, interest in church music (especially children's and youth choirs), and interest in ministry of church music as a vocation.

Financial data: The stipend is $1,500 per year.
Duration: 1 year; recipients may reapply.
Number awarded: 1 or more each year.
Deadline: January of each year.

1492 RUTH KEELING HEMMINGWAY HISTORY SCHOLARSHIP

Florida Society Colonial Dames XVII Century
c/o Jo Dell Coning
1043 Dundee Circle
Leesburg, FL 34788–7684

Summary: To provide financial assistance to upper–division and graduate students working on a degree in history at Florida colleges and universities.

Eligibility: Open to juniors, seniors, and graduate students working on a degree in history at colleges and universities in Florida. Applicants must be enrolled full time and have a GPA of 3.0 or higher. Along with their application, they must submit 2 letters of recommendation, a short biographical resume that includes their goals, and a short essay about American history and why it is their major. Financial need is not considered in the selection process.

Financial data: The stipend is $1,000.
Duration: 1 year.
Number awarded: 1 each year.
Deadline: March of each year.

1493 $$ RUTH WHITNEY SCHOLARSHIP

New York Women in Communications, Inc.
Attn: NYWICI Foundation
355 Lexington Avenue, 15th Floor
New York, NY 10017–6603
Phone: (212) 297–2133; Fax: (212) 370–9047;
Email: nywicipr@nywici.org
Web: www.nywici.org/foundation/scholarships

Summary: To provide financial assistance to female residents of designated eastern states who are interested in preparing for a career in magazine journalism or publishing at a college or graduate school in any state.

Eligibility: Open to women who are residents of New York, New Jersey, Connecticut, or Pennsylvania and enrolled as undergraduate or graduate students at a college or university in any state. Graduate students must be members of New York Women in Communications, Inc. (NYWICI). Also eligible are women who reside outside the 4 states but are currently enrolled at a college or university within 1 of the 5 boroughs of New York City. Applicants must have some experience in writing, reporting, or design and be preparing for a career in magazine journalism or publishing. Along with their application, they must submit a 2–page resume that includes school and extracurricular activities, significant achievements, academic honors and awards, and community service work; a personal essay of 300 to 500 words on their choice of an assigned topic that changes annually; 2 letters of recommendation; and an official transcript. Selection is based on academic record, need, demonstrated leadership, participation in school and community activities, honors, work experience, goals and aspirations, and unusual personal and/or family circumstances. U.S. citizenship is required.

Financial data: The stipend ranges up to $10,000.
Duration: 1 year.
Number awarded: 1 each year.
Deadline: January of each year.

1494 $ SABIAN, LTD. LARRIE LONDIN MEMORIAL SCHOLARSHIP

Percussive Arts Society
110 West Washington Street, Suite A
Indianapolis, IN 46204
Phone: (317) 974–4488; Fax: (317) 974–4499;
Email: percarts@pas.org
Web: www.pas.org/experience/grantsscholarships.aspx

Summary: To provide financial assistance to young drummers interested in furthering their drumset studies.

Eligibility: Open to drummers in 2 categories: those 17 years of age and under and those from 18 to 24 years of age. Applicants must submit 1) a DVD, up to 3 minutes in length, that demonstrates their ability to perform different drumming styles; 2) an essay (from 100 to 200 words in length) on why they feel they qualify for a scholarship and how the money would be used (e.g., college, summer camp, private teacher); and 3) a supporting letter of recommendation verifying their age and school attendance. Students in the age 18 to 24 category must be enrolled in, or apply funds to an accredited, structured music education program. Financial need is not considered in the selection process.

Financial data: The stipend is $2,000 for students in the 18 to 24 age category or $1,000 for students under 17.
Duration: 1 year.
Number awarded: 2 each year: 1 in each age category.
Deadline: March of each year.

1495 $$ SAMSUNG MOBILE INNOVATION AND LEADERSHIP IN ADVERTISING INTERNSHIP AND SCHOLARSHIP

American Advertising Federation–District 10
Attn: Executive Director
16080 Gardendale Road
Gardendale, TX 79758
Phone: (800) 808–4473; Fax: (800) 232–9891;
Email: dobbsprt@nts–online.net
Web: www.aaf10.org

Summary: To provide financial assistance and work experience to upper–division and graduate students working on degree in a field related to advertising at a school in designated states.

Eligibility: Open to juniors, seniors, and graduate students at colleges and universities in Arkansas, Louisiana, Oklahoma, and Texas. Applicants must be working on a bachelor's or master's degree in advertising, commercial art, communications, film, marketing, public relations, radio, or television. They must have a GPA of 3.0 or higher. Preference is given to students who demonstrate 1) enthusiasm for mobile technology or consumer electronics; 2) understanding of measurement techniques and methodologies for communications; 3) understanding of communications channels, including traditional media, social media, and internal communications; and 4) strong writing and editing skills. Along with their application, they must submit 3 to 5 samples of their work, 1 to

3 letters of recommendation, transcripts, and financial information. They must be available for an internship with Samsung Mobile in Dallas, Texas during the summer following receipt of the award.
Financial data: The student selected for this award receives a stipend from Samsung Mobile and $1,500 from the Tenth District of the American Advertising Federation to defray expenses for the internship, a stipend of $1,750 paid to the school for the following fall, and a stipend of $1,750 paid to the school for the following spring.
Duration: 1 year.
Number awarded: 1 each year.
Deadline: April of each year.

1496 SAMUEL ROBINSON AWARD

Presbyterian Church (USA)
Attn: Office of Financial Aid for Studies
100 Witherspoon Street, Room M–052
Louisville, KY 40202–1396
Phone: (502) 569–5224; (800) 728–7228, ext. 5224; Fax: (502) 569–8766;
TDD: (800) 833–5955;
Email: finaid@pcusa.org
Web: gamc.pcusa.org
Summary: To recognize and reward students in Presbyterian colleges who write essays on religious topics.
Eligibility: Open to juniors and seniors enrolled full time in 1 of the 64 colleges related to the Presbyterian Church (USA). Applicants must successfully recite the answers to the Westminster Shorter Catechism and write a 2,000–word original essay on an assigned topic related to the Shorter Catechism.
Financial data: Awards are $5,000 or $2,000.
Duration: 1 year; nonrenewable.
Number awarded: Up to 20 each year, including 2 at $5,000 and the remainder at $2,000.
Deadline: March of each year.

1497 $$ SAN ANTONIO POST SAME SCHOLARSHIPS

Society of American Military Engineers–San Antonio Post
Attn: Scholarship Awards Committee
20770 U.S. Highway 281 N, Suite 108
PMB 451
San Antonio, TX 78258–7500
Phone: (210) 828–9494; Fax: (210) 828–7282;
Email: jlgerman@pbsj.com
Web: www.same–satx.org
Summary: To provide financial assistance to students (especially those participating in ROTC) who are majoring in designated fields at colleges and universities in Texas.
Eligibility: Open to full–time students majoring in architecture, community planning, construction science or management, engineering, physical science, or a related program at a college or university in Texas. Preference is given to students participating in an ROTC program and planning a career in the U.S. Army, Navy, Marine Corps, Coast Guard, or Air Force. Selection is based on academic achievement, leadership, professionalism, participation in extracurricular activities, and service to university and/or local community. Financial need is not considered, but students receiving a full scholarship from another source are not eligible.
Financial data: Stipends range from $1,000 to $5,000.
Duration: 1 year; nonrenewable.
Number awarded: Each year, this program awards 6 scholarships at $5,000 each (including the named scholarships) and a varying number of other scholarships at $1,000 to $4,000.
Deadline: October of each year.

1498 $$ SAN FRANCISCO SWEA SCHOLARSHIPS

Swedish Women's Educational Association International–San Francisco Chapter
c/o Lotta Askerlund, Scholarship Committee
2121 26th Street, Unit 201
San Francisco, CA 94107–4407
Email: scholarship@sweasanfrancisco.org
Web: sweasanfrancisco.org/?page_id=14
Summary: To provide financial assistance to students from the western United States who are interested in studying or conducting research on topics related to Sweden.
Eligibility: Open to residents of the western United States who are interested in working on an academic or artistic project with particular relevance to Sweden. Applicants must submit a detailed description of the project in English or Swedish; if knowledge of the Swedish language has a bearing on the project, the description must be written in Swedish. The project may include, but is not limited to, the study of such areas as Swedish culture, history, art, literature, media, or science. The scholarship is not awarded for language study or participation in exchange programs.
Financial data: The stipend is $5,000.
Duration: 1 year.
Number awarded: 1 each year.
Deadline: June of each year.

1499 SAVELE SYRJALA SCHOLARSHIP

Finlandia Foundation–Boston Chapter
c/o Edith Eash
80 Potter Road
Lexington, MA 02421
Phone: (781) 652–0154;
Email: syrjalaeash@rcn.net
Web: sites.google.com/site/finlandiafoundationboston/scholarships
Summary: To provide financial assistance to residents of New England who are of Finnish heritage and studying journalism or communications.
Eligibility: Open to students from the New England states who have a Finnish–American heritage. Applicants must be studying journalism or communications. Along with their application, they must submit information on their college experience, background and performances, extracurricular and work activities (especially those related to their interest in journalism or communications), language proficiency, and Finnish ancestry.
Financial data: The stipend is $1,000.
Duration: 1 year.
Number awarded: 1 each year.
Deadline: May of each year.

1500 SBO ESSAY CONTEST

School Band and Orchestra Magazine
Attn: Student Scholarships
21 Highland Circle, Suite One
Needham, MA 02494
Phone: (781) 453–9310; (800) 964–5150; Fax: (781) 453–9389
Web: www.sbomagazine.com/essay–contest
Summary: To recognize and reward, with college scholarships, elementary and high school students who submit outstanding essays on playing a musical instrument.
Eligibility: Open to public and private school students in grades 4 through 12. Applicants must submit an essay of up to 250 words on a topic that changes annually but relates to music; recently, students were invited to write a letter to a member of their school board on why they need music education in their schools.
Financial data: The award is a $1,000 college scholarship.
Duration: The competition is held annually.
Number awarded: 10 each year: 5 to students in grades 4–8 and 5 to students in grades 9–12.
Deadline: December of each year.

1501 SCANDIGITAL STUDENT PHOTOGRAPHY SCHOLARSHIP

ScanDigital
680 Knox Street, Suite 150
Torrance, CA 90502
Phone: (310) 341–0172; (888) 333–2808;
Email: info@scandigital.com
Web: www.scandigital.com/photography–scholarship.php
Summary: To provide financial assistance to high school seniors and current undergraduates who demonstrate interest in preparing for a career in photography or journalism.
Eligibility: Open to graduating high school seniors and students already enrolled at a college or university. Applicants must be interested in a career in photography or journalism. Along with their application, they must submit 200–word essays on the industry they plan to enter, how they feel they will contribute to the growth of that industry, and why they think they are deserving of this scholarship.
Financial data: The stipend is $1,000.

Duration: 1 year.
Number awarded: 1 each year.
Deadline: December of each year.

1502 SCHOLARSHIP IN BOOK PRODUCTION AND PUBLISHING

Publishing Professionals Network
Attn: Scholarship Committee
9328 Elk Grove Boulevard, Suite 105–250
Elk Grove, CA 95624
Phone: (916) 320–0638;
Email: michael@laserwords.com
Web: www.bookbuilders.org/wordpress/?page_id=663

Summary: To recognize and reward outstanding sample book projects created by students in the western states.

Eligibility: Open to students currently enrolled at a college, university, or technical school in the western states (Alaska, Arizona, California, Colorado, Hawaii, Idaho, Montana, Nevada, New Mexico, Oregon, Utah, Washington, and Wyoming). They must intend to prepare for a career in the field of book production or publishing, have at least a 2.0 GPA, and submit a sample book project (which usually comes from a course assignment). In addition to identifying and describing the subject book, the project submission should include the following items: a brief summary of the concept of the book selected for design and production; a definition of the design objective for the cover, interior, and any special features (e.g., slipcase); written design specifications for the cover, title page, table of contents, sample chapter opening, and interior text pages; a dummy that includes sample pages for the items listed above; and (optionally) a hand binding of the sample pages, slipcases, and other packaging. The project is judged in terms of creativity, meeting defined design objectives, and presentation of material.

Financial data: The stipend ranges up to $1,000.

Duration: 1 year.

Number awarded: Varies each year; recently, 6 of these scholarships were awarded: 1 at $1,000, 2 at $750, and 3 at $500.

Deadline: May of each year.

1503 SCHOLARSHIP OF THE ARTS

Boomer Esiason Foundation
c/o Jerry Cahill
483 Tenth Avenue, Suite 300
New York, NY 10018
Phone: (646) 292–7930; Fax: (646) 292–7945;
Email: jcahill@esiason.org
Web: esiason.org/thriving–with–cf/scholarships.php

Summary: To provide financial assistance to undergraduate and graduate students who have cystic fibrosis (CF) and are working on a degree in the arts.

Eligibility: Open to CF patients who are working on an undergraduate or graduate degree in the arts. Applicants must submit a sample of their work (video, painting, sketching, sculpture), a letter from their doctor confirming the diagnosis of CF and a list of daily medications, information on financial need, a detailed breakdown of tuition costs from their academic institution, transcripts, and a 2–page essay on 1) their postgraduation goals; and 2) the importance of compliance with CF therapies and what they practice on a daily basis to stay healthy. Selection is based on academic ability, character, leadership potential, service to the community, and financial need.

Financial data: Stipends range from $500 to $1,000. Funds are paid directly to the academic institution to assist in covering the cost of tuition and fees.

Duration: 1 year; nonrenewable.

Number awarded: 1 each year.

Deadline: May of each year.

1504 $ SCHOLARSHIPS SUPPORTING POST–SECONDARY EDUCATION FOR A CAREER IN THE AUDIOVISUAL INDUSTRY

InfoComm International
International Communications Industries Foundation
11242 Waples Mill Road, Suite 200
Fairfax, VA 22030
Phone: (703) 273–7200; (800) 659–7469; Fax: (703) 278–8082;
Email: jhardwick@infocomm.org
Web: www.infocomm.org/cps/rde/xchg/infocomm/hs.xsl/7163.htm

Summary: To provide financial assistance to undergraduate and graduate students who are interested in preparing for a career in the audiovisual (AV) industry.

Eligibility: Open to second–year students at 2–year colleges, juniors and seniors at 4–year institutions, and graduate students. Applicants must have a GPA of 2.75 or higher and be majoring or planning to major in audiovisual subjects or related fields, including audio, video, audiovisual, radio/television/film, or other field related to a career in the audiovisual industry. Students in other programs, such as journalism, may be eligible if they can demonstrate a relationship to career goals in the AV industry. Along with their application, they must submit 1) an essay of 150 to 200 words on the career path they plan to pursue in the audiovisual industry in the next 5 years; and 2) an essay of 250 to 300 words on the experience or person influencing them the most in selecting the audiovisual industry as their career of choice. Minority and women candidates are especially encouraged to apply. Selection is based on the essays, presentation of the application, GPA, AV–related experience, work experience, and letters of recommendation.

Financial data: The stipend is $4,000. Funds are sent directly to the school.

Duration: 1 year.

Number awarded: Varies each year.

Deadline: April of each year.

1505 $$ SCHOLASTIC ART AWARDS

Scholastic, Inc.
Attn: Alliance for Young Artists & Writers, Inc.
557 Broadway
New York, NY 10012
Phone: (212) 343–6730; Fax: (212) 389–3939;
Email: info@artandwriting.org
Web: www.artandwriting.org/Scholarships/AllianceScholarships

Summary: To recognize and reward, with college scholarships, outstanding middle school and high school artists and photographers.

Eligibility: Open to all students in grades 7–12 who are currently enrolled in public, parochial, private, or home schools in the United States, U.S. territories, Canada, or U.S.–sponsored schools abroad. They may submit art work in 1 or more of these categories: architecture, comic art, ceramics and glass, digital art, design (commercial and applied arts), drawing, fashion, film and animation, jewelry, mixed media, painting, photography, printmaking, sculpture, and video games. Participants who are graduating seniors planning to attend college may submit an art portfolio of 8 works from any category or a photography portfolio of 8 works from any category. Those entries are eligible for Portfolio Gold Awards or Portfolio Silver Medals with Distinction. Special awards, available to all entries, include: the New York Life Awards, presented for outstanding folios that deal with loss or bereavement; the Creativity and Citizenship Awards, presented for works that deal with bullying; the AMD Game Changer Awards, presented to the top winners in the video game design category; the Prismacolor Awards, presented to the top winners in the categories of architecture, comic art, fashion, drawing, and mixed media; and the Best in Grade Awards are presented to the highest–ranked entries from each grade level and in each category.

Financial data: The Portfolio Gold Awards are $10,000 scholarships and the Portfolio Silver Medals with Distinction are $1,000. The New York Life Awards are $1,000, the Creativity and Citizenship Awards are $1,000, the AMD Game Changer Awards are $1,000, the Prismacolor Awards are $1,000, and the Best in Grade (B.I.G.) Awards are $500. In addition, teachers of the Portfolio Gold Award winners receive Portfolio Gold Teacher Awards of $1,000 and teachers of the Portfolio Silver Medals receive Portfolio Silver Medal with Distinction Teacher Awards of $250. The teacher who submits the most outstanding group of entries in any category receives the Ovation Inspired Teaching Award of $1,000.

Number awarded: At the national level, 15 Portfolio Gold Awards are presented in the art, photography, and general writing categories. The teachers of those 15 winners receive Portfolio Teacher Awards. In addition, 30 Portfolio Silver Medals with Distinction are presented and each of those teachers receives an award. New York Life Awards are presented to 6 artists and writers, Creativity and Citizenship Awards are presented to 3 artists and writers, 5 AMD Game Changer Awards are presented, and 5 Prismacolor Awards (1 to the winner in each of the eligible categories) are presented. The Ovation Inspired Teaching Award is presented to 1 teacher.

Deadline: January of each year.

1506 $$ SCHOLASTIC WRITING AWARDS

Scholastic, Inc.
Attn: Alliance for Young Artists & Writers, Inc.
557 Broadway
New York, NY 10012
Phone: (212) 343–6730; Fax: (212) 389–3939;
Email: info@artandwriting.org
Web: www.artandwriting.org

Summary: To recognize and reward outstanding middle school and high school writers.

Eligibility: Open to all students in grades 7–12 who are currently enrolled in public, private, parochial, or home schools in the United States, U.S. territories, U.S.–sponsored schools abroad, and Canada. Competitions are held in the following categories: dramatic script, flash fiction (formerly short short story), humor, journalism, novel writing, personal essay/memoir, persuasive writing, poetry, science fiction/fantasy, and short story. Participants who are graduating seniors planning to attend college may submit a portfolio of 4 to 8 works from any category; the maximum number of words for a portfolio is 24,000. Those entries are eligible for Portfolio Gold Awards or Portfolio Silver Medals with Distinction. Special awards, available to all entries, include: the New York Life Awards, presented for outstanding folios that deal with loss or bereavement; the Creativity and Citizenship Awards, presented for works that deal with bullying; and the Best in Grade Awards are presented to the highest–ranked entries from each grade level and in each category.

Financial data: The Portfolio Gold Awards are $10,000 scholarships and the Portfolio Silver Medals with Distinction are $1,000. The New York Life Awards are $1,000, the Creativity and Citizenship Awards are $1,000, and the Best in Grade (B.I.G.) Awards are $500. In addition, teachers of the Portfolio Gold Award winners receive Portfolio Gold Teacher Awards of $1,000 and teachers of the Portfolio Silver Medals receive Portfolio Silver Medal with Distinction Teacher Awards of $250. The teacher who submits the most outstanding group of entries in any category receives the Ovation Inspired Teaching Award of $1,000.

Number awarded: At the national level, 15 Portfolio Gold Awards are presented in the art, photography, and general writing categories. The teachers of those 15 winners receive Portfolio Teacher Awards. In addition, 30 Portfolio Silver Medals with Distinction are presented and each of those teachers receives an award. New York Life Awards are presented to 6 artists and writers and Creativity and Citizenship Awards are presented to 3 artists and writers. The Ovation Inspired Teaching Award is presented to 1 teacher.

Deadline: January of each year.

1507 SEATTLE PROFESSIONAL CHAPTER SCHOLARSHIPS

Association for Women in Communications–Seattle Professional Chapter
c/o Pam Love, Scholarship Chair
3417 30th Avenue West
Seattle, WA 98199
Phone: (425) 280–1968;
Email: pamlove@grappanetwork.og
Web: www.seattleawc.org/about/student–chapter

Summary: To provide financial assistance to female upper–division and graduate students in Washington who are preparing for a career in the communications industry.

Eligibility: Open to female Washington state residents who are enrolled at a 4–year college or university in the state as a junior, senior, or graduate student (sophomores at 2–year colleges applying to a 4–year institution are also eligible). Applicants must be majoring, or planning to major, in a communications program, including print and broadcast journalism, television and radio production, film, advertising, public relations, marketing, graphic design, multimedia design, photography, or technical communication. Selection is based on demonstrated excellence in communications; contributions made to communications on campus and in the community; scholastic achievement; financial need; and writing samples from journalism, advertising, public relations, or broadcasting.

Financial data: The stipend is $1,500. Funds are paid directly to the recipient's school and must be used for tuition and fees.

Duration: 1 year.

Number awarded: 2 each year.

Deadline: April of each year.

1508 $ SEHAR SALEHA AHMAD AND ABRAHIM EKRAMULLAH ZAFAR FOUNDATION SCHOLARSHIP

Oregon Student Access Commission
Attn: Grants and Scholarships Division
1500 Valley River Drive, Suite 100
Eugene, OR 97401–2146
Phone: (541) 687–7395; (800) 452–8807, ext. 7395; Fax: (541) 687–7414; TDD: (800) 735–2900;
Email: awardinfo@osac.state.or.us
Web: www.oregonstudentaid.gov/scholarships.aspx

Summary: To provide financial assistance to female high school seniors in Oregon who are interested in studying English at a college in the state.

Eligibility: Open to women who are graduating seniors from high schools in Oregon (including GED recipients and home–schooled students). Applicants must be planning to major in English at a 4–year college or university in the state. They must have a GPA of 3.5 or higher and be able to demonstrate financial need.

Financial data: Stipends for scholarships offered by the Oregon Student Access Commission (OSAC) range from $200 to $10,000 but recently averaged $2,300.

Duration: 1 year; may be renewed if the recipient shows satisfactory academic progress and continued financial need.

Number awarded: 1 or more each year.

Deadline: February of each year.

1509 SHERWOOD COLLINS PLAYWRITING CONTEST

Massachusetts Educational Theater Guild
P.O. Box 93
Chelmsford, MA 01824
Phone: (978) 456–3454;
Email: metg@metg.org
Web: metg.org/contests/playwriting–contest

Summary: To recognize and reward high school students in Massachusetts who submit outstanding scripts for a play.

Eligibility: Open to students in grades 9–12 at high schools in Massachusetts. Applicants must prepare a script for a 1–act play, up to 40 minutes in length. Scripts must be written for stage presentation; musicals, screen plays, teleplays, and adaptations of another author's work are not accepted.

Financial data: Cash prizes are awarded (amount not specified).

Duration: The contest is held annually.

Number awarded: Varies each year; recently, 3 of these awards were presented.

Deadline: January of each year.

1510 SIKH COALITION DIVERSITY VIDEO COMPETITION

Sikh Coalition
Attn: Director of Programs
40 Exchange Place, Suite 728
New York, NY 10005
Phone: (212) 655–3095, ext. 83;
Email: amar@sikhcoalition.org
Web: sikhcoalition.org/Video_Competition.asp

Summary: To recognize and reward high school and college students who submit outstanding essays on topics related to diversity and faith.

Eligibility: Open to students at high schools and colleges in all countries. Applicants are invited to submit a 5–minute video on a topic that changes annually but relates to issues involving civil rights of minorities, especially Sikhs. Recently, students were invited to submit entries that dealt with bullying and harassment in schools, with special reference to the Sikh experience. Selection is based on creativity and originality, effective conveyance of the message, technical and cinematographic quality, versatility with a focus on multiple minority communities, and compliance with film length limit and other requirements.

Financial data: Prizes are $1,000 for first place, $500 for second, and $250 for third.

Duration: The competition is held annually.

Number awarded: 3 cash prizes are awarded each year.

Deadline: August of each year.

1511 SKOKIE VALLEY SYMPHONY YOUNG ARTIST COMPETITION

Skokie Valley Symphony Orchestra
9501 Skokie Boulevard
Skokie, IL 60077
Phone: (847) 679–9501, ext. 3014; Fax: (847) 679–1879;
Email: info@svso.org
Web: www.svso.org/YAC.html

Summary: To recognize and reward outstanding young musicians.

Eligibility: Open to pianists and other orchestral instrumentalists (including string, woodwind, brass, percussion, piano, and classical guitar) between the ages of 16 and 22 who are not professional musicians. Applicants participate in a competition on the campus of Northeastern Illinois University in which they play a memorized movement of a concerto. Previous winners of the competition are ineligible.

Financial data: First prize is $1,000 and second is $600.

Number awarded: 2 each year.

Deadline: April of each year.

1512 SOCIETY OF MAYFLOWER DESCENDANTS IN THE STATE OF NEW JERSEY

Society of Mayflower Descendants in the State of New Jersey Scholarship
c/o Mark C. Fulcomer, Education Committee
48 Trainor Circle
Bordentown, NJ 08505
Email: eNJN@njmayflower.org

Summary: To provide financial assistance to high school seniors in New Jersey who plan to major in U.S. history at a college in the state.

Eligibility: Open to seniors graduating from high schools in New Jersey who rank in the top quarter or their class or have SAT or ACT scores at or above the 75th percentile. Applicants must be planning to enroll at a 4–year college or university in New Jersey and major in a field related to U.S. history. Each high school in the state may nominate 1 student for this award. Financial need is not considered in the selection process.

Financial data: The stipend is $1,500.

Duration: 1 year.

Number awarded: 3 each year.

Deadline: March of each year.

1513 $$ SOUTH CAROLINA VOCATIONAL REHABILITATION DEPARTMENT JOURNALISM CONTEST

South Carolina Vocational Rehabilitation Department
Attn: Public Information Office
1410 Boston Avenue
P.O. Box 15
West Columbia, SC 29171–0015
Phone: (803) 896–6503; (866) 247–8354; TDD: (803) 896–6553
Web: scvrd.net/journalism

Summary: To recognize and reward, with college scholarships, high school students in South Carolina who submit outstanding newspaper articles on topics related to the employment of people with disabilities.

Eligibility: Open to South Carolina residents between 16 and 19 years of age enrolled as juniors or seniors in high school or otherwise qualified to begin postsecondary education no later than 2 years after the contest. Applicants are not required to have a disability, but they must submit a newspaper article, up to 3 pages in length, on a topic that changes annually but relates to the employment of people with disabilities. A recent topic was "Profit by investing in workers with disabilities." Articles should use correct grammar and sentence structure and follow standard journalistic practice of the 5 Ws (who, what, where, when, and why).

Financial data: The winner receives full payment of tuition and fees at a South Carolina state–supported institution. Some schools include room and board as part of tuition and fees.

Duration: 4 years, provided the recipient meets general scholastic and conduct standards.

Number awarded: 1 each year.

Deadline: January of each year.

1514 SPECIAL CABLE DEALS SCHOLARSHIP CONTEST

Digital Landing
9675 N.W. 117th Avenue
Miami, FL 33178
Phone: (305) 265–0136; Fax: (304) 267–1651;
Email: scholarship@specialcabledeals.com
Web: www.specialcabledeals.com/best–cable–promotions.html

Summary: To recognize and reward, with scholarships for continuing study, undergraduate and graduate students who submit outstanding essays on topics that relate to television or movies.

Eligibility: Open to undergraduate and graduate students currently enrolled at an accredited university or private career school. Applicants must submit an essay, at least 750 words in length, on why people love to be scared by television and movies. They must be U.S. citizens or visa holders. Financial need and GPA are not considered in the selection process.

Financial data: The award is a $1,000 scholarship. Funds are made payable to the winner's school of attendance.

Duration: The competition is held annually.

Number awarded: 1 each year.

Deadline: December.

1515 $ ST. ANDREW'S SOCIETY OF WASHINGTON SCHOLARSHIPS

Summary: To provide financial assistance for college or graduate school to students in Scotland and to U.S. students of Scottish descent who live in the mid–Atlantic states.

See Listing #889.

1516 STEPHEN AND SANDY SHELLER SCHOLARSHIP

Pennsylvania State System of Higher Education Foundation, Inc.
Attn: Foundation Manager
2986 North Second Street
Harrisburg, PA 17110
Phone: (717) 720–4065; Fax: (717) 720–7082;
Email: eshowers@thePAfoundation.org
Web: www.thepafoundation.org/scholarships/index.asp

Summary: To provide financial assistance to upper–division students at institutions of the Pennsylvania State System of Higher Education (PASSHE) who are preparing for a career in law or art therapy.

Eligibility: Open to full–time students currently working on an undergraduate degree leading to a career in law or in art therapy at 1 of the 14 institutions within the PASSHE. Applicants must have completed at least 60 credits with a GPA of 3.5 or higher. Along with their application, they must submit an essay of 500 to 800 words on a quotation from Winston Churchill regarding the importance of giving. Financial need is considered in the selection process.

Financial data: The stipend is $1,000.

Duration: 1 year; nonrenewable.

Number awarded: 4 each year.

Deadline: May of each year.

1517 $$ STEPHEN G. KING PLAY ENVIRONMENTS SCHOLARSHIP

Landscape Architecture Foundation
Attn: Leadership in Landscape Scholarship Program
818 18th Street, N.W., Suite 810
Washington, DC 20006–3520
Phone: (202) 331–7070; Fax: (202) 331–7079;
Email: scholarships@lafoundation.org
Web: www.lafoundation.org

Summary: To provide financial assistance to upper–division and graduate students who wish to study landscape architecture with an emphasis on play environments.

Eligibility: Open to landscape architecture students in the final 2 years of undergraduate study or in graduate school. Applicants must have a demonstrated interest and aptitude in the design of play environments, including integrating playgrounds into parks, schools, and other play environments and understanding the significant social and educational value of play. Along with their application, they must submit 2 letters of recommendation, a plan and details of a play environment of their design, and an essay of 300 to 500 words on their views of the significant social and educational value of play and the value of integrating playgrounds into play and recreation environments. Selection is based on financial need, creativity, openness to innovation, and demonstrated interest in park and playground planning.

Financial data: The stipend is $5,000.

Duration: 1 year.

Number awarded: 1 each year.

Deadline: February of each year.

1518 $$ STORYTELLERS PHOTOGRAPHY COMPETITION

The Art Institutes International, Inc.
Free Markets Center
210 Sixth Avenue, 33rd Floor
Pittsburgh, PA 15222–2603
Phone: (412) 995–7685; (888) 624–0300; Fax: (412) 918–2598
Web: www.artinstitutes.edu/competitions/photography–storytellers.aspx

Summary: To recognize and reward (with scholarships to participating Art Institutes) high school seniors and graduates who are winners in a photography competition.

Eligibility: Open to residents of the United States and Puerto Rico who are high school seniors or graduates and interested in attending an Art Institute that offers a photography program. Applicants must have a high school GPA of 2.0 or higher. They must apply through the Art Institute they plan to attend and submit 1) 6 photographs (submitted as JPEGs) that reflect the competition theme of "Storytelling Through the Lens" and that have a relationship to each other to tell a story; and 2) a statement of 500 to 800 words that describes their purpose and intent of producing the work, what they intend to communicate, and their approach. Those entries are judged on the basis of photographic technical acuity, including (but not limited to) color, balance, tonality range, exposure, and focus (30%); composition (30%); articulation of theme (30%); and adherence to entry requirements (10%). Semifinalists are selected at each Art Institute to advance to national finals. At that level, selection is based on photographic technical acuity (30%), composition (30%), and articulation of theme (40%).

Financial data: For high school seniors, local prizes are $3,000 tuition scholarships to the Art Institute they plan to attend; national prizes are tuition scholarships of $10,000 per year for 4 years as a grand prize, $5,000 per year for 4 years as a first prize, and $2,500 per year for 4 years as a second prize. For high school graduates, local prizes are $1,000 tuition scholarships to the Art Institute they plan to attend; the national prize is a tuition scholarship of $10,000 for 1 year.
Duration: The competition is held annually.
Number awarded: Recently, 39 Art Institutes participated in this program and each awarded 1 scholarship to a high school senior and 1 to a high school graduate. In addition, 3 high school seniors and 1 high school graduate received national prizes.
Deadline: February of each year.

1519 $$ STUDENT ACADEMY AWARDS

Academy of Motion Picture Arts and Sciences
Attn: Academy Foundation
8949 Wilshire Boulevard
Beverly Hills, CA 90211–1972
Phone: (310) 247–3000, ext. 1131; Fax: (310) 859–9619;
Email: rmiller@oscars.org
Web: www.oscars.org/awards/saa/index.html

Summary: To recognize and reward student filmmakers who have no previous professional experience.
Eligibility: Open to student filmmakers who are enrolled in degree–granting programs at accredited colleges and universities as full–time students and have no previous professional experience. Applicants must submit films that they have completed within the past year as part of a teacher–student relationship within the curricular structure of their institution. There are 4 award categories: alternative, animation, narrative, and documentary. Entries must be submitted in DVD–R format and be no longer than 60 minutes. Selection is based on resourcefulness, originality, entertainment, and production quality, without regard to cost of production or subject matter.
Financial data: Gold, silver, and bronze awards in each category are $5,000, $3,000, and $2,000, respectively.
Duration: The awards are presented annually.
Number awarded: Up to 12 awards may be presented each year: 3 in each of the 4 categories.
Deadline: March of each year.

1520 $$ STUDENT COMPOSER AWARDS

Broadcast Music Inc.
Attn: BMI Foundation, Inc.
7 World Trade Center
250 Greenwich Street
New York, NY 10007–0030
Phone: (212) 220–3000;
Email: info@bmifoundation.org
Web: www.bmifoundation.org/program/bmi_student_composer_awards

Summary: To recognize and reward outstanding student composers from the Western Hemisphere.
Eligibility: Open to citizens of countries in North, Central, or South America, the Caribbean Island nations, or the Hawaiian Islands who are younger than 28 years of age. Applicants must be 1) enrolled in accredited public, private, or parochial secondary schools; 2) enrolled in accredited colleges or conservatories of music; or 3) engaged in the private study of music with recognized and established teachers (other than a relative). Any composer having won the award 3 times previously is not eligible to enter the contest again. Compositions may be for vocal, instrumental, electronic, or any combination of those. There are no limitations on medium, instrumentation, or length of the work. Manuscripts may be submitted either on usual score paper or reproduced by a generally accepted reproduction process. Electronic music and recordings of graphic works that cannot adequately be presented in score may be submitted on cassette or CD. Selection is based on evidence of creative talent. Academic finesse is considered, but that is secondary to vital musicality and clarity of expression of the composer's work. Judges consider 1) formal content of the composition; 2) melodic, harmonic, and rhythmic idioms, but only in terms of their consistency and suitability for the intent of the particular composition; 3) suitability of the choice and use of instruments or voices to the ideas presented in the composition; and 4) age of the composer (if 2 compositions are of equal merit, preference is given to the younger contestant).
Financial data: Prizes range from $500 to $5,000.
Duration: The competition is held annually.
Number awarded: Varies each year; recently, 11 of these awards were presented. A total of $20,000 in prizes is awarded each year.
Deadline: February of each year.

1521 $ STUDENT CORRUGATED PACKAGING DESIGN COMPETITION

Association of Independent Corrugated Converters
Attn: AICC Student Design Competition
113 South West Street, Third Floor
P.O. Box 25708
Alexandria, VA 22313
Phone: (703) 836–AICC; (877) 836–AICC; Fax: (703) 836–2795;
Email: info@aiccbox.org
Web: www.aiccbox.org/Student

Summary: To recognize and reward college students who submit outstanding corrugated packaging designs.
Eligibility: Open to undergraduate students enrolled in packaging courses at colleges, universities, and/or technical schools in Canada and the United States. Individual and team entries are accepted. Applicants construct, develop, and/or manufacture packaging designs using corrugated as the primary medium. Entries are accepted in 3 categories: structural, graphics, and corrugated as art. In the selection process, heavy emphasis is placed on a written essay describing the project. The first– and second–place winners in the structural and graphics categories compete in a "Best of the Best" program in which they make a presentation about their entry as they might to a prospective customer.
Financial data: In each of the categories, first place is $500, second $250, and third $100. The first–place winners in the structural and graphics categories also receive all–expense paid trips to the sponsor's annual fall meeting and trade fair in September. In the "Best of the Best" program, the prize is $1,500, second $1,000, third $750, and fourth $500.
Duration: The competition is held annually.
Number awarded: 9 winners (3 in each category) are selected in the first level of competition; 4 additional prizes are awarded for the "Best of the Best" program.
Deadline: June of each year.

1522 STUDENT DESIGN COMPETITION IN ACOUSTICS

Robert Bradford Newman Student Award Fund
c/o Acoustical Society of America
2 Huntington Quadrangle, Suite 1NO1
Melville, NY 11747–4502
Phone: (516) 576–2360; Fax: (516) 576–2377;
Email: asa@aip.org
Web: www.newmanfund.org

Summary: To recognize and reward undergraduate and graduate students who submit outstanding entries in an acoustics design competition.
Eligibility: Open to undergraduate and graduate students who enter as individuals or as members of teams of up to 3 students. Applicants must submit an acoustics design for a problem given by the competition. Selection is based on technical merit, design vision, adherence to the design prompt and program requirements, and effectiveness of the presentation.
Financial data: The prize for the winning individual or team is $1,250. Commendation awards are $700.
Duration: The competition is held annually.
Number awarded: 1 winner and 4 commendation awards are presented each year.
Deadline: Students must register by April of each year.

1523 STUDENT DESIGN PROJECT COMPETITION

American Society of Heating, Refrigerating and Air–Conditioning Engineers
Attn: Assistant Manager of Student Activities
1791 Tullie Circle, N.E.
Atlanta, GA 30329–2305
Phone: (678) 539–1212; Fax: (678) 539–2212;
Email: tholman@ashrae.org
Web: www.ashrae.org/studentzone/design_competition

Summary: To recognize and reward outstanding student designs in a competition involving heating, ventilating, and air conditioning (HVAC) engineering.
Eligibility: Open to undergraduate architecture and engineering students. They are invited to submit entries in 3 categories: integrated sustainable building design (ISBD), HVAC system selection, and HVAC design calculations. Teams entering the ISBD category should include students in engineering, architecture, technology, and other allied fields; they are asked to design their own building that approaches a sustainable or "net zero" energy level. Teams entering the HVAC system selection category should involve students who have a solid HVAC base; they are asked to use the life–cycle cost process to select the building HVAC systems. Teams entering the HVAC design calculations category should consist of students who have attending at least 2 HVAC courses; they are asked to conduct design calculations required to provide an energy–efficient design for the facility that complies with ASHRAE standards. Judging criteria are, for ISBD:

design brief development phase (10%), pre–design phase (10%), conceptual design phase (20%), description (15%), approaching zero energy building and sustainability (15%), and communication of results (20%); for HVAC system selection: system selection criteria matrix (10%), low life cycle (10%), low environmental impact (10%), comfort and health (10%), synergy with architecture (10%), creative high performance green design (10%), and communication of results (40%); for HVAC design calculations: system sizing (30%), ASHRAE standards (20%), creativity (20%), and communication of results (30%).

Financial data: In each of the 3 categories, the first–place team receives $1,500 and 1 of its representatives receives free transportation, 2 nights' lodging, and up to $100 in expense reimbursement to attend the ASHRAE winter meeting where the award is presented. The second–place and third–place team in each category also are entitled to send a representative to that meeting, with ASHRAE covering transportation, 2 nights' lodging, and up to $100 in expenses.

Duration: The competition is held annually.

Number awarded: 3 teams (1 in each category) receive cash prizes; 9 individual team members (3 in each category) receive funds to attend the meeting.

Deadline: May of each year.

1524 STUDENT JOURNALISM IMPACT AWARD

Journalism Education Association
c/o Kansas State University
103 Kedzie Hall
Manhattan, KS 66506–1505
Phone: (785) 532–5532; (866) JEA–5JEA; Fax: (785) 532–5563;
Email: jea@spub.ksu.edu
Web: jea.org/category/awards

Summary: To recognize and reward high school students who, through the practice of journalism, have made a significant difference in the lives of others.

Eligibility: Open to secondary school students (or teams of students who worked on the same entry) who, through the study and practice of journalism, have made a significant difference in their own life, the lives of others, or the students' school and/or community. The entry should contain: 1) the article, series of articles, or mass communication media (radio, broadcast, video, etc.) that made the impact; 2) a narrative of at least 250 words explaining why the piece was produced and how the entry impacted the individual, others, the school, and/or the community; and 3) letters from the adviser, a school administrator, and a professional journalist describing the impact of the work. The entry must be original student work and must have been published within 2 years preceding the deadline. The applicant's teacher/adviser must be a member of the Journalism Education Association. In the selection process, the focus is on the impact of the work, not on the author(s).

Financial data: The award is $1,000.

Duration: The competition is held annually.

Number awarded: 1 each year.

Deadline: February of each year.

1525 $$ TADEUSZ SENDZIMIR ACADEMIC YEAR AWARDS

Connecticut Community Foundation
43 Field Street
Waterbury, CT 06702–1906
Phone: (203) 753–1315; Fax: (203) 756–3054;
Email: grants@conncf.org
Web: www.conncf.org/scholarships

Summary: To provide financial assistance to Connecticut residents (especially those of Polish descent) who are working on an undergraduate or graduate degree in a field related to Polish studies at a college in the United States or Poland.

Eligibility: Open to residents of Connecticut who are currently enrolled at an accredited college or university in the United States or Poland. Preference is given to students of Polish descent. Graduate students must be working on a degree in Slavic studies with an emphasis on Polish culture. Undergraduates must be taking classes in Polish history, culture, or language.

Financial data: The stipend is $5,000.

Duration: 1 year.

Number awarded: Varies each year.

Deadline: March of each year.

1526 $$ TCADVANCE SCHOLARSHIPS FOR TURKISH AMERICAN STUDENTS

Turkish Coalition of America
1510 H Street, N.W., Suite 900
Washington, DC 20005
Phone: (202) 370–1399; Fax: (202) 370–1398;
Email: info@tc–america.org
Web: www.turkishcoalition.org/scholarships

Summary: To provide financial assistance to Turkish–Americans entering or continuing an undergraduate or graduate program in fields related to public affairs.

Eligibility: Open to Turkish Americans who are graduating high school seniors, current undergraduates, or entering or continuing graduate students. Applicants must be enrolled or planning to enroll full time to work on a degree in law, public policy, public affairs, political science, international relations, communications, journalism, or public relations. They must have a GPA of 3.3 or higher. Along with their application, they must submit an essay of 500 words or less on how they have been able to achieve success both academically and socially, the major obstacles they have faced, how they have been able to overcome those obstacles, and how they plan to contribute to the Turkish American community, to U.S.–Turkey relations, and to Turkey. Selection is based on academic achievement, interest in Turkish American issues as demonstrated by involvement in Turkish American community affairs, and individual leadership qualities conducive to preparing for a career in public affairs, media, or public relations. Financial need is not required, but special consideration is given to applicants who provide information about and prove financial need. Preference is given to students who are admitted to top national universities or liberal arts colleges. U.S. citizenship or permanent resident status is required.

Financial data: The stipend is $5,000 per year.

Duration: 1 year; may be renewed as long as the recipient maintains a GPA of 3.3 or higher.

Number awarded: Up to 15 each year.

Deadline: June of each year.

1527 TERRY WALKER SCHOLARSHIP

Classical Association of the Empire State
c/o Ellyn S. Bibik, Scholarship Chair
P.O. Box 100
Verona, NY 13478
Email: ebibik@nhart.org
Web: wwww.caesny.org/p/scholarships–and–awards.html

Summary: To provide financial assistance to students from New York who are preparing to teach Latin in school.

Eligibility: Open to students who are currently enrolled in college in at least the sophomore year and graduated from a high school in New York and/or are currently attending college in New York. Preference is given to students who are preparing to teach Latin on the elementary or secondary school level. Applicants must submit a self–evaluation essay in which they describe their competence in Latin, speaking skills, arguments for the retention and expansion of Latin in the schools, and ideas for the motivation and instruction of students. Selection is based on that essay, character, scholarship, and intention to teach Latin on the elementary and/or secondary level.

Financial data: The stipend is $1,000.

Duration: 1 year; recipients may reapply.

Number awarded: 1 each year.

Deadline: March of each year.

1528 TEXAS CHORAL DIRECTORS ASSOCIATION STUDENT SCHOLARSHIPS

Texas Choral Directors Association
Attn: Executive Director
7900 Centre Park Drive, Suite A
Austin, TX 78754
Phone: (512) 474–2801; Fax: (512) 474–7873;
Email: tcda@tcda.net
Web: tcda.net/scholarship.html

Summary: To provide financial assistance to upper–division and graduate students from any state who are working on a degree in choral music or church music at a college or university in Texas.

Eligibility: Open to upper–division undergraduates and graduate students from any state who are enrolled at a college or university in Texas. Applicants must have at least a 3.0 GPA and be enrolled in a program of study that will lead to a degree in elementary or secondary choral music or church music. Selection is based on musical contributions and accomplishments, potential for success in the choral music profession, and personal qualifications.

Financial data: The stipend is $1,000.

Duration: 1 year.

Number awarded: Varies each year; recently, 12 of these scholarships were awarded.

Deadline: April of each year.

1529 THE ART INSTITUTES CULINARY SCHOLARSHIP COMPETITION

The Art Institutes International, Inc.
Free Markets Center
210 Sixth Avenue, 33rd Floor
Pittsburgh, PA 15222–2603
Phone: (412) 995–7685; (888) 624–0300; Fax: (412) 918–2598
Web: www.artinstitutes.edu

Summary: To recognize and reward (with scholarships to participating Art Institutes) high school graduates who are winners in a culinary competition.

Eligibility: Open to residents of the United States, Puerto Rico, and Canada who are high school graduates and interested in attending an Art Institute that offers a culinary arts program. Students currently enrolled at an Art Institute are not eligible. Applicants must submit 1) their favorite recipe in standardized format; 2) a 250–word essay on why they would like to study the culinary arts at their participating Art Institute; 3) a copy of their high school transcript or proof of high school graduation; and 4) (if applicable) transcripts from all colleges previously attended. Those entries are judged on the basis of presentation, creative use of ingredients, ease of preparation, quality of essay in conveying the applicant's desire to study the culinary arts, and academic performance. Semifinalists are selected at each Art Institute to compete in local cook–offs. In the cook–offs, winners are selected on the basis of technical skills (such as knife skills), safety and sanitation, mise en place, cooking techniques, and clean–up (45%); and judges' scores in taste and flavor, texture and doneness, portion size, temperature, and presentation (55%).

Financial data: The first–prize winner at each participating Arts Institutes International culinary school receives a $1,500 tuition scholarship to that school.

Duration: The competition is held annually.

Number awarded: Recently, 38 Art Institutes (37 in the United States and 1 in Canada) participated in this program and each awarded 1 scholarship.

Deadline: February of each year.

1530 THE WESLEYAN CHURCH LOAN/GRANT ASSISTANCE

The Wesleyan Church
13300 Olio Road
P.O. Box 50434
Indianapolis, IN 46250
Phone: (317) 774–3911; Fax: (317) 774–3915;
Email: education@wesleyan.org
Web: www.wesleyan.org/em/loan_grant

Summary: To provide money for college to upper–division and graduate students preparing for ordained ministry within the North American General Conference of The Wesleyan Church.

Eligibility: Open to 1) juniors and seniors currently enrolled at colleges and universities of The Wesleyan Church; and 2) graduate students enrolled for theological training leading to a M.Div. degree or its equivalent. Applicants must be members of a local Wesleyan church of the North American General Conference and have been recommended by their local church conference to the district for license as a ministerial student. They must have a GPA of 2.0 or higher.

Financial data: A loan is awarded (amount not specified). No interest is charged while the recipient remains in school. For students who serve in a qualifying ministerial appointment of The Wesleyan Church following graduation, 20% of the loan principal plus interest is cancelled for each year of full–time serving. For students who do not serve The Wesleyan Church following graduation, interest of 10% per year is charged; the full loan must be repaid within 5 years at the rate of 20% of the amount borrowed per year.

Duration: 1 year; may be renewed.

Number awarded: Varies each year.

Deadline: October of each year for fall semester or quarter; January of each year for winter quarter; February of each year for spring semester or quarter; May of each year for summer session.

1531 THEATRE FOR YOUNG AUDIENCES AWARD

John F. Kennedy Center for the Performing Arts
Education Department
Attn: Kennedy Center American College Theater Festival
2700 F Street, N.W.
Washington, DC 20566
Phone: (202) 416–8857; Fax: (202) 416–8860;
Email: KCACTF@kennedy–center.org
Web: www.kcactf.org/KCACTF.ORG_NATIONAL/Kanin_Playwriting.html

Summary: To recognize and reward the student authors of plays on themes that appeal to young people.

Eligibility: Open to students at an accredited junior or senior college in the United States. They are eligible to compete, provided their college agrees to participate in the Kennedy Center American College Theater Festival (KCACTF). Undergraduate students must be carrying at least 6 semester hours, graduate students must be enrolled in at least 3 semester hours, and continuing part–time students must be enrolled in a regular degree or certificate program. These awards are presented to the best student–written plays based on a theme appealing to young people from kindergarten through grade 12.

Financial data: The prize is $1,000. The winner also receives payment of all expenses to attend the Kennedy Center's New Visions/New Voices development laboratory.

Duration: The award is presented annually.

Number awarded: 1 each year.

Deadline: November of each year.

1532 $ THOMAS M. LEMONS SCHOLARSHIP

International Association of Lighting Designers
Attn: Education Trust Fund
440 North Wells Street, Suite 210
Chicago, IL 60654
Phone: (312) 527–3677; Fax: (312) 527–3680;
Email: iald@iald.org
Web: www.iald.org/trust/programs.asp?altlink=152

Summary: To provide financial assistance to U.S. citizens working on an undergraduate or graduate degree in architectural lighting design.

Eligibility: Open to juniors, seniors, and graduate student who are pursuing architectural lighting design as a course of study. Applicants must be U.S. citizens enrolled at a college or university in the United States. Along with their application, they must submit 1) a 2–page resume; 2) an official transcript; 3) 2 letters of reference; 4) up to 10 images of their artwork that show their design ability; and 5) a personal statement, up to 2 pages, on their experience with lighting, why they want to study lighting, or why they should receive this scholarship. Selection is based on those submissions; financial need is not considered.

Financial data: The stipend is $4,000 per year.

Duration: 2 years.

Number awarded: 1 each year.

Deadline: March of each year.

1533 $ THOMAS R. KEATING FEATURE WRITING COMPETITION

Indianapolis Press Club Foundation Inc.
Attn: Scholarship Committee
P.O. Box 40923
Indianapolis, IN 46240–0923
Phone: (317) 701–1130; Fax: (317) 844–5805;
Email: jlabalme.indypress@att.net
Web: indypressfoundation.typepad.com

Summary: To recognize and reward journalism students in Indiana who submit outstanding entries in a writing competition.

Eligibility: Open to students enrolled at colleges and universities in Indiana. Applicants first submit 3 samples of their writing. from which finalists are selected. They are invited to a newsroom in the state where they are given approximately 4 hours to develop a feature story under deadline pressure. Stories are judged the day of the competition and prizes are awarded at a banquet that evening.

Financial data: Prizes vary; recently, the first–place winner received $2,500, second $1,250, and third $750.

Duration: The competition is held annually.

Number awarded: 3 each year.

Deadline: Initial entries must be submitted in September of each year.

1534 $ TILE CONTRACTORS' ASSOCIATION OF AMERICA ARCHITECTURE SCHOLARSHIP

Tile Contractors' Association of America
Attn: Scholarship Program
10434 Indiana Avenue
Kansas City, MO 64137
Phone: (816) 508–9900; Fax: (816) 767–0194;
Email: info@tcaainc.org
Web: www.tcaainc.org/scholarships.php

Summary: To provide financial assistance to students working on a bachelor's or master's degree in architecture.

Eligibility: Open to students working on a professional degree in architecture and enrolled in 1) the third or fourth year of a 5–year program that results in a B.Arch. degree or equivalent; 2) the fourth or fifth year of a 6–year program that results in an M.Arch. degree or equivalent; or 3) the first, second, or third year of a 3– to 4–year program that results in a M.Arch degree. Applicants must submit 500–word essays on their ideas on where and how they feel ceramic tile and/or stone products would further the goal of sustainability (Green Architecture) in commercial and residential construction beyond the traditional applications; and 2) their educational goals as related to their future professional career. Selection is based on those essays, academic performance, and recommendations.

Financial data: The stipend is $2,000.

Duration: 1 year; nonrenewable.

Number awarded: 2 each year.

Deadline: April of each year.

1535 $$ TLMI FOUR YEAR COLLEGE DEGREE SCHOLARSHIP PROGRAM

Tag and Label Manufacturers Institute, Inc.
Attn: Scholarship Committee
1 Blackburn Center
Gloucester, MA 01930
Phone: (978) 282–1400; Fax: (978) 282–3238;
Email: office@tlmi.com
Web: tlmi.com/about–tlmi/scholarships

Summary: To provide financial assistance to upper–division college students who are preparing for a career in the tag and label manufacturing industry.

Eligibility: Open to full–time students entering their junior or senior year and preparing for a career in the tag and label manufacturing industry. Applicants must be majoring in management, production, graphic arts, sales and marketing, and graphic design. They must have a GPA of 3.0 or higher. Along with their application, they must submit 3 references and a 1–page personal statement describing their financial circumstances, career and/or educational goals, employment experience, and reasons why they should be selected for the award. A personal interview may be required. Selection is based on that statement, academic achievement, demonstrated interest in entering the industry, and an interview.

Financial data: The stipend is $5,000. Funds are sent to the recipient's school and paid in 2 equal installments.

Duration: 1 year.

Number awarded: Up to 6 each year.

Deadline: March of each year.

1536 TLMI TWO YEAR COLLEGE DEGREE SCHOLARSHIP PROGRAM

Tag and Label Manufacturers Institute, Inc.
Attn: Scholarship Committee
1 Blackburn Center
Gloucester, MA 01930
Phone: (978) 282–1400; Fax: (978) 282–3238;
Email: office@tlmi.com
Web: tlmi.com/about–tlmi/scholarships

Summary: To provide financial assistance and work experience to students at 2–year and technical colleges who are preparing for a career in the tag and label manufacturing industry.

Eligibility: Open to students enrolled full time in a flexographic printing program at a 2–year college or a technical school that grants degrees and preparing for a career in the tag and label manufacturing industry. Applicants must have a GPA of 3.0 or higher. Along with their application, they must submit a 1–page personal statement describing their financial circumstances, career and/or educational goals, employment experience, and reasons why they should be selected for the award. Selection is based on that statement, academic achievement, and demonstrated interest in entering the industry.

Financial data: The stipend is $1,000. Funds are sent to the recipient's school and paid in 2 equal installments.

Duration: 1 year.

Number awarded: Up to 4 each year.

Deadline: March of each year.

1537 TONY TORRICE PROFESSIONAL DEVELOPMENT GRANT

International Furnishings and Design Association
Attn: IFDA Educational Foundation
2700 East Grace Street
Richmond, VA 23223
Phone: (804) 644–3946; Fax: (804) 644–3834;
Email: colleaguesinc@earthlink.net
Web: www.ifdaef.org/grants.php

Summary: To provide funding to professionals working in the interior furnishing industry who are interested in advancing their career through independent or academic study.

Eligibility: Open to professionals working in the interior furnishing industry in the areas of design, marketing, education, writing and publishing, retailing, or manufacturing. Applicants must be interested in advancing their professional development and career through independent or academic study. Along with their application, they must submit an essay of 300 to 500 words explaining their reasons for wanting to pursue independent or academic study, how they will use the grant funds (a budget), and why they believe they are deserving of the award.

Financial data: The grant is $1,500.

Duration: 1 year.

Number awarded: 1 each year.

Deadline: June of each year.

1538 TRAINING AWARDS FOR RELIGIOUS LEADERSHIP

Order of the Eastern Star
Attn: Right Worthy Grand Secretary
1618 New Hampshire Avenue, N.W.
Washington, DC 20009–2549
Phone: (202) 667–4737; (800) 648–1182; Fax: (202) 462–5162;
Email: RWGSecretary@easternstar.org
Web: www.easternstar.org

Summary: To provide financial assistance for college to individuals who are willing to dedicate their lives to full–time religious service.

Eligibility: Open to applicants preparing for leadership in various fields of religious service, including ministers, missionaries, directors of church music, directors of religious education, and counselors of youth leadership. They need not be affiliated with the Masonic Fraternity or the Order of the Eastern Star. Specific eligibility is determined by each Grand Jurisdiction (state or province) and each chapter under jurisdiction of the General Grand Chapter.

Financial data: The amounts are determined by each jurisdiction or committee on the basis of funds available, number of applicants, and needs of the individual. Funds are paid directly to the recipient's school and may be used, as needed, for books, tuition, board, or medical aid.

Duration: 1 year; may be renewed.

Number awarded: Varies each year.

Deadline: Deadlines vary by jurisdiction or committee; check with the unit in your area for details.

1539 TUSKEGEE AIRMEN SCHOLARSHIPS

Tuskegee Airmen Scholarship Foundation
P.O. Box 83395
Los Angeles, CA 90045
Phone: (310) 215–3985;
Email: anoldwarrior@msn.com
Web: www.taisf.org/scholar.htm

Summary: To provide financial assistance for college to high school seniors and graduates who submit an essay on the history of Tuskegee Airmen, a group of African Americans who served as pilots in World War II.

Eligibility: Open to students who have graduated or will graduate from high school in the current year with a GPA of 3.0 or higher. Applicants must submit a 1–page essay entitled "The Tuskegee Airmen" that reflects an overview of their history. They must also submit documentation of financial need and a 2–page essay that includes a brief autobiographical sketch, educational aspirations, career goals, and an explanation of why financial assistance is essential. Applications must be submitted to individual chapters of Tuskegee Airmen, Inc. which verify them as appropriate, evaluate them, and forward those considered worthy of further consideration to the national competition. Selection is based on academic achievement, extracurricular and community activities, financial need, recommendations, and both essays.

Financial data: The stipend is $1,500.

Duration: 1 year; nonrenewable.

Number awarded: 40 each year.

Deadline: January of each year.

1540 $ UNDERGRADUATES EXPLORING MINISTRY PROGRAM

The Fund for Theological Education, Inc.
Attn: Partnership for Excellence
825 Houston Mill Road, Suite 100
Atlanta, GA 30329
Phone: (404) 727–1450; Fax: (404) 727–1490

Web: www.fteleaders.org/pages/undergrad
Summary: To provide financial assistance to undergraduate students who are considering the ministry as a career.
Eligibility: Open to full–time students entering their junior or senior year at accredited North American colleges and universities. Applicants must be considering ministry as a career. They must be nominated by a college faculty member, administrator, campus minister or chaplain, or current pastor. Nominees must have a GPA of 3.0 or higher and be U.S. or Canadian citizens under 29 years of age. Along with their application, they must submit a 3–page essay in which they discuss the ways in which their core Christian commitments shape their engagement with the world, the community of faith, and the exploration of vocation. Financial need is not considered in the selection process.
Financial data: The stipend is $2,000.
Duration: 1 year.
Number awarded: Up to 50 each year.
Deadline: Nominations must be submitted by January of each year.

1541 $ VIDEO CONTEST FOR COLLEGE STUDENTS

The Christophers
Attn: Youth Department Coordinator
5 Hanover Square, 11th Floor
New York, NY 10004
Phone: (212) 759–4050; (888) 298–4050; Fax: (212) 838–5073;
Email: youth@christophers.org
Web: www.christophers.org/Page.aspx?pid=273
Summary: To recognize and reward videos produced by undergraduate and graduate students that best illustrate the motto of The Christophers, "It's better to light one candle than to curse the darkness."
Eligibility: Open to currently–enrolled undergraduate and graduate students. They are invited to submit films or videos on the theme: "One Person Can Make a Difference." They may use any style or format to express this theme in 5 minutes or less. Entries may be created using film or video, but they must be submitted as region 1 or regionless DVDs or on standard, full–sized VHS in NTSC format. Selection is based on overall impact, effectiveness in conveying the theme, artistic merit, and technical proficiency.
Financial data: First prize is $2,000, second $1,000, third $500, and honorable mentions $100.
Number awarded: 8 each year: 1 each for first, second, and third place plus 5 honorable mentions.
Deadline: June of each year.

1542 $ VIRGINIA MUSEUM OF FINE ARTS UNDERGRADUATE FELLOWSHIPS

Virginia Museum of Fine Arts
Attn: Fellowship Program Coordinator
200 North Boulevard
Richmond, VA 23220–4007
Phone: (804) 204–2685; Fax: (804) 204–2675;
Email: elizabeth.cruickshanks@vmfa.museum
Web: www.vmfa.museum/fellowships
Summary: To offer financial support to residents of Virginia who are interested in working on an undergraduate degree in the arts at a school in any state.
Eligibility: Open to residents of Virginia who are enrolled or planning to enroll full time at an accredited college, university, or school of the arts in any state. Students attending schools in Virginia and paying in–state tuition qualify as residents. Applications are accepted for work or study in the following artistic fields: crafts, drawing, painting, film/video, mixed media, printmaking, photography, or sculpture. Applicants may apply in only 1 of these categories. Only non–commercial, non–instructional projects over which the applicant had control and primary creative responsibility will be considered. Applications must be accompanied by work samples, a resume, transcripts, and a 200–word artistic statement about the work being submitted. Awards are made to those applicants with the highest artistic merit. U.S. citizenship or permanent resident status is required.
Financial data: The stipend is $4,000.
Duration: 1 year.
Number awarded: Varies each year; recently, 12 of these fellowships were awarded.
Deadline: November of each year.

1543 VIVIAN D. TILLMAN SCHOLARSHIP

Sigma Gamma Rho Sorority, Inc.
Attn: National Education Fund
1000 Southhill Drive, Suite 200
Cary, NC 27513
Phone: (919) 678–9720; (888) SGR–1922; Fax: (919) 678–9721;
Email: info@sgrho1922.org
Web: www.sgrho1922.org/nef
Summary: To provide financial assistance to undergraduate students working on a degree in journalism or communications.
Eligibility: Open to undergraduates working on a degree in journalism or communications. The sponsor is a traditionally African American sorority, but support is available to males and females of all races. Applicants must have a GPA of "C" or higher and be able to demonstrate financial need. Along with their application, they must submit a 500–word essay on how they will use their communication or journalism skills for the betterment of the country.
Financial data: A stipend is awarded (amount not specified).
Duration: 1 year.
Number awarded: 1 each year.
Deadline: April of each year.

1544 $$ VSA INTERNATIONAL YOUNG SOLOISTS AWARD

John F. Kennedy Center for the Performing Arts
Attn: Department of VSA and Accessibility
2700 F Street, N.W.
Washington, DC 20566
Phone: (202) 416–8898; (800) 444–1324; Fax: (202) 416–4840; TDD: (202) 416–8728;
Email: vasinfo@kennedy–center.org
Web: www.kennedy–center.org/education/vsa/programs/young_soloists.cfm
Summary: To recognize and reward young musicians from any country who are physically or mentally challenged.
Eligibility: Open to musicians between 14 and 25 years of age who have a disability. Musical ensembles of 2 to 5 performers are also eligible if at least 1 member has a disability and all members are between 14 and 25 years of age. Applicants must be either 1) U.S. citizens or permanent residents; or 2) citizens of other countries living in the United States (as on a student visa). They may be performers in any type of music, including, but not limited to, rock, alt rock, pop, indie, classical, country, folk, jazz, R&B/blues, hip hop, rap, Latin, and world. Along with their application, they must submit recordings of 3 musical selections (audio or video) and a 1–page personal narrative that describes why they should be selected to receive this award. Tapes are evaluated on the basis of technique, tone, intonation, rhythm, and interpretation.
Financial data: The award is $5,000. Funds must be used to assist the recipients' music career.
Duration: The competition is held annually.
Number awarded: 4 each year: 2 from the United States and 2 from other countries.
Deadline: January of each year.

1545 $$ VSA/VOLKSWAGEN GROUP OF AMERICA EXHIBITION PROGRAM

John F. Kennedy Center for the Performing Arts
Attn: Department of VSA and Accessibility
2700 F Street, N.W.
Washington, DC 20566
Phone: (202) 416–8898; (800) 444–1324; Fax: (202) 416–4840; TDD: (202) 416–8728;
Email: vasinfo@kennedy–center.org
Web: www.kennedy–center.org/education/vsa/programs/momentum.cfm
Summary: To recognize and reward emerging visual artists who have a disability.
Eligibility: Open to visual artists between 16 and 25 years of age who have a disability. Applicants must submit samples of their work along with a brief essay on the theme "Momentum" that examines the vital creative spark behind their work. Their essays should describe the force that drives their artistic interest and informs the path they take each day as they move toward their future.
Financial data: Awards are $20,000 for the grand award, $10,000 for the first award, $6,000 for the second award, and $2,000 for each award of excellence.
Duration: The competition is held annually.
Number awarded: 15 each year: 1 grand award, 1 first award, 1 second award, and 12 awards of excellence.
Deadline: June of each year.

1546 WALLY WIKOFF SCHOLARSHIP FOR EDITORIAL LEADERSHIP

National Scholastic Press Association
2221 University Avenue, S.E., Suite 121

Minneapolis, MN 55414
Phone: (612) 625–8335; Fax: (612) 626–0720;
Email: contests@studentpress.org
Web: www.studentpress.org/nspa/contests.html
Summary: To provide financial assistance for college to high school journalists.
Eligibility: Open to high school seniors who have worked on the staff of a student newspaper that is a member of the National Scholastic Press Association (NSPA). Applicants must have a GPA of 3.5 or higher and must submit 3 published editorials and a brief recommendation from the program's adviser.
Financial data: The stipend is $1,000.
Duration: 1 year.
Number awarded: 1 each year.
Deadline: February of each year.

1547 WALTER S. PATTERSON SCHOLARSHIPS

Broadcast Education Association
Attn: Scholars
1771 N Street, N.W.
Washington, DC 20036–2891
Phone: (202) 429–3935; (888) 380–7222; Fax: (202) 775–2981;
Email: BEAMemberServices@nab.org
Web: www.beaweb.org/scholarships.htm
Summary: To provide financial assistance to upper–division and graduate students who are interested in preparing for a career in radio.
Eligibility: Open to juniors, seniors, and graduate students enrolled full time at a college or university where at least 1 department is an institutional member of the Broadcast Education Association (BEA). Applicants must be studying for a career in radio. Selection is based on evidence that the applicant possesses high integrity, superior academic ability, potential to be an outstanding electronic media professional, and a sense of personal and professional responsibility.
Financial data: The stipend is $1,750.
Duration: 1 year; nonrenewable.
Number awarded: 2 each year.
Deadline: October of each year.

1548 $ WASHINGTON FASHION GROUP INTERNATIONAL SCHOLARSHIP

Fashion Group International of Washington
c/o Jean Nathlich, Awards Committee
P.O. Box 20862
Baltimore, MD 21209
Email: jbnathlich@gmail.com
Web: washingtondc.fgi.org/index.php?news=2114
Summary: To provide financial assistance to residents of Maryland, Virginia, and Washington, D.C. interested in preparing for a career in fashion or a fashion–related field at a college or graduate school in any state.
Eligibility: Open to residents of Washington, D.C. and all cities and counties in Maryland and Virginia who are graduating high school seniors or current undergraduate or graduate students. Applicants must be enrolled at a college or university in any state in a fashion or fashion–related degree program (e.g., fashion merchandising, fashion journalism, fashion photography, fashion illustration, textiles and clothing design, interior design, graphic and commercial arts). They must submit a 200–word personal statement on their career goals and motivation for entering a fashion–related career. Selection is based on that statement, academic achievement, 3 to 6 samples of supporting portfolio materials, extracurricular activities, honors and awards, and 2 letters of reference.
Financial data: The maximum stipend is $2,000.
Duration: 1 year; nonrenewable.
Number awarded: 1 or more each year.
Deadline: March of each year.

1549 $ WAYNE ALEXANDER MEMORIAL SCHOLARSHIP

Electronic Document Systems Foundation
Attn: EDSF Scholarship Awards
1845 Precinct Line Road, Suite 212
Hurst, TX 76054
Phone: (817) 849–1145; Fax: (817) 849–1185;
Email: info@edsf.org
Web: www.edsf.org/what_we_do/scholarships/index.html
Summary: To provide financial assistance to undergraduate and graduate students from any country who are working on a degree in the field of document management and graphic communications.
Eligibility: Open to full–time undergraduate and graduate students from any country who demonstrate a strong interest in preparing for a career in the document management and graphic communications industry, including computer science and engineering (e.g., web design, webmaster, software development, materials engineer, applications specialist, information technology designer, systems analyst); graphic and media communications (e.g., graphic designer, illustrator, color scientist, print production, prepress imaging specialist, workflow specialist, document preparation, production and/or document distribution, content management, e–commerce, imaging science, printing, web authoring, electronic publishing, archiving, security); or business (e.g., sales, marketing, trade shows, customer service, project or product development, management). Preference is given to graduate students and upper–division undergraduates, but freshmen and sophomores who can show interest, experience, and/or commitment to the document management and graphic communication industry are encouraged to apply. Special consideration is given to students who attend the University of Central Florida. Applicants must have a GPA of 3.0 or higher. Along with their application, they must submit 2 essays on assigned topics that change annually but relate to the document management and graphic communication industries. Selection is based on the essays, academic excellence, participation in school activities, community service, honors and organizational affiliations, education goals, and recommendations; financial need is not considered.
Financial data: The stipend is $2,000.
Duration: 1 year.
Number awarded: 1 each year.
Deadline: April of each year.

1550 WHY EDUCATION MATTERS ESSAY CONTEST

Fagen Friedman & Fulfrost LLP
Attn: F3 Education Awards Foundation
6300 Wilshire Boulevard, Suite 1700
Los Angeles, CA 90048
Phone: (323) 330–6300; Fax: (323) 330–6311;
Email: nmchugh@fagenfriedman.com
Web: www.fagenfriedman.com/page.php?id=85
Summary: To recognize and reward high school juniors and seniors in California who submit outstanding photographs on specified themes.
Eligibility: Open to seniors at public high schools in California who plan to attend a community college or 4–year university in any state. Applicants must submit essays, up to 700 words in length, that are solely their original work. Their essay must explain how they define success, the role education plays in aiding them to achieve it, their unique passions, and how education helps them to unite those personal passions with professional endeavors. Selection is based on content and style, including passion; clear, articulate, and logical organization; development of ideas; insight; creativity; completeness and consistency in the use of language; variety in sentence structure; range of vocabulary; and use of proper grammar, spelling, and punctuation.
Financial data: Prizes are $1,000. Funds must be used for educational purposes.
Duration: The contest is held annually.
Number awarded: 5 each year.
Deadline: January of each year.

1551 $ WILLIAM D. GREENLEE SCHOLARSHIP

Pennsylvania State System of Higher Education Foundation, Inc.
Attn: Foundation Manager
2986 North Second Street
Harrisburg, PA 17110
Phone: (717) 720–4065; Fax: (717) 720–7082;
Email: eshowers@thePAfoundation.org
Web: www.thepafoundation.org/scholarships/index.asp
Summary: To provide financial assistance to upper–division students at institutions of the Pennsylvania State System of Higher Education (PASSHE) who are majoring in communications, journalism, or political science.
Eligibility: Open to full–time students currently working on an undergraduate degree at 1 of the 14 institutions within the PASSHE. Applicants must have completed at least 60 credits with a major in communications, journalism, or political science and a GPA of 3.0 or higher. Along with their application, they must submit an essay of 500 to 700 words on a quotation from Tom Brokaw regarding the need to make a difference. Financial need is considered in the selection process.
Financial data: The stipend is $2,500.
Duration: 1 year; nonrenewable.
Number awarded: 4 each year.
Deadline: May of each year.

1552 $$ WOMEN'S JEWELRY ASSOCIATION SCHOLARSHIP

Women's Jewelry Association
Attn: Scholarship Chair
52 Vanderbilt Avenue, 19th Floor
New York, NY 10017–3827
Phone: (212) 687–2722; (877) 224–5421; Fax: (212) 355–0219;
Email: lisa@lisaslovis.com
Web: wjamarion.memberlodge.com/Scholarships_and_Grants

Summary: To provide financial assistance for college to women who are interested in careers in jewelry.

Eligibility: Open to women who are enrolled at a college or university and taking classes in fine jewelry and watch design. Applicants in the designer category must submit images (e.g., CAD, drawings of finished work they have created. Applicants in the designer/creator category must submit images of finished pieces that they have designed and created. Applicants in the non–designer category must be interested in preparing for a career as a bench jeweler, appraiser, gemologist, watch–maker, or retailer; they must submit a 2–page essay on the program for which they are applying, what motivated them to attend this program, why they think they deserve a scholarship, why they wish to prepare for a career in jewelry or watches, their goals and aspirations for the future, and how the jewelry industry will benefit from their receiving this scholarship. Financial need is not considered in the selection process.

Financial data: Stipends range from $500 to $7,000.

Duration: 1 year.

Number awarded: Varies each year; recently, 10 of these scholarships, with a total value of $19,300, were awarded.

Deadline: April of each year.

1553 $$ YOUNG AMERICAN CREATIVE PATRIOTIC ART AWARDS

Ladies Auxiliary to the Veterans of Foreign Wars
c/o National Headquarters
406 West 34th Street
Kansas City, MO 64111
Phone: (816) 561–8655; Fax: (816) 931–4753;
Email: info@ladiesauxvfw.org
Web: www.ladiesauxvfw.org/programs/scholarships.html

Summary: To recognize and reward high school students who submit outstanding works of art on patriotic themes.

Eligibility: Open to students in grades 9–12 at high schools in the United States. Home–schooled students are eligible; foreign exchange students are not. Entrants may submit art on paper or canvas using water color, pencil, pastel, charcoal, tempera, crayon, acrylic, pen–and–ink, or oil. Digital art is not accepted. Competitions are held in individual Veterans of Foreign Wars (VFW) Auxiliaries, then at the department level, and finally at the national level. Students must be sponsored by an Auxiliary; they must attend school in the same state as the sponsoring Auxiliary. Entries are judged on the originality of concept, presentation, and patriotism expressed; content, how it relates to patriotism, and clarity of ideas; design technique; total impact of work; and uniqueness.

Financial data: National awards are $10,000 for first prize, $5,000 for second, $2,500 for third, $1,500 for fourth, and $500 for fifth through eighth. Funds must be used for continued art education or for art supplies.

Number awarded: 8 national winners are selected each year.

Deadline: April of each year.

1554 $$ YOUNGARTS COMPETITION AWARDS

National Foundation for Advancement in the Arts
Attn: YoungArts Program
777 Brickell Avenue, Suite 370
Miami, FL 33131
Phone: (305) 377–1140; (800) 970–ARTS; Fax: (305) 377–1149;
Email: info@YoungArts.org
Web: www.youngarts.org/about

Summary: To recognize and reward outstanding high school students and other young people in the arts.

Eligibility: Open to U.S. citizens and permanent residents who are in grades 10–12 in high school, or, if not enrolled in high school, are between 15 and 18 years of age. Applicants may enter competitions in cinematic arts, dance, jazz, music, photography, theater, visual arts, voice, or writing by submitting samples of their work online. On the basis of those entries, award winners are invited to Miami for the final competitions.

Financial data: The gold award is $10,000, silver awards are $5,000, first level awards are $3,000 each, second level $1,500, and third level $1,000. Honorable mentions are $250 and merit awards are $100, but those winners are not invited to Miami.

Duration: The competition is held annually.

Number awarded: Recently, 152 finalists were invited to Miami, including 7 in cinematic arts, 22 in dance, 5 in jazz, 21 in music, 5 in photography, 22 in theater, 28 in visual arts, 20 in voice, and 22 in writing); in addition, 174 honorable mentions and 271 merit awards were made to candidates who were not invited to Miami. Total awards were approximately $500,000, including 5 gold awards, 40 silver awards, 44 first level awards, 43 second level awards, and 20 third level awards.

Deadline: October of each year.

1555 $ YVAR MIKHASHOFF PIANIST/COMPOSER COMMISSIONING PROJECT

Yvar Mikhashoff Trust for New Music
152 Russell Street
Buffalo, NY 14214
Phone: (716) 474–1635;
Email: info@mikhashofftrust.org
Web: www.mikhashofftrust.org

Summary: To recognize and reward young composers and pianists who collaborate on the performance of new works.

Eligibility: Open to teams consisting of a composer and a pianist, each of whom must be younger than 34 years of age. The composer must create a new work for piano solo (with or without electronics) of at least 12 minutes in duration; the pianist must perform the work. Pianists who are composers may not apply to commission themselves. Pianists may not apply to commission a work that is already in progress or has been publicly presented either in part or whole. Composers must submit a 1–page biography, a representative list of works and performances, a signed letter of commitment to the project, and a CD with 3 recent compositions. Pianists must submit a 1–page biography, a list of solo piano pieces and concertos in their repertoire composed since 1950, a demonstration CD with performances of a total of 3 pieces chosen from the repertoire list, copies of 3 programs of past solo piano recitals with at least 50% of the music composed since 1950, a CD or DVD documenting 1 of those recital programs, and a proposal for the premiere of the commissioned piece, including a letter of agreement with the presenting organization for a concert. The application for the competition must be submitted jointly by the pianist and composer.

Financial data: Each award is $3,000.

Duration: The competition is held annually.

Number awarded: 2 each year: 1 composer and 1 pianist.

Deadline: November of each year.

1556 $$ ZIMMER GUNSUL FRASCA ARCHITECTURAL SCHOLARSHIP

Zimmer Gunsul Frasca Architects
Attn: Scholarship
1223 S.W. Washington Street, Suite 200
Portland, OR 97205
Phone: (503) 863–2295;
Email: scholarship@zgf.com
Web: www.zgf.com/pages/zgf_main.php?navloc=firm

Summary: To provide financial assistance to fifth–year and master's degree architecture students at selected schools in designated states.

Eligibility: Open to architecture students who are either entering their fifth year of undergraduate study or enrolled in a master's degree program at an NAAB–accredited program. They must be recommended by the dean of their school; each school may recommend 2 students. Along with their application, they must submit a portfolio with 5 examples of their work and a 1–page essay discussing the design intent of the work shown in the portfolio. Financial need is not considered in the selection process.

Financial data: The stipend is $10,000.

Duration: 1 year.

Number awarded: 1 each year.

Deadline: April of each year.

1557 $ A NURSE I AM SCHOLARSHIP PROGRAM

Cherokee Uniforms
9800 DeSoto Avenue
Chatsworth, CA 91311
Phone: (818) 671–2100; (800) 283–7272, ext. 2117; Fax: (818) 671–2101;
Email: ANurseIAm–Feedback@cherokeeuniforms.com
Web: www.anurseiam.com/application.php

Summary: To provide financial assistance to nursing students who view the film "A Nurse I Am" as part of their program.

Eligibility: Open to nursing students who attend any of the 340 schools of nursing that show the film "A Nurse I Am" as part of their curriculum. Applicants must submit an essay on which of the attributes of the nurses who appear in the film they would most like to emulate and why.

Financial data: The stipend is $2,000.

Duration: 1 year.

Number awarded: 10 each year.

Deadline: February of each year.

1558 AAAE FOUNDATION SCHOLARSHIP

American Association of Airport Executives Foundation
Attn: AAAE Foundation Scholarship Program
601 Madison Street, Suite 400
Alexandria, VA 22314
Phone: (703) 824–0500, ext. 148; Fax: (703) 820–1395;
Email: cindy.dewitt@aaae.org
Web: www.aaae.org/about_aaae/aaae_foundationscholarship_program

Summary: To provide financial assistance to upper–division college students who are majoring in aviation.

Eligibility: Open to full–time college juniors or seniors who are enrolled in an aviation program and have a GPA of 3.0 or higher. Selection is based on academic record, financial need, participation in school and community activities, work experience, and a personal statement.

Financial data: The stipend is $1,000.

Duration: 1 year.

Number awarded: 10 each year.

Deadline: March of each year.

1559 AABB–FENWAL SPECIALIST IN BLOOD BANK SCHOLARSHIP AWARDS

AABB
Attn: Scholarship Coordinator
8101 Glenbrook Road
Bethesda, MD 20814–2749
Phone: (301) 215–6483; Fax: (301) 907–6895;
Email: tjohnson@aabb.org
Web: www.aabb.org

Summary: To recognize and reward essays by students enrolled in programs accredited by AABB (formerly the American Association of Blood Banks).

Eligibility: Open to students enrolled in an accredited program for the education of Specialists in Blood Banking (SBB). Applicants must submit 1 of the following types of entries: 1) a scientific paper reporting experimental work (the work may be an original concept, extension of a major concept, or application of a procedure in blood substitutes, IV immune globulin, hemophilia, or other transfusion medicine topics); 2) an analytical or interpretational review suitable for publication in a professional journal; or 3) an innovative educational syllabus using traditional or advanced technology modalities. The essays or scientific papers must be less than 3,000 words on a subject pertaining to blood banking or a related field. Scientific papers should describe materials and methods used, including experimental design, in sufficient detail to enable other scientists to evaluate or duplicate the work. Reviews should analyze or interpret the subject and not just restate the literature. Educational entries should include a brief summary covering the need for the program, how the program is innovative, and a list of references. A student may submit more than 1 entry; however, no student may receive more than 1 award.

Financial data: The award is $1,500.

Duration: The competition is held annually.

Number awarded: 2 each year.

Deadline: June of each year.

1560 $$ ABLE FLIGHT CAREER TRAINING SCHOLARSHIPS

Able Flight, Inc.
Attn: Scholarships
91 Oak Leaf Lane
Chapel Hill, NC 27516
Phone: (919) 942–4699;
Email: info@ableflight.org
Web: ableflight.org/scholarships

Summary: To provide financial assistance to people who have a physical disability and wish to attend college or technical school to prepare for a career in aviation.

Eligibility: Open to U.S. citizens who use wheelchairs because of spinal cord injury, have congenital birth defects, have lost limbs, or have other physical disabilities. Applicants must be interested in enrolling in a program of career training at a facility selected and approved by the sponsor. They must be working on 1) an FAA–issued Repairman Certificate (Light Sport Aircraft) with Maintenance Rating; 2) an FAA Dispatcher License; or 3) an academic degree related to an aviation career (e.g., aviation management, air traffic control). Along with their application, they must submit an essay of 300 to 500 words describing how they feel this scholarship will change their life and a statement from their attending physician describing the nature of their disability and the effects of the disability upon their level of physical activity.

Financial data: Scholarships cover course fees, testing fees, and travel and lodging as required.

Duration: Most training programs for FAA licenses last 23 to 25 days. The length of academic degree programs is determined by the sponsor on an individual basis.

Number awarded: Varies each year.

Deadline: Applications may be submitted at any time.

1561 $ ABRAHAM ANSON MEMORIAL SCHOLARSHIP

American Society for Photogrammetry and Remote Sensing
Attn: Scholarship Administrator
5410 Grosvenor Lane, Suite 210
Bethesda, MD 20814–2160
Phone: (301) 493–0290, ext. 101; Fax: (301) 493–0208;
Email: scholarships@asprs.org
Web: www.asprs.org/Awards–and–Scholarships

Summary: To provide financial assistance to undergraduate students interested in a program of study to prepare for a career related to geospatial science.

Eligibility: Open to students planning to enroll or currently enrolled as undergraduates at a college or university in the United States. Applicants must be interested in a program of study to prepare for a career in geospatial science or technology, surveying and mapping, photogrammetry, or remote sensing. Along with their application, they must submit a 2–page statement describing their plans for continuing studies towards becoming a professional in a field that uses photogrammetry, remote sensing, surveying and mapping, or land and/or geospatial information science or technology as a key part of its performance. Financial need is not considered in the selection process.

Financial data: The stipend is $2,000. A 1–year student membership in the American Society for Photogrammetry and Remote Sensing (ASPRS) is also provided.

Duration: 1 year.

Number awarded: 1 each year.

Deadline: October of each year.

1562 $ ACCENTURE SWE SCHOLARSHIPS

Society of Women Engineers
Attn: Scholarship Selection Committee
203 North LaSalle Street, Suite 1675
Chicago, IL 60601–1269
Phone: (312) 596–5223; (877) SWE–INFO; Fax: (312) 644–8557;
Email: scholarships@swe.org
Web: societyofwomenengineers.swe.org/index.php/scholarships

Summary: To provide financial assistance to undergraduate women majoring in designated engineering specialties.

Eligibility: Open to women who are entering their sophomore or junior year at a 4–year ABET–accredited college or university. Applicants must be working full time on a degree in computer science or chemical, civil, computer, electrical, industrial, or mechanical engineering and have a GPA of 3.2 or higher. They must be U.S. citizens or permanent residents. Selection is based on merit.

Financial data: The stipend is $2,000.

Duration: 1 year.

Number awarded: 5 each year: 2 to sophomores and 3 to juniors.
Deadline: February of each year.

1563 ADA DENTAL ASSISTING SCHOLARSHIPS

American Dental Association
Attn: ADA Foundation
211 East Chicago Avenue
Chicago, IL 60611
Phone: (312) 440–2547; Fax: (312) 440–3526;
Email: adaf@ada.org
Web: www.ada.org/applyforassistance.aspx
Summary: To provide financial assistance to currently–enrolled dental assisting students.
Eligibility: Open to full–time students entering a dental assisting program accredited by the Commission on Dental Accreditation. They must have a GPA of 3.0 or higher and be able to demonstrate financial need of at least $1,000. U.S. citizenship is required. Selection is based on academic achievement, a written summary of personal and professional goals, letters of reference, and financial need.
Financial data: Stipends range up to $1,000 per year. Funds are to be used to cover school expenses (tuition, fees, books, supplies, living expenses) and are paid in 2 equal installments to the recipient's school.
Duration: 1 year.
Number awarded: Varies each year; recently, 7 of these scholarships were awarded.
Deadline: October of each year.

1564 $$ ADA I. PRESSMAN SCHOLARSHIP

Society of Women Engineers
Attn: Scholarship Selection Committee
203 North LaSalle Street, Suite 1675
Chicago, IL 60601–1269
Phone: (312) 596–5223; (877) SWE–INFO; Fax: (312) 644–8557;
Email: scholarships@swe.org
Web: societyofwomenengineers.swe.org/index.php/scholarships
Summary: To provide financial assistance to women working on an undergraduate or graduate degree in engineering or computer science.
Eligibility: Open to women who will be sophomores, juniors, seniors, or graduate students at ABET–accredited colleges and universities. Applicants must be U.S. citizens or permanent residents working full time on a degree in computer science or engineering and have a GPA of 3.0 or higher. Selection is based on merit.
Financial data: The stipend is $5,000.
Duration: 1 year.
Number awarded: 7 each year.
Deadline: February of each year.

1565 $$ ADECCO ENGINEERING AND TECHNICAL FUTURE ENGINEERS SCHOLARSHIP

Center for Scholarship Administration, Inc.
Attn: Tribble Foundation Scholarship Fund
4320 Wade Hampton Boulevard, Suite G
P.O. Box 1465
Taylors, SC 29687–0031
Phone: (864) 268–3363; Fax: (864) 268–7160;
Email: sallyking@bellsouth.net
Web: www.scholarshipprograms.org/adeng/index.htm
Summary: To provide financial assistance to high school seniors who are interested in studying engineering at a college in any state.
Eligibility: Open to graduating high school seniors who plan to enroll full time at an accredited 2– or 4–year college or university in any state to work on a degree in engineering. Applicants must have a GPA of 3.0 or higher. Along with their application, they must submit a 1–page essay on their vision of the workplace of the 2030s and how they see themselves impacting the engineering industry at large. Selection is based on academic ability, educational goals, and career ambitions.
Financial data: The stipend is $5,000.
Duration: 1 year; nonrenewable.
Number awarded: 1 each year.
Deadline: April of each year.

1566 ADMIRAL GRACE MURRAY HOPPER MEMORIAL SCHOLARSHIPS

Society of Women Engineers
Attn: Scholarship Selection Committee
203 North LaSalle Street, Suite 1675
Chicago, IL 60601–1269
Phone: (312) 596–5223; (877) SWE–INFO; Fax: (312) 644–8557;
Email: scholarships@swe.org
Web: societyofwomenengineers.swe.org/index.php/scholarships
Summary: To provide financial assistance to women who will be entering college as freshmen and are interested in studying engineering or computer science.
Eligibility: Open to women who are entering college as freshmen with a GPA of 3.5 or higher. Applicants must be U.S. citizens or permanent residents planning to enroll full time at an ABET–accredited 4–year college or university and major in computer science or engineering. Selection is based on merit. Preference is given to students in computer–related engineering.
Financial data: The stipend is $1,500.
Duration: 1 year.
Number awarded: 3 each year.
Deadline: May of each year.

1567 AEMP FOUNDATION SCHOLARSHIPS

Association of Equipment Management Professionals
Attn: AEMP Foundation
P.O. Box 1368
Glenwood Springs, CO 81602
Phone: (970) 384–0510, ext. 205; Fax: (970) 384–0512;
Email: sara@aemp.org
Web: www.aemp.org/the–aemp–foundation/for–students
Summary: To provide financial assistance to high school seniors interested in preparing for a career as a heavy equipment technician.
Eligibility: Open to graduating seniors who have maintained a GPA of 2.0 or higher throughout high school. Applicants must be planning to prepare for a career as a heavy equipment technician by attending a college or vocational/technical program that offers a diesel technology program. Along with their application, they must submit brief essays on 1) their career goals; 2) their technical interests; 3) what they consider to the elements of a good work ethic; 4) their idea of a successful work day; 5) their experiences with technology; 6) what intrigues them about a technical career; 7) what they have done thus far to pursue their career goals; and 8) why they think they should receive a scholarship. Financial need is not considered in the selection process.
Financial data: The stipend is $500 per semester ($1,000 per year).
Duration: Up to 4 semesters, provided the recipient remains enrolled full time with a GPA of 3.0 or higher.
Number awarded: 1 or more each year.
Deadline: April of each year.

1568 AFRO–ACADEMIC, CULTURAL, TECHNOLOGICAL AND SCIENTIFIC OLYMPICS (ACT–SO)

Summary: To recognize and reward (with college scholarships) outstanding African American high school students who distinguish themselves in the Afro–Academic, Cultural, Technological and Scientific Olympics (ACT–SO) program.
See Listing #1090.

1569 $ AFSA HIGH SCHOOL SENIOR SCHOLARSHIP CONTEST

American Fire Sprinkler Association
12750 Merit Drive, Suite 350
Dallas, TX 75251
Phone: (214) 349–5965; Fax: (214) 343–8898;
Email: scholarship@firesprinkler.org
Web: www.afsascholarship.org/hsinformation.html
Summary: To recognize and reward, with college scholarships, high school seniors who take an online examination on fire sprinklers.
Eligibility: Open to seniors at high schools in the United States who are U.S. citizens or permanent residents. Home–schooled students are eligible if their course of study is equivalent to that of a senior in high school. Applicants must download an essay of approximately 3,000 words on fire sprinklers. They then submit their answers to a 10–question, multiple–choice, open–book examination. For each question they answer correctly, they are entered into a drawing for a college scholarship. Scholarship winners are selected in a random drawing.

Financial data: The prizes are $2,000 college scholarships. Funds are paid directly to the recipient's institution.
Duration: The competition is held annually.
Number awarded: 10 each year.
Deadline: April of each year.

1570 $ AFTERCOLLEGE/AACN NURSING SCHOLARSHIP FUND

American Association of Colleges of Nursing
One Dupont Circle, N.W., Suite 530
Washington, DC 20036
Phone: (202) 463–6930; Fax: (202) 785–8320;
Email: scholarship@aacn.nche.edu
Web: www.aacn.nche.edu/students/scholarships
Summary: To provide financial assistance to students at institutions that are members of the American Association of Colleges of Nursing (AACN).
Eligibility: Open to students working on a baccalaureate, master's, or doctoral degree at an AACN member school. Special consideration is given to applicants who are 1) enrolled in a master's or doctoral program to prepare for a nursing faculty career; 2) completing an R.N. to baccalaureate (B.S.N.) or master's (M.S.N) program; or 3) enrolled in an accelerated baccalaureate or master's degree nursing program. Applicants must submit a 250–word essay on their goals and aspirations as related to their education, career, and future plans. They must also register and submit their resume to AfterCollege.com.
Financial data: The stipend is $2,500.
Duration: 1 year.
Number awarded: Up to 8 each year: 2 for each application deadline.
Deadline: January, April, July, or October of each year.

1571 $ AGC UNDERGRADUATE SCHOLARSHIPS

Associated General Contractors of America
Attn: AGC Education and Research Foundation
2300 Wilson Boulevard, Suite 400
Arlington, VA 22201
Phone: (703) 837–5342; Fax: (703) 837–5451;
Email: patricianm@agc.org
Web: www.agc.org/cs/about/foundation/scholarship_program
Summary: To provide financial assistance to undergraduate students in a field related to construction.
Eligibility: Open to 1) second–year students at 2–year institutions planning to transfer to a 4–year program; 2) rising college sophomores or juniors in 4–year programs; and 3) rising seniors in 5–year programs. Applicants must be enrolled or planning to enroll full–time in an ABET– or ACCE–accredited construction management or construction–related engineering program and have a GPA of 2.0 or higher. They must be preparing for a career in construction. Financial need is not considered in the selection process. Finalists are interviewed. U.S. citizenship or permanent resident status is required.
Financial data: The stipend is $2,500 per year.
Duration: 1 year; may be renewed for up to 2 additional years.
Number awarded: More than 100 each year.
Deadline: October of each year.

1572 AICHE FUELS AND PETROCHEMICALS DIVISION SCHOLARSHIPS

American Institute of Chemical Engineers
Attn: Fuels and Petrochemicals Division
Three Park Avenue
New York, NY 10016–5991
Phone: (646) 495–1348; Fax: (646) 495–1504;
Email: communications@aiche–fpd.org
Web: www.aiche.org/community/awards/division–forum–awards
Summary: To provide financial assistance to high school seniors who plan to study engineering or science in college.
Eligibility: Open to graduating high school seniors who are sponsored by a member of the Fuels and Petrochemicals Division of the American Institute of Chemical Engineers (AIChE). Each member may sponsor 2 students. Applicants must be planning to attend a 4–year college or university and major in engineering or science. Along with their application, they must submit a 1,000–word essay that discusses a current event regarding the fuels and petrochemicals industry. Selection is based on that essay, honors and awards, extracurricular activities, and academic merit.
Financial data: The stipend is $1,000.
Duration: 1 year; nonrenewable.
Number awarded: 2 each year.
Deadline: January of each year.

1573 $$ AIR FORCE ROTC BIOMEDICAL SCIENCES CORPS

U.S. Air Force
Attn: Headquarters AFROTC/RRUC
551 East Maxwell Boulevard
Maxwell AFB, AL 36112–5917
Phone: (334) 953–2091; (866) 4–AFROTC; Fax: (334) 953–6167;
Email: afrotc1@maxwell.af.mil
Web: afrotc.com
Summary: To provide financial assistance to students who are interested in joining Air Force ROTC in college and preparing for a career as a physical therapist, optometrist, or pharmacist.
Eligibility: Open to U.S. citizens who are freshmen or sophomores in college and interested in a career as a physical therapist, optometrist, or pharmacist. Applicants must have a GPA of 2.0 or higher and meet all other academic and physical requirements for participation in AFROTC. At the time of their Air Force commissioning, they may be no more than 31 years of age. They must agree to serve for at least 4 years as non–line active–duty Air Force officers following graduation from college.
Financial data: Awards are type 2 AFROTC scholarships that provide for payment of tuition and fees, to a maximum of $18,000 per year, plus an annual book allowance of $900. All recipients are also awarded a tax–free subsistence allowance for 10 months of each year that is $350 per month during their sophomore year, $450 during their junior year, and $500 during their senior year.
Duration: 2 or 3 years, provided the recipient maintains a GPA of 2.0 or higher.
Deadline: June of each year.

1574 $ AIST FOUNDATION SCHOLARSHIPS

Association for Iron & Steel Technology
Attn: AIST Foundation
186 Thorn Hill Road
Warrendale, PA 15086–7528
Phone: (724) 814–3044; Fax: (724) 814–3001;
Email: lwharrey@aist.org
Web: www.aistfoundation.org/scholarships/scholarships.htm
Summary: To provide financial assistance for college to students interested in preparing for a career in the iron and steel or steel–related industries.
Eligibility: Open to full–time students entering their sophomore, junior, or senior year at accredited universities in North America (Canada, Mexico, and the United States). Applicants must be majoring in metallurgy, materials science, or engineering (chemical, computer, electrical, environmental, mechanical, or industrial) and have a GPA of 3.0 or higher. Along with their application, they must submit a 2–page essay on their professional goals, explaining why they are interested in a career in the steel industry and how their skills could be applied to enhance the industry. Selection is based on GPA (20%); demonstrated interest in the iron and steel industry (35%); 3 letters of recommendation (30%); and a resume with work experience and extracurricular activities, noting any leadership positions (15%).
Financial data: The stipend is $3,000.
Duration: 1 year; recipients may reapply.
Number awarded: 8 each year.
Deadline: March of each year.

1575 $$ ALABAMA CONCRETE INDUSTRIES ASSOCIATION SCHOLARSHIPS

Summary: To provide financial assistance to students from any state majoring in architecture, building sciences, or engineering in Alabama.
See Listing #1097.

1576 ALABAMA HOME BUILDERS SCHOLARSHIPS

Home Builders Association of Alabama
Attn: Alabama Home Builders Foundation
7515 Halcyon Summit Drive, Suite 200
P.O. Box 241305
Montgomery, AL 36124–1305
Phone: (334) 834–3006; (800) 745–4222;
Email: info@hbaa.org
Web: hbaa.org/wp/foundation–2/scholarships
Summary: To provide financial assistance for college to Alabama residents interested in preparing for a career in the home building industry.

Eligibility: Open to residents of Alabama enrolled in, or attending, a junior college, technical school, or university in the state. Applicants must be working on a certificate or degree in a construction–related field. They must be able to demonstrate financial need.
Financial data: A stipend is awarded (amount not specified).
Duration: 1 year.
Number awarded: Varies each year.
Deadline: March of each year.

1577 $$ ALASKA CHAPTER COLLEGE SCHOLARSHIP

Safari Club International–Alaska Chapter
Attn: Scholarship Committee
P.O. Box 770511
Eagle River, AK 99577
Phone: (907) 980–9018;
Email: Admin@aksafariclub.org
Web: www.aksafariclub.org/#!education/cr4j
Summary: To provide financial assistance to high school seniors in Alaska who have participated in hunting activities and plan to major in a field related to wildlife management in college.
Eligibility: Open to graduating high school seniors in Alaska who have an excellent academic record, have participated in hunting activities, can demonstrate financial need, and plan to major in a field related to wildlife management, wildlife biology, or natural resource management in college. Applicants must be U.S. citizens and able to document participation in local or national conservation activities. Selection is based on academic achievement, leadership, financial need, planned major, and participation in conservation activities, shooting sports programs, and hunting sports.
Financial data: The stipend is $5,000. Funds, which are paid to the student's institution, must be used for tuition, fees, books, supplies, or required equipment.
Duration: 1 year.
Number awarded: 1 each year.
Deadline: March of each year.

1578 $ ALBERT E. AND FLORENCE W. NEWTON NURSING SCHOLARSHIP

Rhode Island Foundation
Attn: Funds Administrator
One Union Station
Providence, RI 02903
Phone: (401) 427–4017; Fax: (401) 331–8085;
Email: lmonahan@rifoundation.org
Web: www.rifoundation.org
Summary: To provide financial assistance to students, especially residents of Rhode Island, working on a degree in nursing.
Eligibility: Open to 1) students enrolled in a baccalaureate nursing program; 2) students in a diploma nursing program; 3) students in a 2–year associate degree nursing program; and 4) active practicing R.N.s working on a bachelor's degree in nursing. Applicants must be studying at a nursing school on a full– or part–time basis and able to demonstrate financial need. They may be enrolled at a school in any state, but preference is given to residents of Rhode Island. Along with their application, they must submit an essay, up to 300 words, on their career goals, particularly as they relate to practicing in or advancing the field of nursing in Rhode Island.
Financial data: The stipend ranges from $500 to $2,000.
Duration: 1 year; may be renewed.
Number awarded: Varies each year; recently, 8 of these scholarships were awarded: 3 new awards and 5 renewals.
Deadline: April of each year.

1579 $ ALFRED G. AND ELMA M. MILOTTE SCHOLARSHIP

Summary: To provide financial assistance to high school seniors or graduates from Washington who wish to attend college or graduate school in any state to work on a degree in a field related to the artistic portrayal of wilderness areas.
See Listing #1102.

1580 $$ ALFRED T. GRANGER STUDENT ART FUND

Summary: To provide financial assistance to residents of Vermont who are interested in working on an undergraduate or graduate degree in a field related to design at a school in any state.
See Listing #1103.

1581 ALICE/JEANNE WAGNER ENDOWMENT SCHOLARSHIP

Epsilon Sigma Alpha International
Attn: ESA Foundation
363 West Drake Road
Fort Collins, CO 80526
Phone: (970) 223–2824; Fax: (970) 223–4456;
Email: esainfo@epsilonsigmaalpha.org
Web: www.epsilonsigmaalpha.org/scholarships–and–grants
Summary: To provide financial assistance to students interested in working on a nursing degree in college.
Eligibility: Open to nursing students who are 1) graduating high school seniors with a GPA of 3.0 or higher or with minimum scores of 22 on the ACT or 1030 on the combined critical reading and mathematics SAT; 2) enrolled in college with a GPA of 3.0 or higher; 3) enrolled at a technical school or returning to school after an absence for retraining of job skills or obtaining a degree; or 4) engaged in online study through an accredited college, university, or vocational school. Selection is based on character (10%), leadership (20%), service (10%), financial need (30%), and scholastic ability (30%).
Financial data: The stipend is $1,000.
Duration: 1 year; may be renewed.
Number awarded: 2 each year.
Deadline: January of each year.

1582 $$ ALICE M. YARNOLD AND SAMUEL YARNOLD SCHOLARSHIP

Alice M. Yarnold and Samuel Yarnold Scholarship Trust
c/o Stephen H. Roberts, Trustee
P.O. Box 2303
Dover, NH 03821–2303
Phone: (603) 436–0666;
Email: sroberts@hpgrlaw.com
Summary: To provide financial assistance to currently–enrolled students in New Hampshire who are majoring in nursing, medicine, or social work at a college or university in any state.
Eligibility: Open to residents of New Hampshire who are enrolled at a college or university in any state and working on a degree in nursing, medicine, or social work. Applicants must be able to demonstrate financial need. Along with their application, they must submit their FAFSA, a copy of their latest transcript, and 2 letters of recommendation.
Financial data: Stipends range from $2,000 to $5,000 annually.
Duration: 1 year; may be renewed up to 3 additional years.
Deadline: April of each year.

1583 $ ALLEN W. PLUMB SCHOLARSHIP

New Hampshire Land Surveyors Foundation
Attn: Scholarship Committee
77 Main Street
P.O. Box 689
Raymond, NH 03077–0689
Phone: (603) 895–4822; (800) 698–5447; Fax: (603) 462–0343;
Email: info@nhlsa.org
Web: www.nhlsa.org/scholarship.htm
Summary: To provide financial assistance to residents of New Hampshire who are studying forestry at a college in any state as preparation for a career in land surveying.
Eligibility: Open to New Hampshire residents enrolled in the second, third, or fourth year of a 2– or 4–year program in forestry at a college or university in any state. Applicants must have shown serious interest, capability, and outstanding accomplishments in surveying courses and must be preparing for a career in land surveying. Along with their application, they must submit an essay about their professional aspirations, their goals in college and afterwards, and factors that make them particularly deserving of support. Financial need is not required.
Financial data: The stipend is $2,000.
Duration: 1 year.
Number awarded: 1 each year.
Deadline: November of each year.

1584 $$ ALMOND SCHOLARSHIP

Syngenta Crop Protection, LLC
410 Swing Road
P.O. Box 18300

Greensboro, NC 27419
Phone: (919) 870–5718; (800) 334–9481;
Email: cmiller@gibbs–soell.com
Web: www.farmassist.com/promo/almonds

Summary: To recognize and reward, with college scholarships, students from California who are involved in almond growing or are members of FFA or 4–H and submit outstanding essays on agriculture.

Eligibility: Open to high school seniors and college freshmen, sophomores, and juniors who either live in California or attend school there. Applicants must either be involved in the almond–growing industry or be members of FFA or 4–H. They must submit an essay, up to 700 words in length, on a topic that changes annually but relates to the future of agriculture in this country and what farmers can do to improve prospects for the industry. Selection is based on 1) creativity and uniqueness of the idea (30 points), flow and organization of the essay (30 points), functionality and professional appeal (20 points), and absence of grammatical or typographical errors (20 points).

Financial data: The prize is a $5,000 scholarship.

Duration: The competition is held annually.

Number awarded: 1 each year.

Deadline: August of each year.

1585 ALPHA MU TAU UNDERGRADUATE SCHOLARSHIPS

Alpha Mu Tau Fraternity
c/o American Society for Clinical Laboratory Science
2025 M Street, N.W., Suite 800
Washington, DC 20036
Phone: (202) 367–1174;
Email: alphamutaujoe@yahoo.com
Web: www.ascls.org/?page=Awards_AMTF

Summary: To provide financial assistance to undergraduate students in the clinical laboratory sciences.

Eligibility: Open to U.S. citizens and permanent residents accepted into or currently enrolled in an undergraduate program in clinical laboratory science, including cytotechnology, histotechnology, clinical laboratory science/medical technology, or clinical laboratory technician/medical laboratory technician. Applicants must be entering their last year of study. Along with their application, they must submit a 500–word statement describing their interest and reasons for preparing for a career in clinical laboratory science. Financial need is also considered in the selection process.

Financial data: The stipend is $1,500.

Duration: 1 year.

Number awarded: Several each year.

Deadline: March of each year.

1586 $$ ALTRIA SCHOLARS

Virginia Foundation for Independent Colleges
Attn: Director of Development
8010 Ridge Road, Suite B
Richmond, VA 23229–7288
Phone: (804) 288–6609; (800) 230–6757; Fax: (804) 282–4635;
Email: info@vfic.org
Web: www.vfic.org/scholarships/scholarships_vfic.html

Summary: To provide financial assistance to students majoring in designated fields at a college or university that is a member of the Virginia Foundation for Independent Colleges (VFIC).

Eligibility: Open to sophomores who are enrolled as full–time second–semester sophomores at 1 of the 15 VFIC member institutions. Applicants must be nominated by their institution. They must have a GPA of 3.0 or higher and a declared major in accounting, biology, business management, business, chemistry, computer science, economics, engineering, finance, marketing, or physics. Selection is based on merit and financial need. Special consideration is given to underserved populations. U.S. citizenship is required.

Financial data: The stipend is $5,000 per year.

Duration: 1 year (the junior year). May be renewed for the senior year, provided the recipient maintains a GPA of 3.0 or higher and a record of good citizenship and conduct.Funding for this program, established in 2001, is provided by Altria Group (parent company of Philip Morris USA). Recipients also have an opportunity to apply for paid internships with Altria. The 15 member institutions are Bridgewater College, Emory and Henry College, Hampden–Sydney College, Hollins University, Lynchburg College, Mary Baldwin College, Marymount University, Randolph College, Randolph–Macon College, Roanoke College, Shenandoah University, Sweet Briar College, University of Richmond, Virginia Wesleyan College, and Washington and Lee University.

Number awarded: 10 each year.

Deadline: October of each year.

1587 $$ ALTRIA SCHOLARSHIPS OF THE THURGOOD MARSHALL COLLEGE FUND

Thurgood Marshall College Fund
Attn: Campus Relations Associate
901 F Street, N.W., Suite 300
Washington, DC 20004
Phone: (202) 747–7183; Fax: (202) 652–2934;
Email: janay.hawkins@tmcfund.org
Web: www.thurgoodmarshallfund.net/current–scholarships

Summary: To provide financial assistance to African American upper–division students working on a degree in designated fields at public Historically Black Colleges and Universities (HBCUs) that are members of the Thurgood Marshall College Fund (TMCF).

Eligibility: Open to students currently enrolled as juniors at any of the 47 TMCF member institutions. Some awards are designated for students at Florida A&M University, North Carolina A&T State University, or Winston–Salem State University. Applicants must be majoring in accounting, business, economics, engineering, finance, mathematics, science, or technology. They must have a GPA of 3.5 or higher and be able to demonstrate financial need. Along with their application, they must submit a 500–word essay on 1 of the following topics: 1) a significant setback, challenge, or opportunity in their life and the impact it has had on them; 2) what inspired them to pursue a degree in their current field of study and the impact it will have on our society; or 3) what it means to be the first person in their family to receive a college degree. U.S. citizenship or permanent resident status is required.

Financial data: The stipend is $3,100 per semester ($6,200 per year).

Duration: 1 year; nonrenewable.

Number awarded: 17 each year.

Deadline: April of each year.

1588 $ ALWIN B. NEWTON SCHOLARSHIP

American Society of Heating, Refrigerating and Air–Conditioning Engineers
Attn: Scholarship Administrator
1791 Tullie Circle, N.E.
Atlanta, GA 30329–2305
Phone: (404) 539–1120; Fax: (404) 539–2120;
Email: lbenedict@ashrae.org
Web: www.ashrae.org/students/page/1271

Summary: To provide financial assistance to undergraduate engineering students interested in heating, ventilating, air conditioning, and refrigeration (HVAC&R).

Eligibility: Open to undergraduate engineering students working on a bachelor's degree in a program recognized as accredited by the American Society of Heating, Refrigerating and Air–Conditioning Engineers (ASHRAE). Applicants must be enrolled full time in a course of study that has traditionally been preparatory for the profession of HVAC&R. They must have a GPA of 3.0 or higher and a standing in the top 30% of their class. Selection is based on potential service to the HVAC&R profession, financial need, leadership ability, recommendations from instructors, and work ethics.

Financial data: The stipend is $3,000.

Duration: 1 year.

Number awarded: 1 each year.

Deadline: November of each year.

1589 $$ AMERICAN ASSOCIATION OF BLACKS IN ENERGY NATIONAL SCHOLARSHIPS

American Association of Blacks in Energy
Attn: Scholarship Committee
1625 K Street, N.W., Suite 405
Washington, DC 20006
Phone: (202) 371–9530; Fax: (202) 371–9218;
Email: info@aabe.org
Web: aabe.org/index.php?component=pages&id=4

Summary: To provide financial assistance to underrepresented minority high school seniors who are interested in majoring in business, engineering, mathematics, or physical science in college.

Eligibility: Open to members of minority groups underrepresented in energy–related fields (African Americans, Hispanics, and Native Americans) who are graduating high school seniors. Applicants must have a "B" academic average overall and a "B" average in mathematics and science courses. They must be planning to attend an accredited college or university to major in business, engineering, mathematics, technology, or the physical sciences. Along with their application, they must submit a transcript, 2 letters of reference, and documentation of financial need. The applicant who demonstrates the most outstanding

achievement and promise is presented with the Premier Award. All applications must be submitted to the local office of the sponsoring organization in the student's state. For a list of local offices, contact the scholarship committee at the national office.
Financial data: The stipends are $3,000. The Premier Award is an additional $5,000. All funds are paid directly to the students upon proof of enrollment at an accredited college or university.
Duration: 1 year; nonrenewable.
Number awarded: 6 each year (1 in each of the organization's regions); of those 6 winners, 1 is chosen to receive the Premier Award.
Deadline: March of each year.

1590 $ AMERICAN ASSOCIATION OF OCCUPATIONAL HEALTH NURSES FOUNDATION ACADEMIC SCHOLARSHIPS

American Association of Occupational Health Nurses, Inc.
Attn: AAOHN Foundation
7794 Grow Drive
Pensacola, FL 32514
Phone: (850) 474–6963; (800) 241–8014; Fax: (850) 484–8762;
Email: aaohn@aaohn.org
Web: www.aaohn.org/grants/research–grants.html
Summary: To provide financial assistance to registered nurses who are working on a bachelor's or graduate degree to prepare for a career in occupational and environmental health.
Eligibility: Open to registered nurses who are enrolled in a baccalaureate or graduate degree program. Applicants must demonstrate an interest in, and commitment to, occupational and environmental health. Along with their application, they must submit a 500–word narrative on their professional goals as they relate to the academic activity and the field of occupational and environmental health. Selection is based on that essay (50%), impact of education on applicant's career (20%), and 2 letters of recommendation (30%).
Financial data: The stipend is $2,500.
Duration: 1 year; may be renewed up to 2 additional years.
Number awarded: 2 each year.
Deadline: January of each year.

1591 AMERICAN ASSOCIATION ON HEALTH AND DISABILITY SCHOLARSHIPS

American Association on Health and Disability
Attn: Scholarship Committee
110 North Washington Street, Suite 328–J
Rockville, MD 20850
Phone: (301) 545–6140, ext. 206; Fax: (301) 545–6144;
Email: contact@aahd.us
Web: www.aahd.us/page.php?pname=ScholarshipProgram
Summary: To provide financial assistance to undergraduate and graduate students who have a disability, especially those studying a field related to health and disability.
Eligibility: Open to high school graduates who have a documented disability and are enrolled in an accredited 4–year college or university as a full–time undergraduate or full– or part–time graduate student. Preference is given to students working on a degree in public health, disability studies, health promotion, or other field related to health and disability. Along with their application, they must submit a 3–page personal statement that includes a personal history, educational and career goals, extracurricular activities, and reasons why they should be selected to receive this scholarship. U.S. citizenship or permanent resident status is required.
Financial data: Stipends range up to $1,000.
Duration: 1 year.
Number awarded: 2 each year.
Deadline: November of each year.

1592 $$ AMERICAN CHEMICAL SOCIETY SCHOLARS PROGRAM

American Chemical Society
Attn: Scholars Program
1155 16th Street, N.W.
Washington, DC 20036
Phone: (202) 872–6250; (800) 227–5558, ext. 6250; Fax: (202) 872–4361;
Email: scholars@acs.org
Web: portal.acs.org
Summary: To provide financial assistance to underrepresented minority students who have a strong interest in chemistry and a desire to prepare for a career in a chemically–related science.
Eligibility: Open to 1) college–bound high school seniors; 2) freshmen, sophomores, and juniors enrolled full time at an accredited college or university; 3) community college students planning to transfer to a 4–year school; and 4) community college students working on a 2–year degree. Applicants must be African American, Hispanic/Latino, or Native American. They must be majoring or planning to major in chemistry, biochemistry, chemical engineering, or other chemically–related fields, such as environmental science, materials science, or toxicology, in preparation for a career in the chemical sciences or chemical technology. Students planning careers in medicine or pharmacy are not eligible. U.S. citizenship or permanent resident status is required. Selection is based on academic record (GPA of 3.0 or higher), career objective, leadership ability, participation in school activities, community service, and financial need.
Financial data: Annual stipends are $2,500 for freshmen, $3,000 for sophomores, or $5,000 for seniors. Funds are sent directly to the recipient's college or university.
Duration: 1 year; may be renewed.
Number awarded: Approximately 135 new awards are granted each year.
Deadline: February of each year.

1593 $ AMERICAN COUNCIL OF INDEPENDENT LABORATORIES ACADEMIC SCHOLARSHIPS

American Council of Independent Laboratories
Attn: ACIL Scholarship Alliance
1875 I Street, N.W., Suite 500
Washington, DC 20006
Phone: (202) 887–5872; Fax: (202) 887–0021;
Email: info@acil.org
Web: www.acil.org/displaycommon.cfm?an=13
Summary: To provide financial assistance to upper–division and graduate students working on a degree in the natural or physical sciences.
Eligibility: Open to college juniors, seniors, and graduate students working on a degree in physics, chemistry, engineering, geology, biology, or environmental sciences. Applicants must submit a brief resume or personal statement outlining their activities in college, including their field of study and future plans. Selection is based on academic achievement, career goals, leadership, and financial need. Children and grandchildren of employees of member companies of the American Council of Independent Laboratories (ACIL) who are planning scientific or engineering careers are especially encouraged to apply.
Financial data: Stipends range from $1,000 to $4,000.
Duration: 1 year.
Number awarded: Varies each year.
Deadline: April of each year.

1594 AMERICAN FLORAL ENDOWMENT VOCATIONAL SCHOLARSHIPS

American Floral Endowment
1601 Duke Street
Alexandria, VA 22314
Phone: (703) 838–5211; Fax: (703) 838–5212;
Email: afe@endowment.org
Web: endowment.org/floriculture–scholarshipsinternships.html
Summary: To provide financial assistance to vocational students in horticulture.
Eligibility: Open to students who have been accepted in a 1– or 2–year vocational program. Applicants must have a major interest in horticulture and intentions of becoming a grower or greenhouse manager. They must by U.S. or Canadian citizens or permanent residents and have a GPA of 2.0 or higher. Along with their application, they must submit a statement describing their career goals and the academic, work–related, and/or life experiences that support those goals. Financial need is considered in the selection process.
Financial data: The stipend varies each year; recently, it was $1,350.
Duration: 1 year.
Number awarded: 1 each year.
Deadline: April of each year.

1595 AMERICAN HELICOPTER SOCIETY STUDENT DESIGN COMPETITION

American Helicopter Society
Attn: Deputy Director
217 North Washington Street

Alexandria, VA 22314–2538
Phone: (703) 684–6777; Fax: (703) 739–9279;
Email: Staff@vtol.org
Web: www.vtol.org/education/student–design–competition

Summary: To recognize and reward undergraduate and graduate students who submit outstanding designs for a helicopter.

Eligibility: Open to undergraduate and graduate students who may enter as individuals or as teams up to 10 members. Undergraduates and graduate students compete in separate categories. A third category is limited to new entrants from schools (graduate or undergraduate) that have not participated in at least 2 of the prior 3 competitions. Applicants must submit a completed design for a helicopter that meets annual competition specifications; recently, the program called for a rotary winged pylon racer. Selection is based on technical content (40 points), application and feasibility (25 points), originality (20 points), and organization and presentation (15 points).

Financial data: Awards in the graduate category are $1,300 for first place and $700 for second. In the undergraduate category, first place is $800 and second $400. The best new entrant receives $300. The sponsor also reimburses up to $1,000 in travel expenses for the team member who presents a technical summary of the design at the international forum.

Duration: The competition is held annually.

Number awarded: 5 awards are presented each year: 2 to undergraduates, 2 to graduate students, and 1 to a new entry.

Deadline: Letters of intent must be submitted by February of each year.

1596 $$ AMERICAN INSTITUTE OF STEEL CONSTRUCTION EDUCATION FOUNDATION SCHOLARSHIPS

American Institute of Steel Construction
Attn: Director of University Relations
1 East Wacker Drive, Suite 700
Chicago, IL 60601–1802
Phone: (312) 670–5408; Fax: (312) 670–5403;
Email: gavlin@aisc.com
Web: www.aisc.org/content.aspx?id=716

Summary: To provide financial assistance to upper–division and graduate engineering students at schools in any state who demonstrate an interest in structural steel.

Eligibility: Open to full–time students entering their junior or senior year or working on a master's degree at universities in any state. Applicants must be working on a degree in engineering (architectural, construction, or civil) or construction management. Along with their application, they must submit a 1–page essay that demonstrates either 1) steel–related course work and/or thesis research with a strong structural steel orientation; or 2) a proposed course work plan of study and/or proposed thesis concentration in structural steel. Selection is based on that essay, academic performance, and a faculty recommendation. U.S. citizenship is required.

Financial data: The stipend is $5,000.

Duration: 1 year.

Number awarded: 9 each year.

Deadline: April of each year.

1597 $ AMERICAN PUBLIC TRANSPORTATION FOUNDATION SCHOLARSHIP AWARDS PROGRAM

American Public Transportation Association
Attn: American Public Transportation Foundation
1666 K Street, N.W., Suite 1100
Washington, DC 20006
Phone: (202) 496–4803; Fax: (202) 496–4323;
Email: yconley@apta.com
Web: www.aptfd.org/work/scholarship.htm

Summary: To provide financial assistance to undergraduate and graduate students who are preparing for a career in public transportation.

Eligibility: Open to college sophomores, juniors, seniors, and graduate students who are preparing for a career in the transit industry, either with a transit agency or a transit business member organization. Any member organization of the American Public Transportation Association (APTA) can nominate and sponsor candidates for this scholarship. Nominees must be enrolled in a fully–accredited institution, have and maintain at least a 3.0 GPA, and be either employed by or demonstrate a strong interest in entering the public transportation industry. They must submit a 1,000–word essay on the topic, "In what segment of the public transportation industry will you make a career and why?" Selection is based on demonstrated interest in the transit field as a career, need for financial assistance, academic achievement, essay content and quality, and involvement in extracurricular citizenship and leadership activities. The Donald C. Hyde Memorial Essay Award is presented to the applicant who submits the best response to the required essay component of the program.

Financial data: The stipend is $2,500. The winner of the Donald C. Hyde Memorial Essay Award receives an additional $500.

Duration: 1 year; may be renewed.

Number awarded: At least 2 each year.

Deadline: May of each year.

1598 $ AMERICAN ROYAL SCHOLARS

American Royal Association
1701 American Royal Court
Kansas City, MO 64102
Phone: (816) 221–9800; Fax: (816) 221–8189;
Email: ALD@americanroyal.com
Web: www.americanroyal.com/p/About/158

Summary: To provide financial assistance to students at colleges in designated midwestern states, especially those who demonstrate an interest in agriculture.

Eligibility: Open to residents of any state who are enrolled at 4–year colleges and universities in Illinois, Iowa, Kansas, Minnesota, Missouri, Nebraska, Oklahoma, or South Dakota. Special consideration is given to students working on a degree in a field related to agriculture. Applicants must have completed at least 32 credit hours in a bachelor's or higher degree program, have a GPA of 2.5 or higher, and be younger than 24 years of age. Along with their application, they must submit 500–word essays on 1) what they see as the greatest challenge facing agriculture in the next 10 years and how they would address that challenge; and 2) the challenges that young people have to make to become successful, contributing, and well–rounded members of society. Financial need is not considered in the selection process.

Financial data: The stipend is $2,500.

Duration: 1 year; nonrenewable.

Number awarded: 6 each year.

Deadline: June of each year.

1599 AMERICAN SOCIETY FOR ENOLOGY AND VITICULTURE SCHOLARSHIPS

American Society for Enology and Viticulture
Attn: Scholarship Committee
1784 Picasso Avenue, Suite D
P.O. Box 1855
Davis, CA 95617–1855
Phone: (530) 753–3142; Fax: (530) 753–3318;
Email: society@asev.org
Web: www.asev.org/scholarship–program

Summary: To provide financial assistance to graduate and undergraduate students interested in working on a degree in enology, viticulture, or another area related to the wine and grape industry.

Eligibility: Open to upper–division and graduate students working on a degree in enology, viticulture, or another field emphasizing a science basic to the wine and grape industry. Applicants must be enrolled or accepted full time at a 4–year accredited college or university. They must reside in North America (including Canada and Mexico) and have a GPA of 3.0 or higher as undergraduates or 3.2 as graduate students. Along with their application, they must supply a written statement of intent to prepare for a career in the wine or grape industry. Financial need is not considered in the selection process.

Financial data: The awards are not in predetermined amounts and may vary from year to year.

Duration: Students receive quarter or semester stipends. Recipients are eligible to reapply each year in open competition with new applicants.

Number awarded: Varies each year; recently, 13 of these scholarships were awarded.

Deadline: February of each year.

1600 AMERICAN SOCIETY FOR HORTICULTURAL SCIENCE SCHOLARS AWARD

American Society for Horticultural Science
1018 Duke Street
Alexandria, VA 22314
Phone: (703) 836–4606; Fax: (703) 836–2024;
Email: tforbes@ashs.org
Web: www.ashs.org/db/awards/record_detail.lasso?x=39

Summary: To provide financial assistance to undergraduate students majoring in horticulture.

Eligibility: Open to full–time undergraduate students of any class standing who are actively working on a degree in horticulture at a 4–year college or university. Applicants must be nominated by the chair of the department in which they are majoring; each department may nominate only 1 student. They must submit transcripts, 3 letters of reference, a complete resume and/or vitae, and an essay of 250 to 500 words on their reasons for interest in horticulture and for selecting their intended field of work after graduation. Selection is based on academic excellence in the major and supporting areas of science; participation in extracurricular, leadership, and research activities relating to horticulture; participation in university and community service; demonstrated commitment to the horticultural science profession and related career fields; and related horticultural experiences. Financial need is not considered.
Financial data: The stipend is $1,500.
Duration: 1 year.
Number awarded: 2 each year.
Deadline: February of each year.

1601 AMERICAN SOCIETY OF CRIME LABORATORY DIRECTORS SCHOLARSHIP PROGRAM

American Society of Crime Laboratory Directors
Scholarship Application
139K Technology Drive
Garner, NC 27529
Phone: (919) 773–2044; Fax: (919) 861–9930
Web: www.ascld.org/content/student–resources
Summary: To provide financial assistance to students preparing for careers in forensic science.
Eligibility: Open to juniors, seniors, and graduate students who are working on a degree in forensic science, forensic chemistry, or physical or natural science. Current forensic science laboratory employees working on a graduate degree are not eligible. Applicants must submit a statement describing their motivation for applying for this award, including their interest in specific forensic disciplines, career goals, past projects, financial need, or any other topic that will help explain their situation. Selection is based on that statement, overall scholastic record, scholastic record in forensic science course work, motivation or commitment to a forensic science career, and recommendations.
Financial data: The stipend is $1,000.
Duration: 1 year.
Number awarded: 1 or more each year.
Deadline: April of each year.

1602 $ AMERICAN SOCIETY OF HEATING, REFRIGERATING AND AIR–CONDITIONING ENGINEERS GENERAL SCHOLARSHIPS

American Society of Heating, Refrigerating and Air–Conditioning Engineers
Attn: Scholarship Administrator
1791 Tullie Circle, N.E.
Atlanta, GA 30329–2305
Phone: (404) 539–1120; Fax: (404) 539–2120;
Email: lbenedict@ashrae.org
Web: www.ashrae.org/students/page/1271
Summary: To provide financial assistance to undergraduate engineering students interested in heating, ventilating, air conditioning, and refrigeration (HVAC&R).
Eligibility: Open to undergraduate engineering students working on a bachelor's degree in a program recognized as accredited by the American Society of Heating, Refrigerating and Air–Conditioning Engineers (ASHRAE). Applicants must be enrolled full time in a course of study that has traditionally been preparatory for the profession of HVAC&R. They must have a GPA of 3.0 or higher and a standing in the top 30% of their class. Selection is based on potential service to the HVAC&R profession, financial need, leadership ability, recommendations from instructors, and work ethics.
Financial data: The stipend is $3,000.
Duration: 1 year.
Number awarded: 2 each year.
Deadline: November of each year.

1603 $ AMERICAN SOCIETY OF NAVAL ENGINEERS SCHOLARSHIP PROGRAM

American Society of Naval Engineers
Attn: Scholarship Committee
1452 Duke Street
Alexandria, VA 22314–3458
Phone: (703) 836–6727; Fax: (703) 836–7491;
Email: asnehq@navalengineers.org
Web: www.navalengineers.org
Summary: To provide financial assistance to undergraduate and graduate students who are interested in the field of naval engineering.
Eligibility: Open to students entering the final year of a full–time undergraduate program or starting the first year of full–time graduate study at an accredited college or university. Scholarships are not available to doctoral candidates or to persons who already have an advanced degree. Applicants must be U.S. citizens who have demonstrated an interest in a career in naval engineering. Eligible programs of study include naval architecture; aeronautical, civil, electrical, electronic, environmental, marine, mechanical, ocean, or structural engineering; or other relevant military and civilian fields. Graduate student candidates must be members of the American Society of Naval Engineers (ASNE). Selection is based on academic record, work history, professional promise, interest in naval engineering, extracurricular activities, and recommendations. Financial need may also be considered.
Financial data: The stipends are $3,000 per year for undergraduates or $4,000 per year for graduate students. Funds may be used for the payment of tuition, fees, and school–related expenses.
Duration: 1 year.
Number awarded: Varies each year; since the program was established, it has awarded 421 of these scholarships.
Deadline: February of each year.

1604 $$ AMERICAN SYSTEMS HBCU SCHOLARSHIPS

Armed Forces Communications and Electronics Association
Attn: AFCEA Educational Foundation
4400 Fair Lakes Court
Fairfax, VA 22033–3899
Phone: (703) 631–6138; (800) 336–4583, ext. 6138; Fax: (703) 631–4693;
Email: scholarshipsinfo@afcea.org
Web: www.afcea.org
Summary: To provide funding to students majoring in fields of science, technology, engineering, or mathematics (STEM) at an Historically Black College or University (HBCU).
Eligibility: Open to sophomores and juniors enrolled full time at an accredited 2– or 4–year HBCU or in a distance learning or online degree program affiliated with those institutions. They must be working toward a bachelor's degree in such STEM fields as engineering (aerospace, computer, electrical, or systems), computer science, computer engineering technology, computer information systems, mathematics, physics, information systems management, or other field directly related to the support of U.S. intelligence or homeland security enterprises. Special consideration is given to military enlisted personnel and veterans.
Financial data: The stipend is $5,000.
Duration: 1 year; may be renewed.
Number awarded: At least 2 each year.
Deadline: April of each year.

1605 $$ AMERICAN WELDING SOCIETY DISTRICT SCHOLARSHIPS

American Welding Society
Attn: AWS Foundation, Inc.
550 N.W. LeJeune Road
Miami, FL 33126
Phone: (305) 445–6628; (800) 443–9353, ext. 212; Fax: (305) 443–7559;
Email: found@aws.org
Web: www.aws.org/w/a/foundation/district_scholarships.html
Summary: To provide financial assistance to students interested in studying in a vocational training, community college, or degree program in welding or a related field of study.
Eligibility: Open to students enrolled in a welding–related educational or training program. Applicants must be a high school graduate or possess a GED certificate. Selection is based on transcripts; a personal statement of ambitions, goals, background, and other factors that indicate a commitment to pursuing welding education; and financial need.
Financial data: Stipends are intended to cover tuition, books, supplies, and related institutional charges.
Duration: 1 year; recipients may reapply.
Number awarded: Varies each year; recently, 208 of these scholarships were awarded.
Deadline: February of each year.

1606 AMFA SCHOLARSHIP

AMTSociety
Attn: Scholarship Program
801 Cliff Road East, Suite 201
Burnsville, MN 55337
Email: jhawkins@mtsu.edu
Web: www.amtsociety.org/scholarships.jsp

Summary: To provide financial assistance to students interested in preparing for a career as a licensed aircraft maintenance technician (AMT).

Eligibility: Open to U.S. citizens who have completed at least 1 semester of training at an FAA compliant that will prepare them to become a professional aircraft maintenance technician. Applicants must have a GPA of 3.0 or higher. Along with their application, they must submit a 500–word essay on the advantages of a craft specific union as compared to an industrial union for aircraft mechanics.

Financial data: The stipend is $1,500.

Duration: Scholarship funds must be used within 1 year.

Number awarded: 1 each year.

Deadline: December of each year.

1607 $ AMS FRESHMAN UNDERGRADUATE SCHOLARSHIPS

American Meteorological Society
Attn: Development and Student Program Manager
45 Beacon Street
Boston, MA 02108–3693
Phone: (617) 227–2426, ext. 3907; Fax: (617) 742–8718;
Email: dFernandez@ametsoc.org
Web: www.ametsoc.org/amsstudentinfo/scholfeldocs/index.html

Summary: To provide financial assistance to high school seniors planning to attend college to prepare for a career in the atmospheric or related oceanic or hydrologic sciences.

Eligibility: Open to high school seniors entering their freshman year of college to work on a bachelor's degree in the atmospheric or related oceanic or hydrologic sciences. Applicants must be U.S. citizens or permanent residents planning to enroll full time. Along with their application, they must submit a 500–word essay on how they believe their college education, and what they learn in the atmospheric and related sciences, will help them to serve society during their professional career. Selection is based on performance in high school, including academic records, recommendations, scores from a national examination, and the essay. Financial need is not considered. The sponsor specifically encourages applications from women, minorities, and students with disabilities who are traditionally underrepresented in the atmospheric and related oceanic sciences.

Financial data: The stipend is $2,500 per academic year.

Duration: 1 year; may be renewed for the second year of college study.

Number awarded: Varies each year; recently, 14 of these scholarships were awarded.

Deadline: February of each year.

1608 $ ANDREA PATTERSON SCHOLARSHIP

Board of Registered Polysomnographic Technologists
Attn: Scholarship Committee
8400 Westpark Drive, Second Floor
McLean, VA 22102
Phone: (703) 610–9020; Fax: (703) 610–0229;
Email: info@brpt.org
Web: www.brpt.org/default.asp?contentID=58

Summary: To provide financial assistance to students interested in sleep technology and preparing for a career as a polysomnographic technologist.

Eligibility: Open to students working on or planning to work on a polysomnographic technologist credential. Applicants must submit a 750–word biography on their experience, interest in sleep, academic abilities, and why they deserve this scholarship. Selection is based on that biography, involvement in professional sleep organizations, work experience, and letters of recommendation.

Financial data: The stipend is $2,500. Funds may be used only for payment of tuition.

Duration: 1 year.

Number awarded: 1 each year.

Deadline: October of each year.

1609 $$ ANITA BORG MEMORIAL SCHOLARSHIPS

Google Inc.
Attn: Scholarships
1600 Amphitheatre Parkway
Mountain View, CA 94043–8303
Phone: (650) 253–0000; Fax: (650) 253–0001;
Email: anitaborgscholarship@google.com
Web: www.google.com/intl/en/anitaborg/us

Summary: To provide financial assistance to women working on a bachelor's or graduate degree in a computer–related field.

Eligibility: Open to women who are entering their senior year of undergraduate study or are enrolled in a graduate program in computer science, computer engineering, or a closely–related field. Applicants must be full–time students at a university in the United States and have a GPA of 3.5 or higher. They must submit essays of 400 to 600 words on 1) a significant technical project on which they have worked; 2) their leadership abilities; 3) what they would do if someone gave them the funding and resources for a 3– to 12–month project to investigate a technical topic of their choice; and 4) what they would do if someone gave them $1,000 to plan an event or project to benefit women in technical fields. Citizens, permanent residents, and international students are eligible. Selection is based on academic background and demonstrated leadership.

Financial data: The stipend is $10,000 per year.

Duration: 1 year; recipients may reapply.

Number awarded: Varies each year; recently, 25 of these scholarships were awarded.

Deadline: January of each year.

1610 $ ANNA N. DOSEN SERBIAN EDUCATIONAL FUND

Pittsburgh Foundation
Attn: Scholarship Coordinator
Five PPG Place, Suite 250
Pittsburgh, PA 15222–5414
Phone: (412) 394–2649; Fax: (412) 391–7259;
Email: turnerd@pghfdn.org
Web: www.pittsburghfoundation.org/node/1543

Summary: To provide financial assistance to undergraduate students of Serbian background interested in studying the health sciences or engineering in college.

Eligibility: Open to students of Serbian background who are attending or planning to attend a 2– or 4–year accredited college or university to major in health sciences or engineering. Applicants must submit a 1–page essay explaining why they chose their particular field of study and what accomplishments they hope to achieve in that field. Financial need is also considered in the selection process.

Financial data: Recently, the stipend was $4,500 per year.

Duration: 4 years, provided the recipient maintains a GPA of 2.0 or higher.

Number awarded: 1 or more each year.

Deadline: March of each year.

1611 $$ ANNE MAUREEN WHITNEY BARROW MEMORIAL SCHOLARSHIP

Society of Women Engineers
Attn: Scholarship Selection Committee
203 North LaSalle Street, Suite 1675
Chicago, IL 60601–1269
Phone: (312) 596–5223; (877) SWE–INFO; Fax: (312) 644–8557;
Email: scholarships@swe.org
Web: societyofwomenengineers.swe.org/index.php/scholarships

Summary: To provide financial assistance to women interested in studying engineering or computer science in college.

Eligibility: Open to women who are enrolled or planning to enroll full time at an ABET–accredited 4–year college or university. Applicants must be planning to major in engineering or computer science. Entering freshmen must have a GPA of 3.5 or higher; current undergraduates must have a GPA of 3.0 or higher. Selection is based on merit.

Financial data: The stipend is $7,000 per year.

Duration: 1 year; may be renewed for 4 additional years.

Number awarded: 1 every 5 years.

Deadline: May of the years in which it is offered.

1612 $$ ANNIE'S SUSTAINABLE AGRICULTURE SCHOLARSHIPS

Annie's Homegrown, Inc.
Attn: Scholarship Committee
1610 Fifth Street
Berkeley, CA 94710

Phone: (800) 288–1089;
Email: scholarships@annies.com
Web: www.annies.com/doing–good

Summary: To provide financial assistance to entering or enrolled undergraduate and graduate students working on a degree in sustainable agriculture.

Eligibility: Open to full–time undergraduate and graduate students beginning or returning to an accredited 2– or 4–year college or university and working on a degree in a field related to sustainable and organic agriculture. International students at U.S. universities are also eligible. Applicants must submit a personal statement of 2 to 3 pages that discusses why they have chosen their field of study, their vision of the meaning of the phrase "sustainable agriculture," their plans for the future, and how they think their work will impact the Earth and consumers. Selection is based on that statement, academic course work, awards and honors, extracurricular activities, and work experience. Financial need is not considered.

Financial data: Stipends are $10,000 or $2,500.

Duration: 1 year.

Number awarded: Varies each year; recently, 6 undergraduate scholarships (3 at $10,000 and 3 at $2,500) and 6 graduate scholarships (3 at $10,000 and 3 at $2,500) were awarded.

Deadline: December of each year.

1613 ANTHEM BLUE CROSS BLUE SHIELD OF WISCONSIN NURSING SCHOLARSHIPS

Wisconsin League for Nursing
P.O. Box 136
Long Lake, WI 54542–0136
Phone: (888) 755–3329; Fax: (888) 755–3329;
Email: info@wisconsinwln.org
Web: www.wisconsinwln.org/Scholarships.htm

Summary: To provide financial assistance to residents of Wisconsin attending a school of nursing in the state.

Eligibility: Open to residents of Wisconsin who are enrolled at an accredited school of nursing in the state in an L.P.N., A.D.N., B.S.N., M.S.N., D.N.P., or Ph.D. program. Applicants must have completed at least half the credits needed for graduation. Ethnic minority students are especially encouraged to apply. Students must submit their applications to their school, not directly to the sponsor. Each school may nominate 4 graduate students, 6 students in an R.N. program, and 2 L.P.N. students. Selection is based on scholastic ability, professional abilities and/or community service, understanding of the nursing profession, goals upon graduation, and financial need.

Financial data: Stipends are $500 for L.P.N. students or $1,000 for all other students.

Duration: 1 year.

Number awarded: 2 graduate, 26 undergraduate, and 2 L.P.N. scholarships are awarded each year.

Deadline: February of each year.

1614 ANTOINETTE C. HODES SCHOLARSHIP

Mental Health America of Kentucky
120 Sears Avenue, Suite 213
Louisville, KY 40207
Phone: (502) 893–0460; (888) 705–0463;
Email: mhaky@mhaky.org
Web: www.mhaky.org/scholarships.php

Summary: To provide financial assistance to undergraduate and graduate students at colleges and universities in Kentucky who are preparing for a career in mental health and have performed volunteer service in a mental health setting.

Eligibility: Open to residents of any state who are currently enrolled as undergraduate or graduate students at colleges and universities in Kentucky. Applicants must be working on a degree in a field related to mental health (e.g., allied health, medicine, nursing, psychology, social work). They must have performed volunteer service in a mental health setting. Along with their application, they must submit a 200–word essay on their motivation for considering a career in mental health, 2 letters of recommendation, and college transcripts. Financial need is not considered in the selection process.

Financial data: The stipend is $1,000.

Duration: 1 year.

Number awarded: 1 each year.

Deadline: August of each year.

1615 AORN FOUNDATION SCHOLARSHIPS

Association of periOperative Registered Nurses
Attn: AORN Foundation
2170 South Parker Road, Suite 400
Denver, CO 80231–5711
Phone: (303) 755–6300; (800) 755–2676; Fax: (303) 755–4219;
Email: foundation@aorn.org
Web: www.aorn.org/AORNFoundation

Summary: To provide financial assistance to students who wish to work on an advanced degree in a field of interest to the Association of periOperative Registered Nurses (AORN).

Eligibility: Open to registered nurses who are committed to perioperative nursing and are currently enrolled in an accredited baccalaureate, master's, or doctoral degree program. Applicants must have a GPA of 3.0 or higher. International students are eligible. Selection is based on academic record, an essay, accurate completion of the application, and financial need.

Financial data: A stipend is awarded (amount not specified); funds are intended to be used for payment of tuition, related fees, and books.

Duration: 1 year.

Number awarded: Varies each year; recently, 67 of these scholarships were awarded: 14 for bachelor's degree students, 46 for master's degree students, and 7 for doctoral students.

Deadline: June of each year.

1616 $$ APPLIED COMPUTER SECURITY ASSOCIATES CYBERSECURITY SCHOLARSHIP

Society of Women Engineers
Attn: Scholarship Selection Committee
203 North LaSalle Street, Suite 1675
Chicago, IL 60601–1269
Phone: (312) 596–5223; (877) SWE–INFO; Fax: (312) 644–8557;
Email: scholarships@swe.org
Web: societyofwomenengineers.swe.org/index.php/scholarships

Summary: To provide financial assistance to women working on an undergraduate or graduate degree in a field of engineering related to cybersecurity.

Eligibility: Open to women who will be juniors, seniors, or graduate students at ABET–accredited colleges and universities. Applicants must be U.S. citizens or permanent residents working full time on a degree in computer science, cybersecurity, computer security, or software engineering. They must have a GPA of 3.0 or higher and a demonstrated interest in security, as evidenced by course work, outside study, and work experience. Selection is based on merit.

Financial data: The stipend is $10,000.

Duration: 1 year.

Number awarded: 1 each year.

Deadline: February of each year.

1617 APPLIED INSECT ECOLOGISTS FOUNDATION SCHOLARSHIPS

Association of Applied IPM Ecologists
Attn: Applied Insect Ecologists Foundation
Scholarship Committee
P.O. Box 1119
Coarsegold, CA 93614
Phone: (559) 761–1064;
Email: director@aaie.net
Web: aaie.net/index.php?id=18

Summary: To provide financial assistance to undergraduate and graduate students working on a degree in a field related to integrated pest management (IPM).

Eligibility: Open to full–time undergraduate and graduate students enrolled or accepted at an accredited college or university. Applicants must be working on a degree in a field emphasizing pest management, including plant pathology, entomology, nematology, acarology, and weed science. Undergraduates must have a GPA of 3.0 or higher; graduate students must have at least a 3.2 GPA. Along with their application, they must submit a written statement of intent relating to a future career in applied ecology and IPM, a statement on how they became interested in and the efforts they have made to become familiar with the industry and/or research, transcripts, and 2 letters of recommendation. Financial need is considered in the selection process.

Financial data: The stipend is $1,500 for graduate students or $750 for undergraduates.

Duration: 1 year.

Number awarded: At least 2 each year (1 undergraduate and 1 graduate student).

Deadline: November of each year.

1618 APWA SCHOLARSHIP FUND

Community Foundation of Greater Jackson
525 East Capitol Street, Suite 5B
Jackson, MS 39201
Phone: (601) 974–6044; Fax: (601) 974–6045;
Email: info@cfgj.org
Web: www.cfgreaterjackson.org/scholarships.html

Summary: To provide financial assistance to undergraduate students in Mississippi who are preparing for a career in the field of public works.

Eligibility: Open to full–time juniors and seniors at public universities in Mississippi who are preparing to enter the field of public works. Applicants must have graduated from a high school in Mississippi. Eligible majors include civil engineering, electrical engineering, environmental engineering, public administration, biology, or chemistry. Selection is based on merit and need.

Financial data: The stipend ranges up to $1,000.

Duration: 1 year.

Number awarded: 1 or more each year.

Deadline: April of each year.

1619 $$ ARC OF WASHINGTON TRUST FUND STUDENT GRANTS

ARC of Washington Trust Fund
Attn: Policy and Advocacy Coordinator
2638 State Avenue N.E.
Olympia, WA 98506–4880
Phone: (360) 357–5596; (888) 754–8798; Fax: (360) 357–3279;
Email: diana@arcwa.org
Web: www.arcwa.org/student_grants.htm

Summary: To provide financial assistance to undergraduate and graduate students in northwestern states who have a career interest in work relating to developmental disabilities.

Eligibility: Open to upper–division and graduate students who are residents of or enrolled at institutions of higher education in Washington, Oregon, Alaska, or Idaho. Applicants must have a demonstrated interest in the field of intellectual or other developmental disabilities. Along with their application, they must submit a statement of their interest in the field of intellectual or other developmental disabilities, academic and other qualifications, achievements, and immediate and long–term goals. Financial need is not considered in the selection process.

Financial data: The stipend is $5,000 per year, paid in 4 equal installments. Funds are sent to the recipient's school and must be used for tuition, books, and general living expenses.

Duration: 1 year.

Number awarded: Several each year.

Deadline: February of each year.

1620 ARC WELDING AWARDS–DIVISION I

James F. Lincoln Arc Welding Foundation
Attn: Secretary
22801 Saint Clair Avenue
P.O. Box 17188
Cleveland, OH 44117–9949
Phone: (216) 481–8100; Fax: (216) 486–1751;
Email: innovate@lincolnelectric.com
Web: www.jflf.org/awards/division1.asp

Summary: To recognize and reward students younger than 18 years of age who submit written descriptions of outstanding arc welding projects.

Eligibility: Open to students 18 years of age or younger who enrolled in a shop course at any time during their school or training program. Applicants must submit a paper, 3 to 13 pages in length, describing an arc welding project they have completed during the previous 12–month period. The project may be 1) home, artistic, or recreational equipment; 2) a shop tool, machine, or mechanical device; 3) a structure; 4) agricultural equipment; or 5) a repair. Illustrations and photographs are encouraged, but models or specimens may not be submitted. Students may enter as individuals or groups of up to 5 persons. Selection is based on the appearance of the paper and how clearly the project or problem was described; the effort, skill, and ability with which the project or problem was completed; and how well the use and knowledge of welding was applied.

Financial data: At the regional level, gold awards are $500, silver awards are $250, bronze awards are $100, and merit awards are $50. At the national level, the gold award is $1,000, the silver award is $750, and the bronze award is $500.

Duration: The competition is held annually.

Number awarded: In each of 4 geographic regions, 1 gold award, 2 silver awards, and 3 bronze awards are presented. A total of 40 merit awards are presented, regardless of region. At the national level, 3 students receive awards (1 each of gold, silver, and bronze).

Deadline: June of each year.

1621 ARC WELDING AWARDS–DIVISION II

James F. Lincoln Arc Welding Foundation
Attn: Secretary
22801 Saint Clair Avenue
P.O. Box 17188
Cleveland, OH 44117–9949
Phone: (216) 481–8100; Fax: (216) 486–1751;
Email: innovate@lincolnelectric.com
Web: www.jflf.org/awards/division2.asp

Summary: To recognize and reward career students 19 years of age and older who submit written descriptions of outstanding arc welding problems.

Eligibility: Open to students 19 years of age and older who are other than college students studying for a bachelor's or master's degree. Applicants may be enrolled in evening adult classes, high schools, vocational schools, private trade schools, in–plant training classes, technical institutes, apprenticeship programs, junior colleges, community colleges, or other 2–year college courses. They must submit a paper, 3 to 13 pages in length, describing an arc welding project they have completed during the previous 12–month period. The project may be 1) home, artistic, or recreational equipment; 2) a shop tool, machine, or mechanical device; 3) a structure; 4) agricultural equipment; or 5) a repair. Illustrations and photographs are encouraged, but models or specimens may not be submitted. Students may enter as individuals or groups of up to 5 persons. Selection is based on the appearance of the paper and how clearly the project or problem was described; the effort, skill, and ability with which the project or problem was completed; and how well the use and knowledge of welding was applied.

Financial data: The gold award is $1,000, the silver award is $500, the bronze award is $250, and merit awards are $50.

Duration: The competition is held annually.

Number awarded: 1 gold award, 2 silver awards, 3 bronze awards, and 40 merit awards are presented each year.

Deadline: June of each year.

1622 ARC WELDING AWARDS–DIVISION IV

James F. Lincoln Arc Welding Foundation
Attn: Secretary
22801 Saint Clair Avenue
P.O. Box 17188
Cleveland, OH 44117–9949
Phone: (216) 481–8100; Fax: (216) 486–1751;
Email: innovate@lincolnelectric.com
Web: www.jflf.org/awards/division4.asp

Summary: To recognize and reward engineering and technology students who are working on an associate degree and submit outstanding papers involving the knowledge or application of arc welding.

Eligibility: Open to students enrolled in a 2–year associate degree program related to welding at an accredited college in the United States. Participants must submit papers, from 3 to 13 pages in length, representing their work on design, engineering, or manufacturing relating to 1) any type of building, bridge, structure, machine, product, or mechanical apparatus; or 2) arc welding research, testing, procedure, or process development. They may participate as individuals or in groups of up to 6 students. Papers must represent work completed within the past 12 months. Selection is based on originality or ingenuity, feasibility, results achieved or expected, engineering competence, and clarity of the presentation. All applicants are also considered for the Chairman's Award, which is presented for a paper that significantly advances the art or science of welding relative to quality, safety, or productivity.

Financial data: Awards are $1,000 for the first–place gold award, $750 for silver, $500 for bronze, or $250 for merit. The Chairman's Award, if presented, is $1,000.

Duration: The competition is held annually.

Number awarded: Each year, 1 gold award, 2 silver awards, 3 bronze awards, and 3 or more merit awards are presented; if a paper meets the criteria, 1 Chairman's Award may also be presented.

Deadline: June of each year.

1623 ARC WELDING AWARDS–DIVISION V

James F. Lincoln Arc Welding Foundation
Attn: Secretary

22801 Saint Clair Avenue
P.O. Box 17188
Cleveland, OH 44117–9949
Phone: (216) 481–8100; Fax: (216) 486–1751;
Email: innovate@lincolnelectric.com
Web: www.jflf.org/awards/division5.asp

Summary: To recognize and reward engineering and technology students who are working on a bachelor's or graduate degree and submit outstanding papers involving the knowledge or application of arc welding.

Eligibility: Open to students enrolled in a bachelor's or graduate degree program related to welding at an accredited college or university in the United States. Participants must submit papers, from 3 to 13 pages in length, representing their work on design, engineering, or manufacturing relating to 1) any type of building, bridge, structure, machine, product, or mechanical apparatus; or 2) arc welding research, testing, procedure, or process development. They may participate as individuals or in groups of up to 6 students. Papers must represent work completed within the past 12 months. Selection is based on originality or ingenuity, feasibility, results achieved or expected, engineering competence, and clarity of the presentation. All applicants are also considered for the Chairman's Award, which is presented for a paper that significantly advances the art or science of welding relative to quality, safety, or productivity.

Financial data: Awards are $1,000 for the first–place gold award, $750 for silver, $500 for bronze, or $250 for merit. The Chairman's Award, if presented, is $1,000.

Duration: The competition is held annually.

Number awarded: Each year, 1 gold award, 2 silver awards, 3 bronze awards, and 3 or more merit awards are presented; if a paper meets the criteria, 1 Chairman's Award may also be presented.

Deadline: June of each year.

1624 ARIZONA CATTLE INDUSTRY SCHOLARSHIP

Arizona Cattlemen's Association
Attn: Arizona Cattle Industry Research and Education Foundation
1401 North 24th Street, Suite 4
Phoenix, AZ 85008
Phone: (602) 267–1129; Fax: (602) 220–9833
Web: www.azcattlemensassoc.org/arizonacattleindustryfoundation.aspx

Summary: To provide financial assistance to residents of Arizona who are interested in attending college in any state to study a field related to the cattle industry.

Eligibility: Open to Arizona residents who are high school seniors or undergraduates enrolled full time at a college or university in any state. Applicants must be interested in studying topics or subjects directly or indirectly related to the cattle industry and have a GPA of 2.5 or higher. Along with their application, they must submit a 3–page letter of intent that covers their career plans and goals; plans upon graduation; achievements and activities, including awards, extracurricular activities, offices held, and honors and scholarships received; participation with equine, ranching, agriculture, or related activities and accomplishments; and financial need. Special consideration is given to applicants whose families are engaged in agriculture.

Financial data: A stipend is awarded (amount not specified).

Duration: 1 year.

Number awarded: 1 or more each year.

Deadline: March of each year.

1625 $ ARIZONA FEDERATION OF GARDEN CLUBS SCHOLARSHIPS

Arizona Federation of Garden Clubs
c/o Mary Jo Wall
3701 East Poinsettia Drive
Phoenix, AZ 85028–1433
Phone: (602) 996–3509;
Email: maryjo.wall@cox.net
Web: azgardenclubs.com/home/scholarship

Summary: To provide financial assistance to residents of Arizona working on an undergraduate or graduate degree in a field related to gardening at a school in any state.

Eligibility: Open to Arizona residents who are either 1) sophomores, juniors, seniors, fifth–year landscape architecture students, or master's degree students at colleges and universities in any state; or 2) students at community colleges in the state. Applicants must be working on a degree in agricultural education, horticulture (including fruit science), floriculture, landscape design, botany, biology, plant pathology and science, forestry, agronomy, economics, environmental concerns, environmental engineering, environmental law, city (rural and urban) planning, wildlife science, habitat or forest systems ecology, land management, or an allied subject. They must have a GPA of 3.25 or higher and be able to demonstrate financial need. Along with their application, they must submit a personal letter discussing their background, future goals, financial need, and future career goals. Selection is based on that letter (30%), academic record (40%), listing of honors, extracurricular activities, and work experience (10%), financial need (15%), and recommendations (5%). U.S. citizenship or permanent resident status is required; international and foreign exchange students are not eligible.

Financial data: Stipends are $3,500 for students at 4–year colleges and universities or $500 for students at community colleges.

Duration: 1 year.

Number awarded: Varies each year.

Deadline: February.

1626 $ ARIZONA HYDROLOGICAL SOCIETY SCHOLARSHIPS

Arizona Hydrological Society
Attn: Executive Director
P.O. Box 1882
Higley, AZ 85236
Phone: (480) 270–4937;
Email: azhydrosoc.dir@gmail.com
Web: www.azhydrosoc.org/scholarships.html

Summary: To provide financial assistance to upper–division and graduate students working on a degree in a field related to water resources at a college or university in Arizona.

Eligibility: Open to juniors, seniors, and graduate students enrolled full time at Arizona colleges and universities. Applicants must be studying hydrology, hydrogeology, or any other field related to water resources. Along with their application, they must submit a letter describing their interests and career goals in hydrology and water resources. Selection is based on that letter, GPA, letters of recommendation, background in hydrology and water resources related activities, and financial need.

Financial data: The stipend is $2,000.

Duration: 1 year.

Number awarded: 3 each year.

Deadline: May of each year.

1627 $ ARIZONA NURSERY ASSOCIATION FOUNDATION SCHOLARSHIPS

Arizona Nursery Association
Attn: ANA Foundation Endowment for Research and Scholarship
1430 West Broadway, Suite 110
Tempe, AZ 85282
Phone: (480) 966–1610; Fax: (480) 966–0923;
Email: scholarship@azna.org
Web: azna.org/scholarship–program

Summary: To provide financial assistance to students from Arizona who are enrolled or planning to enroll in a horticulture–related curriculum at a college in any state.

Eligibility: Open to Arizona residents who are currently enrolled, or planning to enroll, in a horticulture–related curriculum at a university, community college, or continuing education program at a college or university in any state. Applicants must be currently employed in or have an interest in the nursery industry as a career. They must have an above average GPA or at least 2 years of work experience in the nursery industry. Involvement in extracurricular activities related to the nursery industry must also be demonstrated. Financial need is not considered in the selection process.

Financial data: Stipends range from $500 to $3,000.

Duration: 1 year.

Number awarded: Varies each year.

Deadline: April of each year.

1628 $ ARKANSAS GAME AND FISH SCHOLARSHIP

Arkansas Game and Fish Commission
Attn: Education and Information Division
Two Natural Resources Drive
Little Rock, AR 72205
Phone: (501) 223–6317; (800) 364–4263
Web: www.agfc.com

Summary: To provide financial assistance to high school seniors, undergraduates, and graduate students from Arkansas interested in preparing for a career in natural resource conservation.

Eligibility: Open to Arkansas residents who are high school seniors, college undergraduates, or graduate students attending or planning to attend a college or university in the state and paying in–state tuition. Applicants must be interested in preparing for a career in the field of natural resource conservation; approved majors include agriculture, animal science, biology, botany, conservation management, criminal justice, education, environmental management and regulatory science, environmental management/geographic information systems technician, environmental science, fisheries and wildlife biology, fisheries management, forestry, political science, recreation and park administration, wildlife management, and zoology. They must be full–time students and have a GPA of 2.5 or higher. Along with their application, they must submit 4 essays: 150 words on how their field of study relates to natural resource conservation and their choice as a possible career; 200 words on their accomplishments in leadership roles; 100 words on their outdoor–related work or volunteer experience; and 300 words on their philosophy of fish and wildlife conservation as it relates to environmental stewardship. Selection is based solely on merit.

Financial data: The stipend is $1,000 per semester. Funds are to be used for tuition, books, fees, and lodging.

Duration: 1 semester; may be renewed for up to 7 additional semesters.

Number awarded: 25 each year.

Deadline: June of each year for fall semester; January of each year for second semester.

1629 $ ARKANSAS POST SAME SCHOLARSHIPS

Summary: To provide financial assistance to Arkansas high school seniors interested in studying architecture or engineering at a college in any state.

See Listing #1120.

1630 ARKANSAS PUBLIC HEALTH ASSOCIATION COLLEGE SCHOLARSHIP

Arkansas Public Health Association
Attn: Scholarship Chair
P.O. Box 250327
Little Rock, AR 72225–0327
Email: ar_apha@yahoo.com
Web: www.arkpublichealth.org/scholarships.php

Summary: To provide financial assistance to residents of Arkansas working on a degree in public health at a college in any state.

Eligibility: Open to Arkansas residents currently enrolled as at least a sophomore at a college, university, or approved vocational/technical institute in any state. Applicants must be working on a degree in public health and have a GPA of 2.5 or higher. Selection is based on GPA (4 points), goals in public health (7 points), honors and volunteer activity with health–related organizations (7 points), a letter from a major professor (3 points), a personal reference letter (3 points), present or past public health experience (3 points), full–time student (2 points), part–time student (1 point), and financial need (5 points).

Financial data: The stipend is $1,000.

Duration: 1 year.

Number awarded: 1 or more each year.

Deadline: March of each year.

1631 $ ARMY NURSE CORPS ASSOCIATION SCHOLARSHIPS

Army Nurse Corps Association
Attn: Education Committee
P.O. Box 39235
San Antonio, TX 78218–1235
Phone: (210) 650–3534; Fax: (210) 650–3494;
Email: education@e–anca.org
Web: e–anca.org/ANCAEduc.htm

Summary: To provide financial assistance to students who have a connection to the Army and are interested in working on an undergraduate or graduate degree in nursing.

Eligibility: Open to U.S. citizens attending colleges or universities that have accredited programs offering associate, bachelor's, master's, or doctoral degrees in nursing. Applicants must be 1) nursing or anesthesia students who plan to enter a component of the U.S. Army and are not participating in a program funded by a component of the U.S. Army; 2) nursing or anesthesia students who have previously served in a component of the U.S. Army; 3) Army Nurse Corps officers enrolled in an undergraduate or graduate nursing program not funded by a component of the U.S. Army; 4) enlisted soldiers in a component of the U.S. Army who are working on a baccalaureate degree in nursing not funded by a component of the U.S. Army; or 5) nursing or anesthesia students whose parent(s), spouse, and/or children are serving or have served in a component of the U.S. Army. Along with their application, they must submit a personal statement on their professional career objectives, reasons for applying for this scholarship, financial need, special considerations, personal and academic interests, and why they are preparing for a nursing career.

Financial data: The stipend is $3,000. Funds are sent directly to the recipient's school.

Duration: 1 year.

Number awarded: 1 or more each year.

Deadline: March of each year.

1632 $ ARNE ENGEBRETSEN SCHOLARSHIPS

Wisconsin Mathematics Council
W175 N11117 Stonewood Drive, Suite 204
Germantown, WI 53022
Phone: (262) 437–0174; Fax: (262) 532–2430;
Email: wmc@wismath.org
Web: www.wismath.org/awards–scholarships

Summary: To provide financial assistance to high school seniors in Wisconsin interested in attending college to prepare for a career as a mathematics teacher.

Eligibility: Open to seniors graduating from high schools in Wisconsin who have shown a significant interest in preparing for a career as a K–12 educator. Applicants must be planning to study mathematics with the goal of becoming a mathematics teacher. Along with their application, they must submit a 2–page essay that covers the personal experiences that have influenced their decision to teach mathematics, why teaching mathematics is important to them, how they envision using technology in their own classroom, and how they will continue the Arne Engebretsen legacy. Selection is based on that essay (40%), academic achievement (30%), and a letter of support (30%).

Financial data: The stipend is $2,000.

Duration: 1 year.

Number awarded: 1 each year.

Deadline: February of each year.

1633 ARNOLD SADLER MEMORIAL SCHOLARSHIP

American Council of the Blind
Attn: Coordinator, Scholarship Program
2200 Wilson Boulevard, Suite 650
Arlington, VA 22201
Phone: (202) 467–5081; (800) 424–8666; Fax: (703) 465–5085;
Email: info@acb.org
Web: www.acb.org/scholarship

Summary: To provide financial assistance to undergraduate or graduate students who are blind and are interested in studying in a field of service to persons with disabilities.

Eligibility: Open to undergraduate and graduate students in rehabilitation, education, law, or other fields of service to persons with disabilities. Applicants must be legally blind in both eyes. Along with their application, they must submit verification of legal blindness in both eyes; SAT, ACT, GRE, or similar scores; information on extracurricular activities (including involvement in the American Council of the Blind); employment record; and a 500–word autobiographical sketch that includes their personal goals, strengths, weaknesses, hobbies, honors, achievements, and reasons for choice of field or courses of study. A cumulative GPA of 3.3 or higher is generally required. Financial need is not considered in the selection process.

Financial data: The stipend is $1,500.

Duration: 1 year.

Number awarded: 1 each year.

Deadline: February of each year.

1634 $ ARSHAM AMIRIKIAN ENGINEERING SCHOLARSHIP

American Welding Society
Attn: AWS Foundation, Inc.
550 N.W. LeJeune Road
Miami, FL 33126
Phone: (305) 445–6628; (800) 443–9353, ext. 212; Fax: (305) 443–7559;
Email: found@aws.org
Web: www.aws.org/w/a/foundation/scholarships/arsham.html

Summary: To provide financial assistance to college students working on a degree in civil engineering as related to welding.

Eligibility: Open to full–time undergraduate students who are working on a 4–year bachelor's degree in structural and civil engineering as related to welding at an accredited university. Applicants must have an overall GPA of 3.0 or higher and be able to demonstrate financial need. U.S. citizenship is required.
Financial data: The stipend is $2,500 per year.
Duration: 4 years, provided the recipient maintains a GPA of 3.0 or higher.
Number awarded: 1 each year.
Deadline: February of each year.

1635 $ ARTHUR AND DOREEN PARRETT SCHOLARSHIP

Arthur and Doreen Parrett Scholarship Foundation
c/o U.S. Bank of Washington
Attn: Trust Group
1420 Fifth Avenue, Suite 2100
Seattle, WA 98101–2613
Phone: (206) 344–3683; Fax: (206) 344–3738
Summary: To provide financial assistance to residents of Washington who are interested in studying science, engineering, medicine, or dentistry at a university in any state.
Eligibility: Open to full–time sophomores, juniors, seniors, master's degree students, doctoral students, and first professional degree students. Applicants must be residents of Washington with a major or career interest in general science, engineering, medicine, or dentistry. Selection is based on academic achievement and financial need.
Financial data: The stipends range from $1,000 to $3,500; funds are paid to the recipient's school and may be used for tuition and books, room and board, or travel in connection with education.
Duration: 1 year.
Number awarded: Approximately 15 each year.
Deadline: January of each year.

1636 ARTHUR C. PIKE SCHOLARSHIP IN METEOROLOGY

National Weather Association
Attn: Executive Director
228 West Millbrook Road
Raleigh, NC 27609–4304
Phone: (919) 845–1546; Fax: (919) 845–2956;
Email: exdir@nwas.org
Web: www.nwas.org/committees/ed_comm/application/index.php
Summary: To provide financial assistance to students working on an undergraduate or graduate degree in meteorology.
Eligibility: Open to students who are either entering their junior or senior year of undergraduate study or enrolled as graduate students. Applicants must be working on a degree in meteorology. Along with their application, they must submit a 1–page statement explaining why they are applying for this scholarship. Selection is based on that statement, academic achievement, and 2 letters of recommendation.
Financial data: The stipend is $1,000.
Duration: 1 year.
Number awarded: 1 each year.
Deadline: October of each year.

1637 $$ ARTHUR E. COTE SCHOLARSHIP

National Fire Protection Association
Attn: Fire Safety Educational Memorial Fund Committee
1 Batterymarch Park
Quincy, MA 02169–7471
Phone: (617) 984–7244; Fax: (617) 984–7110;
Email: cellis@nfpa.org
Web: www.nfpa.org
Summary: To provide financial assistance to undergraduate students enrolled in fire protection engineering programs.
Eligibility: Open to students who are nominated by colleges and universities in the United States and Canada. Each college is invited to nominate up to 2 undergraduate students enrolled in a fire protection engineering program. Nominees must submit a letter describing their achievements, leadership abilities, volunteerism, interest in fire protection engineering, and specific long–range goals. Financial need is not considered in the selection process.
Financial data: The stipend is at least $5,000.
Duration: 1 year.
Number awarded: 1 each year.
Deadline: March of each year.

1638 $ ARTHUR W. PENSE SCHOLARSHIP

NYSARC, Inc.
Attn: Scholarship and Awards Committee
393 Delaware Avenue
Delmar, NY 12054
Phone: (518) 439–8311; Fax: (518) 439–1893;
Email: info@nysarc.org
Web: www.nysarc.org
Summary: To provide financial assistance to college students in New York working on a degree in occupational or physical therapy.
Eligibility: Open to students enrolled at a college or university in New York in a 4– or 5–year degree program in occupational or physical therapy. Nominations must be submitted by the college; each school in the state may submit only 1 nomination. Students must supply a list of work experience with people who have intellectual and other developmental disabilities and a 1–page autobiographical sketch indicating their interest in the field and their plans after graduation. Financial need is not considered in the selection process.
Financial data: The stipend is $1,000 per semester.
Duration: 3 semesters (the final semesters of study).
Number awarded: 1 each year.
Deadline: Nominations must be submitted by December of each year.

1639 ARTS AND SCIENCES AWARDS

Summary: To provide financial aid to hearing impaired students who are participating in extracurricular activities in arts and sciences.
See Listing #1123.

1640 ASCLS EDUCATION AND RESEARCH FUND UNDERGRADUATE SCHOLARSHIPS

Alpha Mu Tau Fraternity
c/o American Society for Clinical Laboratory Science
2025 M Street, N.W., Suite 800
Washington, DC 20036
Phone: (202) 367–1174;
Email: alphamutaujoe@yahoo.com
Web: www.ascls.org/?page=Awards_AMTF
Summary: To provide financial assistance to undergraduate students in the clinical laboratory sciences.
Eligibility: Open to U.S. citizens and permanent residents accepted into or currently enrolled in a program in clinical laboratory science, including cytotechnology, histotechnology, clinical laboratory science/medical technology, or clinical laboratory technician/medical laboratory technician. Applicants must be entering their last year of study. Along with their application, they must submit a 500–word statement describing their interest and reasons for preparing for a career in clinical laboratory science. Financial need is also considered in the selection process.
Financial data: The stipend is $1,500.
Duration: 1 year.
Number awarded: Several each year.
Deadline: March of each year.

1641 $$ ASHADO SCHOLARSHIP

The Race for Education
Attn: Student Services Manager
1818 Versailles Road
P.O. Box 11355
Lexington, KY 40575
Phone: (859) 252–8648; Fax: (859) 252–8030;
Email: info@raceforeducation.org
Web: raceforeducation.org/scholarships
Summary: To provide financial assistance to female undergraduate students working on an equine–related degree.
Eligibility: Open to female undergraduate students under 24 years of age working on an equine–related degree, including (but not limited to) pre–veterinary medicine (equine practice only), equine science, equine business management, racetrack management, or other equine– or agriculture–related program. Applicants must have a GPA of 2.85 or higher and a household income of less than $50,000 per year. Along with their application, they must submit a 500–word essay on 1 of the following topics: 1) the last book they read for enjoyment only, why they chose it, and what they learned from it; 2) a facet of thoroughbred racing that interests them and why; or 3) their interests outside the equine industry or chosen career field.

Financial data: The stipend covers payment of tuition, to a maximum of $6,000 per year. The student is responsible for all other fees.
Duration: 1 year; may be renewed up to 3 additional years, provided the recipient maintains a GPA of 3.0 or higher.
Number awarded: 1 or more each year.
Deadline: February of each year.

1642 $ ASLA COUNCIL OF FELLOWS SCHOLARSHIPS

Summary: To provide financial assistance to upper–division students, especially those from disadvantaged and underrepresented groups, working on a degree in landscape architecture.
See Listing #1126.

1643 $ ASNT ENGINEERING UNDERGRADUATE AWARDS

American Society for Nondestructive Testing, Inc.
Attn: Administrative Assistant
1711 Arlingate Lane
P.O. Box 28518
Columbus, OH 43228–0518
Phone: (614) 274–6003; (800) 222–2768; Fax: (614) 274–6899;
Email: sdille@asnt.org
Web: www.asnt.org/keydocuments/awards/engineering.htm
Summary: To provide financial assistance to undergraduate engineering students who are interested in nondestructive testing and evaluation.
Eligibility: Open to undergraduate students enrolled in an engineering program at an ABET–accredited university who show an active interest in the field of nondestructive testing and evaluation. Students must be nominated. Nominations must include the official transcript of the student, 3 letters of recommendation from faculty members, and an essay by the student describing the role nondestructive testing and evaluation will play in their career.
Financial data: The stipend is $3,000.
Duration: 1 year.
Number awarded: Up to 3 each year.
Deadline: December of each year.

1644 $ ASSOCIATE DEGREE ENGINEERING TECHNOLOGY SCHOLARSHIP

American Society of Heating, Refrigerating and Air–Conditioning Engineers
Attn: Scholarship Administrator
1791 Tullie Circle, N.E.
Atlanta, GA 30329–2305
Phone: (404) 539–1120; Fax: (404) 539–2120;
Email: lbenedict@ashrae.org
Web: www.ashrae.org/students/page/1271
Summary: To provide financial assistance to engineering technology students interested in heating, ventilating, air conditioning, and refrigeration (HVAC&R).
Eligibility: Open to engineering technology students enrolled full time in a program leading to an associate degree. Applicants must be engaged in a course of study that traditionally has been preparatory for the profession of HVAC&R. They must have a GPA of 3.0 or higher and a standing in the top 30% of their class. Selection is based on potential service to the HVAC&R profession, financial need, leadership ability, recommendations from instructors, and work ethics.
Financial data: The stipend is $3,000.
Duration: 1 year.
Number awarded: 2 each year.
Deadline: April of each year.

1645 $$ ASSOCIATION FOR WOMEN GEOSCIENTISTS MINORITY SCHOLARSHIP

Association for Women Geoscientists
Attn: AWG Foundation
12000 North Washington Street, Suite 285
Thornton, CO 80241
Phone: (303) 412–6219; Fax: (303) 253–9220;
Email: minorityscholarship@awg.org
Web: www.awg.org/EAS/scholarships.html
Summary: To provide financial assistance to underrepresented minority women who are interested in working on an undergraduate degree in the geosciences.
Eligibility: Open to women who are African American, Hispanic, or Native American (including Eskimo, Hawaiian, Samoan, or American Indian). Applicants must be full–time students working on, or planning to work on, an undergraduate degree in the geosciences (including geology, geophysics, geochemistry, hydrology, meteorology, physical oceanography, planetary geology, or earth science education). They must submit a 500–word essay on their academic and career goals, 2 letters of recommendation, high school and/or college transcripts, and SAT or ACT scores. Financial need is not considered in the selection process. U.S. citizenship is required.
Financial data: A total of $6,000 is available for this program each year.
Duration: 1 year; may be renewed.
Number awarded: 1 or more each year.
Deadline: June of each year.

1646 ASSOCIATION FOR WOMEN IN ARCHITECTURE SCHOLARSHIPS

Summary: To provide financial assistance to women undergraduates in California who are interested in preparing for a career in architecture.
See Listing #1130.

1647 $ ASSOCIATION OF COMPUTER PROFESSIONALS SCHOLARSHIPS

Association of Computer Professionals
Attn: Scholarship Committee
P.O. Box 6053
Portland, OR 97228–6053
Phone: (253) 891–6085; Fax: (253) 891–6091;
Email: scholarship@acpenw.org
Web: www.acpenw.org/home/awards.html
Summary: To provide financial assistance to high school seniors in Washington and Oregon who plan to attend college in any state to study a technology–related field.
Eligibility: Open to seniors graduating from high schools in Washington or Oregon who have been actively involved in the use of technology during their high school careers. Applicants must be planning to attend college in any state to work on at least a 2–year degree in a technology–related field. They must have a grade average of "C+" or higher. Along with their application, they must submit 500–word statements describing 1) their involvement with technology during their high school career; 2) their community and school involvement and how that involvement includes technology; 3) their plans for postsecondary education, including the school they plan to attend to obtain their technology–related degree; 4) any additional information that would distinguish them as an applicant; and 5) the URL to their web–based technology project they have completed. Financial need is not considered in the selection process.
Financial data: The stipend is $2,500.
Duration: 1 year.
Number awarded: 4 each year.
Deadline: February of each year.

1648 $ ASSOCIATION OF CUBAN ENGINEERS SCHOLARSHIPS

Association of Cuban Engineers
c/o Dr. Helena Solo–Gabriele
University of Miami, College of Engineering
1251 Memorial Drive, EB252
Coral Gables, FL 33146
Phone: (305) 284–2908; Fax: (305) 284–3492;
Email: hmsolo@miami.edu
Web: aic–ace.com
Summary: To provide financial assistance to undergraduate and graduate students of Cuban American heritage who are interested in preparing for a career in engineering.
Eligibility: Open to U.S. citizens and legal residents who have completed at least 30 units of college work in the United States and are working on an undergraduate or graduate degree in engineering. Applicants must be attending an ABET–accredited college or university within the United States or Puerto Rico as a full–time student and have a GPA of 3.0 or higher. They must be of Cuban or other Hispanic heritage (at least 1 grandparent Cuban or other Hispanic nationality). Along with their application, they must submit brief essays on their family history, professional goals, extracurricular activities, work experience,

and how they will help other Cuban and Hispanic engineering students in the future. Financial need is not considered in the selection process.
Financial data: Stipends range from $500 to $2,000.
Duration: 1 year; may be renewed.
Number awarded: Varies each year; recently, 10 of these scholarships were awarded.
Deadline: November of each year.

1649 $ ASSOCIATION OF ENERGY ENGINEERS SCHOLARSHIPS

Association of Energy Engineers
Attn: Foundation
4025 Pleasantdale Road, Suite 420
Atlanta, GA 30340
Phone: (770) 447–5083, ext. 221; Fax: (770) 446–3969;
Email: info@aeecenter.org
Web: www.aeefoundation.org/scholarships/
Summary: To provide financial assistance to undergraduate and graduate students interested in taking courses directly related to energy engineering or energy management.
Eligibility: Open to undergraduate and graduate students who are enrolled in engineering or management programs at accredited colleges and universities and who would be interested in taking courses directly related to energy engineering or energy management (preferably within a curriculum leading to a major or minor in energy engineering). Qualified students are invited to submit their applications to the association's local chapter, along with transcripts and letters of recommendation. Along with their application, they must submit an essay of 50 to 100 words explaining why they wish to study energy engineering or energy management.
Financial data: Stipends are $2,000, $1,000, $500, or $125. The 2 most outstanding candidates receive the Victor Ottaviano Scholarship and the Al Thumann Scholarship.
Duration: 1 year.
Number awarded: Varies each year; recently, 53 of these scholarships were awarded: 1 at $2,000 (the Al Thumann Scholarship), 1 at $1,000 (the Victor Ottaviano Scholarship), 48 at $500, and 3 at $125. Since the program was established, it has awarded more than $600,000 in scholarships to 1,115 students.
Deadline: April of each year.

1650 $$ ASSOCIATION OF FEDERAL COMMUNICATIONS CONSULTING ENGINEERS SCHOLARSHIPS

Association of Federal Communications Consulting Engineers
P.O. Box 19333
Washington, DC 20036
Email: scholarships@afcce.org
Web: www.afcce.org
Summary: To provide financial assistance to upper–division and graduate students working on an engineering or science degree related to telecommunications.
Eligibility: Open to juniors, seniors, and graduate students who are working full time on a degree in engineering or science related to telecommunications. Applicants must be sponsored by a member of the Association of Federal Communications Consulting Engineers (AFCCE). Along with their application, they must submit a statement of 250 to 500 words describing their career goals, areas of strong interest, and how they anticipated either working as or in collaboration with radio communications consulting engineers, including broadcast and wireless telecommunication engineers. Financial need is considered in the selection process.
Financial data: The stipend ranges from $1,000 to $2,500 per semester.
Duration: 1 semester.
Number awarded: Up to 2 each semester.
Deadline: Deadline not specified.

1651 ASSOCIATION OF FOOD AND DRUG OFFICIALS SCHOLARSHIP AWARDS

Association of Food and Drug Officials
Attn: Awards Committee Chair
2550 Kingston Road, Suite 311
York, PA 17402–3734
Phone: (717) 757–2888; Fax: (717) 650–3650;
Email: afdo@afdo.org
Web: www.afdo.org/afdo/awards/scholarships.cfm
Summary: To provide financial assistance to upper–division students who are preparing for a career in an aspect of food, drug, or consumer product safety.
Eligibility: Open to students entering their senior year of college who have a GPA of 3.0 or higher for the first 2 years. Applicants should be interested in preparing to serve in a career of research, regulatory work, quality control, or teaching in an area related to some aspect of food, drug, or consumer product safety. Along with their application, they must submit transcripts, 2 letters of recommendation, and a 1–page biographical sketch that includes their choice of major and future career plans. Selection is based on those submissions and demonstrated leadership capabilities.
Financial data: The stipend is $1,500.
Duration: 1 year.
Number awarded: 3 each year.
Deadline: January of each year.

1652 ASSOCIATION OF PERIOPERATIVE REGISTERED NURSES FOUNDATION NURSING STUDENT SCHOLARSHIPS

Association of periOperative Registered Nurses
Attn: AORN Foundation
2170 South Parker Road, Suite 400
Denver, CO 80231–5711
Phone: (303) 755–6300; (800) 755–2676; Fax: (303) 755–4219;
Email: foundation@aorn.org
Web: www.aorn.org/AORNFoundation
Summary: To provide financial assistance to students interested in preparing for a career in perioperative nursing.
Eligibility: Open to students currently enrolled in an accredited nursing program leading to initial licensure as an R.N. High school students just entering college are not eligible. Applicants must have a GPA of 3.0 or higher. Along with their application, they must submit an essay that clearly indicates an interest in perioperative nursing. International students are eligible. Selection is based on academic record, the essay, accurate completion of the application, and financial need.
Financial data: A stipend is awarded (amount not specified); funds are intended to be used for payment of tuition, related fees, and books.
Duration: 1 year.
Number awarded: Varies each year; recently, 5 of these scholarships were awarded.
Deadline: June of each year.

1653 $ ASSOCIATION OF PHYSICIAN ASSISTANTS IN ONCOLOGY STUDENT SCHOLARSHIP

Association of Physician Assistants in Oncology
c/o Dayne Alonso, Scholarship Committee
7265 S.W. 89th Street, Apartment 311
Miami, FL 33156
Email: apaoscholarship@gmail.com
Web: www.apao.cc/displaycommon.cfm?an=1&subarticlenbr=13
Summary: To provide financial assistance to physician assistant students who have an interest in oncology.
Eligibility: Open to students who have completed the basic science courses of an accredited physician assistant program in the United States or Canada and have a GPA of 3.0 or higher. Applicants must be members of the American Academy of Physician Assistants (AAPA) or have applied for membership. They must have a strong interest in preparing for a career in the oncology field and must have completed or plan to complete a clinical rotation in an oncology specialty. Along with their application, they must submit brief statements on 1) their motivation for choosing to work in oncology as a physician assistant; and 2) how they will impact oncology patients in their career as a physician assistant.
Financial data: The stipend is $2,000. The winner also receives up to $500 for reimbursement of travel expenses to attend the annual meeting of the sponsoring organization.
Duration: 1 year.
Number awarded: 1 each year.
Deadline: April of each year.

1654 $$ ASSOCIATION OF STATE DAM SAFETY OFFICIALS SCHOLARSHIPS

Association of State Dam Safety Officials
Attn: Scholarship Coordinator
450 Old Vine Street, Second Floor
Lexington, KY 40507

Phone: (859) 257–5140; Fax: (859) 323–1958;
Email: info@damsafety.org
Web: www.damsafety.org

Summary: To provide financial assistance to college seniors working on a degree in fields related to dam safety.

Eligibility: Open to full–time college seniors who have a GPA of 2.5 or higher and are studying civil engineering or a related field. They must have a demonstrated interest in preparing for a career in hydraulics, hydrology, or geotechnical disciplines related to the design, construction, and operation of dams. Along with their application, they must submit a 500–word essay on their proposed course of study and why dam safety is important. Selection is based on that essay, academic achievement, work experience and activities, and financial need. U.S. citizenship is required.

Financial data: The stipend is $10,000 per year.

Duration: 1 year; junior recipients may reapply for their senior year.

Number awarded: 2 or 3 each year.

Deadline: March of each year.

1655 $$ ASTRONAUT SCHOLARSHIP FOUNDATION SCHOLARSHIPS

Astronaut Scholarship Foundation
Attn: Executive Director
6225 Vectorspace Boulevard
Titusville, FL 32780
Phone: (321) 455–7011; Fax: (321) 264–9176;
Email: Linn@astronautscholarship.org
Web: www.astronautscholarship.org

Summary: To provide financial assistance to upper–division students in science and engineering.

Eligibility: Open to full–time students entering their junior or senior year with a major in engineering, the natural or applied sciences (e.g., astronomy, biology, chemistry, computer science, earth science, physics), or mathematics. Candidates must be nominated by faculty or staff at 1 of 27 participating universities; each may nominate 2 students. Students intending to practice professional medicine are not eligible, but those intending to do biomedical research are considered. No special consideration is given to aeronautical or astronautical engineering students or those intending to prepare for a career as astronauts. Special consideration is given, however, to applicants who have shown initiative, creativity, and excellence in their field. U.S. citizenship is required.

Financial data: The stipend is $10,000.

Duration: 1 year.

Number awarded: Normally 27 each year: 1 at each of the participating universities.

Deadline: Deadline not specified.

1656 $ ATCA STUDENT SCHOLARSHIP PROGRAM

Air Traffic Control Association
Attn: Scholarship Fund
1101 King Street, Suite 300
Alexandria, VA 22314
Phone: (703) 299–2430; Fax: (703) 299–2437;
Email: info@atca.org
Web: www.atca.org/ATCA–Scholarship

Summary: To provide financial assistance to students working on a bachelor's degree or higher in aviation.

Eligibility: Open to half– or full–time students who are U.S. citizens, enrolled or accepted for enrollment in an accredited college or university, taking classes to prepare for an aviation–related career, working on a bachelor's or graduate degree, registered for at least 6 hours, and at least 30 semester or 45 quarter hours away from graduation. Applicants must submit an essay, up to 500 words, on how their educational efforts will enhance their potential contribution to aviation. Financial need is considered in the selection process.

Financial data: Stipends range from $1,500 to $2,500.

Duration: 1 year; may be renewed.

Number awarded: Varies each year; recently, 6 of these scholarships were awarded.

Deadline: April of each year.

1657 AUTOMOTIVE AFTERMARKET ASSOCIATION SOUTHEAST EDUCATIONAL FOUNDATION SCHOLARSHIPS

Automotive Aftermarket Association Southeast
Attn: AAAS Educational Foundation
11245 Chantilly Parkway Court
Montgomery, AL 36117–7585
Phone: (334) 834–1848; (800) 239–7779; Fax: (334) 834–1818;
Email: randal@aaas.us
Web: www.aaas.us/member–programs/aaas–educational–foundation.aspx

Summary: To provide financial assistance to residents of designated southeastern states interested in attending college or technical school in any state to prepare for a career in the automotive aftermarket industry.

Eligibility: Open to residents of Alabama, Florida, Georgia, and Mississippi who are graduating high school seniors, recent high school graduates, or holders of a GED certificate. Applicants must be enrolled or planning to enroll full time at an accredited college, university, technical institute, or automotive technical program certified by the National Automotive Technicians Education Foundation–National Institute for Automotive Service Excellence (NATEF–ASE) in any state. They must be sponsored by a member of the Automotive Aftermarket Association Southeast (AAAS). Priority is given to 1) students planning to work on a degree or certificate in an automotive–related curriculum (e.g., engineering, computer science, accounting, marketing, business); and 2) AAAS members, employees of members, or family of members or employees. Along with their application, they must submit a 250–word essay on their career goals, how this scholarship will help them, and why they are considering a career in the automotive aftermarket. Financial need is not considered in the selection process.

Financial data: A stipend is awarded (amount not specified).

Duration: 1 year; recipients may reapply.

Number awarded: Varies each year; recently, 4 of these scholarships were awarded.

Deadline: March of each year.

1658 AUTOMOTIVE SCHOLARSHIPS

Iowa Automobile Dealers Association
Attn: IAD Foundation for Education
1111 Office Park Road
West Des Moines, IA 50265
Phone: (515) 440–7625; (800) 869–1900; Fax: (515) 226–1988;
Email: mcason@iada.com
Web: www.iada.com/FoundationForEducation.aspx

Summary: To provide financial assistance to high school seniors in Iowa who are interested in attending college to prepare for a career in the automobile industry.

Eligibility: Open to seniors graduating from high schools in Iowa. Applicants must be planning to attend a postsecondary institution to study an automotive– or truck–related area, including technician training, body shop/collision repair, diesel, new vehicle sales, parts sales, accounting, or business administration. Selection is based on interest and commitment to the automotive industry and, in part, on financial need. Preference is given to applicants who plan to attend an Iowa college or university.

Financial data: Stipends average more than $1,000.

Duration: 1 year.

Number awarded: Varies each year; recently, 16 of these scholarships were awarded.

Deadline: February of each year.

1659 $ AVIATION AND PROFESSIONAL DEVELOPMENT SCHOLARSHIPS

Airport Minority Advisory Council
Attn: AMAC Educational and Scholarship Program, Inc.
2345 Crystal Drive, Suite 902
Arlington, VA 22202
Phone: (703) 414–2622; Fax: (703) 414–2686;
Email: amac.info@amac–org.com
Web: www.amac–org.com/scholarship/ScholarshipAwards.html

Summary: To provide financial assistance to undergraduates who are preparing for a career in the aviation industry and interested in participating in activities of the Airport Minority Advisory Council (AMAC).

Eligibility: Open to students at the sophomore or higher level who have a GPA of 3.0 or higher and a record of involvement in community and extracurricular activities. Applicants must be working on a bachelor's degree in accounting, architecture, aviation, business administration, engineering, or finance as preparation for a career in the aviation or airport industry. They must be interested in participating in the AMAC program, including having an endorsement from a current AMAC member, becoming a member if they are awarded a scholarship, and communicating with AMAC once each semester during the term of the scholarship. Along with their application, they must submit a 1–

page essay on their career goals and why they have chosen their particular field of study. Financial need is not considered in the selection process. U.S. citizenship is required.
Financial data: The stipend is $2,000 per year.
Duration: 1 year; recipients may reapply.
Number awarded: 4 or more each semester.
Deadline: August of each year for fall semester; January of each year for spring semester.

1660 $ BACHELOR DEGREE ENGINEERING TECHNOLOGY SCHOLARSHIP

American Society of Heating, Refrigerating and Air–Conditioning Engineers
Attn: Scholarship Administrator
1791 Tullie Circle, N.E.
Atlanta, GA 30329–2305
Phone: (404) 539–1120; Fax: (404) 539–2120;
Email: lbenedict@ashrae.org
Web: www.ashrae.org/students/page/1271
Summary: To provide financial assistance to engineering technology students interested in heating, ventilating, air conditioning, and refrigeration (HVAC&R).
Eligibility: Open to engineering technology students enrolled full time in an ABET–accredited program leading to a bachelor's degree. Applicants must be engaged in a course of study that traditionally has been preparatory for the profession of HVAC&R. They must have a GPA of 3.0 or higher and a standing in the top 30% of their class. Selection is based on potential service to the HVAC&R profession, financial need, leadership ability, recommendations from instructors, and work ethics.
Financial data: The stipend is $3,000.
Duration: 1 year.
Number awarded: 1 each year.
Deadline: April of each year.

1661 BAKER SCHOLARSHIP

Garden Club Federation of Massachusetts, Inc.
Attn: Scholarship Secretary
219 Washington Street
Wellesley Hills, MA 02481
Phone: (781) 237–0336; Fax: (781) 237–0336;
Email: gcfmscholarship@aol.com
Web: www.gcfm.org/Education/Scholarships/GCFMScholarships.aspx
Summary: To provide financial assistance to residents of Massachusetts interested in working on an undergraduate or graduate degree in a field related to horticulture at a college in any state.
Eligibility: Open to high school seniors, undergraduates, and graduate students who have been residents of Massachusetts for at least 1 year. Applicants must be working on or planning to work on a degree in a field related to horticulture, including floriculture, landscape design, conservation, forestry, agronomy, city planning, environmental studies, land management, botany, or biology. They must have a GPA of 3.0 or higher. Along with their application, they must submit official transcripts; a brief essay about their goals, aspirations, and career plans; a list of their activities, including special honors and/or leadership positions; 3 letters of recommendation; and documentation of financial need.
Financial data: The stipend is $1,000.
Duration: 1 year.
Number awarded: 1 each year.
Deadline: February of each year.

1662 $ BALL HORTICULTURAL COMPANY SCHOLARSHIP

American Floral Endowment
1601 Duke Street
Alexandria, VA 22314
Phone: (703) 838–5211; Fax: (703) 838–5212;
Email: afe@endowment.org
Web: endowment.org/floriculture–scholarshipsinternships.html
Summary: To provide financial assistance to undergraduates interested in a career in commercial floriculture.
Eligibility: Open to undergraduate students at 4–year colleges and universities who are entering their junior or senior year. Applicants must be horticulture majors who intend to prepare for a career in commercial floriculture. They must be U.S. or Canadian citizens or permanent residents and have a GPA of 2.0 or higher. Along with their application, they must submit a statement describing their career goals and the academic, work–related, and/or life experiences that support those goals. Financial need is considered in the selection process.
Financial data: The stipend varies each year.
Duration: 1 year.
Number awarded: 1 each year.
Deadline: April of each year.

1663 $$ BARRY M. GOLDWATER SCHOLARSHIPS

Barry M. Goldwater Scholarship and Excellence in Education Foundation
Springfield Corporate Center
6225 Brandon Avenue, Suite 315
Springfield, VA 22150–2519
Phone: (703) 756–6012; Fax: (703) 756–6015;
Email: goldh2o@vacoxmail.com
Web: www.act.org/goldwater
Summary: To provide financial assistance to upper–division students planning careers in mathematics, engineering, or the natural sciences.
Eligibility: Open to full–time students enrolled as sophomores or juniors who are in the top quarter of their class and have a GPA of at least 3.0. Applicants must be majoring in mathematics, engineering (aerospace, chemical, electrical, environmental, nuclear), or the natural sciences (astrophysics, biochemistry, biology, botany, chemistry, computer science, entomology, environmental science, geology, microbiology, molecular genetics, natural resources management, neurobiology, physics, zoology). Students intending to enter medical school are eligible if they plan a career in research rather than private practice. Status as a U.S. citizen, national, or resident alien is also required. Students must be nominated by their institutions; 4–year colleges and universities may nominate up to 4 current sophomores or juniors and 2–year colleges may nominate up to 2 sophomores. Applicants must submit a 2–page essay on a significant issue or problem in their field of study that is of particular interest to them. Selection is based on academic performance and demonstrated potential for and commitment to a career in mathematics, engineering, or the natural sciences.
Financial data: Scholarships cover the cost of tuition, fees, books, and room and board up to a maximum of $7,500 per year.
Duration: Students who receive scholarships as juniors are eligible for 2 years of support or until they complete their baccalaureate degree; students who receive scholarships as seniors are eligible for 1 year of support or until they complete their baccalaureate degree.
Number awarded: Up to 300 each year.
Deadline: Institutions set their own deadlines; they must submit nominations to the foundation by January of each year.

1664 BARTLETT TREE FOUNDATION SCHOLARSHIPS

Bartlett Tree Foundation
Attn: Scholarship Fund
P.O. Box 3067
Stamford, CT 06905
Phone: (203) 323–1131; (877) BARTLET
Web: www.bartletttreefoundation.org/scholarship–application.cfm
Summary: To provide financial assistant to college students preparing for a career in arboriculture.
Eligibility: Open to students currently enrolled full time at a 2– or 4–year college or university. Applicants must be majoring in arboriculture, horticulture, or urban forestry as preparation for a career in arboriculture. Along with their application, they must submit a 500–word narrative outlining their accomplishments, academic record, awards, career aspirations, and future goals. Financial need is considered in the selection process.
Financial data: The stipend is $1,000.
Duration: 1 year.
Number awarded: 4 each year.
Deadline: September of each year for fall; January of each year for spring.

1665 BBG COMMUNICATIONS AWARD

Breylan Communications
3000 John Hawkins Parkway
Hoover, AL 35244
Phone: (205) 383–1753;
Email: james.bath@breylancommunications.com
Web: www.breylancommunications.com
Summary: To recognize and reward, with college scholarships, students who submit outstanding essays on topics related to communications technology.

Eligibility: Open to U.S. and Canadian citizens who are enrolled or planning to enroll at a college or university and have at least 1 full year of postsecondary studies remaining. Applicants must be between 16 and 21 years of age and have a GPA of 2.5 or higher. Along with their application, they must submit essays of 1,500 words each on 1) what they think is the greatest advancement in the information and communications technology industry (including information technology, telephony, broadcast media, audio and video processing and transmission) over the last 10 years; and 2) why they think a college or university education is important. Selection is based primarily on those essays.
Financial data: The award is a $1,000 college scholarship.
Duration: The competition is held annually.
Number awarded: 1 each year.
Deadline: June of each year.

1666 BEEF INDUSTRY SCHOLARSHIP PROGRAM

National Cattlemen's Beef Association
Attn: National Cattlemen's Foundation
9110 East Nichols Avenue, Suite 300
Centennial, CO 80112
Phone: (303) 694–0305; Fax: (303) 770–7745;
Email: ncf@beef.org
Web: www.nationalcattlemensfoundation.org

Summary: To provide financial assistance to students who are interested in preparing for a career in the beef industry.
Eligibility: Open to graduating high school seniors and full–time undergraduate students enrolled at a 2– or 4–year academic institution. Applicants must have demonstrated a commitment to a career in an area of the beef industry, through classes, internships, or life experiences. They must write a 1–page letter indicating what role they see themselves playing in the beef industry after graduation; write an essay (up to 750 words) on an issue confronting the beef industry and offering their solution; and submit 2 letters of reference. Essays are judged on the basis of clarity of expression, persuasiveness, originality, accuracy, relevance, and solutions offered. A career in the beef industry may include: education, communications, production, research, or other related areas. Selection is based on the letter (20%), the essay (70%), and the letters of recommendation (10%).
Financial data: The stipend is $1,500.
Duration: 1 year.
Number awarded: 10 each year.
Deadline: November of each year.

1667 $ BERNARD AND CAROLYN TORRACO MEMORIAL NURSING SCHOLARSHIPS

UNICO National
Attn: UNICO Foundation, Inc.
271 U.S. Highway 46 West, Suite A–108
Fairfield, NJ 07004
Phone: (973) 808–0035; (800) 877–1492; Fax: (973) 808–0043;
Email: uniconational@unico.org
Web: www.unico.org/scholarships.asp

Summary: To provide financial assistance to nursing students of all ethnicities.
Eligibility: Open to students currently enrolled in a prelicensure or graduate nursing program in any state. Applicants must have a GPA of 3.0 or higher and be able to demonstrate financial need. They may be of any ethnicity, but they must be U.S. citizens.
Financial data: The stipend is $2,500 per year.
Duration: 1 year; recipients may reapply.
Number awarded: 2 each year.
Deadline: April of each year.

1668 BERNICE PICKENS PARSONS FUND SCHOLARSHIPS

Greater Kanawha Valley Foundation
Attn: Scholarship Program Officer
1600 Huntington Square
900 Lee Street East, 16th Floor
Charleston, WV 25301
Phone: (304) 346–3620; (800) 467–5909; Fax: (304) 346–3640;
Email: shoover@tgkvf.org
Web: www.tgkvf.org/page.aspx?pid=409

Summary: To provide financial assistance to residents of West Virginia who are interested in studying designated fields at a school in any state.
Eligibility: Open to residents of West Virginia who are working or planning to work full time on a degree or certificate in the fields of library science, nursing, or paraprofessional legal work at a college or university in any state. Applicants must have an ACT score of 20 or higher, be able to demonstrate good moral character and financial need, and have a GPA of 2.5 or higher. Preference is given to residents of Jackson County.
Financial data: Stipends average $1,000 per year.
Duration: 1 year; may be renewed.
Number awarded: Varies each year; recently, 7 of these scholarships were awarded.
Deadline: January of each year.

1669 BERTHA LAMME MEMORIAL SCHOLARSHIP

Society of Women Engineers
Attn: Scholarship Selection Committee
203 North LaSalle Street, Suite 1675
Chicago, IL 60601–1269
Phone: (312) 596–5223; (877) SWE–INFO; Fax: (312) 644–8557;
Email: scholarships@swe.org
Web: societyofwomenengineers.swe.org/index.php/scholarships

Summary: To provide financial assistance to women who will be entering college as freshmen and are interested in studying electrical engineering.
Eligibility: Open to women who are entering college as freshmen with a GPA of 3.5 or higher. Applicants must be U.S. citizens or permanent residents planning to enroll full time at an ABET–accredited 4–year college or university and major in electrical engineering. Selection is based on merit.
Financial data: The stipend is $1,200.
Duration: 1 year.
Number awarded: 1 each year.
Deadline: May of each year.

1670 $ BERTHA P. SINGER SCHOLARSHIP

Oregon Student Access Commission
Attn: Grants and Scholarships Division
1500 Valley River Drive, Suite 100
Eugene, OR 97401–2146
Phone: (541) 687–7395; (800) 452–8807, ext. 7395; Fax: (541) 687–7414; TDD: (800) 735–2900;
Email: awardinfo@osac.state.or.us
Web: www.oregonstudentaid.gov/scholarships.aspx

Summary: To provide financial assistance to residents of Oregon who are interested in studying nursing at a school in the state.
Eligibility: Open to residents of Oregon who are studying nursing at a college in the state and have a cumulative GPA of 3.0 or higher. Applicants must provide documentation of enrollment in the third year of a 4–year nursing degree program or the second year of a 2–year associate degree nursing program. Financial need is considered in the selection process.
Financial data: Stipends for scholarships offered by the Oregon Student Access Commission (OSAC) range from $200 to $10,000 but recently averaged $2,300.
Duration: 1 year.
Number awarded: Varies each year.
Deadline: February of each year.

1671 BETTIE UNDERWOOD DENTAL ASSISTING SCHOLARSHIP

California Dental Association
Attn: CDA Foundation, Grants Administrator
1201 K Street, Suite 1511
Sacramento, CA 95814
Phone: (916) 443–3382, ext. 4929; (800) 232–7645, ext. 4929; Fax: (916) 498–6182;
Email: Jolene.Murray@cda.org
Web: www.cdafoundation.org/receive/dental_education_&_scholarships

Summary: To provide financial assistance to dental assisting students in California.
Eligibility: Open to students who are interested in becoming a dental assistant and enrolled or accepted at an institution in California. Applicants must submit a personal statement describing their career goals and what they hope to accomplish through their education. They must be able to demonstrate academic achievement, financial need, and a strong desire for a career in the dental field; a strong record of volunteer service is not required but is highly valued.

Financial data: The stipend is $1,000. Funds may be paid directly to the student or the school, at the student's request.
Duration: 1 year.
Number awarded: 1 each year.
Deadline: March of each year.

1672 BETTY BARRICK NON–TRADITIONAL STUDENT SCHOLARSHIP

Kentucky Energy and Environment Cabinet
Attn: Department for Natural Resources
Division of Conservation
375 Versailles Road
Frankfort, KY 40601
Phone: (502) 573–3080; Fax: (502) 573–1692;
Email: Angie.Wingfield@ky.gov
Web: conservation.ky.gov/Pages/Scholarships.aspx
Summary: To provide financial assistance to nontraditional students who are residents of Kentucky and interested in majoring in agriculture or conservation of natural resources at a college in any state.
Eligibility: Open to residents of Kentucky who are at least 25 years of age and attending a college or university in any state. Applicants must be working on or planning to work on an undergraduate degree in agriculture or a field related to the conservation of natural resources. Along with their application, they must submit an essay of 200 to 300 words on how their chosen profession will contribute to saving Kentucky's dwindling family farms. Selection is based on the essay (15 points), academic record (30 points), leadership (30 points), and extracurricular activities or jobs (25 points).
Financial data: The stipend is $1,000.
Duration: 1 year; nonrenewable.
Number awarded: 1 each year.
Deadline: February of each year.

1673 BETTY MONTOYA GIFT OF LIFE SCHOLARSHIP

Organ Transplant Awareness Program of New Mexico
P.O. Box 37217
Albuquerque, NM 87176
Phone: (505) 345–3740;
Email: otapscholarships@hotmail.com
Web: www.otapnm.org
Summary: To provide financial assistance to high school seniors in New Mexico who plan to attend college in any state, especially those planning to major in a health–related field.
Eligibility: Open to seniors graduating from high schools in New Mexico who plan to enroll at an accredited 2– or 4–year college, university, or vocational/technical school in any state. Applicants may be planning to study any field, but preference is given to those preparing for a health–related career. They must have a GPA of 2.0 or higher. Along with their application, they must submit either a personal story or an informative essay on organ transplant or tissue donation. Selection is based primarily on that story or essay; financial need is not considered.
Financial data: Stipends are $1,000 or $500. Funds are sent directly to the recipient's institution.
Duration: 1 year.
Number awarded: 4 each year: 2 at $1,000 and 2 at $500.
Deadline: February of each year.

1674 BILL KANE UNDERGRADUATE SCHOLARSHIP

American Association for Health Education
Attn: Scholarship Committee
1900 Association Drive
Reston, VA 20191–1599
Phone: (703) 476–3437; (800) 213–7193, ext. 437; Fax: (703) 476–9527;
Email: aahe@aahperd.org
Web: www.aahperd.org/aahe/events/scholarships.cfm
Summary: To provide financial assistance to undergraduates who are currently enrolled in a health education program.
Eligibility: Open to undergraduate students who are enrolled full time in a health education program at a 4–year college or university in the United States or its territories. Applicants must have a GPA of 3.25 or higher as a sophomore, junior, or senior. Along with their application, they must submit an essay of 400 to 450 words on what they hope to accomplish as a health educator (during training and in the future) and the attributes and aspirations they bring to the field of health education. Selection is based on evidence of leadership potential, academic talent, and activity in health education profession–related activities or organizations at the college, university, and/or community level.
Financial data: The stipend is $1,000 plus a 1–year complimentary student membership in the association.
Duration: 1 year; nonrenewable.
Number awarded: 1 each year.
Deadline: November of each year.

1675 $ BIOQUIP UNDERGRADUATE SCHOLARSHIP

Entomological Society of America
Attn: Entomological Foundation
9332 Annapolis Road, Suite 210
Lanham, MD 20706–3150
Phone: (301) 459–9082; Fax: (301) 459–9084;
Email: melodie@entfdn.org
Web: www.entfdn.org/awards_education.php
Summary: To provide financial assistance to upper–division students working on a degree in entomology.
Eligibility: Open to undergraduate students majoring in entomology at a college or university in the United States, Canada, or Mexico; if their school does not offer a degree in entomology, they must be preparing for a career as an entomologist through their studies. Applicants must have accumulated at least 90 semester hours and have either completed 2 junior–level entomology courses or have a research project in entomology. Along with their application, they must submit a 2–page statement on their interest in entomology, career goals, financial need, and other pertinent factors that illustrate qualifications for the scholarship. Selection is based on that statement (10 points); academic credentials (10 points); extracurricular activities including research, meeting presentations, awards and honors, and professional memberships and affiliations (10 points); letters of recommendation (10 points); and enthusiasm for entomology (10 points).
Financial data: The stipend is $2,000.
Duration: 1 year.
Number awarded: 1 each year.
Deadline: June of each year.

1676 BIOWORKS IPM/SUSTAINABLE PRACTICES SCHOLARSHIP

American Floral Endowment
1601 Duke Street
Alexandria, VA 22314
Phone: (703) 838–5211; Fax: (703) 838–5212;
Email: afe@endowment.org
Web: endowment.org/floriculture–scholarshipsinternships.html
Summary: To provide financial assistance to undergraduate students working on a degree in floriculture, especially those interested in the use of integrated pest management (IPM).
Eligibility: Open to undergraduate students who are working on a degree in horticulture and are interested in preparing for a career in floriculture. Preference is given to applicants who are interested in furthering the use of IPM or sustainable practices. They must be U.S. or Canadian citizens or permanent residents and have a GPA of 3.0 or higher. Along with their application, they must submit a statement describing their career goals and the academic, work–related, and/or life experiences that support those goals. Financial need is considered in the selection process.
Financial data: The stipend varies each year; recently, it was $1,150.
Duration: 1 year.
Number awarded: 1 each year.
Deadline: April of each year.

1677 B.J. HARROD SCHOLARSHIPS

Society of Women Engineers
Attn: Scholarship Selection Committee
203 North LaSalle Street, Suite 1675
Chicago, IL 60601–1269
Phone: (312) 596–5223; (877) SWE–INFO; Fax: (312) 644–8557;
Email: scholarships@swe.org
Web: societyofwomenengineers.swe.org/index.php/scholarships
Summary: To provide financial assistance to women who will be entering college as freshmen and are interested in studying engineering or computer science.

Eligibility: Open to women who are entering college as freshmen with a GPA of 3.5 or higher. Applicants must be planning to enroll full time at an ABET–accredited 4–year college or university and major in computer science or engineering. Selection is based on merit.
Financial data: The stipend is $1,500.
Duration: 1 year.
Number awarded: 2 each year.
Deadline: May of each year.

1678 $ B.K. KRENZER MEMORIAL REENTRY SCHOLARSHIP

Society of Women Engineers
Attn: Scholarship Selection Committee
203 North LaSalle Street, Suite 1675
Chicago, IL 60601–1269
Phone: (312) 596–5223; (877) SWE–INFO; Fax: (312) 644–8557;
Email: scholarships@swe.org
Web: societyofwomenengineers.swe.org/index.php/scholarships
Summary: To provide financial assistance to women interested in returning to college or graduate school to study engineering or computer science.
Eligibility: Open to women who are planning to enroll at an ABET–accredited 4–year college or university. Applicants must have been out of the engineering workforce and school for at least 2 years and must be planning to return as an undergraduate or graduate student to work on a degree in computer science or engineering. They must have a GPA of 3.0 or higher. Selection is based on merit. Preference is given to engineers who already have a degree and are planning to reenter the engineering workforce after a period of temporary retirement.
Financial data: The stipend is $2,000.
Duration: 1 year.
Number awarded: 1 each year.
Deadline: February of each year.

1679 $$ BLACK & VEATCH–MAKING A DIFFERENCE SCHOLARSHIP

American Water Works Association
Attn: Scholarship Coordinator
6666 West Quincy Avenue
Denver, CO 80235–3098
Phone: (303) 347–6201; (800) 926–7337; Fax: (303) 795–7603;
Email: lmoody@awwa.org
Web: www.awwa.org
Summary: To provide funding to undergraduate students interested in preparing for a career in the drinking water field.
Eligibility: Open to students working on an undergraduate degree at an institution of higher education located in Canada, Guam, Puerto Rico, Mexico, or the United States. Applicants must be preparing for a career in the drinking water field. Along with their application, they must submit a 2–page resume, official transcripts, 3 letters of recommendation, a proposed curriculum of study, a 1–page statement of educational plans and career objectives demonstrating an interest in the drinking water field, and a 3–page proposed plan of research. Selection is based on academic record and potential to provide leadership in the field of water supply and treatment.
Financial data: The stipend is $5,000.
Duration: 1 year; nonrenewable.
Number awarded: 1 each year.
Deadline: January of each year.

1680 $$ BLACKS AT MICROSOFT SCHOLARSHIPS

Blacks at Microsoft
Attn: BAM Scholarship
One Microsoft Way
Redmond, WA 98052
Email: bamship@microsoft.com
Web: www.microsoft.com
Summary: To provide financial assistance to African American high school seniors who plan to major in engineering, computer science, or a business–related field in college.
Eligibility: Open to seniors of African descent graduating from high school and planning to attend a 4–year college or university. Applicants must be planning to work on a bachelor's degree in engineering, computer science, computer information systems, or selected business fields (such as finance, business administration, or marketing). They must be able to demonstrate a "passion for technology," leadership at school or in the community, a need for financial assistance to attend college, and a GPA of 3.3 or higher. Along with their application, they must submit a 500–word essay on how they plan to engage in the technology industry in their future career and a 250–word essay on their financial need for this scholarship.
Financial data: The stipend is $5,000 per year.
Duration: 1 year; may be renewed up to 3 additional years.
Number awarded: 2 each year.
Deadline: March of each year.

1681 BMW/SAE ENGINEERING SCHOLARSHIP

Society of Automotive Engineers
Attn: Scholarships and Loans Program
400 Commonwealth Drive
Warrendale, PA 15096–0001
Phone: (724) 776–4790; (877) 606–7323; Fax: (724) 776–0790;
Email: scholarships@sae.org
Web: students.sae.org/awdscholar/scholarships/bmw
Summary: To provide financial support to high school seniors interested in studying engineering in college.
Eligibility: Open to U.S. citizens who intend to earn an ABET–accredited degree in engineering. Applicants must be high school seniors with a GPA of 3.75 or higher who rank in the 90th percentile in both mathematics and critical reading on the SAT or in the composite ACT. Selection is based on high school transcripts; SAT or ACT scores; school–related extracurricular activities; non–school related activities; academic honors, civic honors, and awards; and a 250–word essay on their goals, plans, experiences, and interests in mobility engineering. Financial need is not considered.
Financial data: The stipend is $1,500 per year.
Duration: 1 year; may be renewed up to 3 additional years, provided the recipient maintains a GPA of 3.0 or higher.
Number awarded: 1 each year.
Deadline: January of each year.

1682 $ BREAKTHROUGH TO NURSING SCHOLARSHIPS

National Student Nurses' Association
Attn: Foundation
45 Main Street, Suite 606
Brooklyn, NY 11201
Phone: (718) 210–0705; Fax: (718) 797–1186;
Email: nsna@nsna.org
Web: www.nsna.org/FoundationScholarships/FNSNAScholarships.aspx
Summary: To provide financial assistance to minority undergraduate and graduate students who wish to prepare for careers in nursing.
Eligibility: Open to students currently enrolled in state–approved schools of nursing or pre–nursing associate degree, baccalaureate, diploma, generic master's, generic doctoral, R.N. to B.S.N., R.N. to M.S.N., or L.P.N./L.V.N. to R.N. programs. Graduating high school seniors are not eligible. Support for graduate education is provided only for a first degree in nursing. Applicants must be members of a racial or ethnic minority underrepresented among registered nurses (American Indian or Alaska Native, Hispanic or Latino, Native Hawaiian or other Pacific Islander, Black or African American, or Asian). They must be committed to providing quality health care services to underserved populations. Along with their application, they must submit a 200–word description of their professional and educational goals and how this scholarship will help them achieve those goals. Selection is based on academic achievement, financial need, and involvement in student nursing organizations and community health activities. U.S. citizenship or permanent resident status is required.
Financial data: Stipends range from $1,000 to $2,500.
Duration: 1 year.
Number awarded: Varies each year; recently, 13 of these scholarships were awarded: 10 sponsored by the American Association of Critical–Care Nurses and 3 sponsored by the Mayo Clinic.
Deadline: January of each year.

1683 BRIAN MORDEN MEMORIAL SCHOLARSHIP

Summary: To provide financial assistance to students, including cancer survivors, who are interested in studying computer science, medicine, or music in college.
See Listing #1155.

1684 BRILL FAMILY SCHOLARSHIP

Society of Women Engineers
Attn: Scholarship Selection Committee
203 North LaSalle Street, Suite 1675

Chicago, IL 60601–1269
Phone: (312) 596–5223; (877) SWE–INFO; Fax: (312) 644–8557;
Email: scholarships@swe.org
Web: societyofwomenengineers.swe.org/index.php/scholarships
Summary: To provide financial assistance to undergraduate women majoring in designated engineering specialties.
Eligibility: Open to women who are entering their sophomore, junior, or senior year at an ABET–accredited 4–year college or university. Applicants must be working full time on a degree in computer science or aeronautical or biomedical engineering and have a GPA of 3.0 or higher. Selection is based on merit.
Financial data: The stipend is $1,000.
Duration: 1 year.
Number awarded: 1 each year.
Deadline: February of each year.

1685 BROADCAST METEOROLOGY SCHOLARSHIP

National Weather Association
Attn: Executive Director
228 West Millbrook Road
Raleigh, NC 27609–4304
Phone: (919) 845–1546; Fax: (919) 845–2956;
Email: exdir@nwas.org
Web: www.nwas.org/committees/ed_comm/application/index.php
Summary: To provide financial assistance to undergraduate students working on a degree in broadcast meteorology.
Eligibility: Open to students who are entering their sophomore or higher year of undergraduate study. Applicants must be working on a degree in broadcast meteorology. Along with their application, they must submit 1) a 1–page statement explaining why they want to be a broadcast meteorologist and their vision for the future; and 2) a DVD that includes 2 full on–camera weathercasts, with all graphics and show elements prepared by them. Selection is based on that statement, the DVD, academic achievement, and 2 letters of recommendation.
Financial data: The stipend is $1,000.
Duration: 1 year.
Number awarded: 1 each year.
Deadline: March of each year.

1686 BUD GLOVER MEMORIAL SCHOLARSHIP

Aircraft Electronics Association
Attn: AEA Educational Foundation
3570 N.E. Ralph Powell Road
Lee's Summit, MO 64064
Phone: (816) 347–8400; Fax: (816) 347–8405;
Email: info@aea.net
Web: www.aea.net/educationalfoundation/scholarships.asp
Summary: To provide financial assistance to students interested in preparing for a career in avionics or aircraft maintenance.
Eligibility: Open to high school seniors and currently–enrolled college students who are attending (or planning to attend) an accredited postsecondary institution in an avionics or aircraft maintenance program. Applicants must submit an official transcript (cumulative GPA of 2.5 or higher), a statement about their career plans, a description of their involvement in school and community activities, and a 300–word essay on the most important issues the career field of avionics and aviation maintenance are facing today. Selection is based on merit.
Financial data: The stipend is $1,000.
Duration: 1 year.
Number awarded: 1 each year. The sponsor also awards a number of other named scholarships each year for students preparing for a career in avionics or aircraft maintenance.
Deadline: February of each year.

1687 $$ BUICK ACHIEVERS SCHOLARSHIP PROGRAM

Summary: To provide financial assistance to students entering college for the first time and planning to major in specified fields related to design, engineering, or business.
See Listing #1157.

1688 $ CALCOT–SEITZ FOUNDATION SCHOLARSHIPS

Calcot–Seitz Foundation
Attn: Scholarship Committee
1900 East Brundage Lane
P.O. Box 259
Bakersfield, CA 93302–0259
Phone: (661) 395–6874; Fax: (661) 861–9870;
Email: mcunningham@calcot.com
Web: www.calcot.com/calcotseitz.asp?post=scholarships&flag=calcotseitz
Summary: To provide financial assistance to students from cotton–growing areas of selected southwestern states who are interested in majoring in an agricultural–related field at a college in any state.
Eligibility: Open to students from cotton–growing areas of Arizona, California, New Mexico, and Texas who are working or planning to work full time on a degree in agriculture at a 4–year college or university in any state. Applicants may be high school seniors or currently–enrolled college students who are continuing their studies. They must have a GPA of 3.0 or higher. Along with their application, they must submit a 150–word essay on their educational objectives, their future in agriculture, and what they consider to be some of the main problems in agriculture at present. Selection is based on scholastic aptitude and performance, leadership potential, demonstrated capability, financial need, and a personal interview.
Financial data: Stipends range from $1,000 to $3,000 per year.
Duration: 3 years.
Number awarded: Varies each year; recently, 24 of these scholarships were awarded: 6 at $3,000, 6 at $2,000 and 12 at $1,000.
Deadline: March of each year.

1689 $ CALIFORNIA GARDEN CLUBS SCHOLARSHIPS

California Garden Clubs, Inc.
c/o Albert Chang, Scholarship Co–Chair
12010 Susan Drive
Granada Hills, CA 91344–2641
Phone: (602) 418–2900;
Email: AFChangUSA@gmail.com
Web: californiagardenclubs.com/CGCI_scholarships
Summary: To provide financial assistance to upper–division and graduate students from California who are working on a degree in a field related to horticulture at a school in any state.
Eligibility: Open to California residents who are enrolled as full–time juniors, seniors, or graduate students at a college or university in any state and have a GPA of 3.25 or higher. Applicants must be preparing for a career in horticulture, floriculture, landscape design, botany, forestry, agronomy, conservation, plant pathology, environmental concerns, city planning, or allied subjects. Along with their application, they must submit a 2–page letter discussing their goals, background, financial need, and personal commitment to their career choice. Selection is based on academic record (40%), the letter (30%), a list of honors, extracurricular activities, and work experience (10%), financial need (15%), and recommendations (5%).
Financial data: The stipend is $2,000.
Duration: 1 year.
Number awarded: 2 each year.
Deadline: January of each year.

1690 CALIFORNIA GROUNDWATER ASSOCIATION WATER SCHOLARSHIP

California Groundwater Association
P.O. Box 14369
Santa Rosa, CA 95402
Phone: (707) 578–4408; Fax: (707) 546–4906;
Email: wellguy@groundh2o.org
Web: www.groundh2o.org/programs/scholarship.html
Summary: To provide financial assistance to California residents who are interested in studying a field related to ground water at a college in any state.
Eligibility: Open to residents of California currently enrolled or accepted at a college or university in any state. Applicants must be interested in working on a degree in a field of study related to ground water. Along with their application, they must submit a 500–word essay demonstrating their interest in ground water technology. Financial need is not considered in the selection process.
Financial data: The stipend is $1,000.
Duration: 1 year.
Number awarded: 1 each year.
Deadline: March of each year.

1691 $ CALIFORNIA LEGION AUXILIARY PAST PRESIDENTS' PARLEY NURSING SCHOLARSHIPS

American Legion Auxiliary
Department of California

Veterans War Memorial Building
401 Van Ness Avenue, Room 113
San Francisco, CA 94102–4586
Phone: (415) 861–5092; Fax: (415) 861–8365;
Email: calegionaux@calegionaux.org
Web: www.calegionaux.org/scholarships.htm

Summary: To provide financial assistance to California residents who are current military personnel, veterans, or members of their families and interested in studying nursing at a school in the state.

Eligibility: Open to California residents who are currently serving on active military duty, veterans who served during war time, or the spouse, widow(er), or child of such a veteran. Applicants must be entering or continuing students of nursing at an accredited institution of higher learning in California. Selection is based on the application (25%), scholarship (25%), character and leadership (25%), and financial need (25%).

Financial data: Stipends range up to $2,000.

Duration: 1 year.

Number awarded: Varies each year.

Deadline: March of each year.

1692 CALIFORNIA MARINE SCIENCES SCHOLARSHIP

Central California Council of Diving Clubs
c/o James L. Kaller, Scholarship Director
155 Montgomery Street, Suite 1004
San Francisco, CA 94104–4115
Phone: (415) 362–9134, ext. 12; Fax: (415) 434–1880;
Email: jameskaller@batnet.com
Web: www.cencal.org/scholarship.html

Summary: To provide financial assistance to undergraduate and graduate students in California engaged in the study of underwater habitats.

Eligibility: Open to California residents who are enrolled full time in a California academic institute, are at least 18 years of age, are a certified diver holding current national certification, and have at least a 3.0 GPA. Applicants must be working on an undergraduate or graduate degree related to underwater habitats. Aquatic–related programs in the disciplines of biology, physical sciences, marine education, maritime archaeology, historical and social aspects of marine resources, and the science of diving are considered relevant for this program. Along with their application, they must submit a 300–word description of their professional goals. Financial need is not considered in the selection process.

Financial data: The stipend is $1,000.

Duration: 1 year.

Number awarded: 1 each year.

Deadline: October of each year.

1693 CALIFORNIA TRANSPORTATION FOUNDATION TRANSPORTATION SCHOLARSHIP

California Department of Transportation
Attn: Division of Human Resources
Equal Employment Opportunity Program (MS 90)
P.O. Box 168037
Sacramento, CA 95816–8037
Phone: (916) 227–1823;
Email: steve_perez@dot.ca.gov
Web: www.dot.ca.gov/hq/jobs/scholarships.htm

Summary: To provide financial assistance to undergraduate students in California who are preparing for a career in transportation.

Eligibility: Open to sophomores and juniors enrolled at a college or university in California and preparing for a career in transportation. Applicants must be majoring in a field other than civil engineering. They must be a U.S. citizen, permanent resident, or documented international student. Along with their application, they must submit a 500–word essay on why they are interested in a career in transportation. Selection is based on academic record, current job skills, and commitment to a career in transportation; financial need may be considered but is not a primary factor.

Financial data: The stipend is $1,000.

Duration: 1 year.

Number awarded: 1 each year.

Deadline: May of each year.

1694 CALIFORNIA–NEVADA SECTION AWWA SCHOLARSHIPS

American Water Works Association–California–Nevada Section
Attn: Scholarship Program
10574 Acacia Street, Suite D6
Rancho Cucamonga, CA 91730
Phone: (909) 481–7200; Fax: (909) 481–4688;
Email: info@ca–nv–awwa.org
Web: ca–nv–awwa.org

Summary: To provide financial assistance to residents of California and Nevada who are working on an undergraduate degree in a field related to water supply and treatment.

Eligibility: Open to residents of California and Nevada who are currently enrolled full or part time at a 4–year college or university in those states. Applicants must be preparing for a career in a field related to water supply and treatment. Along with their application, they must submit a 300–word statement on their educational plans and career objectives as those relate to the water utility industry. Selection is based on academic record, career goals, relation of academic program to the water supply and treatment industry, and financial need.

Financial data: The stipend is $1,000.

Duration: 1 year.

Number awarded: 2 each year.

Deadline: May of each year.

1695 CALLE BUSER MEMORIAL SCHOLARSHIPS

California Transportation Foundation
c/o Bob Davies
Buser Memorial Scholarship Coordinator
1727 30th Street, MS 35
Sacramento, CA 95816
Phone: (916) 227–9441;
Email: bob.davies@dot.ca.gov
Web: www.transportationfoundation.org/scholarships

Summary: To provide financial assistance to students working on undergraduate degrees in land surveying at colleges and universities in California.

Eligibility: Open to students enrolled or planning to enroll at a college or university in California as a freshman, sophomore, junior, or senior. Applicants must be working on a degree or enrolled in a program related to land surveying. They must have a GPA of 2.5 or higher. Along with their application, they must submit an essay of 500 to 600 words on what they see as the future of surveying, especially as it pertains to transportation organizations. Selection is based on that essay (25%); professional activities (20%); professional organization memberships (15%); cumulative GPA (15%); extracurricular activities (10%); overall application presentation (10%); and scholarships, awards, and academic honors (5%).

Financial data: The stipend is $1,000. Funds are paid directly to the student.

Duration: 1 year.

Number awarded: 4 each year: 1 each to a freshman, sophomore, junior, and senior.

Deadline: November of each year.

1696 $ CAMPUSRN SCHOLARSHIPS

CampusCareerCenter.com
2454 Massachusetts Avenue
Cambridge, MA 02140
Phone: (617) 661–2613; Fax: (617) 812–8585
Web: www.campusrn.com/network/scholarship_program

Summary: To provide financial assistance to students working on a degree or certificate in nursing at a school that is registered with CampusRN.

Eligibility: Open to students working on a nursing degree or certificate at any academic level. Applicants must be attending a school that is registered with CampusRN. Along with their application, they must submit an essay of 200 to 500 words on their goals and aspirations as they relate to their educational, career, and future plans. Financial need is not considered in the selection process.

Financial data: The stipend is $2,500.

Duration: 1 year.

Number awarded: 6 each year: 1 in each region of the country.

Deadline: March of each year.

1697 $$ CAPTAIN JASON DAHL SCHOLARSHIP

Captain Jason Dahl Scholarship Fund
9956 West Remington Place, Unit A–10, Suite 93
Littleton, CO 80128
Web: dahlfund.org/?page_id=389

Summary: To provide financial assistance to aviation students who are specializing in pilot–related studies.

Eligibility: Open to full–time students at accredited universities who are majoring in aviation with an emphasis in pilot–related studies. Applicants must submit a 1,000–word essay describing their desire to prepare for a career as a professional pilot or in aviation.
Financial data: The stipend is $5,000.
Duration: 1 year.
Number awarded: 2 each year.
Deadline: March of each year.

1698 $$ CAPTAIN SEAN P. GRIMES PHYSICIAN ASSISTANT EDUCATIONAL SCHOLARSHIP AWARD

Society of Army Physician Assistants
c/o Harold Slusher
6762 Candlewood Drive
P.O. Box 07490
Fort Myers, FL 33919
Phone: (239) 482–2162; Fax: (239) 482–2162;
Email: hal.shusher@juno.com
Web: www.sapa.org/SeanScholarshipPage.htm
Summary: To provide financial assistance to current and former Army personnel interested in seeking training as a physician assistant.
Eligibility: Open to Army veterans, Army active–duty soldiers, Army National Guard soldiers, and Army Reservists. Soldiers may be of any enlisted or officer rank from E–5 through O–4. Applicants may be seeking initial training as a physician assistant or current physician assistants working on a baccalaureate, master's, or doctoral degree. They must have a GPA of 2.5 or higher. Candidates for initial training must be enrolled in an ARC–PA approved program. Other candidates must be enrolled at an accredited college or university. Financial need is considered in the selection process.
Financial data: The stipend is $6,000.
Duration: 1 year.
Number awarded: 1 each year.
Deadline: January of each year.

1699 CAREER ADVANCEMENT SCHOLARSHIPS

Business and Professional Women's Foundation
Attn: Scholarship Program
1718 M Street, N.W., Suite 148
Washington, DC 20036
Phone: (202) 293–1100; Fax: (202) 861–0298;
Email: foundation@bpwfoundation.org
Web: www.bpwfoundation.org/index.php/about/scholarships
Summary: To provide financial assistance for college to mature women who are interested in completing a bachelor's degree in a field of science, technology, engineering, or mathematics (STEM).
Eligibility: Open to women who are at least 25 years of age, citizens of the United States, and within 2 years of completing a bachelor's degree in a field of STEM. They must apply through a participating partner organization of the Business and Professional Women's (BPW) Foundation at the state or local level. Selection is based on academics (20%), career objectives (25%), responsibility and involvement, e.g., paid employment, domestic or family responsibilities (15%), disadvantage, e.g., financial, situational, physical or mental, medical (35%), and special considerations, e.g., military veteran (5%).
Financial data: Stipends are at least $1,000.
Duration: 1 year.
Number awarded: Varies each year; recently, 12 of these scholarships (including 1 for a veteran) were awarded.
Deadline: Each partner organization sets its own deadline.

1700 $$ CAREFIRST BLUECROSS BLUESHIELD HEALTH AND LIFE SCIENCES SCHOLARS PROGRAM

Independent College Fund of Maryland
Attn: Director of Programs and Scholarships
3225 Ellerslie Avenue, Suite C–160
Baltimore, MD 21218–3519
Phone: (443) 997–5700; Fax: (443) 997–2740;
Email: Ifund@jhu.edu
Web: i–fundinfo.org/scholarships/emerging–technology–scholarships.html
Summary: To provide financial assistance to students from any state at member institutions of the Independent College Fund of Maryland who are majoring in designated fields of science.
Eligibility: Open to students from any state currently entering their sophomore, junior, or senior year at member institutions. Applicants must be majoring in or have demonstrated a career interest in the biological sciences, biochemistry, biophysics, microbiology, or related scientific fields, including chemistry, computer science, physics, or environmental health. They must have a GPA of 3.0 or higher.
Financial data: The stipend is $5,000.
Duration: 1 year.
Number awarded: 1 or more each year.
Deadline: Deadline not specified.

1701 $ CARGILL SCHOLARSHIP PROGRAM FOR TRIBAL COLLEGES

American Indian College Fund
Attn: Scholarship Department
8333 Greenwood Boulevard
Denver, CO 80221
Phone: (303) 426–8900; (800) 776–FUND; Fax: (303) 426–1200;
Email: scholarships@collegefund.org
Web: www.collegefund.org/content/full_circle_scholarships_listings
Summary: To provide financial assistance to Native American college students from any state who are working on a bachelor's degree in specified fields at Tribal Colleges and Universities (TCUs) in selected states.
Eligibility: Open to American Indians who have proof of enrollment or descendancy. Applicants must be enrolled full time at an eligible TCU in Kansas, Minnesota, North Dakota, South Dakota, or Wisconsin and be working on a bachelor's degree in agricultural studies, business, engineering, finance, mathematics, science, or technology. They must have a GPA of 3.0 or higher and a record of leadership and service to the Native American community. Applications are available only online and include required essays on specified topics. Selection is based on exceptional academic achievement. U.S. citizenship is required.
Financial data: Stipends range from $2,000 to $4,000.
Duration: 1 year.
Number awarded: 1 or more each year.
Deadline: May of each year.

1702 CAROL BOND UNIVERSITY STUDENT SCHOLARSHIPS

North Carolina American Water Works Association and Water Environment Association
3725 National Drive, Suite 217
Raleigh, NC 27612
Phone: (919) 784–9030; Fax: (919) 784–9032
Web: www.ncsafewater.org/resources_/for_students_educators
Summary: To provide financial assistance to upper–division students at colleges in North Carolina who are majoring in environmental sciences or environmental engineering.
Eligibility: Open to U.S. citizens from any state entering their junior or senior year at a 4–year college or university in North Carolina. Applicants must be working on a bachelor's degree in environmental sciences or environmental engineering. They must have a GPA of 2.75 or higher. Along with their application, they must submit an essay of 500 to 750 words on why they should receive a scholarship. Selection is based on academic record and potential to provide leadership in the environmental sciences and environmental engineering fields.
Financial data: The stipend is $1,000.
Duration: 1 year.
Number awarded: 2 each year.
Deadline: March of each year.

1703 CAROL JORGENSEN SCHOLARSHIP FOR ENVIRONMENTAL STEWARDSHIP

Society of American Indian Government Employees
c/o Luke Jones
U.S. Environmental Protection Agency
American Indian Environmental Office (2690–M)
1200 Pennsylvania Avenue, N.W.
Washington, DC 20460
Phone: (202) 564–0303; Fax: (202) 564–0298;
Email: jones.luke@epa.gov
Web: www.saige.org/scholar/scholarships.html
Summary: To provide financial assistance to Native Americans working on an undergraduate degree in a field related to environmental stewardship.

Eligibility: Open to full–time undergraduate students who are affiliated with a federally–recognized tribe of Native Americans. Tribal enrollment is not required, but tribal affiliation must be verified by a letter of support from a current or former tribal government official or respected member of the tribal community. Applicants must be working on a degree in an environmental stewardship discipline (e.g., environmental studies, natural resource management, the natural sciences, public policy or administration with an environmental focus). Along with their application, they must submit a 2–page personal statement that describes how their undergraduate studies support their commitment to environmental stewardship.
Financial data: The stipend is $1,000.
Duration: 1 year.
Number awarded: 1 each year.
Deadline: June of each year.

1704 $ CAROLINAS AGC SCHOLARSHIPS

Carolinas AGC
Attn: CAGC Foundation, Inc.
1100 Euclid Avenue
P.O. Box 30277
Charlotte, NC 28230–0277
Phone: (704) 372–1450; Fax: (704) 332–5032;
Email: cmills@carolinasagc.org
Web: www.cagc.org/edu_training/careers_scholarships.cfm
Summary: To provide financial assistance to undergraduate students working on a degree in construction in North or South Carolina.
Eligibility: Open to students attending 1 of the 5 major universities in North or South Carolina with an accredited construction department.
Financial data: The stipend is $2,500.
Duration: 1 year.
Number awarded: 5 each year.
Deadline: Deadline not specified.

1705 $ CAROLINAS GOLF ASSOCIATION SCHOLARSHIPS

Carolinas Golf Association
Attn: Foundation
135 North Trade Street
P.O. Box 319
West End, NC 27376
Phone: (910) 673–1000; Fax: (910) 673–1001;
Email: info@carolinasgolf.org
Web: www.carolinasgolf.org
Summary: To provide financial assistance to students working on a degree in turfgrass management at colleges and universities in North and South Carolina.
Eligibility: Open to students enrolled at colleges and universities in North and South Carolina. Applicants must be preparing for a career as a golf superintendent or turfgrass manager in the Carolinas.
Financial data: The stipend is $2,000.
Duration: 1 year.
Number awarded: Varies each year. Recently, 2 of these scholarships were awarded.
Deadline: Deadline not specified.

1706 CARVILLE M. AKEHURST MEMORIAL SCHOLARSHIP

Summary: To provide financial assistance to residents of Maryland, Virginia, and West Virginia working on an undergraduate or graduate degree in landscape architecture or horticulture at a school in any state.
See Listing #1163.

1707 $ CATERPILLAR SWE SCHOLARSHIPS

Society of Women Engineers
Attn: Scholarship Selection Committee
203 North LaSalle Street, Suite 1675
Chicago, IL 60601–1269
Phone: (312) 596–5223; (877) SWE–INFO; Fax: (312) 644–8557;
Email: scholarships@swe.org
Web: societyofwomenengineers.swe.org/index.php/scholarships
Summary: To provide financial assistance to women who are working on an undergraduate or graduate degree in selected fields of engineering or computer science.
Eligibility: Open to women who are sophomores, juniors, seniors, or graduate students at ABET–accredited 4–year colleges and universities. Applicants must be working full time on a degree in computer science or agricultural, chemical, electrical, industrial, manufacturing, materials, or mechanical engineering. They must be U.S. citizens or authorized to work in the United States and have a GPA of 3.0 or higher. Selection is based on merit.
Financial data: The stipend is $2,400.
Duration: 1 year.
Number awarded: 3 each year.
Deadline: February of each year.

1708 $ CBC SCHOLARSHIPS

Summary: To provide financial assistance to high school seniors in Connecticut who are interested in studying a field related to the construction industry at a college in any state.
See Listing #1164.

1709 $$ CERTIFIEDBACKGROUND.COM–AACN NURSING SCHOLARSHIP FUND

American Association of Colleges of Nursing
One Dupont Circle, N.W., Suite 530
Washington, DC 20036
Phone: (202) 463–6930; Fax: (202) 785–8320;
Email: scholarship@aacn.nche.edu
Web: www.aacn.nche.edu/students/scholarships
Summary: To provide financial assistance to students at institutions that are members of the American Association of Colleges of Nursing (AACN) affiliated with CertifiedBackground.com.
Eligibility: Open to students working on a baccalaureate, master's, or doctoral degree at an AACN member school affiliated with CertifiedBackground.com. Applicants must have a GPA of 3.2 or higher. Along with their application, they must submit a 250–word essay on their goals and aspirations as related to their education, career, and future plans.
Financial data: The stipend is $5,000.
Duration: 1 year.
Number awarded: Up to 8 each year: 2 for each application deadline.
Deadline: January, April, July, or October of each year.

1710 $ CHARLES S. GARDNER MEMORIAL SCHOLARSHIP IN FOREST RESOURCES

Mill Operations Technical Advancement Group (MOTAG) South
c/o Mike Grist, Scholarship Chair
Mead Westvaco
104 East Riverside Street
Covington, VA 24426–0950
Phone: (540) 969–5368;
Email: mvg@meadwestvaco.com
Web: www.andritzwoodprocessing.com/motag/south/html/scholarship.html
Summary: To provide financial assistance to students working on a degree in a wood fiber related field at a university in the South.
Eligibility: Open to students entering their sophomore year at a college or university in the Southeast or South Central states. Applicants must be planning to major in a field related to wood fiber (e.g., forestry, silviculture, land management) and have a GPA of 3.0 or higher for their freshman year. Financial need is considered in the selection process.
Financial data: The stipend is $2,000 per year.
Duration: 1 year; may be renewed up to 3 additional years, provided the recipient maintains a GPA of 3.0 or higher.
Number awarded: 1 each year.
Deadline: June of each year.

1711 CHARLES SKOCH SCHOLARSHIP

Florida Sea Grant
c/o University of Florida
Building 803 McCarty Drive
P.O. Box 110400
Gainesville, FL 32611–0400
Phone: (352) 392–5870; Fax: (352) 392–5113
Web: www.flseagrant.org/students/scholarships–fellowships

Summary: To provide financial assistance to high school seniors in Florida who plan to major in a coastal–related field at a college or university in the state.
Eligibility: Open to seniors graduating from high schools in Florida who plan to attend a college or university in the state. Applicants must be planning to major in marine biology, zoology, oceanography, ocean and coastal engineering, fisheries, aquaculture, seafood technology, or a social science with a marine studies option. They must apply through the Florida Annual State Science and Engineering Fair conducted by the Florida Foundation for Future Scientists.
Financial data: The stipend is $1,000.
Duration: 1 year; nonrenewable.
Number awarded: 1 each year.
Deadline: October of each year.

1712 $$ CHARLES W. RILEY FIRE AND EMERGENCY MEDICAL SERVICES TUITION REIMBURSEMENT PROGRAM

Maryland Higher Education Commission
Attn: Office of Student Financial Assistance
6 North Liberty Street, Ground Suite
Baltimore, MD 21201
Phone: (410) 767–3300; (800) 974–0203; Fax: (410) 332–0250; TDD: (800) 735–2258;
Email: osfamail@mhec.state.md.us
Web: www.mhec.state.md.us/financialAid/descriptions.asp
Summary: To provide financial assistance for college and graduate school to firefighters, ambulance personnel, and rescue squad members in Maryland.
Eligibility: Open to firefighters, ambulance personnel, and rescue squad members who are enrolled as full–time or part–time undergraduate or graduate students at an accredited institution of higher education in Maryland in a degree or certificate program for fire service technology or emergency medical technology. Applicants must have received at least a grade of "C" in any course required for completion of their program. They must be serving a Maryland community while they are taking college courses.
Financial data: Awards provide full reimbursement of tuition charges the student has paid, up to the equivalent annual tuition of a resident undergraduate students at a 4–year public institution within the University System of Maryland.
Duration: 1 year; may be renewed if the recipient maintains satisfactory academic progress and remains enrolled in an eligible program.
Number awarded: Varies each year.
Deadline: June of each year.

1713 $$ CHESAPEAKE UROLOGY ASSOCIATES SCHOLARSHIP

Central Scholarship Bureau
1700 Reisterstown Road, Suite 220
P.O. Box 37064
Baltimore, MD 21297–3064
Phone: (410) 415–5558; Fax: (410) 415–5501;
Email: contact@centralsb.org
Web: www.centralsb.org/html/ChesapeakeUrologyAssocSF.htm
Summary: To provide financial assistance to residents of Maryland working on a degree in a health–related field at a college in any state.
Eligibility: Open to residents of Maryland who are enrolled full time at a college or university in any state. Applicants must be working on a degree in pre–medicine, pre–nursing, or an ancillary health field. They must have a GPA of 3.0 or higher and a family income less than $90,000 per year. Selection is based on demonstrated commitment to the medical field, academic achievement, and financial need. U.S. citizenship or permanent resident status is required.
Financial data: The stipend is $5,000.
Duration: 1 year.
Number awarded: 3 each year.
Deadline: May of each year.

1714 CHS FOUNDATION HIGH SCHOOL SCHOLARSHIP PROGRAM

CHS Foundation
Attn: Scholarship Program
5500 Cenex Drive, MS 407
Inver Grove Heights, MN 55077
Phone: (651) 355–5129; (800) 814–0506; Fax: (651) 355–5073;
Email: info@chsfoundation.org
Web: www.chsfoundation.org/scholarshipprog.html
Summary: To provide financial assistance to high school seniors planning to study a field related to agriculture at a college or university in any state.
Eligibility: Open to seniors who are graduating from high schools in the United States and planning to enroll at a 2– or 4–year college or university. Applicants must be planning to major in an agriculture–related field, including agribusiness and economics, agronomy, land use planning, agricultural communications, animal science, biotechnology, international agriculture, environmental science, or agricultural engineering. Along with their application, they must submit 500–word essays on 1) the role of the U.S. agricultural industry in a global economy; and 2) a leader whom they admire, the leadership qualities that he or she exhibits, and why they look up to him or her. Financial need is not considered in the selection process. U.S. citizenship is required.
Financial data: The stipend is $1,000.
Duration: 1 year; nonrenewable.
Number awarded: 50 each year.
Deadline: March of each year.

1715 CHS FOUNDATION TWO–YEAR SCHOLARSHIP PROGRAM

CHS Foundation
Attn: Scholarship Program
5500 Cenex Drive, MS 407
Inver Grove Heights, MN 55077
Phone: (651) 355–5129; (800) 814–0506; Fax: (651) 355–5073;
Email: info@chsfoundation.org
Web: www.chsfoundation.org/scholarshipprog.html
Summary: To provide financial assistance to students enrolled at 2–year colleges who are interested in studying an agriculture–related program.
Eligibility: Open to students who are completing their first year at a 2–year college in the United States. Applicants must be studying an agriculture–related field. Along with their application, they must submit 1,000–word essays on 1) their career ambitions, why they chose that path, and how they are preparing for their career; and 2) their opinion on the value of cooperative–based business in the agricultural industry. Financial need is not considered in the selection process. U.S. citizenship is required.
Financial data: The stipend is $1,000.
Duration: 1 year; nonrenewable.
Number awarded: 5250 each year.
Deadline: March of each year.

1716 CHUCK PEACOCK MEMORIAL SCHOLARSHIP

Aircraft Electronics Association
Attn: AEA Educational Foundation
3570 N.E. Ralph Powell Road
Lee's Summit, MO 64064
Phone: (816) 347–8400; Fax: (816) 347–8405;
Email: info@aea.net
Web: www.aea.net/educationalfoundation/scholarships.asp
Summary: To provide financial assistance to students interested in preparing for a career in aviation management.
Eligibility: Open to high school seniors and currently–enrolled college students who are attending (or planning to attend) an accredited postsecondary institution in an aviation management program. Applicants must submit an official transcript (cumulative GPA of 2.5 or higher), a statement about their career plans, a description of their involvement in school and community activities, and a 300–word essay on the most important issues the career field of avionics and aviation maintenance are facing today. Selection is based on merit.
Financial data: The stipend is $1,000.
Duration: 1 year.
Number awarded: 1 each year.
Deadline: February of each year.

1717 CHUCK REVILLE, K3FT, MEMORIAL SCHOLARSHIP

Foundation for Amateur Radio, Inc.
Attn: Scholarship Committee
P.O. Box 911
Columbia, MD 21044–0911
Phone: (410) 552–2652; Fax: (410) 981–5146;
Email: dave.prestel@gmail.com
Web: www.farweb.org/scholarships
Summary: To provide funding to licensed radio amateurs who are interested in studying engineering or the physical sciences in college.

Eligibility: Open to radio amateurs who are interested in working full time on a bachelor's degree in a branch of engineering or the physical sciences. There are no restrictions on license class or residence area. Financial need is considered in the selection process.
Financial data: The stipend is $1,000.
Duration: 1 year.
Number awarded: 1 each year.
Deadline: April of each year.

1718 $ CLAMPITT PAPER SCHOLARSHIP

Summary: To provide financial assistance to undergraduate and graduate students at schools in designated states, especially those who are working on a degree in the field of document management and graphic communications.
See Listing #1175.

1719 $ CLARK–PHELPS SCHOLARSHIP

Oregon Student Access Commission
Attn: Grants and Scholarships Division
1500 Valley River Drive, Suite 100
Eugene, OR 97401–2146
Phone: (541) 687–7395; (800) 452–8807, ext. 7395; Fax: (541) 687–7414; TDD: (800) 735–2900;
Email: awardinfo@osac.state.or.us
Web: www.oregonstudentaid.gov/scholarships.aspx
Summary: To provide financial assistance to residents of Oregon and Alaska who are interested in studying nursing, dentistry, or medicine at schools in Oregon.
Eligibility: Open to residents of Oregon and Alaska who are currently enrolled or planning to enroll at a public college or university in Oregon. Applicants must be interested in working on a 4–year or graduate degree in nursing, a doctoral degree in dentistry, or a doctoral degree in medicine. Preference is given to applicants who are interested in studying at Oregon Health and Science University, including the nursing programs at Eastern Oregon University, Southern Oregon University, and Oregon Institute of Technology. Financial need is considered in the selection process.
Financial data: Stipends for scholarships offered by the Oregon Student Access Commission (OSAC) range from $200 to $10,000 but recently averaged $2,300.
Duration: 1 year; recipients may reapply.
Number awarded: Varies each year.
Deadline: February of each year.

1720 $$ CLAY MAITLAND SCHOLARSHIP

U.S. Coast Guard
Attn: Office of Work–Life (CG–111)
2100 Second Street, S.W., Stop 7902
Washington, DC 20593–7902
Phone: (202) 475–5140; (800) 872–4957; Fax: (202) 475–5907;
Email: HQS.SMB.FamilySupportServices@uscg.mil
Web: www.uscg.mil/worklife/scholarship.asp
Summary: To provide financial assistance to the dependent children of Coast Guard enlisted personnel who are interested in studying marine science in college.
Eligibility: Open to the dependent children of enlisted members of the U.S. Coast Guard on active duty, retired, or deceased and of enlisted personnel in the Coast Guard Reserve currently on extended active duty 180 days or more. Applicants must be high school seniors or current undergraduates enrolled or planning to enroll full–time at a 4–year college, university, or vocational school with a major in marine science. They must be under 24 years of age and registered in the Defense Enrollment Eligibility Reporting System (DEERS) system. Along with their application, they must submit their SAT or ACT scores, a letter of recommendation, transcripts, a financial information statement, and a 500–word essay on their personal and academic achievements, extracurricular activities, contributions to the community, and academic plans and career goals.
Financial data: The stipend is $5,000.
Duration: 1 year; nonrenewable.
Number awarded: 1 each year.
Deadline: March of each year.

1721 $ CLIFFORD H. "TED" REES, JR. SCHOLARSHIP

Air–Conditioning, Heating, and Refrigeration Institute
Attn: Clifford H. "Ted" Rees, Jr. Scholarship Foundation
2111 Wilson Boulevard, Suite 500
Arlington, VA 22201
Phone: (703) 524–8800; Fax: (703) 528–3816;
Email: mneufcourt@ahrinet.org
Web: www.ahrinet.org/rees+scholarship.aspx
Summary: To provide financial assistance to students preparing for a career as a heating, ventilation, air–conditioning, and refrigeration (HVACR) technician.
Eligibility: Open to U.S. citizens, nationals, and permanent residents who are enrolled in a program for preparation for a career in residential air–conditioning and heating, light commercial air–conditioning and heating, or commercial refrigeration. They must be enrolled in a training program at an institutionally accredited school. Along with their application, they must submit an essay of 150 to 200 words on why this scholarship should be awarded to them.
Financial data: The stipend is $2,000.
Duration: 1 year; nonrenewable.
Number awarded: Approximately 15 each year. Since the program was established, it has awarded nearly $175,000 to 97 students.
Deadline: June of each year.

1722 $$ COLLEGIATE INVENTORS COMPETITION

Invent Now
Attn: Collegiate Inventors Competition
3701 Highland Park N.W.
North Canton, OH 44720
Phone: (330) 849–6887; (800) 968–4332;
Email: collegiate@invent.org
Web: www.invent.org/collegiate/overview.html
Summary: To recognize and reward outstanding inventions by college or graduate students in the fields of science, engineering, and technology.
Eligibility: Open to undergraduate and graduate students who are (or have been) enrolled full time at least part of the 12–month period prior to entry in a college or university in the United States or Canada. Entries may also be submitted by teams, up to 4 members, of whom at least 1 must meet the full–time requirement and all others must have been enrolled at least half time sometime during the preceding 24–month period. Entries must be original ideas and the work of a student or team and a university adviser; the invention should be reproducible and may not have been 1) made available to the public as a commercial product or process; 2) described in detail in a publication more than 1 year prior to submission for this competition; or 3) patented more than 1 year prior to submission. Entries are first reviewed by a committee of judges that selects the finalists. Judges come from the fields of mathematics, engineering, biology, chemistry, physics, information technology, materials science, and medicine. Selection is based on the degree of originality and inventiveness of the new idea, process, or technology; potential value to society (economically, environmentally, and socially); and the scope of use.
Financial data: The top graduate prize is $15,000 and the top undergraduate prize is $10,000. Other prizes are awarded to select finalists.
Duration: The competition is held annually.
Number awarded: 12 finalists are selected each year; of those, at least 2 individuals or teams (1 graduate and 1 undergraduate) win prizes.
Deadline: June of each year.

1723 $ COLORADO FEDERATION OF GARDEN CLUBS SCHOLARSHIPS

Summary: To provide financial assistance to upper–division and graduate students in horticulture, landscape design, and related disciplines.
See Listing #1179.

1724 COLORADO LEGION AUXILIARY PAST PRESIDENT'S PARLEY NURSE'S SCHOLARSHIP

American Legion Auxiliary
Department of Colorado
7465 East First Avenue, Suite D
Denver, CO 80230
Phone: (303) 367–5388; Fax: (303) 367–5388;
Email: dept–sec@alacolorado.com
Web: www.alacolorado.com/index_files/Forms.htm
Summary: To provide financial assistance to wartime veterans and their descendants in Colorado who are interested in attending school in the state to prepare for a career in nursing.
Eligibility: Open to 1) daughters, sons, spouses, granddaughters, and great–granddaughters of veterans; and 2) veterans who served in the armed forces during eligibility dates for membership in the American Legion. Applicants must be Colorado residents who have been accepted by an accredited school of

nursing in the state. Along with their application, they must submit a 500–word essay on the topic, "Americanism." Selection is based on that essay (25%), scholastic ability (25%), financial need (25%), references (13%), and dedication to chosen field (12%).
Financial data: Stipends range from $500 to $1,000.
Duration: 1 year; nonrenewable.
Number awarded: Varies each year, depending on the availability of funds.
Deadline: April of each year.

1725 COLORADO WEED MANAGEMENT ASSOCIATION SCHOLARSHIP

Colorado Weed Management Association
c/o Laurie Mingen, Executive Director
P.O. Box 364
Paonia, CO 80124
Phone: (970) 361–8262; Fax: (720) 880–3051;
Email: contact@cwma.org
Web: www.cwma.org/scholarships.html
Summary: To provide financial assistance to upper–division and graduate students in any state who are interested in weed management.
Eligibility: Open to juniors, seniors, and graduate students who are working full time on a degree in a weed, range, or agricultural science field. Applicants may be enrolled at a college or university in any state, but they must have completed an internship or summer job emphasizing noxious weed management within Colorado. Along with their application, they must submit an essay on how their summer work benefited and/or related to the state mission of the Colorado Weed Management Association. Selection is based on that essay, academic excellence, and overall achievement.
Financial data: The stipend is $1,000 per year.
Duration: 1 year; recipients may reapply.
Number awarded: 2 each year.
Deadline: February of each year.

1726 $$ COLVIN SCHOLARSHIP PROGRAM

Summary: To provide financial assistance to upper–division students working on a degree related to the beef industry.
See Listing #1181.

1727 COMMITMENT TO AGRICULTURE SCHOLARSHIP PROGRAM

National FFA Organization
Attn: Scholarship Office
6060 FFA Drive
P.O. Box 68960
Indianapolis, IN 46268–0960
Phone: (317) 802–4419; Fax: (317) 802–5419;
Email: scholarships@ffa.org
Web: www.ffa.org
Summary: To provide financial assistance to high school students from farm families who plan to study agriculture in college.
Eligibility: Open to high school seniors whose families are actively engaged in corn, cotton, grain sorghum, production agriculture, soybean, vegetable production, or wheat. Applicants must be planning to study an agricultural field in college on a full–time basis and prepare for a career in agriculture. They must have a GPA of 3.0 or higher and an ACT composite score of 18 or higher or an SAT score of 1320 or higher (or 850 out of 1600). Along with their application, they must submit an essay on the importance of innovation to U.S. agriculture. If they are a member of FFA, they must also include a statement from their adviser evaluating their involvement in FFA activities and indicating special circumstances, such as financial need, that should be considered. If they are not FFA members, they must provide documentation of other school, community, leadership, and work activities.
Financial data: The stipend is $1,500.
Duration: 1 year; nonrenewable.
Number awarded: 100 each year.
Deadline: February of each year.

1728 COMPOSITES DIVISION/HAROLD GILES SCHOLARSHIP

Society of Plastics Engineers
Attn: SPE Foundation
13 Church Hill Road
Newtown, CT 06740
Phone: (203) 740–5447; Fax: (203) 775–1157;
Email: foundation@4spe.org
Web: www.4spe.org/spe–foundation
Summary: To provide financial assistance to undergraduate and graduate students who have a career interest in the plastics industry, especially composites.
Eligibility: Open to full–time undergraduate and graduate students at 4–year colleges or in 2–year technical programs. Applicants must be majoring in or taking courses that would be beneficial to a career in the plastics or polymer industry (e.g., plastics engineering, packaging, polymer sciences, chemistry, physics, chemical engineering, mechanical engineering, industrial engineering). Along with their application, they must submit 3 letters of recommendation; a high school and/or college transcript; a 1– to 2–page statement telling why they are applying for the scholarship, their qualifications, and their educational and career goals in the plastics industry; their employment history; a list of current and past school activities and community activities and honors; information on their financial need; and a statement detailing their experience in the composites industry (courses taken, research conducted, or jobs held).
Financial data: The stipend is $1,000. Funds are paid directly to the recipient's school.
Duration: 1 year.
Number awarded: 1 each year.
Deadline: February of each year.

1729 $ COMTO ROSA L. PARKS SCHOLARSHIPS

Conference of Minority Transportation Officials
Attn: National Scholarship Program
1875 I Street, N.W., Suite 500
Washington, DC 20006
Phone: (703) 234–4072; Fax: (202) 318–0364
Web: www.comto.org/?page=Scholarships
Summary: To provide financial assistance for college to children of members of the Conference of Minority Transportation Officials (COMTO) and to other students working on a bachelor's or master's degree in transportation.
Eligibility: Open to 1) college–bound high school seniors whose parent has been a COMTO member for at least 1 year; 2) undergraduates who have completed at least 60 semester credit hours in a transportation discipline; and 3) students working on a master's degree in transportation who have completed at least 15 credits. Applicants must have a GPA of 3.0 or higher. Along with their application, they must submit a cover letter with a 500–word statement of career goals. Financial need is not considered in the selection process. U.S. citizenship or legal resident status is required.
Financial data: The stipend is $4,500. Funds are paid directly to the recipient's college or university.
Duration: 1 year.
Number awarded: 1 each year.
Deadline: May of each year.

1730 $ CONCRETE REINFORCING STEEL INSTITUTE FOUNDATION UNDERGRADUATE SCHOLARSHIP PROGRAM

Concrete Reinforcing Steel Institute
Attn: CRSI Education & Research Foundation
933 North Plum Grove Road
Schaumburg, IL 60173–4758
Phone: (847) 517–1200; Fax: (847) 517–1206;
Email: lkelly@crsi.org
Web: www.crsi–foundation.org/index.cfm/scholarships/programs
Summary: To provide financial assistance to undergraduate students in civil, construction, or architectural engineering who are interested in preparing for a career in reinforced concrete construction.
Eligibility: Open to U.S. citizens who are entering their senior year as a full–time student in an ABET–accredited program in civil, construction, or architectural engineering. Applicants must demonstrate a career goal of employment in the reinforced concrete construction industry. They must have a GPA of 3.25 or higher. Preference is given to students who have shown an interest, either through their educational program or by work experience, in a phase of that industry. Students having "hands–on" experience from full–time, part–time, or co–op work in the industry are especially encouraged to apply. Financial need is not considered in the selection process.
Financial data: The stipend is $3,000.
Duration: 1 year.
Number awarded: Varies each year; recently, 10 of these scholarships were awarded.
Deadline: September of each year.

1731 CONNECTICUT ASSOCIATION OF LAND SURVEYORS SCHOLARSHIPS

Connecticut Association of Land Surveyors, Inc.
78 Beaver Road
Wethersfield, CT 06109
Phone: (860) 563–1990; Fax: (860) 529–9700
Web: ctsurveyors.org/scholars.htm

Summary: To provide financial assistance to residents of Connecticut working on a degree in surveying.

Eligibility: Open to residents of Connecticut enrolled in a program leading to a degree in surveying or a related field (engineering, sciences, geography). Applicants must be able to demonstrate 1) an interest in being a part of the surveying profession; and 2) a proven record of surveying employment. Financial need is not considered in the selection process.

Financial data: A stipend is awarded (amount not specified).

Duration: 1 year.

Number awarded: Several each year.

Deadline: May of each year.

1732 $ CONNECTICUT CHAPTER HEALTHCARE FINANCIAL MANAGEMENT SCHOLARSHIPS

Healthcare Financial Management Association–Connecticut Chapter
c/o Cassandra L. Mitchell, Scholarship Committee Chair
UConn Health Center/John Dempsey Hospital
263 Farmington Avenue
Farmington, CT 06030–5355
Phone: (860) 679–2916; Fax: (860) 679–3071;
Email: mitchellc@uchc.edu
Web: www.cthfma.org/site/epage/18079_473.htm

Summary: To recognize and reward, with scholarships, undergraduate and graduate students in fields related to health care financial management at colleges and universities in Connecticut who submit outstanding essays on topics in the field.

Eligibility: Open to full– and part–time undergraduate and graduate students at colleges and universities in Connecticut, children of members of the Connecticut chapter of the Healthcare Financial Management Association (HFMA) attending a school in any state, residents of Connecticut commuting to a college or university in New England, Connecticut health care industry employees who are currently attending college, and students attending accredited colleges and universities in New England who were residents of Connecticut for at least 5 years. Applicants must be enrolled in a business, finance, accounting, or information systems program and have an interest in health care or be enrolled in a nursing or allied health program. They must submit an essay, up to 5 pages, on a topic that changes annually but relates to financing of health care. Finalists may be interviewed.

Financial data: The first–place winner (undergraduate or graduate) receives a $4,000 award and the second–place winner (undergraduate or graduate) receives a $1,000 award. Both winners also receive membership in the Connecticut chapter of HFMA, a 1–year subscription to *Healthcare Financial Management,* and waiver of chapter program fees for 1 year.

Duration: 1 year.

Number awarded: 2 each year: 1 for an undergraduate and 1 for a graduate student.

Deadline: August of each year.

1733 CONNECTICUT CHAPTER SCHOLARSHIP

Air & Waste Management Association–Connecticut Chapter
c/o Steve Bailey, Education Chair
69 Old North Road
Barkhamsted, CT 06063
Phone: (860) 724–9777;
Email: steve.bailey@ct.gov
Web: awmanewengland.org/connecticut_chapter.htm

Summary: To provide financial assistance to residents of Connecticut who are interested in studying fields related to air and waste management at a college in any state.

Eligibility: Open to 1) seniors graduating from high schools in Connecticut who plan to enroll full time in college; and 2) Connecticut residents already enrolled full time in college. Applicants must be interested in working on a degree in science or engineering leading to careers in the environmental field, especially air pollution control or waste management. Selection is based on academic record, proposed plan of study, career goals, extracurricular activities, and recommendations; financial need is not considered.

Financial data: The stipend is $1,000.

Duration: 1 year; recipients may reapply.

Number awarded: 1 each year.

Deadline: April of each year.

1734 $$ CONNECTICUT NURSERYMEN'S FOUNDATION SCHOLARSHIP

Connecticut Nurserymen's Foundation
Attn: Scholarship Committee
44 Hillcrest Avenue
Watertown, CT 06795
Phone: (860) 274–5269; Fax: (860) 567–3507;
Email: TBodnar@whiteflowerfarm.com
Web: www.flowersplantsinct.com/cnla_cnf.htm

Summary: To provide financial assistance to high school seniors in Connecticut who are interested in studying fields related to horticulture at a college in any state.

Eligibility: Open to seniors graduating from high schools in Connecticut who plan to attend a 4–year or 2–year college or university in any state. Applicants must be planning to enrolled in a program of study beneficial to the horticulture industry, including, but not limited to, ornamental horticulture, landscape design, nursery management, or greenhouse management. Along with their application, they must submit a brief statement about themselves, why they want to pursue their education, and why they think a career path in horticulture is right for them. Selection is based on academic achievement, non–school work related to horticulture, and financial need.

Financial data: The stipend is $5,000 per year.

Duration: 1 year; may be renewed if the recipient maintains a GPA of 3.0 or higher.

Number awarded: 1 each year.

Deadline: March of each year.

1735 CONNECTICUT SOCIETY FOR RESPIRATORY CARE SCHOLARSHIP

Connecticut Society for Respiratory Care
c/o John Duquette, President
39 White Rock Drive
Windsor, CT 06095
Web: www.ctsrc.org/index2.php

Summary: To provide financial assistance to residents of any state who are entering or enrolled in a respiratory care program at a Connecticut college.

Eligibility: Open to U.S. citizens from any state who are either incoming or continuing students at an institution in Connecticut. Applicants must be preparing for a career in respiratory care. They must have a GPA of 2.75 or higher. Along with their application, they must submit an essay on their choice of an assigned topic relating to the respiratory care profession. Financial need is not considered in the selection process.

Financial data: The stipend is $1,000.

Duration: 1 year.

Number awarded: 1 or more each year.

Deadline: June of each year.

1736 CONSTANCE H. SMITH ENDOWED SCHOLARSHIP

Garden Club Federation of Pennsylvania
c/o Lee Ann Stine, Secretary
1525 Cedar Cliff Drive, Suite 103
Camp Hill, PA 17011–7775
Phone: (717) 737–8219; Fax: (717) 737–8219;
Email: GCFP2@aol.com
Web: www.pagardenclubs.org/scholarshipinfor.html

Summary: To provide financial assistance to residents of Pennsylvania who are working on an undergraduate or graduate degree in a field related to horticulture at a college in any state.

Eligibility: Open to Pennsylvania residents who are sponsored by a Federated Garden Club. Special consideration is given to children, grandchildren, or legal dependents of club members. Applicants may be undergraduates or graduate students who are enrolled at a college or university in any state. They must be working on a degree in agriculture education, agronomy, biology, botany, city (urban or rural) planning, conservation, environmental control, floriculture, forestry, horticulture, land management, landscape architecture, plant pathology, wildlife science, or an allied field. Selection is based on academic record, character, initiative, personal recommendations, and financial need.

Financial data: The stipend is $1,000 per year.

Duration: 1 year; recipients may reapply, as long as they maintain their academic standing and financial need.
Number awarded: 1 each year.
Deadline: February of each year.

1737 $ CONSTRUCTION MANAGEMENT ASSOCIATION OF AMERICA FOUNDATION SCHOLARSHIPS

Construction Management Association of America
Attn: CMAA Foundation
7926 Jones Branch Drive, Suite 800
McLean, VA 22101–3303
Phone: (703) 356–2622; Fax: (703) 356–6388;
Email: foundation@cmaanet.org
Web: www.cmaafoundation.org/scholarships/application–process
Summary: To provide financial assistance to undergraduate and graduate students working on a degree in construction management.
Eligibility: Open to full–time undergraduate and graduate students who have completed at least 1 year of study and have at least 1 full year remaining. Applicants must be working on a bachelor's or master's degree in construction management or a related field. Along with their application, they must submit an essay on why they are interested in a career in construction management and why they should be awarded this scholarship. Selection is based on that essay (20%), academic performance (40%), recommendation of the faculty adviser (15%), and extracurricular activities (25%).
Financial data: The stipend is $3,000. Funds are disbursed directly to the student's university.
Duration: 1 year.
Number awarded: 3 undergraduates and 1 graduate student receive these scholarships each year. In addition, a number of chapters also offer scholarships to students.
Deadline: June of each year.

1738 COPERNICUS AWARD

Polanki, The Polish Women's Cultural Club of Milwaukee
Attn: College Achievement Awards
P.O. Box 341458
Milwaukee, WI 53234
Phone: (414) 858–9357;
Email: polanki@polanki.org
Web: www.polanki.org/scholar–main.html
Summary: To recognize and reward upper–division and graduate students in Wisconsin who have a Polish connection and demonstrate academic excellence in science.
Eligibility: Open to college juniors, seniors, and graduate students who are Wisconsin residents or attending college in the state. Applicants must be 1) of Polish heritage; or 2) non–Polish students significantly engaged with Polish culture. They must have a GPA of 3.0 or higher. Along with their application, they must submit 1) an essay of 500 to 600 words on a topic that changes annually but relates to Poland; and 2) a paragraph of 100 to 150 words on their personal, academic, and professional plans for the future. This award is reserved for a student a field of the sciences. U.S. citizenship or permanent residence is required.
Financial data: Awards range from $750 to $1,500.
Duration: The awards are presented annually.
Number awarded: 1 each year.
Deadline: January of each year.

1739 CORRIE WHITLOCK MEMORIAL SCHOLARSHIP

National Garden Clubs, Inc.–South Atlantic Region
c/o Betsy Steele, Scholarship Committee Chair
P.O. Box 339
Richburg, SC 29729
Phone: (803) 789–5451;
Email: BetsySteele@Truvista.net
Web: www.southatlanticregiongardenclubs.org/scholarships–2
Summary: To provide financial assistance to residents of designated south Atlantic states who are working on an undergraduate degree in a field related to gardening at a college in any state.
Eligibility: Open to residents of Kentucky, North Carolina, South Carolina, Virginia, and West Virginia who are entering their junior or senior year at a college in any state. Applicants must be majoring in horticulture, floriculture, landscape design, botany, plant pathology, biology, forestry, agronomy, environmental concerns, city planning, land management, or a related subject. Along with their application, they must submit a letter discussing their background, goals, personal commitment, and financial need. Selection is based on that letter (30%), academic record (40%), a list of honors, extracurricular activities, and work experience (10%), financial need (15%), and recommendations (5%).
Financial data: The stipend is $1,000.
Duration: 1 year.
Number awarded: 1 each year.
Deadline: Applications must be received by the chair of the appropriate National Garden Club state scholarship committee by January of each year.

1740 $ CORRUGATED PACKAGING DIVISION SCHOLARSHIPS

Technical Association of the Pulp and Paper Industry
Attn: Scholarship Department
15 Technology Parkway South
Norcross, GA 30092
Phone: (770) 209–7276; (800) 332–8686; Fax: (770) 446–6947;
Email: standards@tappi.org
Web: www.tappi.org/About–TAPPI/TAPPI–Scholarships.aspx
Summary: To provide financial assistance to students who are interested in preparing for a career in the paper industry, with a focus on the manufacture and use of corrugated, solid fiber, and associated packaging materials and products.
Eligibility: Open to 1) full– or part–time employees in the box business who are working on a graduate or undergraduate degree; and 2) students who are attending college full time, have a GPA of 3.0 or higher, are able to demonstrate an interest in the corrugated container industry, and are recommended and endorsed by an instructor or faculty member. Selection is based on financial need, overall scholarship, maturity, job potential, and current and future contribution to the corrugated container industry.
Financial data: The stipend is either $2,000 or $1,000.
Duration: 1 year.
Number awarded: Varies each year; recently, 4 of these scholarships were awarded.
Deadline: February of each year.

1741 $$ COURTLAND PAUL SCHOLARSHIP

Summary: To provide financial assistance to upper–division students working on a degree in landscape architecture.
See Listing #1185.

1742 CRA OUTSTANDING UNDERGRADUATE RESEARCH AWARD

Computing Research Association
1828 L Street, N.W., Suite 800
Washington, DC 20036–5104
Phone: (202) 234–2111; Fax: (202) 667–1066;
Email: awards@cra.org
Web: www.cra.org/awards/undergrad
Summary: To recognize and reward undergraduate students who show exceptional promise in an area of importance to computing research.
Eligibility: Open to undergraduates at colleges and universities in North America who show outstanding research potential in computing research. Students must be nominated by 2 faculty members and recommended by their department chair. Nomination packages must include the nominee's resume (up to 2 pages), the nominee's transcript, a verification statement signed by the department chair, 2 letters of support, and a 1–page description of the student's research or other achievements. Selection is based primarily on the significance of the student's research contributions; consideration is also given to academic record and service to the computing or broader community. Women and men are judged separately.
Financial data: The award is $1,000.
Duration: The awards are presented annually.
Number awarded: 2 cash prizes (1 to a woman and 1 to a man) and a number of certificates of honorable mention are presented each year.
Deadline: October of each year.

1743 CUMMINS SCHOLARSHIPS

Society of Women Engineers
Attn: Scholarship Selection Committee
203 North LaSalle Street, Suite 1675
Chicago, IL 60601–1269

Phone: (312) 596–5223; (877) SWE–INFO; Fax: (312) 644–8557;
Email: scholarships@swe.org
Web: societyofwomenengineers.swe.org/index.php/scholarships

Summary: To provide financial assistance to women working on an undergraduate or graduate degree in computer science or designated engineering specialties.

Eligibility: Open to women who are sophomores, juniors, seniors, or graduate students at 4–year ABET–accredited colleges and universities. Applicants must be working full time on a degree in computer science or automotive, chemical, computer, electrical, industrial, manufacturing, materials, or mechanical engineering and have a GPA of 3.5 or higher. Preference is given to members of groups underrepresented in engineering or computer science. Selection is based on merit. U.S. citizenship or permanent resident status is required.

Financial data: The stipend is $1,000.

Duration: 1 year.

Number awarded: 2 each year.

Deadline: February of each year.

1744 CUSTOM BUILDERS INC./EPS BUILDINGS SCHOLARSHIP

Iowa Foundation for Agricultural Advancement
Attn: Winner's Circle Scholarships
c/o SGI
30805 595th Avenue
Cambridge, IA 50046
Phone: (515) 291–3941;
Email: linda@slweldon.net
Web: www.iowastatefair.org

Summary: To provide financial assistance to Iowa high school seniors who have been involved in livestock and/or equine exhibiting and plan to major in animal science or a related field at a college in the state.

Eligibility: Open to residents of Iowa who will be incoming freshmen at a college or university in the state in the following fall. Applicants must be planning to major in animal science or a program in agriculture or human sciences that is related to the animal industry. They must have a strong background in livestock and/or equine exhibiting, projects, and activities. Along with their application, they must submit a 250–word essay summarizing their experiences with their agricultural and livestock projects. Selection is based on that essay and participation in agricultural and livestock projects (50%); activities, leadership, and recognition in 4–H, FFA, and other high school and community activities (25%); academic record (15%); and curriculum plans for college and career plans after graduation as they relate to the agricultural industry in general (10%).

Financial data: The stipend is $1,000.

Duration: 1 year; nonrenewable.

Number awarded: 1 each year.

Deadline: April of each year.

1745 D. ANITA SMALL SCIENCE AND BUSINESS SCHOLARSHIP

Business and Professional Women of Maryland
Attn: BPW Foundation of Maryland
c/o Joyce Draper, Chief Financial Officer
615 Fairview Avenue
Frederick, MD 21701
Web: www.bpwmaryland.org

Summary: To provide financial assistance to women in Maryland who are interested in working on an undergraduate or graduate degree in a science or business–related field.

Eligibility: Open to women who are at least 21 years of age and have been accepted to a bachelor's or advanced degree program at an accredited Maryland academic institution. Applicants must be preparing for a career in 1 of the following or a related field: accounting, aeronautics, business administration, computer sciences, engineering, finance, information technology, mathematics, medical sciences (including nursing, laboratory technology, therapy, etc.), oceanography, or physical sciences. They must have a GPA of 3.0 or higher and be able to demonstrate financial need.

Financial data: The stipend is $1,000 per year.

Duration: 1 year.

Number awarded: 1 or more each year.

Deadline: July of each year.

1746 $ DAEDALIAN ACADEMIC MATCHING SCHOLARSHIP PROGRAM

Daedalian Foundation
Attn: Scholarship Committee
55 Main Circle, Building 676
P.O. Box 249
Randolph AFB, TX 78148–0249
Phone: (210) 945–2113; Fax: (210) 945–2112;
Email: kristi@daedalians.org
Web: www.daedalians.org/foundation/scholarships.htm

Summary: To provide financial assistance to ROTC and other college students who wish to become military pilots.

Eligibility: Open to students who are attending or have been accepted at an accredited 4–year college or university and have demonstrated the desire and potential to become a commissioned military pilot. Usually, students in ROTC units of all services apply to local chapters (Flights) of Daedalian; if the Flight awards a scholarship, the application is forwarded to the Daedalian Foundation for 1 of these matching scholarships. College students not part of a ROTC program are eligible to apply directly to the Foundation if their undergraduate goals and performance are consistent with Daedalian criteria. Selection is based on intention to pursue a career as a military pilot, demonstrated moral character and patriotism, scholastic and military standing and aptitude, and physical condition and aptitude for flight. Financial need may also be considered. Additional eligibility criteria may be set by a Flight Scholarship Selection Board.

Financial data: The amount awarded varies but is intended to serve as matching funds for the Flight scholarship. Generally, the maximum awarded is $2,000.

Number awarded: Up to 99 each year.

Deadline: Students who are members of Daedalian Flights must submit their applications by November of each year; students who apply directly to the Daedalian Foundation must submit their applications by July of each year.

1747 $ DAIRY STUDENT RECOGNITION PROGRAM

National Dairy Shrine
Attn: Executive Director
P.O. Box 725
Denmark, WI 54208
Phone: (920) 863–6333; Fax: (920) 863–6333;
Email: info@dairyshrine.org
Web: www.dairyshrine.org/scholarships.php

Summary: To recognize and reward outstanding college seniors who are planning a career related to dairy or production agriculture.

Eligibility: Open to graduating college seniors who are planning a career related to dairy (e.g., production agriculture, manufacturing, marketing, agricultural law, business, veterinary medicine, or environmental sciences). Each university may nominate 2 students for the awards. Selection is based on leadership ability and extracurricular activities (35 points), academic standing (10 points), interest and experience in the dairy industry (35 points), and plans for the future (20 points).

Financial data: First prize is $2,000, second $1,500, and third through seventh $1,000.

Duration: The awards are presented annually.

Number awarded: 7 each year.

Deadline: April of each year.

1748 $$ DAKOTA CORPS SCHOLARSHIP PROGRAM

South Dakota Board of Regents
Attn: Dakota Corps Scholarship Program
306 East Capitol Avenue, Suite 200
Pierre, SD 57501–2545
Phone: (800) 874–9033;
Email: DakotaCorps@sdbor.edu
Web: www.sdbor.edu/dakotacorps/whatisdakotacorps.html

Summary: To provide money for college to high school seniors in South Dakota who plan to attend a college or university in the state and work in the state in nursing or other critical need occupation following graduation.

Eligibility: Open to seniors graduating from high schools in South Dakota who are U.S. citizens or nationals. Applicants must plan to attend a participating college, university, technical college, or tribal college in the state and major in a field to prepare for a career in a critical need occupation; currently, those are 1) teaching K–12 music, special education, or foreign language in a public, private, or parochial school; 2) teaching high school mathematics or science in a public, private, or parochial school; 3) working as a licensed practical nurse, registered nurse, or other allied health care provider; or 4) working as a large

animal veterinarian. They must have a GPA of 2.8 or higher and an ACT score of at least 24 (or the SAT equivalent). Applications must be submitted within 1 year after high school graduation or release from active duty of a component of the U.S. armed forces. Along with their application, they must submit a short essay explaining what has attracted them to their profession and to remaining in South Dakota for employment. Selection is based on that essay, GPA, test scores, activities, honors, and community service.
Financial data: At public colleges, universities, technical colleges, and tribal colleges, awards provide full payment of tuition and generally–applicable fees up to 16 credit hours. At private colleges and universities, awards provide the same amount as at a public 4–year college; the remaining tuition and generally–applicable fees must be covered by the participating college through an institutional scholarship or tuition waiver. This is a scholarship loan program; recipients must commit to work in a critical need occupation in South Dakota for a period of time equal to the number of years of scholarship support received plus 1 additional year. If recipients fail to complete their commitment, the scholarship converts to a low–interest loan that must be repaid.
Duration: 1 year; may be renewed up to 3 additional years, provided the recipient maintains a GPA of 2.8 or higher and remains enrolled full time.
Number awarded: A limited number each year.
Deadline: January of each year.

1749 $ DALLAS AND DONNA LIPSCOMB SCHOLARSHIP

American Academy of Physician Assistants–Veterans Caucus
Attn: Veterans Caucus
P.O. Box 362
Danville, PA 17821–0362
Phone: (570) 271–0292; Fax: (570) 271–5850;
Email: admin@veteranscaucus.org
Web: www.veteranscaucus.org
Summary: To provide financial assistance to veterans who are single parents or Air Force veterans and studying to become physician assistants.
Eligibility: Open to U.S. citizens who are currently enrolled in a physician assistant program. The program must be approved by the Commission on Accreditation of Allied Health Education. Applicants must be honorably discharged members of the armed forces who are a single parent; if no single parent applies, the award is presented to a veteran of the U.S. Air Force. Selection is based on military honors and awards received, civic and college honors and awards received, professional memberships and activities, and GPA. An electronic copy of the applicant's DD Form 214 must accompany the application.
Financial data: The stipend is $2,000.
Duration: 1 year.
Number awarded: 1 each year.
Deadline: February of each year.

1750 DAVID E. LUMLEY YOUNG SCIENTIST SCHOLARSHIP

American Geophysical Union
Attn: Development Assistant
2000 Florida Avenue, N.W.
Washington, DC 20009–1277
Phone: (202) 777–7434; (800) 966–2481; Fax: (202) 328–0566;
Email: grants@agu.org
Web: education.agu.org/grants/scholarships
Summary: To provide financial assistance to high school seniors and undergraduates interested in preparing for a career in energy or environmental science.
Eligibility: Open to graduating high school seniors and current undergraduates. Applicants must be interested in preparing for a career that will enable them to work on problems of global importance in both the energy and environmental sectors of industry and academia.
Financial data: The stipend is $1,000. The winner also receives $500 to attend the fall meeting of the American Geophysical Union (AGU) and up to $500 in value of AGU products or services.
Number awarded: 1 each year.
Deadline: September of each year.

1751 $ DAVID HERMANCE HYBRID TECHNOLOGIES SCHOLARSHIP

Society of Automotive Engineers
Attn: Scholarships and Loans Program
400 Commonwealth Drive
Warrendale, PA 15096–0001
Phone: (724) 776–4790; (877) 606–7323; Fax: (724) 776–0790;
Email: scholarships@sae.org
Web: students.sae.org/awdscholar/scholarships/hermance
Summary: To provide financial support to entering college juniors working on a degree in engineering.
Eligibility: Open to U.S. citizens who are sophomores at a 2– or 4–year college or university and planning to continue as juniors in an ABET–accredited program in engineering. Applicants must have a GPA of 3.50 or higher. Along with their application, they must submit an essay of 250 to 300 words describing their interest in preparing for an engineering career in the field of advanced technology vehicles, including hybrids, fuel cells, alternative fueled vehicles, and advanced powertrains. Financial need is not considered in the selection process.
Financial data: The stipend is $2,500.
Duration: 1 year; nonrenewable.
Number awarded: 1 each year.
Deadline: February of each year.

1752 DAVID HONEYCUTT MEMORIAL SCHOLARSHIP

Summary: To provide financial assistance to students preparing for a career in a field related to construction.
See Listing #1192.

1753 $ DAVID HOODS MEMORIAL SCHOLARSHIP

Summary: To provide financial assistance to undergraduate and graduate students from any country interested in preparing for a career in document management and graphic communications, especially those interested in marketing and public relations.
See Listing #1193.

1754 $ DAVID LAINE MEMORIAL SCHOLARSHIP

North American Die Casting Association
241 Holbrook Drive
Wheeling, IL 60090–5809
Phone: (847) 279–0001; Fax: (847) 279–0002
Web: www.diecasting.org/scholarship
Summary: To provide financial assistance to undergraduate students who are interested in preparing for a career in the die casting industry.
Eligibility: Open to full–time undergraduate engineering students who are citizens of the United States, Canada, or Mexico, Applicants must have worked in the die casting industry for at least 3 months within the past year. Along with their application, they must submit a paper on their activities and results from their work in the die casting industry.
Financial data: The stipend is $3,000.
Duration: 1 year.
Number awarded: Varies each year; recently, 3 of these scholarships were awarded.
Deadline: September of each year.

1755 $ DAVID M. CLINE SCHOLARSHIP

Harry Hampton Memorial Wildlife Fund, Inc.
P.O. Box 2641
Columbia, SC 29202
Phone: (803) 600–1570;
Email: jim.goller@hamptonwildlifefund.org
Web: www.hamptonwildlifefund.org/scholarship.html
Summary: To provide financial assistance to high school seniors in South Carolina who plan to major in a field related to law enforcement or natural resources at a college or university in the state.
Eligibility: Open to seniors graduating from high schools in South Carolina who plan to attend an institution of higher learning in the state. Applicants must be planning to major in 1) law enforcement; or 2) a field related to natural resources (e.g., wildlife, fisheries, biology, zoology, forestry, marine science, environmental science). Along with their application, they must submit a brief autobiography that includes 1) a description of their career ambitions in law enforcement or the natural resources field; 2) why they desire a college education; 3) their interest in wildlife resources, the environment, coastal resources, or related topics; and 4) why they will be a good investment if they are awarded this scholarship. Financial need is also considered in the selection process.
Financial data: The stipend is $2,000.
Duration: 1 year; nonrenewable.
Number awarded: 1 each year.
Deadline: January of each year.

1756 DAVID MANN SCHOLARSHIP

American Mensa Education and Research Foundation
1229 Corporate Drive West
Arlington, TX 76006–6103
Phone: (817) 607–5577; (800) 66–MENSA; Fax: (817) 649–5232;
Email: info@mensafoundation.org
Web: www.mensafoundation.org/what–we–do/scholarships

Summary: To provide financial assistance for undergraduate or graduate study in aeronautical engineering or an aerospace field.

Eligibility: Open to students who are enrolled or planning to enroll in a degree program at an accredited American institution of postsecondary education with a major or career plans in aeronautical engineering or an aerospace field. Membership in Mensa is not required, but applicants must be U.S. citizens or permanent residents. There are no restrictions as to age, race, gender, level of postsecondary education, GPA, or financial need. Selection is based on a 550–word essay that describes the applicant's career, vocational, or academic goals.

Financial data: The stipend is $1,000.

Duration: 1 year; nonrenewable.

Number awarded: 1 each year.

Deadline: January of each year.

1757 DAVID R. WOODLING MEMORIAL SCHOLARSHIP

Albuquerque Community Foundation
Attn: Scholarship Program
624 Tijeras Avenue, N.W.
P.O. Box 25266
Albuquerque, NM 87125–5266
Phone: (505) 883–6240; Fax: (505) 883–3629;
Email: foundation@albuquerquefoundation.org
Web: www.albuquerquefoundation.org/student_aid

Summary: To provide financial assistance to residents of New Mexico interested in working on an associate degree or certificate in metals technology at a school in the state.

Eligibility: Open to applicants who have been residents of New Mexico for at least 1 year and are working on or planning to work full time on an associate degree or certificate in metals technology at an accredited nonprofit or public educational institution in the state. They must be 1) a high school senior graduating from high school with a GPA of 2.5 or higher; 2) receiving a GED diploma or certificate; 3) a current undergraduate student; or 4) a nontraditional student with a high school diploma or GED certificate. Along with their application, they must submit a personal essay that describes their career goals, any relevant experience, why they have chosen metals technology as a field of study, and how they plan to use their skills to better themselves, their families, and their community. Financial need is also considered in the selection process.

Financial data: The stipend ranges from $500 to $1,000.

Duration: 1 year.

Number awarded: Varies each year.

Deadline: June of each year.

1758 DAVID SANKEY MINORITY SCHOLARSHIP IN METEOROLOGY

National Weather Association
Attn: Executive Director
228 West Millbrook Road
Raleigh, NC 27609–4304
Phone: (919) 845–1546; Fax: (919) 845–2956;
Email: exdir@nwas.org
Web: www.nwas.org/committees/ed_comm/application/index.php

Summary: To provide financial assistance to members of minority groups working on an undergraduate or graduate degree in meteorology.

Eligibility: Open to members of minority ethnic groups who are either entering their sophomore or higher year of undergraduate study or enrolled as graduate students. Applicants must be working on a degree in meteorology. Along with their application, they must submit a 1–page statement explaining why they are applying for this scholarship. Selection is based on that statement, academic achievement, and 2 letters of recommendation.

Financial data: The stipend is $1,000.

Duration: 1 year.

Number awarded: 1 each year.

Deadline: April of each year.

1759 $$ DEED TECHNICAL DESIGN PROJECT

American Public Power Association
Attn: DEED Administrator
1875 Connecticut Avenue, N.W., Suite 1200
Washington, DC 20009–5715
Phone: (202) 467–2960; (800) 515–2772; Fax: (202) 467–2910;
Email: DEED@PublicPower.org
Web: www.publicpower.org

Summary: To recognize and reward undergraduate and graduate students who develop and demonstrate outstanding projects related to energy innovation.

Eligibility: Open to undergraduate and graduate students or groups of students in energy–related disciplines at accredited colleges and universities in the United States and Canada. Applicants must complete a technical design project and submit a final report on the project, describing activities, cost, sources used, achievements, problems, results, and recommendations. The project must relate to energy innovation, improving efficiencies, and lowering the cost of providing energy services to the customers of publicly–owned electric utilities. Selection is based on the applicability of benefits to public power systems, the applicant's major in an academic field related to the electric power or energy service industries, academic performance, generalizable methodologies, and promotion of energy efficiency.

Financial data: The award is $5,000. An additional $3,000 is available to pay for travel expenses to attend the engineering and operations technical conference of the American Public Power Association (APPA) and present their project. If more than 1 student is involved in a project, the award funds are split among all participants.

Duration: This competition is held annually.

Number awarded: 1 each year.

Deadline: October of each year.

1760 $ DEEP SOUTH REGION SCHOLARSHIP

National Garden Clubs, Inc.–Deep South Region
c/o Mary W. Summerville, Scholarship Committee Chair
P.O. Box 680636
Fort Payne, AL 35968–1607
Phone: (205) 845–4121;
Email: msummer1@att.net
Web: www.dsregion.org/scholarship.html

Summary: To provide financial assistance to high school seniors and college students in the Deep South who are interested in studying a field related to gardening.

Eligibility: Open to 1) seniors graduating from high schools in Alabama, Florida, Georgia, Louisiana, Mississippi, or Tennessee; and 2) students enrolled at colleges or universities in those states. Applicants must be interested in working on a degree in a garden or environmental–related field. They must be able to demonstrate financial need.

Financial data: The stipend is $2,000.

Duration: 1 year.

Number awarded: 1 each year.

Deadline: Applications must be received by the chair of the appropriate National Garden Club state scholarship committee by January of each year.

1761 $$ DELAWARE NURSING INCENTIVE PROGRAM

Delaware Department of Education
Attn: Higher Education Office
401 Federal Street
Dover, DE 19901–3639
Phone: (302) 735–4120; (800) 292–7935; Fax: (302) 739–4654;
Email: dheo@doe.k12.de.us
Web: www.doe.k12.de.us/infosuites/students_family/dheo/default.shtml

Summary: To provide scholarship/loans to Delaware residents who are interested in studying nursing at a school in any state.

Eligibility: Open to residents of Delaware who are enrolled or planning to enroll full time in an accredited program in any state leading to certification as an R.N. or L.P.N. Nurses who already have R.N. certification and 5 or more years of state service may enroll in a B.S.N. program on a full– or part–time basis. High school seniors must rank in the upper half of their class and have a cumulative GPA of 2.5 or higher. Current undergraduate students must be enrolled full time and have a GPA of 2.5 or higher. Also eligible are 1) current state employees (they are not required to be Delaware residents and may enroll part time); and 2) registered nurses with 5 or more years of state service (they must be working on a bachelor of science in nursing degree, but they may enroll full or part time). U.S. citizenship or eligible noncitizen status is required.

Financial data: Awards up to the cost of tuition, fees, and other direct educational expenses are available. This is a scholarship/loan program; if the recipient performs required service at a state–owned hospital or clinic in Delaware, the loan is forgiven at the rate of 1 year of service for each year of assistance. Recipients who fail to perform the required service must repay the loan in full.
Duration: 1 year; may be renewed for up to 3 additional years, provided the recipient maintains a GPA of 2.75 or higher.
Number awarded: Up to 50 each year.
Deadline: March of each year.

1762 $ DELAWARE VALLEY CHAPTER AWMA SCHOLARSHIP

Air & Waste Management Association–Delaware Valley Chapter
c/o Marjorie J. Fitzpatrick
IES Engineers
1720 Walton Road
Blue Bell, PA 19422
Phone: (610) 828–3078; Fax: (610) 828–7842;
Email: mfitzpatrick@iesengineers.com
Web: www.mass–awma.net/DVC/Scholarship.html
Summary: To provide financial assistance to undergraduate and graduate students from the area served by the Delaware Valley Chapter of the Air & Waste Management Association (AWMA) who are working on a degree in an environmental field.
Eligibility: Open to full– and part–time undergraduate and graduate students who are either attending school in Delaware, southern New Jersey, or Pennsylvania east of the Susquehanna River or residents of that area attending school in any state. Applicants must be preparing for a career in environmental sciences, environmental engineering, environmental management, or a related field. Selection is based on academic background related to the environmental field, interest in preparing for a career in the environmental field (as demonstrated through course work, extracurricular activities, volunteer activities, jobs, etc.), and a letter of recommendation.
Financial data: Stipends range from $500 to $2,000.
Duration: 1 year.
Number awarded: 1 or more each year.
Deadline: February of each year.

1763 $ DELL COMPUTER CORPORATION SCHOLARSHIPS

Society of Women Engineers
Attn: Scholarship Selection Committee
203 North LaSalle Street, Suite 1675
Chicago, IL 60601–1269
Phone: (312) 596–5223; (877) SWE–INFO; Fax: (312) 644–8557;
Email: scholarships@swe.org
Web: societyofwomenengineers.swe.org/index.php/scholarships
Summary: To provide financial assistance to upper–division women majoring in computer science or designated engineering specialties.
Eligibility: Open to women who are entering their junior or senior year at an ABET–accredited college or university. Applicants must be working full time on a degree in computer science or electrical, computer, or mechanical engineering and have a GPA of 3.0 or higher. Financial need is considered in the selection process.
Financial data: The stipend is $2,250.
Duration: 1 year.
Number awarded: 2 each year.
Deadline: February of each year.

1764 $ DELORAS JONES RN SCHOLARSHIP PROGRAM

Kaiser Permanente
Attn: Student Financial Aid
P.O. Box 24522
Oakland, CA 94623–1522
Phone: (866) 232–2934;
Email: sfap@kp.org
Web: nursingpathways.kp.org/scal/learning/finaid/scholarships.html
Summary: To provide financial assistance to nursing students in California who are working on an undergraduate or graduate degree.
Eligibility: Open to 1) students enrolled in a California BRN–approved program for an associate degree in nursing (A.D.N.), bachelor of science in nursing (B.S.N.), or entry–level master of science in nursing (M.S.N./M.N.); 2) residents of California enrolled in a CCNE–accredited postgraduate master of science in nursing (M.S.N./M.N.) or doctoral program in nursing (Ph.D./D.N.Sc./D.N.P.). Applicants must meet the minimum GPA requirement in applicable nursing program course work, including at least 1 clinical nursing course with a clinical rotation (not a laboratory course), and expect to graduate no earlier than March of the following year; the minimum GPA requirement depends on the type of program in which the applicant is enrolled, including 2.5 for the affiliate schools awards, 3.8 for the academic excellence in pre–licensure awards, or 3.0 for the graduate or doctoral studies awards. Both need– and merit–based scholarships are available. U.S. citizenship or permanent resident status is required; student visas or temporary employment authorizations are not accepted.
Financial data: Stipends range from $1,000 to $3,000.
Duration: 1 year.
Number awarded: Varies each year; recently, 188 students (100 in southern California and 88 in northern California) received $319,500 ($179,500 in southern California and $140,000 in northern California) in funding from this program. Since it began, it has awarded more than $4 million to 2,130 students statewide.
Deadline: September of each year.

1765 DENTAL HYGIENE SCHOLARSHIPS

American Dental Association
Attn: ADA Foundation
211 East Chicago Avenue
Chicago, IL 60611
Phone: (312) 440–2547; Fax: (312) 440–3526;
Email: adaf@ada.org
Web: www.ada.org/applyforassistance.aspx
Summary: To provide financial assistance to currently–enrolled dental hygiene students.
Eligibility: Open to students entering their final year of full–time study at a dental hygiene program accredited by the Commission on Dental Accreditation. They must have a GPA of 3.0 or higher and be able to demonstrate financial need of at least $1,000. U.S. citizenship is required. Selection is based on academic achievement, a written summary of personal and professional goals, letters of reference, and financial need.
Financial data: Stipends range up to $1,000 per year. Funds are to be used to cover school expenses (tuition, fees, books, supplies, living expenses) and are paid in 2 equal installments to the recipient's school.
Duration: 1 year.
Number awarded: Varies each year; recently, 18 of these scholarships were awarded.
Deadline: October of each year.

1766 DENTAL LABORATORY TECHNOLOGY SCHOLARSHIPS

American Dental Association
Attn: ADA Foundation
211 East Chicago Avenue
Chicago, IL 60611
Phone: (312) 440–2547; Fax: (312) 440–3526;
Email: adaf@ada.org
Web: www.ada.org/applyforassistance.aspx
Summary: To provide financial assistance to currently–enrolled dental laboratory technology students.
Eligibility: Open to students entering their final year of full–time study at a dental laboratory technology program accredited by the Commission on Dental Accreditation. They must have a GPA of 3.0 or higher and be able to demonstrate financial need of at least $1,000. U.S. citizenship is required. Selection is based on academic achievement, a written summary of personal and professional goals, letters of reference, and financial need.
Financial data: Stipends range up to $1,000 per year. Funds are to be used to cover school expenses (tuition, fees, books, supplies, living expenses) and are paid in 2 equal installments to the recipient's school.
Duration: 1 year.
Number awarded: Varies each year; recently, 5 of these scholarships were awarded.
Deadline: October of each year.

1767 DESK AND DERRICK EDUCATION TRUST SCHOLARSHIPS

Association of Desk and Derrick Clubs
Attn: Desk and Derrick Educational Trust
3930 Waverly Bend
Katy, TX 77450

Phone: (281) 392–7181; Fax: (318) 671–8887;
Email: info@theeducationaltrust.org
Web: www.theeducationaltrust.org/scholarships

Summary: To provide financial assistance to currently–enrolled college students who are planning a career in the petroleum or an allied industry.

Eligibility: Open to full–time undergraduate and graduate students who have completed at least 2 years of college or are currently enrolled in the second year of undergraduate study. Applicants must have a GPA of 3.2 or higher and be able to demonstrate financial need. They must be preparing for a career in the petroleum, energy, or an allied industry; qualifying majors include geology, geophysics, petroleum engineering, chemical engineering, mechanical engineering, nuclear engineering, and energy management. Students working on degrees in research and development of alternate energy sources (e.g., coal, electric, solar, wind, hydroelectric, nuclear, ethanol) are also eligible. U.S. or Canadian citizenship is required. Some of the awards are designated for women.

Financial data: Stipends range from $1,000 to $1,500.

Duration: 1 year.

Number awarded: Varies each year; recently, 12 of these scholarships (including 9 designated for women) were awarded.

Deadline: March of each year.

1768 $ DISABLED WAR VETERANS SCHOLARSHIPS

Armed Forces Communications and Electronics Association
Attn: AFCEA Educational Foundation
4400 Fair Lakes Court
Fairfax, VA 22033–3899
Phone: (703) 631–6138; (800) 336–4583, ext. 6138; Fax: (703) 631–4693;
Email: scholarshipsinfo@afcea.org
Web: www.afcea.org/education/scholarships/military

Summary: To provide financial assistance to disabled military personnel and veterans who are majoring in specified scientific fields in college.

Eligibility: Open to active–duty service personnel and honorably discharged U.S. military veterans, Reservists, and National Guard members who are disabled because of wounds received during service in Enduring Freedom (Afghanistan) or Iraqi Freedom operations. Applicants must be enrolled full or part time at an accredited 2– or 4–year college or university or in a distance learning or online degree program. They must be working toward a degree in engineering (aerospace, computer, electrical, or systems), computer science, computer engineering technology, computer network systems, computer information systems, electronics engineering technology, mathematics, physics, information systems management, information systems security, technology management, or other field directly related to the support of U.S. intelligence or national security enterprises. Selection is based on demonstrated academic excellence, leadership, and financial need.

Financial data: The stipend is $2,500.

Duration: 1 year.

Number awarded: 2 each year: 1 for spring and 1 for fall.

Deadline: March of each year for fall; November of each year for spring.

1769 DIVISION OF ENGINEERING SERVICES ENGINEERING/ ARCHITECTURAL SCHOLARSHIP

Summary: To provide financial assistance to high school seniors in California who plan to study engineering or architecture at a college or university in the state.

See Listing #1200.

1770 DONALD G. WILLEMS SCHOLARSHIP

American Water Works Association–Montana Section
Attn: Executive Secretary
P.O. Box 582
Seeley Lake, MT 59868
Phone: (406) 546–5496;
Email: info@montana–awwa.org
Web: www.montana–awwa.org/scholarships

Summary: To provide financial assistance to students from Montana who are working on an undergraduate or graduate degree in a water–related field.

Eligibility: Open to 1) high school seniors planning to attend a college or university in Montana; and 2) students currently enrolled at colleges and universities in Montana. Applicants must be working on or planning to work on an associate, bachelor's, or graduate degree in a field that will lead to employment in the water and wastewater fields, including water treatment and distribution, wastewater treatment and collection, water resources, watershed protection, groundwater remediation, and related subdisciplines. They must have a GPA of 2.0 or higher. Along with their application, they must submit 3 references, a resume, and a 1,000–word statement on their professional goals. Financial need is not considered.

Financial data: The stipend is $1,000.

Duration: 1 year.

Number awarded: 1 or 2 each year.

Deadline: March of each year.

1771 DOROTHY C. WISNER SCHOLARSHIP

P.E.O. Foundation–California State Chapter
c/o Carol Born, Scholarship Committee Chair
718 Via La Paloma
Riverside, CA 92507–6403
Phone: (951) 686–2728
Web: www.peocalifornia.org/dcw.html

Summary: To provide financial assistance to women from California who are interested in working on an undergraduate degree in the medical field at a school in any state.

Eligibility: Open to female residents of California who have completed at least their first year of undergraduate work in the broad field of medicine. Graduate students are not eligible. Applicants may be studying in any state. They must submit a personal narrative that describes their background, interests, scholastic achievements, extracurricular activities, service, talents, and goals. Selection is based on character, integrity, academic excellence, and financial need.

Financial data: The stipend ranges from $500 to $1,000 per year.

Duration: 1 year; recipients may reapply.

Number awarded: 1 each year.

Deadline: January of each year.

1772 $ DOROTHY LEMKE HOWARTH SCHOLARSHIPS

Society of Women Engineers
Attn: Scholarship Selection Committee
203 North LaSalle Street, Suite 1675
Chicago, IL 60601–1269
Phone: (312) 596–5223; (877) SWE–INFO; Fax: (312) 644–8557;
Email: scholarships@swe.org
Web: societyofwomenengineers.swe.org/index.php/scholarships

Summary: To provide financial assistance to lower–division women majoring in computer science or engineering.

Eligibility: Open to women who are entering their sophomore year at a 4–year ABET–accredited college or university. Applicants must be U.S. citizens or permanent residents who are working full time on a degree in computer science or engineering and have a GPA of 3.0 or higher. Selection is based on merit.

Financial data: The stipend is $2,500.

Duration: 1 year.

Number awarded: 6 each year.

Deadline: February of each year.

1773 $ DOROTHY M. AND EARL S. HOFFMAN SCHOLARSHIPS

Society of Women Engineers
Attn: Scholarship Selection Committee
203 North LaSalle Street, Suite 1675
Chicago, IL 60601–1269
Phone: (312) 596–5223; (877) SWE–INFO; Fax: (312) 644–8557;
Email: scholarships@swe.org
Web: societyofwomenengineers.swe.org/index.php/scholarships

Summary: To provide financial assistance to women who will be entering college as freshmen and are interested in studying engineering or computer science.

Eligibility: Open to women who are entering college as freshmen with a GPA of 3.5 or higher. Applicants must be planning to enroll full time at an ABET–accredited 4–year college or university and major in computer science or engineering. Selection is based on merit. Preference is given to students at Bucknell University and Rensselaer Polytechnic Institute.

Financial data: The stipend is $3,000 per year.

Duration: 1 year; may be renewed for up to 3 additional years.

Number awarded: Varies each year; recently, 8 of these scholarships were awarded.

Deadline: May of each year.

1774 $ DOROTHY MORRISON UNDERGRADUATE SCHOLARSHIP

Alpha Mu Tau Fraternity
c/o American Society for Clinical Laboratory Science
2025 M Street, N.W., Suite 800
Washington, DC 20036
Phone: (202) 367–1174;
Email: alphamutaujoe@yahoo.com
Web: www.ascls.org/?page=Awards_AMTF

Summary: To provide financial assistance to undergraduate students in the clinical laboratory sciences.

Eligibility: Open to U.S. citizens and permanent residents accepted into or currently enrolled in a program in clinical laboratory science, including cytotechnology, histotechnology, clinical laboratory science/medical technology, or clinical laboratory technician/medical laboratory technician. Applicants must be entering their last year of study. Along with their application, they must submit a 500–word statement describing their interest and reasons for preparing for a career in clinical laboratory science. Financial need is also considered in the selection process.

Financial data: The stipend is $2,000.

Duration: 1 year.

Number awarded: 1 each year.

Deadline: March of each year.

1775 $ DOUGLAS BARTON MEMORIAL SCHOLARSHIP

Technical Association of the Pulp and Paper Industry
Attn: Scholarship Department
15 Technology Parkway South
Norcross, GA 30092
Phone: (770) 209–7276; (800) 332–8686; Fax: (770) 446–6947;
Email: standards@tappi.org
Web: www.tappi.org/About–TAPPI/TAPPI–Scholarships.aspx

Summary: To provide financial assistance to students who are interested in preparing for a career in the paper industry, with a focus on environmental control as it relates to the pulp, paper, and allied industries.

Eligibility: Open to students who are attending college full time, are at least sophomores, are enrolled at an ABET–accredited or equivalent college, have a GPA of 3.0 or higher, and are able to demonstrate a strong desire to prepare for a career in environmental control as it relates to the pulp, paper, and allied industries. Applicants may be interviewed.

Financial data: The stipend is $2,500.

Duration: 1 year.

Number awarded: At least 1 each year.

Deadline: February of each year.

1776 $$ DR. ALMA S. ADAMS SCHOLARSHIP

Summary: To provide financial assistance to undergraduate or graduate students in selected fields who have engaged in community service or visual arts activities to reduce smoking in communities designated as especially vulnerable to the tobacco industry.

See Listing #1203.

1777 DR. AND MRS. H.H. NININGER METEORITE AWARD

Arizona State University
Attn: Center for Meteorite Studies
P.O. Box 871404
Tempe, AZ 85287–1404
Phone: (480) 965–6511;
Email: meteorites@asu.edu
Web: meteorites.asu.edu/nininger

Summary: To recognize and reward outstanding student papers dealing with aspects of meteoritic investigation.

Eligibility: Open to both undergraduate and graduate students. They are invited to submit a paper (under 10,000 words) reflecting an aspect of meteoritic investigation. Research topics may include (but are not limited to) physical and chemical properties of meteorites, origin of meteoritic material, and cratering. Observational, experimental, statistical, and theoretical investigations are allowed. Students must be the first author of the paper, but they do not have to be the sole author. Papers must have been written, submitted, or published during the first 10 and a half months of the calendar year. They must cover original research conducted by the student.

Financial data: The award is $1,000.

Duration: The award is granted annually.

Number awarded: 1 each year.

Deadline: November of each year.

1778 DR. GORDON P. BOUTWELL, JR. MEMORIAL SCHOLARSHIP

Louisiana Solid Waste Association
Attn: Scholarship Committee
P.O. Box 309
Amite, LA 70422
Phone: (985) 878–4403; Fax: (985) 878–2361;
Email: info@lswa.us
Web: www.lswa.us

Summary: To provide financial assistance to high school seniors, high school graduates, and current undergraduates who are residents of Louisiana or attending college in the state and preparing for a career in the environmental industry.

Eligibility: Open to residents of Louisiana and students currently enrolled at a college or university in the state. Applicants must be high school seniors, high school graduates, and current undergraduates interested in preparing for a career within the environmental industry as an environmental engineer, environmental consultant, waste industry employee, or related professional. Along with their application, they must submit an essay of 150 to 200 words about themselves, their educational goals, their professional aspirations, how this award would help them to achieve those goals, and why they should receive this award. Selection is based on that essay, academic records and awards, field of study, and community service.

Financial data: A stipend is awarded (amount not specified). Funds are paid directly to the recipient's college or university.

Duration: 1 year.

Number awarded: Varies each year; recently, 3 of these scholarships were awarded.

Deadline: January of each year.

1779 DR. HELEN L. SCHEIBNER LIFE SCIENCE AND PUBLIC HEALTH SCHOLARSHIP

Indiana Public Health Foundation
Attn: Scholarship Committee
3512 Rockville Road, Suite 159–D
Indianapolis, IN 46222
Phone: (317) 888–8664; Fax: (317) 889–0399;
Email: helenscheibner@netscape.net
Web: www.iphf.us/scholarship.htm

Summary: To provide financial assistance to upper–division and graduate students who are Indiana residents working on a health–related degree at a college in any state.

Eligibility: Open to Indiana residents who are entering their junior or senior year or a graduate program at an accredited 4–year college or university in any state. Applicants must be working on a degree in a life science or public health field, defined to include (but not limited to) medicine, dentistry, nursing, allied health sciences (e.g., physical therapy, occupational therapy, dental hygiene, physician assistant), and the science of public health. Along with their application, they must submit 1–page statements on 1) their desire to become a professional in the field of "life science" or "public health;" and 2) a summary of their reasons for choosing that career. Selection is based on academic standing and interest in their chosen career path.

Financial data: The stipend is $1,000. Funds are paid jointly to the student and the school.

Duration: 1 year.

Number awarded: 1 each year.

Deadline: August of each year.

1780 DR. IVY M. PARKER MEMORIAL SCHOLARSHIP

Society of Women Engineers
Attn: Scholarship Selection Committee
203 North LaSalle Street, Suite 1675
Chicago, IL 60601–1269
Phone: (312) 596–5223; (877) SWE–INFO; Fax: (312) 644–8557;
Email: scholarships@swe.org
Web: societyofwomenengineers.swe.org/index.php/scholarships

Summary: To provide financial assistance to upper–division women majoring in computer science or engineering.

Eligibility: Open to women who are entering their junior or senior year at an ABET–accredited college or university. Applicants must be working full time on a degree in computer science or engineering and have a GPA of 3.0 or higher. Financial need is considered in the selection process.
Financial data: The stipend is $1,500.
Duration: 1 year.
Number awarded: 1 each year.
Deadline: February of each year.

1781 $ DR. ROBERT W. SIMS MEMORIAL SCHOLARSHIP

Florida Association of Educational Data Systems
c/o Betsy Wetzel, Scholarship Chair
Brevard Community College
1519 Clearlake Road
Cocoa, FL 32922
Phone: (321) 433–7400;
Email: wetzelb@brevardcc.edu
Web: www.faeds.org/scholarships.cfm
Summary: To provide financial assistance to students attending a Florida college or university and majoring in computer science or information technology.
Eligibility: Open to residents of Florida enrolled full time at a private or public college or university in the state. Applicants must have a GPA of 2.5 or higher and be majoring or planning to major in computer science or information technology. Along with their application, they must submit a 2–page autobiography that includes their academic success and course work in technology–related areas, why they selected their major, and how they intend to use it in the future. Financial need is not considered in the selection process. U.S. citizenship is required.
Financial data: The stipend is $3,000.
Duration: 1 year.
Number awarded: Varies each year; recently, 2 of these scholarships were awarded.
Deadline: February of each year.

1782 DR. RODERICK A. SCOFIELD SCHOLARSHIP IN METEOROLOGY

National Weather Association
Attn: Executive Director
228 West Millbrook Road
Raleigh, NC 27609–4304
Phone: (919) 845–1546; Fax: (919) 845–2956;
Email: exdir@nwas.org
Web: www.nwas.org/committees/ed_comm/application/index.php
Summary: To provide financial assistance to students working on an undergraduate or graduate degree in meteorology.
Eligibility: Open to students who are either entering their junior or senior year of undergraduate study or enrolled as graduate students. Applicants must be working on a degree in meteorology or a related field. Along with their application, they must submit a 1–page statement explaining why they are applying for this scholarship. Selection is based on that statement, academic achievement, and 2 letters of recommendation.
Financial data: The stipend is $1,000.
Duration: 1 year.
Number awarded: 1 each year.
Deadline: May of each year.

1783 DR. ROE B. LEWIS MEMORIAL SCHOLARSHIPS

Southwest Indian Agricultural Association
P.O. Box 93524
Phoenix, AZ 85070–3524
Phone: (520) 562–6722; Fax: (520) 562–2840;
Email: swiaa@g.com
Web: www.swindianag.com/construction.html
Summary: To provide financial assistance to American Indians working on an undergraduate or graduate degree in a field related to agriculture or natural resources.
Eligibility: Open to American Indians enrolled in a federally–recognized band, nation, or tribe. Applicants must be working on an undergraduate or graduate degree in agriculture or natural resources at an accredited college, university, or vocational/technical school. Along with their application, they must submit an essay explaining how they plan to use their education to promote, educate, and/or improve agriculture on southwest reservations. First–year undergraduates must have a GPA of 2.5 or higher; all other students must have a GPA of 3.0 or higher. Financial need is not considered in the selection process.
Financial data: The stipend is $1,000.
Duration: 1 year.
Number awarded: 3 each year: 2 to undergraduates and 1 to a graduate student.
Deadline: November of each year.

1784 DR. S. BRADLEY BURSON MEMORIAL SCHOLARSHIP

American Council of the Blind
Attn: Coordinator, Scholarship Program
2200 Wilson Boulevard, Suite 650
Arlington, VA 22201
Phone: (202) 467–5081; (800) 424–8666; Fax: (703) 465–5085;
Email: info@acb.org
Web: www.acb.org/scholarship
Summary: To provide financial assistance to blind students who are working on an undergraduate or graduate degree in designated fields of science.
Eligibility: Open to undergraduate or graduate students working on a degree in the "pure" sciences (i.e., biology, chemistry, physics, and engineering, but not computer science). Applicants must be legally blind in both eyes. Along with their application, they must submit verification of legal blindness in both eyes; SAT, ACT, GRE, or similar scores; information on extracurricular activities (including involvement in the American Council of the Blind); employment record; and a 500–word autobiographical sketch that includes their personal goals, strengths, weaknesses, hobbies, honors, achievements, and reasons for choice of field or courses of study. A cumulative GPA of 3.3 or higher is generally required. Financial need is not considered in the selection process.
Financial data: The stipend is $1,000.
Duration: 1 year.
Number awarded: 1 each year.
Deadline: February of each year.

1785 DUPONT SCHOLARSHIPS

Society of Women Engineers
Attn: Scholarship Selection Committee
203 North LaSalle Street, Suite 1675
Chicago, IL 60601–1269
Phone: (312) 596–5223; (877) SWE–INFO; Fax: (312) 644–8557;
Email: scholarships@swe.org
Web: societyofwomenengineers.swe.org/index.php/scholarships
Summary: To provide financial assistance to women interested in studying chemical or mechanical engineering at a college or university in the East or Midwest.
Eligibility: Open to women entering their sophomore, junior, or senior year as a full–time student at an ABET–accredited 4–year college or university in an eastern or midwestern state. Applicants must have a GPA of 3.0 or higher and be planning to major in chemical or mechanical engineering. Selection is based on merit.
Financial data: The stipend is $1,000.
Duration: 1 year.
Number awarded: 2 each year.
Deadline: February of each year.

1786 $$ DWIGHT DAVID EISENHOWER HISTORICALLY BLACK COLLEGES AND UNIVERSITIES TRANSPORTATION FELLOWSHIP PROGRAM

Summary: To provide financial assistance to undergraduate and graduate students working on a degree in a transportation–related field at an Historically Black College or University (HBCU).
See Listing #1207.

1787 DWIGHT WELLER, KB3LA, MEMORIAL SCHOLARSHIP

Foundation for Amateur Radio, Inc.
Attn: Scholarship Committee
P.O. Box 911
Columbia, MD 21044–0911
Phone: (410) 552–2652; Fax: (410) 981–5146;
Email: dave.prestel@gmail.com
Web: www.farweb.org/scholarships

Summary: To provide funding to licensed radio amateurs who are interested in studying engineering or the physical sciences in college.
Eligibility: Open to radio amateurs who are interested in working full time on a bachelor's degree in a branch of engineering or the physical sciences. There are no restrictions on license class or residence area. Financial need is considered in the selection process.
Financial data: The stipend is $1,000.
Duration: 1 year.
Number awarded: 1 each year.
Deadline: April of each year.

1788 $ E. NOEL LUDDY SCHOLARSHIP

Association of Federal Communications Consulting Engineers
P.O. Box 19333
Washington, DC 20036
Email: scholarships@afcce.org
Web: www.afcce.org
Summary: To provide financial assistance to upper–division and graduate students working on an engineering or other degree related to the broadcast and telecommunications industries.
Eligibility: Open to juniors, seniors, and graduate students who are working full time on a degree in engineering or another field related to the broadcast and telecommunications industries. Applicants must be sponsored by a member of the Association of Federal Communications Consulting Engineers (AFCCE). Along with their application, they must submit a statement of 250 to 500 words describing their career goals, areas of strong interest, and how they anticipated either working as or in collaboration with radio communications consulting engineers, including broadcast and wireless telecommunication engineers. Financial need is considered in the selection process.
Financial data: The stipend is $2,500.
Duration: 1 year.
Number awarded: 1 each year.
Deadline: Deadline not specified.

1789 EARL DEDMAN MEMORIAL SCHOLARSHIP

American Floral Endowment
1601 Duke Street
Alexandria, VA 22314
Phone: (703) 838–5211; Fax: (703) 838–5212;
Email: afe@endowment.org
Web: endowment.org/floriculture–scholarshipsinternships.html
Summary: To provide financial assistance to residents of northwestern states who are working on an undergraduate degree in horticulture at colleges and universities in any state.
Eligibility: Open to sophomores, juniors, and seniors who are residents of northwestern states enrolled at colleges or universities in any state. Applicants must be horticulture majors with a specific interest in becoming a greenhouse grower. They must be U.S. citizens or permanent residents and have a GPA of 2.0 or higher. Along with their application, they must submit a statement describing their career goals and the academic, work–related, and/or life experiences that support those goals. Financial need is considered in the selection process.
Financial data: The stipend varies each year; recently, it was $1,850.
Duration: 1 year.
Number awarded: 1 each year.
Deadline: April of each year.

1790 EAST MICHIGAN CHAPTER SCHOLARSHIPS

Air & Waste Management Association–East Michigan Chapter
c/o Kay F. Bedenis, Scholarship Committee Chair
12467 Beacon Hill Drive
Plymouth, MI 48170
Email: kbedenis@yahoo.com
Web: www.emawma.org/archives.php
Summary: To provide financial assistance to undergraduate and graduate students in Michigan who are interested in preparing for a career in air and waste management.
Eligibility: Open to students enrolled in or entering their junior or senior year of undergraduate study or any year of graduate or professional school at a college or university in Michigan. They must be full–time students preparing for a career in air pollution control, toxic and/or hazardous waste management, or another environmental area. Preferred courses of study include engineering, physical or natural sciences, public health, law, and natural resources. Selection is based on academic achievement (at least a 3.0 GPA), a paper (between 500 and 600 words) on career interests and objectives, extracurricular activities, and financial need.
Financial data: The stipend is $1,500. Winners also receive a 1–year student membership in the Air & Waste Management Association (A&WMA).
Duration: 1 year; may be renewed.
Number awarded: Up to 4 each year.
Deadline: February of each year.

1791 EAST TEXAS GEOLOGICAL SOCIETY SCHOLARSHIP

East Texas Communities Foundation
Attn: Scholarship Coordinator
315 North Broadway, Suite 210
Tyler, TX 75702
Phone: (903) 533–0208; (866) 533–ETCF; Fax: (903) 533–0258;
Email: llauderdale@etcf.org
Web: www.etcf.org/sch20.htm
Summary: To provide financial assistance to students working on a bachelor's or master's degree in geology at a college or university in Texas.
Eligibility: Open to students enrolled at colleges and universities in Texas as a sophomore or higher. Applicants must be working on a degree in geology and have a GPA of 3.0 or higher. Preference is given to students who attended high school in east Texas. Along with their application, they must submit a 2–page essay on their motivation to prepare for a career in geology. Financial need is not considered in the selection process. A personal interview may be requested.
Financial data: A stipend is awarded (amount not specified).
Duration: 1 year; may be renewed 1 additional year, provided the recipient remains enrolled full time with a GPA of 3.0 or higher.
Number awarded: 1 or more each year.
Deadline: March of each year.

1792 E.B. MILLER MEMORIAL SCHOLARSHIP

Ohio Forestry Association, Inc.
1100–H Brandywine Boulevard
Zanesville, OH 43701–7303
Phone: (614) 497–9580; (888) 38–TREES; Fax: (614) 497–9581;
Email: info@ohioforest.org
Web: www.ohioforest.org
Summary: To provide financial assistance to residents of Ohio who are interested in working on an undergraduate degree in forest resources.
Eligibility: Open to high school seniors and current undergraduate students who are residents of Ohio. Applicants must be interested in preparing for a career in forest resource management. Along with their application, they must submit brief essays on their goals and plans for a career, the challenges facing the forest resources profession, and additional information relevant to their consideration for this scholarship. Preference is given to students attending colleges and universities in Ohio. U.S. citizenship is required. Financial need is not considered in the selection process.
Financial data: Stipends range from $500 to $1,000 per year.
Duration: 1 year.
Number awarded: Varies each year; recently, 4 of these scholarships were awarded.
Deadline: April of each year.

1793 EDITH M. ALLEN SCHOLARSHIPS

United Methodist Church
Attn: General Board of Higher Education and Ministry
Office of Loans and Scholarships
1001 19th Avenue South
P.O. Box 340007
Nashville, TN 37203–0007
Phone: (615) 340–7344; Fax: (615) 340–7367;
Email: umscholar@gbhem.org
Web: www.gbhem.org
Summary: To provide financial assistance to Methodist students who are African American and working on an undergraduate or graduate degree in specified fields.
Eligibility: Open to full–time undergraduate and graduate students at Methodist colleges and universities (preferably Historically Black United Methodist colleges) who have been active, full members of a United Methodist Church for at least 3 years prior to applying. Applicants must be African

Americans working on a degree in education, social work, medicine, and/or other health professions. They must have at least a "B+" average and be recognized as a person whose academic and vocational contributions will help improve the quality of life for others.
Financial data: Stipends average $1,000.
Duration: 1 year; recipients may reapply.
Number awarded: Varies each year.
Deadline: February of each year.

1794 $$ EDSA MINORITY SCHOLARSHIP

Summary: To provide financial assistance to minority college students who are interested in studying landscape architecture.
See Listing #1210.

1795 EDWARD D. BURKETT SCHOLARSHIP PROGRAM

American Public Works Association–Florida Chapter
c/o Perry Lopez, Scholarship Chair
Town of Belleair
901 Ponce de Leon Boulevard
Belleair, FL 33765
Phone: (727) 588–3769, ext. 402;
Email: plopez@townofbelleair.net
Web: florida.apwa.net/resources/scholarships/76
Summary: To provide financial assistance to undergraduate and graduate students in Florida who are preparing for a career in public works.
Eligibility: Open to undergraduate and graduate students at colleges and universities in Florida. Undergraduates must have completed at least 60 credit hours of work on a bachelor's degree in civil engineering or a related field; graduate students must be working on an advanced degree in public works engineering, management, public administration, or other field related to public works. Applicants must submit transcripts and information on their financial situation.
Financial data: Stipends range up to $1,000.
Duration: 1 year.
Number awarded: Varies each year; recently, 6 of these scholarships were awarded.
Deadline: January of each year.

1796 EDWARD D. HENDRICKSON/SAE ENGINEERING SCHOLARSHIP

Society of Automotive Engineers
Attn: Scholarships and Loans Program
400 Commonwealth Drive
Warrendale, PA 15096–0001
Phone: (724) 776–4790; (877) 606–7323; Fax: (724) 776–0790;
Email: scholarships@sae.org
Web: students.sae.org/awdscholar/scholarships/hendrickson
Summary: To provide financial support to high school seniors interested in studying engineering in college.
Eligibility: Open to U.S. citizens who intend to earn an ABET–accredited degree in engineering. Applicants must be high school seniors with a GPA of 3.75 or higher who rank in the 90th percentile in both mathematics and critical reading on the SAT or in the composite ACT. Selection is based on high school transcripts; SAT or ACT scores; school–related extracurricular activities; non–school related activities; academic honors, civic honors, and awards; and a 250–word essay on their goals, plans, experiences, and interests in mobility engineering. Financial need is not considered.
Financial data: The stipend is $1,000 per year.
Duration: 1 year; may be renewed up to 3 additional years, provided the recipient maintains a GPA of 3.0 or higher.
Number awarded: 1 each year.
Deadline: January of each year.

1797 $ EDWARD J. AND VIRGINIA M. ROUTHIER NURSING SCHOLARSHIP

Rhode Island Foundation
Attn: Funds Administrator
One Union Station
Providence, RI 02903
Phone: (401) 427–4017; Fax: (401) 331–8085;
Email: lmonahan@rifoundation.org
Web: www.rifoundation.org
Summary: To provide financial assistance to undergraduate and graduate students enrolled in nursing programs in Rhode Island.
Eligibility: Open to students enrolled or accepted at an accredited nursing program in Rhode Island. Applicants must be 1) registered nurses (R.N.s) enrolled in a nursing baccalaureate degree program; 2) students enrolled in a baccalaureate nursing program; or 3) R.N.s working on a graduate degree (master's or Ph.D.). They must be able to demonstrate financial need and a commitment to practice in Rhode Island. Along with their application, they must submit an essay, up to 300 words, on their career goals, particularly as they relate to practicing in or advancing the field of nursing in Rhode Island.
Financial data: The stipend ranges from $500 to $3,000 per year.
Duration: 1 year; may be renewed.
Number awarded: Varies each year; recently, 11 of these scholarships were awarded: 6 new awards and 5 renewals.
Deadline: April of each year.

1798 $ EDWARD J. BRADY SCHOLARSHIP

American Welding Society
Attn: AWS Foundation, Inc.
550 N.W. LeJeune Road
Miami, FL 33126
Phone: (305) 445–6628; (800) 443–9353, ext. 212; Fax: (305) 443–7559;
Email: found@aws.org
Web: www.aws.org/w/a/foundation/scholarships/brady.html
Summary: To provide financial assistance to college students majoring in welding engineering or welding engineering technology.
Eligibility: Open to undergraduate students who are working on a 4–year bachelor's degree in welding engineering or welding engineering technology; preference is given to students in welding engineering. Applicants must have a minimum GPA of 2.5, provide a letter of reference indicating previous hands–on welding experience, be U.S. citizens, submit an essay of 300 to 500 words on "Why I Want to Pursue a Career in Welding," and be able to demonstrate financial need.
Financial data: The stipend is $2,500.
Duration: 1 year; recipients may reapply.
Number awarded: 1 each year.
Deadline: February of each year.

1799 $ ELECTRONIC DOCUMENT SYSTEMS FOUNDATION BOARD OF DIRECTORS SCHOLARSHIPS

Summary: To provide financial assistance to undergraduate and graduate students from any country interested in preparing for a career in document management and graphic communications.
See Listing #1213.

1800 $ ELECTRONICS DIVISION LEWIS C. HOFFMAN SCHOLARSHIP

American Ceramic Society
Attn: Electronics Division
600 North Cleveland Avenue, Suite 210
Westerville, OH 43082
Phone: (614) 794–5821; (866) 721–3322; Fax: (614) 794–5882;
Email: mstout@ceramics.org
Web: ceramics.org/acers–community/award–winners–resources
Summary: To provide financial assistance to undergraduate students in a field related to ceramic science.
Eligibility: Open to juniors enrolled in a program related to ceramics/materials science and engineering. Applicants must submit a 500–word essay on a topic that changes annually; recently, the topic was "Environmentally benign electronic ceramics." Selection is based on the essay, extracurricular activities, a letter of recommendation from a faculty adviser, PSAT/SAT/ACT scores, and GPA (cumulative and in science courses).
Financial data: The stipend is $2,000. Funds are to be used to assist in payment of tuition.
Duration: 1 year.
Number awarded: 1 each year.
Deadline: July of each year.

1801 $$ ELEKTA RADIATION THERAPY SCHOLARSHIPS

American Society of Radiologic Technologists
Attn: ASRT Education and Research Foundation
15000 Central Avenue, S.E.
Albuquerque, NM 87123–3909
Phone: (505) 298–4500, ext. 2541; (800) 444–2778, ext. 2541; Fax: (505) 298–5063;
Email: foundation@asrt.org
Web: www.asrtfoundation.org/Content/Scholarships_and_Awards

Summary: To provide financial assistance to entry–level students preparing for a career in radiation therapy.

Eligibility: Open to students enrolled in an accredited radiologic science program at the entry level. Applicants must be able to finish their radiation therapy degree or certificate in the year for which they are applying. They must be U.S. citizens, nationals, or permanent residents have a GPA of 3.0 or higher. Along with their application, they must submit 9 essays of 200 words each on assigned topics related to their personal situation and interest in a career as a radiation therapist. Selection is based on those essays, academic and professional achievements, recommendations, and financial need.

Financial data: The stipend is $5,000. Funds are paid directly to the recipient's institution.

Duration: 1 year.

Number awarded: 4 each year.

Deadline: January of each year.

1802 ELIZABETH LOWELL PUTNAM PRIZE

Mathematical Association of America
1529 18th Street, N.W.
Washington, DC 20036–1358
Phone: (202) 387–5200; (800) 741–9415; Fax: (202) 265–2384;
Email: maahq@maa.org
Web: www.maa.org/awards/putnam.html

Summary: To recognize and reward outstanding women participants in a mathematics competition.

Eligibility: Open to women at colleges and universities in Canada and the United States. Entrants participate in an examination containing mathematics problems designed to test originality as well as technical competence. The woman with the highest score receives this prize.

Financial data: The prize is $1,000.

Duration: The competition is held annually.

Number awarded: 1 each year.

Deadline: Deadline not specified.

1803 ELIZABETH MCLEAN MEMORIAL SCHOLARSHIP

Society of Women Engineers
Attn: Scholarship Selection Committee
203 North LaSalle Street, Suite 1675
Chicago, IL 60601–1269
Phone: (312) 596–5223; (877) SWE–INFO; Fax: (312) 644–8557;
Email: scholarships@swe.org
Web: societyofwomenengineers.swe.org/index.php/scholarships

Summary: To provide financial assistance to undergraduate women majoring in civil engineering.

Eligibility: Open to women who are entering their sophomore, junior, or senior year at an ABET–accredited 4–year college or university. Applicants must be working full time on a degree in civil engineering and have a GPA of 3.0 or higher. Selection is based on merit.

Financial data: The stipend is $1,500.

Duration: 1 year.

Number awarded: 1 each year.

Deadline: February of each year.

1804 ELSIE BORCK HEALTH CARE SCHOLARSHIP

Kansas Federation of Business & Professional Women's Clubs, Inc.
Attn: Kansas BPW Educational Foundation, Inc.
c/o Kathy Niehoff, Executive Secretary
605 East 15th
Ottawa, KS 66067
Phone: (785) 242–9319; Fax: (785) 242–1047;
Email: kathyniehoff@sbcglobal.net
Web: kansasbpw.memberlodge.org/Default.aspx?pageId=450103

Summary: To provide financial assistance to residents of Kansas who are preparing for a career in a health profession in the state.

Eligibility: Open to Kansas residents (men and women) who are at least a college freshman and working on an associate or higher degree in a health profession at a school in the state. Applicants must submit a 3–page personal biography in which they express their career goals, the direction they want to take in the future, their proposed field of study, their reason for selecting that field, the institutions they plan to attend and why, their circumstances for reentering school (if a factor), and what makes them uniquely qualified for this scholarship. They must also be able to document financial need. Applications must be submitted through a local organization of the sponsor.

Financial data: A stipend is awarded (amount not specified).

Duration: 1 year.

Number awarded: 1 or more each year.

Deadline: December of each year.

1805 $$ EMERGENCY NURSES ASSOCIATION NON–R.N. SCHOLARSHIPS

Emergency Nurses Association
Attn: ENA Foundation
915 Lee Street
Des Plaines, IL 60016–6569
Phone: (847) 460–4100; (800) 900–9659, ext. 4100; Fax: (847) 460–4004;
Email: foundation@ena.org
Web: www.ena.org/foundation/scholarships/Pages/Default.aspx

Summary: To provide financial assistance to rescue workers enrolled in an undergraduate degree program in nursing.

Eligibility: Open to pre–hospital care providers, firefighters, and police officers who are working on an associate or baccalaureate nursing degree. Rescue workers from all states are eligible. Applicants must have a GPA of 3.0 or higher and be a member of a state or national professional EMT, firefighter, or police officer association. They are not required to be a member of the Emergency Nurses Association (ENA), but they must submit a letter of reference from an ENA member. Along with their application, they must submit a 1–page statement on their professional and educational goals and how this scholarship will help them attain those goals. Selection is based on content and clarity of the goal statement (45%), professional association involvement (35%), presentation of the application (10%), and letters of reference (10%).

Financial data: The stipend is $5,000 or $2,500.

Duration: 1 year.

Number awarded: Varies each year; recently, 7 of these scholarships were awarded: 1 at $5,000 and 6 at $2,500.

Deadline: May of each year.

1806 $ EMERGING DIVERSITY EDUCATION FUND SCHOLARSHIPS

Decisive Magazine
Attn: Emerging Diversity Education Fund
8201 Corporate Drive, Suite 500
Landover, MD 20785
Phone: (301) 850–2858
Web: www.decisivemagazine.com

Summary: To provide financial assistance to minority students interested in preparing for a career in an automotive–related profession.

Eligibility: Open to minority (African American, Asian Indian American, Asian Pacific American, Hispanic American, or Native American) high school seniors or students who are currently enrolled full time at a college, university, or technical school. Applicants must be interested in preparing for a career in the automotive industry. They must have a GPA of 2.7 or higher. Along with their application, they must submit 250–word essays on 1) what diversity in the automotive industry means to them; and 2) how their automotive profession or endeavors will have an impact on diversity. Financial need is not considered in the selection process. U.S. citizenship is required.

Financial data: Stipends range from $1,000 to $2,500.

Duration: 1 year.

Deadline: December of each year.

1807 EMILY M. HEWITT MEMORIAL SCHOLARSHIP

Calaveras Big Trees Association
P.O. Box 1196
Arnold, CA 95223–1196

Phone: (209) 795–3840; Fax: (209) 795–6680;
Email: cbtvc@goldrush.com
Web: www.bigtrees.org/events–programs/scholarship–fund

Summary: To provide financial assistance to students at California colleges and universities who are working on an undergraduate or graduate degree in an environmental field.

Eligibility: Open to full–time upper–division and graduate students currently enrolled at a California college or university. Applicants must have demonstrated an educational and career commitment to the study of environment and the need to practice conservation. They must be able to document financial need and active commitment to nature and conservation. Eligible fields of study include environmental protection, forestry, wildlife and fisheries biology, parks and recreation, park management, environmental law, public policy, environmental art, and California history.

Financial data: The stipend is $1,000.

Duration: 1 year.

Number awarded: 1 or more each year.

Deadline: April of each year.

1808 $ E.N. ROBERTS SCHOLARSHIP

New Hampshire Land Surveyors Foundation
Attn: Scholarship Committee
77 Main Street
P.O. Box 689
Raymond, NH 03077–0689
Phone: (603) 895–4822; (800) 698–5447; Fax: (603) 462–0343;
Email: info@nhlsa.org
Web: www.nhlsa.org/scholarship.htm

Summary: To provide financial assistance to residents of New Hampshire who are studying civil engineering at a college in any state as preparation for a career in land surveying.

Eligibility: Open to New Hampshire residents enrolled in the second, third, or fourth year of a 2–year college program in civil engineering technology or surveying or a 4–year college program in civil engineering. Applicants must have shown serious interest, capability, and outstanding accomplishments in surveying courses and must be preparing for a career in land surveying. They may be attending college in any state Along with their application, they must submit an essay about their professional aspirations, their goals in college and afterwards, and factors that make them particularly deserving of support. Financial need is not required.

Financial data: The stipend is $2,000.

Duration: 1 year.

Number awarded: 1 each year.

Deadline: November of each year.

1809 ENCOURAGE MINORITY PARTICIPATION IN OCCUPATIONS WITH EMPHASIS ON REHABILITATION

Courage Center
Attn: EMPOWER Scholarship Program
3915 Golden Valley Road
Minneapolis, MN 55422
Phone: (763) 520–0214; (888) 8–INTAKE; Fax: (763) 520–0562; TDD: (763) 520–0245;
Email: empower@couragecenter.org
Web: www.couragecenter.org/ContentPages/empower_details.aspx

Summary: To provide financial assistance to students of color from Minnesota and western Wisconsin interested in attending college in any state to prepare for a career in the medical rehabilitation field.

Eligibility: Open to ethnically diverse students accepted at or enrolled in an institution of higher learning in any state. Applicants must be residents of Minnesota or western Wisconsin (Burnett, Pierce, Polk, and St. Croix counties). They must be able to demonstrate a career interest in the medical rehabilitation field by a record of volunteer involvement related to health care and must have a GPA of 2.0 or higher. Along with their application, they must submit a 1–page essay that covers their experiences and interactions to date with the area of volunteering, what they have accomplished and gained from those experiences, how those experiences will assist them in their future endeavors, why education is important to them, how this scholarship will help them with their financial need and their future career goals.

Financial data: The stipend is $1,500.

Duration: 1 year.

Number awarded: 2 each year.

Deadline: May of each year.

1810 $ ENGINEERS FOUNDATION OF WISCONSIN SCHOLARSHIPS

Wisconsin Society of Professional Engineers
Engineers Foundation of Wisconsin
7044 South 13th Street
Oak Creek, WI 53154
Phone: (414) 908–4950, ext. 450; Fax: (414) 768–8001;
Email: wspe@wspe.org
Web: www.wspe.org/efw.html

Summary: To provide financial assistance to high school seniors in Wisconsin who are interested in majoring in engineering at a college in any state.

Eligibility: Open to seniors graduating from high schools in Wisconsin who intend to enroll in an accredited engineering undergraduate program in any state, earn a degree in engineering, and enter the practice of engineering after graduation. Applicants must have a GPA of 3.0 or higher and an ACT composite score of 24 or higher. Along with their application, they must submit a 250–word essay on how and when they became interested in engineering, the field of engineering that is most interesting to them and why, and why they want to become a practicing engineer. U.S. citizenship is required. Special consideration is given to applicants who can identify extenuating circumstances that will require financial assistance for them to continue their education.

Financial data: Recently, stipends were $2,000 or $1,500.

Duration: 1 year.

Number awarded: Varies each year; recently, 7 of these scholarships were awarded: 3 at $2,000 and 4 at $1,500.

Deadline: December of each year.

1811 $ ENVIRONMENTAL CAREER SCHOLARSHIP

New York Water Environment Association
Attn: Executive Director
525 Plum Street, Suite 102
Syracuse, NY 13204
Phone: (315) 422–7811; (877) 55–NYWEA; Fax: (315) 422–3851;
Email: pcr@nywea.org
Web: nywea.org/scholarship

Summary: To provide financial assistance to high school seniors in New York who are planning to enroll in an environmentally–related program at a college in any state.

Eligibility: Open to seniors graduating from high schools in New York who plan to enroll full time at a college or university in any state. Applicants must be planning to work on a bachelor's degree in an environmental field, including (but not limited to) environmental engineering, civil engineering with an environmental minor, chemical engineering with an environmental minor, hydrogeology with an environmental emphasis, or biology or microbiology with an environmental emphasis. Along with their application, they must submit 2 essays of 500 to 600 words each on 1) the personal efforts and initiatives they might take or have taken to ensure the protection of water as a resource for future generations; and 2) either the actions they have taken to affect or initiate change with respect to the environment, or how their career choice would positively impact the environment. Selection is based on the essays, transcripts, and 2 letters of recommendation; financial need is not considered.

Financial data: The stipend is $1,000 for the first year, $2,000 for the second year, $3,000 for the third year, and $4,000 for the fourth year.

Duration: 4 years. Renewal requires the recipient to maintain a GPA of 2.5 or higher for year 1, 2.7 or higher for years 1 through 2, and 3.0 or higher for years 1 through 3.

Number awarded: 1 each year.

Deadline: January of each year.

1812 EPOC SCHOLARSHIP FUND

Environmental Professionals' Organization of Connecticut
Attn: Executive Director
P.O. Box 176
Amston, CT 06231–0176
Phone: (860) 537–0337; Fax: (860) 537–3572;
Email: sjm@epoc.org
Web: www.epoc.org/Default.aspx?pageId=751601

Summary: To provide financial assistance to upper–division and graduate students from Connecticut attending college in any state to prepare for a career as an environmental professional.

Eligibility: Open to Connecticut residents who are preparing for a career as an environmental professional in the state. Applicants must be enrolled as juniors, seniors, or graduate students at a college or university in any state. They must be working on a degree in a relevant field, including biology, chemistry, earth science, ecology, engineering (agricultural, chemical, civil, environmental, mechanical), environmental science, environmental studies, geology, hydrogeology, hydrology, natural resource management, soil sciences, toxicology, water resources, or wetland science. Along with their application, they must submit an essay of 400 to 500 words on their reasons for choosing their major, what they expect from a career in that field of study, and why this scholarship is important to them. Financial need is not considered in the selection process.

Financial data: A stipend is awarded (amount not specified).

Duration: 1 year.

Number awarded: Varies each year; recently, 4 of these scholarships were awarded.

Deadline: July of each year.

1813 $$ ERNEST F. HOLLINGS UNDERGRADUATE SCHOLARSHIP PROGRAM

National Oceanic and Atmospheric Administration
Attn: Office of Education
1315 East–West Highway
SSMC3, Room 10703
Silver Spring, MD 20910
Phone: (301) 713–9437, ext. 206; Fax: (301) 713–9465;
Email: StudentScholarshipPrograms@noaa.gov
Web: www.oesd.noaa.gov/scholarships/hollings.html

Summary: To provide financial assistance and summer research experience to upper–division students who are working on a degree in a field of interest to the National Oceanic and Atmospheric Administration (NOAA).

Eligibility: Open to full–time students entering their junior year at an accredited college or university in the United States or its territories. Applicants must be majoring in a discipline related to oceanic and atmospheric science, research, technology, and education, and supportive of the purposes of NOAA's programs and mission. Eligible areas of interest include (but are not limited to) atmospheric, biological, environmental, and oceanic sciences; mathematics; engineering; remote sensing technology; social and physical sciences such as geography, geomatics, hydrology, or physics; or teacher education. They must have a GPA of 3.0 or higher. As part of their program, they must be interested in participating in summer research and development activities at NOAA headquarters (Silver Spring, Maryland) or field centers. U.S. citizenship is required.

Financial data: This program provides a stipend of $8,000 per academic year and $650 per week during the research internship, a housing subsidy and limited travel reimbursement for round–trip transportation to the internship site, and travel expenses to the scholarship program conference at the completion of the internship.

Duration: 2 academic years plus 10 weeks during the intervening summer.

Number awarded: Approximately 100 each year.

Deadline: January of each year.

1814 ERNIE AYER AVIATION SCHOLARSHIP

Ernie Ayer Aviation Education Foundation
5 Rogers Court
Midland Park, NJ 07432
Phone: (201) 447–4164;
Email: TAyer73352@aol.com

Summary: To provide financial assistance to students enrolled or planning to enroll in an aviation program.

Eligibility: Open to students who have been accepted to a professional aviation training program, aviation institution of higher learning, or aviation technical school. Students accepted to a college or technical program must submit transcripts and proof of enrollment and attendance at classes. Students in a recognized flight school receive the award in installments following the achievement of certain goals (i.e., after the first solo, after the first solo cross-country flight, after the written FAA examination is passed, and after the pilot certificate is received). For students seeking advanced ratings, selection is based on records, experience, potential, and demonstrated commitment to aviation. Applicants for all types of training must submit essays on 2 topics: 1) their goals in aviation and how receiving a scholarship would help them to realize those goals; and 2) a significant person or event in their life that has been a major influence in their decision to prepare for a career in aviation. Financial need is not considered in the selection process.

Financial data: The stipend is $1,000.

Duration: 1 year.

Number awarded: 2 each year.

Deadline: April of each year.

1815 $ EUNICE FIORITO MEMORIAL SCHOLARSHIP

American Council of the Blind
Attn: Coordinator, Scholarship Program
2200 Wilson Boulevard, Suite 650
Arlington, VA 22201
Phone: (202) 467–5081; (800) 424–8666; Fax: (703) 465–5085;
Email: info@acb.org
Web: www.acb.org/scholarship

Summary: To provide financial assistance to undergraduate or graduate students who are blind and are interested in studying in a field of advocacy or service for persons with disabilities.

Eligibility: Open to undergraduate and graduate students in rehabilitation, education, law, or other fields of service or advocacy for persons with disabilities. Applicants must be legally blind in both eyes. Along with their application, they must submit verification of legal blindness in both eyes; SAT, ACT, GRE, or similar scores; information on extracurricular activities (including involvement in the American Council of the Blind); employment record; and a 500–word autobiographical sketch that includes their personal goals, strengths, weaknesses, hobbies, honors, achievements, and reasons for choice of field or courses of study. A cumulative GPA of 3.3 or higher is generally required. Financial need is not considered in the selection process. Preference is given to students with little or no vision.

Financial data: The stipend is $2,000.

Duration: 1 year.

Number awarded: 1 each year.

Deadline: February of each year.

1816 EVAN AND KATHERINE HARROD SCHOLARSHIP

Mental Health America of Kentucky
120 Sears Avenue, Suite 213
Louisville, KY 40207
Phone: (502) 893–0460; (888) 705–0463;
Email: mhaky@mhaky.org
Web: www.mhaky.org/scholarships.php

Summary: To provide financial assistance to undergraduate and graduate students at colleges and universities in Kentucky who come from a rural community in any state and are preparing for a career in mental health.

Eligibility: Open to residents of any state who are currently enrolled as undergraduate or graduate students at colleges and universities in Kentucky. Applicants must be working on a degree in a field related to mental health (e.g., allied health, medicine, nursing, psychology, social work). They must come from a rural area. Along with their application, they must submit a 200–word essay on their motivation for considering a career in mental health, 2 letters of recommendation, and college transcripts. Financial need is not considered in the selection process.

Financial data: The stipend is $1,000.

Duration: 1 year.

Number awarded: 1 each year.

Deadline: August of each year.

1817 EVELYN R. COLE SCHOLARSHIP

Garden Club Federation of Massachusetts, Inc.
Attn: Scholarship Secretary
219 Washington Street
Wellesley Hills, MA 02481
Phone: (781) 237–0336; Fax: (781) 237–0336;
Email: gcfmscholarship@aol.com
Web: www.gcfm.org/Education/Scholarships/GCFMScholarships.aspx

Summary: To provide financial assistance to residents of Massachusetts interested in working on an undergraduate or graduate degree in a field related to environmental science at a college in any state.

Eligibility: Open to high school seniors, undergraduates, and graduate students who have been residents of Massachusetts for at least 1 year. Applicants must be working on or planning to work on a degree in a field related to environmental science, including floriculture, landscape design, horticulture, forestry, agronomy, city planning, land management, botany, or biology. They must have a GPA of 3.0 or higher. Along with their application, they must submit official transcripts; a brief essay about their goals, aspirations, and career plans; a list of their activities, including special honors and/or leadership positions; 3 letters of recommendation; and documentation of financial need.

Financial data: The stipend is $1,000.

Duration: 1 year.

Number awarded: 1 each year.

Deadline: February of each year.

1818 EVIE WOLLMAN MEMORIAL SCHOLARSHIP

Maryland Academy of Physician Assistants
Attn: Scholarships
P.O. Box 1726
Annapolis, MD 21404–1726
Phone: (888) 357–3360; Fax: (443) 283–4086
Web: www.mdapa.org/cme/Student.asp

Summary: To provide financial assistance to residents of Maryland who are enrolled in a physician assistant program in any state.

Eligibility: Open to residents of Maryland who are enrolled in the second year of a physician assistant program in any state. Applicants must be members of the Maryland Academy of Physician Assistants (MAPA) or have applied for membership. Along with their application, they must submit a 500–word essay on how their community service or volunteer experience has shaped them personally and how it has prepared them to become a physician assistant. Financial need is not considered in the selection process.

Financial data: A stipend is awarded (amount not specified).

Duration: 1 year.

Number awarded: 1 each year.

Deadline: August of each year.

1819 EXELON SCHOLARSHIPS

Society of Women Engineers
Attn: Scholarship Selection Committee
203 North LaSalle Street, Suite 1675
Chicago, IL 60601–1269
Phone: (312) 596–5223; (877) SWE–INFO; Fax: (312) 644–8557;
Email: scholarships@swe.org
Web: societyofwomenengineers.swe.org/index.php/scholarships

Summary: To provide financial assistance to women who will be entering college as freshmen and are interested in studying electrical or mechanical engineering or computer science.

Eligibility: Open to women who are entering college as freshmen with a GPA of 3.5 or higher. Applicants must be planning to enroll full time at an ABET–accredited 4–year college or university and major in computer science, electrical engineering, or mechanical engineering. Selection is based on merit.

Financial data: The stipend is $1,000.

Duration: 1 year.

Number awarded: 5 each year.

Deadline: May of each year.

1820 $$ EXXONMOBIL BERNARD HARRIS MATH AND SCIENCE SCHOLARSHIPS

Council of the Great City Schools
1301 Pennsylvania Avenue, N.W., Suite 702
Washington, DC 20004
Phone: (202) 393–2427; Fax: (202) 393–2400
Web: www.cgcs.org/Page/47

Summary: To provide financial assistance to African American and Hispanic high school seniors interested in studying science, technology, engineering, or mathematics (STEM) in college.

Eligibility: Open to African American and Hispanic seniors graduating from high schools in a district that is a member of the Council of the Great City Schools, a coalition of 65 of the nation's largest urban public school systems. Applicants must be planning to enroll full time at a 4–year college or university and major in a STEM field of study. They must have a GPA of 3.0 or higher. Along with their application, they must submit 1–page essays on 1) how mathematics and science education has impacted their lives so far; and 2) why they have chosen to prepare for a career in a STEM field. Selection is based on those essays; academic achievement; extracurricular activities, community service, or other experiences that demonstrate commitment to a career in a STEM field; and 3 letters of recommendation. Financial need is not considered. Males and females are judged separately.

Financial data: The stipend is $5,000.

Duration: 1 year; nonrenewable.

Number awarded: 4 each year: an African American male and female and an Hispanic male and female.

Deadline: May of each year.

1821 $ F. ATLEE DODGE MAINTENANCE SCHOLARSHIP

Alaska Airmen's Association
Attn: Scholarship Committee
4200 Floatplane Drive
Anchorage, AK 99502
Phone: (907) 245–1251; (800) 464–7030; Fax: (907) 245–1259;
Email: info@alaskaairmen.org
Web: www.alaskaairmen.org/index.php?pagename=scholarships

Summary: To provide financial assistance to residents of Alaska who are interested in attending a school in any state to prepare for a professional career in aircraft maintenance.

Eligibility: Open to residents of Alaska who are currently enrolled in an aviation–related program at an accredited college, university, trade school, or approved training center. Applicants must have completed at least 25% of the work for an airframe and powerplant (A&P) certificate and have a GPA of 3.0 or higher. They must intend to use their training to work in Alaska. Along with their application, they must submit essays of 250 words or less on each of the following: 1) why they are applying for this scholarship and how the funds will increase their ability to achieve their career goals; 2) their 5–year career plan; 3) why they selected their current degree field or training goal; 4) their monthly income and expenses; and 5) why they are the best candidate for this award.

Financial data: The stipend is $2,500. Funds are disbursed directly to the recipient's educational institution or training facility for payment of tuition, specified laboratories, books, or training manuals only.

Duration: Funds must be used within 2 years.

Number awarded: 1 or more each year.

Deadline: March of each year.

1822 F. CARROLL SARGENT SCHOLARSHIP

Garden Club Federation of Massachusetts, Inc.
Attn: Scholarship Secretary
219 Washington Street
Wellesley Hills, MA 02481
Phone: (781) 237–0336; Fax: (781) 237–0336;
Email: gcfmscholarship@aol.com
Web: www.gcfm.org/Education/Scholarships/GCFMScholarships.aspx

Summary: To provide financial assistance to residents of Massachusetts interested in working on an undergraduate or graduate degree in a field related to horticulture at a college in any state.

Eligibility: Open to high school seniors, undergraduates, and graduate students who have been residents of Massachusetts for at least 1 year. Applicants must be working on or planning to work on a degree in a field related to horticulture, including floriculture, landscape design, conservation, forestry, agronomy, city planning, environmental studies, land management, botany, or biology. They must have a GPA of 3.0 or higher. Along with their application, they must submit official transcripts; a brief essay about their goals, aspirations, and career plans; a list of their activities, including special honors and/or leadership positions; 3 letters of recommendation; and documentation of financial need.

Financial data: The stipend is $1,000.

Duration: 1 year.

Number awarded: 1 each year.

Deadline: February of each year.

1823 FARM CREDIT SERVICES OF HAWAII SCHOLARSHIP

Farm Credit Services of Hawaii, ACA
Attn: Branch Manager, Hilo
988 Kinoole Street
P.O. Box 5059
Hilo, HI 96720
Phone: (808) 961–3781; (800) 894–4996, ext. 0 (within HI); Fax: (808) 961–5494
Web: www.hawaiifarmcredit.com/scholarship.html

Summary: To provide financial assistance to high school seniors and graduates in Hawaii who are interested in majoring in agriculture at a college in any state.

Eligibility: Open to graduating seniors and recent graduates of high schools in Hawaii who are attending or planning to attend an accredited college, university, or trade school in any state. Applicants must intend to work on an undergraduate degree in a field related to agriculture. Along with their application, they must submit 2 letters of recommendation, a transcript, a short essay (up to 500 words) on "What future does Tropical Agriculture have for the young," and a list of agriculturally–related activities (e.g., 4–H, FFA) in which they have been involved. Selection is based on recommendations, academics, the essay, and agricultural activities.

Financial data: The stipend is $1,500.

Duration: 1 year; nonrenewable.

Number awarded: 2 each year.

Deadline: May of each year.

1824 $ FARM KIDS FOR COLLEGE SCHOLARSHIPS

National Farmers
Attn: National Scholarship Coordinator
528 Billy Sunday Road, Suite 100
Ames, IA 50010
Phone: (800) 247–2110, ext. 4670;
Email: hbergren@nfo.org
Web: www.nfo.org/Scholarships/Default.aspx

Summary: To provide financial assistance to high school seniors who plan to study agriculture in college.

Eligibility: Open to high school seniors to plan to major in an agricultural field at an accredited college or university. Applicants must submit an essay of 850 to 1,200 words on a topic that changes annually but relates to agriculture; recently, students were invited to write on how marketing production with other farmers and ranchers can improve prices for grain, dairy, and livestock, and how niche marketing, risk management, and price negotiation can impact the prices that producers receive. Selection is based on plans for the future, involvement in agriculture, high school activities and honors, and community activities and honors; financial need is not considered.

Financial data: The stipend is $1,000.

Duration: 1 year.

Number awarded: 3 each year.

Deadline: March of each year.

1825 $ FEDERATED GARDEN CLUBS OF CONNECTICUT SCHOLARSHIP

Federated Garden Clubs of Connecticut, Inc.
14 Business Park Drive
P.O. Box 854
Branford, CT 06405–0854
Phone: (203) 488–5528; Fax: (203) 488–5528;
Email: info@ctgardenclubs.org
Web: www.ctgardenclubs.org/scholarship.html

Summary: To provide financial assistance to Connecticut residents who are interested in majoring in horticulture–related fields at a Connecticut college or graduate school.

Eligibility: Open to legal residents of Connecticut who are studying at a college or university in the state in agronomy, botany, city planning, conservation, environmental studies, floriculture, forestry, horticulture, land management, landscape design, plant pathology, or related subjects. They must be entering their junior or senior year of college or be a graduate student, have a GPA of 3.0 or higher, and be able to demonstrate financial need.

Financial data: Stipends are generally about $3,000 each. Funds are sent to the recipient's school in 2 equal installments.

Duration: 1 year.

Number awarded: Varies each year; recently, 2 of these scholarships were awarded.

Deadline: June of each year.

1826 $ FEDERATED GARDEN CLUBS OF MARYLAND SCHOLARSHIP

Federated Garden Clubs of Maryland, Inc.
Attn: Scholarship Chair
4915 Greenspring Avenue
Baltimore, MD 21209–4542
Phone: (410) 396–4842;
Email: office@fgcofmd.org
Web: www.fgcofmd.org/SCHOLARSHIP_PROGRAMS.html

Summary: To provide financial assistance to Maryland residents who are interested in working on an undergraduate or graduate degree in a field related to horticulture or landscape design at a school in any state.

Eligibility: Open to Maryland residents who are full–time juniors, seniors, or master's degree students at an accredited college or university in the United States. Applicants must be interested in working on a degree in agricultural education, agronomy, biology, botany, city (urban and rural) planning, economics, environmental concerns, environmental conservation (including environmental engineering and environmental law), floriculture, forestry, habitat or forest systems ecology, horticulture, landscape design, land management, plant pathology, wildlife science, or an allied subject. They must have a GPA of 3.25 or higher and be legal residents of the United States.

Financial data: Stipends range up to $2,500.

Duration: 1 year.

Number awarded: 1 or more each year.

Deadline: April of each year.

1827 FEDERATED GARDEN CLUBS OF NEW YORK STATE SCHOLARSHIPS

Federated Garden Clubs of New York State
104 F Covent Gardens
Guilderland, NY 12084
Phone: (518) 869–6311; Fax: fgcnys@nycap.rr.com
Web: www.gardencentral.org/fgcny/fgcnysscholarship

Summary: To provide financial assistance to residents of New York majoring in fields related to gardening at colleges in any state.

Eligibility: Open to residents of New York completing their first or second year at a 2– or 4–year college or university in any state. Applicants must be studying horticulture, floriculture, landscape design, botany, plant pathology, forestry, conservation, agronomy, environmental studies, city planning, land management, wildlife science, or a related field. They must have a GPA of 2.5 or higher. Along with their application, they must submit a 250–word essay on why they chose their course of study and what they expect their overall contribution to that field will be. Selection is based on that essay, academic record, financial need, commitment to career, and involvement in college and community activities.

Financial data: The stipend is $1,000.

Duration: 1 year.

Number awarded: 2 each year.

Deadline: February of each year.

1828 FEEDING TOMORROW FRESHMAN SCHOLARSHIPS

Institute of Food Technologists
Attn: Feeding Tomorrow Office
525 West Van Buren, Suite 1000
Chicago, IL 60607
Phone: (312) 782–8424; Fax: (312) 782–8348;
Email: info@ift.org
Web: www.ift.org/knowledge–center/learn–about–food–science.aspx

Summary: To provide financial assistance to students who are high school seniors or college freshmen and interested in studying food science or food technology.

Eligibility: Open to graduating high school seniors and current college freshmen interested in working full time on a bachelor's degree in food science or food technology at an educational institution in the United States or Canada. Applicants must have a GPA of 3.0 or higher. Along with their application, they must submit a 250–word list of academic and professional awards, honors, and scholarships they have received at the high school and college freshman level; a 250–word outline of their employment experience, including internships and part–time or full–time work; a 250–word list of community service and extracurricular activities within clubs and organizations; a 250–word list of honors classes and/or advanced placement courses and scores; a 250–word essay on what they feel distinguishes them among other candidates for this scholarship; and a 300–word essay on why they want to pursue an education in food science and the aspects of food science they find most interesting. Financial need is not considered in the selection process.

Financial data: The stipend is $1,000 per year.

Duration: 1 year; recipients may reapply.

Number awarded: 15 each year.

Deadline: March of each year.

1829 $$ FERROUS METALLURGY EDUCATION TODAY (FEMET) SCHOLARSHIPS

Association for Iron & Steel Technology
Attn: AIST Foundation
186 Thorn Hill Road
Warrendale, PA 15086–7528
Phone: (724) 814–3044; Fax: (724) 814–3001;
Email: lwharrey@aist.org
Web: www.aistfoundation.org/scholarships/scholarships.htm

Summary: To provide financial assistance and work experience to college juniors working on a degree in metallurgy or materials sciences engineering.

Eligibility: Open to full–time students entering their junior year in a metallurgy or materials science program at a college or university in North America (Canada, Mexico, and the United States). Applicants must have a GPA of 3.0 or higher and a demonstrated interest in the iron and steel industry. They must be available for employment at a steel company during the summer after their junior year; students unable to accept an internship will not be considered. Along with their application, they must submit a 2–page essay on their professional goals, why they are interested in a career in the steel industry, and how their skills could be applied to enhance the industry. Selection is based on steel

industry interest (35%), letters of recommendation (30%), grades (20%), and extracurricular activities (15%).
Financial data: The program provides a stipend of $5,000 for the junior year, a paid internship during the following summer, and a stipend of $5,000 for the senior year.
Duration: 2 years.
Number awarded: 10 each year.
Deadline: March of each year.

1830 $ FESTIVAL OF TREES SCHOLARSHIP FUND

New Hampshire Charitable Foundation
37 Pleasant Street
Concord, NH 03301–4005
Phone: (603) 225–6641; (800) 464–6641; Fax: (603) 225–1700;
Email: info@nhcf.org
Web: www.nhcf.org/page.aspx?pid=472
Summary: To provide financial assistance to students, preferably those from New Hampshire, working on a degree in natural resources or horticulture at a school in that state.
Eligibility: Open to students who have completed at least 1 semester of work on a degree in natural resources or horticulture at a college or university in New Hampshire. Applicants must have a GPA of 2.5 or higher, be able to demonstrate involvement in school and community activities, and have some work experience that supports their career goals and aspirations in life. Preference is given to residents of the seacoast region of New Hampshire. Financial need is not considered in the selection process.
Financial data: The stipend ranges up to $2,000.
Duration: 1 year.
Number awarded: 1 or more each year.
Deadline: April of each year.

1831 $ FFTA SCHOLARSHIP COMPETITION

Summary: To provide financial assistance for college to students interested in a career in flexography.
See Listing #1224.

1832 $ FLEMING/BLASZCAK SCHOLARSHIP

Society of Plastics Engineers
Attn: SPE Foundation
13 Church Hill Road
Newtown, CT 06740
Phone: (203) 740–5447; Fax: (203) 775–1157;
Email: foundation@4spe.org
Web: www.4spe.org/spe–foundation
Summary: To provide financial assistance to Mexican American undergraduate and graduate students who have a career interest in the plastics industry.
Eligibility: Open to full–time undergraduate and graduate students of Mexican descent who are enrolled at a 4–year college or university. Applicants must be U.S. citizens or legal residents. They must be majoring in or taking courses that would be beneficial to a career in the plastics or polymer industry (e.g., plastics engineering, packaging, polymer sciences, chemistry, physics, chemical engineering, mechanical engineering, industrial engineering). Along with their application, they must submit 3 letters of recommendation; a high school and/or college transcript; a 1– to 2–page statement telling why they are applying for the scholarship, their qualifications, and their educational and career goals in the plastics industry; their employment history; a list of current and past school activities and community activities and honors; information on their financial need; and documentation of their Mexican heritage.
Financial data: The stipend is $2,000. Funds are paid directly to the recipient's school.
Duration: 1 year.
Number awarded: 1 each year.
Deadline: February of each year.

1833 $ FLEXIBLE PACKAGING INDUSTRY SCHOLARSHIP/INTERNSHIP PROGRAM

Flexible Packaging Association
Attn: Scholarship/Internship Program
971 Corporate Boulevard, Suite 403
Linthicum, MD 21090
Phone: (410) 694–0800; Fax: (410) 694–0900;
Email: fpa@flexpack.org
Web: www.flexpack.org
Summary: To provide financial assistance and work experience to students interested in preparing for a career in the flexible packaging industry.
Eligibility: Open to students working on an associate, bachelor's, or master's degree to prepare for a career in the packaging converting industry. Applicants must have completed at least 24 credit hours (including at least 9 credits in packaging–related course work) with a GPA of 2.7 or higher. They must have been accepted as an intern for a participating flexible packaging manufacturer. Along with their application, they must submit a 500–word essay on how they expect to apply what they have learned in their course work to an internship with a flexible packaging converter. Financial need is not considered in the selection process.
Financial data: The scholarship stipend is $3,000. For the internship, participants receive a competitive salary.
Duration: The scholarship is for 1 year; the internship is for 1 summer.
Number awarded: 10 each year.
Deadline: February of each year.

1834 FLORENCE MARGARET HARVEY MEMORIAL SCHOLARSHIP

American Foundation for the Blind
Attn: Scholarship Committee
2 Penn Plaza, Suite 1102
New York, NY 10121
Phone: (212) 502–7661; (800) AFB–LINE; Fax: (888) 545–8331;
Email: afbinfo@afb.net
Web: www.afb.org/Section.asp?Documentid=2962
Summary: To provide financial assistance to blind undergraduate and graduate students who wish to study in the field of rehabilitation and/or education of the blind.
Eligibility: Open to legally blind juniors, seniors, or graduate students. U.S. citizenship is required. Applicants must be studying in the field of rehabilitation and/or education of visually impaired and blind persons. Along with their application, they must submit 200–word essays on 1) their past and recent achievements and accomplishments; 2) their intended field of study and why they have chosen it; and 3) the role their visual impairment has played in shaping their life. Financial need is considered in the selection process.
Financial data: The stipend is $1,000.
Duration: 1 year.
Number awarded: 1 each year.
Deadline: April of each year.

1835 $ FLORIDA CHAPTER OF THE WILDLIFE SOCIETY SCHOLARSHIP

Wildlife Society–Florida Chapter
c/o Holly Ober, Scholarship Committee Chair
North Florida Research and Education Center
155 Research Road
Quincy, FL 32351
Phone: (850) 875–7150;
Email: holly.ober@ufl.edu
Web: fltws.org/scholarships.php
Summary: To provide financial assistance to upper–division students working on a degree in wildlife ecology and/or management at a Florida college.
Eligibility: Open to students entering their junior or senior year at a 4–year college or university in Florida. Applicants must be interested in preparing for a career in wildlife ecology and/or management. They must have a GPA of 2.5 or higher. Along with their application, they must submit a letter describing their professional goals and financial need. Selection is based on goals as expressed in the letter, extracurricular activities, demonstrated leadership, professional potential, and financial need.
Financial data: The stipend is $2,000.
Duration: 1 year.
Number awarded: 1 each year.
Deadline: November of each year.

1836 FLORIDA CHAPTER UNDERGRADUATE SCHOLARSHIPS

American Public Works Association–Florida Chapter
c/o Russell Ketchem, Scholarship Chair
City of Pompano Beach
1190 N.E. Third Avenue

Pompano Beach, FL 33060
Phone: (954) 913–3442;
Email: Russell.Ketchem@copbfl.com
Web: florida.apwa.net/resources/scholarships/79
Summary: To provide financial assistance to undergraduate students in Florida who are working on a degree in civil engineering.
Eligibility: Open to students who have earned at least 60 units at an ABET–accredited school in Florida. Applicants must be working on a bachelor's degree in civil engineering or a related field. Along with their application, they must submit a 2–page personal statement about their career goals and background, transcripts, and information on their financial situation.
Financial data: The stipend is $1,000.
Duration: 1 year.
Number awarded: Varies each year; recently, 3 of these scholarships were awarded.
Deadline: March of each year.

1837 $ FLORIDA FEDERATION OF GARDEN CLUBS SCHOLARSHIPS

Florida Federation of Garden Clubs, Inc.
Attn: Scholarship Chair
1400 South Denning Drive
Winter Park, FL 32789–5662
Phone: (407) 647–7016; Fax: (407) 647–5479;
Email: ffgc@earthlink.net
Web: ffgc.org/awards–scholarships/scholarships/index.html
Summary: To provide financial assistance to Florida residents who are interested in working on an undergraduate or graduate degree in a field related to gardening at a college in the state.
Eligibility: Open to residents of Florida who are graduating high school seniors or students already enrolled full time as sophomores, juniors, seniors, or graduate students at a college or university in the state. Applicants must be working on a degree in agriculture, biology, botany, city planning, conservation, ecology, forestry, horticulture, landscape design, or an allied subject. They must have a GPA of 3.0 or higher and be able to demonstrate financial need. U.S. citizenship is required.
Financial data: The stipend ranges from $1,000 to $2,000. The funds are sent directly to the recipient's school.
Duration: 1 year.
Number awarded: 1 or more each year.
Deadline: April of each year.

1838 $ FLORIDA PUBLIC TRANSPORTATION ASSOCIATION SCHOLARSHIP

American Public Transportation Association
Attn: American Public Transportation Foundation
1666 K Street, N.W., Suite 1100
Washington, DC 20006
Phone: (202) 496–4803; Fax: (202) 496–4323;
Email: yconley@apta.com
Web: www.aptfd.org/work/scholarship.htm
Summary: To provide financial assistance to undergraduate and graduate students from Florida who are preparing for a career in public transportation.
Eligibility: Open to college sophomores, juniors, seniors, and graduate students at colleges and universities in Florida who are preparing for a career in the transit industry. Any member organization of the Florida Public Transportation Association (FPTA) can nominate and sponsor candidates for this scholarship. Nominees must be enrolled in a fully–accredited institution, have and maintain at least a 3.0 GPA, and be either employed by or demonstrate a strong interest in entering the public transportation industry. They must submit a 1,000–word essay on the topic, "In what segment of the public transportation industry will you make a career and why?" Selection is based on demonstrated interest in the transit field as a career, need for financial assistance, academic achievement, essay content and quality, and involvement in extracurricular citizenship and leadership activities.
Financial data: The stipend is $2,500.
Duration: 1 year; may be renewed.
Number awarded: 1 each year.
Deadline: May of each year.

1839 $ FORD MOTOR COMPANY SCHOLARSHIPS

American Indian College Fund
Attn: Scholarship Department
8333 Greenwood Boulevard
Denver, CO 80221
Phone: (303) 426–8900; (800) 776–FUND; Fax: (303) 426–1200;
Email: scholarships@collegefund.org
Web: www.collegefund.org/content/full_circle_scholarships_listings
Summary: To provide financial assistance to Native American college students who are majoring in designated fields at mainstream colleges and universities, especially those in Michigan.
Eligibility: Open to American Indians and Alaska Natives who have proof of enrollment or descendancy and are enrolled full time in a bachelor's degree program at a mainstream institution; first preference is given to students at colleges and universities in Michigan. Applicants must have a GPA of 3.0 or higher and be able to demonstrate exceptional academic achievement or financial need. They must have declared a major in accounting, computer science, engineering, finance, marketing, or operations management. Applications are available only online and include required essays on specified topics. U.S. citizenship is required.
Financial data: The stipend is $3,000 per year.
Duration: 1 year; may be renewed.
Number awarded: Varies each year.
Deadline: May of each year.

1840 FORD MOTOR COMPANY SWE UNDERGRADUATE SCHOLARSHIPS

Society of Women Engineers
Attn: Scholarship Selection Committee
203 North LaSalle Street, Suite 1675
Chicago, IL 60601–1269
Phone: (312) 596–5223; (877) SWE–INFO; Fax: (312) 644–8557;
Email: scholarships@swe.org
Web: societyofwomenengineers.swe.org/index.php/scholarships
Summary: To provide financial assistance to undergraduate women majoring in designated engineering specialties.
Eligibility: Open to women who are entering their sophomore or junior year at a 4–year ABET–accredited college or university. Applicants must be working full time on a degree in automotive, electrical, industrial, or mechanical engineering and have a GPA of 3.5 or higher. Selection is based on merit and leadership potential.
Financial data: The stipend is $1,000.
Duration: 1 year.
Number awarded: 3 each year: 1 to a sophomore and 2 to juniors.
Deadline: February of each year.

1841 $ FORD MOTOR COMPANY TRIBAL COLLEGE SCHOLARSHIP

American Indian College Fund
Attn: Scholarship Department
8333 Greenwood Boulevard
Denver, CO 80221
Phone: (303) 426–8900; (800) 776–FUND; Fax: (303) 426–1200;
Email: scholarships@collegefund.org
Web: www.collegefund.org/content/full_circle_scholarships_listings
Summary: To provide financial assistance to Native Americans who are attending a Tribal College or University (TCU) and majoring in specified fields.
Eligibility: Open to American Indians or Alaska Natives who are enrolled full time at an eligible TCU; first preference is given to students at TCUs in Michigan. Applicants must have a GPA of 3.0 or higher and be able to demonstrate exceptional academic achievement or financial need. They must have declared a major in mathematics, science, engineering, business, teacher training, or environmental science. Applications are available only online and include required essays on specified topics. U.S. citizenship is required.
Financial data: The stipend is $3,000.
Duration: 1 year.
Number awarded: 1 or more each year.
Deadline: May of each year.

1842 FORREST BASSFORD STUDENT AWARD

Summary: To provide financial assistance to students majoring in agricultural communications or related fields.
See Listing #1233.

1843 FORT DETRICK POST SAME SCHOLARSHIPS

Summary: To provide financial assistance to students working on a bachelor's degree in specified fields related to architecture or engineering, especially at colleges and universities in the service area of the Fort Detrick Post of the American Society of Military Engineers (SAME).

See Listing #1234.

1844 FORT WORTH POST SAME SCHOLARSHIP

Summary: To provide financial assistance to engineering, architecture, and science college and graduate students, especially those at colleges and universities in Texas.

See Listing #1235.

1845 FORUM FOR CONCERNS OF MINORITIES SCHOLARSHIPS

American Society for Clinical Laboratory Science
Attn: Forum for Concerns of Minorities
2025 M Street, N.W., Suite 800
Washington, DC 20036
Phone: (202) 367–1174;
Email: ascls@ascls.org
Web: www.ascls.org/?page=Awards_FCM

Summary: To provide financial assistance to minority students in clinical laboratory scientist and clinical laboratory technician programs.

Eligibility: Open to minority students who are enrolled in a program in clinical laboratory science, including clinical laboratory science/medical technology (CLS/MT) and clinical laboratory technician/medical laboratory technician (CLT/MLT). Applicants must be able to demonstrate financial need. Membership in the American Society for Clinical Laboratory Science is encouraged but not required.

Financial data: Stipends depend on the need of the recipients and the availability of funds.

Duration: 1 year.

Number awarded: 2 each year: 1 to a CLS/MT student and 1 to a CLT/MLT student.

Deadline: March of each year.

1846 FRAN JOHNSON NON–TRADITIONAL SCHOLARSHIP

American Floral Endowment
1601 Duke Street
Alexandria, VA 22314
Phone: (703) 838–5211; Fax: (703) 838–5212;
Email: afe@endowment.org
Web: endowment.org/floriculture–scholarshipsinternships.html

Summary: To provide financial assistance to nontraditional undergraduate students interested in studying horticulture.

Eligibility: Open to undergraduate students interested in working on a degree in horticulture (with a specific interest in bedding plants or other floral crops). Applicants must be reentering the academic setting after an absence of at least 5 years. They must be U.S. or Canadian citizens or permanent residents and have a GPA of 2.0 or higher. Along with their application, they must submit a statement describing their career goals and the academic, work–related, and/or life experiences that support those goals. Financial need is considered in the selection process.

Financial data: The stipend varies each year; recently, it was $1,050.

Duration: 1 year.

Number awarded: 1 each year.

Deadline: April of each year.

1847 $$ FRAN O'SULLIVAN WOMEN IN LENOVO LEADERSHIP (WILL) SCHOLARSHIP

Society of Women Engineers
Attn: Scholarship Selection Committee
203 North LaSalle Street, Suite 1675
Chicago, IL 60601–1269
Phone: (312) 596–5223; (877) SWE–INFO; Fax: (312) 644–8557;
Email: scholarships@swe.org
Web: societyofwomenengineers.swe.org/index.php/scholarships

Summary: To provide financial assistance to women working on an undergraduate or graduate degree in computer science or engineering.

Eligibility: Open to women who are entering full–time freshmen, sophomores, juniors, seniors, or graduate students at an ABET–accredited 4–year college or university. Applicants must be interested in studying computer science or engineering and have a GPA of 3.5 or higher (for entering freshmen) or 3.0 or higher (for all other students). Selection is based on merit.

Financial data: The stipend is $7,500. The award includes a travel grant for the recipient to attend the national conference of the Society of Women Engineers.

Duration: 1 year.

Number awarded: 1 each year.

Deadline: February of each year for continuing students; May of each year for entering freshmen.

1848 FRANCES W. HARRIS SCHOLARSHIP

New England Regional Black Nurses Association, Inc.
P.O. Box 190690
Boston, MA 02119
Phone: (617) 524–1951
Web: www.nerbna.org/org/scholarships.html

Summary: To provide financial assistance to nursing students from New England who have contributed to the African American community.

Eligibility: Open to residents of the New England states who are enrolled full time in a NLN–accredited generic diploma, associate, or bachelor's nursing program in any state. Applicants must have at least 1 full year of school remaining. Along with their application, they must submit a 3–page essay that covers their career aspirations in the nursing profession; how they have contributed to the African American or other communities of color in such areas as work, volunteering, church, or community outreach; an experience that has enhanced their personal and/or professional growth; and any financial hardships that may hinder them from completing their education.

Financial data: A stipend is awarded (amount not specified).

Duration: 1 year.

Number awarded: 1 or more each year.

Deadline: February of each year.

1849 $ FRANCIS H. MOFFITT MEMORIAL SCHOLARSHIP

American Society for Photogrammetry and Remote Sensing
Attn: Scholarship Administrator
5410 Grosvenor Lane, Suite 210
Bethesda, MD 20814–2160
Phone: (301) 493–0290, ext. 101; Fax: (301) 493–0208;
Email: scholarships@asprs.org
Web: www.asprs.org/Awards–and–Scholarships

Summary: To provide financial assistance to undergraduate and graduate students interested in a program of study to prepare for a career in the geospatial mapping profession.

Eligibility: Open to students planning to enroll or currently enrolled in an upper–division or graduate program at an accredited college or university in the United States or Canada. Applicants must be working on a degree in surveying or photogrammetry leading to a career in the geospatial mapping profession. Along with their application, they must submit a 2–page statement describing their educational and/or research goals that relate to the advancement of surveying, photogrammetry, and related geospatial information technologies and the applications of those technologies. Financial need is not considered in the selection process.

Financial data: The stipend is $4,000. A 1–year student or associate membership in the American Society for Photogrammetry and Remote Sensing (ASPRS) is also provided.

Duration: 1 year.

Number awarded: 1 each year.

Deadline: October of each year.

1850 $ FRANCIS M. KEVILLE MEMORIAL SCHOLARSHIP

Construction Management Association of America
Attn: CMAA Foundation
7926 Jones Branch Drive, Suite 800
McLean, VA 22101–3303
Phone: (703) 356–2622; Fax: (703) 356–6388;
Email: foundation@cmaanet.org
Web: www.cmaafoundation.org/scholarships/application–process

Summary: To provide financial assistance to minority and female undergraduate and graduate students working on a degree in construction management.

Eligibility: Open to women and members of minority groups who are enrolled as full–time undergraduate or graduate students. Applicants must have completed at least 1 year of study and have at least 1 full year remaining for a bachelor's or master's degree in construction management or a related field. Along with their application, they must submit essays on why they are interested in a career in construction management and why they should be awarded this scholarship. Selection is based on that essay (20%), academic performance (40%), recommendation of the faculty adviser (15%), and extracurricular activities (25%).
Financial data: The stipend is $3,000. Funds are disbursed directly to the student's university.
Duration: 1 year.
Number awarded: 1 each year.
Deadline: June of each year.

1851 FRANK AND BRENNIE MORGAN PRIZE

Mathematical Association of America
1529 18th Street, N.W.
Washington, DC 20036–1358
Phone: (202) 387–5200; (800) 741–9415; Fax: (202) 265–2384;
Email: maahq@maa.org
Web: www.maa.org/awards/morgan.html
Summary: To recognize and reward outstanding mathematical research papers by undergraduate students.
Eligibility: Open to students at colleges and universities in Canada, Mexico, and the United States and its possessions. Either the student or a professor may submit a nomination that consists of a single research paper or several papers. The paper or papers must be submitted while the student is an undergraduate, not after the student's graduation. Publication of the research is not required. Selection is based on the quality of completed research projects in mathematics.
Financial data: The prize is $1,200.
Duration: The prize is awarded annually.
Number awarded: 1 each year.
Deadline: Nominations must be submitted by June of each year.

1852 FRANK L. DAUTRIEL MEMORIAL SCHOLARSHIP FUND

Louisiana Environmental Health Association
Attn: Awards Chair
P.O. Box 2661
Baton Rouge, LA 70821
Phone: (225) 219–3392;
Email: Claudia.Richard@la.gov
Web: www.leha.net/leha/awards.asp
Summary: To provide financial assistance to undergraduate and graduate students from Louisiana who are working on a degree in a field related to environmental health.
Eligibility: Open to residents of Louisiana who are enrolled full time in an undergraduate or graduate program in environmental health, environmental science, environmental engineering, or public health. Applicants must have a GPA of 2.75 or higher and be able to demonstrate financial need. Along with their application, they must submit a short summary of their professional goals and their reasons for preparing for a career in environmental health.
Financial data: The stipend is $1,000.
Duration: 1 year.
Number awarded: 2 each year: 1 to an undergraduate and 1 to a graduate student.
Deadline: October of each year.

1853 $ FRANK LANZA MEMORIAL SCHOLARSHIPS

Phi Theta Kappa
Attn: Scholarship Programs Department
1625 Eastover Drive
Jackson, MS 39211
Phone: (601) 987–5741; (800) 946–9995; Fax: (601) 984–3550;
Email: lanza@ptk.org
Web: www.ptkfoundation.org/become–a–member/scholarships/lanza
Summary: To provide financial assistance to community college students who are working on an associate degree in registered nursing, respiratory care, or emergency medical services.
Eligibility: Open to full–time students, part–time students, and international students who have completed at least 50% of the course work for an associate degree in registered nursing, respiratory care, or emergency medical services at an accredited community college. Pre–major students and certificate students are not eligible. Applicants must have a GPA of 3.0 or higher and be able to demonstrate financial need.
Financial data: The stipend is $2,500.
Duration: 1 year.
Number awarded: Up to 20 each year.
Deadline: March of each year.

1854 $ FRANK T. MARTIN LEADERSHIP SCHOLARSHIP

Conference of Minority Transportation Officials
Attn: National Scholarship Program
1875 I Street, N.W., Suite 500
Washington, DC 20006
Phone: (703) 234–4072; Fax: (202) 318–0364
Web: www.comto.org/?page=Scholarships
Summary: To provide financial assistance to undergraduate and graduate minority students working on a degree in transportation or a related field.
Eligibility: Open to full–time undergraduate and graduate students who are working on a degree in transportation, engineering, planning, or a related discipline. They must be able to demonstrate leadership and active commitment to community service. Along with their application, they must submit a cover letter with a 500–word statement of career goals. Financial need is not considered in the selection process. U.S. citizenship or legal resident status is required.
Financial data: The stipend is $3,000. Funds are paid directly to the recipient's college or university.
Duration: 1 year.
Number awarded: 1 each year.
Deadline: May of each year.

1855 FRED M. YOUNG SR./SAE ENGINEERING SCHOLARSHIP

Society of Automotive Engineers
Attn: Scholarships and Loans Program
400 Commonwealth Drive
Warrendale, PA 15096–0001
Phone: (724) 776–4790; (877) 606–7323; Fax: (724) 776–0790;
Email: scholarships@sae.org
Web: students.sae.org/awdscholar/scholarships/young
Summary: To provide financial support to high school seniors interested in studying engineering in college.
Eligibility: Open to U.S. citizens who intend to earn an ABET–accredited degree in engineering. Applicants must be high school seniors with a GPA of 3.75 or higher who rank in the 90th percentile in both mathematics and critical reading on the SAT or in the composite ACT. Selection is based on high school transcripts; SAT or ACT scores; school–related extracurricular activities; non–school related activities; academic honors, civic honors, and awards; and a 250–word essay on their goals, plans, experiences, and interests in mobility engineering. Financial need is not considered.
Financial data: The stipend is $1,000 per year.
Duration: 1 year; may be renewed up to 3 additional years, provided the recipient maintains a GPA of 3.0 or higher.
Number awarded: 1 each year.
Deadline: January of each year.

1856 GABRIEL A. HARTL SCHOLARSHIP

Air Traffic Control Association
Attn: Scholarship Fund
1101 King Street, Suite 300
Alexandria, VA 22314
Phone: (703) 299–2430; Fax: (703) 299–2437;
Email: info@atca.org
Web: www.atca.org/ATCA–Scholarship
Summary: To provide financial assistance to students enrolled in an air traffic control program.
Eligibility: Open to half– or full–time students who are U.S. citizens, enrolled in a 2– or 4–year air traffic control program at an institution approved and/or listed by the Federal Aviation Administration (FAA) as directly supporting its college and training initiative. Applicants must be registered for at least 6 hours and be at least 30 semester or 45 quarter hours away from graduation. They must submit an essay, up to 500 words, on how their educational efforts will enhance their potential contribution to aviation. Financial need is considered in the selection process.

Financial data: The amount of the award depends on the availability of funds and the number, qualifications, and need of the applicants.
Duration: 1 year; may be renewed.
Number awarded: Varies each year; recently, 3 of these scholarships were awarded.
Deadline: April of each year.

1857 GARDEN CLUB COUNCIL OF WINSTON-SALEM AND FORSYTH COUNTY SCHOLARSHIP

Summary: To provide financial assistance to residents of North Carolina who are interested in working on an undergraduate degree in horticulture or landscape architecture at a school in the state.
See Listing #1240.

1858 $ GARDEN CLUB FEDERATION OF MAINE HORTICULTURE SCHOLARSHIP

Garden Club Federation of Maine
c/o Mary Blackstone, Scholarship Chair
5 Christian Ridge Road
Ellsworth, ME 04605
Email: Mary.Blackstone@uregina.ca
Web: www.mainegardenclubs.org/GCFM_Hort_Scholarship.html
Summary: To provide financial assistance to Maine residents who are upper-division or graduate students working on a degree in horticulture or a related field at a college in any state.
Eligibility: Open to juniors, seniors, and master's degree students who are residents of Maine enrolled at a college or university in any state. Applicants must be working on a degree in horticulture, floriculture, landscape design, conservation, forestry, botany, agronomy, plant pathology, environmental control, city planning, or other garden-related field. Along with their application, they must submit a 2-page personal letter discussing their goals, background, extracurricular activities, personal commitment, and financial need. Selection is based on aptitude in the field, academic record, character, avocational interest, vocational potential, and financial need.
Financial data: The stipend is $3,300.
Duration: 1 year.
Number awarded: 1 each year.
Deadline: February of each year.

1859 GARDEN CLUB FEDERATION OF PENNSYLVANIA SCHOLARSHIPS

Garden Club Federation of Pennsylvania
c/o Lee Ann Stine, Secretary
1525 Cedar Cliff Drive, Suite 103
Camp Hill, PA 17011-7775
Phone: (717) 737-8219; Fax: (717) 737-8219;
Email: GCFP2@aol.com
Web: www.pagardenclubs.org/scholarshipinfor.html
Summary: To provide financial assistance to residents of Pennsylvania who are interested in working on an undergraduate or graduate degree in a field related to horticulture at a college in any state.
Eligibility: Open to Pennsylvania residents who are sponsored by a Federated Garden Club. Special consideration is given to children, grandchildren, or legal dependents of club members. Applicants may be high school seniors, undergraduates, or graduate students who are enrolled or planning to enroll at a college or university in any state. They must be working on or planning to work on a degree in agriculture education, agronomy, biology, botany, city (urban or rural) planning, conservation, environmental control, floriculture, forestry, horticulture, land management, landscape architecture, plant pathology, wildlife science, or an allied field. Selection is based on academic record, character, initiative, personal recommendations, and financial need.
Financial data: The stipend is $1,000 per year.
Duration: 1 year; recipients may reapply, as long as they maintain their academic standing and financial need.
Number awarded: 6 each year.
Deadline: February of each year.

1860 $ GARDEN CLUB OF NEW JERSEY SCHOLARSHIPS

Garden Club of New Jersey
c/o Onnolee Allieri
552 Powerville Road
Boonton Township, NJ 07005-9440
Phone: (973) 335-8249;
Email: callieri@aol.com
Web: njclubs.esiteasp.com/gcnj/scholarships.nxg
Summary: To provide financial assistance to New Jersey residents interested in working on an undergraduate or graduate degree in a field related to gardening.
Eligibility: Open to residents of New Jersey who are high school seniors, undergraduates, or graduate students. Applicants must be studying or planning to study horticulture, floriculture, landscape design, botany, plant pathology, agronomy, environmental science, city planning, land management, or a related subject. Along with their application, they must submit a personal letter that discusses their goals, background, personal commitment to chosen field, and financial need. Selection is based on academic excellence, evidence of future contribution to the field of study, extracurricular activities, work experience, academic honors, and financial need.
Financial data: Stipends range from $250 to $3,000.
Duration: 1 year.
Number awarded: Varies each year.
Deadline: February of each year.

1861 $ GARDEN CLUB OF NORTH CAROLINA SCHOLARSHIPS

Garden Club of North Carolina, Inc.
Attn: Scholarship Chair
4415 Beryl Road, Room 102
P.O. Box 33520
Raleigh, NC 27636-3520
Phone: (919) 834-0686; Fax: (919) 834-4571;
Email: theGCofNC1@aol.com
Web: www.gardenclubofnc.org/index.php/scholarships
Summary: To provide financial assistance to North Carolina residents working on an undergraduate or graduate degree in a field related to gardening.
Eligibility: Open to residents of North Carolina enrolled full time as juniors, seniors, or graduate students at public universities in the state. Applicants must be working on a degree in botany, environmental studies, forestry, landscape architecture, horticulture, recreation resources administration, or a related field. They must have a GPA of 3.0 or higher and be able to demonstrate financial need. U.S. citizenship is required.
Financial data: Stipends range up to $3,500 per year.
Duration: 1 year; may be renewed.
Number awarded: Varies each year; recently, 6 of these scholarships were awarded.
Deadline: February of each year.

1862 GARDEN CLUB OF OHIO SCHOLARSHIPS

Garden Club of Ohio, Inc.
c/o Cleo Lehman, Scholarship Committee Chair
2440 State Street N.E.
Canton, OH 44721-1036
Phone: (330) 608-0919;
Email: clehman6@neo.rr.com
Web: www.gardenclubofohio.org/gardenclubofohio/Scholarships.html
Summary: To provide financial assistance to Ohio residents who are working on an undergraduate or graduate degree in horticulture or related fields at a school in any state.
Eligibility: Open to residents of Ohio who are 1) first-year students at a 2-year institution; or 2) juniors, college seniors, or graduate students at a 4-year college or university in any state. Applicants must have a GPA of 3.0 or higher and be working on a degree in 1 of the following: agricultural education, agronomy, biology, botany, city (rural and urban) planning, environmental concerns, environmental conservation (including engineering and law), floriculture, forestry, habitat or forest systems ecology, horticulture, land management, landscape design, plant pathology, or an allied subject. Along with their application, they must submit a transcript, a completed financial aid form, a personal statement of financial need and career goals, a list of extracurricular activities, 3 letters of recommendation, and a recent photograph.
Financial data: Stipends are generally $1,000 or more per year.
Duration: 1 year.
Number awarded: Varies each year; recently, 17 of these scholarships, worth $21,300, were awarded.
Deadline: February of each year.

1863 $ GARDEN WRITERS ASSOCIATION FOUNDATION GENERAL SCHOLARSHIPS

Summary: To provide financial assistance to upper–division students working on a degree in horticulture, plant science, or journalism.

See Listing #1241.

1864 GARY WAGNER, K3OMI, SCHOLARSHIP

American Radio Relay League
Attn: ARRL Foundation
225 Main Street
Newington, CT 06111–1494
Phone: (860) 594–0397; Fax: (860) 594–0259;
Email: foundation@arrl.org
Web: www.arrl.org/scholarship–descriptions

Summary: To provide financial assistance to licensed radio amateurs, particularly from selected states, who are interested in working on a bachelor's degree in engineering.

Eligibility: Open to ARRL members who are licensed radio amateurs of novice class or higher. Preference is given to residents of Maryland, North Carolina, Tennessee, Virginia, or West Virginia who are enrolled at a 4–year college or university in those states. Applicants must be working on a bachelor's degree in engineering. Along with their application, they must submit an essay on the role amateur radio has played in their lives and provide documentation of financial need.

Financial data: The stipend is $1,000.

Duration: 1 year.

Number awarded: 1 each year.

Deadline: January of each year.

1865 $$ GATES MILLENNIUM SCHOLARS PROGRAM

Bill and Melinda Gates Foundation
P.O. Box 10500
Fairfax, VA 22031–8044
Phone: (877) 690–GMSP; Fax: (703) 205–2079
Web: www.gmsp.org

Summary: To provide financial assistance to outstanding low–income minority students, particularly those interested in majoring in specific fields in college.

Eligibility: Open to African Americans, Alaska Natives, American Indians, Hispanic Americans, and Asian Pacific Islander Americans who are graduating high school seniors with a GPA of 3.3 or higher. Principals, teachers, guidance counselors, tribal higher education representatives, and other professional educators are invited to nominate students with outstanding academic qualifications, particularly those likely to succeed in the fields of computer science, education, engineering, library science, mathematics, public health, or science. Nominees should have significant financial need and have demonstrated leadership abilities through participation in community service, extracurricular, or other activities. U.S. citizenship, nationality, or permanent resident status is required. Nominees must be planning to enter an accredited college or university as a full–time, degree–seeking freshman in the following fall.

Financial data: The program covers the cost of tuition, fees, books, and living expenses not paid for by grants and scholarships already committed as part of the recipient's financial aid package.

Duration: 4 years or the completion of the undergraduate degree, if the recipient maintains at least a 3.0 GPA.

Number awarded: 1,000 new scholarships are awarded each year.

Deadline: January of each year.

1866 $ G.C. MORRIS/PAUL RUPP MEMORIAL EDUCATIONAL TRUST

Automotive Parts and Services Association
425 East McCarty
P.O. Box 1049
Jefferson City, MO 65102
Phone: (800) 375–2968; Fax: (573) 635–3215;
Email: clrackers@suddenlink.net
Web: apsassociation.com/educational/scholarships/morris–rupp

Summary: To provide financial assistance to residents of designated states who are interested in attending college or technical school in any state to prepare for a career in the automotive aftermarket industry.

Eligibility: Open to residents of Arkansas, Colorado, Iowa, Kansas, Missouri, Nebraska, New Mexico, Oklahoma, Texas, and Wyoming who are graduating high school seniors, recent high school graduates, or holders of a GED certificate. Applicants must be enrolled or planning to enroll full time at an accredited college, university, or technical institute in any state to work on a degree or certificate in an automotive–related curriculum (e.g., engineering, computer science, accounting, marketing, business). Priority is given to students sponsored by a member of the Automotive Parts and Services Association (APSA). Along with their application, they must submit a 1–page essay on their career goals, how this scholarship will help them, and why they are considering a career in the automotive aftermarket. Financial need is not considered in the selection process.

Financial data: Stipends are $2,000 or $1,000. Funds are paid directly to the recipient's school.

Duration: 1 year; nonrenewable.

Number awarded: Varies each year; recently, 11 of these scholarships were awarded: 3 at $2,000 and 8 at $1,000.

Deadline: March of each year.

1867 $ GCA ZONE VI FELLOWSHIP IN URBAN FORESTRY

Garden Club of America
Attn: Scholarship Committee
14 East 60th Street, Third Floor
New York, NY 10022–1006
Phone: (212) 753–8287; Fax: (212) 753–0134;
Email: scholarships@gcamerica.org
Web: www2.gcamerica.org/scholarships.cfm

Summary: To provide financial assistance to upper–division and graduate students interested in working on a degree in a field related to urban forestry.

Eligibility: Open to advanced undergraduates and graduate students working on a degree in urban forestry, environmental studies, horticulture, forestry, or related courses of study with an emphasis on the urban forest. Applicants must be enrolled at a 4–year college or university in the United States. Along with their application, they must submit brief statements on their career goals and how this fellowship will benefit them and help to further their academic and career goals. Financial need is not considered in the selection process.

Financial data: The stipend is $4,000.

Duration: 1 year; may be renewed 1 additional year.

Number awarded: Varies each year; recently, 6 of these fellowships were awarded.

Deadline: January of each year.

1868 $ GENERAL AVIATION MANUFACTURERS ASSOCIATION SCHOLARSHIP

International Council of Air Shows
Attn: ICAS Foundation
750 Miller Drive, S.E., Suite F–3
Leesburg, VA 20175
Phone: (703) 779–8510; Fax: (703) 779–8511;
Email: scholarships@icasfoundation.org
Web: www.icasfoundation.org/scholarship–gama

Summary: To provide financial assistance to college students working on a degree in a field related to aviation.

Eligibility: Open to students who have completed at least 2 semesters of college with a major in a field related to aviation (e.g., professional pilot, maintenance or engineering, airport administration). Applicants must submit a 1–page essay on why they want to receive this scholarship, how the funds will be used, and their aviation career goals. Selection is based that essay, academic record, extracurricular and community participation, other activities that distinguish the applicants from their peers, and passion of their approach toward aviation career goals.

Financial data: The stipend is $2,000.

Duration: 1 year.

Number awarded: 1 or more each year.

Deadline: December of each year.

1869 $ GENERAL EMMETT PAIGE SCHOLARSHIPS

Armed Forces Communications and Electronics Association
Attn: AFCEA Educational Foundation
4400 Fair Lakes Court
Fairfax, VA 22033–3899
Phone: (703) 631–6138; (800) 336–4583, ext. 6138; Fax: (703) 631–4693;
Email: scholarshipsinfo@afcea.org
Web: www.afcea.org/education/scholarships/military

Summary: To provide financial assistance to veterans, military personnel, and their family members who are majoring in specified scientific fields in college.
Eligibility: Open to veterans, persons on active duty in the uniformed military services, and their spouses or dependents who are currently enrolled full time in an accredited 4–year college or university in the United States. Graduating high school seniors are not eligible, but veterans entering college as freshmen may apply. Spouses or dependents must be sophomores or juniors. Applicants must be U.S. citizens, be of good moral character, have demonstrated academic excellence, be motivated to complete a college education, and be working toward a degree in engineering (aerospace, computer, electrical, or systems), computer engineering technology, electronics engineering technology, computer network systems, mathematics, physics, information systems security, information systems management, technology management, computer science, or other field directly related to the support of U.S. intelligence enterprises or national security. They must have a GPA of 3.0 or higher. Along with their application, they must provide a copy of Discharge Form DD214, Certificate of Service, or facsimile of their current Department of Defense or Coast Guard Identification Card. Financial need is not considered in the selection process.
Financial data: The stipend is $2,500 per year.
Duration: 1 year; may be renewed.
Number awarded: Varies each year; recently, 5 of these scholarships were awarded.
Deadline: April of each year.

1870 GENERAL FEDERATION OF WOMEN'S CLUBS OF IOWA PRESIDENT'S SCHOLARSHIP

General Federation of Women's Clubs of Iowa
Attn: Scholarship Chair
3839 Merle Hay Road, Suite 201
Des Moines, IA 50310–1321
Phone: (515) 276–0510;
Email: gfwciowa@qwestoffice.net
Web: www.gfwciowa.org/id21.html
Summary: To provide financial assistance to high school seniors in Iowa who plan to study radiology technology at a college in the state.
Eligibility: Open to seniors graduating from high schools in Iowa and planning to enroll at a college or university in the state. Applicants must be planning to work on a degree in radiology technology. Along with their application, they must submit a personal letter about themselves and their family, reasons for applying, goals, and accomplishments; transcripts; letter of sponsorship from a local club member of the General Federation of Women's Clubs of Iowa; ACT or SAT scores; and information on their financial situation.
Financial data: The stipend is $1,000.
Duration: 1 year.
Number awarded: 1 each year.
Deadline: February of each year.

1871 $ GENERAL JOHN A. WICKHAM SCHOLARSHIPS

Armed Forces Communications and Electronics Association
Attn: AFCEA Educational Foundation
4400 Fair Lakes Court
Fairfax, VA 22033–3899
Phone: (703) 631–6138; (800) 336–4583, ext. 6138; Fax: (703) 631–4693;
Email: scholarshipsinfo@afcea.org
Web: www.afcea.org/education/scholarships/undergraduate/pub2.asp
Summary: To provide financial assistance to undergraduate students who are working full time on a degree in engineering or the sciences.
Eligibility: Open to full–time students entering their junior or senior year at an accredited degree–granting 4–year college or university in the United States. Applicants must be U.S. citizens working toward a degree in engineering (aerospace, chemical, computer, electrical, or systems), mathematics, physics, science or mathematics education, management information systems, technology management, computer science, or other field directly related to the support of U.S. intelligence enterprises or national security. They must have a GPA of 3.5 or higher. Selection is based on academic achievement, patriotism, and potential to contribute to the American workforce. Financial need is not considered.
Financial data: The stipend is $2,000.
Duration: 1 year; may be renewed.
Number awarded: Varies each year; recently, 8 of these scholarships were awarded.
Deadline: April of each year.

1872 $$ GENERATION GOOGLE SCHOLARSHIPS

Google Inc.
Attn: Scholarships
1600 Amphitheatre Parkway
Mountain View, CA 94043–8303
Phone: (650) 253–0000; Fax: (650) 253–0001;
Email: generationgoogle@google.com
Web: www.google.com
Summary: To provide financial assistance to members of underrepresented groups planning to work on a bachelor's degree in a computer–related field.
Eligibility: Open to high school seniors planning to enroll full time at a college or university in the United States or Canada. Applicants must be members of a group underrepresented in computer science: African Americans, Hispanics, American Indians, women, or people with a disability. They must be interested in working on a bachelor's degree in computer science, computer engineering, software engineering, or a related field. Selection is based on academic achievement (GPA of 3.2 or higher), leadership, commitment to and passion for computer science and technology through involvement in their community, and financial need.
Financial data: The stipend is $10,000 per year for U.S. students or $C5,000 for Canadian students.
Duration: 1 year; may be renewed for up to 3 additional years or until graduation, whichever comes first.
Number awarded: Varies each year.
Deadline: February of each year.

1873 GENEVIEVE CHRISTEN DISTINGUISHED UNDERGRADUATE STUDENT AWARD

American Dairy Science Association
Attn: Awards Coordinator
2441 Village Green Place
Champaign, IL 61822
Phone: (217) 356–5146, ext. 141; Fax: (217) 398–4119;
Email: adsa@adsa.org
Web: www.adsa.org/awarddesc.asp
Summary: To recognize and reward undergraduate students who have participated in dairy science activities.
Eligibility: Open to undergraduate students nominated by a faculty member at their institution; only 1 student may be nominated by a college or university each year. The nominator must be a member of the American Dairy Science Association (ADSA). Selection is based on demonstrated leadership ability (25 points), academic standing (15 points), interest and experience in the dairy industry (20 points), participation in ADSA Student Affiliate Division and local club activities (30 points), and a statement of their plans for the future (10 points).
Financial data: The award consists of a plaque and a $1,000 honorarium.
Duration: The award is presented annually.
Number awarded: 1 each year.
Deadline: Nominations must be submitted by December of each year.

1874 GEORGE AND LEOLA SMITH AWARD

David and Dovetta Wilson Scholarship Fund, Inc.
115–67 237th Street
Elmont, NY 11003–3926
Phone: (516) 285–4573;
Email: DDWSF4@aol.com
Web: www.wilsonfund.org/GeorgeLeolaSmith.html
Summary: To provide financial assistance to high school seniors who are interested in studying nursing or business in college.
Eligibility: Open to graduating high school seniors who plan to attend an accredited college or university and study business or nursing. Applicants must be U.S. citizens or permanent residents and have a GPA of 3.0 or higher. Along with their application, they must submit 3 letters of recommendation, high school transcripts, and an essay (up to 250 words) on "How My College Education Will Help Me Make a Positive Impact on My Community." Selection is based on community involvement, desire to prepare for a career in the field of business or nursing, and financial need.
Financial data: The stipend is $1,000.
Duration: 1 year; nonrenewable.
Number awarded: 1 each year.
Deadline: March of each year.

1875 GEORGE B. BOLAND NURSES TRAINING TRUST FUND

National Forty and Eight
Attn: Voiture Nationale
777 North Meridian Street
Indianapolis, IN 46204–1170
Phone: (317) 634–1804; Fax: (317) 632–9365;
Email: voiturenationale@msn.com
Web: www.fortyandeight.org/boland–trust–fund

Summary: To provide financial assistance to students working on an undergraduate degree in nursing.

Eligibility: Open to students working full time on an associate or bachelor's degree in nursing. Applications must be submitted to the local Voiture of the Forty and Eight in the county of the student's permanent residence; if the county organization has exhausted all of its nurses training funds, it will provide the student with an application for this scholarship. Students who are receiving assistance from the Eight and Forty Lung and Respiratory Disease Nursing Scholarship Program of the American Legion are not eligible. Financial need must be demonstrated.

Financial data: Grants may be used to cover tuition, required fees, room and board or similar living expenses, and other school–related expenses.

Number awarded: Varies each year; recently, 2,131 students received more than $1,100,000 in these scholarships.

Deadline: Deadline not specified.

1876 GEORGE CRAFTON MEMORIAL SCHOLARSHIP

Kentucky Energy and Environment Cabinet
Attn: Department for Natural Resources
Division of Conservation
375 Versailles Road
Frankfort, KY 40601
Phone: (502) 573–3080; Fax: (502) 573–1692;
Email: Angie.Wingfield@ky.gov
Web: conservation.ky.gov/Pages/Scholarships.aspx

Summary: To provide financial assistance to high school seniors in Kentucky who are interested in majoring in conservation or agriculture at a college in any state.

Eligibility: Open to seniors graduating from high schools in Kentucky and planning to attend a college or university in any state. Applicants must be interested in majoring in agriculture or a field related to the conservation of natural resources. Along with their application, they must submit an essay of 200 to 300 words on what they foresee as the future of agriculture and the important issues facing the industry. Selection is based on the essay (15 points), scholarship, including ACT score, GPA, and class rank (30 points), leadership (30 points), and extracurricular activities or jobs (25 points).

Financial data: The stipend is $1,000.

Duration: 1 year; nonrenewable.

Number awarded: 1 each year.

Deadline: February of each year.

1877 $$ GEORGE D. MILLER SCHOLARSHIP

National Fire Protection Association
Attn: NFPA Fire Safety Educational Memorial Fund
1 Batterymarch Park
Quincy, MA 02169–7471
Phone: (617) 984–7244; Fax: (617) 984–7110;
Email: cellis@nfpa.org
Web: www.nfpa.org

Summary: To provide financial assistance to undergraduate and graduate students enrolled in fire service or public administration programs.

Eligibility: Open to students at colleges and universities in the United States and Canada. Each college is invited to nominate up to 2 full– or part–time students working on a bachelor's or master's degree in fire service or public administration. Nominees must submit a letter describing their achievements, leadership abilities, volunteerism, interest in fire service or public administration, and specific long–range goals. Financial need is not considered in the selection process.

Financial data: The stipend is at least $5,000.

Duration: 1 year.

Number awarded: 1 each year.

Deadline: March of each year.

1878 $ GEORGE V. SOULE SCHOLARSHIP

Ruffed Grouse Society–Maine Chapter
c/o Bill Richards
6 Sturbridge Lane
Cumberland, ME 04021
Phone: (207) 829–4269;
Email: crichar2@maine.rr.com
Web: www.ruffedgrousemaine.com/scholarship.html

Summary: To provide financial assistance to residents of Maine enrolled or entering college in any state to major in a field related to conservation.

Eligibility: Open to residents of Maine who are entering or already enrolled in an undergraduate program at a college or university in any state. Applicants must be majoring or planning to major in wildlife conservation, forest management, conservation law enforcement, or a related field and have a GPA of 3.0 or higher. They must be preparing for a career in those fields, preferably as a practitioner in Maine. Along with their application, they must submit a brief essay that includes information about their educational, career, and personal goals, especially as they pertain to preparation for a profession in the fields of wildlife management, conservation law enforcement, forestry, or a related field, and how this scholarship will help them achieve those goals. Financial need is also considered in the selection process.

Financial data: The stipend is $3,000.

Duration: 1 year.

Number awarded: 2 each year.

Deadline: March of each year.

1879 GEORGIA ASSOCIATION OF PHYSICIAN ASSISTANTS STUDENT SCHOLARSHIPS

Georgia Association of Physician Assistants
1905 Woodstock Road, Suite 2150
Roswell, GA 30075
Phone: (770) 640–1920; (888) 811–GAPA; Fax: (770) 640–1095;
Email: info@gapa.net
Web: www.gapa.net/index.php/about–gapa/students/278–scholarships

Summary: To provide financial assistance to physician assistant students who have ties to Georgia.

Eligibility: Open to students who are members of the Georgia Association of Physician Assistants (GAPA) or have applied for membership. Applicants must have completed the didactic portion of an accredited physician assistant program in any state. Along with their application, they must submit 1) a 200–word essay on how they plan to impact the physician assistant profession after graduation; 2) a list of their extracurricular and volunteer activities in school, the community, and the profession; and 3) and 2 letters of reference. Financial need is not considered in the selection process.

Financial data: The stipend is $1,500.

Duration: 1 year.

Number awarded: 2 each year.

Deadline: June of each year.

1880 $ GEORGIA ASSOCIATION OF WATER PROFESSIONALS H2OPPORTUNITY UNDERGRADUATE SCHOLARSHIP

Georgia Association of Water Professionals
1655 Enterprise Way
Marietta, GA 30067
Phone: (770) 618–8690; Fax: (770) 618–8695;
Email: jdozier@gawp.org
Web: www.gawp.org

Summary: To provide financial assistance to undergraduate students who are residents of Georgia or attending college in the state and preparing for a career in the water profession.

Eligibility: Open to 1) residents of Georgia interested in attending a recognized college, university, or technical training school in any state; and 2) residents of other states attending an institution in Georgia. Applicants must be working on or planning to work on an undergraduate degree to prepare for a career in the water profession. Neither they nor their parents may have an individual membership (except a student membership) in the Georgia Association of Water Professionals (GAWP) and they may not work for a corporate or utility member of that association. Along with their application, they must submit a 1,500–word essay on their interest in and intended course of studies leading to a career in the water profession. Selection is based on that essay, academic record (measured by GPA and SAT/ACT scores), extracurricular and civic activities, and community service. Work experience or an internship in a water–related field is recommended but not required.

Financial data: The stipend is $2,000.

Duration: 1 year; recipients may reapply.
Number awarded: 1 each year.
Deadline: February of each year.

1881 GEORGIA BEEF INDUSTRY SCHOLARSHIP CHALLENGE

Georgia Junior Cattlemen's Association
100 Cattlemen's Drive
P.O. Box 27990
Macon, GA 31221
Phone: (478) 474–6560; (877) 444–BEEF; Fax: (478) 474–5732;
Email: katlin@gabeef.org
Web: www.gabeef.org/gjca/contest.html

Summary: To recognize and reward, with scholarships for college in any state, teams of high school juniors and seniors from southeastern states who demonstrate knowledge about the beef industry in a competition.
Eligibility: Open to teams of 3 members who are juniors or seniors at high schools in Alabama, Florida, Georgia, Louisiana, Mississippi, North Carolina, South Carolina, and Tennessee. A separate junior competition is held for teams limited to freshmen and sophomores only. Preference is given to teams from Georgia, who must be members of the Georgia Junior Cattlemen's Association. Team members do not have to be from the same high school or county. Students enter as teams that work through 10 stations in a 25–minute rotation. At each station, team members are given an opportunity to demonstrate their knowledge of the beef industry. The stations cover 1) handling and health; 2) nutrition; 3) marketing; 4) credit and finance 5) seedstock merchandising with keep–cull replacement heifers; 6) job interview; 7) beef industry issues; 8) reproduction; 9) meat identification; and 10) beef management challenge. Teams receive points at each station based on their performance or knowledge of issues. Team members who are seniors receive scholarships; team members who are juniors may complete again as seniors unless they are on the first–place team.
Financial data: Team prizes are $3,000 for first, $2,100 for second, $1,500 for third, $900 for fourth, $750 for fifth, $600 for sixth, $450 for seventh, $300 for eighth, $200 for ninth, and $200 for tenth. The junior champion team receives $300. Prizes are in the form of scholarships that can be redeemed at any college in the nation.
Duration: The competition is held annually.
Number awarded: 10 teams of juniors and seniors are admitted to the competition and all receive a scholarship prize.
Deadline: May of each year.

1882 $$ GEORGIA ENGINEERING FOUNDATION SCHOLARSHIPS

Georgia Engineering Foundation, Inc.
Attn: Scholarship and Loan Committee
233 Peachtree Street, Suite 700
Atlanta, GA 30303
Phone: (404) 521–2324; Fax: (404) 521–0283;
Email: Alicia.sosebee@gaengineers.org
Web: www.gefinc.org

Summary: To provide financial assistance to undergraduate and graduate students from Georgia who are attending or entering an approved engineering program in any state.
Eligibility: Open to residents of Georgia who are attending or accepted at an ABET–accredited engineering or engineering technology program in any state. Applications from incoming freshmen must include a high school transcript with final senior grades, SAT scores, 2 letters of recommendation, and a brief essay on why they want to prepare for a career in engineering. Applications from college and graduate students must include a transcript of all college grades and a brief essay on why they want to prepare for a career in engineering. U.S. citizenship is required. Selection is based on demonstrated competence in mathematics, science, and communications skills; interest in a career in engineering or engineering technology; and financial need.
Financial data: Stipends range from $1,000 to $5,000 per year.
Duration: 1 year.
Number awarded: Between 35 and 50 each year.
Deadline: August of each year.

1883 GEORGIA LEGION AUXILIARY PAST PRESIDENT'S PARLEY NURSING SCHOLARSHIP

American Legion Auxiliary
Department of Georgia
3035 Mt. Zion Road
Stockbridge, GA 30281–4101
Phone: (678) 289–8446; Fax: (678) 289–9496;
Email: secretary@galegionaux.org
Web: www.galegionaux.org

Summary: To provide financial assistance to daughters of veterans in Georgia who are interested in attending college in any state to prepare for a career in nursing.
Eligibility: Open to George residents who are 1) interested in nursing education; and 2) the daughters of veterans. Applicants must be sponsored by a local unit of the American Legion Auxiliary. Selection is based on a statement explaining why they want to become a nurse and why they need a scholarship, a transcript of all high school or college grades, and 4 letters of recommendation (1 from a high school principal or superintendent, 1 from the sponsoring American Legion Auxiliary local unit, and 2 from other responsible people).
Financial data: The amount of the award depends on the availability of funds.
Number awarded: Varies, depending upon funds available.
Deadline: April of each year.

1884 GET IT GIRL COLLEGE TECHNOLOGY SCHOLARSHIP PROGRAM

Michigan Council of Women in Technology Foundation
Attn: Scholarship Committee
19011 Norwich Road
Livonia, MI 48152
Phone: (248) 654–3697; Fax: (248) 281–5391;
Email: info@mcwtf.org
Web: www.mcwtf.org/Scholarships_149.html

Summary: To provide financial assistance to female high school seniors from Michigan who have participated in the GET IT Girl program and are interested in working on a degree in a field related to information technology at a school in any state.
Eligibility: Open to women graduating from high schools in Michigan who have participated in the sponsor's GET IT Girl program. Applicants must be planning to work on a degree in business applications, computer science, computer engineering, graphics design, health technology, information security, information systems, instructional technology, music technology, or software engineering at a college or university in any state. They must have a GPA of 2.5 or higher. Along with their application, they must submit an essay of 200 to 400 words on why they are preparing for a career in information technology, the accomplishments in which they take the most pride, why they should be selected for this scholarship, and what constitutes success for them in this program and/or their future career and life mission. Selection is based on that essay, GPA, participation in the GET IT Girl program, technology related activities, community service, letters of recommendation, and completeness of the application. U.S. citizenship is required.
Financial data: The stipend is $1,000 per year; funds are sent directly to the financial aid office at the college or university where the recipient is enrolled.
Duration: 1 year; may be renewed for up to 3 additional years.
Number awarded: 1 each year.
Deadline: January of each year.

1885 $ GETCHELL AND ROTC SCHOLARSHIPS

Daedalian Foundation
Attn: Scholarship Committee
55 Main Circle (Building 676)
P.O. Box 249
Randolph AFB, TX 78148–0249
Phone: (210) 945–2113; Fax: (210) 945–2112;
Email: kristi@daedalians.org
Web: www.daedalians.org/foundation/scholarships.htm

Summary: To provide financial assistance to ROTC students who wish to become military pilots.
Eligibility: Open to students who are currently enrolled in an ROTC program at their college or university. Applicants must be interested in preparing for a career as a military pilot. They must apply through their ROTC detachment. Selection is based on intention to pursue a career as a military pilot, demonstrated moral character and patriotism, scholastic and military standing and aptitude, and physical condition and aptitude for flight. Financial need may also be considered.
Financial data: The stipend is $2,000.
Duration: 1 year.
Number awarded: 19 each year: 5 designated as Getchell Scholarships, 8 for Air Force ROTC cadets, 3 for Army ROTC cadets, and 3 for Navy/Marine ROTC midshipmen.
Deadline: November of each year.

1886 $ GLENN B. HUDSON SCHOLARSHIP

Central Ohio Golf Course Superintendents Association
c/o Don Sutton
4031 Meadow Knoll Road
Delaware, OH 43015
Phone: (613) 554–3316;
Email: mrawlins@clover.net
Web: www.cogcsa

Summary: To provide financial assistance to students from any state working on an undergraduate degree in turfgrass management at a college or university in Ohio.

Eligibility: Open to undergraduates at colleges and universities in Ohio who have completed at least 20 hours of course work, including at least 10 hours in turfgrass management. Applicants must have a cumulative GPA of 2.5 or higher and a GPA of 2.75 or higher in the major. Selection is based on scholarship and academic achievement to date, dedication to the golf course management field, and desire and need for financial assistance to further educational goals.

Financial data: The stipend is $4,000.

Duration: 1 year.

Number awarded: 1 each year.

Deadline: February of each year.

1887 $ GO RED MULTICULTURAL SCHOLARSHIP FUND

American Heart Association
Attn: Go Red for Women
7272 Greenville Avenue
Dallas, TX 75231–4596
Phone: (800) AHA–USA1;
Email: GoRedScholarship@heart.org
Web: www.goredforwomen.org/goredscholarship.aspx

Summary: To provide financial assistance to women from multicultural backgrounds who are preparing for a career in a field of health care.

Eligibility: Open to women who are currently enrolled at an accredited college, university, health care institution, or program and have a GPA of 3.0 or higher. Applicants must be undergraduates of Hispanic, African American, or other minority origin. They must be preparing for a career as a nurse, physician, or allied health care worker. Selection is based on community involvement, a personal letter, transcripts, and 2 letters of recommendation.

Financial data: The stipend is $2,500.

Duration: 1 year.

Number awarded: Varies each year; recently, 16 of these scholarships were awarded.

Deadline: November of each year.

1888 $$ GOOGLE LIME SCHOLARSHIPS FOR STUDENTS WITH DISABILITIES

Lime Connect, Inc.
590 Madison Avenue, 21st Floor
New York, NY 10022
Phone: (212) 521–4469; Fax: (212) 521–4099;
Email: info@limeconnect.com
Web: www.limeconnect.com

Summary: To provide financial assistance to students with disabilities working on a bachelor's or graduate degree in a computer–related field at a college or university in Canada or the United States.

Eligibility: Open to students at colleges and universities in the United States or Canada who have a disability and are entering their junior or senior year of undergraduate study or are enrolled as graduate students. International students with disabilities enrolled at universities in the United States or Canada are also eligible. Applicants must be working full time on a degree in computer science, computer engineering, or a closely–related technical field. Along with their application, they must submit 2 essays of 400 to 600 words each on 1) their academic accomplishments in terms of the technical projects on which they have worked; and 2) the issue about which they are passionate, what they have done to fulfill that passion, or what they dream of doing to fulfill it. Financial need is not considered in the selection process.

Financial data: The stipend is $10,000 for students at U.S. universities or $C5,000 for students at Canadian universities.

Duration: 1 year.

Number awarded: Varies each year.

Deadline: February of each year.

1889 $$ GOOGLE–SVA SCHOLARSHIP

Student Veterans of America
P.O. Box 77673
Washington, DC 20013
Email: SVA@studentveterans.org
Web: www.studentveterans.org/?page=Programs

Summary: To provide financial assistance to veterans who are working on a bachelor's or graduate degree in a computer–related field.

Eligibility: Open to sophomores, juniors, seniors, and graduate students at U.S. colleges and universities who are veterans (must possess a DD–214) and were honorably discharged or are still in good standing with their branch of service. Applicants must be working full time on a degree in computer science, computer engineering, or a closely–related technical field (e.g., software engineering, electrical engineering with a heavy computer science course load, information systems, information technology, applied networking, system administration). Along with their application, they must submit a 1,000–word personal statement that covers their reasons for applying for this scholarship, their reasons for choosing their major, their professional objectives as they relate to their degree, their role as a leader in their community and/or chapter, and any additional community service initiatives in which they have been involved. Financial need is not considered in the selection process.

Financial data: The stipend is $10,000.

Duration: 1 year.

Number awarded: 8 each year.

Deadline: March of each year.

1890 $$ GORDON & JUNE ITO FOUNDATION SCHOLARSHIP

Gordon & June Ito Foundation
919 Lehua Avenue
Pearl City, HI 96782
Phone: (808) 455–2646;
Email: ciwai@itofamilyfoundation.org
Web: www.itofamilyfoundation.org/scholarship.html

Summary: To provide financial assistance to nursing students entering their senior year at a public college or university in Hawaii.

Eligibility: Open to nursing students entering their senior year at a 4–year accredited public college or university in Hawaii. Applicants must submit information on their scholastic record, academic or nursing honors or awards, extracurricular activities and community involvement, and financial circumstances, along with a 2–page essay on their nursing career goals.

Financial data: The stipend is $10,000.

Duration: 1 year.

Number awarded: 1 each year.

Deadline: March of each year.

1891 GORDON M. ROBINSON MEMORIAL SCHOLARSHIP

Greater Kansas City Community Foundation
Attn: Scholarship Coordinator
1055 Broadway, Suite 130
Kansas City, MO 64105–1595
Phone: (816) 842–0944; Fax: (816) 842–8079;
Email: scholarships@gkccf.org
Web: www.gkccf.org/scholarships

Summary: To provide financial assistance to residents of Missouri who are interested in studying computer science at a college in the state.

Eligibility: Open to graduating high school seniors and current undergraduate students under 21 years of age who are residents of Missouri. Applicants must be enrolled or planning to enroll full time at a 4–year public college or university in Missouri and major in computer science. Preference is given to seniors and graduates of Truman High School in Independence, Missouri and to students at Missouri University of Science and Technology, but all Missouri students and residents are welcome to apply. Financial need is considered in the selection process.

Financial data: The stipend is $1,000 per year.

Duration: 1 year; may be renewed up to 3 additional years, provided the recipient maintains a GPA of 2.75 or higher.

Number awarded: 1 or more each year.

Deadline: March of each year.

1892 GREAT PLAINS CHAPTER ICRI SCHOLARSHIP

International Concrete Repair Institute–Great Plains Chapter
c/o Mike Murray
8329 Monticello

Shawnee, KS 66227
Phone: (913) 422–4443;
Email: mike@murraydecorative.com
Web: www.icrigreatplains.com/scholarships.html

Summary: To provide financial assistance to upper–division students from any state working on a degree related to concrete repair and restoration at universities within the area served by the Great Plains Chapter of the International Concrete Repair Institute (ICRI).

Eligibility: Open to residents of any state entering their junior or senior year at a college or university in Kansas, Missouri, or Nebraska. Applicants must be majoring in civil engineering, architectural engineering, construction management, construction technology, or construction science; strong preference is given to students preparing for a career in concrete restoration, concrete strengthening methods, concrete repair material research, or related fields in concrete design or construction. Along with their application, they must submit a cover letter describing their qualifications and why they should be selected, including personal and professional information. Financial need is not considered. An interview is required.

Financial data: The stipend is $1,000.

Duration: 1 year.

Number awarded: 3 each year.

Deadline: May of each year.

1893 GREATER KANAWHA VALLEY MATH AND SCIENCE SCHOLARSHIP

Greater Kanawha Valley Foundation
Attn: Scholarship Program Officer
1600 Huntington Square
900 Lee Street East, 16th Floor
Charleston, WV 25301
Phone: (304) 346–3620; (800) 467–5909; Fax: (304) 346–3640;
Email: shoover@tgkvf.org
Web: www.tgkvf.org/page.aspx?pid=409

Summary: To provide financial assistance to residents of West Virginia who are working on a degree in a mathematics or science field at a school in any state.

Eligibility: Open to residents of West Virginia who are working full time on a degree in mathematics, science (chemistry, physics, or biology), or engineering at a college or university anywhere in the country. Applicants must have an ACT score of 20 or higher, be able to demonstrate good moral character, and have a GPA of 2.5 or higher. Financial need is not considered in the selection process.

Financial data: The stipend is $1,000 per year.

Duration: 1 year; may be renewed.

Number awarded: Varies each year; recently, 4 of these scholarships were awarded.

Deadline: January of each year.

1894 GREATER PITTSBURGH GOLF COURSE SUPERINTENDENTS ASSOCIATION

Greater Pittsburgh Golf Course Superintendents Association
Attn: Scholarship Committee
2993 Amy Drive
South Park, PA 15129–9349
Phone: (412) 714–8707; Fax: (412) 650–8155;
Email: gpgcsa@comcast.net
Web: www.gpgcsa.org/scholarship_program.php

Summary: To provide financial assistance to undergraduate students preparing for a career as a golf course superintendent.

Eligibility: Open to full–time undergraduates at universities throughout the country who plan to enter the profession of golf course superintendent. Applicants must be enrolled in an agricultural major emphasizing turfgrass management. They must have a GPA of 2.0 or higher. Along with their application, they must submit 100–word essays on 1) what stimulated their initial interest in golf and this profession; 2) why they chose their current major; 3) what they expect from a career as a superintendent; 4) their goals for the next 10 years; 5) the special contribution they could make to the profession; and 6) what sets them apart and more deserving than other applicants. Financial need is not considered in the selection process.

Financial data: The stipend is $1,000.

Duration: 1 year.

Number awarded: 2 each year.

Deadline: July of each year.

1895 $$ GREATER RESEARCH OPPORTUNITIES (GRO) FELLOWSHIPS FOR UNDERGRADUATE ENVIRONMENTAL STUDY

Environmental Protection Agency
Attn: National Center for Environmental Research
Ariel Rios Building
1200 Pennsylvania Avenue, N.W.
Washington, DC 20460
Phone: (202) 347–8049; (800) 490–9194;
Email: boddie.georgette@epa.gov
Web: epa.gov/ncer/rfa

Summary: To provide financial assistance and summer internships to undergraduates who are enrolled at colleges and universities that receive limited federal funding and who are interested in majoring in fields related to the environment.

Eligibility: Open to U.S. citizens or permanent residents who are enrolled full time at a college or university in this country that receives less than $35 million in federal research and development expenditures. Students attending eligible institutions with significant minority enrollment (defined as Minority–Serving Institutions) are particularly encouraged to apply. Applicants must have at least 2 years remaining for completion of a bachelor's degree in an environmentally–related field, such as physics, biology, health, the social sciences, or engineering. They must be available to work as interns at an EPA facility during the summer between their junior and senior years. A goal of the program is to meet the need for scientists from diverse cultural backgrounds, so the sponsor strongly encourages women, minorities, and persons with disabilities to apply. A minimum average of "B" overall is required.

Financial data: The fellowship provides up to $19,700 per year, including up to $10,000 for tuition and academic fees, a stipend of $7,200 ($200 per month for 9 months), and an expense allowance of up to $2,500 for items and activities for the direct benefit of the student's education, such as books, supplies, and travel to professional conferences and workshops. The summer internship grant is $9,500, including a stipend of $7,000 for living expenses, an allowance of $1,000 for travel to and from the site, and an allowance of $1,500 for travel while at the site.

Duration: The final 2 years of baccalaureate study, including 12 weeks during the summer between those years.

Number awarded: Approximately 40 each year.

Deadline: December of each year.

1896 GREATLAND SWE SECTION SCHOLARSHIPS

Society of Women Engineers–Greatland Section
c/o Maria Kampsen, Scholarship Chair
DOWL HKM
4041 B Street
Anchorage, AK 99503
Phone: (907) 562–2000; Fax: (907) 563–3953;
Email: mkampsen@dowlhkm.com
Web: www.swealaska.org/scholarships.html

Summary: To provide financial assistance to female high school seniors in Alaska who plan to major in engineering at a college in any state.

Eligibility: Open to women graduating from high schools in Alaska and planning to enroll in an ABET–accredited engineering program at a 4–year college or university in any state. Applicants must submit a 2–page essay discussing their interest in engineering, their major area of study or specialization, the job they wish to pursue after receiving their college degree, their long–term goals, and how they hope to achieve those. Selection is based on that essay, academic performance, activities and work experience, recommendations, honors and awards, application presentation, and financial need.

Financial data: The stipend is $1,500 or $1,000.

Duration: 1 year.

Number awarded: 3 each year: 2 at $1,500 and 1 at $1,000.

Deadline: February of each year.

1897 $ GROGAN MEMORIAL SCHOLARSHIP

American Academy of Physician Assistants–Veterans Caucus
Attn: Veterans Caucus
P.O. Box 362
Danville, PA 17821–0362
Phone: (570) 271–0292; Fax: (570) 271–5850;
Email: admin@veteranscaucus.org
Web: www.veteranscaucus.org

Summary: To provide financial assistance to veterans and their dependents who are studying to become physician assistants.

Eligibility: Open to U.S. citizens who are currently enrolled in a physician assistant program. The program must be approved by the Commission on Accreditation of Allied Health Education. Applicants must be honorably discharged members of any branch of the military or the dependents of those members. Selection is based on military honors and awards received, civic and college honors and awards received, professional memberships and activities, and GPA. An electronic copy of the applicant's DD Form 214 must accompany the application.
Financial data: The stipend is $2,000.
Duration: 1 year.
Number awarded: 1 each year.
Deadline: February of each year.

1898 GULF COAST HURRICANE SCHOLARSHIPS

Society of Plastics Engineers
Attn: SPE Foundation
13 Church Hill Road
Newtown, CT 06740
Phone: (203) 740–5447; Fax: (203) 775–1157;
Email: foundation@4spe.org
Web: www.4spe.org/spe–foundation
Summary: To provide financial assistance to undergraduate students from Gulf Coast states who are attending college in the area to prepare for a career in the plastics industry.
Eligibility: Open to residents of Alabama, Florida, Louisiana, Mississippi, and Texas who are enrolled or planning to enroll at a university, college, or technical institute in their home state in a program that supports the plastics industry. Applicants must be majoring in or taking courses that would be beneficial to a career in the plastics or polymer industry (e.g., plastics engineering, packaging, polymer sciences, chemistry, physics, chemical engineering, mechanical engineering, industrial engineering). Along with their application, they must submit 3 letters of recommendation; a high school and/or college transcript; a 1– to 2–page statement telling why they are applying for the scholarship, their qualifications, and their educational and career goals in the plastics industry; their employment history; a list of current and past school activities and community activities and honors; and information on their financial need.
Financial data: Total stipends are $6,000 at 4–year institutions or $2,000 at 2–year institutions. Funds are paid on an annual basis directly to the recipient's school.
Duration: 1 year; may be renewed up to 3 additional years at 4–year institutions or 1 additional year at 2–year institutions. Renewal depends on the recipient's maintaining a GPA of 2.0 or higher and enrollment in at least 5 credit hours per term.
Number awarded: 3 each year: 1 to a 4–year student and 2 to 2–year students.
Deadline: February of each year.

1899 $$ GUS ARCHIE MEMORIAL SCHOLARSHIPS

Society of Petroleum Engineers
Attn: Student Activities Manager
2552 Summit Avenue, Suite 406
P.O. Box 833836
Richardson, TX 75083–3836
Phone: (972) 952–9452; (800) 456–6863; Fax: (972) 952–9435;
Email: service@spe.org
Web: www.spe.org/scholarships/archie.php
Summary: To provide financial assistance to high school seniors interested in preparing for a career in petroleum engineering.
Eligibility: Open to graduating high school seniors who have a score of at least 1800 on the SAT or 27 on the ACT and are planning to enroll in a petroleum engineering program at an accredited college or university. Selection is based on academic record, career plans, and financial need.
Financial data: The stipend is $6,000 per year.
Duration: 1 year; may be renewed for up to 3 additional years, provided the recipient maintains full–time enrollment and a GPA of 3.0 or higher both cumulatively and for the current semester.
Number awarded: 1 or more each year.
Deadline: April of each year.

1900 $$ GUS LARSON SCHOLARSHIP

American Society of Heating, Refrigerating and Air–Conditioning Engineers–Wisconsin Chapter
c/o Marty Herrick
Ring & DuChateau, Inc.
10101 Innovation Drive, Suite 200
Milwaukee, WI 53226
Phone: (414) 778–7411;
Email: mherrick@ringdu.com
Web: www.ashrae–wi.org/gus_larson_scholarship.html
Summary: To provide financial assistance to seniors at universities in Wisconsin who are preparing for a career in the field of heating, ventilating, air conditioning, and refrigeration engineering.
Eligibility: Open to engineering students entering their senior year at a college or university in Wisconsin. Applicants must submit information on the courses they plan to pursue in the field of heating, ventilating, air conditioning, and refrigeration during the coming year and the area of the industry that holds the most interest for them. Financial need is considered in the selection process.
Financial data: A total of $5,000 is available for this program each year.
Duration: 1 year.
Number awarded: 1 to 3 each year.
Deadline: May of each year.

1901 H. JAMES HARRINGTON SCHOLARSHIPS

American Society for Quality
Attn: Inspection Division
600 North Plankinton Avenue
P.O. Box 3005
Milwaukee, WI 53201–3005
Phone: (414) 272–8575; (800) 248–1946; Fax: (414) 272–1734;
Email: help@asq.org
Web: asq.org/inspect/about/INSPECT_SCHOLARSHIPS
Summary: To provide financial assistance to students at all levels interested working on a degree in a field related to quality.
Eligibility: Open to high school seniors, undergraduates, graduate students, and professionals returning to college who are nominated or sponsored by a member of the Inspection Division of the American Society for Quality (ASQ). Applicants must be interested in studying a field related to quality. Along with their application, they must submit a transcript, a copy of their sponsor's current membership card in the ASQ, and a 750–word essay on how they can use their degree to enhance quality. Selection is based on the essay, academic achievement, extracurricular activities, honors and awards, and leadership qualities and personality. Financial need is not considered.
Financial data: The stipend is $1,500 or $500.
Duration: 1 year.
Number awarded: Varies each year; recently, 4 of these scholarships were awarded: 1 at $1,500 and 3 at $500.
Deadline: February of each year.

1902 HAROLD BETTINGER MEMORIAL SCHOLARSHIP

American Floral Endowment
1601 Duke Street
Alexandria, VA 22314
Phone: (703) 838–5211; Fax: (703) 838–5212;
Email: afe@endowment.org
Web: endowment.org/floriculture–scholarshipsinternships.html
Summary: To provide financial assistance to undergraduate and graduate students interested in the business of horticulture.
Eligibility: Open to undergraduate and graduate students working on a degree in either 1) horticulture with a business and/or marketing emphasis; or 2) business and/or marketing with the intent to apply it to a horticulture–related business. Applicants must be U.S. or Canadian citizens or permanent residents and have a GPA of 2.0 or higher. Along with their application, they must submit a statement describing their career goals and the academic, work–related, and/or life experiences that support those goals. Financial need is considered in the selection process.
Financial data: The stipend varies each year; recently, it was $1,875.
Duration: 1 year.
Number awarded: 1 each year.
Deadline: April of each year.

1903 $ HAROLD E. ENNES SCHOLARSHIP

Society of Broadcast Engineers
Attn: Scholarship Committee
9102 North Meridian Street, Suite 150
Indianapolis, IN 46260
Phone: (317) 846–9000; Fax: (317) 846–9120

Web: www.sbe.org/sections/edu_ennes_scholarships.php
Summary: To provide financial assistance for college to students interested in the technical aspects of broadcasting.
Eligibility: Open to applicants who have a career interest in the technical aspects of broadcasting and are recommended by 2 members of the Society of Broadcast Engineers (SBE). They must submit 1) a brief autobiography that includes their interest and goals in broadcasting; 2) a summary of the technical changes they anticipate in broadcasting within the next 5 years; and 3) transcripts. Preference is given to members of the SBE and to students currently employed at least part time in broadcast engineering. Both new students just entering college and students already enrolled in college may apply. Financial need is not considered in the selection process.
Financial data: The stipend ranges from $1,000 to $3,000, depending on the availability of funds. Awards may be used for 1) tuition, room, board, or textbook costs at postsecondary educational institutions; or 2) other technical training programs approved by the sponsor.
Duration: 1 year.
Number awarded: 1 each year.
Deadline: June of each year.

1904 $ HARRY HAMPTON FUND SCHOLARSHIP

Harry Hampton Memorial Wildlife Fund, Inc.
P.O. Box 2641
Columbia, SC 29202
Phone: (803) 600–1570;
Email: jim.goller@hamptonwildlifefund.org
Web: www.hamptonwildlifefund.org/scholarship.html
Summary: To provide financial assistance to high school seniors in South Carolina who plan to major in a field related to natural resources at a college or university in the state.
Eligibility: Open to seniors graduating from high schools in South Carolina who plan to attend an institution of higher learning in the state. Applicants must be planning to major in a field related to natural resources, including wildlife, fisheries, biology, zoology, forestry, marine science, or environmental science. Along with their application, they must submit a brief autobiography that includes 1) a description of their career ambitions in the natural resources field; 2) why they desire a college education; 3) their interest in wildlife resources, the environment, coastal resources, or related topics; and 4) why they will be a good investment if they are awarded this scholarship. Financial need is also considered in the selection process.
Financial data: The stipend is $2,500 per year.
Duration: 1 year; may be renewed up to 3 additional years, provided the recipient maintains a GPA of 2.5 or higher.
Number awarded: 1 each year.
Deadline: January of each year.

1905 $ HAWAII CHAPTER/DAVID T. WOOLSEY SCHOLARSHIP

Summary: To provide financial assistance to residents of Hawaii who are working on an undergraduate or graduate degree in landscape architecture at a school in any state.
See Listing #1255.

1906 $ HAWAII LAND SURVEYORS ASSOCIATION SCHOLARSHIP

Hawaii Land Surveyors Association
P.O. Box 2981
Honolulu, HI 96802
Email: admin@hlsa–hawaii.org
Web: www.hlsa–hawaii.org/displaycommon.cfm?an=1&subarticlenbr=17
Summary: To provide financial assistance to high school seniors in Hawaii who are interested in working on a baccalaureate degree in land surveying at a college in any state.
Eligibility: Open to seniors graduating from high schools in Hawaii who have a GPA of 3.0 or higher. Applicants must be planning to attend an ABET–accredited college or university in any state to work on a baccalaureate degree in land surveying. Along with their application, they must submit an essay of 1 to 5 pages on their goals (including plans for a formal education and career), merit (e.g., awards, GPA, membership in honor societies), work history, extracurricular activities, work history, and financial need.
Financial data: The stipend is $3,000.
Duration: 1 year.
Number awarded: 1 each year.
Deadline: March of each year.

1907 HEALTH FOCUS OF SOUTHWEST VIRGINIA SCHOLARSHIPS

Health Focus of Southwest Virginia
Attn: Scholarship Committee
1902 Braeburn Drive
Salem, VA 24153
Phone: (540) 444–2925, ext. 202; Fax: (540) 444–2927;
Email: channah@healthfocusswva.org
Web: www.healthfocusswva.org
Summary: To provide financial assistance to students who are residents of or attending school in Virginia and interested in preparing for a health career.
Eligibility: Open to high school seniors, high school graduates and currently–enrolled college students who are interested in preparing for a health career (broadly defined). The vast majority of funds are awarded to Virginia residents and then to students attending Virginia schools. Applicants must have been accepted into a health program; students taking prerequisite courses (e.g., pre–nursing, pre–occupational therapy) are not eligible. Along with their application, they must submit a 1–page summary explaining why they need financial assistance. A GPA of 2.75 or higher is required. Selection is based on financial need and potential for completing a health career program.
Financial data: The stipend is $1,000 per year. Funds may be used to pay for tuition, book supplies, and uniforms.
Duration: 1 year; recipients may reapply.
Number awarded: Varies each year; recently 162 of these scholarships were awarded.
Deadline: November of each year.

1908 $ HEART OF AMERICA GOLF COURSE SUPERINTENDENTS ASSOCIATION ACADEMIC SCHOLARSHIPS

Heart of America Golf Course Superintendents Association
Attn: Scholarship and Research Committee
638 West 39th Street
P.O. Box 419264
Kansas City, MO 64141–6264
Phone: (816) 561–5323; Fax: (816) 561–1991;
Email: kweitzel@swassn.com
Web: www.hagcsa.org/academic–scholarships
Summary: To provide financial assistance to undergraduate and graduate students from any state working on a degree in turfgrass management at a school in Missouri or Kansas.
Eligibility: Open to undergraduate and graduate students working on a degree in turfgrass management at colleges and universities in Kansas and Missouri. Applicants must submit brief essays on what stimulated their initial interest in golf and the turf profession, why they believe the sponsor should grant them a scholarship, their goals upon graduation, and their professional goals with their degree as a golf course superintendent or other management position. Financial need is not considered in the selection process.
Financial data: Stipends are $2,500, $1,500, or $1,000.
Duration: 1 year.
Number awarded: Up to 5 each year; a total of $5,000 is available for this program annually.
Deadline: October of each year.

1909 $ HEIDELBERG USA SCHOLARSHIP

Summary: To provide financial assistance to undergraduate and graduate students from any country interested in preparing for a career in document management and graphic communications, especially those who have experience with printing equipment.
See Listing #1261.

1910 $ HESSIE T. MORRAH HORTICULTURE SCHOLARSHIP

Garden Club of South Carolina, Inc.
c/o Sandra Hamann
405 East Seven Oaks Drive
Greenville, SC 29605
Phone: (864) 235–9709;
Email: dasaham@charter.net
Web: www.gardenclubofsc.org/projects/scholarships/default.htm
Summary: To provide financial assistance to residents of South Carolina interested in studying a horticulture–related field at a college in any state.
Eligibility: Open to residents of South Carolina who are high school seniors, undergraduates, or master's degree students. Applicants must be enrolled or

planning to enroll full time at a college, university, or technical school in any state and have a GPA of 3.0 or higher. They must be interested in working on a degree in agriculture, agronomy, botany, city planning, floriculture, forestry, horticulture, land management, landscape design, plant pathology, or related fields. Along with their application, they must submit a 2–page essay discussing their goals, commitment to their chosen field of study, financial concerns, background, activities, and honors.
Financial data: The stipend is $2,000.
Duration: 1 year.
Number awarded: 1 or more each year.
Deadline: January of each year.

1911 $ HIGH SCHOOL SENIOR SCHOLARSHIPS

American Society of Heating, Refrigerating and Air–Conditioning Engineers
Attn: Scholarship Administrator
1791 Tullie Circle, N.E.
Atlanta, GA 30329–2305
Phone: (404) 539–1120; Fax: (404) 539–2120;
Email: lbenedict@ashrae.org
Web: www.ashrae.org/students/page/1271
Summary: To provide financial assistance to high school seniors who are entering college to work on a bachelor's degree in heating, ventilating, air conditioning, and refrigeration (HVAC&R).
Eligibility: Open to high school seniors who are entering an ABET–accredited program in engineering, pre–engineering, or engineering technology. Applicants must be planning to work on a bachelor's degree in a course of study that has traditionally been preparatory for the profession of HVAC&R. They must have a GPA of 3.0 or higher and a standing in the top 30% of their class. Selection is based on potential service to the HVAC&R profession, financial need, leadership ability, recommendations from instructors, and work ethics.
Financial data: The stipend is $3,000.
Duration: 1 year.
Number awarded: 1 each year.
Deadline: April of each year.

1912 HIGHMARK SCHOLARSHIP

Pennsylvania State System of Higher Education Foundation, Inc.
Attn: Foundation Manager
2986 North Second Street
Harrisburg, PA 17110
Phone: (717) 720–4065; Fax: (717) 720–7082;
Email: eshowers@thePAfoundation.org
Web: www.thepafoundation.org/scholarships/index.asp
Summary: To provide financial assistance to freshmen entering institutions of the Pennsylvania State System of Higher Education (PASSHE) who plan to major in a health care–related field.
Eligibility: Open to freshmen entering 1 of the 14 institutions within the PASSHE. Applicants must be planning to major in a field of health care, including (but not limited to) nursing, pre–physician assistant, pre–medicine, biology, health science, audiology, speech pathology, health services administration, health education, medical imagery, or exercise science. Each PASSHE university establishes its own selection criteria.
Financial data: The stipend is $1,000.
Duration: 1 year; nonrenewable.
Number awarded: 140 each year: 10 at each PASSHE university.
Deadline: Each PASSHE university sets its own deadline.

1913 HISTORY AND PHILOSOPHY OF GEOLOGY STUDENT AWARD

Summary: To recognize and reward undergraduate and graduate students who submit outstanding papers on the history of geology.
See Listing #1266.

1914 $$ HONEYWELL INTERNATIONAL SCHOLARSHIPS

Society of Women Engineers
Attn: Scholarship Selection Committee
203 North LaSalle Street, Suite 1675
Chicago, IL 60601–1269
Phone: (312) 596–5223; (877) SWE–INFO; Fax: (312) 644–8557;
Email: scholarships@swe.org
Web: societyofwomenengineers.swe.org/index.php/scholarships
Summary: To provide financial assistance to women interested in studying specified fields of engineering in college.
Eligibility: Open to women who are graduating high school seniors or rising college sophomores, juniors, or seniors. Applicants must be enrolled or planning to enroll full time at an ABET–accredited 4–year college or university and major in computer science or aerospace, chemical, computer, electrical, industrial, manufacturing, materials, or mechanical engineering. They must have a GPA of 3.5 or higher. Preference is given to members of groups underrepresented in computer science and engineering. U.S. citizenship or permanent resident status is required. Financial need is considered in the selection process.
Financial data: The stipend is $5,000.
Duration: 1 year.
Number awarded: 3 each year.
Deadline: February of each year for current college students; May of each year for high school seniors.

1915 $ HORIZONS–MICHIGAN SCHOLARSHIP

Women in Defense–Michigan Chapter
Attn: Scholarship Director
P.O. Box 4744
Troy, MI 48099
Email: scholarships@wid–mi.org
Web: www.wid–mi.org/scholarships.aspx
Summary: To provide financial assistance to women in Michigan who are upper–division or graduate students working on a degree related to national defense.
Eligibility: Open to women who are residents of Michigan and enrolled either full or part time at a college or university in the state. Applicants must be juniors, seniors, or graduate students and have a GPA of 3.25 or higher. They must be interested in preparing for a career related to national security or defense. Relevant fields of study include security studies, military history, government relations, engineering, computer science, physics, mathematics, business (as related to national security or defense), law (as related to national security or defense), international relations, political science, or economics; other fields may be considered if the applicant can demonstrate relevance to a career in national security or defense. Along with their application, they must submit brief statements on their interest in a career in national security or defense, the principal accomplishments in their life that relate to their professional goals, and the objectives of their educational program. Selection is based on those statements, academic achievement, participation in defense and national security activities, field of study, work experience, recommendations, and financial need. U.S. citizenship is required.
Financial data: Stipends have averaged at least $3,000.
Duration: 1 year.
Number awarded: Varies each year; recently, 6 of these scholarships were awarded.
Deadline: September of each year.

1916 HOUSTON AREA SECTION FIRST SCHOLARSHIP

Society of Women Engineers–Houston Area Section
Attn: Vice President Outreach
P.O. Box 1355
Houston, TX 77251–1355
Email: VP_Outreach@swehouston.org
Web: www.swehouston.org/education/Scholarships.php
Summary: To provide financial assistance to high school women, especially those in Texas, interested in studying engineering at a college in any state.
Eligibility: Open to female high school seniors planning to attend an ABET–accredited 4–year college or university to major in engineering. Preference is given to students attending high school in Texas, but applicants may be planning to enroll at a college in any state. They must have completed at least 1 regional FIRST (For Inspiration and Recognition of Science and Technology) competition. Along with their application, they must submit transcripts; a 1–page essay on why they would like to be an engineer, how they believe they will make a difference as an engineer, and what influenced them to study engineering; a letter of reference regarding their scholastic ability, general character, attitude, ambition, motivation, and leadership characteristics; and a resume. Information on financial situation is purely voluntary and is not used in the selection process.
Financial data: The stipend is $1,000.
Duration: 1 year; nonrenewable.
Number awarded: 1 each year.
Deadline: February of each year.

1917 $ HOWARD YOUNG AND FRANK BAKER SCHOLARSHIPS

Arkansas Cattlemen's Association
310 Executive Court
Little Rock, AR 72205
Phone: (501) 224–2114; Fax: (501) 224–5377;
Email: info@arbeef.org
Web: www.arbeef.org/scholarships.aspx

Summary: To provide financial assistance to upper–division students from Arkansas who are preparing for a career in the cattle industry.

Eligibility: Open to residents of Arkansas entering their junior or senior year at an accredited 4–year college or university. Applicants must be preparing for a career in or related to the cattle industry. They must have a GPA of 2.5 or higher. Preference is given to children and grandchildren of members of the Arkansas Cattlemen's Association. Selection is based on achievement, individual character, career plans, and leadership potential.

Financial data: The stipend is $2,000.

Duration: 1 year.

Number awarded: Up to 5 each year.

Deadline: May of each year.

1918 HUBERT J. BYRD SR. SCHOLARSHIP

Soil Science Society of America
5585 Guilford Road
Madison, WI 53711–5801
Phone: (608) 273–8080; Fax: (608) 273–2021;
Email: awards@sciencesocieties.org
Web: www.soils.org/awards/award/detail/?a=59

Summary: To provide financial assistance to upper–division and graduate students in soil science.

Eligibility: Open to 1) undergraduates completing their sophomore or junior years with a declared major in soil science or a closely–related degree program; and 2) undergraduates completing their senior year and entering a master's degree program in soil science. Applicants must have a GPA of 2.5 or higher. They must be able to demonstrate strong interest in science and business, with practical applications of their knowledge and skills. Along with their application, they must submit a letter of interest that includes their background, strengths and accomplishments, community and extracurricular activities, interests in sciences (particularly soil science), significant work or volunteer experience, and future career goals.

Financial data: The stipend is $1,000.

Duration: 1 year.

Number awarded: 2 each year.

Deadline: March of each year.

1919 $ HUBERTUS W.V. WILLEMS SCHOLARSHIP FOR MALE STUDENTS

National Association for the Advancement of Colored People
Attn: Education Department
4805 Mt. Hope Drive
Baltimore, MD 21215–3297
Phone: (410) 580–5760; (877) NAACP–98;
Email: youth@naacpnet.org
Web: www.naacp.org/pages/naacp–scholarships

Summary: To provide funding to males who are interested in undergraduate or graduate education in selected scientific fields.

Eligibility: Open to males who are high school seniors, college students, or graduate students. Applicants must be majoring (or planning to major) in 1 of the following fields: engineering, chemistry, physics, or mathematics. Membership and participation in the NAACP are highly desirable. The required minimum GPA is 2.5 for graduating high school seniors and undergraduate students or 3.0 for graduate students. Undergraduates must be enrolled full time but graduate students may be full– or part–time students. Applicants must be able to demonstrate financial need, defined as a family income of less than $16,245 for a family of 1 ranging to less than $49,905 for a family of 7. Along with their application, they must submit a 1–page essay on their interest in their major and a career, their life's ambition, what they hope to accomplish in their lifetime, and what position they hope to attain. Full–time enrollment is required for undergraduate students, although graduate students may be enrolled full or part time. U.S. citizenship is required.

Financial data: The stipend is $2,000 per year for undergraduate students or $3,000 per year for graduate students.

Duration: 1 year; may be renewed.

Number awarded: Varies each year; recently, 7 of these scholarships were awarded.

Deadline: March of each year.

1920 $ HURST REVIEW SERVICES/AACN NURSING SCHOLARSHIP FUND

American Association of Colleges of Nursing
One Dupont Circle, N.W., Suite 530
Washington, DC 20036
Phone: (202) 463–6930; Fax: (202) 785–8320;
Email: scholarship@aacn.nche.edu
Web: www.aacn.nche.edu/students/scholarships

Summary: To provide financial assistance to entry–level nursing students at institutions that are members of the American Association of Colleges of Nursing (AACN).

Eligibility: Open to entry–level students working on their first professional degree in a prelicensure program at an AACN member school. Applicants must submit a 250–word essay on their goals and aspirations as related to their education, career, and future plans. Selection is based on academic performance.

Financial data: The stipend is $2,500.

Duration: 1 year.

Number awarded: Up to 4 each year: 2 for each application deadline.

Deadline: January or July of each year.

1921 HURST REVIEW SERVICES/N–OADN FOUNDATION SCHOLARSHIP

National Organization for Associate Degree Nursing
Attn: Foundation
7794 Grow Drive
Pensacola, FL 32514
Phone: (850) 484–6948; (877) 966–6236; Fax: (850) 484–8762;
Email: noadn@dancyamc.com
Web: www.noadn.org

Summary: To provide financial assistance to students working on an Associate Degree in Nursing (A.D.N.).

Eligibility: Open to students currently enrolled or entering their second year of a state–approved A.D.N. program. Applicants must have earned a GPA of 3.0 or higher and be active in a local, state, or national student nurse association. Along with their application, they must submit a 500–word essay on the code of conduct they will follow as a professional nurse. Financial need is not considered.

Financial data: The stipend is $1,000.

Duration: 1 year.

Number awarded: 5 each year.

Deadline: January or August of each year.

1922 $ IAD FOUNDATION FOR EDUCATION SCHOLARSHIPS

Iowa Automotive Dealers Association
Attn: IAD Foundation for Education
1111 Office Park Road
West Des Moines, IA 50265
Phone: (515) 440–7625; (800) 869–1900; Fax: (515) 226–1988;
Email: mcason@iada.com
Web: iada.com/FoundationForEducation.aspx

Summary: To provide financial assistance to high school seniors in Iowa who plan to attend college in any state to study an automotive–related field.

Eligibility: Open to seniors graduating from high schools in Iowa and planning to attend a 2– or 4–year postsecondary institution in any state. Applicants must be planning to study an automotive–related field; in the past, most recipients have prepared for a career as an automotive technician, although some have studied collision repair and others have pursued diesel training. Financial need is considered for some scholarships, but others are awarded on the basis of academic excellence.

Financial data: The stipend is $2,000.

Duration: 1 year.

Number awarded: Varies each year; recently, 16 of these scholarships were awarded.

Deadline: February of each year.

1923 IAGER DAIRY SCHOLARSHIP

National Dairy Shrine
Attn: Executive Director
P.O. Box 725
Denmark, WI 54208
Phone: (920) 863–6333; Fax: (920) 863–6333;
Email: info@dairyshrine.org
Web: www.dairyshrine.org/scholarships.php

Summary: To provide financial assistance to 2–year college students majoring in animal or dairy science.

Eligibility: Open to students completing their first year at a 2–year agricultural school and preparing for a career in the dairy industry. Applicants must have a GPA of 2.5 or higher. Along with their application, they must submit a 500–word essay on why they are interested in the dairy industry and their plans for the future. Selection is based on that essay, academic standing, leadership ability, extracurricular activities, and interest in the dairy industry.

Financial data: The stipend is $1,000.

Duration: 1 year.

Number awarded: 1 each year.

Deadline: April of each year.

1924 IBM CORPORATION SWE SCHOLARSHIPS

Society of Women Engineers
Attn: Scholarship Selection Committee
203 North LaSalle Street, Suite 1675
Chicago, IL 60601–1269
Phone: (312) 596–5223; (877) SWE–INFO; Fax: (312) 644–8557;
Email: scholarships@swe.org
Web: societyofwomenengineers.swe.org/index.php/scholarships

Summary: To provide financial assistance to undergraduate women majoring in designated engineering specialties.

Eligibility: Open to women who are entering their sophomore or junior year at a 4–year ABET–accredited college or university. Applicants must be working full time on a degree in computer science or electrical or computer engineering and have a GPA of 3.4 or higher. Preference is given to members of groups underrepresented in engineering or computer science. Selection is based on merit. U.S. citizenship or permanent resident status is required.

Financial data: The stipend is $1,000.

Duration: 1 year.

Number awarded: 5 each year.

Deadline: February of each year.

1925 $ IDA AND MAY REILLY GRADUATE OR UNDERGRADUATE SCHOLARSHIP

Alpha Mu Tau Fraternity
c/o American Society for Clinical Laboratory Science
2025 M Street, N.W., Suite 800
Washington, DC 20036
Phone: (202) 367–1174;
Email: alphamutaujoe@yahoo.com
Web: www.ascls.org/?page=Awards_AMTF

Summary: To provide financial assistance to undergraduate or graduate students in the clinical laboratory sciences.

Eligibility: Open to U.S. citizens and permanent residents accepted into or currently enrolled in a program in clinical laboratory science, including clinical laboratory education or management programs for graduate students or cytotechnology, histotechnology, clinical laboratory science/medical technology, or clinical laboratory technician/medical laboratory technician for undergraduates. Undergraduate applicants must be entering their last year of study. Graduate students must be members of the American Society for Clinical Laboratory Science (ASCLS). Along with their application, they must submit a 500–word statement describing their interest and reasons for preparing for a career in clinical laboratory science. Financial need is also considered in the selection process.

Financial data: The stipend is $3,000.

Duration: 1 year.

Number awarded: 1 or more each year.

Deadline: March of each year.

1926 IDAHO EDUCATION INCENTIVE LOAN FORGIVENESS

Idaho State Board of Education
Len B. Jordan Office Building
650 West State Street, Room 307
P.O. Box 83720
Boise, ID 83720–0037
Phone: (208) 332–1574; Fax: (208) 334–2632;
Email: scholarshiphelp@osbe.idaho.gov
Web: www.boardofed.idaho.gov/scholarship/st_loan_forgive.asp

Summary: To provide funding to Idaho students who wish to prepare for a teaching or nursing career in Idaho.

Eligibility: Open to students who graduated from a secondary school in Idaho within the previous 2 years and rank within the upper 15% of their graduating high school class or have earned a cumulative GPA in college of 3.0 or higher. They must enroll full time at an Idaho public college or university and work on a degree that will qualify them to receive an Idaho teaching certificate or licensure by the Board of Nursing for a registered nurse.

Financial data: This is a scholarship/loan program. Loans are forgiven if the recipient pursues a teaching or nursing career within Idaho for at least 2 years.

Duration: 1 year; renewable.

Number awarded: Approximately 45 each year.

Deadline: Deadline not specified.

1927 IDAHO LEGION AUXILIARY NURSES SCHOLARSHIP

American Legion Auxiliary
Department of Idaho
905 Warren Street
Boise, ID 83706–3825
Phone: (208) 342–7066;
Email: idalegionaux@msn.com
Web: idahoala.org/scholarships.aspx

Summary: To provide financial assistance to Idaho veterans and their descendants who are interested in studying nursing at a school in any state.

Eligibility: Open to student nurses who are veterans or the children or grandchildren of veterans and are residents of Idaho. Applicants must be attending or planning to attend a school of nursing in any state. They may be traditional or nontraditional students between 17 and 35 years of age. Selection is based on financial need, scholarship, and deportment.

Financial data: The stipend is $1,000.

Duration: 1 year.

Number awarded: 1 each year.

Deadline: May of each year.

1928 IDAHO NURSING AND HEALTH PROFESSIONS SCHOLARSHIP

Idaho Community Foundation
Attn: Scholarship Coordinator
210 West State Street
Boise, ID 83702
Phone: (208) 342–3535; (800) 657–5357; Fax: (208) 342–3577;
Email: edavis@idcomfdn.org
Web: www.idcomfdn.org/pages/scho_general.htm

Summary: To provide financial assistance to residents of any state who have been accepted to a nursing or health professions program in Idaho.

Eligibility: Open to students who may be residents of any state but have been accepted to an accredited Idaho nursing or health professions program (e.g., respiratory therapy, physical therapy). Applicants must be able to demonstrate financial need. Along with their application, they must submit a brief statement of their educational and career goals and objectives. Preference is given to students in the top third of their class.

Financial data: A stipend is awarded (amount not specified).

Duration: 1 year.

Number awarded: 1 or more each year.

Deadline: March of each year.

1929 $$ IFMA FOUNDATION SCHOLARSHIPS

Summary: To provide financial assistance to undergraduate and graduate students working on a degree in facility management or a related field.

See Listing #1277.

1930 $$ ILLINOIS ALLIED HEALTH CARE PROFESSIONAL SCHOLARSHIP PROGRAM

Illinois Department of Public Health
Attn: Center for Rural Health
535 West Jefferson Street

Springfield, IL 62761
Phone: (217) 782–1624; Fax: (217) 782–3987; TDD: (800) 547–0466;
Email: DPH.MAILUS@illlinois.gov
Web: www.idph.state.il.us/about/rural_health/rural_scholarship.htm

Summary: To provide funding to Illinois students preparing for a career as a nurse practitioner, physician assistant, or certified nurse midwife and interested in practicing in areas of the state that have insufficient numbers of primary care providers.

Eligibility: Open to Illinois residents who are enrolled or accepted for enrollment at an accredited school located in the state and preparing for a career as a nurse practitioner, physician assistant, or certified nurse midwife. Applicants must be able to demonstrate financial need. They must agree to practice full time in a designated shortage area as an allied health care professional for 1 year for each year of scholarship funding received. Along with their application, they must submit proof of enrollment or acceptance for admission and documentation of financial need. An interview may be required. Preference is given to applicants demonstrating 1) interest in obtaining a degree or licensure as a nurse practitioner, physician assistant, or certified nurse midwife; 2) previous experience with medically underserved populations; 3) previous experience with practice in rural areas, especially in primary care; 4) greatest financial need; and 5) academic capabilities.

Financial data: The stipend is $7,500 per year. This is a scholarship/loan program. Recipients repay scholarships by practicing as nurse practitioners, physician assistants, and certified nurse midwives in areas of Illinois determined by the Illinois Department of Public Health to be designated shortage areas. They must practice full time, 1 year for each year of scholarship support received. If they fail to meet that service requirement, they must reimburse the state 3 times the amount received plus 7% interest.

Duration: 1 year; may be renewed 1 additional year.

Number awarded: Approximately 12 each year.

Deadline: June of each year.

1931 $ ILLINOIS CHAPTER ASHRAE SCHOLARSHIP

American Society of Heating, Refrigerating and Air–Conditioning Engineers–Illinois Chapter
P.O. Box 428020
Evergreen Park, IL 60805–8020
Phone: (708) 636–5819; Fax: (708) 636–5847;
Email: dkdoherty@sbcglobal.net
Web: www.illinoisashrae.org

Summary: To provide financial assistance to high school seniors and current undergraduates in Illinois who are working on or planning to work on a degree in engineering, science, or mathematics as preparation for a career in the heating, ventilating, refrigeration, and air conditioning field.

Eligibility: Open to students entering or attending a college or university in Illinois. Applicants must be interested in preparing for a career in the heating, ventilating, air conditioning, and refrigeration (HVAC&R) field by majoring in a relevant field of engineering, science, or mathematics. Along with their application, they must submit 250–word essays on 1) their school, community, and volunteer activities; and 2) their career aspirations and interest in the HVAC&R industry. Selection is based on academic merit, stewardship, and participation in American Society of Heating, Refrigerating and Air–Conditioning Engineers (ASHRAE) activities.

Financial data: Stipends are $3,000 or $1,500.

Duration: 1 year.

Number awarded: 4 each year: 2 at $3,000 and 2 at $1,500.

Deadline: January of each year.

1932 $ ILLINOIS ELKS CHILDREN'S CARE CORPORATION PHYSICAL AND OCCUPATIONAL THERAPY SCHOLARSHIP

Illinois Elks
Attn: Children's Care Corporation
1201 North Main
P.O. Box 222
Chatham, IL 62629–0222
Phone: (217) 483–3020; (800) 272–0074;
Email: scholarships@illinois–elks.org
Web: www.illinois–elks.org/ccc/scholarship/index.htm

Summary: To provide financial assistance to residents of Illinois interested in preparing for a career as a physical or occupational therapist at a school in any state.

Eligibility: Open to residents of Illinois enrolled or planning to enroll full time at a college or university in any state. Applicants must be preparing for a career in physical or occupational therapy by enrolling in a professional program, a pre–therapy course of studies, or a therapy assistant program. They must have a grade average of "B" or better and be able to document financial need. Along with their application, they must submit an essay on what they plan to do with their training in physical or occupational therapy. Selection is based on academic qualifications (40%), personality and desire (20%), and financial need (40%).

Financial data: Stipends are $1,000 for the first year, $1,500 for the second year, $2,000 for the third year, and $2,500 per year for the fourth through sixth years.

Duration: 1 year; may be renewed up to 5 additional years.

Number awarded: 1 or more each year.

Deadline: March of each year.

1933 $$ ILLINOIS NURSING EDUCATION SCHOLARSHIPS

Illinois Department of Public Health
Attn: Center for Rural Health
535 West Jefferson Street
Springfield, IL 62761
Phone: (217) 782–1624; Fax: (217) 782–3987; TDD: (800) 547–0466;
Email: DPH.MAILUS@illlinois.gov
Web: www.idph.state.il.us/about/rural_health/rural_scholarship.htm

Summary: To provide funding to residents of Illinois who are interested in working on a degree or diploma in nursing.

Eligibility: Open to U.S. citizens who have resided in Illinois for at least 1 year. Applicants must be enrolled or accepted for enrollment in an Illinois associate degree in nursing program, hospital–based diploma in nursing program, baccalaureate degree in nursing program, certificate in practical nursing program, or graduate degree in nursing. They must agree to repay the loans in cash or through service. Financial need must be documented. In the selection process, highest priority is given, in order, to applicants 1) with the greatest financial need; 2) studying on a full–time basis; 3) having the fewest number of credit hours remaining; 4) who already have a certificate in practical nursing, a hospital–based diploma in nursing, or an associate degree in nursing and are working on a higher degree; and 5) with the highest cumulative GPA.

Financial data: Students working full time on an associate, bachelor's, or graduate degree at a public college or university receive $4,942 for tuition and fees and $5,943 as a living expense stipend. Students working full time on an associate degree or hospital–based diploma at a community college receive $1,603 for tuition and fees or $5,943 as a living expense stipend. Students in a practical nursing program receive 75% of the average tuition and fees charged at all practical nursing programs and $5,943 as a living expense stipend. Students attending private institutions receive the same amount as students attending public institutions. Awards for part–time students are prorated. Repayment of loans must begin 6 months following withdrawal from school or completion of the degree. Loans are forgiven if the recipient documents either 1) substantially full–time professional nursing practice in direct patient care or (for graduate nursing students) service as a nurse educator at an approved institution in Illinois for a number of years equal to the number of years loan funds were received; or 2) substantially half–time professional nursing practice in direct patient care at an approved institution in Illinois for twice the number of years as the number of years loan funds were received. Recipients who fail to perform the service requirement must repay the loans with 7% interest; repayment must be completed within 6 years.

Duration: Support is available for a total of 1 year for certificate in practical nursing students, 2 years for associate degree students, 3 years for hospital–based diploma students, 4 years for baccalaureate degree students, or 5 years for graduate degree students.

Number awarded: Varies each year; at least 40% of the scholarships are reserved for students working on a baccalaureate degree, 30% for students working on an associate degree or hospital–based diploma, 20% for students working on a graduate degree in nursing, and 10% for students working on a certificate in practical nursing.

Deadline: May of each year.

1934 INCOMING FRESHMAN SCHOLARSHIPS

American Nuclear Society
Attn: Scholarship Coordinator
555 North Kensington Avenue
La Grange Park, IL 60526–5535
Phone: (708) 352–6611; (800) 323–3044; Fax: (708) 352–0499;
Email: outreach@ans.org
Web: www.new.ans.org/honors/scholarships

Summary: To provide financial assistance to students entering their freshman year of college and planning to prepare for a career in nuclear science or nuclear engineering.

Eligibility: Open to graduating high school seniors who have enrolled as a full–time college student. Applicants must be taking science, mathematics, or technical courses with an interest in working in nuclear science and technology.

They must be U.S. citizens or permanent residents. Along with their application, they must submit a 500–word essay on their academic and career goals. Selection is based on that essay, high school academic achievement, freshmen college courses enrolled in, and letters of recommendation.
Financial data: The stipend is $1,000.
Duration: 1 year; nonrenewable.
Number awarded: Up to 10 each year.
Deadline: March of each year.

1935 $$ INDIANA NURSING SCHOLARSHIP FUND PROGRAM

State Student Assistance Commission of Indiana
Attn: Grants and Scholarships
W462 Indiana Government Center South
402 West Washington Street
Indianapolis, IN 46204
Phone: (317) 232–2355; (888) 528–4719 (within IN); Fax: (317) 232–3260;
Email: grants@ssaci.in.gov
Web: www.in.gov/ssaci/2343.htm
Summary: To provide funding to Indiana residents who are interested in attending college in the state to prepare for a career as a nurse.
Eligibility: Open to Indiana residents who are admitted to an eligible Indiana school as a full– or part–time student to work on a certificate or bachelor's degree in nursing, are able to demonstrate financial need, are U.S. citizens, and have a GPA of 2.0 or higher. They must agree to work as a nurse in Indiana in 1 of the following locations: acute care or specialty hospital, long–term care facility, rehabilitation care facility, home health care entity, hospice program, mental health facility, or a facility located in a shortage area.
Financial data: The stipend is $5,000 per year. Funds may be used only for tuition and fees. Recipients agree in writing to work as a nurse in a health care setting in Indiana for at least the first 2 years after graduation. If they fail to fulfill that service obligation, they will be required to reimburse the state of Indiana.
Duration: 1 year; may be renewed up to 3 additional years, but recipients must complete the nursing program within 6 years from the time the first scholarship is awarded.
Number awarded: Varies each year.
Deadline: Each participating college or university establishes its own filing deadline for this program.

1936 $ INFORMATION SYSTEMS COMMUNITY OF PRACTICE GLOBAL SCHOLARSHIP FUND

Project Management Institute
Attn: PMI Educational Foundation
14 Campus Boulevard
Newtown Square, PA 19073–3299
Phone: (610) 356–4600, ext. 7004; Fax: (610) 356–0357;
Email: pmief@pmi.org
Web: www.pmi.org/pmief/scholarship/scholarships.asp
Summary: To provide financial assistance to undergraduate or graduate students from any state who are working on a degree in a field related to information systems or project management.
Eligibility: Open to residents of any state enrolled as an undergraduate or graduate student at a college or university. First priority is given to members of the Project Management Institute (PMI) working on or planning to work on a degree in information systems, information technology, or project management; second priority is given to all students working on or planning to work on a degree in information systems, information technology, or project management; third priority is given to all students working on or planning to work on a degree in a field benefitting from project management. Along with their application, they must submit 1) a 500–word essay on why they want to be a project manager; and 2) a 250–word essay on how a code of ethics is important to project management. Financial need is not considered in the selection process.
Financial data: The stipend is $2,000.
Duration: 1 year.
Number awarded: 1 each year.
Deadline: May of each year.

1937 $ INJECTION MOLDING DIVISION SCHOLARSHIP

Society of Plastics Engineers
Attn: SPE Foundation
13 Church Hill Road
Newtown, CT 06740
Phone: (203) 740–5447; Fax: (203) 775–1157;
Email: foundation@4spe.org
Web: www.4spe.org/spe–foundation
Summary: To provide college scholarships to students who have a career interest in the plastics industry and experience in the injection molding industry.
Eligibility: Open to full–time undergraduate students at 4–year colleges and 2–year technical programs and to graduate students. Applicants must have experience in the injection molding industry, through courses taken, research conducted, or jobs held. They must be majoring in or taking courses that would be beneficial to a career in the plastics or polymer industry (e.g., plastics engineering, packaging, polymer sciences, chemistry, physics, chemical engineering, mechanical engineering, industrial engineering). Along with their application, they must submit 3 letters of recommendation; a high school and/or college transcript; a 1– to 2–page statement telling why they are applying for the scholarship, their qualifications, and their educational and career goals in the plastics industry; their employment history; a list of current and past school activities and community activities and honors; and information on their financial need.
Financial data: The stipend is $3,000. Funds are paid directly to the recipient's school.
Duration: 1 year.
Number awarded: 1 each year.
Deadline: February of each year.

1938 $$ INTEL INTERNATIONAL SCIENCE AND ENGINEERING FAIR

Society for Science & the Public
Attn: Director of Youth Programs
1719 N Street, N.W.
Washington, DC 20036
Phone: (202) 785–2255; Fax: (202) 785–1243;
Email: src@scienceforsociety.org
Web: www.societyforscience.org/isef
Summary: To recognize and reward outstanding high school students who enter a science and engineering competition.
Eligibility: Open to students from grades 9–12 who first compete in approximately 540 affiliated science and engineering fairs around the world. Each fair then sends 2 individuals and 1 team (up to 3 members) to compete in the ISEF in 1 of 17 categories: animal sciences, behavioral and social sciences, biochemistry, cellular and molecular biology, chemistry, computer science, earth and planetary sciences, electrical and mechanical engineering, environmental management, materials engineering and bioengineering, energy and transportation, environmental science, mathematical sciences, medicine and health, microbiology, physics and astronomy, and plant sciences. Each entry consists of a science project and a 250–word abstract that summarizes the project. Judging of individual projects is based on creative ability (30%), scientific thought or engineering goals (30%), thoroughness (15%), skill (15%), and clarity (10%).
Financial data: The student whose project is judged most outstanding receives the Gordon E. Moore Award of $75,000. The next 2 most outstanding projects receive Intel Foundation Young Scientist Awards of $50,000 each. In each of the categories, the first awards are $3,000, second awards $1,500, third awards $1,000, and fourth awards $500. The Intel Best of Category Awards, for the project that exemplifies the best in each scientific category that has also won a first–place in the category, are a $5,000 scholarship to the students, $1,000 to their schools, and $1,000 to their science fair. Winners also qualify for all–expense paid trips to attend the Stockholm International Youth Science Seminar that includes the Nobel Prize Ceremony in Stockholm, Sweden, and the European Union Contest for Young Scientists. Special prizes, worth more than $1.5 million, include scholarships from individual colleges and universities, all–expense paid trips to scientific and engineering installations or national conventions, summer jobs at research institutes, and laboratory equipment provided by Intel. Many professional organizations award prizes for projects that meet specified criteria.
Duration: The fair is held annually. The Intel Foundation Young Scientist Awards are paid in 8 equal installments. Most other awards are for 1 year.
Number awarded: 1 Gordon E. Moore Award and 2 Intel Foundation Young Scientist Awards are presented each year. The number of cash awards varies; recently, a total of 346 were presented, including 37 first awards, 70 second awards, 106 third awards, and 133 fourth awards. Other prizes include 17 Intel Best of Category Awards, other special awards, regional awards, and scholarships from individual colleges. A total of $4 million in scholarship and prizes is presented each year.
Deadline: The fair is always held in May.

1939 $$ INTEL SCIENCE TALENT SEARCH SCHOLARSHIPS

Society for Science & the Public
Attn: Director of Youth Programs

1719 N Street, N.W.
Washington, DC 20036
Phone: (202) 785–2255; Fax: (202) 785–1243;
Email: sts@societyforscience.org
Web: www.societyforscience.org/sts

Summary: To recognize and reward outstanding high school seniors who are interested in attending college to prepare for a career in mathematics, engineering, or any of the sciences.

Eligibility: Open to high school seniors in the United States and its territories, as well as U.S. citizens attending Department of Defense dependents schools and accredited overseas American and international schools. Applicants must complete an independent research project and submit a written report of up to 20 pages. The project may be in the following fields: animal sciences, behavioral and social sciences, biochemistry, bioengineering, bioinformatics and genomics, chemistry, computer science, earth and planetary science, engineering, environmental science, mathematics, medicine and health, microbiology, materials science, physics and space science, and plant sciences. Based on those reports, 300 students are designated as semifinalists, and from those 40 are chosen as finalists. Selection is based on individual research ability, scientific originality, and creative thinking.

Financial data: Semifinalists and their schools each receive $1,000 awards. Among the finalists, first place is a $100,000 scholarship, second place a $75,000 scholarship, third place a $50,000 scholarship, fourth place a $40,000 scholarship, fifth place a $30,000 scholarship, sixth and seventh places $25,000 scholarships, and eighth through tenth places $20,000 scholarships. In addition, 30 other finalists receive at least $7,500 scholarships. The first 10 awards are paid in 8 equal installments.

Duration: The competition is held annually. Scholarships given to the first 10 prize winners are for 4 years. The scholarships of the other 30 finalists are for 1 year.

Number awarded: Each year, 300 semifinalists are selected, and from those 40 are designated as finalists. Scholarships for finalists include 1 at $100,000, 1 at $75,000, 1 at $50,000, 3 at $25,000, 4 at $20,000, and 30 at $5,000.

Deadline: November of each year.

1940 $$ INTELLIGENCE AND CYBER SECURITY SCHOLARSHIPS

Summary: To provide financial assistance to undergraduate and graduate students working on a degree in a field related to intelligence.

See Listing #1282.

1941 INTERMOUNTAIN SECTION AWWA DIVERSITY SCHOLARSHIP

American Water Works Association–Intermountain Section
3430 East Danish Road
Sandy, UT 94093
Phone: (801) 712–1619; Fax: (801) 487–6699;
Email: nicoleb@ims–awwa.org
Web: www.ims–awwa.org/scholarships/Scholarship_Apps.html

Summary: To provide financial assistance to female and minority undergraduate and graduate students working on a degree in the field of water quality, supply, and treatment at a university in Idaho or Utah.

Eligibility: Open to 1) women; and 2) students who identify as Hispanic or Latino, Black or African American, Native Hawaiian or other Pacific Islander, Asian, or American Indian or Alaska Native. Applicants must be entering or enrolled in an undergraduate or graduate program at a college or university in Idaho or Utah that relates to water quality, supply, or treatment. Along with their application, they must submit a 2–page essay on their academic interests and career goals and how those relate to water quality, supply, or treatment. Selection is based on that essay, letters of recommendation, and potential to contribute to the field of water quality, supply, and treatment in the Intermountain West.

Financial data: The stipend is $1,000. The winner also receives a 1–year student membership in the Intermountain Section of the American Water Works Association (AWWA) and a 1–year subscription to *Journal AWWA*.

Duration: 1 year; nonrenewable.

Number awarded: 1 each year.

Deadline: October of each year.

1942 INTERMOUNTAIN SECTION AWWA UNDERGRADUATE SCIENCE AND ENGINEERING SCHOLARSHIP

American Water Works Association–Intermountain Section
3430 East Danish Road
Sandy, UT 94093
Phone: (801) 712–1619; Fax: (801) 487–6699;
Email: nicoleb@ims–awwa.org
Web: www.ims–awwa.org/scholarships/Scholarship_Apps.html

Summary: To provide financial assistance to undergraduate students working on a degree in the field of water quality, supply, and treatment at a university in Idaho or Utah.

Eligibility: Open to students entering or enrolled in an undergraduate science or engineering program at a college or university in Idaho or Utah. Applicants must be working on a degree related to water quality, supply, or treatment. Along with their application, they must submit a 2–page essay on their academic interests and career goals and how those relate to water quality, supply, or treatment. Selection is based on that essay, letters of recommendation, and potential to contribute to the field of water quality, supply, and treatment in the Intermountain West.

Financial data: The stipend is $1,000. The winner also receives a 1–year student membership in the Intermountain Section of the American Water Works Association (AWWA) and a 1–year subscription to *Journal AWWA*.

Duration: 1 year; nonrenewable.

Number awarded: 1 each year.

Deadline: October of each year.

1943 $$ INTERNATIONAL FUTURE ENERGY CHALLENGE STUDENT COMPETITION

Institute of Electrical and Electronics Engineers
Power Electronics Society
Attn: Chris Mi, IFEC Competition Administrator
University of Michigan at Dearborn
226 ELB
Dearborn, MI 48128
Phone: (313) 583–6434; Fax: (313) 583–6336;
Email: chrismi@umich.edu
Web: www.energychallenge.org

Summary: To recognize and reward undergraduate engineering students who design and build prototype equipment related to power systems.

Eligibility: Open to teams of undergraduate students enrolled in an engineering program at a college or university that is ABET–accredited or equivalent. Applicants must have a faculty adviser and the support of the school's administration to design and build a prototype of a device that meets the particular specifications of the competition for that year. Recently, students were invited to submit their proposals for 1) a highly efficient microinverter for photovoltaic panels; or 2) a low power off–line light–emitting diode driver with long lifetime. Selection is based on cost effectiveness, performance, quality of the prototype and other results, engineering reports, adherence to rules and deadlines, innovation, future promise, and other criteria related to the specific topic.

Financial data: Prizes vary each year, depending on the funding available from sponsors. Recently, the prize for the high score among all entries was $10,000. Scores for specific topic areas (e.g., engineering achievement, innovation, educational impact, presentations) ranged from $1,000 to $5,000.

Duration: The competition is held biennially, extending from mid–February of each odd–numbered year through July of the next odd–numbered year.

Number awarded: Varies each year.

Deadline: Initial proposals must be submitted by June of each even–numbered year.

1944 $ IOWA FOUNDATION FOR AGRICULTURAL ADVANCEMENT SCHOLARSHIPS

Iowa Foundation for Agricultural Advancement
Attn: Winner's Circle Scholarships
c/o SGI
30805 595th Avenue
Cambridge, IA 50046
Phone: (515) 291–3941;
Email: linda@slweldon.net
Web: www.iowastatefair.org

Summary: To provide financial assistance to Iowa high school seniors who have been involved in livestock activities and plan to major in animal science or a related field at a college in the state.

Eligibility: Open to residents of Iowa who will be incoming freshmen at a college or university in the state in the following fall. Applicants must be planning to major in animal science or a program in agriculture or human sciences that is related to the animal industry. They must have a strong background in 4–H leadership and livestock projects. Along with their application, they must submit a 250–word essay summarizing their experiences with their agricultural and livestock projects. Selection is based on that essay and participation in

agricultural and livestock projects (50%); activities, leadership, and recognition in 4–H, FFA, and other high school and community activities (25%); academic record (15%); and curriculum plans for college and career plans after graduation as they relate to the agricultural industry in general (10%).
Financial data: The stipend is $2,000.
Duration: 1 year; nonrenewable.
Number awarded: 9 each year: 6 for excellence in overall livestock project participation and 1 each for excellence in beef, swine, and sheep.
Deadline: April of each year.

1945 IOWA PHYSICIAN ASSISTANT SOCIETY SCHOLARSHIP

Iowa Physician Assistant Society
525 S.W. Fifth Street, Suite A
Des Moines, IA 50309
Phone: (515) 282–8192; Fax: (515) 282–9117;
Email: info@iapasociety.org
Web: www.iapasociety.org
Summary: To provide financial assistance to physician assistant students in Iowa.
Eligibility: Open to students enrolled in an approved physician assistant program in Iowa. Applicants must submit a 1–page narrative on any topic that the student believes will aid the committee's decision. Selection is based on demonstrated leadership in school and community activities (20 points); demonstrated professionalism in prior medical experience, training, and community activities (20 points); academic achievement (20 points); understanding of the physician assistant concept (20 points); involvement and dedication in student, civic, and professional organizations (15 points); and other intangibles (5 points).
Financial data: The stipend is $1,000.
Duration: 1 year.
Number awarded: 2 each year.
Deadline: September of each year.

1946 IOWA PORK FOUNDATION SCHOLARSHIPS

Iowa Pork Producers Association
Attn: Iowa Pork Foundation
1636 N.W. 114th Street
P.O. Box 71009
Clive, IA 50325
Phone: (515) 225–7675; (800) 372–7675; Fax: (515) 225–0563;
Email: info@iowapork.org
Web: www.iowapork.org/IAPorkYouthTeam/tabid/692/Default.aspx
Summary: To provide financial assistance to high school seniors and current college students in Iowa interested in majoring in swine production or a related field at a college in the state.
Eligibility: Open to graduating high school seniors and current college students who are residents of Iowa with a GPA of 2.5 or higher. Applicants must be attending or planning to attend a 2– or 4–year college or university in the state and major in a agriculture–related field with an emphasis on swine production. Along with their application, they must submit an essay on why they are applying for this scholarship. Financial need is not considered in the selection process.
Financial data: The stipend is $1,000. Funds are paid directly to the recipient's college or university.
Duration: 1 year.
Number awarded: 4 each year: 2 to high school seniors and 2 to current college students.
Deadline: April of each year.

1947 IOWA PORK PRODUCERS SCHOLARSHIP

Iowa Foundation for Agricultural Advancement
Attn: Winner's Circle Scholarships
c/o SGI
30805 595th Avenue
Cambridge, IA 50046
Phone: (515) 291–3941;
Email: linda@slweldon.net
Web: www.iowastatefair.org
Summary: To provide financial assistance to Iowa high school seniors who have been involved in swine activities and plan to major in animal science or a related field at a college in the state.
Eligibility: Open to residents of Iowa who will be incoming freshmen at a college or university in the state in the following fall. Applicants must be planning to major in animal science or a program in agriculture or human sciences that is related to the animal industry. They must have a strong background in swine projects and activities. Along with their application, they must submit a 250–word essay summarizing their experiences with their agricultural and livestock projects. Selection is based on that essay and participation in agricultural and livestock projects (50%); activities, leadership, and recognition in 4–H, FFA, and other high school and community activities (25%); academic record (15%); and curriculum plans for college and career plans after graduation as they relate to the agricultural industry in general (10%). Preference is given to applicants who show a desire to remain active in the swine industry after graduation.
Financial data: The stipend is $1,000.
Duration: 1 year; nonrenewable.
Number awarded: 1 each year.
Deadline: April of each year.

1948 IOWA POULTRY ASSOCIATION SCHOLARSHIP

Iowa Foundation for Agricultural Advancement
Attn: Winner's Circle Scholarships
c/o SGI
30805 595th Avenue
Cambridge, IA 50046
Phone: (515) 291–3941;
Email: linda@slweldon.net
Web: www.iowastatefair.org
Summary: To provide financial assistance to Iowa high school seniors who have been involved in poultry activities and plan to major in animal science or a related field at a college in the state.
Eligibility: Open to residents of Iowa who will be incoming freshmen at a college or university in the state in the following fall. Applicants must be planning to major in animal science or a program in agriculture or human sciences that is related to the animal industry. They must have a strong background in poultry and a desire to remain active in the poultry industry after graduation. Along with their application, they must submit a 250–word essay summarizing their experiences with their agricultural and livestock projects. Selection is based on that essay and participation in agricultural and livestock projects (50%); activities, leadership, and recognition in 4–H, FFA, and other high school and community activities (25%); academic record (15%); and curriculum plans for college and career plans after graduation as they relate to the agricultural industry in general (10%).
Financial data: The stipend is $1,000.
Duration: 1 year; nonrenewable.
Number awarded: 1 each year.
Deadline: April of each year.

1949 IOWA PUREBRED SWINE COUNCIL SCHOLARSHIP

Iowa Foundation for Agricultural Advancement
Attn: Winner's Circle Scholarships
c/o SGI
30805 595th Avenue
Cambridge, IA 50046
Phone: (515) 291–3941;
Email: linda@slweldon.net
Web: www.iowastatefair.org
Summary: To provide financial assistance to Iowa high school seniors who have been involved in swine activities and plan to major in animal science or a related field at a college in the state.
Eligibility: Open to residents of Iowa who will be incoming freshmen at a college or university in the state in the following fall. Applicants must be planning to major in animal science or a program in agriculture or human sciences that is related to the animal industry. They must have a strong background in swine projects and activities. Along with their application, they must submit a 250–word essay summarizing their experiences with their agricultural and livestock projects. Selection is based on that essay and participation in agricultural and livestock projects (50%); activities, leadership, and recognition in 4–H, FFA, and other high school and community activities (25%); academic record (15%); and curriculum plans for college and career plans after graduation as they relate to the agricultural industry in general (10%). Preference is given to applicants who show a desire to remain active in the purebred swine industry after graduation.
Financial data: The stipend is $1,500.
Duration: 1 year; nonrenewable.
Number awarded: 1 each year.
Deadline: April of each year.

1950 IOWA READY MIXED CONCRETE ASSOCIATION SCHOLARSHIP PROGRAM

Iowa Ready Mixed Concrete Association
Attn: Scholarship Committee
380 S.E. Delaware Avenue
Ankeny, IA 50021
Phone: (515) 965–4575; Fax: (515) 963–4010;
Email: irmca@iowareadymix.org
Web: www.iowareadymix.org

Summary: To provide financial assistance to undergraduates at colleges and universities in Iowa who are preparing for a career in the concrete, construction, or engineering industries.

Eligibility: Open to U.S. citizens who have achieved at least sophomore status at a 2– or 4–year college or university in Iowa. Applicants must be working on a degree in an area that will prepare them for a career in the ready mixed concrete or construction and engineering industries. Preference is given to applicants who are residents of Iowa, related to an employee of a member company of the Iowa Ready Mixed Concrete Association, and experienced in the ready mixed concrete industry. Along with their application, they must submit a short essay explaining why they might consider employment in the ready mixed concrete, construction, or engineering fields. Selection is based on academic achievement, area of study as it relates to the industry, other achievements and activities, and financial need.

Financial data: The stipend is $1,000.

Duration: 1 year.

Number awarded: At least 5 each year.

Deadline: November of each year.

1951 $$ IOWA SELECT FARMS SCHOLARSHIP

Iowa Foundation for Agricultural Advancement
Attn: Winner's Circle Scholarships
c/o SGI
30805 595th Avenue
Cambridge, IA 50046
Phone: (515) 291–3941;
Email: linda@slweldon.net
Web: www.iowastatefair.org

Summary: To provide financial assistance to Iowa high school seniors who have been involved in swine activities and plan to major in animal science or a related field at a college in the state.

Eligibility: Open to residents of Iowa who will be incoming freshmen at a college or university in the state in the following fall. Applicants must be planning to major in animal science or a program in agriculture or human sciences that is related to the animal industry. They must have a strong agricultural background involving 4–H and/or FFA with an emphasis on swine. Along with their application, they must submit a 250–word essay summarizing their experiences with their agricultural and livestock projects. Selection is based on that essay and participation in agricultural and livestock projects (50%); activities, leadership, and recognition in 4–H, FFA, and other high school and community activities (25%); academic record (15%); and curriculum plans for college and career plans after graduation as they relate to the agricultural industry in general (10%). Preference is given to applicants who show a desire to remain active in the swine production industry after graduation.

Financial data: The stipend is $5,000.

Duration: 1 year; nonrenewable.

Number awarded: 1 each year.

Deadline: April of each year.

1952 IRENE STRAUS SCHOLARSHIP

Wisconsin Garden Club Federation
c/o Carolyn A. Craig, Scholarship Chair
900 North Shore Drive
New Richmond, WI 54017–9466
Phone: (715) 246–6242;
Email: cacraig@frontiernet.net
Web: www.wisconsingardenclub.org/education/college–scholarship–program

Summary: To provide financial assistance to upper–division and graduate students from any state who are working on a degree related to gardening at a school in Wisconsin.

Eligibility: Open to juniors, seniors, and graduate students from any state who are enrolled at colleges and universities in Wisconsin. Applicants must be working on a degree in horticulture, floriculture, landscape design/architecture, botany, forestry, agronomy, plant pathology, environmental studies, city planning, land management, or a related field. They must have a GPA of 3.0 or higher. Selection is based on academic record (50%), character (25%), and occupational objective (25%).

Financial data: The stipend is $1,000.

Duration: 1 year.

Number awarded: 1 each year.

Deadline: February of each year.

1953 $ ITW SCHOLARSHIPS

Society of Women Engineers
Attn: Scholarship Selection Committee
203 North LaSalle Street, Suite 1675
Chicago, IL 60601–1269
Phone: (312) 596–5223; (877) SWE–INFO; Fax: (312) 644–8557;
Email: scholarships@swe.org
Web: societyofwomenengineers.swe.org/index.php/scholarships

Summary: To provide financial assistance to undergraduate women majoring in designated engineering specialties.

Eligibility: Open to women who are entering their junior year at a 4–year ABET–accredited college or university. Applicants must be working full time on a degree in computer science, electrical or mechanical engineering, or polymer science. They must have a GPA of 3.0 or higher. Preference is given to members of groups underrepresented in engineering or computer science. Selection is based on merit. U.S. citizenship or permanent resident status is required.

Financial data: The stipend is $2,500 per year.

Duration: 1 year; may be renewed 1 additional year.

Number awarded: 2 each year.

Deadline: February of each year.

1954 J. FIELDING REED SCHOLARSHIP

American Society of Agronomy
5585 Guilford Road
Madison, WI 53711–5801
Phone: (608) 273–8080; Fax: (608) 273–2021;
Email: awards@sciencesocieties.org
Web: www.agronomy.org/awards/award/detail/?a=6

Summary: To provide financial assistance to undergraduate students preparing for a career in soil or plant sciences.

Eligibility: Open to undergraduates who are preparing for a career in the plant or soil sciences. Applicants must have a GPA of 3.0 or higher and be able to document a history of community and campus leadership activities, particularly in agriculture. They must be planning to graduate sometime in the current calendar year.

Financial data: The stipend is $1,000.

Duration: 1 year.

Number awarded: 1 each year.

Deadline: March of each year.

1955 J. GAIL MCGREW AND JOHN J. FRUECHT SCHOLARSHIP

American Mensa Education and Research Foundation
1229 Corporate Drive West
Arlington, TX 76006–6103
Phone: (817) 607–5577; (800) 66–MENSA; Fax: (817) 649–5232;
Email: info@mensafoundation.org
Web: www.mensafoundation.org/what–we–do/scholarships

Summary: To provide financial assistance to residents of designated southeastern states who are interested in studying physics or chemistry at a college in any state.

Eligibility: Open to residents of Alabama, Georgia, Mississippi, North Carolina, South Carolina, and Tennessee who are enrolled or planning to enroll at an accredited American institution of postsecondary education. Applicants must 1) be interested in undergraduate or graduate study of physics or chemistry; or 2) have been out of formal education for a period of 5 or more years. Membership in Mensa is not required, but applicants must be U.S. citizens or permanent residents. There are no restrictions as to age, race, gender, level of postsecondary education, GPA, or financial need. Selection is based on a 550–word essay that describes the applicant's career, vocational, or academic goals.

Financial data: The stipend is $1,000.

Duration: 1 year; nonrenewable.

Number awarded: 1 each year.

Deadline: January of each year.

1956 $ J.A. AND FLOSSIE MAE SMITH SCHOLARSHIP

San Diego Foundation
Attn: Community Scholarship Program
2508 Historic Decatur Road, Suite 200
San Diego, CA 92106
Phone: (619) 235–2300; Fax: (619) 239–1710;
Email: scholarships@sdfoundation.org
Web: www.sdfoundation.org/GrantsScholarships/Scholarships.aspx

Summary: To provide financial assistance to undergraduate or graduate students interested in majoring in agriculture.

Eligibility: Open to graduating high school seniors, current college and university students, and adult reentry students who are attending or planning to attend an accredited 2– or 4–year college or university, graduate school, or licensed trade or vocational school in any state. Applicants may be interested in working on a degree in agriculture. A personal interview is required. Selection is based on academic ability and financial need.

Financial data: The maximum stipend awarded is $2,500 per year. Funds may be paid either to the recipient or to the recipient's school.

Duration: 1 year; may be renewed up to a maximum of 6 years.

Number awarded: 1 or more each year.

Deadline: February of each year.

1957 $ JACK CRAMER SCHOLARSHIP

National Athletic Trainers' Association
2952 Stemmons Freeway, Suite 200
Dallas, TX 75247–6103
Phone: (214) 637–6282; (800) 879–6282; Fax: (214) 637–2206
Web: www.nata.org/jack–cramer–scholarship

Summary: To provide financial aid to high school seniors who plan to attend college to prepare for a career as an athletic trainer.

Eligibility: Open to graduating high school seniors who have a GPA of 3.0 or higher. Applicants must be planning to enroll full time at a college or university to work on a baccalaureate degree in athletic training. They must be sponsored by an athletic trainer at their school who is a member of the National Athletic Trainers' Association (NATA) and under whose supervision they have accumulated at least 200 hours of observation in an athletic training room setting. Along with their application, they must submit 1) a 500–word essay on why they wish to become a certified athletic trainer, why they wish to work in the secondary school setting as an athletic trainer, how they will prepare themselves as a viable employee in the secondary school setting, and their role as a health care provider to high school athletes; 2) a 100–word essay on what they plan to be doing in 5 years; and 3) a 300–word essay on their vision of their future athletic training program. Financial need is not considered in the selection process.

Financial data: The stipend is $2,000.

Duration: 1 year.

Number awarded: 1 each year.

Deadline: December of each year.

1958 $ JACK R. GILSTRAP SCHOLARSHIP

American Public Transportation Association
Attn: American Public Transportation Foundation
1666 K Street, N.W., Suite 1100
Washington, DC 20006
Phone: (202) 496–4803; Fax: (202) 496–4323;
Email: yconley@apta.com
Web: www.aptfd.org/work/scholarship.htm

Summary: To provide financial assistance to undergraduate and graduate students who are preparing for a career in public transportation.

Eligibility: Open to college sophomores, juniors, seniors, and graduate students who are preparing for a career in the transit industry. Any member organization of the American Public Transportation Association (APTA) can nominate and sponsor candidates for this scholarship. Nominees must be enrolled in a fully–accredited institution, have and maintain at least a 3.0 GPA, and be either employed by or demonstrate a strong interest in entering the public transportation industry. They must submit a 1,000–word essay on "In what segment of the public transportation industry will you make a career and why?" Selection is based on demonstrated interest in the transit field as a career, need for financial assistance, academic achievement, essay content and quality, and involvement in extracurricular citizenship and leadership activities. This award is presented to the applicant receiving the highest overall score.

Financial data: The stipend is $2,500.

Duration: 1 year; may be renewed.

Number awarded: 1 each year.

Deadline: May of each year.

1959 JACKSON FAMILY SCHOLARSHIP

Orange County Community Foundation
Attn: Scholarship Associate
4041 MacArthur Boulevard, Suite 510
Newport Beach, CA 92660
Phone: (949) 553–4202, ext. 46; Fax: (949) 553–4211;
Email: alee@oc–cf.org
Web: www.oc–cf.org/Page.aspx?pid=869

Summary: To provide financial assistance to residents of California who are currently enrolled in an accredited nursing program in any state.

Eligibility: Open to residents of California who have completed at least 2 semesters of study in an accredited nursing program in any state. Applicants must be 1) students seeking to enter the nursing profession; or 2) current nursing professionals upgrading their standing (e.g., L.V.N. to R.N., R.N. to nurse practitioner). They must have a GPA of 3.0 or higher and be able to demonstrate financial need. U.S. citizenship is required.

Financial data: The stipend is $1,000 per year.

Duration: 1 year; may be renewed.

Number awarded: 1 or more each year.

Deadline: March of each year.

1960 JACOB AND RITA VAN NAMEN MARKETING SCHOLARSHIP

American Floral Endowment
1601 Duke Street
Alexandria, VA 22314
Phone: (703) 838–5211; Fax: (703) 838–5212;
Email: afe@endowment.org
Web: endowment.org/floriculture–scholarshipsinternships.html

Summary: To provide financial assistance to undergraduates preparing for a career in the business of horticulture.

Eligibility: Open to sophomores, juniors, and seniors who are horticulture majors and have a career interest in agribusiness marketing and distribution of floral products. Applicants must be U.S. or Canadian citizens or permanent residents and have a GPA of 2.0 or higher. Along with their application, they must submit a statement describing their career goals and the academic, work–related, and/or life experiences that support those goals. Financial need is considered in the selection process.

Financial data: The stipend varies each year; recently, it was $1,025.

Duration: 1 year.

Number awarded: 1 each year.

Deadline: April of each year.

1961 $ JAMES A. HOLEKAMP MEMORIAL SCHOLARSHIP IN FOREST RESOURCES

Mill Operations Technical Advancement Group (MOTAG) South
c/o Mike Grist, Scholarship Chair
Mead Westvaco
104 East Riverside Street
Covington, VA 24426–0950
Phone: (540) 969–5368;
Email: mvg@meadwestvaco.com
Web: www.andritzwoodprocessing.com/motag/south/html/scholarship.html

Summary: To provide financial assistance to students working on a degree in a wood fiber related field at a university in the South.

Eligibility: Open to students entering their sophomore year at a college or university in the Southeast or South Central states. Applicants must be planning to major in a field related to wood fiber (e.g., forestry, silviculture, land management) and have a GPA of 3.0 or higher for their freshman year. Financial need is considered in the selection process.

Financial data: The stipend is $2,000 per year.

Duration: 1 year; may be renewed up to 3 additional years, provided the recipient maintains a GPA of 3.0 or higher.

Number awarded: 1 each year.

Deadline: June of each year.

1962 JAMES E. ROBERTS ENGINEERING SCHOLARSHIP

California Department of Transportation
Attn: Division of Human Resources
Equal Employment Opportunity Program (MS 90)
P.O. Box 168037

Sacramento, CA 95816–8037
Phone: (916) 227–1823;
Email: steve_perez@dot.ca.gov
Web: www.dot.ca.gov/hq/jobs/scholarships.htm

Summary: To provide financial assistance to high school seniors in California who plan to major in civil engineering at a college in the state.

Eligibility: Open to seniors graduating from high schools in California and planning to enroll at a community college, state college, or university in the state. Applicants must be planning to major in civil engineering to prepare for a career in transportation. They must be a U.S. citizen, permanent resident, or documented international student. Along with their application, they must submit a 1–page personal statement on their college and career plans and how they believe they can make a contribution to the California Department of Transportation as a civil engineer in the transportation field. Selection is based on academic record, current job skills, community and school involvement, work and/or volunteer experience, commitment to a career in transportation, and financial need.

Financial data: The stipend is $1,000.

Duration: 1 year.

Number awarded: 4 each year.

Deadline: May of each year.

1963 JAMES F. REVILLE SCHOLARSHIP

NYSARC, Inc.
Attn: Scholarship and Awards Committee
393 Delaware Avenue
Delmar, NY 12054
Phone: (518) 439–8311; Fax: (518) 439–1893;
Email: info@nysarc.org
Web: www.nysarc.org

Summary: To provide financial assistance to college students in New York majoring in a field related to intellectual and other development disabilities.

Eligibility: Open to students enrolled full time at a college or university in New York. Applicants must be working on a degree in a field related to intellectual and other development disabilities. They must be nominated by a chapter of NYSARC, Inc. Students must submit brief statements on 1) how they became interested in becoming a professional in a field related to people who have intellectual and other developmental disabilities; 2) their experiences with people who have intellectual and other developmental disabilities; 3) any memberships in organizations concerned with people who have intellectual and other developmental disabilities; and 4) their career plans and how they relate to people who have intellectual and other developmental disabilities. Financial need is not considered in the selection process.

Financial data: The stipend is $1,500 per year.

Duration: 2 years.

Number awarded: 1 each year.

Deadline: January of each year.

1964 $ JAMES H. DAVIS MEMORIAL SCHOLARSHIP

National Foliage Foundation
c/o Florida Nursery, Growers and Landscape Association
1533 Park Center Drive
Orlando, FL 32835–5705
Phone: (407) 295–7994; (800) 375–3642; Fax: (407) 295–1619;
Email: info@nationalfoliagefoundation.org
Web: www.nationalfoliagefoundation.org/scholarship/scholarship–info

Summary: To provide financial assistance to undergraduate and graduate students from any state who are interested in attending school in Florida to prepare for a career in the horticulture industry.

Eligibility: Open to undergraduate and graduate students from any state entering or enrolled at a college, university, community college, or other postsecondary program in Florida. Applicants must enroll full time in a horticulture program or related field with the intent to graduate in that field. They must have a GPA of 2.0 or higher. Along with their application, they must submit a short essay about themselves that includes their work and classroom experience with horticulture or related field, the area of horticulture or related field that they are interested in pursuing, what they plan to do after graduation, and why they are qualified to receive the scholarship. Selection is based on the essay, 2 letters of recommendation, transcripts, and financial need.

Financial data: The amount of the stipend varies; recently, the average was more than $2,000.

Duration: 1 year.

Number awarded: Varies each year; recently, 9 of these scholarships were awarded.

Deadline: January of each year.

1965 JAMES L. ALLHANDS ESSAY COMPETITION

Associated General Contractors of America
Attn: AGC Education and Research Foundation
2300 Wilson Boulevard, Suite 400
Arlington, VA 22201
Phone: (703) 837–5342; Fax: (703) 837–5451;
Email: patricianm@agc.org
Web: www.agc.org

Summary: To recognize and reward outstanding student essays on a topic related to construction or civil engineering.

Eligibility: Open to college seniors who are enrolled full time in a 4– or 5–year ABET– or ACCE–accredited construction or construction–related engineering degree program. Applicants must submit an essay, up to 10 pages in length, on a topic that changes annually; recently, it was "Setting the Standard for Ethical Behavior and Legal Compliance." Selection is based on clarity; use of specific examples to support opinions; grammar, spelling, and punctuation; neatness; adherence to format and MLA standards; originality and uniqueness of ideas; and adherence to competition guidelines for essay length, abstract, bibliography, and submission deadline.

Financial data: The first–prize winner receives $1,000 and a trip to the annual convention of the Associated General Contractors (AGC) of America; the second–prize winner receives $500; the third–prize winner receives $300. In addition, the faculty sponsor of the first–prize winner receives $500 and a trip to the AGC convention.

Duration: The competition is held annually.

Deadline: November of each year.

1966 $$ JAMES L. AND GENEVIEVE H. GOODWIN MEMORIAL SCHOLARSHIPS

Hartford Foundation for Public Giving
Attn: Donor Services Officer
10 Columbus Boulevard, Eighth Floor
Hartford, CT 06106
Phone: (860) 548–1888; Fax: (860) 524–8346;
Email: scholarships@hfpg.org
Web: www.hfpgscholarships.org/Scholarships/Home/tabid/305/Default.aspx

Summary: To provide financial assistance to residents of Connecticut interested in working on an undergraduate or graduate degree in forestry or forest management at a school in any state.

Eligibility: Open to Connecticut residents who are graduating high school seniors, currently enrolled in college, or graduate students. Applicants must be attending or planning to attend a college or university in any state and studying silviculture or forest management. Selection is based on financial need, academic record, and a personal statement on why the applicant is interested in forestry or forest management.

Financial data: Stipends range from $1,000 to $5,000 per year. Funds may be used for tuition or living costs. Payment is made only to the recipient's institution.

Duration: 1 year; may be renewed.

Number awarded: 5 to 10 each year.

Deadline: March of each year.

1967 $ JAMES M. AND VIRGINIA M. SMYTH SCHOLARSHIP FUND

Summary: To provide financial assistance to high school seniors, especially those from designated states, who are interested in majoring in selected fields at colleges in any state.

See Listing #1294.

1968 $ JAMES MONTAG, JR. SCHOLARSHIP

Tennessee Academy of Physician Assistants
Attn: Tennessee Physician Assistant Foundation
P.O. Box 150785
Nashville, TN 37215–0785
Phone: (615) 463–0026; Fax: (615) 463–0036;
Email: info@tnpa.com
Web: www.tnpa.com/scholarships.php

Summary: To provide financial assistance to physician assistant students from Tennessee who are serving or have served in the military.

Eligibility: Open to students in the first or second year of a physician assistant program who are either 1) enrolled at an approved program in Tennessee; or 2) residents of Tennessee enrolled at an approved school in another state.

Applicants must be serving on active or Reserve duty in any branch of the military or the National Guard or have an honorable discharge; Air Force medics are particularly encouraged to apply. Along with their application, they must submit an essay of 2 to 3 pages on their professional career and lifetime goals. Financial need is not considered in the selection process.
Financial data: Recently, the stipend was $2,000.
Duration: 1 year.
Number awarded: 1 each year.
Deadline: September of each year.

1969 $ JAMES W. HUNT, JR. COMMUNITY HEALTH AND PUBLIC SERVICE SCHOLARSHIP

Massachusetts League of Community Health Centers
40 Court Street, Tenth Floor
Boston, MA 02108
Phone: (617) 426–2225; Fax: (617) 426–0097;
Email: massleague@massleague.org
Web: www.massleague.org
Summary: To provide financial assistance to undergraduate students from Massachusetts who are interested in community and public health.
Eligibility: Open to undergraduate students from Massachusetts who display a genuine interest in community and public health through academic study or volunteer service. Applicants must submit a 2–page essay expressing their interest in community health or public service. They may also submit letters of support and documentation of financial need, but those are optional.
Financial data: The stipend is $2,000.
Duration: 1 year.
Number awarded: 1 or more each year.
Deadline: March of each year.

1970 JANET CULLEN TANAKA SCHOLARSHIP

Association for Women Geoscientists
Attn: AWG Foundation
12000 North Washington Street, Suite 285
Thornton, CO 80241
Phone: (303) 412–6219; Fax: (303) 253–9220;
Email: scholarship@awg–ps.org
Web: www.awg.org/EAS/scholarships.html
Summary: To provide financial assistance to women from any state who are working on an undergraduate degree in geoscience at a college or university in Oregon or Washington.
Eligibility: Open to undergraduate women from any state who are working on a bachelor's degree and committed to preparing for a career or graduate work in the geosciences, including geology, environmental or engineering geology, geochemistry, geophysics, hydrogeology, or hydrology. Applicants must be currently enrolled in a 2– or 4–year college or university in Oregon or Washington and have a GPA of 3.2 or higher. Along with their application, they must submit a 1–page essay summarizing their commitment to a career in the geosciences. Selection is based on potential for professional success, academic achievements, and financial need.
Financial data: The stipend is $1,000.
Duration: 1 year.
Number awarded: 1 each year.
Deadline: November of each year.

1971 $ JAY KAPLAN MEMORIAL SCHOLARSHIP

Vermont Student Assistance Corporation
Attn: Scholarship Programs
10 East Allen Street
P.O. Box 2000
Winooski, VT 05404–2601
Phone: (802) 654–3798; (888) 253–4819; Fax: (802) 654–3765; TDD: (800) 281–3341 (within VT);
Email: info@vsac.org
Web: services.vsac.org/wps/wcm/connect/VSAC/vsac/pay+for+college
Summary: To provide financial assistance to residents of Vermont, especially those with disabilities, who are interested in working on a degree in science or finance at a college in any state.
Eligibility: Open to residents of Vermont who are attending or planning to attend a college or university in any state. Applicants must be seeking training or education related to science or finance. Preference is given to students who have a documented disability (must submit school 504 or IEP plan). Along with their application, they must submit 1) a 100–word essay on their interest in and commitment to pursuing their chosen career or vocation; and 2) any significant barriers that limit their access to education. Selection is based on those essays, a letter of recommendation, and financial need.
Financial data: The stipend is $2,000.
Duration: 1 year; nonrenewable.
Number awarded: 2 each year.
Deadline: March of each year.

1972 JEANNE MOWLDS DISTINGUISHED LIFETIME SERVICE AWARD

Summary: To provide financial assistance to undergraduate and graduate students from any country interested in preparing for a career in document management and graphic communications.
See Listing #1304.

1973 JENNET COLLIFLOWER KEYS NURSING SCHOLARSHIP

The Miami Foundation
Attn: Development Officer
200 South Biscayne Boulevard, Suite 505
Miami, FL 33131–5330
Phone: (305) 371–2711; Fax: (305) 371–5342;
Email: jbenzaquen@miamifoundation.org
Web: miamifoundation.org/scholarships.aspx
Summary: To provide financial assistance to upper–division students in Florida who are working on a degree in nursing at a school in the state.
Eligibility: Open to students entering their junior or senior year of an undergraduate nursing program. Applicants must be Florida residents enrolled full time in a public or private university in the state. Selection is based on academic achievement, a personal statement of career goals, and financial need. U.S. citizenship or permanent resident status is required.
Financial data: The stipend is $1,000.
Duration: 1 year.
Number awarded: 2 each year.
Deadline: April of each year.

1974 $ JEREMIAH TENHET US ARMY MILITARY INTELLIGENCE SCHOLARSHIP

American Academy of Physician Assistants–Veterans Caucus
Attn: Veterans Caucus
P.O. Box 362
Danville, PA 17821–0362
Phone: (570) 271–0292; Fax: (570) 271–5850;
Email: admin@veteranscaucus.org
Web: www.veteranscaucus.org
Summary: To provide financial assistance to Army veterans who served in Afghanistan and their dependents who are studying to become physician assistants.
Eligibility: Open to U.S. citizens who are currently enrolled in a physician assistant program. The program must be approved by the Commission on Accreditation of Allied Health Education. Applicants must be honorably discharged members of the United States Army who served in Afghanistan or the dependents of those members. Selection is based on military honors and awards received, civic and college honors and awards received, professional memberships and activities, and GPA. An electronic copy of the applicant's DD Form 214 must accompany the application.
Financial data: The stipend is $2,000.
Duration: 1 year.
Number awarded: 1 each year.
Deadline: February of each year.

1975 $ JERMAN–CAHOON STUDENT SCHOLARSHIP

American Society of Radiologic Technologists
Attn: ASRT Education and Research Foundation
15000 Central Avenue, S.E.
Albuquerque, NM 87123–3909
Phone: (505) 298–4500, ext. 2541; (800) 444–2778, ext. 2541; Fax: (505) 298–5063;
Email: foundation@asrt.org
Web: www.asrtfoundation.org/Content/Scholarships_and_Awards

Summary: To provide financial assistance to entry–level students preparing for a career in a field related to radiologic science.
Eligibility: Open to students enrolled in an accredited entry–level program in radiography, sonography, magnetic resonance, or nuclear medicine. Applicants must be able to finish their degree or certificate in the year for which they are applying. They must be U.S. citizens, nationals, or permanent residents have a GPA of 3.0 or higher. Along with their application, they must submit 9 essays of 200 words each on assigned topics related to their personal situation and interest in a career in radiologic science. Selection is based on those essays, academic and professional achievements, recommendations, and financial need.
Financial data: The stipend is $2,500. Funds are paid directly to the recipient's institution.
Duration: 1 year.
Number awarded: 5 each year.
Deadline: January of each year.

1976 JESSICA M. BLANDING MEMORIAL SCHOLARSHIP

New England Regional Black Nurses Association, Inc.
P.O. Box 190690
Boston, MA 02119
Phone: (617) 524–1951
Web: www.nerbna.org/org/scholarships.html
Summary: To provide financial assistance to licensed practical nurses from New England who are working on a degree and have contributed to the African American community.
Eligibility: Open to residents of the New England states who are licensed practical nurses working on an associate or bachelor's degree in nursing at a school in any state. Applicants must have at least 1 full year of school remaining. Along with their application, they must submit a 3–page essay that covers their career aspirations in the nursing profession; how they have contributed to the African American or other communities of color in such areas as work, volunteering, church, or community outreach; an experience that has enhanced their personal and/or professional growth; and any financial hardships that may hinder them from completing their education.
Financial data: A stipend is awarded (amount not specified).
Duration: 1 year.
Number awarded: 1 or more each year.
Deadline: February of each year.

1977 JILL S. TIETJEN P.E. SCHOLARSHIP

Society of Women Engineers
Attn: Scholarship Selection Committee
203 North LaSalle Street, Suite 1675
Chicago, IL 60601–1269
Phone: (312) 596–5223; (877) SWE–INFO; Fax: (312) 644–8557;
Email: scholarships@swe.org
Web: societyofwomenengineers.swe.org/index.php/scholarships
Summary: To provide financial assistance to women working on an undergraduate degree in engineering or computer science.
Eligibility: Open to women who will be sophomores, juniors, or seniors at ABET–accredited colleges and universities. Applicants must be U.S. citizens or permanent residents working full time on a degree in computer science or engineering and have a GPA of 3.0 or higher. Selection is based on merit.
Financial data: The stipend is $1,500.
Duration: 1 year.
Number awarded: 1 each year.
Deadline: February of each year.

1978 JIM KIBLER AGRICULTURE FUND

Blue Mountain Community Foundation
8 South Second Street, Suite 618
P.O. Box 603
Walla Walla, WA 99362–0015
Phone: (509) 529–4371; Fax: (509) 529–5284;
Email: bmcf@bluemountainfoundation.org
Web: www.bluemountainfoundation.org/scholarship–funds.php
Summary: To provide financial assistance to students, especially residents of Idaho, Oregon, or Washington, who are working on a degree in an agriculture–related field at a school in any state.
Eligibility: Open to students currently enrolled at a college or specialized vocational agribusiness program in any state. Applicants must be preparing for a career in farming, animal science (including veterinary medicine), natural resources management, agricultural technology, agricultural marketing, or agricultural management. Preference is given to residents of Idaho, Oregon, or Washington who have a farming or cattle–raising background.
Financial data: The amount awarded varies, depending upon the availability of funds.
Duration: 1 year; recipients may reapply.
Number awarded: 1 or more each year.
Deadline: February of each year.

1979 JIMMY A. YOUNG MEMORIAL EDUCATION RECOGNITION AWARD

American Association for Respiratory Care
Attn: American Respiratory Care Foundation
9425 North MacArthur Boulevard, Suite 100
Irving, TX 75063–4706
Phone: (972) 243–2272; Fax: (972) 484–2720;
Email: info@arcfoundation.org
Web: www.arcfoundation.org/awards/undergraduate/young.cfm
Summary: To provide financial assistance to college students, especially minorities, interested in becoming respiratory therapists.
Eligibility: Open to students who are enrolled in an accredited respiratory therapy program, have completed at least 1 semester/quarter of the program, and have a GPA of 3.0 or higher. Preference is given to nominees of minority origin. Applications must include 6 copies of an original referenced paper on some aspect of respiratory care and letters of recommendation. The foundation prefers that the candidates be nominated by a school or program, but any student may initiate a request for sponsorship by a school (in order that a deserving candidate is not denied the opportunity to compete simply because the school does not initiate the application).
Financial data: The stipend is $1,000. The award also provides airfare, 1 night's lodging, and registration for the association's international congress.
Duration: 1 year.
Number awarded: 1 each year.
Deadline: June of each year.

1980 JOE D. SIMMONS MEMORIAL SCHOLARSHIP

American Society for Quality
Attn: Measurement Quality Division
600 North Plankinton Avenue
P.O. Box 3005
Milwaukee, WI 53201–3005
Phone: (414) 272–8575; (800) 248–1946; Fax: (414) 272–1734;
Email: help@asq.org
Web: asq.org/measure/about/awards–measure.html
Summary: To provide financial assistance to undergraduate and graduate students working on a degree in a field related to metrology and quality.
Eligibility: Open to undergraduate and graduate students who are working on a degree in a field of study related to measurement science and quality. Applicants must submit a 1,000–word essay describing the metrology and quality concepts they have learned and applied in academic or work settings and their career aspirations. Financial need is also considered in the selection process.
Financial data: The stipend is $1,500.
Duration: 1 year.
Number awarded: 1 or more each year.
Deadline: April of each year.

1981 $ JOE J. WELKER MEMORIAL SCHOLARSHIP

Delaware Engineering Society
c/o Stacy Ziegler
Duffield Associates, Inc.
5400 Limestone Road
Wilmington, DE 19808
Phone: (302) 239–6634; Fax: (302) 239–8485;
Email: sziegler@duffnet.com
Web: www.desonline.us
Summary: To provide financial assistance to high school seniors in Delaware who are interested in majoring in engineering in college.
Eligibility: Open to graduating high school seniors in Delaware who are residents of the state and interested in majoring in engineering at an ABET–accredited college or university. Applicants must have SAT scores of 600 or higher in mathematics, 500 or higher in critical reading, and 500 or higher in writing (or

ACT scores of 29 or higher in mathematics and 25 or higher in English). They must submit an essay (up to 500 words) on their interest in engineering, their major area of study and area of specialization, the occupation they propose to pursue after graduation, their long–term goals, and how they hope to achieve them. Selection is based on the essay, academic record, honors and scholarships, volunteer activities, work experience, and letters of recommendation. Financial need is not required.

Financial data: The stipend ranges from $1,500 to $2,000.

Duration: 1 year; nonrenewable.

Number awarded: Varies each year; recently, 3 of these scholarships were awarded.

Deadline: December of each year.

1982 JOEL CARTUN SCHOLARSHIP

Summary: To provide financial assistance to undergraduate and graduate students from any country interested in preparing for a career in document management and graphic communications.

See Listing #1311.

1983 $ JOHN AND ALICE EGAN MULTI–YEAR MENTORING SCHOLARSHIP PROGRAM

Daedalian Foundation
Attn: Scholarship Committee
55 Main Circle (Building 676)
P.O. Box 249
Randolph AFB, TX 78148–0249
Phone: (210) 945–2113; Fax: (210) 945–2112;
Email: kristi@daedalians.org
Web: www.daedalians.org/foundation/scholarships.htm

Summary: To provide financial assistance to college students who are participating in a ROTC program and wish to become military pilots.

Eligibility: Open to students who have completed at least the freshman year at an accredited 4–year college or university and have a GPA of 3.0 or higher. Applicants must be participating in an ROTC program and be medically qualified for flight training. They must plan to apply for and be awarded a military pilot training allocation at the appropriate juncture in their ROTC program. Selection is based on intention to prepare for a career as a military pilot, demonstrated moral character and patriotism, scholastic and military standing and aptitude, and physical condition and aptitude for flight. Financial need may also be considered.

Financial data: The stipend is $2,500 per year, including $500 provided by a local Flight of the organization and $2,000 as a matching award provided by the foundation.

Duration: 1 year; may be renewed up to 2 or 3 additional years, provided the recipient maintains a GPA of 3.0 or higher and is enrolled in an undergraduate program.

Number awarded: Up to 11 each year.

Deadline: July of each year.

1984 $ JOHN D. SPURLING, O.B.E., SCHOLARSHIPS

American Kennel Club
Attn: AKC Humane Fund, Inc.
260 Madison Avenue
New York, NY 10016
Phone: (212) 696–8243;
Email: dxs@akc.org
Web: www.akc.org/humane_fund/grants.html

Summary: To provide financial assistance to college students working on a degree in a field that advances responsible pet ownership.

Eligibility: Open to full–time students enrolled in a degree or certification program at an accredited U.S. institution. Applicants must be studying a field that advances responsible pet ownership. Along with their application, they must submit brief statements 1) describing the course of study for which they are applying for this scholarship; 2) explaining why they are pursuing that course of study; 3) identifying the outcomes they wish to achieve with that course of study; and 4) describing their involvement in organizations and clubs that advance responsible pet ownership. Selection is based on those statements, academic merit, community experience with responsible pet ownership, and letters of recommendation.

Financial data: The stipend is $2,000.

Duration: 1 year.

Number awarded: 5 each year.

Deadline: May of each year.

1985 $ JOHN FARMER SCHOLARSHIPS

Washington Association of Wine Grape Growers
Attn: Washington Wine Industry Foundation
203 Mission Avenue, Suite 107
P.O. Box 716
Cashmere, WA 98815–0716
Phone: (509) 782–1108; Fax: (509) 782–1203;
Email: info@washingtonwinefoundation.org
Web: www.washingtonwinefoundation.org/index.php?page_id=6

Summary: To provide financial assistance to residents of Washington who are interested in studying viticulture and/or enology at a college in the state.

Eligibility: Open to residents of Washington who are enrolled or planning to enroll at a college or university in the state to study viticulture and/or enology. Applicants must submit a 500–word essay on why they should receive this scholarship, including their career goals, interests and experiences in the wine grape industry, and plans to improve or enhance the industry. Selection is based on academic merit, leadership abilities, interest in the study of enology and/or viticulture, and financial need.

Financial data: Stipends range from $500 to $2,000.

Duration: 1 year.

Number awarded: Varies each year; recently, 6 of these scholarships were awarded: 1 at $2,000, 1 at $1,000, and 4 at $500.

Deadline: May of each year.

1986 $$ JOHN J. MCKETTA UNDERGRADUATE SCHOLARSHIP

American Institute of Chemical Engineers
Attn: Awards Administrator
Three Park Avenue
New York, NY 10016–5991
Phone: (646) 495–1348; Fax: (646) 495–1504;
Email: awards@aiche.org
Web: www.aiche.org/community/awards/student–awards–competitions

Summary: To provide financial assistance to upper–division students majoring in chemical engineering.

Eligibility: Open to students entering their junior or senior year of a 4–year program in chemical engineering (or equivalent for a 5–year co–op program). Applicants must be attending an ABET–accredited school in the United States, Canada, or Mexico and have a GPA of 3.0 or higher. Along with their application, they must submit a 3–page essay outlining their career goals in the chemical engineering process industries. Preference is given to student members of the American Institute of Chemical Engineers (AIChE) and to applicants who can show leadership or activity in either their school's AIChE student chapter or other university–sponsored campus activity. Financial need is not considered in the selection process.

Financial data: The stipend is $5,000.

Duration: 1 year.

Number awarded: 1 each year.

Deadline: June of each year.

1987 $$ JOHN KITT MEMORIAL SCHOLARSHIP

American Association of Candy Technologists
711 West Water Street
P.O. Box 266
Princeton, WI 54968
Phone: (920) 295–6969; Fax: (920) 295–6843;
Email: aactinfo@gomc.com
Web: www.aactcandy.org/aactscholarship.asp

Summary: To provide financial assistance to college students interested in preparing for a career in confectionery technology.

Eligibility: Open to students who are entering their sophomore, junior, or senior year of college and have demonstrated an interest in confectionary technology (through research projects, work experience, or formal study). Applicants must be attending an accredited 4–year college or university in North America; be majoring in a food science, chemical science, biological science, or related area; and have a GPA of 3.0 or higher. Selection is based on academic activities (including those relating to confectionary technology; experience (e.g., work, internships, volunteer activities); other activities; honors and awards; and a short statement of personal and professional goals.

Financial data: The stipend is $5,000.

Duration: 1 year; nonrenewable.

Number awarded: 1 or more each year.

Deadline: April of each year.

1988 JOHN M. CHAMBERS STATISTICAL SOFTWARE AWARD

American Statistical Association
Attn: Statistical Computing Section
732 North Washington Street
Alexandria, VA 22314–1943
Phone: (703) 684–1221; (888) 231–3473; Fax: (703) 684–2037;
Email: asainfo@amstat.org
Web: stat–computing.org/awards/jmc/index.html

Summary: To recognize and reward undergraduate and graduate students who have written outstanding statistical software.

Eligibility: Open to undergraduate or graduate students who have designed and implemented a piece of statistical software, working either as an individual or as a team of up to 3 students. Applicants must have begun the development while students, and they must either currently be students or have completed all requirements for their last degree within the past 2 years. They must submit a current curriculum vitae for each team member; a letter from a faculty mentor at their academic institution confirming that the software is their work and discussing its importance to statistical practice; and a brief description of the software, summarizing what it does, how it does it, and why it is an important contribution. They must also provide the award committee members with access to the software for their use on inputs of their choosing.

Financial data: The award includes an honorarium of $1,000 (to be divided among members of the team) and a substantial allowance for travel and housing at the JSM (paid to 1 member of the team who will be presented the award).

Duration: The award is presented annually.

Number awarded: 1 each year.

Deadline: February of each year.

1989 JOHN MABRY FORESTRY SCHOLARSHIP

Railway Tie Association
Attn: Education and Information Committee
115 Commerce Drive, Suite C
Fayetteville, GA 30214
Phone: (770) 460–5553; Fax: (770) 460–5573;
Email: ties@rta.org
Web: www.rta.org/Default.aspx?tabid=120

Summary: To provide financial aid to college students who are enrolled in accredited forestry schools.

Eligibility: Open to second–year students at accredited 2–year technical schools and juniors and seniors at accredited 4–year colleges and universities. Applicants must be working on a degree in forestry. Along with their application, they must submit an essay of more than 1 page on their present and future educational focus, research projects or school activities with which they are or have been involved, postgraduate plans, why and how they have chosen to major in forestry, and how they think their career path might ultimately be beneficial to the hardwood industry that serves the railroads. Selection is based on academic achievement (60%), leadership qualities (30%), career objectives (25%), and financial need (10%).

Financial data: The stipend is $1,500 per year.

Duration: 1 year.

Number awarded: 2 each year: 1 for a student at a 2–year institution and 1 for a student at a 4–year institution.

Deadline: June of each year.

1990 $ JOHN O. BEHRENS INSTITUTE FOR LAND INFORMATION (ILI) MEMORIAL SCHOLARSHIP

American Society for Photogrammetry and Remote Sensing
Attn: Scholarship Administrator
5410 Grosvenor Lane, Suite 210
Bethesda, MD 20814–2160
Phone: (301) 493–0290, ext. 101; Fax: (301) 493–0208;
Email: scholarships@asprs.org
Web: www.asprs.org/Awards–and–Scholarships

Summary: To provide financial assistance to undergraduate students interested in a program of study to prepare for a career related to land information systems or records.

Eligibility: Open to students planning to enroll or currently enrolled as undergraduates at a college or university in the United States. Applicants must be interested in a program of study to prepare for a career in land information systems or records or in geospatial science or technology. Along with their application, they must submit a 2–page statement describing their plans for continuing studies towards becoming a professional in a field that uses land and/or geospatial information as a key part of its performance. Financial need is not considered in the selection process.

Financial data: The stipend is $2,000. A 1–year student membership in the American Society for Photogrammetry and Remote Sensing (ASPRS) is also provided.

Duration: 1 year.

Number awarded: 1 each year.

Deadline: October of each year.

1991 $ JOHN P. "PAT" HEALY SCHOLARSHIP

Delaware Department of Education
Attn: Higher Education Office
401 Federal Street
Dover, DE 19901–3639
Phone: (302) 735–4120; (800) 292–7935; Fax: (302) 739–4654;
Email: dheo@doe.k12.de.us
Web: www.doe.k12.de.us/infosuites/students_family/dheo/default.shtml

Summary: To provide financial assistance to high school seniors and college students in Delaware who are interested in majoring in engineering or environmental sciences at a college in the state.

Eligibility: Open to high school seniors and full–time college freshman and sophomores who are Delaware residents and majoring in either environmental engineering or environmental sciences at a Delaware college. Applicants must submit a 500–word essay on "What would you do to protect the environment?" Selection is based on financial need, academic performance, community and school involvement, and leadership ability. U.S. citizenship or eligible noncitizen status is required.

Financial data: The stipend is $2,000.

Duration: 1 year; automatically renewed for 3 additional years if a GPA of 3.0 or higher is maintained.

Number awarded: 1 or more each year.

Deadline: March of each year.

1992 $ JOHN R. LILLARD VAOC SCHOLARSHIP

Virginia Airport Operators Council
c/o Virginia Department of Aviation
Attn: Betty Wilson
5702 Gulfstream Road
Richmond, VA 23250–2422
Phone: (804) 236–3624; (800) 292–1034 (within VA); Fax: (804) 236–3635;
Email: Betty.Wilson@doav.virginia.gov
Web: www.doav.virginia.gov/scholarship_lillard.htm

Summary: To provide financial assistance to high school seniors in Virginia who are interested in attending college in any state to prepare for a career in aviation.

Eligibility: Open to seniors graduating from high schools in Virginia who have a GPA of 3.75 or higher and are planning a career in the field of aviation. Applicants must have been accepted to an aviation–related program at an accredited college in any state. They must submit an essay of 350 to 500–words on why they wish to prepare for a career in aviation. Selection is based on the essay (30%), academic achievement (35%), accomplishment and leadership (20%), and financial need (15%).

Financial data: The stipend is $3,000.

Duration: 1 year.

Number awarded: 1 each year.

Deadline: March of each year.

1993 JOHN W. AUSTIN MEMORIAL SCHOLARSHIP

Maine Motor Transport Association
Attn: President
142 Whitten Road
P.O. Box 857
Augusta, ME 04332–0857
Phone: (207) 623–4128; Fax: (207) 623–4096;
Email: bparke@mmta.com
Web: www.mmta.com

Summary: To provide financial assistance to high school seniors in Maine who are interested in attending college in any state to prepare for a career in the trucking industry.

Eligibility: Open to seniors graduating from high schools in Maine who are planning to attend a college, university, or technical college in any state. Applicants must be seeking higher education or technical training in areas relevant to the motor transportation industry. Selection is based on prior academic

performance, recommendations from instructors, demonstrated skills relevant to the motor transportation industry, and financial need.
Financial data: The stipend is $1,000.
Duration: 1 year; nonrenewable.
Number awarded: 10 each year.
Deadline: May of each year.

1994 JOSE A. VILA SCHOLARSHIP

Cuban–American Association of Civil Engineers
Attn: President
10305 N.W. 41st Street, Suite 115
Doral, FL 33178
Phone: (305) 525–3915;
Email: CMGil@apcte.com
Web: www.c–aace.org/html/scholarships.htm
Summary: To provide financial assistance to Cuban American undergraduates from any state who are studying civil engineering at a college in Florida.
Eligibility: Open to students from any state who have completed at least 80 credits in a civil engineering program at a college or university in Florida. Applicants must be Cuban, of Cuban descent, or of Hispanic heritage and able to speak, read, and write Spanish fluently. The must have a GPA of 3.0 or higher and be able to demonstrate financial need. Along with their application, they must submit a 500–word essay on why they think they deserve this scholarship.
Financial data: The stipend is $1,000.
Duration: 1 year.
Number awarded: 1 or more each year.
Deadline: September of each year.

1995 $ JOSEPH A. MCALINDEN DIVERS' SCHOLARSHIP

Navy–Marine Corps Relief Society
Attn: Education Division
875 North Randolph Street, Suite 225
Arlington, VA 22203–1757
Phone: (703) 696–4960; Fax: (703) 696–0144;
Email: education@nmcrs.org
Web: www.nmcrs.org/education.html
Summary: To provide financial assistance to current and former Navy and Marine Corps divers and their families who are interested in working on an undergraduate degree in a field related to ocean agriculture.
Eligibility: Open to Navy and Marine Corps active–duty and retired divers (includes Reservists serving on active duty for more than 90 days), their children under 23 years of age, and their spouses. Applicants must be working full time on their first undergraduate degree in oceanography, ocean agriculture, aquaculture, or a related field; they may also be engaged in advanced diver training, certification, or recertification. Financial need is considered in the selection process.
Financial data: The stipend ranges from $500 to $3,000, depending on the need of the recipient.
Duration: 1 year.
Number awarded: 1 or more each year.
Deadline: Applications may be submitted at any time.

1996 JOSEPH FRASCA EXCELLENCE IN AVIATION SCHOLARSHIP

University Aviation Association
3410 Skyway Drive
Auburn, AL 36830–6444
Phone: (334) 844–2434; Fax: (334) 844–2432;
Email: uaamail@uaa.aero
Web: www.uaa.aero/default.aspx?scid=LVE776fHv6g=&mp=0
Summary: To provide financial assistance to upper–division college students majoring in aviation.
Eligibility: Open to juniors or seniors who are currently enrolled at a school affiliated with the University Aviation Association (UAA). Applicants must have earned a GPA of 3.0 or higher in their college courses; have Federal Aviation Administration certification/qualifications in either aviation maintenance or flight; be a member of at least 1 aviation organization (e.g., Alpha Eta Rho, National Intercollegiate Flying Association's Flying Team, Experimental Aircraft Association, Warbirds of America); and have a record of aviation activities, projects, or events that demonstrates an interest and an enthusiasm for aviation. Preference is given to applicants who can document interest or experience in aviation simulation, work experience in aviation, interest or experience in aircraft restoration, work experience while in school, interest or experience in aerobatics, or financial need. They may also submit an optional 250–word essay on their personal philosophy of excellence in aviation, especially as it relates to flying, aerobatics, aircraft mechanics and restoration, and aviation simulation; completion of the essay enhances their application but non–completion does not eliminate them from consideration.
Financial data: The stipend is $1,000.
Duration: 1 year.
Number awarded: 2 each year.
Deadline: April of each year.

1997 $ JOSEPH P. AND HELEN T. CRIBBINS SCHOLARSHIP

Association of the United States Army
Attn: Executive Assistant
2425 Wilson Boulevard
Arlington, VA 22201
Phone: (703) 841–4300, ext. 2652; (800) 336–4570, ext. 2652;
Email: ausa–info@ausa.org
Web: www.ausa.org/about/scholarships/Pages/CribbinsScholarship.aspx
Summary: To provide financial assistance to active–duty and honorably–discharged soldiers interested in studying engineering in college.
Eligibility: Open to 1) soldiers currently serving in the active Army, Army Reserve, or Army National Guard of any rank; and 2) honorably–discharged soldiers from any component of the total Army. Applicants must have been accepted at an accredited college or university to work on a degree in engineering or a related field (e.g., computer science, biotechnology). Along with their application, they must submit a 1–page autobiography, 2 letters of recommendation, and a transcript of high school or college grades (depending on which they are currently attending). Selection is based on academic merit and personal achievement. Financial need is not normally a selection criterion but in some cases of extreme need it may be used as a factor; the lack of financial need, however, is never a cause for non–selection.
Financial data: The stipend is $2,000; funds are sent directly to the recipient's college or university.
Duration: 1 year.
Number awarded: 1 or more each year.
Deadline: June of each year.

1998 $ JOSEPH ROEDER ASSISTIVE TECHNOLOGY SCHOLARSHIP

National Industries for the Blind
Attn: Scholarship Program
1310 Braddock Place
Alexandria, VA 22314–1691
Phone: (703) 310–0343;
Email: kgallagher@nib.org
Web: www.nib.org/content/scholarship–application
Summary: To provide financial assistance to upper–division and graduate students who are 1) blind and 2) preparing for a career in assistive technology.
Eligibility: Open to blind college juniors, seniors, and graduate students working on a degree in computer science, information systems, or a related field to prepare for a career in assistive technology. Applicants must submit information about their work experience, community activities, years of experience using a screen reader, years of experience using a text magnification program, the adaptive technology they use, and an essay of 200 to 300 words on their career history and future career goals.
Financial data: The stipend is $2,500.
Duration: 1 year.
Number awarded: 1 each year.
Deadline: July of each year.

1999 $ JOSEPH SHINODA MEMORIAL SCHOLARSHIP

Joseph Shinoda Memorial Scholarship Foundation Inc.
Attn: Executive Secretary
234 Via La Paz
San Luis Obispo, CA 93401
Phone: (805) 544–0717;
Email: info@shinodascholarship.org
Web: www.shinodascholarship.org
Summary: To provide financial assistance to undergraduates working on a degree in floriculture.

Eligibility: Open to undergraduates entering their sophomore, junior, or senior year at an accredited 4–year college or university in the United States or at a community college in California. Applicants must be majoring in a degree program related to floriculture (production, distribution, research, or retail) and be planning to work in a phase of commercial floriculture after graduation. Financial need is considered in the selection process.
Financial data: Stipends range from $1,500 to $3,500.
Duration: 1 year.
Number awarded: Varies each year; recently, 8 of these scholarships were awarded. Since the foundation was established, it has awarded more than $682,000 to 593 floriculture students.
Deadline: March of each year.

2000 J.R. POPALISKY SCHOLARSHIP

American Water Works Association–Missouri Section
c/o Chester Bender, Scholarship Committee Chair
Ponzer Youngquist, P.A.
227 East Dennis Avenue
Olathe, KS 66061
Phone: (913) 782–0541;
Email: cbender@pyengineers.com
Web: www.awwa–mo.org/site/?page_id=10
Summary: To provide financial assistance to students from any state working on an undergraduate or graduate degree related to water supply at a college or university in Missouri.
Eligibility: Open to U.S. citizens currently enrolled at 2– and 4–year colleges and universities in Missouri. Applicants must be working on an undergraduate or graduate degree in a field related to water supply, such as civil or environmental engineering or environmental science. Along with their application, they must submit a 2–page essay on their course of study and the occupation in which they plan to use their education. Selection is based on the relationship of their program to the water supply field (30 points), GPA (20 points), financial need (20 points), the essay (10 points), a letter of recommendation (10 points), and professional activities, offices held, and work experience (10 points).
Financial data: The stipend is $1,000.
Duration: 1 year.
Number awarded: 1 or more each year.
Deadline: March of each year.

2001 $ KAISER PERMANENTE COLORADO DIVERSITY SCHOLARSHIP PROGRAM

Kaiser Permanente
Attn: Physician Recruitment Services
10350 East Dakota Avenue
Denver, CO 80231–1314
Phone: (303) 344–7299; (866) 239–1677; Fax: (303) 344–7818;
Email: co–diversitydevelopment@kp.org
Web: scholarselect.com
Summary: To provide financial assistance to Colorado residents who come from diverse backgrounds and are interested in working on an undergraduate or graduate degree in a health care field at a public college in the state.
Eligibility: Open to all residents of Colorado, including those who identify as 1 or more of the following: African American, Asian Pacific, Latino, lesbian, gay, bisexual, transgender, intersex, Native American, U.S. veteran, and/or a person with a disability. Applicants must be enrolled or planning to enroll full time at a publicly–funded college, university, or technical school in Colorado as 1) a graduating high school senior with a GPA of 2.7 or higher; 2) a GED recipient with a GED score of 520 or higher; 3) an undergraduate student; or 4) a graduate or doctoral student. They must be preparing for a career in health care (e.g., athletic training, audiology, cardiovascular perfusion technology, clinical medical assisting, cytotechnology, dental assisting, dental hygiene, diagnostic medicine, dietetics, emergency medical technology, medicine, nursing, occupational therapy, pharmacy, phlebotomy, physical therapy, physician assistant, radiology, respiratory therapy, social work, sports medicine, surgical technology). Along with their application, they must submit 300–word essays on 1) a brief story from their childhood and the aspects of their experience that will contribute to their become a good health care provided; 2) what giving back to the community means to them and their experiences in community involvement that demonstrate their commitment to health care; and 3) what they consider the most pressing issue in health care today. Selection is based on academic achievement, character qualities, community outreach and volunteering, and financial need. U.S. citizenship is required.
Financial data: Stipends range from $1,400 to $2,600.
Duration: 1 year.
Number awarded: Varies each year; recently, 17 of these scholarships were awarded.
Deadline: February of each year.

2002 $ KAISER PERMANENTE NORTHWEST HEALTH CARE CAREER SCHOLARSHIPS

Kaiser Permanente Northwest
c/o Oregon Health Career Center
Attn: Scholarship Program Coordinator
25195 S.W. Parkway Avenue, Suite 204
Wilsonville, OR 97070
Phone: (503) 682–1300, ext. 113; Fax: (503) 682–1311;
Email: kpnwscholarship@gmail.com
Web: info.kaiserpermanente.org
Summary: To provide financial assistance to seniors at more than 100 designated high schools in Oregon and Washington who plan to attend college in any state to prepare for a career as a health care professional.
Eligibility: Open to seniors graduating from approved high schools in Oregon and Washington and planning to enroll full time at a college or university in any state. Applicants must be planning to prepare for a career as a medical or dental health care professional. They must be a U.S. citizen, national, or permanent resident and have a GPA of 2.5 or higher. Preference is given to students who 1) can demonstrate financial need; 2) are the first member of their family to attend college; 3) are bilingual; or 4) are a member of an ethnic or racial group underrepresented in the health professions.
Financial data: The stipend is $2,000 per year.
Duration: 1 year (the freshman year of college); recipients may apply for 1 additional year (the junior year of college) of funding.
Number awarded: At least 1 at each of the 113 approved high schools.
Deadline: January of each year.

2003 KANSAS ASSOCIATED GARDEN CLUBS SCHOLARSHIP GRANT

Kansas Associated Garden Clubs
c/o Ann L. Becker, Scholarship Chair
6428 East Murdock
Wichita, KS 67026
Phone: (316) 686–6250;
Email: annlbecker@aol.com
Web: www.ksgardenclub.com
Summary: To provide financial assistance to residents of Kansas who are working on an undergraduate or graduate degree in a garden–related field at a college or university in any state.
Eligibility: Open to residents of Kansas currently enrolled as sophomores, juniors, seniors, or master's degree students at a college or university in any state. Applicants must be working on a degree in conservation, ecology, floriculture, horticulture, landscape architecture, or a related field. They must have a GPA of 3.0 or higher and be able to demonstrate financial need.
Financial data: The stipend is $1,000.
Duration: 1 year.
Number awarded: 1 each year.
Deadline: February of each year.

2004 $$ KANSAS CITY IFMA SCHOLARSHIP

Summary: To provide financial assistance to students from any state who are working on an undergraduate or graduate degree in a field related to facility management at a school in Kansas or Missouri.
See Listing #1330.

2005 $ KANSAS NURSING SERVICE SCHOLARSHIPS

Kansas Board of Regents
Attn: Student Financial Assistance
1000 S.W. Jackson Street, Suite 520
Topeka, KS 66612–1368
Phone: (785) 296–3518; Fax: (785) 296–0983;
Email: dlindeman@ksbor.org
Web: www.kansasregents.org/scholarships_and_grants
Summary: To provide funding to Kansas residents who are interested in preparing for a nursing career.

Eligibility: Open to students in Kansas who are committed to practicing nursing (L.P.N. or R.N.) in the state. Applicants must be accepted at a Kansas nursing program (pre–nursing students are ineligible). They must locate a sponsor (defined as a licensed adult care home, psychiatric hospital, medical care facility, home health agency, local health department, or state agency that employs L.P.N.s or R.N.s) that is willing to provide up to half of the scholarship and to provide full–time employment to the recipient after licensure. Financial need is considered if there are more applicants than available funding.
Financial data: Stipends are $2,500 per year for students in L.P.N. programs or $3,500 per year for students in R.N. (associate or bachelor's degree) programs. Sponsors pay from $1,000 to one half of the scholarship and the State of Kansas pays the remaining amount. This is a scholarship/loan program; recipients must work for the sponsor the equivalent of full time for 1 year for each year of scholarship support received. If the recipient changes majors or decides not to work for the sponsor as a nurse, the scholarship becomes a loan, with interest at 5% above the federal PLUS loan rate.
Duration: 1 year; may be renewed.
Number awarded: Up to 50 for L.P.N. students; up to 200 for R.N. students, of which 100 are reserved for applicants whose sponsors are located in rural counties.
Deadline: April of each year.

2006 $ KAREN ANN SHOPIS–FOX MEMORIAL SCHOLARSHIP

Summary: To provide financial assistance to residents of Connecticut interested in working on an undergraduate or graduate degree in landscape architecture at a college or university in any state.
See Listing #1332.

2007 $ KATHARINE M. GROSSCUP SCHOLARSHIP

Garden Club of America
Attn: Scholarship Committee
14 East 60th Street, Third Floor
New York, NY 10022–1006
Phone: (212) 753–8287; Fax: (212) 753–0134;
Email: scholarships@gcamerica.org
Web: www2.gcamerica.org/scholarships.cfm
Summary: To provide financial assistance to undergraduate and graduate students, especially those from designated states, working on a degree in horticulture or other field related to gardening.
Eligibility: Open to college juniors, seniors, and master's degree students interested in working on a degree in horticulture or other subjects related to the field of gardening. Applicants must have a GPA of 3.5 or higher. Along with their application, they must submit a statement of their career goals, why those are important to them, and how their proposed course of student will support them in their endeavor. Preference is given to students from Ohio, Pennsylvania, West Virginia, Michigan, Kentucky, and Indiana. A personal interview is required.
Financial data: The stipend is $3,000.
Duration: 1 year.
Number awarded: Several each year.
Deadline: January of each year.

2008 $ KEITH DWIGHT MILLIS SCHOLARSHIP

Foundry Educational Foundation
1695 North Penny Lane
Schaumburg, IL 60173
Phone: (847) 490–9200; Fax: (847) 890–6270;
Email: info@fefoffice.org
Web: www.fefinc.org/students/scholarships/KeithDwightMillis.php
Summary: To provide financial assistance to undergraduate and graduate students who are interested in preparing for a career in the ductile iron industry.
Eligibility: Open to full–time undergraduate and graduate students who are citizens of any country, are enrolled in a college or university in the United States, and have a demonstrated interest in ductile iron. Applicants must be registered with the Foundry Educational Foundation (FEF), but they are not required to attend FEF schools. As part of their application, they must explain their interest in ductile iron.
Financial data: The stipend is $2,500.
Duration: 1 year.
Number awarded: 1 each year.
Deadline: October of each year.

2009 KELLIE CANNON MEMORIAL SCHOLARSHIP

American Council of the Blind
Attn: Coordinator, Scholarship Program
2200 Wilson Boulevard, Suite 650
Arlington, VA 22201
Phone: (202) 467–5081; (800) 424–8666; Fax: (703) 465–5085;
Email: info@acb.org
Web: www.acb.org/scholarship
Summary: To provide financial assistance to students who are blind and interested in preparing for a career in the computer field.
Eligibility: Open to high school seniors, high school graduates, and college students who are blind and interested in majoring in computer information systems or data processing. Applicants must submit verification of legal blindness in both eyes; SAT or ACT scores; information on extracurricular activities (including involvement in the American Council of the Blind); employment record; and a 500–word autobiographical sketch that includes their personal goals, strengths, weaknesses, hobbies, honors, achievements, and reasons for choice of field or courses of study. A cumulative GPA of 3.3 or higher is generally required. Financial need is not considered in the selection process, but the severity of the applicant's visual impairment and his/her study methods are taken into account.
Financial data: The stipend is $1,000.
Duration: 1 year.
Number awarded: 1 each year.
Deadline: February of each year.

2010 $ KEN YOST MEMORIAL SCHOLARSHIP

American Public Works Association–Missouri Chapter
c/o John M. Collins
City of Ellisville
1 Weis Avenue
Ellisville, MO 63011
Phone: (636) 227–9660;
Email: jcollins@ellisville.mo.us
Web: missouri.apwa.net/resources/scholarships
Summary: To provide financial assistance to high school seniors in Missouri who plan to attend college in any state to prepare for a career in a field related to public works.
Eligibility: Open to seniors graduating from high schools in Missouri and planning to enroll at a college or university in any state. Applicants must be planning to major in engineering, public administration, public works management, construction management, facilities management, or other field related to a career in public works. They must be a U.S. citizen. Along with their application, they must submit statements on their career objectives, their contributions to their school and community, what public works means to them, and what they plan to contribute to the field of public works. Financial need is not considered in the selection process.
Financial data: The stipend is $2,000.
Duration: 1 year.
Number awarded: 1 each year.
Deadline: March of each year.

2011 $ KENNETH J. OSBORN MEMORIAL SCHOLARSHIP

American Society for Photogrammetry and Remote Sensing
Attn: Scholarship Administrator
5410 Grosvenor Lane, Suite 210
Bethesda, MD 20814–2160
Phone: (301) 493–0290, ext. 101; Fax: (301) 493–0208;
Email: scholarships@asprs.org
Web: www.asprs.org/Awards–and–Scholarships
Summary: To provide financial assistance to undergraduate students who are preparing for a career in surveying, mapping, geospatial information and technology, or photogrammetry.
Eligibility: Open to students planning to enroll or currently enrolled in an undergraduate program in an accredited college or university in the United States. Applicants must be preparing for a career in the general area of geospatial information and technology, surveying, mapping, or photogrammetry. Along with their application, they must submit a 2–page statement detailing their plans for continuing studies towards becoming a professional in geospatial information and technology, surveying, mapping, or photogrammetry; 2 faculty reference forms; papers, research reports, or other items they have produced; transcripts and lists of courses taken; and a statement of work experience. Selection is based on those submissions; financial need is not considered.

Financial data: The stipend is $2,000. A 1–year new or renewal student membership in the American Society for Photogrammetry and Remote Sensing (ASPRS) is also provided.
Duration: 1 year.
Number awarded: 1 each year.
Deadline: October of each year.

2012 $ KENTUCKY EDUCATIONAL EXCELLENCE SCHOLARSHIPS

Summary: To provide financial assistance to Kentucky residents who achieve high GPAs and ACT scores in high school and plan to attend college in the state.
See Listing #425.

2013 KENTUCKY NATURAL RESOURCES SCHOLARSHIP

Kentucky Energy and Environment Cabinet
Attn: Department for Natural Resources
Division of Conservation
375 Versailles Road
Frankfort, KY 40601
Phone: (502) 573–3080; Fax: (502) 573–1692;
Email: Angie.Wingfield@ky.gov
Web: conservation.ky.gov/Pages/Scholarships.aspx
Summary: To provide financial assistance to residents of Kentucky who are majoring in agriculture or conservation of natural resources at a college in any state.
Eligibility: Open to residents of Kentucky who are working on an undergraduate degree in agriculture or a field related to the conservation of natural resources at a college or university in any state. Along with their application, they must submit an essay of 200 to 300 words on how their chosen profession will contribute to saving Kentucky's dwindling family farms. Selection is based on the essay (15 points), academic record (30 points), leadership (30 points), and extracurricular activities or jobs (25 points).
Financial data: The stipend is $1,000.
Duration: 1 year; nonrenewable.
Number awarded: 1 each year.
Deadline: February of each year.

2014 KENTUCKY SCHOOL PLANT MANAGERS ASSOCIATION SCHOLARSHIPS

Kentucky School Plant Managers Association
Attn: Scholarship Chair
3213 Marston Place
Lexington, KY 40503
Email: jrgilber@fayette.k12.ky.us
Web: www.kspma.org/scholarship.htm
Summary: To provide financial assistance to high school seniors in Kentucky who are interested in attending college to prepare for a career in school plant operations.
Eligibility: Open to residents of Kentucky who are graduating high school seniors or students completing a GED. Applicants must be planning to attend a postsecondary program with a major in a trade area related to school plant operations (e.g., heating and air conditioning, industrial electronics, mechanical engineering). Along with their application, they must submit a 250–word essay on why they want to receive this scholarship, the course of study and major they plan to follow, their proposed occupation or profession, and what they want to accomplish upon completion of their studies. Selection is based on that essay, ACT and/or SAT scores, GPA, curriculum, attendance, honors, extracurricular and work activities, and financial need.
Financial data: The stipend is $500 per semester ($1,000 per year).
Duration: 2 years.
Number awarded: Up to 5 each year.
Deadline: April of each year.

2015 $ K.K. WANG SCHOLARSHIP

Society of Plastics Engineers
Attn: SPE Foundation
13 Church Hill Road
Newtown, CT 06740
Phone: (203) 740–5447; Fax: (203) 775–1157;
Email: foundation@4spe.org
Web: www.4spe.org/spe–foundation
Summary: To provide college scholarships to students who have a career interest in the plastics industry and experience in injection molding and computer–aided engineering.
Eligibility: Open to full–time undergraduate students at 4–year colleges and 2–year technical programs and to graduate students. Applicants must have experience in injection molding and computer–aided engineering (CAE), such as courses taken, research conducted, or jobs held. They must be majoring in or taking courses that would be beneficial to a career in the plastics or polymer industry (e.g., plastics engineering, packaging, polymer sciences, chemistry, physics, chemical engineering, mechanical engineering, industrial engineering). Along with their application, they must submit 3 letters of recommendation; a high school and/or college transcript; a 1– to 2–page statement telling why they are applying for the scholarship, their qualifications, and their educational and career goals in the plastics industry; their employment history; a list of current and past school activities and community activities and honors; information on their financial need; and a statement detailing their experience in injection molding and CAE.
Financial data: The stipend is $2,000. Funds are paid directly to the recipient's school.
Duration: 1 year.
Number awarded: 1 each year.
Deadline: February of each year.

2016 KLUSSENDORF/MCKOWN SCHOLARSHIPS

National Dairy Shrine
Attn: Executive Director
P.O. Box 725
Denmark, WI 54208
Phone: (920) 863–6333; Fax: (920) 863–6333;
Email: info@dairyshrine.org
Web: www.dairyshrine.org/scholarships.php
Summary: To provide financial assistance to college students majoring in dairy science at a college or university in the United States or Canada.
Eligibility: Open to students who are completing their first, second, or third year at a 2– or 4–year college or university in the United States or Canada. Applicants must be majoring in dairy science, animal science, agribusiness, or other field that will help prepare them for a career in the dairy industry. They must submit 200–word essays on 1) their dairy cattle experiences; 2) their dairy–related participation in 4–H, FFA, judging, breed association, and other student–related activities; 3) their leadership roles; and 4) why they want to be part of the U.S. or Canadian dairy industry's future. Financial need is not considered in the selection process.
Financial data: The stipend is $1,500.
Duration: 1 year.
Number awarded: 7 each year.
Deadline: April of each year.

2017 LAND SURVEYORS' ASSOCIATION OF WASHINGTON FOUNDATION SCHOLARSHIP

Land Surveyors' Association of Washington
Attn: LSAW Foundation
41 Griffin View Lane
Friday Harbor, WA 98250
Phone: (360) 378–4578;
Email: vickit@rockisland.com
Web: www.lsawfoundation.org/scholarships.html
Summary: To provide financial assistance to undergraduate students who are preparing for a career as a professional land surveyor in the state of Washington.
Eligibility: Open to students who are enrolled full time in 1) a 4–year degree program in land surveying with the intent of becoming a professional land surveyor; or 2) a 2–year survey technician program. Applicants must submit an essay on their financial situation, what they plan to do in the future, and if they plan to practice or work in Washington in the surveying field after they graduate.
Financial data: A stipend is awarded (amount not specified).
Duration: 1 year.
Number awarded: Varies each year.
Deadline: June of each year.

2018 LANDSCAPE DESIGN CRITICS COUNCIL SCHOLARSHIP

Garden Club Federation of Massachusetts, Inc.
Attn: Scholarship Secretary

219 Washington Street
Wellesley Hills, MA 02481
Phone: (781) 237–0336; Fax: (781) 237–0336;
Email: gcfmscholarship@aol.com
Web: www.gcfm.org/Education/Scholarships/GCFMScholarships.aspx

Summary: To provide financial assistance to residents of Massachusetts interested in working on an undergraduate or graduate degree in a field related to landscape architecture at a college in any state.

Eligibility: Open to high school seniors, undergraduates, and graduate students who have been residents of Massachusetts for at least 1 year. Applicants must be working on or planning to work on a degree in city planning, landscape architecture, or a related field, including horticulture and conservation. They must have a GPA of 3.0 or higher. Along with their application, they must submit official transcripts; a brief essay about their goals, aspirations, and career plans; a list of their activities, including special honors and/or leadership positions; 3 letters of recommendation; and documentation of financial need.

Financial data: The stipend is $1,000.

Duration: 1 year.

Number awarded: 1 each year.

Deadline: February of each year.

2019 $ LANDSCAPE EDUCATIONAL ADVANCEMENT FOUNDATION SCHOLARSHIPS

Summary: To provide financial assistance to students in California who are majoring in ornamental horticulture.

See Listing #1344.

2020 $ LANDSCAPE FORMS DESIGN FOR PEOPLE SCHOLARSHIP

Summary: To provide financial assistance to undergraduate landscape architecture students who demonstrate interest in design of public spaces.

See Listing #1345.

2021 $ LARRY WILSON SCHOLARSHIP FOR CIVIL ENGINEERING UNDERGRADUATES

Arkansas Environmental Federation
Attn: Communications Director
1400 West Markham, Suite 302
Little Rock, AR 72201
Phone: (501) 374–0263; Fax: (501) 374–8752;
Email: ecullen@environmentark.org
Web: netforum.avectra.com/eWeb/DynamicPage.aspx?Site=AEF&WebCode=Sch

Summary: To provide financial assistance to residents of Arkansas working on an undergraduate degree in civil engineering (with an environmental emphasis) at a college or university in the state.

Eligibility: Open to Arkansas residents who have completed at least 40 credit hours as a full–time undergraduate student at a college or university in the state. Applicants must be majoring in civil engineering with an environmental emphasis and have a GPA of 2.8 or higher. Along with their application, they must submit an essay of 1 to 3 pages explaining their professional career goals relating to the field of environmental health and safety. U.S. citizenship is required. Financial need is not considered in the selection process.

Financial data: The stipend is $2,500.

Duration: 1 year.

Number awarded: 1 each year.

Deadline: April of each year.

2022 $ LARRY WILSON SCHOLARSHIP FOR ENVIRONMENTAL STUDIES

Arkansas Environmental Federation
Attn: Communications Director
1400 West Markham, Suite 302
Little Rock, AR 72201
Phone: (501) 374–0263; Fax: (501) 374–8752;
Email: ecullen@environmentark.org
Web: netforum.avectra.com/eWeb/DynamicPage.aspx?Site=AEF&WebCode=Sch

Summary: To provide financial assistance to residents of Arkansas working on an undergraduate or graduate degree in environmental studies at a college or university in the state.

Eligibility: Open to Arkansas residents who have completed at least 40 credit hours as a full–time undergraduate or graduate student at a college or university in the state. Applicants must be working on a degree in a field related to environmental studies, including agriculture with an environmental emphasis, chemical engineering with an environmental emphasis, civil engineering with an environmental emphasis, environmental engineering, environmental health science, fisheries and wildlife biology, forestry, geology, or wildlife management. They must have a GPA of 2.8 or higher. Along with their application, they must submit an essay of 1 to 3 pages explaining their professional career goals relating to the field of environmental health and safety. U.S. citizenship is required. Financial need is not considered in the selection process.

Financial data: The stipend is $2,500.

Duration: 1 year.

Number awarded: 1 each year.

Deadline: April of each year.

2023 $ LAURENCE R. FOSTER MEMORIAL SCHOLARSHIPS

Oregon Student Access Commission
Attn: Grants and Scholarships Division
1500 Valley River Drive, Suite 100
Eugene, OR 97401–2146
Phone: (541) 687–7395; (800) 452–8807, ext. 7395; Fax: (541) 687–7414; TDD: (800) 735–2900;
Email: awardinfo@osac.state.or.us
Web: www.oregonstudentaid.gov/scholarships.aspx

Summary: To provide financial assistance to residents of Oregon who are enrolled at a college or graduate school in any state to prepare for a public health career.

Eligibility: Open to residents of Oregon who are enrolled at least half time at a 4–year college or university in any state to prepare for a career in public health (not private practice). Preference is given first to applicants from diverse environments; second to persons employed in, or graduate students working on a degree in, public health; and third to juniors and seniors majoring in a health program (e.g., nursing, medical technology, physician assistant). Applicants must be able to demonstrate financial need. Along with their application, they must submit essays of 250 to 350 words on 1) what public health means to them; 2) the public health aspect they intend to practice and the health and population issues impacted by that aspect; and 3) their experience living or working in diverse environments.

Financial data: Stipends for scholarships offered by the Oregon Student Access Commission (OSAC) range from $200 to $10,000 but recently averaged $2,300.

Duration: 1 year.

Number awarded: Varies each year; recently, 6 of these scholarships were awarded.

Deadline: February of each year.

2024 $ LAWRENCE E. AND THELMA J. NORRIE MEMORIAL SCHOLARSHIP

Foundation for Amateur Radio, Inc.
Attn: Scholarship Committee
P.O. Box 911
Columbia, MD 21044–0911
Phone: (410) 552–2652; Fax: (410) 981–5146;
Email: dave.prestel@gmail.com
Web: www.farweb.org/scholarships

Summary: To provide funding to licensed radio amateurs who are interested in working on an undergraduate or graduate degree in engineering or the sciences.

Eligibility: Open to licensed radio amateurs who are currently enrolled full time as college juniors, seniors, or graduate students. Applicants may be working on a degree in science or engineering. They must have a GPA of 3.0 or higher. Financial need is considered in the selection process.

Financial data: The stipend is $2,500.

Duration: 1 year.

Number awarded: 1 each year.

Deadline: April of each year.

2025 $ LAWRENCE GINOCCHIO AVIATION SCHOLARSHIPS

National Business Aviation Association, Inc.
Attn: Director of Operations
1200 18th Street, N.W., Suite 400
Washington, DC 20036–2527

Phone: (202) 783–9250; Fax: (202) 331–8364;
Email: scholarships@nbaa.org
Web: www.nbaa.org/prodev/scholarships

Summary: To provide financial assistance to undergraduates majoring in aviation at participating colleges and universities.

Eligibility: Open to U.S. citizens enrolled full time at the sophomore, junior, or senior level in an aviation–related program of study at an institution belonging to the National Business Aviation Association (NBAA) and the University Aviation Association (UAA). Applicants must have at least a 3.0 GPA. Along with their application they must submit an official transcript, an essay of 500 to 1,000 words on their interest in and goals for a career in the business aviation industry, 2 letters of recommendation, and a resume.

Financial data: The stipend is $4,500. Checks are made payable to the recipient's institution.

Duration: 1 year.

Number awarded: 5 each year.

Deadline: July of each year.

2026 $ LEADING EDGE STUDENT DESIGN COMPETITION

Summary: To recognize and reward undergraduate and graduate students who submit outstanding zero–net energy entries in a design competition.

See Listing #1348.

2027 $$ LEGACY OF LIFE SCHOLARSHIPS

Washington Regional Transplant Consortium
7619 Little River Turnpike, Suite 900
Annandale, VA 22003–2628
Phone: (703) 641–0100; (866) 232–3666; Fax: (703) 658–0711;
Email: contactwrtc@wrtc.org
Web: www.beadonor.org

Summary: To recognize and reward, with college scholarships, high school seniors in the Washington, D.C. area who submit outstanding essays on organ, eye, and tissue donations.

Eligibility: Open to high school seniors in the District of Columbia; the Virginia counties of Arlington, Fairfax, Fauquier, Loudoun, Prince William, and Stafford; the Virginia cities of Alexandria, Falls Church, Fairfax, Manassas, and Manassas Park; and the Maryland counties of Charles, Montgomery, and Prince George's. Applicants must submit an essay, up to 1,000 words in length, on the theme, "Organ & Tissue Donation: Persuade Someone to Give the Gift of a Lifetime." Entries must be a persuasive argument in either fiction or nonfiction. Selection is based on originality, persuasiveness of the argument, proper grammar and spelling, adherence to the topic, and up–to–date citations.

Financial data: The first–place winner receives $5,000, the second–place winner receives $3,000 and each runner–up receives $1,000. All awards are in the form of college scholarships. Funds are paid directly to the college or university that the winner selects.

Duration: The competition is held annually.

Number awarded: 8 each year: 1 first–place winner, 1 second–place winner, and 6 runners–up.

Deadline: March of each year.

2028 $ LEO BOURASSA SCHOLARSHIP

Virginia Lakes and Watershed Association
Attn: Scholarship Committee
4229 Lafayette Center Drive
Chantilly, VA 20151
Phone: (757) 671–6222;
Email: scholarship@vlwa.org
Web: www.vlwa.org/leo.aspx

Summary: To provide financial assistance to residents of Virginia working on an undergraduate or graduate degree related to water resources at a university in the state.

Eligibility: Open to residents of Virginia who are enrolled at a college or university in the state as a 1) full–time undergraduate with at least 2 semesters of study completed; or 2) full– or part–time graduate student. Applicants must be working on a degree in a field related to water resources, including (but not limited to) biology, conservation, ecology, engineering, environmental science, geology, hydrology, limnology, stormwater management, water quality, or wildlife studies. Along with their application, they must submit brief statements on their experiences related to water resources and watershed management, a list of clubs and organizations related to water resources to which they belong, and why they are deserving of this scholarship. Selection is based on academic performance, educational plans, and contribution to the field of water resources.

Financial data: The stipend is $2,500 per year.

Duration: 1 year; recipients may reapply.

Number awarded: 2 each year: 1 to an undergraduate and 1 to a graduate student.

Deadline: May of each year.

2029 $ LEOPOLD AND ELIZABETH MARMET SCHOLARSHIPS

Greater Kanawha Valley Foundation
Attn: Scholarship Program Officer
1600 Huntington Square
900 Lee Street East, 16th Floor
Charleston, WV 25301
Phone: (304) 346–3620; (800) 467–5909; Fax: (304) 346–3640;
Email: shoover@tgkvf.org
Web: www.tgkvf.org/page.aspx?pid=409

Summary: To provide financial assistance to residents of West Virginia who are interested in working on an undergraduate or graduate degree in science, energy, or natural resources.

Eligibility: Open to residents of West Virginia who are attending or planning to attend a college or university in any state. Applicants must be planning to study science, the production or conservation of energy, or natural resources. Both undergraduate and graduate students are eligible, but preference is given to graduate students. Financial need is not considered in the selection process.

Financial data: Recently, stipends averaged $3,000 per year.

Duration: 1 year; may be renewed.

Number awarded: Varies each year; recently, 12 of these scholarships were awarded.

Deadline: January of each year.

2030 LEWIS CENKER SCHOLARSHIP

Home Builders Association of Georgia
Attn: Scholarship Fund
3015 Camp Creek Parkway
Atlanta, GA 30344
Phone: (404) 763–2453; (800) 248–2453 (within GA); Fax: (404) 559–1531
Web: www.hbag.org/page.asp?pg=Lewis%20Cenker%20Award

Summary: To provide financial assistance to residents of Georgia who are interested in attending college in any state to prepare for a career in the home building industry.

Eligibility: Open to residents of Georgia who are entering or enrolled full time at an accredited college, university, or certified technical school in any state. Applicants must be interested in pursuing courses of study designed to train them in an area directly related to the home building industry. They must have a grade average of "C" or higher. Along with their application, they must submit a 200–word narrative that covers their decision to pursue a postsecondary course of study in a residential construction–related field, their reasons for applying for this scholarship, their ultimate career goals, and their reasons for those. Applications must be submitted through a builder member or associate member of the Home Builders Association of Georgia. Selection is based on academic excellence, career goals, letters of recommendation, other activities or services, and financial need.

Financial data: A stipend is awarded (amount not specified).

Duration: 1 year; requests for extensions may be considered, provided the student still meets all eligibility requirements.

Number awarded: 1 or more each year.

Deadline: February of each year.

2031 LIBBIE H. HYMAN MEMORIAL SCHOLARSHIP

Society for Integrative and Comparative Biology
Attn: Division of Invertebrate Zoology
1313 Dolley Madison Boulevard, Suite 402
McLean, VA 22101
Phone: (703) 790–1745; (800) 955–1236; Fax: (703) 790–2672;
Email: sicb@BurkInc.com
Web: sicb.org/grants/hyman

Summary: To provide funding to advanced undergraduates and beginning graduate students interested in studying or conducting research in invertebrate zoology.

Eligibility: Open to 1) advanced undergraduates; and 2) first– and second–year graduate students. Applicants must be interested in taking courses in invertebrate zoology or conducting a research project in that area at a marine, freshwater, or terrestrial field station. Along with their application, they must

submit information on their proposed course work or research, any previous experience working at field stations, a brief budget, and institutional or other sources of support.
Financial data: The grant amount varies but recently was $1,100.
Duration: 1 year.
Number awarded: 1 each year.
Deadline: February of each year.

2032 $$ LIFE TECHNOLOGIES SCHOLARSHIPS

Society of Women Engineers
Attn: Scholarship Selection Committee
203 North LaSalle Street, Suite 1675
Chicago, IL 60601–1269
Phone: (312) 596–5223; (877) SWE–INFO; Fax: (312) 644–8557;
Email: scholarships@swe.org
Web: societyofwomenengineers.swe.org/index.php/scholarships
Summary: To provide financial assistance to undergraduate women who are majoring in designated engineering specialties.
Eligibility: Open to society members who are entering their sophomore, junior, or senior year at an ABET–accredited 4–year college or university. Applicants must be working full time on a degree in computer science or biomedical, chemical, civil, computer, electrical, industrial, manufacturing, materials, mechanical, or software engineering and have a GPA of 3.0 or higher. They must be U.S. citizens or permanent residents. Selection is based on merit. Preference is given to groups underrepresented in computer science and engineering.
Financial data: The stipend is $7,500 or $2,500.
Duration: 1 year.
Number awarded: 3 each year: 1 at $7,500 and 2 at $2,500.
Deadline: February of each year.

2033 LILLIAN CAMPBELL MEDICAL SCHOLARSHIP

Wisconsin Veterans of Foreign Wars
P.O. Box 6128
Monona, WI 53716–0128
Phone: (608) 221–5276; Fax: (608) 221–5277;
Email: wivfw@att.net
Web: vfwofwi.com/?w=wisconsin
Summary: To provide financial assistance to students working on a degree in a medical field in Wisconsin who served in the military or are related to a person who did.
Eligibility: Open to students who have completed at least 1 year of study in Wisconsin in a program in nursing, pharmacy, physician assistant, medical or surgical technology, physical or occupational therapy, dental assisting, radiology, or other related medical profession. Applicants or a member of their immediate family (parent, sibling, child, spouse, or grandparent) must have served in the military. They must have a high school diploma or GED but may be of any age. Along with their application, they must submit a 200–word essay on why they are studying this medical profession. Financial need is considered in the selection process.
Financial data: The stipend is $1,000.
Duration: 1 year.
Number awarded: 1 or more each year.
Deadline: April of each year.

2034 $$ LILLIAN MOLLER GILBRETH MEMORIAL SCHOLARSHIP

Society of Women Engineers
Attn: Scholarship Selection Committee
203 North LaSalle Street, Suite 1675
Chicago, IL 60601–1269
Phone: (312) 596–5223; (877) SWE–INFO; Fax: (312) 644–8557;
Email: scholarships@swe.org
Web: societyofwomenengineers.swe.org/index.php/scholarships
Summary: To provide financial assistance to upper–division women majoring in computer science or engineering.
Eligibility: Open to women who are entering their junior or senior year at an ABET–accredited 4–year college or university. Applicants must be working full time on a degree in computer science or engineering and have a GPA of 3.0 or higher. Selection is based on merit.
Financial data: The stipend is $10,000 per year.
Duration: 1 year; may be renewed 1 additional year.
Number awarded: 1 each year.
Deadline: February of each year.

2035 LINK FOUNDATION SCHOLARSHIP

Florida Foundation for Future Scientists
Attn: Executive Director
P.O. Box 67
Goldenrod, FL 32733
Phone: (407) 473–8475;
Email: nbesley@floridassef.net
Web: www.floridassef.net
Summary: To provide financial assistance to high school seniors in Florida who submit a project related to specified fields to the State Science and Engineering Fair of Florida (SSEF) and plan to attend college in the state.
Eligibility: Open to seniors graduating from high schools in Florida who have a project for the SSEF related to marine biology, ocean engineering, oceanography, aviation, or energy conservation and research. Applicants must be planning to enroll at a college or university in the state. They must be nominated by a teacher at their school. Selection is based on the SSEF project and transcripts.
Financial data: The stipend is $1,000.
Duration: 1 year.
Number awarded: 1 each year.
Deadline: April of each year.

2036 $ L.L. WATERS SCHOLARSHIP PROGRAM

American Society of Transportation and Logistics, Inc.
Attn: Scholarship Judging Panel
P.O. Box 3363
Warrenton, VA 20188
Phone: (202) 580–7270; Fax: (202) 962–3939;
Email: info@astl.org
Web: www.astl.org/i4a/pages/index.cfm?pageid=3293
Summary: To provide financial assistance to advanced undergraduate and graduate students in the field of transportation.
Eligibility: Open to undergraduate students in their junior year at fully–accredited 4–year colleges or universities who are majoring in transportation, logistics, or physical distribution. Students in graduate school in the same areas are also eligible. Applicants must submit a letter explaining why they have chosen transportation, logistics, or physical distribution as their field of study and describing their professional objectives. Selection is based on scholastic performance and potential as well as commitment to a professional career in the field. Financial need is not considered.
Financial data: The stipend is $2,000.
Duration: 1 year; recipients may apply again but not in consecutive years.
Number awarded: 1 or more each year.
Deadline: September of each year.

2037 $ LOCKHEED MARTIN SCHOLARSHIPS

Society of Women Engineers
Attn: Scholarship Selection Committee
203 North LaSalle Street, Suite 1675
Chicago, IL 60601–1269
Phone: (312) 596–5223; (877) SWE–INFO; Fax: (312) 644–8557;
Email: scholarships@swe.org
Web: societyofwomenengineers.swe.org/index.php/scholarships
Summary: To provide financial assistance to women working on an undergraduate or graduate degree in computer science, computer engineering, or electrical engineering.
Eligibility: Open to women who are entering full–time freshmen, sophomores, juniors, seniors, or graduate students at an ABET–accredited 4–year college or university. Applicants must be interested in studying computer science, computer engineering, or electrical engineering and have a GPA of 3.5 or higher (for entering freshmen) or 3.2 or higher (for all other students). Selection is based on merit.
Financial data: The stipend is $2,000. The award includes a travel grant for the recipient to attend the national conference of the Society of Women Engineers.
Duration: 1 year.
Number awarded: 4 each year: 2 for entering freshmen and 2 for other students.
Deadline: February of each year for continuing students; May of each year for entering freshmen.

2038 $ LOIS BRITT MEMORIAL PORK INDUSTRY SCHOLARSHIPS

National Pork Producers Council
P.O. Box 10383
Des Moines, IA 50306–9960
Phone: (515) 278–8012; Fax: (515) 278–8014;
Email: pork@nppc.org
Web: www.nppc.org/programs/scholarships

Summary: To provide financial assistance to college students interested in preparing for a career in the pork industry.

Eligibility: Open to students who are currently enrolled in a 2–year swine program or 4–year undergraduate agricultural program. Applicants must submit a 750–word essay on an issue confronting the U.S. pork industry today or in the future, a letter indicating the role they see themselves playing in the pork industry after graduation, and 2 letters of reference. Financial need is not considered in the selection process.

Financial data: The stipend is $2,500.

Duration: 1 year.

Number awarded: 4 each year.

Deadline: January of each year.

2039 $ LOUIS T. KLAUDER SCHOLARSHIP

American Public Transportation Association
Attn: American Public Transportation Foundation
1666 K Street, N.W., Suite 1100
Washington, DC 20006
Phone: (202) 496–4803; Fax: (202) 496–4323;
Email: yconley@apta.com
Web: www.aptfd.org/work/scholarship.htm

Summary: To provide financial assistance to undergraduate and graduate students who are preparing for a career in public transportation as an electrical or mechanical engineer.

Eligibility: Open to college sophomores, juniors, seniors, and graduate students who are preparing for an career in the rail transit industry as a mechanical or electrical engineer. Any member organization of the American Public Transportation Association (APTA) can nominate and sponsor candidates for this scholarship. Nominees must be enrolled in a fully–accredited institution, have and maintain at least a 3.0 GPA, and be either employed by or demonstrate a strong interest in entering the public transportation industry as an electrical or mechanical engineer. They must submit a 1,000–word essay on the topic, "In what segment of the public transportation industry will you make a career and why?" Selection is based on demonstrated interest in the transit field as a career, need for financial assistance, academic achievement, essay content and quality, and involvement in extracurricular citizenship and leadership activities.

Financial data: The stipend is $2,500.

Duration: 1 year; may be renewed.

Number awarded: 1 each year.

Deadline: May of each year.

2040 $$ LOUISE MORITZ MOLITORIS LEADERSHIP AWARD

Women's Transportation Seminar
Attn: WTS Foundation
1701 K Street, N.W., Suite 800
Washington, DC 20006
Phone: (202) 955–5085; Fax: (202) 955–5088;
Email: wts@wtsinternational.org
Web: www.wtsinternational.org/education/scholarships

Summary: To provide financial assistance to undergraduate women interested in a career in transportation.

Eligibility: Open to women who are working on an undergraduate degree in transportation or a transportation–related field (e.g., transportation engineering, planning, finance, or logistics). Applicants must have a GPA of 3.0 or higher. Along with their application, they must submit a 500–word statement about their career goals after graduation and why they think they should receive the scholarship award; their statement should specifically address the issue of leadership. Applications must be submitted first to a local chapter; the chapters forward selected applications for consideration on the national level. Minority women are especially encouraged to apply. Selection is based on transportation involvement and goals, job skills, academic record, and leadership potential; financial need is not considered.

Financial data: The stipend is $5,000.

Duration: 1 year.

Number awarded: 1 each year.

Deadline: Applications must be submitted by November to a local WTS chapter.

2041 LOUISIANA SECTION AWMA SCHOLARSHIP AWARD

Air & Waste Management Association–Louisiana Section
c/o Karen J. Blakemore
Phelps Dunbar, LLP
445 North Boulevard, Suite 501
P.O. Box 4412
Baton Rouge, LA 70821–4412
Phone: (225) 346–0285; Fax: (225) 381–9197;
Email: karen.blakemore@phelps.com
Web: la–awma.org/education/scholarships

Summary: To provide financial assistance to upper–division and master's degree students working on a degree in an environmental field at a university in the area served by the Louisiana Section of the Air & Waste Management Association (AWMA).

Eligibility: Open to juniors, seniors, and master's degree students at colleges and universities in Louisiana and the Sabine River Region of eastern Texas. Applicants must be working full time on a degree in an environmental field, including engineering, physical or natural science, law, or public health and have a GPA of 3.0 or higher. They must be able to demonstrate through course work, projects, or personal interest a desire to promote air pollution control and/or solid or hazardous waste management. A personal interview is required. Selection is based on academic record, plan of study, career goals, recommendations, and financial status.

Financial data: The stipend is $1,000.

Duration: 1 year; nonrenewable.

Number awarded: 2 or more each year.

Deadline: March of each year.

2042 $ LT. COL. DAVID H. GWINN SCHOLARSHIP

American Academy of Physician Assistants–Veterans Caucus
Attn: Veterans Caucus
P.O. Box 362
Danville, PA 17821–0362
Phone: (570) 271–0292; Fax: (570) 271–5850;
Email: admin@veteranscaucus.org
Web: www.veteranscaucus.org

Summary: To provide financial assistance to Air Force veterans who are studying to become physician assistants.

Eligibility: Open to U.S. citizens who are currently enrolled in a physician assistant program. The program must be approved by the Commission on Accreditation of Allied Health Education. Applicants must be honorably discharged members of the United States Air Force. Selection is based on military honors and awards received, civic and college honors and awards received, professional memberships and activities, and GPA. An electronic copy of the applicant's DD Form 214 must accompany the application.

Financial data: The stipend is $2,000.

Duration: 1 year.

Number awarded: 1 each year.

Deadline: February of each year.

2043 $ LT. COL. ROMEO AND JOSEPHINE BASS FERRETTI SCHOLARSHIP

Air Force Association
Attn: Manager, National Aerospace Awards
1501 Lee Highway
Arlington, VA 22209–1198
Phone: (703) 247–5800, ext. 4807; (800) 727–3337, ext. 4807; Fax: (703) 247–5853;
Email: lcross@afa.org
Web: www.afa.org/aef/aid/Ferretti.asp

Summary: To provide financial assistance to dependents of Air Force enlisted personnel who are high school seniors planning to attend college to major in a field of science, technology, engineering, or mathematics (STEM).

Eligibility: Open to dependents of Air Force active duty, Reserve, or Air National Guard enlisted personnel who are graduating high school seniors. Applicants must be planning to enroll full time at an accredited institute of higher education to work on an undergraduate degree in any area of STEM. Selection is based on academic achievement, character, and financial need.

Financial data: The stipend is $2,500.

Duration: 1 year; nonrenewable.

Number awarded: Varies each year; recently, 4 of these scholarships were awarded.

Deadline: June of each year.

2044 $$ LTK SCHOLARSHIP

Conference of Minority Transportation Officials
Attn: National Scholarship Program
1875 I Street, N.W., Suite 500
Washington, DC 20006
Phone: (703) 234–4072; Fax: (202) 318–0364
Web: www.comto.org/?page=Scholarships

Summary: To provide financial assistance to minority upper–division and graduate students in engineering or other field related to transportation.

Eligibility: Open to full–time minority juniors, seniors, and graduate students in engineering of other technical transportation–related disciplines. Applicants must have a GPA of 3.0 or higher. Along with their application, they must submit a cover letter with a 500–word statement of career goals. Financial need is not considered in the selection process. U.S. citizenship or legal resident status is required.

Financial data: The stipend is $6,000. Funds are paid directly to the recipient's college or university.

Duration: 1 year.

Number awarded: 1 or more each year.

Deadline: May of each year.

2045 $ LUBRIZOL CORPORATION SCHOLARSHIP PROGRAM

College Now Greater Cleveland, Inc.
Attn: Managed Scholarships
200 Public Square, Suite 3820
Cleveland, OH 44114
Phone: (216) 241–5587; Fax: (216) 241–6184;
Email: info@collegenowgc.org
Web: www.collegenowgc.org

Summary: To provide financial assistance to women and minorities working on a degree in specified fields of science and business at college in any state.

Eligibility: Open to members of minority ethnic groups (American Indians, African Americans, Asian Pacific Americans, and Hispanic Americans) and women. Applicants must be enrolled full time at a 4–year college or university in any state and majoring in chemistry, computer information systems, computer science, engineering (chemical, computer, or mechanical), business, marketing, accounting, or finance. They must have a GPA of 3.0 or higher and be able to demonstrate financial need. Along with their application, they must submit a 500–word essay describing their academic and career goals.

Financial data: The stipend is $4,000 per year.

Duration: 1 year; may be renewed, provided the recipient maintains a GPA of 3.0 or higher.

Number awarded: Varies each year.

Deadline: March of each year.

2046 MABEL MAYFORTH SCHOLARSHIP

Federated Garden Clubs of Vermont, Inc.
c/o Jennifer Hanlon, State Scholarship Chair
676 Arthur John Road
Island Pond, VT 05846
Phone: (802) 723–4002;
Email: flora2u@earthlink.net
Web: vermontfgcv.com/FGCV–Scholarship.php

Summary: To provide financial assistance to upper–division or incoming graduate students from Vermont who are majoring in horticulture or allied subjects at a college in any state.

Eligibility: Open to Vermont residents who are currently enrolled as full–time juniors, seniors, or master's degree students at a college or university in any state. Applicants must be majoring in horticulture, floriculture, landscape design, conservation, forestry, agronomy, plant pathology, or biology with a special interest in plants, ecology, and allied subjects. They must have a GPA of 3.0 or higher. Along with their application, they must submit a 2–page letter on their goals, background, financial need, and commitment to their field of study. Selection is based on that letter, academic achievement, extracurricular activities, financial need, and letters of recommendation.

Financial data: The stipend is $1,000.

Duration: 1 year; recipients may reapply.

Number awarded: 1 each year.

Deadline: February of each year.

2047 MAINE METAL PRODUCTS ASSOCIATION SCHOLARSHIP

Maine Education Services
Attn: MES Foundation
One City Center, 11th Floor
Portland, ME 04101
Phone: (207) 791–3600; (800) 922–6352; Fax: (207) 791–3616;
Email: info@mesfoundation.com
Web: www.mesfoundation.com

Summary: To provide financial assistance to students in Maine who are interested in furthering their education in the machine or related metal working trades.

Eligibility: Open to residents of Maine who have been accepted into a metal trade program at a college in the state. The field of specialization may be mechanical engineering, machine tool technology, sheet metal fabrication, welding, or CADCAM for metals industry. Applicants must submit an essay on their goals, aspirations, and accomplishments; why and how they decided on a career in metal working; and why they think they should receive this scholarship. They will be interviewed by a member of the association. Selection is based on aptitude or demonstrated ability in the metal working trades; high school and postsecondary scholastic and extracurricular records; personal qualifications of attitude, initiative, and seriousness of intent; and overall impression.

Financial data: A stipend is awarded (amount not specified); funds may be applied toward the costs of tuition and textbooks only.

Duration: 1 year; may be renewed, provided the recipient remains enrolled full time and maintains a "C" average or higher.

Number awarded: Varies each year; recently, 9 of these scholarships were awarded.

Deadline: April of each year.

2048 MAINE SOCIETY OF LAND SURVEYORS MERIT SCHOLARSHIPS

Maine Society of Land Surveyors
Attn: Executive Director
126 Western Avenue
PMB 211
Augusta, ME 04330
Phone: (207) 882–5200;
Email: director@msls.org
Web: www.msls.org/resources.html

Summary: To provide financial assistance to Maine residents interested in attending college in the state to prepare for a career as a surveyor.

Eligibility: Open to residents of Maine who are graduating high school seniors or students currently enrolled in college. Applicants must be interested in preparing for a career as a surveyor. Along with their application, they must submit an essay on their professional aspirations, their goals during and after college, the kind of work they want to do after graduation, and where they want to work. Financial need is considered in the selection process.

Financial data: The stipend is $1,000.

Duration: 1 year.

Number awarded: Varies each year; recently, 4 of these scholarships were awarded.

Deadline: November of each year.

2049 $ MAINE SOCIETY OF PROFESSIONAL ENGINEERS SCHOLARSHIPS

Maine Society of Professional Engineers
c/o Colin C. Hewett, Scholarship Committee Chair
P.O. Box 318
Winthrop, ME 04364
Phone: (207) 967–3741; Fax: (207) 967–3741;
Email: chewett@hwengineers.com
Web: mespe.org/Scholarships.htm

Summary: To provide financial assistance to high school seniors in Maine who are interested in majoring in engineering at a college in any state.

Eligibility: Open to seniors graduating from high schools in Maine and planning to enroll in an ABET–accredited engineering program at a college or university in any state. Applicants must have scores of at least 600 on SAT mathematics, 500 on SAT critical reading, 500 on SAT writing, 29 on ACT mathematics, and 25 on ACT English. Along with their application, they must submit a 250–word essay on how they became interested in engineering, the field of engineering that interests them the most, and why they want to become a practicing engineer. Selection is based on that essay (20 points), GPA (20 points), SAT/ACT scores (20 points), activities (15 points), recommendations (15 points), and composite application (10 points).

Financial data: The stipend is $2,500.

Duration: 1 year.

Number awarded: 2 each year.
Deadline: February of each year.

2050 $ MALCOLM BALDRIGE SCHOLARSHIP

Connecticut Community Foundation
43 Field Street
Waterbury, CT 06702–1906
Phone: (203) 753–1315; Fax: (203) 756–3054;
Email: grants@conncf.org
Web: www.conncf.org/scholarships

Summary: To provide financial assistance to Connecticut residents who are interested in attending college in the state to major in a field related to manufacturing or international business.

Eligibility: Open to residents of Connecticut who are entering or attending a college or university in the state. Applicants must be majoring or planning to major in a field related to manufacturing or international business or trade. Students majoring in international business or trade must be able to demonstrate fluency in or formal study of a foreign language. Selection is based on academic excellence. U.S. citizenship is required.

Financial data: The stipend ranges from $2,000 to $4,000. Funds are paid directly to the recipient's school.
Duration: 1 year.
Number awarded: Varies each year.
Deadline: March of each year.

2051 MARGARET A. PEMBERTON SCHOLARSHIP FUND

Black Nurses' Association of Greater Washington, D.C. Area, Inc.
Attn: Scholarship Committee Chair
P.O. Box 55285
Washington, DC 20040
Phone: (202) 291–8866
Web: www.bnaofgwdca.org/scholarships.html

Summary: To provide financial assistance to African American high school seniors in the Washington, D.C. area who are interested in working on a baccalaureate degree in nursing at a school in any state.

Eligibility: Open to African American seniors graduating from high schools in the District of Columbia or adjoining counties in Maryland (Anne Arundel, Calvert, Charles, Howard, Montgomery, and Prince George's). Applicants must be U.S. citizens or permanent residents and have a GPA of 2.8 or higher. They must have been accepted into a baccalaureate nursing program at a college or university in the United States. Along with their application, they must submit a 1–page essay that describes their personal and educational goals, reasons why they should be selected (including evidence of financial need), and current and projected contributions to the community (including high school service and/or volunteer activities).

Financial data: A stipend is awarded (amount not specified).
Duration: 1 year.
Number awarded: 1 each year.
Deadline: April of each year.

2052 MARGARET BENT PATTERSON SCHOLARSHIP

Garden Club Federation of Massachusetts, Inc.
Attn: Scholarship Secretary
219 Washington Street
Wellesley Hills, MA 02481
Phone: (781) 237–0336; Fax: (781) 237–0336;
Email: gcfmscholarship@aol.com
Web: www.gcfm.org/Education/Scholarships/GCFMScholarships.aspx

Summary: To provide financial assistance to residents of Massachusetts interested in working on an undergraduate or graduate degree in a field related to horticulture or landscape architecture at a college in any state.

Eligibility: Open to high school seniors, undergraduates, and graduate students who have been residents of Massachusetts for at least 1 year. Applicants must be working on or planning to work on a degree in horticulture, landscape architecture, or a related field (e.g., agronomy, biology, botany, city planning, conservation, floriculture, forestry, land management). They must have a GPA of 3.0 or higher. Along with their application, they must submit official transcripts; a brief essay about their goals, aspirations, and career plans; a list of their activities, including special honors and/or leadership positions; 3 letters of recommendation; and documentation of financial need.

Financial data: The stipend is $1,000.
Duration: 1 year.
Number awarded: 1 each year.
Deadline: February of each year.

2053 MARIA BLAHA MEDICAL GRANT

The Resource Center
16362 Wilson Boulevard
Masaryktown, FL 34604–7335
Phone: (352) 799–1381;
Email: dblaha@innet.com

Summary: To provide financial assistance for college to students interested in a medical field.

Eligibility: Open to students currently enrolled or planning to enroll in college to study a medical field. Along with their application, they must submit a 250–word essay on how they can make a difference. GPA and financial need are not considered in the selection process.

Financial data: The stipend is $1,000.
Duration: 1 year.
Number awarded: 2 each year: 1 in spring and 1 in fall.
Deadline: June or December of each year.

2054 $ MARSHALL E. MCCULLOUGH SCHOLARSHIPS

Summary: To provide financial assistance to graduating high school students interested in a career in dairy journalism.
See Listing #1372.

2055 MARTIN DEVLIN SCHOLARSHIP GRANT

Physician Assistant Academy of Vermont
45 Lyme Road, Suite 304
Hanover, NH 03755
Phone: (603) 643–2325; Fax: (603) 643–1444;
Email: paav@conmx.net
Web: www.paav.org/scholarship.html

Summary: To provide financial assistance to residents of Vermont enrolled in a physician assistant training program in any state and to physician assistants in Vermont who have educational loans.

Eligibility: Open to 1) residents of Vermont currently enrolled full time in an approved physician assistant program in any state; and 2) physician assistants employed or seeking employment in Vermont and in need of assistance to repay educational loans. Applicants must submit an essay that covers such questions as how they intend to use the scholarship, if they hope to return to Vermont to work as a physician assistant, how they will contribute to the physician assistant profession, their professional goals. Students should also explain if they anticipate coming back to Vermont to work. Physician assistants should also explain what brought them to Vermont. Financial need is also considered in the selection process.

Financial data: The stipend is $1,000. Funds may be used by students for payment of tuition or other educational expenses or by current physician assistants for repayment of educational loans.
Duration: 1 year; nonrenewable.
Number awarded: 1 each year.
Deadline: June of each year.

2056 $ MARTIN SMILO UNDERGRADUATE SCHOLARSHIP

California Environmental Health Association
110 South Fairfax, A11–175
Los Angeles, CA 90036
Phone: (323) 634–7698; Fax: (323) 571–1889;
Email: support@ceha.org
Web: www.ceha.org/~cehaor5/awards

Summary: To provide financial assistance to undergraduates from California interested in preparing for a career in the sciences, especially environmental health.

Eligibility: Open to California students who have completed at least 48 semester units of undergraduate study, including at least 12 semester units in science, with a GPA of 3.0 or higher. Applicants must be enrolled full time at an accredited 4–year college or university in any state with an intention to work on a degree and prepare for a career in science. Preference is given to students in environmental health. Along with their application, they must submit a 3–page essay on 1 of 3 assigned topics related to public health and the role of professional organizations. Financial need is not considered in the selection process.

Financial data: The stipend is $2,500.

Duration: 1 year.
Number awarded: 1 or 2 each year.
Deadline: January of each year.

2057 MARY ANNE WILLIAMS SCHOLARSHIP

United Daughters of the Confederacy–Virginia Division
c/o Barbara Joyner, Second Vice President
8219 Seaview Drive
Chesterfield, VA 23838–5163
Email: bobbielou–udc@comcast.net
Web: vaudc.org/gift.html

Summary: To provide financial assistance to Confederate descendants from Virginia who are interested in working on an undergraduate or graduate degree in engineering or medicine at a school in the state.

Eligibility: Open to residents of Virginia who are 1) lineal descendants of Confederates; or 2) collateral descendants and also members of the Children of the Confederacy or the United Daughters of the Confederacy. Applicants must be interested in working on an undergraduate or graduate degree in medicine or engineering at a college or university in Virginia. They must submit proof of the Confederate military record of at least 1 ancestor, with the company and regiment in which he served. They must also submit a personal letter pledging to make the best possible use of the scholarship; describing their health, social, family, religious, and fraternal connections within the community; and reflecting on what a Southern heritage means to them (using the term "War Between the States" in lieu of "Civil War"). They must have a GPA of 3.0 or higher and be able to demonstrate financial need.

Financial data: The amount of the stipend depends on the availability of funds. Payment is made directly to the college or university the recipient attends.

Duration: 1 year; may be renewed up to 3 additional years if the recipient maintains a GPA of 3.0 or higher.

Number awarded: This scholarship is offered whenever a prior recipient graduates or is no longer eligible.

Deadline: April of the years in which the scholarship is available.

2058 $ MARY EILEEN DIXEY SCHOLARSHIP

American Occupational Therapy Foundation
Attn: Scholarship Coordinator
4720 Montgomery Lane
P.O. Box 31220
Bethesda, MD 20824–1220
Phone: (301) 652–6611, ext. 2550; Fax: (301) 656–3620; TDD: (800) 377–8555;
Email: JCooper@aotf.org
Web: www.aotf.org/scholarshipsgrants/scholarshipprogram.aspx

Summary: To provide financial assistance to students in New Hampshire who are working on an associate or professional degree in occupational therapy in the state.

Eligibility: Open to New Hampshire residents who are enrolled in an accredited occupational therapy educational program in the state at the associate or professional master's degree level. Applicants must be able to demonstrate a sustained record of outstanding scholastic performance. Selection is based on academic merit and leadership potential; financial need is not considered.

Financial data: The stipend is $2,000.

Duration: 1 year.

Number awarded: 1 each year.

Deadline: November of each year.

2059 MARY ELIZA MAHONEY SCHOLARSHIP

New England Regional Black Nurses Association, Inc.
P.O. Box 190690
Boston, MA 02119
Phone: (617) 524–1951
Web: www.nerbna.org/org/scholarships.html

Summary: To provide financial assistance to high school seniors New England who have contributed to the African American community and are interested in studying nursing at a school in any state.

Eligibility: Open to seniors graduating from high schools in New England who are planning to enroll full time in an NLN–accredited baccalaureate program in nursing in any state. Applicants must have at least 1 full year of school remaining. Along with their application, they must submit a 3–page essay that covers their career aspirations in the nursing profession; how they have contributed to the African American or other communities of color in such areas as work, volunteering, church, or community outreach; an experience that has enhanced their personal and/or professional growth; and any financial hardships that may hinder them from completing their education.

Financial data: A stipend is awarded (amount not specified).

Duration: 1 year.

Number awarded: 1 or more each year.

Deadline: February of each year.

2060 $ MARY GUNTHER MEMORIAL SCHOLARSHIP

Society of Women Engineers
Attn: Scholarship Selection Committee
203 North LaSalle Street, Suite 1675
Chicago, IL 60601–1269
Phone: (312) 596–5223; (877) SWE–INFO; Fax: (312) 644–8557;
Email: scholarships@swe.org
Web: societyofwomenengineers.swe.org/index.php/scholarships

Summary: To provide financial assistance to women interested in studying engineering or computer science in college.

Eligibility: Open to women who are enrolled or planning to enroll full time at an ABET–accredited 4–year college or university. Applicants must be planning to major in engineering or computer science; preference is given to students majoring in architectural or environmental engineering. Entering freshmen must have a GPA of 3.5 or higher; current undergraduates must have a GPA of 3.0 or higher. Selection is based on merit.

Financial data: The stipend is $2,000.

Duration: 1 year.

Number awarded: 4 each year: 2 for entering freshmen and 2 for continuing undergraduates.

Deadline: February of each year for continuing undergraduates; May of each year for entering freshmen.

2061 MARY LOU MARKS SMITH SCHOLARSHIP

Garden Club Federation of Maine
c/o Mary Blackstone, Scholarship Chair
5 Christian Ridge Road
Ellsworth, ME 04605
Email: Mary.Blackstone@uregina.ca
Web: www.mainegardenclubs.org/Mary_Lou_Smith_Scholarsh.html

Summary: To provide financial assistance to Maine residents who are enrolled or planning to enroll at a community college in the state to study horticulture or a related field.

Eligibility: Open to residents of Maine who are graduating high school seniors planning to enroll at a community college in the state or students already enrolled at such a college. Applicants must be planning to major in horticulture, floral design, or a related field. Along with their application, they must submit a 2–page personal letter discussing their goals, background, extracurricular activities, personal commitment, and financial need. Selection is based on aptitude in the field, academic record, character, and financial need.

Financial data: The stipend is $1,000.

Duration: 1 year.

Number awarded: 1 each odd–numbered year.

Deadline: February of each odd–numbered year.

2062 MARY M. CONLEY SCHOLARSHIP

Garden Club Federation of Massachusetts, Inc.
Attn: Scholarship Secretary
219 Washington Street
Wellesley Hills, MA 02481
Phone: (781) 237–0336; Fax: (781) 237–0336;
Email: gcfmscholarship@aol.com
Web: www.gcfm.org/Education/Scholarships/GCFMScholarships.aspx

Summary: To provide financial assistance to residents of Massachusetts interested in working on an undergraduate or graduate degree in a field related to horticulture at a college in any state.

Eligibility: Open to high school seniors, undergraduates, and graduate students who have been residents of Massachusetts for at least 1 year. Applicants must be working on or planning to work on a degree in horticulture, landscape design, environmental science, or a related field (e.g., agronomy, biology, botany, city planning, floriculture, forestry, land management). They must have a GPA of 3.0 or higher. Along with their application, they must submit official transcripts; a brief essay about their goals, aspirations, and career plans; a list of their activities, including special honors and/or leadership positions; 3 letters of recommendation; and documentation of financial need.

Financial data: The stipend is $1,000.
Duration: 1 year.
Number awarded: 1 each year.
Deadline: February of each year.

2063 $ MARY MARSHALL NURSING SCHOLARSHIP PROGRAM FOR REGISTERED NURSES

Virginia Department of Health
Attn: Office of Minority Health and Public Health Policy
109 Governor Street, Suite 1016 East
Richmond, VA 23219
Phone: (804) 864–7435; Fax: (804) 864–7440;
Email: IncentivePrograms@vdh.virginia.gov
Web: www.vdh.state.va.us

Summary: To provide funding to nursing students in Virginia who are willing to practice as nurses in the state following graduation.

Eligibility: Open to residents of Virginia who are enrolled or accepted for enrollment full or part time at a school of nursing in the state (graduate students working on degrees not offered in Virginia may attend school in another state). Applicants must submit a narrative in which they explain the significance of the scholarship in pursuing their educational goals and their plans for professional practice following graduation. They must have a GPA of at least 3.0 in required courses. Selection is based primarily on financial need, although scholastic achievement is also considered.

Financial data: The amount of the award depends on the availability of funds and the number of qualified applicants; recently, stipends averaged $2,222. Scholarship recipients must agree to engage in full–time nursing practice in Virginia for 1 month for every $100 received. The required service must begin within 90 days of the recipient's licensure date. If the recipient fails to complete the course of study, or pass the licensing examination, or provide the required service, all scholarship funds received must be repaid with interest.

Duration: 1 year; may be renewed for up to 3 additional years.

Number awarded: Varies each year; recently, 72 of these scholarships were awarded.

Deadline: June of each year.

2064 $$ MARYLAND ASSOCIATION OF PRIVATE COLLEGES AND CAREER SCHOOLS SCHOLARSHIPS

Summary: To provide financial assistance to students interested in attending selected private career schools in Maryland.
See Listing #1373.

2065 $ MARYLAND LEGION AUXILIARY PAST PRESIDENTS' PARLEY NURSING SCHOLARSHIP

American Legion Auxiliary
Department of Maryland
1589 Sulphur Spring Road, Suite 105
Baltimore, MD 21227
Phone: (410) 242–9519; Fax: (410) 242–9553;
Email: hq@alamd.org
Web: www.alamd.org/Home/Scholarships.html

Summary: To provide financial assistance to the female descendants of Maryland veterans who wish to study nursing at a school in any state.

Eligibility: Open to Maryland residents who are the daughters, granddaughters, great–granddaughters, step–daughters, step–granddaughters, or step–great–granddaughters of ex–servicewomen (or of ex–servicemen, if there are no qualified descendants of ex–servicewomen). Applicants must be interested in attending a school in any state to become a registered nurse and be able to show financial need. They must submit a 300–word essay on the topic "What a Nursing Career Means to Me."

Financial data: The stipend is $2,000. Funds are sent directly to the recipient's school.

Duration: 1 year; may be renewed for up to 3 additional years if the recipient remains enrolled full time.

Number awarded: 1 each year.

Deadline: April of each year.

2066 $$ MARYLAND WORKFORCE SHORTAGE STUDENT ASSISTANCE GRANT PROGRAM

Maryland Higher Education Commission
Attn: Office of Student Financial Assistance
6 North Liberty Street, Ground Suite
Baltimore, MD 21201
Phone: (410) 767–3300; (800) 974–0203; Fax: (410) 332–0250; TDD: (800) 735–2258;
Email: osfamail@mhec.state.md.us
Web: www.mhec.state.md.us/financialAid/descriptions.asp

Summary: To provide money for college to Maryland residents interested in a career in specified workforce shortage areas.

Eligibility: Open to residents of Maryland who are high school seniors, undergraduates, or graduate students. Applicants must be enrolled or planning to enroll at a 2– or 4–year Maryland college or university. They may major in the following service areas: 1) child development or early childhood education; 2) human services; 3) education; 4) nursing; 5) physical therapy or occupational therapy; 6) law; or 8) public service. Applicants are ranked by GPA and then by need within each occupational field. Students with the greatest need within each GPA range are awarded first.

Financial data: Awards are $4,000 per year for full–time undergraduate and graduate students at 4–year institutions, $2,000 per year for part–time undergraduate and graduate students at 4–year institutions, $2,000 per year for full–time students at community colleges, or $1,000 per year for part–time students at community colleges. The total amount of all state awards may not exceed the cost of attendance as determined by the school's financial aid office or $19,000, whichever is less. Within 1 year of graduation, recipients must provide 1 year of service in Maryland in their field of study for each year of financial aid received under this program; failure to comply with that service obligation will require them to repay the scholarship money with interest.

Duration: 1 year; may be renewed up to 4 additional years, provided the recipient continues to meet eligibility requirements.

Number awarded: Varies each year.

Deadline: June of each year.

2067 MAS FAMILY SCHOLARSHIP PROGRAM

Summary: To provide financial assistance to students of Cuban descent who are working on an undergraduate or graduate degree in selected subject areas.
See Listing #1374.

2068 $$ MASONIC–RANGE SCIENCE SCHOLARSHIP

Society for Range Management
10030 West 27th Avenue
Wheat Ridge, CO 80215–6601
Phone: (303) 986–3309; Fax: (303) 986–3892;
Email: info@rangelands.org
Web: www.rangelands.org/masonicscholarship

Summary: To provide financial assistance to students who are interested in majoring in range science in college.

Eligibility: Open to high school seniors and college freshmen and sophomores who are interested in majoring in range science in college. Applicants must be sponsored by a member of the Society for Range Management, the National Association of Conservation Districts, or the Soil and Water Conservation Society. Along with their application, they must submit an essay on why they are interested in a career in range science, including any experiences that have led them to choose a range science major. Selection is based on that essay, letters of reference, academic record, leadership experience, community service, and honors and awards.

Financial data: The amount awarded each year varies; recently, the stipend was $5,000.

Duration: 1 year; may be renewed provided the recipient maintains a GPA of 2.5 or higher for the first 2 years of college and 3.0 or higher thereafter.

Number awarded: 1 each year.

Deadline: December of each year.

2069 MASSACHUSETTS EDUCATIONAL SCHOLARSHIP FOR CAREER ADVANCEMENT

Massachusetts Federation of Business and Professional Women's Clubs, Inc.
P.O. Box 352
Maynard, MA 01754
Phone: (413) 545–0721;
Email: bpwmass@yahoo.com
Web: www.bpwma.org/scholarship–information

Summary: To provide financial assistance to mature women from Massachusetts who are working on a bachelor's degree in a field of science, technology, engineering, or mathematics (STEM).

Eligibility: Open to women who are residents of Massachusetts, 25 years of age or older, and interested in returning to college in the state to work full or part time on a bachelor's degree in a field of STEM. Applicants must be within 2 years of completing their degree and have a scheduled time frame in which they expect to achieve their educational goals. They must be able to demonstrate financial need and clear career plans. U.S. citizenship is required. Membership in the sponsoring organization is not required and members receive no special consideration. A personal interview is required.
Financial data: The stipend is $1,000.
Duration: 1 year.
Number awarded: 1 or more each year.
Deadline: July of each year.

2070 $$ MASSACHUSETTS HIGH TECHNOLOGY SCHOLAR/INTERN TUITION WAIVER PROGRAM

Massachusetts Office of Student Financial Assistance
454 Broadway, Suite 200
Revere, MA 02151
Phone: (617) 391–6070; Fax: (617) 727–0667;
Email: osfa@osfa.mass.edu
Web: www.osfa.mass.edu/default.asp?page=highTechWaiver
Summary: To provide financial assistance to students at Massachusetts public institutions of higher education who are participating in a high technology scholar/intern program.
Eligibility: Open to students at Massachusetts public institutions who are participating as interns in a computer, information technology, or engineering program approved by the Massachusetts Board of Higher Education. Applicants must be U.S. citizens or permanent residents and residents of Massachusetts. Their institution must have obtained scholarship funding from business and industry.
Financial data: The awards match industry scholarships up to the resident undergraduate tuition rate at the participating institution.
Duration: Up to 4 academic years.
Number awarded: Varies each year.
Deadline: April of each year.

2071 MASWE SCHOLARSHIPS

Society of Women Engineers
Attn: Scholarship Selection Committee
203 North LaSalle Street, Suite 1675
Chicago, IL 60601–1269
Phone: (312) 596–5223; (877) SWE–INFO; Fax: (312) 644–8557;
Email: scholarships@swe.org
Web: societyofwomenengineers.swe.org/index.php/scholarships
Summary: To provide financial assistance to undergraduate women majoring in computer science or engineering.
Eligibility: Open to women who are entering their sophomore, junior, or senior year at a 4–year ABET–accredited college or university. Applicants must be working full time on a degree in computer science or engineering and have a GPA of 3.0 or higher. Financial need is considered in the selection process.
Financial data: The stipend is $1,500.
Duration: 1 year.
Number awarded: 4 each year.
Deadline: February of each year.

2072 $ MATERIALS AND ENERGY RECOVERY DIVISION UNDERGRADUATE SCHOLARSHIP PROGRAM

ASME International
Attn: Materials and Energy Recovery Division
Three Park Avenue
New York, NY 10016–5990
Phone: (212) 591–8234; (800) THE–ASME; Fax: (212) 591–7671;
Email: FrederickJ@asme.org
Web: divisions.asme.org/MER/Scholarships.cfm
Summary: To provide financial assistance to undergraduate students working on a degree in solid waste management.
Eligibility: Open to undergraduate students in any branch of engineering who are currently enrolled full time in a solid waste management program. They must attend or plan to attend a college or university in North America (including Alaska, Canada, Hawaii, Mexico, and Puerto Rico). Along with their application, they must submit a statement of intent to pursue a branch of engineering as a career or professional certification, a 1– to 2–page statement of interest in solid waste management, information on any experience in the solid waste management field, and copies of any papers they have written on solid waste management. Financial need is not considered in the selection process.
Financial data: The award is $4,000. One half is given to the student and the other half is given to the recipient's school for support of its solid waste management program.
Duration: 1 year.
Number awarded: 1 each year.
Deadline: June of each year.

2073 $ MATTIE J.T. STEPANEK CAREGIVING SCHOLARSHIP

Rosalynn Carter Institute for Caregiving
c/o Georgia Southwestern State University
800 GSW Drive
Americus, GA 31709–4379
Phone: (229) 928–1234; Fax: (229) 931–2663
Web: www.rosalynncarter.org/Mattie%20Stepanek
Summary: To provide financial assistance to caregivers interested in additional training.
Eligibility: Open to family, professional, or paraprofessional caregivers of any age who are seeking training or education in specific skills, procedures, and strategies that lead to more effective care. Applicants must submit a resume that includes community and volunteer service experience; a statement describing their plans to pursue a specific course of training or education; and 2 letters of recommendation.
Financial data: The stipend is $2,500.
Duration: 1 year.
Number awarded: 4 each year.
Deadline: May of each year.

2074 MAURICE E. CORE SCHOLARSHIP

National Dairy Shrine
Attn: Executive Director
P.O. Box 725
Denmark, WI 54208
Phone: (920) 863–6333; Fax: (920) 863–6333;
Email: info@dairyshrine.org
Web: www.dairyshrine.org/scholarships.php
Summary: To provide financial assistance to college freshmen working on a bachelor's degree in animal or dairy science.
Eligibility: Open to college freshmen working on a bachelor's degree in animal science, dairy science, or other field that will prepare them for a career in the dairy industry. Applicants must have a GPA of 2.5 or higher. Along with their application, they must submit a 300–word essay on their plans for the future and how this scholarship will assist them in meeting their goals. Selection is based on that essay, academic standing, high school leadership and activities, college and dairy club activities, awards and honors, and promotion and volunteer activities for the dairy industry.
Financial data: The stipend is $1,000.
Duration: 1 year.
Number awarded: 1 each year.
Deadline: April of each year.

2075 $ MAX ZAR SCHOLARSHIP

Structural Engineers Association of Illinois
Attn: Structural Engineers Foundation
134 North LaSalle Street, Suite 1910
Chicago, IL 60602
Phone: (312) 726–4165; Fax: (312) 277–1991;
Email: office@seaol.org
Web: www.seaoi.org/sef.htm
Summary: To provide financial assistance to upper–division and graduate students at universities in Illinois who are interested in a career in structural engineering.
Eligibility: Open to students 1) entering their third or higher year of an undergraduate program; or 2) entering or continuing a graduate program. Applicants must be enrolled in a civil or architectural engineering program at a university in Illinois and planning to continue with a structural engineering specialization. Students enrolled in structural engineering technology programs are also eligible if they are qualified to take the Fundamentals of Engineering and Principles and Practice licensure examinations in their home state upon graduation. U.S. citizenship or permanent resident status is required. Selection is

based on a statement giving reasons why the applicant should receive the award (including plans for continued formal education), academic performance, and potential for development and leadership. Financial need is not considered.
Financial data: The stipend is $2,000.
Duration: 1 year; nonrenewable.
Number awarded: 1 or more each year.
Deadline: April of each year.

2076 MAXINE V. FENNELL MEMORIAL SCHOLARSHIP

New England Regional Black Nurses Association, Inc.
P.O. Box 190690
Boston, MA 02119
Phone: (617) 524–1951
Web: www.nerbna.org/org/scholarships.html

Summary: To provide financial assistance to licensed practical nurses from New England who are studying to become a registered nurse (R.N.) and have contributed to the African American community.
Eligibility: Open to residents of the New England states who are licensed practical nurses and currently enrolled in an NLN–accredited R.N. program (diploma, associate, baccalaureate) at a school in any state. Applicants must have at least 1 full year of school remaining. Along with their application, they must submit a 3–page essay that covers their career aspirations in the nursing profession; how they have contributed to the African American or other communities of color in such areas as work, volunteering, church, or community outreach; an experience that has enhanced their personal and/or professional growth; and any financial hardships that may hinder them from completing their education.
Financial data: A stipend is awarded (amount not specified).
Duration: 1 year.
Number awarded: 1 or more each year.
Deadline: February of each year.

2077 MCCOLLUM SCHOLARSHIP

Kansas Dietetic Association
Attn: Executive Director
8921 Quail Ridge Lane
Lenexa, KS 66220–3445
Phone: (913) 499–0977;
Email: director@eatrightks.org
Web: www.eatrightks.org

Summary: To provide financial assistance to upper–division students at universities in Kansas who are enrolled in a program in dietetics.
Eligibility: Open to juniors and seniors at colleges and universities in Kansas who either 1) are enrolled in a Coordinated Program in Dietetics; or 2) have a declared undergraduate major in dietetics. Applicants must submit a 1–page personal letter describing their goals and plans for attaining those goals. Selection is based on that letter (15%), academic achievement (20%), a faculty evaluation (10%), leadership in dietetics (15%), financial need (20%), and an overall evaluation (20%).
Financial data: A stipend is awarded (amount not specified).
Duration: 1 year.
Number awarded: 1 or more each year.
Deadline: February of each year.

2078 $ MCKESSON SCHOLARSHIPS

National Student Nurses' Association
Attn: Foundation
45 Main Street, Suite 606
Brooklyn, NY 11201
Phone: (718) 210–0705; Fax: (718) 797–1186;
Email: nsna@nsna.org
Web: www.nsna.org/FoundationScholarships/FNSNAScholarships.aspx

Summary: To provide financial assistance to nursing students enrolled in programs leading to licensure as a registered nurse (R.N.).
Eligibility: Open to students currently enrolled in state–approved schools of nursing and working on an associate degree, baccalaureate degree, or diploma leading to licensure as an R.N. Graduating high school seniors are not eligible. Applicants must submit a 200–word description of their professional and educational goals and how this scholarship will help them achieve those goals. Selection is based on academic achievement, financial need, and involvement in student nursing organizations and community health activities. U.S. citizenship or permanent resident status is required.
Financial data: Stipends range from $1,000 to $2,500.
Duration: 1 year.
Number awarded: Varies each year; recently, 12 of these scholarships were awarded.
Deadline: January of each year.

2079 $ MCKIM & CREED SCHOLARSHIP

Professional Engineers of North Carolina
Attn: PENC Educational Foundation
1015 Wade Avenue, Suite A
Raleigh, NC 27605
Phone: (919) 834–1144; Fax: (919) 834–1148;
Email: exec@penc.org
Web: www.penc.org/scholarships.aspx

Summary: To provide financial assistance to upper–division students from any state working on a degree in civil engineering at a campus of the University of North Carolina (UNC).
Eligibility: Open to residents of any state entering their junior year at a campus of the UNC system that has an ABET–accredited program in civil engineering. Applicants must submit a 500–word essay that discusses their interest in civil engineering, their major area of study and specialization, the occupation they propose to pursue after graduation, their financial need, their long–term goals, how the scholarship could help them achieve those goals, and their interest in an internship. Preference is given to members of the National Society of Professional Engineers (NSPE). U.S. citizenship is required.
Financial data: The stipend is $2,000 per year.
Duration: 2 years.
Number awarded: 1 or more each year.
Deadline: April of each year.

2080 $$ MEDICAL PROFESSIONALS OF TOMORROW SCHOLARSHIP

U.S. Medical Supplies
3901A Commerce Park Drive
Raleigh, NC 27610
Phone: (800) 790–4792; Fax: (919) 231–4217
Web: www.usmedicalsupplies.com/scholarship

Summary: To provide financial assistance to undergraduate and graduate students preparing for a career in a medical field.
Eligibility: Open to legal residents of the United States currently enrolled full time in a 2–year, 4–year, or graduate program of study. Applicants must be preparing for a career as a doctor, nurse, physical therapist, anesthesiologist, radiologist, or other medical position. They must like the sponsor on Facebook or +1 it on Google+. Along with their application, they must submit a 500–word essay on the person or event that inspired them to prepare for a career in a medical field and how they plan to capitalize on that experience in their field. Financial need is not considered in the selection process.
Financial data: The stipend is $5,000.
Duration: 1 year.
Number awarded: 1 each year.
Deadline: December of each year.

2081 MEDICAL/RESEARCH SCHOLARSHIP OF THE JUVENILE DIABETES RESEARCH FOUNDATION

Diabetes Scholars Foundation
2118 Plum Grove Road, Suite 356
Rolling Meadows, IL 60008
Phone: (312) 215–9861; Fax: (847) 991–8739;
Email: collegescholarships@diabetesscholars.org
Web: www.diabetesscholars.org/college.html

Summary: To provide financial assistance to high school seniors who have diabetes and plan to major in a health care field in college.
Eligibility: Open to graduating high school seniors who have Type 1 diabetes and plan to attend an accredited 4–year university, college, or technical/trade school in any state. Applicants must be planning to major in a health care field. They must be able to demonstrate active involvement in the diabetes community, academic performance, participation in community and/or extracurricular activities, and successful management of the challenges of living with diabetes. Financial need is not considered in the selection process. U.S. citizenship or permanent resident status is required.
Financial data: The stipend is $1,000.
Duration: 1 year.

Number awarded: 1 each year.
Deadline: May of each year.

2082 $ MERIDITH THOMS MEMORIAL SCHOLARSHIPS

Society of Women Engineers
Attn: Scholarship Selection Committee
120 South LaSalle Street, Suite 1515
Chicago, IL 60603–3572
Phone: (312) 596–5223; (877) SWE–INFO; Fax: (312) 644–8557;
Email: scholarshipapplication@swe.org
Web: societyofwomenengineers.swe.org/index.php/scholarships

Summary: To provide financial assistance to undergraduate women majoring in computer science or engineering.
Eligibility: Open to women who are entering their sophomore, junior, or senior year at a 4–year ABET–accredited college or university. Applicants must be working full time on a degree in computer science or engineering and have a GPA of 3.0 or higher. Selection is based on merit.
Financial data: The stipend is $2,000.
Duration: 1 year.
Number awarded: 5 each year.
Deadline: February of each year.

2083 $ MERITER MINORITY HEALTH CAREERS SCHOLARSHIP

Meriter Health Services
Attn: Human Resources
202 South Park Street
Madison, WI 53715–1596
Phone: (608) 417–6567;
Email: rthrall@meriter.com
Web: www.meriter.com/wordpress/?p=2241

Summary: To provide financial assistance to members of minority groups who are preparing for a career in a health care occupation.
Eligibility: Open to members of minority groups (African American, Hispanic, Asian or Pacific Islander, and Native American) who are U.S. citizens or permanent residents. Applicants must have completed at least 1 semester in a college or technical school and be working on a college degree, professional degree, or certification in a health care occupation. Along with their application, they must submit a 2–page essay on their reasons for selecting a health career, any unique experiences that have prepared them for such a career, and how their contributions to the health care field can enhance the fabric of life in our community. Selection is based on demonstrated history of academic success and demonstrated commitment to community service.
Financial data: The stipend is $4,000. Funds are paid directly to the student for assistance with tuition.
Duration: 1 year.
Number awarded: 1 or more each year.
Deadline: April of each year.

2084 $$ MESBEC PROGRAM

Catching the Dream
8200 Mountain Road, N.E., Suite 203
Albuquerque, NM 87110–7835
Phone: (505) 262–2351; Fax: (505) 262–0534;
Email: NScholarsh@aol.com
Web: www.catchingthedream.org/Scholarship.htm

Summary: To provide financial assistance to American Indian students who are interested in working on an undergraduate or graduate degree in selected fields.
Eligibility: Open to American Indians who can provide proof that they have at least one–quarter Indian blood and are a member of a U.S. tribe that is federally–recognized, state–recognized, or terminated. Applicants must be enrolled or planning to enroll full time and major in 1 of the following fields: mathematics, engineering, science (including medicine), business administration, education, or computer science. They may be entering freshmen, undergraduate students, graduate students, or Ph.D. candidates. Along with their application, they must submit documentation of financial need, 3 letters of recommendation, copies of applications and responses for all other sources of funding for which they are eligible, official transcripts, standardized test scores (ACT, SAT, GRE, MCAT, LSAT, etc.), and an essay explaining their goals in life, college plans, and career plans (especially how those plans include working with and benefiting Indians). Selection is based on merit and potential for improving the lives of Indian people.
Financial data: Stipends range from $500 to $5,000 per year.
Duration: 1 year; may be renewed.
Number awarded: Varies; generally, 30 to 35 each year.
Deadline: April of each year for fall term; September of each year for spring and winter terms; March of each year for summer school.

2085 $$ METROPOLITAN WASHINGTON CHAPTER ARCS FOUNDATION SCHOLAR AWARDS

ARCS Foundation, Inc.–Metropolitan Washington Chapter
P.O. Box 60868
Potomac, MD 20859–0868
Email: washington@arcsfoundation.org
Web: www.arcsfoundation.org/metro_washington

Summary: To provide financial assistance to undergraduate and graduate students in the sciences, medicine, and engineering at designated universities in the metropolitan Washington, D.C. area.
Eligibility: Open to full–time undergraduate and graduate students at George Washington University, Johns Hopkins University, Georgetown University, University of Maryland, and University of Virginia. Applicants must have completed at least 1 year of work on a degree in the sciences, medicine, or engineering. They must be U.S. citizens and have a GPA of 3.5 or higher. Recipients are selected by the participating schools on the basis of their ability in science, and research, character, community involvement, and financial need. U.S. citizenship is required.
Financial data: The stipend is $5,000 per year for undergraduates or $15,000 per year for graduate students.
Duration: 1 year; may be renewed.
Number awarded: Varies each year; recently, 20 of these scholarships were awarded: 4 at George Washington, 3 at Johns Hopkins, 5 at Georgetown, 4 at University of Maryland, and 4 at University of Virginia.
Deadline: Deadline not specified.

2086 $$ MHEFI SCHOLARSHIP PROGRAM

Material Handling Industry of America
Attn: Material Handling Education Foundation, Inc.
8720 Red Oak Boulevard, Suite 201
Charlotte, NC 28217–3992
Phone: (704) 676–1190; (800) 722–6832; Fax: (704) 676–1199;
Email: vwheeler@mhia.org
Web: www.mhia.org/about/mhefi/scholarship

Summary: To provide financial assistance to undergraduate or graduate students who are studying material handling.
Eligibility: Open to 1) students at 4–year colleges and universities who have completed at least 2 years of undergraduate study; and 2) graduate students enrolled in a program leading to a master's or doctoral degree. Students from junior or community colleges are eligible if they have been accepted as a transfer student into a 4–year program. Applicants must be U.S. citizens; be attending an academic institution that has been prequalified for foundation funding; have earned a GPA of 3.0 or higher in college; and be enrolled full time in a course of study relevant to the material handling industry, including engineering (civil, computer, industrial, electrical, or mechanical), engineering technology, computer science, or business administration with an emphasis on production management, industrial distribution, supply chain, and/or logistics. Along with their application, they must submit 3 letters of recommendation, official transcripts, documentation of financial need, and a 600–word essay on how their course of study, work experience, and career goals make them an appropriate candidate for this scholarship.
Financial data: Stipends range from $1,500 to $9,000.
Duration: 1 year.
Number awarded: Varies each year; recently, 29 of these scholarships, with a total value of $87,100, were awarded.
Deadline: February of each year.

2087 MICHAEL A. SHUTT ACADEMIC SCHOLARSHIP

American Association of Airport Executives–Southwest Chapter
Attn: Executive Director
107 South Southgate Drive
Chandler, AZ 85226
Phone: (480) 403–4604; Fax: (480) 893–7775;
Email: info@swaaae.org
Web: www.swaaae.org/displaycommon.cfm?an=1&subarticlenbr=10

Summary: To provide financial assistance to undergraduate or graduate students from the Southwest working on a degree in an aviation–related field.

Eligibility: Open to students working on an undergraduate or graduate degree in airport or transportation engineering, environmental studies, planning, or airport management. Applicants must be attending a college or university in Arizona, California, Hawaii, Nevada, or Utah or have a permanent address in those states. Along with their application, they must submit an autobiography (not to exceed 1 page) and a statement of their interest in aviation (not to exceed 1 page). Selection is based on academic record, extracurricular activities, and financial need.
Financial data: The stipend is $1,500; the sponsor also provides a $1,000 travel allowance for recipients to attend the awards ceremony.
Duration: 1 year.
Number awarded: 1 each year.
Deadline: November of each year.

2088 $$ MICHAEL KIDGER MEMORIAL SCHOLARSHIP

SPIE–The International Society for Optical Engineering
Attn: Michael Kidger Memorial Scholarship
1000 20th Street
P.O. Box 10
Bellingham, WA 98227–0010
Phone: (360) 676–3290; Fax: (360) 647–1445;
Email: scholarships@spie.org
Web: www.kidger.com/mkms_home.html
Summary: To provide financial assistance to undergraduate and graduate students who are preparing for a career in optical design.
Eligibility: Open to students of optical design from any country at the undergraduate and graduate level. Applicants must have at least 1 more year, after the award, to complete their current course of study. They must submit 2 letters of recommendation and a 5–page essay on their academic background and interest in pursuing training or research in optical design. Financial need is not considered in the selection process.
Financial data: The stipend is $5,000.
Duration: 1 year.
Number awarded: 1 or more each year.
Deadline: March of each year.

2089 $$ MICHIGAN COUNCIL OF WOMEN IN TECHNOLOGY FOUNDATION SCHOLARSHIPS

Michigan Council of Women in Technology Foundation
Attn: Scholarship Committee
19011 Norwich Road
Livonia, MI 48152
Phone: (248) 654–3697; Fax: (248) 281–5391;
Email: info@mcwtf.org
Web: www.mcwtf.org/Scholarships_149.html
Summary: To provide financial assistance to women from Michigan who are interested in working on an undergraduate or graduate degree in a field related to information technology at a school in any state.
Eligibility: Open to female residents of Michigan who are graduating high school seniors, current undergraduates, or graduate students. Applicants must be planning to work on a degree in business applications, computer science, computer engineering, graphics design, health technology, information security, information systems, instructional technology, music technology, or software engineering at a college or university in any state. They must have a GPA of 2.8 or higher. Along with their application, they must submit an essay of 200 to 400 words on why they are preparing for a career in information technology, the accomplishments in which they take the most pride, why they should be selected for this scholarship, and what constitutes success for them in this program and/or their future career and life mission. Selection is based on that essay, GPA, technology related activities, community service, letters of recommendation, and completeness of the application. U.S. citizenship is required.
Financial data: The stipend is $5,000 per year; funds are sent directly to the financial aid office at the college or university where the recipient is enrolled.
Duration: 1 year; may be renewed for up to 3 additional years for high school seniors or 2 additional years for undergraduate and graduate students.
Number awarded: 3 each year: 1 each to a high school senior, an undergraduate, and a graduate student.
Deadline: January of each year.

2090 MICHIGAN PA FOUNDATION SCHOLARSHIP AWARD

Michigan Academy of Physician Assistants
Attn: Michigan Physician Assistant Foundation
1390 Eisenhower Place
Ann Arbor, MI 48108–3282
Phone: (734) 353–4752; (877) YES–MAPA; Fax: (734) 677–2407;
Email: mapa@michiganpa.org
Web: www.mipaf.com/SchApp/SApplication.htm
Summary: To provide financial assistance to students enrolled in a physician assistant program at a college or university in Michigan.
Eligibility: Open to students currently enrolled in their final clinical year of a physician assistant program in Michigan. Applicants must submit a brief essay that includes their past, present, and future plans to serve their community in volunteer work; their involvement in activities sponsored by student professional academies and organizations; honors, awards, or special recognition that they have received; their academic record; and their financial need. Selection is based on scholarship, professional involvement, community service, and financial need.
Financial data: A stipend is awarded (amount not specified).
Duration: 1 year.
Number awarded: 1 or more each year.
Deadline: July of each year.

2091 MIKE AND FLO NOVOVESKY SCHOLARSHIP

American Floral Endowment
1601 Duke Street
Alexandria, VA 22314
Phone: (703) 838–5211; Fax: (703) 838–5212;
Email: afe@endowment.org
Web: endowment.org/floriculture–scholarshipsinternships.html
Summary: To provide financial assistance to undergraduate and graduate students who are married and working on a degree in horticulture.
Eligibility: Open to undergraduate and graduate students who are married and holding a job to put themselves through college. Applicants must working on a degree in horticulture. They must be U.S. or Canadian citizens or permanent residents and have a GPA of 2.5 or higher. If no married students apply, consideration may be given to undergraduates who are working their way through college. Along with their application, they must submit a statement describing their career goals and the academic, work–related, and/or life experiences that support those goals. Financial need is considered in the selection process.
Financial data: The stipend varies each year; recently, it was $1,150.
Duration: 1 year.
Number awarded: 1 each year.
Deadline: April of each year.

2092 MIKE CRAPO MATH AND SCIENCE SCHOLARSHIPS

Idaho Community Foundation
Attn: Scholarship Coordinator
210 West State Street
Boise, ID 83702
Phone: (208) 342–3535; (800) 657–5357; Fax: (208) 342–3577;
Email: edavis@idcomfdn.org
Web: www.idcomfdn.org/pages/scho_general.htm
Summary: To provide financial assistance to residents of Idaho who are entering college in the state to work on a degree in mathematics or science.
Eligibility: Open to residents of Idaho who are entering freshmen as full–time students at public and private 4–year colleges and universities in the state. Applicants must be planning to major in mathematics or science (including engineering) and have a GPA of 3.0 or higher. Along with their application, they must submit 4 letters of reference, transcripts, ACT and/or SAT scores, and a 300–word essay on the value of mathematics and science to them as individuals and to society as a whole. Financial need is not considered in the selection process.
Financial data: A stipend is awarded (amount not specified).
Duration: 1 year; nonrenewable.
Number awarded: 1 or more each year.
Deadline: March of each year.

2093 $ MILDRED COLLINS NURSING/HEALTH SCIENCE/ MEDICINE SCHOLARSHIP

African–American/Caribbean Education Association, Inc.
P.O. Box 1224
Valley Stream, NY 11582–1224
Phone: (718) 949–6733;
Email: aaceainc@yahoo.com
Web: www.aaceainc.com/Scholarships.html

Summary: To provide financial assistance to high school seniors of African American or Caribbean heritage who plan to study a field related to nursing, health science, or medicine in college.
Eligibility: Open to graduating high school seniors who are U.S. citizens of African American or Caribbean heritage. Applicants must be planning to attend a college or university and major in a field related to nursing, health science, or medicine. They must have completed 4 years of specified college preparatory courses with a grade of 90 or higher and have an SAT score of at least 1790. They must also have completed at least 200 hours of community service during their 4 years of high school, preferably in the field that they plan to study in college. Financial need is not considered in the selection process. New York residency is not required, but applicants must be available for an interviews in the Queens, New York area.
Financial data: The stipend ranges from $1,000 to $2,500. Funds are paid directly to the recipient.
Duration: 1 year.
Number awarded: 1 each year.
Deadline: April of each year.

2094 $ MINNESOTA ASSOCIATION OF ASPHALT PAVING TECHNOLOGISTS SCHOLARSHIP

Minnesota Association of Asphalt Paving Technologists
c/o Associated General Contractors of Minnesota
Capitol Office Building
525 Park Street, Suite 110
St. Paul, MN 55103–2186
Phone: (651) 796–2187; (800) 552–7670; Fax: (651) 632–8928;
Email: jsanem@agcmn.org
Web: www.agcmn.org/i4a/pages/index.cfm?pageid=3519
Summary: To provide financial assistance to students in Minnesota preparing for a career in asphalt pavement technology.
Eligibility: Open to residents of Minnesota enrolled at colleges and universities in the state. Applicants must be studying civil engineering, construction management, or civil technology with an interest in asphalt pavement technology. Along with their application, they must submit a personal statement that includes information on their work–related experience, involvement in student or community organizations, honors or awards they have received, their financial situation, and other appropriate information. Selection is based on academic standing (20%), career objectives (20%), financial need (20%), personal information (20%), and overall application clarity (20%).
Financial data: Stipends range from $500 to $2,500.
Duration: 1 year.
Number awarded: 8 to 10 each year.
Deadline: May of each year.

2095 MINNESOTA CHAPTER SCHOLARSHIP

Healthcare Information and Management Systems Society–Minnesota Chapter
Attn: Scholarship Chair
P.O. Box 2331
Minneapolis, MN 55402–0331
Phone: (612) 325–9014;
Email: studentaffairs@himss–mn.org
Web: www.himss–mn.org/information/information.html
Summary: To provide financial assistance to undergraduate and graduate students with a Minnesota connection who are working on a degree in health care information or management.
Eligibility: Open to full– and part–time students who are either residents of Minnesota or enrolled at a Minnesota institution of higher education. Applicants must be working on an undergraduate, master's, or Ph.D. degree in a field related to health care information or management systems, including industrial engineering, operations research, health care informatics, computer science and information systems, mathematics, and quantitative programs in business administration or hospital administration. Membership in the Minnesota Chapter of the Healthcare Information and Management Systems Society (HIMSS) is not required, but applicants are provided with a complimentary 1–year local student membership as soon as their application is completed. Selection is based on academic achievement, demonstration of leadership potential, communication skills, and participation in HIMSS activities.
Financial data: The stipend is $1,000.
Duration: 1 year; nonrenewable.
Number awarded: 2 each year: 1 to an undergraduate and 1 to a graduate student.
Deadline: March of each year.

2096 $ MINORITY AND UNDERREPRESENTED ENVIRONMENTAL LITERACY PROGRAM

Missouri Department of Higher Education
Attn: Minority and Underrepresented Environmental Literacy Program
205 Jefferson Street
P.O. Box 1469
Jefferson City, MO 65102–1469
Phone: (573) 751–2361; (800) 473–6757; Fax: (573) 751–6635;
Email: info@dhe.mo.gov
Web: dhe.mo.gov/ppc/grants/muelp_0310_final.php
Summary: To provide financial assistance to underrepresented and minority students from Missouri who are or will be working on a bachelor's or master's degree in an environmental field.
Eligibility: Open to residents of Missouri who are high school seniors or current undergraduate or graduate students enrolled or planning to enroll full time at a college or university in the state. Priority is given to members of the following underrepresented minority ethnic groups: African Americans, Hispanic or Latino Americans, Native Americans and Alaska Natives, and Native Hawaiians and Pacific Islanders. Applicants must be working on or planning to work on a bachelor's or master's degree in 1) engineering (civil, chemical, environmental, mechanical, or agricultural); 2) environmental studies (geology, biology, wildlife management, natural resource planning, natural resources, or a closely–related course of study); 3) environmental chemistry; or 4) environmental law enforcement. They must be U.S. citizens or permanent residents or otherwise lawfully present in the United States. Graduating high school seniors must have a GPA of 3.0 or higher; students currently enrolled in college or graduate school must have a GPA of 2.5 or higher. Along with their application, they must submit a 1–page essay on their environmental education and career goals, 3 letters of recommendation, a resume of school and community activities, and transcripts that include SAT or ACT scores. Financial need is not considered in the selection process.
Financial data: Stipends vary each year; recently, they averaged approximately $3,996 per year.
Duration: 1 year; may be renewed if the recipient maintains a GPA of 2.5 or higher and full–time enrollment.
Number awarded: Varies each year.
Deadline: May of each year.

2097 $ MINORITY NURSE MAGAZINE SCHOLARSHIP PROGRAM

Minority Nurse Magazine
c/o Alloy Education
2 LAN Drive, Suite 100
Westford, MA 01886
Phone: (877) ASK–ALLO;
Email: editor@minoritynurse.com
Web: www.minoritynurse.com
Summary: To provide financial assistance to members of minority groups who are working on a bachelor's or master's degree in nursing.
Eligibility: Open to racial and ethnic minority nursing students currently enrolled in 1) the third or fourth year of an accredited B.S.N. program; 2) an accelerated program leading to a B.S.N. degree (e.g., R.N. to B.S.N., B.A. to B.S.N.); or 3) an accelerated master's entry nursing program (e.g., B.A. to M.S.N.) for students with bachelor's degrees in fields other than nursing. Graduate students who already have a bachelor's degree in nursing are not eligible. Along with their application, they must submit a 250–word essay on their academic and personal accomplishments, community service, and goals for their future nursing career. Selection is based on academic excellence (GPA of 3.0 or higher), demonstrated commitment of service to the student's minority community, and financial need. U.S. citizenship of permanent resident status is required.
Financial data: The stipends are $3,000 or $1,000.
Duration: 1 year.
Number awarded: 3 each year: 1 at $3,000 and 2 at $1,000.
Deadline: January of each year.

2098 $ MISSISSIPPI HEALTH CARE PROFESSIONS LOAN/SCHOLARSHIP PROGRAM

Mississippi Office of Student Financial Aid
3825 Ridgewood Road
Jackson, MS 39211–6453
Phone: (601) 432–6997; (800) 327–2980 (within MS); Fax: (601) 432–6527;
Email: sfa@mississippi.edu
Web: www.mississippi.edu/riseupms/financialaid–state.php

Summary: To provide funding to Mississippi residents who are working on an undergraduate degree in speech pathology or psychology at a school in the state.
Eligibility: Open to Mississippi residents who are enrolled full time as a junior or senior in an approved training program in speech pathology or psychology at a school in the state. Applicants must agree to provide service at a state–operated health institution in Mississippi. The highest priority is given to renewal students.
Financial data: The stipend is $1,500 per year. This is a scholarship/loan program. Obligation can be discharged on the basis of 1 year's service in the health profession at a state–operated health institution in Mississippi for 1 year's scholarship/loan award. In the event the recipient fails to fulfill the service obligation, repayment of principal and interest is required.
Duration: 1 year; may be renewed 1 additional year, provided the recipient maintains a GPA of 2.5 or higher.
Number awarded: 1 or more each year.
Deadline: March of each year.

2099 $ MISSISSIPPI NURSING EDUCATION LOAN/ SCHOLARSHIP PROGRAM–BSN

Mississippi Office of Student Financial Aid
3825 Ridgewood Road
Jackson, MS 39211–6453
Phone: (601) 432–6997; (800) 327–2980 (within MS); Fax: (601) 432–6527;
Email: sfa@mississippi.edu
Web: www.mississippi.edu/riseupms/financialaid–state.php
Summary: To provide funding to Mississippi residents who are interested in working on a bachelor's degree in nursing.
Eligibility: Open to Mississippi residents working on a B.S.N. degree as a full– or part–time junior or senior at an accredited school of nursing in the state. Applicants must have earned a GPA of 2.5 or higher on all previous college work. They must agree to employment in professional nursing (patient care) in Mississippi.
Financial data: Scholarship/loans are $4,000 per academic year for up to 2 years or a total of $8,000 (prorated over 3 years for part–time participants). For each year of service in Mississippi as a professional nurse (patient care), 1 year's loan will be forgiven. For nurses who received prorated funding over 3 years, the length of service required is 2 years. In the event the recipient fails to fulfill the service obligation, repayment of principal and interest is required.
Duration: 1 year; may be renewed up to 1 additional year of full–time study or 2 years of part–time study, provided the recipient maintains a GPA of 2.5 or higher each semester.
Number awarded: Varies each year; recently, 226 students received more than $760,000 in assistance from this program.
Deadline: March of each year.

2100 $ MISSOURI APWA CHAPTER TECHNOLOGY SCHOLARSHIP

American Public Works Association–Missouri Chapter
c/o John M. Collins
City of Ellisville
1 Weis Avenue
Ellisville, MO 63011
Phone: (636) 227–9660;
Email: jcollins@ellisville.mo.us
Web: missouri.apwa.net/resources/scholarships
Summary: To provide financial assistance to high school seniors in Missouri who plan to attend a technical school in the state to prepare for a career in a field related to public works.
Eligibility: Open to seniors graduating from high schools in Missouri and planning to enroll at a technical school in the state. Applicants must be planning to study such fields as construction technology; surveying; heavy equipment operation; parks, grounds, and building maintenance; fleet maintenance; or other field related to a career in public works. They must be a U.S. citizen. Along with their application, they must submit statements on their career objectives, what public works means to them, and what they plan to contribute to the field of public works. Financial need is not considered in the selection process.
Financial data: The stipend is $2,500.
Duration: 1 year.
Number awarded: 1 each year.
Deadline: March of each year.

2101 $ MISSOURI CHAPTER CONTINUING EDUCATION SCHOLARSHIP

American Public Works Association–Missouri Chapter
c/o John M. Collins
City of Ellisville
1 Weis Avenue
Ellisville, MO 63011
Phone: (636) 227–9660;
Email: jcollins@ellisville.mo.us
Web: missouri.apwa.net/resources/scholarships
Summary: To provide financial assistance to students at 2–year colleges in Missouri who are completing a pre–engineering program and planning to transfer to a 4–year institution in the state to complete a degree in public administration or engineering.
Eligibility: Open to residents of Missouri who are completing a 2–year pre–engineering program at a college in the state. Applicants must be planning to transfer to a college or university in the state to complete a degree in engineering or public administration. They must be a U.S. citizen. Along with their application, they must submit statements on their career objectives, their contributions to their school and community, what public works means to them, and what they plan to contribute to the field of public works. Financial need is not considered in the selection process.
Financial data: The stipend is $2,500.
Duration: 1 year.
Number awarded: 1 each year.
Deadline: March of each year.

2102 $ MISSOURI MINORITY TEACHING SCHOLARSHIP PROGRAM

Missouri Department of Higher Education
Attn: Student Financial Assistance
205 Jefferson Street
P.O. Box 1469
Jefferson City, MO 65102–1469
Phone: (573) 526–7958; (800) 473–6757; Fax: (573) 751–6635;
Email: info@dhe.mo.gov
Web: www.dhe.mo.gov/ppc/grants/minorityteaching.php
Summary: To provide scholarships and other funding to minority high school seniors, high school graduates, and college students in Missouri who are interested in preparing for a teaching career in mathematics or science.
Eligibility: Open to Missouri residents who are African American, Asian American, Hispanic American, or Native American. Applicants must be 1) high school seniors, college students, or returning adults (without a degree) who rank in the top 25% of their high school class and scored at or above the 75th percentile on the ACT or SAT examination (recently, that meant a composite score of 24 or higher on the ACT or 1340 or higher on the composite critical reading and mathematics SAT); 2) individuals who have completed 30 college hours and have a cumulative GPA of 3.0 or better; or 3) baccalaureate degree–holders who are returning to an approved mathematics or science teacher education program. They must be a U.S. citizen or permanent resident or otherwise lawfully present in the United States. All applicants must be enrolled full time in an approved teacher education program at a community college, 4–year college, or university in Missouri. Selection is based on high school class rank, ACT or SAT scores, school and community activities, career interest in teaching, leadership skills, employment experience, and recommendations.
Financial data: The stipend is $3,000 per year, of which $2,000 is provided by the state as a forgivable loan and $1,000 is provided by the school as a scholarship. Recipients must commit to teaching in a Missouri public elementary or secondary school for 5 years following graduation. If they fail to fulfill that obligation, they must repay the state portion of the scholarship with interest at 9.5%.
Duration: Up to 4 years.
Number awarded: Up to 100 each year.
Deadline: June of each year.

2103 MONTANA CATTLEWOMEN SCHOLARSHIP

Montana CattleWomen, Inc.
420 North California
Helena, MT 59601
Phone: (406) 442–3420; Fax: (406) 449–5105
Web: www.montanacattlewomen.org/scholarship.html
Summary: To provide financial assistance to Montana residents working on a degree, especially in a field related to the livestock industry, at a college or university in the state.
Eligibility: Open to residents of Montana who are enrolled at a postsecondary institution in the state at least at the sophomore level. Applicants must have a GPA of 2.7 or higher and be able to demonstrate financial need. Preference is given to students who are 1) majoring in a field beneficial to the livestock

industry; 2) from an agriculture–oriented family; or 3) members or children of members of Montana CattleWomen, Inc. Along with their application, they must submit a 300–word essay on a topic of interest to the livestock industry that discusses their potential to affect this and/or other issues for the benefit of agriculture and the livestock industry.
Financial data: The stipend is $1,000.
Duration: 1 year.
Number awarded: 1 each year.
Deadline: March of each year.

2104 MONTANA FEDERATION OF GARDEN CLUBS LIFE MEMBERS SCHOLARSHIP

Montana Federation of Garden Clubs, Inc.
c/o Susan Woods, Life Members Chair
390 Cayuse Trail
Bozeman, MT 59718–8050
Phone: (406) 586–7533;
Email: edsue@wispwest.net
Web: wwww.mtfgc.org
Summary: To provide financial assistance to residents of Montana majoring in a horticulture–related field at a college in the state.
Eligibility: Open to Montana residents who are enrolled at least as sophomores at a college or university in the state. Applicants must be majoring in a horticulture–related field (e.g. agriculture education, agronomy, biology, botany, environmental conservation, floriculture, forestry, habitat or forest systems ecology, land management, landscape design, plant pathology). They must have a GPA of 2.7 or higher and be able to demonstrate financial need. Along with their application, they must submit a letter that includes a short autobiography and a statement of future plans.
Financial data: The stipend is $1,000.
Duration: 1 year.
Number awarded: 1 or more each year.
Deadline: April of each year.

2105 MONTANA GOVERNOR'S "BEST AND BRIGHTEST" NEED–BASED SCHOLARSHIPS

Summary: To provide financial assistance to Montana residents who are attending or planning to attend designated institutions in the state and can demonstrate financial need.
See Listing #592.

2106 MORAN FAMILY SCHOLARSHIPS

New Hampshire Land Surveyors Foundation
Attn: Scholarship Committee
77 Main Street
P.O. Box 689
Raymond, NH 03077–0689
Phone: (603) 895–4822; (800) 698–5447; Fax: (603) 462–0343;
Email: info@nhlsa.org
Web: www.nhlsa.org/scholarship.htm
Summary: To provide financial assistance to high school seniors in New Hampshire who plan to study surveying in college.
Eligibility: Open to seniors graduating from high schools in New Hampshire who plan to enroll in a college program in surveying. Applicants must submit an essay about their professional aspirations, their goals in college and afterwards, and factors that make them particularly deserving of support. In the selection process, first consideration is given to financial need, second to the likelihood that the applicant will become a surveyor, and third to grades.
Financial data: The stipend is $1,000.
Duration: 1 year.
Number awarded: 2 each year.
Deadline: March of each year.

2107 MORTON B. DUGGAN, JR. MEMORIAL EDUCATION RECOGNITION AWARD

American Association for Respiratory Care
Attn: American Respiratory Care Foundation
9425 North MacArthur Boulevard, Suite 100
Irving, TX 75063–4706
Phone: (972) 243–2272; Fax: (972) 484–2720;
Email: info@arcfoundation.org
Web: www.arcfoundation.org/awards/undergraduate/duggan.cfm
Summary: To provide financial assistance to college students, especially those from Georgia and South Carolina, interested in becoming respiratory therapists.
Eligibility: Open to U.S. citizens who are enrolled in an accredited respiratory care program and have a GPA of 3.0 or higher. Candidates must submit an original referenced paper on an aspect of respiratory care, an official transcript, and letters of recommendation. Nominations are accepted from all states, but preference is given to applicants from Georgia and South Carolina. Financial need is not considered in the selection process.
Financial data: The stipend is $1,000. The award also provides airfare, 1 night's lodging, and registration for the international congress of the association.
Duration: 1 year.
Number awarded: 1 each year.
Deadline: June of each year.

2108 $ MOSMILLER INTERN SCHOLARSHIP PROGRAM

American Floral Endowment
1601 Duke Street
Alexandria, VA 22314
Phone: (703) 838–5211; Fax: (703) 838–5212;
Email: afe@endowment.org
Web: endowment.org/floriculture–scholarshipsinternships.html
Summary: To provide financial assistance and work experience to students working on an undergraduate degree in floriculture or business.
Eligibility: Open to U.S. citizens who are currently enrolled full time in a 2– or 4–year college or university in the United States in a floriculture, environmental horticulture, or business program. Applicants must be making satisfactory progress in a degree or certificate program and have a GPA of "C" or better. They must be interested in interning at a wholesale, retail, or allied trade company located in the United States away from their home and school. Following completion of the internship, they receive a grant for continued study.
Financial data: Employers must agree to pay a fair market wage for the geographic area and position. In addition, students receive a grant of $2,000 following completion of the internship.
Duration: Internships are for 10 to 14 weeks. Preference is given to fall or spring internships, but summer internships are allowed if the location can provide valuable experience.
Number awarded: Varies each year; recently, 5 of these internships were awarded.
Deadline: February or September of each year.

2109 $ MTS STUDENT SCHOLARSHIPS FOR GRADUATING HIGH SCHOOL SENIORS

Marine Technology Society
Attn: Student Scholarships
1100 H Street, N.W., Suite LL–100
Washington, DC 20005
Phone: (202) 717–8705; Fax: (202) 347–4305;
Email: scholarships@mtsociety.org
Web: www.mtsociety.org/education/scholarships.aspx
Summary: To provide financial assistance to high school seniors planning to work on a degree in a field related to marine science.
Eligibility: Open to high school seniors accepted into a full–time undergraduate program. Applicants must be planning to work on a degree in marine technology, marine engineering, or marine science. Along with their application, they must submit a 500–word essay on their interest in marine technology, how their interest in marine technology relates to their current field of study, and how they plan to use their degree. Selection is based on that essay, honors received, marine–oriented activities, extracurricular school activities, and community service activities. Membership in the Marine Technology Society (MTS) is not required.
Financial data: The stipend is $2,000. Funds are sent directly to the recipient's college bursar's office.
Duration: 1 year.
Number awarded: Varies each year; recently, 8 of these scholarships were awarded.
Deadline: April of each year.

2110 MUGGETS SCHOLARSHIP

Summary: To provide financial assistance to students working on an undergraduate or graduate degree in landscape architecture or horticulture.
See Listing #1396.

2111 MW ISA CHAPTER SCHOLARSHIPS

International Society of Arboriculture–Midwestern Chapter
c/o Gerri Makay, North Dakota Forest Service
NDSU Research Extension Center
P.O. Box 219
Carrington, ND 58421
Phone: (701) 652–2951;
Email: Gerri.Makay@ndsu.edu
Web: www.mwisa.org/scholarship–program

Summary: To provide financial assistance to undergraduate and graduate students working on a degree in a field related to arboriculture at a college or university in designated midwestern states.

Eligibility: Open to undergraduate and graduate students entering or currently enrolled at 2– and 4–year colleges and universities in Iowa, Kansas, Missouri, Nebraska, North Dakota, Oklahoma, and South Dakota. Applicants must be interested in preparing for a career in arboriculture, urban and commercial forestry, horticulture, or a closely–related field. Along with their application, they must submit a 500–word essay on how they will benefit from a degree in forestry or arboriculture and how good arboricultural practices can affect the quality of life in the community where they live. Selection is based on that essay, citizenship, employment history in the field of arboriculture or forestry, career goals, and why the scholarship is important to the applicant.

Financial data: The stipend is $1,000.

Duration: 1 year.

Number awarded: Varies each year; recently, 12 of these scholarships were awarded.

Deadline: November of each year.

2112 NACME PRE–ENGINEERING STUDENT SCHOLARSHIPS

National Action Council for Minorities in Engineering
Attn: University Programs
440 Hamilton Avenue, Suite 302
White Plains, NY 10601–1813
Phone: (914) 539–4010; Fax: (914) 539–4032;
Email: scholarships@nacme.org
Web: www.nacmebacksme.org/NBM_C.aspx?pageid=153

Summary: To provide financial assistance to underrepresented minority high school seniors interested in studying engineering or related fields in college.

Eligibility: Open to African American, Latino, and American Indian high school seniors who are in the top 10% of their graduating class and have demonstrated academic excellence, leadership skills, and a commitment to science and engineering as a career. Candidates must have been accepted as a full–time student at an ABET–accredited engineering program. They must be nominated by their school (each high school may nominate only 1 student). Fields of study include all areas of engineering as well as computer science, materials science, mathematics, operations research, or physics. Letters of nomination must be accompanied by a transcript, SAT or ACT report form, resume, and 100–word statement of why the student should receive this scholarship.

Financial data: The stipend is $1,500. Funds are sent directly to the recipient's university.

Duration: 1 year.

Number awarded: Varies each year; recently, 95 of these scholarships were awarded.

Deadline: April of each year.

2113 $ NADCA INDIANA CHAPTER 25 SCHOLARSHIP

Foundry Educational Foundation
1695 North Penny Lane
Schaumburg, IL 60173
Phone: (847) 490–9200; Fax: (847) 890–6270;
Email: info@fefoffice.org
Web: www.fefinc.org/students/scholarships/NADCA.php

Summary: To provide financial assistance to college students in Indiana and adjoining states who are interested in preparing for a career in the die casting industry.

Eligibility: Open to students preparing for a career in the die casting industry with first preference to residents of central Indiana, then to residents of Indiana outside the central area, then to residents of states adjacent to Indiana. Preference is also given to students attending an Indiana college or university with an agreement with the Foundry Educational Foundation (FEF), then to students attending school in Indiana, then to students attending an FEF school in an adjacent state. Preference is also given to applicants pursuing programs deemed most useful to the die–casting industry, then to candidates with the best scholastic record. In addition, preference is given (in order) to applicants who are currently participating in a co–op program involving the die–casting industry, who have work experience in the die–casting industry, who have work experience in the cast metal industry, and who have any manufacturing work experience. Finally, preference is given to applicants who know or have worked for or with a member of Indiana Chapter 25 of the North American Die Casting Association (NADCA).

Financial data: The stipends range from $500 to $2,500 per year.

Duration: 1 year.

Number awarded: 1 each year.

Deadline: May of each year.

2114 NAMEPA BEGINNING FRESHMEN AWARD

National Association of Multicultural Engineering Program Advocates, Inc.
Attn: National Scholarship Selection Committee Chair
1430 Duke Street
Alexandria, VA 22314
Phone: (703) 562–3650; Fax: (202) 207–3518;
Email: namepa@namepa.org
Web: www.namepa.org/student–scholarships

Summary: To provide financial assistance to underrepresented minority high school seniors who are planning to major in engineering.

Eligibility: Open to African American, Latino, and American Indian high school seniors who have been approved for admission to an engineering program at an institution affiliated with the National Association of Multicultural Engineering Program Advocates (NAMEPA). For a list of affiliated schools, write to the sponsor. Applicants must have a GPA of 2.7 or higher and minimum cumulative scores of 25 on the ACT or 1000 on the critical reading and mathematics SAT. They must submit a copy of their high school transcript; test scores; letter of recommendation; and 1–page essay on why they have chosen engineering as a profession, why they think they should be selected, and an overview of their future aspirations as an engineer. Selection is based on that essay, course work while in high school, activities, course distribution, and recommendations.

Financial data: The stipend is $1,000, paid in 2 equal installments.

Duration: 1 year; nonrenewable.

Number awarded: Varies each year; recently, NAMEPA awarded a total of 20 scholarships for its Beginning Freshman Awards and its Transfer Engineering Awards.

Deadline: May of each year.

2115 NANCY WILLIAMS DIDACTIC PROGRAM IN DIETETICS SCHOLARSHIP

North Carolina Dietetic Association
Attn: NCDA Foundation
c/o Christie Nicholson, First Vice Chair
P.O. Box 383
Greenville, NC 27835
Phone: (252) 759–0721;
Email: foodandyou@aol.com
Web: www.eatrightnc.org

Summary: To provide financial assistance to residents of North Carolina who are interested in participating in a Didactic Program in Dietetics (DPD) at a school in the state.

Eligibility: Open to residents of North Carolina who are currently attending a college or university in the state. Applicants must be able to satisfy the didactic requirements established by the Academy of Nutrition and Dietetics during the current academic year (e.g., a rising senior who is enrolled in a DPD program, a first–year graduate student in a coordinated master's program, a graduate student in a master's degree program who will complete the DPD requirements). They must have a GPA of 3.0 or higher, a record of leadership activities in the university or community, and potential as a professional dietitian as determined by a letter of recommendation. Along with their application, they must submit a 250–word statement on how this scholarship will help them reach their educational goals. Financial need is not considered in the selection process.

Financial data: The stipend is $1,000.

Duration: 1 year.

Number awarded: 1 or more each year.

Deadline: February of each year.

2116 NAOMI BRACK SCHOLARSHIP

National Organization for Associate Degree Nursing
Attn: Foundation
7794 Grow Drive

Pensacola, FL 32514
Phone: (850) 484–6948; (877) 966–6236; Fax: (850) 484–8762;
Email: noadn@dancyamc.com
Web: www.noadn.org
Summary: To provide financial assistance to students working on an Associate Degree in Nursing (A.D.N.).
Eligibility: Open to students currently enrolled or entering their second year of a state–approved A.D.N. program. Applicants must have earned a GPA of 3.0 or higher and be active in a local, state, or national student nurse association. Along with their application, they must submit a 500–word essay on where they see themselves as a professional nurse in 10 years. Financial need is not considered.
Financial data: The stipend is $1,000.
Duration: 1 year.
Number awarded: 1 each year.
Deadline: August of each year.

2117 $$ NAPA RESEARCH AND EDUCATION FOUNDATION SCHOLARSHIP PROGRAM

National Asphalt Pavement Association
Attn: NAPA Research and Education Foundation
5100 Forbes Boulevard
Lanham, MD 20706–4413
Phone: (301) 731–4748, ext. 127; (888) HOT–MIXX; Fax: (301) 731–4621;
Email: cwilson@asphaltpavement.org
Web: www.asphaltpavement.org
Summary: To provide financial assistance to undergraduate and graduate engineering students interested in preparing for a career in the asphalt industry.
Eligibility: Open to undergraduate and graduate students interested in preparing for a career in the asphalt industry, especially the hot mix asphalt (HMA) industry. Applicants must be U.S. citizens and enrolled full time in a civil engineering, construction management, or construction engineering program at an accredited 4–year college or university or at a 2–year technical institution. The applicant's institution must offer at least 1 course in HMA technology. Financial need is not considered in the selection process; awards are based on academic performance, future potential, leadership and participation in school and community activities, work experience, career and educational aspirations, goals, unusual personal or family circumstances, and an outside appraisal.
Financial data: Stipends range from $1,000 to $5,000 per year.
Duration: 1 year; may be renewed for up to 2 years or until graduation, whichever occurs first.
Number awarded: Approximately 100 each year.
Deadline: Deadline not specified.

2118 NARRAGANSETT BAY POST SAME SCHOLARSHIP

Summary: To provide financial assistance to residents of New England interested in working on a bachelor's degree in construction–related fields at colleges in any state.
See Listing #1401.

2119 $$ NASA AERONAUTICS UNDERGRADUATE SCHOLARSHIP PROGRAM

American Society for Engineering Education
Attn: NASA Aeronautics Scholarship Program
1818 N Street, N.W., Suite 600
Washington, DC 20036–2479
Phone: (202) 331–3546; Fax: (202) 265–8504;
Email: nasa.asp@asee.org
Web: nasa.asee.org/undergraduate_program
Summary: To provide financial assistance and summer research experience at National Aeronautics and Space Administration (NASA) facilities to undergraduate students majoring in designated fields of science and engineering.
Eligibility: Open to U.S. citizens and nationals who are working on an undergraduate degree and have at least 2 years of full–time study remaining. Applicants must be majoring in computer sciences, mathematics, physics, or engineering (aeronautical and aerospace, chemical, civil, computer, electrical and electronic, energy, engineering mechanics, engineering science, industrial, materials, mechanical, metallurgical, polymer, or systems). They must be available for an internship at a NASA center performing aeronautical research during the summer between their junior and senior years. Along with their application, they must submit an essay describing what they think are the greatest technical challenges in aeronautics during the next 20 to 25 years and why. Financial need is not considered in the selection process.
Financial data: The academic stipend is $15,000 per year; funds must be used for educational related expenses. The salary for the summer internship is $10,000.
Duration: 2 years.
Number awarded: 20 each year.
Deadline: January of each year.

2120 $$ NASCAR/WENDELL SCOTT AWARD

Hispanic Association of Colleges and Universities
Attn: National Scholarship Program
8415 Datapoint Drive, Suite 400
San Antonio, TX 78229
Phone: (210) 692–3805; Fax: (210) 692–0823; TDD: (800) 855–2880;
Email: scholarships@hacu.net
Web: www.hacu.net/hacu/Scholarships.asp?SnID=899378480
Summary: To provide financial assistance to undergraduate and graduate students majoring in specified fields at member institutions of the Hispanic Association of Colleges and Universities (HACU) in designated states.
Eligibility: Open to full–time undergraduate and graduate students at 4–year HACU member institutions in Florida, Georgia, and North Carolina. Applicants must be working on a degree in business, engineering, marketing, mass media, marketing management and technology, public relations, or sports marketing. They must have a GPA of 3.0 or higher and be able to demonstrate financial need. Along with their application, they must submit an essay that focuses on their personal motivation for applying to this scholarship program, their academic and/or career goals, and the skills they could bring to an employer.
Financial data: The stipend is $12,100.
Duration: 1 year.
Number awarded: 1 or more each year.
Deadline: June of each year.

2121 $ NATIONAL ACADEMY FOR NUCLEAR TRAINING SCHOLARSHIP PROGRAM

National Academy for Nuclear Training
Attn: Scholarship Program
301 ACT Drive
P.O. Box 4030
Iowa City, IA 52243–4030
Phone: (800) 294–7492;
Email: nant@act.org
Web: www.nei.org/nantscholarships
Summary: To provide financial assistance for college to students interested in careers in the nuclear power industry.
Eligibility: Open to U.S. citizens who are full–time students entering their junior or senior year at accredited 4–year institutions with a GPA of 3.0 or higher. Applicants must be majoring in nuclear–fission or electric power–related fields, including 1) nuclear, mechanical, or electrical engineering, 2) power generation health physics, or 3) chemical engineering with a nuclear or power option. They must have work experience at an Institute of Nuclear Power Operations (INPO) member utility and must be nominated by a utility manager or executive. Selection is based on academic performance, motivation and ability to complete a rigorous course of study, and expressed interest and desire to work in the nuclear power industry.
Financial data: The stipend is $2,500 per year. Funds are paid directly to the college or university.
Duration: 1 year; may be renewed for up to 2 additional years.
Number awarded: Approximately 120 new and renewal scholarships are awarded each year.
Deadline: February of each year.

2122 $ NATIONAL AMBUCS SCHOLARSHIP PROGRAM

National AMBUCS, Inc.
Attn: National Scholarship Committee
P.O. Box 5127
High Point, NC 27262
Phone: (800) 838–1845; Fax: (336) 852–6830;
Email: ambucs@ambucs.org
Web: www.ambucs.com/scholars
Summary: To provide financial assistance to upper–division and graduate students working on a degree in a therapy–related field.

Eligibility: Open to students in their junior or senior year of a bachelor's degree program or in a graduate program leading to a master's or doctoral degree. Applicants must be enrolled in an accredited program in physical therapy, occupational therapy, speech language pathology, or hearing audiology. Assistant programs are not eligible. U.S. citizenship is required. Selection is based on academic accomplishment, character for compassion and integrity, career objectives, commitment to local community, and financial need.
Financial data: Stipends range from $500 to $1,500, although 1 scholarship is for $3,000 per year.
Duration: Up to 2 years.
Number awarded: Varies each year; recently, 251 students received a total of $183,625 from this program. Since it began, it has awarded more than $7.6 million to more than 14,000 students.
Deadline: April of each year.

2123 $ NATIONAL ASSOCIATION OF WATER COMPANIES NEW JERSEY SCHOLARSHIP

National Association of Water Companies–New Jersey Chapter
c/o Gail Brady
49 Howell Drive
Verona, NJ 07044
Phone: (973) 669–5807; Fax: (973) 669–8327;
Email: gbradygbconsult@verizon.net
Web: www.nawc.org
Summary: To provide financial assistance to New Jersey residents who are interested in working on an undergraduate or graduate degree at a school in the state to prepare for a career in the water utility industry.
Eligibility: Open to graduating high school seniors, undergraduates, and graduate students who have been residents of New Jersey for at least 5 years. Applicants must be attending or planning to attend a college or university in the state to work full or part time on a degree in a field related to the water utility industry (e.g., accounting, biology, business administration, chemistry, communications, computer sciences, consumer affairs, engineering, environmental sciences, finance, human resources, law, natural resource management). They must have a GPA of 3.0 or higher. Along with their application, they must submit a 1–page essay that describes their career objectives, their interest in the water utility industry or a field related to it, their financial need, and why they believe they should be selected for this scholarship.
Financial data: The stipend is $2,500.
Duration: 1 year.
Number awarded: 2 each year.
Deadline: March of each year.

2124 $ NATIONAL BEEF AMBASSADOR PROGRAM

American National CattleWomen, Inc.
Attn: National Beef Ambassador Coordinator
9110 East Nichols Avenue, Suite 302
P.O. Box 3881
Centennial, CO 80112
Phone: (303) 694–0313; Fax: (303) 694–2390;
Email: ancw@beef.org
Web: www.nationalbeefambassador.org
Summary: To recognize and reward, with college scholarships, young people who can serve as spokespersons for the beef industry.
Eligibility: Open to students between 17 and 20 years of age who are able to serve as spokespersons for the beef industry within their schools and their communities. Students first compete on the state level. Each state sends 1 winner to the national competition. At the national event, students compete in 4 categories: 1) an issues response, in which they compose a 150–word response to a recently–published news article about the beef industry; 2) a consumer demonstration, in which they serve as demonstrators at a mock consumer promotion event and answer questions about beef posed by other students; 3) a youth presentation, describing 3 presentations they have made to young people in their community with a lesson plan, teachers' evaluation forms, pictures of them making presentations, and examples of items used in their presentations; and 4) a mock media interview. Winners are selected on the basis of their performance in those activities.
Financial data: Awards are $2,500 for first place, $1,200 for second, $800 for third, $250 for fourth, and $250 for fifth. In addition, scholarships of $1,000 are presented to the first–place winner, $750 to the second–place winner, and $500 to the third–place winner.
Duration: The competition is held annually.
Number awarded: 5 cash awards and 3 scholarships are presented each year.
Deadline: August of each year.

2125 NATIONAL CAPITAL AREA GARDEN CLUBS SCHOLARSHIPS

National Capital Area Garden Clubs, Inc.
Attn: Scholarship Chair
3501 New York Avenue, N.E.
Washington, DC 20002–1958
Phone: (202) 399–5958;
Email: scholarship@ncagardenclubs.org
Web: ncagardenclubs.org/scholarship.html
Summary: To provide financial assistance to undergraduate and graduate students who live in the Washington, D.C. area and are working on a degree in a field related to gardening at a school in any state.
Eligibility: Open to residents of Washington, D.C., as well as Montgomery County, Maryland; Prince George's County, Maryland; Arlington, Virginia; Alexandria, Virginia; Fairfax County, Virginia; and Prince William County, Virginia. Applicants must be working full time on an undergraduate or graduate degree in biology, botany, city planning, conservation, environmental concerns, floriculture, forestry, horticulture, landscape design, plant pathology, or related subjects. They must have a GPA of 3.0 or higher. Along with their application, they must submit a personal letter discussing their background, career goals, financial need, and commitment to their chosen field of study; undergraduate and graduate transcripts; a list of extracurricular activities and honors; documentation of financial need; and 3 letters of recommendation.
Financial data: A stipend is awarded (amount not specified).
Duration: 1 year.
Number awarded: Varies each year.
Deadline: February of each year.

2126 $ NATIONAL CAPITAL CHAPTER CMAA SCHOLARSHIPS

Construction Management Association of America–National Capital Chapter
c/o Christopher J. Payne, Student Liaison Committee and Scholarship
3040 Williams Drive, Suite 300
Fairfax, VA 22031
Phone: (703) 641–9088;
Email: cpayne@mbpce.com
Web: www.cmaancc.com
Summary: To provide financial assistance to undergraduate and graduate students at colleges and universities in the area served by the National Capital Chapter of the Construction Management Association of America (CMAA) who are working on a degree in construction management or a related field.
Eligibility: Open to undergraduate and graduate students from any state attending colleges and universities in the local area served by the National Capital Chapter. Applicants must be working on an ACCE–accredited construction management or related degree. They must have completed at least 1 full year of study and be in good academic standing. Selection is based on academic excellence, the adviser's evaluation, extracurricular activities, and employment experience (if applicable); financial need is not considered.
Financial data: The stipend is $2,000.
Duration: 1 year; nonrenewable.
Number awarded: 1 or more each year.
Deadline: March of each year.

2127 $$ NATIONAL COMMISSION FOR COOPERATIVE EDUCATION SCHOLARSHIPS

Summary: To provide financial assistance to students participating or planning to participate in cooperative education projects at designated colleges and universities.
See Listing #612.

2128 NATIONAL DAIRY SHRINE/DMI MILK MARKETING SCHOLARSHIPS

National Dairy Shrine
Attn: Executive Director
P.O. Box 725
Denmark, WI 54208
Phone: (920) 863–6333; Fax: (920) 863–6333;
Email: info@dairyshrine.org
Web: www.dairyshrine.org/scholarships.php
Summary: To provide financial assistance to college students enrolled in a dairy science program who are preparing for careers in the marketing of dairy products.

Eligibility: Open to college sophomores or juniors who have a cumulative GPA of 2.5 or higher. They must be majoring in dairy science, animal science, agricultural economics, agricultural communications, agricultural marketing, milk product development and testing, or food and nutrition. Selection is based on student organizational activities (15%), other organizational activities (10%), academic standing and course work associated with marketing (25%), honors and awards (10%), marketing experiences (10%), and a 500–word essay on why they are interested in dairy product development or marketing, including their plans for the future (30%).
Financial data: Stipends are $1,500 or $1,000.
Duration: 1 year.
Number awarded: 7 each year: 1 at $1,500 and 6 at $1,000.
Deadline: April of each year.

2129 NATIONAL FFA SCHOLARSHIPS FOR UNDERGRADUATES IN THE SCIENCES

National FFA Organization
Attn: Scholarship Office
6060 FFA Drive
P.O. Box 68960
Indianapolis, IN 46268–0960
Phone: (317) 802–4419; Fax: (317) 802–5419;
Email: scholarships@ffa.org
Web: www.ffa.org
Summary: To provide financial assistance to FFA members who wish to study agriculture and related fields in college.
Eligibility: Open to current and former members of the organization who are working or planning to work full time on a degree in fields related to agriculture; this includes: agricultural mechanics and engineering, agricultural technology, animal science, conservation, dairy science, equine science, floriculture, food science, horticulture, irrigation, lawn and landscaping, and natural resources. For most of the scholarships, applicants must be high school seniors; others are open to students currently enrolled in college. The program includes a large number of designated scholarships that specify the locations where the members must live, the schools they must attend, the fields of study they must pursue, or other requirements. Some consider family income in the selection process, but most do not. Selection is based on academic achievement (10 points for GPA, 10 points for SAT or ACT score, 10 points for class rank), leadership in FFA activities (30 points), leadership in community activities (10 points), and participation in the Supervised Agricultural Experience (SAE) program (30 points). U.S. citizenship is required.
Financial data: Stipends vary, but most are at least $1,000.
Duration: 1 year or more.
Number awarded: Varies; generally, a total of approximately 1,000 scholarships are awarded annually by the association.
Deadline: February of each year.

2130 NATIONAL FOLIAGE FOUNDATION GENERAL SCHOLARSHIPS

National Foliage Foundation
c/o Florida Nursery, Growers and Landscape Association
1533 Park Center Drive
Orlando, FL 32835–5705
Phone: (407) 295–7994; (800) 375–3642; Fax: (407) 295–1619;
Email: info@nationalfoliagefoundation.org
Web: www.nationalfoliagefoundation.org/scholarship/scholarship–info
Summary: To provide financial assistance to undergraduate and graduate students who are interested in a career in the horticulture industry.
Eligibility: Open to undergraduate and graduate students attending or planning to attend a college, university, community college, or other postsecondary program. Applicants must enroll full time in a horticulture program or related field with the intent to graduate in that field. They must have a GPA of 2.5 or higher. Along with their application, they must submit a short essay about themselves that includes their work and classroom experience with horticulture or related field, the area of horticulture or a related field that they are interested in pursuing, what they plan to do after graduation, and why they are qualified to receive the scholarship. Selection is based on the essay, 2 letters of recommendation, transcripts, and financial need.
Financial data: A stipend is awarded (amount not specified).
Duration: 1 year.
Number awarded: 1 or more each year.
Deadline: January of each year.

2131 NATIONAL GARDEN CLUBS HIGH SCHOOL ESSAY CONTEST

National Garden Clubs, Inc.
4401 Magnolia Avenue
St. Louis, MO 63110–3492
Phone: (314) 776–7574; Fax: (314) 776–5108;
Email: headquarters@gardenclub.org
Web: www.gardenclub.org/Youth/Contests/EssayContest.aspx
Summary: To recognize and reward, with college scholarships, high school students who submit outstanding essays on a topic related to horticulture.
Eligibility: Open to high school students in grades 9–12. Each year, students are invited to submit an essay, between 600 and 700 words in length, on a topic that changes annually but relates to horticulture. Recently, the topic was "Ways We Can Protect Aquatic Ecosystems." The contest must be sponsored by a garden club that is a member of the National Garden Clubs, a group of member clubs, a council or district, or a state garden club. State winners are forwarded to regional chairs; regional winners are then entered in the national competition. Selection is based on knowledge of subject (25 points), practicality of proposal (10 points), originality (15 points), clarity of presentation (15 points), vocabulary (15 points), conformance to length (10 points), and quality of manuscript (10 points).
Financial data: The national winner receives a $1,000 scholarship. Second prize is $100. If the national winner is an underclassman, the prize is held until the student graduates from high school. At that time, the funds are forwarded to the college that the student enters.
Duration: The contest is held annually.
Number awarded: 2 each year.
Deadline: Each state sets its own deadline; most are in October. State winners must be forwarded to the regional chair by December of each year.

2132 $ NATIONAL GARDEN CLUBS SCHOLARSHIPS

Summary: To provide financial assistance to upper–division and graduate students in horticulture, landscape design, and related disciplines.
See Listing #1406.

2133 $ NATIONAL HYDROPOWER ASSOCIATION PAST PRESIDENTS' LEGACY SCHOLARSHIP

National Hydropower Association
25 Massachusetts Avenue, N.W., Suite 450
Washington, DC 20001
Phone: (202) 682–1700; Fax: (202) 682–9478;
Email: help@hydro.org
Web: hydro.org/about–nha/awards
Summary: To provide financial assistance to undergraduate and graduate students working on a degree in a field related to the hydropower industry.
Eligibility: Open to juniors, seniors, and graduate students who are enrolled full time at an accredited 4–year college or university or vocational/technical school. Applicants must be working on a degree in a program of study related to the hydropower industry: engineering (civil, earth sciences, electrical, mechanical, systems); science (biology, fisheries, hydrology); communications (public administration, public policy, public relations); or environmental (environmental studies, environmental management, renewable energy). They must have a cumulative GPA of 2.5 or higher. Along with their application, they must submit a brief statement on their plans as they relate to their educational objectives, career objectives, and long–term goals, especially their desire and intent to work in the hydropower industry. U.S. citizenship or permanent resident status is required. Financial need is not considered in the selection process.
Financial data: The stipend is $2,500.
Duration: 1 year.
Number awarded: 1 each year.
Deadline: February of each year.

2134 $$ NATIONAL OCEANIC AND ATMOSPHERIC ADMINISTRATION EDUCATIONAL PARTNERSHIP PROGRAM WITH MINORITY SERVING INSTITUTIONS UNDERGRADUATE SCHOLARSHIPS

National Oceanic and Atmospheric Administration
Attn: Office of Education
1315 East–West Highway
SSMC3, Room 10703
Silver Spring, MD 20910

Phone: (301) 713–9437, ext. 150; Fax: (301) 713–9465;
Email: studentscholarshipprograms@noaa.gov
Web: www.epp.noaa.gov/ssp_undergrad_page.html

Summary: To provide financial assistance and work experience to undergraduate students at Minority Serving Institutions who are majoring in scientific fields of interest to the National Oceanic and Atmospheric Administration (NOAA).

Eligibility: Open to full–time juniors at Minority Serving Institutions, including Hispanic Serving Institutions (HSIs), Historically Black Colleges and Universities (HBCUs), and Tribal Colleges and Universities (TCUs). Applicants must have a GPA of 3.0 or higher and a major in atmospheric science, biology, computer science, engineering, environmental science, geography, hydrology, mathematics, oceanography, physical science, physics, remote sensing, social science, or other field that supports NOAA's programs and mission. They must also be interested in participating in a research internship at an NOAA site. Selection is based on relevant course work (30%), education plan and statement of career interest (40%), recommendations (20%), and additional experience related to diversity of education, extracurricular activities, honors and awards, non–academic and volunteer work, and communication skills (10%). U.S. citizenship is required.

Financial data: This program provides payment of tuition and fees (to a maximum of $8,000 per year) and a stipend during the internship of $650 per week.

Duration: 2 academic years and 2 summer internships.

Number awarded: Up to 15 each year.

Deadline: February of each year.

2135 $ NATIONAL RICE MONTH SCHOLARSHIP PROGRAM

USA Rice Federation
Attn: Kim Broome
2101 Wilson Boulevard, Suite 610
Arlington, VA 22201
Phone: (703) 236–1446; Fax: (703) 236–2301;
Email: kbroome@usarice.com
Web: www.usarice.com

Summary: To recognize and reward, with college scholarships, high school seniors in rice–growing counties of designated states who produce an activity to promote National Rice Month.

Eligibility: Open to seniors graduating from high schools in rice–growing counties of Arkansas, California, Louisiana, Mississippi, Missouri, and Texas. Applicants must produce a promotional activity to be conducted in September (National Rice Month) that presents the nutritional benefits, culinary versatility, economic importance, and environmental benefits of the U.S. rice industry. Entries must provide details of the promotion, including (but not limited to) a full description, photographs (digital or print), sample promotional materials, and pre– and post–event publicity; preference is given to digital or electronic submissions, but all entries are judged equally whether electronic or hard copy.

Financial data: First place is $4,000, second $3,000, and third $1,500. All prizes are in the form of scholarships that are disbursed upon proof of enrollment in college.

Duration: The competition is held annually.

Number awarded: 3 each year.

Deadline: October of each year.

2136 $$ NATIONAL SECURITY SCHOLARSHIPS OF THE INDEPENDENT COLLEGE FUND OF MARYLAND

Summary: To provide financial assistance to students from any state enrolled at member institutions of the Independent College Fund of Maryland and majoring in a field related to national security.

See Listing #1414.

2137 NATIONAL SPACE GRANT COLLEGE AND FELLOWSHIP PROGRAM

National Aeronautics and Space Administration
Attn: Office of Education
300 E Street, S.W.
Mail Suite 6M35
Washington, DC 20546–0001
Phone: (202) 358–1069; Fax: (202) 358–7097;
Email: Diane.D.DeTroye@nasa.gov
Web: www.nasa.gov

Summary: To provide financial assistance to undergraduate and graduate students interested in preparing for a career in a space–related field.

Eligibility: Open to undergraduate and graduate students at colleges and universities that participate in the National Space Grant program of the U.S. National Aeronautics and Space Administration (NASA) through their state consortium. Applicants must be interested in a program of study and/or research in a field of science, technology, engineering, or mathematics (STEM) related to space. A specific goal of the program is to recruit and train U.S. citizens, especially underrepresented minorities, women, and persons with disabilities, for careers in aerospace science and technology. Financial need is not considered in the selection process.

Financial data: Each consortium establishes the terms of the fellowship program in its state.

Number awarded: Varies each year.

Deadline: Each consortium sets its own deadlines.

2138 NATIONAL STRENGTH AND CONDITIONING ASSOCIATION WOMEN'S SCHOLARSHIPS

National Strength and Conditioning Association
Attn: Grants and Scholarships Program
1885 Bob Johnson Drive
Colorado Springs, CO 80906–4000
Phone: (719) 632–6722, ext. 152; (800) 815–6826; Fax: (719) 632–6367;
Email: foundation@nsca–lift.org
Web: www.nsca–lift.org/NSCAFoundation/grants.shtml

Summary: To provide financial assistance to women who are interested in working on an undergraduate or graduate degree in strength training and conditioning.

Eligibility: Open to women who are 17 years of age or older. Applicants must have been accepted into an accredited postsecondary institution to work on an undergraduate or graduate degree in the strength and conditioning field. Along with their application, they must submit a 500–word essay on their personal and professional goals and how receiving this scholarship will assist them in achieving those goals. Selection is based on that essay, academic achievement, strength and conditioning experience, honors and awards, community involvement, letters of recommendation, and involvement in the National Strength and Conditioning Association (NSCA).

Financial data: The stipend is $1,500.

Duration: 1 year.

Number awarded: 4 each year.

Deadline: March of each year.

2139 $ NATIONAL STUDENT NURSES' ASSOCIATION CAREER MOBILITY SCHOLARSHIPS

National Student Nurses' Association
Attn: Foundation
45 Main Street, Suite 606
Brooklyn, NY 11201
Phone: (718) 210–0705; Fax: (718) 797–1186;
Email: nsna@nsna.org
Web: www.nsna.org/FoundationScholarships/FNSNAScholarships.aspx

Summary: To provide financial assistance to nurses interested in pursuing additional education.

Eligibility: Open to 1) registered nurses enrolled in programs leading to a baccalaureate or master's degree in nursing or 2) licensed practical and vocational nurses enrolled in programs leading to licensure as a registered nurse. Graduating high school seniors are not eligible. Applicants must submit a 200–word description of their professional and educational goals and how this scholarship will help them achieve those goals. Selection is based on academic achievement, financial need, and involvement in student nursing organizations and community activities related to health care. U.S. citizenship or permanent resident status is required.

Financial data: Stipends range from $1,000 to $2,500.

Duration: 1 year.

Number awarded: Varies each year; recently, 2 of these scholarships were awarded, both sponsored by Anthony J. Jannetti, Inc.

Deadline: January of each year.

2140 $ NATIONAL STUDENT NURSES' ASSOCIATION GENERAL SCHOLARSHIPS

National Student Nurses' Association
Attn: Foundation
45 Main Street, Suite 606
Brooklyn, NY 11201

Phone: (718) 210–0705; Fax: (718) 797–1186;
Email: nsna@nsna.org
Web: www.nsna.org/FoundationScholarships/FNSNAScholarships.aspx
Summary: To provide financial assistance to nursing or pre–nursing students.
Eligibility: Open to students currently enrolled in state–approved schools of nursing or pre–nursing associate degree, baccalaureate, diploma, generic master's, generic doctoral, R.N. to B.S.N., R.N. to M.S.N., or L.P.N./L.V.N. to R.N. programs. Graduating high school seniors are not eligible. Support for graduate education is provided only for a first degree in nursing. Applicants must submit a 200–word description of their professional and educational goals and how this scholarship will help them achieve those goals. Selection is based on academic achievement, financial need, and involvement in student nursing organizations and community health activities. U.S. citizenship or permanent resident status is required.
Financial data: Stipends range from $1,000 to $2,500. A total of approximately $125,000 is awarded each year by the foundation for all its scholarship programs.
Duration: 1 year.
Number awarded: Varies each year; recently, 68 of these scholarships were awarded.
Deadline: January of each year.

2141 $ NATIONAL STUDENT NURSES' ASSOCIATION SPECIALTY SCHOLARSHIPS

National Student Nurses' Association
Attn: Foundation
45 Main Street, Suite 606
Brooklyn, NY 11201
Phone: (718) 210–0705; Fax: (718) 797–1186;
Email: nsna@nsna.org
Web: www.nsna.org/FoundationScholarships/FNSNAScholarships.aspx
Summary: To provide financial assistance to nursing students in designated specialties.
Eligibility: Open to students currently enrolled in state–approved schools of nursing or pre–nursing associate degree, baccalaureate, diploma, generic master's, generic doctoral, R.N. to B.S.N., R.N. to M.S.N., or L.P.N./L.V.N. to R.N. programs. Graduating high school seniors are not eligible. Support for graduate education is provided only for a first degree in nursing. Applicants must designate their intended specialty, which may be anesthesia nursing, critical care, emergency, gerontology, informatics, nephrology, nurse educator, oncology, orthopedic, perioperative, nurse manager, or infusion nursing. Along with their application, they must submit a 200–word description of their professional and educational goals and how this scholarship will help them achieve those goals. Selection is based on academic achievement, financial need, and involvement in student nursing organizations and community activities related to health care. U.S. citizenship or permanent resident status is required.
Financial data: Stipends range from $1,000 to $2,500. A total of approximately $125,000 is awarded each year by the foundation for all its scholarship programs.
Duration: 1 year.
Number awarded: Varies each year; recently 16 of these scholarships were awarded.
Deadline: January of each year.

2142 NATIVE AMERICAN HEALTH EDUCATION FUND SCHOLARSHIP

Triangle Community Foundation
Attn: Scholarship and Special Projects Coordinator
324 Blackwell Street, Suite 1220
Durham, NC 27701
Phone: (919) 474–8370, ext. 134; Fax: (919) 941–9208;
Email: info@trianglecf.org
Web: www.trianglecf.org/grants_support/view_scholarships
Summary: To provide financial assistance to Native Americans who are attending college or graduate school to prepare for a career in a health–related field.
Eligibility: Open to Native American students currently enrolled at a college or graduate school. Applicants must be preparing for a career in medicine, nursing, dietetics and nutrition, medical technology, physical therapy, pharmacy, social work, medical research (biochemistry), or other health–related fields. They must be able to demonstrate a desire to return to their community or Reservation to improve health care.
Financial data: A stipend is awarded (amount not specified).
Duration: 1 year.
Number awarded: Varies each year. Since the program began, it has awarded 106 scholarships.
Deadline: June of each year.

2143 $ NAVIGATE YOUR FUTURE SCHOLARSHIP

National Air Transportation Foundation
Attn: Manager, Education and Training
4226 King Street
Alexandria, VA 22302
Phone: (703) 845–9000, ext. 125; (800) 808–6282; Fax: (703) 845–8176;
Email: Safety1st@nata.aero
Web: www.nata.aero/About–NATA/Scholarships.aspx
Summary: To provide financial assistance to high school seniors planning to attend college to prepare for a career in general aviation.
Eligibility: Open to graduating high school seniors who have been accepted into an aviation–related program at an accredited college or university. Applicants must be able to demonstrate an interest in a career in general aviation (not the major commercial airlines). Along with their application, they must submit a 250–word essay on their educational and career goals in general aviation. Selection is based on that essay, academic record, and letter of recommendation.
Financial data: The stipend is $2,500.
Duration: 1 year.
Number awarded: 1 each year.
Deadline: June of each year.

2144 $$ NAVY COLLEGE ASSISTANCE/STUDENT HEADSTART (NAVY–CASH) PROGRAM

U.S. Navy
Attn: Navy Personnel Command
5722 Integrity Drive
Millington, TN 38054–5057
Phone: (901) 874–3070; (888) 633–9674; Fax: (901) 874–2651;
Email: nukeprograms@cnrc.navy.mil
Web: www.cnrc.navy.mil/nucfield/college/enlisted_options.htm
Summary: To provide financial assistance to high school seniors and current college students interested in attending college for a year and then entering the Navy's nuclear program.
Eligibility: Open to applicants who are able to meet the specific requirements of the Navy's Enlisted Nuclear Field Program. They must be enrolled or accepted for enrollment at an accredited 2–year community or junior college or 4–year college or university.
Financial data: While they attend school, participants are paid a regular Navy salary at a pay grade up to E–3 (starting at $1,303.50 per month). They are also eligible for all of the Navy's enlistment incentives (such as the Loan Repayment Program) and an enlistment bonus up to $12,000.
Duration: 12 months.
Number awarded: Varies each year.
Deadline: Deadline not specified.

2145 $$ NAVY NURSE CANDIDATE PROGRAM

U.S. Navy
Attn: Navy Medicine Professional Development Center
Code OH
8901 Wisconsin Avenue, Building 1, 13th Floor, Room 13132
Bethesda, MD 20889–5611
Phone: (301) 295–1217; (800) USA–NAVY; Fax: (301) 295–6865;
Email: oh@med.navy.mil
Web: www.med.navy.mil
Summary: To provide financial assistance for nursing education to students interested in serving in the Navy.
Eligibility: Open to full–time students in a bachelor of science in nursing program who are U.S. citizens under 40 years of age. Prior to or during their junior year of college, applicants must enlist in the U.S. Navy Nurse Corps Reserve. Following receipt of their degree, they must be willing to serve on active duty as a nurse in the Navy.
Financial data: This program pays a $10,000 initial grant upon enlistment (paid in 2 installments of $5,000 each) and a stipend of $1,000 per month. Students are responsible for paying all school expenses.
Duration: Up to 24 months.
Number awarded: Varies each year.
Deadline: Deadline not specified.

2146 $$ NAVY NURSE CORPS NROTC SCHOLARSHIP PROGRAM

U.S. Navy
Attn: Naval Education and Training Command
NSTC OD2
250 Dallas Street, Suite A
Pensacola, FL 32508–5268
Phone: (850) 452–4941, ext. 29395; (800) NAV–ROTC, ext. 29395; Fax: (850) 452–2486;
Email: pnsc_nrotc.scholarship@navy.mil
Web: www.nrotc.navy.mil/nurse.aspx

Summary: To provide financial assistance to graduating high school seniors who are interested in joining Navy ROTC and majoring in nursing in college.

Eligibility: Open to graduating high school seniors who have been accepted at a college with a Navy ROTC unit on campus or a college with a cross–enrollment agreement with such a college. Applicants must be U.S. citizens between the ages of 17 and 23 who plan to study nursing in college and are willing to serve for 4 years as active–duty Navy officers in the Navy Nurse Corps following graduation from college. They must not have reached their 27th birthday by the time of college graduation and commissioning; applicants who have prior active–duty military service may be eligible for age adjustments for the amount of time equal to their prior service, up to a maximum of 36 months. They must have minimum SAT scores of 530 in critical reading and 520 in mathematics or minimum ACT scores of 22 in English and 21 in mathematics.

Financial data: This scholarship provides payment of full tuition and required educational fees, as well as $375 per semester for textbooks, supplies, and equipment. The program also provides a stipend for 10 months of the year that is $250 per month as a freshman, $300 per month as a sophomore, $350 per month as a junior, and $400 per month as a senior.

Duration: 4 years.

Number awarded: Varies each year.

Deadline: January of each year.

2147 $ NEBRASKA ACTUARIES CLUB SCHOLARSHIPS

Nebraska Actuaries Club
c/o Alicia Loftus
Blue Cross Blue Shield of Nebraska
1919 Aksarben Drive
P.O. Box 3428
Omaha, NE 68180–0001
Phone: (402) 982–8862; (800) 422–2763;
Email: Alicia.loftus@nebraskablue.com
Web: n–a–c.org

Summary: To provide financial assistance to residents of any state who are planning to attend college in Nebraska to prepare for an actuarial career.

Eligibility: Open to seniors graduating from high schools in any state and planning to attend a college or university in Nebraska. Applicants must intend to major in actuarial science, mathematics, statistics, or economics and prepare for a career as an actuary. They must be able to demonstrate mathematical ability. Along with their application, they must submit an essay on their interest in actuarial science and why they would like to be an actuary. Financial need is not considered in the selection process.

Financial data: The stipend is $2,000 per year for students at campuses of the University of Nebraska or $1,000 per year for students at other colleges and universities in the state.

Duration: 1 year; the scholarships at the University of Nebraska system may be renewed 1 additional year, provided the recipient maintains a GPA of 3.33 or higher.

Number awarded: 3 each year: 2 to students attending the University of Nebraska system (designated Madden Scholarships and supported by the Nebraska Insurance Federation) and 1 to a student attending another college or university in the state (supported by the Nebraska Actuaries Club).

Deadline: March of each year.

2148 NEBRASKA AVIATION TRADES ASSOCIATION SCHOLARSHIPS

Nebraska Aviation Trades Association
c/o Judy McDowell
192 West Lakeshore Drive
Lincoln, NE 68528
Phone: (402) 475–NATA;
Email: nata@windstream.net
Web: gonata.net

Summary: To provide financial assistance to residents of Nebraska who submit outstanding essays on agricultural aviation and are interested in attending college in any state.

Eligibility: Open to residents of Nebraska who are graduating high school seniors or students currently enrolled full time at colleges and universities in any state. Applicants must submit a 400–word essay on a topic that changes annually but relates to agricultural aviation; recently, students were asked to write on how agricultural aviation helps the entire U.S. economy. They must be recommended by a member of the Nebraska Aviation Trades Association (NATA). Selection is based on the essay, academic achievements (including SAT and ACT scores), and leadership.

Financial data: Stipends are $1,000 or $500.

Duration: 1 year; nonrenewable.

Number awarded: 2 each year: 1 at $1,000 and 1 at $500.

Deadline: March of each year.

2149 NEBRASKA CHAPTER ASHRAE SCHOLARSHIPS

American Society of Heating, Refrigerating and Air–Conditioning Engineers–Nebraska Chapter
c/o Scott Murray, Student Activities Chair
9545 Western Circle
Omaha, NE 68114–6717
Phone: (402) 490–0528;
Email: s.murray@sensusmi.com
Web: cmdept.unl.edu/ne–ashrae

Summary: To provide financial assistance to students in Nebraska working on a degree in the field related to the interests of the American Society of Heating, Refrigerating and Air–Conditioning Engineers (ASHRAE).

Eligibility: Open to students at colleges and universities in Nebraska working on a degree in a field related to the interests of ASHRAE. Applicants must submit a list of college activities and hobbies, a list of any offices held in professional or honorary societies, a brief resume of work experience, a statement of their particular interest in the field covered by ASHRAE, the extent to which they have participated in ASHRAE–related activities, an essay on which they should be awarded this scholarship, and information on their financial situation.

Financial data: The stipend is $1,000.

Duration: 1 year.

Number awarded: 4 each year.

Deadline: January of each year.

2150 $ NEED SCHOLARSHIP AWARD FOR COMMUNITY COLLEGE AND TRADE SCHOOL STUDENTS

American Nuclear Society
Attn: Scholarship Coordinator
555 North Kensington Avenue
La Grange Park, IL 60526–5535
Phone: (708) 352–6611; (800) 323–3044; Fax: (708) 352–0499;
Email: outreach@ans.org
Web: www.new.ans.org/honors/scholarships

Summary: To provide financial assistance to community college and trade school students who can demonstrate financial need and are preparing for a career in the nuclear power industry.

Eligibility: Open to students working on a 2–year associate degree at a community college or trade school in the United States in nuclear science, nuclear engineering, or a nuclear–related field. Applicants must be able to demonstrate financial need. They must be sponsored by a local section, plant branch, student section, or member of the American Nuclear Society (ANS). U.S. citizenship is not required.

Financial data: The stipend is $2,500.

Duration: 1 year; nonrenewable.

Number awarded: Up to 4 each year.

Deadline: March of each year.

2151 NEIL AND PAT KILPATRICK MEMORIAL SCHOLARSHIP

Tennessee Academy of Physician Assistants
Attn: Tennessee Physician Assistant Foundation
P.O. Box 150785
Nashville, TN 37215–0785
Phone: (615) 463–0026; Fax: (615) 463–0036;
Email: info@tnpa.com
Web: www.tnpa.com/scholarships.php

Summary: To provide financial assistance to physician assistant students from Tennessee.

Eligibility: Open to students enrolled in the first or second year of a physician assistant program who are either 1) enrolled at an approved program in Tennessee; or 2) residents of Tennessee enrolled at an approved in another state. Applicants must submit an essay of 2 to 3 pages on their professional career and lifetime goals. Financial need is not considered in the selection process.

Financial data: Stipends are $1,000 or $500.

Duration: 1 year.

Number awarded: Varies each year; recently, 5 of these scholarships were awarded: 1 at $1,000 and 4 at $500.

Deadline: September of each year.

2152 $ NEIL HAMILTON MEMORIAL SCHOLARSHIP

Oregon Fire Marshal's Association
Attn: Scholarship Committee
1284 Court Street N.E.
Salem, OR 97301
Phone: (503) 378–0595; Fax: (503) 364–9910;
Email: mary.ofma.net
Web: www.ofma.net/Scholarships.html

Summary: To provide financial assistance to residents of Oregon who are interested in studying fire science at a community college in the state.

Eligibility: Open to graduates of high schools in Oregon, including GED recipients and home–schooled graduates. Applicants must be enrolled or planning to enroll at least half time at a community college in the state and majoring in fire science or fire suppression/protection. They must have a GPA of 2.5 or higher or a GED score of at least 2500. Financial need is not required, but it is considered in the selection process.

Financial data: Stipends for scholarships offered by the Oregon Student Access Commission (OSAC) range from $200 to $10,000 but recently averaged $2,300.

Duration: 1 year; nonrenewable.

Number awarded: Varies each year.

Deadline: February of each year.

2153 NEUROSCIENCE RESEARCH PRIZE FOR HIGH SCHOOL STUDENTS

American Academy of Neurology
Attn: Program Manager, Scientific Programs
1080 Montreal Avenue
St. Paul, MN 55116–2325
Phone: (651) 695–2704; (800) 879–1960; Fax: (651) 695–2791;
Email: ejackson@aan.com
Web: www.aan.com/go/science/awards

Summary: To recognize and reward high school students who submit outstanding laboratory reports in neuroscience.

Eligibility: Open to students enrolled in grades 9–12 in the United States. Applicants must submit an original laboratory research report, up to 10 pages in length, that represents their own written work. Research on all aspects of the brain or nervous system is eligible, including (but not limited to) anatomy, physiology, pathology, function, and behavior. The report should be written in the style of a scientific paper, describing actual laboratory or field research experiments or observations performed, the results obtained, and the interpretation of those results. Selection criteria include the paper's relevance to neuroscience, creativity, communication skills, and interpretation of data.

Financial data: Winners receive a $1,000 prize and an all–expense paid trip to a professional neuroscience conference where they present their projects. The winners' teachers are also invited to the conferences, with all their expenses paid.

Duration: The prizes are awarded annually.

Number awarded: 4 each year; 3 winners receive trips to the AAN meeting and 1 to the CNS meeting.

Deadline: October of each year.

2154 NEW ENGLAND CHAPTER ISA EDUCATIONAL SCHOLARSHIP PROGRAM

International Society of Arboriculture–New England Chapter
Attn: Executive Assistant
Norwell, MA 02061
Phone: (978) 844–0441;
Email: heather@newenglandisa.org
Web: www.newenglandisa.org/scholarships.html

Summary: To provide financial assistance to undergraduates from New England interested in attending college to prepare for a career in a plant material–oriented field.

Eligibility: Open to 1) students enrolled full time at a 2– or 4–year college or university in the New England states; and 2) residents of those states enrolled full time at a 2– or 4–year college or university in any state. Applicants must have completed at least 1 semester of study for a degree or career in a plant material–oriented program, such as arboriculture, botany, entomology, horticulture, plant pathology, urban forestry, or a related field. Along with their application, they must submit a 500–word essay about their reasons for preparing for a career in their chosen field; their involvement in related extracurricular activities, jobs, or internships; their goals and objectives; and why they should be chosen for this scholarship. Financial need is not considered in the selection process.

Financial data: The stipend is $1,500.

Duration: 1 year.

Number awarded: 2 each year.

Deadline: April of each year.

2155 $ NEW HAMPSHIRE GOLF COURSE SUPERINTENDENTS ASSOCIATION SCHOLARSHIP

New Hampshire Golf Course Superintendents Association
Attn: Scholarship Award
P.O. Box 784
Auburn, NH 03032
Phone: (603) 674–1163;
Email: nhgcsa@comcast.net
Web: nhgcsa.com/Scholarship.html

Summary: To provide financial assistance to residents of New Hampshire who are interested in majoring in turfgrass management at a college in any state.

Eligibility: Open to New Hampshire residents currently enrolled or planning to enroll full time at an accredited institution of higher education in any state. Applicants must in interested in a major in turf–related studies. Along with their application, they must submit a 500–word essay on their personal achievements and why they are a deserving candidate for this scholarship. Selection is based on the essay, academic achievement, extracurricular activities, community involvement, leadership, and outside employment. Financial need is not considered.

Financial data: Stipends range from $500 to $2,000, depending upon available funds.

Duration: 1 year; recipients may reapply.

Number awarded: 1 or more each year.

Deadline: August of each year.

2156 NEW JERSEY CLINICAL LABORATORY SCIENCE SCHOLARSHIPS

American Society for Clinical Laboratory Science–New Jersey
c/o Martha M. Smith, Scholarship Committee Chair
56 Gregory Lane
Franklin Park, NJ 08823
Phone: (609) 406–6830;
Email: Martha_smith@doh.state.nj.us
Web: ascls–nj.org/Documents.html

Summary: To provide financial assistance to members of the American Society for Clinical Laboratory Science (ACLS) from any state who are enrolled in a medical laboratory science (MLS) program in New Jersey.

Eligibility: Open to ACLS members from any state enrolled in their final year of an MLS program at a New Jersey institution accredited by the National Accrediting Agency for Clinical Laboratory Sciences. Applicants must submit a personal statement explaining why they have chosen the field of clinical laboratory science and describing their proposed career. Selection is based on academic record, awards and honors, extracurricular activities, professional activities, and letters of recommendation.

Financial data: The stipend is $1,000.

Duration: 1 year.

Number awarded: 2 each year.

Deadline: February of each year.

2157 NEW JERSEY LEGION AUXILIARY PAST PRESIDENTS' PARLEY NURSES SCHOLARSHIPS

American Legion Auxiliary
Department of New Jersey

c/o Lucille M. Miller, Secretary/Treasurer
1540 Kuser Road, Suite A–8
Hamilton, NJ 08619
Phone: (609) 581–9580; Fax: (609) 581–8429

Summary: To provide financial assistance to New Jersey residents who are the descendants of veterans and interested in studying nursing at a school in any state.

Eligibility: Open to the children, grandchildren, and great–grandchildren of veterans who served in the U.S. armed forces during specified periods of war time. Applicants must be graduating high school seniors who have been residents of New Jersey for at least 2 years. They must be planning to study nursing at a school in any state. Along with their application, they must submit a 1,000–word essay on a topic that changes annually; recently, students were asked to write on the topic, "The Importance of Helping Military Families in Your Community." Selection is based on academic achievement (40%), character (15%), leadership (15%), Americanism (15%), and financial need (15%).

Financial data: A stipend is awarded (amount not specified).

Duration: 1 year.

Number awarded: 1 or more each year.

Deadline: April of each year.

2158 NEW JERSEY POST SAME SCHOLARSHIP

Summary: To provide financial assistance to students in New Jersey working on an undergraduate degree in architecture, engineering, or a related field.

See Listing #1425.

2159 NEW JERSEY SECTION DRINKING WATER CAREERS SCHOLARSHIP

American Water Works Association–New Jersey Section
Attn: Section Manager
38 East Ridgewood Avenue
PMB 183
Ridgewood, NJ 07450
Phone: (646) 831–1882; (866) 436–1120; Fax: (718) 728–8469;
Email: mona@njawwa.org
Web: www.njawwa.org/education_scholarships.php

Summary: To provide financial assistance to upper–division and graduate students from New Jersey who are preparing for a career in the water industry.

Eligibility: Open to residents of New Jersey and students enrolled at a college or university in the state. Applicants must be entering their junior or senior year of undergraduate study or enrolled as graduate students. They must be working full time on a degree in a field related to drinking water supply, treatment, or distribution. Along with their application, they must submit a 500–word essay on their educational plans or career objectives that demonstrate their interest in the water industry. Financial need is not considered in the selection process.

Financial data: The stipend is $1,500.

Duration: 1 year; recipients may reapply.

Number awarded: 1 or more each year.

Deadline: April of each year.

2160 $ NEW JERSEY SWE SCHOLARSHIP

Society of Women Engineers
Attn: Scholarship Selection Committee
203 North LaSalle Street, Suite 1675
Chicago, IL 60601–1269
Phone: (312) 596–5223; (877) SWE–INFO; Fax: (312) 644–8557;
Email: scholarships@swe.org
Web: societyofwomenengineers.swe.org/index.php/scholarships

Summary: To provide financial assistance to women from New Jersey who will be entering freshmen at a college in any state and are interested in studying engineering or computer science.

Eligibility: Open to women who are entering college in any state as freshmen with a GPA of 3.5 or higher. Applicants must be residents of New Jersey planning to enroll full time at an ABET–accredited 4–year college or university in any state and major in computer science or engineering. Selection is based on merit.

Financial data: The stipend is $2,000.

Duration: 1 year.

Number awarded: 1 each year.

Deadline: May of each year.

2161 $$ NEW MEXICO ALLIED HEALTH STUDENT LOAN–FOR–SERVICE PROGRAM

New Mexico Higher Education Department
Attn: Financial Aid Division
2048 Galisteo Street
Santa Fe, NM 87505–2100
Phone: (505) 476–8411; (800) 279–9777; Fax: (505) 476–8454;
Email: feliz.romerol@state.nm.us
Web: hed.state.nm.us/Allied.aspx

Summary: To provide funding to health professions students willing to work in underserved areas of New Mexico.

Eligibility: Open to residents of New Mexico interested in preparing for a career as a health professional in the following fields: physical therapy, occupational therapy, speech–language pathology, audiology, pharmacy, nutrition, respiratory care, laboratory technology, mental health services, emergency medical services, dental hygiene, or other licensed or certified health profession as defined by the commission. Applicants must be enrolled at least half time or accepted in an accredited program at a New Mexico public postsecondary institution. They must declare an intent to practice in a designated shortage area of New Mexico for at least 1 year after completing their education. Along with their application, they must submit a brief essay on why they want to enter their chosen health field and obligate themselves to a rural practice in New Mexico. U.S. citizenship or eligible noncitizen status is required.

Financial data: The award depends on the financial need of the recipient, to a total of $12,000 per year. This is a loan–for–service program; loans are forgiven if the student performs the required professional service as a health professional in a designated shortage area in New Mexico. For every year of service, a portion of the loan is forgiven. If the entire service agreement is fulfilled, 100% of the loan is eligible for forgiveness. Penalties may be assessed if the service agreement is not satisfied.

Duration: 1 year; may be renewed up to 3 additional years.

Number awarded: Varies each year, depending on the availability of funds.

Deadline: June of each year.

2162 NEW MEXICO LEGION AUXILIARY PAST PRESIDENTS PARLEY SCHOLARSHIPS

American Legion Auxiliary
Department of New Mexico
1215 Mountain Road, N.E.
Albuquerque, NM 87102–2716
Phone: (505) 242–9918; Fax: (505) 247–0478;
Email: alauxnm@netscape.com

Summary: To provide financial assistance to residents of New Mexico who are the children of veterans and studying nursing or a related medical field at a school in any state.

Eligibility: Open to New Mexico residents who are attending college in any state. Applicants must be the children of veterans who served during specified periods of war time. They must be studying nursing or a related medical field. Selection is based on scholarship, character, leadership, Americanism, and financial need.

Financial data: A stipend is awarded (amount not specified).

Deadline: April of each year.

2163 $$ NEW MEXICO NURSING LOAN–FOR–SERVICE PROGRAM

New Mexico Higher Education Department
Attn: Financial Aid Division
2048 Galisteo Street
Santa Fe, NM 87505–2100
Phone: (505) 476–8411; (800) 279–9777; Fax: (505) 476–8454;
Email: feliz.romerol@state.nm.us
Web: hed.state.nm.us/Nurse.aspx

Summary: To provide funding to nursing students from New Mexico willing to work in underserved areas of the state after graduation.

Eligibility: Open to residents of New Mexico interested in preparing for a career as a nurse (including a licensed practical nursing certificate, associate degree in nursing, bachelor of science in nursing, master of science in nursing, or advanced practice nurse). Applicants must be enrolled at least half time or accepted in an accredited program at a New Mexico public postsecondary institution. As a condition of the loan, they must declare an intent to practice in a designated shortage area of New Mexico for at least 1 year after completing their education. Along with their application, they must submit a brief essay on why they want to enter the field of nursing and obligate themselves to a rural practice in New Mexico. U.S. citizenship or eligible noncitizen status is required.

Financial data: The amount awarded depends on the financial need of the recipient, to a total of $12,000 per year. This is a loan–for–service program; for every year of service as a nurse in New Mexico, a portion of the loan is forgiven. If the entire service agreement is fulfilled, 100% of the loan is eligible for forgiveness. Penalties may be assessed if the service agreement is not satisfied.
Duration: 1 year; may be renewed up to 3 additional years.
Number awarded: Varies each year, depending on the availability of funds.
Deadline: June of each year.

2164 NEW YORK LEGION AUXILIARY PAST PRESIDENTS PARLEY STUDENT SCHOLARSHIP IN MEDICAL FIELD

American Legion Auxiliary
Department of New York
112 State Street, Suite 1310
Albany, NY 12207
Phone: (518) 463–1162; (800) 421–6348; Fax: (518) 449–5406;
Email: alanyterry@nycap.rr.com
Web: www.deptny.org/Scholarships.htm

Summary: To provide financial assistance to descendants of wartime veterans in New York who are interested in attending college in any state to prepare for a career in a medical field.
Eligibility: Open to residents of New York who are high school seniors or graduates and attending or planning to attend an accredited college or university in any state to prepare for a career in a medical field. Applicants must be the children, grandchildren, or great–grandchildren of veterans who served during specified periods of war time. Along with their application, they must submit a 500–word essay on why they selected the medical field. Selection is based on character (30%), Americanism (20%), leadership (10%), scholarship (20%), and financial need (20%). U.S. citizenship is required.
Financial data: The stipend is $1,000. Funds are paid directly to the recipient's school.
Duration: 1 year.
Number awarded: 2 each year.
Deadline: February of each year.

2165 NEW YORK STATE GOLF ASSOCIATION SCHOLARSHIPS

New York State Golf Association
Attn: Executive Director
P.O. Box 15333
Syracuse, NY 13215–0333
Phone: (315) 471–6979; (888) NYSGA–23 (within NY); Fax: (315) 471–1372;
Email: nysga@nysga.org
Web: www.nysga.org/scholarship–program.html

Summary: To provide financial assistance to residents of New York working on a degree in a field related to golf course management at a school in any state.
Eligibility: Open to New York residents enrolled full time at a 2– or 4–year college or university in any state. Applicants must be studying agronomy, turfgrass management, professional golf and country club management, or a related field. Along with their application, they must submit an essay about themselves. Financial need is considered in the selection process.
Financial data: The stipend is $1,500.
Duration: 1 year.
Number awarded: Varies each year; recently, 11 of these scholarships were awarded.
Deadline: May of each year.

2166 $ NICK WINTER MEMORIAL SCHOLARSHIP

Association of State Floodplain Managers
Attn: ASFPM Foundation
2809 Fish Hatchery Road, Suite 204
Madison, WI 53713
Phone: (608) 441–3003; Fax: (608) 274–0696;
Email: asfpmfoundation@floods.org
Web: www.asfpmfoundation.org/winters.htm

Summary: To provide funding to undergraduate and graduate students working on a degree in a field related to floodplain or stormwater management.
Eligibility: Open to U.S. citizens who are enrolled or planning to enroll at an accredited U.S. college or university as full–time juniors or seniors or as graduate students. Applicants must be working on a degree in a field related to floodplain or stormwater management (e.g., civil or environmental engineering, planning, emergency management, environmental sciences). Along with their application, they must submit a 500–word essay on their interest in floodplain and stormwater management and their professional and career goals. In the selection process, preference is given to students who can demonstrate financial need and a record of civic or volunteer service.
Financial data: The stipend is $2,000.
Duration: 1 year.
Deadline: April of each year.

2167 NICOLE MARIE GOULART MEMORIAL SCHOLARSHIP

Luso–American Education Foundation
Attn: Administrative Director
7080 Donlon Way, Suite 202
P.O. Box 2967
Dublin, CA 94568
Phone: (925) 828–3883; Fax: (925) 828–3883;
Email: education@luso–american.org
Web: www.luso–american.org/laef

Summary: To provide financial assistance to undergraduate students of Portuguese descent who are majoring in designated fields.
Eligibility: Open to U.S. residents who are sophomores, juniors, and seniors at 4–year colleges and universities and of Portuguese descent. Applicants must be majoring in medicine/health, neurology, nursing, pharmacology, emergency medical technology, or protective services. They must have a GPA of 3.5 or higher. Selection is based on promise of success in college, financial need, leadership, vocational promise, and sincerity of purpose.
Financial data: A stipend is awarded (amount not specified).
Duration: 1 year; renewable.
Number awarded: 1 each year.
Deadline: February of each year.

2168 $ NIGHTINGALE SCHOLARSHIP

American Society for Quality
Attn: Healthcare Division
600 North Plankinton Avenue
P.O. Box 3005
Milwaukee, WI 53201–3005
Phone: (414) 272–8575; (800) 248–1946; Fax: (414) 272–1734;
Email: help@asq.org
Web: asq.org/health/about/awards–health.html

Summary: To provide financial assistance to undergraduate and graduate students working on a degree in a field related to health care and quality.
Eligibility: Open to undergraduate and graduate students who are working on a degree in a field of study related to health care quality. Applicants must be a member of the Healthcare Division of the American Society for Quality (ASQ) or nominated by a member. Along with their application, they must submit 1) a 1–page personal profile describing their work experience, professional society involvement, current program of study, area of interest in health care quality, and future career plans; 2) official transcripts; 3) 3 letters of recommendation (including 1 from the sponsoring Healthcare Division member); and 4) an essay up to 6 pages on the topic, "Quality in Healthcare: Reducing Adverse Outcomes, Costs, or Both While Improving Quality of Care." Selection is based on that essay (40 points), letters of recommendation (30 points), academic standing (10 points, with preference for students in a graduate or professional program), employment experience (10 points), and professional society activity (10 points).
Financial data: The stipend is $2,000.
Duration: 1 year.
Number awarded: 1 each year.
Deadline: February of each year.

2169 N–OADN FOUNDATION/AFTERCOLLEGE SCHOLARSHIP

National Organization for Associate Degree Nursing
Attn: Foundation
7794 Grow Drive
Pensacola, FL 32514
Phone: (850) 484–6948; (877) 966–6236; Fax: (850) 484–8762;
Email: noadn@dancyamc.com
Web: www.noadn.org

Summary: To provide financial assistance to students working on an Associate Degree in Nursing (A.D.N.).
Eligibility: Open to students currently enrolled or entering their second year of a state–approved A.D.N. program. Applicants must have earned a GPA of 3.0 or higher and be active in a local, state, or national student nurse association.

Along with their application, they must submit a 500–word essay on how nursing is a unique profession within the health care system. Financial need is not considered.

Financial data: The stipend is $1,000.

Duration: 1 year.

Number awarded: 4 each year.

Deadline: January or August of each year.

2170 NONWOVENS DIVISION SCHOLARSHIP

Technical Association of the Pulp and Paper Industry
Attn: Scholarship Department
15 Technology Parkway South
Norcross, GA 30092
Phone: (770) 209–7276; (800) 332–8686; Fax: (770) 446–6947;
Email: standards@tappi.org
Web: www.tappi.org/About–TAPPI/TAPPI–Scholarships.aspx

Summary: To provide financial assistance to undergraduate students who are interested in preparing for a career in the paper industry.

Eligibility: Open to students who are attending a state–accredited college full time, have earned a GPA of 3.0 or higher, are enrolled in a program preparatory to a career in the nonwovens industry or can demonstrate an interest in the areas covered by the Nonwovens Division of the Technical Association of the Pulp and Paper Industry, and are recommended and endorsed by an instructor or faculty member. Applicants must be interested in preparing for a career in the paper industry with a focus on the materials, equipment, and processes for the manufacture and use of nonwovens. Selection is based on the candidates' potential career contributions to the pulp and paper industry as it relates to nonwovens; financial need is not considered.

Financial data: The stipend is $1,000.

Duration: 1 year.

Number awarded: 1 each year.

Deadline: February of each year.

2171 NORINE FRIELL SERVICE AWARD

Wisconsin Academy of Physician Assistants
Attn: WAPA Foundation
563 Carter Court, Suite B
Kimberly, WI 54136
Phone: (920) 560–5630; (800) 762–8965; Fax: (920) 882–3655;
Email: wapa@wapa.org
Web: www.wapa.org/About–WAPA/WAPA–Foundation/Awards–and–Nominations

Summary: To recognize and reward physician assistant (PA) students in Wisconsin who demonstrate outstanding community service.

Eligibility: Open to students enrolled in their final year of a PA program in Wisconsin. Applicants must demonstrate outstanding community service at the state, local, and community level. Along with their application, they must submit a personal statement listing and describing the depth and time of community service provided. Selection is based on that statement and 2 letters of recommendation.

Financial data: The award is $1,000.

Duration: 1 year.

Number awarded: 1 each year.

Deadline: June of each year.

2172 $ NORTH AMERICAN MEAT ASSOCIATION SCHOLARSHIPS

North American Meat Association
Attn: NAMA Scholarship Foundation
1970 Broadway, Suite 825
Oakland, CA 94612
Phone: (510) 763–1533; Fax: (510) 763–6186;
Email: info@meatassociation.com
Web: meatscholars.org

Summary: To provide financial assistance to undergraduate students preparing for a career in the meat industry.

Eligibility: Open to undergraduates majoring in meat science, animal science, poultry science, agricultural engineering, or other field oriented toward post–harvest processing of meat and poultry food products. Applicants must be considering a career in the meat industry. The highest–ranked applicant receives the Frank DeBenedetti Memorial Scholarship.

Financial data: Stipends are $2,500 or $2,250.

Duration: 1 year.

Number awarded: Varies each year; recently, 10 of these scholarships were awarded: 1 at $2,500 (the Frank DeBenedetti Memorial Scholarship) and 9 at $2,250.

Deadline: May of each year.

2173 NORTH AMERICAN SURVEYING HISTORY SCHOLARSHIP

Summary: To provide financial assistance to upper–division surveying students in North America who have demonstrated an interest in history.

See Listing #1428.

2174 $$ NORTH CAROLINA FORGIVABLE EDUCATION LOANS FOR SERVICE

College Foundation of North Carolina
Attn: College Foundation, Inc.
2917 Highwoods Boulevard
P.O. Box 41966
Raleigh, NC 27629–1966
Phone: (888) 234–6400; Fax: (919) 821–3139
Web: www.cfnc.org/FELS

Summary: To provide forgivable loans to residents of North Carolina who wish to attend school in any state to prepare for a career in specified fields of education, health care, medicine, or nursing and to practice in North Carolina.

Eligibility: Open to North Carolina residents who are enrolled or planning to enroll at least half time at a college or university in any state. Applicants must be interested in working on a degree in 1) education (biology, chemistry, comprehensive science, English as a second language, mathematics, middle grades, physics, or special education); 2) health care (chiropractic care, clinical laboratory sciences, cytotechnology, dental hygiene, emergency medical science, emergency medical technology, imaging, medical technology, occupational therapy, occupational therapy assistant, optometry, pharmacy, pharmacy technician, physical therapy, physical therapy assistant, physician assistant, radiography, radiology, radiology technician, sonography, social work, or speech–language pathology); 3) medicine (dentistry, medical doctor, osteopathy, podiatry, or psychology); or 4) nursing (nurse educator, nurse practitioner, nursing). They must have a minimum GPA of 3.0 as a graduating high school senior, 2.8 as an undergraduate in an associate or bachelor's program, or 3.2 as a graduate or professional student.

Financial data: Annual stipends are $3,000 for candidates for a certificate or associate degree, $3,000 for freshmen and sophomores in a bachelor's degree program, $7,000 for juniors and seniors in a bachelor's degree program, $10,000 for master's degree students, or $14,000 for doctoral students. This is a forgivable loan program; 1 year of full–time work in their chosen profession in North Carolina cancels 1 year of support under this program. Recipients who fail to honor the work obligation must repay the balance plus 8% interest. Loan forgiveness must be completed within 10 years of graduation.

Duration: 1 year; may be renewed 1 additional year by candidates for a certificate or associate degree, up to 3 additional years by candidates for a bachelor's degree, 1 additional year by master's degree students, or 3 additional years by doctoral students.

Number awarded: Varies each year.

Deadline: Deadline not specified.

2175 NORTH CAROLINA HEALTH CAREER SCHOLARSHIPS

North Carolina Community College System
Attn: North Carolina Community Colleges Foundation
200 West Jones Street
5016 Mail Service Center
Raleigh, NC 27699–5016
Phone: (919) 807–7195; Fax: (919) 807–7173;
Email: hickmanm@nccommunitycolleges.edu
Web: www.nccommunitycolleges.edu/pr/Awards/index.htm

Summary: To provide financial assistance to North Carolina residents enrolled at a community college in the state and preparing for a career in designated fields of health care.

Eligibility: Open to North Carolina residents who are enrolled full time in the second year at a community college in the state and have a GPA of 3.0 or higher. Applicants must be working on an associate degree in a field of high demand that will prepare them for a health care profession. Eligible fields vary each year, but may be selected from among the following: associate degree nursing, dental hygiene, emergency medical science, health information technology, medical assisting, medical laboratory technology, pharmacy technology, physical therapist assistant, respiratory therapy, or veterinary medical technology. Along with

their application, they must submit a 500–word statement on their career goals. Selection is based on personal commitment to the health profession, academic performance, and financial need.
Financial data: The stipend is $1,000.
Duration: 1 year.
Number awarded: Varies each year; recently, 15 of these scholarships, limited to students completing an associated degree in nursing.
Deadline: September of each year.

2176 $$ NORTH CAROLINA UNDERGRADUATE NURSE SCHOLARS PROGRAM

North Carolina State Education Assistance Authority
Attn: Nurse Scholars Program
10 T.W. Alexander Drive
P.O. Box 13663
Research Triangle Park, NC 27709–3663
Phone: (919) 549–8614; (800) 700–1775; Fax: (919) 248–4687;
Email: information@ncseaa.edu
Web: www.ncseaa.edu/NSP.htm
Summary: To provide funding to residents of North Carolina who wish to attend school in the state to prepare for a career in nursing.
Eligibility: Open to high school seniors, high school graduates, or currently–enrolled college students who are U.S. citizens, North Carolina residents, and interested in becoming a nurse. Applicants must be enrolled or planning to enroll at a North Carolina college, university, or hospital that prepares them for licensure as a registered nurse. They must have a GPA of 3.0 or higher. Selection is based on academic achievement, leadership potential, and the promise of service as a registered nurse in North Carolina; financial need is not considered.
Financial data: Annual stipends are $3,000 for candidates for an associate degree, $3,000 for candidates for a diploma in nursing, $5,000 for full–time students in a B.S.N. program, or $2,500 for part–time students in a B.S.N. program. This is a loan–for–service program; 1 year of full–time work as a nurse in North Carolina cancels 1 year of support under this program. Recipients who fail to honor the work obligation must repay the balance plus 10% interest. They have up to 7 years to repay the loan in service or 10 years to repay in cash.
Duration: 1 year; may be renewed 1 additional year by candidates for an associate degree, registered nurses completing a B.S.N. degree, and community college transfer students and juniors in a B.S.N. program, or for 3 additional years by freshmen and nontraditional students in a B.S.N. program.
Number awarded: Varies; generally, up to 450 new undergraduate degree awards are made each year; recently, a total of 805 students were receiving $3,502,775 through this program.
Deadline: February of each year for B.S.N. programs; May of each year for A.D.N. and diploma students.

2177 NORTH CAROLINA WILDLIFE FEDERATION SCHOLARSHIP GRANTS

North Carolina Wildlife Federation
Attn: Scholarships
2155 McClintock Road
Charlotte, NC 28205
Phone: (704) 332–5696;
Email: scholarships@ncwf.org
Web: www.ncwf.org/Scholarships
Summary: To provide financial assistance to full–time undergraduate or graduate students in North Carolina working on a degree in wildlife, the environment, or related areas.
Eligibility: Open to undergraduate and graduate students enrolled full time at accredited colleges (including 2–year colleges) and universities in North Carolina. Applicants must be working on a degree in the areas of environmental science, wildlife, fisheries, forestry, or conservation and have a GPA of 2.5 or higher. Selection is based on financial need, academic record, and extracurricular activities.
Financial data: The stipend is $1,000.
Duration: 1 year.
Number awarded: Up to 7 each year.
Deadline: June of each year.

2178 $$ NORTHROP GRUMMAN FOUNDATION SCHOLARSHIP

Society of Women Engineers
Attn: Scholarship Selection Committee
203 North LaSalle Street, Suite 1675
Chicago, IL 60601–1269
Phone: (312) 596–5223; (877) SWE–INFO; Fax: (312) 644–8557;
Email: scholarships@swe.org
Web: societyofwomenengineers.swe.org/index.php/scholarships
Summary: To provide financial assistance to female undergraduates at designated universities who are interested in studying specified fields of engineering.
Eligibility: Open to women who entering their sophomore, junior, or senior year as a full-time student at a designated ABET–accredited 4–year college or university. Applicants must have a GPA of 3.0 or higher and be majoring in computer science or aerospace, computer, electrical, industrial, mechanical, or systems engineering. Selection is based on merit. U.S. citizenship or permanent resident status is required.
Financial data: The stipend is $5,000.
Duration: 1 year.
Number awarded: 5 each year.
Deadline: February of each year.

2179 $$ NORWEGIAN COMMERCIAL CLUB FISHERIES SCHOLARSHIP

Norwegian Commercial Club
2245 N.W. 57th Street
Seattle, WA 98107
Phone: (206) 783–1274
Web: www.norwegiancommercialclub.com
Summary: To provide financial assistance for undergraduate or graduate study in fisheries management or research in the Pacific Northwest or Alaska.
Eligibility: Open to high school seniors and currently–enrolled graduate students in the Pacific Northwest who "have a background in American–Norwegian ideals." Applicants must be interested in preparing for a career in fisheries management or research in the Pacific Northwest or Alaska. Students in fishery technical schools, such as the Maritime Academy, are also eligible. Along with their application, they must submit a 300–word essay on their plans for furthering their education or vocation and why they think they qualify for this scholarship. Selection is based on financial need, academic capability, and activities of the applicant.
Financial data: The stipend is approximately $5,000. Funds are paid directly to the recipient's school.
Duration: 1 year.
Number awarded: 1 each year.
Deadline: March of each year.

2180 $ NPCA EDUCATIONAL FOUNDATION SCHOLARSHIPS

National Precast Concrete Association
Attn: NPCA Educational Foundation
1320 City Center Drive, Suite 200
Carmel, IN 46032
Phone: (317) 571–9500; (800) 366–7731; Fax: (317) 571–0041;
Email: npca@precast.org
Web: precast.org/foundation
Summary: To provide financial assistance for college to students interested in preparing for a career in fields related to the precast concrete industry.
Eligibility: Open to high school seniors, high school graduates, and undergraduate students who plan to enroll full time at a college, university, or community college. Applicants must be interested in majoring in architecture, civil engineering, or other field related to the building, construction, or precast concrete industry. They must submit an essay of 300 to 500 words on a topic of their choice related to the precast concrete industry, a description of their anticipated career, a transcript of high school and/or college grades (including ACT/SAT scores), a letter of recommendation from a faculty member, and a letter of sponsorship from a firm that is a member of the National Precast Concrete Association (NPCA). Financial need is not considered in the selection process.
Financial data: The stipend is $2,200 per year.
Duration: 1 year; may be renewed up to 3 additional years, provided the recipient remains enrolled full time and maintains a GPA of 2.8 or higher.
Number awarded: Varies each year; recently, 4 of these scholarships were awarded.
Deadline: December of each year.

2181 $ NPFDA SCHOLARSHIPS

National Poultry and Food Distributors Association
Attn: NPFDA Scholarship Foundation

2014 Osborne Road
Saint Marys, GA 31558
Phone: (770) 535–9901; Fax: (770) 535–7385;
Email: info@npfda.org
Web: www.npfda.org

Summary: To provide financial assistance to upper–division students enrolled in fields related to the poultry industry.

Eligibility: Open to full–time students entering their junior or senior year of college. Applicants must be studying a field related to the poultry industry (e.g., poultry science, food science, agricultural economics, animal science, food marketing, agricultural business, pre–veterinary science). Along with their application, they must submit a 1–page narrative on their professional goals and objectives. Selection is based on that narrative, transcripts, and a letter of recommendation; financial need is not considered.

Financial data: Stipends range from $1,500 to $2,000.

Duration: 1 year.

Number awarded: Varies each year; recently, 5 of these scholarships were awarded.

Deadline: May of each year.

2182 NSCA HIGH SCHOOL SCHOLARSHIPS

National Strength and Conditioning Association
Attn: Grants and Scholarships Program
1885 Bob Johnson Drive
Colorado Springs, CO 80906–4000
Phone: (719) 632–6722, ext. 152; (800) 815–6826; Fax: (719) 632–6367;
Email: foundation@nsca–lift.org
Web: www.nsca–lift.org/NSCAFoundation/grants.shtml

Summary: To provide financial assistance for undergraduate study in strength training and conditioning to high school seniors.

Eligibility: Open to high school students preparing to enter college. Applicants must have a GPA of 3.0 or higher and be planning to major in a strength and conditioning field. Along with their application, they must submit a 500–word essay on their personal and professional goals and how receiving this scholarship will assist them in achieving those goals. Selection is based on that essay, academic achievement, strength and conditioning experience, honors and awards, community involvement, letters of recommendation, and involvement in the National Strength and Conditioning Association (NSCA).

Financial data: The stipend is $1,500.

Duration: 1 year; nonrenewable.

Number awarded: 3 each year.

Deadline: March of each year.

2183 NSCA MINORITY SCHOLARSHIPS

National Strength and Conditioning Association
Attn: Grants and Scholarships Program
1885 Bob Johnson Drive
Colorado Springs, CO 80906–4000
Phone: (719) 632–6722, ext. 152; (800) 815–6826; Fax: (719) 632–6367;
Email: foundation@nsca–lift.org
Web: www.nsca–lift.org/NSCAFoundation/grants.shtml

Summary: To provide financial assistance to minorities who are interested in working on an undergraduate or graduate degree in strength training and conditioning.

Eligibility: Open to Blacks, Hispanics, Asian Americans, and Native Americans who are 17 years of age and older. Applicants must have been accepted into an accredited postsecondary institution to work on an undergraduate or graduate degree in the strength and conditioning field. Along with their application, they must submit a 500–word essay on their personal and professional goals and how receiving this scholarship will assist them in achieving those goals. Selection is based on that essay, academic achievement, strength and conditioning experience, honors and awards, community involvement, letters of recommendation, and involvement in the National Strength and Conditioning Association (NSCA).

Financial data: The stipend is $1,500.

Duration: 1 year.

Number awarded: 3 each year.

Deadline: March of each year.

2184 $$ NUCLEAR PROPULSION OFFICER CANDIDATE (NUPOC) PROGRAM

U.S. Navy
Attn: Navy Personnel Command
5722 Integrity Drive
Millington, TN 38054–5057
Phone: (901) 874–3070; (888) 633–9674; Fax: (901) 874–2651;
Email: nukeprograms@cnrc.navy.mil
Web: www.cnrc.navy.mil/nucfield/college/officer_options.htm

Summary: To provide financial assistance to college juniors and seniors who wish to serve in the Navy's nuclear propulsion training program following graduation.

Eligibility: Open to U.S. citizens who are entering their junior or senior year of college as a full–time student. Strong technical majors (mathematics, physics, chemistry, or an engineering field) are encouraged. Applicants must have completed at least 1 year of calculus and 1 year of physics and must have earned a grade of "C" or better in all mathematics, science, and technical courses. Normally, they must be 26 years of age or younger at the expected date of commissioning, although applicants for the design and research specialty may be up to 29 years old.

Financial data: Participants become Active Reserve enlisted Navy personnel and receive a salary of up to $2,500 per month; the exact amount depends on the local cost of living and other factors. A bonus of $10,000 is also paid at the time of enlistment and another $2,000 upon completion of nuclear power training.

Duration: Up to 30 months, until completion of a bachelor's degree.

Number awarded: Varies each year.

Deadline: Deadline not specified.

2185 $$ NURSING HOME ABUSE AWARENESS AND PREVENTION SCHOLARSHIP

National Association to Stop Nursing Home Abuse
100 Jackson Street, Suite 240
Houston, TX 77002
Email: NHAscholarship@educationaid.org
Web: www.nursinghomeabuse.net/scholarship

Summary: To provide financial assistance to nursing and other students who are preparing for a career that will enable them to help combat nursing home abuse.

Eligibility: Open to U.S. citizens who are currently working on a degree in nursing (preferably geriatrics), social work, psychology, or health care administration. Applicants must be planning to work with the senior citizen population and to help combat nursing home abuse. They must be currently attending an accredited postsecondary institution and receiving some type of financial aid.

Financial data: The stipend is $5,000. Funds must be used for expenses other than tuition, such as rent, child care, books and supplies, travel and gas expenses, utilities, and groceries.

Duration: 1 year.

Number awarded: 1 each year.

Deadline: February of each year.

2186 NUTS, BOLTS AND THINGAMAJIGS TRADE OR TECHNICAL SCHOOL SCHOLARSHIPS

Fabricators and Manufacturers Association, International
Attn: FMA Foundation
833 Featherstone Road
Rockford, IL 61107–6302
Phone: (815) 399–8700; (888) 394–4362; Fax: (815) 484–7738;
Email: foundation@fmanet.org
Web: www.nutsandboltsfoundation.org/scholarships

Summary: To provide financial assistance to students entering or continuing in a trade school or technical or community college to prepare for a career in manufacturing technology.

Eligibility: Open to students enrolled or planning to enroll full time at a 2–year trade school or technical or community college to major in an engineering or related program that may lead to a career in the manufacturing technology industry. Applicants must have a GPA of 2.5 or higher. They must become a student member of the Fabricators and Manufacturers Association, International (FMA), the Tube and Pipe Association, International (TPA), or the Outside Processors Council (OPC), unless they are already 1) a student or basic member; 2) the child of a basic member; 3) an employee of an Advantage–level member company; or 4) the child of an employee of an Advantage–level member company. Along with their application, they must submit 350–word essays on the following topics: 1) their educational and career goals; 2) the experiences that have influenced their decision to prepare for a career in manufacturing and why they want to work in the technology industry; 3) any personal, sporting, educational, and/or clubs, competitions, or extracurricular activities in which they are participating; and 4) any academic or community honors or awards they have received. Financial need is not considered in the selection process.

Financial data: The stipend is $1,500.
Duration: 1 year.
Number awarded: 20 each year.
Deadline: March of each year.

2187 NWA/ACCUWEATHER UNDERGRADUATE SCHOLARSHIP IN METEOROLOGY

National Weather Association
Attn: Executive Director
228 West Millbrook Road
Raleigh, NC 27609–4304
Phone: (919) 845–1546; Fax: (919) 845–2956;
Email: exdir@nwas.org
Web: www.nwas.org/committees/ed_comm/application/index.php
Summary: To provide financial assistance to undergraduate students working on a degree in operational meteorology.
Eligibility: Open to students who are entering their sophomore or higher year of undergraduate study. Applicants must be working on a degree in operational meteorology (forecasting, broadcasting, consulting). Along with their application, they must submit a 1–page statement explaining why they are applying for this scholarship. Selection is based on that statement, academic achievement, and 2 letters of recommendation.
Financial data: The stipend is $1,000.
Duration: 1 year; nonrenewable.
Number awarded: 1 each year.
Deadline: May of each year.

2188 NYWEA SCHOLARSHIPS

New York Water Environment Association
Attn: Executive Director
525 Plum Street, Suite 102
Syracuse, NY 13204
Phone: (315) 422–7811; (877) 55–NYWEA; Fax: (315) 422–3851;
Email: pcr@nywea.org
Web: nywea.org/scholarship
Summary: To provide financial assistance to students who are enrolled or planning to enroll in an environmentally–related program in college.
Eligibility: Open to 3 categories of students: 1) children of members of the New York Water Environment Association (NYWEA) who are enrolled or planning to enroll full time at a college or university in any state in a program that will prepare them for a professional career in the environmental field; 2) students enrolled full time in a program that will prepare them for a professional career in the environmental field at a college or university that has an NYWEA student chapter; and 3) high school seniors who plan to enroll in an environmentally–related program at a 4–year college or university in any state. All applicants must submit essays, from 200 to 300 words in length, on 1) their interest in the environment and how that interest influences their career goals; and 2) a current environmental issue that impacts their life and their community and how it affects them. Selection is based on career objective, academic potential, other activities, character, and environmental interest.
Financial data: The stipend is $1,500.
Duration: 1 year.
Number awarded: 6 each year: 2 in each of the 3 categories.
Deadline: January of each year.

2189 OCCUPATIONAL/PHYSICAL THERAPY SCHOLARSHIP

Summary: To provide financial assistance to students working on an undergraduate degree in occupational, physical, art, or music therapy.
See Listing #1436.

2190 $ OHIO AGGREGATES & INDUSTRIAL MINERALS SCHOLARSHIP PROGRAM

Ohio Aggregates & Industrial Minerals Association
Attn: Executive Director
162 North Hamilton Road
Gahanna, OH 43230
Phone: (614) 428–7954; (800) OH–ROCKS; Fax: (614) 428–7919;
Email: patj@oaima.org
Web: www.oaima.org/aws/OAIMA/pt/sp/teacher
Summary: To provide financial assistance to upper–division and graduate students at universities in Ohio who are interested in preparing for a career in the industrial minerals industry.
Eligibility: Open to U.S. citizens from any state who are entering their junior, senior, or fifth undergraduate year at a college or university in Ohio. Applicants must be able to demonstrate interest in a career in the Ohio industrial minerals industry. They must be working on a bachelor's degree in civil engineering, construction materials, or a related field. Graduate students at universities in Ohio whose major focus of study is related to construction materials with an emphasis on mining are also eligible. In the selection process, outstanding academic ability is not required, but students must be in good academic standing with their university; financial need is not required, but students may indicate if they require financial assistance; extracurricular and philanthropic activities are considered.
Financial data: The stipend is at least $2,000.
Duration: 1 year.
Number awarded: 1 or more each year.
Deadline: October of each year.

2191 $ OHIO ASPHALT SCHOLARSHIP PROGRAM

Flexible Pavements of Ohio
Attn: Ohio Asphalt Scholarship Fund
525 Metro Place North, Suite 101
Dublin, OH 43017–5504
Phone: (614) 791–3600; (888) 4–HOTMIX; Fax: (614) 791–4800;
Email: info@flexiblepavements.org
Web: www.flexiblepavements.org/scholarships/hma–scholarships–program
Summary: To provide financial assistance to undergraduate and graduate students at colleges and universities in Ohio who are interested in preparing for a career in a field related to asphalt pavement technology.
Eligibility: Open to students entering their junior, senior, or fifth year of study in a civil engineering, construction management, or construction engineering curriculum at a participating university in Ohio. Applicants should be able to demonstrate interest in a career in the transportation industry. Preference is given to students who show an interest in the design and construction of Ohio's highways and transportation facilities. The university must offer, and the student must take, at least 1 course on hot mix asphalt technology. Graduate students with their major focus of study related to asphalt and attending an Ohio university or college are also considered. All applicants must be full–time students and U.S. citizens. Selection is based on past academic performance and future potential, leadership and participation in school and community activities, work experience, level of career and educational aspirations in the transportation industry, goals, and special personal or family circumstances. Although it is not a requirement, applicants should indicate if there is a need for financial assistance.
Financial data: The stipend is $1,200 per year for undergraduates or $2,000 for graduate students.
Duration: 1 year; may be renewed for up to 2 years or until graduation, whichever comes first.
Number awarded: Varies each year; recently, 24 undergraduate scholarships and 1 graduate fellowship were awarded.
Deadline: January of each year.

2192 OHIO NURSE EDUCATION ASSISTANCE LOAN PROGRAM FOR NURSES

Ohio Board of Regents
Attn: State Grants and Scholarships
30 East Broad Street, 36th Floor
Columbus, OH 43215–3414
Phone: (614) 466–3561; (888) 833–1133; Fax: (614) 466–5866;
Email: hotline@regents.state.oh.us
Web: ohiohighered.org/nealp
Summary: To provide funding to students in Ohio who intend to study nursing.
Eligibility: Open to Ohio residents who are enrolled at least half time in an approved nursing education program in Ohio. Applicants must demonstrate financial need and intend to engage in direct clinical practice as a registered nurse or licensed practical nurse following graduation. U.S. citizenship or permanent resident status is required.
Financial data: The maximum award is currently $1,500 per year. This is a scholarship/loan program; up to 100% of the loan may be forgiven at the rate of 20% per year if the recipient serves as a nurse under specified conditions for up to 5 years. If the loan is not repaid with service, it must be repaid in cash with interest at the rate of 8% per year.
Duration: 1 year; renewable for up to 3 additional years.

Number awarded: Varies each year; recently, 35 students received benefits through this program.
Deadline: July of each year.

2193 OHIO OCCUPATIONAL THERAPY ASSOCIATION SCHOLARSHIPS

American Occupational Therapy Foundation
Attn: Scholarship Coordinator
4720 Montgomery Lane
P.O. Box 31220
Bethesda, MD 20824–1220
Phone: (301) 652–6611, ext. 2550; Fax: (301) 656–3620; TDD: (800) 377–8555;
Email: JCooper@aotf.org
Web: www.aotf.org/scholarshipsgrants/scholarshipprogram.aspx
Summary: To provide financial assistance to students in Ohio who are working on an associate or professional master's degree in occupational therapy.
Eligibility: Open to Ohio residents who are enrolled in an accredited occupational therapy educational program in the state at the associate or professional master's degree level. Applicants must be able to demonstrate a sustained record of outstanding scholastic performance. Selection is based on academic merit and leadership potential; financial need is not considered.
Financial data: The stipend is $1,000.
Duration: 1 year.
Number awarded: 2 each year: 1 to an associate degree student and 1 to a professional master's degree student.
Deadline: November of each year.

2194 $$ OHIO SOYBEAN COUNCIL FOUNDATION UNDERGRADUATE SCHOLARSHIPS

Ohio Soybean Council
Attn: Foundation
918 Proprietors Road, Suite A
Worthington, OH 43085
Phone: (614) 476–3100; (888) SOY–OHIO; Fax: (614) 476–9576;
Email: tfontana@soyohio.org
Web: associationdatabase.com/aws/OHSOY/pt/sp/osc_foundation_programs
Summary: To provide financial assistance to residents of Ohio enrolled at a college in the state and preparing for a career in science and technology as related to agriculture.
Eligibility: Open to residents of Ohio enrolled full time at colleges and universities in the state as sophomores or higher. Applicants must be preparing for a career focused on the application of science and technology to agriculture. They must have a GPA of 3.0 or higher. Eligible majors include agricultural science, agricultural engineering, agricultural communications, agricultural business, biochemistry, bioengineering, chemical engineering, or a related field. Selection is based on merit. The highest ranked applicant receives the Bhima Vijayendran Scholarship.
Financial data: Stipends are $5,000 or $3,000. Funds are paid directly to the recipients' institutions.
Duration: 1 year; recipients may reapply.
Number awarded: 5 each year: 1 at $5,000 (the Bhima Vijayendran Scholarship) and 4 at $3,000.
Deadline: January of each year.

2195 OKLAHOMA CATTLEWOMEN'S SCHOLARSHIP

Oklahoma CattleWomen, Inc.
P.O. Box 82395
Oklahoma City, OK 73148
Phone: (405) 235–4391; Fax: (405) 235–3608
Web: okcattlewomen.org/scholarships
Summary: To provide financial assistance to upper–division students working on a food–related degree at colleges in Oklahoma.
Eligibility: Open to juniors and seniors at colleges and universities in Oklahoma. Applicants must be majoring in food and nutrition, food science, or other food–related field with an interest in the production and consumption of beef. They must have a GPA of 3.0 or higher and be able to demonstrate financial need. Along with their application, they must submit an essay, up to 50 words in length, on why beef is important for a well–balanced diet.
Financial data: The stipend is $1,250.
Duration: 1 year.
Number awarded: 1 each year.
Deadline: April of each year.

2196 OKLAHOMA SOCIETY OF LAND SURVEYORS SCHOLARSHIPS

Oklahoma Society of Land Surveyors
Attn: Scholarship Fund
13905 Twin Ridge Road
Edmonds, OK 73034
Phone: (405) 202–5792; Fax: (405) 330–3432;
Email: osls@osls.org
Web: www.osls.org/displaycommon.cfm?an=1&subarticlenbr=7
Summary: To provide financial assistance to Oklahoma high school seniors who are interested in studying surveying at a college in any state.
Eligibility: Open to seniors graduating from high schools in Oklahoma. Applicants must be interested in preparing for a career as a Registered Professional Land Surveyor. They must have a GPA of 2.5 or higher and an ACT score of 19 or higher with a strong emphasis on mathematics. Also eligible are associate members of the Oklahoma Society of Land Surveyors who are currently working under the direct supervision of a Registered Professional Surveyor. Applicants must submit short essays on how they became interested in land surveying, their long–term goals in the field of land surveying, what they can contribute to the Oklahoma Society of Land Surveyors, and how they will take a leadership role in the future of surveying. Financial need is not considered in the selection process.
Financial data: A stipend is awarded (amount not specified).
Duration: 1 year.
Number awarded: Varies each year.
Deadline: April of each year.

2197 OLIVE LYNN SALEMBIER MEMORIAL REENTRY SCHOLARSHIP

Society of Women Engineers
Attn: Scholarship Selection Committee
203 North LaSalle Street, Suite 1675
Chicago, IL 60601–1269
Phone: (312) 596–5223; (877) SWE–INFO; Fax: (312) 644–8557;
Email: scholarships@swe.org
Web: societyofwomenengineers.swe.org/index.php/scholarships
Summary: To provide financial assistance to women interested in returning to college or graduate school to study engineering or computer science.
Eligibility: Open to women who are planning to enroll at an ABET–accredited 4–year college or university. Applicants must have been out of the engineering workforce and school for at least 2 years and must be planning to return as an undergraduate or graduate student to major in computer science or engineering. They must have a GPA of 3.0 or higher. Selection is based on merit.
Financial data: The award is $1,500.
Duration: 1 year; may be renewed up to 3 additional years.
Number awarded: 1 each year.
Deadline: February of each year.

2198 $ OLIVER JOEL AND ELLEN PELL DENNY HEALTHCARE SCHOLARSHIP FUND

Winston–Salem Foundation
Attn: Student Aid Department
860 West Fifth Street
Winston–Salem, NC 27101–2506
Phone: (336) 714–3445; (866) 227–1209; Fax: (336) 727–0581;
Email: StudentAid@wsfoundation.org
Web: www.wsfoundation.org/netcommunity/page.aspx?pid=854
Summary: To provide financial assistance to residents of North Carolina working on a degree or certificate in fields related to health care at a college or university in the state.
Eligibility: Open to North Carolina residents working on a certificate, diploma, or bachelor's or associate degree in health care fields, including (but not limited to) registered nursing, licensed practical nursing, nuclear medicine, radiography, and respiratory therapy. Applicants must be attending or planning to attend a 2– or 4–year college or university in North Carolina as a traditional or nontraditional student. They must have a cumulative GPA of 2.5 or higher in health care classes and be able to demonstrate financial need. Preference is given to residents of Davidson, Davie, Forsyth, Stokes, Surry, and Yadkin counties. Some of the scholarships are set aside for eligible noncitizens.
Financial data: The stipend ranges up to $3,000 per year.
Duration: 1 year; may be renewed.
Number awarded: 1 or more each year, including 5 scholarships set aside for eligible noncitizens.
Deadline: August of each year.

2199 $$ OLIVIA M. SAYLOR SCHOLARSHIP

The Race for Education
Attn: Student Services Manager
1818 Versailles Road
P.O. Box 11355
Lexington, KY 40575
Phone: (859) 252–8648; Fax: (859) 252–8030;
Email: info@raceforeducation.org
Web: raceforeducation.org/scholarships

Summary: To provide financial assistance to residents of New York attending college in the state to prepare for a career in the equine industry.

Eligibility: Open to undergraduate students under 24 years of age who are residents of New York. Applicants must be attending a college or university in the state to prepare for a career in the thoroughbred industry. Fields of study may include (but are not limited to) equine science, equine business management, farrier school, or equine–related agriculture programs. They must have a GPA of 2.85 or higher and a household income of less than $75,000 per year. Along with their application, they must submit a 500–word essay on 1 of the following topics: 1) the last book they read for enjoyment only, why they chose it, and what they learned from it; 2) a facet of thoroughbred racing that interests them and why; or 3) their interests outside the equine industry or chosen career field.

Financial data: The stipend covers payment of tuition, to a maximum of $6,000 per year. The student is responsible for all other fees.

Duration: 1 year; may be renewed up to 3 additional years, provided the recipient maintains a GPA of 3.0 or higher.

Number awarded: 1 each year.

Deadline: March of each year.

2200 $$ OLMSTED SCHOLARS PROGRAM

Summary: To provide financial assistance to upper–division and graduate students in landscape architecture who demonstrate outstanding potential for leadership.

See Listing #1441.

2201 OMAHA VOLUNTEERS FOR HANDICAPPED CHILDREN SCHOLARSHIPS

Summary: To provide financial assistance to Nebraska residents who have a physical disability or are preparing for a career related to people with orthopedic impairments or physical disabilities and are interested in attending college in any state.

See Listing #727.

2202 OMEGA MASON/MAUDE BISSON NURSING SCHOLARSHIP

Auxiliary to the National Medical Association
8403 Colesville Road, Suite 920
Silver Spring, MD 20910
Phone: (301) 495–3779; Fax: (301) 495–0037;
Email: anmanationaloffice@earthlink.net
Web: www.anmanet.org

Summary: To provide financial assistance to African American nursing students.

Eligibility: Open to African Americans who are currently enrolled in an accredited nursing school, have earned a GPA of 3.2 or higher, are able to demonstrate financial need, and have a record of community involvement. For 2–year nursing programs, applicants must be second–year students; for 4–year programs, applicants must be entering their third year. In addition to completing a formal application, students must submit a 1–page essay detailing their educational goals and reasons for requesting this scholarship. The scholarship is awarded to a student nurse in the city where the national convention of the Auxiliary to the National Medical Association (ANMA) is held each year.

Financial data: A stipend is awarded (amount not specified).

Duration: 1 year.

Number awarded: 1 each year.

Deadline: April of each year.

2203 $ ONCOLOGY NURSING CERTIFICATION CORPORATION BACHELOR'S SCHOLARSHIPS

Oncology Nursing Society
Attn: ONS Foundation
125 Enterprise Drive
Pittsburgh, PA 15275–1214
Phone: (412) 859–6100; (866) 257–4ONS; Fax: (412) 859–6163;
Email: info@onsfoundation.org
Web: www.onsfoundation.org/apply/ed/Bachelors

Summary: To provide financial assistance to nurses and other students who are interested in working on a bachelor's degree in oncology nursing.

Eligibility: Open to students who are accepted to or currently enrolled in a bachelor's degree program at an NLN– or CCNE–accredited school of nursing. Applicants must be able to demonstrate an interest in and commitment to oncology nursing. They may 1) already have a current license to practice as a registered nurse (R.N.); 2) currently have a postsecondary degree at some level but not be an R.N.; or 3) have only a high school diploma. Along with their application, they must submit 1) an essay of 250 words or less on their role or interest in caring for persons with cancer; and 2) a statement of their professional goals and the relationship of those goals to the advancement of oncology nursing. Non–R.N. applicants must be in the nursing component of the B.S.N. program. High school students and individuals in the liberal arts component of a B.S.N. program are not eligible. Financial need is not considered in the selection process.

Financial data: The stipend is $2,000.

Duration: 1 year; nonrenewable.

Number awarded: Varies each year; recently, 8 of these scholarships were awarded.

Deadline: January of each year.

2204 $ ONCOLOGY PRACTICE ALLIANCE SCHOLARSHIP

Oncology Nursing Society
Attn: ONS Foundation
125 Enterprise Drive
Pittsburgh, PA 15275–1214
Phone: (412) 859–6100; (866) 257–4ONS; Fax: (412) 859–6163;
Email: info@onsfoundation.org
Web: www.onsfoundation.org/apply/ed/Bachelors

Summary: To provide financial assistance to residents of Ohio and West Virginia who are interested in working on a bachelor's degree in oncology nursing.

Eligibility: Open to residents of Ohio and West Virginia who are currently enrolled in the nursing component of a bachelor's degree program at an NLN–accredited school of nursing. Applicants must be able to demonstrate an interest in and commitment to oncology nursing. Along with their application, they must submit 1) an essay of 250 words or less on their interest in caring for persons with cancer; and 2) a statement of their professional goals and the relationship of those goals to the advancement of oncology nursing. High school students and individuals in the liberal arts component of a B.S.N. program are not eligible. Financial need is not considered in the selection process.

Financial data: The stipend is $2,000.

Duration: 1 year; nonrenewable.

Number awarded: 1 each year.

Deadline: January of each year.

2205 $ OREGON FOUNDATION FOR BLACKTAIL DEER OUTDOOR AND WILDLIFE SCHOLARSHIP

Oregon Student Access Commission
Attn: Grants and Scholarships Division
1500 Valley River Drive, Suite 100
Eugene, OR 97401–2146
Phone: (541) 687–7395; (800) 452–8807, ext. 7395; Fax: (541) 687–7414; TDD: (800) 735–2900;
Email: awardinfo@osac.state.or.us
Web: www.oregonstudentaid.gov/scholarships.aspx

Summary: To provide financial assistance to high school seniors in Oregon interested in studying fields related to wildlife management at a college in the state.

Eligibility: Open to seniors graduating from high schools in Oregon and planning to attend college in the state. Applicants must be interested in majoring in forestry, biology, wildlife science, or a related field to prepare for a career in wildlife management. They must be able to demonstrate financial need. As part of the application process, they must submit a 250–word essay on "Challenges of Wildlife Management in the Coming 10 Years" and a copy of their previous year's hunting license.

Financial data: Stipends for scholarships offered by the Oregon Student Access Commission (OSAC) range from $200 to $10,000 but recently averaged $2,300.

Duration: 1 year.

Number awarded: Varies each year; recently, 4 of these scholarships were awarded.
Deadline: February of each year.

2206 OREGON LEGION AUXILIARY DEPARTMENT NURSES SCHOLARSHIP

American Legion Auxiliary
Department of Oregon
30450 S.W. Parkway Avenue
P.O. Box 1730
Wilsonville, OR 97070–1730
Phone: (503) 682–3162; Fax: (503) 685–5008;
Email: contact@alaoregon.org
Web: www.alaoregon.org

Summary: To provide financial assistance to the wives, widows, and children of Oregon veterans who are interested in studying nursing at a school in any state.
Eligibility: Open to Oregon residents who are the wives or children of veterans with disabilities or the widows of deceased veterans. Applicants must have been accepted by an accredited hospital or university school of nursing in any state. Selection is based on ability, aptitude, character, determination, seriousness of purpose, and financial need.
Financial data: The stipend is $1,500.
Duration: 1 year; may be renewed.
Number awarded: 1 each year.
Deadline: May of each year.

2207 OREGON SHEEP GROWERS ASSOCIATION SCHOLARSHIP

Oregon Sheep Growers Association, Inc.
1270 Chemeketa Street, N.E.
Salem, OR 97301–4145
Phone: (503) 364–5462; Fax: (503) 585–1921
Web: www.sheeporegon.com/scholarship.html

Summary: To provide financial assistance to Oregon residents who are attending college in any state to prepare for a career in the sheep industry.
Eligibility: Open to Oregon residents who are currently enrolled in a college or university in any state as an undergraduate sophomore or above or as a graduate student. Applicants must be working on a degree in agricultural science or veterinary medicine and be interested in a career in the sheep industry. Financial need is not considered in the selection process.
Financial data: Stipends range up to $1,000 per year. Funds are to be used to pay for tuition, books, or academic fees. Checks are made payable jointly to the recipient and the recipient's institution.
Duration: 1 year.
Number awarded: Up to 2 each year.
Deadline: June of each year.

2208 OUTPUTLINKS SUSTAINABILITY/STEWARDSHIP AWARD

Summary: To provide financial assistance to undergraduate and graduate students from any country who are working on a degree in the field of document management and graphic communications, especially those who are involved in environmental sustainability project or who have a record of leadership and community involvement.
See Listing #1445.

2209 $$ OUTPUTLINKS WOMAN OF DISTINCTION AWARD

Summary: To provide financial assistance to female undergraduate and graduate students from any country interested in preparing for a career in document management and graphic communications.
See Listing #1446.

2210 OUTREACH SCHOLARSHIP OF THE JUVENILE DIABETES RESEARCH FOUNDATION

Diabetes Scholars Foundation
2118 Plum Grove Road, Suite 356
Rolling Meadows, IL 60008
Phone: (312) 215–9861; Fax: (847) 991–8739;
Email: collegescholarships@diabetesscholars.org
Web: www.diabetesscholars.org/college.html

Summary: To provide financial assistance to high school seniors who have diabetes and plan to major in a field related to mental health in college.
Eligibility: Open to graduating high school seniors who have Type 1 diabetes and plan to attend an accredited 4–year university, college, or technical/trade school in any state. Applicants must be planning to major in psychology, social work, or other field related to mental health. They must be able to demonstrate active involvement in the diabetes community, academic performance, participation in community and/or extracurricular activities, and successful management of the challenges of living with diabetes. Financial need is not considered in the selection process. U.S. citizenship or permanent resident status is required.
Financial data: The stipend is $1,000.
Duration: 1 year.
Number awarded: 1 each year.
Deadline: May of each year.

2211 PACIFIC NORTHWEST CHAPTER ARPAS SCHOLARSHIP

American Registry of Professional Animal Scientists–Pacific Northwest Chapter
c/o Joe Harrison
Washington State University at Puyallup
Department of Animal Sciences
2606 West Pioneer
Puyallup, WA 98371
Phone: (253) 445–4638;
Email: jhharison@wsu.edu

Summary: To provide financial assistance to upper–division students at colleges in the Pacific Northwest who are preparing for a career in animal nutrition.
Eligibility: Open to juniors and seniors at universities in the Pacific Northwest who are majoring in animal science or dairy science. Applicants must have demonstrated an interest in preparing for a career in animal nutrition or the livestock feed industry; work experience in those areas is highly desirable. They must have a GPA of 3.2 or higher. Along with their application, they must submit a statement of their career goals. Financial need is not considered in the selection process.
Financial data: The stipend is $1,000.
Duration: 1 year.
Number awarded: 1 each year.
Deadline: May of each year.

2212 $ PACIFIC NORTHWEST SECTION AWWA SCHOLARSHIP

American Water Works Association–Pacific Northwest Section
c/o Dave Leland, Public Health Division Chair
Oregon Drinking Water Program
800 N.E. Oregon Avenue
Portland, OR 97232
Phone: (971) 673–0415; Fax: (971) 673–0457;
Email: david.e.leland@state.or.us
Web: www.pnws–awwa.org/files/scholarships.html

Summary: To provide financial assistance to students who reside or attend college or graduate school in the states served by the Pacific Northwest Section of the American Water Works Association (AWWA) and are preparing for a career in the water works profession.
Eligibility: Open to residents of Idaho, Oregon, and Washington and to students attending college or graduate school in those states. Applicants must be preparing for a career in the water works profession as a second–year student at a community college, a second– or third–year undergraduate, or a graduate student. Along with their application, they must submit 1–paragraph statements on 1) their educational goals; 2) their career goals and any relevant experience; and 3) why they deserve a scholarship. Selection is based on those statements, academic record, and community service.
Financial data: Stipends vary; recently, they averaged approximately $2,500.
Duration: 1 year.
Number awarded: Varies each year; recently, 9 students received scholarships worth $22,750.
Deadline: February of each year.

2213 PACIFIC REGION OF NATIONAL GARDEN CLUBS SCHOLARSHIP

National Garden Clubs, Inc.–Pacific Region
c/o Kristie Livreri, Scholarship Chair
5608 Great Gorge Court

Las Vegas, NV 89107
Email: Info@PacificRegionGardenClubs.org
Web: www.pacificregiongardenclubs.org/scholarship.htm
Summary: To provide financial assistance to residents of states that are part of the Pacific Region of the National Garden Clubs who are working on an undergraduate or graduate degree in a field related to horticulture.
Eligibility: Open to full–time college juniors, seniors, and master's degree students who are residents of Alaska, Arizona, California, Hawaii, Idaho, Nevada, Oregon, or Washington (the states that comprise the Pacific Region of National Garden Clubs). Applicants must be working on a degree in horticulture, floriculture, landscape design, conservation, forestry, botany, agronomy, plant pathology, environmental control, city planning, land management, alternative energy, or allied subjects. They may be enrolled at a college or university in any state, but they must have a GPA of 3.25 or higher. Along with their application, they must submit a 2–page letter discussing their career goals, educational background, financial need, and personal commitment to their chosen field of study. Selection is based on academic record (40%), the letter (25%), a list of honors, extracurricular activities, and work experience (10%), financial need (20%), and recommendations (5%).
Financial data: The stipend is $1,000.
Duration: 1 year.
Number awarded: 1 each year.
Deadline: Applications must be submitted to the appropriate state garden club scholarship chair by January of each year.

2214 $$ PALADIN BUILDING SCIENCES SCHOLARSHIP

Summary: To provide financial assistance to students transferring from an institution within the Kentucky Community and Technical College System (KCTCS) to a 4–year university in Kentucky and majoring in the building sciences.
See Listing #1450.

2215 $ PARSONS BRICKERHOFF–JIM LAMMIE SCHOLARSHIP

American Public Transportation Association
Attn: American Public Transportation Foundation
1666 K Street, N.W., Suite 1100
Washington, DC 20006
Phone: (202) 496–4803; Fax: (202) 496–4323;
Email: yconley@apta.com
Web: www.aptfd.org/work/scholarship.htm
Summary: To provide financial assistance to undergraduate and graduate students who are preparing for a career in public transportation engineering.
Eligibility: Open to college sophomores, juniors, seniors, and graduate students who are preparing for an engineering career in the transit industry. Any member organization of the American Public Transportation Association (APTA) can nominate and sponsor candidates for this scholarship. Nominees must be enrolled in a fully–accredited institution, have and maintain at least a 3.0 GPA, and be either employed by or demonstrate a strong interest in entering the public transportation industry as an engineer. They must submit a 1,000–word essay on the topic, "In what segment of the public transportation industry will you make a career and why?" Selection is based on demonstrated interest in the transit field as a career, need for financial assistance, academic achievement, essay content and quality, and involvement in extracurricular citizenship and leadership activities.
Financial data: The stipend is $2,500.
Duration: 1 year; may be renewed.
Number awarded: 1 each year.
Deadline: May of each year.

2216 PATRICIA SONNTAG MEMORIAL SCHOLARSHIP

California Association for Postsecondary Education and Disability
Attn: Executive Assistant
71423 Biskra Road
Rancho Mirage, CA 92270
Phone: (760) 346–8206; Fax: (760) 340–5275; TDD: (760) 341–4084;
Email: caped2000@aol.com
Web: www.caped.net/scholarships.html
Summary: To provide financial assistance to students enrolled at 4–year college and universities in California who have a disability and are involved in activities or classes related to providing services to people with disabilities.
Eligibility: Open to students at 4–year colleges and universities in California who have a disability. Applicants must have completed at least 6 semester credits with a GPA of 2.5 or higher. They must be majoring in a field related to policy formulation or service delivery to students with disabilities or be actively engaged in advocacy or leadership in campus, community, or governmental organizations that benefit individuals with disabilities, regardless of their major. Along with their application, they must submit a 1–page personal letter that demonstrates their writing skills, progress towards meeting their educational and vocational goals, management of their disability, and involvement in community activities. They must also submit a letter of recommendation from a faculty member, verification of disability, official transcripts, proof of current enrollment, and documentation of financial need.
Financial data: The stipend is $1,000.
Duration: 1 year.
Number awarded: 1 each year.
Deadline: September of each year.

2217 $ PAUL A. WHELAN AVIATION SCHOLARSHIP

University Aviation Association
3410 Skyway Drive
Auburn, AL 36830–6444
Phone: (334) 844–2434; Fax: (334) 844–2432;
Email: uaamail@uaa.aero
Web: www.uaa.aero/default.aspx?scid=LVE776fHv6g=&mp=0
Summary: To provide financial assistance to students working on an undergraduate or graduate degree in aviation or a space–related field.
Eligibility: Open to sophomores, juniors, seniors, and graduate students who are currently enrolled at a college, university, or community college affiliated with the University Aviation Association (UAA). Applicants must be majoring in aviation or a space–related field and have a GPA of 2.5 or higher overall and 3.0 in their aviation courses. They must be able to demonstrate a love of aviation, extracurricular and community involvement, and leadership. Preference is given to applicants who have Federal Aviation Administration certification as a pilot or mechanic; former or current military service through active duty, ROTC, Air National Guard, or Reserves while in school; or membership in an aviation–related association or professional group. U.S. citizenship is required.
Financial data: The stipend is $2,000.
Duration: 1 year.
Number awarded: 1 each year.
Deadline: May of each year.

2218 PAUL AND ELLEN RUCKES SCHOLARSHIP

American Foundation for the Blind
Attn: Scholarship Committee
2 Penn Plaza, Suite 1102
New York, NY 10121
Phone: (212) 502–7661; (800) AFB–LINE; Fax: (888) 545–8331;
Email: afbinfo@afb.net
Web: www.afb.org/Section.asp?Documentid=2962
Summary: To provide financial assistance to legally blind students who wish to work on a graduate or undergraduate degree in engineering or computer, physical, or life sciences.
Eligibility: Open to legally blind undergraduate or graduate students who are U.S. citizens working or planning to work full time on a degree in engineering or the computer, physical, or life sciences. Along with their application, they must submit 200–word essays on 1) their past and recent achievements and accomplishments; 2) their intended field of study and why they have chosen it; and 3) the role their visual impairment has played in shaping their life. Financial need is considered in the selection process.
Financial data: The stipend is $1,000.
Duration: 1 year.
Number awarded: 1 each year.
Deadline: April of each year.

2219 PAUL AND HELEN L. GRAUER SCHOLARSHIP

Summary: To provide financial assistance to licensed radio amateurs, especially those from designated midwestern states, who are interested in working on an undergraduate or graduate degree, preferably in electronics or communications.
See Listing #1452.

2220 PAUL COLE SCHOLARSHIP AWARD

Society of Nuclear Medicine and Molecular Imaging
Attn: Grants and Awards
1850 Samuel Morse Drive
Reston, VA 20190–5316

Phone: (703) 708–9000, ext. 1253; Fax: (703) 708–9015;
Email: kpadleyh@snmmi.org
Web: www.snm.org/index.cfm?pageid=1083

Summary: To provide financial support to students seeking training in nuclear medicine technology.

Eligibility: Open to students in baccalaureate, associate, or certificate programs in nuclear medicine technology. Applicants must have a cumulative GPA of 2.5 or higher. Selection is based on financial need and academic achievement.

Financial data: The stipend is $1,000.

Duration: 1 year.

Number awarded: Varies each year; recently, 15 of these scholarships were awarded: 8 for students working on a bachelor's degree, 3 for students working on an associate degree, and 4 for students working on a certificate.

Deadline: April of each year.

2221 PAUL S. ROBINSON LEADERSHIP AWARD

Wisconsin Academy of Physician Assistants
Attn: WAPA Foundation
563 Carter Court, Suite B
Kimberly, WI 54136
Phone: (920) 560–5630; (800) 762–8965; Fax: (920) 882–3655;
Email: wapa@wapa.org
Web: www.wapa.org/About–WAPA/WAPA–Foundation/Awards–and–Nominations

Summary: To recognize and reward physician assistant (PA) students in Wisconsin who demonstrate outstanding leadership.

Eligibility: Open to students enrolled in their final year of a PA program in Wisconsin. Applicants must demonstrate outstanding leadership in the community, profession, program, or campus. Along with their application, they must submit a personal statement listing and describing the depth and time of leadership provided. Selection is based on that statement and 2 letters of recommendation.

Financial data: The award is $1,000.

Duration: 1 year.

Number awarded: 1 each year.

Deadline: June of each year.

2222 $ PCI ENGINEERING STUDENT DESIGN "BIG BEAM" COMPETITION

Precast/Prestressed Concrete Institute
Attn: Director of Educational Activities
200 West Adams Street, Suite 2100
Chicago, IL 60606
Phone: (312) 360–3219; Fax: (312) 621–1114
Web: pci.org/cms/index.cfm/education/big_beam/index

Summary: To recognize and reward engineering students who submit outstanding entries in a competition for precast concrete beams.

Eligibility: Open to students enrolled in a 2–year degree program, a 4– or 5–year bachelor's degree program, or a graduate degree program in any of the following areas: civil engineering (including all sub–disciplines) or technology; construction engineering or technology; architecture, architectural engineering, or technology; or building sciences or technology. Students enter as teams, preferably of 3 or 4 members, although any size is acceptable; graduate and undergraduate students and/or students from different degree programs within a university or college may be on the same team. Each team must work with a producer member of the Precast/Prestressed Concrete Institute (PCI) to build a precast concrete beam that is 18 feet long and tested as a 16–foot span. Points are awarded in 7 categories (design accuracy, lowest cost, lowest weight, largest measured deflection at maximum total applied load, most accurate prediction of cracking load and deflection at maximum load, report quality, and practicality/innovation). Prizes are awarded to teams with the highest scores. The open division accepts entries that do not conform to the traditional standards but utilize innovative and original designs.

Financial data: Prizes range up to $2,000.

Duration: The competition is held annually.

Number awarded: Prizes are awarded to individual zone winners and overall winners from 7 zones and to the winners in the open division.

Deadline: March of each year.

2223 $ PDEF MICKEY WILLIAMS MINORITY STUDENT SCHOLARSHIPS

Society of Nuclear Medicine and Molecular Imaging
Attn: Grants and Awards
1850 Samuel Morse Drive
Reston, VA 20190–5316
Phone: (703) 708–9000, ext. 1253; Fax: (703) 708–9015;
Email: kpadleyh@snmmi.org
Web: www.snm.org/index.cfm?pageid=1083

Summary: To provide financial support to minority students working on an associate or bachelor's degree in nuclear medicine technology.

Eligibility: Open to students accepted or enrolled in a baccalaureate or associate degree program in nuclear medicine technology. Applicants must be members of a minority group: African American, Native American (including American Indian, Eskimo, Hawaiian, and Samoan), Hispanic American, Asian American, or Pacific Islander. They must have a cumulative GPA of 2.5 or higher and be able to demonstrate financial need. Along with their application, they must submit an essay on their reasons for entering the nuclear medicine technology field, their career goals, and their financial need. U.S. citizenship or permanent resident status is required.

Financial data: The stipend is $2,500.

Duration: 1 year; may be renewed for 1 additional year.

Number awarded: Varies each year; recently, 2 of these scholarships were awarded.

Deadline: April of each year.

2224 PEG GRINNUS SCHOLARSHIP

Virginia Federation of Garden Clubs
c/o Lisa Robinson, Scholarship Chair
315 Tulip Tree Lane
Moneta, VA 24121–2011
Phone: (540) 266–3083;
Email: gardenlisa@r22sml.com
Web: www.virginiagardenclubs.org/VFGC/Scholarships.html

Summary: To provide financial assistance to residents of Virginia who are enrolled at a university in any state and working on a degree in landscape design.

Eligibility: Open to undergraduate and graduate students enrolled at colleges and universities in any state who are residents of Virginia. Applicants must be working on a degree in landscape design and have a garden–related career goal. Along with their application, they must submit a letter discussing their goals, background, personal commitment, and financial need.

Financial data: A stipend is awarded (amount not specified).

Duration: 1 year.

Number awarded: 1 each year.

Deadline: January of each year.

2225 $ PENNSYLVANIA SCITECH SCHOLARSHIPS

Pennsylvania Higher Education Assistance Agency
Attn: Special Programs
1200 North Seventh Street
P.O. Box 8157
Harrisburg, PA 17105–8157
Phone: (717) 720–2800; (800) 692–7392; Fax: (717) 720–5786; TDD: (800) 654–5988;
Email: nets@pheaa.org
Web: www.pheaa.org

Summary: To provide funding to residents of Pennsylvania who are interested in studying approved science or technology fields at a public or private college or university in the state and then working in the state after graduation.

Eligibility: Open to residents of Pennsylvania who graduated from a high school in the state and are currently enrolled full time as at least a sophomore at an approved Pennsylvania public or private college or university. Applicants must be working on a bachelor's degree in an approved science or technology field and have a GPA of 3.0 or higher. They must apply for a federal Pell Grant and a Pennsylvania State Grant, but financial need is not considered in the selection process. Funds are awarded on a first–come, first–served basis.

Financial data: Scholarships provide up to $3,000 per year.

Duration: Up to 3 years, provided the recipient maintains a GPA of 3.0 or higher and full–time enrollment.

Number awarded: Varies each year.

Deadline: December of each year for first–time applicants; September of each year for renewal applicants.

2226 PERENNIAL PLANT ASSOCIATION SCHOLARSHIPS

Perennial Plant Association
Attn: Executive Director

3383 Schirtzinger Road
Hilliard, OH 43026
Phone: (614) 771–8431; Fax: (614) 876–5238;
Email: ppa@perennialplant.org
Web: www.perennialplant.org/education.asp
Summary: To provide financial assistance to undergraduates studying horticulture or a related subject.
Eligibility: Open to college students in a 2– or 4–year program majoring or minoring in horticulture or a related subject. Applicants should have at least 1 quarter or semester remaining, should have at least a 3.0 GPA, and must be able to attend the annual perennial plant symposium. Along with their application, they must submit a statement of purpose, college transcript, and recommendation letters. An interest in perennials is preferred but not required. Financial need is not considered in the selection process.
Financial data: The stipend is $1,000 per year. Funds are sent directly to the recipient's school. Winners also receive complimentary registration and lodging to attend the symposium.
Duration: 1 year.
Number awarded: 5 each year.
Deadline: February of each year.

2227 PETROLEUM DIVISION HIGH SCHOOL SCHOLARSHIPS
International Petroleum Technology Institute
Attn: Student Scholarship Program
11757 Katy Freeway, Suite 865
Houston, TX 77079
Phone: (281) 493–3491; Fax: (281) 493–3493;
Email: watsona@asme.org
Web: asme–ipti.org/petroleum–division/scholarships
Summary: To provide financial assistance to high school seniors planning to major in engineering in college and prepare for a career in the petroleum industry.
Eligibility: Open to high school seniors who have indicated a pre–declared major in the mechanical engineering field on their application to college. Applicants must have a GPA of 3.0 or higher. Along with their application, they must submit a 2–page essay on their interest in the petroleum industry, the challenges the industry offers them, and the value they may add to the industry. Financial need is not considered in the selection process.
Financial data: The stipend is $1,000.
Duration: 1 year.
Number awarded: 8 each year.
Deadline: October of each year.

2228 PFATS–NFL CHARITIES MINORITY SCHOLARSHIPS
Professional Football Athletic Trainers Society
c/o Britt Brown, ATC, Associate Athletic Trainer
Dallas Cowboys
One Cowboys Parkway
Irving, TX 75063
Phone: (972) 556–9992;
Email: bbrown@dallascowboys.net
Web: pfats.com/about/scholarships.aspx
Summary: To provide financial assistance to ethnic minority undergraduate and graduate students working on a degree in athletic training.
Eligibility: Open to ethnic minority students who are working on an undergraduate or graduate degree in athletic training. Applicants must have a GPA of 2.5 or higher. Along with their application, they must submit a cover letter, a curriculum vitae, and a letter of recommendation from their supervising athletic trainer.
Financial data: A stipend is awarded (amount not specified).
Duration: 1 year.
Number awarded: 1 or more each year.
Deadline: March of each year.

2229 $ PHCC EDUCATIONAL FOUNDATION NEED–BASED SCHOLARSHIP
Plumbing–Heating–Cooling Contractors–National Association
Attn: PHCC Educational Foundation
180 South Washington Street
P.O. Box 6808
Falls Church, VA 22040–6808
Phone: (703) 237–8100; (800) 533–7694; Fax: (703) 237–7442;
Email: foundation@naphcc.org
Web: foundation.phccweb.org
Summary: To provide financial assistance to undergraduate students who are interested in the plumbing, heating, and cooling industry and can demonstrate financial need.
Eligibility: Open to 1) full–time undergraduate students (entering or continuing) who are majoring in a field related to plumbing, heating, and cooling (e.g., business management, construction management with a specialization in mechanical construction, mechanical engineering) at a 4–year college or university; 2) students enrolled full time in an approved certificate or degree program at a 2–year technical college, community college, or trade school in business management, mechanical CAD design, construction management with a specialty in mechanical construction, or plumbing or HVACR installation, service, and repair; and 3) full–time employees of a licensed plumbing or HVAC contractor (must be a member of the Plumbing–Heating–Cooling Contractors–National Association–PHCC) who are enrolled in an apprenticeship program in plumbing or HVACR installation, service, and repair. Students majoring in accounting, architecture, computer engineering, construction–related engineering, civil engineering, electrical engineering, or environmental engineering are not eligible. Applicants must have a GPA of 2.0 or higher. Along with their application, they must submit a letter of recommendation from a PHCC member; a copy of school transcripts; SAT and/or ACT scores; documentation of financial need; and a letter of recommendation from a school principal, counselor, or dean. U.S. or Canadian citizenship is required.
Financial data: The stipend is $2,500.
Duration: 1 year.
Number awarded: 1 each year.
Deadline: April of each year.

2230 $ PHCC EDUCATIONAL FOUNDATION SCHOLARSHIP PROGRAM
Plumbing–Heating–Cooling Contractors–National Association
Attn: PHCC Educational Foundation
180 South Washington Street
P.O. Box 6808
Falls Church, VA 22040–6808
Phone: (703) 237–8100; (800) 533–7694; Fax: (703) 237–7442;
Email: foundation@naphcc.org
Web: foundation.phccweb.org
Summary: To provide financial assistance to undergraduate students interested in the plumbing, heating, and cooling industry.
Eligibility: Open to 1) full–time undergraduate students (entering or continuing) who are majoring in a field related to plumbing, heating, and cooling (e.g., business management, construction management with a specialization in mechanical construction, mechanical engineering) at a 4–year college or university; 2) students enrolled full time in an approved certificate or degree program at a 2–year technical college, community college, or trade school in business management, mechanical CAD design, construction management with a specialty in mechanical construction, or plumbing or HVACR installation, service, and repair; and 3) full–time employees of a licensed plumbing or HVAC contractor (must be a member of the Plumbing–Heating–Cooling Contractors–National Association–PHCC) who are enrolled in an apprenticeship program in plumbing or HVACR installation, service, and repair. Students majoring in accounting, architecture, computer engineering, construction–related engineering, civil engineering, electrical engineering, or environmental engineering are not eligible. Applicants must have a GPA of 2.0 or higher. Along with their application, they must submit a letter of recommendation from a PHCC member; a copy of school transcripts; SAT and/or ACT scores; and a letter of recommendation from a school principal, counselor, or dean. U.S. or Canadian citizenship is required. Financial need is not considered in the selection process.
Financial data: Stipends range from $1,000 to $4,000.
Duration: Up to 4 years for students at a 4–year college or university or 2 years for students at a 2–year technical college, community college, or trade school or enrolled in an apprenticeship program.
Number awarded: Varies each year; recently, 22 of these scholarships were available: 1 at $4,000, 4 at $3,000, 13 at $2,500, and 4 at $1,000.
Deadline: April of each year.

2231 $ PHILLIP M. FIELDS SCHOLARSHIP
South Carolina Aquatic Plant Management Society
c/o Steve de Kozlowski, Scholarship Chair
South Carolina Department of Natural Resources
P.O. Box 167

Columbia, SC 29201
Phone: (803) 734–9114;
Email: sdekoz2@gmail.com
Web: www.scapms.org/scapmsscholarship.htm

Summary: To provide funding for study or research to undergraduate and graduate students interested in the biology, ecology, or management of aquatic plants in the Southeast.

Eligibility: Open to full–time undergraduate and graduate students at accredited colleges and universities in the United States. Preference is given to students at southeastern and South Carolina academic institutions. Applicants must be involved in course work or research related to the biology, ecology, or management of aquatic plants in the Southeast. Selection is based on relevant test scores (ACT, SAT, GRE, etc.), high school and/or college grades, quality and relevance of course work or research, a proposed budget, information obtained from references, and other related considerations.

Financial data: The grant is $3,000. Funds may be used by the recipient to cover costs associated with education and research expenses.

Duration: 1 year.

Number awarded: 1 each year.

Deadline: April of each year.

2232 PHILLIPS FAMILY UNDERGRADUATE SCHOLARSHIP FOR METEOROLOGY

National Weather Association
Attn: Executive Director
228 West Millbrook Road
Raleigh, NC 27609–4304
Phone: (919) 845–1546; Fax: (919) 845–2956;
Email: exdir@nwas.org
Web: www.nwas.org/committees/ed_comm/application/index.php

Summary: To provide financial assistance to undergraduate students working on a degree in operational meteorology.

Eligibility: Open to students who are enrolled in any year of undergraduate study. Applicants must be working on a degree in meteorology. Along with their application, they must submit a 1–page statement explaining why they are applying for this scholarship. Selection is based on that statement, academic achievement, and 2 letters of recommendation.

Financial data: The stipend is $1,000.

Duration: 1 year.

Number awarded: 1 each year.

Deadline: October of each year.

2233 $$ PHOENIX POST SAME SCHOLARSHIPS

Summary: To provide financial assistance to residents of Arizona who are interested in working on an undergraduate degree in a field related to the built environment at a college in the state.

See Listing #1459.

2234 PIONEERS OF FLIGHT SCHOLARSHIP PROGRAM

National Air Transportation Foundation
Attn: Manager, Education and Training
4226 King Street
Alexandria, VA 22302
Phone: (703) 845–9000, ext. 125; (800) 808–6282; Fax: (703) 845–8176;
Email: Safety1st@nata.aero
Web: www.nata.aero/About–NATA/Scholarships.aspx

Summary: To provide financial assistance for college to students planning careers in general aviation.

Eligibility: Open to students intending to enroll full time at an accredited 4–year college or university as a junior or senior. Applicants must demonstrate an interest in a career in general aviation (not the major commercial airlines) and have a GPA of 3.0 or higher. Along with their application, they must submit a 250–word essay on their educational and career goals in general aviation. Selection is based on that essay, academic record, and letter of recommendation.

Financial data: The stipend is $1,000.

Duration: 1 year; may be renewed 1 additional year if the recipient maintains a 3.0 GPA and full–time enrollment.

Number awarded: 1 each year.

Deadline: December of each year.

2235 PISCATAQUA POST SAME SCHOLARSHIPS

Summary: To provide financial assistance to residents of Maine, New Hampshire, and Vermont, especially those with ties to the military, who are majoring in designated fields at their state universities.

See Listing #1463.

2236 $ PLANET AEF SCHOLARSHIPS

Summary: To provide financial assistance to students at colleges and universities that have a connection to the Professional Landcare Network (PLANET).

See Listing #1464.

2237 $ PLASTICS PIONEERS ASSOCIATION SCHOLARSHIPS

Society of Plastics Engineers
Attn: SPE Foundation
13 Church Hill Road
Newtown, CT 06740
Phone: (203) 740–5447; Fax: (203) 775–1157;
Email: foundation@4spe.org
Web: www.4spe.org/spe–foundation

Summary: To provide financial assistance to undergraduate students who have a career interest in becoming "hands–on" workers in the plastics industry.

Eligibility: Open to full–time undergraduate students at 4–year colleges or in 2–year technical programs. Applicants must be committed to becoming "hands–on" workers in the plastics industry with a dedication to careers as plastics technicians or engineers. They must be majoring in or taking courses that would be beneficial to a career in the plastics or polymer industry (e.g., plastics engineering, packaging, polymer sciences, chemistry, physics, chemical engineering, mechanical engineering, industrial engineering). Along with their application, they must submit 3 letters of recommendation; a high school and/or college transcript; a 1– to 2–page statement telling why they are applying for the scholarship, their qualifications, and their educational and career goals in the plastics industry; their employment history; a list of current and past school activities and community activities and honors; and information on their financial need. U.S. citizenship is required.

Financial data: The stipend is $3,000. Funds are paid directly to the recipient's school.

Duration: 1 year.

Number awarded: Varies each year; recently, 5 of these scholarships were awarded.

Deadline: February of each year.

2238 $ P.O. PISTILLI SCHOLARSHIPS

Design Automation Conference
c/o Andrew B. Kahng, Scholarship Director
University of California at San Diego–Jacobs School of Engineering
Jacobs Hall, EBU3B, Rpp, 2134
9500 Gilman Drive
La Jolla, CA 92093–0404
Phone: (858) 822–4884; Fax: (858) 534–7029;
Email: abk@cs.ucsd.edu
Web: www.dac.com/p_o_+pistilli+undergraduate+scholarship.aspx

Summary: To provide financial assistance to female, minority, or disabled high school seniors who are interested in preparing for a career in computer science or electrical engineering.

Eligibility: Open to graduating high school seniors who are members of underrepresented groups: women, African Americans, Hispanics, Native Americans, and persons with disabilities. Applicants must be interested in preparing for a career in electrical engineering, computer engineering, or computer science. They must have at least a 3.0 GPA, have demonstrated high achievements in math and science courses, have demonstrated involvement in activities associated with the underrepresented group they represent, and be able to demonstrate significant financial need. U.S. citizenship is not required, but applicants must be U.S. residents when they apply and must plan to attend an accredited U.S. college or university. Along with their application, they must submit 3 letters of recommendation, official transcripts, ACT/SAT and/or PSAT scores, a personal statement outlining future goals and why they think they should receive this scholarship, and documentation of financial need.

Financial data: Stipends are $4,000 per year. Awards are paid each year in 2 equal installments.

Duration: 1 year; may be renewed up to 4 additional years.

Number awarded: 2 to 7 each year.

Deadline: January of each year.

2239 POCKET NURSE SCHOLARSHIP FUND

Pittsburgh Foundation
Attn: Scholarship Coordinator
Five PPG Place, Suite 250
Pittsburgh, PA 15222–5414
Phone: (412) 394–2649; Fax: (412) 391–7259;
Email: turnerd@pghfdn.org
Web: www.pittsburghfoundation.org/node/1695

Summary: To provide financial assistance to residents of any state who are working on a degree in allied health, nursing, or nursing education.

Eligibility: Open to residents of any state who are enrolled in an accredited allied health program, an accredited nursing program, or a nursing graduate program in preparation for a career as a nursing faculty member. Applicants must have a GPA of 3.0 or higher. Along with their application, they must submit a 500–word essay describing a community project related to health care in which they have participated within the past 2 years.

Financial data: A stipend is awarded (amount not specified).

Duration: 1 year.

Number awarded: 3 each year: 1 each in allied health, nursing, and nursing education.

Deadline: May of each year.

2240 $ POLYMER MODIFIERS AND ADDITIVES DIVISION SCHOLARSHIPS

Society of Plastics Engineers
Attn: SPE Foundation
13 Church Hill Road
Newtown, CT 06740
Phone: (203) 740–5447; Fax: (203) 775–1157;
Email: foundation@4spe.org
Web: www.4spe.org/spe–foundation

Summary: To provide financial assistance to undergraduate students who have a career interest in the plastics industry.

Eligibility: Open to full–time undergraduate students at 4–year colleges or in 2–year technical programs. Applicants must be majoring in or taking courses that would be beneficial to a career in the plastics or polymer industry (e.g., plastics engineering, packaging, polymer sciences, chemistry, physics, chemical engineering, mechanical engineering, industrial engineering). Along with their application, they must submit 3 letters of recommendation; a high school and/or college transcript; a 1– to 2–page statement telling why they are applying for the scholarship, their qualifications, and their educational and career goals in the plastics industry; their employment history; a list of current and past school activities and community activities and honors; and information on their financial need.

Financial data: The stipend is $4,000. Funds are paid directly to the recipient's school.

Duration: 1 year.

Number awarded: 4 each year.

Deadline: February of each year.

2241 PORTLAND CHAPTER SCHOLARSHIP

Data Processing Management Association–Portland Chapter
Attn: Scholarship Chair
P.O. Box 61493
Vancouver, WA 98666
Email: wyeaw@phoenixtecnology.us
Web: www.dpmapc.com/scholarship.htm

Summary: To provide financial assistance to high school seniors in Oregon and Clark County, Washington who are interested in studying information technology at a college in those states.

Eligibility: Open to seniors graduating from high schools Oregon or Clark County, Washington. Applicants must be planning to attend college in Oregon or Washington and major in a field directly related to information technology (e.g., CS, CIS). Selection is based on academic performance; career goals related to information technology; counselor or instructor recommendations; previous experience and interest in information technology; completeness, neatness, and presentation of the application; and financial need.

Financial data: The stipend is $1,000.

Duration: 1 year; may be renewed at $500 per year.

Number awarded: At least 1 each year.

Deadline: May of each year.

2242 $$ POTATO SCHOLARSHIP

Syngenta Crop Protection, LLC
410 Swing Road
P.O. Box 18300
Greensboro, NC 27419
Phone: (919) 870–5718; (800) 334–9481;
Email: cmiller@gibbs–soell.com
Web: www.farmassist.com/promo/potato

Summary: To recognize and reward, with college scholarships, students from designated potato–producing states who are involved in potato growing or are members of FFA or 4–H and submit outstanding essays on agriculture.

Eligibility: Open to high school seniors and college freshmen, sophomores, and juniors who either live or attend school in the following potato–producing states: Colorado, Idaho, Maine, Michigan, North Dakota, Oregon, Washington, or Wisconsin. Applicants must either be involved in the potato–growing industry or be members of FFA or 4–H. They must submit an essay, up to 700 words in length, on a topic that changes annually but relates to agriculture in this country; recently, students were asked to give their ideas on how younger people can be motivated to continue their farming legacies. Selection is based on 1) creativity and uniqueness of the idea (30 points), flow and organization of the essay (30 points), functionality and professional appeal (20 points), and absence of grammatical or typographical errors (20 points).

Financial data: The prize is a $5,000 scholarship.

Duration: The competition is held annually.

Number awarded: 1 each year.

Deadline: August of each year.

2243 PRAXAIR SCHOLARSHIPS

Society of Women Engineers
Attn: Scholarship Selection Committee
203 North LaSalle Street, Suite 1675
Chicago, IL 60601–1269
Phone: (312) 596–5223; (877) SWE–INFO; Fax: (312) 644–8557;
Email: scholarships@swe.org
Web: societyofwomenengineers.swe.org/index.php/scholarships

Summary: To provide financial assistance to undergraduate women who are majoring in chemical or mechanical engineering.

Eligibility: Open to society members who are entering their sophomore, junior, or senior year at an ABET–accredited 4–year college or university. Applicants must be working full time on a degree in computer science or chemical or mechanical engineering and have a GPA of 3.2 or higher. Selection is based on merit. Preference is given to groups underrepresented in computer science and engineering.

Financial data: The stipend is $1,000.

Duration: 1 year.

Number awarded: 10 each year.

Deadline: February of each year.

2244 $ PRESSURE VESSELS AND PIPING DIVISION STUDENT PAPER COMPETITION

ASME International
Attn: Pressure Vessels and Piping Division
Three Park Avenue
New York, NY 10016–5990
Phone: (212) 591–7052; (800) THE–ASME; Fax: (212) 591–7671;
Email: McComieJ@asme.org
Web: divisions.asme.org/PVP/Student_Activities.cfm

Summary: To recognize and reward outstanding student papers on pressure vessels and piping.

Eligibility: Open to senior undergraduate and graduate students in engineering or physical sciences. Applicants submit previously unpublished papers that present new knowledge or experience in a field related to pressure vessels and piping. The paper must be technically correct and should be of interest to a reasonable number of people working in the field. It may be theoretical or may present the results of laboratory studies, and it may state or analyze a problem. The paper may also be a review–type paper, but it must be of significant value to the technical field. Applicants first submit abstracts; based on those abstracts, finalists and honorable mentions are invited to present papers at the annual Pressure Vessels and Piping Conference, where the winning papers are selected on the basis of written technical content (70%) and presentation effectiveness (30%). Judging is conducted in 2 categories: 1 for bachelor's and master's degree students and 1 for Ph.D. students.

Financial data: Travel allowances of $1,000 are awarded to the presenting author of each finalist paper and $700 to the presenting author of each honorable mention paper. In addition, in each category, $1,000 is awarded to the presenting author of the outstanding paper, $800 to the presenting author of the first runner–up student paper, and $500 to the presenting author of the second runner–up student paper.
Duration: The competition is held annually.
Number awarded: The number of finalists and honorable mentions varies each year; 6 of them receive additional prizes.
Deadline: Abstracts must be submitted by November of each year.

2245 $ PROFESSIONAL ENGINEERS OF NORTH CAROLINA SCHOLARSHIP

Professional Engineers of North Carolina
Attn: PENC Educational Foundation
1015 Wade Avenue, Suite A
Raleigh, NC 27605
Phone: (919) 834–1144; Fax: (919) 834–1148;
Email: exec@penc.org
Web: www.penc.org/scholarships.aspx

Summary: To provide financial assistance to upper–division students from any state working on a degree in engineering at a campus of the University of North Carolina (UNC).
Eligibility: Open to residents of any state entering their junior or senior year at a campus of the UNC system that has an ABET–accredited program in engineering. Applicants must submit a 500–word essay that discusses their interest in engineering, their major area of study and specialization, the occupation they propose to pursue after graduation, their financial need, their long–term goals, and how the scholarship could help them achieve those goals. Preference is given to members of the National Society of Professional Engineers (NSPE). U.S. citizenship is required.
Financial data: The stipend is $2,000.
Duration: 1 year.
Number awarded: 1 or more each year.
Deadline: March of each year.

2246 $ PROFESSIONAL LAND SURVEYORS OF OREGON SCHOLARSHIP

Oregon Student Access Commission
Attn: Grants and Scholarships Division
1500 Valley River Drive, Suite 100
Eugene, OR 97401–2146
Phone: (541) 687–7395; (800) 452–8807, ext. 7395; Fax: (541) 687–7414; TDD: (800) 735–2900;
Email: awardinfo@osac.state.or.us
Web: www.oregonstudentaid.gov/scholarships.aspx

Summary: To provide financial assistance to students in Oregon interested in a career in land surveying.
Eligibility: Open to residents of Oregon enrolled at colleges and universities in the state. Applicants must be enrolled in a program leading to a career as a land surveyor, including community college applicants who intend to transfer to eligible 4–year schools or complete a degree in land surveying at the community college level. They must intend to take the Fundamentals of Land Surveying (FLS) examination. Along with their application, they must submit a brief essay on what led them to prepare for a land surveying career and what surveying means to them. Financial need is considered in the selection process.
Financial data: Stipends for scholarships offered by the Oregon Student Access Commission (OSAC) range from $200 to $10,000 but recently averaged $2,300.
Duration: 1 year.
Number awarded: Varies each year; recently, 5 of these scholarships were awarded.
Deadline: February of each year.

2247 $ PROMISE OF NURSING SCHOLARSHIPS

National Student Nurses' Association
Attn: Foundation
45 Main Street, Suite 606
Brooklyn, NY 11201
Phone: (718) 210–0705; Fax: (718) 797–1186;
Email: nsna@nsna.org
Web: www.nsna.org/FoundationScholarships/FNSNAScholarships.aspx

Summary: To provide financial assistance to nursing or pre–nursing students at schools in selected geographic locations.
Eligibility: Open to students currently enrolled in state–approved schools of nursing or pre–nursing associate degree, baccalaureate, diploma, generic master's, generic doctoral, R.N. to B.S.N., R.N. to M.S.N., or L.P.N./L.V.N. to R.N. programs. Graduating high school seniors are not eligible. Support for graduate education is provided only for a first degree in nursing. Applicants must be attending school in the Houston/Galveston area of Texas (Austin, Brazoria, Chambers, Colorado, Fort Bend, Galveston, Harris, Liberty, Matagorda, Montgomery, Walker, Waller, and Wharton counties) or the states of Louisiana, Maryland, Tennessee, or Washington. Selection is based on academic achievement, financial need, and involvement in student nursing organizations and community health activities.
Financial data: Stipends range from $1,000 to $2,500.
Duration: 1 year.
Number awarded: Varies each year.
Deadline: January of each year.

2248 $$ PROTON ONSITE SCHOLARSHIP

Proton OnSite
Attn: Scholarship Program
10 Technology Drive
Wallingford, CT 06492
Phone: (203) 678–2000;
Email: scholarshipinfo@protononsite.com
Web: protononsitescholarship.com/about.asp

Summary: To provide financial assistance to high school seniors interested in studying specified fields of science and technology in college.
Eligibility: Open to U.S. citizens who are graduating high school seniors planning to enroll full time at a college or university. Applicants must have a GPA of 3.6 or higher. Their proposed major must be in the area of science and technology, including biological sciences, chemical technology, computer science and engineering, geosciences, engineering, material science, engineering technology, mathematical sciences, and physics. Selection is based on academic performance, ability, and promise; commitment to further education and a career in a field of science or technology; strength of application; demonstrated leadership, work ethic, and community involvement; and financial need.
Financial data: Stipends range up to $25,000 per year.
Duration: The winner's scholarship may be renewed for up to 3 additional years.
Number awarded: Varies each year; recently, 3 of these scholarships were awarded.
Deadline: February of each year.

2249 $ QUESTEX MEDIA GROUP SCHOLARSHIP

Summary: To provide financial assistance to undergraduate and graduate students from any country who are working on a degree in the field of document management and graphic communications, especially those who are interested in journalism, trade show management, or marketing communications.
See Listing #1471.

2250 QUIT SMOKING ACADEMIC SCHOLARSHIP

Quit Smoking
3675 Glennvale Court
Cumming, GA 30041
Phone: (702) 765–4848;
Email: scholarship@quitsmoking.com
Web: www.quitsmoking.com/scholarship

Summary: To recognize and reward, with scholarships for further study, undergraduate and graduate students who submit outstanding essays on their interest in a career in behavior modification and what they have done to help other students quit smoking.
Eligibility: Open to undergraduate and graduate students who are working on a degree in medicine, physiology, psychology, or other field related to behavior modification. Applicants must submit an essay, from 500 to 1,000 words in length, that covers such topics as their passion and commitment to helping others overcome tobacco or other addiction, why they want to be a doctor or professional in addiction management or behavior modification, current ideas for helping others overcome addiction, their motives for studying behavior modification, their goals for the next 5 to 10 years, and what it means to overcome addiction. Selection is based on the essay's creativity, specificity, and basic grammar.

Financial data: The award is $1,000, paid directly to the winner's college or university.
Duration: The award is presented annually.
Number awarded: 1 each year.
Deadline: September of each year.

2251 RADIO CLUB OF AMERICA SCHOLARSHIPS

Foundation for Amateur Radio, Inc.
Attn: Scholarship Committee
P.O. Box 911
Columbia, MD 21044–0911
Phone: (410) 552–2652; Fax: (410) 981–5146;
Email: dave.prestel@gmail.com
Web: www.farweb.org/scholarships
Summary: To provide funding to licensed radio amateurs who are interested in studying electrical engineering in college.
Eligibility: Open to college juniors and seniors who have a general class amateur radio license and are working full time on a bachelor's degree. Applicants must be majoring in electrical engineering; preference is given to students taking courses in wireless communications. U.S. citizenship is required. Financial need is considered in the selection process.
Financial data: The stipend is $1,000.
Duration: 1 year.
Number awarded: 3 each year.
Deadline: April of each year.

2252 $ RAIN BIRD INTELLIGENT USE OF WATER SCHOLARSHIP

Summary: To provide financial assistance to landscape architecture, horticulture, and irrigation science students who demonstrate commitment to those professions.
See Listing #1474.

2253 RALPH A. KLUCKEN SCHOLARSHIP

Technical Association of the Pulp and Paper Industry
Attn: Scholarship Department
15 Technology Parkway South
Norcross, GA 30092
Phone: (770) 209–7276; (800) 332–8686; Fax: (770) 446–6947;
Email: standards@tappi.org
Web: www.tappi.org/About–TAPPI/TAPPI–Scholarships.aspx
Summary: To provide financial assistance for college or graduate school to students who are interested in preparing for a career in the pulp and paper industry.
Eligibility: Open to high school seniors, undergraduates, and graduate students who are either enrolled full time or working full time and attending night school as a part–time student. Applicants must be able to demonstrate responsibility and maturity through a history of part–time and summer employment; an interest in the technological areas covered by the Polymers, Laminations, Adhesives, Coatings and Extrusions (PLACE) Division of the Technical Association of the Pulp and Paper Industry (TAPPI); and a GPA of 3.0 or higher. Selection is based on the candidates' potential career contributions to the pulp and paper industry; financial need is not considered.
Financial data: The stipend is $1,000.
Duration: 1 year. A student may apply for the scholarship each year, but the award will not be given to the same person twice consecutively.
Number awarded: 1 each even–numbered year.
Deadline: February of each even–numbered year.

2254 $ RALPH HALE RUPPERT MEMORIAL SCHOLARSHIPS

California Scottish Rite Foundation
Attn: Secretary
855 Elm Avenue
Long Beach, CA 90813–4414
Phone: (562) 435–6061; Fax: (562) 435–3302;
Email: secy.csrf@verizon.net
Web: www.casr–foundation.org/scholarships/ruppert–scholarship
Summary: To provide financial assistance to California residents interested in attending college in any state to major in designated fields.
Eligibility: Open to California residents between 17 and 25 years of age who are attending or planning to attend an accredited college or university in any state as a full–time student. Applicants must be preparing for a career in medicine, engineering, forestry, or public school administration. They must be able to demonstrate high ideals and ability, strong grades in school (GPA of 3.0 or higher), financial need, and part–time employment. No affiliation with a Masonic–related organization is required. Along with their application, they must submit brief statements on their 1) belief in a Supreme Being; 2) ideas about separation of church and state; and 3) career goals.
Financial data: The stipend is $2,000 per year.
Duration: 1 year; may be renewed up to 3 additional years.
Number awarded: Varies each year. Since the program was established, it has awarded more than $1,000,000 in scholarships.
Deadline: February of each year.

2255 RALPH K. HILLQUIST HONORARY SAE SCHOLARSHIP

Society of Automotive Engineers
Attn: Scholarships and Loans Program
400 Commonwealth Drive
Warrendale, PA 15096–0001
Phone: (724) 776–4970; (877) 606–7323; Fax: (724) 776–0790;
Email: scholarships@sae.org
Web: students.sae.org/awdscholar/scholarships/hillquist
Summary: To provide financial assistance to college juniors who are majoring in mechanical or automotive engineering.
Eligibility: Open to juniors enrolled full time at U.S. universities. Applicants must have a declared major in mechanical engineering or an automotive–related engineering discipline, with preference given to those who have completed studies or courses in the areas of expertise related to noise and vibration (e.g., statics, dynamics, physics, vibration). They must be U.S. citizens with a GPA of 3.0 or higher and significant academic and leadership achievements. Along with their application, they must submit a 300–word essay on the single experience that most strongly convinced them or confirmed their decision to prepare for a career in engineering. Financial need is not considered in the selection process.
Financial data: The stipend is $1,000.
Duration: 1 year; nonrenewable.
Number awarded: 1 each odd–numbered year.
Deadline: January of each odd–numbered year.

2256 $ RANDALL MATHIS SCHOLARSHIP FOR ENVIRONMENTAL STUDIES

Arkansas Environmental Federation
Attn: Communications Director
1400 West Markham, Suite 302
Little Rock, AR 72201
Phone: (501) 374–0263; Fax: (501) 374–8752;
Email: ecullen@environmentark.org
Web: netforum.avectra.com/eWeb/DynamicPage.aspx?Site=AEF&WebCode=Sch
Summary: To provide financial assistance to residents of Arkansas working on an undergraduate or graduate degree in environmental studies at a college or university in the state.
Eligibility: Open to Arkansas residents who have completed at least 40 credit hours as a full–time undergraduate or graduate student at a college or university in the state. Applicants must be majoring in a field related to environmental studies, including agriculture with an environmental emphasis, chemical engineering with an environmental emphasis, civil engineering with an environmental emphasis, environmental engineering, environmental health science, fisheries and wildlife biology, forestry, geology, or wildlife management. They must have a GPA of 2.8 or higher. Along with their application, they must submit an essay of 1 to 3 pages on their professional career goals relating to the fields of environmental health and safety. U.S. citizenship is required. Financial need is not considered in the selection process.
Financial data: The stipend is $2,500.
Duration: 1 year.
Number awarded: 1 each year.
Deadline: April of each year.

2257 $$ RANELIUS SCHOLARSHIP PROGRAM

Minnesota Turkey Growers Association
Attn: Scholarship Selection Committee
108 Marty Drive

Buffalo, MN 55313–9338
Phone: (763) 682–2171; Fax: (763) 682–5546;
Email: lara@minnesotaturkey.com
Web: minnesotaturkey.com/education

Summary: To provide financial assistance to residents of Minnesota who are interested in attending college in the state to prepare for a career in the poultry industry.

Eligibility: Open to residents of Minnesota who are enrolled or planning to enroll in a postsecondary educational program in the state that will prepare them for employment in some phase of the poultry industry. Applicants may be majoring in any field or program as long as it provides them with suitable training for their career goals. Preference is given to members of the Minnesota Turkey Growers Association (MTGA), family members or employees of members of the MTGA, and applicants who have not previously received this scholarship. Selection is based on academic record, experience, honors received, and demonstrated interest in the poultry industry.

Financial data: A total of $5,000 is available for this program each year.

Duration: 1 year.

Number awarded: 1 or more each year.

Deadline: February of each year.

2258 $ RAYMOND G. ALVINE MEMORIAL SCHOLARSHIP

Alvine Engineering
1102 Douglas on the Mall
Omaha, NE 68102
Phone: (402) 346–7007; Fax: (402) 346–9576;
Email: alvine@alvine.com
Web: rgascholarship.org

Summary: To provide financial assistance to residents of Iowa, Kansas, and Nebraska interested in studying specified fields of engineering at public universities in those states.

Eligibility: Open to students who are entering as full–time freshmen, sophomores, or juniors at the University of Iowa, Iowa State University, Kansas State University, or any campus of the University of Nebraska system. Applicants must be preparing for a career in architectural, electrical, or mechanical engineering and have a GPA of 3.0 or higher. They must have taken the ACT and scored 21 or higher or the SAT and scored 800 or higher. Along with their application, they must submit a 2–page essay that covers their specific interest in engineering, their leadership qualities, their personal and career goals, and the event or individual that made the biggest impact on who they are today. Financial need is also considered in the selection process.

Financial data: Stipends range from $500 to $3,000.

Duration: 1 year.

Number awarded: 1 or more each year.

Deadline: March of each year.

2259 $ RBC WEALTH MANAGEMENT COLORADO SCHOLARSHIPS

Denver Foundation
Attn: Scholarships and Special Projects
55 Madison Street, Eighth Floor
Denver, CO 80206
Phone: (303) 996–7328; Fax: (303) 300–6547;
Email: information@denverfoundation.org
Web: www.denverfoundation.org

Summary: To provide financial assistance to high school seniors from Colorado who plan to study science or engineering at a college in any state.

Eligibility: Open to seniors graduating from high schools in Colorado who have a GPA of 3.75 or higher and plan to attend a college or university in any state. Applicants must be planning to study science, mathematics, or engineering and must have completed all college preparatory course work in their proposed field of study. They must be able to demonstrate that they stand out from their peers in terms of academics and/or achievement in the arts, athletics, community service, leadership, or other areas. Selection is based on academic excellence, leadership in school and community activities, personal achievements, significant challenges that have been overcome, and financial need. A personal interview may be required.

Financial data: The stipend is $3,000.

Duration: 1 year.

Number awarded: 5 each year.

Deadline: March of each year.

2260 $$ RICHARD B. FISHER SCHOLARSHIP

Morgan Stanley
Attn: Diversity Recruiting
1585 Broadway
New York, NY 10036
Phone: (212) 762–0211; Fax: (212) 507–4972;
Email: richardbfisherprogram@morganstanley.com
Web: www.morganstanley.com/about/careers/ischolarships_na.html

Summary: To provide financial assistance and work experience to members of underrepresented groups who are preparing for a career in technology within the financial services industry.

Eligibility: Open to African American, Hispanic, Native American and lesbian/gay/bisexual/transgender students who are enrolled in their sophomore or junior year of college (or the third or fourth year of a 5–year program). Applicants must be enrolled full time and have a GPA of 3.3 or higher. They must be willing to commit to a paid summer internship in the Morgan Stanley Information Technology Division. All majors and disciplines are eligible, but preference is given to students preparing for a career in technology within the financial services industry. Along with their application, they must submit 1–page essays on 1) why they are applying for this scholarship and why they should be selected as a recipient; 2) a technical project on which they worked, either through a university course or previous work experience, their role in the project, and how they contributed to the end result; and 3) a software, hardware, or new innovative application of existing technology that they would create if they could and the impact it would have. Financial need is not considered in the selection process.

Financial data: The stipend is $7,500 per year.

Duration: 1 year (the junior year); may be renewed for the senior year.

Number awarded: 1 or more each year.

Deadline: January of each year.

2261 $ RICHARD GOOLSBY SCHOLARSHIP

Foundation for the Carolinas
Attn: Vice President, Scholarships
220 South Tryon Street
Charlotte, NC 28202
Phone: (704) 973–4537; (800) 973–7244; Fax: (704) 973–4935;
Email: tcapers@fftc.org
Web: www.fftc.org/page.aspx?pid=958

Summary: To provide financial assistance to undergraduate and graduate students in North and South Carolina who are preparing for a career in the plastics industry.

Eligibility: Open to residents of South Carolina, central North Carolina, or western North Carolina. Applicants must be entering their sophomore, junior, or senior year at a 2– or 4–year college or university in North or South Carolina or be a graduate student in those states. They must be working full time on a degree in a subject that will prepare them for a career in the plastics industry (e.g., chemistry, physics, chemical engineering, mechanical engineering, industrial engineering, business administration). Along with their application, they must submit a 1– to 2–page statement explaining why they are applying for the scholarship, their qualifications, and their educational and career goals in the plastics industry. Selection is based on academic performance, demonstrated interest in the plastics industry, financial need, school and community involvement, and personal achievements.

Financial data: Stipends range up to $4,000 per year. Funds are paid directly to the recipient's school to be used for tuition, required fees, books, and supplies.

Duration: 1 year; recipients may reapply, provided they remain enrolled full time and meet all qualifying requirements.

Number awarded: 1 or more each year.

Deadline: February of each year.

2262 RICHARD J. SCHNELL MEMORIAL SCHOLARSHIPS

Community Foundation of Northern Illinois
Attn: Program and Scholarship Officer
946 North Second Street
Rockford, IL 61107
Phone: (815) 962–2110, ext. 11; Fax: (815) 962–2116;
Email: jpatterson@cfnil.org
Web: www.cfnil.org/apply/scholarships/online–applications

Summary: To provide financial assistance to residents of any state who are entering or enrolled in a dental, dental hygiene, or dental postdoctoral program in any state.

Eligibility: Open to residents of any state who have been accepted into or are enrolled in a dental, dental hygiene, or dental graduate postdoctoral program

in any state. Applicants must be able to demonstrate financial need. Their program must be accredited by the American Dental Association. U.S. citizenship is required.
Financial data: The stipend is $1,000.
Duration: 1 year.
Number awarded: Varies each year; recently, 5 of these scholarships were awarded.
Deadline: June of each year.

2263 $ RICHARD JENSEN SCHOLARSHIP

National Alliance of Independent Crop Consultants
Attn: Foundation for Environmental Agriculture Education
349 East Nolley Drive
Collierville, TN 38017
Phone: (901) 861–0511; Fax: (901) 861–0512;
Email: JonesNAICC@aol.com
Web: www.naicc.org/FEAE/scholarship.cfm
Summary: To provide financial assistance to agriculture students specializing in crop production.
Eligibility: Open to students entering their third year of college. Applicants must be working on a 4–year degree in agriculture with a major in crop production, including soil sciences, agronomy, entomology, horticulture, plant pathology, or weed science. Financial need is not considered in the selection process.
Financial data: The stipend is $2,000.
Duration: 1 year.
Number awarded: 1 each year.
Deadline: September of each year.

2264 RICK PANKOW FOUNDATION SCHOLARSHIP

Summary: To provide financial assistance to high school seniors in Washington who are interested in majoring in horticulture or landscape architecture at a college in any state.
See Listing #1481.

2265 RITA LOWE COLLEGE SCHOLARSHIPS

Washington State Mathematics Council
c/o Pat Reistroffer, Scholarship Chair
146 Scenic View Drive
Longview, WA 98632
Phone: (360) 636–5125;
Email: preistrof@aol.com
Web: www.wsmc.net/scholarship
Summary: To provide financial assistance to students from any state majoring in mathematics education at colleges and universities in Washington.
Eligibility: Open to residents of any state currently attending a college or university in Washington and majoring in mathematics education. Applicants must be preparing for teaching certification in order to become a professional educator teaching mathematics at the elementary or secondary level. They must submit a transcript (from the ninth grade to the date of application), a 300–word statement on their experience with and interest in mathematics, and 2 letters of recommendation. Selection is based on academic achievement, demonstrated intent to become a mathematics educator, character, academic potential, and leadership potential.
Financial data: The stipend is $1,000.
Duration: 1 year.
Number awarded: 2 each year.
Deadline: February of each year.

2266 RITA LOWE HIGH SCHOOL SCHOLARSHIP

Washington State Mathematics Council
c/o Pat Reistroffer, Scholarship Chair
146 Scenic View Drive
Longview, WA 98632
Phone: (360) 636–5125;
Email: preistrof@aol.com
Web: www.wsmc.net/scholarship
Summary: To provide financial assistance to high school seniors in Washington planning to major in mathematics education at a college or university in the state.
Eligibility: Open to seniors graduating from high schools in Washington and planning to attend a college or university in the state to major in mathematics education. Applicants must be preparing for teaching certification in order to become a professional educator teaching mathematics at the elementary or secondary level. They must submit a transcript (from the ninth grade to the date of application), a 300–word statement on their experience with and interest in mathematics, and 2 letters of recommendation. Selection is based on academic achievement, demonstrated intent to become a mathematics educator, character, academic potential, and leadership potential.
Financial data: The stipend is $1,000.
Duration: 1 year.
Number awarded: 2 each year.
Deadline: February of each year.

2267 RITA M. COSTELLO SCHOLARSHIP

Virginia Federation of Garden Clubs
c/o Lisa Robinson, Scholarship Chair
315 Tulip Tree Lane
Moneta, VA 24121–2011
Phone: (540) 266–3083;
Email: gardenlisa@r22sml.com
Web: www.virginiagardenclubs.org/VFGC/Scholarships.html
Summary: To provide financial assistance to residents of Virginia who are upper–division or graduate students at a university in any state and working on a degree in horticulture.
Eligibility: Open to juniors, seniors, and graduate students at colleges and universities in any state who are residents of Virginia. Applicants must be working on a degree in a horticulture–related field and have a garden–related career goal. Along with their application, they must submit a letter discussing their goals, background, personal commitment, and financial need.
Financial data: A stipend is awarded (amount not specified).
Duration: 1 year.
Number awarded: 1 each year.
Deadline: January of each year.

2268 $ ROBERT B. OLIVER ASNT SCHOLARSHIPS

American Society for Nondestructive Testing, Inc.
Attn: Administrative Assistant
1711 Arlingate Lane
P.O. Box 28518
Columbus, OH 43228–0518
Phone: (614) 274–6003; (800) 222–2768; Fax: (614) 274–6899;
Email: sdille@asnt.org
Web: www.asnt.org/keydocuments/awards/oliver.htm
Summary: To recognize and reward undergraduate students who submit outstanding papers in the field of nondestructive testing.
Eligibility: Open to students who are enrolled in a program related to nondestructive testing that leads to an undergraduate degree, associate degree, or postsecondary certificate. The award is offered to students submitting the best original manuscript (up to 5,000 words) on the topic. The manuscript should develop an original concept and may be based on practical experience, laboratory work, or library research. Papers may be classroom assignments in courses outside the area of nondestructive testing, such as an English class. Applicants must be currently enrolled in school and should submit 4 copies of their paper, their curriculum, a transcript of grades, and a letter from a school official verifying the student's enrollment. Selection is based on creativity (10 points), content (50 points), format and readability (25 points), and the student's hands–on involvement in the project (15 points).
Financial data: The award is $2,500.
Duration: The award is presented annually.
Number awarded: Up to 3 each year.
Deadline: February of each year.

2269 $ ROBERT D. GREENBERG SCHOLARSHIP

Society of Broadcast Engineers
Attn: Scholarship Committee
9102 North Meridian Street, Suite 150
Indianapolis, IN 46260
Phone: (317) 846–9000; Fax: (317) 846–9120
Web: www.sbe.org/sections/edu_ennes_scholarships.php
Summary: To provide financial assistance for college to students interested in the technical aspects of broadcasting.
Eligibility: Open to students who have a career interest in the technical aspects of broadcasting and are recommended by 2 members of the Society of Broadcast

Engineers (SBE). They must submit 1) a brief autobiography that includes their interest and goals in broadcasting; 2) a summary of the technical changes they anticipate in broadcasting within the next 5 years; and 3) transcripts. Preference is given to members of the SBE and to students currently employed at least part time in broadcast engineering. Both new students just entering college and students already enrolled in college may apply. Financial need is not considered in the selection process.
Financial data: The stipend ranges from $1,000 to $3,000, depending on the availability of funds. Awards may be used for 1) tuition, room, board, or textbook costs at postsecondary educational institutions; or 2) other technical training programs approved by the sponsor.
Duration: 1 year.
Number awarded: 1 each year.
Deadline: June of each year.

2270 ROBERT E. CRAMER/PRODUCT DESIGN AND DEVELOPMENT DIVISION/MID–MICHIGAN SECTION SCHOLARSHIP

Society of Plastics Engineers
Attn: SPE Foundation
13 Church Hill Road
Newtown, CT 06740
Phone: (203) 740–5447; Fax: (203) 775–1157;
Email: foundation@4spe.org
Web: www.4spe.org/spe–foundation
Summary: To provide financial assistance to undergraduate students who have a career interest in the plastics industry.
Eligibility: Open to full–time undergraduate students at 4–year colleges or in 2–year technical programs. Applicants must be majoring in or taking courses that would be beneficial to a career in the plastics or polymer industry (e.g., plastics engineering, packaging, polymer sciences, chemistry, physics, chemical engineering, mechanical engineering, industrial engineering). Along with their application, they must submit 3 letters of recommendation; a high school and/or college transcript; a 1– to 2–page statement telling why they are applying for the scholarship, their qualifications, and their educational and career goals in the plastics industry; their employment history; a list of current and past school activities and community activities and honors; and information on their financial need.
Financial data: The stipend is $1,000. Funds are paid directly to the recipient's school.
Duration: 1 year.
Number awarded: 1 each year.
Deadline: February of each year.

2271 $$ ROBERT E. DOUGHERTY SCHOLARSHIPS

Composite Panel Association
Attn: Robert E. Dougherty Educational Foundation
19465 Deerfield Avenue, Suite 306
Leesburg, VA 20176
Phone: (703) 724–1128; (866) 4COMPOSITES; Fax: (703) 724–1588
Web: www.pbmdf.com/index.asp?bid=1052
Summary: To provide financial assistance to upper–division and graduate students preparing for a career in the composite panel and affiliated industries.
Eligibility: Open to U.S. and Canadian citizens who are entering their junior or senior year of undergraduate study or enrolled in graduate school. Applicants must be nominated by a company or educational institution that is a member of the Robert E. Dougherty Educational Foundation. They must be working on a degree in forest products, wood science or technology, chemistry, mechanical engineering, or industrial engineering. Along with their application, they must submit brief essays on why they selected their major, what they see as the biggest challenge facing the North American composite panel or related industries, and their career aspirations in the field of the composite panel and related industries. Financial need is not considered in the selection process.
Financial data: The stipend is $5,000 per year.
Duration: 1 year; may be renewed 1 additional year.
Number awarded: Up to 5 each year.
Deadline: February of each year.

2272 $ ROBERT G. DAILEY/DETROIT SECTION SCHOLARSHIP

Society of Plastics Engineers
Attn: SPE Foundation
13 Church Hill Road
Newtown, CT 06740
Phone: (203) 740–5447; Fax: (203) 775–1157;
Email: foundation@4spe.org
Web: www.4spe.org/spe–foundation
Summary: To provide financial assistance to undergraduate students who have a career interest in the plastics industry.
Eligibility: Open to full–time undergraduate students at 4–year colleges or in 2–year technical programs. Applicants must be majoring in or taking courses that would be beneficial to a career in the plastics or polymer industry (e.g., plastics engineering, packaging, polymer sciences, chemistry, physics, chemical engineering, mechanical engineering, industrial engineering). Along with their application, they must submit 3 letters of recommendation; a high school and/or college transcript; a 1– to 2–page statement telling why they are applying for the scholarship, their qualifications, and their educational and career goals in the plastics industry; their employment history; a list of current and past school activities and community activities and honors; and information on their financial need.
Financial data: The stipend is $4,000. Funds are paid directly to the recipient's school.
Duration: 1 year.
Number awarded: 1 each year.
Deadline: February of each year.

2273 $$ ROBERT LEWIS BAKER SCHOLARSHIP

Summary: To provide financial assistance to Maryland residents who are interested in working on an undergraduate or graduate degree in ornamental horticulture or landscape design at a school in any state.
See Listing #1486.

2274 $ ROBERT M. LAWRENCE, MD EDUCATION RECOGNITION AWARD

American Association for Respiratory Care
Attn: American Respiratory Care Foundation
9425 North MacArthur Boulevard, Suite 100
Irving, TX 75063–4706
Phone: (972) 243–2272; Fax: (972) 484–2720;
Email: info@arcfoundation.org
Web: www.arcfoundation.org/awards/undergraduate/lawrence.cfm
Summary: To provide financial assistance to upper–division students working on a bachelor's degree in respiratory therapy.
Eligibility: Open to students who have completed at least 2 years in an accredited respiratory care bachelor's degree program. Applicants must submit 1) an original referenced paper on an aspect of respiratory care; and 2) an essay of at least 1,200 words describing how the award will assist them in reaching their objective of a baccalaureate degree and their ultimate goal of leadership in health care. Selection is based on academic performance.
Financial data: The stipend is $2,500. The award also provides airfare, 1 night's lodging, and registration for the international congress of the association.
Duration: 1 year.
Number awarded: 1 each year.
Deadline: June of each year.

2275 $$ ROBERT NOYCE SCHOLARSHIPS OF PENNSYLVANIA

Pennsylvania State System of Higher Education Foundation, Inc.
Attn: Foundation Manager
2986 North Second Street
Harrisburg, PA 17110
Phone: (717) 720–4065; Fax: (717) 720–7082;
Email: eshowers@thePAfoundation.org
Web: www.thepafoundation.org/scholarships/index.asp
Summary: To provide financial assistance to upper–division students and professionals at institutions of the Pennsylvania State System of Higher Education (PASSHE) who are majoring in a discipline of science, technology, engineering, or mathematics (STEM) and planning to become a high school science and mathematics teacher in Pennsylvania.
Eligibility: Open to 1) juniors and seniors enrolled at 1 of the 14 institutions within the PASSHE and majoring in a STEM discipline; and 2) post–baccalaureate students who have a bachelor's degree in science or mathematics and have returned to college to receive additional training. Applicants must be interested in completing certification requirements for secondary science and mathematics education and be willing to commit to teaching at a high school in Pennsylvania. They must have a GPA of 3.0 or higher (preferably 3.5 or higher); transfer students and post–baccalaureates must complete a semester or more

of course work at a State System university to establish the 3.0 qualifying GPA. Along with their application, they must submit a 2–page essay on their personal and professional goals, commitment to teaching, and personal philosophy of teaching. Selection is based on that essay (20 points), GPA (30 points for 3.0 or higher; 40 points for 3.5 or higher), letters of recommendation (15 points), resume quality (15 points), evidence of leadership experiences and/or abilities (15 points), and professionalism of the application packet (10 points).
Financial data: Stipends range from $7,500 to $10,000 per year; funds are paid directly to the recipient's university account to be used for educational expenses.
Duration: 1 semester; may be renewed up to 3 additional semesters, provided the recipient remains enrolled full time, maintains a GPA of 3.0 or higher, and provides specified services for the program.
Number awarded: Varies each year, depending on the availability of funds.
Deadline: April of each year for fall awards; October of each year for spring awards.

2276 $ ROBERTA PIERCE SCOFIELD BACHELOR'S SCHOLARSHIPS

Oncology Nursing Society
Attn: ONS Foundation
125 Enterprise Drive
Pittsburgh, PA 15275–1214
Phone: (412) 859–6100; (866) 257–4ONS; Fax: (412) 859–6163;
Email: info@onsfoundation.org
Web: www.onsfoundation.org/apply/ed/Bachelors
Summary: To provide financial assistance to nurses and other students who are interested in working on a bachelor's degree in oncology nursing.
Eligibility: Open to students who are accepted to or currently enrolled in a bachelor's degree program at an NLN– or CCNE–accredited school of nursing. Applicants must be able to demonstrate an interest in and commitment to oncology nursing. They may 1) already have a current license to practice as a registered nurse (R.N.); 2) currently have a postsecondary degree at some level but not be an R.N.; or 3) have only a high school diploma. Along with their application, they must submit 1) an essay of 250 words or less on their role or interest in caring for persons with cancer; and 2) a statement of their professional goals and the relationship of those goals to the advancement of oncology nursing. Non–R.N. applicants must be in the nursing component of the B.S.N. program. High school students and individuals in the liberal arts component of a B.S.N. program are not eligible. Financial need is not considered in the selection process.
Financial data: The stipend is $2,000.
Duration: 1 year; nonrenewable.
Number awarded: 1 or more each year.
Deadline: January of each year.

2277 $ ROCKEFELLER STATE WILDLIFE SCHOLARSHIP

Louisiana Office of Student Financial Assistance
602 North Fifth Street
P.O. Box 91202
Baton Rouge, LA 70821–9202
Phone: (225) 219–1012; (800) 259–LOAN, ext. 1012; Fax: (225) 208–1496;
Email: custserv@osfa.state.la.us
Web: www.osfa.state.la.us
Summary: To provide financial assistance to upper–division and graduate students in Louisiana who are interested in working on a degree in forestry, wildlife, or marine science.
Eligibility: Open to U.S. citizens and eligible noncitizens who have been residents of Louisiana for at least 1 year. Applicants must be enrolled full time at a public university in Louisiana to work on an undergraduate or graduate degree in forestry, wildlife, or marine science. Undergraduates must have completed at least 60 hours of college credit and have a cumulative GPA of 2.5 or higher. Graduate students must have a GPA of 3.0 or higher for all graduate credits earned. This is a merit–based award; financial need is not considered.
Financial data: The stipend is $2,000 per year for undergraduates or $3,000 per year for graduate students.
Duration: Support is provided for up to 3 years of undergraduate and 2 years of graduate study, provided the recipient remains enrolled full time with a GPA of 2.5 or higher as an undergraduate or 3.0 as a graduate student.
Number awarded: Varies each year.
Deadline: June of each year.

2278 $ ROCKWELL AUTOMATION SCHOLARSHIPS

Society of Women Engineers
Attn: Scholarship Selection Committee
203 North LaSalle Street, Suite 1675
Chicago, IL 60601–1269
Phone: (312) 596–5223; (877) SWE–INFO; Fax: (312) 644–8557;
Email: scholarships@swe.org
Web: societyofwomenengineers.swe.org/index.php/scholarships
Summary: To provide financial assistance to upper–division women majoring in computer science or selected engineering specialties.
Eligibility: Open to women who are entering their junior year at an ABET–accredited college or university. Applicants must be working full time on a degree in computer science or computer, electrical, industrial, manufacturing, mechanical, or software engineering and have a GPA of 3.0 or higher. Selection is based on merit and demonstrated leadership potential. Preference is given to students attending designated universities and to members of groups underrepresented in computer science and engineering.
Financial data: The stipend is $2,500.
Duration: 1 year.
Number awarded: 2 each year.
Deadline: February of each year.

2279 ROCKY MOUNTAIN CHAPTER ASHRAE SCHOLARSHIPS

American Society of Heating, Refrigerating and Air–Conditioning Engineers–Rocky Mountain Chapter
c/o Craig Wanklyn, Student Activities Committee Chair
M–E Engineers, Inc.
10055 West 43rd Avenue
Wheat Ridge, CO 80033
Phone: (303) 421–6655;
Email: craig.wanklyn@me–engineers.com
Web: www.rockymtnashrae.com
Summary: To provide financial assistance to students at colleges and universities in Colorado and Wyoming who are preparing for a career in heating, ventilating, air conditioning, and refrigeration (HVAC&R).
Eligibility: Open to undergraduates from any state who are attending a college or university in Colorado or Wyoming and are preparing for a career in HVAC&R. Applicants must submit 1) a 2–page cover letter describing their interests, professional goals, internship experience, and financial need; 2) a 1–page current resume; and 3) a 1–page document describing their academic achievement.
Financial data: The stipend is $1,000.
Duration: 1 year.
Number awarded: 4 each year.
Deadline: October of each year.

2280 ROCKY MOUNTAIN CHAPTER ICRI SCHOLARSHIP AWARD

International Concrete Repair Institute–Rocky Mountain Chapter
c/o Mike Kerker
DRS Engineering Contractors
12905 South Division Street, Unit C
Littleton, CO 80125
Phone: (303) 306–9200, ext. 12;
Email: mkerker@drscorp.net
Web: www.icri.org/Chapters/chap_details.asp?id=RM
Summary: To provide financial assistance to residents of designated Rocky Mountain states who are interested in working on a degree related to engineering or construction management in the field of concrete at a school in any state.
Eligibility: Open to residents of Colorado, New Mexico, Utah, and Wyoming who are enrolled or planning to enroll at an accredited college, university, or vocational school in any state. Applicants must be interested in working on an associate or bachelor's degree related to concrete design, materials, construction, or any combination of those areas. They must be U.S. citizens and capable in English. Along with their application, they must submit essays on 1) the reasons that support and justify their application for this award (financial need is not considered); 2) their interest in concrete design, materials, construction, or combination of those; and 3) their plan for completing their college education.
Financial data: A stipend is awarded (amount not specified).
Duration: 1 year.
Number awarded: 1 of each year.
Deadline: March of each year.

2281 ROCKY MOUNTAIN SECTION COLLEGE SCHOLARSHIPS

Society of Women Engineers–Rocky Mountain Section
Attn: Collegiate Scholarship Committee Chair

P.O. Box 260692
Lakewood, CO 80226–0692
Phone: (303) 751–0741; Fax: (303) 751–2581;
Email: christi.wisleder@gmail.copm
Web: www.societyofwomenengineers.org/RockyMountain/scholarships.html

Summary: To provide financial assistance to women from any state who are working on an undergraduate or graduate degree in engineering at colleges and universities in Colorado and Wyoming.

Eligibility: Open to women from any state who are enrolled as an undergraduate or graduate engineering student in an ABET–accredited engineering or computer science program in Colorado or Wyoming (excluding zip codes 80800–81599). Applicants must have a GPA of 3.0 or higher. Along with their application, they must submit an essay on why they have chosen an engineering major, what they will accomplish or how they believe they will make a difference as an engineer, and who or what influenced them to study engineering. Selection is based on merit.

Financial data: The stipend is $1,250.

Duration: 1 year.

Number awarded: 3 each year.

Deadline: January of each year.

2282 $ ROCKY MOUNTAIN STEEL CONSTRUCTION ASSOCIATION FELLOWSHIP

American Institute of Steel Construction
Attn: Director of University Relations
1 East Wacker Drive, Suite 700
Chicago, IL 60601–1802
Phone: (312) 670–5408; Fax: (312) 670–5403;
Email: gavlin@aisc.com
Web: www.aisc.org/content.aspx?id=716

Summary: To provide financial assistance to upper–division and graduate engineering students at universities in Colorado and Wyoming who demonstrate an interest in structural steel.

Eligibility: Open to full–time civil or architectural engineering students entering their senior year or working on a master's degree at universities in Colorado and Wyoming. Applicants must submit a 1–page essay that demonstrates either 1) steel–related course work and/or thesis research with a strong structural steel orientation; or 2) a proposed course work plan of study and/or proposed thesis concentration in structural steel. Selection is based on that essay, academic performance, and a faculty recommendation. U.S. citizenship is required.

Financial data: The stipend is $3,000.

Duration: 1 year.

Number awarded: 1 each year.

Deadline: April of each year.

2283 $$ ROSSINI FLEXOGRAPHIC SCHOLARSHIP COMPETITION

Summary: To recognize and reward, with funding for research, undergraduate students who propose an outstanding project related to flexography.

See Listing #1488.

2284 $$ ROV SCHOLARSHIPS

Marine Technology Society
Attn: Student Scholarships
1100 H Street, N.W., Suite LL–100
Washington, DC 20005
Phone: (202) 717–8705; Fax: (202) 347–4305;
Email: scholarships@mtsociety.org
Web: www.mtsociety.org/education/scholarships.aspx

Summary: To provide financial assistance to entering and continuing undergraduate and graduate students working on a degree related to remotely–operated vehicles (ROVs) in marine science.

Eligibility: Open to 1) high school seniors accepted into a full–time undergraduate program; and 2) current undergraduate and graduate students who are members of the Marine Technology Society (MTS). Applicants must be interested in ROVs or work that supports ROVs in a marine–related field. Along with their application, they must submit a 1–page essay on their interest in ROVs or underwater work that furthers the use of ROVs; a biographical sketch; an official transcript; a recommendation from a current teacher or counselor in a marine–related field; and 3 personal letters of reference. Financial need is not considered in the selection process.

Financial data: The stipend ranges up to $10,000. Funds are sent directly to the recipient's college.

Duration: 1 year.

Number awarded: 1 or more each year.

Deadline: April of each year.

2285 ROY A. WALLACE BEEF IMPROVEMENT FEDERATION MEMORIAL SCHOLARSHIP

Beef Improvement Federation
c/o Joe Cassady, Executive Director
North Carolina State University
Department of Animal Science
P.O. Box 7621
Raleigh, NC 27695–7621
Phone: (919) 513–0262; Fax: (919) 513–6884;
Email: joe_cassady@ncsu.edu
Web: www.beefimprovement.org/awardwinners.html

Summary: To provide financial assistance to undergraduate and graduate students working on a degree related to the beef cattle industry.

Eligibility: Open to undergraduate and graduate students currently working full time on a degree related to the beef cattle industry. Preference is given to students who are interested in the areas of beef breeding, genetics, and reproduction. Applicants must submit a 1–page essay on their involvement in the beef industry, ambitions, goals, background, and other relevant information. Selection is based on demonstrated interest in beef cattle improvement (40%), service to the beef industry (30%), academic performance (20%), and community involvement (10%).

Financial data: The stipend is $1,250.

Duration: 1 year.

Number awarded: 2 each year: 1 for an undergraduate and 1 for a graduate student.

Deadline: March of each year.

2286 $$ ROY G. POST FOUNDATION SCHOLARSHIPS

Roy G. Post Foundation
P.O. Box 27646
Tempe, AZ 85285–7646
Fax: (480) 557–0263;
Email: post@wmarizona.org
Web: www.roygpost.org/scholarshippoc.html

Summary: To provide financial assistance to upper–division and graduate students from any country interested in working on a degree related to the safe management of nuclear material.

Eligibility: Open to students from any country entering their third year of undergraduate study or any year of graduate study. Applicants must be working on a degree related to the safe management of nuclear material. Along with their application, they must submit a personal statement on their academic and career objectives and areas of interest in the nuclear or radioactive waste management industry or related field. Financial need is also considered in the selection process.

Financial data: The stipend is $5,000.

Duration: 1 year.

Number awarded: Varies each year; recently, 10 of these scholarships were awarded.

Deadline: December of each year.

2287 $ ROY W. LIKINS SCHOLARSHIPS

American Water Works Association–Florida Section
Attn: Administrative Assistant
1300 Ninth Street, Suite B–124
St. Cloud, FL 34769
Phone: (407) 957–8448; Fax: (407) 957–8415;
Email: fsawwa@gmail.com
Web: www.fsawwa.org/displaycommon.cfm?an=1&subarticlenbr=143

Summary: To provide financial assistance to students from any state who are working on an undergraduate or graduate degree in a field related to the drinking water industry at colleges in Florida.

Eligibility: Open to upper–division and graduate students currently enrolled at colleges and universities in Florida. Applicants must be majoring in an area related to the drinking water industry. They must have a GPA of 3.0 or higher. Along with their application, they must submit information on their drinking water industry–related activities, involvement in non–technical civil and

community activities, special recognition and academic honors, and employment. Financial need is not considered in the selection process.
Financial data: Stipends are $2,000 or $1,000.
Duration: 1 year; nonrenewable.
Number awarded: 3 each year.
Deadline: May of each year.

2288 $ ROYCE OSBORN MINORITY STUDENT SCHOLARSHIPS

American Society of Radiologic Technologists
Attn: ASRT Education and Research Foundation
15000 Central Avenue, S.E.
Albuquerque, NM 87123–3909
Phone: (505) 298–4500, ext. 2541; (800) 444–2778, ext. 2541; Fax: (505) 298–5063;
Email: foundation@asrt.org
Web: www.asrtfoundation.org/Content/Scholarships_and_Awards
Summary: To provide financial assistance to minority students enrolled in entry–level radiologic sciences programs.
Eligibility: Open to Blacks or African Americans, American Indians or Alaska Natives, Hispanics or Latinos, Asians, and Native Hawaiians or other Pacific Islanders who are enrolled in an accredited entry–level program in radiography, sonography, magnetic resonance, or nuclear medicine. Applicants must be able to finish their degree or certificate in the year for which they are applying. They must be U.S. citizens, nationals, or permanent residents have a GPA of 3.0 or higher. Along with their application, they must submit 9 essays of 200 words each on assigned topics related to their personal situation and interest in a career in radiologic science. Selection is based on those essays, academic and professional achievements, recommendations, and financial need.
Financial data: The stipend is $4,000. Funds are paid directly to the recipient's institution.
Duration: 1 year.
Number awarded: 5 each year.
Deadline: January of each year.

2289 ROYCE WATSON SCHOLARSHIP

Alpha Mu Tau Fraternity
c/o American Society for Clinical Laboratory Science
2025 M Street, N.W., Suite 800
Washington, DC 20036
Phone: (202) 367–1174;
Email: alphamutaujoe@yahoo.com
Web: www.ascls.org/?page=Awards_AMTF
Summary: To provide financial assistance to undergraduate students in the clinical laboratory sciences.
Eligibility: Open to U.S. citizens and permanent residents accepted into or currently enrolled in a program in clinical laboratory science, including cytotechnology, histotechnology, clinical laboratory science/medical technology, or clinical laboratory technician/medical laboratory technician. Applicants must be entering their last year of study. Along with their application, they must submit a 500–word statement describing their interest and reasons for preparing for a career in clinical laboratory science. Financial need is also considered in the selection process.
Financial data: The stipend is $1,500.
Duration: 1 year.
Number awarded: Several each year.
Deadline: March of each year.

2290 $ RUBINOS–MESIA SCHOLARSHIP

Structural Engineers Association of Illinois
Attn: Structural Engineers Foundation
134 North LaSalle Street, Suite 1910
Chicago, IL 60602
Phone: (312) 726–4165; Fax: (312) 277–1991;
Email: office@seaol.org
Web: www.seaoi.org/sef.htm
Summary: To provide financial assistance to upper–division and graduate students of Hispanic descent interested in a career in structural engineering.
Eligibility: Open to students of Hispanic descent who are 1) entering their third or higher year of an undergraduate program; or 2) entering or continuing a graduate program. Applicants must be enrolled in a civil or architectural engineering program and planning to continue with a structural engineering specialization. Students enrolled in structural engineering technology programs are also eligible if they are qualified to take the Fundamentals of Engineering and Principles and Practice licensure examinations in their home state upon graduation. U.S. citizenship or permanent resident status is required. Students enrolled in military academies or ROTC programs are not eligible. Selection is based on a statement giving reasons why the applicant should receive the award (including plans for continued formal education), academic performance, and potential for development and leadership. Financial need is not considered.
Financial data: The stipend is $2,000.
Duration: 1 year; nonrenewable.
Number awarded: 1 or more each year.
Deadline: April of each year.

2291 $ RUDOLPH DILLMAN MEMORIAL SCHOLARSHIP

American Foundation for the Blind
Attn: Scholarship Committee
2 Penn Plaza, Suite 1102
New York, NY 10121
Phone: (212) 502–7661; (800) AFB–LINE; Fax: (888) 545–8331;
Email: afbinfo@afb.net
Web: www.afb.org/Section.asp?Documentid=2962
Summary: To provide financial assistance to legally blind undergraduate or graduate students studying in the field of rehabilitation and/or education of visually impaired and blind persons.
Eligibility: Open to legally blind U.S. citizens who have been accepted to an accredited undergraduate or graduate training program within the broad field of rehabilitation and/or education of blind and visually impaired persons. Along with their application, they must submit 200–word essays on 1) their past and recent achievements and accomplishments; 2) their intended field of study and why they have chosen it; and 3) the role their visual impairment has played in shaping their life. Financial need is considered for 1 of the scholarships.
Financial data: The stipend is $2,500 per year.
Duration: 1 academic year; previous recipients may not reapply.
Number awarded: 4 each year: 3 without consideration to financial need and 1 based on financial need.
Deadline: April of each year.

2292 RUSS BRANNEN/KENT FEEDS MEMORIAL BEEF SCHOLARSHIP

Iowa Foundation for Agricultural Advancement
Attn: Winner's Circle Scholarships
c/o SGI
30805 595th Avenue
Cambridge, IA 50046
Phone: (515) 291–3941;
Email: linda@slweldon.net
Web: www.iowastatefair.org
Summary: To provide financial assistance to Iowa high school seniors who have been involved in beef activities and plan to major in animal science or a related field at a college in the state.
Eligibility: Open to residents of Iowa who will be incoming freshmen at a college or university in the state in the following fall. Applicants must be planning to major in animal science or a program in agriculture or human sciences that is related to the animal industry. They must have a strong background in beef projects and activities. Along with their application, they must submit a 250–word essay summarizing their experiences with their agricultural and livestock projects. Selection is based on that essay and participation in agricultural and livestock projects (50%); activities, leadership, and recognition in 4–H, FFA, and other high school and community activities (25%); academic record (15%); and curriculum plans for college and career plans after graduation as they relate to the agricultural industry in general (10%). Preference is given to applicants who have been active in beef cattle expositions and showmanship contests.
Financial data: The stipend is $1,000.
Duration: 1 year; nonrenewable.
Number awarded: 1 each year.
Deadline: April of each year.

2293 $$ RUSTICI LIVESTOCK AND RANGELAND SCHOLARSHIP

California Farm Bureau Scholarship Foundation
Attn: Scholarship Foundation
2300 River Plaza Drive
Sacramento, CA 95833

Phone: (916) 561–5520; (800) 698–FARM (within CA); Fax: (916) 561–5699;
Email: dlicciardo@cfbf.com
Web: www.cfbf.com/programs/scholar/rustici.cfm

Summary: To provide financial assistance for college to residents of California who are interested in preparing for a career in rangeland management.

Eligibility: Open to students entering or attending a California 4–year accredited college or university or a 2–year community college. Applicants must be planning to prepare for a career that benefits the beef cattle or sheep industry by studying a field with a focus on rangeland management. Preference is given to students who plan to return to the family ranch. They must have a GPA of 2.0 or higher, although grades are not a primary factor in the selection process. Along with their application, they must submit a 500–word essay on why they have chosen the field of beef cattle or sheep ranching or range management, their goals, and how their past, present, and future activities make the accomplishment of those goals possible. Financial need is not considered in the selection process.

Financial data: The stipend is $5,000 per year for students at 4–year colleges or universities or $2,500 per year for students at 2–year community colleges.

Duration: 1 year; may be renewed, provided the recipient remains enrolled full time and maintains a GPA of 2.0 or higher.

Number awarded: 1 each year.

Deadline: February of each year.

2294 RUTH I. CLEVELAND SCHOLARSHIP

Summary: To provide financial assistance to residents of Massachusetts interested in working on an undergraduate or graduate degree in the arts and/or sciences.

See Listing #1490.

2295 S. EVELYN LEWIS MEMORIAL SCHOLARSHIP IN MEDICAL HEALTH SCIENCES

Zeta Phi Beta Sorority, Inc.
Attn: National Education Foundation
1734 New Hampshire Avenue, N.W.
Washington, DC 20009
Phone: (202) 387–3103; Fax: (202) 232–4593;
Email: scholarship@ZPhiBNEF.org
Web: www.zphib1920.org/nef

Summary: To provide financial assistance to women interested in studying medicine or health sciences on the undergraduate or graduate school level.

Eligibility: Open to women enrolled full time in a program on the undergraduate or graduate school level leading to a degree in medicine or health sciences. Proof of enrollment is required. Applicants need not be members of Zeta Phi Beta Sorority. Along with their application, they must submit a 150–word essay on their educational goals and professional aspirations, how this award will help them to achieve those goals, and why they should receive the award. Financial need is not considered in the selection process.

Financial data: The stipend ranges from $500 to $1,000. Funds are paid directly to the college or university.

Duration: 1 academic year.

Number awarded: 1 or more each year.

Deadline: January of each year.

2296 $$ SABAN MILITARY WIFE EDUCATIONAL SCHOLARSHIPS

Operation Homefront
8930 Fourwinds Drive, Suite 340
San Antonio, TX 78239
Phone: (210) 659–7756; (800) 722–6098; Fax: (210) 566–7544
Web: www.operationhomefront.net/scholarship

Summary: To provide financial assistance to wives of military personnel who are interested in studying a medical–related field at a vocational school.

Eligibility: Open to wives of military members currently serving on active duty, including Reserve and National Guard members who have served at least 180 combined days of full–time military duty since January 1, 2008. Applicants must be enrolled or planning to enroll in a vocational training program as a dental assistance, medical assistant, medical billing and coding specialist, medical insurance technician, patient care assistant/technician, nurse assistant, vocational nurse, or medical transcriber. Along with their application, they must submit a 300–word essay on how, besides being a military wife, they have contributed to making their community a better place. Selection is based on the essay and commitment to volunteerism.

Financial data: Maximum stipends are $30,000, $10,000, or $8,500. Funds may be used for tuition only; books and other fees are not covered.

Duration: The program of study must be completed within 48 months.

Number awarded: 22 each year: 2 at $30,000 (for nursing students only), 5 at $10,000, and 15 at $8,500.

Deadline: April of each year.

2297 SAD SACKS NURSING SCHOLARSHIP

AMVETS–Department of Illinois
2200 South Sixth Street
Springfield, IL 62703
Phone: (217) 528–4713; (800) 638–VETS (within IL); Fax: (217) 528–9896
Web: www.ilamvets.org/prog_scholarships.cfm

Summary: To provide financial assistance for nursing education to Illinois residents, especially descendants of disabled or deceased veterans.

Eligibility: Open to seniors at high schools in Illinois who have been accepted to an approved nursing program and students already enrolled in an approved school of nursing in Illinois. Priority is given to dependents of deceased or disabled veterans. Selection is based on academic record, character, interest and activity record, and financial need. Preference is given to students in the following order: third–year students, second–year students, and first–year students.

Financial data: A stipend is awarded (amount not specified).

Duration: 1 year.

Number awarded: Varies each year; recently, 2 of these scholarships were awarded.

Deadline: February of each year.

2298 $$ SAE/FORD PAS SCHOLARSHIP

Society of Automotive Engineers
Attn: Scholarships and Loans Program
400 Commonwealth Drive
Warrendale, PA 15096–0001
Phone: (724) 776–4790; (877) 606–7323; Fax: (724) 776–0790;
Email: scholarships@sae.org
Web: students.sae.org/awdscholar/scholarships/ford

Summary: To provide financial support to graduating high school seniors who participated in the Ford Partnership for Advanced Studies (Ford PAS) program and are interested in studying engineering in college.

Eligibility: Open to graduating high school seniors who are past or present students in a Ford PAS program at their high school or in a Ford PAS after–school/weekend/summer/college program. Applicants must be planning to work on an associate or bachelor's degree in engineering or technology at an accredited college or university. They must have a GPA of 3.0 or higher and a rank in the 90th percentile on SAT 1 or composite ACT. Along with their application, they must submit 2 letters of recommendation (1 from a Ford PAS instructor) and a 250–word essay on their goals, plans, experiences, and interests in mobility engineering. Financial need is not considered. U.S. citizenship is required.

Financial data: The stipend is $5,000.

Duration: 1 year; nonrenewable.

Number awarded: 1 each year.

Deadline: January of each year.

2299 $ SAE WOMEN ENGINEERS COMMITTEE SCHOLARSHIP

Society of Automotive Engineers
Attn: Scholarship Administrator
400 Commonwealth Drive
Warrendale, PA 15096–0001
Phone: (724) 776–4970; Fax: (724) 776–3049;
Email: scholarships@sae.org
Web: students.sae.org/awdscholar/scholarships/wec

Summary: To provide financial support to female graduating high school seniors interested in studying engineering in college.

Eligibility: Open to female U.S. citizens who intend to earn an ABET–accredited degree in engineering. Applicants must be high school seniors with a GPA of 3.0 or higher. Selection is based on high school transcripts; SAT or ACT scores; school–related extracurricular activities; non–school related activities; academic honors, civic honors, and awards; and a 250–word essay on their goals, plans, experiences, and interests in mobility engineering. Financial need is not considered.

Financial data: The stipend is $2,000.

Duration: 1 year; nonrenewable.

Number awarded: 1 each year.

Deadline: January of each year.

2300 SAFARI CLUB INTERNATIONAL FOUNDATION FOUR–YEAR CONSERVATION SCHOLARSHIPS

Safari Club International
SCI Foundation
Attn: Education Department
4800 West Gates Pass Road
Tucson, AZ 85745–9490
Phone: (520) 620–1220, ext. 231; (800) 377–5399; Fax: (520) 622–1205
Web: www.safariclubfoundation.org

Summary: To provide financial assistance to entering college freshmen interested in studying a field related to conservation.

Eligibility: Open to graduating high school seniors who have been accepted into an accredited 4–year college or university. Preference is given to students planning to work on a degree in a field related to conservation (e.g., natural resource management, forestry, environmental studies, conservation education, outdoor education and recreation, or animal science). Applicants must be recommended by a Safari Club International Chapter. They must be able to demonstrate academic ability and a concern for their school and community. Along with their application, they must submit a 500–word essay describing their commitment to a conservation–related field, citing how their past experiences (academic accomplishments, volunteer or paid work, and life experience) support their career goals. Financial need is not considered.

Financial data: The stipend is $1,200 per year.
Duration: 4 years.
Number awarded: Up to 4 each year.
Deadline: April of each year.

2301 $ SAFARI CLUB INTERNATIONAL FOUNDATION'S UPPER–LEVEL COLLEGE SCHOLARSHIPS

Safari Club International
SCI Foundation
Attn: Education Department
4800 West Gates Pass Road
Tucson, AZ 85745–9490
Phone: (520) 620–1220, ext. 231; (800) 377–5399; Fax: (520) 622–1205
Web: www.safariclubfoundation.org

Summary: To provide financial assistance to entering college juniors interested in studying a field related to conservation.

Eligibility: Open to college students entering their junior year at an accredited 4–year college or university who have a GPA of 3.0 or higher. Preference is given to students working on a degree in a field related to conservation (e.g., wildlife or range management, forestry, wildlife law enforcement, conservation education). Applicants must be recommended by their college or university faculty adviser. They must be able to demonstrate academic ability, fishing and hunting activities, and a pro–hunting viewpoint on wildlife management and land use. Along with their application, they must submit a 500–word essay describing their commitment to a conservation–related field, citing how their past experiences (academic accomplishments, volunteer or paid work, and life experience) support their career goals, describing their active hunting experiences, and stating their pro–hunting viewpoint. Financial need is not considered.

Financial data: The stipend is $2,200 per year.
Duration: 2 years.
Number awarded: Up to 4 each year.
Deadline: April of each year.

2302 $$ SAN ANTONIO POST SAME SCHOLARSHIPS

Summary: To provide financial assistance to students (especially those participating in ROTC) who are majoring in designated fields at colleges and universities in Texas.

See Listing #1497.

2303 SANDRA R. SPAULDING MEMORIAL SCHOLARSHIPS

California Nurses Association
Attn: California Nurses Foundation
2030 Franklin Street, Suite 610
Oakland, CA 94612
Phone: (510) 622–8311; Fax: (510) 663–4825;
Email: info@calnursesfoundation.org
Web: www.nationalnursesunited.org/pages/1074

Summary: To provide financial assistance to students from diverse ethnic backgrounds who are enrolled in an associate degree in nursing (A.D.N.) program in California.

Eligibility: Open to students who have been admitted to a second–year accredited A.D.N. program in California and plan to complete the degree within 2 years. Along with their application, they must submit a 1–page essay describing their personal and professional goals. Selection is based on that essay, commitment and active participation in nursing and health–related organizations, professional vision and direction, and financial need. A goal of this scholarship program is to encourage ethnic and socioeconomic diversity in nursing.

Financial data: A stipend is awarded (amount not specified).
Duration: 1 year; nonrenewable.
Number awarded: 1 or more each year.
Deadline: July of each year.

2304 $$ SAP NORTH AMERICA SCHOLARSHIPS

SAP America, Inc.
Attn: Director, University Alliances
3999 West Chester Pike
Newton Square, PA 19073
Phone: (610) 661–1000; (800) 872–1727;
Email: SAPScholarship@easymatch.com
Web: www.sap.com/about–sap/csr/scholarshipprogram/index.epx

Summary: To provide financial assistance to upper–division students working on a degree related to enterprise technology.

Eligibility: Open to full–time students entering their junior or senior year at a college or university in the United States or Canada that is an active member of the SAP University Alliances program. Applicants must be majoring in business, computer science, engineering, or mathematics. They must have a GPA of 3.5 or higher. Along with their application, they must submit transcripts, a resume, a letter of recommendation, and confirmation of community service. Selection is based on academic achievement, the quality of the application, the resume and letter of recommendation, community service and volunteerism, and demonstration of understanding of enterprise technology; financial need is not considered.

Financial data: The stipend is $5,000.
Duration: 1 year; nonrenewable.
Number awarded: Up to 15 each year.
Deadline: May of each year.

2305 SAPA SCHOLARSHIP AND EXCELLENCE IN EDUCATION PROGRAM

Sino–American Pharmaceutical Professionals Association
Attn: Scholarship Office
P.O. Box 292
Nanuet, NY 10954
Email: sapa_scholarship@yahoo.com
Web: www.sapaweb.org/new/index.htm

Summary: To provide financial assistance to high school seniors who plan to major in life sciences in college.

Eligibility: Open to graduating high school seniors who have a GPA of 3.3 or higher, a class rank in the top 10% of their class, and an SAT score of at least 2000. Applicants must be planning to enroll full time at a college or university in any state and major in a life science. Eligible fields include biochemistry, biology, botany, chemical engineering, chemistry, computer science, entomology, environmental engineering, environmental science, mathematics, mechanical engineering, microbiology, molecular genetics, pharmacy/pharmacology, physics, physiology, and zoology. They must be U.S. citizens or permanent residents. Along with their application, they must submit a 600–word essay on why they want to prepare for a life science–related career. Selection is based on academic performance and demonstrated potential for and commitment to a career in life science.

Financial data: The stipend is $1,000.
Duration: 1 year.
Number awarded: 2 or more each year.
Deadline: April of each year.

2306 $ S.C. INTERNATIONAL ACTUARIAL SCIENCE SCHOLARSHIPS

S.C. International, Ltd.
1315 Butterfield Road, Suite 224
Downers Grove, IL 60515
Phone: (630) 963–3033; (800) 543–2553; Fax: (630) 963–3170;
Email: search@scinternational.com
Web: www.scinternational.com/scholarship_application.asp

Summary: To provide financial assistance to college seniors majoring in actuarial science or mathematics.

Eligibility: Open to students entering their senior year of undergraduate study in actuarial science or mathematics. Applicants must have passed at least 1 actuarial examination and have a GPA of 3.0 or higher both in their major and overall. They must be eligible to work in the United States.

Financial data: The stipend is $1,000 or $500 per semester.

Duration: 1 semester (nonrenewable).

Number awarded: 4 each year (2 each semester: 1 at $1,000 and 1 at $500).

Deadline: May of each year for the fall semester; December of each year for the spring semester.

2307 SCHLUTZ FAMILY BEEF BREEDING SCHOLARSHIP

Iowa Foundation for Agricultural Advancement
Attn: Winner's Circle Scholarships
c/o SGI
30805 595th Avenue
Cambridge, IA 50046
Phone: (515) 291–3941;
Email: linda@slweldon.net
Web: www.iowastatefair.org

Summary: To provide financial assistance to Iowa high school seniors who have been involved in beef activities and plan to major in animal science or a related field at a college in the state.

Eligibility: Open to residents of Iowa who will be incoming freshmen at a college or university in the state in the following fall. Applicants must be planning to major in animal science or a program in agriculture or human sciences that is related to the animal industry. They must have a strong background in beef projects and activities. Along with their application, they must submit a 250–word essay summarizing their experiences with their agricultural and livestock projects. Selection is based on that essay and participation in agricultural and livestock projects (50%); activities, leadership, and recognition in 4–H, FFA, and other high school and community activities (25%); academic record (15%); and curriculum plans for college and career plans after graduation as they relate to the agricultural industry in general (10%). Preference is given to applicants who show a desire to remain active in the beef cattle industry after graduation.

Financial data: The stipend is $1,000.

Duration: 1 year; nonrenewable.

Number awarded: 1 each year.

Deadline: April of each year.

2308 $ SCHOLARSHIPS SUPPORTING POST–SECONDARY EDUCATION FOR A CAREER IN THE AUDIOVISUAL INDUSTRY

Summary: To provide financial assistance to undergraduate and graduate students who are interested in preparing for a career in the audiovisual (AV) industry.

See Listing #1504.

2309 $$ SCIENCE, MATHEMATICS, AND RESEARCH FOR TRANSFORMATION (SMART) DEFENSE SCHOLARSHIP FOR SERVICE PROGRAM

American Society for Engineering Education
Attn: SMART Defense Scholarship Program
1818 N Street, N.W., Suite 600
Washington, DC 20036–2479
Phone: (202) 331–3544; Fax: (202) 265–8504;
Email: smart@asee.org
Web: smart.asee.org

Summary: To provide funding and work experience to undergraduate and graduate students in designated science, technology, engineering, or mathematics (STEM) disciplines that are of interest to the U.S. Department of Defense (DoD).

Eligibility: Open to full–time undergraduate and graduate students working on a degree in any of the following fields: aeronautical and astronautical engineering; biosciences; chemical engineering; chemistry; civil engineering; cognitive, neural, and behavioral sciences; computer and computational sciences; electrical engineering; geosciences, including terrain, water, and air; industrial and systems engineering (technical tracks only); information sciences; materials science and engineering; mathematics; mechanical engineering; naval architecture and ocean engineering; nuclear engineering, oceanography; operations research (technical tracks only); or physics. Applicants must be U.S. citizens who have a GPA of 3.0 or higher. They must be available to work as interns at DoD laboratories during the summer months. Selection is based on academic records, personal statements, letters of recommendation, and ACT/SAT or GRE scores.

Financial data: The program provides 1) full payment of tuition and related educational fees at the recipient's institution; 2) a stipend ranging from $25,000 to $41,000 per year, depending on prior educational experience, for the academic year and summer internship; 3) a book allowance of $1,000 per year; and 4) health insurance reimbursement up to $1,200 per calendar year. This is a scholarship/loan program; recipients must agree to serve for 1 year per year of support received as a civilian employee of the DoD in a science and engineering position. If they fail to fulfill that service obligation, they must reimburse the federal government for all funds they received.

Duration: Until completion of a degree (to a maximum of 4 years for a bachelor's, 2 years for a master's, or 5 years for a Ph.D.).

Number awarded: Varies each year; recently, 30 of these scholarships were awarded.

Deadline: December of each year.

2310 SEALANT, WATERPROOFING AND RESTORATION FOUNDATION SCHOLARSHIPS

Sealant, Waterproofing and Restoration Institute
Attn: SWR Foundation
400 Admiral Boulevard
Kansas City, MO 64106
Phone: (816) 472–7974; Fax: (816) 472–7765;
Email: info@swrionline.org
Web: www.swrionline.org/resources/scholarship.asp

Summary: To provide financial assistance to students interested in preparing for a career in construction, especially the sealant, waterproofing, and restoration industry.

Eligibility: Open to students enrolled or planning to enroll as an undergraduate at a college or university. Applicants must be studying a field to prepare for a career in the sealant, waterproofing, and restoration construction industry. Along with their application, they must submit 1) a 500–word description of their activities, interests, anticipated employment, prospective field of study, and career path; 2) an outline of their proposed program of study, indicating their intent to pursue an education in the field of construction (specifically, the sealant, waterproofing, and restoration industry); 3) transcripts; and 4) letters of recommendation from instructors or employees of firms in the sealant, waterproofing, and restoration industry who are knowledgeable about the applicant's interest and involvement in that industry. Selection is based on those submissions and financial need.

Financial data: The maximum stipend is $1,500. Funds are paid directly to the recipient's college or university.

Duration: 1 year.

Number awarded: Varies each year; recently, 7 of these scholarships were awarded.

Deadline: August of each year for fall semester; January of each year for spring semester.

2311 SEE EDUCATION FOUNDATION SCHOLARSHIPS

International Society of Explosives Engineers
Attn: SEE Education Foundation
30325 Bainbridge Road
Cleveland, OH 44139
Phone: (440) 349–4400; Fax: (440) 349–3788;
Email: isee@isee.org
Web: www.isee.org

Summary: To provide financial assistance to undergraduate and graduate engineering students interested in preparing for a career involving the use of explosives.

Eligibility: Open to students working on a technical undergraduate, graduate, or doctoral degree as a full–time student at an accredited college or university. Applicants must be preparing for a career in a field related to the commercial explosives industry, such as mining, construction, forestry, manufacturing, automotives, or aerospace. Selection is based on a career resume, a statement of personal goals, academic potential, written communications, ability to overcome personal challenges, and financial need.

Financial data: A stipend is awarded (amount not specified). Funds are sent directly to the educational institution.

Duration: 1 year; may be renewed.

Number awarded: Varies each year; since the program was established, it has awarded more than 90 scholarships.

Deadline: May of each year.

2312 $ SEED COMPANIES SCHOLARSHIP

American Floral Endowment
1601 Duke Street
Alexandria, VA 22314
Phone: (703) 838–5211; Fax: (703) 838–5212;
Email: afe@endowment.org
Web: endowment.org/floriculture–scholarshipsinternships.html

Summary: To provide financial assistance to upper–division and graduate students in horticulture.

Eligibility: Open to undergraduate students entering their junior or senior year and to graduate students. Applicants must be working on a degree in horticulture and intending to prepare for a career in the seed industry, including research, breeding, sales, and marketing. They must be U.S. or Canadian citizens or permanent residents and have a GPA of 1.0 or higher. Along with their application, they must submit a statement describing their career goals and the academic, work–related, and/or life experiences that support those goals. Financial need is considered in the selection process.

Financial data: The stipend varies each year; recently, it was $2,300.

Duration: 1 year.

Number awarded: 1 each year.

Deadline: April of each year.

2313 $ SGNA RN GENERAL EDUCATION SCHOLARSHIP

Society of Gastroenterology Nurses and Associates, Inc.
Attn: Awards Committee
401 North Michigan Avenue
Chicago, IL 60611–4267
Phone: (312) 321–5165; (800) 245–SGNA; Fax: (312) 673–6694;
Email: sgna@smithbucklin.com
Web: www.sgna.org/AboutUs/AwardsandScholarships.aspx

Summary: To provide financial assistance to full–time students working toward licensure as a registered nurse (R.N.).

Eligibility: Open to students currently enrolled full time in an accredited nursing program with a GPA of 3.0 or higher. Applicants must be studying to become an R.N. Along with their application, they must submit a 2–page essay on a challenging situation they see in the health care environment today and how they, as an R.N., would best address and meet that challenge. Financial need is not considered in the selection process.

Financial data: The stipend is $2,500. Funds are issued as reimbursement after the recipient has completed the proposed course work with a GPA of 3.0 or higher.

Duration: 1 year.

Number awarded: 1 or more each year.

Deadline: July of each year.

2314 $$ SHARON D. BANKS MEMORIAL UNDERGRADUATE SCHOLARSHIP

Women's Transportation Seminar
Attn: WTS Foundation
1701 K Street, N.W., Suite 800
Washington, DC 20006
Phone: (202) 955–5085; Fax: (202) 955–5088;
Email: wts@wtsinternational.org
Web: www.wtsinternational.org/education/scholarships

Summary: To provide financial assistance to undergraduate women interested in a career in transportation.

Eligibility: Open to women who are working on an undergraduate degree in transportation or a transportation–related field (e.g., transportation engineering, planning, finance, or logistics). Applicants must have a GPA of 3.0 or higher and be interested in a career in transportation. Along with their application, they must submit a 500–word statement about their career goals after graduation and why they think they should receive the scholarship award. Applications must be submitted first to a local chapter; the chapters forward selected applications for consideration on the national level. Minority women are especially encouraged to apply. Selection is based on transportation involvement and goals, job skills, and academic record; financial need is not considered.

Financial data: The stipend is $5,000.

Duration: 1 year.

Number awarded: 1 each year.

Deadline: Applications must be submitted by November to a local WTS chapter.

2315 SHARPS SCHOLARSHIP ESSAY CONTEST

Sharps Compliance, Inc.
9220 Kirby Drive, Suite 500
Houston, TX 77054
Phone: (713) 432–0300; Fax: (713) 838–0508;
Email: scholarship@sharpsinc.com
Web: www.sharpsinc.com/learning–center/scholarships

Summary: To recognize and reward, with college scholarships, students in health–related fields who submit outstanding essays on topics related to disposal of medical waste.

Eligibility: Open to U.S. and Canadian citizens who are enrolled or planning to enroll at an accredited college or university in a field of study related to health care. Applicants must submit an essay of 1,250 to 1,500 words on a topic that varies each semester but relates to the disposal of medical waste; recently, students were invited to write on accidental needle–stick injuries outside of the hospital and health care setting, including their ideas about measures that could have been taken to prevent such injuries.

Financial data: Prizes are $1,500 for first, $1,000 for second, and $740 for third. Funds are paid directly to the recipient's college or university.

Duration: This program began in 2011.

Number awarded: 6 each year: 3 in the fall contest and 3 in the spring contest.

Deadline: April of each year for the fall contest; October of each year for the spring contest.

2316 SHEENA M. TAYLOR MEMORIAL SCHOLARSHIP FUND

Pittsburgh Foundation
Attn: Scholarship Coordinator
Five PPG Place, Suite 250
Pittsburgh, PA 15222–5414
Phone: (412) 394–2649; Fax: (412) 391–7259;
Email: turnerd@pghfdn.org
Web: www.pittsburghfoundation.org/node/1711

Summary: To provide financial assistance to residents of western Pennsylvania and West Virginia (and of the United Kingdom) who are attending a school of nursing in those states.

Eligibility: Open to residents of western Pennsylvania, West Virginia, or the United Kingdom who are nursing students not yet qualified to practice as registered nurses. Applicants must be enrolled in a college or hospital program in western Pennsylvania or West Virginia. They must have a GPA of 2.0 or higher and be able to demonstrate financial need.

Financial data: The stipend varies each year; recently, $1,850 was available for this program.

Duration: 1 year; nonrenewable.

Number awarded: 1 each year.

Deadline: February of each year.

2317 $$ SHELL INCENTIVE FUND SCHOLARSHIPS

Shell Oil Company
Attn: Scholarship Administrator
910 Louisiana, Suite 4476C
Houston, TX 77002
Phone: (713) 241–6314
Web: www.shell.us

Summary: To provide financial assistance to underrepresented minority students majoring in specified engineering and geosciences fields at designated universities.

Eligibility: Open to students enrolled full time as sophomores, juniors, or seniors at 22 participating universities. Applicants must be U.S. citizens or authorized to work in the United States and members of a race or ethnicity underrepresented in the technical and scientific academic areas (Black, Hispanic/Latino, American Indian, or Alaskan Native). They must have a GPA of 3.2 or higher with a major in engineering (chemical, civil, electrical, geological, geophysical, mechanical, or petroleum) or geosciences (geology, geophysics, or physics). Along with their application, they must submit a 100–word essay on the kind of work they plan to be doing in 10 years, both in their career and in their community. Financial need is not considered in the selection process.

Financial data: The stipend is $5,000 per year.

Duration: 1 year; may be renewed up to 3 additional years, provided the recipient remains qualified and accepts a Shell Oil Company internship (if offered).

Number awarded: Approximately 20 each year.

Deadline: February of each year.

2318 SHELL OIL COMPANY PROCESS TECHNOLOGY SCHOLARSHIP

Center for the Advancement of Process Technology
Attn: College of the Mainland Foundation
1200 Amburn Road
Texas City, TX 77591
Phone: (409) 933–9508; Fax: (409) 933–8015;
Email: moneal@com.edu
Web: www.captech.org/students/scholarships.php

Summary: To provide financial assistance to students interested in working on a 2–year degree in process technology.

Eligibility: Open to students currently enrolled or planning to enroll in a 2–year degree program in process/production technology, petroleum technology, compressor/compression technology, electrical/electronics technology, industrial maintenance technology, instrumentation/analyzer technology, or machinist/mechanical technology. Applicants must have a GPA of 2.5 or higher. They must be U.S. citizens or authorized to work full time in the United States. Along with their application, they must submit a 1–page essay on why they should be considered for this scholarship and selected over other qualified, worthy applicants. Selection is based on scholastic performance; financial need is not considered.

Financial data: Stipends are $750 per semester for full–time students or $500 per semester for part–time students. Eligible expenses are limited to tuition, books, fees, and educational supplies.

Duration: Recipients have up to 3 years to complete the 2–year process technology degree program. The maximum amount of support they may receive is $2,200.

Number awarded: 1 or more each year.

Deadline: February of each year.

2319 $$ SHELL OIL COMPANY TECHNICAL SCHOLARSHIP PROGRAM FOR COLLEGE STUDENTS

Shell Oil Company
Attn: Scholarship Administrator
910 Louisiana, Suite 4476C
Houston, TX 77002
Email: ariana.robinson@shell.com
Web: www.shell.us

Summary: To provide financial assistance to undergraduate students majoring in specified engineering and geosciences fields at designated universities.

Eligibility: Open to students enrolled full time as sophomores, juniors, or seniors at 22 participating universities. Applicants must have a GPA of 3.2 or higher with a major in engineering (chemical, civil, electrical, geological, geophysical, mechanical, or petroleum) or geosciences (geology, geophysics, or physics). They must be U.S. citizens or authorized to work in the United States. Along with their application, they must submit a 100–word essay on the kind of work they plan to be doing in 10 years, both in their career and in their community. Financial need is not considered in the selection process.

Financial data: The stipend is $5,000 per year.

Duration: 1 year; may be renewed up to 3 additional years, provided the recipient remains qualified and accepts a Shell Oil Company internship (if offered).

Number awarded: Approximately 20 each year.

Deadline: February of each year.

2320 $ SHELL OIL COMPANY TECHNICAL SCHOLARSHIP PROGRAM FOR HIGH SCHOOL SENIORS

Shell Oil Company
Attn: Scholarship Administrator
910 Louisiana, Suite 4476C
Houston, TX 77002
Phone: (713) 241–6314
Web: www.shell.us

Summary: To provide financial assistance to high school seniors planning to major in specified engineering and geosciences fields at designated universities.

Eligibility: Open to graduating high school seniors planning to enroll full time at 22 participating universities. Applicants must be planning to major in engineering (chemical, civil, electrical, geological, geophysical, mechanical, or petroleum) or geosciences (geology, geophysics, or physics). They must be U.S. citizens or authorized to work in the United States. Along with their application, they must submit a 100–word essay on the kind of work they plan to be doing in 10 years, both in their career and in their community; they should comment specifically on how they could potentially contribute to the petrochemical industry. Financial need is not considered in the selection process.

Financial data: The stipend is $2,500.

Duration: 1 year; nonrenewable, although recipients may apply to the Shell Oil Company Technical Scholarship Program for College Students to cover the remaining years of their undergraduate program.

Number awarded: Approximately 20 each year.

Deadline: February of each year.

2321 SHELL PROCESS TECHNOLOGY SCHOLARSHIPS

Shell Oil Company
Attn: Scholarship Administrator
910 Louisiana, Suite 4476C
Houston, TX 77002
Email: ariana.robinson@shell.com
Web: www.shell.us

Summary: To provide financial assistance to students working on or planning to work on a 2–year degree in process technology.

Eligibility: Open to students enrolled or planning to enroll in the following 2–year degree programs: process/production technology, petroleum technology, compressor/compression technology, electrical/electronics technology, industrial maintenance technology, instrumentation/analyzer technology, or machinist/mechanical technology. Applicants must be students already enrolled in a relevant degree program or high school seniors entering such a program. They must be U.S. citizens or authorized to work in the United States. Along with their application, they must submit a 100–word essay on the kind of work they plan to be doing in 10 years, both in their career and in their community. Financial need is not considered in the selection process.

Financial data: Full–time students may receive up to $750 per semester and part–time students up to $500 per semester. All students are limited to a lifetime total of $2,000.

Duration: All work must be completed within a 3–year period.

Number awarded: Varies each year.

Deadline: February of each year.

2322 SHERYL KRATZ MEMORIAL SCHOLARSHIP

California Groundwater Association
P.O. Box 14369
Santa Rosa, CA 95402
Phone: (707) 578–4408; Fax: (707) 546–4906;
Email: wellguy@groundh2o.org
Web: www.groundh2o.org/programs/scholarship.html

Summary: To provide financial assistance to women in California who are interested in attending college in any state and plan to major in a field related to ground water.

Eligibility: Open to female residents of California currently enrolled or accepted at a college or university in any state. Applicants must either 1) have a family affiliation with a CGA member (including employees of business members) and be interested in working on a degree in any field; or 2) be interested in working on a degree in a field of study related to ground water. Along with their application, they must submit a 500–word essay demonstrating their interest in either their chosen field of interest or in ground water technology. Financial need is not considered in the selection process.

Financial data: The stipend is $1,000.

Duration: 1 year.

Number awarded: 1 each year.

Deadline: March of each year.

2323 SIDNEY B. MEADOWS SCHOLARSHIPS

Southern Nursery Association
Attn: Sidney B. Meadows Scholarship Endowment Fund
P.O. Box 801513
Acworth, GA 30101
Phone: (678) 813–1880; Fax: (678) 813–1881;
Email: info@sbmsef.org
Web: www.sbmsef.org

Summary: To provide financial assistance to upper–division and graduate students from designated southern states who are interested in preparing for a career in horticulture.

Eligibility: Open to residents of Alabama, Arkansas, Florida, Georgia, Kentucky, Louisiana, Maryland, Mississippi, Missouri, North Carolina, Oklahoma, South Carolina, Tennessee, Texas, Virginia, and West Virginia. Applicants must be college juniors, seniors, or graduate students enrolled full time in an accredited ornamental horticulture program or related discipline at a school in any state. They must have a GPA of 2.75 or higher (for undergraduates) or 3.0 or higher (for graduate students). Preference is given to applicants who plan to work in an aspect of the industry (including owning their own business) and those in financial need. U.S. citizenship is required.

Financial data: The stipend is $1,500 per year.

Duration: 1 year; may be renewed up to 1 additional year.

Number awarded: 12 each year.

Deadline: May of each year.

2324 $$ SIEMENS AWARDS FOR ADVANCED PLACEMENT

Siemens Foundation
170 Wood Avenue South
Iselin, NJ 08830
Phone: (877) 822–5233; Fax: (732) 603–5890;
Email: foundation.us@siemens.com
Web: www.siemens–foundation.org/en/advanced_placement.htm

Summary: To recognize and reward high school students with exceptional scores on the Advanced Placement (AP) examinations in mathematics and the sciences.

Eligibility: Open to all students in U.S. high schools (as well as home–schooled students and those in U.S. territories). Each fall, the College Board identifies the male and female seniors in each state who have earned the highest number of scores of 5 on 8 AP exams: biology, calculus BC, chemistry, computer science A, environmental science, physics C mechanics, physics C electricity and magnetism, and statistics. Males and females are considered separately. Students with the highest scores nationally receive separate awards. The program also provides awards to teachers who demonstrate excellence in teaching AP mathematics and science.

Financial data: State scholarships are $2,000; in addition, national winners receive $5,000 scholarships. State awards for teachers high schools are $1,000; the National AP Teacher of the Year receives $5,000.

Duration: The awards are presented annually.

Number awarded: 100 state scholarships (1 female and 1 male from each state) and 2 national scholarships (1 female and 1 male) are awarded each year. In addition, 50 teachers (1 from each state) receive awards and 1 of those is designated the National AP Teacher of the Year.

Deadline: There is no application or nomination process for these awards. The College Board identifies the students and teachers for the Siemens Foundation.

2325 $$ SIEMENS COMPETITION IN MATH, SCIENCE AND TECHNOLOGY AWARDS

Siemens Foundation
170 Wood Avenue South
Iselin, NJ 08830
Phone: (877) 822–5233; Fax: (732) 603–5890;
Email: foundation.us@siemens.com
Web: www.siemens–foundation.org/en/competition.htm

Summary: To recognize and reward outstanding high school seniors who have undertaken individual or team research projects in science, mathematics, and technology (or in combinations of those disciplines).

Eligibility: Open to high school and home–schooled seniors who are legal or permanent U.S. residents and live in the United States, Puerto Rico, Guam, Virgin Islands, American Samoa, Wake and Midway Islands, or the Marianas. U.S. high school students enrolled in a Department of Defense dependents school, an accredited overseas American or international school, a foreign school as an exchange student, or a foreign school because their parent(s) live and work abroad are also eligible. Research projects may be submitted in mathematics, engineering, or the biological or physical sciences, or involve combinations of disciplines, such as astrophysics, biochemistry, bioengineering, biology, biophysics, botany, chemical engineering, chemistry, computer science, civil engineering, earth and atmospheric science, electrical engineering, environmental science and engineering, genetics, geology, materials science/nanoscience, mathematics, mechanical engineering, microbiology, nutritional science, physics, or toxicology. Both individual and team projects (2 or 3 members) may be entered. Competition entrants must submit a detailed report on their research project, including a description of the purpose of the research, rationale for the research, pertinent scientific literature, methodology, results, discussion, and conclusion. All projects must be endorsed by a sponsoring high school and have a project adviser or mentor. There are 3 judging phases to the competition. An initial review panel selects outstanding research projects from 6 different regions of the country. The highest–rated projects from each region are selected and the students who submitted them are recognized as regional finalists. They are offered all–expense paid trips to the regional competition on the campus of a regional university partner, and are required to make an oral presentation. The top–rated individual and team project in each region are selected to represent the region in the national competition. At each phase, selection is based on clarity of expression, comprehensiveness, creativity, field knowledge, future work, interpretation, literature review, presentation, scientific importance, and validity.

Financial data: At the regional level, finalists receive $1,000 scholarships, both as individuals and members of teams. Individual regional winners receive $3,000 scholarships. Winning regional teams receive $6,000 scholarships to be divided among the team members. Those regional winners then receive additional scholarships as national finalists. In the national competition, the first–place individual winner receives an additional $100,000 scholarship and members of the first–place team winner share an additional $100,000 in scholarships. Other individual winners receive scholarships of $50,000 for second, $40,000 for third, $30,000 for fourth, $20,000 for fifth, and $10,000 for sixth. Other team winners share an additional $50,000 for second, $40,000 for third, $30,000 for fourth, $20,000 for fifth, and $10,000 for sixth. Scholarship money is sent directly to the recipient's college or university to cover undergraduate and/or graduate educational expenses.

Duration: The competition is held annually.

Number awarded: In the initial round of judging, up to 300 regional semifinalists (up to 50 in each region) are selected. Of those, 60 are chosen as regional finalists (5 individuals and 5 teams in each of the 6 regions). Then 12 regional winners (1 individual and 1 team) are selected in each regional competition, and they become the national finalists.

Deadline: September of each year.

2326 SISTER HELEN MARIE PELLICER SCHOLARSHIP

Florida Dietetic Association
Attn: Scholarship Chair
P.O. Box 12608
Tallahassee, FL 32317–2608
Phone: (850) 386–8850; Fax: (850) 386–7918;
Email: info@eatrightflorida.org
Web: www.eatrightflorida.org

Summary: To provide financial assistance to upper–division students in Florida preparing for a career in the field of dietetics.

Eligibility: Open to Florida residents enrolled full time as upper–division undergraduates in a program that will prepare them to practice in the field of dietetics. Applicants must be members of the Florida Dietetic Association and the Academy of Nutrition and Dietetics or enrolled in a program leading to eligibility for membership. They must have a GPA of 2.5 or higher. Along with their application, they must submit a brief statement of their professional goals and reason for choosing the field of dietetics. U.S. citizenship or permanent resident status is required. Selection is based on academics, professional involvement and potential, and financial need.

Financial data: The stipend is $1,000.

Duration: 1 year.

Number awarded: 1 each year.

Deadline: October of each year.

2327 $ SISTER MARY PETRONIA VAN STRATEN SCHOLARSHIP

Wisconsin Mathematics Council
W175 N11117 Stonewood Drive, Suite 204
Germantown, WI 53022
Phone: (262) 437–0174; Fax: (262) 532–2430;
Email: wmc@wismath.org
Web: www.wismath.org/awards–scholarships

Summary: To provide financial assistance to students from Wisconsin preparing for a career as a mathematics teacher.

Eligibility: Open to residents of Wisconsin currently enrolled in an undergraduate or graduate teacher education program in the state. Applicants must be enrolled in or have completed a course in methods of teaching mathematics and have a GPA of 3.0 or higher. If they are a secondary education major, they must have completed 16 credits of mathematics; a statistics and a computer programming or technology application course must be part of their undergraduate or graduate program. If they are an elementary education major, their program must include 6 credits of mathematics; some statistics concepts and some computer/technology knowledge must be part of their undergraduate or graduate program. Selection is based on college performance, recommendations, and potential contributions to mathematics education in Wisconsin.

Financial data: The stipend is $2,000.

Duration: 1 year.

Number awarded: 1 each year.

Deadline: February of each year.

2328 SOCIETY FOR PHYSICIAN ASSISTANTS IN PEDIATRICS SCHOLARSHIPS

Society for Physician Assistants in Pediatrics
P.O. Box 121
Schertz, TX 78154–0121
Phone: (210) 722–7622; Fax: (210) 568–6375;
Email: spapmail@gmail.com
Web: www.spaponline.org

Summary: To provide financial assistance to physician assistant students who have an interest in pediatrics.

Eligibility: Open to students currently enrolled in a physician assistant program. Applicants must submit a 500–word on how they intend to contribute to pediatrics as a physician assistant, including personal and professional activities related to their interest in pediatrics and their future professional goals.

Financial data: A stipend is awarded (amount not specified).

Duration: 1 year.

Number awarded: 1 or more each year.

Deadline: June of each year.

2329 $ SOCIETY FOR PROTECTIVE COATINGS COLLEGE SCHOLARSHIP PROGRAM

Society for Protective Coatings
Attn: Scholarship Committee
40 24th Street, Sixth Floor
Pittsburgh, PA 15222–4656
Phone: (412) 281–2331; (877) 281–7772; Fax: (412) 281–9992;
Email: info@sspc.org
Web: www.sspc.org/College–Scholarship–Program

Summary: To provide financial assistance to students interested in studying a field related to protective coatings at a designated university or trade school.

Eligibility: Open to graduating high school seniors and students already enrolled full time at 1 of 10 approved universities or trade schools. Applicants must be studying or planning to study a program that deals with protective coatings. They must have a GPA of 2.0 or higher. Along with their application, they must submit 1) a 250–word paragraph on why they feel they deserve this scholarship; and 2) a 500–word essay on their future plans and goals, including how they intend to use their college education to achieve their goals in the coatings field. Financial need is not considered in the selection process.

Financial data: The stipend is $2,500.

Duration: 1 year.

Number awarded: 2 each year.

Deadline: Deadline not specified.

2330 $ SOCIETY OF ARMY PHYSICIAN ASSISTANTS SCHOLARSHIP

American Academy of Physician Assistants–Veterans Caucus
Attn: Veterans Caucus
P.O. Box 362
Danville, PA 17821–0362
Phone: (570) 271–0292; Fax: (570) 271–5850;
Email: admin@veteranscaucus.org
Web: www.veteranscaucus.org

Summary: To provide financial assistance to Army veterans who are studying to become physician assistants.

Eligibility: Open to U.S. citizens who are currently enrolled in a physician assistant program. The program must be approved by the Commission on Accreditation of Allied Health Education. Applicants must be honorably discharged members of the United States Army. Selection is based on military honors and awards received, civic and college honors and awards received, professional memberships and activities, and GPA. An electronic copy of the applicant's DD Form 214 must accompany the application.

Financial data: The stipend is $2,000.

Duration: 1 year.

Number awarded: 1 each year.

Deadline: February of each year.

2331 $ SOCIETY OF BROADCAST ENGINEERS YOUTH SCHOLARSHIP

Society of Broadcast Engineers
Attn: Scholarship Committee
9102 North Meridian Street, Suite 150
Indianapolis, IN 46260
Phone: (317) 846–9000; Fax: (317) 846–9120
Web: www.sbe.org/sections/edu_ennes_scholarships.php

Summary: To provide financial assistance for college to high school seniors interested in the technical aspects of broadcasting.

Eligibility: Open to graduating high school seniors who intend to enroll at a technical school, college, or university the following fall. Applicants must have a serious interest in preparing for a career in broadcast engineering or a closely–related field. Along with their application, they must submit a brief autobiography that includes their interests and goals in broadcasting, a brief written statement explaining their career goals and education plans after high school, and transcripts. Financial need is not considered in the selection process.

Financial data: The award ranges from $1,000 to $3,000, depending on the availability of funds.

Duration: 1 year.

Number awarded: 1 each year.

Deadline: June of each year.

2332 $$ SOCIETY OF EXPLORATION GEOPHYSICISTS SCHOLARSHIP PROGRAM

Society of Exploration Geophysicists
Attn: SEG Foundation
8801 South Yale, Suite 500
P.O. Box 702740
Tulsa, OK 74170–2740
Phone: (918) 497–5500; Fax: (918) 497–5557;
Email: scholarships@seg.org
Web: www.seg.org/web/foundation/programs/scholarship

Summary: To provide financial assistance to high school seniors, undergraduates, and graduate students who are preparing for a career in applied geophysics.

Eligibility: Open to 1) high school students planning to enter college in the fall; and 2) undergraduate or graduate students whose grades are above average. Applicants must intend to work on a degree directed toward a career in applied geophysics or a closely–related field (e.g., geosciences, physics, geology, or earth and environmental sciences). Along with their application, they must submit a 150–word essay on how they plan to use geophysics in their future. Financial need is not considered in the selection process. Some of the scholarships are set aside for students at recognized colleges or universities in countries outside of the United States.

Financial data: The stipends generally range from $500 to $14,000 per year and average $2,500 per year.

Duration: 1 academic year; may be renewable, based on scholastic standing, availability of funds, and continuance of a course of study leading to a career in applied geophysics.

Number awarded: Varies each year; recently, a total of 118 scholarships, with a value of $434,150, were awarded.

Deadline: February of each year.

2333 $ SOCIETY OF INDEPENDENT PROFESSIONAL EARTH SCIENTISTS SCHOLARSHIPS

Society of Independent Professional Earth Scientists
Attn: SIPES Foundation
4925 Greenville Avenue, Suite 1106
Dallas, TX 75206–4019
Phone: (214) 363–1780; Fax: (214) 363–8195;
Email: sipes@sipes.org
Web: www.sipes.org

Summary: To provide financial assistance to upper–division and graduate students working on a degree in earth science or engineering.

Eligibility: Open to U.S. citizens who are upper–division or graduate students. Applicants must be working on a degree in any field of earth science or engineering. They must have a GPA of 3.5 or higher. Along with their application, they must submit a short statement on their career goals and information on their financial situation.

Financial data: Stipends range up to $2,300.

Duration: 1 year.

Number awarded: Varies each year; recently, 7 of these scholarships were awarded: 1 at $2,300 and 6 at $2,000.

Deadline: July of each year.

2334 $ SOCIETY OF PLASTICS ENGINEERS FOUNDATION SCHOLARSHIPS

Society of Plastics Engineers
Attn: SPE Foundation
13 Church Hill Road

Newtown, CT 06740
Phone: (203) 740–5447; Fax: (203) 775–1157;
Email: foundation@4spe.org
Web: www.4spe.org/spe–foundation
Summary: To provide financial assistance to undergraduate and graduate students who have a career interest in the plastics industry.
Eligibility: Open to full–time undergraduate students at 4–year colleges and 2–year technical programs and to graduate students. Applicants must be majoring in or taking courses that would be beneficial to a career in the plastics or polymer industry (e.g., plastics engineering, packaging, polymer sciences, chemistry, physics, chemical engineering, mechanical engineering, industrial engineering). Along with their application, they must submit 3 letters of recommendation; a high school and/or college transcript; a 1– to 2–page statement telling why they are applying for the scholarship, their qualifications, and their educational and career goals in the plastics industry; their employment history; a list of current and past school activities and community activities and honors; and information on their financial need.
Financial data: Stipends range up to $4,000 per year. Funds are paid directly to the recipient's school.
Duration: 1 year; may be renewed for up to 3 additional years.
Number awarded: 1 or more each year.
Deadline: February of each year.

2335 SOCIETY OF WOMEN ENGINEERS MID–HUDSON SECTION SCHOLARSHIP

Society of Women Engineers
Attn: Scholarship Selection Committee
203 North LaSalle Street, Suite 1675
Chicago, IL 60601–1269
Phone: (312) 596–5223; (877) SWE–INFO; Fax: (312) 644–8557;
Email: scholarships@swe.org
Web: societyofwomenengineers.swe.org/index.php/scholarships
Summary: To provide financial assistance to women, especially those from New York, who are working on an undergraduate or graduate degree in engineering or computer science.
Eligibility: Open to women who will be full–time sophomores, juniors, seniors, or graduate students at ABET–accredited colleges and universities. Applicants must be working on a degree in computer science or engineering and have a GPA of 3.0 or higher. Selection is based on merit. Preference is given to applicants who reside and attend school in New York.
Financial data: The stipend is $1,000.
Duration: 1 year.
Number awarded: 1 each year.
Deadline: February of each year.

2336 SOCIETY OF WOMEN ENGINEERS PAST PRESIDENTS SCHOLARSHIPS

Society of Women Engineers
Attn: Scholarship Selection Committee
203 North LaSalle Street, Suite 1675
Chicago, IL 60601–1269
Phone: (312) 596–5223; (877) SWE–INFO; Fax: (312) 644–8557;
Email: scholarships@swe.org
Web: societyofwomenengineers.swe.org/index.php/scholarships
Summary: To provide financial assistance to women working on an undergraduate or graduate degree in engineering or computer science.
Eligibility: Open to women who will be sophomores, juniors, seniors, or graduate students at ABET–accredited colleges and universities. Applicants must be U.S. citizens or permanent residents working full time on a degree in computer science or engineering and have a GPA of 3.0 or higher. Along with their application, they must submit a 1–page essay on why they want to be an engineer or computer scientist, how they believe they will make a difference as an engineer or computer scientist, and what influenced them to study engineering or computer science. Selection is based on merit.
Financial data: The stipend is $1,500.
Duration: 1 year.
Number awarded: 2 each year.
Deadline: February of each year.

2337 SOCIETY OF WOMEN ENGINEERS–DELMAR SECTION SCHOLARSHIP AWARD

Delaware Engineering Society
c/o Stacy Ziegler
Duffield Associates, Inc.
5400 Limestone Road
Wilmington, DE 19808
Phone: (302) 239–6634; Fax: (302) 239–8485;
Email: sziegler@duffnet.com
Web: www.desonline.us
Summary: To provide financial assistance to female high school seniors in the DelMar area who are interested in majoring in engineering in college.
Eligibility: Open to female high school seniors in Delaware and Maryland who will be enrolling in an engineering program at an ABET–accredited college or university. Applicants must have SAT scores of 600 or higher in mathematics, 500 or higher in critical reading, and 500 or higher in writing (or ACT scores of 29 or higher in mathematics and 25 or higher in English). They must submit an essay (up to 500 words) on their interest in engineering, their major area of study and area of specialization, the occupation they propose to pursue after graduation, their long–term goals, and how they hope to achieve them. Selection is based on the essay, academic record, honors and scholarships, volunteer activities, work experience, and letters of recommendation. Financial need is not required.
Financial data: A stipend is awarded (amount not specified).
Duration: 1 year (freshman year); nonrenewable.
Number awarded: Varies each year.
Deadline: December of each year.

2338 $ SOIL AND WATER CONSERVATION SCHOLARSHIP

Soil Science Society of America
Attn: Soil and Water Management and Conservation Division
5585 Guilford Road
Madison, WI 53711–5801
Phone: (608) 273–8080; Fax: (608) 273–2021;
Email: awards@sciencesocieties.org
Web: www.soils.org/membership/divisions/S06/awards/scholarship
Summary: To provide financial assistance to students at universities in North America working on a bachelor's or master's degree in a field related to soil and water conservation.
Eligibility: Open to students enrolled as juniors, seniors, or master's degree students at universities in Canada, Mexico, or the United States. Preference is given to students enrolled at land grant universities or at other universities that have an equivalent agricultural curriculum. Applicants must exhibit classroom activities, special studies, or work experience in the field of soil and water conservation and be working on a degree and career in that field. Selection is based on academic accomplishments, career goals in soil and water conservation, work experience in the field, and major professor's support.
Financial data: The stipend is $3,000. The recipient's major professor receives a grant of $500 to encourage the continued mentoring of the student and to accompany the student to attend the annual meeting where the scholarship is awarded.
Duration: 1 year.
Number awarded: 1 each year.
Deadline: March of each year.

2339 SOLAR TURBINES SCHOLARSHIP

Society of Women Engineers
Attn: Scholarship Selection Committee
203 North LaSalle Street, Suite 1675
Chicago, IL 60601–1269
Phone: (312) 596–5223; (877) SWE–INFO; Fax: (312) 644–8557;
Email: scholarships@swe.org
Web: societyofwomenengineers.swe.org/index.php/scholarships
Summary: To provide financial assistance to women who will be entering college as freshmen and are interested in studying computer science or specified fields of engineering.
Eligibility: Open to women who are entering college as freshmen with a GPA of 3.5 or higher. Applicants must be planning to enroll full time at a designated ABET–accredited 4–year college or university and major in computer science or aeronautical, chemical, electrical, industrial, manufacturing, materials, mechanical, metallurgical, or petroleum engineering. Selection is based on merit.
Financial data: The stipend is $1,000. The award includes a travel grant for the recipient to attend the national conference of the Society of Women Engineers (SWE).
Duration: 1 year.
Number awarded: 1 each year.
Deadline: May of each year.

2340 SOUTH CAROLINA COACHES ASSOCIATION OF WOMEN'S SPORTS AND TROPHIES BY "M" SCHOLARSHIP

South Carolina Coaches Association of Women's Sports
c/o Amy Boozer, Executive Secretary
P.O. Box 261
Newberry, SC 29108
Phone: (803) 321–2628;
Email: amy_caws@yahoo.com
Web: www.hometeamsonline.com/teams/?u=SCCAWS&t=c&s=htosports&p=home

Summary: To provide financial assistance to female high school senior athletes in South Carolina who plan to study at medical field at a college in any state.

Eligibility: Open to women graduating from high schools in South Carolina who have participated in at least 1 athletic team. Applicants must be planning to attend a college or university in any state to prepare for a career in medicine. They must have minimum scores of 1000 on the SAT and/or 22 on the ACT. Along with their application, they must submit a 1–page essay on why they want to enter the medical field and the area of specialization they plan to pursue. Selection is based on that essay, academic achievement, participation in athletic and non–athletic extracurricular activities, and financial need.

Financial data: The stipend is $1,000.

Duration: 1 year; nonrenewable.

Number awarded: 1 each year.

Deadline: March of each year.

2341 SOUTHEASTERN AIRPORT MANAGERS' ASSOCIATION SCHOLARSHIP PROGRAM

American Association of Airport Executives–Southeast Chapter
Attn: Southeastern Airport Managers' Association Educational Foundation
c/o Scholarship Managers
307 Provincetown Road
P.O. Box 2810
Cherry Hill, NJ 08034
Phone: (856) 573–9400; Fax: (856) 573–9799;
Email: secaaae@aol.com
Web: secaaae.org/scholarships.htm

Summary: To provide financial assistance to full–time students majoring in aviation at selected schools in the South.

Eligibility: Open to residents of southeastern states who are enrolled full time at 1 of the following 9 participating schools: Auburn University in Alabama, Delta State University in Mississippi, Eastern Kentucky University, Fairmont State College in West Virginia, Florida Institute of Technology, Middle Georgia College, Hampton University in Virginia, Louisiana Tech University, or Middle Tennessee State University. They must be classified as a junior or above, have a strong interest in aviation (preferably airport management), have at least a 3.0 GPA in their major, and be able to demonstrate financial need. Selection is based on academic record, participation in school and community activities, work experience, a statement of goals and aspirations, financial need, and a recommendation.

Financial data: The stipend is $1,500. Funds are paid jointly to the student and the school and must be used for tuition, books, lab fees, or other related educational expenses. The scholarship may not be used to pay for room or board.

Duration: 1 year; nonrenewable.

Number awarded: Varies each year.

Deadline: May of each year.

2342 $ SOUTHERN ASSOCIATION OF STEEL FABRICATORS SCHOLARSHIP

American Institute of Steel Construction
Attn: Director of University Relations
1 East Wacker Drive, Suite 700
Chicago, IL 60601–1802
Phone: (312) 670–5408; Fax: (312) 670–5403;
Email: gavlin@aisc.com
Web: www.aisc.org/content.aspx?id=716

Summary: To provide financial assistance to undergraduate engineering students from southern states who are interested in the structural field, especially structural steel.

Eligibility: Open to full–time civil or architectural engineering students entering their junior or senior year at universities in Alabama, Florida, Georgia, Kentucky, Louisiana, Mississippi, and Tennessee. Preference is given to students who have selected a concentration in the structural field, with particular emphasis on structural steel. Along with their application, they must submit a 2–page essay on their overall career objective and an original sample structural steel analysis/design solution, with calculations. Selection is based on those submissions, academic performance, and a faculty recommendation. U.S. citizenship is required.

Financial data: The stipend is $2,500.

Duration: 1 year.

Number awarded: 1 each year.

Deadline: April of each year.

2343 SOUTHWEST PARK AND RECREATION TRAINING INSTITUTE STUDENT SCHOLARSHIPS

Southwest Park and Recreation Training Institute
Attn: Scholarship Chair
P.O. Box 330154
Fort Worth, TX 76163–0154
Phone: (817) 292–8974; Fax: (817) 361–8515;
Email: scholarship@swprti.org
Web: www.swprti.org/scholarships.html

Summary: To provide financial assistance to undergraduate and graduate students preparing for a career in the park and recreation profession at universities in designated southwestern states.

Eligibility: Open to sophomores, juniors, seniors, and graduate students at universities within the network states of the Southwest Park and Recreation Training Institute (SWPRTI): Arkansas, Colorado, Kansas, Louisiana, Missouri, New Mexico, Oklahoma, and Texas. Applicants must be working on a degree in park administration, recreation and park administration, landscape architecture, recreation with a minor in park administration, horticulture, natural resources, or a related degree. They must demonstrate a high degree of professional competence through extracurricular activities and potential contribution to the field of parks and recreation. They must also have a GPA of 2.0 or higher overall or 2.5 or higher in their major and be able to demonstrate financial need.

Financial data: The stipend is $1,000.

Duration: 1 year.

Number awarded: 3 each year: 2 for undergraduates and 1 for a graduate student.

Deadline: December of each year.

2344 SPIRIT OF APOLLO SCHOLARSHIP

American Institute of Aeronautics and Astronautics–Houston Section
Attn: Rafael E. Munoz, Scholarship Committee Chair
P.O. Box 57524
Webster, TX 77598
Web: www.aiaa–houston.org/SpiritOfApolloScholarship.aspx

Summary: To provide financial assistance to students from any state working on a degree in a field related to aerospace at colleges and universities in Texas.

Eligibility: Open to students from any state who have completed at least 1 academic year of full–time study at a college or university in Texas and have a GPA of 3.0 or higher. Applicants must be majoring in a field of engineering, mathematics, or science (e.g., physical science, physics, computer science) that is relevant to the technical activities of the American Institute of Aeronautics and Astronautics (AIAA). Along with their application, they must submit an essay of 500 to 1,000 words on their career objectives and the academic program required to achieve those objectives. Selection is based on that essay (15%), academic achievement (40%), letters of recommendation (15%), extracurricular activities (10%), work experience (10%), and financial need (10%). U.S. citizenship or permanent resident status is required.

Financial data: The stipend is $1,000.

Duration: 1 year; recipients may reapply.

Number awarded: 1 or more each year.

Deadline: May of each year.

2345 SPRING MEADOW NURSERY SCHOLARSHIP

American Nursery and Landscape Association
Attn: Horticultural Research Institute
1200 G Street, N.W., Suite 800
Washington, DC 20005
Phone: (202) 695–2474; Fax: (888) 761–7883;
Email: scholarships@hriresearch.org
Web: www.hriresearch.org/index.cfm?page=Content&categoryID=167

Summary: To provide financial assistance to students working on an undergraduate or graduate degree in landscape architecture or horticulture.

Eligibility: Open to students enrolled full time in a landscape or horticulture undergraduate or graduate program at an accredited 2– or 4–year college or university. Students enrolled in a vocational agriculture program are also eligible. Applicants must be at least in their sophomore year of undergraduate study or any year of graduate study and have a minimum GPA of 2.25 overall and 2.7 in their major. They must be interested in woody plant production, woody plant propagation, wood plant breeding, and/or horticultural sales and marketing.
Financial data: The stipend is $1,500.
Duration: 1 year; may be renewed.
Number awarded: 1 each year.
Deadline: May of each year.

2346 ST. FRANCIS SCHOOL OF NURSING ALUMNI OF PITTSBURGH, PA SCHOLARSHIP FUND

Pittsburgh Foundation
Attn: Scholarship Coordinator
Five PPG Place, Suite 250
Pittsburgh, PA 15222–5414
Phone: (412) 394–2649; Fax: (412) 391–7259;
Email: turnerd@pghfdn.org
Web: www.pittsburghfoundation.org/node/1713
Summary: To provide financial assistance to students working on an undergraduate or graduate degree in nursing.
Eligibility: Open to 1) students working on their first academic degree or diploma that leads to professional licensure as a registered nurse; and 2) licensed registered nurses working on an advanced degree in nursing. Applicants must have a GPA of 3.0 or higher and be able to demonstrate financial need. Along with their application, they must submit brief essays on their prior work experience, prior education, financial obligations, extracurricular activities and volunteer work, past achievements related to nursing, and career goals. U.S. citizenship is required.
Financial data: A stipend is awarded (amount not specified).
Duration: 1 year.
Number awarded: 1 or more each year.
Deadline: December of each year.

2347 $ STAN BECK FELLOWSHIP

Entomological Society of America
Attn: Entomological Foundation
9332 Annapolis Road, Suite 210
Lanham, MD 20706–3150
Phone: (301) 459–9082; Fax: (301) 459–9084;
Email: melodie@entfdn.org
Web: www.entfdn.org/awards_education.php
Summary: To assist "needy" students working on an undergraduate or graduate degree in entomology who are nominated by members of the Entomological Society of America (ESA).
Eligibility: Open to students working on an undergraduate or graduate degree in entomology at a college or university in Canada, Mexico, or the United States. Candidates must be nominated by members of the society. They must be "needy" students; for the purposes of this program, need may be based on physical limitations, or economic, minority, or environmental conditions.
Financial data: The stipend is $2,000 per year.
Duration: 1 year; may be renewed up to 3 additional years.
Number awarded: 1 each year.
Deadline: June of each year.

2348 $ STANLEY W. STREW EDUCATIONAL FUND SCHOLARSHIPS

California Association of Pest Control Advisers
Attn: Scholarship Committee
2300 River Plaza Drive, Suite 120
Sacramento, CA 95833
Phone: (916) 928–1625, ext. 200; Fax: (916) 928–0705;
Email: lien@capca.com
Web: capca.com/scholarshipinformation
Summary: To provide financial assistance to residents of California who are upper–division or graduate students working on a degree in horticulture or agriculture and planning to prepare for a career in pest management.
Eligibility: Open to California residents who are currently enrolled at a college or university as an entering junior, senior, or graduate student. Applicants must be working on a degree in an agricultural or horticultural program to prepare for a career in pest management. They must have a GPA of 2.5 or higher. Selection is based on academic record (25%), extracurricular activities (15%), pest management experience (20%), professional and career goals (20%), financial need (10%), and class standing (10%). Students working on a bachelor's degree are given priority.
Financial data: The stipend is $3,000 or $2,000.
Duration: 1 year.
Number awarded: 3 each year: 2 at $3,000 and 1 at $2,000.
Deadline: May of each year.

2349 $$ STEEL ENGINEERING EDUCATION LINK (STEEL) SCHOLARSHIPS

Association for Iron & Steel Technology
Attn: AIST Foundation
186 Thorn Hill Road
Warrendale, PA 15086–7528
Phone: (724) 814–3044; Fax: (724) 814–3001;
Email: lwharrey@aist.org
Web: www.aistfoundation.org/scholarships/scholarships.htm
Summary: To provide financial assistance and work experience to college juniors working on a degree in specified fields of engineering.
Eligibility: Open to full–time students entering their junior year in a program in chemical, computer, electrical, environmental, industry, or mechanical engineering at a college or university in North America (Canada, Mexico, and the United States). Applicants must have a GPA of 3.0 or higher and a demonstrated interest in the iron and steel industry. They must be available for employment at a steel company during the summer after their junior year; students unable to accept an internship will not be considered. Along with their application, they must submit a 2–page essay on their professional goals, why they are interested in a career in the steel industry, and how their skills could be applied to enhance the industry. Selection is based on steel industry interest (35%), letters of recommendation (30%), grades (20%), and extracurricular activities (15%).
Financial data: The program provides a stipend of $5,000 for the junior year, a paid internship during the following summer, and a stipend of $5,000 for the senior year.
Duration: 2 years.
Number awarded: 10 each year.
Deadline: February of each year.

2350 STELLA GRIFFIN MEMORIAL SCHOLARSHIP

American Society for Clinical Laboratory Science–Ohio
c/o Sondra Sutherland, Scholarship Chair
Jefferson Community College
4000 Sunset Boulevard
Steubenville, OH 43952
Phone: (740) 264–5591, ext. 165; Fax: (740) 264–9504;
Email: ssutherlan@jcc.edu
Web: ascls–ohio.org/Scholarships.htm
Summary: To provide financial assistance to college students in Ohio who are interested in preparing for a career in clinical laboratory science.
Eligibility: Open to Ohio residents who are enrolled in the clinical laboratory science curriculum of an Ohio college or school of medical technology. They must have at least a 2.5 GPA, be in need of financial assistance, and have the following personal characteristics: an inquiring mind, an aptitude for science, initiative, adaptability to people and situations, patience, consideration for and an interest in others, a sense of responsibility, honesty, and integrity.
Financial data: The stipend is $1,000. Funds are paid directly to the recipient.
Duration: 1 year; recipients may reapply.
Number awarded: 1 each year.
Deadline: March of each year.

2351 $$ STEPHEN G. KING PLAY ENVIRONMENTS SCHOLARSHIP

Summary: To provide financial assistance to upper–division and graduate students who wish to study landscape architecture with an emphasis on play environments.
See Listing #1517.

2352 STEVE WAGNER SCHOLARSHIP

Saginaw Community Foundation
1 Tuscola, Suite 100

Saginaw, MI 48607
Phone: (989) 755–0545; Fax: (989) 755–6524;
Email: info@saginawfoundation.org
Web: www.saginawfoundation.org/grants_and_scholarships/scholarships
Summary: To provide financial assistance to high school seniors in Michigan who plan to work on an undergraduate degree in civil engineering or land surveying at a school in any state.
Eligibility: Open to seniors graduating from high schools in Michigan who have a GPA of 3.0 or higher. Applicants must be planning to work full time on an undergraduate degree in civil engineering or land surveying in an ABET–accredited program in any state. Along with their application, they must submit an essay describing their personal and educational goals, including their plans for a major, why they have chosen that field, and what they plan to do with their degree. Selection is based on academic record (10 points), community service (40 points), recommendations (20 points), and overall involvement in community, school, and work activities (30 points). Special consideration is given to students who have worked for a firm that is a member of the American Council of Engineering Companies (ACEC) in the last 24 months.
Financial data: A stipend is awarded (amount not specified).
Duration: 1 year.
Number awarded: 1 or more each year.
Deadline: January of each year.

2353 $ STRUCTURAL ENGINEERS ASSOCIATION OF COLORADO SCHOLARSHIPS

Structural Engineers Association of Colorado
SEAC Scholarship Fund
c/o Neujahr and Gorman, Inc.
88 Steele Street, Suite 200
Denver, CO 80206
Phone: (303) 377–2732;
Email: SEACscholarship@jvajva.com
Web: www.seacolorado.org/scholarship
Summary: To provide financial assistance to residents of Colorado who are working on an undergraduate or graduate degree in structural engineering at a college in any state.
Eligibility: Open to residents of Colorado who are entering their junior, senior, or fifth year of undergraduate study or any year of graduate study at a college or university in any state. Applicants must be enrolled full time in a program in structural engineering with an intent to return to practice in Colorado. Along with their application, they must submit transcripts, a letter expressing their intent to return to Colorado, a letter of recommendation, and a 300–word essay on their view of the role of the structural engineer in society. Financial need is considered in the selection process.
Financial data: The stipend is $2,000.
Duration: 1 year.
Number awarded: 2 each year.
Deadline: Deadline not specified.

2354 $ STRUCTURAL ENGINEERS ASSOCIATION OF OREGON SCHOLARSHIPS

Structural Engineers Association of Oregon
Attn: Scholarship Foundation
9220 S.W. Barbur Boulevard, Suite 119
PMB 336
Portland, OR 97219
Phone: (503) 753–3075; Fax: (503) 214–8142;
Email: jane@seao.org
Web: www.seaosf.org/recipients
Summary: To provide financial assistance to residents of Oregon and Clark County, Washington who are working on a bachelor's or master's degree in civil engineering at a school in any state.
Eligibility: Open to full–time in an ABET–accredited civil engineering program at a college or university in any state who have been residents of Oregon and Clark County, Washington for at least 4 years. Applicants must be working on a bachelor's or master's degree and have completed at least 2 terms of junior–level civil engineering classes during the previous academic year. They must have a cumulative GPA of 3.0 or higher and be able to demonstrate financial need. Along with their application, they must submit brief statements on 1) their interest and goals related to structural engineering; and 2) other experiences (e.g., student groups, community service, military service) that will supplement their engineering education. U.S. citizenship or permanent resident status is required. The highest–ranked applicant receives the Don Kramer Memorial Scholarship.
Financial data: Stipends are $2,500 or $2,000.
Duration: 1 year.
Number awarded: Varies each year: at least 1 at $2,500 (the Don Kramer Memorial Scholarship) and 2 or more at $2,000.
Deadline: April of each year.

2355 $ STRUCTURAL ENGINEERS ASSOCIATION OF SOUTHERN CALIFORNIA SCHOLARSHIPS

Structural Engineers Association of Southern California
Attn: Executive Director
1105 South Euclid Street, D409
Fullerton, CA 92832
Phone: (562) 908–6131; Fax: (562) 692–3425;
Email: seaosc@seaosc.org
Web: www.seaosc.org/events_students.cfm
Summary: To provide financial assistance to undergraduate students at universities in southern California who are majoring in structural engineering.
Eligibility: Open to students currently enrolled as undergraduates at 11 designated universities in southern California and working on a degree in civil engineering with an emphasis on structural engineering. They must be nominated by a professor at their university. Nominees must submit 1) a statement of purpose describing their interest in studying structural engineering; 2) a resume of achievements and activities; and 3) a letter of recommendation from the nominating professor or their lead teacher. Financial need is not considered in the selection process.
Financial data: Stipends range from $1,000 to $2,500.
Duration: 1 year.
Number awarded: Varies each year; normally, at least 1 student at each university receives a scholarship.
Deadline: December of each year.

2356 $ STRUCTURAL ENGINEERS ASSOCIATION OF WASHINGTON SCHOLARSHIPS

Structural Engineers Association of Washington
Attn: Public Information Committee
P.O. Box 44
Olympia, WA 98507
Phone: (206) 682–6026; Fax: (360) 753–1838;
Email: seaw@seaw.org
Web: www.seaw.org/resources_education.cfm
Summary: To provide financial assistance to residents of Washington working on an undergraduate or graduate degree in structural engineering at a school in any state.
Eligibility: Open to residents of Washington enrolled as seniors or graduate students at a college or university in any state. Applicants must be working on a degree in structural engineering and committed to preparing for a career in that field. Along with their application, they must submit a 500–word essay on 1 of the following subjects: 1) their favorite structural course; 2) an interesting structural problem; 3) a significant structural accomplishment; or 4) whether steel or concrete is better. U.S. citizenship is required.
Financial data: The stipend is $3,000.
Duration: 1 year.
Number awarded: 2 each year.
Deadline: March of each year.

2357 $ STRUCTURAL ENGINEERS FOUNDATION SCHOLARSHIPS

Structural Engineers Association of Illinois
Attn: Structural Engineers Foundation
134 North LaSalle Street, Suite 1910
Chicago, IL 60602
Phone: (312) 726–4165; Fax: (312) 277–1991;
Email: office@seaol.org
Web: www.seaoi.org/sef.htm
Summary: To provide financial assistance to upper–division and graduate students interested in a career in structural engineering.
Eligibility: Open to students 1) entering their third or higher year of an undergraduate program; or 2) entering or continuing a graduate program. Applicants must be enrolled in a civil or architectural engineering program and planning to continue with a structural engineering specialization. Students enrolled in structural engineering technology programs are also eligible if they are qualified to take the Fundamentals of Engineering and Principles and Practice licen-

sure examinations in their home state upon graduation. U.S. citizenship or permanent resident status is required. Students enrolled in military academies or ROTC programs are not eligible. Selection is based on a statement giving reasons why the applicant should receive the award (including plans for continued formal education), academic performance, and potential for development and leadership. Financial need is not considered.
Financial data: The stipend is $2,000.
Duration: 1 year; nonrenewable.
Number awarded: 1 or more each year.
Deadline: April of each year.

2358 STUDENT ASSOCIATION GEORGE R. FOSTER MEMORIAL SCHOLARSHIP

Institute of Food Technologists
Attn: Feeding Tomorrow Office
525 West Van Buren, Suite 1000
Chicago, IL 60607
Phone: (312) 782–8424; Fax: (312) 782–8348;
Email: info@ift.org
Web: www.ift.org/knowledge–center/learn–about–food–science.aspx
Summary: To provide financial assistance to students who are high school seniors or college freshmen and interested in studying food science or food technology.
Eligibility: Open to graduating high school seniors and current college freshmen interested in working full time on a bachelor's degree in food science or food technology at an educational institution in the United States or Canada. Applicants must have a GPA of 3.0 or higher. Along with their application, they must submit a 250–word list of academic and professional awards, honors, and scholarships they have received at the high school and college freshman level; a 250–word outline of their employment experience, including internships and part–time or full–time work; a 250–word list of community service and extracurricular activities within clubs and organizations; a 250–word list of honors classes and/or advanced placement courses and scores; a 250–word essay on what they feel distinguishes them among other candidates for this scholarship; and a 300–word essay on why they want to pursue an education in food science and the aspects of food science they find most interesting. Financial need is not considered in the selection process.
Financial data: The stipend is $1,000 per year.
Duration: 1 year; recipients may reapply.
Number awarded: 1 each year.
Deadline: March of each year.

2359 $ STUDENT CORRUGATED PACKAGING DESIGN COMPETITION

Summary: To recognize and reward college students who submit outstanding corrugated packaging designs.
See Listing #1521.

2360 STUDENT DESIGN COMPETITION IN ACOUSTICS

Summary: To recognize and reward undergraduate and graduate students who submit outstanding entries in an acoustics design competition.
See Listing #1522.

2361 STUDENT DESIGN PROJECT COMPETITION

Summary: To recognize and reward outstanding student designs in a competition involving heating, ventilating, and air conditioning (HVAC) engineering.
See Listing #1523.

2362 $ STUDENT SAFETY INNOVATION CHALLENGE

ASME International
Attn: Safety Engineering and Risk Analysis Division
Three Park Avenue
New York, NY 10016–5990
Phone: (212) 591–7052; (800) THE–ASME; Fax: (212) 591–7671;
Email: McComieJ@asme.org
Web: divisions.asme.org/SERAD/Student_Activities.cfm
Summary: To recognize and reward outstanding safety engineering design papers by undergraduate and graduate students.
Eligibility: Open to undergraduate and graduate students enrolled in an ABET–accredited mechanical engineering curriculum. Applicants must submit a senior design or other in–class project that relates either to safety or risk; recently, the assigned topic for safety was safety improvement using engineering concepts and the topics for risk was analytical approaches to risk management. The recommended length of papers is 4 pages of text and 2 pages of figures.
Financial data: Prizes are $500 for the winning student and $250 for the sponsoring professor.
Duration: The competition is held annually.
Number awarded: 1 each year.
Deadline: Abstracts must be submitted by June of each year.

2363 SUGARBEET SCHOLARSHIP

Syngenta Crop Protection, LLC
410 Swing Road
P.O. Box 18300
Greensboro, NC 27419
Phone: (919) 648–6700; (800) 334–9481;
Email: ereynolds@gibbs–soell.com
Web: www.farmassist.com/promo/sugarbeets
Summary: To recognize and reward, with college scholarships, students from designated sugarbeet–producing states who are involved in the sugarbeet industry or are members of FFA or 4–H and submit outstanding essays on agriculture.
Eligibility: Open to high school seniors and college freshmen, sophomores, and juniors who either live or attend school in the following sugarbeet–producing regions: 1) Idaho, Washington, and Oregon; 2) North Dakota and Minnesota; 3) Colorado, Montana, Nebraska, and Wyoming; and 4) Michigan. Applicants must either be involved in the sugarbeet industry or be members of FFA or 4–H. They must submit an essay, up to 700 words in length, on a topic that changes annually but relates to the sugarbeet industry. Selection is based on 1) creativity and uniqueness of the idea (30 points), flow and organization of the essay (30 points), functionality and professional appeal (20 points), and absence of grammatical or typographical errors (20 points).
Financial data: The prize is a $1,500 scholarship.
Duration: The competition is held annually.
Number awarded: 4 each year: 1 in each of the regions.
Deadline: June of each year.

2364 SUSAN AND TOM LUSTY MEMORIAL SCHOLARSHIP

American Association of Surgical Physician Assistants
Attn: Chair, Student Scholarship Committee
P.O. Box 781688
Sebastian, FL 32978–1688
Phone: (772) 388–0498; Fax: (772)388–3457;
Email: aaspa@aaspa.com
Web: www.aspa.com/page.asp?tid=155&name=AASPA–Scholarships&navid=54
Summary: To provide financial assistance to physician assistant students preparing for a career in surgery.
Eligibility: Open to students enrolled in either the didactic or clinical year of an accredited physician assistant program. Applicants must be able to demonstrate financial need and an interest in surgical practice. Along with their application, they must submit a 500–word narrative describing their career goals and their desire to practice in surgery. They must either be members of the American Association of Surgical Physician Assistants (AASPA) or submit an application for membership.
Financial data: The stipend is $1,000.
Duration: 1 year.
Number awarded: 1 or more each year.
Deadline: June of each year.

2365 SUSAN LINDAHL MEMORIAL SCHOLARSHIP

Physician Assistants in Orthopaedic Surgery
Attn: Scholarships
P.O. Box 10781
Glendale, AZ 85318–0781
Phone: (800) 804–7267; Fax: (623) 581–0085;
Email: info@paos.org
Web: www.paos.org/susan–lindahl–memorial–scholarship
Summary: To provide financial assistance to physician assistant students who have an interest in orthopedic surgery.

Eligibility: Open to students in approved physician assistant programs who are enrolled in their first or second year and have an interest in orthopedic surgery. Applicants must submit a letter that describes their interest in preparing for an orthopedic career, involvement in supporting activities, prior education, and other experience.
Financial data: The stipend is $1,000.
Duration: 1 year.
Number awarded: 3 each year.
Deadline: September of each year.

2366 SUSAN MISZKOWICZ MEMORIAL SCHOLARSHIP

Society of Women Engineers
Attn: Scholarship Selection Committee
203 North LaSalle Street, Suite 1675
Chicago, IL 60601–1269
Phone: (312) 596–5223; (877) SWE–INFO; Fax: (312) 644–8557;
Email: scholarships@swe.org
Web: societyofwomenengineers.swe.org/index.php/scholarships
Summary: To provide financial assistance to undergraduate women majoring in computer science or engineering.
Eligibility: Open to women who are entering their sophomore, junior, or senior year at a 4–year ABET–accredited college or university. Applicants must be working full time on a degree in computer science or engineering and have a GPA of 3.0 or higher. Selection is based on merit.
Financial data: The stipend is $1,500.
Duration: 1 year.
Number awarded: 1 each year.
Deadline: February of each year.

2367 SUSAN VINCENT MEMORIAL SCHOLARSHIP

DownEast Association of Physician Assistants
30 Association Drive
P.O. Box 190
Manchester, ME 04351
Phone: (207) 620–7577; Fax: (207) 622–3332;
Email: info@deapa.com
Web: www.deapa.com/career/scholarship.php
Summary: To provide financial assistance to residents of Maine enrolled in a program for physician assistants in any state.
Eligibility: Open to Maine residents who are attending a physician assistant program in any state. Applicants must submit a brief statement describing why they deserve and need this scholarship.
Financial data: The stipend is $1,000.
Duration: 1 year.
Number awarded: 1 each year.
Deadline: May of each year.

2368 $ S.W. (BILL) PRESTON SCHOLARSHIP

Washington Association of Wine Grape Growers
Attn: Washington Wine Industry Foundation
203 Mission Avenue, Suite 107
P.O. Box 716
Cashmere, WA 98815–0716
Phone: (509) 782–1108; Fax: (509) 782–1203;
Email: info@washingtonwinefoundation.org
Web: www.washingtonwinefoundation.org/index.php?page_id=6
Summary: To provide financial assistance to residents of any state who are interested in studying viticulture and/or enology at a college in Washington.
Eligibility: Open to students who are enrolled or planning to enroll at a college or university to study viticulture and/or enology. Applicants may be residents of any state, but they must attend a college or university in Washington. Along with their application, they must submit a 500–word essay on why they should receive this scholarship, including their career goals, interests and experiences in the wine grape industry, and plans to improve or enhance the industry. Selection is based on academic merit, leadership abilities, and interest in the study of enology and/or viticulture; financial need is not considered.
Financial data: The stipend is $3,000.
Duration: 1 year.
Number awarded: 1 each year.
Deadline: May of each year.

2369 TAFFORD UNIFORMS NURSING SCHOLARSHIPS

Tafford Uniforms
Attn: Customer Service
104 Park Drive
Montgomeryville, PA 18936
Phone: (800) 697–3321;
Email: customerservice@tafford.com
Web: www.tafford.com/t–scholarship.aspx
Summary: To provide financial assistance to students working on a certificate or degree in nursing.
Eligibility: Open to students currently enrolled in an accredited nursing school in the United States. Applicants must be working on associate degree, licensed vocational nurse (L.V.N.) certificate, licensed practical nurse (L.P.N.) certificate, bachelor's degree (B.S.N.), or master's degree (M.S.N.). They must have a GPA of 2.5 or higher. Along with their application, they must submit a 250–word essay on their reasons for entering the profession of nursing.
Financial data: The stipend is $1,000.
Duration: 1 year.
Number awarded: 4 each year: 2 in the spring and 2 in the fall.
Deadline: June of each year.

2370 TAU BETA PI/SAE ENGINEERING SCHOLARSHIP

Society of Automotive Engineers
Attn: Scholarships and Loans Program
400 Commonwealth Drive
Warrendale, PA 15096–0001
Phone: (724) 776–4790; (877) 606–7323; Fax: (724) 776–0790;
Email: scholarships@sae.org
Web: students.sae.org/awdscholar/scholarships/taubetapi
Summary: To provide financial support to high school seniors interested in studying engineering in college.
Eligibility: Open to U.S. citizens who intend to earn an ABET–accredited degree in engineering. Applicants must be high school seniors who have a GPA of 3.75 or higher and a rank in the 90th percentile in both mathematics and critical reading on the SAT or the composite ACT. Selection is based on high school transcripts; SAT or ACT scores; school–related extracurricular activities; non–school related activities; academic honors, civic honors, and awards; and a 250–word essay on their goals, plans, experiences, and interests in mobility engineering. Financial need is not considered.
Financial data: The stipend is $1,000.
Duration: 1 year; nonrenewable.
Number awarded: 6 each year.
Deadline: January of each year.

2371 $ TED AND RUTH NEWARD SCHOLARSHIPS

Society of Plastics Engineers
Attn: SPE Foundation
13 Church Hill Road
Newtown, CT 06740
Phone: (203) 740–5447; Fax: (203) 775–1157;
Email: foundation@4spe.org
Web: www.4spe.org/spe–foundation
Summary: To provide financial assistance to undergraduate and graduate students who have a career interest in the plastics industry.
Eligibility: Open to full–time undergraduate students at 4–year colleges and 2–year technical programs and to graduate students. Applicants must be majoring in or taking courses that would be beneficial to a career in the plastics or polymer industry (e.g., plastics engineering, packaging, polymer sciences, chemistry, physics, chemical engineering, mechanical engineering, industrial engineering). Along with their application, they must submit 3 letters of recommendation; a high school and/or college transcript; a 1– to 2–page statement telling why they are applying for the scholarship, their qualifications, and their educational and career goals in the plastics industry; their employment history; a list of current and past school activities and community activities and honors; and information on their financial need. U.S. citizenship is required.
Financial data: The stipend is $3,000. Funds are paid directly to the recipient's school.
Duration: 1 year.
Number awarded: 3 each year.
Deadline: February of each year.

2372 $$ TENNESSEE RURAL HEALTH LOAN FORGIVENESS PROGRAM

Tennessee Student Assistance Corporation
Parkway Towers
404 James Robertson Parkway, Suite 1510
Nashville, TN 37243–0820
Phone: (615) 741–1346; (800) 342–1663; Fax: (615) 741–6101;
Email: TSAC.Aidinfo@tn.gov
Web: www.tn.gov/collegepays/mon_college/ruralhealth.html

Summary: To provide funding to residents of Tennessee who are working on a degree at a school in the state to prepare for a career as a physician, dentist, physician assistant, or nurse practitioner and practice in an underserved area of the state.

Eligibility: Open to students currently enrolled full time at a postsecondary educational institution in Tennessee that has a school of medicine that offers an M.D. degree, a school of osteopathic medicine that offers a D.O. degree, a school of dentistry that offers a D.D.S. or D.M.D. degree, a physician assistant program, or a master's or doctoral degree as a nurse practitioner. Applicants must have been residents of Tennessee for at least 1 year. They must agree to practice their profession in a health resource shortage area following completion of their program of study for 1 year per year of support received.

Financial data: The maximum loan is $12,000 per year or the cost of tuition, mandatory fees, books, and equipment, whichever is less. Funds are disbursed directly to the educational institution. If recipients fail to fulfill their service agreement, they must repay all funds received in cash with 9% interest.

Duration: 1 year; may be renewed up to 4 additional years or until completion of the program.

Number awarded: 50 each year.

Deadline: August of each year.

2373 TERRY L. MCKANNA SCHOLARSHIP

American Water Works Association–Kansas Section
c/o Lester Estelle, Scholarship Committee Chair
City of Olathe
600 South Curtis
Olathe, KS 66062
Phone: (913) 971–9123; Fax: (913) 971–9099;
Email: lestelle@olatheks.org
Web: www.ksawwa.org

Summary: To provide financial assistance to undergraduate and graduate students from any state enrolled at a college in Kansas to prepare for a career in the water works industry.

Eligibility: Open to undergraduate and graduate students enrolled full time at a 2– or 4–year college or university in Kansas. Applicants must be interested in preparing for a career in a field associated with the water works industry. Their program must include courses related to civil or environmental engineering or environmental science. U.S. citizenship is required. Selection is based on relation of program to the waterworks industry (30 points), GPA (30 points), an essay on career plans (20 points), a recommendation by a professor (10 points), and professional activities, offices held, and/or work experience (10 points).

Financial data: The stipend is $1,000.

Duration: 1 year.

Number awarded: 1 each year.

Deadline: July of each year.

2374 TEXAS AMERICAN LEGION AUXILIARY PAST PRESIDENT'S PARLEY SCHOLARSHIPS

American Legion Auxiliary
Department of Texas
P.O. Box 140407
Austin, TX 78714–0407
Phone: (512) 476–7278; Fax: (512) 482–8391;
Email: alatexas@txlegion.org
Web: alatexas.org/scholarship/ppp.html

Summary: To provide financial assistance to descendants of Texas veterans who wish to study a field related to medicine at a school in the state.

Eligibility: Open to the children, grandchildren, and great–grandchildren of veterans who served during specified periods of war time. Applicants must be residents of Texas studying or planning to study a medical field at a postsecondary institution in the state. Selection is based on need, goals, character, citizenship, and objectives.

Financial data: The stipend is $1,000.

Duration: 1 year.

Number awarded: 1 or more each year.

Deadline: April of each year.

2375 TEXAS ASPHALT PAVEMENT SCHOLARSHIPS

Texas Asphalt Pavement Association
Attn: Scholarship Program
149 Commercial Drive
P.O. Box 1468
Buda, TX 78610
Phone: (512) 312–2099; Fax: (512) 312–5043;
Email: sbuckberry@txhotmix.org
Web: texasasphalt.org/education–d/scholarships

Summary: To provide financial assistance to civil engineering students in Texas who are interested in the hot mix asphalt concrete field.

Eligibility: Open to residents of any state who are full–time students enrolled, at the sophomore level or above, in a baccalaureate or graduate degree program in civil engineering, construction science, or technology at a college or university in Texas. Applicants must have demonstrated a strong interest in the hot mix asphalt concrete field; preference is given to applicants who have demonstrated their interest in the field through summer or part–time employment. Selection is based on academic record; financial need is not considered. U.S. citizenship is required.

Financial data: The stipend is approximately $1,500 per year.

Duration: 1 year; recipients may reapply.

Number awarded: Varies each year; recently, 10 of these scholarships were awarded.

Deadline: September of each year.

2376 TEXAS CATTLEWOMEN IVOMEC GENERATIONS OF EXCELLENCE SCHOLARSHIP

Texas CattleWomen, Inc.
Attn: Erin Worrell, Scholarship Chair
657 Blue Oak Trail
Harper, TX 78631–6371
Phone: (830) 864–5161;
Email: erin@theranchersresource.com
Web: www.txcattlewomen.org/programsactivities.html

Summary: To provide financial assistance to residents of Texas who are upper–division or graduate students at a school in any state and preparing for a career in the beef industry.

Eligibility: Open to residents of Texas who are graduates of high schools in the state currently enrolled as college juniors, seniors, or graduate students at a college or university in any state. Applicants must come from an agricultural background in the beef industry and be returning to the beef industry after graduation. They must have a GPA of 2.5 or higher. Along with their application, they must submit a 500–word essay on their background, their financial need, their interest in and willingness to support the production and consumption of beef, and how they plan to make an impact on the future.

Financial data: The stipend is $1,000 per year. Funds may be used for any educational expense.

Duration: 1 year.

Number awarded: 1 each year.

Deadline: January of each year.

2377 $$ TEXAS ENGINEERING SCHOLARSHIP PROGRAM

Texas Higher Education Coordinating Board
Attn: Grants and Special Programs
1200 East Anderson Lane
P.O. Box 12788
Austin, TX 78711–2788
Phone: (512) 427–6340; (800) 242–3062; Fax: (512) 427–6420;
Email: grantinfo@thecb.state.tx.us
Web: www.collegeforalltexans.com/apps/financialaid/tofa2.cfm?ID=400

Summary: To provide financial assistance to residents of Texas who are working on an undergraduate degree in engineering at a university in the state.

Eligibility: Open to residents of Texas who are enrolled as sophomores in an engineering program at a public or private 4–year college or university in the state. Applicants must have graduated from high school in the top 20% of their class and with a GPA of 3.5 or higher in mathematics and science courses offered under the recommended or advanced high school program. Financial need is not considered in the selection process.

Financial data: The stipend is $5,000 per year.
Duration: 1 year; recipients may reapply as long as they maintain an overall GPA of 3.0 or higher.
Number awarded: Varies each year.
Deadline: Deadline not specified.

2378 TEXAS EXEMPTION PROGRAM FOR CLINICAL PRECEPTORS AND THEIR CHILDREN

Summary: To provide financial assistance for additional study at institutions in Texas to residents of the state who are working as clinical preceptors in nursing programs in the state and to their children.
See Listing #946.

2379 $$ TEXAS FIREFIGHTER EXEMPTION PROGRAM

Texas Higher Education Coordinating Board
Attn: Grants and Special Programs
1200 East Anderson Lane
P.O. Box 12788
Austin, TX 78711–2788
Phone: (512) 427–6340; (800) 242–3062; Fax: (512) 427–6420;
Email: grantinfo@thecb.state.tx.us
Web: www.collegeforalltexans.com/apps/financialaid/tofa2.cfm?ID=506
Summary: To provide educational assistance to firefighters who are enrolled in fire science courses in Texas.
Eligibility: Open to Texas residents employed as a paid firefighter by a political subdivision of the state or serving as active members of volunteer fire departments. Applicants must be enrolled in fire science courses offered as part of a fire science curriculum at a public college or university in Texas.
Financial data: Eligible firefighters are exempted from the payment of all dues, fees, and tuition charges at publicly–supported colleges and universities in Texas.
Duration: 1 year; nonrenewable.
Number awarded: Varies each year.
Deadline: Deadline not specified.

2380 TEXAS GARDEN CLUBS SCHOLARSHIPS

Texas Garden Clubs, Inc.
Attn: Vice President, Scholarship
3111 Old Garden Road
Fort Worth, TX 76107–3498
Phone: (817) 332–6602; Fax: (817) 332–3802;
Email: TGCFW@texasgardenclubs.org
Web: www.texasgardenclubs.org/scholarship.html
Summary: To provide financial assistance to upper–division and graduate students from Texas who are working on a degree in a field related to gardening.
Eligibility: Open to residents of Texas enrolled at colleges and universities in the state as juniors, seniors, and graduate students. Applicants must be majoring in horticulture, floriculture, landscape design, botany, biology, plant pathology, forestry, environmental concerns, city planning, land management, agronomy, or an allied subject. They must have a GPA of 3.25 or higher. Along with their application, they must submit a personal statement about their goals, financial need, and career commitment.
Financial data: Stipends are $2,000, $1,500, or $1,000.
Duration: 1 year.
Number awarded: Varies each year; recently, 4 of these scholarships were awarded: 2 at $2,000, 1 at $1,500, and 1 at $1,000.
Deadline: September of each year.

2381 $ THE FRUIT COMPANY GIFT BASKET ENTREPRENEUR AWARD

The Fruit Company
2900 Van Horn Drive
Hood River, OR 97031
Phone: (541) 387–3100; (800) 387–3100; Fax: (541) 387–3104;
Email: scholarship@thefruitcompany.com
Web: www.thefruitcompany.com/page/scholarship
Summary: To provide financial assistance to entering college freshmen interested in studying agriculture or business to prepare for a career in the online gifting industry.
Eligibility: Open to graduates of high schools in any state who are entering freshmen at a college or university. Applicants must be planning to major in business or agriculture as preparation for a career in the online gifting industry, with an interest in search marketing, social media, and online business. Along with their application, they must submit a 500–word statement of career objectives and a 1,000–word essay on how the Internet has changed the way we work, play, communicate, and shop, and how they would bridge the gap between traditional advertising and modern technology to reach a new and younger generation of consumers. Financial need is not considered in the selection process.
Financial data: The stipend is $4,000. Funds are paid directly to the recipient's college or university.
Duration: 1 year.
Number awarded: 1 each year.
Deadline: April of each year.

2382 $$ THE HONORABLE JOHN W. WARNER STEM TEACHER'S SCHOLARSHIP

Armed Forces Communications and Electronics Association
Attn: AFCEA Educational Foundation
4400 Fair Lakes Court
Fairfax, VA 22033–3899
Phone: (703) 631–6138; (800) 336–4583, ext. 6138; Fax: (703) 631–4693;
Email: scholarshipsinfo@afcea.org
Web: www.afcea.org
Summary: To provide financial assistance to undergraduate and graduate students at colleges and universities in Virginia who are preparing for a career as a teacher of science and mathematics.
Eligibility: Open to full–time sophomores, juniors, seniors, and graduate students at accredited colleges and universities in Virginia. Applicants must be U.S. citizens preparing for a career as a teacher of science, information technology, engineering, or mathematics (STEM) at a middle or secondary school. They must have a GPA of 3.0 or higher. Financial need is not considered in the selection process.
Financial data: The stipend is $5,000. Recipients are also entitled to STEM Teaching Tools grants of $1,000 per year for 3 years after they begin teaching a STEM subject.
Duration: 1 year.
Number awarded: 1 each year.
Deadline: March of each year.

2383 $$ THE LAND CONSERVANCY OF NEW JERSEY SCHOLARSHIPS

The Land Conservancy of New Jersey
Attn: Scholarship Program
19 Boonton Avenue
Boonton, NJ 07005
Phone: (973) 541–1010; Fax: (973) 541–1131;
Email: info@tlc–nj.org
Web: www.tlc–nj.org/scholarship.html
Summary: To provide financial assistance to undergraduate and graduate students from New Jersey who are working on a degree in an environmental field at a school in any state.
Eligibility: Open to New Jersey residents who have completed at least 15 credits at a college or university in any state offering a degree in environmental science, natural resource management, conservation, horticulture, park administration, or a related field. Applicants must have a cumulative GPA of 3.0 or higher. They must be considering a career in New Jersey in an environmental field. Along with their application, they must submit a 500–word essay on their career goals and how those will advance the effort of land conservation. Financial need is not considered in the selection process.
Financial data: The stipend is $7,000.
Duration: 1 year.
Number awarded: 2 each year.
Deadline: March of each year.

2384 THE MASCHHOFFS INC. PORK INDUSTRY SCHOLARSHIP

Iowa Foundation for Agricultural Advancement
Attn: Winner's Circle Scholarships
c/o SGI
30805 595th Avenue
Cambridge, IA 50046

Phone: (515) 291–3941;
Email: linda@slweldon.net
Web: www.iowastatefair.org

Summary: To provide financial assistance to Iowa high school seniors who have been involved in swine activities and plan to major in animal science or a related field at a college in the state.

Eligibility: Open to residents of Iowa who will be incoming freshmen at a college or university in the state in the following fall. Applicants must be planning to enroll full time and major in animal science or a program in agriculture or human sciences that is related to the animal industry. They must have a strong background in swine projects and activities. Along with their application, they must submit a 250–word essay summarizing their experiences with their agricultural and livestock projects. Selection is based on that essay and participation in agricultural and livestock projects (50%); activities, leadership, and recognition in 4–H, FFA, and other high school and community activities (25%); academic record (15%); and curriculum plans for college and career plans after graduation as they relate to the agricultural industry in general (10%). Preference is given to applicants who express an interest in working in the pork industry after graduation.

Financial data: The stipend is $1,000.

Duration: 1 year; nonrenewable.

Number awarded: 1 each year.

Deadline: April of each year.

2385 $$ THE RACE FOR EDUCATION THOROUGHBRED SCHOLARSHIPS

The Race for Education
Attn: Student Services Manager
1818 Versailles Road
P.O. Box 11355
Lexington, KY 40575
Phone: (859) 252–8648; Fax: (859) 252–8030;
Email: info@raceforeducation.org
Web: raceforeducation.org/scholarships

Summary: To provide financial assistance to undergraduate students working on an equine–related or agriculture–related degree.

Eligibility: Open to undergraduate students under 24 years of age working on an equine–related degree, including (but not limited to) pre–veterinary medicine (equine practice only), equine science, equine business management, racetrack management, or other equine– or agriculture–related program. Applicants must have a GPA of 2.85 or higher and a household income of less than $50,000 per year. Along with their application, they must submit a 500–word essay on 1 of the following topics: 1) the last book they read for enjoyment only, why they chose it, and what they learned from it; 2) a facet of thoroughbred racing that interests them and why; or 3) their interests outside the equine industry or chosen career field.

Financial data: The stipend covers payment of tuition, to a maximum of $6,000 per year. The student is responsible for all other fees.

Duration: 1 year; may be renewed up to 3 additional years, provided the recipient maintains a GPA of 3.0 or higher.

Number awarded: 1 or more each year.

Deadline: February of each year.

2386 THELMA W. UTT SCHOLARSHIP

Virginia Federation of Garden Clubs
c/o Lisa Robinson, Scholarship Chair
315 Tulip Tree Lane
Moneta, VA 24121–2011
Phone: (540) 266–3083;
Email: gardenlisa@r22sml.com
Web: www.virginiagardenclubs.org/VFGC/Scholarships.html

Summary: To provide financial assistance to residents of Virginia who are upper–division or graduate students at a university in any state and working on a degree in horticulture.

Eligibility: Open to juniors, seniors, and graduate students at colleges and universities in any state who are residents of Virginia. Applicants must be working on a degree in a horticulture–related field and have a garden–related career goal. Along with their application, they must submit a letter discussing their goals, background, personal commitment, and financial need.

Financial data: A stipend is awarded (amount not specified).

Duration: 1 year.

Number awarded: 1 each year.

Deadline: January of each year.

2387 $ THEODORE MAIMAN STUDENT PAPER COMPETITION

Optical Society of America
Attn: OSA Foundation
2010 Massachusetts Avenue, N.W.
Washington, DC 20036–1012
Phone: (202) 416–1464; Fax: (202) 416–6130;
Email: Foundation@osa.org
Web: www.osa–foundation.org/maimancompetition

Summary: To recognize and reward students from any country who submit outstanding papers to the Conference on Lasers and Electro–Optics (CLEO).

Eligibility: Open to undergraduate and graduate students who are listed as first presenting author of papers submitted for presentation at CLEO. Students must be enrolled at least half time at a college or university in any country. The paper must be submitted and accepted during the regular call for papers for the conference and must be presented to a panel of judges in a private session during the conference. Selection is based on innovation, research excellence, and presentation skills.

Financial data: The winner receives a prize of $3,000; honorable mentions receive a certificate.

Duration: The awards are presented annually.

Number awarded: 1 winner and 2 honorable mentions are selected each year.

Deadline: March of each year.

2388 $$ THERMOFORMING DIVISION MEMORIAL SCHOLARSHIPS

Society of Plastics Engineers
Attn: SPE Foundation
13 Church Hill Road
Newtown, CT 06740
Phone: (203) 740–5447; Fax: (203) 775–1157;
Email: foundation@4spe.org
Web: www.4spe.org/spe–foundation

Summary: To provide college scholarships to students who have a career interest in the plastics industry and experience in the thermoforming industry.

Eligibility: Open to full–time undergraduate and graduate students at either a 4–year college or in a 2–year technical program. Applicants must have experience in the thermoforming industry, such as courses taken, research conducted, or jobs held. They must be majoring in or taking courses that would be beneficial to a career in the plastics or polymer industry (e.g., plastics engineering, packaging, polymer sciences, chemistry, physics, chemical engineering, mechanical engineering, industrial engineering). Along with their application, they must submit 3 letters of recommendation; a high school and/or college transcript; a 1– to 2–page statement telling why they are applying for the scholarship, their qualifications, and their educational and career goals in the plastics industry; their employment history; a list of current and past school activities and community activities and honors; information on their financial need; and a statement detailing their exposure to the thermoforming industry.

Financial data: The maximum stipend is $5,000. Funds are paid directly to the recipient's school.

Duration: 1 year.

Number awarded: Varies each year; recently, 2 of these scholarships were awarded.

Deadline: February of each year.

2389 $ THERMOPLASTIC ELASTOMERS SPECIAL INTEREST GROUP SCHOLARSHIP

Society of Plastics Engineers
Attn: SPE Foundation
13 Church Hill Road
Newtown, CT 06740
Phone: (203) 740–5447; Fax: (203) 775–1157;
Email: foundation@4spe.org
Web: www.4spe.org/spe–foundation

Summary: To provide college scholarships to students who have a career interest in the plastics industry and experience in the thermoplastic elastomers industry.

Eligibility: Open to full–time undergraduate students at 4–year colleges and 2–year technical programs and to graduate students. Applicants must have experience in the thermoplastic elastomers industry, such as courses taken, research conducted, or jobs held. They must be majoring in or taking courses that would be beneficial to a career in the plastics or polymer industry (e.g., plastics engineering, packaging, polymer sciences, chemistry, physics, chemical engineering, mechanical engineering, industrial engineering). Along with their application, they must submit 3 letters of recommendation; a high school and/

or college transcript; a 1– to 2–page statement telling why they are applying for the scholarship, their qualifications, and their educational and career goals in the plastics industry; their employment history; a list of current and past school activities and community activities and honors; information on their financial need; and a statement detailing their exposure to the thermoplastic elastomers industry.
Financial data: The stipend is $2,500. Funds are paid directly to the recipient's school.
Duration: 1 year.
Number awarded: 1 each year.
Deadline: February of each year.

2390 $ THERMOPLASTIC MATERIALS AND FOAMS DIVISION SCHOLARSHIP

Society of Plastics Engineers
Attn: SPE Foundation
13 Church Hill Road
Newtown, CT 06740
Phone: (203) 740–5447; Fax: (203) 775–1157;
Email: foundation@4spe.org
Web: www.4spe.org/spe–foundation
Summary: To provide financial assistance to undergraduate students who have a career interest in the thermoplastic materials and foams industry.
Eligibility: Open to full–time undergraduate students at 4–year colleges or in 2–year technical programs. Applicants must have experience in the thermoplastic materials and foams industry, such as courses taken, research conducted, or jobs held. They must be majoring in or taking courses that would be beneficial to a career in the plastics or polymer industry (e.g., plastics engineering, packaging, polymer sciences, chemistry, physics, chemical engineering, mechanical engineering, industrial engineering). Along with their application, they must submit 3 letters of recommendation; a high school and/or college transcript; a 1– to 2–page statement telling why they are applying for the scholarship, their qualifications, and their educational and career goals in the plastics industry; their employment history; a list of current and past school activities and community activities and honors; information on their financial need; and a statement detailing their exposure to the thermoplastic materials and foams industry.
Financial data: The stipend is $2,500. Funds are paid directly to the recipient's school.
Duration: 1 year.
Number awarded: 1 each year.
Deadline: February of each year.

2391 $ THERMOSET DIVISION SCHOLARSHIPS

Society of Plastics Engineers
Attn: SPE Foundation
13 Church Hill Road
Newtown, CT 06740
Phone: (203) 740–5447; Fax: (203) 775–1157;
Email: foundation@4spe.org
Web: www.4spe.org/spe–foundation
Summary: To provide financial assistance to undergraduate and graduate students who have a career interest in the plastics industry and experience in the thermoset industry.
Eligibility: Open to full–time undergraduate and graduate students at either a 4–year college or in a 2–year technical program. Applicants must have experience in the thermoset industry, such as courses taken, research conducted, or jobs held. They must be majoring in or taking courses that would be beneficial to a career in the plastics or polymer industry (e.g., plastics engineering, packaging, polymer sciences, chemistry, physics, chemical engineering, mechanical engineering, industrial engineering). Along with their application, they must submit 3 letters of recommendation; a high school and/or college transcript; a 1– to 2–page statement telling why they are applying for the scholarship, their qualifications, and their educational and career goals in the plastics industry; their employment history; a list of current and past school activities and community activities and honors; information on their financial need; and a statement detailing their exposure to the thermoset industry.
Financial data: The stipend is $2,500 per year. Funds are paid directly to the recipient's school.
Duration: 1 year.
Number awarded: 2 each year: 1 to an undergraduate and 1 to a graduate student.
Deadline: February of each year.

2392 THOMARA LATIMER CANCER FOUNDATION SCHOLARSHIPS

Thomara Latimer Cancer Foundation
Attn: Scholarship Committee
Franklin Plaza Center
29193 Northeastern Highway, Suite 528
Southfield, MI 48034–1006
Phone: (248) 557–2346; Fax: (248) 557–8063;
Email: scholarships@thomlatimercares.org
Web: www.thomlatimercares.org
Summary: To provide financial assistance to African American residents of Michigan, especially those who have had cancer, interested in studying a medically–related field at a college in any state.
Eligibility: Open to African American residents of Michigan between 17 and 30 years of age. Applicants must be 1) a high school senior accepted at an accredited college or university in any state in a medically–related program (e.g., medical technician, physician assistant); or 2) a student admitted to a medically–related professional program (e.g., nursing, medicine, physical or occupational therapy) at a college or university in any state. They must have a GPA of 3.0 or higher. Along with their application, they must submit a brief essay on why they should be awarded this scholarship. Financial need is not considered in the selection process. Special consideration is given to students who are cancer survivors.
Financial data: The stipend is $1,000.
Duration: 1 year; may be renewed 1 additional year.
Number awarded: 10 each year.
Deadline: December of each year.

2393 $ THOMAS E. POWERS/DETROIT SECTION SCHOLARSHIP

Society of Plastics Engineers
Attn: SPE Foundation
13 Church Hill Road
Newtown, CT 06740
Phone: (203) 740–5447; Fax: (203) 775–1157;
Email: foundation@4spe.org
Web: www.4spe.org/spe–foundation
Summary: To provide financial assistance to undergraduate students who have a career interest in the plastics industry.
Eligibility: Open to full–time undergraduate students at 4–year colleges or in 2–year technical programs. Applicants must be majoring in or taking courses that would be beneficial to a career in the plastics or polymer industry (e.g., plastics engineering, packaging, polymer sciences, chemistry, physics, chemical engineering, mechanical engineering, industrial engineering). Along with their application, they must submit 3 letters of recommendation; a high school and/or college transcript; a 1– to 2–page statement telling why they are applying for the scholarship, their qualifications, and their educational and career goals in the plastics industry; their employment history; a list of current and past school activities and community activities and honors; and information on their financial need.
Financial data: The stipend is $4,000. Funds are paid directly to the recipient's school.
Duration: 1 year.
Number awarded: 1 each year.
Deadline: February of each year.

2394 THOMAS HALBERT SCHOLARSHIP

Community Foundation of the Ozarks
Attn: Scholarship Coordinator
421 East Trafficway
P.O. Box 8960
Springfield, MO 65801–8960
Phone: (417) 864–6199; (888) 266–6815; Fax: (417) 864–8344;
Email: jbillings@cfozarks.org
Web: www.cfozarks.org/cfo–grantmaking–programs/scholarship–programs
Summary: To provide financial assistance to students, especially African Americans, at nursing schools in Springfield, Missouri who have been admitted to a degree program.
Eligibility: Open to residents of any state who are attending or entering a nursing school in Springfield, Missouri and who have been accepted to work on a nursing degree. Applicants must submit a high school transcript with cumulative GPA and ACT/SAT scores or a college transcript with cumulative GPA. Preference is given to qualified African American candidates. In the selection process, primary consideration is given to financial need; secondary

consideration is given to academic achievement, leadership abilities, and moral character.
Financial data: The stipend is $1,200 per year.
Duration: 1 year; recipients may reapply.
Number awarded: 1 each year.
Deadline: March of each year.

2395 $ THROLSON AMERICAN BISON FOUNDATION SCHOLARSHIPS

National Bison Association
Attn: Throlson American Bison Foundation
8690 Wolff Court, Suite 200
Westminster, CO 80031
Phone: (303) 292–2833; Fax: (303) 845–9081;
Email: jim@bisoncentral.com
Web: www.bisoncentral.com/about–nba/throlson–american–bison–foundation
Summary: To provide financial assistance to upper–division and graduate students studying bison or fields related to the bison industry.
Eligibility: Open to full–time college juniors, seniors, and graduate students in a recognized livestock, animal science, veterinary, agriculture, or human nutrition program in the United States or Canada. Applicants must be preparing for a career related to the bison or bison industry. Selection is based on essays on the following topics: how they may play a role in the growth of the bison industry in the next 15 years (30 points); community and professional organizations to which they belong and their involvement with them (10 points); their livestock, veterinary, biological, zoological, human nutrition, agribusiness, or agricultural work experience (10 points); their hobbies and leisure activities (5 points); their philosophy of bison in today's environment (10 points); what they believe to be the most critical issue affecting their field of study during the next 10 years (10 points); and their career goals and objectives (25 points).
Financial data: The stipend is either $2,000 or $1,000.
Duration: 1 year; nonrenewable.
Number awarded: 3 each year: 1 at $2,000 and 2 at $1,000.
Deadline: September of each year.

2396 TIDEWATER CHAPTER ROTC SCHOLARSHIP PROGRAM

Armed Forces Communications and Electronics Association–Tidewater Chapter
Attn: Scholarship Program
P.O. Box 65337
Langley AFB, VA 23665–0337
Phone: (757) 846–0037;
Email: makeva.flowers@yahoo.com
Web: www.afceatidewater.com
Summary: To provide financial assistance to students enrolled in ROTC who are majoring in selected areas of science and engineering.
Eligibility: Open to students at colleges and universities in the United States who are enrolled in at least the first year of an ROTC program. U.S. citizenship is required. Applicants must be working full time on a degree in electrical engineering, aerospace engineering, computer engineering, mathematics, computer science, electronics, telecommunications, or physics. They must be nominated by their professor of military science, naval science, or aerospace studies. Membership in AFCEA is not required. Along with their application, they must submit a 1–page essay on: "How the AFCEA Scholarship Can Benefit My Education." Selection is based on academic achievement, participation in extracurricular activities, and financial need.
Financial data: A stipend is awarded (amount not specified). Funds are sent directly to the recipient's university.
Duration: 1 year.
Deadline: April of each year.

2397 $ TIMOTHY BIGELOW AND PALMER W. BIGELOW, JR. SCHOLARSHIPS

American Nursery and Landscape Association
Attn: Horticultural Research Institute
1200 G Street, N.W., Suite 800
Washington, DC 20005
Phone: (202) 695–2474; Fax: (888) 761–7883;
Email: scholarships@hriresearch.org
Web: www.hriresearch.org/index.cfm?page=Content&categoryID=167
Summary: To provide financial support to residents of New England interested in working on an undergraduate or graduate degree in landscape architecture or horticulture.
Eligibility: Open to full–time students enrolled in an accredited landscape or horticulture program in 1) the final year of a 2–year curriculum; 2) the third year of a 4–year curriculum; or 3) a graduate program. Applicants must have a minimum GPA of 2.25 as undergraduates or 3.0 as graduate students. They must be a resident of 1 of the 6 New England states, although attendance at an institution within those states is not required. Preference is given to applicants who plan to work in an aspect of the nursery industry, including a business of their own, and to applicants who demonstrate financial need.
Financial data: The stipend is $2,000.
Duration: 1 year; nonrenewable.
Number awarded: Up to 3 each year.
Deadline: March of each year.

2398 $ TIMOTHY J. O'LEARY SCHOLARSHIPS

American Public Works Association–New England Chapter
Attn: Secretary–Treasurer
404 Woodland Road
Storrs, CT 06268
Phone: (860) 429–3332; Fax: (860) 429–6863;
Email: HultgrenLR@MansfieldCT.org
Web: newengland.apwa.net/resources/scholarships
Summary: To provide financial assistance to undergraduate and graduate students from New England interested in preparing for a career in the public works profession.
Eligibility: Open to students who are enrolled or accepted for enrollment as a full– or part–time student at an accredited trade school, college, or graduate school in any state. Applicants must be working on a degree in highway and traffic engineering, structural engineering, civil engineering, public administration, business administration, environmental engineering and science, horticulture, GIS, or other related field. They are not required to be members of the American Public Works Association (APWA), but they must be sponsored by a member of the New England APWA chapter and committed to a career in the public works profession. Along with their application, they must submit an essay of 200 to 300 words on their reasons for furthering their education. Selection is based on that essay, a transcript, a letter of recommendation, and financial need. U.S. citizenship is required.
Financial data: The stipend is $2,200.
Duration: 1 year.
Number awarded: 2 each year.
Deadline: April of each year.

2399 $$ TK FOUNDATION MARITIME SCHOLARSHIP

Orange County Community Foundation
Attn: Scholarship Associate
4041 MacArthur Boulevard, Suite 510
Newport Beach, CA 92660
Phone: (949) 553–4202, ext. 46; Fax: (949) 553–4211;
Email: alee@oc–cf.org
Web: www.oc–cf.org/Page.aspx?pid=869
Summary: To provide financial assistance to residents of any state attending college to prepare for a career in the maritime industry.
Eligibility: Open to students entering their sophomore, junior, or senior year at a 4–year college or university in any state. Applicants must be preparing for a career in the maritime industry. Relevant majors include, but are not limited to, marine biology, marine engineering, marine science, marine transportation, maritime law enforcement, maritime studies, naval architecture, Navy/Marine Corps ROTC, ocean engineering, or oceanography. They must have a GPA of 3.0 or higher and be able to demonstrate financial need.
Financial data: The stipend ranges from $3,000 to $5,000.
Duration: 1 year.
Number awarded: 1 or more each year.
Deadline: March of each year.

2400 TMC/SAE DONALD D. DAWSON TECHNICAL SCHOLARSHIP

Society of Automotive Engineers
Attn: Scholarships and Loans Program
400 Commonwealth Drive
Warrendale, PA 15096–0001

Phone: (724) 776–4790; (877) 606–7323; Fax: (724) 776–0790;
Email: scholarships@sae.org
Web: students.sae.org/awdscholar/scholarships/undesignated

Summary: To provide financial support to students interested in working on a college degree in engineering.

Eligibility: Open to U.S. citizens who intend to earn an ABET–accredited degree in engineering. Applicants must be 1) high school seniors with a GPA of 3.25 or higher and minimum SAT scores of 600 in mathematics and 550 in critical reading or ACT scores of 27 or higher; 2) transfer students from 4–year colleges or universities with a GPA of 3.0 or higher; or 3) transfer students from postsecondary technical or vocational schools with a GPA of 3.5 or higher. Selection is based on school transcripts; evidence of some type of hands–on technical experience or activity (e.g., rebuilding engines, working on cars or trucks); SAT or ACT scores; school–related extracurricular activities; non–school related activities; academic honors, civic honors, and awards; and a 250–word essay on their goals, plans, experiences, and interests in mobility engineering. Financial need is not considered.

Financial data: The stipend is $1,500 per year.

Duration: 1 year; may be renewed up to 3 additional years if the recipient maintains a GPA of 3.0 or higher.

Number awarded: 1 each year.

Deadline: January of each year.

2401 $ TNLA SCHOLARSHIP PROGRAM

Texas Nursery and Landscape Association
Attn: Education and Research Foundation
7730 South IH–35
Austin, TX 78745–6698
Phone: (512) 280–5182; (800) 880–0343; Fax: (512) 280–3012;
Email: education@tnlaonline.org
Web: www.tnlaonline.org/EandRFoundation/index.php

Summary: To provide financial assistance to high school seniors and returning undergraduate and graduate students in Texas who are majoring in horticulture.

Eligibility: Open to Texas residents who are either high school seniors or returning undergraduate or graduate students. Applicants must be majoring or planning to major in horticulture at their choice of 22 approved colleges in Texas (for a list, contact the sponsor). Along with their application, they must submit a statement on why they are applying for the scholarship and their career objectives as they relate to the field of horticulture and the nursery and landscape industry. Financial need is not considered in the selection process.

Financial data: The standard award is $1,000, divided into a $500 payment per semester. Other scholarships, ranging from $500 to $2,000, are also available.

Duration: The standard award is for 1 year.

Number awarded: Varies each year; recently, 18 of these scholarships were awarded.

Deadline: April of each year.

2402 $ TOM MOUSLEY SCHOLARSHIPS

Society of Commercial Arboriculture
Attn: Scholarships
P.O. Box 3129
Champaign, IL 61826–3129
Phone: (217) 355–9411, ext. 209; (888) 472–8733; Fax: (217) 355–9516;
Email: isa@isa–arbor.com
Web: www.isa–arbor.com

Summary: To provide financial assistance to college students majoring in arboriculture, urban forestry, or horticulture.

Eligibility: Open to students who are enrolled full time in college, have at least 3 months of work experience (preferably in commercial arboriculture), and are majoring in arboriculture, urban forestry, or horticulture. Along with their application, they must submit a 1–page statement describing their goals and aspirations and what makes them an ideal candidate for a scholarship in commercial arboriculture. Selection is not based on need or grades but on career goals and work experience.

Financial data: The stipend is $2,000 for students in 4–year programs or $1,000 for students in 2–year programs; funds are sent to the student upon receipt of proof of enrollment.

Duration: 1 year.

Number awarded: 1 or more each year.

Deadline: May of each year.

2403 $ TRAILBLAZER SCHOLARSHIP

Conference of Minority Transportation Officials
Attn: National Scholarship Program
1875 I Street, N.W., Suite 500
Washington, DC 20006
Phone: (703) 234–4072; Fax: (202) 318–0364
Web: www.comto.org/?page=Scholarships

Summary: To provide financial assistance to undergraduate and graduate minority students working on a degree in a field related to transportation.

Eligibility: Open to undergraduate and graduate students who are working (either full or part time) on a degree in a field related to transportation and have a GPA of 2.5 or higher. Along with their application, they must submit a cover letter with a 500–word statement of career goals. Financial need is not considered in the selection process. U.S. citizenship or legal resident status is required.

Financial data: The stipend is $2,500. Funds are paid directly to the recipient's college or university.

Duration: 1 year.

Number awarded: 1 each year.

Deadline: May of each year.

2404 TRANSFER ENGINEERING STUDENT AWARD

National Association of Multicultural Engineering Program Advocates, Inc.
Attn: National Scholarship Selection Committee Chair
1430 Duke Street
Alexandria, VA 22314
Phone: (703) 562–3650; Fax: (202) 207–3518;
Email: namepa@namepa.org
Web: www.namepa.org/student–scholarships

Summary: To provide financial assistance to underrepresented minority college transfer students who are planning to major in engineering.

Eligibility: Open to African American, Latino, and American Indian college transfer students who are coming from a junior college, community college, or 3/2 dual–degree program. Applicants must be transferring to an engineering program at an institution affiliated with the National Association of Multicultural Engineering Program Advocates (NAMEPA). For a list of affiliated schools, write to the sponsor. They must have a GPA of 2.7 or higher. Along with their application, they must submit a copy of their college transcript, a letter of recommendation, and a 1–page essay on why they have chosen engineering as a profession, why they think they should be selected, and an overview of their future aspirations as an engineer. Financial need is not considered in the selection process.

Financial data: The stipend is $1,000, paid in 2 equal installments.

Duration: 1 year; nonrenewable.

Number awarded: Varies each year; recently, NAMEPA awarded a total of 20 scholarships for its Beginning Freshman Awards and its Transfer Engineering Awards.

Deadline: May of each year.

2405 $ TWIN CITY AFS MEMORIAL SCHOLARSHIP

Foundry Educational Foundation
1695 North Penny Lane
Schaumburg, IL 60173
Phone: (847) 490–9200; Fax: (847) 890–6270;
Email: info@fefoffice.org
Web: www.fefinc.org/students/scholarships/AFSTwinCityMemorial.php

Summary: To provide financial assistance to undergraduate students from Minnesota, Wisconsin, and Iowa who are interested in preparing for a career in the die casting industry.

Eligibility: Open to full–time undergraduate students who are U.S. citizens, have taken or plan to take courses in the die–casting process, and can demonstrate their intention to prepare for a career in the die–casting industry. Preference is given first to residents of Minnesota, then to residents of western Wisconsin, then to residents of northern Iowa. Preference is also given to students attending a college or university with an agreement with the Foundry Educational Foundation (FEF) and to students enrolled in foundry–related courses.

Financial data: The stipends range from $500 to $2,500 per year.

Duration: 1 year.

Number awarded: 1 each year.

Deadline: October of each year.

2406 $ TWISTER SCHOLARSHIP

Women in Technology of Tennessee
c/o Barbara Webb
330 Franklin Road, Suite 135A–538
Brentwood, TN 37027
Phone: (615) 202–5840;
Email: barbara.webb@level3.com
Web: www.wittn.org/scholarship–outreach/scholarship–program.html

Summary: To provide financial assistance to female high school seniors in Tennessee who are interested in attending college in any state to prepare for a career in science, technology, engineering, or research.

Eligibility: Open to women who are graduating from a Tennessee public high school, approved private high school, or home school. Applicants must be interested in attending college in any state to prepare for a career in science, technology, engineering, or research. They must have a GPA of 3.0 or higher. Along with their application, they must submit a 2–page essay on a topic that changes annually but relates to science, technology, or engineering. Financial need is not considered in the selection process.

Financial data: Stipends are $2,500 and $1,000.

Duration: 1 year.

Number awarded: 2 each year: 1 at $2,500 and 1 at $1,000.

Deadline: February of each year.

2407 $$ TYLENOL FUTURE CARE SCHOLARSHIPS

McNeil Consumer Healthcare
c/o International Scholarship and Tuition Services, Inc.
1321 Murfreesboro Road, Suite 800
Nashville, TN 37217
Phone: (615) 320–3149; (855) 670–ISTS; Fax: (615) 320–3151;
Email: contactus@applyists.com
Web: www.tylenol.com/page.jhtml?id=tylenol/news/subptyschol.inc

Summary: To provide financial assistance for college or graduate school to students intending to prepare for a career in a health–related field.

Eligibility: Open to students who have completed at least 1 year of an undergraduate or graduate course of study at an accredited 2– or 4–year college, university, or vocational/technical school. Applicants must be working on a degree in health education, medicine, nursing, pharmacy, or public health. Along with their application, they must submit 1) a 500–word essay on the experiences or persons that have contributed to their plans to prepare for a career in a health–related field; and 2) a 100–word summary of their professional plans. Selection is based on the essays, academic record, community involvement, and college GPA.

Financial data: Stipends are $10,000 or $5,000.

Duration: 1 year.

Number awarded: 40 each year: 10 at $10,000 and 30 at $5,000.

Deadline: May of each year.

2408 UAA JANICE K. BARDEN AVIATION SCHOLARSHIPS

National Business Aviation Association, Inc.
Attn: Director of Operations
1200 18th Street, N.W., Suite 400
Washington, DC 20036–2527
Phone: (202) 783–9250; Fax: (202) 331–8364;
Email: scholarships@nbaa.org
Web: www.nbaa.org/prodev/scholarships

Summary: To provide financial assistance to undergraduates majoring in aviation.

Eligibility: Open to U.S. citizens enrolled full time at the sophomore, junior, or senior level in an aviation–related program of study at an institution belonging to the National Business Aviation Association (NBAA) and the University Aviation Association (UAA). Applicants must have a cumulative GPA of 3.0 or higher. Along with their application they must submit an official transcript, a 250–word essay on their interest in and goals for a career in the business aviation industry, a letter of recommendation from a member of the aviation department faculty, and a 1–page resume. Financial need is not considered in the selection process.

Financial data: The stipend is $1,000. Checks are made payable to the recipient's institution.

Duration: 1 year.

Number awarded: 5 each year.

Deadline: October of each year.

2409 $ UNITED HEALTH FOUNDATION HACU SCHOLARSHIP

Hispanic Association of Colleges and Universities
Attn: National Scholarship Program
8415 Datapoint Drive, Suite 400
San Antonio, TX 78229
Phone: (210) 692–3805; Fax: (210) 692–0823; TDD: (800) 855–2880;
Email: scholarships@hacu.net
Web: www.hacu.net/hacu/Scholarships.asp?SnID=899378480

Summary: To provide financial assistance to undergraduate and graduate students who are working on a degree in a health–related field at institutions that belong to the Hispanic Association of Colleges and Universities (HACU).

Eligibility: Open to full–time undergraduate and graduate students who are enrolled at a 2– or 4–year HACU member institution. Applicants must have a declared major in clinical psychology, dental technician, nursing, pre–optometry, pre–dental, pre–medicine, pre–pharmacy, physician assistant, public health, mental health, or behavioral health. They must have a GPA of 3.0 or higher and be able to demonstrate financial need. Along with their application, they must submit an essay that focuses on their personal motivation for applying to this scholarship program, their academic and/or career goals, and the skills they could bring to an employer.

Financial data: The stipend is $2,000.

Duration: 1 year; nonrenewable.

Number awarded: Varies each year.

Deadline: June of each year.

2410 $$ UNITED HEALTH FOUNDATION SCHOLARSHIPS OF THE THURGOOD MARSHALL COLLEGE FUND

Thurgood Marshall College Fund
Attn: Campus Relations Associate
901 F Street, N.W., Suite 300
Washington, DC 20004
Phone: (202) 747–7183; Fax: (202) 652–2934;
Email: janay.hawkins@tmcfund.org
Web: www.thurgoodmarshallfund.net/current–scholarships

Summary: To provide financial assistance to African American upper–division students working on a degree in health–related fields at public Historically Black Colleges and Universities (HBCUs) that are members of the Thurgood Marshall College Fund (TMCF).

Eligibility: Open to students currently enrolled as juniors at any of the 47 TMCF member institutions. Applicants must be majoring in a health–related field. They must have a GPA of 3.0 or higher and be able to demonstrate financial need. Along with their application, they must submit a 500–word essay on 1 of the following topics: 1) a significant setback, challenge, or opportunity in their life and the impact it has had on them; 2) what inspired them to pursue a degree in their current field of study and the impact it will have on our society; or 3) what it means to be the first person in their family to receive a college degree. U.S. citizenship or permanent resident status is required.

Financial data: The stipend $6,200.

Duration: 1 year; nonrenewable.

Number awarded: Varies each year.

Deadline: April of each year.

2411 $$ UNITED STATES STEEL CORPORATION SCHOLARSHIPS

Society of Women Engineers
Attn: Scholarship Selection Committee
203 North LaSalle Street, Suite 1675
Chicago, IL 60601–1269
Phone: (312) 596–5223; (877) SWE–INFO; Fax: (312) 644–8557;
Email: scholarships@swe.org
Web: societyofwomenengineers.swe.org/index.php/scholarships

Summary: To provide financial assistance to members of the Society of Women Engineers (SWE) majoring in computer science or engineering at designated universities.

Eligibility: Open to members of the society who are entering their junior year or fourth year of a 5–year program at a designated ABET–accredited college or university. Applicants must be U.S. citizens or permanent residents who are working full time on a degree in computer science or engineering and have a GPA of 3.0 or higher. Selection is based on merit and interest in manufacturing.

Financial data: The stipend is $5,000.

Duration: 1 year.

Number awarded: 6 each year.

Deadline: February of each year.

2412 $$ U.S. AIR FORCE ROTC NURSING SCHOLARSHIPS

U.S. Air Force
Attn: Headquarters AFROTC/RRUC
551 East Maxwell Boulevard
Maxwell AFB, AL 36112–5917
Phone: (334) 953–2091; (866) 4–AFROTC; Fax: (334) 953–6167;
Email: afrotc1@maxwell.af.mil
Web: afrotc.com/admissions/professional–programs/nursing

Summary: To provide financial assistance to college students who are interested in a career as a nurse, are interested in joining Air Force ROTC, and are willing to serve as Air Force officers following completion of their bachelor's degree.

Eligibility: Open to U.S. citizens who are freshmen or sophomores in college and interested in a career as a nurse. Applicants must have a cumulative GPA of 2.5 or higher at the end of their freshman year and meet all other academic and physical requirements for participation in AFROTC. They must be interested in working on a nursing degree from an accredited program. At the time of Air Force commissioning, they may be no more than 31 years of age. They must be able to pass the Air Force Officer Qualifying Test (AFOQT) and the Air Force ROTC Physical Fitness Test.

Financial data: Awards are type 1 AFROTC scholarships that provide for full payment of tuition and fees plus an annual book allowance of $900. All recipients are also awarded a tax–free subsistence allowance for 10 months of each year that is $350 per month during their sophomore year, $450 during their junior year, and $500 during their senior year.

Duration: 2 or 3 years, provided the recipient maintains a GPA of 2.5 or higher.

Deadline: June of each year.

2413 $$ U.S. ARMY ROTC NURSE PROGRAM

U.S. Army
ROTC Cadet Command
Attn: Scholarship Branch
204 1st Cavalry Regiment Road, Building 1002
Fort Knox, KY 40121
Phone: (502) 624–7371; (888) 550–ARMY; Fax: (502) 624–6937;
Email: train2lead@usacc.army.mil
Web: www.rotc.usaac.army.mil/scholarships.aspx

Summary: To provide financial assistance to high school seniors or graduates who are interested in enrolling in Army ROTC and majoring in nursing in college.

Eligibility: Open to students who meet the requirements for the Army Reserve Officers' Training Corps (ROTC) Nurse program: 1) be a U.S. citizen; 2) be at least 17 years of age by October of the year in which they are seeking a scholarship; 3) be no more than 27 years of age when graduating from college after 4 years; 4) score at least 1050 on the combined mathematics and critical reading SAT or 21 on the ACT; 5) have a high school GPA of 3.0 or higher; and 6) meet medical and other regulatory requirements. This program is open to ROTC scholarship applicants who wish to enroll in a nursing program at 1 of approximately 100 designated partner colleges and universities and become Army nurses after graduation.

Financial data: This scholarship provides financial assistance toward college tuition and educational fees up to an annual amount of $17,000. In addition, a flat rate of $1,000 is provided for the purchase of textbooks, classroom supplies, and equipment. Recipients are also awarded a stipend for up to 10 months of each year that is $300 per month during their freshman year, $350 per month during their sophomore year, $450 per month during their junior year, and $500 per month during their senior year.

Duration: 4 years, until completion of a baccalaureate degree. A limited number of 2–year and 3–year scholarships are also available to students who are already attending an accredited B.S.N. program on a campus affiliated with ROTC.

Number awarded: A limited number each year.

Deadline: November of each year.

2414 UTAH ACADEMY OF NUTRITION AND DIETETICS SCHOLARSHIPS

Utah Academy of Nutrition and Dietetics
Attn: Executive Assistant
P.O. Box 767
Layton, UT 84041–0767
Phone: (801) 363–1359;
Email: utah@eatrightutah.org
Web: www.eatrightutah.org/uda.cfm?page=scholarships

Summary: To provide financial assistance to upper–division dietetic students in Utah.

Eligibility: Open to 1) juniors in a Coordinated Program in dietetics; and 2) seniors in an approved Didactic Program planning to complete an internship the following year. Applicants may be residents of any state, but they must be enrolled at a qualified school in Utah and have a GPA of 3.0 or higher. Along with their application, they must submit a 200–word personal statement on their professional goals, 2 letters of support, an official transcript, and documentation of financial need.

Financial data: The stipend is $1,000.

Duration: 1 year.

Number awarded: 3 each year.

Deadline: February of each year.

2415 UTAH CHAPTER ASHRAE SCHOLARSHIPS

American Society of Heating, Refrigerating and Air–Conditioning Engineers–Utah Chapter
c/o Adam Evertsen, Student Activities Chair
GSC
668 West Confluence Avenue
Murray, UT 84123
Phone: (801) 288–1000; Fax: (801) 288–1085;
Email: student/utahashrae.org
Web: utahashrae.org/students

Summary: To provide financial assistance to upper–division students at colleges and universities in Utah who are interested in a career in heating, ventilating, and air conditioning (HVAC).

Eligibility: Open to students entering their junior or senior year at a college or university in Utah. Applicants must have an interest or background in thermodynamics, psychometrics, fluid mechanics, indoor air quality, energy, building automation or controls, or HVAC principles. Along with their application, they must submit a resume of their relevant classes and/or work experience relating to those areas; a list of classes in those areas that they have completed or are planning to take; and a letter stating how this scholarship will help them in their education that may lead to a career in the building sciences, energy, or HVAC areas.

Financial data: The stipend is $1,000.

Duration: 1 year.

Number awarded: 3 each year.

Deadline: February of each year.

2416 $$ VADM SAMUEL L. GRAVELY, JR., USN (RET.) MEMORIAL SCHOLARSHIPS

Armed Forces Communications and Electronics Association
Attn: AFCEA Educational Foundation
4400 Fair Lakes Court
Fairfax, VA 22033–3899
Phone: (703) 631–6138; (800) 336–4583, ext. 6138; Fax: (703) 631–4693;
Email: scholarshipsinfo@afcea.org
Web: www.afcea.org/education/scholarships/undergraduate/Gravely.asp

Summary: To provide funding to students majoring in specified scientific fields at an Historically Black College or University (HBCU).

Eligibility: Open to sophomores and juniors enrolled full or part time at an accredited 2– or 4–year HBCU or in a distance learning or online degree program affiliated with those institutions. They must be working toward a bachelor's degree in engineering (aerospace, computer, electrical, or systems), computer science, computer engineering technology, computer information systems, mathematics, physics, information systems management, or other field directly related to the support of U.S. intelligence or homeland security enterprises. Special consideration is given to military enlisted personnel and veterans.

Financial data: The stipend is $5,000.

Duration: 1 year; may be renewed.

Number awarded: At least 2 each year.

Deadline: April of each year.

2417 $ VERIZON SCHOLARSHIPS OF THE SOCIETY OF WOMEN ENGINEERS

Society of Women Engineers
Attn: Scholarship Selection Committee
203 North LaSalle Street, Suite 1675
Chicago, IL 60601–1269
Phone: (312) 596–5223; (877) SWE–INFO; Fax: (312) 644–8557;
Email: scholarships@swe.org
Web: societyofwomenengineers.swe.org/index.php/scholarships

Summary: To provide financial assistance to women working on an undergraduate or graduate degree in designated engineering specialties.
Eligibility: Open to women who are enrolling as sophomores, juniors, seniors, or graduate students at an ABET–accredited 4–year college or university. Applicants must be working full time on a degree in computer science or computer, electrical, industrial, or mechanical engineering and have a GPA of 3.0 or higher. Preference is given to students attending specified colleges and universities, to students enrolled in an ROTC program, and to disabled veterans. Selection is based on merit. U.S. citizenship or permanent resident status is required.
Financial data: The stipend is $3,000.
Duration: 1 year.
Number awarded: 10 each year.
Deadline: February of each year.

2418 $ VETERANS CAUCUS SCHOLARSHIPS

American Academy of Physician Assistants–Veterans Caucus
Attn: Veterans Caucus
P.O. Box 362
Danville, PA 17821–0362
Phone: (570) 271–0292; Fax: (570) 271–5850;
Email: admin@veteranscaucus.org
Web: www.veteranscaucus.org
Summary: To provide financial assistance to veterans of any of the uniformed services who are studying to become physician assistants.
Eligibility: Open to U.S. citizens who are currently enrolled in a physician assistant program. The program must be approved by the Commission on Accreditation of Allied Health Education. Applicants must be honorably discharged members of 1 of the 7 uniformed services of the United States. Selection is based on military honors and awards received, civic and college honors and awards received, professional memberships and activities, and GPA. An electronic copy of the applicant's DD Form 214 must accompany the application.
Financial data: The stipend is $2,000.
Duration: 1 year.
Number awarded: Varies each year.
Deadline: February of each year.

2419 $ VETERANS OF ENDURING FREEDOM (AFGHANISTAN) AND IRAQI FREEDOM SCHOLARSHIP

Armed Forces Communications and Electronics Association
Attn: AFCEA Educational Foundation
4400 Fair Lakes Court
Fairfax, VA 22033–3899
Phone: (703) 631–6138; (800) 336–4583, ext. 6138; Fax: (703) 631–4693;
Email: scholarshipsinfo@afcea.org
Web: www.afcea.org/education/scholarships/undergraduate/military.asp
Summary: To provide financial assistance to veterans and military personnel who served in Afghanistan or Iraq and are working on an undergraduate degree in fields related to the support of U.S. intelligence enterprises.
Eligibility: Open to active–duty and honorably discharged U.S. military members (including Reservists and National Guard personnel) who served in Enduring Freedom (Afghanistan) or Iraqi Freedom operations. Applicants must be enrolled at a 2– or 4–year institution in the United States and working on an undergraduate degree in computer engineering technology, computer information systems, computer network systems, computer science, electronics engineering technology, engineering (aerospace, computer, electrical, or systems), information systems management, information systems security, mathematics, physics, technology management, or other field directly related to the support of U.S. intelligence enterprises or national security. Along with their application, they must submit an essay that includes a brief synopsis of relevant work experience (including military assignments), a brief statement of career goals after graduation, and an explanation of how their academic and career goals will contribute to the areas related to communications, intelligence and/or information systems, and the mission of the Armed Forces Communications and Electronics Association (AFCEA). Financial need is also considered in the selection process.
Financial data: The stipend is $2,500.
Duration: 1 year.
Number awarded: 12 each year: 6 for the fall semester and 6 for the spring semester.
Deadline: March of each year for fall semester; October of each year for spring semester.

2420 $$ VIC AND MARGARET BALL INTERN SCHOLARSHIP

American Floral Endowment
1601 Duke Street
Alexandria, VA 22314
Phone: (703) 838–5211; Fax: (703) 838–5212;
Email: afe@endowment.org
Web: endowment.org/floriculture–scholarshipsinternships.html
Summary: To provide financial assistance and work experience to students working on an undergraduate degree in floriculture.
Eligibility: Open to U.S. citizens who are currently enrolled full time in a 2– or 4–year college or university in the United States in a floriculture or environmental horticulture program. Applicants must be maintaining satisfactory progress in a degree or certificate program and a GPA of "C" or better. They must be interested in gaining additional training by interning at a commercial production greenhouse or nursery of sufficient size to support a well–rounded internship program away from their home and school community.
Financial data: Employers must agree to pay a fair market wage for the geographic area and position. In addition, students receive a scholarship of $6,000 for a 6–month internship, $3,000 for a 4–month internship, or $1,500 for a 3–month summer internship.
Duration: 6 months, 4 months, or 3 summer months.
Number awarded: Varies each year; recently, 6 of these interns were appointed.
Deadline: February or September of each year.

2421 VICTOR VALLEY GEM AND MINERAL CLUB SCHOLARSHIPS

Victor Valley Gem and Mineral Club
Attn: Scholarship Chair
15056–B Seventh Street
Victorville, CA 92395
Phone: (760) 243–2330
Web: www.vvgmc.org/education.html
Summary: To provide financial assistance to upper–division students majoring in earth or natural sciences.
Eligibility: Open to undergraduate students entering their junior or senior year at a college or university and majoring in earth or natural sciences. Applicants must have a GPA of 3.0 or higher. Along with their application, they must submit an essay describing their educational and career goals. Financial need is not considered in the selection process.
Financial data: The stipend is $1,000.
Duration: 1 year.
Number awarded: Several each year.
Deadline: February of each year.

2422 $ VINYL PLASTICS DIVISION SCHOLARSHIP

Society of Plastics Engineers
Attn: SPE Foundation
13 Church Hill Road
Newtown, CT 06740
Phone: (203) 740–5447; Fax: (203) 775–1157;
Email: foundation@4spe.org
Web: www.4spe.org/spe–foundation
Summary: To provide financial assistance to undergraduate students who have a career interest in the vinyl plastics industry.
Eligibility: Open to full–time undergraduate students at 4–year colleges or in 2–year technical programs. Applicants must be majoring in or taking courses that would be beneficial to a career in the plastics or polymer industry (e.g., plastics engineering, packaging, polymer sciences, chemistry, physics, chemical engineering, mechanical engineering, industrial engineering). Along with their application, they must submit 3 letters of recommendation; a high school and/or college transcript; a 1– to 2–page statement telling why they are applying for the scholarship, their qualifications, and their educational and career goals in the plastics industry; their employment history; a list of current and past school activities and community activities and honors; and information on their financial need. Preference is given to applicants with experience in the vinyl industry, such as courses taken, research conducted, or jobs held.
Financial data: The stipend is $3,000. Funds are paid directly to the recipient's school.
Duration: 1 year.
Number awarded: 1 each year.
Deadline: February of each year.

2423 VIOLET E. MACLAREN CONSERVATION SCHOLARSHIP

Garden Club Federation of Massachusetts, Inc.
Attn: Scholarship Secretary
219 Washington Street
Wellesley Hills, MA 02481
Phone: (781) 237–0336; Fax: (781) 237–0336;
Email: gcfmscholarship@aol.com
Web: www.gcfm.org/Education/Scholarships/GCFMScholarships.aspx

Summary: To provide financial assistance to residents of Massachusetts interested in working on an undergraduate or graduate degree in a field related to conservation at a college in any state.

Eligibility: Open to high school seniors, undergraduates, and graduate students who have been residents of Massachusetts for at least 1 year. Applicants must be working on or planning to work on a degree in a field related to conservation, including floriculture, landscape design, horticulture, forestry, agronomy, city planning, environmental studies, land management, botany, or biology. They must have a GPA of 3.0 or higher. Along with their application, they must submit official transcripts; a brief essay about their goals, aspirations, and career plans; a list of their activities, including special honors and/or leadership positions; 3 letters of recommendation; and documentation of financial need.

Financial data: The stipend is $1,000.

Duration: 1 year.

Number awarded: Varies each year.

Deadline: February of each year.

2424 $ VIP WOMEN IN TECHNOLOGY SCHOLARSHIPS

Visionary Integration Professionals
80 Iron Point Circle, Suite 100
Folsom, CA 95630
Phone: (916) 985–9625; (800) 434–2673; Fax: (916) 985–9632;
Email: WITS@vipconsulting.com
Web: www.vipconsulting.com

Summary: To provide financial assistance to women preparing for a career in information technology.

Eligibility: Open to women who are enrolled at or accepted into a 2– or 4–year college or university to prepare for a career in information technology or a related field. Applicants must have a cumulative GPA of 3.0 or higher. Along with their application, they must submit a 1,000–word essay in which they define a specific problem that they see in their community related to information technology and recommend a solution that is thoughtful and likely to make an impact on the problem. Selection is based on that essay, academic performance, and participation in community service and/or extracurricular activities.

Financial data: The stipend is $2,500.

Duration: 1 year.

Number awarded: Varies each year; recently, 9 of these scholarships were awarded.

Deadline: March of each year.

2425 VIRGINIA ELIZABETH AND ALMA VANE TAYLOR NURSING SCHOLARSHIP

Winston–Salem Foundation
Attn: Student Aid Department
860 West Fifth Street
Winston–Salem, NC 27101–2506
Phone: (336) 714–3445; (866) 227–1209; Fax: (336) 727–0581;
Email: StudentAid@wsfoundation.org
Web: www.wsfoundation.org/netcommunity/page.aspx?pid=854

Summary: To provide financial assistance to residents of North Carolina interested in studying nursing at a school in the state.

Eligibility: Open to traditional and nontraditional students in North Carolina who are interested in working on an associate or baccalaureate degree in nursing, preferably a first–time degree, at a school in the state. Applicants must have a high school or college cumulative GPA of 2.5 or higher and be able to demonstrate financial need. Preference is given to residents of Davidson, Davie, Forsyth, Stokes, Surry, and Yadkin counties. Some of the scholarships are set aside for eligible noncitizens.

Financial data: A stipend is awarded (amount not specified).

Duration: 1 year; may be renewed.

Number awarded: 1 or more each year, including 5 scholarships set aside for eligible noncitizens.

Deadline: August of each year.

2426 VIRGINIA LEGION AUXILIARY NURSES SCHOLARSHIP

American Legion Auxiliary
Department of Virginia
Attn: Education Chair
1708 Commonwealth Avenue
Richmond, VA 23230
Phone: (804) 355–6410; Fax: (804) 353–5246
Web: vaauxiliary.org

Summary: To provide financial assistance to descendants of veterans in Virginia who plan to study nursing at a college in any state.

Eligibility: Open to seniors graduating from high schools in Virginia and to graduates of those high schools who have not yet attended a postsecondary institution. Applicants must be the children or grandchildren of veterans who served during eligibility dates for membership in the American Legion. They must be planning to attend college in any state to study nursing. Along with their application, they must submit a 500–word essay on a topic of their choice. Selection is based on academics, character, and Americanism.

Financial data: The stipend is $1,000.

Duration: 1 year.

Number awarded: 1 each year.

Deadline: April of each year.

2427 $$ VIRGINIA NURSE PRACTITIONER/NURSE MIDWIFE SCHOLARSHIP PROGRAM

Virginia Department of Health
Attn: Office of Minority Health and Public Health Policy
109 Governor Street, Suite 1016 East
Richmond, VA 23219
Phone: (804) 864–7435; Fax: (804) 864–7440;
Email: IncentivePrograms@vdh.virginia.gov
Web: www.vdh.state.va.us

Summary: To provide money for college to nursing students in Virginia who are willing to work as nurse practitioners and/or midwives in the state following graduation.

Eligibility: Open to residents of Virginia who are enrolled or accepted for enrollment full or part time at a nurse practitioner program in the state or a nurse midwifery program in Virginia or a nearby state. Applicants must have a cumulative GPA of at least 3.0 in undergraduate and/or graduate courses. Preference is given to 1) residents of designated medically underserved areas of Virginia; 2) students enrolled in family practice, obstetrics and gynecology, pediatric, adult health, and geriatric nurse practitioner programs; and 3) minority students. Selection is based on scholastic achievement, character, and stated commitment to postgraduate employment in a medically underserved area of Virginia.

Financial data: The stipend is $5,000 per year. Recipients must agree to serve in a designated medically underserved area of Virginia for a period of years equal to the number of years of scholarship support received. The required service must begin within 2 years of the recipient's graduation and must be in a facility that provides services to persons who are unable to pay for the service and that participates in all government–sponsored insurance programs designed to assure full access to medical care service for covered persons. If the recipient fails to complete the course of study, or pass the licensing examination, or provide the required service, all scholarship funds received must be repaid with interest and a penalty.

Duration: 1 year; may be renewed for 1 additional year.

Number awarded: Up to 5 each year.

Deadline: June of each year.

2428 VIRGINIA NURSES FOUNDATION SCHOLARSHIP

Virginia Nurses Association
Attn: Virginia Nurses Foundation
7113 Three Chopt Road, Suite 204
Richmond, VA 23226
Phone: (804) 282–1808; (800) 868–6877; Fax: (804) 282–4916;
Email: admin@virginianurses.com
Web: www.virginianurses.com/displaycommon.cfm?an=9

Summary: To provide financial assistance to registered nurses in Virginia working on a bachelor's degree at a school in any state.

Eligibility: Open to registered nurses who are residents of Virginia. Applicants must be enrolled in an R.N. to B.S.N. program at a school in any state and have a GPA of 3.0 or higher. They must intend to practice in Virginia. Selection is based on academic achievement, commitment to nursing, and clinical and leadership abilities.

Financial data: The stipend is $1,000.

Duration: 1 year.
Number awarded: 1 each year.
Deadline: August of each year.

2429 $ VIRGINIA TUITION ASSISTANCE GRANT PROGRAM

Summary: To provide financial assistance to undergraduate and graduate students attending private colleges or universities in Virginia.
See Listing #1012.

2430 WAAIME SCHOLARSHIPS

Woman's Auxiliary to the American Institute of Mining, Metallurgical and Petroleum Engineers
c/o Society for Mining, Metallurgy, and Exploration, Inc.
Scholarship Coordinator
12999 East Adam Aircraft Circle
Englewood, CO 80112
Phone: (303) 948–4208; (800) 763–3132; Fax: (303) 973–3845;
Email: membership@smenet.org
Web: www.smenet.org/scholarships
Summary: To provide financial assistance to upper–division and graduate students working on a degree in earth sciences as related to the minerals industry.
Eligibility: Open to full–time upper–division and graduate students who are working on a degree in earth sciences as related to and supporting the efforts of the minerals industry. Relevant areas of study include chemical engineering, geological sciences, materials science and engineering, metallurgy, mineral sciences, mining economics, petroleum engineering, and other related fields. Preference is given to undergraduate applicants. Applicants must submit a 1–page autobiography detailing their background, studies, and reasons for selecting this career path; 2 letters of reference; a resume detailing past education and work experience; transcripts; a list of other awards or scholarships received for the academic year; and information on financial need.
Financial data: Recently, stipends averaged approximately $1,420.
Duration: 1 year; may be renewed.
Number awarded: Varies each year; recently, more than 80 students received $115,000 in support from this program.
Deadline: November of each year.

2431 WALLACE F. PATE SCHOLARSHIP

Harry Hampton Memorial Wildlife Fund, Inc.
P.O. Box 2641
Columbia, SC 29202
Phone: (803) 600–1570;
Email: jim.goller@hamptonwildlifefund.org
Web: www.hamptonwildlifefund.org/scholarship.html
Summary: To provide financial assistance to high school seniors in South Carolina who plan to major in a field related to natural resources at a college or university in the state.
Eligibility: Open to seniors graduating from high schools in South Carolina who plan to attend an institution of higher learning in the state. Applicants must be planning to major in a field related to natural resources, including wildlife, fisheries, biology, zoology, forestry, marine science, or environmental science. Along with their application, they must submit a brief autobiography that includes 1) a description of their career ambitions in the natural resources field; 2) why they desire a college education; 3) their interest in wildlife resources, the environment, coastal resources, or related topics; and 4) why they will be a good investment if they are awarded this scholarship. Financial need is also considered in the selection process.
Financial data: The stipend is $1,500.
Duration: 1 year; nonrenewable.
Number awarded: 1 each year.
Deadline: January of each year.

2432 $ WALTER C. AND MARIE C. SCHMIDT SCHOLARSHIP

Oregon Student Access Commission
Attn: Grants and Scholarships Division
1500 Valley River Drive, Suite 100
Eugene, OR 97401–2146
Phone: (541) 687–7395; (800) 452–8807, ext. 7395; Fax: (541) 687–7414; TDD: (800) 735–2900;
Email: awardinfo@osac.state.or.us
Web: www.oregonstudentaid.gov/scholarships.aspx
Summary: To provide financial assistance for the study of nursing to residents of Oregon who are attending school in any state to prepare for a career in geriatric health care.
Eligibility: Open to residents of Oregon who are enrolled at least half time in a program at a school in any state to become a registered nurse. Applicants must submit an essay on their desire to prepare for a nursing career in geriatric health care. First preference is given to students at Lane Community College; second preference is given to students at other 2–year college nursing programs. Financial need is considered in the selection process.
Financial data: Stipends for scholarships offered by the Oregon Student Access Commission (OSAC) range from $200 to $10,000 but recently averaged $2,300.
Duration: 1 year.
Number awarded: Varies each year.
Deadline: February of each year.

2433 $ WALTER J. CLORE SCHOLARSHIPS

Washington Association of Wine Grape Growers
Attn: Washington Wine Industry Foundation
203 Mission Avenue, Suite 107
P.O. Box 716
Cashmere, WA 98815–0716
Phone: (509) 782–1108; Fax: (509) 782–1203;
Email: info@washingtonwinefoundation.org
Web: www.washingtonwinefoundation.org/index.php?page_id=6
Summary: To provide financial assistance to residents of Washington who are interested in studying viticulture and/or enology in college.
Eligibility: Open to students who are enrolled or planning to enroll at a college or university to study viticulture and/or enology. Preference is given to residents of Washington, although they may study in any state. Applicants must submit a 500–word essay on why they should receive this scholarship, including their career goals, interests and experiences in the wine grape industry, and plans to improve or enhance the industry. Selection is based on academic merit, leadership abilities, and interest in the study of enology and/or viticulture; financial need is not considered.
Financial data: Stipends range from $500 to $2,000.
Duration: 1 year.
Number awarded: Varies each year; recently, 8 of these scholarships were awarded.
Deadline: May of each year.

2434 WANDA MUNN SCHOLARSHIP

Society of Women Engineers
Attn: Scholarship Selection Committee
203 North LaSalle Street, Suite 1675
Chicago, IL 60601–1269
Phone: (312) 596–5223; (877) SWE–INFO; Fax: (312) 644–8557;
Email: scholarships@swe.org
Web: societyofwomenengineers.swe.org/index.php/scholarships
Summary: To provide financial assistance to women from selected northwestern states interested in returning to college or graduate school to study engineering or computer science.
Eligibility: Open to women who are planning to enroll at an ABET–accredited 4–year college or university. Applicants must have been out of the engineering workforce and school for at least 2 years and must be planning to return as an undergraduate or graduate student to work on a degree in computer science or engineering. They must be residents of are attending school in Alaska, Idaho, Montana, Oregon, or Washington and have a GPA of 3.0 or higher. Selection is based on merit. Preference is given to engineers who already have a degree and are planning to reenter the engineering workforce after a period of temporary retirement.
Financial data: The stipend is $1,500.
Duration: 1 year.
Number awarded: 1 each year.
Deadline: February of each year.

2435 $ WARNER N. PLUMMER SCHOLARSHIP

New Hampshire Land Surveyors Foundation
Attn: Scholarship Committee
77 Main Street
P.O. Box 689
Raymond, NH 03077–0689

Phone: (603) 895–4822; (800) 698–5447; Fax: (603) 462–0343;
Email: info@nhlsa.org
Web: www.nhlsa.org/scholarship.htm

Summary: To provide financial assistance to residents of New Hampshire who are preparing for a career in land surveying.

Eligibility: Open to New Hampshire residents enrolled in the second, third, or fourth year of a 4–year program in surveying or surveying engineering at a college or university in the United States or Canada. Applicants must have shown serious interest, capability, and outstanding accomplishments in surveying courses and must be preparing for a career in land surveying. Along with their application, they must submit an essay about their professional aspirations, their goals in college and afterwards, and factors that make them particularly deserving of support. Financial need is not required.

Financial data: The stipend is $2,000.

Duration: 1 year.

Number awarded: 1 each year.

Deadline: November of each year.

2436 $$ WASHINGTON STATE OPPORTUNITY SCHOLARSHIPS

College Success Foundation
1605 N.W. Sammamish Road, Suite 200
Issaquah, WA 98027–5388
Phone: (425) 416–2000; (877) 899–5002; Fax: (425) 416–2001;
Email: SPollack@collegesuccessfoundation.org
Web: waopportunityscholarship.org

Summary: To provide financial assistance to high school seniors and college freshmen and sophomores in Washington who plan to work on a bachelor's degree in a field related to science, technology, engineering, or mathematics (STEM) or health care at a college in the state.

Eligibility: Open to residents of Washington who are either graduating high school seniors or freshmen or sophomores at a 4–year college or university in the state. Applicants must be planning to work full time on a bachelor's degree in a field of STEM or health care. They must have a GPA of 2.75 or higher and have a family income less than 125% of the median Washington state family income. Along with their application, they must submit an affidavit verifying their status and pledging to seek permanent resident status when legally permitted to do so.

Financial data: Participants receive $1,000 per year as freshmen and sophomores and $5,000 per year as juniors, seniors, or fifth–year students (if necessary to graduate).

Duration: 1 year; may be renewed up to 4 additional years. Renewal requires the recipient to demonstrate satisfactory academic progress, continued financial need, and enrollment in an eligible program.

Number awarded: 3,000 new and renewal scholarships are awarded each year.

Deadline: June of each year.

2437 $$ WASHINGTON STATE THOROUGHBRED FOUNDATION SCHOLARSHIP

The Race for Education
Attn: Student Services Manager
1818 Versailles Road
P.O. Box 11355
Lexington, KY 40575
Phone: (859) 252–8648; Fax: (859) 252–8030;
Email: info@raceforeducation.org
Web: raceforeducation.org/scholarships

Summary: To provide financial assistance to residents of Washington or students attending college in the state who are preparing for a career in the equine industry.

Eligibility: Open to undergraduate students who are residents of Washington or attending a college or university in the state to prepare for a career in the equine industry. Fields of study may include (but are not limited to) equine science, pre–veterinary medicine (equine practice only), equine business management, racetrack management, pasture management as it relates to horse farms, or other related field. They must have a GPA of 2.85 or higher and a household income of less than $75,000. Along with their application, they must submit a 500–word essay on 1 of the following topics: 1) the last book they read for enjoyment only, why they chose it, and what they learned from it; 2) a facet of thoroughbred racing that interests them and why; or 3) their interests outside the equine industry or chosen career field.

Financial data: The stipend is $5,000.

Duration: 1 year.

Number awarded: 1 each year.

Deadline: March of each year.

2438 WATDA TECHNICIAN SCHOLARSHIPS

Wisconsin Automobile and Truck Dealers Association
Attn: Foundation
150 East Gilman, Suite A
P.O. Box 5345
Madison, WI 53705–0345
Phone: (608) 251–4631; Fax: (608) 251–4379;
Email: jolson@watda.org
Web: www.watda.org/index.php?module=cms&page=31

Summary: To provide financial assistance to students attending or planning to attend an automotive, diesel, or auto collision technician program in Wisconsin.

Eligibility: Open to Wisconsin residents enrolled or planning to enroll as an automotive, auto collision, or diesel technician student at a certified Wisconsin technical college. Applicants must be planning to prepare for a career in the automotive, diesel, or auto collision industry. They must have completed a series of assessment evaluations relevant to their field of interest. Finalists must participate in a personal interview.

Financial data: Stipend amounts vary and range up to full payment of tuition. Snap–On Corporation of Kenosha, Wisconsin also provides tools valued at more than $3,000 to scholarship recipients.

Duration: 1 semester; may be renewed up to 3 additional semesters provided the recipient remains enrolled full time with a GPA of 2.8 or higher.

Number awarded: 1 or more each year.

Deadline: January of each year.

2439 $ WAYNE ALEXANDER MEMORIAL SCHOLARSHIP

Summary: To provide financial assistance to undergraduate and graduate students from any country who are working on a degree in the field of document management and graphic communications.

See Listing #1549.

2440 $$ WAYNE V. BLACK SCHOLARSHIP AWARD

Energy Telecommunications and Electrical Association
Attn: Sales/Operations Coordinator
5005 Royal Lane, Suite 116
Irving, TX 75063
Phone: (888) 503–8700, ext. 205; Fax: (972) 915–6040;
Email: tiffany@entelec.org
Web: www.entelec.org

Summary: To provide financial assistance to undergraduates working on a degree in a field related to telecommunications.

Eligibility: Open to full–time undergraduates at accredited colleges and universities in the United States and Canada. Applicants must be working on a bachelor's degree in engineering or engineering technology, computer science or management information systems, pre–law, political science, or telecommunications or information technology. They must be citizens or permanent residents of the United States or citizens of Canada. Along with their application, they must submit a 1–page autobiography and a 5–page essay on a topic that changes annually but relates to telecommunications and similar technologies. Financial need is not considered in the selection process.

Financial data: The stipend is $5,000.

Duration: 1 year.

Number awarded: 1 each year.

Deadline: January of each year.

2441 $$ WEISMAN SCHOLARSHIPS

Connecticut Office of Financial and Academic Affairs for Higher Education
Attn: Student Financial Aid
61 Woodland Street
Hartford, CT 06105–2326
Phone: (860) 947–1853; (800) 842–0229 (within CT); Fax: (860) 947–1314;
Email: mtip@ctdhe.org
Web: www.ctohe.org/SFA/default.htm

Summary: To provide financial assistance to minority upper–division college students from any state who are enrolled at a college in Connecticut and interested in teaching mathematics or science at public middle and high schools in the state.

Eligibility: Open to residents of any state who are enrolled full time as juniors or seniors at Connecticut colleges and universities and preparing to become a mathematics or science teacher at the middle or high school level. Applicants must be members of a minority group, defined as African American, Hispanic/

Latino, Asian American, or Native American. They must be nominated by the education dean at their institution.
Financial data: The maximum stipend is $5,000 per year. In addition, if recipients complete a credential and begin teaching mathematics or science at a public school in Connecticut within 16 months of graduation, they may receive up to $2,500 per year, for up to 4 years, to help pay off college loans.
Number awarded: Varies each year.
Deadline: October of each year.

2442 WEST COAST EQUINE FOUNDATION FRESHMAN SCHOLARSHIP

West Coast Equine Foundation
7200 Lone Pine Drive
Rancho Murieta, CA 95683
Phone: (916) 354–2119; Fax: (916) 354–2127;
Email: maryann@murietaequestriancenter.com
Web: www.westcoastequinefoundation.org/scholarship.html
Summary: To provide financial assistance to high school seniors in designated western states, particularly those who are preparing for a career in the equine or agricultural industry, who are interested in attending college in any state.
Eligibility: Open to seniors graduating from high schools in California, Nevada, Oregon, and Washington who are planning to enroll full time at a college, university, vocational school, or business school in any state. Applicants must have a GPA of 3.0 or higher. Along with their application, they must submit a 300–word personal statement on their educational plans, career goals, and financial need. Preference is given to applicants who are focusing on a future in the equine or agricultural field.
Financial data: A stipend is awarded (amount not specified). Funds are mailed to the recipient's institution.
Duration: 1 year.
Number awarded: 1 or more each year.
Deadline: June of each year.

2443 WEST COAST EQUINE FOUNDATION STUDENTS SCHOLARSHIP

West Coast Equine Foundation
7200 Lone Pine Drive
Rancho Murieta, CA 95683
Phone: (916) 354–2119; Fax: (916) 354–2127;
Email: maryann@murietaequestriancenter.com
Web: www.westcoastequinefoundation.org/scholarship.html
Summary: To provide financial assistance to residents of designated western states, particularly those who are preparing for a career in the equine or agricultural industry, who are currently enrolled at a college in any state.
Eligibility: Open to residents of California, Nevada, Oregon, and Washington who are currently enrolled at a college, university, vocational school, or business school in any state. Applicants must be enrolled full time and have a GPA of 3.0 or higher. Along with their application, they must submit a 300–word personal statement on their educational plans, career goals, and financial need. Preference is given to applicants who are focusing on a future in the equine or agricultural field.
Financial data: A stipend is awarded (amount not specified). Funds are mailed to the recipient's institution.
Duration: 1 year.
Number awarded: 1 or more each year.
Deadline: June of each year.

2444 $ WEST MICHIGAN CHAPTER AWMA SCHOLARSHIPS

Air & Waste Management Association–West Michigan Chapter
c/o Phil Komar, Scholarship Chair
P.O. Box 465
Ada, MI 49301
Phone: (616) 846–9528; Fax: (616) 846–9541;
Email: komarp@trimatrixlabs.com
Web: www.wmawma.org
Summary: To provide financial assistance to upper–division and master's degree students in Michigan who are interested in preparing for a career in an environmental field.
Eligibility: Open to 1) students currently enrolled full time at an accredited college or university in Michigan; and 2) members of the West Michigan Chapter of the Air & Waste Management Association (AWMA) and their children who are enrolled full time at an accredited college or university in any state. Applicants must be entering their junior or senior year of undergraduate studies or enrolled in a master's degree program and preparing for a career in air pollution control, waste management, or other environmental management field. Preferred courses of study include environmental engineering, physical or natural sciences, or natural resources. Selection is based on academic achievement (GPA of 3.0 or higher), an essay of 500 to 600 words on interests and objectives, and participation in extracurricular activities.
Financial data: The stipend is $2,000.
Duration: 1 year; recipients may reapply.
Number awarded: Up to 3 each year.
Deadline: January of each year.

2445 WESTERN FEDERATION OF PROFESSIONAL SURVEYORS SCHOLARSHIPS

Western Federation of Professional Surveyors
Attn: Executive Director
526 South E Street
Santa Rosa, CA 95404
Phone: (707) 578–1130; Fax: (707) 578–4406;
Email: admin@wfps.org
Web: www.wfps.org/files/scholarsh.html
Summary: To provide financial assistance to upper–division students majoring in surveying at colleges and universities in 13 designated western states.
Eligibility: Open to students attending accredited private and public colleges that 1) offer a program leading to a 4–year bachelor's degree with a land surveying major; and 2) are in the states of Alaska, Arizona, California, Colorado, Hawaii, Idaho, Montana, Nevada, New Mexico, Oregon, Utah, Washington, or Wyoming. Applicants must have completed at least 2 years of study. Community college students must be planning to transfer to an eligible 4–year school. Along with their application, they must submit a 1–page essay on their educational goals, career goals, and why their qualifications justify their receiving this scholarship. Selection is based on the quality and neatness of the essay, academic achievement, professional qualifications, college activities, community activities, work experience, and letters of recommendation.
Financial data: The stipend is $1,200.
Duration: 1 year; recipients may reapply.
Number awarded: Varies each year; recently, 3 of these scholarships were awarded.
Deadline: March of each year.

2446 WESTERN PLASTIC PIONEER SCHOLARSHIP

Society of Plastics Engineers
Attn: SPE Foundation
13 Church Hill Road
Newtown, CT 06740
Phone: (203) 740–5447; Fax: (203) 775–1157;
Email: foundation@4spe.org
Web: www.4spe.org/spe–foundation
Summary: To provide financial assistance to undergraduate students from any state who are attending college in designated western states and have a career interest in the plastics industry.
Eligibility: Open to full–time undergraduate students from any state who are enrolled at 4–year colleges or in 2–year technical programs in Arizona, California, Oregon, or Washington. Applicants must be majoring in or taking courses that would be beneficial to a career in the plastics or polymer industry (e.g., plastics engineering, packaging, polymer sciences, chemistry, physics, chemical engineering, mechanical engineering, industrial engineering). Along with their application, they must submit 3 letters of recommendation; a high school and/or college transcript; a 1– to 2–page statement telling why they are applying for the scholarship, their qualifications, and their educational and career goals in the plastics industry; their employment history; a list of current and past school activities and community activities and honors; and information on their financial need.
Financial data: The stipend is $1,000. Funds are paid directly to the recipient's school.
Duration: 1 year.
Number awarded: 1 each year.
Deadline: February of each year.

2447 WESTERN POULTRY SCHOLARSHIPS

Pacific Egg and Poultry Association
Attn: Western Poultry Scholarship and Research Foundation
1521 "I" Street

Sacramento, CA 95814
Phone: (916) 441–0801; Fax: (916) 446–1063;
Email: info@pacificegg.org
Web: www.pacificegg.org/scholarship.html

Summary: To provide financial assistance to undergraduate and graduate students at institutions in western states and Canadian provinces who are interested in preparing for a career in the poultry industry.

Eligibility: Open to high school seniors, undergraduates, and graduate students (including veterinary students) who are enrolled or planning to enroll full time at a college or university in the 11 western states (Alaska, Arizona, California, Colorado, Hawaii, Idaho, Montana, Nevada, Oregon, Utah, and Washington) or the western provinces of Canada that offer a poultry curriculum. Selection is based on academic achievement, financial need, and interest (current and future) in the poultry industry.

Financial data: The stipend is $1,000 for high school seniors or $1,350 for students currently enrolled at a college or university.

Duration: 1 year.

Number awarded: Varies each year; recently, 17 of these scholarships were awarded.

Deadline: January of each year.

2448 WIA/DASSAULT FALCON JET CORPORATION SCHOLARSHIP

Women in Aviation, International
Attn: Scholarships
Morningstar Airport
3647 State Route 503 South
West Alexandria, OH 45381–9354
Phone: (937) 839–4647; Fax: (937) 839–4645;
Email: scholarships@wai.org
Web: www.wai.org/education/scholarships.cfm

Summary: To provide financial assistance to women who are working on an undergraduate or graduate degree in a field related to aviation.

Eligibility: Open to women who are working on an undergraduate or graduate degree in an aviation–related field. Applicants must be U.S. citizens, be fluent in English, and have a GPA of 3.0 or higher. Along with their application, they must submit 2 letters of recommendation; a 1–page essay on their current educational status, what they hope to achieve by working on a degree in aviation, and their aspirations in the field; a resume; copies of all aviation licenses and medical certificates; and the last 3 pages of their pilot logbook (if applicable). Selection is based on achievements, attitude toward self and others, commitment to success, dedication to career, financial need, motivation, reliability, responsibility, and teamwork.

Financial data: The stipend is $1,000.

Duration: 1 year.

Number awarded: 1 each year. The sponsor also offers a number of other corporate and named scholarships to members (primarily) and other women interested in preparing for a career in the field of aviation.

Deadline: November of each year.

2449 $ WILDLIFE LEADERSHIP AWARDS

Rocky Mountain Elk Foundation
Attn: Director of Human Relations
5705 Grant Creek
P.O. Box 8249
Missoula, MT 59807–8249
Phone: (406) 523–4555; (800) CALL ELK, ext. 555; Fax: (406) 523–4581;
Email: bbennett@rmef.org
Web: www.rmef.org/Conservation/ConEd/EdPrograms/Awards

Summary: To provide financial assistance to upper–division students who are majoring in wildlife studies.

Eligibility: Open to students enrolled in a recognized wildlife program at a 4–year college or university in the United States or Canada. Applicants must be juniors or seniors, have at least 1 semester or 2 quarters remaining in their degree program, and be scheduled to enroll as full–time students the following fall semester/quarter. Previous recipients of this award are ineligible. Selection is based on a 100–word list of their hobbies and leisure activities (5 points), a 500–word essay on their leadership activities that relate to wildlife or natural resources (35 points), employment experience (5 points), a 300–word essay on what they believe to be the most important conservation issues facing North America during the next 10 years (20 points), a 250–word essay on the role of hunting in conservation (25 points), a 100–word statement on their career goals and objectives (5 points), and a 100–word statement describing their financial need (5 points).

Financial data: The stipend is $2,000. In addition, recipients are given an engraved plaque and a 1–year membership in the foundation.

Duration: 1 year; nonrenewable.

Number awarded: Up to 10 each year. Since the program was established, it has awarded $227,000 to 145 students.

Deadline: February of each year.

2450 $ WILLARD AND MARJORIE SCHEIBE NURSING SCHOLARSHIP

Rhode Island Foundation
Attn: Funds Administrator
One Union Station
Providence, RI 02903
Phone: (401) 427–4017; Fax: (401) 331–8085;
Email: lmonahan@rifoundation.org
Web: www.rifoundation.org

Summary: To provide financial assistance to residents of Rhode Island studying nursing at a school in any state.

Eligibility: Open to residents of Rhode Island who are working on an L.P.N., R.N., or advanced nursing degree at a school in any state. Applicants must be able to demonstrate financial need and a commitment to practice in Rhode Island. Along with their application, they must submit an essay, up to 300 words, on their career goals, particularly as they relate to practicing in or advancing the field of nursing in Rhode Island.

Financial data: The stipend ranges from $500 to $3,000 per year.

Duration: 1 year; may be renewed.

Number awarded: Varies each year.

Deadline: April of each year.

2451 WILLARD G. PLENTL AVIATION SCHOLARSHIP

Virginia Department of Aviation
Attn: Betty Wilson
5702 Gulfstream Road
Richmond, VA 23250–2422
Phone: (804) 236–3624; (800) 292–1034 (within VA); Fax: (804) 236–3635;
Email: Betty.Wilson@doav.virginia.gov
Web: www.doav.virginia.gov/scholarship_plentl.htm

Summary: To provide financial assistance to high school seniors in Virginia who are interested in preparing for a career in a field of aviation not related to engineering.

Eligibility: Open to seniors graduating from high schools in Virginia who have a GPA of 3.5 or higher and are planning a career in a field of aviation not related to engineering (e.g., pilot, aviation maintenance technician, aviation manager). Applicants must have been accepted to an aviation–related program at an accredited college. They must submit an essay of 350 to 500–words on why they wish to prepare for a career in aviation. Financial need is also considered in the selection process.

Financial data: The stipend is $1,000.

Duration: 1 year; nonrenewable.

Number awarded: 1 each year.

Deadline: February of each year.

2452 $$ WILLIAM FOSTER TICHENOR TUITION SCHOLARSHIPS

Kentucky Community and Technical College System
Attn: Financial Aid
300 North Main Street
Versailles, KY 40383
Phone: (859) 256–3100; (877) 528–2748 (within KY)
Web: www.kctcs.edu

Summary: To provide financial assistance to sophomores working on a degree in nursing at an institution within the Kentucky Community and Technical College System (KCTCS).

Eligibility: Open to KCTCS students entering their sophomore year with a GPA of 2.5 or higher. Applicants must have completed at least 30 hours of a nursing program and be able to demonstrate financial need. Along with their application, they must submit a 1–page essay on their career choice and personal values.

Financial data: Stipends vary at each participating college but are intended to provide full payment of tuition and required fees.

Duration: 1 year.

Number awarded: Varies each year.
Deadline: September of each year.

2453 $ WILLIAM J. ENGLISH MEMORIAL SCHOLARSHIP

Florida Association of Educational Data Systems
c/o Betsy Wetzel, Scholarship Chair
Brevard Community College
1519 Clearlake Road
Cocoa, FL 32922
Phone: (321) 433–7400;
Email: wetzelb@brevardcc.edu
Web: www.faeds.org/scholarships.cfm

Summary: To provide financial assistance to high school seniors in Florida planning to attend a college or university in the state and major in computer science or information technology.

Eligibility: Open to high school and vocational school seniors in Florida who have a GPA of 2.5 or higher. Applicants must be planning to enroll full time at a Florida private or public college and major in computer science or information technology. Along with their application, they must submit a 2–page autobiography that includes their academic success and course work in technology–related areas, why they selected their major, and how they intend to use it in the future. Financial need is not considered in the selection process. U.S. citizenship is required.

Financial data: The stipend is $3,000.

Duration: 1 year.

Number awarded: Varies each year; recently, 3 of these scholarships were awarded.

Deadline: February of each year.

2454 $$ WILLIAM J. FEINGOLD SCHOLARSHIP

American Society for Quality
Attn: Biomedical Division
600 North Plankinton Avenue
P.O. Box 3005
Milwaukee, WI 53201–3005
Phone: (414) 272–8575; (800) 248–1946; Fax: (414) 272–1734;
Email: help@asq.org
Web: asq.org/biomed/about/awards–biomed.html

Summary: To provide financial assistance to undergraduate and graduate students working on a degree in a field related to quality in the biomedical community.

Eligibility: Open to students who have completed at least 2 years of study in a technical, engineering, or scientific course of study that is applicable to the biomedical community. Applicants must have a GPA of 3.0 or higher. Along with their application, they must submit essays on 1) their career objectives and how they relate to quality issues within the biomedical community; and 2) why quality systems are important in the biomedical community. Graduate students are eligible, but preference is given to undergraduates. Priority is given to students who 1) are enrolled in a technical or scientific course of study related to medical products; 2) have contributed to or participated in activities related to quality in the biomedical community; and 3) have a higher GPA or more compelling essay.

Financial data: The stipend is $5,000 per year.

Duration: 1 year; may be renewed 1 additional year.

Number awarded: Varies each year; recently, 3 of these scholarships were awarded.

Deadline: Applications may be submitted at any time.

2455 $ WILLIAM L. CULLISON SCHOLARSHIP

Technical Association of the Pulp and Paper Industry
Attn: TAPPI Foundation
15 Technology Parkway South
Norcross, GA 30092
Phone: (770) 209–7536; (800) 332–8686; Fax: (770) 446–6947;
Email: standards@tappi.org
Web: www.tappi.org/About–TAPPI/TAPPI–Scholarships.aspx

Summary: To provide financial assistance to college students who are interested in preparing for a career in the pulp and paper industry.

Eligibility: Open to full–time students who have completed the first 2 years at a designated university with a pulp and paper program and have a GPA of 3.5 or better. Applicants must demonstrate outstanding leadership abilities and a significant interest in the pulp and paper industry. They must submit 50–word essays on the persons who have influenced them most deeply and why, what attracts them to a career in the pulp and paper industry, the extent to which they have participated in activities related to the pulp and paper industry, and why they think they are more likely to make a major contribution to the pulp and paper industry than other engineers or scientists. Financial need is not considered in the selection process.

Financial data: The stipend is $4,000 per year.

Duration: 1 year (the junior year); may be renewed for the senior year if the recipient maintains at least a 3.0 GPA and pursues courses in the pulp and paper curriculum.

Number awarded: 1 or 2 each year.

Deadline: April of each year.

2456 $ WILLIAM LOWELL PUTNAM COMPETITION

Mathematical Association of America
1529 18th Street, N.W.
Washington, DC 20036–1358
Phone: (202) 387–5200; (800) 741–9415; Fax: (202) 265–2384;
Email: maahq@maa.org
Web: www.maa.org/awards/putnam.html

Summary: To recognize and reward outstanding collegiate participants in a mathematics competition.

Eligibility: Open to undergraduate students at colleges and universities in Canada and the United States. Entrants take a test containing mathematics problems designed to measure originality as well as technical competence. Institutions with at least 3 registered participants obtain a team ranking based on the scores of 3 designated individuals. Awards are presented to both individuals and teams.

Financial data: In the individual competition, the 5 individuals with the highest scores receive $2,500 each, the next 10 receive $1,000 each, and the next 10 receive $250 each. In the team competition, the university of the first–place team receives $25,000 and each team member receives $1,000; the university of the second–place team receives $20,000 and each team member receives $800; the university of the third–place team receives $15,000 and each team member receives $600; the university of the fourth–place team receives $10,000 and each team member receives $400; the university of the fifth–place team receives $5,000 and each team member receives $200.

Duration: The competition is held annually.

Number awarded: 25 individuals and 5 teams and their members win cash prizes each year.

Deadline: October of each year.

2457 $ WILLIAM M. FANNING MAINTENANCE SCHOLARSHIP

National Business Aviation Association, Inc.
Attn: Director of Operations
1200 18th Street, N.W., Suite 400
Washington, DC 20036–2527
Phone: (202) 783–9250; Fax: (202) 331–8364;
Email: scholarships@nbaa.org
Web: www.nbaa.org/prodev/scholarships

Summary: To provide financial assistance to students who are preparing for a career as an aviation maintenance technician.

Eligibility: Open to applicants who are either 1) a student currently enrolled in an accredited airframe and powerplant (A&P) program at an approved FAR Part 147 school; or 2) an individual who is not currently enrolled but who has been accepted for enrollment in an A&P program. They must be U.S. citizens. Along with their application, they must submit 1) an official transcript from their program or school or a letter of acceptance; 2) a 250–word essay on their career goals in the aviation maintenance field; 3) a letter of recommendation from either a faculty member or other individual familiar with the applicant's abilities; and 4) a 1–page resume.

Financial data: The stipend is $2,500.

Duration: 1 year.

Number awarded: 2 each year: 1 for a student who is already enrolled and 1 for a student who has been accepted for enrollment.

Deadline: July of each year.

2458 $$ WILLIAM R. GOLDFARB MEMORIAL SCHOLARSHIP

American Radio Relay League
Attn: ARRL Foundation
225 Main Street
Newington, CT 06111–1494

Phone: (860) 594–0397; Fax: (860) 594–0259;
Email: foundation@arrl.org
Web: www.arrl.org/scholarship–descriptions

Summary: To provide financial assistance to high school seniors who are licensed radio amateurs and interested in working on an undergraduate degree in selected fields.

Eligibility: Open to licensed radio amateurs of any class who are graduating high school seniors planning to attend an accredited institution of higher education. Preference is given to students planning to work on a bachelor's degree in computers, medicine, nursing, engineering, science, or a business–related field. Applicants must submit an essay on the role amateur radio has played in their lives and provide documentation of financial need.

Financial data: The stipend is at least $10,000.

Duration: 1 year.

Number awarded: 1 each year.

Deadline: January of each year.

2459 $ WILLIAM SAMBER SR. AVIATION/MATH AND SCIENCE SCHOLARSHIP

African–American/Caribbean Education Association, Inc.
P.O. Box 1224
Valley Stream, NY 11582–1224
Phone: (718) 949–6733;
Email: aaceainc@yahoo.com
Web: www.aaceainc.com/Scholarships.html

Summary: To provide financial assistance to high school seniors of African American or Caribbean heritage who plan to study a field related to aviation, mathematics, or science in college.

Eligibility: Open to graduating high school seniors who are U.S. citizens of African American or Caribbean heritage. Applicants must be planning to attend a college or university and major in a field related to a career in aviation, mathematics, or science. They must have completed 4 years of specified college preparatory courses with a grade of 90 or higher and have an SAT score of at least 1790. They must also have completed at least 200 hours of community service during their 4 years of high school, preferably in the field that they plan to study in college. Financial need is not considered in the selection process. New York residency is not required, but applicants must be available for an interview in the Queens, New York area.

Financial data: The stipend ranges from $1,000 to $2,500. Funds are paid directly to the recipient.

Duration: 1 year.

Number awarded: 2 each year.

Deadline: April of each year.

2460 $ WILLIAM W. BURGIN, JR. MD EDUCATION RECOGNITION AWARD

American Association for Respiratory Care
Attn: American Respiratory Care Foundation
9425 North MacArthur Boulevard, Suite 100
Irving, TX 75063–4706
Phone: (972) 243–2272; Fax: (972) 484–2720;
Email: info@arcfoundation.org
Web: www.arcfoundation.org/awards/undergraduate/burgin.cfm

Summary: To provide financial assistance to college students working on an associate degree in respiratory therapy.

Eligibility: Open to students who are in their second year of an accredited respiratory care program leading to an associate degree. Applicants must submit 1) an original referenced paper on an aspect of respiratory care; and 2) an essay of at least 1,200 words describing how the award will assist them in reaching their objective of an associate degree and their ultimate goal of leadership in health care. Selection is based on academic performance.

Financial data: The stipend is $2,500. The award also provides 1 night's lodging and registration for the international congress of the association.

Duration: 1 year.

Number awarded: 1 each year.

Deadline: June of each year.

2461 $$ WILLIS H. CARRIER SCHOLARSHIPS

American Society of Heating, Refrigerating and Air–Conditioning Engineers
Attn: Scholarship Administrator
1791 Tullie Circle, N.E.
Atlanta, GA 30329–2305
Phone: (404) 539–1120; Fax: (404) 539–2120;
Email: lbenedict@ashrae.org
Web: www.ashrae.org/students/page/1271

Summary: To provide financial assistance to undergraduate engineering students interested in heating, ventilating, air conditioning, and refrigeration (HVAC&R).

Eligibility: Open to undergraduate engineering students working on a bachelor's degree in a program recognized as accredited by the American Society of Heating, Refrigerating and Air–Conditioning Engineers (ASHRAE). Applicants must be enrolled full time in a course of study that has traditionally been preparatory for the profession of HVAC&R. They must have a GPA of 3.0 or higher and a standing in the top 30% of their class. Selection is based on potential service to the HVAC&R profession, financial need, leadership ability, recommendations from instructors, and work ethics.

Financial data: The stipend is $10,000.

Duration: 1 year; nonrenewable.

Number awarded: 2 each year.

Deadline: November of each year.

2462 WINDSTAR FOUNDATION ENVIRONMENTAL STUDIES SCHOLARSHIPS

Windstar Foundation
2317 Snowmass Creek Road
Snowmass, CO 81654
Phone: (970) 927–5430; (866) 927–5430;
Email: WindstarCO@wstar.org
Web: www.wstar.org

Summary: To provide financial assistance to upper–division and graduate students working on a degree in environmental studies or engineering.

Eligibility: Open to students at colleges and universities in the United States and working on a degree in environmental studies, environmental engineering, or other field focused on environmental studies. Undergraduates must be entering their junior or senior year of college; graduate students must be entering their second year of graduate school. Applicants must have a college GPA of 3.0 or higher. They must select an environmental issue that has been of concern to them and submit a 500–word essay describing the actions they have taken relative to that issue. Financial need is not considered in the selection process.

Financial data: Stipends are $500 for undergraduates and $1,000 for graduate students.

Duration: 1 year.

Number awarded: 3 each year: 2 to undergraduates and 1 to a graduate student.

Deadline: May of each year.

2463 $$ WIRE REINFORCEMENT INSTITUTE EDUCATION FOUNDATION SCHOLARSHIPS

Wire Reinforcement Institute Education Foundation
Attn: Scholarship Selection Committee
942 Main Street, Suite 300
Hartford, CT 06103
Phone: (860) 240–9545; (800) 552–4WRI; Fax: (860) 808–3009;
Email: admin@wirereinforcementinstitute.org
Web: www.wirereinforcementinstitute.org

Summary: To provide financial assistance to undergraduate and graduate students working on a degree in civil or structural engineering.

Eligibility: Open to high school seniors, high school graduates, undergraduates, and graduate students enrolled or planning to enroll full time at a 4–year college or university in the United States or Canada. Applicants must be planning to work on a degree in structural and/or civil engineering. Along with their application, they must submit brief essays on 1) their anticipated career plans; and 2) a topic of their choice related to the field of structural and/or civil engineering and why they selected that as their course of undergraduate or graduate study. Financial need is not considered in the selection process.

Financial data: Stipends range from $2,500 to $5,000. Funds are paid directly to the recipient's college or university.

Duration: 1 year.

Number awarded: Varies each year; recently, 4 of these scholarships were awarded.

Deadline: April of each year.

2464 WISCONSIN CHAPTER ASSE SCHOLARSHIP

American Society of Safety Engineers–Wisconsin Chapter
c/o Nicole Tubeszewski

Diversified Insurance Services
100 North Corporate Drive, Suite 100
Brookfield, WI 53045
Phone: (262) 439–4752;
Email: ntubeszewski@div–ins.com
Web: wisconsin.asse.org

Summary: To provide financial assistance to residents of Wisconsin who are majoring in a safety or related program at a university in the state.

Eligibility: Open to residents of Wisconsin who are enrolled in a safety or related program at a university in the state. Applicants may be undergraduate or graduate students, but they must have a GPA of 2.5 or higher. Along with their application, they must submit brief statements on how they will use their safety degree, their goals as a safety professional, and how they will use the scholarship.

Financial data: The stipend is $1,000.

Number awarded: 1 each year.

Deadline: March of each year.

2465 WISCONSIN DIETETIC ASSOCIATION SCHOLARSHIPS

Wisconsin Dietetic Association
Attn: Scholarship Chair
563 Carter Court, Suite B
Kimberly, WI 54136
Phone: (920) 560–5619; (888) 232–8631; Fax: (920) 882–3655;
Email: eatrightwisc@gmail.com
Web: www.eatrightwisc.org

Summary: To provide financial assistance to undergraduate and graduate students in dietetics programs at colleges and universities in Wisconsin.

Eligibility: Open to students at colleges, universities, and technical schools in Wisconsin who are working on an undergraduate or graduate degree in dietetics or a certificate as a dietetic technician. Applicants must submit a brief summary of their professional and career goals and what they hope to bring to the profession of dietetics, 3 letters of reference, official transcripts, and a financial statement.

Financial data: Stipends are $1,000 or $500.

Duration: 1 year.

Number awarded: Up to 8 each year: 3 for undergraduates at $1,000 each, the Ada B. Lothe Student Grant at $1,000, 1 at $1,000 for a full–time graduate student, 1 at $500 for a part–time graduate student, 1 at $500 for a dietetic technician student, and the Jo Saunders Student Scholarship at $500.

Deadline: February of each year.

2466 WISCONSIN GARDEN CLUB FEDERATION SCHOLARSHIPS

Wisconsin Garden Club Federation
c/o Carolyn A. Craig, Scholarship Chair
900 North Shore Drive
New Richmond, WI 54017–9466
Phone: (715) 246–6242;
Email: cacraig@frontiernet.net
Web: www.wisconsingardenclub.org/education/college–scholarship–program

Summary: To provide financial assistance to upper–division and graduate students from any state who are working on a degree related to gardening at a school in Wisconsin.

Eligibility: Open to juniors, seniors, and graduate students from any state who are enrolled at colleges and universities in Wisconsin. Applicants must be working on a degree in horticulture, floriculture, landscape design/architecture, botany, forestry, agronomy, plant pathology, environmental studies, city planning, land management, or a related field. They must have a GPA of 3.0 or higher. Selection is based on academic record (50%), financial need (30%), character (10%), and occupational objective (10%).

Financial data: The stipend is $1,000.

Duration: 1 year.

Number awarded: 3 each year.

Deadline: February of each year.

2467 WISCONSIN LABORATORY ASSOCIATION SCHOLARSHIPS

Wisconsin Laboratory Association
c/o Gina Steiner
P.O. Box 808
Fort Atkinson, WI 53538–0808
Phone: (800) 563–1004;
Email: ginas@jonesdairyfarm.com
Web: www.wisconsinlabassociation.org/scholarships.htm

Summary: To provide financial assistance to technical, undergraduate, and graduate students in Wisconsin who are preparing for a career in a non–medical laboratory.

Eligibility: Open to students currently attending an accredited college or university in Wisconsin as a technical, undergraduate, or graduate student. Applicants must be enrolled in a curriculum that will prepare them for a career in a field related to non–medical laboratories. They must have a GPA of 3.0 or higher. Along with their application, they must submit a personal statement that may include school or community activities, hobbies, special interests, and reasons for choosing laboratory related studies. Financial need is not considered in the selection process.

Financial data: The stipend is $1,000.

Duration: 1 year.

Number awarded: 2 each year.

Deadline: July of each year.

2468 WISCONSIN LEAGUE FOR NURSING SCHOLARSHIPS

Wisconsin League for Nursing
P.O. Box 136
Long Lake, WI 54542–0136
Phone: (888) 755–3329; Fax: (888) 755–3329;
Email: wln@wisconsinwln.org
Web: www.wisconsinwln.org/Scholarships.htm

Summary: To provide financial assistance to residents of Wisconsin attending a school of nursing in the state.

Eligibility: Open to residents of Wisconsin who working on a graduate, B.S.N., or A.D.N. degree at an accredited school of nursing in the state. Applicants must have completed at least half the credits needed for graduation. They must submit their applications to their school, not directly to the sponsor. Each school may nominate 4 graduate students, 6 students in an R.N. program, and 2 students in an L.P.N. program. Selection is based on scholastic ability, professional activities and/or community service, understanding of the nursing profession, goals upon graduation, and financial need.

Financial data: Stipends are $500 for L.P.N. students or $1,000 for all other students.

Duration: 1 year.

Number awarded: Varies each year.

Deadline: February of each year.

2469 WISCONSIN LEGION AUXILIARY PAST PRESIDENTS PARLEY HEALTH CAREER SCHOLARSHIPS

American Legion Auxiliary
Department of Wisconsin
Attn: Education Chair
2930 American Legion Drive
P.O. Box 140
Portage, WI 53901–0140
Phone: (608) 745–0124; (866) 664–3863; Fax: (608) 745–1947;
Email: alawi@amlegionauxwi.org
Web: www.amlegionauxwi.org/Scholarships.htm

Summary: To provide financial assistance for health–related education at a school in any state to the dependents and descendants of veterans in Wisconsin.

Eligibility: Open to the children, wives, and widows of veterans who are attending or entering a hospital, university, or technical school in any state to prepare for a health–related career. Grandchildren and great–grandchildren of veterans are eligible if they are members of the American Legion Auxiliary. Applicants must be residents of Wisconsin and have a GPA of 3.5 or higher. Along with their application, they must submit a 300–word essay on "The Importance of Health Careers Today." Financial need is considered in the selection process.

Financial data: The stipend is $1,200.

Duration: 1 year; nonrenewable.

Number awarded: 2 each year.

Deadline: March of each year.

2470 WISCONSIN LEGION AUXILIARY PAST PRESIDENTS PARLEY REGISTERED NURSE SCHOLARSHIPS

American Legion Auxiliary
Department of Wisconsin
Attn: Education Chair

2930 American Legion Drive
P.O. Box 140
Portage, WI 53901–0140
Phone: (608) 745–0124; (866) 664–3863; Fax: (608) 745–1947;
Email: alawi@amlegionauxwi.org
Web: www.amlegionauxwi.org/Scholarships.htm

Summary: To provide financial assistance to the dependents and descendants of Wisconsin veterans who are interested in studying nursing at a school in any state.

Eligibility: Open to the wives, widows, and children of Wisconsin veterans who are enrolled or have been accepted in an accredited school of nursing in any state to prepare for a career as a registered nurse. Grandchildren and great–grandchildren of veterans are also eligible if they are American Legion Auxiliary members. Applicants must be Wisconsin residents and have a GPA of 3.5 or higher. Along with their application, they must submit a 300–word essay on "The Need for Trained Nurses Today." Financial need is considered in the selection process.

Financial data: The stipend is $1,200.

Duration: 1 year.

Number awarded: 3 each year.

Deadline: March of each year.

2471 $ WISCONSIN NURSING STUDENT LOANS

Wisconsin Higher Educational Aids Board
131 West Wilson Street, Suite 902
P.O. Box 7885
Madison, WI 53707–7885
Phone: (608) 267–2209; Fax: (608) 267–2808;
Email: peter.zammuto@wisconsin.gov
Web: heab.state.wi.us/programs.html

Summary: To provide money for college to nursing students in Wisconsin who are interested in working in the state following licensure.

Eligibility: Open to Wisconsin residents who are enrolled at least half time at an eligible institution in the state that prepares them to be licensed as nurses, either R.N. or L.P.N. Applicants must agree to be employed as a licensed nurse in Wisconsin following completion of their program. Financial need is considered in the selection process.

Financial data: Loans are provided up to $3,000 per year. For each of the first 2 years the recipient works as a nurse and meets the eligibility criteria, 25% of the loan is forgiven. The balance remaining after forgiveness must be repaid at an interest rate up to 5%. If the student does not practice nursing and meet the eligibility criteria, the entire loan must be repaid at an interest rate up to 5%.

Duration: 1 year; may be renewed up to 4 additional years.

Number awarded: Varies each year.

Deadline: Deadline dates vary by institution; check with your school's financial aid office.

2472 WISCONSIN SCHOLARSHIPS OF THE AMERICAN OCCUPATIONAL THERAPY FOUNDATION

American Occupational Therapy Foundation
Attn: Scholarship Coordinator
4720 Montgomery Lane
P.O. Box 31220
Bethesda, MD 20824–1220
Phone: (301) 652–6611, ext. 2550; Fax: (301) 656–3620; TDD: (800) 377–8555;
Email: JCooper@aotf.org
Web: www.aotf.org/scholarshipsgrants/scholarshipprogram.aspx

Summary: To provide financial assistance to residents of Wisconsin who are working on an associate, professional, or advanced degree in occupational therapy.

Eligibility: Open to Wisconsin residents who are enrolled in an accredited occupational therapy professional master's degree program in the state. Applicants must be working on 1) an associate degree; 2) a professional degree at the master's level; or 3) a post–professional degree at the master's or doctoral level. They must be able to demonstrate a sustained record of outstanding scholastic performance. Selection is based on academic merit and leadership potential; financial need is not considered.

Financial data: The stipend is $2,500 for professional master's degree and post–professional students or $2,000 for students at the associate degree level.

Duration: 1 year.

Number awarded: 3 each year: 1 for each academic level of student.

Deadline: November of each year.

2473 W.J. FOURNET SCHOLARSHIP

Louisiana Rural Water Association
1325 Third Avenue
P.O. Box 180
Kinder, LA 70648
Phone: (337) 738–2896; Fax: (337) 738–5620;
Email: larwa@centurytel.net
Web: www.lrwa.org/LRWAScholarship.html

Summary: To provide financial assistance to high school seniors in Louisiana who live on a water system that is a member of the Louisiana Rural Water Association (LRWA) and who plan to attend college in any state to prepare for a career in the field of water or wastewater.

Eligibility: Open to seniors graduating from high schools in Louisiana and planning to enroll at an approved college or university in any state. Applicants must reside on a water and/or wastewater system that is a member of LRWA and be planning to prepare for a career in the field of water and/or wastewater. They must be U.S. citizens or permanent residents. Along with their application, they must submit a 250–word essay on their goals as those related to their education, career, and future plans. Selection is based on that essay; academic record; awards and honors; number, length of commitment, and quality of leadership responsibilities in community and school activities; and financial need.

Financial data: The stipend is $1,000 per year.

Duration: 2 years, provided the recipient maintains a GPA of 2.0 or higher.

Number awarded: 2 each year: 1 from southern Louisiana and 1 from northern Louisiana.

Deadline: February of each year.

2474 WOMEN@MICROSOFT HOPPERS SCHOLARSHIP

Fargo–Moorhead Area Foundation
Attn: Finance/Program Assistant
502 First Avenue North, Suite 202
Fargo, ND 58102–4804
Phone: (701) 234–0756; Fax: (701) 234–9724;
Email: Stanna@areafoundation.org
Web: areafoundation.org/index.php/scholarships

Summary: To provide financial assistance to women who are interested in studying computer science at a college or university in Minnesota or the Dakotas.

Eligibility: Open to women who are accepted or enrolled at a college or university in Minnesota, North Dakota, or South Dakota. Applicants must be undergraduates with a declared major in either computer science or a related discipline and a GPA of 3.0 or higher. Along with their application, they must submit essays, up to 500 words each, on 2 of the following topics: 1) What do you see as the computer industry's primary shortcomings? If you were a leader in the technical world today, in what direction would you guide technology and why? 2) Why have you chosen a degree in the discipline you are currently pursuing? 3) Describe a coding, class, or work project related to your field of study that you significantly contributed towards; describe your contribution and what impact this project had on you or others. Selection is based on the essays, academic achievement, character, qualities of leadership, and financial need.

Financial data: The stipend is $1,500.

Duration: 1 year.

Number awarded: 1 each year.

Deadline: April of each year.

2475 WYOMING ASSOCIATION OF PHYSICIAN ASSISTANTS SCHOLARSHIPS

Wyoming Association of Physician Assistants
P.O. Box 4009
Cheyenne, WY 82002
Phone: (307) 635–2424;
Email: scholarships@wapa.net
Web: www.wapa.net/scholarships.html

Summary: To provide financial assistance to residents of Wyoming who are enrolled in a physician assistant program in any state.

Eligibility: Open to Wyoming residents who have been accepted at an accredited physician assistant program in any state. Applicants must submit a brief essay describing why they feel they should receive this scholarship, including school, work, and personal experiences; achievements; personal goals; and financial need.

Financial data: The stipend is $1,000.

Duration: 1 year.

Number awarded: At least 2 each year.

Deadline: February of each year.

2476 YANMAR/SAE SCHOLARSHIP

Society of Automotive Engineers
Attn: Scholarships and Loans Program
400 Commonwealth Drive
Warrendale, PA 15096–0001
Phone: (724) 776–4970; (877) 606–7323; Fax: (724) 776–0790;
Email: scholarships@sae.org
Web: students.sae.org/awdscholar/scholarships/yanmar

Summary: To provide financial support for study or research to college seniors and graduate students working on a degree in engineering or conservation.

Eligibility: Open to students entering their senior year of full–time study in an undergraduate engineering program or enrolled in a graduate engineering or related science program at a college or university in Canada, Mexico, or the United States. They must be pursuing a course of study or research related to the internal combustion engine, the conservation of energy in transportation, agriculture, construction, or power generation. Emphasis is placed on research or study related to the internal combustion engine. Canadian, Mexican, or U.S. citizenship is required. Selection is based on academic and leadership achievement related to engineering or science, scholastic performance and special study or honors in the field of the award, and an essay of 250 to 300 words on how their study or research relates to the field of their award. Financial need is not considered.

Financial data: The stipend is $1,000 per year.

Duration: 1 year; may be renewed 1 additional year.

Number awarded: 1 each year.

Deadline: February of each year.

2477 $ YASME FOUNDATION SCHOLARSHIPS

American Radio Relay League
Attn: ARRL Foundation
225 Main Street
Newington, CT 06111–1494
Phone: (860) 594–0397; Fax: (860) 594–0259;
Email: foundation@arrl.org
Web: www.arrl.org/scholarship–descriptions

Summary: To provide financial assistance to licensed radio amateurs who are interested in working on an undergraduate degree in science or engineering.

Eligibility: Open to undergraduate students who are licensed radio amateurs of technician class or higher. Applicants must be enrolled or planning to enroll at an accredited 4–year college or university. They must submit an essay on the role amateur radio has played in their lives and provide documentation of financial need. Preference is given to 1) students majoring in science or engineering; 2) high school seniors ranked in the top 5% to 10% of their class; 3) college students ranked in the top 10% of their class; and 4) students who have participated in a local amateur radio club and community service activities.

Financial data: The stipend is $2,000 per year.

Duration: 1 year; the program includes 2 awards that may be renewed for up to 3 additional years or until successful completion of undergraduate study.

Number awarded: 5 each year.

Deadline: January of each year.

2478 $ YOUNG ENTREPRENEUR SCHOLARSHIP

Armed Forces Communications and Electronics Association
Attn: AFCEA Educational Foundation
4400 Fair Lakes Court
Fairfax, VA 22033–3899
Phone: (703) 631–6138; (800) 336–4583, ext. 6138; Fax: (703) 631–4693;
Email: scholarshipsinfo@afcea.org
Web: www.afcea.org

Summary: To provide financial assistance to young professionals who are working on an undergraduate or graduate degree in specified science or technology disciplines.

Eligibility: Open to young (under 40 years of age) professionals who are enrolled part time at a 2–year community college or accredited university while employed by a small business. Applicants may be undergraduates who are at least second–year students or master's degree students who have completed at least 2 graduate–level classes. They must be working on a degree in engineering (chemical, communications, computer, electrical, or systems), computer science, computer information systems, management information systems, mathematics, physics, or technology management; business majors with a minor in science or technology are also eligible. U.S. citizenship and a GPA of 3.0 or higher are required.

Financial data: The stipend is $2,000.

Duration: 1 year.

Number awarded: 1 or more each year.

Deadline: March of each year.

2479 $ YOUNG NATURALIST AWARDS

American Museum of Natural History
Attn: National Center for Science Literacy, Education, and Technology
Central Park West at 79th Street
New York, NY 10024–5192
Phone: (212) 496–3498;
Email: yna@amnh.org
Web: www.amnh.org/nationalcenter/youngnaturalistawards

Summary: To recognize and reward high school students who develop outstanding science projects.

Eligibility: Open to students in grades 7–12 currently enrolled in a public, private, parochial, or home school in the United States, Canada, the U.S. territories, or U.S.–sponsored schools abroad. Applicants are invited to submit reports of observation–based projects on a scientific topic of their own selection. Entries must be between 500 and 2,000 words for grades 7 and 8, between 750 and 2,500 words for grades 9 and 10, or between 1,000 and 3,000 words for grades 11 and 12. Students must include photographs. Entries are judged by grade level. Selection is based on focus of investigation, procedure, analysis and interpretation, documentation of research materials, personal voice, clarity and style, and use of visuals.

Financial data: This program provides scholarships of $2,500 for grade 12, $2,000 for grade 11, $1,500 for grade 10, $1,000 for grade 9, $750 for grade 8, or $500 for grade 7.

Duration: Awards are presented annually.

Number awarded: 12 awards are presented each year: 2 for each grade level.

Deadline: March of each year.

2480 $ ACADEMIC SCHOLARSHIPS FOR UNDERGRADUATE, PROSTART ALUMNI, AND MANAGEFIRST STUDENTS

National Restaurant Association Educational Foundation
Attn: Scholarships Program
175 West Jackson Boulevard, Suite 1500
Chicago, IL 60604–2814
Phone: (312) 715–1010, ext. 738; (800) 765–2122, ext. 6738; Fax: (312) 566–9733;
Email: scholars@nraef.org
Web: www.nraef.org/scholarships

Summary: To provide financial assistance to undergraduate students who are interested in preparing for a career in the hospitality industry.

Eligibility: Open to full–time and substantial part–time college students, especially those who have completed the National Restaurant Association ProStart Program or are participating in its ManageFirst Program. Applicants must have completed at least 1 term of a food service–related program at an accredited culinary school, college, or university. They must be U.S. citizens or permanent residents. Along with their application, they must submit 1) an essay of 200 to 300 words on their career goals in the restaurant/food service industry, their background and educational and work experience, how their background and experience will help them achieve their career goals, and what they need to do to achieve their career goals; and 2) an essay of 350 to 750 words on either profitability and entrepreneurship in the restaurant and food service industry or social responsibility in that industry. Selection is based on the essays, presentation of the application, industry–related work experience, letters of recommendation, and food service certificates (such as the ProStart National Certificate of Achievement or a ManageFirst certificate).

Financial data: The stipend is $2,500.

Duration: 1 year.

Number awarded: Approximately 200 each year.

Deadline: March of each year.

2481 ACCOUNTING CAREERS FOR DUMMIES SCHOLARSHIPS

Accounting Careers for Dummies
c/o Vertical Response Group, LLC
171 Main Street, Suite 245
Los Altos, CA 94022
Phone: (650) 948–4324; Fax: (415) 946–3370
Web: www.accountingcareersfordummies.com

Summary: To provide financial assistance to high school seniors in designated states who plan to study accounting at a college in any state.

Eligibility: Open to seniors graduating from high schools in California, Florida, Illinois, and Texas. Applicants must be planning to enroll at a college or university in any state and work on a degree in accounting. Along with their application, they must submit an essay of 500 to 1,000 words on the area of accounting that interests them the most and why. Selection is based on that essay and academic record.

Financial data: The stipend is $1,000.

Duration: 1 year; nonrenewable.

Number awarded: 4 each year: 1 in each of the participating states.

Deadline: May of each year.

2482 $ ACI–NA COMMISSIONERS SCHOLARSHIPS

Airports Council International–North America
1775 K Street, N.W., Suite 500
Washington, DC 20006
Phone: (202) 293–8500; (888) 424–7767; Fax: (202) 331–1362
Web: www.aci–na.org/content/aci–na–scholarships

Summary: To provide financial support to undergraduate or graduate students preparing for a career in airport management or airport operations.

Eligibility: Open to students enrolled in an undergraduate or graduate program that focuses on airport management or airport operations at an accredited college or university in the United States or Canada. Students in flight–related majors are not eligible. Applicants must have a GPA of 3.0 or higher. Along with their application, they must submit a personal statement (from 350 to 500 words) on their interest in airport management or airport operations. Selection is based on academic excellence, leadership, expected impact on the airport industry, and financial need.

Financial data: The stipend is $2,500.

Duration: 1 year; recipients may reapply.

Number awarded: Up to 6 each year.

Deadline: April or December of each year.

2483 $ ACTUARIAL DIVERSITY SCHOLARSHIPS

Actuarial Foundation
Attn: Actuarial Education and Research Fund Committee
475 North Martingale Road, Suite 600
Schaumburg, IL 60173–2226
Phone: (847) 706–3535; Fax: (847) 706–3599;
Email: scholarships@actfnd.org
Web: www.actuarialfoundation.org

Summary: To provide financial assistance to minority undergraduate and graduate students who are preparing for a career in actuarial science.

Eligibility: Open to members of minority groups, defined as having at least 1 birth parent who is Black/African American, Hispanic, or Native North American. Applicants must be graduating high school seniors or current full–time undergraduate or graduate students working on or planning to work on a degree at an accredited 2– or 4–year college or university that may lead to a career in the actuarial profession. They must have a GPA of 3.0 or higher; high school seniors must also have a minimum score of 28 on the ACT mathematics examination or 600 on the SAT mathematics examination. Along with their application, they must submit a 1– or 2–page personal statement that covers why they are interested in becoming an actuary, the steps they are taking to enter the actuarial profession, participation in actuarial internships, and participation in extracurricular activities. Financial need is not considered in the selection process.

Financial data: Annual stipends are $1,000 for high school seniors applying for freshman year, $2,000 for college freshmen applying for sophomore year and for college sophomores applying for junior year, $3,000 for college juniors applying for senior year, or $3,000 for college seniors applying for graduate school or continuing graduate students.

Duration: 1 year; may be renewed, provided the recipient remains enrolled full time, in good academic standing, in a course of study that may lead to a career in the actuarial profession, and (for college juniors and higher) passes actuarial examinations.

Number awarded: Varies each year; recently, 23 of these scholarships were awarded.

Deadline: May of each year.

2484 $ ADVANCING WOMEN IN ACCOUNTING SCHOLARSHIP

Illinois CPA Society
Attn: CPA Endowment Fund of Illinois
550 West Jackson, Suite 900
Chicago, Il 60661–5716
Phone: (312) 993–0407; (800) 993–0407 (within IL); Fax: (312) 993–9954
Web: www.icpas.org/hc–students.aspx?id=2724

Summary: To provide financial assistance to female residents of Illinois who will be enrolled as seniors or graduate students in an accounting program in the state.

Eligibility: Open to women in Illinois who plan to enroll as seniors or graduate students in an accounting program at a college or university in the state. Applicants must be planning to complete the educational requirements needed to sit for the C.P.A. examination in Illinois. They must have at least a 3.0 GPA and be able to demonstrate financial need or special circumstances; the society is especially interested in assisting students who, because of limited options or opportunities, may not have alternative means of support. U.S. citizenship or permanent resident status is required. Selection is based on academic achievement and financial need.

Financial data: The maximum stipend is $4,000 for payment of tuition and fees. Awards include up to $500 in expenses for books and required classroom materials.

Duration: 1 year (fifth year for accounting students planning to become a C.P.A.).

Number awarded: Varies each year; recently, 3 of these scholarships were awarded.

Deadline: March of each year.

2485 ADVOCACY SCHOLARSHIP OF THE JUVENILE DIABETES RESEARCH FOUNDATION

Diabetes Scholars Foundation
2118 Plum Grove Road, Suite 356
Rolling Meadows, IL 60008

Phone: (312) 215–9861; Fax: (847) 991–8739;
Email: collegescholarships@diabetesscholars.org
Web: www.diabetesscholars.org/college.html

Summary: To provide financial assistance to high school seniors who have diabetes and plan to major in political science in college.

Eligibility: Open to graduating high school seniors who have Type 1 diabetes and plan to attend an accredited 4–year university, college, or technical/trade school in any state. Applicants must be planning to major in political science. They must be able to demonstrate active involvement in the diabetes community, academic performance, participation in community and/or extracurricular activities, and successful management of the challenges of living with diabetes. Financial need is not considered in the selection process. U.S. citizenship or permanent resident status is required.

Financial data: The stipend is $1,000.

Duration: 1 year.

Number awarded: 1 each year.

Deadline: May of each year.

2486 AFDA SCHOLARSHIP

Alabama Funeral Directors Association
Attn: Executive Director
7956 Vaughn Road
PMB 380
Montgomery, AL 36116
Phone: (334) 956–8000; Fax: (334) 956–8001;
Email: afda06@bellsouth.net
Web: www.alabamafda.org/Scholarships.htm

Summary: To provide financial assistance to residents of Alabama who are attending an accredited mortuary science school.

Eligibility: Open to residents of Alabama who have been accepted by an accredited mortuary science school in any state and have an overall GPA of 2.5 or higher. Applicants must be sponsored by an active member of the Alabama Funeral Directors Association (AFDA) and must submit a 500–word essay on "A Career in Funeral Service." They must be planning to return to Alabama to serve the public in their chosen profession. Selection is based on academic record and evaluation of the required essay; financial need is not considered.

Financial data: The stipend is $1,000. Funds are paid directly to the school the recipient attends.

Duration: 1 year.

Number awarded: 2 each year.

Deadline: April of each year.

2487 $ AFSA NATIONAL HIGH SCHOOL ESSAY CONTEST

American Foreign Service Association
Attn: National High School Essay Contest
2101 E Street, N.W.
Washington, DC 20037
Phone: (202) 338–4045; (800) 704–AFSA; Fax: (202) 338–6820;
Email: green@afsa.org
Web: www.afsa.org/essay_contest.aspx

Summary: To recognize and reward high school students who submit essays on a topic related to U.S. foreign relations.

Eligibility: Open to students in grades 9–12 attending a public, private, parochial, or home school or participating in a high school correspondence program in any of the 50 states, the District of Columbia, or the U.S. territories. U.S. citizens attending schools overseas are also eligible. Students whose parents are members of the U.S. Foreign Service or have served on the Advisory Committees are not eligible. Applicants must submit an essay of 1,000 to 1,250 words on a topic that changes annually. Recently, participants were invited to explain what they would do as a diplomat in the U.S. Foreign Service to improve the relations between the United States and a designated country. Selection is based on the quality of research, quality of analysis, and style and mechanics.

Financial data: The winner receives $2,500 and an all–expense paid trip to Washington, D.C. for the awards ceremony.

Duration: The competition is held annually.

Number awarded: 1 each year.

Deadline: April of each year.

2488 $ AL SCHUMAN ECOLAB FIRST–TIME FRESHMAN ENTREPRENEURIAL SCHOLARSHIPS

National Restaurant Association Educational Foundation
Attn: Scholarships Program
175 West Jackson Boulevard, Suite 1500
Chicago, IL 60604–2814
Phone: (312) 715–1010, ext. 738; (800) 765–2122, ext. 6738; Fax: (312) 566–9733;
Email: scholars@nraef.org
Web: www.nraef.org/scholarships

Summary: To provide financial assistance to students entering selected universities throughout the country who have demonstrated entrepreneurship relevant to the food service industry.

Eligibility: Open to U.S. citizens and permanent residents who are first–time entering freshmen at any of 15 designated universities. Applicants must be planning to enroll full time for at least 2 consecutive terms in a restaurant and/or food service program. They must have a GPA of 3.0 or higher or a GED average standard score of 470 or higher. Along with their application, they must submit a 750–word essay describing a food service–related entrepreneurial project (e.g., starting a new restaurant, developing a new product or menu) that they have completed or that they plan to undertake in the future. Selection is based on that essay, presentation of the application, letters of recommendation, and industry–related work experience.

Financial data: The stipend is $3,500 or $3,000.

Duration: 1 year.

Number awarded: 2 each year: 1 at $3,500 and 1 at $3,000.

Deadline: August of each year.

2489 $$ AL SCHUMAN ECOLAB UNDERGRADUATE ENTREPRENEURIAL SCHOLARSHIPS

National Restaurant Association Educational Foundation
Attn: Scholarships Program
175 West Jackson Boulevard, Suite 1500
Chicago, IL 60604–2814
Phone: (312) 715–1010, ext. 738; (800) 765–2122, ext. 6738; Fax: (312) 566–9733;
Email: scholars@nraef.org
Web: www.nraef.org/scholarships

Summary: To provide financial assistance to students currently enrolled at selected universities throughout the country who have demonstrated entrepreneurship relevant to the food service industry.

Eligibility: Open to U.S. citizens and permanent residents who have completed at least 1 grading term at any of 15 designated universities. Applicants must be enrolled full time in a restaurant and/or food service program and have a GPA of 3.0 or higher. Along with their application, they must submit a 750–word essay describing a food service–related entrepreneurial project (e.g., starting a new restaurant, developing a new product or menu) that they have completed or that they plan to undertake in the future. Selection is based on that essay, presentation of the application, letters of recommendation, and industry–related work experience.

Financial data: The stipend is $5,500 or $3,000.

Duration: 1 year.

Number awarded: 2 each year: 1 at $5,500 and 1 at $3,000.

Deadline: March of each year.

2490 $ ALABAMA SOCIETY OF CERTIFIED PUBLIC ACCOUNTANT GENERAL SCHOLARSHIPS

Alabama Society of Certified Public Accountants
Attn: ASCPA Educational Foundation
1103 South Perry Street
P.O. Box 5000
Montgomery, AL 36103
Phone: (334) 834–7650; (800) 227–1711
Web: www.ascpa.org

Summary: To provide financial assistance to accounting students at colleges and universities in Alabama.

Eligibility: Open to residents of any state enrolled at least half time at colleges and universities in Alabama with at least 1 full year of school remaining. Applicants must have declared a major in accounting and have completed intermediate accounting courses. They must have a GPA of 3.0 or higher overall and in all accounting classes. Along with their application, they must submit a 25–word essay on why the scholarship is important to them. Financial need is not considered in the selection process. Preference is given to students who have a strong interest in a career as a C.P.A. in Alabama. U.S. citizenship or permanent resident status is required.

Financial data: The stipend is $2,500.

Duration: 1 year.

Number awarded: 23 each year: 1 at each accredited accounting program in Alabama.

Deadline: March of each year.

2491 $$ ALAN H. CONKLIN BUSINESS AVIATION MANAGEMENT SCHOLARSHIP

National Business Aviation Association, Inc.
Attn: Director of Operations
1200 18th Street, N.W., Suite 400
Washington, DC 20036–2527
Phone: (202) 783–9250; Fax: (202) 331–8364;
Email: scholarships@nbaa.org
Web: www.nbaa.org/prodev/scholarships

Summary: To provide financial assistance to undergraduates preparing for a career in business aviation management.

Eligibility: Open to sophomores, juniors, and seniors currently enrolled full time at a college or university that belongs to the University Aviation Association (UAA). Applicants must have at least a 3.0 GPA and be working on a degree in a field related to business aviation management. Along with their application they must submit an official transcript, a 500–word essay on their interest in and goals for a career in business aviation, 2 letters of recommendation, and a resume. U.S. citizenship or permanent resident status is required. Financial need is not considered in the selection process.

Financial data: The stipend is $5,000. Checks are made payable to the recipient's institution.

Duration: 1 year.

Number awarded: 1 each year.

Deadline: July of each year.

2492 ALASKA AIRLINES SCHOLARSHIP

Tourism Cares
Attn: Academic Scholarship Program
275 Turnpike Street, Suite 307
Canton, MA 02021
Phone: (781) 821–5990; Fax: (781) 821–8949;
Email: scholarships@tourismcares.org
Web: www.tourismcares.org

Summary: To provide financial assistance to undergraduate students working on a degree in travel and tourism or hospitality–related fields.

Eligibility: Open to U.S. and Canadian citizens and permanent residents who are 1) entering the second year at an accredited 2–year college; or 2) entering their junior or senior year at an accredited 4–year college or university. Applicants must be enrolled full or part time in a travel and tourism or hospitality–related program of study. They must have a GPA of 3.0 or higher. Along with their application, they must submit an essay on the segment of the travel and tourism or hospitality industry their current program of study emphasizes, the opportunities they are utilizing as they prepare for a career in the industry, and their academic and extracurricular activities. Financial need is not considered in the selection process.

Financial data: The stipend is $1,000.

Duration: 1 year.

Number awarded: 1 each year.

Deadline: March of each year.

2493 ALEXANDER HARRIS SCHOLARSHIP

Tourism Cares
Attn: Academic Scholarship Program
275 Turnpike Street, Suite 307
Canton, MA 02021
Phone: (781) 821–5990; Fax: (781) 821–8949;
Email: scholarships@tourismcares.org
Web: www.tourismcares.org

Summary: To provide financial assistance to undergraduate students working on a degree in travel and tourism or hospitality–related fields.

Eligibility: Open to U.S. citizens and permanent residents who are 1) entering the second year at an accredited 2–year college; or 2) entering their junior or senior year at an accredited 4–year college or university. Applicants must be enrolled full or part time in a travel and tourism or hospitality–related program of study. They must have a GPA of 3.0 or higher. Along with their application, they must submit an essay on the segment of the travel and tourism or hospitality industry their current program of study emphasizes, the opportunities they are utilizing as they prepare for a career in the industry, and their academic and extracurricular activities. Financial need is not considered in the selection process.

Financial data: The stipend is $1,000.

Duration: 1 year.

Number awarded: 1 each year.

Deadline: March of each year.

2494 $ ALICE L. HALTOM EDUCATIONAL FUND SCHOLARSHIPS

Alice L. Haltom Educational Fund
P.O. Box 70530
Houston, TX 77270
Email: contact@alhef.org
Web: www.alhef.org

Summary: To provide financial assistance to students working on an undergraduate or advanced degree in a field related to information and records management.

Eligibility: Open to citizens of the United States, Canada, and Mexico working on a graduate, bachelor's, or associate degree in a field related to information and records management. Applicants must submit an essay of 300 words or less on their career–related interest in information and records management. Selection is based on that essay, academic achievement, work experience, and financial need.

Financial data: Stipends are $2,000 for students working on a bachelor's or advanced degree or $1,000 for students working on an associate degree.

Duration: 1 year.

Number awarded: Varies each year; recently, 20 of these scholarships were awarded.

Deadline: April of each year.

2495 $$ ALICE M. YARNOLD AND SAMUEL YARNOLD SCHOLARSHIP

Summary: To provide financial assistance to currently–enrolled students in New Hampshire who are majoring in nursing, medicine, or social work at a college or university in any state.

See Listing #1582.

2496 ALMA EXLEY SCHOLARSHIP

Community Foundation of Greater New Britain
Attn: Scholarship Manager
74A Vine Street
New Britain, CT 06052–1431
Phone: (860) 229–6018, ext. 305; Fax: (860) 225–2666;
Email: cfarmer@cfgnb.org
Web: www.cfgnb.org/Scholarships/ScholarshipList/tabid/622/Default.aspx

Summary: To provide financial assistance to minority college students in Connecticut who are interested in preparing for a teaching career.

Eligibility: Open to students of color (African Americans, Asian Americans, Hispanic Americans, and Native Americans) enrolled in a teacher preparation program in Connecticut. Applicant must 1) have been admitted to a traditional teacher preparation program at an accredited 4–year college or university in the state; or 2) be participating in the Alternate Route to Certification (ARC) program sponsored by the Connecticut Department of Higher Education.

Financial data: The stipend is $1,500 per year for students at a 4–year college or university or $500 for a student in the ARC program.

Duration: 2 years for students at 4–year colleges or universities; 1 year for students in the ARC program.

Number awarded: 2 each year: 1 to a 4–year student and 1 to an ARC student.

Deadline: October of each year.

2497 $ ALOHA CHAPTER SCHOLARSHIPS

American Society of Military Comptrollers–Aloha Chapter
Attn: Scholarship Chair
P.O. Box 29564
Honolulu, HI 96820
Phone: (808) 473–8000, ext. 6320;
Email: mary.c.garcia@navy.mil
Web: chapters.asmconline.org/aloha/category/education

Summary: To provide financial assistance to high school seniors and recent graduates in Hawaii interested in attending college in any state to prepare for a career in financial management.

Eligibility: Open to seniors graduating from high schools in Hawaii and to people who graduated from those high schools during the preceding 6 months. Applicants must be planning to enter college in any state in a field of study directly related to financial resource management, including business administration, economics, public administration, accounting, or finance. Selection is based on scholastic achievement, leadership ability, extracurricular activities, career and academic goals, and financial need.

Financial data: Stipends recently ranged from $1,000 to $2,000.

Duration: 1 year.
Number awarded: Varies each year; recently, 3 of these scholarships were awarded: 1 each at $2,000, $1,500, and $1,000.
Deadline: February of each year.

2498 $ ALPHA DELTA KAPPA SCHOLARSHIP

Oregon Student Access Commission
Attn: Grants and Scholarships Division
1500 Valley River Drive, Suite 100
Eugene, OR 97401–2146
Phone: (541) 687–7395; (800) 452–8807, ext. 7395; Fax: (541) 687–7414; TDD: (800) 735–2900;
Email: awardinfo@osac.state.or.us
Web: www.oregonstudentaid.gov/scholarships.aspx
Summary: To provide financial assistance to Oregon residents working on an undergraduate or graduate degree in education at a school in the state.
Eligibility: Open to residents of Oregon who are U.S. citizens or permanent residents and enrolled at a college or university in the state. Applicants must be college seniors or fifth–year students majoring in elementary or secondary education, or graduate students in their fifth year working on an elementary or secondary certificate. Full–time enrollment and financial need are required.
Financial data: Stipends for scholarships offered by the Oregon Student Access Commission (OSAC) range from $200 to $10,000 but recently averaged $2,300.
Duration: 1 year.
Number awarded: 1 or more each year.
Deadline: February of each year.

2499 $$ ALTRIA SCHOLARS

Summary: To provide financial assistance to students majoring in designated fields at a college or university that is a member of the Virginia Foundation for Independent Colleges (VFIC).
See Listing #1586.

2500 $$ ALTRIA SCHOLARSHIPS OF THE THURGOOD MARSHALL COLLEGE FUND

Summary: To provide financial assistance to African American upper–division students working on a degree in designated fields at public Historically Black Colleges and Universities (HBCUs) that are members of the Thurgood Marshall College Fund (TMCF).
See Listing #1587.

2501 $$ AMERICAN ASSOCIATION OF BLACKS IN ENERGY NATIONAL SCHOLARSHIPS

Summary: To provide financial assistance to underrepresented minority high school seniors who are interested in majoring in business, engineering, mathematics, or physical science in college.
See Listing #1589.

2502 $ AMERICAN EDUCATIONAL LEADERS PRIVATE ENTERPRISE ESSAY CONTEST

American Educational Leaders
P.O. Box 1287
Monrovia, CA 91017
Phone: (626) 357–7733;
Email: aelmain@americanism.org
Web: www.americanism.org/pages/contest/college.htm
Summary: To recognize and reward undergraduate students who submit outstanding essays on topics related to current political and economic issues.
Eligibility: Open to undergraduate students currently enrolled at colleges and universities in the United States. Applicants must submit essays of 1,500 to 2,000 words on assigned topics that change annually but involve issues of current political and economic interest. Recently, students were invited to provide their answers to the following topics: 1) should there be a mandatory requirement that legislators must produce a timely, balanced budget without deficits or surpluses; 2) would a reading and civic knowledge test before a person is eligible to vote be beneficial; 3) enumerate and explain tax loopholes to be eliminated; or 4) how can an unemployed person become productive without disturbing the economy. Selection is based on internal logic, coherence, originality, thoughtfulness, and evidence of sound research.
Financial data: Prizes are $3,000 for first, $1,250 for second, and $1,000 for third. The professors of the top 2 finishers receive a $250 honorarium.
Duration: The competition is held annually.
Number awarded: 3 students and 2 professors receive awards each year.
Deadline: April of each year.

2503 AMERICAN INDIAN FELLOWSHIP IN BUSINESS SCHOLARSHIP

National Center for American Indian Enterprise Development
Attn: Event Specialist
953 East Juanita Avenue
Mesa, AZ 85204
Phone: (800) 462–2433, ext. 250; Fax: (480) 545–4208;
Email: Shawna.Benally@ncaied.org
Web: www.ncaied.org/the–ncaied/scholarships
Summary: To provide financial assistance to American Indians and Alaska Natives working on a bachelor's or master's degree in business.
Eligibility: Open to enrolled members of American Indian tribes and Alaska Native villages. Applicants must be enrolled full time as a junior, senior, or master's degree student in business at a college or university in the United States. Along with their application, they must submit 3 essays of 150 to 250 words each on their community involvement, personal challenges, or business experience (paid or volunteer). Selection is based on the quality of those essays (5%), grades (30%), community involvement (30%), personal challenges (25%), and business experience (10%).
Financial data: A stipend is awarded (amount not specified).
Duration: 1 year.
Number awarded: Varies each year; recently, 10 of these scholarships were awarded.
Deadline: August of each year.

2504 AMERICAN SOCIETY FOR INDUSTRIAL SECURITY STUDENT WRITING COMPETITION

American Society for Industrial Security
Attn: ASIS Foundation
1625 Prince Street
Alexandria, VA 22314–2818
Phone: (703) 518–1441; Fax: (703) 519–6299;
Email: foundation@asisonline.org
Web: www.asisonline.org
Summary: To recognize and reward undergraduate and graduate students in fields related to industrial security who submit outstanding academic papers.
Eligibility: Open to full– and part–time students working on an associate, bachelor's, or master's degree at an accredited institution. Applicants must submit a research paper, from 3,000 to 6,000 words in length, on an issue relevant to the security and assets protection profession. Selection is based on relevance of the content and specific subject matter to the topic, creativity in addressing the issue at hand, organization and overall quality of the written product, and applicability of analysis and the conclusions presented.
Financial data: Awards are $1,000 for the winning undergraduate and $1,500 for the winning graduate student.
Duration: The competition is held annually.
Number awarded: 2 each year: 1 undergraduate and 1 graduate student.
Deadline: November of each year.

2505 $$ ANGUS ROBINSON, JR. MEMORIAL FOUNDATION SCHOLARSHIPS

The Angus Robinson, Jr. Memorial Foundation
c/o Jackie Hayes, Odyssey Reinsurance Company
300 First Stamford Place
Stamford, CT 06902
Phone: (203) 977–8070; Fax: (203) 356–0196;
Email: info@angusrobinsonfoundation.org
Web: angusrobinsonfoundation.org/foundation
Summary: To provide financial assistance to undergraduate students who are working on a degree in an insurance–related field.
Eligibility: Open to students currently enrolled full time at a 4–year college or university in the United States or Canada. Applicants must be majoring in insurance, risk management, or actuarial science and have a GPA of 3.0 or higher. Along with their application, they must submit a 500–word personal statement on what the scholarship means to them, why they are interested in a career in the insurance industry, and the specific field within the industry

they hope to pursue. Selection is based on that essay, cumulative GPA, letters of recommendation, demonstrated commitment to the pursuit of a career in the insurance industry, and financial need.
Financial data: Stipends range up to $5,000.
Duration: 1 year; recipients may reapply.
Number awarded: Varies each year; since the foundation was established, it has awarded 477 scholarships to 388 students attending 33 colleges in the United States and Canada.
Deadline: January of each year.

2506 $$ ANNE SOWLES CALHOUN MEMORIAL SCHOLARSHIP

Summary: To provide financial assistance for college to women who want to prepare for a career in the printing or publishing industry.
See Listing #1116.

2507 $ ANTHONY "TONY" GOBAR JUVENILE JUSTICE SCHOLARSHIP FUND

Community Foundation of Greater Jackson
525 East Capitol Street, Suite 5B
Jackson, MS 39201
Phone: (601) 974–6044; Fax: (601) 974–6045;
Email: info@cfgj.org
Web: www.cfgreaterjackson.org/scholarships.html
Summary: To provide financial assistance to upper–division students in Mississippi and Louisiana who are preparing for a career in the field of juvenile justice.
Eligibility: Open to full–time juniors and seniors at public universities in Mississippi and at Southern University in Louisiana who are preparing to enter the field of juvenile justice. Applicants must have demonstrated a strong commitment to community and public service. They must be U.S. citizens and have a GPA of 2.5 or higher. Eligible majors include criminal justice, counseling, and political science. Selection is based on merit and need.
Financial data: The stipend ranges up to $2,500.
Duration: 1 year.
Number awarded: 1 each year.
Deadline: April of each year.

2508 APPLEGATE/JACKSON/PARKS FUTURE TEACHER SCHOLARSHIP

National Institute for Labor Relations Research
Attn: Future Teacher Scholarships
5211 Port Royal Road, Suite 510
Springfield, VA 22151
Phone: (703) 321–9606; Fax: (703) 321–7342;
Email: research@nilrr.org
Web: www.nilrr.org/resources/scholarship–application
Summary: To provide financial assistance to students majoring in education who oppose compulsory unionism in the education community.
Eligibility: Open to undergraduate and graduate students majoring in education at institutions of higher learning in the United States. Applicants must demonstrate the potential to complete a degree program in education and receive a teaching license. Along with their application, they must submit an essay of approximately 500 words demonstrating an understanding of the principles of voluntary unionism and the problems of compulsory unionism in relation to education. Selection is based on scholastic ability and a demonstrated interest in the work of the sponsoring organization to promote voluntary unionism.
Financial data: The stipend is $1,000.
Duration: 1 year.
Number awarded: 1 each year.
Deadline: December of each year.

2509 APPRAISAL INSTITUTE EDUCATION TRUST UNDERGRADUATE SCHOLARSHIP

Appraisal Institute
Attn: Appraisal Institute Education Trust
200 West Madison Street, Suite 1500
Chicago, IL 60606
Phone: (312) 335–4133; Fax: (312) 335–4134;
Email: educationtrust@appraisalinstitute.org
Web: www.appraisalinstitute.org/education/scholarship.aspx
Summary: To provide financial assistance to undergraduate students majoring in real estate or allied fields.
Eligibility: Open to U.S. citizens who are full– or part–time sophomores, juniors, or seniors working on an associate or bachelor's degree in real estate appraisal, land economics, real estate, or related fields. Applicants must submit a 200–word personal statement discussing their academic achievements, career aspirations, involvement in the real estate field, financial need and any other relevant qualifications.
Financial data: The stipend is $1,000. Funds are paid directly to the recipient's academic institution.
Duration: 1 year.
Number awarded: At least 1 each year.
Deadline: March of each year.

2510 APPRAISAL INSTITUTE MINORITIES AND WOMEN EDUCATIONAL SCHOLARSHIP PROGRAM

Appraisal Institute
Attn: Appraisal Institute Education Trust
200 West Madison Street, Suite 1500
Chicago, IL 60606
Phone: (312) 335–4133; Fax: (312) 335–4134;
Email: educationtrust@appraisalinstitute.org
Web: www.appraisalinstitute.org/education/scholarship.aspx
Summary: To provide financial assistance to women and minority undergraduate students majoring in real estate or allied fields.
Eligibility: Open to members of groups underrepresented in the real estate appraisal profession. Those groups include women, American Indians, Alaska Natives, Asians and Pacific Islanders, Blacks or African Americans, and Hispanics. Applicants must be full– or part–time students enrolled in real estate courses within a degree–granting college, university, or junior college. They must have a GPA of 2.5 or higher and be able to demonstrate financial need. U.S. citizenship is required.
Financial data: The stipend is $1,000. Funds are paid directly to the recipient's institution to be used for tuition and fees.
Duration: 1 year.
Number awarded: At least 1 each year.
Deadline: April of each year.

2511 APWA SCHOLARSHIP FUND

Summary: To provide financial assistance to undergraduate students in Mississippi who are preparing for a career in the field of public works.
See Listing #1618.

2512 $$ ARC OF WASHINGTON TRUST FUND STUDENT GRANTS

Summary: To provide financial assistance to undergraduate and graduate students in northwestern states who have a career interest in work relating to developmental disabilities.
See Listing #1619.

2513 $$ ARMED FORCES COMMUNICATIONS AND ELECTRONICS ASSOCIATION STEM TEACHER'S SCHOLARSHIP

Armed Forces Communications and Electronics Association
Attn: AFCEA Educational Foundation
4400 Fair Lakes Court
Fairfax, VA 22033–3899
Phone: (703) 631–6138; (800) 336–4583, ext. 6138; Fax: (703) 631–4693;
Email: scholarshipsinfo@afcea.org
Web: www.afcea.org
Summary: To provide financial assistance to undergraduate and graduate students who are preparing for a career as a teacher of science and mathematics.
Eligibility: Open to full–time sophomores, juniors, seniors, and graduate students at accredited colleges and universities in the United States. Applicants must be U.S. citizens preparing for a career as a teacher of science, information technology, engineering, or mathematics (STEM) at a middle or secondary school. They must have a GPA of 3.0 or higher. Financial need is not considered in the selection process.

Financial data: The stipend is $5,000. Recipients are also entitled to STEM Teaching Tools grants of $1,000 per year for 3 years after they begin teaching a STEM subject.
Duration: 1 year.
Number awarded: 50 each year.
Deadline: March of each year.

2514 $ ARNE ENGEBRETSEN SCHOLARSHIPS

Summary: To provide financial assistance to high school seniors in Wisconsin interested in attending college to prepare for a career as a mathematics teacher.
See Listing #1632.

2515 ARNOLD SADLER MEMORIAL SCHOLARSHIP

Summary: To provide financial assistance to undergraduate or graduate students who are blind and are interested in studying in a field of service to persons with disabilities.
See Listing #1633.

2516 $ ARTHUR H. GOODMAN MEMORIAL SCHOLARSHIPS

CDC Small Business Finance
Attn: Scholarship Program
2448 Historic Decatur Road, Suite 200
San Diego, CA 92106
Phone: (619) 291–3594; (800) 611–5170; Fax: (619) 291–6954
Web: cdcloans.com/scholar.htm

Summary: To provide financial assistance to women and minority college students from California who are interested in preparing for a career related to community development.
Eligibility: Open to women and minorities who are residents of or attending school in California. Applicants must have completed 2 years of community college study with a GPA of 3.0 or higher and be ready to transfer to a 4–year college or university. They must be interested in preparing for a career in business, government, nonprofit, public service, or other profession that will improve their community. Along with their application, they must submit a 3–page personal statement on their community involvement and volunteerism, why they volunteer, how it has influenced them personally and their career goals, how their volunteerism has impacted individuals or the community, an individual or event that has influenced their decision to attend college and/or select their desired career, their future goals and how they include community involvement, and why they feel they are a strong candidate for this scholarship. Financial need is considered in the selection process.
Financial data: Stipends range from $1,500 to $3,000.
Duration: 1 year.
Number awarded: Approximately 4 each year.
Deadline: April of each year.

2517 $ ASMC NATIONAL SCHOLARSHIP PROGRAM

American Society of Military Comptrollers
Attn: National Awards Committee
415 North Alfred Street
Alexandria, VA 22314
Phone: (703) 549–0360; (800) 462–5637; Fax: (703) 549–3181;
Email: lindaryan_asmchsscholarships@yahoo.com
Web: awards.asmconline.org

Summary: To provide financial assistance to high school seniors and recent graduates interested in preparing for a career in financial management.
Eligibility: Open to high school seniors and to people who graduated from high school during the preceding 6 months. Applicants must be planning to enter college in a field of study directly related to financial resource management, including business administration, economics, public administration, accounting, or finance. They must be endorsed by a chapter of the American Society of Military Comptrollers (ASMC). Selection is based on scholastic achievement, leadership ability, extracurricular activities, career and academic goals, and financial need.
Financial data: Stipends are $2,000 or $1,000 per year.
Duration: 1 year; recipients of the $2,000 scholarships may reapply and receive up to $1,000 per year for 3 additional years.
Number awarded: 10 each year: 5 at $2,000 and 5 at $1,000.
Deadline: March of each year.

2518 $ ASPARAGUS CLUB SCHOLARSHIPS

Baton Rouge Area Foundation
Attn: Scholarship Program Officer
402 North Fourth Street
Baton Rouge, LA 70802
Phone: (225) 381–7084; (877) 387–6126; Fax: (225) 387–6153;
Email: efargason@braf.org
Web: www.braf.org/index.cfm/page/3/n/2

Summary: To provide financial assistance to undergraduate and graduate students interested in preparing for a career in the grocery industry.
Eligibility: Open to upper–division and graduate students who are working on a degree in an academic discipline relevant to the grocery industry. Their field of study may relate to retailing, wholesaling, or processing/manufacturing aspects of the food distribution industry (supermarket management and ownership, convenience store management, advertising and public relations, computer technology, food safety, consumer affairs, food plant management, purchasing management, financial planning, or traffic management). Applicants must submit a letter of recommendation from a professor in the food management and/or business school, a statement of 250 to 500 words on why they are preparing for a career in the grocery industry, transcripts, ACT and/or SAT scores, and documentation of financial need. The student judged to be the most meritorious receives the Thomas K. Zaucha Asparagus Club Scholarship.
Financial data: Stipends range up to $3,000 per year. The Thomas K. Zaucha Asparagus Club Scholar receives an additional $1,000 in their first year. Funds are sent directly to the recipients with a check payable to them and their universities to be used for tuition and fees.
Duration: 1 year; may be renewed if the recipient remains enrolled full time and maintains a GPA of 2.5 or higher.
Number awarded: Up to 10 each year.
Deadline: April of each year.

2519 ASPIRING MUSIC TEACHER SCHOLARSHIP

Summary: To provide financial assistance to residents of Vermont who are interested in attending college in any state to study music education or piano pedagogy.
See Listing #1127.

2520 $ ASSOCIATED CHINESE UNIVERSITY WOMEN SCHOLARSHIPS

Summary: To provide financial assistance to residents of Hawaii who are of Chinese ancestry and interested in majoring in education or Chinese studies at a college in any state.
See Listing #1128.

2521 ASSOCIATION OF FOOD AND DRUG OFFICIALS SCHOLARSHIP AWARDS

Summary: To provide financial assistance to upper–division students who are preparing for a career in an aspect of food, drug, or consumer product safety.
See Listing #1651.

2522 ASSOCIATION OF GOLF MERCHANDISERS SCHOLARSHIPS

Association of Golf Merchandisers
P.O. Box 7247
Phoenix, AZ 85011–7247
Phone: (602) 604–8250; Fax: (602) 604–8251;
Email: info@agmgolf.org
Web: www.agmgolf.org

Summary: To provide financial assistance to college students interested in a career in golf merchandising.
Eligibility: Open to students who are currently enrolled at a college, university, or technical institute and are actively preparing for a golf merchandising career. Applicants must have completed at least their sophomore year with a GPA of 3.0 or higher.
Financial data: The stipend is $1,000.
Duration: 1 year.
Number awarded: Several each year.
Deadline: Deadline not specified.

2523 ASWA UNDERGRADUATE SCHOLARSHIPS

American Society of Women Accountants
Attn: Educational Foundation
1760 Old Meadow Road, Suite 500
McLean, VA 22102
Phone: (703) 506–3265; (800) 326–2163; Fax: (703) 506–3266;
Email: foundation@aswa.org
Web: www.aswa.org/PageDisplay.asp?p1=1386

Summary: To provide financial assistance to undergraduates interested in preparing for a career in accounting or finance.

Eligibility: Open to women and men who are entering their third, fourth, or fifth year of undergraduate study at a college, university, or professional school of accounting. Applicants must have completed at least 60 semester hours with a declared major in accounting or finance and a GPA of 3.0 or higher. Along with their application, they must submit an essay of 150 to 250 words on their career goals and objectives, the impact they want to have on the accounting world, community involvement, and leadership examples. Selection is based on leadership, character, communication skills, scholastic average, and financial need. Membership in the American Society of Women Accountants (ASWA) is not required. Applications must be submitted to a local ASWA chapter.

Financial data: A stipend is awarded (amount not specified).

Duration: 1 year; recipients may reapply.

Number awarded: Varies each year.

Deadline: Local chapters must submit their candidates to the national office by March of each year.

2524 $$ ATLANTA CHAPTER RIMS SCHOLARSHIP

Spencer Educational Foundation, Inc.
c/o Risk Insurance and Management Society
1065 Avenue of the Americas, 13th Floor
New York, NY 10018
Phone: (212) 286–9292;
Email: asabatino@spencered.org
Web: www.spencered.org

Summary: To provide financial assistance to upper–division students from Georgia who are preparing for a career in risk management.

Eligibility: Open to residents of Georgia who are enrolled as full–time students entering their junior or senior year at a college or university in any state with a major or minor in a risk management discipline. Applicants must have a career objective in risk management and relevant work experience. They must have a GPA of 3.0 or higher. Along with their application, they must submit a 500–word essay on their chosen career path and goals. Selection is based on merit.

Financial data: The stipend is $5,000.

Duration: 1 year.

Number awarded: 2 each year.

Deadline: January of each year.

2525 ATLANTA CHAPTER UNDERGRADUATE/GRADUATE SCHOLARSHIPS

American Society of Women Accountants–Atlanta Chapter
Attn: Teresa Edelman
P.O. Box 11422
Birmingham, AL 35202
Email: TEdelman@BrooksMcGinnis.com
Web: www.aswaatlanta.org/scholarships

Summary: To provide financial assistance to residents of any state working on an undergraduate or graduate degree in accounting or finance at a college or university in Georgia.

Eligibility: Open to women and men from any state who are working on a bachelor's or master's degree in accounting or finance at a college or university in Georgia. Applicants must have completed at least 60 semester hours and have a GPA of 3.0 or higher. They are not required to be members of the American Society of Women Accountants (ASWA). Along with their application, they must submit an essay of 150 to 250 words on their career goals and objectives, the impact they want to have on the accounting world, community involvement, and leadership examples. Selection is based on that essay, leadership, character, communication skills, academic average, and financial need.

Financial data: A stipend is awarded (amount not specified).

Duration: 1 year.

Number awarded: 1 or more each year.

Deadline: February of each year.

2526 $$ ATLAS SHRUGGED ESSAY CONTEST

Ayn Rand Institute
Attn: Essay Contests
2121 Alton Parkway, Suite 250
P.O. Box 57044
Irvine, CA 92619–7044
Phone: (949) 222–6550, ext. 247; Fax: (949) 222–6558;
Email: essays@aynrand.org
Web: essaycontest.aynrandnovels.com/AtlasShrugged.aspx?theme=blue

Summary: To recognize and reward outstanding essays written by high school seniors, undergraduates, and graduate students on Ayn Rand's novel, *Atlas Shrugged.*

Eligibility: Open to high school seniors and part– or full–time undergraduate or graduate students. Applicants must submit an essay on questions selected each year from Ayn Rand's novel, *Atlas Shrugged.* The essay must be between 800 and 1,600 words. Selection is based on style and content. Judges look for writing that is clear, articulate, and logically organized. To win, an essay must demonstrate an outstanding grasp of the philosophic meaning of the novel.

Financial data: First prize is $10,000; second prizes are $2,000; third prizes are $1,000, finalist prizes are $100, and semifinalist prizes are $50.

Duration: The competition is held annually.

Number awarded: 84 each year: 1 first prize, 3 second prizes, 5 third prizes, 25 finalist prizes, and 50 semifinalist prizes.

Deadline: September of each year.

2527 AUTOMOTIVE AFTERMARKET ASSOCIATION SOUTHEAST EDUCATIONAL FOUNDATION SCHOLARSHIPS

Summary: To provide financial assistance to residents of designated southeastern states interested in attending college or technical school in any state to prepare for a career in the automotive aftermarket industry.

See Listing #1657.

2528 AUTOMOTIVE SCHOLARSHIPS

Summary: To provide financial assistance to high school seniors in Iowa who are interested in attending college to prepare for a career in the automobile industry.

See Listing #1658.

2529 $ AVIATION AND PROFESSIONAL DEVELOPMENT SCHOLARSHIPS

Summary: To provide financial assistance to undergraduates who are preparing for a career in the aviation industry and interested in participating in activities of the Airport Minority Advisory Council (AMAC).

See Listing #1659.

2530 $ AVIATION COUNCIL OF PENNSYLVANIA SCHOLARSHIP

Aviation Council of Pennsylvania
Attn: Scholarship Committee
3111 Arcadia Avenue
Allentown, PA 18103–6903
Phone: (610) 797–6911; Fax: (610) 797–8238;
Email: info@acpfly.com
Web: www.acpfly.com/scholarship_education.htm

Summary: To provide financial assistance for college to students from Pennsylvania preparing for a career in aviation or aviation management.

Eligibility: Open to residents of Pennsylvania who are interested in preparing for a career in aviation technology, aviation management, or the professional pilot field. Applicants for the aviation management scholarship may attend college in any state. Applicants for the aviation technology and professional pilot scholarships must attend school in Pennsylvania. They may be currently enrolled in high school, a 2– or 4–year college program, or an aviation technology program. Financial need is considered in the selection process.

Financial data: Stipends range from $500 to $2,000.

Duration: 1 year.

Number awarded: 4 each year: 1 for aviation technology, 1 for aviation management, and 2 for professional pilots.

Deadline: October of each year.

2531 BACHELOR'S DEGREE SCHOLARSHIP IN BUSINESS

DegreeDirectory.org
100 View Street, Suite 202
Mountain View, CA 94041
Phone: (650) 488–5017;
Email: moreinformation@degreedirectory.org
Web: degreedirectory.org/pages/business_scholarship.html

Summary: To provide financial assistance to undergraduates working on a bachelor's degree in a business–related field.

Eligibility: Open to students working full time on a bachelor's degree in accounting, business administration, entrepreneurship, finance, human resource management, information systems management, or marketing. Applicants must submit an essay on how their degree program is preparing them to achieve their dreams. Selection is based on academic history, extracurricular activities, and employment history; financial need is not considered.

Financial data: The stipend is $1,000.

Duration: 1 year; recipients may reapply for 1 additional year.

Number awarded: At least 1 each year.

Deadline: March of each year.

2532 BALTIMORE CHAPTER SCHOLARSHIPS

American Society for Industrial Security–Baltimore Chapter
c/o A.J. Wells, Education Chair
AlliedBarton Security Services
7939 Honeygo Boulevard
Nottingham, MD 21236
Phone: (410) 931–5061; Fax: (410) 931–3370;
Email: aj.wells@alliedbarton.com
Web: www.baltimoreasis.com

Summary: To provide financial assistance to undergraduate and graduate students working on a degree in a security–related field at a college in Maryland.

Eligibility: Open to students enrolled full or part time in an undergraduate or graduate degree program in security, law enforcement, or emergency management at a college or university in Maryland. Applicants must be members of the American Society for Industrial Security (ASIS) or referred by a member. They must have a GPA of 3.0 or higher. Along with their application, they must submit 250–word essays on 1) the prime benefit they want to achieve through completion of their degree; 2) how they feel their degree will prepare them for success, both in their intended major and in general; 3) how they will be financing their college education and how a scholarship will impact their plans; and 4) any other information they want the sponsor to know about themselves.

Financial data: Full scholarships are $1,000, partial scholarships are $500, and book scholarships are $250.

Duration: 1 year.

Number awarded: Varies each year.

Deadline: Deadline not specified.

2533 BATYA LEWTON AWARD OF INSPIRATION

David and Dovetta Wilson Scholarship Fund, Inc.
115–67 237th Street
Elmont, NY 11003–3926
Phone: (516) 285–4573;
Email: DDWSF4@aol.com
Web: www.wilsonfund.org/Batya_Lewton.html

Summary: To provide financial assistance to high school seniors who are interested in studying education in college.

Eligibility: Open to graduating high school seniors who plan to attend an accredited college or university and major in education. Applicants must be U.S. citizens or permanent residents and have a GPA of 3.0 or higher. Along with their application, they must submit 3 letters of recommendation, high school transcripts, and an essay (up to 250 words) on "How My College Education Will Help Me Make a Positive Impact on My Community." Selection is based on community involvement, desire to prepare for a career in the field of education, and financial need.

Financial data: The stipend is $1,000.

Duration: 1 year; nonrenewable.

Number awarded: 1 each year.

Deadline: March of each year.

2534 BENJAMIN POMEROY MEMORIAL SCHOLARSHIPS

National Defense Transportation Association–San Francisco Bay Area Chapter
Attn: Scholarship Committee
600 Rock Oak Road
Walnut Creek, CA 94598
Email: c_madison@msn.com
Web: ndta–sf.com/schlrgrnt_info

Summary: To provide financial assistance to residents of California who are majoring in a field related to transportation at a school in any state.

Eligibility: Open to residents of California who are enrolled or planning to enroll in an undergraduate or vocational program at an accredited institution in any state with a major in transportation, logistics, business, marketing, engineering, planning, or environment. Applicants must be preparing for a career related to transportation. Along with their application, they must submit a certified copy of their high school, vocational school, or college transcript; 3 letters of recommendation; and a 1–page essay detailing their career goals and ambitions (with an emphasis on transportation and related areas). U.S. citizenship is required. Selection is based on academic ability, professional interest, potential, and character.

Financial data: The stipend is $1,000.

Duration: 1 year.

Number awarded: 1 or more each year.

Deadline: May of each year.

2535 BERNICE PICKENS PARSONS FUND SCHOLARSHIPS

Summary: To provide financial assistance to residents of West Virginia who are interested in studying designated fields at a school in any state.

See Listing #1668.

2536 BETTER BUSINESS BUREAU OF ALASKA, OREGON, AND WESTERN WASHINGTON STUDENTS OF INTEGRITY SCHOLARSHIPS

Better Business Bureau of Alaska, Oregon, and Western Washington
Attn: Marketing Coordinator
1000 Station Drive, Suite 222
P.O. Box 1000
DuPont, WA 98327
Phone: (253) 830–2924; Fax: (253) 830–2925;
Email: BBBFoundation@thebbb.org
Web: alaskaoregonwesternwashington.bbb.org/scholarship

Summary: To provide financial assistance to high school seniors in Alaska, Oregon, and western Washington who submit outstanding essays on ethics in business and plan to attend college in any state.

Eligibility: Open to seniors graduating from high schools in Alaska, Oregon, and western Washington and planning to enroll at a college or university in any state. Applicants must have a GPA of 3.5 or higher. Along with their application, they must submit an essay, up to 1,000 words in length, on sustainable business practices and their relationship to ethics. Essays are judged on the basis of relevance to the theme, spelling and grammar, readability and clarity, organization, overall portrayal of ideas, and creativity in presentation. Financial need is not considered.

Financial data: The stipend is $1,000.

Duration: 1 year.

Number awarded: 3 each year: 1 in each of the participating states.

Deadline: December of each year.

2537 BETTY RENDEL SCHOLARSHIPS

National Federation of Republican Women
Attn: Scholarships and Internships
124 North Alfred Street
Alexandria, VA 22314–3011
Phone: (703) 548–9688; Fax: (703) 548–9836;
Email: mail@nfrw.org
Web: www.nfrw.org/programs/scholarships.htm

Summary: To provide financial assistance to undergraduate Republican women who are majoring in political science, government, or economics.

Eligibility: Open to women who have completed at least 2 years of college. Applicants must be majoring in political science, government, or economics. Along with their application, they must submit 3 letters of recommendation, an official transcript, a 1–page essay on why they should be considered for the scholarship, and a 1–page essay on career goals. Applications must be submitted to the Republican federation president in the applicant's state. Each president chooses 1 application from her state to submit for scholarship consideration. Financial need is not a factor in the selection process. U.S. citizenship is required.

Financial data: The stipend is $1,000.

Duration: 1 year; nonrenewable.
Number awarded: 3 each year.
Deadline: Applications must be submitted to the state federation president by May of each year.

2538 BILL KANE UNDERGRADUATE SCHOLARSHIP

Summary: To provide financial assistance to undergraduates who are currently enrolled in a health education program.
See Listing #1674.

2539 $ BILL OF RIGHTS ESSAY CONTEST

National Foundation for Women Legislators, Inc.
910 16th Street, N.W., Suite 100
Washington, DC 20006
Phone: (202) 293–3040; Fax: (202) 293–5430;
Email: events@womenlegislators.org
Web: www.womenlegistors.org/events/scholarship–program.php
Summary: To recognize and reward, with college scholarships, the best essays written by female high school juniors or seniors on a topic related to the Bill of Rights.
Eligibility: Open to female high school juniors or seniors. Applicants are invited to write an essay of 400 to 600 words on a topic (changes annually) related to the Bill of Rights; recently, the topic related to the impact of the first amendment on women leaders and social media. In addition to the essay, candidates must submit 2 personal reference letters.
Financial data: Each winner receives a $3,000 unrestricted scholarship to use toward college tuition at any U.S. college or university and an all–expense paid trip to the foundation's annual conference.
Duration: The competition is held annually.
Number awarded: Varies each year; recently, 9 of these scholarships were awarded.
Deadline: June of each year.

2540 BILLINGS CHAPTER UNDERGRADUATE SCHOLARSHIPS

American Society of Women Accountants–Billings Chapter
Attn: Meghan Ekholt, Scholarship Chair
P.O. Box 20593
Billings, MT 59104–0593
Email: mrekholt@gmail.com
Web: www.billingsaswa.org/Scholarships.html
Summary: To provide financial assistance to women working on an bachelor's degree in accounting at a college or university in Montana.
Eligibility: Open to women working on a bachelor's degree in accounting or finance at a college or university in Montana. Applicants must have completed at least 60 semester hours and have a GPA of 3.0 or higher. Along with their application, they must submit an essay of 150 to 250 words on their career goals and objectives, the impact they want to have on the accounting world, their community involvement, and leadership examples. Selection is based on leadership, character, scholastic average, communication skills, and financial need.
Financial data: The stipend is $1,500.
Duration: 1 year.
Number awarded: 2 each year.
Deadline: March of each year.

2541 $ BILLY DON SIMS SCHOLARSHIP

Association for Education and Rehabilitation of the Blind and Visually Impaired–Alabama Chapter
c/o Julie Brock, Scholarship Committee Chair
P.O. Box 19888
Birmingham, AL 35219–0888
Phone: (205) 290–4451;
Email: juliabrock11@aol.com
Web: www.alabamaaer.com/Scholarship.html
Summary: To provide financial assistance to residents of Alabama who are working on a degree in a field related to education and rehabilitation of the blind and visually impaired at a school in any state.
Eligibility: Open to residents of Alabama who are currently enrolled at a college or university in any state. Applicants must be preparing for a career in 1 of the following fields: rehabilitation teaching, orientation and mobility; teaching the visually impaired; or rehabilitation counseling. They must submit a brief statement of their purpose for applying for this scholarship.
Financial data: The stipend is $2,000.
Duration: 1 year.
Number awarded: 1 each year.
Deadline: June of each year.

2542 BIRMINGHAM CHAPTER SCHOLARSHIPS

American Society of Women Accountants–Birmingham Chapter
P.O. Box 11422
Birmingham, AL 35202
Email: general@birminghamaswa.org
Web: www.birminghamaswa.org/scholarships.html
Summary: To provide financial assistance to residents of any state working on an undergraduate or graduate degree in accounting or finance at a college or university in Alabama.
Eligibility: Open to women and men from any state who are working full time on a bachelor's or master's degree in accounting or finance at Alabama colleges and universities. Applicants must have completed at least 60 semester hours and have a GPA of 3.0 or higher. They are not required to be members of the American Society of Women Accountants (ASWA). Along with their application, they must submit an essay of 150 to 250 words on their career goals and objectives, the impact they want to have on the accounting world, community involvement, and leadership examples. Selection is based on that essay, letters of reference, college transcripts, extracurricular activities, and financial need.
Financial data: The stipend ranges from $500 to $1,500.
Duration: 1 year.
Number awarded: 1 or more each year.
Deadline: March of each year.

2543 $$ BLACKS AT MICROSOFT SCHOLARSHIPS

Summary: To provide financial assistance to African American high school seniors who plan to major in engineering, computer science, or a business–related field in college.
See Listing #1680.

2544 $$ BMO CAPITAL MARKETS LIME CONNECT EQUITY THROUGH EDUCATION SCHOLARSHIPS FOR STUDENTS WITH DISABILITIES

Lime Connect, Inc.
590 Madison Avenue, 21st Floor
New York, NY 10022
Phone: (212) 521–4469; Fax: (212) 521–4099;
Email: info@limeconnect.com
Web: www.limeconnect.com/opportunities
Summary: To provide financial assistance to students with disabilities working on a bachelor's or graduate degree in a business–related field at a college or university in Canada or the United States.
Eligibility: Open to sophomores and graduate students at 4–year colleges and universities in the United States or Canada who have a disability. International students with disabilities enrolled at universities in the United States or Canada are also eligible. Applicants must be working full time on a degree in a business–related field. Along with their application, they must submit an essay on their career goals and why they believe they should be selected to receive this scholarship. Financial need is not considered in the selection process.
Financial data: The stipend is $10,000 for students at U.S. universities or $C5,000 for students at Canadian universities.
Duration: 1 year.
Number awarded: Varies each year.
Deadline: May of each year.

2545 $ BOATING INDUSTRY SCHOLARSHIPS

Michigan Boating Industries Association
Attn: Recreational Boating Industries Educational Foundation
32398 Five Mile Road
Livonia, MI 48154–6109
Phone: (734) 261–0123, ext. 201; Fax: (734) 261–0880;
Email: dneedham@mbia.org
Web: www.mbia.org/content.aspx?page=programs_rbief
Summary: To provide financial assistance to students, especially those in Michigan, who are interested in preparing for a career in the boating industry.

Eligibility: Open to high school seniors and students currently enrolled at an accredited college or university; preference is given to students at colleges and universities in Michigan. Applicants may be interested in majoring in any field, but priority is given to those who are preparing for a career in the Michigan boating industry and are working on a degree in fields of study that are applicable to industry needs (e.g., marketing, advertising, retail sales, management, product distribution, product repair, marina management, facility design, naval architecture, construction). Along with their application, they must submit a copy of their high school and/or college transcript, 2 letters of reference, and an essay (200 to 300 words) on their boating industry career goals and why they feel they are deserving of a boating industry scholarship. Financial need is considered in the selection process.
Financial data: Stipends range from $500 to $2,500.
Duration: 1 year; recipients may reapply.
Number awarded: 10 to 15 each year.
Deadline: March of each year.

2546 BOB HERSH MEMORIAL SCHOLARSHIP

Mary M. Gooley Hemophilia Center
Attn: Scholarship Selection Committee
1415 Portland Avenue, Suite 500
Rochester, NY 14621
Phone: (585) 922–5700; Fax: (585) 922–5775;
Email: Kristina.Ritchie@rochestergeneral.org
Web: www.hemocenter.org/site/PageServer?pagename=programs_scholarships
Summary: To provide financial assistance to people with a bleeding disorder and their families who plan to attend college to prepare for a career in a teaching or helping profession.
Eligibility: Open to people who are affected directly or indirectly by hemophilia, von Willebrand Disease, hereditary bleeding disorder, or hemochromatosis. Applicants must be enrolled or planning to enroll at an accredited 2– or 4–year college or university, vocational/technical school, or certified training program. They must be preparing for a career in a teaching or helping profession. Along with their application, they must submit 1) a 1,000–word essay on their goals and aspirations, their biggest challenge and how they met it, and anything else they want the selection committee to know about them; and 2) a 250–word essay on any unusual family or personal circumstances that have affected their achievement in school, work, or participation in school and community activities, including how their bleeding disorder or that of their family member has affected their life. Selection is based on the essays, academic performance, participation in school and community activities, work or volunteer experience, personal or family circumstances, recommendations, and financial need.
Financial data: The stipend is $1,000.
Duration: 1 year.
Number awarded: 1 each year.
Deadline: March of each year.

2547 BOSTON AFFILIATE SCHOLARSHIP

American Woman's Society of Certified Public Accountants–Boston Affiliate
c/o Andrea Costantino
Oxford Bioscience Partners
222 Berkeley Street, Suite 1650
Boston, MA 02116
Phone: (617) 357–7474;
Email: acostantino@oxbio.com
Web: www.awscpa.org/affiliate_scholarships/boston.html
Summary: To provide financial assistance to women from any state who are working on an undergraduate or graduate degree in accounting at a college or university in New England.
Eligibility: Open to women from any state who are attending a college in New England and majoring in accounting. Applicants must have completed at least 12 semester hours of accounting or tax courses and have a cumulative GPA of 3.0 or higher. They must be planning to graduate between May of next year and May of the following year or, for the 15–month graduate program, before September of the current year. Along with their application, they must submit a brief essay on why they feel they would be a good choice for this award. Selection is based on that essay, academic achievement, work experience, extracurricular activities, scholastic honors, career plans, and financial need.
Financial data: The stipend is $1,000.
Duration: 1 year.
Number awarded: 2 each year.
Deadline: September of each year.

2548 $$ BOSTON SWEA SCHOLARSHIP

Summary: To provide financial assistance to women who are working on an undergraduate or graduate degree in Swedish studies at a university in New England and interested in visiting Sweden for a study, work/study, or research program.
See Listing #1152.

2549 $ BRENDA RENEE HORN MEMORIAL SCHOLARSHIP

Funeral Service Foundation
Attn: Executive Director
13625 Bishop's Drive
Brookfield, WI 53005
Phone: (262) 789–1880; (877) 402–5900; Fax: (262) 789–6977;
Email: info@funeralservicefoundation.org
Web: www.funeralservicefoundation.org/scholarships/index.htm
Summary: To provide financial assistance to mortuary science students who submit outstanding essays on a topic related to the profession.
Eligibility: Open to students who are currently enrolled in an accredited program of mortuary science. Applicants must submit an essay and video on a topic that changes annually but requires them to express their personal views on current issues facing the funeral industry. Selection is based primarily on that essay and academic achievement; financial need is not considered.
Financial data: The stipend is $3,000.
Duration: 1 year.
Number awarded: 1 each year.
Deadline: March of each year.

2550 $$ BRIAN CUMMINS MEMORIAL SCHOLARSHIP

National Federation of the Blind of Connecticut
477 Connecticut Boulevard, Suite 217
East Hartford, CT 06108
Phone: (860) 289–1971;
Email: info@nfbct.org
Web: www.nfbct.org/html/bcmsch.htm
Summary: To provide financial assistance to residents of Connecticut who plan to become a teacher of the blind and visually impaired.
Eligibility: Open to graduate and undergraduate students enrolled full time at colleges and universities in Connecticut who are preparing for a career in the state as a certified teacher of the blind and visually impaired. Along with their application, they must submit a letter on their career goals and how the scholarship might help them achieve those. Applicants do not need to be blind or members of the National Federation of the Blind of Connecticut. Selection is based on academic quality, service to the community, and financial need.
Financial data: The stipend is $5,000.
Duration: 1 year.
Number awarded: 1 each year.
Deadline: September of each year.

2551 $ BRIGHT FUTURES AWARDS

Bright Horizons Family Solutions
Attn: Human Resources
200 Talcott Avenue, South
Watertown, MA 02472
Phone: (617) 673–8000;
Email: brightfutures@brighthorizons.com
Web: www.brighthorizons.com/careers/brightfutures.aspx
Summary: To provide financial assistance to teachers of young children who are interested in completing an undergraduate or graduate degree in that field.
Eligibility: Open to people who 1) have at least 9 months of experience working with children under 8 years of age and are interested in working full time on an associate or bachelor's degree in the field of early childhood education; or 2) have at least 1 year of teaching or directing experience at a program accredited by the National Association for the Education of Young Children (NAEYC) and are interested in working on a master's degree in early childhood education. Applicants must submit 1) a personal history that includes their education, honors and awards, employment, career goals, and extracurricular activities and/or special interests; 2) a personal essay of 500 to 800 words that focuses on why they are passionate and committed to their education; and 3) a resume of work experience. Financial need is not considered in the selection process.
Financial data: Stipends are $1,500 for students working on an associate degree and $2,500 for students working on a bachelor's or master's degree.

Duration: 1 year.
Number awarded: 3 each year.
Deadline: May of each year.

2552 BROOME AND ALLEN SCHOLARSHIP FUND

Summary: To provide financial assistance to Sephardic Jews for undergraduate or graduate study in America.
See Listing #1156.

2553 $$ BUICK ACHIEVERS SCHOLARSHIP PROGRAM

Summary: To provide financial assistance to students entering college for the first time and planning to major in specified fields related to design, engineering, or business.
See Listing #1157.

2554 $ CAC EDUCATIONAL SCHOLARSHIPS

California Association of Collectors, Inc.
Attn: CAC Educational Scholarship Foundation
1455 Response Road, Suite 240
Sacramento, CA 95815
Phone: (916) 929–2125; Fax: (916) 929–7682;
Email: scholarship@calcollectors.net
Web: www.cacesf.org

Summary: To recognize and reward, with scholarships for college study in any area, high school seniors in California who submit outstanding essays on credit.
Eligibility: Open to seniors graduating from high schools in California who plan to attend an accredited public or private college, university, or trade school in any state. Applicants must submit an essay, from 700 to 1,000 words in length, on a topic that changes annually but relates to the use of credit; recently, students were invited to write on "Importance of Establishing and Maintaining Good Credit During Your College Years."
Financial data: Awards, in the form of college scholarships, are $2,500 for first place, $2,000 for second, and $1,500 for third.
Duration: The competition is held annually.
Number awarded: 3 each year.
Deadline: January of each year.

2555 CAEOP HIGH SCHOOL SENIOR SCHOLARSHIPS

California Association of Educational Office Professionals
c/o Linda Rush, Scholarship/Awards Chair
Hemet Unified School District
1791 West Acacia Avenue
Hemet, CA 92545
Phone: (951) 765–5100, ext. 3301; Fax: (951) 765–5119;
Email: lrush@hemetusd.k12.ca.us
Web: www.caeop.org/index.php?option=com_content&view=article&id=121

Summary: To provide financial assistance to high school seniors and recent graduates in California who are interested in attending college in any state to prepare for a career in business administration or education.
Eligibility: Open to seniors graduating from high schools in California and recent graduates already enrolled in college. Applicants must be majoring or planning to major in education or business administration. They must have an overall GPA of 2.0 or higher in high school. Along with their application, they must submit a 1–page essay on "Why I am Choosing a Career in Business or Education." Selection is based on the essay (20%), financial need (30%), academic record (30%), school and extracurricular activities (10%), and recommendations (10%).
Financial data: The stipend is $1,000.
Duration: 1 year.
Number awarded: 1 or more each year.
Deadline: January of each year.

2556 CAEYC TUITION AWARD

Colorado Association for the Education of Young Children
Attn: Tuition Award Committee
P.O. Box 631326
Highlands Ranch, CO 80163–1326
Phone: (303) 791–2772; (888) 892–4453 (within CO); Fax: (303) 791–7597;
Email: caeyc@ColoradoAEYC.org
Web: coloradoaeyc.org/awards/caeyc–award

Summary: To provide financial assistance to upper–division college students in Colorado who are majoring in early childhood education.
Eligibility: Open to Colorado residents who are U.S. citizens, have been accepted for full–time study as a junior or senior at a Colorado college or university, are majoring in early childhood education, and have a GPA of 3.0 or higher. Along with their application, they must submit 5 essays: a resume of their work experiences with children, their academic goal and when they expect to attain it, why they are going into early childhood education, what they see themselves doing in 5 years, and their philosophy in working with young children. Selection is based on academic ability, awards and honors, strength of character, leadership potential, emotional maturity, and special interest and commitment to the early childhood education field; financial need is not considered.
Financial data: A stipend is awarded (amount not specified).
Duration: 1 year; renewable upon reapplication.
Number awarded: Varies each year, depending upon the number of qualified applicants.
Deadline: March of each year.

2557 CALIFORNIA ASSOCIATION OF FAMILY AND CONSUMER SCIENCES–SAN DIEGO CHAPTER SCHOLARSHIPS

San Diego Foundation
Attn: Community Scholarship Program
2508 Historic Decatur Road, Suite 200
San Diego, CA 92106
Phone: (619) 235–2300; Fax: (619) 239–1710;
Email: scholarships@sdfoundation.org
Web: www.sdfoundation.org/GrantsScholarships/Scholarships.aspx

Summary: To provide financial assistance to residents of California who are interested in working on an undergraduate or graduate degree in a field related to family and consumer sciences at a school in any state.
Eligibility: Open to high school seniors, current college students, and current graduate students who are residents of California and attending or planning to attend an accredited 2– or 4–year college, university, or licensed trade–vocational school in the United States. Applicants must be working on or planning to work on a degree in food sciences; dietetics; nutrition; food services; hospitality; human, child, and family development; apparel, fashion, and textile services; housing and interiors; consumer economics; management and resources; or family and consumer science education. They must have a GPA of 2.5 or higher. Undergraduates must be enrolled full time; graduate students may be enrolled full or part time.
Financial data: A stipend is awarded (amount not specified). Funds may be used for tuition, books, and fees.
Duration: 1 year; recipients may reapply. This program includes the Ellen Ferguson Snyder Scholarships and the Henry R. Hague, J.D. Scholarship.
Number awarded: Varies each year; recently, 9 of these scholarships were awarded.
Deadline: February of each year.

2558 $ CALIFORNIA ASSOCIATION OF REALTORS SCHOLARSHIPS

California Association of Realtors
Attn: Scholarship Foundation
525 South Virgil Avenue
Los Angeles, CA 90020–1403
Phone: (213) 739–8200; Fax: (213) 480–7724;
Email: scholarship@car.org
Web: www.car.org/aboutus/carscholarships

Summary: To provide financial assistance to undergraduate and graduate students in California who are interested in a career related to real estate.
Eligibility: Open to undergraduate and graduate students enrolled at California colleges and universities who are interested in studying real estate brokerage, real estate finance, real estate management, real estate development, real estate appraisal, real estate planning, real estate law, or other related areas of study. Applicants must have completed at least 12 units prior to applying, be currently enrolled for at least 6 units per semester or term, have a cumulative GPA of 2.6 or higher, and have been legal residents of California for at least 1 year. Real estate licensees who wish to pursue advanced real estate designations, degrees, or credentials are also eligible.
Financial data: The stipend is $4,000 for students at 4–year colleges or universities or $2,000 for students at 2–year colleges.
Duration: 1 year; may be renewed 1 additional year.

Number awarded: Varies each year; recently, 9 of these scholarships were awarded.
Deadline: March or September of each year.

2559 $ CALIFORNIA CHILD DEVELOPMENT GRANT PROGRAM

California Student Aid Commission
Attn: Child Development Grant Program
10811 International Drive, Suite 100
P.O. Box 419029
Rancho Cordova, CA 95741–9029
Phone: (916) 526–8276; (888) CA–GRANT; Fax: (916) 464–8240;
Email: specialized@csac.ca.gov
Web: www.csac.ca.gov/doc.asp?id=110

Summary: To provide funding to college students in California who are preparing for a career in child development.
Eligibility: Open to college students in California who plan to teach or supervise at a licensed children's center. Applicants must be California residents working on a child development permit at the teacher, master teacher, site supervisor, or program director level; be a U.S. citizen or eligible noncitizen; be able to demonstrate financial need; and be nominated by an eligible postsecondary institution. Selection is based on demonstrated financial need and academic achievement.
Financial data: The annual stipend is $1,000 for students enrolled in 2–year colleges or $2,000 for students enrolled in 4–year colleges. This is a scholarship/loan program; recipients must teach full time in a licensed California children's center for 1 year for each year of grant assistance.
Duration: 1 year; may be renewed if the recipient maintains at least half time enrollment and satisfactory academic progress. The maximum total benefit is $6,000.
Number awarded: Up to 100 each year.
Deadline: June of each year.

2560 CALIFORNIA/NEVADA/ARIZONA AUTOMOTIVE WHOLESALERS' ASSOCIATION SCHOLARSHIPS

California/Nevada/Arizona Automotive Wholesalers' Association
Attn: Automotive Education Memorial Fund
11460 Sun Center Drive
Rancho Cordova, CA 95670
Phone: (916) 635–9774; (800) 332–2292; Fax: (916) 635–9995;
Email: programs@cawa.org
Web: www.cawa.org/train.htm

Summary: To provide financial assistance to students from California, Nevada, and Arizona who are interested in preparing for a career in the automotive aftermarket.
Eligibility: Open to high school seniors and college undergraduates enrolled full time in a college or vocational program and working on a degree or accreditation in the automotive aftermarket. Applicants must be residents of and/or attending school in California, Nevada, or Arizona. They must be sponsored by a member of the California/Nevada/Arizona Automotive Wholesalers' Association (CAWA). Along with their application, they must submit a 250–word essay on their career goals, how this scholarship will help them, and why they are considering a career in the automotive aftermarket. Financial need is not considered in the selection process.
Financial data: A stipend is awarded (amount not specified).
Duration: 1 year.
Number awarded: Varies each year; recently, 25 of these scholarships were awarded.
Deadline: March of each year.

2561 $ CALIFORNIA RESTAURANT ASSOCIATION EDUCATIONAL FOUNDATION SCHOLARSHIPS

Summary: To provide financial assistance to California residents enrolled or planning to enroll in a postsecondary culinary program at a school in any state.
See Listing #1160.

2562 $ CAMERON E. WILLIAMS MEMORIAL SCHOLARSHIP

Griffith Insurance Education Foundation
623 High Street
Worthington, OH 43085
Phone: (614) 880–9870; Fax: (614) 880–9872;
Email: info@griffithfoundation.org
Web: www.griffithfoundation.org/higher–ed/scholarships

Summary: To provide financial assistance to students working on an undergraduate degree in a field related to insurance.
Eligibility: Open to U.S. citizens enrolled full time at a college or university in the United States with a GPA of 3.0 or higher. Applicants must be at least sophomores and enrolled in an insurance, risk management, actuarial science, business, computer science, finance, or other insurance–related program. They must be planning to enter an insurance–related field after graduation. Preference is given to 1) children, stepchildren, or legally adopted children of The Motorists Insurance Group employees and agents; and 2) students recommended by a Motorists employee or retiree. Selection is based on academic achievement, extracurricular activities and honors, work experience, 3 letters of recommendation, and financial need.
Financial data: The stipend is $2,000.
Duration: 1 year.
Number awarded: 1 each year.
Deadline: March of each year.

2563 CANE CERTIFICATION SCHOLARSHIP

Classical Association of New England
c/o Katy Ganino Reddick, Chair, Committee on Scholarships
Strong Middle School
191 Main Street
Durham, CT 06422–2108
Phone: (860) 349–7222; Fax: (860) 349–7225;
Email: kreddick@rsd13.org
Web: www.caneweb.org

Summary: To provide financial assistance to upper–division and graduate students in New England who are working on certification as a teacher of Latin or Greek.
Eligibility: Open to junior and senior undergraduates at colleges and universities in New England and to holders of master's degrees. Applicants must be preparing for secondary school certification as a teacher of Latin or Greek or both in a New England state. Full–time, part–time, and summer programs qualify. Along with their application, they must submit 2 letters of recommendation from college classicists, a letter attesting to their ability to communicate and work with young people and inspire them to high levels of achievement, a 1,000–word personal statement explaining why they are preparing for a career as a pre–collegiate classicist, college transcripts, and a description of their program and the expenses involved.
Financial data: The stipend is $1,500. Funds are intended to cover tuition and fees.
Duration: 1 year or summer session.
Number awarded: 1 each year.
Deadline: January of each year.

2564 $ CARGILL SCHOLARSHIP PROGRAM FOR TRIBAL COLLEGES

Summary: To provide financial assistance to Native American college students from any state who are working on a bachelor's degree in specified fields at Tribal Colleges and Universities (TCUs) in selected states.
See Listing #1701.

2565 CAROL MURPHY MEMORIAL ENDOWMENT SCHOLARSHIP

Epsilon Sigma Alpha International
Attn: ESA Foundation
363 West Drake Road
Fort Collins, CO 80526
Phone: (970) 223–2824; Fax: (970) 223–4456;
Email: esainfo@epsilonsigmaalpha.org
Web: www.epsilonsigmaalpha.org/scholarships–and–grants

Summary: To provide financial assistance to mature residents of designated states who plan to major in business or education at a college in any state.
Eligibility: Open to residents of Indiana, Missouri, or Texas who are at least 25 years of age. Applicants must be 1) enrolled in college with a GPA of 3.0 or higher; 2) enrolled at a technical school or returning to school after an absence for retraining of job skills or obtaining a degree; or 3) engaged in online study through an accredited college, university, or vocational school. They may be attending or planning to attend an accredited school anywhere in the United States and major in education or business. Selection is based on character

(10%), leadership (10%), service (5%), financial need (50%), and scholastic ability (25%).
Financial data: The stipend is $1,000.
Duration: 1 year; may be renewed.
Number awarded: 1 each year.
Deadline: January of each year.

2566 CARROLL A. LAMBTON MEMORIAL FUND

Pittsburgh Foundation
Attn: Scholarship Coordinator
Five PPG Place, Suite 250
Pittsburgh, PA 15222–5414
Phone: (412) 394–2649; Fax: (412) 391–7259;
Email: turnerd@pghfdn.org
Web: www.pittsburghfoundation.org/node/1554
Summary: To provide financial assistance to residents of designated states who have a connection to the U.S. Department of Energy (DOE) or the National Contract Management Association (NCMA) and are interested in working on an undergraduate or graduate degree in a field related to contracting at a college in any state.
Eligibility: Open to 1) DOE employees and their children; and 2) NCMA members and their children. Applicants must be residents of Ohio, Pennsylvania, or West Virginia and enrolled or planning to enroll at a 2– or 4–year college or university in any state. They must be interested in working on an undergraduate or graduate degree in contracting, procurement, or a related field. Along with their application, they must submit a 1–page essay about their purpose in pursuing advanced education, their career objectives, their future goals, and why they feel they should be selected to receive this scholarship.
Financial data: A stipend is awarded (amount not specified).
Duration: 1 year.
Number awarded: 1 or more each year.
Deadline: April of each year.

2567 $ CAS TRUST SCHOLARSHIP PROGRAM

Casualty Actuarial Society
Attn: CAS Trust Scholarship Coordinator
4350 North Fairfax Drive, Suite 250
Arlington, VA 22203
Phone: (703) 276–3100; Fax: (703) 276–3108;
Email: moneill@casact.org
Web: www.casact.org/academic/index.cfm?fa=scholarship
Summary: To provide financial assistance to U.S. and Canadian students who are preparing for a career in the property and casualty actuarial profession.
Eligibility: Open to U.S. and Canadian citizens and permanent residents who are enrolled full time at a college or university in the United States or Canada. Incoming freshmen and first–year students are not eligible. Applicants must be preparing for a career in the property and casualty actuarial profession and pursuit of the Casualty Actuarial Society (CAS) designations. They must have demonstrated high scholastic achievement, strong interest in the casualty actuarial profession, mathematics aptitude, and communication skills. Preference is given to students who have passed an actuarial examination and who have not yet won this or another scholarship from this sponsor or the Society of Actuaries. Selection is based on individual merit.
Financial data: The stipend is $2,000.
Duration: 1 year.
Number awarded: Up to 3 each year.
Deadline: February of each year.

2568 CASUALTY ACTUARIES OF THE SOUTHEAST SCHOLARSHIP PROGRAM

Casualty Actuaries of the Southeast
c/o Zachery M. Ziegler, Vice President of College Relations
FTI Consulting
4505 Country Club Road, Suite 200
Winston–Salem, NC 27104
Phone: (336) 768–8217; Fax: (336) 768–2185;
Email: zachery.ziegler@fticonsulting.com
Web: www.casact.org/affiliates/case/index.cfm?fa=scholarmemo
Summary: To provide financial assistance to residents of any state current attending college in designated southeastern states to prepare for a career in the casualty actuarial profession.
Eligibility: Open to students currently enrolled full time at a college or university in Alabama, Arkansas, Florida, Georgia, Kentucky, Louisiana, Mississippi, North Carolina, South Carolina, Tennessee, or Virginia. Applicants must be able to demonstrate mathematical aptitude, communication skills, and interest in the actuarial profession, by having sat for and/or passed an actuarial examination, taken and excelled in actuarial science courses, or completed an actuarial internship. They must have a GPA of 3.0 or higher. Along with their application, they must submit a 1–page essay on why they are interested in becoming a casualty actuary. Financial need is not considered in the selection process.
Financial data: The stipend is $1,500.
Duration: 1 year.
Number awarded: 2 each year.
Deadline: April of each year.

2569 $ CATRALA–HAWAII SCHOLARSHIPS

CATRALA–Hawaii
Attn: Scholarship Selection Committee
707 Richards Street, Suite 525
Honolulu, HI 96813–4623
Phone: (808) 952–4287;
Email: catralahawaii@yahoo.com
Summary: To provide financial assistance to high school seniors in Hawaii who plan to study a field related to travel industry management at a college in any state.
Eligibility: Open to seniors graduating from high schools in Hawaii who plan to enroll full time at an accredited 4–year college or university in any state. Applicants must be planning to work on a degree in travel industry management or other business–related course of study. They must have a GPA of 2.5 or higher and be able to demonstrate financial need.
Financial data: The stipend is $2,000 per year.
Duration: 4 years, provided the recipient remains enrolled full time and maintains a GPA of 2.5 or higher.
Number awarded: 2 or 3 each year.
Deadline: April of each year.

2570 $$ CENTER FOR ALCOHOL POLICY ESSAY CONTEST

Center for Alcohol Policy
Attn: Essay Contest
1101 King Street, Suite 600–A
Alexandria, VA 22314
Phone: (703) 519–3090;
Email: essay@centerforalcoholpolicy.org
Web: www.centerforalcoholpolicy.org/essay–contest
Summary: To recognize and reward people who submit outstanding essay on alcohol policy.
Eligibility: Open to all persons over 18 years of age, including students, academics, practicing attorneys, policymakers, and members of the general public. Applicants must submit an essay up to 25 pages in length on a topic related to alcohol policy; recently, entrants were asked to give their answer to the question, "If a country were starting alcohol regulation from scratch, what regulatory framework would you advise it to create and why?" Selection is based on the analysis of the question, depth of the analysis, readiness of the essay for publication, quality of the writing, originality, and thoroughness of the research.
Financial data: First prize is $5,000, second $2,500, and third $1,250.
Duration: The competition is held annually.
Number awarded: 3 each year.
Deadline: December of each year.

2571 CENTRAL FLORIDA PMI CHAPTER SCHOLARSHIP

Project Management Institute
Attn: PMI Educational Foundation
14 Campus Boulevard
Newtown Square, PA 19073–3299
Phone: (610) 356–4600, ext. 7004; Fax: (610) 356–0357;
Email: pmief@pmi.org
Web: www.pmi.org/pmief/scholarship/scholarships.asp
Summary: To provide financial assistance to undergraduate and graduate students, especially those from central Florida, interested in working on a degree in a field related to project management.
Eligibility: Open to undergraduate and graduate students who are working on or planning to work on a degree in project management or a related field benefitting from project management. First priority is given to residents of central

Florida attending or planning to attend an accredited college or university in any state or residents of any state attending or planning to attend an accredited college or university in central Florida; second priority is given to residents of Florida attending or planning to attend an accredited college or university in any state or residents of any state attending or planning to attend an accredited college or university in Florida; third priority is given to residents of any state attending or planning to attend an accredited college or university in any state. Along with their application, they must submit 1) a 500–word essay on why they want to be a project manager; and 2) a 250–word essay on how a code of ethics is important to project management. Financial need is not considered in the selection process.
Financial data: The stipend is $1,000.
Duration: 1 year.
Number awarded: 1 each year.
Deadline: May of each year.

2572 $ CENTRAL IOWA PMI CHAPTER SCHOLARSHIP

Project Management Institute
Attn: PMI Educational Foundation
14 Campus Boulevard
Newtown Square, PA 19073–3299
Phone: (610) 356–4600, ext. 7004; Fax: (610) 356–0357;
Email: pmief@pmi.org
Web: www.pmi.org/pmief/scholarship/scholarships.asp
Summary: To provide financial assistance to residents of any state who are working on an undergraduate or graduate degree in project management at a school in Iowa.
Eligibility: Open to residents of any state who are attending or planning to attend a college or university in Iowa. Applicants must be interested in working on an undergraduate or graduate degree in a field related to project management. Along with their application, they must submit 1) a 500–word essay on why they want to be a project manager; and 2) a 250–word essay on how a code of ethics is important to project management. Financial need is not considered in the selection process.
Financial data: The stipend is $2,500.
Duration: 1 year.
Number awarded: 1 each year.
Deadline: May of each year.

2573 CENTRAL OHIO INSURANCE EDUCATION DAY SCHOLARSHIPS

Griffith Insurance Education Foundation
623 High Street
Worthington, OH 43085
Phone: (614) 880–9870; Fax: (614) 880–9872;
Email: info@griffithfoundation.org
Web: www.griffithfoundation.org/higher–ed/scholarships
Summary: To provide financial assistance to undergraduate students from Ohio who are preparing for a career in a field related to insurance.
Eligibility: Open to U.S. citizens from Ohio who are attending a college or university in any state. Applicants must be studying actuarial science, business, computer science, finance, risk management, or other insurance–related area and be planning to enter an insurance–related field upon graduation. They must have a GPA of 3.5 or higher. Selection is based on academic achievement, extracurricular activities and honors, work experience, 3 letters of recommendation, and financial need.
Financial data: The stipend is $1,500.
Duration: 1 year.
Number awarded: 3 each year.
Deadline: March or November of each year.

2574 $$ CFA INSTITUTE 11 SEPTEMBER MEMORIAL SCHOLARSHIP

CFA Institute
Attn: Research Foundation
560 Ray C. Hunt Drive
P.O. Box 2082
Charlottesville, VA 22902–2082
Phone: (434) 951–5499; (800) 237–8132; Fax: (434) 951–5240;
Email: rf@cfainstitute.org
Web: www.cfainstitute.org
Summary: To provide financial assistance to individuals and their families who were disabled or killed in the September 11, 2001 terrorist attacks and who wish to major in business–related fields in college.
Eligibility: Open to residents of any state or country who either 1) were permanently disabled in the attacks of September 11, 2001; or 2) are the spouses, domestic partners, or children of anyone killed or permanently disabled in the attacks. Applicants must be working full or part time on an undergraduate degree in finance, economics, accounting, or business ethics. Selection is based on demonstrated leadership and good citizenship, academic record, and financial need.
Financial data: Stipends range up to $25,000 per year, depending on the need of the recipient.
Duration: 1 year; renewable up to 4 additional years.
Number awarded: Varies each year; recently, 12 of these scholarships were awarded.
Deadline: May of each year.

2575 CHARLES MCDANIEL TEACHER SCHOLARSHIPS

Georgia Student Finance Commission
Attn: Scholarships and Grants Division
2082 East Exchange Place, Suite 200
Tucker, GA 30084–5305
Phone: (770) 724–9000; (800) 505–GSFC; Fax: (770) 724–9089;
Email: gacollege411@gsfc.org
Web: www.gacollege411.org
Summary: To provide financial assistance to Georgia residents who wish to prepare for a career as a teacher.
Eligibility: Open to residents of Georgia who graduated from a public high school in the state and are currently enrolled as full–time juniors or seniors in a college or department of education within an approved Georgia public institution. Each of the public colleges in Georgia that offers a teaching degree may nominate 1 student for these scholarships. Nominees must be working toward an initial baccalaureate degree, have a GPA of 3.25 or higher, and indicate a strong desire to prepare for a career as an elementary or secondary school teacher. They must submit an essay discussing their professional goals, reasons for pursuing a teaching career at the elementary or secondary level, and accomplishments, experiences, and honors that relate to teaching. Selection is based on merit. U.S. citizenship or status as a national or permanent resident is required.
Financial data: The stipend is $1,000 per year.
Duration: 1 year.
Number awarded: Normally, 3 each year.
Deadline: July of each year.

2576 $$ CHICAGO CHAPTER RIMS SCHOLARSHIP

Spencer Educational Foundation, Inc.
c/o Risk Insurance and Management Society
1065 Avenue of the Americas, 13th Floor
New York, NY 10018
Phone: (212) 286–9292;
Email: asabatino@spencered.org
Web: www.spencered.org
Summary: To provide financial assistance to upper–division students from any state who are preparing for a career in risk management at a college in designated Midwestern states.
Eligibility: Open to residents of any state who are enrolled as full–time students entering their junior or senior year at a college or university in Illinois, Indiana, Iowa, Michigan, or Wisconsin. Applicants must have a major or minor in a risk management discipline and a career objective in that field. They must have a GPA of 3.0 or higher and relevant work experience. Along with their application, they must submit a 500–word essay on their chosen career path and goals. Selection is based on merit.
Financial data: The stipend is $5,000.
Duration: 1 year.
Number awarded: 1 each year.
Deadline: January of each year.

2577 $ CHRISTA MCAULIFFE FIELD OF EDUCATION SCHOLARSHIP

American Legion
Department of New Hampshire
State House Annex

25 Capitol Street, Room 431
Concord, NH 03301–6312
Phone: (603) 271–2211; (800) 778–3816; Fax: (603) 271–5352;
Email: adjutantnh@amlegion.state.nh.us
Web: www.nhlegion.org/Legion%20Scholarships/Index%20Page.htm

Summary: To provide financial assistance to high school seniors in New Hampshire who are interested in studying education at a college in any state.

Eligibility: Open to seniors graduating from high schools in New Hampshire who have been residents of the state for at least 3 years. Applicants must be entering their first year at an accredited 4–year college or university in any state to work on a bachelor's degree in the field of education. They must have a GPA of 3.0 or higher in their junior and senior high school years. Financial need is considered in the selection process.

Financial data: The stipend is $2,000.

Duration: 1 year.

Number awarded: 1 each year.

Deadline: April of each year.

2578 CHRISTA MCAULIFFE SCHOLARSHIP

Baltimore Community Foundation
Attn: Grants and Scholarships Administrator
2 East Read Street, Ninth Floor
Baltimore, MD 21202
Phone: (410) 332–4172, ext. 171; Fax: (410) 837–4701;
Email: aknoeller@bcf.org
Web: www.bcf.org

Summary: To provide financial assistance to residents of Maryland who are interested in attending a college or university in the state to prepare for a career as a teacher.

Eligibility: Open to high school seniors and currently–enrolled college students who have been residents of Maryland for at least 6 months. Applicants must be attending or planning to attend a college or university in Maryland to prepare for a career as a teacher in the state. They must have a GPA of 3.0 or higher. Along with their application, they must submit 300–word essays on 1) why they want to be a teacher; and 2) the special talents and abilities they possess that will be helpful in a teaching career. Financial need is considered in the selection process.

Financial data: The stipend is $1,250 per year.

Duration: 1 year; recipients may reapply.

Number awarded: Varies each year; recently, 2 of these scholarships were awarded.

Deadline: February of each year for early applications; March of each year for standard applications.

2579 $$ CHRISTA MCAULIFFE TEACHER INCENTIVE PROGRAM

Delaware Department of Education
Attn: Higher Education Office
401 Federal Street
Dover, DE 19901–3639
Phone: (302) 735–4120; (800) 292–7935; Fax: (302) 739–4654;
Email: dheo@doe.k12.de.us
Web: www.doe.k12.de.us/infosuites/students_family/dheo/default.shtml

Summary: To provide funding for teacher training to Delaware residents with outstanding academic records.

Eligibility: Open to Delaware residents who are enrolled or accepted for enrollment at a college or university in the state in a program leading to teacher qualification. Preference is given to applicants planning to teach in an area of critical need. High school seniors must rank in the top half of their class and have a combined score of at least 1570 on the SAT; applicants who are already enrolled in college must have a cumulative GPA of 2.75 or higher. Selection is based on academic achievement. U.S. citizenship or eligible noncitizen status is required.

Financial data: Funds up to the cost of tuition, fees, and other direct educational expenses are provided. This is a forgivable loan program; if the recipient performs required service at a school in Delaware, the loan is forgiven at the rate of 1 year of assistance for each year of service.

Duration: 1 year; may be renewed for up to 3 additional years, provided the recipient maintains a GPA of 2.75 or higher.

Number awarded: Up to 50 each year.

Deadline: March of each year.

2580 CHRISTINE O. GREGOIRE YOUTH/YOUNG ADULT AWARD

American Legacy Foundation
1724 Massachusetts Avenue, N.W.
Washington, DC 20036
Phone: (202) 454–5555;
Email: awards@legacyforhealth.org
Web: www.legacyforhealth.org/awards

Summary: To recognize and reward young people who contribute to the health of the public through use of tobacco documents.

Eligibility: Open to people under 24 years of age who use documents provided by the tobacco industry to further the goals of tobacco prevention and control. Nominees must have 1) made a remarkable research, policy, or advocacy contribution with the use of tobacco industry documents; and/or 2) employed innovative, creative approaches to the employment of tobacco industry documents that result in an improvement in the health or public awareness of a community or nation. They may be nominated by colleagues, peers, coworkers, instructors or professors, governments, or community–based organizations.

Financial data: A cash award is presented.

Duration: The award is presented annually.

Number awarded: 1 each year.

Deadline: March of each year.

2581 CHUCK PEACOCK MEMORIAL SCHOLARSHIP

Summary: To provide financial assistance to students interested in preparing for a career in aviation management.
See Listing #1716.

2582 $ CIRILO MCSWEEN (NEW YORK LIFE) SCHOLARSHIP

PUSH Excel
Attn: General Offices
930 East 50th Street
Chicago, IL 60615
Phone: (773) 373–3366;
Email: pushexcel@rainbowpush.org
Web: www.pushexcel.org/?page_id=63

Summary: To provide financial assistance to high school seniors who plan to major in business and are willing to help promote the scholarship program of PUSH–Excel.

Eligibility: Open to seniors graduating from high school and planning to major in business at an accredited 4–year college or university. Applicants must be U.S. citizens and have a GPA of 3.0 or higher. Along with their application, they must submit a 500–word essay that identifies 5 prerequisites for success, explains their personal philosophy for the pursuit of excellence, and explains how they will use their college education to achieve this pursuit of excellence. They must also agree to cooperate with the scholarship committee of PUSH–Excel by promoting its program, participating in its public relations activities, and attending its Annual National Conference luncheon and Education Leadership Conference. Selection is based on the essay, academic preparation to attend college and succeed, and ability to overcome obstacles to achieve academic and personal goals.

Financial data: The stipend is $2,500 per year.

Duration: 1 year; may be renewed up to 3 additional years if the recipient maintains a GPA of 3.0 or higher and fulfills the obligations to PUSH–Excel.

Number awarded: 1 or more each year.

Deadline: June of each year.

2583 $ CLAMPITT PAPER SCHOLARSHIP

Summary: To provide financial assistance to undergraduate and graduate students at schools in designated states, especially those who are working on a degree in the field of document management and graphic communications.
See Listing #1175.

2584 $$ CLAN MACBEAN FOUNDATION GRANTS

Summary: To provide financial assistance to college students interested in studying subjects or conducting research relating to 1) Scottish culture; or 2) the liberal arts and sciences as related to the "Human Family."
See Listing #1176.

2585 $ CLAUDE E. POPE SCHOLARSHIP

Mortgage Bankers Association of the Carolinas, Inc.
P.O. Box 2588
Mount Pleasant, SC 29465
Phone: (843) 303–5705; Fax: (704) 625–7195;
Email: rbm@mbac.org
Web: www.mbac.org/committeeinvolvement.php

Summary: To provide financial assistance to upper–division students who are preparing for a career in mortgage banking at colleges and universities in the Carolinas.

Eligibility: Open to rising juniors at 4–year accredited colleges and universities in North Carolina or South Carolina who are working on a degree related to mortgage banking or mortgage financing (e.g., real estate, banking, economics). Applicants must be residents of North Carolina or South Carolina, although they may attend school in either state. They must have a GPA of 3.0 or higher. Financial need is not considered in the selection process.

Financial data: The stipend is $2,500 per year.

Duration: 2 years.

Number awarded: 2 each year.

Deadline: March of each year.

2586 $$ COLLEGE FED CHALLENGE

Federal Reserve Bank of New York
Attn: Director of School Programs
33 Liberty Street
New York, NY 10045–0001
Phone: (212) 720–7966; (877) FED–CHLG;
Email: fedchallenge@ramapo.edu
Web: www.ny.frb.org/education/fedchallenge_college.html

Summary: To recognize and reward outstanding students who participate in the College Fed Challenge economics competition.

Eligibility: Open to students at colleges and community colleges in participating Federal Reserve Districts. Currently, 3 of the 12 Federal Reserve Banks participate in the competition: Boston (which serves the New England states), New York (which serves New York, northern New Jersey, and southwestern Connecticut), and Richmond (which serves Maryland, North Carolina, South Carolina, Virginia, Washington, D.C., and West Virginia). Teams of 3 to 5 undergraduates make a 15–minute presentation followed by a 15–minute question–and–answer session with a panel of judges. Presentations should include discussion of current economic and financial conditions; near–term forecast of economic and financial conditions that affect monetary policy; identification of risks that threaten the economic well–being of the country; and recommendation as to the action the Federal Reserve System should take with regard to short–term interest rates. Selection is based on 1) knowledge about the Federal Reserve's role in developing and implementing monetary policy; 2) responses to judges' questions; 3) presentation skills; 4) quality of research and analysis; and 5) evidence of teamwork and cooperation. Competitions are held in each district and then at the interdistrict level.

Financial data: In the interdistrict competition, the first–place team wins $15,000 and its department receives $10,000, the second–place team wins $10,000 and its department receives $5,000, the third–place team wins $5,000 and its department receives $2,500, and the honorable mention team wins $3,000 and its department receives $1,500. In the community college competition, the first–place team wins $3,000 and its department receives $2,000 and the second–place team wins $1,500 and its department receives $1,000.

Duration: The competition is held annually.

Number awarded: 6 teams (including 1 from community colleges) win interdistrict prizes. Additional prizes are awarded by the 3 participating Federal Reserve Banks within their Districts.

Deadline: Each of the 3 participating Federal Reserve Banks sets its own deadlines.

2587 COLONEL SULLY H. DE FONTAINE SCHOLARSHIP

Association of Former Intelligence Officers
Attn: Scholarships Committee
6723 Whittier Avenue, Suite 200
McLean, VA 22101–4533
Phone: (703) 790–0320; Fax: (703) 991–1278;
Email: afio@afio.com
Web: www.afio.com/13_scholarships.htm

Summary: To provide financial assistance to undergraduate students who have a career interest in intelligence and national security.

Eligibility: Open to undergraduates who are entering their sophomore or junior year and preparing for a career within the U.S. intelligence community. Applicants must be working on a degree in intelligence, foreign affairs, and/or national security. Along with their application, they must submit a cover letter that describes any relevant prior experience as well as their future plans. Selection is based on merit, character, estimated future potential, background, and relevance of their studies to the full spectrum of national security interests and career ambitions. U.S. citizenship is required.

Financial data: The stipend is $1,200.

Duration: 1 year.

Number awarded: 1 each year.

Deadline: June of each year.

2588 $$ COLORADO SUPPLEMENTAL LEVERAGING EDUCATIONAL ASSISTANCE PARTNERSHIP (SLEAP)

Colorado Commission on Higher Education
1560 Broadway, Suite 1600
Denver, CO 80202
Phone: (303) 866–2723; Fax: (303) 866–4266;
Email: cche@state.co.us
Web: highered.colorado.gov

Summary: To provide funding to Colorado undergraduate education students who need assistance in paying for college while they are working as student teachers.

Eligibility: Open to residents of Colorado who are enrolled in an undergraduate or post–baccalaureate teacher education program in the states. Applicants must be engaged full time in a student teaching assignment as preparation for teacher education licensure. They must be able to demonstrate substantial financial need. U.S. citizenship or permanent resident status is required.

Financial data: The amount of assistance varies, to a maximum of $5,000 per year.

Duration: 1 year.

Number awarded: Varies each year.

Deadline: Each participating institution sets its own deadlines.

2589 $ COLUMBIA RIVER BASIN PMI CHAPTER ACADEMIC SCHOLARSHIP

Project Management Institute
Attn: PMI Educational Foundation
14 Campus Boulevard
Newtown Square, PA 19073–3299
Phone: (610) 356–4600, ext. 7004; Fax: (610) 356–0357;
Email: pmief@pmi.org
Web: www.pmi.org/pmief/scholarship/scholarships.asp

Summary: To provide financial assistance to undergraduate students with a tie to the Columbia River Basin Chapter of the Project Management Institute (PMI) who are interested in working on a degree in project management.

Eligibility: Open to undergraduate students interested in working on a degree in a field related to project management at a college or university in any state. First priority is given to members of the Columbia River Basin Chapter of PMI and their immediate family; second priority is given to residents of the Columbia River Basin in central Washington; third priority is given to residents of Washington. Along with their application, they must submit 1) a 500–word essay on why they want to be a project manager; and 2) a 250–word essay on how a code of ethics is important to project management. Financial need is not considered in the selection process.

Financial data: The stipend is $2,000.

Duration: 1 year.

Number awarded: 1 each year.

Deadline: May of each year.

2590 $$ COLVIN SCHOLARSHIP PROGRAM

Summary: To provide financial assistance to upper–division students working on a degree related to the beef industry.

See Listing #1181.

2591 $ COMMUNITY SERVICE SCHOLARSHIPS

Association of Government Accountants
Attn: National Awards Committee
2208 Mount Vernon Avenue
Alexandria, VA 22301–1314

Phone: (703) 684–6931; (800) AGA–7211, ext. 321; Fax: (703) 548–9367;
Email: lkapelewski@agacgfm.org
Web: www.agacgfm.org/membership/awards

Summary: To provide financial assistance to high school seniors, undergraduates, and graduate students who are interested in majoring in financial management and are involved in community service.

Eligibility: Open to graduating high school seniors, high school graduates, college and university undergraduates, and graduate students. Applicants must be working on or planning to work on a degree in a financial management discipline, including accounting, auditing, budgeting, economics, finance, electronic data processing, information resources management, or public administration. They must have a GPA of 2.5 or higher and be actively involved in community service projects. Along with their application, they must submit a 2–page essay on "My community service accomplishments," high school or college transcripts, and a reference letter from a community service organization. Selection is based on community service involvement and accomplishments; financial need is not considered.

Financial data: The stipend is $3,000 per year.

Duration: 1 year; renewable.

Number awarded: 1 each year.

Deadline: March of each year.

2592 $ CONNECTICUT CHAPTER HEALTHCARE FINANCIAL MANAGEMENT SCHOLARSHIPS

Summary: To recognize and reward, with scholarships, undergraduate and graduate students in fields related to health care financial management at colleges and universities in Connecticut who submit outstanding essays on topics in the field.

See Listing #1732.

2593 CONNECTICUT CHAPTER SCHOLARSHIP

American Society of Women Accountants–Connecticut Chapter
c/o Karen M. Desautelle, Scholarship Committee Chair
129 Sunset Drive
Glastonbury, CT 06033
Phone: (860) 659–4663;
Email: scholarship@aswact.org
Web: www.aswact.org

Summary: To provide financial assistance to women from Connecticut working on an undergraduate degree in accounting at a school in the state.

Eligibility: Open to women who are residents of Connecticut and enrolled at a college or university in the state as a sophomore, junior, or senior. Applicants must be preparing for a career in accounting. Along with their application, they must submit a short statement on their career goals and objectives. Financial need is considered in the selection process.

Financial data: Stipends range from $500 to $1,500. Funds are paid directly to the student.

Duration: 1 year.

Number awarded: Varies each year; recently, 2 of these scholarships were awarded.

Deadline: October of each year.

2594 CONNECTICUT FUNERAL DIRECTORS ASSOCIATION MORTUARY SCIENCE SCHOLARSHIP

Connecticut Funeral Directors Association
364 Silas Deane Highway
Wethersfield, CT 06109
Phone: (860) 721–0234; (800) 919–CFDA; Fax: (860) 257–3617;
Email: connfda@aol.com
Web: www.ctfda.org/html/scholarship–mortuary.html

Summary: To provide financial assistance to residents of Connecticut who are working on a degree in mortuary science at a school in any state.

Eligibility: Open to residents of Connecticut who are enrolled in an accredited mortuary science school in any state. Applicants must be planning to complete their education and serve the public in their chosen profession in Connecticut. Along with their application, they must submit essays on 1) the process they used and the experiences they underwent in their decision to enter the funeral service profession; and 2) more about themselves. Selection is based on the essays and academic record; financial need is not considered.

Financial data: The stipend is $1,000.

Duration: 1 year.

Number awarded: Up to 2 each year.

Deadline: October of each year.

2595 CONNECTICUT HOSPITALITY EDUCATIONAL FOUNDATION SCHOLARSHIPS

Summary: To provide financial assistance to Connecticut high school seniors interested in preparing for a career in the food service industry at a school in any state.

See Listing #1182.

2596 $$ CONNECTICUT MINORITY TEACHER INCENTIVE PROGRAM

Connecticut Office of Financial and Academic Affairs for Higher Education
Attn: Student Financial Aid
61 Woodland Street
Hartford, CT 06105–2326
Phone: (860) 947–1853; (800) 842–0229 (within CT); Fax: (860) 947–1314;
Email: mtip@ctdhe.org
Web: www.ctohe.org/SFA/default.htm

Summary: To provide financial assistance and loan repayment to minority upper–division college students in Connecticut who are interested in teaching at public schools in the state.

Eligibility: Open to juniors and seniors enrolled full time in Connecticut college and university teacher preparation programs. Applicants must be members of a minority group, defined as African American, Hispanic/Latino, Asian American, or Native American. They must be nominated by the education dean at their institution.

Financial data: The maximum stipend is $5,000 per year. In addition, if recipients complete a credential and begin teaching at a public school in Connecticut within 16 months of graduation, they may receive up to $2,500 per year, for up to 4 years, to help pay off college loans.

Duration: Up to 2 years.

Number awarded: Varies each year.

Deadline: October of each year.

2597 $ CONNECTICUT MORTGAGE BANKERS SOCIAL AFFAIRS FUND

Hartford Foundation for Public Giving
Attn: Donor Services Officer
10 Columbus Boulevard, Eighth Floor
Hartford, CT 06106
Phone: (860) 548–1888; Fax: (860) 524–8346;
Email: scholarships@hfpg.org
Web: www.hfpgscholarships.org/Scholarships/Home/tabid/305/Default.aspx

Summary: To provide financial assistance to residents of Connecticut who are working on a finance–related degree at a college in any state.

Eligibility: Open to graduates of high schools in Connecticut who are currently enrolled at a college or university in any state. Applicants must be working on a degree in business, finance, or real estate.

Financial data: The stipend is $3,000 per year.

Duration: 1 year; may be renewed up to 3 additional years.

Number awarded: 1 each year.

Deadline: January of each year.

2598 CONSTITUTIONAL OFFICERS' ASSOCIATION OF GEORGIA SCHOLARSHIPS

Constitutional Officers' Association of Georgia, Inc.
P.O. Box 1644
Decatur, GA 30031
Phone: (404) 377–1364; Fax: (404) 378–7831;
Email: Suzanne.cross@coag.info
Web: www.coag.info

Summary: To provide financial assistance to residents of Georgia who are interested in working on a degree related to government, business, or law enforcement at a college in the state.

Eligibility: Open to seniors graduating from high schools in Georgia and undergraduates currently enrolled at a college, university, junior college, or technical school in the state. Applicants must be working on or planning to work on a degree in government, political science, law enforcement, accounting, finance, business, or pre–law. Along with their application, they must submit a 1,000–word essay on a topic that changes annually but relates to constitutional officers in Georgia; recently, students were asked to explain why electing constitutional officers, rather than appointing them, is advantageous to the communities they serve. Financial need is not considered in the selection process.

Financial data: The stipend is $1,000.
Duration: 1 year.
Number awarded: 2 each year.
Deadline: March of each year.

2599 $$ CREW NETWORK SCHOLARSHIPS

Commercial Real Estate Women (CREW) Network
1201 Wakarusa Drive, Suite C3
Lawrence, KS 66049
Phone: (785) 832–1808; Fax: (785) 832–1551;
Email: crewnetwork@crewnetwork.org
Web: crewnetwork.org/CZ_scholarships.aspx?id=257

Summary: To provide financial assistance to women who are attending college to prepare for a career in commercial real estate.
Eligibility: Open to women who are enrolled as full–time juniors, seniors, or graduate students at a college or university that has an accredited real estate program. If their institution does not have a real estate program, they may be studying another field, as long as they are preparing for a career in commercial real estate. They must have a GPA of 3.0 or higher and be U.S. or Canadian citizens. Along with their application, undergraduates must submit a brief statement about their interest in commercial real estate and their career objectives; graduate students must submit a statement that explains why they are interested in the commercial real estate industry, their experiences and insights into that industry and how those have impacted them, the impact they expect to make in the commercial real estate industry, and how their long–term career objectives make them uniquely qualified for this scholarship. Financial need is not considered in the selection process.
Financial data: The stipend is $5,000.
Duration: 1 year.
Number awarded: 10 each year.
Deadline: April of each year.

2600 $ CTBA SCHOLARSHIPS

Summary: To provide financial assistance to Connecticut residents who are interested in attending college in any state to prepare for a career in broadcasting.
See Listing #1187.

2601 D. ANITA SMALL SCIENCE AND BUSINESS SCHOLARSHIP

Summary: To provide financial assistance to women in Maryland who are interested in working on an undergraduate or graduate degree in a science or business–related field.
See Listing #1745.

2602 $$ DAKOTA CORPS SCHOLARSHIP PROGRAM

Summary: To provide money for college to high school seniors in South Dakota who plan to attend a college or university in the state and work in the state in nursing or other critical need occupation following graduation.
See Listing #1748.

2603 $$ DALLAS/FORT WORTH RIMS CHAPTER SCHOLARSHIP

Spencer Educational Foundation, Inc.
c/o Risk Insurance and Management Society
1065 Avenue of the Americas, 13th Floor
New York, NY 10018
Phone: (212) 286–9292;
Email: asabatino@spencered.org
Web: www.spencered.org

Summary: To provide financial assistance to upper–division students from Texas who are preparing for a career in risk management.
Eligibility: Open to residents of Texas who are enrolled as full–time students entering their junior or senior year at a college or university in any state with a major or minor in a risk management discipline. Applicants must have a career objective in risk management and relevant work experience. They must have a GPA of 3.0 or higher. Along with their application, they must submit a 500–word essay on their chosen career path and goals. Selection is based on merit.
Financial data: The stipend is $5,000.
Duration: 1 year.
Number awarded: 1 each year.
Deadline: January of each year.

2604 DAMON P. MOORE SCHOLARSHIP

Indiana State Teachers Association
Attn: Scholarships
150 West Market Street, Suite 900
Indianapolis, IN 46204–2875
Phone: (317) 263–3369; (800) 382–4037; Fax: (800) 777–6128;
Email: mshoup@ista–in.org
Web: www.ista–in.org/dynamic.aspx?id=1212

Summary: To provide financial assistance to ethnic minority high school seniors in Indiana who are interested in studying education in college.
Eligibility: Open to ethnic minority public high school seniors in Indiana who are interested in studying education in college. Selection is based on academic achievement, leadership ability as expressed through co–curricular activities and community involvement, recommendations, and a 300–word essay on their educational goals and how they plan to use this scholarship.
Financial data: The stipend is $1,000.
Duration: 1 year; may be renewed for 2 additional years if the recipient maintains at least a "C+" average.
Number awarded: 1 each year.
Deadline: February of each year.

2605 $ DAN M. REICHARD, JR. SCHOLARSHIP

American Public Transportation Association
Attn: American Public Transportation Foundation
1666 K Street, N.W., Suite 1100
Washington, DC 20006
Phone: (202) 496–4803; Fax: (202) 496–4323;
Email: yconley@apta.com
Web: www.aptfd.org/work/scholarship.htm

Summary: To provide financial assistance to undergraduate and graduate students who are preparing for a career in the business administration or management area of the public transportation industry.
Eligibility: Open to college sophomores, juniors, seniors, and graduate students who are preparing for a career in the business administration or management area of the transit industry. Any member organization of the American Public Transportation Association (APTA) can nominate and sponsor candidates for this scholarship. Nominees must be enrolled in a fully–accredited institution, have and maintain at least a 3.0 GPA, and be either employed by or demonstrate a strong interest in entering the business administration or management area of the public transportation industry. They must submit a 1,000–word essay on the topic, "In what segment of the public transportation industry will you make a career and why?" Selection is based on demonstrated interest in the transit field as a career, need for financial assistance, academic achievement, essay content and quality, and involvement in extracurricular citizenship and leadership activities.
Financial data: The stipend is $2,500.
Duration: 1 year; may be renewed.
Number awarded: 1 each year.
Deadline: May of each year.

2606 DAN WHITWORTH MEMORIAL SCHOLARSHIP

Texas Amateur Athletic Federation
Attn: Scholarship Application
421 North IH 35
P.O. Box 1789
Georgetown, TX 78627–1789
Phone: (512) 863–9400; Fax: (512) 869–2393;
Email: mark@taaf.com
Web: www.taaf.com/index.cfm?load=page&page=44

Summary: To provide financial assistance to residents of Texas who are entering and continuing undergraduate and graduate students at institutions in the state and interested in preparing for a career in the parks and recreation profession.
Eligibility: Open to residents of Texas who are enrolled or planning to enroll full time at a college or university in an accredited bachelor's, master's, or doctoral degree program in sports sciences, kinesiology, conservation, physical education, recreation and tourism, and/or another major relating to the field of parks and recreation. Preference is given to students attending a Texas college

or university. Graduating high school seniors must have a class rank in the top quarter, a GPA of 2.5 or higher, a combined mathematics and critical reading SAT score of 850 or higher, or an ACT score of 21 or higher. Students already enrolled in college or graduate school must have a GPA of 2.5 or higher. In addition to grades and test scores, selection is based on honors and awards from, and participation in, activities, endeavors, volunteerism, and work related to athletics and/or the field of parks and recreation. Financial need is not considered.
Financial data: A stipend is awarded (amount not specified).
Duration: 1 year.
Number awarded: 1 or more each year.
Deadline: April of each year.

2607 $$ DANIEL LADNER SCHOLARSHIPS

Summary: To provide financial assistance to female upper–division and graduate students who reside in designated eastern states and are interested in preparing for a career in financial or political communications at a college or graduate school in any state.
See Listing #1190.

2608 DANIEL T. MULHERAN MEMORIAL SCHOLARSHIP

Maryland State Funeral Directors Association
Attn: Memorial Scholarship
311 Crain Highway, S.E.
Glen Burnie, MD 21061
Phone: (410) 553–9106; (888) 459–9693; Fax: (410) 553–9107;
Email: msfda@msfda.net
Web: www.msfda.net/?page=scholarships
Summary: To provide financial assistance to Maryland residents who are interested in preparing for a career in funeral service.
Eligibility: Open to residents of Maryland who have completed two–thirds of the educational requirements at an accredited mortuary science school in any state or have graduated within the past 6 months. Applicants must have no "D" grade in any required class and an overall GPA of 2.5 or higher. They must be eligible for licensure in the state of Maryland. Along with their application, they must submit 500–word essays on 1) the process they used and the experiences they underwent in their decision to enter the funeral service profession and their perception of the value of the funeral; and 2) more about themselves, such as books that interest them, experiences that have impacted them, civic or church activities, or what they like to do on their own time. Selection is based on the essays, application information, and academic record.
Financial data: The stipend is $1,000.
Duration: 1 year.
Number awarded: 1 each year.
Deadline: September of each year.

2609 $$ DANTE PETRIZZO MEMORIAL SCHOLARSHIP

Spencer Educational Foundation, Inc.
c/o Risk Insurance and Management Society
1065 Avenue of the Americas, 13th Floor
New York, NY 10018
Phone: (212) 286–9292;
Email: asabatino@spencered.org
Web: www.spencered.org
Summary: To provide financial assistance to upper–division students from Connecticut, New Jersey, and New York who are preparing for a career in risk management.
Eligibility: Open to residents of the tri–state area of Connecticut, New Jersey, and New York who are enrolled as full–time students entering their junior or senior year at a college or university in any state with a major or minor in a risk management discipline. Applicants must have a career objective in risk management and relevant work experience. They must have a GPA of 3.0 or higher. Along with their application, they must submit a 500–word essay on their chosen career path and goals. Selection is based on merit.
Financial data: The stipend is $5,000.
Duration: 1 year.
Number awarded: 1 each year.
Deadline: January of each year.

2610 DAVE HERREN MEMORIAL SCHOLARSHIP

Tourism Cares
Attn: Academic Scholarship Program
275 Turnpike Street, Suite 307
Canton, MA 02021
Phone: (781) 821–5990; Fax: (781) 821–8949;
Email: scholarships@tourismcares.org
Web: www.tourismcares.org
Summary: To provide financial assistance to upper–division and graduate students who are working on a degree in travel and tourism or hospitality–related fields.
Eligibility: Open to citizens and permanent residents of the United States who are enrolled full time at a 4–year college or university. Applicants must be entering their junior or senior year or be enrolled or entering graduate school. They must have a GPA of 3.0 or higher and be working on a degree in a travel or tourism or hospitality–related field. Undergraduates must submit an essay on the segment of the travel and tourism or hospitality industry their current program of study emphasizes, the opportunities they are utilizing as they prepare for a career in the industry, and their academic and extracurricular activities. Graduate students must submit an essay on the changes they have observed thus far in the travel and tourism or hospitality industry, the changes they anticipate in the future of the industry, and where they see their future potential in the industry. Financial need is not considered in the selection process.
Financial data: The stipend is $1,000.
Duration: 1 year.
Number awarded: 1 each year.
Deadline: March of each year.

2611 $ DAVID HOODS MEMORIAL SCHOLARSHIP

Summary: To provide financial assistance to undergraduate and graduate students from any country interested in preparing for a career in document management and graphic communications, especially those interested in marketing and public relations.
See Listing #1193.

2612 $ DAVID M. CLINE SCHOLARSHIP

Summary: To provide financial assistance to high school seniors in South Carolina who plan to major in a field related to law enforcement or natural resources at a college or university in the state.
See Listing #1755.

2613 $ DAVID MEADOR HOSPITALITY–FOOD SERVICE SCHOLARSHIPS

New England Club Managers Association
Attn: Scholarship Chair
P.O. Box 20008
Worcester, MA 01602–0008
Email: scholarships@necma.org
Web: www.necma.org
Summary: To provide financial assistance to undergraduates at college in New England who are preparing for a career in hospitality management.
Eligibility: Open to students enrolled full time at a 4–year college or university in New England. Applicants must have completed at least 1 year with a major or minor in hospitality and a GPA of 3.0 or higher. They must have worked at least 1 season as a private club and be able to demonstrate an interest in preparing for a career in hospitality management. Along with their application, they must submit a 2–page essay on their career goals, their interest in the hospitality industry, and why they feel they deserve this scholarship. Financial need is not considered in the selection process.
Financial data: Stipend amounts vary; recently, they averaged approximately $2,000.
Duration: 1 year.
Number awarded: Varies each year; recently, 2 of these scholarships were awarded.
Deadline: September of each year.

2614 DAVIDSON AND JONES HOTEL CORPORATION SCHOLARSHIP

North Carolina Restaurant and Lodging Association
Attn: NC Hospitality Education Foundation
6036 Six Forks Road
Raleigh, NC 27609
Phone: (919) 844–0098; (800) 582–8750; Fax: (919) 844–0190;
Email: alyssab@ncrla.biz

Web: www.ncrla.biz/displaycommon.cfm?an=1&subarticlenbr=95
Summary: To provide financial assistance to residents of North Carolina who are enrolled in a program related to the culinary or hospitality industry at a college in the state.
Eligibility: Open to residents of North Carolina enrolled full time at an accredited 4–year college, university, or culinary program in the state. Applicants must be entering the junior year of a culinary or hospitality program. Financial need is considered in the selection process.
Financial data: The stipend is $1,000.
Duration: 1 year; nonrenewable.
Number awarded: 1 each year. In addition, the sponsor also offers a number of other, similar scholarships, including the ALSCO Scholarship, the Daren Restaurants Partner Scholarship, and the Davidson and Jones Hotel Corporation Scholarship.
Deadline: February of each year.

2615 DEEN TERRY MEMORIAL SCHOLARSHIP

Summary: To provide financial assistance to residents of Georgia interested in studying culinary arts or hospitality at a school in any state.
See Listing #1197.

2616 DELAWARE SCHOOL NUTRITION ASSOCIATION SCHOLARSHIPS

Delaware School Nutrition Association
c/o Dee Greenwood, Continuing Education and Scholarships
Child Nutrition Programs
82 Monrovia Avenue
Smyrna, DE 19977
Phone: (302) 653–8585;
Email: GreenwoodDee@smyrna.k12.de.us
Web: www.deschoolnutrition.org/shopexd.asp?id=778&bc=no
Summary: To provide financial assistance to high school seniors in Delaware who plan to study nutrition or food service management at a college in any state.
Eligibility: Open to seniors graduating from high schools in Delaware who plan to enroll at an accredited 2– or 4–year college or university in any state. Applicants must be planning to major in a field related to nutrition or food service management. Along with their application, they must submit a 500–word essay on a topic that changes annually but relates to nutrition. Selection is based on that essay, academic achievement, participation in school activities and clubs, and participation in community and volunteer activities; financial need is not considered.
Financial data: The stipend is $1,000.
Duration: 1 year.
Number awarded: 3 each year: 1 to a student from each Delaware county.
Deadline: April of each year.

2617 $ DELAWARE SHRM STUDENT SCHOLARSHIPS

Society for Human Resource Management–Delaware Chapter
c/o Monterry "Terry" Luckey
47 Anderson Court
Bear, DE 19701
Email: monterryluckey@comcast.net
Web: www.shrmde.org
Summary: To provide financial assistance to students from Delaware working on a bachelor's or master's degree in human resources.
Eligibility: Open to 1) undergraduate students enrolled in a human resources program or related program; and 2) graduate students currently enrolled in a master's degree program with an emphasis on human resources or related areas. Applicants must live or work in Delaware or attend a Delaware college or university. They must have a GPA of 3.0 or higher. Along with their application, they must submit a 2–page essay on their future objectives in the human resources field and why they chose this profession. Selection is based on total achievements and need.
Financial data: The stipend is $2,500.
Duration: 1 year.
Number awarded: 3 each year.
Deadline: September of each year.

2618 $$ DELAWARE TEACHER CORPS PROGRAM

Delaware Department of Education
Attn: Higher Education Office
401 Federal Street
Dover, DE 19901–3639
Phone: (302) 735–4120; (800) 292–7935; Fax: (302) 739–4654;
Email: dheo@doe.k12.de.us
Web: www.doe.k12.de.us/infosuites/students_family/dheo/default.shtml
Summary: To provide money for college to Delaware residents interested in preparing for a career as a teacher at a public institution in the state.
Eligibility: Open to Delaware residents who are enrolled or accepted for enrollment in an undergraduate or graduate program leading to teacher qualification at a public college or university in the state. Applicants must be planning to teach in an area of critical need, currently defined to include art, bilingual education, business education, English, foreign languages, English to speakers of other languages, mathematics, music, reading, science, school librarianship, special education, and technology education. First priority is given to students who intend to teach middle and high school mathematics and science; second priority is given to students who intend to teach special education in a content area. High school seniors must rank in the top half of their class and have a combined score of at least 1570 on the SAT; undergraduates must have a cumulative GPA of 2.75 or higher. Selection is based on academic achievement. U.S. citizenship or eligible noncitizen status is required.
Financial data: The maximum loan is equal to the cost of tuition at a public college or university in Delaware. This is a scholarship/loan program; if the recipient performs required service at a school in Delaware, the loan is forgiven at the rate of 1 year of assistance for each year of service.
Duration: 1 year; may be renewed for up to 3 additional years, provided the recipient maintains a GPA of 2.75 or higher.
Number awarded: Varies each year.
Deadline: March of each year.

2619 $ DELOITTE SCHOLARS PROGRAM

Hispanic Association of Colleges and Universities
Attn: National Scholarship Program
8415 Datapoint Drive, Suite 400
San Antonio, TX 78229
Phone: (210) 692–3805; Fax: (210) 692–0823; TDD: (800) 855–2880;
Email: scholarships@hacu.net
Web: www.hacu.net/hacu/Scholarships.asp?SnID=899378480
Summary: To provide financial assistance to undergraduate and graduate students working on a degree in accounting at member institutions of the Hispanic Association of Colleges and Universities (HACU).
Eligibility: Open to sophomores, juniors, and first–year master's degree students at 4–year HACU member institutions who are working full time on a degree in accounting. Applicants must have a GPA of 3.5 or higher and be able to demonstrate financial need. They must be interested in a career with Deloitte. Along with their application, they must submit an essay that focuses on their personal motivation for applying for this scholarship, their academic and/or career goals, and the skills they could bring to an employer.
Financial data: The stipend is $2,200.
Duration: 1 year.
Number awarded: 1 or more each year.
Deadline: June of each year.

2620 $ DELTA NU ALPHA FOUNDATION SCHOLARSHIPS

Delta Nu Alpha
Attn: Foundation
c/o Tom Bock, Scholarship Committee Chair
4123 Apple Blossom Road
Lutz, FL 33558
Phone: (813) 545–1104;
Email: dnafoundation@cableone.net
Web: www.deltanualphafoundation.org
Summary: To provide financial assistance to undergraduate students working on a degree in the fields of transportation, logistics, or supply chain management.
Eligibility: Open to students working on an associate or bachelor's degree in the fields of transportation, logistics, or supply chain management. Applicants must submit essays on their career interests and objectives; any special school projects, papers, and/or internships related to their major field of study; and how this award will help them, including why they feel they should be considered for this scholarship. Selection is based on scholastic achievement, career goals, related transportation and logistics interests, and financial need.
Financial data: Stipends range from $1,000 to $2,000.
Duration: 1 year.

Number awarded: Varies each year; recently, 3 of these scholarships were awarded.
Deadline: May of each year.

2621 DENVER CHAPTER SCHOLARSHIPS

American Society of Women Accountants–Denver Chapter
c/o Nicolette Rounds, Scholarship Trustee
3773 Cherry Creek Drive North, Suite 575
Denver, CO 80209
Phone: (303) 377–4282;
Email: roundscpa@qwestoffice.net
Web: www.aswadenver.org/scholarship_info.htm
Summary: To provide financial assistance to women working on a degree in accounting at a college or university in Colorado.
Eligibility: Open to women who have completed at least 60 semester hours toward a degree in accounting with a GPA of 3.0 or higher. Applicants must be attending a college or university in Colorado. Membership in the American Society of Women Accountants (ASWA) is not required. Selection is based on academic achievement, extracurricular activities and honors, a statement of career goals and objectives, 3 letters of recommendation, and financial need.
Financial data: A stipend is awarded (amount not specified).
Duration: 1 year.
Number awarded: Several each year; a total of $7,000 is available for this program annually.
Deadline: June of each year.

2622 $$ DEREK HUGHES SCHOLARSHIP

National Association of Professional Surplus Lines Offices, Ltd.
Attn: Educational Foundation
200 N.E. 54th Street, Suite 200
Kansas City, MO 64118
Phone: (816) 741–3910; Fax: (816) 741–5409;
Email: foundation@napslo.org
Web: www.napslo.org/imispublic/AM/Template.cfm/Section=Foundation
Summary: To provide financial assistance to undergraduate and graduate students who are enrolled or accepted for enrollment in a program that will lead to a career in the insurance industry.
Eligibility: Open to students enrolled or accepted for enrollment in an undergraduate or graduate degree program in actuarial science, business, economics, finance, insurance, management, risk management, or statistics. Entering freshmen must rank in the top 25% of their high school class or have a GPA of 3.0 or higher; other students must have a GPA or 3.0 or higher. Applicants must be preparing for a career in the insurance industry. Along with their application, they must submit a 1– or 2–page essay summarizing their career objectives, academic accomplishments, work experience, pertinent extracurricular activities, and reasons for applying for this scholarship; if they wish to have financial need considered in the selection process, they must also explain the reasons.
Financial data: The stipend is $5,000.
Duration: 1 year.
Number awarded: Varies each year; recently, 14 of these scholarships were awarded.
Deadline: May of each year.

2623 DETROIT CHAPTER RIMS SCHOLARSHIPS

Risk and Insurance Management Society–Detroit Chapter
c/o Laura Quigley, Scholarship Committee
Kelly Services
1301 West Long Lake Road, Suite 160
Troy, MI 48098
Phone: (248) 822–9585; Fax: (248) 641–8690;
Email: quigllp@kellyservices.com
Web: Detroit.rims.org/Detroit/AboutUs/Detroit_RIMS_Awards/Scholarships
Summary: To provide financial assistance to Michigan college students who are preparing for a career in insurance and risk management.
Eligibility: Open to residents of Michigan enrolled at a college or university in the state. Applicants must be preparing for a career within the risk management and insurance industry.
Financial data: A stipend is awarded (amount not specified).
Duration: 1 year.
Number awarded: 1 or more each year.
Deadline: October of each year.

2624 $$ DIRECT MARKETING EDUCATIONAL FOUNDATION SCHOLARSHIPS

Direct Marketing Association
Attn: Educational Foundation
1120 Avenue of the Americas
New York, NY 10036
Phone: (212) 768–7277, ext. 1817; Fax: (212) 790–1561;
Email: sbasuk@directworks.org
Web: www.directworks.org/Students/Default.aspx?id=292
Summary: To provide financial assistance to undergraduate and graduate students working on a degree in direct marketing.
Eligibility: Open to undergraduates at 4–year colleges and universities who have at least 1 semester of study remaining and to graduate students. Applicants must be working on a degree related to the field of direct or interactive marketing. They must be U.S. citizens or permanent residents. Along with their application, they must submit an essay of 250 to 500 words on why they are applying for this scholarship, including information on courses they have taken and/or work experience that has led to their interest in direct or interactive marketing. Financial need is not considered in the selection process.
Financial data: Stipends range from $1,000 to $5,000.
Duration: 1 year.
Number awarded: Varies each year; recently, 25 of these scholarships were awarded.
Deadline: May of each year.

2625 $ DIVERSITY SCHOLARSHIPS

Alabama Society of Certified Public Accountants
Attn: ASCPA Educational Foundation
1103 South Perry Street
P.O. Box 5000
Montgomery, AL 36103
Phone: (334) 834–7650; (800) 227–1711
Web: www.ascpa.org
Summary: To provide financial assistance to minority accounting students at colleges and universities in Alabama.
Eligibility: Open to minority (Black or African American, Hispanic or Latino, Native American, or Asian) residents of any state enrolled at least half time at colleges and universities in Alabama with at least 1 full year of school remaining. Applicants must have declared a major in accounting and have completed intermediate accounting courses. They must have a GPA of 3.0 or higher overall and in all accounting classes. Along with their application, they must submit a 25–word essay on why the scholarship is important to them. Financial need is not considered in the selection process. Preference is given to students who have a strong interest in a career as a C.P.A. in Alabama. U.S. citizenship or permanent resident status is required.
Financial data: The stipend is $2,500.
Duration: 1 year.
Number awarded: 4 each year.
Deadline: March of each year.

2626 $ DIXON HUGHES GOODMAN SCHOLARSHIP

Virginia Society of Certified Public Accountants
Attn: Educational Foundation
4309 Cox Road
Glen Allen, VA 23060
Phone: (804) 612–9427; (800) 733–8272; Fax: (804) 273–1741;
Email: info@vscpafoundation.com
Web: www.vscpa.com/content/Ed_Found/SA/Scholarships.aspx
Summary: To provide financial assistance to upper–division students enrolled in an accounting program in Virginia.
Eligibility: Open to juniors and seniors currently enrolled in a Virginia college or university accounting program. Applicants must be U.S. citizens, be intending to take the C.P.A. examination, and have a GPA of 3.0 or higher. Along with their application, they must submit a 500–word essay on assigned topics. Selection is based on the essay, their most recent transcript, a current resume, a faculty letter of recommendation, and financial need.
Financial data: The stipend is $3,000.
Duration: 1 year.
Number awarded: 1 each year. The sponsor also awards a number of other named scholarships for upper–division students.
Deadline: March of each year.

2627 $$ DR. ALMA S. ADAMS SCHOLARSHIP

Summary: To provide financial assistance to undergraduate or graduate students in selected fields who have engaged in community service or visual arts activities to reduce smoking in communities designated as especially vulnerable to the tobacco industry.

See Listing #1203.

2628 $ DR. AURA–LEE A. AND JAMES HOBBS PITTENGER AMERICAN HISTORY SCHOLARSHIP

Summary: To provide financial assistance to high school seniors planning to major in American history or government in college.

See Listing #1204.

2629 $ DR. GEORGE M. SMERK SCHOLARSHIP

American Public Transportation Association
Attn: American Public Transportation Foundation
1666 K Street, N.W., Suite 1100
Washington, DC 20006
Phone: (202) 496–4803; Fax: (202) 496–4323;
Email: yconley@apta.com
Web: www.aptfd.org/work/scholarship.htm

Summary: To provide financial assistance to undergraduate and graduate students who are preparing for a career in the management area of the public transportation industry.

Eligibility: Open to college sophomores, juniors, seniors, and graduate students who are preparing for a career in the management area of the transit industry. Any member organization of the American Public Transportation Association (APTA) can nominate and sponsor candidates for this scholarship. Nominees must be enrolled in a fully–accredited institution, have and maintain at least a 3.0 GPA, and be either employed by or demonstrate a strong interest in entering the management area of the public transportation industry. They must submit a 1,000–word essay on the topic, "In what segment of the public transportation industry will you make a career and why?" Selection is based on demonstrated interest in the transit field as a career, need for financial assistance, academic achievement, essay content and quality, and involvement in extracurricular citizenship and leadership activities.

Financial data: The stipend is $2,500.

Duration: 1 year; may be renewed.

Number awarded: 1 each year.

Deadline: May of each year.

2630 DR. JOSEPH C. BASILE, II MEMORIAL SCHOLARSHIP

Greater Kanawha Valley Foundation
Attn: Scholarship Program Officer
1600 Huntington Square
900 Lee Street East, 16th Floor
Charleston, WV 25301
Phone: (304) 346–3620; (800) 467–5909; Fax: (304) 346–3640;
Email: shoover@tgkvf.org
Web: www.tgkvf.org/page.aspx?pid=409

Summary: To provide financial assistance to residents of West Virginia who are working on a degree in education at a school in the state.

Eligibility: Open to residents of West Virginia who are working or planning to work full time on a degree in the field of education at a college or university in the state. Applicants must have an ACT score of 20 or higher, be able to demonstrate good moral character and financial need, and have a GPA of 2.5 or higher.

Financial data: Recently, stipends averaged $1,200.

Duration: 1 year; nonrenewable.

Number awarded: Varies each year; recently, 1 of these scholarships was awarded.

Deadline: January of each year.

2631 DR. JULIANNE MALVEAUX SCHOLARSHIP

Summary: To provide financial assistance to African American women studying journalism, economics, or a related field in college.

See Listing #1206.

2632 $ DREAM DEFERRED ESSAY CONTEST

American Islamic Congress
Attn: Hands Across the Mideast Support Alliance
1718 M Street, N.W., Suite 243
Washington, DC 20036
Phone: (202) 595–3160; Fax: (202) 315–5838;
Email: essay@aicongress.org
Web: www.hamsaweb.org/essay

Summary: To recognize and reward young people who live in the United States or the Middle East and submit outstanding essays on civil rights.

Eligibility: Open to residents of the United States or the Middle East (defined as the member states of the Arab League, Iran, and Afghanistan) who are younger than 25 years of age. There is no minimum age requirement and entrants do not need to be students. Applicants must submit an essay of 600 to 1,500 words on their choice of a list of 7 topics assigned for residents of the Middle East and 7 different topics assigned for residents of the United States. For Americans, recent topics included 1) how the past year has changed their view of individual rights in the Middle East; 2) a profile of a Middle East civil rights reformer and ways that Americans can help support their work; 3) a profile of an American assisting Middle East reform; 4) what they can do in their community or campus to support Middle East civil rights efforts; 5) their "dream deferred" vision of Americans helping to protect individual rights in the Middle East; 6) what they would do if Iranian women organized a protest by walking down the street with their hair uncovered and were arrested; or 7) a sample script for a video about individual rights in the Middle East. Essays may not focus on U.S. government policy or regional geopolitics (e.g., the Iraq war, the Arab–Israeli–Iranian conflict, Iran's nuclear program). They should focus on issues of individual rights (e.g., free expression, women's equality, minority rights, religious freedom, economic liberty, artistic freedom) within Middle Eastern societies.

Financial data: For each of the competition areas (Middle East and the United States), first prize is $2,000, second prize is $1,500, and runner–up prizes are $500. All prizes are paid in cash.

Duration: The competition is held annually.

Number awarded: 10 each year: 1 first prize, 1 second prize, and 3 runners–up in the United States and the same in the Middle East.

Deadline: May of each year.

2633 $ D.W. SIMPSON & COMPANY ACTUARIAL SCIENCE SCHOLARSHIPS

D.W. Simpson & Company
1800 West Larchmont Avenue
Chicago, IL 60613
Phone: (312) 951–8386; (800) 837–8338; Fax: (312) 951–8386;
Email: scholarship@dwsimpson.com
Web: www.dwsimpson.com/scholar.html

Summary: To provide financial assistance to college seniors majoring in actuarial science.

Eligibility: Open to students who are entering their senior year of undergraduate study in actuarial science. Applicants must have a GPA of 3.0 or higher overall and 3.2 or higher in their major, have passed at least 1 actuarial examination, and be eligible to work in the United States. Along with their application, they must submit 1) a list of internships, scholarships, honors, and extracurricular activities; and 2) an essay on their long–term career goals. Financial need is not considered in the selection process.

Financial data: The stipend is $1,000 per semester.

Duration: 1 semester; nonrenewable.

Number awarded: 2 each year (1 per semester).

Deadline: April of each year for the fall scholarship; October of each year for the spring scholarship.

2634 $$ DWIGHT DAVID EISENHOWER HISTORICALLY BLACK COLLEGES AND UNIVERSITIES TRANSPORTATION FELLOWSHIP PROGRAM

Summary: To provide financial assistance to undergraduate and graduate students working on a degree in a transportation–related field at an Historically Black College or University (HBCU).

See Listing #1207.

2635 DWIGHT P. JACOBUS SCHOLARSHIPS

Association of School Business Officials of Maryland and the District of Columbia
Attn: Executive Director
P.O. Box 6602
Lutherville, MD 21093–9998
Phone: (410) 608–09111;
Email: asbomddc1@gmail.com
Web: www.asbo.org/scholarships.asp

Summary: To provide financial assistance to the residents of Maryland and the District of Columbia who are interested in majoring in business or education at a college or university in the area.

Eligibility: Open to students who have been residents of Maryland or the District of Columbia for at least 1 year, have been accepted as a full–time student at an accredited institution of higher education within Maryland or the District, are able to demonstrate financial need, and have a GPA of 3.0 or higher. Both high school seniors and currently–enrolled college students may apply. They must be preparing for a career in business or in education. Selection is based on scholastic achievement, financial need, SAT or ACT scores, and quality of extracurricular achievements.

Financial data: The stipend is $1,000. Funds are paid directly to the recipient's school.

Duration: 1 year; may be renewed up to 3 additional years, provided the recipient remains enrolled full time with a GPA of 3.0 or higher.

Number awarded: 4 each year; at least 1 of these will go to a student enrolled in an approved program leading to teacher certification.

Deadline: February of each year.

2636 EDITH M. ALLEN SCHOLARSHIPS

Summary: To provide financial assistance to Methodist students who are African American and working on an undergraduate or graduate degree in specified fields.

See Listing #1793.

2637 $ EDUCATORS FOR MAINE PROGRAM

Finance Authority of Maine
Attn: Education Finance Programs
5 Community Drive
P.O. Box 949
Augusta, ME 04332–0949
Phone: (207) 623–3263; (800) 228–3734; Fax: (207) 623–0095; TDD: (207) 626–2717;
Email: education@famemaine.com
Web: www.famemaine.com/Education_Home.aspx

Summary: To provide forgivable loans to residents of Maine who are interested in attending college in any state to prepare for a career as a teacher.

Eligibility: Open to residents of Maine who are graduating high school seniors, currently–enrolled college students, or students accepted into a graduate program. Applicants must be enrolled or planning to enroll at a college or university in any state in a program leading to certification as a teacher, including speech pathology or child care. They must have a GPA of 3.0 or higher. Selection is based on academic performance, relevant activities, awards and special honors, and an essay; financial need is not considered. Preference is given to applicants planning to teach an underserved subject area.

Financial data: Full–time undergraduate students receive $3,000 per academic year; graduate students receive $2,000 per academic year. This is a forgivable loan program. Recipients may receive 1 year of loan forgiveness by completing 1 year of full–time teaching in a Maine public or private elementary or secondary school or child care center. The repayment option can be accelerated to 2 years of loan forgiveness for each year of teaching if the service is conducted in an educator shortage area or underserved subject area. If the loan recipient does not meet the service obligation, the total amount borrowed must be repaid with interest at 5%.

Duration: 1 year; may be renewed up to 3 additional years if the recipient remains a Maine resident and maintains a cumulative GPA of 2.5 or higher.

Deadline: April of each year.

2638 EDWARD D. BURKETT SCHOLARSHIP PROGRAM

Summary: To provide financial assistance to undergraduate and graduate students in Florida who are preparing for a career in public works.

See Listing #1795.

2639 EFWA/IMA UNDERGRADUATE SCHOLARSHIP

Educational Foundation for Women in Accounting
Attn: Foundation Administrator
136 South Keowee Street
Dayton, OH 45402
Phone: (937) 424–3391; Fax: (937) 222–5749;
Email: info@efwa.org
Web: www.efwa.org/scholarships_ima.php

Summary: To provide financial support to women who are working on an undergraduate accounting degree.

Eligibility: Open to women who are enrolled at any stage in an accounting degree program at an accredited college or university. Applicants may be completing a fifth–year requirement through general studies. Selection is based on aptitude for accounting and business, commitment to the goal of working on a degree in accounting (including evidence of continued commitment after receiving this award), clear evidence that the candidate has established goals and a plan for achieving those goals (both personal and professional), financial need, and a demonstration of how the scholarship will impact her life. U.S. citizenship is required.

Financial data: The stipend is $1,000.

Duration: 1 year.

Number awarded: 1 each year. In addition, a number of individual chapters award scholarships to students attending school in their state.

Deadline: April of each year.

2640 $ ELEANORE KLINE MEMORIAL SCHOLARSHIP

Michigan Association of Certified Public Accountants
Attn: Michigan Accountancy Foundation
5480 Corporate Drive, Suite 200
Troy, MI 48098–2642
Phone: (248) 267–3723; (888) 877–4CPE (within MI); Fax: (248) 267–3737;
Email: maf@michcpa.org
Web: www.michcpa.org/Content/22461.aspx

Summary: To provide financial assistance to single mothers at Michigan colleges and universities who are working on a degree in accounting.

Eligibility: Open to single mothers enrolled full time at accredited Michigan colleges and universities with a declared concentration in accounting. Applicants must be seniors planning to enter the fifth or graduate year of their school's program. They must intend to or have successfully passed the Michigan C.P.A. examination and intend to practice public accounting in the state. Along with their application, they must submit a 500–word statement about their educational and career aspirations, including internships and/or other employment, volunteer and community activities, professional affiliations, and full–time employment. Documentation of financial need may also be included. U.S. citizenship or eligibility for permanent employment in the United States is required.

Financial data: The stipend is $4,000 per year; funds are disbursed directly to the recipient's college or university.

Duration: 1 year.

Number awarded: 1 each year.

Deadline: January of each year.

2641 $ ELECTRONIC DOCUMENT SYSTEMS FOUNDATION BOARD OF DIRECTORS SCHOLARSHIPS

Summary: To provide financial assistance to undergraduate and graduate students from any country interested in preparing for a career in document management and graphic communications.

See Listing #1213.

2642 ELSIE M. VOGLER AND LOIS E. CARTER MEMORIAL TEACHING SCHOLARSHIP

Epsilon Sigma Alpha International
Attn: ESA Foundation
363 West Drake Road
Fort Collins, CO 80526
Phone: (970) 223–2824; Fax: (970) 223–4456;
Email: esainfo@epsilonsigmaalpha.org
Web: www.epsilonsigmaalpha.org/scholarships–and–grants

Summary: To provide financial assistance to residents of Arizona or Michigan preparing for a career in education.

Eligibility: Open to residents of Arizona and Michigan who are 1) graduating high school seniors with a GPA of 3.0 or higher or with minimum scores of 22 on the ACT or 1030 on the combined critical reading and mathematics SAT; 2) enrolled in college with a GPA of 3.0 or higher; 3) enrolled at a technical school or returning to school after an absence for retraining of job skills or obtaining a degree; or 4) engaged in online study through an accredited college, university, or vocational school. Applicants may be attending or planning to attend school in any state to major in education. Selection is based on character (20%), leadership (20%), service (20%), financial need (20%), and scholastic ability (20%).

Financial data: The stipend is $1,000.

Duration: 1 year; may be renewed.
Number awarded: 1 each year.
Deadline: January of each year.

2643 $ EMERGING DIVERSITY EDUCATION FUND SCHOLARSHIPS

Summary: To provide financial assistance to minority students interested in preparing for a career in an automotive–related profession.
See Listing #1806.

2644 ENID HALL GRISWOLD MEMORIAL SCHOLARSHIP

Summary: To provide financial assistance to upper–division college students majoring in selected social science fields.
See Listing #1216.

2645 $ ERIC JENNETT FOUNDERS SCHOLARSHIP

Project Management Institute
Attn: PMI Educational Foundation
14 Campus Boulevard
Newtown Square, PA 19073–3299
Phone: (610) 356–4600, ext. 7004; Fax: (610) 356–0357;
Email: pmief@pmi.org
Web: www.pmi.org/pmief/scholarship/scholarships.asp
Summary: To provide financial assistance to undergraduate students from any state who are working on a bachelor's degree in project management.
Eligibility: Open to residents of any state enrolled at an accredited college or university. Applicants must be working on a bachelor's degree in project management or a related field. Along with their application, they must submit 1) a 500–word essay on why they want to be a project manager; and 2) a 250–word essay on how a code of ethics is important to project management. Financial need is not considered in the selection process.
Financial data: The stipend is $2,000.
Duration: 1 year.
Number awarded: 1 each year.
Deadline: May of each year.

2646 $$ ESTHER R. SAWYER RESEARCH AWARD

Institute of Internal Auditors Research Foundation
Attn: Research Administrator
247 Maitland Avenue
Altamonte Springs, FL 32701–4201
Phone: (407) 937–1111; Fax: (407) 937–1101;
Email: research@theiia.org
Web: https://na.theiia.org/iiarf/pages/grants–and–awards.aspx
Summary: To recognize and reward upper–division and graduate students who submit essays on a theme related to modern internal auditing.
Eligibility: Open to juniors, seniors, and graduate students enrolled in a program in internal auditing at a school endorsed by the Institute of Internal Auditors (IIA). Applicants must write and submit an original manuscript of 3,000 to 5,000 words on a specific topic that changes annually but is related to modern internal auditing. Selection is based on the manuscript's responsiveness to the assigned research topic, relevance to readers who are familiar with internal audit issues, originality, coherence of organization, clarity, conciseness and focus, and appropriate application of English.
Financial data: The award is $5,000. In addition, the IIA–endorsed school with which the winner is or was affiliated receives up to $3,000 for use in the program or the purchase of materials related to internal auditing.
Duration: The competition is held annually.
Number awarded: 1 each year.
Deadline: February of each year.

2647 $ ETHEL A. NEIJAHR SCHOLARSHIP

Wisconsin Mathematics Council
W175 N11117 Stonewood Drive, Suite 204
Germantown, WI 53022
Phone: (262) 437–0174; Fax: (262) 532–2430;
Email: wmc@wismath.org
Web: www.wismath.org/awards–scholarships
Summary: To provide financial assistance to students from Wisconsin preparing for a career as a mathematics teacher.
Eligibility: Open to residents of Wisconsin currently enrolled in an undergraduate or graduate teacher education program in the state. Applicants must be enrolled in or have completed a course in methods of teaching mathematics and have a GPA of 3.0 or higher. If they are a secondary education major, they must have completed 16 credits of mathematics; a statistics and a computer programming or technology application course must be part of their undergraduate or graduate program. If they are an elementary education major, their program must include 6 credits of mathematics; some statistics concepts and some computer/technology knowledge must be part of their undergraduate or graduate program. Selection is based on college performance, recommendations, and potential contributions to mathematics education in Wisconsin.
Financial data: The stipend is $2,000.
Duration: 1 year.
Number awarded: 1 each year.
Deadline: February of each year.

2648 ETHEL LEE HOOVER ELLIS SCHOLARSHIP

National Association of Negro Business and Professional Women's Clubs
Attn: Scholarship Committee
1806 New Hampshire Avenue, N.W.
Washington, DC 20009–3206
Phone: (202) 483–4206; Fax: (202) 462–7253;
Email: education@nanbpwc.org
Web: www.nanbpwc.org/scholarship_applications0.aspx
Summary: To provide financial assistance to African American women from designated southern states studying business at a college in any state.
Eligibility: Open to African Americans women who are residents of Alabama, Florida, Georgia, Mississippi, North Carolina, South Carolina, Tennessee, or West Virginia. Applicants must be enrolled at an accredited college or university in any state as a sophomore or junior. They must have a GPA of 3.0 or higher and be majoring in business. Along with their application, they must submit an essay, up to 750 words in length, on the topic, "Business and Community United." U.S. citizenship is required.
Financial data: A stipend is awarded (amount not specified).
Duration: 1 year.
Number awarded: 1 or more each year.
Deadline: February of each year.

2649 $ EUNICE FIORITO MEMORIAL SCHOLARSHIP

Summary: To provide financial assistance to undergraduate or graduate students who are blind and are interested in studying in a field of advocacy or service for persons with disabilities.
See Listing #1815.

2650 $$ EWI SCHOLARSHIP PROGRAM

Summary: To provide financial assistance for college to high school juniors with outstanding business and general leadership potential.
See Listing #238.

2651 F. GRANT WAITE, CPA, MEMORIAL SCHOLARSHIP

Massachusetts Society of Certified Public Accountants
Attn: MSCPA Educational Foundation
105 Chauncy Street, Tenth Floor
Boston, MA 02111
Phone: (617) 556–4000; (800) 392–6145; Fax: (617) 556–4126;
Email: info@mscpaonline.org
Web: www.cpatrack.com/scholarships
Summary: To provide financial assistance to college juniors and seniors from any state majoring in accounting at a Massachusetts college or university.
Eligibility: Open to residents of any state who are entering their junior or senior year of an accounting program at a college or university in Massachusetts. Applicants must be enrolled in school on a full–time basis. They must demonstrate superior academic standing, financial need, and an intention to seek a career in a public accounting firm in Massachusetts. Special consideration is given to married students with children.
Financial data: The stipend is $1,000.
Duration: 1 year.
Number awarded: 1 each year.
Deadline: March of each year.

2652 $$ FAITH C. AI LAI HEA SCHOLARSHIPS

Hawaii Education Association
Attn: Scholarship Committee
1953 South Beretania Street, Suite 5C
Honolulu, HI 96826
Phone: (808) 949–6657; (866) 653–9372; Fax: (808) 944–2032;
Email: hea.office@heaed.com
Web: www.heaed.com/HEA_Scholarships.html

Summary: To provide financial assistance to student teachers who are residents of Hawaii and enrolled in an undergraduate or post–baccalaureate program in the state.

Eligibility: Open to residents of Hawaii who are enrolled in a student teaching semester and seeking financial assistance so they will not need to be employed and can instead concentrate their efforts on their student teaching. Applicants must be enrolled full time in an undergraduate or post–baccalaureate program at an accredited institution of higher learning in Hawaii. They must have a GPA of 3.5 or higher. Along with their application, they must submit a 300–word personal statement on their reasons for choosing teaching as a career and their experiences in activities related to teaching. Selection is based on that statement (15 points), ability (10 points), financial need (15 points), and faculty recommendation (10 points).

Financial data: The stipend is $5,000.

Duration: 1 year.

Number awarded: Up to 3 each year.

Deadline: March of each year.

2653 $ FICPA EDUCATIONAL FOUNDATION SCHOLARSHIPS

Florida Institute of CPAs
Attn: FICPA Educational Foundation
325 West College Avenue
P.O. Box 5437
Tallahassee, FL 32314
Phone: (850) 224–2727, ext. 0; (800) 342–3197, ext. 0 (within FL); Fax: (850) 222–8190;
Email: wilsonb@ficpa.org
Web: www.ficpa.org/Content/EdFoundation/Scholarships.aspx

Summary: To provide financial assistance to upper–division students in Florida who are majoring in accounting at a school in the state.

Eligibility: Open to Florida residents who are fourth– or fifth–year accounting students enrolled full time in an accounting program at a Florida college or university. A faculty member in the accounting department of their college must nominate them. Applicants should be planning to sit for the C.P.A. exam and indicate a desire to work in Florida. Selection is based on financial need, educational achievement, and demonstrated professional, social, and charitable activities. U.S. citizenship or permanent resident status is required.

Financial data: The stipend is $2,000 or $1,000.

Duration: 1 year; recipients may reapply for 1 additional year of support.

Number awarded: Varies each year; recently, 71 of these scholarships were awarded.

Deadline: April of each year.

2654 $ FINANCIAL NEED SCHOLARSHIPS

Alabama Society of Certified Public Accountants
Attn: ASCPA Educational Foundation
1103 South Perry Street
P.O. Box 5000
Montgomery, AL 36103
Phone: (334) 834–7650; (800) 227–1711
Web: www.ascpa.org

Summary: To provide financial assistance to minority accounting students at colleges and universities in Alabama who can demonstrate financial need.

Eligibility: Open to residents of any state enrolled at least half time at colleges and universities in Alabama with at least 1 full year of school remaining. Applicants must have declared a major in accounting and have completed intermediate accounting courses. They must have a GPA of 3.0 or higher overall and in all accounting classes and be able to demonstrate financial need. Along with their application, they must submit a 25–word essay on why the scholarship is important to them. Preference is given to students who have a strong interest in a career as a C.P.A. in Alabama. U.S. citizenship or permanent resident status is required.

Financial data: The stipend is $2,500.

Duration: 1 year.

Number awarded: 2 each year.

Deadline: March of each year.

2655 $$ FLEET RESERVE ASSOCIATION AMERICANISM ESSAY CONTEST

Fleet Reserve Association
Attn: National Committee on Americanism–Patriotism
125 North West Street
Alexandria, VA 22314–2754
Phone: (703) 683–1400; (800) FRA–1924; Fax: (703) 549–6610;
Email: fra@fra.org
Web: www.fra.org/Content/fra/AboutFRA/EssayContest/default.cfm

Summary: To recognize and reward outstanding high school student essays on Americanism.

Eligibility: Open to students in grades 7–12. The contest is not restricted to children of the Fleet Reserve Association (FRA) or its Ladies Auxiliary. However, each entrant must be sponsored by an FRA member, branch, or Ladies Auxiliary unit. Essays must be on the annual theme (recently: "What Freedom of Speech Means to Me") and cannot exceed 350 words. Students may submit only 1 entry per year. Essays are first graded on the FRA branch level and the top essays from each branch are forwarded to the regional level. From there, the top essays in each region are sent to the national level to be graded.

Financial data: The Grand National Prize is a $10,000 U.S. savings bond. For each grade level, first place is a $5,000 U.S. savings bond, second place is a $3,000 U.S. savings bond, and third place is a $2,000 U.S. savings bond. Additional prizes are awarded to students winning at local branch and regional levels of competition.

Duration: The competition is held annually.

Number awarded: 1 Grand Prize and 18 grade–level prizes (3 for each grade from 7 through 12) are offered on the national level. Many smaller prizes are awarded on the local and regional levels.

Deadline: November of each year.

2656 FLORENCE MARGARET HARVEY MEMORIAL SCHOLARSHIP

Summary: To provide financial assistance to blind undergraduate and graduate students who wish to study in the field of rehabilitation and/or education of the blind.

See Listing #1834.

2657 $ FLORIDA BANKERS EDUCATIONAL FOUNDATION SCHOLARSHIP/LOANS

Florida Bankers Association
Attn: Florida Bankers Educational Foundation
1001 Thomasville Road, Suite 201
P.O. Box 1360
Tallahassee, FL 32302–1360
Phone: (850) 224–2265, ext. 139; Fax: (850) 224–2423;
Email: lnewton@floridabankers.com
Web: www.floridabankers.com

Summary: To provide money for college to upper–division and graduate students who are interested in preparing for a career in Florida banking.

Eligibility: Open to college juniors, seniors, and graduate students who are interested in preparing for a career in Florida banking. Applicants must be Florida residents, registered at 1 of 26 participating colleges or universities in the state, and taking banking–related classes. They must have a GPA of 2.5 or higher. Along with their application, they must submit a report signed by an authorized banker in the state who interviewed the applicant. Selection is based on interest in Florida banking, scholastic achievement, aptitude, ability, leadership, personality, and character.

Financial data: The amount of assistance is based on the number of semester hours the student has remaining until graduation. The maximum award is $1,500 per year or a total of $3,000 as an undergraduate and $3,000 as a graduate student. This is a loan forgiveness program. When recipients complete 1 year of continuous full–time employment in Florida banking, they are released from their financial obligation to repay the loan. Students who do not work for a Florida bank must repay the loan.

Duration: Up to 2 years as an undergraduate and another 2 years as a graduate student.

Number awarded: Several each year.

Deadline: February, May, August, or November of each year.

2658 $ FLORIDA EDUCATIONAL FACILITIES PLANNERS' ASSOCIATION ASSISTANTSHIP

Florida Educational Facilities Planners' Association, Inc.
c/o Bob Griffith, Selection Committee Chair
Florida International University

University Park, CSC 236
Miami, FL 33199
Phone: (305) 348–4090; Fax: (305) 348–4010;
Email: griffith@fiu.edu
Web: www.fefpa.org/assist.html
Summary: To provide financial assistance to undergraduate and graduate students in Florida who are preparing for a career in educational facilities management.
Eligibility: Open to full–time sophomores, juniors, seniors, and graduate students who are enrolled in a degree program at an accredited community college or university in Florida. Applicants must be Florida residents and majoring in facilities planning or in a field related to facilities planning with a GPA of 3.0 or higher. Part–time students with full–time employment are considered if they are working on a degree in a field related to facilities planning. Along with their application, they must submit transcripts, SAT scores, a 1–page essay on why they deserve this scholarship, and a completed appraisal form from their issuing professor, supervisor, or department head. Selection is based on financial need, academic excellence, community involvement, references, employment, the appraisal form, and the essay.
Financial data: The stipend is $3,000 per year, paid in 2 equal installments ($1,500 per semester). Funds are sent directly to the recipients.
Duration: 1 year.
Number awarded: 2 each year.
Deadline: May of each year.

2659 $$ FLORIDA REALTORS SCHOLARSHIP/ESSAY CONTEST

Florida Realtors
Attn: Media Center
7025 Augusta National Drive
P.O. Box 725025
Orlando, FL 32872–5025
Phone: (407) 438–1400, ext. 2326;
Email: media@floridarealtors.org
Web: media.floridarealtors.org/scholarshipinfo.htm
Summary: To recognize and reward, with college scholarships, high school seniors in Florida who submit outstanding essays on realtors.
Eligibility: Open to seniors graduating from high schools in Florida. Applicants must submit essays (up to 500 words in length) on the topic, "How Does a Realtor Professional Benefit the Community?" They must be planning to attend a college, university, technical school, or other institution of higher education in any state. Selection is based on understanding of the topic (30 points), clarity and effectiveness of style and organization (20 points), originality (30 points), ability to establish a coherent and convincing response to the topic (10 points), and adherence to rules (10 points).
Financial data: The winner in each of the sponsor's 13 districts receives a $1,000 scholarship. Those winners are then entered into a statewide competition, and the authors of the top 3 essays receive an additional scholarship of $5,000.
Duration: The competition is held annually.
Number awarded: 13 each year, of whom 3 are selected to receive additional scholarships.
Deadline: February of each year.

2660 FLORIDA STATE ASSOCIATION OF SUPERVISORS OF ELECTIONS SCHOLARSHIP

Florida State Association of Supervisors of Elections
225 South Adams Street, Suite 250
P.O. Box 350
Tallahassee, FL 32302
Phone: (850) 599–9120; Fax: (850) 561–6834–5185;
Email: melrod@bplawfirm.net
Web: www.myfloridaelections.org/index.php?id=21&Spanish=N
Summary: To provide financial assistance to Florida residents who are interested in majoring in business, political science, or communications in college.
Eligibility: Open to residents of Florida who have completed 2 years of undergraduate study and are enrolled or planning to enroll full time at a 4–year college or university in the state. Applicants must be majoring in business administration, political science/public administration, or journalism/mass communications and have a GPA of 2.0 or higher. They must be U.S. citizens registered to vote in Florida. Along with their application, they must submit 2 letters of recommendation, a resume of high school and/or college activities, and documentation of financial need. Applications should be submitted to the student's county Supervisor of Elections. Each county's supervisor will review the applications received and select 1 finalist to be sent to the association for consideration.
Financial data: The stipend is $1,200.
Duration: 1 year.
Number awarded: 1 each year.
Deadline: March of each year.

2661 $ FORD MOTOR COMPANY SCHOLARSHIPS

Summary: To provide financial assistance to Native American college students who are majoring in designated fields at mainstream colleges and universities, especially those in Michigan.
See Listing #1839.

2662 $ FORD MOTOR COMPANY TRIBAL COLLEGE SCHOLARSHIP

Summary: To provide financial assistance to Native Americans who are attending a Tribal College or University (TCU) and majoring in specified fields.
See Listing #1841.

2663 $$ FORECLOSURE.COM SCHOLARSHIP PROGRAM

Active Data Group, Inc.
Attn: Foreclosure.com
1095 Broken South Parkway, N.W., Suite 200
Boca Raton, FL 33487
Phone: (561) 988–9669, ext. 7397;
Email: scholarship@foreclosure.com
Web: www.foreclosure.com/scholarship
Summary: To recognize and reward, with scholarships for continuing study, college students who submit outstanding essays related to the foreclosure of real estate.
Eligibility: Open to residents of the 50 United States, the U.S. territories, the District of Columbia, and Puerto Rico who are currently enrolled at an accredited postsecondary institution of higher learning. Applicants must submit an essay of 800 to 2,000 words on a topic that relates to foreclosure of real estate; recently, students were asked to assume that they have acquired $150,000 in cash for a distressed real estate purchase and then to outline a detailed strategy that ensures the maximum return on investment (in terms of financial profit, personal satisfaction, or both). Selection is based on writing ability (25%), creativity (25%), originality (25%), and overall excellence (25%).
Financial data: The winner receives a top prize of $5,000 and the second–through fifth–place winners receive prizes of $1,000 each. Funds are paid directly to the winners' college, university, or trade school.
Duration: The competition is held annually.
Number awarded: 5 each year: 1 top prize and 4 other prizes.
Deadline: November of each year.

2664 FRANCIS A. HERZOG SCHOLARSHIP

Griffith Insurance Education Foundation
623 High Street
Worthington, OH 43085
Phone: (614) 880–9870; Fax: (614) 880–9872;
Email: info@griffithfoundation.org
Web: www.griffithfoundation.org/higher–ed/scholarships
Summary: To provide financial assistance to students from Ohio working on an undergraduate degree in a field related to insurance.
Eligibility: Open to U.S. citizens who are either Ohio residents attending a college or university in any state or residents of other states attending a college or university in Ohio. Applicants must be full–time juniors or seniors with a GPA of 2.5 or higher and enrolled in an insurance, risk management, actuarial science, business, computer science, finance, or other insurance–related program. They must be planning to enter an insurance–related field after graduation. Preference is given to 1) children, stepchildren, or legally adopted children of members of Independent Insurance Agents of Ohio (Ohio Big I); and 2) students recommended by an Ohio Big I member or retiree. Selection is based on academic achievement, extracurricular activities and honors, work experience, 3 letters of recommendation, and financial need.
Financial data: The stipend is $1,000.
Duration: 1 year.
Number awarded: 1 each year.
Deadline: March of each year.

2665 $$ FRANK L. GREATHOUSE GOVERNMENT ACCOUNTING SCHOLARSHIP

Government Finance Officers Association
Attn: Scholarship Committee
203 North LaSalle Street, Suite 2700
Chicago, IL 60601–1210
Phone: (312) 977–9700; Fax: (312) 977–4806
Web: www.gfoa.org

Summary: To provide financial assistance to undergraduate and graduate students who are preparing for a career in public accounting.

Eligibility: Open to 1) undergraduates who are completing at least their junior year of college; and 2) graduate students. Applicants must be enrolled full time in an accounting program and preparing for a career in state and local government finance. They must be citizens or permanent residents of the United States or Canada and able to provide a letter of recommendation from their academic adviser or the chair of their accounting program. Along with their application, they must submit a statement of their proposed career plan in state and local government finance and, if applicable, a plan of graduate study. Selection is based on that statement, strength of past course work and present plan of study, letters of recommendation, and undergraduate and graduate GPA. Financial need is not considered.

Financial data: The stipend is $5,000.

Duration: 1 year.

Number awarded: 1 each year.

Deadline: February of each year.

2666 $$ FREEDOM IN ACADEMIA ESSAY CONTEST

Foundation for Individual Rights in Education
601 Walnut Street, Suite 510
Philadelphia, PA 19106
Phone: (215) 717–FIRE; Fax: (215) 717–3440;
Email: fire@thefire.org
Web: www.thefire.org/takeaction/students/essaycontest

Summary: To recognize and reward, with college scholarships, high school seniors who submit outstanding essays on individual rights in colleges and universities.

Eligibility: Open to graduating high school seniors who plan to attend a college or university. Applicants are invited to view 2 online videos describing incidents in which the sponsoring organization defended free speech on particular campuses. Based on those videos, they write an essay of 800 to 1,000 words in which they discuss the issues involved and explain how the universities violated constitutional rights of free expression. The essay should focus on why such practices are incompatible with higher education and why free speech is important in our nation's colleges and universities.

Financial data: Prizes, all in the form of college scholarships, are $5,000 for first place, $2,500 for second place, or $1,000 for runners–up.

Duration: The contest is held annually.

Number awarded: 7 each year: 1 first place, 1 second place, and 5 runners–up.

Deadline: November of each year.

2667 $$ FRIENDS OF OREGON STUDENTS PROGRAM

Oregon Student Access Commission
Attn: Grants and Scholarships Division
1500 Valley River Drive, Suite 100
Eugene, OR 97401–2146
Phone: (541) 687–7395; (800) 452–8807, ext. 7395; Fax: (541) 687–7414; TDD: (800) 735–2900;
Email: awardinfo@osac.state.or.us
Web: www.oregonstudentaid.gov/scholarships.aspx

Summary: To provide financial assistance to students in Oregon who are employed while working on an undergraduate or graduate degree in teaching at a school in any state.

Eligibility: Open to residents of Oregon who are working and will continue to work at least 20 hours per week while enrolled as an undergraduate or graduate student at a 4–year college or university in any state at least half time. Applicants must be interested in preparing for a career in teaching. They must be able to demonstrate a cumulative GPA of 2.5 or higher and volunteer or work experience relevant to their chosen profession. Preference is given to applicants who are 1) nontraditional students (e.g., older, returning, single parents); or 2) the first generation in their family to attend college. Along with their application, they must submit essays and letters of reference on how they balance school, work, and personal life as well as their experiences in overcoming obstacles. Selection is based on work experience, community service and volunteer activities, responses to essay questions, letters of reference, interviews, and financial need; academic promise (as indicated by GPA and SAT/ACT scores) is also considered.

Financial data: Stipends range from $3,000 to $5,000 per year.

Duration: 1 year; may be renewed.

Number awarded: Varies each year; recently, 28 of these scholarships were awarded.

Deadline: February of each year.

2668 GAIL BURNS–SMITH "DARE TO DREAM" SCHOLARSHIPS

Hartford Foundation for Public Giving
Attn: Donor Services Officer
10 Columbus Boulevard, Eighth Floor
Hartford, CT 06106
Phone: (860) 548–1888; Fax: (860) 524–8346;
Email: scholarships@hfpg.org
Web: www.hfpgscholarships.org/Scholarships/Home/tabid/305/Default.aspx

Summary: To provide financial assistance to residents of Connecticut who have participated in sexual violence prevention activities and are interested in attending college in any state to continue their involvement in the field.

Eligibility: Open to Connecticut residents who are attending a high school or college in the state. Applicants must have paid or volunteer work experience in the field of women's issues or sexual violence prevention or advocacy. They must be planning to continue work in the field of sexual violence prevention or advocacy.

Financial data: The stipend is $1,000.

Duration: 1 year.

Number awarded: 1 each year.

Deadline: February of each year.

2669 $$ GATES MILLENNIUM SCHOLARS PROGRAM

Summary: To provide financial assistance to outstanding low–income minority students, particularly those interested in majoring in specific fields in college.

See Listing #1865.

2670 $ G.C. MORRIS/PAUL RUPP MEMORIAL EDUCATIONAL TRUST

Summary: To provide financial assistance to residents of designated states who are interested in attending college or technical school in any state to prepare for a career in the automotive aftermarket industry.

See Listing #1866.

2671 $ GENERAL JOHN A. WICKHAM SCHOLARSHIPS

Summary: To provide financial assistance to undergraduate students who are working full time on a degree in engineering or the sciences.

See Listing #1871.

2672 GENERATIONS FOR PEACE ESSAY CONTEST

Generations for Peace
c/o St. James Lutheran Church
1315 S.W. Park Avenue
Portland, OR 97201
Phone: (503) 222–2194
Web: stjamespdx.org

Summary: To recognize and reward, with college scholarships, outstanding essays on the general subject of peace written by high school students.

Eligibility: Open to all 11th and 12th grade students who are citizens and residents of the United States. Each year, the exact subject of the essay changes, but it always deals with the theme of peace. Essays may not be more than 750 words.

Financial data: The first–place essay receives a $2,000 college scholarship. Funds are paid directly to the winner's school.

Duration: The competition is held annually.

Number awarded: 2 each year.

Deadline: April of each year.

2673 GEORGE AND DONNA NIGH PUBLIC SERVICE SCHOLARSHIP

Oklahoma State Regents for Higher Education
Attn: Director of Scholarship and Grant Programs
655 Research Parkway, Suite 200
P.O. Box 108850
Oklahoma City, OK 73101–8850
Phone: (405) 225–9239; (800) 858–1840; Fax: (405) 225–9230;
Email: studentinfo@osrhe.edu
Web: www.okcollegestart.org

Summary: To provide financial assistance to residents in Oklahoma who are interested in attending college in the state to prepare for a career in public service.

Eligibility: Open to residents of Oklahoma who are enrolled full time in an undergraduate program at a public or private college or university in the state. Applicants must be enrolled in a degree program leading to a career in public service (as determined by the institution). Selection is based on academic achievement, including GPA, class rank, national awards, honors, teachers' recommendations, and participation in extracurricular activities. Each participating college or university may nominate 1 student each year.

Financial data: The stipend is $1,000.

Duration: 1 year; nonrenewable.

Number awarded: Varies each year.

Deadline: Deadline not specified.

2674 GEORGE AND LEOLA SMITH AWARD

Summary: To provide financial assistance to high school seniors who are interested in studying nursing or business in college.

See Listing #1874.

2675 $$ GEORGE D. MILLER SCHOLARSHIP

Summary: To provide financial assistance to undergraduate and graduate students enrolled in fire service or public administration programs.

See Listing #1877.

2676 GEORGE E. REGER MEMORIAL SCHOLARSHIP

West Virginia Funeral Directors Association
Attn: Scholarship Fund
400 Allen Drive, Suite 20
Charleston, WV 25302
Phone: (304) 345–4711; (855) 345–4711 (within WV); Fax: (304) 346–6416;
Email: info@wvfda.org
Web: www.wvfda.org/aws/WVFDA/pt/sp/scholarships

Summary: To provide financial assistance to residents of West Virginia who are currently enrolled in a mortuary school.

Eligibility: Open to students who have completed at least half of an accredited mortuary science program at a school in any state and have a GPA of 2.5 or higher. Applicants must have been residents of West Virginia for at least 2 years. Along with their application, they must submit a letter of recommendation from a member of the funeral profession. Selection is based on academic performance, extracurricular and/or community involvement, and financial need.

Financial data: The stipend is $1,000.

Duration: 1 year.

Number awarded: 1 each year.

Deadline: March of each year.

2677 GEORGE L. PATT SCHOLARSHIP

Illinois Association of Realtors
Attn: Illinois Real Estate Educational Foundation
522 South Fifth Street
P.O. Box 2607
Springfield, IL 62708
Phone: (866) 854–REEF; Fax: (217) 241–9935;
Email: lclayton@iar.org
Web: www.ilreef.org/Scholarships.htm

Summary: To provide financial assistance to veterans in Illinois who are preparing for a career in real estate at a college or university in the state.

Eligibility: Open to U.S. veterans in Illinois who are either 1) working on an undergraduate college or university degree in the field of real estate; or 2) studying real estate administration to establish themselves as an association executive in a realtor organization. Applicants must be Illinois residents studying at a school in the state. Along with their application, they must submit a 1,000–word statement of their general activities and intellectual interests, employment (if any), contemplated line of study, and career they expect to follow. Selection is based on the applicant's record of military service, record of academic achievement, course of study and career goals, references and recommendations, and financial need. Finalists are interviewed.

Financial data: The stipend is $1,000.

Duration: 1 year.

Number awarded: 1 each year.

Deadline: March of each year.

2678 GEORGE PULAKOS SCHOLARSHIP

New Mexico Society of Certified Public Accountants
Attn: Scholarships in Accounting
3400 Menaul Boulevard, N.E.
Albuquerque, NM 87107
Phone: (505) 246–1699; (800) 926–2522; Fax: (505) 246–1686;
Email: corrine@nmscpa.org
Web: www.nmscpa.org/scholarships_application.html

Summary: To provide financial assistance to accounting students at New Mexico universities and colleges.

Eligibility: Open to full–time students at New Mexico colleges and universities who have completed 12 semester hours in accounting, are currently enrolled in 6 or more accounting hours, have completed 75 hours overall, and have a cumulative GPA of 3.0 or higher. Applicants must submit an essay or letter that covers 1) academic achievements in college; 2) the accounting courses in which they are currently enrolled or have completed; 3) extracurricular activities, employment, volunteer service, and any other pertinent activities; 4) reasons for applying for the scholarship, including matters related to financial need; and 5) career objectives and goals in accounting.

Financial data: A stipend is awarded (amount not specified).

Duration: 1 year; may be renewed 2 additional years.

Number awarded: 1 each year.

Deadline: May of each year.

2679 GEORGIA AFFILIATE SCHOLARSHIP

American Woman's Society of Certified Public Accountants–Georgia Affiliate
c/o Amy Knowles–Jones, Scholarship Committee
222 Piedmont Avenue N.E.
Atlanta, GA 30308
Phone: (404) 653–1242; Fax: (404) 653–1575;
Email: aknowles–jones@oxfordinc.com
Web: www.awscpa.org/affiliate_scholarships/georgia.html

Summary: To provide financial assistance to women from any state who are working on an undergraduate or graduate degree in accounting at a college or university in Georgia.

Eligibility: Open to women from any state who are enrolled in a Georgia college or university. Applicants must have completed or be currently enrolled in a course in intermediate accounting II. Along with their application, they must submit a 100–word essay on why they are interested in receiving this scholarship. Financial need is not considered in the selection process.

Financial data: The stipend is $1,000.

Duration: 1 year.

Number awarded: 1 each year.

Deadline: March of each year.

2680 GEORGIA FISCAL MANAGEMENT COUNCIL SCHOLARSHIPS

Georgia Fiscal Management Council
c/o Kendra Mitchell, Scholarship Committee Chair
House Budget Office
Coverdell Legislative Office Building
18 Capitol Square, Room 412
Atlanta, GA 30334
Phone: (404) 656–1780
Web: georgiafmc.com/?page_id=300

Summary: To provide financial assistance to upper–division and graduate students at universities in Georgia majoring in a finance–related field.

Eligibility: Open to rising seniors or graduate students at universities in Georgia who are enrolled full or part time in the following fields of study: government accounting, public administration, or finance. Applicants must be preparing for a career in public service related to fiscal management or administration. They must have a GPA of 3.0 or higher overall and in their major. Along with their application, they must submit a 2–page essay on how they envision using their degree to benefit the state of Georgia, including why they want to prepare for a career in state government and their plans after graduation. Financial need is not considered in the selection process.

Financial data: The stipend is $1,000.

Duration: 1 year.

Number awarded: 2 each year.

Deadline: June of each year.

2681 GEORGIA HEALTH INFORMATION MANAGEMENT ASSOCIATION SCHOLARSHIPS

Georgia Health Information Management Association
Attn: Executive Director
12 Club Drive
Sapphire, NC 28774
Phone: (828) 883–5613; Fax: (828) 883–5613;
Email: centraloffice@ghima.org
Web: www.ghima.org/scholarshipapplication.asp

Summary: To provide financial assistance to residents of Georgia working on an undergraduate or graduate degree in health information management at a school in any state.

Eligibility: Open to residents of Georgia currently working on an associate, bachelor's, or master's degree in health information management at a CAHIM–accredited college or university in any state. Applicants must have a GPA of 3.0 or higher and a record of involvement in such activities as attendance at health information management (HIM) association meetings, service on HIM association committees, employment in an HIM department, participation in school activities, organization of a major class endeavor, or community work. Along with their application, they must submit a transcript, 2 letters of recommendation from HIM professionals, and a resume that includes employment history, school and professional activities and memberships, and community involvement. Selection is based on academic achievement, demonstrated leadership, financial need, and potential as a HIM professional.

Financial data: The stipend is $1,000 for students working on a bachelor's or master's degree or $500 for students working on an associate degree.

Duration: 1 year.

Number awarded: 3 each year: 1 for a bachelor's or master's degree student and 2 for associate degree students.

Deadline: June of each year.

2682 GEORGIA PTA EDUCATIONAL SCHOLARSHIPS

Georgia PTA
Attn: Scholarship Committee
114 Baker Street, N.E.
Atlanta, GA 30308–3366
Phone: (404) 659–0214; Fax: (404) 525–0210;
Email: gapta@bellsouth.net
Web: www.georgiapta.org/leadership–grants–scholarships.html

Summary: To provide financial assistance to high school seniors in Georgia who are interested in attending college in the state to prepare for a career in a youth–related field.

Eligibility: Open to seniors graduating from a Georgia high school with a PTA/PTSA chapter that is in good standing with the Georgia PTA. Applicants must be interested in attending a college or university in the state to prepare to work in a youth–related field. Selection is based on character, academic record, and financial need.

Financial data: Stipends range from $1,000 to $1,500.

Duration: 1 year; nonrenewable.

Number awarded: Varies each year.

Deadline: March of each year.

2683 $$ GEORGIA SOCIETY OF CPAS SCHOLARSHIP PROGRAM

Georgia Society of CPAs
Attn: Educational Foundation
3353 Peachtree Road, N.E., Suite 400
Atlanta, GA 30326–1414
Phone: (404) 231–8676; (800) 330–8889, ext. 2956; Fax: (404) 237–1291;
Email: nhamada@gscpa.org
Web: www.gscpa.org

Summary: To provide financial assistance to upper–division and graduate students who are majoring in accounting in Georgia.

Eligibility: Open to residents of Georgia who have demonstrated a commitment to a career in accounting. Applicants must be 1) rising junior or senior undergraduate accounting majors; or 2) graduate students working on a master's degree in accounting or business administration. They must be enrolled in an accredited public or private college or university in Georgia with a GPA of 3.0 or higher either overall or in their accounting courses. Along with their application, they must submit documentation of financial need, transcripts, a resume, and a 250–word essay on their personal career goals and how this scholarship will help them attain those goals.

Financial data: Stipends range from $500 to $5,000.

Duration: 1 year.

Number awarded: Varies each year; recently, 49 of these scholarships were awarded: 4 at $5,000, 2 at $4,000, 2 at $3,000, 2 at $2,500, 12 at $2,000, 1 at $1,740, 15 at $1,500, 1 at $1,250, 9 at $1,000, and 1 at $500.

Deadline: March of each year.

2684 GERALD M. ROBBINS, SR. SCHOLARSHIP AWARD

Louisiana Funeral Directors Association
Attn: Scholarship Committee
P.O. Box 82531
Baton Rouge, LA 70884
Phone: (225) 767–7640; Fax: (225) 767–7648;
Email: lfda@lfdaweb.org
Web: www.lfdaweb.org/pages/default.asp?p1=237

Summary: To provide financial assistance to residents of Louisiana who are attending a college of mortuary science in any state.

Eligibility: Open to students currently enrolled at a college of mortuary science in any state who have been residents of Louisiana for at least 2 years. Applicants must have earned a GPA of 2.5 or higher while in high school and be able to meet the requirements of the Louisiana State Board of Embalmer and Funeral Directors. Along with their application, they must submit 3 letters of recommendation, high school transcripts that include ACT scores, and a 250–word essay that describes the processes used and the experiences they underwent in their decision to enter the funeral service profession. Selection is based on academic excellence.

Financial data: A stipend is awarded (amount not specified).

Duration: 1 year; may be renewed, provided the recipient remains enrolled full time and maintains a GPA of 2.5 or higher.

Number awarded: 1 or more each year.

Deadline: March of each year.

2685 $$ GOLDEN APPLE SCHOLARS OF ILLINOIS

Golden Apple Foundation
Attn: Scholars Program
8 South Michigan Avenue, Suite 700
Chicago, IL 60603–3463
Phone: (312) 407–0006; Fax: (312) 407–0344;
Email: info@goldenapple.org
Web: www.goldenapple.org/becoming_a_scholar/30.php

Summary: To provide funding to high school seniors in Illinois who wish to study education at an Illinois college and teach in the state.

Eligibility: Open to high school seniors at schools in Illinois. Students must be nominated by a teacher, principal, guidance counselor, or other non–family adult; self–nominations are also accepted. Nominees must be committed to teaching as a profession and must be interested in attending 1 of 53 designated colleges and universities in Illinois. A limited number of openings are also available to sophomores at those designated Illinois institutions. The program strongly encourages nomination of prospective teachers for which there is currently a shortage, especially minority and bilingual teachers. Selection is based on 7 essays included on the application, ACT scores and transcripts, letters of reference, and an interview.

Financial data: Scholars receive a scholarship/loan of $2,500 per year for their freshman and sophomore year and $5,000 per year for their junior and senior year. They also receive a stipend of $2,000 per year for participating in a summer teaching internship. If they complete a bachelor's degree and teach for 5 years in an Illinois school of need, the loan is forgiven. Schools of need are defined as those either having Chapter I status by the U.S. Department of Education or having mediocre to poor PSAE or ISAT scores.

Duration: 4 years, provided the recipient maintains a GPA of 2.0 or higher during the freshman year and 2.5 or higher in subsequent years. Students who enter the program as sophomores receive 2 years of support.

Number awarded: Varies each year; recently, 110 of these scholarships were awarded.

Deadline: Nominations must be submitted by November of each year.

2686 $$ GOLDMAN SACHS SCHOLARSHIP FOR EXCELLENCE

Goldman Sachs
Attn: Human Capital Management
30 Hudson Street, 34th Floor
Jersey City, NJ 07302
Phone: (212) 902–1000;
Email: Julie.Mantilla@gs.com
Web: www2.goldmansachs.com/careers/our–firm/diversity/index.html

Summary: To provide financial assistance and work experience to underrepresented minority students preparing for a career in the financial services industry.

Eligibility: Open to undergraduate students of Black, Latino, or Native American heritage. Applicants must be entering their sophomore or junior year with a GPA of 3.4 or higher. Students with all majors and disciplines are encouraged to apply, but they must be able to demonstrate an interest in the financial services industry. Along with their application, they must submit 2 essays of 500 words or fewer on the following topics: 1) why they are interested in the financial services industry; and 2) how they have demonstrated team–oriented leadership through their involvement with a campus–based or community–based organization. Selection is based on academic achievement, interest in the financial services industry, community involvement, and demonstrated leadership and teamwork capabilities.

Financial data: Sophomores receive a stipend of $5,000, a summer internship at Goldman Sachs, an opportunity to receive a second award upon successful completion of the internship, and an offer to return for a second summer internship. Juniors receive a stipend of $10,000 and a summer internship at Goldman Sachs.

Duration: Up to 2 years.

Number awarded: 1 or more each year.

Deadline: December of each year.

2687 $ GRANT M. MACK MEMORIAL SCHOLARSHIP

American Council of the Blind
Attn: Coordinator, Scholarship Program
2200 Wilson Boulevard, Suite 650
Arlington, VA 22201
Phone: (202) 467–5081; (800) 424–8666; Fax: (703) 465–5085;
Email: info@acb.org
Web: www.acb.org/scholarship

Summary: To provide financial assistance to blind students who are working on an undergraduate or graduate degree in business or management.

Eligibility: Open to undergraduate and graduate students working on a degree in business or management. Applicants must submit verification of legal blindness in both eyes; SAT, ACT, GMAT, or similar scores; information on extracurricular activities (including involvement in the American Council of the Blind); employment record; and a 500–word autobiographical sketch that includes their personal goals, strengths, weaknesses, hobbies, honors, achievements, and reasons for choice of field or courses of study. A cumulative GPA of 3.3 or higher is generally required. Financial need is not considered in the selection process. U.S. citizenship or permanent resident status is required.

Financial data: The stipend is $2,000.

Duration: 1 year.

Number awarded: 1 each year.

Deadline: February of each year.

2688 $ GREAT FALLS ADVERTISING FEDERATION HIGH SCHOOL MARKETING/COMMUNICATION SCHOLARSHIP

Great Falls Advertising Federation
Attn: Advertising Scholarship Committee
609 Tenth Avenue South, Suite B
P.O. Box 634
Great Falls, MT 59403
Phone: (406) 761–6453; (800) 803–3351; Fax: (406) 453–1128;
Email: gfaf@gfaf.com
Web: www.gfaf.com/Scholarships.html

Summary: To provide financial assistance to high school seniors in Montana planning to attend college in any state to prepare for a career in a field related to marketing.

Eligibility: Open to seniors graduating from high schools in Montana who plan to enroll at a postsecondary educational or training program in any state. Applicants must intend to pursue a program of study that will prepare them for a career in advertising, communications, marketing, or a related field. Along with their application, they must submit 1) a resume that includes work experience, volunteer experience, extracurricular activities, and honors and awards; 2) letters of recommendation; and 3) a hypothetical marketing plan that they have developed. Financial need is not considered in the selection process.

Financial data: The stipend is $2,000.

Duration: 1 year.

Number awarded: 1 each year.

Deadline: February of each year.

2689 $$ GREATER RESEARCH OPPORTUNITIES (GRO) FELLOWSHIPS FOR UNDERGRADUATE ENVIRONMENTAL STUDY

Summary: To provide financial assistance and summer internships to undergraduates who are enrolled at colleges and universities that receive limited federal funding and who are interested in majoring in fields related to the environment.

See Listing #1895.

2690 H. JAMES HARRINGTON SCHOLARSHIPS

Summary: To provide financial assistance to students at all levels interested working on a degree in a field related to quality.

See Listing #1901.

2691 $ HAROLD AND MARIA RANSBURG AMERICAN PATRIOT SCHOLARSHIPS

Association of Former Intelligence Officers
Attn: Scholarships Committee
6723 Whittier Avenue, Suite 200
McLean, VA 22101–4533
Phone: (703) 790–0320; Fax: (703) 991–1278;
Email: afio@afio.com
Web: www.afio.com/13_scholarships.htm

Summary: To provide financial assistance to undergraduate and graduate students who have a career interest in intelligence and national security.

Eligibility: Open to undergraduates who are entering their sophomore or junior year and graduate students who apply in their senior undergraduate year or first graduate year. Applicants must share the sponsor's educational mission on behalf of "national security, patriotism, and loyalty to the constitution." They must be working on a degree in intelligence, foreign affairs, and/or national security. Along with their application, they must submit a cover letter that explains their need for assistance, their career goals and dreams, and their views of U.S. world standing and its intelligence community. Selection is based on merit, character, estimated future potential, background, and relevance of their studies to the full spectrum of national security interests and career ambitions. U.S. citizenship is required.

Financial data: The stipend is $2,000.

Duration: 1 year.

Number awarded: 8 each year.

Deadline: June of each year.

2692 HAROLD BETTINGER MEMORIAL SCHOLARSHIP

Summary: To provide financial assistance to undergraduate and graduate students interested in the business of horticulture.

See Listing #1902.

2693 HARRIET IRSAY SCHOLARSHIP GRANT

Summary: To provide financial assistance to Polish American and other students interested in working on an undergraduate or graduate degree in selected fields.

See Listing #1253.

2694 $ HARRIET SIMMONS SCHOLARSHIP

Oregon Student Access Commission
Attn: Grants and Scholarships Division
1500 Valley River Drive, Suite 100
Eugene, OR 97401–2146
Phone: (541) 687–7395; (800) 452–8807, ext. 7395; Fax: (541) 687–7414; TDD: (800) 735–2900;
Email: awardinfo@osac.state.or.us
Web: www.oregonstudentaid.gov/scholarships.aspx

Summary: To provide financial assistance to Oregon residents majoring in education on the undergraduate or graduate level at a school in the state.
Eligibility: Open to residents of Oregon who are U.S. citizens or permanent residents. Applicants must be college seniors or fifth–year students majoring in elementary or secondary education, or graduate students in their fifth year working on an elementary or secondary certificate. They must be enrolled at a school in the state. Full–time enrollment and financial need are required.
Financial data: Stipends for scholarships offered by the Oregon Student Access Commission (OSAC) range from $200 to $10,000 but recently averaged $2,300.
Duration: 1 year; nonrenewable.
Number awarded: 1 or more each year.
Deadline: February of each year.

2695 $ HASSON/NEWMAN MEMORIAL SCHOLARSHIP

Oregon Collectors Association, Inc.
Attn: ORCA Scholarship Fund
1814 N.E. 123rd Avenue
Vancouver, WA 98684
Phone: (503) 201–0858; Fax: (360) 882–3622;
Email: dcj@PandHBilling.com
Web: www.orcascholarshipfund.com/oc
Summary: To recognize and reward, with scholarships for college study in Oregon of any subject, high school seniors in the state who submit essays related to credit.
Eligibility: Open to seniors graduating from high schools in Oregon who submit an essay of 1,000 to 1,500 word entitled "Credit in the 21st Century." Children and grandchildren of owners and officers of collection agencies registered in Oregon are not eligible. Applicants must be planning to enroll full time at a college, university, or vocational school in Oregon.
Financial data: Awards are $3,000 for first place, $2,000 for second, or $1,000 for third. Funds must be used for tuition and other educational expenses at a college or vocational school in Oregon.
Duration: The award, presented annually, may not be renewed.
Number awarded: 3 each year.
Deadline: February of each year.

2696 $ HEIDELBERG USA SCHOLARSHIP

Summary: To provide financial assistance to undergraduate and graduate students from any country interested in preparing for a career in document management and graphic communications, especially those who have experience with printing equipment.
See Listing #1261.

2697 $ HERMAN J. NEAL SCHOLARSHIP PROGRAM

Illinois CPA Society
Attn: CPA Endowment Fund of Illinois
550 West Jackson, Suite 900
Chicago, Il 60661–5716
Phone: (312) 993–0407; (800) 993–0407 (within IL); Fax: (312) 993–9954
Web: www.icpas.org/hc–students.aspx?id=2724
Summary: To provide financial assistance to African American residents of Illinois enrolled as upper–division or graduate students in accounting at a college or university in the state.
Eligibility: Open to African American residents of Illinois enrolled as juniors, seniors, or graduate student at a college or university in the state. Applicants must be studying accounting and have a GPA of 3.0 or higher. They must be able to demonstrate a commitment to becoming a C.P.A. and financial need. U.S. citizenship or permanent resident status is required.
Financial data: The maximum stipend is $4,000 for payment of tuition and fees. Awards include up to $500 in expenses for books and required classroom materials.
Duration: 1 year.
Number awarded: Varies each year; recently, 4 of these scholarships were awarded.
Deadline: March of each year.

2698 $ HIROSHI AND BARBARA KIM YAMASHITA HEA SCHOLARSHIP

Hawaii Education Association
Attn: Scholarship Committee
1953 South Beretania Street, Suite 5C
Honolulu, HI 96826
Phone: (808) 949–6657; (866) 653–9372; Fax: (808) 944–2032;
Email: hea.office@heaed.com
Web: www.heaed.com/HEA_Scholarships.html
Summary: To provide financial assistance to undergraduate education majors who plan to teach in Hawaii public schools.
Eligibility: Open to full–time undergraduate students majoring in education who have a GPA of 3.2 or higher. Applicants must be planning to teach in a Hawaii public school at the elementary or secondary level. Along with their application, they must submit a 300–word personal statement on their reasons for selecting education as a major, including their future plans, employment experience, extracurricular activities, and community service. Selection is based on that statement (5 points), college transcript (10 points), financial need (10 points), and recommendations (5 points).
Financial data: The stipend is $2,000, paid in 2 equal installments.
Duration: 1 year.
Number awarded: 1 each year.
Deadline: March of each year.

2699 HOLLAND AMERICA LINE UNDERGRADUATE SCHOLARSHIP

Tourism Cares
Attn: Academic Scholarship Program
275 Turnpike Street, Suite 307
Canton, MA 02021
Phone: (781) 821–5990; Fax: (781) 821–8949;
Email: scholarships@tourismcares.org
Web: www.tourismcares.org
Summary: To provide financial assistance to undergraduate students working on a degree in travel and tourism or hospitality–related fields.
Eligibility: Open to U.S. and Canadian citizens and permanent residents who are 1) entering the second year at an accredited 2–year college; or 2) entering their junior or senior year at an accredited 4–year college or university. Applicants must be enrolled full or part time in a travel and tourism or hospitality–related program of study. They must have a GPA of 3.0 or higher. Along with their application, they must submit an essay on their expectations for the future of the cruise industry. Financial need is not considered in the selection process.
Financial data: The stipend is $1,500.
Duration: 1 year.
Number awarded: 1 each year.
Deadline: March of each year.

2700 $ HONORABLE ERNESTINE WASHINGTON LIBRARY SCIENCE/ENGLISH LANGUAGE ARTS SCHOLARSHIP

Summary: To provide financial assistance to high school seniors of African American or Caribbean heritage who plan to study a field related to library science or English language arts in college.
See Listing #1268.

2701 $ HORIZONS–MICHIGAN SCHOLARSHIP

Summary: To provide financial assistance to women in Michigan who are upper–division or graduate students working on a degree related to national defense.
See Listing #1915.

2702 $ HSMAI FOUNDATION SCHOLARSHIPS

Hospitality Sales and Marketing Association International
Attn: HSMAI Foundation
1760 Old Meadow Road, Suite 500
McLean, VA 22102
Phone: (703) 506–3280; Fax: (703) 506–3266;
Email: info@hsmai.org
Web: www.hsmai.org/Resources/scholarships.cfm
Summary: To provide financial assistance to undergraduate and graduate students who are preparing for a career in hospitality sales and marketing.
Eligibility: Open to students working full or part time on an associate, bachelor's, or graduate degree in hospitality sales and marketing or revenue management and preparing for a career in the field. Along with their application, they must submit 3 essays: their interest in the hospitality industry and their career goals, the personal characteristics that will enable them to succeed in reaching those goals, and a situation in which they faced a challenge or were in

a leadership role and how they dealt with the situation. Selection is based on the essays, industry–related work experience, GPA, extracurricular involvement, 2 letters of recommendation, and involvement in the Hospitality Sales and Marketing Association International (HSMAI).

Financial data: The stipend is $2,000 for baccalaureate/graduate degree students or $500 for associate degree students.

Duration: 1 year.

Number awarded: Varies each year; recently, 5 of these scholarships were awarded.

Deadline: June of each year.

2703 $$ HUMANE STUDIES FELLOWSHIPS

Summary: To provide financial assistance to undergraduate and graduate students in the United States or abroad who intend to prepare for scholarly careers and have demonstrated an interest in classical liberal principles.

See Listing #1272.

2704 IDAHO ASSOCIATION OF EDUCATIONAL OFFICE PROFESSIONALS STUDENT SCHOLARSHIP

Idaho Association of Educational Office Professionals
c/o Kelley Davis, Scholarship Committee
1910 University Drive
Boise, ID 83725–1840
Web: www.idahoaeop.org/programs_services.htm

Summary: To provide financial assistance to high school seniors in Idaho who plan to attend college in any state to study an office–related business program.

Eligibility: Open to seniors graduating from high schools in Idaho who have completed 2 or more business education classes from among the following: computer classes, keyboarding, accounting, office practices, and/or bookkeeping. Applicants must be planning to enroll at a 2– or 4–year college, university, business college, or vocational/technical school in any state. They must be recommended by a local affiliate of the sponsoring organization. Along with their application, they must submit an autobiographical essay on their educational goals, chosen career, plan for accomplishment, and specific reasons why they need financial aid for college. Selection is based on that essay (40%), academic record (40%), extracurricular and other activities (10%), and recommendations (10%).

Financial data: The stipend is $1,000.

Duration: 1 year; nonrenewable.

Number awarded: 1 each year.

Deadline: January of each year.

2705 IDAHO EDUCATION INCENTIVE LOAN FORGIVENESS

Summary: To provide funding to Idaho students who wish to prepare for a teaching or nursing career in Idaho.

See Listing #1926.

2706 IDAHO SOCIETY OF CPAS SCHOLARSHIPS

Idaho Community Foundation
Attn: Scholarship Coordinator
210 West State Street
Boise, ID 83702
Phone: (208) 342–3535; (800) 657–5357; Fax: (208) 342–3577;
Email: edavis@idcomfdn.org
Web: www.idcomfdn.org/pages/scho_general.htm

Summary: To provide financial assistance to residents of Idaho working on a degree in accounting at a college in the state.

Eligibility: Open to residents of Idaho who are currently enrolled full time as juniors or seniors at a public or private college or university in the state. Applicants must be majoring in accounting and have a GPA of 2.75 or higher. Along with their application, they must submit brief essays on why they should be awarded this scholarship, what sparked their interest in accounting, and what excites them about the profession. Selection is based on desire for further education or training, individual achievement (as evidenced through participation in outside interests and activities, leadership roles, and/or work experience), and academic standing (not the primary determinant). Financial need is not considered.

Financial data: The stipend is $1,000.

Duration: 1 year.

Number awarded: 1 or more each year.

Deadline: April of each year.

2707 $ IFEC SCHOLARSHIPS

Summary: To provide financial assistance to undergraduate or graduate students who are interested in preparing for a career in communications in the food service industry.

See Listing #1276.

2708 $$ IFMA FOUNDATION SCHOLARSHIPS

Summary: To provide financial assistance to undergraduate and graduate students working on a degree in facility management or a related field.

See Listing #1277.

2709 ILLINOIS ASSOCIATION OF EDUCATIONAL OFFICE PROFESSIONALS STUDENT SCHOLARSHIP

Illinois Association of Educational Office Professionals
c/o Sherry Johnson, Student Scholarship Chair
I–KAN Regional Office of Education
189 East Court Street, Suite 600
Kankakee, IL 60901
Phone: (815) 937–3949
Web: www.iaeop.com/awards.htm

Summary: To provide financial assistance to high school seniors in Illinois who plan to attend college in any state to study an office–related business program.

Eligibility: Open to seniors graduating from high schools in Illinois who have completed 2 or more business education classes from among the following: computer classes, keyboarding/typing, marketing, business communication, accounting, office practices, bookkeeping, desktop publishing, and/or business law. Applicants must be planning to enroll full time at a 2– or 4–year college, university, business college, or vocational/technical school in any state. They must be recommended by a local affiliate of the sponsoring organization. Along with their essay, they must submit a 1–page essay on why they are choosing an office–related career or vocation. Selection is based on that essay (10%), academic record (40%), recommendations (10%), school and extracurricular activities (10%), and financial need (30%).

Financial data: A stipend is awarded (amount not specified).

Duration: 1 year.

Number awarded: 1 each year.

Deadline: January of each year.

2710 ILLINOIS REAL ESTATE EDUCATIONAL FOUNDATION ACADEMIC SCHOLARSHIPS

Illinois Association of Realtors
Attn: Illinois Real Estate Educational Foundation
522 South Fifth Street
P.O. Box 2607
Springfield, IL 62708
Phone: (866) 854–REEF; Fax: (217) 241–9935;
Email: lclayton@iar.org
Web: www.ilreef.org/Scholarships.htm

Summary: To provide financial assistance to Illinois residents who are preparing for a career in real estate.

Eligibility: Open to applicants who are U.S. citizens, Illinois residents, attending a 2– or 4–year college or university in the state on a full–time basis, and working on a degree with an emphasis in real estate. They must have completed at least 30 credits. Along with their application, they must submit a 1,000–word statement of their general activities and intellectual interests, employment (if any), contemplated line of study, and career they expect to follow. Selection is based on the applicant's indication of interest in preparing for a career in real estate or an allied field (e.g., construction, land use planning, mortgage banking, property management, real estate appraising, real estate assessing, real estate brokerage, real estate development, real estate investment counseling, real estate law, and real estate syndication), academic achievement, references and recommendations, and financial need. Finalists are interviewed.

Financial data: The stipend is $1,000.

Duration: 1 year.

Number awarded: 1 or more each year.

Deadline: March of each year.

2711 $$ ILLINOIS SPECIAL EDUCATION TEACHER TUITION WAIVER PROGRAM

Illinois Student Assistance Commission
Attn: Scholarship and Grant Services

1755 Lake Cook Road
Deerfield, IL 60015–5209
Phone: (847) 948–8550; (800) 899–ISAC; Fax: (847) 831–8549; TDD: (800) 526–0844;
Email: isac.studentservices@isac.illinois.gov
Web: www.collegeillinois.org
Summary: To provide funding to students in Illinois who are interested in training or retraining for a career in special education.
Eligibility: Open to Illinois residents who are enrolled or planning to enroll at an Illinois 4–year public institution of higher education to prepare for a career as a public, private, or parochial elementary or secondary school teacher in the state. Applicants must be undergraduate or graduate students seeking certification in an area of special education. They must rank in the upper half of their Illinois high school graduating class. Current teachers who have a valid teaching certificate that is not in the discipline of special education are also eligible. Selection of high school seniors is based on ACT or SAT scores; selection of current college students and teachers returning to school to study special education is determined in a lottery. U.S. citizenship or eligible noncitizenship status is required.
Financial data: This program waives tuition and fees at 12 participating Illinois public 4–year universities. Recipients must agree to teach full time in a special education discipline at an Illinois public, private, or parochial school for 2 of the 5 years immediately following graduation or termination of enrollment. That teaching requirement may be postponed if the recipient serves in the U.S. armed forces, enrolls full time in a graduate or postgraduate program, becomes temporarily disabled, is unable to find employment as a teacher, or withdraws from a course of study leading to a teacher certification in special education but remains enrolled full time in another academic discipline. Participants who fail to fulfill that teaching requirement must repay the entire amount of the tuition waiver prorated to the fraction of the teaching requirement not completed, plus interest at a rate of 5% per year.
Duration: Up to 4 continuous calendar years.
Number awarded: 250 each year: 105 graduating high school seniors, 105 current college students, and 40 teachers returning to school to study special education.
Deadline: February of each year.

2712 INDIANA AMERICAN LEGION AMERICANISM AND GOVERNMENT TEST

American Legion
Department of Indiana
777 North Meridian Street
Indianapolis, IN 46204
Phone: (317) 630–1200; Fax: (317) 630–1277
Web: www.indlegion.org/?page_id=252
Summary: To recognize and reward, with college scholarships, high school students in Indiana who score highest on a test on Americanism.
Eligibility: Open to Indiana students in grades 10–12. They are eligible to take a written test on Americanism and government. Scholarships are awarded to the students with the highest scores. Girls and boys compete separately.
Financial data: The award is a $1,000 scholarship.
Duration: The awards are presented annually.
Number awarded: 6 each year: 3 are set aside for girls in grades 10, 11, and 12 respectively and 3 to a boy in each of the participating grades.
Deadline: Schools that wish to have their students participate must order the tests by October of each year.

2713 INDIANA CPA SOCIETY SCHOLARSHIP GRANTS

Independent Colleges of Indiana
3135 North Meridian Street
Indianapolis, IN 46208
Phone: (317) 236–6090; Fax: (317) 236–6086;
Email: info@icindiana.org
Web: www.icindiana.org
Summary: To provide financial assistance to residents of Indiana who are enrolled at private colleges and universities in the state and preparing for a career in accounting and finance.
Eligibility: Open to residents of Indiana currently enrolled at private colleges and universities that are members of Independent Colleges of Indiana (ICI). Applicants must be working on a degree in accounting or other field that will prepare them for a career in the accounting and finance field. They must be on target to graduate within the next 2 years. Along with their application, they must submit a list of campus activities and involvement, a brief statement of career aspirations after college, and a brief statement as to why they want or need this scholarship.
Financial data: The stipend is $1,000.
Duration: 1 year; nonrenewable.
Number awarded: 3 each year.
Deadline: April of each year.

2714 INDIANAPOLIS CHAPTER HIGH SCHOOL SCHOLARSHIPS

American Society of Military Comptrollers–Indianapolis Chapter
Attn: Markita Carrol, Scholarship Committee
8899 East 56th Street
Indianapolis, IN 46249
Phone: (317) 212–6199;
Email: markita.carroll@dfas.mil
Web: indyasmc.org/Awards.aspx
Summary: To provide financial assistance to high school seniors and recent graduates in Indiana interested in preparing for a career in financial management.
Eligibility: Open to seniors graduating from high schools in Indiana and to people who graduated from those high schools during the preceding 6 months. Applicants must be planning to enter college in any state in a field of study directly related to financial resource management, including business administration, economics, public administration, accounting, or finance. They must be sponsored by a member of the Indianapolis chapter of the American Society of Military Comptrollers (ASMC). Along with their application, they must submit a 250–word essay on their career and academic goals, their financial need, what they want to accomplish, and the circumstances that prompt the need for financial support. Selection is based on scholastic achievement, leadership ability, extracurricular activities, career and academic goals, and financial need.
Financial data: Stipends range from $500 to $1,000.
Duration: 1 year.
Number awarded: 3 each year: 1 each at $1,000, $750, and $500.
Deadline: March of each year.

2715 $ INFORMATION SYSTEMS COMMUNITY OF PRACTICE GLOBAL SCHOLARSHIP FUND

Summary: To provide financial assistance to undergraduate or graduate students from any state who are working on a degree in a field related to information systems or project management.
See Listing #1936.

2716 $$ INSTITUTIONAL EQUITY WOMEN'S COLLEGE FELLOWSHIP PROGRAM

Morgan Stanley
Attn: Diversity Recruiting
1585 Broadway
New York, NY 10036
Phone: (212) 762–0211; Fax: (212) 507–4972;
Email: iedwomenscollegefellowship@morganstanley.com
Web: www.morganstanley.com/about/careers/ischolarships_na.html
Summary: To provide financial assistance and work experience to college sophomore women who are interested in a career in the institutional equities business.
Eligibility: Open to women who are currently enrolled as sophomores at a 4–year college or university with a GPA of 3.3 or higher. Applicants may be majoring in any field, but they must desire to work within the institutional equities business. Selection is based on academic achievement, extracurricular activities, leadership qualities, and an on–site interview.
Financial data: The program provides a stipend of $12,500 during the spring semester of their junior year, a paid internship at Morgan Stanley's Institutional Equity Division during the summer between their junior and senior years, and another stipend of $12,500 for the fall semester of the senior year.
Duration: 1 year; may be renewed for a second year, providing the student maintains a GPA of 3.3 or higher and completes the summer internship following the junior year.
Number awarded: 1 or more each year.
Deadline: April of each year.

2717 $ INSURANCE ACCOUNTING AND SYSTEMS ASSOCIATION SCHOLARSHIPS

Insurance Accounting and Systems Association
Attn: Director of Customer Relations

P.O. Box 51340
Durham, NC 27717–1340
Phone: (919) 489–0991, ext. 211;
Email: khuber@iasa.org
Web: www.iasa.org/Members/AM/Template.cfm?Section=Scholarship_Program
Summary: To provide financial assistance to students working on an undergraduate or graduate degree in specified fields to prepare for a career in the insurance industry.
Eligibility: Open to students who are enrolled as sophomores or higher at a 4–year college or university and have a GPA of 3.0 or higher. Applicants must be working on a bachelor's or higher degree in accounting, actuarial science, information technology, or risk management as preparation for a career in the insurance industry. Along with their application, they must submit 500–word essays on 1) their short–term personal and career goals and objectives; and 2) how the scholarship would help them achieve their goals. Financial need is considered in the selection process.
Financial data: Stipends range up to $2,500. Funds are paid directly to the recipient's institution.
Duration: 1 year.
Number awarded: Varies each year; recently, 8 of these scholarships were awarded.
Deadline: February of each year.

2718 INSURANCE SCHOLARSHIP FOUNDATION OF AMERICA AWARD OF EXCELLENCE

National Association of Insurance Women
Attn: Insurance Scholarship Foundation of America
P.O. Box 866
Hendersonville, NC 28793–0866
Phone: (828) 243–5001;
Email: foundation@inssfa.org
Web: www.inssfa.org/college.html
Summary: To provide financial assistance to college and graduate students working on a degree in insurance and risk management.
Eligibility: Open to candidates for a bachelor's degree or higher with a major or minor in insurance, risk management, or actuarial science. Applicants must 1) be completing or have completed their second year of college; 2) have an overall GPA of 3.0 or higher; 3) have successfully completed at least 2 insurance, risk management, or actuarial science courses; and 4) not be receiving full reimbursement for the cost of tuition, books, or other educational expenses from their employer or any other outside source. Selection is based on academic record and honors, extracurricular and personal activities, work experience, 3 letters of recommendation, and a 500–word essay on career path and goals. This award is presented at the discretion of the foundation to an applicant who demonstrates the qualities necessary to excel in the industry.
Financial data: The award is $1,000; funds are paid jointly to the institution and to the student.
Duration: 1 year.
Number awarded: Generally, 1 each year.
Deadline: October or March of each year.

2719 $$ INSURANCE SCHOLARSHIP FOUNDATION OF AMERICA COLLEGE SCHOLARSHIPS

National Association of Insurance Women
Attn: Insurance Scholarship Foundation of America
P.O. Box 866
Hendersonville, NC 28793–0866
Phone: (828) 243–5001;
Email: foundation@inssfa.org
Web: www.inssfa.org/college.html
Summary: To provide financial assistance to college and graduate students working on a degree in insurance and risk management.
Eligibility: Open to candidates for a bachelor's degree or higher with a major or minor in insurance, risk management, or actuarial science. Applicants must 1) be completing or have completed their second year of college; 2) have an overall GPA of 3.0 or higher; 3) have successfully completed at least 2 insurance, risk management, or actuarial science courses; and 4) not be receiving full reimbursement for the cost of tuition, books, or other educational expenses from their employer or any other outside source. Selection is based on academic record and honors, extracurricular and personal activities, work experience, 3 letters of recommendation, and a 500–word essay on career path and goals.
Financial data: Stipends range from $500 to $5,000; funds are paid jointly to the institution and to the student.
Duration: 1 year.
Number awarded: Varies each year; recently, 6 of these scholarships were awarded.
Deadline: October or March of each year.

2720 $$ INTEL INTERNATIONAL SCIENCE AND ENGINEERING FAIR

Summary: To recognize and reward outstanding high school students who enter a science and engineering competition.
See Listing #1938.

2721 $$ INTEL SCIENCE TALENT SEARCH SCHOLARSHIPS

Summary: To recognize and reward outstanding high school seniors who are interested in attending college to prepare for a career in mathematics, engineering, or any of the sciences.
See Listing #1939.

2722 ISABEL M. HERSON SCHOLARSHIP IN EDUCATION

Zeta Phi Beta Sorority, Inc.
Attn: National Education Foundation
1734 New Hampshire Avenue, N.W.
Washington, DC 20009
Phone: (202) 387–3103; Fax: (202) 232–4593;
Email: scholarship@ZPhiBNEF.org
Web: www.zphib1920.org/nef
Summary: To provide financial assistance to undergraduate and graduate students interested in preparing for a career in education.
Eligibility: Open to students enrolled full time in an undergraduate or graduate program leading to a degree in either elementary or secondary education. Proof of enrollment is required. Along with their application, they must submit a 150–word essay on their educational goals and professional aspirations, how this award will help them to achieve those goals, and why they should receive the award. Financial need is not considered in the selection process.
Financial data: The stipend ranges from $500 to $1,000.
Duration: 1 academic year.
Number awarded: 1 or more each year.
Deadline: January of each year.

2723 $ IVA MCCANTS SCHOLARSHIP

National Association of Federal Education Program Administrators
c/o Rick Carder, President
125 David Drive
Sutter Creek, CA 95685
Phone: (916) 669–5102; Fax: (888) 487–6441;
Email: rickc@sia–us.com
Web: www.nafepa.org
Summary: To provide financial assistance to high school seniors and college freshmen who are interested in working on a degree in education or another field.
Eligibility: Open to graduating high school seniors and graduates already enrolled in the first year of college. Applicants must be working on or planning to work on a degree in education or another field of their choice. They must be nominated by their state affiliate of the sponsoring organization. Along with their application, they must submit a 300–word personal narrative explaining why they are applying for this scholarship, including their awards, interests, leadership activities within the community, and future goals. Selection is based on that essay (20 points), a high school or college transcript from the current semester (20 points), extracurricular and leadership activities within the community or church (20 points), 3 letters of recommendation (20 points), and financial need (20 points).
Financial data: The stipend is $2,500.
Duration: 1 year.
Number awarded: 1 each year.
Deadline: Each state affiliate sets its own deadline; for a list of those, contact the sponsor.

2724 $ J. SPARGO AND ASSOCIATES TEACHER'S SCHOLARSHIP

Armed Forces Communications and Electronics Association
Attn: AFCEA Educational Foundation
4400 Fair Lakes Court

Fairfax, VA 22033–3899
Phone: (703) 631–6138; (800) 336–4583, ext. 6149; Fax: (703) 631–4693;
Email: scholarship@afcea.org
Web: www.afcea.org

Summary: To provide financial assistance to undergraduate and graduate students who are preparing for a career as a teacher of science and mathematics.

Eligibility: Open to full–time sophomores, juniors, seniors, and graduate students at accredited colleges and universities in the United States. Applicants must be U.S. citizens preparing for a career as a teacher of science, mathematics, or information technology at a middle or secondary school. They must have a GPA of 3.0 or higher. Financial need is not considered in the selection process.

Financial data: The stipend is $2,500.

Duration: 1 year.

Number awarded: 1 each year.

Deadline: March of each year.

2725 JACOB AND RITA VAN NAMEN MARKETING SCHOLARSHIP

Summary: To provide financial assistance to undergraduates preparing for a career in the business of horticulture.

See Listing #1960.

2726 $ JAMES CARLSON MEMORIAL SCHOLARSHIP

Oregon Student Access Commission
Attn: Grants and Scholarships Division
1500 Valley River Drive, Suite 100
Eugene, OR 97401–2146
Phone: (541) 687–7395; (800) 452–8807, ext. 7395; Fax: (541) 687–7414; TDD: (800) 735–2900;
Email: awardinfo@osac.state.or.us
Web: www.oregonstudentaid.gov/scholarships.aspx

Summary: To provide financial assistance to Oregon residents majoring in education on the undergraduate or graduate school level at a school in any state.

Eligibility: Open to residents of Oregon who are U.S. citizens or permanent residents and enrolled at a college or university in any state. Applicants must be either 1) college seniors or fifth–year students majoring in elementary or secondary education; or 2) graduate students working on an elementary or secondary certificate. Full–time enrollment and financial need are required. Priority is given to 1) students who come from diverse environments and submit an essay of 250 to 350 words on their experience living or working in diverse environments; 2) dependents of members of the Oregon Education Association; and 3) applicants committed to teaching autistic children.

Financial data: Stipends for scholarships offered by the Oregon Student Access Commission (OSAC) range from $200 to $10,000 but recently averaged $2,300.

Duration: 1 year.

Number awarded: Varies each year; recently, 3 of these scholarships were awarded.

Deadline: February of each year.

2727 JAMES F. REVILLE SCHOLARSHIP

Summary: To provide financial assistance to college students in New York majoring in a field related to intellectual and other development disabilities.

See Listing #1963.

2728 JAMES L. MCCOY SCHOLARSHIPS

North Carolina Association of Certified Public Accountants
Attn: North Carolina CPA Foundation, Inc.
3100 Gateway Centre Boulevard
P.O. Box 80188
Raleigh, NC 27623–0188
Phone: (919) 469–1040, ext. 130; (800) 722–2836; Fax: (919) 378–2000;
Email: jtahler@ncacpa.org
Web: ncacpa.org/Member_Connections/Students/Scholarships.aspx

Summary: To provide financial assistance to students majoring in accounting at colleges and universities in North Carolina.

Eligibility: Open to North Carolina residents majoring in accounting at a college or university in the state. Applicants must have completed at least 36 semester hours, including at least 1 college or university–level accounting course, and have a GPA of 3.0 or higher. They must be sponsored by an accounting faculty member. Along with their application, they must submit an essay of 500 to 1,000 words on a topic that changes annually but relates to the public accounting profession; recently, students were asked for their ideas on the 3 most important skills someone in the accounting field should have and why. Selection is based on academic achievement and financial need.

Financial data: The stipend is $1,000.

Duration: 1 year; may be renewed up to 2 additional years.

Number awarded: Varies each year; recently, 15 of these scholarships were awarded.

Deadline: February of each year.

2729 $ JAMES M. AND VIRGINIA M. SMYTH SCHOLARSHIP FUND

Summary: To provide financial assistance to high school seniors, especially those from designated states, who are interested in majoring in selected fields at colleges in any state.

See Listing #1294.

2730 JANET DZIADULEWICZ BRANDEN MEMORIAL AWARD

Summary: To recognize and reward upper–division and graduate students in Wisconsin who have a Polish connection and demonstrate academic excellence in Polish studies.

See Listing #1296.

2731 $ JAY KAPLAN MEMORIAL SCHOLARSHIP

Summary: To provide financial assistance to residents of Vermont, especially those with disabilities, who are interested in working on a degree in science or finance at a college in any state.

See Listing #1971.

2732 JEAN LEE/JEFF MARVIN COLLEGIATE SCHOLARSHIPS

Summary: To provide financial assistance to upper–division students in Indiana who are majoring in health education, physical education, recreation, or dance.

See Listing #1302.

2733 JEANNE MOWLDS DISTINGUISHED LIFETIME SERVICE AWARD

Summary: To provide financial assistance to undergraduate and graduate students from any country interested in preparing for a career in document management and graphic communications.

See Listing #1304.

2734 JEFFREY WHITEHEAD MEMORIAL AWARD

David and Dovetta Wilson Scholarship Fund, Inc.
115–67 237th Street
Elmont, NY 11003–3926
Phone: (516) 285–4573;
Email: DDWSF4@aol.com
Web: www.wilsonfund.org/Jeffrey_Whitehead.html

Summary: To provide financial assistance to high school seniors who are interested in going to college to prepare for a career in social service.

Eligibility: Open to graduating high school seniors who plan to attend an accredited college or university to prepare for a career in social service. Applicants must be U.S. citizens or permanent residents and have a GPA of 3.0 or higher. Along with their application, they must submit 3 letters of recommendation, high school transcripts, and an essay (up to 250 words) on "How My College Education Will Help Me Make a Positive Impact on My Community." Selection is based on community involvement, desire to prepare for a career in the field of social service, and financial need.

Financial data: The stipend is $1,000.

Duration: 1 year; nonrenewable.

Number awarded: 1 each year.

Deadline: March of each year.

2735 $ JEROME C. PREMO SCHOLARSHIP

American Public Transportation Association
Attn: American Public Transportation Foundation

1666 K Street, N.W., Suite 1100
Washington, DC 20006
Phone: (202) 496–4803; Fax: (202) 496–4323;
Email: yconley@apta.com
Web: www.aptfd.org/work/scholarship.htm
Summary: To provide financial assistance to upper–division and graduate students who are preparing for a career in the public transportation industry.
Eligibility: Open to college juniors, seniors, and graduate students who are preparing for a career in the transit industry. Any member organization of the American Public Transportation Association (APTA) can nominate and sponsor candidates for this scholarship. Nominees must be enrolled in a fully–accredited institution, have and maintain at least a 3.0 GPA, and be either employed by or demonstrate a strong interest in entering the business administration or management area of the public transportation industry. They must submit a 1,000–word essay on the topic, "In what segment of the public transportation industry will you make a career and why?" Selection is based on demonstrated interest in the transit field as a career, need for financial assistance, academic achievement, essay content and quality, and involvement in extracurricular citizenship and leadership activities.
Financial data: The stipend is $2,500.
Duration: 1 year; may be renewed.
Number awarded: 1 each year.
Deadline: May of each year.

2736 JERRY WHEELER SCHOLARSHIPS

South Dakota Retailers Association
320 East Capitol Avenue
P.O. Box 638
Pierre, SD 57501
Phone: (605) 224–5050; (800) 658–5545; Fax: (605) 224–2059;
Email: donna@sdra.org
Web: www.sdra.org/scholarship
Summary: To provide financial assistance to South Dakota residents who are interested in preparing for a career in retailing.
Eligibility: Open to residents of South Dakota who are interested in a career in a retail or business field. Examples of eligible fields include, but are not limited to, accounting, agribusiness, animal science/veterinary technician, apparel merchandising, auto mechanics, automotive technology, banking, business administration, business management, collision repair, computer science, culinary arts, commercial baking, diesel mechanics, electrical maintenance, heating and ventilation, hotel and restaurant management, landscape design, pharmacy, photography, printing industries, refrigeration, sales and marketing management, and tourism industry management. Applicants must have graduated from a South Dakota high school but they may be enrolled in a vocational school, college, or university in any state. They must have completed at least 1 year of full–time college study or 1 semester of full–time vocational school. Selection is not based solely on financial need or on outstanding scholarship.
Financial data: Stipends range from $500 to $1,000.
Duration: 1 year.
Number awarded: Varies each year; recently, 13 of these scholarships, with a total value of $8,100, were awarded.
Deadline: April of each year.

2737 $$ JEWELL L. TAYLOR NATIONAL UNDERGRADUATE SCHOLARSHIPS

American Association of Family and Consumer Sciences
Attn: Senior Manager, Awards and Governance
400 North Columbus Street, Suite 202
Alexandria, VA 22314
Phone: (703) 706–4608; (800) 424–8080, ext. 4608; Fax: (703) 706–4663;
Email: staff@aafcs.org
Web: www.aafcs.org/Recognition/scholarshipseven.asp
Summary: To provide financial assistance to undergraduate students in the field of family and consumer sciences.
Eligibility: Open to U.S. citizens and permanent residents working on an undergraduate degree in an area of family and consumer sciences. Selection is based on ability to pursue undergraduate study (10 points); enrollment in undergraduate study in family and consumer sciences (10 points); experience in relation to preparation for study in proposed field (10 points); special recognition and awards (5 points); voluntary participation in professional and community organizations and activities (10 points); evidence (or degree) of professional commitment and leadership (10 points); significance of proposed area of study to families and individuals (15 points); professional goals (10 points); written communication (5 points); and recommendations (15 points). Special consideration is given to applicants who have been members of the American Association of Family and Consumer Sciences (AAFCS) for up to 2 years (3 points) or for 2 or more years (5 points).
Financial data: The award provides a stipend of $5,000 and financial support of up to $1,000 for 1 year of AAFCS membership and participation in its annual conference and exposition.
Duration: 1 year; recipients may reapply.
Number awarded: 1 each year.
Deadline: January of each year.

2738 JIM AND CAROLYN FERN MUSIC EDUCATION SCHOLARSHIP

Summary: To provide financial assistance to residents of any state who are working on a degree in music education at a college in Kentucky.
See Listing #1308.

2739 JIM KIBLER AGRICULTURE FUND

Summary: To provide financial assistance to students, especially residents of Idaho, Oregon, or Washington, who are working on a degree in an agriculture–related field at a school in any state.
See Listing #1978.

2740 $ JOE PERDUE SCHOLARSHIPS

Club Foundation
Attn: Scholarship Coordinator
1733 King Street
Alexandria, VA 22314–2720
Phone: (703) 739–9500; Fax: (703) 739–0124;
Email: joeperduescholarship@clubfoundation.org
Web: www.clubfoundation.org/joePerdueScholarship.htm
Summary: To provide financial assistance for college to students planning a career in private club management.
Eligibility: Open to students who are currently attending an accredited 4–year college or university and are actively preparing for a managerial career in the private club industry. Applicants must have completed their freshman year with a GPA of 2.5 or higher. Along with their application, they must submit an essay of 500 to 1,000 words on their career objectives and goals, the characteristics they possess that will allow them to succeed as a club manager, their perception of the Club Managers Association of America (CMAA) and the private club industry, their specific interests within the private club management field, and why they feel the Club Foundation should select them as a scholarship recipient. Selection is based on the essay (20 points), academic record (20 points), extracurricular activities (15 points), and employment record (15 points). Additional points are awarded for CMAA student chapter members.
Financial data: The stipend is $2,500 per year. Funds are paid directly to the recipient's college or university.
Duration: 1 year.
Number awarded: Varies each year; since the Foundation was established, it has awarded more than 155 of these scholarships, worth more than $270,000.
Deadline: April of each year.

2741 JOEL CARTUN SCHOLARSHIP

Summary: To provide financial assistance to undergraduate and graduate students from any country interested in preparing for a career in document management and graphic communications.
See Listing #1311.

2742 $ JOHN CULVER WOODDY SCHOLARSHIPS

Actuarial Foundation
Attn: Actuarial Education and Research Fund Committee
475 North Martingale Road, Suite 600
Schaumburg, IL 60173–2226
Phone: (847) 706–3535; Fax: (847) 706–3599;
Email: scholarships@actfnd.org
Web: www.actuarialfoundation.org/programs/actuarial/jcwoody.shtml
Summary: To provide financial assistance to undergraduate students who are preparing for a career in actuarial science.
Eligibility: Open to undergraduate students who will have senior standing in the semester after receiving the scholarship. Students must be nominated. Nominees must rank in the top quartile of their class and have successfully

completed 1 actuarial examination. Each university may nominate only 1 student. Preference is given to candidates who have demonstrated leadership potential by participating in extracurricular activities. Financial need is not considered in the selection process.
Financial data: The stipend is $2,000.
Duration: 1 year.
Number awarded: Varies each year; recently, 14 of these scholarships were awarded.
Deadline: June of each year.

2743 $ JOHN J. KILLIAN SCHOLARSHIP

Kansas Society of Certified Public Accountants
Attn: Educational Foundation
100 S.E. Ninth Street, Suite 502
Topeka, KS 66612–1213
Phone: (785) 272–4366; (800) 222–0452 (within KS); Fax: (785) 262–4468;
Email: info@kscpa.org
Web: www.kscpa.org/up_and_coming_professionals/scholarships
Summary: To provide financial assistance to students in Kansas who are majoring in accounting at independent colleges.
Eligibility: Open to residents of any state who are enrolled full time as accounting majors in their junior year at independent colleges and universities in Kansas. Each college may nominate 1 candidate. In the selection process, emphasis is placed on the nominee's grades in English and rhetoric subjects as well as courses in business and economics. Other criteria include involvement in leadership activities, willingness to comply with standards of professional responsibility, and overall moral character; financial need is not considered.
Financial data: The stipend is $2,500.
Duration: 1 year.
Number awarded: 1 each year.
Deadline: March of each year.

2744 $ JOHN SWAIN MEMORIAL SCHOLARSHIP

Summary: To provide financial assistance to residents of any state who are enrolled as upper–division students at colleges and universities in the mid–Atlantic region and have an interest in direct marketing.
See Listing #1317.

2745 $$ JOHN T. LOCKTON MEMORIAL SCHOLARSHIPS

Spencer Educational Foundation, Inc.
c/o Risk Insurance and Management Society
1065 Avenue of the Americas, 13th Floor
New York, NY 10018
Phone: (212) 286–9292;
Email: asabatino@spencered.org
Web: www.spencered.org
Summary: To provide financial assistance to upper–division students who are preparing for a career in risk management.
Eligibility: Open to full–time students entering their junior or senior year at a college or university in any state with a major or minor in a business administration, insurance, or risk management discipline. Applicants must have a career objective in risk management and relevant work experience. They must have a GPA of 3.0 or higher. Along with their application, they must submit a 500–word essay on their chosen career path and goals. Selection is based on merit.
Financial data: The stipend is $5,000.
Duration: 1 year.
Number awarded: 10 each year.
Deadline: January of each year.

2746 $ JOHN W. AND MARY D. NICHOLS SCHOLARSHIP

Summary: To provide financial assistance to high school seniors in Oklahoma who demonstrate knowledge and appreciation of the state's history and geography and plan to attend college in the state.
See Listing #1318.

2747 JOHN W. AUSTIN MEMORIAL SCHOLARSHIP

Summary: To provide financial assistance to high school seniors in Maine who are interested in attending college in any state to prepare for a career in the trucking industry.
See Listing #1993.

2748 $ JOSEPH AND MARION GREENBAUM JUDAIC STUDIES SCHOLARSHIP

Summary: To provide financial assistance to 1) Jewish residents of Delaware and adjacent communities interested in taking courses in Jewish studies at a college in any state and 2) Jewish residents of other states interested in studying in Delaware.
See Listing #1319.

2749 $ JOSEPH E. HAGAN MEMORIAL SCHOLARSHIP

Funeral Service Foundation
Attn: Executive Director
13625 Bishop's Drive
Brookfield, WI 53005–6607
Phone: (262) 789–1880; (877) 402–5900; Fax: (262) 789–6977;
Email: info@funeralservicefoundation.org
Web: www.funeralservicefoundation.org
Summary: To provide financial assistance to mortuary science students.
Eligibility: Open to full–time students who are currently enrolled or accepted for enrollment in a program of mortuary science accredited by the American Board of Funeral Service Education. Applicants must submit an essay of 500 to 1,000 words on a topic that changes annually but relates to the funeral profession; recently, students were asked to describe the changes that they see in funeral service today that will have a positive impact for their career. Selection is based primarily on that essay and academic achievement; financial need is not considered.
Financial data: The stipend is $2,500.
Duration: 1 year; nonrenewable.
Number awarded: 2 each year.
Deadline: June of each year.

2750 JOSEPH T. WEINGOLD SCHOLARSHIP

NYSARC, Inc.
Attn: Scholarship and Awards Committee
393 Delaware Avenue
Delmar, NY 12054
Phone: (518) 439–8311; Fax: (518) 439–1893;
Email: info@nysarc.org
Web: www.nysarc.org
Summary: To provide financial assistance to college students in New York majoring in special education.
Eligibility: Open to sophomores enrolled at colleges and universities in New York and working on certification in special education. They must be nominated by their institution. Students must provide a list of work experience with people who have intellectual and other developmental disabilities and a 1–page autobiographical sketch indicating their interest in the field and their plans after graduation. Financial need is not considered in the selection process.
Financial data: The stipend is $1,500 per year.
Duration: 2 years.
Number awarded: 1 each year.
Deadline: January of each year.

2751 $ JOSH TURNER SCHOLARSHIP FUND

Summary: To provide financial assistance to high school seniors in rural areas of South Carolina who are interested in attending college in any state to prepare for a career in the music business or the arts.
See Listing #1322.

2752 JOURNALISM EDUCATION ASSOCIATION FUTURE TEACHER SCHOLARSHIP

Summary: To provide financial assistance to upper–division and master's degree students working on a degree in education who intend to teach journalism.
See Listing #1323.

2753 JOYCE V. LAWRENCE SCHOLARSHIP

North Carolina Federation of Business and Professional Women's Club, Inc.
Attn: BPW/NC Foundation
P.O. Box 276
Carrboro, NC 27510
Web: www.bpw–nc.org/Default.aspx?pageId=837230

Summary: To provide financial assistance to students attending North Carolina colleges or community colleges and majoring in education.
Eligibility: Open to students currently enrolled in either a North Carolina community college or North Carolina 4–year college and majoring in a field related to education. They must be endorsed by a local BPW unit and have a GPA of 3.0 or higher. Along with their application, they must submit a 1–page statement that summarizes their career goals, previous honors, or community activities and justifies their need for this scholarship. U.S. citizenship is required.
Financial data: The stipend is $1,000. Funds are paid directly to the recipient's school.
Duration: 1 year; recipients may reapply.
Number awarded: 1 each year.
Deadline: April of each year.

2754 JUDITH CARY MEMORIAL SCHOLARSHIP

P. Buckley Moss Society
74 Poplar Grove Lane
Mathews, VA 23109
Phone: (540) 932–1728; (800) 430–1320;
Email: society@mosssociety.org
Web: www.mosssociety.org/page.php?id=29
Summary: To provide financial assistance to students working on a bachelor's or master's degree in special education.
Eligibility: Open to students who have completed at least 2 years of undergraduate study and are working on a bachelor's or master's degree in special education. They must be nominated by a member of the P. Buckley Moss Society. The nomination packet must include proof of acceptance into a specific program to teach special needs students, 2 letters of recommendation, a short essay on school and community work activities and achievements, and an essay of 250 to 500 words on their career goals, teaching philosophies, reasons for choosing this career, and ways in which they plan to make a difference in the lives of special needs students. Financial need is not considered in the selection process.
Financial data: The stipend is $1,000. Funds are paid to the recipient's college or university.
Duration: 1 year.
Number awarded: 1 each year.
Deadline: March of each year.

2755 KANSAS CITY CHAPTER SCHOLARSHIPS

American Society of Women Accountants–Kansas City Chapter
c/o Mary Roach, Scholarship Committee Co–Chair
1404 S.W. Highland Drive
Lees Summit, MO 64081–3510
Phone: (816) 443–2100;
Email: mary.roach@pdqts.com
Web: aswadc.org/page/scholarship–information
Summary: To provide financial assistance to residents of any state working on an undergraduate degree in accounting or finance at a college or university in Kansas and western Missouri.
Eligibility: Open to residents of any state who are working on a bachelor's degree in accounting or finance at a college or university in Kansas or western Missouri. Applicants must be entering their third, fourth, or fifth year of study and have a GPA of 3.0 or higher. Along with their application, they must submit an essay of 150 to 250 words on their career goals and objectives, the impact they want to have on the accounting world, community involvement, and leadership examples. Membership in the American Society of Women Accountants (ASWA) is not required. Selection is based on leadership, character, communication skills, and scholastic average; financial need is not considered, although students who wish to be considered for scholarships offered by the national organization of the American Society of Women Accountants may include information on their financial situation.
Financial data: A stipend is awarded (amount not specified).
Duration: 1 year.
Number awarded: Varies each year; recently, 4 of these scholarships were awarded.
Deadline: February of each year.

2756 $$ KANSAS CITY IFMA SCHOLARSHIP

Summary: To provide financial assistance to students from any state who are working on an undergraduate or graduate degree in a field related to facility management at a school in Kansas or Missouri.
See Listing #1330.

2757 KANSAS FUNERAL DIRECTORS ASSOCIATION FOUNDATION SCHOLARSHIP

Kansas Funeral Directors Association
Attn: KFDA Foundation
1200 South Kansas Avenue
P.O. Box 1904
Topeka, KS 66601–1904
Phone: (913) 232–7789; Fax: (913) 232–7791;
Email: kfda@kfda.kscoxmail.com
Web: www.ksfda.org
Summary: To provide financial assistance to Kansas residents who are currently enrolled in a school of mortuary science in any state.
Eligibility: Open to Kansas residents who are currently enrolled full time at a mortuary school in any state. They must have at least 1 but not more than 2 semesters of schooling left and be registered with the Kansas State Board of Mortuary Arts. Along with their application, they must submit an essay that covers their reasons for choosing funeral service as a profession, any experience or exposure they have had with the funeral profession, their plans for employment after graduation, and their reasons for seeking financial assistance. Selection is based on that essay, academic achievement, leadership qualities, financial need, and special abilities. Preference is given to applicants who intend to practice in Kansas.
Financial data: Stipends range from $250 to $1,000.
Duration: 1 year.
Number awarded: 2 to 4 each year.
Deadline: March or September of each year.

2758 $$ KANSAS TEACHER SERVICE SCHOLARSHIPS

Kansas Board of Regents
Attn: Student Financial Assistance
1000 S.W. Jackson Street, Suite 520
Topeka, KS 66612–1368
Phone: (785) 296–3518; Fax: (785) 296–0983;
Email: dlindeman@ksbor.org
Web: www.kansasregents.org/scholarships_and_grants
Summary: To provide funding to high school seniors, current undergraduates, licensed teachers, and selected graduate students who are interested in teaching specified disciplines or in designated areas of Kansas.
Eligibility: Open to Kansas residents who are attending a postsecondary institution in the state. Applicants must be 1) accepted for admission to, or currently enrolled in, a course of instruction leading to licensure as a teacher in a hard–to–fill discipline (recently defined as special education, mathematics, science, foreign language, and English as a Second Language) or an underserved geographic area of Kansas (recently defined as Topeka, Kansas City, Wichita, and the western third of the state); 2) currently licensed as a teacher and enrolled in a course of instruction leading to endorsement in a hard–to–fill discipline or teaching in an underserved geographic area of Kansas; or 3) currently licensed as a teacher and accepted for admission or enrolled in a course of instruction leading to a master's degree in a field of education as a teacher in a hard–to–fill discipline or in an underserved geographic area of the state. They must submit evidence of completion of the Kansas Scholars Curriculum (4 years of English, 4 years of mathematics, 3 years of science, 3 years of social studies, 2 years of foreign language, and 1 year of computer technology), ACT or SAT scores, high school GPA, high school class rank, and (if relevant) college transcripts and letters of recommendation from a college or university official.
Financial data: The stipend is $5,396 per year for full–time students or prorated amounts for part–time students. This is a scholarship/loan program. Recipients must teach a hard–to–fill discipline or in an underserved geographic area of Kansas for the period of time they received support, or they must repay the amount received with interest (currently, 12.9%).
Duration: 1 year; may be renewed for up to 3 additional years or up to 4 additional years for designated 5–year courses of study requiring graduate work.
Number awarded: Approximately 100 each year.
Deadline: April of each year.

2759 $ KATHLEEN M. PEABODY, C.P.A., MEMORIAL SCHOLARSHIP

Massachusetts Society of Certified Public Accountants
Attn: MSCPA Educational Foundation
105 Chauncy Street, Tenth Floor
Boston, MA 02111
Phone: (617) 556–4000; (800) 392–6145; Fax: (617) 556–4126;
Email: info@mscpaonline.org
Web: www.cpatrack.com/scholarships

Summary: To provide financial assistance to upper–division students majoring in accounting at a Massachusetts college or university.
Eligibility: Open to Massachusetts residents who are entering their junior or senior year of an accounting program at a college or university in the state. Applicants must be enrolled in school on a full–time basis. They must demonstrate superior academic standing, financial need, and an intention to seek a career in a public accounting firm.
Financial data: The stipend is $2,500.
Duration: 1 year.
Number awarded: 1 each year.
Deadline: March of each year.

2760 KATHRYN M. DAUGHERTY EDUCATION SCHOLARSHIP

Business and Professional Women of Maryland
Attn: BPW Foundation of Maryland
c/o Joyce Draper, Chief Financial Officer
615 Fairview Avenue
Frederick, MD 21701
Web: www.bpwmaryland.org
Summary: To provide financial assistance to residents of Maryland who are majoring in education at a school in the state.
Eligibility: Open to residents of Maryland who are majoring in education at an academic institution in the state, with preference given to majors in elementary education. Applicants must be registered full time and entering their sophomore year in college. They must have a GPA of 3.0 or higher and be able to demonstrate financial need. Graduate study, correspondence courses, and nondegree programs are not eligible. Along with their application, they must submit a 200–word statement on how they expect the proposed training or education to add to their opportunities for advancement or employment. Selection is based on financial need (50%) and academic performance (50%); a bonus of 15% is added for elementary education majors.
Financial data: The stipend is $1,000 for the sophomore year and $250 per year for the junior and senior years.
Duration: 1 year; may be renewed for 2 additional years, provided the recipient maintains a GPA of 3.0 or higher and enrollment in an education program.
Number awarded: 1 or more each year.
Deadline: July of each year.

2761 $$ KEMPER SCHOLARS GRANT PROGRAM

James S. Kemper Foundation
20 North Wacker Drive, Suite 1823
Chicago, IL 60606
Phone: (312) 332–3114;
Email: dmattison@jskemper.org
Web: www.jskemper.org/scholars.html
Summary: To provide financial assistance and work experience to freshmen at selected colleges and universities who are interested in preparing for a career in business and/or administration.
Eligibility: Open to students enrolled as full–time freshmen at 1 of 16 participating colleges and universities. Applicants must be interested in preparing for a career in administration and/or business and must have a record of academic achievement, extracurricular activity, community service, and leadership ability. They must be willing to participate in community service by engaging in campus activities, exploring their vocational calling outside the classroom, participating in a full–time work program with a nonprofit organization in Chicago for 1 summer, and conducting an independent project during the next summer.
Financial data: The stipend for the school year ranges from $3,000 to $10,000 per year, depending on the need of the recipient. For the summer following their sophomore year, scholars receive a stipend of at least $6,000 for their work with a major nonprofit organization in Chicago. For the summer following their junior year, they receive a grant for an independent project that ranges from $2,000 to $6,000, depending on the expenses associated with the project.
Duration: 3 years, as long as the scholar maintains a GPA of 3.0 or higher each academic term.
Number awarded: Varies each year; recently, 19 of these grants were awarded.
Deadline: Deadlines vary at each institution.

2762 $ KEN YOST MEMORIAL SCHOLARSHIP

Summary: To provide financial assistance to high school seniors in Missouri who plan to attend college in any state to prepare for a career in a field related to public works.
See Listing #2010.

2763 $ KENTUCKY ASSOCIATION OF SCHOOL BUSINESS OFFICIALS SCHOLARSHIPS

Kentucky Association of School Business Officials
c/o Debbie Frazier, Scholarship Chair
Madison County Board of Education
550 South Keenland Drive
P.O. Box 768
Richmond, KY 40476–0768
Phone: (859) 624–4500;
Email: debbie.frazier@madison.kyschools.us
Web: kasbo.com/scholarships.html
Summary: To provide financial assistance to high school seniors in Kentucky who plan to major in business or education at a college in the state.
Eligibility: Open to seniors graduating from high schools in Kentucky and planning to major in business or education at a college or university in the state. Applicants must submit information on their extracurricular activities, honors and awards, voluntary or paid service activities, leadership roles, and family financial situation.
Financial data: The stipend is $2,500.
Duration: 1 year.
Number awarded: 3 each year.
Deadline: February of each year.

2764 KENTUCKY EARLY CHILDHOOD DEVELOPMENT SCHOLARSHIPS

Kentucky Higher Education Assistance Authority
Attn: Student Aid Branch
100 Airport Road
P.O. Box 798
Frankfort, KY 40602–0798
Phone: (502) 696–7392; (800) 928–8926, ext. 7392; Fax: (502) 696–7373;
TDD: (800) 855–2880;
Email: studentaid@kheaa.com
Web: www.kheaa.com/website/kheaa/ecds?main=1
Summary: To provide financial assistance to Kentucky residents who are working on a degree or certificate in early childhood education on a part–time basis while they are employed in the field.
Eligibility: Open to Kentucky residents who are U.S. citizens, nationals, or permanent residents enrolled at a participating institution in the state for less than 9 credit hours per academic term. Applicants must be working on 1) an associate degree in early childhood education; 2) a bachelor's degree in interdisciplinary early childhood education or an approved related program; 3) a Kentucky Early Childhood Development Director's Certificate; or 4) a child development associate credential. They must be employed at least 20 hours per week in a participating early childhood facility or provide training in early childhood development for an approved organization. They may have no unpaid financial obligation and may not be eligible to receive state or federal training funds through Head Start, a public preschool program, or First Steps.
Financial data: Stipends are the lesser of the tuition actually charged by the institution or $1,800 per year. Funds are either credited to the student's account or, if the student has already paid the tuition, disbursed to the student at the beginning of each school term by the institution.
Duration: 1 year; may be renewed if funds permit.
Number awarded: Varies each year; recently, 960 students received these scholarships.
Deadline: Deadline not specified.

2765 $ KENTUCKY LABOR–MANAGEMENT CONFERENCE BOARD OF DIRECTORS' SCHOLARSHIP

Kentucky Labor–Management Conference, Inc.
Attn: Scholarship Award
P.O. Box 4248
Frankfort, KY 40604
Phone: (502) 564–3203; Fax: (502) 696–1897;
Email: jodie.craig@ky.gov
Web: www.labor.ky.gov/dows/lmrm/Pages/Labor–Management–Conference.aspx
Summary: To provide financial assistance to residents of Kentucky working on an undergraduate or graduate degree in labor relations at a school in any state.
Eligibility: Open to residents of Kentucky who are working on an associate, bachelor's, or graduate degree or technical certification at a college or university in any state. Applicants must have completed 1 year of a 2–year program or 2 years of a 4–year program and have a GPA of 2.5 or higher. They must be preparing for a career in a labor–relations related field or an apprenticeship trade. Along

with their application, they must submit an essay of approximately 1,000 words on a topic that changes annually but relates to an issue of current interest in labor relations. Selection is based on merit, including interest in a labor relations–related field as a career, leadership characteristics, and academic achievement.
Financial data: Stipends are $1,000 for students in 2–year associate or technical programs, $1,500 for students in 4–year undergraduate programs, and $2,000 for graduate students.
Duration: 1 year.
Number awarded: Up to 2 each year.
Deadline: July of each year.

2766 KENTUCKY LIBRARY ASSOCIATION SCHOLARSHIP FOR MINORITY STUDENTS

Kentucky Library Association
c/o Executive Secretary
1501 Twilight Trail
Frankfort, KY 40601
Phone: (502) 223–5322; Fax: (502) 223–4937;
Email: info@kylibasn.org
Web: www.kylibasn.org/scholarships965.cfm
Summary: To provide financial assistance to members of minority groups who are residents of Kentucky or attending school there and are working on an undergraduate or graduate degree in library science.
Eligibility: Open to members of minority groups (defined as American Indian, Alaskan Native, Black, Hispanic, Pacific Islander, or other ethnic group) who are entering or continuing at a graduate library school accredited by the American Library Association (ALA) or an undergraduate library program accredited by the National Council of Teacher Education (NCATE). Applicants must be residents of Kentucky or a student in a library program in the state. Along with their application, they must submit a statement of their career objectives, why they have chosen librarianship as a career, and their reasons for applying for this scholarship. Selection is based on that statement, cumulative undergraduate and graduate GPA (if applicable), academic merit and potential, and letters of recommendation. U.S. citizenship or permanent resident status is required.
Financial data: The stipend is $1,000.
Duration: 1 year; nonrenewable.
Number awarded: 1 or more each year.
Deadline: June of each year.

2767 $$ KENTUCKY MINORITY EDUCATOR RECRUITMENT AND RETENTION SCHOLARSHIPS

Kentucky Department of Education
Attn: Minority Educator Recruitment and Retention
500 Mero Street, 8th Floor
Frankfort, KY 40601
Phone: (502) 564–1479, ext. 4014; Fax: (502) 564–6952; TDD: (502) 564–4970;
Email: monica.davis@education.ky.gov
Web: www.education.ky.gov
Summary: To provide funding to minority undergraduate and graduate students enrolled in Kentucky public institutions who want to become teachers.
Eligibility: Open to residents of Kentucky who are undergraduate or graduate students pursuing initial teacher certification at a public university or community college in the state. Applicants must have a GPA of 2.5 or higher and either maintain full–time enrollment or be a part–time student within 18 semester hours of receiving a teacher education degree. They must be U.S. citizens and meet the Kentucky definition of a minority student.
Financial data: Stipends are $5,000 per year at the 8 state universities in Kentucky or $2,000 per year at community and technical colleges. This is a scholarship/loan program. Recipients are required to teach 1 semester in Kentucky for each semester or summer term the scholarship is received. If they fail to fulfill that requirement, the scholarship converts to a loan with severe penalties for non–payment.
Duration: 1 year; may be renewed up to 3 additional years.
Number awarded: Varies each year.
Deadline: Each state college of teacher education sets its own deadline.

2768 KENTUCKY RESTAURANT ASSOCIATION ACADEMIC SCHOLARSHIPS

Kentucky Restaurant Association
Attn: Educational Foundation
133 Evergreen Road, Suite 201
Louisville, KY 40243
Phone: (502) 896–0464; (800) 896–0414; Fax: (502) 896–0465;
Email: info@kyra.org
Web: www.kyra.org/mx/hm.asp?id=scholarship
Summary: To provide financial assistance to residents in Kentucky who are preparing for a career in the food service industry at a school in any state.
Eligibility: Open to applicants who are Kentucky residents (or have been residing within 25 miles of Kentucky's borders) for the past 18 months. They must be enrolled or planning to enroll full time at an accredited college in any state to work on an associate, bachelor's, or master's degree in food service. Work experience in food service is required. Financial need is considered in the selection process.
Financial data: Stipend amounts vary, depending on tuition and fees at the school the recipient attends.
Duration: 1 year; may be renewed.
Number awarded: Varies; generally, up to 25 each year.
Deadline: June or December of each year.

2769 $ KENTUCKY SOCIETY OF CERTIFIED PUBLIC ACCOUNTANTS COLLEGE SCHOLARSHIPS

Kentucky Society of Certified Public Accountants
Attn: Educational Foundation
1735 Alliant Avenue
Louisville, KY 40299–6326
Phone: (502) 266–5272; (800) 292–1754 (within KY); Fax: (502) 261–9512;
Email: backerman@kycpa.org
Web: www.cpa2be.org/mx/hm.asp?id=scholarc
Summary: To provide financial assistance to undergraduate and graduate students in Kentucky who are interested in majoring in accounting.
Eligibility: Open to residents or Kentucky who are currently enrolled as a sophomore, junior, senior, or graduate student at a Kentucky college or university. Applicants must have an overall GPA of at least 2.75 and an accounting GPA of at least 3.0. They must have completed the "principles of accounting" course, be currently enrolled in or have completed intermediate accounting, indicate plans to sit for the C.P.A. examination, and intend to stay and work in Kentucky after graduation. Along with their application, they must submit a 1–page essay on their career goals, reasons for choosing accounting, how they are financing their education, and why they should receive this scholarship. Financial need is not considered in the selection process.
Financial data: The stipend ranges from $1,000 to $2,500.
Duration: 1 year.
Number awarded: Approximately 35 each year.
Deadline: January of each year.

2770 $$ KENTUCKY TEACHER SCHOLARSHIP PROGRAM

Kentucky Higher Education Assistance Authority
Attn: Student Aid Branch
100 Airport Road
P.O. Box 798
Frankfort, KY 40602–0798
Phone: (502) 696–7391; (800) 928–8926, ext. 7391; Fax: (502) 696–7373;
TDD: (800) 855–2880;
Email: studentaid@kheaa.com
Web: www.kheaa.com/website/kheaa/teacher?main=1
Summary: To provide funding to Kentucky high school seniors, high school graduates, college students, and graduate students who are interested in preparing for a career as a teacher.
Eligibility: Open to U.S. citizens who are Kentucky residents enrolled or accepted for enrollment as full–time students (unless they are enrolled for their final term and less than full–time enrollment is required to complete the program) at an eligible Kentucky institution of higher education. They must be studying in an undergraduate or graduate program of teacher education which is preparatory to initial teacher certification but does not lead to a certificate, diploma, or degree in theology, divinity, or religious education. Financial need must be demonstrated. Awards are granted according to the following priorities: 1) prior recipients applying for renewal; 2) teachers who are eligible for the "Best in Class" program administered by the Kentucky Higher Education Student Loan Corporation; 3) highly qualified applicants who have been unconditionally admitted to a teacher education program by their college, ranked in ascending order by Expected Family Contribution (EFC); 4) highly qualified applicants who have not yet been admitted to a teacher education program but who meet the standards and requirements for admission, ranked in ascending order by EFC; and 5) otherwise eligible applicants seeking admission to a teacher education program, ranked in ascending order by EFC.

Financial data: Freshmen and sophomores may receive up to $1,250 per academic year and $325 per summer. Juniors, seniors, post–baccalaureates, and graduate students may receive up to $5,000 per academic year and $1,250 per summer. The total amount a student may receive is $12,500 as an undergraduate or $7,500 as a graduate student. This is a scholarship/loan program. Recipients must provide 1 semester of qualified teaching service in Kentucky for each semester or summer scholarship received; recipients who teach in a critical shortage area must provide 1 semester of qualified teaching service as repayment for 2 scholarships received. If any of those requirements are not met in the prescribed time, the scholarship converts immediately to a loan bearing interest at the rate of 6%.

Duration: 1 semester; may be renewed if the recipient remains enrolled in an eligible program of study and makes satisfactory academic progress.

Number awarded: Varies each year; recently, 520 of these scholarship/loans were issued.

Deadline: April of each year.

2771 $ KEVIN AND KELLY PERDUE MEMORIAL SCHOLARSHIP

Summary: To provide funding to licensed radio amateurs who are interested in studying humanities or the social sciences in college.

See Listing #1336.

2772 KLUSSENDORF/MCKOWN SCHOLARSHIPS

Summary: To provide financial assistance to college students majoring in dairy science at a college or university in the United States or Canada.

See Listing #2016.

2773 $$ KRISTEN A. SANCHEZ AND JORGE A. CABALLERO DELOITTE STUDENT AND LEADER OF THE YEAR SCHOLARSHIPS

Hispanic Association of Colleges and Universities
Attn: National Scholarship Program
8415 Datapoint Drive, Suite 400
San Antonio, TX 78229
Phone: (210) 692–3805; Fax: (210) 692–0823; TDD: (800) 855–2880;
Email: scholarships@hacu.net
Web: www.hacu.net/hacu/Scholarships.asp?SnID=899378480

Summary: To provide financial assistance to undergraduate and graduate students working on a degree in accounting at member institutions of the Hispanic Association of Colleges and Universities (HACU).

Eligibility: Open to juniors and first–year master's degree students at 4–year HACU member institutions who are working full time on a degree in accounting. Applicants must have a GPA of 3.5 or higher and be able to demonstrate financial need. They must be interested in a career with Deloitte. Along with their application, they must submit an essay that focuses on their personal motivation for applying for this scholarship, their academic and/or career goals, and the skills they could bring to an employer.

Financial data: The stipend is $10,000.

Duration: 1 year.

Number awarded: 1 or more each year.

Deadline: June of each year.

2774 $ KRISTEN SCHROEDER MEMORIAL SCHOLARSHIP

Minnesota Association of Administrators of State and Federal Education Programs
c/o Matthew Mohs, Treasurer
2140 Timmy Street
St. Paul, MN 55120
Phone: (651) 632–3787;
Email: matthew.mohs@spps.org
Web: www.maasfep.org/scholarships.shtml

Summary: To provide financial assistance to high school seniors in Minnesota who have participated in a Title I program and plan to major in education or criminal justice at a college in any state.

Eligibility: Open to seniors graduating from high schools in Minnesota who have participated in a Title I program while in high school. Applicants must be planning to attend a 4–year college or university in any state and major in education or criminal justice. They must have a GPA of 2.5 or higher. Along with their application, they must submit 1) a 100–word essay on how the Title I program helped them with their education; 2) a 100–word essay on their plans for the future; and 3) a 250–word essay on a challenging experience they have had in their life and how they overcame it. Selection is based on those essays, desire for education beyond high school, study habits, positive attitude, and interest in school, community, and/or work–related activities.

Financial data: The stipend is $2,000.

Duration: 1 year.

Number awarded: 1 each year.

Deadline: January of each year.

2775 $ KSCPA COLLEGE SCHOLARSHIPS

Kansas Society of Certified Public Accountants
Attn: Educational Foundation
100 S.E. Ninth Street, Suite 502
Topeka, KS 66612–1213
Phone: (785) 272–4366; (800) 222–0452 (within KS); Fax: (785) 262–4468;
Email: info@kscpa.org
Web: www.kscpa.org/up_and_coming_professionals/scholarships

Summary: To provide financial assistance to college students in Kansas who are majoring in accounting.

Eligibility: Open to upper–division students at each of the 6 regent institutions in Kansas and at Washburn University. Applicants must be studying accounting.

Financial data: The stipend is $2,250.

Duration: 1 year.

Number awarded: 7 each year: 1 at each of the participating institutions.

Deadline: June of each year.

2776 KSCPA HIGH SCHOOL MERIT SCHOLARSHIPS

Kansas Society of Certified Public Accountants
Attn: Educational Foundation
100 S.E. Ninth Street, Suite 502
Topeka, KS 66612–1213
Phone: (785) 272–4366; (800) 222–0452 (within KS); Fax: (785) 262–4468;
Email: info@kscpa.org
Web: www.kscpa.org/up_and_coming_professionals/scholarships

Summary: To provide financial assistance to high school seniors in Kansas who plan to major in accounting at a college in the state.

Eligibility: Open to seniors graduating from high schools in Kansas and planning to enter a college or university in the state to study accounting. Applicants must submit a short essay on their impression of the accounting profession. Selection is based on ACT or SAT scores.

Financial data: Stipends are $1,300, $900, $800, $700, $600, or $500.

Duration: 1 year.

Number awarded: 20 each year: 1 each at $1,300, $900, $800, $700, and $600, plus 15 at $500.

Deadline: Test scores must be submitted by March of each year; applications are due in April.

2777 $ LAURA E. SETTLE SCHOLARSHIPS

California Retired Teachers Association
Attn: Laura E. Settle Foundation
800 Howe Avenue, Suite 370
Sacramento, CA 95825
Phone: (916) 923–2200; (800) 523–2782; Fax: (916) 923–1910;
Email: admin@calrta.org
Web: calrta.org/explore–calrta/scholarship

Summary: To provide financial assistance to undergraduate and graduate students majoring in education in California.

Eligibility: Open to juniors, seniors, and graduate students majoring in education at a campus of the University of California (UC) or the California State University (CSU) system. Students interested in applying must contact the department of teacher education at their campus.

Financial data: The stipend is $2,000.

Duration: 1 year.

Number awarded: 30 each year: 1 at each UC and CSU campus with a teacher education program.

Deadline: Deadline not specified.

2778 $ LAW IN SOCIETY AWARD COMPETITION

Virginia State Bar
Attn: Law in Society Award Competition
707 East Main Street, Suite 1500

Richmond, VA 23219–2800
Phone: (804) 775–0594; Fax: (804) 775–0582; TDD: (804) 775–0502;
Email: lawinsociety@vsb.org
Web: www.vsb.org/site/public/law–in–society

Summary: To recognize and reward high school students in Virginia who submit outstanding essays on the role of law in society.

Eligibility: Open to students enrolled at a Virginia high school in grades 9–12 who are 19 years of age or younger. Home–schooled students at equivalent grade and age levels are also eligible. Applicants must submit an essay, between 750 and 1,000 words in length, on a topic that changes annually but relates to a hypothetical situation on the role of law in society. Awards are presented to students whose essays show a superior understanding of the role and value of our legal system in our everyday lives.

Financial data: Prizes vary annually, but recently were $2,300 for first, $1,850 for second, $1,350 for third, and $250 for honorable mention. All prizes are paid in cash.

Duration: The competition is held annually.

Number awarded: 8 each year: 1 first prize, 1 second prize, 1 third prize, and 5 honorable mentions.

Deadline: February of each year.

2779 LCPA EDUCATIONAL FOUNDATION SCHOLARSHIPS

Society of Louisiana Certified Public Accountants
Attn: LCPA Education Foundation
2400 Veterans Boulevard, Suite 500
Kenner, LA 70062–4739
Phone: (504) 464–1040; (800) 288–5272; Fax: (504) 469–7930
Web: www.lcpa.org/LCPAScholarships.html

Summary: To provide financial assistance to undergraduate and graduate students in Louisiana who are interested in becoming Certified Public Accountants (C.P.A.s).

Eligibility: Open to Louisiana residents who are currently enrolled full time in an accounting program at a 4–year college or university in the state. Applicants must be upper–division, fifth–year, or graduate students and have a GPA of 2.5 or higher. Along with their application, they must submit a 1–page essay on a topic that changes annually but relates to the C.P.A. profession; recently, students were asked to give their ideas on the most important issues in the accounting profession today. Selection is based on academic merit and the essay. At least 1 scholarship is reserved for a graduate student working on a doctoral degree.

Financial data: Stipends range from $500 to $1,000.

Duration: 1 year.

Number awarded: Varies each year; recently, 20 of these scholarships were awarded: 15 at $500, 3 at $750, and 2 at $1,000.

Deadline: January of each year.

2780 $$ LEADERSHIP SPEECH CONTEST

National Management Association
Attn: Leadership Speech Contest
2210 Arbor Boulevard
Dayton, OH 45439–1580
Phone: (937) 294–0421; Fax: (937) 294–2374;
Email: nma@nma1.org
Web: nma1.org/Speech_Contest/Speech_Contest.html

Summary: To recognize and reward high school students who deliver outstanding speeches on leadership.

Eligibility: Open to students in grades 9–12 in a high school or home school within an area of a sponsoring chapter of the National Management Association (NMA). Contestants prepare speeches of 4 to 6 minutes on a topic related to leadership. Non–leadership issues (e.g., social, medical, environmental, political) should not be used unless integrated into how leadership plays a role. No audio/visual aids are allowed with the presentations, and speeches may not be read verbatim, although notes are allowed. Winners of the chapter contests advance to council competitions, from which winners proceed to compete at either the East or the West Leadership Development Council (LDC) of the NMA. The first– and second–place LDC winners then compete in the national contest. Speeches are judged on the basis of content (50%), delivery (30%), and language (20%).

Financial data: Chapter awards are determined by each chapter, up to a maximum of $300 for the first–place winner; each council also determines its own awards, to a maximum of $500 for the first–place winner. At each LDC, first prize is $1,000 and second is $500. In the national contest, first prize is $4,000, second $1,000, third $500, and fourth $500.

Number awarded: 4 LDC winners are selected each year and compete for the national prizes; the number of chapter and council prizes awarded varies.

Deadline: Chapter contests are held in January or early February of each year, council contests in February or March, LDC contests in April or May, and the national contest in September or October.

2781 $ LENDIO BROCK BLAKE STUDENT ENTREPRENEUR OF THE YEAR

Lendio, Inc.
10235 South Jordan Parkway, Suite 410
South Jordan, UT 84095
Phone: (801) 858–3611; (855) 8–LENDIO;
Email: scholarship@lendio.com
Web: www.lendio.com/scholarship

Summary: To recognize and reward, with scholarships for continued study, entering and continuing undergraduates who submit outstanding essays on their desire to become an entrepreneur.

Eligibility: Open to students who are currently enrolled at a college or university or who will be attending within 1 year. Applicants must submit an essay, from 500 to 1,000 words in length, that covers such topics as their passion and commitment to being an entrepreneur, the challenge of juggling a startup with academics, why they want to be an entrepreneur, current business plans or ideas, their motives for being a business owner, their goals for the next 5 to 10 years, and what it means to be an entrepreneur. Selection is based on the essay's creativity, specificity, and basic grammar.

Financial data: The award is $2,500; funds are paid directly to the winner's college or university.

Duration: The award is presented annually.

Number awarded: 1 each year.

Deadline: June of each year.

2782 LEO BROWN SCHOLARSHIP

Alabama Association of Federal Program Administrators
c/o Karen Calvert
Blount County Board of Education
204 Second Avenue East
P.O. Box 578
Oneonta, AL 35121
Phone: (205) 625–4102;
Email: kcalvert@blountboe.net
Web: www.aafepa.org

Summary: To provide financial assistance to high school seniors and college freshmen from Alabama interested in working on a college degree in education.

Eligibility: Open to students currently enrolled as seniors at high schools in Alabama or freshmen at accredited colleges or universities in the state. Applicants must be interested in working on a degree in education. They must be able to demonstrate 1) a GPA of 3.0 or higher; 2) a commitment to learning; and 3) a successful experience working with children or young people. Along with their application, they must submit a 300–word essay outlining their leadership activities and future goals. Financial need is considered in the selection process.

Financial data: The stipend is $1,500.

Duration: 1 year.

Number awarded: 1 each year.

Deadline: October of each year.

2783 LEON B. PENNINGTON MEMORIAL SCHOLARSHIP

Maryland Association of Educational Office Professionals
c/o Winopa Mbakop
Baltimore County Public Schools
6901 Charles Street
Towson, MD 21204
Phone: (410) 887–4556;
Email: info@maeop.org
Web: www.maeop.org/generated/ingen/disp.cgi?id=5

Summary: To provide financial assistance to high school seniors in Maryland who plan to attend college in any state to prepare for an office–related career, preferably in the education field.

Eligibility: Open to seniors graduating from high schools in Maryland who have taken at least 2 business education classes from among the following: computers, keyboarding, typing, shorthand, accounting, office practices and procedures, or bookkeeping. Applicants must be planning to enroll full time at a 2– or 4–year college or university, business college or school, or vocational/technical institute. They must be preparing for an office–related career, especially in the

field of education. Along with their application, they must submit a 500–word essay on why they are choosing an office–related career or vocation. Selection is based on that essay (10%), academic record (40%), school and extracurricular activities (10%), recommendations (10%), and financial need (30%).
Financial data: The stipend is $1,000.
Duration: 1 year.
Number awarded: 1 each year.
Deadline: April of each year.

2784 LETITIA B. CARTER SCHOLARSHIP AWARD

Restaurant Association of Maryland Education Foundation
Attn: Senior Director of Development and ProStart
6301 Hillside Court
Columbia, MD 21046
Phone: (410) 290–6800, ext. 1015; Fax: (410) 290–6882;
Email: LaDeana@ramef.org
Web: www.ramef.org/displaycommon.cfm?an=1&subarticlenbr=6
Summary: To provide financial assistance to Maryland residents who are food service or hospitality students, teachers, or professionals interested in further course work.
Eligibility: Open to residents of Maryland who are 1) high school or college students; 2) high school, college, or corporate instructors or teachers; or 3) hospitality industry professionals. Applicants must be interested in taking courses in a professional development program or a food service or hospitality program recognized by the Restaurant Association of Maryland Education Foundation (RAMEF). Students must have a GPA of 3.0 or higher and at least 400 documented hours of industry experience. Instructors, teachers, and professionals must have at least 1,500 hours of documented industry experience. All applicants must submit essays on 1) their personal skills and characteristics that will help them meet the future challenges of the food service or hospitality industry; and 2) the person who was most influential in helping them choose a career in the food service or hospitality industry. Students must also be able to demonstrate financial need.
Financial data: A stipend is awarded (amount not specified).
Duration: 1 year.
Number awarded: 1 or more each year.
Deadline: April of each year.

2785 LILA M. VAN SWERINGEN STUDENT SCHOLARSHIP

Educational Office Professionals of Ohio
c/o Cindy Goga, Scholarship Chair
Educational Service Center of Cuyahoga County
5811 Canal Road
Valley View, OH 44125
Phone: (216) 524–3000;
Email: cindy.goga@esc–cc.org
Web: www.eopo–oh.org/sscholar.html
Summary: To provide financial assistance to Ohio residents who are interested in attending college in the state to prepare for an office–related career.
Eligibility: Open to residents of Ohio who are attending a high school or college in the state. Applicants must be preparing for an office–related career. Along with their application, they must submit brief statements on how they plan to finance their education, their ideas about a good office manager, their goals, and a biographical sketch on why they are choosing an office–related career as a vocation.
Financial data: The stipend is $1,000.
Duration: 1 year.
Number awarded: 1 each year.
Deadline: February of each year.

2786 LILLIAN WALL SCHOLARSHIP

Zonta Club of Bangor
c/o Barbara A. Cardone
P.O. Box 1904
Bangor, ME 04402–1904
Web: www.zontaclubofbangor.org/?area=scholarship
Summary: To provide financial assistance to women attending or planning to attend college in Maine and major in special education or a related field.
Eligibility: Open to women who are attending or planning to attend an accredited 2– or 4–year college in Maine. Applicants must major in special education or a related field. Along with their application, they must submit brief essays on 1) their goals in seeking higher education and their plans for the future; and 2) any school and community activities that have been of particular importance to them and why they found them worthwhile. Financial need may be considered in the selection process.
Financial data: The stipend is $1,000.
Duration: 1 year.
Number awarded: 1 each year.
Deadline: March of each year.

2787 $ L.L. WATERS SCHOLARSHIP PROGRAM

Summary: To provide financial assistance to advanced undergraduate and graduate students in the field of transportation.
See Listing #2036.

2788 LOS ANGELES CIVIC CENTER CHAPTER SCHOLARSHIP

Association of Government Accountants–Los Angeles Civic Center Chapter
c/o Samitha Wijayaratne, Scholarship Committee
17030 Index Street
Granada Hills, CA 91344
Phone: (213) 978–0954;
Email: samitha.wijayaratne@lacity.org
Web: www.agalacivic.org
Summary: To provide financial assistance to residents of any state enrolled as upper–division students at a school in California and working on a degree in accounting or a related field.
Eligibility: Open to U.S. citizens and permanent residents who are enrolled as full–time juniors or seniors at a college or university in California. Applicants must be majoring in accounting, business management, economics, finance, information systems, marketing, or public administration. Along with their application, they must submit a 1–page essay on their career plans, including why it is important to consider public service as a career. Financial need is not considered in the selection process.
Financial data: The stipend is $1,000.
Duration: 1 year.
Number awarded: 2 each year.
Deadline: October of each year.

2789 $ LOTUS YEE CHEIGH SCHOLARSHIP

American Society of Women Accountants–Honolulu Chapter
Attn: Fe Velasco, Scholarship Chair
P.O. Box 4374
Honolulu, HI 96812
Phone: (808) 921–6535; Fax: (808) 921–6644;
Email: fevelasco327@yahoo.com
Web: aswahawaii.org/Scholarship.htm
Summary: To provide financial assistance to undergraduate and graduate female accounting students in Hawaii.
Eligibility: Open to women working full or part time on a bachelor's or master's degree in accounting at a college, university, or professional school of accounting in Hawaii. Applicants must have completed at least 60 semester hours with a GPA of 2.7 or higher. They are not required to be a member of the American Society of Women Accountants (ASWA). Along with their application, they must submit a personal statement of 150 to 250 words on their career goals. Selection is based on that statement, extracurricular activities and honors, communication skills, GPA, and financial needs and circumstances.
Financial data: Stipends range from $1,000 to $2,000. Funds are paid directly to the recipient's school.
Duration: 1 year; nonrenewable.
Number awarded: 1 each year.
Deadline: March of each year.

2790 $$ LOUISE MORITZ MOLITORIS LEADERSHIP AWARD

Summary: To provide financial assistance to undergraduate women interested in a career in transportation.
See Listing #2040.

2791 $$ LTG JAMES F. MCCALL SCHOLARSHIP

American Society of Military Comptrollers
Attn: National Awards Committee
415 North Alfred Street

Alexandria, VA 22314
Phone: (703) 549–0360; (800) 462–5637; Fax: (703) 549–3181;
Email: lindaryan_asmchsscholarships@yahoo.com
Web: awards.asmconline.org

Summary: To provide financial assistance to high school seniors interested in preparing for a career in financial management.

Eligibility: Open to high school seniors who demonstrate exemplary leadership abilities, an interest in the financial management career field, and academic promise. Applicants must be planning to enter college in a field of study directly related to financial resource management, including business administration, economics, public administration, accounting, or finance. They must be endorsed by a chapter of the American Society of Military Comptrollers (ASMC). Selection is based on scholastic achievement, leadership ability, extracurricular activities, career and academic goals, and financial need.

Financial data: The stipend is $3,000 per year.

Duration: 1 year; the recipient may reapply and receive up to $1,500 per year for 3 additional years.

Number awarded: 1 each year.

Deadline: March of each year.

2792 $ LUBRIZOL CORPORATION SCHOLARSHIP PROGRAM

Summary: To provide financial assistance to women and minorities working on a degree in specified fields of science and business at college in any state.

See Listing #2045.

2793 LULLELIA W. HARRISON SCHOLARSHIP IN COUNSELING

Zeta Phi Beta Sorority, Inc.
Attn: National Education Foundation
1734 New Hampshire Avenue, N.W.
Washington, DC 20009
Phone: (202) 387–3103; Fax: (202) 232–4593;
Email: scholarship@ZPhiBNEF.org
Web: www.zphib1920.org/nef

Summary: To provide financial assistance to undergraduate and graduate students interested in preparing for a career in counseling.

Eligibility: Open to students enrolled full time in an undergraduate or graduate program leading to a degree in counseling. Proof of enrollment is required. Along with their application, they must submit a 150–word essay on their educational goals and professional aspirations, how this award will help them to achieve those goals, and why they should receive the award. Financial need is not considered in the selection process.

Financial data: The stipend ranges from $500 to $1,000.

Duration: 1 academic year.

Number awarded: 3 or more each year.

Deadline: January of each year.

2794 $ LYDIA MILLER SPECIAL EDUCATION SCHOLARSHIP

Illinois Elks
Attn: Children's Care Corporation
1201 North Main
P.O. Box 222
Chatham, IL 62629–0222
Phone: (217) 483–3020; (800) 272–0074;
Email: scholarships@illinois–elks.org
Web: www.illinois–elks.org/ccc/scholarship/index.htm

Summary: To provide financial assistance to residents of Illinois interested in preparing for a career in special education at a school in the state.

Eligibility: Open to residents of Illinois enrolled as full–time juniors, seniors, or graduate students at a college or university in the state. Applicants must be working on a degree in special education. They must have a grade average of "B" or better and be able to document financial need. Along with their application, they must submit a 1,000–word statement on their goals in the field of special education, how they became interested in the field, what they wish to accomplish, and any particular area in which they are planning to concentrate; if they have been working in another field, they should explain what prompted them to return to school in special education.

Financial data: Stipends are $2,500 for juniors or $3,000 for seniors and graduate students.

Duration: 1 year.

Number awarded: 9 each year: 3 juniors, 3 seniors, and 3 graduate students.

Deadline: May of each year.

2795 MACDONALD SCHOLARSHIPS

Maine Society of Certified Public Accountants
Attn: Education and Scholarship Committee
153 U.S. Route 1, Suite 8
Scarborough, ME 04074–9053
Phone: (207) 883–6090; (800) 660–2721 (within ME); Fax: (207) 883–6211
Web: www.mecpa.org/students

Summary: To provide financial assistance to upper–division and graduate students in Maine working on a degree in accounting.

Eligibility: Open to residents of Maine enrolled full time as a junior, senior, or master's degree student at a college or university in the state. Applicants must be working on a degree in accounting and be committed to preparing for a career as a Certified Public Accountant (C.P.A.). They must have a GPA of 3.25 or higher overall and 3.5 or higher in accounting courses. Along with their application, they must submit a 250–word essay on their personal career goals. Financial need is not considered in the selection process.

Financial data: The stipend is $1,000.

Duration: 1 year.

Number awarded: 3 each year.

Deadline: April of each year.

2796 $ MALCOLM BALDRIGE SCHOLARSHIP

Summary: To provide financial assistance to Connecticut residents who are interested in attending college in the state to major in a field related to manufacturing or international business.

See Listing #2050.

2797 MARCIA S. HARRIS LEGACY FUND SCHOLARSHIP

Summary: To provide financial assistance to Maryland residents who are students or teachers of culinary arts or hospitality management and interested in attending a college or university in any state.

See Listing #1368.

2798 MARGARET KELDIE SCHOLARSHIP

American Society of Women Accountants–Chicago Chapter
c/o Pamela Metz, Scholarship Fund Secretary
1957 North Dayton Street, Number 1
Chicago, IL 60614
Phone: (312) 480–8566;
Email: MKSF_aswa@yahoo.com
Web: www.aswachicago.org/scholarship–info

Summary: To provide financial assistance to women from any state working on an undergraduate or graduate degree in accounting at a college or university in Illinois.

Eligibility: Open to women from any state who are currently enrolled full or part time at an accredited 4–year college or university in Illinois. Applicants must be working on an undergraduate or graduate degree in accounting and have a cumulative grade average of "B" or higher. They must have indicated an intention to prepare for an accounting career. Undergraduates must have completed at least 60 semester hours. Financial need is not considered in the selection process.

Financial data: Stipends are $1,500 for full–time students or $800 for part–time students.

Duration: 1 year.

Number awarded: 1 or more each year. Since the program was established, it has awarded nearly $135,000 in scholarships to more than 250 women.

Deadline: February of each year.

2799 MARION T. WOOD STUDENT SCHOLARSHIPS

National Association of Educational Office Professionals
Attn: NAEOP Foundation
1841 South Eisenhower Court
P.O. Box 12619
Wichita, KS 67277–2619
Phone: (316) 942–4822, ext. 140; Fax: (316) 942–7100;
Email: foundation@naeop.org
Web: www.naeop.org/foundation.htm

Summary: To provide financial assistance to students interested in preparing for an office–related career.

Eligibility: Open to graduating high school seniors and current college students who are enrolled or planning to enroll full time. Applicants must have completed 2 or more business education courses (4 semesters, whether in high school, college, or a combination of both) from among the following: computer classes, keyboarding/typing, marketing, business communication, accounting, office practices and procedures, bookkeeping, desktop publishing, and/or business law. They must be planning to prepare for an office–related career, preferably in the field of education. Along with their application, they must submit a 500–word essay on why they are choosing an office–related career or vocation. Selection is based on that essay (10%), academic record (40%), recommendations (10%), school and extracurricular activities (10%), and financial need (30%).
Financial data: The stipend is $1,000.
Duration: 1 year.
Number awarded: Varies each year.
Deadline: March of each year.

2800 $ MARK J. SMITH SCHOLARSHIP

Colorado Society of Certified Public Accountants
Attn: Educational Foundation
7979 East Tufts Avenue, Suite 1000
Denver, CO 80237–2847
Phone: (303) 773–2877; (800) 523–9082 (within CO); Fax: (303) 773–6344;
Email: gmantz@cocpa.org
Web: www.want2bcpa.com/get–started/cscpa–scholarships.html

Summary: To provide financial assistance to upper–division and graduate students in Colorado who are studying accounting and come from a single–parent household.
Eligibility: Open to upper–division and graduate students at colleges and universities in Colorado who have completed at least 6 semester hours of accounting courses and have a GPA of 3.0 or higher. Applicants must be from a single–parent household or be attending college as a single parent. They must be U.S. citizens or noncitizens legally living and studying in Colorado with a valid visa that enables them to become employed. Selection is based on academics and financial need.
Financial data: The stipend is $2,500. Funds are paid directly to the recipient's school to be used for books, C.P.A. review materials, tuition, fees, and dormitory room and board.
Duration: 1 year; recipients may reapply.
Number awarded: 1 each year.
Deadline: May of each year for fall semester or quarter; November of each year for winter quarter or spring semester.

2801 MARK JEFFREY PHEBUS ENDOWED SCHOLARSHIP

Texas Department of Public Safety Officers' Association
Attn: Texas DPS Troopers Foundation
5821 Airport Boulevard
Austin, TX 78752
Phone: (512) 451–0582; (800) 933–7762; Fax: (512) 451–0709;
Email: info@dpstf.org
Web: www.dpstf.org/programs–2/scholarship–grants

Summary: To provide financial assistance to residents of Texas working on a degree in law enforcement at a college in the state.
Eligibility: Open to residents of Texas currently enrolled full time in the second or third year at a college or university in the state. Applicants must be working on a degree in a law enforcement–related major. They must have a GPA of 2.75 or higher. Along with their application, they must submit a narrative description of their achievements, leadership skills, extracurricular activities, career goals, and need for financial assistance.
Financial data: A stipend is awarded (amount not specified).
Duration: 1 year.
Number awarded: 1 each year.
Deadline: June of each year.

2802 MARK LIERMAN MEMORIAL SCHOLARSHIPS

Hawaii Geographic Information Coordinating Council
P.O. Box 1174
Honolulu, HI 96807–1174
Email: scholarship@higicc.org
Web: higicc.camp8.org/awards

Summary: To provide financial assistance to undergraduate and graduate students from Hawaii interested in learning about and/or using geographic information systems (GIS).
Eligibility: Open to undergraduate and graduate students who graduated from a high school in Hawaii or are attending a college or university in the state. Applicants must be working on an associate, bachelor's, master's, or doctoral degree in geospatial data or GIS. Along with their application, they must submit official transcripts, 2 letters of recommendation, and a 500–word essay on their past experience with geospatial data (academically, professionally, or personally) and how they hope to use geospatial data to achieve their future goals. Financial need is not considered in the selection process.
Financial data: The stipend is $1,000. Funds may be used for general tuition and other educational expenses or for costs associated with a specified proposal.
Duration: 1 year.
Number awarded: 2 each year: 1 for an undergraduate and 1 for a graduate student.
Deadline: May of each year.

2803 MARLA BOUMA MEMORIAL TUITION AWARD

Colorado Association for the Education of Young Children
Attn: Tuition Award Committee
P.O. Box 631326
Highlands Ranch, CO 80163–1326
Phone: (303) 791–2772; (888) 892–4453 (within CO); Fax: (303) 791–7597;
Email: caeyc@ColoradoAEYC.org
Web: coloradoaeyc.org/awards/the–marla–bouma–memorial–award

Summary: To provide financial assistance to undergraduate and graduate school students in Colorado who have taken courses in early childhood education.
Eligibility: Open to Colorado residents who are U.S. citizens, are full– or part–time undergraduate or graduate students at a Colorado college or university, have taken at least 6 hours of early childhood–related courses, are interested in taking additional courses in early childhood education, and have a GPA of 3.0 or higher. Along with their application, they must submit 5 essays: a resume of their work experiences with children, their academic goal and when they expect to attain it, why they are going into early childhood education, what they see themselves doing in 5 years, and their philosophy in working with young children. Selection is based on academic ability, awards and honors, strength of character, leadership potential, emotional maturity, and special interest and commitment to the early childhood education field; financial need is not considered.
Financial data: A stipend is awarded (amount not specified).
Duration: 1 year; renewable upon reapplication.
Number awarded: Varies each year, depending upon the number of qualified applicants.
Deadline: November of each year.

2804 $$ MARRIOTT SCHOLARS PROGRAM

Summary: To provide financial assistance to Hispanic American undergraduate students who are interested in preparing for a career in the hospitality industry.
See Listing #1371.

2805 $$ MARSH COLLEGE SCHOLARSHIPS

National Association of Insurance Women
Attn: Insurance Scholarship Foundation of America
P.O. Box 866
Hendersonville, NC 28793–0866
Phone: (828) 243–5001;
Email: foundation@inssfa.org
Web: www.inssfa.org/college.html

Summary: To provide financial assistance to college and graduate students working on a degree in insurance and risk management.
Eligibility: Open to candidates for a bachelor's degree or higher with a major or minor in insurance, risk management, or actuarial science. Applicants must 1) be completing or have completed their second year of college; 2) have an overall GPA of 3.0 or higher; 3) have successfully completed at least 2 insurance, risk management, or actuarial science courses; and 4) not be receiving full reimbursement for the cost of tuition, books, or other educational expenses from their employer or any other outside source. Selection is based on academic record and honors, extracurricular and personal activities, work experience, 3 letters of recommendation, and a 500–word essay on career path and goals.

Financial data: Stipends range from $500 to $5,000; funds are paid jointly to the institution and to the student.
Duration: 1 year.
Number awarded: Varies each year; recently, 2 of these scholarships were awarded.
Deadline: October or March of each year.

2806 MARTIN LUTHER KING JR. SCHOLARSHIP AWARDS

American Correctional Association
Attn: Scholarship Award Committee
206 North Washington Street, Suite 200
Alexandria, VA 22314
Phone: (703) 224–0000; (800) ACA–JOIN; Fax: (703) 224–0179;
Email: jenniferb@aca.org
Web: www.aca.org/pastpresentfuture/awards.asp
Summary: To provide financial assistance for undergraduate or graduate study to minorities interested in a career in the criminal justice field.
Eligibility: Open to minority undergraduates or graduate students interested in preparing for a career in the criminal justice field. The must be nominated by members of the American Correctional Association (ACA). Nominees do not need to be ACA members, but they must have been accepted to or be enrolled in an undergraduate or graduate program in criminal justice at a 4–year college or university. Along with the nomination package, they must submit a 250–word essay describing their reflections on the ideals and philosophies of Dr. Martin Luther King and how they have attempted to emulate those qualities in their lives. They must provide documentation of financial need, academic achievement, and commitment to the principles of Dr. King.
Financial data: A stipend is awarded (amount not specified). Funds are paid directly to the recipient's college or university.
Number awarded: 1 each year.
Deadline: May of each year.

2807 $$ MARVIN DODSON–CARL PERKINS SCHOLARSHIP

Kentucky Education Association
Attn: Student Program
401 Capital Avenue
Frankfort, KY 40601
Phone: (800) 231–4532, ext. 315; Fax: (502) 227–8062;
Email: cmain@kea.org
Web: www.kea.org/kea_student_program/scholarships.aspx
Summary: To provide financial assistance to upper–division and master's degree students in Kentucky who plan to become teachers in the state.
Eligibility: Open to juniors, seniors, post–baccalaureate, and M.A.T. students at Kentucky colleges and universities. Applicants must be participating in the Kentucky Education Association's student program and planning to teach in the state. They must have a GPA of 3.0 or higher and be able to demonstrate financial need. Along with their application, they must submit a 500–word essay on why they are applying for this scholarship, why they want to be a teacher, and any special circumstances or obstacles they have overcome.
Financial data: Up to $6,000 is available for this program each year.
Duration: 1 year.
Number awarded: 1 or more each year.
Deadline: January of each year.

2808 MARYLAND ASSOCIATION OF CERTIFIED PUBLIC ACCOUNTANTS SCHOLARSHIP PROGRAM

Maryland Association of Certified Public Accountants
Attn: MACPA Educational Foundation
901 Dulaney Valley Road, Suite 710
Towson, MD 21204–2683
Phone: (410) 296–6250; (800) 782–2036; Fax: (410) 296–8713;
Email: info@macpa.org
Web: www.tomorrowscpa.org/college/scholarships.html
Summary: To provide financial assistance to residents of Maryland working on an undergraduate or graduate degree in accounting at a school in the state.
Eligibility: Open to Maryland residents enrolled as a full–time undergraduate or graduate student in accounting at a college or university in the state. Applicants must have completed at least 60 total credit hours at the time of the award, including at least 6 hours in accounting courses. They must have a GPA of 3.0 or higher and be able to demonstrate financial need. U.S. citizenship is required.
Financial data: Stipends are at least $1,000. The exact amount of the award depends upon the recipient's financial need.
Duration: 1 year; may be renewed until completion of the 150–hour requirement and eligibility for sitting for the C.P.A. examination in Maryland. Renewal requires continued full–time enrollment and a GPA of 3.0 or higher.
Number awarded: Varies each year; recently, 22 of these scholarships were awarded.
Deadline: April of each year.

2809 $$ MARYLAND ASSOCIATION OF PRIVATE COLLEGES AND CAREER SCHOOLS SCHOLARSHIPS

Summary: To provide financial assistance to students interested in attending selected private career schools in Maryland.
See Listing #1373.

2810 MARYLAND CORRECTIONAL ADMINISTRATORS ASSOCIATION MEMORIAL SCHOLARSHIPS

Maryland Correctional Administrators Association
c/o Milton M. Crump, Memorial Scholarship Committee Chair
Calvert County Detention Center
P.O. Box 9
Barstow, MD 20610
Phone: (410) 535–4300;
Email: crumpmm@co.cal.md.us
Web: www.mdle.net/mcaa/scholarships.htm
Summary: To provide financial assistance to residents of Maryland interested in working on an undergraduate or graduate degree in a field related to corrections at a school in any state.
Eligibility: Open to residents of Maryland who are graduating high school seniors, undergraduates, or graduate students. Applicants must be interested in attending a college or university in any state to work on a degree in corrections or a closely–related criminal justice field. Along with their application, they must submit a 500–word essay describing their interest in corrections and criminal justice and why they are the best candidate for the scholarship. Their application must be endorsed by a sponsoring member of the Maryland Correctional Administrators Association (MCAA).
Financial data: A stipend is awarded (amount not specified).
Duration: 1 year; recipients may reapply.
Number awarded: Varies each year; recently, 11 of these scholarships were awarded.
Deadline: April of each year.

2811 $$ MARYLAND WORKFORCE SHORTAGE STUDENT ASSISTANCE GRANT PROGRAM

Summary: To provide money for college to Maryland residents interested in a career in specified workforce shortage areas.
See Listing #2066.

2812 MAS FAMILY SCHOLARSHIP PROGRAM

Summary: To provide financial assistance to students of Cuban descent who are working on an undergraduate or graduate degree in selected subject areas.
See Listing #1374.

2813 $$ MASSACHUSETTS INCENTIVE PROGRAM FOR ASPIRING TEACHERS

Massachusetts Office of Student Financial Assistance
454 Broadway, Suite 200
Revere, MA 02151
Phone: (617) 391–6070; Fax: (617) 727–0667;
Email: osfa@osfa.mass.edu
Web: www.osfa.mass.edu/default.asp?page=aspireTeachersWaiver
Summary: To provide funding to students at colleges and universities in Massachusetts who are interested in becoming teachers in the state following graduation.
Eligibility: Open to students enrolled in their third or fourth year of a Massachusetts state–approved teacher certification program field with teacher shortages. Applicants must 1) have been residents of Massachusetts for at least 1 year and 2) be U.S. citizens or permanent residents. They must be attending 1 of the 9 Massachusetts state colleges or the 4 campuses of the University of

Massachusetts and have a cumulative GPA of 3.0 or higher. A condition of the program is that they must commit to teaching for 2 years in a public school in Massachusetts upon successful completion of a bachelor's degree.

Financial data: Eligible students are entitled to a tuition waiver equal to the resident tuition rate at the state college or university campus where they are enrolled. If they do not complete their college education within 4 years of entering the program, or if they fail to complete their 2–year teaching commitment within 4 years following graduation from college, they must pay the state the full amount of the tuition waivers granted, with interest.

Duration: 2 years, provided the recipient maintains a GPA of 3.0 or higher.

Number awarded: Varies each year.

Deadline: April of each year.

2814 $$ MASSACHUSETTS PARAPROFESSIONAL TEACHER PREPARATION GRANT PROGRAM

Massachusetts Office of Student Financial Assistance
454 Broadway, Suite 200
Revere, MA 02151
Phone: (617) 391–6070; Fax: (617) 727–0667;
Email: osfa@osfa.mass.edu
Web: www.osfa.mass.edu/default.asp?page=paraprofessional

Summary: To provide funding to students and educational paraprofessionals in Massachusetts who are interested in completing a college degree and becoming certified as teachers.

Eligibility: Open to Massachusetts residents who 1) are working on a degree in an area of high need (recently defined as bilingual education, foreign languages, mathematics, science, and special education); or 2) have been employed as paraprofessionals in public schools in the state for at least 2 years. Applicants must be enrolled full time in an undergraduate degree program leading to teacher certification at a Massachusetts public institution. U.S. citizenship or permanent resident status is required. Applicants must submit a Free Application for Federal Student Aid (FAFSA), but financial need is not required.

Financial data: Grants depend on the type of institution attended. At public universities, the maximum award is $625 per credit, to a total of $7,500 per academic year. At state colleges, the maximum award is $450 per credit, to a total of $6,000 per academic year. At community colleges, the maximum award is $250 per credit, to a total of $4,000 per academic year. At private universities and colleges, the maximum award is $625 per credit, to a total of $7,500 per academic year. This is a scholarship/loan program. Recipients must agree to teach in a Massachusetts public school 1 year for each year that a full or partial grant was received. If they fail to complete that teaching obligation, they must repay the amount of the grant received.

Duration: Until completion of an undergraduate degree, provided the recipient maintains satisfactory academic progress.

Number awarded: Varies each year.

Deadline: June of each year.

2815 $$ MASSMUTUAL SCHOLARS PROGRAM

Massachusetts Mutual Life Insurance Company
1295 State Street
Springfield, MA 01111–0001
Phone: (800) 542–6767
Web: www.act.org/massmutual

Summary: To provide financial assistance to minority undergraduates preparing for a career in the insurance and financial services industry.

Eligibility: Open to full–time students of African American, Asian/Pacific Islander, or Hispanic descent who are entering their sophomore, junior, senior, or fifth–year senior year at an accredited college or university in the United States, Puerto Rico, U.S. Virgin Islands, or Guam. Applicants must be U.S. citizens or permanent residents and have a GPA of 3.0 or higher. They may be majoring in any field, but preference is given to students who demonstrate 1) an interest in preparing for a career in the insurance and financial services industry; and 2) leadership and participation in extracurricular activities. Financial need is considered in the selection process.

Financial data: The stipend is $5,000.

Duration: 1 year.

Number awarded: 30 each year.

Deadline: May of each year.

2816 $ MATTHEW H. PARRY MEMORIAL SCHOLARSHIP

Project Management Institute
Attn: PMI Educational Foundation
14 Campus Boulevard
Newtown Square, PA 19073–3299
Phone: (610) 356–4600, ext. 7004; Fax: (610) 356–0357;
Email: pmief@pmi.org
Web: www.pmi.org/pmief/scholarship/scholarships.asp

Summary: To provide financial assistance to undergraduate students from any state who are working on a degree in project management.

Eligibility: Open to residents of any state enrolled as an undergraduate at a degree–granting institution of higher education. Applicants must demonstrate an interest in project management as a potential career. Along with their application, they must submit 1) a 500–word essay on why they want to be a project manager; and 2) a 250–word essay on how a code of ethics is important to project management. Financial need is not considered in the selection process.

Financial data: The stipend is $2,000.

Duration: 1 year.

Number awarded: 1 each year.

Deadline: May of each year.

2817 $ MAY AND HUBERT EVERLY HEA SCHOLARSHIP

Hawaii Education Association
Attn: Scholarship Committee
1953 South Beretania Street, Suite 5C
Honolulu, HI 96826
Phone: (808) 949–6657; (866) 653–9372; Fax: (808) 944–2032;
Email: hea.office@heaed.com
Web: www.heaed.com/HEA_Scholarships.html

Summary: To provide financial assistance to education majors in Hawaii who plan to teach in the state.

Eligibility: Open to currently–enrolled college students who are attending an accredited institution of higher learning in Hawaii. Applicants must be majoring in education and be planning to teach in the state at the K–12 level. Along with their application, they must submit a 300–word essay on their reasons for choosing education as a career, including future plans, extracurricular activities, community services, membership in clubs and positions held, and past and present employment records. Selection is based on that statement (5 points), official transcript (5 points), recommendations (5 points), and financial need (10 points).

Financial data: The stipend is $2,000, paid in 2 equal installments. Funds are sent directly to the recipient's institution.

Duration: 1 year.

Number awarded: 1 each year.

Deadline: March of each year.

2818 MEDIA FELLOWS PROGRAM

Summary: To provide financial assistance to upper–division students who are preparing for a career in a media–related field.

See Listing #1376.

2819 $ MEDIA PLAN CASE COMPETITION

Summary: To recognize and reward, with scholarships for continuing study, undergraduate students who develop outstanding strategic media plans in a case competition.

See Listing #1377.

2820 $$ MESBEC PROGRAM

Summary: To provide financial assistance to American Indian students who are interested in working on an undergraduate or graduate degree in selected fields.

See Listing #2084.

2821 $ MG EUGENE C. RENZI, USA (RET.)/MANTECH INTERNATIONAL CORPORATION TEACHER'S SCHOLARSHIP

Armed Forces Communications and Electronics Association
Attn: AFCEA Educational Foundation
4400 Fair Lakes Court
Fairfax, VA 22033–3899
Phone: (703) 631–6138; (800) 336–4583, ext. 6138; Fax: (703) 631–4693;
Email: scholarshipsinfo@afcea.org
Web: www.afcea.org

Summary: To provide financial assistance to undergraduate and graduate students who are preparing for a career as a teacher of science and mathematics.

Eligibility: Open to full–time sophomores, juniors, seniors, and graduate students at accredited colleges and universities in the United States. Applicants must be U.S. citizens preparing for a career as a teacher of science, mathematics, or information technology at a middle or secondary school. They must have a GPA of 3.0 or higher. In the selection process, first consideration is given to wounded or disabled veterans, then to honorably discharged veterans. Financial need is not considered.
Financial data: The stipend is $2,500.
Duration: 1 year.
Number awarded: 1 each year.
Deadline: March of each year.

2822 $$ MHEFI SCHOLARSHIP PROGRAM

Summary: To provide financial assistance to undergraduate or graduate students who are studying material handling.
See Listing #2086.

2823 $ MICHAEL BENDIX SUTTON SCHOLARSHIPS

Michael Bendix Sutton Foundation
c/o Marion B. Sutton
300 Martine Avenue
White Plains, NY 10601–3459
Summary: To provide financial assistance to people with hemophilia who are pre–law students.
Eligibility: Open to pre–law students who have hemophilia.
Financial data: The stipend is $2,000.
Duration: 1 year.
Number awarded: 2 each year.
Deadline: March of each year.

2824 MICHELE L. MCDONALD SCHOLARSHIP

Educational Foundation for Women in Accounting
Attn: Foundation Administrator
136 South Keowee Street
Dayton, OH 45402
Phone: (937) 424–3391; Fax: (937) 222–5749;
Email: info@efwa.org
Web: www.efwa.org/scholarships_McDonald.php
Summary: To provide financial support to women who are returning to college from the workforce or after raising their family to work on a degree in accounting.
Eligibility: Open to women who are returning to college from the workforce or after raising children. Applicants must be planning to begin a program of study for a college degree in accounting. Selection is based on aptitude for accounting and business, commitment to the goal of working on a degree in accounting (including evidence of continued commitment after receiving this award), clear evidence that the candidate has established goals and a plan for achieving those goals (both personal and professional), and financial need. U.S. citizenship is required.
Financial data: The stipend is $1,000 per year.
Duration: 1 year; may be renewed 1 additional year if the recipient completes at least 12 hours each semester.
Number awarded: 1 each year.
Deadline: April of each year.

2825 $ MICHIGAN ASSOCIATION OF REALTORS SCHOLARSHIPS

Michigan Association of Realtors
Attn: Scholarship Trust
720 North Washington Avenue
P.O. Box 40725
Lansing, MI 48901–7925
Phone: (517) 372–8890; (800) 454–7842; Fax: (517) 334–5568
Web: www.mirealtors.com/content/ScholarshipsAndAwards.htm
Summary: To provide financial assistance to upper–division and graduate students from Michigan who are working on a degree in real estate at a school in any state.
Eligibility: Open to residents of Michigan who are enrolled full time at a major college or university in any state with an academic major related to real estate. Applicants must be undergraduates entering their junior or senior year or graduate students and taking courses related to real estate, including business, finance, and law. They must have a GPA of 2.0 or higher and be able to show other evidence of academic achievement. Along with their application, they must submit a statement of their reasons for preparing for a career in real estate. Financial need is also considered in the selection process.
Financial data: The stipend is $2,000.
Duration: 1 year.
Number awarded: Varies each year; recently, 2 of these scholarships were awarded.
Deadline: June of each year.

2826 $$ MICHIGAN MORTUARY SCIENCE FOUNDATION SCHOLARSHIP

Michigan Funeral Directors Association
Attn: Michigan Mortuary Science Foundation
2420 Science Parkway
Okemos, MI 48864
Phone: (517) 349–9565; (888) 955–6332; Fax: (517) 349–9819;
Email: mmsf@mfda.org
Web: www.mfda.org
Summary: To provide financial assistance to Michigan residents who are interested in preparing for a career in mortuary science.
Eligibility: Open to students entering or attending a school of mortuary science in any state. Applicants must have been residents of Michigan for at least 12 months. Along with their application, they must submit transcripts, a letter of recommendation from a member of the sponsoring organization, and an essay (between 250 and 500 words) explaining their decision to pursue a funeral service education. They must also view a 5–minute video on You Tube and submit their responses to 3 questions raised by the video: 1) the difference between empathy and sympathy and the role they play as a funeral director; 2) their plans for getting started in the funeral profession; and 3) a discussion on a funeral–related topic. Selection is based on the submitted material; financial need is not considered.
Financial data: Stipends range from $1,000 to $5,000. Funds are sent directly to the recipient's school to be used to help pay for tuition.
Duration: 1 year.
Number awarded: 1 or more each year.
Deadline: April of each year.

2827 $ MIEF COLLEGE SCHOLARSHIPS

Missouri Insurance Education Foundation
Attn: Scholarship Administrator
P.O. Box 1654
Jefferson City, MO 65102
Phone: (573) 893–4234;
Email: miis@midamerica.net
Web: www.mief.org
Summary: To provide financial assistance to upper–division students from Missouri who are working on a degree in insurance at a college or university in the state.
Eligibility: Open to juniors and seniors majoring in insurance or a related area at a Missouri college or university. Applicants must be enrolled full time, have a GPA of 2.5 or higher, and be residents of Missouri. Preference is given to students who can demonstrate financial need. Finalists may be interviewed. The top–ranked applicant receives the C. Lawrence Leggett Scholarship.
Financial data: Stipends are $2,500 or $2,000.
Duration: 1 year.
Number awarded: 6 each year: 1 at $2,500 (the C. Lawrence Leggett Scholarship) and 5 at $2,000.
Deadline: March of each year.

2828 MIEF HIGH SCHOOL SCHOLARSHIPS

Missouri Insurance Education Foundation
Attn: Scholarship Administrator
P.O. Box 1654
Jefferson City, MO 65102
Phone: (573) 893–4234;
Email: miis@midamerica.net
Web: www.mief.org
Summary: To provide financial assistance to high school seniors from Missouri who plan to major in insurance or a related field at a college or university in the state.

Eligibility: Open to seniors graduating from high schools in Missouri who plan to attend a college or university in the state. Applicants must be planning to major in insurance, risk management, or actuarial science as a full–time student. Selection is based on academic achievement, participation in school and outside activities and organizations, honors and awards, and work experience; financial need is not considered.
Financial data: The stipend is $1,500.
Duration: 1 year.
Number awarded: 4 each year.
Deadline: March of each year.

2829 MILWAUKEE CHAPTER SCHOLARSHIPS

American Society of Women Accountants–Milwaukee Chapter
c/o Sue Heaton, Scholarship Chair
9310 North 107th Street
Milwaukee, WI 53224
Phone: (414) 446–9098; Fax: (414) 365–9138;
Email: sheaton1@wi.rr.com
Web: www.aswamilwaukee.org/Scholarship.html
Summary: To provide financial assistance to women from any state who are majoring in accounting at a college in Wisconsin.
Eligibility: Open to women who are entering their second year at a 2–year college or their senior year at a 4–year college or university in Wisconsin. Applicants must be majoring in accounting. Along with their application, they must submit an essay on their career goals and objectives. Selection is based on the essay, grades, extracurricular activities, life experience, and financial need.
Financial data: The stipend is $1,500 for students in a 4–year program or $500 for students in a 2–year program.
Duration: 1 year.
Number awarded: 1 or more each year.
Deadline: October of each year for students in a 2–year program or November of each year for students in a 4–year program.

2830 MINNESOTA CHAPTER SCHOLARSHIP

Summary: To provide financial assistance to undergraduate and graduate students with a Minnesota connection who are working on a degree in health care information or management.
See Listing #2095.

2831 $$ MINORITIES IN GOVERNMENT FINANCE SCHOLARSHIP

Government Finance Officers Association
Attn: Scholarship Committee
203 North LaSalle Street, Suite 2700
Chicago, IL 60601–1210
Phone: (312) 977–9700; Fax: (312) 977–4806
Web: www.gfoa.org
Summary: To provide financial assistance to minority upper–division and graduate students who are preparing for a career in state and local government finance.
Eligibility: Open to upper–division and graduate students who are preparing for a career in public finance by working on a degree in public administration, accounting, finance, political science, economics, or business administration (with a specific focus on government or nonprofit management). Applicants must be members of a minority group, citizens or permanent residents of the United States or Canada, and able to provide a letter of recommendation from a representative of their school. Selection is based on career plans, academic record, plan of study, letters of recommendation, and GPA. Financial need is not considered.
Financial data: The stipend is $5,000.
Duration: 1 year.
Number awarded: 1 or more each year.
Deadline: February of each year.

2832 $$ MINORITY TEACHERS OF ILLINOIS SCHOLARSHIP PROGRAM

Illinois Student Assistance Commission
Attn: Scholarship and Grant Services
1755 Lake Cook Road
Deerfield, IL 60015–5209
Phone: (847) 948–8550; (800) 899–ISAC; Fax: (847) 831–8549; TDD: (800) 526–0844;
Email: isac.studentservices@isac.illinois.gov
Web: www.collegeillinois.org
Summary: To provide funding to minority students in Illinois who plan to become teachers at the preschool, elementary, or secondary level.
Eligibility: Open to Illinois residents who are U.S. citizens or eligible noncitizens, members of a minority group (African American/Black, Hispanic American, Asian American, or Native American), and high school graduates or holders of a General Educational Development (GED) certificate. They must be enrolled at least half time as an undergraduate or graduate student, have a GPA of 2.5 or higher, not be in default on any student loan, and be enrolled or accepted for enrollment in a teacher education program.
Financial data: Grants up to $5,000 per year are awarded. This is a scholarship/loan program. Recipients must agree to teach full time 1 year for each year of support received. The teaching agreement may be fulfilled at a public, private, or parochial preschool, elementary school, or secondary school in Illinois; at least 30% of the student body at those schools must be minority. It must be fulfilled within the 5–year period following the completion of the undergraduate program for which the scholarship was awarded. The time period may be extended if the recipient serves in the U.S. armed forces, enrolls full time in a graduate program related to teaching, becomes temporarily disabled, is unable to find employment as a teacher at a qualifying school, or takes additional courses on at least a half–time basis to obtain certification as a teacher in Illinois. Recipients who fail to honor this work obligation must repay the award with 5% interest.
Duration: 1 year; may be renewed for a total of 8 semesters or 12 quarters.
Number awarded: Varies each year.
Deadline: Priority consideration is given to applications received by February of each year.

2833 MIRIAM HOFFMAN SCHOLARSHIPS

Summary: To provide financial assistance to undergraduate and graduate Methodist students who are preparing for a music–related career.
See Listing #1385.

2834 MISSISSIPPI CRITICAL NEEDS TEACHER LOAN/SCHOLARSHIP PROGRAM

Mississippi Office of Student Financial Aid
3825 Ridgewood Road
Jackson, MS 39211–6453
Phone: (601) 432–6997; (800) 327–2980 (within MS); Fax: (601) 432–6527;
Email: sfa@mississippi.edu
Web: www.mississippi.edu/riseupms/financialaid–state.php
Summary: To provide funding to students in Mississippi interested in preparing for a career as a teacher and willing to work in selected areas of the state or teach in specified subject areas.
Eligibility: Open to juniors and seniors at Mississippi 4–year colleges and universities. Mississippi residency is not required. Applicants must have passed Praxis I or had an ACT score of 21 or higher with a minimum of 18 on all subscores. They must enroll in a program of study leading to a bachelor's degree and a Class "A" teacher educator license; agree to employment immediately after completing their degree as a full–time classroom teacher in a Mississippi public school located in a critical teacher shortage area of the state or in a subject shortage area; and have a cumulative GPA of 2.5 or higher.
Financial data: Full–time students receive an award equal to the highest cost of tuition, room, and board at a public institution in the state; part–time students receive a prorated amount. This is a scholarship/loan program; recipients must sign a contract agreeing to teach 1 year for each year the award is received in an accredited public school or public school district in a critical teacher geographic shortage area of Mississippi as defined at the time of graduation. If the recipient fails to remain enrolled in a teacher education program or fails to fulfill the service obligation, repayment of principal and interest is required.
Duration: 1 year; may be renewed 1 additional year if the recipient maintains a GPA of 2.5 or higher, meets the satisfactory academic progress standards of their institution, and remains enrolled in a program of study leading to a Class "A" teacher educator license.
Number awarded: Varies each year; recently, 151 of these scholarship loans, with a total value of more than $1.8 million were awarded.
Deadline: March of each year.

2835 $ MISSISSIPPI SOCIETY OF CERTIFIED PUBLIC ACCOUNTANTS UNDERGRADUATE SCHOLARSHIP

Mississippi Society of Certified Public Accountants
Attn: MSCPA Education Foundation
The Commons, Highland Colony Parkway
306 Southampton Row
Ridgeland, MS 39157

Phone: (601) 856–4244; (800) 772–1099 (within MS); Fax: (601) 856–8255;
Email: mail@ms–cpa.org
Web: www.ms–cpa.org/foundation.asp?id=44

Summary: To provide financial assistance to upper–division students majoring in accounting at designated 4–year institutions in Mississippi.

Eligibility: Open to residents of Mississippi who have completed or are completing their junior year of college, are majoring in accounting, have completed at least 6 hours of accounting courses above the principles or introductory level, and are attending 1 of the following schools in Mississippi: Alcorn State University, Belhaven University, Delta State University, Jackson State University, Millsaps College, Mississippi College, Mississippi State University, Mississippi University for Women, Mississippi Valley State University, University of Mississippi, University of Southern Mississippi, or William Carey University. They must be nominated by their academic institution. Nominees must submit a completed application form, transcripts, and a 1–page essay explaining why they plan a career in public accounting. Selection is based on the essay, academic excellence (GPA of 3.0 or higher both overall and in accounting classes), recommendations, financial need, and campus involvement.

Financial data: The stipend is $2,000. Checks are made payable to the recipient's school.

Duration: 1 year.

Number awarded: 1 or more each year.

Deadline: June of each year.

2836 $ MISSOURI CHAPTER CONTINUING EDUCATION SCHOLARSHIP

Summary: To provide financial assistance to students at 2–year colleges in Missouri who are completing a pre–engineering program and planning to transfer to a 4–year institution in the state to complete a degree in public administration or engineering.

See Listing #2101.

2837 $ MISSOURI MINORITY TEACHING SCHOLARSHIP PROGRAM

Summary: To provide scholarships and other funding to minority high school seniors, high school graduates, and college students in Missouri who are interested in preparing for a teaching career in mathematics or science.

See Listing #2102.

2838 $$ MORGAN STANLEY SCHOLARS PROGRAM

American Indian College Fund
Attn: Scholarship Department
8333 Greenwood Boulevard
Denver, CO 80221
Phone: (303) 426–8900; (800) 776–FUND; Fax: (303) 426–1200;
Email: scholarships@collegefund.org
Web: www.collegefund.org/content/full_circle_scholarships_listings

Summary: To provide financial assistance to American Indian students at mainstream 4–year institutions who are preparing for a career in the business and financial services industry.

Eligibility: Open to American Indians or Alaska Natives who are currently enrolled full time in a bachelor's degree program at a mainstream institution in the United States. Applicants must be interested in preparing for a career in the business or financial services industry. They must have a GPA of 3.0 or higher and a demonstrated commitment to the American Indian community. Applications are available only online and include required essays on specified topics. Selection is based on exceptional academic achievement. U.S. citizenship is required.

Financial data: The stipend is $5,000.

Duration: 1 year.

Number awarded: 5 each year.

Deadline: May of each year.

2839 $ MORGAN STANLEY TRIBAL SCHOLARS PROGRAM

American Indian College Fund
Attn: Scholarship Department
8333 Greenwood Boulevard
Denver, CO 80221
Phone: (303) 426–8900; (800) 776–FUND; Fax: (303) 426–1200;
Email: scholarships@collegefund.org
Web: www.collegefund.org/content/full_circle_scholarships_listings

Summary: To provide financial assistance to Native American students currently enrolled full time at a Tribal College or University (TCU) to prepare for a career in business and the financial services industry.

Eligibility: Open to American Indians and Alaska Natives who are enrolled full time at an eligible TCU. Applicants must have declared a major in business or a field related to the financial services industry and have a GPA of 3.0 or higher. They must be able to demonstrate a commitment to the American Indian community. Applications are available only online and include required essays on specified topics. Selection is based on exceptional academic achievement. U.S. citizenship is required.

Financial data: The stipend is $2,500.

Duration: 1 year.

Number awarded: 10 each year.

Deadline: May of each year.

2840 $ MOSMILLER INTERN SCHOLARSHIP PROGRAM

Summary: To provide financial assistance and work experience to students working on an undergraduate degree in floriculture or business.

See Listing #2108.

2841 MOSS ADAMS FOUNDATION SCHOLARSHIP

Educational Foundation for Women in Accounting
Attn: Foundation Administrator
136 South Keowee Street
Dayton, OH 45402
Phone: (937) 424–3391; Fax: (937) 222–5749;
Email: info@efwa.org
Web: www.efwa.org/scholarships_MossAdams.php

Summary: To provide financial support to women, including minority women, who are working on an accounting degree.

Eligibility: Open to women who are enrolled in an accounting degree program at an accredited college or university. Applicants must meet 1 of the following criteria: 1) women pursuing a fifth–year requirement either through general studies or within a graduate program; 2) women returning to school as current or reentry juniors or seniors; or 3) minority women. Selection is based on aptitude for accounting and business, commitment to the goal of working on a degree in accounting (including evidence of continued commitment after receiving this award), clear evidence that the candidate has established goals and a plan for achieving those goals (both personal and professional), financial need, and a demonstration of how the scholarship will impact her life. U.S. citizenship is required.

Financial data: The stipend is $1,000.

Duration: 1 year.

Number awarded: 1 each year.

Deadline: April of each year.

2842 $ MSCPA FIRM SCHOLARSHIPS

Massachusetts Society of Certified Public Accountants
Attn: MSCPA Educational Foundation
105 Chauncy Street, Tenth Floor
Boston, MA 02111
Phone: (617) 556–4000; (800) 392–6145; Fax: (617) 556–4126;
Email: info@mscpaonline.org
Web: www.cpatrack.com/scholarships

Summary: To provide financial assistance to residents of Massachusetts working on an undergraduate degree in accounting at a college or university in the state.

Eligibility: Open to Massachusetts residents enrolled at a college or university in the state. Applicants must have completed the first semester of their junior year and be able to demonstrate financial need, academic excellence, and an intention to prepare for a career as a Certified Public Accountant (C.P.A.) at a firm in Massachusetts.

Financial data: The stipend is $2,500.

Duration: 1 year.

Number awarded: Varies each year; recently, 15 of these scholarships were awarded.

Deadline: March of each year.

2843 $$ MULTI–YEAR SCHOLARSHIPS FOR UNDERGRADUATES

Pennsylvania Institute of Certified Public Accountants
Attn: Careers in Accounting Team
1801 Market Street, Suite 2400

Philadelphia, PA 19103
Phone: (215) 496–9272; (888) CPA–2001 (within PA); Fax: (215) 496–9212;
Email: schools@picpa.org
Web: www.picpa.org/Content/38801.aspx

Summary: To provide financial assistance to Pennsylvania undergraduates majoring in accounting.

Eligibility: Open to full–time undergraduate students majoring in accounting at a Pennsylvania college or university. Applicants must have completed at least 36 credit hours and have a GPA of 3.0 or higher. Selection is based on intellectual capacity, leadership potential, intent to prepare for a career in accounting, and financial need.

Financial data: Stipends range from $1,000 to $5,000 per year.

Duration: 1 year; most may be renewed until completion of an undergraduate degree, provided the recipient maintains a GPA of 3.0 or higher and full–time enrollment in an accounting program.

Number awarded: Varies each year; recently, 99 of these scholarships (55 first–time and 44 renewal) were awarded.

Deadline: March of each year.

2844 $$ NASCAR/WENDELL SCOTT AWARD

Summary: To provide financial assistance to undergraduate and graduate students majoring in specified fields at member institutions of the Hispanic Association of Colleges and Universities (HACU) in designated states.

See Listing #2120.

2845 $ NATIONAL ASSOCIATION OF WATER COMPANIES NEW JERSEY SCHOLARSHIP

Summary: To provide financial assistance to New Jersey residents who are interested in working on an undergraduate or graduate degree at a school in the state to prepare for a career in the water utility industry.

See Listing #2123.

2846 NATIONAL CAPITAL AREA CHAPTER SCHOLARSHIP PROGRAM

Healthcare Information and Management Systems Society–National Capital Area Chapter
c/o Wanda Gamble, Scholarship Chair
Vangent Inc.
4250 North Fairfax Drive, Suite 1200
Arlington, VA 22203
Phone: (703) 502–1119;
Email: wanda_gamble@vangent.com
Web: www.himss–nca.org/resources/resources1.html

Summary: To provide financial assistance to residents of any state enrolled at colleges and universities in the Washington, D.C. metropolitan area and working on an undergraduate or graduate degree in fields related to the health or management information systems field.

Eligibility: Open to residents of any state enrolled at a college or university in the Washington, D.C. metropolitan area and working on an associate, bachelor's, master's, or Ph.D. degree or post–degree certification. Applicants must be studying health information, health management, or information systems management. They must have a GPA of 3.0 or higher. Along with their application, they must submit a 500–word essay on why they have chosen the field of information management/information technology (IM/IT), why IM/IT is important to health care today, and a major issue facing the community today and how IM/IT can address that issue. Selection is based on that essay, academic achievement, recommendations, professional achievements, and participation in professional associations such as the National Capital Area (NCA) chapter of the Healthcare Information and Management Systems Society (HIMSS).

Financial data: A stipend is awarded (amount not specified).

Duration: 1 year; nonrenewable.

Number awarded: 4 each year: 1 each to an associate degree student, undergraduate student, a graduate student, and post–degree certification student.

Deadline: April of each year.

2847 NATIONAL CONFERENCE OF CPA PRACTITIONERS SCHOLARSHIPS FOR GRADUATING HIGH SCHOOL SENIORS

National Conference of CPA Practitioners, Inc.
Attn: Scholarship Committee
22 Jericho Turnpike, Suite 110
Mineola, NY 11501
Phone: (516) 333–8282; (888) 488–5400; Fax: (516) 333–4099;
Email: execdir@nccpap.org
Web: www.nccpap.org/about–us/scholarships

Summary: To provide financial assistance to high school seniors planning to attend college to prepare for a career as a Certified Public Accountant (C.P.A.).

Eligibility: Open to seniors graduating from high school with a GPA of 3.3 or higher. Applicants must be planning to attend a 2– or 4–year college or university as a full–time student to prepare for a career as a C.P.A. Along with their application, they must submit a 200–word essay that explains why they desire to prepare for a career as a C.P.A. Financial need is not considered in the selection process.

Financial data: The stipend is $1,000.

Duration: 1 year.

Number awarded: Varies each year; recently, 11 of these scholarships were awarded.

Deadline: December of each year.

2848 NATIONAL ESSAY SCHOLARSHIP CONTEST

Chapel of Four Chaplains
The Navy Yard, Building 649
1201 Constitution Avenue
Philadelphia, PA 19112–1307
Phone: (215) 218–1943; (866) 400–0975; Fax: (215) 218–1949;
Email: chapel@fourchaplains.org
Web: www.fourchaplains.org/programs.html

Summary: To recognize and reward, with college scholarships, high school seniors who submit outstanding essays on a topic related to public service.

Eligibility: Open to public and private high school seniors. The children of members of the Chapel of Four Chaplains, youth committee, board of directors, or trustees are ineligible. The topic of the essay changes periodically; recently, students were invited to identify a compelling problem, need, or unresolved conflict (e.g., racial discrimination, religious community injustice, public indifference, civic discord, societal ignorance) that, through caring intervention, can be transformed and corrected. Essays must be no more than 450 words in length. Selection is based on imaginative creativity, correct grammar and spelling, clarity, relevance, and logical presentation.

Financial data: Prizes are scholarships of $1,000 for first, $750 for second, $500 for third, $400 for fourth, and $300 for fifth.

Duration: The competition is held annually.

Number awarded: 5 each year.

Deadline: November of each year.

2849 $$ NATIONAL FEDERATION OF INDEPENDENT BUSINESS YOUNG ENTREPRENEUR AWARDS

National Federation of Independent Business
Attn: NFIB Young Entrepreneur Foundation
1201 F Street, N.W., Suite 200
Washington, DC 20004
Phone: (202) 314–2055; (800) NFIB–NOW;
Email: yef@nfib.org
Web: www.nfib.com/yef/yef–programs/young–entrepreneur–awards

Summary: To provide financial assistance for college to high school seniors who are running their own business.

Eligibility: Open to graduating high school seniors who plan to enroll as a full–time freshman at an accredited 2– or 4–year college, university, or vocational/technical institute. Applicants must be running their own established business. They must meet or exceed academic standards, using standardized test scores (ACT/SAT), class rank, and GPA as indicators. Along with their application, they must submit a 1,000–word essay describing their entrepreneurial experience and their involvement with small business. Selection is based on that essay, academic record, extracurricular activities, leadership activities, and small business experience; evidence of entrepreneurial spirit and initiative is given special consideration.

Financial data: The highest–ranked applicant receives $10,000 and 4 other finalists receive $5,000. Other stipends are $1,000.

Duration: 1 year; some awards may be renewed.

Number awarded: Varies each year; recently, 131 of these scholarships were awarded: 1 at $10,000, 4 at $5,000, and 126 at $1,000. Since the program began, it has awarded more than $2.5 million in scholarships to more than 2,200 students.

Deadline: December of each year.

2850 NATIONAL FFA SCHOLARSHIPS FOR UNDERGRADUATES IN THE SOCIAL SCIENCES

National FFA Organization
Attn: Scholarship Office
6060 FFA Drive
P.O. Box 68960
Indianapolis, IN 46268–0960
Phone: (317) 802–4419; Fax: (317) 802–5419;
Email: scholarships@ffa.org
Web: www.ffa.org

Summary: To provide financial assistance to FFA members who wish to study agribusiness and related fields in college.

Eligibility: Open to current and former members of the organization who are working or planning to work full time on a degree in fields related to business and the social sciences; this includes: agribusiness, agricultural economics, agricultural education, agricultural finance, and agricultural marketing. For most of the scholarships, applicants must be high school seniors; others are open to students currently enrolled in college. The program includes a large number of designated scholarships that specify the locations where the members must live, the schools they must attend, the fields of study they must pursue, or other requirements. Some consider family income in the selection process, but most do not. Selection is based on academic achievement (10 points for GPA, 10 points for SAT or ACT score, 10 points for class rank), leadership in FFA activities (30 points), leadership in community activities (10 points), and participation in the Supervised Agricultural Experience (SAE) program (30 points). U.S. citizenship is required.

Financial data: Stipends vary, but most are at least $1,000.

Duration: 1 year or more.

Number awarded: Varies; generally, a total of approximately 1,000 scholarships are awarded annually by the association.

Deadline: February of each year.

2851 $$ NATIONAL HIGH SCHOOL ORATORICAL CONTEST

American Legion
Attn: Americanism and Children & Youth Division
700 North Pennsylvania Street
P.O. Box 1055
Indianapolis, IN 46206–1055
Phone: (317) 630–1249; Fax: (317) 630–1223;
Email: acy@legion.org
Web: legion.org/oratorical

Summary: To recognize and reward, with college scholarships, high school students who participate in an oratorical contest on a theme related to the U.S. Constitution.

Eligibility: Open to U.S. citizens and permanent residents under 20 years of age who are currently enrolled in junior high or high school (grades 9–12). Students enter the contest through their Department (state) American Legion. Each department chooses 1 contestant to enter the regional contest. Regional winners compete in sectional contests; sectional winners compete on the national level. In all competitions, participants are evaluated on both the content and presentation of their prepared and extemporaneous speeches, which must deal with an aspect of the American Constitution or principles of government under the Constitution.

Financial data: Scholarship awards are presented to the 3 finalists in the national contest: $18,000 to the first–place winner; $16,000 to the second–place winner; and $14,000 to the third–place winner. Each Department (state) winner who participates in the first round of the national contest receives a $1,500 scholarship; each first–round winner who advances to and participates in the second round, but does not advance to the final round, receives an additional $1,500 scholarship.

Duration: The competition is held annually.

Number awarded: 3 national winners; hundreds of sectional, regional, and departmental winners.

Deadline: The dates of departmental competitions vary; check with your local American Legion post. The national competition is generally held in April.

2852 $ NATIONAL HYDROPOWER ASSOCIATION PAST PRESIDENTS' LEGACY SCHOLARSHIP

Summary: To provide financial assistance to undergraduate and graduate students working on a degree in a field related to the hydropower industry.

See Listing #2133.

2853 $ NATIONAL INDIAN GAMING ASSOCIATION TRIBAL COLLEGE SCHOLARSHIPS

American Indian College Fund
Attn: Scholarship Department
8333 Greenwood Boulevard
Denver, CO 80221
Phone: (303) 426–8900; (800) 776–FUND; Fax: (303) 426–1200;
Email: scholarships@collegefund.org
Web: www.collegefund.org/content/full_circle_scholarships_listings

Summary: To provide financial assistance to Native American students enrolled at a Tribal College or University (TCU), especially those majoring in business-related fields.

Eligibility: Open to American Indians and Alaska Natives who are enrolled full time at an eligible TCU. Applicants may be studying any field, but preference is given to business, hospitality, information technology, or marketing majors. They must have a GPA of 3.0 or higher. Applications are available only online and include required essays on specified topics. U.S. citizenship is required.

Financial data: The stipend is $2,000.

Duration: 1 year.

Number awarded: 1 or more each year.

Deadline: May of each year.

2854 $$ NATIONAL ITALIAN AMERICAN FOUNDATION GENERAL CATEGORY II SCHOLARSHIPS

Summary: To provide financial assistance for college or graduate school to students interested in majoring in Italian language, Italian studies, or Italian American studies.

See Listing #1407.

2855 $$ NATIONAL MILITARY INTELLIGENCE FOUNDATION SCHOLARSHIPS

National Military Intelligence Association
Attn: National Military Intelligence Foundation
P.O. Box 6844
Arlington, VA 22206
Phone: (434) 542–5929;
Email: ffrank54@comcast.net
Web: www.nmia.org/?page=Scholarship

Summary: To provide financial assistance to upper–division and graduate students working on a degree in a field of interest to the intelligence community.

Eligibility: Open to full– and part–time juniors, seniors, and graduate students who are preparing for a career in a field related to the military or national intelligence community. Applicants must submit 4 essays that discuss their interest in a career in the intelligence community and how this scholarship will contribute to that career. Selection is based on academic excellence, demonstrated commitment to a career in the intelligence community, and financial need. The most outstanding applicant receives the LTG James A. Williams Scholarship.

Financial data: The stipend is $5,000 for the winner of the LTG James A. Williams Scholarship, $3,000 for other full–time students, or $2,000 for part–time students.

Duration: 1 year; nonrenewable.

Number awarded: 9 each year: the LTG James A. Williams Scholarship at $5,000, 4 for full–time students at $3,000 each, and 4 for part–time students at $2,000 each.

Deadline: November each year.

2856 $$ NATIONAL SECURITY SCHOLARSHIPS OF THE INDEPENDENT COLLEGE FUND OF MARYLAND

Summary: To provide financial assistance to students from any state enrolled at member institutions of the Independent College Fund of Maryland and majoring in a field related to national security.

See Listing #1414.

2857 $$ NATIVE AMERICAN FINANCE OFFICERS ASSOCIATION STUDENT SCHOLARSHIP FUND

Native American Finance Officers Association
Attn: Christina Morbelli, Program Coordinator
P.O. Box 50637
Phoenix, AZ 85076–0637

Phone: (602) 466–8697; Fax: (201) 447–0945;
Email: christina@nafoa.org
Web: www.nafoa.org/education.html
Summary: To provide financial assistance to Native Americans and Alaska Natives who are studying a business–related field in college or graduate school.
Eligibility: Open to Native American and Alaska Native students working on an associate, bachelor's, master's, or Ph.D. degree at an accredited university. Applicants must be working on a degree in a finance–related discipline, including (but not limited to) accounting, business, economics, finance, or marketing. Selection is based on academic merit, interest in business and finance, and evidence of commitment to their Native community.
Financial data: Stipends range from $10,000 to $22,000.
Duration: 1 year.
Number awarded: Varies each year; recently, 22 of these scholarships were awarded, including 5 students at tribal colleges, 10 undergraduates, and 7 graduate students.
Deadline: October of each year.

2858 $$ NATIVE AMERICAN LEADERSHIP IN EDUCATION (NALE) PROGRAM

Catching the Dream
8200 Mountain Road, N.E., Suite 203
Albuquerque, NM 87110–7835
Phone: (505) 262–2351; Fax: (505) 262–0534;
Email: NScholarsh@aol.com
Web: www.catchingthedream.org/Scholarship.htm
Summary: To provide financial assistance to American Indian paraprofessionals in the education field who wish to return to college or graduate school.
Eligibility: Open to paraprofessionals who are working in Indian schools and who plan to return to college or graduate school to complete their degree in education, counseling, or school administration. Applicants must be able to provide proof that they are at least one–quarter Indian blood and a member of a U.S. tribe that is federally–recognized, state–recognized, or terminated. Along with their application, they must submit documentation of financial need, 3 letters of recommendation, copies of applications and responses from all other sources of funding for which they are eligible, official transcripts, standardized test scores (ACT, SAT, GRE, MCAT, LSAT, etc.), and an essay explaining their goals in life, college plans, and career plans (especially how those plans include working with and benefiting Indians). Selection is based on merit and potential for improving the lives of Indian people.
Financial data: Stipends range from $500 to $5,000 per year.
Duration: 1 year; may be renewed.
Number awarded: Varies; generally, 15 or more each year.
Deadline: April of each year for fall term; September of each year for spring and winter terms; March of each year for summer school.

2859 $ NCSEAA UNDERGRADUATE CRIMINAL JUSTICE SCHOLARSHIPS

North Carolina State Education Assistance Authority
Attn: Grants, Training, and Outreach Department
10 T.W. Alexander Drive
P.O. Box 13663
Research Triangle Park, NC 27709–3663
Phone: (919) 549–8614; (800) 700–1775; Fax: (919) 248–4687;
Email: information@ncseaa.edu
Web: www.ncseaa.edu/Ncsheriffs.htm
Summary: To provide financial assistance to residents of North Carolina, especially children of deceased or disabled law enforcement officers, who are majoring in criminal justice at a college in the state.
Eligibility: Open to North Carolina residents enrolled full time in a criminal justice program at any of the 10 state institutions offering that major: Appalachian State University, East Carolina University, Elizabeth City State University, Fayetteville State University, North Carolina Central University, North Carolina State University, the University of North Carolina at Charlotte, the University of North Carolina at Pembroke, the University of North Carolina at Wilmington, and Western Carolina University. First priority in selection is given to children of law enforcement officers killed in the line of duty; second priority is given to children of sheriffs or deputy sheriffs who are deceased, retired (regular or disability), or currently active in law enforcement in North Carolina; third priority is given to other resident criminal justice students meeting their institution's academic and financial need criteria.
Financial data: The stipend is $2,000 per year.
Duration: 1 year; nonrenewable.
Number awarded: Up to 10 each year: 1 at each of the participating universities.
Deadline: Deadline not specified.

2860 $ NEBRASKA ACTUARIES CLUB SCHOLARSHIPS

Summary: To provide financial assistance to residents of any state who are planning to attend college in Nebraska to prepare for an actuarial career.
See Listing #2147.

2861 NEBRASKA EDUCATIONAL OFFICE PROFESSIONALS ASSOCIATION STUDENT SCHOLARSHIP

Nebraska Educational Office Professionals Association
P.O. Box 83872
Lincoln, NE 68501–3872
Fax: (402) 466–0882
Web: neopa.unl.edu/awards.html
Summary: To provide financial assistance to residents of Nebraska who are enrolled at a school in any state to prepare for an office–related career.
Eligibility: Open to residents of Nebraska who are graduating high school seniors or students currently enrolled in a postsecondary educational institution. Applicants must have completed 2 or more business education courses (in high school, college, or a combination) from among the following: computer classes, keyboarding, typing, short hand, accounting, office practices and procedures, and/or bookkeeping. Along with their application, they must submit a 1–page essay on why they are choosing an office–related career or vocation, 3 letters of recommendation, and high school or college transcripts. Selection is based on academic achievement, initiative of the student, and financial need.
Financial data: The stipend is $1,000.
Duration: 1 year.
Number awarded: 1 each year.
Deadline: January of each year.

2862 $ NEBRASKA SOCIETY OF CERTIFIED PUBLIC ACCOUNTANTS GENERAL SCHOLARSHIPS

Nebraska Society of Certified Public Accountants
Attn: Foundation
635 South 14th Street, Suite 330
Lincoln, NE 68508
Phone: (402) 476–8482; (800) 642–6178; Fax: (402) 476–8731;
Email: society@nescpa.org
Web: www.nescpa.org/scholarships.php
Summary: To provide financial assistance to upper–division accounting students at colleges and universities in Nebraska.
Eligibility: Open to students who are majoring in accounting and have completed their junior year at a Nebraska college or university. Applicants must have the interest in and capabilities of becoming a successful C.P.A., be considering an accounting career in Nebraska, and be planning to take the C.P.A. examination. They must be nominated by accounting faculty members. Selection is based on scholarship, leadership, and character; the highest scholastic average is not necessarily required.
Financial data: Stipends range from $750 to $2,500.
Duration: July of each year.
Number awarded: Varies each year; recently, 34 of these scholarships were awarded.
Deadline: July of each year.

2863 NEBRASKANS OF WORLD WAR II SCHOLARSHIPS

Nebraska State Historical Society Foundation
Attn: Executive Director
Kinman–Oldfield Suite 1010
128 North 13th Street
Lincoln, NE 68508–1565
Phone: (402) 435–3535; (888) 515–3535; Fax: (402) 435–3986;
Email: info@nshsf.org
Web: www.nshsf.org
Summary: To provide financial assistance to high school seniors in Nebraska who submit essays on World War II and plan to attend college in any state.
Eligibility: Open to seniors graduating from high schools in Nebraska with a GPA of 3.5 or higher. Applicants must be planning to enroll full time at a 4–year college or university in any state. Along with their application, they must submit a 1– to 2–page essay on the significance of the history of World War II to them and their community.
Financial data: The stipend is $1,000.
Duration: 1 year; nonrenewable.
Number awarded: Up to 6 each year.
Deadline: January of each year.

2864 $ NEDMA FOUNDATION DIRECT MARKETING SCHOLARSHIP

Summary: To provide financial assistance and work experience to upper–division students in New England who are preparing for a career in direct marketing.

See Listing #1419.

2865 $$ NEEBC SCHOLARSHIP PROGRAM

New England Employee Benefits Council
240 Bear Hill Road, Suite 102
Waltham, MA 02451
Phone: (781) 684–8700; Fax: (781) 684–9200;
Email: info@neebc.org
Web: www.neebc.org/scholar/index.php

Summary: To provide financial assistance to residents and students in New England who are working on an undergraduate or graduate degree in a field related to employee benefits.

Eligibility: Open to undergraduate and graduate students who are residents of New England or enrolled at a college in the region. Applicants must be interested in preparing for a career in the employee benefits field; specific interests include, but are not limited to, actuarial sciences, ERISA and legal aspects of employee benefits, pension design and planning, work and family issues, or corporate benefits design, analysis, and management. Along with their application, they must submit an essay (up to 300 words) describing why they are interested in entering the employee benefits field and what careers within the field are of interest to them and why. Selection is based on 1) study, activities, and goals related to employee benefits; 2) school and community activities; 3) work experience; and 4) academic performance and potential.

Financial data: The stipend is $5,000 per year.

Duration: 1 year; may be renewed up to 3 additional years or until completion of a degree.

Number awarded: 1 or more each year.

Deadline: March of each year.

2866 $ NEHRA FUTURE STARS IN HR SCHOLARSHIPS

Northeast Human Resources Association
Attn: Scholarship Awards
303 Wyman Street, Suite 285
Waltham, MA 02451–1253
Phone: (781) 235–2900; Fax: (781) 237–8745;
Email: info@nehra.com
Web: www.nehra.com

Summary: To provide financial assistance to undergraduate and graduate students at colleges and universities in New England who are preparing for a career in human resources.

Eligibility: Open to full–time undergraduate and graduate students at accredited colleges and universities in New England. Applicants must have completed at least 1 course related to human resources and have a GPA of 3.0 or higher. Along with their application, they must submit a 1–page essay on why they are interested in becoming a human resources professional. Selection is based on interest in becoming a human resources professional, academic success, leadership skills, and participation in non–academic activities. The applicant who is judged most outstanding receives the John D. Erdlen Scholarship Award.

Financial data: Stipends are $3,000 or $2,500 per year.

Duration: 1 year; may be renewed.

Number awarded: 2 each year: 1 at $3,000 (the John D. Erdlen Scholarship Award) and 1 at $2,500.

Deadline: April of each year.

2867 $$ NELSON BROWN AWARD

Summary: To provide financial assistance to Connecticut residents who are interested in attending college in any state to prepare for a career in broadcasting.

See Listing #1421.

2868 $ NEW HAMPSHIRE DUNKIN' DONUTS SCHOLARSHIPS

New Hampshire Charitable Foundation
37 Pleasant Street
Concord, NH 03301–4005
Phone: (603) 225–6641; (800) 464–6641; Fax: (603) 225–1700;
Email: info@nhcf.org
Web: www.nhcf.org/page.aspx?pid=477

Summary: To provide financial assistance to high school seniors in New Hampshire who plan to attend college in any state, especially those interested in preparing for a career related to the food service industry.

Eligibility: Open to seniors graduating from high schools in New Hampshire who are planning to attend a 2– or 4–year college, university, or technical school in any state. Applicants must have a GPA of 3.25 or higher. Preference is given to students preparing for a career in business, hospitality, or the food service industries. Selection is based on academic merit, involvement in school activities, volunteer or community service, paid work experience, and financial need.

Financial data: The stipend is $2,500.

Duration: 1 year.

Number awarded: 10 each year.

Deadline: April of each year.

2869 NEW JERSEY AFFILIATE SCHOLARSHIPS

American Woman's Society of Certified Public Accountants–New Jersey Affiliate
Attn: Scholarship Committee
P.O. Box 143
Roseland, NJ 07068
Email: awscpa.nj@comcast.net
Web: www.awscpa.org/nj/index.html

Summary: To provide financial assistance to women from any state who are working on an undergraduate degree in accounting at a college or university in New Jersey.

Eligibility: Open to women from any state who are enrolled at a college or university in New Jersey and have a cumulative GPA of "B" or higher. Applicants must be majoring in accounting and preparing for a career as a Certified Public Accountant (C.P.A.). They must be a member of the New Jersey affiliate of the American Woman's Society of Certified Public Accountants (AWSCPA). In the selection process, preference is given to students who can demonstrate involvement in school, community, professional, and/or charitable organizations; financial need is not considered.

Financial data: The stipend is $1,500.

Duration: 1 year.

Number awarded: 2 each year.

Deadline: April of each year.

2870 NEW JERSEY FUNERAL SERVICE EDUCATION CORPORATION SCHOLARSHIPS

New Jersey State Funeral Directors Association
Attn: New Jersey Funeral Service Education Corporation
P.O. Box L
Manasquan, NJ 08736
Phone: (732) 974–9444; Fax: (732) 974–8144;
Email: njsfda@njsfda.org
Web: www.njsfda.org/public/Home/CareerSeekers/tabid/74/Default.aspx

Summary: To provide financial assistance to New Jersey residents who are currently enrolled in a mortuary science program.

Eligibility: Open to New Jersey residents who are currently enrolled in a mortuary science program, currently registered as an intern, and planning to enter the field of funeral service in the state after graduation. Applicants must have a college GPA of 3.0 or higher. They must submit an essay on either 1) why they have chosen funeral service as a career; or 2) what they feel they can contribute to funeral service. A personal interview is required. Selection is based on the essay, academic record and commitment to funeral service as a career; financial need is considered after personal and academic accomplishments.

Financial data: A stipend is awarded (amount not specified).

Duration: 1 year.

Number awarded: 1 or more each year.

Deadline: June of each year.

2871 NEW JERSEY SCHOOLWOMEN'S CLUB SCHOLARSHIPS

New Jersey Schoolwomen's Club
c/o Arlene Rogers
13 Ryerson Drive
Hamilton, NJ 08690

Summary: To provide financial assistance to female high school seniors in New Jersey who plan to attend college in any state to prepare for a career in education.
Eligibility: Open to women graduating from high schools in New Jersey who plan to attend a college or university in any state to work on a baccalaureate degree and certification in education. Applicants must have a GPA of 2.5 or higher and scores of at least 1460 on the SAT or 24 on the ACT. Along with their application, they must submit 500–word essays on why they have chosen the field of education as a career, what they anticipate their area of concentration will be, and the contributions they expect to make to their students and to the profession during their career. Financial need is not considered in the selection process.
Financial data: Stipends are $1,000 or $500.
Duration: 1 year.
Number awarded: 4 each year: 2 at $1,000 (the 2 named scholarships) and 2 at $500.
Deadline: February of each year.

2872 $$ NEW JERSEY SOCIETY OF CERTIFIED PUBLIC ACCOUNTANTS COLLEGE SCHOLARSHIP PROGRAM

New Jersey Society of Certified Public Accountants
Attn: Student Programs Coordinator
425 Eagle Rock Avenue, Suite 100
Roseland, NJ 07068–1723
Phone: (973) 226–4494, ext. 241; Fax: (973) 226–7425;
Email: lmatullo@njscpa.org
Web: www.njscpa.org/index/students/scholarships/college
Summary: To provide financial assistance to upper–division and graduate students in New Jersey who are preparing for a career as a Certified Public Accountant (C.P.A.).
Eligibility: Open to residents of New Jersey who are attending a college or university in the state. Applicants must be 1) juniors who are majoring or concentrating in accounting and have completed at least 12 units in accounting; or 2) graduate students enrolled in or entering an accounting–related program. They must have a GPA of 3.2 or higher. Along with their application, they must submit a 500–word essay on why they chose accounting, the activities and experiences that have influenced their commitment to the profession, and how they plan to utilize their studies and experiences to achieve a career in accounting. Financial need is not considered in the selection process.
Financial data: The stipend is $5,000.
Duration: 1 year.
Number awarded: Varies each year; recently, 51 of these scholarships were awarded.
Deadline: January of each year.

2873 $ NEW JERSEY SOCIETY OF CERTIFIED PUBLIC ACCOUNTANTS HIGH SCHOOL SCHOLARSHIP PROGRAM

New Jersey Society of Certified Public Accountants
Attn: Student Programs Coordinator
425 Eagle Rock Avenue, Suite 100
Roseland, NJ 07068–1723
Phone: (973) 226–4494, ext. 241; Fax: (973) 226–7425;
Email: lmatullo@njscpa.org
Web: www.njscpa.org/index/students/scholarships/high–school
Summary: To provide financial assistance to seniors in New Jersey high schools who are interested in preparing for a career as a Certified Public Accountant (C.P.A.) at a college in any state.
Eligibility: Open to seniors graduating from high schools in New Jersey and planning to major in accounting at a 2– or 4–year college or university in any state. Applicants must have 1) a GPA of 3.0 or higher; 2) an SAT score of 1500 or higher; or 3) an ACT score of 23 or higher. Along with their application, they must submit a 500–word essay on a topic that changes annually but relates to the C.P.A. profession; recently, students were asked to write on specialties within the profession and the 1 that interests them the most. Financial need is not considered in the selection process.
Financial data: Stipends range up to $2,125 per year.
Duration: 1 year; may be renewed up to 3 additional years if the recipient maintains a GPA of 2.75 or higher in the freshman year and 3.2 or higher in subsequent years.
Number awarded: Varies each year; recently, 23 of these scholarships were awarded.
Deadline: December of each year.

2874 $ NEW MEXICO TEACHER LOAN–FOR–SERVICE PROGRAM

New Mexico Higher Education Department
Attn: Financial Aid Division
2048 Galisteo Street
Santa Fe, NM 87505–2100
Phone: (505) 476–8411; (800) 279–9777; Fax: (505) 476–8454;
Email: feliz.romero1@state.nm.us
Web: hed.state.nm.us
Summary: To provide funding to residents of New Mexico who are interested in becoming teachers in the state.
Eligibility: Open to residents of New Mexico who are enrolled at least half time in an undergraduate, graduate, or alternative licensure teacher preparation program at an approved college or university in the state. Applicants must intend to practice as a teacher at a public school in New Mexico. They must be able to demonstrate financial need. Along with their application, they must submit an essay on why they want to become a teacher and obligate themselves to teach in New Mexico. U.S. citizenship or eligible noncitizenship status is required.
Financial data: Loans range up to $4,000 per year, depending on financial need. This is a loan–for–service program; for every year of service as a teacher in New Mexico, a portion of the loan is forgiven. If the entire service agreement is fulfilled, 100% of the loan is eligible for forgiveness. Penalties may be assessed if the service agreement is not satisfied.
Duration: 1 year; may be renewed up to 4 additional consecutive years.
Number awarded: Varies each year.
Deadline: June of each year.

2875 $ NEW YORK EXCELLENCE IN ACCOUNTING SCHOLARSHIP

New York State Society of Certified Public Accountants
Attn: Foundation for Accounting Education
3 Park Avenue, 18th Floor
New York, NY 10016–5991
Phone: (212) 719–8383; (800) 537–3635; Fax: (212) 719–3364;
Email: pfederowicz@nysscpa.org
Web: www.nysscpa.org/page/future–cpas/college–students
Summary: To provide financial assistance to New York residents who are entering the third or fourth year of an accounting program at a college or university in the state.
Eligibility: Open to residents or New York enrolled at colleges and universities in the state with an approved 150–hour accounting curriculum. Applicants must be entering the third or fourth year of a 4–year or 5–year accounting program with a GPA of 3.0 or higher. They must have completed 72 credit hours and be planning to enter the accounting profession. Each school may nominate up to 3 candidates. Selection is based on scholarship and financial need. U.S. citizenship or permanent resident status is required.
Financial data: The stipend is $2,500 for full–time students or $1,250 for part–time students. Payment is made co–payable to the student and the school.
Duration: 1 year; recipients may reapply.
Number awarded: Varies each year; recently, 44 of these scholarships were awarded.
Deadline: March of each year.

2876 NEW YORK STATE GOLF ASSOCIATION SCHOLARSHIPS

Summary: To provide financial assistance to residents of New York working on a degree in a field related to golf course management at a school in any state.
See Listing #2165.

2877 $$ NEW YORK STATE MATH AND SCIENCE TEACHING INCENTIVE SCHOLARSHIPS

New York State Higher Education Services Corporation
Attn: Student Information
99 Washington Avenue
Albany, NY 12255
Phone: (518) 473–1574; (888) NYS–HESC; Fax: (518) 473–3749; TDD: (800) 445–5234;
Email: webmail@hesc.com
Web: www.hesc.com/content.nsf/SFC/Grants_Scholarships_and_Awards
Summary: To provide funding to undergraduate and graduate students in New York who agree to teaching secondary science or mathematics in the state following graduation.

Eligibility: Open to residents of any state accepted or enrolled as a full–time undergraduate or graduate student at a college or university in New York. Applicants must be preparing for a career as a secondary education science or mathematics teacher in the state and have a cumulative GPA of 2.5 or higher. They are not required to be New York residents, but they must agree to a service contract of full–time employment for 5 years as a science or mathematics teacher at a secondary school (grades 7–12) in the state. U.S. citizenship or eligible noncitizen status is required. Financial need is not considered in the selection process.

Financial data: The maximum stipend is $5,295 per year or actual tuition, whichever is less. Funds are paid directly to the schools the recipients attend. If they fail to honor the service contract in any way, the award converts to a 10–year student loan and must be repaid with interest at the FFELP PLUS loan rate (currently, 8.5%).

Duration: This program is available for 4 years of undergraduate study or 1 year of graduate study, provided the recipient remains enrolled full time and maintains a GPA of 2.5 or higher.

Number awarded: Varies each year.

Deadline: March of each year.

2878 $ NOLAN MOORE MEMORIAL EDUCATION FOUNDATION SCHOLARSHIP

Printing and Imaging Association of MidAmerica
Attn: Nolan Moore Memorial Education Foundation
1349 Empire Central Drive, Suite 220
Dallas, TX 75247
Phone: (214) 630–8871; (800) 788–2040;
Email: info@piamidam.org
Web: www.piamidam.org/nolan–moore–foundation

Summary: To provide financial assistance to residents of designated states who are attending college to prepare for a career in the printing industry.

Eligibility: Open to students enrolled or planning to enroll in an educational institution in any state that offers a 2– or 4–year degree in printing technology, printing management, or a related field. Applicants must be residents of Kansas, Missouri, Oklahoma, or Texas. They must be interested in preparing for a career in the printing and graphic arts industry, including production, management, production control, sales, or variable data imaging; students interested in a career in commercial graphics, advertising, or photography are not eligible. Along with their application, they must submit a 1–page statement outlining their career goals and a letter of endorsement from their faculty sponsor that reinforces their stated intention to prepare for a career in the graphic arts industry. Selection is based on interest in the industry and GPA; financial need is not considered.

Financial data: The stipend ranges from $1,500 to $2,500 per year.

Duration: 1 year; may be renewed if the recipient remains enrolled full time with a GPA of 2.5 or higher.

Number awarded: Varies each year; recently, 7 of these scholarships were awarded.

Deadline: February of each year.

2879 $ NORA WEBB–MCKINNEY SCHOLARSHIP

American Council of the Blind of Ohio
Attn: Executive Director
P.O. Box 307128
Gahanna, OH 43230–7128
Phone: (614) 221–6688; (800) 835–2226 (within OH);
Email: mary.hiland@wowway.com
Web: www.acbohio.org/scholarships/scholarship–requirements.php

Summary: To provide financial assistance to Ohio students who are interested in working on an undergraduate or graduate degree involving service to blind people.

Eligibility: Open to 1) residents of Ohio who are high school seniors or current undergraduate or graduate students; and 2) undergraduate and graduate students from any state enrolled at colleges and universities in Ohio. Applicants must be interested in working on or planning to work on a degree in a field related to blindness (e.g., special education, rehabilitation teaching or counseling, orientation and mobility, or a concentration on programs serving people who are blind). They may be blind or sighted. Along with their application, they must submit transcripts (must have a GPA of 3.0 or higher) and an essay of 250 to 500 words on their career objectives, future plans, personal goals, other academic or personal qualities, and why they believe they are qualified to receive this scholarship. Financial need is not the sole factor considered in the selection process.

Financial data: The stipend is $2,000 per year.

Duration: 1 year; recipients may reapply.

Number awarded: 1 each year.

Deadline: August of each year.

2880 NORTH AMERICA SCHOLARSHIPS OF THE NATIONAL TOUR ASSOCIATION

Tourism Cares
Attn: Academic Scholarship Program
275 Turnpike Street, Suite 307
Canton, MA 02021
Phone: (781) 821–5990; Fax: (781) 821–8949;
Email: scholarships@tourismcares.org
Web: www.tourismcares.org

Summary: To provide financial assistance to upper–division and graduate students who are working on a degree in travel and tourism or hospitality–related fields.

Eligibility: Open to citizens and permanent residents of the United States and Canada who are enrolled full or part time at a 4–year college or university. Applicants must be entering their junior or senior year or be enrolled or entering graduate school. They must have a GPA of 3.0 or higher and be working on a degree in a travel or tourism or hospitality–related field. Undergraduate must submit an essay on the segment of the travel and tourism or hospitality industry their current program of study emphasizes, the opportunities they are utilizing as they prepare for a career in the industry, and their academic and extracurricular activities. Graduate students must submit an essay on the changes they have observed thus far in the travel and tourism or hospitality industry, the changes they anticipate in the future of the industry, and where they see their future potential in the industry. Financial need is not considered in the selection process.

Financial data: The stipend is $1,000.

Duration: 1 year.

Number awarded: 13 each year. Also, Tourism Cares also offers a number of National Tour Association scholarships for students residing in several individual states.

Deadline: March of each year.

2881 $ NORTH CAROLINA CHAPTER SCHOLARSHIP

Project Management Institute
Attn: PMI Educational Foundation
14 Campus Boulevard
Newtown Square, PA 19073–3299
Phone: (610) 356–4600, ext. 7004; Fax: (610) 356–0357;
Email: pmief@pmi.org
Web: www.pmi.org/pmief/scholarship/scholarships.asp

Summary: To provide financial assistance to undergraduate or graduate students with a tie to North Carolina who are working on a degree in project management.

Eligibility: Open to students working on or planning to work on an undergraduate or graduate degree in a field related to project management. First priority is given to residents of North Carolina attending or planning to attend a college or university in any state; second priority is given to residents of any state attending or planning to attend a college or university in North Carolina; third priority is given to residents of any state attending or planning to attend a college or university in the tri–state area of North Carolina, South Carolina, or Virginia; fourth priority is given to residents of any state attending or planning to attend a college or university in any state. Along with their application, they must submit 1) a 500–word essay on why they want to be a project manager; and 2) a 250–word essay on how a code of ethics is important to project management. Financial need is not considered in the selection process.

Financial data: The stipend is $2,500.

Duration: 1 year.

Number awarded: 1 each year.

Deadline: May of each year.

2882 $$ NORTH CAROLINA CPA FOUNDATION SCHOLARSHIPS

North Carolina Association of Certified Public Accountants
Attn: North Carolina CPA Foundation, Inc.
3100 Gateway Centre Boulevard
P.O. Box 80188
Raleigh, NC 27623–0188
Phone: (919) 469–1040, ext. 130; (800) 722–2836; Fax: (919) 378–2000;
Email: jtahler@ncacpa.org
Web: ncacpa.org/Member_Connections/Students/Scholarships.aspx

Summary: To provide financial assistance to students majoring in accounting at colleges and universities in North Carolina.

Eligibility: Open to North Carolina residents majoring in accounting at a college or university in the state. Applicants must have completed at least 36 semester hours, including at least 1 college or university–level accounting course, and have a GPA of 3.0 or higher. They must be sponsored by an accounting faculty member. Along with their application, they must submit an essay of 500 to 1,000 words on a topic that changes annually but relates to the public accounting profession; recently, students were asked for their ideas on the 3 most important skills someone in the accounting field should have and why. Selection is based on extracurricular activities (30%), essay content (35%), and essay grammar (35%).

Financial data: Stipends range from $1,000 to $5,000.

Duration: 1 year; may be renewed up to 2 additional years.

Number awarded: Varies each year; recently, 46 of these scholarships, with a total value of $57,000, were awarded.

Deadline: February of each year.

2883 $$ NORTH CAROLINA FORGIVABLE EDUCATION LOANS FOR SERVICE

Summary: To provide forgivable loans to residents of North Carolina who wish to attend school in any state to prepare for a career in specified fields of education, health care, medicine, or nursing and to practice in North Carolina.

See Listing #2174.

2884 NORTHERN COLORADO/SOUTHERN WYOMING CHAPTER SCHOLARSHIP

American Society for Industrial Security–Northern Colorado/Southern Wyoming Chapter
c/o Verne H. McClurg, Scholarship Chair
2407 Merino Court
Fort Collins, CO 80526–1431
Phone: (970) 407–7340;
Email: doc_bullseye@comcast.net
Web: www.nocoasis.org/Scholarship_Program.html

Summary: To provide financial assistance to undergraduate and graduate students working on a degree in a field related to industrial security at a college in Colorado or Wyoming.

Eligibility: Open to undergraduate and graduate students enrolled full or part time at an accredited college or university in Colorado or Wyoming. Applicants must be working on a degree in security, criminal justice, or sociology/criminology. They must have a GPA of 3.5 or higher. Along with their application, they must submit a 250–word narrative that describes their plans for a career as a security professional or in the field of criminal justice.

Financial data: Stipends range from $500 to $1,500.

Duration: 1 year.

Number awarded: Several each year.

Deadline: September of each year.

2885 $ NRAEF ACADEMIC SCHOLARSHIPS FOR FIRST–TIME FRESHMEN, GED GRADUATES AND PROSTART STUDENTS

Summary: To provide financial assistance to high school seniors, GED graduates, ProStart students, and first–time freshmen entering college to prepare for a career in the hospitality industry.

See Listing #1432.

2886 NSA ANNUAL SCHOLARSHIP AWARDS

National Society of Accountants
Attn: NSA Scholarship Foundation
1010 North Fairfax Street
Alexandria, VA 22314–1574
Phone: (703) 549–6400, ext. 1307; (800) 966–6679, ext. 1307; Fax: (703) 549–2984;
Email: sbrasse@nsacct.org
Web: www.nsacct.org

Summary: To provide financial assistance to undergraduate students majoring in accounting.

Eligibility: Open to undergraduate students enrolled full or part time in an accounting degree program at an accredited 2– or 4–year college or university with a GPA of 3.0 or better. Students in 2–year colleges may apply during their first year or during their second year if transferring to a 4–year institution, provided they have committed themselves to a major in accounting throughout the remainder of their college career; students in 4–year colleges may apply for a scholarship for their second, third, or fourth year of studies, provided they have committed themselves to a major in accounting through the remainder of their college career. Only U.S. or Canadian citizens attending a U.S. accredited business school, college, or university may apply. Selection is based on academic attainment, demonstrated leadership ability, and financial need.

Financial data: The stipend is usually $500 per year for students entering their second year of studies or usually $1,000 per year for students entering their third or fourth year.

Duration: 1 year.

Number awarded: Approximately 32 each year.

Deadline: March of each year.

2887 $$ NURSING HOME ABUSE AWARENESS AND PREVENTION SCHOLARSHIP

Summary: To provide financial assistance to nursing and other students who are preparing for a career that will enable them to help combat nursing home abuse.

See Listing #2185.

2888 OHIO CLASSICAL CONFERENCE SCHOLARSHIP FOR PROSPECTIVE LATIN TEACHERS

Summary: To provide financial assistance to Ohio residents preparing for a career as a Latin teacher.

See Listing #1437.

2889 OHIO FUNERAL DIRECTORS ASSOCIATION SCHOLASTIC ASSISTANCE

Ohio Funeral Directors Association
Attn: Scholastic Assistance Committee
2501 North Star Road
P.O. Box 21760
Columbus, OH 43221–0760
Phone: (614) 486–5339; (800) 589–6332; Fax: (614) 486–5358;
Email: Melissa@OFDAonline.org
Web: www.ohio–fda.org

Summary: To provide financial assistance to residents of Ohio interested in attending a college of mortuary science in any state.

Eligibility: Open to residents of Ohio who are attending or planning to attend a college or mortuary science in any state. Applicants must submit brief statements on their personal experience in the funeral service profession, why they chose a career in funeral service, how their friends and family have responded to their interest in funeral service, how funeral service provides value, where they see funeral service in the future and the changes they would like to see made to the profession, and how they would rate the funeral service professional in their community. Selection is based on those statements, academic transcripts, participation in community activities, honors or recognition received, 3 letters of recommendation (including 1 from a licensed funeral service professional), and (especially) financial need.

Financial data: A stipend is awarded (amount not specified).

Duration: 1 year.

Number awarded: 1 or more each year.

Deadline: July of each year.

2890 OKLAHOMA FUNERAL DIRECTORS ASSOCIATION SCHOLARSHIP

Oklahoma Funeral Directors Association
Attn: Scholarship Committee
6801 North Broadway, Suite 106
Oklahoma City, OK 73116
Phone: (405) 843–0730; (800) 256–6332; Fax: (405) 843–5404;
Email: ofda@wavelinx.net
Web: www.okfda.com/scholarship.htm

Summary: To provide financial assistance to Oklahoma residents who are attending a mortuary college in any state.

Eligibility: Open to students currently enrolled in a mortuary science program at a school in any state who have been residents of Oklahoma for at least 2 years. Applicants must have a GPA of 2.0 or higher in high school and in any mortuary studies to date. They must be recommended by a member of the sponsoring organization, meet the educational requirements of the Oklahoma Funeral

Board, and possess the following personal characteristics: an acute mind, a pleasing personality, good character, ambition, and positive qualities of leadership. Financial need is not considered in the selection process.
Financial data: The maximum stipend is $1,500. Funds are sent to the recipient's school and must be used only for tuition and books.
Duration: 1 year; may be renewed if the recipient continues to do satisfactory work.
Number awarded: 1 or more each year.
Deadline: Deadline not specified.

2891 OKLAHOMA FUTURE TEACHERS SCHOLARSHIP PROGRAM

Oklahoma State Regents for Higher Education
Attn: Director of Scholarship and Grant Programs
655 Research Parkway, Suite 200
P.O. Box 108850
Oklahoma City, OK 73101–8850
Phone: (405) 225–9239; (800) 858–1840; Fax: (405) 225–9230;
Email: studentinfo@osrhe.edu
Web: www.okcollegestart.org
Summary: To provide funding to Oklahoma residents who are interested in teaching in designated shortage fields in the state.
Eligibility: Open to residents of Oklahoma who are enrolled as undergraduate or graduate students at institutions of higher education in the state and are nominated by their school. Nominees must meet 1 of the following criteria: 1) rank in the top 15% of their high school graduating class; 2) have an ACT or SAT score ranking in the top 15% for high school graduates of the same year; 3) have been admitted into a professional education program at an accredited Oklahoma institution of higher education; or 4) have achieved an undergraduate record of outstanding success as defined by the institution. Both part–time and full–time students are eligible, but preference is given to full–time students. Applicants must be interested in teaching in critical shortage areas in the state upon graduation. These areas change periodically but recently have included mathematics, science, music, social studies, and early childhood education.
Financial data: Full–time students receive up to $1,500 per year if they have completed 60 hours or more or up to $1,000 if they have completed fewer than 60 hours; part–time students receive up to $750 per year if they have completed 60 hours or more or up to $500 per year if they have completed fewer than 60 hours. Funds are paid directly to the institution on the student's behalf. This is a forgivable loan program; recipients must agree to teach in Oklahoma public schools for 3 years following graduation and licensure.
Duration: 1 year; may be renewable for up to 3 additional years, provided the recipient maintains a GPA of 2.5 or higher.
Number awarded: Varies each year; recently, 136 students received support through this program.
Deadline: Each eligible institution establishes its own deadline.

2892 OKLAHOMA HERITAGE COUNTY SCHOLARSHIPS

Summary: To recognize and reward, with college scholarships, high school students in Oklahoma who achieve high scores on a test about the state's history and geography.
See Listing #1440.

2893 $ OMAHA CHAPTER SCHOLARSHIPS

American Society of Women Accountants–Omaha Chapter
c/o Chris Carlson, Scholarship Committee
13609 California Street
Omaha, NE 68069
Email: ccarlson@aureusgroup.com
Web: www.aswaomaha.org/scholarships.html
Summary: To provide financial assistance to women from any state working on an undergraduate degree in accounting at a school in Nebraska.
Eligibility: Open to women from any state enrolled part or full time in an associate, bachelor's, or master's degree program in accounting or finance at a college or university in Nebraska. Applicants must have completed at least 15 semester hours of a 2–year program or 60 semester hours of a 4– or 5–year program. They must have a GPA of 3.0 or higher. Membership in the American Society of Women Accountants (ASWA) is not required. Along with their application, they must submit an essay of 150 to 250 words on their career goals and objectives, the impact they want to have on the accounting world, community involvement, and leadership examples. Selection is based on leadership, character, communication skills, scholastic average, and financial need.
Financial data: The stipend is $2,000.
Duration: 1 year.
Number awarded: Varies each year; recently, 3 of these scholarships (2 for undergraduates and 1 for a graduate student) were awarded.
Deadline: February of each year.

2894 OMAHA HEARTLAND CHAPTER SCHOLARSHIPS

American Society for Industrial Security–Omaha Heartland Chapter
c/o James M. Van Lent, Scholarship Chair
First National Bank of Omaha
1620 Dodge Street
Omaha, NE 68197–2155
Phone: (402) 633–7450;
Email: jvanlent@fnni.com
Web: asisomaha.org/content.php?page=Scholarship
Summary: To provide financial assistance to students enrolled at a college in the service area of the Omaha Heartland Chapter of the American Society for Industrial Security (ASIS) and working on an undergraduate or graduate degree in a security–related field.
Eligibility: Open to undergraduate and graduate students currently enrolled full or part time at a college or university in Nebraska, western Iowa, or southern South Dakota. Applicants must be preparing for a career in the security profession. They must have completed at least 1 year of study and have a GPA of 3.0 or higher. Along with their application, they must submit brief statements on their future career plans, future academic plans, academic and/or professional memberships, and interest in the security profession. Financial need is not considered in the selection process.
Financial data: The chapter awards a stipend of $500. If the recipient is an ASIS member, the International Foundation provides an additional $1,000. If the recipient is not a member, the matching amount is $500.
Duration: 1 year.
Number awarded: 1 or more each year.
Deadline: November of each year.

2895 OMAHA VOLUNTEERS FOR HANDICAPPED CHILDREN SCHOLARSHIPS

Summary: To provide financial assistance to Nebraska residents who have a physical disability or are preparing for a career related to people with orthopedic impairments or physical disabilities and are interested in attending college in any state.
See Listing #727.

2896 $ OREGON ASSOCIATION OF INDEPENDENT ACCOUNTANTS SCHOLARSHIPS

Oregon Association of Independent Accountants
Attn: OAIA Scholarship Foundation
1804 N.E. 43rd Avenue
Portland, OR 97213–1404
Phone: (503) 282–7247; Fax: (503) 292–7406;
Email: info@oaia.net
Web: www.oaia.net
Summary: To provide financial assistance to Oregon residents interested in majoring in accounting at a college in the state.
Eligibility: Open to Oregon residents who are enrolled full time or accepted for enrollment at an accredited school in the state for the study of accounting. Applicants must submit an essay on why they have chosen to study and prepare for a career in accounting. Selection is based on financial need, scholastic achievement, personal qualifications, and professional promise.
Financial data: Stipends range from $1,000 to $2,000. Checks are made payable to the recipient and the recipient's college. Funds may be used for tuition, fees, books, or other academic expenses during the year.
Duration: 1 year; renewable.
Deadline: March of each year.

2897 $ OSCPA EDUCATIONAL FOUNDATION COLLEGE SCHOLARSHIPS

Oregon Society of Certified Public Accountants
Attn: OSCPA Educational Foundation
10206 S.W. Laurel Street
P.O. Box 4555
Beaverton, OR 97076–4555

Phone: (503) 597–5471, ext. 29; (800) 255–1470, ext. 29; Fax: (503) 626–2942;
Email: edfound@orcpa.org
Web: https://secure.orcpa.org/educational_foundation/scholarships
Summary: To provide financial assistance to currently–enrolled undergraduate and graduate students in Oregon who are working on a degree in accounting.
Eligibility: Open to full–time students at Oregon colleges and universities, and community colleges who are enrolled in an undergraduate, post–baccalaureate, or master's degree program in accounting. Applicants must have a GPA of 3.2 or higher in accounting/business classes and overall. Along with their application, they must submit 3 letters of recommendation and a recent transcript. Selection is based on scholastic ability and intent to enter the accounting profession in Oregon.
Financial data: For students at 4–year colleges and universities, stipends range from $1,000 to $3,000. For students at community colleges, the stipend is $500.
Duration: 1 year.
Number awarded: Varies each year; recently, this foundation awarded 58 scholarships worth $107,525.
Deadline: January of each year.

2898 OUTPUTLINKS MARKETING PROFESSIONS SCHOLARSHIPS

Electronic Document Systems Foundation
Attn: EDSF Scholarship Awards
1845 Precinct Line Road, Suite 212
Hurst, TX 76054
Phone: (817) 849–1145; Fax: (817) 849–1185;
Email: info@edsf.org
Web: www.edsf.org/what_we_do/scholarships/index.html
Summary: To provide financial assistance to undergraduate students at schools in any country who are working on a degree in marketing.
Eligibility: Open to full–time undergraduate students at 2– and 4–year colleges and universities in any country. Applicants must be working on a degree in marketing. They must have a GPA of 3.0 or higher. Along with their application, they must submit 2 essays on assigned topics that change annually but relate to the graphic arts and communication industries. Selection is based on the essays, academic excellence, participation in school activities, community service, honors and organizational affiliations, education goals, and recommendations; financial need is not considered.
Financial data: The stipend is $1,000.
Duration: 1 year.
Number awarded: 2 each year.
Deadline: April of each year.

2899 OUTPUTLINKS SUSTAINABILITY/STEWARDSHIP AWARD

Summary: To provide financial assistance to undergraduate and graduate students from any country who are working on a degree in the field of document management and graphic communications, especially those who are involved in environmental sustainability project or who have a record of leadership and community involvement.
See Listing #1445.

2900 $$ OUTPUTLINKS WOMAN OF DISTINCTION AWARD

Summary: To provide financial assistance to female undergraduate and graduate students from any country interested in preparing for a career in document management and graphic communications.
See Listing #1446.

2901 OUTREACH SCHOLARSHIP OF THE JUVENILE DIABETES RESEARCH FOUNDATION

Summary: To provide financial assistance to high school seniors who have diabetes and plan to major in a field related to mental health in college.
See Listing #2210.

2902 $$ PASSION FOR FASHION COMPETITION

Summary: To recognize and reward (with scholarships to participating Art Institutes) high school seniors who participate in competitions in fashion design and in fashion marketing and merchandising.
See Listing #1451.

2903 PATRICIA SONNTAG MEMORIAL SCHOLARSHIP

Summary: To provide financial assistance to students enrolled at 4–year college and universities in California who have a disability and are involved in activities or classes related to providing services to people with disabilities.
See Listing #2216.

2904 $ PAUL HAGELBARGER MEMORIAL SCHOLARSHIP

Alaska Society of Certified Public Accountants
341 West Tudor Road, Suite 105
Anchorage, AK 99503
Phone: (907) 562–4334; (800) 478–4334; Fax: (907) 562–4025;
Email: akcpa@ak.net
Web: www.akcpa.org/careers/students
Summary: To provide financial assistance to upper–division and graduate students at colleges and universities in Alaska who are preparing for a career in public accounting.
Eligibility: Open to juniors, seniors, and graduate students majoring in accounting at 4–year colleges and universities in Alaska. Applicants must submit brief essays on their educational goals, career goals, and financial need. Selection is based on academic achievement, intent to prepare for a career in public accounting in Alaska, and financial need.
Financial data: The stipend is at least $2,000.
Duration: 1 year.
Number awarded: 1 or more each year.
Deadline: November of each year.

2905 $ PAUL K. TAFF SCHOLARSHIP AWARD

Summary: To provide financial assistance to Connecticut residents who are interested in attending college in any state to prepare for a career in broadcasting.
See Listing #1454.

2906 PAYCHEX INC. ENTREPRENEUR SCHOLARSHIP

Massachusetts Society of Certified Public Accountants
Attn: MSCPA Educational Foundation
105 Chauncy Street, Tenth Floor
Boston, MA 02111
Phone: (617) 556–4000; (800) 392–6145; Fax: (617) 556–4126;
Email: info@mscpaonline.org
Web: www.cpatrack.com/scholarships
Summary: To provide financial assistance to residents of Massachusetts working on an undergraduate degree in accounting at a college or university in the state.
Eligibility: Open to Massachusetts residents enrolled full time at a college or university in the state with a cumulative GPA of 3.0 or higher. Applicants must be entering their junior year and be able to demonstrate both financial need and a commitment to preparing for a career as a Certified Public Accountant (C.P.A.).
Financial data: The stipend is $1,000.
Duration: 1 year.
Number awarded: 1 each year.
Deadline: March of each year.

2907 $ PENNSYLVANIA AFL–CIO SCHOLARSHIP ESSAY CONTEST

Pennsylvania AFL–CIO
Attn: Director of Education
319 Market Street, Third Floor
Harrisburg, PA 17101–2207
Phone: (717) 231–2843; (800) 242–3770; Fax: (717) 238–8541;
Email: cdillinger@paaflcio.org
Web: www.paaflcio.org
Summary: To recognize and reward high school and college students in Pennsylvania who submit outstanding essays on a labor topic.
Eligibility: Open to 1) graduating seniors at high schools in Pennsylvania; 2) students currently enrolled at accredited postsecondary school programs in the state; and 3) affiliated union members attending an accredited institution. Applicants must submit essays on topics that change annually but relate to labor unions. Recently, high school seniors were asked to write on how organized labor built the middle class and created family sustaining jobs. College students were to write on how "Right to Work" laws affect workers and the community.

Union members were to write on how politics affects union workers. In each competition, all essays must be at least 1,500 words in length and include 3 references, of which at least 1 must be from a labor organization.
Financial data: In each category, first prize is $2,000, second $1,000, and third $500.
Duration: The competition is held annually.
Number awarded: 9 each year: 3 in each of the 3 categories.
Deadline: January of each year.

2908 $ PENNSYLVANIA AMERICAN LEGION HIGH SCHOOL ESSAY CONTEST

American Legion
Department of Pennsylvania
Attn: Scholarship Secretary
P.O. Box 2324
Harrisburg, PA 17105–2324
Phone: (717) 730–9100; Fax: (717) 975–2836;
Email: hq@pa–legion.com
Web: www.pa–legion.com/programs/student–programs/essay
Summary: To recognize and reward, with college scholarships, high school students in Pennsylvania who submit outstanding essays on a patriotic topic.
Eligibility: Open to students who are currently enrolled in grades 9–12 in a Pennsylvania public, parochial, private, or home school. Applicants must submit an essay, from 500 to 1,000 words, on a topic that changes annually but relates to a patriotic theme; a recent topic was "Is the Stimulus Package Worthwhile?" Competitions are held at the level of local American Legion post, county, district, inter–district, sectional, and then state. Selection is based on proper English structure, accuracy, extent of information, and originality.
Financial data: At the state level, the first–place winner receives a $3,500 scholarship, second a $3,000 scholarship, and third a $2,500 scholarship. If winners choose not to attend college, prizes are $300 for first place, $200 for second, and $200 for third. Local posts, counties, districts, and sections also offer awards.
Duration: The competition is held annually.
Number awarded: 3 state winners are selected each year.
Deadline: Applications must be submitted to the local American Legion post by February of each year.

2909 $ PENNSYLVANIA SOCIETY OF PUBLIC ACCOUNTANTS SCHOLARSHIPS

Pennsylvania Society of Public Accountants
Attn: Executive Office
20 Erford Road, Suite 200A
Lemoyne, PA 17043
Phone: (800) 270–3352; Fax: (717) 737–6847;
Email: info@pspa–state.org
Web: www.pspa–state.org/consumers/scholarships.aspx
Summary: To provide financial assistance to accounting majors in Pennsylvania.
Eligibility: Open to Pennsylvania residents who have completed at least 36 credit hours at a college or university in the state with a major in accounting and a GPA of 3.0 or higher. Applicants must be enrolled as full–time undergraduates. Along with their application, they must submit a brief statement on their plans upon completion of their degree. Selection is based primarily on academic merit, but leadership potential, extracurricular activities, and financial need may be considered in the selection process. The highest–ranked applicant receives the Robert T. Zaleski Memorial Scholarship.
Financial data: The stipend is $2,000 or $1,000.
Duration: 1 year.
Number awarded: 3 each year: 1 at $2,000 and 2 at $1,000.
Deadline: May of each year.

2910 PERSONNEL PREPARATION SCHOLARSHIPS

Association for Education and Rehabilitation of the Blind and Visually Impaired of Ohio
c/o Jan Jasko
7012 Beresford Avenue
Parma Heights, OH 44130–5050
Phone: (440) 888–6236
Web: www.aerohio.org/scholarships
Summary: To provide financial assistance to Ohio residents who are working on an undergraduate or graduate degree in a field related to rehabilitation of the blind.
Eligibility: Open to juniors, seniors, and graduate students in rehabilitation counseling, rehabilitation teaching, orientation and mobility, or education of students with visual disabilities. Applicants must be residents of Ohio, although they may be studying in any state. They must have a GPA of 3.0 or higher. Along with their application, they must submit 1) a 250–word essay explaining why they have chosen their specific field as their profession and what they would like to contribute to the field; 2) a short description of volunteer or paid involvement with individuals with visual disabilities or any other disability; 3) transcripts; and 4) 3 letters of recommendation.
Financial data: The stipend is $1,000.
Duration: 1 year; nonrenewable.
Number awarded: 1 each year.
Deadline: April of each year.

2911 $ PETER W. JASIN SCHOLARSHIPS

Association of Former Intelligence Officers
Attn: Scholarships Committee
6723 Whittier Avenue, Suite 200
McLean, VA 22101–4533
Phone: (703) 790–0320; Fax: (703) 991–1278;
Email: afio@afio.com
Web: www.afio.com/13_scholarships.htm
Summary: To provide financial assistance to undergraduate and graduate students who are preparing for a career in the U.S. intelligence community.
Eligibility: Open to undergraduates who are entering their sophomore or junior year and graduate students who apply in their senior undergraduate year or first graduate year. Applicants must be able to demonstrate a goal of serving in the U.S. intelligence community following graduation. They must be working on a degree in counterterrorism, homeland security, intelligence, counterintelligence, or other intelligence–related discipline. Along with their application, they must submit a cover letter that explains their need for assistance, their career goals and dreams, and their views of U.S. world standing and its intelligence community. Selection is based on merit, character, estimated future potential, background, and relevance of their studies to the full spectrum of national security interests and career ambitions. U.S. citizenship is required.
Financial data: The stipend is $4,000.
Duration: 1 year.
Number awarded: 7 each year.
Deadline: June of each year.

2912 PHOENIX CHAPTER SCHOLARSHIP

Association of Government Accountants–Phoenix Chapter
c/o Michelle Brooks, Scholarships Committee Chair
P.O. Box 64911
Phoenix, AZ 85082–4911
Email: scholarships@agaphoenix.org
Web: www.agaphoenix.org/id17.html
Summary: To provide financial assistance to undergraduate and graduate students from any state working on a degree in accounting or finance at a college in Arizona.
Eligibility: Open to residents of any state working on a bachelor's or master's degree in accounting or finance at a college or university in Arizona. Applicants must be at least sophomores. Along with their application, they must submit a 1–page essay on why they are interested in a career in public financial management. Financial need is not considered in the selection process.
Financial data: The stipend is $1,000.
Duration: 1 year.
Number awarded: 1 each year.
Deadline: December of each year.

2913 PHOENIX PROJECT MANAGEMENT INSTITUTE CHAPTER SCHOLARSHIP

Project Management Institute
Attn: PMI Educational Foundation
14 Campus Boulevard
Newtown Square, PA 19073–3299
Phone: (610) 356–4600, ext. 7004; Fax: (610) 356–0357;
Email: pmief@pmi.org
Web: www.pmi.org/pmief/scholarship/scholarships.asp
Summary: To provide financial assistance to residents of Arizona interested in working on an undergraduate or graduate degree in a field related to project management.

Eligibility: Open to residents of Arizona who are working on or planning to work on an undergraduate or graduate degree in project management or a related field at a college or university in any state. Applicants must submit 1) a 500–word essay on why they want to be a project manager; and 2) a 250–word essay on how a code of ethics is important to project management. Financial need is not considered in the selection process.
Financial data: The stipend is $1,000.
Duration: 1 year.
Number awarded: 1 each year.
Deadline: May of each year.

2914 $ PICATINNY CHAPTER SCHOLARSHIP

American Society of Military Comptrollers–Picatinny Chapter
Attn: Cathy Heslin
P.O. Box 943
Wharton, NJ 07885
Phone: (973) 724–5439;
Email: cheslin@optonline.net
Web: picatinnyasmc.com
Summary: To provide financial assistance to high school seniors and recent graduates in New Jersey interested in attending college in any state to prepare for a career in financial management.
Eligibility: Open to seniors graduating from high schools in New Jersey and to people who graduated from those high schools during the preceding 6 months. Applicants must be planning to enter college in any state in a field of study directly related to financial resource management, including business administration, economics, public administration, accounting, or finance. Along with their application, they must submit official transcripts with SAT or ACT scores attached, a letter of recommendation from a school official, a list of leadership abilities and extracurricular activities, and a 1–page essay on their career and academic goals that includes their financial need.
Financial data: Stipends range from $750 to $2,000.
Duration: 1 year; nonrenewable.
Number awarded: Up to 4 each year.
Deadline: March of each year.

2915 $ PICPA STUDENT WRITING COMPETITION

Pennsylvania Institute of Certified Public Accountants
Attn: Careers in Accounting Team
1801 Market Street, Suite 2400
Philadelphia, PA 19103
Phone: (215) 496–9272; (888) CPA–2001 (within PA); Fax: (215) 496–9212;
Email: journal@picpa.org
Web: www.picpa.org/Content/38798.aspx
Summary: To recognize and reward outstanding essays written by students in Pennsylvania on an accounting topic that changes annually.
Eligibility: Open to 1) accounting and business majors at Pennsylvania colleges and universities; and 2) Pennsylvania residents who attend college out–of–state. Candidates are invited to submit an essay on an issue (changes annually) that affects the accounting profession. Recently, the topic related to fraud and the global business environment. Essays should be from 1,000 to 1,500 words in length and include a 50– to 75–word abstract. Selection is based on content, method of presentation, and writing style.
Financial data: First place is $3,000, second $1,800, and third $1,200.
Duration: The competition is held annually.
Number awarded: 3 each year.
Deadline: April of each year.

2916 POLANKI COLLEGE ACHIEVEMENT AWARDS

Summary: To recognize and reward upper–division and graduate students in Wisconsin who have a Polish connection and demonstrate academic excellence.
See Listing #780.

2917 $ PRINCESS CRUISES SCHOLARSHIP

Tourism Cares
Attn: Academic Scholarship Program
275 Turnpike Street, Suite 307
Canton, MA 02021
Phone: (781) 821–5990; Fax: (781) 821–8949;
Email: scholarships@tourismcares.org
Web: www.tourismcares.org
Summary: To provide financial assistance to undergraduate students working on a degree in travel and tourism or hospitality–related fields.
Eligibility: Open to U.S. and Canadian citizens and permanent residents who are 1) entering the second year at an accredited 2–year college; or 2) entering their junior or senior year at an accredited 4–year college or university. Applicants must be enrolled full or part time in a travel and tourism or hospitality–related program of study. They must have a GPA of 3.0 or higher. Along with their application, they must submit an essay on 1) the customer service or product features a travel supplier needs to offer to gain a competitive edge in the vacation market; and 2) the program of study or extracurricular activities they are pursuing to learn about the trends that could apply to a job in the travel and tourism or hospitality industry. Financial need is not considered in the selection process.
Financial data: The stipend is $2,500.
Duration: 1 year.
Number awarded: 1 each year.
Deadline: March of each year.

2918 PRIVATE UNIVERSITY AND COMMUNITY COLLEGE SCHOLARSHIPS

Arizona Society of Certified Public Accountants
Attn: Foundation for Education and Innovation
4801 East Washington Street, Suite 225–B
Phoenix, AZ 85034
Phone: (602) 252–4144, ext. 214; (888) 237–0700, ext. 214 (within AZ); Fax: (602) 252–1511;
Email: mwitt@ascpa.com
Web: secure.ascpa.com/future_cpas/scholarships
Summary: To provide financial assistance to students majoring in accounting at a community college or private university in Arizona.
Eligibility: Open to residents of Arizona who are enrolled full time at a community college or private university in the state and have completed at least 12 credit hours. Applicants must be majoring in accounting and have completed at least 1 accounting course. They must have a GPA of 3.0 or higher. Along with their application, they must submit a 1–page essay on their future career interests and professional goals. Selection is based on academic achievement, community involvement, leadership potential, and likelihood of the student's becoming a C.P.A. and remaining in Arizona. U.S. citizenship or permanent resident status is required.
Financial data: The stipend is $1,000. Funds are paid directly to the college or university.
Duration: 1 year.
Number awarded: 2 each year.
Deadline: February of each year.

2919 $$ PROFILE IN COURAGE ESSAY CONTEST

Summary: To recognize and reward high school authors of essays on public officials who have demonstrated political courage.
See Listing #1468.

2920 PROOF–READING.COM SCHOLARSHIP PROGRAM

Proof–Reading, Inc.
12 Geary Street, Suite 806
San Francisco, CA 94108–5720
Phone: (866) 4–EDITOR;
Email: scholarships@proof–reading.com
Web: www.proof–reading.com/proof–reading_scholarship_program.asp
Summary: To recognize and reward, with scholarships for continuing study, college students who submit outstanding essays on a topic of national concern.
Eligibility: Open to full–time students at 4–year colleges and universities in the United States. Applicants must submit an essay of at least 1,500 words on a topic that changes each year but relates to issues of national concern; recently, students were required to write on the controversy over raising the debt limit of the U.S. government. Selection is based on grammar and clarity of presentation of ideas.
Financial data: The award is a $1,500 scholarship.
Duration: The competition is held annually.
Number awarded: 1 each year.
Deadline: May of each year.

2921 PUGET SOUND CHAPTER SCHOLARSHIP

American Society for Industrial Security–Puget Sound Chapter
c/o Don Pilker, Scholarship Committee

Virginia Mason Medical Center
1100 Ninth Avenue
Mailstop G3–SE
Seattle, WA 98101
Phone: (206) 625–7373, ext. 63199
Web: www.asispugetsound.com/scholarship

Summary: To provide financial assistance to undergraduate and graduate students from Washington working on a degree in a field related to security.
Eligibility: Open to residents of any state who have completed at least 1 year of study at an accredited college, university, or community college in Washington. Applicants must be working full or part time on an undergraduate or graduate degree in a field related to security. They must have a GPA of 3.0 or higher. Along with their application, they must submit a brief essay on their interest in the security profession. Financial need is not considered in the selection process.
Financial data: The stipend ranges from $500 to $1,500.
Duration: 1 year.
Number awarded: 1 each year.
Deadline: July of each year.

2922 $ PWC EXCEED SCHOLARSHIP PROGRAM

PricewaterhouseCoopers LLP
Attn: Campus Recruiting Manager
125 High Street
Boston, MA 02110
Phone: (617) 530–5349; Fax: (813) 741–8595
Web: www.pwc.com

Summary: To provide financial assistance to underrepresented minority undergraduate students interested in preparing for a career in public accounting.
Eligibility: Open to African American, Native American, and Hispanic American students entering their sophomore, junior, or senior year of college. Applicants must have a GPA of 3.4 or higher, be able to demonstrate interpersonal skills and leadership ability, and be working on a bachelor's degree in accounting, computer information systems, management information systems, finance, economics, or actuarial science. Along with their application, they must submit a 300–word essay on how they have demonstrated the core values of PricewaterhouseCoopers (PwC) of achieving excellence, developing teamwork, and inspiring leadership in their academic and/or professional career.
Financial data: The stipend is $3,000.
Duration: 1 year; nonrenewable.
Number awarded: Varies each year; recently, 81 of these scholarships were awarded.
Deadline: December of each year.

2923 QUENTIN N. BURDICK MEMORIAL SCHOLARSHIP

Fargo–Moorhead Area Foundation
Attn: Finance/Program Assistant
502 First Avenue North, Suite 202
Fargo, ND 58102–4804
Phone: (701) 234–0756; Fax: (701) 234–9724;
Email: Stanna@areafoundation.org
Web: areafoundation.org/index.php/scholarships

Summary: To provide financial assistance high school seniors in North Dakota who are interested in attending college in any state to prepare for a career in public service.
Eligibility: Open to seniors graduating from high schools in North Dakota and planning to attend a college or university in any state. Applicants must be interested in preparing for a career in public service. Along with their application, they must submit a 500–word essay on how individuals can make a difference in their community and how they hope to become involved in public or community service.
Financial data: A stipend is awarded (amount not specified).
Duration: 1 year.
Number awarded: 1 each year.
Deadline: April of each year.

2924 $ QUESTEX MEDIA GROUP SCHOLARSHIP

Summary: To provide financial assistance to undergraduate and graduate students from any country who are working on a degree in the field of document management and graphic communications, especially those who are interested in journalism, trade show management, or marketing communications.
See Listing #1471.

2925 QUIT SMOKING ACADEMIC SCHOLARSHIP

Summary: To recognize and reward, with scholarships for further study, undergraduate and graduate students who submit outstanding essays on their interest in a career in behavior modification and what they have done to help other students quit smoking.
See Listing #2250.

2926 $$ R. GENE RICHTER SCHOLARSHIP

Institute for Supply Management
Attn: Richter Scholarship Program
2055 East Centennial Circle
P.O. Box 22160
Tempe, AZ 85285–2160
Phone: (480) 752–6276, ext. 3023; (800) 888–6276, ext. 3023; Fax: (480) 752–7890;
Email: jkellerman@ism.ws
Web: www.ism.ws

Summary: To provide financial support to college seniors working on a degree in supply management.
Eligibility: Open to undergraduates entering their senior year of a full–time program in supply management or a related field (e.g., supply chain management, purchasing, procurement). Applicants must be U.S. or Canadian citizens or possess a valid green card. Along with their application, they must submit essays on 1) how they have led or worked within a group of achieve a common goal; 2) an ethical dilemma that they faced and how they resolved their difficulty; and 3) why they have chosen the field of supply chain management. Selection is based on academic achievement, leadership ability, ethical standards, and commitment to preparing for a career in the field of supply chain management.
Financial data: The stipend is $5,000.
Duration: 1 year.
Number awarded: 10 each year.
Deadline: February of each year.

2927 $ RACHEL RAY'S YUM–O! ORGANIZATION SCHOLARSHIPS

National Restaurant Association Educational Foundation
Attn: Scholarships Program
175 West Jackson Boulevard, Suite 1500
Chicago, IL 60604–2814
Phone: (312) 715–1010, ext. 738; (800) 765–2122, ext. 6738; Fax: (312) 566–9733;
Email: scholars@nraef.org
Web: www.nraef.org/scholarships

Summary: To provide financial assistance to high school seniors, GED graduates, ProStart students, and first–time freshmen entering college to prepare for a career in the hospitality industry.
Eligibility: Open to graduating high school seniors, GED graduates enrolling in college for the first time, students who have participated in the ProStart program of the National Restaurant Association, and high school graduates enrolling in college for the first time. Applicants must be planning to enroll either full time or substantial part time at an accredited culinary school, college, or university to major in culinary, restaurant management, or other food service–related field of study. They must be U.S. citizens or permanent residents. Along with their application, they must submit an essay of 350 to 1,000 words on their career goals in the restaurant/food service industry, their background and educational and work experience, how their background and experience will help them to achieve their career goals, what they need to do to reach their career goals, and the person or experience that most influenced them in selecting restaurant and food service as a career. Selection is based on the essays, presentation of the application, industry–related work experience, letters of recommendation, and food service certificates such as the ProStart National Certificate of Achievement.
Financial data: The stipend is $2,500.
Duration: 1 year.
Number awarded: 1 or more each year.
Deadline: August of each year.

2928 $ RALPH HALE RUPPERT MEMORIAL SCHOLARSHIPS

Summary: To provide financial assistance to California residents interested in attending college in any state to major in designated fields.
See Listing #2254.

2929 $ RANZY GAMMAL MEMORIAL SCHOLARSHIP

Project Management Institute
Attn: PMI Educational Foundation
14 Campus Boulevard
Newtown Square, PA 19073–3299
Phone: (610) 356–4600, ext. 7004; Fax: (610) 356–0357;
Email: pmief@pmi.org
Web: www.pmi.org/pmief/scholarship/scholarships.asp

Summary: To provide financial assistance to undergraduate or graduate students from areas of the mid–Atlantic region who are interested in working on a degree in project management or a related field at a college in any state.

Eligibility: Open to undergraduate or graduate students attending or planning to attend a college or university in any state and work on a degree in project management or a field that benefits from project management (e.g., architecture, business administration, construction, educational administration, engineering, hotel management, human resources, information technology, pharmaceuticals, science). First priority is given to residents of the Hampton Roads area of Virginia (the counties of Accomack, Isle of Wight, Northampton, and York and the cities of Chesapeake, Hampton, Newport News, Norfolk, Poquoson, Portsmouth, Suffolk, Virginia Beach, and Williamsburg); second priority is given to residents of Virginia; third priority is given to residents of the mid–Atlantic region (Delaware, Maryland, New Jersey, New York, Pennsylvania, Virginia, Washington, D.C., and West Virginia). Along with their application, they must submit 1) a 500–word essay on why they want to be a project manager; and 2) a 250–word essay on how a code of ethics is important to project management. Financial need is not considered in the selection process.

Financial data: The stipend is $2,500.

Duration: 1 year.

Number awarded: 1 each year.

Deadline: May of each year.

2930 RAY PIPER GLOBAL PROJECT MANAGEMENT EDUCATION SCHOLARSHIP

Project Management Institute
Attn: PMI Educational Foundation
14 Campus Boulevard
Newtown Square, PA 19073–3299
Phone: (610) 356–4600, ext. 7004; Fax: (610) 356–0357;
Email: pmief@pmi.org
Web: www.pmi.org/pmief/scholarship/scholarships.asp

Summary: To provide financial assistance to undergraduate students from any country who are interested in working on a degree in project management.

Eligibility: Open to residents of any country enrolled or planning to enroll as an undergraduate at a degree–granting institution of higher education. Applicants must demonstrate an interest in project management as a potential career. Along with their application, they must submit 1) a 500–word essay on why they want to be a project manager; and 2) a 250–word essay on how a code of ethics is important to project management. Financial need is not considered in the selection process.

Financial data: The stipend is $1,000.

Duration: 1 year.

Number awarded: 1 each year.

Deadline: May of each year.

2931 $ RAYMOND C. MILLER SCHOLARSHIP

American Public Transportation Association
Attn: American Public Transportation Foundation
1666 K Street, N.W., Suite 1100
Washington, DC 20006
Phone: (202) 496–4803; Fax: (202) 496–4323;
Email: yconley@apta.com
Web: www.aptfd.org/work/scholarship.htm

Summary: To provide financial assistance to undergraduate and graduate students who are preparing for a career in transit marketing.

Eligibility: Open to college sophomores, juniors, seniors, and graduate students who are preparing for a career in public transportation marketing. Any member organization of the American Public Transportation Association (APTA) can nominate and sponsor candidates for this scholarship. Nominees must be enrolled in a fully–accredited institution, have and maintain at least a 3.0 GPA, and be either employed by or demonstrate a strong interest in preparing for a career in public transportation marketing. They must submit a 1,000–word essay on the topic, "In what segment of the public transportation industry will you make a career and why?" Selection is based on demonstrated interest in the transit field as a career, need for financial assistance, academic achievement, essay content and quality, and involvement in extracurricular citizenship and leadership activities.

Financial data: The stipend is $2,500.

Duration: 1 year; may be renewed.

Number awarded: 1 each year.

Deadline: May of each year.

2932 $ REBA MALONE SCHOLARSHIP

American Public Transportation Association
Attn: American Public Transportation Foundation
1666 K Street, N.W., Suite 1100
Washington, DC 20006
Phone: (202) 496–4803; Fax: (202) 496–4323;
Email: yconley@apta.com
Web: www.aptfd.org/work/scholarship.htm

Summary: To provide financial assistance to undergraduate and graduate students who are preparing for a career in transit marketing or communications.

Eligibility: Open to college sophomores, juniors, seniors, and graduate students who are preparing for an career in transit or transportation marketing or communications. Any member organization of the American Public Transportation Association (APTA) can nominate and sponsor candidates for this scholarship. Nominees must be enrolled in a fully–accredited institution, have and maintain at least a 3.0 GPA, and be either employed by or demonstrate a strong interest in preparing for a career in transit or transportation marketing or communications. They must submit a 1,000–word essay on the topic, "In what segment of the public transportation industry will you make a career and why?" Selection is based on demonstrated interest in the transit field as a career, need for financial assistance, academic achievement, essay content and quality, and involvement in extracurricular citizenship and leadership activities.

Financial data: The stipend is $2,500.

Duration: 1 year; may be renewed.

Number awarded: 1 each year.

Deadline: May of each year.

2933 REJESTA V. PERRY SCHOLARSHIP

Sigma Gamma Rho Sorority, Inc.
Attn: National Education Fund
1000 Southhill Drive, Suite 200
Cary, NC 27513
Phone: (919) 678–9720; (888) SGR–1922; Fax: (919) 678–9721;
Email: info@sgrho1922.org
Web: www.sgrho1922.org/nef

Summary: To provide financial assistance to undergraduate students working on a degree in education.

Eligibility: Open to undergraduates working on a degree in education. The sponsor is a traditionally African American sorority, but support is available to males and females of all races. Applicants must have a GPA of "C" or higher and be able to demonstrate financial need.

Financial data: A stipend is awarded (amount not specified).

Duration: 1 year.

Number awarded: 1 each year.

Deadline: April of each year.

2934 RHODE ISLAND HEALTHCARE FINANCIAL MANAGEMENT SCHOLARSHIP PROGRAM

Healthcare Financial Management Association–Massachusetts–Rhode Island Chapter
411 Waverley Oaks Road, Suite 331B
Waltham, MA 02452
Phone: (781) 647–4422; Fax: (781) 647–7222;
Email: Admin@ma–ri–hfma.org
Web: www.ma–ri–hfam.org/index.htm?content=content/scholarships.inc

Summary: To provide financial assistance to residents of Rhode Island who are working on a bachelor's or master's degree in a field related to health care financial management at a school in any state.

Eligibility: Open to residents of Rhode Island who are currently working on a bachelor's or master's degree at an accredited college or university in any state. Preference is given to students concentrating in finance or accounting, but applicants in such fields as health care administration or public health are also eligible. Along with their application, they must submit an essay that covers benefit to be received from enrolling in the program and its relevance to the health care field, desire to further education, prior academic achievement, and (if applicable) financial need.

Financial data: The stipend is $1,000.
Duration: 1 year.
Number awarded: 1 each year.
Deadline: September of each year for fall semester; January of each year for spring semester.

2935 RICHARD D. WIEGERS SCHOLARSHIP

Illinois Association of Realtors
Attn: Illinois Real Estate Educational Foundation
522 South Fifth Street
P.O. Box 2607
Springfield, IL 62708
Phone: (866) 854–REEF; Fax: (217) 241–9935;
Email: lclayton@iar.org
Web: www.ilreef.org/Scholarships.htm
Summary: To provide financial assistance to residents of Illinois working on an undergraduate or graduate degree in specified fields at a college or university in the state.
Eligibility: Open to Illinois residents who are attending or planning to attend a college or university in the state. Applicants must be working on or planning to work on 1) an undergraduate degree in business, law, or finance; or 2) a graduate degree in business. Along with their application, they must submit a 1,000–word statement on their general activities and intellectual interests, any employment experience, their proposed line of study, and the career they expect to follow. Selection is based on that statement, academic achievement, recommendations, and financial need.
Financial data: The stipend is $1,000.
Duration: 1 year.
Number awarded: 1 or more each year.
Deadline: March of each year.

2936 $ RICHARD J. BOUCHARD SCHOLARSHIP

American Public Transportation Association
Attn: American Public Transportation Foundation
1666 K Street, N.W., Suite 1100
Washington, DC 20006
Phone: (202) 496–4803; Fax: (202) 496–4323;
Email: yconley@apta.com
Web: www.aptfd.org/work/scholarship.htm
Summary: To provide financial assistance to undergraduate and graduate students who are preparing for a career in public transportation planning and development.
Eligibility: Open to college sophomores, juniors, seniors, and graduate students who are preparing for an career in public transportation planning and development. Any member organization of the American Public Transportation Association (APTA) can nominate and sponsor candidates for this scholarship. Nominees must be enrolled in a fully–accredited institution, have and maintain at least a 3.0 GPA, and be either employed by or demonstrate a strong interest in preparing for a career in public transportation planning and development. They must submit a 1,000–word essay on the topic, "In what segment of the public transportation industry will you make a career and why?" Selection is based on demonstrated interest in the transit field as a career, need for financial assistance, academic achievement, essay content and quality, and involvement in extracurricular citizenship and leadership activities.
Financial data: The stipend is $2,500.
Duration: 1 year; may be renewed.
Number awarded: 1 each year.
Deadline: May of each year.

2937 RICHARD PODLESAK MEMORIAL SCHOLARSHIP

Association of Certified Fraud Examiners–Heartland Chapter
Attn: Scholarship Committee Chair
P.O. Box 460726
Papillion, NE 68046–0726
Phone: (402) 563–5936; Fax: (402) 563–5380;
Email: jwcarte@nppd.com
Web: www.heartlandacfe.com/Scholarship_Information
Summary: To provide financial assistance to undergraduate and graduate students in Iowa, Nebraska, and South Dakota who are working on a degree in fields related to detecting, deterring, and preventing fraud.
Eligibility: Open to full–time undergraduates and part–time graduate students at colleges and universities in Iowa, Nebraska, and South Dakota. Applicants must be working on a degree in accounting, business, criminal justice, or other fields related to detecting, deterring, and preventing fraud and white–collar crime and have a GPA of 3.0 or higher. Along with their application, they must submit a brief essay on why they desire to receive the scholarship and how fraud awareness will enhance their professional career. Selection is based on the essay, academic achievement, letters of recommendation, and an interview.
Financial data: Stipends range from $500 to $1,000.
Duration: 1 year.
Number awarded: 1 or more each year.
Deadline: January of each year.

2938 RITA LOWE COLLEGE SCHOLARSHIPS

Summary: To provide financial assistance to students from any state majoring in mathematics education at colleges and universities in Washington.
See Listing #2265.

2939 RITA LOWE HIGH SCHOOL SCHOLARSHIP

Summary: To provide financial assistance to high school seniors in Washington planning to major in mathematics education at a college or university in the state.
See Listing #2266.

2940 $$ RITCHIE–JENNINGS MEMORIAL SCHOLARSHIPS PROGRAM

Association of Certified Fraud Examiners
Attn: Scholarships Program Coordinator
The Gregor Building
716 West Avenue
Austin, TX 78701–2727
Phone: (512) 478–9000; (800) 245–3321; Fax: (512) 478–9297;
Email: scholarships@ACFE.com
Web: www.acfe.com/scholarship.aspx
Summary: To provide financial assistance to undergraduate and graduate students working on a degree related to finance or criminal justice.
Eligibility: Open to students working full time on an undergraduate or graduate degree in accounting, business administration, finance, or criminal justice at a 4–year college or university in any country. Applicants must submit an essay of 250 to 500 words on why they deserve the award and how fraud awareness will affect their professional career development. Selection is based on the essay, academic achievement, and 3 letters of recommendation (including at least 1 from a certified fraud examiner for students in Canada and the United States or 1 from a major professor for students from outside North America).
Financial data: The stipend ranges from $1,000 to $10,000. Funds are paid directly to the student's university.
Duration: 1 year.
Number awarded: 30 each year: 1 at $10,000, 2 at $5,000, 4 at $2,500, and 23 at $1,000.
Deadline: January of each year.

2941 $$ ROBERT C. BYRD MEMORIAL SCHOLARSHIPS

Summary: To provide financial assistance to Turkish–Americans from Appalachian area states who are entering or continuing an undergraduate or graduate program in fields related to public affairs.
See Listing #1484.

2942 $ ROBERT J. YOURZAK SCHOLARSHIP AWARD

Project Management Institute
Attn: PMI Educational Foundation
14 Campus Boulevard
Newtown Square, PA 19073–3299
Phone: (610) 356–4600, ext. 7004; Fax: (610) 356–0357;
Email: pmief@pmi.org
Web: www.pmi.org/pmief/scholarship/scholarships.asp
Summary: To provide financial assistance to undergraduate or graduate students from any state who are working on a degree in a field related to project management.
Eligibility: Open to residents of any state enrolled as an undergraduate or graduate student at a college or university. Applicants must be working on a degree in project management or a related field. Along with their application, they

must submit 1) a 500–word essay on why they want to be a project manager; and 2) a 250–word essay on how a code of ethics is important to project management. Financial need is not considered in the selection process.
Financial data: The stipend is $2,000.
Duration: 1 year.
Number awarded: 1 each year.
Deadline: May of each year.

2943 $$ ROBERT NOYCE SCHOLARSHIPS OF PENNSYLVANIA

Summary: To provide financial assistance to upper–division students and professionals at institutions of the Pennsylvania State System of Higher Education (PASSHE) who are majoring in a discipline of science, technology, engineering, or mathematics (STEM) and planning to become a high school science and mathematics teacher in Pennsylvania.
See Listing #2275.

2944 ROBERT R. ROBINSON SCHOLARSHIP

Michigan Townships Association
Attn: Robert R. Robinson Memorial Scholarship Fund
512 Westshire Drive
P.O. Box 80078
Lansing, MI 48908–0078
Phone: (517) 321–6467; Fax: (517) 321–8908;
Email: debra@michigantownships.org
Web: www.michigantownships.org/rrrschol.asp
Summary: To provide financial assistance to upper–division and graduate students majoring in fields related to public administration at a college or university in Michigan.
Eligibility: Open to juniors, seniors, and graduate students enrolled in a Michigan college or university and working on a degree in public administration, public affairs management, or some other field closely related to local government administration. Applicants must be considering a career in local government administration. They must submit a letter of recommendation from a professor or instructor, a copy of a resolution of support from a Michigan township board (resolutions from other types of entities or from individual public officials are not sufficient), and a short essay on an important issue facing local government. Selection is based on academic achievement, community involvement, and commitment to a career in local government administration.
Financial data: Stipends range from $500 to $1,000.
Duration: 1 year.
Number awarded: 1 or more each year.
Deadline: May of each year.

2945 $ ROGER BUCHOLZ MEMORIAL CPA CANDIDATE SCHOLARSHIPS

Wisconsin Institute of Certified Public Accountants
Attn: WICPA Educational Foundation
235 North Executive Drive, Suite 200
Brookfield, WI 53005
Phone: (262) 785–0445; (800) 772–6939 (within WI); Fax: (262) 785–0838;
Email: tammy@wicpa.org
Web: www.wicpa.org
Summary: To provide financial assistance to students in Wisconsin working on an undergraduate degree in accounting.
Eligibility: Open to residents of Wisconsin who are working on an undergraduate degree in accounting at a college or university in the state. Selection is based on academic achievement, a personal statement, and letters of recommendation.
Financial data: The stipend is $4,000 or $2,000.
Duration: 1 year.
Number awarded: Varies each year; recently, 4 of these scholarships were awarded: 2 at $4,000 and 2 at $2,000.
Deadline: February of each year.

2946 RONALD A. SANTANA MEMORIAL SCHOLARSHIPS

Tourism Cares
Attn: Academic Scholarship Program
275 Turnpike Street, Suite 307
Canton, MA 02021
Phone: (781) 821–5990; Fax: (781) 821–8949;
Email: scholarships@tourismcares.org
Web: www.tourismcares.org
Summary: To provide financial assistance to undergraduate students from the United States, Guam, and Puerto Rico who are majoring in travel and tourism or a hospitality–related field.
Eligibility: Open to citizens and permanent residents of the United States, Guam, and Puerto Rico entering the second year of a 2–year program or the junior or senior year of a 4–year program at an accredited college or university. Applicants must be working full or part time on a degree in travel and tourism or a hospitality–related program and have a GPA of 3.0 or higher. Along with their application, they must submit an essay on the segment of the travel and tourism industry their current program of study emphasizes, the opportunities they are utilizing as they prepare for a career in the industry, and their academic and extracurricular activities. Financial need is not considered in the selection process.
Financial data: The stipend is $1,000.
Duration: 1 year.
Number awarded: 5 each year.
Deadline: March of each year.

2947 $ ROSA PARKS PLAYWRITING AWARD

Summary: To recognize and reward the student and faculty authors of plays that relate to civil rights and/or social justice.
See Listing #1487.

2948 $ ROSS N. AND PATRICIA PANGERE FOUNDATION SCHOLARSHIPS

American Council of the Blind
Attn: Coordinator, Scholarship Program
2200 Wilson Boulevard, Suite 650
Arlington, VA 22201
Phone: (202) 467–5081; (800) 424–8666; Fax: (703) 465–5085;
Email: info@acb.org
Web: www.acb.org/scholarship
Summary: To provide financial assistance to blind students working on an undergraduate or graduate degree in business.
Eligibility: Open to undergraduate and graduate students working on a degree in business. Applicants must submit verification of legal blindness in both eyes; SAT, ACT, GMAT, or similar scores; information on extracurricular activities (including involvement in the American Council of the Blind); employment record; and a 500–word autobiographical sketch that includes their personal goals, strengths, weaknesses, hobbies, honors, achievements, and reasons for choice of field or courses of study. A cumulative GPA of 3.3 or higher is generally required. Financial need is not considered in the selection process.
Financial data: The stipend is $2,500.
Duration: 1 year.
Number awarded: 2 each year.
Deadline: February of each year.

2949 RUBY J. DARENSBOURG–COOK MEMORIAL SCHOLARSHIP FUND

Baton Rouge Area Foundation
Attn: Scholarship Program Officer
402 North Fourth Street
Baton Rouge, LA 70802
Phone: (225) 381–7084; (877) 387–6126; Fax: (225) 387–6153;
Email: efargason@braf.org
Web: www.braf.org/index.cfm/page/3/n/2
Summary: To provide financial assistance to high school seniors in Louisiana interested in attending college in the state to prepare for a career in education.
Eligibility: Open to seniors graduating from high schools in Louisiana and planning to enroll full time at an accredited college or university in the state. Applicants must intend to work on a degree in education, preferably elementary education or early childhood education. Along with their application, they must submit 1) an essay about their life experience and the challenges they have had to overcome; 2) a resume that includes their goals for the future, extracurricular activities, academic and other educational honors and awards, leadership positions, a record of distinctive and significant contributions to the school and/or community, and anticipated graduation date; 3) letters of recommendation; 4) transcripts; and 5) ACT and/or SAT scores. Financial need is not considered in the selection process.

Financial data: The stipend is $500 per semester ($1,000 per year). Funds must be used in the following order of priority: tuition and fees; room and board; books and supplies; and commuting expenses.
Duration: 1 year; may be renewed up to 3 additional years, provided the recipient remains enrolled full time and has an overall GPA of 2.5 or higher each semester and a GPA of 3.0 or higher for courses in their major course of study.
Number awarded: 1 or more each year.
Deadline: April of each year.

2950 $ RUDOLPH DILLMAN MEMORIAL SCHOLARSHIP

Summary: To provide financial assistance to legally blind undergraduate or graduate students studying in the field of rehabilitation and/or education of visually impaired and blind persons.
See Listing #2291.

2951 RUTH MOSS EASTERLING SCHOLARSHIP

North Carolina Federation of Business and Professional Women's Club, Inc.
Attn: BPW/NC Foundation
P.O. Box 276
Carrboro, NC 27510
Web: www.bpw–nc.org/Default.aspx?pageId=837230
Summary: To provide financial assistance to students attending North Carolina colleges or community colleges and majoring in political science or related fields.
Eligibility: Open to students currently enrolled in either a North Carolina community college or North Carolina 4–year college and majoring in law (including legal secretary), public administration, or political science. They must be endorsed by a local BPW unit and have a GPA of 3.0 or higher. Along with their application, they must submit a 1–page statement that summarizes their career goals, previous honors, or community activities and justifies their need for this scholarship. U.S. citizenship is required.
Financial data: The stipend is $1,000. Funds are paid directly to the recipient's school.
Duration: 1 year; recipients may reapply.
Number awarded: 1 each year.
Deadline: April of each year.

2952 $$ SAN FRANCISCO SWEA SCHOLARSHIPS

Summary: To provide financial assistance to students from the western United States who are interested in studying or conducting research on topics related to Sweden.
See Listing #1498.

2953 $$ SAP NORTH AMERICA SCHOLARSHIPS

Summary: To provide financial assistance to upper–division students working on a degree related to enterprise technology.
See Listing #2304.

2954 $ S.C. INTERNATIONAL ACTUARIAL SCIENCE SCHOLARSHIPS

Summary: To provide financial assistance to college seniors majoring in actuarial science or mathematics.
See Listing #2306.

2955 $ SEATTLE CHAPTER SCHOLARSHIP

Educational Foundation for Women in Accounting
Attn: Foundation Administrator
136 South Keowee Street
Dayton, OH 45402
Phone: (937) 424–3391; Fax: (937) 222–5749;
Email: info@efwa.org
Web: www.efwa.org/scholarships_seattle.php
Summary: To provide financial support to women who are enrolled in an undergraduate or graduate accounting degree program at a school in Washington.
Eligibility: Open to women from any state who are working on a bachelor's or master's degree in accounting at an accredited school in Washington. Selection is based on aptitude for accounting and business, commitment to the goal of working on a degree in accounting (including evidence of continued commitment after receiving this award), clear evidence that the candidate has established goals and a plan for achieving those goals (both personal and professional), and financial need. U.S. citizenship is required.
Financial data: The stipend is $2,000 per year.
Duration: 1 year; may be renewed 1 additional year if the recipient completes at least 12 hours each semester.
Number awarded: 1 each year.
Deadline: April of each year.

2956 $$ SEATTLE CHAPTER SCHOLARSHIPS

American Society of Women Accountants–Seattle Chapter
c/o Janet Stebbins
MASInc.
604 West Meeker Street, Suite 202
Kent, WA 98032
Phone: (206) 467–8645;
Email: scholarship@aswaseattle.com
Web: www.aswaseattle.com/scholarships.cfm
Summary: To provide financial assistance to female students from any state working on a bachelor's or master's degree in accounting at a college or university in Washington.
Eligibility: Open to female residents of any state who are working part time or full time on an associate, bachelor's, or master's degree in accounting at a college or university in Washington. Applicants must have completed at least 30 semester hours and have maintained a GPA of at least 2.5 overall and 3.0 in accounting. Membership in the American Society of Women Accountants (ASWA) is not required. Selection is based on career goals, communication skills, GPA, personal circumstances, and financial need.
Financial data: Stipends range from $1,500 to $5,000.
Duration: 1 year.
Number awarded: May of each year.
Deadline: Varies each year; recently, 6 of these scholarships were awarded: 1 at $5,000, 1 at $3,000, 2 at $2,000, and 2 at $1,500.

2957 $ SECURE INDIANA SCHOLARSHIP

Indiana Homeland Security Foundation
c/o Indiana Department of Homeland Security
Attn: Council Coordinator
302 West Washington Street, Room E220
Indianapolis, IN 46204
Phone: (317) 234–6219; Fax: (317) 233–5006;
Email: mafields@dhs.in.gov
Web: www.in.gov/dhs/foundationscholarship.htm
Summary: To provide financial assistance to residents of Indiana interested in working on an undergraduate degree in public safety at a college in the state.
Eligibility: Open to residents of Indiana who are enrolled or planning to enroll as an undergraduate at a college or university in the state. Applicants must be interested in working on a degree in public safety. They must have a GPA of 2.8 or higher and a record of volunteer service at a public safety organization in the state. Along with their application, they must submit a 500–word essay describing why they are applying for this scholarship and why they wish to prepare for a career in public safety. Financial need is not considered in the selection process.
Financial data: The stipend is $2,000 for full–time students or $1,000 for part–time students.
Duration: 1 year.
Number awarded: Varies each year; at least 1 scholarship is awarded in each of Indiana's 100 legislative districts.
Deadline: November of each year.

2958 $$ SHARON D. BANKS MEMORIAL UNDERGRADUATE SCHOLARSHIP

Summary: To provide financial assistance to undergraduate women interested in a career in transportation.
See Listing #2314.

2959 $ SHIRLEY DELIBERO SCHOLARSHIP

American Public Transportation Association
Attn: American Public Transportation Foundation
1666 K Street, N.W., Suite 1100

Washington, DC 20006
Phone: (202) 496–4803; Fax: (202) 496–4323;
Email: yconley@apta.com
Web: www.aptfd.org/work/scholarship.htm

Summary: To provide financial assistance to African American undergraduate and graduate students who are preparing for a career in the public transportation industry.

Eligibility: Open to African American sophomores, juniors, seniors, and graduate students who are preparing for a career in the transit industry. Any member organization of the American Public Transportation Association (APTA) can nominate and sponsor candidates for this scholarship. Nominees must be enrolled in a fully–accredited institution, have and maintain at least a 3.0 GPA, and be either employed by or demonstrate a strong interest in entering the business administration or management area of the public transportation industry. They must submit a 1,000–word essay on the topic, "In what segment of the public transportation industry will you make a career and why?" Selection is based on demonstrated interest in the transit field as a career, need for financial assistance, academic achievement, essay content and quality, and involvement in extracurricular citizenship and leadership activities.

Financial data: The stipend is $2,500.

Duration: 1 year; may be renewed.

Number awarded: 1 each year.

Deadline: May of each year.

2960 SIKH COALITION DIVERSITY VIDEO COMPETITION

Summary: To recognize and reward high school and college students who submit outstanding essays on topics related to diversity and faith.

See Listing #1510.

2961 SIOUX FALLS RETIRED TEACHERS ASSOCIATION SCHOLARSHIP

Sioux Falls Area Community Foundation
Attn: Scholarship Coordinator
300 North Phillips Avenue, Suite 102
Sioux Falls, SD 57104–6035
Phone: (605) 336–7055, ext. 20; Fax: (605) 336–0038;
Email: pgale@sfacf.org
Web: www.sfacf.org/ScholarshipDetails.aspx?CategoryID=6

Summary: To provide financial assistance to upper–division students from any state who are working on a degree in education at a college or university in South Dakota.

Eligibility: Open to residents of any state who are entering their junior or senior year at an accredited South Dakota college or university. Applicants must be majoring in education. They must have a GPA of 2.5 or higher and be able to demonstrate a record of participation in school and community affairs, motivation and commitment to the teaching profession, and financial need.

Financial data: The stipend is $1,000 per year. Funds are to be used for tuition, fees, and/or books.

Duration: 1 year; may be renewed.

Number awarded: 1 each year.

Deadline: January of each year.

2962 $ SISTER MARY PETRONIA VAN STRATEN SCHOLARSHIP

Summary: To provide financial assistance to students from Wisconsin preparing for a career as a mathematics teacher.

See Listing #2327.

2963 $ SOCIETY OF LOUISIANA CERTIFIED PUBLIC ACCOUNTANTS MEMORIAL SCHOLARSHIPS

Society of Louisiana Certified Public Accountants
Attn: LCPA Education Foundation
2400 Veterans Boulevard, Suite 500
Kenner, LA 70062–4739
Phone: (504) 464–1040; (800) 288–5272; Fax: (504) 469–7930
Web: www.lcpa.org/LCPAScholarships.html

Summary: To provide financial assistance to undergraduate and graduate students in Louisiana who are interested in becoming Certified Public Accountants (C.P.A.s).

Eligibility: Open to Louisiana residents who are currently enrolled full time in an accounting program at a 4–year college or university in the state. Applicants must be upper–division, fifth–year, or graduate students and have a GPA of 2.5 or higher. Along with their application, they must submit a 1–page essay on a topic that changes annually but relates to the C.P.A. profession; recently, students were asked to give their ideas on the most important issues in the accounting profession today. Selection is based on academic merit and the essay.

Financial data: Stipends recently ranged from $750 to $2,400.

Duration: 1 year.

Number awarded: Varies each year; recently, 6 of these scholarships were awarded: 1 at $750, 4 at $1,000, and 1 at $2,400.

Deadline: January of each year.

2964 $ SOCIETY OF SPONSORS OF THE UNITED STATES NAVY CENTENNIAL SCHOLARSHIP

Navy–Marine Corps Relief Society
Attn: Education Division
875 North Randolph Street, Suite 225
Arlington, VA 22203–1757
Phone: (703) 696–4960; Fax: (703) 696–0144;
Email: education@nmcrs.org
Web: www.nmcrs.org/education.html

Summary: To provide financial assistance to Navy and Marine Corps veterans who were wounded in combat in Iraq or Afghanistan and are interested in preparing to become a teacher.

Eligibility: Open to Navy and Marine Corps veterans who were injured in combat in Operations Enduring Freedom, Iraqi Freedom, or New Dawn. Applicants must be enrolled full time in an undergraduate program leading to a bachelor's degree and teacher licensure. They must have a GPA of 2.5 or higher. Along with their application, they must submit a 1–page essay describing the factors in their background and military experience that convinced them to prepare for a career in education and the special qualities they will bring to the classroom that will have a positive impact on the youth of America. Financial need is not considered in the selection process.

Financial data: The stipend is $3,000 per year. Funds are paid directly to the student.

Duration: 1 year; recipients may reapply.

Number awarded: Up to 5 each year.

Deadline: Applications may be submitted at any time.

2965 $ SOUTH CAROLINA ASSOCIATION OF CPA'S SCHOLARSHIP PROGRAM

South Carolina Association of Certified Public Accountants
Attn: Educational Fund, Inc.
570 Chris Drive
West Columbia, SC 29169
Phone: (803) 791–4181, ext. 107; (888) 557–4814 (within SC); Fax: (803) 791–4196;
Email: gosier@scacpa.org
Web: www.scacpa.org

Summary: To provide financial assistance to upper–division and graduate students working on a degree in accounting in South Carolina.

Eligibility: Open to South Carolina residents who are working on a bachelor's or master's degree in accounting at a college or university in the state. Applicants must be juniors, seniors, or graduate students with a GPA of 3.25 or higher overall and 3.5 or higher in accounting. They must submit their college transcripts, a listing of awards and other scholarships, 2 letters of reference, a resume, a 250–word essay on their personal career goals, and certification of their accounting major. Financial need is not considered in the selection process.

Financial data: Stipends range from $500 to $2,000. Funds are paid to the recipient's school.

Duration: 1 year.

Number awarded: Varies each year; recently, 20 of these scholarships, worth more than $20,500, were awarded.

Deadline: May of each year.

2966 SOUTH DAKOTA BANKERS ASSOCIATION SCHOLARSHIPS

South Dakota Bankers Association
Attn: Foundation
109 West Missouri Avenue
P.O. Box 1081
Pierre, SD 57501–1081

Phone: (605) 224–1653; (800) 726–7322; Fax: (605) 224–7835;
Email: jchambers@sdba.com
Web: www.sdba.com/SDBA/Foundation/scholarships.htm
Summary: To provide financial assistance to students at South Dakota colleges or universities who are preparing for a career in banking, finance, or business.
Eligibility: Open to juniors at colleges or universities in South Dakota who have expressed an interest in banking, finance, or business. Applicants must submit brief statements on 1) their career goals and their interest in a career in business, finance, or banking; 2) how they have guided, inspired, or directed others in their personal, community, or academic life; 3) their participation in up to 3 unpaid volunteer activities; and 4) other qualifications that make them stand out for these scholarships, especially challenges (economic, emotional, physical, or geographic) that required courage, self–reliance, and determination. Financial need is not considered in the selection process.
Financial data: The stipend is $1,000.
Duration: 1 year.
Number awarded: 4 each year.
Deadline: March of each year.

2967 SOUTHWEST CHAPTER ACADEMIC SCHOLARSHIPS

American Association of Airport Executives–Southwest Chapter
Attn: Executive Director
107 South Southgate Drive
Chandler, AZ 85226
Phone: (480) 403–4604; Fax: (480) 893–7775;
Email: info@swaaae.org
Web: www.swaaae.org/displaycommon.cfm?an=1&subarticlenbr=10
Summary: To provide financial assistance to residents of any state working on an undergraduate or graduate degree in airport management at a college or university in the Southwest.
Eligibility: Open to residents of any state working on an undergraduate or graduate degree in airport management at colleges and universities in Arizona, California, Hawaii, Nevada, or Utah. Applicants must submit an autobiography (not to exceed 1 page) and a statement of their interest in aviation and airport management (not to exceed 1 page). Selection is based on academic record, extracurricular activities, and financial need.
Financial data: The stipend is $1,500; the sponsor also provides a $1,000 travel allowance for recipients to attend the awards ceremony.
Duration: 1 year.
Number awarded: 2 each year.
Deadline: November of each year.

2968 SOUTHWEST OHIO CHAPTER SCHOLARSHIP

Project Management Institute
Attn: PMI Educational Foundation
14 Campus Boulevard
Newtown Square, PA 19073–3299
Phone: (610) 356–4600, ext. 7004; Fax: (610) 356–0357;
Email: pmief@pmi.org
Web: www.pmi.org/pmief/scholarship/scholarships.asp
Summary: To provide financial assistance to undergraduate or graduate students from any state who are interested in working on a degree in project management at a college in Indiana, Kentucky, or Ohio.
Eligibility: Open to residents of any state working on or planning to work on an undergraduate or graduate degree in a field related to project management. Applicants must be attending or planning to attend an accredited college or university in the tri–state area of Indiana, Kentucky, and Ohio. Along with their application, they must submit 1) a 500–word essay on why they want to be a project manager; and 2) a 250–word essay on how a code of ethics is important to project management. Selection is based on relation of the applicant's college program and career goals to project management, academic performance, extracurricular activities, and completeness and neatness of application.
Financial data: The stipend is $1,000.
Duration: 1 year.
Number awarded: 1 each year.
Deadline: May of each year.

2969 SOUTHWEST PARK AND RECREATION TRAINING INSTITUTE STUDENT SCHOLARSHIPS

Summary: To provide financial assistance to undergraduate and graduate students preparing for a career in the park and recreation profession at universities in designated southwestern states.
See Listing #2343.

2970 $$ SPENCER EDUCATIONAL FOUNDATION UNDERGRADUATE SCHOLARSHIPS

Spencer Educational Foundation, Inc.
c/o Risk Insurance and Management Society
1065 Avenue of the Americas, 13th Floor
New York, NY 10018
Phone: (212) 286–9292;
Email: asabatino@spencered.org
Web: www.spencered.org
Summary: To provide financial assistance to upper–division students who are preparing for a career in risk management.
Eligibility: Open to full–time students entering their junior or senior year with a major or minor in a risk management discipline. Applicants must have a career objective in risk management and relevant work experience. They must have a GPA of 3.0 or higher. Along with their application, they must submit a 500–word essay on their chosen career path and goals. Selection is based on merit. The applicant with the highest GPA receives the Douglas Barlow Scholarship, sponsored by Royal & SunAlliance of Great Britain.
Financial data: The Douglas Barlow Scholarship is $7,500. Stipends for all other scholarships are $5,000.
Duration: 1 year.
Number awarded: Varies each year; recently, 24 of these scholarships were awarded.
Deadline: January of each year.

2971 $ STANLEY MCFARLAND SCHOLARSHIP

National Association of Federal Education Program Administrators
c/o Rick Carder, President
125 David Drive
Sutter Creek, CA 95685
Phone: (916) 669–5102; Fax: (888) 487–6441;
Email: rickc@sia–us.com
Web: www.nafepa.org
Summary: To provide financial assistance to high school seniors and college freshmen who are interested in working on a degree in education.
Eligibility: Open to graduating high school seniors and graduates already enrolled in the first year of college. Applicants must be working on or planning to work on a degree in education. They must be nominated by their state affiliate of the sponsoring organization. Along with their application, they must submit a 300–word personal narrative explaining why they are applying for this scholarship, including their awards, interests, leadership activities within the community, and future goals. Selection is based on that essay (20 points), a high school or college transcript from the current semester (20 points), extracurricular and leadership activities within the community or church (20 points), 3 letters of recommendation (20 points), and financial need (20 points).
Financial data: The stipend is $2,500.
Duration: 1 year.
Number awarded: 1 each year.
Deadline: Each state affiliate sets its own deadline; for a list of those, contact the sponsor.

2972 STEPHEN AND SANDY SHELLER SCHOLARSHIP

Summary: To provide financial assistance to upper–division students at institutions of the Pennsylvania State System of Higher Education (PASSHE) who are preparing for a career in law or art therapy.
See Listing #1516.

2973 $ STEPHEN W. CAVANAUGH SCHOLARSHIP FUND

Baton Rouge Area Foundation
Attn: Scholarship Program Officer
402 North Fourth Street
Baton Rouge, LA 70802
Phone: (225) 381–7084; (877) 387–6126; Fax: (225) 387–6153;
Email: efargason@braf.org
Web: www.braf.org/index.cfm/page/3/n/2
Summary: To provide financial assistance to residents of Louisiana interested in attending college in the state to prepare for a career in the insurance industry.
Eligibility: Open to residents of Louisiana who are enrolled or planning to enroll full time at a college, university, or community college in the state. Applicants must intend to major in an insurance–related field. Along with their application, they must submit a transcript, ACT and/or SAT scores, a letter of recommendation from a teacher or professor, and a statement of 250 to

500 words explaining why they are preparing for a career within the insurance industry. Selection is based on extracurricular activities, community and public service, leadership potential, and ability to make satisfactory academic progress toward a degree or a major in an academic discipline related to the insurance industry.
Financial data: The stipend is $1,000 per semester ($2,000 per year). Funds must be used in the following order of priority: tuition and fees; room and board; books and supplies; and commuting expenses.
Duration: 1 year; may be renewed up to 3 additional years, provided the recipient remains enrolled full time and has a GPA of 2.5 or higher each semester.
Number awarded: 1 or more each year.
Deadline: April of each year.

2974 $$ STUART A. ROBERTSON MEMORIAL SCHOLARSHIP

Actuarial Foundation
Attn: Actuarial Education and Research Fund Committee
475 North Martingale Road, Suite 600
Schaumburg, IL 60173–2226
Phone: (847) 706–3535; Fax: (847) 706–3599;
Email: scholarships@actfnd.org
Web: www.actuarialfoundation.org/programs/actuarial/robertson.shtml
Summary: To provide financial assistance to undergraduate students who are preparing for a career in actuarial science.
Eligibility: Open to full–time students who are entering their sophomore, junior, or senior year at an accredited college or university. Applicants must have a GPA of 3.0 or higher and have successfully completed 2 actuarial examinations. Along with their application, they must submit a 500–word essay that answers questions on 1) how their work experiences have prepared them for an actuarial career; 2) the qualifications and abilities that have helped them succeed in college and will help them succeed in an actuarial career; 3) the extracurricular activities they have enjoyed the most and how those will help them in their career; and 4) the college courses they have enjoyed the most/least and why. Financial need is not considered in the selection process.
Financial data: The stipend is $7,500.
Duration: 1 year.
Number awarded: 1 each year.
Deadline: May of each year.

2975 STUDENT EDUCATION FUND SCHOLARSHIPS

Arkansas Society of Certified Public Accountants
Attn: Student Education Fund
11300 Executive Center Drive
Little Rock, AR 72211–4352
Phone: (501) 664–8739; (800) 482–8739 (within AR); Fax: (501) 664–8320;
Email: bangel@arcpa.org
Web: www.arcpa.org/Content/60012.aspx
Summary: To provide financial assistance to students at colleges and universities in Arkansas who are majoring in accounting.
Eligibility: Open to accounting majors at 4–year colleges and universities in Arkansas. Applicants must have completed at least 84 semester hours of course work (including 15 semester hours of accounting) with a GPA of 3.5 or higher in accounting classes. They must certify that they are pursuing the requirements to sit for the C.P.A. examination and intend to pursue the C.P.A. professional certification. Each accounting department at an Arkansas 4–year college or university offering an accounting degree may nominate 1 student per faculty member who is a regular or associate member in good standing of the Arkansas Society of Certified Public Accountants. Selection is based on academic achievement, professional promise, and commitment to pursuing a C.P.A. credential.
Financial data: Recently, the stipend was $1,300.
Duration: 1 year.
Number awarded: Varies each year; recently, 21 of these scholarships were awarded.
Deadline: February of each year.

2976 SUE AND VIRGINIA HESTER SPECIAL EDUCATION SCHOLARSHIP

Alabama Federation of Women's Clubs
Attn: Scholarship Chair
2728 Niazuma Avenue
Birmingham, AL 35205
Phone: (205) 323–2392; Fax: (205) 323–8443
Web: www.gfwc–alabama.org/Scholarships.html
Summary: To provide financial assistance to women who are residents of Alabama and interested in studying special education at a public university in the state.
Eligibility: Open to female residents of Alabama who are attending or planning to attend a public university in the state. Applicants must be interested in majoring in special education. Along with their application, they must submit a personal letter on their educational goals, 3 letters of recommendation, and transcripts. Financial need is not considered in the selection process.
Financial data: The stipend is $1,000.
Duration: 1 year.
Number awarded: 1 each year.
Deadline: Deadline not specified.

2977 $ SURETY AND FIDELITY INDUSTRY SCHOLARSHIP PROGRAM

The Surety Foundation
Attn: Scholarship Program for Minority Students
1101 Connecticut Avenue, N.W., Suite 800
Washington, DC 20036
Phone: (202) 463–0600; Fax: (202) 463–0606;
Email: scarradine@surety.org
Web: www.thesuretyfoundation.org/scholarshipprogram.html
Summary: To provide financial assistance to minority undergraduates working on a degree in a field related to insurance.
Eligibility: Open to full–time undergraduates who are U.S. citizens and members of a minority group (Black, Native American/Alaskan Native, Asian/Pacific Islander, Hispanic). Applicants must have completed at least 30 semester hours of study at an accredited 4–year college or university and have a declared major in insurance/risk management, accounting, business, or finance. They must have a GPA of 3.0 or higher and be able to demonstrate financial need. Along with their application, they must submit an essay of 500 to 1,000 words on the role of surety bonding and the surety industry in public sector construction.
Financial data: The stipend is $2,500 per year.
Duration: 1 year; recipients may reapply.
Number awarded: Varies each year.
Deadline: April of each year.

2978 TAER PROFESSIONAL PREPARATION SCHOLARSHIP

Texas Association for Education and Rehabilitation of the Blind and Visually Impaired
c/o Michael Munro
Stephen F. Austin State University
Department of Human Services
Teacher Preparation–Visual Impairment
P.O. Box 13019
Nacogdoches, TX 75962
Phone: (936) 468–1036; Fax: (936) 468–1342;
Email: munromicha@sfasu.edu
Web: www.txaer.org/Scholarships_Awards/scholaraward.htm
Summary: To provide financial assistance to residents of Texas who are interested in attending college in any state to study rehabilitation or education of people with visual impairments.
Eligibility: Open to residents of Texas who are enrolled or planning to enroll at a college or university in any state. Applicants be interested in majoring in a field related to rehabilitation or education of people with visual impairments. They must be able to demonstrate financial need. Along with their application, they must submit a letter regarding the goal of their education.
Financial data: The stipend is $1,000.
Duration: 1 year.
Number awarded: 1 or more each year.
Deadline: February of each year.

2979 $ TAX SCHOLARS PROGRAM

Hispanic Association of Colleges and Universities
Attn: National Scholarship Program
8415 Datapoint Drive, Suite 400
San Antonio, TX 78229
Phone: (210) 692–3805; Fax: (210) 692–0823; TDD: (800) 855–2880;
Email: scholarships@hacu.net
Web: www.hacu.net/hacu/Scholarships.asp?SnID=899378480

Summary: To provide financial assistance to undergraduate and graduate students working on a degree in accounting with an emphasis on taxes at member institutions of the Hispanic Association of Colleges and Universities (HACU).
Eligibility: Open to sophomores, juniors, and first–year master's degree students at 4–year HACU member institutions who are working full time on a degree in accounting with an emphasis on taxes. Applicants must have a GPA of 3.5 or higher and be able to demonstrate financial need. They must be interested in a career with Deloitte in its taxation activities. Along with their application, they must submit an essay that focuses on their personal motivation for applying for this scholarship, their academic and/or career goals, and the skills they could bring to an employer.
Financial data: The stipend is $2,200.
Duration: 1 year.
Number awarded: 1 or more each year.
Deadline: June of each year.

2980 $$ TCADVANCE SCHOLARSHIPS FOR TURKISH AMERICAN STUDENTS

Summary: To provide financial assistance to Turkish–Americans entering or continuing an undergraduate or graduate program in fields related to public affairs.
See Listing #1526.

2981 $ TEACHER EDUCATION ASSISTANCE FOR COLLEGE AND HIGHER EDUCATION (TEACH) GRANTS

Department of Education
Attn: Federal Student Aid Information Center
P.O. Box 84
Washington, DC 20044–0084
Phone: (319) 337–5665; (800) 4–FED–AID; TDD: (800) 730–8913
Web: studentaid.ed.gov/types/grants–scholarships
Summary: To provide scholarship/loans to undergraduate and graduate students interested in completing a degree in education and teaching in a high–need field at a school that serves low–income students.
Eligibility: Open to U.S. citizens and eligible noncitizens who are enrolled as an undergraduate, post–baccalaureate, or graduate student at a postsecondary educational institution that has chosen to participate in this program. Applicants must be enrolled in course work that will prepare them for a career in teaching. They must meet certain academic achievement requirements (scoring above the 75th percentile on a college admissions test or maintaining a cumulative GPA of 3.25 or higher). The program requires that they sign an agreement to provide service as a teacher in 1) designated high–need fields, currently defined as bilingual education and English language acquisition, foreign language, mathematics, reading specialist, science, or special education; and 2) at a school serving low–income students at the elementary or secondary level.
Financial data: The maximum grant is $4,000 per year. This is a scholarship/loan program; recipients must teach a high–need field at a school serving low–income students for at least 4 academic years per year of grant support they receive. If they fail to complete the service obligation, the grant is converted to a Federal Direct Unsubsidized Stafford Loan and must be repaid with interest from the date the grant was disbursed.
Duration: Up to 2 years.
Number awarded: Varies each year; recently, nearly 32,000 of these grants, worth nearly $80 million, were awarded.
Deadline: Deadline not specified.

2982 TEACHERS OF ACCOUNTING AT TWO YEAR COLLEGES SCHOLARSHIPS

Teachers of Accounting at Two Year Colleges
c/o Lori Hatchell
Aims Community College
5401 West 20th Street
Greeley, CO 80632
Phone: (970) 339–6215;
Email: scholarship@tactyc.org
Web: www.tactyc.org/scholarships
Summary: To provide financial assistance to students enrolled at or graduating from 2–year colleges who are preparing for a career in accounting.
Eligibility: Open to students who are 1) graduating from a 2–year college and transferring to a 4–year school to work on a bachelor's degree in accounting; or 2) enrolled at a 2–year college and working on a degree in accounting. Applicants must have completed at least 30 college credits (including at least 6 in accounting) with an overall GPA of 3.3 or higher and a GPA in accounting courses of 3.5 or higher. They must be committed to a career in accounting. Along with their application, they must submit a 1–page self–description of their academic and professional goals and a 2–page essay on an accounting problem. Financial need is not considered in the selection process.
Financial data: The stipend is $1,000.
Duration: 1 year.
Number awarded: 4 each year: 2 for graduating students planning to work on a bachelor's degree and 2 for students working on a 2–year degree.
Deadline: February of each year.

2983 TED BRIDGES HOSPITALITY SCHOLARSHIP

Vermont Student Assistance Corporation
Attn: Scholarship Programs
10 East Allen Street
P.O. Box 2000
Winooski, VT 05404–2601
Phone: (802) 654–3798; (888) 253–4819; Fax: (802) 654–3765; TDD: (800) 281–3341 (within VT);
Email: info@vsac.org
Web: services.vsac.org
Summary: To provide financial assistance to Vermont residents who are interested in working on a degree in hospitality and tourism at a school in any state.
Eligibility: Open to high school seniors, high school graduates, and currently–enrolled college students in Vermont who are enrolled or planning to enroll at a college or university in any state. Applicants must be interested in preparing for a career in hospitality and tourism. Along with their application, they must submit 1) a 100–word essay on their interest in and commitment to pursuing their chosen career or vocation; and 2) a 250–word essay on their short– and long–term academic, educational, career, vocational, and/or employment goals. Selection is based on those essays, academic achievement (GPA of 3.1 or higher), and financial need (expected family contribution less than $23,360).
Financial data: The stipend is $1,000.
Duration: 1 year; nonrenewable.
Number awarded: 1 each year.
Deadline: March of each year.

2984 TENNESSEE FUNERAL DIRECTORS ASSOCIATION MEMORIAL SCHOLARSHIP PROGRAM

Tennessee Funeral Directors Association
Attn: Scholarship Committee
1616 Church Street, Suite A
Nashville, TN 37203
Phone: (615) 321–8792; (800) 537–1599 (within TN); Fax: (615) 321–8794;
Email: tnfda@tnfda.comcastbiz.net
Web: www.tnfda.org
Summary: To provide financial assistance to Tennessee residents who are preparing for a career in funeral service.
Eligibility: Open to U.S. citizens who are Tennessee residents, enrolled full time, and have completed 1 semester at a college in any state accredited by the American Board of Funeral Service Education. They must have expressed the intent to enter funeral service in Tennessee upon graduation. Along with their application, they must submit the latest family federal income tax return, college transcripts, 2 letters of recommendation, and a 2–page essay on why they decided to enter funeral service and what the word "service" means to them. Selection is based on financial need, academic record, recommendations, extracurricular and community activities, and the required essay.
Financial data: The stipend is $1,000.
Duration: 1 year.
Number awarded: 2 each year.
Deadline: Deadline not specified.

2985 $$ TENNESSEE MINORITY TEACHING FELLOWS PROGRAM

Tennessee Student Assistance Corporation
Parkway Towers
404 James Robertson Parkway, Suite 1510
Nashville, TN 37243–0820
Phone: (615) 741–1346; (800) 342–1663; Fax: (615) 741–6101;
Email: TSAC.Aidinfo@tn.gov
Web: www.tn.gov/collegepays/mon_college/minority_teach.htm
Summary: To provide funding to minority residents of Tennessee who wish to attend college in the state to prepare for a career in the teaching field.

Eligibility: Open to minority residents of Tennessee who are either high school seniors planning to enroll full time at a college or university in the state or continuing college students at a Tennessee college or university. High school seniors must have a GPA of 2.75 or higher and an ACT score of at least 18 or a combined mathematics and critical reading SAT score of at least 860. Continuing college students must have a college GPA of 2.5 or higher. All applicants must agree to teach at the K–12 level in a Tennessee public school following graduation from college. Along with their application, they must submit a 250–word essay on why they chose teaching as a profession. U.S. citizenship is required.
Financial data: The scholarship/loan is $5,000 per year. Recipients incur an obligation to teach at the preK–12 level in a Tennessee public school 1 year for each year the award is received.
Duration: 1 year; may be renewed for up to 3 additional years, provided the recipient maintains full–time enrollment and a cumulative GPA of 2.5 or higher.
Number awarded: 20 new awards are granted each year.
Deadline: April of each year.

2986 $ TENNESSEE TEACHING SCHOLARS PROGRAM

Tennessee Student Assistance Corporation
Parkway Towers
404 James Robertson Parkway, Suite 1510
Nashville, TN 37243–0820
Phone: (615) 741–1346; (800) 342–1663; Fax: (615) 741–6101;
Email: TSAC.Aidinfo@tn.gov
Web: www.tn.gov/collegepays/mon_college/tn_teach_sch.htm
Summary: To provide funding to residents of Tennessee who are attending college in the state to prepare for a teaching career.
Eligibility: Open to college juniors, seniors, and post–baccalaureate students in approved teacher education programs in Tennessee. Applicants must be U.S. citizens, be Tennessee residents, have a GPA of 2.75 or higher, and agree to teach at the public preschool, elementary, or secondary level in Tennessee. Undergraduates must be enrolled full time; graduate students must be enrolled at least half time.
Financial data: Loans up to $4,500 per year are available. For each year of teaching in Tennessee, 1 year of the loan is forgiven.
Duration: 1 year; may be renewed for up to 3 additional years, provided the recipient maintains a GPA of 2.75 or higher.
Number awarded: 185 each year.
Deadline: April of each year.

2987 TERRY WALKER SCHOLARSHIP

Summary: To provide financial assistance to students from New York who are preparing to teach Latin in school.
See Listing #1527.

2988 TEXAS AMATEUR ATHLETIC FEDERATION ATHLETE SCHOLARSHIPS

Texas Amateur Athletic Federation
Attn: Scholarship Application
421 North IH 35
P.O. Box 1789
Georgetown, TX 78627–1789
Phone: (512) 863–9400; Fax: (512) 869–2393;
Email: mark@taaf.com
Web: www.taaf.com/index.cfm?load=page&page=44
Summary: To provide financial assistance to undergraduate and graduate students who have participated in activities of the Texas Amateur Athletic Federation (TAAF) and are interested in preparing for a career in the parks and recreation profession.
Eligibility: Open to past and present Texas Amateur Athletic Federation (TAAF) athletes who have competed in 1 or more state level competitions or tournaments. Applicants must be enrolled or planning to enroll at a college or university, preferably in Texas, in an accredited bachelor's, master's, or doctoral degree program in sports sciences, kinesiology, conservation, physical education, recreation and tourism, and/or another major relating to the field of parks and recreation. They must have a GPA of 2.5 or higher. Selection is based on honors and awards from, and participation in, activities, endeavors, volunteerism, and work related to athletics and/or the field of parks and recreation. Financial need is not considered.
Financial data: A stipend is awarded (amount not specified).
Duration: 1 year.
Number awarded: 1 or more each year.
Deadline: April of each year.

2989 $$ TEXAS EXEMPTION FOR PEACE OFFICERS ENROLLED IN LAW ENFORCEMENT OR CRIMINAL JUSTICE COURSES

Texas Higher Education Coordinating Board
Attn: Grants and Special Programs
1200 East Anderson Lane
P.O. Box 12788
Austin, TX 78711–2788
Phone: (512) 427–6340; (800) 242–3062; Fax: (512) 427–6420;
Email: grantinfo@thecb.state.tx.us
Web: www.collegeforalltexans.com/apps/financialaid/tofa2.cfm?ID=589
Summary: To provide educational assistance to Texas peace officers who are working on an undergraduate degree in a field related to their employment.
Eligibility: Open to peace officers employed by the state of Texas or by a political subdivision of the state. Applicants must be enrolled or planning to enroll at a public college or university in Texas in an undergraduate (certificate, associate, baccalaureate) program in law enforcement or criminal justice.
Financial data: Eligible students are exempted from the payment of tuition and laboratory fees for law enforcement or criminal justice courses that relate to the major requirements of the program. Courses not directly related to law enforcement or criminal justice are not eligible for reimbursement, even though they may be required for completion of the certificate or degree.
Duration: 1 semester; may be renewed as long as the student makes satisfactory academic progress.
Number awarded: Varies each year.
Deadline: Applications may be submitted at any time, but they must be received at least 1 week before the last day of the institution's regular registration period.

2990 $ THE FRUIT COMPANY GIFT BASKET ENTREPRENEUR AWARD

Summary: To provide financial assistance to entering college freshmen interested in studying agriculture or business to prepare for a career in the online gifting industry.
See Listing #2381.

2991 $$ THE HONORABLE JOHN W. WARNER STEM TEACHER'S SCHOLARSHIP

Summary: To provide financial assistance to undergraduate and graduate students at colleges and universities in Virginia who are preparing for a career as a teacher of science and mathematics.
See Listing #2382.

2992 $ THOMAS F. SEAY SCHOLARSHIP

Illinois Association of Realtors
Attn: Illinois Real Estate Educational Foundation
522 South Fifth Street
P.O. Box 2607
Springfield, IL 62708
Phone: (866) 854–REEF; Fax: (217) 241–9935;
Email: lclayton@iar.org
Web: www.ilreef.org/Scholarships.htm
Summary: To provide financial assistance to Illinois residents who are preparing for a career in real estate at a college or university in any state.
Eligibility: Open to applicants who are U.S. citizens and Illinois residents, attending a college or university in any state on a full–time basis, and working on a degree with an emphasis in real estate. They must have completed at least 30 credits with a GPA of 3.5 or higher. Along with their application, they must submit a 1,000–word statement of their general activities and intellectual interests, employment (if any), contemplated line of study, and career they expect to follow. Selection is based on the applicant's indication of interest in preparing for a career in real estate or an allied field (e.g., construction, land use planning, mortgage banking, property management, real estate appraising, real estate assessing, real estate brokerage, real estate development, real estate investment counseling, real estate law, and real estate syndication), academic achievement, references and recommendations, and financial need. Finalists are interviewed.
Financial data: The stipend is $2,000.
Duration: 1 year.
Number awarded: 1 each year.
Deadline: March of each year.

2993 $$ THOMAS R. PICKERING FOREIGN AFFAIRS FELLOWSHIPS

Woodrow Wilson National Fellowship Foundation
Attn: Foreign Affairs Fellowship Program
5 Vaughn Drive, Suite 300
P.O. Box 2437
Princeton, NJ 08543–2437
Phone: (609) 452–7007; Fax: (609) 452–0066;
Email: pickeringfaf@woodrow.org
Web: www.woodrow.org

Summary: To provide funding for the final year of undergraduate study and the first year of graduate study to students interested in preparing for a career with the Department of State's Foreign Service.

Eligibility: Open to U.S. citizens in the junior year of undergraduate study at an accredited college or university who have a cumulative GPA of 3.2 or higher. Applicants must plan to continue on to graduate school and prepare for a career in the Foreign Service with a major in such fields as international affairs, management, communications, history, political science, economics, or foreign languages. Special consideration is given to students who can demonstration leadership skills, academic achievement, and financial need.

Financial data: The program pays for tuition, room, board, books, mandatory fees, and 1 round trip ticket from the fellow's residence to academic institution, to a maximum of $40,000 per academic year. Participating schools provide additional financial support for the second year of graduate study, based on financial need. For the internships, travel expenses and stipends are paid.

Duration: 2 years: the senior year of college and the first year of graduate work (provided the student maintains a GPA of 3.2 or higher).

Number awarded: Approximately 20 each year.

Deadline: February of each year.

2994 $$ THOMAS REGAN MEMORIAL SCHOLARSHIP

Spencer Educational Foundation, Inc.
c/o Risk Insurance and Management Society
1065 Avenue of the Americas, 13th Floor
New York, NY 10018
Phone: (212) 286–9292;
Email: asabatino@spencered.org
Web: www.spencered.org

Summary: To provide financial assistance to upper–division students from Connecticut, New Jersey, and New York who are preparing for a career in risk management.

Eligibility: Open to residents of the tri–state area of Connecticut, New Jersey, and New York who are enrolled as full–time students entering their junior or senior year at a college or university in any state with a major or minor in a risk management discipline. Applicants must have a career objective in risk management and relevant work experience. They must have a GPA of 3.0 or higher. Along with their application, they must submit a 500–word essay on their chosen career path and goals. Selection is based on merit.

Financial data: The stipend is $5,000.

Duration: 1 year.

Number awarded: 1 each year.

Deadline: January of each year.

2995 TIM SMITH MEMORIAL SCHOLARSHIP

Colorado Fiscal Managers Association
Attn: Scholarship Committee Chair
1550 Larimer Street, Number 242
Denver, CO 80202
Phone: (303) 866–2659;
Email: cfma@live.com
Web: colofma.com/index.php?p=1_10_Scholarships

Summary: To provide financial assistance to Colorado students majoring in accounting, finance, or related fields.

Eligibility: Open to residents of Colorado entering their sophomore, junior, or senior year at an accredited state–supported higher education institution in the state. Applicants must be enrolled in a degree program with a declared major in accounting, finance, or other financial management study. Part–time students are encouraged to apply. Selection is based on academic achievement, involvement in extracurricular organizations and/or activities, work experience, and community involvement.

Financial data: The stipend is $1,000 or a pro–rated amount for part–time students.

Duration: 1 year.

Number awarded: At least 3 each year.

Deadline: June of each year.

2996 $ TIMOTHY J. O'LEARY SCHOLARSHIPS

Summary: To provide financial assistance to undergraduate and graduate students from New England interested in preparing for a career in the public works profession.

See Listing #2398.

2997 $$ TLMI FOUR YEAR COLLEGE DEGREE SCHOLARSHIP PROGRAM

Summary: To provide financial assistance to upper–division college students who are preparing for a career in the tag and label manufacturing industry.

See Listing #1535.

2998 TONY TORRICE PROFESSIONAL DEVELOPMENT GRANT

Summary: To provide funding to professionals working in the interior furnishing industry who are interested in advancing their career through independent or academic study.

See Listing #1537.

2999 TRAINING AWARDS FOR RELIGIOUS LEADERSHIP

Summary: To provide financial assistance for college to individuals who are willing to dedicate their lives to full–time religious service.

See Listing #1538.

3000 $$ TRIBAL BUSINESS MANAGEMENT (TBM) PROGRAM

Catching the Dream
8200 Mountain Road, N.E., Suite 203
Albuquerque, NM 87110–7835
Phone: (505) 262–2351; Fax: (505) 262–0534;
Email: NScholarsh@aol.com
Web: www.catchingthedream.org/Scholarship.htm

Summary: To provide financial assistance for college to American Indian undergraduate and graduate students interested in studying a field related to economic development for tribes.

Eligibility: Open to American Indians who can provide proof that they are at least one–quarter Indian blood and a member of a U.S. tribe that is federally–recognized, state–recognized, or terminated. Applicants must be enrolled or planning to enroll full time and major in the 1 of the following fields: business administration, finance, management, economics, banking, hotel management, or other fields related to economic development for tribes. They may be entering freshmen, undergraduate students, graduate students, or Ph.D. candidates. Along with their application, they must submit documentation of financial need, 3 letters of recommendation, copies of applications and responses for all other sources of funding for which they are eligible, official transcripts, standardized test scores (ACT, SAT, GRE, MCAT, LSAT, etc.), and an essay explaining their goals in life, college plans, and career plans (especially how those plans include working with and benefiting Indians). Selection is based on merit and potential for improving the lives of Indian people.

Financial data: Stipends range from $500 to $5,000 per year.

Duration: 1 year.

Number awarded: Varies; generally, 30 to 35 each year.

Deadline: April of each year for fall term; September of each year for spring and winter terms; March of each year for summer school.

3001 $ TRIBUTE FOUNDATION SCHOLARSHIPS

New York State Funeral Directors Association
Attn: New York State Tribute Foundation
426 New Karner Road
Albany, NY 12205
Phone: (518) 452–8230; (800) 291–2629; Fax: (518) 452–8667;
Email: tribute@tributefoundation.org
Web: www.tributefoundation.org/tributescholarship.htm

Summary: To provide financial assistance to residents of New York who are interested in attending school in any state to prepare for a career in funeral service.
Eligibility: Open to residents of New York who are 1) high school seniors or graduates accepted to an accredited mortuary science program in any state; 2) first– or second–year students at such a school; 3) students enrolled in an accredited online mortuary studies program; or 4) mortuary science students working on a bachelor's degree in mortuary science at an accredited college or university. Applicants must submit a 500–word essay on a topic that depends on their educational level but relates to their interest in a career in funeral service. They must intend to serve their residency in New York. Financial need is not considered in the selection process.
Financial data: The stipend is $3,000 per year.
Duration: 1 year; may be renewed 1 additional year.
Number awarded: 4 each year.
Deadline: June of each year.

3002 UNIVERSITY JUNIOR STANDING SCHOLARSHIPS

Arizona Society of Certified Public Accountants
Attn: Foundation for Education and Innovation
4801 East Washington Street, Suite 225–B
Phoenix, AZ 85034
Phone: (602) 252–4144, ext. 214; (888) 237–0700, ext. 214 (within AZ); Fax: (602) 252–1511;
Email: mwitt@ascpa.com
Web: secure.ascpa.com/future_cpas/scholarships
Summary: To provide financial assistance to students entering the junior year of an accounting program at a public university in Arizona.
Eligibility: Open to students entering their junior year at a public university in Arizona. Applicants must be majoring in accounting, have completed the first introductory accounting course, and have a GPA of 3.5 or higher. They must be nominated by the accounting department at their university. Nominees are asked to prepare a statement of career goals and a formal resume. U.S. citizenship or permanent resident status is required.
Financial data: The stipend is $1,000.
Duration: 1 year.
Number awarded: 6 each year: 2 at each of the 3 public universities in Arizona.
Deadline: Deadline not specified.

3003 UTAH CHAPTER SCHOLARSHIPS

Chartered Property Casualty Underwriters Society–Utah Chapter
c/o Neal Westover, Scholarship Committee Chair
Workers Compensation Fund
100 West Towne Ridge Parkway
Sandy, UT 84070
Phone: (800) 446–2667;
Email: nwestove@wcfgroup.com
Web: utah.cpcusociety.org/page/154687/index.v3page
Summary: To provide financial assistance to high school seniors in Utah who plan to attend college in any state to prepare for a career in the insurance industry.
Eligibility: Open to seniors graduating from high schools in Utah and planning to enroll at a college or university in any state. Applicants must be preparing for a career in the insurance industry. Along with their application, they must submit an essay on why they are preparing for a career in insurance, how their selected major will prepare them for a successful career, why they feel they should receive this scholarship, their 3 top priority goals today, and what they want to be doing 2 and 6 years from now. Selection is based on that essay, academic record, participation in community or school activities, letters of reference, and (if they wish financial need to be considered) financial information.
Financial data: A stipend is awarded (amount not specified).
Duration: 1 year.
Number awarded: Varies each year; recently, 4 of these scholarships were awarded.
Deadline: April of each year.

3004 VCOPS COLLEGE SCHOLARSHIP PROGRAM

Virginia Coalition of Police and Deputy Sheriffs
Attn: Scholarship Competition
3204 Cutshaw Avenue
Richmond, VA 23230
Web: www.virginiacops.org/Programs/Scholar/Scholarship.htm
Summary: To recognize and reward, with scholarships for college study in any state, high school seniors in Virginia who submit outstanding essays on law enforcement.
Eligibility: Open to seniors graduating from high schools in Virginia and planning to attend college in any state. Applicants must submit an essay, up to 1,500 words in length, on Virginia law enforcement and the general theme, "Virginia Law Enforcement: A Commitment to Community." They must also include a 150–word statement on their plans for college.
Financial data: The award is a $1,000 scholarship. Funds are paid directly to the winners' college or university account.
Duration: The competition is held annually.
Number awarded: 1 winner is selected each year.
Deadline: April of each year.

3005 $$ VERDE DICKEY MEMORIAL SCHOLARSHIP

United Methodist Higher Education Foundation
Attn: Scholarships Administrator
60 Music Square East, Suite 350
P.O. Box 340005
Nashville, TN 37203–0005
Phone: (615) 649–3990; (800) 811–8110; Fax: (615) 649–3980;
Email: umhefscholarships@umhef.org
Web: www.umhef.org/scholarship–info
Summary: To provide financial assistance to upper–division students at schools affiliated with the United Methodist Church who are preparing for a career as a teacher or coach.
Eligibility: Open to full–time students entering their junior or senior year at a United Methodist–related college or university. Applicants must have been active, full members of a United Methodist Church for at least 1 year prior to applying. They must 1) be majoring in education or physical education; 2) be planning to become teachers or coaches; 3) have a GPA of 3.0 or higher; 4) be able to demonstrate financial need; and 5) be a citizen or permanent resident of the United States.
Financial data: The stipend is $7,500.
Duration: 1 year.
Number awarded: 2 each year.
Deadline: February of each year.

3006 VERMONT ASSOCIATION OF EDUCATIONAL OFFICE PROFESSIONALS STUDENT SCHOLARSHIP

Vermont Association of Educational Office Professionals
c/o Pat Cahill, Student Scholarship Chair
Windsor Southwest Supervisory Union
89 Vermont Route 103 South
Chester, VT 05143
Phone: (802) 875–6678;
Email: pcahill@wswsu.org
Web: www.vaeop.org/membership.htm
Summary: To provide financial assistance to residents of Vermont who are interested in attending college in any state to prepare for an educational office–related career.
Eligibility: Open to residents of Vermont who are graduating high school seniors or full–time students at an institution of higher education in any state. Applicants must be preparing for an educational office–related career. They must have completed at least 4 semesters of study (in high school and/or college) from among the following business education courses: computer classes, software applications, marketing, business communication, accounting, office practices and procedures, bookkeeping, and/or business law. Along with their application, they must submit a 1–page essay on why they are choosing an office–related career or vocation. Selection is based on that essay (10%), academic record (40%), school and extracurricular activities (10%), recommendations (10%), and a biographical and financial need statement (30%).
Financial data: The stipend is $1,000.
Duration: 1 year.
Number awarded: 1 each year.
Deadline: March of each year.

3007 $ VETERANS OF ENDURING FREEDOM (AFGHANISTAN) AND IRAQI FREEDOM SCHOLARSHIP

Summary: To provide financial assistance to veterans and military personnel who served in Afghanistan or Iraq and are working on an undergraduate degree in fields related to the support of U.S. intelligence enterprises.
See Listing #2419.

3008 VIRGINIA ASSOCIATION OF LEGAL STAFF SCHOLARSHIP

Virginia Association of Legal Staff
c/o Nancy E. Stewart, Scholarship Chair
Woods Rogers PLC
10 South Jefferson Street, Suite 1400
P.O. Box 14125
Roanoke, VA 24038–4125
Phone: (540) 983–7600; Fax: (540) 983–7711;
Email: invovals@gmail.com
Web: www.v–a–l–s.org/education.htm

Summary: To provide financial assistance to residents of Virginia interested in attending college in any state to prepare for a career in the legal field.
Eligibility: Open to residents of Virginia who are enrolled or planning to enroll at a postsecondary school in any state. Applicants must submit brief statements on 1) their career goals, specifically including an interest or major in the legal field; 2) why they wish to prepare for their chosen career; and 3) why they desire this award.
Financial data: The stipend is $1,500.
Duration: 1 year.
Number awarded: 1 each year.
Deadline: March of each year.

3009 VIRGINIA PTA ANNUAL CITIZENSHIP ESSAY PROJECT

Virginia Congress of Parents and Teachers
1027 Wilmer Avenue
Richmond, VA 23227–2419
Phone: (804) 264–1234; (866) 4VA–KIDS; Fax: (804) 264–4014;
Email: info@vapta.org
Web: www.vapta.org

Summary: To recognize and reward outstanding essays on patriotic themes written by middle school and high school students in Virginia.
Eligibility: Open to students in grades 6–12 in Virginia. Their school must have a PTA/PTSA unit in good standing. Students are invited to write an essay (at least 500 words for grades 6–8, at least 750 words for grades 9–12) on a theme that changes annually but relates to patriotism; recently, the theme was: "Character or Citizenship."
Financial data: First place is a $1,000 savings bond, second a $500 savings bond, and third a $250 savings bond.
Duration: The competition is held annually.
Number awarded: 3 prizes are awarded each year.
Deadline: January of each year.

3010 VIRGINIA PTA SCHOLARSHIPS

Virginia Congress of Parents and Teachers
1027 Wilmer Avenue
Richmond, VA 23227–2419
Phone: (804) 264–1234; (866) 4VA–KIDS; Fax: (804) 264–4014;
Email: info@vapta.org
Web: www.vapta.org

Summary: To provide financial assistance to high school seniors in Virginia who are interested in preparing for a teaching or related career.
Eligibility: Open to seniors graduating from public high schools in Virginia that have a PTA or PTSA association in good standing. Applicants must be planning to attend a college or university in Virginia to prepare for a career in teaching or another youth–serving profession. They must have a GPA of 2.5 or higher. Selection is based on academic achievement and financial need.
Financial data: The stipend is either $1,000 or $1,200 (for the 2 named scholarships) per year.
Duration: 1 year.
Number awarded: Varies each year; recently, 19 of these scholarships were awarded: the 2 named scholarships at $1,200 and 17 scholarships at $1,000.
Deadline: February of each year.

3011 VIRGINIA SHERIFFS' INSTITUTE SCHOLARSHIP PROGRAM

Virginia Sheriffs' Institute
701 East Franklin Street, Suite 706
Richmond, VA 23219
Phone: (804) 225–7152; Fax: (804) 225–7162;
Email: vsavsi@virginiasheriffs.org
Web: vasheriffsinstitute.org/scholarship

Summary: To provide financial assistance to Virginia residents who are majoring or planning to major in law enforcement or criminal justice at a college in the state.
Eligibility: Open to Virginia residents who live in areas where the sheriffs 1) are members of the Virginia Sheriffs' Institute; and 2) authorized the Institute to conduct a direct mail special appeal to raise funds for the scholarship program. Applicants must be attending or planning to attend a college or university in Virginia and major in law enforcement or criminal justice. Along with their application, they must submit a short essay on their proposed course of college study, how they reached that decision, what they expect to gain from college, and their personal goals and ambitions. Financial need is not considered in the selection process.
Financial data: A stipend is awarded (amount not specified). Checks are made payable directly to the recipient's educational institution.
Duration: 1 year; may be renewed.
Number awarded: Varies each year.
Deadline: April of each year.

3012 VIRGINIA SOCIETY FOR HEALTHCARE HUMAN RESOURCES ADMINISTRATION SCHOLARSHIP

Virginia Society for Healthcare Human Resources Administration
c/o Cyndi Derricott, Scholarship Chair
Bon Secours Richmond Health System
8580 Magellan Parkway
Richmond, VA 23227
Phone: (540) 627–5003;
Email: cyndi_derricott@bshsi.org
Web: www.vashhra.org

Summary: To provide financial assistance to undergraduate and graduate students in Virginia working on a degree in human relations and interested in a career in a health care setting.
Eligibility: Open to residents of Virginia currently enrolled in an accredited college or university in the state and working on an undergraduate or graduate degree in human resources administration or a related field. Applicants must be at least a second–semester sophomore when the application is submitted and have a demonstrated interest in working in a health care setting. Along with their application, they must submit a 1–page statement on their contribution to the human resources profession to date, their future goals as a human resources professional, and how this scholarship would help them to achieve those goals. Selection is based on that statement, work experience, 2 letters of recommendation from faculty members, and financial need.
Financial data: The stipend is $1,000.
Duration: 1 year; nonrenewable.
Number awarded: 1 each year.
Deadline: October of each year.

3013 VIRGINIA SOCIETY OF CERTIFIED PUBLIC ACCOUNTANTS UNDERGRADUATE ACCOUNTING SCHOLARSHIPS

Virginia Society of Certified Public Accountants
Attn: Educational Foundation
4309 Cox Road
Glen Allen, VA 23060
Phone: (804) 612–9427; (800) 733–8272; Fax: (804) 273–1741;
Email: info@vscpafoundation.com
Web: www.vscpa.com/content/Ed_Found/SA/Scholarships.aspx

Summary: To provide financial assistance to students enrolled in an undergraduate accounting program in Virginia.
Eligibility: Open to students who are currently enrolled in a Virginia college or university undergraduate accounting program. They must be U.S. citizens, be majoring in accounting, have completed at least 3 hours of accounting, be currently registered for 3 more credit hours of accounting, and have a GPA of 3.0 or higher. Along with their application, they must submit a 500–word essay on assigned topics. Selection is based on the essay, their most recent transcript, a current resume, a faculty letter of recommendation, and financial need.
Financial data: The stipend is generally $1,000.
Duration: 1 year.
Number awarded: Up to 5 each year.
Deadline: March of each year.

3014 $$ VOICE OF DEMOCRACY SCHOLARSHIP PROGRAM

Veterans of Foreign Wars of the United States
VFW Building
406 West 34th Street

Kansas City, MO 64111
Phone: (816) 968–1117; Fax: (816) 968–1149;
Email: KHarmer@vfw.org
Web: www.vfw.org/Community/Voice–of–Democracy

Summary: To recognize and reward, with college scholarships, outstanding high school students in a national broadcast scriptwriting competition dealing with freedom and democracy.

Eligibility: Open to students in grades 9–12 at public, private, and parochial high schools and home schools in the United States, its territories and possessions, and U.S. military and civilian dependent overseas schools. Contestants prepare a script, from 3 to 5 minutes in length, on a topic chosen annually but related to freedom and democracy; a recent theme was "Is Our Constitution Still Relevant?" Students record the script themselves on a CD and submit it for sponsorship by a local post or auxiliary of the Veterans of Foreign Wars (VFW). Scripts must reflect the entrant's own original thinking. Selection is based on delivery (35 points), content (35 points), and originality (30 points).

Financial data: A total of $152,000 in national scholarships is awarded each year; first place is $30,000, second $16,000, third $10,000, and fourth $7,000. Other state winners receive scholarships that may vary each year but range from $1,000 to $5,000. Winners in each state also receive an all–expense paid trip to Washington, D.C. for the national competition.

Duration: The competition is held annually.

Number awarded: Recently, a total of 54 of these scholarships were awarded. In addition to the 4 top winners, other scholarships included 2 at $5,000, 1 at $4,000, 1 at $3,500, 2 at $3,000, 2 at $2,500, 15 at $2,000, 7 at $1,500, and 20 at $1,000.

Deadline: October of each year.

3015 $$ W. GREGOR MACFARLAN EXCELLENCE IN CONTRACT MANAGEMENT RESEARCH AND WRITING PROGRAM

National Contract Management Association
Attn: Awards and Honors Committee
21740 Beaumeade Circle, Suite 125
Ashburn, VA 20147
Phone: (571) 382–0082; (800) 344–8096; Fax: (703) 448–0939;
Email: awards@ncmahq.org
Web: www.ncmahq.org

Summary: To recognize and reward undergraduates, graduate students, and professionals who submit outstanding papers related to contract management.

Eligibility: Open to authors of theoretical and empirical papers relevant to the practice of contract management, including those from such disciplines as business, finance, marketing, management, accounting, management information systems, public administration, economics, and related fields. Entries are accepted in 3 categories: 1) undergraduates enrolled full or part time who submit papers that may be, but are not required to be, based on research; 2) graduate students enrolled full or part time who submit papers based on research that will advance the body of knowledge of the practice of contract management (faculty collaboration is allowed); and 3) professionals who specialize in business research and consulting and submit papers based on research that will advance the body of knowledge of the practice of contract management (sponsorship by a third party is allowed). Papers may be no longer than 6,000 words and must have been written within the past 2 years.

Financial data: Awards are $1,500 for undergraduates, $5,000 for graduate students, and $5,000 for professionals.

Duration: The award is presented annually.

Number awarded: 3 each year: 1 for each category.

Deadline: February of each year.

3016 WALLACE S. AND WILMA K. LAUGHLIN FOUNDATION TRUST SCHOLARSHIPS

Nebraska Funeral Directors Association
Attn: Laughlin Trust Committee
6201 South 58th Street, Suite B
Lincoln, NE 68516
Phone: (402) 423–8900; Fax: (402) 420–0031;
Email: staff@nefda.org
Web: www.nefda.org/careers

Summary: To provide financial assistance to residents of Nebraska who are interested in preparing for a career in mortuary science.

Eligibility: Open to residents of Nebraska who are graduates of a high school in the state and have met the pre–mortuary academic requirements set by the state prior to entering a mortuary science college. Students planning to attend a 1–year course of study must apply prior to entering an accredited mortuary school. Students planning a 4–year course of study must apply prior to entering the third year of study. Applicants must be recommended by a member of the Nebraska Funeral Directors Association. Interviews are required. Financial need is not considered in the selection process.

Financial data: Stipends are at least $1,000 per year. Funds are paid directly to the recipient's school.

Duration: 1 year.

Number awarded: Varies, depending upon the funds available.

Deadline: June of each year.

3017 WALTER FRESE MEMORIAL SCHOLARSHIP

Association of Government Accountants–Boston Chapter
c/o William A. Muench
10 Jordan Road
Hopkinton, MA 01748–2650
Phone: (978) 796–3637;
Email: wmuench@dcaa.mil
Web: www.agaboston.org/Scholarships.html

Summary: To provide financial assistance to high school seniors, undergraduates, or graduate students from New England or attending school in New England who are working on a degree in financial management.

Eligibility: Open to graduating high school seniors, undergraduates, and graduate students entering or enrolled in a program related to financial management, including (but not limited to) accounting, business administration, economics, finance, or information systems. Applicants must be residents of New England or attending school in the area. Graduate students may be working in a government accounting, auditing, or finance position. Selection is based on scholastic achievement, leadership qualities, extracurricular activities, recommendations, writing ability, and an expressed interest in the field of government accounting, auditing, or financial management. Financial need may also be considered if the applicant provides relevant information.

Financial data: The stipend is $1,000.

Duration: 1 year.

Number awarded: 1 each year.

Deadline: April of each year.

3018 WASA/PEMCO 21ST CENTURY EDUCATOR SCHOLARSHIP

Washington Association of School Administrators
825 Fifth Avenue, S.E.
Olympia, WA 98501
Phone: (360) 943–5717; (800) 859–9272; Fax: (360) 352–2043;
Email: admin@wasa–oly.org
Web: www.wasa–oly.org

Summary: To provide financial assistance to minority and other high school seniors in the state of Washington who are interested in majoring in education in college.

Eligibility: Open to high school seniors who are enrolled in a Washington public or accredited private school, have a GPA of 3.0 or higher, and intend to major and prepare for a career in K–12 education. Applicants must submit a completed application form, a criteria essay, a goals essay, 3 reference letters, and an official grades transcript. They compete in 3 applicant pools: eastern Washington, western Washington, and minority. Along with their application, they must submit a 1–page essay on why they have chosen K–12 education as their future profession. Selection is based on that essay, leadership, community service, honors and awards, and student activities.

Financial data: The stipend is $1,000 per year.

Duration: 4 years.

Number awarded: 3 each year: 1 to a student from eastern Washington, 1 to a student from western Washington, and 1 to a minority student.

Deadline: March of each year.

3019 WASHINGTON CHAPTER SCHOLARSHIPS

American Society of Military Comptrollers–Washington Chapter
Attn: Matt Ernest, Scholarship Chair
P.O. Box 16237
Arlington, VA 22215–1237
Phone: (703) 692–4185;
Email: Scholarships@Washington–ASMC.org
Web: www.washington–asmc.org/stuaward.htm

Summary: To provide financial assistance to high school seniors in the Washington, D.C. area who plan to work on an undergraduate degree related to financial operations.

Eligibility: Open to seniors graduating from high schools in Maryland, Virginia, and Washington, D.C. Applicants must be entering a field of study directly related to financial operations (e.g., business administration, economics, public administration, operations research related to financial management, accounting, finance). Along with their application, they must submit 3 letters of recommendation, an official transcript, and SAT or ACT scores. Selection is based on academic achievement, leadership ability, extracurricular activities, and career goals.

Financial data: The stipend is $1,000.

Duration: 1 year; the top 3 recipients may renew their award for up to 3 additional years.

Number awarded: Varies each year; recently, 10 of these scholarships were awarded.

Deadline: February of each year.

3020 $ WASHINGTON CPA FOUNDATION ACCOUNTING STUDENT SCHOLARSHIPS

Washington Society of Certified Public Accountants
Attn: Washington CPA Foundation
902 140th Avenue N.E.
Bellevue, WA 98005–3480
Phone: (425) 644–4800; (800) 272–8273 (within WA); Fax: (425) 562–8853;
Email: memberservices@wscpa.org
Web: www.discovercpa.org/discovercpa/scholarships/index.cfm

Summary: To provide financial assistance to undergraduate and graduate students in Washington who are working on a degree in accounting.

Eligibility: Open to accounting majors in Washington who have completed at least their sophomore year at an accredited 4–year institution or have completed an associate degree and been accepted into a 4–year institution. Fifth–year and graduate students are encouraged to apply. Preference is given to residents of Washington, but residents of other states may be eligible if they attend school in the state and plan to take the C.P.A. examination and practice in the state. International students are eligible if they have the same intentions. Applicants must have a GPA of 3.0 or higher in accounting classes and overall. Along with their application, they must submit essays on 1) the skills or abilities they will bring to the accounting profession that will be a positive force; 2) why they are preparing for a career in accounting; 3) their career goals; 4) their involvement in an extracurricular organization or community service experience and how it affected their life; 5) why they should be awarded a scholarship; and 6) any reasons why their GPA does not tell the entire story of their academic capability or achievement. Selection is based on the essays, academic achievement, campus and/or community activities, work history, 2 letters of recommendation, and probability of obtaining a C.P.A. license. Financial need is not considered.

Financial data: The stipend is $2,000.

Duration: 1 year; nonrenewable.

Number awarded: Up to 20 each year.

Deadline: February of each year.

3021 $ WAYNE ALEXANDER MEMORIAL SCHOLARSHIP

Summary: To provide financial assistance to undergraduate and graduate students from any country who are working on a degree in the field of document management and graphic communications.

See Listing #1549.

3022 $$ WAYNE V. BLACK SCHOLARSHIP AWARD

Summary: To provide financial assistance to undergraduates working on a degree in a field related to telecommunications.

See Listing #2440.

3023 W.E. HAMMOND SCHOLARSHIP

New Mexico Society of Certified Public Accountants
Attn: Scholarships in Accounting
3400 Menaul Boulevard, N.E.
Albuquerque, NM 87107
Phone: (505) 246–1699; (800) 926–2522; Fax: (505) 246–1686;
Email: corrine@nmscpa.org
Web: www.nmscpa.org/scholarships_application.html

Summary: To provide financial assistance to accounting students at New Mexico universities and colleges.

Eligibility: Open to full–time students at New Mexico colleges and universities who have completed 12 semester hours in accounting, are currently enrolled in 6 or more accounting hours, have completed 75 hours overall, and have a cumulative GPA of 3.0 or higher. Applicants must submit an essay or letter that covers 1) academic achievements in college; 2) the accounting courses in which they are currently enrolled or have completed; 3) extracurricular activities, employment, volunteer service, and any other pertinent activities; 4) reasons for applying for the scholarship, including matters related to financial need; and 5) career objectives and goals in accounting.

Financial data: The stipend is $1,500.

Duration: 1 year; may be renewed 2 additional years.

Number awarded: 1 each year.

Deadline: May of each year.

3024 $$ WEISMAN SCHOLARSHIPS

Summary: To provide financial assistance to minority upper–division college students from any state who are enrolled at a college in Connecticut and interested in teaching mathematics or science at public middle and high schools in the state.

See Listing #2441.

3025 $ WESTRAN INSURANCE SCHOLARSHIPS

Westran Insurance Scholarship Foundation
c/o Carol Ann Breed, Olivet College
Mott Building, Room 408A
320 South Main Street
Olivet, MI 49076
Phone: (269) 749–7664;
Email: CBreed@Olivetcollege.edu
Web: www.westranscholarship.org

Summary: To provide financial assistance to entering or continuing undergraduate students, especially those from designated Great Lakes area states, who are preparing for a career in the insurance industry.

Eligibility: Open to students enrolled or planning to enroll full time in a degree program, including majoring or concentrating in actuarial science, insurance, loss control, or risk management. Applicants with other majors or study concentrations may also be considered if they can demonstrate a career goal in an insurance–related field. Entering freshmen must have a high school GPA of 3.0 or higher; current college students must have a GPA of 2.7 or higher overall and 3.0 or higher in insurance and other business courses. Preference is given to 1) residents of the Great Lakes Region (Illinois, Indiana, Michigan, Ohio, and Wisconsin); and 2) applicants who can submit documentation of examinations taken for professional insurance designations (e.g., ARM, CIC, CPCU, IIA) or licenses. Applications must be accompanied by a 500–word essay on chosen career path and goals, a 1–page resume, transcripts, 2 letters of recommendation, and information on financial need.

Financial data: Stipends range from $1,000 to $2,000.

Duration: 1 year.

Number awarded: Varies each year; since the program was established, it has awarded more than 400 scholarships.

Deadline: March of each year.

3026 WHY EDUCATION MATTERS ESSAY CONTEST

Summary: To recognize and reward high school juniors and seniors in California who submit outstanding photographs on specified themes.

See Listing #1550.

3027 WICHITA CHAPTER SCHOLARSHIPS

American Society of Women Accountants–Wichita Chapter
c/o Jen Church, Scholarship Chair
P.O. Box 397
Wichita, KS 67030
Email: jchurch@kcoe.com
Web: www.wichitaaswa.org/Scholarship/Requirements.aspx

Summary: To provide financial assistance to women working on an undergraduate or graduate degree in accounting or finance at a college or university in Kansas.

Eligibility: Open to women working full or part time on an associate, bachelor's, or master's degree in accounting or finance at a college or university in Kansas. Applicants must have completed at least 15 semester hours in a 2–year program or 60 semester hours in a 4–year program. They must have a cumulative GPA of 3.0 or higher. Membership in the American Society of Women Accountants (ASWA) is not required. Along with their application, they must submit an essay of 150 to 250 words on their career goals and objectives, the impact they want to have on the accounting world, community involvement,

and leadership examples. Selection is based on leadership, character, communication skills, GPA, and financial need.
Financial data: The stipend is $1,000.
Duration: 1 year.
Number awarded: Varies each year; recently, 4 of these scholarships were awarded.
Deadline: February of each year.

3028 WILFRED M. "WILEY" POST SCHOLARSHIP

American Association of Airport Executives–Northeast Chapter
Attn: Executive Secretary
P.O. Box 8
West Milford, NJ 07480–0008
Phone: (973) 728–6760; Fax: (973) 728–6760
Web: www.necaaae.org/cfiles/about_sgi.php
Summary: To provide financial assistance to upper–division students majoring in airport management.
Eligibility: Open to college juniors and seniors who are majoring in airport management. Preference is given to those with a permanent residence in the northeast region. Students preparing for a career as commercial pilots are not eligible. Applicants must indicate how they will benefit from the grant and provide documentation of financial need.
Financial data: The stipend is $1,000.
Duration: 1 year.
Number awarded: 4 each year.
Deadline: February of each year.

3029 $ WILLA S. BELLAMY SCHOLARSHIP

Government Finance Officers Association of South Carolina
Attn: Scholarship Committee
P.O. Box 8840
Columbia, SC 29202
Email: info@gfoasc.org
Web: gfoasc.org
Summary: To provide financial assistance to South Carolina residents who are majoring in accounting, finance, or business administration at a college in the state.
Eligibility: Open to residents of South Carolina who are currently enrolled as a rising sophomore, junior, or senior at a public college or university in the state. Applicants must be enrolled full time and have a GPA of 3.0 or higher and a major in finance, accounting, or business administration with a concentration in accounting or finance. Financial need is not considered in the selection process.
Financial data: The stipend is $2,000.
Duration: 1 year.
Number awarded: 1 each year.
Deadline: April of each year.

3030 WILLIAM B. BRANDT MEMORIAL SCHOLARSHIPS

Nebraska Bankers Association
Attn: Educational Foundation
233 South 13th Street, Suite 700
P.O. Box 80008
Lincoln, NE 68501–0008
Phone: (402) 474–1555; Fax: (402) 474–2946;
Email: karen.miller@nebankers.org
Web: www.nebankers.org/index/php/scholarships.html
Summary: To provide financial assistance to Nebraska residents working on a degree in business at a college or university in the state.
Eligibility: Open to residents of Nebraska who are enrolled as full–time juniors or seniors at a college or university in the state (except for the University of Nebraska). Applicants must be working on a bachelor of science in business administration with an emphasis on finance, accounting, or economics and have a GPA of 3.0 or higher. Along with their application, they must submit an essay of 100 to 200 words on how the banking industry has impacted their community or the role they expect the banking industry to play in their future. Financial need is not considered in the selection process.
Financial data: The stipend is $1,000.
Duration: 1 year.
Number awarded: Up to 12 each year.
Deadline: January of each year.

3031 $ WILLIAM D. GREENLEE SCHOLARSHIP

Summary: To provide financial assistance to upper–division students at institutions of the Pennsylvania State System of Higher Education (PASSHE) who are majoring in communications, journalism, or political science.
See Listing #1551.

3032 WILLIAM HUNT SCHOLARSHIPS

Tourism Cares
Attn: Academic Scholarship Program
275 Turnpike Street, Suite 307
Canton, MA 02021
Phone: (781) 821–5990; Fax: (781) 821–8949;
Email: scholarships@tourismcares.org
Web: www.tourismcares.org
Summary: To provide financial assistance to residents of northwestern states who are preparing for a career in the travel and tourism or hospitality industry at a school in any state.
Eligibility: Open to U.S. citizens and permanent residents who are residents of Alaska, Idaho, Montana, Oregon, or Washington and 1) entering the second year at an accredited 2–year college; or 2) entering their junior or senior year at an accredited 4–year college or university. Applicants must be enrolled full or part time in a travel and tourism or hospitality–related program of study at a college or university in any state. They must have a GPA of 3.0 or higher. Along with their application, they must submit an essay on the segment of the travel and tourism or hospitality industry their current program of study emphasizes, the opportunities they are utilizing as they prepare for a career in the industry, and their academic and extracurricular activities. Financial need is not considered in the selection process.
Financial data: The stipend is $1,500.
Duration: 1 year.
Number awarded: 2 each year.
Deadline: March of each year.

3033 $ WILLIAM MILLAR SCHOLARSHIP

American Public Transportation Association
Attn: American Public Transportation Foundation
1666 K Street, N.W., Suite 1100
Washington, DC 20006
Phone: (202) 496–4803; Fax: (202) 496–4323;
Email: yconley@apta.com
Web: www.aptfd.org/work/scholarship.htm
Summary: To provide financial assistance to undergraduate and graduate students who are preparing for a career in the public transportation industry.
Eligibility: Open to college sophomores, juniors, seniors, and graduate students who are preparing for a career in the transit industry. Any member organization of the American Public Transportation Association (APTA) can nominate and sponsor candidates for this scholarship. Nominees must be enrolled in a fully–accredited institution, have and maintain at least a 3.0 GPA, and be either employed by or demonstrate a strong interest in entering the business administration or management area of the public transportation industry. They must submit a 1,000–word essay on the topic, "In what segment of the public transportation industry will you make a career and why?" Selection is based on demonstrated interest in the transit field as a career, need for financial assistance, academic achievement, essay content and quality, and involvement in extracurricular citizenship and leadership activities.
Financial data: The stipend is $2,500.
Duration: 1 year; may be renewed.
Number awarded: 1 each year.
Deadline: May of each year.

3034 $$ WILLIAM R. GOLDFARB MEMORIAL SCHOLARSHIP

Summary: To provide financial assistance to high school seniors who are licensed radio amateurs and interested in working on an undergraduate degree in selected fields.
See Listing #2458.

3035 WILLIAM T. MCDERMOTT SCHOLARSHIPS

Virginia Society of Certified Public Accountants
Attn: Educational Foundation
4309 Cox Road
Glen Allen, VA 23060

Phone: (804) 612–9427; (800) 733–8272; Fax: (804) 273–1741;
Email: info@vscpafoundation.com
Web: www.vscpa.com/content/Ed_Found/SA/Scholarships.aspx

Summary: To provide financial assistance to students enrolled in an undergraduate accounting program in Virginia, especially those interested in taxation.

Eligibility: Open to students who are currently enrolled in a Virginia college or university undergraduate accounting program. They must be U.S. citizens, be majoring in accounting, have completed at least 3 hours of accounting, be currently registered for 3 more credit hours of accounting, and have a GPA of 3.0 or higher; preference is given to students interested in a career in taxation. Along with their application, they must submit a 500–word essay on assigned topics, including their interest in taxation. Selection is based on the essay, their most recent transcript, a current resume, a faculty letter of recommendation, and financial need.

Financial data: The stipend is $1,000.

Duration: 1 year.

Number awarded: 3 each year.

Deadline: March of each year.

3036 $ WILLIAM WINTER TEACHER SCHOLAR LOAN PROGRAM

Mississippi Office of Student Financial Aid
3825 Ridgewood Road
Jackson, MS 39211–6453
Phone: (601) 432–6997; (800) 327–2980 (within MS); Fax: (601) 432–6527;
Email: sfa@mississippi.edu
Web: www.mississippi.edu/riseupms/financialaid–state.php

Summary: To provide money for college to Mississippi residents working on a Class "A" teacher educator license.

Eligibility: Open to Mississippi residents who are enrolled full time as juniors or seniors at an accredited Mississippi 4–year public or private college or university. Applicants must be working on a bachelor's degree in a program of study leading to a Class "A" teacher educator license and have a cumulative GPA of 2.5 or higher. They must be able to document that they have passed Praxis I or have an ACT score of 21 or higher with a minimum of 18 on all sub–scores. Programs of study that do not qualify include, but are not limited to, speech and language pathology, psychological and counseling services, and recreational therapy.

Financial data: Loans are provided up to $4,000 per academic year. For each year of service as a full–time classroom teacher in an accredited public school or public school district in Mississippi, 1 year's loan will be forgiven.

Duration: 1 year; may be renewed 1 additional year if the recipient maintains a GPA of 2.5 or higher, remains enrolled full time in a program of study leading to a Class "A" teacher educator license, exhibits satisfactory academic progress, and documents that Praxis II has been passed after no more than 3 semesters of participation in this program.

Number awarded: Varies each year; recently, 456 of these scholarship/loans, with a total value greater than $1.6 million, were awarded.

Deadline: March of each year.

3037 WILMA D. HOYAL/MAXINE CHILTON SCHOLARSHIPS

American Legion Auxiliary
Department of Arizona
4701 North 19th Avenue, Suite 100
Phoenix, AZ 85015–3727
Phone: (602) 241–1080; Fax: (602) 604–9640;
Email: secretary@aladeptaz.org
Web: aladeptaz.org/Scholarships.html

Summary: To provide financial assistance to veterans, dependents of veterans, and other students who are majoring in selected subjects at Arizona public universities.

Eligibility: Open to second–year or upper–division full–time students majoring in political science, public programs, or special education at public universities in Arizona (the University of Arizona, Northern Arizona University, or Arizona State University). Applicants must have been Arizona residents for at least 1 year. They must have a GPA of 3.0 or higher. U.S. citizenship is required. Honorably–discharged veterans and immediate family members of veterans receive preference. Selection is based on scholarship (25%), financial need (40%), character (20%), and leadership (15%).

Financial data: The stipend is $1,000.

Duration: 1 year; renewable.

Number awarded: 3 each year: 1 to each of the 3 universities.

Deadline: May of each year.

3038 $ WISCONSIN MINORITY TEACHER LOANS

Wisconsin Higher Educational Aids Board
131 West Wilson Street, Suite 902
P.O. Box 7885
Madison, WI 53707–7885
Phone: (608) 267–2212; Fax: (608) 267–2808;
Email: deanna.schulz@wisconsin.gov
Web: heab.state.wi.us/programs.html

Summary: To provide money for college to minorities in Wisconsin who are interested in teaching in Wisconsin school districts with large minority enrollments.

Eligibility: Open to residents of Wisconsin who are African Americans, Hispanic Americans, American Indians, or southeast Asians (students who were admitted to the United States after December 31, 1975 and who are a former citizen of Laos, Vietnam, or Cambodia or whose ancestor was a citizen of 1 of those countries). Applicants must be enrolled at least half time as juniors, seniors, or graduate students at an independent or public institution in the state in a program leading to teaching licensure and have a GPA of 2.5 or higher. They must agree to teach in a Wisconsin school district in which minority students constitute at least 29% of total enrollment or in a school district participating in the inter–district pupil transfer program. Financial need is not considered in the selection process.

Financial data: Loans are provided up to $2,500 per year. For each year the student teaches in an eligible school district, 25% of the loan is forgiven; if the student does not teach in an eligible district, the loan must be repaid at an interest rate of 5%.

Duration: 1 year; may be renewed 1 additional year.

Number awarded: Varies each year.

Deadline: Deadline dates vary by institution; check with your school's financial aid office.

3039 WISCONSIN PROFESSIONAL POLICE ASSOCIATION SCHOLARSHIP PROGRAM

Wisconsin Professional Police Association
Attn: Scholarship Committee
660 John Nolen Drive, Suite 300
Madison, WI 53713
Phone: (608) 273–3840; (800) 362–8838; Fax: (608) 273–3904;
Email: palmer@wppa.com
Web: www.wppa.com/resources/scholarship_program.htm

Summary: To provide financial assistance to residents of Wisconsin and the upper peninsula of Michigan who are entering or attending a program in law enforcement in any state.

Eligibility: Open to residents of Wisconsin and the upper peninsula of Michigan who are enrolled or planning to enroll in a 2– or 4–year program in police science, criminal justice, or a related field of law enforcement at a school in any state. Applicants must submit an essay on why they have chosen a career in law enforcement, including any special projects relating to their interest in the field. Financial need is not considered in the selection process.

Financial data: Stipends range from $500 to $1,000; funds are sent directly to the recipient.

Duration: 1 year.

Number awarded: Approximately 10 each year.

Deadline: January of each year.

3040 $$ WISCONSIN TEACHER OF THE VISUALLY IMPAIRED LOANS

Wisconsin Higher Educational Aids Board
131 West Wilson Street, Suite 902
P.O. Box 7885
Madison, WI 53707–7885
Phone: (608) 267–2213; Fax: (608) 267–2808;
Email: nancy.wilkison@wi.gov
Web: heab.state.wi.us/programs.html

Summary: To provide money for college to residents of Wisconsin who are interested in teaching the visually impaired at a school in Wisconsin or an adjacent state.

Eligibility: Open to residents of Wisconsin who are enrolled at least half time in a program that prepares them to be licensed as teachers of the visually impaired or as orientation and mobility instructors. Applicants must be attending an institution that offers such a program in Wisconsin or in an adjacent state (Illinois, Iowa, Michigan, or Minnesota). They must agree to be a licensed teacher or an orientation and mobility instructor in a Wisconsin school district,

the Wisconsin Center for the Blind and Visually Impaired, or a cooperative educational service agency. Financial need is considered in the selection process.
Financial data: Scholarship/loans are provided up to $10,000 per year, or a lifetime maximum of $40,000. For each of the first 2 years the student teaches and meets the eligibility criteria, 25% of the loan is forgiven; for the third year, 50% of the loan is forgiven. If the student does not teach and meet the eligibility criteria, the loan must be repaid at an interest rate of 5%.
Duration: 1 year; may be renewed up to 3 additional years.
Number awarded: Varies each year.
Deadline: Deadline dates vary by institution; check with your school's financial aid office.

3041 $ WISCONSIN WOMEN IN GOVERNMENT UNDERGRADUATE SCHOLARSHIPS

Wisconsin Women in Government, Inc.
Attn: Scholarship Committee
P.O. Box 2543
Madison, WI 53701
Phone: (608) 848–2321;
Email: info@wiscwomeningovernment.org
Web: www.wiscwomeningovernment.org/scholarships.cfm
Summary: To provide financial assistance to women in Wisconsin interested in attending a college or university in the state to prepare for a career in public service.
Eligibility: Open to women in Wisconsin who are enrolled full or part time at an institution that is a member of the University of Wisconsin system, the Wisconsin Technical College System, or the Wisconsin Association of Independent Colleges and Universities. Applicants must have a grade average of "C" or higher and be able to demonstrate financial need. They must possess leadership potential, initiative, and excellent communication skills and have an interest in public service, government, and the political process. Juniors and seniors must have declared a major. Selection is based on leadership, demonstrated ability to handle responsibility, initiative, communication skills, academic achievement, community involvement, and commitment to public service.
Financial data: The stipend is $3,000 per year. Funds may be used for tuition, school supplies, child care, or to reduce loan burden.
Duration: 1 year; may be renewed.
Number awarded: 6 each year.
Deadline: April of each year.

3042 $ WOMEN IN TRANSITION ACCOUNTING SCHOLARSHIP

Educational Foundation for Women in Accounting
Attn: Foundation Administrator
136 South Keowee Street
Dayton, OH 45402
Phone: (937) 424–3391; Fax: (937) 222–5749;
Email: info@efwa.org
Web: www.efwa.org/scholarships_women_in_transition.php
Summary: To provide financial support to women who have become the sole support of their family and wish to begin work on an undergraduate accounting degree.
Eligibility: Open to women who, either through divorce or death of a spouse, have become the sole source of support for themselves and their family. Women who are single parents as a result of other circumstances are also considered. Applicants should be incoming or current freshmen, or they may be returning to school with sufficient credits to qualify for freshman status. Selection is based on aptitude for accounting, commitment to the goal of working on a degree in accounting (including evidence of continued commitment after receiving this award), clear evidence that the candidate has established goals and a plan for achieving those goals (both personal and professional), and financial need. U.S. citizenship is required.
Financial data: The stipend is $4,000 per year.
Duration: 1 year; may be renewed 3 additional years if the recipient completes at least 12 hours each semester and maintains a GPA of 3.0 or higher.
Number awarded: 1 each year.
Deadline: April of each year.

3043 $ WOMEN'S BUSINESS ALLIANCE SCHOLARSHIP PROGRAM

Choice Hotels International
Attn: Women's Business Alliance
4225 East Windrose Drive
Phoenix, AZ 85032
Phone: (602) 953–4478
Web: www.choicehotels.com/en/about–choice/wba
Summary: To provide financial assistance to women interested in preparing for a career in the hospitality industry.
Eligibility: Open to female high school seniors, undergraduates, and graduate students. Applicants must be U.S. citizens or permanent residents interested in preparing for a career in the hospitality industry. They must submit an essay of 500 words or less on why they are interested in a career in the hospitality industry, the area of the industry that appeals to them the most, and some of their major accomplishments and/or personal characteristics that will benefit their work in the hospitality industry. Selection is based on that essay, academic record, and 2 letters of recommendation.
Financial data: The stipend is $2,000.
Duration: 1 year; recipients may reapply.
Number awarded: 2 or more each year.
Deadline: January of each year.

3044 $$ WOMEN'S JEWELRY ASSOCIATION SCHOLARSHIP

Summary: To provide financial assistance for college to women who are interested in careers in jewelry.
See Listing #1552.

3045 WORDA RUSSELL MEMORIAL ENDOWMENT SCHOLARSHIPS

Epsilon Sigma Alpha International
Attn: ESA Foundation
363 West Drake Road
Fort Collins, CO 80526
Phone: (970) 223–2824; Fax: (970) 223–4456;
Email: esainfo@epsilonsigmaalpha.org
Web: www.epsilonsigmaalpha.org/esa–foundation/scholarships
Summary: To provide financial assistance to students from any state planning to attend college to prepare for a teaching career.
Eligibility: Open to students who are 1) graduating high school seniors with a GPA of 3.0 or higher or with minimum scores of 22 on the ACT or 1030 on the combined critical reading and mathematics SAT; 2) enrolled in college with a GPA of 3.0 or higher; 3) enrolled at a technical school or returning to school after an absence for retraining of job skills or obtaining a degree; or 4) engaged in online study through an accredited college, university, or vocational school. Applicants must be planning to prepare for a teaching career. They may attend school in any state. Selection is based on character (10%), leadership (20%), service (10%), financial need (30%), and scholastic ability (30%).
Financial data: The stipend is $1,000.
Duration: 1 year; may be renewed.
Number awarded: 1 each year.
Deadline: January of each year.

3046 WORTHY GOAL SCHOLARSHIP FUND

International Food Service Executives Association
Attn: Coordinator
4955 Miller Street, Suite 107
Wheat Ridge, CO 80033
Phone: (800) 893–5499;
Email: hq@ifsea.com
Web: www.ifsea.com/programs_inside.cfm?catid=3087
Summary: To provide financial aid to students interested in majoring in college in a field related to food service.
Eligibility: Open to full–time students in a food service–related major at a 2– or 4–year college or university. Applicants must submit a personal financial statement, a 500–word statement on their personal background, a description of their work experience, a listing of their memberships in professional student organizations, a 250–word statement on how the scholarship will help them in achieving their goals, a transcript of grades from high school or college, and 3 letters of recommendation. Selection is based on food service work experience, membership in professional organizations, financial need, interest in food service as a career, contribution of this scholarship to personal goals, academic ability, and letters of recommendation.
Financial data: Stipends range from $500 to $1,500 per year.
Duration: 1 year.
Number awarded: Varies each year.
Deadline: January of each year.

3047 $ WSAJ AMERICAN JUSTICE ESSAY SCHOLARSHIP CONTEST

Washington State Association for Justice
1809 Seventh Avenue, Suite 1500
Seattle, WA 98101–1328
Phone: (206) 464–1011; Fax: (206) 464–0703;
Email: wsja@washingtonjustice.org
Web: www.washingtonjustice.org

Summary: To recognize and reward, with scholarships for college in any state, high school students in Washington who submit an essay on a topic related to the role of the civil justice system in our society.

Eligibility: Open to students attending high school in the state of Washington. Applicants must submit an essay, from 4 to 5 pages in length, on a topic that changes annually; recently, students were invited to select 3 rights guaranteed by the U.S. constitution and write an essay explaining why those should be included in the constitution of a hypothetical new country. They must be interested in attending college in any state.

Financial data: Awards range from $1,000 to $3,000, to be used when the recipient attends college. Funds are paid directly to the winners' institutions, to be used for tuition, room, board, or fees.

Duration: The competition is held annually.

Number awarded: Up to 3 each year.

Deadline: March of each year.

3048 WYOMING ASSOCIATION OF PUBLIC ACCOUNTANTS SCHOLARSHIP

Wyoming Association of Public Accountants
c/o Jarvis Windom, Scholarship Chair
1064 Gilchrist Street
Wheatland, WY 82201
Phone: (307) 322–3433; (800) 491–3028;
Email: jarvis@windom.org
Web: www.wyopa.com/scholarship.htm

Summary: To provide financial assistance to residents of Wyoming interested in working on a degree in business or accounting at a school in the state.

Eligibility: Open to residents of Wyoming who are enrolled or planning to enroll full time at an accredited college or university in the state. Applicants must be majoring or planning to major in accounting or business. Along with their application, they must submit a brief paragraph on their reasons for wishing to study in the professional field of accounting. Financial need is considered in the selection process.

Financial data: A stipend is awarded (amount not specified).

Duration: 1 year.

Number awarded: 1 each year.

Deadline: Deadline not specified.

3049 $$ YELLOW RIBBON SCHOLARSHIP

Tourism Cares
Attn: Academic Scholarship Program
275 Turnpike Street, Suite 307
Canton, MA 02021
Phone: (781) 821–5990; Fax: (781) 821–8949;
Email: scholarships@tourismcares.org
Web: www.tourismcares.org

Summary: To provide financial assistance for college or graduate school to students with disabilities who are planning a career in the travel and tourism or hospitality industry.

Eligibility: Open to citizens and permanent residents of the United States and Canada who have a physical or sensory disability. Applicants must be enrolled full time and 1) entering the second year at an accredited 2–year college; 2) entering their junior or senior year at an accredited 4–year college or university; or 3) be enrolled or entering graduate school. They must have a GPA of 2.5 or higher and be working on a degree in a travel or tourism or hospitality–related field at a college or university in Canada or the United States. Undergraduates must submit an essay on the segment of the travel and tourism or hospitality industry their current program of study emphasizes, the opportunities they are utilizing as they prepare for a career in the industry, and their academic and extracurricular activities. Graduate students must submit an essay on the changes they have observed thus far in the travel and tourism or hospitality industry, the changes they anticipate in the future of the industry, and where they see their future potential in the industry. Financial need is not considered in the selection process.

Financial data: The stipend is $5,000.

Duration: 1 year.

Number awarded: 1 each year.

Deadline: March of each year.

3050 $ YOUNT, HYDE & BARBOUR SCHOLARSHIP

Virginia Society of Certified Public Accountants
Attn: Educational Foundation
4309 Cox Road
Glen Allen, VA 23060
Phone: (804) 612–9427; (800) 733–8272; Fax: (804) 273–1741;
Email: info@vscpafoundation.com
Web: www.vscpa.com/content/Ed_Found/SA/Scholarships.aspx

Summary: To provide financial assistance to upper–division students enrolled in an accounting program in Virginia.

Eligibility: Open to juniors and seniors currently enrolled in a Virginia college or university accounting program. Applicants must be U.S. citizens, be intending to take the C.P.A. examination, and have a GPA of 3.0 or higher. Along with their application, they must submit a 500–word essay on assigned topics. Selection is based on the essay, their most recent transcript, a current resume, a faculty letter of recommendation, and financial need.

Financial data: The stipend is $2,500.

Duration: 1 year.

Number awarded: 1 each year.

Deadline: March of each year.

Subject Index

Use this index when you want to identify funding programs by subject. To help you pinpoint your search, we've also included hundreds of "see" and "see also" references. In addition to looking for terms that represent your specific subject interests, be sure to check the "General programs" entry; hundreds of programs are listed there that can be used to support study in any subject area (although the programs may be restricted in other ways). Remember: the numbers cited in this index refer to book entry numbers, not page numbers in the book.

Residency Index

Some programs listed in this book are restricted to residents of a particular city, county, state, or region. Others are open to students wherever they live. The Residency Index will help you pinpoint programs available only to residents in your area as well as programs that have no residency restrictions (these are listed under the term "United States"). To use this index, look up the geographic areas that apply to you (always check the listings under "United States"), jot down the entry numbers listed after the subject areas that interest you, and use those numbers to find the program descriptions in the directory. To help you in your search, we've provided some "see also" references in each index entry. Remember: the numbers cited here refer to program entry numbers, not to page numbers in the book.

Tenability Index

Some programs listed in this book can be used only in specific cities, counties, states, or regions. Others may be used anywhere in the United States (or even abroad). The Tenability Index will help you locate funding that is restricted to a specific area as well as funding that has no tenability restrictions (these are listed under the term "United States"). To use this index, look up the geographic areas where you'd like to go (always check the listings under "United States"), jot down the entry numbers listed under the subject areas that interest you, and use those numbers to find the program descriptions in the directory. To help you in your search, we've provided some "see also" references in each index entry. Remember: the numbers cited here refer to program entry numbers, not to page numbers in the book.

Sponsoring Organization Index

The Sponsoring Organization Index makes it easy to identify agencies that offer college funding. In this index, sponsoring organizations are listed alphabetically, word by word. In addition, we've used a code (within parentheses) to help you identify which programs sponsored by these organizations fall within your scope of interest: U = Unrestricted by Subject Area; H = Humanities; S = Sciences; SS = Social Sciences. Here's how the codes work: if an organization's name is followed by (U) 41, the program sponsored by that organization is described in entry 41, in the Unrestricted by Subject Area section. If that sponsoring organization's name is followed by another entry number—for example, (SS) 2649—the same or a different program is described in entry 2649, in the Social Sciences section. Remember: the numbers cited here refer to program entry numbers, not to page numbers in the book.

Calendar Index

Since most financial aid programs have specific deadline dates, some may have already closed by the time you begin to look for funding. You can use the Calendar Index to identify which programs are still open. To do that, look at the subject categories that interest you, think about when you'll be able to complete your application forms, go to the appropriate months, jot down the entry numbers listed there, and use those numbers to find the program descriptions in the directory. Keep in mind that the numbers cited here refer to program entry numbers, not to page numbers in the book.

Social Sciences